Selected Highlights

Chapter	You Make the Call	Current Happenings	Using the Information	Did You Know?
<14>	• Engineer • Farmer • Teacher	• Declining dividends • Reporting income • Stock options	• Earnings per share • Dividend yield • Price-earnings	• Buybacks explode • Earnings expectations • Fortunes in options
<15>	• Bond rater • Retailer • Bond investor	• Return of junk bonds • Convertible bonds • Amortization software	• Bond vs stock financing • Collateral agreements • Analyzing pledged assets	• Muni bonds • Bond quotes • Rating bonds
<16>	• Money manager • Home builder • Retailer	• Classifying investments • International investments • Reporting investments	• Interpreting investments • Foreign exchange rates • Return on total assets	• Trading secrets • Mob on Wall Street • Tinseltown securities
<17>	• Reporter • Community activist	• Measuring cash flows • Classifying cash flows • Reporting cash flows	• Cash vs net income • Analyzing sources & uses • Cash flow on total assets	• Cash valuation • E-cash • Free cash flow
<18>	• Banker • Auditor	• Data from the Web • Building blocks of analysis • Reporting analysis results	• Horizontal analysis • Vertical analysis • Ratio analysis	• Chips and brokers • Ticker prices • Bears and bulls
<19>	• Budget officer • Purchases manager • Salesperson	• Customer orientation • Global economy • Manuf. mgmt. principles	• Classifying costs • Quality management • Contribution margin	• Airline quality • Banished to overhead • Continuous improvement
<20>	• Mgmt. consultant • Sales director • Systems consultant	• Manufacturing activities • Job order manufacturing • Job order documents	• Applying overhead • Analyzing cost flows • Multiple overhead rates	• Build-to-order PCs • Job order colleges • Software modules
<21>	• Budget officer • Process manager • General manager	• Customer-interaction software • Flexibility & standardization • Process cost summary	• Analyzing process cost • Cost per equivalent unit • Spoiled units	• Training programs • Service companies • Teamwork
<22>	• Operations manager • Officer • Center manager	• Responsibility accounting • Activity-based costing • Contribution reporting	• Assigning overhead • Allocating joint costs • Analyzing centers	• Overhead kills • Healthcare costing • Nonfinancial measures
<23>	• Trainee • Operations manager • Marketing manager	• Cost-volume-profit analysis • Cost behavior • Multiproduct analysis	• Estimating costs • Break-even • Operating leverage	• Compaq's break-even • Price-cutting • Graphical analysis
<24>	• Environmental manager • Budget staffer • Sales manager	• Administering budgets • Master budgeting • Linking budgets	• Expense planning • Managing cash • Zero-based budgeting	• Budget calendar • Budgeting acquisitions • Activity/Process budgeting
<25>	• Human Resource Mgr. • Sales manager • Internal auditor	• Standard costing • Management by exception • Performance reports	• Cost variances • Flexible budgeting • Sales variances	• Setting standard costs • Strategic partnerships • Benchmarking
<26>	• Systems manager • Production manager • Investment manager	• Using payback • Analyzing rate of return • Net present value	• Capital budgeting • Relevant costs • Break-even time	• The winner is ... • Deciding new products • 'Make or Buy' services

Fundamental Accounting Principles

Fifteenth Edition

Kermit D. Larson
University of Texas at Austin

John J. Wild
University of Wisconsin at Madison

Barbara Chiappetta
Nassau Community College

Boston Burr Ridge, IL Dubuque, IA Madison, WI
New York San Francisco St. Louis
Bangkok Bogotá Caracas Lisbon London Madrid Mexico City
Milan New Delhi Seoul Singapore Sydney Taipei Toronto

To the Instructor

Changes in accounting education have led to the most significant revision in the history of **Fundamental Accounting Principles**. The call for change in introductory accounting is upon us, and we responded. This fifteenth edition gives you more flexibility and options for innovation than preceding editions. At the same time, it maintains the rich content that has made it a market-leading textbook in accounting principles. See the Preface and its "To the Instructor" comments to learn more about this new and exciting edition and all its supporting materials. We know you will enjoy teaching from this new edition.

To the Student

Accounting is one of the most valuable subjects you will study. Understanding accounting—the language of business—is essential for business success. **Fundamental Accounting Principles** gives you this understanding. Its content, features, and insights make learning accounting exciting and relevant. Please see the preface's "To the Student" comments to learn more about this book and how it can help you achieve success. Described in the preface are many student supplements that will help you succeed. We are confident you will find this book relevant and fun.

To my wife **Nancy.**
To my wife **Gail** and children, **Kimberly, Jonathan, Stephanie,** and **Trevor.**
To my husband **Bob,** my sons **Michael** and **David,** and my **mother.**

McGraw-Hill
A Division of The ***McGraw-Hill*** *Companies*

FUNDAMENTAL ACCOUNTING PRINCIPLES

This book is printed on acid-free paper.

International 1 2 3 4 5 6 7 8 9 0 VNH/VNH 9 3 2 1 0 9 8
Domestic 1 2 3 4 5 6 7 8 9 0 VNH/VNH 9 3 2 1 0 9 8

ISBN 0-256-25534-2
ISBN 0-07-366125-2
ISBN 0-07-366126-0
ISBN 0-07-366127-9
ISBN 0-07-365857-X
ISBN 0-07-365858-8
ISBN 0-07-030722-9
ISBN 0-07-030723-7
ISBN 0-07-366315-8

Vice president and editorial director: *Michael W. Junior*
Publisher: *Jeffrey J. Shelstad*
Developmental editor: *Tracey Klein Douglas/Jackie Scruggs/Burrston House*
Senior marketing manager: *Rhonda Seelinger*
Senior project manager: *Denise Santor-Mitzit*
Production supervisor: *Lori Koetters*
Interior Designer: *Ellen Pentengell*
Cover Design: *Z Graphics*
Cover photos: *Front image: © Tony Stone Images, Chris Specdic;*
Back image: Tony Stone Images, David Madison
Senior photo research coordinator: *Keri Johnson*
Supplement coordinator: *Rose Hepburn*
Compositor: *York Graphic Services, Inc.*
Typeface: *10.5/12 Times Roman*
Printer: *Von Hoffmann Press, Inc.*

INTERNATIONAL EDITION

When ordering the title, use ISBN 0-07-115818-9

http://www.mhhe.com

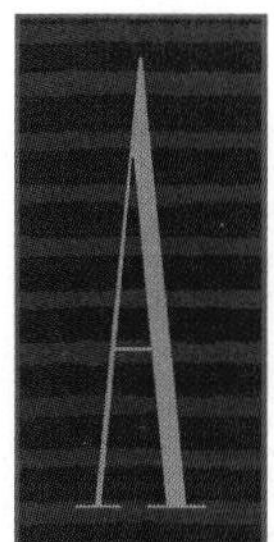

About the Authors

A progressive new authoring team further establishes F.A.P.'s market leadership . . .

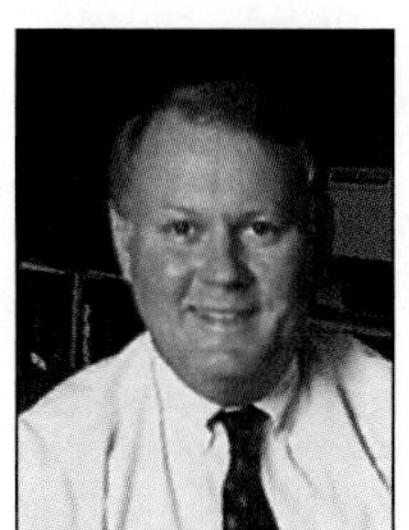

Kermit D. Larson

Kermit D. Larson is the Arthur Andersen & Co. Alumni Professor of Accounting Emeritus at the University of Texas at Austin. He served as chairman of the University of Texas, Department of Accounting and was visiting associate professor at Tulane University. His scholarly articles have been published in a variety of journals, including *The Accounting Review, Journal of Accountancy,* and *Abacus.* He is the author of several books, including *Financial Accounting* and *Fundamentals of Financial and Managerial Accounting,* both published by Irwin/McGraw-Hill.

Professor Larson is a member of the American Accounting Association, the Texas Society of CPAs, and the American Institute of CPAs. His positions with the AAA have included vice president, southwest regional vice president, and chairperson of several committees, including the Committee of Concepts and Standards. He was a member of the committee that planned the first AAA doctoral consortium and served as its director.

Professor Larson served as president of the Richard D. Irwin Foundation. He also served on the Accounting Accreditation Committee and on the Accounting Standards Committee of the AACSB. He was a member of the Constitutional Drafting Committee of the Federation of Schools of Accountancy and a member of the Commission on Professional Accounting Education. He has been an expert witness on cases involving mergers, antitrust litigation, consolidation criteria, franchise taxes, and expropriation of assets by foreign governments. Professor Larson served on the Board of Directors and Executive Committee of Tekcon, Inc., and on the National Accountants Advisory Board of Safe-Guard Business Systems. In his leisure time, he enjoys skiing and is an avid sailor and golfer.

John J. Wild

John J. Wild is a professor of business and the Vilas Research Scholar at the University of Wisconsin at Madison. He has previously held appointments at Michigan State University and the University of Manchester in England. He received his BBA, MS, and PhD from the University of Wisconsin.

Professor Wild teaches courses at both the undergraduate and graduate levels. He has received the Mable W. Chipman Excellence-in-Teaching Award and the departmental Excellence-in-Teaching Award at the University of Wisconsin. He also received the Beta Alpha Psi and Roland F. Salmonson Excellence-in-Teaching Award from Michigan State University. Professor Wild is a past KPMG Peat Marwick National Fellow and is a recipient of fellowships from the American Accounting Association and the Ernst and Young Foundation.

Professor Wild is an active member of the American Accounting Association and its sections. He has served on several committees of these organizations, including the Outstanding Accounting Educator Award, National Program Advisory, Publications, and Research Committees. Professor Wild is author of *Financial Statement Analysis* published by Irwin/McGraw-Hill. His research appears in *The Accounting Review, Journal of Accounting Research, Journal of Accounting and Economics, Contemporary Accounting Research, Journal of Accounting, Auditing and Finance, Journal of Accounting and Public Policy,* and other business periodicals. He is associate editor of *Contemporary Accounting Research* and has served on several editorial boards including *The Accounting Review.*

Professor Wild, his wife, and four children enjoy travel, music, sports, and community activities.

Barbara Chiappetta

Barbara Chiappetta received her BBA in Accountancy and MS in Education from Hofstra University and is a tenured full professor at Nassau Community College. For the past 17 years, she has been an active executive board member of the Teachers of Accounting at Two-Year Colleges (TACTYC), serving 10 years as vice president and currently as president since the fall of 1993. As an active member of the American Accounting Association, she has served on the Northeast Regional Steering Committee, chaired the Curriculum Revision Committee of the Two-Year Section, and participated in numerous national committees.

In April 1998, Professor Chiappetta was inducted into the American Accounting Association Hall of Fame for the Northeast Region. She received the Nassau Community College dean of instruction's Faculty Distinguished Achievement Award in the spring of 1995. Professor Chiappetta was honored with the State University of New York Chancellor's Award for Teaching Excellence in 1997. As a confirmed believer in the benefits of the active learning pedagogy, Professor Chiappetta has authored *Student Learning Tools*, an active learning workbook for a first-year accounting course, published by Irwin/McGraw-Hill.

In her leisure time, Professor Chiappetta enjoys tennis and participates on a U.S.T.A. team. She also enjoys the challenge of bridge. Her husband, Robert, is an entrepreneur in the leisure sport industry. She has two sons — Michael, a lawyer, currently manages David's rock band called Blindman's Sun.

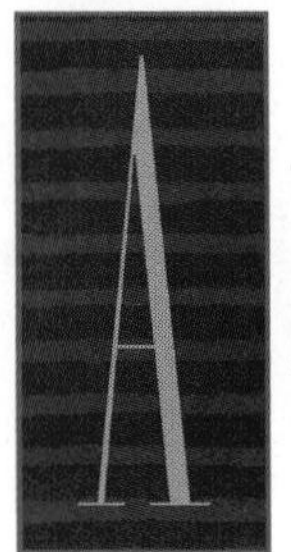

About the Contributors

An expert set of contributors complements the authors' rich experiences and success . . .

Jo Lynne Koehn

Jo Lynne Koehn received her PhD and Master's of Accountancy from the University of Wisconsin at Madison and is an associate professor at Central Missouri State University. Her scholarly articles have been published in a variety of journals including *The CPA Journal, Accounting Enquiries,* and *The MSCPA casebook.* Professor Koehn is a member of the American Accounting Association and the American Institute of CPAs. She also holds a Certified Financial Planning license and is active in developing a financial planning curriculum at Central Missouri State University. In the spring of 1997, she received the Faculty Excellence in Teaching Award from the Harmon College of Business Administration's Advisory Board. In her leisure time, Professor Koehn indulges her passion for golf and participates in the Executive Women's Golf Association of Kansas City. Professor Koehn also enjoys reading, traveling, and visiting bookstores.

Suresh Kalagnanam

Suresh Kalagnanam is an associate professor of accounting at the University of Saskatchewan in Canada. He received his B.Eng. from the University of Madras, MBA from Gujarat University (both in India), MBA and MSc in Accounting from the University of Saskatchewan, and PhD from the University of Wisconsin at Madison. His scholarly articles have been published in *Accounting, Organizations and Society, The Journal of Cost Management,* and *Management Accounting*. He has also written a teaching case which has been published by the Institute of Management Accountants. Dr. Kalagnanam is a member of the American Accounting Association, American Society for Quality, Canadian Academic Accounting Association, and the Institute of Management Accountants, and is an associate member of the Society of Management Accountants of Saskatchewan. Dr. Kalagnanam has two children, Pallavi and Siddharth. His wife, Viji, is a homemaker and a part-time university student.

Thomas L. Zeller

Thomas L. Zeller is associate professor of accountancy and university scholar/teacher in the Department of Accounting at Loyola University, Chicago. He received his Doctor of Philosophy from Kent State University. He has published numerous articles addressing managerial accounting, financial statement analysis, and health care financial measurement issues. His research has appeared in several journals, including *Business Horizons, Healthcare Financial Management, Journal of Accounting and Public Policy, Business and Economic Review,* and *Journal of Applied Business Research*. Dr. Zeller is a member of the American Accounting Association and the American Institute of Certified Public Accountants.

Carol Yacht

Carol Yacht received her MA in business and Economic Education from California State University, Los Angeles and BS in Business Education from the University of New Mexico. She is the author of Irwin/McGraw-Hill's *Computer Accounting with Peachtree for Microsoft Windows* books, and is a recognized expert in payroll accounting and reporting. She has worked as an educational consultant for IBM Corporation, an accounting instructor at Yavapai College, and a business education department chair at Beverly Hills High School in California. She chairs the Distance Learning Committee of the Computer Education Task Force, National Business Education Association. Professor Yacht's son, Matthew, is completing his accounting degree at Northern Arizona University. Her husband, Brice Wood, is an artist and part owner of a fine arts gallery. She is active in community activities and chairs the Planning and Zoning Commission of her town.

Preface

Let's Talk

Through extensive market-based surveys, focus groups, reviews, and personal correspondence with instructors and students, we discovered several interests and needs in accounting education today. In a nutshell, these desires can be grouped into eight pedagogical areas: (1) motivation, (2) organization, (3) preparation, analysis, and use; (4) ethics, (5) technology, (6) real world; (7) active learning, and (8) flexibility. Our main goal in this edition of Fundamental Accounting Principles (F.A.P.) is to address these needs and create the most contemporary, exciting, relevant, and flexible principles book in the market. A quick summary of these areas follows.

Motivation. Motivation drives learning. From the chapter's opening article and its focus on young entrepreneurs to the decision-making prompted by You Make the Call, **F.A.P.** motivates readers. It brings accounting and business to life and demonstrates that this material can make a difference in your life.

Organization. Organization serves the learning process, and **F.A.P.**'s outstanding organization aids that process. From "Chapter Linkages" and learning objectives organized by the *CAP Model*™ to its chapter outline and Flashbacks, **F.A.P.** is the leader in lending readers a helping hand in learning about accounting and business.

Preparation, Analysis, and Use. Accounting involves preparing, analyzing, and using information. **F.A.P.** balances each of these important roles in explaining and illustrating topics. From the unique Using the Information section to the creative Hitting the Road projects, **F.A.P.** shows all aspects of accounting.

Ethics. Ethics is fundamental to accounting. **F.A.P.** highlights the roles of ethics and social responsibility in modern businesses. From the Judgment and Ethics decision-making feature to its Ethics Challenge assignments, **F.A.P.** alerts readers to relevant and important ethical concerns.

Technology. Technology continues to change business and accounting, creating new and exciting accounting opportunities. **F.A.P.** is the leader in applying and showing technology in accounting. From the innovative Taking It to the Net projects to its Web-based assignments, **F.A.P.** pushes the accounting frontiers.

Real World. Accounting is important to the information age. From features and assignments that highlight companies like NIKE, Reebok, and America Online to the Teamwork in Action and Communication in Practice activities, **F.A.P.** shows accounting in a modern, global context. It also engages both accountants and nonaccountants. From the exciting Did You Know? features to its *Business Week* Activities, **F.A.P.** shows accounting is relevant to everyone.

Active Learning. Active learning implies active inquiry and interaction. **F.A.P.**'s instructor's edition (F.A.S.T.) gives new annotated links to pedagogical materials for those interested in applying active learning activities. **F.A.P.** is the undisputed leader in offering a strong pedagogical support package for active learning. Also, the *MHLA* service is a new, special addition to our support package.

Flexibility. Accounting involves conceptual, analytical, and procedural aspects. **F.A.P.** offers a new CAP Model to help choose the preferred teaching or learning approach. The CAP Model establishes color-coded learning objectives as either Conceptual, Analytical, or Procedural, and assigns them to chapter content, assignments, and test items. This gives maximum flexibility and choice in teaching and learning structure.

This is just a sneak preview of **F.A.P.**'s new and exciting features. From communication, interpersonal, and critical thinking skills to the development of ethical and global awareness, **F.A.P.** is the leader. We invite you to take a complete look at these and other special features in the remainder of this preface to see why **F.A.P.** is the *first choice* in accounting principles books.

To Instructor

F.A.P. gives Web addresses for current follow-ups to articles, excerpts, and financial statements, and for a real world flavor.

To Student

The chapter's opening article and its *You Make the Call* features drive home the relevance of accounting and business.

Motivation

Motivation is a main goal of **F.A.P.** We know information retention is selective—if it doesn't apply to the lives of readers, they typically aren't motivated to learn. **F.A.P.** explains and illustrates how accounting applies to the reader. Here is a sampling of materials that motivates the reader.

The **Chapter Opening Article** sets the stage and shows how the chapter's contents are relevant to the reader. Articles often focus on young entrepreneurs in business who benefit from preparing, analyzing, and using accounting information. These articles bring the material to life in concrete terms.

Tax Cop

DETROIT, MI—Carmen Benish and her two comrades jump out of their battered Zhiguli and walk briskly to the door of a bicycle sales and services shop in the Moscow suburb of Podolsk. Ducking under bicycle frames hanging from the ceiling, they approach a salesclerk and flash their badges. A few days earlier, an undercover colleague made a purchase that wasn't reported. Benish, Mikail Nikolas, and Val Yaroslav are investigating whether the business is underreporting sales to avoid paying

You Make the Call features develop critical thinking and decision-making skills by requiring decisions using accounting information. Each chapter contains two to four of these features. They are purposely chosen to reflect different kinds of users. Examples are investors, consultants, programmers, financial planners, engineers, appraisers, and political and community activists. Guidance answers are provided.

Entrepreneur
You are the owner of a small retail store. You are considering allowing customers to purchase merchandise using credit cards. Until now, your store only accepted cash and checks. What form of analysis do you use to make this decision?

You Make the Call

Company Excerpts call attention to well-known organizations to illustrate accounting topics. These excerpts are often accompanied by a photo drawing attention to the nature of the business and its relevance to readers.

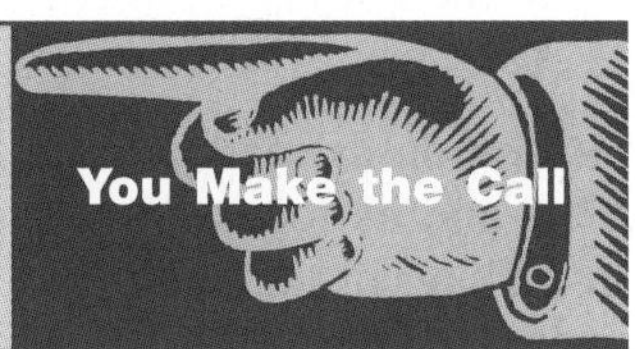

Sales are generally recorded by the Corporation when products are shipped to independent dealers.
General Motors

Financial Statements of familiar companies are used to acquaint readers with the format, content, and use of accounting information. The financial statements for NIKE, Reebok, and America Online are reproduced in the book and referenced often.

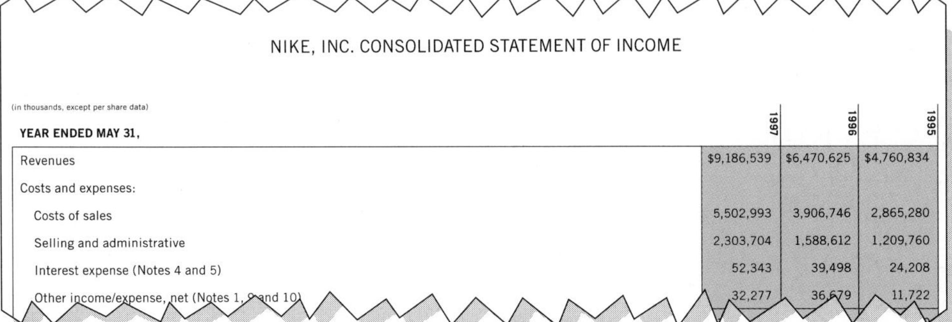

NIKE, INC. CONSOLIDATED STATEMENT OF INCOME

(in thousands, except per share data)

YEAR ENDED MAY 31,	1997	1996	1995
Revenues	$9,186,539	$6,470,625	$4,760,834
Costs and expenses:			
Costs of sales	5,502,993	3,906,746	2,865,280
Selling and administrative	2,303,704	1,588,612	1,209,760
Interest expense (Notes 4 and 5)	52,343	39,498	24,208
Other income/expense, net (Notes 1, 9 and 10)	32,277	36,679	11,722

Organization

Organization is crucial to effective learning. If it isn't well-organized or linked with previous knowledge, learning is less effective. **F.A.P.** helps readers organize and link accounting concepts, procedures, and analyses. A **Preview** kicks off each chapter. It introduces the importance and relevance of the materials. It also links these materials to the opening article to further motivate the reader. Here are some additional materials to enhance learning effectiveness.

To Instructor

Use the *CAP Model*™ and its link to learning objectives to help structure the course and assignment material to your instructional style.

To Student

Study each of these helpful organizational aids to increase your understanding and learning of accounting and business.

A Look Back

Chapter 1 began by considering the role of accounting in the information age. We described accounting for different organizations and identified users and uses of accounting. We saw that ethics and social responsibility are crucial to accounting.

A Look Ahead

Chapter 3 explains the recording of transactions. We introduce the double-entry accounting system and show how T-accounts are helpful in analyzing transactions. Journals and trial balances are also identified and explained.

Chapter linkages launch a chapter and establish bridges between prior, current, and upcoming chapters. Linkages greatly assist readers in effectively learning the materials and help them link concepts across topics.

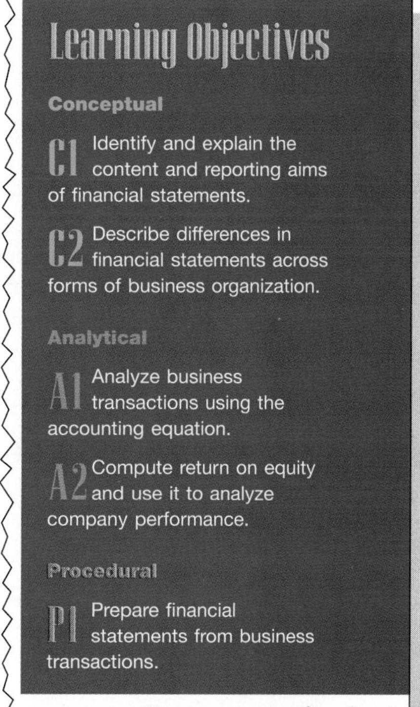

Learning Objectives
Conceptual
C1 Identify and explain the content and reporting aims of financial statements.
C2 Describe differences in financial statements across forms of business organization.
Analytical
A1 Analyze business transactions using the accounting equation.
A2 Compute return on equity and use it to analyze company performance.
Procedural
P1 Prepare financial statements from business transactions.

Learning Objectives are shown at the beginning of the chapter to help focus and organize the materials. Each objective is repeated in the chapter at the point it is described and illustrated. Self-contained summaries for learning objectives are provided at the end of the chapter.

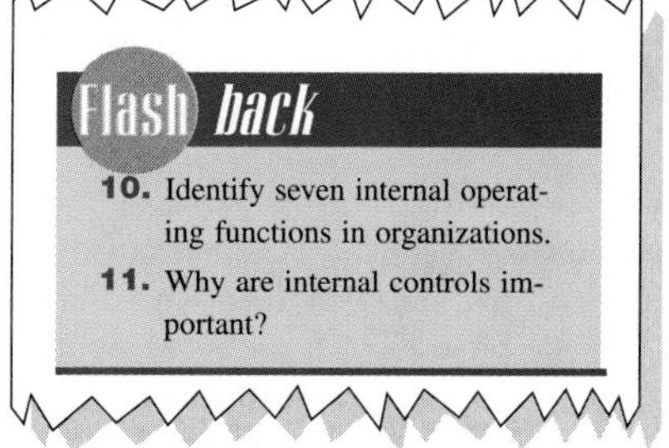

Flash back
10. Identify seven internal operating functions in organizations.
11. Why are internal controls important?

A series of **Flashbacks** in the chapter reinforce the immediately preceding materials. Flashbacks allow the reader to momentarily stop and reflect on the topics described. They give immediate feedback on the reader's comprehension before going on to new topics. Answers are provided.

Chapter Outline

- **Communicating with Financial Statements**
  - Previewing Financial Statements
  - Financial Statements and Forms of Organization
- **Transactions and the Accounting Equation**
  - Transaction Analysis—Part I
  - Transaction Analysis—Part II
  - Summary of Transactions

A color-coded **Chapter Outline** is provided for the chapter. This gives a mental and visual framework to help readers learn the material.

To Instructor

A focus on *Using the Information* section is a great way to develop analytical thinking.

To Student

Learning accounting principles greatly increases your understanding of articles such as those in *Business Week*—the world's best-selling business magazine.

Preparation, Analysis, and Use

Accounting is a service focused on preparing, analyzing, and using information. **F.A.P.** presents a balanced approach to these three crucial aspects of accounting. The preparation aspect of **F.A.P.** is well established and highly regarded. A new and progressive emphasis on analysis and use continues to put **F.A.P.** on the frontier of practice. Here's a sampling of new or revised textual materials on analysis and use:

The **Accounting Equation** (Assets = Liabilities + Equity) is used as a tool to evaluate each journal entry. The accounting equation is especially useful in learning and understanding the impacts of business transactions and events on financial statements. **F.A.P.** is a pioneer in showing this additional analysis tool.

Aug. 31	Cash	6,300		
	Sales		6,000	Assets = Liabilities + Equity
	Sales Taxes Payable ($6,000 × 0.05)		300	+6,300 +300 +6,000
	To record cash sales and 5% sales tax.			

The **Using the Information** section wraps up each chapter and emphasizes critical-thinking and decision-making skills. Each section introduces one or more tools of analysis. It applies these tools to actual companies and interprets the results. The section often focuses on use of ratio analyses to study and compare the performance and financial condition of competitors.

> **Return on Investment** — USING THE INFORMATION
>
> **A4** Compute and interpret return on investment.
>
> We introduced return on investment in assessing return and risk earlier in the chapter. Return on investment is also useful in evaluating management, analyzing and forecasting profits, and planning future activities. **Dell Computer** has its marketing department compute return on investment for *every* mailing. "We spent 15 months educating people about return on invested capital," says Dell's Chief Financial Offi-

Hitting the Road is a unique addition to the chapter's assignment material. This activity requires readers to work outside the book and often requires application of interpersonal and communication skills. Tasks range from visits to local merchandisers and Social Security headquarters to conducting phone interviews and Web searches. These activities help readers understand and appreciate the relevance of accounting.

> **Hitting the Road** C2
>
> Select a company in your community that you can visit in person or interview on the telephone. Call ahead to the company to arrange a time when you can interview an employee (often an accountant) who helps prepare the annual financial statements for the company. During the interview inquire about the following aspects of the company's accounting cycle:

A ***Business Week* Activity** requires the reader to apply the chapter's material to read and interpret a *Business Week* article. It also aids in developing reading comprehension skills and gives exposure to business happenings. Students can purchase **F.A.P.** with a special *Business Week* subscription package.

> ***Business Week* Activity** A3
>
> Read the article "Michael Dell: Whirlwind on the Web" in the April 7, 1997, issue of *Business Week.* Answer the following questions:
>
> **1.** How many days of sales does Dell have in inventory?
>
> **2.** How does Dell's days of sales in inventory compare with one of its chief competitors?

Ethics

Ethics is the most fundamental accounting principle. Without ethics, information and accounting cease to be useful. **F.A.P.** is the leader in bringing ethics into accounting and demonstrating its importance. From the first chapter's opening article to the ethics codes at the end of the book, **F.A.P.** sets the standard in emphasizing ethical behavior and its consequences. Here's a sampling of how we sensitize readers to ethical concerns and decision making:

To Instructor

The *Judgment and Ethics* feature raises the role of ethics in accounting and develops critical thinking skills.

To Student

Use these features and book materials to remind us that accounting and business decisions affect peoples' lives.

The **Judgment and Ethics** feature requires readers to make accounting and business decisions with ethical consequences. It uses role-playing to show the interaction of judgment and ethics, the need for ethical awareness, and the impact of ethics. Guidance answers are provided.

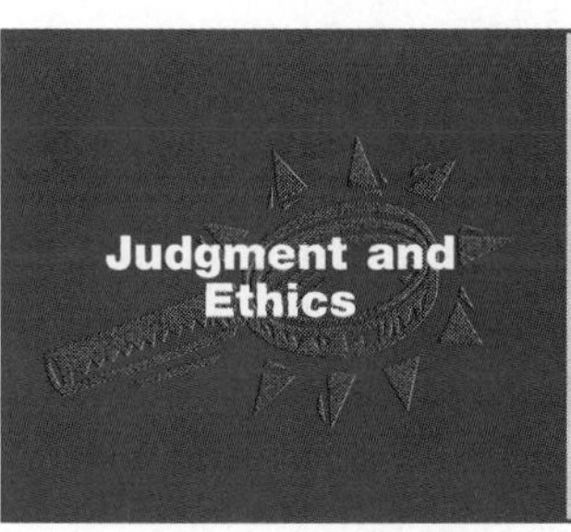

Certified Public Accountant
You are a CPA consulting with a client. This client's business has grown to the point where its accounting system must be updated to handle both the volume of transactions and management's needs for information. Your client requests your advice in purchasing new software for its accounting system. You have been offered a 10% commission by a software company for each purchase of its system by one of your clients. Do you think your evaluation of software is affected by this commission arrangement? Do you think this commission arrangement is appropriate? Do you tell your client about the commission arrangement before making a recommendation?

A new **Ethics Challenge** is provided in the *Beyond the Numbers* section. It confronts ethical concerns based on material from the chapter. Many of these challenges involve actions where the ethical path is blurred.

Ethics Challenge
P2

Randy Meyer is the chief executive officer of a medium-size company in Wichita, Kansas. Several years ago Randy persuaded the board of directors of his company to base a percent of his compensation on the net income the company earns each year. Each December, Randy estimates year-end financial figures in anticipation of the bonus he will receive. If the bonus is not as high as he would like he offers several accounting recommendations to his controller for year-end adjustments. One of his favorite recommendations is for the controller to reduce the estimate of doubtful accounts. Randy has used this

Social Responsibility is a major emphasis of progressive organizations. **F.A.P.** is unique in introducing this important topic in Chapter 1. We describe social responsibility and accounting's role in both reporting on and assessing its impact. **F.A.P.** also introduces social audits and reports on social responsibility.

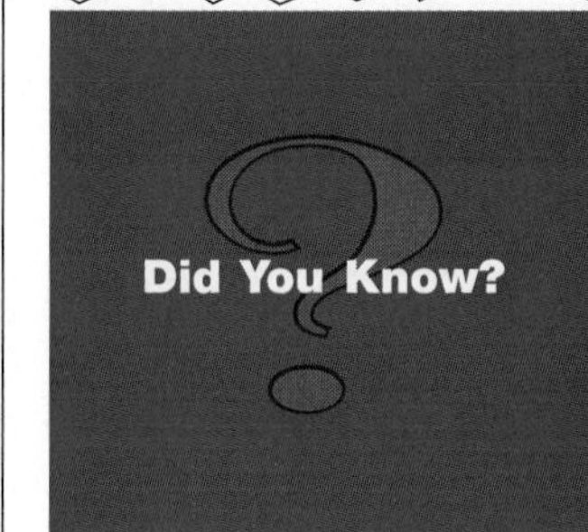

In Pursuit of Profit
How far can companies go in pursuing profits? **Converse** proposed to name a new footwear product Run N' Gun. This sparked debate on ethics, social responsibility, and profits. Converse says Run N' Gun is a basketball and football team. Critics claim it invites youth violence and links with the gun culture. To the credit of Converse, it changed the name from Run N' Gun to Run N' Slam prior to its sale to consumers.

To Instructor

PowerPoint presentation slides can be customized for your instructional style and are great visual aids to lecture materials.

To Student

Use **F.A.P.**'s Home Page for current updates, hot links to important sites, and much more . . .

A **Student Software CD** provides several technology-assisted educational activities. These include (1) *Essentials*—reviewing the entire accounting cycle, (2) *PeachTree Templates*—uses leading software for accounting support, (3) *Tutorial*—interactive review of topics, and (4) *GLAS* and (5) *SPATS*—instructional software to solve problems.

Technology

Technology and innovation can be exciting and fun. **F.A.P.** makes the transition to new technologies easy. It is the leader in demonstrating the relevance of technology and showing readers how to use it. Here's a sampling of items pushing the technology frontier:

F.A.P.'s **Home Page,** www.mhhe.com/business/accounting/fap, is the starting point for accessing accounting and business resources on the Web. The book's Web site harnesses technological resources to provide the most up-to-date and powerful Web services available.

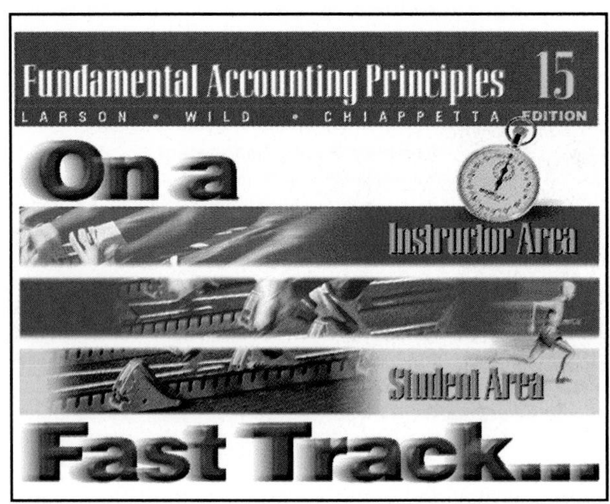

Taking It to the Net requires accessing a Web site and obtaining information relevant to the chapter. It aims to make readers comfortable with Web technology, familiar with information available, and aware of the power of Web technology.

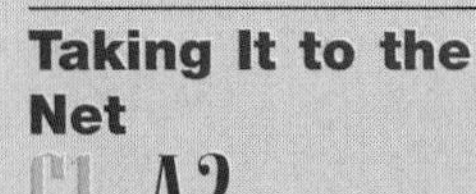

Taking It to the Net
C1, A2

Access the Cannondale promotional Web site at http://www.cannondale.com. Visit several hotlinks on the site to get a feel for the company's products.

1. What is the primary product that Cannondale sells?
2. Review the Cannondale 10K—this is the annual financial data required by the SEC. You can access this from the SEC's Edgar system (see this book's Web page). (Hint: Edgar Web site lists numerous

PowerPoint® Presentations and Supplements augment each chapter with colorful graphics, interesting charts, innovative presentations, and interactive activities. The PowerPoint® materials are flexible and can be customized for any use.

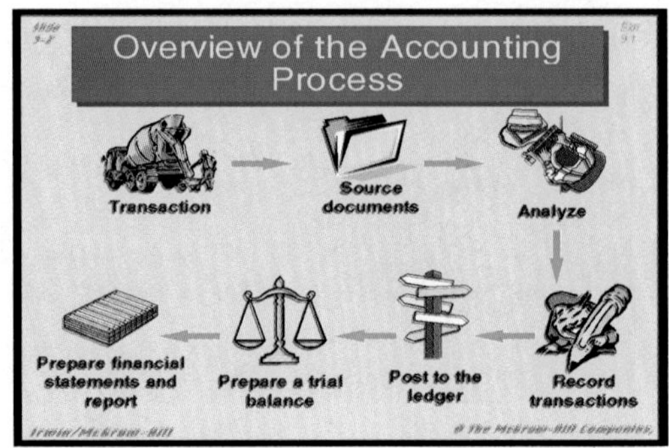

Real World

Showing readers that accounting matters is part of an effective learning package. **F.A.P.** is the leader in real world instructional materials. It offers unique assignments challenging the reader to apply knowledge learned in practical and diverse ways. These challenges include analytical problems, research requirements, comparative analysis, teamwork assignments, and communication exercises. They also allow greater emphasis on conceptual, analytical, communication, and interpersonal skills. Here's a sampling of these materials:

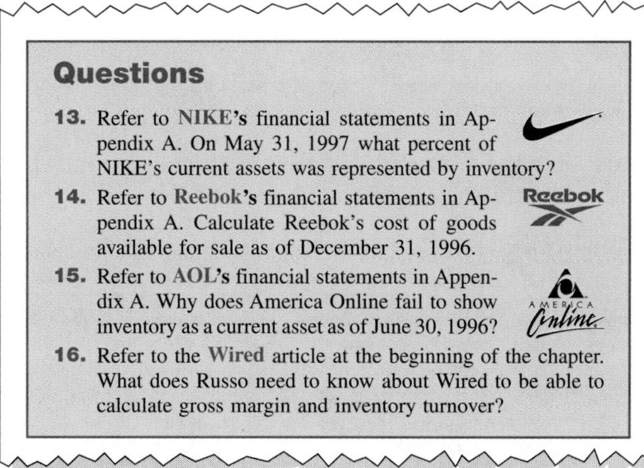

Questions

13. Refer to **NIKE's** financial statements in Appendix A. On May 31, 1997 what percent of NIKE's current assets was represented by inventory?

14. Refer to **Reebok's** financial statements in Appendix A. Calculate Reebok's cost of goods available for sale as of December 31, 1996.

15. Refer to **AOL's** financial statements in Appendix A. Why does America Online fail to show inventory as a current asset as of June 30, 1996?

16. Refer to the **Wired** article at the beginning of the chapter. What does Russo need to know about Wired to be able to calculate gross margin and inventory turnover?

To Instructor and Student

The **glossary** gives complete and accurate definitions of key terms. A key term is set in bold when first introduced, and the glossary references this page number. It also gives synonyms for key terms.

A **summary** describes the chapter in terms of its learning objectives. It assists in understanding of key concepts, procedures, and analyses.

Questions give readers quick feedback on their understanding of key chapter topics.

Quick studies are effective checks on concepts, procedures, and analyses. They help build the reader's confidence with the material. Each are keyed to usually one learning objective.

Exercises focus on one or more learning objectives. They are mildly challenging and are an effective way to launch into more challenging problems.

Check Figures serve as an aid to readers.

Reporting in Action requires analysis and use of NIKE's annual report information. The unique *Swoosh Ahead* feature allows use of the most current information in the marketplace.

Reporting in Action
A1, A3, A4

NIKE designs, produces, markets, and sells sports footwear and apparel. Key financial figures for NIKE's fiscal year ended May 31, 1997 are:

Key figure	In millions
Financing (liabilities + equity)	$5,361
Profit	796
Sales	9,187

Required

1. What is the total amount of assets invested in NIKE?

2. What is NIKE's return on investment? NIKE's assets at May 31, 1996 equal $3,952 (in millions).

3. How much are total expenses for NIKE?

Analysis component:

4. Does NIKE's return on investment seem satisfactory if competitors average a 5% return?

Swoosh Ahead

5. Obtain NIKE's most recent annual report. You can also access NIKE's annual report at its Web site **(www.nike.com)** or at the SEC's Web site **(www.sec.gov).** Compute NIKE's return on investment using this updated annual report information you obtain. Compare the May 31, 1997, fiscal year-end return on investment to any subsequent years' returns you are able to compute.

Comparative Analysis compares the performance and financial condition of NIKE and Reebok using the accounting knowledge obtained from the chapter. These activities help develop analytical skills.

Comparative Analysis

A2

Both **NIKE** and **Reebok** design, produce, market, and sell sports footwear and apparel. Key comparative figures ($ millions) for these two organizations follow:

Key figures*	NIKE	Reebok
Total liabilities	$2,205	$1,405
Total equity	$3,156	$ 381

* NIKE figures are from its annual report for the fiscal year ended May 31,1997. Reebok figures are from its annual report for the fiscal year ended December 31, 1996.

Comprehensive and Serial Problems are included in several chapters and focus on multiple learning objectives from multiple chapters. They help integrate and summarize key principles.

Comprehensive Problem

Alpine Company

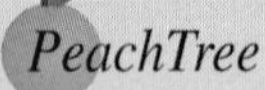

Assume it is Monday, May 1, the first business day of the month, and you have just been hired as the accountant for Alpine Corporation, which operates with monthly accounting periods. All of the company's accounting work has been completed through the end of April and its ledgers show April 30 balances. During your first month on the job, you record the following transactions:

May 1 Issued Check No. 3410 to S&M Management Co. in payment of the May rent, $3,710. (Use two lines to record the transaction. Charge 80% of the rent to Rent Expense—Selling Space and the balance to Rent Expense—Office Space.)

2 Sold merchandise on credit to Essex Company, Invoice No. 8785, $6,100. (The terms of all credit sales are 2/10, n/30.)

2 Issued a $175 credit memorandum to Nabors, Inc., for defective merchandise sold on April 28 and returned for credit. The total selling price (gross) was $4,725.

Problems often cover multiple learning objectives and usually require preparing, analyzing, and using information. They are paired with **Alternate Problems** (at the end of the book) for further review of the same topics. Problems are supported with software and other technology options. Many include an **Analytical Component** focusing on financial statement consequences and interpretations.

Problem 7-3A
Income comparisons and cost flows—periodic

A1, P4

Green Jeans, Inc., sold 5,500 units of its product at $45 per unit during 1999, and incurred operating expenses of $6 per unit in selling the units. It began the year with 600 units and made successive purchases of the product as follows:

January 1 (beginning inventory) . . .	600 units @ $18 per unit
Purchases:	
February 20	1,500 units @ $19 per unit
May 16	700 units @ $20 per unit
October 3	400 units @ $21 per unit
December 11	3,300 units @ $22 per unit
	6,500 units

Required

Preparation Component

Check Figure Net income (LIFO), $69,020

1. Prepare a comparative income statement for the company, showing in adjacent columns the net incomes earned from the sale of the product, assuming the company uses a periodic inventory system and prices its ending inventory on the basis of: *(a)* FIFO, *(b)* LIFO, and *(c)* weighted average. Assume an income tax rate of 30%.

A **Demonstration Problem** is at the end of the chapter. It illustrates important topics and shows how to apply concepts in preparing, analyzing, and using information. A problem-solving strategy helps guide the reader.

Demonstration Problem

On July 14, 1999, Tulsa Company paid $600,000 to acquire a fully equipped factory. The purchase involved the following assets (we include additional facts related to each):

Asset	Appraised Value	Estimated Salvage Value	Estimated Useful Life	Depreciation Method
Land	$160,000			Not depreciated
Land improvements ...	80,000	$ -0-	10 years	Straight line
Building	320,000	100,000	10 years	Double-declining balance
Machinery	240,000	20,000	10,000 units	Units of production*
Total	$800,000			

*The machinery is used to produce 700 units in 1999 and 1,800 units in 2000.

Required

1. Allocate the total $600,000 cost among the separate assets.

Infographics and Artwork aid in visual learning of key accounting and business topics. Photos, color, highlighting, and authentic documents all help with visual learning.

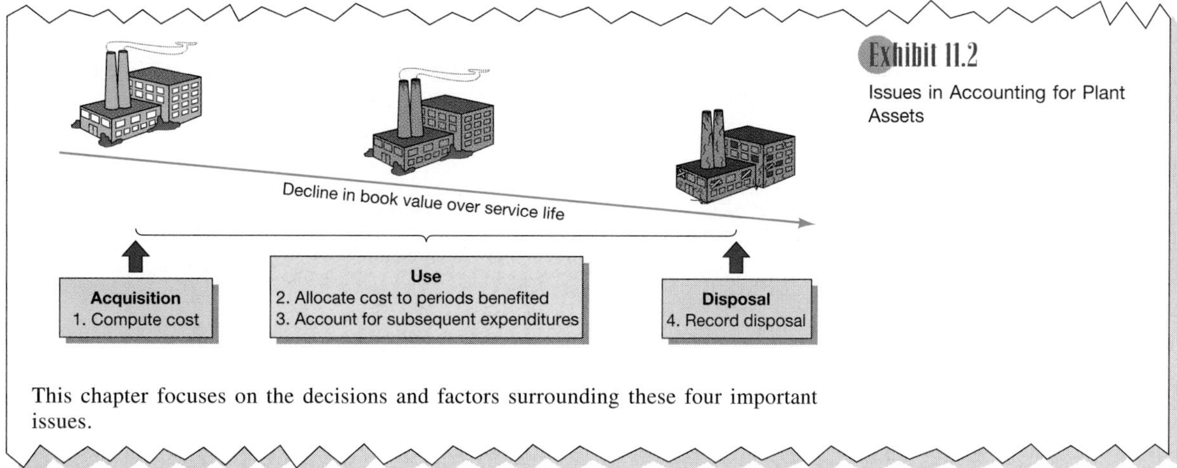

Exhibit 11.2

Issues in Accounting for Plant Assets

This chapter focuses on the decisions and factors surrounding these four important issues.

To Instructor

Teamwork in Action and Communicating in Practice are excellent starting points in developing an active learning environment. Both develop communication and interpersonal skills.

To Student

Team-building, collaborative effort skills are usually crucial to career success.

Active Learning

Active learning requires effective assignments. **F.A.P.** is the student-proven and instructor-tested leader in assignment materials. Proven and thoughtful assignments not only facilitate but motivate effective and active learning. Many assignments include writing components. Here's a sampling of relevant assignment materials:

Teamwork in Action assignments require preparing, analyzing, and using information in teams. They can be completed in or outside of class. These active learning activities reinforce understanding of key topics and develop interpersonal skills.

Teamwork in Action

P2

A team will be called upon to personify the operation of a voucher system. Yet all teams must prepare for the potential to be selected by doing the following:

1. Each team is to identify the documents in a voucher system. The team leader will play the voucher, and each team member is to assume "the role" of one or more documents.

2. To prepare for your individual role you are to:
   a. Find an illustration for the document within the chapter.
   b. Write down your documents function, where you originate, and how you flow through the voucher system.

3. Rehearse the role playing of operating the system. You may use text illustrations as props, and for visual effect you may wear a nametag identifying the part you play.

Communicating in Practice exercises aim at applying accounting knowledge to develop written and verbal communication skills.

Communicating in Practice

A2

The class is divided into teams. Teams are to select an industry, and each team member is to select a different company in that industry. Each team member is to acquire the annual report of the company selected. Annual reports can be obtained in many ways including accessing this book's Web page or through the SEC's EDGAR database **[www.sec.gov]**. Use the annual report to compute total asset turnover. Communicate with teammates via a meeting, e-mail, or telephone to discuss the meaning of this ratio, how different companies compare to each other, and the industry norm. The team must prepare a single memo reporting the ratios for each company and identify the conclusions reached during the team's discussion. The memo is to be duplicated and distributed to the instructor and all classmates.

Student Learning Tools (SLT) is a pedagogical support package aimed at helping in the teaching and learning process geared to active learning. The instructor's F.A.S.T. Edition offers links to SLT and its related Instructor's Manual (IM) when appropriate.

Fast Hint **Active Learning:** *SLT* provides Activity 29 for introducing plant asset disposals in an active learning environment (see pp. 132–136 in *SLT* and notes in *IM*).

Flexibility

Learning and instructing requires flexibility. **F.A.P.** offers flexibility in meeting the unique demands of individual students and teachers. From the conventional classroom to the active learning environment, **F.A.P.**'s new edition and its pedagogical package give more flexibility and options for innovation in learning and instruction. It does this while maintaining the rich content that has made it the market-leading book in accounting principles.

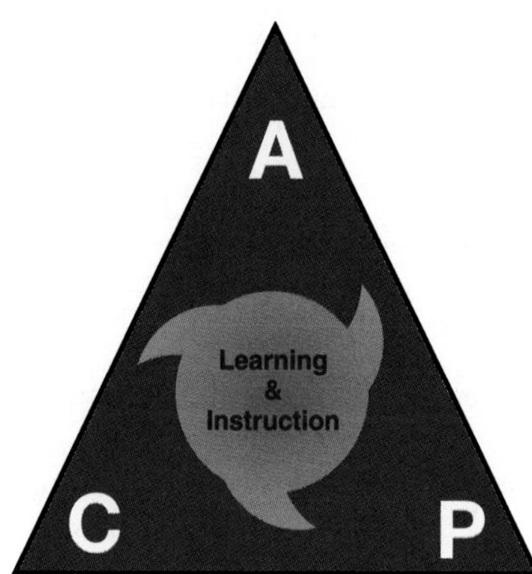

CAP Model

The new **CAP Model,** as already discussed, allows courses to be specially designed to meet instructional and learning needs—whether they be conceptual, analytical, procedural, or some combination of the three. The CAP Model recognizes the strength of each approach. Its identification of learning objectives, textual material, assignments, and test material by **C, A,** or **P** provides the flexibility to readily adapt **F.A.P.** to the preferred instructional and learning emphasis. It also allows the instructor to vary the emphasis by topic.

Packaging Options

Unique **packaging options** support **F.A.P.**'s flexibility. Nobody matches Irwin/McGraw-Hill when it comes to packaging options for accounting principles. Drawing on user feedback, we offer several new options with this edition:

- Hardcover splits—with a special introductory price and exciting packages. This new option is a hit with both instructors and students.
- *Business Week* Editions—The new *Business Week* Edition gives students a 16-week subscription for under $10! *Business Week* excerpts in the book further peak student interest in both accounting and business.
- F.A.S.T. Edition splits—with a two-volume Instructor's Edition to "lighten the load". The F.A.S.T. annotations have been revised by Barbara Chiappetta and offer added value.

To Instructor

F.A.P. supports all instructional and learning styles.
Additional Supporting Materials:
Instructor's Resource Manual
Solutions Manual
Test Bank
Transparencies
Student Learning Tools (SLT) and its Instructor's Manual (IM)

To Student

Working Papers, Study Guide, and Ready Notes are helpful in your accounting course.

Innovations and Enhancements

In preparing this edition, we asked questions of instructors and students. We asked what topics to add, delete, or change in emphasis. We asked what pedagogical aids would help in teaching and learning. We wanted to know what innovations and enhancements would help instructors and maintain **F.A.P.** leadership in accounting principles. From these questions came several requests. We listened, and this edition is the result. We've already described major content and pedagogical changes. This section identifies many other chapter-by-chapter innovations and enhancements:

Chapter 1

- New focus on the information age and the relevance of accounting.
- Early introduction to income, revenues, and expenses using Nike.
- New discussion of return and risk as part of all business decisions.
- New introduction to the Web with reference to **F.A.P.**'s homepage.
- New description of business activities: financing, investing, and operating.
- New and unique presentation of ethics and social responsibility.

Chapter 2

- ***FASTForward,*** an athletic service company, introduced as the new focus company for Chapters 2–5.
- New company transactions to add realism and interest.
- Revised discussion and presentation of accounting principles.
- Added analysis of each transaction using the accounting equation.
- New presentation and integration of cash flow statement with other financial statements.
- New description of reporting differences between proprietorships, partnerships, and corporations.

Chapter 3

- Revised presentation of transactions and source documents.
- New exhibits on the accounting equation and double-entry accounting.
- New exhibits and discussion linking transactions to financial statements, including the statement of cash flows.
- Revised discussion and exhibits for recording transactions.
- Expanded discussion of debt ratio with new comparative analyses.

Chapter 4

- New discussion of the accounting period and the motivation for adjusting accounts.
- New framework for preparing and analyzing adjustments.
- Several new exhibits and graphics illustrating adjusting accounts.
- New presentation linking adjustments to financial statements.
- Several new features highlighting current happenings in revenue recognition and the role of technology.
- Revised discussion of profit margin using Ben & Jerry's along with comparative analyses.

Chapter 5

- Revised presentation and new exhibits for the closing process.
- New contemporary presentation of the work sheet using Excel®. [*A traditional acetate overlay presentation is available in full color teaching transparencies. PowerPoint slides mimic the overlay.*]
- Revised presentation and discussion of the statement of cash flows as an integral part of the full set of financial statements.
- New exhibits presenting the accounting cycle.
- New presentation of the classified balance sheet.
- Revised current ratio discussion using Harley-Davidson and industry analyses.

Chapter 6

- New discussion comparing a service company and a merchandiser.
- New presentation of the operating cycle of a merchandiser with credit or cash sales.
- New design of source documents including an invoice and debit and credit memoranda.
- Revised presentation of merchandising sales and purchases using the perpetual inventory system.
- Revised discussion on the transfer of ownership for inventory.
- New discussion and presentation of merchandising cost flows across periods.
- New comparison of cash and accrual measures of sales and costs.
- Revised acid-test ratio and gross margin discussion using J.C. Penney and industry analyses.
- New appendix on accounting for merchandising sales and purchases under both the periodic and perpetual inventory systems.

Chapter 7

- Revised presentation of assigning costs to inventory using the perpetual inventory system.
- Revised discussion of inventoriable items and costs.
- New explanation of both financial and tax reporting for inventory.
- New exhibits illustrating statement effects of inventory errors.
- Revised presentation of alternative inventory valuation methods.
- New appendix presentation assigning costs to inventory using the periodic inventory system.
- Expanded merchandise turnover and days' sales in inventory ratio discussion using Toys 'R' Us and industry analyses.

Chapter 8

- New section on fundamental system principles.
- Contemporary and streamlined presentation on components of accounting systems.
- Revised discussion of hardware and software for systems.
- Contemporary presentation of Special Journals.
- Revised discussion of technology-based accounting systems.
- Revised layout for Special Journals reflecting current practice.
- New discussion of *enterprise-application software,* including SAP and Oracle.
- New analysis of business segments using a contribution matrix and Woolworth's data.

Chapter 9

- New sections on the purpose of internal control and its limitations.
- Revised discussion on the principles of internal control.
- New feature boxes involving current technological developments.
- Revised discussion on control of cash.
- New presentation and exhibits on the voucher system of control.
- New depictions of important source documents.
- New presentation on using banking activities as controls, including the bank reconciliation.
- Revised discussion of days' sales uncollected using comparative analyses of Hasbro and Mattel.

Chapter 10

- New organization focuses on receivables first and short-term investments second.
- Revised discussion of credit sales, including use of credit cards.
- New presentation on accounting for accounts receivables.
- New ordering of (simpler) write-off method before (more complex) allowance method.
- New presentation and exhibits for estimating bad debts.
- Revised presentation and exhibits for notes receivable.
- Streamlined accounting for investments including unrealized gains and losses.
- Revised discussion of accounts receivable turnover using comparative analyses of Dell and Compaq.

Chapter 11

- New introduction and motivation on accounting for plant assets.
- New discussion to describe and illustrate depreciation.
- Streamlined MACRS depreciation for tax reporting.
- Revised presentation and exhibits for disposals of plant assets.
- New discussion on natural resources and intangible assets.
- New discussion on the cash flow impacts of long-term assets.
- Revised total asset turnover illustration using Coors and Anheuser-Busch.

Chapter 12

- New introduction on accounting for liabilities.
- Revised presentation of known (determinable) liabilities.
- New exhibits and discussion on promissory notes.
- Revised presentation and exhibits for payroll-related liabilities.
- Revised discussion of accounting for long-term liabilities.
- Transfer of present value discussion of liabilities to Chapter 15.
- New appendix on **Payroll Accounting and Reports**.
- New exhibits, including form 941, W-2, payroll register, check, and withholding table.
- Use of **PeachTree**® to generate payroll-related reports.
- Revised presentation of times interest earned with application to Best Buy.

Chapter 13

- Reorganized chapter with partnerships first and corporations second.
- New discussion of LPs, LLPs, S Corporations, and LLCs.
- New discussion of partnerships, including financial statements, admission/withdrawal, and liquidation.
- New exhibits include the Boston Celtics' partnership report.
- Revised corporation coverage to focus on its characteristics and both common and preferred stock.
- New summary exhibit highlighting differences across alternative forms of organization.
- New exhibits including Green Bay Packer stock certificate.
- Streamlined coverage of stock subscriptions.

- Transfer of cash dividends discussion to Chapter 14.
- Revised book value per share discussion with references to Anheuser-Busch and Ride (snowboard manufacturer).

Chapter 14

- Reorganization into four main sections: dividends; treasury stock; reporting income; and retained earnings.
- New dividend presentation with new exhibits and infographics.
- Revised and streamlined discussion on treasury stock.
- Streamlined presentation on reporting income information.
- Revised earnings per share discussion to reflect new standard.
- New section on accounting for stock options.
- Revised presentation of reporting retained earnings.
- New presentation of dividend yield and price-earnings ratios using The GAP, Microsoft, Chevron, and Philip Morris.

Chapter 15

- New introduction to bond (long-term debt) financing.
- Revised bond presentation with new exhibits and infographics.
- New layout for effective interest amortization tables.
- Revised presentation of accounting for bond retirements.
- Revised presentation for notes payable.
- New explanation of present value concepts.
- New discussion on computing present values using interest tables.
- New discussion of collateral agreements for bonds and notes.
- Revised presentation of pledged assets to secured liabilities with reference to Chock Full O'Nuts.

Chapter 16

- Streamlined coverage of investments and international accounting.
- Reorganized into 3 sections: classification of investments; long-term investments in securities; and international investments.
- New exhibits and infographics on accounting for securities.
- Revised presentation of accounting for international investments.
- New presentation on the components of return on total assets with application to Reebok and Nike.

Chapter 17

- New presentation on the motivation for cash flow reporting.
- New exhibits on the format of the statement of cash flows.
- Revised discussion on cash flows from operating activities—both direct and indirect methods.
- New flexible presentation allows coverage of either or both direct or indirect methods.
- New exhibits summarize adjustments for both the direct and indirect methods.
- Revised discussion of cash flows from investing activities.
- Revised discussion of cash flows from financing activities.
- Revised presentation of analysis of cash sources and uses.
- New presentation of cash flow on total assets ratio with references to Nike, PepsiCo, Wal-Mart, and Wendy's.

Chapter 18

- New discussion on the basics of financial statement analysis.
- New explanation of the building blocks of analysis.
- Revised discussion on analysis tools and standards for comparisons.
- Revised presentation of horizontal and vertical analysis.
- New application of financial statement analysis to Nike.
- New comparative analysis of Nike and Reebok along with other competitors (Converse, LA Gear, Stride Rite).
- Revised graphical analysis using pie charts and bar graphs.
- Revised summary exhibit of financial statement analysis ratios.
- New section on analysis reporting.

Chapter 19

- New introduction to managerial accounting.
- New section and exhibit on the purpose of managerial accounting.
- Revised presentation of reporting manufacturing activities.
- New section on cost accounting concepts emphasizing cost identification and classification.
- New discussion of manufacturing management principles.
- New introduction to important managerial topics including prime, conversion, product, and period costs.
- New infographics augment many new and revised topics.
- Transfer of discussion of a manufacturing statement and a general accounting system to Chapter 20.
- New presentation on unit contribution margin with illustrations using a bike manufacturer.

Chapter 20

- New focus on manufacturing and job order cost accounting.
- Revised presentation of manufacturing activities and reporting.
- Revised discussion of job order cost accounting system.
- Streamlined discussion of underapplied and overapplied overhead.
- New presentation on multiple overhead allocation rates.

- Revised discussion of general accounting system (periodic) in a new appendix.

Chapter 21

- Revised introduction and motivation for a process manufacturing system.
- New exhibit and discussion comparing job order and process manufacturing systems.
- New exhibit to explain process manufacturing operations.
- Revised discussion of computing and using equivalent units.
- New discussion on the physical flow of units and preparation of a cost reconciliation.
- New presentation on spoilage in process costing and its effects on costs per equivalent unit.

Chapter 22

- New section and exhibits on two-stage cost allocation.
- New presentation and exhibits for activity-based costing.
- Transfer of activity-based costing upfront to link with Chapter 21.
- Revised discussion of decision making relevance of cost allocation and performance measurement.
- Revised discussion of departmental expense allocation.
- New exhibit and presentation of joint costs.
- New presentation of return on assets by investment centers.
- Transfer of discussion of "eliminating an unprofitable department" to Chapter 26.

Chapter 23

- Revised discussion on describing and identifying cost behavior.
- Revised presentation and comparison of the high-low, scatter diagram, and regression methods.
- Revised presentation on applying cost-volume-profit analysis.
- New presentation of operating leverage and its role in determining income.

Chapter 24

- New presentation of the budget calendar.
- New exhibit showing the master budget sequence.
- Expanded discussion and new exhibits of production and manufacturing budgets.
- Revised discussion motivated by new material on planning objectives.
- New presentation on zero-based budgeting.

Chapter 25

- New discussion and exhibit on the process of budgetary control.
- Revised emphasis on a decision making role for budgets and standard costs.
- New presentation of standard costs and the standard cost card.
- Revised organization of variance analysis.
- New presentation of and visual orientation to variance analysis.
- New separate analysis of variable and fixed overhead variances.
- New presentation on sales variances with illustrations.

Chapter 26

- Revised presentation of capital budgeting.
- New exhibits illustrating capital budgeting and its computations.
- New presentation of the internal rate of return for capital budgeting.
- New section comparing methods of analyzing investments using capital budgeting.
- New section on managerial decision making, information, and relevant costs.
- Revised presentation of short-term managerial decision tools.
- New section on qualitative factors in managerial decisions.
- New presentation of break-even time with illustrations.

Supplements

Instructor

Fully Annotated Support for Teaching Edition

Marginal annotations labeled **Fast Hints** have been revised and expanded. These annotations include: *Points* of interest or emphasis; *Discussion* suggestions; *Terminology,* offering alternate terminology; *Application,* referencing end-of-chapter quick studies and exercises; *Tools,* referencing instructional visuals found in the Instructor's Resource Manual; *Critical Thinking* questions; *Active Learning,* referencing class activities and team presentation assignments; and *Hint,* offering teaching suggestions.

Instructor's Resource Manual

By Barbara Chiappetta, Nassau Community College, and Jeannie Folk, College of DuPage. This manual contains materials for managing an active learning environment and provides new instructional visuals. Each chapter provides a Lecture Outline, a chart linking Learning Objectives to end-of-chapter material, a list of relevant active learning activities, transparency masters, and digital files on disk. For instructors' convenience, student copies of these visuals are provided in the *study guide.*

Solutions Manual

The manuals, prepared by John J. Wild, along with Suresh Kalagnanam, Jo Lynne Koehn, Marilyn Sagrillo, and Thomas Zeller, contain solutions for all assignment materials. An electronic version and transparencies in large, boldface type are also available.

Test Bank

Prepared by Jane G. Wiese of Valencia Community College and Robert Landry of Massassoit Community College. The Test Bank contains a wide variety of questions, including true-false, multiple-choice, matching, short essay, quantitative problems, and completion problems of varying levels of difficulty. All Test Bank materials are grouped according to learning objective. A computerized version is also available in Macintosh and Windows.

Ready Shows, Ready Slides, Ready Notes

These teaching enhancement packages were prepared by Jon A. Booker, Charles W. Caldwell, Susan C. Galbreath, Richard S. Rand, all of Tennessee Technological University.

Ready Shows. This is a package of multimedia lecture enhancement aids that uses PowerPoint® software to illustrate chapter concepts. It includes a viewer so that they can be shown with or without Microsoft PowerPoint® software.

Ready Slides. These selected four-color teaching transparencies are derived from the Ready Shows presentation screens. The package also includes a booklet of black and white transparency masters.

Instructor's Manual for Student Learning Tools.

This manual illustrates how to approach a traditional accounting principles curriculum and meet the objectives set forth by the AECC. The approach employs a concept and user focus and aims at developing intellectual, communication, and interpersonal skills. Active learning strategies and structures, group formation, and assessment techniques are discussed. Transparency masters for instructional visuals to facilitate mini-lectures are also provided.

Presentation CD-ROM

This integrated CD-ROM allows you to maneuver from PowerPoint® slides to solutions to test bank questions and much more. Now the disk supplements that come with the text are packaged in one convenient CD-ROM.

Distance Learning

McGraw-Hill Learning Architecture

This Web-based learning environment distributes product course materials for viewing on any PC compatible or Macintosh computer. This on-line learning center is packed with dynamically generated pages of text, graphics, PowerPoint® slides, exercises, and more. Customization possibilities are easily implemented.

LeCroy Center (Dallas Community College District) Telecourse

An exciting new Telecourse is being developed in partnership with the LeCroy Center, the world leader in Telecourse education. Approximately 13 hours of new videos will be developed for **F.A.P.,** as well as a student Telecourse Guide and additional Web support. Consult your Irwin/McGraw-Hill representative for more details.

Videos

Lecture Enhancement Video Series. These short, action-oriented videos provide the impetus for lively classroom discussion. There are separate *Financial Accounting* and *Managerial Accounting* libraries.

Student Software CD

Achievement Tests

Student

Working Papers

These new volumes are prepared by John J. Wild to match end-of-chapter assignment material. They include papers that can be used to solve all quick studies, exercises, serial problems, comprehensive problems, and Beyond the Numbers activities. Each chapter contains one set of papers that can be used for either the problems or the alternate problems.

Study Guide

By Barbara Chiappetta, Nassau Community College, and Jeannie Folk, College of DuPage. For each chapter and appendix, these guides review the learning objectives and the summaries, outline the chapter, and provide a variety of practice problems and solutions. Several chapters also contain visuals to illustrate key chapter concepts.

Student Learning Tools

Written by Barbara Chiappetta, this supplement contains material for creating an active learning environment in the classroom. Class activities, writing assignments, and team presentation assignments are provided; suggestions for their implementation and evaluation are provided in the accompanying instructor's manual. Accounting working papers are also provided for duplication.

Ready Notes

These note-taking tools contain printouts of the text-specific Ready Shows (PowerPoint®) presentation screens.

Software CD-ROM

Five pieces of software on one CD-ROM enable students to practice accounting applications such as journal entries and spreadsheets as well as take a self-test on text vocabulary, procedures, and concepts.

GLAS (General Ledger Applications Software) by Jack E. Terry, ComSource Associates, Inc.

SPATS (Spreadsheet Applications Template Software) by Jack E. Terry, ComSource Associates, Inc.

Peachtree Problems by Jack E. Terry, ComSource Associates, Inc.

Tutorial Software by Leland Mansuetti and Keith Weidkamp, Sierra College

Essentials of Financial Accounting: A Multimedia Approach

Manual Practice Sets

FastMart, Inc.

Republic Lighting Company

Republic Lighting Company, Extended Version

Cogg Hill Camping Equipment

Freewheel Corporation, Inc.

KJC Manufacturing Company, Inc.

Computerized Practice Sets

From Leland Mansuetti and Keith Weidkamp, both of Sierra College

Business Simulations for Microsoft® Windows®

Granite Bay Jet Ski, Level 1

Granite Bay Jet Ski, Level 2

Wheels Exquisite, Inc., Level 1

Practice Set for Microsoft® Windows® by Donald V. Saftner, University of Toledo *and* Rosalind Cranor, Virginia Polytechnic Institute and State University.

Acknowledgments

We are thankful for the encouragement, suggestions, and counsel provided by the many instructors, professionals, and students in preparing the 15th edition. This new edition reflects the pedagogical needs and innovative ideas of both instructors and students of accounting principles. It has been a team effort and we recognize the contributions of many individuals. We especially thank and recognize those individuals who provided valuable comments and suggestions to further improve this edition, including:

Patricia Ayres	*Arapahoe Community College*
Russell Baker	*Florida Metropolitan University*
Bill Barribeau	*Fox Valley Technical College*
Abdul Baten	*North Virginia Community College—Manassas*
Irene Bembenista	*Davenport College*
Judy Benish	*Fox Valley Technical College*
James Beisel	*Longview Community College*
Stuart Brown	*Bristol Community College*
Ed Browning	*Northwest Missouri State University*
Jo Ann Buchmann	*Rockland Community College*
Don Bush	*Regis University*
Howard Clampman	*Bronx Community College*
Ronald Clute	*Metropolitan State College of Denver*
Robert Coburn	*Franklin Pierce College*
Kenneth Coffey	*Johnson County Community College*
Jim Crowther	*Kirkwood Community College*
Lyle Dehning	*Metropolitan State College of Denver*
Paul Donohue	*Delaware County Community College*
Thomas Edmonds	*Regis University*
Brad Farr	*Arapahoe Community College*
Thomas Franco	*Wayne County Community College*
Linda Frye	*Northwest Missouri State University*
John Gorham	*Bronx Community College*
Jerry C.Y. Han	*SUNY—Buffalo*
David Hancock	*Northwest Missouri State University*
Sara Harris	*Arapahoe Community College*
Ken Kettelhohn	*Milwaukee Area Technical College*
Shirley Kleiner	*Johnson County Community College*
Judy Korb	*Johnson County Community College*
Frank Korman	*Dallas Community College District*
Charles Lacey	*Henry Ford Community College*
John Lacey	*Montgomery County Community College*
Bruce Leauby	*La Salle University*
Tuan Luong	*Northern Virginia Community College—Woodbridge*
Florence McGovern	*Bergen County College*
Rosalie Morgan	*Delaware County Community College*
Ali Naggar	*West Chester University*
Don Noseworthy	*Hesser College*
Lynn Pape	*Northwest Virginia Community College*
Sam Pedregon	*Pueblo Community College*
Clarence Perkins	*Bronx Community College*
Ann Price	*Shepherd College*
Tae Ryu	*Metropolitan State College*
Mary Scott	*Northwest Missouri State University*
Carl Smith	*West Chester University*
Dennis Smith	*Consumnes River College*
Thomas Szczurek	*Delaware County Community College*
Jim Thomas	*Consumnes River College*
Tom Thompson	*Madison Area Technical College*
Marilyn Uecker	*Fox Valley Technical College*
Martin E. Ward	*DeVry Institute of Technology*
Henry Weiman	*Bronx Community College*
Kenneth L. Wild	*University of London*
Rahnl Wood	*Northwest Missouri State University*
Orville Wright	*Morgan State University*
Mike Zematis	*Davenport College*

We also wish to thank our accuracy checkers, Barbara Schnathorst of The Write Solution Inc. and Marilyn Sagrillo of the University of Wisconsin—Green Bay, and also our supplement proofreader, Kalista A. Johnston of Nash KalistaAnn Graphics Inc.

Kermit D. Larson
John J. Wild
Barbara Chiappetta

Contents in Brief

Contents

Accounting in the Information Age

A Look at This Chapter

Accounting plays a crucial role in the information age. In this chapter, we discuss the importance of accounting to different types of organizations and describe its many users and uses. We see that ethics and social responsibility are crucial to accounting, and that the information age provides many new accounting opportunities.

A Look Ahead

While Chapter 1 presents an overview of accounting, Chapter 2 introduces financial statements and the principles underlying them. Chapter 2 also describes and analyzes business transactions. Chapters 2 through 5 emphasize the accounting cycle and show how financial statements capture transactions and events. Many important financial and managerial accounting topics are examined throughout the book.

Chapter Outline

Winning at Giving

PITTSBURGH, PA—Just a few years ago, Stephanie Williams was working as a salesclerk, but spent much of her time dreaming about getting a degree and a better job. In September of that year, her dreams came true. She quit her job and returned to college. Yet no one would have predicted that Williams, now 25, would soon be living the American Dream.

Williams signed up for her first accounting course with no idea of what to expect. "I took accounting because people I trusted said it would be useful," says Williams. "What I got in return was a career, lots of friends, and a partner!" Her accounting course included a community service requirement. Students had to pair up and help less advantaged individuals.

My partner, Brett Fulwood, and I volunteered our services to a senior citizens community." Williams and Fulwood never looked back. On their first visit, Williams says they helped more than a dozen seniors, fielding questions on reading bank statements, interpreting pension checks, and analyzing financial reports of companies in which a few had invested their modest savings. "It was great," says Williams. "I saw the relevance of accounting and I was able to give something to others."

In the weeks that followed, Williams and Fulwood answered several follow-up questions. "We even got a call from a woman's nephew in Harrisburg asking if we could help with recordkeeping in the family trucking business," says Williams. "He offered to pay us a decent fee if we'd do it," added Fulwood. "That's when we knew we were onto something."

Today, Williams and Fulwood are running their own business, **W&F Financial Services.** "We still visit with seniors on the second Saturday of every month with free financial advice," says Williams. "It's the most rewarding work I do."

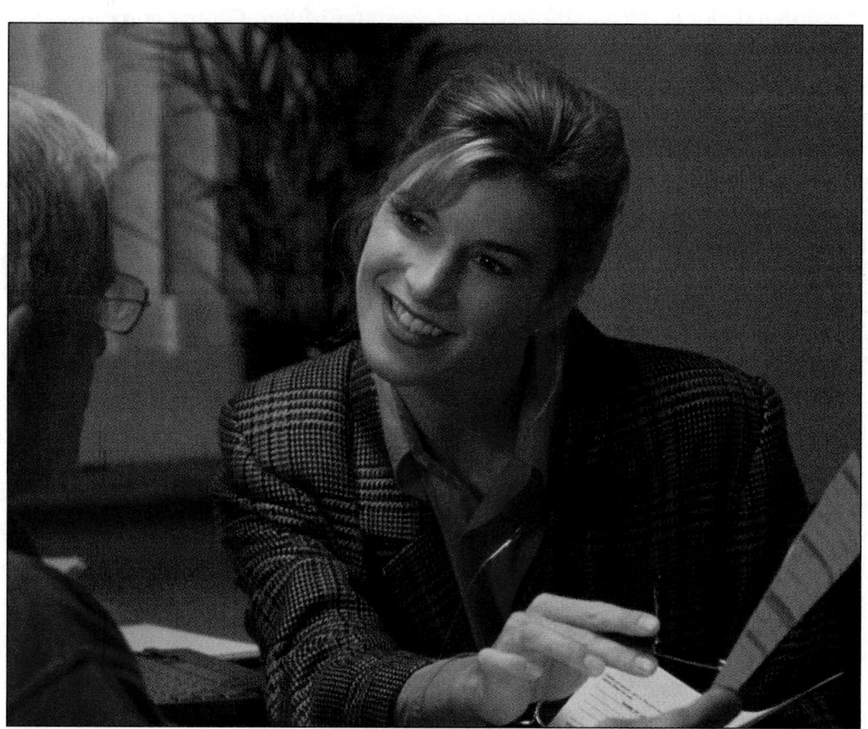

Learning Objectives

Conceptual

C1 Explain the aim and power of accounting in the information age.

C2 Identify forms of organization and their characteristics.

C3 Identify and describe the three major activities in organizations.

C4 Identify users and uses of accounting.

C5 Explain why ethics and social responsibility are crucial to accounting.

C6 Identify opportunities in accounting and related fields.

Analytical

A1 Describe profit and its two major components.

A2 Explain the relation between return and risk.

A3 Explain and interpret the accounting equation.

A4 Compute and interpret return on investment.

CHAPTER PREVIEW

Accounting in the information age is about people like Stephanie Williams and Brett Fulwood. Today's world is one of information—its preparation, communication, analysis, and use. Accounting is at the heart of the information age. Knowledge of accounting gives us opportunities and the insight to benefit from them. By studying this course and this book, you will learn about many concepts, procedures, and analyses that are useful in our everyday lives. This knowledge reduces our reliance on hunches, guesses, and intuition and, in turn, improves decision making.

In this chapter we describe accounting in the information age, the users and uses of accounting information, the forms and activities of organizations, and the importance of ethics and social responsibility. We also explain several important accounting concepts, procedures, and analyses. This chapter provides a foundation for those who have little or no understanding of business. Chapter 2 will build on this foundation when we consider transactions and financial statements.

Living in the Information Age

We live in the **information age**—a time of communication, data, news, facts, access, and commentary. The information age encourages timeliness, independence, and freedom of expression. Access to and understanding of information affect how we live, whom we associate with, and the opportunities we have. We use information to pick and choose among products and services like cars, bikes, clothes, computers, hotels, and restaurants. We pay people to analyze information for us. Examples are product rankings (*Consumer Reports*), medicinal advice (*American Medical Association*), and credit rating (*Standard & Poor's*).

Communication with and access to data are a major part of the information age and make up much of the *information superhighway*. The information superhighway has redefined communication, especially business communication. Global computer networks and telecommunications equipment allow us access to all types of business information. As it did for Stephanie Williams and Brett Fulwood (mentioned in the opening article), information provides us with powerful tools and opportunities. To take advantage of these, we need knowledge of the information system.

An information system is the collecting, processing, and reporting of information to decision makers. Knowing the information system means personal opportunities and real increases in pay. Two-year degree graduates with this knowledge can make upwards of 20 to 30 percent more than high school graduates, and bachelor degree graduates can make at least 55 percent more than high school graduates.[1] This added pay is due to an ability to understand and process information. Understanding and processing information is the core of accounting.

To get the most from our education and opportunities in life, we must know accounting. Your instructor will provide you with many assignments from this book and related materials to help you master accounting. We also encourage you to join us on the information superhighway to explore the opportunities awaiting you. For your help, we devote an entire Web site solely for your use and enjoyment with this book. You can access this site at **[www.mhhe.com/business/accounting/fap].** The time and effort you spend in this course will repay you many times over.

Power of Accounting

C1 Explain the aim and power of accounting in the information age

One of the most important roles of the information superhighway is the reporting of business activities. Providing information about what businesses own, what they owe, and how they perform is the aim of accounting. **Accounting** is an information and mea-

[1] "The Diploma Dividend," *Washington Post,* July 22, 1994, p. D1.

surement system that identifies, records, and communicates relevant, reliable, and comparable information about an organization's economic activities. It helps people make better decisions, including assessing opportunities, products, investments, and social and community responsibilities. Opportunities abound and accounting opens our eyes to new and exciting possibilities.

Completing this course can be one of your most important learning experiences. It will help you apply information in a way you can use in your everyday life. The use of information is not limited to accountants or even to people in business. Often the greatest benefits from understanding accounting come to those outside of accounting and business. We can use accounting to get a loan for a house or to start a business. We can use accounting to make better investment decisions. We are able to use accounting knowledge wherever we go and in whatever career we choose.

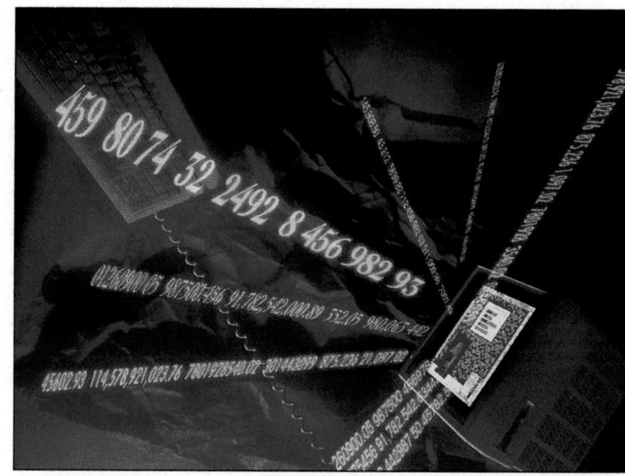

The World Wide Web is a part of our lives. This book is supported by a website homepage to help you in your studies.

Business and Investment

A1 Describe profit and its two major components.

A **business** is one or more individuals selling products or services for profit. Products such as athletic apparel **(NIKE, Reebok, Converse),** computers **(Packard-Bell, Hewlett-Packard, Apple)** and clothing (Levis, REI, GAP) are part of our lives. Services like information communication **(America Online, CompuServe, Prodigy, Microsoft),** dining **(McDonald's, Burger King, Wendy's),** and car rental **(Hertz, Budget, Alamo)** make our lives easier. A business can be as small as an in-home child care service or as massive as **Wal-Mart.** Nearly 1 million new businesses are started in the United States each year, no different than **W&S Financial Services** in the opening article. Most of these are started by people who want freedom from ordinary jobs, a new challenge in life, or the advantage of extra money.

Business Profit

A common feature of all businesses is the desire for profit. **Profit,** also called **net income** or **earnings,** is the amount a business earns after subtracting all expenses related to its sales. **Sales,** also called **revenues,** are the amounts earned from selling products and services. **Expenses** are the costs incurred with sales. For **W&F Financial Services,** profit is the amount earned from consulting with clients less expenses such as travel, meals, advertising, and promotion. Not all businesses make profits. A **loss** arises when expenses are more than sales. Many new businesses incur losses in their first several months or years of business. Yet no business can continually experience losses and stay in business.

Let's look at **NIKE**'s profit breakdown in Exhibit 1.1. If we pay $100 for a pair of **NIKE** athletic footwear, $8.66 is profit to **NIKE.** The rest goes to cover expenses such as materials and labor ($53.51) and advertising ($10.65). **NIKE** also pays $5.43 per pair in total taxes. One question confronting our society today is what is the "right" amount of profit. Should business pay more for charitable giving or community services? Are taxes too high or too low? For us to even begin to consider important questions like these we must understand accounting.

Exhibit 1.1

Where Our Money Goes When Buying a Pair of NIKEs

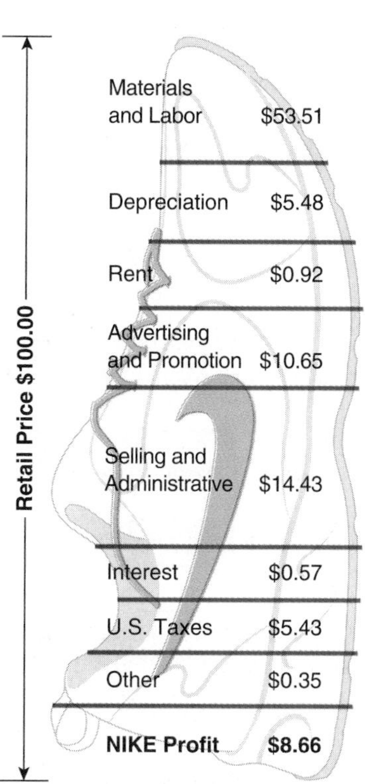

Return and Risk

Profit is often linked to **return.** The term *return* derives from the idea of getting something back from an investment, or return on investment. **Return on investment** is often stated in ratio form as profit divided by amount invested. For example, banks or savings and loans often report our return from a savings account in the form of an interest rate of return on investment. For example, we might have a 4% savings account or invest our college money in an 8% money market fund.

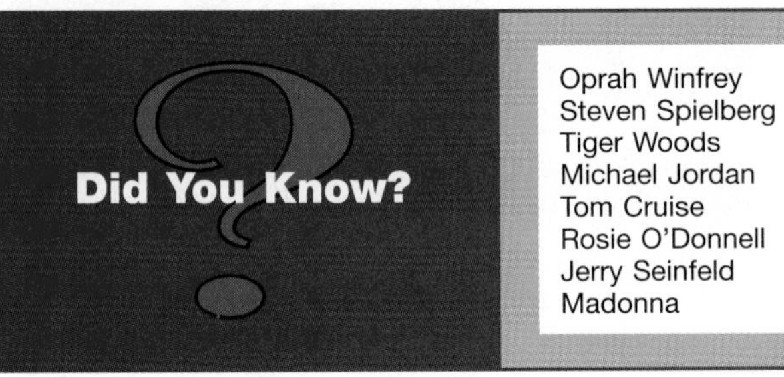

Oprah Winfrey	27%
Steven Spielberg	19
Tiger Woods	15
Michael Jordan	14
Tom Cruise	8
Rosie O'Donnell	5
Jerry Seinfeld	4
Madonna	2

Celebrity Investment
How do fame and fortune translate into return and risk? A poll asked people which celebrity is the best investment. Similar to business investments, people named relatively young performers with years of earning power ahead. Oprah came out on top with high return and low risk. Source: *Business Week,* March 24, 1997.

Did You Know is a feature that extends throughout the book. This feature highlights important and interesting cases from practice.

A2 Explain the relation between return and risk.

We can invest our money in many ways. If we invest it in a savings account or in U.S. government treasury bills, we get a return of around 3% to 7%. We could also invest in a company's stock, or even start our own business like Williams and Fulwood. How do we decide among these investment options? Our answer rests on the trade-off between return and risk.

Risk is the amount of uncertainty about the return we expect to earn. All business decisions involve risk. But some decisions involve more risk than others. The lower the risk of an investment, the lower is our expected return. The reason why savings accounts pay such a low return is the low risk of our not being repaid with interest. The government guarantees most savings accounts from default. Also, U.S. government bonds pay a low return because of the low risk of the U.S. government's defaulting on its payments. But if we buy a share of NIKE or any other company, there is no guarantee of any return. There is even the risk of loss.

The bar graph in Exhibit 1.2 shows returns for bonds with different risks. **Bonds** are written promises by organizations to repay amounts loaned with interest. U.S. treasury bonds provide us a low expected return of 6.49%, but they also offer low risk since they are backed by the U.S. government. High-risk corporate bonds offer a much larger expected return (8.52%) but with much greater risk.

The trade-off between return and risk is a normal part of business. Higher risk implies higher, but more risky, expected returns. To help us make better business decisions,

Returns for Bonds with Different Risks

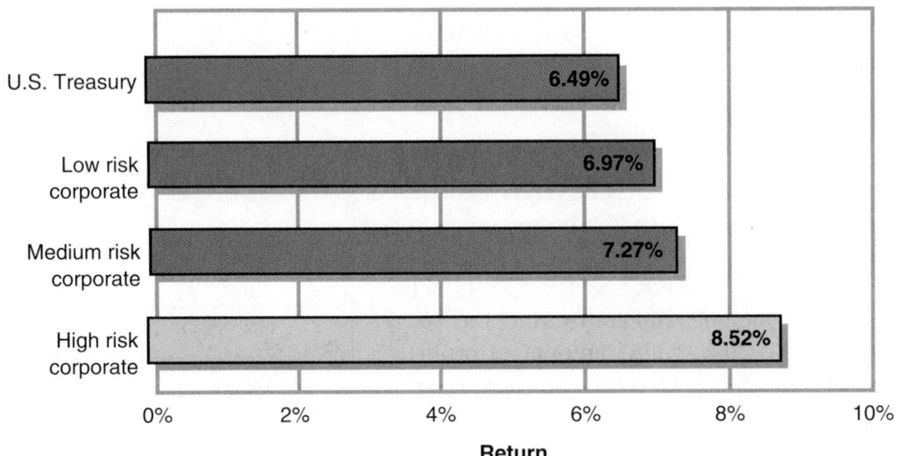

Source: *The Wall Street Journal,* August 4, 1997.

we use accounting information in measuring both return and risk. We decide on our desired level of return and risk and use accounting information to help achieve it.

Answer—p. 27

Programmer
You are considering two job offers. Both require your computer programming skills. One is with a new start-up Internet provider at an annual salary of $31,000; the other is with an established medical supply company for $25,500 a year. Which offer do you accept? *[Note: Guidance answers to "You Make the Call" are at the end of chapter.]*

"You Make the Call" are role-playing exercises extending throughout the book. These exercises stress the relevance of accounting for people in and outside of business.

Accounting Information

Factors of production are the means businesses use to make profit. *Land, labor,* and *plant and equipment* are the traditional factors of production. Today's information age suggests we add accounting information to these traditional factors of production. Accounting information gives us knowledge to make better decisions, and good decision making is key to business success.

If we analyze recent business performance, we see it is not the traditional factors driving success. For example, we see **GTE** with its factors of production worth well over $40 billion reporting a recent loss of more than $2 billion. We see **Kmart,** which employs more than 250,000 employees, reporting a recent loss of $571 million. Other giants like **IBM, Woolworth,** and **Tandy** struggle to consistently yield a 5% or 10% return on investment. Yet smaller companies like **GAP, NIKE,** and **Mattel** consistently yield a 15% or greater return on investment. The common denominator in the success stories is relevant and reliable information.

Focus of Accounting

We need to guard against a narrow view of accounting. Accounting affects many parts of our lives and is crucial to modern society. Our most obvious contact with accounting is through credit approvals, checking accounts, tax forms, and payroll. Yet these experiences are limited and tend to focus on the recordkeeping parts of accounting. **Recordkeeping** or **bookkeeping,** is the recording of financial transactions and events, either manually or electronically. While recordkeeping is essential to data reliability in our information age, accounting is this and much more.

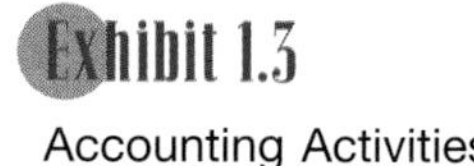
Exhibit 1.3
Accounting Activities

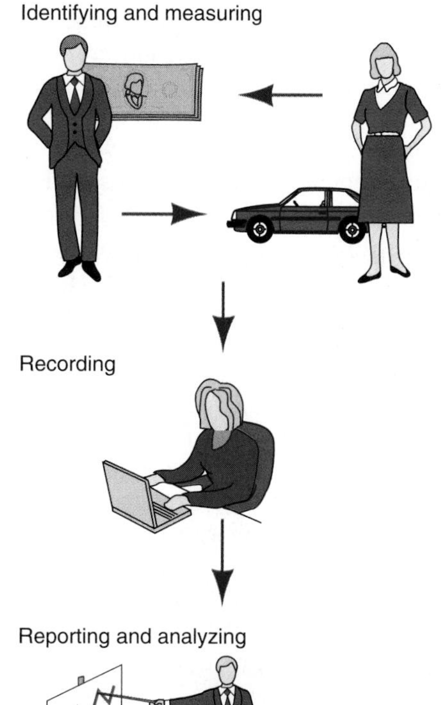

The primary objective of accounting is to provide useful information for decision making as shown in Exhibit 1.3. Accounting activities include identifying, measuring, recording, reporting, and analyzing economic events and transactions. They also involve interpreting information and designing information systems to provide useful reports that monitor and control an organization's activities. Whatever our career path, accounting is part of it. We benefit by understanding how accounting information is prepared and used. To gain this understanding, we need to know certain recordkeeping skills. This book provides opportunities for you to learn these skills. This knowledge helps us read and interpret financial data. Our opportunities are greater if we understand accounting and are able to use information effectively.

Accounting and Technology

Technology is a key part of our modern society and business practices. It also plays a major role in accounting. Computing technology reduces the time, effort, and cost of recordkeeping while improving clerical accuracy. While some smaller organizations continue to perform various accounting tasks manually, they are still impacted by information technology.

As technology has changed the way we store, process, and summarize large masses of data, accounting has been freed to expand its field. Major consulting, planning, and other financial services are quickly becoming part of accounting. Now more than ever we need people who can quickly sort through masses of data, interpret their meaning, identify key factors, and analyze their implications.

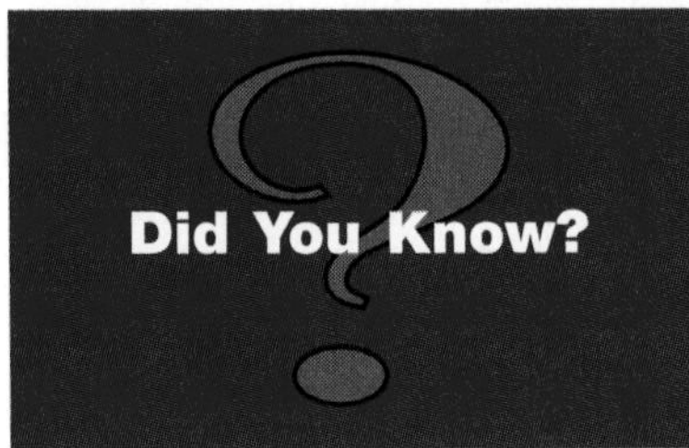

Accounting Web

Technology is changing the face of business and accounting. Many organizations maintain their own Web pages that include substantial accounting information. You might want to visit **NIKE**'s **(www.nike.com)** or **Reebok**'s **(www.reebok.com)** Web site to see for yourself. You can also search the SEC's on-line database called **EDGAR (www.sec.gov).** EDGAR has accounting information for thousands of companies.

Setting Accounting Rules

There are rules for reporting on an organization's performance and current condition. These rules increase the usefulness of reports, including their reliability and comparability. The rules that make up acceptable accounting practices are determined by many individuals and groups and are referred to as **generally accepted accounting principles,** or **GAAP.** Since accounting is a service activity, these rules reflect our society's needs and not those of accountants or any other single constituency. This is reinforced by the federal government, which regulates organizations that sell shares of ownership to the public. The **Securities and Exchange Commission** (**SEC**) is charged by Congress with the authority to set reporting rules for these organizations. For the most part, the SEC passes authority to set accounting rules to professionals in practice.

The **Financial Accounting Standards Board** (**FASB**) is currently responsible for setting accounting rules. The FASB is an independent group of seven full-time members with a large staff. It has issued six statements of accounting concepts to help guide accounting standard setting. Many interested groups and individuals involve themselves in setting accounting rules and lobby the FASB in their self-interests. They include unions, investors, government agencies, lenders, politicians, and other business and nonbusiness organizations. Individuals and leaders in these organizations must understand accounting information and any proposed rules to chart and defend a position in their best interests. The **American Institute of Certified Public Accountants** (**AICPA**)**,** the largest and most influential national professional organization of certified public accountants, is especially active in the process of setting accounting rules.

Flashbacks *give you a chance to stop and reflect on key points in the book. Guidance answers to* Flashbacks *are given at the end of the chapter.*

Flash back

1. What is the aim of accounting?
2. Describe profit, sales, and expenses.
3. Explain the trade-off between return and risk.
4. What is the relation between accounting and recordkeeping?
5. Who sets accounting rules?

Answers—p. 27

Exhibit 1.4

Forms of Organizations

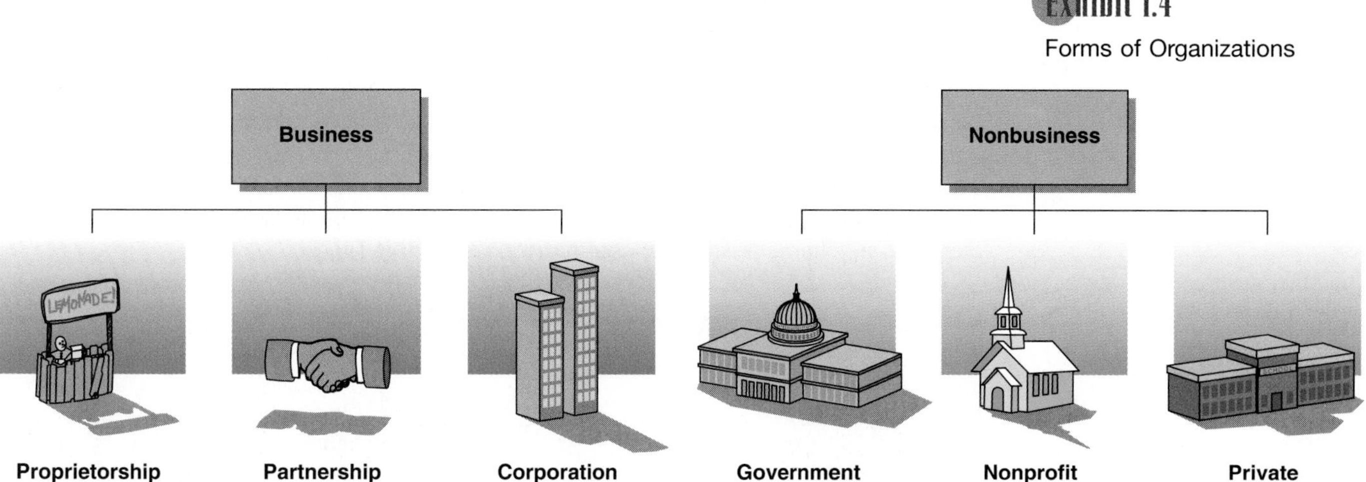

Forms of Organization

C2 Identify forms of organization and their characteristics.

Organizations can be classified as either business or nonbusiness as shown in Exhibit 1.4. Typically, businesses are organized for profit, while nonbusinesses serve us in ways not always measured by profit.

Most organizations engage in economic activities. These can include the usual business activities of purchasing materials and labor and of selling products and services. They can also involve nonbusiness activities like collecting money through taxes, dues, contributions, investments, or borrowings. A common feature in all these organizations is the power and use of accounting.

Business Organization

A business is organized and operated to make a profit. Because of this, a business is often called a *profit-oriented organization.* A principle that must be followed in accounting for organizations is the **business entity principle.** This principle means every organization is accounted for separately from its owner's personal activities. It also means that a set of accounting records and reports refer only to the transactions and events of that one organization. We will discuss this and other important accounting principles in the next chapter.

Businesses take one of three legal forms: a *sole proprietorship*, a *partnership,* or a *corporation*. Exhibit 1.5 gives us the proportion and revenues from these different organization forms.

Exhibit 1.5

Different Business Organizations and Their Revenues

Forms of businesses

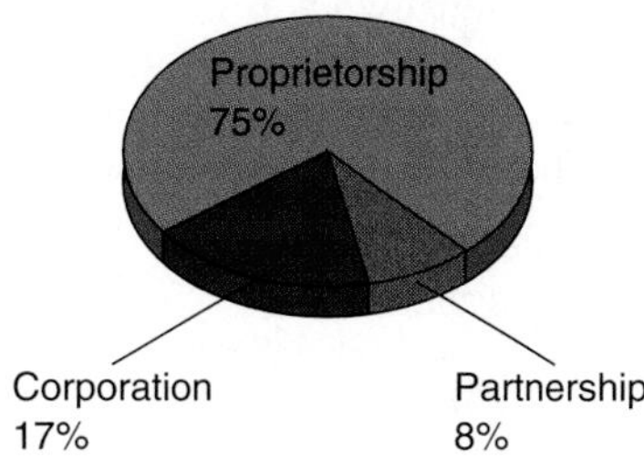

Source: *Statistical Abstract of the United States,* U.S. Bureau of the Census

Revenues of businesses

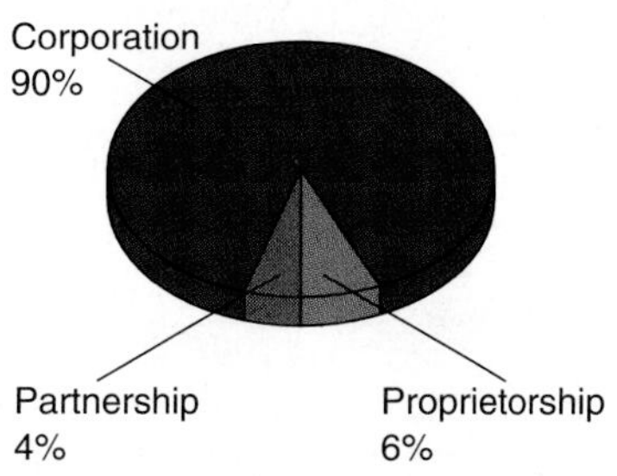

Source: *Statistical Abstract of the United States,* U.S. Bureau of the Census

Sole Proprietorship

A **sole proprietorship,** or **single proprietorship,** is a business owned by one person. No special legal requirements must be met to start a sole proprietorship. While it is a separate entity for accounting purposes, it is *not* a separate legal entity from its owner. This means, for example, a court can order an owner to sell personal belongings to pay a proprietorship's debt. An owner is even responsible for debts that exceed an owner's net investment in the proprietorship. This *unlimited liability* of a proprietorship is sometimes a disadvantage.

Tax authorities do not separate a proprietorship from its owner. This means the profits of a proprietorship are not subject to a business income tax, but must be reported and taxed on the owner's personal income tax return. The rate of tax on a proprietorship's income depends on the level of total income from all sources that the owner had for the year. Small retail stores and service businesses often are organized as proprietorships. Sole proprietorships are by far the most common form of business organization in our society and its characteristics are summarized in Exhibit 1.6.

Exhibit 1.6

Characteristics of Business Organizations

	Proprietorship	Partnership	Corporation
Business entity	yes	yes	yes
Legal entity	no	no	yes
Limited liability	no	no	yes
Unlimited life	no	no	yes
Business taxed	no	no	yes
One owner allowed	yes	no	yes

Partnership

A **partnership** is a business owned by two or more people, called *partners*. Like a proprietorship, no special legal requirements must be met in starting a partnership. All that is required is an agreement between partners to run a business together. The agreement can be either oral or written and usually indicates how profits and losses are shared. A written agreement is preferred as it can help partners avoid or resolve disputes. A partnership, like a proprietorship, is *not* legally separate from its owners. This means that each partner's share of profits is reported and taxed on that partner's tax return. It also means *unlimited liability* for its partners.

There are two types of partnerships that limit liability. A *limited partnership* includes a general partner(s) with unlimited liability and a limited partner(s) with liability restricted to the amount invested. A *limited liability partnership* restricts partners' liabilities to their own acts and the acts of individuals under their control. This protects an innocent partner from the negligence of another partner. Yet all partners remain responsible for partnership debts. There are about one-tenth as many partnerships as proprietorships. **NIKE** began as a partnership and was originally called **Blue Ribbon Sports.** The partners, Philip Knight and Bill Bowerman, each contributed $500 and shipped shoes out of Knight's basement.

Corporation

A **corporation** is a business legally separate from its owners. This means a corporation is responsible for its own acts and its own debts. It can enter into its own contracts, and it can buy, own, and sell property. It can also sue and be sued. Separate legal status means a corporation can conduct business with the rights, duties, and responsibilities of a person. A corporation acts through its managers, who are its legal agents. Separate legal status also means its owners, who are called *shareholders,* are not personally liable for corporate acts and debts. Shareholders are legally distinct from the business and their loss is limited to their net investment in shares purchased. This limited liability is a key to why corporations can raise resources from shareholders who are not active in managing the business. It also encourages more risky investment with higher expected returns.

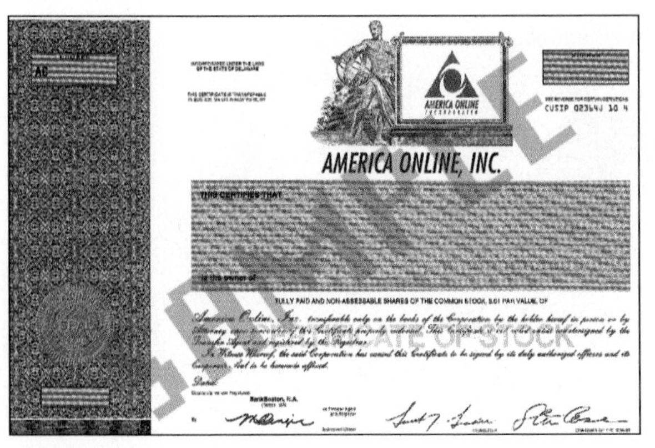

A corporation is legally chartered (*incorporated*) under state or federal law. Separate legal status results in a corporation having unlimited life. Ownership, or *equity*, of all corporations is divided into units called **shares** or **stock.** Owners of shares are called **shareholders** or **stock-**

holders. A shareholder can sell or transfer shares to another person without affecting the operations of a corporation. When a corporation issues only one class of stock, we call it **common stock,** or *capital stock.*

A corporation is subject to *double taxation.* This means a corporation is taxed on its net income. Any distribution of corporate earnings to its owners is also taxed as part of their personal income. An exception to this is an S corporation. An *S corporation* is a corporation with certain characteristics that give it special tax status.[2] This special tax status removes its double taxation. Instead, shareholders of S corporations report their share of corporate income or loss as part of their personal income.[3]

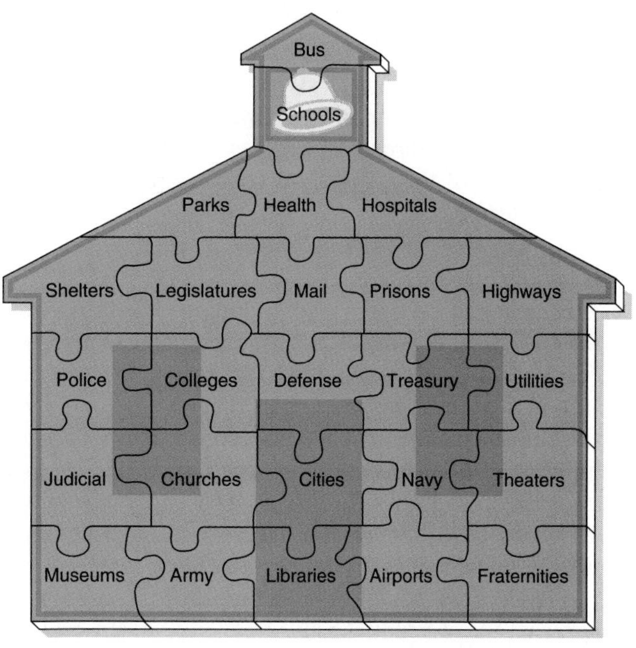

Exhibit 1.7

Partial List of Nonbusinesses

Nonbusiness Organization

Nonbusiness organizations plan and operate for goals other than profit. These goals often are met by government or nonprofit organizations and include security, health, education, transportation, judicial, and religious services and cultural and social activities. Examples are public schools meeting the needs of citizens and community care groups meeting the needs of the poor.

Nonbusiness organizations lack an identifiable owner. Still the demand for accounting information in nonbusiness organizations is high because they are accountable to their sponsors. Governments need to report receipts and expenditures of tax money, and colleges need to explain tuition increases. These organizations are accountable to taxpayers, donors, lenders, legislators, regulators, or other constituents. Accounting for these organizations is usually a *fund-based* system, but the basic principles are similar to accounting for business organizations.

Exhibit 1.7 lists a wide range of nonbusiness organizations affected by the power of accounting. This list is but a sampling of the roughly one-third of U.S. economic activity done by nonbusiness organizations. Some of these organizations, such as hospitals, are often run as private, nonprofit, or government operations. In all of these organizations, accounting captures key information about their activities.

Entrepreneur

You and a friend develop a new design for mountain bikes that improves speed and performance by 25% to 40%. You plan to form a small business to manufacture and market these bikes. You and your friend want to minimize taxes, but your prime concern is potential lawsuits from individuals who will "push the limit" on these bikes and be injured. What form of organization do you set up?

Answer—p. 27

[2] The required characteristics are listed in the *Internal Revenue Code.* These characteristics include: no more than 75 shareholders (not counting spouses), only one class of stock, and all shareholders are U.S. citizens or residents.

[3] A *limited liability company* (or LLC) is a new alternative form of business organization. It offers the limited liability of a corporation and the tax treatment of a partnership (or proprietorship).

Activities in Organizations

C3 Identify and describe the three major activities in organizations.

Organizations carry out their activities in many different ways. These differences extend to their products, services, goals, organization form, management style, worker compensation, and community giving. Yet the major activities of organizations are similar. We discuss the three major types of business activities: financing, investing, and operating. Each of these activities requires planning.

Planning

All organizations begin with planning. **Planning** involves defining the ideas, goals, and actions of an organization. Strategies and tactics need to be laid out. Employees must be informed and motivated. Managers must be credible and display leadership and vision. All of these tasks are part of planning and are the duty of *executive management.* Executive management sets the organization's strategic goals and policies that are captured in an *organization plan.* The owner or owners take on this duty in most organizations. Responsibility for this duty often carries with it the title of president, chief executive officer, or chairman of the board of directors. In nonprofit organizations the title for top managers is often executive director.

Planning assists an organization in focusing its efforts and identifying opportunities. External users benefit from knowledge of an organization's plans. They look for clues on tactics, market demands, competitors, promotion, pricing, innovations, and projections. Much of this information, both for internal and external users, is provided in accounting reports. **NIKE** (and most other public corporations) uses the Management Discussion and Analysis section in its annual report for this purpose:

> the Company is positioning itself to continue to expand markets and gain market share on a worldwide basis . . . The Company intends to continue to invest in growth opportunities and worldwide marketing and advertising in order to ensure the successful sell-through of the high level of orders.

It is important to remember that planning involves change and reaction to it. It is not cast in stone. This adds *risk* to both the development and analysis of an organization's plans. Accounting information can reduce this risk through more informed and better decision making. Both internal and external accounting reports affect the plans, decisions, and actions of management.

Financing

An organization requires financing to begin and operate according to its plans. **Financing activities** are the means organizations use to pay for resources like land, buildings, and machines to carry out plans. Organizations are careful in acquiring and managing financing activities because of their potential to determine success or failure.

There are two main sources of financing: owner and nonowner. *Owner financing* refers to resources contributed by the owner and any profits that the owner chooses to leave in the organization. *Nonowner* (or *creditor*) *financing* refers to resources contributed by creditors (lenders) that are called liabilities. Creditors can include banks, savings and loans, and other financial institutions. *Financial management* is the task of planning how to obtain these resources and to set the right mix between the amounts of owner and creditor financing. Government organizations can also acquire resources with taxes and fees, and nonprofit organizations can acquire resources from contributions by donors. **NIKE**'s total 1997 financing equaled \$5,361 (in millions). It comprised \$3,156 in owner financing and \$2,205 in creditor financing.

Investing

Investing activities are the acquiring and disposing of resources (assets) that an organization uses to sell its products or services. These assets are funded by an organization's financing. **Assets** are economic resources that are expected to produce future benefits. They include land, buildings, equipment, inventories, supplies, cash, and all investments needed for operating an organization. **NIKE**'s 1997 assets totaled $5,361 (in millions). Organizations differ on the amount and makeup of their assets. Some organizations require land and factories to operate. Others might only need an office. Determining the amount and type of assets for organizations to operate is called *asset management.*

It is important to see that an organization's investing and financing totals are *always* equal. Invested amounts are referred to as *assets,* and financing is made up of creditor and owner financing. Creditors and owners hold claims, or rights, in assets. Creditors' claims are called **liabilities** and the owner's claim is called **owner's equity** (or simply *equity*). This equality can be written as:

Assets = Liabilities + Equity

A3 Explain and interpret the accounting equation.

This equality is called the **accounting equation. NIKE**'s 1997 assets of $5,361 equaled its liabilities of $2,205 plus its owner's equity of $3,156 (in millions):

Assets = Liabilities + Equity
$5,361 = $2,205 + $3,156

The accounting equation works for all organizations. It is an important part of accounting. We will return to and use the accounting equation in our analysis of transactions in the next several chapters.

Operating

An organization's main purpose is operating activities. **Operating activities** are the carrying out of an organization's plans and involve using assets to research, develop, purchase, produce, distribute, and market products and services. They include management activities like worker supervision and compliance with laws. Operating activities aim at selling the organization's products and services. Sales and revenues are the inflow of assets from selling products and services. Costs and expenses are the outflow of assets necessary to support operating activities. Examples of costs and expenses are salaries, rent, electricity, and supplies. *Strategic management* is the process of determining the right mix of operating activities for the type of organization, its plans, and its market. How well the organization carries out its operating activities determines its success and return.

Exhibit 1.8 summarizes these activities. Planning is part of every activity and is the common link between activities. Planning gives the activities meaning and focus. Investing (assets) and financing (liabilities and equity) are set opposite each other to stress their balance. Operating activities are shown below investing and financing activities. This is to emphasize that operating activities are the result of investing and financing. Financing, investing, and operating activities and the planning involved in all three are constantly changing to reflect the actions of an organization.

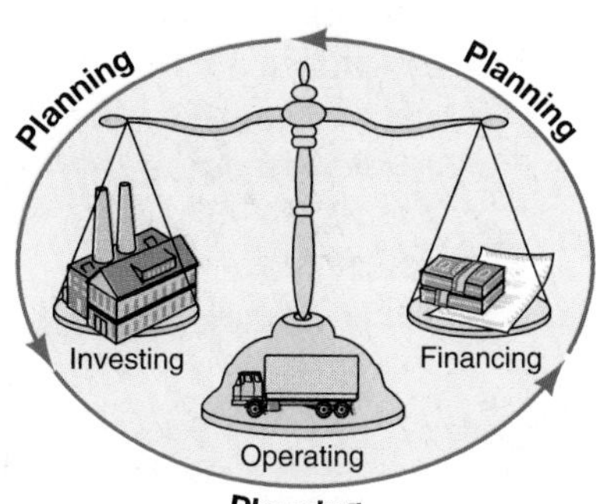

Exhibit 1.8
Activities in Organizations

Flash *back*

6. What are the three common forms of business organizations?
7. Can you identify examples of nonbusiness organizations?
8. What are the three major activities in organizations?

Answers—p. 28

Users of Accounting Information

C4 Identify users and uses of accounting.

Organizations set up accounting information systems to help them and others make better decisions. Every organization uses some type of information system to report on its activities. The accounting information system is a service activity as shown in Exhibit 1.9. It serves the information needs of many kinds of users (or stakeholders) including managers, lenders, suppliers, customers, directors, auditors, employees, and current and potential investors. Knowledge of accounting improves their decisions.

External Information Users

External users of accounting information are *not* directly involved in running the organization. They include shareholders, lenders, directors, customers, suppliers, regulators, lawyers, brokers, and the press. Yet these users are affected by, and sometimes affect, the organization. External users rely on accounting information to make better decisions in pursuing their goals. For example, lenders are less likely to make bad loans or shareholders bad investments when they know current and past profits of a business.

Financial accounting is the area of accounting aimed at serving external users. Its primary objective is to provide external reports called financial statements to help users analyze an organization's activities. External users have limited access to an organization's valuable information. Their own success depends on getting external reports that are reliable, relevant, and comparable. Some governmental and regulatory agencies have the power to get reports in specific forms. But most external users must rely on *general-purpose financial statements*. The term *general-purpose* refers to the broad range of purposes for which external users rely on these statements. Generally accepted accounting principles are important in increasing the usefulness of financial statements to users. We discuss these principles along with financial statements in the next chapter.

Each external user has special information needs depending on the kinds of decisions one must make. These decisions involve getting answers to key questions, answers that are often available in accounting reports. This section describes several external users and questions they confront. Your accounting course will provide you many insights into where answers can be found.

Exhibit 1.9

Users of Accounting Information

Internal users

- Managers
- Officers
- Internal auditors
- Sales managers
- Budget officers
- Controller

External users

- Lenders
- Shareholders
- Government
- Labor unions
- External auditors
- Customers

Lenders (Creditors)

Lenders loan money or other resources to an organization. Lenders include banks, savings and loans, co-ops, and mortgage and finance companies. Lenders look for information to help them assess whether an organization is likely to repay its loan with interest. External reports help them answer questions about organizations such as:

- Has it promptly paid past loans?
- Can it repay current loans?
- What are its current risks?
- What is its profit outlook?

The questions can change between short- and long-term lending decisions. The more long-term a loan, the more a lender's questions look like those of an owner.

Shareholders (Owners)

Shareholders have legal control over part or all of a corporation. They are the owners of corporations and in many cases are not part of management. Owners are exposed to the greatest return and risk. Risk is high because there is no promise of either repayment or a return on investment. They can lose their entire investment. Yet owners have a claim on assets after a business pays its debts. Many businesses do not give all or most of their profits back to owners but invest them in more assets to enable the company to grow. External reports aim to help answer shareholder (owner) questions such as:

- What is the income for current and past periods?
- Are assets adequate to meet business plans?
- Do expenses fit the level and type of sales?
- Are customers' bills paid promptly?
- Do loans seem large or unusual?

Corporations typically have a board of directors. *Directors* are elected representatives of shareholders and are charged to oversee their interests in an organization. Because directors are responsible to shareholders, their questions are similar. **NIKE**'s 1997 board of directors had 13 members.

External Auditors

External (or *independent*) auditors examine and provide an opinion on whether financial statements are prepared according to generally accepted accounting principles. External reports of competing organizations are used by auditors to help assess the reasonableness of a client's reports. **NIKE**'s independent auditor is **Price Waterhouse LLP.**

Employees

Employees, or their union representatives, have a special interest in an organization. They are interested in judging the fairness of their wages and in assessing future job prospects. External reports provide information useful in addressing these needs. External reports are also used in bargaining for better wages when an organization is successful.

Regulators

Regulators often have legal authority or significant influence over the activities of organizations. The Internal Revenue Service and other tax authorities require organizations to use various reports in computing taxes. These taxes include income, unemployment, sales, and social security. Tax reports usually require special forms and supporting records. Government and nongovernment agencies also use financial reports. Examples include utility boards that use accounting information to set utility rates and securities regulators that require special filings for businesses with publicly traded securities.

Other Important External Users

Accounting serves the needs of many other important external users. Voters, legislators, and elected officials use accounting information to monitor and evaluate a government's receipts and expenses. Contributors to nonprofit organizations use accounting information to evaluate the use and impact of their donations. Suppliers use accounting information to judge the soundness of a business before making sales on credit. Customers use external reports to assess the staying power of potential suppliers and the extent of products returned.

Internal Information Users

Internal users of accounting information are those individuals directly involved in managing and operating an organization. They include managers, officers, and other important internal decision makers. Internal users make the strategic and operating decisions for an organization. The internal role of accounting is to provide information to help improve the efficiency or effectiveness of an organization in delivering products or services. In this way, accounting helps businesses reach their goals.

Management accounting is the area of accounting aimed at serving the decision-making needs of internal users. Management accounting provides internal reports to help internal users improve an organization's activities. Internal reports are not subject to the same rules as external reports. This is because decisions of internal users are not constrained by the need to keep certain information private from external users because of competitive concerns. Internal users often have access to a lot of private and valuable information. Costs in preparing internal reports are usually the only constraint on internal reporting. Internal reports aim to answer questions like:

- What are manufacturing costs per product?
- What is the most profitable mix of services?
- What level of sales is necessary to break even?
- Which service activities are most profitable?
- What costs vary with sales?

Information to help answer these questions is very important for success. This book provides many tools to help in this task.

The responsibilities and duties of internal users extend to every function of an organization. There are at least seven functions common to most organizations. Accounting is essential to the smooth operation of each of these functions. The internal operating functions are shown in Exhibit 1.10 and include: research and development, purchasing, human resources, production, distribution, marketing, and servicing. The larger the business, the more likely these operating functions are separate units in the business. Each unit often has its own internal user (manager) who is responsible for decisions. Depending on the type of business, not all of these operating functions are necessary. For example, publishing companies usually don't require separate research and development units, and banks don't require production units. Less frequently used functions are often combined. We briefly describe the information needs of these internal users for each operating function:

- **Research and development** Research and development is aimed at creating or improving a company's products or services. Managers need information about current and projected costs and potential sales to decide on research and development projects.
- **Purchasing** Purchasing involves acquiring and managing materials needed for operations. Managers need to know what, when, and how much to purchase.
- **Human resources** Human resource management aims to locate, screen, hire, train, compensate, promote, and counsel employees. Managers need information about current and potential employees, payroll costs, employee benefits, and other performance and compensation data.

- **Production** Production is the mix of the factors of production to produce products and services. Good production methods depend on information to monitor costs and ensure quality.
- **Distribution** Distribution involves timely and accurate delivery of products and services. Relevant information is often key to quality distribution including its cost.
- **Marketing** Marketing is the promotion and advertising of products and services. Marketing managers use accounting reports about sales and costs to effectively target consumers and set pricing. Marketing also uses accounting to monitor consumer needs, tastes, and price concerns.
- **Servicing** Servicing customers after selling products or services is often key to success and includes training, assistance, installation, warranties, and maintenance. Information is needed on both the costs and benefits of servicing.

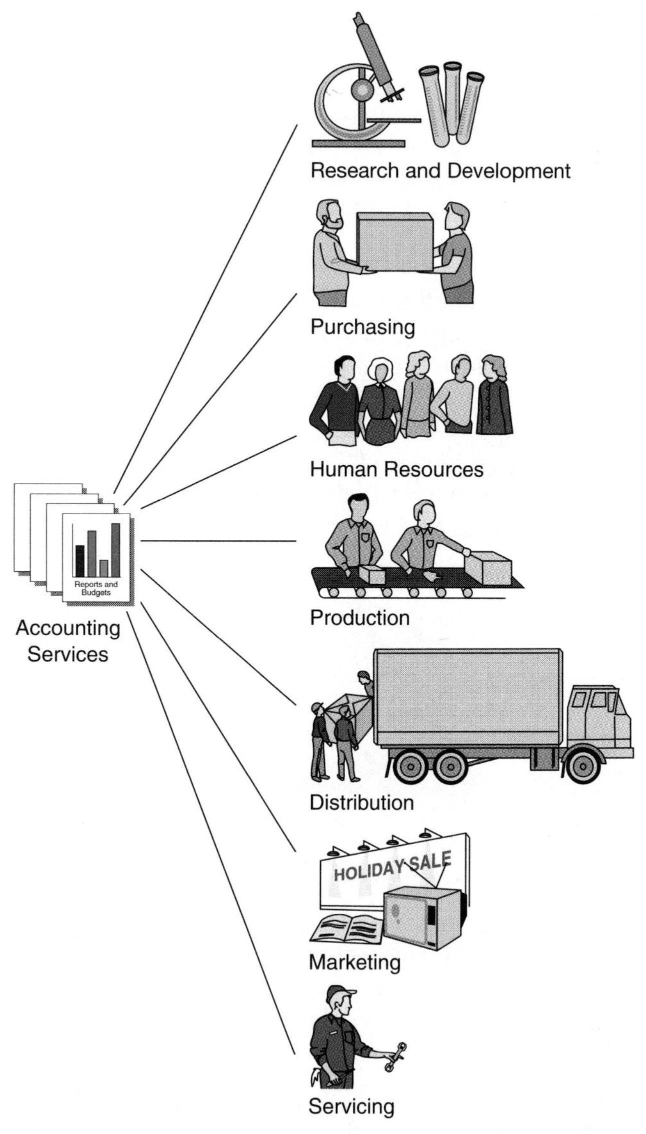

Exhibit 1.10
Internal Operating Functions

Both internal and external users rely on internal controls to monitor these operating functions. **Internal controls** are procedures set up to protect assets, ensure reliable accounting reports, promote efficiency, and encourage adherence to company policies.

Ethics and Social Responsibility

C5 Explain why ethics and social responsibility are crucial to accounting.

Ethics and ethical behavior are important. We are reminded of this when we run across disappointing stories in the media or witness wrongful actions by individuals such as cheating, harassment, misconduct, and bribery. Such cases make it more difficult for people to trust one another. If trust is missing, our lives are more difficult, inefficient, and unpleasant.

This section explains the meaning of ethics and describes how ethics affect organizations. We take up ethics early in our study because of their importance to organizations, accounting, and everyday living. The goal of accounting is to provide useful information for decision making. For information to be useful, it must be trusted. This demands ethics in accounting. This section also discusses social responsibility for organizations.

Understanding Ethics

Ethics are beliefs that separate right from wrong. They are known as accepted standards of good and bad behavior. Ethics and laws often coincide, with the result that many unethical actions (such as theft and physical violence) are also illegal. Yet other actions are not against the law but are considered unethical, such as not helping people in need. Because of differences between laws and ethics, we cannot look to laws to keep people ethical.

Identifying the ethical path is sometimes difficult. The preferred ethical path is to take a course of action that avoids casting doubt on one's decision. For example, accounting users are less likely to trust an auditor's report on the fairness of accounting if the auditor's pay depends on the success of the reporting organization. To avoid questions and concerns of this type, ethics rules are often set. Auditors are indeed banned from any direct investment in their client, regardless of amount.[4] Auditors also cannot accept pay that depends on figures reported in a client's accounting reports.[5] These ethics rules are aimed at preventing conflicts of interest or even the appearance that an auditor is not independent. Exhibit 1.11 gives us guidelines for making ethical decisions.

Exhibit 1.11

Guidelines for Ethical Decision Making

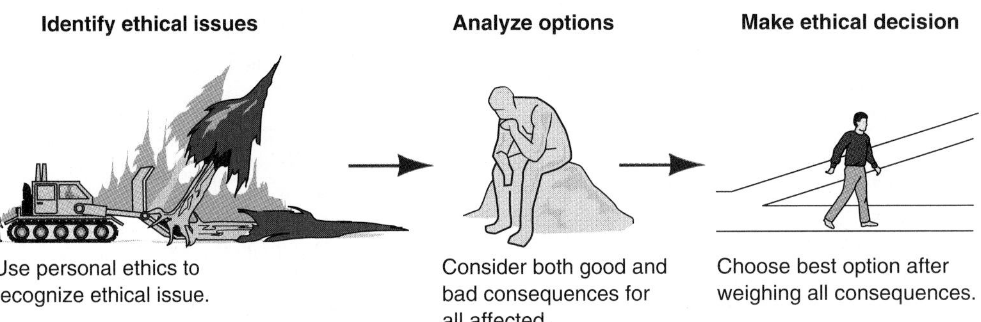
Identify ethical issues
Analyze options
Make ethical decision
Use personal ethics to recognize ethical issue.
Consider both good and bad consequences for all affected.
Choose best option after weighing all consequences.

Throughout our lives we will continue to face decisions with ethical aspects. These arise in our school, our workplace, and our personal relationships. A commitment to ethical behavior requires us to think carefully before we act, to be certain we are making ethical choices. Our success in making these choices affects how we feel about ourselves and how others feel about us. Ethics are not a personal matter. Our combined individual choices affect the quality of our community and the experiences of all of us.

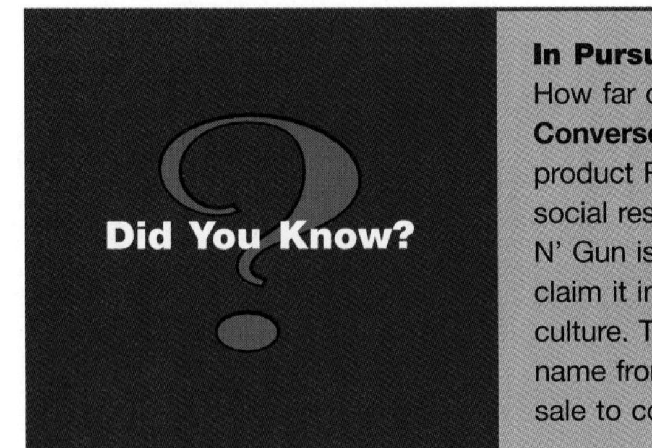
Did You Know?

In Pursuit of Profit

How far can companies go in pursuing profits? **Converse** proposed to name a new footwear product Run N' Gun. This sparked debate on ethics, social responsibility, and profits. Converse says Run N' Gun is a basketball and football team. Critics claim it invites youth violence and links with the gun culture. To the credit of Converse, it changed the name from Run N' Gun to Run N' Slam prior to its sale to consumers.

Organizational Ethics

Organizational ethics are likely learned through example and leadership. Companies like **McDonald's**, **Marriott**, **Ben & Jerry's Homemade Ice Cream**, and **IBM** work hard at instilling ethics in employees. Yet we still hear people express concern about what

---

[4] *AICPA Code of Professional Conduct,* Rule 101.

[5] *AICPA Code of Professional Conduct,* Rule 301.

they see as low ethics in organizations. A survey of more than 1,100 executives, educators, and legislators showed that 94% of the participants agreed with the comment that "the business community is troubled by ethical problems."[6] Yet this survey revealed that the vast majority of participants believe high ethical standards are followed by organizations that are successful over the long run. This finding confirms an old saying: *Good ethics is good business*. Ethical practices build trust, which promotes loyalty and long-term relationships with customers, suppliers, and employees. Because of this and the public interest in ethics, many organizations have their own codes of ethics. These codes set standards for internal activities and for relationships with customers, suppliers, regulators, the public, and even competitors.

Accounting Ethics

Ethics are crucial in accounting. Providers of accounting information often face ethical choices as they prepare financial reports. Their choices can affect both the use and receipt of money, including taxes owed and money shared with owners. It can affect the price a buyer pays and the wages paid to workers. It can even affect the success of products, services, and divisions. Misleading information can lead to a wrongful closing of a division where workers, customers, and suppliers are seriously harmed.

Because of the importance of accounting ethics, codes of ethics are set up and enforced. These codes include those of the American Institute of Certified Public Accountants and the Institute of Management Accountants. These codes are presented at the end of the book and can help us when confronting ethical dilemmas. For example, organizations often pay managers bonuses based on the amount of income reported. Managers can benefit from using accounting in ways to increase their pay. These choices can reduce the money available for employee wages, training programs, community giving, and other supported programs such as the **United Way.**

Ethics codes can also help in dealing with confidential information. For example, auditors have access to confidential salaries and an organization's strategies. Organizations can be harmed if auditors pass this information to others. To prevent this, auditors' ethics codes require them to keep information confidential.[7] Internal accountants are also not to use confidential information for personal gain.[8] These examples show the practical value of ethical codes. They provide guidance in knowing what action to take.

Ethical Challenge

In our lives we will encounter many situations needing ethical decisions. You will face many such situations in this book. We need to remember that accounting must be done ethically if it is to be useful. Ethics is the most fundamental of accounting principles. We are all in control of our ethics and the ethical decisions we make.

Social Responsibility

Social responsibility is a concern for the impact of our actions on society as a whole. Social responsibility is a concern for all of us. Organizations, too, are increasingly concerned with their social responsibility. **Reebok** proclaims in its annual report:

> We have a deep-felt commitment to operate in a socially responsible way and we stand for human rights throughout the world.

[6] Touche Ross & Co., *Ethics in American Business* (New York, 1988), pp. 1–2.

[7] *AICPA Code of Professional Conduct,* Rule 301.

[8] *Institute of Management Accountants Standards of Ethical Conduct.*

Our society is increasing the pressure on organizations to give something back. Socially conscious employees, customers, investors, and others see to it that organizations back up rhetoric with actions. There are several ways that organizations give something back. This section describes some of these programs and discusses social auditing as a means to monitor social responsibility.

Social Programs

An organization's social responsibility extends in many directions. It can include donations to nonprofit organizations such as hospitals, colleges, community programs, and law enforcement. It can also include programs to reduce pollution, increase product safety, improve worker conditions, support continuing education, and better use our natural resources. Yet most organizations are more likely to invest in their own social programs. For example, **NIKE** invests in its *P.L.A.Y. (Participate in the Lives of America's Youth)* program. It is aimed at activism, especially providing opportunities and facilities for kids to pursue fitness and fun. **Xerox** offers its workers up to a one-year leave to work for a nonprofit organization. During their leave, workers receive full salary and benefits and return to their same positions when the leave is finished. Many other organizations offer similar social programs. We are aware of well over 1,000 businesses that offer social programs to their employees to pursue community service activities. **Boeing**'s corporate citizenship is described in its annual report as follows:

> In 1996 . . . Company and employee contributions totaled nearly $60 million to support a full spectrum of community programs in the areas of education, health and human services, civic participation, and the arts. Boeing employees and retirees also volunteered more than one million hours of their own time to serve their communities.

A more detailed social responsibility report is that of **AT&T** shown in Exhibit 1.12. These programs are not limited to large companies. For example, many independently owned movie theaters and leisure sports businesses offer discounts to students and senior citizens. Still others help sponsor events such as the Special Olympics and summer reading programs with the local library.

Support for all of these types of social programs by organizations is not universal. Some argue that organizations are not unbiased in supporting social programs. There is a concern that an organization's interests might be quite different from its workers', customers', or the public's. It is sometimes argued that an organization should increase pay to its workers so that they can contribute to their own community concerns. While there will be continuing debate and disagreement with the charitable giving of organizations, the new era of social responsibility is here to stay.

Exhibit 1.12

AT&T's "Social Responsibility" Report

Commitment to Making a Difference

- The AT&T CARES program is granting 130,400 AT&T people a paid workday by the end of 1997 in which they may perform community service work. Our efforts can generate more than 1 million hours of volunteer local service. To date, some 10,000 employees have participated in projects that include planting trees, cleaning playgrounds and helping build houses.
- The AT&T Foundation donated $49 million in 1996 through our Matching Gift Program, the United Way and local contributions.
- Last year, 8.7 percent of AT&T's total purchases came from minority- and women-owned businesses (MWBE). We received the Distinguished Corporate Award from the U.S. Department of Commerce and U.S. Small Business Administration, while the Asian Entrepreneurs organization awarded AT&T its Corporate Advocate Award.

Returns on Social Responsibility
Virtue isn't always its own reward. Compare the **S&P 500,** which includes companies selling weapons, alcohol, and tobacco, with the **Domini Social Index** which covers 400 companies that don't, and have good records of social responsibility. Notice that returns for companies with socially responsible behavior are at least as large if not higher than those of the S&P 500.
Source: *Business Week,* May 26, 1997.

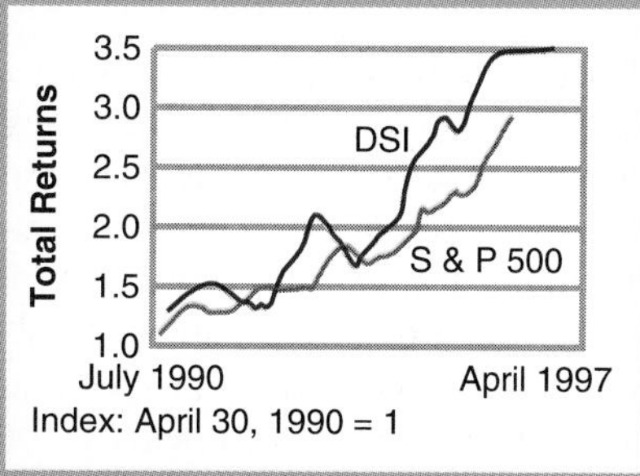

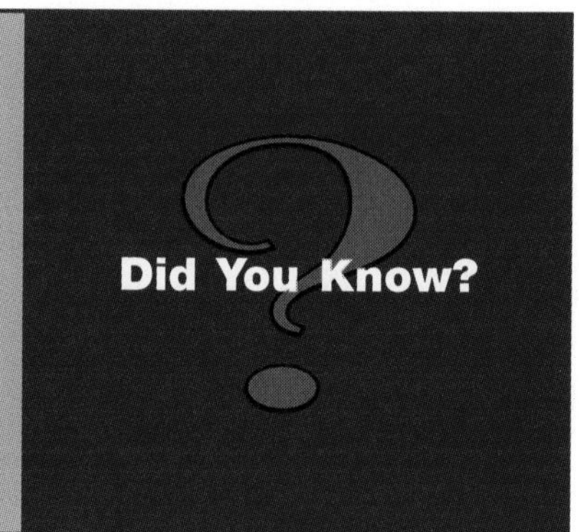

Social Auditing

How do we measure and evaluate an organization's activities aimed at social responsibility? **Chiquita** declares in its annual report:

> The **Chiquita Environmental Charter** is to protect the rainforest; to maintain clean water; to minimize the use of agrichemicals; to reduce, re-use and recycle waste; to support environmental education; and to ensure our workforce is well-trained and works safely.

While it is difficult to compute a net social contribution measure for declarations like these, we can use social auditing to help us out. A **social audit** is an analysis of an organization's success in carrying out programs that are socially responsible and responsive. There are different approaches in practice. But organizations that report these activities usually stick with disclosing *positive* actions (contributions, pollution reduction, minority business).

Flash back

9. Who are the internal and external users of accounting information?
10. Identify seven internal operating functions in organizations.
11. Why are internal controls important?
12. What are the guidelines in helping us make ethical decisions?
13. Why are ethics and social responsibility valuable to organizations?
14. Why are ethics crucial to accounting?

Answers—p. 28

Opportunities in Practice

C6 Identify opportunities in accounting and related fields.

Accounting information affects many aspects of our lives. The organizations we work for, the work we do, and the lives we live are impacted by accounting. When we earn money, pay taxes, invest savings, budget earnings, and plan for the future, we are influenced by accounting. Accounting helps us better perform and compete in society. To help us understand the opportunities for us in accounting, this section discusses four areas: financial, managerial, taxation, and accounting related. These areas differ by the kinds of information provided to and demanded by decision makers. Exhibit 1.13 lists selected opportunities for each of these areas. We also discuss unique aspects of these areas in business and nonbusiness organizations. These activities demand the work of millions of individuals employed in accounting or accounting-related areas.

Financial Accounting

Financial accounting provides information to decision makers not involved in the daily operations of an organization. These decision makers include customers, suppliers, planners, investors, and lenders. Information is normally reported through general-purpose financial statements. Financial statements describe the condition of an organization and its major transactions and events for a period of time. The process of preparing financial statements often demands the input of many individuals within and outside of accounting. They include lawyers, statisticians, doctors, artists, and photographers.

Exhibit 1.13 shows a demand for auditing in financial accounting. Many financial statements are issued with an *audit report* from a public accountant. An **audit** is a check of an organization's accounting systems and records using various tests. It increases the credibility of financial statements. Banks usually require audits of financial statements when companies apply for large loans. Also, federal and state laws require companies to have audits before their securities (stocks and bonds) are sold to the public. An auditor's objective is to decide whether the statements reflect the company's financial position and operating results using generally accepted accounting principles. When an audit is complete, an auditor writes a report expressing a professional *opinion* about whether the financial statements are fairly presented. It is an opinion because an auditor uses samples to examine the statements and does not verify every transaction and event. The auditor's reports accompanying the statements of **NIKE, Reebok,** and **America Online** are shown in Appendix A near the end of this book.

Government organizations such as the SEC are involved with regulating financial accounting practices and information issued to the public. SEC employees review companies' financial reports to be sure they comply with securities regulations. Employees who work for other regulatory agencies such as the Federal Trade Commission often review reports filed by businesses subject to the agencies' authority. They also help organizations understand and comply with regulations. Some government employees investigate and pursue violations of laws. Employees of the SEC investigate crimes related to securities, and others investigate financial frauds and white-collar crimes in their duties as agents of the Federal Bureau of Investigation (FBI). The FBI is a major employer of accounting-related professionals.

Managerial Accounting

Managerial accounting provides information to an organization's decision makers, or internal users. Managerial accounting reports often include much of the information in financial accounting. But managerial accounting reports also include information not reported outside the company. These reports generally fall within one of five major areas.

Opportunities in Practice

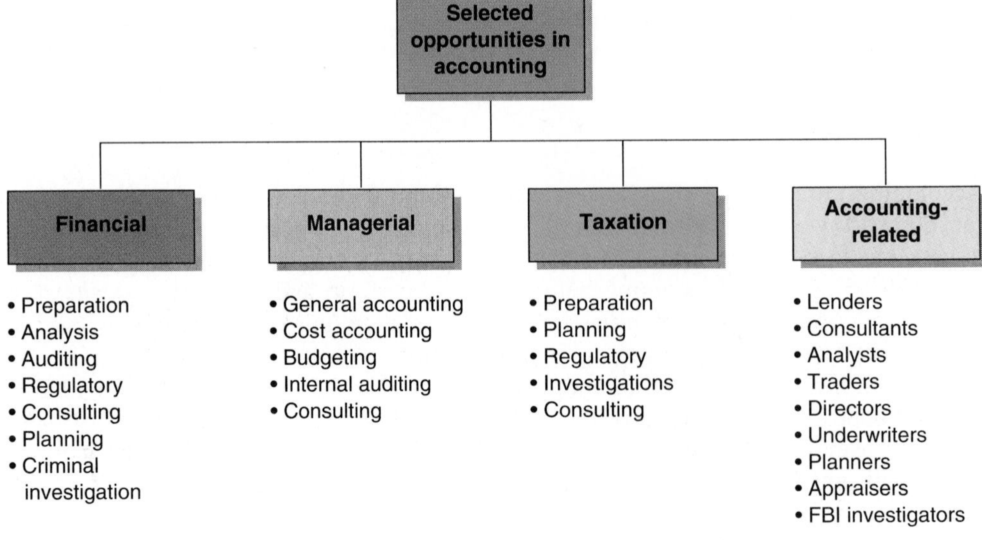

General Accounting

General accounting is the recording of transactions, the processing of data, and the preparing of reports for internal use. General accounting also includes preparing financial statements that companies issue to external users. An organization's own employees usually design the necessary information system, often with help from outsiders. The general accounting area is supervised by a chief accounting officer called the **controller.** This title reflects the fact that accounting information is used to control an organization's activities.

Cost Accounting

To plan and control operations, managers need information about the nature of costs incurred. **Cost accounting** is a process of accumulating the information managers need about costs. It helps managers identify, measure, and control costs. For example, **America Online** uses cost accounting in disclosing in its annual report that:

> The increase in cost of revenues was primarily attributable to an increase in data communication costs, customer support costs and royalties paid to information and service providers.

Cost accounting involves accounting for the costs of products, services, and other activities. Cost accounting information is especially useful for evaluating a manager's performance.

Budgeting

The process of developing formal plans for an organization's future activities is called **budgeting.** One goal of budgeting is to give individual managers an understanding of how their activities affect the entire organization. After the budget is adopted, it provides a basis for evaluating actual performance.

Internal Auditing

Organizations often employ individuals in **internal auditing** to add credibility to reports produced and used within the organization. **Reebok** includes a Report of Management in its annual report that states:

> The Company maintains an internal auditing program that monitors and assesses the effectiveness of the internal control system and recommends possible improvements thereto.

The value of internal auditors often goes beyond an examination of recordkeeping. Internal auditors assess whether managers are following established operating procedures and evaluate the efficiency of operating procedures.

Management Consulting

Individuals with knowledge of accounting are in demand by organizations that desire **management consulting** (or advisory) services. They include organizations like **Andersen Consulting, McKinsey,** and **Standard & Poor's.** Independent auditors gain a deep understanding of a client's accounting and operating procedures when they conduct their tests. As a result, auditors are in an excellent position to offer suggestions for improving an organization's activities. Most clients expect these suggestions as a useful by-product of an audit. Consultants with accounting knowledge often help organizations design and install new accounting and control systems, develop budgeting procedures, and set up employee benefit plans.

Tax Accounting

Taxes raised by federal, state, and local governments are usually based on income earned by taxpayers. These taxpayers include both individuals and organizations. The amount of taxes is computed on what the law defines as income. **Tax accounting** practitioners help taxpayers comply with the law by preparing their tax returns. **H&R Block** is one of the largest of such organizations. It claims that:

> **H&R Block** now processes the taxes for one out of every seven Americans who file returns.

Another tax accounting activity is planning future transactions to minimize taxes. Large organizations usually have employees who are responsible for tax returns and tax planning. But they often consult with other tax accounting experts when needing tax advice. Small organizations especially rely on these experts for much of their tax accounting. Nonbusinesses are major employers of tax services, especially the Internal Revenue Service **(IRS).** The IRS is responsible for collecting federal taxes and enforcing tax law. IRS employees review tax returns filed by taxpayers. IRS employees also offer assistance to taxpayers, help write regulations, and investigate possible violations of tax law.

Accounting Specialization

The majority of accounting professionals work in **private** businesses as seen in Exhibit 1.14. A large business can employ 100 or more accounting professionals, but most have less. Another large number of accounting professionals are employed as **public accountants** whose services are available to the public. Many in public accounting are self-employed, while others work for public accounting firms that have a few or even several thousand employees. Another large number of accounting professionals work in nonbusiness organizations, with many of these in federal, state, or local government. *Government accountants* perform accounting services for government units, including business regulation and investigation of law violations. Many other accounting specialists are employed in education. Since accounting is a crucial service activity in modern society, there is a demand for educators who can teach accounting to a wide range of users.

Accounting specialists are highly regarded and require special abilities, including integrity and fairness. The professional standing of an accounting specialist often is denoted by a certificate. Certified Public Accountants **(CPAs)** are licensed in every state in the United States, the District of Columbia, Guam, Puerto Rico, and the Virgin Islands. The licensing process helps ensure a high standard of professional service. Individuals can legally identify themselves as CPAs only if they hold the license. To become licensed, an individual must meet education and experience requirements, pass the CPA examination, and exhibit ethical character. Most states require a college degree with the equivalent of a major in accounting. Some states allow persons to substitute experience for part of the education requirements. The CPA examination covers topics in financial and managerial accounting, taxation, auditing, and business law.

Exhibit 1.14

Accounting Jobs by Area

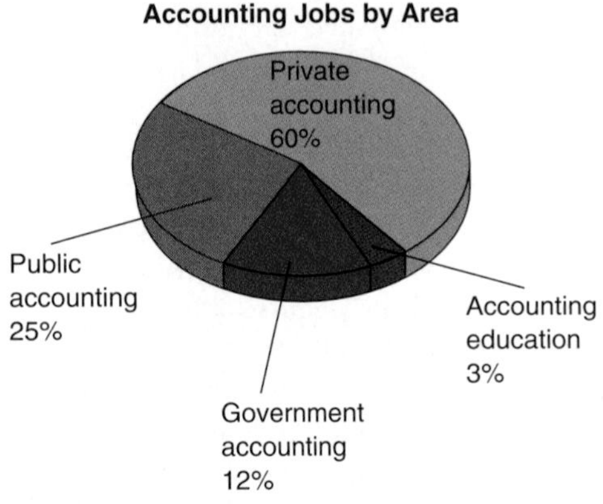

Source: Institute of Management Accountants

Many accounting specialists hold certificates in addition to or instead of the CPA license. Two of the most common are the Certificate in Management Accounting **(CMA)** and the Certified Internal Auditor **(CIA).** Holders of these certificates must meet examination, education, and experience requirements similar to those of a CPA. The CMA is awarded by the Institute of Management Accountants and the CIA is granted by the Institute of Internal Auditors. Another prestigious certificate is the Chartered Financial Analyst **(CFA).** It is awarded by the Association for Investment Management and Research (AIMR), an international nonprofit organization of investment practitioners and educators.

Accounting-Related Opportunities

Accounting-related opportunities are great. Accounting is the common language of financial communications. It spans professions, continents, and economies. Exhibit 1.13 lists several accounting-related opportunities including lenders, consultants, managers, and planners. Less traditional ones include community activist, political consultant, reporter, salesperson, union official, entrepreneur, programmer, engineer, and mechanic. All of these professions are made easier with a working knowledge of accounting. This course provides that knowledge.

Return on Investment

USING THE INFORMATION

A4 Compute and interpret return on investment.

We introduced return on investment in assessing return and risk earlier in the chapter. Return on investment is also useful in evaluating management, analyzing and forecasting profits, and planning future activities. **Dell Computer** has its marketing department compute return on investment for *every* mailing. "We spent 15 months educating people about return on invested capital," says Dell's Chief Financial Officer T.J. Meredith.[9] This section describes return on investment and how it can help us with these tasks.

Return on investment (ROI), also commonly called *return on assets (ROA),* measures performance independent of its financing sources. It is viewed as an indicator of operating efficiency. We compute **return on investment** as shown in Exhibit 1.15.

Exhibit 1.15

Return on Investment

$$\textbf{Return on investment} = \frac{\textbf{Net income}}{\textbf{Average total assets}}$$

Average total assets is usually computed by adding beginning and ending year amounts and dividing by two. For illustrative purposes, let's consider **Reebok.** Reebok reports net income of $138.95 in 1996 (in millions). At the beginning of 1996, Reebok's total assets are $1,651.619 and at the end of 1996 they total $1,786.184 (in millions). Reebok's return on investment for 1996 is:

$$\text{Return on investment} = \frac{\$138.95}{(\$1{,}651.619 + \$1{,}786.184)/2} = 8.08\%$$

Is an 8.08% return on investment good or bad for **Reebok?** To help answer this question and others like it, we can compare **Reebok's** return on investment with its prior performance, the returns of similar companies (such as **NIKE, Converse,** and **L.A.Gear**), and returns from alternative investments. Reebok's return on investment for each of the prior six years is reported in the second column

[9] Gary McWilliams, "Michael Dell: Whirlwind on the Web," *Business Week,* April 7, 1997.

Exhibit 1.16

Reebok, NIKE, and Industry Returns

Year	Reebok's Return on Investment	NIKE's Return on Investment	Industry Return on Investment
1996	8.1%	15.6%	2%
1995	10.0	14.5	4
1994	16.7	13.1	9
1993	16.3	18.0	7
1992	8.3	18.4	6
1991	16.7	20.5	7

of Exhibit 1.16. Reebok's return on investment for this period ranges from 16.7% in 1991 to 8.1% in 1996. This pattern suggests a recent decline in Reebok's efficiency in using its assets. We can also compare **Reebok** to a similar company such as **NIKE,** whose return on investment is shown in the third column of Exhibit 1.16. In five of six years, **NIKE's** return exceeds **Reebok's** and its average return is higher for this period. We can also compare Reebok's return to the normal return for manufacturers of athletic footwear. Industry averages are available from services like **Dun & Bradstreet's** (D&B) *Industry Norms and Key Ratios* and **Robert Morris Associates'** (RMA) *Annual Statement Studies.* Ratios computed from a select group of similar manufacturers are shown in the fourth column.[10] When compared to their competitors both **Reebok** and **NIKE** perform well.

Exhibit 1.17

Return on Investment for Other Companies

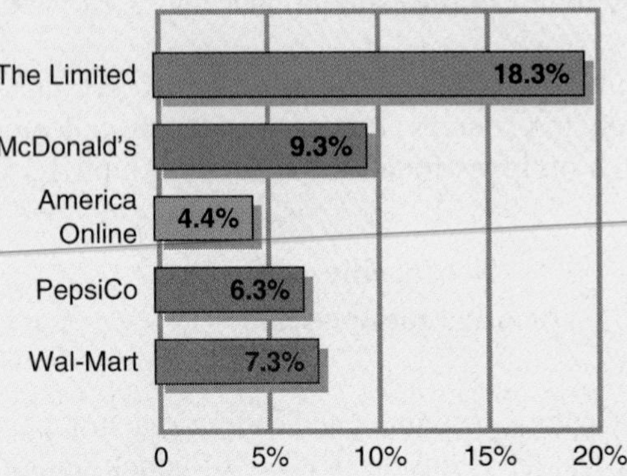

Another useful analysis is to compare returns to alternative investments. Exhibit 1.17 shows recent returns for five familiar companies. **The Limited** and **McDonald's** performed better than Reebok, while **AOL, PepsiCo,** and **Wal-Mart** did not. Using this information, Reebok's performance is probably "good." While not equal to NIKE, it is similar to the norm as judged by the returns of competitors both in and outside its business.

Summary

C1 Explain the aim and power of accounting in the information age. Accounting is an information and measurement system that aims to identify, record, and communicate relevant, reliable, and comparable information about economic activities. It helps us better assess opportunities, products, investments, and social and community responsibilities. The power of accounting is in opening our eyes to new and exciting opportunities. The greatest benefits from understanding accounting often come to those outside of accounting.

C2 Identify forms of organization and their characteristics. Organizations can be classified as either businesses or nonbusinesses. Businesses are organized for profit, while nonbusinesses serve us in ways not always measured by profit. Businesses take one of three forms: sole proprietorship, partnership, or corporation. These forms of organization have characteristics that hold important implications for legal liability, taxation, continuity, number of owners, and legal status.

C3 Identify and describe the three major activities in organizations. Organizations carry out three major activities: financing, investing, and operating. These activities are tied together by an organization's plans, including its ideas, goals, and strategies. Financing is the means used to pay for resources like land, buildings, and machines. Investing refers to the buying and selling of resources used in selling products and services. Operating activities are those necessary for carrying out the organization's plans.

[10] The industry ratio is the median value computed from 11 competitors including Fila, Converse, L. A. Gear, and Stride Rite, among others.

C4 **Identify users and uses of accounting.** There are both internal and external users of accounting. Some users and uses of accounting include: (a) managers in controlling, monitoring, and planning; (b) lenders for measuring the risk and return of loans; (c) shareholders for assessing the return and risk in acquiring shares; (d) directors for overseeing management; and (e) employees for judging employment opportunities. Other users are auditors, consultants, officers, regulators, analysts, unions, suppliers, and appraisers.

C5 **Explain why ethics and social responsibility are crucial to accounting.** The goal of accounting is to provide useful information for decision making. For information to be useful it must be trusted. This demands ethics and socially responsible behavior in accounting.

C6 **Identify opportunities in accounting and related fields.** Opportunities in accounting include traditional ones such as financial, managerial, and tax accounting. They also include accounting-related fields such as lending, consulting, managing, and planning. Nontraditional opportunities with accounting knowledge include careers as a community activist, political consultant, reporter, salesperson, union official, entrepreneur, programmer, and engineer.

A1 **Describe profit and its two major components.** Profit is the amount a business earns after subtracting all expenses necessary for its sales (Sales − Expenses = Profit). Sales are the amounts earned from selling products and services. Expenses are the costs incurred with sales. A loss arises when expenses are more than sales.

A2 **Explain the relation between return and risk.** Return refers to profit, and risk is the uncertainty about the return we hope to make. All business decisions involve risk. The lower the risk of an investment, the lower is its expected return. Higher expected return offsets higher risk. Higher risk means higher, but more risky, expected return.

A3 **Explain and interpret the accounting equation.** Investing activities are funded by an organization's financing activities. An organization cannot have more or less assets than its financing and, similarly, it cannot have more or less nonowner (liabilities) and owner (equity) financing than its total assets. This basic relation gives us the accounting equation: Assets = Liabilities + Owner's equity.

A4 **Compute and interpret return on investment.** Return on investment is commonly computed as profit, also called net income or earnings, divided by amount invested. For example, if we have an average balance in our savings account of $100 and it earns interest of $5 for the year, then our return on investment is $5/$100, or 5%. Return on investment is also called return on assets, where the amount invested is measured by the average assets for the period.

Guidance Answers to **"You Make the Call"**

Programmer

As the computer programmer, you are confronting a trade-off between return (salary) and risk (dependable employment). The new start-up company has an uncertain future and is willing to increase your pay to balance the added risk you have in working for them (this company could fail). The established medical supply company pays less, but you are assured of employment. If you or others are totally dependent on your income, the risk of the start-up company might be too high. Yet if you and others do not depend on your salary, the increased pay might be worth the risk.

Entrepreneur

You should probably form your business as a corporation if potential lawsuits are of prime concern. The corporate form of organization protects your personal property from lawsuits directed at the business and would place only the corporation's resources at risk. A downside of the corporate form is double taxation—the corporation must pay taxes on earnings and you must pay taxes on any money distributed to you from the business (even though the corporation already paid taxes on this money). You should also examine the ethical and socially responsible aspects of starting a business where you anticipate injuries to others.

Guidance Answers to Flash*backs*

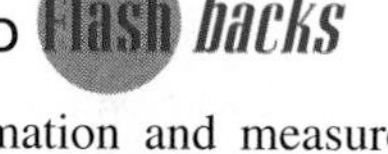

1. Accounting is an information and measurement system that identifies, records, and communicates relevant information to people that helps them make better decisions. It helps people in business identify and react to investment opportunities. It also helps us better assess opportunities, products, investments, and social and community responsibilities.
2. Profit is the money a business earns after paying for all expenses necessary for its sales. Sales, also called revenues, are the amounts earned from selling products and services. Expenses are the costs incurred with sales.
3. The trade-off between return and risk is a normal part of business. The lower the risk of an investment, the lower is our expected return. Similarly, higher expected return offsets higher risk. Remember that *actual* return usually differs from *expected* return. Higher risk implies higher, but more risky, expected returns.
4. Recordkeeping is the recording of financial transactions and events, either manually or electronically. While recordkeeping is essential to data reliability, accounting is this and much more. Accounting includes identifying, measuring, recording, reporting, and analyzing economic events and transactions. It involves interpreting information and designing information systems to provide useful reports that monitor and control an organization's activities.
5. Accounting rules are determined by many individuals and groups. Since accounting is a service activity, these rules reflect our society's needs and not those of accountants or any other single constituency. Major participants in setting rules include the Securities and Exchange Commission (SEC), the Financial Accounting Standards Board (FASB), and the American Institute of Certified Public Accountants (AICPA).

6. The three common forms of business organizations are sole proprietorships, partnerships, and corporations.
7. Nonbusiness organizations often include airports, libraries, national defense, museums, churches, cities, police, mail, colleges, bus lines, utilities, highways, fraternities, shelters, parks, hospitals, and schools.
8. Organizations pursue financing, investing, and operating activities. These three major activities all require planning.
9. External users of accounting information are not directly involved in running the organization and include lenders, shareholders, directors, customers, suppliers, regulators, lawyers, brokers, and the press. Internal users of accounting information are those individuals directly involved in managing and operating an organization. They include managers, officers, and other important internal decision makers involved with the strategic and operating decisions.
10. The internal operating functions are: research and development, purchasing, human resources, production, distribution, marketing, and servicing.
11. Internal controls are procedures set up to protect assets, ensure reliable accounting reports, promote efficiency, and encourage adherence to company policies. Internal controls are crucial if accounting reports are to provide relevant and reliable information.
12. Ethical guidelines are threefold: (1) identify ethical issues using personal ethics; (2) analyze options considering both good and bad consequences for all individuals affected; and (3) make ethical decisions choosing the best option after weighing all consequences.
13. Ethics and social responsibility are important for us because without them our lives are more difficult, inefficient, and unpleasant. They are equally important to organizations for these same reasons. In addition, they often translate into higher profits and a better working environment.
14. Accounting aims to provide useful information for decision making. For information to be useful it must be trusted. Trust of information demands ethics in accounting.

Glossary

Accounting an information and measurement system that identifies, records, and communicates relevant information about a company's economic activities to people to help them make better decisions. (p. 4).

Accounting equation the equality where Assets = Liabilities + Owner's Equity. (p. 13).

American Institute of Certified Public Accountants (AICPA) the largest and most influential national professional organization of certified public accountants. (p. 8).

Assets economic resources that are expected to produce future benefits. (p. 13).

Audit a check of an organization's accounting systems and records using various tests. (p. 22).

Bonds written promises by organizations to repay amounts loaned with interest. (p. 6).

Bookkeeping the part of accounting that involves recording economic transactions and events, either electronically or manually (also known as *recordkeeping*). (p. 7).

Budgeting the process of developing formal plans for future activities, often serving as a basis for evaluating actual performance. (p. 23).

Business one or more individuals selling products or services for profit. (p. 5).

Business entity principle every business is accounted for separately from its owner's personal activities. (p. 9).

CFA Chartered Financial Analyst; a certification from the Association for Investment Management and Research that an individual is professionally competent in the area of investments. (p. 25).

CIA Certified Internal Auditor; a certification from the Institute of Internal Auditors that an individual is professionally competent in internal auditing. (p. 24).

CMA Certificate in Management Accounting; a certification from the Institute of Management Accountants that an individual is professionally competent in managerial accounting. (p. 24).

Common stock the name for a corporation's stock when only one class of stock is issued (also called *capital stock*). (p. 11).

Controller the chief accounting officer of an organization. (p. 23).

Corporation a business that is a separate legal entity under state or federal laws with owners that are called shareholders or stockholders. (p. 10).

Cost accounting a managerial accounting activity designed to help managers identify, measure, and control operating costs. (p. 23).

CPA Certified Public Accountant; an accountant who has met examination, education, and experience requirements; CPAs are licensed by state boards to practice in public accounting. (p. 24).

Earnings the amount a business earns after subtracting all expenses necessary for its sales (also called *net income* or *profit*). (p. 5).

Ethics codes of conduct by which actions are judged as right or wrong, fair or unfair, honest or dishonest. (p. 18).

Expenses the costs incurred to earn sales. (p. 5).

External users persons using accounting information who are not directly involved in the running of the organization; examples include shareholders, customers, regulators, and suppliers. (p. 14).

Factors of production the means businesses use to make profit; land, labor, and plant and equipment are the traditional factors of production. (p. 7).

Financial accounting the area of accounting aimed at serving external users. (p. 14).

Financial Accounting Standards Board (FASB) an independent group of seven full-time members who are currently responsible for setting accounting rules. (p. 8).

Financing activities the means organizations use to pay for resources like land, building, and machines. (p. 12).

General accounting the task of recording transactions, processing data, and preparing reports for managers; includes preparing financial statements for disclosure to external users. (p. 23).

Generally accepted accounting principles (GAAP) the rules that indicate acceptable accounting practice. (p. 8).

Information age a time period that emphasizes communication, data, news, facts, access, and commentary. (p. 4).

Internal auditing activity conducted by employees within organizations to assess whether managers are following established operating procedures and to evaluate the efficiency of operating procedures. (p. 23).

Internal controls procedures set up to protect assets, ensure reliable accounting reports, promote efficiency, and encourage adherence to company policies. (p. 17).

Internal users persons using accounting information who are directly involved in managing and operating an organization; examples include managers and officers. (p. 16).

Investing activities the buying and selling of resources that an organization uses to sell its products or services. (p. 13.)

IRS Internal Revenue Service; the federal agency that has the duty of collecting federal taxes and otherwise enforcing tax laws. (p. 24).

Liabilities creditors' claims on an organization's assets. (p. 13).

Loss arises when expenses are more than sales, or revenues. (p. 5).

Management accounting the area of accounting aimed at serving the decision-making needs of internal users. (p. 16).

Management consulting activity in which suggestions are offered for improving a company's procedures; the suggestions may concern new accounting and internal control systems, new computer systems, budgeting, and employee benefit plans (also called *advisory services*). (p. 23).

Net income the amount a business earns after subtracting all expenses necessary for its sales (also called *profits* or *earnings*). (p. 5).

Operating activities the use of assets to carry out an organization's plans in the areas of research, development, purchasing, production, distribution, and marketing. (p. 13).

Owner's equity the owner's claim on an organization's assets. (p. 13).

Partnership a business that is owned by two or more people that is not organized as a corporation. (p. 10).

Planning the term for defining the ideas, goals, and actions of an organization. (p. 12).

Private accountants accountants who work for a single employer other than the government. (p. 24).

Profit the amount a business earns after subtracting all expenses necessary for its sales (also called *net income* or *earnings*). (p. 5).

Public accountants accountants who provide their services to many different clients. (p. 24).

Recordkeeping the recording of financial transactions and events, either manually or electronically (also known as *bookkeeping*). (p. 7).

Return derives from the idea of getting something back from an investment in a business. (p. 6).

Return on investment a financial ratio serving as an indicator of operating efficiency; net income divided by average total assets. (p. 6, 25).

Revenues the amounts earned from selling products or services (also called *sales*). (p. 5).

Risk the amount of uncertainty about the return to be earned. (p. 6).

Sales the amounts earned from selling products or services (also called *revenues*). (p. 5).

Securities and Exchange Commission (SEC) the federal agency charged by Congress to set reporting rules for organizations that sell ownership shares to the public. (p. 8).

Shareholders the owners of a corporation (also called *stockholders*). (p. 10).

Shares equity of a corporation divided into units (also called *stock*). (p. 10).

Single proprietorship a business owned by one individual that is not organized as a corporation (also called *sole proprietorship*). (p. 9).

Social audit an analysis of an organization's success in carrying out programs that are socially responsible and responsive. (p. 21).

Social responsibility involves considering and being accountable for the impact actions might have on society. (p. 19).

Sole proprietorship a business owned by one person that is not organized as a corporation (also called *single proprietorship*). (p. 9).

Stock equity of a corporation divided into units (also called *shares*). (p. 10).

Stockholders the owners of a corporation (also called *shareholders*). (p. 10).

Tax accounting the field of accounting that includes preparing tax returns and planning future transactions to minimize the amount of tax; involves private, public, and government accountants. (p. 24).

Questions

1. Identify four external users and their uses of accounting information.
2. Identify three types of organizations that can be formed as either profit-oriented businesses, government units, or nonprofit establishments.
3. What type of accounting information might be useful to those who carry out the marketing activities of a business?
4. Explain return and risk. Discuss the trade-off between return and risk.
5. What is the purpose of accounting in society?
6. Describe the internal role of accounting for organizations.
7. Explain business profit and its computation.
8. What are at least three questions business owners might answer by looking at accounting information?
9. Technology is increasingly used to process accounting data. Why then should we study accounting?
10. Define and explain return on investment (assets).
11. Why do organizations license and monitor accounting and accounting-related professionals?
12. What is the relation between accounting and the information superhighway?
13. Identify three types of services typically offered by accounting professionals.
14. Describe three forms of business organizations and their characteristics.
15. An organization's chief accounting officer is often called the controller. Why?
16. Identify at least four managerial accounting tasks performed by both private and government accountants.
17. Describe three important activities in organizations.
18. Identify at least two management advisory services offered by public accounting professionals.
19. Explain why investing (assets) and financing (liabilities and equity) totals are always equal.
20. List at least three examples of the types of tasks performed by government accounting professionals.
21. Identify three businesses that offer services and three businesses that offer products.
22. What work do tax accounting professionals perform in addition to preparing tax returns?
23. Why is accounting described as a service activity?
24. What is a social responsibility report?
25. What ethical issues might accounting professionals face in dealing with confidential information?
26. Identify the chief financial officer for **NIKE** from its financial statements in Appendix A. How many directors does **NIKE** have?

27. Identify the auditing firm that audited the financial statements of **NIKE** in Appendix A. What responsibility does the independent auditor claim regarding these financial statements?
28. The chapter's opening article discussed **W&F Financial Services.** This business is organized as a partnership. Identify important characteristics of partnerships and their implications.

Quick Study exercises give readers a brief test of key elements in every chapter.

Quick Study

QS 1-1
Identifying transactions and events

Accounting provides information about an organization's economic transactions and events. Identify examples of economic transactions and events.

QS 1-2
Identifying planning activities

Identify three responsibilities in the overall *executive management* (planning) activity of organizations.

QS 1-3
Explaining internal control

An important responsibility of many accounting professionals is to design and implement internal control procedures for organizations. Explain the purpose of internal control procedures.

QS 1-4
Accounting opportunities

C6

Identify at least three main areas of work for accounting professionals. For each accounting area identify at least three accounting-related opportunities in practice.

QS 1-5
Identifying ethical concerns
C5

Accounting professionals must sometimes choose between two or more acceptable methods of accounting for certain transactions and events. Explain why these situations can involve difficult matters of ethical concern.

QS 1-6
Identifying and computing assets, liabilities, and equity
A3

Use **America Online's** 1996 annual report printed in Appendix A near the end of the book to answer the following:

a. Identify the dollar amounts of America Online's 1996 (1) assets, (2) liabilities, and (3) equity.

b. Using America Online's amounts from (a), verify that: Assets = Liabilities + Equity.

Exercises

Exercise 1-1
Distinguishing business organizations

Presented below are descriptions of several different business organizations. Determine whether the situation described refers to a sole proprietorship, partnership, or corporation.

a. Ownership of Cola Company is divided into 1,000 shares of stock.

b. TexTech is owned by Kimberly Fisher, who is personally liable for the debts of the business.

c. Jerry Forrentes and Susan Montgomery own Financial Services, a financial services provider. Neither Forrentes nor Montgomery has personal responsibility for the debts of Financial Services.

d. Nancy Kerr and Frank Levens own Runners, a courier service. Both Kerr and Levens are personally liable for the debts of the business.

e. MRC Consulting Services does not have separate legal existence apart from the one person who owns it.

f. Biotech Enterprises has one owner and does not pay taxes.

g. Tennessee Technologies has two owners and pays its own taxes.

Exercise 1-2
Determining internal operating functions

Select the internal operating function from the two choices provided that is most likely to regularly use the information described. While the information is likely used in both functions, it is most relevant to one.

a. Which internal operating function is most likely to use payroll information: marketing or human resources?

b. Which internal operating function is most likely to use sales report information: marketing or research and development?

c. Which internal operating function is most likely to use cash flow information: finance or human resources?

d. Which internal operating function is most likely to use financial statement, budget, and performance report information: research and development or executive management?

e. Which internal operating function is most likely to use product quality information: finance or production?

Exercise 1-3
Identifying accounting users and uses
C4

Identify at least three external users of accounting information and indicate some questions they might seek to answer through their use of accounting information.

Exercise 1-4
Describing accounting responsibilities

Many accounting professionals work in one of the following three areas:

A. Financial accounting **B.** Managerial accounting **C.** Tax accounting

Identify the area of accounting that is most involved in each of the following responsibilities:

_____ **1.** Auditing financial statements.	_____ **5.** Reviewing reports for SEC compliance.
_____ **2.** Planning transactions to minimize taxes.	_____ **6.** Budgeting.
_____ **3.** Cost accounting.	_____ **7.** Internal auditing.
_____ **4.** Preparing financial statements.	_____ **8.** Investigating violations of tax laws.

Exercise 1-5
Identifying ethical concerns
C5

Assume the following role and describe a situation where ethical considerations play an important part in guiding your action:

a. You are a student in an accounting principles course.
b. You are a manager with responsibility for several employees.
c. You are an accounting professional preparing tax returns for clients.
d. You are an accounting professional with audit clients that are competitors in business.

Exercise 1-6
Learning the language of business
C1–C6

Indicate which term best fits each of the following descriptions:

A. Audit **C.** Cost accounting **E.** Ethics **G.** Budgeting
B. Controller **D.** GAAP **F.** General accounting **H.** Tax accounting

_____ **1.** An accounting area that includes planning future transactions to minimize taxes paid.
_____ **2.** A managerial accounting process designed to help managers identify, measure, and control operating costs.
_____ **3.** Principles that determine whether an action is right or wrong.
_____ **4.** An examination of an organization's accounting system and records that adds credibility to financial statements.
_____ **5.** The task of recording transactions, processing recorded data, and preparing reports and financial statements.
_____ **6.** The chief accounting officer of an organization.

Exercise 1-7
Learning the language of business
A1, A2, C4, C6

Indicate which term best fits each of the following descriptions:

A. Government accountants **C.** IRS **E.** CIA **G.** Risk **I.** AICPA
B. Internal auditing **D.** SEC **F.** Profit **H.** Public accountants **J.** CMA

_____ **1.** Responsibility of an organization's employees that involves examining the organization's recordkeeping processes, assessing whether managers are following established operating procedures, and appraising the efficiency of operating procedures.
_____ **2.** Amount of uncertainty associated with an expected return.
_____ **3.** Money a business earns after paying all expenses associated with its sales.
_____ **4.** Federal agency responsible for collecting federal taxes and enforcing tax law.
_____ **5.** Accounting professionals who provide services to many different clients.
_____ **6.** Accounting professionals employed by federal, state, or local branches of government.

Exercise 1-8
Using the accounting equation
A3

Answer the following questions. (*Hint*: Use the accounting equation.)

a. Doug Stockton's medical supplies business has assets equal to $123,000 and liabilities equal to $53,000 at the end of the year. What is the total of the owner's equity for Stockton's business at the end of the year?
b. At the beginning of the year, ParFour Company's assets are $200,000, and its owner's equity is $150,000. During the year, assets increase $70,000 and liabilities increase $30,000. What is the owner's equity at the end of the year?
c. At the beginning of the year, Navy Company's liabilities equal $60,000. During the year assets increase by $80,000 and at year-end they equal $180,000. Liabilities decrease $10,000 during the year. What are the beginning and ending amounts of owner's equity?

Exercise 1-9
Calculating return on investment
A4

Java Jimmies reports net income of $20,000 for 1999. At the beginning of 1999, Java Jimmies had $100,000 in assets. By the end of 1999 assets had grown to $140,000. What is Java Jimmies' return on investment?

Exercise 1-10
Using the accounting equation
A3

Determine the amount missing from each accounting equation below.

	Assets	=	Liabilities	+	Equity
a.	?	=	$30,000	+	$65,000
b.	$ 89,000	=	22,000	+	?
c.	132,000	=	?	+	20,000

Problems

Problem 1-1
Determining profits, sales, costs, and returns

A1, A3, A4

Bell Systems manufactures, markets, and sells cellular telephones. The average amount invested, or average total assets, in Bell Systems is $250,000. In its most recent year, Bell earned a profit of $55,000 on sales of $455,000.

Required

1. What is Bell Systems' return on investment?
2. Does return on investment seem satisfactory for Bell Systems when its competitors average a 12% return on investment?
3. What are total expenses for Bell Systems in its most recent year?
4. What is the average total amount of financing (liabilities plus equity) for Bell Systems?

Problem 1-2
Computing and interpreting return on investment

A4

Coke Company and Sprite Company both produce and market beverages and are direct competitors. Key financial figures (in $ millions) for these businesses over the past four years are:

Key figures	Coke Company	Sprite Company
Sales	$400	$250
Profit	$50	$37.5
Average invested (assets)	$625	$312.5

Required

1. Compute return on investment for *(a)* Coke Company and *(b)* Sprite Company.
2. Which company is more successful in sales to consumers?
3. Which company is more successful in earning profits from its amount invested?

Analysis component:

4. Write a brief memo explaining which company you would invest your money in and why.

Problem 1-3
Identifying risk and return

A2

All business decisions involve risk and return.

Required

Identify the risk and return in the following activities:

1. Investing $1,000 in a 4% saving account.
2. Placing a $1,000 bet on your favorite sports team.
3. Investing $10,000 in America Online stock.
4. Taking a $10,000 college loan to study accounting.

Problem 1-4
Describing organizational activities

C3

Write a description of an organization's three major activities.

Problem 1-5
Describing organizational activities.

C3

A new startup company often engages in the following transactions during its first year of operations. Classify these transactions within one of the three major categories of an organization's business activities.

A. Financing **B.** Investing **C.** Operating

_____ **1.** Leaving profits in the business.
_____ **2.** Obtaining necessary licenses.
_____ **3.** Purchasing land.
_____ **4.** Obtaining credit at bank.
_____ **5.** Purchasing equipment.
_____ **6.** Distributing products.
_____ **7.** Conducting an advertising campaign.

BEYOND THE NUMBERS

Reporting in Action

A1, A3, A4

NIKE designs, produces, markets, and sells sports footwear and apparel. Key financial figures for NIKE's fiscal year ended May 31, 1997 are:

Key figure	In millions
Financing (liabilities + equity)	$5,361
Profit	796
Sales	9,187

Required

1. What is the total amount of assets invested in NIKE?
2. What is NIKE's return on investment? NIKE's assets at May 31, 1996 equal $3,952 (in millions).
3. How much are total expenses for NIKE?

Analysis component:

4. Does NIKE's return on investment seem satisfactory if competitors average a 5% return?

Swoosh Ahead

5. Obtain NIKE's most recent annual report. You can also access NIKE's annual report at its Web site **(www.nike.com)** or at the SEC's Web site **(www.sec.gov).** Compute NIKE's return on investment using this updated annual report information you obtain. Compare the May 31, 1997, fiscal year-end return on investment to any subsequent years' returns you are able to compute.

Comparative Analysis

A1, A3, A4

Both NIKE and Reebok design, produce, market, and sell sports footwear and apparel. Key comparative figures ($ millions) for these two organizations follow:

Key figure*	NIKE	Reebok
Financing (liabilities + equity)	$5,361	$1,786
Profit	796	139
Sales	9,187	3,483

*NIKE figures are from its annual report for fiscal year-end May 31, 1997.
Reebok figures are from its annual report for fiscal year-end December 31, 1996.

Required

1. What is the total amount of assets invested in *(a)* NIKE and *(b)* Reebok?
2. What is the return on investment for *(a)* NIKE and *(b)* Reebok? NIKE's beginning assets equal $3,952 (in millions) and Reebok's beginning assets equal $1,652 (in millions).
3. How much are expenses for *(a)* NIKE and *(b)* Reebok?

Analysis components:

4. Is return on investment satisfactory for *(a)* NIKE and *(b)* Reebok [competitors average a 5% return]?
5. What can you conclude about NIKE and Reebok from these computations?

Ethics Challenge

C5

Rupert Jones works in a public accounting firm and hopes to eventually be a partner. The management of ShadowTech Company invites Jones to prepare a bid to audit ShadowTech's financial statements. In discussing the audit's fee, ShadowTech's management suggests a fee range where the fee amount depends on the reported profit of ShadowTech. The higher its profit, the higher the audit fee paid to Jones' firm.

Required

1. Identify the parties potentially affected by this situation.
2. What are the ethical factors in this situation?
3. Would you recommend that Jones accept this audit fee arrangement? Why or why not?
4. Describe some ethical considerations guiding your recommendation.

Communicating in Practice

A2, C2

Refer to this chapter's opening article about **W&F Financial Services.** Before establishing the business, Williams and Fulwood met with a loan officer of a Pittsburgh bank to discuss a loan.

Required

1. Prepare a brief report outlining the information you would request from Williams and Fulwood if you were the loan officer.
2. Indicate whether the information you request, and your loan decision, are affected by the form of business organization for **W&F Financial Services.**

Taking It to the Net

C1, C4

There is extensive accounting and business information available on the Internet. This includes the SEC's on-line database referred to as EDGAR **(www.sec.gov)** and numerous other Web sites offering access to financial statement information or related data. Examples are the AICPA **(www.aicpa.org),** the IRS **(www.irs.ustreas.gov),** and the AAA **(AAA-edu.org).** You can access the Web site devoted to this book **(www.mhhe.com/business/accounting/fap)** for updated links to several of these databases in case Web addresses change.

Required

Access at least one of the Web sites, selected by either you or your instructor, and answer the following:

1. Write a brief report describing the types of relevant information available at this Web site.
2. How would you rate the importance of the information available at this Web site for accounting and business?

Teamwork in Action

C1

Effectively implementing a team approach in both business and education requires scheduling team meetings and maintaining ongoing communication between team members. Cooperation and support are key elements in effective teams. As part of a team, you have the right to receive assistance from your teammates when you need or request it, and you have the responsibility to provide it when possible. This activity is designed to open channels of communication to provide ongoing opportunities to fulfill team rights and responsibilities.

Required:

1. Open a team discussion and determine a regular time and place where your team will meet between each scheduled class meeting.
2. Develop a list of telephone numbers and/or e-mail addresses of your teammates.
3. Notify your instructor, via a memo or e-mail message, as to when and where your team will hold regularly scheduled meetings.

Hitting the Road

C2

You are to interview a local business owner. (This can be a friend or relative.) Opening lines of communication with members of the business community can provide personal benefits of business networking. If you do not know the owner, you should call ahead to introduce yourself and explain your position as a student and your assignment requirements. You should request an appointment for a face-to-face or phone discussion to discuss the form of organization and operations of the business. Be prepared to make a good impression.

Required:

1. Identify and describe the primary operating activity and the form of organization for this business.
2. Determine and explain why the owner(s) chose this particular form of organization.
3. Identify any special advantages and/or disadvantages the owner(s) experiences in operating with this form of business organization.

Business Week Activity

C1

Business Week publishes a ranking of the top 1,000 companies based on several performance measures. This issue is called the **BUSINESS WEEK 1000.** Obtain the March 25, 1996 (or more recent) publication of this issue (***Business Week*** also maintains a web site with access to its articles at **www.businessweek.com/**).

Required

1. What are the top 10 performing companies on the basis of sales?
2. What are the top 10 performing companies on the basis of profits?
3. What are the top 10 performing companies on the basis of assets?

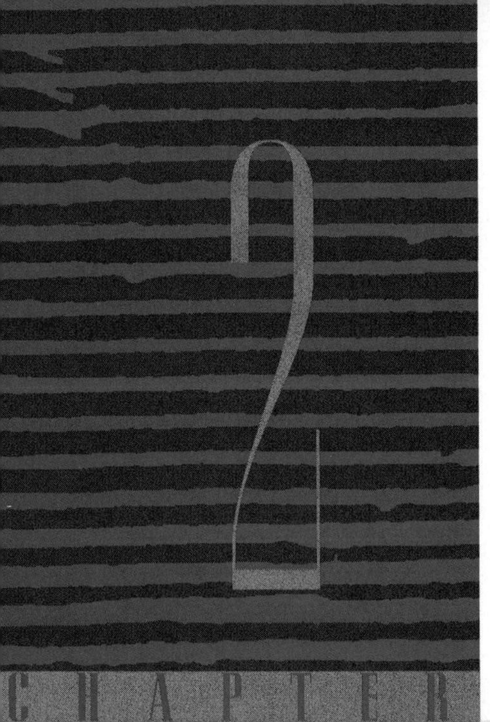

Financial Statements and Accounting Transactions

A Look Back

Chapter 1 began by considering the role of accounting in the information age. We described accounting for different organizations and identified users and uses of accounting. We saw that ethics and social responsibility are crucial to accounting.

A Look at This Chapter

In this chapter, we describe financial statements and the accounting principles guiding their preparation. An important part of this chapter is transaction analysis using the accounting equation. We prepare and analyze financial statements based on transaction analysis.

A Look Ahead

Chapter 3 explains the recording of transactions. We introduce the double-entry accounting system and show how T-accounts are helpful in analyzing transactions. Journals and trial balances are also identified and explained.

Chapter Outline

Shoes on Trial

LOS ANGELES—Tucked along an oceanside street, **FastForward** could be another trendy sports shop. But its small back lot, where Chuck Taylor runs up grassy mounds, through sand pits, and in mud, makes clear this is something far different. These obstacles are product research tools.

FastForward consults on athletic footwear. In just one year, Chuck Taylor has become a consultant sought after by sports clubs, schools, and athletes. In the first six months of 1998, his company's profits are rising at a 35% rate.

FastForward's story is the envy of every entrepreneur. Taylor, 29, loved sports—but he hated his shoes. He never seemed to have the right shoes for the right conditions. Independent tests of shoe performance were either nonexistent or outdated.

So in September 1997, Taylor had an idea. He went out and purchased 21 pairs of the best basketball shoes on the market. He ran the shoes through a battery of tests under many different court conditions. His results were striking. Many lower priced, lesser known shoes performed on par or better than many big ticket, big name shoes. He carried his findings to athletic teams and athletes, and got a welcome reception and payment for his services.

In November 1997, Taylor quit his job to devote full time to his new business. "I instantly needed accounting skills to keep track of receipts, bills, everything," says Taylor. "When I later applied for a loan, the bank couldn't believe my poor accounting records. But what'd you expect from a sports junkie!"

Taylor eventually cleaned up his accounting and got the loan. To boost growth, **FastForward** is now moving into the testing of soccer, track, and football shoes. "We are meeting a market need and making people happy," added Taylor. And you can count Taylor as one of the happy.

Learning Objectives

Conceptual

C1 Identify and explain the content and reporting aims of financial statements.

C2 Describe differences in financial statements across forms of business organization.

C3 Explain the financial reporting environment.

C4 Identify those responsible for setting accounting and auditing principles.

C5 Identify, explain, and apply accounting principles.

Analytical

A1 Analyze business transactions using the accounting equation.

A2 Compute return on equity and use it to analyze company performance.

Procedural

P1 Prepare financial statements from business transactions.

CHAPTER PREVIEW

Financial statements report on the financial performance and condition of an organization. They are one of the most important products of accounting, and are useful to both internal and external decision makers. Chuck Taylor of **Fast-Forward** recognized the importance of accounting reports in running his own business and in applying for a loan. Financial statements are the way business people communicate. Knowledge of their preparation, organization, and analysis is important.

In this chapter, we describe the kind of information captured and revealed in financial statements. We also discuss the principles and assumptions guiding their preparation. This discussion includes the organizations that regulate and influence accounting. An important goal of this chapter is to illustrate how transactions are reflected in financial statements and how they impact our analysis. This helps us see the immediate usefulness of financial statements. Special attention is devoted to a discussion of **FastForward,** whose first month's transactions are the focus of our analysis.

Communicating with Financial Statements

C1 Identify and explain the content and reporting aims of financial statements.

In Chapter 1 we discussed how accounting provides information to help people make better decisions. These decision makers include investors, lenders, managers, suppliers, and customers. Many organizations report their accounting information to internal and external users in the form of financial statements. These statements are useful in revealing an organization's financial health and performance in a summarized and easy to read format. They give an overall view of an organization's financing, investing, and operating activities. They also are the primary means of financial communication.

Previewing Financial Statements

There are four major financial statements: income statement, balance sheet, statement of changes in owner's equity, and statement of cash flows. We begin our study of these statements with a brief description of these statements. We cover all four statements in detail by the end of this chapter. How these statements are linked in time is illustrated in Exhibit 2.1.

A balance sheet reports on an organization's financial position at a *point in time*. The income statement, statement of changes in owner's equity, and statement of cash flows

Exhibit 2.1

Links between Financial Statements

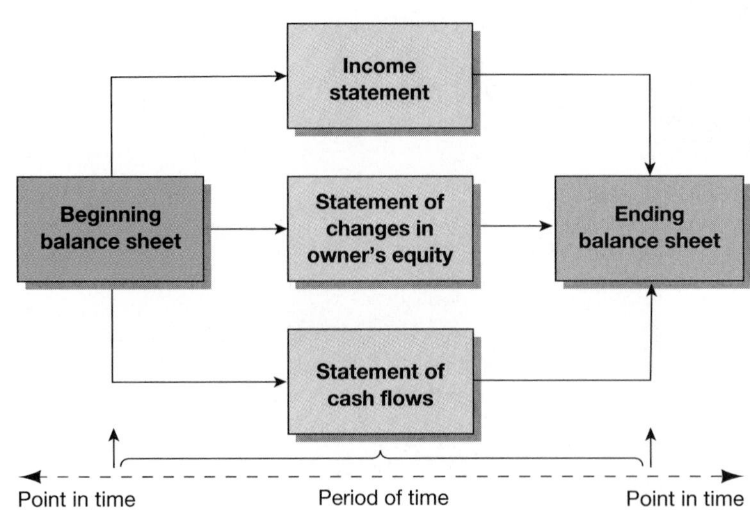

report on performance over a *period of time*. The three statements in the middle column of Exhibit 2.1 link balance sheets from the beginning to the end of a reporting period. They explain how the financial position of an organization changes from one point to another.[1]

Selection of a reporting period is up to preparers and users (including regulatory agencies). A one-year, or annual, reporting period is common, as are semiannual, quarterly, and monthly periods. The one-year reporting period is also known as the *accounting,* or *fiscal, year*. Businesses whose accounting year begins on January 1 and ends on December 31 are known as *calendar year* companies. But many companies choose a fiscal year ending on a date other than December 31. **NIKE** is a *noncalendar year* company as reflected in the headings of its May 31 year-end financial statements shown in Appendix A. Some companies choose a fiscal year-end when sales and inventory are low. For example, the **GAP's** 1997 fiscal year-end is February 1, after the holiday season.

Income Statement

An **income statement** reports revenues earned and expenses incurred by a business over a period of time. Expenses are subtracted from revenues on the income statement to show whether the business earned a net income. A **net income** means revenues exceed expenses. A **net loss,** or simply *loss,* means expenses exceed revenues.

The income statement for FastForward's first month of operations is shown in Exhibit 2.2 (FastForward is a sole proprietorship). An income statement does not simply report net income or net loss. It lists the types and amounts of both revenues and expenses. This is crucial information for users as it helps in understanding and predicting company performance. For example, **Walt Disney** classifies its revenues and expenses in three categories: theme parks, filmed entertainment, and consumer products. Also **McDonald's** separates its revenues into two groups: company-operated restaurants and franchised and affiliated restaurants. This information is more useful for making decisions than simply an income or loss number.

Exhibit 2.2

Income Statement

FASTFORWARD **Income Statement** **For Month Ended December 31, 1997**		
Revenues:		
Consulting revenue	$3,800	
Rental revenue	300	
Total revenues		$4,100
Expenses:		
Rent expense	$1,000	
Salaries expense	700	
Total expenses		1,700
Net income		$2,400

Revenues

Revenues are inflows of assets in exchange for products and services provided to customers as part of a company's primary operations.[2] Assets include cash, land, equipment, and buildings. The income statement in Exhibit 2.2 shows that FastForward earned total revenues of $4,100 during December from consulting services and rental revenue.

[1] Some view Exhibit 2.1 like a motion picture where points in time are freeze frames and periods of time are the actions occurring between freeze frames.

[2] Financial Accounting Standards Board, *Statement of Financial Accounting Concepts No. 6,* "Elements of Financial Statements" (Norwalk, CT, 1985), par. 78.

Expenses

Expenses are outflows or the using up of assets from providing products and services to customers.[3] The income statement in Exhibit 2.2 shows FastForward used up some of its assets in paying for rented store space. The $1,000 expense for store space is reported in the income statement as rent expense. FastForward also paid for an employee's wages at a cost of $700. This is reported on the income statement as salaries expense. The income statement heading identifies the company, the type of statement, and the time period covered. Knowledge of the time period is important in judging whether a company's performance is satisfactory. In assessing whether FastForward's $2,400 net income is satisfactory, we must remember it earned this amount during a one-month period.

Answer—p. 63

Chef

You are working as a chef at a restaurant and feel your wages are too low. You decide to ask the owner for a raise. How can you use the income statement of the restaurant to help in your request?

Statement of Changes in Owner's Equity

The **statement of changes in owner's equity** reports on changes in equity over the reporting period. This statement starts with beginning equity and adjusts it for events that (1) increase it—investments by the owner and net income, and (2) decrease it—net loss and owner withdrawals.

The statement of changes in owner's equity for FastForward's first month of operations is shown in Exhibit 2.3. This statement describes events that changed owner's equity during the month. It shows $30,000 of equity created by Taylor's initial investment. It also shows $2,400 of net income earned during the month, and Taylor's $600 withdrawal. FastForward's equity balance at the end of the month is $31,800.[4]

Statement of Changes in Owner's Equity

FASTFORWARD Statement of Changes in Owner's Equity For Month Ended December 31, 1997		
C.Taylor, capital, December 1, 1997		$ 0
Add: Investment by owner	$30,000	
Net income	2,400	32,400
Total		$32,400
Less: Withdrawal by owner		(600)
C.Taylor, capital, December 31, 1997		$31,800

Balance Sheet

The **balance sheet** reports the financial position of a company at a point in time, usually at the end of a month or year. Because of its emphasis on financial position it is also called the **statement of financial position.** The balance sheet describes financial

[3] Ibid., par. 80.

[4] The beginning capital balance in the statement of changes in owner's equity is rarely zero. An exception is for the first period of a company's operations. Since FastForward began operations in December 1997, its beginning capital balance for the month of December is zero. But the beginning capital balance in January 1998 for FastForward will be $31,800 (this is December's ending balance).

Balance Sheet

FASTFORWARD Balance Sheet December 31, 1997			
Assets		**Liabilities**	
Cash	$ 8,400	Accounts payable	$ 1,100
Supplies	3,600	Note payable	5,100
Equipment	26,000	Total liabilities	$ 6,200
		Owner's Equity	
		C.Taylor, capital	31,800
Total assets	$38,000	Total liabilities and owner's equity	$38,000

position by listing the types and dollar amounts of assets, liabilities, and equity. Exhibit 2.4 shows the balance sheet for FastForward as of December 31, 1997. The balance sheet heading lists the company, the statement, and the specific date on which assets, liabilities, and equity are identified and measured. The amounts in the balance sheet are measured as of the close of business on that specific date.

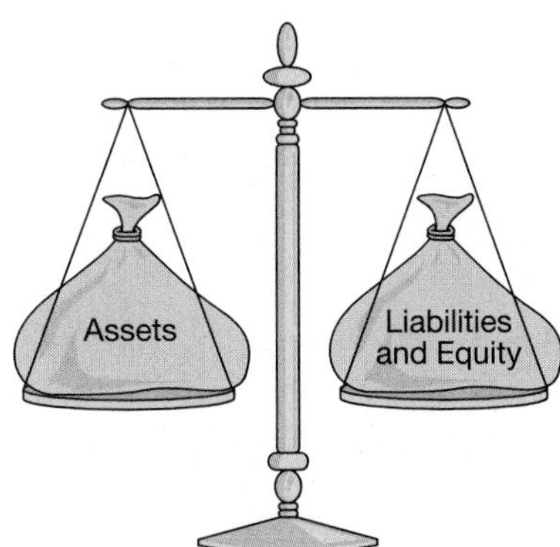

The balance sheet for FastForward shows it owns three different assets at the close of business on December 31, 1997. The assets are cash, supplies, and equipment. The total dollar amount for these assets is $38,000. The balance sheet also shows total liabilities of $6,200. Owner's equity is $31,800. Equity is the difference between assets and liabilities. The total amounts on each side of the balance sheet are equal (assets = liabilities + equity). This equality is why the statement is named a *balance sheet.* This name also reflects the reporting of asset, liability, and equity *balances* in the statement.

Assets

Assets are resources owned or controlled by a company. A common characteristic of assets is their ability to provide future benefits to the company.[5] Assets are of many types. A familiar asset is cash. Another is accounts receivable. An **account receivable** is an asset created by selling products or services on credit. It reflects amounts owed to a company by its credit customers. These customers and other individuals and organizations who owe a company are called its **debtors.** Other common assets include merchandise held for sale, supplies, equipment, buildings, and land. Assets also can be intangible rights such as those granted by a patent or copyright.

Personal Assets

Assets of U.S. households have more than tripled in the past 15 years. They now exceed $20 trillion. But as Wall Street has soared and inflation has cooled, the asset mix has changed. Where we once saw savings and money market accounts, we now see stocks, mutual funds, and pension assets.

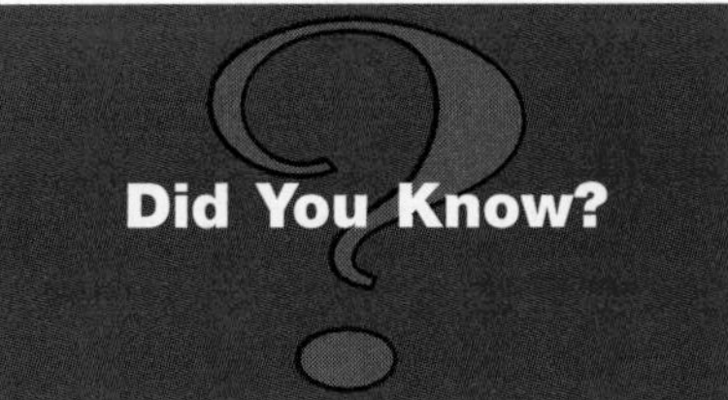

[5] Financial Accounting Standards Board, *Statement of Financial Accounting Concepts No. 6,* "Elements of Financial Statements" (Norwalk, CT, 1985), par. 25.

Liabilities

Liabilities are obligations of a business. They are claims of others against the assets of the business. A common characteristic of liabilities is their potential for reducing future assets or requiring future services or products.[6] Liabilities take many forms. Familiar liabilities are accounts payable and notes payable. An **account payable** is a liability created by buying products or services on credit. It reflects amounts owed to others. A **note payable** is a liability expressed by a written promise to make a future payment at a specific time. Other familiar liabilities are salaries and wages owed to employees and interest payable.

Individuals and organizations who own the right to receive payments from a business are called its **creditors.** Creditors own the right to be paid by a business. One entity's payable is another entity's receivable. If a business fails to pay its obligations, the law gives creditors a right to force the sale of business assets to obtain the money to meet creditors' claims. When assets are sold under these conditions, creditors are paid first, but only up to the amount of their claims. Any remaining money, the residual, goes to the owner of the business. Creditors often use a balance sheet to help decide whether to loan money to a business. They compare the amounts of liabilities and assets. A loan is less risky if liabilities are small in comparison to assets. This is because there are more resources than claims on resources. A loan is more risky if liabilities are large compared to assets.

Equity

Equity is the owner's claim on the assets of a business. It is the *residual interest* in the assets of a business after deducting liabilities.[7] Equity also is called **net assets.** Since FastForward is a sole proprietorship, the equity heading of its balance sheet in Exhibit 2.4 is *owner's equity*. If it was organized as a corporation, its owner would be a shareholder and equity would be called *shareholders',* or *stockholders', equity.*

Owner's equity is increased by owner investments and by revenues. It is decreased by owner withdrawals and by expenses. Exhibit 2.5 shows these important relations. Owner investments are assets put into the business by the owner. Owner withdrawals are assets taken from the business by the owner. These changes in owner's equity are reported in the statement of changes in owner's equity and give us the ending balance of owner's equity. This ending balance is also reported in the balance sheet.

Exhibit 2.5

Flow of Money In and Out of Owner's Equity

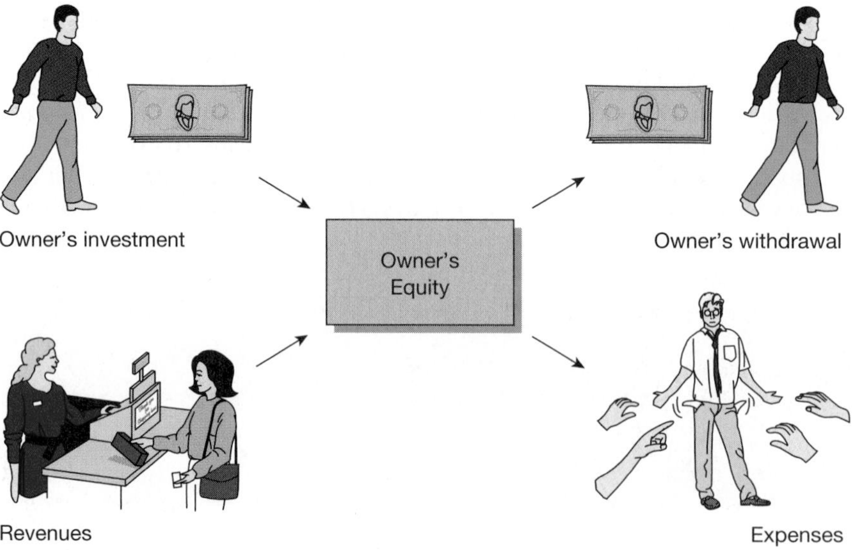

[6] Ibid., par. 35.

[7] Ibid., par. 49.

Exhibit 2.6

Statement of Cash Flows

FASTForward

FASTFORWARD Statement of Cash Flows For Month Ended December 31, 1997		
Cash flows from operating activities:		
Cash received from clients	$4,100	
Cash paid for supplies	(2,500)	
Cash paid for rent	(1,000)	
Cash paid to employee	(700)	
Net cash used by operating activities		$ (100)
Cash flows from investing activities:		
Purchase of equipment	$(20,000)	
Net cash used by investing activities		(20,000)
Cash flows from financing activities:		
Investment by owner	$ 30,000	
Partial repayment of note	(900)	
Withdrawal by owner	(600)	
Net cash provided by financing activities		28,500
Net increase in cash		$ 8,400
Cash balance, December 1, 1997		0
Cash balance, December 31, 1997		$ 8,400

Statement of Cash Flows

The **statement of cash flows** describes the sources (inflows) and uses (outflows) of cash for a reporting period. It also reports the amount of cash at both the beginning and end of a period. The statement of cash flows is organized by a company's major activities: operating, investing, and financing. Since a company must carefully manage cash if it is to survive and prosper, cash flow information is important.

FastForward's statement of cash flows for December is shown in Exhibit 2.6. The first section shows cash outflows from operating activities equal to $100. This is the result of $4,100 of cash received from customers less $4,200 paid for supplies, rent, and salaries. The second section reports on investing activities and shows a $20,000 cash outflow for buying equipment. The third section reports a $28,500 cash inflow from financing activities. FastForward's financing activities included an owner investment, a loan repayment, and an owner withdrawal.

Financial Statements and Forms of Organization

C2 Describe differences in financial statements across forms of business organization.

Chapter 1 described three different forms of business organization: proprietorships, partnerships, and corporations. While there are many differences between these forms of business organization, financial statements for these organizations are very similar.

Probably the most important difference in financial statements is in the equity section of the balance sheet. A proprietorship's balance sheet lists the equity balance beside the owner's name as in Exhibit 2.4. A partnership's balance sheet uses the same approach, unless there are too many owners for their names to fit in the available space. For example, if Chuck Taylor is part of an equal partnership with his sister Jane, then the equity section of the balance sheet would look like the one in Exhibit 2.7.

Exhibit 2.7

Equity Section of a Partnership Balance Sheet

FASTFORWARD Partial Balance Sheet December 31, 1997	
Partners' Equity	
Chuck Taylor, capital	$15,900
Jane Taylor, capital	15,900
Total partners' equity	$31,800

Exhibit 2.8

Equity Section of a Corporation Balance Sheet

FASTFORWARD Partial Balance Sheet December 31, 1997	
Shareholders' Equity	
Contributed capital:	
Common stock	$30,000
Retained earnings	1,800
Total shareholders' equity ...	$31,800

A corporation's balance sheet does not list the names of its shareholders. Instead, equity is divided into **contributed capital** (also called **paid-in capital**) and **retained earnings.** Contributed capital reflects shareholders' investments. Retained earnings are the corporation's profits that have not been distributed to shareholders. For example, assume Chuck Taylor had set up FastForward as a corporation in which he was the sole shareholder. If he is issued common stock for his $30,000 investment, then the equity section of the balance sheet would look like the one in Exhibit 2.8.

Retained earnings is a corporation's accumulated net income (loss) for all prior periods' operations that has not been distributed to shareholders. FastForward has earned $2,400, of which $600 was distributed to Taylor as a dividend, leaving $1,800 in retained earnings.

When an owner of a proprietorship or a partnership takes cash or other assets from a company, the distributions are called **withdrawals.** When owners of a corporation receive cash or other assets from a company, the distributions are called **dividends.** Withdrawals and dividends are not reported as part of the income statement because they are *not* expenses incurred to generate revenues. Also, when the owner of a proprietorship is its manager, no salary expense is reported on the income statement for these services. The same is true for a partnership. But since a corporation is a separate legal entity, salaries paid to its managers are always reported as expenses on its income statement. This different treatment of owners' salaries requires special consideration when analyzing an income statement. We explain one special adjustment near the end of this chapter.

The emphasis in the early chapters of this book is on sole proprietorships. This allows us to focus on important measurement and reporting issues in accounting without getting caught up in the complexities of organizational form. We do discuss forms of organization and provide examples when appropriate. Chapters 13 and 14 return to this topic and provide details about the financial statements of partnerships and corporations.

Flash back

1. What are the four major financial statements?
2. Describe revenues and expenses.
3. Explain assets, liabilities, and equity.
4. What are three differences in financial statements for different forms of organizations?

Answers—p. 63

Generally Accepted Accounting Principles

We explained in Chapter 1 how financial accounting practice is governed by rules called *generally accepted accounting principles,* or *GAAP.* For us to use and interpret financial statements effectively, we need an understanding of these principles. A primary purpose of GAAP is to make information in financial statements relevant, reliable, and comparable. Relevant information affects the decisions of its users. Information must be reliable so decision makers can depend on it. Information is comparable for different companies if the companies use similar practices. GAAP impose limits on the range of accounting practices companies can use. We describe in this section the current process for setting GAAP and many of the most important accounting principles.

Financial Reporting Environment

C3 Explain the financial reporting environment.

Generally accepted accounting principles are developed in response to the needs of users. While accounting professionals prepare financial statements, independent auditors (CPAs) often examine them and prepare an audit report to give users more assurance in the statements' reliability. Statements along with an audit report then are distributed to users.

Exhibit 2.9 shows how accounting principles, auditing standards, and various parties interact in the financial reporting environment. Accounting principles are applied in preparing financial statements. Preparers use preferred procedures in accounting for business transactions and events. Audits are performed in accordance with **generally accepted auditing standards (GAAS),** which are the accepted rules for conducting audits of financial statements. Both accounting and auditing help assure users that financial statements include relevant, reliable, and comparable information. An audit does not ensure success, and does not reduce the risk that a company's products and services will be unsuccessful or that adverse factors will cause it to fail. Instead, it tells us the statements are prepared using accepted accounting principles. **Ernst and Young** says in its audit report of **Harley-Davidson:**

> In our opinion, the consolidated financial statements . . . present fairly, in all material respects . . . in conformity with generally accepted accounting principles.

Setting Accounting Principles

Accounting principles were historically developed through common usage. A principle was acceptable if it was permitted by most professionals. This history is reflected in the phrase *generally accepted.* As business transactions became more complex, users were less satisfied with the lack of more concrete guidance. Many of these users desired more

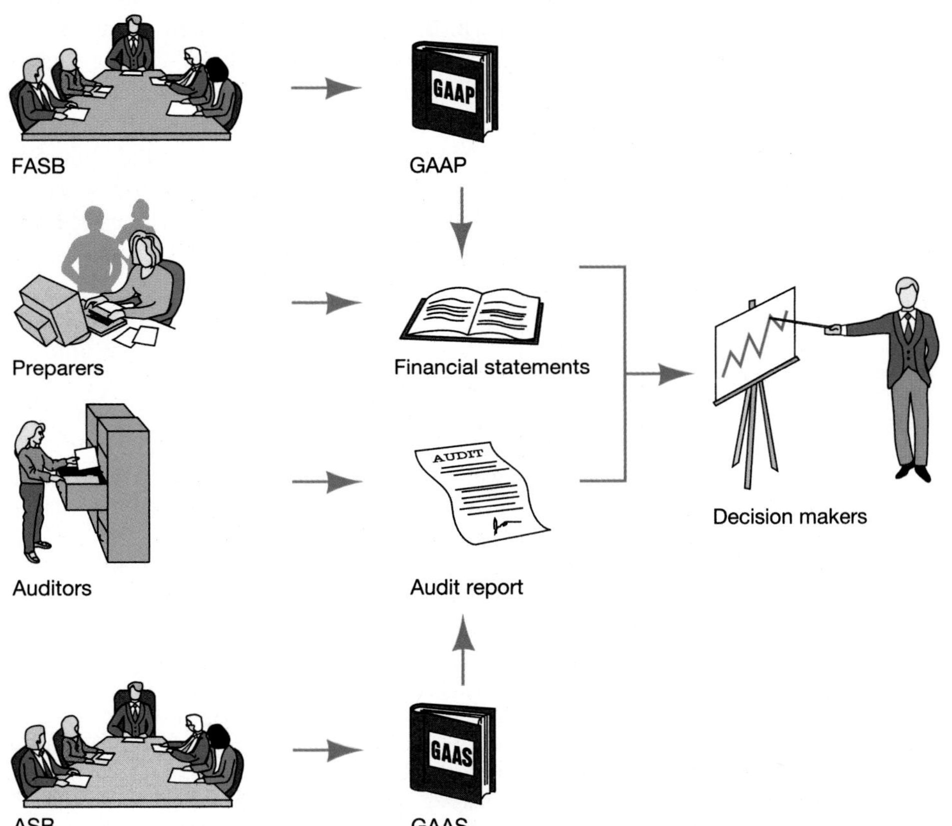

Exhibit 2.9
Financial Reporting Environment

C4 Identify those responsible for setting accounting and auditing principles.

uniformity in practice. Authority for developing accepted principles was eventually assigned to a select group of professionals in the field. These committees or boards have authority to establish GAAP. The authority of these groups has increased over time.

We show two organizations in Exhibit 2.9 that are the primary authoritative sources of GAAP and GAAS. The Financial Accounting Standards Board (FASB) is the primary authoritative source of GAAP. It is a nonprofit organization with a large research staff to help identify accounting problems and solutions. The Board seeks advice from all users and often holds public hearings for this purpose. Its goal is to improve financial reporting and balance the interests of all users. The FASB communicates its decisions in various publications. Most notable are **Statements of Financial Accounting Standards (SFAS).** These statements set generally accepted accounting principles in the United States and often affect international practices.[8]

The FASB draws its authority from two major sources. The first is the Securities and Exchange Commission (SEC). Congress created the SEC to regulate securities markets, including the flow of information from companies to the public. The SEC designates the FASB as its primary authority for setting GAAP. It can overrule the FASB but rarely does so. The second source of authority is state boards that license CPAs. Independent auditors assure us that financial statements comply with FASB rules. State ethics codes require CPAs that audit reports to disclose any areas where statements fail to comply. If CPAs fail to report noncompliance, they can lose their licenses to practice. The AICPA's Code of Professional Conduct includes a similar provision. A member of the AICPA can be expelled from the institute for not objecting to financial statements that fail to comply with FASB rules.[9]

Authority for generally accepted auditing standards (GAAS) belongs to the **Auditing Standards Board (ASB).** The ASB is a special committee of the AICPA with unpaid volunteer members. The SEC is an important source of the ASB's authority.[10]

International Accounting Principles

In today's global economy, people in different countries increasingly do business with each other. It is common for companies in the United States to sell products and services around the world. We see examples of companies in countries such as Russia selling their shares to American and Japanese investors and borrowing from lenders in places such as Saudi Arabia and Germany. **Marriott** is a United States company providing lodging and contract services. While many of **Marriott's** operations are in the United States, it recently opened or scheduled to open businesses in Aruba, the Bahamas, Egypt, Lebanon, Puerto Rico, Costa Rica, Ecuador, Germany, Guatemala, Indonesia, Malaysia, Mexico, and Thailand. Also, **NIKE** says the following about its global operations:

> All NIKE regions outside the U.S. experienced revenue increases greater than 30%. Europe increased 33%, Asia Pacific, 41%, and the Americas, 35%. The most significant increases were in Japan, Italy, United Kingdom, Korea, and Canada.

Despite our growing global economy, countries continue to maintain their unique set of acceptable accounting practices. Consider a Singapore company selling stock to foreign investors. Should it prepare financial statements that comply with Singapore ac-

[8] Predecessors to the FASB were the Accounting Principles Board (APB) and the Committee on Accounting Procedure (CAP).

[9] Many other professional organizations support the FASB, including the American Accounting Association (AAA), Financial Executives Institute (FEI), Institute of Management Accountants (IMA), Association for Investment Management and Research (AIMR), and Securities Industry Association (SIA). They increase the Board's credibility by participating in its process for setting GAAP.

[10] Working alongside the FASB is the Governmental Accounting Standards Board (GASB), which identifies special accounting principles to be applied in preparing financial statements for state and local governments.

counting standards or with the standards of the United States, Japan, Saudi Arabia, or Germany? Should it prepare five different sets of reports to gain access to financial markets in all five countries? This is a difficult and pressing problem.

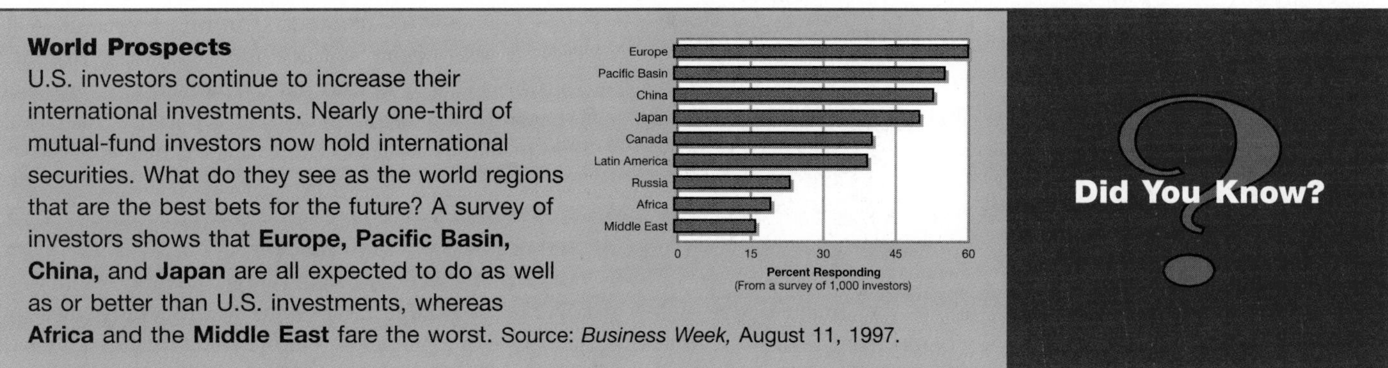

World Prospects
U.S. investors continue to increase their international investments. Nearly one-third of mutual-fund investors now hold international securities. What do they see as the world regions that are the best bets for the future? A survey of investors shows that Europe, Pacific Basin, China, and Japan are all expected to do as well as or better than U.S. investments, whereas Africa and the Middle East fare the worst. Source: Business Week, August 11, 1997.
Europe
Pacific Basin
China
Japan
Canada
Latin America
Russia
Africa
Middle East
0
15
30
45
60
Percent Responding
(From a survey of 1,000 investors)
Did You Know?

One response has been to create an **International Accounting Standards Committee (IASC).** The IASC issues *International Accounting Standards* that identify preferred accounting practices and encourages their worldwide acceptance. By narrowing the range of alternative practices, the IASC hopes to create more harmony among accounting practices of different countries. If standards are harmonized, a single set of financial statements can be used by one company in all financial markets. Many countries' standard setters support the IASC. Both the FASB and the SEC provide support and technical assistance. Yet the IASC does not have authority to impose its standards on companies. While interest is growing in moving United States GAAP toward the IASC's preferred practices, authority to make such changes rests with the FASB and the SEC.

Flash back

5. What organization sets GAAP? From where does it draw authority?
6. What is GAAS? What organization sets GAAS?
7. How are U.S. companies with international operations affected by international accounting standards?

Answers—p. 63

Principles of Accounting

C5 Identify, explain, and apply accounting principles.

Accounting principles are both general and specific. General principles are the basic assumptions, concepts, and guidelines for preparing financial statements. Specific principles are detailed rules used in reporting business transactions and events. General principles stem from long-used accounting practices. Specific principles arise more often from the rulings of authoritative groups.

We need an understanding of both general and specific principles to effectively use accounting information. Because general principles are especially crucial in using accounting information, we emphasize them in the early chapters of this book. The general principles described in this chapter include: business entity, objectivity, cost, going-concern, monetary unit, and revenue recognition. General principles described in later chapters (with their relevant chapter in parentheses) include: time period (4), matching (4), materiality (9), full-disclosure (9), consistency (10), and conservatism (10).[11] The specific principles are especially important for understanding individual items in financial statements and are portrayed as the building blocks for the *House of GAAP* in

[11] General principles are also commonly called *concepts, theories, assumptions,* or *postulates.*

Exhibit 2.10

Building Blocks for the House of GAAP

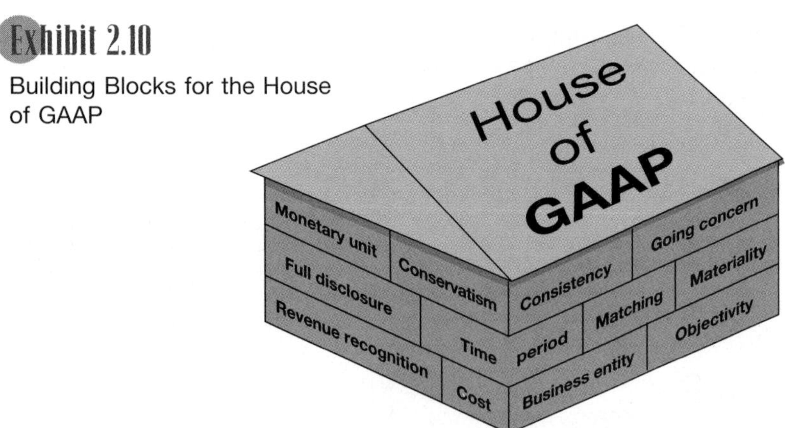

Exhibit 2.10. They are described throughout the book as we come to them.

Business Entity Principle

The **business entity principle** means that a business is accounted for separately from its owner or owners. It also means we account separately for each business that is controlled by the same owner. The reason for this principle is that separate information about each business is relevant to the decisions of its users.

We use FastForward to illustrate the importance of the business entity principle. Suppose Chuck Taylor, the owner, wants to know how well the business is doing. For financial statements to address his need, FastForward's transactions must be separate from Taylor's personal transactions. For example, Taylor's personal expenses (such as entertainment and clothes) must not be subtracted from FastForward's revenues on its income statement because they are not incurred as part of FastForward's business. A company's statements must not reflect its owner's *personal* transactions, assets, and liabilities. It also must not reflect the transactions, assets, and liabilities of *another business.* For reports and decision making to be effective, businesses must follow the entity principle.

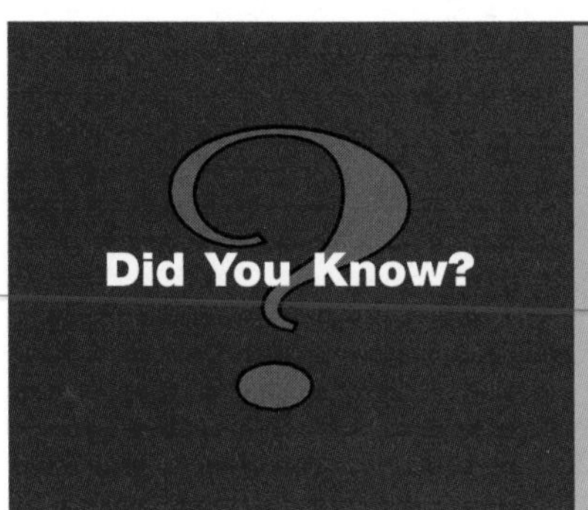

Penthouse Suspicions

Abuse of the business entity principle brought down executives at **Allegheny International.** Allegheny's executives turned in expenses not part of business activities. The worst? More than $1 million was spent to renovate and pay for a lavish penthouse for the CEO's son.

Source: Securities and Exchange Commission, AAER No. 151.

Objectivity Principle

The **objectivity principle** means that financial statement information is supported by independent, unbiased evidence. It involves more than one person's opinion. Information is not reliable if it is based only on what a preparer thinks might be true. A preparer can be too optimistic or pessimistic. An unethical preparer might even try to mislead users by intentionally misrepresenting the truth. The objectivity principle is intended to make financial statements useful by ensuring they report reliable and verifiable information.

Cost Principle

The **cost principle** means financial statements are based on actual costs incurred in business transactions. **Business transactions** are exchanges of economic consideration between two parties. Sales and purchases are examples of business transactions. Economic consideration can include products, services, money, and rights to collect money. Cost is measured on a cash or equal-to-cash basis. This means if cash is given for an asset or service, its cost is measured as the amount of cash paid. If something besides cash is exchanged (such as a car traded for a truck), cost is measured as the cash equal of what is given up or received.[12]

The cost principle is accepted by users because of its emphasis on reliability and relevance. Cost is the amount given up to purchase an asset or service. It approximates market

[12] FASB, *Accounting Standards—Current Text* (Norwalk, CT, 1995), sec. N35.105. First published as *APB Opinion No. 29,* par. 18.

value of an asset or service when it is acquired. Most users consider cost information as relevant to their decisions. The cost principle is also consistent with *objectivity* in that information based on cost is considered objective. For example, reporting purchases of assets and services at cost is more objective than reporting a manager's estimate of their value.

To illustrate this principle, suppose FastForward pays $5,000 for equipment. The cost principle tells us to record this purchase at $5,000. It would make no difference if Chuck Taylor thinks this equipment is really worth $7,000. The cost principle requires that this purchase be recorded at a cost of $5,000.

Going-Concern Principle

The **going-concern principle,** also called the *continuing-concern principle,* means financial statements reflect an assumption that the business will continue operating instead of being closed or sold. This means a balance sheet does not report liquidation values of assets held for long-term use. Instead, these assets are reported at cost. Since costs change, a balance sheet seldom reflects a company's exact worth. If a company is to be bought or sold, buyers and sellers should obtain additional information from other sources.[13] Neither the going-concern principle nor the cost principle is appropriate if a company is expected to fail or be liquidated. Instead, market values are most relevant.

Monetary Unit Principle

The **monetary unit principle** means we can express transactions and events in monetary, or money, units. Money is the common denominator in business. Expressing transactions and events in money helps us use financial statements for communication in business. Examples of monetary units are the dollar in the United States, Canada, Australia, and Singapore, pound sterling in the United Kingdom, and peso in Mexico, the Philippines, and Chile. An *exchange rate* expresses the value of one currency relative to another. Exchange rates change frequently and are tied to many economic and political factors. The chart below is a partial listing of exchange rates in terms of U.S. dollars:

Country	U.S. $ equivalent†	Country	U.S. $ equivalent†
Canada (dollar)	0.70	United Kingdom (pound)	1.67
Taiwan (dollar)	0.03	Mexico (peso)	0.12
Germany (mark)	0.54	Philippines (peso)	0.03

†Rates as of April 2, 1998.

The monetary unit used by an organization usually depends on the country where it operates. But we are seeing more companies expressing financial statements in more than one monetary unit. For example, an excerpt in Exhibit 2.11 from **Nintendo's** financial statements shows results reported in *both* yen and dollars.

Exhibit 2.11

Nintendo's Financial Highlights in Both Dollars and Yen

NINTENDO'S FINANCIAL HIGHLIGHTS
Years Ended March 31, 1997 and 1996

	Yen (¥) in Millions		U.S. ($000s) Dollars	
	1997	1996	1997	1996
Total revenues	¥462,922	¥400,707	$3,733,249	$3,231,512
Net income	65,481	59,870	528,077	482,828
Total assets	735,620	649,840	5,932,422	5,240,650
Total equity	563,718	512,524	4,546,120	4,133,260

[13] In *SFAS 107,* the FASB requires supplemental disclosures (in notes to financial statements) of the current market values of many assets and liabilities.

Accounting generally assumes a *stable* monetary unit. This means we expect the value of a currency to not change. The more changes in the monetary unit, the more difficult it is for us to use and interpret financial statements, especially across time.

Flash back

8. Why is the business entity principle important?
9. How are the objectivity and cost principles related?

Answers—p. 63

Transactions and the Accounting Equation

A1 Analyze business transactions using the accounting equation.

We know financial statements reflect the business activities of a company. We also know many of these activities, such as purchases and sales, involve business transactions. To understand information in financial statements, we need to know how an accounting system captures relevant data about transactions, classifies and records data, and reports data in financial statements. This section starts us on an important path that continues through Chapter 5.

The basic tool of modern accounting systems is the **accounting equation** as shown in Exhibit 2.12.

Exhibit 2.12
Accounting Equation

Assets = Liabilities + Owner's equity

The accounting equation is also called the **balance sheet equation** because of its link to the balance sheet. Like any mathematical equation, the accounting equation can be modified by rearranging terms. Moving liabilities to the left side of the equality, for example, gives us an equation for owner's equity in terms of assets and liabilities:

Assets − Liabilities = Owner's equity

We next show how to use the accounting equation to keep track of changes in a company's assets, liabilities, and owner's equity in a way that provides us useful information.

Transaction Analysis—Part I

A business transaction is an exchange of economic consideration between two parties. Examples of economic consideration include products, services, money, and rights to collect money. Because two parties are exchanging assets and liabilities, a transaction affects the components of the accounting equation. It is important to remember that each transaction leaves the equation in balance. Assets *always* equal the sum of liabilities and equity. We show how this equality is preserved by looking at the transactions of Fast-Forward in its first month of operations.

Transaction 1: Investment by Owner

On December 1, 1997, Chuck Taylor formed an athletic shoe consulting business. He set it up as a proprietorship. Taylor is the manager of the business as well as its owner. The marketing plan for the business is to focus primarily on consulting with schools, sports clubs, athletes, and others who place orders of athletic shoes with manufacturers. Taylor invests $30,000 cash in the new company and deposits it in a bank account opened under the name of **FastForward.** After this transaction, the cash (an asset) and the owner's equity (called *C. Taylor, Capital*) each equal $30,000. The effect of this transaction on the accounting equation is:

	Assets	=	Liabilities	+	Owner's Equity
	Cash	=			C.Taylor, Capital
(1)	+$30,000	=			+$30,000 Investment

The accounting equation is in balance. It reveals that FastForward has one asset, cash, equal to $30,000. It also reveals no liabilities and an owner's equity of $30,000. The source of increase in equity is also identified as an investment to distinguish it from revenues.

Transaction 2: Purchase Supplies for Cash

FastForward uses $2,500 of its cash to buy supplies of brand name athletic shoes for testing. This transaction is an exchange of cash, an asset, for another kind of asset, supplies. The transaction produces no expense because no value is lost. It merely changes the form of assets from cash to supplies. The decrease in cash is exactly equal to the increase in supplies. The equation remains in balance.

	Assets			=	Liabilities	+	Owner's Equity
	Cash	+	Supplies	=			C.Taylor, Capital
Old Bal.	$30,000			=			$30,000
(2)	−2,500		+2,500				
New Bal.	$27,500	+	$2,500	=			$30,000
	$30,000				$30,000		

Transaction 3: Purchase Equipment for Cash

FastForward spends $20,000 to acquire equipment for testing athletic shoes. Like transaction 2, transaction 3 is an exchange of one asset, cash, for another asset, equipment. It is not an expense because no value is lost. This purchase changes the makeup of assets but does not change the asset total. The equation remains in balance.

	Assets					=	Liabilities	+	Owner's Equity
	Cash	+	Supplies	+	Equipment	=			C.Taylor, Capital
Old Bal.	$27,500	+	$2,500			=			$30,000
(3)	−20,000				+20,000				
New Bal.	$7,500	+	$2,500	+	$20,000	=			$30,000
			$30,000				$30,000		

Transaction 4: Purchase Equipment and Supplies on Credit

Taylor decides he needs more testing equipment and supplies of brand name athletic shoes. These purchases total $7,100. But as we see from the accounting equation in transaction 3, FastForward has only $7,500 in cash. Concerned that these purchases would use nearly all of FastForward's cash, Taylor arranges to purchase them on credit from CalTech Supply Company. This means FastForward acquires these items in exchange for a promise to pay for them later. Supplies of athletic shoes cost $1,100, the new testing equipment cost $6,000, and the total liability to CalTech Supply is $7,100. The effects of this purchase on the accounting equation are:

	Assets					=	Liabilities			+	Owner's Equity
	Cash	+	Supplies	+	Equipment	=	Accounts Payable	+	Note Payable	+	C.Taylor, Capital
Old Bal.	$7,500	+	$2,500	+	$20,000	=					$30,000
(4)		+	1,100	+	6,000		+$1,100	+	$6,000		
New Bal.	$7,500	+	$3,600	+	$26,000	=	$1,100	+	$6,000	+	$30,000
			$37,100						$37,100		

This purchase increases assets by $7,100 while liabilities (called *accounts payable* and *note payable)* increase by the same amount. Both of these payables are promises by Taylor to repay its debt, but the note payable reflects a more formal, written agreement. A note payable is often necessary when the repayment period is longer than a month or two. We discuss these liabilities in detail in later chapters.

Transaction 5: Services Rendered for Cash

A main objective of a business is to increase its owner's wealth. This goal is met when a business produces *net income.* Net income is reflected in the accounting equation as an increase in owner's equity. FastForward earns revenues by consulting with clients about test results on athletic shoes. FastForward earns a net income only if its revenues are greater than the expenses incurred in earning them.

We see how the accounting equation is affected by earning consulting revenues in transaction 5. FastForward provides consulting services to a Los Angeles athletic club on December 10 and immediately collects $2,200 cash. The accounting equation shows an increase in cash by $2,200 and in owner's equity by $2,200. This increase in equity is identified in the far right column as a revenue because it is earned by providing services. These explanations are useful in later preparing and interpreting a statement of changes in owner's equity and an income statement.

	Assets			= Liabilities		+ Owner's Equity	
	Cash	+ Supplies	+ Equipment	= Accounts Payable	+ Note Payable	+ C.Taylor, Capital	
Old Bal.	$7,500	+ $3,600	+ $26,000	= $1,100	+ $6,000	+ $30,000	
(5)	+ 2,200					+ 2,200	Consulting Revenue
New Bal.	$9,700	+ $3,600	+ $26,000	= $1,100	+ $6,000	+ $32,200	
	$39,300			$39,300			

Transactions 6 and 7: Payment of Expenses in Cash

FastForward pays $1,000 rent on December 10 to the landlord of the building where its store is located. Paying this amount allows FastForward to occupy the space for the entire month of December. The effects of this event on the accounting equation are shown below as transaction 6. On December 12, FastForward pays the $700 salary of the company's only employee. This event is reflected in the accounting equation as transaction 7.

	Assets			= Liabilities		+ Owner's Equity	
	Cash	+ Supplies	+ Equipment	= Accounts Payable	+ Note Payable	+ C.Taylor, Capital	
Old Bal.	$9,700	+ $3,600	+ $26,000	= $1,100	+ $6,000	+ $32,200	Rent Expense
(6)	−1,000					− 1,000	
Bal.	$8,700	+ $3,600	+ $26,000	= $1,100	+ $6,000	+ $31,200	Salary Expense
(7)	− 700					− 700	
New Bal.	$8,000	+ $3,600	+ $26,000	= $1,100	+ $6,000	+ $30,500	
	$37,600			$37,600			

Both transactions 6 and 7 are expenses for FastForward. They use up cash for the purpose of providing services to clients. Unlike the asset purchases in transactions 2 and 3, the cash payments in transactions 6 and 7 acquire services. The benefits of these services do *not* last beyond the end of this month. The accounting equation shows both transactions reduce cash and Taylor's equity. The accounting equation remains in balance after each event. The far right column identifies these decreases as expenses.

Summary of Part I Transactions

FastForward has net income when its revenues exceed its expenses. Net income increases owner's equity. If expenses exceed revenues, a net loss occurs and equity is decreased. Net income or loss is not affected by transactions between a business and its owner. This means Taylor's initial investment of $30,000 is not income to FastForward, even though it increased equity.

To stress that revenues and expenses yield changes in equity, we add revenues directly to owner's equity and subtract expenses directly from owner's equity in this chapter. In practice and in later chapters, information about revenues and expenses is compiled separately. These amounts are later added to or subtracted from owner's equity at the end of the period. We describe this process in Chapters 3–5. Because of the importance of properly recognizing revenues for a business, we interrupt our analysis of FastForward's transactions to describe the revenue recognition principle.

10. How can a transaction not affect liability and equity accounts?

11. Describe a transaction increasing owner's equity and one decreasing it.

Answers—pp. 63, 64

Revenue Recognition Principle

Preparers need guidance in deciding when to recognize revenue. *Recognize* means to record a transaction or event for the purpose of reporting its effects in financial statements. If revenue is recognized too early, the income statement reports net income sooner than it should and the business looks more profitable than it is. If revenue is recognized late, the earlier income statement shows lower amounts of revenue and net income than it should and the business looks less profitable than it is. In both cases, the income statement does not provide decision makers with the most useful information about company success.

The **revenue recognition principle** provides guidance on when revenue should be recognized on the income statement. Recognition is also sometimes called *realization*. The recognition principle includes three important guidelines:

1. *Revenue is recognized when earned.* Preparing to provide services, finding customers, and promoting sales all contribute to earning revenue. Yet the revenue earned at any point in this process usually cannot be determined reliably until the process is complete, that is, when the business acquires the right to collect the selling price. This means revenue is usually not recognized on the income statement until the earnings process is complete. The earnings process is normally complete when services are rendered or the seller transfers ownership of products sold to the buyer. To illustrate, suppose a customer pays in advance of taking delivery of a product or service. Because the earnings process is not complete, the seller must not recognize revenue. The seller must complete the earnings process before recognizing revenue.[14] This practice is called *sales basis of revenue recognition.*
2. *Assets received from selling products and services do not have to be in cash.* A common noncash asset acquired by the seller in a revenue transaction is a customer's promise to pay at a future date. The seller views the customer's promise as an account receivable. These transactions are called *credit sales* and are often convenient for customers in purchasing products or services and paying for them later.

[14] FASB, *Accounting Standards—Current Text* (Norwalk, CT, 1995), sec. R75.101. First published as *APB Opinion No. 10,* par. 12.

FastForward did this in transaction 4 when it bought supplies and equipment on credit. If objective evidence shows that a seller has earned the right to collect from a customer, this seller should recognize an account receivable as an asset and record revenue earned. When cash is collected later, no additional revenue is recognized. Collecting the cash simply changes the makeup of assets from a receivable to cash.

3. *Revenue recognized is measured by cash received plus the cash equivalent (market) value of other assets received.* This means, for example, if a transaction creates an account receivable, the seller recognizes revenue equal to the value of the receivable, which usually is the amount of cash expected to be collected.

Notes to financial statements should include an explanation of the revenue recognition method used by a company. **General Motors,** for instance, reports in its annual report that:

> Sales are generally recorded by the Corporation when products are shipped to independent dealers.

Transaction Analysis—Part II

We return to the transactions of FastForward to show how revenue recognition works in practice.

Transaction 8: Services and Rental Rendered for Credit

FastForward provides consulting services of $1,600 and rental of test facilities for $300 to a small college sports team. The rental involves allowing selected team members to try recommended shoes at FastForward's testing grounds. The sports team is billed for $1,900. This transaction results in a new asset, account receivable from a client. The $1,900 increase in assets produces an equal increase in owner's equity. The increase in equity is identified as two revenue components in the far right column of the accounting equation:

	Assets				= Liabilities		+ Owner's Equity	
	Cash	+ Accounts Receivable	+ Supplies	+ Equipment	= Accounts Payable	+ Note Payable	+ C.Taylor, Capital	
Old Bal.	$8,000	+	+ $3,600	+ $26,000	= $1,100	+ $6,000	+ $30,500	
(8)		+ 1,900					+ 1,600	Consulting Revenue
							+ 300	Rental Revenue
New Bal.	$8,000	+ $1,900	+ $3,600	+ $26,000	= $1,100	+ $6,000	+ $32,400	
	$39,500				$39,500			

Transaction 9: Receipt of Cash on Account

An amount of $1,900 is received from the client 10 days after being billed for consulting services in transaction 8. Transaction 9 does not change the amount of assets and does not affect liabilities or equity. It converts the receivable to cash. It does not create new revenue. Revenue was recognized when FastForward rendered the services, not when the cash is now collected. This emphasis on the earnings process instead of cash flows is a goal of the revenue recognition principle and yields useful information to users. The new balances are:

	Assets				= Liabilities		+ Owner's Equity
	Cash	+ Accounts Receivable	+ Supplies	+ Equipment	= Accounts Payable	+ Note Payable	+ C.Taylor, Capital
Old. Bal.	$8,000	+ $1,900	+ $3,600	+ $26,000	= $1,100	+ $6,000	+ $32,400
(9)	+ 1,900	−1,900					
New. Bal.	$9,900	+ $ 0	+ $3,600	+ $26,000	= $1,100	+ $6,000	+ $32,400
		$39,500				$39,500	

Transaction 10: Payment on Note Payable

FastForward pays $900 to CalTech Supply on December 24. The $900 payment is for the earlier $6,000 purchase of testing equipment from CalTech, leaving $5,100 unpaid. The $1,100 amount due CalTech for supplies remains unpaid. The accounting equation shows this transaction decreases FastForward's cash by $900 and decreases its liability to CalTech Supply by the same amount. As a result, owner's equity does not change. This event does not create an expense even though cash flows out of FastForward.

	Assets				= Liabilities		+ Owner's Equity
	Cash	+ Accounts Receivable	+ Supplies	+ Equipment	= Accounts Payable	+ Note Payable	+ C.Taylor, Capital
Old Bal.	$9,900	+ $ 0	+ $3,600	+ $26,000	= $1,100	+ $6,000	+ $32,400
(10)	− 900					− 900	
New Bal.	$9,000	+ $ 0	+ $3,600	+ $26,000	= $1,100	+ $5,100	+ $32,400
		$38,600				$38,600	

Transaction 11: Withdrawal of Cash by Owner

Taylor withdraws $600 in cash from FastForward for personal living expenses. A proprietorship's distribution of cash, or other assets, to its owner is called a *withdrawal.* This decrease in owner's equity is not an expense. Withdrawals are not expenses because they are not part of the company's earnings process. Since withdrawals are not expenses, they are not used in calculating net income.

	Assets				= Liabilities		+ Owner's Equity	
	Cash	+ Accounts Receivable	+ Supplies	+ Equipment	= Accounts Payable	+ Note Payable	+ C.Taylor, Capital	
Old Bal.	$9,000	+ $ 0	+ $3,600	+ $26,000	= $1,100	+ $5,100	+ $32,400	
(11)	− 600						− 600	Withdrawal
New Bal.	$8,400	+ $ 0	+ $3,600	+ $26,000	= $1,100	+ $5,100	+ $31,800	
		$38,000				$38,000		

Summary of Transactions

FastForward engaged in transactions with five major entities: the owner, suppliers, an employee, customers, and the landlord. We identify the specific transactions by number with the specific entity in Exhibit 2.13.

We also summarize in Exhibit 2.14 the effects of all eleven transactions of FastForward using the accounting equation. Three points should be noted. First, the accounting equation remains in balance after each transaction. Second, transactions can be analyzed

FastForward's Transactions Grouped by Entities

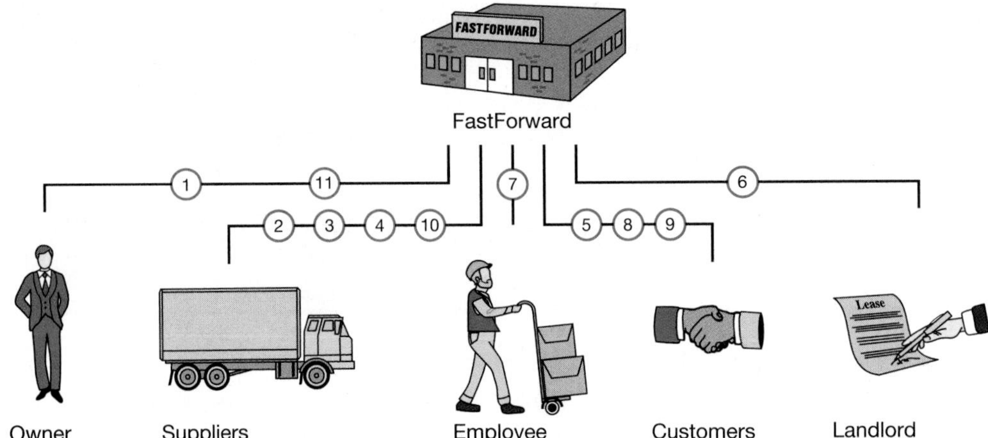

by their effects on components of the accounting equation. For example, total assets and equity increased by equal amounts in transactions 1, 5, and 8. In transactions 2, 3, and 9, one asset increased while another decreased by equal amounts. For transaction 4, we see equal increases in assets and liabilities. Both assets and equity decrease by equal amounts in transactions 6, 7, and 11. In transaction 10, we see equal decreases in an asset and a liability. Third, the equality of effects in the accounting equation is crucial to the double-entry accounting system. We discuss this system in the next chapter.

Summary of transactions using the Accounting Equation

	Assets				= Liabilities		+ Owner's Equity	
	Cash	+ Accounts Receivable	+ Supplies	+ Equipment	= Accounts Payable	+ Note Payable	+ C.Taylor, Capital	
(1)	$30,000						$30,000	Investment
(2)	− 2,500		+$2,500					
Bal.	$27,500		$2,500				$30,000	
(3)	−20,000			+$20,000				
Bal.	$ 7,500		$2,500	$20,000			$30,000	
(4)			+1,100	+ 6,000	+$1,100	+ $6,000		
Bal.	$ 7,500		$3,600	$26,000	$1,100	$6,000	$30,000	
(5)	+ 2,200						+$2,200	Consulting Revenue
Bal.	$ 9,700		$3,600	$26,000	$1,100	$6,000	$32,200	
(6)	− 1,000						− 1,000	Rent Expense
Bal.	$ 8,700		$3,600	$26,000	$1,100	$6,000	$31,200	
(7)	− 700						− 700	Salary Expense
Bal.	$ 8,000		$3,600	$26,000	$1,100	$6,000	$30,500	
(8)		+$1,900					+ 1,600	Consulting Revenue
							+ 300	Rental Revenue
Bal.	$ 8,000	$1,900	$3,600	$26,000	$1,100	$6,000	$32,400	
(9)	+ 1,900	−1,900						
Bal.	$ 9,900	$ 0	$3,600	$26,000	$1,100	$6,000	$32,400	
(10)	− 900					− 900		
Bal.	$ 9,000	$ 0	$3,600	$26,000	$1,100	$5,100	$32,400	
(11)	− 600						− 600	Withdrawal
Bal.	$ 8,400	+$ 0	+$3,600	+ $26,000	= $1,100	+ $5,100	+ $31,800	

Flash back

12. Why is the revenue recognition principle important?

13. Identify a transaction decreasing both assets and liabilities.

14. When is the accounting equation in balance and what does it mean?

Answers—p. 64

Financial Statements

P1 Prepare financial statements from business transactions.

We described financial statements at the beginning of this chapter. These statements are required under GAAP. In this section we show how financial statements are prepared from business transactions. Recall that the four major financial statements and their purposes are:

1. *Income statement* describes a company's revenues and expenses along with the resulting net income or loss over a period of time. It helps explain how owner's equity changes during a period due to earnings activities.
2. *Statement of changes in owner's equity* explains changes in equity due to items such as net income and an owner's investments and withdrawals over a period of time.
3. *Statement of cash flows* identifies cash inflows (receipts) and outflows (payments) over a period of time. It explains how the cash balance on the balance sheet changed from the beginning to the end of a period.
4. *Balance sheet* describes a company's financial position (assets, liabilities, and equity) at a point in time.

We now show how to prepare these financial statements using the transactions of FastForward.

Income Statement

FastForward's income statement is shown at the top of Exhibit 2.17. It is prepared from the December transactions of FastForward. These transactions and information about revenues and expenses are conveniently taken from the owner's equity column of Exhibit 2.14.

Revenues of $4,100 are reported first on the income statement. They include consulting revenues of $3,800 resulting from transactions 5 and 8, and rental revenue of $300 from transaction 8. Pie charts shown in Exhibits 2.15 and 2.16 are often helpful in analyzing the makeup of revenues and expenses. If FastForward earned other kinds of revenues, they would be shown separately to help users better understand the company's activities.

Revenue sources for FastForward

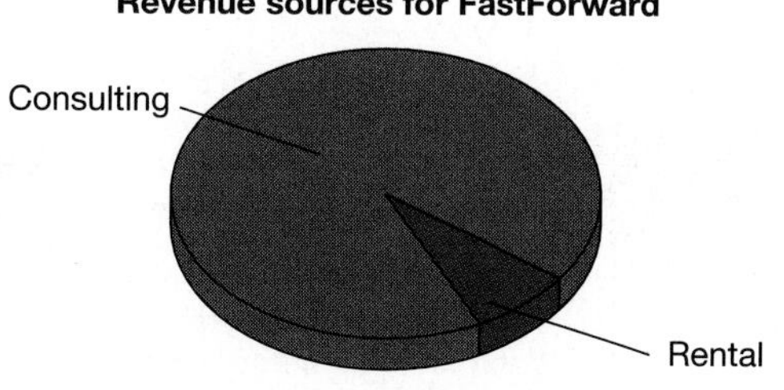

Exhibit 2.15

Pie Chart Analysis of Revenues

Expense sources for FastForward

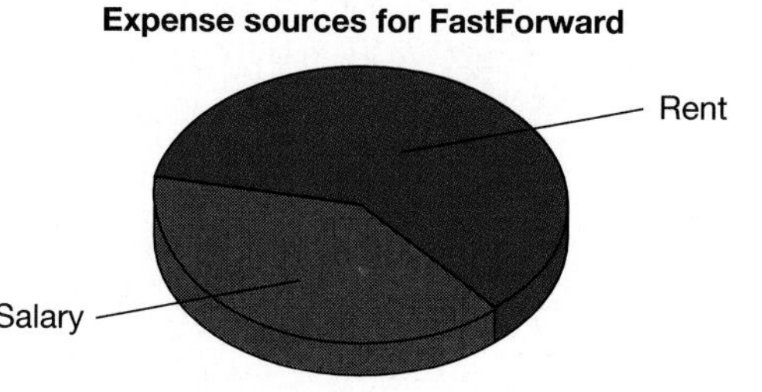

Exhibit 2.16

Pie Chart Analysis of Expenses

Expenses follow revenues. We can list expenses in different ways. For convenience in this chapter, we list larger amounts first. Rent and salary expenses are from transactions 6 and 7. Expenses help users interpret events of the time period. Net income is reported at the bottom and is the amount earned during December. Owner's investments and withdrawals are *not* part of measuring income.

Financial Statements and Their Links

FASTFORWARD
Income Statement
For Month Ended December 31, 1997

Revenues:		
Consulting revenue	$3,800	
Rental revenue	300	
Total revenues		$4,100
Expenses:		
Rent expense	1,000	
Salaries expense	700	
Total expenses		1,700
Net income		$2,400

FASTFORWARD
Statement of Changes in Owner's Equity
For Month Ended December 31, 1997

C.Taylor, capital, December 1, 1997		$ 0
Plus: Investment by owner	$30,000	
Net income	2,400	32,400
Total		$32,400
Less: Withdrawal by owner		(600)
C.Taylor, capital, December 31, 1997		$31,800

FASTFORWARD
Balance Sheet
December 31, 1997

Assets		Liabilities	
Cash	$ 8,400	Accounts payable	$ 1,100
Supplies	3,600	Note payable	5,100
Equipment	26,000	Total liabilities	$ 6,200
		Owner's Equity	
		C.Taylor, capital	31,800
		Total liabilities and	
Total assets	$38,000	owner's equity	$38,000

FASTFORWARD
Statement of Cash Flows
For Month Ended December 31, 1997

Cash flows from operating activities:		
Cash received from clients	$ 4,100	
Cash paid for supplies	(2,500)	
Cash paid for rent	(1,000)	
Cash paid to employee	(700)	
Net cash used by operating activities		$ (100)
Cash flows from investing activities:		
Purchase of equipment	(20,000)	
Net cash used by investing activities		(20,000)
Cash flows from financing activities:		
Investment by owner	30,000	
Partial repayment of note	(900)	
Withdrawal by owner	(600)	
Net cash provided by financing activities		28,500
Net increase in cash		$ 8,400
Cash balance, December 1, 1997		0
Cash balance, December 31, 1997		$ 8,400

Statement of Changes in Owner's Equity

The statement of changes in owner's equity reports information about changes in equity over the reporting period. This statement shows beginning equity, events that increase it (investments by owner and net income), and events that decrease it (withdrawals and net loss). Ending owner's equity is computed from this statement and is carried over and reported on the balance sheet.

The second report in Exhibit 2.17 is the statement of changes in owner's equity for FastForward. Its heading lists the month of December 1997 because this statement describes events that happened during that month. The beginning balance of equity is measured as of the start of business on December 1. It is zero only because FastForward did not exist before then. An existing business reports the beginning balance as of the end of the prior reporting period (such as November 30). FastForward's statement shows $30,000 of equity is created by Taylor's initial investment. It also shows the $2,400 of net income earned during the month. This item links the income statement to the statement of changes in owner's equity. The statement also reports Taylor's $600 withdrawal and FastForward's $31,800 equity balance at the end of the month.

Balance Sheet

FastForward's balance sheet is the third report listed in Exhibit 2.17. Its heading tells us the statement refers to FastForward's financial condition at the close of business on December 31, 1997.

The left side of the balance sheet lists FastForward's assets: cash, supplies, and equipment. The right side of the balance sheet shows FastForward owes $6,200 to creditors. This is made up of $1,100 for accounts payable and $5,100 for a note payable. If any other liabilities had existed (such as a bank loan) they would be listed here. The equity section shows an ending balance of $31,800. Note the link between the ending balance from the statement of changes in owner's equity and the equity balance here.

Supplier
You open your own wholesale business selling home entertainment equipment to small retail outlets. You quickly find that most of your potential customers demand to buy on credit. How can you use the balance sheet in deciding which customers you extend credit to?

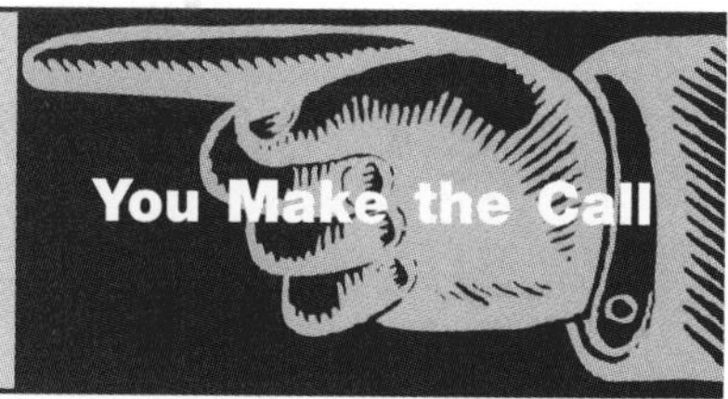

Answer—p. 63

Statement of Cash Flows

The final report in Exhibit 2.17 is FastForward's statement of cash flows. This statement describes where FastForward's cash came from and where it went during December. It also shows the amount of cash at the beginning of the period and the amount left at the end. This information is important for users because a company must carefully manage cash if it is to survive and grow. **Delta Air Lines** reported net losses of more than $1.3 billion for the three-year period ending June 30, 1994. But Delta avoided bankruptcy by carefully managing its cash by delaying spending, increasing borrowings, and issuing stock. Delta earned a profit of $408 million in 1995 and $156 million in 1996.

Cash Flows from Operating Activities

The first section of the statement of cash flows reports cash flows from *operating activities.* The $4,100 of cash received from customers equals total revenue on the income statement only because FastForward collected all of its revenues in cash. If some credit sales are not collected, or if credit sales from a prior period are collected this period, the amount of cash received from customers will not equal the revenues reported on the income statement for this period.

This section also lists cash paid for supplies, rent, and salaries. These cash flows are from transactions 2, 6, and 7. We put these amounts in parentheses to indicate they are subtracted. Amounts for rent and salaries equal the expenses on FastForward's income statement because it paid expenses in cash. The payment for supplies is an operating activity because they are expected to be used up in short-term operations.

Cash used by operating activities for December is $100. If cash received exceeded cash paid for operating activities, we would call it "cash from operating activities." Decision makers are especially interested in the operating section of the statement of cash flows. This information allows users to answer questions such as how much of operating income is in the form of cash.

Cash Flows from Investing Activities

The second section of the statement of cash flows describes *investing activities.* Investing activities involve the buying and selling of assets such as land and equipment that are held for long-term use in the business. FastForward's only investing activity is the $20,000 purchase of equipment in transaction 3.

Decision makers are interested in this section of the statement because it describes how a company is preparing for its future. If it is spending cash on productive assets, it should be able to grow. But a user is also concerned that a company does not overly spend on productive assets and face a cash shortage. If a company is selling its productive assets, it is downsizing its operations.

Cash Flows from Financing Activities

The third section of this statement shows cash flows related to *financing activities.* Financing activities include borrowing and repaying cash from lenders, and cash investments or withdrawals by the owner. The statement of cash flows in Exhibit 2.17 shows FastForward received $30,000 from Chuck Taylor's initial investment in transaction 1. If the business had borrowed cash, that amount would appear here as an increase in cash. The financing section also shows $900 paid for the note to CalTech Supply from transaction 10 and the $600 owner withdrawal in transaction 11. The total effect of financing activities was a $28,500 net inflow of cash. The financing section shows us why FastForward did not run out of cash even though it spent $20,000 on assets and used $100 in its operating activities. Namely, it used the owner's investment and a note from a supplier. Decision makers are interested in the financing section because excessive borrowing can burden a company and reduce its potential for growth.

The final part of the statement of cash flows is the net increase or decrease in cash. It shows FastForward increased its cash balance by $8,400 in December. Because it started with no cash, the ending balance is also $8,400. This ending amount is the link from the statement of cash flows to the balance sheet. We give a more detailed explanation of the statement of cash flows in Chapter 17.

Flash back

15. Explain the link between an income statement and the statement of changes in owner's equity.

16. Describe the link between a balance sheet and the statement of changes in owner's equity.

17. Discuss the three major sections of the statement of cash flows.

Answers—p. 64

USING THE INFORMATION | Return on Equity

A2 Compute return on equity and use it to analyze company performance.

An important reason for recording and reporting information about assets, liabilities, equity, and income is to help an owner judge the company's success compared to other business or personal opportunities. One measure of success is the **return on eq-**

uity ratio. This ratio is computed by taking net income for a period and dividing it by average owner's equity as shown in Exhibit 2.18.

$$\text{Return on equity} = \frac{\text{Net income}}{\text{Average owner's equity}}$$

Exhibit 2.18
Return on Equity

Chuck Taylor's return on equity is computed as:

$$\text{Return on equity} = \frac{\$2{,}400}{[\$30{,}000 + \$31{,}800] \div 2} = 7.8\%$$

This shows Taylor earned a return on equity of 7.8% for the month of December.[15]

Taylor's return for December is very high compared to most investments, especially for the first month of operations. But we must remember that net income for a proprietorship does not include an expense for the effort exerted by the owner in managing its operations. To take this into consideration, we compute a **modified return on equity** for proprietorships and partnerships. This modified return on equity reduces net income by the value of the owner's efforts and is computed as shown in Exhibit 2.19.

$$\text{Modified return on equity} = \frac{\text{Net income} - \text{Value of owner's efforts}}{\text{Average owner's equity}}$$

Exhibit 2.19
Modified Return on Equity

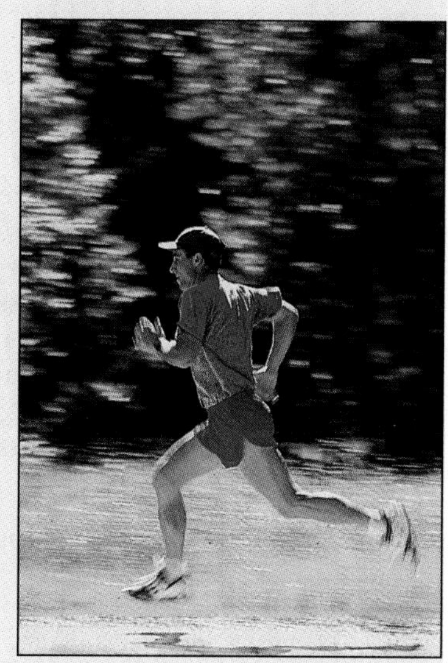

Other employment opportunities suggest that Taylor's efforts are valued at $1,800 per month. Taylor's modified return on equity is then computed as:

$$\text{Modified return on equity} = \frac{\$2{,}400 - \$1{,}800}{[\$30{,}000 + \$31{,}800] \div 2} = 1.9\%$$

This modified return for Taylor of 1.9% per month is quite different from the 7.8% above.

Taylor compares this return with other opportunities to determine whether it is adequate. Examples of other opportunities are savings accounts, government bonds, and company stock. Because 1.9% per month is more than 20% per year,[16] it is likely Taylor will continue to operate FastForward. For further comparison, we graph in Exhibit 2.20 the return on equity for seven different industries. FastForward's return exceeds each of these.

Three additional points need mention. First, an evaluation of returns should also recognize risk. Risk can differ considerably across investment alternatives. Second, income can vary from month to month. Income variation is related to risk. Third, because of company, business, and economic fluctuations, a better measure of return is obtained by computing it over a longer period such as one year.

[15] A simple average equals the sum of beginning and ending equity balances divided by two, or [$30,000 + $31,800] ÷ 2. Since this is the company's first month of operations, we use the owner's initial investment as its beginning balance.

[16] The annual rate is approximated by taking the 1.9% monthly rate and multiplying by the 12 months in a year, or 22.8%.

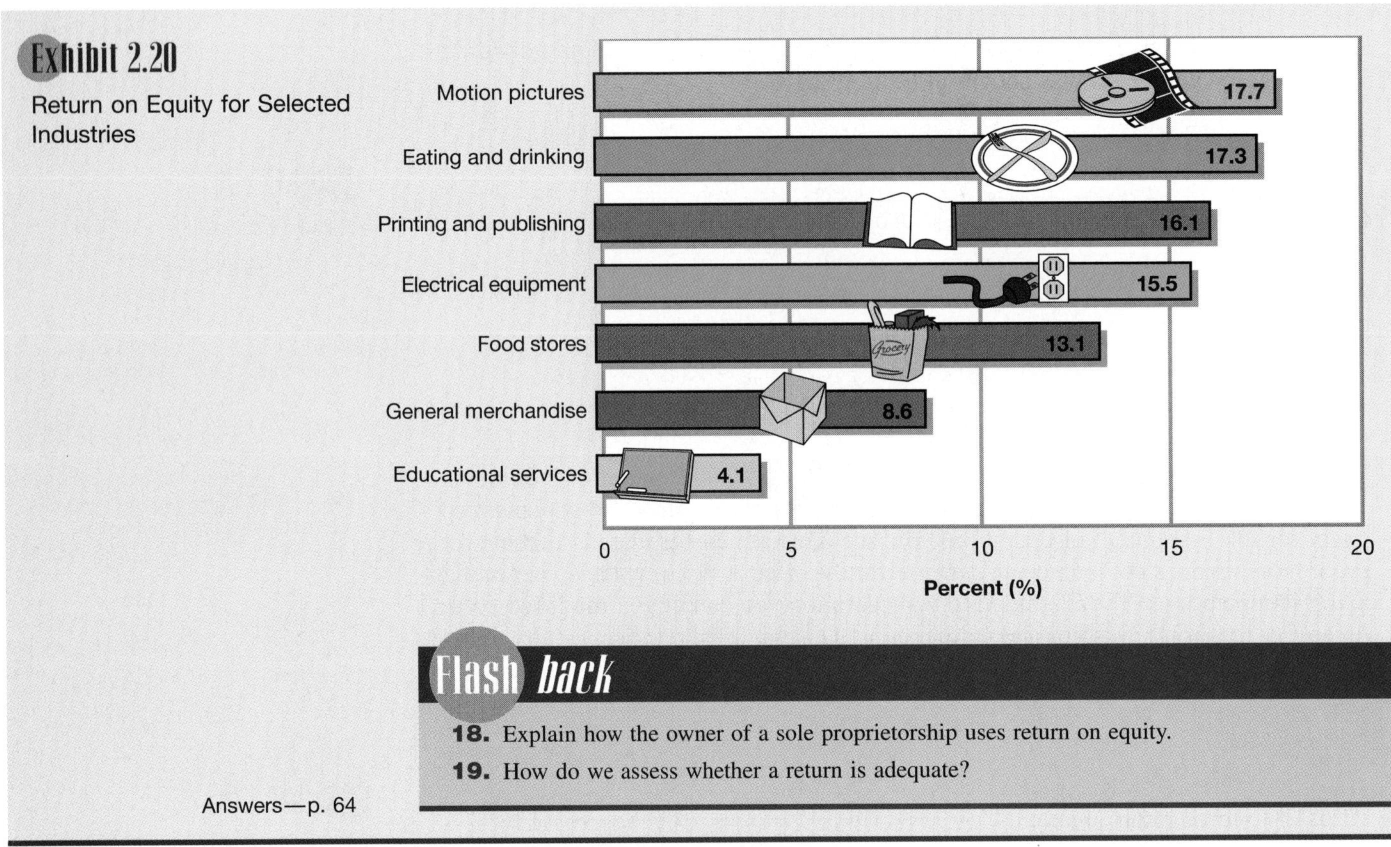

Exhibit 2.20

Return on Equity for Selected Industries

Flash back

18. Explain how the owner of a sole proprietorship uses return on equity.

19. How do we assess whether a return is adequate?

Answers—p. 64

Summary

C1 Identify and explain the content and reporting aims of financial statements. The major financial statements are: income statement, balance sheet, statement of changes in owner's equity, and statement of cash flows. An income statement shows a company's profitability including revenues, expenses, and net income (loss). A balance sheet reports on a company's financial position including assets, liabilities, and owner's equity. A statement of changes in owner's equity explains how owner's equity changes from the beginning to the end of a period, and the statement of cash flows identifies all cash inflows and outflows for the period.

C2 Describe differences in financial statements across forms of business organization. One important difference is in the equity section of the balance sheet. Proprietorship and partnership balance sheets list the equity balance beside the owner's name. Names of a corporation's shareholders are not listed in a balance sheet. Another difference is with the term used to describe distributions by a business to its owners. When an owner of a proprietorship or a partnership takes cash or other assets from a company, the distributions are called *withdrawals.* When owners of a corporation receive cash or other assets from a company, the distributions are called *dividends.* Recording payments to managers when managers are also owners is another difference. When the owner of a proprietorship or partnership is its manager, no salary expense is reported. But since a corporation is a separate legal entity, salaries paid to its managers are always reported as expenses on its income statement.

C3 Explain the financial reporting environment. Accounting professionals prepare financial statements, independent auditors often examine them and prepare an audit report, and users rely on them for making important decisions. Preparers use GAAP to decide what procedures are most appropriate for accounting for business transactions and events, and for proper reporting of statements. GAAS guide auditors in deciding on the audit procedures useful in determining whether financial statements comply with GAAP. Applying both GAAP and GAAS helps ensure that financial statements include relevant, reliable, and comparable information for users.

C4 Identify those responsible for setting accounting and auditing principles. The FASB is the primary authoritative source of GAAP. The FASB draws its authority from two major sources: the SEC and state boards that license CPAs. Authority for GAAS belongs to the ASB. The SEC is an important source of the ASB's authority.

C5 Identify, explain, and apply accounting principles. Accounting principles aid in producing relevant, reliable, and comparable information. The general principles described in this chapter include: business entity, objectivity, cost, going-concern, monetary unit, and revenue recognition. We will discuss others in later chapters. The business entity principle means that a business is accounted for separately from its owner. The objectivity principle means information is supported by independent, objective evidence. The cost principle means financial statements are based on actual costs incurred in business transactions. The monetary unit principle assumes transactions and events can be captured in money terms and that the monetary unit is stable over time. The going-concern principle means financial statements reflect an assumption that the business will continue to operate. The revenue recognition principle means revenue is recognized when earned, that assets received from selling products and services do not have to be in cash, and that revenue recognized is measured by cash received plus the cash equivalent (market) value of other assets received.

A1 **Analyze business transactions using the accounting equation.** A transaction is an exchange of economic consideration between two parties. Examples of economic considerations include products, services, money, and rights to collect money. Because two different parties exchange assets and liabilities, transactions affect the components of the accounting equation. The accounting equation is: Assets = Liabilities + Owner's equity. Business transactions always have at least two effects on the components of the accounting equation. The equation is always in balance when business transactions are properly recorded.

A2 **Compute return on equity and use it to analyze company performance.** Return on equity is computed as net income divided by average owner's equity. A modified return on equity for proprietorships and partnerships, that values the owner's efforts, is often useful and is computed as net income less the value of the owner's efforts and this quantity divided by average owner's equity. Return should be compared with other investment alternatives and opportunities to determine whether it is adequate. We should remember that net income can fluctuate and is a source of risk.

P1 **Prepare financial statements from business transactions.** Business transactions can be summarized using the accounting equation. Once transaction data are organized by the accounting equation we can readily prepare financial statements. The balance sheet uses the ending balances in the accounting equation at a point in time. The statement of changes in owner's equity and the income statement use data from the owner's equity account for the period. The statement of cash flows uses the numbers in the cash account for the period.

Guidance Answers to **You Make the Call**

Chef

A chef's efforts are often reflected in the income statement. This statement reports information on the revenues and expenses associated with operating activities. If operating activities are successful and you can point to specific contributions such as increased sales or reduced expenses, then you are much more likely to be successful in getting a wage increase.

Supplier

We can use the accounting equation to help us identify risky customers to whom we would not want to extend credit. The accounting equation is: Assets = Liabilities + Owner's equity. A balance sheet provides us with amounts for each of these key components. The lower owner's equity is, the less likely you should be to extend credit. A low owner's equity means there is little value in the business that does not already have claims on it from other creditors.

Guidance Answers to Flash *backs*

1. The four major financial statements are: income statement, balance sheet, statement of changes in owner's equity, and statement of cash flows.
2. Revenues are inflows of assets in exchange for products or services provided to customers as part of the primary operations of a business. Expenses are outflows or the using up of assets that result from providing products or services to customers.
3. Assets are the resources owned by a business. Liabilities are the obligations of a business, representing the claims of others against the assets of a business. Equity is the owner's claim on the assets of the business after deducting liabilities.
4. Three differences are: (*a*) A proprietorship's balance sheet lists the equity balance beside the owner's name. Partnerships use the same approach, unless there are too many owners for listing purposes. Names of a corporation's owners, or shareholders, are not listed in the balance sheet. (*b*) Distributions of cash or other assets to owners of a proprietorship or partnership are called withdrawals. Distributions of cash or other assets to owners of a corporation are called dividends. (*c*) When the owner of a single proprietorship is also its manager, no salary expense is reported on the income statement. The same is true for a partnership. But salaries paid to a corporation's managers are always reported as expenses on its income statement.
5. The FASB sets GAAP. Its most notable decisions are reported in *Statements of Financial Accounting Standards.* The FASB draws authority from two main sources: the SEC and state boards that license CPAs.
6. GAAS refer to generally accepted auditing standards and are the guidelines for performing audits of financial statements. GAAS are set by the Auditing Standards Board (ASB).
7. U.S. companies with international operations are not directly affected by international accounting standards. International standards are put forth as preferred accounting practices. However, there is growing pressure by stock exchanges and other parties to narrow differences in worldwide accounting practices. International accounting standards are playing an important role in that process.
8. Users desire information about the performance of a specific entity. If information is mixed between two or more entities, its usefulness decreases. It is important for the usefulness of accounting that the business entity principle be followed.
9. The objectivity principle means that financial statement information is supported by independent, unbiased evidence. The cost principle means financial statements are based on actual costs incurred in business transactions. The objectivity and cost principles are related in that most users consider information based on cost as objective. Information prepared using both principles is considered highly reliable and often relevant.
10. A transaction that changes the makeup of assets would not affect any liability and equity accounts. Both transactions 2 and 3 offer examples. Each involves exchanging one asset for another asset.

11. Earning revenue by performing services for a customer, such as in transaction 5, increases the owner's equity (and assets). Incurring expenses while servicing clients, such as in transactions 6 and 7, decreases the owner's equity (and assets). Other examples include owner investments that increase equity, and owner withdrawals that decrease equity.

12. The revenue recognition principle gives preparers guidelines on when to recognize (record) revenue. This is important since if revenue is recognized too early, the income statement reports net income sooner than it should and the business looks more profitable than it is. If revenue is recognized too late, the income statement shows lower amounts of revenue and net income than it should and the business looks less profitable than it is. In both cases the income statement is less useful to users.

13. Payment of a liability with an asset reduces both asset and liability totals. An example is transaction 10 where a note payable is reduced by paying cash.

14. The accounting equation is: Assets = Liabilities + Owner's equity. This equation is always in balance, both before and after every transaction. *Balance* refers to the equality in this equation and it is always maintained.

15. An income statement presents a company's revenues and expenses along with the resulting net income or loss. A statement of changes in owner's equity shows changes in equity, including net income. Also, both statements report transactions occurring over a period of time.

16. A balance sheet describes a company's financial position (assets, liabilities, and equity) at a point in time. The owner's equity account in the balance sheet is obtained from the statement of changes in owner's equity.

17. The statement of cash flows reports cash inflows and outflows in three sections: operating, investing, and financing activities. Cash flows from operating activities include revenues and expenses from the primary business the company is engaged in. Cash flows from investing activities involve transactions from the buying and selling of assets. Cash flows from financing activities include borrowing cash or other assets from lenders and the investments or withdrawals of the owner. The net figure in the statement of cash flows is the increase or decrease in cash for the business over the period. This net figure links the statement of cash flows to the balance sheet.

18. An owner of a proprietorship uses return on equity to measure the success of the business. This return is compared to alternative investment opportunities an owner could engage in. If the owner also works in the business, a modified return on equity is appropriate. This modified return subtracts the value of the owner's effort from net income in the numerator of the return on equity formula.

19. The return should be compared with other investment alternatives to determine whether it is adequate. Investment alternatives include savings accounts, government bonds, stocks, and other business ventures. These alternatives should be compared on the basis of both return and risk.

Demonstration Problem

After several months of planning, Barbara Schmidt started a haircutting business called The Cutlery. The following events occurred during its first month:

a. On August 1, Schmidt put $3,000 cash into a checking account in the name of The Cutlery. She also invested $15,000 of equipment that she already owned.

b. On August 2, she paid $600 cash for furniture for the shop.

c. On August 3, she paid $500 cash to rent space in a strip mall for August.

d. On August 4, she purchased some new equipment for the shop that she bought on credit for $1,200. This amount is to be repaid in three equal payments at the end of August, September, and October.

e. On August 5, The Cutlery opened for business. Receipts from services provided for cash in the first week and a half of business (ended August 15) were $825.

f. On August 15, Schmidt provided haircutting services on account for $100.

g. On August 17, Schmidt received a $100 check for services previously rendered on account.

h. On August 17, Schmidt paid $125 to an assistant for working during the grand opening.

i. Cash receipts from services provided during the second half of August were $930.

j. On August 31, Schmidt paid an installment on the account payable.

k. On August 31, she withdrew $900 cash for her personal use.

Required

1. Arrange the following asset, liability, and owner's equity titles in a table similar to the one in Exhibit 2.14: Cash, Accounts Receivable, Furniture, Store Equipment, Accounts Payable, and Barbara Schmidt, Capital. Show the effects of each transaction on the equation. Explain each of the changes in owner's equity.
2. Prepare an income statement for August.
3. Prepare a statement of changes in owner's equity for August.
4. Prepare a balance sheet as of August 31.
5. Prepare a statement of cash flows for August.
6. Determine the return on equity ratio for August.

7. Determine the modified return on equity ratio for August, assuming that Schmidt's management efforts were worth $1,000.

Planning the Solution

- Set up a table with the appropriate columns, including a final column for describing the events that affect owner's equity.
- Analyze each transaction and show its effects as increases or decreases in the appropriate columns. Be sure the accounting equation remains in balance after each transaction.
- To prepare the income statement, find the revenues and expenses in the last column. List those items on the statement, calculate the difference, and label the result as *net income* or *net loss.*
- Use the information in the Explanation of Change column to prepare the statement of changes in owner's equity.
- Use the information in the last row of the table to prepare the balance sheet.
- To prepare the statement of cash flows, include all events listed in the Cash column of the table. Classify each cash flow as operating, investing, or financing. Follow the example in Exhibit 2.17.
- Calculate the return on equity by dividing net income by the average equity. Calculate the modified return by subtracting the $1,000 value of Schmidt's efforts from the net income, and then dividing the difference by the average equity.

Solution to Demonstration Problem

1.

	Assets				= Liabilities +	Owner's Equity	
	Cash +	Accounts Receivable +	Furniture +	Store Equipment =	Accounts Payable +	Barbara Schmidt, Capital	Explanation of Change
a.	$3,000			$15,000		$18,000	Investment
b.	− 600		+$600				
Bal.	$2,400		$600	$15,000		$18,000	
c.	− 500					− 500	Rent Expense
Bal.	$1,900		$600	$15,000		$17,500	
d.				+ 1,200	+$1,200		
Bal.	$1,900		$600	$16,200	$1,200	$17,500	
e.	+ 825					+ 825	Haircutting Services Revenue
Bal.	$2,725		$600	$16,200	$1,200	$18,325	
f.		+$100				+ 100	Haircutting Services Revenue
Bal.	$2,725	$100	$600	$16,200	$1,200	$18,425	
g.	+ 100	− 100					
Bal.	$2,825	$ 0	$600	$16,200	$1,200	$18,425	
h.	− 125					− 125	Salaries Expense
Bal.	$2,700	$ 0	$600	$16,200	$1,200	$18,300	
i.	+ 930					+ 930	Haircutting Services Revenue
Bal.	$3,630		$600	$16,200	$1,200	$19,230	
j.	− 400				− 400		
Bal.	$3,230		$600	$16,200	$800	$19,230	
k.	− 900					− 900	Withdrawal
Bal.	$2,330 +		$600 +	$16,200 =	$800 +	$18,330	

2.

THE CUTLERY
Income Statement
For Month Ended August 31

Revenues:		
Haircutting services revenue		$1,855
Operating expenses:		
Rent expense	$500	
Salaries expense	125	
Total operating expenses		625
Net income		$1,230

3.

THE CUTLERY
Statement of Changes in Owner's Equity
For Month Ended August 31

Barbara Schmidt, capital, August 1		$ 0
Plus: Investments by owner	$18,000	
Net income	1,230	19,230
Total		$19,230
Less withdrawals by owner		(900)
Barbara Schmidt, capital, August 31		$18,330

4.

THE CUTLERY
Balance Sheet
August 31

Assets		**Liabilities**	
Cash	$ 2,330	Accounts payable	$ 800
Furniture	600	**Owner's Equity**	
Store equipment	16,200	Barbara Schmidt, capital	18,330
		Total liabilities and	
Total assets	$19,130	owner's equity	$19,130

5.

THE CUTLERY
Statement of Cash Flows
For Month Ended August 31

Cash flows from operating activities:		
Cash received from customers	$1,855	
Cash paid for rent	(500)	
Cash paid for wages	(125)	
Net cash provided by operating activities		$1,230
Cash flows from investing activities:		
Cash paid for furniture		(600)
Cash flows from financing activities:		
Cash received from owner	$3,000	
Cash paid to owner	(900)	
Repayment of debt	(400)	
Net cash provided by financing activities		1,700
Net increase in cash		$2,330
Cash balance, August 1		0
Cash balance, August 31		$2,330

6.

$$\text{Return on equity} = \frac{\text{Net income}}{\text{Average owner's equity}} = \frac{\$1,230}{\$18,165} = \mathbf{6.77\%}$$

Average owner's equity is ($18,000 + $18,330)/2 = $18,165

7.

$$\text{Modified return on equity} = \frac{\text{Net income} - \text{Owner's efforts}}{\text{Average owner's equity}} = \frac{\$230}{\$18,165} = \mathbf{1.27\%}$$

Glossary

Accounting equation a description of the relation between a company's assets, liabilities, and equity; expressed as Assets = Liabilities + Owner's equity; also called the *balance sheet equation*. (p. 50).

Account payable a liability created by buying goods or services on credit. (p. 42).

Account receivable an asset created by selling products or services on credit. (p. 41).

Assets resources owned or controlled by the business; more precisely, resources with an ability to provide future benefits to the business. (p. 41).

Auditing Standards Board (ASB) the authoritative committee of the AICPA that identifies generally accepted auditing standards. (p. 46).

Balance sheet a financial statement providing information that helps users understand a company's financial status; lists the types and dollar amounts of assets, liabilities, and equity as of a specific date; also called the *statement of financial position.* (p. 40).

Balance sheet equation another name for the accounting equation. (p. 50).

Business entity principle the principle that requires every business to be accounted for separately from its owner or owners; based on the goal of providing relevant information about each business separately to users. (p. 48).

Business transaction an economic event that changes the financial position of an organization; often takes the form of an exchange of economic consideration (such as goods, services, money, or rights to collect money) between two parties. (p. 48).

Continuing-concern principle another name for the *going-concern principle.* (p. 48).

Contributed capital the category of equity created by shareholders' investments; also called *paid-in capital.* (p. 44).

Cost principle the accounting principle that requires financial statement information to be based on actual costs incurred in business transactions; it requires assets and services to be recorded initially at the cash or cash equivalent amount given in exchange. (p. 48).

Creditors individuals or organizations entitled to receive payments from a company. (p. 42).

Debtors individuals or organizations that owe money to a business. (p. 41).

Dividends distributions of assets by a corporation to its owners. (p. 44).

Equity owner's claim on the assets of a business; more precisely, the residual interest in the assets of an entity that remains after deducting its liabilities; also called *net assets.* (p. 42).

Expenses outflows or the using up of assets as a result of the primary operations of a business. (p. 40).

Financial statements the most important products of accounting; include the balance sheet, income statement, statement of changes in owner's equity, and the statement of cash flows. (p. 38).

Generally accepted auditing standards (GAAS) rules adopted by the accounting profession as guides for conducting audits of financial statements. (p. 45).

Going-concern principle rule that requires financial statements to reflect the assumption that the business will continue operating, unless evidence shows it will not continue; also called *continuing-concern principle.* (p. 49).

Income statement a financial statement in which expenses are subtracted from revenues to show whether the business earned a profit; it lists the types and amounts of revenues earned and expenses incurred by a business over a period of time; also called *profit and loss statement.* (p. 39).

International Accounting Standards Committee (IASC) a committee that attempts to create more harmony among the accounting practices of different countries by identifying preferred practices and encouraging their worldwide acceptance. (p. 47).

Liabilities debts owed by a business or organization; claims by others that will reduce the future assets of a business or require services or products. (p. 42).

Modified return on equity the ratio of net income minus the value of owner's effort to average owner's equity. (p. 61).

Monetary unit principle the expression of transactions and events in money units; examples include units such as the dollar, peso, and pound sterling. (p. 49).

Net assets another name for equity. (p. 42).

Net income the excess of revenues over expenses for a period. (p. 39).

Net loss the excess of expenses over revenues for a period. (p. 39).

Note payable a liability expressed by a written promise to make a future payment at a specific time. (p. 42).

Objectivity principle accounting guideline that requires financial statement information to be supported by independent, unbiased evidence rather than someone's opinion; objectivity adds to the reliability, verifiability, and usefulness of information. (p. 48).

Paid-in capital another name for contributed capital. (p. 44).

Retained earnings shareholders' equity that results from a corporation's profits that have not been distributed to shareholders. (p. 44).

Return on equity ratio of net income to average stockholders' equity; used to judge a business's success compared to other activities or investments. (p. 60).

Revenue recognition principle provides guidance on when revenue should be reflected on the income statement; the rule includes three guidelines: (1) revenue must be recognized at the time it is earned; (2) the inflow of assets associated with revenue may be in a form other than cash; and (3) the amount of revenue is measured as the cash plus the cash equivalent value of any noncash assets received from customers in exchange for goods or services. (p. 53).

Revenues inflows of assets received in exchange for goods or services provided to customers as part of the major or primary operations of the business. (p. 39).

Statement of cash flows a financial statement that describes where a company's cash came from (receipts) and where it went during a period (payments); cash flows are arranged by an organization's activities: operating, investing, and financing. (p. 43).

Statement of changes in owner's equity reports the changes in equity over the reporting period; beginning equity is adjusted for increases (owner investment and net income) and for decreases (owner withdrawals and net loss). (p. 40).

Statement of financial position another name for the balance sheet. (p. 40).

Statements of Financial Accounting Standards (SFAS) the publications of the FASB that establish generally accepted accounting principles in the United States. (p. 46).

Withdrawal a payment of cash or other assets from a proprietorship or partnership to its owner or owners. (p. 44).

Questions

1. What information is reported in an income statement?
2. What do accountants mean by the term *revenue?*
3. Why does the user of an income statement need to know the time period that it covers?
4. What information is reported in a balance sheet?
5. Define *(a)* assets, *(b)* liabilities, *(c)* equity, and *(d)* net assets.
6. Identify two categories of accounting principles.
7. What FASB pronouncements identify generally accepted accounting principles?

8. What does the objectivity principle require for information reported in financial statements? Why?
9. A business shows office stationery on the balance sheet at its $430 cost, although it cannot be sold for more than $10 as scrap paper. Which accounting principle justifies this treatment?
10. Why is the revenue recognition principle needed? What does it require?
11. What events or transactions change owner's equity?
12. Identify the four main financial statements that a business reports to its owners and other users.
13. What should a company's return on equity ratio be compared with to determine whether the owner has made a good investment?
14. Find the financial statements of **NIKE**, in Appendix A. To what level of significance are the dollar amounts rounded? What time period does the income statement cover?
15. Review the balance sheet of **Reebok** in Appendix A. What is the amount of total assets reported at December 31, 1996? Prove the accounting equation for Reebok for December 31, 1996.
16. Find **America Online's** income statement in Appendix A. How is the name of this statement different from FastForward's income statement? How does AOL's 1996 net income compare to the previous year's?
17. Review **FastForward's** financial statements presented in the chapter for the month ended December 31, 1997. Review the balance sheet and determine the business form Chuck Taylor has chosen to organize his business. How much cash did FastForward generate from the total of its operating, investing, and financing activities in December 1997?

In solving the assignment materials in this and later chapters, assume no income taxes unless they are specifically mentioned.

Quick Study

QS 2-1
Identifying financial statement items
C1

Identify the financial statement on which each of the following items appears:

a. Office supplies
b. Service fees earned
c. Cash received from customers
d. Owner, withdrawals
e. Office equipment
f. Accounts payable
g. Repayment of bank loan
h. Utilities expense

QS 2-2
Identifying accounting principles
C5

Identify which general accounting principle is best described by each of the following practices:

a. Tracy Regis owns Second Time Around Clothing and also owns Antique Accents, both of which are sole proprietorships. In preparing financial statements for Antique Accents, Regis should be sure that the expense transactions of Second Time Around are excluded from the statements.
b. In December, 2000, Classic Coverings received a customer's order to install carpet and tile in a new house that would not be ready for completion until March 2001. Classic Coverings should record the revenue for the order in March 2001, not in December 2000.
c. If $30,000 cash is paid to buy land, the land should be reported on the purchaser's balance sheet at $30,000.

QS 2-3
Applying the accounting equation
A1

Determine the missing amount for each of the following equations:

	Assets	=	Liabilities	+	Equity
a.	$ 75,000	=	$ 40,500	+	?
b.	$300,000	=	?	+	85,500
c.	?	=	$187,500	+	$95,400

QS 2-4
Applying the accounting equation
A1

Use the accounting equation to determine the:

a. Owner's equity in a business that has $374,700 of assets and $252,450 of liabilities.
b. Liabilities of a business having $150,900 of assets and $126,000 of owner's equity.
c. Assets of a business having $37,650 of liabilities and $112,500 of owner's equity.

QS 2-5
Computing return on equity
A2

In a recent year's financial statements, **Boeing Company,** which is the largest aerospace company in the United States, reported the following:

Sales and other operating revenues	$21,924 million
Net income	856 million
Total assets	21,463 million
Total beginning-of-year equity	8,983 million
Total end-of-year equity	9,700 million

Calculate Boeing's return on equity.

Exercises

Exercise 2-1
Effects of transactions on accounting equation
A1

The table below shows the effects of five transactions *a* through *e* on the assets, liabilities, and equity of Pace Design. Write short descriptions of the probable nature of each transaction.

	Assets								= Liabilities	+ Owner's Equity
	Cash	+	Accounts Receivable	+	Office Supplies	+	Land	=	Accounts Payable	+ C. Pace Capital
	$7,500				$2,500		$14,500			$24,500
a.	−3,000						+3,000			
	$4,500				$2,500		$17,500			$24,500
b.					+ 400				+$400	
	$4,500				$2,900		$17,500		$400	$24,500
c.			+$1,050							+ 1,050
	$4,500		$1,050		$2,900		$17,500		$400	$25,550
d.	− 400								−400	
	$4,100		$1,050		$2,900		$17,500		$ 0	$25,550
e.	+1,050		−1,050							
	$5,150	+	$ 0	+	$2,900	+	$17,500	=	$ 0	+ $25,550

Exercise 2-2
Analysis using the accounting equation
A1

Carter Stark began a new consulting firm on January 3. The accounting equation showed the following balances after each of the company's first five transactions. Analyze the equations and describe each of the five transactions with their amounts.

	Assets				= Liabilities	+ Owner's Equity
Transaction	Cash	+ Accounts Receivable	+ Office Supplies	+ Office Furniture	= Accounts Payable	+ C. Stark, Capital
a.	$30,000	$ 0	$ 0	$ 0	$ 0	$30,000
b.	29,000	0	1,750	0	750	30,000
c.	21,000	0	1,750	8,000	750	30,000
d.	21,000	2,000	1,750	8,000	750	32,000
e.	20,500	2,000	1,750	8,000	750	31,500

Exercise 2-3
Computing net income
C1, C5

A business had the following amounts of assets and liabilities at the beginning and end of a recent year:

	Assets	Liabilities
Beginning of the year	$ 75,000	$30,000
End of the year	120,000	46,000

Determine the net income earned or net loss incurred by the business during the year under each of the following unrelated assumptions:

a. Owner made no additional investments in the business and withdrew no assets during the year.

b. Owner made no additional investments in the business during the year but withdrew $1,750 per month to pay personal living expenses.

c. Owner withdrew no assets during the year but invested an additional $32,500 cash.

d. Owner withdrew $1,750 per month to pay personal living expenses and invested an additional $25,000 cash in the business.

Exercise 2-4
Effects of transactions on accounting equation and computing return on equity

A1, A2

Linda Champion began a professional practice on May 1 and plans to prepare financial statements at the end of each month. During May, Champion completed these transactions:

a. Invested $50,000 cash along with equipment that had a $10,000 fair market value.

b. Paid $1,600 rent for office space for the month.

c. Purchased $12,000 of additional equipment on credit.

d. Completed work for a client and immediately collected the $2,000 cash earned.

e. Completed work for a client and sent a bill for $7,000 to be paid within 30 days.

f. Purchased $8,000 of additional equipment for cash.

g. Paid an assistant $2,400 as wages for the month.

h. Collected $5,000 of the amount owed by the client described in transaction *e*.

i. Paid for the equipment purchased in transaction *c*.

j. Withdrew $500 for personal use.

Required

Create a table like the one in Exhibit 2.14, using the following headings for columns: Cash; Accounts Receivable; Equipment; Accounts Payable; and L. Champion, Capital. Then, use additions and subtractions to show the effects of the transactions on the elements of the accounting equation. Show new totals after each transaction. Determine the modified return on Champion's initial investment, assuming that her management efforts during the month have a value of $3,000.

Check Figure Net income, $5,000

Exercise 2-5
Effects of transactions on the accounting equation

A1

Seven pairs of changes in items of the accounting equation are described below in *a* through *g*. Provide an example of a transaction that creates the described effects.

a. Decreases a liability and increases a liability.

b. Increases an asset and decreases an asset.

c. Decreases an asset and decreases equity.

d. Increases a liability and decreases equity.

e. Increases an asset and increases a liability.

f. Increases an asset and increases equity.

g. Decreases an asset and decreases a liability.

Exercise 2-6
Income statement

C1, P1

On November 1, Joseph Grayson organized a new consulting firm called The Grayson Group. On November 30, the company's records showed the following items. Use this information to prepare a November income statement for the business.

Cash	$12,000	Owner's withdrawals	$ 3,360
Accounts receivable	15,000	Consulting fees earned	15,000
Office supplies	2,250	Rent expense	2,550
Automobiles	36,000	Salaries expense	6,000
Office equipment	28,000	Telephone expense	660
Accounts payable	7,500	Miscellaneous expenses	680
Owner's investments	84,000		

Check Figure Net income, $5,110

Exercise 2-7
Statement of changes in owner's equity

Use the facts in Exercise 2-6 to prepare a November statement of changes in owner's equity for The Grayson Group.

Exercise 2-8
Balance sheet
C1, P1

Use the facts in Exercise 2-6 to prepare a November 30 balance sheet for The Grayson Group.

Exercise 2-9
Reporting financial statement items
C1, P1

Match each of the numbered items below with the financial statement or statements on which it should be reported. Indicate your answer by writing the letter or letters for the correct statement in the blank space next to each item.

A. Income statement
B. Statement of changes in owner's equity
C. Balance sheet
D. Statement of cash flow

_____ **1.** Cash received from customers
_____ **2.** Office supplies
_____ **3.** Rent expense incurred and paid in cash
_____ **4.** Consulting fees earned and received in cash
_____ **5.** Accounts payable
_____ **6.** Investments of cash by owner
_____ **7.** Accounts receivable
_____ **8.** Cash withdrawals by owner

Exercise 2-10
Statement of changes in owner's equity
C1, P1

Compute the amount of the missing item in each of the following separate cases *a* through *d*:

	a	b	c	d
Owner's equity, January 1	$ 0	$ 0	$ 0	$ 0
Owner's investments during the year	120,000	?	63,000	75,000
Owner's withdrawals during the year	?	(54,000)	(30,000)	(31,500)
Net income (loss) for the year	31,500	81,000	(9,000)	?
Owner's equity, December 31	102,000	99,000	?	85,500

Exercise 2-11
Accounting principles
C5, C3

Match each of the numbered descriptions below with the principle it best illustrates. Indicate your answer by writing the letter for the correct principle in the blank space next to each description.

A. General principle
B. Cost principle
C. Business entity principle
D. Revenue recognition principle
E. Specific principle
F. Objectivity principle
G. Going-concern principle

_____ **1.** Requires every business to be accounted for separately from its owner or owners.
_____ **2.** Requires financial statement information to be supported by evidence other than someone's opinion or belief.
_____ **3.** Usually created by a pronouncement from an authoritative body.
_____ **4.** Requires financial statement information to be based on costs incurred in transactions
_____ **5.** Derived from long-used and accepted accounting practices.
_____ **6.** Requires financial statements to reflect the assumption that the business will continue operating.
_____ **7.** Requires revenue to be recorded only when the earnings process is complete.

Exercise 2-12
Return on equity
A2

Use information for each of the following separate cases *a* through *d* to calculate the company's return on equity and its modified return on equity:

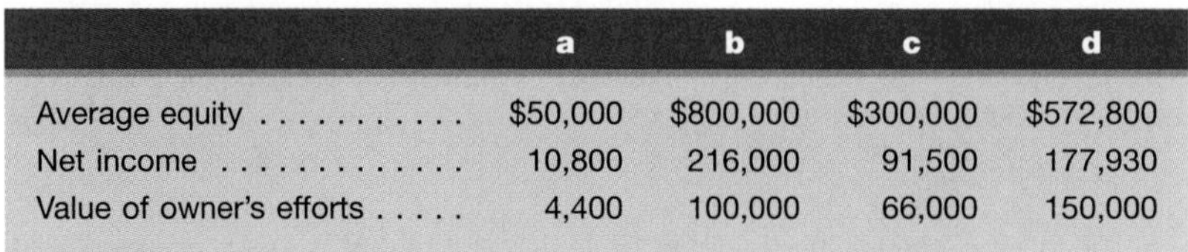

	a	b	c	d
Average equity	$50,000	$800,000	$300,000	$572,800
Net income	10,800	216,000	91,500	177,930
Value of owner's efforts	4,400	100,000	66,000	150,000

Exercise 2-13
Statement of cash flows

Indicate the section in which each of the following cash flows would appear on the statement of cash flows.

A. Cash flow from operating activity **C.** Cash flow from financing activity
B. Cash flow from investing activity

_____ **1.** Cash paid to suppliers
_____ **2.** Withdrawal by owner
_____ **3.** Cash paid to employee
_____ **4.** Purchase of equipment
_____ **5.** Cash paid for rent
_____ **6.** Investment by owner
_____ **7.** Repayment of note
_____ **8.** Cash received from customers

Problems

Problem 2-1
Analyzing effects of transactions and computing return on equity

C5, A1, A2

George Hemphill started a new business called Hemphill Enterprises and completed the following transactions during its first month of operations:

a. Hemphill invested $60,000 cash along with office equipment valued at $30,000 in the business.
b. Paid $300,000 for a building to be used as an office. Paid $50,000 in cash and signed a note payable promising to pay the balance over several years.
c. Purchased $4,000 of office supplies for cash.
d. Purchased $36,000 of office equipment on credit.
e. Performed services and billed the client $4,000 to be received at a later date.
f. Paid a local newspaper $1,000 for an advertisement of the new business.
g. Performed services for a client and collected $18,000 cash.
h. Made a $2,000 payment on the equipment purchased in transaction *d*.
i. Received $3,000 from the client described in transaction *e*.
j. Paid $2,500 cash for the office secretary's wages.
k. Withdrew $1,800 cash from the company bank account to pay personal living expenses.

Required

Preparation Component

1. Create a table like the one in Exhibit 2.14, using the following headings for the columns: Cash; Accounts Receivable; Office Supplies; Office Equipment; Building; Accounts Payable; Notes Payable; and George Hemphill, Capital. Leave space for an explanation column to the right of the Capital column. Identify revenues and expenses by name in the explanation column.
2. Use additions and subtractions to show the transactions' effects on the elements of the accounting equation. Show new totals after each transaction. Indicate next to each change in the owner's equity whether it was caused by an investment, a revenue, an expense, or a withdrawal.
3. Once you have completed the table, determine the company's net income.

Check Figure Net income, $18,500

Analysis Component

4. Determine the return on Hemphill's average owner's equity. Also, assume Hemphill could have earned $6,000 for the period from another job and determine the modified return on equity for the period. State whether you think the business is a good use of Hemphill's money if an alternative investment would have returned 9% for the same period.

Problem 2-2
Preparing a balance sheet, an income statement, and a statement of changes in owner's equity

Kelly Young started a new business called Resource Consulting Co. and began operations on April 1. Young completed the following transactions during the month:

Apr.	1	Invested $60,000 cash in the business.
	1	Rented a furnished office and paid $3,200 cash for April's rent.
	3	Purchased office supplies for $1,680 cash.
	5	Paid $800 cash for the month's cleaning services.
	8	Provided consulting services for a client and immediately collected $4,600 cash.
	12	Provided consulting services for a client on credit, $3,000.
	15	Paid $850 cash for an assistant's salary for the first half of the month.
	20	Received payment in full for the services provided on April 12.
	22	Provided consulting services on credit, $2,800.
	23	Purchased additional office supplies on credit, $1,000.

28 Received full payment for the services provided on April 22.
29 Paid for the office supplies purchased on April 23.
30 Purchased advertising for $60 in the local paper. The payment is due May 1.
30 Paid $200 cash for the month's telephone bill.
30 Paid $480 cash for the month's utilities.
30 Paid $850 cash for an assistant's salary for the second half of the month.
30 Purchased insurance protection for the next 12 months (beginning May 1) by paying a $3,000 premium. Because none of this insurance protection had been used up, it was considered to be an asset called Prepaid Insurance.
30 Withdrew $1,200 cash from the business for personal use.

Required

1. Arrange the following asset, liability, and owner's equity titles in a table like Exhibit 2.14: Cash; Accounts Receivable; Prepaid Insurance; Office Supplies; Accounts Payable; and Kelly Young, Capital. Include an Explanation column for changes in owner's equity. Identify revenues and expenses by name in the explanation column.
2. Show effects of the transactions on the elements of the equation by recording increases and decreases in the appropriate columns. Do not determine new totals for the items of the equation after each transaction. Next to each change in owner's equity, state whether it was caused by an investment, a revenue, an expense, or a withdrawal. Determine the final total for each item and verify that the equation is in balance.
3. Prepare an income statement for April, a statement of changes in owner's equity for April, and an April 30 balance sheet.

Check Figure Ending owner's equity, $62,760

Problem 2-3
Computing net income, preparing a balance sheet, and calculating return on equity

The accounting records of Goodall Delivery Services show the following assets and liabilities as of the end of 1999 and 2000:

	December 31	
	1999	2000
Cash	$ 52,500	$ 18,750
Accounts receivable	28,500	22,350
Office supplies	4,500	3,300
Trucks	54,000	54,000
Office equipment	138,000	147,000
Building		180,000
Land		45,000
Accounts payable	7,500	37,500
Notes payable		105,000

Late in December 2000 (just before the amounts in the second column were calculated), Travis Goodall, the owner, purchased a small office building and moved the business from rented quarters to the new building. The building and the land it occupies cost $225,000. The business paid $120,000 in cash and a note payable was signed for the balance. Goodall had to invest $35,000 cash in the business to enable it to pay the $120,000. The business earned a satisfactory net income during 2000, which enabled Goodall to withdraw $3,000 per month from the business for personal expenses.

Required

1. Prepare balance sheets for the business as of the end of 1999 and the end of 2000. (Remember that owner's equity equals the difference between assets and liabilities.)
2. By comparing owner's equity amounts from the balance sheets and using the additional information presented in this problem, prepare a calculation to show how much net income was earned by the business during 2000.
3. Calculate the 2000 return on equity for the business. Also, calculate the modified return on equity assuming that Goodall's efforts were worth $40,000 for the year.

Check Figure Modified return on equity, 6.3%

Problem 2-4
Analyzing transactions, preparing financial statements, and calculating return on equity
C1, A1, A2, P1

Stan Frey started a new business and completed these transactions during November:

Nov. 1 Stan Frey transferred $56,000 out of a personal savings account to a checking account in the name of Frey Electrical Co.
1 Rented office space and paid cash for the month's rent of $800.
3 Purchased electrical equipment from an electrician who was going out of business for $14,000 by paying $3,200 in cash and agreeing to pay the balance in six months.
5 Purchased office supplies by paying $900 cash.
6 Completed electrical work and immediately collected $1,000 for doing the work.
8 Purchased $3,800 of office equipment on credit.
15 Completed electrical work on credit in the amount of $4,000.
18 Purchased $500 of office supplies on credit.
20 Paid for the office equipment purchased on November 8.
24 Billed a client $600 for electrical work completed; the balance is due in 30 days.
28 Received $4,000 for the work completed on November 15.
30 Paid the assistant's salary of $1,200.
30 Paid the monthly utility bills of $440.
30 Withdrew $700 from the business for personal use.

Required

Preparation Component

1. Arrange the following asset, liability, and owner's equity titles in a table like Exhibit 2.14: Cash; Accounts Receivable; Office Supplies; Office Equipment; Electrical Equipment; Accounts Payable; and Stan Frey, Capital. Leave space for an explanation column to the right of Stan Frey, Capital. Identify revenues and expenses by name in the explanation column.
2. Use additions and subtractions to show the effects of each transaction on the items in the equation. Show new totals after each transaction. Next to each change in owner's equity, state whether the change was caused by an investment, a revenue, an expense, or a withdrawal.
3. Use the increases and decreases in the last column of the table from part 2 to prepare an income statement and a statement of changes in owner's equity for the month. Also prepare a balance sheet as of the end of the month.
4. Calculate the return on average owner's equity for the month.

Check Figure Ending owner's equity, $58,460

Analysis Component

5. Assume the investment transaction on November 1 was $40,000 instead of $56,000 and that Frey obtained the $16,000 difference by borrowing it from a bank. Explain the effect of this change on total assets, total liabilities, owner's equity, and return on equity.

Problem 2-5
Calculating missing information using accounting knowledge
C1, A1

The following financial statement information is known about five unrelated companies:

	Company A	Company B	Company C	Company D	Company E
December 31, 1999:					
Assets	$45,000	$35,000	$29,000	$80,000	$123,000
Liabilities	23,500	22,500	14,000	38,000	?
December 31, 2000:					
Assets	48,000	41,000	?	125,000	112,500
Liabilities	?	27,500	19,000	64,000	75,000
During 2000:					
Owner investments	5,000	1,500	7,750	?	4,500
Net income	7,500	?	9,000	12,000	18,000
Owner withdrawals	2,500	3,000	3,875	0	9,000

Required

1. Answer the following questions about Company A:
   a. What was the owner's equity on December 31, 1999?
   b. What was the owner's equity on December 31, 2000?
   c. What was the amount of liabilities owed on December 31, 2000?
2. Answer the following questions about Company B:
   a. What was the owner's equity on December 31, 1999?
   b. What was the owner's equity on December 31, 2000?
   c. What was the net income for 2000?
3. Calculate the amount of assets owned by Company C on December 31, 2000.
4. Calculate the amount of owner investments in Company D made during 2000.
5. Calculate the amount of liabilities owed by Company E on December 31, 1999.

Check Figure Co. C, Dec. 31, 2000, assets, $46,875

Problem 2-6
Identifying effects of transactions on financial statements
C1, A1

Identify how each of the following transactions affects the company's financial statements. For the balance sheet, identify how each transaction affects total assets, total liabilities, and owner's equity. For the income statement, identify how each transaction affects net income. For the statement of cash flows, identify how each transaction affects cash flows from operating activities, cash flows from financing activities, and cash flows from investing activities. If there is an increase, place a "+" in the column or columns. If there is a decrease, place a "−" in the column or columns. If there is both an increase and a decrease, place a "+/−" in the column or columns. The line for the first transaction is completed as an example.

		Balance Sheet			Income Statement	Statement of Cash Flows		
	Transaction	Total Assets	Total Liab.	Owner's Equity	Net Income	Operating	Financing	Investing
1	Owner invests cash	+		+			+	
2	Perform services for cash							
3	Purchase services on credit							
4	Pay wages with cash							
5	Owner withdraws cash							
6	Borrow cash with note payable							
7	Perform services on credit							
8	Buy office equipment for cash							
9	Collect cash on receivable from (7)							
10	Buy asset with note payable							

Problem 2-7
Preparing a statement of cash flows
C1, P1

A new business, Do You Copy, has the following beginning cash balance and cash flows for the month of December:

Cash balance, December 1	$ 0
Withdrawals by owner	500
Cash received from customers . .	4,000
Repayment of debt	1,000
Cash paid for store supplies	2,600
Purchase of equipment	21,000
Cash paid for rent	2,000
Cash paid to employee	800
Investment by owner	32,000

Required

Prepare a statement of cash flows for Do You Copy for the month of December.

Check Figure Cash bal., Dec. 31, $8,100

BEYOND THE NUMBERS

Reporting in Action
C1, A2

NIKE designs, produces, markets, and sells sports footwear and apparel. The financial statements and other information from NIKE's May 31, 1997, annual report are included in Appendix A at the end of the book. Use information from that report to answer the following questions:

1. Examine NIKE's consolidated balance sheet. To what level are the dollar amounts rounded?
2. What is the closing date of NIKE's most recent annual reporting period?
3. What amount of net income did NIKE earn for the fiscal year ended May 31, 1997?
4. How much cash (and equivalents) did NIKE hold at fiscal year-end May 31, 1997?
5. What was the net amount of cash provided by the company's operating activities during fiscal year ended May 31, 1997?
6. Did the company's investing activities for fiscal year ended May 31, 1997, create a net cash inflow or outflow? What was the amount of the net flow?
7. Compare fiscal year-end 1997's results to 1996's results to determine whether the company's total revenues increased or decreased. What was the amount of the increase or decrease?
8. What was the change in the company's net income between fiscal year-end 1997 and 1996?
9. What amount was reported as total assets at fiscal year-end 1997?
10. Calculate the return on equity that NIKE achieved for the fiscal year ended May 31, 1997.

Swoosh Ahead

11. Obtain access to NIKE's annual report for fiscal years ending after May 31, 1997. You can gain access to NIKE's annual report at its web site [**www.nike.com**] or through the SEC's EDGAR database [**www.sec.gov**]. Recompute NIKE's return on equity with the updated annual report information you obtain. Compare the May 31, 1997, fiscal year-end return on investment to any subsequent year's return you are able to calculate. Also compare how NIKE's total assets, total revenues, and net income have changed since May 31, 1997.

Comparative Analysis

A2

Both **NIKE** and **Reebok** design, produce, market, and sell sports footwear and apparel. Key comparative figures ($ millions) for these two organizations follow:

Key figures	NIKE	Reebok
Beginning equity	$2431.4	$895.3
Ending equity	$3155.8	$381.2
Net income	$ 795.8	$139.0

Required

1. What is the return on equity for (a) NIKE and (b) Reebok?
2. Is return on equity satisfactory for (a) NIKE and (b) Reebok if competitors average a 26% return?
3. Would it be appropriate to calculate the modified return on equity for Reebok and Nike?
4. What can you conclude about NIKE and Reebok from these computations?

Ethics Challenge

C5

BJ Crist is a new entry-level accountant for a mail order company that specializes in supplying skateboards and accessories for the sport. At the end of the fiscal period, BJ is advised by a supervisor to include as revenue for the period any orders that have been charged by phone but not yet fulfilled by shipping the product. BJ is also advised to include as revenue any orders received by mail with checks enclosed that are also pending fulfillment.

Required

1. Identify relevant accounting principles that BJ should be aware of in view of the supervisor's instructions.
2. What are the ethical factors in this situation?
3. Would you recommend that Crist follow the supervisor's directions?
4. What alternatives might be available to Crist other than following the supervisor's directions?

Communicating in Practice

Understanding and using financial information is important in a wide range of careers. You are to obtain a copy of the article, "Why Neil Simon Decided to Turn His Back on Broadway" by Donald G. McNeil, Jr., ***The New York Times,*** November 21, 1994, pp. C9 and C13. After reading the article, prepare a brief written report that includes responses to the following questions.

1. How does this article illustrate the importance for Neil Simon, a playwright, of understanding financial statements?
2. Summarize and explain the financial considerations that brought Neil Simon and his producer to the conclusion it was a financially wise decision to produce off-Broadway. Do you agree with their conclusion? Why or why not?
3. Using the figures in the article, at what point does the decision to produce off-Broadway prove less profitable than the alternative one? Explain.

Taking It to the Net

C1, C5

Access the **Reebok** Web site (**http://www.Reebok.com**). After you arrive at Reebok's home page, click on the *company* hotlink. This link should take you to http://www.Reebok.com/company/company.html. Now click on *REEBOK CHARTER.*

Required

1. What does Reebok identify as its greatest asset in the Charter?
2. Using your knowledge of accounting principles write a brief memo listing reasons why Reebok has not included this "greatest asset" on its balance sheet.

Teamwork in Action

C5, A1

This activity is aimed at generating a team discussion of business transactions. Understanding transactions provides the necessary background for dealing with more complex transactions later in the book.

Required

1. Each team member should write down as many different transactions they can think of that fall into one of the following categories:
   a. Transactions affecting assets.
   b. Transactions affecting liabilities.
   c. Transactions affecting owner's equity but not affecting revenues and expenses.
   d. Transactions affecting revenues and/or expenses.
2. Team members should exchange lists and write down the analysis of each transaction on the list received.
3. Each team member is to report the analysis in part 2 to other team members. If all members of the team agree with the analysis presented, they should proceed to other transactions and team members' reports. If there is disagreement, team members should discuss differences and consult the book in reaching a decision. If the discussion does not result in agreement, team members should consult the instructor.

Hitting the Road

C1

Use the Edgar database **[http://www.sec.gov]** and obtain the toll-free 800 number of a company that you are interested in learning more about. Once you have obtained the 800 number call the company and ask to speak to the Investor Relations department. Request a copy of that company's most recent annual report from the Investor Relations phone representative. You should receive the requested report within 1-3 weeks. Once you have received your report consult it throughout the term to see the principles you are learning in the classroom applied in practice.

Business Week Activity

A2

Business Week periodically publishes a ranking of the top 1,000 businesses in the world based on market performance. This issue contains charts labeled BUSINESS WEEK GLOBAL 1000. Obtain the most recent publication of this issue.

Required

1. Is the company that is ranked number 1 in the world a United States company?
2. Of the top 10 global businesses, how many are United States companies?
3. What is the return on equity for the number 1 company in the world?
4. What is the industry of the number 1 company in the world?

Analyzing and Recording Transactions

A Look Back

We explained the value of accounting in the information age. We showed how financial statements, prepared according to accounting principles, communicate useful information. We also analyzed and prepared financial statements from transactions.

A Look at This Chapter

This chapter focuses on the accounting process. We describe transactions and source documents as inputs for analysis. We explain analysis and recording of transactions for preparing financial statements. T-accounts, postings, ledgers, and trial balances are shown as useful tools in carrying out these important steps.

A Look Ahead

Chapter 4 extends our focus on processing information. We explain the importance of adjusting accounts and procedures in preparing financial statements.

Chapter Outline

Spinning an Accounting Web

HOUSTON—Maria Sanchez's second year on the job was nearly her last. She was working as a staff accountant for a small medical center where she was assigned to payroll and accounts receivable. In late December of her second year, she was instructed to add 1% to all employees' end-of-year paychecks as a bonus. Instead, she keyed an extra zero and gave everyone a 10% bonus. "The controller was furious," says Sanchez. "To top it off, the employees were so grateful that the controller and board couldn't do anything but keep quiet, accept the error, and congratulate everyone."

Today, Sanchez accepts blame for the error. But it wasn't always that way. "I still partly blame our accounting technology. It was awful," says Sanchez. It was this experience that led Sanchez to add technology skills to her accounting background. While taking evening classes in computing, Sanchez became convinced that accounting packages could be more user friendly. She also foresaw the power of the Web.

Sanchez, 29, is now the owner of **RecordLink,** an accounting software firm that provides recordkeeping services for small businesses. It is unique in that it relies on the Web. This means there is no need for software purchases or special computing hardware requirements for small business. Clients link into her Web servers for their computing needs.

The convenience of clients having access to their accounting information anytime, anywhere, is attracting new clients. "We offer 24-hour accounting and computing advice, and we are expanding our software options to include strategic planning, budget analyses, and other sophisticated programs that few small businesses can individually afford." RecordLink spreads these costs over all its clients.

Sanchez sees recordkeeping services for small business as a lucrative and underserved market. She plans to expand her business to Dallas and San Antonio by year-end. So far, her creativity has been a hit with clients. Last year, RecordLink's revenues went over $850,000. Adds Sanchez, "Not bad for a high-tech recordkeeper!"

Learning Objectives

Conceptual

C1 Explain the steps in processing transactions.

C2 Describe source documents and their purpose.

C3 Describe an account and its use in recording information about transactions.

C4 Describe a ledger and a chart of accounts.

C5 Define debits and credits and explain their role in double-entry accounting.

Analytical

A1 Analyze the impact of transactions on accounts and financial statements.

A2 Compute the debt ratio and describe its use in analyzing company performance.

Procedural

P1 Record transactions in a journal and post entries to a ledger.

P2 Prepare and explain the use of a trial balance.

HAPTER PREVIEW

The accounting process is crucial to producing useful financial information. We explained in Chapter 2 how the accounting equation (Assets = Liabilities + Equity) helps us understand and analyze transactions and events. In this chapter we describe how transactions are processed and how their effects are recorded in accounts. All accounting systems use procedures similar to those described here. These procedures are important steps leading to financial statements. Maria Sanchez of **RecordLink** uses a Web-based system, but the accounting procedures are essentially identical for manual systems.

We begin by describing how source documents provide crucial information about transactions. We then describe accounts and explain their purpose. Debits and credits are introduced and identified as valuable tools in helping us understand and process transactions. This background then enables us to describe the process of recording events in a journal and posting them to a ledger. We return to transactions of **FastForward,** first introduced in Chapter 2, to illustrate many of these procedures. We conclude the chapter by describing how to use a company's debt ratio to assess its risk.

Transactions and Documents

C1 Explain the steps in processing transactions.

We explained in Chapter 1 how accounting provides information to help people make better decisions. This information is the result of an accounting process that captures business transactions and events, analyzes and records their effects, and summarizes and prepares information in reports and financial statements. These reports and statements are used for making investing, lending, and other important decisions. We illustrate the steps in the accounting process in Exhibit 3.1.

Transactions and events are the starting points in the accounting process. Relying on source documents, we analyze transactions and events using the accounting equation to understand how they affect organization performance and financial position. These effects are recorded in accounting records, informally referred to as the *accounting books,* or simply the *books.* Additional processing steps such as posting and preparing a trial balance help us summarize and classify the effects of transactions and events. A final step in the accounting process is to provide information in useful reports or financial statements to decision makers. We begin our overview of the accounting process with a discussion of transactions and events.

Transactions and Events

Business activities can be described in terms of transactions and events. We know from Chapter 2 that business transactions are exchanges of economic consideration between two parties. We also know that the accounting equation is affected by transactions and events.

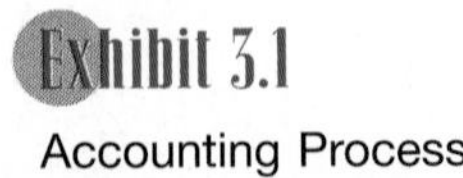

Exhibit 3.1

Accounting Process

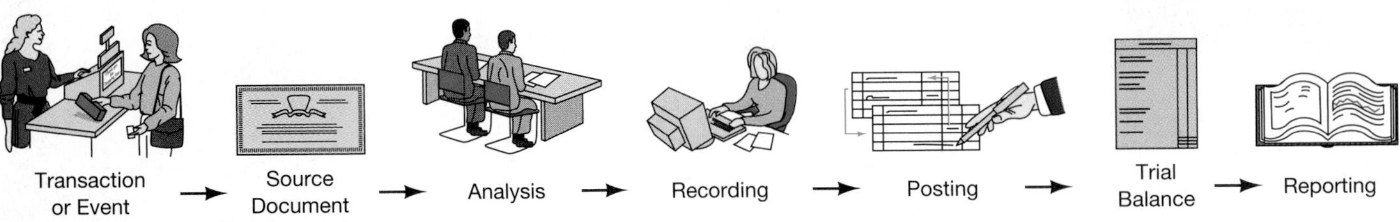

Transactions and events are the starting point in the accounting process. **External transactions** are exchanges between an organization and another person or organization. External transactions yield changes in the accounting equation. **Internal transactions** are exchanges within an organization. Internal transactions can also affect the accounting equation. One example is a company using equipment in its operating activities. As the equipment is used, its costs are reported as expenses.

Events are happenings that both affect an organization's financial position and can be reliably measured. These include financial events such as changes in the market value of certain assets and liabilities, and natural events such as floods and fires that destroy assets and create losses. The analysis and recording of events are explained in the next chapter.

Source Documents

C2 Describe source documents and their purpose.

Organizations use various documents when doing business. **Source documents,** or *business papers,* identify and describe transactions and events entering the accounting process. They are the sources of accounting information and can be in either hard copy or electronic form. Examples are sales tickets, checks, purchase orders, charges to customers, bills from suppliers, employee earnings records, and bank statements.

When we buy an item on credit, the store usually prepares at least two copies of a sales invoice. One copy is given to you. Another is sent to the store's accounting department and gives rise to an entry in the information system to record a sale. This copy is often sent electronically. Also, for both cash and credit sales, the item is usually rung up on a register that records and stores the amount of each sale. Many registers record this information for each sale on a tape or electronic file locked inside the register. Total sales for a day or for any time period can be obtained immediately from these registers. This record is used as a source document for recording sales in the accounting records.

The accounting procedures when buying an item are part of an information system designed to ensure the accounting records include all transactions. They also help prevent mistakes and theft. To encourage employees to follow procedures such as these, stores often give discounts or free goods if a customer is not provided a receipt. This is part of internal control procedures.

Cashier
You are a cashier at a cash-and-carry retail store. When hired, the manager explained to you the policy of immediately ringing up each sale. Recently, lunch hour traffic has increased dramatically and the assistant manager asks you to avoid delays by taking customers' cash and making change without ringing up sales. The assistant manager says she will add up cash and ring up sales equal to the cash amount after lunch. She says that in this way the register will always be accurate when the manager arrives at three o'clock. What do you do?

Answer—p. 109

Both buyers and sellers use sales invoices as source documents. Sellers use them for recording sales and for control purposes. Buyers use them for recording purchases and for monitoring purchasing activity. In both cases, a copy of the invoice is a source document.

Source documents, especially if obtained from outside the organization, provide objective evidence about both transactions and events, and their amounts. As we explained in the prior chapter, objective evidence is important because it makes information more reliable and useful.

There are still many accounting systems that require manual (pencil and paper) recording and processing of transaction data. These are mostly limited to small businesses. In today's information age, computers assist us in recording and processing data. Yet computers are only part of the process, and modern technology still demands human insight and understanding of transactions. In our discussion of the steps making up the accounting process, we use a manual system for presentation. The fundamental concepts of the manual system are identical to those of a computerized information system.

Flash back

1. Describe external and internal transactions.
2. Identify examples of accounting source documents.
3. Explain the importance of source documents.

Answers—p. 109

Accounts and Double-Entry Accounting

This section explains an *account* and its importance to accounting and business. We also describe several crucial elements that support an accounting system. These include ledgers, T-accounts, debits and credits, and double-entry accounting.

The Account

C3 Describe an account and its use in recording information about transactions.

An **account** is a detailed record of increases and decreases in a specific asset, liability, equity, revenue, or expense. Information is taken from accounts, analyzed, summarized, and presented in reports and financial statements useful for decision makers. A separate account is maintained for items of importance to information users. This means that separate accounts are kept for each important asset, liability, and equity item. It also means separate accounts are kept for important revenue and expense items. Important changes in owner's withdrawals and contributions are also captured in separate accounts.[1]

A **ledger** is a record containing all accounts used by a business. This is often in electronic form and is what we mean when we refer to the *books.* While most companies' ledgers contain similar accounts, there are often several accounts that are unique to a company because of its individual type of operations. Accounts are arranged into three general categories using the accounting equation as shown in Exhibit 3.2.

Accounting Equation

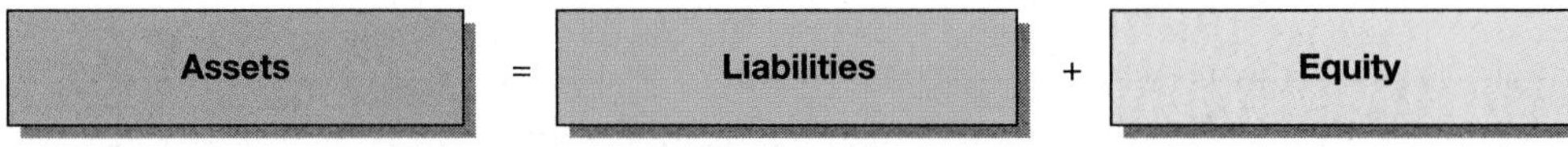

These accounts directly affect the preparation of financial reports and statements. The remainder of this section introduces accounts that are common to most organizations.

Asset Accounts

Assets are resources controlled by an organization that carry current and future benefits. Most accounting systems include separate accounts for the assets described here.

Cash

Increases and decreases in the amount of cash are recorded in a *Cash* account. A cash account includes money and any medium of exchange that a bank accepts for deposit. Examples are coins, currency, checks, money orders, and checking account balances.

Accounts Receivable

Products and services are often sold to customers in return for promises to pay in the future. These transactions are called *credit sales* or *sales on account.* The promises from buyers are called *accounts receivable* to sellers. Accounts receivable are increased by new credit sales and are decreased by customer payments. A company needs to know

[1] As an example of an account, see Exhibit 3.5 showing the Cash account for **FastForward.**

the amount currently due from each customer to send bills. A separate record for each customer's purchases and payments is necessary for this purpose. We describe the system for maintaining these records in Chapters 6 and 7. For now, we use the simpler practice of recording all increases and decreases in receivables in a single account called Accounts Receivable. The importance of accounts receivable, like many other accounts, depends on the nature of a company's operations as shown in this excerpt from practice:

ShowBiz Pizza Time's accounts receivable amount to less than 2% of its assets. In comparison, **NIKE**'s accounts receivable amount to more than 30% of its assets.

Notes Receivable

A **note receivable,** or **promissory note,** is a written promise to pay a definite sum of money on a specified future date(s). A company holding a promissory note signed by another party has an asset. This asset is recorded in a Notes Receivable account.

Prepaid Expenses

Prepaid Expenses is an asset account containing payments made for assets that are not used until later. As these assets are used up, the costs of these used assets become expenses. Common examples of prepaid expenses include office supplies, store supplies, prepaid insurance, prepaid rent, and advance payments for legal and accounting services. An asset's cost can be initially recorded as an expense *if* it is used up before the end of the period when statements are prepared. If an asset will not be used before the end of the reporting period, then its cost is recorded in an asset account. Prepaid expenses that are more crucial to the business are often accounted for in separate assets accounts. We describe three of the more common accounts: insurance, office supplies, and store supplies.

Prepaid Insurance

Insurance contracts provide us with protection against losses caused by fire, theft, accidents, and other events. An insurance policy often requires the fee, called a *premium,* to be paid in advance. Protection can be purchased for almost any time period, including month, year, or even several years. When an insurance premium is paid in advance, the cost is typically recorded in an asset account called *Prepaid Insurance.* Over time the expiring portion of the insurance cost is removed from this asset account and reported in expenses on the income statement. The unexpired portion remains in Prepaid Insurance and is reported on the balance sheet as an asset.

Office Supplies

All companies use office supplies such as stationery, paper, and pens. These supplies are assets until they are used. When they are used up, their cost is reported as an expense. The cost of unused supplies is an asset and is recorded in an Office Supplies account.

Store Supplies

Many stores keep supplies for wrapping and packaging purchases for customers. These include plastic and paper bags, gift boxes, cartons, and ribbons. The cost of these unused supplies is recorded in a Store Supplies account. Supplies are reported as expenses as they are used.

Equipment

Most organizations own computers, printers, desks, chairs, and other office equipment. Costs incurred to buy this equipment are recorded in an *Office Equipment* account. The costs of assets used in a store such as counters, showcases, and cash registers are recorded in a *Store Equipment* account.

Building

A building owned by an organization can provide space for a store, an office, a warehouse, or a factory. Buildings are assets because they provide benefits. Their costs are recorded in a Buildings account. When several buildings are owned, separate accounts are sometimes used for each of them.

Land

A Land account records the cost of land owned by a business. The cost of land is separated from the cost of buildings located on the land to provide more useful information in financial statements.

Liability Accounts

Liabilities are obligations to transfer assets or provide services to other entities. An organization often has several different liabilities, each represented by a separate account. The more common liability accounts are described here.

Accounts Payable

Purchases of merchandise, supplies, equipment, or services made by an oral or implied promise to pay later produce liabilities called *payables.* Accounting systems keep separate records about purchases from and payments to each creditor. We describe these individual records in Chapters 6 and 7. For now, we use the simpler practice of recording all increases and decreases in payables in a single account, Accounts Payable.

Notes Payable

When an organization formally recognizes a promise to pay by signing a *promissory note,* the resulting liability is a *note payable.* Its recording in either a Short-Term Notes Payable account or a Long-Term Notes Payable account depends on when it must be repaid. We explain details of account classification in Chapter 5.

Unearned Revenues

Chapter 2 explained that the *revenue recognition principle* requires revenues be reported on the income statement when earned. This principle means we must be careful with transactions where customers pay in advance for products or services. Because cash from these transactions is received before revenues are earned, the seller considers them **unearned revenues.** Unearned revenue is a liability that is satisfied by delivering products or services in the future. Examples of unearned revenue include magazine subscriptions collected in advance by a publisher, sales of gift certificates by stores, and rent collected in advance by a landlord. **Reader's Digest** reported unearned revenues of $408 million as of December 31, 1997.

When cash is received in advance for products and services, the seller records it in a liability account such as Unearned Subscriptions, Unearned Rent, or Unearned Professional Fees. When products and services are delivered, the now earned portion of the unearned revenues is transferred to revenue accounts such as Subscription Fees, Rent Earned, or Professional Fees.[2]

---

[2] There are variations in account titles in practice. As one example, Subscription Fees is sometimes called Subscription Fees Revenue, Subscription Fees Earned, or Earned Subscription Fees. As another example, Rent Earned is sometimes called Rent Revenue, Rental Revenue, or Earned Rent Revenue. We must use our good judgment when reading financial statements since titles can differ even within the same industry. For example, product sales are called revenues at **NIKE** and **K. Swiss,** but net sales at **Reebok** and **Converse.** The term *revenues* or *fees* is more commonly used with service businesses, and *net sales* or *sales* with product businesses.

Accrued Liabilities

Common accrued liabilities include wages payable, taxes payable, and interest payable. Each of these is often recorded in a separate liability account. If they are not large in amount, one or more of them may be added and reported as a single amount on the balance sheet.

The liabilities section of **Harley-Davidson's** balance sheet at the end of 1997 included accrued liabilities of more than $160 million.

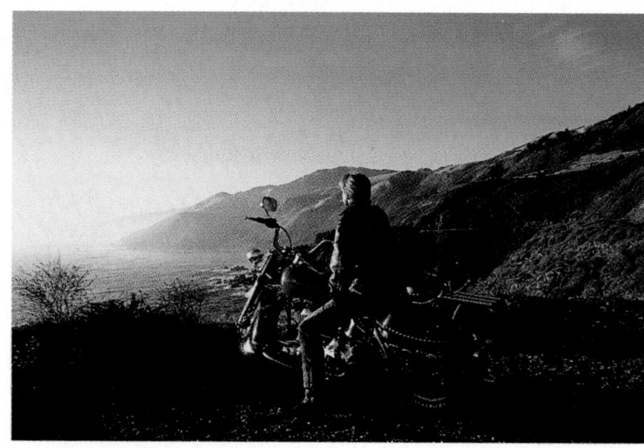

Equity Accounts

We described in the prior chapter the four types of transactions that affect owner's equity. They are (1) investments by the owner, (2) withdrawals by the owner, (3) revenues, and (4) expenses. We entered all equity transactions in a single column under the owner's name in Chapter 2. When we later prepared the income statement and the statement of changes in owner's equity, we reviewed the items in that column to classify them in financial statements.

A preferred approach is to use four separate accounts. They are: owner's capital, owner's withdrawals, revenues, and expenses. We show this visually in Exhibit 3.3 by expanding the accounting equation.

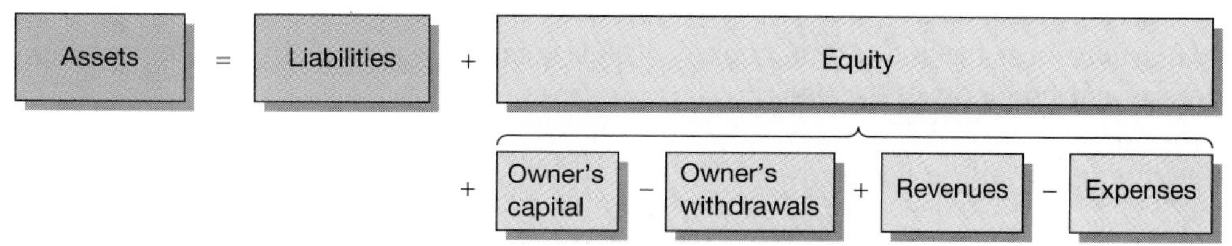

Exhibit 3.3

Expanded Accounting Equation

Information in these separate accounts is readily used to prepare financial statements without further analysis. We describe these four accounts below.

Owner's Capital

When a person invests in a proprietorship, the invested amount is recorded in an account identified by the owner's name and the title Capital. An account called *Chuck Taylor, Capital,* can be used to record Taylor's original investment in FastForward. Any further investments by the owner also are recorded in the owner's capital account.

Owner's Withdrawals

Owner's equity increases when a business earns income. The owner can leave this equity intact or can withdraw assets from the business. When the owner withdraws assets, perhaps to cover personal living expenses, the withdrawal decreases both the company's assets and owner's equity.

It is common for owners of proprietorships to withdraw regular weekly or monthly amounts of cash. We know that owners of proprietorships cannot receive salaries because they are not legally separate from their companies. Also, they cannot enter into salary (or any other) contracts with themselves. These withdrawals are neither income to the owners nor expenses of the business. They are simply the opposite of investments by owners.

Most accounting systems use an account with the name of the owner and the word *withdrawals* in recording withdrawals by the owner. An account called *Chuck Taylor, Withdrawals,* is used to record Taylor's withdrawals from FastForward. The owner's withdrawals account also is sometimes called the owner's *personal* account or *drawing* account.

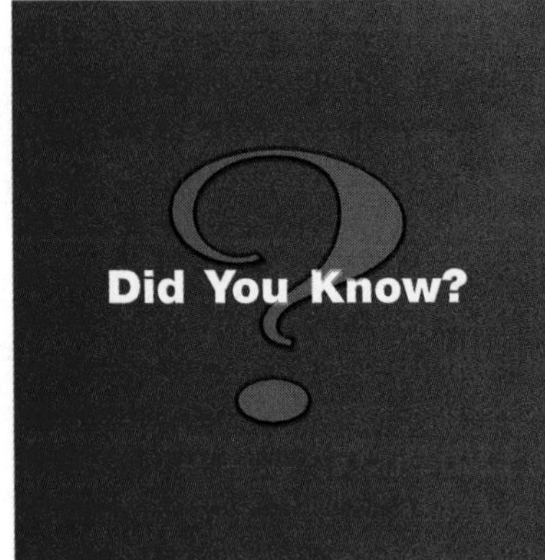

NBA Accounting

The **Boston Celtics** report the following major revenue and expense accounts:

Revenues:	Basketball ticket sales
	TV and radio broadcast fees
	Advertising revenues
Expenses:	Team salaries
	Game costs
	NBA franchise costs

Source: Boston Celtics' Financial Statements.

Revenues and Expenses

Decision makers often want information about revenues earned and expenses incurred for a period. Businesses use a variety of revenue and expense accounts to report this information on income statements. Different companies have different kinds of revenue and expense accounts reflecting their own important activities. Examples of revenue accounts are Sales, Commissions Earned, Professional Fees Earned, Rent Earned, and Interest Earned. Examples of expense accounts are Advertising Expense, Store Supplies Expense, Office Salaries Expense, Office Supplies Expense, Rent Expense, Utilities Expense, and Insurance Expense.

We can get an idea of the variety of revenues and expenses by looking at the *chart of accounts* near the end of this book. It lists accounts needed to solve some of the exercises and problems in the book.[3]

Ledger and Chart of Accounts

C4 Describe a ledger and a chart of accounts.

The actual recording of accounts can differ depending on the system. Computerized systems store accounts in files on electronic storage devices. Clients of **RecordLink,** as explained in the opening article, store their accounts on-line at another location. Manual systems often record accounts on separate pages in a special booklet. The collection of all accounts for an information system is called a ledger. If accounts are in files on a hard disk, those files are the ledger. If the accounts are pages in a booklet, then the booklet is the ledger. A ledger simply refers to the group of accounts.

A company's size and diversity of operations affect the number of accounts needed in its accounting system. A small company may get by with as few as 20 or 30 accounts, while a large company may need several thousand. The **chart of accounts** is a list of all accounts used by a company. The chart includes an identification number assigned to each account. Companies assign account identification numbers in an orderly manner. A small business might use the following numbering system for its accounts:

101–199	Asset accounts
201–299	Liability accounts
301–399	Owner's equity accounts
401–499	Revenue accounts
501–699	Expense accounts

[3] Different companies sometimes use different account titles than those in this book's chart of accounts. For example, a company might use Interest Revenue instead of Interest Earned, or Rental Expense instead of Rent Expense. It is only important that an account title describe the item it represents.

While this particular system provides for 99 asset accounts, a company may not use all of them. These numbers also provide a three-digit code that is useful in recordkeeping. In this case the first digit assigned to asset accounts is a 1, while the first digit assigned to liability accounts is a 2, and so on. The second and third digits also relate to the accounts' categories. A partial chart of accounts is shown below for FastForward.

Account Number	Account Name	Account Number	Account Name
101	Cash	301	C. Taylor, Capital
106	Accounts receivable	302	C. Taylor, Withdrawals
128	Prepaid insurance	403	Consulting revenue
125	Supplies	406	Rental revenue
167	Equipment	641	Rent expense
201	Accounts payable	622	Salaries expense
236	Unearned consulting revenue	690	Utilities expense
240	Note payable		

Ledger Bytes

What does technology mean for accounting information processing? **Sears Roebuck** provides an answer. For its annual financial plan, Sears at one time used a 100-square-foot flow chart with more than 300 steps. Using computing technology, this plan is now 25 steps on *one* 8½-by-11-inch sheet of paper! Technology also allows Sears' analysts to view and analyze budgets and financial plans on their PCs. Sears says it has slashed $100 million in costs. [Source: *Business Week,* October 28, 1996.]

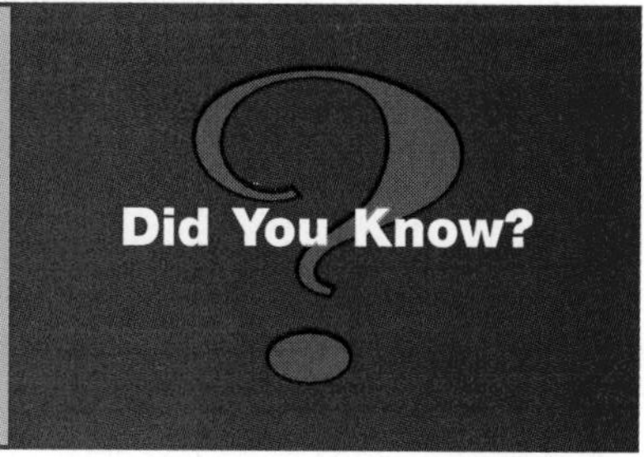

T-Account

A **T-account** is a helpful tool in showing the effects of transactions and events on individual accounts. The T-account gets its name from its shape. Its shape looks like the letter "T" and is shown in Exhibit 3.4.

Exhibit 3.4

The T-Account

Account Title	
(Left side) *Debit*	(Right side) *Credit*

The format of a T-account includes (1) the account title on top, (2) a left, or debit, side, and (3) a right, or credit, side. A T-account provides one side for recording increases in the item and the other side for decreases. As we will discuss later, whether increases are recorded on the right or the left side depends on the type of account. The T-account for FastForward's Cash account after recording the transactions in Chapter 2 is shown in Exhibit 3.5.

Exhibit 3.5

Cash T-Account for FastForward

Cash			
Investment by owner	30,000	Purchase of supplies	2,500
Consulting services revenue earned	2,200	Purchase of equipment	20,000
Collection of account receivable	1,900	Payment of rent	1,000
		Payment of salary	700
		Payment of note payable	900
		Withdrawal by owner	600

Balance of an Account

An **account balance** is the difference between the increases and decreases recorded in an account. For example, the balance of a liability account is the amount owed on the date the balance is computed.

Putting increases on one side of an account and decreases on the other helps in computing an account's balance. To determine the balance, we start with the beginning balance and then (1) compute the total increases shown on one side, (2) compute the total decreases shown on the other side, and (3) subtract the sum of the decreases from the sum of the increases. The total increases in FastForward's Cash account are $34,100, the total decreases are $25,700, and the account balance is $8,400. The T-account in Exhibit 3.6 shows how we calculate the $8,400 balance.

Exhibit 3.6

Computing the Balance of a T-Account

Cash			
Investment by owner	30,000	Purchase of supplies	2,500
Consulting services revenue earned	2,200	Purchase of equipment	20,000
Collection of account receivable	1,900	Payment of rent	1,000
		Payment of salary	700
		Payment of note payable	900
		Withdrawal by owner	600
Total increases	**34,100**	Total decreases	**25,700**
Less decreases	**−25,700**		
Balance	**8,400**		

Debits and Credits

C5 Define debits and credits and explain their role in double-entry accounting.

The left side of a T-account is called the **debit** side, often abbreviated *Dr* (*or Db*). The right side is called the **credit** side, abbreviated *Cr.*[4] To enter amounts on the left side of an account is to *debit* the account. To enter amounts on the right side is to *credit* the account. The difference between total debits and total credits for an account is the account balance. When the sum of debits exceeds the sum of credits, the account has a *debit balance*. It has a *credit balance* when the sum of credits exceeds the sum of debits. When the sum of debits equals the sum of credits, the account has a *zero balance*.

We must guard against the error of thinking that the terms *debit* and *credit* mean increase or decrease. Whether a debit is an increase or decrease depends on the account. Similarly, whether a credit is an increase or decrease depends on the account. But in every account, a debit and a credit have opposite effects. In an account where a debit is an increase, the credit is a decrease. And, in an account where a debit is a decrease, the credit is an increase. Identifying the account is the key to understanding the effects of debits and credits.

We must remember in working with T-accounts that a debit means an entry on the left side and a credit means an entry on the right side. To emphasize this, Exhibit 3.7 shows how Taylor's initial investment in FastForward is recorded in the Cash and Capital T-accounts:

Debits and Credits in T-Accounts

Cash	
Investment 30,000	

C.Taylor, Capital	
	Investment 30,000

The cash increase is recorded on the *left side* of the Cash account with a $30,000 debit entry. The corresponding increase in owner's equity is recorded on the *right side* of the

[4] These abbreviations are remnants of 18th-century English recordkeeping practices where the terms *debitor* and *creditor* were used instead of *debit* and *credit*. The abbreviations use the first and last letters of these terms, just as we still do for Saint (St.) and Doctor (Dr.).

capital account with a $30,000 credit entry. This dual method of recording transactions on both the left and right sides is an essential feature of *double-entry accounting*, the topic of the next section.

Flash *back*

4. Classify each of the following accounts as either an asset, liability, or equity: (a) Prepaid Rent, (b) Unearned Fees, (c) Building, (d) Retained Earnings, (e) Wages Payable, and (f) Office Supplies.
5. What is an account? What is a ledger?
6. What determines the number and types of accounts used by a company?
7. Does debit always mean increase and credit always mean decrease?

Answers—p. 109

Double-Entry Accounting

Double-entry accounting means every transaction affects and is recorded in at least two accounts. This means the *total amount debited must equal the total amount credited* for each transaction. Since each transaction is recorded with total debits equal to total credits, the sum of the debits for all entries must equal the sum of the credits for all entries. The sum of debit account balances in the ledger must equal the sum of credit account balances. The only reason the sum of debit balances would not equal the sum of credit balances is that an error has occurred. Double-entry accounting helps prevent errors by assuring that debits and credits for each transaction are equal.

The system for recording debits and credits follows from the accounting equation in Exhibit 3.8. Assets are on the left side of this equation. Liabilities and equity are on the right side. Two points are important here. First, like any mathematical relation, increases or decreases on one side have equal effects on the other side. For example, the net increase in assets must be accompanied by an identical net increase in the liabilities and equity side. Recall that some transactions only affect one side of the equation. This means that two or more accounts on one side are affected, but their net effect on this one side is zero. Second, we treat the left side as the *normal balance* side for assets, and the right side as the *normal balance* for liabilities and equity. This matches their layout in the accounting equation.

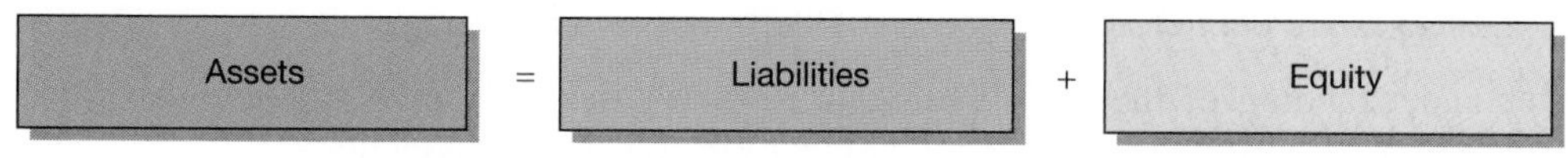

Exhibit 3.8
Accounting Equation

The normal debit balances of asset accounts and the normal credit balances of liability and equity accounts again follow from the accounting equation. This means that increases in asset accounts are recorded with debits, while increases in liability and equity accounts are recorded with credits. These important relations are captured in Exhibit 3.9.

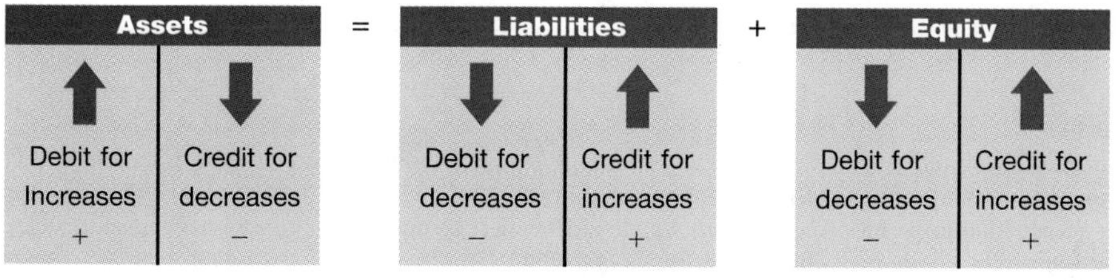

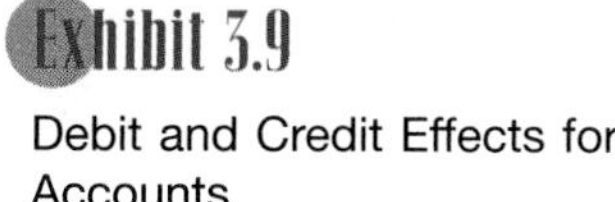

Exhibit 3.9
Debit and Credit Effects for Accounts

Three important rules for recording transactions in a double-entry accounting system follow from the diagram in Exhibit 3.9:

1. Increases in assets are debits to asset accounts. Decreases in assets are credits to asset accounts.
2. Increases in liabilities are credits to liability accounts. Decreases in liabilities are debits to liability accounts.
3. Increases in owner's equity are credits to owner's equity accounts. Decreases in owner's equity are debits to owner's equity accounts.

We explained in Chapter 2 how owner's equity increases from owner's investments and revenues. We also described how owner's equity decreases from expenses and withdrawals. These important owner's equity relations are conveyed by expanding the accounting equation as shown in Exhibit 3.10.

Components of the Accounting Equation

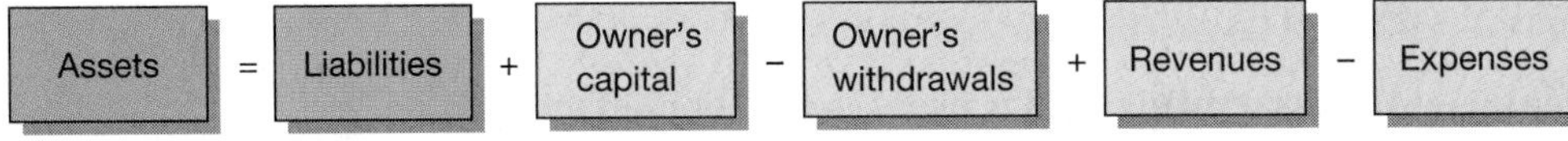

Exhibit 3.11

Debit and Credit Effects for Component Accounts

We can extend Exhibit 3.10 to include debits and credits in double-entry form as shown in Exhibit 3.11.

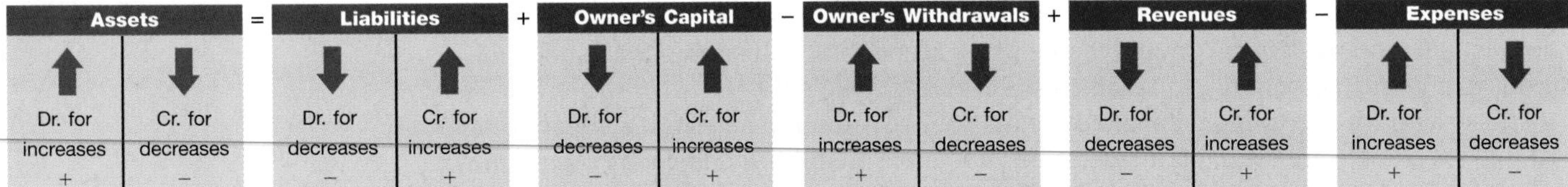

Increases in capital or revenues increase owner's equity, while increases in withdrawals or expenses *decrease* owner's equity. These relations are reflected in the following important rules:

1. Investments are credited to owner's capital because they increase equity.
2. Withdrawals are debited to owner's withdrawals because they decrease equity.
3. Revenues are credited to revenue accounts because they increase equity.
4. Expenses are debited to expense accounts because they decrease equity.

Our understanding of these diagrams and rules is crucial to analyzing and recording transactions. It also helps us prepare and analyze financial statements.[5]

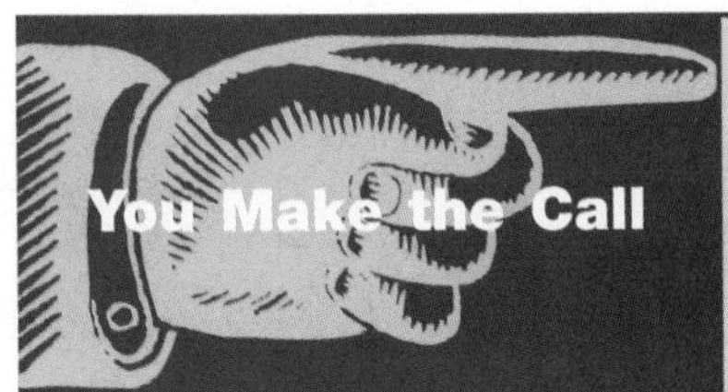

Marketing Manager
You are a company's marketing manager and you want to know your company's revenues for the current period. Financial statements are not yet available. Where do you direct your search for this information? Would the general journal or the ledger be more useful to you in getting revenue figures?

[Answer—p. 109]

[5] We can use good judgment to our advantage in applying double-entry accounting. For example, revenues and expenses normally (but not always) accumulate in business. This means they increase and rarely decrease during an accounting period. Accordingly, we should be alert to decreases in these accounts (such as debit revenues or credit expenses) to be certain this is our intent.

Analyzing Transactions

A1 Analyze the impact of transactions on accounts and financial statements.

FASTForward

We return to the activities of **FastForward** to show how debit and credit rules and double-entry accounting are useful in analyzing and processing transactions. We analyze FastForward's transactions in two steps. Step one analyzes a transaction and its source document(s). Step two applies double-entry accounting to identify the impact of a transaction on account balances. We include in step two an analysis of statement links to identify the financial statements impacted by a transaction. Exhibit 3.13 shown later in this chapter summarizes these links. Three additional steps are necessary to fully process transactions. We identify and describe these three additional steps after we complete steps one and two.

We should study each transaction thoroughly before proceeding to the next transaction. The first 11 transactions are familiar to us from Chapter 2. We expand our analysis of these transactions and consider five other transactions (numbered 12 through 16) of FastForward that were omitted from Chapter 2.

1. Investment by Owner

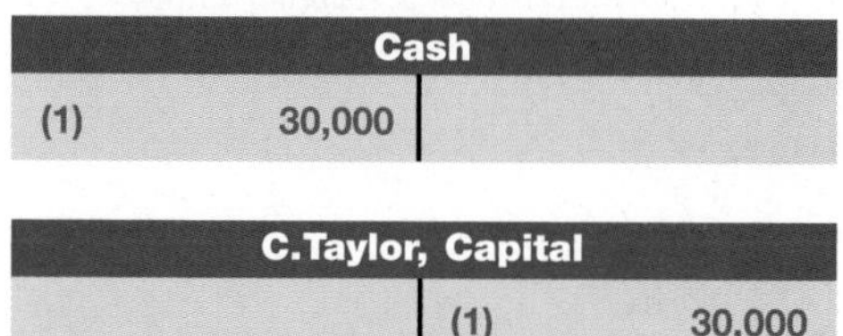

Cash			
(1)	30,000		

C.Taylor, Capital			
		(1)	30,000

Transaction. Chuck Taylor invests $30,000 in FastForward on December 1.
Analysis. Assets increase. Owner's equity increases.
Double-entry. Debit the Cash asset account for $30,000. Credit Taylor's Capital account in owner's equity for $30,000.
Statements affected.[6] BS, SCF, and SCOE

2. Purchase Supplies for Cash

Supplies			
(2)	2,500		

Cash			
(1)	30,000	(2)	2,500

Transaction. FastForward pays $2,500 cash for supplies.
Analysis. Assets increase. Assets decrease. This changes the composition of assets but does not change the total amount of assets.
Double-entry. Debit the Supplies asset account for $2,500. Credit the Cash asset account for $2,500.
Statements affected. BS and SCF

3. Purchase Equipment for Cash

Equipment			
(3)	20,000		

Cash			
(1)	30,000	(2)	2,500
		(3)	20,000

Transaction. FastForward pays $20,000 cash for equipment.
Analysis. Assets increase. Assets decrease. This changes the composition of assets but does not change the total amount of assets.
Double-entry. Debit the Equipment asset account for $20,000. Credit the Cash asset account for $20,000.
Statements affected. BS and SCF

4. Purchase Equipment and Supplies on Credit

Supplies			
(2)	2,500		
(4)	1,100		

Equipment			
(3)	20,000		
(4)	6,000		

Accounts Payable			
		(4)	1,100

Note Payable			
		(4)	6,000

Transaction. FastForward purchases $1,100 of supplies and $6,000 of equipment on credit. FastForward signs a promissory note for the $6,000 of equipment.
Analysis. Assets increase. Liabilities increase.
Double-entry. Debit two asset accounts: Supplies for $1,100 and Equipment for $6,000. Credit two liability accounts: Accounts Payable for $1,100 and Note Payable for $6,000.
Statements affected. BS

[6] We use abbreviations for the statements: Income Statement (IS); Balance Sheet (BS); Statement of Cash Flows (SCF); and Statement of Changes in Owner's Equity (SCOE).

5. Provide Services for Cash

Cash			
(1)	30,000	(2)	2,500
(5)	2,200	(3)	20,000

Consulting Revenue			
		(5)	2,200

Transaction. FastForward provides consulting services to a customer and immediately collects $2,200 cash.
Analysis. Assets increase. Owner's equity increases from revenue.
Double-entry. Debit the Cash asset account for $2,200. Credit the Consulting Revenue account for $2,200 (this increases owner's equity).
Statements affected. BS, IS, SCF, and SCOE

6. Payment of Expense in Cash

Rent Expense			
(6)	1,000		

Cash			
(1)	30,000	(2)	2,500
(5)	2,200	(3)	20,000
		(6)	1,000

Transaction. FastForward pays $1,000 cash for December rent.
Analysis. Assets decrease. Owner's equity decreases from expense.
Double-entry. Debit the Rent Expense account for $1,000 (this decreases owner's equity). Credit the Cash asset account for $1,000.
Statements affected. BS, IS, SCF, and SCOE

7. Payment of Expense in Cash

Salaries Expense			
(7)	700		

Cash			
(1)	30,000	(2)	2,500
(5)	2,200	(3)	20,000
		(6)	1,000
		(7)	700

Transaction. FastForward pays $700 cash for employee's salary for the pay period ending on December 12.
Analysis. Assets decrease. Owner's equity decreases from expense.
Double-entry. Debit the Salaries Expense account for $700 (this decreases owner's equity). Credit the Cash asset account for $700.
Statements affected. BS, IS, SCF, and SCOE

8. Provide Consulting and Rental Services on Credit

Accounts Receivable			
(8)	1,900		

Consulting Revenue			
		(5)	2,200
		(8)	1,600

Rental Revenue			
		(8)	300

Transaction. FastForward provides consulting services of $1,600 and rents test facilities for $300 to a customer (both services are part of FastForward's normal operations). The customer is billed $1,900 for the services and FastForward expects to collect this money in the near future.
Analysis. Assets increase. Owner's equity increases from revenue.
Double-entry. Debit the Accounts Receivable asset account for $1,900. Credit two revenue accounts: Consulting Revenue for $1,600 (this increases owner's equity) and Rental Revenue for $300 (this increases owner's equity).
Statements affected. BS, IS, and SCOE

9. Receipt of Cash on Account

Cash			
(1)	30,000	(2)	2,500
(5)	2,200	(3)	20,000
(9)	1,900	(6)	1,000
		(7)	700

Accounts Receivable			
(8)	1,900	(9)	1,900

Transaction. An amount of $1,900 is received from the client in transaction 8 on the 10th day after being billed for the services and facilities provided.
Analysis. Assets increase. Assets decrease. This changes the composition of assets but does not change the total amount of assets.
Double-entry. Debit the Cash asset account for $1,900. Credit Accounts Receivable asset account for $1,900.
Statements affected. BS and SCF

10. Partial Payment of Note Payable

Note Payable			
(10)	900	(4)	6,000

Cash			
(1)	30,000	(2)	2,500
(5)	2,200	(3)	20,000
(9)	1,900	(6)	1,000
		(7)	700
		(10)	900

Transaction. FastForward pays CalTech Supply $900 cash toward the note payable of $6,000 owed from the purchase of equipment in transaction 4.

Analysis. Assets decrease. Liabilities decrease.

Double-entry. Debit the Note Payable liability account for $900. Credit the Cash asset account for $900.

Statements affected. BS and SCF

11. Withdrawal of Cash by Owner

C.Taylor, Withdrawals			
(11)	600		

Cash			
(1)	30,000	(2)	2,500
(5)	2,200	(3)	20,000
(9)	1,900	(6)	1,000
		(7)	700
		(10)	900
		(11)	600

Transaction. Chuck Taylor withdraws $600 from FastForward for personal living expenses.

Analysis. Assets decrease. Owner's equity decreases.

Double-entry. Debit the owner's equity withdrawal account for $600. Credit the Cash asset account for $600.

Statements affected. BS, SCF, and SCOE

12. Receipt of Cash for Future Services

Cash			
(1)	30,000	(2)	2,500
(5)	2,200	(3)	20,000
(9)	1,900	(6)	1,000
(12)	3,000	(7)	700
		(10)	900
		(11)	600

Unearned Consulting Revenue			
		(12)	3,000

Transaction. FastForward enters into (signs) a contract with a customer to provide future consulting. FastForward receives $3,000 cash in advance of providing these consulting services.

Analysis. Assets increase. Liabilities increase. Accepting $3,000 cash obligates FastForward to perform future services and is a liability. No revenue is earned until services are provided.

Double-entry. Debit the Cash asset account for $3,000. Credit an Unearned Consulting Revenue liability account for $3,000.

Statements affected. BS and SCF

13. Pay Cash for Future Insurance Coverage

Prepaid Insurance			
(13)	2,400		

Cash			
(1)	30,000	(2)	2,500
(5)	2,200	(3)	20,000
(9)	1,900	(6)	1,000
(12)	3,000	(7)	700
		(10)	900
		(11)	600
		(13)	2,400

Transaction. FastForward pays $2,400 cash (premium) for a two-year insurance policy. Coverage begins on December 1.

Analysis. Assets increase. Assets decrease. This changes the composition of assets from cash to a "right" to insurance coverage. This does not change the total amount of assets. Expense is incurred as insurance coverage expires.

Double-entry. Debit the Prepaid Insurance asset account for $2,400. Credit the Cash asset account for $2,400.

Statements affected. BS and SCF

14. Purchase Supplies for Cash

Supplies			
(2)	2,500		
(4)	1,100		
(14)	120		

Cash			
(1)	30,000	(2)	2,500
(5)	2,200	(3)	20,000
(9)	1,900	(6)	1,000
(12)	3,000	(7)	700
		(10)	900
		(11)	600
		(13)	2,400
		(14)	120

Transaction. FastForward pays $120 cash for supplies.
Analysis. Assets increase. Assets decrease. This changes the composition of assets.
Double-entry. Debit the Supplies asset account for $120. Credit the Cash asset account for $120.
Statements affected. BS and SCF

15. Payment of Expense in Cash

Utilities Expense			
(15)	230		

Cash			
(1)	30,000	(2)	2,500
(5)	2,200	(3)	20,000
(9)	1,900	(6)	1,000
(12)	3,000	(7)	700
		(10)	900
		(11)	600
		(13)	2,400
		(14)	120
		(15)	230

Transaction. FastForward pays $230 cash for December utilities.
Analysis. Assets decrease. Owner's equity decreases from expense.
Double-entry. Debit the Utilities Expense account for $230 (this decreases owner's equity). Credit the Cash asset account for $230.
Statements affected. BS, IS, SCF, and SCOE

16. Payment of Expense in Cash

Salaries Expense			
(7)	700		
(16)	700		

Cash			
(1)	30,000	(2)	2,500
(5)	2,200	(3)	20,000
(9)	1,900	(6)	1,000
(12)	3,000	(7)	700
		(10)	900
		(11)	600
		(13)	2,400
		(14)	120
		(15)	230
		(16)	700

Transaction. FastForward pays $700 cash for employee's salary for the two-week pay period ending on December 26.
Analysis. Assets decrease. Owner's equity decreases from expense.
Double-entry. Debit the Salaries Expense account for $700 (this decreases owner's equity). Credit the Cash asset account for $700.
Statements affected. BS, IS, SCE, and SCOE

Accounting Equation Analysis

Exhibit 3.12 shows the accounts of FastForward after all 16 transactions are recorded and the balances computed. The accounts are grouped into three major columns.

These columns represent the terms in the accounting equation: assets, liabilities, and equity.

Exhibit 3.12 highlights several important points. First, as with each transaction, the totals for the three columns must obey the accounting equation: Assets = Liabilities + Equity. Specifically, assets equal $40,070 ($7,950 + $0 + $2,400 + $3,720 + $26,000); liabilities are $9,200 ($1,100 + $3,000 + $5,100); and equity is $30,870 ($30,000 − $600 + $3,800 + $300 − $1,000 − $1,400 − $230). These numbers obey the accounting equation: $40,070 = $9,200 + $30,870. Second, the withdrawals, revenue, and expense accounts reflect the events that change owner's equity. Their ending balances make up the statement of changes in owner's equity. Third, the revenue and expense account balances are summarized and reported in the income statement. Fourth, components of the cash account make up the elements reported in the statement of cash flows.

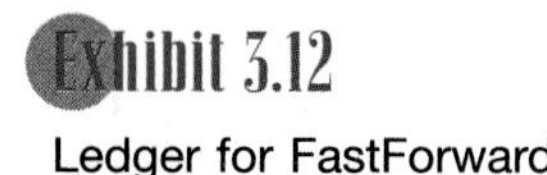

Ledger for FastForward

Assets = Liabilities + Owner's Equity

Assets

Cash			
(1)	30,000	(2)	2,500
(5)	2,200	(3)	20,000
(9)	1,900	(6)	1,000
(12)	3,000	(7)	700
		(10)	900
		(11)	600
		(13)	2,400
		(14)	120
		(15)	230
		(16)	700
Total	37,100	Total	29,150
	−29,150		
Balance	**7,950**		

Accounts Receivable			
(8)	1,900	(9)	1,900
Balance	**0**		

Prepaid Insurance			
(13)	**2,400**		

Supplies			
(2)	2,500		
(4)	1,100		
(14)	120		
Balance	**3,720**		

Equipment			
(3)	20,000		
(4)	6,000		
Balance	**26,000**		

Liabilities

Accounts Payable			
		(4)	**1,100**

Unearned Consulting Revenue			
		(12)	**3,000**

Note Payable			
(10)	900	(4)	6,000
		Balance	**5,100**

Owner's Equity

C. Taylor, Capital			
		(1)	**30,000**

C. Taylor, Withdrawals			
(11)	**600**		

Consulting Revenue			
		(5)	2,200
		(8)	1,600
		Bal.	**3,800**

Rental Revenue			
		(8)	**300**

Rent Expense			
(6)	**1,000**		

Salaries Expense			
(7)	700		
(16)	700		
Balance	**1,400**		

Utilities Expense			
(15)	**230**		

Accounts in this white area reflect increases and decreases in owner's equity. Their balances are reported on the income statement or the statement of changes in owner's equity.

$40,070 = $9,200 + $30,870

Financial Statement Links

Exhibit 3.13 extends the analysis and summarizes how transactions and their related accounts impact financial statements. Some transactions such as purchasing supplies on credit (no. 4) impact only one statement. Others such as receiving cash for services performed (no. 5) impacts all of the statements. We should review this exhibit and understand how transactions link to financial statements. We return to explain the details of these links in Chapter 5, including the adjusting and closing processes required.

Flash back

8. What kinds of transactions increase owner's equity? What kinds decrease owner's equity?

9. Why are most accounting systems called *double-entry?*

10. Double-entry accounting requires:

- **a.** All transactions that create debits to asset accounts must create credits to liability or owner's equity accounts.
- **b.** A transaction with a debit to a liability account must create a credit to an asset account.
- **c.** Every transaction to be recorded with total debits must equal total credits.

Answers—p. 109

Transactions		Balance Sheet (BS)										
		Assets					=	Liabilities			+	Equity
No.	Description	Cash	+ Accts. Rec.	+ Prepd. Insur.	+ Supp.	+ Equip.	=	Accts. Pay.	+ Unearned Rev.	+ Note Pay.	+	Taylor Capital
1	Owner investment	30,000					=				+	30,000
2	Purch. supp.	(2,500)			2,500		=				+	
3	Purch. equip.	(20,000)				20,000	=				+	
4	Credit purch.				1,100	6,000	=	1,100		6,000	+	
5	Services for cash	2,200					=				+	2,200
6	Rent exp.	(1,000)					=				+	(1,000)
7	Salary exp.	(700)					=				+	(700)
8	Services for credit		1,900				=				+	1,600 300
9	Cash rec'd. on Acct. Rec.	1,900	(1,900)				=				+	
10	Payment of Note Pay	(900)					=			(900)	+	
11	Owner Withdrawals	(600)					=				+	(600)
12	Cash for future service	3,000					=		3,000		+	
13	Payment of future insur.	(2,400)		2,400			=				+	
14	Purch. supp.	(120)			120		=				+	
15	Util exp.	(230)					=				+	(230)
16	Salary exp.	(700)					=				+	(700)
	Total	7,950	0	2,400	3,720	26,000	=	1,100	3,000	5,100	+	30,870

Recording and Posting Transactions

P1 Record transactions in a journal and post entries to a ledger.

We used double-entry accounting in the prior section to show how transactions affect accounts. This process of analyzing transactions and recording their effects directly in accounts is useful in understanding the accounting system. Yet accounting systems rarely record transactions directly in accounts. This is to avoid the potential for error and the difficulty in tracking mistakes.

Instead, the accounting process includes a *third step* where we record transactions in a journal before recording them in accounts. A **journal** gives us a complete record of each transaction in one place. It also links directly the debits and credits for each transaction. The process of recording transactions in a journal is called **journalizing.**

Step four of the accounting process is to transfer (or **post**) entries from the journal to the ledger. This step occurs only after debits and credits for each transaction are entered into a journal. This process leaves a helpful trail in checking for accuracy. It also helps us avoid errors. The process of transferring journal entry information to the ledger is called **posting.** This section describes both journalizing and posting of transactions. *Step five,* preparing a trial balance, is explained in the next section. Each of these steps in processing transactions is depicted in Exhibit 3.14.

Exhibit 3.13

Financial Statement Links to Transactions

Income Statement (IS)					Statement of Cash Flows (SCF)							Transactions	
Rev.	−	Exp.	=	Net Inc.	Oper. Cash Flow	+	Inv. Cash Flow	+	Fin. Cash Flow	=	Net Cash Flow	No.	Description
	−		=						30,000	=	30,000	1	Owner investment
	−		=		(2,500)					=	(2,500)	2	Purch. supp.
	−		=				(20,000)			=	(20,000)	3	Purch. equip.
	−		=							=		4	Credit purch.
2,200	−		=	2,200	2,200					=	2,200	5	Services for cash
	−	1,000	=	(1,000)	(1,000)					=	(1,000)	6	Rent exp.
	−	700	=	(700)	(700)					=	(700)	7	Salary exp.
1,600	−		=	1600								8	Services
300	−		=	300									for credit
	−		=		1,900					=	1,900	9	Cash rec'd. on Acct. Rec.
	−		=						(900)	=	(900)	10	Payment of Note Pay
	−		=						(600)	=	(600)	11	Owner Withdrawals
	−		=		3,000					=	3,000	12	Cash for future service
	−		=		(2,400)					=	(2,400)	13	Payment of future insur.
	−		=		(120)					=	(120)	14	Purch. supp.
	−	230	=	(230)	(230)					=	(230)	15	Util exp.
	−	700	=	(700)	(700)					=	(700)	16	Salary exp.
4,100	−	2,630	=	1,470	(550)	+	(20,000)	+	28,500	=	7950		Total

Exhibit 3.14

Steps in Processing Transactions

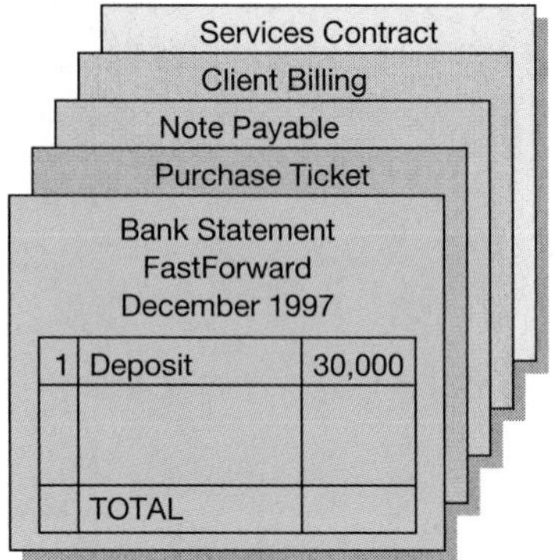

Step 1: Analyze transactions and source documents.

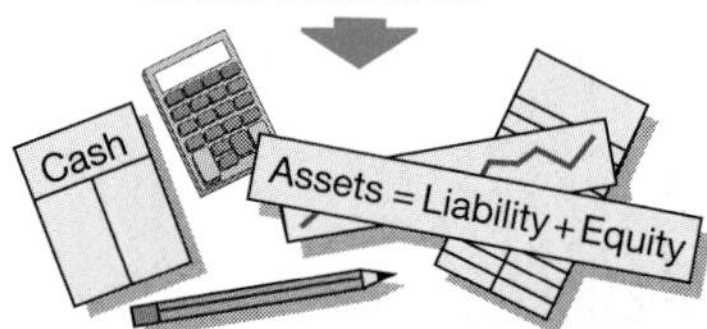

Step 2: Apply double-entry accounting.

General Journal				
Dec.	1	Cash	30,000	
		Taylor, Capital		30,000
Dec.	2	Supplies	2,500	
		Cash		2,500

Step 3: Record journal entry.

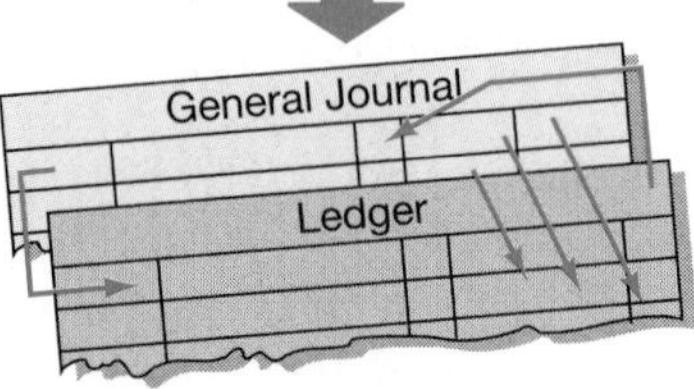

Step 4: Post entry to ledger.

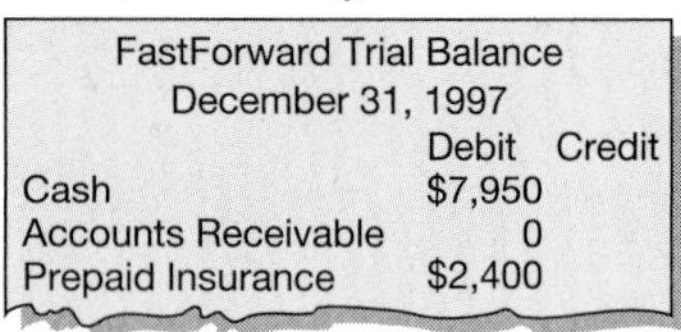

FastForward Trial Balance
December 31, 1997

	Debit	Credit
Cash	$7,950	
Accounts Receivable	0	
Prepaid Insurance	$2,400	

Step 5: Prepare trial balance.

The Journal Entry

The **general journal** shows the debits and credits of transactions and it can be used to record any transaction. A general journal entry includes the following information about each transaction:

1. Date of transaction.
2. Titles of affected accounts.
3. Dollar amount of each debit and credit.
4. Explanation of transaction.

Exhibit 3.15 shows how the first four transactions of FastForward are recorded in a general journal. A journal is often referred to as the *book of original entry.* The accounting process is similar for manual and computerized systems. Many computer programs even copy the look of a paper journal.

The fourth entry in Exhibit 3.15 uses four accounts. There are debits to the two assets purchased—supplies and equipment. There are also credits to the two sources of payment—accounts payable and note payable. A transaction affecting three or more accounts is called a **compound journal entry.**

Journalizing Transactions

There are standard procedures for recording entries in a general journal. We can identify nine steps in journalizing. It is helpful to review the entries in Exhibit 3.15 when studying these steps.

1. Enter the year on the first line at the top of the first column.
2. Enter the month in column one on the first line of the journal entry. Later entries for the same month and year on the same page of the journal do not require reentering the same month and year.
3. Enter the day of the transaction in column two on the first line of each entry.
4. Enter titles of accounts debited. Account titles are taken from the chart of accounts and are aligned with the left margin of the "Account Titles and Explanation" column.
5. Enter debit amounts in the "Debit" column on the same line as the accounts debited.
6. Enter titles of accounts credited. Account titles are taken from the chart of accounts and are indented from the left margin of the "Account Titles and Explanation" column to distinguish them from debited accounts.
7. Enter credit amounts in the "Credit" column on the same line as the accounts credited.
8. Enter a brief explanation of the transaction on the line below the entry (it is often a reference to a source document). This explanation is indented about half as far as the credited account titles to avoid confusing an explanation with accounts. We italicize explanations.
9. Skip a line between each journal entry for clarity.

A complete journal entry gives a useful description of a transaction and its effects.

The **posting reference (PR) column** is left blank when a transaction is initially recorded. Individual account numbers are later entered into the PR column when entries are posted to the ledger.

Computerized Journals

Journals in computerized and manual systems serve the same purposes. Computerized journals are often designed to look like a manual journal page as in Exhibit 3.15. Maria Sanchez of **RecordLink** in the opening article designed her Web-based system to look exactly like the paper-based system. Computerized systems typically include error-check-

Date		General Journal Account Titles and Explanation	PR	Debit	Page 1 Credit
1997 Dec.	1	Cash		30,000	
		C.Taylor, Capital			30,000
		Investment by owner.			
	2	Supplies		2,500	
		Cash			2,500
		Purchased store supplies for cash.			
	3	Equipment		20,000	
		Cash			20,000
		Purchased copy equipment for cash.			
	6	Supplies		1,100	
		Equipment		6,000	
		Accounts Payable			1,100
		Note Payable			6,000
		Purchased supplies and equipment on credit.			

Exhibit 3.15

Partial General Journal for FastForward

ing routines that ensure debits equal credits for each entry. Shortcuts often allow recordkeepers to enter account numbers instead of names, and to enter account names and numbers with pull-down menus.

Balance Column Account

T-accounts are simple and direct means to show how the accounting process works. They allow us to omit less relevant details and concentrate on main ideas. Accounting systems in practice need more structure and use **balance column accounts.** Exhibit 3.16 is an example.

		Cash			Account No. 101	
Date		Explanation	PR	Debit	Credit	Balance
1997	1		G1	30,000		30,000
	2		G1		2,500	27,500
	3		G1		20,000	7,500
	10		G1	2,200		9,700

Exhibit 3.16

Cash Account in Balance Column Format

The balance column account format is similar to a T-account in having columns for debits and credits. It is different in having a transaction's date and explanation. It also has a third column with the balance of the account after each entry is posted. This means the amount on the last line in this column is the account's current balance. For example, FastForward's Cash account in Exhibit 3.16 is debited on December 1 for the $30,000 investment by Taylor. The account then shows a $30,000 debit balance. The account is credited on December 2 for $2,500, and its new $27,500 balance is shown in the third column. On December 3, it is credited again, this time for $20,000, and its balance is reduced to $7,500. The Cash account is debited for $2,200 on December 10, and its balance increases to $9,700.

When a balance column account is used, the heading of the Balance column does not show whether it is a debit or credit balance. This omission is no problem because every account has a *normal balance.* The normal balance of each account (asset, liability, equity, revenue, or expense) refers to the left or right (debit or credit) side where increases are recorded. The earlier diagrams in this chapter highlight this. Exhibit 3.17 shows normal balances for accounts to emphasize their importance.

Exhibit 3.17

Normal Balances for Accounts

Assets		=	Liabilities		+	Owner's Capital		−	Owner's Withdrawals		+	Revenues		−	Expenses	
Dr. for increases	Cr. for decreases		Dr. for decreases	Cr. for increases		Dr. for decreases	Cr. for increases		Dr. for increases	Cr. for decreases		Dr. for decreases	Cr. for increases		Dr. for increases	Cr. for decreases
+	−		−	+		−	+		+	−		−	+		+	−
Normal				**Normal**			**Normal**		**Normal**				**Normal**		**Normal**	

Abnormal Balance

Unusual events can sometimes temporarily give an abnormal balance for an account. An *abnormal balance* refers to a balance on the side where decreases are recorded. For example, a customer might mistakenly overpay a bill. This gives that customer's account receivable an abnormal (credit) balance. An abnormal balance is often identified by circling it or by entering it in red or some other unusual color. Computerized systems often provide a code beside a balance such as *dr.* or *cr.* to identify its balance.

Zero Balance

A zero balance for an account is usually shown by writing zeros or a dash in the Balance column. This practice avoids confusion between a zero balance and one omitted in error.

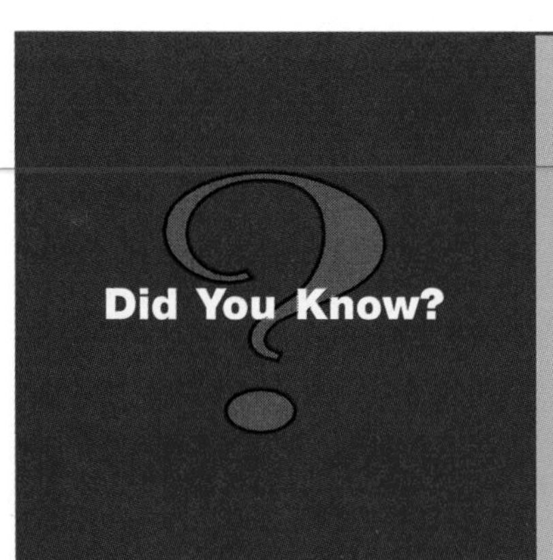

STAR CFOs: The Next Generation

What are likely duties for the next generation of accounting professionals? A recent article on chief financial officers (CFOs) gives us a peek. CFOs were once perceived as: bean counters; nonplayers in corporate strategy; narrowly focused; and preoccupied with costs. CFOs are now major players in: long-term planning; revenue strategies; using technology; and interpreting accounting information. This suggests the next generation of accounting professionals will require more analytical and conceptual skills. [Source: *Business Week,* October 28, 1996.]

Posting Journal Entries

Exhibit 3.14 shows that journal entries are posted to ledger accounts. To ensure that the ledger is up to date, entries are posted as soon as possible. This might be daily, weekly, or when time permits. All entries must be posted to the ledger by the end of a reporting period. This is necessary so account balances are current when financial statements are prepared. It is why the ledger is referred to as the *book of final entry.*

When entries are posted to the ledger, the debits in journal entries are copied into ledger accounts as debits, and credits are copied into ledger accounts as credits. Exhibit 3.18 shows six steps of manual systems to post each debit and credit from a journal entry.

The usual process is to post in order debits and then credits. The steps in posting are:

1. Identify the ledger account that was debited in the journal entry.
2. Enter the date of the journal entry in this ledger account.
3. Enter the source of the debit in the PR column of the ledger, both the journal and page. The letter *G* shows it came from the general journal.[7]

[7] Other journals are identified by their own letters. We discuss other journals later in the book.

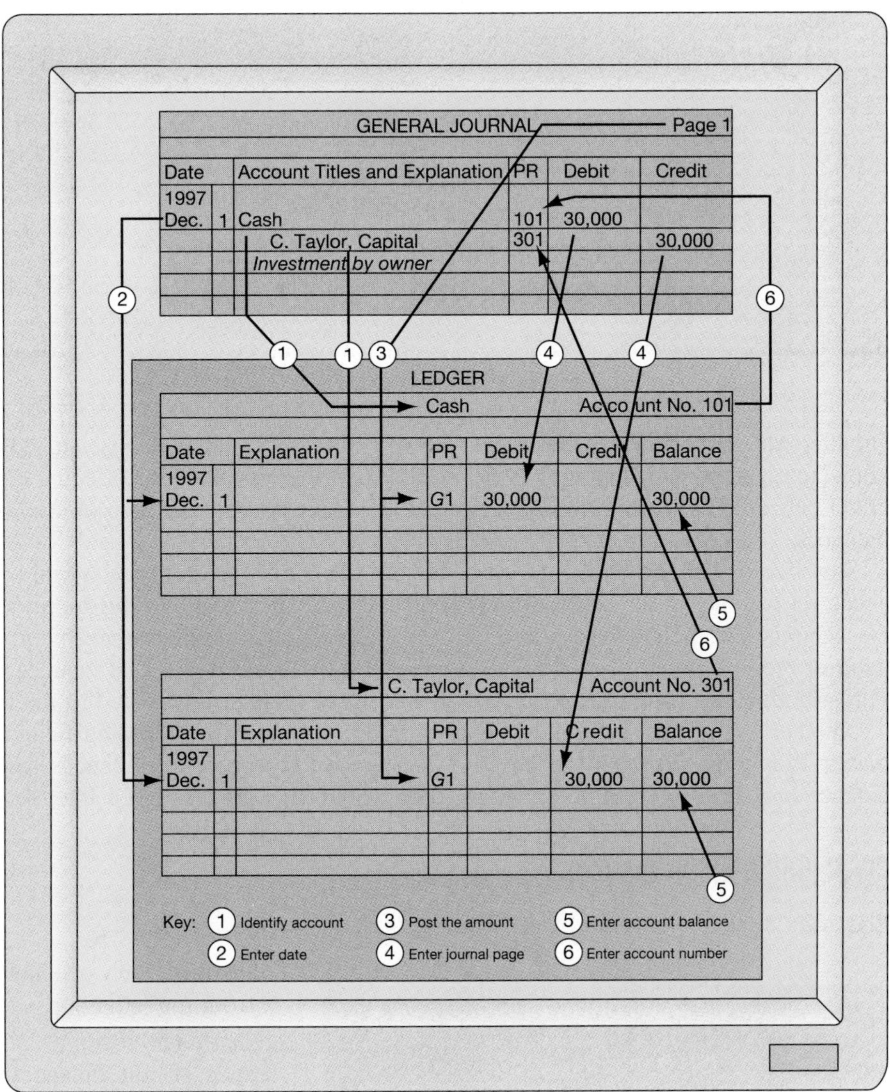

Exhibit 3.18

Posting an entry to the ledger

4. Enter the amount debited from the journal entry into the Debit column of the ledger account.
5. Compute and enter the account's new balance in the Balance column.
6. Enter the ledger account number in the PR column of the journal entry.
7. Repeat the six steps for credit amounts and Credit columns.

Step 6 in the posting process for both debit and credit amounts of an entry inserts the account number in the journal's PR column. This creates a link between the ledger and the journal entry. This link is a useful cross-reference for tracing an amount from one record to another. It also readily shows the stage of completion in the posting process. This permits one to easily start and stop the posting process.

Posting in Computerized Systems

Computerized systems require no added effort to post journal entries to the ledger. These systems automatically transfer debit and credit entries from the journal to the ledger. Journal entries are posted directly to ledger accounts. Many systems, including those of **RecordLink,** have programs testing the reasonableness of a journal entry and the account balance when recorded. For example, the payroll program might alert a preparer to hourly rates exceeding $500.

Flash back

11. When Maria Sanchez set up RecordLink, she invested $15,000 cash and equipment with a market value of $23,000. RecordLink also took responsibility for an $18,000 note payable issued to finance the purchase of equipment. Prepare the journal entry to record Sanchez's investment.

12. Explain what a compound journal entry is.

13. Why are posting reference numbers entered in the journal when entries are posted to accounts?

Answers—p. 109

Trial Balance

P2 Prepare and explain the use of a trial balance.

Double-entry accounting records every transaction with equal debits and credits. We know an error exists if the sum of debit entries in the ledger does not equal the sum of credit entries. The sum of debit account balances must equal the sum of credit account balances.

Step five of the accounting process shown in Exhibit 3.14 is to use a trial balance to check on whether debit and credit account balances are equal. A **trial balance** is a list of accounts and their balances at a point in time. Account balances are reported in the debit or credit column of a trial balance. Exhibit 3.19 shows the trial balance for Fast-Forward after the 16 entries described earlier in the chapter are posted to the ledger.

Another use of the trial balance is as an internal report for preparing financial statements. Preparing statements is easier when we can take account balances from a trial balance instead of searching the ledger. We explain this process in Chapter 4.

Preparing a Trial Balance

Preparing a trial balance involves five steps:

Exhibit 3.19

Trial Balance

FASTFORWARD
Trial Balance
December 31, 1997

	Debit	Credit
Cash	$ 7,950	
Prepaid insurance	2,400	
Supplies	3,720	
Equipment	26,000	
Accounts payable		$ 1,100
Unearned consulting revenue		3,000
Note payable		5,100
C. Taylor, Capital		30,000
C. Taylor, Withdrawals	600	
Consulting revenue		3,800
Rental revenue		300
Rent expense	1,000	
Salaries expense	1,400	
Utilities expense	230	
Total	$43,300	$43,300

1. Identify each account balance from the ledger.
2. List each account and its balance. Debit balances are entered in the Debit column and credit balances in the Credit column.[8]
3. Compute the total of debit balances.
4. Compute the total of credit balances.
5. Verify total debit balances equal total credit balances.

The total debit balances equal the total credit balances for the trial balance in Exhibit 3.19. If these two totals were not equal, we would know that one or more errors exist. Equality of these two totals does not guarantee no errors were made.

[8] If an account has a zero balance, it can be listed in the trial balance with a zero in the column for its normal balance.

Using a Trial Balance

We know one or more errors exist when a trial balance does not balance (when its columns are not equal). When one or more errors exist they often arise from one of the following steps in the accounting process: (1) preparing journal entries, (2) posting entries to the ledger, (3) computing account balances, (4) copying account balances to the trial balance, or (5) totaling the trial balance columns.

When a trial balance does balance, the accounts are likely free of the kinds of errors that create unequal debits and credits. Yet errors may still exist. One example is when a debit or credit of a correct amount is made to a wrong account. This can occur when either journalizing or posting. The error would produce incorrect balances in two accounts but the trial balance would balance. Another error is to record equal debits and credits of an incorrect amount. This error produces incorrect balances in two accounts but again the debits and credits are equal. We give these examples to show that when a trial balance does balance, it does not prove all journal entries are recorded and posted correctly.

Searching for Errors

At least one error exists if the trial balance does not balance. The error (or errors) must be found and corrected before preparing financial statements. Searching for the error is more efficient if we check the journalizing, posting, and trial balance preparation process in *reverse order.* Otherwise we would need to look at every transaction until the error is found.

Several steps are involved. Step one is to verify that the trial balance columns are correctly added. If step one fails to find the error, then step two is to verify that account balances are accurately copied from the ledger. Our third step in identifying the error is to see if a debit or credit balance is mistakenly listed in the trial balance as a credit or debit. A clue to this kind of error is when the difference between total debits and total credits in the trial balance equals twice the amount of the incorrect account balance.

If the error is still undiscovered, our fourth step is to recompute each account balance. Our fifth step if the error remains is to verify that each journal entry is properly posted to ledger accounts. Our sixth step is to verify that the original journal entry has equal debits and credits.

One frequent error is called a *transposition.* This error occurs when two digits are switched, or transposed, within a number. If transposition is the only error, then it yields a difference between two trial balance columns that is evenly divisible by nine. For example, assume a $691 debit in a journal entry is incorrectly posted to the ledger as $619. Total credits in the trial balance are then larger than total debits by $72 ($691 − $619). The $72 error is *evenly* divisible by 9 ($72/9 = 8). The first digit of the quotient (in our example it is 8) equals the difference between the digits of the two transposed numbers (i.e., between the 9 and the 1). The number of digits in the quotient also tells the location of the transposition. Because the quotient in our example had only one digit (8), it tells us the transposition is in the first digit of the transposed numbers, starting from the right.[9]

Correcting Errors

If errors are discovered in either the journal or the ledger, they must be corrected. Our approach to correcting errors depends on the kind of error and when it is discovered.

If an error in a journal entry is discovered before the error is posted, it can be corrected in a manual system by drawing a line through the incorrect information. The cor-

[9] Consider another example where a transposition error involves posting $961 instead of the correct $691. The difference in these numbers is $270, and its quotient is $30 ($270/9). Because the quotient has two digits, it tells us to check the second digits from the right for a transposition of two numbers that have a difference of 3.

rect information is written above it to create a record of change for the auditor. Many computerized systems allow the operator to replace the incorrect information directly. If a correct amount in the journal is posted incorrectly to the ledger, we can correct it the same way.

Another case occurs when an error in a journal entry is not discovered until after it is posted. We usually do not strike through both erroneous entries in the journal and ledger. Instead, the usual practice is to correct the error in the original journal entry by creating *another* journal entry. This *correcting entry* removes the amount from the wrong account and records it to the correct account. As an example, suppose we recorded a purchase of office supplies in the journal with an incorrect debit to Office Equipment:

Assets = Liabilities + Equity
+1,600
−1,600

Oct. 14	Office Equipment	1,600	
	Cash		1,600
	To record the purchase of office supplies.		

We then post this entry to the ledger. The Office Supplies ledger account balance is understated by $1,600 and the Office Equipment ledger account balance is overstated by the same amount. When we discover the error three days later, the following correcting entry is made:

Assets = Liabilities + Equity
+1,600
−1,600

Oct. 17	Office Supplies	1,600	
	Office Equipment		1,600
	To correct the entry of October 14 that incorrectly debited Office Equipment instead of Office Supplies.		

The credit in the correcting entry removes the error from the first entry. The debit correctly records the supplies. The explanation reports exactly what happened.

Computerized systems often use similar correcting entries. The exact procedure depends on the system used and management policy. Yet nearly all systems include controls to show when and where a correction is made.

Did You Know?

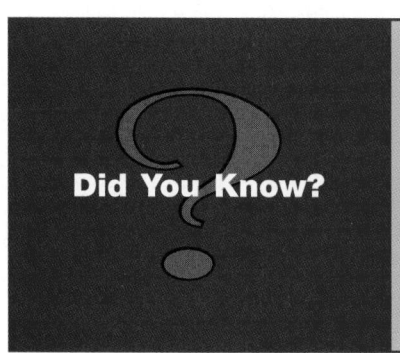

Window on Accounting

Manual and computerized accounting systems mirror each other. Computerized systems often take on many routine tasks in accounting. They also give regular updating (batch time) or continuous (real time) processing of information. Many programs point out errors like unequal debits and credits or the transposing of numbers. They usually look like the paper-based ledger and general journal. Computerized systems have freed accounting professionals to spend more time and effort on analyzing and interpreting information for users. [Source: *Business Week,* September 16, 1996.]

Formatting Conventions

Dollar signs are not used in journals and ledgers. They do appear in financial statements and other reports, including trial balances. This book follows the usual practice of putting a dollar sign beside the first amount in each column of numbers and the first amount appearing after a ruled line indicating that an addition or subtraction has been performed. The financial statements in Exhibit 2.17 demonstrate how dollar signs are used in this book. Different companies use various conventions for dollar signs. For example, dollar signs are usually printed beside only the first and last numbers in columns of the financial statements for **NIKE.**

When amounts are entered manually in a journal, ledger, or trial balance, commas are not needed to indicate thousands, millions, and so forth. However, commas are used in financial statements and other reports. It is common for companies to round amounts to the nearest dollar, and even to a higher level for certain accounts. **NIKE** is typical of many companies in that it rounds its financial statement amounts to the nearest thousand dollars. But it continues to report its income per share amount in dollars with cents. NIKE's decision is usually linked with the perceived importance of rounding for users' decisions.

Flash back

14. Explain a chart of accounts.

15. When are dollar signs typically used in accounting reports?

16. If a $4,000 debit to Equipment in a journal entry is incorrectly posted to the ledger as a $4,000 credit, and the ledger account has a resulting debit balance of $20,000, what is the effect of this error on the trial balance column totals?

Answers—p. 110

Debt Ratio

USING THE INFORMATION

A2 Compute the debt ratio and describe its use in analyzing company performance.

Accounting records are designed to provide useful information to users of financial statements. One important objective for many users is gathering information to help them assess a company's risk of failing to pay its debts when they are due. This section describes the debt ratio and how it can help in this task.

Most companies finance a portion of their assets with liabilities and the remaining portion with equity. A company that finances a relatively large portion of its assets with liabilities is said to have a high degree of *financial leverage.* While we will discuss more about financial leverage in Chapter 14, we should understand that higher financial leverage involves greater risk. This is because liabilities must be repaid and often require regular interest payments. The risk is that a company may not be able to meet required payments. This risk is higher if a company has more liabilities (more highly leveraged).

One way to assess the risk associated with a company's use of liabilities is to compute and analyze the debt ratio. The **debt ratio** describes the relation between a company's liabilities and its assets, and is defined in Exhibit 3.20.

Exhibit 3.20
Debt Ratio

$$\textbf{Debt ratio} = \frac{\textbf{Total liabilities}}{\textbf{Total assets}}$$

To see how we apply the debt ratio, let's look at **Stride Rite**'s liabilities and assets (in millions) for 1992–1996. Stride Rite is the maker of Keds, Pro-Keds, and other footwear. Using these data, we compute in Exhibit 3.21 the debt ratio for Stride Rite at the end of each year.

Exhibit 3.21
Computation and Analysis of Debt Ratio

	1996	1995	1994	1993	1992
a. Total liabilities	$103	$99	$104	$110	$112
b. Total assets	$364	$367	$397	$412	$384
c. **Debt ratio**	.283	.270	.262	.267	.292
d. Industry debt ratio*	.64	.47	.52	.50	.47

* Industry debt ratio is the median value from ten of Stride Rite's competitors including NIKE, Reebok, Fila, Converse, L. A. Gear, and others.

Evaluating a company's debt ratio depends on several factors such as the nature of its operations, its ability to generate cash flows, its industry, and economic conditions. It is not possible to say that a specific debt ratio is good or bad for all companies. As we already discussed, we need to compare performance over time and across companies both in and outside of the industry.

We note that **Stride Rite's** debt ratio is stable over recent years, ranging from a low of .262 to a high of .292. This is low for most companies as evidenced by comparisons with industry figures. It is also unusual for a company like Stride Rite to carry no long-term debt as pointed out in its 1996 annual report:

> . . . the Company had no long-term debt as the final payment on the Company's Senior Notes will be made during 1997.

This analysis implies a low risk from financial leverage for Stride Rite. There are other risk factors we need to examine and we will do this in later chapters.

Investor

You are considering buying stock in **Converse.** As part of your analysis, you compute the debt ratio of Converse for 1994, 1995, and 1996: 0.80, 1.10, and 1.17, respectively.* Based on these debt ratios, is Converse a low risk investment? Has the risk of buying Converse stock increased or decreased from 1994 to 1996?

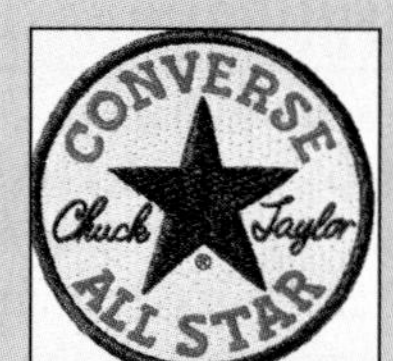

*Converse's equity balances are negative in 1995 and 1996 because of losses.

Answer—p. 109

Summary

C1 Explain the steps in processing transactions. The accounting process captures business transactions and events, analyzes and records their effects, and summarizes and prepares information useful in making decisions. Transactions and events are the starting points in the accounting process. Source documents help in analyzing them. The effects of transactions and events are recorded in the accounting books. Postings and the trial balance help summarize and classify these effects. The final step is providing this information in useful reports or financial statements to decision makers.

C2 Describe source documents and their purpose. Source documents are business papers that identify and describe transactions and events. Examples are sales tickets, checks, purchase orders, bills, and bank statements. Source documents help ensure accounting records reflect all transactions. They also help prevent mistakes and theft, and are important to internal control. Source documents provide objective evidence making information more reliable and useful.

C3 Describe an account and its use in recording information about transactions. An account is a detailed record of increases and decreases in a specific asset, liability, equity, revenue, or expense item. Information is taken from accounts, analyzed, summarized, and presented in reports and financial statements for use by decision makers.

C4 Describe a ledger and a chart of accounts. A ledger is a record containing all accounts used by a company. This is what is referred to as the *books.* The chart of accounts is a listing of all accounts and usually includes an identification number assigned to each account.

C5 Define debits and credits and explain their role in double-entry accounting. Debit refers to left, and credit refers to right. Debits increase assets, withdrawals, and expenses, while credits decrease them. Credits increase liabilities, capital, and revenues, while debits decrease them. Double-entry accounting means every transaction affects at least two accounts and has at least one debit and one credit. The total amount debited must equal the total amount credited for each transaction. The system for recording debits and credits follows from the accounting equation. The left side of a T-account is the normal balance for assets, and the right side is the normal balance for liabilities and equity.

A1 Analyze the impact of transactions on accounts and financial statements. We analyze transactions using concepts of double-entry accounting. This analysis is performed by determining a transaction's effects on accounts. These effects are recorded in journals and posted to ledgers.

A2 Compute the debt ratio and describe its use in analyzing company performance. A company's debt ratio is computed as total liabilities divided by total assets. It tells us how much of the assets are financed by creditor (nonowner or liability) financing. The higher this ratio, the more risk a company faces in using liabilities to finance assets. This is because liabilities must be repaid.

P1 **Record transactions in a journal and post entries to a ledger.** We record transactions in a journal to give a record of their effects. Each entry in a journal is posted to the accounts in the ledger. This provides information in accounts that is used to produce financial statements. Balance column ledger accounts are widely used and include columns for debits, credits, and the account balance after each entry.

P2 **Prepare and explain the use of a trial balance.** A trial balance is a list of accounts in the ledger showing their debit and credit balances in separate columns. The trial balance is a convenient summary of the ledger's contents and is useful in preparing financial statements. It reveals errors of the kind that produce unequal debit and credit account balances.

Guidance Answer to **Judgment and Ethics**

Cashier

There are advantages to the process proposed by the assistant manager. They include improved customer service, less delays, and less work for you. However, you should have serious concerns about control and the potential for fraud. In particular, there is no control over the possibility of embezzlement by the assistant manager. The assistant manager could steal cash and simply ring up less sales to match the remaining cash. You should reject her suggestion without approval by the manager. Moreover, you should have an ethical concern about the assistant manager's suggestion to ignore store policy.

Guidance Answers to **You Make the Call**

Marketing Manager

You direct your search to the accounting information system. The general journal contains all the revenue information you desire. The difficulty in working with the journal is that you must go through all entries, identify revenues, and compute the total. The ledger also contains the information you desire and is a preferred source as it keeps a running balance of each account and would directly answer your question.

Investor

The debt ratio suggests the stock of Converse is of higher risk than normal and that this risk is rising. Industry ratios reported along with Stride Rite's debt ratios in the chapter further support the conclusion that Converse is of higher risk. In particular, the debt ratio for Converse has been steadily increasing and is now more than double the industry norm of about 0.50. Also, a debt ratio larger than 1.0 indicates negative equity. Excessive losses for Converse led to its negative equity.

Guidance Answers to Flash *backs*

1. External transactions are exchanges between an organization and some other person or organization. Internal transactions are exchanges within an organization, for example, a company using equipment in its operating activities.
2. Examples of source documents are sales tickets, checks, purchase orders, charges to customers, bills from suppliers, employee earnings records, and bank statements.
3. Source documents serve many purposes including recordkeeping and internal control. Source documents, especially if obtained from outside the organization, provide objective evidence about transactions and their amounts for recording. Objective evidence is important because it makes information more reliable and useful.
4.

Assets	Liabilities	Equity
a,c,f	b,e	d

5. An account is a record in an accounting system where increases and decreases in a specific asset, liability, owner's equity, revenue, or expense are recorded and stored. A ledger is a collection of all accounts used by a business.
6. A company's size and diversity affect the number of accounts needed in its accounting system. The types of accounts used by a business depend on information the business needs to both effectively operate and report its activities in financial statements.
7. No. Debit and credit both can mean increase or decrease. The particular meaning in a circumstance depends on the *type of account.* For example, a debit increases the balance of asset and expense accounts but decreases the balance of liability, equity, and revenue accounts.
8. Owner's equity is increased by revenues and by an owner's investments. Owner's equity is decreased by expenses and by an owner's cash withdrawals.
9. The name *double-entry* is used because all transactions affect at least two accounts. There must be at least one debit in one account and at least one credit in another.
10. Answer is *(c)*.
11. The entry is:

Cash	15,000	
Equipment	23,000	
Note Payable		18,000
Sanchez, Capital		20,000

12. A compound journal entry is one that affects three or more accounts.
13. Posting reference numbers are entered in the journal when posting to the ledger as a control over the posting process. They provide a cross-reference that allows the recordkeeper or au-

ditor to trace debits and credits from one record to another. They also create a marker in case the posting process is interrupted.

14. A chart of accounts is a listing of all of a company's accounts and their identifying numbers.

15. Dollar signs are used in financial statements and other reports to identify the kind of currency being used in the reports. At a minimum, they are placed beside the first and last numbers in each column. Some companies place dollar signs beside any amount that appears after a ruled line to indicate that an addition or subtraction has taken place.

16. The effect of this error is to understate the trial balance's debit column total by $4,000 and overstate the credit column total by $4,000. This results in an $8,000 difference between the two totals.

Demonstration Problem

This demonstration problem is based on the same facts as the demonstration problem at the end of Chapter 2. The following events occurred during the first month of Barbara Schmidt's new haircutting business called The Cutlery:

a. On August 1, Schmidt put $3,000 cash into a checking account in the name of The Cutlery. She also invested $15,000 of equipment that she already owned.

b. On August 2, she paid $600 cash for furniture for the shop.

c. On August 3, she paid $500 cash to rent space in a strip mall for August.

d. On August 4, she furnished the shop by installing the old equipment and some new equipment that she bought on credit for $1,200. This amount is to be repaid in three equal payments at the end of August, September, and October.

e. On August 5, The Cutlery opened for business. Cash receipts from haircutting services provided in the first week and a half of business (ended August 15) were $825.

f. On August 15, Schmidt provided haircutting services on account for $100.

g. On August 17, Schmidt received a $100 check in the mail for services previously rendered on account.

h. On August 17, Schmidt paid $125 to an assistant for working during the grand opening.

i. Cash receipts from haircutting services provided during the second half of August were $930.

j. On August 31, Schmidt paid an installment on the accounts payable from (d).

k. On August 31, she withdrew $900 cash for her personal use.

Required

1. Prepare general journal entries for the preceding transactions.
2. Open the following accounts: Cash (101); Accounts Receivable (102); Furniture (161); Store Equipment (165); Accounts Payable (201); Barbara Schmidt, Capital (301); Barbara Schmidt, Withdrawals (302); Haircutting Services Revenue (403); Wages Expense (623); and Rent Expense (640).
3. Post the journal entries from (1) to the ledger accounts.
4. Prepare a trial balance as of August 31.

Extended Analysis

5. In the coming months, The Cutlery will experience an even greater variety of business transactions. Identify which accounts are debited and credited for the transactions that follow. (Hint: You may have to use some accounts not listed in (2) above.)

a. Purchases supplies with cash.

b. Pays cash for future insurance coverage.

c. Receives cash for services to be provided in the future.

Planning the Solution

- Analyze each transaction to identify the accounts affected by the transaction and the amount of each effect.
- Use the debit and credit rules to prepare a journal entry for each transaction.

- Post each debit and each credit in the journal entries to the appropriate ledger accounts and cross-reference each amount in the Posting Reference columns in the journal and account.
- Calculate each account balance and list the accounts with their balances on a trial balance.
- Verify that the total debits in the trial balance equal total credits.
- Analyze future transactions to identify the accounts affected and apply debit and credit rules.

Solution to Demonstration Problem

1. General journal entries:

Date	Account Titles and Explanations	PR	Debit	Credit
Aug. 1	Cash	101	3,000	
	Store Equipment	165	15,000	
	Barbara Schmidt, Capital	301		18,000
	Owner's initial investment.			
2	Furniture	161	600	
	Cash	101		600
	Purchased furniture for cash.			
3	Rent Expense	640	500	
	Cash	101		500
	Paid rent for August.			
4	Store Equipment	165	1,200	
	Accounts Payable	201		1,200
	Purchased additional equipment on credit.			
15	Cash	101	825	
	Haircutting Services Revenue	403		825
	Cash receipts from 10 days of operations.			
15	Accounts Receivable	102	100	
	Haircutting Services Revenue	403		100
	To record revenue for services provided on account.			
17	Cash	101	100	
	Accounts Receivable	102		100
	To record cash received as payment on account.			
17	Wages Expense	623	125	
	Cash	101		125
	Paid wages to assistant.			
31	Cash	101	930	
	Haircutting Services Revenue	403		930
	Cash receipts from second half of August.			
31	Accounts Payable	201	400	
	Cash	101		400
	Paid an installment on accounts payable.			
31	Barbara Schmidt, Withdrawals	302	900	
	Cash	101		900
	Owner withdrew cash from the business.			

2. & 3. Open ledger accounts and post journal entries:

Cash — Account No. 101

Date		Explanation	PR	Debit	Credit	Balance
Aug.	1		G1	3,000		3,000
	2		G1		600	2,400
	3		G1		500	1,900
	15		G1	825		2,725
	17		G1	100		2,825
	17		G1		125	2,700
	31		G1	930		3,630
	31		G1		400	3,230
	31		G1		900	2,330

Accounts Receivable — Account No. 102

Date		Explanation	PR	Debit	Credit	Balance
Aug.	15		G1	100		100
	17		G1		100	0

Furniture — Account No. 161

Date		Explanation	PR	Debit	Credit	Balance
Aug.	2		G1	600		600

Store Equipment — Account No. 165

Date		Explanation	PR	Debit	Credit	Balance
Aug.	1		G1	15,000		15,000
	4		G1	1,200		16,200

Accounts Payable — Account No. 201

Date		Explanation	PR	Debit	Credit	Balance
Aug.	4		G1		1,200	1,200
	31		G1	400		800

Barbara Schmidt, Capital — Account No. 301

Date		Explanation	PR	Debit	Credit	Balance
Aug.	1		G1		18,000	18,000

Barbara Schmidt, Withdrawals — Account No. 302

Date		Explanation	PR	Debit	Credit	Balance
Aug.	31		G1	900		900

Haircutting Services Revenue					Account No. 403	
Date		Explanation	PR	Debit	Credit	Balance
Aug.	15		G1		825	825
	15		G1		100	925
	31		G1		930	1,855

Wages Expense					Account No. 623	
Date		Explanation	PR	Debit	Credit	Balance
Aug.	17		G1	125		125

Rent Expense					Account No. 640	
Date		Explanation	PR	Debit	Credit	Balance
Aug.	3		G1	500		500

4. Prepare trial balance:

THE CUTLERY
Trial Balance
August 31, 2000

	Debit	Credit
Cash	$ 2,330	
Accounts Receivable	0	
Furniture	600	
Store equipment	16,200	
Accounts payable		$ 800
Barbara Schmidt, capital		18,000
Barbara Schmidt, withdrawals	900	
Haircutting services revenue		1,855
Wages expense	125	
Rent expense	500	
Totals	$20,655	$20,655

5a. Supplies debited
Cash credited
5b. Prepaid Insurance debited
Cash credited
5c. Cash debited
Unearned Services Revenue credited

Glossary

Account a place or location within an accounting system in which the increases and decreases in a specific asset, liability, equity, revenue, or expense are recorded and stored. (p. 84).

Account balance the difference between the increases (including the beginning balance) and decreases recorded in an account. (p. 90).

Balance column account an account with debit and credit columns for recording entries and a third column for showing the balance of the account after each entry is posted. (p. 101).

Chart of accounts a list of all accounts used by a company; includes the identification number assigned to each account. (p. 88).

Compound journal entry a journal entry that affects at least three accounts. (p. 100).

Credit an entry that decreases asset and expense accounts or increases liability, equity, and revenue accounts; recorded on the right side of a T-account. (p. 90).

Debit an entry that increases asset and expense accounts or decreases liability, equity, and revenue accounts; recorded on the left side of a T-account. (p. 90).

Debt ratio the ratio of a company's total liabilities to its total assets; used to describe the risk associated with the company's debts. (p. 107).

Double-entry accounting an accounting system where every transaction affects at least two accounts and has at least one debit and one credit; the sum of the debits for each entry must equal the sum of the credits for each entry. (p. 91).

Events happenings that both affect an organization's financial position and can be reliably measured. (p. 83).

External transactions exchanges of economic consideration between an entity and another person or organization. (p. 83).

General journal a record of the debits and credits of transactions; can be used to record any transaction. (p. 100).

Internal transactions exchanges within an organization that can also affect the accounting equation. (p. 83).

Journal a record where transactions are recorded before they are recorded in accounts; amounts are posted from the journal to the ledger; also called the *book of original entry.* (p. 99).

Journalizing the process of recording transactions in a journal. (p. 99).

Ledger a record containing all accounts used by a business. (p. 84).

Note payable an unconditional written promise to pay a definite sum of money on demand or on a defined future date(s); also called a *promissory note.* (p. 85).

Posting the process of transferring journal entry information to the ledger. (p. 99).

Posting reference (PR) column a column in journals where individual account numbers are entered when entries are posted to the ledger. (p. 100).

Promissory note an unconditional written promise to pay a definite sum of money on demand or on a defined future date(s); also called a *note payable* (or *note receivable*). (p. 85).

Source documents another name for *business papers*; these documents are the source of information recorded with accounting entries and can be in either paper or electronic form. (p. 83).

T-account a simple account form used as a helpful tool in showing the effects of transactions and events on specific accounts. (p. 89).

Trial balance a list of accounts and their balances at a point in time; the total debit balances should equal the total credit balances. (p. 104).

Unearned revenues liabilities created when customers pay in advance for products or services; created when cash is received before revenues are earned; satisfied by delivering the products or services in the future. (p. 86).

Questions

1. Discuss the steps in the accounting process.
2. What is the difference between a note receivable and an account receivable?
3. If assets are valuable resources and asset accounts have debit balances, why do expense accounts have debit balances?
4. Why does the recordkeeper prepare a trial balance?
5. Should a transaction be recorded first in a journal or the ledger? Why?
6. Are debits or credits listed first in general journal entries? Are the debits or the credits indented?
7. What kinds of transactions can be recorded in a general journal?
8. If a wrong amount is journalized and posted to the accounts, how should the error be corrected?
9. Review the NIKE balance sheet for fiscal year-end 5/31/97 in Appendix A. Identify three accounts on the balance sheet that carry debit balances and three accounts on the balance sheet that carry credit balances.
10. Review the Reebok balance sheet for fiscal year-end 12/31/96 in Appendix A. Identify four different liability accounts that include the word *payable* in the account title.
11. Locate AOL's income statement in Appendix A. What account titles are used for revenue accounts? Describe these revenue accounts.
12. Reread the chapter's opening scenario describing Maria Sanchez's company, RecordLink. Last year RecordLink's revenues exceeded $850,000. Suggest an appropriate account title for RecordLink's revenue account.

Quick Study

QS 3-1 Identifying source documents C2

Select the items from the following list that are likely to serve as source documents:

- **a.** Income statement
- **b.** Trial balance
- **c.** Telephone bill
- **d.** Invoice from supplier
- **e.** Owner's withdrawals account
- **f.** Balance sheet
- **g.** Bank statement
- **h.** Sales ticket

QS 3-2 Classifying accounts in financial statements A1

Indicate the financial statement on which each of the following accounts appears. Use IS for income statement, SCOE for the statement of changes in owner's equity, and BS for balance sheet:

- **a.** Buildings
- **b.** Interest Earned
- **c.** Owner, Withdrawals
- **d.** Equipment
- **e.** Prepaid Insurance
- **f.** Interest Payable
- **g.** Accounts Receivable
- **h.** Salaries Expense
- **i.** Office Supplies
- **j.** Repair Services Revenue

QS 3-3 Linking debit or credit with normal balance C5

Indicate whether a debit or credit is necessary to *decrease* the normal balance of each of the following accounts:

- **a.** Buildings
- **b.** Interest Earned
- **c.** Owner, Withdrawals
- **d.** Owner, Capital
- **e.** Prepaid Insurance
- **f.** Interest Payable
- **g.** Accounts Receivable
- **h.** Salaries Expense
- **i.** Office Supplies
- **j.** Repair Services Revenue

QS 3-4 Analyzing debit or credit by account C5

Identify whether a debit or credit is necessary to result in the indicated change for each of the following accounts:

- **a.** To increase Notes Payable.
- **b.** To decrease Accounts Receivable.
- **c.** To increase Owner, Capital.
- **d.** To decrease Unearned Fees.
- **e.** To decrease Prepaid Insurance.
- **f.** To decrease Cash.
- **g.** To increase Utilities Expense.
- **h.** To increase Fees Earned.
- **i.** To increase Store Equipment.
- **j.** To increase Owner, Withdrawals.

QS 3-5 Preparing journal entries A1

Prepare journal entries for the following transactions:

- **a.** On January 15, Stan Adams opened a landscaping business by investing $60,000 cash and equipment having a $40,000 fair value.
- **b.** On January 20, purchased office supplies on credit for $340.
- **c.** On January 28, received $5,200 in return for providing landscaping services to a customer.

QS 3-6 Identifying a posting error P2

A trial balance has total debits of $21,000 and total credits of $25,500. Which one of the following errors would create this imbalance? Explain.

- **a.** A $4,500 debit to Salaries Expense in a journal entry was incorrectly posted to the ledger as a $4,500 credit, leaving the Salaries Expense account with a $750 debit balance.
- **b.** A $2,250 credit to Consulting Fees Earned in a journal entry was incorrectly posted to the ledger as a $2,250 debit, leaving the Consulting Fees Earned account with a $6,300 credit balance.
- **c.** A $2,250 debit to Rent Expense in a journal entry was incorrectly posted to the ledger as a $2,250 credit, leaving the Rent Expense account with a $3,000 debit balance.

Exercises

Exercise 3-1

Increases, decreases, and normal balances of accounts

C3, C5

Complete the following table by (1) identifying the type of account as an asset, liability, equity, revenue, or expense, (2) entering *debit* or *credit* to identify the kind of entry that would increase or decrease the account balance, and (3) identifying the normal balance of the account.

	Account	Type of Account	Debit or Credit		Normal Balance
			Increase	Decrease	
a.	Land				
b.	H. Cooper, Capital				
c.	Accounts receivable				
d.	H. Cooper, Withdrawals				
e.	Cash				
f.	Equipment				
g.	Unearned revenue				
h.	Accounts payable				
i.	Postage expense				
j.	Prepaid insurance				
k.	Wages expense				
l.	Fees earned				

Exercise 3-2

Analyzing effects of transactions on accounts

A1

Jan Garret recently notified a client that it would have to pay a $48,000 fee for accounting services. Unfortunately, the client did not have enough cash to pay the entire bill. Garret agreed to accept the following items in full payment: (1) $7,500 cash, (2) computer equipment worth $75,000, and (3) assume responsibility for a $34,500 note payable related to the equipment. The entry Garret would make to record this transaction would include which one or more of the following items?

a. $34,500 increase in a liability account.
b. $7,500 increase in the Cash account.
c. $7,500 increase in a revenue account.
d. $48,000 increase in the Jan Garret, Capital, account.
e. $48,000 increase in a revenue account.

Exercise 3-3

Recording effects of transactions in T-accounts

A1

Open the following T-accounts: Cash; Accounts Receivable; Office Supplies; Office Equipment; Accounts Payable; Steve Moore, Capital; Steve Moore, Withdrawals; Fees Earned; and Rent Expense. Record the transactions of Moore Company by recording the debit and credit entries directly in T-accounts. Use the letters beside each transaction to identify entries. Determine the balance of each T-account.

a. Steve Moore invested $12,750 cash in the business.
b. Purchased $375 of office supplies for cash.
c. Purchased $7,050 of office equipment on credit.
d. Received $1,500 cash as fees for services provided to a customer.
e. Paid for the office equipment purchased in transaction *c*.
f. Billed a customer $2,700 as fees for services.
g. Paid the monthly rent with $525 cash.
h. Collected $1,125 of the account receivable created in transaction *f*.
i. Withdrew $1,000 cash from the business.

Exercise 3-4
Preparing a trial balance
P2

After recording the transactions of Exercise 3-3 in T-accounts and calculating the balance of each account, prepare a trial balance. Use May 31, 2000, as its date.

Exercise 3-5
Effects of posting errors on the trial balance
A1, P2

For each of the listed posting errors, enter in column (1) the amount of the difference the error would create between the two trial balance columns (show a zero if the columns would balance). If there is a difference between the two columns, identify in column (2) the trial balance column that is larger. Identify the account(s) affected in column (3) and the amount by which the account(s) is under- or overstated in column (4). The answer for the first error is shown as an example.

	Description of Posting Error	(1) Difference between Debit and Credit Columns	(2) Column with the Larger Total	(3) Identify Account(s) Incorrectly Stated	(4) Amount that Account(s) Is Over- or Understated
a.	A $2,400 debit to Rent Expense was posted as a $1,590 debit.	$810	credit	Rent Expense	Rent Expense is understated by $810
b.	A $42,000 debit to Machinery was posted as a debit to Accounts Payable.				
c.	A $4,950 credit to Services Revenue was posted as a $495 credit.				
d.	A $1,440 debit to Store Supplies was not posted at all.				
e.	A $2,250 debit to Prepaid Insurance was posted as a debit to Insurance Expense.				
f.	A $4,050 credit to Cash was posted twice as two credits to the Cash account.				
g.	A $9,900 debit to the owner's withdrawals account was debited to the owner's capital account.				

Exercise 3-6
Analyzing a trial balance error

As the accountant for a company, you are told the column totals in the trial balance are not equal. After going through a careful analysis, you discover only one error. Specifically, the balance of the Office Equipment account has a debit balance of $23,400 on the trial balance. But you discover that a correctly recorded credit purchase of a computer for $5,250 was posted from the journal to the ledger with a $5,250 debit to Office Equipment and another $5,250 debit to Accounts Payable. Answer each of the following questions and show the dollar amount of any misstatement:

a. Is the balance of the Office Equipment account overstated, understated, or correctly stated in the trial balance?

b. Is the balance of the Accounts Payable account overstated, understated, or correctly stated in the trial balance?

c. Is the debit column total of the trial balance overstated, understated, or correctly stated?

d. Is the credit column total of the trial balance overstated, understated, or correctly stated?

e. If the debit column total of the trial balance is $360,000 before correcting the error, what is the total of the credit column?

Exercise 3-7
Preparing a corrected trial balance
P2

On January 1, Jan Taylor started a new business called The Party Place. Near the end of the year, she hired an accountant without making a careful reference check. As a result, a number of mistakes were made in preparing the following trial balance:

THE PARTY PLACE
Trial Balance
December 31, 2000

	Debit	Credit
Cash	$ 5,500	
Accounts receivable		$ 7,900
Office supplies	2,650	
Office equipment	20,500	
Accounts payable		9,465
Jan Taylor, capital	16,745	
Services revenue		22,350
Wages expense		6,000
Rent expense		4,800
Advertising expense		1,250
Totals	$45,395	$52,340

Taylor's analysis of the situation reveals:

a. The sum of the debits in the Cash account is $37,175 and the sum of its credits is $30,540.
b. A $275 payment from a credit customer was posted to Cash but was not posted to Accounts Receivable.
c. A credit purchase of office supplies for $400 was completely unrecorded.
d. A transposition error occurred in copying the balance of the Services Revenue account to the trial balance. The correct amount was $23,250.
e. Errors were made in assigning account balances to the debit and credit columns of the trial balance, and in computing totals of the columns.

Use this information to prepare a correct trial balance.

Exercise 3-8
Analyzing account entries and balances
A1

Use the information in each of the following situations to calculate the unknown amount:

1. During October, Ridgeway Company had $97,500 of cash receipts and $101,250 of cash disbursements. The October 31 Cash balance was $16,800. Determine how much cash the company had on hand at the close of business on September 30.
2. On September 30, Ridgeway had a $97,500 balance in Accounts Receivable. During October, the company collected $88,950 from its credit customers. The October 31 balance in Accounts Receivable was $100,500. Determine the amount of sales on account that occurred in October.
3. Ridgeway had $147,000 of accounts payable on September 30 and $136,500 on October 31. Total purchases on account during October were $270,000. Determine how much cash was paid on accounts payable during October.

Exercise 3-9
Describing transactions from T-accounts
A1

Seven transactions were posted to these T-accounts. Provide a short description of each transaction. Include the amounts in your descriptions.

Cash

(a)	7,000	(b)	3,600
(e)	2,500	(c)	600
		(f)	2,400
		(g)	700

Office Supplies

(c)	600		
(d)	200		

Prepaid Insurance

(b)	3,600		

Equipment

(a)	5,600		
(d)	9,400		

Automobiles

(a)	11,000		

Accounts Payable

(f)	2,400	(d)	9,600

Jerry Steiner, Capital

		(a)	23,600

Delivery Services Revenue

		(e)	2,500

Gas and Oil Expense

(g)	700		

Exercise 3-10
General journal entries
A1

Use information from the T-accounts in Exercise 3-9 to prepare general journal entries for the seven transactions (a) through (g).

Exercise 3-11
Preparing general journal entries
A1

Prepare general journal entries for the following transactions of a new business called PhotoFinish.

Aug.	1	Hannah Young, the owner, invested $7,500 cash and photography equipment valued at $32,500.
	1	Rented a studio, paying $3,000 for the next three months in advance.
	5	Purchased office supplies for $1,400 cash.
	20	Received $2,650 in photography fees earned.
	31	Paid $875 for August utilities.

Exercise 3-12
Preparing T-accounts and the trial balance
P2

Use the information provided in Exercise 3-11 to prepare an August 31 trial balance for Photo-Finish. Open these T-accounts: Cash; Office Supplies; Prepaid Rent; Photography Equipment; Hannah Young, Capital; Photography Fees Earned; and Utilities Expense. Post the general journal entries to the T-accounts, and prepare a trial balance.

Exercise 3-13
Analyzing and journalizing revenue transactions
A1

Examine the following transactions and identify those that create revenues for Jarrell Services, a sole proprietorship owned by John Jarrell. Prepare general journal entries to record those transactions and explain why the other transactions did not create revenues.

a. John Jarrell invested $38,250 cash in the business.
b. Provided $1,350 of services on credit.
c. Received $1,575 cash for services provided to a client.
d. Received $9,150 from a client in payment for services to be provided next year.
e. Received $4,500 from a client in partial payment of an account receivable.
f. Borrowed $150,000 from the bank by signing a promissory note.

Exercise 3-14
Analyzing and journalizing expense transactions
A1

Examine the following transactions and identify those that create expenses for Jarrell Services. Prepare general journal entries to record those transactions and explain why the other transactions did not create expenses.

a. Paid $14,100 cash for office supplies purchased 3 months previously.
b. Paid the $1,125 salary of the receptionist.
c. Paid $45,000 cash for equipment.
d. Paid utility bill with $930 cash.
e. Withdrew $5,000 from the business for personal use.

Exercise 3-15
Computing and interpreting the debt ratio
A2

1. Calculate the debt ratio for each of the following six seperate cases:

Case	Assets	Liabilities	Owner's Equity
Company 1	$ 88,500	$ 11,000	$ 77,500
Company 2	62,000	46,000	16,000
Company 3	30,500	25,500	5,000
Company 4	145,000	55,000	90,000
Company 5	90,000	30,000	60,000
Company 6	102,500	50,500	52,000

2. Of the six cases, which business relies most heavily on creditor financing?
3. Of the six cases, which business relies most heavily on equity financing?
4. Which two companies indicate the greatest risk?

Problems

Problem 3-1

Recording transactions in T-accounts; preparing a trial balance

A1, P2

Business transactions completed by Kevin Smith during the month of November are as follows:

- **a.** Kevin Smith invests $80,000 cash and office equipment valued at $30,000 in a new sole proprietorship named Apex Consulting.
- **b.** Purchased land and a small office building. The land was worth $30,000, and the building was worth $170,000. The purchase price was paid with $40,000 cash and a long-term note payable for $160,000.
- **c.** Purchased $2,400 of office supplies on credit.
- **d.** Kevin Smith transferred title of his personal automobile to the business. The automobile had a value of $18,000 and was to be used exclusively in the business.
- **e.** Purchased $6,000 of additional office equipment on credit.
- **f.** Paid $1,500 salary to an assistant.
- **g.** Provided services to a client and collected $6,000 cash.
- **h.** Paid $800 for this month's utilities.
- **i.** Paid account payable created in transaction *c*.
- **j.** Purchased $20,000 of new office equipment by paying $18,600 cash and trading in old equipment with a recorded net cost of $1,400.
- **k.** Completed $5,200 of services for a client. This amount is to be paid within 30 days.
- **l.** Paid $1,500 salary to an assistant.
- **m.** Received $3,800 payment on the receivable created in transaction *k*.
- **n.** Withdrew $6,400 cash from the business for personal use.

Required

1. Open the following T-accounts: Cash; Accounts Receivable; Office Supplies; Automobiles; Office Equipment; Building; Land; Accounts Payable; Long-Term Notes Payable; Kevin Smith, Capital; Kevin Smith, Withdrawals; Fees Earned; Salaries Expense; and Utilities Expense.
2. Record the transactions above by entering debits and credits directly in T-accounts. Use the transaction letters to identify each debit and credit entry.
3. Determine the balance of each account and prepare a trial balance as of November 30.

Check Figure
Totals in trial balance, $305,200

Problem 3-2

Recording transactions in T-accounts, preparing a trial balance, and computing a debt ratio

A1, A2, P2

Forest Engineering, a sole proprietorship, completed the following transactions during the month of July:

- **a.** Stephen Forest, the owner, invested $105,000 cash, office equipment with a value of $6,000, and $45,000 of drafting equipment in the business.
- **b.** Purchased land for an office. The land was worth $54,000, and is paid with $5,400 cash and a long-term note payable for $48,600.
- **c.** Purchased a portable building with $75,000 cash and moved it onto the land.
- **d.** Paid $6,000 cash for the premiums on two one-year insurance policies.
- **e.** Completed and delivered a set of plans for a client and collected $5,700 cash.
- **f.** Purchased additional drafting equipment for $22,500. Paid $10,500 cash and signed a long-term note payable for the $12,000 balance.
- **g.** Completed $12,000 of engineering services for a client. This amount is to be paid within 30 days.
- **h.** Purchased $2,250 of additional office equipment on credit.
- **i.** Completed engineering services for $18,000 on credit.
- **j.** Received a bill for rent on equipment that was used on a completed job. The $1,200 rent must be paid within 30 days.
- **k.** Collected $7,200 from the client described in transaction *g*.
- **l.** Paid $1,500 wages to a drafting assistant.
- **m.** Paid the account payable created in transaction *h*.
- **n.** Paid $675 cash for some repairs to an item of drafting equipment.
- **o.** Stephen Forest withdrew $9,360 cash from the business for personal use.
- **p.** Paid $1,500 wages to a drafting assistant.
- **q.** Paid $3,000 cash to advertise in the local newspaper.

Required

1. Open the following T-accounts: Cash; Accounts Receivable; Prepaid Insurance; Office Equipment; Drafting Equipment; Building; Land; Accounts Payable; Long-Term Notes Payable; Stephen Forest, Capital; Stephen Forest, Withdrawals; Engineering Fees Earned; Wages Expense; Equipment Rental Expense; Advertising Expense; and Repairs Expense.
2. Record the transactions by entering debits and credits directly in T-accounts. Use the transaction letters to identify each debit and credit. Prepare a trial balance as of July 31.
3. Calculate the company's debt ratio. Use $236,265 as the ending total assets. Are the assets of the company financed more by debt or equity?

Check Figure
Totals in trial balance, $253,500

Problem 3-3
Preparing and posting general journal entries and preparing a trial balance
A1, P1, P2

Hector Mendez opened a computer consulting business called Capital Consultants and completed the following transactions during May:

May	1	Mendez invested $100,000 in cash and office equipment valued at $24,000 in the business.
	1	Prepaid $7,200 cash for three months' rent for an office.
	2	Made credit purchases of office equipment for $12,000 and office supplies for $2,400.
	6	Completed services for a client and immediately received $2,000 cash.
	9	Completed an $8,000 project for a client, who will pay within 30 days.
	10	Paid the account payable created on May 2.
	19	Paid $6,000 cash for the annual premium on an insurance policy.
	22	Received $6,400 as partial payment for the work completed on May 9.
	25	Completed work for another client for $2,640 on credit.
	31	Withdrew $6,200 cash from the business for personal use.
	31	Purchased $800 of additional office supplies on credit.
	31	Paid $700 for the month's utility bill.

Required

1. Prepare general journal entries to record the transactions.
2. Open the following accounts (use the balance column format): Cash (101); Accounts Receivable (106); Office Supplies (124); Prepaid Insurance (128); Prepaid Rent (131); Office Equipment (163); Accounts Payable (201); Hector Mendez, Capital (301); Hector Mendez, Withdrawals (302); Services Revenue (403); and Utilities Expense (690).
3. Post entries to the accounts and enter the balance after each posting.
4. Prepare a trial balance as of the end of this month.

Check Figure
Cash account balance, $73,900

Problem 3-4
Interpreting journals, posting, and analyzing trial balance errors
A1, P1, P2

Art Platt started a business called Able Movers and began operations in July. His accounting skills are weak, and he needs help gathering information at the end of the month. He recorded the following journal entries during July:

July	1	Cash	60,000	
		Trucks	44,000	
		Art Platt, Capital		104,000
	2	Office Supplies	1,292	
		Cash		1,292
	4	Moving Equipment	12,800	
		Accounts Payable		12,800
	8	Cash	2,000	
		Accounts Receivable	10,000	
		Moving Fees Earned		12,000
	12	Cash	1,600	
		Moving Fees Earned		1,600
	15	Prepaid Insurance	2,700	
		Cash		2,700

21	Cash	10,000	
	Accounts Receivable		10,000
23	Accounts Payable	12,800	
	Cash		12,800
25	Office Equipment	18,800	
	Art Platt, Capital		18,800
29	Office Supplies	2,908	
	Accounts Payable		2,908
31	Art Platt, Withdrawals	4,912	
	Cash		4,912
31	Wages Expense	6,280	
	Cash		6,280

Based on these entries, Platt prepared the following trial balance:

ABLE MOVERS
Trial Balance
For Month Ended July 31, 2000

	Debit	Credit
Cash	$ 45,616	
Accounts receivable	0	
Office supplies	2,400	
Prepaid insurance	2,700	
Trucks	44,000	
Office equipment	18,800	
Moving equipment		$ 12,800
Accounts payable		29,080
Art Platt, capital		122,800
Art Platt, withdrawals	491	
Moving fees earned		13,600
Wages expense	6,280	
Totals	$120,287	$178,280

Preparation Component

1. Platt remembers something about trial balances and realizes the preceding one has at least one error. To help him find the mistakes, set up the following balance column accounts and post entries to them: Cash (101); Accounts Receivable (106); Office Supplies (124); Prepaid Insurance (128); Trucks (153); Office Equipment (163); Moving Equipment (167); Accounts Payable (201); Art Platt, Capital (301); Art Platt, Withdrawals (302); Moving Fees Earned (401); and Wages Expense (623).

Analysis Components

2. Although Platt's journal entries are correct, he forgot to provide explanations. Analyze each entry and present a reasonable explanation of what happened.
3. Prepare a correct trial balance and describe the errors that Platt made.

Check Figure
Totals in trial balance, $139,308

Problem 3-5
Analyzing account balances and reconstructing transactions
A1, P2

Carlos Young started an engineering firm called Young Engineering. He began operations in March and completed seven transactions, including his initial investment of $17,000 cash. After these transactions, the ledger included the following accounts with their normal balances:

Cash	$26,660
Office supplies	660
Prepaid insurance	3,200
Office equipment	16,500
Accounts payable	16,500
Carlos Young, capital	17,000
Carlos Young, withdrawals	3,740
Engineering fees earned	24,000
Rent expense	6,740

Required

Preparation Component

1. Prepare a trial balance for the business.

Analysis Components

2. Analyze the accounts and their balances and prepare a list that describes each of the seven most likely transactions and their amounts.

3. Present a schedule that shows how the seven transactions in *2* resulted in the $26,660 Cash balance.

Problem 3-6
Classifying accounts in financial statements

A1

Travis McAllister operates a surveying company. For the first few months of the company's life (through April), the accounting records were maintained by an outside accounting service. According to those records, McAllister's owner's equity balance was $75,000 as of April 30. To save on expenses, McAllister decided to keep the records himself. He managed to record May's transactions properly but he had problems properly classifying accounts in financial statements. His first versions of the balance sheet and income statement follow. Using the information contained in these financial statements, prepare revised statements, including a statement of changes in owner's equity, for the month of May.

McALLISTER SURVEYING
Income Statement
For Month Ended May 31, 2000

Revenue:		
Investments by owner		$ 3,000
Unearned surveying fees		6,000
Total revenues		$ 9,000
Operating expenses:		
Rent expense	$3,100	
Telephone expense	600	
Surveying equipment	5,400	
Advertising expense	3,200	
Utilities expense	300	
Insurance expense	900	
Withdrawals by owner	6,000	
Total operating expenses		19,500
Net income (loss)		$(10,500)

McALLISTER SURVEYING
Balance Sheet
For May 31, 2000

Assets		Liabilities	
Cash	$ 3,900	Accounts payable	$ 2,400
Accounts receivable	2,700	Surveying fees earned	18,000
Prepaid insurance	1,800	Short-term notes payable	48,000
Prepaid rent	4,200	Total liabilities	$ 68,400
Office supplies	300		
Buildings	81,000		
Land	36,000	**Owner's Equity**	
Salaries expense	3,000	Travis McAllister, capital	64,500
		Total liabilities and	
Total assets	$132,900	owner's equity	$132,900

Serial Problem
Echo Systems

(This comprehensive problem starts in this chapter and continues in Chapters 4, 5, and 6. Because of its length, this problem is most easily solved if you use the Working Papers that accompany this text.)

On October 1, 2000, Mary Graham organized a computer service company called **Echo Systems.** Echo Systems is organized as a sole proprietorship and will provide consulting services, computer system installations, and custom program development. Graham has adopted the calendar year for reporting and expects to prepare the company's first set of financial statements as of December 31, 2000. The initial chart of accounts for the accounting system includes these items:

Account	No.	Account	No.
Cash	101	Mary Graham, Capital	301
Accounts Receivable	106	Mary Graham, Withdrawals	302
Computer Supplies	126	Computer Services Revenue	403
Prepaid Insurance	128	Wages Expense	623
Prepaid Rent	131	Advertising Expense	655
Office Equipment	163	Mileage Expense	676
Computer Equipment	167	Miscellaneous Expenses	677
Accounts Payable	201	Repairs Expense, Computer	684

Required

1. Prepare journal entries to record each of the following transactions for Echo Systems.
2. Open balance column accounts for the company and post journal entries to them.

Oct.	1	Mary Graham invested $45,000 cash, an $18,000 computer system, and $9,000 of office equipment in the business.
	2	Paid $4,500 for four months' rent.
	3	Purchased computer supplies on credit for $1,320 from Abbott Office Products.
	5	Paid $2,160 cash for one year's premium on a property and liability insurance policy.
	6	Billed Capital Leasing $3,300 for installing a new computer.
	8	Paid for the computer supplies purchased from Abbott Office Products.
	10	Hired Carly Smith as a part-time assistant for $100 per day, as needed.
	12	Billed Capital Leasing another $1,200 for services.
	15	Received $3,300 from Capital Leasing on their account.
	17	Paid $705 to repair computer equipment damaged when moving into the new office.
	20	Paid $1,860 for an advertisement in the local newspaper.
	22	Received $1,200 from Capital Leasing on their account.
	28	Billed Decker Company $3,225 for services.
	31	Paid Carly Smith for seven days' work.
	31	Withdrew $3,600 cash from the business for personal use.
Nov.	1	Reimbursed Mary Graham's business automobile mileage for 1,000 miles at $0.25 per mile.
	2	Received $4,650 cash from Elite Corporation for computer services.
	5	Purchased $960 of computer supplies from Abbott Office Products.
	8	Billed Fostek Co. $4,350 for services.
	13	Received notification from Alamo Engineering Co. that Echo's bid of $3,750 for an upcoming project was accepted.
	18	Received $1,875 from Decker Company against the bill dated October 28.
	22	Donated $750 to the United Way in the company's name.
	24	Completed work for Alamo Engineering Co. and sent them a bill for $3,750.
	25	Sent another bill to Decker Company for the past due amount of $1,350.
	28	Reimbursed Mary Graham's business automobile mileage for 1,200 miles at $0.25 per mile.
	30	Paid Carly Smith for 14 days' work.
	30	Withdrew $1,800 cash from the business for personal use.

BEYOND THE NUMBERS

Reporting in Action
C3, A2

Refer to the financial statements and related information for **NIKE** in Appendix A.

Required

Answer the following questions by analyzing the information in NIKE's statements:

1. How many revenue categories does NIKE report on its consolidated statement of income?
2. What five current assets are reported on NIKE's consolidated balance sheet?
3. What five current liabilities are reported on its balance sheet?
4. What dollar amounts of income taxes are reported on its income statements for the annual reporting periods ending in 1997 and 1996?
5. During the annual reporting period ended May 31, 1997, how much cash did NIKE pay in dividends?
6. What is NIKE's debt ratio at May 31, 1997? (Hint: Use Liabilities = Assets − Stockholders' equity.) How does this compare to its ratio at May, 31 1996?

Swoosh Ahead

7. Obtain access to NIKE's annual report for fiscal years ending after May 31, 1997. You can gain access to NIKE's annual report at its web site **[www.nike.com]** or through the SEC's EDGAR database **[www.sec.gov].** Recompute NIKE's debt ratio with the updated annual report information you have obtained. Compare the May 31, 1997, fiscal year-end debt ratio to any subsequent year's debt ratio that you are able to calculate. Also compare how NIKE's income tax expense has changed since May 31, 1997.

Comparative Analysis
A2

Both **NIKE** and **Reebok** design, produce, market, and sell sports footwear and apparel. Key comparative figures ($ millions) for these two organizations follow:

Key Figures*	NIKE	Reebok
Total liabilities	$2,205	$1,405
Total equity	$3,156	$ 381

* NIKE figures are from its annual report for the fiscal year ended May 31,1997. Reebok figures are from its annual report for the fiscal year ended December 31, 1996.

Required

Use the information in the table above to answer the following questions:

1. What are the total assets for (a) NIKE and (b) Reebok?
2. What is the debt ratio for (a) NIKE and (b) Reebok?
3. Which of the two companies has the higher degree of financial leverage?

Ethics Challenge*
C2

Review the **Judgment and Ethics** from the first section of this chapter. Join a class discussion on the nature of the dilemma in this case. The guidance answer suggests that you should not comply with the assistant manager's request.

Required

Evaluate at least two other courses of action you might consider and why.

Communicating in Practice A2

The class should be divided into teams. Teams are to select an industry, and each team member is to select a different company in that industry. Each team member is to acquire the annual report of the company selected. Annual reports can be obtained in many ways, including accessing this book's Web page or through the SEC's EDGAR database **[www.sec.gov].**

Required

1. Use the annual report to compute the debt ratio.
2. Communicate with teammates via a meeting, e-mail, or telephone to discuss the meaning of this ratio, how different companies compare to each other, and the industry norm. The team must prepare a single memo reporting the ratios for each company and identify the conclusions or consensus of opinion reached during the team's discussion. The memo is to be duplicated and distributed to the instructor and all classmates.

Taking it to the Net

Visit the **NIKE** annual report Web site at **www.nike.com.** Select the link to visit the financial highlights of NIKE.

Required

1. Of the financial highlights NIKE reports, identify terms you have already discussed in Chapters 1 through 3. Which terms are unfamiliar to you?
2. As a highlight, NIKE reports its stock price at fiscal year-end. Visit the **Yahoo Quote Service** at **quote.yahoo.com.** Use this quote service to locate NIKE's most recent stock price. NIKE's ticker symbol that you will need to use in the quote service is NIKE. How has the price changed since May 31, 1997 when its price was $57.50?

Teamwork in Action A1

The general ledger shown below reflects the transactions for Musician Makers, a business that provides music lessons for individuals, for the month of November. Your team must validate the accuracy of the information reported. You can divide responsibilities among team members. In rotation, team members must explain to the team how they derived the information required.

MUSICIAN MAKERS
General Ledger

Cash

Beg. Bal.	3900		
(a)	5000	(b)	1000
(c)	400	(g)	500
(d)	50	(h)	120
(j)	120	(i)	200

Accounts Payable

		(e)	125

A. Melody, Capital

		Beg. Bal.	3075
		(a)	5000

Unearned Lesson Revenue

		(j)	120

A. Melody, Withdrawals

(i)	200		

Notes Payable

(b)	1000	Beg. Bal	1000
		(g)	1500

Lesson Revenue

		(c)	400
		(f)	80

Accounts Receivable

Beg. Bal.	75	(d)	50
(f)	80		

Wage Expense		
(h)	120	

Supplies		
Beg. Bal.	100	
(e)	125	

Equipment		
(g)	2000	

Required

1. A brief description of each transaction (a) through (j).
2. Compute net income or net loss for November.
3. Compute ending owner's equity.
4. Prove the accounting equation is in balance. Compute the debt ratio.
5. A schedule of cash flows by activities.
6. Prove that the schedule in (5) agrees with the change in the cash account.
7. Explain why cash flow from operating activities doesn't agree with net income.

Hitting the Road

Obtain a recent copy of the most prominent newspaper distributed in your area. Research the classified section and prepare a report answering the following questions (attach relevant classified clippings to your report). Alternatively, you may want to search the Web for the required job information. One suitable Web site is: **www.ajb.dni.us.** For documentation, you should print copies of Web sites accessed.

1. Identify the number of listings for accounting positions and the various accounting job titles.
2. Identify the number of listings for other job titles, with examples, that require or prefer accounting knowledge/experience but are not specifically accounting positions.
3. Specify the salary range for the accounting and accounting-related positions if provided.
4. Indicate the job that appeals to you, the reason for its appeal, and its requirements.

Business Week Activity

C3, A1

Read the article "Answered Prayers for America Online" in the September 22, 1997, issue of *Business Week.*

Required

1. Identify three setbacks that AOL has suffered in the year preceding the time the article was written. Do any of these setbacks deal with accounting practices at AOL? Why would a company consider doing something potentially offensive to its customers?
2. Compare the number of AOL subscribers as of June 30, 1997, to June 30, 1995.
3. A measure of the reliability of the AOL network is the number of simultaneous users it can service. How many users was AOL simultaneously servicing as of August 31, 1997?
4. The article reports that AOL has proposed a deal in which they will exchange part of their company (ANS Communications) for subscribers of the CompuServe service. How many subscribers would AOL gain access to if the deal is completed? Would these new subscribers be shown as assets on AOL's balance sheet?

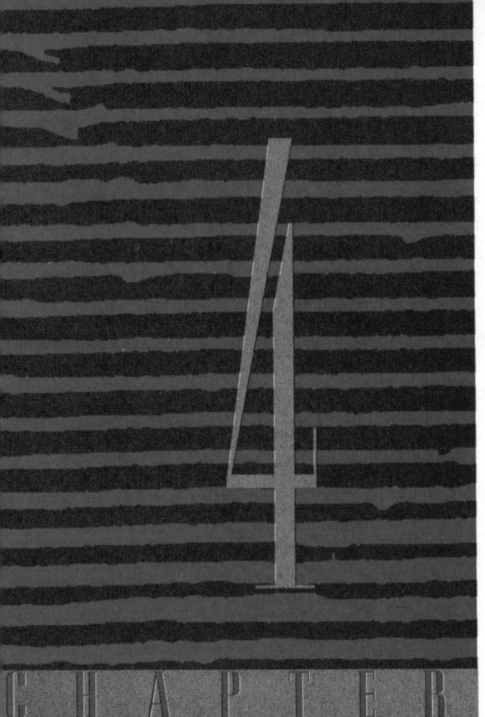

Adjusting Accounts for Financial Statements

A Look Back

Chapter 3 explained the analysis and recording of transactions. We showed how to work with source documents, T-accounts, double-entry accounting, ledgers, postings, and trial balances. These are important parts of the accounting process leading to financial statements.

A Look at This Chapter

This chapter focuses on the timing of reports and the need to adjust accounts. Adjusting accounts is important for recognizing revenues and expenses in the proper period. We describe why adjustments are necessary, how to record them, and their effects on financial statements. We also explain the adjusted trial balance and how we use it to prepare financial statements.

A Look Ahead

Chapter 5 highlights the completion of the accounting cycle. We explain the important final steps in obtaining reliable, relevant, and comparable accounting information. These include closing procedures, post-closing trial balances, and reversing entries.

Chapter Outline

Bad Boys Need Money

NEW YORK—In New York, a mecca for professional and amateur sports teams, there is a new team on the block. It's the **Bronx Bombers,** the "bad boys" of rugby. The Bombers are organized and owned by Rob Burston, a 28-year-old player/coach.

Burston has always been driven. He took just three years to finish college. And he did it while working part-time as a salesperson. So it's no surprise the Bombers, a team Burston organized three years ago, are moving just as fast, topping their division and winning the playoffs. "To take the championship in only our third year is incredible," says Burston proudly. "We wanted it bad, and we believed in each other."

So far, that belief has been a hit on the field and in the stands. Attendance has skyrocketed. This year, between ticket sales, promotional advertising, and other revenues, the Bombers took in over $490,000 in revenues. Just this month, Burston's team signed an exclusive deal with an athletic shoe company to market rugby shoes and apparel. He won't reveal the figure, but the smile on his face is revealing enough.

Burston's next move? He wants to upgrade the facilities and field. "Rugby is a great spectator sport," insists Burston. "And if we do it right, the sky's the limit." Still, it's likely to be a battle. Burston needs money to fund his ideas, and bankers and investors are not accustomed to funding sports teams. A banker, whom Burston has negotiated with, warns of hurdles. "How do you predict income and cash flows in rugby? When do you recognize season ticket sales, promotional revenues, and exclusive contracts? Are facility and field costs expenses or assets? You must overcome these financial hurdles."

Such hurdles don't frighten Burston, who grew up poor with a "can't make it" label. Yet he is a realist who's now working with financial advisors in preparing pro forma statements to see his dream come true. But count on this: Burston and the bad boys of rugby are gunning for the big boys.

Learning Objectives

Conceptual

C1 Explain the importance of periodic reporting and the time period principle.

C2 Describe the purpose of adjusting accounts at the end of a period.

C3 Explain accrual accounting and how it adds to the usefulness of financial statements.

C4 Identify the types of adjustments and their purpose.

Analytical

A1 Explain how accounting adjustments link to financial statements.

A2 Compute profit margin and describe its use in analyzing company performance.

Procedural

P1 Prepare and explain adjusting entries for prepaid expenses, depreciation, and unearned revenues.

P2 Prepare and describe adjusting entries for accrued expenses and accrued revenues.

P3 Explain and prepare an adjusted trial balance.

P4 Prepare financial statements from an adjusted trial balance.

P5 Record and describe entries for later periods that result from accruals.

CHAPTER PREVIEW

Financial statements reflect revenues when earned and expenses when incurred. This is known as *accrual accounting.* Accrual accounting requires several steps. We described many of these steps in Chapter 3. We showed how companies use accounting systems to collect information about *external* transactions and events. We also explained how journals, ledgers, and other procedures are useful in preparing financial statements.

This chapter emphasizes the accounting process for producing useful information involving *internal* transactions and events. An important part of this process is adjusting the account balances, which are then reported in financial statements. Adjusting of accounts is necessary so that financial statements at the end of a reporting period reflect the effects of all transactions. We also identify and explain an important measure of company performance drawn from these statements (profit margin) and how users put it to work.

Timing and Reporting

Regular, or periodic, reporting is an important part of the accounting process. The point in time or the period of time to which a report refers impacts this process. This section describes the more important impacts of accounting time periods.

The Accounting Period

C1 Explain the importance of periodic reporting and the time period principle.

The value of information is often linked to its timeliness. Useful information must reach decision makers frequently and promptly. To provide timely information, accounting systems prepare reports at regular intervals. This results in an accounting process impacted by the time period (or periodicity) principle. The **time period principle** assumes that an organization's activities can be divided into specific time periods such as a month, a three month quarter, or a year as shown in Exhibit 4.1.

"Nike today announced quarterly earnings per share of . . ."

Financial statements are prepared for time periods that are considered important for decision making and regulatory purposes. Time periods covered by statements are called **accounting,** or *reporting,* **periods.** Most organizations use a year as their

Exhibit 4.1

Accounting Periods

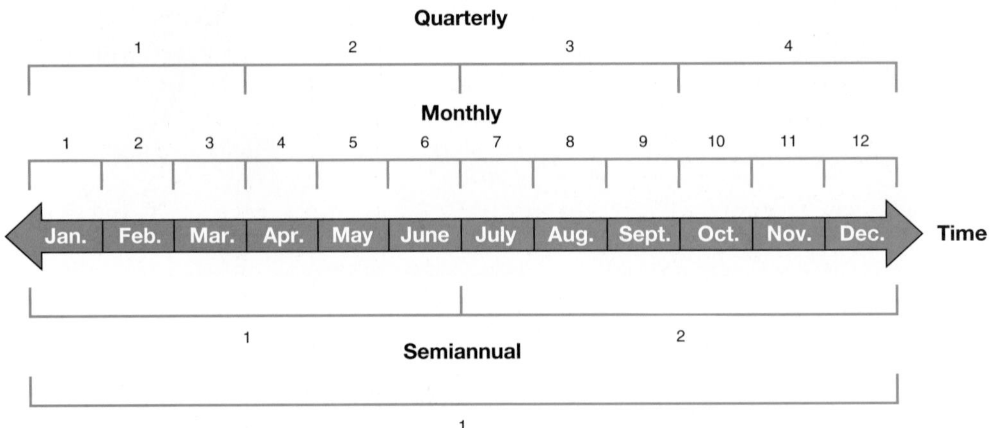

primary accounting period. Reports covering a one-year period are known as **annual financial statements.** Many organizations also prepare **interim financial statements** covering one, three, or six months of activity.

The annual reporting period is not always a calendar year ending on December 31. An organization can adopt a **fiscal year** consisting of any 12 consecutive months. It is also acceptable to adopt an annual reporting period of 52 weeks. For example, **The GAP**'s 1997 fiscal year ended on February 1, its 1996 year on February 3, and its 1995 year on January 28.

Companies not experiencing much seasonal variation in sales volume within the year often choose the calendar year as their fiscal year. For example, the financial statements of **Alcoa** reflect a fiscal year that ends on December 31. Companies experiencing seasonal variations in sales often choose a fiscal year corresponding to their natural business year. The **natural business year** ends when sales activities are at their lowest point during the year. The natural business year for retailers ends around January 31, after the holiday season. Examples of these companies include **Wal-Mart, Kmart,** and **Dell.** They start their annual accounting periods on or near February 1.

Purpose of Adjusting

C2 Describe the purpose of adjusting accounts at the end of a period.

The usual accounting process is to record external transactions and events (with outside parties) during an accounting period. After external transactions are recorded, several accounts in the ledger need adjustments before their balances appear in financial statements. This need arises because internal transactions and events remain unrecorded.

An example is the cost of certain assets that expire as time passes. The Prepaid Insurance account of **FastForward** is one of these. FastForward's trial balance shown in Exhibit 4.2 shows Prepaid Insurance with a balance of $2,400. This amount is the premium for two years of insurance protection beginning on December 1, 1997. By December 31, 1997, one month's coverage is used up, and $2,400 is no longer an accurate amount for the remaining 23 months' prepaid insurance. Because the coverage costs an average of $100 per month ($2,400/24 months), the Prepaid Insurance account balance must be reduced by one month's cost. The income statement must report this $100 cost as insurance expense for December.

Another example is the $3,720 balance in Supplies. This account includes the cost of supplies that were used in December. The cost of the supplies used must be reported as a December expense. The balances of both Prepaid Insurance and Supplies accounts must be adjusted before they are reported on the December 31 balance sheet.

Another adjustment necessary for FastForward relates to one month's usage of equipment. Also, the balances of Unearned Consulting Revenue, Consulting Revenue, and Salaries Expense accounts often need adjusting before appearing on the December statements. We explain in the next section how this adjusting process is carried out.

Recognizing Revenues and Expenses

Decision makers need timely financial information. We use the time period principle in dividing a company's activities into specific time periods. Yet because of the need for regular reporting of information, not all activities are complete at the time financial state-

Trial Balance

FASTFORWARD Trial Balance December 31, 1997	Debit	Credit
Cash	$ 7,950	
Accounts receivable	0	
Prepaid insurance	2,400	
Supplies	3,720	
Equipment	26,000	
Accounts payable		$ 1,100
Unearned consulting revenue		3,000
Note payable		5,100
C.Taylor, capital		30,000
C.Taylor, withdrawals	600	
Consulting revenue		3,800
Rental revenue		300
Rent expense	1,000	
Salaries expense	1,400	
Utilities expense	230	
Total	$43,300	$43,300

ments are prepared. This means we must make some adjustments in reporting to not mislead decision makers.

We rely on two principles in the adjusting process—*revenue recognition* and *matching*. Chapter 2 explains that the revenue recognition principle requires that revenue be reported when earned, not before and not after. Revenue is earned for most companies when services and products are delivered to customers. If FastForward provides consulting to a client in December, the revenue is earned in December. This means it must be reported on the December income statement, even if the client paid for the services in a month other than December. A major goal of the adjusting process is to have revenue recognized (reported) in the time period when it is earned.

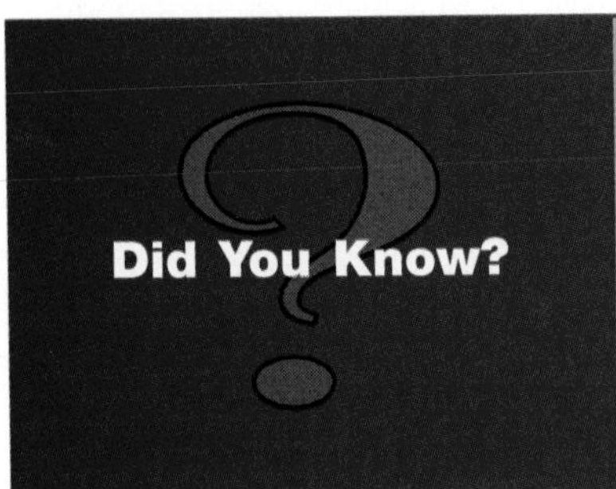

Is It Revenue, or Is It Not?

Centennial Technology, like many companies, recognizes revenue when products are shipped. What is not common is that the CEO of Centennial shipped products to the warehouses of friends and reported it as revenue. **Informix,** a database software maker, also recorded revenue when products were passed to distributors. It admits now that there were "errors in the way revenues had been recorded," and its CEO is in jail. These and other risky revenue recognition practices are often revealed by a large increase in accounts receivable relative to sales ratio.

The **matching principle** aims to report expenses in the same accounting period as the revenues that are earned as a result of these expenses. This matching of costs (expenses) with benefits (revenues) is a major part of the adjusting process. A common example is a business like FastForward that earns monthly revenues while operating out of rented store space. The earning of revenues required rented space. The matching principle tells us that rent must be reported on the income statement for December, even if rent is paid in a month either before or after December. This ensures the rent expense for December is matched with December's revenues.

Matching expenses with revenues often requires us to predict certain events. When we use financial statements we must understand that they involve estimates. This means they include measures that are not precise. **Walt Disney**'s annual report explains that its film and television production costs from movies such as *The Absent-Minded Professor* and *Hercules* are matched to revenues based on a ratio of current revenues from the show divided by its predicted total revenues.

Accrual Basis Compared to Cash Basis

C3 Explain accrual accounting and how it adds to the usefulness of financial statements.

Accrual basis accounting uses the adjusting process to recognize revenues when earned and to match expenses with revenues. This means the economic effects of revenues and expenses are recorded when earned or incurred, not when cash is received or paid.

Cash basis accounting means revenues are recognized when cash is received and that expenses are recorded when cash is paid. If a business earns revenue in December but cash is not received from clients until January, then cash basis accounting reports this revenue in January. Because revenues are reported when cash is received and expenses are deducted when cash is paid, the cash basis net income for a period is the difference between revenues received in cash (called *receipts*) and expenses paid in cash (called *expenditures* or *disbursements*).

Cash basis accounting for the income statement, balance sheet, and statement of changes in owner's equity is not consistent with accepted accounting principles. It is commonly held that accrual accounting provides a better indication of business performance than information about current cash receipts and payments.[1] Accrual accounting also increases the *comparability* of financial statements from one period to another. Yet many companies and users of statements still find cash basis accounting useful for several internal reports and decisions.

To see the impact of these different accounting systems, let's consider the Prepaid Insurance of FastForward. FastForward paid $2,400 for two years of insurance coverage beginning on December 1. Accrual accounting means that $100 of insurance expense is reported on December's income statement. Another $1,200 of expense is reported in 1998, and the remaining $1,100 is reported as expense in the first 11 months of 1999. This allocation of insurance cost across these three fiscal years is illustrated in Exhibit 4.3.

A cash basis income statement for December 1997 reports insurance expense of $2,400 as shown in Exhibit 4.4. The income statements for 1998 and 1999 report no insurance expense from this policy.

Exhibit 4.3

Accrual Basis Accounting for Prepaid Insurance

December *Transaction:* Purchase 24 months' insurance beginning December 1997 →

Insurance Expense 1997			
Jan $0	Feb $0	Mar $0	Apr $0
May $0	June $0	July $0	Aug $0
Sept $0	Oct $0	Nov $0	Dec $100

Insurance Expense 1998			
Jan $100	Feb $100	Mar $100	Apr $100
May $100	June $100	July $100	Aug $100
Sept $100	Oct $100	Nov $100	Dec $100

Insurance Expense 1999			
Jan $100	Feb $100	Mar $100	Apr $100
May $100	June $100	July $100	Aug $100
Sept $100	Oct $ 100	Nov $100	Dec $0

[1] *Statement of Financial Accounting Concepts No. 1,* "Objectives of Financial Reporting by Business Enterprises" (Norwalk, CT, 1978), par. 44.

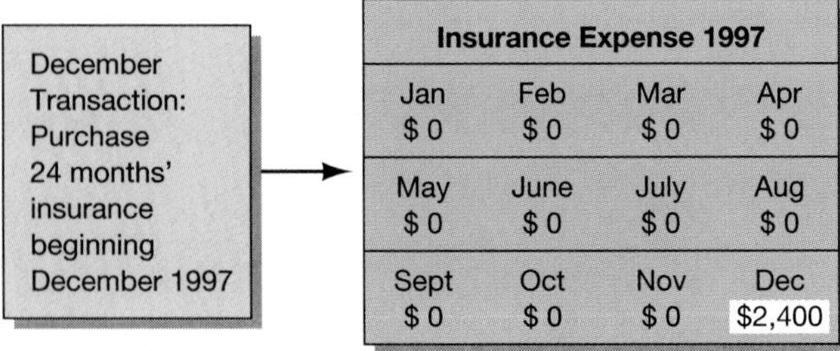

Insurance Expense 1997			
Jan $0	Feb $0	Mar $0	Apr $0
May $0	June $0	July $0	Aug $0
Sept $0	Oct $0	Nov $0	Dec $2,400

Insurance Expense 1998			
Jan $0	Feb $0	Mar $0	Apr $0
May $0	June $0	July $0	Aug $0
Sept $0	Oct $0	Nov $0	Dec $0

Insurance Expense 1999			
Jan $0	Feb $0	Mar $0	Apr $0
May $0	June $0	July $0	Aug $0
Sept $0	Oct $0	Nov $0	Dec $0

Exhibit 4.4

Cash Basis Accounting for Prepaid Insurance

The accrual basis balance sheet reports any unexpired premium as a Prepaid Insurance asset. The cash basis never reports this asset. The cash basis information is less useful for most decisions because reported income for 1997–1999 fails to match the cost of insurance with the benefits received for those years.

Accrual basis accounting is generally accepted for external reporting. Yet information about cash flows is also useful and is why companies reporting financial statements according to generally accepted accounting principles must include a statement of cash flows.

Flash back

1. Describe a company's annual reporting period.
2. Why do companies prepare interim financial statements?
3. What accounting principles most directly propel the adjusting process?
4. Is cash basis accounting consistent with the matching principle? Why or why not?
5. If your company pays a $4,800 premium on April 1, 1998, for two years' insurance coverage, how much insurance expense is reported in 1999 using cash basis accounting?

Answers—p. 151

Adjusting Accounts

C4 Identify the types of adjustments and their purpose.

The process of adjusting accounts is similar to our process of analyzing and recording transactions in the prior chapter. We must analyze each account balance and the transactions and events that affect it to determine any needed adjustments. An **adjusting entry** is recorded to bring an asset or liability account balance to its proper amount when an adjustment is needed. This entry also updates the related expense or revenue account. Adjusting entries are posted to accounts like any other entry. This section explains why adjusting entries are needed to provide useful information. We also show the mechanics of adjusting entries and their links to financial statements.

Framework for Adjustments

Adjustments are necessary for transactions and events that extend over more than one period. It is helpful to group adjustments by the timing of cash receipt or payment in relation to the recognition of the related revenues or expenses. Exhibit 4.5 identifies the five main adjustments. These involve both expenses and revenues.

Prepaid expenses, depreciation, and unearned revenues each reflect transactions where cash is paid or received *before* a related expense or revenue is recognized.[2] Accrued expenses and accrued revenues reflect transactions where cash is paid or received *after* a related expense or revenue is recognized. Adjusting entries are necessary for each of

[2] Prepaids are also called *deferrals* because the recognition of an expense or revenue is *deferred* until after the related cash is paid or received.

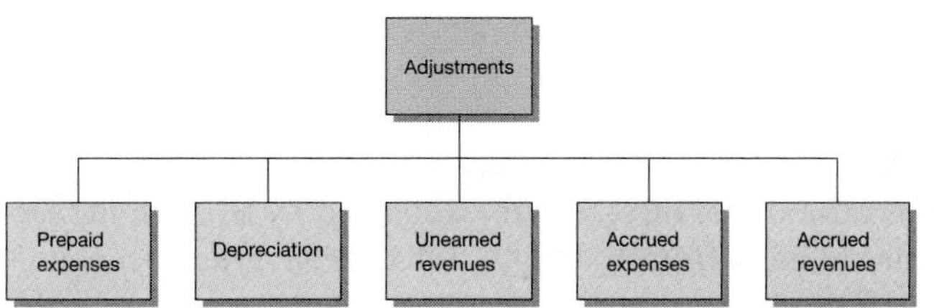

Exhibit 4.5
Framework for Adjustments

these so that revenues, expenses, assets, and liabilities are correctly reported. It is helpful to remember that each adjusting entry affects one or more income statement accounts *and* one or more balance sheet accounts. Also note that an adjusting entry *never* involves the Cash account.

Adjusting Prepaid Expenses

P1 Prepare and explain adjusting entries for prepaid expenses, depreciation, and unearned revenues.

Prepaid expenses refer to items *paid for* in advance of receiving their benefits. Prepaid expenses, also called *deferred expenses,* are assets. As these assets are used, their costs become expenses. Adjusting entries for prepaids involve increasing (debiting) expenses and decreasing (crediting) assets as shown in Exhibit 4.6.

"Here is the first 24 months' insurance in advance."

Adjustments are made to reflect transactions and events (including passage of time) that impact the amount of prepaid expenses. This section describes the accounting for three common prepaid expenses: insurance, supplies, and depreciation.

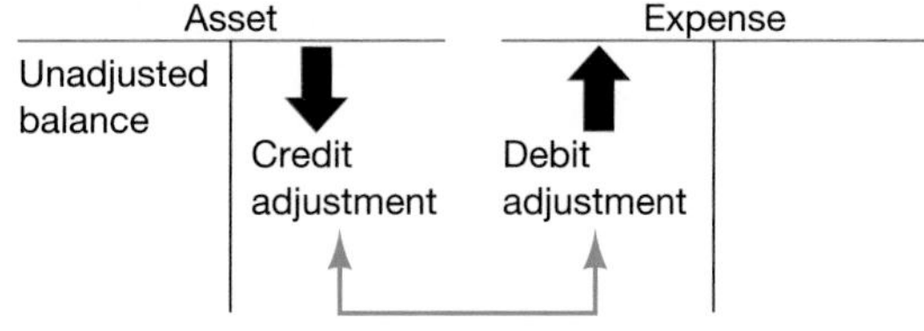

Exhibit 4.6
Adjusting for Prepaid Expenses

Prepaid Insurance

We illustrate prepaid insurance using FastForward's payment of $2,400 for two years of insurance protection beginning on December 1, 1997. The cash payments are illustrated in Exhibit 4.4 for 1997–1999. With the passage of time, the benefit of the insurance protection gradually expires and a portion of the Prepaid Insurance asset becomes expense. For instance, one month's insurance coverage expires by December 31, 1997. This expense is $100, or 1/24 of $2,400. Our adjusting entry to record this expense and reduce the asset is:

	Adjustment (a)		
Dec. 31	Insurance Expense	100	
	Prepaid Insurance		100
	To record expired insurance.		

Assets = Liabilities + Equity
−100 −100

Posting this adjusting entry affects the accounts as shown in Exhibit 4.7.

Exhibit 4.7
Insurance Accounts after Adjusting for Prepaids

Prepaid Insurance			
Dec. 26	2,400	**Dec. 31**	**100**
	−100		
Balance	2,300		

Insurance Expense			
Dec. 31	**100**		

After posting, the $100 balance in Insurance Expense and the $2,300 balance in Prepaid Insurance are ready for reporting in financial statements. If the adjustment is *not* made at December 31, then (a) expenses are understated by $100 and net income overstated by $100 for the December income statement, and (b) both Prepaid Insurance and owner's equity (because of net income) are overstated by $100 in the December 31 balance sheet. It is also evident from Exhibit 4.3 that 1998 adjustments must transfer a total of $1,200 from Prepaid Insurance to Insurance Expense, and 1999 adjustments must transfer the remaining $1,100 to Insurance Expense.

Supplies

Supplies are another prepaid expense often requiring adjustment. FastForward purchased $3,720 of supplies in December and used some of them during this month. Consuming these supplies creates expenses equal to their cost. Daily usage of supplies was not recorded in FastForward's accounts because this information was not needed. Also, when we report account balances in financial statements only at the end of a month, record-keeping costs can be reduced by making only one adjusting entry at that time. This entry needs to record the total cost of all supplies used in the month.

Because we prepare an income statement for December, the cost of supplies used during this month must be recognized as an expense. FastForward computes (takes inventory of) the remaining unused supplies. The cost of the remaining supplies is then deducted from the cost of the purchased supplies to compute the amount used. FastForward has $2,670 of supplies remaining out of the $3,720 purchased in December. The $1,050 difference between these two amounts is the cost of the consumed supplies. This amount is December's supplies expense. Our adjusting entry to record this expense and reduce the Supplies asset account is:

Assets	= Liabilities	+ Equity
−1,050		−1,050

Adjustment (b)

Dec. 31	Supplies Expense	1,050	
	Supplies		1,050
	To record supplies used.		

Posting this adjusting entry affects the accounts shown in Exhibit 4.8.

The balance of the supplies account is $2,670 after posting and equals the cost of remaining supplies. If the adjustment is *not* made at December 31, then (a) expenses are understated by $1,050 and net income overstated by $1,050 for the December income statement, and (b) both Supplies and owner's equity are overstated by $1,050 in the December 31 balance sheet.

Exhibit 4.8

Supplies Accounts after Adjusting for Prepaids

Supplies			
Dec. 2	2,500	Dec. 31	1,050
6	1,100		
26	120		
Total	3,720	Total	1,050
	−1,050		
Balance	2,670		

Supplies Expense		
Dec. 31	1,050	

Other Prepaid Expenses

There are other prepaid expenses, such as Prepaid Rent, that are accounted for exactly like Insurance and Supplies above. We should also note that some prepaid expenses are both paid for and fully used up within a single accounting period. One example is when a company pays monthly rent on the first day of each month. The payment creates a prepaid expense on the first day of each month that fully expires by the end of the month. In these special cases we can record the cash paid with a debit to the expense account instead of an asset account. This practice is described more completely later in the chapter.

Appraiser
You are hired as an appraiser to estimate the value of a small publishing company. This company recently signed a well-known athlete to write a book. The company agreed to pay the athlete $500,000 to sign plus future royalties on the book. Your analysis of the company's financial statements finds the $500,000 is not reported as an expense. Instead, it is reported as part of Prepaid Expenses. A note to the statement says "prepaid expenses include author signing fees that are matched against future expected sales." Is this accounting for the $500,000 signing bonus acceptable? How does it affect your analysis?

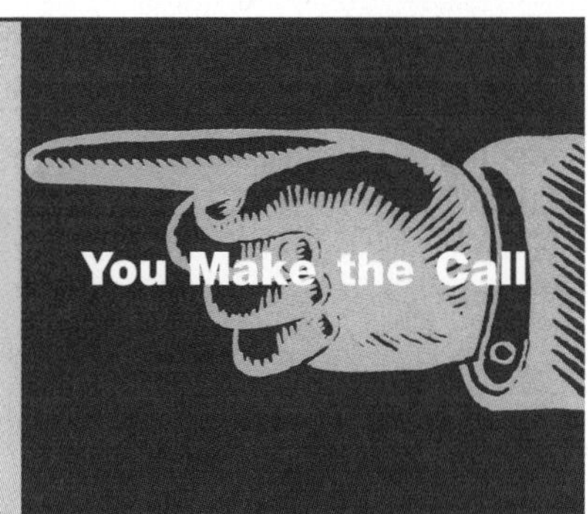

Answer—p. 151

Adjusting for Depreciation

Plant and equipment refers to long-term tangible assets used to produce and sell products and services. These assets are expected to provide benefits for more than one period. Examples of plant and equipment are land, buildings, machines, vehicles, and fixtures. All plant and equipment assets, except for land, eventually wear out or decline in usefulness. The costs of these assets are deferred, but gradually reported as expenses in the income statement over the assets' useful lives (benefit periods). **Depreciation** is the process of computing expense by allocating the cost of these assets over their expected useful lives. Depreciation expense is recorded with an adjusting entry similar to that for prepaid expenses.

FastForward uses equipment in earning revenue. This equipment's cost must be depreciated. Recall that FastForward made two purchases of equipment, one for $20,000 and the other for $6,000, in early December. Chuck Taylor expects this equipment to have a useful life (benefit period) of four years. Taylor expects to sell the equipment for about $8,000 at the end of four years. This means the net cost expected to expire over the useful life is $18,000 ($26,000 − $8,000).[3]

There are several methods we can use to allocate this $18,000 net cost to expense. FastForward uses a method called straight-line depreciation.[4] The **straight-line depreciation method** allocates equal amounts of an asset's cost to depreciation during its useful life. When the $18,000 net cost is divided by the 48 months in the asset's useful life, we get an average monthly cost of $375 ($18,000/48). Our adjusting entry to record monthly depreciation expense is:

	Adjustment (c)		
Dec. 31	Depreciation Expense	375	
	Accumulated Depreciation—Equipment . .		375
	To record monthly depreciation on equipment.		

Assets	=	Liabilities	+	Equity
−375				−375

Posting this adjusting entry affects the accounts shown in Exhibit 4.9.

After posting the adjustment, the Equipment account less its Accumulated Depreciation—Equipment account equals the December 31 balance sheet amount for this asset. The balance in the Depreciation Expense—Equipment account is the expense reported

[3] For simplicity, we treat this equipment as "one", with a net cost of $18,000. Chapter 11 will explain how we deal with depreciation and its many factors.

[4] We explain the details of depreciation methods in Chapter 11. We briefly describe the straight-line method here to help us understand the adjusting process.

Equipment		
Dec. 3	20,000	
6	6,000	
Bal.	26,000	

Accumulated Depreciation—Equipment		
	Dec. 31	375

Depreciation Expense—Equipment		
Dec. 31	375	

Exhibit 4.9

Accounts after Depreciation Adjustments

in the December income statement. If the adjustment is *not* made at December 31, then (a) expenses are understated by $375 and net income overstated by $375 for the December income statement, and (b) both assets and owner's equity are overstated by $375 in the December 31 balance sheet.

It is common for decreases in an asset account to be recorded with a credit to the account. But this procedure is *not* followed when recording depreciation. Instead, depreciation is recorded in a contra account. A **contra account** is an account linked with another account and having an opposite normal balance. It is reported as a subtraction from the other account's balance. For instance, FastForward's contra account for Accumulated Depreciation—Equipment is subtracted from the equipment account in the balance sheet.

The use of contra accounts allows balance sheet readers to know both the cost of assets and the total amount of depreciation charged to expense. By knowing both these amounts, decision makers can better assess a company's productive capacity and any need to replace assets. FastForward's balance sheet shows both the $26,000 original cost of equipment and the $375 balance in the accumulated depreciation contra account. This information reveals that the equipment is close to new. If FastForward only reports equipment at its net amount of $25,625, users cannot assess the equipment's age or its need for replacement.

The title of this contra account is *Accumulated Depreciation.* It means the account includes total depreciation expense for all prior periods during which the assets were being used. For instance, FastForward's Equipment and Accumulated Depreciation accounts would appear as shown in Exhibit 4.10 on February 28, 1998, after three monthly adjusting entries.

Exhibit 4.10

Accounts after 3 Months of Depreciation Adjustments

Equipment		
Dec. 3	20,000	
6	6,000	
Total	**26,000**	

Accumulated Depreciation—Equipment		
	Dec. 31	375
	Jan. 31	375
	Feb. 28	375
	Total	**1,125**

These account balances are reported in the assets section on the February 28 balance sheet as shown in Exhibit 4.11.

Exhibit 4.11

Equipment and Accumulated Depreciation Contra Accounts in the Balance Sheet

Assets		
Cash		$
⋮		
Equipment	**$26,000**	
Less accumulated depreciation	**(1,125)**	**24,875**
Total Assets		$

Small Business Owner
You are preparing to make an offer to purchase a small family-run restaurant. The manager gives you a copy of her depreciation schedule for the restaurant's building and equipment. It shows costs of $75,000 and accumulated depreciation of $55,000. This leaves a net total for building and equipment of $20,000. Is this information valuable in deciding on a purchase offer for the restaurant?

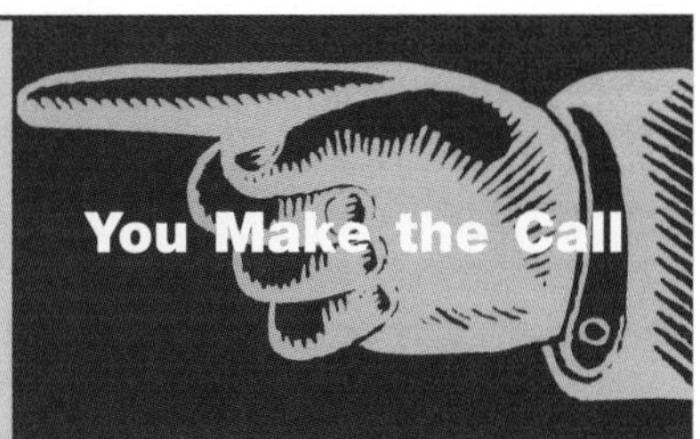

Answer—p. 151

Adjusting Unearned Revenues

Unearned revenues refer to cash *received* in advance of providing products and services. Unearned revenues, also known as *deferred revenues,* are a liability. When cash is accepted, an obligation to provide products and services is accepted. As products and services are provided, the unearned revenues become *earned* revenues. Adjusting entries for unearned revenues involve increasing (crediting) revenues and decreasing (debiting) unearned revenues as shown in Exhibit 4.12.

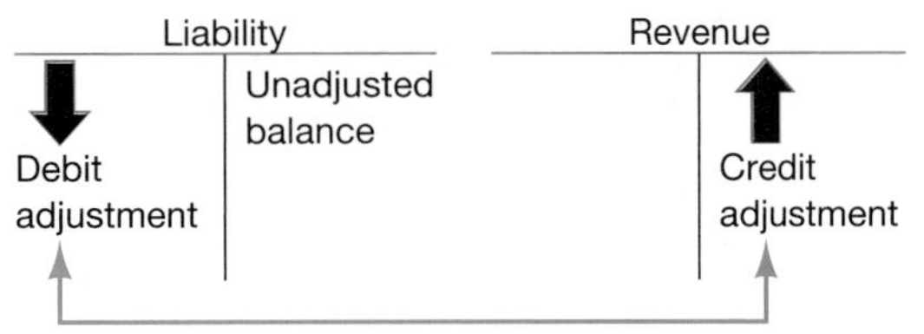

Exhibit 4.12
Adjusting for Unearned Revenues

These adjustments reflect transactions and events (including passage of time) that impact unearned revenues.

An example of unearned revenues is in **America Online**'s annual report in Appendix A. AOL reports Deferred Revenue of $37.95 million among the liabilities on its balance sheet. Another example is **The New York Times,** which reports unexpired (unearned) subscriptions in 1996 of more than $90 million.

> Proceeds from subscriptions . . . are deferred at the time of sale and are included in . . . Income on a pro rata basis over the terms of the subscription.

Unearned revenues are over 10% of total current liabilities for both companies.

Money Is Celtic Green
Game day for the **Boston Celtics** includes adjusting accounts. When the Celtics receive cash from tickets sales and broadcast fees, it is recorded in an unearned revenue account called "Deferred Game Revenues." The Celtics recognize this unearned revenue on a game-by-game basis. Because the NBA regular season begins in October and ends in April, revenue recognition is mainly limited to this period. For the 1997 season, the Celtics' quarterly (3-month) revenues (in millions) are: $0 for July–Sept.; $21 for Oct.–Dec.; $34 for Jan.–Mar.; and $9 for April–June. [Source: Boston Celtics, Annual & Quarterly Reports.]

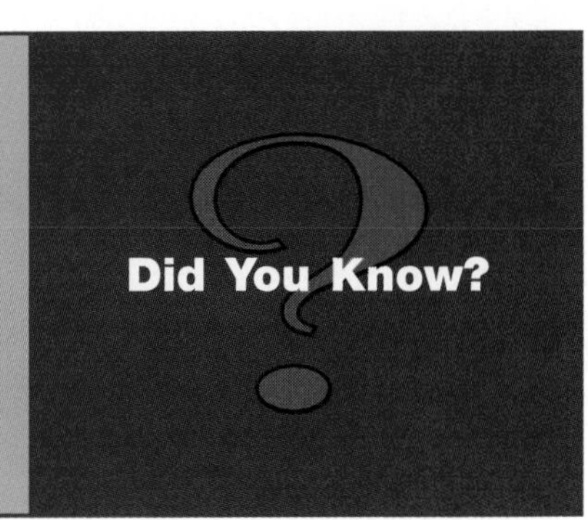

FastForward has unearned revenues. FastForward agreed on December 26 to provide consulting services to a client for a fixed fee of $1,500 per month. On that same day, this client paid the first two months' fees in advance, covering the period December 27 to February 24. The entry to record the cash received in advance is:

Assets = Liabilities + Equity
+3,000 +3,000

Dec. 26	Cash	3,000	
	Unearned Consulting Revenue		3,000
	Received advance payment for services over the next two months.		

This advance payment increases cash and creates an obligation to do consulting work over the next two months. As time passes, FastForward will earn this payment. There are no external transactions linked with this earnings process. By December 31, FastForward provides five days' service and earns one-sixth of the $1,500 revenue for the first month. This amounts to $250 ($1,500 × 5/30). The *revenue recognition principle* implies that $250 of unearned revenue is reported as revenue on the December income statement. The adjusting entry to reduce the liability account and recognize earned revenue is:

Assets = Liabilities + Equity
−250 +250

	Adjustment (d)		
Dec. 31	Unearned Consulting Revenue	250	
	Consulting Revenue ($1,500 × 5/30)		250
	To record earned revenue received in advance.		

After posting the adjusting entry the accounts appear as in Exhibit 4.13.

The adjusting entry transfers $250 out of unearned revenue (a liability account) to a revenue account. If the adjustment is *not* made, then (a) revenue and net income are understated by $250 in the December income statement, and (b) Unearned Revenue is overstated and owner's equity understated by $250 on the December 31 balance sheet.

Exhibit 4.13

Revenue Accounts after Adjusting for Prepaids

Unearned Consulting Revenue			
Dec. 31	250	Dec. 26	3,000
			−250
		Balance	2,750

Consulting Revenue			
		Dec. 10	2,200
		12	1,900
		31	250
		Total	4,350

Adjusting Accrued Expenses

P2 Prepare and describe adjusting entries for accrued expenses and accrued revenues.

Accrued expenses refer to costs that are incurred in a period but are both unpaid and unrecorded. Accrued expenses are incurred expenses that must be reported on the income statement. When costs are incurred in acquiring products and services, there is an obligation to pay for them. The costs of products and services acquired but not yet paid are accrued expenses. Adjusting entries for recording accrued expenses involve increasing (debiting) expenses and increasing (crediting) liabilities as shown in Exhibit 4.14.

Exhibit 4.14

Adjusting for Accrued Expenses

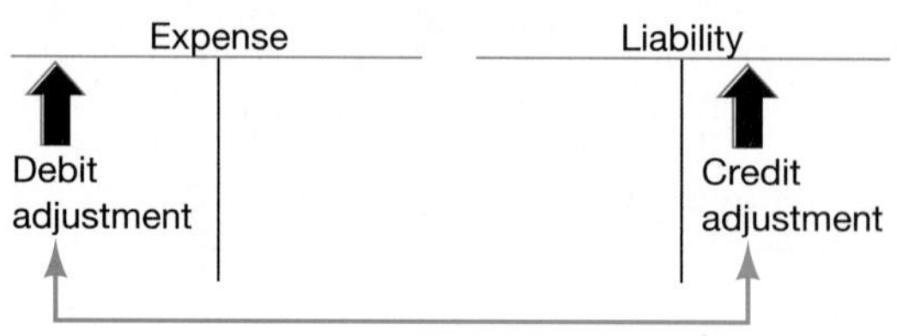

This adjustment recognizes expenses incurred in a period but not yet paid. Common examples of accrued expenses are salaries, interest, rent, and taxes. We use salaries and interest to show how to adjust accounts for accrued expenses.

Accrued Salaries Expense

FastForward's employee earns $70 per day, or $350 for a five-day workweek beginning on Monday and ending on Friday. This employee gets paid every two weeks on Friday.

On December 12 and 26, the wages are paid, recorded in the journal, and posted to the ledger. The *unadjusted* Salaries Expense and Cash paid for salaries appear as shown in Exhibit 4.15:

Salaries Expense		
Dec. 12	700	
26	700	

Cash		
	Dec. 12	700
	26	700

Exhibit 4.15

Salary and Cash Accounts Before Adjusting

The calendar in Exhibit 4.16 shows three working days after the December 26 payday (29, 30, and 31). This means the employee earns three days' salary by the close of business on Wednesday, December 31. While this salary cost has been incurred, it is not yet paid or recorded.

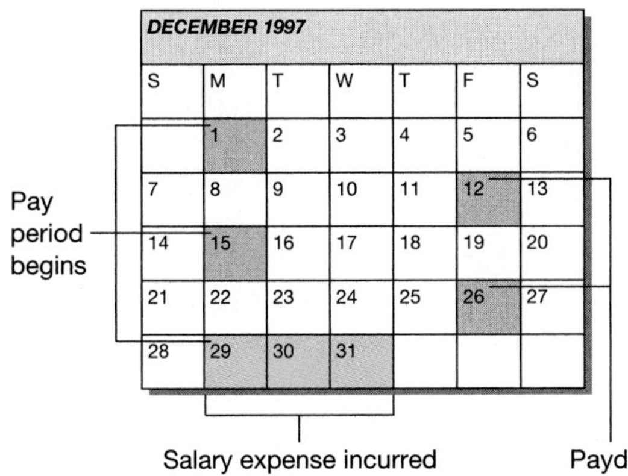

JANUARY 1998						
S	M	T	W	T	F	S
				1	2	3
4	5	6	7	8	9	10
11	12	13	14	15	16	17
18	19	20	21	22	23	24
25	26	27	28	29	30	31

Payday

Exhibit 4.16

Salary Accrual and Paydays

The year-end financial statements are incomplete if FastForward fails to report both the added expense and the liability to the employee for unpaid salary. The year-end adjusting entry to account for accrued salaries is:

	Adjustment (e)		
Dec. 31	Salaries Expense	210	
	Salaries Payable		210
	To record three days' accrued salary (3 × $70).		

Assets = Liabilities + Equity
+210 −210

After the adjusting entry is posted, the expense and liability accounts appear as shown in Exhibit 4.17:

Salaries Expense		
Dec. 12	700	
26	700	
31	**210**	
Total	1,610	

Salaries Payable		
	Dec. 31	**210**

Exhibit 4.17

Salary Accounts After Accrual Adjustments

This means $1,610 of salaries expense is reported on the income statement and that a $210 salaries payable (liability) is reported in the balance sheet. If the adjustment is *not* made, then (a) Salaries Expense is understated and net income overstated by $210 in the December income statement, and (b) Salaries Payable is understated and owner's equity overstated by $210 on the December 31 balance sheet.

Accrued Interest Expense

It is common for companies to have accrued interest expense on notes payable and certain other liabilities at the end of a period. Interest expense is incurred with the passage of time. Unless interest is paid on the last day of an accounting period, we need to adjust accounts for interest expense incurred but not yet paid. This means we must accrue interest cost from the most recent payment date up to the end of the period.[5] We fully describe computation of interest expense later in the book. The adjusting entry is similar to the one for accruing unpaid salary, with a debit to Interest Expense and a credit to Interest Payable (liability).

Adjusting Accrued Revenues

"You can pay me when I finish."

Accrued revenues refer to revenues earned in a period that are both unrecorded and not yet received. Accrued revenues are earned revenues that must be reported on the income statement. An example is a house painter who bills customers when the job is done. If one-third of a house is painted by the end of a period, then one-third of the painter's billing is recorded as revenue in the period even though it is not yet billed or collected. When products and services are delivered, we expect to receive payment for them. Adjusting entries recognize accrued revenues for the value of products and services delivered that are both unrecorded and not yet collected. The adjusting entries increase (debit) assets and increase (credit) revenues as shown in Exhibit 4.18.

Exhibit 4.18

Adjusting for Accrued Revenues

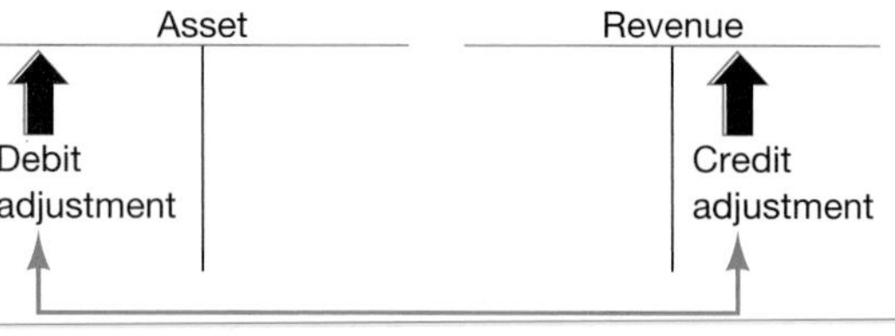

This adjustment recognizes revenues earned in a period but not yet received in cash. Common examples of accrued revenues arise from services, products, interest, and rent. We use service fees and interest to show how to adjust accounts for accrued revenues.

Accrued Services Revenue

Many revenues are recorded when cash is received from a customer or when products and services are sold on credit. Accrued revenues are not recorded until adjusting entries are made at the end of the accounting period. These accrued revenues are earned but unrecorded because either the customer has not yet paid for them or the seller has not yet billed the customer.

FastForward provides us one example. In the second week of December, FastForward agreed to provide consulting services to the athletic department of a college for a fixed fee of $2,700 per month. The terms of the initial agreement call for FastForward to provide services from December 12, 1997 through January 10, 1998, or 30 days of service. The athletic department agrees to pay $2,700 cash to FastForward on January 10, 1998, when the service period is complete.

At December 31, 1997, 20 days of services are already provided to the college. Since the contracted services are not yet entirely provided, the college is not yet billed nor has FastForward recorded the services already provided. FastForward has earned two-thirds of the one-month fee, or $1,800 ($2,700 × 20/30). The *revenue recognition principle* implies we must report the $1,800 on the December income statement because it was earned in December. The balance sheet also must report that this college owes FastForward $1,800. The year-end adjusting entry to account for accrued services revenue is:

[5] The formula for computing accrued interest is: Payable amount × Annual interest rate × Fraction of year since last payment date.

	Adjustment (f)		
Dec. 31	Accounts Receivable	1,800	
	Consulting Revenue		1,800
	To record 20 days' accrued revenue.		

Assets = Liabilities + Equity
+1,800 +1,800

The debit to accounts receivable reflects the amount owed to FastForward from the college for consulting services already provided. After the adjusting entry is posted, the affected accounts appear as shown in Exhibit 4.19.

Exhibit 4.19

Receivable and Revenue Accounts after Accrual Adjustments

Accounts Receivable			
Dec. 12	1,900	Dec. 22	1,900
31	**1,800**		
Total	3,700	Total	1,900
	−1,900		
Balance	1,800		

Consulting Revenue			
		Dec. 10	2,200
		12	1,600
		31	250
		31	**1,800**
		Total	5,850

Accounts receivable are reported on the balance sheet at $1,800, and $5,850 of revenues are reported on the income statement. If the adjustment is *not* made, then (a) both Consulting Revenue and net income are understated by $1,800 in the December income statement, and (b) both Accounts Receivable and owner's equity are understated by $1,800 on the December 31 balance sheet.

Loan Officer

You are a loan officer when an owner of a stereo components store applies for a business loan from your bank. Your analysis of the store's financial statements reveals a record increase in revenues and profits for the current year. Further analysis shows nearly all of this increase is due to a promotional campaign where consumers bought now and pay nothing until January 1 of next year. The store recorded all of these sales as accrued revenue. Do you see any concerns in approving a loan to this store?

Answer—p. 151

Accrued Interest Revenue

In addition to the accrued interest expense we described earlier, interest can yield an accrued revenue when a company is owed money (or other assets) from a debtor. If a company is holding notes or accounts receivable that produce interest revenue, we must adjust the accounts to record any earned and yet uncollected interest revenue. The adjusting entry is similar to the one for accruing services revenue, with a debit to Interest Receivable (asset) and a credit to Interest Revenue.

Answer—p. 151

Financial Officer

You are the financial officer for a retail outlet company. At year-end when you are reviewing adjusting entries to record accruals, you are called into the president's office. The president asks about accrued expenses and instructs you to not record these expenses until next year because they will not be paid until January or later. The president also asks how much current year's revenues increased by the recent purchase order from a new customer. You state there is no effect on sales until next year because the purchase order says merchandise is to be delivered after January 15 and that is when your company plans to make delivery. The president points out that the order already has been received, that your company is ready to make delivery, and tells you to record this sale in the current year. Your company would report a net income instead of a net loss if you carried out the president's orders for adjusting accruals. What do you do?

Summary of Adjustments and Financial Statement Links

Type	Before Adjusting: Balance Sheet Account	Before Adjusting: Income Statement Account	Adjusting Entry
Prepaid expense	Asset overstated	Expense understated	Dr. Expense Cr. Asset
Depreciation	Asset overstated	Expense understated	Dr. Expense Cr. Contra Asset
Unearned revenues	Liability overstated	Revenue understated	Dr. Liability Cr. Revenue
Accrued Expenses	Liability understated	Expense understated	Dr. Expense Cr. Liability
Accrued Revenues	Asset understated	Revenue understated	Dr. Asset Cr. Revenue

Adjustments and Financial Statements

A1 Explain how accounting adjustments link to financial statements.

The process of adjusting accounts is intended to bring an asset or liability account balance to its correct amount. The adjusting entry also updates a related expense or revenue account. These adjustments are necessary for transactions and events that extend over more than one period. Adjusting entries are posted like any other entry.

Exhibit 4.20 lists the five major types of transactions requiring adjustment. Adjusting entries are necessary for each. Understanding this exhibit is important to understanding the adjusting process and its importance to financial statements. Remember each adjusting entry affects one or more income statement accounts *and* one or more balance sheet accounts. Note that an adjusting entry never affects cash.

Exhibit 4.21 summarizes the adjusting entries of FastForward on December 31. The posting of adjusting entries to individual ledger accounts was shown when we described

Exhibit 4.21

Journalizing Adjusting Entries

Date	GENERAL JOURNAL Account Titles and Explanation	PR	Debit	Page # Credit
1997	Adjusting Entries			
Dec. 31	Insurance Expense		100	
	Prepaid Insurance			100
	To record expired insurance.			
31	Supplies Expense		1,050	
	Supplies			1,050
	To record supplies used.			
31	Depreciation Expense—Equipment		375	
	Accumulated Depreciation—Equipment			375
	To record monthly depreciation on equipment.			
31	Unearned Consulting Revenue		250	
	Consulting Revenue			250
	To record earned revenue received in advance.			
31	Salaries Expense		210	
	Salaries Payable			210
	To record three days' accrued salary.			
31	Accounts Receivable		1,800	
	Consulting Revenue			1,800
	To record 20 days' accrued revenue.			

each of the transactions and is not repeated here. Adjusting entries are often set apart from other journal entries with the caption Adjusting Entries.

Flash back

6. If you omit an adjusting entry for accrued service revenues of $200 at year-end, what is the effect of this error on the income statement and balance sheet?
7. What is a contra account? Explain.
8. What is an accrued expense? Give an example.
9. Describe how an unearned revenue arises. Give an example.

Answers—p. 152

Adjusted Trial Balance

P3 Explain and prepare an adjusted trial balance.

An **unadjusted trial balance** is a listing of accounts and balances prepared *before* adjustments are recorded. An **adjusted trial balance** is a list of accounts and balances prepared *after* adjusting entries are recorded and posted to the ledger. Exhibit 4.22 shows the unadjusted and adjusted trial balances for FastForward at December 31, 1997. Notice several new accounts arising from the adjusting entries. The listing of accounts is also slightly changed to match the order in the chart of account numbers listed near the end of the book.

Exhibit 4.22

Unadjusted and Adjusted Trial Balances

FASTForward

FASTFORWARD
Trial Balances
December 31, 1997

	Unadjusted Trial Balance		Adjusted Trial Balance	
	Dr.	Cr.	Dr.	Cr.
Cash	$ 7,950		$ 7,950	
Accounts receivable			1,800	
Supplies	3,720		2,670	
Prepaid insurance	2,400		2,300	
Equipment	26,000		26,000	
Accumulated depreciation—Equipment				$ 375
Accounts payable		$ 1,100		1,100
Salaries payable				210
Unearned consulting revenue		3,000		2,750
Note payable		5,100		5,100
Chuck Taylor, capital		30,000		30,000
Chuck Taylor, withdrawals	600		600	
Consulting revenue		3,800		5,850
Rental revenue		300		300
Depreciation expense—Equipment			375	
Salaries expense	1,400		1,610	
Insurance expense			100	
Rent expense	1,000		1,000	
Supplies expense			1,050	
Utilities expense	230		230	
Totals	$43,300	$43,300	$45,685	$45,685

Preparing Financial Statements

P4 Prepare financial statements from an adjusted trial balance.

We can prepare financial statements directly from information in the *adjusted* trial balance. An adjusted trial balance includes all balances appearing in financial statements. We know that a trial balance summarizes information in the ledger by listing accounts and their balances. This summary is easier to work from than the entire ledger when preparing financial statements.

Exhibit 4.23 shows how FastForward's revenue and expense balances are transferred from the adjusted trial balance to the (1) income statement and (2) statement of changes in owner's equity. Note how we use the net income and withdrawals account to prepare the statement of changes in owner's equity.

Exhibit 4.24 shows how FastForward's asset and liability balances on the adjusted trial balance are transferred to the balance sheet. The ending owner's equity is determined on the statement of changes in owner's equity and transferred to the balance sheet. There are different formats for the balance sheet. The **account form** lists assets on the left and liabilities and owner's equity on the right side of the balance sheet. Its name comes from its link to the accounting equation, Assets = Liabilities + Equity. The balance sheet in Exhibit 2.17 is in account form. The **report form** balance sheet lists items vertically as shown in Exhibit 4.24. **NIKE** uses a report form. Both forms are widely used and are considered equally helpful to users.

We usually prepare financial statements in the order shown: income statement, statement of changes in owner's equity, and balance sheet.[6] This order makes sense since the balance sheet uses information in the statement of changes in owner's equity, which in turn uses information from the income statement.

Exhibit 4.23

Preparing the Income Statement and Statement of Changes in Owner's Equity from the Adjusted Trial Balance

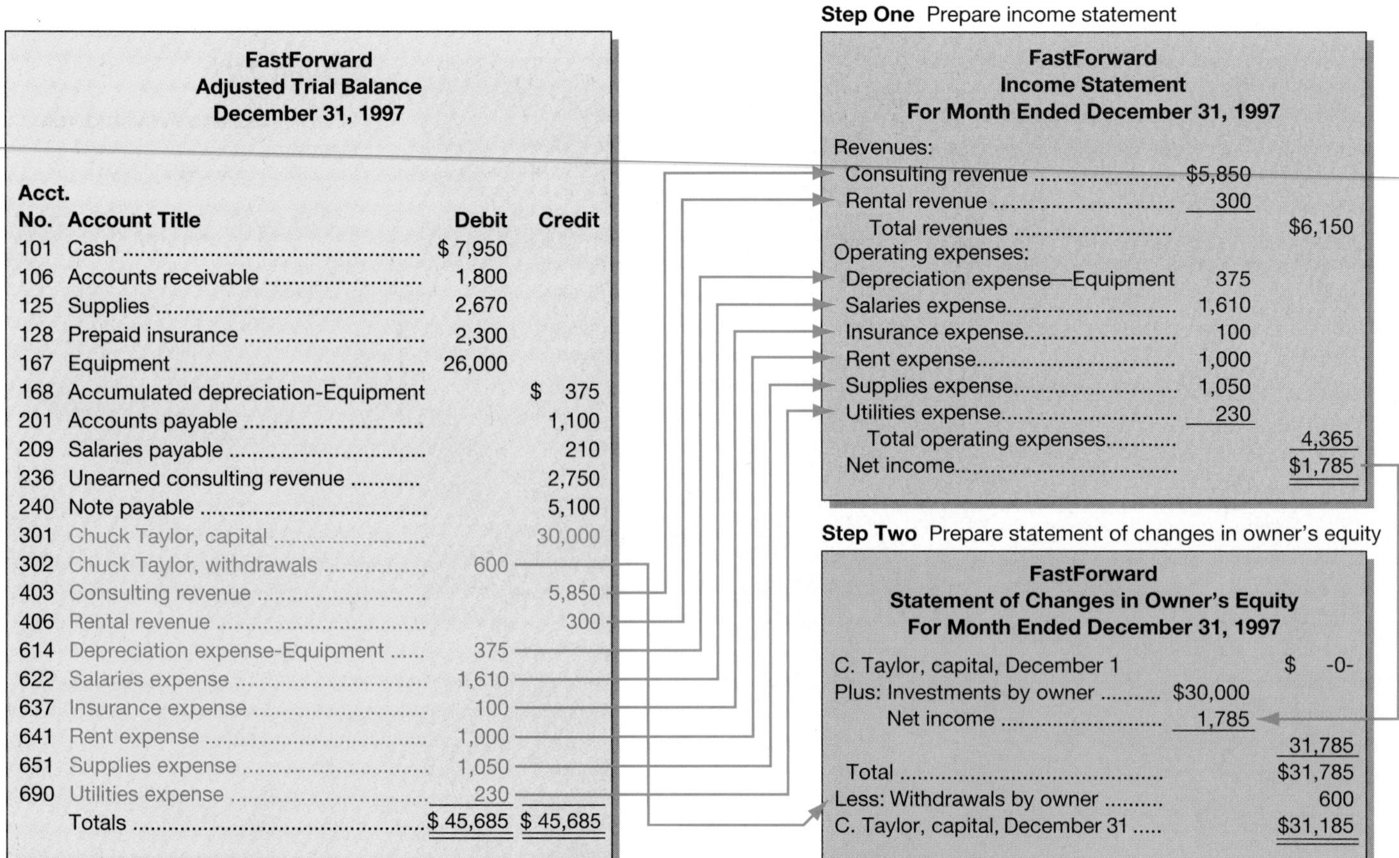

FastForward
Adjusted Trial Balance
December 31, 1997

Acct. No.	Account Title	Debit	Credit
101	Cash	$ 7,950	
106	Accounts receivable	1,800	
125	Supplies	2,670	
128	Prepaid insurance	2,300	
167	Equipment	26,000	
168	Accumulated depreciation-Equipment		$ 375
201	Accounts payable		1,100
209	Salaries payable		210
236	Unearned consulting revenue		2,750
240	Note payable		5,100
301	Chuck Taylor, capital		30,000
302	Chuck Taylor, withdrawals	600	
403	Consulting revenue		5,850
406	Rental revenue		300
614	Depreciation expense-Equipment	375	
622	Salaries expense	1,610	
637	Insurance expense	100	
641	Rent expense	1,000	
651	Supplies expense	1,050	
690	Utilities expense	230	
	Totals	$ 45,685	$ 45,685

Step One Prepare income statement

FastForward
Income Statement
For Month Ended December 31, 1997

Revenues:		
Consulting revenue	$5,850	
Rental revenue	300	
Total revenues		$6,150
Operating expenses:		
Depreciation expense—Equipment	375	
Salaries expense	1,610	
Insurance expense	100	
Rent expense	1,000	
Supplies expense	1,050	
Utilities expense	230	
Total operating expenses		4,365
Net income		$1,785

Step Two Prepare statement of changes in owner's equity

FastForward
Statement of Changes in Owner's Equity
For Month Ended December 31, 1997

C. Taylor, capital, December 1		$ -0-
Plus: Investments by owner	$30,000	
Net income	1,785	31,785
Total		$31,785
Less: Withdrawals by owner		600
C. Taylor, capital, December 31		$31,185

[6] The statement of cash flows is often the final statement prepared. The cash ledger account is very helpful for this purpose. Its preparation is illustrated in the next chapter.

Preparing the Balance Sheet from the Adjusted Trial Balance

FastForward
Adjusted Trial Balance
December 31, 1997

Acct. No.	Account Title	Debit	Credit
101	Cash	$ 7,950	
106	Accounts receivable	1,800	
125	Supplies	2,670	
128	Prepaid insurance	2,300	
167	Equipment	26,000	
168	Accumulated depreciation—Equipment		$ 375
201	Accounts payable		1,100
209	Salaries payable		210
236	Unearned consulting revenue		2,750
240	Note payable		5,100
301	Chuck Taylor, capital		30,000
302	Chuck Taylor, withdrawals	600	
403	Consulting revenue		5,850
406	Rental revenue		300
614	Depreciation expense—Equipment	375	
622	Salaries expense	1,610	
637	Insurance expense	100	
641	Rent expense	1,000	
651	Supplies expense	1,050	
690	Utilities expense	230	
	Totals	$ 45,685	$ 45,685

Step Three Prepare balance sheet

FastForward
Balance Sheet
December 31, 1997

Assets		
Cash		$ 7,950
Accounts receivable		1,800
Supplies		2,670
Prepaid insurance		2,300
Equipment	$ 26,000	
Less accumulated depreciation	(375)	25,625
Total assets		$ 40,345
Liabilities		
Accounts payable	$ 1,100	
Salaries payable	210	
Unearned consulting revenue	2,750	
Note payable	5,100	
Total liabilities		$ 9,160
Owner's Equity		
C. Taylor, capital, December 31, 1997		$ 31,185
Total liabilities and owner's equity		$ 40,345

From statement of changes in owner's equity in Exhibit 4.23

Flash back

10. Jordan Air has the following information in its unadjusted and adjusted trial balances:

	Unadjusted		Adjusted	
	Debit	Credit	Debit	Credit
Prepaid insurance	$6,200		$5,900	
Salaries payable				$1,400

What are the adjusting entries that Jordan Air likely recorded?

11. What accounts are taken from the adjusted trial balance to prepare an income statement?

12. In preparing financial statements from an adjusted trial balance, what statement is usually prepared second?

Answers—p. 152

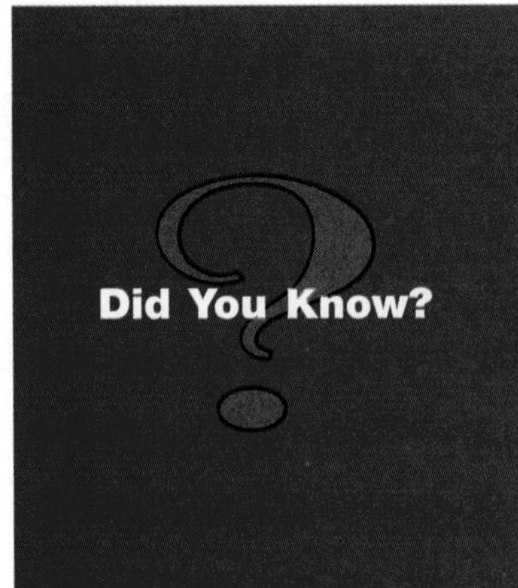

SUN Shines on Accounting

Only three years ago **Sun Microsystems** took almost a month to prepare statements after the end of an accounting period. Today, it takes only 24 hours to deliver preliminary figures to key decision makers at Sun. This gives Sun a big jump on strategic planning for the next period. What is Sun's secret? Transactions are entered in a network of Sun computers so everyone can share and manage data faster. This frees its accounting professionals to take a more active role in managing and strategizing. [Source: *Business Week*, October 28, 1996.]

Accrual Adjustments in Later Periods

P5 Record and describe entries for later periods that result from accruals.

Accrued revenues at the end of one accounting period often result in cash *receipts* from customers in the next period. Also, accrued expenses at the end of one accounting period often result in cash *payments* in the next period. This section explains how we account for these cash receipts or payments in later periods.

Paying Accrued Expenses

FastForward recorded three days of accrued salaries for its employee with this adjusting entry:

Assets = Liabilities + Equity
+210 −210

Dec. 31	Salaries Expense	210	
	Salaries Payable		210
	To record three days' accrued salary (3 × $70).		

When the first payday of the next period arrives on Friday, January 9, the following entry settles the accrued liability (salaries payable) and records additional salaries expense for work in January:

Assets = Liabilities + Equity
−700 −210 −490

Jan. 9	Salaries Payable (3 days at $70)	210	
	Salaries Expense (7 days at $70)	490	
	Cash		700
	Paid two weeks' salary including three days accrued in December.		

The first debit in the January 9 entry records the payment of the liability for the three days' salary accrued on December 31. The second debit records the salary for January's first seven working days (including the New Year's Day holiday) as an expense of the new accounting period. The credit records the total amount of cash paid to the employee.

Receiving Accrued Revenues

FastForward made the following adjusting entry to record 20 days' accrued revenue earned from its consulting contract with a college:

Assets = Liabilities + Equity
+1,800 +1,800

Dec. 31	Accounts Receivable	1,800	
	Consulting Revenue		1,800
	To record 20 days' accrued revenue.		

When the first month's fee is received on January 10, FastForward makes the following entry to remove the accrued asset (accounts receivable) and recognize the additional revenue earned in January:

Jan. 10	Cash	2,700	
	Accounts Receivable		1,800
	Consulting Revenue		900
	Received cash for accrued asset and earned consulting revenue.		

Assets	= Liabilities	+ Equity
+2,700		+900
−1,800		

The debit reflects the cash received. The first credit reflects the removal of the receivable, and the second credit records the earned revenue.

13. Music-Mart records $1,000 of accrued salaries on December 31. Five days later on January 5 (the next payday), salaries of $7,000 are paid. What is the January 5 entry?

Answer—p. 152

Profit Margin

USING THE INFORMATION

A2 Compute profit margin and describe its use in analyzing company performance.

Preparers of information want financial statements to reflect relevant information about a company's financial performance and condition. A primary goal of this effort is to provide information to help internal and external decision makers evaluate a company's performance during a reporting period. This includes evaluating management's success in producing profits. This type of information can suggest ways to improve operations and helps users in predicting future results.

In using accounting information to evaluate operating results, one helpful measure is the ratio of a company's net income to sales. This ratio is called the **profit margin,** or **return on sales,** and is computed as shown in Exhibit 4.25.

Exhibit 4.25
Profit Margin

$$\textbf{Profit margin} = \frac{\textbf{Net income}}{\textbf{Revenues}}$$

This ratio can be interpreted as reflecting the portion of profit in each dollar of revenue.

To illustrate how we compute and use the profit margin, we look at the results of **Ben & Jerry's Homemade Ice Cream** in Exhibit 4.26. Profit margin is one measure we can use to evaluate Ben & Jerry's performance during the past few years.

Exhibit 4.26
Ben & Jerry's Profit Margin

	Year Ended					
Accounting measures	**12/28/96**	**12/30/95**	**12/31/94**	**12/30/93**	**12/29/92**	**12/30/91**
Net income (in thousands)	$ 3,926	$ 5,948	$ (1,869)	$ 7,201	$ 6,675	$ 3,739
Net sales (in thousands)	167,155	155,333	148,802	140,328	131,969	96,997
Profit margin	2.3%	3.8%	(1.3%)	5.1%	5.1%	3.9%
Industry profit margin	**2.%**	**2.%**	**3.%**	**5.%**	**4.%**	**4.%**

Ben & Jerry's average profit margin is 3.15% over this period. Year 1994 stands out as the only year with a loss. This is due to a large increase in operating expenses. The profit margin returns to a positive level in both 1995 and 1996. Also note the steady increase in Ben & Jerry's sales, from less than $100 million in 1991 to more than $167 million in 1996.

Our analysis can benefit from a comparison of profit margins with other companies (see last line of Exhibit 4.26). Ben & Jerry's is a relatively small competitor in the super-premium ice cream industry. As a result of selling in this segment of the market, the company's historical profit margins tend to be at or better than those of its competitors. Competition from larger super-premium companies keeps Ben & Jerry's from enjoying a higher margin.

When we evaluate profit margin of a sole proprietorship, we need to modify the above formula by subtracting from net income the value of the owner's efforts. To illustrate this for FastForward, let's assume the efforts of Chuck Taylor, the owner, are worth $1,500 per month. **FastForward's** profit margin for December 1997 is then computed as shown in Exhibit 4.27.

Exhibit 4.27

Modified profit margin

$$\textbf{Modified profit margin} = \frac{\textbf{Net income} - \textbf{Value of owner's efforts}}{\textbf{Revenues}} = \frac{\$1{,}785 - \$1{,}500}{\$6{,}150} = 4.6\%$$

Flash back

14. Define and interpret the profit margin ratio.

15. If Fila's profit margin is 22.5% and its net income is $1,012,500, what are Fila's total revenues for the reporting period?

Answers—p. 152

Summary

C1 Explain the importance of periodic reporting and the time period principle. The value of information is often linked to its timeliness. Useful information must reach decision makers frequently and promptly. To provide timely information, accounting systems prepare periodic reports at regular intervals. The time period principle assumes that an organization's activities can be divided into specific time periods such as a month, a three-month quarter, or a year for periodic reporting.

C2 Describe the purpose of adjusting accounts at the end of a period. After external transactions and events are recorded, several accounts in the ledger often need adjusting for correct balances to appear in financial statements. This need arises because internal transactions and events remain unrecorded. The purpose of adjusting accounts at the end of a period is to recognize revenues earned and expenses incurred during the period that are not yet recorded.

C3 Explain accrual accounting and how it adds to the usefulness of financial statements. Accrual accounting recognizes revenue when earned and expenses when incurred. Accrual accounting reports the effects of transactions and events when they occur, not necessarily when cash inflows and outflows occur. This information is viewed as valuable in assessing a company's financial position and performance. Yet cash flow information is also useful.

C4 Identify the types of adjustments and their purpose. Adjustments can be grouped according to the timing of cash receipts or payments relative to when they're recognized as revenues or expenses. There are five groups: prepaid expenses, depreciation, unearned revenues, accrued expenses, and accrued revenues. Adjusting entries are necessary for each of these groups so that revenues, expenses, assets, and liabilities are correctly reported for each period.

A1 Explain how accounting adjustments link to financial statements. Accounting adjustments bring an asset or liability account balance to its correct amount. They also update related expense or revenue accounts. Every adjusting entry affects one or more income statement accounts *and* one or more balance sheet accounts. An adjusting entry never affects cash. Adjustments are necessary for transactions and events that extend over more than one period. Exhibit 4.20 summarizes financial statement links by type of adjustment.

A2 Compute profit margin and describe its use in analyzing company performance. Profit margin is defined as the reporting period's net income divided by revenues for the same period. Profit margin reflects a company's earnings activities by showing how much profit is in each dollar of revenue. Analyzing company performance using this ratio is helped by computing similar ratios for competitors.

P1 Prepare and explain adjusting entries for prepaid expenses, depreciation, and unearned revenues. Prepaid expenses refer to items paid for in advance of receiving their benefits. Prepaid expenses are assets. As a prepaid asset is used, its cost becomes an expense. Adjusting entries for prepaids involve increasing (debiting) expenses and decreasing (crediting) assets. Unearned (or prepaid) revenues refer to cash received in advance of providing products and services. Unearned revenues are a liability. As products and services are provided, the amount of unearned revenues becomes earned revenues. Adjusting entries for unearned revenues involve increasing (crediting) revenues and decreasing (debiting) unearned revenues.

P2 Prepare and describe adjusting entries for accrued expenses and accrued revenues. Accrued expenses refer to costs incurred in a period that are both unpaid and unrecorded. Accrued expenses are incurred expenses and are reported on the income statement. Adjusting entries for recording accrued expenses involve increasing (debiting) expenses and increasing (crediting) liabilities. Accrued revenues refer to revenues earned in a period that are both unrecorded and not yet received in cash. Accrued revenues are part of revenues and reported on the income statement. Adjusting entries for recording accrued revenues involve increasing (debiting) assets and increasing (crediting) revenues.

P3 Explain and prepare an adjusted trial balance. An adjusted trial balance is a list of accounts and balances prepared after adjusting entries are recorded and posted to the ledger. Financial statements are often prepared from the adjusted trial balance.

P4 Prepare financial statements from an adjusted trial balance. We can prepare financial statements directly from the adjusted trial balance. Revenue and expense balances are transferred to the income statement and statement of changes in owner's equity. Asset, liability, and owner's equity balances are transferred to the balance sheet. We usually prepare statements in the following order: income statement, statement of changes in owner's equity, and balance sheet.

P5 Record and describe entries for later periods that result from accruals. Accrued revenues at the end of one accounting period usually result in cash receipts from customers in later periods. Accrued expenses at the end of one accounting period usually result in cash payments in later periods. When cash is received or paid in these later periods, the entries must account for the accrued assets or liabilities initially recorded.

Guidance Answers to **You Make the Call**

Appraiser

Prepaid expenses are items paid for in advance of receiving their benefits. They also are assets and are expensed as they are used up. The publishing company's treatment of the signing bonus is acceptable provided there are future book sales that we can match against the $500,000 expense. As an appraiser, you are concerned about the likelihood of future book sales and the risks involved. The most conservative appraiser would adjust the records used for analysis so that all $500,000 is treated as an expense for the period when the athlete signs. The more risky the likelihood of future book sales is, the more likely your analysis treats the $500,000 as an expense and not a prepaid expense (asset).

Small Business Owner

Depreciation is a process of cost allocation, not asset valuation. Knowing the depreciation schedule of the restaurant is not especially useful in your estimation of what the restaurant's building and equipment are currently worth. Your assessment of the age, quality, and usefulness of the building and equipment is much more important. You would also use the current market values of similar assets in estimating the value of this restaurant's building and equipment.

Loan Officer

Your concern in lending to this store arises from analysis of current year sales. While increased revenues and profits are great, your concern is with the collectibility of these promotional sales. If the owner sold products to customers with poor records of paying bills, then collectibility of these sales is low. Your analysis must assess this possibility and recognize any expected losses. If the owner sold only to financially secure customers, then you can reliably count on receiving these accrued revenues.

Guidance Answer to **Judgment and Ethics**

Financial Officer

It appears you must make a choice between following the president's orders or not. The requirements of acceptable practice are clear. Omitting adjustments and early recognition of revenue can mislead users of financial statements (including managers, owners, and lenders). One action is to request a second meeting with the president where you explain that accruing expenses when incurred and recognizing revenue when earned are required practices. You should also mention the ethical implications of not complying with accepted practice. Point out that the president's orders involve intentional falsification of the statements. If the president persists, you might discuss the situation with legal counsel and any auditors involved. Your ethical action might cost you this job. But the potential pitfalls of falsification of statements, reputation loss, personal integrity, and other costs are too great.

Guidance Answers to  backs

1. An annual reporting (or accounting) period covers one year and refers to the preparation of annual financial statements. The annual reporting period is not always the same as a calendar year that ends on December 31. An organization can adopt a fiscal year consisting of any 12 consecutive months. It is also acceptable to adopt an annual reporting period of 52 weeks.
2. Interim (less than one year) financial statements are prepared to provide decision makers information frequently and promptly.
3. The revenue recognition principle and the matching principle lead most directly to the adjusting process.
4. No. Cash basis accounting is not consistent with the matching principle because it does not always report expenses in the same period as the revenues earned as a result of those expenses.
5. No expense is reported in 1999. Under cash basis accounting the entire $4,800 is reported as expense in 1998 when the premium is paid.

6. If the accrued services revenue adjustment of $200 is not made, then both revenue and net income are understated by $200 on the current year's income statement, and assets and owner's equity are understated by $200 on the balance sheet.

7. A contra account is an account that is subtracted from the balance of a related account. Use of a contra account often provides more complete information than simply reporting a net amount.

8. An accrued expense refers to a cost incurred in a period that is both unpaid and unrecorded prior to adjusting entries. One example is salaries earned by employees but not yet paid at the end of a period.

9. An unearned revenue arises when cash (or other assets) is received from a customer before the services and products are delivered to the customer. Magazine subscription receipts in advance are one example.

10. The probable adjusting entries of Jordan Air are:

Insurance Expense	300	
Prepaid Insurance		300
To record insurance expired.		
Salaries Expense	1,400	
Salaries Payable		1,400
To record accrued salaries.		

11. Revenue accounts and expense accounts.

12. Statement of changes in owner's equity.

13. The January 5 entry to settle the accrued salaries and to pay for the additional salaries from January is:

Jan. 5	Salaries Payable	1,000	
	Salaries Expense	6,000	
	Cash		7,000
	Paid salary including accrual from December.		

14. Profit margin is defined as net income divided by revenues. It can be interpreted as the portion of profit in each dollar of revenue.

15. Fila's profit margin of 22.5% equals $1,012,500 ÷ Revenues. Solving for revenues, we get revenues equal to $4,500,000 (computed as $1,012,500 ÷ 22.5%).

Demonstration Problem

The following information relates to Best Electronics on December 31, 2001. The company uses the calendar year as its annual reporting period. The company initially records prepaid and unearned items in balance sheet accounts.

a. The company's weekly payroll is $8,400, paid every Friday for a five-day workweek. December 31, 2001, falls on a Monday, but the employees will not be paid until Friday, January 4, 2002.

b. Eighteen months earlier, on July 1, 2000, the company purchased equipment that cost $10,000 and had no salvage value. Its useful life is predicted to be five years.

c. On October 1, 2001, the company agreed to work on a new housing development. For installing alarm systems in 24 new homes, the company was paid $144,000 in advance. When the $144,000 cash was received on October 1, that amount was credited to the Unearned Revenue account. Between October 1 and December 31, work on 18 homes was completed.

d. On September 1, 2001, the company purchased a one-year insurance policy for $1,200. The transaction was recorded with a $1,200 debit to Prepaid Insurance.

e. On December 29, 2001, the company renders a $5,000 service which has not been billed as of December 31, 2001.

Required

1. Prepare adjusting entries needed on December 31, 2001, to record the previously unrecorded effects of these transactions and events.

2. Prepare T-accounts for accounts affected by adjusting entries. Post adjusting entries to T-accounts. Determine the adjusted balances for the Unearned Revenue account and the Prepaid Insurance account.

3. Complete the following table describing the effects of your adjusting entries on the 2001 income statement and the December 31, 2001, balance sheet. Use up (down) arrows to indicate an increase (decrease).

Entry	Amount in the Entry	Effect on Net Income	Effect on Total Assets	Effect on Total Liabilities	Effect on Owner's Equity
a					
b					
c					
d					
e					

Planning the Solution

- Analyze information for each situation to determine which accounts need to be updated with an adjustment.
- Calculate the size of each adjustment and prepare the necessary journal entries.
- Show the amount entered by each adjustment in the designated accounts, determine the adjusted balance, and then determine the balance sheet classification that the account falls within.
- Determine each entry's effect on net income for the year and on total assets, total liabilities, and owner's equity at the end of the year.

Solution to Demonstration Problem

1. Adjusting journal entries.

a. Dec. 31	Wages Expense	1,680	
	Wages Payable		1,680
	To accrue wages for the last day of the year ($8,400 × 1/5).		
b. Dec. 31	Depreciation Expense—Equipment	2,000	
	Accumulated Depreciation—Equipment . .		2,000
	To record depreciation expense for the year ($10,000/5 = $2,000).		
c. Dec. 31	Unearned Revenue	108,000	
	Services Revenue		108,000
	To recognize revenues earned ($144,000 × 18/24).		
d. Dec. 31	Insurance Expense	400	
	Prepaid Insurance		400
	To adjust for expired portion of insurance ($1,200 × 4/12).		
e. Dec. 31	Accounts Receivable	5,000	
	Services Revenue		5,000
	To record revenues earned.		

2. T-accounts for adjusting journal entries *a* through *e*.

Wages Expense			
(a)	1,680		

Wages Payable			
		(a)	1,680

Depreciation Expense—Equipment

(b)	2,000		

Accumulated Depreciation—Equipment

		(b)	2,000

Unearned Revenue

Balance			144,000
(c)	108,000		
		Balance	36,000

Services Revenue

		(c)	108,000
		(e)	5,000
		Balance	113,000

Insurance Expense

(d)	400		

Prepaid Insurance

Balance	1,200	(d)	400
Balance	800		

Accounts Receivable

(e)	5,000		

3. Financial statement effects of adjusting journal entries.

Entry	Amount in the Entry	Effect on Net Income	Effect on Total Assets	Effect on Total Liabilities	Effect on Owner's Equity
a	$1,680	$1,680 ↓	No effect	$1,680 ↑	$1,680 ↓
b	$2,000	$2,000 ↓	$2,000 ↓	No effect	$2,000 ↓
c	$108,000	$108,000 ↑	No effect	$108,000 ↓	$108,000 ↑
d	$400	$400 ↓	$400 ↓	No effect	$400 ↓
e	$5,000	$5,000 ↑	$5,000 ↑	No effect	$5,000 ↑

Alternatives in Accounting for Prepaids

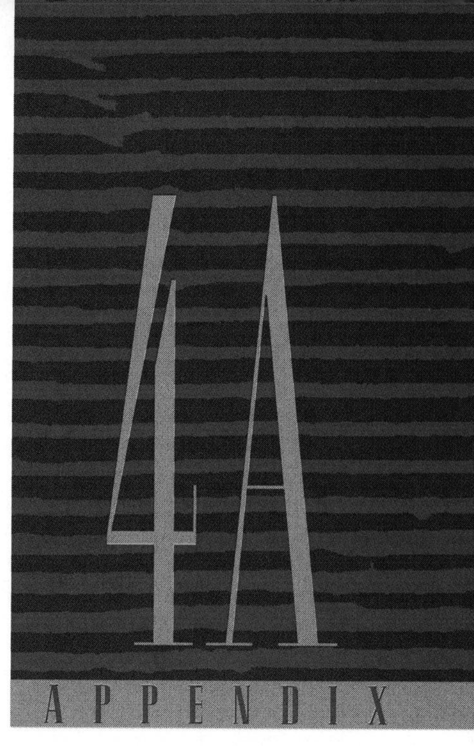

This section explains two alternatives in accounting for prepaid expenses and prepaid (unearned) revenues. We show the accounting for both alternatives.

Learning Objectives

Procedural

P6 Identify and explain two alternatives in accounting for prepaids.

Recording Prepaid Expenses in Expense Accounts

We explained that prepaid expenses are assets when they are purchased and are recorded with debits to asset accounts. Adjusting entries transfer the costs that expire to expense accounts at the end of an accounting period. We also explained that some prepaid expenses are purchased and fully expire before the end of an accounting period. In these cases, we can avoid adjusting entries by charging the prepaid items to expense accounts when purchased.

P6 Identify and explain two alternatives in accounting for prepaids.

There is an alternative practice of recording *all* prepaid expenses with debits to expense accounts. If any prepaids remain unused or unexpired at the end of an accounting period, then adjusting entries must transfer the cost of the unused portions from expense accounts to prepaid expense (asset) accounts. This alternative practice is acceptable. The financial statements are identical under either procedure, but the adjusting entries are different.

To illustrate the accounting differences between these two practices, let's look at FastForward's cash payment of December 26 for 24 months of insurance coverage beginning on December 1. FastForward recorded that payment with a debit to an asset account. But it could have recorded a debit to an expense account. These alternatives are shown in Exhibit 4A.1.

Exhibit 4A.1

Initial Entry for Prepaid Expenses for Two Alternatives

		Payment Recorded as Asset		Payment Recorded as Expense	
Dec. 26	Prepaid Insurance	2,400			
	Cash		2,400		
26	Insurance Expense			2,400	
	Cash				2,400

At the end of the accounting period on December 31, insurance protection for one month is expired. This means $100 ($2,400/24) of the asset expires and becomes an expense for December. The adjusting entry depends on how the original payment is recorded. This is shown in Exhibit 4A.2.

When these entries are posted to the accounts we can see that these two alternatives give identical results. The December 31 adjusted account balances in Exhibit 4A.3 show prepaid insurance of $2,300 and insurance expense of $100 for both methods.

Exhibit 4A.2

Adjusting Entry for Prepaid Expenses for Two Alternatives

		Payment Recorded as Asset		Payment Recorded as Expense	
Dec. 31	Insurance Expense	100			
	Prepaid Insurance		100		
31	Prepaid Insurance			2,300	
	Insurance Expense				2,300

Exhibit 4A.3

Account balances under Two Alternatives for Recording Prepaid Expenses

Payment Recorded as Asset

Prepaid Insurance			
Dec. 26	2,400 −100	Dec. 31	100
Balance	2,300		

Insurance Expense			
Dec. 31	100		

Payment Recorded as Expense

Prepaid Insurance			
Dec. 31	2,300		

Insurance Expense			
Dec. 26	2,400 −2,300	Dec. 31	2,300
Balance	100		

Recording Unearned Revenues in Revenue Accounts

Unearned (prepaid) revenues are liabilities requiring delivery of products and services. We explained how unearned revenues are recorded as credits to liability accounts when cash and other assets are received. Adjusting entries at the end of an accounting period transfer to revenue accounts the earned portion of unearned revenues. Some unearned revenues are received and fully earned before the end of an accounting period. In these cases, we can avoid adjusting entries by recording unearned revenues into revenue accounts when received.

As with prepaid expenses, there is an alternative practice of recording *all* unearned revenues with credits to revenue accounts. If any revenues are unearned at the end of an accounting period, then adjusting entries must transfer the unearned portions from revenue accounts to unearned revenue (liability) accounts. This alternative practice is acceptable. While the adjusting entries are different for these two alternatives, the financial statements are identical.

To illustrate the accounting differences between these two practices, let's look at FastForward's December 26 receipt of $3,000 for consulting services covering the period December 27 to February 24. FastForward recorded this transaction with a credit to a liability account. The alternative is to record it with a credit to a revenue account as shown in Exhibit 4A.4.

By the end of the accounting period (December 31), FastForward earns $250 of this revenue. This means $250 of the liability is satisfied. Depending on how the initial receipt is recorded, the adjusting entry is as shown in Exhibit 4A.5.

Exhibit 4A.4

Initial Entry for Unearned Revenues for Two Alternatives

		Receipt Recorded as Liability		Receipt Recorded as Revenue	
Dec. 26	Cash	3,000			
	Unearned Consulting Revenue		3,000		
26	Cash			3,000	
	Consulting Revenue				3,000

Exhibit 4A.5 Adjusting Entry for Unearned Revenues for Two Alternatives

		Receipt Recorded as Liability		Receipt Recorded as Revenue	
Dec. 31	Unearned Consulting Revenue	250			
	Consulting Revenue		250		
31	Consulting Revenue			2,750	
	Unearned Consulting Revenue				2,750

After adjusting entries are posted, the two alternatives give identical results. The December 31 adjusted account balances in Exhibit 4A.6 show unearned consulting revenue of $2,750 and consulting revenue of $250 for both methods.

Exhibit 4A.6 Account Balances under Two Alternatives for Recording Unearned Revenues

Receipt Recorded as Liability

Unearned Consulting Revenue			
Dec. 31	250	Dec. 26	3,000
			−250
		Balance	2,750

Consulting Revenue			
		Dec. 31	250

Receipt Recorded as Revenue

Unearned Consulting Revenue			
		Dec. 31	2,750

Consulting Revenue			
Dec. 31	2,750	Dec. 26	3,000
			−2,750
		Balance	250

Flash back

16. Miller Company records cash receipts of unearned revenues and cash payments of prepaid expenses in balance sheet accounts. Bud Company records these items in income statement accounts. Explain any difference in the financial statements of these two companies from their alternative accounting for prepaids.

Answer—p. 157

Summary of Appendix 4A

P6 Identify and explain two alternatives in accounting for prepaids. It is acceptable to charge all prepaid expenses to expense accounts when they are purchased. When this is done, adjusting entries must transfer any unexpired amounts from expense accounts to asset accounts. It is also acceptable to credit all unearned revenues to revenue accounts when cash is received. In this case the adjusting entries must transfer any unearned amounts from revenue accounts to unearned revenue accounts.

Guidance Answer to Flash backs

16. When adjusting entries are correctly prepared, it does not make any difference whether cash receipts of unearned revenues and cash payments of prepaid expenses are recorded in balance sheet accounts or in income statement accounts. The financial statements of these companies are identical under both methods.

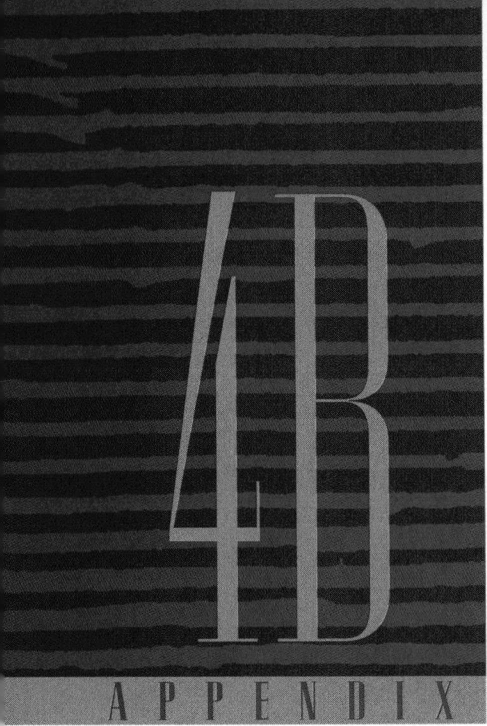

Work Sheet Format for Adjusted Trial Balance

We show in the next chapter how to prepare an adjusted trial balance and financial statements from a work sheet. To focus on the important aspects of the adjusting process in this chapter, we did not introduce the work sheet format. Yet some users prefer this format in introducing the adjusted trial balance, and we present it in Exhibit 4B.1.

Exhibit 4B.1

Work Sheet Format for Preparing the Adjusted Trial Balance

	Unadjusted Trial Balance		Adjustments		Adjusted Trial Balance	
	Dr.	Cr.	Dr.	Cr.	Dr.	Cr.
Cash	$ 7,950				$ 7,950	
Accounts receivable			*(f)* 1,800		1,800	
Supplies	3,720			*(b)* 1,050	2,670	
Prepaid insurance	2,400			*(a)* 100	2,300	
Equipment	26,000				26,000	
Accumulated depreciation—Equipment				*(c)* 375		$ 375
Accounts payable		$ 1,100				1,100
Salaries payable				*(e)* 210		210
Unearned consulting revenue		3,000	*(d)* 250			2,750
Note payable		5,100				5,100
Chuck Taylor, capital		30,000				30,000
Chuck Taylor, withdrawals	600				600	
Consulting revenue		3,800		*(d)* 250		5,850
				(f) 1,800		
Rental revenue		300				300
Depreciation expense—Equipment			*(c)* 375		375	
Salaries expense	1,400		*(e)* 210		1,610	
Insurance expense			*(a)* 100		100	
Rent expense	1,000				1,000	
Supplies expense			*(b)* 1,050		1,050	
Utilities expense	230				230	
Totals	$43,300	$43,300	$ 3,785	$ 3,785	$45,685	$45,685

Glossary

Account form balance sheet a balance sheet that lists assets on the left and liabilities and owner's equity on the right side. (p. 146).

Accounting period the length of time covered by financial statements and other reports; also called *reporting period.* (p. 130).

Accrual basis accounting the approach to preparing financial statements that uses the adjusting process to recognize revenues when earned and expenses when incurred; the basis for generally accepted accounting principles. (p. 133).

Accrued expenses costs incurred in a period that are both unpaid and unrecorded; adjusting entries for recording accrued expenses involve increasing (debiting) expenses and increasing (crediting) liabilities. (p. 140).

Accrued revenues revenues earned in a period that are both unrecorded and not yet received in cash (or other assets); adjusting entries for recording accrued revenues involve increasing (debiting) assets and increasing (crediting) revenues. (p. 142).

Adjusted trial balance a listing of accounts and balances prepared after adjustments are recorded and posted to the ledger. (p. 145).

Adjusting entry a journal entry at the end of an accounting period to bring an asset or liability account balance to its proper amount while also updating the related expense or revenue account. (p. 134).

Annual financial statements financial statements covering a one year period; often based on a calendar year, but any twelve consecutive month period is acceptable. (p. 131).

Cash basis accounting revenues are recognized when cash is received and expenses are recorded when cash is paid. (p. 133).

Contra account an account linked with another account and having an opposite normal balance; reported as a subtraction from the other account's balance to provide more complete information than simply the net amount. (p. 138).

Depreciation the expense created by allocating the cost of plant and equipment to the periods in which they are used; represents the expense of using the assets. (p. 137).

Fiscal year the 12 consecutive months (or 52 weeks) chosen as an organization's annual accounting period. (p. 131).

Interim financial statements financial statements covering periods of less than one year; usually based on one- or three- or six-month periods. (p. 131).

Matching principle the principle that requires expenses to be reported in the same period as the revenues that were earned as a result of the expenses. (p. 132).

Natural business year a 12-month period that ends when a company's sales activities are at their lowest point. (p. 131).

Plant and equipment tangible long-lived assets used to produce goods or services. (p. 137).

Prepaid expenses items paid for in advance of receiving their benefits; classified as assets. (p. 135).

Profit margin the ratio of a company's net income to its revenues; measures the portion of profit in each dollar of revenue. (p. 149).

Report form balance sheet a balance sheet that lists items vertically with assets above the liabilities and owner's equity. (p. 146).

Return on sales another name for *profit margin.* (p. 149).

Straight-line depreciation method allocates equal amounts of an asset's net cost to depreciation expense during its useful life. (p. 137).

Time period principle a principle that assumes an organization's activities can be divided into specific time periods such as months, quarters, or years. (p. 130).

Unadjusted trial balance a listing of accounts and balances prepared before adjustments are recorded and posted to the ledger. (p. 145).

Unearned revenues cash received in advance of providing products and services; a liability. (p. 139).

The superscript letter ^{A} identifies assignment material based on Appendix 4A; the superscript letter ^{B} identifies material based on Appendix 4B.

Questions

1. What type of business is most likely to select a fiscal year that corresponds to the natural business year instead of the calendar year?

2. What kind of assets requires adjusting entries to record depreciation?

3. What contra account is used when recording and reporting the effects of depreciation? Why is it used?

4. Where is an unearned revenue reported in the financial statements?

5. What is an accrued revenue? Give an example.

6. What is the difference between the cash and accrual bases of accounting?

7. Where is a prepaid expense reported in the financial statements?

8. Why is the accrual basis of accounting preferred over the cash basis?

9^{A}. If a company initially records prepaid expenses with debits to expense accounts, what type of account is debited in the adjusting entries for prepaid expenses?

10. Why does a sole proprietorship require special procedures in calculating the profit margin?

11. Review the consolidated balance sheet of NIKE in Appendix A. Identify two asset accounts that require adjustment before annual financial statements can be prepared. What would the effect on the income statement be if these two asset accounts were not adjusted?

12. Review the consolidated balance sheet of Reebok in Appendix A. As a simplification, assume that the company did not sell or purchase any property, plant, and equipment during 1996. How much depreciation was recorded in the adjusting entry for depreciation at the end of 1996?

13. What current asset account on America Online's balance sheet in Appendix A was probably adjusted before the financial statements were prepared as of June 30, 1996? As of June 30, 1995?

14. Review the chapter's opening scenario, *Bad Boys Need Money*. Identify two current sources of revenue for the Bronx Bombers. Identify two additional sources of revenue that the Bronx Bombers might be able to develop. What does it mean when the article states that Burston is currently preparing pro forma financial statements?

Quick Study

QS 4-1
Accrual and cash accounting
C3

In its first year of operations, Harris Co. earned $39,000 in revenues and received $33,000 cash from customers. The company incurred expenses of $22,500 but had not paid $2,250 of them at year-end. In addition, Harris prepaid $3,750 for expenses that would be incurred the next year. Calculate the first year's net income under both cash basis and accrual basis accounting.

QS 4-2
Preparing adjusting entries
C4

In recording its transactions during the year, Stark Company records prepayments of expenses in asset accounts and receipts of unearned revenues in liability accounts. At the end of its annual accounting period, the company must make three adjusting entries. They are: (a) accrue salaries expense, (b) adjust the Unearned Services Revenue account to recognize earned revenue, and (c) record the earning of services revenue for which cash will be received the following period. For each of these adjusting entries (a), (b), and (c), use the numbers assigned to the following accounts to indicate the correct account to be debited and the correct account to be credited.

1. Prepaid Salaries Expense
2. Cash
3. Salaries Payable
4. Accounts Receivable
5. Salaries Expense
6. Services Revenue Earned
7. Unearned Services Revenue

QS 4-3
Effects of adjusting entries
C4, A1

In making adjusting entries at the end of its accounting period, Carter Consulting Agency failed to record $1,400 of insurance premiums that had expired. This cost had been initially debited to the Prepaid Insurance account. The company also failed to record accrued salaries payable of $800. As a result of these two oversights, the financial statements for the reporting period will: [choose the best alternative from the following] *(a)* understate assets by $1,400; *(b)* understate expenses by $2,200; *(c)* understate net income by $800; or *(d)* overstate liabilities by $800.

QS 4-4
Intrpreting adjusting entries
C4

The following information is taken from Shank Company's unadjusted and adjusted trial balances:

	Unadjusted		Adjusted	
	Debit	Credit	Debit	Credit
Prepaid insurance	$3,100		$2,950	
Interest payable				$700

Given this information, which of the following items must be included among the adjusting entries?

a. A $150 debit to Insurance Expense and a $700 debit to Interest Expense.
b. A $150 credit to Prepaid Insurance and a $700 debit to Interest Payable.
c. A $150 debit to Insurance Expense and a $700 debit to Interest Payable.

QS 4-5[A]
Preparing adjusting entries
C4, P6

Foster Consulting Company initially records prepaid and unearned items in income statement accounts. Given Foster Consulting Company's practices, which of the following choices applies to the preparation of adjusting entries at the end of the company's first accounting period?

a. Unpaid salaries will be recorded with a debit to Prepaid Salaries and a credit to Salaries Expense.

b. The cost of unused office supplies will be recorded with a debit to Supplies Expense and a credit to Office Supplies.

c. Unearned fees will be recorded with a debit to Consulting Fees Earned and a credit to Unearned Consulting Fees.

d. Earned but unbilled consulting fees will be recorded with a debit to Unearned Consulting Fees and a credit to Consulting Fees Earned.

QS 4-6
Analyzing profit margin
A2

Revell Company had net income of $37,925 and revenue of $390,000 for the year ended December 31, 2000. Calculate Revell's profit margin. Interpret the profit margin calculation.

QS 4-7
Identifying accounting adjustments
C4

Classify the following adjusting entries as involving prepaid expenses (P), depreciation (D), unearned revenues (U), accrued expenses (E), or accrued revenues (R).

a. _____ Entry to record annual depreciation expense.

b. _____ Entry to show wages earned but not yet paid.

c. _____ Entry to show revenue earned but not yet billed.

d. _____ Entry to show expiration of prepaid insurance.

e. _____ Entry to show revenue earned that was previously received as cash in advance.

QS 4-8
Recording and analyzing adjusting entries
A1

Adjusting entries affect at least one balance sheet account and at least one income statement account. For the entries listed below, identify the account to be debited and the account to be credited. Indicate which of the two accounts is the income statement account and which is the balance sheet account.

a. Entry to record annual depreciation expense.

b. Entry to record wages earned but not yet paid.

c. Entry to record revenue earned but not yet billed.

d. Entry to record expiration of prepaid insurance.

e. Entry to record revenue earned that was previously received as cash in advance.

Exercises

Exercise 4-1
Preparing adjusting entries
P1

Prepare adjusting journal entries for the financial statements for the year ended December 31, 2000, for each of these independent situations. Assume prepaid expenses are initially recorded in asset accounts. Also, assume fees collected in advance of work are initially recorded as liabilities.

a. Depreciation on the company's equipment for year 2000 is computed to be $16,000.

b. The Prepaid Insurance account had a $7,000 debit balance at December 31, 2000, before adjusting for the costs of any expired coverage. An analysis of the company's insurance policies showed that $1,040 of unexpired insurance remained in effect.

c. The Office Supplies account had a $300 debit balance on January 1, 2000; $2,680 of office supplies were purchased during the year; and the December 31, 2000, physical count showed that $354 of supplies are on hand.

d. One-half of the work for a $10,000 fee received in advance was performed this period.

e. The Prepaid Insurance account had a $5,600 debit balance at December 31, 2000, before adjusting for the costs of any expired coverage. An analysis of the company's insurance policies showed that $4,600 of coverage had expired.

f. Wages of $4,000 have been earned by workers but not paid as of December 31, 2000.

Exercise 4-2
Adjusting and paying accrued wages

Resource Management has five part-time employees, each of whom earns $100 per day. They are normally paid on Fridays for work completed on Monday through Friday of the same week. They were all paid in full on Friday, December 28, 2001. The next week, all five of the employees worked only four days because New Year's Day was an unpaid holiday. Show the adjusting entry that would be recorded on Monday, December 31, 2001, and the journal entry that would be made to record paying the employees' wages on Friday, January 4, 2002.

Exercise 4-3
Adjusting entry classification

In the blank space beside each of these adjusting entries, enter the letter of the explanation that most closely describes the entry:

a. To record this period's depreciation expense.
b. To record accrued salaries expense.
c. To record this period's consumption of a prepaid expense.
d. To record accrued interest income.
e. To record accrued interest expense.
f. To record the earning of previously unearned income.

			Debit	Credit
_____	**1.**	Unearned Professional Fees	18,450	
		Professional Fees Earned		18,450
_____	**2.**	Interest Receivable	2,700	
		Interest Earned		2,700
_____	**3.**	Depreciation Expense	49,500	
		Accumulated Depreciation		49,500
_____	**4.**	Salaries Expense	16,400	
		Salaries Payable		16,400
_____	**5.**	Interest Expense	3,800	
		Interest Payable		3,800
_____	**6.**	Insurance Expense	4,200	
		Prepaid Insurance		4,200

Exercise 4-4
Determining cost flows through accounts
P1

Determine the missing amounts in each of these four independent situations *a* through *d*:

	a	b	c	d
Supplies on hand—January 1	$ 300	$1,600	$1,360	?
Supplies purchased during the year	2,100	5,400	?	$6,000
Supplies on hand—December 31	750	?	1,840	800
Supplies expense for the year	?	1,300	9,600	6,575

Exercise 4-5
Adjusting and paying accrued expenses
P2

The following three situations require adjusting journal entries to prepare financial statements as of April 30. For each situation, present the adjusting entry and the entry that would be made to record the payment of the accrued liability during May.

a. The company has a $780,000 note payable that requires 0.8% interest to be paid each month on the 20th of the month. The interest was last paid on April 20 and the next payment is due on May 20.
b. The total weekly salaries expense for all employees is $9,000. This amount is paid at the end of the day on Friday of each week with five working days. April 30 falls on Tuesday of this year, which means that the employees had worked two days since the last payday. The next payday is May 3.
c. On April 1, the company retained an attorney at a flat monthly fee of $2,500. This amount is payable on the 12th of the following month.

Exercise 4-6
Assets and expenses for accrual and cash accounting
C3

On March 1, 1999, a company paid a $16,200 premium on a three-year insurance policy for protection beginning on that date. Fill in the blanks in the following table:

	Balance Sheet Asset under the:			Insurance Expense under the:	
	Accrual Basis	Cash Basis		Accrual Basis	Cash Basis
12/31/1999	$_______	$_______	1999	$_______	$_______
12/31/2000	_______	_______	2000	_______	_______
12/31/2001	_______	_______	2001	_______	_______
12/31/2002	_______	_______	2002	_______	_______
			Total	$_______	$_______

Exercise 4-7
Unearned and accrued revenues
P1, P2

Landmark Properties owns and operates an apartment building and prepares annual financial statements based on a March 31 fiscal year.

a. The tenants of one of the apartments paid five months' rent in advance on November 1, 1999. The rent is $1,500 per month. The journal entry credited the Unearned Rent account when the payment was received. No other entry had been recorded prior to March 31, 2000. Give the adjusting journal entry that should be recorded on March 31, 2000.

b. On January 1, 2000, the tenants of another apartment moved in and paid the first month's rent. The $1,350 payment was recorded with a credit to the Rent Earned account. However, the tenants have not paid the rent for February or March. They have agreed to pay it as soon as possible. Give the adjusting journal entry that should be recorded on March 31, 2000.

c. On April 2, 2000, the tenants described in part *b* paid $4,050 rent for February, March, and April. Give the journal entry to record the cash collection.

Exercise 4-8
Analyzing and preparing adjusting entries
A1, A2, P1, P2

Following are two income statements for Pemberton Company for the year ended December 31. The left column was prepared before any adjusting entries were recorded and the right column includes the effects of adjusting entries. The company records cash receipts and disbursements related to unearned and prepaid items in balance sheet accounts. Analyze the statements and prepare the adjusting entries that must have been recorded. Thirty percent of the $6,000 adjustment for Fees Earned was earned but not billed and the other 70% was earned by performing services that the customers had paid for in advance.

PEMBERTON CO.
Income Statements
For Year Ended December 31

	Before Adjustments	After Adjustments
Revenues:		
Fees earned	$24,000	$30,000
Commissions earned	42,500	42,500
Total revenues	$66,500	$72,500
Operating expenses:		
Depreciation expense, computers		$ 1,500
Depreciation expense, office furniture		1,750
Salaries expense	$12,500	14,950
Insurance expense		1,300
Rent expense	4,500	4,500
Office supplies expense		480
Advertising expense	3,000	3,000
Utilities expense	1,250	1,320
Total operating expenses	$21,250	$28,800
Net income	$45,250	$43,700

Exercise 4-9^A
Adjustments for prepaids recorded in expense and revenue accounts
P6

Classic Customs began operations on December 1. In setting up its accounting procedures, the company decided to debit expense accounts when the company prepays its expenses and to credit revenue accounts when customers pay for services in advance. Prepare journal entries for items *a* through *d* and adjusting entries as of December 31 for items *e* through *g*:

a. Supplies are purchased on December 1 for $3,000.
b. The company prepaid insurance premiums of $1,440 on December 2.
c. On December 15, the company receives an advance payment of $12,000 from a customer for remodeling work.
d. On December 28, the company receives $3,600 from a second customer for remodeling work to be performed in January.
e. By a physical count on December 31, Classic Customs determines that $1,920 of supplies are on hand.
f. An analysis of the insurance policies in effect on December 31 shows that $240 of insurance coverage had expired.
g. As of December 31, only one project is completed. The $6,300 fee for this project had been received in advance.

Exercise 4-10^A
Recording and reporting revenues received in advance
P6

Pavillion Company experienced the following events and transactions during July:

July	1	Received $2,000 in advance of performing work for Andrew Renking.
	6	Received $8,400 in advance of performing work for Matt Swarbuck.
	12	Completed the job for Andrew Renking.
	18	Received $7,500 in advance of performing work for Drew Sayer.
	27	Completed the job for Matt Swarbuck.
	31	The job for Drew Sayer is still unfinished.

a. Give journal entries (including any adjusting entry as of the end of the month) to record these events using the procedure of initially crediting the Unearned Fees account when payment is received from a customer in advance of performing services.
b. Give journal entries (including any adjusting entry as of the end of the month) to record these events using the procedure of initially crediting the Fees Earned account when payment is received from a customer in advance of performing services.
c. Under each method, determine the amount of earned fees reported on the income statement for July and the amount of unearned fees reported on the balance sheet as of July 31.

Exercise 4-11
Computing and interpreting profit margin
A2

Use the following information to calculate the profit margin for each unrelated company *a* through *e*:

	Net Income	Revenues
a.	$ 3,490	$ 31,620
b.	96,744	394,953
c.	110,204	252,786
d.	55,026	1,350,798
e.	79,264	433,914

Which of the five companies is the most profitable according to the profit margin ratio? Interpret the profit margin ratio of the most profitable company.

Problems

Problem 4-1
Adjusting and subsequent journal entries
A1, P1, P2, P5

Garza Company's annual accounting period ends on December 31, 2002. Garza follows the practice of recording prepaid expenses and unearned revenues in balance sheet accounts. The following information concerns the adjusting entries to be recorded as of that date:

a. The Office Supplies account started the year with a $3,000 balance. During 2002, the company purchased supplies at a cost of $12,400, which was added to the Office Supplies account. The inventory of supplies on hand at December 31 had a cost of $2,640.

b. An analysis of the company's insurance policies provided these facts:

Policy	Date of Purchase	Years of Coverage	Total Cost
1	April 1, 2001	2	$15,840
2	April 1, 2002	3	13,068
3	August 1, 2002	1	2,700

The total premium for each policy was paid in full at the purchase date, and the Prepaid Insurance account was debited for the full cost.

c. The company has 15 employees who earn a total of $2,100 in salaries for every working day. They are paid each Monday for their work in the five-day workweek ending on the previous Friday. December 31, 2002, falls on Tuesday, and all 15 employees worked the first two days of the week. Because New Year's Day is a paid holiday, they will be paid salaries for five full days on Monday, January 6, 2003.

d. The company purchased a building on August 1, 2002. The building cost $855,000 and is expected to have a $45,000 salvage value at the end of its predicted 30-year life.

e. Because the company is not large enough to occupy the entire building, it arranged to rent some space to a tenant at $2,400 per month, starting on November 1, 2002. The rent was paid on time on November 1, and the amount received was credited to the Rent Earned account. However, the tenant has not paid the December rent. The company has worked out an agreement with the tenant, who has promised to pay both December's and January's rent in full on January 15. The tenant has agreed not to fall behind again.

f. On November 1, the company rented space to another tenant for $2,175 per month. The tenant paid five months' rent in advance on that date. The payment was recorded with a credit to the Unearned Rent account.

Required

1. Use the information to prepare adjusting entries as of December 31, 2002.

2. Prepare journal entries to record the first subsequent cash transactions for parts *c* and *e*.

Check Figure Insurance expense, $12,312

Problem 4-2
Adjusting entries, financial statements, and profit margin
P1, P2, P4, A1, A2

Southwest Careers, a school owned by S. Carr, provides training to individuals who pay tuition directly to the school. The school also offers training to groups in off-site locations. The school's unadjusted trial balance as of December 31, 1999 follows. Southwest Careers follows the practice of initially recording prepaid expenses and unearned revenues in balance sheet accounts. Items that require adjusting entries on December 31, 1999, are shown after the trial balance.

SOUTHWEST CAREERS Unadjusted Trial Balance December 31, 1999		
Cash	$ 26,000	
Accounts receivable		
Teaching supplies	10,000	
Prepaid insurance	15,000	
Prepaid rent	2,000	
Professional library	30,000	
Accumulated depreciation—Professional library		$ 9,000
Equipment	70,000	
Accumulated depreciation—Equipment		16,000
Accounts payable		36,000
Salaries payable		
Unearned training fees		11,000
S. Carr, capital		63,600
S. Carr, withdrawals	40,000	
Tuition fees earned		102,000
Training fees earned		38,000
Depreciation expense—Equipment		
Depreciation expense—Professional library		
Salaries expense	48,000	
Insurance expense		
Rent expense	22,000	
Teaching supplies expense		
Advertising expense	7,000	
Utilities expense	5,600	
Totals	$275,600	$275,600

Additional Items

a. An analysis of the company's insurance policies shows that $3,000 of coverage has expired.

b. An inventory shows that teaching supplies costing $2,600 are on hand at the end of the year.

c. Annual depreciation on the equipment is $12,000.

d. Annual depreciation on the professional library is $6,000.

e. On November 1, the company agreed to do a special six-month course for a client. The contract calls for a monthly fee of $2,200, and the client paid the first five months' fees in advance. When the cash was received, the Unearned Training Fees account was credited.

f. On October 15, the school agreed to teach a four-month class for an individual for $3,000 tuition per month payable at the end of the class. The services are being provided as agreed, and no payment has been received.

g. The school's two employees are paid weekly. As of the end of the year, two days' wages have accrued at the rate of $100 per day for each employee.

h. The balance in the Prepaid Rent account represents rent for December.

Required

1. Prepare T-accounts with the balances listed from the unadjusted trial balance.

2. Prepare adjusting journal entries for items *a* through *h* and post them to the T-accounts.

3. Update the balances in T-accounts for the adjusting entries and prepare an adjusted trial balance.

4. Prepare Southwest Careers' income statement and statement of changes in owner's equity for 1999 and prepare its balance sheet as of December 31, 1999.

5. Calculate the company's profit margin for the year.

Check Figure Ending owner's equity, $62,100

Problem 4-3B
Interpreting unadjusted and adjusted trial balances, preparing financial statements, and calculating profit margin

P1, P2, P4, A1, A2

A six-column table for RPE Company is shown below. The first two columns contain the unadjusted trial balance for the company as of July 31, 1999. The last two columns contain the adjusted trial balance as of the same date.

	Unadjusted Trial Balance		Adjustments		Adjusted Trial Balance	
Cash	$ 27,000				$ 27,000	
Accounts receivable	12,000				22,460	
Office supplies	18,000				3,000	
Prepaid insurance	7,320				4,880	
Office equipment	92,000				92,000	
Accum. depreciation— Office equipment		$12,000				$18,000
Accounts payable		9,300				10,200
Interest payable						800
Salaries payable						6,600
Unearned consulting fees		16,000				14,300
Long-term notes payable		44,000				44,000
R. P. Edds, capital		28,420				28,420
R. P. Edds, withdrawals	10,000				10,000	
Consulting fees earned		156,000				168,160
Depreciation expense— Office equipment					6,000	
Salaries expense	71,000				77,600	
Interest expense	1,400				2,200	
Insurance expense					2,440	
Rent expense	13,200				13,200	
Office supplies expense					15,000	
Advertising expense	13,800				14,7000	
Totals	$265,720	$265,720			$290,480	$290,480

Required

Preparation Component

1. Prepare this company's income statement and its statement of changes in owner's equity for the year ended July 31, 1999.

2. Prepare the company's balance sheet as of July 31, 1999.

3. Calculate the company's profit margin for the year.

Check Figure Profit margin, 22%

Analysis Component

4. Analyze the differences between the unadjusted and adjusted trial balances to determine the adjustments that must have been made. Show the results of your analysis by inserting amounts from the adjusting journal entries that must have been recorded by the company in the two middle columns. Label each entry with a letter, and provide a short description of the purpose for recording it.

Problem 4-4
Computing accrual income from cash income
C3

The records for Urban Landscape Co. are kept on the cash basis instead of the accrual basis. But the company is now applying for a loan and the bank wants to know what its net income for year 2000 is under generally accepted accounting principles. Here is the income statement for year 2000 under the cash basis:

URBAN LANDSCAPE CO. Income Statement (Cash Basis) For Year Ended December 31, 2000	
Revenues	$525,000
Expenses	330,000
Net income	$195,000

Additional information was gathered to help convert the income statement to the accrual basis:

	As of 12/31/1999	As of 12/31/2000
Accrued revenues	$12,000	$16,500
Unearned revenues	66,000	21,000
Accrued expenses	14,700	9,000
Prepaid expenses	27,000	20,700

All prepaid expenses from the beginning of the year are consumed or expired, all unearned revenues from the beginning of the year are earned, and all accrued expenses and revenues from the beginning of the year are paid or collected.

Required

Prepare an accrual basis income statement for this company for year 2000. Provide schedules that explain how you converted from cash revenues and expenses to accrual revenues and expenses.

Check Figure Net Income, $243,900

Problem 4-5
Identifying adjusting and subsequent entries
C4, P5

For these adjusting and transaction entries, enter the letter of the explanation that most closely describes the adjustment or transaction in the space beside each entry. (You can use letters more than once.)

a. To record receipt of unearned revenue.
b. To record the earning of previously unearned revenue.
c. To record payment of an accrued expense.
d. To record receipt of an accrued revenue.
e. To record an accrued expense.
f. To record an accrued revenue.
g. To record this period's use of a prepaid expense.
h. To record payment of a prepaid expense.
i. To record this period's depreciation expense.

_____	**1.**	Depreciation Expense	3,000	
		Accumulated Depreciation		3,000
_____	**2.**	Unearned Professional Fees	2,000	
		Professional Fees Earned		2,000
_____	**3.**	Rent Expense	1,000	
		Prepaid Rent		1,000
_____	**4.**	Interest Expense	4,000	
		Interest Payable		4,000

____ 5.	Prepaid Rent	3,500	
	Cash		3,500
____ 6.	Salaries Expense	5,000	
	Salaries Payable		5,000
____ 7.	Insurance Expense	6,000	
	Prepaid Insurance		6,000
____ 8.	Salaries Payable	1,500	
	Cash		1,500
____ 9.	Cash	6,500	
	Unearned Professional Fees		6,500
____ 10.	Cash	9,000	
	Interest Receivable		9,000
____ 11.	Interest Receivable	7,000	
	Interest Earned		7,000
____ 12.	Cash	8,000	
	Accounts Receivable		8,000

Problem 4-6
Preparing financial statements from the adjusted trial balance and calculating profit margin
P4, A1, A2

The adjusted trial balance below is for Conquest Company as of December 31, 2000:

	Debit	Credit
Cash	$ 22,000	
Accounts receivable	44,000	
Interest receivable	10,000	
Notes receivable (due in 90 days)	160,000	
Office supplies	8,000	
Automobiles	160,000	
Accumulated depreciation—Automobiles		$ 42,000
Equipment	130,000	
Accumulated depreciation—Equipment		10,000
Land	70,000	
Accounts payable		88,000
Interest payable		12,000
Salaries payable		11,000
Unearned fees		22,000
Long-term notes payable		130,000
J. Conroe, capital		247,800
J. Conroe, withdrawals	38,000	
Fees earned		420,000
Interest earned		16,000
Depreciation expense—Automobiles	18,000	
Depreciation expense—Equipment	10,000	
Salaries expense	180,000	
Wages expense	32,000	
Interest expense	24,000	
Office supplies expense	26,000	
Advertising expense	50,000	
Repairs expense—Automobiles	16,800	
Total	$998,800	$998,800

Check Figure Total assets, $552,000

Required

1. Use the information in the trial balance to prepare *(a)* the income statement for the year ended December 31, 2000; *(b)* the statement of changes in owner's equity for the year ended December 31, 2000; and *(c)* the balance sheet as of December 31, 2000.
2. Assume that the value of J. Conroe's services as owner are valued at $30,000 for the year. Calculate the modified profit margin for year 2000.

Problem 4-7[A]

Recording prepaid expenses and unearned revenues

P1, P2, P6

Trex Company had the following transactions in the last two months of its fiscal year ended December 31:

Nov.	1	Paid $1,500 for future newspaper advertising.
	1	Paid $2,160 for insurance through October 31 of the following year.
	30	Received $3,300 for future services to be provided to a customer.
Dec.	1	Paid $2,700 for the services of a consultant, to be received over the next three months.
	15	Received $7,650 for future services to be provided to a customer.
	31	Of the advertising paid for on November 1, $900 worth had not yet been published by the newspaper.
	31	Part of the insurance paid for on November 1 had expired.
	31	Services worth $1,200 had not yet been provided to the customer who paid on November 30.
	31	One-third of the consulting services paid for on December 1 had been received.
	31	The company has performed $3,000 of services that the customer paid for on December 15.

Required

Preparation Component

1. Prepare entries for the above transactions under the method that records prepaid expenses as assets and records unearned revenues as liabilities. Also, prepare adjusting entries at the end of the year.
2. Prepare entries for the above transactions under the method that records prepaid expenses as expenses and records unearned revenues as revenues. Also, prepare adjusting entries at the end of the year.

Analysis Component

3. Explain why the alternative sets of entries in requirements 1 and 2 do not result in different financial statement amounts.

Serial Problem

Echo Systems

(This serial problem involving Echo Systems was introduced in Chapter 3 and continues in Chapters 5 and 6. If the Chapter 3 segment has not been completed, the assignment can begin at this point. You need to use the facts presented for the serial problem at the end of Chapter 3. Because of its length, this problem is best solved if you use the Working Papers that accompany this book.)

After the success of its first two months, Mary Graham decides to continue operating Echo Systems. (Transactions that occurred in these first two months are described in Chapter 3.) On December 1, Graham adds these new accounts to the chart of accounts for the ledger:

Account	No.
Accumulated Depreciation—Office Equipment	164
Accumulated Depreciation—Computer Equipment	168
Wages Payable	210
Unearned Computer Services Revenue	236
Depreciation Expense—Office Equipment	612
Depreciation Expense—Computer Equipment	613
Insurance Expense	637
Rent Expense	640
Computer Supplies Expense	652

Required

1. Prepare journal entries to record each of the following transactions for Echo Systems. Post entries to the accounts in the ledger.
2. Prepare adjusting entries to record the transactions and events described on December 31. Post these entries to the accounts in the ledger.
3. Prepare an adjusted trial balance as of December 31, 2000.
4. Prepare an income statement for the three months ended December 31, 2000.
5. Prepare a statement of changes in owner's equity for the three months ended December 31, 2000.
6. Prepare a balance sheet as of December 31, 2000.

Transactions and other information:

Dec.	2	Paid $1,050 to Lakeshore Mall for Echo Systems' share of mall advertising costs.
	3	Paid $600 to repair the company's computer.
	4	Received $3,750 from Alamo Engineering Co. for the receivable from the prior month.
	10	Paid Carly Smith for six days' work at the rate of $100 per day.
	14	Notified by Alamo Engineering Co. that Echo's bid of $6,000 on a proposed project was accepted. Alamo paid an advance of $1,500.
	15	Purchased $1,155 of computer supplies on credit from Abbott Office Products.
	16	Sent a reminder to Fostek Co. to pay the fee for services originally recorded on November 8.
	20	Completed project for Elite Corporation and received $5,625 cash.
	22–26	Took the week off for the holidays.
	28	Received $2,850 from Fostek Co. on their receivable.
	29	Reimbursed Mary Graham's business automobile mileage of 600 miles at $0.25 per mile.
	31	Mary Graham withdrew $1,800 cash from the business.
	31	The following *additional facts* were collected for use in adjusting entries prior to preparing financial statements for the company's first three months:

Additional Facts

a. The December 31 inventory of computer supplies was $720.
b. Three months have passed since the annual insurance premium was paid.
c. As of the end of the year, Carly Smith has not been paid for four days of work at the rate of $100 per day.
d. The computer is expected to have a four-year life with no salvage value.
e. The office equipment is expected to have a three-year life with no salvage value.
f. Prepaid rent for three of the four months has expired.

BEYOND THE NUMBERS

Reporting in Action

C4, A1, A2

Refer to the financial statements and related information for **NIKE** in Appendix A. Answer the following questions by analyzing the NIKE information:

1. What are the major items making up NIKE's prepaid expenses?
2. What is the total amount recorded as property, plant, and equipment and what is the amount of accumulated depreciation as of May 31, 1997? How do these totals compare to May 31, 1996?
3. What is NIKE's profit margin for 1997 and 1996?

Swoosh Ahead

4. Obtain access to NIKE's annual report for fiscal years ending after May 31, 1997. You can gain access to NIKE's annual report at its web site **[www.nike.com]** or through the SEC's EDGAR database **[www.sec.gov].** Compare the May 31, 1997, fiscal year profit margin to any subsequent year's profit margin that you are able to calculate. Also compare how NIKE's net amount of property, plant, and equipment has changed since May 31, 1997.

Comparative Analysis

A2

Both **NIKE** and **Reebok** design, produce, market, and sell sports footwear and apparel. Key comparative figures ($ millions) for these two organizations follow:

Key figures*	NIKE		Reebok	
	1997	1996	1996	1995
Net income	$ 796	$ 553	$ 139	$ 165
Net sales	$9,187	$6,471	$3,479	$3,481

*NIKE figures are from its annual reports for fiscal years ended May 31,1997 and 1996.
Reebok figures are from its annual reports for fiscal years ended December 31, 1996 and 1995.

Required

1. Compute profit margins for (a) NIKE and (b) Reebok for the two years of data shown above.
2. Which company is more successful on the basis of profit margin?
3. For each company write the following sentence: For every one dollar of sales generated (insert NIKE or Reebok) makes an average profit of _______ cents.
4. Would it be appropriate to calculate the modified profit margin for NIKE or Reebok?

Ethics Challenge

A1

Jackie Houston is a new accountant for Seitzer company. She is learning on the job from Bob Welch, who already has worked several years for Seitzer. Jackie and Bob are preparing adjusting journal entries in anticipation of producing annual financial statements. Jackie has calculated depreciation expense for the fiscal year and records it as:

Depreciation Expense—Equipment	$123,546	
Accumulated Depreciation—Equipment . .		$123,546

Bob is rechecking the numbers and says he agrees with her computation. But he says the credit entry should be directly to the equipment account. He argues that while accumulated depreciation is taught in the classroom, "it is a lot less hassle not to use a contra account and just credit the equipment account directly for the annual allocation of depreciation. And, besides, the balance sheet shows the same amount for total assets under both methods."

Required:

1. How should depreciation be recorded? Do you support Jackie or Bob?
2. Evaluate the strengths and weaknesses of Bob's reasons for preferring his method.
3. Indicate whether the situation faced by Jackie is an ethical problem.

Communicating in Practice

C1, C2, A1

Failure to apply accounting principles properly can have significant influence on reported profits as well as on the success or failure of a business. Obtain a copy of the article "KnowledgeWare Accounting Practices Are Questioned," by Timothy O'Brien, ***The Wall Street Journal,*** September 7, 1994. Read the article and write a summary that includes the following:

1. Identification of the specific accounting principle that this article discusses and an explanation of what this principle requires and prohibits.
2. A description of the accounting practice for **KnowledgeWare** that is questioned in the article.
3. Identification of who has the authority to investigate the challenged practices.
4. Identification of the stakeholders in this case and possible consequences of the questioned accounting practice.
5. An explanation of how this relates to the material in this chapter.

Taking It to the Net

C1, A2

Access the **Cannondale** promotional Web site at http://www.cannondale.com. Visit several hotlinks on the site to get a feel for the company's products.

1. What is the primary product that Cannondale sells?
2. Review the Cannondale 10K—this is the annual financial data required by the SEC. You can access this from the SEC's Edgar system (see this book's Web page). (Hint: Edgar Web site lists numerous recent reports filed with the SEC; click on the one labeled 10K. You will need to scroll down in the 10K report to find the financial statements.)

a. What is the fiscal year-end of Cannondale? Does it appear that Cannondale uses a 12-month or 52-week annual reporting period?

b. What are net sales for Cannondale for the annual accounting period ended June 29, 1996?

c. What is net income for Cannondale for the annual accounting period ended June 29, 1996?

d. Compute profit margin for Cannondale for the annual accounting period ended June 29, 1996.

e. Why do you think Cannondale is employing a fiscal year-end of late June or early July? Does it relate to their natural business year?

Teamwork in Action

C4, A1

Each member of a team will have the responsibility to become a resident expert on a specific type of accounting adjustment. This expertise will be used to facilitate their teammates' understanding of the concepts relevant to the adjustments process and that specific adjustment. Follow the procedures below:

1. Refer to Exhibit 4.20. Each team member is to select their area of expertise by choosing one type of adjustment listed in the exhibit. You have approximately two minutes to make your choices.

2. Learning teams are to disburse and expert teams are to be formed. Expert teams are made up of students who have selected the same area of expertise. The instructor will identify the location where each expert team will meet.

3. Expert teams will collaborate to develop a presentation of items *a–e* listed below. Students must write up the presentations in a format they can show to their learning teams.

   a. A specific example (with amounts and dates) of a transaction or event requiring adjustment.

   b. The adjusting journal entry for this example with posting as illustrated in T-accounts.

   c. Identification and description of the relevant accounting principle bearing on the example.

   d. Description of what the post-adjustment account balances reflect, and identification of the statement(s) these balances are reported on.

   e. Explanation of how failure to make adjustments affects financial statements.

4. Regroup to original teams. In rotation, experts make the presentations developed in (3) to their own team members. Experts are to encourage and respond to questions.

Hitting the Road

C1

Pair up with a classmate. Visit the business area of your community or a shopping mall. Identify 10 businesses that operate in the area. Try to construct your list so that it contains a mix of retail and service businesses. Predict whether the companies operate on a 12-month fiscal period that coincides with the calendar year-end or whether they use a natural business fiscal year. Visit each shop in turn, introduce yourself to the employee you are visiting, and try to confirm whether you made a correct determination of the fiscal year-end for the store. In some instances, the personnel available for questioning may not know the answer to your question. If you cannot confirm the answer, thank the employee and note that you could not test your prediction of fiscal year-end. After the visits are complete, compute the percent of fiscal year-ends that you correctly anticipated.

Business Week Activity

A2

Read the short article, "Porsche is back—and then some," in the September 15, 1997, issue of ***Business Week***.

Required

1. Contrast the profitability of **Porsche** in 1992 to five years later in 1997.

2. When does Porsche's fiscal year end?

3. What is the amount of sales for Porsche in the 1997 fiscal year?

4. Calculate Porsche's profit margin for the 1997 fiscal year.

5. Despite its recent profitability, what does the article identify as Porsche's weaknesses?

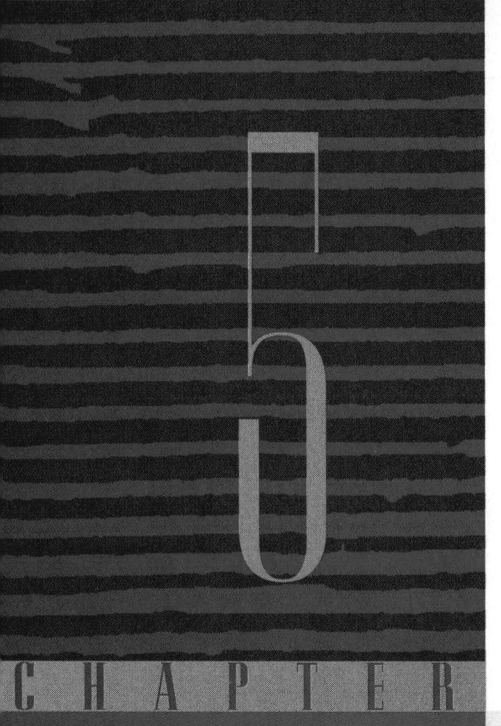

CHAPTER 5

Completing the Accounting Cycle

A Look Back

Chapter 4 explained the timing of reports. We described why adjusting accounts is important for recognizing revenues and expenses in the proper period. We explained how to prepare an adjusted trial balance and use it in preparing financial statements.

A Look at This Chapter

This chapter emphasizes the final steps in the accounting process and reviews the entire accounting cycle. We explain the closing process, including accounting procedures and the use of a post-closing trial balance. We describe a work sheet and other tools that help in the preparation of financial statements. A classified balance sheet and its usefulness as a tool in analyzing information are explained.

A Look Ahead

Chapter 6 looks at accounting for merchandising activities. We describe the sale and purchase of merchandise and its implications for preparing and analyzing financial statements.

Chapter Outline

Accounting Edge

Washington, DC—Janet Wittes wasn't trying to jump on the latest management bandwagon. But when she founded **Statistics Collaborative** in 1993 to analyze clinical trials of drug companies, her son did her company's accounting. When demand for her services grew—and her son went off to become a journalist—Wittes knew she needed outside accounting help. She lacked work sheets, financial reports, and other tools needed for business decisions. "I realized how little I knew—like not even knowing how to bill clients or pay salaries," said Wittes.

For support, Wittes turned her books over to a local firm called **BusinessMatters.** The firm took care of her basic accounting needs, but it also told her something that shocked her. She was consistently underestimating her expenses—sometimes by as much as 75%. Today, BusinessMatters is not only keeping Wittes' books, it is helping with strategic analyses. Wittes says her profits have doubled since she started using accounting information.

Wittes relies on outsourcing, contracting out accounting services she once did in-house. More business owners are using outsourcing as a strategic tool. Instead of simply looking for cost savings, they seek accounting services at a higher quality than they can do themselves. Providers review every part of the accounting cycle using work sheets and other tools such as what-if and ratio analyses.

A recent survey of executives showed the top two reasons for outsourcing are to improve company focus and reach company potential. Effectively managing data and preparing classified financial reports are important steps in achieving these goals. Coopers & Lybrand found companies that effectively used these services had 22% more revenues than those that didn't and also greater profit margins and cash flows.

Accounting is the gold mine of outsourcers. They look for ways companies can better manage and analyze financial data. The surprise is they tackle tasks with tools readily available to us. The tasks include payroll, recordkeeping, statement preparation, and computing. They now are experimenting with inventory, pensions, and sales—even customer service. There are enormous accounting opportunities for graduates in managing and analyzing data. As one consultant put it, "I have data everywhere but not a drop of information." Work sheets and other analysis tools are one remedy. [Source: *Business Week,* May 13, 1996]

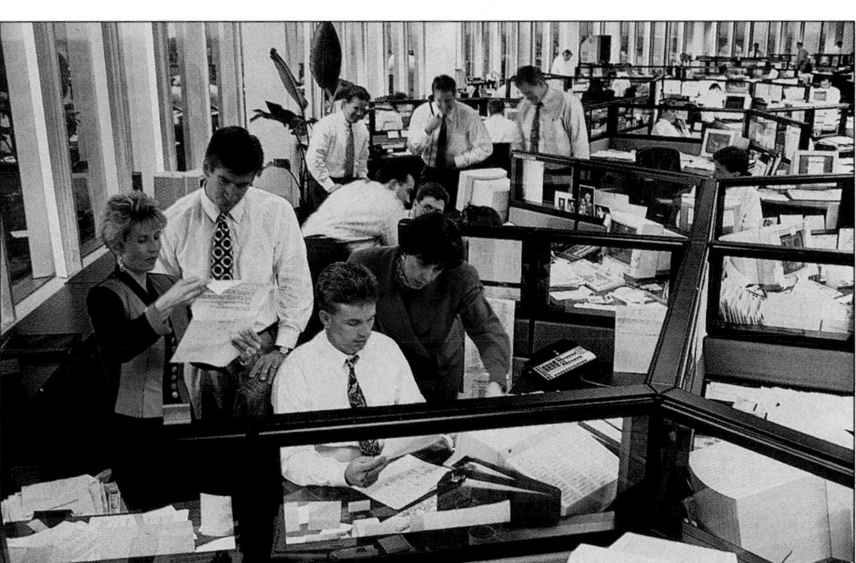

Learning Objectives

Conceptual

C1 Explain why temporary accounts are closed each period.

C2 Identify steps in the accounting cycle.

C3 Explain and prepare a classified balance sheet.

Analytical

A1 Compute the current ratio and describe what it reveals about a company's financial condition.

Procedural

P1 Describe and prepare closing entries.

P2 Explain and prepare a post-closing trial balance.

P3 Prepare a work sheet and explain its usefulness.

HAPTER PREVIEW

Financial statement preparation is a major purpose of accounting. Many of the important steps leading to financial statements are explained in earlier chapters. We described how transactions and events are analyzed, journalized, and posted. We also described important adjustments that are often necessary to properly reflect revenues when earned and expenses when incurred.

This chapter describes the final steps in the accounting process leading to financial statements. It includes the closing process that prepares revenue, expense, and withdrawal accounts for the next reporting period and updates the owner's capital account. A work sheet is shown as a useful tool in preparing financial statements. We explain how accounts are classified on a balance sheet to give more useful information to decision makers. We also describe the current ratio and explain how it is used by decision makers to assess a company's ability to pay its liabilities in the near future. These tools for managing and analyzing data are the kind Janet Wittes refers to in the opening article. Such tools improve their decision making.

Closing Process

C1 Explain why temporary accounts are closed each period.

The **closing process** is an important step at the end of an accounting period. It prepares accounts for recording the transactions and events of the *next* period. In the closing process we must:

1. Identify accounts for closing.
2. Record and post the closing entries.
3. Prepare a post-closing trial balance.

The purpose of the closing process is twofold. First, it resets revenue, expense, and withdrawal account balances to zero at the end of every period. This is done so that these accounts can measure income and withdrawal amounts for the next period. This is important if we wish to know how a company performs during a period of time. Second, it helps in summarizing a period's revenues and expenses. We use an Income Summary account for this purpose. This section explains the three steps in the closing process.

Temporary and Permanent Accounts

Temporary Accounts

Revenues
Expenses
Withdrawals
Income Summary

Temporary, or **nominal, accounts** accumulate data related to one accounting period. They include all income statement accounts, withdrawal accounts, and Income Summary. They are temporary because the accounts are opened at the beginning of a period, used to record events for that period, and then closed at the end of the period. They are nominal because the accounts describe events or changes that have occurred rather than conditions that exist at the end of the period. *The closing process applies only to temporary accounts.*

Permanent Accounts

Assets
Liabilities
Owner's Capital

Permanent, or **real, accounts** report on activities related to one or more future accounting periods. They carry their ending balances into the next period and include all balance sheet accounts. Asset, liability, and owner's equity accounts are not closed as long as a company continues to own the assets, owe the liabilities, and have owner's equity. They are real because they describe existing conditions.

Recording and Posting Closing Entries

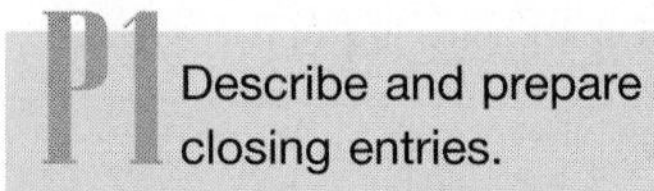
P1
Describe and prepare closing entries.

Recording and posting **closing entries** is to transfer the end-of-period balances in revenue, expense, and withdrawal accounts to the permanent owner's capital account. Closing entries are a necessary step at the end of a period after financial statements are prepared because:

- Revenue, expense, and withdrawal accounts must begin the next period with zero balances.

- The owner's capital account must reflect (a) increases from revenues and (b) decreases from both expenses and withdrawals.

An income statement aims to report revenues earned and expenses incurred during one accounting period. It is prepared from information recorded in revenue and expense accounts. The statement of changes in owner's equity aims to report changes in the owner's capital account during one period. It uses information on revenues and expenses along with amounts accumulated in the withdrawal account. Because revenue, expense, and withdrawal accounts accumulate information for only one period, they must start each period with zero balances.

To close revenue and expense accounts, we transfer their balances first to an account called Income Summary. **Income Summary** is a temporary account that contains a credit for the sum of all revenues and a debit for the sum of all expenses. Its balance equals net income or net loss and is transferred to the owner's capital account. We then transfer the withdrawal account balance to the owner's capital account. After these closing entries are posted, the revenue, expense, Income Summary, and withdrawal accounts have zero balances. These accounts are then said to be *closed* or *cleared.* This process is illustrated in Exhibit 5.1.

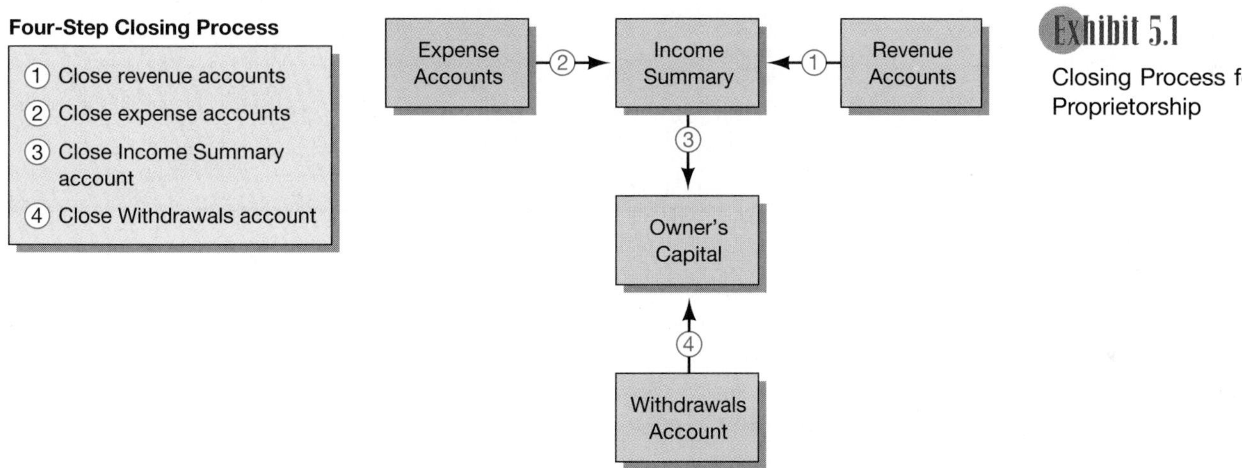

Exhibit 5.1

Closing Process for a Proprietorship

FastForward's adjusted trial balance on December 31, 1997, is shown in Exhibit 5.2. Exhibit 5.3 uses the adjusted account balances from Exhibit 5.2 to show the four types of entries necessary to close FastForward's revenue, expense, Income Summary, and withdrawal accounts. We explain each of these four types.

Step 1: Close Credit Balances in Revenue Accounts to Income Summary

The first closing entry transfers credit balances in revenue accounts to the Income Summary account. We get accounts with credit balances to zero by debiting them. For FastForward, this journal entry is:

Dec. 31	Consulting Revenue	5,850	
	Rental Revenue	300	
	Income Summary		6,150
	To close revenue accounts.		

This entry closes revenue accounts and leaves them with zero balances. They are now ready to record new revenues for the next period.

The Income Summary account is created and used only for the closing process. The current $6,150 credit balance in Income Summary equals total revenues for the period.

Exhibit 5.2

Adjusted Trial Balance

FASTFORWARD
Adjusted Trial Balance
December 31, 1997

Cash	$ 7,950	
Accounts receivable	1,800	
Supplies	2,670	
Prepaid insurance	2,300	
Equipment	26,000	
Accumulated depreciation—Equipment		$ 375
Accounts payable		1,100
Salaries payable		210
Unearned consulting revenue		2,750
Note payable		5,100
Chuck Taylor, capital		30,000
Chuck Taylor, withdrawals	600	
Consulting revenue		5,850
Rental revenue		300
Depreciation expense—Equipment	375	
Salaries expense	1,610	
Insurance expense	100	
Rent expense	1,000	
Supplies expense	1,050	
Utilities expense	230	
Totals	$45,685	$45,685

Exhibit 5.3

Closing entries for FastForward

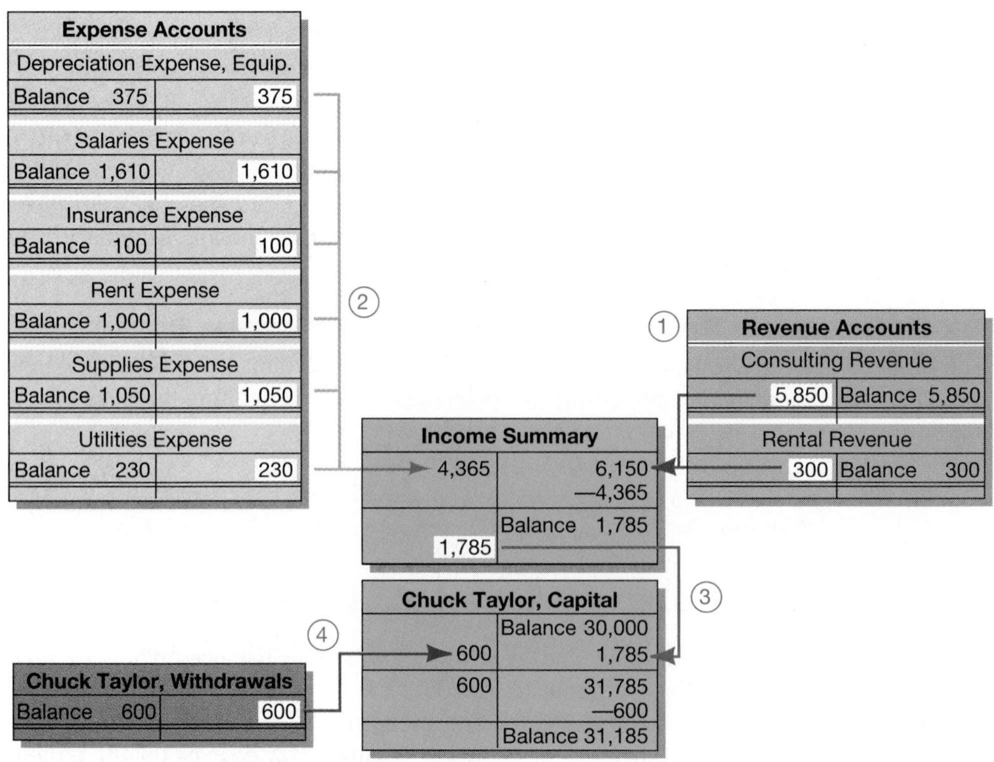

Step 2: Close Debit Balances in Expense Accounts to Income Summary

The second closing entry transfers debit balances in expense accounts to the Income Summary account. This step gathers all the expense account debit balances in the Income Summary account. We get expense accounts' debit balances to zero by crediting them. This allows these accounts to accumulate a record of new expenses in the next period. This second closing entry for FastForward is:

Dec. 31	Income Summary	4,365	
	Depreciation Expense—Equipment		375
	Salaries Expense		1,610
	Insurance Expense		100
	Rent Expense		1,000
	Supplies Expense		1,050
	Utilities Expense		230
	To close expense accounts.		

Exhibit 5.3 shows that posting this entry gives each expense account a zero balance. This prepares each account for expense entries for the next period. The entry makes the balance of Income Summary equal to December's net income of $1,785. All debit and credit balances related to expense and revenue accounts have now been collected in the Income Summary account as shown in Exhibit 5.4.

Income Summary	
4,365	6,150

Exhibit 5.4

Income Summary after Closing Revenue and Expense Accounts

Step 3: Close Income Summary to Owner's Capital

The third closing entry transfers the balance of the Income Summary account to the owner's capital account. This entry closes the Income Summary account and adds the company's net income to the owner's capital account:

Dec. 31	Income Summary	1,785	
	Chuck Taylor, Capital		1,785
	To close the Income Summary account.		

The Income Summary account has a zero balance after posting this entry. It continues to have a zero balance until the closing process occurs at the end of the next period. The owner's capital account has now been increased by the amount of net income. Because the normal balance of owner's capital is a credit, increases to owner's capital from net income are credits.

Step 4: Close Withdrawals Account to Owner's Capital

The fourth closing entry transfers any debit balance in the withdrawals account to the owner's capital account. This entry for FastForward is:

Dec. 31	Chuck Taylor, Capital	600	
	Chuck Taylor, Withdrawals		600
	To close the withdrawals account.		

This entry gives the withdrawals account a zero balance, and the account is ready to accumulate next period's payments to owner. This entry also reduces the capital account balance to the $31,185 amount reported on the balance sheet.

Sources of Closing Entry Information

We can identify the accounts needing to be closed and the amounts in the closing entries by looking to individual revenue, expense, and withdrawal accounts in the ledger.

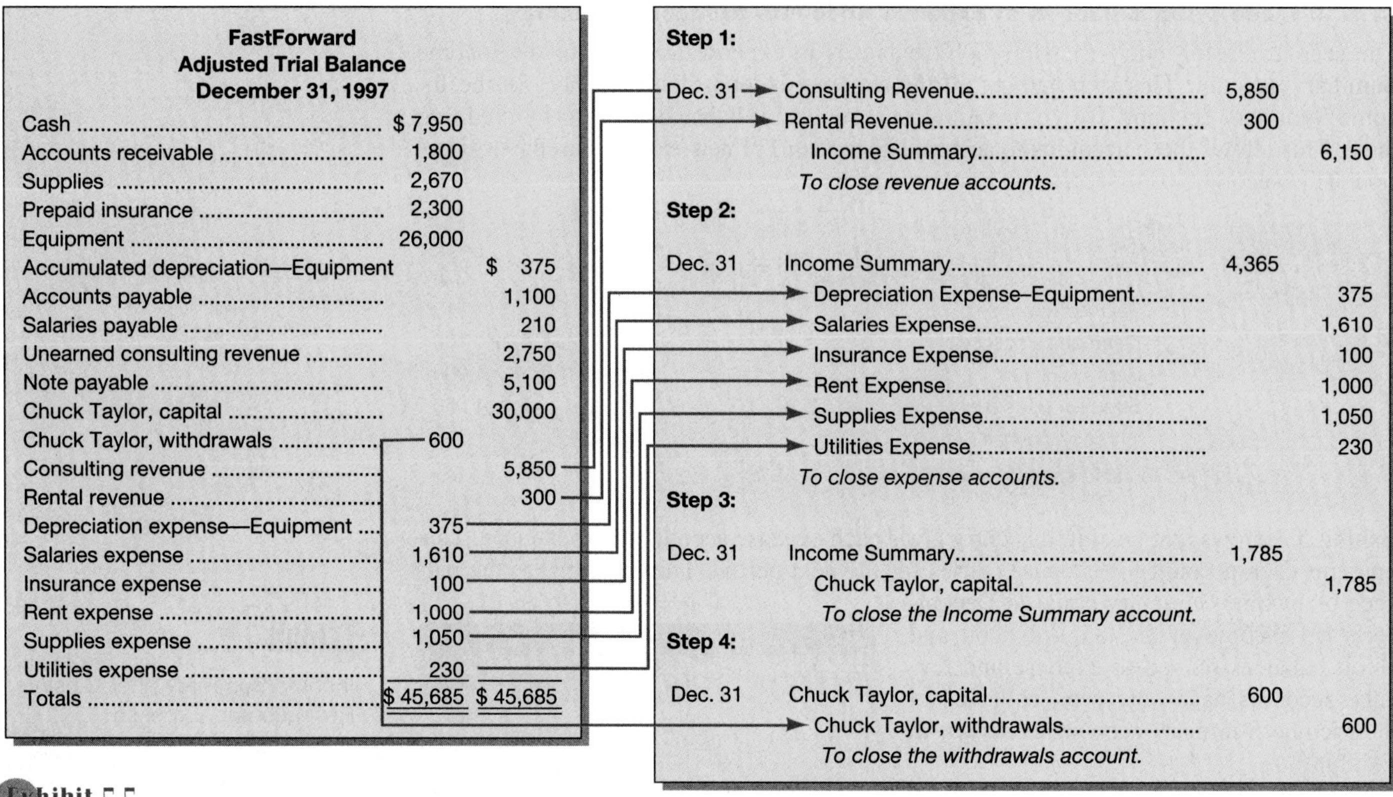

FastForward
Adjusted Trial Balance
December 31, 1997

Account	Debit	Credit
Cash	$ 7,950	
Accounts receivable	1,800	
Supplies	2,670	
Prepaid insurance	2,300	
Equipment	26,000	
Accumulated depreciation—Equipment		$ 375
Accounts payable		1,100
Salaries payable		210
Unearned consulting revenue		2,750
Note payable		5,100
Chuck Taylor, capital		30,000
Chuck Taylor, withdrawals	600	
Consulting revenue		5,850
Rental revenue		300
Depreciation expense—Equipment	375	
Salaries expense	1,610	
Insurance expense	100	
Rent expense	1,000	
Supplies expense	1,050	
Utilities expense	230	
Totals	$ 45,685	$ 45,685

Date	Account	Debit	Credit
Step 1:			
Dec. 31	Consulting Revenue	5,850	
	Rental Revenue	300	
	Income Summary		6,150
	To close revenue accounts.		
Step 2:			
Dec. 31	Income Summary	4,365	
	Depreciation Expense–Equipment		375
	Salaries Expense		1,610
	Insurance Expense		100
	Rent Expense		1,000
	Supplies Expense		1,050
	Utilities Expense		230
	To close expense accounts.		
Step 3:			
Dec. 31	Income Summary	1,785	
	Chuck Taylor, capital		1,785
	To close the Income Summary account.		
Step 4:			
Dec. 31	Chuck Taylor, capital	600	
	Chuck Taylor, withdrawals		600
	To close the withdrawals account.		

Exhibit 5.5

Preparing Closing Entries from an Adjusted Trial Balance

If we prepare an adjusted trial balance after the adjusting process, the information for closing entries is easily taken from the trial balance. This is illustrated in Exhibit 5.5 where we show how to prepare closing entries using only the adjusted trial balance.

We are not usually able to make all adjusting and closing entries on the last day of each period. This is because information about certain transactions and events that require adjusting is not always available until several days or even weeks later. This means that some adjusting and closing entries are recorded later but dated as of the last day of the period.

One example is a company that receives a utility bill on January 14 for costs incurred for the month of December. When the bill is received, the company records the expense and the payable as of December 31. Other examples include long-distance phone usage and costs of many Web billings. The income statement for December reflects these additional expenses incurred and the December 31 balance sheet includes these payables even though the amounts are not actually known on December 31.

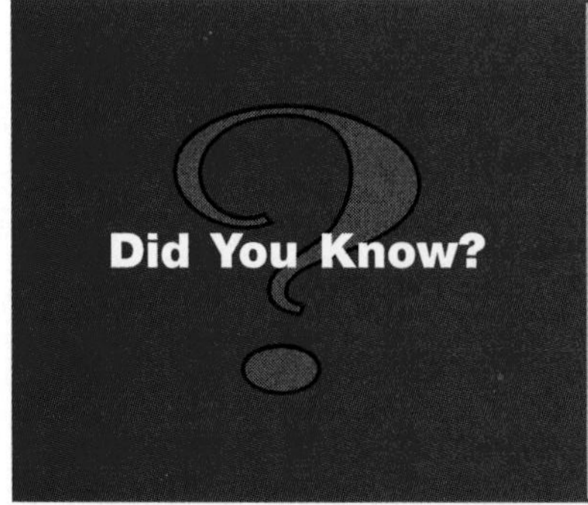

Virtual Financial Statements

Leading-edge companies venturing into the Information Age are seeing major changes in the accounting process. Quantum leaps in computing technology are increasing the importance of accounting analysis and interpretation. We are moving toward what Clark Johnson, chief financial officer of **Johnson & Johnson,** calls the "virtual financial statement." This means with a click of a mouse we can get up-to-date financials and slash thousands of hours now required in the closing process. Those with knowledge of the accounting process have a competitive edge. [Source: *Business Week,* October 28, 1996.]

Post-Closing Trial Balance

A **post-closing trial balance** is a list of permanent accounts and their balances from the ledger after all closing entries are journalized and posted. It is a list of balances for all accounts not closed. These accounts are a company's assets, liabilities, and owner's equity, and are identical to those in the balance sheet. The aim of a post-closing trial balance is to verify that (1) total debits equal total credits for permanent accounts, and (2) all temporary accounts have zero balances.

P2 Explain and prepare a post-closing trial balance.

FastForward's post-closing trial balance is shown in Exhibit 5.6. The post-closing trial balance is the last step in the accounting process. Like the unadjusted and adjusted trial balances, the post-closing trial balance does not tell us all transactions are recorded or that the ledger is correct.

Exhibit 5.6

Post-Closing Trial Balance

FASTFORWARD Post-Closing Trial Balance December 31, 1997		
Cash	$ 7,950	
Accounts receivable	1,800	
Supplies	2,670	
Prepaid insurance	2,300	
Equipment	26,000	
Accumulated depreciation—Equipment		$ 375
Accounts payable		1,100
Salaries payable		210
Unearned consulting revenue		2,750
Note payable		5,100
Chuck Taylor, capital		31,185
Totals	$40,720	$40,720

Exhibit 5.7 shows the entire ledger of FastForward as of December 31, 1997. We should note that the temporary accounts (revenue, expense, and withdrawal accounts) have balances equal to zero.

Closing Entries for Corporations

Our discussion to this point regarding closing entries relates to activities and accounts of a proprietorship. Closing entries for a partnership are similar to a proprietorship, but some are different for a corporation. The first two closing entries for a corporation are exactly the same. That is, a corporation's revenue and expense accounts are closed to the Income Summary account. The last two closing entries for a corporation are different.

Recall that a corporation's balance sheet shows shareholders' equity as contributed capital and retained earnings. This means the third closing entry for a corporation closes the Income Summary account to the Retained Earnings account. As an example, **Hershey Foods** reported net income of $336 million in 1997. This means the credit balance in the Income Summary account after the revenue and expense accounts are closed is $336 million. **Hershey**'s third closing entry, to update its Retained Earnings account, is (in millions):

Dec. 31	Income Summary	336	
	Retained Earnings		336
	To close Income Summary to Retained Earnings.		

Ledger after the Closing Process for FastForward*

General Ledger

Asset Accounts

Cash — Acct. No. 101

Date	Explan.	PR	Debit	Credit	Balance
1997 Dec. 1		G1	30,000		30,000
2		G1		2,500	27,500
3		G1		20,000	7,500
10		G1	2,200		9,700
12		G1		1,000	8,700
12		G1		700	8,000
22		G1	1,900		9,900
24		G1		900	9,000
24		G1		600	8,400
26		G1	3,000		11,400
26		G1		2,400	9,000
26		G1		120	8,880
26		G1		230	8,650
26		G1		700	**7,950**

Accounts Receivable — Acct. No. 106

Date	Explan.	PR	Debit	Credit	Balance
1997 Dec. 12		G1	1,900		1,900
22		G1		1,900	0
31	Adj.	G1	1,800		**1,800**

Supplies — Acct. No. 125

Date	Explan.	PR	Debit	Credit	Balance
1997 Dec. 2		G1	2,500		2,500
6		G1	1,100		3,600
26		G1	120		3,720
31	Adj.	G1		1,050	**2,670**

Prepaid Insurance — Acct. No. 128

Date	Explan.	PR	Debit	Credit	Balance
1997 Dec. 26		G1	2,400		2,400
31	Adj.	G1		100	**2,300**

Equipment — Acct. No. 167

Date	Explan.	PR	Debit	Credit	Balance
1997 Dec. 3		G1	20,000		20,000
6		G1	6,000		**26,000**

Accumulated Depreciation—Equipment — Acct. No. 168

Date	Explan.	PR	Debit	Credit	Balance
1997 Dec. 31	Adj.	G1		375	**375**

Liability and Equity Accounts

Accounts Payable — Acct. No. 201

Date	Explan.	PR	Debit	Credit	Balance
1997 Dec. 6		G1		1,100	**1,100**

Salaries Payable — Acct. No. 209

Date	Explan.	PR	Debit	Credit	Balance
1997 Dec. 31	Adj.	G1		210	**210**

Unearned Consulting Revenue — Acct. No. 236

Date	Explan.	PR	Debit	Credit	Balance
1997 Dec. 26		G1		3,000	3,000
31	Adj.	G1	250		**2,750**

Note Payable — Acct. No. 240

Date	Explan.	PR	Debit	Credit	Balance
1997 Dec. 6		G1		6,000	6,000
24		G1	900		**5,100**

Chuck Taylor, capital — Acct. No. 301

Date	Explan.	PR	Debit	Credit	Balance
1997 Dec. 1		G1		30,000	30,000
31	Closing	G1		1,785	31,785
31	Closing	G1	600		**31,785**

Chuck Taylor, withdrawals — Acct. No. 302

Date	Explan.	PR	Debit	Credit	Balance
1997 Dec. 24		G1	600		600
31	Closing	G1		600	**0**

*Explanations are omitted for brevity.

Exhibit 5.7 *(continued)*

Revenue and Expense Accounts (including Income Summary)

Consulting Revenue — Acct. No. 403

Date	Explan.	PR	Debit	Credit	Balance
1997 Dec. 10		G1		2,200	2,200
12		G1		1,600	3,800
31	Adj.	G1		250	4,050
31	Adj.	G1		1,800	5,850
31	Closing	G1	5,850		**0**

Rental Revenue — Acct. No. 406

Date	Explan.	PR	Debit	Credit	Balance
1997 Dec. 12		G1		300	300
31	Closing	G1	300		**0**

Depreciation Expense, Equipment — Acct. No. 614

Date	Explan.	PR	Debit	Credit	Balance
1997 Dec. 31	Adj.	G1	375		375
31	Closing	G1		375	**0**

Salaries Expense — Acct. No. 622

Date	Explan.	PR	Debit	Credit	Balance
1997 Dec. 12		G1	700		700
26		G1	700		1,400
31	Adj.	G1	210		1,610
31	Closing	G1		1,610	**0**

Insurance Expense — Acct. No. 637

Date	Explan.	PR	Debit	Credit	Balance
1997 Dec. 31	Adj.	G1	100		100
31	Closing	G1		100	**0**

Rent Expense — Acct. No. 641

Date	Explan.	PR	Debit	Credit	Balance
1997 Dec. 12		G1	1,000		1,000
31	Closing	G1		1,000	**0**

Supplies Expense — Acct. No. 651

Date	Explan.	PR	Debit	Credit	Balance
1997 Dec. 31	Adj.	G1	1,050		1,050
31	Closing	G1		1,050	**0**

Utilities Expense — Acct. No. 690

Date	Explan.	PR	Debit	Credit	Balance
1997 Dec. 26		G1	230		230
31	Closing	G1		230	**0**

Income Summary — Acct. No. 901

Date	Explan.	PR	Debit	Credit	Balance
1997 Dec. 31	Closing	G1		6,150	6,150
31	Closing	G1	4,365		1,785
31	Closing	G1	1,785		**0**

The fourth closing entry for a corporation uses a Dividends Declared account instead of a withdrawal account. **Hershey** declared $122 million in cash dividends. Its fourth closing entry, to update Retained Earnings, is (in millions):

Dec. 31	Retained Earnings	122	
	Dividends Declared		122
	To close Dividends Declared to Retained Earnings.		

Dividends are normally a return of earnings. They are accounted for by reducing the retained earnings of the corporation. We explain and show entries for paying dividends in Chapter 14.

Flash *back*

1. What are the four major closing entries?
2. Why are revenue and expense accounts called temporary? Are there other temporary accounts?
3. What accounts are listed on the post-closing trial balance?

Answers—p. 196

Work Sheet as a Tool

P3 Prepare a work sheet and explain its usefulness.

Accountants use various analyses and internal documents when organizing information for reports to internal and external decision makers. Internal documents are important and are often called **working papers.** One widely used working paper is the **work sheet.** The work sheet is a useful tool for preparers in working with accounting information. It is not usually given to decision makers.

Benefits of a Work Sheet

A work sheet is *not* a required financial report. When a business has only a few accounts and adjustments, preparing a work sheet is unnecessary. Also, computerized accounting systems generate financial statements without the need to generate a work sheet. Yet there are several potential benefits from using a manual or electronic work sheet:

1. It helps preparers avoid errors when working with accounting systems involving many accounts and adjustments.
2. It captures the entire accounting process, linking transactions and events to their effects in financial statements.
3. Auditors of financial statements often use a work sheet for planning and organizing the audit. It can be used to reflect any adjustments necessary as a result of the audit.
4. It is useful in preparing interim (monthly or quarterly) financial statements when journalizing and posting adjusting entries are postponed until the year-end.
5. It is helpful in showing the effects of proposed or "what-if" transactions.

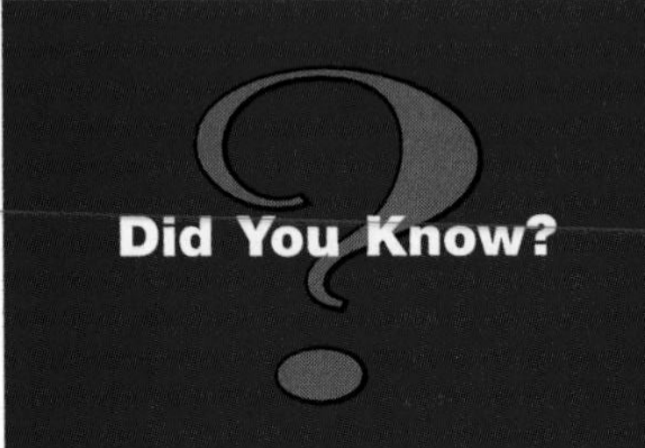

Silicon Accounting
An electronic work sheet is increasingly common in business. Popular spreadsheet software such as **Excel** and **Lotus 1-2-3** is putting electronic work sheets and their benefits within the reach of small business owners. This technology allows us to easily change numbers, assess the impact of alternative strategies, and ease the recordkeeping burden. It can also dramatically decrease the time devoted to the accounting process and other procedures required at the end of a period.

Using a Work Sheet

A work sheet can simplify efforts in preparing financial statements. It is prepared before making adjusting entries at the end of a reporting period. The work sheet stores information about accounts, their needed adjustments, and the financial statements. A complete work sheet contains all information recorded in the journals and shown in the statements. Exhibit 5.8 shows the form of a work sheet and the 5 steps in preparing it.

The multicolumn work sheet provides two columns each for: the unadjusted trial balance, the adjustments, the adjusted trial balance, the income statement, and the balance sheet and statement of changes in owner's equity. A work sheet sometimes has two separate columns for the statement of changes in owner's equity and two separate columns for the balance sheet. Because the statement of changes in owner's equity often includes only a few items, this usually is not done.

We use the information of FastForward to describe and interpret the work sheet. Important steps in preparing the work sheet are explained below. Each step, 1 through 5, is color-coded and explained with reference to Exhibit 5.9.[1]

(1) *Step 1. Enter Unadjusted Trial Balance*

Refer to Exhibit 5.9, Step 1. The first step in using a work sheet is to list the title of every account with a balance in the company's ledger. The unadjusted debit or credit

[1] A traditional acetate overlay presentation is available in *full color* teaching transparencies. A new PowerPoint presentation mimics this overlay option.

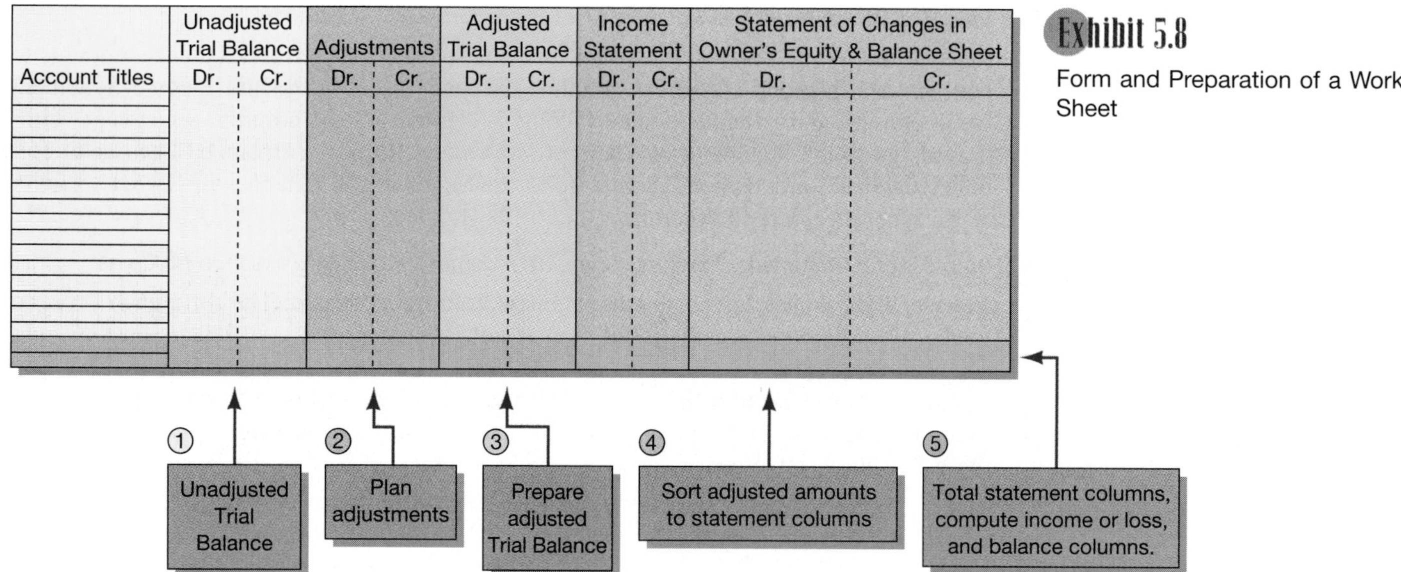

Exhibit 5.8

Form and Preparation of a Work Sheet

balances for accounts in the ledger are then recorded in the two columns of the unadjusted trial balance. The totals of these two columns must be equal. Exhibit 5.9 shows FastForward's work sheet after completing this first step.

The unadjusted trial balance in Exhibit 5.9 reflects the account balances after the December transactions are recorded but *before any adjusting entries are journalized or posted.* Sometimes blank lines are left on the worksheet based on past experience where lines will be needed for adjustments to certain accounts. Exhibit 5.9 shows Accumulated Depreciation as one example. An alternative is to squeeze adjustments on one line or to combine the effects of two or more adjustments in one amount.

② *Step 2. Enter Adjustments*

Refer to Exhibit 5.9, Step 2. The second step in preparing a work sheet is to enter adjustments in the columns labeled Adjustments, as shown in Exhibit 5.9. The adjustments shown are the same ones we discussed in Chapter 4. An identifying letter relates the debit and credit of each adjustment. This is called *keying* the adjustments. After preparing a work sheet, we still must enter adjusting entries in the journal and post them to the ledger. The identifying letters help match correctly the debit and credit of each adjusting entry. Exhibit 5.9 shows six adjustments for FastForward that we explained in Chapter 4:

a. Expiration of $100 of prepaid insurance.
b. Use of $1,050 of supplies.
c. Depreciation of $375 on equipment.
d. Earning $250 of previously unearned revenue.
e. Accrual of $210 of salaries owed to an employee.
f. Accrual of $1,800 of revenue from a customer.

In entering adjustments, we sometimes identify additional accounts that need to be inserted on the work sheet. The additional accounts can be inserted below the initial list.

③ *Step 3. Prepare Adjusted Trial Balance*

Refer to Exhibit 5.9, Step 3. The adjusted trial balance is prepared by combining the adjustments with the unadjusted balances for each account. As an example, the Prepaid Insurance account has a $2,400 debit balance in the Unadjusted Trial Balance columns. This $2,400 debit is combined with the $100 credit in the Adjustments columns to give Prepaid Insurance a $2,300 debit in the Adjusted Trial Balance columns. The totals of the Adjusted Trial Balance columns confirm the equality of debits and credits.

④ *Step 4. Sort Adjusted Trial Balance Amounts to Financial Statements*

Refer to Exhibit 5.9, Step 4. This step involves sorting adjusted trial balance amounts to their proper financial statement columns. Expense items go to the Income Statement Debit column and revenues to the Income Statement Credit column. Assets and withdrawals go to the Statement of Changes in Owner's Equity & Balance Sheet Debit column. Liabilities and owner's capital go to the Statement of Changes in Owner's Equity & Balance Sheet Credit column.

⑤ *Step 5. Total Statement Columns, Compute Income or Loss, and Balance Columns*

Refer to Exhibit 5.9, Step 5. Each statement column is totaled. The difference between totals of the Income Statement columns is net income or net loss. This is because revenues are entered in the Credit column and expenses in the Debit column. If the Credit total exceeds the Debit total, there is net income. If the Debit total exceeds the Credit total, there is a net loss. For FastForward, the Credit total exceeds the Debit total, giving a $1,785 net income.

The net income from the Income Statement columns is added to the Statement of Changes in Owner's Equity & Balance Sheet Credit column. Adding net income to the last Credit column implies it is to be added to owner's capital. If a loss occurs, it is added to the Debit column. This implies it is to be subtracted from owner's capital. While the ending balance of owner's capital does not appear in the last two columns as a single amount, it is computed as the owner's capital account balance *plus* net income (or minus net loss) and *minus* the withdrawals account balance.

Exhibit 5.9

Worksheet for FastForward

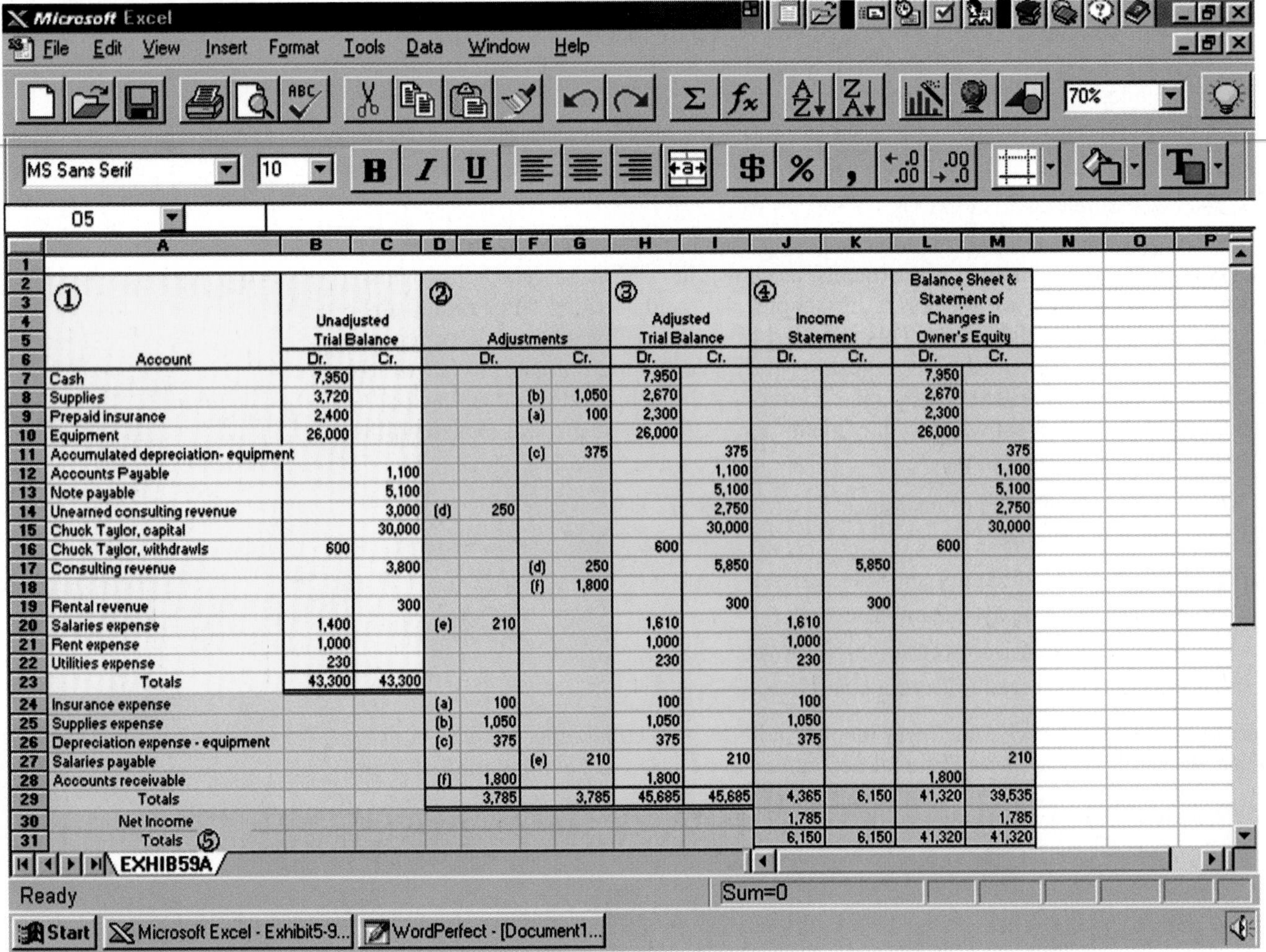

① Account	Unadjusted Trial Balance Dr.	Unadjusted Trial Balance Cr.	② Adjustments Dr.	Adjustments Cr.	③ Adjusted Trial Balance Dr.	Adjusted Trial Balance Cr.	④ Income Statement Dr.	Income Statement Cr.	Balance Sheet & Statement of Changes in Owner's Equity Dr.	Balance Sheet & Statement of Changes in Owner's Equity Cr.
Cash	7,950				7,950				7,950	
Supplies	3,720			(b) 1,050	2,670				2,670	
Prepaid insurance	2,400			(a) 100	2,300				2,300	
Equipment	26,000				26,000				26,000	
Accumulated depreciation- equipment				(c) 375		375				375
Accounts Payable		1,100				1,100				1,100
Note payable		5,100				5,100				5,100
Unearned consulting revenue		3,000	(d) 250			2,750				2,750
Chuck Taylor, capital		30,000				30,000				30,000
Chuck Taylor, withdrawls	600				600				600	
Consulting revenue		3,800		(d) 250		5,850		5,850		
				(f) 1,800						
Rental revenue		300				300		300		
Salaries expense	1,400		(e) 210		1,610		1,610			
Rent expense	1,000				1,000		1,000			
Utilities expense	230				230		230			
Totals	43,300	43,300								
Insurance expense			(a) 100		100		100			
Supplies expense			(b) 1,050		1,050		1,050			
Depreciation expense - equipment			(c) 375		375		375			
Salaries payable				(e) 210		210				210
Accounts receivable			(f) 1,800		1,800				1,800	
Totals			3,785	3,785	45,685	45,685	4,365	6,150	41,320	39,535
Net Income							1,785			1,785
Totals ⑤							6,150	6,150	41,320	41,320

Step 1: ☐ Prepare unadjusted trial balance; Step 2: ☐ Enter adjustments; Step 3: ☐ Prepare adjusted trial balance; Step 4: ☐ Sort adjusted trial balance amounts to financial statement columns; Step 5: ☐ Total statement columns, compute income or loss, and balance column.

Exhibit 5.10

Financial Statements from the Work Sheet

FASTFORWARD
Income Statement
For Month Ended December 31, 1997

Revenues:		
Consulting revenue	$ 5,850	
Rental revenue	300	
Total revenues		$ 6,150
Expenses:		
Depreciation expense—Equipment	$ 375	
Salaries expense	1,610	
Insurance expense	100	
Rent expense	1,000	
Supplies expense	1,050	
Utilities expense	230	
Total expenses		4,365
Net income		$ 1,785

FASTFORWARD
Statement of Changes in Owner's Equity
For Month Ended December 31, 1997

C.Taylor, capital, December 1, 1997		$ 0
Add: Investment by owner	$30,000	
Net income	1,785	31,785
Total		$31,785
Less: Withdrawal by owner		600
C.Taylor, capital, December 31, 1997		$31,185

FASTFORWARD
Balance Sheet
December 31, 1997

Assets		
Cash		$ 7,950
Accounts receivable		1,800
Supplies		2,670
Prepaid Insurance		2,300
Equipment	26,000	
Accumulated depreciation—Equipment	(375)	25,625
Total assets		$40,345
Liabilities		
Accounts payable		$ 1,100
Salaries payable		210
Unearned consulting revenue		2,750
Note payable		5,100
Total liabilities		$ 9,160
Owner's Equity		
Chuck Taylor, capital		31,185
Total liabilities and owner's equity		$40,345

When net income or net loss is added to the proper Statement of Changes in Owner's Equity & Balance Sheet column, the totals of the last two columns must balance. If they do not balance, one or more errors were made. The error can be mathematical or can involve error in sorting one or more amounts to columns. A balance in the last two columns is not proof of no errors.

Entering adjustments in the Adjustments columns of a work sheet does not adjust the ledger accounts. Adjusting entries still must be entered in the general journal and posted to ledger accounts. The work sheet helps because its Adjustments columns provide the information for these entries. The adjustments in Exhibit 5.9 are the same as the adjusting entries we described in Chapter 4. In addition, all items in the Income Statement columns must be closed to Income Summary. The net income or net loss shown on the work sheet must be closed to owner's capital. The withdrawals account in the last Debit column must be closed to owner's capital.

Auditor

You are auditing the financial statements of a food service client. This client owns and operates her own restaurant. You ask and receive a printout of her electronic work sheet used to prepare financial statements. There is no depreciation adjustment, yet this client owns a large amount of food service equipment. Does the lack of depreciation adjustment concern you?

Answer—p. 196

Work Sheet Application and Analysis

A work sheet does not substitute for financial statements. The work sheet is a tool we use at the end of an accounting period to help organize and manage data. We use the information in it to prepare financial statements. The financial statements of FastForward are shown in Exhibit 5.10. Its income statement amounts are taken from the Income Statement columns of the work sheet. Similarly, amounts for the statement of changes in owner's equity and the balance sheet are taken from the Statement of Changes in Owner's Equity & Balance Sheet columns of the work sheet. FastForward's statement of cash flows is discussed in the next section and is prepared from the Cash account and supporting documents.

While we can prepare all the statements at this point, we must remember that adjusting entries must be journalized and posted before moving to the closing process. A work sheet is a useful tool, but it is not a substitute for adjusting entries and postings to ledger accounts. These procedures must still be performed as described in Chapter 4.

Work sheets are also useful in analyzing the effects of proposed, or what-if, transactions. This is done by entering their adjusted financial statement amounts in the first two columns, arranging them in the form of financial statements. Proposed transactions are entered in the second two columns. Extended amounts in the last columns show the effects of these proposed transactions on financial statements. These final columns are called **pro forma statements** because they show the statements *as if* the proposed transactions occurred.

Flash back

4. Where do we get the amounts to enter in the Unadjusted Trial Balance columns of a work sheet?

5. What are the advantages of using a work sheet in helping us prepare adjusting entries?

Answers—p. 196

Statement of Cash Flows

All of FastForward's cash receipts and cash payments are recorded in its Cash account in the ledger. This Cash account holds information about cash flows from operating, investing, and financing activities. The Cash account for FastForward is shown in Exhibit 5.11.

Cash Account of FastForward

Cash			
Investment by owner (1)	30,000	Purchase of supplies (2)	2,500
Consulting revenue (5)	2,200	Purchase of equipment (3)	20,000
Collection of account receivable (9)	1,900	Payment of rent (6)	1,000
Receipts for future services (12)	3,000	Payment of salary (7)	700
		Payment of note payable (10)	900
		Withdrawal by owner (11)	600
		Payment of insurance (13)	2,400
		Purchase of supplies (14)	120
		Payment of utilities (15)	230
		Payment of salary (16)	700
Total increases	37,100	Total decreases	29,150
Less decreases	−29,150		
Balance	7,950		

The Cash account reports individual cash transactions by types of receipts and payments. These amounts are keyed according to the transactions (1) through (16) from Chapter 3. Adjustments never affect the Cash account; they are not cash-related activities. To prepare the statement of cash flows, we must determine whether a cash inflow or outflow is an operating, investing, or financing activity. We then report amounts in their proper category on the statement of cash flows. FastForward's statement of cash flows is shown in Exhibit 5.12.

Statement of Cash Flows

FASTForward

FASTFORWARD Statement of Cash Flows For Month Ended December 31, 1997		
Cash flows from operating activities:		
Cash received from clients	$ 7,100	
Cash paid for supplies	(2,620)	
Cash paid for rent	(1,000)	
Cash paid for insurance	(2,400)	
Cash paid for utilities	(230)	
Cash paid to employee	(1,400)	
Net cash used by operating activities		$ (550)
Cash flows from investing activities:		
Purchase of equipment	$(20,000)	
Net cash used by investing activities		(20,000)
Cash flows from financing activities:		
Investment by owner	$ 30,000	
Partial repayment of note payable	(900)	
Withdrawal by owner	(600)	
Net cash provided by financing activities		28,500
Net increase in cash		$ 7,950
Cash balance, December 1, 1997		0
Cash balance, December 31, 1997		$ 7,950

Our analysis of the Cash account provides us a direct means to prepare the statement of cash flows. But there are two limitations with this method. First, companies often have so many individual cash receipts and disbursements that it is often difficult to review them all. Second, the Cash account often does not contain a description of each cash transaction. Later in this book we show how we can prepare the statement of cash flows when facing these limitations.

Reviewing the Accounting Cycle

C2 Identify steps in the accounting cycle.

The **accounting cycle** refers to the steps in preparing financial statements. It is called a cycle because the steps are repeated each reporting period. Exhibit 5.13 shows the 10 steps in the cycle. They are shown in order, beginning with analyzing transactions and ending with a post-closing trial balance or reversing entries.

Steps 1 through 3 usually occur regularly as a company enters into transactions. Steps 4 through 9 are done at the end of a period. Reversing entries in step 10 are optional and are explained in the appendix to this chapter. Detailed descriptions for all of these steps are in Chapters 3, 4, and 5.

Exhibit 5.13

Steps in the Accounting Cycle*

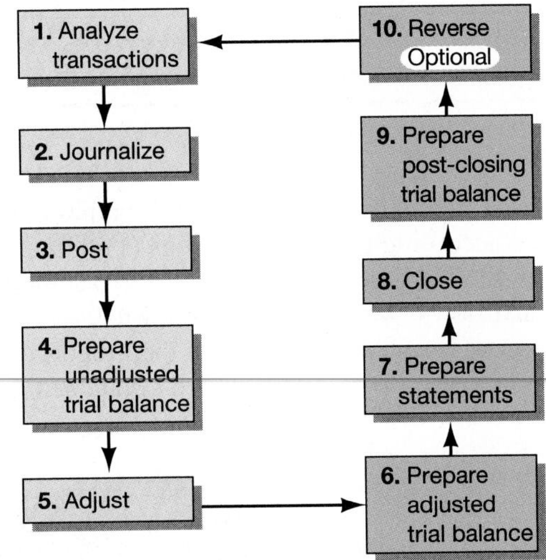

*Steps 4 and 6 can be done on a work sheet. A work sheet is especially useful in planning adjustments and in projecting an adjusted trial balance. But adjustments must always be journalized and posted.

We briefly describe these steps in Exhibit 5.14 to emphasize their importance in providing users relevant and reliable information for decision making.

Exhibit 5.14

Summary of Steps in Accounting Cycle

1. Analyze transaction	Analyze transactions in preparation for journalizing.
2. Journalize	Record debits and credits in a journal.
3. Post	Transfer debits and credits from the journal to the ledger.
4. Prepare unadjusted trial balance	Summarize ledger accounts and amounts.
5. Adjust	Record adjustments to bring account balances up to date; journalize and post adjusting entries.
6. Prepare adjusted trial balance	Summarize adjusted ledger accounts and amounts.
7. Prepare statements	Use adjusted trial balance to prepare statements.
8. Close	Journalize and post entries to close temporary accounts and update the owner's capital account.
9. Prepare post-closing trial balance	Test clerical accuracy of adjusting and closing steps.
10. Reverse (optional)	Reverse certain adjustments in the next period — optional step; see Appendix 5A.

Flash back

6. What are the benefits of a work sheet?
7. What steps in the accounting cycle are optional?

Answers—p. 196

Classified Balance Sheet

C3 Explain and prepare a classified balance sheet.

Our discussion to this point has been limited to *unclassified financial statements*. But companies also prepare classified financial statements. This section focuses on a classified balance sheet. Later in the book we discuss other classified financial statements.

An **unclassified balance sheet** is one where its items are broadly grouped into assets, liabilities and owner's equity. One example is FastForward's balance sheet in Exhibit 5.10. A **classified balance sheet** organizes assets and liabilities into important subgroups. The information in a balance sheet is more useful to decision makers if assets and liabilities are classified into subgroups. One example is information to distinguish liabilities that are due soon from those not due for several years. This information helps us assess a company's ability to meet liabilities when they come due.

Classification Structure

There is no required layout for a classified balance sheet. Yet a classified balance sheet often contains common groupings as shown in Exhibit 5.15.

Exhibit 5.15

Sections of a Classified Balance Sheet

Assets	Liabilities and Equity
Current assets	Current liabilities
Long-term investments	Long-term liabilities
Plant and equipment	Owner's equity
Intangible assets	

One of the more important classifications is the separation between current and noncurrent items for both assets and liabilities. Current items are those expected to come due (both collected and owed) within the longer of one year or the company's normal operating cycle. An operating cycle is the length of time between (1) purchases of services or products from suppliers to carry out a company's plans and (2) the sale of services or products to customers. The length of a company's operating cycle depends on its activities.

Exhibit 5.16 shows the steps of an operating cycle for both a service company and a merchandising company. For a service company, the **operating cycle** is the average time between (1) paying employees who do the services and (2) receiving cash from customers. For a company selling products, the operating cycle is the average time between (1) paying suppliers for merchandise and (2) receiving cash from customers.

Most operating cycles are less than one year. This means most companies use a one-year period in deciding which assets and liabilities are current. Yet there are companies with an operating cycle longer than one year. For instance, there are companies that routinely allow customers to take more than one year to pay for purchases. Also, producers of certain beverages and products that require aging for several years have operating cycles longer than one year. These companies use their operating cycle in deciding which balance sheet items are current.[2]

[2] In these uncommon situations, companies provide supplemental information about their current assets and liabilities to allow users to compare them with other companies.

Exhibit 5.16

Operating Cycles for a Service Company and a Merchandise Company

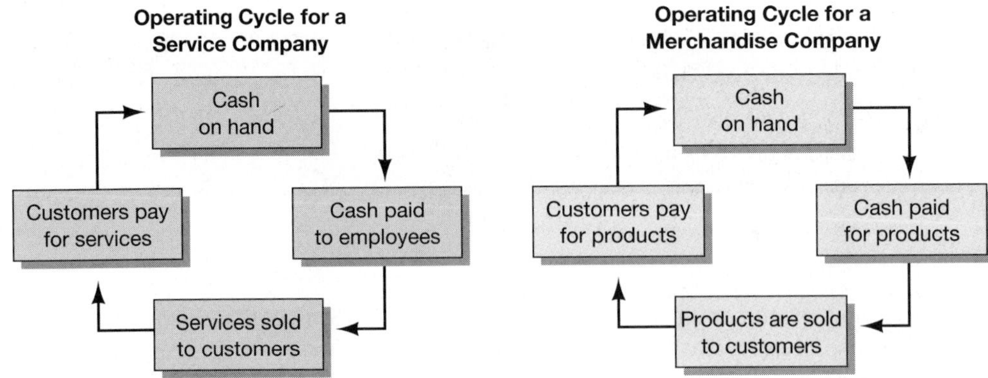

A balance sheet usually lists current assets before long-term assets, and current liabilities before long-term liabilities. This consistency in presentation allows users to quickly identify current assets that are most easily converted to cash, and current liabilities that are shortly coming due. Items in the current group are usually listed in the order of how quickly they will be converted to or paid in cash.

Classification Example

The balance sheet for **Music Components** is shown in Exhibit 5.17. It shows the most commonly used groupings. Its assets are classified as (1) current assets, (2) investments, (3) plant and equipment, and (4) intangible assets. Its liabilities are classified as either current or long term. Not all companies use the same categories of assets and liabilities on their balance sheets. **Compaq**'s balance sheet lists only three asset classes: current assets; property, plant and equipment; and other assets.

Classification Groups

This section describes the most common groups in a classified balance sheet.

Current Assets

Current assets are cash and other resources that are expected to be sold, collected, or used within the longer of one year or the company's operating cycle.[3] Examples are cash, short-term investments in marketable securities, accounts receivable, notes receivable, goods for sale to customers (called *merchandise* or *inventory*), and prepaid expenses. **Wal-Mart**'s 1997 current assets are reported in Exhibit 5.18.

Exhibit 5.18

Current Assets Section

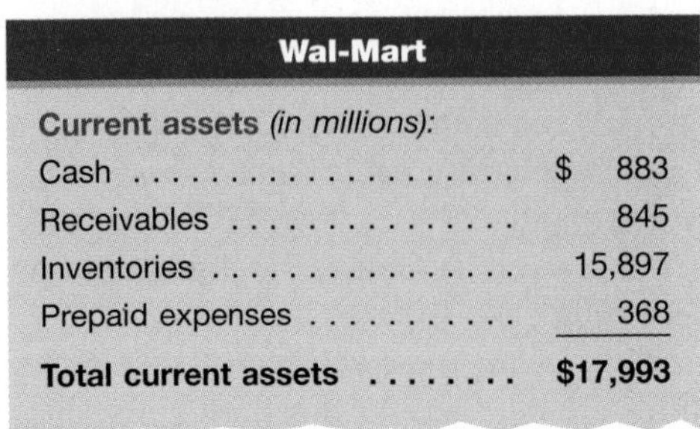

Wal-Mart	
Current assets *(in millions):*	
Cash	$ 883
Receivables	845
Inventories	15,897
Prepaid expenses	368
Total current assets	**$17,993**

A company's prepaid expenses are usually small compared to other assets and are often combined and shown as a single item. It is likely the prepaid expenses in both Exhibit 5.17 and 5.18 include items such as prepaid insurance, prepaid rent, office supplies, and store supplies. Prepaid expenses are usually listed last because they will not be converted to cash.

Long-Term Investments

A second major balance sheet classification often is **long-term investments.** Notes receivable and investments in stocks and bonds are in many cases long-term assets. This

[3] FASB, *Accounting Standards—Current Text* (Norwalk, CT, 1995), Sec. B05.105. First published as *Accounting Research Bulletin No. 43*, Chapter 3A, par. 4.

Classified Balance Sheet

MUSIC COMPONENTS Balance Sheet January 31, 2000			
Assets			
Current assets:			
Cash		$ 6,500	
Short-term investments		2,100	
Accounts receivable		4,400	
Notes receivable		1,500	
Merchandise inventory		27,500	
Prepaid expenses		2,400	
Total current assets			$ 44,400
Long-term investments:			
Disney common stock		18,000	
Land held for future expansion		48,000	
Total investments			66,000
Plant and equipment:			
Store equipment	$ 33,200		
Less accumulated depreciation	8,000	25,200	
Buildings	170,000		
Less accumulated depreciation	45,000	125,000	
Land		73,200	
Total plant and equipment			223,400
Intangible assets:			
Trademark			10,000
Total assets			$343,800
Liabilities			
Current liabilities:			
Accounts payable	$ 15,300		
Wages payable	3,200		
Notes payable	3,000		
Current portion of long-term liabilities	7,500		
Total current liabilities		$ 29,000	
Long-term liabilities:			
Notes payable (net of current portion)		150,000	
Total liabilities			$179,000
Owner's Equity			
D. Bowie, capital			164,800
Total liabilities and owner's equity			$343,800

is because they are held for more than one year or the operating cycle. The *short-term* investments in Exhibit 5.15 are current assets and not shown as long-term investments. We explain the differences between short- and long-term investments later in this book.

Plant and Equipment

Plant and equipment, also called **plant assets,** are tangible long-lived assets used to produce or sell products and services. Examples are equipment, vehicles, buildings, and land. It is important that items in this group are both *long-lived* and *used to produce or sell products and services.* Land held for future expansion is *not* a plant and equipment

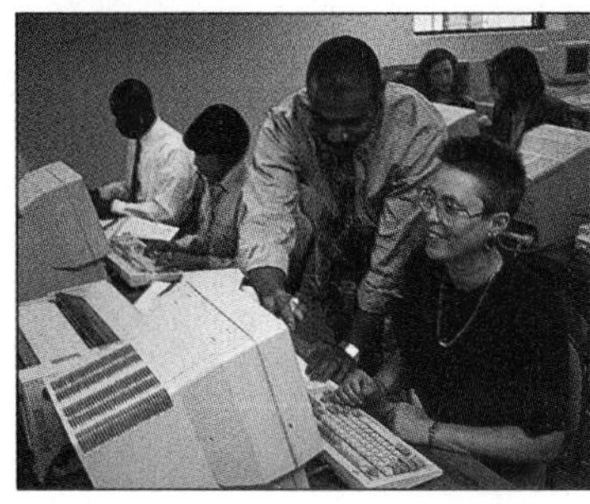

asset because it is not used to produce or sell products and services. Plant and equipment assets are also called *property, plant, and equipment* or *land, buildings, and equipment.* The order of listing plant assets within this category varies.

Intangible Assets

Intangible assets are long-term resources used to produce or sell products and services. They lack physical form and their benefits are uncertain. Examples are patents, trademarks, copyrights, franchises, and goodwill. Their value comes from the privileges or rights granted to or held by the owner. **Wang Laboratories** reports intangible assets for 1997 as shown in Exhibit 5.19.

Exhibit 5.19

Intangible Assets Section

Wang Laboratories	
Intangible assets, net (in millions)	$313

Wang's intangibles include software, licenses, trademarks, and patents.

Current Liabilities

Current liabilities are obligations due to be paid or settled within the longer of one year or the operating cycle. They are usually settled by paying out current assets. Current liabilities include accounts payable, notes payable, wages payable, taxes payable, interest payable, and unearned revenues. Any portion of a long-term liability due to be paid within the longer of one year or the operating cycle is a current liability. Exhibit 5.15 shows how the current portion of long-term liabilities is usually reported. Unearned revenues are current liabilities when they will be settled by delivering products or services within the longer of the year or the operating cycle. While practice varies, current liabilities are often reported in the order of those to be settled first.

Long-Term Liabilities

Long-term liabilities are obligations not due within the longer of one year or the operating cycle. Notes payable, mortgages payable, bonds payable, and lease obligations are common long-term liabilities. If a company has both short- and long-term items in one of these accounts, it is common to separate them in the ledger for later reporting.

Owner's Equity

Owner's equity is the owner's claim on the assets of a company. It is reported in the equity section with an owner's capital account for a proprietorship. For a partnership, the equity section reports a capital account for each partner. For a corporation, the equity section is called Shareholders' Equity and is divided into two main subsections: Capital Stock and Retained Earnings. Chapter 2 described these alternative organization forms in detail.

Flash back

8. Identify which of the following assets are classified as (1) current assets or (2) plant and equipment: *(a)* land used in operations; *(b)* office supplies; *(c)* receivables from customers due in 10 months; *(d)* insurance protection for the next nine months; *(e)* trucks used to provide services to customers; *(f)* trademarks used in advertising the company's services.
9. Name two examples of assets classified as investments on the balance sheet.
10. Explain an operating cycle for a service company.

Answers—p. 197

Current Ratio

USING THE INFORMATION

A1 Compute the current ratio and describe what it reveals about a company's financial condition.

An important use of financial statements is as an aid in assessing a company's ability to pay its debts in the near future. This type of analysis affects decisions by suppliers in allowing a company to buy on credit. It affects decisions by creditors about lending money to a company. For instance, it can affect creditors' decision about loan terms, including the interest rate, due date, and any requirements for collateral for the loan. An assessment of the ability to pay debts can also affect an internal manager's decisions about using cash to pay existing debts when they come due.

The **current ratio** is one important measure used to evaluate a company's ability to pay its short-term obligations. It is computed by dividing current assets by current liabilities:

$$\textbf{Current ratio} = \frac{\textbf{Current assets}}{\textbf{Current liabilities}}$$

Exhibit 5.20

Current Ratio Formula

Using financial information for **Harley-Davidson,** we compute its annual current ratios for the time period 1993–1996. These results are shown in Exhibit 5.21.

Exhibit 5.21

Harley-Davidson's Current Ratio

(in Millions)	Harley-Davidson 1996	1995	1994	1993
Total current assets	$429	$332	$406	$334
Total current liabilities	$264	$233	$216	$191
Current ratio	**1.63**	**1.42**	**1.88**	**1.75**
Industry current ratio	2.1	1.8	2.2	1.9

Harley's current ratio dipped to 1.42 in 1995 compared to higher ratios for the prior two years, but it rebounded in 1996 to 1.63. The current ratio for all of these years suggests that Harley's short-term obligations can be covered with short-term assets on hand. If the ratio moved closer to 1, Harley would expect to face more problems in covering liabilities. We often look to a company's sales to see if there are sufficient cash inflows to cover liabilities. If the ratio were *less* than 1, it would mean that Harley's current liabilities exceed its current assets, and it would likely face serious problems in covering current liabilities. Harley's current ratio favorably compares with the industry average. Although it appears to be at the lower end of the industry, Harley's ability to pay short-term obligations is good.

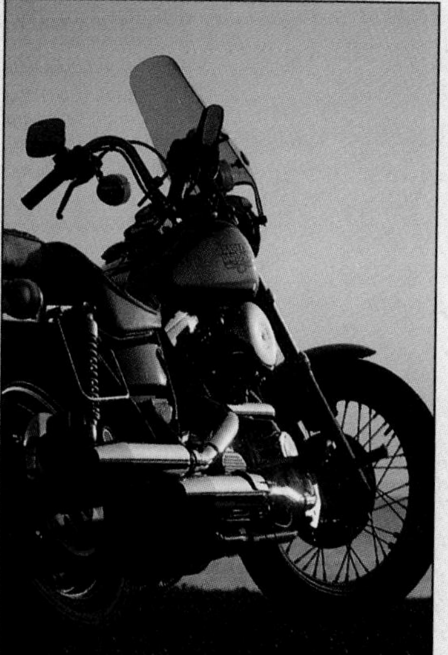

Answer—p. 196

Analyst
You are analyzing the financial condition of a sports and fitness club. Your main goal is to assess the club's ability to meet upcoming loan payments in the next period. You compute its current ratio and it is 1.2. You also find a major portion of Accounts Receivable is due from one client who has not made any payments in the past 12 months. Removing this accounts receivable from current assets drops the current ratio to 0.7. What do you conclude?

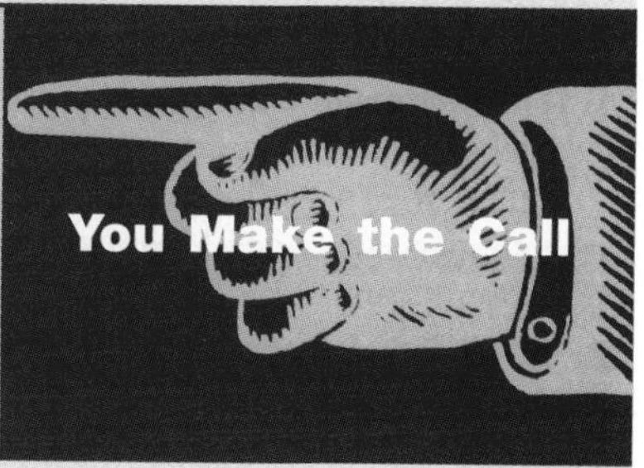

11. If a company misclassifies a portion of liabilities as long-term when they are short-term, how does this affect its current ratio?

Answer—p. 197

Summary

C1 Explain why temporary accounts are closed each period. Temporary accounts are closed at the end of each accounting period for two main reasons. First, the closing process updates the owner's capital account to include the effects of all transactions and events recorded for the period. Second, it prepares revenue, expense, and withdrawal accounts for the next reporting period by giving them zero balances.

C2 Identify steps in the accounting cycle. The accounting cycle consists of 10 steps: (1) analyze transactions, (2) journalize, (3) post, (4) prepare an unadjusted trial balance, (5) adjust accounts, (6) prepare an adjusted trial balance, (7) prepare statements, (8) close, (9) prepare a post-closing trial balance, and (10) prepare (optional) reversing entries. If a work sheet is prepared, it covers steps 4 and 6.

C3 Explain and prepare a classified balance sheet. Classified balance sheets usually report four groups of assets: current assets, long-term investments, plant and equipment, and intangible assets. They include at least two groups of liabilities: current and long-term. Owner's equity for proprietorships and partners' equity for partnerships both report the capital account balances. A corporation separates shareholders' equity into contributed capital and retained earnings.

A1 Compute the current ratio and describe what it reveals about a company's financial condition. A company's current ratio is defined as current assets divided by current liabilities. We use it to evaluate a company's ability to pay its current liabilities out of current assets.

P1 Describe and prepare closing entries. Recording and posting closing entries involve transferring the end-of-period balances in revenue, expense, and withdrawal accounts to the owner's capital account. Closing entries involve four steps: (1) close credit balances in revenue accounts to income summary, (2) close debit balances in expense accounts to income summary, (3) close income summary to owner's capital, and (4) close withdrawal account to owner's capital.

P2 Explain and prepare a post-closing trial balance. A post-closing trial balance is a list of permanent accounts and their balances after all closing entries are journalized and posted. Permanent accounts are asset, liability, and owner's equity accounts. The purpose of a post-closing trial balance is to verify that (1) total debits equal total credits for permanent accounts and (2) all temporary accounts have zero balances.

P3 Prepare a work sheet and explain its usefulness. A work sheet can be a useful tool in preparing and analyzing financial statements. It is helpful at the end of a period in preparing adjusting entries, an adjusted trial balance, and financial statements. A work sheet often contains five pairs of columns: unadjusted trial balance, adjustments, adjusted trial balance, income statement, and statement of changes in owner's equity & balance sheet.

Guidance Answers to **You Make the Call**

Auditor

You are concerned about the absence of a depreciation adjustment. Equipment does depreciate, and financial statements recognize this occurrence. Its absence suggests an error or a misrepresentation. You must follow up and require management to adjust the statements for depreciation. Also, if fraud is suggested, you must substantially expand your audit tests, obtain legal advice, and prepare to withdraw from the audit engagement.

Analyst

A current ratio of 1.2 suggests sufficient current assets to cover upcoming current liabilities. But a ratio of 1.2 does not give you much of a buffer in case of error in measuring current assets or current liabilities. Removing tardy receivables further reduces the current ratio to 0.7. This suggests current assets cannot cover current liabilities. Your assessment is that the sports and fitness club will have difficulty meeting upcoming loan payments.

Guidance Answers to Flash *backs*

1. The four major closing entries consist of closing: (1) credit balances in revenue accounts to Income Summary, (2) debit balances in expense accounts to Income Summary, (3) Income Summary to owner's capital, and (4) withdrawal account to owner's capital.
2. Revenue and expense accounts are called temporary because they are opened and closed every reporting period. The Income Summary and owner's withdrawal accounts are also temporary accounts.
3. Permanent accounts are listed on the post-closing trial balance. These accounts are the asset, liability, and owner's equity accounts.
4. Amounts in the Unadjusted Trial Balance columns are taken from account balances in the ledger.
5. A work sheet offers the advantage of listing on one page all of the necessary information to make adjusting entries.
6. A worksheet can help in: (a) avoiding errors, (b) linking transactions and events to their effects in financial statements, (c)

showing adjustments for audit purposes, (d) preparing interim financial statements, and (e) showing effects from proposed, or what-if, transactions.

7. Reversing entries is an optional step in the accounting cycle. Also, a worksheet is an optional tool in completing steps 4 and 6.

8. Current assets: *b, c, d.* Plant and equipment: *a, e.* Item *f* is an intangible asset.

9. Investment in common stock, investment in bonds, land held for future expansion.

10. The length of a company's operating cycle depends on its activities. For a service company, the operating cycle is the average time between (1) paying employees who do the services and (2) receiving cash from customers from services provided.

11. Since the current ratio is defined as current assets divided by current liabilities, ignoring a portion of current liabilities (1) decreases the reported amount of current liabilities and (2) erroneously increases the current ratio because current assets are now divided by a smaller number.

Demonstration Problem

This partial work sheet shows the December 31, 2000, adjusted trial balance of Westside Appliance Repair Company:

	Adjusted Trial Balance		Income Statement		Statement of Owner's Equity and Balance Sheet	
Cash	$ 83,300					
Notes receivable	60,000					
Prepaid insurance	19,000					
Prepaid rent	5,000					
Equipment	165,000					
Accumulated depreciation—Equipment		$ 52,000				
Accounts payable		37,000				
Long-term notes payable		58,000				
B. Westside, capital		173,500				
B. Westside, withdrawals	25,000					
Repair services revenue		294,000				
Interest earned		6,500				
Depreciation expense—Equipment	26,000					
Wages expense	155,000					
Rent expense	71,000					
Insurance expense	7,000					
Interest expense	4,700					
Totals	$621,000	$621,000				

Required

1. Complete the work sheet by extending the adjusted trial balance totals to the appropriate financial statement columns.

2. Prepare closing entries for Westside Appliance Repair Company.

3. Set up Income Summary and B. Westside, Capital, accounts in the general ledger and post the closing entries to these accounts.

4. Determine the balance of the B. Westside, Capital, account to be reported on the December 31, 2000, balance sheet.

Planning the Solution

- Extend the adjusted trial balance account balances to the appropriate financial statement columns.
- Prepare entries to close the revenue accounts to Income Summary, to close the expense accounts to Income Summary, to close Income Summary to the capital account, and to close the withdrawal account to the capital account.

- Post the first and second closing entries to the Income Summary account. Examine the balance of income summary and verify that it agrees with the net income shown on the work sheet.
- Post the third and fourth closing entries to the capital account.

Solution to Demonstration Problem

1. Completing the work sheet:

	Adjusted Trial Balance		Income Statement		Statement of Changes in Owner's Equity and Balance Sheet	
Cash	$ 83,300				$ 83,300	
Notes receivable	60,000				60,000	
Prepaid insurance	19,000				19,000	
Prepaid rent	5,000				5,000	
Equipment	165,000				165,000	
Accumulated depreciation—Equipment		$ 52,000				$ 52,000
Accounts payable		37,000				37,000
Long-term notes payable		58,000				58,000
B. Westside, capital		173,500				173,500
B. Westside, withdrawals	25,000				25,000	
Repair services revenue		294,000		$294,000		
Interest earned		6,500		6,500		
Depreciation expense—Equipment	26,000		$ 26,000			
Wages expense	155,000		155,000			
Rent expense	71,000		71,000			
Insurance expense	7,000		7,000			
Interest expense	4,700		4,700			
Totals	$621,000	$621,000	$263,700	$300,500	$357,300	$320,500
Net Income			36,800			36,800
Totals			$300,500	$300,500	$357,300	$357,300

2. Closing entries:

Dec. 31	Repair Services Revenue	294,000	
	Interest Earned	6,500	
	Income Summary		300,500
	To close revenue accounts.		
Dec. 31	Income Summary	263,700	
	Depreciation Expense—Equipment		26,000
	Wages Expense		155,000
	Rent Expense		71,000
	Insurance Expense		7,000
	Interest Expense		4,700
	To close expense accounts.		
Dec. 31	Income Summary	36,800	
	B. Westside, capital		36,800
	To close the Income Summary account.		
Dec. 31	B. Westside, capital	25,000	
	B. Westside, withdrawals		25,000
	To close the withdrawals account.		

3. Set up Income Summary and Capital ledger accounts and post the closing entries.

Income Summary — Account No. 999

Date	Explanation	PR	Debit	Credit	Balance
2000 Jan. 1	Beginning balance				0
Dec. 31	Close revenue accounts			300,500	300,500
31	Close expense accounts		263,700		36,800
31	Close income summary		36,800		0

B. Westside, Capital — Account No. 301

Date	Explanation	PR	Debit	Credit	Balance
2000 Jan. 1	Beginning balance				173,500
Dec. 31	Close Income Summary			36,800	210,300
31	Close B. Westside, withdrawals		25,000		185,300

4. The final capital balance of $185,300 (from part 3) will be reported on the December 31, 2000, balance sheet. The final capital balance reflects the increase due to the net income earned during the year and the decrease for the owner's withdrawals during the year.

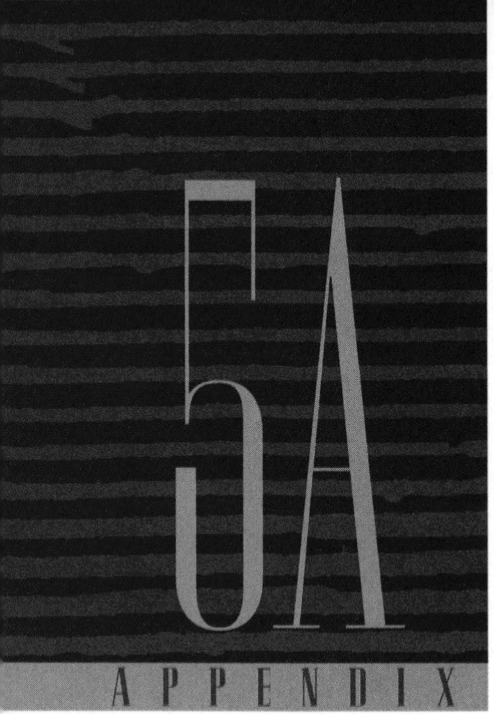

APPENDIX

Reversing Entries and Account Numbering

Learning Objectives

Procedural

P4 Prepare reversing entries and explain their purpose.

This appendix describes both reversing entries and the account numbering system applied in companies.

Reversing Entries

Reversing entries are optional entries. They are linked to any accrued assets and liabilities that were created by adjusting entries at the end of a reporting period. Reversing entries are used to simplify a company's recordkeeping.

Exhibit 5A.1 shows how reversing entries work for **FastForward.** The top of the exhibit shows the adjusting entry FastForward recorded on December 31, 1997, for the employee's earned but unpaid salary. The entry recorded three days' salary to increase December's total salary expense to $1,610. The entry also recognized a liability of $210. The expense is reported on December's income statement. The expense account is then closed. As a result, the ledger on January 1, 1998, reflects a $210 liability and a zero balance in the Salaries Expense account. At this point, the choice is made between using or not using reversing entries.

Accounting without Reversing Entries

The path down the left side of Exhibit 5A.1 is described in detail in Chapter 4. To summarize here, when the next payday occurs on January 9, we record payment with a compound entry that debits both the expense and liability accounts and credits cash. Posting that entry creates a $490 balance in the expense account and reduces the liability account balance to zero because the debt has been settled.

The disadvantage of this approach is the slightly more complex entry required on January 9. Paying the accrued liability means this entry differs from the routine entries made on all other paydays. To construct the proper entry on January 9, we must recall the effect of the adjusting entry. Reversing entries overcome this disadvantage.

P4 Prepare reversing entries and explain their purpose.

Accounting with Reversing Entries

The right side of Exhibit 5A.1 shows how a reversing entry on January 1 overcomes the disadvantage of the January 9 entry from not using reversing entries. A reversing entry is the exact opposite of an adjusting entry. In our example, the Salaries Payable liability

Exhibit 5A.1

Reversing Entries for Accrued Expenses

Accrue salaries expense on December 31, 1997

Salaries Expense 210
Salaries Payable 210

Salaries Expense

Date	Expl.	Debit	Credit	Balance
1997				
Dec. 12	(7)	700		700
26	(16)	700		1,400
31	*(e)*	210		1,610

Salaries Payable

Date	Expl.	Debit	Credit	Balance
1997				
Dec. 31	*(e)*		210	210

— OR —

No reversing entry recorded on January 1, 1998

NO ENTRY

Salaries Expense

Date	Expl.	Debit	Credit	Balance
1998				

Salaries Payable

Date	Expl.	Debit	Credit	Balance
1997				
Dec. 31	*(e)*		210	210
1998				

Reversing entry recorded on January 1, 1998

Salaries Payable 210
Salaries Expense 210

Salaries Expense

Date	Expl.	Debit	Credit	Balance
1998				
Jan. 1			210	(210)

Salaries Payable

Date	Expl.	Debit	Credit	Balance
1997				
Dec. 31	*(e)*		210	210
1998				
Jan. 1		210		0

Pay the accrued and current salaries on January 9, the first payday in 1998

Salaries Expense 490
Salaries Payable 210
Cash 700

Salaries Expense

Date	Expl.	Debit	Credit	Balance
1998				
Jan. 9		490		490

Salaries Payable

Date	Expl.	Debit	Credit	Balance
1997				
Dec. 31	*(e)*		210	210
1998				
Jan. 9		210		0

Salaries Expense 700
Cash 700

Salaries Expense

Date	Expl.	Debit	Credit	Balance
1998				
Jan. 1			210	(210)
Jan. 9		700		490

Salaries Payable

Date	Expl.	Debit	Credit	Balance
1997				
Dec. 31	*(e)*		210	210
1998				
Jan. 1		210		0

Under both approaches, the expense and liability accounts have identical balances after the cash payment on January 9.

Salaries Expense $490
Salaries Payable .... $ 0

is debited for $210, meaning that this account now has a zero balance after the entry is posted. The Salaries Payable account temporarily understates the liability, but this is not a problem since financial statements are not prepared before the liability is settled on January 9. The credit to the Salaries Expense account is unusual because it gives the account an *abnormal credit balance.* We highlight an abnormal balance by circling it.

Because of the reversing entry, the January 9 entry to record payment is straightforward. This entry debits the Salaries Expense account and credits Cash for the full $700 paid. It is the same as all other entries made to record 10 days' salary for the employee.

We should also look at the accounts on the lower right side of Exhibit 5A.1. After the payment entry is posted, Salaries Expense account has a $490 balance that reflects seven days' salary of $70 per day. The zero balance in the Salaries Payable account is now correct.

The lower section of Exhibit 5A.1 shows that the expense and liability accounts have exactly the same balances whether reversing occurs or not. This means either approach produces identical results.

As a general rule, adjusting entries that create new asset or new liability accounts are likely candidates for reversing.

12. How are financial statements affected by a decision to make reversing entries?

Answer—p. 203

Account Numbering System

We described a three-digit account numbering system in Chapter 3. In such a system, the code number assigned to an account both identifies the account and gives information about the account's financial statement category.

In this section we describe a more detailed system, although we see many different systems in practice. The first digit in an account's number identifies its primary balance sheet or income statement category. For example, account numbers beginning with a 1 are assigned to asset accounts and account numbers beginning with a 2 are assigned to liability accounts. Exhibit 5A.2 shows how numbers can be assigned to the accounts of a company that buys and sells merchandise.

Exhibit 5A.2

Account Numbering for a Merchandiser

101–199	Asset accounts
201–299	Liability accounts
301–399	Owner's equity (including withdrawals)
401–499	Sales or revenue accounts
501–599	Cost of goods sold accounts (These are discussed in Chapter 6.)
601–699	Operating expense accounts
701–799	Accounts that reflect unusual and/or infrequent gains
801–899	Accounts that reflect unusual and/or infrequent losses

The second digit of each account number identifies its classification within the primary category. Exhibit 5A.3 shows this identification.

Exhibit 5A.3

Second Digit Account Numbering

101–199	**Assets**
101–139	Current assets (second digit is 0, 1, 2, or 3)
141–149	Long-term investments (second digit is 4)
151–179	Plant assets (second digit is 5, 6, or 7)
181–189	Natural resources (second digit is 8)
191–199	Intangible assets (second digit is 9)
201–299	**Liabilities**
201–249	Current liabilities (second digit is 0, 1, 2, 3, or 4)
251–299	Long-term liabilities (second digit is 5, 6, 7, 8, or 9)

The third digit completes the unique code for each account. Specific current asset accounts might be assigned the numbers shown in Exhibit 5A.4.

An extensive list of accounts using this code is provided near the end of this book. A three-digit account numbering system is often adequate for smaller businesses. A numbering system for more complex businesses might use four, five, or even more digits.

101–199	Assets
101–139	Current assets
101	Cash
106	Accounts Receivable
110	Rent Receivable
128	Prepaid Insurance

Three-Digit Account Numbering

Summary of Appendix 5A

P3 Prepare reversing entries and explain their purpose. Reversing entries are an optional step. They are applied to accrued assets and liabilities. The purpose of reversing entries is to simplify subsequent journal entries. Financial statements are unaffected by the choice to use or not use reversing entries.

Guidance Answer to 

12. Financial statements are unchanged by the choice between using or not using reversing entries.

Glossary

Accounting cycle recurring steps performed each accounting period, starting with analyzing transactions and continuing through the post-closing trial balance. (p. 182).

Classified balance sheet a balance sheet that presents assets and liabilities in relevant subgroups. (p. 188).

Closing entries journal entries recorded at the end of each accounting period that transfer the end-of-period balances in revenue, expense, and withdrawal accounts to the owner's capital account to prepare for the upcoming period and update the owner's capital account. (p. 176).

Closing process steps to prepare accounts for recording the transactions of the next period. (p. 176).

Current assets cash or other assets that are expected to be sold, collected, or used within the longer of one year or the company's operating cycle. (p. 192).

Current liabilities obligations due to be paid or settled within the longer of one year or the operating cycle. (p. 194).

Current ratio a ratio that is used to evaluate a company's ability to pay its short-term obligations, calculated by dividing current assets by current liabilities. (p. 195).

Income Summary a temporary account used only in the closing process to which the balances of revenue and expense accounts are transferred; its balance equals net income or net loss and is transferred to the owner's capital account or the Retained Earnings account for a corporation. (p. 177).

Intangible assets long-term assets (resources) used to produce or sell products or services; these assets lack physical form and their benefits are uncertain. (p. 194).

Long-term investments Assets such as notes receivable or investments in stocks and bonds that are held for more than one year or the operating cycle. (p. 192).

Long-term liabilities obligations that are not due to be paid within the longer of one year or the operating cycle. (p. 194).

Nominal accounts another name for *temporary accounts.* (p. 176).

Operating cycle of a business the average time between paying cash for employee salaries or merchandise and receiving cash from customers. (p. 191).

Owner's equity the owner's claim on the assets of a company. (p. 194).

Permanent accounts accounts that are used to report activities related to one or more future accounting periods; their balances are carried into the next period and include all balance sheet accounts; these balances are not closed as long as the company continues to own the assets, owe the liabilities, and have owner's equity; also called *real accounts.* (p. 176).

Plant and equipment are tangible long-lived assets used to produce or sell products and services; also called *plant assets.* (p. 193).

Post-closing trial balance a list of permanent accounts and their balances from the ledger after all closing entries are journalized and posted; a list of balances for all accounts not closed. (p. 181).

Pro forma statements statements that show the effects of the proposed transactions as if the transactions had already occurred. (p. 187).

Real accounts another name for *permanent accounts.* (p. 176).

Reversing entries optional entries recorded at the beginning of a new year that prepare the accounts for simplified journal entries subsequent to accrual adjusting entries. (p. 200).

Temporary accounts accounts that are used to describe revenues, expenses, and owner's withdrawals for one accounting period; they are closed at the end of the reporting period; also called *nominal accounts.* (p. 176).

Unclassified balance sheet a balance sheet that broadly groups the assets, liabilities, and owner's equity. (p. 188).

Working papers analyses and other informal reports prepared by accountants when organizing the information for formal reports to internal and external decision makers. (p. 184).

Work sheet a 10-column spreadsheet used to draft a company's unadjusted trial balance, adjusting entries, adjusted trial balance, and financial statements; an optional step in the accounting process. (p. 184).

A superscript letter [A] identifies assignment material based on Appendix 5A.

Questions

1. What two purposes are accomplished by recording closing entries?
2. What are the four closing entries?
3. What accounts are affected by closing entries? What accounts are not affected?
4. Describe the similarities and differences between adjusting and closing entries.
5. What is the purpose of the Income Summary account?
6. Explain whether an error has occurred if a post-closing trial balance includes the account: Depreciation Expense—Building.
7. How is an unearned revenue classified on the balance sheet?
8. What classes of assets and liabilities are shown on a typical classified balance sheet?
9. What is a company's operating cycle?
10. What are the characteristics of plant and equipment?
11. What tasks are aided by a work sheet?
12. Why are the debit and credit entries in the Adjustments columns of the work sheet identified with letters?
13. How do reversing entries simplify a company's record-keeping efforts?
14. [A] If a company accrued unpaid salaries expense of $500 at the end of a fiscal year, what reversing entry could be made? When would it be made?
15. Refer to the May 31, 1997, consolidated balance sheet for **NIKE** in Appendix A. What percent of NIKE's long-term debt is coming due before May 31, 1998?
16. Refer to **Reebok's** Consolidated Statements of Stockholders' Equity in Appendix A. What journal entry was likely recorded as of December 31, 1996, to close the Dividends Declared account?
17. Refer to the financial statements of **America Online** in Appendix A. What journal entry was likely recorded as of June 30, 1996, to close the company's Income Summary account?
18. What are three reasons why a company might wish to outsource services previously performed by a business in-house? Identify five common services that businesses may outsource.

Quick Study

QS 5-1
Effects of closing entries

Jontil Company began the current period with a $14,000 balance in the Peter Jontil, capital, account. At the end of the period, the company's adjusted account balances include the following temporary accounts with normal balances:

Service fees earned	$35,000
Salaries expense	19,000
Depreciation expense	4,000
Interest earned	3,500
Peter Jontil, withdrawals	6,000
Utilities expense	2,300

After closing revenue and expense accounts, what will be the balance of the Income Summary account? After all closing entries are journalized and posted, what will be the balance of the Peter Jontil, capital, account?

QS 5-2
Explaining the accounting cycle

List the following steps of the accounting cycle in their proper order:

a. Preparing the unadjusted trial balance.
b. Preparing the post-closing trial balance.
c. Journalizing and posting adjusting entries.
d. Journalizing and posting closing entries.
e. Preparing the financial statements.
f. Journalizing transactions.
g. Posting the transaction entries.
h. Preparing the adjusted trial balance.
i. Analyze transactions.

QS 5-3
Classifying balance sheet items
C3

The following are common categories on a classified balance sheet:

A. Current assets
B. Investments
C. Property, plant, and equipment
D. Intangible assets
E. Current liabilities
F. Long-term liabilities

For each of the following items, select the letter that identifies the balance sheet category in which the item should appear.

_____ **1.** Store equipment
_____ **2.** Wages payable
_____ **3.** Cash
_____ **4.** Notes payable (due in three years)
_____ **5.** Land not currently used in operations
_____ **6.** Accounts receivable
_____ **7.** Trademarks

QS 5-4
Computing current ratio
A1

Compute Tucker Company's current ratio from the following information about its assets and liabilities:

Accounts receivable	$15,000
Accounts payable	10,000
Buildings	42,000
Cash	6,000
Long-term notes payable	20,000
Office supplies	1,800
Prepaid insurance	2,500
Unearned services revenue	4,000

QS 5-5
Applying a work sheet
P3

In preparing a work sheet, indicate the financial statement debit column to which a normal balance of each of the following accounts should be extended. Use IS for the Income Statement Debit column and BS for the Statement of Changes in Owner's Equity or Balance Sheet Debit column.

_____ **1.** Equipment
_____ **2.** Owner, withdrawals
_____ **3.** Insurance expense
_____ **4.** Prepaid rent
_____ **5.** Accounts receivable
_____ **6.** Depreciation expense—Equipment

QS 5-6
Interpreting a work sheet
P3

The following information is taken from the work sheet for Hascal Company as of December 31, 1999. Using this information, determine the amount for S. Hascal, capital, that should be reported on its December 31, 1999, balance sheet.

	Income Statement		Statement of Changes in Owner's Equity and Balance Sheet	
	Dr.	Cr.	Dr.	Cr.
S. Hascal, capital				65,000
S. Hascal, withdrawals			32,000	
Totals	115,000	174,000		

QS 5-7A
Reversing entries
P4

On December 31, 1999, Yacht Management Co. prepared an adjusting entry for $6,700 of earned but unrecorded management fees. On January 16, 2000, Ace received $15,500 of management fees which included the fees earned in 1999. Assuming the company uses reversing entries, prepare the reversing entry and the January 16, 2000, entry.

Exercises

Exercise 5-1
Preparing closing entries
C1, P1

The following adjusted trial balance contains the accounts and balances of Painters Company as of December 31, 2000, the end of its fiscal year:

No.	Account Title	Debit	Credit
101	Cash	$18,000	
126	Supplies	12,000	
128	Prepaid insurance	2,000	
167	Equipment	23,000	
168	Accumulated depreciation—Equipment		$ 6,500
301	R. Tanner, capital		46,600
302	R. Tanner, withdrawals	6,000	
404	Services revenue		36,000
612	Depreciation expense—Equipment	2,000	
622	Salaries expense	21,000	
637	Insurance expense	1,500	
640	Rent expense	2,400	
652	Supplies expense	1,200	
	Totals	$89,100	$89,100

Prepare closing entries for Painters Company.

Exercise 5-2
Preparing closing entries and a post-closing trial balance
P1, P2

The adjusted trial balance for West Marketing Co. is shown below. Prepare a table with two columns under each of the following headings: Adjusted Trial Balance, Closing Entries, and Post-Closing Trial Balance. Complete the table by providing four closing entries and the post-closing trial balance.

No.	Account Title	Adjusted Trial Balance	
101	Cash	$ 8,200	
106	Accounts receivable	24,000	
153	Equipment	41,000	
154	Accumulated depreciation—Equip.		$ 16,500
193	Franchise	30,000	
201	Accounts payable		14,000
209	Salaries payable		3,200
233	Unearned fees		2,600
301	F. West, capital		64,500
302	F. West, withdrawals	14,400	
401	Marketing fees earned		79,000
611	Depreciation expense—Equip.	11,000	
622	Salaries expense	31,500	
640	Rent expense	12,000	
677	Miscellaneous expenses	7,700	
901	Income summary		
	Totals	$179,800	$179,800

Exercise 5-3
Closing entries for a corporation
P1

The following balances of the Retained Earnings and temporary accounts are from High Rider's adjusted trial balance:

Account Title	Debit	Credit
Retained earnings		$42,100
Cash dividends declared	$ 7,500	
Services revenue		32,000
Interest earned		5,300
Salaries expense	25,400	
Insurance expense	3,800	
Rental expense	6,400	
Supplies expense	3,100	
Depreciation expense—Trucks	10,600	

Required

a. Prepare the closing entries.

b. Determine the amount of retained earnings to be reported on the company's balance sheet.

Exercise 5-4
Preparing and posting closing entries
P1

Open the following T-accounts with the provided balances. Prepare closing journal entries and post them to the T-accounts.

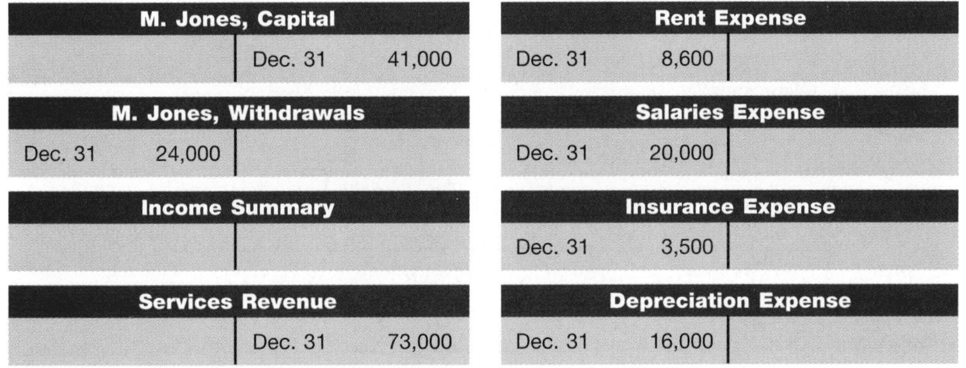

M. Jones, Capital			
		Dec. 31	41,000

M. Jones, Withdrawals			
Dec. 31	24,000		

Income Summary	

Services Revenue			
		Dec. 31	73,000

Rent Expense		
Dec. 31	8,600	

Salaries Expense		
Dec. 31	20,000	

Insurance Expense		
Dec. 31	3,500	

Depreciation Expense		
Dec. 31	16,000	

Exercise 5-5
Preparing a classified balance sheet
C3

Use the following adjusted trial balance of Hanson Trucking Company to prepare a classified balance sheet as of December 31, 2000.

Account Title	Debit	Credit
Cash	$ 7,000	
Accounts receivable	16,500	
Office supplies	2,000	
Trucks	170,000	
Accumulated depreciation—Trucks		$ 35,000
Land	75,000	
Accounts payable		11,000
Interest payable		3,000
Long-term notes payable		52,000
S. Hanson, capital		161,000
S. Hanson, withdrawals	19,000	
Trucking fees earned		128,000
Depreciation expense—Trucks	22,500	
Salaries expense	60,000	
Office supplies expense	7,000	
Repairs expense—Trucks	11,000	
Total	$390,000	$390,000

Exercise 5-6
Preparing a 10-column worksheet
P3

The following unadjusted trial balance contains the accounts and balances of the Deshaw Delivery Company as of December 31, 2000. Use the following information about the company's adjustments to complete a 10-column worksheet for Deshaw Delivery.

a. Depreciation of equipment for the year is $35,000.
b. The amount of incurred but unpaid Interest expense at the end of the year is $8,000.
c. The cost of unused office supplies on hand at the end of the year is $1,000.

Account Title	Debit	Credit
Cash	$ 14,000	
Accounts receivable	33,000	
Office supplies	4,000	
Trucks	340,000	
Accumulated depreciation—Trucks		$ 70,000
Land	150,000	
Accounts payable		22,000
Interest payable		6,000
Long-term notes payable		104,000
S. Deshaw, capital		322,000
S. Deshaw, withdrawals	38,000	
Delivery fees earned		256,000
Depreciation expense—Trucks	45,000	
Salaries expense	120,000	
Office supplies expense	14,000	
Interest expense	6,000	
Repairs expense, trucks	16,000	
Total	$780,000	$780,000

Exercise 5-7
Computing current ratio
A1

Use the information in the adjusted trial balance reported in Exercise 5-5 to compute the current ratio as of the balance sheet date.

Exercise 5-8
Computing current ratio
A1

Calculate the current ratio in each of the following separate cases:

	Current Assets	Current Liabilities
Case 1	$ 78,000	$31,000
Case 2	104,000	75,000
Case 3	44,000	48,000
Case 4	84,500	80,600
Case 5	60,000	99,000

Exercise 5-9
Extending adjusted account balances on a work sheet
P3

These accounts are from the Adjusted Trial Balance columns of a company's 10-column work sheet. In the blank space beside each account, write the letter of the appropriate financial statement column to which a normal account balance is extended.

A. Debit column for the income statement.
B. Credit column for the income statement.
C. Debit column for the statement of changes in owner's equity and balance sheet.
D. Credit column for the statement of changes in owner's equity and balance sheet.

_____ **1.** Service Fees Revenue
_____ **2.** Insurance Expense
_____ **3.** Accumulated Depreciation
_____ **4.** Interest Earned
_____ **5.** Accounts Receivable
_____ **6.** Rent Expense
_____ **7.** Depreciation Expense
_____ **8.** Cash
_____ **9.** Office Supplies
_____ **10.** Accounts Payable
_____ **11.** Owner, capital
_____ **12.** Wages Payable
_____ **13.** Machinery
_____ **14.** Interest Receivable
_____ **15.** Interest Expense
_____ **16.** Owner, withdrawals

Exercise 5-10
Preparing adjusting entries from work sheet
P3

Use the following information from the Adjustments columns of a 10-column work sheet to prepare the necessary adjusting journal entries:

		Adjustments	
No.	**Account Title**	**Debit**	**Credit**
109	Interest receivable	*(d)* $ 580	
124	Office supplies		*(b)* $ 1,650
128	Prepaid insurance		*(a)* 900
164	Accumulated depreciation—Office equipment		*(c)* 3,300
209	Salaries payable		*(e)* 660
409	Interest earned		*(d)* 580
612	Depreciation expense—Office equipment	*(c)* 3,300	
620	Office salaries expense	*(e)* 660	
636	Insurance expense, office equipment	*(a)* 432	
637	Insurance expense, store equipment	*(a)* 468	
650	Office supplies expense	*(b)* 1,650	
	Totals	$ 7,090	$ 7,090

Exercise 5-11
Completing the income statement columns and preparing closing entries
P3

These partially completed Income Statement columns from a 10-column work sheet are for WinSail Rental Co. Use the information to determine the amount that should be entered on the net income line of the work sheet. In addition, prepare closing entries for WinSail Rental. The owner, Jack Cooper, did not make any withdrawals.

Account Title	Debit	Credit
Rent earned		102,000
Salaries expense	45,300	
Insurance expense	6,400	
Dock rental expense	15,000	
Boat supplies expense	3,200	
Depreciation expense, boats	19,500	
Totals		
Net income		
Totals		

Exercise 5-12
Extending accounts in a work sheet
P3

The Adjusted Trial Balance columns of a 10-column work sheet for Plummer Company are shown below. Complete the work sheet by extending the account balances into the appropriate financial statement columns and by entering the amount of net income for the reporting period.

No.	Account Title	Adjusted Trial Balance	
101	Cash	$ 6,000	
106	Accounts receivable	26,200	
153	Trucks	41,000	
154	Accumulated depreciation—Trucks		$ 16,500
193	Franchise	30,000	
201	Accounts payable		14,000
209	Salaries payable		3,200
233	Unearned fees		2,600
301	F. Plummer, capital		64,500
302	F. Plummer, withdrawals	14,400	
401	Plumbing fees earned		79,000
611	Depreciation expense—Trucks	5,500	
622	Salaries expense	37,000	
640	Rent expense	12,000	
677	Miscellaneous expenses	7,700	
	Totals	$179,800	$179,800

Exercise 5-13A
Reversing entries
P4

Breaker Company records prepaid assets and unearned revenues in balance sheet accounts. The following information was used to prepare adjusting entries for Breaker Corporation as of August 31, the end of the company's fiscal year:

a. The company has earned $5,000 of unrecorded service fees.
b. The expired portion of prepaid insurance is $2,700.
c. Earned $1,900 of the total balance of the Unearned Fees account balance.
d. Depreciation expense for office equipment is $2,300.
e. Employees have earned but have not been paid salaries of $2,400.

Prepare the necessary reversing entries assuming Breaker uses reversing entries in its accounting system.

Exercise 5-14A
Reversing entries
P4

The following two events occured for Maxit Co. on October 31, 2000, the end of its fiscal year:

a. Maxit rents a building from its owner for $3,200 per month. By a prearrangement, the company delayed paying October's rent until November 5. On this date, the company paid the rent for both October and November.
b. Maxit rents space in a building it owns to a tenant for $750 per month. By prearrangement, the tenant delayed paying the October rent until November 8. On this date, the tenant paid the rent for both October and November.

Required

1. Prepare adjusting entries that Maxit must record for these events as of October 31.
2. Assuming Maxit does *not* use reversing entries, prepare journal entries to record Maxit's payment of rent on November 5 and the collection of rent on November 8 from Maxit's tenant.
3. Assuming Maxit does use reversing entries, prepare reversing entries and the journal entries to record Maxit's payment of rent on November 5 and collection of rent on November 8 from Maxit's tenant.

Problems

Problem 5-1

Closing entries, financial statements, and current ratio

C3, A1, P1

Bradshaw Repairs' adjusted trial balance on December 31, 2000, is shown below:

BRADSHAW REPAIRS Adjusted Trial Balance December 31, 2000			
No.	**Account Title**	**Debit**	**Credit**
101	Cash	$ 13,000	
124	Office supplies	1,200	
128	Prepaid insurance	1,950	
167	Equipment	48,000	
168	Accumulated depreciation—Equipment		$ 4,000
201	Accounts payable		12,000
210	Wages payable		500
301	H. Bradshaw, capital		40,000
302	H. Bradshaw, withdrawals	15,000	
401	Repair fees earned		77,750
612	Depreciation expense—Equipment	4,000	
623	Wages expense	36,500	
637	Insurance expense	700	
640	Rent expense	9,600	
650	Office supplies expense	2,600	
690	Utilities expense	1,700	
	Totals	$134,250	$134,250

Required

Preparation Component

1. Prepare an income statement and a statement of changes in owner's equity for the year 2000 and a classified balance sheet at the end of the year. There were no owner investments during the year.

Check Figure Ending capital balance, $47,650

2. Enter the adjusted trial balance in the first two columns of a six-column table that has middle columns for closing entries and the last two columns for a post-closing trial balance. Insert an Income Summary account as the last item in the trial balance.

3. Enter closing entries in the six-column table and prepare journal entries for them.

4. Determine the company's current ratio.

Analysis Component

5. Assume we collect the following two additional information items related to the adjusted trial balance shown above:

a. None of the $700 insurance expense had expired during the year. Instead, it is a prepayment of future insurance protection.

b. There were no earned and unpaid wages at the end of the year.

Describe the changes in financial statements that would result from these two information items.

Problem 5-2
Closing entries, financial statements, and ratios
C3, A1, P1

The adjusted trial balance for Graw Construction as of December 31, 2000, is shown below:

GRAW CONSTRUCTION
Adjusted Trial Balance
December 31, 2000

No.	Account Title	Debit	Credit
101	Cash	$ 4,000	
104	Short-term investments	22,000	
126	Supplies	7,100	
128	Prepaid insurance	6,000	
167	Equipment	39,000	
168	Accumulated depreciation—Equipment		$ 20,000
173	Building	130,000	
174	Accumulated depreciation—Building		55,000
183	Land	45,000	
201	Accounts payable		15,500
203	Interest payable		1,500
208	Rent payable		2,500
210	Wages payable		1,500
213	Property taxes payable		800
233	Unearned professional fees		6,500
251	Long-term notes payable		66,000
301	T. Graw, capital		82,700
302	T. Graw, withdrawals	12,000	
401	Professional fees earned		96,000
406	Rent earned		13,000
407	Dividends earned		1,900
409	Interest earned		1,000
606	Depreciation expense—Building	10,000	
612	Depreciation expense—Equipment	5,000	
623	Wages expense	31,000	
633	Interest expense	4,100	
637	Insurance expense	9,000	
640	Rent expense	12,400	
652	Supplies expense	6,400	
682	Postage expense	3,200	
683	Property taxes expense	4,000	
684	Repairs expense	7,900	
688	Telephone expense	2,200	
690	Utilities expense	3,600	
	Totals	$363,900	$363,900

An analysis of other information reveals that Graw Construction is required to make a $6,600 payment on its long-term note payable during 2001. Also, T. Graw invested $50,000 cash at the beginning of year 2000.

Required

Check Figure Total assets, $178,100

1. Prepare the income statement, statement of changes in owner's equity, and classified balance sheet.
2. Prepare the closing entries at the end of the year 2000.
3. Use the information in the financial statements to calculate these ratios:
   a. Return on equity.
   b. Modified return on equity assuming the owner's efforts are valued at $12,000 for the year.
   c. Debt ratio.
   d. Profit margin (use total revenues as the denominator).
   e. Current ratio.

Problem 5-3
Applying the accounting cycle
C2, P1, P2
S

On June 1, 2000, Jennifer Farrow created a new travel agency called Worldwide Tours. The company records prepaid and unearned items in balance sheet accounts. These transactions occurred during the company's first month:

June 1 Farrow invested $20,000 cash and computer equipment worth $40,000.
2 Rented furnished office space by paying $1,700 rent for the first month.
3 Purchased $1,100 of office supplies for cash.
10 Paid $3,600 for the premium on a one-year insurance policy. Insurance coverage began on June 10.
14 Paid $1,800 for two weeks' salaries to employees.
24 Collected $7,900 of commissions from airlines on tickets obtained for customers.
28 Paid another $1,800 for two weeks' salaries.
29 Paid the month's $650 telephone bill.
30 Paid $250 cash to repair the company's computer.
30 Farrow withdrew $1,500 cash from the business for personal use.

The company's chart of accounts included these accounts:

101	Cash	405	Commissions Earned
106	Accounts Receivable	612	Depreciation Expense—Computer Equipment
124	Office Supplies		
128	Prepaid Insurance	622	Salaries Expense
167	Computer Equipment	637	Insurance Expense
168	Accumulated Depreciation—Computer Equipment	640	Rent Expense
		650	Office Supplies Expense
209	Salaries Payable	684	Repairs Expense
301	J. Farrow, Capital	688	Telephone Expense
302	J. Farrow, Withdrawals	901	Income Summary

Required

1. Use the balance-column format to create each of the listed accounts.
2. Prepare journal entries to record the transactions for June and post them to the accounts.
3. Prepare an unadjusted trial balance as of June 30.
4. Use the following information to journalize and post adjusting entries for the month:
   a. Two-thirds of one month's insurance coverage was consumed.
   b. There were $700 of office supplies on hand at the end of the month.
   c. Depreciation on the computer equipment was estimated to be $600.
   d. The employees had earned $320 of unpaid and unrecorded salaries.
   e. The company had earned $1,650 of commissions that had not yet been billed.
5. Prepare an income statement, a statement of changes in owner's equity, and a balance sheet.
6. Prepare journal entries to close the temporary accounts and post them to the accounts.
7. Prepare a separate post-closing trial balance.

Check Figure Ending capital balance, $60,330

Problem 5-4
Balance sheet classifications
C3

In the blank space beside each numbered balance sheet item, enter the letter of its balance sheet classification. If the item should not appear on the balance sheet, enter a *z* in the blank.

a. Current assets **e.** Current liabilities
b. Investments **f.** Long-term liabilities
c. Plant and equipment **g.** Owner's equity
d. Intangible assets **h.** Stockholders' equity

_____ **1.** Depreciation expense, trucks
_____ **2.** L. Hale, capital
_____ **3.** Interest receivable
_____ **4.** L. Hale, withdrawals
_____ **5.** Automobiles
_____ **6.** Notes payable—due in three years

_____ **7.** Accounts payable
_____ **8.** Prepaid insurance
_____ **9.** Common stock
_____ **10.** Unearned services revenue
_____ **11.** Accumulated depreciation—Trucks
_____ **12.** Cash
_____ **13.** Building
_____ **14.** Retained earnings
_____ **15.** Office equipment
_____ **16.** Land (used in operations)
_____ **17.** Repairs expense
_____ **18.** Prepaid property taxes
_____ **19.** Current portion of long-term note payable
_____ **20.** Investment in Chrysler common stock (long-term holding)

Problem 5-5
Work sheet, journal entries, financial statements, and current ratio
C3, A1, P3

This unadjusted trial balance is for Whiten Construction Co. as of the end of its 1999 fiscal year. The beginning balance of the owner's capital was $52,660 and the owner invested another $25,000 cash in the company during the year.

WHITEN CONSTRUCTION CO.
Unadjusted Trial Balance
April 30, 1999

No.	Account Title	Debit	Credit
101	Cash	$ 17,500	
126	Supplies	8,900	
128	Prepaid insurance	6,200	
167	Equipment	131,000	
168	Accumulated depreciation—Equipment		$ 25,250
201	Accounts payable		5,800
203	Interest payable		
208	Rent payable		
210	Wages payable		
213	Property taxes payable		
251	Long-term notes payable		24,000
301	R. Whiten, capital		77,660
302	R. Whiten, withdrawals	30,000	
401	Construction fees earned		134,000
612	Depreciation expense—Equipment		
623	Wages expense	45,860	
633	Interest expense	2,640	
637	Insurance expense		
640	Rent expense	13,200	
652	Supplies expense		
683	Property taxes expense	4,600	
684	Repairs expense	2,810	
690	Utilities expense	4,000	
	Totals	$266,710	$266,710

Required

Preparation Component

1. Prepare a 10-column work sheet for 1999, starting with the unadjusted trial balance and including adjustments based on these additional facts:

a. The supplies on hand at the end of the year had a cost of $3,200.

b. The cost of expired insurance for the year is $3,900.

c. Annual depreciation on equipment is $8,500.

d. The April utilities expense of $550 is not included in the unadjusted trial balance because the bill arrived after it was prepared. The $550 amount owed needs to be recorded.

e. The company's employees have earned $1,600 of accrued wages.

f. The lease for the office requires the company to pay total rent for the year ended April 30 equal to 10% of the company's annual revenues. Rent has been estimated and is being paid to the building owner with monthly payments of $1,100. If the annual rent owed exceeds the total monthly estimated payments, the company must pay the excess before May 31. If the total owed is less than the amount previously paid, the building owner will refund the difference by May 31.

g. Additional property taxes of $900 have been assessed on the equipment but have not been paid or recorded in the accounts.

h. The long-term note payable bears interest at 1% per month, which the company is required to pay by the 10th of the following month. The balance of the Interest Expense account equals the amount paid for the first 11 months of the past fiscal year. The interest for April has not yet been paid or recorded. In addition, the company is required to make a $5,000 payment on the note on June 30, 1999.

2. Use the work sheet to journalize the adjusting and closing entries.

3. Prepare an income statement, a statement of changes in owner's equity, and a classified balance sheet. Calculate the company's current ratio.

Check Figure Total assets, $120,250

Analysis Component

4. Analyze the following errors and describe how each would affect the 10-column work sheet. Explain whether the error is likely to be discovered in completing the work sheet and, if not, the effect of the error on the financial statements.

a. Assume the adjustment for supplies consumption credited Supplies for $3,200 and debited the same amount to Supplies Expense.

b. When completing the adjusted trial balance in the work sheet, the $17,500 cash balance is incorrectly entered in the Credit column.

Problem 5-6[A]
Adjusting, reversing, and subsequent entries
P3, P4

The unadjusted trial balance for Shooting Ranges as of December 31, 2000, is shown below:

SHOOTING RANGES
Unadjusted Trial Balance
December 31, 2000

Cash	$ 13,000	
Accounts receivable		
Supplies	5,500	
Equipment	130,000	
Accumulated depreciation—Equipment		$ 25,000
Interest payable		
Salaries payable		
Unearned membership fees		14,000
Notes payable		50,000
S. Becker, capital		58,250
S. Becker, withdrawals	20,000	
Membership fees earned		53,000
Depreciation expense—Equipment		
Salaries expense	28,000	
Interest expense	3,750	
Supplies expense		
Totals	$200,250	$200,250

Required

1. Prepare a six-column table with two columns under each of the following headings: Unadjusted Trial Balance, Adjustments, and Adjusted Trial Balance. Complete the table by entering adjustments that reflect the following information:
   a. As of December 31, employees have earned $900 of unpaid and unrecorded salaries. The next payday is January 4, and the total amount of salaries to be paid is $1,600.
   b. The cost of supplies on hand at December 31 is $2,700.
   c. The note payable requires an interest payment to be made every three months. The amount of unrecorded accrued interest at December 31 is $1,250, and the next payment is due on January 15. This payment will be $1,500.
   d. An analysis of the unearned membership fees shows $5,600 remains unearned at December 31.
   e. In addition to the membership fees included in the revenue account balance, the company has earned another $9,100 in fees that will be collected on January 21. The company is also expected to collect $8,000 on the same day for new fees earned during January.
   f. Depreciation expense for the year is $12,500.
2. Prepare journal entries for the adjustments entered in the six-column table.
3. Prepare journal entries to reverse the effects of the adjusting entries that involve accruals.
4. Prepare journal entries to record the cash payments and collections that are described for January.

Check Figure Total debits in adjusted trial balance, $224,000

Serial Problem

Echo Systems

(The first two segments of this serial problem were in Chapters 3 and 4, and the final segment is presented in Chapter 6. If the Chapter 3 and 4 segments have not been completed, the assignment can begin at this point. It is recommended you use the Working Papers that accompany this book because they reflect the account balances that resulted from posting the entries required in Chapters 3 and 4.)

The transactions of Echo Systems for October through December 2000 have been recorded in the problem segments in Chapters 3 and 4, as well as the year-end adjusting entries. Prior to closing the revenue and expense accounts for year 2000, the accounting system is modified to include the Income Summary account, which is given the account number 901.

Check Figure Total credits in post-closing trial balance, $78,560.

Required

1. Record and post the necessary closing entries.
2. Prepare a post-closing trial balance.

BEYOND THE NUMBERS

Reporting in Action

P1

Refer to the financial statements and related information for **NIKE** in Appendix A. Find answers to the following questions by analyzing the information in its report:

Required

1. For the fiscal year ended May 31, 1997, what amount will be credited to Income Summary to summarize NIKE's revenues earned for the period?
2. For the fiscal year ended May 31, 1997, what amount will be debited to Income Summary to summarize NIKE's expenses incurred for the period?
3. For the fiscal year ended May 31, 1997, what will be the balance of the Income Summary account before it is closed to Retained Earnings?
4. Consult the Consolidated Statement of Cash Flows for the year ended May 31, 1997. What amount of cash was paid in dividends to common and preferred stockholders?

Swoosh Ahead

5. Obtain access to NIKE's annual report for fiscal years ending after May 31, 1997. You can gain access to NIKE's annual report at its web site **[www.nike.com]** or through the SEC's EDGAR data-

base **[www.sec.gov].** How has the amount of net income closed to Income Summary changed in the fiscal years ending after May 31, 1997? How has the amount of cash paid as dividends changed in the fiscal years ending after May 31, 1997?

Comparative Analysis

A1

Both **NIKE** and **Reebok** design, produce, market, and sell sports footwear and apparel. Key comparative figures ($ millions) for these two organizations follow:

Key Figures*	NIKE		Reebok	
	1997	*1996*	*1996*	*1995*
Current assets	$3,831	$2,727	$1,463	$1,333
Current liabilities	$1,867	$1,467	$ 517	$ 432

*NIKE figures are from its annual reports for fiscal years ended May 31, 1997 and 1996. Reebok figures are from its annual reports for fiscal years ended December 31, 1996 and 1995.

Required

1. Compute the current ratios for both years for both companies.
2. Which company has the better ability to pay short-term obligations according to the current ratio?
3. Comment on each company's current ratios for the past two years.
4. How do NIKE's and Reebok's current ratios compare to their industry average ratio of about 1.6?

Ethics Challenge

C2

On January 20, 2000, Jennifer Nelson, the staff accountant for Newby Enterprises, is feeling pressure to complete the preparation of the annual financial statements. The president of the company has said he needs up-to-date financial statements to share with several bankers on January 21 at a dinner meeting that has been called to discuss the possibility of Newby obtaining loan financing for a special building project. Jennifer knows that she won't be able to gather all the needed information in the next 24 hours to prepare the entire set of adjusting entries that must be posted before the financial statements accurately portray the company's performance and financial position for the fiscal period just ended December 31, 1999. Jennifer ultimately decides to estimate several expense accruals at the last minute. When deciding on estimates for the expenses, Jennifer uses low estimates as she doesn't want to make the financial statements look worse than they are. Jennifer finishes the financial statements before the deadline and gives them to the president without mentioning that several accounts use estimated balances as of December 31, 1999.

Required

1. Identify several courses of action that Jennifer could have taken instead of the one she decided on.
2. If you were in Jennifer's situation what would you have done? Briefly justify your response.

Communicating in Practice

C1

Assume one of your classmates said that the *going-concern,* or *continuing-concern, principle* states that the books of a company should be ongoing and therefore not closed until that business is terminated. This classmate does not understand the objective of the closing process or the meaning of the going-concern principle. Write a memo to this classmate that explains the concept of the closing process by drawing analogies between (a) a scoreboard for an athletic event and the revenue and expense accounts of a business or (b) a sports team's record book and the capital account. (Hint: Think about what would happen if the scoreboard was not cleared before the start of a new game.) Your memo should also clarify the meaning of the going-concern principle.

Taking it to the Net

A1

Visit **The Gap's** homepage at **www.gap.com.**

Required

1. Use the hotlink *Company History* to read the story of Gap's creation and evolution. To what does the name "The Gap" refer?

2. Chronicle the new types of stores that The Gap has opened throughout the 1980s and 1990s.
3. Access The Gap's annual financial report by using the hotlink provided. (Hint: If an adobe reader is required and the computer you are using is not so equipped, you may alternatively read the annual report information at www.sec.gov). Compute the current ratio for The Gap for the three years 1995–1997 (the most recent for the year ending January 31, 1998). Comment on the company's trend in liquidity.

Teamwork in Action

P1

The unadjusted trial balance and information for accounting adjustments of Noseworthy Investigators are shown below. Each team member involved in this project is to assume one of the responsibilities listed after the data. After completing each of these responsibilities, the team should work together to prove the accounting equation utilizing information from teammates (1 and 4). If your equation does not balance, you are to work as a team to resolve the error. The team's goal is to complete the task as quickly and accurately as possible.

Unadjusted Trial Balance

Account Title	Debit	Credit
Cash	$ 15,000	
Supplies	11,000	
Prepaid Insurance	2,000	
Equipment	24,000	
Accumulated Depreciation—Equipment		$ 6,000
Accounts Payable		2,000
D. Noseworthy, capital		31,000
D. Noseworthy, withdrawals	5,000	
Investigation fees earned		32,000
Rent expense	14,000	
Totals	$71,000	$71,000

Additional Year-End Information

a. Expired insurance is $1,200.
b. Equipment depreciation is $3,000.
c. Unused supplies total $4,000.
d. Services in the amount of $500 have been provided and have not been billed or collected.

Responsibilities for individual Team Members

1. Determine the accounts and adjusted balances to be extended to the balance sheet columns of a work sheet. Also, determine total assets and total liabilities.
2. Determine the adjusted revenue account balance and prepare the entry to close this account.
3. Determine the adjusted expense account balances and prepare the entry to close these accounts.
4. Prepare a T-account for D. Noseworthy, Capital, that reflects the unadjusted trial balance amount, and a T-account for Income Summary. Prepare the third closing entry without amounts and the fourth closing entry with amounts. Ask teammates assigned to parts *2* and *3* for the postings for Income Summary. Obtain amounts to complete the third closing entry and post both the third and fourth closing entries. Provide the team with the ending Capital account balance.
5. The entire team should prove the accounting equation.

Hitting the Road

C2

Select a company in your community that you can visit in person or interview on the telephone. Call ahead to the company to arrange a time when you can interview an employee (often an accountant) who helps prepare the annual financial statements for the company. During the interview inquire about the following aspects of the company's accounting cycle:

1. Does the company prepare interim financial statements? What time period is used for the interim statements?
2. Does the company use the cash or accrual basis of accounting?
3. Does the company use a work sheet to aid in the preparation of the financial statements? Why or why not?
4. Does the company use a spreadsheet program to construct the work sheet? If so, which software program is used?
5. How long does it usually take after the end of the 12-month fiscal period to complete annual financial statements?

Business Week Activity

C3, A1

Read "An Enormous Temptation to Waste" in the February 10, 1997, issue of *Business Week.*

Required

1. What are possible advantages and disadvantages of stockpiling cash?
2. What are some of the reasons for the growth in cash for the companies highlighted in the article?
3. Under what asset subgroup does cash appear on a classified balance sheet?
4. What ratio does the article use to target the companies with the greatest relative amounts of cash?
5. How would the current ratio for the companies be affected by the stockpiling of cash?

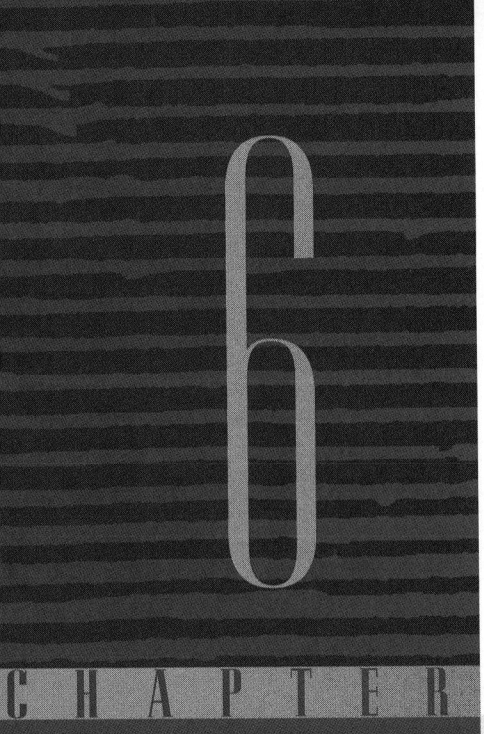

Accounting for Merchandising Activities

A Look Back

Chapter 5 focused on the final steps of the accounting process. We explained the importance of proper revenue and expense recognition and described the closing process. We also showed how to prepare financial statements from accounting records.

A Look at This Chapter

This chapter emphasizes merchandising activities. We explain how the reporting of merchandising activities differs from the reporting of service activities. Both the perpetual and periodic inventory systems are described. We also analyze and record merchandise purchases and sales transactions and explain adjustments and the closing process for merchandising companies.

A Look Ahead

Chapter 7 extends our analysis of merchandising activities. We focus on the valuation of inventory. Topics include the items in inventory, costs assigned, costing methods used, and inventory estimation techniques.

Chapter Outline

Fizzling Inventory

BOSTON—By June of last year, 27-year-old Jason Walker was living his dream. He'd just opened **Exotic Fruit Drinks,** a small retail outlet devoted to serving the quirky tastes of young and old alike. But within months, this young entrepreneur's dream had become a nightmare.

Exotic Fruit Drinks started out with a bang. Customers raved about its stock of exotic and unique beverage products. Profit margins on successful drinks far outweighed the costs of unsold products. "We were ready to take on **Nantucket Nectars**," boasted Walker. Within 2 months, however, Walker lost control of inventory, and margins were being squeezed. What happened? Was Exotic Fruit Drinks soon to be another flash in the pan?

Two problems emerged. One was Walker's selection of the periodic inventory system. This system reports inventory levels at periodic intervals such as once a month. This means the inventory system couldn't give Walker up-to-date information on sales and inventory he'd need for stocking and ordering. "Our popular brands were being sold out and nothing was in inventory," says Walker. "We were turning away too many customers." Hardly a ticket for success. The second problem was Walker's lack of negotiating ability regarding purchase contracts. Purchase discounts and returns left too much power and too many decisions with suppliers.

But Walker fought back. With the help of a consultant, he installed a perpetual inventory system and renegotiated purchase contracts. His new inventory system gives up-to-date details on sales and inventory. "We now know what's hot and what's not," says Walker, "And we don't turn away customers." Also, his new contracts allow him to return unsold inventories and to deeply discount others. "This time," claims Walker, "we'll not disappoint!" And the future of Exotic Fruit Drinks looks downright bubbly.

Learning Objectives

Conceptual

C1 Describe merchandising activities and identify business examples.

C2 Identify and explain the components of income for a merchandising company.

C3 Identify and explain the inventory asset of a merchandising company.

C4 Describe both periodic and perpetual inventory systems.

C5 Analyze and interpret cost flows and operating activities of a merchandising company.

Analytical

A1 Analyze and interpret accruals and cash flows for merchandising activities.

A2 Compute the acid-test ratio and explain its use as an indicator of liquidity.

A3 Compute the gross margin ratio and explain its use as an indicator of profitability.

Procedural

P1 Analyze and record transactions for merchandise purchases using a perpetual system.

P2 Analyze and record transactions for sales of merchandise using a perpetual system.

P3 Prepare adjustments and close accounts for a merchandising company.

P4 Define and prepare multiple-step and single-step income statements.

CHAPTER PREVIEW

Merchandising activities are a major part of modern business. Consumers expect a wealth of products, discount prices, inventory on demand, and high quality. This chapter introduces the business and accounting practices used by companies engaged in merchandising activities. These companies buy products and then resell them to customers. We show how financial statements capture these merchandising activities. The new financial statement elements created by merchandising activities are explained. We also analyze and record merchandise purchases and sales transacted by these companies. Adjustments and the closing process for merchandising companies are explained. An understanding of these important topics is what Jason Walker of Exotic Fruit Drinks needed to avoid the problems he encountered.

Merchandising Activities

C1 Describe merchandising activities and identify business examples.

Our emphasis in previous chapters was on the accounting and reporting activities of companies providing services such as **Greyhound Lines, Merrill Lynch, America West Airlines, Avis,** and **Marriott.** In return for services provided to its customers, a service company receives commissions, fares, or fees as revenue. Its net income for a reporting period is the difference between its revenues and the operating expenses incurred in providing services.

A merchandising company's activities are different from those of a service company. A **merchandiser** earns net income by buying and selling merchandise. **Merchandise** consists of products, also called *goods,* that a company acquires for the purpose of reselling them to customers. Merchandisers are often identified as either wholesalers or retailers.

A **wholesaler** is a *middleman* that buys products from manufacturers or other wholesalers and sells them to retailers or other wholesalers. Wholesalers provide promotion, market information, and financial assistance to retailers. They also provide a sales force, reduced inventory costs, less risk, and market information to manufacturers. Wholesalers include companies such as **Fleming, SuperValu, McKesson,** and **Sysco.** A **retailer** is a middleman that buys products from manufacturers or wholesalers and sells them to consumers. Examples of retailers include **The Gap, Oakley, CompUSA, Wal-Mart,** and **Musicland.** Retailers such as **Best Buy** often sell both products and services.

Reporting Financial Performance

C2 Identify and explain the components of income for a merchandising company.

Net income to a merchandiser implies that revenue from selling merchandise exceeds both the cost of merchandise sold to customers and the cost of other operating expenses for the period (see Exhibit 6.1). The usual accounting term for revenues from selling merchandise is *sales* and the term used for the cost of buying and preparing the merchandise is *cost of goods sold.*[1] A merchandiser's expenses are often called *operating expenses.*

Exhibit 6.1

Computing Income for Both a Merchandising Company and a Service Company

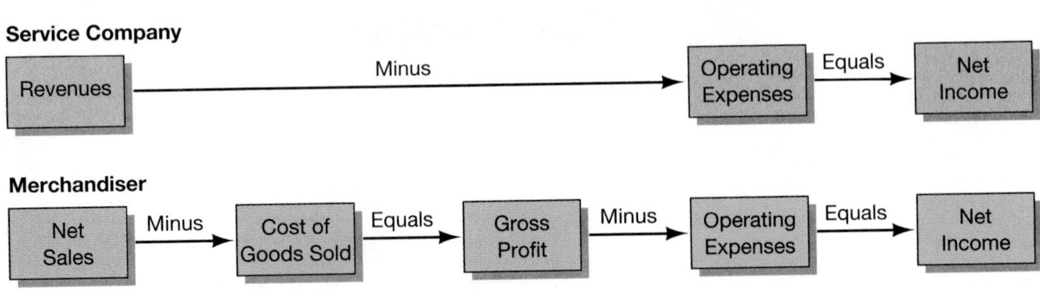

[1] Many service companies use the term *sales* in their income statements to describe revenues. **Marriott** is one example. Cost of goods sold is often called *cost of sales* and is described as an operating expense.

The condensed income statement for Z-Mart in Exhibit 6.2 shows how these three elements of net income are related. This statement shows Z-Mart sold products acquired at a cost of $230,400 to customers for $314,700. This yields a $84,300 gross profit. **Gross profit,** also called **gross margin,** equals net sales less cost of goods sold. Gross profit is important to the profitability of merchandisers. Changes in gross profit often greatly impact a merchandiser's operations since gross profit must cover all other expenses plus yield a return for the owner. Z-Mart, for instance, used gross profit to cover $71,400 of other expenses. This left $12,900 in net income for the year 1999.

Exhibit 6.2

Condensed Income Statement for a Merchandiser

Z-MART Condensed Income Statement For Year Ended December 31, 1999	
Net sales	$314,700
Cost of goods sold	**(230,400)**
Gross profit from sales	**$84,300**
Total other expenses	(71,400)
Net income	$ 12,900

Reporting Financial Condition

A merchandising company's balance sheet includes an item not on the balance sheet of a service company—a current asset called merchandise inventory. **Merchandise inventory** refers to products a company owns for the purpose of selling to customers. Exhibit 6.3 shows the classified balance sheet for Z-Mart, including merchandise inventory of $21,000. The cost of this asset includes the cost incurred to buy the goods, ship them to the store, and make them ready for sale. Although companies usually hold inventories of other items such as supplies, most companies simply refer to merchandise inventory as *inventory.*

C3 Identify and explain the inventory asset of a merchandising company.

Exhibit 6.3

Classified Balance Sheet for a Merchandiser

Z-MART Balance Sheet December 31, 1999			
Assets			
Current assets:			
Cash		$ 8,200	
Accounts receivable		11,200	
Merchandise inventory		**21,000**	
Prepaid expenses		1,100	
Total current assets			$41,500
Plant and equipment:			
Office equipment	$ 4,200		
Less accumulated depreciation	1,400	2,800	
Store equipment	30,000		
Less accumulated depreciation	6,000	24,000	
Total plant and equipment			26,800
Total assets			$68,300
Liabilities			
Current liabilities:			
Accounts payable		$16,000	
Salaries payable		800	
Total liabilities			$16,800
Owner's Equity			
K. Marty, capital			51,500
Total liabilities and owner's equity			$68,300

Operating Cycle

A merchandising company's operating cycle begins with the purchase of merchandise and ends with the collection of cash from the sale of merchandise. An example is a merchandiser who buys products at wholesale and distributes and sells them to consumers at retail. The length of an operating cycle differs across the types of businesses. Department stores such as **Sears** and **Dayton Hudson** commonly have operating cycles from three to five months. But operating cycles for grocery merchants such as **Kroger** and **Safeway** usually range from 1 to 2 months.

Exhibit 6.4 illustrates an operating cycle for a merchandiser with (1) cash sales and (2) credit sales. The cash sales cycle moves from (a) merchandise purchases to (b) inventory for sale to (c) cash sales. The credit sales cycle moves from (a) merchandise purchases to (b) inventory for sale to (c) credit sales and (d) accounts receivable to (e) cash. Credit sales delay the receipt of cash until the account receivable is paid by the customer. Companies always try to shorten their operating cycles. Assets tied up in inventory or receivables are not productive assets.

Exhibit 6.4

Operating Cycle of a Merchandiser*

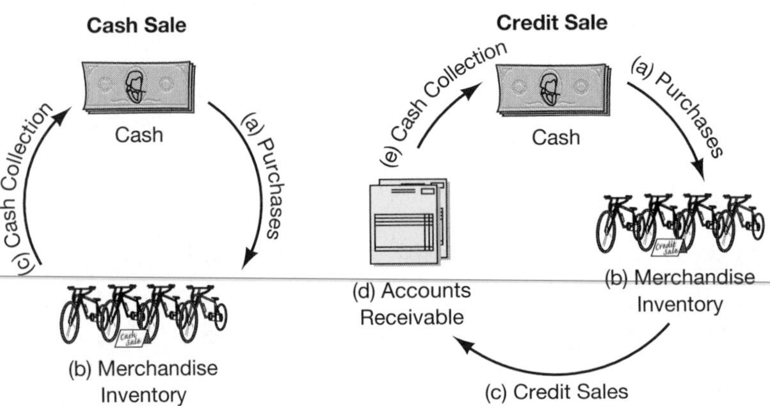

* This exhibit assumes cash purchases. Credit purchases would involve inserting accounts payable before merchandise inventory in the cycle.

Inventory Systems

We explained that a merchandising company's income statement includes an item called *cost of goods sold* and its balance sheet includes a current asset called *inventory*. **Cost of goods sold** is the cost of merchandise sold to customers during a period. It is often the largest single deduction on the income statement of a merchandiser. **Inventory** is products a company owns and expects to sell in its normal operations. These items are part of merchandising activities captured in Exhibit 6.5. This exhibit shows that a company's merchandise available for sale is a combination of what it begins with (beginning inventory) and what it purchases (net cost of purchases). The merchandise available is either sold (cost of goods sold) or kept for future sales (ending inventory).

Exhibit 6.5

Merchandising Cost Flow

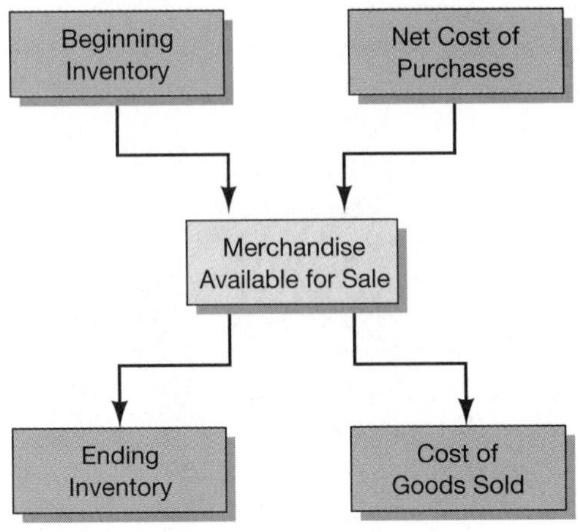

There are two inventory accounting systems used to collect information about cost of goods sold and cost of inventory on hand. The two systems are called *periodic* and *perpetual.*

C4 Describe both periodic and perpetual inventory systems.

Periodic Inventory System

A **periodic inventory system** requires updating the inventory account only at the *end of a period* to reflect the quantity and cost of both goods on hand and goods sold. It does not require continual updating of the inventory account. The company records the cost of new merchandise in a temporary *Purchases* account. When merchandise is sold, revenue is recorded but the cost of the merchandise sold is *not* yet recorded as a cost. When financial statements are prepared, the company takes a *physical count of inventory* by counting the quantities of merchandise on hand. Cost of merchandise on hand is determined by relating the quantities on hand to records showing each item's original cost. The cost of merchandise on hand is then used to compute cost of goods sold. The inventory account is adjusted to reflect the amount computed from the physical count of inventory.

Periodic systems were historically used by companies such as hardware, drug, and department stores that sold large quantities of low-value items. Without today's computers and scanners, it was not feasible for accounting systems to track such small items as pencils, toothpaste, paper clips, socks, and toothpicks through inventory and into customers' hands.

Perpetual Inventory System

A **perpetual inventory system** keeps a continual record of the amount of inventory on hand. A perpetual system accumulates the net cost of merchandise purchases in the inventory account and subtracts the cost of each sale from the same inventory account. When an item is sold, its cost is recorded in a *Cost of Goods Sold* account. With a perpetual system we can find out the cost of merchandise on hand at any time by looking at the balance of the inventory account. We can also find out the current balance of cost of goods sold anytime during a period by looking in the Cost of Goods Sold account.

Before advancements in computing technology, a perpetual system was often limited to businesses making a limited number of daily sales such as automobile dealers and major appliance stores. Because there were relatively few transactions, a perpetual system was feasible. In today's information age, with widespread use of computing technology, the use of a perpetual system has dramatically grown. Also, the number of companies using a perpetual system continues to increase.

Perpetual Information
Today's information technology is transforming merchandising activities. Computers and perpetual inventory systems are taking the guesswork out of wholesale buying, slashing inventory cycles, keeping popular items in stock, and cutting return rates. These advances have "totally changed the industry from a push industry to a pull industry," says the chairman of **Western Merchandisers,** a supplier of more than 1,000 **Wal-Marts.** Are supermarkets next? A recent study says grocers can cut prices by 11% or more with similar changes in accounting for inventory. [Source: *Business Week,* June 6, 1994.]

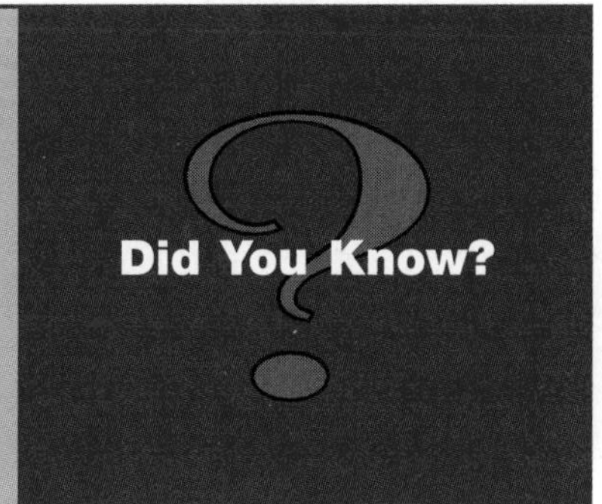

Because a perpetual inventory system gives users more timely information and is widely used in practice, our discussion in the chapter emphasizes a perpetual system. At **Wal-Mart,** for instance, a majority of suppliers get point-of-sale data. Yet we analyze and record merchandising transactions using *both* periodic and perpetual inventory systems in the appendix to this chapter.

Flash back

1. Describe a merchandiser's cost of goods sold.
2. What is gross profit for a merchandising company?
3. Explain why use of the perpetual inventory system has grown dramatically.

Answers—p. 249

Accounting for Merchandise Purchases

Assets = Liabilities + Equity
+1,200
−1,200

P1 Analyze and record transactions for merchandise purchases using a perpetual system.

We explained that with a perpetual inventory system, the cost of merchandise bought for resale is recorded in the Merchandise Inventory asset account. Z-Mart records a $1,200 cash purchase of merchandise on November 2 with this entry:

Nov. 2	Merchandise Inventory	1,200	
	Cash		1,200
	Purchased merchandise for cash.		

The invoice for this merchandise is shown in Exhibit 6.6. The buyer usually receives the original, while the seller keeps a copy. This source document serves as the purchase invoice of Z-Mart (buyer) and the sales invoice for Trex (seller). The amount recorded for merchandise inventory includes its purchase cost, shipping fees, taxes, and any other costs necessary to make it ready for sale.

To compute the total cost of merchandise purchases, we must adjust the invoice cost for (1) any discounts given to a purchaser by a supplier, (2) any returns and allowances for unsatisfactory items received from a supplier, and (3) any required freight costs paid by a purchaser. This section explains how these items affect our recorded cost of merchandise purchases.

Exhibit 6.6

Invoice

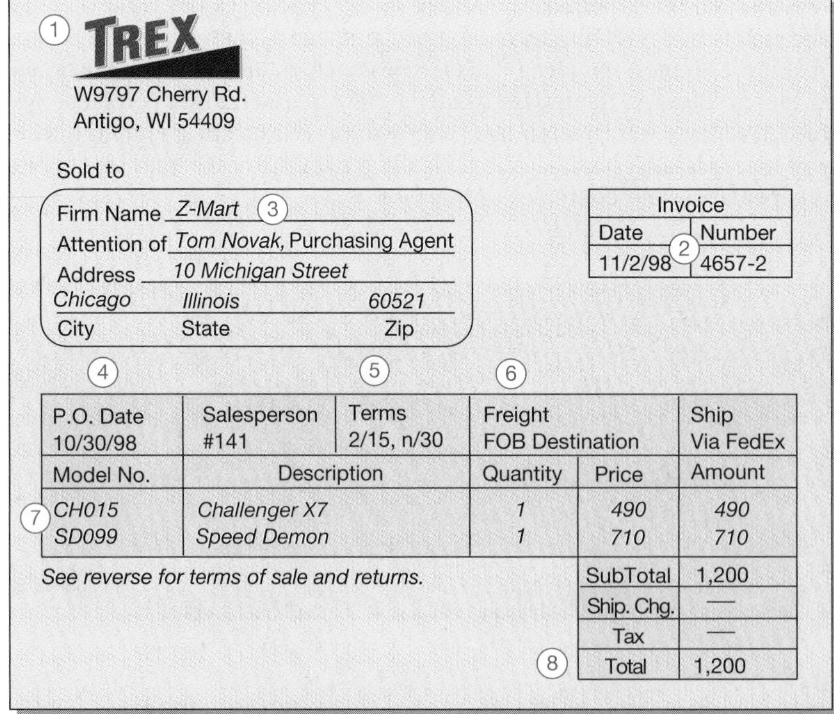

(1) TREX
W9797 Cherry Rd.
Antigo, WI 54409

Sold to

Firm Name *Z-Mart* (3)
Attention of *Tom Novak,* Purchasing Agent
Address *10 Michigan Street*
Chicago *Illinois* *60521*
City State Zip

Invoice	
Date	Number
11/2/98 (2)	4657-2

P.O. Date (4)	Salesperson	Terms (5)	Freight (6)		Ship
10/30/98	#141	2/15, n/30	FOB Destination		Via FedEx
Model No.	Description		Quantity	Price	Amount
(7) *CH015*	*Challenger X7*		*1*	*490*	*490*
SD099	*Speed Demon*		*1*	*710*	*710*
See reverse for terms of sale and returns.				SubTotal	1,200
				Ship. Chg.	—
				Tax	—
			(8)	Total	1,200

(1) Seller (2) Invoice date (3) Purchaser (4) Order date (5) Credit terms
(6) Freight terms (7) Goods (8) Total invoice amount

Trade Discounts

When a manufacturer or wholesaler prepares a catalog of items it has for sale, each item is usually given a **list price,** also called a *catalog price.* List price often is not the intended selling price of an item. Instead, the intended selling price equals list price minus a given percent called a **trade discount.**

The amount of trade discount usually depends on whether a buyer is a wholesaler, retailer, or final consumer. A wholesaler buying in large quantities is often granted a larger discount than a retailer buying in smaller quantities. A trade discount reduces a list price and is used to compute the actual selling price of the goods.

Trade discounts are commonly used by manufacturers and wholesalers to change selling prices without republishing their catalogs. When a seller wants to change selling prices, it can notify its customers merely by sending them a new table of trade discounts that they can apply to catalog prices.

Because a list price is not intended to reflect actual selling price of merchandise, a buyer does not enter list prices and trade discounts in its accounts. Instead, a buyer records the net amount of list price minus trade discount. In the November 2 purchase of merchandise by Z-Mart, it received a 40% trade discount for this item that was listed in the seller's catalog at $2,000. Z-Mart's purchase price is $1,200, computed as $2,000 − (40% × $2,000).

Purchase Discounts

The purchase of goods on credit requires a clear statement of expected amounts and dates of future payments to avoid misunderstandings. **Credit terms** for a purchase are a listing of the amounts and timing of payments between a buyer and a seller. Credit terms usually reflect the practices in an industry. In some industries, purchasers expect terms requiring payment within 10 days after the end of a month where purchases occur. These credit terms are entered on sales invoices or tickets as "n/10 EOM." The **EOM** refers to "end of month." In some other industries, invoices are often due and payable 30 calendar days after the invoice date. These credit terms are entered as "n/30." The 30-day period is called the **credit period.** Exhibit 6.7 portrays credit terms.

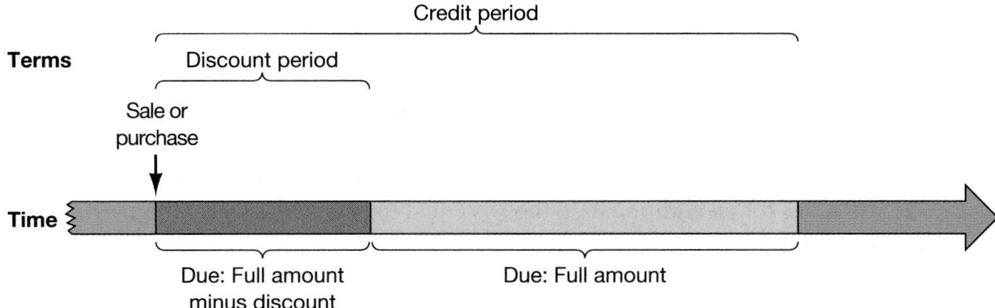

Exhibit 6.7
Credit Terms

Sellers often grant a **cash discount** when the credit period is long and buyers pay within a certain period. A buyer views a cash discount as a **purchase discount.** A seller views a cash discount as a **sales discount.** If cash discounts for early payment exist, they are described in the credit terms on an invoice. As an example, credit terms of "2/10, n/60" mean there is a 60-day credit period before full payment is due. But the seller allows a buyer to deduct 2% of the invoice amount from the payment if it is paid within 10 days of the invoice date. Sellers do this to encourage early payment. A **discount period** is the period where the reduced payment can be made.

To illustrate how a buyer accounts for a purchase discount, we assume Z-Mart's purchase of merchandise for $1,200 was on credit with terms of 2/10, n/30. Z-Mart's entry to record this credit purchase is:[2]

Assets = Liabilities + Equity
+1,200 +1,200

(a) Nov. 2	Merchandise Inventory	1,200	
	Accounts Payable		1,200
	Purchased merchandise on credit, invoice dated November 2, terms 2/10, n/30.		

If Z-Mart takes advantage of the discount and pays the amount due on November 12, the entry to record payment is:

Assets = Liabilities + Equity
−24 −1,200
−1,176

(b) Nov. 12	Accounts Payable	1,200	
	Merchandise Inventory (2% × $1,200) . . .		24
	Cash		1,176
	Paid for the purchase of November 2 less the discount.		

Z-Mart's Merchandise Inventory account now reflects the net cost of merchandise purchased. Its Accounts Payable account shows a zero balance, meaning the debt is satisfied.

Merchandise Inventory			
Nov. 2	1,200	Nov. 12	24
Balance	1,176		

Accounts Payable			
Nov. 12	1,200	Nov. 2	1,200
		Balance	0

Companies' buying practices involving inventory can impact gross profit. **Home Depot,** for instance, reported an increase in gross profit for 1996 over 1995. It explained in its Management Discussion and Analysis section that:

> The improvement resulted primarily from more effective buying practices, which resulted in lowering the cost of merchandise.
>
> **Home Depot**

Managing Discounts

A buyer's failure to pay within a discount period is often quite expensive. If Z-Mart does not pay within the 10-day discount period, it delays the payment by 20 more days. This delay costs Z-Mart an added 2% to the cost of merchandise. Most buyers try to take advantage of purchase discounts. We can approximate Z-Mart's annual rate of interest attached to not paying within the discount period. For Z-Mart's terms of 2/10, n/30, missing the 2% discount for an additional 20 days is equal to an annual interest rate of 36.5%, computed as (365 days ÷ 20 days) × 2%.

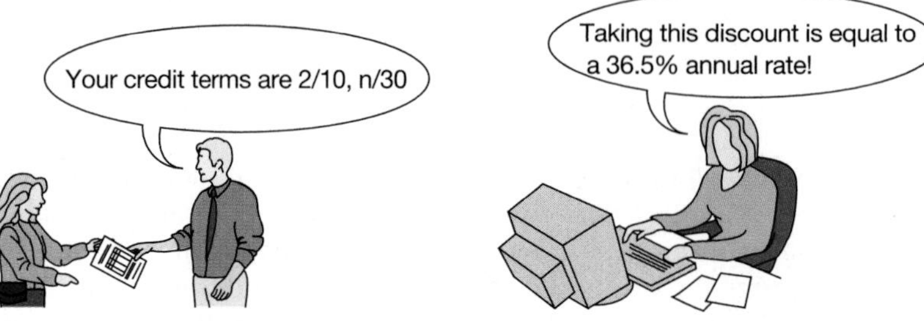

Nov. 2. Credit purchase. Nov. 12. Cash paid in discount period.

[2] Appendix 6A repeats journal entries *(a)* through *(f)* using a periodic inventory system.

Purchasing Agent
You're the purchasing agent for a merchandising company. You purchase a batch of CDs on terms of 3/10, n/90, but your company has limited cash and you must borrow funds at an 11% annual rate if you are to pay within the discount period. Do you take advantage of the purchase discount?

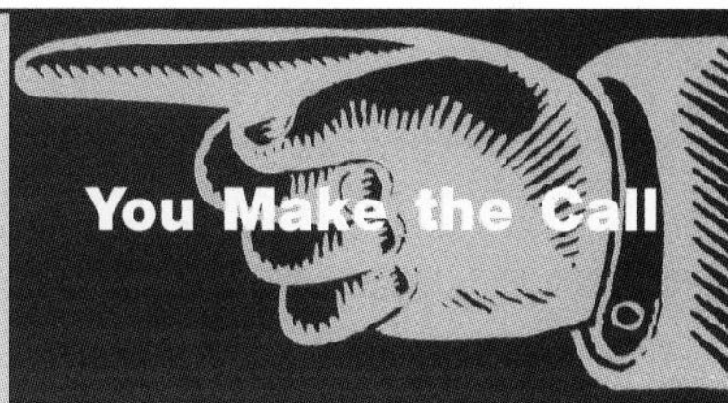

Answer—p. 249

Most companies set up a system to pay invoices with favorable discounts within the discount period. Careful cash management means that no invoice is paid until the last day of a discount period. One technique to achieve this goal is to file each invoice so that it automatically comes up for payment on the last day of its discount period. A simple manual system uses 31 folders, one for each day in a month. After an invoice is recorded, it is placed in the folder matching the last day of its discount period. If the last day of an invoice's discount period is November 12, it is filed in folder number 12. This invoice and other invoices in the same folder are removed and paid on November 12. Computerized systems achieve the same result by using a code identifying the last date in the discount period. When that date occurs, the system automatically identifies accounts to be paid.

Credit Manager
You are the new credit manager for a merchandising company that purchases its merchandise on credit. You are trained for your new job by the outgoing employee. You are to oversee payment of payables to maintain the company's credit standing with suppliers and to take advantage of favorable cash discounts. The outgoing employee explains that the computer system is programmed to prepare checks for amounts net of favorable cash discounts, and checks are dated the last day of the discount period. But you are told checks are not mailed until five days later. "It's simple," this employee explains. "Our company gets free use of cash for an extra five days, and our department looks better. When a supplier complains, we blame the computer system and the mailroom." Your first invoice arrives with a 10-day discount period for a $10,000 purchase. This transaction occurs on April 9 with credit terms of 2/10, n/30. Do you mail the $9,800 check on April 19 or April 24?

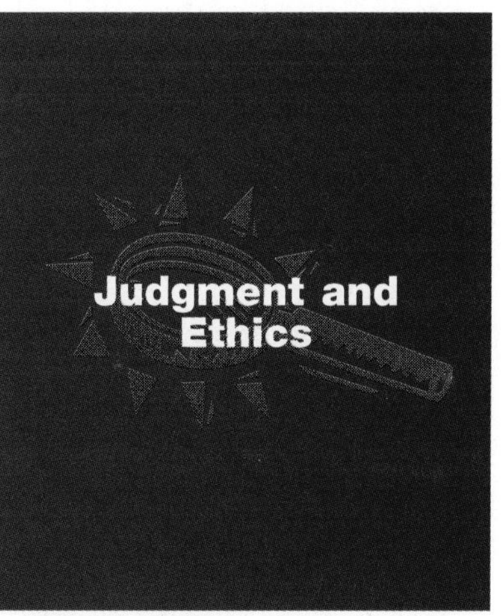

Answer—p. 249

Purchase Returns and Allowances

Purchase returns are merchandise received by a purchaser but returned to the supplier. A *purchase allowance* is a reduction in the cost of defective merchandise received by a purchaser from a supplier. Purchasers will often keep defective but still marketable merchandise if the supplier grants an acceptable allowance.

The purchaser usually informs the supplier in writing of any returns and allowances. This is often with a letter or a debit memorandum. A **debit memorandum** is a form issued by the purchaser to inform the supplier of a debit made to the supplier's account, including the reason for a return or allowance. The purchaser sends the debit memorandum to the supplier and also keeps a copy. Exhibit 6.8 shows a debit memorandum prepared by Z-Mart requesting an allowance from Trex for the defective *SpeedDemon* mountain bike. The purchaser's accounting for a debit memorandum requires updating the Merchandise Inventory account to reflect returns and allowances. The November 15 entry by Z-Mart for the purchase allowance requested in the debit memorandum is:

(c) Nov. 15	Accounts Payable	300	
	Merchandise Inventory		300
	Returned defective merchandise.		

Assets = Liabilities + Equity
−300 −300

Debit Memorandum

Case: Z-Mart (buyer) proposes $300 allowance for defective merchandise from Trex (seller)

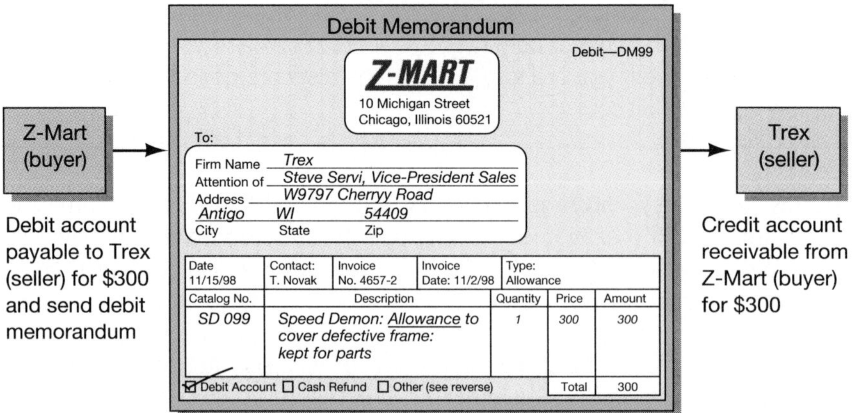

Debit Memorandum

Debit—DM99

Z-MART
10 Michigan Street
Chicago, Illinois 60521

To:
Firm Name Trex
Attention of Steve Servi, Vice-President Sales
Address W9797 Cherry Road
Antigo WI 54409
City State Zip

Date	Contact:	Invoice	Invoice	Type:		
11/15/98	T. Novak	No. 4657-2	Date: 11/2/98	Allowance		
Catalog No.	Description			Quantity	Price	Amount
SD 099	Speed Demon: Allowance to cover defective frame: kept for parts			1	300	300
☑ Debit Account ☐ Cash Refund ☐ Other (see reverse)					Total	300

If this had been a return, then the recorded cost of the defective merchandise would have been entered.[3] Z-Mart's agreement with this supplier says the cost of returned and defective merchandise is offset against Z-Mart's next purchase or its current account payable balance. Some agreements with suppliers involve refunding the cost to a buyer. If there is a refund of cash, then the Cash account is debited for $300 instead of Accounts Payable.

Discounts and Returns

When goods are returned within the discount period, a buyer can take the discount only on the remaining balance of the invoice. As an example, suppose Z-Mart purchases $1,000 of merchandise offered with a 2% cash discount. Two days later, Z-Mart returns $100 of goods before the invoice is paid. When Z-Mart later pays within the discount period, it can take the 2% discount only on the $900 balance. The discount is $18 (2% × $900) and the cash payment is $882 ($900 − $18).

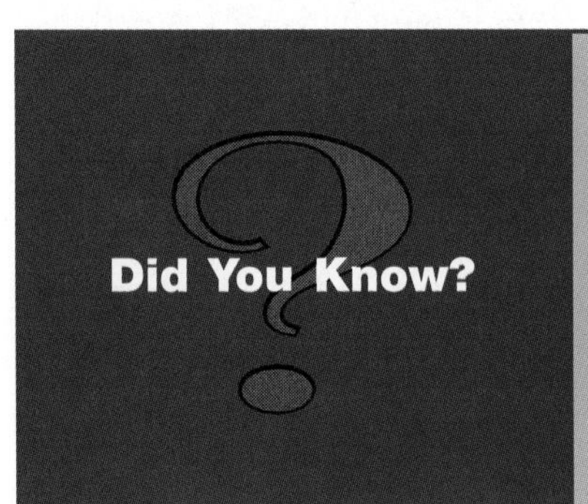

Clout!
Merchandising companies are unleashing a barrage of demands on suppliers. These include special discounts for new stores, payment of fines for shipping errors, and huge numbers of free samples. One merchandiser warned **Totes** it would impose a fine of $30,000 for errors in bar-coding on products Totes shipped. Merchandisers' goals are to slash inventories, shorten lead times, and eliminate error. [Source: *Business Week*, December 21, 1992.]

Transportation Costs

Depending on terms negotiated with sellers, a merchandiser is sometimes responsible for paying shipping costs on purchases, often called *transportation-in* or *freight-in* costs. Z-Mart's $1,200 purchase on November 2 is on terms of FOB destination. This means Z-Mart is not responsible for paying transportation costs.

A different situation arises when a merchandiser is responsible for paying transportation costs. Such costs are sometimes made to an independent carrier but are also sometimes directly made to the seller. Transportation costs are often included on the invoice when owed to the seller. Transportation costs owed to an independent carrier usually are

[3] Recorded cost is the cost reported in an account minus any discounts.

not included on the invoice. The cost principle requires these transportation costs be included as part of the cost of purchased merchandise. This means a separate entry is necessary when they are *not* listed on the invoice. For example, Z-Mart's entry to record a $75 freight charge to an independent carrier for merchandise purchased FOB shipping point is:

(d) Nov. 24	Merchandise Inventory	75	
	Cash		75
	Paid freight charges on purchased merchandise.		

Assets = Liabilities + Equity
+75
−75

Transportation-in costs are different from the costs of shipping goods to customers. Transportation-in costs are included in the cost of merchandise inventory whereas the costs of shipping goods to customers are not. The costs of shipping goods to customers are recorded in a Delivery Expense account when the seller is responsible for these costs. Delivery Expense, also called *freight-out* or *transportation-out*, is reported as a selling expense in the income statement.

Transfer of Ownership

The buyer and seller must reach agreement on who is responsible for paying any freight costs and who bears the risk of loss during transit for merchandising transactions. This is essentially the same as asking at what point does ownership transfer from the seller to the buyer. The point of transfer is called the **FOB** point, where FOB stands for *free on board.* The point when ownership transfers from the seller to the buyer determines who pays transportation costs (and other incidental costs of transit such as insurance).

Exhibit 6.9 identifies two alternative points of transfer. The first is FOB shipping point. *FOB shipping point,* also called *FOB factory*, means the buyer accepts ownership at the seller's place of business. The buyer is then responsible for paying shipping costs and bears the risk of damage or loss when goods are in transit. The goods are part of the buyer's inventory when they are in transit since ownership has transferred to the buyer.

Exhibit 6.9

Identifying Transfer of Ownership

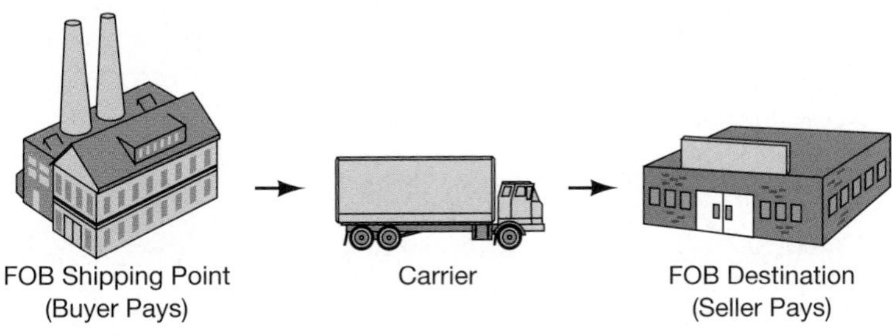

	Ownership transfers when goods passed to	Transportation costs paid by
FOB Shipping Point	Carrier	Buyer
FOB Destination	Buyer	Seller

Midway Games is a leader in entertainment software and uses FOB shipping point. Midway has released many outstanding games including Mortal Kombat, Cruis'n USA, Cruis'n World, NBA Jam, Joust, Defender, Pacman, and Space Invaders. Its subsidiary, Atari, has had similar success. Midway is given the right by Nintendo and Sega to self-manufacture cartridges for its platforms. Midway often uses manufacturers in Mexico where the platforms are purchased on an "as is" and "where is" basis. This means they "are delivered to the Company FOB place of manufacture and shipped at the Company's own expense and risk." Shipping usually takes 3 to 10 days, "depending on the mode of transport and location of manufacturer."[4]

The second point of transfer is FOB destination. *FOB destination* means ownership of the goods transfers to the buyer at the buyer's place of business. The seller is responsible for paying shipping charges and bears the risk of damage or loss in transit. The seller does not record revenue from this sale until the goods arrive at the destination because this transaction is not complete before that point.

Compaq Computer previously shipped its products FOB shipping point. Compaq found delivery companies to be undependable in picking up shipments at scheduled times, which caused backups at the plant, missed deliveries, and unhappy consumers. Compaq then changed its agreements to FOB destination, and its problems were eliminated.

There are situations when the party not responsible for shipping costs pays the carrier. In these cases, the party paying these costs either bills the party responsible or, more commonly, adjusts its account payable or receivable with the other party. For example, a buyer who pays a carrier when terms are FOB destination can decrease its account payable to the seller by the amount of shipping cost. Similarly, a seller who pays a carrier when terms are FOB shipping point can increase its account receivable from the buyer by the amount of shipping cost.

Recording Purchases Information

We explained how purchase discounts, purchase returns and allowances, and transportation-in are included in computing the total cost of merchandise inventory. Purchases are initially recorded as debits to Merchandise Inventory. Any later purchase discounts, returns, and allowances are credited to Merchandise Inventory. Transportation-in is debited to Merchandise Inventory. Z-Mart's 1999 total cost of merchandise purchases is made up of the items listed in Exhibit 6.10.

Exhibit 6.10

Total Cost of Merchandise Purchases Computation

Z-MART
Total Cost of Merchandise Purchases
For Year Ended December 31, 1999

Invoice cost of merchandise purchases	$235,800
Less: Purchase discounts received	(4,200)
Purchase returns and allowances received	(1,500)
Add: Cost of transportation-in	2,300
Total cost of merchandise purchases	**$232,400**

Combining these costs in the Merchandise Inventory account means this account reflects the net cost of purchased merchandise according to the *cost principle.* Recall that the Merchandise Inventory account is updated after each transaction affecting the cost of goods purchased. We later explain how this account is also updated each time merchandise is sold. These timely updates of the Merchandise Inventory account reflect a perpetual inventory system.

The accounting system described here does not provide separate records for total purchases, total purchase discounts, total purchase returns and allowances, and total transportation-in. Yet managers usually need this information to evaluate and control each of these cost elements. Many companies collect this information in supplementary records. **Supplementary records,** also called *supplemental records,* are a register of information outside the usual accounting records and accounts. We explain in Chapter 8 a process where supplementary records can be maintained.

[4] Midway Games Inc., *Form 10-K405* (6-30-97).

Flash back

4. How long are both the credit and discount periods when credit terms are 2/10, n/60?
5. Identify items subtracted from the *list* amount when computing purchase price: *(a)* freight-in; *(b)* trade discount; *(c)* purchase discount; *(d)* purchase return and/or allowance.
6. Explain the meaning of *FOB*. What does *FOB destination* mean?

Answers—p. 249

Accounting for Merchandise Sales

We explained how companies buying merchandise for resale need to account for purchases, purchase discounts, and purchase returns and allowances. Merchandising companies also must account for sales, sales discounts, sales returns and allowances, and cost of goods sold. A merchandising company such as Z-Mart reports these items in the gross profit section of an income statement as shown in Exhibit 6.11.

Exhibit 6.11

Gross Profit Section of income statement

Z-MART **Computation of Gross Profit** **For Year Ended December 31, 1999**		
Sales		$321,000
Less: Sales discounts	$4,300	
Sales returns and allowances	2,000	6,300
Net sales		$314,700
Cost of goods sold		(230,400)
Gross profit		**$ 84,300**

This section explains how information in this computation is derived from transactions involving sales, sales discounts, and sales returns and allowances.

P2 Analyze and record transactions for sales of merchandise using a perpetual system.

Sales Transactions

Each sales transaction for a seller of merchandise involves two related parts. One part is the revenue received in the form of an asset from a customer. The second part is recognizing the cost of merchandise sold to a customer. Accounting for a sales transaction means capturing information about both parts.

Sales transactions of merchandisers usually include both sales for cash and sales on credit. Whether a sale is for cash or on credit, a sales transaction requires two entries: one for revenue and one for cost. As an example, Z-Mart sold $2,400 of merchandise on credit on November 3. The revenue part of this transaction is recorded as:

(e) Nov. 3	Accounts Receivable	2,400	
	Sales		2,400
	Sold merchandise on credit.		

Assets	=	Liabilities	+	Equity
+2,400				+2400

This entry reflects an increase in Z-Mart's assets in the form of an account receivable. It also shows the revenue from the credit sale.[5] If the sale is for cash, the debit is to Cash instead of Accounts Receivable. The cost of the merchandise Z-Mart sold on November 3 is $1,600. We explain in Chapter 7 how the cost of this merchandise is computed. The

[5] We describe in Chapter 8 how companies account for sales to customers who use third-party credit cards such as those issued by banks and other organizations.

entry to record the cost part of this sales transaction (under a perpetual inventory system) is:

(e) Nov. 3	Cost of Goods Sold	1,600	
	Merchandise Inventory		1,600
	To record the cost of Nov. 3 sale.		

Since the cost part is recorded each time a sale occurs, the Merchandise Inventory account reflects the cost of the remaining merchandise on hand.

Sales Discounts

Selling goods on credit demands that expected amounts and dates of future payments be made clear to avoid misunderstandings. We explained earlier in this chapter how credit terms often include a discount to encourage early payment. Companies granting cash discounts to customers refer to these as sales discounts. Sales discounts can benefit a seller by decreasing the delay in receiving cash. Prompt payments also reduce future efforts and costs of billing customers.

A seller does not know whether a customer will pay within the discount period and take advantage of a cash discount at the time of a credit sale. This means a sales discount is usually not recorded until a customer pays within the discount period. As an example, Z-Mart completed a credit sale for $1,000 on November 12, subject to terms of 2/10, n/60. The entry to record this sale is:

Assets = Liabilities + Equity
+1,000 +1,000

Nov. 12	Accounts Receivable	1,000	
	Sales		1,000
	Sold merchandise under terms of 2/10, n/60.		

This entry records the receivable and the revenue as if the full amount will be paid by the customer.

But the customer has two options. One option is to wait 60 days until January 11 and pay the full $1,000. In this case, Z-Mart would record the payment as:

Assets = Liabilities + Equity
+1,000
−1,000

Jan. 11	Cash	1,000	
	Accounts Receivable		1,000
	Received payment for November 12 sale.		

The customer's second option is to pay $980 within a 10-day period running through November 22. If the customer pays on or before November 22, Z-Mart would record the payment as:

Assets = Liabilities + Equity
+980 −20
−1,000

Nov. 22	Cash	980	
	Sales Discounts	20	
	Accounts Receivable		1,000
	Received payment for November 12 sale less the discount.		

Sales discounts are recorded in a contra-revenue account called Sales Discounts. This is so management can monitor sales discounts to assess their effectiveness and cost. The Sales Discounts account is deducted from the Sales account when computing a company's net sales (see Exhibit 6.11). While information about sales discounts is useful, it is seldom reported on income statements distributed to external users.

Discount Miscount
Sales and purchases discounts are a major item for many merchandisers. **Penquin Books** admitted that unauthorized discounts were given to some of its merchandisers. This led to a $163 million charge against Penquin's 1996 income. [Source: *Business Week,* April 14, 1997.]

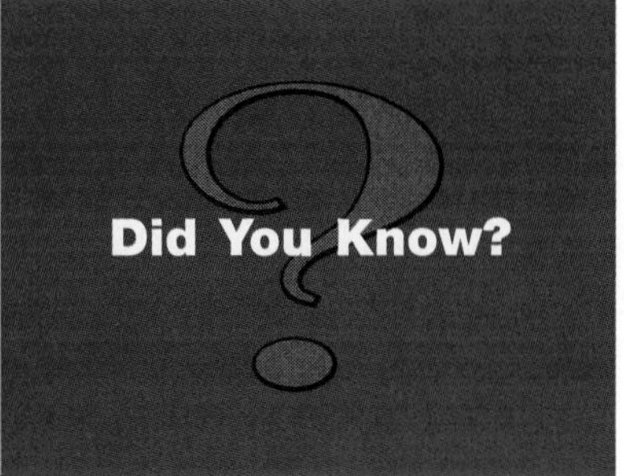

Sales Returns and Allowances

Sales returns refer to merchandise that customers return to the seller after a sale. Many companies allow customers to return merchandise for a full refund. *Sales allowances* refer to reductions in the selling price of merchandise sold to customers. This can occur with damaged merchandise that a customer is willing to purchase with a decrease in selling price. Sales returns and allowances involve dissatisfied customers and the possibility of lost future sales. Managers need information about returns and allowances to monitor these problems. Many accounting systems record returns and allowances in a separate contra-revenue account for this purpose.

Recall Z-Mart's sale of merchandise on November 3. As already recorded, the merchandise is sold for $2,400 and cost $1,600. But what if the customer returns part of the merchandise on November 6, where returned items sell for $800 and cost $600? The revenue part of this transaction must reflect the decrease in sales from the customer's return of merchandise:

(f) Nov. 6	Sales Returns and Allowances	800	
	Accounts Receivable		800
	Customer returned merchandise.		

Assets = Liabilities + Equity
−800 −800

Z-Mart can record this return with a debit to the Sales account instead of Sales Returns and Allowances. This method provides the same net sales, but does not provide information managers need in monitoring returns and allowances. By using the Sales Returns and Allowances contra account, this information is available. Published income statements usually omit this detail and show only net sales.

MegaBooks and MegaHeadaches
Book merchandisers such as **Barnes & Noble** and **Borders Books** can return unsold books to publishers at purchase price. Publishers say returns of new hardcover books are now running between 35% and 50%. This compares with 15% to 25% ten years ago. Also, competition for big hits is prompting huge author advances that together with returns are depressing publishers' earnings. [Source: *Business Week, April 14,* 1997.]

Name	Advances (in millions)	Book
Jonathan Kellerman	$20–$25	Five-book deal (Random House)
Marcia Clark	$4.2	*Without a Doubt* (Viking)
George Stephanpoulos	$2.75	*White House Memoir* (Little, Brown)
Dick Morris	$2.5	*Behind the Oval Office* (Random House)

Data: *Publishers Weekly;* Simon & Schuster; Joni Evans
By Hardy Green in New York, Superstores, Megabooks—and Humongous Headaches 04/14/97.

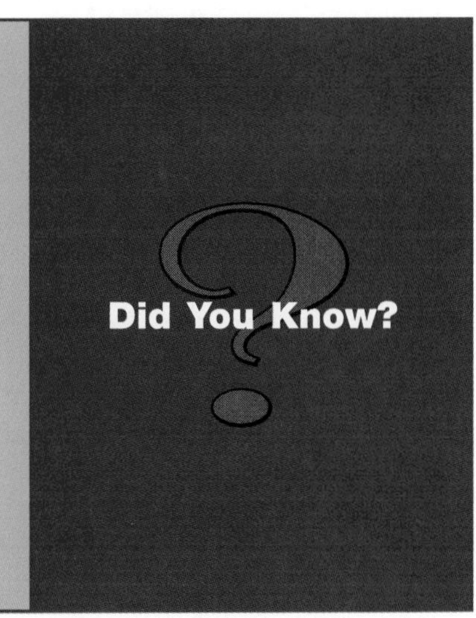

If merchandise returned to Z-Mart is not defective and can be resold to another customer, then Z-Mart returns these goods to its inventory. The entry necessary to restore the cost of these goods to the Merchandise Inventory account is:

Assets = Liabilities + Equity
+600 +600

Nov. 6	Merchandise Inventory	600	
	Cost of Goods Sold		600
	Returned goods to inventory.		

But if the merchandise returned is defective, the seller may discard the returned items. In this case, the cost of returned merchandise is not restored to the Merchandise Inventory account. Instead, most companies leave the cost of defective merchandise in the Cost of Goods Sold account.[6]

Another possibility is that $800 of the merchandise Z-Mart sold on November 3 is defective but the customer decides to keep it because Z-Mart grants the customer a price reduction of $500. The only entry Z-Mart must make in this case is one to reflect the decrease in expected revenue and assets:

Assets = Liabilities + Equity
−500 −500

Nov. 6	Sales Returns and Allowances	500	
	Accounts Receivable		500
	To record sales allowance.		

The seller usually prepares a credit memorandum to confirm a customer's return or allowance. A **credit memorandum** informs a customer of a credit to its Account Receivable account from a sales return or allowance. The information in a credit memorandum is similar to that of a debit memorandum. Z-Mart's credit memorandum issued to the customer for the return of $800 of merchandise on November 6 is shown in Exhibit 6.12.

Credit Memorandum

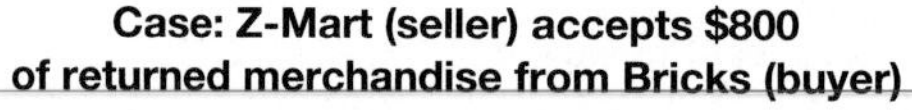

Case: Z-Mart (seller) accepts $800
of returned merchandise from Bricks (buyer)

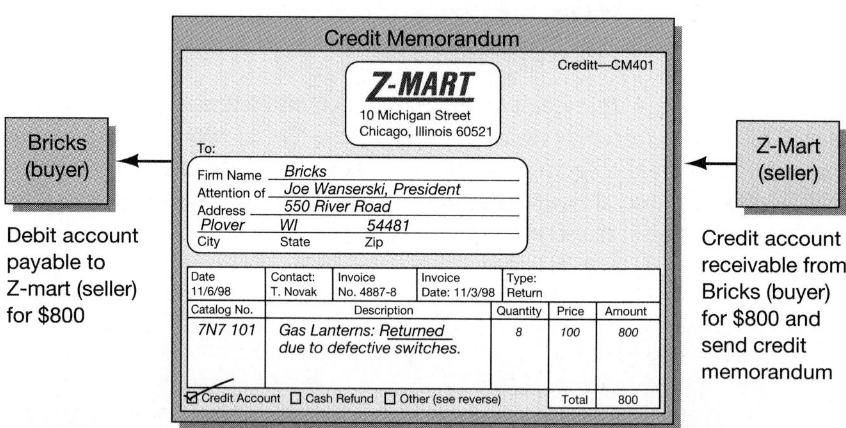

Flash back

7. Why are sales discounts and sales returns and allowances recorded in contra-revenue accounts instead of directly in the Sales account?
8. Under what conditions are two entries necessary to record a sales return?
9. When merchandise is sold on credit and the seller notifies the buyer of a price reduction, does the seller send a credit memorandum or a debit memorandum?

Answers—p. 249

[6] When managers want to monitor the cost of defective merchandise, a better method is to remove their cost from Cost of Goods Sold and charge it to a Loss from Defective Merchandise account.

Additional Merchandising Issues

This section identifies and explains how merchandising activities affect other accounting processes. We address cost and price adjustments, preparation of adjusting and closing entries, and relations between important accounts.

Cost and Price Adjustments

Buyers and sellers often find they need to adjust the amount owed between them. Such adjustment occurs when purchased merchandise does not meet specifications, unordered goods are received, different quantities are received than were ordered and billed, and errors occur in billing. The original balance can sometimes be adjusted by the buyer without negotiation. For example, when a seller makes an error on an invoice and the buyer discovers it, the buyer can make an adjustment and notify the seller by sending a debit or a credit memorandum. Sometimes adjustments can be made only after negotiations between the buyer and seller. An example is a buyer claims that some merchandise does not meet specifications. In these cases, the amount of allowance given by the seller is usually arrived at only after discussion.

Adjusting Entries

P3 Prepare adjustments and close accounts for a merchandising company.

Most adjusting entries are the same for both merchandising companies and service companies. The adjustments for both types of companies involve prepaid expenses, depreciation, accrued expenses, unearned revenues, and accrued revenues.

A merchandising company using a perpetual inventory system is often required to make one additional adjustment. This adjustment updates the Merchandise Inventory account to reflect any losses of merchandise. Merchandising companies can lose merchandise in several ways, including theft and deterioration. **Shrinkage** refers to the loss of inventory for merchandising companies.

While a perpetual inventory system tracks all goods as they move in and out of the company, a perpetual system is unable to directly measure shrinkage. Yet we can compute shrinkage by comparing a physical count of the inventory with recorded quantities. A physical count is usually performed at least once annually to verify the Merchandise Inventory account. Most companies record any necessary adjustment due to shrinkage by charging it to Cost of Goods Sold, assuming shrinkage is not abnormally large.

As an example, Z-Mart's Merchandise Inventory account at the end of 1999 had a balance of $21,250. But a physical count of inventory revealed only $21,000 inventory on hand. The adjusting entry to record this $250 shrinkage is:

Dec. 31	Cost of Goods Sold	250	
	Merchandise Inventory		250
	To adjust for $250 shrinkage revealed by a physical count of inventory.		

Assets	=	Liabilities	+	Equity
−250				−250

Wanted for Shrinkage
Shrinkage can be a sizable cost for many merchandisers. Recent examples of annual losses due to shrinkage are:

MusicLand	**$22 Million**
Sports Authority	**9 Million**

Companies often invest considerable resources in reducing shrinkage costs.

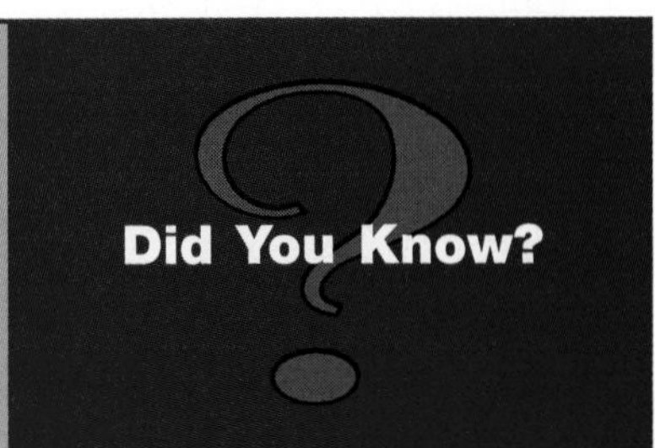

Closing Entries

Closing entries are similar for merchandising companies and service companies when using a perpetual system. The one difference is we must close temporary accounts re-

Adjusted Trial Balance

Z-MART
Adjusted Trial Balance
December 31, 1999

Cash	$ 8,200	
Accounts receivable	11,200	
Merchandise inventory	21,000	
Office supplies	550	
Store supplies	250	
Prepaid insurance	300	
Office equipment	4,200	
Accumulated depreciation—Office equipment		$ 1,400
Store equipment	30,000	
Accumulated depreciation—Store equipment		6,000
Accounts payable		16,000
Salaries payable		800
K. Marty, capital		42,600
K. Marty, withdrawals	4,000	
Sales		321,000
Sales discounts	4,300	
Sales returns and allowances	2,000	
Cost of goods sold	230,400	
Depreciation expense—Store equipment	3,000	
Depreciation expense—Office equipment	700	
Office salaries expense	25,300	
Sales salaries expense	18,500	
Insurance expense	600	
Rent expense, office space	900	
Rent expense, selling space	8,100	
Office supplies expense	1,800	
Store supplies expense	1,200	
Advertising expense	11,300	
Totals	$387,800	$387,800

lated to merchandising activities. We show the closing process for Z-Mart using its 1999 adjusted trial balance in Exhibit 6.13.

Z-Mart's trial balance includes several accounts unique to merchandising companies. These include: Merchandise Inventory, Sales, Sales Discounts, Sales Returns and Allowances, and Cost of Goods Sold. Their existence in the ledger means the four closing entries for a merchandiser are slightly different from the ones described in Chapter 5 for a service company. These differences are bolded in the closing entries in Exhibit 6.14.

Merchandising Cost Flows

C5 Analyze and interpret cost flows and operating activities of a merchandising company.

Exhibit 6.15 shows the relations between inventory, purchases, and cost of goods sold across periods. We already explained how the net cost of purchases captures trade discounts, purchase discounts granted, and purchase returns and allowances. These items constituting the cost of purchases are recorded in the Merchandise Inventory account when using a perpetual system. When each sale occurs, the cost of items sold is transferred from Merchandise Inventory to the Cost of Goods Sold account. Cost of goods sold is reported on the income statement. The ending balance in Merchandise Inventory is reported on the balance sheet.

The Merchandise Inventory account balance at the end of period one is the amount of beginning inventory in period two. The sequence of events during period two (and every period) is the same as during period one. The cost of each purchase is added to

Exhibit 6.14

Closing Entries for a Merchandiser

Step1: Close Credit Balances in Temporary Accounts to Income Summary.

The first entry closes temporary accounts having credit balances. Z-Mart has one temporary account with a credit balance and it is closed with the entry:

Dec. 31	**Sales**	**321,000**	
	Income Summary		321,000
	To close temporary accounts having credit balances.		

Posting this entry to the ledger gives a zero balance to the Sales account and opens the Income Summary account.

Step 2: Close Debit Balances in Temporary Accounts to Income Summary.

The second entry closes temporary accounts having debit balances. These include Cost of Goods Sold, Sales Discounts, and Sales Returns and Allowances. This entry also yields the amount of net income as the balance in the Income Summary account. Z-Mart's second closing entry is:

Dec. 31	Income Summary	308,100	
	Sales Discounts		**4,300**
	Sales Returns and Allowances		**2,000**
	Cost of Goods Sold		**230,400**
	Depreciation Expense—Store Equipment . .		3,000
	Depreciation Expense—Office Equipment .		700
	Office Salaries Expense		25,300
	Sales Salaries Expense		18,500
	Insurance Expense		600
	Rent Expense—Office Space		900
	Rent Expense—Selling Space		8,100
	Office Supplies Expense		1,800
	Store Supplies Expense		1,200
	Advertising Expense		11,300
	To close temporary accounts having debit balances.		

Step 3: Close Income Summary to Owner's Capital.

The third closing entry is the same for a merchandising company and a service company. It closes the Income Summary account and updates the owner's capital account for income or loss. Z-Mart's third closing entry is:

Dec. 31	Income Summary	12,900	
	K. Marty, capital		12,900
	To close the Income Summary account.		

The $12,900 amount in the entry is net income reported on the income statement in Exhibit 6.2.

Step 4: Close Withdrawals Account to Owner's Capital.

The fourth closing entry for a merchandising company is the same as the fourth closing entry for a service company. It closes the withdrawals account and reduces the owner's capital account balance to the amount shown on the balance sheet. The fourth closing entry for Z-Mart is:

Dec. 31	K. Marty, capital 4,000		
	K. Marty, withdrawals	4,000	
	To close the withdrawals account.		

When this entry is posted, all temporary accounts are cleared and ready to record events for the year 2000. The Owner's Capital account also is updated and reflects transactions of 1999.

Exhibit 6.15

Merchandising Cost Flow Across Periods*

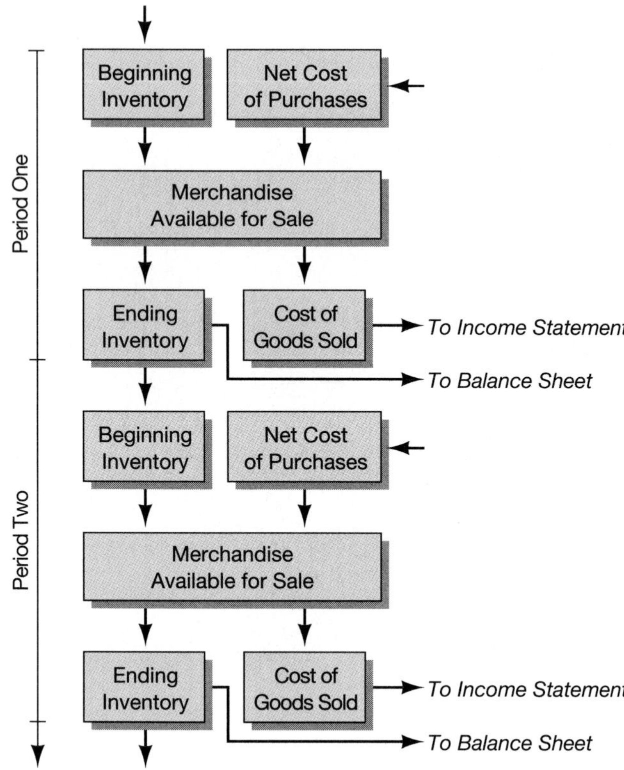

*Cost of goods sold is reported on the Income statement. Ending Inventory is reported on the balance sheet. One period's ending inventory is the next period's beginning inventory.

the Merchandise Inventory account and the cost of each sale is transferred from Merchandise Inventory to Cost of Goods Sold. At the end of the period, the Merchandise Inventory balance is reported on the balance sheet.

Merchandising Cost Accounts

To explain how merchandising transactions affect the Merchandise Inventory and Cost of Goods Sold accounts, we list Z-Mart's merchandising activities during 1999 in Exhibit 6.16 and show the impact of these activities in ledger T-accounts of Exhibit 6.17. The amounts in these exhibits are linked by superscripts *a* through *h*.

We explained how the perpetual inventory accounting system does not include separate accounts for purchases, purchase discounts, purchase returns and allowances, and transportation-in. But Z-Mart, like many companies, keeps supplementary records about these items. These supplementary records are used to accumulate the information in Exhibit 6.16. Z-Mart also keeps a separate record for the cost of merchandise returned by customers and restored in inventory.

The Merchandise Inventory and Cost of Goods Sold T-accounts in Exhibit 6.17 reflect the effects of these merchandising activities for Z-Mart. Most amounts in these T-accounts are summary representations of several entries during the year 1999.

The Cost of Goods Sold balance of $230,400 is the amount reported on the income statement in Exhibit 6.2. The Merchandise Inventory balance of $21,000 is the amount reported as a current asset on the balance sheet in Exhibit 6.3. These amounts also appeared on Z-Mart's adjusted trial balance in Exhibit 6.13.

Exhibit 6.16

Summary of Merchandising Activities

Z-Mart's Merchandising Activities for 1999	
Z-Mart's beginning inventory on January 1, 1999	19,000[a]
Invoice cost of merchandise purchases	$235,800[b]
Cost of freight to bring merchandise to Z-Mart's store	2,300[c]
Purchase discounts Z-Mart received from making payments within discount periods	4,200[d]
Refunds and credit granted to Z-Mart from purchase returns and allowances	1,500[e]
Cost of merchandise sold to customers	231,550[f]
Cost of merchandise returned by customers and restored to Z-Mart's inventory	1,400[g]
Cost of inventory shrinkage computed by physical count of inventory at year-end	250[h]

Flash back

10. When a merchandiser uses a perpetual inventory system, why is it often necessary to adjust the Merchandise Inventory balance with an adjusting entry?

11. What temporary accounts do you expect to find in a merchandising business but not in a service business?

12. Describe the closing entries normally made by a merchandising company.

Answers—p. 249

Exhibit 6.17

Merchandising Transactions Reflected in T-Accounts

Merchandise Inventory			
Dec. 31, 1998, balance	19,000[a]		
Purchases of merchandise	235,800[b]	Purchase discounts in 1999	4,200[d]
Merchandise returned by customers and restored to inventory in 1999	1,400[g]	Purchase returns and allowances in 1999	1,500[e]
Transportation-in costs for 1999	2,300[c]	Cost of sales transactions in 1999	231,550[f]
Total	258,500 −237,250	Total	237,250
Dec. 31, 1999 unadjusted balance	21,250	Dec. 31 Shrinkage	250[h]
Total	21,250 −250	Total	250
Dec. 31, 1999 adjusted balance	21,000		

Cost of Goods Sold			
Cost of sales transactions	231,550[a]	Merchandise returned by customers and restored to inventory in 1999	1,400[g]
Inventory shrinkage at Dec. 31, 1999, adjusting entry	250[h]		
Total	231,800 −1,400	Total	1,400
Balance (before closing)	230,400		

Income Statement Formats

P4 Define and prepare multiple-step and single-step income statements.

Generally accepted accounting principles do not require companies to use any one format for financial statements. We see many different formats in practice. The first part of this section describes two common income statement formats using Z-Mart's data: multiple-step and single-step. The final part of this section compares accrual and cash flow measures of gross profit for merchandising activities.

Multiple-Step Income Statement

Multiple-step income statements often contain more detail than simply a listing of revenues and expenses. There are two general types of multiple-step income statement. The usual format we see in external reports is what people commonly call the *multiple-step* format. A more detailed format is also available but usually seen only in internal documents. It is called the *classified, multiple-step* format. Both formats can be used in either a perpetual or periodic system.

Classified, Multiple-Step Format

Exhibit 6.18 shows a **classified, multiple-step income statement** for Z-Mart. This format shows detailed computations of net sales and cost of goods sold. Operating expenses are classified separately as selling expenses or general and administrative expenses. This format reports subtotals for various classes of items. This is why it is called a *classified* format.

Z-Mart's sales section is the same as shown earlier in the chapter. The cost of goods sold section draws on supplementary records Z-Mart keeps for merchandise purchases, purchase discounts, purchase returns and allowances, and transportation-in. The difference between net sales and cost of goods sold is Z-Mart's gross profit. Its operating ex-

Classified, Multiple-Step Income Statement

Z-MART
Income Statement
For Year Ended December 31, 1999

Sales			$321,000
Less: Sales discounts		$ 4,300	
Sales returns and allowances		2,000	6,300
Net sales			$314,700
Cost of goods sold:			
Merchandise inventory, December 31, 1998		$ 19,000	
Total cost of merchandise purchases*		232,400	
Goods available for sale		$251,400	
Merchandise inventory, December 31, 1999		21,000	
Cost of goods sold			230,400
Gross profit from sales			$ 84,300
Operating expenses:			
Selling expenses:			
Depreciation expense, store equipment	$ 3,000		
Sales salaries expense	18,500		
Rent expense, selling space	8,100		
Store supplies expense	1,200		
Advertising expense	11,300		
Total selling expenses		$ 42,100	
General and administrative expenses:			
Depreciation expense, office equipment	$ 700		
Office salaries expense	25,300		
Insurance expense	600		
Rent expense, office space	900		
Office supplies expense	1,800		
Total general and administrative expenses		29,300	
Total operating expenses			71,400
Net income			$ 12,900

* Using *supplementary records,* the total cost of merchandise purchases is composed of: invoice cost of merchandise (235,800) − discounts (4,200) − returns and allowances (1,500) + freight (2,300). See Exhibit 6.10 and related discussion for further explanation.

penses are classified into two categories. **Selling expenses** include the expenses of promoting sales through displaying and advertising merchandise, making sales, and delivering goods to customers. **General and administrative expenses** support the overall operations of a company and include expenses related to accounting, human resource management, and financial management.

Expenses are often divided between categories when they contribute to more than one activity. Exhibit 6.18 shows that Z-Mart allocates the rent expense of $9,000 for its store building between two categories—$8,100 to selling expense and $900 to general and administrative expense.[7]

Multiple-Step Format

Exhibit 6.19 shows a multiple-step income statement format common in external reports. In comparison to Exhibit 6.18, a multiple-step statement leaves out detailed computations of net sales and cost of goods sold. Selling expenses are also combined with general and administrative expenses.

[7] These expenses can be recorded in a single ledger account or in two separate accounts. If they are recorded in one account, we allocate its balance between the two expenses when preparing statements.

Z-MART Income Statement For Year Ended December 31, 1999		
Net sales		$314,700
Cost of goods sold		230,400
Gross profit from sales		$ 84,300
Operating expenses:		
Depreciation expense	$ 3,700	
Salaries expense	43,800	
Rent expense	9,000	
Insurance expense	600	
Supplies expense	3,000	
Advertising expense	11,300	
Total operating expenses		71,400
Net income		$ 12,900

Exhibit 6.19

Multiple-Step Income Statement

We frequently see more condensed formats in practice. For example, **Reebok's** income statement in Appendix A shows a single line item titled *Selling, general and administrative expenses.* But its annual report includes management's discussion and analysis of these expenses.

Single-Step Income Statement

A **single-step income statement** is another widely used format. This format is shown in Exhibit 6.20 for Z-Mart. This simple format includes cost of goods sold as an operating expense and shows only one subtotal for total expenses. Operating expenses are highly summarized.

Z-MART Income Statement For Year Ended December 31, 1999		
Net sales		$314,700
Cost of goods sold	$230,400	
Selling expenses	42,100	
General and admin. expenses	29,300	
Total expenses		301,800
Net income		$ 12,900

Exhibit 6.20

Single-Step Income Statement

Many companies use formats that combine features of both the single- and multiple-step statements. As long as income statement items are shown sensibly, management can choose the format it wants.[8] Similar options are available for the statement of changes in owner's equity and statement of cash flows for both merchandising companies and service companies.

Merchandising Cash Flows

A1 Analyze and interpret accruals and cash flows for merchandising activities.

Another aspect of effectively reporting on merchandising activities relates to their cash flow impacts. Merchandising sales and costs reported in the income statement usually differ from their cash receipts and payments for the period. This is because an income

[8] We describe some items in later chapters, such as extraordinary gains and losses, that must be shown in certain locations on the income statement.

statement is prepared using accrual accounting, not cash flows. Recognition of sales earned is rarely equal to cash received from customers. Also, recognition of cost of goods sold incurred is rarely equal to cash paid to suppliers.

We use Z-Mart's data in Exhibit 6.21 to illustrate this point. Z-Mart's net sales in the income statement total $314,700. Yet cash receipts from customers are only $309,200 (shown on the right side of Exhibit 6.21). This difference reflects a $5,500 *increase* in Accounts Receivable during 1999 for Z-Mart.

Exhibit 6.21

Analysis of Merchandising Cash Flows

Z-MART For Year Ended December 31, 1999			
Income Statement		**Statement of Cash Flows**	
Net sales	$314,700	Receipts from customers	$309,200
Cost of goods sold . .	230,400	Payments to suppliers	240,900
Gross profit	84,300	Net cash flows from customers and suppliers . .	68,300

An increase in accounts receivable means a delay in Z-Mart's receipt of cash from customers. It also means cash received from customers this period is less than net sales. To see this, recall that net sales and cash received are the same if all net sales are cash sales. But when some or all net sales are credit sales, then net sales and cash are likely different amounts. Since Accounts Receivable increased during the period, we know cash received is less than net sales. But if Accounts Receivable had decreased, then cash received would be greater than net sales. For Z-Mart, this relation is revealed as follows:

Net sales	$314,700
Less increase in accounts receivable . .	5,500
Cash received from customers	$309,200

We apply similar analysis to cost of goods sold. Z-Mart's cost of goods sold reported in its income statement totals $230,400. Yet cash paid to suppliers is $240,900. The difference between cost of goods sold and cash paid to suppliers reflects *two* items: (1) *change in inventory* and (2) *change in accounts payable*. An increase in inventory implies more goods were purchased than sold this period. But a decrease in inventory implies less goods were purchased than sold this period. An increase in accounts payable suggests less cash is paid to suppliers than the cost of this period's purchases. But a decrease in accounts payable suggests more cash is paid to suppliers than the cost of this period's purchases. We know from Exhibit 6.21 that the cash paid to suppliers is $10,500 more than cost of goods sold. This $10,500 difference reflects a $2,000 *increase* in inventory (purchased *more* than sold) and a $8,500 *decrease* in accounts payable (paid for *more* than current purchases) in 1999 for Z-Mart.

Recall that cost of goods sold and cash paid are the same if inventory and account payable levels don't change during the period. But when one or both account balances change, then cost of goods sold and cash paid are likely different amounts. For Z-Mart, this relation for 1999 is shown as follows:

Cost of goods sold	$230,400
Add increase in Inventory	2,000
Add decrease in accounts payable . .	8,500
Cash paid to suppliers	$240,900

Buying and selling merchandise is the most important activity for a merchandiser such as Z-Mart. We need to analyze both accrual and cash flows of this activity for signs of opportunity or problems. The increase in accounts receivable reflects an attempt by Z-Mart to meet competition and increase sales. It is trying to expand its sales by extending credit to more customers. But extending credit to customers who don't pay their bills can backfire. For effective decision making, we must always analyze important differences in accrual and cash flow figures and identify their causes.

Acid-Test and Gross Margin

USING THE INFORMATION

Companies with merchandising activities have at least two major differences from service companies. First, merchandise inventory often makes up a large part of assets, especially current assets. Second, merchandising activities result in cost of goods sold. Cost of goods sold is often the largest cost for these companies. Companies with merchandising activities change the way we use ratio analysis. This is especially the case with the current ratio (see Chapter 5) and the profit margin ratio (see Chapter 4). This section describes adjustments to these ratios to help us analyze merchandising companies.

Acid-Test Ratio

Merchandise inventory is a current asset. For many merchandising companies, inventory makes up a large portion of current assets. This often means a large part of current assets is not readily available for paying liabilities. This is because inventory must be sold and any resulting accounts receivable must be collected before cash is available.

A2 Compute the acid-test ratio and explain its use as an indicator of liquidity.

Information about current assets is important since we use it in assessing a company's ability to pay its current liabilities. We explained how the current ratio, defined as current assets divided by current liabilities, is useful in assessing a company's ability to pay current liabilities. Yet since it is sometimes unreasonable to assume inventories are a source of payment for current liabilities, we look to another measure.

One measure used to help us assess a company's ability to pay its current liabilities is the acid-test ratio. The acid-test ratio differs from the current ratio by excluding less liquid current assets such as inventory. *Liquidity* refers to how quickly an item is converted to cash. The less liquid assets or liabilities are those that will take longer to convert to cash. The **acid-test ratio,** also called *quick ratio,* is defined as *quick assets* (cash, short-term investments, and current receivables) divided by current liabilities. This is similar to the current ratio except that the numerator omits inventory and prepaid expenses. Exhibit 6.22 shows both the acid-test and current ratios of **J.C. Penney** for 1993 through 1996.

Exhibit 6.22

J.C. Penney's Acid-Test and Current Ratios

(in millions)	1996	1995	1994	1993
J.C. Penney:				
Total quick assets	$ 5,888	$5,380	$5,420	$4,852
Total current assets	$11,712	$9,409	$9,369	$8,565
Total current liabilities	$ 7,966	$4,020	$4,481	$3,883
Acid-test ratio	0.74	1.34	1.21	1.25
Current ratio	1.47	2.34	2.09	2.21
Industry:				
Industry acid-test ratio	1.1	1.3	1.3	1.2
Industry current ratio	3.6	3.9	3.9	3.4

The formula for the acid-test ratio is shown in Exhibit 6.23.

Exhibit 6.23
Acid-Test Ratio

$$\textbf{Acid-test ratio} = \frac{\textbf{Quick assets}}{\textbf{Current liabilities}}$$

We compute **Penney's** 1996 acid-test ratio by using information in Exhibit 6.22:

$$\frac{\$5,888}{\$7,966} = 0.74$$

Penney's acid-test and current ratios dropped in 1996 compared with prior years. While the industry ratios also dropped, neither declined to the extent of Penney's ratios. Penney's current ratios for 1993–1996 suggest its short-term obligations can be covered with short-term assets. Yet the acid-test ratio raises a concern in 1996. An acid-test ratio less than 1 means Penney's current liabilities exceed its quick assets. Penney is likely facing some problems in covering current liabilities with liquid assets. This is mainly due to a sharp increase in accounts payable and accrued expenses.

A common rule of thumb is that the acid-test ratio should have a value of at least 1.0 to conclude that a company is unlikely to face liquidity problems in the near future. A value less than 1.0 suggests a liquidity problem unless a company can generate enough cash from sales or if the accounts payable are not due until late in the next period. Similarly, a value greater than 1.0 can hide a liquidity problem if payables are due shortly and receivables won't be collected until late in the next period. Our analysis of Penney's emphasizes that one ratio is seldom enough to reach a conclusion as to strength or weakness. The power of a ratio is often its ability to identify areas we need to analyze in more detail.

Supplier
You're a supplier of building materials. A retail store asks you for credit on future purchases of materials. You have no prior experience with this store. You ask and receive the store's financial statements to assess its ability to make payment on purchases. The store's current ratio is 2.1 and its acid-test ratio is 0.5. You find inventory makes up most of current assets. Do you extend credit to this store?

Answer—p. 249

A3 Compute the gross margin ratio and explain its use as an indicator of profitability.

Gross Margin Ratio

A major cost of merchandising companies is its cost of goods sold. For many merchandising companies, cost of goods sold makes up the majority of its costs. This means success for merchandising companies often depends on the relation between sales and cost of goods sold.

We described the importance of the profit margin ratio in Chapter 4. Gross profit, also called *gross margin,* is a major part of the profit margin of merchandising companies. To help us focus on this important item, users often compute a gross margin ratio. Without sufficient gross profit, a merchandising company will likely fail. The gross margin ratio differs from the profit margin ratio by excluding all costs except cost of goods sold. The **gross margin ratio** is defined as gross margin (net sales minus cost of goods sold) divided by net sales. Exhibit 6.24 shows the gross margin ratios of **J.C. Penney** for 1993–1996.

(in millions)	1996	1995	1994	1993
Gross margin	$ 7,606	$ 7,086	$ 7,112	$ 6,581
Net sales	$23,649	$21,419	$21,082	$19,578
Gross margin ratio	**32.2%**	**33.1%**	**33.7%**	**33.6%**

Exhibit 6.24

J.C. Penney's Gross Margin Ratio

The formula for the gross margin ratio is shown in Exhibit 6.25.

$$\textbf{Gross margin ratio} = \frac{\textbf{Gross margin}}{\textbf{Net sales}}$$

Exhibit 6.25

Gross Margin Ratio

This ratio reflects the gross margin in each dollar of sales. To illustrate how we compute and use the gross margin ratio, we look at the results of J.C. Penney for the past few years as reported in Exhibit 6.24. From the information in this exhibit, we can compute Penney's 1996 gross margin ratio as:

$$\frac{\$7,606}{\$23,649} = 0.32$$

This ratio result means that each $1 of sales for J.C. Penney yields about 32¢ in gross margin to cover all other expenses and still produce a profit for the company.

Results in Exhibit 6.24 show Penney gross margin ratio declined from 1994 to 1996. The 1996 gross margin ratio, for instance, declined to 32.2% from 33.1% in 1995. This nearly 1% decline is an important development. Success for merchandisers such as Penney depends on maintaining an adequate gross margin. Data in this exhibit also reveal that Penney's sales are increasing over this period while its gross margin is decreasing. This shows costs of sales are rising faster than sales.

Chief Financial Officer

You're a chief financial officer of a merchandising company. You're analyzing profitability for your company and compute a 36% gross margin ratio and a 17% net profit margin ratio. Industry averages are 44% for gross margin and 16% for net profit margin. Do these ratios concern you?

Answer—p. 249

Flash *back*

13. What income statement format shows detailed computations for net sales and cost of goods sold? What format gives no subtotals except total expenses?

14. Which assets are quick assets in computing the acid-test ratio?

15. What ratio is a more strict test of a company's ability to meet its short-term obligations, the acid-test ratio or current ratio?

Answers—p. 249

Summary

C1 Describe merchandising activities and identify business examples. Operations of merchandising companies involve buying products and reselling them. Examples of merchandisers include Wal-Mart, Home Depot, Woolworth, Limited, Circuit City, and Barnes & Noble.

C2 Identify and explain the components of income for a merchandising company. A merchandiser's costs on an income statement include an amount for cost of goods sold. Gross profit, or gross margin, equals sales minus cost of goods sold.

C3 Identify and explain the inventory asset of a merchandising company. The current asset section of a merchandising company's balance sheet includes merchandise inventory. Merchandise inventory refers to the products a merchandiser sells and are on hand at the balance sheet date.

C4 Describe both periodic and perpetual inventory systems. A perpetual inventory system continuously tracks the cost of goods on hand and the cost of goods sold. A periodic system accumulates the cost of goods purchased during the period and does not compute the amount of inventory on hand or the cost of goods sold until the end of a period.

C5 Analyze and interpret cost flows and operating activities of a merchandising company. Net costs of merchandise purchases flow into Merchandise Inventory and from there to Cost of Goods Sold on the income statement. Any remaining Merchandise Inventory balance is reported as a current asset on the balance sheet. This is the beginning inventory for the next period.

A1 Analyze and interpret accruals and cash flows for merchandising activities. Merchandising sales and costs of sales reported in the income statement usually differ from their corresponding cash receipts and payments for the period. Cash received from customers equals net sales less the increase (or plus the decrease) in Accounts Receivable during the period. Cash paid to suppliers equals cost of goods sold less the increase (or plus the decrease) in Accounts Payable and less the decrease (or plus the increase) in Inventory during the period.

A2 Compute the acid-test ratio and explain its use as an indicator of liquidity. The acid-test ratio is computed as quick assets (cash, short-term investments, and current receivables) divided by current liabilities. It is an indicator of a company's ability to pay its current liabilities with its existing quick assets. A ratio equal to or greater than one is often considered adequate.

A3 Compute the gross margin ratio and explain its use as an indicator of profitability. The gross margin (or gross profit) ratio is computed as gross margin (sales minus cost of goods sold) divided by sales. It is an indicator of a company's profitability in merchandising absent operating expenses. A gross margin ratio must be large enough to cover operating expenses and give an adequate net profit margin.

P1 Analyze and record transactions for merchandise purchases using a perpetual system. For a perpetual inventory system, purchases net of trade discounts are added (debited) to the Merchandise Inventory account. Purchase discounts and purchase returns and allowances are subtracted (credited) from Merchandise Inventory, and transportation-in costs are added (debited) to Merchandise Inventory. Many companies keep supplementary records to accumulate information about the total amounts of purchases, purchase discounts, purchase returns and allowances, and transportation-in.

P2 Analyze and record transactions for sales of merchandise using a perpetual system. A merchandiser records sales at list price less any trade discounts. The cost of items sold is transferred from Merchandise Inventory to Cost of Goods Sold. Refunds or credits given to customers for unsatisfactory merchandise are recorded (debited) in Sales Returns and Allowances, a contra account to Sales. If merchandise is returned and restored to inventory, the cost of this merchandise is removed from Cost of Goods Sold and transferred back to Merchandise Inventory. When cash discounts from the sales price are offered and customers pay within the discount period, the seller records (debits) discounts in Sales Discounts, a contra account to Sales. Debit and credit memoranda are documents sent between buyers and sellers to communicate that the sender is either debiting or crediting an account of the recipient.

P3 Prepare adjustments and close accounts for a merchandising company. With a perpetual inventory system, it is often necessary to make an adjustment for inventory shrinkage. This is computed by comparing a physical count of inventory with the Merchandise Inventory account balance. Shrinkage is normally charged to Cost of Goods Sold. Temporary accounts of merchandising companies include Sales, Sales Discounts, Sales Returns and Allowances, and Cost of Goods Sold. Each is closed to Income Summary.

P4 Define and prepare multiple-step and single-step income statements. Multiple-step income statements include greater detail for sales and expenses than do single-step income statements. Classified multiple-step income statements are usually limited to internal use. They show computations of net sales and cost of goods sold. The multiple-step statement reports expenses in categories reflecting different activities. Income statements published for external parties can be either multiple-step or single-step.

Guidance Answers to **You Make the Call**

Purchasing Agent

Delaying payment for 90 days costs your company an additional 3%. You can approximate the annual rate of interest attached to not paying within the discount period. For terms of 3/10, n/90, missing the 3% discount for an additional 80 days is equal to an annual interest rate of 13.69%, computed as (365 days ÷ 80 days) × 3%. Since you can borrow funds at 11% (assuming no other processing costs), it is better to borrow and pay within the discount period. You save 2.69% (13.69% − 11%) in interest costs by not delaying payment.

Supplier

A current ratio of 2.1 suggests there are sufficient current assets to cover current liabilities. But an acid-test ratio of 0.5 is low for most businesses. This says quick assets can only cover about one-half of current liabilities. This implies the store depends on profits from sales of inventory to pay current liabilities. If sales of inventory stall or profit margins decrease, then the likelihood of this store defaulting on its payments increases. Your decision is probably not to extend credit to the store. If you do extend credit, then you are likely to closely monitor the store's financial condition.

Chief Financial Officer

Your company's net profit margin is about equal to the industry average and suggests typical industry performance. However, gross margin reveals a markedly different picture. This ratio indicates your company is paying far more in cost of goods sold or receiving far less in sales than competitors. Your attention must be directed to finding the problem with cost of goods sold, sales, or both. One positive note is that your company's expenses make up 19% of sales (36% − 17%). This favorably compares with competitors' expenses making up 28% of sales (44% − 16%).

Guidance Answer to **Judgment and Ethics**

Credit Manager

Your decision is whether to comply with prior policy or to create a new policy and not abuse discounts offered by suppliers. Your first step should be to meet with your superior to find out if the automatic late payment policy is the actual policy and, if so, its rationale. It is possible the prior employee was reprimanded because of this behavior. If it is the policy to pay late, then you must apply your own sense of right and wrong. One point of view is that the late payment policy is unethical. A deliberate plan to make late payments means the company lies when it pretends to make purchases within the credit terms. There is the potential that your company can lose its ability to get future credit. Another view is that the late payment policy is acceptable. There may exist markets where attempts to take discounts through late payments are accepted as a continued phase of price negotiation. Also, your company's suppliers can respond by billing your company for the discounts not accepted because of late payments. This is a dubious viewpoint, especially given that the old employee proposes you cover up late payments as computer or mail problems, and given that some suppliers have previously complained.

Guidance Answers to 

1. Cost of goods sold is the cost of merchandise that was purchased from a supplier and is sold to customers during a period.
2. Gross profit (or gross margin) is the difference between net sales and cost of goods sold.
3. Widespread use of computing and related technology in today's information age has dramatically increased use of the perpetual inventory system in practice.
4. Under credit terms of 2/10, n/60, the credit period is 60 days and the discount period is 10 days.
5. *b*
6. FOB means free on board. It is used in identifying the point where ownership transfers from seller to buyer. *FOB destination* means the seller does not transfer ownership of goods to the buyer until they arrive at the buyer's place of business. The seller is responsible for paying shipping charges and bears the risk of damage or loss during shipment.
7. Recording sales discounts and sales returns and allowances separate from sales gives useful information to managers for internal monitoring and decision making.
8. When a customer returns merchandise and the seller restores the merchandise to inventory, two entries are necessary. One entry records the decrease in revenue and credits the customer's account. The second entry debits inventory and reduces cost of goods sold.
9. A credit memorandum.
10. Merchandise Inventory balance may need adjusting to reflect shrinkage.
11. Sales, Sales Discounts, Sales Returns and Allowances, and Cost of Goods Sold.
12. Four closing entries: (1) close credit balances in temporary accounts to Income Summary, (2) close debit balances in temporary accounts to Income Summary, (3) close Income Summary to owner's capital, and (4) close withdrawals account to owner's capital.
13. Classified, multiple-step income statement. Single-step income statement.
14. Cash, short-term investments, and current receivables.
15. Acid-test ratio.

Demonstration Problem

Use the following adjusted trial balance and additional information to complete the requirements:

IOWA ANTIQUES Adjusted Trial Balance December 31, 1999		
Cash	$ 19,000	
Merchandise inventory	50,000	
Store supplies	1,000	
Equipment	44,600	
Accumulated depreciation—Equipment		$ 16,500
Accounts payable		8,000
Salaries payable		1,000
Dee Rizzo, capital		69,000
Dee Rizzo, withdrawals	8,000	
Sales		325,000
Sales discounts	6,000	
Sales returns and allowances	5,000	
Cost of goods sold	148,000	
Depreciation expense—Store equipment	4,000	
Depreciation expense—Office equipment	1,500	
Sales salaries expense	28,000	
Office salaries expense	32,000	
Insurance expense	12,000	
Rent expense (70% is store, 30% is office)	24,000	
Store supplies expense	6,000	
Advertising expense	30,400	
Totals	$419,500	$419,500

Iowa Antiques' *supplementary records* for 1999 reveal the following merchandising activities:

Invoice cost of merchandise purchases	$140,000
Purchase discounts received	3,500
Purchase returns and allowances received	2,600
Cost of transportation-in	4,000

Required

1. Use the supplementary records to compute the cost of merchandise purchases for 1999.
2. Prepare a 1999 classified, multiple-step income statement for internal use. The beginning inventory at January 1, 1999 is $60,100.
3. Prepare a single-step income statement for 1999 similar to the one in Exhibit 6.20.
4. Prepare closing entries for Iowa Antiques at the end of 1999.
5. Compute the acid-test ratio and the gross margin ratio. Explain the meaning of each ratio and interpret them for Iowa Antiques.

Planning the Solution

- Compute the total cost of merchandise purchases for 1999.
- Compute net sales. Then, to compute cost of goods sold, add the net cost of merchandise purchases for the year to beginning inventory and subtract the cost of ending inventory. Subtract cost of goods sold from net sales to get gross profit. Then, classify operating expenses as selling expenses or general administrative expenses.

- To prepare the single-step income statement, begin with net sales. Then, list and subtract the operating expenses.
- The first closing entry debits all temporary accounts with credit balances and opens the Income Summary account. The second closing entry credits all temporary accounts with debit balances. The third entry closes the Income Summary account to the owner's capital account, and the fourth closing entry closes the withdrawals account to the capital account.
- Identify the quick assets on the adjusted trial balance. Compute the acid-test ratio by dividing the quick assets by the amount of current liabilities. Compute the gross margin ratio by dividing the gross profit found in requirement 2 by net sales. Explain and interpret each ratio.

Solution to Demonstration Problem

1.

Invoice cost of merchandise purchases	$140,000
Less: Purchases discounts received	(3,500)
Purchase returns and allowances received	(2,600)
Add: Cost of transportation-in	4,000
Total cost of merchandise purchases	$137,900

2. Classified, multiple-step income statement

IOWA ANTIQUES
Income Statement
For Year Ended December 31, 1999

Sales			$325,000
Less: Sales discounts		$ 6,000	
Sales returns and allowances		5,000	11,000
Net sales			$314,000
Cost of goods sold:			
Merchandise inventory, December 31, 1998		$ 60,100	
Invoice cost of merchandise purchases	$140,000		
Less: Purchase discounts received	(3,500)		
Purchase returns and allowances received	(2,600)		
Add: Cost of transportation-in	4,000		
Total cost of merchandise purchases		137,900	
Goods available for sale		$198,000	
Merchandise inventory, December 31, 1999		50,000	
Cost of goods sold			148,000
Gross profit from sales			$166,000

(continued)

Operating expenses:			
Selling expenses:			
Depreciation expense—Store equipment	$ 4,000		
Sales salaries expense	28,000		
Rent expense—Selling space	16,800		
Store supplies expense	6,000		
Advertising expense	30,400		
Total selling expenses		$ 85,200	
General and administrative expenses:			
Depreciation expense—Office equipment	$ 1,500		
Office salaries expense	32,000		
Insurance expense	12,000		
Rent expense—Office space	7,200		
Total general and administrative expenses		52,700	
Total operating expenses			137,900
Net income			$ 28,100

3. Single-step income statement

IOWA ANTIQUES
Income Statement
For Year Ended December 31, 1999

Net sales		$314,000
Operating expenses:		
Cost of goods sold	$148,000	
Selling expenses	85,200	
General and administrative expenses	52,700	285,900
Net income		$ 28,100

4.

Dec. 31	Sales	325,000	
	Income Summary		325,000
	To close temporary accounts with credit balances.		
Dec. 31	Income Summary	296,900	
	Sales Discounts		6,000
	Sales Returns and Allowances		5,000
	Cost of Goods Sold		148,000
	Depreciation Expense—Store Equipment		4,000
	Depreciation Expense—Office Equipment		1,500
	Sales Salaries Expense		28,000
	Office Salaries Expense		32,000
	Insurance Expense		12,000
	Rent Expense		24,000
	Store Supplies Expense		6,000
	Advertising Expense		30,400
	To close temporary accounts with debit balances.		

Dec. 31	Income Summary	28,100	
	Dee Rizzo, capital		28,100
	To close the Income Summary account.		
Dec. 31	Dee Rizzo, capital	8,000	
	Dee Rizzo, withdrawals		8,000
	To close the withdrawals account.		

5. Acid test ratio = Cash /(Accounts payable + Salaries payable)

= \$19,000/(\$8,000 + \$1,000) = \$19,000/\$9,000 = 2.11

Gross margin ratio = Gross profit/Net sales = \$166,000/\$314,000 = 0.53

Iowa Antiques has a healthy acid-test ratio of 2.11. This means it has over \$2.00 in liquid assets to satisfy each \$1.00 in current liabilities. (Neither supplies nor inventory are considered liquid assets readily convertible into cash for use in satisfying short-term obligations.) The gross margin of .53 shows that Iowa Antiques spends 47 cents of every dollar of net sales on the costs of acquiring the merchandise it sells. This leaves 53 cents of every dollar of net sales to cover other expenses incurred in the business and to provide for a profit.

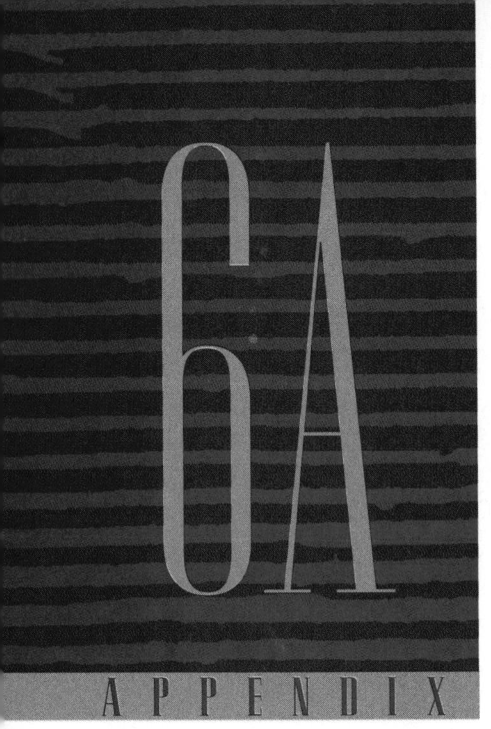

Periodic and Perpetual Inventory Systems: Accounting Comparisons

Learning Objectives

Procedural

P5 Record and compare merchandising transactions using both periodic and perpetual inventory systems.

Recall that under a perpetual system, the Merchandise Inventory account is updated after each purchase and each sale. The Cost of Goods Sold account also is updated after each sale so that during the period the account balance reflects the period's total cost of goods sold to date.

Under a periodic inventory system, the Merchandise Inventory account is updated only once each accounting period. This update occurs at the *end* of the period. During the next period, the Merchandise Inventory balance remains unchanged. It reflects the beginning inventory balance until it is updated again at the end of the period. Similarly, in a periodic inventory system, cost of goods sold is not recorded as each sale occurs. Instead, the total cost of goods sold during the period is computed at the end of the period.

Recording Merchandise Transactions

Under a perpetual system, each purchase, purchase return and allowance, purchase discount, and transportation-in transaction is recorded in the Merchandise Inventory account. Under a periodic system, a separate temporary account is set up for each of these items. At the end of a period, each of these temporary accounts is closed and the Merchandise Inventory account is updated. To illustrate the differences, we use parallel columns to show journal entries for the most common transactions using both periodic and perpetual inventory systems (we drop explanations for simplicity).

Purchases

Z-Mart purchases merchandise for $1,200 on credit with terms of 2/10, n/30. Z-Mart's entry to record this credit purchase is:

(a)

Periodic			Perpetual		
Purchases	1,200		Merchandise Inventory	1,200	
Accounts Payable . .		1,200	Accounts Payable		1,200

The periodic system uses a temporary *Purchases* account that accumulates the cost of all purchase transactions during the period.

Purchase Discounts

When Z-Mart pays the supplier for the previous purchase in (a) within the discount period, the required payment is $1,176 ($1,200 × 98%) and is recorded as:

(b)

Periodic		
Accounts Payable	1,200	
Purchase Discounts .		24
Cash		1,176

Perpetual		
Accounts Payable	1,200	
Merchandise Inventory . .		24
Cash		1,176

The periodic system uses a temporary *Purchase Discounts* account that accumulates discounts taken on purchase transactions during the period. If payment is delayed until after the discount period expires, the entry under both methods is to debit Accounts Payable and credit Cash for $1,200 each.

Purchase Returns and Allowances

Z-Mart returns merchandise purchased on November 2 because of defects. If the recorded cost of the defective merchandise is $300, Z-Mart records the return with this entry:[9]

(c)

Periodic		
Accounts Payable	300	
Purchase Returns and Allowances		300

Perpetual		
Accounts Payable	300	
Merchandise Inventory . .		300

This entry is the same if Z-Mart is granted a price reduction (allowance) instead of returning the merchandise. In the periodic system, the temporary Purchase Returns and Allowances account accumulates the cost of all returns and allowances transactions during a period.

Transportation-In

Z-Mart paid a $75 freight charge to haul merchandise to its store. In the periodic system, this cost is charged to a temporary Transportation-In account.

(d)

Periodic		
Transportation-In	75	
Cash		75

Perpetual		
Merchandise Inventory	75	
Cash		75

Sales

Z-Mart sold $2,400 of merchandise on credit and Z-Mart's cost of this merchandise is $1,600:

(e)

Periodic		
Accounts Receivable ...	2,400	
Sales		2,400

Perpetual		
Accounts Receivable	2,400	
Sales		2,400
Cost of Goods Sold	1,600	
Merchandise Inventory . .		1,600

Under the periodic system the cost of goods sold is not recorded at the time of sale. We later show how the total cost of goods sold at the end of a period is computed under the periodic system.

---

[9] Recorded cost is the cost recorded in the account after any discounts.

Sales Returns

A customer returns part of the merchandise from the previous transaction in (e), where returned items sell for $800 and cost $600. Z-Mart restores the merchandise to inventory and records the return as:

(f)

Periodic		
Sales Returns and Allowances	800	
Accounts Receivable		800

Perpetual		
Sales Returns and Allowances	800	
Accounts Receivable . . .		800
Merchandise Inventory	600	
Cost of Goods Sold		600

The periodic system records only the revenue reduction.

Adjusting and Closing Entries

The periodic and perpetual inventory systems show differences in the adjusting and closing entries. Z-Mart's unadjusted trial balances at the end of 1999 under each system are shown in Exhibit 6A.1.

The Merchandise Inventory balance is $19,000 under the periodic system and $21,250 under the perpetual system. Because the periodic system does not revise the Merchandise Inventory balance during the period, the $19,000 amount is the beginning inventory. The $21,250 balance under the perpetual system is the recorded ending inventory before adjusting for any inventory shrinkage.

A physical count of inventory taken at the end of the period disclosed $21,000 of merchandise on hand. We then know inventory shrinkage is: $21,250 − $21,000 = $250. The adjusting entry for shrinkage along with closing entries under the two systems is shown in Exhibit 6A.2.

The periodic system does not require an adjusting entry to record inventory shrinkage. Instead, the periodic system puts the ending inventory of $21,000 in the Merchandise Inventory account in the first closing entry, and removes the $19,000 beginning inventory balance from the account in the second closing entry.

By updating Merchandise Inventory and closing Purchases, Purchase Discounts, Purchase Returns and Allowances, and Transportation-In, the periodic system transfers the cost of goods sold amount to Income Summary. Review the periodic side of Exhibit 6A.2 and notice the color items affect Income Summary as follows:

Credited to Income Summary in the first closing entry:	
Merchandise inventory	$ 21,000
Purchase discounts	4,200
Purchase returns and allowances	1,500
Debited to Income Summary in the second closing entry:	
Merchandise inventory	(19,000)
Purchases	(235,800)
Transportation-in	(2,300)
Net effect on Income Summary	**($230,400)**

Exhibit 6A.1

Comparison of Unadjusted Trial Balances—Periodic and Perpetual

Z-MART
Unadjusted Trial Balance
December 31, 1999
Periodic

Cash	$ 8,200	
Accounts receivable	11,200	
Merchandise inventory	19,000	
Office supplies	550	
Store supplies	250	
Prepaid insurance	300	
Office equipment	4,200	
Accumulated depreciation—Office eq.		$ 1,400
Store equipment	30,000	
Accumulated depreciation—Store eq.		6,000
Accounts payable		16,000
Salaries payable		800
K. Marty, capital		42,600
K. Marty, withdrawals	4,000	
Sales		321,000
Sales discounts	4,300	
Sales returns and allowances	2,000	
Purchases	235,800	
Purchase discounts		4,200
Purchase returns and allowances		1,500
Transportation-in	2,300	
Depreciation expense—Store eq.	3,000	
Depreciation expense—Office eq.	700	
Office salaries expense	25,300	
Sales salaries expense	18,500	
Insurance expense	600	
Rent expense—Office space	900	
Rent expense—Selling space	8,100	
Office supplies expense	1,800	
Store supplies expense	1,200	
Advertising expense	11,300	

Z-MART
Unadjusted Trial Balance
December 31, 1999
Perpetual

Cash	$ 8,200	
Accounts receivable	11,200	
Merchandise inventory	21,250	
Office supplies	550	
Store supplies	250	
Prepaid insurance	300	
Office equipment	4,200	
Accumulated depreciation—Office eq.		$ 1,400
Store equipment	30,000	
Accumulated depreciation—Store eq.		6,000
Accounts payable		16,000
Salaries payable		800
K. Marty, capital		42,600
K. Marty, withdrawals	4,000	
Sales		321,000
Sales discounts	4,300	
Sales returns and allowances	2,000	
Cost of goods sold	230,150	
Depreciation expense—Store eq.	3,000	
Depreciation expense—Office eq.	700	
Office salaries expense	25,300	
Sales salaries expense	18,500	
Insurance expense	600	
Rent expense—Office space	900	
Rent expense—Selling space	8,100	
Office supplies expense	1,800	
Store supplies expense	1,200	
Advertising expense	11,300	

Exhibit 6A.2

Comparison of Adjusting and Closing Entries—Periodic and Perpetual

Periodic			Perpetual		
Adjusting entries			**Adjusting entries**		
			Cost of Goods Sold	250	
			Merchandise Inventory		250
Closing entries			**Closing entries**		
(1) Sales	321,000		(1) Sales	321,000	
Merchandise inventory	21,000		Income Summary		321,000
Purchase discounts	4,200				
Purchase returns and allowances	1,500				
Income Summary		347,700			
(2) Income Summary	334,800		(2) Income Summary	308,100	
Sales discounts		4,300	Sales discounts		4,300
Sales returns and allowances		2,000	Sales returns and allowances		2,000
Merchandise inventory		19,000	Cost of Goods Sold		230,400
Purchases		235,800			
Transportation-In		2,300			
Depreciation Expense—Store eq.		3,000	Depreciation Expense—Store eq.		3,000
Depreciation Expense—Office eq.		700	Depreciation Expense—Office eq.		700
Office Salaries Expense		25,300	Office Salaries Expense		25,300
Sales Salaries Expense		18,500	Sales Salaries Expense		18,500
Insurance Expense		600	Insurance Expense		600
Rent Expense—Office space		900	Rent Expense—Office space		900
Rent Expense—Selling space		8,100	Rent Expense—Selling space		8,100
Office Supplies Expense		1,800	Office Supplies Expense		1,800
Store Supplies Expense		1,200	Store Supplies Expense		1,200
Advertising Expense		11,300	Advertising Expense		11,300
(3) Income Summary	12,900		(3) Income Summary	12,900	
K. Marty, capital		12,900	K. Marty, capital		12,900
(4) K. Marty, capital	4,000		(4) K. Marty, capital	4,000	
K. Marty, withdrawals		4,000	K. Marty, withdrawals		4,000

This $230,400 effect on Income Summary is the cost of goods sold amount. This figure is confirmed as follows:

Beginning inventory		$ 19,000
Purchases	$235,800	
Less purchase discounts	(4,200)	
Less purchase returns and allowances	(1,500)	
Plus transportation-in	2,300	
Net cost of goods purchased		232,400
Cost of goods available for sale		$251,400
Less ending inventory		(21,000)
Cost of goods sold		**$230,400**

The periodic system transfers cost of goods sold to the Income Summary account but does not use a Cost of Goods Sold account.

The periodic system does not measure shrinkage. Instead it computes cost of goods available for sale, subtracts the cost of ending inventory, and defines the difference as cost of goods sold. This difference, called the *cost of goods,* includes shrinkage.

Adjusting Entry Method to Record Changes in Merchandise Inventory

In our discussion of the periodic system, the change in the Merchandise Inventory account is recorded as part of the closing process. The closing entry method is common in practice. Yet an alternative method, called the *adjusting entry method,* also is commonly used.[10] The *adjusting entry method* records the change in the Merchandise Inventory account with adjusting entries. Under this method, the first two closing entries do not include changes in the Merchandise Inventory account.

Adjusting Entries

Under the adjusting entry method of the periodic system, Z-Mart removes the beginning balance from the Merchandise Inventory account by recording this adjusting entry at the end of 1999:

Dec. 31	Income Summary	19,000	
	Merchandise Inventory		19,000
	To remove the beginning balance from the Merchandise Inventory account.		

A second adjusting entry gives the correct ending balance in the Merchandise Inventory account:

Dec. 31	Merchandise Inventory	21,000	
	Income Summary		21,000
	To insert the correct ending balance in the Merchandise Inventory account.		

After these entries are posted, the Merchandise Inventory account has a $21,000 debit balance:

Merchandise Inventory			
Beg. bal.	19,000		
		19,000	Adj.
Adj.	21,000		
End. bal.	21,000		

These adjustments leave the Income Summary account with a $2,000 credit balance.

Closing Entries

If the adjusting entry method for inventory is used, the closing entries differ only by not including the Merchandise Inventory account. In particular, entries *(1)* and *(2)* in Exhibit 6A.2 are the same except for removing the Merchandise Inventory account and its balance from both entries. Entry *(3)* to close Income Summary is also unchanged. The only difference is that the adjusting entry method took us four entries instead of two to get the net income of $12,900.

[10] The adjusting entry method also is used by some computerized accounting systems that do not allow the Merchandise Inventory account (a permanent account) to be changed in the closing process.

Flash back

16. What account is used in a perpetual inventory system but not in a periodic system?

17. Which of the following accounts are temporary accounts under a periodic system? (a) Merchandise Inventory; (b) Purchases; (c) Transportation-In.

18. How is cost of goods sold computed under a periodic inventory accounting system?

19. Do reported amounts of ending inventory and net income differ if the adjusting entry method of recording the change in inventory is used instead of the closing entry method?

Answers—p. 260

Summary of Appendix 6A

P5 Record and compare merchandising transactions using both periodic and perpetual inventory systems. Transactions involving the sale and purchase of merchandise are recorded and analyzed under both the periodic and perpetual inventory systems. Adjusting and closing entries for both inventory systems are also illustrated and explained.

Guidance Answers to  *backs*

16. Cost of Goods Sold.

17. (b) Purchases and (c) Transportation-In.

18. Under a periodic inventory system, the cost of goods sold is determined at the end of an accounting period by adding the net cost of goods purchased to the beginning inventory and subtracting the ending inventory.

19. Both methods report the same ending inventory and net income.

Glossary

Acid-test ratio a ratio used to assess the company's ability to settle its current debts with its most liquid assets; it is the ratio between a company's quick assets (cash, short-term investments, and current receivables) and its current liabilities. (p. 245)

Cash discount a reduction in the price of merchandise that is granted by a seller to a purchaser in exchange for the purchaser's making payment within a specified period of time called the *discount period.* (p. 227)

Classified, multiple-step income statement an income statement format that shows intermediate totals between sales and net income and detailed computations of net sales and cost of goods sold. (p. 241)

Cost of goods sold the cost of merchandise sold to customers during a period. (p. 224)

Credit memorandum a notification that the sender has entered a credit in the recipient's account maintained by the sender. (p. 236)

Credit period the time period that can pass before a customer's payment is due. (p. 227)

Credit terms the description of the amounts and timing of payments that a buyer agrees to make in the future. (p. 227)

Debit memorandum a notification that the sender has entered a debit in the recipient's account maintained by the sender. (p. 229)

Discount period the time period in which a cash discount is available and a reduced payment can be made by the buyer. (p. 227)

EOM the abbreviation for *end-of-month*; used to describe credit terms for some transactions. (p. 227)

FOB the abbreviation for *free on board*; the designated point at which ownership of goods passes to the buyer; FOB shipping point (or factory) means that the buyer pays the shipping costs and accepts ownership of the goods at the seller's place of business; FOB destination means that the seller pays the shipping costs and the ownership of the goods transfers to the buyer at the buyer's place of business. (p. 231)

General and administrative expenses expenses that support the overall operations of a business and include the expenses of such activities as providing accounting services, human resource management, and financial management. (p. 242)

Gross margin the difference between net sales and the cost of goods sold; also called *gross profit.* (p. 223)

Gross margin ratio gross margin (sales minus cost of goods sold) divided by sales; also called *gross profit ratio.* (p. 246).

Gross profit the difference between net sales and the cost of goods sold; also called *gross margin.* (p. 223)

Inventory products a company owns and expects to sell in its normal operations. (p. 224)

List price the catalog price of an item before any trade discount is deducted. (p. 227)

Merchandise products, also called *goods,* that a company acquires for the purpose of reselling them to customers. (p. 222)

Merchandiser earns net income by buying and selling merchandise. (p. 222).

Merchandiser inventory products that a company owns for the purpose of selling them to customers. (p. 223).

Periodic inventory system a method of accounting that records the cost of inventory purchased but does not track the quantity on hand or sold to customers; the records are updated at the end of each period to reflect the results of physical counts of the items on hand. (p. 225)

Perpetual inventory system a method of accounting that maintains continuous records of the cost of inventory on hand and the cost of goods sold. (p. 225)

Purchase discount a term used by a purchaser to describe a cash discount granted to the purchaser for paying within the discount period. (p. 227)

Retailer a middleman that buys products from manufacturers or wholesalers and sells them to consumers. (p. 222)

Sales discount a term used by a seller to describe a cash discount granted to customers for paying within the discount period. (p. 227)

Selling expenses the expenses of promoting sales by displaying and advertising the merchandise, making sales, and delivering goods to customers. (p. 242)

Shrinkage inventory losses that occur as a result of shoplifting or deterioration. (p. 237)

Single-step income statement an income statement format that includes cost of goods sold as an operating expense and shows only one subtotal for total expenses. (p. 243)

Supplementary records a register of information outside the usual accounting records and accounts; also called *supplemental records.* (p. 232)

Trade discount a reduction below a list or catalog price that may vary in amount for wholesalers, retailers, and final consumers. (p. 227)

Wholesaler a middleman that buys products from manufacturers or other wholesalers and sells them to retailers or other wholesalers. (p. 222)

The superscript letter [A] identifies assignment material based on Appendix 6A.

Questions

1. What items appear in the financial statements of merchandising companies but not in the statements of service companies?
2. Explain how a business can earn a gross profit on its sales and still have a net loss.
3. Why would a company offer a cash discount?
4. What is the difference between a sales discount and a purchase discount?
5. Distinguish between cash discounts and trade discounts. Is the amount of a trade discount on purchased merchandise recorded in the Purchase Discounts account?
6. How does a company that uses a perpetual inventory system determine the amount of inventory shrinkage?
7. Why would a company's manager be concerned about the quantity of its purchase returns if its suppliers allow unlimited returns?
8. Does the sender of a debit memorandum record a debit or a credit in the account of the recipient? Which does the recipient record?
9. What is the difference between single-step and multiple-step income statement formats?
10. In comparing the accounts of a merchandising company with those of a service company, what additional accounts would the merchandising company be likely to use, assuming it employs a perpetual inventory system?
11. Refer to the income statement for **NIKE** in Appendix A. What term is used instead of cost of goods sold? Does the company present a detailed calculation of the cost of goods sold?
12. Refer to the balance sheet for **Reebok** in Appendix A. How does Reebok refer to the inventory account? What is an alternate name that could be used?
13. Refer to the income statement of **America Online** in Appendix A. Does the AOL income statement report a gross profit figure?

14. Jason Walker in the opening article talks about the need to be skillful in negotiating purchase contracts with suppliers. What type of shipping terms should Jason Walker attempt to negotiate to minimize his freight-in costs?

Quick Study

QS 6-1

Contrast periodic and perpetual systems

C4

For each description below, identify whether the reference best applies to a periodic or perpetual inventory system.

a. Requires a physical count of inventory to determine the amount of inventory to report on the balance sheet.
b. Records cost of goods sold each time a sales transaction occurs.
c. Provides more timely information to managers.

d. Traditionally used by drug and department stores that sold large quantities of low-valued items.
e. Requires an adjusting entry to record inventory shrinkage.

QS 6-2
Purchases entries—perpetual system
P1

Prepare journal entries to record each of the following transactions of a merchandising company. Show any supporting calculations. Assume a perpetual inventory system.

Mar. 5 Purchased 500 units of product with a list price of $5 per unit. The purchaser was granted a trade discount of 20% and the terms of the sale were 2/10, n/60.
Mar. 7 Returned 50 defective units from the March 5 purchase and received full credit.
Mar. 15 Paid the amount due resulting from the March 5 purchase, less the return on March 7.

QS 6-3
Sales entries—perpetual system
P2

Prepare journal entries to record each of the following transactions of a merchandising company. Show any supporting calculations. Assume a perpetual inventory system.

Apr. 1 Sold merchandise for $2,000, granting the customer terms of 2/10, EOM. The cost of the merchandise was $1,400.
Apr. 4 The customer in the April 1 sale returned merchandise and received credit for $500. The merchandise, which had cost $350, was returned to inventory.
Apr. 11 Received payment for the amount due from the April 1 sale less the return on April 4.

QS 6-4
Accounting for shrinkage—perpetual system
P3

Beamer Company's ledger on July 31, the end of its fiscal year, includes the following accounts that have normal balances:

Merchandise inventory	$ 34,800
J. Beamer, capital	115,300
J. Beamer, withdrawals	4,000
Sales	157,200
Sales discounts	1,700
Sales returns and allowances	3,500
Cost of goods sold	102,000
Depreciation expense	7,300
Salaries expense	29,500
Miscellaneous expenses	2,000

A physical count of the inventory discloses that the cost of the merchandise on hand is $32,900. Prepare the entry to record this information.

QS 6-5[A]
Closing entries
P3

Refer to QS 6-4 and prepare the entries to close the balances in temporary accounts. Do not forget to take into consideration the entry that was made to solve QS 6-4.

QS 6-6
Gross margin analysis
C2, A3

Compute net sales, gross profit, and the gross margin ratio in each of the following situations:

	a	b	c	d
Sales	$130,000	$512,000	$35,700	$245,700
Sales discounts	4,200	16,500	400	3,500
Sales returns and allowances	17,000	5,000	5,000	700
Cost of goods sold	76,600	326,700	21,300	125,900

Interpret the gross margin ratio for situation *a*.

QS 6-7
Acid-test ratio and analysis
A2

Use the following information to compute the acid-test ratio. Explain what the acid-test ratio of a company measures. Comment on the ratio you compute.

Cash	$1,200
Accounts receivable	2,700
Inventory	5,000
Prepaid expenses	600
Accounts payable	4,750
Other current liabilities	950

QS 6-8
Contrasting liquidity ratios
A2

Explain the similarities and differences between the acid-test ratio and the current ratio. Compare the two ratios.

Exercises

Exercise 6-1
Merchandising terms
C1, C2

Insert the letter for each term in the blank space beside the definition that it most closely matches:

A. Cash discount **E.** FOB shipping point **H.** Purchase discount
B. Credit period **F.** Gross profit **I.** Sales discount
C. Discount period **G.** Merchandise inventory **J.** Trade discount
D. FOB destination

_____ **1.** An agreement that ownership of goods is transferred at the buyer's place of business.
_____ **2.** The time period in which a cash discount is available.
_____ **3.** The difference between net sales and the cost of goods sold.
_____ **4.** A reduction in a receivable or payable that is granted if it is paid within the discount period.
_____ **5.** A purchaser's description of a cash discount received from a supplier of goods.
_____ **6.** An agreement that ownership of goods is transferred at the seller's place of business.
_____ **7.** A reduction below list or catalog price that is negotiated in setting the price of goods.
_____ **8.** A seller's description of a cash discount granted to customers in return for early payment.
_____ **9.** The time period that can pass before a customer's payment is due.
_____ **10.** The goods that a company owns and expects to sell to its customers.

Exercise 6-2
Recording entries for merchandise purchases

P1

Prepare journal entries to record the following transactions for a retail store. Assume a perpetual inventory system.

Mar. 2 Purchased merchandise from Blanton Company under the following terms: $3,600 invoice price, 2/15, n/60, FOB shipping point.
3 Paid $200 for shipping charges on the purchase of March 2.
4 Returned to Blanton Company unacceptable merchandise that had an invoice price of $600.
17 Sent a check to Blanton Company for the March 2 purchase, net of the discount and the returned merchandise.
18 Purchased merchandise from Fleming Corp. under the following terms: $7,500 invoice price, 2/10, n/30, FOB destination.
21 After negotiations, received from Fleming Corp. a $2,100 allowance on the purchase of March 18.
28 Sent a check to Fleming Corp. paying for the March 18 purchase, net of the discount and the allowance.

Exercise 6-3
Analyzing and recording merchandise transactions—both buyer and seller
P1, P2

On May 11, Wilson Sales accepted delivery of $30,000 of merchandise it purchased for resale. With the merchandise was an invoice dated May 11, with terms of 3/10, n/90, FOB Hostel Corporation's factory. The cost of the goods to Hostel was $20,000. When the goods were delivered, Wilson paid $335 to Express Shipping Service for delivery charges on the merchandise. On May 12, Wilson returned $1,200 of goods to Hostel, who received them one day later and restored them to inventory. The returned goods had cost Hostel $800. On May 20, Wilson mailed a check to Hostel Corporation for the amount owed on that date. It was received by Hostel the following day.

Required

a. Prepare journal entries that Wilson Sales should record for these transactions. Wilson Sales uses a perpetual inventory system.

b. Prepare journal entries that Hostel Corporation should record for these transactions. Hostel uses a perpetual inventory system.

Exercise 6-4
Analyzing and recording merchandise transactions—both buyer and seller
P1, P2

Sundown Company purchased merchandise for resale from Raintree with an invoice price of $22,000 and credit terms of 3/10, n/60. The merchandise had cost Raintree $15,000. Sundown paid within the discount period. Assume that both the buyer and seller use perpetual inventory systems.

Required

a. Prepare entries that the buyer should record for the purchase and payment.

b. Prepare entries that the seller should record for the sale and collection.

c. Assume that the buyer borrowed enough cash to pay the balance on the last day of the discount period at an annual interest rate of 8% and paid it back on the last day of the credit period. Compute how much the buyer saved by following this strategy. (Use a 365-day year.)

Exercise 6-5
Components of cost of goods sold
C5

Using the data provided from the general ledger and supplementary records, determine each of the missing numbers in the following separate situations:

	a	b	c
Invoice cost of merchandise purchases	$90,000	$40,000	$30,500
Purchase discounts received	4,000	?	650
Purchase returns and allowances received	3,000	1,500	1,100
Cost of transportation-in	?	3,500	4,000
Merchandise inventory (beginning of period)	7,000	?	9,000
Total cost of merchandise purchases	89,400	39,500	?
Merchandise inventory (end of period)	4,400	7,500	?
Cost of goods sold	?	41,600	34,130

Exercise 6-6
Calculating expenses and cost of goods sold
C5

Friar Company's ledger and supplementary records at the end of the period reveal the following:

Sales	$340,000
Sales discounts	5,500
Sales returns	14,000
Merchandise inventory (beginning of period)	30,000
Invoice cost of merchandise purchases	175,000
Purchase discounts received	3,600
Purchase returns and allowances received	6,000
Cost of transportation-in	11,000
Gross profit from sales	145,000
Net income	65,000

Required

Calculate *(a)* total operating expenses, *(b)* cost of goods sold, and *(c)* merchandise inventory (end of period).

Exercise 6-7
Calculating revenues, expenses, and income
C2, C5

Fill in the blanks in the following separate income statements. Identify any losses by putting the amount in parentheses.

	a	b	c	d	e
Sales	$60,000	$42,500	$36,000	$?	$23,600
Cost of goods sold:					
Merchandise inventory (beginning)	$ 6,000	$17,050	$ 7,500	$ 7,000	$ 2,560
Total cost of merchandise purchases	36,000	?	?	32,000	5,600
Merchandise inventory (ending)	?	(2,700)	(9,000)	(6,600)	?
Cost of goods sold	$34,050	$15,900	$?	$?	$ 5,600
Gross profit	$?	$?	$ 3,750	$45,600	$?
Expenses	9,000	10,650	12,150	2,600	6,000
Net income (loss)	$?	$15,950	$ (8,400)	$43,000	$?

Exercise 6-8
Sales returns and allowances entries
P2

Travis Parts was organized on June 1, 2000, and made its first purchase of merchandise on June 3. The purchase was for 1,000 units at a price of $10 per unit. On June 5, Travis sold 600 of the units for $14 per unit to Decker Co. Terms of the sale were 2/10, n/60. Prepare entries for Travis to record the June 5 sale and each of the following independent alternatives under a perpetual inventory system.

a. On June 7, Decker returned 100 units because they did not fit the customer's needs. Travis restored the units to its inventory.

b. Decker discovered that 100 units were damaged but of some use and, therefore, kept the units. Travis sent Decker a credit memorandum for $600 to compensate for the damage.

c. Decker returned 100 defective units and Travis concluded that these units could not be resold. As a result, Travis discarded the units.

Exercise 6-9
Purchase returns and allowances entries
P1

Refer to Exercise 6-8 and prepare the appropriate journal entries for Decker Co. to record the purchase and each of the three independent alternatives presented. Decker is a retailer that uses a perpetual inventory system and purchased the units for resale.

Exercise 6-10
Effects of merchandising activities on accounts
C5

The following amounts from supplementary and accounting records summarize Transeer Company's merchandising activities during year 2000. Set up T-accounts for Merchandise Inventory and Cost of Goods Sold. Then record the summarized activities directly in the T-accounts and calculate the account balances.

Cost of merchandise sold to customers in sales transactions	$186,000
Merchandise inventory, December 31, 1999	27,000
Invoice cost of merchandise purchases	190,500
Shrinkage determined on December 31, 2000	700
Cost of transportation-in	1,900
Cost of merchandise returned by customers and restored to inventory	2,200
Purchase discounts received	1,600
Purchase returns and allowances received	4,100

Exercise 6-11[A]
Adjusting and closing entries for a merchandiser
P3

The following list includes some permanent accounts and all of the temporary accounts from the December 31, 2000, unadjusted trial balance of Perry Sales, a business owned by Deborah Perry. Use these account balances along with the additional information to journalize adjusting and closing entries. Perry Sales uses a perpetual inventory system.

	Debit	Credit
Merchandise inventory	$ 28,000	
Prepaid selling expenses	5,000	
Deborah Perry, withdrawals	1,800	
Sales		$429,000
Sales returns and allowances	16,500	
Sales discounts	4,000	
Cost of goods sold	211,000	
Sales salaries expense	47,000	
Utilities expense	14,000	
Selling expenses	35,000	
Administrative expenses	95,000	

Additional Information

Accrued sales salaries amount to $1,600. Prepaid selling expenses of $2,000 have expired. A physical count of merchandise inventory discloses $27,450 of goods on hand.

Exercise 6-12
Acid-test and current ratios
A2

Calculate the current and acid-test ratios in each the following separate cases:

	Case X	Case Y	Case Z
Cash	$ 800	$ 910	$1,100
Short-term investments			500
Receivables		990	800
Inventory	2,000	1,000	4,000
Prepaid expenses	1,200	600	900
Total current assets	$4,000	$3,500	$7,300
Current liabilities	$2,200	$1,100	$3,650

Which company case is in the best position to meet short-term obligations? Explain your choice.

Exercise 6-13
Sales returns and allowances information
C2, P2

Briefly explain why a company's manager would want the accounting system to record a customer's return of unsatisfactory goods in the Sales Returns and Allowances account instead of the Sales account. In addition, explain whether the information would be useful for external decision makers.

Exercise 6-14
Physical count error interpreted as shrinkage
P3

A retail company recently completed a physical count of ending merchandise inventory to use in preparing adjusting entries. In determining the cost of the counted inventory, company employees failed to consider that $2,000 of incoming goods had been shipped by a supplier on December 31 under an FOB shipping point agreement. These goods had been recorded in Merchandise Inventory as a purchase, but they were not included in the physical count because they were not on hand. Explain how this overlooked fact affects the company's financial statements and the following ratios: return on equity, debt ratio, current ratio, profit margin, and acid-test ratio.

Exercise 6-15[A]
Journal entries to contrast the periodic and perpetual systems
P1, P2, P5

Journalize the following merchandising transactions for Scout Systems assuming (a) a periodic system and (b) perpetual system.

1. On November 1 Scout Systems purchases merchandise for $1,400 on credit with terms of 2/10, n/30.
2. On November 5 Scout Systems pays for the previous purchase.
3. On November 7 Scout Systems discovers and returns $100 of defective merchandise that was purchased on November 1 for a cash refund.
4. On November 10 Scout Systems pays $80 to transport merchandise to its store.

5. On November 13 Scout Systems sells merchandise for $1,500 on account. The cost of the merchandise was $750.
6. On November 16 a customer returns merchandise from the November 13 transaction. The returned item sold for $200 and cost $100.

Exercise 6-16
Profitability and merchandising cash flows

A company reports the following balances and activities at year-end:

Net sales	$1,005,000
Cost of goods sold	560,000
Increase in accounts receivable for the period	40,000
Cash payments to suppliers	510,000

Required

1. Calculate gross profit.
2. Calculate cash received from customers.
3. Calculate net cash flows from customers and to suppliers.

Problems

Problem 6-1
Journal entries for merchandising activities (perpetual system)

Prepare journal entries to record the following perpetual system merchandising transactions of Belton Company. (Use a separate account for each receivable and payable; for example, record the purchase on July 1 in Accounts Payable—Jones Company.)

July 1 Purchased merchandise from Jones Company for $6,000 under credit terms of 1/15, n/30, FOB shipping point.
2 Sold merchandise to Terra Co. for $800 under credit terms of 2/10, n/60, FOB shipping point. The merchandise had cost $500.
3 Paid $100 for freight charges on the purchase of July 1.
8 Sold merchandise that cost $1,200 for $1,600 cash.
9 Purchased merchandise from Keene Co. for $2,300 under credit terms of 2/15, n/60, FOB destination.
12 Received a $200 credit memorandum acknowledging the return of merchandise purchased on July 9.
12 Received the balance due from Terra Co. for the credit sale dated July 2, net of the discount.
16 Paid the balance due to Jones Company within the discount period.
19 Sold merchandise that cost $900 to Urban Co. for $1,250 under credit terms of 2/15, n/60, FOB shipping point.
21 Issued a $150 credit memorandum to Urban Co. for an allowance on goods sold on July 19.
22 Received a debit memorandum from Urban Co. for an error that overstated the total sales invoice by $50.
24 Paid Keene Co. the balance due after deducting the discount.
30 Received the balance due from Urban Co. for the credit sale dated July 19, net of the discount.
31 Sold merchandise that cost $3,200 to Terra Co. for $5,000 under credit terms of 2/10, n/60, FOB shipping point.

Problem 6-2
Journal entries for merchandising activities (perpetual system)

Prepare journal entries to record the following perpetual system merchandising transactions of Hanifin Company. (Use a separate account for each receivable and payable; for example, record the purchase on August 1 in Accounts Payable—Dickson Company.)

Aug. 1 Purchased merchandise from Dickson Company for $6,000 under credit terms of 1/10, n/30, FOB destination.
4 At Dickson's request, paid $100 for freight charges on the August 1 purchase, reducing the amount owed to Dickson.
5 Sold merchandise to Griften Corp. for $4,200 under credit terms of 2/10, n/60, FOB destination. The merchandise had cost $3,000.
8 Purchased merchandise from Kendall Corporation for $5,300 under credit terms of 1/10, n/45, FOB shipping point, plus $240 shipping charges. The invoice showed that at Hanifin's request, Kendall had paid $240 shipping charges and added that amount to the bill.

9 Paid $120 shipping charges related to the August 5 sale to Griften Corp.
10 Griften returned merchandise from the August 5 sale that had cost $500 and been sold for $700. The merchandise was restored to inventory.
12 After negotiations with Kendall Corporation concerning problems with the merchandise purchased on August 8, Hanifin received a credit memorandum from Kendall granting a price reduction of $800.
15 Received balance due from Griften Corp. for the August 5 sale less the return on August 10.
18 Paid the amount due Kendall Corporation for the August 8 purchase less the price reduction granted.
19 Sold merchandise to Farley for $3,600 under credit terms of 1/10, n/30, FOB shipping point. The merchandise had cost $2,500.
22 Farley requested a price reduction on the August 19 sale because the merchandise did not meet specifications. Sent Farley a credit memorandum for $600 to resolve the issue.
29 Received Farley's payment of the amount due from the August 19 purchase.
30 Paid Dickson Company the amount due from the August 1 purchase.

Problem 6-3
Income statement computations and formats
P4, A1

Davison Company's adjusted trial balance as of October 31, 2000, the end of its fiscal year, is shown below:

	Debit	Credit
Merchandise inventory	$ 31,000	
Other assets	128,400	
Liabilities		$ 35,000
B. Davison, capital		117,650
B. Davison, withdrawals	16,000	
Sales		212,000
Sales discounts	3,250	
Sales returns and allowances	14,000	
Cost of goods sold	82,600	
Sales salaries expense	29,000	
Rent expense, selling space	10,000	
Store supplies expense	2,500	
Advertising expense	18,000	
Office salaries expense	26,500	
Rent expense, office space	2,600	
Office supplies expense	800	
Totals	$364,650	$364,650

On October 31, 1999, the company's merchandise inventory amounted to $25,000. Supplementary records of merchandising activities during the 2000 fiscal year disclosed the following:

Invoice cost of merchandise purchases	$91,000
Purchase discounts received	1,900
Purchase returns and allowances received	4,400
Cost of transportation-in	3,900

Required

1. Compute the company's net sales for the year.
2. Compute the company's total cost of merchandise purchased for the year.
3. Prepare a classified, multiple-step income statement (see Exhibit 6.18) that lists the company's net sales, cost of goods sold, and gross profit, as well as the components and amounts of selling expenses and general and administrative expenses.
4. Prepare a condensed single-step income statement that lists these costs: cost of goods sold, selling expenses, and general and administrative expenses.
5. Accounts receivable decreased during the period by $30,000. Compute cash received from customers.

Check Figure Part 4, total expenses, $172,000

Problem 6-4
Closing entries and interpreting information about discounts and returns
P3

Use the data for Davison Company in Problem 6-3 to meet the following requirements:

Required

Preparation Component

1. Prepare closing entries for Davison Company as of October 31, 2000.

Analysis Component

2. All of the company's purchases were made on credit and its suppliers uniformly offer a 3% sales discount. Does it appear that the company's cash management system is accomplishing the goal of taking all available discounts? Explain.
3. In prior years, the company experienced a 4% return and allowance rate on its sales, which means approximately 4% of its gross sales were for items that were eventually returned outright or that caused the company to grant allowances to customers. How does this year's results compare to prior years' results?

Check Figure Second closing entry: debit to Income Summary, $189,250

Problem 6-5
Adjusting entries, income statements, and acid-test ratio
A2, P3, P4
S

The following unadjusted trial balance was prepared at the end of the fiscal year for Tinker Sales Company:

TINKER SALES COMPANY
Unadjusted Trial Balance
July 31, 2000

Cash	$ 4,200	
Merchandise inventory	11,500	
Store supplies	4,800	
Prepaid insurance	2,300	
Store equipment	41,900	
Accumulated depreciation—Store equipment		$ 15,000
Accounts payable		9,000
Betsey Tinker, capital		35,200
Betsey Tinker, withdrawals	3,200	
Sales		104,000
Sales discounts	1,000	
Sales returns and allowances	2,000	
Cost of goods sold	37,400	
Depreciation expense—Store equipment		
Salaries expense	31,000	
Insurance expense		
Rent expense	14,000	
Store supplies expense		
Advertising expense	9,900	
Totals	$163,200	$163,200

Rent and salaries expense are equally divided between the selling and the general and administrative functions. Tinker Sales Company uses a perpetual inventory system.

Required

1. Prepare adjusting journal entries for the following:
   a. Store supplies on hand at year-end amount to $1,650.
   b. Expired insurance, an administrative expense, for the year is $1,500.
   c. Depreciation expense, a selling expense, for the year is $1,400.
   d. A physical count of the ending merchandise inventory shows $11,100 of goods on hand.
2. Prepare a multiple-step (not classified) income statement (see Exhibit 6.19).
3. Prepare a single-step income statement (see Exhibit 6.20).
4. Compute the company's current and acid-test ratios as of July 31, 2000.

Check Figure Part 3, total expenses, $98,750

Serial Problem
Echo Systems

(The first three segments of this comprehensive problem were presented in Chapters 3, 4, and 5. If those segments have not been completed, the assignment can begin at this point. You should use the Working Papers that accompany this text because they reflect the account balances that resulted from posting the entries required in Chapters 3, 4, and 5.)

Earlier segments of this problem have described how Mary Graham created Echo Systems on October 1, 2000. The company has been successful, and its list of customers has grown. To accommodate the growth, the accounting system is ready to be modified to set up separate accounts for each customer. The following list of customers includes the account number used for each account and any balance as of the end of year 2000. Graham decided to add a fourth digit with a decimal point to the 106 account number that had been used for the single Accounts Receivable account. This modification allows the company to continue using the existing chart of accounts. The list also includes the balances that two customers owed as of December 31, 2000:

Customer Account	No.	Dec. 31 Balance
Alamo Engineering Co.	106.1	
Buckman Services	106.2	
Capital Leasing	106.3	
Decker Co.	106.4	$1,350
Elite Corporation	106.5	
Fostek Co.	106.6	$1,500
Grandview Co.	106.7	
Hacienda, Inc.	106.8	
Images, Inc.	106.9	

In response to requests from customers, Graham has decided to begin selling computer software. The company also will extend credit terms of 1/10, n/30 to customers who purchase merchandise. No cash discount will be available on consulting fees. The following additional accounts were added to the General Ledger to allow the system to account for the company's new merchandising activities:

Account	No.
Merchandise Inventory	119
Sales	413
Sales Returns and Allowances	414
Sales Discounts	415
Cost of Goods Sold	502

Because the accounting system does not use reversing entries, all revenue and expense accounts have zero balances as of January 1, 2001.

Required

1. Prepare journal entries to record each of the following transactions for Echo Systems.
2. Post the journal entries to the accounts in the company's General Ledger. (Use asset, liability, and equity accounts that start with balances as of December 31, 2000.)
3. Prepare a partial work sheet consisting of the first six columns similar to the one shown in Appendix 4B that shows the unadjusted trial balance, the March 31 adjustments *(a)* through *(g)*, and the adjusted trial balance. Do not prepare closing entries and do not journalize the adjusting entries or post them to the ledger.
4. Prepare an interim income statement for the three months ended March 31, 2001. Use a single-step format like the one in Exhibit 6.20. List all expenses without differentiating between selling expenses and general and administrative expenses.
5. Prepare an interim statement of changes in owner's equity for the three months ended March 31, 2001.
6. Prepare an interim balance sheet as of March 31, 2001.

Transactions

Jan. 4 Paid Carly Smith for five days' work at the rate of $100 per day. Four of the five days are unpaid days of work from the prior year.

5 Mary Graham invested an additional $24,000 cash in the business.

7 Purchased $5,600 of merchandise from Shephard Corp. with terms of 1/10, n/30, FOB shipping point.

9 Received $1,500 from Fostek Co. as final payment on its account.

11 Completed a five-day project for Alamo Engineering Co. and billed them $4,500, which is the total price of $6,000 less the advance payment of $1,500.

13 Sold merchandise with a retail value of $4,200 and a cost of $3,360 to Elite Corporation with terms of 1/10, n/30, FOB shipping point.

15 Paid $700 for freight charges on the merchandise purchased on January 7.

16 Received $3,000 cash from Grandview Co. for computer services.

17 Paid Shephard Corp. for the purchase on January 7, net of the discount.

20 Elite Corporation returned $400 of defective merchandise from its purchase on January 13. The returned merchandise, which had a cost of $320, was discarded.

22 Received the balance due from Elite Corporation net of the discount and the credit for the returned merchandise.

24 Returned defective merchandise to Shephard Corp. and accepted credit against future purchases. Its cost, net of the discount, was $396.

26 Purchased $8,000 of merchandise from Shephard Corp. with terms of 1/10, n/30, FOB destination.

26 Sold merchandise with a cost of $4,640 for $5,800 on credit to Hacienda, Inc.

29 Received a $396 credit memo from Shephard Corp. concerning the merchandise returned on January 24.

31 Paid Carly Smith for 10 days' work at $100 per day.

Feb. 1 Paid $3,375 to the Lakeshore Mall for another three months' rent in advance.

3 Paid Shephard Corp. for the balance due, net of the cash discount, less the $396 amount in the credit memo.

5 Paid $800 to the local newspaper for advertising.

11 Received the balance due from Alamo Engineering Co. for fees billed on January 11.

15 May Graham withdrew $4,800 cash.

23 Sold merchandise with a cost of $2,560 for $3,200 on credit to Grandview Co.

26 Paid Carly Smith for eight days' work at $100 per day.

27 Reimbursed Mary Graham's business automobile mileage for 600 miles at $0.25 per mile.

Mar. 8 Purchased $2,400 of computer supplies from Abbott Office Products on credit.

9 Received the balance due from Grandview Co. for merchandise sold on February 23.

11 Repaired the company's computer at a cost of $860.

16 Received $4,260 cash from Images, Inc., for computing services.

19 Paid the full amount due to Abbott Office Products, including amounts created on December 15 and March 8.

24 Billed Capital Leasing for $5,900 of computing services.

25 Sold merchandise with a cost of $1,002 for $1,800 on credit to Buckman Services.

30 Sold merchandise with a cost of $1,100 for $2,220 on credit to Decker Company.

31 Reimbursed Mary Graham's business automobile mileage for 400 miles at $0.25 per mile.

Information for the March 31 adjustments and financial statements:

a. The March 31 inventory of computer supplies is $2,115.

b. Three more months have passed since the company purchased the annual insurance policy at a cost of $2,160.

c. Carly Smith has not been paid for seven days of work.

d. Three months have passed since any prepaid rent cost has been transferred to expense. The monthly rent is $1,125.

e. Depreciation on the computer for January through March is $1,125.

f. Depreciation on the office equipment for January through March is $750.

g. The March 31 inventory of merchandise is $980.

BEYOND THE NUMBERS

Reporting in Action

A2, C5

Refer to the financial statements and related information for **NIKE** in Appendix A. Answer the following questions by analyzing that information:

1. Assume the amounts reported for inventories and cost of sales reflect items purchased ready for resale. Compute the net cost of goods purchased during the fiscal year ended May 31, 1997.
2. Calculate the current and acid-test ratios as of the end of the fiscal years ended May 31, 1997, and May 31, 1996. Comment on your ratio results.

Swoosh Ahead

3. Obtain access to NIKE's annual report for fiscal years ending after May 31, 1997. You can gain access to NIKE's annual report at its web site **[www.nike.com]** or through the SEC's EDGAR database **[www.sec.gov]**. Recompute the current and acid-test ratios for fiscal years ending after May 31, 1997.

Comparative Analysis

A3

Reebok

Both **NIKE** and **Reebok** design, produce, market, and sell sports footwear and apparel. Key comparative figures ($ millions) for these two organizations follow:

	NIKE		Reebok	
Key figures	**1997**	**1996**	**1996**	**1995**
Net Sales	$9,187	$6,471	$3,479	$3,481
Cost of Sales	5,503	3,907	2,144	2,114

* NIKE figures are from its annual reports for fiscal years ended May 31, 1997 and 1996.
Reebok figures are from its annual reports for fiscal years ended December 31, 1996 and 1995.

Required

1. Compute the dollar amount of gross margin and the gross margin ratio for the two years shown for both companies.
2. Which company earns more in gross margin for each dollar of net sales?
3. Did the gross margin ratios improve or decline for these companies?

Ethics Challenge

P2

Claire Phelps is a student who attends approximately four dances a year at her school. Each dance requires a new dress and accessories that necessitate a financial outlay of $100-$200 per event. Claire's parents inform her that she is "on her own" with respect to financing the dresses. After incurring a major hit to her savings for the first dance in her freshman year, Claire developed a different approach. She buys the dress on credit the week before the dance, wears it to the dance, and returns the dress the next week to the store for a full refund on her charge card.

Required

1. Comment on the ethics exhibited by Claire and possible consequences of her actions.
2. How does the store account for the dresses that Claire returns?

Communicating in Practice

C4, C5, P3

You are the accountant for **Music, Videos, and More,** a retailer that sells goods for home entertainment needs. The owner of the business, Mr. U. Paah, recently reviewed the annual financial statements and sent you an e-mail stating that he is sure you overstated net income. He explains that he makes this claim because, although he has invested a great deal in security, he is sure shoplifting and other forms of inventory shrinkage have still taken place. He does not see any deduction for such loss on the income statement. The store uses a perpetual inventory system.

Required

Prepare a memorandum that responds to the owner's concerns in paper or e-mail format. If the response is to be made via e-mail, you are to assume your instructor is the owner instead of Mr. U. Paah.

Taking It to the Net

C1

The amount of merchandising activity on the Web has grown dramatically. Use a Web search engine (such as Lycos, Yahoo, or Alta Vista) and search for the word *merchandising*. Explore the Web addresses located by the search engine and make a list of at least 10 products that companies or individuals are trying to market and sell using the Web.

Teamwork in Action

C2, C5, A3

World Brands' ledger and supplementary records at the end of the period disclose the following:

Sales	$430,000
Sales returns	18,000
Merchandise inventory (beginning of period)	49,000
Invoice cost of merchandise purchases	180,000
Purchase discounts received	4,500
Sales discounts	6,600
Purchase returns and allowances received	5,500
Cost of transportation-in	11,000
Operating expenses	20,000
Merchandise inventory (end of period)	42,000

Required

1. *Each* member of the team is to assume responsibility for computing *one* of the amounts listed below. You are not to duplicate your teammates' work. Get necessary amounts from teammate. Each member is to explain his or her computation to the team in preparation for reporting to the class.
   a. Net sales
   b. Total cost of merchandise purchases
   c. Cost of goods sold
   d. Gross profit
   e. Net income
2. Check your net income with the instructor. If correct, proceed to (3).
3. Assume a physical inventory disclosed that the actual ending inventory was $38,000. Discuss how this affects previously computed amounts in (1).

Hitting the Road

C1

Arrange an interview (in person or by phone) with the manager of a retail shop in a mall or in the downtown area of your community. Explain to the manager that you are an accounting student studying merchandising operations and the accounting for sales returns and sales allowances. Ask the manager what the store policy is regarding returns. Also find out if sales allowances are ever negotiated with customers. Inquire whether management ever perceives that customers are abusing return policies and what actions management takes to counter the abuses. Be prepared to discuss your findings in class.

Business Week Activity

P4

Read the article "An Adrenalin Rush at Adidas," in the September 29, 1997, issue of *Business Week*.

Required

1. The article identifies Adidas as the number two company in the sporting goods market. What companies are numbers one and three respectively?
2. What new strategy is Adidas using to compete more effectively against its number one rival?
3. After reading the article, do you think the new strategy of Adidas will be effective?
4. Consult the notes of the annual report of NIKE in Appendix A. Determine the advertising and promotion expenses incurred by NIKE. Compare the advertising expenses of NIKE to those incurred by Adidas.
5. Identify where the advertising expenses are reported in the financial statements of NIKE.

Merchandise Inventories and Cost of Sales

A Look Back

Chapter 6 focused on merchandising activities and how they're reported. Both the perpetual and periodic inventory systems were described. We also analyzed and recorded merchandise purchases and sales and explained adjustments and the closing process for merchandising companies.

A Look at This Chapter

This chapter emphasizes accounting for inventory. We describe the methods available for assigning costs to inventory and explain the items and costs making up merchandise inventory. We also analyze the effects of inventory for both financial and tax reporting and discuss other methods of estimating and measuring inventory.

A Look Ahead

In Chapter 8 we discuss information systems and explain how computing technology is expanding accounting opportunities. We also present special journals and describe their importance in the accounting process.

Chapter Outline

Wired in Philly

PHILADELPHIA—Big is not better. Or so says Lenny Russo, the 29-year-old owner of **Wired,** an electronics retailer and service provider. Russo built his business by taking jobs nobody wanted. "Big stores give a hard sell, take your cash, and maybe see you later," says Russo. "Don't get me wrong. They've got a place. It just isn't my place."

What is Russo's place is selling, installing, and servicing home entertainment systems to college students, young families, nightclubs, and other establishments. "I deal with small frys," says Russo. "I give people a great system fitting their needs, and they give me their business." He now has his own store and showroom, and business couldn't be better.

But it wasn't always that way. "The biggest hurdle," bemoans Russo, "was getting the money to get going and to expand." Russo's hurdle was pushing the numbers and getting financial statements together. "The bank wanted to know things like gross margin, turnover, and inventory on hand." Adds Russo, "Til then I thought turnover was something you ate."

The other hurdle Russo faced was measuring inventory. "I started by keeping track of each item sold and recording its cost." But business grew and Russo's system quickly overloaded. He now uses a perpetual system.

Needless to say, Russo has figured a lot of things out in his few years in business. While his tough Philly upbringing shows, he can talk the talk with the best of them. "I can now tell you about turnover, liquidity ratios, and other financial jazz." But, laughs Russo, "don't tell my family!" Somehow, one gets the feeling the Russo family would be proud.

Learning Objectives

Conceptual

C1 Identify the items making up merchandise inventory.

C2 Identify the costs of merchandise inventory.

Analytical

A1 Analyze the effects of inventory methods for both financial and tax reporting.

A2 Analyze the effects of inventory errors on current and future financial statements.

A3 Assess inventory management using both merchandise turnover and days' sales in inventory.

Procedural

P1 Compute inventory in a perpetual system using the methods of specific identification, FIFO, LIFO, and weighted average.

P2 Compute the lower of cost or market amount of inventory.

P3 Apply both the retail inventory and gross profit methods to estimate inventory.

CHAPTER PREVIEW

Activities of merchandising companies involve the purchase and resale of products. We explained accounting for merchandisers in the last chapter and explained how perpetual and periodic inventory systems account for merchandise inventory. In this chapter we extend our study and analysis of inventory by identifying the items making up inventory. We also explain the methods used to assign costs to merchandise inventory *and* cost of goods sold. The assigned costs are not always historical cost.

The principles and methods we describe are used in department stores, grocery stores, and many other merchandising companies that purchase products for resale. These principles and methods affect reported amounts of income, assets, and equity. Understanding these fundamental concepts of inventory accounting increases our ability to analyze and interpret financial statements. As Lenny Russo learned, an understanding of these topics also helps in running one's own business.

Assigning Costs to Inventory

P1 Compute inventory in a perpetual system using the methods of specific identification, FIFO, LIFO, and weighted average.

Accounting for inventory affects both the balance sheet and the income statement. A major goal in accounting for inventory is matching relevant costs against revenues. This is important to properly compute income.[1]

We discussed the *matching principle* in Chapter 4. We use it when accounting for inventory to decide how much of the cost of the goods available for sale is deducted from sales and how much is carried forward as inventory and matched against future sales. Management must make this decision along with several others when accounting for inventory. These decisions include selecting the:

- Costing method (specific identification, FIFO, LIFO, or weighted average)
- Inventory system (perpetual or periodic)
- Items included and their costs
- Use of market or other estimates

Decisions on these factors affect the reported amounts for inventory, cost of goods sold, gross profit, income, current assets, and other accounts. This chapter discusses all of these important issues and their reporting effects.

One of the most important decisions in accounting for inventory is determining the per unit costs assigned to inventory items. When all units are purchased at the same unit cost, this process is simple. But when identical items are purchased at different costs, a question arises as to what amounts are recorded in cost of goods sold when sales occur and what amounts remain in inventory. We must record cost of goods sold and reductions in inventory as sales occur using a perpetual inventory system. A periodic inventory system determines cost of goods sold and inventory amounts at the end of a period (see Appendix 7A). How we assign these costs to inventory and cost of goods sold affects the reported amounts for both systems.

There are four methods commonly used in assigning costs to inventory and cost of goods sold. They are (1) specific identification; (2) first-in, first-out; (3) last-in, first-out; and (4) weighted average. Each method assumes a particular pattern for how costs flow through inventory. Each of the four methods described in this section is acceptable in financial reporting. This is the case whether or not the actual physical flow of goods follows the cost flow assumption.[2] Exhibit 7.1 shows the frequency in use of these methods in practice.

---

[1] FASB, *Accounting Standards—Current Text* (Norwalk, CT, 1995), sec. I78.104. First published as *Accounting Research Bulletin No. 43,* chap. 4, par. 4

[2] Physical flow of goods depends on the type of product and the way it is stored. Perishable goods such as fresh fruit demand that a business attempt to sell them in a first-in, first-out physical flow pattern. Other products such as lanterns or grills can often be sold in a last-in, first-out physical flow pattern. But physical flow and cost flow need not be the same.

We use information from **Trekking,** a sporting goods store, to describe the four methods. Among its many products, Trekking carries one type of mountain bike. Its sales of mountain bikes are directed at biking clubs, and customer purchases are usually in amounts of 10 or more bikes. We use data from Trekking's August 1998 transactions in mountain bikes. Its mountain bike (unit) inventory at the beginning of August and its purchases during August are shown in Exhibit 7.2.

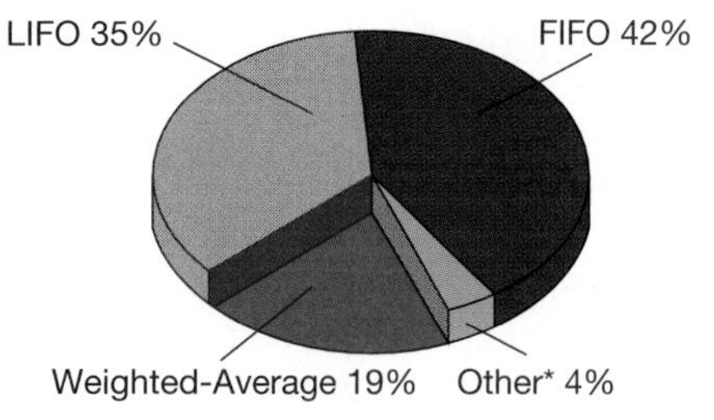

Exhibit 7.1

Frequency in Use of Inventory Methods in Practice

Aug. 1	Beginning inventory	10 units @ $ 91 =	$ 910
Aug. 3	Purchases	15 units @ $106 =	1,590
Aug. 17	Purchases	20 units @ $115 =	2,300
Aug. 28	Purchases	10 units @ $119 =	1,190
Total	. . . .	**55 units**	**$5,990**

Exhibit 7.2

Cost of Goods Available for Sale

Trekking ends August with 12 bikes on hand in inventory. This inventory results after Trekking had two large sales of mountain bikes to two different biking clubs in August as shown in Exhibit 7.3:

Aug. 14	Sales	20 units @ $130 =	$2,600
Aug. 31	Sales	23 units @ $150 =	3,450
Total	. . . .	**43 units**	**$6,050**

Exhibit 7.3

Retail Sales of Goods

Trekking uses the perpetual inventory system. We explained in the last chapter how use of the perpetual inventory system is increasing due to advances in information and computing technology. Widespread use of electronic scanners and product bar codes supports a perpetual inventory system. For these reasons we discuss Trekking's assigning of costs to inventory in a perpetual system. But in Appendix 7A, we also describe the assigning of costs to inventory using a periodic system. A periodic inventory system computes cost of goods available for sale and allocates it between cost of goods sold and ending inventory at the *end of the period.* By assigning an amount to ending inventory and subtracting it from cost of goods available for sale, we get cost of goods sold.[3]

Trekking's use of a perpetual inventory system means the merchandise inventory account is continually updated to reflect purchases and sales. As described in Chapter 6, the important accounting aspects of a perpetual system are:

- Each purchase of merchandise for resale increases (debit) inventory.
- Each sale of merchandise decreases (credit) inventory and increases (debit) costs of goods sold.
- Necessary costs of merchandise such as transportation-in increase (debit) inventory, and cost reductions such as purchase discounts and purchase returns and allowances decrease (credit) inventory.

Except for any inventory shrinkage, the balance in the merchandise inventory account reflects the amount of merchandise on hand at any time.

[3] Similarly, assigning an amount to cost of goods sold also determines the amount of ending inventory.

Specific Identification

When each item in inventory can be directly identified with a specific purchase and its invoice, we can use **specific identification** (also called **specific invoice inventory pricing**) to assign costs. Sales records identify exactly which bikes are sold and when. Trekking's internal documents reveal 6 of the 12 unsold units are from the August 28 purchase and another 6 are from the August 17 purchase. We use this information along with specific identification to assign costs to the goods sold and to ending inventory as shown in Exhibit 7.4.

Specific Identification Computations

Date	Purchases	Cost of Goods Sold	Inventory Balance
Aug. 1	Beginning balance		10 @ $ 91 = $ 910
Aug. 3	15 @ $106 = $1,590		10 @ $ 91 15 @ $106 } = $2,500
Aug. 14		8 @ $ 91 = $ 728 12 @ $106 = $1,272 } = $2,000	2 @ $ 91 3 @ $106 } = $ 500
Aug. 17	20 @ $115 = $2,300		2 @ $ 91 3 @ $106 20 @ $115 } = $2,800
Aug. 28	10 @ $119 = $1,190		2 @ $ 91 3 @ $106 20 @ $115 10 @ $119 } = $3,990
Aug. 31		2 @ $ 91 = $ 182 3 @ $106 = $ 318 14 @ $115 = $1,610 4 @ $119 = $ 476 } = $2,586	6 @ $115 6 @ $119 } = $1,404

When using specific identification, Trekking's cost of goods sold reported on the income statement is **$4,586,** the sum of $2,000 and $2,586 from the third column of Exhibit 7.4. Trekking's ending inventory reported on the balance sheet is **$1,404,** which is the final inventory balance from the fourth column of Exhibit 7.4. *The assignment of costs to cost of goods sold and inventory using specific identification is the same for both the perpetual and periodic systems.*

First-In, First-Out

The first-in, first-out (FIFO) method of assigning cost to inventory and the goods sold assumes inventory items are sold in the order acquired. When sales occur, costs of the earliest units acquired are charged to cost of goods sold. This leaves the costs from the most recent purchases in inventory. Use of FIFO for Trekking means the costs of mountain bikes are assigned to inventory and goods sold as shown in Exhibit 7.5.

Trekking's cost of goods sold reported on the income statement is **$4,570** ($1,970 + $2,600) and its ending inventory reported on the balance sheet is **$1,420.** *The assignment of costs to cost of goods sold and inventory using FIFO is the same for both the perpetual and periodic systems.*

Last-In, First-Out

The **last-in, first-out (LIFO)** method of assigning cost assumes that the most recent purchases are sold first. Their costs are charged to cost of goods sold, and the costs of the earliest purchases are assigned to inventory. Like the other methods, LIFO is acceptable even when the physical flow of goods does not follow a last-in, first-out pattern.

Exhibit 7.5

FIFO Computations—Perpetual System

Date	Purchases	Cost of Goods Sold	Inventory Balance
Aug. 1	Beginning balance		10 @ $ 91 = $ 910
Aug. 3	15 @ $106 = $1,590		10 @ $ 91 15 @ $106 } = $2,500
Aug. 14		10 @ $ 91 = $ 910 10 @ $106 = $1,060 } = **$1,970**	5 @ $106 = $ 530
Aug. 17	20 @ $115 = $2,300		5 @ $106 20 @ $115 } = $2,830
Aug. 28	10 @ $119 = $1,190		5 @ $106 20 @ $115 10 @ $119 } = $4,020
Aug. 31		5 @ $106 = $ 530 18 @ $115 = $2,070 } = **$2,600**	2 @ $115 10 @ $119 } = **$1,420**

Companies commonly replace the inventory items that they sell. This means the sale of goods causes a company to replace inventory. A good matching of costs with revenues suggests we match the costs of replacements with the sales causing the replacements. While costs for the most recent purchases are not exactly replacement costs, they often are close approximations. One appeal of LIFO is that by assigning costs from the most recent purchases to cost of goods sold, LIFO comes closest to matching replacement costs with revenues (compared to FIFO or weighted average).

Use of LIFO for Trekking means costs of mountain bikes are assigned to inventory and goods sold as shown in Exhibit 7.6.

Exhibit 7.6

LIFO Computations—Perpetual System

Date	Purchases	Cost of Goods Sold	Inventory Balance
Aug. 1	Beginning balance		10 @ $ 91 = $ 910
Aug. 3	15 @ $106 = $1,590		10 @ $ 91 15 @ $106 } = $2,500
Aug. 14		15 @ $106 = $1,590 5 @ $ 91 = $ 455 } = **$2,045**	5 @ $ 91 = $ 455
Aug. 17	20 @ $115 = $2,300		5 @ $ 91 20 @ $115 } = $2,755
Aug. 28	10 @ $119 = $1,190		5 @ $ 91 20 @ $115 10 @ $119 } = $3,945
Aug. 31		10 @ $119 = $1,190 13 @ $115 = $1,495 } = **$2,685**	5 @ $ 91 7 @ $115 } = **$1,260**

Trekking's cost of goods sold reported on the income statement is **$4,730** ($2,045 + $2,685) and its ending inventory reported on the balance sheet is **$1,260.** The assignment of costs to cost of goods sold and inventory using LIFO usually gives different results depending on whether a perpetual or periodic system is used. This is because LIFO under a perpetual system assigns the most recent costs to goods sold at the time of each sale, whereas the periodic system waits to assign costs until the end of a period.

Weighted Average

The **weighted average** (also called **average cost**) method of assigning cost requires computing the average cost per unit of merchandise inventory at the time of each sale. Some systems are set up to compute this average after each purchase. The important point is that we compute weighted average cost at the time of each sale by dividing the cost of goods available for sale by the units on hand. Using weighted average for Trekking means the costs of mountain bikes are assigned to inventory and goods sold as shown in Exhibit 7.7.

Exhibit 7.7

Weighted Average Computations—Perpetual System

Date	Purchases	Cost of Goods Sold	Inventory Balance	
Aug. 1	Beginning balance		10 @ $ 91	= $ 910
Aug. 3	15 @ $106 = $1,590		10 @ $ 91 15 @ $106	= $2,500 (or $100 per unit)[a]
Aug. 14		20 @ $100 = $2,000	5 @ $100	= $ 500 (or $100 per unit)[b]
Aug. 17	20 @ $115 = $2,300		5 @ $100 20 @ $115	= $2,800 (or $112 per unit)[c]
Aug. 28	10 @ $119 = $1,190		5 @ $100 20 @ $115 10 @ $119	= $3,990 (or $114 per unit)[d]
Aug. 31		23 @ $114 = **$2,622**	12 @ $114	= **$1,368** (or $114 per unit)[e]

[a] $100 per unit = [$2,500 inventory balance ÷ 25 units in inventory].
[b] $100 per unit = [$ 500 inventory balance ÷ 5 units in inventory].
[c] $112 per unit = [$2,800 inventory balance ÷ 25 units in inventory].
[d] $114 per unit = [$3,990 inventory balance ÷ 35 units in inventory].
[e] $114 per unit = [$1,368 inventory balance ÷ 12 units in inventory].

Trekking's cost of goods sold reported on the income statement is **$4,622** ($2,000 + $2,622) and its ending inventory reported on the balance sheet is **$1,368.** The assignment of costs to cost of goods sold and inventory using weighted average usually gives different results depending on whether a perpetual or periodic system is used. This is because weighted average under a perpetual system recomputes the per unit cost at the time of each sale, whereas under the periodic system the per unit cost is only computed at the end of a period.

Inventory Costing and Technology

A perpetual inventory system can be kept in either electronic or manual form. Using a manual form can make a perpetual inventory system too costly for businesses, especially those with many purchases and sales or many units in inventory. But advances in information and computing technology have greatly reduced the cost of a perpetual inventory system. Many companies are now asking whether they can afford *not* to have a perpetual inventory system because timely access to information is being used strategically by companies to gain a competitive advantage. Scanned sales data, for instance, can reveal crucial information on buying patterns. It can also help companies target promotional and advertising activities. These and other applications have greatly increased the use of the perpetual inventory system.

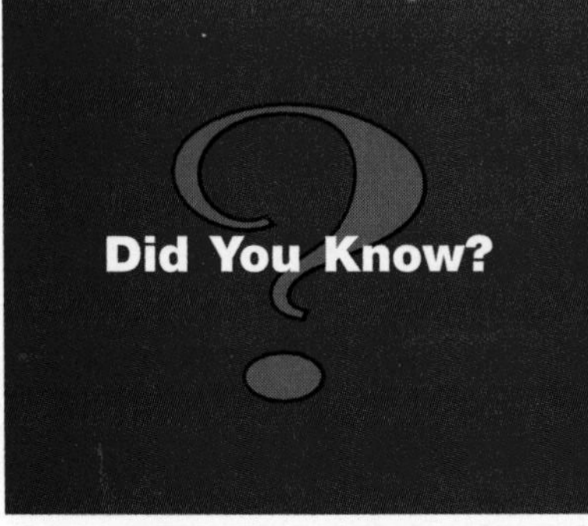

Whirlwind on the Web

From its roots in a college dorm room in 1984, **Dell** now sells several millions of dollars' worth of computers each week from its Web site. "The Internet," says Michael S. Dell, "is the ultimate direct model." Direct buyers now account for a third of the total PC business. The speed of Web technology has allowed Dell to slash inventories so it can underprice rivals by 10% to 15%. Dell's operating cycle is less than 24 hours and its days' sales in inventory is 13 days. "Speed is everything in this business," adds Mr. Dell. With Dell racing past rivals like Sunday drivers on the Information Highway, there may be a new pace for merchandisers in the Age of the Internet: Dell-ocity. [Source: *Business Week,* April 4, 1997.]

Subsidiary Inventory Records

The Merchandise Inventory account is a controlling account for the subsidiary Merchandise Inventory Ledger. This subsidiary ledger contains a separate record for each product, and it can be in electronic or paper form. A typical ledger is shown in Exhibit 7.8. This record shows both the units and costs for each purchase and sale, along with the balance after each purchase and sale. The record also gives the item, its catalog number, and its location (at the top). The subsidiary Merchandise Inventory Ledger is updated after each purchase and sale transaction. This ledger reveals by its computations that a FIFO cost flow assumption is being used for sports bags.

Exhibit 7.8

Subsidiary Inventory Record

Item Leather Sports Bags — **Location code** W18C2
Catalog No. LSB-117 — **Units: Maximum** 25 **Minimum** 5

	Purchases			Cost of Goods Sold			Inventory Balance		
Date	**Units**	**Cost**	**Total**	**Units**	**Cost**	**Total**	**Units**	**Cost**	**Total**
Aug. 1							10	$100	$1,000
Aug. 12				4	$100	$ 400	6	100	600
Aug. 18	20	$110	$2,200				6 20	100 110	2,800
Aug. 30				6 2	100 110	600 220	18	110	1,980
Totals	20		$2,220	12		$ 1,220			

Subsidiary inventory records assist managers in planning and controlling inventory. Exhibit 7.8 reveals a policy of maintaining no more than 25 sports bags to avoid overinvestment in this inventory, and no less than 5 sports bags on hand to avoid out-of-stock occurrences. These records also permit companies to compare a physical count of items on hand to the record. Differences are investigated to identify their cause.

Inventory Items and Costs

This section identifies the items and costs making up merchandise inventory. This identification is important given the major impact of inventory in financial statements. We also describe the importance and methods of taking a physical count of inventory.

Items in Merchandise Inventory

C1 Identify the items making up merchandise inventory.

Merchandise inventory includes all goods owned by a company and held for sale. This rule holds regardless of where goods are located at the time inventory is counted. Most inventory items present no problem when applying this rule. We must simply see that all items are counted and computations are correct. But certain items require special attention. These include goods in transit, goods on consignment, and goods that are damaged or obsolete.

Goods in Transit

Do we include in a purchaser's inventory the goods in transit from a supplier? Our answer depends on whether the rights and risks of ownership have passed from the supplier to the purchaser. If ownership has passed to the purchaser, they are included in the purchaser's inventory. We explained in Chapter 6 how we determine this by looking at the shipping terms—*FOB destination* or FOB *shipping point.* If the purchaser is responsible for paying freight charges, then ownership passes when goods are loaded on the means of transportation. If the supplier is to pay freight charges, ownership passes when goods arrive at their destination.

Goods on Consignment

Goods on consignment are goods shipped by their owner, called the **consignor,** to another party called the **consignee.** A consignee is to sell goods for the owner. Consigned goods are owned by the consignor and are reported in the consignor's inventory. **Score Board,** for instance, pays sports celebrities such as Steve Young and Ken Griffey, Jr., to sign memorabilia. These autographed items (footballs, baseballs, jerseys, photos, etc.) are offered to shopping networks on consignment as well as sold through catalogs and dealers.

Goods Damaged or Obsolete

Damaged goods and obsolete (or deteriorated) goods are not counted in inventory if they are unsalable. If these goods are salable at a reduced price, they are included in inventory at a conservative estimate of their **net realizable value.** Net realizable value is sales price minus the cost of making the sale. The period when damage or obsolescence (or deterioration) occurs is the period when the loss in value is reported.

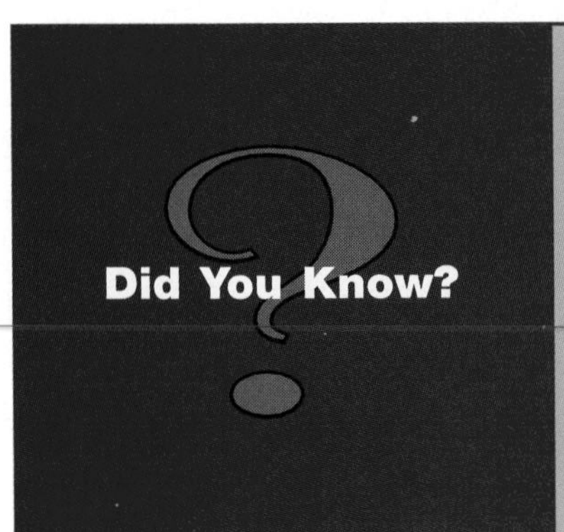

Inventory Online

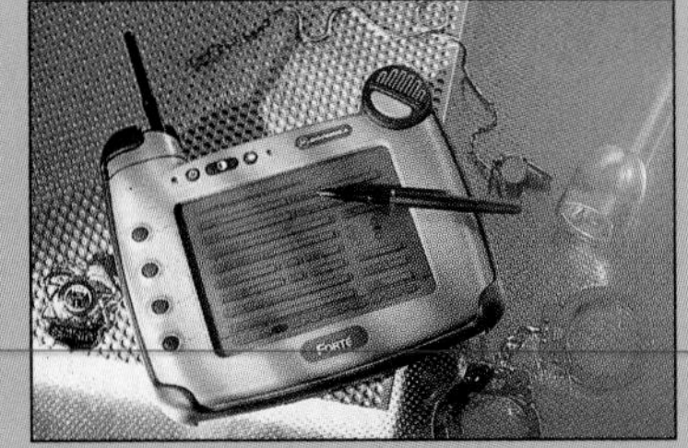

Warehouse inventory clerks can now check in hundreds of boxes by quickly scanning bar codes on merchandise. Thanks to **Motorola,** a new wireless portable computer with a two-way radio allows clerks to send and receive data instantly. It gives managers immediate access to up to date information on inventory. Also, the portable computer can withstand dust and harsh weather, and can be dropped on concrete. [Source: *Business Week,* June 6, 1996.]

Costs of Merchandise Inventory

C2 Identify the costs of merchandise inventory.

Costs included in merchandise inventory are those expenditures necessary, directly or indirectly, to bring an item to a salable condition and location.[4] This means the cost of an inventory item includes its invoice price minus any discount, plus any added or incidental costs necessary to put it in a place and condition for sale. Added or incidental costs can include import duties, transportation-in, storage, insurance, and costs incurred in an aging process (for example, aging of wine and cheese).

Accounting principles imply that incidental costs are assigned to every unit purchased. This is so all inventory costs are properly matched against revenue in the period when inventory is sold. The *materiality principle* or the *cost-to-benefit constraint* is used by some companies to avoid assigning incidental costs of acquiring merchandise to inventory. These companies argue either that incidental costs are immaterial or that the effort in assigning these costs to inventory outweighs the benefits. Such companies price inventory using invoice prices only. When this is done, the incidental costs are allocated to cost of goods sold in the period when they are incurred.

---

[4] FASB, *Accounting Standards—Current Text* (Norwalk, CT, 1995), sec. I78.402. First published as *Accounting Research Bulletin No. 43,* ch. 4, par. 5.

Shopping in the Fast Lane
Bar codes and readers are common business tools for many retailers. Yet the way they are currently used may soon be a thing of the past. Retailers are now experimenting with a bar code reader on shopping carts where the customers simply swipe the product over the reader and it's automatically charged to their credit card. There is no need to stand in any checkout line. Customers simply pass through a gate that checks whether everything in the cart has been scanned. [Source: *Business Week,* June 10, 1996.]

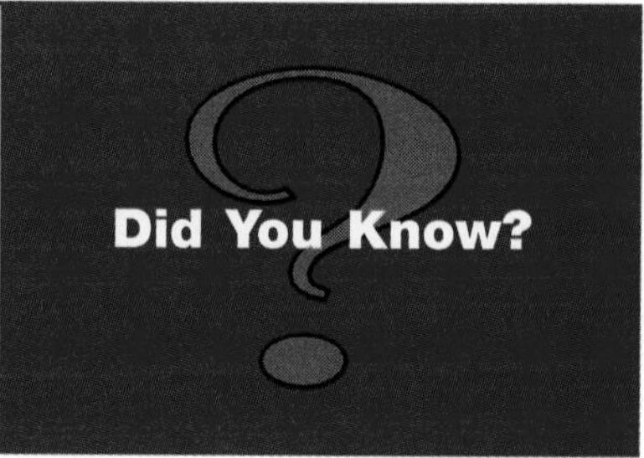

Physical Count of Merchandise Inventory

The Inventory account under a perpetual system is always up to date. Yet events can occur where the Inventory account balance is different from inventory on hand. Such events include theft, loss, damage, and errors. This means nearly all companies take a *physical count of inventory* at least once each year, sometimes called *taking an inventory*. This often occurs at the end of a fiscal year or when inventory amounts are low. This physical count is used to adjust the Inventory account balance to the actual inventory on hand. There is also need for a physical count of inventory under a periodic system (see Appendix 7A).

We determine a dollar amount for the physical count of inventory on hand at the end of a period by: (1) counting the units of each product on hand, (2) multiplying the count for each product by its cost per unit, and (3) adding the costs for all products. When taking a count, items are less likely to be counted more than once or omitted if we use prenumbered inventory tickets. We show a typical inventory ticket in Exhibit 7.9.

Exhibit 7.9

Inventory Ticket

INVENTORY TICKET NO. 1001
Quantity counted ______ Purchase date ______
Sales Price $ ______ Cost price $ ______
Counted by ______ Checked by ______

The process of a physical count is fairly standard. Before beginning a physical count of inventory, we prepare at least one inventory ticket for each product on hand. These tickets are issued to employees doing the count. An employee will count the quantity of a product and obtain information on its purchase date, selling price, and cost. This information is sometimes included with the products but must often be obtained from accounting records or invoices. Once the necessary information is collected, the employee records it on the inventory ticket and signs the form. The inventory ticket is then attached to the counted inventory. Another employee often recounts and rechecks information on the ticket, signs the ticket, and returns it to the manager. To ensure no ticket is lost or missed, internal control procedures verify that all prenumbered tickets are returned. The unit and cost data on inventory tickets are aggregated by multiplying the number of units for each product by its unit cost. This gives us the dollar amount for each product in inventory. The sum total of all products is the dollar amount reported for inventory on the balance sheet.

Flash *back*

1. What accounting principle most governs allocation of cost of goods available for sale between ending inventory and cost of goods sold?
2. If **NIKE** sells goods to **Target** with terms FOB shipping point, does NIKE or Target report these goods in its inventory while they are in transit?
3. An art gallery purchases a painting for $11,400 on terms FOB shipping point. Additional costs in obtaining and offering the artwork for sale include $130 for transportation-in, $150 for import duties, $100 for insurance during shipment, $180 for advertising, $400 for framing, and $800 for sales salaries. For computing inventory, what cost is assigned to the painting?

Answers—p. 296

Inventory Analysis and Effects

This section analyzes and compares the effects of using alternative inventory costing methods. We also analyze the tax effects of inventory methods, examine managers' preferences for an inventory method, and look at the effects of inventory errors.

A1 Analyze the effects of inventory methods for both financial and tax reporting.

Financial Reporting

When purchase prices don't change, the choice of an inventory costing method is unimportant. All methods assign the same cost amounts when prices don't change. But when purchase prices are rising or falling, the methods are likely to assign different cost amounts. We show these differences in Exhibit 7.10 using Trekking's segment income statement for its mountain bike operations.

Exhibit 7.10

Income Statement Effects of Inventory Costing Methods

TREKKING COMPANY
Segment Income Statement—Mountain Bikes
Month Ending August 31

	Specific Identification	FIFO	LIFO	Weighted Average
Sales	$6,050	$6,050	$6,050	$6,050
Cost of goods sold	4,586	4,570	4,730	4,622
Gross profit	$1,464	$1,480	$1,320	$1,428
Operating expenses	450	450	450	450
Income before taxes	$1,014	$1,030	$ 870	$ 978
Income tax expense (30%)	304	309	261	293
Net income	$ 710	$ 721	$ 609	$ 685

The different inventory costing methods show different results for net income. Because Trekking's purchase prices rose in August, FIFO assigned the least amount to cost of goods sold. This led to the highest gross profit and the highest net income. LIFO assigned the highest amount to cost of goods sold. This yields the lowest gross profit and the lowest net income. As expected, amounts from using the weighted average method fell between FIFO and LIFO.[5] The amounts from using specific identification depend on what units are actually sold.

All four inventory costing methods are acceptable in practice. Each method offers certain advantages. One advantage of specific identification is it exactly matches costs and revenues. This is important when each unit has unique features affecting the cost of that unit. An advantage of weighted average is that it tends to smooth out price changes. The advantage of FIFO is it assigns an amount to inventory on the balance sheet that closely approximates current replacement cost. The advantage of LIFO is it assigns the most recent costs incurred to cost of goods sold, and likely better matches current costs with revenues on the income statement.

The choice of an inventory costing method often dramatically impacts amounts on financial statements. **Mobil,** for instance, recently changed its inventory method and reported this change in a news release as follows:

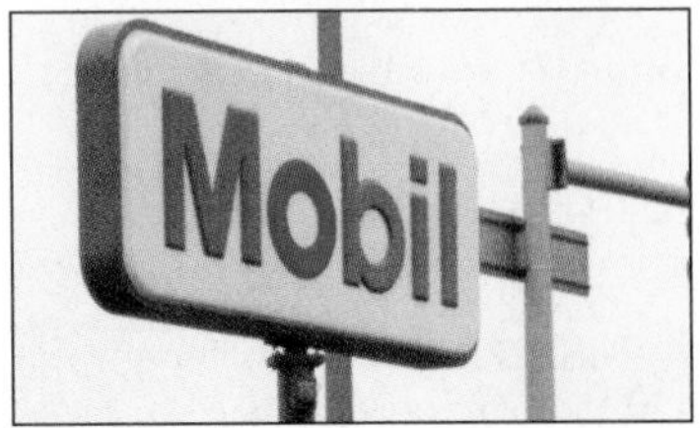

Fairfax, VA—**Mobil Corporation** announced today that it is making a change in its method . . . for crude oil and product inventories. Accordingly, it will reduce . . . year-to-date, net income by a $680 million . . . This inventory accounting change was adopted by Mobil at its board meeting today.

[5] The weighted average amount can be outside the FIFO or LIFO amounts if prices do not steadily increase or decrease but exhibit a cyclical pattern.

Companies disclose the inventory method used in their financial statements or notes. This is required by the *full-disclosure principle.*[6]

It is important for us to know and understand inventory costing in our analysis of financial statements. Some companies' financial statements help our analysis by reporting what the difference would be if another costing method were used. **Kmart,** for instance, reports in its 1997 annual report that:

> Inventories valued on LIFO were $457, $440 and $485 lower than amounts that would have been reported using the first-in, first-out (FIFO) method at year end 1997, 1996 and 1995, respectively.

Financial Planner
You are the financial planner for several clients. Your clients periodically request your advice on analysis of financial statements of companies where they have investments. One of these clients asks you if the merchandise inventory account of a company using FIFO needs any "adjustments" in light of recent inflation. What is your advice? Does your advice depend on changes in the costs of these inventories for the company?

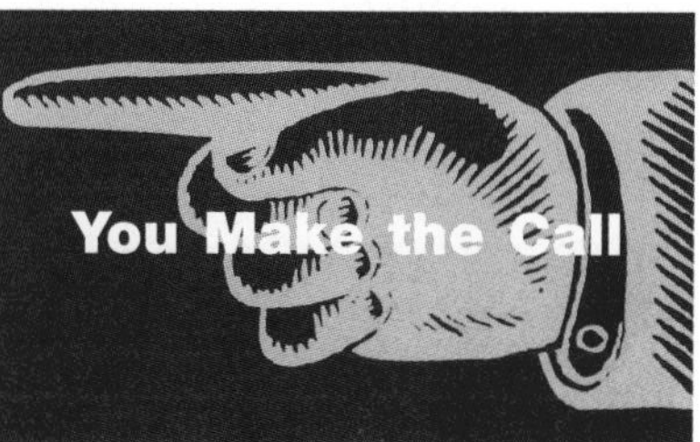

Answer—p. 296

Tax Reporting

Trekking's segment income statement in Exhibit 7.10 reflects the company's formation as a corporation. Its income statement includes income tax expense (at a rate of about 30%). Because inventory costs affect net income, they have potential tax effects. Trekking gains a tax advantage by using LIFO. This advantage occurs because LIFO assigns the largest dollar amounts to cost of goods sold when purchase prices are increasing. Trekking's recent purchases are both more costly and assigned to cost of goods sold. This means less income is reported when LIFO is used and purchase prices are rising. This in turn results in the smallest income tax expense.

The Internal Revenue Service (IRS) identifies several methods that are acceptable for inventory costing in reporting taxable income. It is important to know that companies can and often do use different costing methods for financial reporting and tax reporting. *The only exception is when LIFO is used for tax purposes; in this case the IRS requires it be used in financial statements.* Since costs tend to rise, LIFO usually gives a lower taxable income and a tax advantage. Many companies use LIFO for this reason. Yet managers often have incentives to report greater net income for reasons such as bonus plans, job security, and reputation. FIFO is sometimes preferred in these cases due to its tendency to report a higher income when prices are rising.

Flash back

4. Describe one advantage for each inventory costing method: specific identification, FIFO, LIFO, and weighted average.

5. When costs and prices are rising, does LIFO or FIFO report higher net income?

6. When costs and prices are rising, what effect does LIFO have on a balance sheet compared to FIFO?

Answers—p. 296–297

[6] FASB, *Accounting Standards—Current Text* (Norwalk, CT, 1995), sec. A10.105, 106. First published as *APB Opinion No. 22,* pars. 12, 13.

Consistency in Reporting

Because inventory costing methods can materially affect amounts on financial statements, some managers might be inclined to choose a method most consistent with their hoped-for results each period. These managers' objective might be to pick the method giving the most favorable financial statement amounts. Managers might also be inclined to pick the method giving them the highest bonus since many management bonus plans are based on net income. If managers were allowed to pick the method each period, it would be more difficult for users of financial statements to compare a company's financial statements from one period to the next. If income increased, for instance, a user would need to decide whether it resulted from successful operations or from the accounting method change. The consistency principle is used to avoid this problem.

The **consistency principle** requires a company to use the same accounting methods period after period so the financial statements are comparable across periods.[7] The consistency principle applies to all accounting methods. Whenever a company must choose between alternative methods, consistency requires that the company continue to use the selected method period after period. Users of financial statements can then assume a company uses the same methods across years and they can make comparisons of a company's statements across periods.

The consistency principle *doesn't* require a company to use one method exclusively. It can use different methods to value different categories of inventory. **Harley-Davidson,** for instance, includes the following note in its 1997 annual report:

> Inventories located in the United States are valued using the last-in, first-out (LIFO) method. Other inventories . . . are valued at the lower of cost or market using the first-in, first-out (FIFO) method.

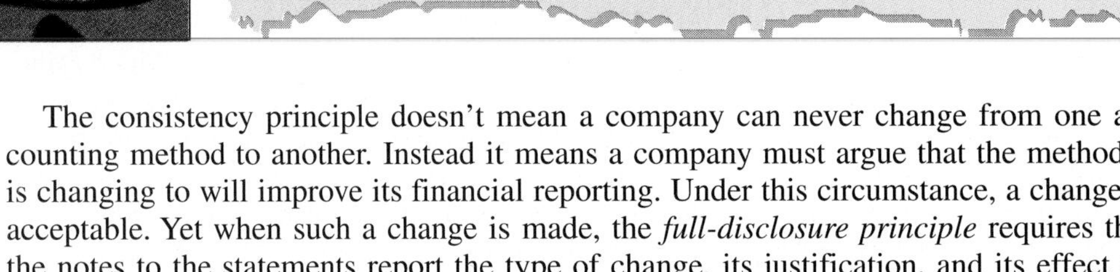

The consistency principle doesn't mean a company can never change from one accounting method to another. Instead it means a company must argue that the method it is changing to will improve its financial reporting. Under this circumstance, a change is acceptable. Yet when such a change is made, the *full-disclosure principle* requires that the notes to the statements report the type of change, its justification, and its effect on net income.[8]

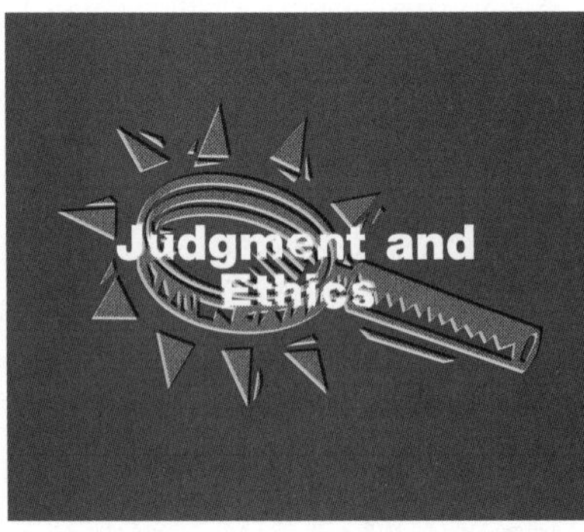

Inventory Manager
You are the inventory manager for a merchandiser. Your compensation includes a bonus plan based on the amount of gross profit reported in the financial statements. Your superior comes to you and asks your opinion in changing the inventory costing method from FIFO to LIFO. Since costs have been rising and are expected to continue to rise, your superior predicts the company will save thousands of dollars by switching to LIFO for tax reporting. This is because LIFO matches higher current costs against sales, thereby lowering gross profit and net income. You realize this proposed change will likely reduce your bonus. What do you recommend?

Answer—p. 296

[7] FASB, *Statement of Financial Accounting Concepts No. 2,* "Qualitative Characteristics of Accounting Information" (Norwalk, CT, 1980), par. 120.

[8] FASB, *Accounting Standards—Current Text* (Norwalk, CT, 1995), sec. A06.113. First published as *APB Opinion No. 20,* par. 17.

Errors in Reporting Inventory

Companies must take care in both computing and taking a physical count of inventory. If inventory is reported in error, it causes misstatements in cost of goods sold, gross profit, net income, current assets, and equity. It also means misstatements will exist in the next period's statements. This is because ending inventory of one period is the beginning inventory of the next. An error carried forward causes misstatements in the next period's cost of goods sold, gross profit, and net income. Misstatements can reduce the usefulness of financial statements.

A2 Analyze the effects of inventory errors on current and future financial statements.

Income Statement Effects

The income statement effects of an inventory error are evident by looking at the components of cost of goods sold as shown in Exhibit 7.11. The effect of an inventory error on cost of goods sold is determined by computing it with the incorrect component amount and comparing it to cost of goods sold when using the correct component amount.

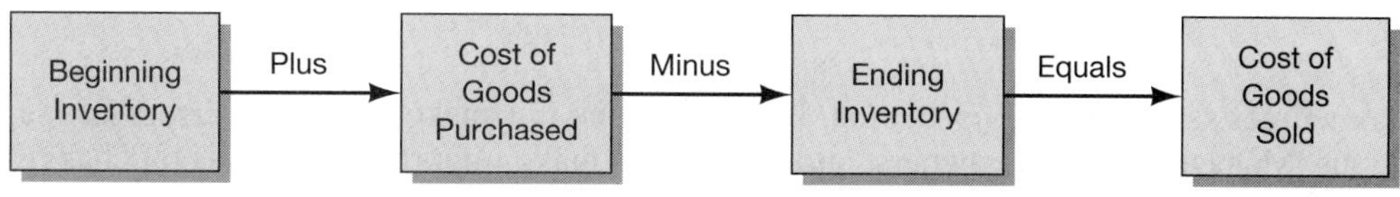

Exhibit 7.11
Cost of Goods Sold Components

We can see, for example, that understating ending inventory will overstate cost of goods sold. An overstatement in cost of goods sold yields an understatement in net income. We can do the same analysis with overstating ending inventory and for an error in beginning inventory. Exhibit 7.12 shows the effects of inventory errors on the current period's income statement amounts.

Inventory Error	Cost of Goods Sold	Net Income
Understate ending inventory	Overstated	Understated
Understate beginning inventory	Understated	Overstated
Overstate ending inventory	Understated	Overstated
Overstate beginning inventory	Overstated	Understated

Exhibit 7.12
Effects of Inventory Errors on This Period's Income Statement

Notice that inventory errors yield opposite effects in cost of goods sold and net income. Inventory errors also carry over to the next period, yielding a reverse effect.

To show these effects, we look at an inventory error for a company with $100,000 in sales for years 1998, 1999, and 2000. If this company maintains a steady $20,000 inventory level during this period and makes $60,000 in purchases in each of these years, then its cost of goods sold is $60,000 and its gross profit is $40,000 each year. But what if this company errs in computing its 1998 ending inventory, and reports $16,000 instead of the correct amount of $20,000? The effects of this error are shown in Exhibit 7.13.

The $4,000 understatement of the 1998 ending inventory causes a $4,000 overstatement in 1998 cost of goods sold and a $4,000 understatement in both 1998 gross profit and 1998 net income. Because 1998 ending inventory becomes the 1999 beginning inventory, this error also causes an understatement in 1999 cost of goods sold and a $4,000 overstatement in both 1999 gross profit and 1999 net income. An inventory error does not affect the third period, year 2000.

If 1998 ending inventory had been overstated, it would have yielded opposite results. In this case the 1998 net income would have been overstated and the 1999 income understated. Because an inventory error causes an offsetting error in the next period, it is

Exhibit 7.13

Effects of Inventory Errors on 3 Periods' Income Statements

Income Statements	1998		1999		2000	
Sales		$100,000		$100,000		$100,000
Cost of goods sold:						
Beginning inventory	$20,000		$16,000*		$20,000	
Cost of goods purchased	60,000		60,000		60,000	
Goods available for sale	$80,000		$76,000		$80,000	
Ending inventory	16,000*		20,000		20,000	
Cost of goods sold		64,000		56,000		60,000
Gross profit		$ 36,000		$ 44,000		$ 40,000
Operating expenses		10,000		10,000		10,000
Net income		$ 26,000		$ 34,000		$ 30,000

*Correct amount is $20,000.

sometimes said to be *self-correcting*. But don't think this makes inventory errors less serious. Managers, lenders, owners, and other users make important decisions on changes in net income and cost of goods sold. Inventory errors must be avoided.

Balance Sheet Effects

Balance sheet effects of an inventory error are evident by looking at the components of the accounting equation in Exhibit 7.14.

Exhibit 7.14

Accounting Equation

Assets = Liabilities + Equity

We can see, for example, that understating ending inventory will understate both current and total assets. An understatement in ending inventory also yields an understatement in equity because of the understatement in net income. We can do the same analysis with overstating ending inventory. Exhibit 7.15 shows the effects of inventory errors on the current period's balance sheet amounts.

Exhibit 7.15

Effects of Inventory Errors on This Period's Balance Sheet

Inventory Error	Assets	Equity
Understate ending inventory	Understated	Understated
Overstate ending inventory	Overstated	Overstated

Errors in beginning inventory do not yield misstatements in the balance sheet, but they do affect the income statement.

Flash back

7. A company takes a physical count of inventory at the end of 1999 and finds ending inventory is overstated by $10,000. Does this error cause cost of goods sold to be overstated or understated in 1999? In year 2000? By how much?

Answer—p. 297

Other Inventory Valuations

This section describes other methods to value inventory. Knowledge of these methods is important for understanding and analyzing financial statements.

Lower of Cost or Market

P2 Compute the lower of cost or market amount of inventory.

We explained how costs are assigned to ending inventory and cost of goods sold using one of four costing methods (FIFO, LIFO, weighted average, or specific identification). Yet the cost of inventory is not necessarily the amount always reported on a balance sheet. *Accounting principles require that inventory be reported at the market value of replacing inventory when market is lower than cost.* Merchandise inventory is then said to be reported on the balance sheet at the **lower of cost or market (LCM).**

Computing the Lower of Cost or Market

In applying LCM, *market* is defined as the current market value (cost) of replacing inventory. It is the current cost of purchasing the same inventory items in the usual manner.[9] It is also important to know that market is *not* defined as the sales price. A decline in market cost reflects a loss of value in inventory. This is because the recorded cost of inventory is higher than the current market cost. When this occurs, a loss is recognized. This is done by recognizing the decline in merchandise inventory from recorded cost to market cost at the end of the period.

LCM is applied in one of three ways: (1) separately to each individual item, (2) to major categories of items, and (3) to the whole of inventory. The less similar the items are that make up inventory, the more likely it is that companies apply LCM to individual items. Advances in technology further encourage the individual item application.

We show how LCM is applied to the ending inventory of a motorsports retailer. Inventory data for this retailer along with LCM computations are shown in Exhibit 7.16.

Exhibit 7.16
Lower of Cost or Market Computations

Inventory Items	Units on Hand	Per Unit Cost	Per Unit Market	Total Cost	Total Market	LCM applied to Items	LCM applied to Categories	LCM applied to Whole
Cycles:								
Roadster	20	$8,000	$7,000	$160,000	$140,000	$140,000		
Sprint	10	5,000	6,000	50,000	60,000	50,000		
Category subtotal				210,000	200,000		200,000	
Off-Road:								
Trax-4	8	5,000	6,500	40,000	52,000	40,000		
Blaz'm	5	9,000	7,000	45,000	35,000	35,000		
Category subtotal				85,000	87,000		85,000	
Total				$295,000	$287,000	$265,000	$285,000	$287,000

When LCM is applied to the *whole* of inventory, the market cost is $287,000. Since this market cost is $8,000 lower than the $295,000 recorded cost, it is the amount reported for inventory on the balance sheet. When LCM is applied to individual *items* of inventory, the market cost is $265,000. Since market is again less than the $295,000 recorded cost, it is the amount reported for inventory. When LCM is applied to the major *categories* of inventory, the market is $285,000. Any one of these three applications of LCM is acceptable. **Best Buy** reports that its:

> Merchandise inventories are recorded at the lower of average cost or market.

[9] Special exceptions to the definition of market as replacement cost do exist but these are unusual.

The *direct method* is a common way of recording inventory at market. The *direct method* substitutes market value for cost in the inventory account. Using LCM applied on the whole of inventory from Exhibit 7.16 we make the following entry to do this: Cost of Goods Sold Dr. $8,000; Merchandise Inventory Cr. $8,000. The Merchandise Inventory account balance is now $287,000, computed as $295,000 minus $8,000.

Conservatism Principle

We explained how accounting rules require recording inventory down to market when market is less than cost. But inventory usually can't be written up to market when market exceeds cost. If recording inventory down to market is acceptable, why can't we record inventory up to market? One reason is a concern that the gain from a market increase isn't realized until a sales transaction verifies the gain. But this problem also applies to when market is less than cost, and it doesn't stop us from recording it down. The primary reason is the conservatism principle.

The **conservatism principle** says when more than one estimate of amounts to be received or paid in the future are about equally likely, then the less optimistic amount should be used.[10] This principle guides accounting professionals in uncertain situations where amounts must be estimated. LCM is often justified with reference to conservatism. Because the value of inventory is uncertain, recording inventory down when its market value falls is the less optimistic estimate of the amount of inventory.

Flash back

8. A company's ending inventory includes the following items:

Product	Units on Hand	Unit Cost	Unit Market Value
A	20	$ 6	$ 5
B	40	9	8
C	10	12	15

Use LCM applied separately to individual items to compute the reported amount for inventory.

Answer—p. 297

Retail Inventory Method

P3 Apply both the retail inventory and gross profit methods to estimate inventory.

Many companies prepare financial statements on a quarterly or monthly basis. Monthly or quarterly statements are called **interim statements** because they are prepared between the traditional annual statements. The cost of goods sold information needed to prepare interim statements is readily available if a perpetual inventory system is used. But a periodic system requires a physical inventory to determine cost of goods sold. To avoid the time-consuming and expensive process of taking a physical inventory each month or quarter, some companies use the **retail inventory method** to estimate cost of goods sold and ending inventory. Some companies even use the retail inventory method to prepare the annual statements. **Home Depot,** for instance, reports in its 1997 annual report that:

> MERCHANDISE INVENTORIES—Inventories are stated at the lower of cost (first-in, first-out) or market, as determined by the retail inventory method.

But all companies should take a physical inventory at least once each year to identify any errors or shortages.

---

[10] FASB, *Statement of Financial Accounting Concepts No. 2* (Norwalk, CT, 1980) par. 95.

Computing the Retail Inventory Estimate

When the retail inventory method is used to estimate inventory, we need to know the amount of inventory a company had at the beginning of the period in both *cost* and *retail* amounts. We already explained the cost of inventory. The retail amount of inventory refers to its dollar amount measured using selling prices of inventory items. We also need the net amount of goods purchased (minus returns, allowances, and discounts) during the period, both at cost and at retail. The amount of net sales at retail is also needed.

A three-step process is used to estimate ending inventory after we compute the amount of goods available for sale during the period both at cost and at retail. This process is shown in Exhibit 7.17.

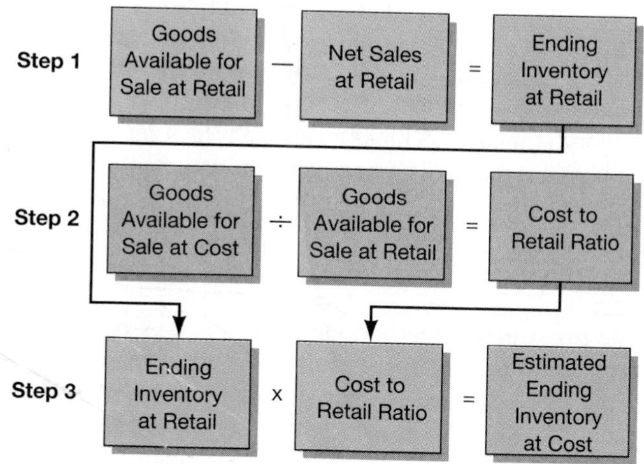

Exhibit 7.17

Inventory Estimation Using Retail Inventory Method

The reasoning behind the retail inventory method is if we can get a good estimate of the cost to retail ratio, then we can apply (multiply) this ratio by ending inventory at retail to estimate ending inventory at cost. We show in Exhibit 7.18 how these steps are applied to estimate ending inventory.

Exhibit 7.18

Computing Ending Inventory Using the Retail Inventory Method

		At Cost	At Retail
	Goods available for sale:		
	Beginning inventory	$20,500	$ 34,500
	Cost of goods purchased	39,500	65,500
	Goods available for sale	$60,000	$100,000
Step 1:	**Deduct net sales at retail**		**70,000**
	Ending inventory at retail		**$130,000**
Step 2:	**Cost to retail ratio: ($60,000 ÷ $100,000) = 60%**		
Step 3:	**Estimated ending inventory at cost ($30,000 × 60%)**	**$18,000**	

Let's recap the steps in Exhibits 7.17 and 7.18 to make certain we understand them. First, there are $100,000 of goods (at retail selling prices) available for sale this period. We see that $70,000 of these goods are sold, leaving $30,000 (retail value) of unsold merchandise in ending inventory. Second, the cost of these goods is 60% of their $100,000 retail value. Third, since cost for this store is 60% of retail, the estimated cost of ending inventory is $18,000.

Estimating Physical Inventory at Cost

Items for sale by retailers usually carry price tags listing selling prices. So when a retailer takes a physical inventory, it commonly totals inventory using selling prices of items on hand. It then reduces the dollar total of this inventory to a cost basis by applying the cost to retail ratio. This is done because selling prices are readily available and by using the cost to retail ratio it eliminates the need to look up invoice prices of items on hand.

To illustrate, assume the company in Exhibit 7.18 estimates its inventory by the retail method and takes a physical inventory using selling prices. If the retail value of this physical inventory is $29,600, then we can compute the cost of this inventory by applying its cost to retail ratio as follows: **$29,600 × 60% = $17,760.** The $17,760 cost figure for ending physical inventory is an acceptable number for annual financial statements. It is also acceptable to the IRS for tax reporting.

Estimating Inventory Shortage at Cost

The inventory estimate in Exhibit 7.18 is an estimate of the amount of goods on hand (at cost). Since it is computed by deducting sales from goods available for sale (at retail), it does not reveal any shrinkage due to breakage, loss, or theft. But we can estimate the amount of shrinkage by comparing the inventory computed in Exhibit 7.18 with the amount from taking a physical inventory. In Exhibit 7.18, for example, we estimated ending inventory at retail as $30,000. But a physical inventory revealed only $29,600 of inventory on hand (at retail). The company has an inventory shortage (at retail) of $400, computed as $30,000 − $29,600. The inventory shortage (at cost) is $240, computed as $400 × 60%.

Gross Profit Method

The **gross profit method** estimates the cost of ending inventory by applying the gross profit ratio to net sales (at retail). A need for this type of estimate can arise when inventory is destroyed, lost, or stolen. These cases need an estimate of inventory so a company can file a claim with its insurer. Users also apply this method to see if inventory amounts from a physical count are reasonable. The gross profit method is useful in these cases. This method uses the historical relation between cost of goods sold and net sales to estimate the proportion of cost of goods sold making up current sales. This cost of goods sold estimate is then subtracted from cost of goods available for sale to give us an estimate of ending inventory at cost. These two steps are shown in Exhibit 7.19.

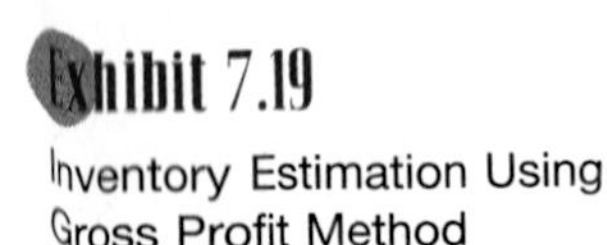

Inventory Estimation Using Gross Profit Method

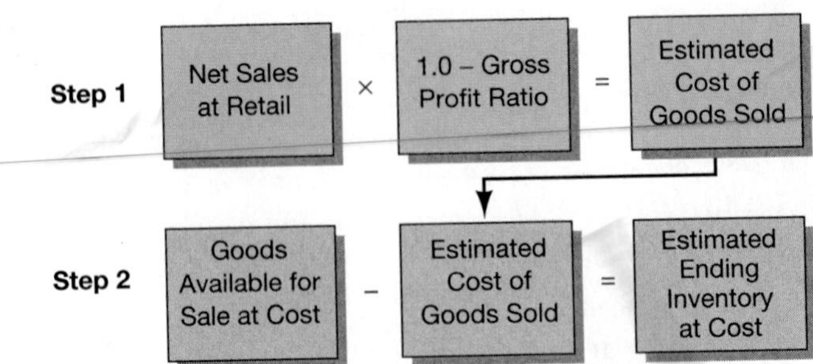

We need certain accounting data to use the gross profit method. This includes the gross profit ratio, beginning inventory (at cost), the net cost of goods purchased, and net sales (at retail). To illustrate, assume a company's inventory is destroyed by fire in March 1999. This company's normal gross profit ratio is 30% of net sales. When the fire occurs, the company's accounts show the following balances:

Sales	$31,500
Sales returns	1,500
Inventory, January 1, 1999	12,000
Net cost of goods purchased	20,500

We can use the gross profit method to estimate this company's inventory loss. We first need to recognize that whatever portion of each dollar of net sales is gross profit, the remaining portion is cost of goods sold. If this company's gross profit ratio is 30%, then 30% of each net sales dollar is gross profit and 70% is cost of goods sold. We show in Exhibit 7.20 how this 70% is used to estimate lost inventory.

Goods available for sale:		
Inventory, January 1, 1999		$12,000
Net cost of goods purchased		20,500
Goods available for sale		32,500
Less estimated cost of goods sold:		
Sales	$31,500	
Less sales returns	(1,500)	
Net sales	$30,000	
Step 1: Estimated cost of goods sold ($30,000 × 70%)		(21,000)
Step 2: Estimated March inventory loss		$11,500

Exhibit 7.20

Computing Inventory using the Gross Profit Method

To help understand Exhibit 7.20, think of subtracting ending inventory from goods available for sale to get the cost of goods sold. In Exhibit 7.20 we estimate ending inventory by subtracting cost of goods sold from the goods available for sale.

Merchandise Turnover and Days' Sales in Inventory

USING THE INFORMATION

A3 Assess inventory management using both merchandise turnover and days' sales in inventory.

This section describes how we use information about inventory to assess a company's short-term liquidity (ability to pay) and its management of inventory. Two measures useful for these assessments are presented.

Merchandise Turnover

We described in prior chapters two important ratios useful in evaluating a company's short-term liquidity: current ratio and acid-test ratio. A merchandiser's ability to pay its short-term obligations also depends on how quickly it sells its merchandise inventory. **Merchandise turnover,** also called *inventory turnover*, is one ratio used to evaluate this and is computed as shown in Exhibit 7.21.

$$\textbf{Merchandise turnover} = \frac{\textbf{Cost of goods sold}}{\textbf{Average merchandise inventory}}$$

Exhibit 7.21

Merchandise Turnover

This ratio tells us how many *times* a company turns over its inventory during a period. Average merchandise inventory is usually computed by adding beginning and ending inventory amounts and dividing the total by two. If a company's sales vary within the year, it is often better to take an average of inventory amounts at the end of each quarter or month.

Users apply merchandise turnover to help analyze short-term liquidity. It is also used to assess whether management is doing a good job controlling the amount of inventory on hand. A ratio that is low compared to competitors' ratios suggests inefficient use of assets. The company may be holding more merchandise than is needed to support its sales volume. Similarly, a ratio that is high compared to those of competitors suggests the amount of inventory is too low. This can mean lost sales because customers must back order merchandise. There is no simple rule with merchandise turnover except to say *a high ratio is preferable provided inventory is adequate to meet demand.*

We know how an inventory costing method such as FIFO, LIFO, or weighted average affects reported amounts of inventory and cost of goods sold. The inventory costing method also affects computation of merchandise turnover. To compare merchandise turnover ratios across companies that use different costing methods can be misleading.

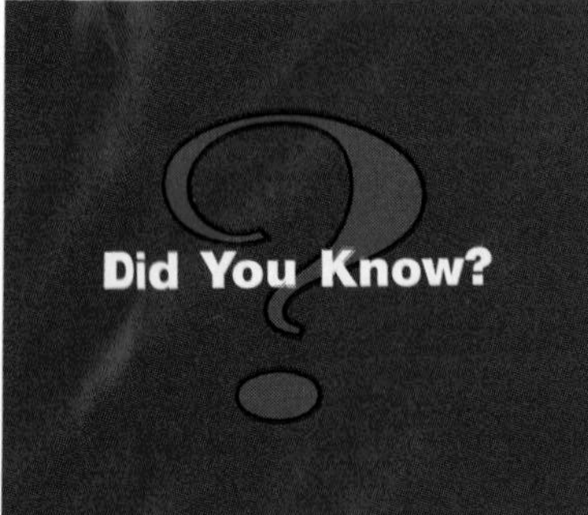

Pentagon Takes Accounting
The Pentagon is applying accounting skills to shrink inventories and speed deliveries. Inventories in inflation-adjusted dollars dropped from $104 billion in 1990 to $76 billion in 1994 and are predicted to plunge to $55 billion by 2001. Delivery time has been slashed from 25 days to 5 days and the Pentagon now offers a 24-hour emergency service. Delivery from factory to foxhole is speeded up by using bar codes, laser cards, radio tags, and accounting databases to track supplies. "We'll have piles of information instead of piles of stock," says Colonel M.D. Russ. Inventory management is the key. [Source: *Business Week*, December 11, 1995.]

Days' Sales in Inventory

To better interpret merchandise turnover, many users look to measure the adequacy of inventory in meeting sales demand. **Days' sales in inventory,** also called *days' stock on hand,* is a ratio that tells us how much inventory we have on hand in terms of days' sales. It can also be interpreted as the number of days we can sell from inventory if no new items are purchased. This ratio is often viewed as a measure of the buffer against out of stock inventory and is useful in evaluating liquidity of inventory. Days' sales in inventory is computed as shown in Exhibit 7.22.

Exhibit 7.22
Days' Sales in Inventory

$$\textbf{Days' sales in inventory} = \frac{\textbf{Ending inventory}}{\textbf{Cost of goods sold}} \times 365$$

The focus of days' sales in inventory is on ending inventory. Days' sales in inventory estimates how many days it will take to convert inventory on hand at the end of the period into accounts receivable or cash. Notice the different focus of days' sales in inventory and merchandise turnover. Days' sales in inventory focuses on *ending* inventory whereas merchandise turnover focuses on *average* inventory.

Analysis of Inventory Management

Inventory management is a major emphasis of most merchandisers. Merchandisers must both plan and control inventory purchases and sales. **Toys "R" Us** is one of those merchandisers. Its merchandise inventory at February 1, 1997, exceeded $2.2 billion. Toys "R" Us' inventory constituted 70% of it current assets and nearly 30% of its total assets. We apply the analysis tools in this section to Toys "R" Us using its February 1, 1997, financial statements. The relevant data and analysis are shown in Exhibit 7.23.

Exhibit 7.23
Merchandise Turnover and Days' Sales in Inventory for Toys "R" Us

	Year Ended		
	Feb. 1, 1997	**Feb. 3, 1996**	**Jan. 28, 1995**
Cost of goods sold	$6,892.5	$6,592.3	$6,008.0
Ending merchandise inventory	$2,214.6	$1,999.5	$1,999.1
Merchandise turnover	**3.27** times	**3.30** times	**3.18** times
Industry merchandise turnover	3.9 times	3.9 times	3.8 times
Days' sales in inventory	**117.3** days	**110.7** days	**121.4** days
Industry days' sales in inventory . . .	93.9 days	101.4 days	95.6 days

The 1997 merchandise turnover of 3.27 for Toys "R" Us is computed as: \$6,892.5 ÷ [(\$2,214.6 + \$1,999.5) ÷ 2]. This means Toys "R" Us turns over its inventory about 3.27 times per year, or about once every 112 days (365 days ÷ 3.27). We prefer merchandise turnover to be high provided inventory is not out of stock and the company is not turning away customers. The 1997 days' sales in inventory of 117.3 for Toys "R" Us helps us assess this likelihood and is computed as: (\$2,214.6 ÷ \$6,892.5) × 365. This tells us Toys "R" Us is carrying more than 117 days of sales in its inventory. This inventory buffer seems more than adequate. Toys "R" Us might benefit from management efforts to increase merchandise turnover. Also, comparisons to 1996 for Toys "R" Us are unfavorable as revealed by a decrease in merchandise turnover and an increase in days' sales in inventory.

Consultant
You are hired as a consultant to analyze inventory management for a retail store. Your preliminary analysis yields a merchandise turnover ratio of 5.0 and a days' sales in inventory measure of 73 days. The industry norm for merchandise turnover is about 4.4 and for days' sales in inventory it is about 74 days. Using this information, where do you direct your attention?

Answer—p. 296

Flash back

9. The following data pertain to a company's inventory during 1999:

	Cost	Retail
Beginning inventory	\$324,000	\$530,000
Cost of goods purchased	195,000	335,000
Net sales		320,000

Using the retail method, estimate the cost of ending inventory.

10. Explain how merchandise turnover and days' sales in inventory are both useful in analyzing inventory.

Answers—p. 297

Summary

C1 **Identify the items making up merchandise inventory.** Merchandise inventory comprises goods owned by a company and held for resale. Three special cases merit our attention. Goods in transit are reported in inventory of the company that holds ownership rights. Goods out on consignment are reported in inventory of the consignor. Goods damaged or obsolete are reported in inventory at a conservative estimate of their net realizable value, computed as sales price minus the cost of making the sale.

C2 **Identify the costs of merchandise inventory.** Costs of merchandise inventory comprise expenditures necessary, directly or indirectly, in bringing an item to a salable condition and location. This means the cost of an inventory item includes its invoice price minus any discount, plus any added or incidental costs necessary to put it in a place and condition for sale.

A1 **Analyze the effects of inventory methods for both financial and tax reporting.** When purchase prices don't change, the choice of an inventory method is unimportant. But when purchase prices are rising or falling, the methods are likely to assign different cost amounts to inventory. Specific identification exactly matches costs and revenues. Weighted average smooths out price changes. FIFO assigns an amount to inventory closely approximating current replacement cost. LIFO assigns the most recent costs incurred to cost of goods sold, and likely better matches current costs with revenues. Because inventory methods are also used in tax reporting, they have potential tax effects.

A2 Analyze the effects of inventory errors on current and future financial statements. An error in the amount of ending inventory affects assets (inventory), net income (cost of goods sold), and equity for that period. Since ending inventory is next period's beginning inventory, an error in ending inventory affects next period's cost of goods sold and net income. The financial statement effects of errors in one period are offset (reverse) in the next.

A3 Assess inventory management using both merchandise turnover and days' sales in inventory. We prefer a high merchandise turnover provided inventory is not out of stock and customers are not being turned away. We use days' sales in inventory to assess the likelihood of inventory being out of stock. We prefer a small number of days' sales in inventory if we can serve customer needs and provide a buffer for uncertainties. Together, each of these ratios helps us assess inventory management and evaluate a company's short-term liquidity.

P1 Compute inventory in a perpetual system using the methods of specific identification, FIFO, LIFO and weighted average. Costs are assigned to the cost of goods sold account *each time* a sale occurs in a perpetual system. Specific identification assigns a cost to each item sold by referring to its actual cost (for example, its net invoice cost). Weighted average assigns a cost to items sold by taking the current balance in the merchandise inventory account and dividing it by the total items available for sale to determine the weighted average cost per unit. We then multiply the number of units sold by this cost per unit to get the cost of each sale. FIFO assigns cost to items sold assuming earliest units purchased are the first units sold. LIFO assigns cost to items sold assuming the most recent units purchased are the first units sold.

P2 Compute the lower of cost or market amount of inventory. Inventory is reported at market value when market is *lower* than cost. This is called the lower of cost or market amount of inventory. Market is typically measured as replacement cost. Lower of cost or market can be applied separately to each item, to major categories of items, or to the whole of inventory.

P3 Apply both the retail inventory and gross profit methods to estimate inventory. The retail inventory method involves three computations: (1) goods available at retail minus net sales at retail gives ending inventory at retail, (2) goods available at cost divided by goods available at retail gives the cost to retail ratio, and (3) ending inventory at retail multiplied by the cost to retail ratio gives estimated ending inventory at cost. The gross profit method involves two computations: (1) net sales at retail multiplied by one minus the gross profit ratio gives estimated cost of goods sold, and (2) goods available at cost minus estimated cost of goods sold gives estimated ending inventory at cost.

Guidance Answers to **You Make the Call**

Financial Planner

The FIFO method means the oldest costs are the first ones recorded in cost of goods sold. This leaves the most recent costs in ending inventory. You report this to your client and note in most cases the ending inventory of a company using FIFO is reported at or near its market replacement cost. This means your client need not in most cases adjust the reported value of inventory. Your answer changes only if there are major increases in replacement cost compared to the cost of recent purchases reported in inventory. When major increases in costs occur, your client might wish to adjust inventory for the difference between the reported cost of inventory and its market replacement cost. (*Note*: Decreases in costs of purchases are recognized under the lower of cost or market adjustment.)

Consultant

Your client's merchandise turnover is markedly higher than the norm, whereas its days' sales in inventory is approximately at the norm. Since your client's turnover is already 14% better than average, you are probably best served by directing attention at days' sales in inventory. You should see if your client can reduce the level of inventory while maintaining its service to customers. Evidence suggests your client can reduce its level of inventory. This is suggested by recognizing that a company can maintain the same level of days' sales in inventory with a much lower turnover. Given your client's higher turnover, it should be able to hold less inventory.

Guidance Answer to **Judgment and Ethics**

Inventory Manager

Your recommendation is a difficult one. On one hand it seems your company can save (or at least postpone) taxes by switching to LIFO. On the other, switching to LIFO is likely to reduce bonus money that you think you've earned and deserve. Since the U.S. tax code requires companies that use LIFO for tax reporting to also use it for financial reporting, your options are even further constrained. Your best decision is to tell your superior about the tax savings with LIFO. But you also should discuss your bonus plan and how this is likely to hurt you unfairly. You might propose to compute inventory under the LIFO method for reporting purposes, but use the FIFO method for your bonus calculations. Another solution is to revise the bonus plan to reflect the company's use of the LIFO method.

Guidance Answers to Flash *backs*

1. The matching principle.
2. Target.
3. Total cost is $12,180, computed as: $11,400 + $130 + $150 + $100 + $400.
4. Specific identification exactly matches costs and revenues. Weighted average tends to smooth out price changes. FIFO assigns an amount to inventory that closely approximates current replacement cost. LIFO assigns the most recent costs incurred to cost of goods sold, and likely better matches current costs with revenues.
5. FIFO. Specifically, FIFO gives a lower cost of goods sold, a higher gross profit, and a higher net income when prices are rising.

6. LIFO gives a lower inventory figure on the balance sheet as compared to FIFO when prices are rising. FIFO's inventory amount will approximate current replacement costs.
7. Cost of goods sold is understated by $10,000 in 1999 and overstated by $10,000 in year 2000.
8. The reported inventory amount is $540, computed as [(20 × $5) + (40 × $8) + (10 × $12)].
9. The estimated ending inventory (at cost) is $327,000 and is computed as:

   Step 1: ($530,000 + $335,000) − $320,000 = $545,000

   Step 2: $\frac{\$324{,}000 + \$195{,}000}{\$530{,}000 + \$335{,}000} = 60\%$

   Step 3: $545,000 × 60% = $327,000
10. We like merchandise turnover to be high provided inventory is not out of stock and customers are not being turned away. We use days' sales in inventory to assess the likelihood of inventory being out of stock. We want days' sales in inventory to be as low as possible but adequate to serve customer needs and provide a buffer for uncertainties. Together these ratios allow us to assess these effects.

Demonstration Problem

Tale Company uses a perpetual inventory system and had the following beginning inventory and purchases during 1999:

Date		Item X Units	Item X Unit Cost
1/1	Inventory	400	$14
3/10	Purchase	200	15
5/9	Purchase	300	16
9/22	Purchase	250	20
11/28	Purchase	100	21

At December 31, 1999, there were 550 units of X on hand. Sales of units were as follows:

Jan. 15	200 units at $30
April 1	200 units at $30
Nov. 1	300 units at $35

Additional data for use in applying the specific identification method: (1) Jan. 15 sale—200 units @ $14, (2) April 1 sale—200 units @ $15, and (3) Nov. 1 sale—200 units @ $14 and 100 units @ $20.

Required

1. Calculate the cost of goods available for sale.
2. Apply the four different methods of inventory costing (FIFO, LIFO, weighted average, and specific identification) to calculate ending inventory and cost of goods sold under each method.
3. In preparing financial statements for 1999, the accountant was instructed to use FIFO but failed to do so and computed the cost of goods sold according to LIFO. Determine the impact on 1999's income from the accountant's error. Also determine the effect of the error on the year 2000 income. Assume no income taxes.
4. The management of the company would like a report showing how net income would change if the company changes from FIFO to another method. Prepare a schedule showing the cost of goods sold amount under each of the four methods. Calculate the amount by which each cost of goods sold total is different from the FIFO cost of goods sold to inform management how net income would change if another method were used.

Planning the Solution

- Make a schedule showing the calculation of the cost of goods available for sale. Multiply the units of beginning inventory and each purchase by the appropriate unit costs to determine the total cost of goods available for sale.
- Prepare a perpetual FIFO schedule showing the composition of beginning inventory and how the composition of inventory changes after each purchase of inventory and after each sale (see Exhibit 7.5).

- Prepare a perpetual LIFO schedule showing the composition of beginning inventory and how the composition of inventory changes after each purchase of inventory and after each sale (see Exhibit 7.6).
- Make a schedule of purchases and sales recalculating the average cost of inventory after each purchase to arrive at the weighted average cost of ending inventory. Add up the average costs associated with each sale to determine the cost of goods sold using the weighted average method (see Exhibit 7.7).
- Prepare a schedule showing the computation of the cost of goods sold and ending inventory using the specific identification method. Use the information provided to determine which specific units were sold and which specific units remain in inventory (see Exhibit 7.4).
- Compare the ending 1999 inventory amounts under FIFO and LIFO to determine the misstatement of 1999 income that resulted from using LIFO. The 1999 and 2000 errors are equal in amount but have opposite effects.
- Create a schedule showing the cost of goods sold under each method and how net income would differ from FIFO net income if an alternate method were to be adopted.

Solution to Demonstration Problem

1. Cost of goods available for sale:

Item X				
Date		**Units**	**Unit Cost**	**Total Cost**
1/1	Inventory	400	$14	$ 5,600
3/10	Purchase	200	15	3,000
5/9	Purchase	300	16	4,800
9/22	Purchase	250	20	5,000
11/28	Purchase	100	21	2,100
Total cost of goods available for sale				$20,500

2a. FIFO perpetual method:

Date	Purchases	Cost of Goods Sold	Inventory Balance
Jan. 1	Beginning balance		400 @ $14 = $ 5,600
Jan. 15		200 @ $14 = $2,800	200 @ $14 = $ 2,800
Mar. 10	200 @ $15 = $3,000		200 @ $14 200 @ $15 } = $ 5,800
April 1		200 @ $14 = $2,800	200 @ $15 = $ 3,000
May 9	300 @ $16 = $4,800		200 @ $15 300 @ $16 } = $ 7,800
Sept. 22	250 @ $20 = $5,000		200 @ $15 300 @ $16 250 @ $20 } = $12,800
Nov . 1		200 @ $15 = $3,000 100 @ $16 = $1,600	200 @ $16 250 @ $20 } = $ 8,200
Nov. 28	100 @ $21 = $2,100		200 @ $16 250 @ $20 100 @ $21 } = $10,300
Total cost of goods sold		**$10,200**	

Note to students: **In a classroom situation,** once cost of goods available for sale is known, we can compute the amount for either cost of goods sold or ending inventory—it is a matter of preference. **But in practice,** the costs of items sold are identified as sales are made and immediately transferred from the inventory account to the cost of goods sold account. This transfer then makes it unnecessary to calculate either account balance at the end of a period. The above solution showing the line-by-line approach illustrates actual application, whereas the alternate solution shown below illustrates that, once the concepts are understood, other solution approaches are available.

Alternate FIFO perpetual solution:

[FIFO Alternate No. 1: Computing cost of goods sold first]

Cost of goods available for sale (from 1.)		$20,500
Cost of goods sold:		
1/15 Sold (200 @ $14)	$ 2,800	
4/1 Sold (200 @ $14)	2,800	
11/1 Sold (200 @ $15 and 100 @ $16)	4,600	10,200
Ending inventory		$10,300

[FIFO Alternate No. 2: Computing ending inventory first]

Cost of goods available for sale (from 1.)		$20,500
Ending inventory*:		
11/28 purchase (100 @ $21)	$2,100	
9/22 purchase (250 @ $20)	5,000	
5/9 purchase (200 @ $16)	3,200	
Ending inventory		10,300
Cost of goods sold		$10,200

*Since FIFO assumes earlier costs relate to items sold, we determine ending inventory by assigning the most recent costs first.

2b. LIFO perpetual method:

Date	Purchases	Cost of Goods Sold	Inventory Balance
Jan. 1	Beginning balance		400 @ $14 = $ 5,600
Jan. 15		200 @ $14 = $2,800	200 @ $14 = $ 2,800
Mar. 10	200 @ $15 = $3,000		200 @ $14 200 @ $15 } = $ 5,800
April 1		200 @ $15 = $3,000	200 @ $14 = $ 2,800
May 9	300 @ $16 = $4,800		200 @ $14 300 @ $16 } = $ 7,600
Sept. 22	250 @ $20 = $5,000		200 @ $14 300 @ $16 250 @ $20 } = $12,600
Nov. 1		250 @ $20 = $5,000 50 @ $16 = $ 800	200 @ $14 250 @ $16 } = $ 6,800
Nov. 28	100 @ $21 = $2,100		200 @ $14 250 @ $16 100 @ $21 } = $ 8,900
Total cost of goods sold		**$11,600**	

Alternate LIFO perpetual solution:

[LIFO Alternate No. 1: Computing cost of goods sold first]

Cost of goods available for sale (from 1.)			$20,500
Cost of goods sold with LIFO perpetual			
1/15	200 units @ $14	$2,800	
4/1	200 units @ $15	$3,000	
11/1	250 units @ $20	$5,000	
	50 units @ $16	$ 800	
Cost of goods sold			11,600
Ending inventory			$ 8,900

[LIFO Alternate No. 2: Computing ending inventory first]

Cost of goods available for sale (from 1.)			$20,500
Ending inventory:			
1/1	inventory (200 @ $14)	$2,800	
5/9	purchase (250 @ $16)	4,000	
11/28	purchase (100 @ $21)	2,100	
Ending inventory			8,900
Cost of goods sold			$11,600

2c. Weighted average perpetual method:

Date	Purchases	Cost of Goods Sold	Inventory Balance
Jan. 1	Beginning balance		400 @ $14 = $5,600
Jan. 15		200 @ $141 = $2,800	200 @ $14 = $2,800
Mar. 10	200 @ $15 = $3,000		200 @ $14 200 @ $15 } = $5,800 (avg. cost is $14.5)
April 1		200 @ $14.5 = $2,900	200 @ $14.5 = $2,900
May 9	300 @ $16 = $4,800		200 @ $14.5 300 @ $16 } = $7,700 (avg. cost is $15.4)
Sept. 22	250 @ $20 = $5,000		200 @ $14.5 300 @ $16 250 @ $20 } = $12,700 (avg. cost is $16.93)
Nov. 1		300 @ $16.93 = $5,079	450 @ $16.93 = $7618.5
Nov. 28	100 @ $21 = $2,100		450 @ $16.93 100 @ $21 } = $9718.5
Total cost of goods sold*		**$10,779**	

*The cost of goods sold ($10,779) plus ending inventory ($9718.5) is slightly less than the cost of goods available for sale ($20,500) due to rounding error.

2d. Specific identification method:

Date	Purchases	Cost of Goods Sold	Inventory Balance
Jan. 1	Beginning balance		400 @ $14 = $ 5,600
Jan. 15		200 @ $14 = $2,800	200 @ $14 = $ 2,800
Mar. 10	200 @ $15 = $3,000		200 @ $14 200 @ $15 } = $ 5,800
April 1		200 @ $15 = $3,000	200 @ $14 = $ 2,800
May 9	300 @ $16 = $4,800		200 @ $14 300 @ $16 } = $ 7,600
Sept. 22	250 @ $20 = $5,000		200 @ $14 300 @ $16 250 @ $20 } = $12,600
Nov. 1		200 @ $14 = $2,800 100 @ $20 = $2,000	300 @ $16 150 @ $20 } = $ 7,800
Nov. 28	100 @ $21 = $2,100		300 @ $16 150 @ $20 100 @ $21 } = $ 9,900
Total cost of goods sold		**$10,600**	

[Specific Identification Alternate No. 1: Computing cost of goods sold first]

Cost of goods available for sale (from 1.)		$20,500
Cost of goods sold:		
1/1 purchase (400 @ $14)	$5,600	
3/10 purchase (200 @ $15)	3,000	
11/28 purchase (100 @ $20)	2,000	
Total cost of goods sold		**10,600**
Ending inventory		**$ 9,900**

[Specific Identification Alternate No. 2: Computing ending inventory first]

Cost of goods available for sale (from 1.)		$20,500
Ending inventory:		
5/9 purchase (300 @ $16)	$4,800	
9/22 purchase (150 @ $20)	3,000	
11/28 purchase (100 @ $21)	2,100	
Total ending inventory		**9,900**
Cost of goods sold		**$10,600**

3. If LIFO was mistakenly used when FIFO should have been used, cost of goods sold in 1999 would be overstated by $1,400, which is the difference between the FIFO and LIFO amounts of ending inventory. Income would be understated in 1999 by $1,400. In year 2000, income would be overstated by $1,400 because of the understatement of the beginning inventory.

4. Analysis of the effects of alternative inventory methods:

	Cost of Goods Sold	Difference from FIFO Cost of Goods Sold	Effect on Net Income if Adopted Instead of FIFO
FIFO	$10,200	—	—
LIFO	$11,600	+$1,400	$1,400 lower
Weighted average	$10,779	+$ 579	$579 lower
Specific identification	$10,600	+$ 400	$400 lower

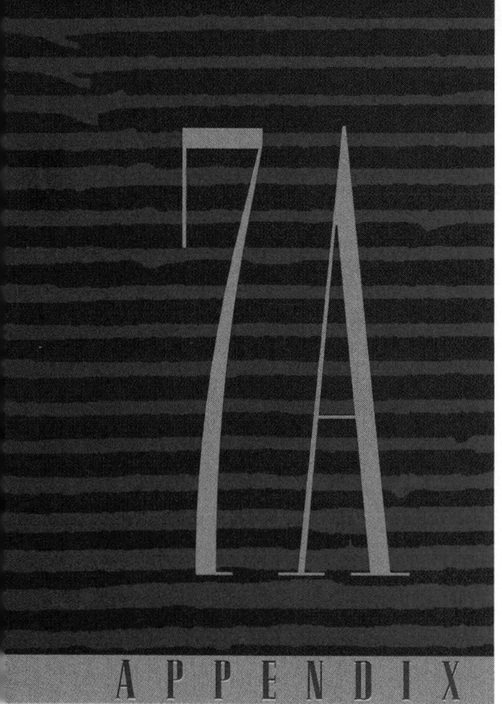

APPENDIX

Assigning Costs to Inventory—Periodic System

Learning Objectives

Procedural

P4 Compute inventory in a periodic system using the methods of specific identification, FIFO, LIFO, and weighted average.

The basic aim of the periodic system is the same as the perpetual system: to assign costs to the inventory and the goods sold. The same four methods are used in assigning costs under the periodic system—specific identification; first-in, first-out; last-in, first-out; and weighted average. We use information from **Trekking** to describe how we assign costs using these four methods with a periodic system. Data for sales and purchases are reported in the chapter (see Exhibits 7.2 and 7.3) and are not repeated here.

We explained the accounting under a periodic system in Appendix 6A. The important accounting aspects of a periodic system are:

- Each purchase of merchandise for resale increases (debit) the Purchases account.
- Cost of merchandise sold is *not* recorded at the time of each sale. A physical count of inventory at the end of the period is used to compute cost of goods sold and inventory amounts.
- Necessary costs of merchandise such as transportation-in and cost reductions such as purchase discounts and purchase returns and allowances are recorded in separate accounts.

Specific Identification

The amount of costs assigned to inventory and cost of goods sold is the same under the perpetual and periodic systems when using specific identification. This is because specific identification precisely defines which units are in inventory and which are sold.

First-In, First-Out

The first-in, first-out (FIFO) method of assigning cost to inventory and goods sold using the periodic system is shown in Exhibit 7A.1:

Exhibit 7A.1

FIFO Computations—Periodic System

Total cost of 55 units available for sale		$5,990
Less ending inventory priced using FIFO:		
10 units from August 28 purchase at $119 each	$1,190	
2 units from August 17 purchase at $115 each	230	
Ending inventory		1,420
Cost of goods sold		$4,570

Trekking's ending inventory reported on the balance sheet is **$1,420**, and its cost of goods sold reported on the income statement is **$4,570.** These amounts are the same as those computed using the perpetual system. This will always occur because the most recent purchases are in ending inventory under both systems.

Last-In, First-Out

The last-in, first-out (LIFO) method of assigning costs to the 12 remaining units in inventory and to cost of goods sold using the periodic system is shown in Exhibit 7A.2:

Exhibit 7A.2

LIFO Computations—Periodic System

Total cost of 55 units available for sale		$5,990
Less ending inventory priced using LIFO:		
10 units in beginning inventory at $ 91 each	$ 910	
2 units from August 3 purchase at $106 each	212	
Ending inventory		1,122
Cost of goods sold		$4,868

Trekking's ending inventory reported on the balance sheet is **$1,122** and its cost of goods sold reported on the income statement is **$4,868.** When LIFO is used with the periodic system, cost of goods sold is assigned costs from the most recent purchases for the period. With a perpetual system, cost of goods sold is assigned costs from the most recent purchases *prior to each sale*.

Weighted Average

The weighted average method of assigning cost involves three important steps. The first two steps are shown in Exhibit 7A.3. First, multiply the per unit cost for beginning inventory and each particular purchase by their corresponding number of units. Second, add these amounts and divide by the total number of units available for sale to find the weighted average cost per unit.

Exhibit 7A.3

Weighted Average Cost per Unit

Step 1:	10 units @ $ 91 =	$ 910
	15 units @ $106 =	1,590
	20 units @ $115 =	2,300
	10 units @ $119 =	1,190
	55	$5,990
Step 2:	$5,990/55 units = **$108.91** weighted average cost per unit	

The third step is to use the weighted average cost per unit to assign costs to inventory and to units sold as shown in Exhibit 7A.4.

Exhibit 7A.4

Weighted Average Computations—Periodic

Step 3:	Total cost of 55 units available for sale	$5,990
	Less **ending inventory** priced on a weighted average cost basis: 12 units at $108.91 each	1,307
	Cost of goods sold	$4,683

Trekking's ending inventory reported on the balance sheet is **$1,307** and its cost of goods sold reported on the income statement is **$4,683.**

Flash back

11. A company reports the following beginning inventory and purchases, and ends the period with 30 units on hand:

	Units	Cost
Beginning Inventory	100	$10
Purchases #1	40	12
#2	20	14

a. Compute ending inventory using the FIFO periodic system.

b. Compute cost of goods sold using the LIFO periodic system.

Answer—p. 304

Summary of Appendix 7A

P4 Compute inventory in a periodic system using the methods of specific identification, FIFO, LIFO, and weighted average. Periodic inventory systems allocate the cost of goods available for sale between cost of goods sold and ending inventory *at the end of a period.* Specific identification and FIFO give identical results whether the periodic or perpetual system is used. LIFO assigns cost to cost of goods sold assuming the last units purchased for the period are the first units sold. The weighted average cost per unit is computed by taking the total cost of both beginning inventory and net purchases and divided by the total number of units available. Then, multiply cost per unit by the number of units sold to give cost of goods sold.

Guidance Answer to 

11. *a.* FIFO periodic ending inventory = (20 × $14) + (10 × $12) = $400.

b. LIFO periodic cost of goods sold = (20 × $14) + (40 × $12) + (70 × $10) = $1,460.

Glossary

Average cost method another name for weighted average inventory pricing. (p. 279).

Conservatism principle the accounting principle that guides accountants to select the less optimistic estimate when two estimates of amounts to be received or paid are about equally likely. (p. 290)

Consignee one who receives and holds goods owned by another party for the purpose of selling the goods for the owner. (p. 282)

Consignor an owner of goods who ships them to another party who will then sell the goods for the owner. (p. 282)

Consistency principle the accounting requirement that a company use the same accounting methods period after period so that the financial statements of succeeding periods will be comparable. (p. 286)

Days' sales in inventory an estimate of how many days it will take to convert the inventory on hand at the end of the period into accounts receivable or cash; calculated by dividing the ending inventory by cost of goods sold and multiplying the result by 365; also called *days' stock on hand.* (p. 294)

First-in, first-out (FIFO) the method of assigning cost to inventory under the assumption that inventory items are sold in the order acquired; the first items received are the first items sold. (p. 278)

Gross profit method a procedure for estimating an ending inventory in which the past gross profit rate is used to estimate cost of goods sold, which is then subtracted from the cost of goods available for sale to determine the estimated ending inventory. (p. 292)

Interim statements monthly or quarterly financial statements prepared in between the traditional, annual statements. (p. 290)

Last-in, first-out (LIFO) the method of assigning cost to inventory under the assumption that costs for the most recent items purchased are sold first and charged to cost of goods sold. (p. 278)

Lower of cost or market (LCM) the required method of reporting merchandise inventory in the balance sheet where market value is reported when market is lower than cost; market value is usually defined as current replacement cost on the date of the balance sheet. (p. 289)

Merchandise turnover—the number of times a company's average inventory is sold during an accounting period; calculated by dividing cost of goods sold by the average merchandise inventory balance; also called *inventory turnover.* (p. 293)

Net realizable value the expected sale price of an item minus the cost of making the sale. (p. 282)

Retail inventory method a method for estimating an ending inventory based on the ratio of the amount of goods for sale at cost to the amount of goods for sale at marked selling prices. (p. 290)

Specific identification method the pricing of inventory where the purchase invoice of each item in the ending inventory is identified and used to determine the cost assigned to the inventory. (p. 278)

Specific invoice inventory pricing another name for specific identification method. (p. 278)

Weighted average the method of assigning cost to inventory in which the unit prices of the items making up the current inventory are weighted by the number of units of each in the current inventory. The total of these amounts is then divided by the total number of units available for sale to find the unit cost of the inventory balance and of the units that were sold. (p. 279)

The superscript letter [A] identifies assignment material based on Appendix 7A.

Questions

1. What accounts are used in a periodic inventory system but not in a perpetual inventory system?
2. What is meant when it is said that inventory errors correct themselves?
3. If inventory errors correct themselves, why be concerned when such errors are made?
4. Where is merchandise inventory disclosed in the financial statements?
5. Why are incidental costs sometimes ignored in pricing inventory? Under what accounting principle is this permitted?
6. Give the meanings of the following when applied to inventory: *(a)* FIFO; *(b)* LIFO; and *(c)* cost.
7. If prices are falling, will the LIFO or the FIFO method of inventory valuation result in the lower cost of goods sold?
8. Can a company change its inventory method each accounting period?
9. Does the accounting principle of consistency preclude any changes from one accounting method to another?
10. What effect does the full-disclosure principle have if a company changes from one acceptable accounting method to another?
11. What guidance for accountants is provided by the principle of conservatism?
12. What is the usual meaning of the word *market* as it is used in determining the lower of cost or market for merchandise inventory?
13. Refer to **NIKE's** financial statements in Appendix A. On May 31, 1997 what percent of NIKE's current assets was represented by inventory?
14. Refer to **Reebok's** financial statements in Appendix A. Calculate Reebok's cost of goods available for sale as of December 31, 1996.
15. Refer to **AOL's** financial statements in Appendix A. Why does America Online fail to show inventory as a current asset as of June 30, 1996?
16. Refer to the **Wired** article at the beginning of the chapter. What does Russo need to know about Wired to be able to calculate gross margin and inventory turnover?

Quick Study

QS 7-1
Inventory ownership

1. At year-end, Carefree Company has shipped $500 of merchandise FOB destination to Stark Company. Which company should include the $500 merchandise that is in transit as part of its inventory at year-end?
2. Carefree Company has shipped $900 of goods to Stark and has an arrangement that Stark will sell the goods for Carefree. Identify the consignor and the consignee. Which company should include any unsold goods as part of inventory?

QS 7-2
Inventory costs

A car dealer acquires a used car for $3,000, terms FOB shipping point. Additional costs in obtaining and offering the car for sale include $150 for transportation-in, $200 for import duties, $50 for insurance during shipment, $25 for advertising, and $250 for sales staff salaries. For computing inventory, what cost is assigned to the used car acquired?

QS 7-3
Calculating cost of goods available for sale

A company has beginning inventory of 10 units at $50 each. Every week for four weeks an additional 10 units are purchased at respective costs of $51, $52, $55, and $60. Calculate the cost of goods available for sale and the units available for sale.

QS 7-4
Inventory ownership
C1

Crafts and More, a distributor of handmade gifts, operates out of owner Scott Arlen's home. At the end of the current accounting period, Arlen reports he has 1,500 units of products in his basement, 30 of which were damaged by water and cannot be sold. He also has another 250 units in his van, ready to deliver to fill a customer order, terms FOB destination, and another 70 units out on consignment to a friend who owns a stationery store. How many units should be included in his company's end-of-period inventory?

QS 7-5
Inventory costs
C2

Rigby & Son, antique dealers, purchased the contents of an estate for a price of $37,500. The terms of the purchase were FOB shipping point, and the cost of transporting the goods to Rigby & Son's warehouse was $1,200. Rigby & Son insured the shipment at a cost of $150. Prior to putting the goods up for sale in the store, they cleaned and refurbished merchandise at a cost of $490. Determine the cost of the inventory acquired from the purchase of the estate's contents.

QS 7-6
Inventory costing methods
P1

A company had the following beginning inventory and purchases during January for a particular item. On January 26, 345 units were sold. What is the cost of the 140 units that remain in the ending inventory, assuming *(a)* FIFO, *(b)* LIFO, and *(c)* weighted average? (Round numbers to the nearest cent.)

	Units	Unit Cost
Beginning inventory on January 1	310	$3.00
Purchase on January 9	75	3.20
Purchase on January 25	100	3.35

QS 7-7
Contrasting inventory costing methods
A1

Identify the inventory costing method most closely described by each of the following separate statements. Assume a period of rising costs.

a. Matches recent costs against revenue.
b. Provides a tax advantage.
c. Understates the current value of inventory on a balance sheet.
d. Results in a balance sheet inventory closest to replacement costs.
e. Fits best when each unit of product has unique features that affect cost.

QS 7-8[A]
Inventory errors
A2

The Weston Company maintains its inventory records on a periodic basis. In taking a physical inventory at the end of year 2000, certain units were counted twice. Explain how this error affects the following: *(a)* 2000 cost of goods sold, *(b)* 2000 gross profit, *(c)* 2000 net income, *(d)* 2001 net income, *(e)* the combined two-year income, and *(f)* income in years after 2001.

QS 7-9
Applying LCM to inventories
P2

Thrifty Trading Co. has the following products in its ending inventory:

Product	Quantity	Cost	Market
Aprons	9	$6.00	$5.50
Bottles	12	3.50	4.25
Candles	25	8.00	7.00

Compute lower of cost or market *(a)* for the inventory as a whole and *(b)* applied separately to each product.

QS 7-10
Estimating inventories
P3

The inventory of Bell Department Store was destroyed by a fire on September 10, 1999. The following 1999 data were available from the accounting records:

Jan. 1 inventory	$180,000
Jan. 1–Sept. 10 purchases (net)	$342,000
Jan. 1–Sept. 10 sales (net)	$675,000
1999 estimated gross profit rate	42%

Estimate the cost of the inventory destroyed in the fire.

Exercises

Exercise 7-1
Inventory costing methods (perpetual)—FIFO and LIFO
P1

Parfour Company made purchases of a particular product in the current year as follows:

Jan. 1	Beginning inventory	100 units @ $10 =	$ 1,000
Mar. 14	Purchased	250 units @ $15 =	3,750
July 30	Purchased	400 units @ $20 =	8,000
Oct. 26	Purchased	600 units @ $25 =	15,000
Units available		1,350 units	
Cost of goods available for sale . . .			$27,750

Parfour Company made sales on the following dates at $40 per unit:

Jan. 10	90 units
Mar. 15	140 units
Oct. 5	300 units
Total sales	530 units

Required

Parfour uses a perpetual inventory system. Determine the costs that should be assigned to the ending inventory and to goods sold under each of the following: *(a)* costs are assigned on the basis of FIFO, and *(b)* costs are assigned on the basis of LIFO. Compute gross margin for each method.

Exercise 7-2
Specific Identification
P1

Refer to the data in Exercise 7–1. Assume ending inventory is made up of the entire March 14 purchase plus 570 units of the October 26 purchase. Using the specific identification method, calculate the costs of goods sold and the gross margin.

Exercise 7-3
Inventory costing methods—perpetual
P1

Trout Company made purchases of a particular product in the current year (1999) as follows:

Jan. 1	Beginning inventory	120 units @ $6.00 =	$ 720
Mar. 7	Purchased	250 units @ $5.60 =	1,400
July 28	Purchased	500 units @ $5.00 =	2,500
Oct. 3	Purchased	450 units @ $4.60 =	2,070
Dec. 19	Purchased	100 units @ $4.10 =	410
	Total	1,420 units	$7,100

Trout Company made sales on the following dates at $15 per unit:

Jan. 10	70 units
Mar. 15	125 units
Oct. 5	600 units
Total	795 units

Required

Trout uses a perpetual inventory system. The ending inventory consists of 625 units, 500 from the July 28 purchase and 125 from the Oct. 3 purchase. Determine the cost assigned to ending inventory and to goods sold under each of the following: *(a)* costs are assigned on the basis of specific identification, *(b)* costs are assigned on a weighted average cost basis, *(c)* costs are assigned on the basis of FIFO, and *(d)* costs are assigned on the basis of LIFO.

Exercise 7-4
Income effects of inventory methods
A1

Use the data in Exercise 7-3 to construct comparative income statements for Trout Company (year-end 1999) similar to those shown in Exhibit 7.10 for the four inventory methods. Assume operating expenses are $1,250. The applicable income tax rate is 30%.

1. Which method results in the highest net income?
2. Does the weighted average net income fall between the FIFO and LIFO net incomes?
3. If costs were rising instead of falling, which method would result in the highest net income?

Exercise 7-5ᴬ
Alternative cost flow assumptions—periodic
P4

Paddington Gifts made purchases of a particular product in the current year as follows:

Jan. 1	Beginning inventory	120 units @ $3.00 =	$ 360
Mar. 7	Purchased	250 units @ $2.80 =	700
July 28	Purchased	500 units @ $2.50 =	1,250
Oct. 3	Purchased	450 units @ $2.30 =	1,035
Dec. 19	Purchased	100 units @ $2.05 =	205
	Total	1,420 units	$3,550

Required

The company uses a periodic inventory system, and its ending inventory consists of 150 units, 50 from each of the last three purchases. Determine the cost assigned to ending inventory and to goods sold under each of the following: *(a)* costs are assigned on the basis of specific identification, *(b)* costs are assigned on a weighted average cost basis, *(c)* costs are assigned on the basis of FIFO, and *(d)* costs are assigned on the basis of LIFO. Assuming the company has enough income to require that it pay income taxes, which method provides a current tax advantage?

Exercise 7-6ᴬ
Alternative cost flow assumptions—periodic
P4

Jasper & Williams Company made purchases of a particular product in the current year as follows:

Jan. 1	Beginning inventory	120 units @ $2.00 =	$ 240
Mar. 7	Purchased	250 units @ $2.30 =	575
July 28	Purchased	500 units @ $2.50 =	1,250
Oct. 3	Purchased	450 units @ $2.80 =	1,260
Dec. 19	Purchased	100 units @ $2.96 =	296
	Total	1,420 units	$3,621

Required

The company uses a periodic inventory system, and its ending inventory consists of 150 units, 50 from each of the last three purchases. Determine the cost assigned to ending inventory and to goods sold under each of the following: *(a)* costs are assigned on the basis of specific identification, *(b)* costs are assigned on a weighted average cost basis, *(c)* costs are assigned on the basis of FIFO, and *(d)* costs are assigned on the basis of LIFO. Assuming the company has enough income to require that it pay income taxes, which method provides a current tax advantage?

Exercise 7-7
Analysis of inventory errors
A2

The John Henry Company had $900,000 of sales during each of three consecutive years 2000–2002, and it purchased merchandise costing $500,000 during each of the years. It also maintained a $200,000 inventory from the beginning to the end of the three-year period. But in accounting for inventory it made an error at the end of year 2000 that caused its ending year 2000 inventory to appear on its statements as $180,000 rather than the correct $200,000.

Required

1. Determine the actual amount of the company's gross profit in each of the years 2000–2002.
2. Prepare comparative income statements as in Exhibit 7.13 to show the effect of this error on the company's cost of goods sold and gross profit in years 2000–2002.

Exercise 7-8
Lower of cost or market
P2

Showtime Company's ending inventory includes the following items:

Product	Units on Hand	Unit Cost	Replacement Cost per Unit
BB	22	$50	$54
FM	15	78	72
MB	36	95	91
SL	40	36	36

Replacement cost is determined to be the best measure of market. Calculate lower of cost or market for the inventory *(a)* as a whole and *(b)* applied separately to each product.

Exercise 7-9
Estimating ending inventory—retail method
P3

During 1999, Harmony Company sold $130,000 of merchandise at marked retail prices. At the end of 1999, the following information was available from its records:

	At Cost	At Retail
Beginning inventory	$31,900	$64,200
Cost of goods purchased	57,810	98,400

Use the retail inventory method to estimate Harmony's 1999 ending inventory at cost.

Exercise 7-10
Reducing physical inventory to cost—retail method
P3

In addition to estimating its ending inventory by the retail method, Harmony Company of Exercise 7–9 took a physical inventory at the marked selling prices of the inventory items at the end of 1999. The total of this physical inventory at marked selling prices was $27,300. Determine *(a)* the estimated amount of this inventory at cost and *(b)* Harmony's 1999 inventory shrinkage at retail and at cost.

Exercise 7-11
Estimating ending inventory—gross profit method
P3

On January 1, The Parts Store had a $450,000 inventory at cost. During the first quarter of the year, it purchased $1,590,000 of merchandise, returned $23,100, and paid freight charges on purchased merchandise totaling $37,600, terms FOB shipping point. During the past several years, the store's gross profit on sales has averaged 30%. Under the assumption the store had $2,000,000 of net sales during the first quarter of the year, use the gross profit method to estimate its inventory at the end of the first quarter.

Exercise 7-12
Merchandise turnover and days' sales in inventory
A3

From the following information for Russo Merchandising Co., calculate merchandise turnover for 2001 and 2000 and days' sales in inventory at December 31, 2001, and 2000. (Round answers to one decimal place.)

	2001	2000	1999
Cost of goods sold	$643,825	$426,650	$391,300
Inventory (December 31)	96,400	86,750	91,500

Comment on Russo's efficiency in using its assets to support increasing sales from 2000 to 2001.

Problems

Problem 7-1
Alternative cost flows—perpetual

Hall Company has the following inventory purchases during the fiscal year ended December 31, 1999:

Beginning	500 units	$45/unit
2/10	250 units	42/unit
3/13	100 units	29/unit
8/21	130 units	50/unit
9/5	245 units	48/unit

Hall Company employs a perpetual inventory system. It had two sales during the period, and the units had a selling price of $75 per unit. The specific units sold are the entire beginning inventory plus 65 units of the 3/13 purchase:

3/15 sales	330 units
9/10 sales	235 units

Required

Preparation Component

1. Calculate cost of goods available for sale and units available for sale.
2. Calculate units remaining in ending inventory.
3. Calculate the dollar value of ending inventory using *(a)* FIFO, *(b)* LIFO, *(c)* specific identification, and *(d)* weighted average.
4. Calculate the gross profit earned by Hall Company under each of the costing methods in (3).

Check Figure Ending inventory (FIFO), $28,930

Analysis Component

5. If the Hall Company's manager earns a bonus based on a percent of gross profit, which method of inventory costing will be preferred?

Problem 7-2ᴬ
Alternative cost flows—periodic

Mill House Company began 1999 with 20,000 units of Product X in its January 1 inventory that cost $15 each, and it made successive purchases of the product as follows:

Mar. 7	28,000 units @ $18 each
May 25	30,000 units @ $22 each
Aug. 1	20,000 units @ $24 each
Nov. 10	33,000 units @ $27 each

The company uses a periodic inventory system. On December 31, 1999, a physical count disclosed that 35,000 units of Product X remained in inventory.

Required

1. Prepare a calculation showing the number and total cost of the units available for sale during 1999.
2. Prepare calculations showing the amounts assigned to the 1999 ending inventory and to cost of goods sold, assuming *(a)* a FIFO basis, *(b)* a LIFO basis, and *(c)* a weighted average basis.

Check Figure Cost of goods sold (FIFO): $1,896,000

Problem 7-3ᴬ
Income comparisons and cost flows—periodic

A1, P4

Green Jeans, Inc., sold 5,500 units of its product at $45 per unit during 1999, and incurred operating expenses of $6 per unit in selling the units. It began the year with 600 units and made successive purchases of the product as follows:

January 1 (beginning inventory) . . .	600 units @ $18 per unit
Purchases:	
February 20	1,500 units @ $19 per unit
May 16	700 units @ $20 per unit
October 3	400 units @ $21 per unit
December 11	3,300 units @ $22 per unit
	6,500 units

Required

Preparation Component

Check Figure Net income (LIFO), $69,020

1. Prepare a comparative income statement for the company, showing in adjacent columns the net incomes earned from the sale of the product, assuming the company uses a periodic inventory system and prices its ending inventory on the basis of: *(a)* FIFO, *(b)* LIFO, and *(c)* weighted average. Assume an income tax rate of 30%.

Analysis Component

2. How would the results from the three alternative inventory costing methods change if Green Jeans had been experiencing declining prices in the acquisition of additional inventory?
3. What specific advantages and disadvantages are offered by using LIFO and by using FIFO, assuming the cost trends continue as shown in the purchases data above?

Problem 7-4
Analysis of inventory errors

The following amounts were reported in Shockley Company's financial statements:

	Financial Statements for Year Ended December 31 1999	2000	2001
(a) Cost of goods sold	$ 715,000	$ 847,000	$ 770,000
(b) Net income	220,000	275,000	231,000
(c) Total current assets	1,155,000	1,265,000	1,100,000
(d) Owner's equity	1,287,000	1,430,000	1,232,000

In making physical counts of inventory, Shockley made the following errors:
Inventory on December 31, 1999: Understated $66,000
Inventory on December 31, 2000: Overstated $30,000

Required

Preparation Component:

1. For each of the preceding financial statement items—*(a)*, *(b)*, *(c)*, and *(d)*—prepare a schedule similar to the following and show the adjustments necessary to correct the reported amounts.

Check Figure Corrected net income (2000), $179,000

	1999	2000	2001
Cost of goods sold:			
Reported	______	______	______
Adjustments: 12/31/1999 error	______	______	______
12/31/2000 error	______	______	______
Corrected	======	======	======

Analysis Component

2. What is the error in aggregate net income for the three-year period that results from the inventory errors? Explain why this result occurs. Also explain why the understatement of inventory by $66,000 at the end of 1999 resulted in an understatement of equity by the same amount that year.

Problem 7-5
Lower of cost or market
P2

A physical inventory of Electronics Unlimited taken at December 31 reveals the following:

Item	Units on Hand	Per Unit Cost	Per Unit Market
Audio equipment:			
Receivers	335	$ 90	$ 98
CD players	250	111	100
Cassette decks	316	86	95
Turntables	194	52	41
Video equipment:			
Televisions	470	150	125
VCRs	281	93	84
Video cameras	202	310	322
Car audio equipment:			
Cassette radios	175	70	84
CD radios	160	97	105

Check Figure Lower of cost or market: (a) $274,702; (b) $270,332; (c) $263,024

Required

Calculate the lower of cost or market *(a)* for the inventory as a whole, *(b)* for the inventory by major category, and *(c)* for the inventory applied separately to each item.

Problem 7-6
Retail inventory method
P3

The records of Basics Company provide the following information for the year ended December 31:

	At Cost	At Retail
January 1 beginning inventory	$ 471,350	$ 927,150
Cost of goods purchased	3,276,030	6,279,350
Sales		5,495,700
Sales returns		44,600

Check Figure Inventory shortage at cost, $41,392

Required

1. Prepare an estimate of the company's year-end inventory by the retail method.
2. The company took a year-end physical inventory at marked selling prices that totaled $1,675,800. Prepare a schedule showing the store's loss from shrinkage at cost and at retail.

Problem 7-7
Gross profit method
P3

Walker Company wants to prepare interim financial statements for the first quarter of 1999. The company would like to avoid making a physical count of inventory each quarter. During the last five years, the company's gross profit rate has averaged 35%. The following information for the first quarter is available from its records:

January 1 beginning inventory	$ 300,260
Net cost of goods purchased	939,050
Sales	1,191,150
Sales returns	9,450

Check Figure Estimated inventory, $471,205

Required

Use the gross profit method to prepare an estimate of the company's first quarter inventory.

BEYOND THE NUMBERS

Reporting in Action

C2, A3

Refer to the financial statements and related information for **NIKE** in Appendix A. Answer the following questions by analyzing the information in NIKE's report:

1. What is the total amount of inventories held as current assets by NIKE on May 31, 1997? On May 31, 1996?
2. Inventories represent what percent of total assets on May 31, 1997? On May 31, 1996?
3. Comment on the relative size of inventories NIKE holds compared to other types of assets.
4. What method did NIKE use to determine the inventory amounts reported on its balance sheet?
5. Calculate merchandise turnover for fiscal year ended May 31, 1997 and days' sales in inventory on May 31, 1997. (Note: Cost of sales is cost of goods sold.)

Swoosh Ahead

6. Obtain access to NIKE's annual report for fiscal years ending after May 31, 1997. You can gain access to NIKE's annual report at its web site **[www.nike.com]** or through the SEC's EDGAR database **[www.sec.gov].** Answer questions 1 through 5 above using the updated NIKE financial information.

Comparative Analysis

A3

Both **NIKE** and **Reebok** design, produce, market, and sell sports footwear and apparel. Key comparative figures ($ millions) for these two companies follow:

	NIKE		Reebok	
Key figures	**1997**	**1996**	**1996**	**1995**
Inventory	$1,339	$ 931	$ 545	$ 635
Cost of sales	5,503	3,907	2,144	2,114

*NIKE figures are from its annual reports for fiscal years ended May 31, 1997 and 1996.
Reebok figures are from its annual reports for fiscal years ended December 31, 1996 and 1995.

Required

1. Calculate merchandise turnover for NIKE (1997) and Reebok (1996).
2. Calculate days' sales in inventory for both companies for the two years shown.
3. Comment on your findings in parts *1* and *2*.

Ethics Challenge

A1

Diversion, Inc., is a retail sports store carrying primarily women's golf apparel and equipment. The store is at the end of its second year of operation and, as new businesses often do, is struggling a bit to be profitable. The cost of inventory items has increased in the short time the store has been in business. In the first year of operations the store accounted for inventory costs using the LIFO method. A loan agreement the store has with Dollar Bank, its prime source of financing, requires that the store maintain a certain profit margin and current ratio. The store's owner, Cindy Foor, is currently looking over Diversion's annual financial statements after its year-end inventory has been taken. The numbers are not very favorable and the only way the store can meet the required financial ratios agreed upon with the bank is to change from the LIFO to FIFO method. The store originally decided upon LIFO for inventory costing because of the tax advantages it would afford. Cindy recalculates the ending inventory using FIFO and submits her income statement and balance sheet to the loan officer at the bank for the required bank review of the loan. As Cindy mails the financial statements to the bank, she thankfully reflects on the latitude she has as manager in choosing an inventory costing method.

Required

1. Why does Diversion's use of FIFO improve its profit margin and current ratio?
2. Is the action by Diversion's owner ethical? Explain.

Communicating in Practice
A1

You are a public accountant working for a wholesale produce business that has just completed its first year of operations. Due to catastrophic weather conditions, resulting in the destruction of crops, the cost of acquiring produce to resell has escalated during the later part of this fiscal period. Your client, Mr. Greenhouse, mentioned that because the business sells perishable goods, he has striven to maintain a first-in, first-out flow of goods. Although sales have been good for a first-year business, the high cost of inventory at the end of the year put the business in a tight cash position. Mr. Greenhouse has expressed concern regarding the ability of the business to meet income tax obligations.

Required

Prepare a memorandum or send an e-mail that explains and justifies the inventory valuation method you recommend that your client, Mr. Greenhouse, adopt. If the response is to be made via e-mail, you are to assume your instructor is the owner instead of Mr. Greenhouse.

Taking It to the Net
A3

Visit the **Bausch and Lomb** Web site at **www.bausch.com.** Access the financial statements and financial statement notes and collect the information you need to answer the following questions. If the Bausch and Lomb Web site is not found, consult the Bausch and Lomb financial information at the Edgar database at **www.sec.gov.**

1. What product does Bausch and Lomb sell that is popular with college students?
2. What inventory costing method does Bausch and Lomb use? (Hint: consult the notes to the financial statements to read about Bausch and Lomb's inventory practices.)
3. Calculate Bausch and Lomb's gross margin and gross margin ratio for the most current year's data found at its Web site.
4. Calculate merchandise turnover and days' sales in inventory for the most current year's data found at its Web site.

Teamwork in Action
P1, A1

Each member of the team has the responsibility to become a resident expert on a specific inventory method. This expertise will be used to facilitate teammates' understanding of the concepts relevant to the method he or she has chosen. Follow the procedure outlined below:

1. Each team member is to select their area for expertise by choosing one of the following inventory methods: specific identification, LIFO, FIFO, or weighted average. You have one minute to make your choices.
2. Learning teams are to disburse and expert teams are to be formed. Expert teams will be made up of students who have all selected the same area of expertise. The instructor will identify the location in the room where each expert team will meet.
3. Using data below, expert teams will collaborate to develop a presentation that illustrates each of the relevant procedures and concepts listed below the data. Each student must write up the presentation in a format that can be shown to the learning teams in the next step in the activity.

   Data:

   Sunmann, Inc., uses a perpetual inventory system. It had the following beginning inventory and current year purchases of a particular product:

Jan. 1	Beginning inventory	50 units @ $10 = $ 500
Jan. 14	Purchased	150 units @ $12 = 1,800
Apr. 30	Purchased	200 units @ $15 = 3,000
Sept. 26	Purchased	300 units @ $20 = 6,000

   Sunmann, Inc., made sales on the following dates at $35 a unit:

Jan. 10	30 units	(actual cost $10)
Feb. 15	100 units	(actual cost $12)
Oct. 5	350 units	(actual cost 100 @ $15 and 250 @ $20)

Procedures and concepts to illustrate in expert presentation:

a. Identify and compute the costs to be assigned to the units sold.
b. Identify and compute the costs to be assigned to the units in ending inventory.
c. How likely is it that this inventory costing method will reflect the actual physical flow of goods? How relevant is that factor in determining if this is an acceptable method to use?
d. What is the impact of this method versus others in determining net income and income taxes?
e. How closely does the valuation of the ending inventory reflect replacement costs for these units?

4. Re-form learning teams. In rotation, each expert is to present to their teams that which they developed in (3). Experts are to encourage and respond to questions.

Hitting the Road

C1, C2

Visit your local mall or downtown retail area with another classmate. Visit five stores. In each store, identify whether the store uses a bar-coding system to help manage its inventory. Try to find at least one store that does not use bar-coding. If a store does not use bar-coding, ask the store's manager or retail clerk whether he or she knows which type of inventory costing method the store employs. Create a table that shows columns for the name of store visited, type of merchandise sold, use or nonuse of bar-coding, and the inventory costing method used if bar-coding is not employed. You might also inquire as to what the store's merchandise turnover is and how often physical inventory is taken.

Business Week Activity

A3

Read the article "Michael Dell: Whirlwind on the Web" in the April 7, 1997, issue of *Business Week.* Answer the following questions:

1. How many days of sales does Dell have in inventory?
2. How does Dell's days of sales in inventory compare with one of its chief competitors?
3. What are three techniques described in the article that Dell uses to improve inventory management?

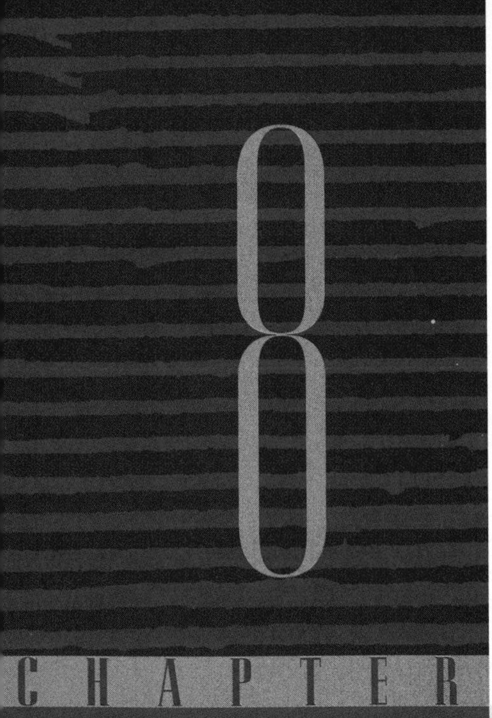

Accounting Information Systems

A Look Back

Chapters 6 and 7 focused on merchandising activities and accounting for inventory. We explained both the perpetual and periodic inventory systems, accounting for inventory transactions, and methods for assigning costs to inventory.

A Look at This Chapter

This chapter emphasizes accounting information systems. We describe fundamental system principles, the system's components, use of special journals and subsidiary ledgers, and technology-based systems. We also discuss segment reporting and how to analyze these data.

A Look Ahead

Chapter 9 focuses on internal controls and accounting for cash and cash equivalents. We explain good internal control procedures and their importance for accounting.

Chapter Outline

Records for Success

MIAMI—It was the worst loss in Maria Lopez's early career as owner of **Outdoors Unlimited.** She'd lobbied hard to carry *REV Sports* products in her sporting goods store. Her rejection letter was harsh, and to the point. "The financial condition and internal controls of Outdoors Unlimited do not support a business relationship at this time . . ." the letter said.

Maria knew she'd pushed the limit in keeping her own records. "I purchased the best accounting software according to small business magazines. But," says Maria, "I didn't have any idea how to use it."

Maria thought she knew how to enter her store's sales and purchases data. Yet it turned out some data were entered in ledgers and not in journals, and vice versa. "The software created lovely reports, but I didn't know if they were correct," admits Maria. "Ledgers, journals, footings, crossfootings—it's all Greek to me!" Most frustrating was that Maria knew her store was doing well, and for unknown reasons, her financials weren't reflecting it.

"I ended up taking an evening course," says Maria. "I learned how to set up an accounting system and to keep special journals. I set up my records as I went through the course."

Maria now regularly creates schedules of accounts payable and accounts receivable. "I use ledgers and aging schedules to identify late-paying customers. I also keep payable records to help me better time payments to suppliers." Maria points out that Outdoors Unlimited now carries *REV*'s products.

And what about that accounting software? "It's great software," says Maria. "But it ought to carry a warning like: *A lack of accounting knowledge can damage your company's health."*

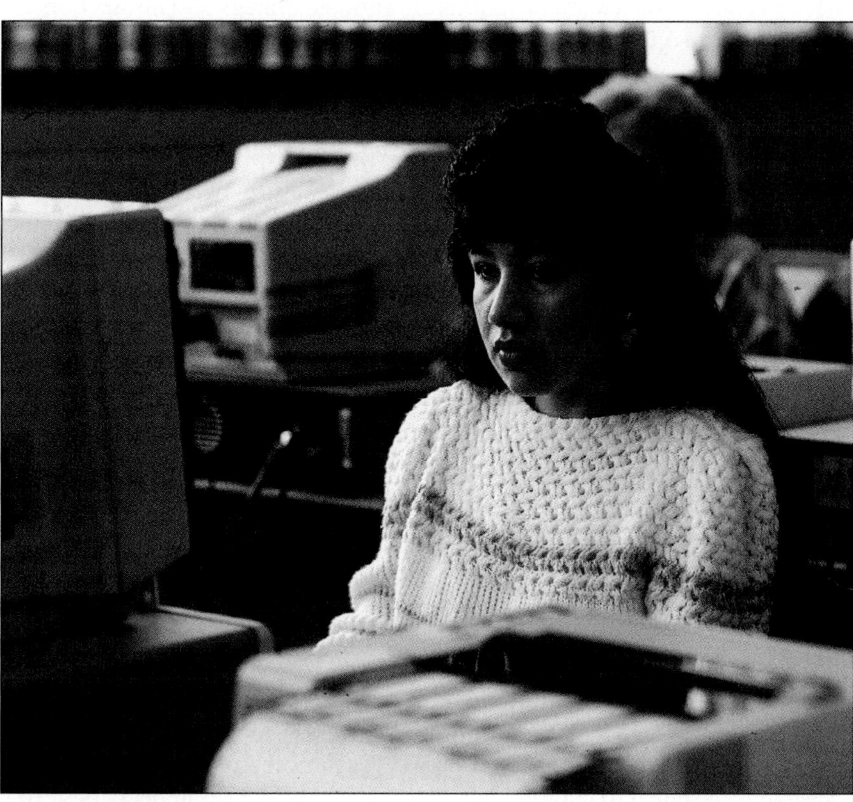

Learning Objectives

Conceptual

C1 Identify fundamental principles of accounting information systems.

C2 Identify components of accounting information systems.

C3 Explain the goals and uses of special journals.

C4 Describe the use of controlling accounts and subsidiary ledgers.

C5 Explain how technology-based information systems impact accounting.

Analytical

A1 Analyze a company's performance and financial condition by business segments.

Procedural

P1 Journalize and post transactions using special journals.

P2 Prepare and test the accuracy of subsidiary ledgers.

CHAPTER PREVIEW

Accounting for business activities requires collecting and processing information. As the number or complexity of business activities rises, demands placed on accounting information systems increase. Accounting information systems must meet this challenge in an efficient and effective manner. In this chapter, we learn about fundamental principles guiding information systems, and we study components making up these systems. We also explain procedures that use special journals and subsidiary ledgers to make accounting information systems more efficient. Our understanding of the details of accounting reports makes us better decision makers when using financial information, and it improves our ability to analyze and interpret financial statements. Like Maria Lopez in the opening article, knowledge of these topics helps in successfully running a company.

Fundamental System Principles

C1 Identify fundamental principles of accounting information systems.

Accounting information systems collect and process data from transactions and events, organize them in useful forms, and communicate results to decision makers. These systems are crucial to effective decision making for both internal and external users of information. With the increasing complexity of business operations and the growing need for information, accounting information systems are more important than ever before.

All decision makers in practice today need to have a basic knowledge of how accounting information systems work. This knowledge gives decision makers a competitive edge as they gain a better understanding of information constraints, measurement limitations, and potential applications. It allows them to make more informed decisions and to better balance the risks and returns of various strategies. This section explains five fundamental principles of accounting information systems, which are shown in Exhibit 8.1.

Exhibit 8.1

System Principles

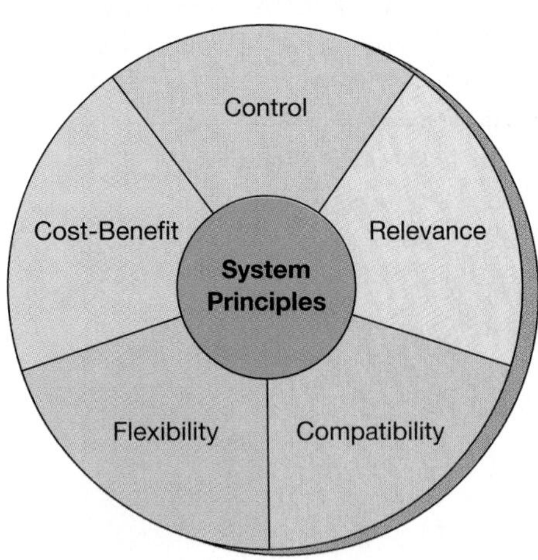

Control Principle

Managers need to control and monitor business activities. To this end, the **control principle** requires an accounting information system to have internal controls. *Internal controls* are methods and procedures allowing managers to control and monitor business activities. They include policies to direct operations toward common goals, procedures to ensure reliable financial reports, safeguards to protect company assets, and methods to achieve compliance with laws and regulations.

Relevance Principle

Decision makers need relevant information to make informed decisions. The **relevance principle** requires that an accounting information system report useful, understandable, timely, and pertinent information for effective decision making. This means an information system is designed to capture data that make a difference in decisions. To ensure this, it is important all decision makers be considered when identifying relevant information for disclosure.

Compatibility Principle

Accounting information systems must be consistent with the aims of a company. The **compatibility principle** requires that an accounting information system conform with a company's activities, personnel, and structure. It also must adapt to the unique characteristics of a company. The system must not be intrusive, but rather work in harmony with and be driven by company goals. **Outdoors Unlimited,** described in the opening article, for example, needs a simple retail information system. **NIKE,** on the other hand, demands both a merchandising and a manufacturing information system able to assemble data from its global operations.

Flexibility Principle

Accounting information systems must be able to adjust to changes. The **flexibility principle** requires that an accounting information system be able to adapt to changes in the company, business environment, and needs of decisions makers. Technological advances, competitive pressures, consumer tastes, regulations, and company activities constantly change. A system must be designed to adapt to these changes.

Cost-Benefit Principle

Accounting information systems must balance costs and benefits. The **cost-benefit principle** requires the benefits from an activity in an accounting information system to outweigh the costs of that activity. The costs and benefits of an activity such as reporting certain information impact the decisions of both external and internal users. They also affect costs of computing, personnel, and other direct and indirect costs. Decisions regarding other systems principles (control, relevance, compatibility, and flexibility) are also affected by the cost-benefit principle.

Components of Accounting Systems

C2 Identify components of accounting information systems.

Accounting information systems consist of people, records, methods, and equipment. The systems are designed to capture information about a company's transactions and to provide output including financial, managerial, and tax reports. Because all accounting information systems have these same goals, they have some basic components. These components apply whether or not a system is heavily computerized. Yet the components of computerized systems usually provide more accuracy, speed, efficiency, and convenience.

There are five basic components of an accounting information system: source documents, input devices, information processors, information storage, and output devices. Exhibit 8.2 shows these components as a series of steps. Yet we know there is a lot of two-way communication between many of these components. We describe each of these key components in this section.

Source Documents

We described source documents in Chapter 3 and explained their importance for both business transactions and information collection. Source documents provide the basic information processed by an accounting system. Most of us are familiar with source documents such as bank statements and checks received from others. Other examples of

Exhibit 8.2

Accounting System Components

source documents include invoices from suppliers, billings to customers, and employee earnings records.

Source documents are often paper-based. Yet increasingly they are taking other forms such as electronic files and Web communications. Also, a growing number of companies are sending invoices directly from their systems to their customers' systems. The Web is playing a major role in this transformation from paper-based to *paperless* systems.

Accurate source documents are crucial to accounting information systems. Input of faulty or incomplete information seriously impairs the reliability and relevance of the information system. We commonly refer to this as "garbage in, garbage out." Information systems are set up with special attention on control procedures to limit the possibility of entering faulty data in the system.

Input Devices

Input devices capture information from source documents and enable its transfer to the information processing component of the system. These devices often involve converting data on source documents from written or electronic form to a form usable for the system. Journal entries, both electronic and paper-based, are a type of input device. If we record transactions using **GLAS, SPATS,** or **PeachTree** software accompanying this book, our input device is a computer keyboard. Keyboards, scanners, and modems are some of the most common input devices in practice today.

Another increasingly common input device is a *bar-code reader.* Commonly used by merchandisers, bar-code readers are growing in importance as input and control devices for military, law enforcement, and special business applications. Bar-code readers capture code numbers and transfer them to the organization's computer for processing. A *scanner* is another popular input device whose applications are expanding. It can capture writing samples and other input directly from source documents.

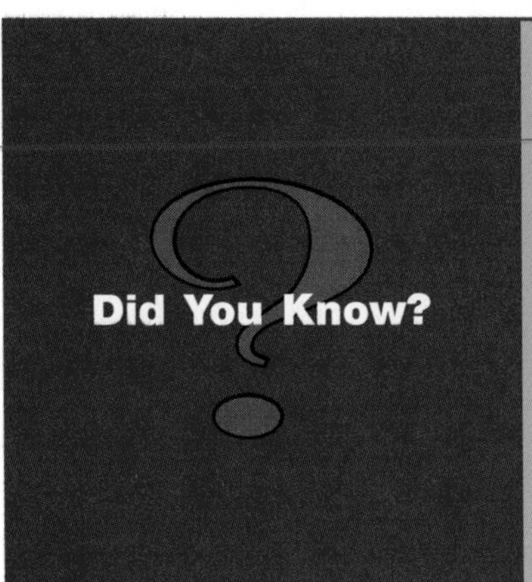

Music-In, Rankings-Out

For decades, merchandisers, radio stations, and consumers saw what was hot and what wasn't in *Billboard* magazine's weekly survey. The survey results were compiled from phone interviews with store owners. But a startup company called **SoundScan** began tracking CD sales electronically at checkout counters, producing more accurate results. Its scanners are now in more than 14,000 stores. Among the surprising findings are that country music and small rap labels are far more popular than record executives imagined. Both now get promoted much more heavily. [Source: *Business Week,* June 6, 1994.]

Accounting information systems encourage accuracy by using consistent methods for inputting data. Controls are also used to ensure that only authorized individuals can input data to the system. Controls increase the reliability of the system. They also allow false information to be traced back to its source.

Information Processor

An **information processor** is a system that interprets, transforms, and summarizes information for use in analysis and reporting. An important part of an information processor in accounting systems is professional judgment. Accounting principles are never so structured that they limit the need for professional judgment. Other parts of an information processor include journals, ledgers, working papers, and posting procedures. Each assists in transforming raw data to useful information.

Increasingly, computer technology is assisting manual information processors. This assistance is freeing accounting professionals to take on greater analysis, interpretive, and managerial roles. This assistance to information processors includes both computing hardware and software. Hardware is the computing equipment, and software is the directions for the hardware. Software consists of computer programs that specify operations performed on data. Software often controls much of the accounting system including input, file management, processing, and output. **Microsoft,** the world's largest software producer, is a major part of this evolution. It reported 1996 revenues of more than $8.6 billion, with much of this from software sales.

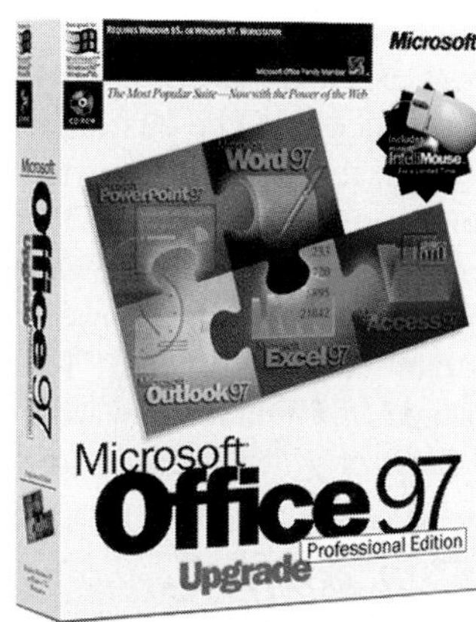

Information Storage

Information storage is the component of an accounting system that keeps data in a form accessible to information processors. After being input and processed, data are usually saved for use in future analysis or reports. This database must be accessible to preparers of periodic financial reports and for other analyses. Information storage is also set up to help in the creation of internal reports. Auditors focus on this database when they audit financial statements. Companies also maintain files of source documents to resolve errors or disputes.

Technology increasingly assists with information storage. While previous systems consisted almost exclusively of paper documents, there is growing use of CDs, hard drives, tapes, and other electronic storage devices. Advances in information storage enable accounting systems to store more detailed data than ever before. This means managers have more data to access and work with in planning and controlling business activities. Information storage can be on-line, meaning data can be accessed whenever it is needed, or it can be off-line, meaning data can't be accessed. Access often requires assistance and authorization. Information storage is increasingly augmented by Web information sources such as SEC databases, FASB standards, and financial and product markets.

Geek Chic
A group of cyberfashion pioneers at **MIT's Media Laboratory** is creating geek chic, a kind of wearable computer. Cyberfashion draws on new technologies. Digital cellular phones mean we can stay connected to the Web wherever we roam. Lithium batteries reduce weight, and miniature monitors are placed at the edge of a pair of glasses. Special conducive thread is woven into clothing to carry low-voltage signals from one part of the system to another and fabric keyboards are sewn into blue jeans. Current offerings include a music synthesizer woven into a dress and a jersey that translates the wearer's words into a foreign language. These creations give new meaning to the term *software.* [Source: *Business Week,* October 20, 1997.]

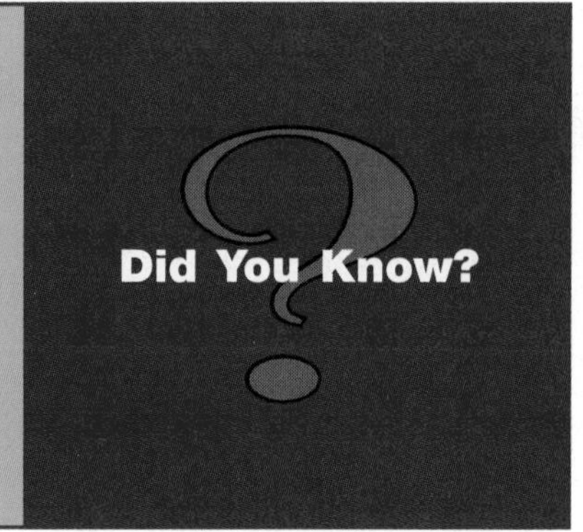

Output Devices

Output devices are the means to take information out of an accounting system and make it available to users. Output devices provide users with a variety of items including graphics, analysis reports, bills to customers, checks to suppliers, employee paychecks, financial statements, and internal reports. The most common output devices are printers and monitors; others include telephones or direct Web communication with the systems of suppliers or customers. When requests for output occur, an information processor takes the needed data from a database and prepares the necessary report. This report is then sent to an output device.

Information can be output in many forms. For example, a touch-tone telephone can serve as an input/output device when a bank customer calls to learn the balance in his or her account. The customer presses buttons to provide requested authorization and then receives the desired information over the phone line. Another kind of output is an electronic fund transfer (EFT) of payroll from the company's bank account to its employees' bank accounts. One output device to accomplish this is an interface that allows a company's accounting system to send payroll data directly to the accounting system of its bank. Still another EFT output device involves a company recording its payroll data on tape or CD and forwarding it to the bank. This tape or disk is then used by the bank to transfer wages earned to employees' accounts.

Flash back

1. Identify the five primary components of an accounting information system.
2. What is the aim of the information processor component of an accounting system?
3. What uses are made of data in the information storage component of an accounting system?

Answers—p. 341

Certified Public Accountant
You are a CPA consulting with a client. This client's business has grown to the point where its accounting system must be updated to handle both the volume of transactions and management's needs for information. Your client requests your advice in purchasing new software for its accounting system. You have been offered a 10% commission by a software company for each purchase of its system by one of your clients. Do you think your evaluation of software is affected by this commission arrangement? Do you think this commission arrangement is appropriate? Do you tell your client about the commission arrangement before making a recommendation?

Answer—p. 341

Special Journals in Accounting

C3 Explain the goals and uses of special journals.

This section describes the underlying records of accounting information systems. Designed correctly, these records support efficiency in processing transactions and events. They are part of all systems in various forms. They are also increasingly electronically based. But even in technologically advanced systems, a basic understanding of the records we describe in this section aids us in using, interpreting, and applying accounting information. It also improves our understanding of the workings of computer-based systems. We must remember that all accounting systems have common purposes and internal workings whether or not they depend on technology.

This section focuses on special journals and subsidiary ledgers that are an important part of accounting systems. We describe how special journals are used to capture transactions, and we explain how subsidiary ledgers are set up to capture details of certain accounts. This section uses selected transactions of **Outdoors Unlimited** to illustrate these important points.

Outdoors Unlimited uses a *periodic* inventory system, so the special journals are set up using this system. The focus on special journals in a periodic system is appropriate because they are more often used in a periodic system than in a perpetual system. Many perpetual systems are computerized, and thus their "special journals" are usually in electronic form and automate several recordkeeping tasks such as posting and preparing accounts receivable and payable schedules. Appendix 8A describes the slight change in special journals required for a *perpetual* system. We also include a note at the bottom of each of the major journals prepared using the periodic system explaining the minor change required if a company uses a perpetual system.

Basics of Special Journals

A General Journal is an all-purpose journal where we can record any transaction. Yet using a General Journal means that each debit and each credit entered must be individually posted to its respective ledger account. This requires time and effort in posting individual debits and credits, especially for less technologically advanced systems. The costs of posting accounts can be reduced by organizing transactions into common groups and providing a separate special journal. A **special journal** is used in recording and posting transactions of similar type. Most transactions of a merchandiser, for instance, fall into four groups: sales on credit, purchases on credit, cash receipts, and cash disbursements. Exhibit 8.3 shows the special journals for these groups. This section assumes the use of these four special journals along with the General Journal.

Exhibit 8.3

Using Special Journals with a General Journal

Sales Journal	Cash Receipts Journal	Purchases Journal	Cash Disbursement Journal	General Journal
For recording credit sales	For recording cash receipts	For recording credit purchases	For recording cash payments	For transactions not in special journals

The General Journal continues to be used for transactions not covered by special journals and for adjusting, closing, and correcting entries. We show in the following discussion how special journals are efficient tools in helping journalize and post transactions. This is done, for instance, by accumulating debits and credits of similar transactions, which allows us to post amounts entered in the columns as column *totals* rather than as individual amounts. The advantage of this system increases as the number of transactions increases. Special journals also allow an efficient division of labor. This can be an effective control procedure.

Subsidiary Ledgers

C4 Describe the use of controlling accounts and subsidiary ledgers.

Special journals are helpful for many reasons including collecting information on accounts making up the *General Ledger.* But to understand the details of special journals, it is necessary to know the workings of a subsidiary ledger. A **subsidiary ledger** is a listing of individual accounts with a common characteristic. A subsidiary ledger supports the General Ledger with detailed information on specific accounts, which removes unnecessary details from the General Ledger.

Accounting information systems often include several subsidiary ledgers. Two of the most important are the amounts due from customers, called *accounts receivable,* and amounts owed to creditors, called *accounts payable.* These two common subsidiary ledgers are known as the:

- *Accounts Receivable Ledger* for storing transaction data with individual customers.
- *Accounts Payable Ledger* for storing transaction data with individual creditors.

Individual accounts in subsidiary ledgers are often arranged alphabetically. We describe accounts receivable and accounts payable ledgers in this section. This knowledge will help us in understanding special journals in the next section when we use both of these ledgers.

Accounts Receivable Ledger

When we recorded credit sales in prior transaction analyses, we usually debited Accounts Receivable. Yet when a company has more than one credit customer, the accounts receivable records must show how much *each* customer purchased, paid, and has yet to pay. This information is collected for companies with credit customers by keeping a separate account receivable for each customer.

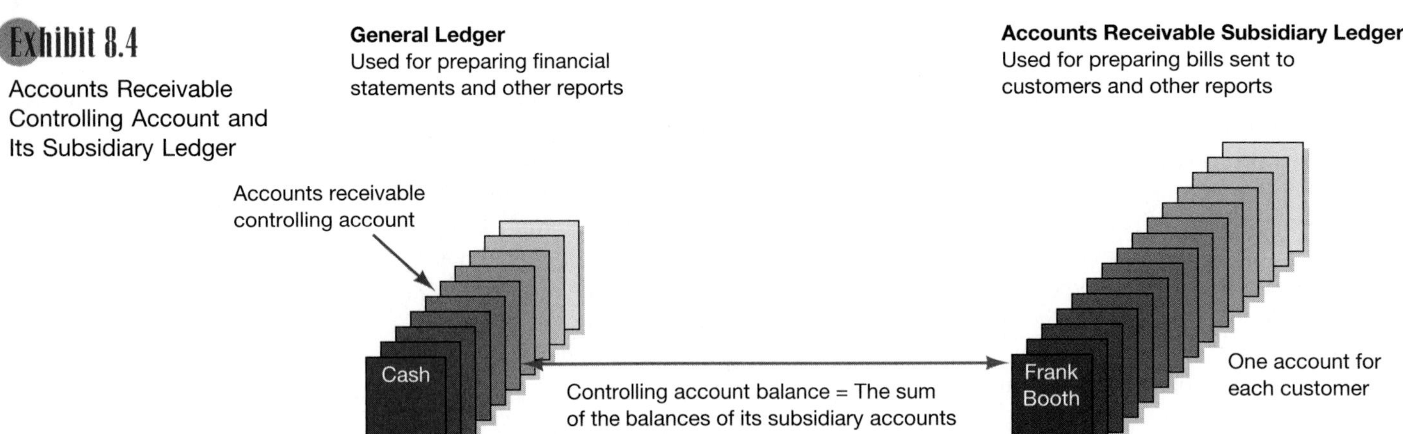

Exhibit 8.4
Accounts Receivable Controlling Account and Its Subsidiary Ledger

A separate account for each customer can be kept in the General Ledger containing the other financial statement accounts. But this is uncommon. Instead, the General Ledger continues to keep a single Accounts Receivable account and a *subsidiary ledger* is set up to keep a separate account for each customer. This subsidiary ledger is called the **Accounts Receivable Ledger** (also called *Accounts Receivable Subsidiary Ledger* or *Customers' Ledger*). Like a General Ledger, a subsidiary ledger can exist in electronic (tape or CD) or paper (book or tray) form. Customer accounts in a subsidiary ledger are kept separate from the Accounts Receivable account in the General Ledger.

Exhibit 8.4 shows the relation between the Accounts Receivable account and its related accounts in the subsidiary ledger. After all items are posted, the balance in the Accounts Receivable account must equal the sum of balances in the customers' accounts. The Accounts Receivable account is said to control the Accounts Receivable Ledger and is called a **controlling account.** Since the Accounts Receivable Ledger is a supplementary record controlled by an account in the General Ledger, it is called a subsidiary ledger.

Accounts Payable Ledger

There are other controlling accounts and subsidiary ledgers. We know, for example, that many companies buy on credit from several suppliers. This means a company must keep a separate account for each creditor. It does this by keeping an Accounts Payable controlling account in the General Ledger and a separate account for each creditor in an **Accounts Payable Ledger** (also called *Accounts Payable Subsidiary Ledger* or *Creditors' Ledger*). The concept of a controlling account and subsidiary ledger as described with accounts receivable also applies to creditor accounts.

Other Subsidiary Ledgers

Subsidiary ledgers are also common for several other accounts. A company with many items of equipment, for example, might keep only one Equipment account in its General Ledger. But this company's Equipment account would control a subsidiary ledger where each item of equipment is recorded in a separate account. Similar treatment is common for investments, inventory, payables, and other large accounts needing separate detailed records.

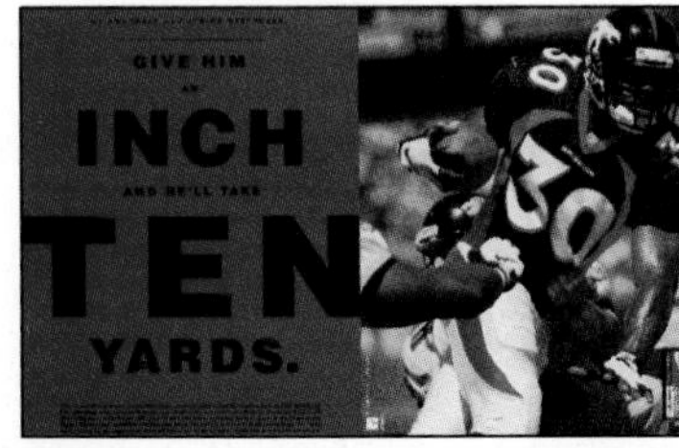

NIKE reports detailed sales information by geographic area in its 1997 annual report presented in Appendix A. Yet NIKE's accounting system most certainly keeps more detailed sales records than reflected in its annual report. NIKE, for instance, sells hundreds of different products and is able to analyze the sales performance of each one of them. This detail can be captured by many different general ledger sales accounts. But it is likely captured by using supplementary records that function like subsidiary ledgers. The concept of a subsidiary ledger can be applied in many different ways to ensure that the accounting system captures sufficient details to support analyses that decision makers need.

Sales Journal

A **sales journal** is used to record sales of merchandise on credit. Sales of merchandise for cash are not recorded in a sales journal but instead are recorded in a cash receipts journal. Sales of nonmerchandise assets on credit are recorded in the general journal.

P1 Journalize and post transactions using special journals.

Journalizing

Credit sale transactions are recorded with information about each sale entered separately in a Sales Journal. This information is often taken from a copy of the sales ticket or invoice prepared at the time of sale. The top of Exhibit 8.5 shows a Sales Journal from

Exhibit 8.5

Sales Journal with Posting*

Outdoors Unlimited Sales Journal

Page 3

Date	Account Debited	Invoice Number	PR	Accounts Receivable Dr./Sales Cr.
Feb. 2	Jason Henry	307	✓	450
7	Albert Co.	308	✓	500
13	Bam Moore	309	✓	350
15	Paul Roth	310	✓	200
22	Jason Henry	311	✓	225
25	Frank Booth	312	✓	175
28	Albert Co.	313	✓	250
28	Total			2,150
				(106/413)

Individual amounts are posted daily to the subsidiary ledger.

Total is posted at the end of the period to General Ledger accounts.

Accounts Receivable Ledger

Frank Booth

Date	PR	Debit	Credit	Balance
Feb. 25	S3	175		175

Jason Henry

Date	PR	Debit	Credit	Balance
Feb. 2	S3	450		450
22	S3	225		675

Bam Moore

Date	PR	Debit	Credit	Balance
Feb. 13	S3	350		350

Paul Roth

Date	PR	Debit	Credit	Balance
Feb. 15	S3	200		200

Albert Co.

Date	PR	Debit	Credit	Balance
Feb. 7	S3	500		500
28	S3	250		750

General Ledger

Accounts Receivable No. 106

Date	PR	Debit	Credit	Balance
Feb. 28	S3	2,150		2,150

Sales No. 413

Date	PR	Debit	Credit	Balance
Feb. 28	S3		2,150	2,150

Customer accounts are in a subsidiary ledger and the financial statement accounts are in the General Ledger. Explanation columns are omitted for brevity.

*Sales Journal in a *perpetual* system requires a new column on the far right titled "Cost of Goods Sold Dr., Inventory Cr." (see Exhibit 8.17).

the sporting goods merchandiser, **Outdoors Unlimited.** The Sales Journal in this exhibit is called a columnar journal because it has columns for recording the date, customer's name, invoice number, posting reference, and amount of each credit sale.[1] A **columnar journal** is a journal with more than one column.

Each transaction recorded in the Sales Journal yields a debit to Accounts Receivable and a credit to Sales. We only need one column for these two accounts. An exception is when managers need more information about taxes, returns, items, and other details of transactions. We do not use the posting reference (PR) column when entering transactions; instead this column is used when posting.

Posting

A Sales Journal is posted as shown with the arrow lines in Exhibit 8.5. Individual transactions in the Sales Journal are posted regularly (typically each day) to customer accounts in the Accounts Receivable Ledger. These postings keep customer accounts up to date. This is important for the person granting credit to customers, who needs to know the amount owed by credit-seeking customers. If this information in the customer's account is out of date, an incorrect decision can be made.

When sales recorded in the Sales Journal are individually posted to customer accounts in the Accounts Receivable Ledger, check marks are entered in the Sales Journal's Posting Reference column. Check marks are usually used rather than account numbers because customer accounts are not always numbered. Customer accounts are arranged alphabetically in the Accounts Receivable Ledger for reference. Note that posting debits to Accounts Receivable twice—once to Accounts Receivable and once to the customer's account—does not violate the accounting equation of debits equal credits. The equality of debits and credits is always maintained in the General Ledger. The Accounts Receivable Ledger is a subsidiary record.

The Sales Journal's dollar amount column is totaled at the end of the period (month of February in this case). The total is debited to Accounts Receivable and credited to Sales. The credit records the period's revenue from sales on account. The debit records the increase in accounts receivable. There is a general rule for all postings to a controlling account: The controlling account is debited periodically for an amount or amounts equal to the sum of the debits to the subsidiary ledger, and it is credited periodically for an amount or amounts equal to the sum of the credits to the subsidiary ledger.

When a company uses more than one journal, it identifies in the Posting Reference column of the *ledgers* the journal and page number from which the amount is taken. We identify a journal by using an initial. Items posted from the Sales Journal carry the initial *S* before their journal page numbers in a Posting Reference column. Likewise, items from the Cash Receipts Journal carry the initial *R*; items from the Cash Disbursements Journal carry the initial *D*; items from the Purchases Journal carry the initial *P*; and items from the General Journal carry the initial *G*.

Testing the Ledger

P2 Prepare and test the accuracy of subsidiary ledgers.

Account balances in the General Ledger and subsidiary ledgers are tested (or proved) for accuracy after posting is complete. We do this by first preparing a trial balance of the General Ledger to confirm debits equal credits (see Chapter 4 for preparing a trial balance). If debits equal credits in the trial balance, the accounts in the General Ledger, including the controlling accounts, are assumed to be correct. Second, we test the subsidiary ledgers by preparing schedules of individual accounts and amounts.

A **schedule of accounts receivable** is a listing of accounts from the Accounts Receivable Ledger with their balances and the sum of all balances. If this total equals the balance of the Accounts Receivable controlling account, the accounts in the Accounts Receivable Ledger are assumed correct. Exhibit 8.6 shows a schedule of accounts receivable drawn from the Accounts Receivable Ledger of Exhibit 8.5.

---

[1] For brevity, we don't record explanations in any of our special journals.

Additional Issues

This section looks at three additional issues with the Sales Journal: (1) recording sales taxes, (2) recording sales returns and allowances, and (3) using sales invoices as a journal.

Exhibit 8.6

Schedule of Accounts Receivable

OUTDOORS UNLIMITED Schedule of Accounts Receivable February 28, 2000	
Frank Booth	$ 175
Jason Henry	675
Bam Moore	350
Paul Roth	200
Albert Co.	750
Total accounts receivable	$2,150

Sales Taxes

Many cities and states require retailers to collect sales taxes from customers and to periodically send these taxes to the city or state treasurer. When using a columnar Sales Journal, we can have a record of taxes collected by adding columns to the journal as shown in Exhibit 8.7 for Outdoors Unlimited.

Exhibit 8.7

Sales Journal with information on Sales Taxes

Outdoors Unlimited Sales Journal Page 3

Date		Account Debited	Invoice Number	PR	Accounts Receivable Dr.	Sales Taxes Payable Cr.	Sales Cr.
Dec.	1	Favre Co.	7-1698		103	3	100

We described how column totals of a Sales Journal are commonly posted at the end of each period (month for Outdoors Unlimited). This now includes crediting the Sales Taxes Payable account for the total of the Sales Taxes Payable column. Individual amounts in the Accounts Receivable column are posted daily to customer accounts in the Accounts Receivable Ledger. Individual amounts in the Sales Taxes Payable and Sales columns are not posted. A company that collects sales taxes on its cash sales can also use a special Sales Taxes Payable column in its Cash Receipts Journal.

Sales Returns and Allowances

A company with only a few sales returns and allowances can record them in a General Journal with an entry like:

Mar. 17	Sales Returns and Allowances	414	175	
	Accounts Receivable—Ray Ball	106/✓		175
	Customer returned merchandise.			

Assets = Liabilities + Equity
−175 −175

The debit in this entry is posted to the Sales Returns and Allowances account. The credit is posted to both the Accounts Receivable controlling account and to the customer's account. We also include the account number and the check mark, 106/✓, in the PR column on the credit line. This means both the Accounts Receivable controlling account in the General Ledger and the Ray Ball account in the Accounts Receivable Ledger are credited for $175. Both are credited because the balance of the controlling account in the General Ledger does not equal the sum of the customer account balances in the subsidiary ledger unless both are credited.

A company with a large number of sales returns and allowances can save costs by recording them in a special Sales Returns and Allowances Journal similar to Exhibit 8.8. A company can design and use a special journal for any group of similar transactions if there are enough transactions to warrant a journal. When using a Sales Returns and Allowances Journal to record returns, amounts in the journal are posted daily to customers' accounts. The journal total is posted as a debit to Sales Returns and Allowances and as a credit to Accounts Receivable at the end of the month.

Exhibit 8.8

Sales Returns and Allowances Journal

Outdoors Unlimited Sales Returns and Allowances Journal

Page 1

Date	Account Credited	Credit Memo No.	PR	Sales Returns & Allowances Dr. Accounts Receivable Cr.
Mar. 7	Robert Moore	203	✓	10
14	James Warren	204	✓	12
18	T.M. Jones	205	✓	6
23	Sam Smith	206	✓	18
31	Total			46
				(414/106)

Sales Invoices as a Sales Journal

To save costs, some merchandisers avoid using Sales Journals for credit sales. Instead they post each sales invoice total directly to the customer's account in the subsidiary Accounts Receivable Ledger. They then put copies of invoices in numerical order in a file. At the end of the month, they total all invoices for that month and make a general journal entry to debit Accounts Receivable and credit Sales for the total. The bound invoice copies essentially act as a Sales Journal. This procedure is called *direct posting of sales invoices.*

Flash back

4. When special journals are used, where are all cash payments by check recorded?
5. How does a columnar journal save posting time and effort?
6. How do debits and credits remain equal when credit sales to customers are posted twice (once to Accounts Receivable and once to the customer's account)?
7. How do we identify the journal from which an amount in a ledger account was posted?

Answers—p. 341

Cash Receipts Journal

A **Cash Receipts Journal** records all receipts of cash. A Cash Receipts Journal is a columnar journal because different accounts are credited when cash is received from different sources.

Journalizing and Posting

Cash receipts usually fall into one of three groups: (1) cash from credit customers in payment of their accounts, (2) cash from cash sales, and (3) cash from other sources. The Cash Receipts Journal in Exhibit 8.9 has a special column for credits when cash is received from one or more of these three sources. We describe how to journalize transactions for each of these three sources in this section. We then describe how to post these transactions.[2]

Cash from Credit Customers

To record cash received in payment of a customer's account, the customer's name is first entered in the Cash Receipts Journal's Account Credited column. Then the amounts debited to Cash and Sales Discount (if any) are entered in their respective journal columns, and the amount credited to the customer's account is entered in the Accounts Receivable Credit column. The February 12 transaction is one example of cash received from credit customers. Note the Accounts Receivable Credit column contains only credits to customer accounts.

[2] We include explanations in the Cash Receipts Journal so the reader knows the source of each cash receipt transaction.

Exhibit 8.9

Cash Receipts Journal with Posting*

Outdoors Unlimited Cash Receipts Journal

Page 2

Date	Accounts Credited	Explanation	PR	Cash Dr.	Sales Discount Dr.	Accounts Receivable Cr.	Sales Cr.	Other Accounts Cr.
Feb. 7	Sales	Cash sales	✓	4,450			4,450	
12	Jason Henry	Invoice, 2/2	✓	441	9	450		
14	Sales	Cash sales	✓	3,925			3,925	
17	Albert Co.	Invoice, 2/7	✓	490	10	500		
20	Notes Payable	Note to bank	245	750				750
21	Sales	Cash sales	✓	4,700			4,700	
22	Interest revenue	Bank account	409	250				250
23	Bam Moore	Invoice, 2/13	✓	343	7	350		
25	Paul Roth	Invoice, 2/15	✓	196	4	200		
28	Sales	Cash sales	✓	4,225			4,225	
28	Totals			19,770	30	1,500	17,300	1,000
				(101)	(415)	(106)	(413)	(✓)

Individual amounts in the other Accounts Credit and Accounts Receivable Credit columns are posted daily.

Column totals, except for Other Accounts column, are posted at the end of the period.

Accounts Receivable Ledger

Frank Booth

Date	PR	Debit	Credit	Balance
Feb. 25	S3	175		175

Jason Henry

Date	PR	Debit	Credit	Balance
Feb. 2	S3	450		450
12	R2		450	0
22	S3	225		225

Bam Moore

Date	PR	Debit	Credit	Balance
Feb. 13	S3	350		350
23	R2		350	0

Paul Roth

Date	PR	Debit	Credit	Balance
Feb. 15	S3	200		200
25	R2		200	0

Albert Co.

Date	PR	Debit	Credit	Balance
Feb. 7	S3	500		500
17	R2		500	0
28	S3	250		250

General Ledger

Cash No. 101

Date	PR	Debit	Credit	Balance
Feb. 28	R2	19,770		19,770

Accounts Receivable No. 106

Date	PR	Debit	Credit	Balance
Feb. 28	S3	2,150		2,150
28	R2		1,500	650

Notes Payable No. 245

Date	PR	Debit	Credit	Balance
Feb. 20	R2		750	750

Sales No. 413

Date	PR	Debit	Credit	Balance
Feb. 28	S3		2,150	2,150
28	R2		17,300	19,450

Sales Discounts No. 415

Date	PR	Debit	Credit	Balance
Feb. 28	R2	30		30

Interest Revenue No. 409

Date	PR	Debit	Credit	Balance
Feb. 22	R2		250	250

*Cash Receipts Journal in a *perpetual* system requires a new column on the far right titled "Cost of Goods Sold Dr., Inventory Cr." (see Exhibit 8.18).

The posting procedure is twofold. First, individual amounts are posted to subsidiary ledger accounts. Second, column totals are posted to General Ledger accounts. Let's look at the Accounts Receivable Credit column as an example. Individual credits are posted regularly (daily) to customer accounts in the subsidiary Accounts Receivable Ledger. The column total is posted at the end of the period (month) as a credit to the Accounts Receivable controlling account.

Cash Sales

When cash sales are collected, the debits to Cash are entered in the Cash Debit column, and the credits in a special column titled Sales Credit. The February 7 transaction is an example of cash sales. By using a separate Sales Credit column, we can post the total cash sales for a period (month) as a single amount, the column total. When recording daily cash sales in the Cash Receipts Journal, we place a check mark in the Posting Reference (PR) column to indicate that no amount is individually posted from that line of the journal. Sometimes companies also use a double check (✓✓) to identify amounts that are not posted to customer accounts from amounts that are posted. Although cash sales are usually journalized daily (or at point of sale) in practice, cash sales are journalized weekly in Exhibit 8.9 for brevity.

Cash from Other Sources

Most cash receipts are from collections of accounts receivable and from cash sales. But other sources of cash include money borrowed from a bank, interest on account, or sale of unneeded assets. The Other Accounts Credit column is for receipts that do not occur often enough to warrant a separate column. This means items entered in this column are few and are posted to a variety of General Ledger accounts. Postings are less apt to be omitted if these items are posted daily. The Cash Receipts Journal's Posting Reference column is used only for daily postings from the Other Accounts and Accounts Receivable columns. The account numbers in the Posting Reference column refer to items that are posted to General Ledger accounts. Check marks indicate that an item (like a day's cash sales) is either not posted or is posted to the subsidiary Accounts Receivable Ledger.

Footing, Crossfooting, and Posting

At the end of a period (month), the amounts in the Cash, Sales Discount, Accounts Receivable, and Sales columns of the Cash Receipts Journal are posted as column totals. The transactions recorded in all journals must result in equal debits and credits to General Ledger accounts. To be sure that total debits and credits in a columnar journal are equal, we often crossfoot column totals before posting them. To *foot* a column of numbers is to add it. To *crossfoot* is to add the debit column totals, add the credit column totals, and then compare the two sums for equality. Footing and crossfooting of the numbers in Exhibit 8.9 yields the schedule in Exhibit 8.10:

Exhibit 8.10

Footing and Crossfooting Journal Amounts

Debit Columns		Credit Columns	
Sales discounts debit	$ 30	Accounts receivable credit	$ 1,500
Cash debit	19,770	Sales credit	17,300
		Other accounts credit	1,000
Total	$19,800	Total	$19,800

After crossfooting the journal to confirm debits equal credits, we post the totals of all but the Other Accounts column. Because individual items in the Other Accounts column are posted daily, this column total is not posted. We place a check mark below the Other Accounts column to indicate that this column total is not posted. The account numbers of the accounts where the remaining column totals are posted are in parentheses below each column. Posting items daily from the Other Accounts column with a delayed posting of the offsetting items in the Cash column (total) causes the General Ledger to be out of balance during the period. But this doesn't matter because posting the Cash column total causes the offsetting amounts to reach the General Ledger before the trial balance or other financial statements are prepared at the end of the period.

Retailer
You are a retailer in computer equipment and supplies. You want to know how promptly customers are paying their bills. This information can help you in deciding whether to extend credit and in planning your own cash payments. Where might you look for this information?

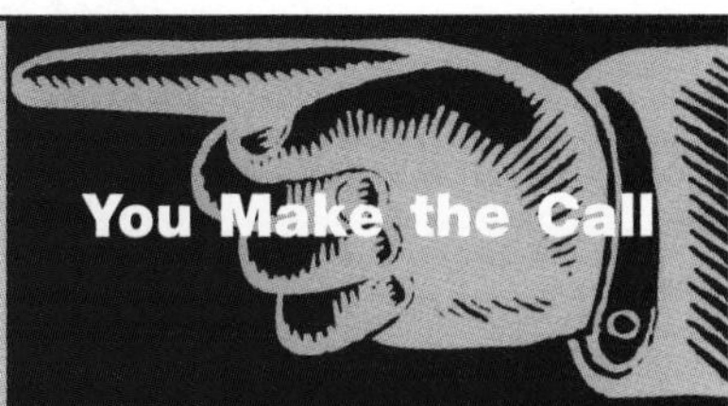

Answer—p. 341

Purchases Journal

A **Purchases Journal** is used to record all purchases on credit. Purchases for cash are recorded in the Cash Disbursements Journal.

Journalizing

A Purchases Journal usually is more useful if it is a multicolumn journal where all credit purchases, not only merchandise, are recorded. Exhibit 8.11 shows a multicolumn Purchases Journal.

Purchase invoices or other source documents are used in recording transactions in the Purchases Journal. The procedure is similar to that for the Sales Journal. We use the invoice date and terms to compute the date when payment for each purchase is due. Merchandise purchases are recorded in the Purchases Debit column. When a purchase involves an amount recorded in the Other Accounts Debit column, we use the Account column to identify the General Ledger account debited. Outdoors Unlimited also includes a separate column for credit purchases of office supplies. A separate column such as this is useful whenever several transactions involve debits to a specific account. Each company uses its own judgment in deciding on the number of separate columns necessary. The Other Accounts Debit column allows the Purchases Journal to be used for all purchase transactions involving credits to Accounts Payable. The Accounts Payable Credit column is used to record the amounts credited to each creditor's account.

Posting

The amounts in the Accounts Payable Credit column are posted regularly (daily) to individual creditor accounts in a subsidiary Accounts Payable Ledger. Each line of the Account column in Exhibit 8.11 shows the subsidiary ledger account that is posted for these amounts in the Accounts Payable Credit column. Individual amounts in the Other Accounts Debit column usually are posted daily to their General Ledger accounts. At the end of the period (month), all column totals except the Other Accounts Debit column are posted to their General Ledger accounts. The balance in the Accounts Payable controlling account must equal the sum of the account balances in the subsidiary Accounts Payable Ledger after posting.

Testing the Ledger

Account balances in the General Ledger and subsidiary ledgers are tested for accuracy after posting of the Purchases Journal is complete. Similar to the procedures followed for testing the ledger for the Sales Journal, two steps are necessary. First, we prepare a trial balance of the General Ledger to confirm debits equal credits. If debits equal credits in the trial balance, the accounts in the General Ledger, including the controlling accounts, are assumed to be correct. Second, we test the subsidiary ledgers by preparing a schedule of accounts payable. A **schedule of accounts payable** is a listing of accounts from the Accounts Payable Ledger with their balances and the sum of all the balances.

Purchases Journal with Posting*

Outdoors Unlimited Purchases Journal

Page 1

Date	Account	Date of Invoice	Terms	PR	Accounts Payable Cr.	Purchases Dr.	Office Supplies Dr.	Other Accounts Dr.
Feb. 3	Horning Supply Co.	2/2	n/30	✓	350	275	75	
5	Ace Mfg. Co.	2/5	2/10, n/30	✓	200	200		
13	Wynet & Co.	2/10	2/10, n/30	✓	150	150		
20	Smite Co.	2/18	2/10, n/30	✓	300	300		
25	Ace Mfg. Co.	2/24	2/10, n/30	✓	100	100		
28	Store Supplies/ITT Co.	2/28	n/30	125/✓	225	125	25	75
28	Totals				1,325	1,150	100	75
					(201)	(505)	(124)	(✓)

Individual amounts in the Other Accounts Debit and Accounts Payable Credit columns are posted daily.

Column totals, except for Other Accounts column, are posted at the end of the period.

Accounts Payable Ledger

Ace Mfg. Company

Date	PR	Debit	Credit	Balance
Feb. 5	P1		200	200
25	P1		100	300

ITT Company

Date	PR	Debit	Credit	Balance
Feb. 28	P1		225	225

Hornung Supply Company

Date	PR	Debit	Credit	Balance
Feb. 3	P1		350	350

Smite Company

Date	PR	Debit	Credit	Balance
Feb. 20	P1		300	300

Wynet and Company

Date	PR	Debit	Credit	Balance
Feb. 13	P1		150	150

General Legder

Office Supplies No. 124

Date	PR	Debit	Credit	Balance
Feb. 28	P1	100		100

Store Supplies No. 125

Date	PR	Debit	Credit	Balance
Feb. 28	P1	75		75

Accounts Payable No. 201

Date	PR	Debit	Credit	Balance
Feb. 28	P1		1,325	1,325

Accounts Payable No. 505

Date	PR	Debit	Credit	Balance
Feb. 28	P1	1,150		1,150

*Purchases Journal in a *perpetual* system replaces "Purchases Dr." with "Inventory Dr." (see Exhibit 8.19).

If this total equals the balance of the Accounts Payable controlling account, the accounts in the Accounts Payable Ledger are assumed correct. Exhibit 8.12 shows a schedule of accounts payable drawn from the Accounts Payable Ledger of Exhibit 8.11.

Cash Disbursements Journal

A **Cash Disbursements Journal,** also called a *Cash Payments Journal,* is used to record all payments of cash. It is a multicolumn journal because cash payments are made for several different purposes.

Journalizing

A Cash Disbursements Journal is like a Cash Receipts Journal except it records repetitive cash payments instead of receipts. Exhibit 8.13 shows the Cash Disbursements Journal for Outdoors Unlimited. We see repetitive credits to the Cash column of this journal. We also commonly see credits to Purchases Discounts and debits to the Accounts Payable account. Many companies purchase merchandise on credit, and therefore, a Purchases column is not often needed. Instead, the occasional cash purchase is recorded in the Other Accounts Debit column and Cash Credit column as illustrated in the February 12 transaction of Exhibit 8.13.

Exhibit 8.12

Schedule of Accounts Payable

OUTDOORS UNLIMITED Schedule of Accounts Payable February 28, 2000	
Ace Mfg. Company	$ 300
ITT Company	225
Hornung Supply Company	350
Smite Company	300
Wynet & Company	150
Total accounts payable	$1,325

The Cash Disbursements Journal has a column titled Ck. No. (check number). For control over cash disbursements, all payments except for very small amounts are made by check.[3] Checks should be prenumbered and entered in the journal in numerical order with each check's number in the column headed Ck. No. This makes it possible to scan the numbers in the column for omitted checks. When a Cash Disbursements Journal has a column for check numbers, it is sometimes called a **Check Register.**

Controller
You are a controller for a merchandising company. You want to analyze your company's cash payments to suppliers, including an analysis of purchases discounts. Where might you look for this information?

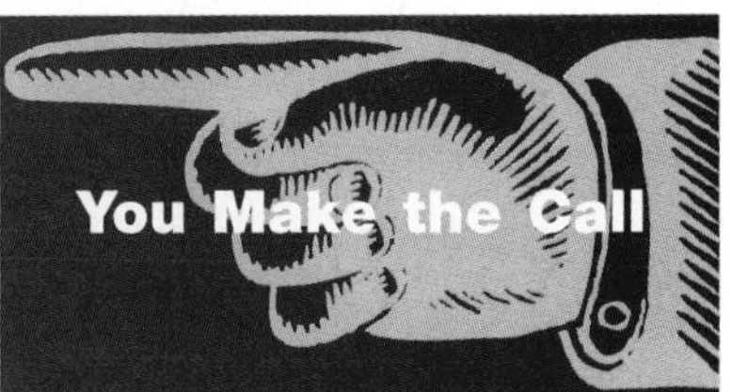

Answer—p. 341

Posting

Individual amounts in the Other Accounts Debit column of a Cash Disbursements Journal are usually posted to their general ledger accounts on a regular (daily) basis. Individual amounts in the Accounts Payable Debit column are also posted regularly (daily) to the specific creditors' accounts in the subsidiary Accounts Payable Ledger. At the end of the period (month), we crossfoot column totals and post the Accounts Payable Debit column total to the Accounts Payable controlling account. Also at the end of the period, the Purchases Discounts Credit column total is posted to the Purchases Discounts account and the Cash Credit column total is posted to the Cash account. The Other Accounts column total is not posted at the end of the period.

Flash back

8. What are the normal recording and posting procedures when using special journals and controlling accounts with subsidiary ledgers?
9. What is the rule for posting to a subsidiary ledger and its controlling account?
10. How do we test the accuracy of account balances in the General Ledger and subsidiary ledgers after posting?

Answers—p. 341

General Journal Transactions

When special journals are used we still need a General Journal for adjusting, closing, and correcting entries, and for transactions not recorded in special journals. These special

[3] We describe a petty cash system for controlling small cash payments in Chapter 9.

Cash Disbursements Journal with Posting*

Outdoors Unlimited Cash Disbursements Journal

Page 2

Date	Ck. No.	Payee	Account Debited	PR	Cash Cr.	Purchases Discounts Cr.	Other Accounts Dr.	Accounts Payable Dr.
Feb. 3	105	L & N Railroad	Transportation-In	508	15		15	
12	106	East Sales Co.	Purchases	505	25		25	
15	107	Ace Mfg. Co.	Ace Mfg. Co.	✓	196	4		200
15	108	Jerry Hale	Salaries Expense	622	250		250	
20	109	Wynet & Co.	Wynet & Co.	✓	147	3		150
28	110	Smite Co.	Smite Co.	✓	294	6		300
28		Totals			927	13	290	650
					(101)	(507)	(✓)	(201)

Column totals, except for Other Accounts column, are posted at the end of the period.

Individual amounts in the Other Accounts column and Accounts Payable column are posted daily.

General Ledger

Cash No. 101

Date	PR	Debit	Credit	Balance
Feb. 28	R2	19,770		19,770
28	D2		927	18,843

Accounts Payable No. 201

Date	PR	Debit	Credit	Balance
Feb. 28	P1		1,325	1,325
28	D2	650		675

Purchases No. 505

Date	PR	Debit	Credit	Balance
Feb. 12	D2	25		25
28	P1	1,150		1,175

Purchases Discounts No. 507

Date	PR	Debit	Credit	Balance
Feb. 28	D2		13	13

Transportation-In No. 508

Date	PR	Debit	Credit	Balance
Feb. 3	D2	15		15

Salaries Expense No. 622

Date	PR	Debit	Credit	Balance
Feb. 15	D2	250		250

Accounts Payable Ledger

Ace Mfg. Company

Date	PR	Debit	Credit	Balance
Feb. 5	P1		200	200
15	D2	200		–0–
25	P1		100	100

ITT Company

Date	PR	Debit	Credit	Balance
Feb. 28	P1		225	225

Hornung Supply Company

Date	PR	Debit	Credit	Balance
Feb. 3	P1		350	350

Smite Company

Date	PR	Debit	Credit	Balance
Feb. 20	P1		300	300
28	D2	300		–0–

Wynet & Company

Date	PR	Debit	Credit	Balance
Feb. 13	P1		150	150
20	D2	150		–0–

*Cash Disbursements Journal in a *perpetual* system replaces "Purchases Discounts Cr." with "Inventory Cr." (see Exhibit 8.20).

transactions include purchases returns and allowances, purchases of plant assets by issuing a note payable, sales returns if a Sales Returns and Allowances Journal is not used, and receiving a note receivable from a customer. We described how transactions are recorded in a General Journal in Chapter 3.

Flash back

11. How are sales taxes recorded in the context of special journals?
12. What is direct posting of sales invoices?
13. Why does a company need a General Journal when using special journals for sales, purchases, cash receipts, and cash disbursements?

Answers—p. 342

Technology-Based Accounting Information Systems

Accounting information systems are supported with technology, which can range from simple calculators to state-of-the-art advanced electronic systems. Because technology is increasingly important in accounting information systems, we discuss in this section the impact of computer technology, how data processing works with accounting data, and the role of computer networks.

Middleware
The latest buzz in information systems is about "middleware." Middleware is software allowing different computer programs used in a company or across companies to work together. It allows transfer of purchase orders, invoices, and other electronic documents between trading partners' accounting systems. It also helps each partner's bank handle the electronic payments. [Source: *Business Week,* June 16, 1997.]

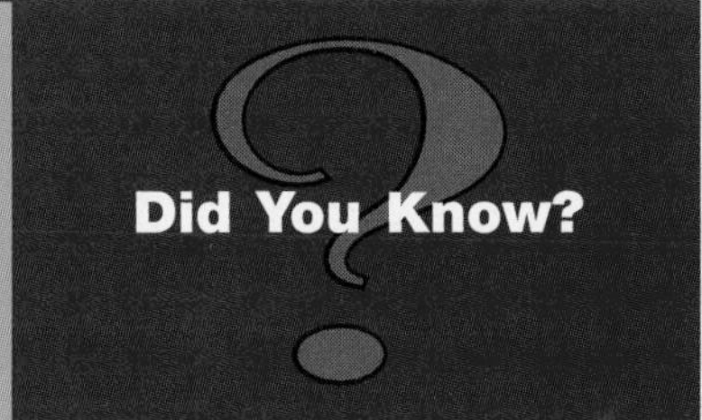

Computer Technology in Accounting

C5 Explain how technology-based information systems impact accounting.

Computer technology can be separated into two broad categories—hardware and software. **Computer hardware** is the physical equipment in a computerized accounting information system. The physical equipment includes processing units, hard drives, RAM, modems, CD-ROM drives, speakers, monitors, workstations, servers, notebooks, printers, scanners, and jukeboxes. Computer hardware increasingly assists accounting and accounting-related professionals in their work. Computer hardware often provides accuracy, speed, efficiency, and convenience in performing accounting tasks.

Computer software comprises the programs that direct the operations of computer hardware. A program is a series of commands directing operations such as data access from input or storage, data processing, or data output. A program can be written, for instance, to process customers' merchandise orders. A typical program works as follows. It creates a shipping order identifying products to be sent to customers. If this shipment causes the quantity on hand to fall below some minimum level, the program creates a purchase order to be approved by a manager. If the quantity on hand is less than what a customer ordered, the program creates a partial shipping order and a report to the customer that the remainder is on back order. If replacements are not on order already, the program creates a purchase order. If no units of the ordered product are on hand, the program creates a notification for the customer of a back order and creates a purchase order if necessary. The program continually processes customer orders as they arrive. This program can also be linked with accounting records for sales and accounts receivable, and it can deal with cash and trade discounts that might be offered to customers.

Widespread use of computer technology has increased the type and power of off-the-shelf programs that are ready to use. Off-the-shelf programs include multipurpose software applications for a variety of computer operations. These include familiar word processing programs such as *Word*® and *WordPerfect*®, spreadsheet programs such as *Excel*® and *Lotus 1-2-3*®, and database management programs such as *dBase*®. Other off-the-shelf programs meet the needs of specialized users. These include accounting programs such as *PeachTree*®, *DacEasy*®, and *QuickBooks*®. Off-the-shelf programs are designed to be user-friendly and guide users through all steps.

Off-the-shelf accounting programs can operate more efficiently as *integrated* systems. In an integrated system, actions taken in one part of the system automatically affect related parts. When a credit sale is recorded in an integrated system, for instance, several parts of the system are automatically updated. First, the system stores transaction data (as in a journal) so that we can review the entire entry at a later time. Second, it automatically updates the Cash and Accounts Receivable accounts. Third, it updates the record of amounts owed by a customer. Fourth, it updates the record of products held for sale to show the number of units sold and the number remaining.

Computer hardware and software can dramatically reduce the time and effort devoted to recordkeeping tasks. Less effort directed at recordkeeping tasks means more time for accounting professionals to concentrate on analysis and managerial type decision making. These advances have created an even greater demand for accounting professionals who understand financial reports and can draw insights and information from mountains of processed data. We must remember the primary demand for accounting knowledge is created by the need for information and not by the need for recordkeeping. Accounting professionals are in increasing demand because of expertise in determining relevant and reliable information for decision making. They are also valuable in analyzing the effects of transactions and events on a company and how they are reflected in financial statements and management reports.

Knowledge of the accounting described in this book enables us to understand and use accounting output. It also enables us to understand the transactions and events driving the output. In this way, and in this way only, can we expect to reap the full benefits of accounting reports. All the reports available can't help the external or internal user who fails to understand the accounting principles and methods determining the information.

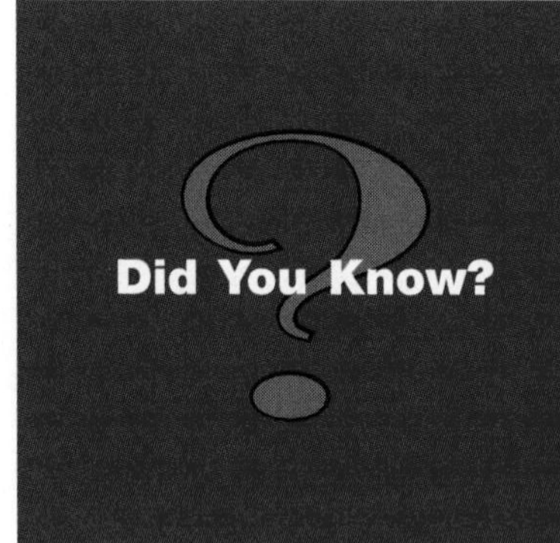

Software CPAs

A new generation of Windows-based accounting software is available. With the touch of a key, users can shift from cash to accrual accounting, and create real-time inventory reports showing all payments, charges, and credit limits at any point in the accounting cycle. Many also include "alert signals" notifying the user when, for example, a large order exceeds a customer's credit limit or purchase orders are needed. This software can also support all four inventory costing methods and do perpetual updating of records as each transaction occurs. **PeachTree Software** is the market leader for small businesses, and most programs cost under $250, with some as low as $50. [Source: *Business Week,* September 1, 1997.]

Data Processing in Accounting

Accounting systems differ in how input is entered and processed. **On-line processing** enters and processes data as soon as source documents are available. This means databases are immediately updated. **Batch processing** accumulates source documents for a period of time and then processes them all at once such as once a day, week, or month.

The advantage of on-line processing is up-to-date databases. This often requires additional costs related to both software and hardware requirements. Common on-line processing in practice includes airline reservations, credit card records, and rapid mail-order processing. The advantage of batch processing is it only requires periodic updating of databases. Records used in sending bills to customers, for instance, might require updating only once a month. The disadvantage of batch processing is the lack of updated databases for management when making business decisions.

Computer Networks in Accounting

Networking, or linking computers with each other, can create technology advantages. **Computer networks** are links among computers giving different users and different computers access to a common database and programs. Many colleges' computer labs, for instance, are networked. A small computer network is called a *local area network (LAN).* This type of network links machines with *hard-wire* hookups. Large computer networks extending over long distances often rely on *modem* communication.

Demand for information sometimes requires advanced networks such as the system used by **Federal Express** for tracking packages and billing customers, and the system used by **Wal-Mart** for monitoring inventory levels in its stores. These networks include many computers (desktops and mainframes) and satellite communications to gather information and to provide ready access to its database from all locations.

Flash *back*

14. Identify an advantage of an integrated computer-based accounting system.

15. What advantages do computer systems offer over manual systems?

16. Identify an advantage of computer networks.

Answers—p. 342

Enterprise-Application Software[4]

The market for enterprise-application software is soaring. **Enterprise-application software** includes the programs that manage a company's vital operations. They extend from order-taking to manufacturing to accounting. When working properly, these integrated programs can speed decision making, slash costs, and give managers control over global operations with the click of a mouse. Many see enterprise-applications emerging as a company's most strategic asset.

For many managers, enterprise-application software is like a lightbulb illuminating the dark recesses of their company's operations. It allows them to scrutinize a global business, identify where inventories are piling up, and see what plants are most efficient. The software is designed to link every part of a company's operations. This software allowed **Monsanto** to slash production planning from six weeks to three, trim inventories, reduce working capital, and increase its bargaining power with suppliers. **Monsanto** estimates this software saves the company $200 million per year.

There are six major enterprise-applications today. **SAP** dominates the market, with **Oracle** a distant second. SAP software runs the back offices of nearly half of the world's 500 largest companies. It links ordering, inventory, production, purchasing, planning, tracking, and human resources. One transaction or event triggers an immediate chain reaction of events throughout the enterprise. It is making companies more efficient and profitable.

Enterprise-applications are pushing into cyberspace. Now companies can share data with customers and suppliers. Applesauce maker **Mott's** is using SAP so that distribu-

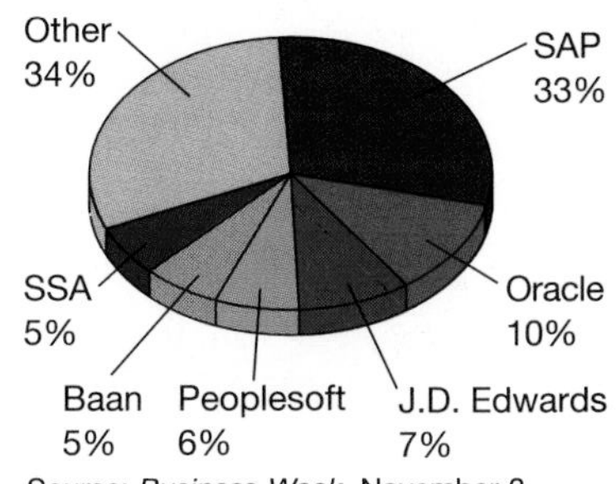

Source: *Business Week,* November 3, 1997.

[4]Source: S. Baker, A. Cortese, and G. Edmondson, "Silicon Valley on the Rhine," *Business Week,* (November 3, 1997).

tors can check the status of orders and place them over the Net, and the **Coca-Cola Company** uses it to ship soda on time. While enterprise-applications may not soon invade small business, it already controls many of our world's largest companies.

USING THE INFORMATION

Business Segments

A1 Analyze a company's performance and financial condition by business segments.

The accounting information system is usually more complex when a company is large and operates in more than one business segment. Special journals and subsidiary ledgers also are usually greater in number and more detailed for these companies.

Information about the business segments of a company is important to both internal and external decision makers. A **business segment** is the part of a company that is separately identified by its products or services or by the geographic market it serves. **NIKE,** for instance, states it operates "in one industry segment," and note 15 of its 1997 annual report shows its four main geographical markets: United States; Europe; Asia/Pacific; and Latin America/Canada. External users of financial statements are especially interested in segment information to better understand a company's business activities.

Information reported about business segments varies in quality and quantity. The full disclosure principle implies we ought to see detailed financial statements for each important segment. But full disclosure by segments is rare because of difficulties in separating segments and management's reluctance to release information that can harm its competitive position.

Companies offering their shares to the public in U.S. stock exchanges must disclose segment information under certain conditions. Accounting standards apply the definition of segments to industries, international activities, export sales, and major customers. A segment is considered important if its sales, operating income, *or* identifiable assets make up 10% or more of their respective totals. Companies are required to report information for these important segments.[5]

Exhibit 8.14 shows the results from a recent survey on the number of companies with business segments. Companies operating in different industries or geographic areas often have different rates of profitability, risk, and growth for these different segments. Evaluating risk and return is a major goal of decision makers, and segment information is useful in this evaluation.

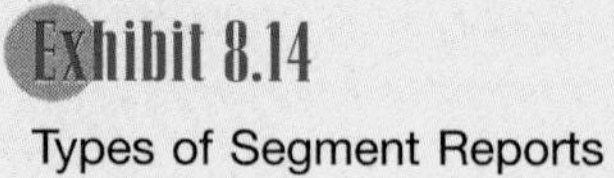

Types of Segment Reports

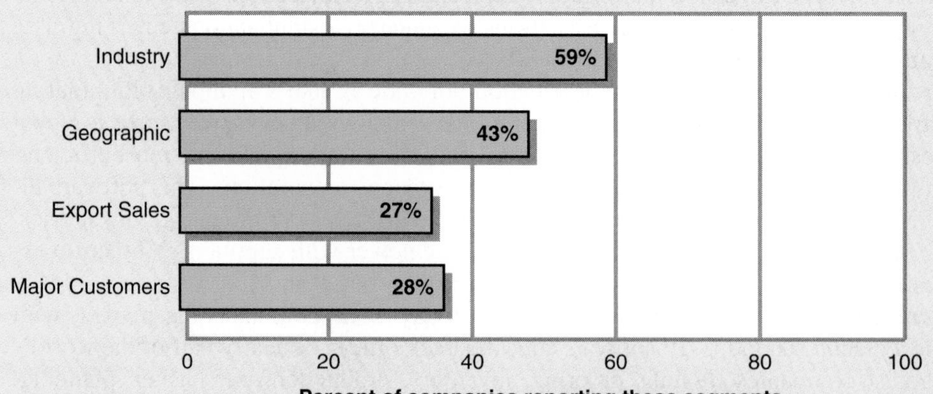

Source: *Accounting Trends & Techniques.* Total exceeds 100% because companies can report one or more segments.

[5] For each industry segment, companies must report: (1) net sales, (2) operating income before interest and taxes, (3) identifiable assets, (4) capital expenditures, and (5) depreciation, depletion, and amortization. Guidelines are given for defining a company's international operations, major customers, and export sales and for segmenting operations by geographic areas. Information similar to that reported for industry segments is required. [FASB, *Accounting Standards Current Text* (Norwalk, CT, 1994), sec. §20.101. First published as *FASB Statement No. 15.*]

Analysis of a company's segments is aided by a segment contribution matrix. A **segment contribution matrix** is a table listing of one or more important measures such as sales by segments. This listing usually includes amounts contributed both in dollars and percents, and its growth rate. We prepare a segment contribution matrix for **Woolworth's** sales in Exhibit 8.15.

Exhibit 8.15

Segment Contribution Matrix

Woolworth's Segment Contribution Matrix for Sales

Segment	Sales Contribution (in millions) 1996	Sales Contribution (in millions) 1995	Sales Contribution (in %) 1996	Sales Contribution (in %) 1995	1-Year Growth Rate Percent
Specialty:					
Athletic Group	$3,615	$3,424	45%	42%	6%
Northern Group	426	367	5%	4%	16%
Specialty Footwear	721	729	9%	9%	−1%
Other Specialty	442	579	5%	7%	−24%
Subtotal	$5,204	$5,099	64%	62%	2%
General Merchandise:					
Germany	$1,624	$1,733	20%	21%	−6%
United States	1,044	1,150	13%	14%	−9%
Other	220	242	3%	3%	−9%
Subtotal	$2,888	$3,125	36%	38%	−8%
Total	$8,092	$8,224	100%	100%	−2%

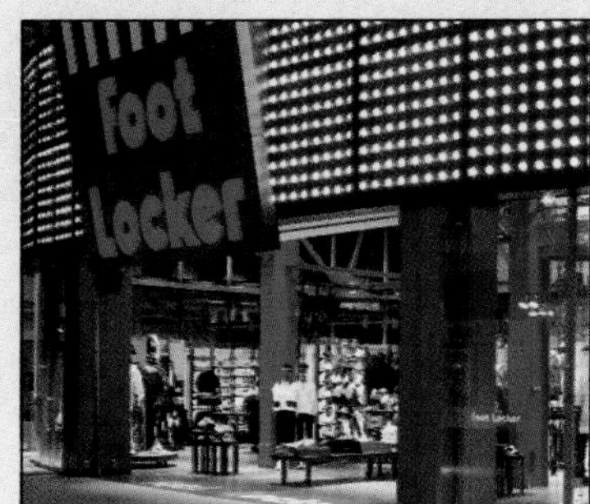

The second and third columns in Exhibit 8.15 list 1996 and 1995 sales data by segment. This data is drawn from Note 4 in Woolworth's 1996 annual report. We see that Woolworth's total 1996 sales were $8,092 million, divided into two major segments: (1) specialty and (2) general merchandise. The specialty segment is divided by a product emphasis, whereas the general merchandise segment is divided by geographic area. Standards permit this latitude. While information in these two columns is useful, several questions remain unanswered. What is the contribution of one segment versus another to total sales? Is there evidence of growth or decline by source? What is the highest growth segment? And which is the lowest? A segment contribution matrix provides us a starting point in answering such crucial questions.

Columns four and five of Exhibit 8.15 give us Woolworth's sales contribution in percent by segment. Each number is computed by taking a segment's sales and dividing by total sales. For example, the 1996 sales contribution in percent for the athletic group is computed as: $3,615 ÷ $8,092 = 0.45 or 45%.

The results tell us specialty merchandise makes up more than 60% of total sales, and most of it comes from its athletic group. This suggests Woolworth's sales are highly dependent on one area, the athletic group. A serious analysis of Woolworth demands special attention to this group. This includes assessing future prospects and the risk of competition for the athletic group. If we reviewed Woolworth's Management's Discussion and Analysis report we'd also find its Athletic Group is dominated by its **Foot Locker** stores and less so by its **Champs Sports** and **Going to the Game!** stores.

The far right column of Exhibit 8.15 shows the one-year growth rate in segment sales. A one-year growth rate is computed as: (Current period sales − Prior period sales) ÷ Prior period sales. For example, Woolworth's one-year growth rate in sales for its athletic group is computed as: ($3,615 − $3,424) ÷ $3,424 = 0.06 or 6%. The growth rates reveal several interesting findings. First, the northern group is growing faster than any other segment. Second, other specialty stores such as **After Thoughts** and **The Best of Times** are markedly declining in sales. Third, Woolworth's general merchandise segment reflects declining sales ranging from 6% to 9%. Fourth, while general merchandise has declined 8% in sales, the specialty segment has increased sales by 2%. We can extend our analysis of segment contribution matrixes to other measures such as operating income and assets. We show pie charts of Woolworth's assets breakdown in Exhibit 8.16 as an example of other analyses available to us.

Exhibit 8.16

Segment Asset Analysis
($ in millions)

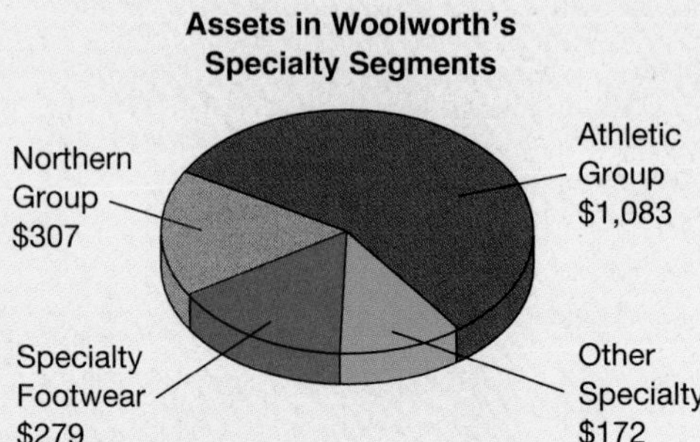

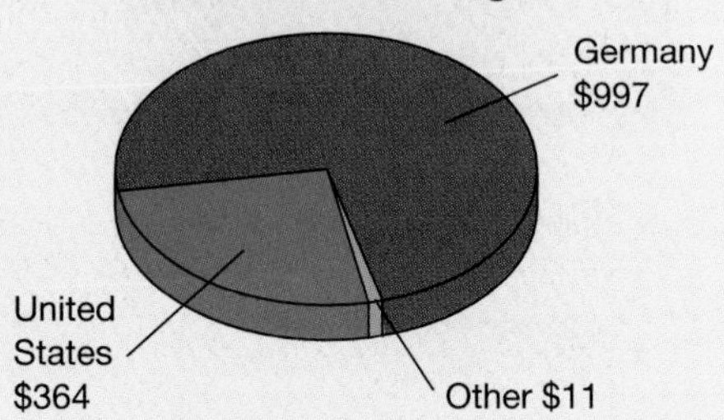

Banker

You are the banker from whom an owner of a merchandiser in mountain bikes requests a loan to expand operations. The merchandiser's financials reveal a solid net income of $220,000, reflecting a 10% increase over the prior year. You also ask about any segments or geographic focus. The owner tells you that $160,000 of net income was from Cuban operations, reflecting a 60% increase over the prior year. The remaining $60,000 of net income was from U.S. operations, reflecting a 40% decrease. The owner is a Cuban immigrant, and he tells of his relationships with family and friends in Cuba. Does this segment information impact your loan decision?

Answer—p. 341

Flash back

17. What are the advantages of using segment information for analysis of a company?

Answer—p. 342

Summary

C1 Identify fundamental principles of accounting information systems. Accounting information systems are governed by five fundamental principles: control, relevance, compatibility, flexibility, and cost-benefit principles.

C2 Identify components of accounting information systems. There are five basic components of an accounting information system: source documents, input devices, information processors, information storage, and output devices.

C3 Explain the goals and uses of special journals. Special journals are used for recording and posting transactions of similar type, each meant to cover one kind of transaction. Four of the most common special journals are the Sales Journal, Cash Receipts Journal, Purchases Journal, and Cash Disbursements Journal. Special journals are efficient and cost-effective tools in the journalizing and posting processes. Special journals allow an efficient division of labor that is also an effective control procedure.

C4 Describe the use of controlling accounts and subsidiary ledgers. A General Ledger keeps controlling accounts such as Accounts Receivable or Accounts Payable, but details on individual accounts making up the controlling account are kept in a subsidiary ledger (such as an Accounts Receivable Ledger). The balance in a controlling account must equal the sum of its subsidiary account balances after posting is complete.

C5 Explain how technology-based information systems impact accounting. Technology-based information systems aim to increase the accuracy, speed, efficiency, and convenience of accounting procedures. Developments in hardware and software, data processing, and networking all impact accounting in varying degrees.

A1 Analyze a company's performance and financial condition by business segments. A business segment is a part of a company that is separately identified by its products or services or by the geographic market it serves. Analysis of a company's segments is aided by a segment contribution matrix listing of one or more accounting measures such as sales by segments. This listing usually includes amounts contributed both in dollars and percents, and the segment's growth rate.

P1 **Journalize and post transactions using special journals.** Special journals are each devoted to similar kinds of transactions. Transactions are journalized on one line of a special journal, with columns devoted to specific accounts, dates, names, posting references, explanations, and other necessary information. Posting is threefold: (1) individual amounts in the Other Accounts column are posted to their General Ledger accounts on a regular (daily) basis, (2) individual amounts in a column that is posted in total to a controlling account at the end of a period (month) are posted regularly (daily) to their account in the subsidiary ledger, and (3) total amounts for all columns except the Other Accounts column are posted at the end of a period (month) to their column's account title.

P2 **Prepare and test the accuracy of subsidiary ledgers.** Account balances in the General Ledger and its subsidiary ledgers are tested for accuracy after posting is complete. This procedure is twofold: (1) prepare a trial balance of the General Ledger to confirm debits equal credits, and (2) prepare a schedule of a subsidiary ledger to confirm the controlling account's balance equals the subsidiary ledger's balance. A schedule is a listing of accounts from a subsidiary ledger with their balances and the sum of all balances.

Guidance Answer to **Judgment and Ethics**

Certified Public Accountant

As a CPA you are guided by the AICPA's Code of Professional Conduct described in Chapter 1 and listed near the end of the book. Here the main issue is whether commissions have an actual or perceived impact on the integrity and objectivity of your advice. The Code says you should not accept a commission arrangement if you either perform an audit or a review of the client's financial statements. The Code also precludes a commission if you compile the client's statements, unless the compilation report discloses a lack of independence. Even in situations where a commission is allowed, the Code requires you tell the client of your commission arrangement. These suggested actions seem appropriate even if you are not bound by the Code. Also, you need to seriously examine the merits of agreeing to a commission arrangement when you are in a position to exploit it.

Guidance Answers to **You Make the Call**

Retailer

The Accounts Receivable Ledger has much of the information you need. It lists detailed information for each customer's account, including the amounts, dates for transactions, and dates of payments. It can be reorganized into an "aging schedule" to show how long customers wait before paying their bills. We describe an aging schedule in Chapter 10.

Controller

Much of the information you need is in the Accounts Payable Ledger. It contains information for each supplier, the amounts due, and when payments are made. This subsidiary ledger along with information on credit terms should enable you to conduct your analyses.

Banker

This merchandiser's segment information is likely to greatly impact your loan decision. The risks associated with this merchandiser's two sources of net income are quite different. While net income is up by 10%, U.S. operations are performing poorly and Cuban operations are subject to many uncertainties. These uncertainties depend on political events, friends and family relationships, Cuban economic conditions, and a host of other risks. While net income results suggested a low-risk loan opportunity, the segment information reveals a high-risk situation.

Guidance Answers to 

1. The five primary components are source documents, input devices, information processors, information storage, and output devices.
2. An information processor interprets, transforms, and summarizes the recorded information so that it can be used in analysis and reports.
3. Data saved in information storage are used to prepare periodic financial reports, special-purpose internal reports, and as source documentation for auditors and other users.
4. All cash payments by check are recorded in the Cash Disbursements Journal.
5. Columnar journals allow us to accumulate repetitive debits and credits and post them as column totals rather than as individual amounts.
6. The equality of debits and credits is kept within the General Ledger. The subsidiary ledger keeps the customer's individual account and is used only for supplementary information.
7. An initial and page number of the journal from which the amount was posted is entered in the Posting Reference column of the ledger account next to the amount.
8. The normal recording and posting procedures are threefold. First, transactions are entered in a special journal column if applicable. Second, individual amounts are posted to the subsidiary ledger accounts. Third, column totals are posted to General Ledger accounts.
9. The controlling account must be debited periodically for an amount or amounts equal to the sum of the debits to the subsidiary ledger, and it must be credited periodically for an amount or amounts equal to the sum of the credits to the subsidiary ledger.

10. Tests for accuracy of account balances in the General Ledger and subsidiary ledgers are twofold. First, we prepare a trial balance of the General Ledger to confirm debits equal credits. Second, we test the subsidiary ledgers by preparing schedules of accounts receivable and accounts payable.
11. A separate column for Sales Taxes Payable can be included in both the Cash Receipts Journal and the Sales Journal.
12. This refers to a procedure of using copies of sales invoices as a Sales Journal. Each invoice total is posted directly to the customer's account, and all invoices are totaled at month-end for posting to the General Ledger accounts.
13. The General Journal is still needed for adjusting, closing, and correcting entries and for special transactions such as sales returns, purchases returns, and plant asset purchases.
14. Integrated systems can save time and minimize errors. This is because actions taken in one part of the system automatically affect and update related parts.
15. Computer systems offer increased accuracy, speed, efficiency, and convenience.
16. Computer networks can create advantages by linking computers, giving different users and different computers access to a common database and programs.
17. Segment information helps us evaluate the risk and return attributes of a company. Companies operating in different business segments often have different rates of profitability, risk, and growth for these segments. This information helps us gain insight into the performance of a segment and its importance for a company's future.

Demonstration Problem

The Pepper Company completed these transactions during March of year 2000:

Mar. 4 Sold merchandise on credit to Jennifer Nelson, Invoice No. 954, $16,800. (Terms of all credit sales are 2/10, n/30.)

6 Purchased office supplies on credit from Mack Company, $1,220. Invoice dated March 3, terms n/30.

6 Sold merchandise on credit to Dennie Hoskins, Invoice No. 955, $10,200.

11 Received merchandise and an invoice dated March 6, terms 2/10, n/30, from Defore Industries, $52,600.

12 Borrowed $26,000 by giving Commerce Bank a long-term promissory note payable.

14 Received payment from Jennifer Nelson for the March 4 sale less the discount.

16 Received a credit memorandum from Defore Industries for unsatisfactory merchandise received on March 11 and returned for credit, $200.

16 Received payment from Dennie Hoskins for the March 6 sale less the discount.

18 Purchased store equipment on credit from Schmidt Supply, invoice dated March 15, terms n/30, $22,850.

20 Sold merchandise on credit to Marjorie Allen, Invoice No. 956, $5,600.

21 Sent Defore Industries Check No. 516 in payment of its March 6 invoice less the returns and the discount.

22 Received merchandise and an invoice dated March 18, terms 2/10, n/30, from the Welch Company, $41,625.

26 Issued a credit memorandum to Marjorie Allen for defective merchandise sold on March 22 and returned for credit $600.

31 Issued Check No. 517, payable to Payroll, in payment of sales salaries for the month, $15,900. Cashed the check and paid the employees.

31 Cash sales for the month were $134,680. (Cash sales are usually recorded daily; however, they are recorded only once in this problem to reduce the repetitive entries.)

31 Post to the customer and creditor accounts. Also, post any amounts that should be posted as individual amounts to General Ledger accounts.

31 Foot and crossfoot the journals and make the month-end postings.

Required

1. Open the following General Ledger accounts: Cash (101), Accounts Receivable (106), Office Supplies (124), Store Equipment (165), Accounts Payable (201), Long-Term Notes Payable (251), Sales (413), Sales Returns and Allowances (414), Sales Discounts (415), Purchases (505), Purchases Returns and Allowances (506), Purchases Discounts (507), and Sales Salaries Expense (621).
2. Open the following Accounts Receivable Ledger accounts: Marjorie Allen, Dennie Hoskins, and Jennifer Nelson.
3. Open the following Accounts Payable Ledger accounts: Defore Industries, Mack Company, Schmidt Supply, and Welch Company.
4. Enter the transactions in a Sales Journal, a Purchases Journal, a Cash Receipts Journal, a Cash Disbursements Journal, and a General Journal similar to the ones illustrated in the chapter. Post at the end of the month. Pepper Co. uses the periodic inventory system.

5. Prepare a trial balance and test the accuracy of subsidiary ledgers by preparing schedules of accounts receivable and accounts payable.

Planning the Solution

- Set up the required general ledger and subsidiary ledger accounts and the five required journals as illustrated in the chapter.
- First read and analyze each transaction and decide in which special journal (or general journal) the transaction is recorded.
- Record each transaction in the proper journal.
- Once you have recorded all transactions, total the journal columns.
- Post from each journal to the appropriate ledger accounts.
- After you have completed posting, prepare a trial balance to prove the equality of the debit and credit balances in your general ledger.
- Prepare schedules of accounts receivable and accounts payable. Compare the total of the schedules to the accounts receivable and accounts payable controlling account balances, making sure that they agree.

Solution to Demonstration Problem

Sales Journal — Page 2

Date		Account Debited	Invoice Number	PR	Accts. Rec. Dr. Sales Cr.
Mar.	4	Jennifer Nelson	954	✓	16,800
	6	Dennie Hoskins	955	✓	10,200
	20	Marjorie Allen	956	✓	5,600
	31	Totals			32,600
					(106/413)

Purchases Journal — Page 3

Date		Account	Date of Invoice	Terms	PR	Accts. Payable Credit	Purchases Debit	Office Supplies Debit	Other Accts. Debit
Mar.	6	Office Supplies/Mack Co	3/3	n/30	✓	1,220		1,220	
	11	Defore Industries	3/6	2/10, n/30	✓	52,600	52,600		
	18	Store Equipment/Schmidt Supp . .	3/15	n/30	165/✓	22,850			22,850
	22	Welch Company	3/18	2/10, n/30	✓	41,625	41,625		
	31	Totals				118,295	94,225	1,220	22,850
						(201)	(505)	(124)	(✓)

Cash Receipts Journal — Page 3

Date		Account Credited	Explanation	PR	Cash Debit	Sales Discount Debit	Accts. Rec. Credit	Sales Credit	Other Accts. Credit
Mar.	12	L.T. Notes Pay . . .	Note to bank . . .	251	26,000				26,000
	14	Jennifer Nelson . . .	Invoice, 3/4	✓	16,464	336	16,800		
	16	Dennie Hoskins . . .	Invoice, 3/6	✓	9,996	204	10,200		
	31	Sales	Cash sales	✓	134,680			134,680	
	31	Totals			187,140	540	27,000	134,680	26,000
					(101)	(415)	(106)	(413)	(✓)

Cash Disbursements Journal — Page 3

Date		Ck. No.	Payee	Account Debited	PR	Cash Credit	Purch. Disc. Credit	Other Accts. Debit	Accts. Payable Debit
Mar.	21	516	Defore Industries . . .	Defore Industries	✓	51,352	1,048		52,400
	31	517	Payroll	Sales Salaries Expense . . .	621	15,900		15,900	
	31		Totals			67,252	1,048	15,900	52,400
						(101)	(507)	(✓)	(201)

General Journal — Page 2

Date	Account	PR	Debit	Credit
Mar. 16	Accounts Payable—Defore Industries	201/✓	200	
	Purchases Returns and Allowances	506		200
26	Sales Returns and Allowances	414	600	
	Accounts Receivable—Marjorie Allen	106/✓		600

Accounts Receivable Ledger

Marjorie Allen

Date	Explanation	PR	Debit	Credit	Balance
Mar. 20		S2	5,600		5,600
26		G2		600	5,000

Dennie Hoskins

Date	Explanation	PR	Debit	Credit	Balance
Mar. 6		S2	10,200		10,200
16		R3		10,200	0

Jennifer Nelson

Date	Explanation	PR	Debit	Credit	Balance
Mar. 4		S2	16,800		16,800
14		R3		16,800	0

Accounts Payable Ledger

Defore Industries

Date	Explanation	PR	Debit	Credit	Balance
Mar. 11		P3		52,600	52,600
16		G2	200		52,400
21		D3	52,400		0

Mack Company

Date	Explanation	PR	Debit	Credit	Balance
Mar. 6		P3		1,220	1,220

Schmidt Supply

Date	Explanation	PR	Debit	Credit	Balance
Mar. 18		P3		22,850	22,850

Welch Company

Date	Explanation	PR	Debit	Credit	Balance
Mar. 22		P3		41,625	41,625

General Ledger

Cash Acct. No. 101

Date	Explanation	PR	Debit	Credit	Balance
Mar. 31		R3	187,140		187,140
31		D4		67,252	119,888

Accounts Receivable Acct. No. 106

Date	Explanation	PR	Debit	Credit	Balance
Mar. 26		G2		600	(600)
31		S2	32,600		32,000
31		R3		27,000	5,000

Office Supplies Acct. No. 124

Date	Explanation	PR	Debit	Credit	Balance
Mar. 31		P3	1,220		1,220

Store Equipment Acct. No. 165

Date	Explanation	PR	Debit	Credit	Balance
Mar. 18		P3	22,850		22,850

Accounts Payable Acct. No. 201

Date	Explanation	PR	Debit	Credit	Balance
Mar. 6		G2	200		(200)
31		P2		118,295	118,095
31		D3	52,400		65,695

Long-Term Notes Payable Acct. No. 251

Date	Explanation	PR	Debit	Credit	Balance
Mar. 12				26,000	26,000

Sales Acct. No. 413

Date	Explanation	PR	Debit	Credit	Balance
Mar. 31		S2		32,600	32,600
31		R3		134,680	167,280

Sales Returns and Allowances Acct. No. 414

Date	Explanation	PR	Debit	Credit	Balance
Mar. 26		G2	600		600

Sales Discounts Acct. No. 415

Date	Explanation	PR	Debit	Credit	Balance
Mar. 31		R3	540		540

Purchases — Acct. No. 505

Date	Explanation	PR	Debit	Credit	Balance
Mar. 31		P2	94,225		94,225

Purchases Returns and Allowances — Acct. No. 506

Date	Explanation	PR	Debit	Credit	Balance
Mar. 6		G2		200	200

Purchases Discounts — Acct. No. 507

Date	Explanation	PR	Debit	Credit	Balance
Mar. 31		D4		1,048	1,048

Sales Salaries Expense — Acct. No. 621

Date	Explanation	PR	Debit	Credit	Balance
Mar. 31		D3	15,900		15,900

PEPPER COMPANY
Trial Balance
March 31, 2000

Cash	$119,888	
Accounts receivable	5,000	
Office supplies	1,220	
Store equipment	22,850	
Accounts payable		$ 65,695
Long-term notes payable		26,000
Sales		167,280
Sales returns and allowances	600	
Sales discounts	540	
Purchases	94,225	
Purchases returns and allowances		200
Purchases discounts		1,048
Sales salaries expense	15,900	
Totals	$260,223	$260,223

PEPPER COMPANY
Schedule of Accounts Receivable
March 31, 2000

Marjorie Allen	$5,000
Total accounts receivable	$5,000

PEPPER COMPANY
Schedule of Accounts Payable
March 31, 2000

Mack Company	$ 1,220
Schmidt Supply	22,850
Welch Company	41,625
Total accounts payable	$65,695

Special Journals under a Perpetual System

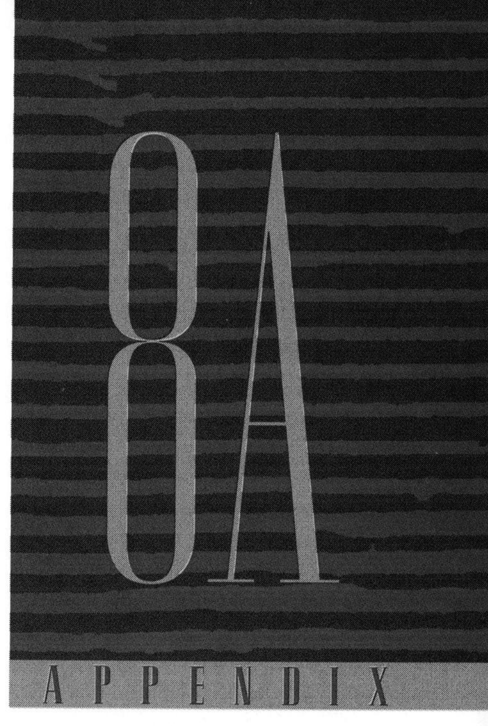

Learning Objective

Procedural

P3 Journalize and post transactions using special journals in a perpetual inventory system.

This appendix shows the special journals under a perpetual inventory system. Each journal is slightly impacted. The Sales Journal and the Cash Receipts Journal each require one new column titled "Cost of Goods Sold Dr., Inventory Cr." The Purchases Journal replaces the "Purchases Dr." column with an "Inventory Dr." column in a perpetual system. The Cash Disbursements Journal replaces the "Purchases Discounts Cr." column with an "Inventory Cr." column in a perpetual system. These changes are illustrated below.

Sales Journal

The Sales Journal for Outdoors Unlimited using the perpetual inventory system is shown in Exhibit 8A.1. The difference in the Sales Journal between the perpetual and periodic system is the addition of a new column to record cost of goods sold and inventory amounts for each sale. The periodic system does not record the increase in cost of goods sold and decrease in inventory at the time of sale. The total of the cost of goods sold and inventory amount column is posted to both of their General Ledger accounts at the end of the period.

Exhibit 8A.1

Sales Journal—Perpetual System

Outdoors Unlimited Sales Journal Page 3

Date	Account Debited	Invoice Number	PR	Accounts Receivable Dr. Sales Cr.	Cost of Goods Sold Dr. Inventory Cr.
Feb. 2	Jason Henry	307	✓	450	315
7	Albert Co.	308	✓	500	355
13	Bam Moore	309	✓	350	260
15	Paul Roth	310	✓	200	150
22	Jason Henry	311	✓	225	155
25	Frank Booth	312	✓	175	95
28	Albert Co.	313	✓	250	170
28	Total			2,150	1,500
				(106/413)	(502/119)

Cash Receipts Journal

The Cash Receipts Journal under the perpetual system is shown in Exhibit 8A.2. Note the addition of a new column on the far right side to record debits to Cost of Goods Sold and credits to Inventory for the cost of merchandise sold. Consistent with the Cash Receipts Journal shown under the periodic system in the chapter, we only show the weekly cash sale entries. But remember that under a perpetual system, these cash sales are recorded at the point of sale. To do that here would make this journal extremely lengthy since Outdoors Unlimited is a retailer with many cash sales every day. Note also that cash received from earlier credit sales does not result in amounts entered in the far right column. This is because the costs for these sales were recorded in the Sales Journal at the point of sale. The total of the cost of goods sold and inventory amount column is posted to both of their General Ledger accounts at the end of the period.

Exhibit 8A.2

Cash Receipts Journal—Perpetual System

Outdoors Unlimited Cash Receipts Journal Page 2

Date	Account Credited	Explanation	PR	Cash Dr.	Sales Discount Cr.	Accounts Receivable Cr.	Sales Cr.	Other Accounts Cr.	Cost of Goods Sold Dr. Inventory Cr.
Feb. 7	Sales	Cash sales	✓	4,450			4,450		3,150
12	Jason Henry	Invoice, 2/2	✓	441	9	450			
14	Sales	Cash sales	✓	3,925			3,925		2,950
17	Albert Co.	Invoice, 2/7	✓	490	10	500			
20	Notes Payable	Note to bank	245	750				750	
21	Sales	Cash sales	✓	4,700			4,700		3,400
22	Interest revenue	Bank account	409	250				250	
23	Bam Moore	Invoice, 2/13	✓	343	7	350			
25	Paul Roth	Invoice, 2/15	✓	196	4	200			
28	Sales	Cash sales	✓	4,225			4,225		3,050
28	Totals			19,770	30	1,500	17,300	1,000	12,550
				(101)	(415)	(106)	(413)	(✓)	(502/119)

Purchases Journal

The Purchases Journal under the perpetual system is shown in Exhibit 8A.3. This journal in a perpetual system includes an Inventory column where the periodic system had a Purchases column. All else is identical under the two systems.

Exhibit 8A.3

Purchases Journal—Perpetual System

Outdoors Unlimited Purchases Journal Page 1

Date	Account	Date of Invoice	Terms	PR	Accounts Payable Cr.	Inventory Dr.	Office Supplies Dr.	Other Accounts Dr.
Feb. 3	Homung Supply Co.	2/2	n/30	✓	350	275	75	
5	Ace Mfg. Co.	2/5	2/10, n/30	✓	200	200		
13	Wynet and Co.	2/10	2/10, n/30	✓	150	150		
20	Smite Co.	2/18	2/10, n/30	✓	300	300		
25	Ace Mfg. Co.	2/24	2/10, n/30	✓	100	100		
28	Store Supplies/ITT Co.	2/28	n/30	125/✓	225	125	25	75
28	Totals				1,325	1,150	100	75
					(201)	(505)	(124)	(✓)

Cash Disbursements Journal

The Cash Disbursements Journal in a perpetual system is shown in Exhibit 8A.4. This journal includes an Inventory column where the periodic system had the Purchases Discounts column. All else is identical under the two systems. When a company has several cash purchases of inventory, it often adds a new column for Inventory Debit entries.

Exhibit 8A.4

Cash Disbursements Journal—Perpetual System

Outdoors Unlimited Cash Disbursements Journal Page 2

Date	Ck. No.	Payee	Account Debited	PR	Cash Cr.	Inventory Cr.	Other Accounts Dr.	Accounts Payable Dr.
Feb. 3	105	L. and N. Railroad	Transportation-In	508	15		15	
12	106	East Sales Co.	Purchases	505	25		25	
15	107	Ace Mfg. Co.	Ace Mfg. Co.	✓	196	4		200
15	108	Jerry Hale	Salaries Expense	622	250		250	
20	109	Wynet and Co.	Wynet and Co.	✓	147	3		150
28	110	Smite Co.	Smite Co.	✓	294	6		300
28		Totals			927	13	290	650
					(101)	(507)	(✓)	(201)

Summary of Appendix 8A

P3 Journalize and post transactions using special journals in a perpetual inventory system. Transactions are journalized and posted using special journals in a perpetual system. The methods are similar to those in a periodic system, with the primary difference being that the cost of goods sold and inventory need adjusting at the time of each sale. This normally results in the addition of one or more columns devoted to these accounts in each special journal.

Glossary

Accounting information system the people, records, methods, and equipment that collect and process data from transactions and events, organize them in useful forms, and communicate results to decision makers. (p. 318).

Accounts Payable Ledger a subsidiary ledger listing individual creditor accounts. (p. 324).

Accounts Receivable Ledger a subsidiary ledger listing individual credit customer accounts. (p. 324).

Batch processing an approach to inputting data that accumulates source documents for a period of time and then processes them all at once such as once a day, week, or month. (p. 336).

Business segment a part of a company that can be separately identified by the products or services that it provides or a geographic market that it serves. (p. 338).

Cash Disbursements Journal the special journal that is used to record all payments of cash; also called *Cash Payments Journal.* (p. 332).

Cash Receipts Journal the special journal that is used to record all receipts of cash. (p. 328).

Check Register another name for a cash disbursements journal when the journal has a column for check numbers. (p. 383).

Columnar journal a journal with more than one column. (p. 326).

Compatibility principle an information system principle that requires an accounting information system conform with a company's activities, personnel, and structure. (p. 319).

Computer hardware the physical equipment in a computerized accounting information system. (p. 335).

Computer network a link among computers giving different users and different computers access to a common database and programs. (p. 337).

Computer software the programs that direct the operations of computer hardware. (p. 335).

Controlling account a General Ledger account, the balance of which (after posting) equals the sum of the balances of the accounts in a related subsidiary ledger. (p. 324).

Control principle an information system principle that requires an accounting information system to aid managers in controlling and monitoring business activities. (p. 318).

Cost-benefit principle an information system principle that requires the benefits from an activity in an accounting information system to outweigh the costs of that activity. (p. 319).

Enterprise-application software programs that manage a company's vital operations which range from order-taking to manufacturing to accounting. (p. 337).

Flexibility principle an information system principle that requires an accounting information system to be able to adapt to changes in the company, business environment, and needs of decision makers. (p. 319).

Information processor the component of an accounting system that interprets, transforms, and summarizes information for use in analysis and reporting. (p. 320).

Information storage the component of an accounting system that keeps data in a form accessible to information processors. (p. 321).

Input device a means of capturing information from source documents that enables its transfer to the information processing component of an accounting system. (p. 320).

On-line processing an approach to inputting data whereby the data on each source document is inputted as soon as the document is available. (p. 336).

Output devices the means by which information is taken out of the accounting system and made available for use. (p. 321).

Purchases Journal a journal that is used to record all purchases on credit. (p. 331).

Relevance principle an information system principle requiring that an accounting information system report useful, understandable, timely, and pertinent information for effective decision making. (p. 318).

Sales Journal a journal used to record sales of merchandise on credit. (p. 325).

Schedule of accounts payable a list of the balances of all the accounts in the Accounts Payable Ledger that is summed to show the total amount of accounts payable outstanding. (p. 331).

Schedule of accounts receivable a list of the balances of all the accounts in the Accounts Receivable Ledger that is summed to show the total amount of accounts receivable outstanding. (p. 326).

Segment contribution matrix a table listing one or more important measures such as sales by segment; usually includes amounts in dollars and percents along with a growth rate. (p. 339).

Special journal any journal that is used for recording and posting transactions of a similar type. (p. 323).

Subsidiary ledger a listing of individual accounts with a common characteristic; linked to a controlling account in the General Ledger. (p. 323).

Questions

1. When special journals are used, separate journals normally are used to record each of four different types of transactions. What are these four types of transactions?
2. Why should sales to and receipts of cash from credit customers be recorded and posted daily?
3. Both credits to customer accounts and credits to miscellaneous accounts are individually posted from a Cash Receipts Journal similar to the one in Exhibit 8.9. Why not put both kinds of credits in the same column and save journal space?
4. Describe the procedures involving the use of copies of a company's sales invoices as a Sales Journal.
5. When a general journal entry is used to record a returned credit sale, the credit of the entry must be posted twice. Does this cause the trial balance to be out of balance? Why or why not?
6. What notations are entered into the Posting Reference column of a ledger account?
7. What are five basic components of an accounting system?
8. What are source documents? Give some examples.
9. What is the purpose of an input device? Give some examples of input devices for computer systems.
10. What is the difference between data that is stored off-line and data that is stored on-line?
11. What purpose is served by the output devices of an accounting system?
12. What is the difference between batch and on-line processing?
13. Locate the footnote that discusses **NIKE's** industry segment and operations by geographic area in Appendix A. What industry segment does NIKE predominantly operate in? Identify the geographic areas for which NIKE discloses revenues, operating income, and assets.
14. Does the income statement of **Reebok** in Appendix A indicate the Net Income earned by Reebok's business segments? If yes, then list them.
15. Does the balance sheet of **America Online** in Appendix A indicate the identifiable assets owned by America Online's business segments? If yes, then list them.

16. Identify all of the special journals that Maria Lopez is now likely keeping for **Outdoors Limited.** What does Maria mean when she says she now keeps an aging schedule on late-paying customers?

Quick Study

QS 8-1
Special journal identification
C3

Trenton Electronics uses a Sales Journal, a Purchases Journal, a Cash Receipts Journal, a Cash Disbursements Journal, and a General Journal. Trenton recently completed the following transactions. List the transaction letters and next to each letter give the name of the journal in which the transaction should be recorded.

a. Sold merchandise on credit.
b. Purchased shop supplies on credit.
c. Paid an employee's salary.
d. Paid a creditor.
e. Purchased merchandise on credit.
f. Borrowed money from the bank.
g. Sold merchandise for cash.

QS 8-2
Entries in the general journal

The Nostalgic Book Shop uses a Sales Journal, a Purchases Journal, a Cash Receipts Journal, a Cash Disbursements Journal, and a General Journal. The following transactions occurred during the month of November. Journalize the November transactions that should be recorded in the General Journal.

Nov.	2	Purchased merchandise on credit for $2,900 from the Ringdol Co., terms 2/10, n/30.
	12	The owner, G. Werthman, contributed an automobile worth $15,000 to the business.
	16	Sold merchandise on credit to R. Wyder for $1,100, terms n/30.
	19	R. Wyder returned $150 of merchandise originally purchased on November 16.

QS 8-3
Accounting information system components

Identify the most likely role in an accounting system played by each of the lettered items *a* through *j* by assigning a number from the list on the left:

1. Source documents	_____ **a.** Bar-code reader
2. Input devices	_____ **b.** Filing cabinet
3. Information processor	_____ **c.** Bank statement
4. Information storage	_____ **d.** Calculator
5. Output devices	_____ **e.** Computer keyboard
	_____ **f.** Floppy diskette
	_____ **g.** Computer monitor
	_____ **h.** Invoice from a supplier
	_____ **i.** Computer software
	_____ **j.** Computer printer

QS 8-4
Accounting information system
C2

Fill in the blanks to complete the following descriptions:

a. A _________ is an input device that captures writing and other input directly from source documents.

b. _______-________ ________ are programs that help manage a company's vital operations, from manufacturing to accounting.

c. With _______ processing, source documents are accumulated for a period of time and then processed all at the same time, such as once a day, week, or month.

d. A computer ________ allows different computer users to share access to data and programs.

QS 8-5
Required segment reporting
A1

Trex is a company with publicly traded securities that operates in more than one industry. Which of the following items of information about each industry segment must the company report?

a. Revenues
b. Net sales
c. Operating income
d. Operating expenses
e. Capital expenditures
f. Amortization and depreciation
g. Cash flows
h. Identifiable assets

QS 8-6
Accounting information system principles
C1

Place the letter for each principle in the blank next to its best description below.

A. Control principle
B. Relevance principle
C. Compatibility principle
D. Flexibility principle
E. Cost-Benefit principle

1. _________ The principle requiring the information system to adapt to the unique characteristics of the company.

2. _________ The principle that affects all other accounting information system principles.

3. _________ The principle requiring the accounting information system to change in response to technological advances and competitive pressures.

4. _________ The principle requiring the accounting information system to help monitor activities.

5. _________ The principle requiring the system to provide timely information for effective decision-making.

Exercises

Exercise 8-1
Sales Journal
P1

Spindle Company uses a Sales Journal, a Purchases Journal, a Cash Receipts Journal, a Cash Disbursements Journal, and a General Journal. The following transactions occurred in the month of February:

Feb. 2 Sold merchandise to S. Mayer for $450 cash, invoice no. 5703.
5 Purchased merchandise on credit from Camp Corp., $2,300.
7 Sold merchandise to J. Eason for $1,150, terms 2/10, n/30, invoice no. 5704.
8 Borrowed $8,000 by giving a note to the bank.
12 Sold merchandise to P. Lathan for $320, terms n/30, invoice no. 5705.
16 Received $1,127 from J. Eason to pay for the purchase of February 7.
19 Sold used store equipment to Whiten, Inc., for $900.
25 Sold merchandise to S. Summers for $550, terms n/30, invoice no. 5706.

Required

Prepare headings for a Sales Journal like the one in Exhibit 8.5. Journalize the February transactions that should be recorded in the Sales Journal.

Exercise 8-2
Cash Receipts Journal

P1

SeaMap Company uses a Sales Journal, a Purchases Journal, a Cash Receipts Journal, a Cash Disbursements Journal, and a General Journal. The following transactions occurred in the month of September:

Sept. 3 Purchased merchandise on credit for $3,100 from Pacer Co.
7 Sold merchandise on credit to J. Namal for $900, subject to a $18 sales discount if paid by the end of the month.
9 Borrowed $2,750 by giving a note to the bank.
13 Received a capital contribution of $4,000 from J. Costeau, the owner of the company.
18 Sold merchandise to B. Baird for $230 cash.
22 Paid Pacer Co. $3,100 for the merchandise purchased on September 3.
27 Received $882 from J. Namal in payment of the September 7 purchase.
30 Paid salaries of $1,600.

Required

Prepare headings for a Cash Receipts Journal like the one in Exhibit 8.9. Journalize the September transactions that should be recorded in the Cash Receipts Journal.

Exercise 8-3
Purchases Journal
P1

Chem Company uses a Sales Journal, a Purchases Journal, a Cash Receipts Journal, a Cash Disbursements Journal, and a General Journal. The following transactions occurred in the month of July:

July 1 Purchased merchandise on credit for $8,100 from Angler, Inc., terms n/30.
8 Sold merchandise on credit to B. Harren for $1,500, subject to a $30 sales discount if paid by the end of the month.
14 Purchased store supplies from Steck Company on credit for $240, terms n/30.
17 Purchased office supplies on credit from Marten Company for $260, terms n/30.
24 Sold merchandise to W. Winger for $630 cash.
28 Purchased store supplies from Hadley's for $90 cash.
29 Paid Angler, Inc., $8,100 for the merchandise purchased on July 1.

Required

Prepare headings for a Purchases Journal like the one in Exhibit 8.11. Journalize the July transactions that should be recorded in the Purchases Journal.

Exercise 8-4
Cash Disbursements Journal
P1

Aeron Supply uses a Sales Journal, a Purchases Journal, a Cash Receipts Journal, a Cash Disbursements Journal, and a General Journal. The following transactions occurred in the month of March:

Mar. 3 Purchased merchandise for $2,750 on credit from Pace, Inc., terms 2/10, n/30.
9 Issued check no. 210 to Narlin Corp. to buy store supplies for $450.
12 Sold merchandise on credit to K. Camp for $670, terms n/30.
17 Issued check no. 211 for $1,500 to repay a note payable to City Bank.
20 Purchased merchandise for $3,500 on credit from LeBaron, terms 2/10, n/30.
29 Issued check no. 212 to LeBaron to pay the amount due for the purchase of March 20, less the discount.
31 Paid salary of $1,700 to E. Brandon by issuing check no. 213.
31 Issued check no. 214 to Pace, Inc., to pay the amount due for the purchase of March 3.

Required

Prepare headings for a Cash Disbursements Journal like the one in Exhibit 8.13. Journalize the March transactions that should be recorded in the Cash Disbursements Journal.

Exercise 8-5
Special journal transactions and error discovery

P1

Simon Pharmacy uses the following journals: Sales Journal, Purchases Journal, Cash Receipts Journal, Cash Disbursements Journal, and General Journal. On June 5, Simon purchased merchandise priced at $12,000, subject to credit terms of 2/10, n/30. On June 14, the pharmacy paid the net amount due. But in journalizing the payment, the accountant debited Accounts Payable for $12,000 and failed to record the cash discount. Cash was credited for the actual amount paid. In what journals would the June 5 and the June 14 transactions have been recorded? What procedure is likely to discover the error in journalizing the June 14 transaction?

Exercise 8-6
Posting to subsidiary ledger accounts

P1, P2

At the end of May, the Sales Journal of Camper Goods appears as follows:

Sales Journal					
Date		Account Debited	Invoice Number	PR	Accounts Receivable Dr. Sales Cr.
May	6	Brad Smithers	190		2,880
	10	Dan Holland	191		1,940
	17	Sanders Farrell	192		850
	25	Dan Holland	193		340
	31	Total			6,010

Camper also recorded the return of certain merchandise with the following entry:

May 20	Sales Returns and Allowances	250	
	Accounts Receivable—Sanders Farrell		250
	Customer returned merchandise.		

Required

1. Open a subsidiary Accounts Receivable Ledger that has a T-account for each customer listed in the Sales Journal. Post to the customer accounts the entries in the Sales Journal and any portion of the general journal entry that affects a customer's account.
2. Open a General Ledger that has T-accounts for Accounts Receivable, Sales, and Sales Returns and Allowances. Post the Sales Journal and any portion of the general journal entry that affects these accounts.
3. Prepare a schedule of the accounts in the subsidiary Accounts Receivable Ledger and add their balances to show that the total equals the balance in the Accounts Receivable controlling account.

Exercise 8-7
Posting from special journals to general and subsidiary ledgers
P1, P2

The condensed journals of Tipper Trophies are shown below. The journal column headings are incomplete and they do not indicate whether the columns are debit or credit columns.

Sales Journal

Account	
Jack Hertz	3,700
Trudy Stone	8,400
Dave Waylon	1,000
Total	13,100

Purchases Journal

Account	
Grass Corp.	5,400
Sulter, Inc.	4,500
McGrew Company	1,700
Total	11,600

Cash Receipts Journal

Account	Cash	Sales Discounts	Accounts Receivable	Sales	Other Accounts
Jack Hertz	3,332	68	3,400		
Sales	2,250			2,250	
Notes Payable	4,500				4,500
Sales	625			625	
Trudy Stone	8,232	168	8,400		
Store Equipment	500				500
Totals	19,439	236	11,800	2,875	5,000

Cash Disbursements Journal

Account	Cash	Purchases Discounts	Other Accounts	Accounts Payable
Prepaid Insurance	850		850	
Sulter, Inc.	4,365	135		4,500
Grass Corp.	4,557	93		4,650
Store Equipment	1,750		1,750	
Totals	11,522	228	2,600	9,150

General Journal

		Account		
		Sales Returns and Allowances	300	
		Accounts Receivable—Jack Hertz		300
		Accounts Payable—Grass Corp.	750	
		Purchases Returns and Allowances		750

Required

1. Prepare T-accounts for the following General Ledger and subsidiary ledger accounts. Separate the accounts of each ledger group as follows:

General Ledger Accounts	Accounts Receivable Ledger Accounts
Cash	Jack Hertz
Accounts Receivable	Trudy Stone
Prepaid Insurance	Dave Waylon
Store Equipment	
Accounts Payable	
Notes Payable	
Sales	**Accounts Payable Ledger Accounts**
Sales Discounts	Grass Corp.
Sales Returns and Allowances	McGrew Company
Purchases	Sulter, Inc.
Purchase Discounts	
Purchase Returns and Allowances	

2. Revise and show complete column headings for the special journals, and post the entries in the journals to their proper T-accounts.

Exercise 8-8
Accounts Receivable Ledger
P1, P2

Skillern Company posts its sales invoices directly and then binds the invoices to make them into a Sales Journal. Skillern had the following sales during January:

Jan.	2	Jay Newton	$ 3,600
	8	Adrian Carr	6,100
	10	Kathy Olivas	13,400
	14	Lisa Mack	20,500
	20	Kathy Olivas	11,200
	29	Jay Newton	7,300
		Total sales	$62,100

Required

1. Open a subsidiary Accounts Receivable Ledger having a T-account for each customer. Post the invoices to the subsidiary ledger.
2. Give the General Journal entry to record the end-of-month total from the Sales Journal.
3. Open an Accounts Receivable controlling T-account and a Sales T-account. Post the General Journal entry from 2.
4. Prepare a schedule of the accounts in the subsidiary Accounts Receivable Ledger and add their balances to show that the total equals the balance in the Accounts Receivable controlling account.

Exercise 8-9
Purchases Journal and error identification
P1

A company that records credit purchases in a Purchases Journal and records purchases returns in a General Journal made the following errors. For each error, indicate when the error should be discovered:

a. Made an addition error in determining the balance of a creditor's account.
b. Made an addition error in totaling the Office Supplies column of the Purchases Journal.
c. Posted a purchases return to the Accounts Payable account and to the creditor's account but did not post to the Purchases Returns and Allowances account.
d. Posted a purchases return to the Purchases Returns and Allowances account and to the Accounts Payable account but did not post to the creditor's account.
e. Correctly recorded a $4,000 purchase in the Purchases Journal but posted it to the creditor's account as a $400 purchase.

Exercise 8-10
Analyzing segment information
A1

Refer to Exhibit 8.15 and complete the segment contribution matrix for Gen X Sports Company. Analyze and interpret the matrix, including identification of segments with the highest and lowest growth rates.

Gen X Sports Company Segment Contribution Matrix for Sales					
	Sales Contribution (in $mil.)		Sales Contribution (in%)		1 Year Growth Rate Percent
Segment	1999	1998	1999	1998	
Segment:					
Skiing Group	$5,235	$3,585			
Skating Group	800	400			
Specialty Footwear	1,200	860			
Other Specialty	975	525			
Subtotal					
General Merchandise:					
South America	$2,725	$1,839			
United States	988	788			
Europe	650	350			
Subtotal					
Total					

Problems

Problem 8-1
Special journals, subsidiary ledgers, and schedule of accounts receivable

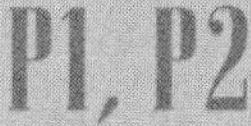

Newton Company completed these transactions during April of the current year:

Apr. 2 Purchased merchandise on credit from Baskin Company, invoice dated April 2, terms 2/10, n/60, $13,300.
3 Sold merchandise on credit to Linda Hobart, Invoice No. 760, $3,000. (The terms of all credit sales are 2/10, n/30.)
3 Purchased office supplies on credit from Eau Claire Inc., $1,380. Invoice dated April 2, terms n/10 EOM.
4 Issued Check No. 587 to *U.S. Times* for advertising expense, $999.
5 Sold merchandise on credit to Paul Abrams, Invoice No. 761, $8,000.
6 Received an $85 credit memorandum from Eau Claire Inc. for office supplies received on April 3 and returned for credit.
9 Purchased store equipment on credit from Frank's Supply, invoice dated April 9, terms n/10 EOM, $11,125.
11 Sold merchandise on credit to Kelly Schaefer, Invoice No. 762, $9,500.
12 Issued Check No. 588 to Baskin Company in payment of its April 2 invoice, less the discount.
13 Received payment from Linda Hobart for the April 3 sale, less the discount.
13 Sold merchandise on credit to Linda Hobart, Invoice No. 763, $4,100.
14 Received payment from Paul Abrams for the April 5 sale, less the discount.
16 Issued Check No. 589, payable to Payroll, in payment of sales salaries for the first half of the month, $9,750. Cashed the check and paid employees.
16 Cash sales for the first half of the month were $50,840. (Cash sales are usually recorded daily from the cash register readings. They are recorded only twice in this problem to reduce repetitive transactions.)
17 Purchased merchandise on credit from Spocket Company, invoice dated April 16, terms 2/10, n/30, $12,750.
18 Borrowed $50,000 from First State Bank by giving a long-term note payable.
20 Received payment from Kelly Schaefer for the April 11 sale, less the discount.
20 Purchased store supplies on credit from Frank's Supply, invoice dated April 19, terms n/10 EOM, $730.
23 Received a $400 credit memorandum from Sprocket Company for defective merchandise received on April 17 and returned to sprocket.
23 Received payment from Linda Hobart for the April 13 sale, less the discount.
25 Purchased merchandise on credit from Baskin Company, invoice dated April 24, terms 2/10, n/60, $10,375.
26 Issued Check No. 590 to Sprocket Company in payment of its April 16 invoice, less the return and the discount.
27 Sold merchandise on credit to Paul Abrams, Invoice No. 764, $3,070.
27 Sold merchandise on credit to Kelly Schaefer, Invoice No. 765, $5,700.

30 Issued Check No. 591, payable to Payroll, in payment of the sales salaries for the last half of the month, $9,750.

30 Cash sales for the last half of the month were $70,975.

Required

Preparation Component

1. Prepare a Sales Journal like Exhibit 8.5 and a Cash Receipts Journal like Exhibit 8.9. Number both journal pages as page 3.
2. Review the transactions of Newton Company and enter those transactions that should be journalized in the Sales Journal and those that should be journalized in the Cash Receipts Journal. Ignore any transactions that should be journalized in a Purchases Journal, a Cash Disbursements Journal, or a General Journal.
3. Open the following General Ledger accounts: Cash, Accounts Receivable, Long-Term Notes Payable, Sales, and Sales Discounts. Also open subsidiary Accounts Receivable Ledger accounts for Paul Abrams, Linda Hobart, and Kelly Schaefer.
4. Post items that should be posted as individual amounts from the journals. (Normally, such items are posted daily; but since they are few in number in this problem you are asked to post them only once.)
5. Foot and crossfoot the journals and make the month-end postings.
6. Prepare a trial balance of the General Ledger and test the accuracy of the subsidiary ledger by preparing a schedule of accounts receivable.

Check Figure Trial balance totals $205,185

Analysis Component

7. Assume the sum of the account balances on the schedule of accounts receivable does not equal the balance of the controlling account in the General Ledger. Describe steps you would take to discover the error(s).

Problem 8-2
Special journals, subsidiary ledgers, schedule of accounts payable

The April transactions of Newton Company are listed in Problem 8–1.

Required

1. Prepare a General Journal, a Purchases Journal like Exhibit 8.11, and a Cash Disbursements Journal like Exhibit 8.13. Number all journal pages as page 3.
2. Review the April transactions of Newton Company and enter those transactions that should be journalized in the General Journal, the Purchases Journal, or the Cash Disbursements Journal. Ignore any transactions that should be journalized in a Sales Journal or Cash Receipts Journal.
3. Open the following General Ledger accounts: Cash, Office Supplies, Store Supplies, Store Equipment, Accounts Payable, Long-Term Notes Payable, Purchases, Purchases Returns and Allowances, Purchases Discounts, Sales Salaries Expense, and Advertising Expense. Enter the March 31 balances of Cash ($167,000) and Long-Term Notes Payable ($167,000). Also open subsidiary Accounts Payable Ledger accounts for Frank's Supply, Baskin Company, Sprocket Company, and Eau Claire Inc.
4. Post items that should be posted as individual amounts from the journals. (Normally, such items are posted daily; but since they are few in number in this problem you are asked to post them only once.)
5. Foot and crossfoot the journals and make the month-end postings.
6. Prepare a trial balance of the General Ledger and a schedule of accounts payable.

Check Figure Trial balance totals, $191,438

Problem 8-3
Special journals, subsidiary ledgers, trial balance

(If the Working Papers that accompany this text are not being used, omit this problem.)
It is December 16 and you have just taken over the accounting work of Saskan Enterprises, whose annual accounting period ends December 31. The company's previous accountant journalized its transactions through December 15 and posted all items that required posting as individual amounts (see the journals and ledgers in the working papers). The company completed these transactions beginning on December 16:

Dec. 16 Sold merchandise on credit to Vickie Foresman, Invoice No. 916, $7,700. (Terms of all credit sales are 2/10, n/30.)

17 Received a $1,040 credit memorandum from Shore Company for merchandise received on December 15 and returned for credit.

17 Purchased office supplies on credit from Brown Supply Company, $615. Invoice dated December 16, terms n/10 EOM.

18 Received a $40 credit memorandum from Brown Supply Company for office supplies received on December 17 and returned for credit.

20 Issued a credit memorandum to Amy Ihrig for defective merchandise sold on December 15 and returned for credit, $500.

21 Purchased store equipment on credit from Brown Supply Company, invoice dated December 21, terms n/10 EOM, $6,700.
22 Received payment from Vickie Foresman for the December 12 sale less the discount.
23 Issued Check No. 623 to Sunshine Company in payment of its December 15 invoice less the discount.
24 Sold merchandise on credit to Bill Grigsby, Invoice No. 917, $1,200.
24 Issued Check No. 624 to Shore Company in payment of its December 15 invoice less the return and the discount.
25 Received payment from Amy Ihrig for the December 15 sale less the return and the discount.
26 Received merchandise and an invoice dated December 25, terms 2/10, n/60, from Sunshine Company, $8,100.
29 Sold a neighboring merchant five boxes of file folders (office supplies) for cash at cost, $50.
30 Ken Shaw, the owner of Saskan Enterprises, used Check No. 625 to withdraw $2,500 cash from the business for personal use.
31 Issued Check No. 626 to Jamie Green, the company's only sales employee, in payment of her salary for the last half of December, $2,020.
31 Issued Check No. 627 to Countywide Electric Company in payment of the December electric bill, $710.
31 Cash sales for the last half of the month were $29,600. (Cash sales are usually recorded daily but are recorded only twice in this problem to reduce the repetitive transactions.)

Required

1. Record the transactions listed above in the journals provided in the working papers.
2. Post to the customer and creditor accounts and also post any amounts that should be posted as individual amounts to the General Ledger accounts. (Normally, these amounts are posted daily, but they are posted only once in this problem because they are few in number.)
3. Foot and crossfoot the journals and make the month-end postings.
4. Prepare a December 31 trial balance and test the accuracy of the subsidiary ledgers by preparing schedules of accounts receivable and accounts payable.

Check Figure Trial balance totals, $221,160

Problem 8-4
Special journals, subsidiary ledgers, trial balance
P1, P2

The Bledsoe Company completed these transactions during March of the current year:

Mar. 2 Sold merchandise on credit to Leroy Hackett, Invoice No. 854, $15,800. (Terms of all credit sales are 2/10, n/30.)
3 Purchased office supplies on credit from Arndt Company, $1,120. Invoice dated March 3, terms n/10 EOM.
3 Sold merchandise on credit to Sam Snickers, Invoice No. 855, $9,200.
5 Received merchandise and an invoice dated March 3, terms 2/10, n/30, from Defore Industries, $42,600.
6 Borrowed $72,000 by giving Commerce Bank a long-term promissory note payable.
9 Purchased office equipment on credit from Jett Supply, invoice dated March 9, terms n/10 EOM, $20,850.
10 Sold merchandise on credit to Marjorie Coble, Invoice No. 856, $4,600.
12 Received payment from Leroy Hackett for the March 2 sale less the discount.
13 Sent Defore Industries Check No. 416 in payment of its March 3 invoice less the discount.
13 Received payment from Sam Snickers for the March 3 sale less the discount.
14 Received merchandise and an invoice dated March 13, terms 2/10, n/30, from the Welch Company, $31,625.
15 Issued Check No. 417, payable to Payroll, in payment of sales salaries for the first half of the month, $15,900. Cashed the check and paid the employees.
15 Cash sales for the first half of the month were $164,680. (Normally, cash sales are recorded daily; however, they are recorded only twice in this problem to reduce the repetitive entries.)
15 Post to the customer and creditor accounts and also post any amounts that should be posted as individual amounts to the General Ledger accounts. (Normally, such items are posted daily; but you are asked to post them on only two occasions in this problem because they are few in number.)
16 Purchased store supplies on credit from Arndt Company, $1,670. Invoice dated March 16, terms n/10 EOM.
17 Received a credit memorandum from the Welch Company for unsatisfactory merchandise received on March 14 and returned for credit, $2,425.
19 Received a credit memorandum from Jett Supply for office equipment received on March 9 and returned for credit, $630.

20 Received payment from Marjorie Coble for the sale of March 10 less the discount.
23 Issued Check No. 418 to the Welch Company in payment of its invoice of March 13 less the return and the discount.
27 Sold merchandise on credit to Marjorie Coble, Invoice No. 857, $13,910.
28 Sold merchandise on credit to Sam Snickers, Invoice No. 858, $5,315.
31 Issued Check No. 419, payable to Payroll, in payment of sales salaries for the last half of the month, $15,900. Cashed the check and paid the employees.
31 Cash sales for the last half of the month were $174,590.
31 Post to the customer and creditor accounts and post any amounts that should be posted as individual amounts to the General Ledger accounts.
31 Foot and crossfoot the journals and make the month-end postings.

Required

1. Open the following General Ledger accounts: Cash, Accounts Receivable, Office Supplies, Store Supplies, Office Equipment, Accounts Payable, Long-Term Notes Payable, Sales, Sales Discounts, Purchases, Purchases Returns and Allowances, Purchases Discounts, and Sales Salaries Expense. Open the following Accounts Receivable Ledger accounts: Marjorie Coble, Leroy Hackett, and Sam Snickers. Open the following Accounts Payable Ledger accounts: Arndt Company, Defore Industries, Jett Supply, and the Welch Company.
2. Enter the transactions listed above in a Sales Journal like Exhibit 8.5, a Purchases Journal like Exhibit 8.11, a Cash Receipts Journal like Exhibit 8.9, a Cash Disbursements Journal like Exhibit 8.13, and a General Journal. Post when instructed to do so.
3. Prepare a trial balance of the General Ledger and test the accuracy of the subsidiary ledgers by preparing schedules of accounts receivable and accounts payable.

Check Figure Trial balance totals, $486,966

Comprehensive Problem

Alpine Company

PeachTree

(If the Working Papers that accompany this text are not available, omit this comprehensive problem.)

Assume it is Monday, May 1, the first business day of the month, and you have just been hired as the accountant for Alpine Company, which operates with monthly accounting periods. All of the company's accounting work has been completed through the end of April and its ledgers show April 30 balances. During your first month on the job, you record the following transactions:

May 1 Issued Check No. 3410 to S&M Management Co. in payment of the May rent, $3,710. (Use two lines to record the transaction. Charge 80% of the rent to Rent Expense—Selling Space and the balance to Rent Expense—Office Space.)
2 Sold merchandise on credit to Essex Company, Invoice No. 8785, $6,100. (The terms of all credit sales are 2/10, n/30.)
2 Issued a $175 credit memorandum to Nabors, Inc., for defective merchandise sold on April 28 and returned for credit. The total selling price (gross) was $4,725.
3 Received a $798 credit memorandum from Parkay Products for merchandise received on April 29 and returned for credit.
4 Purchased on credit from Thompson Supply Co.: merchandise, $37,072; store supplies, $574; and office supplies, $83. Invoice dated May 4, terms n/10 EOM.
5 Received payment from Nabors, Inc., for the remaining balance from the sale of April 28 less the May 2 return and the discount.
8 Issued Check No. 3411 to Parkay Products to pay for the $7,098 of merchandise received on April 29 less the May 3 return and a 2% discount.
9 Sold store supplies to the merchant next door at cost for cash, $350.
10 Purchased office equipment on credit from Thompson Supply Co., invoice dated May 10, terms n/10 EOM, $4,074.
11 Received payment from Essex Company for the May 2 sale less the discount.
11 Received merchandise and an invoice dated May 10, terms 2/10, n/30, from Gale, Inc., $8,800.
12 Received an $854 credit memorandum from Thompson Supply Co. for defective office equipment received on May 10 and returned for credit.
15 Issued Check No. 3412, payable to Payroll, in payment of sales salaries, $5,320, and office salaries, $3,150. Cashed the check and paid the employees.
15 Cash sales for the first half of the month, $59,220. (Such sales are normally recorded daily. They are recorded only twice in this problem to reduce the repetitive entries.)
15 Post to the customer and creditor accounts. Also, post individual items that are not included in column totals at the end of the month to the general ledger accounts. (Such items are normally posted daily, but you are asked to post them only twice each month because they are few in number.)

16 Sold merchandise on credit to Essex Company, Invoice No. 8786, $3,990.
17 Received merchandise and an invoice dated May 14, terms 2/10, n/60, from Chandler Corp., $13,650.
19 Issued Check No. 3413 to Gale, Inc., in payment of its May 10 invoice less the discount.
22 Sold merchandise to Oscar Services, Invoice No. 8787, $6,850, terms 2/10, n/60.
23 Issued Check No. 3414 to Chandler Corp. in payment of its May 14 invoice less the discount.
24 Purchased on credit from Thompson Supply Co.: merchandise, $8,120; store supplies, $630; and office supplies, $280. Invoice dated May 24, terms n/10 EOM.
25 Received merchandise and an invoice dated May 23, terms 2/10, n/30, from Parkay Products, $3,080.
26 Sold merchandise on credit to Deaver Corp., Invoice No. 8788, $14,210.
26 Issued Check No. 3415 to Trinity Power in payment of the April electric bill, $1,283.
29 The owner of Alpine Company, Clint Barry, used Check No. 3416 to withdraw $7,000 from the business for personal use.
30 Received payment from Oscar Services for the May 22 sale less the discount.
30 Issued Check No. 3417, payable to Payroll, in payment of sales salaries, $5,320, and office salaries, $3,150. Cashed the check and paid the employees.
31 Cash sales for the last half of the month were $66,052.
31 Post to the customer and creditor accounts. Also, post individual items that are not included in column totals at the end of the month to the General Ledger accounts.
31 Foot and crossfoot the journals and make the month-end postings.

Required

1. Enter the transactions listed above in a Sales Journal, a Purchases Journal, a Cash Receipts Journal, a Cash Disbursements Journal, and a General Journal. Post when instructed to do so. Use a periodic inventory system.
2. Prepare a trial balance in the Trial Balance columns of the provided work sheet form. Complete the work sheet using the following information (Alpine uses the closing entry approach to record the change in the Merchandise Inventory account):
   a. Expired insurance, $553.
   b. Ending store supplies inventory, $2,632.
   c. Ending office supplies inventory, $504.
   d. Estimated depreciation of store equipment, $567.
   e. Estimated depreciation of office equipment, $329.
   f. Ending merchandise inventory, $176,400.

   Prepare and post adjusting and closing entries.
3. Prepare a May 2000 classified, multiple-step income statement, a May 2000 statement of changes in owner's equity, and a May 31, 2000 classified balance sheet.
4. Prepare a post-closing trial balance. Also test the accuracy of subsidiary ledgers by preparing schedules of accounts receivable and accounts payable. Prepare a list of the Accounts Receivable Ledger accounts and a list of the Accounts Payable Ledger accounts. Total the balances of each schedule to confirm that their totals equal the balances in the controlling accounts.

BEYOND THE NUMBERS

Reporting in Action
A1

Refer to the financial statements and related information for **NIKE** in Appendix A. Answer the following questions by analyzing that information.

1. Identify the note disclosing NIKE's segment information for total revenue and net income.
2. For fiscal year ended May 31, 1997, compute the percent of both total revenue and operating income that NIKE earns from each segment. Comment on your findings, noting whether the segment with the highest percent of total revenue also generates the highest percent of operating income.
3. Compute the percent change in operating income for each segment and in total from the fiscal year ending in 1996 to 1997. Comment on your findings.

Swoosh Ahead

4. Obtain access to NIKE's annual report for fiscal years ending after May 31, 1997. You can gain access to NIKE's annual report at its web site **[www.nike.com]** or through the SEC's EDGAR database **[www.sec.gov].** Fulfill requirements (2) and (3) using the latest data available to you.

Comparative Analysis

A1

Both NIKE and Reebok design, produce, market, and sell sports footwear and apparel. Key comparative figures for these two organizations follow ($ thousands):

NIKE Total Revenue by Segment*	Fiscal Year Ended May 31, 1997	Fiscal Year Ended May 31, 1996
United States	$5,529,132	$3,964,662
Europe	1,833,722	1,334,340
Asia/Pacific	1,245,217	735,094
Latin America/Canada and other	578,468	436,529
Total	$9,186,539	$6,470,625

Reebok Net Sales by Segment*	Fiscal Year Ended Dec. 31, 1996	Fiscal Year Ended Dec, 31, 1995
United States	$1,935,724	$2,027,080
United Kingdom	566,196	492,843
Europe	623,209	642,622
Other countries	353,475	318,905
Total	$3,478,604	$3,481,450

*NIKE figures are from its annual reports for fiscal years ended May 31, 1997 and 1996. Reebok figures are from its annual reports for fiscal years ended December 31, 1996 and 1995.

Required

1. Compute the percent change in total revenue (NIKE) and total net sales (Reebok) for the years given. Comment on your findings.
2. Compute the percent change in revenue by each geographic segment for each company. Comment on your findings.
3. Identify the geographic segment experiencing the largest growth in revenue for each company.

Ethics Challenge

C5

John Harris, CPA, is a sole practitioner. He has been practicing as an auditor for 10 years. Recently a long-standing audit client asked John to design and implement an integrated computer accounting information system. The fees associated with this additional engagement with the client are very attractive. However, John wonders if he can remain objective in his evaluation of the client's accounting system and its records on subsequent audits if he puts himself in the position of auditing a system he was responsible for installing. John knows that the professional auditing standards require him to remain independent in fact and appearance from all of his auditing clients.

Required

1. What do you think auditing standards mean when they require independence in fact? In appearance?
2. Why is it important that auditors remain independent of their clients?
3. Do you think John can accept this engagement and remain independent? Justify your response.

Communicating in Practice

C3, C4

Your friend, Ivanna B. Sweeter, has a small retail operation called "Goodies" that sells candies and nuts. Ivanna acquires her goods from a few select vendors. Purchase orders are generally made by phone and on credit. Sales are primarily for cash. Ivanna keeps her own manual accounting system using a general Journal and a General Ledger. At the end of each business day she records one summary entry for cash sales.

Recently, Ivanna began offering goodies packaged in creative gift packages. This has increased sales substantially and she is now receiving orders from corporate clients and others who order quantities and prefer to buy on credit. Increased sales translate to increased purchases. To expand her gift package selection, Ivanna is considering purchasing packaging supplies from other vendors. As a result of increased credit transactions in both purchases and sales, keeping the accounting records has become extremely time-consuming. Ivanna would like to continue to maintain her own manual system. Ivanna calls you for advice. Write a memo to Ivanna advising her as to how she might modify her current manual accounting system to accommodate the expanded business activities described. She is accustomed to checking her ledger by using a trial balance. Your memo should explain the advantages of what you propose and of any other verification techniques you recommend.

Taking It to the Net

A1

This chapter described the reporting of segment information. Companies have criticized current regulatory discussions that seek to expand the information companies must report on their business segments. To learn more about current FASB deliberations on this topic and others, you should visit the FASB's Web site at **www.rutgers.edu/accounting/raw/fasb.**

Required

1. How is the table of contents for the FASB Web site organized? Identify the topical areas one can visit at this Web site.
2. Visit the Quarterly Plan for the FASB Projects area of the Web site. What accounting issues does FASB hope to discuss in the coming year?

Teamwork in Action

P1, P2

Each member of the team is to assume responsibility for one of the six tasks below.

1. Journalizing in the Purchases Journal.
2. Journalizing in the Cash Disbursements Journal
3. Maintaining and verifying the Accounts Payable Ledger
4. Journalizing in the Sales and General Journal
5. Journalizing in the Cash Receipts Journal
6. Maintaining and verifying the Accounts Receivable Ledger

The team should follow the procedures described below in carrying out responsibilities.

Work Procedures

1. After responsibilities 1–6 are assigned, each member of the team is to quickly read through the list of transactions in Problem 8–4, identifying with initials the journal each transaction is to be recorded in. Upon completion, the team leader is to read transaction dates and the appropriate team member is to vocalize responsibility. Any disagreement between teammates must be resolved within the team.
2. Arrange seating to make it easier to access the necessary data for tasks assigned.
3. Journalize and continually update subsidiary ledgers. Journal recorders should alert subsidiary ledger maintainers when they have an entry to be posted to their subsidiary.
4. Team members responsible for tasks 1, 2, 4, and 5 are to summarize and prove journals, while members responsible for tasks 3 and 6 are to prepare schedules.
5. The team leader is to take charge of the General Ledger, rotating team members to obtain amounts to be posted. The person responsible for a journal must complete posting references in the journal. Other team members should verify accuracy of account balance computations. To avoid any abnormal account balances, post in the following order: P, S, G, R, D. *Note: Posting of any necessary individual General Ledger amounts are done at this time as well.*
6. The team leader is to read out General Ledger account balances while another team member fills in the trial balance form. Concurrently, one member should keep a running balance of debit account balance totals and another credit account balance totals. Verify the final total of the trial balance and the schedules. If necessary, the team is to resolve any errors. Turn in the trial balance and schedules to instructor.

Hitting the Road

C2

Join a classmate and arrange a time when you can conduct a short accounting information systems survey by phone. Select five companies at random from the yellow pages of your community phone book. This survey is probably most easily administered to small service companies in your area. Call each company and ask to speak to a person who is knowledgeable about the accounting system of the company. Explain that you are completing a short phone survey for your accounting class and that it will only take a few minutes to answer your questions. Your survey should ask the following questions:

1. Is the company's accounting system computerized?
2. *If computerized,* what brand of software is used? Is this software a customized program written specifically for the company, or is it a standardized program available to many companies? (Note: Some companies use a combination.)
3. What input device(s) is used to enter transactions into the system?
4. Does the company use on-line or batch processing?
5. Does the company use a network or stand-alone computer workstations?

Business Week Activity

A1

Read the article "Corporate America Is Fed Up with FASB" in the April 21, 1997, edition of *Business Week.*

1. In the article's table, what key reasons are identified for criticisms of the FASB by companies?
2. Why are companies critical of FASB's proposal on segment reporting?
3. In addition to the reasons cited in the article, are there other reasons you can think of why companies do not wish to expand segment reporting beyond what is currently required?

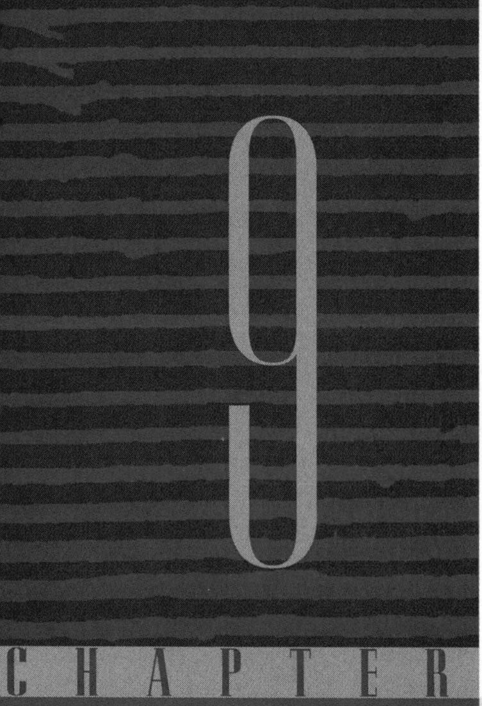

Internal Control and Cash

A Look Back

Chapter 8 focused on accounting information systems. We explained the fundamental principles and components of information systems, the use of special journals and subsidiary ledgers, and technology-based systems. We also discussed segment reporting and how to analyze these data.

A Look at This Chapter

This chapter extends our study of accounting information systems to the area of internal control and accounting for cash. We describe procedures that are good for internal control. We also explain the control of and accounting for cash.

A Look Ahead

Chapter 10 focuses on receivables and short-term investments. These items are the most liquid assets other than cash. We explain how to account and report for these assets.

Chapter Outline

Losing Control

ANN ARBOR, MI—Jason Barron is a 23-year-old entrepreneur and owner of **Barron Sports.** He's one of the people we see toting a cart full of souvenirs, pennants, and other sports items for fans at football games and other sporting events. "I started doing Michigan football games when I was 15," says Barron. "I now sell at all of Michigan's big sporting events. And I hire people to sell my items at games of other colleges."

But Barron is a victim of employee theft and fraud. "I had no idea of what types of controls I needed when I hired people to sell for me," says Barron. "I was learning on the run, and it nearly cost me everything."

Barron's problems grew from his success. Profit margins on items he sold were enormous, and sales were brisk. He quickly hired additional people to sell for him and began covering more events. But he had no real system of control, either for cash or the salable items.

"I didn't know the first thing about recordkeeping, internal control, or cash accounting," admits Barron. "It really hit home when I sent one load of items to a person working for me in Columbus. It was for the Ohio State vs. Penn State game. The items I sent cost me about $2,500, but they sell for about $9,000." But Barron got back only a little more than $6,800 when everything was supposedly sold. What happened? "The person selling for me had lots of excuses—shoplifting, damage, not delivered—you name it. It was clear to me he had ripped me off to a tune of more than $2,000 in one afternoon! That's when I knew things had to change."

Barron responded with several new control procedures. They included making all employees accountable for salable items and making them pay for items lost or stolen. In return, he substantially increased sales commissions. These changes and others cut into profit margins but nearly eliminated the cost of employee theft and fraud.

"Things are back on track," says Barron. "I want to do the major college Bowl games this year and hopefully be at the Final Four basketball finals." Like a good athlete, Barron has cut distractions and is focused on the sales game.

Learning Objectives

Conceptual

C1 Define internal control and its purpose.

C2 Identify principles of internal control.

C3 Define cash and cash equivalents and how they are reported.

C4 Identify control features of banking activities.

Analytical

A1 Compute days' sales uncollected ratio and use it to analyze liquidity.

Procedural

P1 Apply internal control to cash receipts.

P2 Apply the voucher system to control cash disbursements.

P3 Explain and record petty cash fund transactions.

P4 Apply the net method to control purchase discounts.

P5 Prepare a bank reconciliation.

CHAPTER PREVIEW

We all are aware of reports and experiences involving theft and fraud. These occurrences affect us and produce various actions. Actions include locking doors, chaining bikes, reviewing sales receipts, and acquiring alarm systems. A company also takes actions to safeguard, control, and manage what it owns. Experience tells us small companies are most vulnerable. This is usually due to weak internal controls. It is management's responsibility to set up policies and procedures to safeguard a company's assets, especially cash. To do so, management and employees must understand and apply principles of internal control. This chapter describes these principles and how we apply them. We learn about important internal control policies and procedures. We focus special attention on cash. This is because cash is easily transferable and often at high risk of loss. Several controls for cash are explained including a voucher system, petty cash funds, and reconciling bank accounts. This chapter also describes a method of accounting for purchases that helps us decide whether cash discounts on purchases are being lost and, if so, how much is lost. Our understanding of these controls and procedures makes us more secure in carrying out business activities and in assessing those activities of other companies. Like Jason Barron in the opening article, knowledge of these topics is crucial in successfully running a company.

Internal Control

This section describes internal control and its fundamental principles. We also discuss the impact of computing technology on internal control and the limitations of control procedures.

Purpose of Internal Control

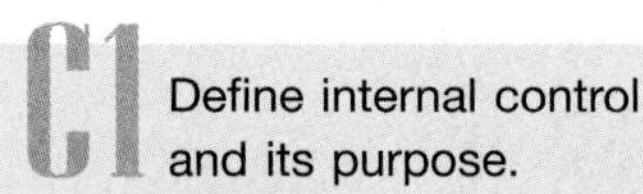
C1 Define internal control and its purpose.

Managers (or owners) of small businesses often control the entire operation. They supervise workers, participate in all activities, and make major decisions. These managers usually buy all the assets and services used in the business. They also hire and manage employees, negotiate all contracts, and sign all checks. These managers know from personal contact and observation whether the business is actually receiving the assets and services paid for. Larger companies find it increasingly difficult to maintain this close personal contact. At some point, managers must delegate responsibilities and rely on formal procedures rather than personal contact in controlling and knowing all operations of the business.

Managers use an internal control system to monitor and control the business's operations. An **internal control system** is all the policies and procedures managers use to:

- Protect assets.
- Ensure reliable accounting.
- Promote efficient operations.
- Urge adherence to company policies.

A properly designed internal control system is a key part of systems design, analysis, and performance. Managers place a high priority on internal control systems because they can prevent avoidable losses, help managers plan operations, and monitor company and human performance. While internal controls don't provide guarantees, they lower the company's risk of loss from not having internal controls.

Access Denied!
Good internal control systems prevent unauthorized access to assets and accounting records by requiring passwords before access is permitted. We all are affected by these control procedures. It takes a password, for instance, to boot up most office PCs these days. Also, logging onto a network calls for another. Then comes voice mail, e-mail, on-line services, and restricted Web pages—not to mention personal ID numbers on phone, credit, and cash cards. Preventing unauthorized access is one of the most difficult and time-consuming tasks for internal control experts. [Source: *Business Week,* May 5, 1997.]

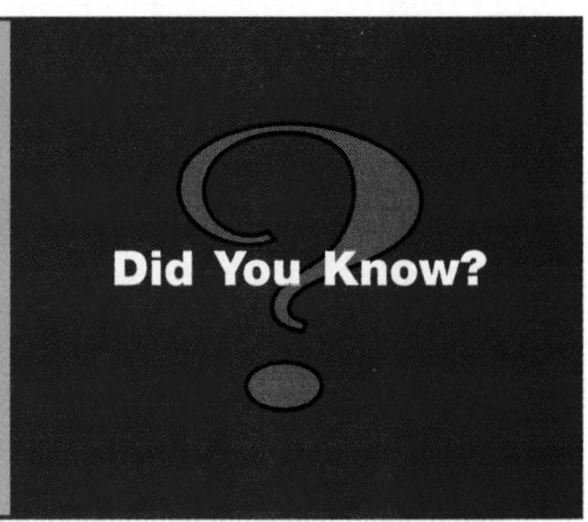
Did You Know?

Principles of Internal Control

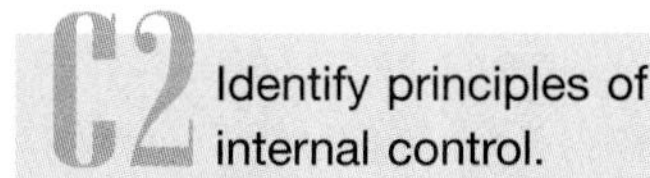
C2
Identify principles of internal control.

Internal control policies and procedures vary from company to company. They depend on factors such as the nature of the business and its size. Yet certain fundamental internal control principles apply to all companies. The **principles of internal control** are:

1. Establish responsibilities.
2. Maintain adequate records.
3. Insure assets and bond key employees.
4. Separate recordkeeping from custody of assets.
5. Divide responsibility for related transactions.
6. Apply technological controls.
7. Perform regular and independent reviews.

We explain these seven principles in this section. We also describe how internal control procedures minimize the risk of fraud and theft. These procedures increase the reliability and accuracy of accounting records.

Establish Responsibilities

Proper internal control means that responsibility for each task is clearly established and assigned to one person. When responsibility is not identified, it is difficult to determine who is at fault when a problem occurs. When two salesclerks share access to the same cash register, for instance, it is difficult to identify which clerk is at fault if there is a cash shortage. Neither clerk can prove or disprove the alleged shortage. To prevent this problem, one clerk might be given responsibility for handling all cash sales. Alternately, a company can use a register with separate cash drawers for each clerk. Most of us have experienced waiting in line at a retail counter during a change of shift while employees swap cash drawers.

Maintain Adequate Records

Good recordkeeping is part of an internal control system. It helps protect assets and ensures that employees use prescribed procedures. Reliable records are also a source of information that management uses to monitor company operations. When detailed records of manufacturing equipment and tools are kept, for instance, items are unlikely to be lost or stolen without the discrepancy's being noticed. Similarly, transactions are less likely to be entered in incorrect accounts if a chart of accounts is set up and used carefully. If this chart is not set up or is used incorrectly, managers might never discover excessive expenses or inflated sales.

Many preprinted forms and internal business papers are also designed for use in a good internal control system. When sales slips are properly designed, for instance, sales personnel can record needed information efficiently with less chance of errors or delays to customers. And when sales slips are prenumbered and controlled, each sales slip issued is the responsibility of one salesperson. This means a salesperson is not able to pocket cash by making a sale and destroying the sales slip. Computerized point-of-sale systems achieve the same control results.

Insure Assets and Bond Key Employees

Good internal control means that assets are adequately insured against casualty, and employees handling cash and negotiable assets are bonded. An employee is *bonded* when a company purchases an insurance policy, or a bond, against losses from theft by that employee. Bonding reduces the risk of loss suffered from theft. It also discourages theft because bonded employees know that an independent bonding company is involved when theft is uncovered, and it is unlikely to be sympathetic with an employee involved in theft.

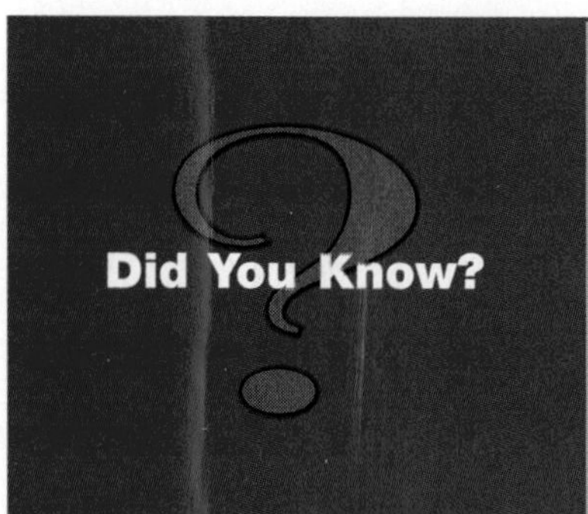

High-Tech Threads

Theft and counterfeiting are concerns of most companies. **Tracer Detection Technology** has developed a technique for permanently marking paper, currency, and all physical assets. Its new technique involves embedding a one-inch-square tag made of nylon fibers with different light-absorbing properties. Each pattern of fibers creates a unique optical signature. They hope to embed tags in everything from compact disks and credit cards to designer clothes and accessories to help fight theft and counterfeiting. Retailers will be able to verify products by running scanners over the fiber tag. [Source: *Business Week*, October 6, 1997.]

Separate Recordkeeping from Custody of Assets

An important principle of internal control is that a person who controls or has access to an asset must not keep that asset's accounting records. This principle reduces the risk of theft or waste of an asset because the person with control over the asset knows that records of the asset are kept by another person. Also the recordkeeper doesn't have access to the asset and has no reason to falsify records. This means that two people must both agree to commit a fraud, called *collusion*, for the asset to be stolen and the theft is hidden from the records. Because collusion is necessary to commit this type of fraud, it is less likely to occur.

Divide Responsibility for Related Transactions

Good internal control divides responsibility for a transaction or a series of related transactions between two or more individuals or departments. This is to ensure that the work of one acts as a check on the other. But this principle, often called *separation of duties*, is not a call for duplication of work. Each employee or department should perform unduplicated effort.

Examples of transactions with divided responsibility are placing purchase orders, receiving merchandise, and paying vendors. These tasks shouldn't be given to one individual or department. Assigning responsibility for any of these tasks to one party creates a case where mistakes and perhaps fraud are more likely to occur. Having an independent person, for example, check incoming goods for quality and quantity encourages more care and attention to detail than having the person who placed the order do the checking. Added protection can result from identifying a third person to approve payment of the invoice. Again the risk of both error and fraud is reduced. We can even designate a fourth person with authority to write checks as another measure of protection.

Apply Technological Controls

Cash registers, check protectors, time clocks, mechanical counters, and personal identification scanners are examples of control devices that can improve internal control. Technology often helps them be used effectively. A cash register with a locked-in tape or electronic file makes a record of each cash sale. A check protector perforates the amount of a check into its face and makes it difficult to alter the amount. A time clock registers the exact time an employee both arrives on and departs from the job. Mechanical change and currency counters quickly and accurately count amounts. And personal scanners limit access to only authorized individuals. Each of these and other technological controls are effective parts of many internal control systems.

Face Codes

We're all familiar with bar codes, but how about "face codes"? Viisage Technology has licensed a powerful face-recognition program from MIT. It snaps a digital picture of the face and converts key facial features—say, the distance between the eyes—into a series of numerical values. These can be stored on an ID or ATM card as a simple bar code. Searching through tens of thousands of faces is a snap. Welfare agencies in Massachusetts are already using the system to identify fraudulent welfare cases. [Source: *Business Week,* May 5, 1997.]

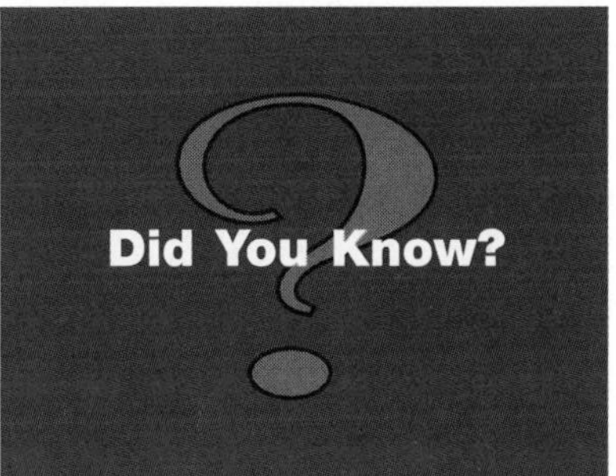

Perform Regular and Independent Reviews

No internal control system is entirely effective. Changes in personnel and technological advances present opportunities for shortcuts and other lapses. So does the stress of time pressures. To counter these changes, regular reviews of internal control systems are needed to ensure that procedures are followed. These reviews are preferably done by internal auditors not directly involved in operations. Their independent perspective encourages an evaluation of the efficiency as well as the effectiveness of the internal control system.

Many companies also pay for audits by independent auditors who are CPAs. These external auditors test the company's financial records and then give an opinion as to whether the company's financial statements are presented fairly in accordance with generally accepted accounting principles. Before external auditors decide on how much testing is needed, they evaluate the effectiveness of the internal control system. In the process of their evaluation, they identify internal controls needing improvement. This information is often helpful to a client.

Political Activist

You are a political activist leading a campaign to improve the health care system. Your funding is limited and you try to hire people who are committed to your cause and who will work for less. A systems analyst recently volunteered her services. One of her recommendations was to require all employees to take at least one week of vacation per year. Why would she recommend a "forced vacation" policy?

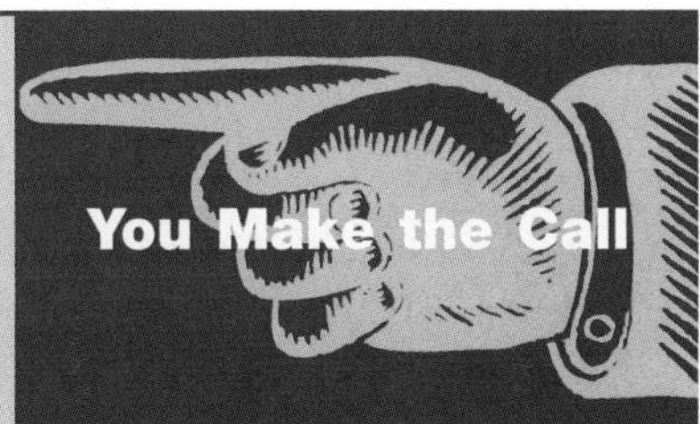

Answer—p. 393

Technology and Internal Control

The fundamental principles of internal control are relevant no matter what the technological state of the accounting system, from purely manual to fully automated systems. Yet technology impacts an internal control system in several important ways. Perhaps the most obvious is that technology allows us quicker access to ever-increasing information databases. Used effectively, technology greatly improves managers' ability to monitor and control business operations. This section describes some technological impacts we must be alert to.

Reduced Processing Errors

Technologically advanced systems reduce the number of errors in processing information. Provided the software and data entry are correct, the risk of mechanical and mathematical errors is nearly eliminated. Yet erroneous data entry does occur and one must be alert to that possibility. The decreasing human involvement in later data processing can cause data entry errors to go undiscovered. Similarly, errors in software can produce consistent erroneous processing of transactions. It is important to continually check and monitor all types of systems.

More Extensive Testing of Records

A company's regular review and audit of electronic records can include more extensive testing when information is easily and rapidly accessed. When accounting records are kept manually, auditors and others likely select only small samples of data to test. But when data are accessible with computer technology, then large samples or even complete data files can be quickly reviewed and analyzed.

Limited Evidence of Processing

Because many data processing steps are increasingly done by computer, fewer hard-copy items of documentary evidence are available for review. Yet technologically advanced systems can store some additional evidence. They can, for instance, record information such as who made the entries, the date and time, and the source of their entry. Technology can also be designed to require use of passwords or other identification before access to the system is granted. This means that internal control depends more on the design and operation of the information system and less on analysis of its resulting documents.

Crucial Separation of Duties

Technological advances in accounting information systems are so efficient that they often require fewer employees. This reduction in workforce carries a risk that separation of crucial responsibilities is lost. Companies that use advanced technology also need employees with special skills to operate programs and equipment. The duties of these employees must be controlled and monitored to minimize risk of error and fraud. Better control is maintained if, for instance, the person designing and programming the system does not serve as the operator. Also, the control over programs and files related to cash receipts and disbursements must be separated. To avoid risk of fraud, check-writing activities should not be controlled by a computer operator. Achieving acceptable separation of duties can be especially difficult and costly in small companies with few employees.

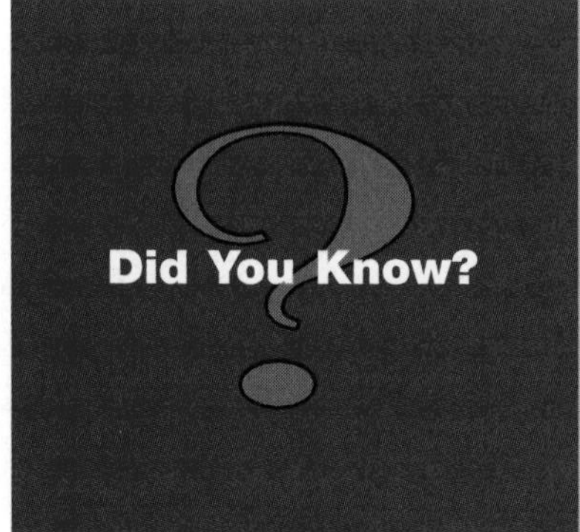

Calling All Techies

Most internal control systems today rely on information technology. A new study estimates 190,000 jobs in information technology stand vacant. Demand far outstrips supply, producing a bidding war for digital talent. **Bay Networks** recently lost a five-year programmer making $80,000 to a consulting company offering $300,000 per year. And starting salaries for new graduates often exceed $45,000. The most prized programmers are those adept at enterprise programs such as SAP or Oracle. But the demand for techies with Web, intranets, and software expertise is also strong. A recent survey cited the shortage of techies as one of the greatest barriers to company growth. [Source: *Business Week,* March 10, 1997.]

Limitations of Internal Control

All internal control policies and procedures have limitations. Probably the most serious source of these limitations is the human element. Internal control policies and procedures are applied by people and often impact other people. This human element creates several potential limitations that we can categorize as either (1) human error or (2) human fraud.

Human error is a factor whenever internal control policies and procedures are carried out by people. *Human error* can occur from negligence, fatigue, misjudgment, or confusion. *Human fraud* involves intent by people to defeat internal controls for personal gain. Fraudulent behavior can defeat many internal controls. This includes collusion to thwart the separation of duties principle as explained above. This human element highlights the importance of establishing an *internal control environment* to convey management's commitment to internal control policies and procedures.

Another important limitation on internal control is the *cost-benefit principle*. This means the costs of internal controls must not exceed their benefits. Analysis of costs and benefits must consider all factors, including the impact on morale. Most companies, for instance, have a legal right to read employees' e-mail. Yet companies seldom exercise that right unless confronted with evidence of potential harm to the company. The same holds for drug testing, phone tapping, and hidden cameras. The bottom line is that no internal control system is perfect, and that managers must establish internal control policies and procedures with a net benefit to the company.

Flash *back*

1. Fundamental principles of internal control include:

- **a.** Responsibility for a series of related transactions (such as placing orders, receiving, and paying for merchandise) should be assigned to one person.
- **b.** Responsibility for specific tasks should be shared by more than one employee so that one serves as a check on the other.
- **c.** Employees who handle cash and negotiable assets should be bonded.

2. What are some impacts of computing technology on internal control?

Answers—p. 393

Control of Cash

Cash is a necessary asset of every company. Most companies also include *cash equivalents*, which are similar to cash, as part of cash. We define cash equivalents later in this section. It is important to apply principles of good internal control to cash and cash equivalents. They are the most liquid of all assets and are easily hidden and moved. A good system of internal control for cash provides adequate procedures for protecting both cash receipts and cash disbursements. These procedures should meet three basic guidelines:

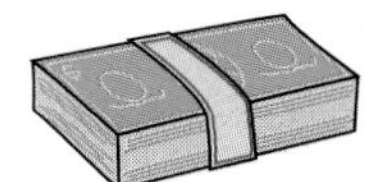

1. Handling of cash is separate from recordkeeping for cash.
2. Cash receipts are promptly (daily) deposited in a bank.
3. Cash disbursements are made by check.

The first guideline aims to minimize errors and fraud by division of duties. When duties are separated, two or more people must collude to steal cash and conceal this action in the accounting records. The second guideline aims to use immediate (daily) deposits of all cash receipts to produce a timely independent test of the accuracy of the count of cash received. It also reduces cash theft or loss, and it reduces the risk of an employee personally using the money before depositing it. The third guideline aims to use payments by check to develop a bank record of cash disbursements. This guideline also reduces the risk of cash theft.

One exception to the third guideline is the disbursement of small amounts of currency and coins from a *petty cash fund*. We describe a petty cash fund later in this section. The deposit of cash receipts and the use of checks for cash disbursements also allows a company to use bank records as a separate external record of cash transactions. We explain how to use bank records to confirm the accuracy of a company's own records later in this section.

The exact procedures used to achieve control over cash vary across companies. They depend on such factors as company size, number of employees, volume of cash transactions, and sources of cash. We must therefore view the procedures described in this section as illustrative of those in practice today.

Cash, Cash Equivalents, and Liquidity

C3 Define cash and cash equivalents and how they are reported.

Cash is an important asset for every company and must be managed. Companies also need to carefully control access to cash by employees and others who are sometimes inclined to take it for personal use. Good accounting systems support both goals by managing how much cash is on hand and controlling who has access to it. The importance of accounting for cash is highlighted by the inclusion of a statement of cash flows in a complete set of financial statements. That statement identifies activities affecting cash.[1] The purpose of this section is to define cash and cash equivalents. It also explains liquidity and its relation to cash and cash equivalents.

Cash Defined

Cash includes currency, coins, and amounts on deposit in bank accounts, checking accounts (also called *demand deposits*), and some savings accounts (also called *time deposits*). Cash also includes items that are acceptable for deposit in these accounts such as customers' checks, cashier's checks, certified checks, and money orders.

Cash Equivalents Defined

To increase their return on investment, many companies invest idle cash in assets called *cash equivalents.* **Cash equivalents** are short-term, highly liquid investment assets meeting two criteria:

1. Readily convertible to a known cash amount.
2. Sufficiently close to their maturity date so that market value is not sensitive to interest rate changes.

Only investments purchased within three months of their maturity dates usually satisfy these criteria.[2] Examples of cash equivalents are short-term investments in U.S. treasury bills, commercial paper such as short-term corporate notes payable, and money market funds.

Reporting Cash and Cash Equivalents

Because cash equivalents are similar to cash, most companies combine them with cash as a single item on the balance sheet. **Ford Motor Company,** for instance, reports the following on its December 31, 1997 balance sheet:

Cash and cash equivalents	$ 6,316 (million)

[1] We described the statement of cash flows in earlier chapters and discussed cash flow relative to various topics. Chapter 17 explains the statement of cash flows in detail.

[2] FASB, *Accounting Standards—Current Text* (Norwalk, CT, 1995), sec. C25.106. First published in *Statement of Financial Accounting Standards No. 95,* par. 8.

Another example is **Mattel**'s December 31, 1997, balance sheet, which reports a Cash balance of $695 (million). There is no balance or mention of cash equivalents in its balance sheet. But Mattel's Note 1 reports:

> Cash includes cash equivalents, which are highly liquid investments with maturities of three months or less when purchased. Because of the short maturities of these instruments, the carrying amount is a reasonable estimate of fair value.

Liquidity

Cash is the usual means of payment when paying for other assets, services, or liabilities. **Liquidity** is how easily an asset can be converted into another asset or be used in paying for services or obligations. All assets can be judged on their liquidity. Cash and similar assets are called **liquid assets** because they are converted easily into other assets or used to pay for services or liabilities. A company needs more than valuable assets to operate. A company must own some liquid assets, for example, so that bills are paid on time and purchases are made for cash when necessary.

Flash back

3. Why must a company own liquid assets?
4. Why does a company own cash equivalent assets in addition to cash?
5. Identify at least two assets that are classified as cash equivalents.

Answers—p. 393

Control of Cash Receipts

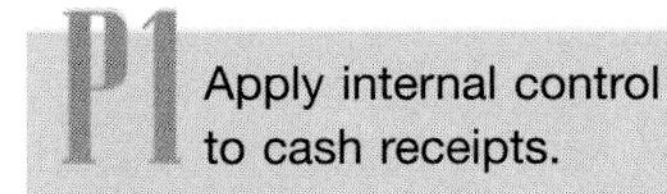

P1 Apply internal control to cash receipts.

Internal control of cash receipts ensures that all cash received is properly recorded and deposited. Cash receipts arise from many transactions including cash sales, collections of customers' accounts, receipts of interest and rent, bank loans, sale of assets, and owner investments. The principles of internal control apply to all types of cash receipts. This section explains internal control over two important types of cash receipts: over-the-counter and by mail.

Over-the-Counter Cash Receipts

For purposes of internal control, over-the-counter cash sales should be recorded on a cash register at the time of each sale. To help ensure that correct amounts are entered, each register should be located so customers can read the amounts entered. Clerks also should be required to both enter each sale before wrapping merchandise and give the customer a receipt for each sale. The design of each cash register should provide a permanent, locked-in record of each transaction. In many systems, the register is directly linked with computing and accounting services. Many software programs accept cash register transactions and enter them in accounting records. Less technology-dependent registers simply print a record of each transaction on a paper tape or electronic file locked inside the register.

One principle of internal control states that custody over cash should be separate from its recordkeeping. For over-the-counter cash sales, this separation begins with the cash register. The clerk who has access to cash in the register should not have access to its locked-in record. At the end of the clerk's work period, the clerk should count the cash in the register, record the amount, and turn over the cash and a record of its amount to an employee in the cashier's office. The employee in the cashier's office, like the clerk, has access to the cash and should not have access to accounting records (or the register tape or file). A third employee compares the record of total register transactions (or the register tape or file) with the cash receipts reported by the cashier's office. This record (or register tape or file) is the basis for a journal entry recording over-the-counter cash sales. The third employee has access to the records for cash but not to the actual cash. The clerk and the employee from the cashier's office have access to cash but not to the accounting records. This means the accuracy of cash records and amounts are automatically checked. None of them can make a mistake or divert cash without the difference being revealed.

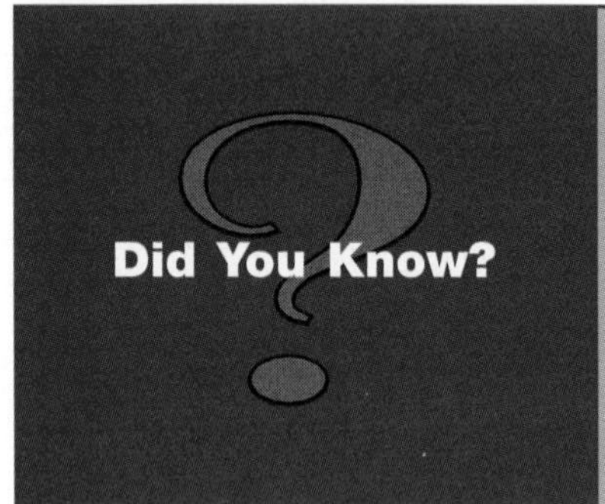

Register Mammoth
Wal-Mart uses an enormous network of information links with its point-of-sale cash registers. With annual sales of more than $100 billion, it uses information systems to coordinate sales, purchases, and distribution. Three Buenos Aires supercenters, for instance, ring up some 15,000 sales on heavy days. Wal-Mart is now the dominant discounter in the U.S., Canada, and Mexico. Yet even it makes mistakes, from a glut of ice-fishing huts in tropical Puerto Rico to a dearth of snowshoes in wintertime Ontario. But using cash register information, it is quick to fix mistakes and to capitalize on sales trends. [Source: *Business Week,* June 23, 1997.]

Cash Over and Short

Sometimes errors in making change are discovered when there are differences between the cash in a cash register and the record of the amount of cash sales. Even though a cashier is careful, one or more customers can be given too much or too little change. This means at the end of a work period, the cash in a cash register might not equal the cash sales entered. This difference is reported in the **Cash Over and Short** account. This account is an income statement account recording the income effects of cash overages and cash shortages from errors in making change and missing petty cash receipts. As an example, if a cash register shows cash sales of $550 but the count of cash in the register is $555, the entry to record cash sales and its overage is:

Assets = Liabilities + Equity
+555 + 5
+550

Cash	555	
Cash Over and Short		5
Sales		550
To record day's cash sales and overage.		

If a cash register shows cash sales of $625 but the count of cash in the register is $621, the entry to record cash sales and its shortage is:

Assets = Liabilities + Equity
+621 − 4
+625

Cash	621	
Cash Over and Short	4	
Sales		625
To record day's cash sales and shortage.		

Because customers are more likely to dispute being shortchanged, the Cash Over and Short account usually has a debit balance at the end of an accounting period. This debit balance reflects an expense. It can be shown on the income statement as an item in general and administrative expenses. But since the amount is usually small, it is often combined with other small expenses and reported as part of *miscellaneous expenses.* If Cash Over and Short has a credit balance at the end of the period, it usually is shown on the income statement as part of *miscellaneous revenues.*

Cash Receipts By Mail

Control of cash receipts that arrive through the mail starts with the person who opens the mail. Preferably, two people are assigned the task of and are present for opening the mail. Because two people are involved, theft of cash receipts by mail usually requires collusion between these two employees. The person opening the mail makes a list (in triplicate) of money received. This list should contain a record of each sender's name, the amount, and an explanation of why the money is sent. The first copy is sent with the money to the cashier. A second copy is sent to the recordkeeper in the accounting area. A third copy is kept by the clerk who opened the mail. The cashier deposits the money in a bank, and the recordkeeper records the amounts received in the accounting records.

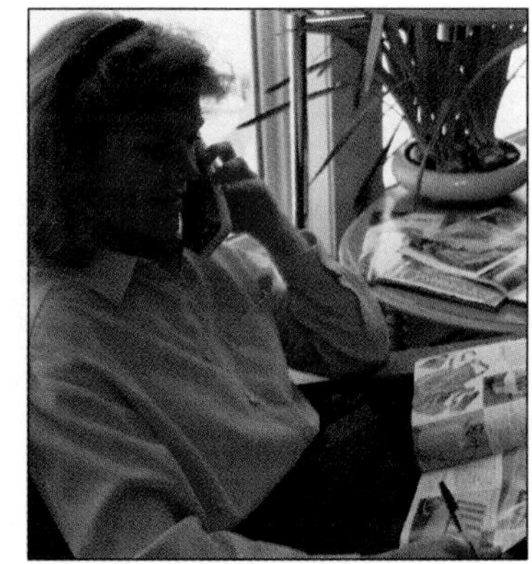

This process reflects excellent internal control. First, when the bank balance is reconciled by another person (explained later in the chapter), errors or fraud by the clerk, the cashier, or the recordkeeper are revealed. They are revealed because the bank's record of cash deposited must agree with the records from each of three people. This arrangement virtually eliminates the possibility of errors and fraud. If the clerk does not report all receipts correctly, for instance, customers will question their account balances. If the cashier does not deposit all receipts, for instance, the bank balance does not agree with the recordkeeper's cash balance. The recordkeeper and the person who reconciles the bank balance do not have access to cash and, therefore, have no opportunity to divert cash to themselves. This system makes errors and fraud highly unlikely. The exception is when employees collude.

Control of Cash Disbursements

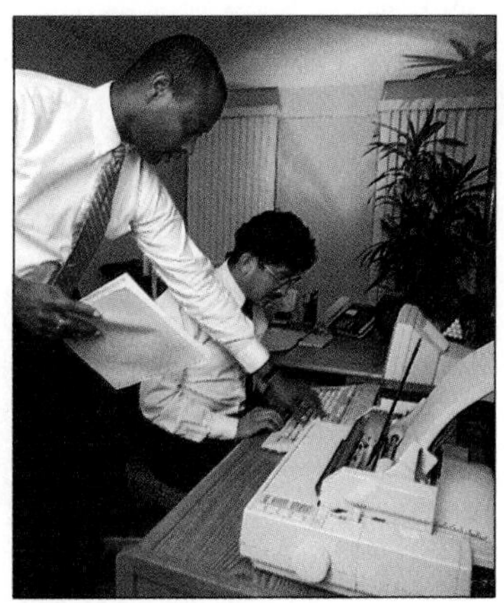

Control of cash disbursements is especially important for companies. Most large thefts occur from payment of fictitious invoices. One key to controlling cash disbursements is to require that all expenditures be made by check. The only exception is small payments made from petty cash. Another key is to deny access to the accounting records to a person other than the owner who has the authority to sign checks. This separation of duties helps prevent an employee from hiding fraudulent disbursements in the accounting records.

The manager of a small business often signs checks and knows from personal contact that the items being paid for are actually received. This arrangement is impossible in large businesses. Instead, internal control procedures must be substituted for personal contact. These procedures are designed to assure the check signer that the obligations recorded were properly incurred and should be paid. These controls are achieved through a voucher system.

This section describes the voucher system, explains the petty cash system, and describes the management of cash disbursements for purchases.

Paper Chase

Paper documents are still common in business today. Yet companies are increasingly converting to electronic documents. The purposes and features of most documents remain basically the same in either system. But the internal control system must change to reflect different risks and concerns. These include issues of confidentiality and competitive sensitive information that are placed at risk in electronic-based systems.

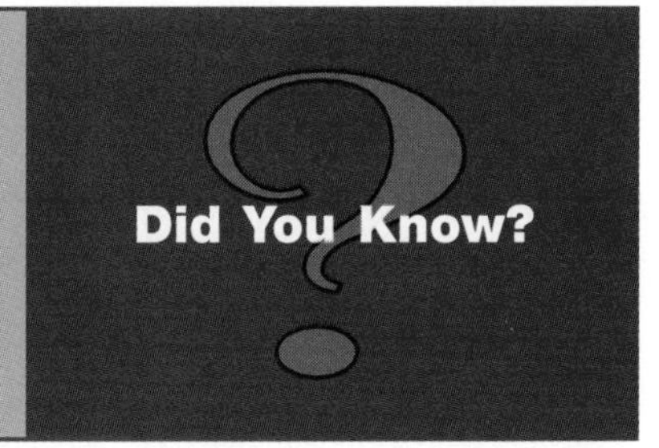

P2 Apply the voucher system to control cash disbursements.

Voucher System of Control

A **voucher system** is a set of procedures and approvals designed to control cash disbursements and acceptance of obligations. The voucher system of control establishes procedures for:

- Accepting obligations resulting in cash disbursements.
- Verifying, approving, and recording obligations.
- Issuing checks for payment of verified, approved, and recorded obligations.
- Requiring obligations be recorded when incurred.
- Treating each purchase as an independent transaction.

A good voucher system follows these procedures for every transaction. This applies even when many purchases are made from the same company during a period.

A voucher system's control over cash disbursements begins when a company incurs an obligation that will result in payment of cash. A key factor in this system is that only approved departments and individuals are authorized to incur such obligations. The system often limits the kind of obligations that a department or individual can incur. In a large retail store, for instance, only a purchasing department should be authorized to incur obligations from merchandise purchases. Another key factor is that procedures for purchasing, receiving, and paying for merchandise are often divided among several departments. These departments include the one requesting the purchase, the purchasing department, the receiving department, and the accounting department. To coordinate and control responsibilities of these departments, several different business papers are used. Exhibit 9.1 shows how these papers are accumulated in a **voucher.** A voucher is an internal business paper (or folder) that is used to accumulate other papers and information needed to control cash disbursements and to ensure a transaction is properly recorded. We next discuss each document entering a voucher. We show how a company uses this system in controlling cash disbursements for merchandise purchases.

Exhibit 9.1

Document Flow in a Voucher System

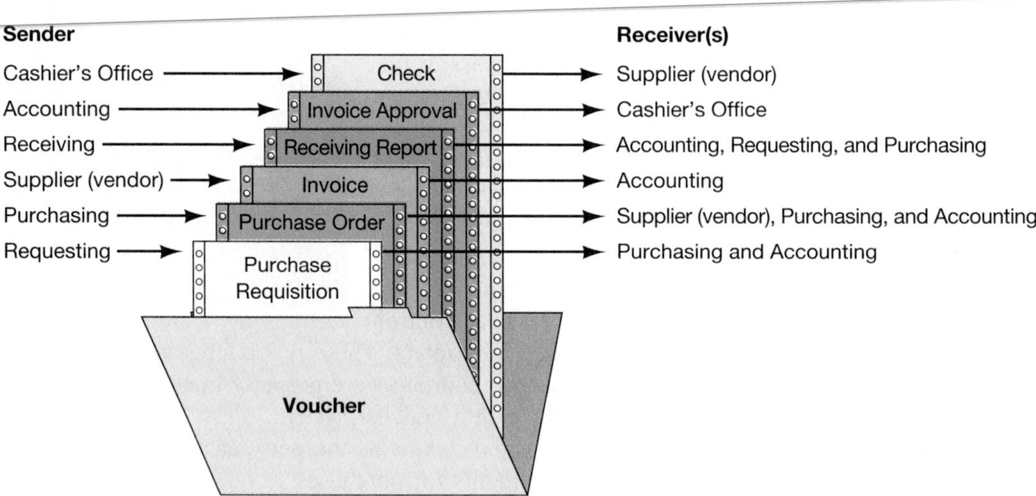

Purchase Requisition

Department managers in larger stores are usually not allowed to place orders directly with suppliers. If each manager deals directly with suppliers, the merchandise purchased and the resulting liabilities are not well controlled. To gain control over purchases and the resulting liabilities, department managers are often required to place all orders through a purchasing department. When merchandise is needed, a department manager must inform the purchasing department of its needs by preparing and signing a purchase requisition. A **purchase requisition** lists the merchandise needed by a department and requests that it be purchased—see Exhibit 9.2. Two copies of the purchase requisition are sent to the purchasing department. The purchasing department sends one copy to the ac-

Purchase Requisition No. 917
Z-Mart

From Sporting Goods Department **Date** October 28, 1998
To Purchasing Department **Preferred Vendor** Trex

Request purchase of the following item(s):

Model No.	Description	Quantity
CH 015	Challenger X7	1
SD 099	SpeedDemon	1

Reason for Request Replenish inventory
Approval for Request J.Z.

For Purchasing Department use only: Order Date 10/30/98 P.O. No. P98

Exhibit 9.2
Purchase Requisition

counting department. When the accounting department receives a purchase requisition, it creates and maintains a voucher for this transaction. A third copy of the requisition is kept by the requesting department as backup.

Purchase Order

A **purchase order** is a business paper used by the purchasing department to place an order with a seller, also called a **vendor.** A vendor usually is a manufacturer or wholesaler. A purchase order authorizes a vendor to ship ordered merchandise at the stated price and terms—see Exhibit 9.3. When the purchasing department receives a purchase requisition, it prepares at least four copies of a purchase order. The copies are distributed as follows: *copy 1* is sent to the vendor as a purchase request and as authority to ship merchandise; *copy 2* is sent, along with a copy of the purchase requisition, to the accounting department where it is entered in the voucher and used in approving payment of the invoice; *copy 3* is sent to the requesting department to inform its manager that action is being taken; and *copy 4* is retained on file by the purchasing department.

Purchase Order No. P98
Z-Mart
10 Michigan Street
Chicago, Illinois 60521

To: Trex
W9797 Cherry Road
Antigo, Wisconsin 54409

Date 10/30/98
FOB Destination
Ship by As soon as possible
Terms 2/15, n/30

Request shipment of the following item(s):

Model No.	Description	Quantity	Price	Amount
CH 015	Challenger X7	1	490	490
SD 099	SpeedDemon	1	710	710

All shipments and invoices must include purchase order number

Ordered by J.W.

Exhibit 9.3
Purchase Order

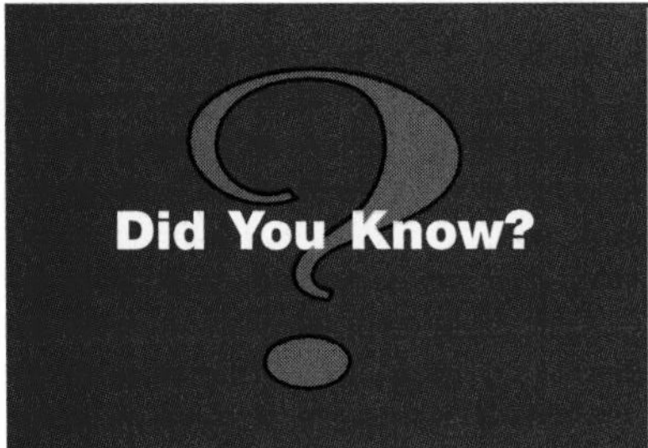

Year 2000

Year 2000 has a special meaning to systems experts. Generations of computer systems are designed to work with dates beginning with 19. This means new software is necessary to make them usable in year 2000 and beyond. Cost estimates at the national level are in the area of $600 billion. Companies in the financial services area are especially hard hit. The SEC requires companies and mutual funds to keep users informed about their year 2000 risk. Source: [*Business Week,* March 10, 1997.]

Invoice

An **invoice** is an itemized statement of goods prepared by the vendor (supplier) listing the customer's name, the items sold, the sales prices, and the terms of sale. An invoice is also a bill sent to the buyer from the supplier. From the vendor's point of view, it is a *sales invoice*. The vendor sends the invoice to a buyer, or **vendee**, who treats it as a *purchase invoice*. When receiving a purchase order, the vendor ships the ordered merchandise to the buyer and includes or mails a copy of the invoice covering the shipment to the buyer. The invoice is sent to the buyer's accounting department where it is placed in the voucher. Exhibit 6.6 shows Z-Mart's purchase invoice.

Receiving Report

Many companies maintain a special department to receive all merchandise or other purchased assets. When each shipment arrives, this receiving department counts the goods and checks them for damage and agreement with the purchase order. It then prepares four or more copies of a receiving report. A **receiving report** is used within the company to notify the appropriate persons that ordered goods have been received and to describe the quantities and condition of the goods. One copy is placed in the voucher. Copies are also sent to the requesting department and the purchasing department to notify them that the goods have arrived. The receiving department retains a copy in its files.

Invoice Approval

When a receiving report arrives, the accounting department should have copies of the following papers on file in the voucher: purchase requisition; purchase order; invoice; and receiving report. With the information in these documents, the accounting department can record the purchase and approve its payment before the end of the discount period. In approving an invoice for payment, the department checks and compares information across all documents. To facilitate this checking and to ensure that no step is omitted, the department often uses an **invoice approval,** also called *check authorization.* Exhibit 9.4 shows an invoice approval form. An invoice approval is a checklist of steps necessary for approving an invoice for recording and payment. It is a separate document either filed in the voucher or preprinted on the voucher. It also is sometimes stamped on the invoice. Exhibit 9.4 shows the invoice approval as a separate document.

Exhibit 9.4

Invoice Approval

Invoice Approval

	No.	By	Date
Purchase requisition	917	TZ	10/28/98
Purchase order	P98	JW	10/30/98
Receiving report	R85	SK	11/3/98
Invoice:	4657		
Price		JK	11/12/98
Calculations		JK	11/12/98
Terms		JK	11/12/98
Approved for payment		BC	11/12/98

As each step in the checklist is approved, the person initials the invoice approval and records the current date. Final approval implies the following steps have occurred:

1. **Requisition check** Items on invoice are requested, as shown on purchase requisition.
2. **Purchase order check** Items on invoice are ordered, as shown on purchase order.
3. **Receiving report check** Items on invoice are received, as shown on receiving report.
4. **Invoice check:** **Price** Invoice prices are as agreed with the vendor.
   Calculations Invoice has no mathematical errors.
   Terms Terms are as agreed with the vendor.

Voucher

Once an invoice is checked and approved, the voucher is complete. A complete voucher is a record summarizing a transaction. The voucher shows a transaction is certified as correct and it authorizes recording an obligation for the buyer. A voucher also contains approval for paying the obligation on an appropriate date. The physical form of vouchers varies across companies. Many are designed so that the invoice and other related source documents are placed inside the voucher, which is often a folder.

Completion of a voucher usually requires a person to enter certain information required on the inside and outside of the voucher. Typical information required on the inside of a voucher is shown in Exhibit 9.5, and that for the outside is shown in Exhibit 9.6. The information is taken from the invoice and the supporting documents filed in the

Exhibit 9.5

Inside of a Voucher

Z-Mart
Chicago, Illinois

Voucher No. 4657

Date Oct. 28, 1998
Pay to Trex
City Antigo City Wisconsin

For the following: (attach all invoices and supporting papers)

Date of Invoice	Terms	Invoice Number and Other Details	Terms
Nov. 2, 1998	2/15. n/30	Invoice No. 4657 Less discount Net amount payable	1,200 24 1,176

Payment approved
N.O. Neal
Auditor

Exhibit 9.6

Outside of a Voucher

Voucher No. 4657

Accounting Distribution

Account Debited	Amount
Merch. Inventory	1,200
Store Supplies	
Office Supplies	
Sales Salaries	
Other	
Total Vouch. Pay. Cr.	1,200

Due Date November 12, 1998
Pay to Trex
City Antigo
State Wisconsin

Summary of charges:
Total charges 1,200
Discount 24
Net payment 1,176

Record of payment:
Paid
Check No.

voucher. A complete voucher is sent to an authorized individual (often called an *auditor*). This person performs a final review, approves the accounts and amounts for debiting (called the *accounting distribution*), and authorizes recording of the voucher.

When a voucher is approved and recorded, it is filed until its due date, when it is sent to the cashier's office for payment. The person issuing checks relies on the approved voucher and its signed supporting documents as proof that an obligation has been incurred and must be paid. The purchase requisition and purchase order confirm the purchase was authorized. The receiving report shows items have been received, and the invoice approval form verifies that the invoice has been checked for errors. There is little chance for error. There is even less chance for fraud without collusion, unless all the documents and signatures are forged.

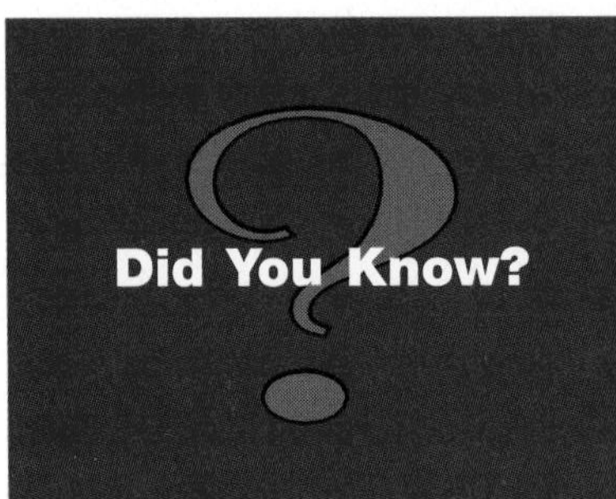

Anyone Smell a Rat?
Weak internal control contributed to a debacle at **Centennial Technologies,** once a high-tech dynamo. Fictitious sales receipts, altered inventory tags, and recording sales that were never shipped are some of the actions carried out by Centennial's management to deceive auditors, investors, and creditors. CEO Emanuel Pinez was eventually indicted on five counts of fraud. Yet many of these accounting shenanigans could have been avoided with better internal control and oversight. [Source: *Business Week,* March 24, 1997.]

Expenses in a Voucher System

Obligations should be approved for payment and recorded as liabilities as soon as possible after they are incurred. This practice should be applied to all purchases. It should also be applied to all expenses. When a company receives a monthly telephone bill, for instance, the charges (especially long distance and costly calls) should be examined for accuracy. A voucher is prepared and the telephone bill is filed inside the voucher. This voucher is then recorded with a journal entry. If the amount is due at once, a check is issued. If not, the voucher is filed for payment on its due date.

Requiring that vouchers be prepared for expenses when they are incurred helps ensure that every expense payment is valid. Yet invoices or bills for such items as repairs are often not received until weeks after work is done. If no records of repairs exist, it can be difficult to determine whether the invoice amount is correct. Also, if no records exist, it is possible for a dishonest employee to collude with a dishonest seller to get more than one payment for an obligation, or for payment of excessive amounts, or for payment for goods and services not received. An effective voucher system helps prevent each of these frauds.

Flash back

6. Good internal control procedures for cash receipts include:
   a. All cash disbursements, other than those for very small amounts, are made by check.
   b. An accounting employee should count cash received from sales and promptly deposit receipts.
   c. Cash receipts by mail should be opened by an accounting employee who is responsible for recording and depositing receipts.

7. Do all companies require a voucher system? At what point in a company's growth do you recommend a voucher system?

Answers—p. 393

Petty Cash System of Control

P3 Explain and record petty cash fund transactions.

A basic principle for controlling cash disbursements is that all payments are made by check. An exception to this rule is made for *petty cash disbursements.* Petty cash disbursements are the small payments required in most companies for items such as postage, courier fees, repairs, and supplies. Any amounts other than small payments are excluded. If firms made all small payments by check, it would require numerous checks for small amounts. This system would be both time-consuming and expensive. To avoid writing checks for small amounts, a company usually sets up a petty cash fund and uses the money in this fund to make small payments.

Operating a Petty Cash Fund

Establishing a petty cash fund requires estimating the total amount of small payments likely to be made during a short period such as a week or month. A check is then drawn by the company cashier for an amount slightly in excess of this estimate. This check is recorded with a debit to the Petty Cash account (an asset) and a credit to Cash. The check is cashed, and the currency is given to an employee designated as the *petty cashier*, also called *petty cash custodian.* The petty cashier is responsible for the safekeeping of the cash, for making payments from this fund, and for keeping accurate records.

The petty cashier should keep petty cash in a locked box in a safe place. As each disbursement is made, the person receiving payment signs a *petty cash receipt*, also called *petty cash ticket*—see Exhibit 9.7. The petty cash receipt is then placed in the petty cashbox with the remaining money. Under this system, the sum of all receipts plus the remaining cash equals the total fund amount. A $100 petty cash fund, for instance, contains any combination of cash and cash receipts that total $100 (examples are $100 cash, or $80 cash plus $20 in receipts, or $10 cash plus $90 in receipts). Each disbursement reduces cash and increases the amount of receipts in the petty cashbox. When the cash is nearly gone, the fund should be reimbursed.

Exhibit 9.7
Petty Cash Receipt

Petty Cash Receipt No. 9
Z-Mart

For Delivery charges — Date 11/5/98
Charge to Merchandise Inventory — Amount $6.75
Approved by *Jim Gibbs* — Received by *Dick Fitch*

When it is time to reimburse the petty cash fund, the petty cashier should sort the paid receipts by the type of expense or other accounts to be debited in recording payments from the fund. The accounts are then totaled, and the totals are used in making the entry to record the reimbursement. The petty cashier presents all paid receipts to the company's cashier. The company's cashier stamps all receipts *paid* so they can't be reused, files them for recordkeeping, and gives the petty cashier a check for their sum. When this check is cashed and the money returned to the cashbox, the total money in the box is restored to its original amount. The fund is now ready to begin a new cycle of operations.

Illustration of a Petty Cash Fund

Z-Mart uses a petty cash fund to avoid writing an excessive number of checks for small amounts. Z-Mart initially established a petty cash fund on November 1, 1998. It designated one of its office employees, Jim Gibbs, as petty cashier. A $75 check was drawn, cashed, and the proceeds turned over to Gibbs. The entry to record the setup of this petty cash fund is:

Assets = Liabilities + Equity
+75
−75

Nov. 1	Petty Cash	75	
	Cash		75
	To establish a petty cash fund.		

This entry transfers $75 from the regular Cash account to the Petty Cash account. After the petty cash fund is established, the Petty Cash account is not debited or credited again unless the size of the total fund is changed. A fund probably should be increased if it is being used up and reimbursed too frequently. If the fund is too large, some of its money should be redeposited in the cash account.

During November, Jim Gibbs, the petty cashier, made several payments from petty cash. He asked each person who received payment to sign a receipt. On November 27, after making a $26.50 payment for repairs to an office computer, only $3.70 cash remained in the fund. Gibbs then summarized and totaled the petty cash receipts as shown in Exhibit 9.8. He gave this summary and all petty cash receipts to the company's cashier in exchange for a $71.30 check to reimburse the fund. Gibbs cashed the check and put the $71.30 cash in the petty cashbox. The company records the reimbursement check as follows:

Assets = Liabilities + Equity
−71.30 −46.50
−15.05
− 5.00
− 4.75

Nov. 27	Miscellaneous Expenses	46.50	
	Merchandise Inventory	15.05	
	Delivery Expense	5.00	
	Office Expense	4.75	
	Cash		71.30
	To reimburse petty cash.		

Information for this entry is from the petty cashier's summary of payments in Exhibit 9.8. The debits in this entry reflect the petty cash payments.

A petty cash fund is often reimbursed at the end of an accounting period even if the petty cash fund is not low on money. This is done to record expenses in the proper period. If the fund is not reimbursed at the end of a period, the financial statements show both an overstated petty cash asset and understated expenses or assets that were paid out of petty cash. Yet the amounts involved are rarely significant to users of financial statements.

Exhibit 9.8

Petty Cash Payments Report

Z-MART
Petty Cash Payments Report

Miscellaneous expenses			
Nov. 2	Washing windows	$10.00	
Nov. 17	Washing windows	10.00	
Nov. 27	Computer repairs	26.50	$46.50
Merchandise inventory (transportation-in)			
Nov. 5	Delivery of merchandise purchased	$ 6.75	
Nov. 20	Delivery of merchandise purchased	8.30	15.05
Delivery expense			
Nov. 18	Customer's package delivered		5.00
Office expense			
Nov. 15	Purchased office supplies		4.75
Total			**$71.30**

Increasing or Decreasing Petty Cash Fund

A decision to increase or decrease a petty cash fund is often made when reimbursing the fund. To illustrate, let's assume Z-Mart decides to *increase* the petty cash fund of Jim Gibbs to $100 on November 27 when it reimburses the fund. This entry is identical to the one above except for two changes: (1) include a debit to Petty Cash for $25 (this increases the fund from $75 to $100), and (2) credit Cash for $96.30 ($71.30 reimbursement of expenses plus $25 increase in the fund).

Alternatively, if Z-Mart *decreases* the petty cash fund from $75 to $55 on November 27, there are two changes required for the entry on this date: (1) include a credit to Petty Cash for $20 (this decreases the fund from $75 to $55), and (2) credit Cash for $51.30 ($71.30 reimbursement of expense minus $20 decrease in the fund).

Internal Auditor
You are an internal auditor for a company. You are currently making surprise counts of three $200 petty cash funds. You arrive at the office of one of the petty cashiers while she is on the telephone. You explain the purpose of your visit, and the petty cashier asks politely that you come back after lunch so that she can finish the business she's conducting by long distance. You agree and return after lunch. The petty cashier opens the petty cashbox and shows you nine new $20 bills with consecutive serial numbers plus receipts totaling $20. Do you take further action or comment on these events in your report to management?

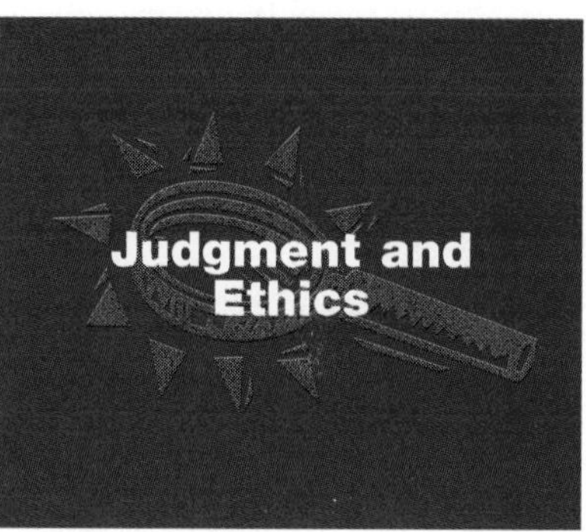

Answer—p. 393

Cash Over and Short

Sometimes a petty cashier fails to get a receipt for payment. When this occurs and the fund is later reimbursed, the petty cashier often won't recall the purpose of the payment. This mistake causes the fund to be *short*. If the petty cash fund is short, this shortage is recorded as an expense in the reimbursing entry with a debit to the Cash Over and Short account. An overage in the petty cash fund is recorded with a credit to Cash Over and Short in the reimbursing entry.

Flash back

8. Why are some cash payments made from a petty cash fund?
9. Why should a petty cash fund be reimbursed at the end of an accounting period?
10. What are two results of reimbursing the petty cash fund?

Answers—p. 393

Control of Purchase Discounts

P4 Apply the net method to control purchase discounts.

This section explains how a company can gain more control over purchase discounts. Chapter 6 described entries to record the receipt and payment of an invoice for a purchase of merchandise under the perpetual inventory system. When Z-Mart purchased merchandise with a $1,200 invoice price with terms of 2/10, n/30, it made the entry:

Nov. 2	Merchandise Inventory	1,200	
	Accounts Payable		1,200
	Purchased merchandise on credit, invoice dated November 2, terms 2/10, n/30.		

Assets = Liabilities + Equity
+1,200 +1,200

When Z-Mart takes advantage of the discount and pays the amount due on November 12, the entry is:

Assets = Liabilities + Equity
−24 −1,200
−1,176

Nov. 12	Accounts Payable	1,200	
	Merchandise Inventory		24
	Cash		1,176
	Paid for the purchase of November 2 less the discount. (2% × $1,200)		

These entries reflect the **gross method** of recording purchases. The gross method records the invoice at its *gross* amount of $1,000 *before* recognizing the cash discount. Many companies record invoices in this way.

Another method of recording purchases is the **net method**. The net method records the invoice at its *net* amount *after* recognizing the cash discount. This method is viewed as providing more useful information to management. If Z-Mart uses the net method of recording purchases, it deducts the potential $24 cash discount from the gross amount and records the initial purchase at the $1,176 net amount:

Assets = Liabilities + Equity
+1,176 +1,176

Nov. 2	Merchandise Inventory	1,176	
	Accounts Payable		1,176
	Purchased merchandise on credit, invoice dated November 2, terms 2/10, n/30.		

If the invoice for this purchase is paid within the discount period, the entry to record the payment debits Accounts Payable and credits Cash for $1,176. But if payment is not made within the discount period and the discount is *lost*, the following entry must be made either on the date the discount is lost or when the invoice is paid:

Assets = Liabilities + Equity
+24 −24

Dec. 2	Discounts Lost	24	
	Accounts Payable		24
	To record the discount lost.		

A check for the full $1,200 invoice amount is then written, recorded, and sent to the creditor.[3]

The net method gives management an advantage in controlling and monitoring purchase discounts. When invoices are recorded at *gross* amounts, the amount of discounts taken is deducted from the balance of the Merchandise Inventory account. This means the amount of any discounts lost is not reported in any account or on the income statement. Discounts lost recorded in this way are unlikely to come to the attention of management. But when purchases are recorded at *net* amounts, a **discounts lost** expense is brought to management's attention as an operating expense on the income statement. Management can then seek to identify the reason for discounts lost such as oversight, carelessness, or unfavorable terms. This practice gives management better control over persons responsible for paying bills to ensure they take advantage of favorable discounts. In this way, it's less likely that favorable discounts are lost.

Banking Activities as Controls

Banks are used for many different services. One of their most important services is helping companies control cash and cash transactions. Banks safeguard cash, provide detailed and independent records of cash transactions, and are a source of cash financing. This section describes services and documents provided by banking activities that increase managers' control over cash.

[3] The discount lost also can be recorded with the payment in a single entry. If financial statements are prepared after a discount is lost, an adjusting entry is required to recognize it if it is not recorded.

Basic Bank Services

This first section explains basic bank services. We include the bank account, the bank deposit, and checking. Each of these services contributes to either or both the control or safeguarding of cash.

C4 Identify control features of banking activities.

Bank Account

A bank account is a record set up by a bank for a customer. It permits this customer to deposit money for safeguarding and check withdrawals. To control access to a bank account, all persons authorized to write checks on the account must sign a **signature card.** Bank employees use signature cards to verify signatures on checks. This lowers the risk of loss from forgery for both banks and customers. Many companies have more than one bank account to serve different needs and handle special transactions such as payroll.

Bank Deposit

Each bank deposit is supported by a deposit ticket. A **deposit ticket** lists the items such as currency, coins, and checks deposited and their corresponding dollar amounts. The bank gives the customer a copy of the deposit ticket or a deposit receipt as proof of the deposit. Exhibit 9.9 shows a deposit ticket.

Exhibit 9.9

Deposit Ticket

Front

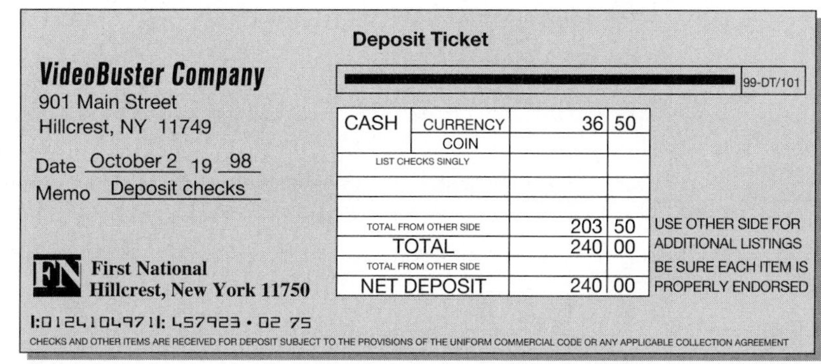

Deposit Ticket

VideoBuster Company
901 Main Street
Hillcrest, NY 11749

99-DT/101

Date October 2 19 98
Memo Deposit checks

CASH	CURRENCY	36	50
	COIN		
LIST CHECKS SINGLY			
TOTAL FROM OTHER SIDE		203	50
TOTAL		240	00
TOTAL FROM OTHER SIDE			
NET DEPOSIT		240	00

USE OTHER SIDE FOR ADDITIONAL LISTINGS
BE SURE EACH ITEM IS PROPERLY ENDORSED

FN First National
Hillcrest, New York 11750

I:0124104971I: 457923 • 02 75

CHECKS AND OTHER ITEMS ARE RECEIVED FOR DEPOSIT SUBJECT TO THE PROVISIONS OF THE UNIFORM COMMERCIAL CODE OR ANY APPLICABLE COLLECTION AGREEMENT

Back

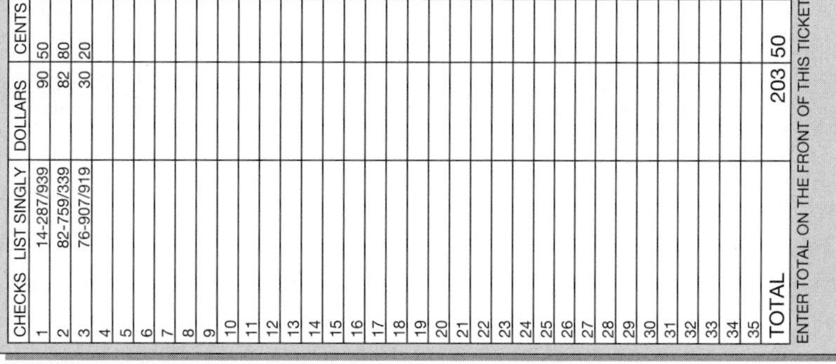

CHECKS	LIST SINGLY	DOLLARS	CENTS
1	14-287/939	90	50
2	82-759/339	82	80
3	76-907/919	30	20
4			
5			
6			
7			
8			
9			
10			
11			
12			
13			
14			
15			
16			
17			
18			
19			
20			
21			
22			
23			
24			
25			
26			
27			
28			
29			
30			
31			
32			
33			
34			
35			
TOTAL		203	50

ENTER TOTAL ON THE FRONT OF THIS TICKET

Booting Up Your Banker

Many companies are now balancing checkbooks and paying bills via PC. The convenience and low cost of wire transfers or checking account balances anytime, anywhere, are attracting thousands of small businesses to banking by PC. The user dials into a private line at the bank or its vendor to access information that is encrypted before it is transferred. Programs offer features such as the ability to stop payment on a check and move money between accounts. Users can also get account balances and identify checks and deposits that have cleared. Even taxes, suppliers, creditors, and employees can be paid electronically using a PC. [Source: *Business Week,* June 20, 1997.]

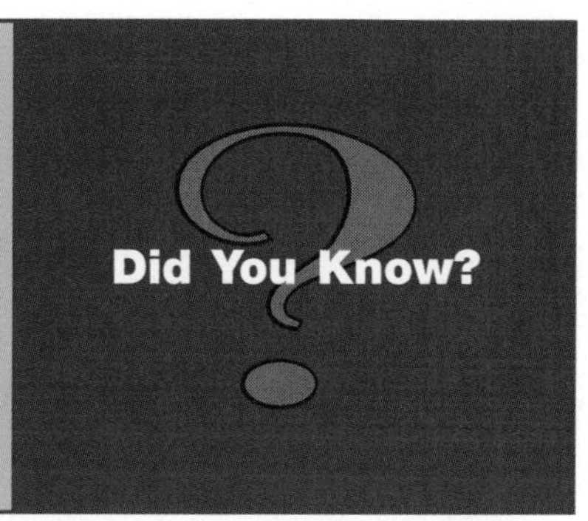

Bank Check

To withdraw money from an account a customer uses a check. A **check** is a document signed by the depositor instructing the bank to pay a specified amount of money to a designated recipient. A check involves three parties: a *maker* who signs the check, a *payee* who is the recipient, and a *bank* (or *payer*) on which the check is drawn. The bank provides a depositor with checks that are serially numbered and imprinted with the name and address of both the depositor and bank. Both checks and deposit tickets are imprinted with identification codes in magnetic ink for computer processing. Exhibit 9.10 shows a check. This check is accompanied with an optional *remittance advice* giving an explanation for the payment. When a remittance advice is unavailable, the *memo* line is often used for a brief explanation.

Check with Remittance Advice

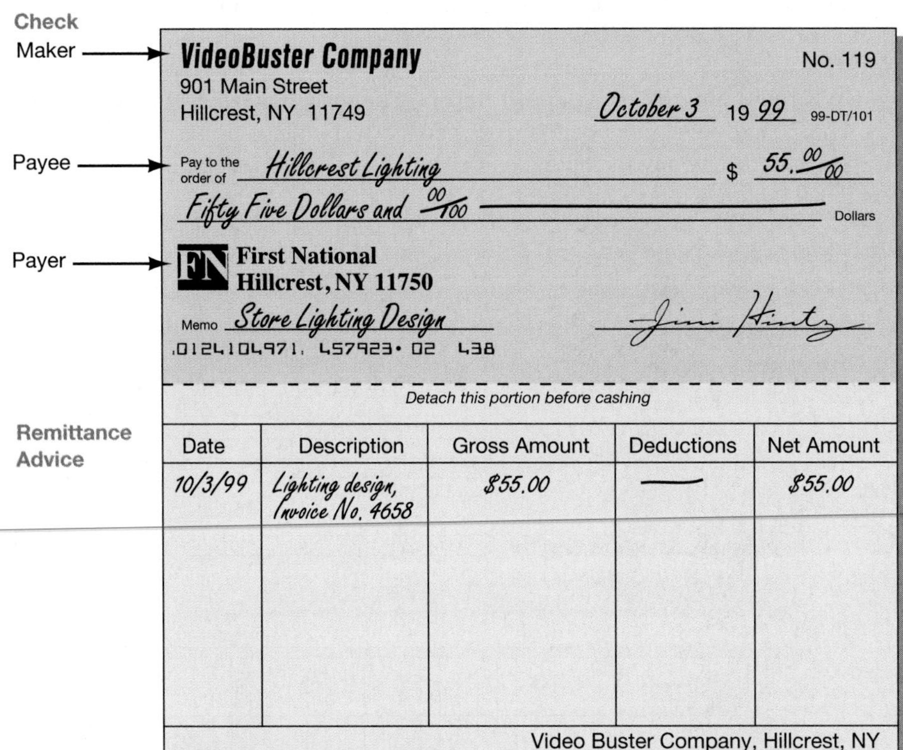

Electronic Funds Transfer

Electronic funds transfer (EFT) is the use of electronic communication to transfer cash from one party to another. No paper documents are necessary. Banks simply transfer cash from one account to another with a journal entry. Companies are increasingly using EFT because of its convenience and low cost. It can cost, for instance, up to a dollar to process a check through the banking system, whereas EFT cost is near zero. We now commonly see items such as payroll, rent, utilities, insurance, and interest payments being handled by EFT. The bank statement lists cash withdrawals by EFT with checks and other deductions. Cash receipts by EFT are listed with deposits and other additions. A bank statement is sometimes a depositor's only notice of an EFT.

Bank Statement

At least once a month, the bank sends each depositor a bank statement showing the activity in that account during the month. Different banks use different formats for their bank statements, yet all of them include the following items of information:

1. Beginning-of-month balance of the depositor's account.

Bank Statement

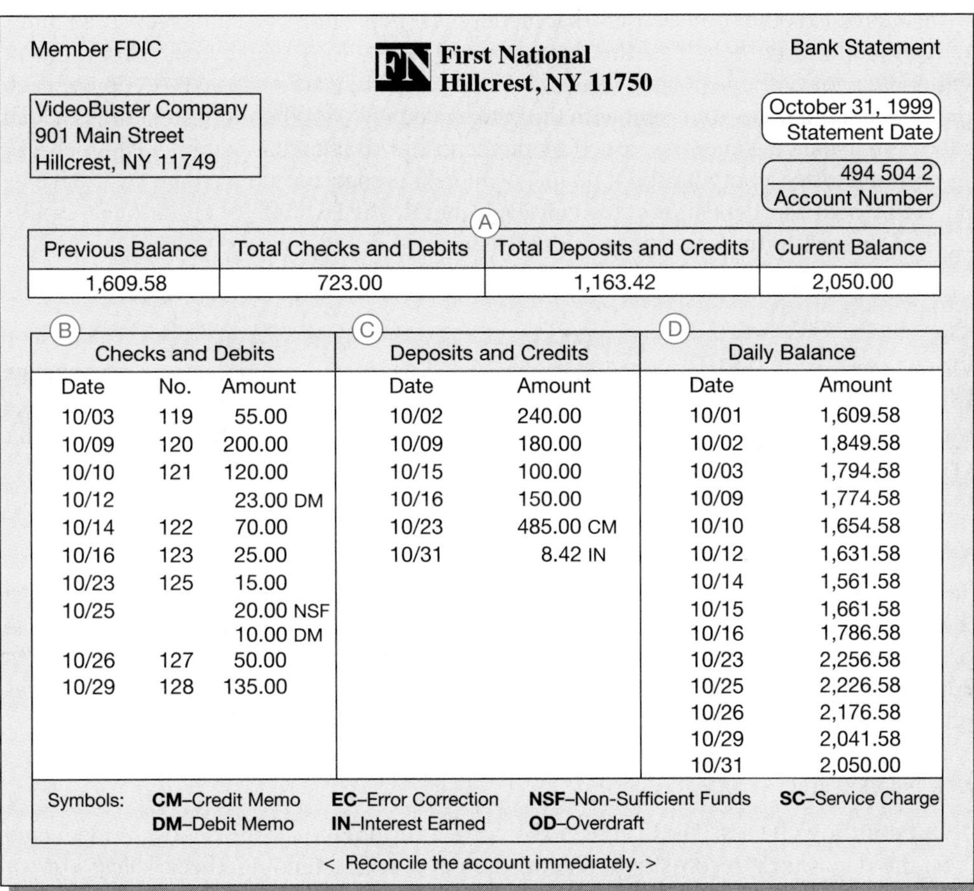

Member FDIC

FN First National
Hillcrest, NY 11750

Bank Statement

VideoBuster Company
901 Main Street
Hillcrest, NY 11749

October 31, 1999
Statement Date

494 504 2
Account Number

(A)

Previous Balance	Total Checks and Debits	Total Deposits and Credits	Current Balance
1,609.58	723.00	1,163.42	2,050.00

(B) Checks and Debits | (C) Deposits and Credits | (D) Daily Balance

Date	No.	Amount	Date	Amount	Date	Amount
10/03	119	55.00	10/02	240.00	10/01	1,609.58
10/09	120	200.00	10/09	180.00	10/02	1,849.58
10/10	121	120.00	10/15	100.00	10/03	1,794.58
10/12		23.00 DM	10/16	150.00	10/09	1,774.58
10/14	122	70.00	10/23	485.00 CM	10/10	1,654.58
10/16	123	25.00	10/31	8.42 IN	10/12	1,631.58
10/23	125	15.00			10/14	1,561.58
10/25		20.00 NSF			10/15	1,661.58
		10.00 DM			10/16	1,786.58
10/26	127	50.00			10/23	2,256.58
10/29	128	135.00			10/25	2,226.58
					10/26	2,176.58
					10/29	2,041.58
					10/31	2,050.00

Symbols: **CM**–Credit Memo **EC**–Error Correction **NSF**–Non-Sufficient Funds **SC**–Service Charge **DM**–Debit Memo **IN**–Interest Earned **OD**–Overdraft

< Reconcile the account immediately. >

2. Checks and other debits decreasing the account during the month.
3. Deposits and other credits increasing the account during the month.
4. End-of-month balance of the depositor's account.

This information reflects the bank's records. Exhibit 9.11 shows a bank statement. Identify each of the four items listed above.

Part A of Exhibit 9.11 summarizes changes in the account. Part B lists paid checks in numerical order along with other debits. Part C lists deposits and credits to the account, and part D shows the daily account balances.

Enclosed with a bank statement are the depositor's canceled checks or images of canceled checks or images of canceled checks along with any debit or credit memoranda affecting the account. **Canceled checks** are checks the bank has paid and deducted from the customer's account during the month. Other deductions also often appear on a bank statement and include: (1) service charges and fees assessed by the bank, (2) customers' checks deposited that are uncollectible, (3) corrections of previous errors, (4) withdrawals through automatic teller machines (ATM), and (5) periodic payments arranged in advance by a depositor.[4] Except for service charges, the bank notifies the depositor of each deduction with a debit memorandum when the bank reduces the balance. A copy of each debit memorandum is usually sent with the monthly statement.[5]

---

[4] Because of a desire to make all disbursements by check, most business checking accounts do not allow ATM withdrawals.

[5] A depositor's account is a liability on the bank's records. This is because the money belongs to the depositor and not the bank. When a depositor increases the account balance, the bank records it with a *credit* to the account. This means that debit memos from the bank produce *credits* on the depositor's books, and credit memos produce *debits* on the depositor's books.

There are also other transactions that increase the depositor's account such as amounts the bank collects on behalf of the depositor and corrections of previous errors. Credit memoranda notify the depositor of all increases when they are recorded. A copy of each credit memorandum is often sent with the bank statement. Another item sometimes added to the bank balance is interest earned by the depositor. Banks that pay interest on checking accounts often compute the amount of interest earned on the average cash balance and credit it to the depositor's account each month. In Exhibit 9.11, the bank credits $8.42 of interest to the account of **VideoBuster.**

Bank Reconciliation

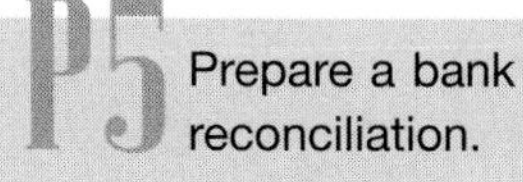
P5
Prepare a bank reconciliation.

When a company deposits all receipts and when all payments except petty cash payments are by check, the bank statement is a device for proving the accuracy of the depositor's cash records. The company tests the accuracy by preparing a bank reconciliation. A **bank reconciliation** explains the difference between the balance of a checking account according to the depositor's records and the balance reported on the bank statement.

Purpose of Bank Reconciliation

The balance of a checking account reported on the bank statement is rarely equal to the balance in the depositor's accounting records. This is usually due to information that one party has that the other does not. We must therefore prove the accuracy of both the depositor's records and those of the bank. This means we must *reconcile* the two balances and explain or account for any differences in these two balances.

Among the factors causing the bank statement balance to differ from the depositor's book balance are:

1. **Outstanding checks.** These are checks written (or drawn) by the depositor, deducted on the depositor's records, and sent to the payees. Outstanding checks have not yet reached the bank for payment and deduction at the time of the bank statement.
2. **Deposits in transit** (also called **outstanding deposits**). These are deposits made and recorded by the depositor but not recorded on the bank statement. For example, companies often make deposits at the end of a business day, after the bank is closed. A deposit in the bank's night depository on the last day of the month is not recorded by the bank until the next business day and doesn't appear on the bank statement for that month. Also, deposits mailed to the bank near the end of a month may be in transit and unrecorded when the statement is prepared.
3. **Deductions for uncollectible items and for services.** A company sometimes deposits a customer's check that is uncollectible. It usually occurs when the balance in a customer's account is not large enough to cover the check. This check is called a *non-sufficient funds (NSF)* check. The bank initially credits the depositor's account for the amount of the deposited check. When the bank learns the check is uncollectible, it debits (reduces) the depositor's account for the amount of that check. The bank may also charge the depositor a fee for processing an uncollectible check and notify the depositor of the deduction by sending a debit memorandum. While each deduction should be recorded by the depositor when a debit memorandum is received, an entry is sometimes not made until the bank reconciliation is prepared.

   Other possible bank charges to a depositor's account reported on a bank statement include the printing of new checks and a service charge for maintaining the account. Notification of these charges is *not* provided until the statement is mailed.
4. **Additions for collections and for interest.** Banks sometimes act as collection agents for their depositors by collecting notes and other items. Banks can also receive electronic fund transfers to the depositor's account. When a bank collects an item it adds it to the depositor's account, less any service fee. It also sends a credit memorandum to notify the depositor of the transaction. When the memorandum is received, it should be recorded by the depositor. Yet they sometimes remain unrecorded until the time of the bank reconciliation.

Many bank accounts earn interest on the average cash balance in the account during the month. If an account earns interest, the bank statement includes a credit for the amount earned during the past month. Notification of earned interest is provided by the bank statement.

5. **Errors.** Both banks and depositors can make errors. Errors by the bank might not be discovered until the depositor prepares the bank reconciliation. Also, the depositor's errors sometimes are not discovered until the bank balance is reconciled.

Steps in Reconciling a Bank Balance

The employee who prepares the bank reconciliation should not be responsible for cash receipts, processing checks, or maintaining cash records. This employee needs to gather information from the bank statement and from other records. A reconciliation requires this person to:

- Compare deposits on the bank statement with deposits in the accounting records. Identify any discrepancies and determine which is correct. List any errors and unrecorded deposits.
- Inspect all additions (credits) on the bank statement and determine whether each is recorded in the books. Examples are collections by the bank, correction of previous bank statement errors, and interest earned by the depositor. List any unrecorded credits.
- Compare canceled checks on the bank statement with actual checks returned with the statement. For each check, make sure the correct amount is deducted by the bank and the returned check is properly charged to the account. List any discrepancies and errors.
- Compare canceled checks on the bank statement with checks recorded in the books. (The bank statement often lists canceled checks in numerical order to help in this step.) List any outstanding checks. Also, while companies with good internal controls rarely write a check without recording it, we should inspect and list any canceled checks unrecorded in the books.
- Identify any outstanding checks listed on the previous month's bank reconciliation that are not included in the canceled checks on this month's bank statement. List these checks that still remain outstanding at the end of the current month. Send the list to the cashier's office for follow-up with the payees to see if the checks were actually received.
- Inspect all deductions (debits) on the bank statement and determine whether each is recorded in the books. Examples are bank charges for newly printed checks, NSF checks, and monthly service charges. List any unrecorded debits.

When this information is gathered, the employee can complete the reconciliation.

Illustrating a Bank Reconciliation

We use the guidelines listed above and follow nine specific steps in preparing the bank reconciliation. It is helpful to refer to the bank reconciliation for VideoBuster shown in Exhibit 9.12 and the steps ① through ⑨ in preparing it. These nine steps are:

① Identify the bank balance of the cash account (*balance per bank*).

② Identify and list any unrecorded deposits and any bank errors understating the bank balance. Add them to the bank balance.

③ Identify and list any outstanding checks and any bank errors overstating the bank balance. Deduct them from the bank balance.

④ Compute the *adjusted bank balance,* also called *corrected* or *reconciled balance.*

⑤ Identify the company's book balance of the cash account (*balance per book*).

⑥ Identify and list any unrecorded credit memoranda from the bank, interest earned, and errors understating the book balance. Add them to the book balance.

VIDEOBUSTER
Bank Reconciliation
October 31, 1999

①	Bank statement balance		$2,050.00	⑤	Book balance		$1,404.58
②	Add:			⑥	Add:		
	Deposit of 10/31 in transit		145.00		Collect $500 note less $15 fee	$485.00	
					Interest earned	8.42	$ 493.42
			$2,195.00				$1,898.00
③	Deduct:			⑦	Deduct:		
	Outstanding checks:				Check printing charge	$ 23.00	
	No. 124	$150.00			NSF check plus service fee	30.00	$ 53.00
	No. 126	200.00	$ 350.00				
④	**Adjusted bank balance**		**$1,845.00**	⑧	**Adjusted book balance**		**$1,845.00**

⑨ Balances are equal (reconciled)

Exhibit 9.12

Bank Reconciliation

⑦ Identify and list any unrecorded debit memoranda from the bank, service charges, and errors overstating the book balance. Deduct them from the book balance.

⑧ Compute the *adjusted book balance*, also called *corrected* or *reconciled balance.*

⑨ Verify that the two adjusted balances from steps 4 and 8 are equal. If yes, they are reconciled. If not, check for mathematical accuracy and missing data.

In preparing to reconcile the bank account, the VideoBuster employee gathers the following data:

- Bank balance shown on the bank statement is $2,050.
- Book balance shown in the accounting records is $1,404.58.
- A $145 deposit placed in the bank's night depository on October 31 is not recorded on the bank statement.
- A comparison of canceled checks with the company's books showed two checks outstanding—No. 124 for $150 and No. 126 for $200.
- Enclosed with the bank statement is a credit memorandum showing the bank collected a note receivable for the company on October 23. The note's proceeds of $500 (minus a $15 collection fee) are credited to the company's account. This credit memorandum is not yet recorded by the company.
- The bank statement shows a credit of $8.42 for interest earned on the average cash balance in the account. There was no prior notification of this item, and it is not yet recorded on the company's books.
- Other debits on the bank statement that are not recorded on the books include *(a)* a $23 charge for checks printed by the bank, and *(b)* a NSF check for $20 plus a related $10 processing fee. The NSF check is from a customer, Frank Heflin, on October 16 and was included in that day's deposit.

The bank reconciliation in Exhibit 9.12 reflects these items. The circled numbers in this reconciliation correspond to the nine steps listed earlier.

When the reconciliation is complete, the employee sends a copy to the accounting department so that any needed journal entries are recorded. For instance, entries are needed for any unrecorded debit and credit memoranda and any company mistakes. Another copy goes to the cashier's office. The cashier's copy is especially important if the bank has made an error needing correction.

High-Tech Recs
High-tech reconciliations are today available on your PC and via the Web. With little or no fee, one can link into financial information that is updated continuously throughout the day—called real-time reconciliations. These programs do automatic bank reconciliations, and the software highlights such mistakes as transposed numbers or checks not previously recorded. Data can be easily downloaded and used in other applications. But one must still be able to analyze and interpret the reconciliation. [Source: *Business Week,* June 20, 1997.]

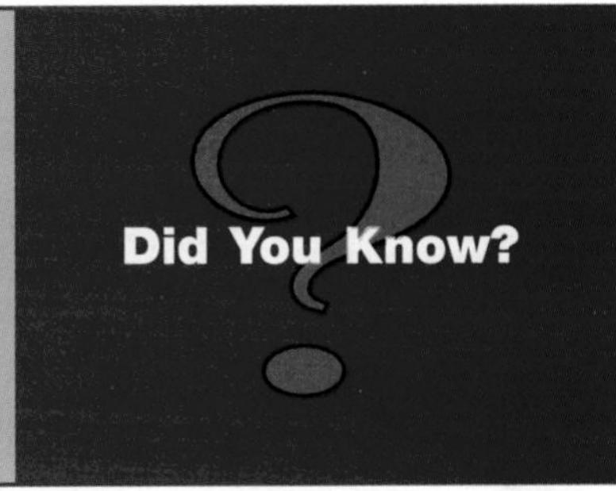

Recording Adjusting Entries from a Bank Reconciliation

A bank reconciliation helps identify errors by both the bank and the depositor. It also identifies unrecorded items that need recording on the company's books. In VideoBuster's reconciliation, the adjusted balance of $1,845 is the correct balance as of October 31. But the company's accounting records show a $1,404.58 balance. We must prepare journal entries to adjust the book balance to the correct balance. It is important to remember that only the items reconciling the book balance require adjustment. A review of Exhibit 9.12 indicates four entries are required for VideoBuster:

Collection of Note

The first entry is to record the net proceeds of VideoBuster's note receivable collected by the bank along with the expense of having the bank perform that service and the reduction in the Notes Receivable account:

Oct. 31	Cash	485	
	Collection Expense	15	
	Notes Receivable		500
	To record collection fee and proceeds of a note collected by the bank.		

Assets = Liabilities + Equity
+485 −15
−500

Interest Earned

The second entry records the interest credited to VideoBuster's account by the bank:

Oct. 31	Cash	8.42	
	Interest Earned		8.42
	To record interest earned on the average cash balance in the checking account.		

Assets = Liabilities + Equity
+8.42 +8.42

Interest earned is a revenue, and the entry recognizes both the revenue and the related increase in Cash.

Check Printing

The third entry debits Miscellaneous Expenses for the check printing charge:

Oct. 31	Miscellaneous Expenses	23	
	Cash		23
	Check printing charge.		

Assets = Liabilities + Equity
−23 −23

NSF Check

The fourth entry records the NSF check that is returned as uncollectible. The $20 check was originally received from Heflin in payment of his account and deposited. The bank charged $10 for handling the NSF check and deducted $30 total from VideoBuster's account. The company must reverse the original entry made when the check was received and also record the $10 fee:

Assets = Liabilities + Equity
+30
−30

Oct. 31	Accounts Receivable—Frank Heflin	30	
	Cash		30
	To charge Heflin's account for NSF check and bank's fee.		

This entry reflects normal business practice by adding the NSF $10 fee to Heflin's account. The company will try to collect the entire $30 from Heflin.

After these four entries are recorded, the balance of cash is increased to the correct amount of $1,845 ($1,404.58 + $485 + $8.42 − $23 − $30).

Flash *back*

11. What is a bank statement?

12. What is the meaning of the phrase *to reconcile a bank balance?*

13. Why do we reconcile the bank statement balance of cash and the depositor's book balance of cash?

14. List at least two items affecting the bank side of a reconciliation and indicate if the items are added or subtracted.

15. List at least three items affecting the book side of a reconciliation and indicate if the items are added or subtracted.

Answers—p. 393

USING THE INFORMATION Days' Sales Uncollected

A1 Compute days' sales uncollected ratio and use it to analyze liquidity.

Many companies attract customers by selling to them on credit. This means that cash flows from customers are delayed until accounts receivable are collected. Users of accounting information often want to know how quickly a company can convert its accounts receivable into cash. This is important for evaluating a company's liquidity.

One way users evaluate the liquidity of receivables is by looking at the **days' sales uncollected,** also called *days' sales in receivables*. This measure is computed by taking the current balance of receivables and dividing by net credit sales over the year just completed, and then multiplying by 365 (number of days in a year). But because the amount of net credit sales usually is not reported to external users, the net sales (or revenues) figure is commonly used in the computation. The formula for days' sales uncollected is shown in Exhibit 9.13.

Exhibit 9.13

Days' Sales Uncollected Formula

$$\textbf{Days' sales uncollected} = \frac{\textbf{Accounts receivable}}{\textbf{Net sales}} \times 365$$

Z-Mart, for instance, reports accounts receivable of $11,200 at the end of 1999 (see Exhibit 6.3) and net sales of $314,700 (see Exhibit 6.2) for the year. By dividing $11,200 by $314,700, we find the receivables balance is 3.56% of that year's sales. Because there are 365 days in a year, the $11,200 balance is 3.56% of 365 days of sales, or 13 days of sales.

We use the number of days' sales uncollected to estimate how much time is likely to pass before we receive cash receipts from credit sales equal to the current amount of accounts receivable. For evaluation purposes, we need to compare this estimate to the days' sales uncollected figures for other companies in the same industry. We also make comparisons between current and prior periods.

To illustrate a more thorough analysis of the number of days' sales uncollected, we select data from the annual reports of two toy manufacturers: **Hasbro** and **Mattel.** The days' sales uncollected figures and their component figures for Hasbro and Mattel are shown in Exhibit 9.14.

Exhibit 9.14

Analysis Using Days' Sales Uncollected

Company	Figure	($ thousands) 1996	1995	1994
Hasbro	Accounts receivable	$ 807	$ 791	$ 718
	Net sales	$3,002	$2,858	$2,670
	Days' sales uncollected	**98 days**	**101 days**	**98 days**
Mattel	Accounts receivable	$ 732	$ 679	$ 762
	Net sales	$3,786	$3,638	$3,205
	Days' sales uncollected	**71 days**	**68 days**	**87 days**

Days' sales uncollected for Hasbro at the end of 1996 is computed as (in thousands):

$$\frac{\$807}{\$3{,}002} \times 365 = \mathbf{98\ days}$$

This means it will take about 98 days to collect cash on ending accounts receivable. This number reflects on one or more of the following factors: a company's ability to collect receivables, the financial health of its customers, customer payment strategies, or sales discount terms.

To better assess this figure for Hasbro, we compare it to the two prior years' numbers and with those of Mattel. We see that Hasbro's days' sales uncollected is steady, varying from 98 to 101 days for the past three years. But in comparison to Mattel, the Hasbro figure is much larger. While Mattel has reduced its days' sales uncollected from 87 days in 1994 to 71 days in 1996, Hasbro has not. This means improved liquidity in receivables for Mattel. Improved liquidity often translates into increased profitability. While we don't show the figures here, the profitability of Mattel exceeds that of Hasbro over 1994–1996. Running a financially successful company requires continuous monitoring of the liquidity of its assets.

Sales Representative

You are a salesperson for a retailer who markets directly to consumers. You and the entire sales staff are told by your accounting division to take action to reduce days' sales uncollected. What can you do to reduce days' sales uncollected?

Answer—p. 393

Flash back

16. Why is the days' sales uncollected computation usually based on net sales instead of credit sales?

Answer—p. 393

Summary

C1 Define internal control and its purpose. An internal control system consists of the policies and procedures managers use to protect assets, ensure reliable accounting, promote efficient operations, and urge adherence to company policies. It is a key part of systems design, analysis, and performance. It can prevent avoidable losses and help managers both plan operations and monitor company and human performance.

C2 Identify principles of internal control. Principles of good internal control include establishing responsibilities, maintaining adequate records, insuring assets and bonding employees, separating recordkeeping from custody of assets, dividing responsibilities for related transactions, applying technological controls, and performing regular independent reviews.

C3 Define cash and cash equivalents and how they are reported. Cash includes currency and coins and amounts on deposit in a bank checking account and some savings accounts. It also includes items that are acceptable for deposit in these accounts. Cash equivalents are short-term, highly liquid investment assets meeting two criteria: readily convertible to a known cash amount and sufficiently close to their maturity date so that market value is not sensitive to interest rate changes. Examples of cash equivalents are short-term investments in U.S. treasury bills, commercial paper, and money market funds. Because cash equivalents are similar to cash, most companies combine them with cash as a single item on the balance sheet. Cash and cash equivalents are liquid assets because they are converted easily into other assets or used in paying for services or liabilities.

C4 Identify control features of banking activities. Banks offer several basic services that promote the control or safeguarding of cash. These involve the bank account, the bank deposit, and checking. A bank account is a record set up by a bank permitting a customer to deposit money for safeguarding and check withdrawals. A bank deposit is money contributed to the account with a deposit ticket as proof. A check is a document signed by the depositor instructing the bank to pay a specified amount of money to a designated recipient. Electronic funds transfer uses electronic communication to transfer cash from one party to another, and it decreases certain risks while exposing others. Companies increasingly use it because of its convenience and low cost.

P1 Apply internal control to cash receipts. Internal control of cash receipts ensures all cash received is properly recorded and deposited. Cash receipts arise from many transactions including cash sales, collections of customers' accounts, receipts of interest and rent, bank loans, sale of assets, and owner investments. Attention is focused on two important types of cash receipts: over-the-counter and by mail. The principles of internal control are applied in both cases. Good internal control for over-the-counter cash receipts includes use of a cash register, customer review, receipts, a permanent transaction record, and separation of the custody of cash from its recordkeeping. Good internal control for cash receipts by mail includes at least two people assigned to open mail and prepare a list with each sender's name, amount, and explanation.

P2 Apply the voucher system to control cash disbursements. A voucher system is a set of procedures and approvals designed to control cash disbursements and acceptance of obligations. The voucher system of control relies on several important documents, including the voucher and many supporting files. A voucher system's control over cash disbursements begins when a company incurs an obligation that will result in payment of cash. A key factor in this system is that only approved departments and individuals are authorized to incur certain obligations. To coordinate and control responsibilities of these departments, several different business documents are used.

P3 Explain and record petty cash fund transactions. Petty cash disbursements are payments of small amounts for items such as postage, courier fees, repairs, and supplies. To avoid writing checks for small amounts, a company usually sets up one or more petty cash funds and uses the money to make small payments. A petty fund cashier is responsible for safekeeping of the cash, for making payments from this fund, and for keeping receipts and records. A Petty Cash account is debited only when the fund is established or increased in size. The cashier presents all paid receipts to the company's cashier for reimbursement. Whenever the fund is replenished, petty cash disbursements are recorded with debits to expense accounts and a credit to cash.

P4 Apply the net method to control purchase discounts. The net method gives management an advantage in monitoring and controlling purchase discounts. When invoices are recorded at gross amounts, the amount of discounts taken is deducted from the balance of the Merchandise Inventory account. This means the amount of any discounts lost is not reported in any account or on the income statement. Discounts lost are unlikely to come to the attention of management. But when purchases are recorded at net amounts, a discounts lost expense is brought to management's attention as an operating expense on the income statement. Management can then seek to identify the reason for discounts lost, such as oversight, carelessness, or unfavorable terms.

P5 Prepare a bank reconciliation. A bank reconciliation is prepared to prove the accuracy of the depositor's and the bank's records. In completing a reconciliation, the bank statement balance is adjusted for such items as outstanding checks and unrecorded deposits made on or before the bank statement date but not reflected on the statement. The depositor's cash account balance also often requires adjustment. These adjustments include items such as service charges, bank collections for the depositor, and interest earned on the account balance.

A1 Compute days' sales uncollected ratio and use it to analyze liquidity. Many companies attract customers by selling to them on credit. This means cash flows from customers are delayed until accounts receivable are collected. Users of accounting information often want to know how quickly a company can convert its accounts receivable into cash. This is important for evaluating a company's liquidity. The days' sales uncollected ratio is one measure reflecting liquidity. It is computed by dividing the current balance of receivables by net sales over the year just completed, and then multiplying by 365. The number of days' sales uncollected is used to estimate how much time is likely to pass before we receive cash receipts from net sales equal to the current amount of accounts receivable. Our analysis needs to compare this estimate with those for other companies in the same industry and with prior years' estimates.

Guidance Answers to **You Make the Call**

Political Activist

A forced vacation policy is part of a good system of internal controls. When employees are forced to take vacations, their ability to hide any fraudulent behavior decreases. This is because someone must take on the responsibilities of the person on vacation, and the replacement employee potentially can uncover fraudulent behavior or records. A forced vacation policy is especially important for employees in more sensitive positions of handling money or easily transferable assets.

Sales Representative

There are several steps a salesperson can take to reduce days' sales uncollected. These include: (1) decreasing the proportion of sales on account to total sales by encouraging more cash sales; (2) identifying customers most delayed in their payments and encouraging earlier payments or cash sales; and (3) implementing stricter credit policies to eliminate credit sales to customers that never pay.

Guidance Answer to **Judgment and Ethics**

Internal Auditor

Your problem is whether to accept the situation or to dig further to see if the petty cashier is abusing petty cash. Since you were asked to postpone your count and the fund consists of nine new $20 bills, you have legitimate concerns on whether money is being used for personal use. You should conduct further investigation. Perhaps the most recent reimbursement of the fund was for $180 (9 × $20) or more. In that case, this reimbursement can leave the fund with sequentially numbered $20 bills. But if the most recent reimbursement was for less than $180, the presence of nine sequentially numbered $20 bills suggests that the new bills were obtained from a bank as replacement for bills that had been removed. Neither situation shows the cashier is stealing money. Yet the second case indicates the cashier "borrowed" the cash and later replaced it after the auditor showed up. In writing your report you must not conclude the cashier is unethical unless evidence along with your knowledge of company policies supports it. Your report must present facts according to the evidence.

Guidance Answers to Flash backs

1. *c*
2. Technology reduces processing errors, allows more extensive testing of records, limits the amount of hard evidence of processing steps, and highlights the importance of maintaining separation of duties.
3. A company owns liquid assets so that it can purchase other assets, buy services, and pay obligations.
4. A company owns cash equivalents because they yield a return greater than what is earned by cash.
5. Examples of cash equivalents are 90-day treasury bills issued by the U.S. government, money market funds, and commercial paper.
6. *a*
7. Not necessarily. A voucher system is used when a manager can no longer control the purchasing procedures through personal supervision and direct participation in business activities.
8. If all cash payments are made by check, numerous checks for small amounts must be written. Because this practice is expensive and time-consuming, a petty cash fund is established for making small cash payments.
9. If the petty cash fund is not reimbursed at the end of an accounting period, the transactions in petty cash are not yet recorded in the accounts and the petty cash asset is overstated. But these amounts are rarely large enough to affect users' decisions based on financial statements.
10. First, when the petty cash fund is reimbursed, the petty cash transactions are recorded in their proper accounts. Second, reimbursement provides money allowing the fund to continue being used. Third, reimbursement identifies any cash shortage or overage in the fund.
11. A bank statement is a report prepared by the bank describing the activities in a depositor's account.
12. To reconcile a bank balance means to explain the difference between the cash balance in the depositor's accounting records and the balance on the bank statement.
13. The purpose of the bank reconciliation is to determine if any errors have been made by the bank or by the depositor and to determine if the bank has completed any transactions affecting the depositor's account that the depositor has not recorded.
14. Outstanding checks—subtracted
Unrecorded deposits—added
15. Bank service charges—subtracted
Debit memos—subtracted
NSF checks—subtracted
Interest earned—added
Credit memos—added
16. The calculation is based on net sales because the amount of credit sales normally is not known by statement readers.

Demonstration Problem

Prepare a bank reconciliation for Jamboree Enterprises for the month ended November 30, 2000. The following information is available to reconcile Jamboree Enterprises' book balance of cash with its bank statement balance as of November 30, 2000:

a. After all posting is complete on November 30, the company's book balance of the Cash account had a $16,380 debit balance, but its bank statement showed a $38,520 balance.

b. Checks No. 2024 for $4,810 and No. 2036 for $5,000 are outstanding.

c. In comparing the canceled checks returned by the bank with the entries in the accounting records, we find that Check No. 2025 in payment of rent is correctly drawn for $1,000 but was erroneously entered in the accounting records as $880.

d. The November 30 deposit of $17,150 was placed in the night depository after banking hours on that date, and this amount did not appear on the bank statement.

e. In reviewing the bank statement, a check belonging to Jumbo Enterprises in the amount of $160 was erroneously drawn against Jamboree's account.

f. A credit memorandum enclosed with the bank statement indicated that the bank collected a $30,000 note and $900 of related interest on Jamboree's behalf. This transaction was not recorded by Jamboree before receiving the statement.

g. A debit memorandum for $1,100 listed a $1,100 NSF check. The check had been received from a customer, Marilyn Welch. Jamboree had not recorded the return of this check before receiving the statement.

h. Bank service charges for November totaled $40. These charges were not recorded by Jamboree before receiving the statement.

Planning the Solution

- Set up a bank reconciliation form as shown below with a bank side and a book side for the reconciliation (also see Exhibit 9.12). Leave room on both sides to add several items and to deduct several items. Each column will result in a reconciled and equal balance.

JAMBOREE ENTERPRISES
Bank Reconciliation
November 30, 2000

Bank statement balance	Book balance of cash . . . .
Add:	Add:
Deduct:	Deduct:
Adjusted bank balance	Adjusted book balance . . . .

- Examine each item *a* through *h* about Jamboree to determine whether it affects the book balance or the bank balance. For each item decide whether it should be added or deducted from the bank or book balance.
- After all items are analyzed, complete the form and arrive at a reconciled balance between the bank side of the reconciliation and the book side.
- For every reconciling item on the book side prepare an appropriate adjusting entry. Additions to the book side require an adjusting entry that debits cash. Deductions on the book side require an adjusting entry that credits cash.

Solution to Demonstration Problem

JAMBOREE ENTERPRISES
Bank Reconciliation
November 30, 2000

Bank statement balance		$38,520	Book balance of cash		$16,380
Add:			Add:		
Deposit of Nov. 30	$17,150		Collection of note . .	$30,000	
Bank error	160	$17,310	Interest earned	900	$30,900
		$55,830			$47,280
Deduct:			Deduct:		
Outstanding checks		9,810	NSF check	$ 1,100	
			Recording error . . .	120	
			Service charge	40	$ 1,260
Adjusted bank balance		**$46,020**	**Adjusted book balance**		**$46,020**

Required Adjusting Entries for Jamboree

Nov. 30	Cash	30,900	
	Notes Receivable		30,000
	Interest Earned		900
	To record collection of note principal and interest.		
Nov. 30	Accounts Receivable—Marilyn Welch	1,100	
	Cash		1,100
	To reinstate account due from an NSF check.		
Nov. 30	Rent Expense	120	
	Cash		120
	To correct recording error on check no. 2025.		
Nov. 30	Bank Service Charges	40	
	Cash		40
	To record bank service charges.		

Glossary

Bank reconciliation an analysis that explains the difference between the balance of a checking account shown in the depositor's records and the balance reported on the bank statement. (p. 386).

Canceled checks checks that the bank has paid and deducted from the customer's account during the month. (p. 385).

Cash includes currency, coins, and amounts on deposit in bank checking or savings accounts. (p. 370).

Cash equivalents short-term, highly liquid investment assets that are readily convertible to a known cash amount and sufficiently close to their maturity date so that market value is not sensitive to interest rate changes. (p. 370).

Cash Over and Short account an income statement account used to record cash overages and cash shortages arising from omitted petty cash receipts and from errors in making change. (p. 372).

Check a document signed by the depositor instructing the bank to pay a specified amount of money to a designated recipient. (p. 384).

Days' sales uncollected a measure of the liquidity of receivables computed by taking the current balance of receivables and dividing by the credit (or net) sales over the year just completed, and then multiplying by 365 (the number of days in a year); also called *days' sales in receivables.* (p. 390).

Deposit ticket lists items such as currency, coins, and checks deposited and their corresponding dollar amounts. (p. 383).

Discounts lost an expense resulting from failing to take advantage of cash discounts on purchases. (p. 382).

Electronic funds transfer (EFT) the use of electronic communication to transfer cash from one party to another. (p. 384).

Gross method a method of recording purchases at the full invoice price without deducting any cash discounts. (p. 382).

Internal control system all the policies and procedures managers use to protect assets, ensure reliable accounting, promote efficient operations, and urge adherence to company policies. (p. 364).

Invoice an itemized statement of goods prepared by the vendor that lists the customer's name, the items sold, the sales prices, and the terms of sale. (p. 376).

Invoice approval a document containing a checklist of steps necessary for approving an invoice for recording and payment; also called *check authorization* (p. 376).

Liquid asset an asset such as cash that is easily converted into other types of assets or used to buy services or pay liabilities. (p. 371).

Liquidity a characteristic of an asset that refers to how easily the asset can be converted into another type of asset or used in paying for services or obligations. (p. 371).

Net method a method of recording purchases at the full invoice price less any cash discounts. (p. 382).

Outstanding checks checks written and recorded by depositor but not yet paid by the bank at the bank statement date (p. 386).

Principles of internal control fundamental principles requiring management to establish responsibility, maintain adequate records, insure assets and bond key employees, separate recordkeeping from custody of assets, divide responsibility for related transactions, apply technological controls, and perform regular and independent reviews. (p. 365).

Purchase order a business document used by the purchasing department to place an order with the seller (vendor); authorizes the vendor to ship the ordered merchandise at the stated price and terms. (p. 375).

Purchase requisition a business document listing merchandise needed by a department and requesting it be purchased. (p. 374).

Receiving report a form used within a company to notify the appropriate persons that ordered goods are received and to describe the quantities and condition of the goods. (p. 376).

Signature card includes the signatures of each person authorized to sign checks on the account. (p. 383).

Vendee the buyer or purchaser of goods or services. (p. 376).

Vendor the seller of goods or services, usually a manufacturer or wholesaler. (p. 375).

Voucher an internal business file (or folder) used to accumulate documents and information needed to control cash disbursements and to ensure that a transaction is properly recorded. (p. 374).

Voucher system a set of procedures and approvals designed to control cash disbursements and acceptance of obligations. (p. 374).

Questions

1. Which of the following assets is most liquid and which is least liquid: merchandise inventory, building, accounts receivable, cash?
2. List the seven broad principles of internal control.
3. Why should the person who keeps the record of an asset not be the person responsible for custody of the asset?
4. Internal control procedures are important in every business, but at what stage in the development of a business do they become especially critical?
5. Why should responsibility for a sequence of related transactions be divided among different departments or individuals?
6. Why should all receipts be deposited on the day of receipt?
7. When merchandise is purchased for a large store, why are department managers not permitted to deal directly with suppliers?
8. What is a petty cash receipt? Who signs a petty cash receipt?
9. **NIKE**'s consolidated statement of cash flows in Appendix A describes the changes in cash and cash equivalents that occurred during the year ended May 31, 1997. What amount was provided by (or used in) investing activities? What amount was provided by (or used in) financing activities?
10. **Reebok**'s balance sheet in Appendix A depicts the cash and cash equivalents of Reebok as of December 31, 1996, and December 31, 1995. Contrast the magnitude of cash and cash equivalents with the other current assets as of December 31, 1996. Compare the cash and cash equivalents on hand as of December 31, 1996, with December 31, 1995.
11. Use **American Online** financial statements in Appendix A to compute the difference in the number of days' sales uncollected on June 30, 1996, and June 30, 1995. (Hint: Use trade accounts receivable only.) Comment on the results.
12. Identify the internal controls that Jason Barron likely implemented to help manage the employee theft he was experiencing. Do you think that increasing the sales commission to employees is a type of internal control? Explain.

Quick Study

QS 9-1
Terminology
C1

What is the difference between the terms *liquidity* and *cash equivalent?*

QS 9-2
Internal control objective
C1, C2

a. What is the main objective of internal control and how is it achieved?
b. Why should recordkeeping for assets be separated from custody over the assets?

QS 9-3
Internal control for cash
P1

A good system of internal control for cash provides adequate procedures for protecting both cash receipts and cash disbursements. Three basic guidelines help achieve this protection. What are these guidelines?

QS 9-4
Petty cash accounting
P3

a. The petty cash fund of the Wee Ones Agency is established at $75. At the end of the month, the fund contained $12.74 and had the following receipts: film rentals, $19.40; refreshments for meetings, $22.81 (both expenditures to be classified as Entertainment Expense); postage, $6.95; and printing, $13.10. Prepare journal entries to record (1) establishment of the fund and (2) reimbursement of the fund at the end of the month.
b. Explain the event(s) causing the Petty Cash account to be credited in a journal entry.

QS 9-5
Bank reconciliation
P5

a. For each of the following items indicate whether its amount (i) affects the bank or book side of the reconciliation and (ii) represents an addition or a subtraction:
   (1) Unrecorded deposits
   (2) Interest on average monthly balance
   (3) Credit memos
   (4) Bank service charges
   (5) Outstanding checks
   (6) Debit memos
   (7) NSF checks
b. Which of the items in *a.* require a journal entry?

QS 9-6
Purchase discounts

P4

Which accounting method uses a Discounts Lost account and what is the advantage of this method?

QS 9-7
Days' sales uncollected

The following account balances are taken from Mountain Snowboards:

	2000	1999
Accounts receivable	$ 75,692	$ 70,484
Net sales	$2,591,933	$2,296,673

What is the difference in the number of days' sales uncollected between years 2000 and 1999? According to this analysis, is the company's collection of receivables improving? Explain your answer.

Exercises

Exercise 9-1
Analyzing internal control

Lombard Company is a start up business that is growing rapidly. The company's recordkeeper, who was hired two years ago, left town suddenly after the company's manager discovered that a large sum of money had disappeared over the past 18 months. An audit disclosed that the recordkeeper had written and signed several checks made payable to the recordkeeper's fiancé and then recorded the checks as salaries expense. The fiancé, who cashed the checks but never worked for the company, left town with the recordkeeper. As a result, the company incurred an uninsured loss of $84,000.

Evaluate Lombard Company's internal control system and indicate which principles of internal control appear to have been ignored in this situation.

Exercise 9-2
Recommending internal control procedures

What internal control procedures would you recommend in each of the following situations?

a. A concession company has one employee who sells T-shirts and sunglasses at the beach. Each day, the employee is given enough shirts and sunglasses to last through the day and enough cash to make change. The money is kept in a box at the stand.

b. An antique store has one employee who is given cash and sent to garage sales each weekend. The employee pays cash for merchandise to be resold at the antique store.

Exercise 9-3
Internal control over cash receipts by mail

Some of Fannin Co.'s cash receipts from customers are sent to the company with the regular mail. Fannin's recordkeeper opens the letters and deposits the cash received each day. What internal control problem exists in this arrangement? What changes do you recommend?

Exercise 9-4
Petty cash fund

Eanes Co. established a $200 petty cash fund on January 1. One week later, the fund contained $27.50 in cash along with receipts for the following expenditures: postage, $64.00; transportation-in, $19.00; store supplies, $36.50; and miscellaneous expenses, $53.00. Eanes uses the perpetual method to account for merchandise inventory. Prepare journal entries to *(a)* establish the fund on January 1 and *(b)* reimburse it on January 8. *(c)* Prepare the journal entry to reimburse the fund and increase it to $500 on January 8 assuming no entry in part *b*.

Exercise 9-5
Petty cash fund with a shortage

Brady Company established a $400 petty cash fund on September 9. On September 30, the fund had $164.25 in cash along with receipts for the following expenditures: transportation-in, $32.45; office supplies, $113.55; and miscellaneous expenses, $87.60. Brady uses the perpetual method to account for merchandise inventory. The petty cashier could not account for the $2.15 shortage in the fund. Prepare *(a)* the September 9 entry to establish the fund and *(b)* the September 30 entry to reimburse the fund and reduce it to $300.

Exercise 9-6
Bank reconciliation
P5

Medline Service Co. deposits all cash receipts on the day when received and makes all cash payments by check. On July 31, 2000, after all posting is complete, its Cash account shows a $11,352 debit balance. Medline's July 31 bank statement shows $10,332 on deposit in the bank on that day. Prepare a bank reconciliation for Medline, using the following information:

a. Outstanding checks total $1,713.

b. The July canceled checks returned by the bank included an $18 debit memorandum for bank services.

c. Check No. 919, returned with the canceled checks, was correctly drawn for $489 in payment of the utility bill and was paid by the bank on July 15. It had been recorded with a debit to Utilities Expense and a credit to Cash in the amount of $498.

d. The July 31 cash receipts of $2,724 were placed in the bank's night depository after banking hours on that date and were unrecorded by the bank when the July bank statement was prepared.

Exercise 9-7
Adjusting entries from bank reconciliation
P5

Give the journal entries that Medline Service Co. must record as a result of having prepared the bank reconciliation in Exercise 9-6.

Exercise 9-8
Bank reconciliation items and adjusting entries
P5

Prepare a table with the following headings for a bank reconciliation as of September 30:

Bank Balance		Book Balance			Not Shown on the Reconciliation
Add	Deduct	Add	Deduct	Adjust	

For each item below, place an *x* in the appropriate columns to indicate whether the item should be added to or deducted from the book or bank balance, or whether it should not appear on the reconciliation. If the book balance is to be adjusted, place a *Dr.* or *Cr.* in the Adjust column to indicate whether the Cash balance should be debited or credited. At the left side of your table, number the entries sequentially to correspond to the numbers in the list.

1. Interest earned on the account.
2. Deposit made on September 30 after the bank was closed.
3. Checks outstanding on August 31 that cleared the bank in September.
4. NSF check from customer returned on September 15 but not recorded by the company.
5. Checks written and mailed to payees on September 30.
6. Deposit made on September 5 that was processed on September 8.
7. Bank service charge.
8. Checks written and mailed to payees on October 5.
9. Checks written by another depositor but charged against the company's account.
10. Principal and interest collected by the bank but not recorded by the company.
11. Special charge for collection of note in No. 10 on company's behalf.
12. Check written against the account and cleared by the bank; erroneously omitted by the company recordkeeper.

Exercise 9-9
Recording invoices at gross or net amounts
P4

Peltier's Imports uses the perpetual method to account for merchandise inventory and had the following transactions during the month of May. Prepare entries to record the transactions assuming Peltier's records invoices *(a)* at gross amounts and *(b)* at net amounts.

May 2 Received merchandise purchased at a $2,016 invoice price, invoice dated April 29, terms 2/10, n/30.

10 Received a $416 credit memorandum (at invoice price) for merchandise received on May 2 and returned for credit.

17 Received merchandise purchased at a $4,480 invoice price, invoice dated May 16, terms 2/10, n/30.
26 Paid for the merchandise received on May 17, less the discount.
28 Paid for the merchandise received on May 2. Payment was delayed because the invoice was mistakenly filed for payment today. This error caused the discount to be lost.

Exercise 9-10
Liquidity of accounts receivable
A1

Federated Merchandise Co. reported net sales for 1999 and 2000 of $565,000 and $647,000. The end-of-year balances of accounts receivable were December 31, 1999, $51,000; and December 31, 2000, $83,000. Calculate the days' sales uncollected at the end of each year and describe any changes in the liquidity of the company's receivables.

Problems

Problem 9-1
Establishing, reimbursing, and increasing petty cash fund
P3

Palladium Art Gallery had the following petty cash transactions in February of the current year:

Feb. 2 Drew a $300 check, cashed it, and gave the proceeds and the petty cash box to Nick Reed, the petty cashier.
5 Purchased paper for the copier, $10.13.
9 Paid $22.50 COD charges on merchandise purchased for resale, terms FOB shipping point. Palladium uses the perpetual method to account for merchandise inventory.
12 Paid $9.95 postage to express mail a contract to a client.
14 Reimbursed Gina Barton, the manager of the business, $58 for business mileage on her car.
20 Purchased stationery, $77.76.
23 Paid a courier $18 to deliver merchandise sold to a customer, terms FOB destination.
25 Paid $15.10 COD charges on merchandise purchased for resale, terms FOB shipping point.
28 Paid $64 for stamps.
28 Reed sorted the petty cash receipts by accounts affected and exchanged them for a check to reimburse the fund for expenditures. There was $21.23 cash in the fund, and he could not account for the shortage. The dollar amount of the petty cash fund was increased to $400.

Required

1. Prepare the journal entry to record establishing the petty cash fund.
2. Prepare a petty cash payments report that has these categories: delivery expense, mileage expense, postage expense, merchandise inventory (transportation-in), and office supplies. Sort the payments into the appropriate categories and total the expenditures in each category.
3. Prepare the journal entry to record the reimbursement and the increase of the fund.

Check Figure February 28, Cash, $378.77 Cr.

Problem 9-2
Establishing, reimbursing, and adjusting petty cash fund; accounting adjustments

El Gatto Co. has only a General Journal in its accounting system and uses it to record all transactions. The company recently set up a petty cash fund to facilitate payments of small items. The following petty cash transactions were reported by the petty cashier as occurring in April (the last month of the company's fiscal year):

Apr. 1 Received a company check for $250 to establish the petty cash fund.
15 Received a company check to replenish the fund for the following expenditures made since April 1 and to increase the fund to $450.
a. Paid $78 for janitorial service.
b. Purchased office supplies for $63.68.
c. Purchased postage stamps for $43.50.
d. Paid $57.15 to *The County Crier* for an advertisement in the newspaper.
e. Counted $11.15 remaining in the petty cash box.
30 The petty cashier reported $293.39 remained in the fund and decided that the April 15 increase in the fund was too large. A company check was drawn to replenish the fund for the following expenditures made since April 15 and to reduce the fund to $400.
f. Purchased office supplies for $48.36.
g. Reimbursed office manager for business mileage, $28.50.
h. Paid $39.75 courier charges to deliver merchandise to a customer, terms FOB destination.

Required

Preparation Component

Check Figure Cash credits: April 15, $438.85; April 30, $106.61

1. Prepare journal entries to record the establishment of the fund on April 1 and its replenishments on April 15 and on April 30 along with any increases or decreases in the fund balance.

Analysis Component

2. Explain how the company's financial statements are affected if the petty cash fund is not replenished and no entry is made on April 30. (Hint: The amount of office supplies that appears on a balance sheet is determined by a physical count of the supplies on hand.)

Problem 9-3
Preparing a bank reconciliation and recording adjustments
P5
S

The following information is available to reconcile Archdale Company's book balance of cash with its bank statement balance as of October 31, 1999:

a. After all posting is completed on October 31, the company's Cash account has a $26,193 debit balance, but its bank statement shows a $28,020 balance.
b. Checks No. 3031 for $1,380 and No. 3040 for $552 were outstanding on the September 30 bank reconciliation. Check No. 3040 was returned with the October canceled checks, but Check No. 3031 was not. Also, Check No. 3065 for $336 and Check No. 3069 for $2,148, both drawn in October, were not among the canceled checks returned with the statement.
c. In comparing the canceled checks returned by the bank with the entries in the accounting records, it was found that Check No. 3056 for the October rent was correctly drawn for $1,250 but was erroneously entered in the accounting records as $1,230.
d. A credit memorandum enclosed with the bank statement indicates the bank collected a $9,000 noninterest-bearing note for Archdale, deducted a $45 collection fee, and credited the remainder to the account. This event was not recorded by Archdale before receiving the statement.
e. A debit memorandum for $805 lists a $795 NSF check plus a $10 NSF charge. The check had been received from a customer, Jefferson Tyler. Archdale had not recorded the return of this check before receiving the statement.
f. Also enclosed with the statement is a $15 debit memorandum for bank services. It had not been recorded because no previous notification had been received.
g. The October 31 cash receipts of $10,152 were placed in the bank's night depository after banking hours on that date and this amount did not appear on the bank statement.

Required

Preparation Component

Check Figure Reconciled balance, $34,308

1. Prepare a bank reconciliation for the company as of October 31, 1999.
2. Prepare the journal entries necessary to bring the company's book balance of cash into conformity with the reconciled balance.

Analysis Component

3. Assume the October 31, 1999, bank reconciliation for the company is prepared and some items are treated incorrectly. For each of the following errors, explain the effect of the error on: (1) the adjusted bank statement balance and (2) the adjusted cash account book balance.
   a. The company's unadjusted cash account balance of $26,193 is listed on the reconciliation as $26,139.
   b. The bank's collection of a $9,000 note less the $45 collection fee is added to the bank statement balance.

Problem 9-4
Preparing a bank reconciliation and recording adjustments
P5

Walburg Company most recently reconciled its bank and book statement balances of cash on August 31 and showed two checks outstanding at that time, No. 5888 for $1,038.05 and No. 5893 for $484.25. The following information is available for the September 30, 1999, reconciliation:

From the September 30 bank statement:

BALANCE OF PREVIOUS STATEMENT ON 8/31/99	16,800.45
6 DEPOSITS AND OTHER CREDITS TOTALING	11,182.85
9 CHECKS AND OTHER DEBITS TOTALING	9,620.05
CURRENT BALANCE AS OF 9/30/99	18,363.55

CHECKING ACCOUNT TRANSACTIONS

DATE	AMOUNT	DESCRIPTION	DATE	AMOUNT	DESCRIPTION
09/05	1,103.75	+Deposit	09/25	2,351.70	+Deposit
09/12	2,226.90	+Deposit	09/30	22.50	+Interest
09/17	588.25	−NSF check	09/30	1,385.00	+Credit memo
09/21	4,093.00	+Deposit			

DATE	CHECK NO	AMOUNT	DATE	CHECK NO	AMOUNT
09/03	5888	1,038.05	09/22	5904	2,080.00
09/07	5901*	1,824.25	09/20	5905	937.00
09/04	5902	731.90	09/28	5907*	213.85
09/22	5903	399.10	09/29	5909*	1,807.65

*Indicates a skip in check sequence.

From Walburg Company's accounting records:

Cash Receipts Deposited

Date			Cash Debit
Sept.	5		1,103.75
	12		2,226.90
	21		4,093.00
	25		2,351.70
	30		1,582.75
			11,358.10

Cash Disbursements

Check No.		Cash Credit
5901		1,824.25
5902		731.90
5903		399.10
5904		2,050.00
5905		937.00
5906		859.30
5907		213.85
5908		276.00
5909		1,807.65
		9,099.05

Cash **Acct. No. 101**

Date		Explanation	PR	Debit	Credit	Balance
Aug.	31	Balance				15,278.45
Sept	30	Total receipts	R12	11,358.10		26,636.55
	30	Total disbursements	D23		9,099.05	17,537.50

Check No. 5904 was correctly drawn for $2,080 to pay for computer equipment; however, the recordkeeper misread the amount and entered it in the accounting records with a debit to Computer Equipment and a credit to Cash of $2,050. The NSF check was originally received from a customer, Delia Hahn, in payment of her account. Its return was not recorded when the bank first notified the company. The credit memorandum resulted from the collection of a $1,400 note for Walburg Company by the bank. The bank deducted a $15 collection fee. The collection and fee have not been recorded.

Required

Preparation Component

Check Figure Reconciled balance, $18,326.75

1. Prepare the September 30 bank reconciliation for this company.
2. Prepare the journal entries to adjust the book balance of cash to the reconciled balance.

Analysis Component

3. The bank statement discloses three places where the canceled checks returned with the bank statement are not numbered sequentially. This means some of the prenumbered checks in the sequence are missing. Several possible situations might explain why canceled checks returned with a bank statement are not numbered sequentially. Describe three of these situations.

Problem 9-5
Analyzing internal control
C2

For the following five scenarios, identify the principle of internal control that is violated. Make a recommendation of what the business should do to ensure adherence to principles of internal control.

1. At Stratford Company, Jill and Joan alternate lunch hours. Normally Jill is the petty cash custodian, but if someone needs petty cash when Jill is at lunch, Joan fills in as custodian.
2. Nadine McDonald does all the posting of patient charges and payments at the Northampton Medical Clinic. Each night Nadine backs up the computerized accounting system to a tape and stores the tape in a locked file at her desk.
3. Jack Mawben prides himself on hiring quality workers who require little supervision. As office manager, Jack gives his employees full discretion over their tasks and has seen no reason to perform independent reviews of their work for years.
4. Bill Clark's manager has told him to reduce overhead. Bill decides to raise the deductible on the plant's property insurance from $5,000 to $10,000. This cuts the property insurance premium in half. In a related move, he decides that bonding of the plant's employees is really a waste of money since the company has not experienced any losses due to employee theft. Bill saves the entire amount of the bonding insurance premium by dropping the bonding insurance.
5. Catherine Young records all incoming customer cash receipts for her employer and also posts the customer payments to their accounts.

BEYOND THE NUMBERS

Reporting in Action
C3, A1

Refer to the financial statements and related information for **NIKE** in Appendix A. Answer the following questions by analyzing information from its statements:

1. For both fiscal year-ends 1997 and 1996, determine the total amount of cash and cash equivalents that NIKE held. Determine the percent this amount represents of total current assets, total current liabilities, total stockholders' equity, and total assets. Comment on any trends.
2. For 1997 use the information in the consolidated statement of cash flows to determine the percent change between the beginning of the year and end of the year amounts of cash and cash equivalents.
3. Compute the days' sales uncollected as of May 31, 1997, and May 31, 1996. Has the collection of receivables improved?

Swoosh Ahead

4. Obtain access to NIKE's annual report for fiscal years ending after May 31, 1997. You can gain access to NIKE's annual report at its web site [**www.nike.com**] or through the SEC's EDGAR database [**www.sec.gov**]. Recompute the days' sales uncollected for any fiscal years ending after May 31, 1997. Compare the days just computed to NIKE's days' sales uncollected in 1997 and 1996.

Comparative Analysis
A1

Both **NIKE** and **Reebok** design, produce, market, and sell sports footwear and apparel. Key comparative figures (in millions) for these two organizations follow:

	NIKE*		Reebok*	
Key Figures	**1997**	**1996**	**1996**	**1995**
Accounts receivable	$1,754	$1,346	$ 591	$ 507
Net sales	$9,187	$6,471	$3,479	$3,481

*NIKE figures are from its annual reports for fiscal years ended May 31, 1997 and 1996. Reebok figures are from its annual reports for fiscal years ended December 31, 1996 and 1995.

Required

Compute days' sales uncollected for both companies for the two years of data provided. Comment on any trends for both companies. Which company has the larger percent change in days' sales uncollected?

Ethics Challenge

C2

Marge Page, Dot Night, and Colleen Walker work for a family physician, Dr. Thomen, who is in private practice. Dr. Thomen is fairly knowledgeable about office management practices and has segregated the cash receipt duties as follows. Marge opens the mail and prepares a triplicate list of money received. She sends one copy of the list to Dot, the cashier, who deposits the receipts daily in the bank. Colleen, the recordkeeper, also receives a copy of the list and posts payments to patients' accounts. About once a month the office clerks decide to have an expensive lunch compliments of Dr. Thomen. Dot endorses a patient's check in Dr. Thomen's name and cashes it at the bank. Marge destroys the remittance advice accompanying the check. Colleen posts payment to the customer's account as a miscellaneous credit. The clerks justify their actions given their relatively low pay and knowing that Dr. Thomen will likely never miss the payment.

Required

1. Who is the best person in Dr. Thomen's office to reconcile the bank statement?
2. Would a bank reconciliation uncover this office fraud?
3. What are some ways to detect this type of fraud?
4. Suggest additional internal controls that Dr. Thomen may want to implement.

Communicating in Practice

P4

You are a business consultant. The owner of a company sends you an e-mail expressing concern that the company is losing money by not taking advantage of discounts offered by vendors. The company currently uses the gross method of recording purchases. The owner is considering requiring a review of all invoices and payment dates from the previous period. But due to the volume of purchases, the owner recognizes this is time-consuming and costly. The owner seeks your advice as to how the business might monitor purchase discounts in the future. Provide a response.

Taking it to the Net

C1, C2

Visit the internal control Web site at **www.duc.auburn.edu/~auaudit.** Explore this Web site and record answers to the following questions.

1. How does this Web site define internal control?
2. What are some controls this Web site suggests as part of your "personal internal control system"?
3. What purposes do internal controls serve in a university environment?
4. Contrast preventative and detective controls.
5. Who is responsible for implementing and maintaining a system of internal controls?

Teamwork in Action

P2

A team will be called upon to personify the operation of a voucher system. Yet all teams must prepare for the potential to be selected by doing the following:

1. Each team is to identify the documents in a voucher system. The team leader will play the voucher, and each team member is to assume "the role" of one or more documents.
2. To prepare for your individual role you are to:
   a. Find an illustration for the document within the chapter.
   b. Write down your document's function, where you originate, and how you flow through the voucher system.
3. Rehearse the role playing of operating the system. You may use text illustrations as props, and for visual effect you may wear a nametag identifying the part you play.

Hitting the Road

C1

Browse through a store in your area. Identify between 5 and 10 internal controls this store is implementing.

Business Week Activity

C1

Read the article "The Heavy Burden of Light Fingers" in the December 16, 1996, issue of *Business Week.*

1. What are some schemes employees use to defraud companies?
2. What is the average amount of loss experienced by companies due to employee fraud?
3. According to the article, how are employee frauds uncovered?

Receivables and Short-Term Investments

A Look Back

Chapter 9 focused on internal control and accounting for cash. We described procedures that are good for internal control, and we explained the accounting for and management of cash.

A Look at This Chapter

This chapter emphasizes receivables and short-term investments. We explain that they are liquid assets and describe how companies account for and report them. We also discuss the importance of estimating uncollectibles and the role of market values in analyzing liquid assets.

A Look Ahead

Chapter 11 focuses on plant assets, natural resources, and intangible assets. We explain how to account for, report, and analyze these long-term assets.

Chapter Outline

Debt into Gold

TULSA, OK—Today's economy runs on credit sales. Credit sales produce accounts receivable that are often the largest current asset a company owns. But not all accounts receivable are paid. Some end up as "bad debts"—accounts that a company can't collect.

Enter William and Kathryn Bartmann. The Bartmanns first started collecting on other companies' bad debt accounts from their kitchen table in Muskogee, Oklahoma. They used something more powerful than technology and pressure tactics to collect money that debtors owed—they used a philosophy of "respect for people."

The Bartmanns know personally the psychology of debtors, having previously been bankrupt themselves. "You've got to be sympathetic; you've got to listen with your heart as well as your head," says William Bartmann.

The Bartmanns "polite persistence" is paying off. Their entrepreneurial spirit led them to create **CFS,** a Tulsa-based company that is now the nation's largest purchaser of bad credit card debts. Last year, their company earned $137 million. And their net profit margin is a cool 67%!

Through all of its success, CFS has maintained its reputation for ethical dealings in an industry still plagued by abusive and questionable tactics. It also keeps a down-to-earth management style. As one recent example, if revenue targets are met, CFS said it will fly all employees and guests to Las Vegas for a mud-wrestling match—William Bartmann vs. one of his executives. Bartmann has also taken all employees to a baseball game in Kansas City. It's vintage Bartmann—bold and flamboyant.

Interestingly, Bartmann recently turned down a huge cash offer for the company. Why? "It wasn't enough. We're going places," he says. It might be the World Series of profits.

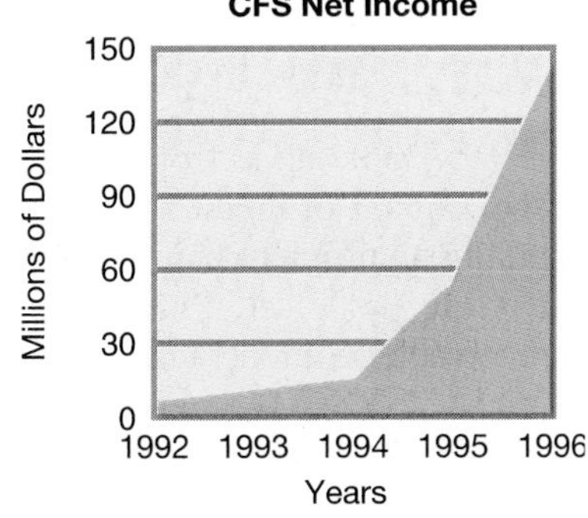

Source: *Business Week,* August 11, 1997

Learning Objectives

Conceptual

C1 Describe accounts receivable and how they occur and are recorded.

C2 Describe a note receivable and the computation of its maturity date and interest.

C3 Explain how receivables can be converted to cash before maturity.

C4 Describe short-term investments in debt and equity securities.

Analytical

A1 Compute accounts receivable turnover and use it to analyze liquidity.

Procedural

P1 Apply the direct write-off and allowance methods to account for accounts receivable.

P2 Estimate uncollectibles using methods based on sales and accounts receivable.

P3 Record the receipt of a note receivable.

P4 Record the honoring and dishonoring of a note and adjustments for interest on a note.

P5 Record the sale of short-term investments.

HAPTER PREVIEW

This chapter focuses on accounts receivable, short-term notes receivable, and short-term investments. We describe each of these assets, their use in practice, and how they are accounted for and reported in financial statements. This knowledge helps us use accounting information to make better decisions. It can also help in predicting bad debts as shown in the opening article.

Accounts Receivable

A *receivable* refers to an amount due from another party. Receivables along with cash, cash equivalents, and short-term investments make up the most liquid assets of a company. The two most common receivables are accounts receivable and notes receivable. Other receivables include interest receivable, rent receivable, tax refund receivable, and amounts due from officers and employees.

Accounts receivable refer to amounts due from customers for credit sales. This section begins by describing how accounts receivable arise and their various sources. These sources include sales when customers use credit cards issued by third parties and when a company gives credit directly to customers. When a company extends credit directly to customers it must (1) maintain a separate account receivable for each customer and (2) account for bad debts from credit sales.

Recognizing Accounts Receivable

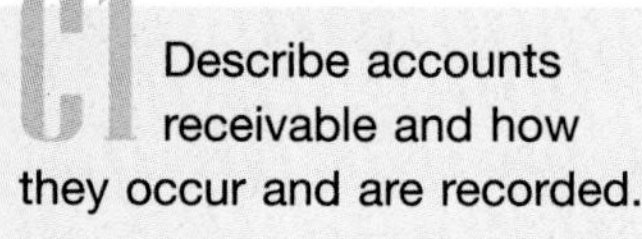

Accounts receivable arise from credit sales to customers by both retailers and wholesalers. The amount of credit sales has increased in recent years, reflecting several factors including an efficient banking system and a sound economy. Retailers such as **The Limited, Chic by H.I.S, Best Buy,** and **CompUSA** hold millions of dollars in accounts receivable. Similar amounts are held by wholesalers such as **NIKE, Reebok, SUPERVALU, SYSCO,** and **Ace Hardware**. Exhibit 10.1 shows the dollar amount of accounts receivable and its percent of total assets for four companies.

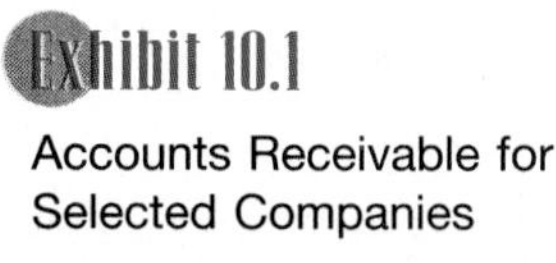

Accounts Receivable for Selected Companies

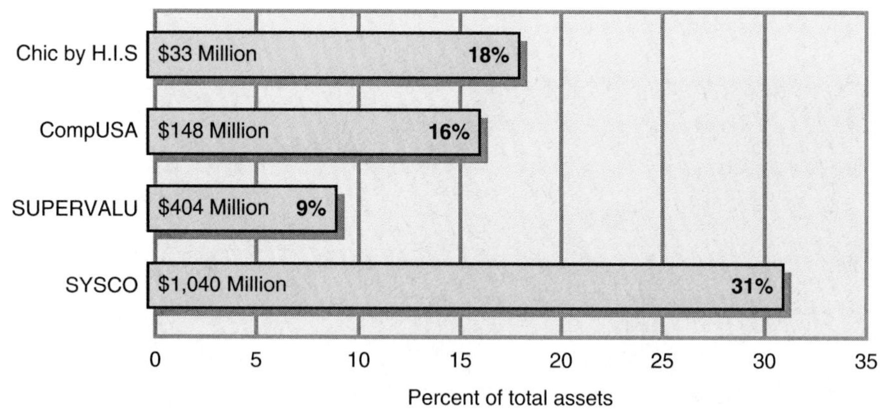

Sales on Credit

We explained in Chapter 8 how credit sales are recorded by debiting an Accounts Receivable account for a specific customer. This is important for showing us how much each customer purchases, how much each customer has paid, and how much each customer still owes. This information provides the basis for sending bills to customers and gives important data for other managerial analyses. To maintain this information, companies that extend credit directly to their customers must maintain a separate account receivable for each of them. The General Ledger continues to report a single Accounts

Receivable amount along with the other financial statement accounts, but a supplementary record is created where a separate account is maintained for each customer. This supplementary record is the *Accounts Receivable Ledger.*.

Exhibit 10.2 shows the relation between the Accounts Receivable account in the General Ledger and the individual customer accounts in the Accounts Receivable Ledger for **TechCom,** a small electronics wholesaler. This exhibit reports the beginning balances of TechCom's accounts receivable for July 15. While TechCom's transactions are mainly in cash, it has two major credit customers: CompStore and RDA Electronics. Exhibit 10.2 shows that the $3,000 total of these two customers' balances in the Accounts Receivable Ledger is equal to the balance of the Accounts Receivable account in the General Ledger.

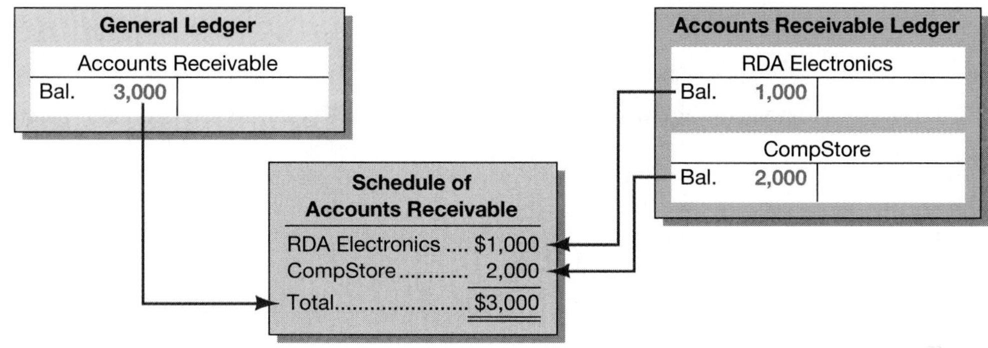

Exhibit 10.2

Accounts Receivable Account and the Accounts Receivable Ledger (before transactions)

To see how accounts receivable from credit sales are recognized in the accounting records, we look at two transactions on July 15 between TechCom and its two major credit customers. The first is a credit sale of $950 to CompStore. A credit sale is posted with both a debit to the Accounts Receivable account in the General Ledger and a debit to the customer account in the Accounts Receivable Ledger. The second transaction is a collection of $720 from RDA Electronics from prior credit sales. Cash receipts from a credit customer are posted with credits to both the Accounts Receivable account in the General Ledger and to the customer account.[1] Both transactions are journalized in Exhibit 10.3.[2]

Exhibit 10.3

Accounts Receivable Transactions

July 15	Accounts Receivable—CompStore	950	
	Sales		950
	To record credit sales.		
July 15	Cash	720	
	Accounts Receivable—RDA Electronics . .		720
	To record collection of credit sales.		

Exhibit 10.4 shows the General Ledger account and the Accounts Receivable Ledger after the two transactions above. The General Ledger account shows the effects of the sale, the collection, and the resulting balance of $3,230. These events are also reflected in the customers' accounts: RDA Electronics has an ending balance of $280 and CompStore now owes $2,950. The $3,230 sum of their accounts equals the debit balance of the General Ledger account.

[1] Posting debits or credits to Accounts Receivable twice does not violate the requirement that debits equal credits. The equality of debits and credits is maintained in the General Ledger. The Accounts Receivable Ledger is a supplementary record providing detailed information on each customer.

[2] We omit the cost of sales entries in order to focus on sales and receivables.

Accounts Receivable Account and the Accounts Receivable Ledger (after transactions)

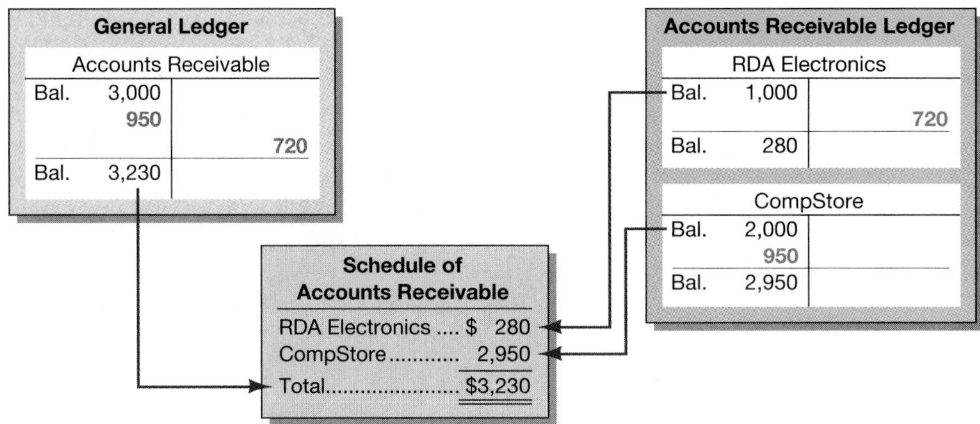

Like many companies, TechCom grants credit directly to qualified customers. Many large retailers such as **Sears** and **J.C. Penney** now maintain their own credit cards. This allows them to grant credit to approved customers and to earn interest on any balance not paid within a specified period of time. It also allows them to avoid the fee charged by credit card companies. The entries in this case are the same as those above except for the possibility of added interest revenue. If a customer owes interest on the bill, then we debit Accounts Receivable and credit Interest Revenue for this amount.

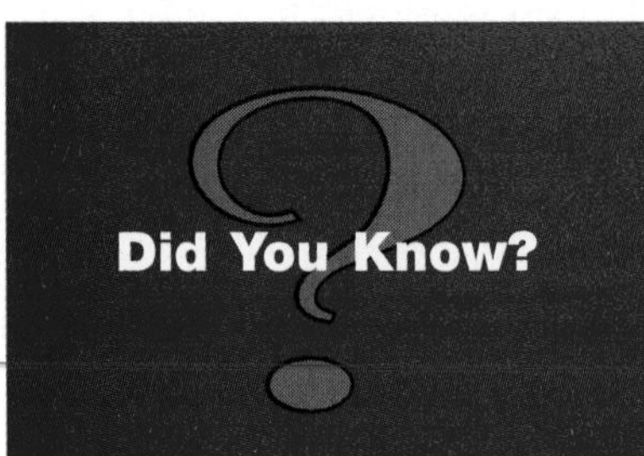

Cyber Receivables

Cyber receivables are the result of new cyber-merchants. Setting up shop in cyberspace is easier than ever. New programs help merchants build Web storefronts quickly and easily. Merchants simply enter product details such as names and prices, and out comes a respectable-looking site complete with order forms. These storefront programs can be listed as part of a cybermall, and they offer secure credit card orders and track sales and site visits. [Source: *Business Week,* June 9, 1997.]

Credit Card Sales

Many companies allow customers to use credit cards such as **Visa, MasterCard,** or **American Express** to charge purchases. This practice gives customers the ability to make purchases without cash or checks. It also allows them to defer their payments to the credit card company. Once credit is established with the credit card company, the customer does not have to open an account with each store. Customers using credit cards can make single monthly payments instead of several to different creditors.

There are good reasons why sellers allow customers to use credit cards instead of granting credit directly. First, the seller does not have to evaluate the credit standing of each customer or make decisions about who gets credit and how much. Second, the seller avoids the risk of extending credit to customers who cannot or do not pay. This risk is transferred to the credit card company. Third, the seller typically receives cash from the credit card company sooner than if it granted credit directly to customers. Fourth, a variety of credit options for customers offers a potential increase in sales volume. **Sears,** one of the nation's largest credit providers among retailers, historically offered credit only to customers using a **SearsCharge** card. Sears recently changed its policy to permit customers to charge purchases to third-party companies. It reported this as follows:

SearsCharge increased its share of Sears retail sales even as the company expanded the payment options available to its customers with the acceptance in 1993 of VISA, MasterCard, and American Express in addition to the Discover Card.

In dealing with some credit cards, usually those issued by banks, the seller deposits a copy of each credit card sales receipt in its bank account just like it deposits a customer's check. The seller receives a credit to its checking account without delay. Some credit cards require the seller to send a copy of each receipt to the credit card company. Until payment is received, the seller has an account receivable from the credit card company. In return for the services provided by the credit card company, the seller pays a fee, often ranging from 2% to 5% of credit card sales. This charge is deducted from the credit to the checking account or the cash payment to the seller.

Entrepreneur
You are the owner of a small retail store. You are considering allowing customers to purchase merchandise using credit cards. Until now, your store only accepted cash and checks. What form of analysis do you use to make this decision?

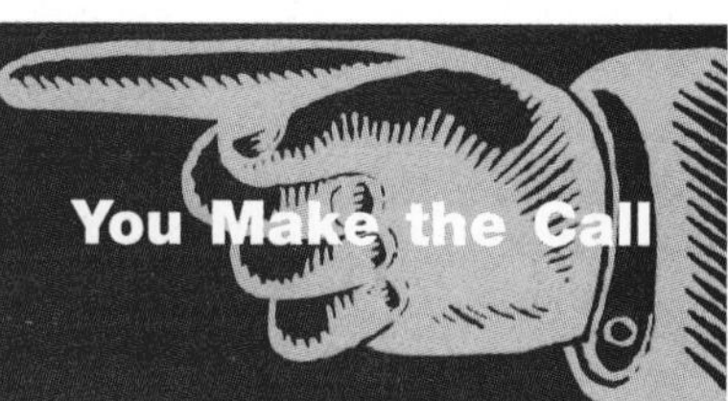

Answer—p. 433

The procedures used in accounting for credit card sales depend on whether cash is received immediately on deposit or is delayed until paid by the credit card company. For instance, if TechCom has $100 of credit card sales with a 4% fee and cash is received immediately on deposit, then the entry is:

July 15	Cash	96	
	Credit Card Expense	4	
	Sales		100
	To record credit card sales less a 4% credit card expense.		

Assets = Liabilities + Equity
+96 −4
+100

If TechCom must send a copy of the credit card sales receipts to a credit card company and wait for payment, then the entry on the date of sale is:

July 15	Accounts Receivable—Credit Card Co.	100	
	Sales		100
	To record credit card sales.		

Assets = Liabilities + Equity
+100 +100

When cash is received from the credit card company, the entry to record the receipt and the deduction of the fee is:

July 30	Cash	96	
	Credit Card Expense	4	
	Accounts Receivable—Credit Card Co. . . .		100
	To record cash receipt less 4% credit card expense.		

Assets = Liabilities + Equity
+96 −4
−100

Note the credit card expense is not recorded until cash is received from the credit card company. This practice is a matter of convenience. By following this practice, the seller avoids computing and recording the credit card expense each time sales are recorded. Instead, the expense related to many sales can be computed once and recorded when cash is received. But the *matching principle* requires reporting credit card expense in the same period as the sale. Therefore, if the sale and cash receipt occur in different periods, we must accrue and report the credit card expense in the period of the sale by using an adjusting entry at the end of the period. If TechCom requires a year-end adjustment of $24 of accrued credit card expense on a $600 receivable that the credit card company has not yet paid, we must make the following entry:

Assets = Liabilities + Equity
−24 −24

Dec. 31	Credit Card Expense	24	
	Accounts Receivable—Credit Card Co. . . .		24
	To accrue credit card expense that is unrecorded at the end of the year.		

The following entry records the cash collection in January:

Assets = Liabilities + Equity
+576
−576

Jan. 5	Cash	576	
	Accounts Receivable—Credit Card Co. . . .		576
	To record collection of amount due from Credit Card Company.		

Some firms report credit card expense in the income statement as a type of discount deducted from sales to get net sales. Other companies classify it as a selling expense or even as an administrative expense. Arguments can be made for all three alternatives.

Flash back

1. In recording credit card sales, when do you debit Accounts Receivable and when do you debit Cash?
2. When are credit card expenses recorded in cases where sales receipts must be accumulated before they can be sent to the credit card company? When are these expenses incurred?
3. If payment for a credit card sale is not received by the end of the accounting period, how do you account for the credit card expense from that sale?

Answers—p. 434

Valuing Accounts Receivable

When a company directly grants credit to its customers, there usually are some customers who do not pay what they promised. The accounts of these customers are **uncollectible accounts,** commonly called **bad debts.** The total amount of uncollectible accounts is an expense of selling on credit. Why do companies sell on credit if they expect some accounts to be uncollectible? The answer is that companies believe granting credit will increase revenues and profits to offset bad debts. They are willing to incur bad debts losses if the net effect is to increase sales and profits.

Two methods are used by companies to account for uncollectible accounts: (1) direct write-off method and (2) allowance method. We describe both of these methods.

Credit Woes
The days of easy money are ending for credit card issuers. Costs of financing credit card operations are rising for all issuers, owing to record default rates. Much of this is the fault of issuers who have flooded the market with offers of credit cards with low "teaser" rates. In response, credit card users have greatly increased their debts, and many are unable to pay them. The table here shows the huge increase in bad debts of major credit card issuers. [Source: *Business Week*, March 31, 1997.]

Write-offs for Bad Credit Card Debt	12/31/96	12/31/95
Banc One	6.8%	N/A
First Chicago	6.7	3.8%
Discover	6.1	4.5
Citicorp	5.5	3.9
Chase	5.1	4.2
Capital One	5.1	2.6
Advanta	5.1	2.6

Did You Know?

Direct Write-Off Method

P1 Apply the direct write-off and allowance methods to account for accounts receivable.

The **direct write-off method** of accounting for bad debts records the loss from an uncollectible account receivable at the time it is determined to be uncollectible. No attempt is made to predict uncollectible accounts or bad debts expense. Bad debts expense is recorded when specific accounts are written off as uncollectible. If TechCom determines on January 23 it can't collect $520 owed to it by its customer Jack Kent, the loss is recognized using the direct write-off method as follows:

Jan. 23	Bad Debts Expense	520	
	Accounts Receivable—Jack Kent		520
	To write off uncollectible account under the direct write-off method.		

Assets = Liabilities + Equity
−520 −520

The debit in this entry charges the uncollectible amount directly to the current year's Bad Debts Expense account. The credit removes the balance of the account from the subsidiary ledger and from the controlling account.

Sometimes an account written off is later collected. This can be due to factors such as continual collection efforts or the good fortune of a customer. If the account of Jack Kent that was written off directly to Bad Debts Expense is later collected in full, the following two entries record this recovery:

Mar. 11	Accounts Receivable—Jack Kent	520	
	Bad Debts Expense		520
	To reinstate account of Jack Kent previously written off.		
Mar. 11	Cash	520	
	Accounts Receivable—Jack Kent		520
	To record full payment of account.		

Assets = Liabilities + Equity
+520 +520

Assets = Liabilities + Equity
+520
−520

Sometimes an amount previously written off directly to Bad Debts Expense is recovered in the year following the write-off. If there is no balance in the Bad Debts Expense account from previous write-offs and no other write-offs are expected, the credit portion of the entry recording the recovery can be made to a Bad Debts Recoveries revenue account.

Companies must weigh at least two principles when considering use of the direct write-off method: (1) matching principle and (2) materiality principle.

Matching Principle Applied to Bad Debts

The **matching principle** requires expenses to be reported in the same accounting period as the sales they helped produce. This means that if extending credit to customers helped produce sales, the bad debts expense linked to those sales is matched and reported in the same period as the sales. The direct write-off method usually doesn't match revenues and expenses. This mismatch occurs because bad debts expense is not recorded until an account becomes uncollectible, which often does not occur during the same period as the credit sale.

Applying the matching principle to bad debts presents challenges. Managers realize that some portion of credit sales results in bad debts. But knowing what specific credit sale is uncollectible doesn't become apparent until later. If a customer fails to pay within the credit period, most companies send out repeated billings and make other efforts to collect. They don't accept that a customer isn't going to pay until every reasonable means of collection is taken. This decision point may not be reached until one or more accounting periods after the period in which the sale was made. Matching bad debts expense with the revenue it produces therefore requires a company to estimate this unknown amount at the end of each period.

Materiality Principle Applied to Bad Debts

The **materiality principle** states that an amount can be ignored if its effect on the financial statements is unimportant to users. The materiality principle permits use of the direct write-off method in accounting for expenses from bad debts when bad debts expenses are very small in relation to a company's other financial statement items such as sales and net income. This requires that bad debts expense be unimportant for decisions made by users of the company's financial statements.

Allowance Method

The **allowance method** of accounting for bad debts matches the *expected* loss from uncollectible accounts receivable against the sales they helped produce. We must use expected losses since management can't exactly identify the customers who won't pay their bills at the time of sale. This means at the end of each period the allowance method requires us to estimate the total bad debts expected to result from that period's sales. An allowance is then recorded for this expected loss. This method has two advantages over the direct write-off method: (1) bad debts expense is charged to the period when the related sales are recognized, and (2) accounts receivable are reported on the balance sheet at the estimated amount of cash to be collected.

Recording Estimated Bad Debts Expense

The allowance method estimates bad debts expense at the end of each accounting period and records it with an adjusting entry. TechCom, for instance, had credit sales of approximately $300,000 during its first year of operations. At the end of the first year, $20,000 of credit sales remained uncollected. Based on the experience of similar businesses, TechCom estimated that $1,500 of the accounts receivable were uncollectible. This estimated expense is recorded with the following adjusting entry:

Assets = Liabilities + Equity
−1,500 −1,500

Dec. 31	Bad Debts Expense	1,500	
	Allowance for Doubtful Accounts		1,500
	To record estimated bad debts.		

The debit in this entry means the estimated bad debts expense of $1,500 from selling on credit is matched on the income statement with the $300,000 sales it helped produce. The credit in this entry is to a contra asset account called **Allowance for Doubtful Accounts.** A contra account is used because at the time of the adjusting entry, the company does not know which customers will not pay. Because specific bad debts accounts are not identifiable at the time of the adjusting entry, they cannot be removed from the subsidiary Accounts Receivable Ledger. Because the customer accounts are left in the subsidiary ledger, the controlling account for Accounts Receivable cannot be reduced. Instead, the Allowance for Doubtful Accounts *must* be credited.

Bad Debts Related Accounts in Financial Statements

The process of evaluating customers and approving them for credit usually is not assigned to the selling department of a company. Given its goal of increasing sales, the selling department might have different motives in approving customers for credit. Because the selling department is not responsible for granting credit, it should not be held responsible for bad debts expense. This means bad debts expense often appears on the income statement as an administrative expense rather than a selling expense.

Recall TechCom has $20,000 of outstanding accounts receivable at the end of its first year of operations. After the bad debts adjusting entry is posted, TechCom's Accounts Receivable and Allowance for Doubtful Accounts look as shown in Exhibit 10.5.

Accounts Receivable			
Dec. 31	20,000		

Allowance for Doubtful Accounts			
		Dec. 31	1,500

Exhibit 10.5

General Ledger Balances after Bad Debts Adjusting Entry

The Allowance for Doubtful Accounts credit balance of $1,500 has the effect of reducing accounts receivable (net of the allowance) to their estimated realizable value. **Realizable value** is the expected proceeds from converting this asset into cash. Although $20,000 is legally owed to TechCom by its credit customers, only $18,500 is expected to be realized in cash collections from customers.

In the balance sheet, the Allowance for Doubtful Accounts is subtracted from Accounts Receivable to show the amount expected to be realized. This information is often reported as shown in Exhibit 10.6.

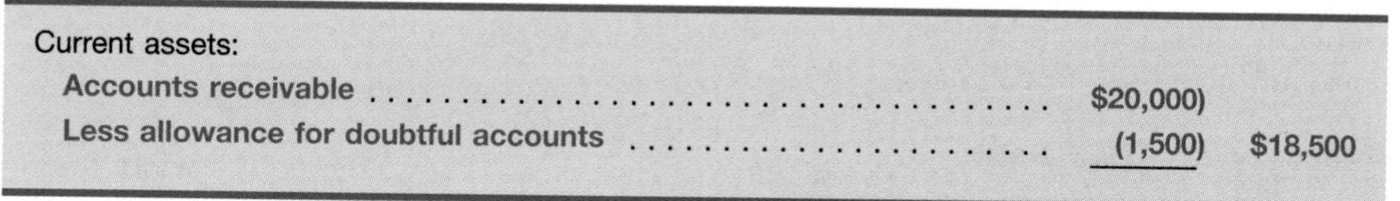

Current assets:		
Accounts receivable	$20,000)	
Less allowance for doubtful accounts	(1,500)	$18,500

Exhibit 10.6

Balance Sheet Presentation of Allowance for Doubtful Accounts

Sometimes the contra assets account to Accounts Receivable is not reported separately. This alternative presentation is shown in Exhibit 10.7.

Accounts receivable (net of $1,500 estimated uncollectible accounts)	$18,500

Exhibit 10.7

Alternative Presentation of Allowance for Doubtful Accounts

Writing Off a Bad Debt

When specific accounts are identified as uncollectible, they are written off against the Allowance for Doubtful Accounts. After spending some time trying to collect from Jack Kent, TechCom decides that Kent's $520 account is uncollectible and makes the following entry to write it off:

Jan. 23	Allowance for Doubtful Accounts	520	
	Accounts Receivable—Jack Kent		520
	To write off an uncollectible account.		

Assets = Liabilities + Equity
+520
−520

Posting the credit of this write-off entry to the Accounts Receivable account removes the amount of the bad debt from the controlling account. Posting it to Jack Kent's account removes the amount of the bad debt from the subsidiary ledger. By removing it from the subsidiary ledger, TechCom avoids the cost of additional collection efforts. After this entry is posted, the General Ledger accounts appear as in Exhibit 10.8 (assuming no changes in the balances of related accounts).

Exhibit 10.8

General Ledger Balances after Write-Off

Accounts Receivable			
Dec. 31	20,000		
		Jan. 23	520

Allowance for Doubtful Accounts			
		Dec. 31	1,500
Jan. 23	520		

Note two aspects of this entry and its related accounts. First, while bad debts are an expense of selling on credit, the allowance account is debited in the write-off. The expense account is not debited. The expense account is not debited because bad debts expense is previously estimated and recorded with an adjusting entry at the end of the period in which the sale occurred. Second, while the write-off removes the amount of the account receivable from the ledgers, it doesn't affect the estimated realizable value of TechCom's net accounts receivable, as shown in Exhibit 10.9.

Exhibit 10.9

Realizable Value before and after Write-Off

	Before Write-Off	After Write-Off
Accounts receivable	$20,000	$19,480
Less allowance for doubtful accounts	1,500	980
Estimated realizable accounts receivable	**$18,500**	**$18,500**

Neither total assets nor net income are affected by the write-off of a specific account. But both total assets and net income are affected by recognizing the year's bad debts expense in the adjusting entry.

Recovery of a Bad Debt

When a customer fails to pay and the account is written off as uncollectible, his or her credit standing is jeopardized. To help restore credit standing, a customer sometimes later chooses to voluntarily pay all or part of the amount owed. When a recovery of a bad debt occurs, it is recorded in the customer's subsidiary account where this information is retained for use in future credit evaluation.

A company makes two entries when collecting an account previously written off. The first is to reverse the original write-off and reinstate the customer's account. The second entry records the collection of the reinstated account. If on March 11, Jack Kent pays in full his account that TechCom previously wrote off, the entries to record this bad debts recovery are:

Assets = Liabilities + Equity
+520
−520

Assets = Liabilities + Equity
+520
−520

Mar. 11	Accounts Receivable—Jack Kent	520	
	Allowance for Doubtful Accounts		520
	To reinstate the account of Kent previously written off.		
Mar. 11	Cash	520	
	Accounts Receivable—Jack Kent		520
	To record full payment of account.		

Jack Kent paid the entire amount previously written off, but in some cases a customer pays only a portion of the amount owed. A question then arises of whether the entire balance of the account is returned to accounts receivable, or just the amount paid. The answer is a matter of judgment. If we believe this customer will later pay in full, the entire amount owed is returned to accounts receivable. But only the amount paid is returned if we expect no further collection.

Flash back

4. Using the matching principle, why must bad debts expenses be estimated?
5. What term describes the balance sheet valuation of accounts receivable less the allowance for doubtful accounts?
6. Why is estimated bad debts expense credited to a contra account rather than to the Accounts Receivable controlling account?

Answers—p. 434

Estimating Bad Debts Expense

P2 Estimate uncollectibles using methods based on sales and accounts receivable.

Companies with direct credit sales estimate bad debts expense. They do this to help them manage their receivables and to set credit policies. The allowance method of accounting for bad debts also requires an estimate of bad debts expense to prepare the adjusting entry at the end of each accounting period. How does a company estimate bad debts expense? There are two common methods. One is based on the income statement relation between bad debts expense and sales. The second is based on the balance sheet relation between accounts receivable and the allowance for doubtful accounts. Both methods require an analysis of past experience.

Percent of Sales Method

The *percent of sales* method uses income statement relations to estimate bad debts. It is based on the idea that a given percent of a company's credit sales for the period are uncollectible.[3] The income statement would then report that percent as the amount of bad debts expense. To illustrate, assume **MusicLand** has credit sales of $400,000 in 1999. Based on past experience and the experience of similar companies, MusicLand estimates 0.6% of credit sales are uncollectible. Using this prediction, MusicLand expects $2,400 of bad debts expense from 1999's sales (computed as $400,000 × 0.006 = $2,400). The adjusting entry to record this estimated expense is:

Dec. 31	Bad Debts Expense	2,400	
	Allowance for Doubtful Accounts		2,400
	To record estimated bad debts.		

Assets	= Liabilities	+ Equity
−2,400		−2,400

This entry doesn't mean the December 31, 1999, balance in Allowance for Doubtful Accounts will be $2,400. A $2,400 balance occurs only if the account had a zero balance prior to posting the adjusting entry. For several reasons, the unadjusted balance of Allowance for Doubtful Accounts is not likely to be zero. Unless a company is in its first period of operations, the allowance account will have a zero balance only if the prior amounts written off as uncollectible *exactly* equal the prior estimated bad debts expenses. And that is not likely.

[3] Note the focus is on *credit* sales. Cash sales don't produce bad debts, and they are generally not used in this estimation. But if cash sales are relatively small compared to credit sales, there is no major impact from including them.

This means we do not expect the Allowance for Doubtful Accounts to have an unadjusted balance of zero at the end of a period. This also means the adjusted balance reported on the balance sheet normally does not equal the amount of expense reported on the income statement. Expressing bad debts expense as a percent of sales is an estimate based on past experience. As new experience is obtained, we often find the percent used is too high or too low. When this happens, we adjust the rate for future periods.

Accounts Receivable Methods

The *accounts receivable* methods use balance sheet relations to estimate bad debts—primarily the relation between accounts receivable and the allowance amount. It is based on the idea that some portion of the end-of-period accounts receivable balance is not collectible. The objective for this bad debts adjusting entry is to make the Allowance for Doubtful Accounts balance equal to the portion of outstanding accounts receivable estimated as uncollectible. To obtain this required balance for the Allowance for Doubtful Accounts, we compare its balance before the adjustment with our estimated balance. The difference between the two is debited to Bad Debts Expense and credited to Allowance for Doubtful Accounts. Estimating this required balance for the allowance account is done in one of two ways: (1) simple estimate of percent uncollectible from the total outstanding accounts receivable and (2) aging accounts receivable.

Percent of Accounts Receivable Method

The *percent of accounts receivable* approach assumes a given percent of a company's outstanding receivables are uncollectible. This estimated percent is based on past experience and the experience of similar companies. It also is impacted by current conditions such as recent economic trends and difficulties faced by customers. The total dollar amount of all outstanding receivables is multiplied by an estimated percent to get the estimated dollar amount of uncollectible accounts. This amount is reported in the balance sheet as the balance for Allowance for Doubtful Accounts. We prepare an adjusting entry debiting Bad Debts Expense and crediting Allowance for Doubtful Accounts. The amount of the adjustment is the amount necessary to give us the required balance in Allowance for Doubtful Accounts.

Assume **MusicLand** has $50,000 of outstanding accounts receivable on December 31, 1999. Past experience suggests 5% of outstanding receivables are uncollectible. This means that after the adjusting entry is posted, we want the Allowance for Doubtful Accounts to show a $2,500 credit balance (computed as 5% of $50,000). Before the adjustment the account appears as:

Allowance for Doubtful Accounts			
		Dec. 31, 1998, bal.	2,000
Feb. 6	800		
July 10	600		
Nov. 20	400		
		Unadjusted bal.	200

The $2,000 beginning balance is from the December 31, 1998, balance sheet. During 1999, accounts of specific customers are written off on February 6, July 10, and November 20. The account has a $200 credit balance prior to the December 31, 1999, adjustment. The adjusting entry to give the allowance the required $2,500 balance is:

Assets = Liabilities + Equity
−2,300 −2,300

Dec. 31	Bad Debts Expense	2,300	
	Allowance for Doubtful Accounts		2,300
	To record estimated bad debts.		

After this entry is posted, the allowance has a $2,500 credit balance as shown in Exhibit 10.10

Allowance for Doubtful Accounts			
		Dec. 31, 1998, bal.	2,000
Feb. 6	800		
July 10	600		
Nov. 20	400		
		Unadjusted bal.	200
		Dec. 31 adjustment	2,300
		Dec. 31, 1999, bal.	2,500

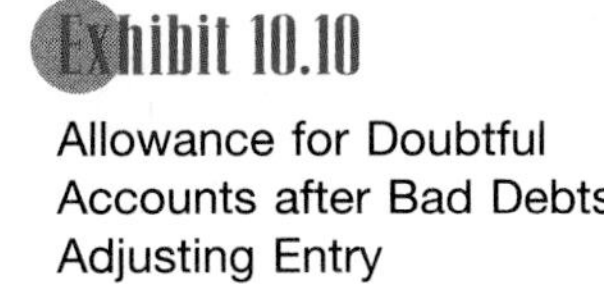

Allowance for Doubtful Accounts after Bad Debts Adjusting Entry

High Tech Estimates
Technology can assist users in estimating bad debts. Both the sales-based and receivables-based methods of estimating bad debts are easily included in computerized information systems. Using current and past data in the system, estimates of bad debts are obtained with adjustments for different assumptions and economic trends. Spreadsheet programs can also be used for estimating bad debts.

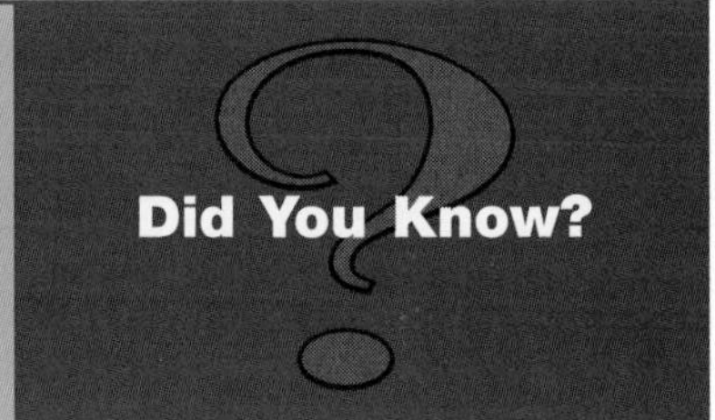

Aging of Accounts Receivable Method

Both the percent of sales (income statement) method and the percent of accounts receivable (balance sheet) method use information from *past* experience to estimate the amount of bad debts expense. Another balance sheet method using receivables information produces a more precise estimate and uses both past experience and current information. The **aging of accounts receivable** method examines *each* account receivable to estimate the amount uncollectible. Receivables are classified by how long they are past their due dates. Then, estimates of uncollectible amounts are made assuming the longer an amount is past due the more likely it is to be uncollectible.

Mining Data and Fool's Gold
Michael Drosnin's best-selling book, *The Bible Code,* claims to find hidden messages in the Bible about dinosaurs, Bill Clinton, and the Land of Magog. The pitfall Drosnin stumbled into reminds us of the dangers of modern technology and "data mining." Done right, data mining can help discover trends, weed out credit card fraud, identify bad credit risks, and estimate uncollectibles. Done wrong, it produces bogus correlations. For instance, historically the single best predictor of the Standard & Poor's 500 stock index was butter production in Bangladesh. The lesson: Use common sense in mining data and beware of fool's gold. [Source: *Business Week,* June 16, 1997.]

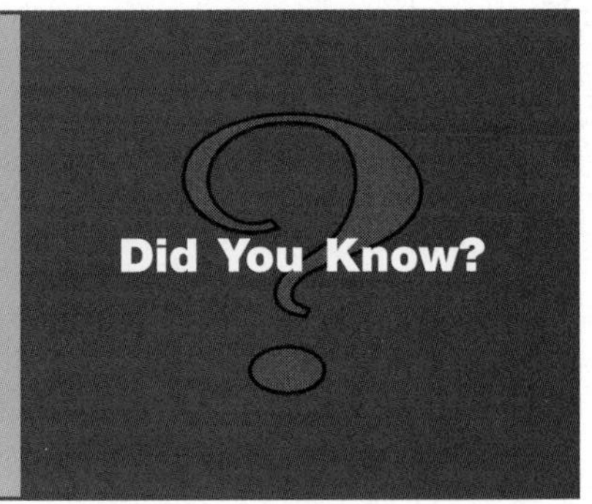

In aging accounts receivable outstanding at the end of a period, we examine each account and classify it by how much time has passed since it was due. Classifications depend on the judgment of a company's management. But classes are often based on 30-day (or one-month) periods. After the outstanding amounts are classified (or aged), past experience is used to estimate the percent of each class that is uncollectible. These percents are applied to the amounts in each class to get the required balance of the Allowance for Doubtful Accounts. This computation is performed by setting up a schedule like Exhibit 10.11 for MusicLand.

Exhibit 10.11

Aging of Accounts Receivable

MUSICLAND Schedule of Accounts Receivable by Age December 31, 1999						
Customer's Name	Total	Not Yet Due	1 to 30 Days Past Due	31 to 60 Days Past Due	61 to 90 Days Past Due	Over 90 Days Past Due
Charles Abbot	$ 450	$ 450				
Frank Allen	710			$ 710		
George Arden	500	300	$ 200			
Paul Baum	740				$ 100	$ 640
ZZ Services	1,000	810	190			
Totals	$49,900	$37,000	$6,500	$3,500	$1,900	$1,000
Percent uncollectible . . .		× 2%	× 5%	× 10%	× 25%	× 40%
Estimated uncollectible .	$ 2,290	$ 740	$ 325	$ 350	$ 475	$ 400

Exhibit 10.11 lists each customer's account with its total balance. Then, each individual balance is assigned to one of five classes based on its days past due. In computerized systems, this task is often programmed. When all accounts are aged, the amounts in each class are totaled and multiplied by the estimated percent of uncollectible accounts for each class. The reasonableness of the percents used is reviewed regularly to reflect changes in the company and economy. The following excerpt from the 1996 annual report of **Sears** shows such a review:

> Provision for uncollectible accounts increased 58.6% and net charge-offs increased 51.1% from 1995. These increases reflect the 12.6% growth in domestic credit card receivables from 1995 levels and the continuing industry-wide trend of increased delinquencies and bankruptcies. The Company has responded to the aforementioned trend by implementing an aggressive action plan which includes enhanced collection efforts and increased investment in technology designed to improve collection staff productivity.

We see in Exhibit 10.11 that MusicLand has $3,500 in accounts receivable that are 31 to 60 days past due. MusicLand's management estimates 10% of the amounts in this age class are not collectible. The dollar amount of uncollectibles in this class is $350 ($3,500 × 10%).

The final total in the first column tells us the adjusted balance in MusicLand's Allowance for Doubtful Accounts is $2,290 ($740 + $325 + $350 + $475 + $400). Because the allowance account has an unadjusted credit balance of $200, the required adjustment to the Allowance for Doubtful Accounts is $2,090. This computation is shown in Exhibit 10.12.

Exhibit 10.12

Computing Required Adjustment for Accounts Receivable Method

Unadjusted balance	$ 200 credit
Required balance	2,290 credit
Required adjustment	**$2,090 credit**

MusicLand records the following end-of-period adjusting entry:

Dec. 31	Bad Debts Expense	2,090	
	Allowance for Doubtful Accounts		2,090
	To record estimated bad debts.		

Assets = Liabilities + Equity
−2,090 −2,090

Alternatively, if MusicLand's allowance had an unadjusted *debit* balance of $500, then its required adjustment is computed as:

Unadjusted balance	$ 500 debit
Required balance	2,290 credit
Required adjustment	**$2,790 credit**

The entry to record this end-of-period adjustment is:

Dec. 31	Bad Debts Expense	2,790	
	Allowance for Doubtful Accounts		2,790
	To record estimated bad debts.		

Assets = Liabilities + Equity
−2,790 −2,790

When the percent of sales (income statement) method is used, MusicLand's bad debts expense for 1999 is estimated at $2,400. When the percent of accounts receivable method is used, the expense is $2,300. And when the aging of accounts receivable method is used, the expense is $2,090. We usually expect these amounts to be different since each method gives only an estimate of future payments. But the aging of accounts receivable method is a more detailed examination of specific accounts and is usually the most reliable.[4] Exhibit 10.13 summarizes the principles guiding all three estimation methods and their focus of analysis.

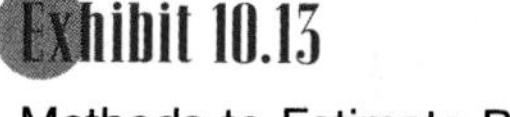

Methods to Estimate Bad Debts

Income Statement Focus	Balance Sheet Focus	Balance Sheet Focus
Percent of Sales Emphasis on Matching Sales ⟷ Bad Debts Expense	Percent of Receivables Emphasis on Realizable Value Accounts Receivable (total) ⟷ Allowance for Doubtful Accounts	Aging of Receivables Emphasis on Realizable Value Accounts Receivable (individual) ⟷ Allowance for Doubtful Accounts

Flash back

7. SnoBoard Company's end of period 12/31/99 balance in the Allowance for Doubtful Accounts is a credit of $440. By aging accounts receivable, it estimates that $6,142 is uncollectible. Prepare SnoBoard's year-end adjusting entry for bad debts.

8. Record entries for the following transactions assuming the allowance method is used:

January 10, 1999	The $300 account of customer Cool Jam is determined uncollectible.
April 12, 1999	Cool Jam pays in full its account that was deemed uncollectible on January 10, 1999.

Answers—p. 434

[4] In many cases, the aging analysis is supplemented with information about specific customers allowing management to decide whether those accounts should be classified as uncollectible. This information often is supplied by the sales and credit department managers.

Installment Accounts Receivable

Many companies allow their credit customers to make periodic payments over several months. When this is done, the selling company's assets may be in the form of installment accounts receivable. *Installment accounts receivable* are amounts owed by customers from credit sales where payment is required in periodic amounts over an extended time period. Source documents for installment accounts receivable include sales slips or invoices describing the sales transactions. When payments are made over several months or if the credit period is long, the customer is usually charged interest. Although installment accounts receivable may have credit periods of more than one year, they should be classified as current assets if the company regularly offers customers such terms.

Companies sometimes allow customers to sign a note receivable for sales. Also, companies sometimes ask for a note to replace an account receivable when a customer requests additional time to pay its past-due account. A note receivable is a written document that promises payment and is signed by the customer. If the credit period is long, the customer is usually charged interest. If the company regularly offers customers this option, these notes receivable are classified as current assets even when their credit period is longer than one year. For legal reasons, sellers generally prefer to receive notes receivable when the credit period is long and the receivable relates to a single sale for a fairly large amount. If a lawsuit is needed to collect from a customer, a note is a written acknowledgment by the buyer of the debt, its amount, and its terms. We explain the details of notes receivable next.

Labor Union Chief
You are representing your employee union in contract negotiations with management. One week prior to contract discussions, management releases financial statements showing zero growth in earnings. This is far below the 10% growth predicted earlier. In your review of the statements, you find the company increased its "allowance for uncollectible accounts" from 1.5% to 4.5% of accounts receivable. Absent this change, earnings would show a 9% growth. Does this information impact your negotiations?

Answer—p. 434

Notes Receivable

C2 Describe a note receivable and the computation of its maturity date and interest.

A **promissory note** is a written promise to pay a specified amount of money either on demand or at a definite future date. Promissory notes are used in many transactions, including paying for products and services, in the lending and borrowing of money, and to pay for accounts receivable.

Exhibit 10.14 shows a promissory note dated July 10, 1999. For this note, Julia Browne promises to pay TechCom or to its order (according to TechCom's instructions) a specified amount of money ($1,000), called the **principal** of the note, at a definite future date (October 8, 1999). As the one who signed the note and promised to pay it at ma-

Promissory Note

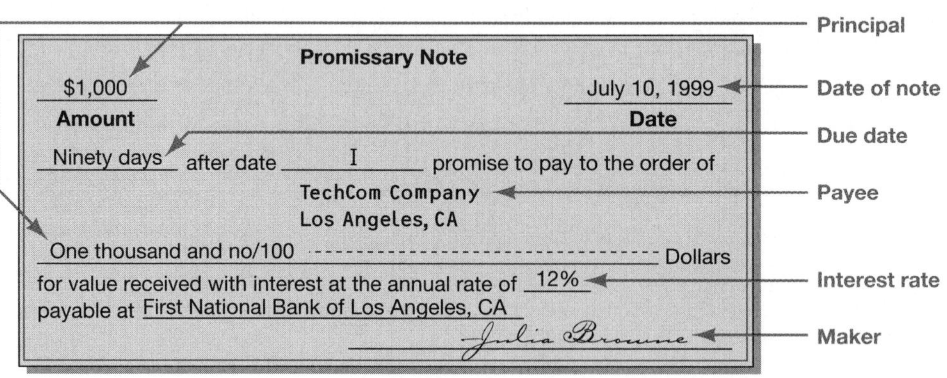

turity, Julia Browne is the **maker** of the note. As the person to whom the note is payable, TechCom is the **payee** of the note. To Julia Browne, the note is a liability called a *note payable.* To TechCom, the same note is an asset called a *note receivable.*

The promissory note in Exhibit 10.14 bears interest at 12%, as written on the note. **Interest** is the charge for using (not paying) the money until a later date. To a borrower, interest is an expense. To a lender, it is a revenue.

Computations for Notes

We need knowledge of certain computations for notes to understand them. This section describes these computations. They include determining maturity date, the period covered, and the interest computation.

Maturity Date and Period

The **maturity date** of a note is the day the note (principal and interest) must be repaid. The *period* of a note is the time from the note's date to its maturity date. Many notes mature in less than a full year, and the period covered by them is often expressed in days. When the time of a note is expressed in days, the maturity date is the specified number of days after the note's date. As an example, a five-day note dated June 15 matures and is due on June 20. A 90-day note dated July 10 matures on October 8. This October 8 due date is computed as shown in Exhibit 10.15.

Exhibit 10.15

Maturity Date Computation

Days in July	31	
Minus the date of the note	10	
Days remaining in July		21
Add days in August		31
Add days in September		30
Days to equal 90 days, or **Maturity Date, October 8**		8
Period of the note in days		90

The period of a note is sometimes expressed in months or years. When months are used, the note matures and is payable in the month of its maturity on the *same day of the month* as its original date. A three-month note dated July 10, for instance, is payable on October 10. The same analysis applies when years are used.

Interest Computation

Interest is the cost of borrowing money for the borrower or the profit from lending money for the lender. Unless otherwise stated, the rate of interest on a note is the rate charged for the use of the principal for one year. The formula for computing interest on a note is shown in Exhibit 10.16.

Computation of Interest Formula

Principal of the note × Annual interest rate × Time expressed in years = Interest

To illustrate, interest on a $1,000, 12%, six-month note is computed as:

$$\$1,000 \times 12\% \times \frac{6}{12} = \$60$$

To simplify interest computations for notes with periods expressed in days, it is common to treat a year as having 360 days. While this practice is not applied as frequently as it used to be, we **treat a year as having 360 days in our examples and in the as-**

signments to keep computations simple. Using the promissory note above where we have a 90-day, 12%, $1,000 note, the interest is computed as:

$$\$1{,}000 \times 12\% \times \frac{90}{360} = \$30$$

Receipt of a Note

P3 Record the receipt of a note receivable.

Notes receivable are usually recorded in a single Notes Receivable account to simplify recordkeeping. We need only one account because the original notes are kept on file. This means the maker, rate of interest, due date, and other information can be learned by examining the actual note.[5]

To illustrate the recording for the receipt of a note, we use the $1,000, 90-day, 12% promissory note in Exhibit 10.14. TechCom receives this note at the time of a product sale to Julia Browne. This transaction is recorded as:

July 10	Notes Receivable	1,000	
	Sales		1,000
	Sold merchandise in exchange for a 90-day, 12% note.		

Assets	= Liabilities	+ Equity
+1,000		+1,000

Companies also sometimes accept a note from an overdue customer as a way of granting a time extension on a past-due account receivable. When this occurs, a company may collect part of the past-due balance in cash. This partial payment forces a concession from the customer, reduces the customer's debt (and the seller's risk), and produces a note for a smaller amount. TechCom, for instance, agreed to accept $232 in cash and a $600, 60-day, 15% note from Jo Cook to settle her $832 past-due account. TechCom made the following entry to record receipt of this cash and note:

Oct. 5	Cash	232	
	Notes Receivable	600	
	Accounts Receivable—Jo Cook		832
	Received cash and note to settle account.		

Assets	= Liabilities	+ Equity
+232		
+600		
−832		

Honoring and Dishonoring a Note

P4 Record the honoring and dishonoring of a note and adjustments for interest on a note.

The principal and interest of a note are due on its maturity date. The maker of the note usually *honors* the note and pays it in full. But sometimes a maker *dishonors* the note and does not pay it at maturity.

Recording an Honored Note

We use the TechCom note transaction above to illustrate the honoring of a note. When Jo Cook pays the note on its due date, TechCom records its receipt as:

Dec. 4	Cash	615	
	Notes Receivable		600
	Interest Earned		15
	Collected Jo Cook note with interest of $600 × 15% × 60/360.		

Assets	= Liabilities	+ Equity
+615		+15
−600		

Interest Earned, also called Interest Revenue, is reported on the current period's income statement.

---

[5] When a company holds a large number of notes, it sometimes sets up a controlling account and a subsidiary ledger for notes.

Recording a Dishonored Note

When a note's maker is unable or refuses to pay at maturity, the note is dishonored. The act of **dishonoring** a note doesn't relieve the maker of the obligation to pay. The payee should use every legitimate means to collect. But how do companies report this event? The balance of the Notes Receivable account normally includes only those notes that have not matured. When a note is dishonored, we therefore remove the amount of this note from the Notes Receivable account and charge it back to an account receivable from its maker. TechCom, for instance, holds an $800, 12%, 60-day note of Greg Hart. At maturity, Hart dishonored the note. TechCom records this dishonoring of its Notes Receivable as follows:

Oct. 14	Accounts Receivable—Greg Hart	816	
	Interest Earned		16
	Notes Receivable		800
	To charge account of G. Hart for a dishonored note and interest of $800 × 12% × 60/360.		

Assets = Liabilities + Equity
+816 +16
−800

Charging a dishonored note back to the account of its maker serves two purposes. First, it removes the amount of the note from the Notes Receivable account, leaving in the account only notes that have not matured. It also records the dishonored note in the maker's account. Second, and more important, if the maker of the dishonored note applies for credit in the future, his or her account will show all past dealings, including the dishonored note. Restoring the account also reminds the company to continue collection efforts. Note that Hart owes both principal and interest. The above entry records the full amount owed in Hart's account and credits the interest to Interest Earned. This ensures that interest is included in efforts to collect from Hart.

End-of-Period Interest Adjustment

When notes receivable are outstanding at the end of an accounting period, accrued interest is computed and recorded. This recognizes both the interest revenue when it is earned and the added asset (interest) owned by the note's holder. For instance, on December 16, TechCom accepted a $3,000, 60-day, 12% note from a customer in granting an extension on a past-due account. When TechCom's accounting period ends on December 31, $15 of interest has accrued on this note ($3,000 × 12% × 15/360). The following adjusting entry records this revenue:

Dec. 31	Interest Receivable	15	
	Interest Earned		15
	To record accrued interest adjustment.		

Assets = Liabilities + Equity
+15 +15

This adjusting entry means interest earned appears on the income statement for the period when it is earned. It also means interest receivable appears on the balance sheet as a current asset.

Receiving Interest Previously Accrued

When the December 16 note above is collected on February 14, TechCom's entry to record the cash receipt is:

Feb. 14	Cash	3,060	
	Interest Earned		45
	Interest Receivable		15
	Notes Receivable		3,000
	Received payment of a note and its interest.		

Assets = Liabilities + Equity
+3,060 +45
−15
−3,000

Total interest earned on this note is $60. This entry's credit to Interest Receivable records collection of the interest accrued in the December 31 adjusting entry. The interest earned is $45 and reflects TechCom's revenue from holding the note from January 1 to February 14 of the current period.

Flash back

9. Wiley purchases $7,000 of merchandise from Stamford Company on December 16, 1999. Stamford accepts Wiley's $7,000, 90-day, 12% note as payment. Stamford's annual accounting period ends on December 31 and it doesn't make reversing entries. Prepare entries for Stamford Company on December 16, 1999, and December 31, 1999.

10. Using the information in Flashback 9., prepare Stamford's March 16, 2000, entry if Wiley dishonors the note.

Answers—p. 434

Converting Receivables to Cash before Maturity

C3 Explain how receivables can be converted to cash before maturity.

Sometimes companies convert receivables to cash before they are due. Reasons for this include the need for cash or a desire to not be involved in collection activities. Converting receivables is usually done either (1) by selling them or (2) by using them as security for a loan. A recent survey showed about 20% of large companies obtain cash from either the sale of receivables or the pledging of receivables as security. In some industries such as textiles and furniture, this is common practice. Recently, this practice has grown to other industries, especially the apparel industry. Also, many small companies use the sale of receivables as an immediate source of cash. This is especially the case for those selling to companies and government agencies that often delay payment.

Selling Accounts Receivable

A company can sell its accounts receivable to a finance company or bank. The buyer, called a *factor*, charges the seller a *factoring fee* and then collects the receivables as they come due. By incurring a factoring fee, the seller receives cash earlier and passes the risk of bad debts to the factor. The seller also avoids costs of billing and accounting for the receivables.

If TechCom, for instance, sells $20,000 of its accounts receivable and is charged a 2% factoring fee, it records this sale as:

Assets	= Liabilities	+ Equity
+19,600		−400
−20,000		

Aug. 15	Cash	19,600	
	Factoring Fee Expense	400	
	Accounts Receivable		20,000
	Sold accounts receivable for cash, less a 2% factoring fee.		

Factoring is a major business today. The **CIT Group** is a large factoring firm with volume of about $8 billion in recent years. Interestingly, about 90% of the factoring industry's business comes from textile and apparel businesses.

Pledging Accounts Receivable

A company can also raise cash by borrowing money and then *pledging* its accounts receivable as security for the loan. Pledging receivables doesn't transfer the risk of bad debts to the lender. The borrower retains ownership of the receivables. But if the borrower defaults on the loan, the lender has a right to be paid from cash receipts when the accounts receivable are collected. When TechCom borrowed $35,000 and pledged its receivables as security, it recorded this transaction as:

Aug. 20	Cash	35,000	
	Notes Payable		35,000
	Borrowed money with a note secured by pledging accounts receivable.		

Assets = Liabilities + Equity
+35,000 +35,000

Because pledged receivables are committed as security for a specific loan, the borrower's financial statements should disclose the pledging of accounts receivable. TechCom, for instance, includes the following note with its financial statements regarding its pledged receivables: *Accounts receivable in the amount of $40,000 are pledged as security for a $35,000 note payable to First National Bank.* Another example is from the notes of **Chock Full O'Nuts:**

> Outstanding borrowings . . . are collateralized by, among other things, the trade accounts receivable.

Cash Poor?
Both **Zenith** and **Packard Bell** used receivables to get much needed cash. **Zenith** obtained a 3-year, $60 million credit agreement by pledging accounts receivable as collateral. **Intel** converted accounts receivable to a note receivable for a major customer—widely assumed to be **Packard Bell.** [Source: *Business Week,* December 11, 1995.]

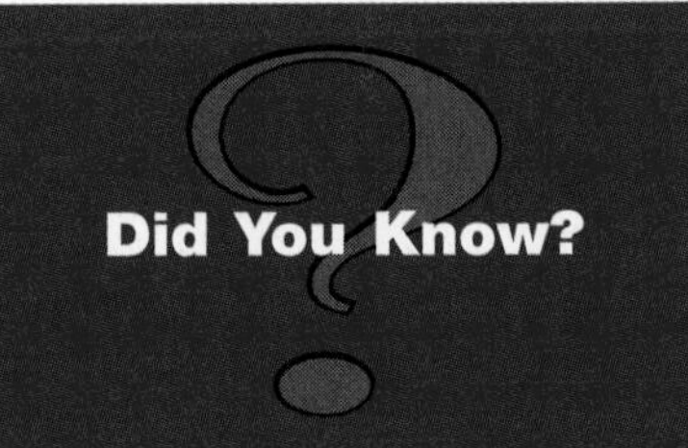

Discounting Notes Receivable

Notes receivable can be converted to cash before they mature. This can be done by discounting notes receivable at a financial institution or bank. TechCom, for instance, discounted a $3,000, 90-day, 10% note receivable at First National Bank. TechCom held the note for 50 of the 90 days before discounting it. The bank applied a 12% rate in discounting the note, and TechCom received proceeds of $3,034 from the bank.[6] It recorded the discounting of this note as:

Aug. 25	Cash	3,034	
	Interest Revenue		34
	Notes Receivable		3,000
	Discounted a note receivable.		

Assets = Liabilities + Equity
+3,034 +34
−3,000

Notes receivable are discounted without recourse or with recourse. When a note is discounted *without recourse,* the bank assumes the risk of a bad debt loss and the original payee doesn't have a contingent liability. A **contingent liability** is an obligation to make

[6] Accounting software and spreadsheet programs are used in practice to compute bank proceeds. TechCom's proceeds from the bank are computed as:

	Principal of Note	$3,000
+	Interest from Note ($3,000 × 10% × 90/360)	75
=	Maturity Value	3,075
−	Bank Discount ($3,075 × 12% × 40/360)	(41)
=	Proceeds	$3,034

a future payment if, and only if, an uncertain future event occurs. A note discounted without recourse is like an outright sale of an asset. If a note is discounted *with recourse* and the original maker of the note fails to pay the bank when it matures, the original payee of the note must pay for it. This means a company discounting a note with recourse has a contingent liability until the bank is paid. A company should disclose contingent liabilities in notes to its financial statements. TechCom included the following note: *The Company is contingently liable for a $3,000 note receivable discounted with recourse.* A similar example of a receivables sale with recourse is from the notes of **Tyco:**

> The Company entered into an agreement pursuant to which it sold . . . receivables. The Company has retained substantially the same risk of credit loss as if the receivables had not been sold.

Full Disclosure

The disclosure of contingencies in notes is consistent with the **full disclosure principle.** This principle requires financial statements (including notes) to report all relevant information about the operations and financial position of a company. Relevance is judged by whether its disclosure impacts users' evaluation of a company. Besides contingent liabilities, other items often reported to satisfy the full disclosure principle are long-term commitments under contracts and accounting methods used.

Contingent Liabilities

In addition to discounted notes, a company should disclose any items where it is contingently liable. Examples are potential tax assessments, debts of others guaranteed by the company, and outstanding lawsuits against the company. Information about these helps users predict events that might affect the company. In October 1994, *The Wall Street Journal* reported "**Pennzoil** said it agreed to pay the IRS $454 million in back taxes and interest to resolve a claim stemming from its 1988 settlement with **Texaco.**" Readers of notes to the financial statements of **Pennzoil** were not surprised since Pennzoil included the following note in its annual report the year before:

> Pennzoil received a letter and examination report from the District Director of the IRS that proposes a tax deficiency based on an audit . . . this proposed adjustment is $550.9 million, net of available offsets.

Long-Term Commitments under Contracts

A company should disclose any long-term commitments under contract. The most common example is signing a long-term lease requiring annual payments, even when the obligation doesn't appear in the accounts. Another case is when a company pledges part of its assets as security for loans. These commitments restrict the flexibility of a company.

Accounting Methods Used

When more than one accounting method can be used, a company must describe the one it uses. This is especially important when the choice can materially impact net income.[7] This information helps users in their analysis of a company.

[7] FASB, Accounting *Standards—Current Text* (Norwalk, CT, 1995), sec. A10.105. First published as *APB Opinion No. 22*, pars. 12, 13.

Short-Term Investments

C4 Describe short-term investments in debt and equity securities.

Recall from Chapter 9 that cash equivalents are investments that are easily converted to known amounts of cash and they generally mature no more than three months after purchase. Yet many investments mature between 3 and 12 months (or the operating cycle). These investments are **short-term investments,** also called *temporary investments,* or *marketable securities.* Management expects to convert them to cash within one year or the current operating cycle of the business, whichever is longer.[8] Short-term investments are current assets and serve a similar purpose to cash equivalents.

Short-term investments can include both debt and equity securities. *Debt securities* reflect a creditor relationship and include investments in notes, bonds, and certificates of deposit. Debt securities are issued by governments, companies, and individuals. *Equity securities* reflect an ownership relationship and include shares of stock issued by companies. In notes to financial statements, companies usually give a description of their short-term investments.

Accounting for Short-Term Investments

This section explains the basics of accounting for short-term investments in both debt and equity securities.

Debt Securities

Short-term investments in both debt and equity securities are recorded at cost when purchased. TechCom, for instance, purchased short-term notes payable of Intel for $4,000 on January 10. TechCom's entry to record this purchase is:

Jan. 10	Short-Term Investments	4,000	
	Cash		4,000
	Bought $4,000 of Intel notes due May 10.		

Assets = Liabilities + Equity
+4,000
−4,000

These notes mature on May 10 and the cash proceeds are $4,000 plus $120 interest. When the proceeds are received, TechCom records this as:

May 10	Cash	4,120	
	Short-Term Investments		4,000
	Interest Earned		120
	Received cash proceeds from matured notes.		

Assets = Liabilities + Equity
+4,120 +120
−4,000

Equity Securities

The cost of an investment includes all necessary costs to acquire it, including commissions paid. TechCom purchased 100 shares of NIKE common stock as a short-term investment. It paid $50 per share plus $100 in commissions. The entry to record this purchase is

June 2	Short-Term Investments	5,100	
	Cash		5,100
	Bought 100 shares of NIKE stock at 50 plus $100 commission.		

Assets = Liabilities + Equity
+5,100
−5,100

The commission is not recorded in a separate account.

[8] FASB, *Accounting Standards—Current Text* (Norwalk, CT, 1995), sec. B05.105. First published as *Accounting Research Bulletin No. 43*, chap. 3A, par. 4.

TechCom received a $0.40 per share cash dividend on its short-term NIKE stock during the current period. This dividend is credited to a revenue account as follows:

Assets = Liabilities + Equity
+40 +40

Dec. 12	Cash	40	
	Dividends Earned		40
	Received dividend of $0.40 per share on 100 shares of NIKE stock.		

Reporting Short-Term Investments

P5 Record the sale of short-term investments.

Companies must report most short-term investments at their fair (market) values.[9] Requirements vary depending on whether short-term investments are classified as (1) held-to-maturity, (2) trading, or (3) available-for-sale securities. This section describes the financial statement presentation for each of these classifications.

Held-to-Maturity Securities

Held-to-maturity securities are *debt securities* that the company has the intent and ability to hold until they mature.[10] **Dairy Queen,** for instance, in notes to its financial statements, stated:

> Management determines the appropriate classification of debt securities at the time of purchase and reevaluates such designation as of each balance sheet date. Debt securities are classified as held-to-maturity because the Company has the positive intent and ability to hold such securities to maturity.

Held-to-maturity securities are reported in current assets if their maturity dates are within one year or the current operating cycle of the company. Held-to-maturity securities are reported at cost.

Trading Securities

Trading securities are either *debt or equity securities* that the company intends to actively trade for profit. These securities are actively managed. This means frequent purchases and sales are made to earn profits on short-term stock price changes. Trading securities are especially common with financial institutions such as banks and insurance companies.

Valuing and Reporting Trading Securities

Companies report the entire set of trading securities at their fair (or market) values with a "fair value adjustment" to the cost of the set. The resulting unrealized holding gains and losses from changes in the market value for the set of securities from one period to another are reported on the income statement as part of net income or loss. Most users believe accounting reports are more useful for decision making when changes in market values for this set of trading securities are reported in income.

To illustrate, TechCom's set of trading securities had a total cost of $11,500 and a fair market value of $13,000 on December 31, 1998. The difference between the $11,500 cost and the $13,000 fair value reflects a $1,500 gain. Because this gain is not yet confirmed by actual sales of these securities, it is called an **unrealized holding gain.** TechCom records this gain as:

---

[9] FASB, "Accounting for Certain Investments in Debt and Equity Securities," *Statement of Financial Accounting Standards No. 115* (Norwalk, CT, 1995). The requirements of *SFAS 115* also apply to long-term investments in debt and marketable equity securities. We discuss this in Chapter 16.

[10] Ibid., par. 7.

Dec. 31	Trading Securities, Fair Value Adjustment	1,500	
	Unrealized Holding Gain (Loss)		1,500
	To reflect a gain in fair values of trading securities.		

Assets = Liabilities + Equity
+1,500 +1,500

The Unrealized Holding Gain (Loss) is reported in Other Revenues and Gains (Expenses and Losses) on the income statement. After posting this entry, TechCom's investment in trading securities is reported in the current assets section of its balance sheet as:

Current Assets:		
Trading securities (at cost)	$11,500	
Trading securities (fair value adjustment)	1,500	
Trading securities (at fair value)		$13,000

The total cost of the entire set of trading securities is maintained in one account and the fair value adjustment is recorded in a separate account. The fair value adjustment is revised at the end of every period to equal the difference between cost and fair value. Keeping the Trading Securities account at cost helps us compute realized gains or losses when securities are sold, which we describe next.

Selling Trading Securities

When individual trading securities are sold, the difference between the net proceeds from the sale (sale price less brokerage fees) and the cost of the individual trading securities sold is recognized as a gain or a loss. When TechCom sells its $5,100 short-term investment in NIKE stock on December 15 for net proceeds of $5,400, it recognizes a gain of $300. The entry to record this sale is:

Dec. 15	Cash	5,400	
	Gain on Sale of Short-Term Investments . .		300
	Short-Term Investments		5,100
	To record sale of 100 shares of NIKE stock.		

Assets = Liabilities + Equity
+5,400 +300
−5,100

This gain is reported in Other Revenues and Gains on the income statement. If a loss is recorded, it is shown in Other Expenses and Losses. At the end of the period, the fair value adjustment for trading securities excludes the cost and fair values of NIKE stock.

Back to the Future
Before 1938, banks reported fair (market) values for their short-term investments but then switched to historical cost. We now see a return to fair-value reporting for many short-term investments that is driven by S&L and banking problems. Ironically, the Great Depression fueled the 1938 conversion from fair values to historical cost. At that time bank examiners were concerned with protecting bank depositors (Federal Deposit Insurance didn't exist). Examiners had to determine market values for bank assets and liabilities to arrive at bank equity. If a bank's liabilities exceeded or even approximated its assets, its capital was considered impaired. Owners of banks with impaired capital then had to add capital, merge with another bank, or close. This led to bank examiners being blamed for excessive bank closings. Bank appraisal methods were then changed to historical cost.[11]

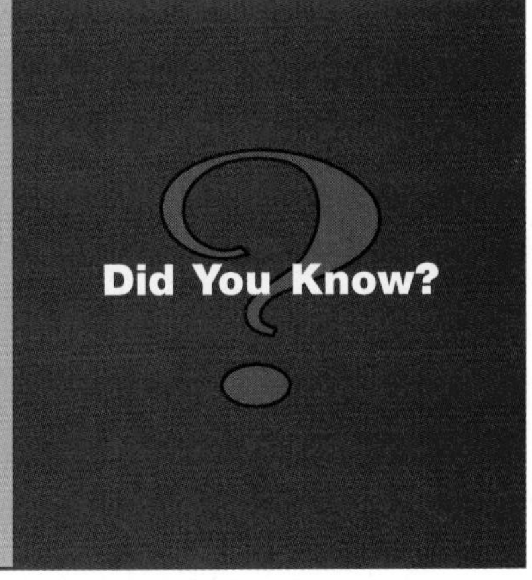

[11] Source: Dan W. Swenson and Thomas E. Buttross, "Return to the Past: Disclosing Market Values of Financial Instruments." Reprinted with permission of the *Journal of Accountancy,* January 1993, pp. 71–77. Copyright © 1993 by the American Institute of Certified Public Accountants, Inc. Opinions of the authors are their own and do not necessarily reflect policies of the AICPA.

Available-for-Sale Securities

Available-for-sale securities are *debt or equity securities not* classified as trading or held-to-maturity securities. Available-for-sale securities are purchased to earn interest, dividends, or increases in market value. They are not actively managed like trading securities. Many companies own available-for-sale securities.

Valuing and Reporting Available-for-Sale Securities

Similar to trading securities, companies adjust the cost of the entire set of available-for-sale securities to reflect changes in fair value with a fair value adjustment to their total cost. The unrealized holding gains and losses from changes in market value for the set of available-for-sale securities from one period to another are *not* reported on the income statement. Instead, they are reported in the equity section of the balance sheet. Many users believe accounting reports are more useful for decision making when changes in market value of the entire set of available-for-sale securities are not reported in income. Since these securities are not actively traded, they believe including changes in market value would unnecessarily increase the variability of income and decrease its usefulness. We describe the reporting of these securities more fully in Chapter 16.

Selling Available-for-Sale Securities

When individual available-for-sale securities are sold, the difference between the cost of the individual securities sold and the net proceeds from the sale (sale price less brokerage fees) is recognized as a gain or loss. Accounting for the sale of individual available-for-sale securities is identical to that described for the sale of trading securities.

Summary of Accounting for Short-Term Investments

Exhibit 10.17 summarizes accounting for short-term investments in debt and equity securities.

Exhibit 10.17

Accounting for Short-Term Investments in Securities

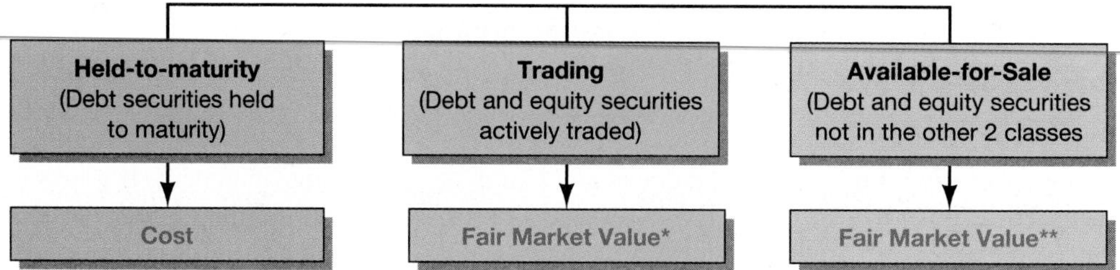

*Unrealized gains or losses reported on income statement.
**Unrealized gains or losses reported in equity section on balance sheet and in comprehensive income.

The balance sheet presentation of short-term investments usually reports the fair market value for the *total* of all three types of securities instead of each individual type. The cost is also usually reported. A typical presentation of short-term securities is shown in Exhibit 10.18.

Exhibit 10.18

Statement Presentation of Short-Term Investments

Current assets:	
Short-term investments, at fair market value (cost is $16,200)	**14,500**

Even though the contra account to Short-Term Investments is not shown, we can determine its balance is $1,700 by comparing the $16,200 cost with the $14,500 net amount. Companies sometimes report separately the market value and cost for each of the three types of short-term securities.

Flash back

11. How are held-to-maturity securities reported on the balance sheet—at cost or fair (market) values?

12. How are trading securities reported on the balance sheet?

13. Unrealized holding gains and losses on available-for-sale securities are reported on what statement?

14. Where are unrealized holding gains and losses on trading securities reported?

Answers—p. 434

Accounts Receivable Turnover

USING THE INFORMATION

A1 Compute accounts receivable turnover and use it to analyze liquidity.

In Chapter 8 we discussed *days' sales uncollected* and how it helps us access a company's short-term liquidity or nearness to cash of its receivables. For companies selling on credit, we want to access both the quality and liquidity of its accounts receivable. *Quality* of receivables refers to the likelihood of collection without loss. Experience shows the longer receivables are outstanding beyond their due date, the lower the likelihood of collection. *Liquidity* of receivables refers to the speed of collection.

The **accounts receivable turnover** is a measure of both the quality and liquidity of accounts receivable. It indicates how often, on average, receivables are received and collected during the period. The formula for this ratio is shown in Exhibit 10.19.

Exhibit 10.19

Accounts Receivable Turnover Formula

$$\textbf{Accounts receivable turnover} = \frac{\textbf{Net sales}}{\textbf{Average accounts receivable}}$$

We prefer net *credit* sales in the numerator because cash sales do not create receivables. But since financial statements rarely report net credit sales, our analysis uses net total sales. The denominator in this turnover formula is the *average* accounts receivable balance during the period. The average is often computed as: (Beginning balance + Ending balance) ÷ 2. This method of estimating the average balance provides a useful result if seasonal changes in the accounts receivable balance during the year are not extreme.

The accounts receivable turnover shows us how often a company converts its average accounts receivable balance into cash during the period. TechCom, for instance, has an accounts receivable turnover of 5.1. This shows its average accounts receivable balance is converted into cash 5.1 times during the year. Exhibit 10.20 shows graphically this turnover activity for TechCom.

Exhibit 10.20

Rate of Accounts Receivable Turnover for TechCom

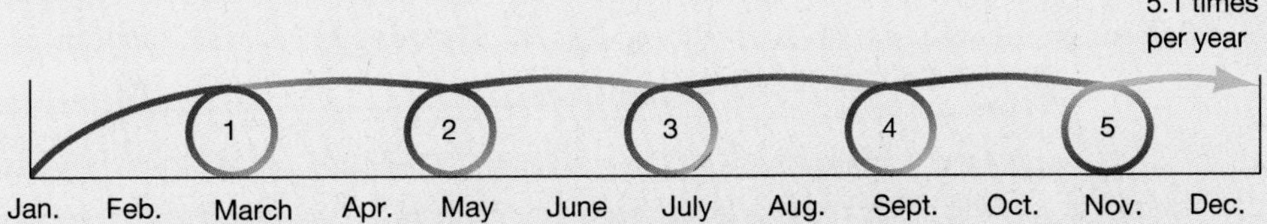

Accounts receivable turnover also helps us evaluate how well management is doing in granting credit to customers in a desire to increase sales revenues. A high turnover in comparison with competitors suggests management should consider using more liberal credit terms to increase sales. A low turnover suggests management should consider stricter credit terms and more aggressive collection efforts to avoid having its resources tied up in accounts receivable.

To illustrate its application, we use data from the annual reports of two competing companies: **Dell Computer** and **Compaq Computer**. Exhibit 10.21 shows results from our computation of accounts receivable turnover for these two companies.

Exhibit 10.21

Analysis Using Accounts Receivable Turnover

Company	Figure ($ millions)	1996	1995	1994
Dell	Net sales	$ 7,759	$ 5,296	$ 3,475
	Average accounts receivable	$ 815	$ 632	$ 475
	Accounts receivable turnover	9.5	8.4	7.3
Compaq	Net sales	$18,109	$14,755	$10,866
	Average accounts receivable	$ 3,155	$ 2,714	$ 1,832
	Accounts receivable turnover	5.7	5.4	5.9

To show how we compute and use accounts receivable turnover, let's look at the numbers for Dell for 1994–1996 as reported in Exhibit 10.21. We compute Dell's 1996 turnover as ($ in millions):

$$\frac{\$7{,}759}{\$815} = 9.5$$

This means Dell's average accounts receivable balance is converted into cash 9.5 times in 1996. Also, Dell's turnover is continually improving over the period 1994–1996, and it is superior to Compaq. Is Dell's turnover too high? Because sales are growing dramatically over this same period, it doesn't appear Dell's turnover is too high. Instead, Dell's management seems to be doing an excellent job at managing receivables. This is especially apparent when compared to Compaq and most of its other competitors. Turnover for Dell's competitors is generally in the range of 6 to 7 over this same period.[12]

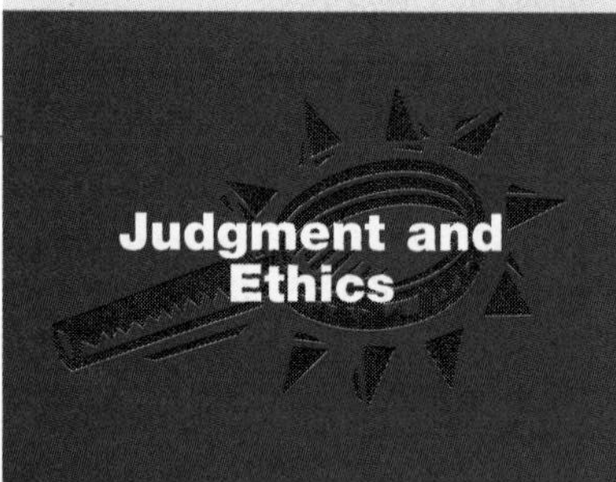

Family Physician

You are a family physician operating a small practice. Your practice has turned less profitable and you hire a health care analyst to examine your financials and to recommend solutions. The analyst's report highlights several problems including accounts receivable. It states "*. . . accounts receivable turnover is too low. Tighter credit policies are recommended along with discontinuing service to those most delayed in payments*." How do you interpret these recommendations? What actions do you take?

Answer—p. 434

Flash back

15. A company needs cash and has substantial accounts receivable. What alternatives are available for getting cash from its accounts receivable prior to receiving payments from credit customers? Show the entry made for each alternative.

16. Compute **Mattel's** accounts receivable turnover for 1994 using the following information:

(In thousands)	1994	1993
Accounts receivable	762,024	580,313
Current assets	1,543,523	1,470,750
Net sales	3,205,025	2,704,448
Net income	255,832	117,208

Answers—p. 434

[12] As an approximation of *average days' sales uncollected* we can compute an estimate of how many days *(on average)* it takes to collect receivables as follows: 365 days ÷ accounts receivable turnover.

Summary

C1 Describe accounts receivable and how they occur and are recorded. Accounts receivable refer to amounts due from customers for credit sales. The subsidiary ledger lists the amounts owed by individual customers. Credit sales arise from at least two sources: (1) sales on credit and (2) credit card sales. Sales on credit refer to a company's granting credit directly to customers. Credit card sales involve use of a third party's issuing a credit card to customers.

C2 Describe a note receivable and the computation of its maturity date and interest. A note receivable is a written promise to pay a specified amount of money either on demand or at a definite future date. The maturity date of a note is the day the note (principal and interest) must be repaid. Interest rates are typically stated in annual terms. When a note's time to maturity is different than one year, the amount of interest on a note is computed by expressing time as a fraction of one year and multiplying the note's principal by this fraction and the annual interest rate.

C3 Explain how receivables can be converted to cash before maturity. There are three usual means to convert receivables to cash before maturity. First, a company can sell accounts receivable to a factor, who charges a factoring fee. Second, a company can borrow money by signing a note payable that is secured by pledging the accounts receivable. Third, notes receivable can be discounted at a bank, with or without recourse. The full disclosure principle requires companies to disclose the amount of receivables pledged and the contingent liability for notes discounted with recourse.

C4 Describe short-term investments in debt and equity securities. Short-term investments can include both debt and equity securities. *Debt securities* reflect a creditor relationship and include investments in notes, bonds, and certificates of deposit. Debt securities are issued by governments, companies, and individuals. *Equity securities* reflect an ownership relationship and include shares of stock issued by companies.

A1 Compute accounts receivable turnover and use it to analyze liquidity. Accounts receivable turnover is a measure of both the quality and liquidity of accounts receivable. Quality of receivables refers to likelihood of collection without loss. Experience shows the longer receivables are outstanding beyond their due date, the lower the likelihood of collection. Liquidity of receivables refers to speed of collection. The accounts receivable turnover measure indicates how often, on average, receivables are received and collected during the period. Accounts receivable turnover is computed as sales divided by average accounts receivable for the period.

P1 Apply the direct write-off and allowance methods to account for accounts receivable. The direct write-off method charges Bad Debts Expense when accounts are written off as uncollectible. This method is acceptable only when the amount of bad debts expense is immaterial. Under the allowance method, bad debts expense is recorded with an adjustment at the end of each accounting period debiting the Expense account and crediting the Allowance for Doubtful Accounts. The uncollectible accounts are later written off with a debit to the Allowance for Doubtful Accounts.

P2 Estimate uncollectibles using methods based on sales and accounts receivable. Uncollectibles are estimated by focusing on either *(a)* the income statement relation between bad debts expense and credit sales or *(b)* the balance sheet relation between accounts receivable and the Allowance for Doubtful Accounts. The first approach emphasizes the matching principle for the income statement. The second approach can include either a simple percent relation with accounts receivable or the aging of accounts receivable. It emphasizes realizable value of accounts receivable for the balance sheet.

P3 Record the receipt of a note receivable. A note is recorded at its principal amount by debiting the Notes Receivable account. The credit amount is to the asset, product, or service provided in return for the note.

P4 Record the honoring and dishonoring of a note and adjustments for interest on a note. When a note is honored, the payee debits the money received and credits both Notes Receivable and Interest Earned. Dishonored notes are credited to Notes Receivable and debited to Accounts Receivable (to the account of the maker in attempts to collect). The interest earned from holding a note is recorded for the amount of time the note was held in the accounting period.

P5 Record the sale of short-term investments. Short-term investments are recorded at cost, and any dividends or interest from these investments are recorded in their income statement accounts. For presentation in financial statements, short-term investments are classified as held-to-maturity securities, trading securities, or available-for-sale securities. Held-to-maturity securities are reported at cost on the balance sheet. Trading securities and available-for-sale securities are reported at their fair (market) values. Unrealized gains and losses on trading securities are reported in income. Unrealized gains and losses on available-for-sale securities are reported as a separate item in the equity section of the balance sheet. When short-term investments are sold, the difference between the net proceeds from the sale (sales price less brokerage fees) and the cost of the trading securities is recognized as a gain or a loss.

Guidance Answers to **You Make the Call**

Entrepreneur

Your analysis of allowing credit card sales should weigh the benefits against the costs. The primary benefit is the potential to increase sales by attracting customers who prefer the convenience of credit cards. The primary cost is the fee charged by the credit card company for providing this service to your store. Your analysis should therefore estimate the expected increase in sales dollars from allowing credit card sales and then subtract (1) the normal costs and expenses and (2) the credit card fees associated with this expected increase in sales dollars. If your analysis shows an increase in profit from allowing credit card sales, your store should probably allow them.

Labor Union Chief

Yes, this information is likely to impact your negotiations. The obvious question is why the company increased the allowance to such a large extent. This major increase in allowance means a substantial increase in bad debts expense *and* a decrease in earnings. Also, this change coming immediately prior to labor contract discussions raises concerns since it reduces the union's bargaining power for increased compensation. You want to ask management for supporting documentation justifying this increase. Also, you want data for two or three prior years, and similar data from competitors. These data should give you some sense of whether the change in the allowance for uncollectibles is justified.

Guidance Answer to **Judgment and Ethics**

Family Physician

The analyst's recommendations are twofold. First, the analyst is suggesting a more stringent screening of patients according to their credit standing. Second, the analyst suggests dropping those patients who are most overdue or delinquent in their payments. You are likely bothered by these suggestions. While they are probably financially wise recommendations, you are troubled by eliminating services to those less able to pay. One possible alternative is to follow the analyst's recommendations while at the same time implementing a care program directed at those patients less able to pay for services. This allows you to continue services to patients less able to pay, and lets you discontinue services to patients able but unwilling to pay for services.

Guidance Answers to 

1. If cash is received as soon as copies of credit card sales receipts are deposited in the bank, the business debits Cash at the time of the sale. If the business does not receive payment until after it submits the receipts to the credit card company, it debits Accounts Receivable at the time of the sale.

2. The credit card expenses are usually *recorded* when the cash is received from the credit card company; however, they are *incurred* at the time of their related sales.

3. An adjusting entry must be made to satisfy the matching principle. The credit card expense must be reported in the same period as their sale.

4. Bad debts expense must be matched with the sales that gave rise to the accounts receivable. This requires that companies estimate bad debts before they learn which accounts are uncollectible.

5. Realizable value (also called net relizable value).

6. The estimated amount of bad debts expense cannot be credited to the Accounts Receivable account because the specific customer accounts that will prove uncollectible cannot be identified and removed from the subsidiary Accounts Receivable Ledger. If the controlling account were credited directly, its balance would not equal the sum of the subsidiary account balances.

7.

1999			
Dec. 31	Bad Debts Expense	5,702	
	Allowance for Doubtful Accounts		5,702

8.

1999			
Jan. 10	Allowance for Doubtful Accounts	300	
	Accounts Receivable—Cool Jam		300
Apr. 12	Accounts Receivable—Cool Jam	300	
	Allowance for Doubtful Accounts		300
Apr. 12	Cash	300	
	Accounts Receivable—Cool Jam		300

9.

1999			
Dec. 16	Notes Receivable	7,000	
	Sales		7,000
Dec. 31	Interest Receivable	35	
	Interest Earned		35
	($7,000 × 12% × 15/360)		

10.

2000			
Mar. 16	Accounts Receivable—Wiley	7,210	
	Interest Earned		175
	Interest Receivable		35
	Notes Receivable		7,000

11. Securities held-to-maturity are reported at cost.

12. Trading securities are reported at fair (market) value.

13. The equity section of the balance sheet (and in comprehensive income).

14. The income statement.

15. Alternatives are (1) selling their accounts receivable to a factor and (2) pledging accounts receivable as loan security. The entries to record these transactions take the following form:

(1) Cash	#	
Factoring Fee Expense	#	
Accounts Receivable		#
(2) Cash	#	
Notes Payable		#

16. Accounts receivable turnover =

$$\frac{3{,}205{,}025}{(762{,}024 + 580{,}313)/2} = 4.78 \text{ times}$$

Demonstration Problem

Garden Company completed the following transactions during 1999:

May 8 Purchased 300 shares of Federal Express common stock as a short-term investment in a security available-for-sale. The cost of $40 per share plus $975 in broker's commissions was paid in cash.

July 14 Wrote off a $750 account receivable arising from a sale to Briggs Company several months ago. (Garden Company uses the allowance method.)

30 Garden Company received a $1,000, 3-month, 10% promissory note for a product sale to Sumrell Company.

Aug. 15 Accepted a $2,000 down payment and a $10,000 note receivable from a customer in exchange for an inventory item that normally sells for $12,000. The note is dated August 15, bears 12% interest, and matures in six months.

Sept. 2 Sold 100 shares of Federal Express stock at $47 per share and continued to hold the other 200 shares. The broker's commission on the sale is $225.

15 Received $9,850 in return for discounting without recourse the $10,000 note (dated August 15) at the local bank.

Oct. 2 Purchased 400 shares of McDonald's stock for $60 per share plus $1,600 in commissions. The stock is held as a short-term investment in a security available-for-sale.

Nov. 1 Made a $200 credit card sale with a 4% fee. The cash is received immediately from the credit card company.

5 Made a $500 credit card sale with a 5% fee. The payment from the credit card company is received on Nov. 7.

15 Received the full amount of $750 from Briggs Company that was previously written off on July 14. Record the bad debts recovery.

20 Sumrell Company refused to pay the note that was due to Garden Company on Oct. 30. Make the journal entry to charge the dishonored note plus accrued interest to Sumrell Company's accounts receivable.

Required

1. Prepare journal entries to record these transactions on the books of Garden Company.
2. Prepare an adjusting journal entry as of December 31, 1999, for the following item:
   a. Bad debts expense is estimated by an aging of accounts receivable. The unadjusted balance of the Allowance for Doubtful Accounts account is a $1,000 debit, while the required balance is estimated to be a $20,400 credit.
   b. Alternatively, assume that bad debts expense is estimated at year-end using a percentage of sales approach. As in (a), assume that the Allowance for Doubtful Accounts account has a $1,000 debit balance before adjustment. The company estimates bad debts to be 1% of credit sales of $2,000,000.

Planning the Solution

- Examine each item to determine which accounts are affected and record the journal entries.
- With respect to the year-end adjustment, record the bad debts expense.

Solution to Demonstration Problem

1.

Date	Account	Debit	Credit
May 8	Short-Term Investments	12,975	
	Cash		12,975
	Purchased 300 shares of Federal Express. Cost is (300 × $40) + $975.		
July 14	Allowance for Doubtful Accounts	750	
	Accounts Receivable—Briggs Company . .		750
	Wrote off an uncollectible account.		

July 30	Notes Receivable—Sumrell Company	1,000	
	Sales		1,000
	Sold merchandise in exchange for a 3-month, 10% note.		
Aug. 15	Cash	2,000	
	Notes Receivable	10,000	
	Sales		12,000
	Sold merchandise to customer for $2,000 cash and $10,000 note receivable.		
Sept. 2	Cash	4,475	
	Gain on Sale of Investment		150
	Short-Term Investments		4,325
	Sold 100 shares of Federal Express for $47 per share less a $225 commission. The original cost is ($12,975 × 100/300).		
Sept. 15	Cash	9,850	
	Loss on Discounting of Notes	150	
	Notes Receivable		10,000
	Discounted note receivable dated August 15.		
Oct. 2	Short-Term Investments	25,600	
	Cash		25,600
	Purchased 400 shares of McDonald's for $60 per share plus $1,600 in commissions.		
Nov. 1	Cash	192	
	Credit Card Expense	8	
	Sales		200
	To record credit card sale less a 4% credit card expense.		
Nov. 5	Accounts Receivable—Credit Card Company . .	500	
	Sales		500
	To record credit card sale.		
Nov. 7	Cash	475	
	Credit Card Expense	25	
	Accounts Receivable—Credit Card Company		500
	To record cash receipt less a 5% credit card expense.		
Nov. 15	Accounts Receivable—Briggs Company	750	
	Allowance for Doubtful Accounts		750
	To reinstate the account of Briggs Company previously written off.		
Nov. 15	Cash	750	
	Accounts Receivable—Briggs Company . .		750
	In full payment of account.		
Nov. 20	Accounts Receivable—Sumrell Company	1,025	
	Interest Earned		25
	Notes Receivable—Sumrell Company . . .		1,000
	To charge account of Sumrell Company for a dishonored note including interest of $1,000 × 10% × 3/12.		

2a.

Dec. 31	Bad Debts Expense	21,400	
	Allowance for Doubtful Accounts		21,400
	To adjust allowance account from $1,000 debit balance to $20,400 credit balance.		

b. Alternate approach:

Dec. 31	Bad Debts Expense	20,000	
	Allowance for Doubtful Accounts		20,000
	To provide for bad debts as 1% x $2,000,000 in credit sales. (Note: disregard any existing balance in the Allowance account when making the entry using the income statement approach.)		

(*Note to students:* Under the income statement approach which requires estimating bad debts as a percent of sales or net credit sales, the Allowance Account balance is not considered when making the adjusting entry. While this might seem arbitrary, it is not. The income statement approach estimates bad debts expense using the relation between bad debts expense and sales. These are both income statement accounts. The allowance account is a balance sheet account. It is therefore logical that its balance is considered when using the balance sheet approach.)

Glossary

Accounts receivable amounts due from customers for credit sales. (p. 406).

Accounts receivable turnover a measure of both the quality and liquidity of accounts receivable; it indicates how often, on average, receivables are received and collected during the period; computed by dividing credit sales (or net sales) by the average accounts receivable balance. (p. 431).

Aging accounts receivable a process of classifying accounts receivable in terms of how long they are past due for the purpose of estimating the amount of uncollectible accounts. (p. 417).

Allowance for Doubtful Accounts a contra asset account with a balance equal to the estimated amount of accounts receivable that will be uncollectible; also called the Allowance for Uncollectible Accounts. (p. 412).

Allowance method of accounting for bad debts an accounting procedure that (1) estimates and reports bad debts expense from credit sales during the period of the sales and (2) reports accounts receivable at the amount of cash proceeds that is expected from their collection (their estimated realizable value). (p. 412).

Available-for-sale securities investments in debt and equity securities that are not classified as trading securities or held-to-maturity securities. (p. 430).

Bad debts the accounts of customers who do not pay what they have promised to pay; the amount is an expense of selling on credit; also called *uncollectible accounts.* (p. 410).

Contingent liability an obligation to make a future payment if, and only if, an uncertain future event actually occurs. (p. 425).

Direct write-off method of accounting for bad debts a method of accounting for bad debts that records the loss from an uncollectible account receivable at the time it is determined to be uncollectible; no attempt is made to estimate uncollectible accounts or bad debts expense. (p. 411).

Dishonoring a note when a note's maker is unable or refuses to pay at maturity. (p. 423).

Full disclosure principle the accounting principle that requires financial statements (including the notes) to report all relevant information about the operations and financial position of the entity. (p. 426).

Held-to-maturity securities debt securities that the company has the intent and ability to hold until they mature. (p. 428).

Interest the charge for using (not paying) money until a later date. (p. 421).

Maker of a note one who signs a note and promises to pay it at maturity. (p. 421).

Matching principle requires expenses to be reported in the same accounting period as the sales they helped produce. (p. 412).

Materiality principle states that an amount may be ignored if its effect on the financial statements is unimportant to their users. (p. 412).

Maturity date of a note the date on which a note and any interest are due and payable. (p. 421).

Payee of a note the one to whom a promissory note is made payable. (p. 421).

Principal of a note the amount that the signer of a promissory note agrees to pay back when it matures, not including the interest. (p. 420).

Promissory note a written promise to pay a specified amount of money either on demand or at a definite future date. (p. 420).

Realizable value the expected proceeds from converting assets into cash. (p. 413).

Short-term investments current assets that serve a similar purpose to cash equivalents; generally mature between 3 and 12 months (or the operating cycle if longer) at which time management expects to convert them into cash; can be either debt or equity securities (also called *temporary investments*). (p. 427).

Trading securities investments in debt and equity securities that the company intends to actively trade for profit; frequent purchases and sales generally are made with the objective of generating profits on short-term changes in price. (p. 428).

Unrealized holding gain (loss) a gain (loss) not yet realized by an actual transaction or event such as a sale. (p. 428).

Questions

1. Under what conditions should investments be classified as current assets?
2. If a short-term investment in securities held for sale costs $6,780 and is sold for $7,500, how should the difference between the two amounts be recorded?
3. On a balance sheet, what valuation must be reported for short-term investments in trading securities?
4. How do businesses benefit from allowing their customers to use credit cards?
5. Explain why writing off a bad debt against the Allowance account does not reduce the estimated realizable value of a company's accounts receivable.
6. Why does the Bad Debts Expense account usually not have the same adjusted balance as the Allowance for Doubtful Accounts?
7. Why does the direct write-off method of accounting for bad debts usually fail to match revenues and expenses?
8. What is the essence of the accounting principle of materiality?
9. Why might a business prefer a note receivable to an account receivable?
10. What does it mean to sell a receivable without recourse?
11. Review the consolidated balance sheet for NIKE in Appendix A. What percent of accounts receivable as of May 31, 1997, has been set aside as an allowance for doubtful accounts? How does the percent compare to the prior year?
12. Review the consolidated balance sheet for Reebok in Appendix A. Does Reebok use the direct write-off method or allowance method to account for doubtful accounts? What is the realizable value of the accounts receivable as of December 31, 1996? What is another name for the Allowance for Doubtful Accounts?
13. America Online shows cash and cash equivalents of $118,421,000 and short-term investments of $10,712,000 on its consolidated balance sheet as of June 30, 1996 in Appendix A. Since both of these items are current assets, why are they reported separately?
14. Who are likely the major customers of CFS?

Quick Study

QS 10-1
Short-term equity investments
C4

On April 18, Kimmell Industries made a short-term investment in 200 shares of Computer Links common stock. The intent is to actively manage these stocks. The purchase price was $42\frac{1}{2}$ and the broker's fee was $350. On June 30, Kimmell received $2 per share in dividends. Prepare the April 18 and June 30 journal entries.

QS 10-2
Credit card sales

Journalize the following transactions:

a. Sold $10,000 in merchandise on MasterCard credit cards. The sales receipts are immediately deposited in the business's bank account. MasterCard charges a 5% fee.

b. Sold $3,000 on miscellaneous credit cards. Cash will be received within 10 days and a 4% fee will be charged.

QS 10-3
Allowance method for bad debts

Foster Corporation uses the allowance method to account for uncollectibles. On October 31, they wrote off a $1,000 account of a customer, Gwen Rowe. On December 9, they received a $200 payment from Rowe.

a. Make the appropriate entry or entries for October 31.

b. Make the appropriate entry or entries for December 9.

QS 10-4
Percent of accounts receivable method

Duncan Company's year-end trial balance shows accounts receivable of $89,000, allowance for doubtful accounts of $500 (credit), and sales of $270,000. Uncollectibles are estimated to be 1.5% of outstanding accounts receivable.

a. Prepare the December 31 year-end adjustment for uncollectibles.

b. What amount would have been used in the year-end adjustment if the allowance account had a year-end debit balance of $200?

c. Assume the same facts, except that Duncan estimates uncollectibles as 1% of sales. What amount would be used in the adjustment?

QS 10-5
Note receivable
P3, P4

On August 2, 2000 SLM Co. received a $5,500, 90-day, 12% note from customer Will Carr as payment on his account. Prepare journal entries for August 2 and the maturity date assuming the note is honored by Carr.

QS 10-6
Note receivable
P3, P4

Seaver Company's December 31 year-end trial balance shows an $8,000 balance in Notes Receivable. This balance is from one note dated December 1, with a period of 45 days and 9% interest. Prepare journal entries for December 31 and the maturity date assuming the note is honored.

QS 10-7
Accounts receivable turnover
A1

The following facts were extracted from the comparative balance sheets of Ernest Blue, P.C.:

	2000	1999
Accounts receivable	$152,900	$133,700
Net sales	754,200	810,600

Compute the accounts receivable turnover for 2000.

Exercises

Exercise 10-1
Short-term investment transactions
C4, P5

Prepare general journal entries to record the following transactions involving the short-term investments of Morton Co., all of which occurred during 1999:

a. On February 15, paid $150,000 to purchase $150,000 of American General's 90-day short-term debt securities, which are dated February 15 and pay 10% interest.

b. On March 22, bought 700 shares of Royal Industries stock at $25\frac{1}{2}$ plus a $250 brokerage fee.

c. On May 16, received a check from American General in payment of the principal and 90 days' interest on the debt securities purchased in transaction *a*.

d. On July 30, paid $50,000 to purchase $50,000 of OMB Electronics' 8% debt securities, dated July 30, 1999, and due January 30, 2000.

e. On September 1, received a $0.50 per share cash dividend on the Royal Industries stock purchased in transaction *b*.

f. On October 8, sold 350 shares of Royal Industries stock for $32 per share, less a $175 brokerage fee.

g. On October 30, received a check from OMB Electronics for three months' interest on the debt securities purchased in transaction *d*.

Exercise 10-2
Credit card sales
C1

Aston Company allows customers to use two credit cards in charging purchases. With the OmniCard, Aston receives an immediate credit when it deposits sales receipts in its checking account. OmniCard assesses a 4% service charge for credit card sales. The second credit card that Aston accepts is Colonial Bank Card. Aston sends its accumulated receipts to Colonial Bank on a weekly basis and is paid by Colonial approximately 10 days later. Colonial Bank charges 2.5% of sales for using its card. Prepare entries in journal form to record the following credit card transactions of Aston Company:

Apr.	6	Sold merchandise for $9,200, accepting the customers' OmniCards. At the end of the day, the OmniCard receipts were deposited in Aston's account at the bank.
	10	Sold merchandise for $310, accepting the customer's Colonial Bank Card.
	17	Mailed $5,480 of credit card receipts to Colonial Bank, requesting payment.
	28	Received Colonial Bank's check for the April 17 billing, less the normal service charge.

Exercise 10-3
Accounts receivable subsidiary ledger

Jenkins Co. recorded the following transactions during November 2000:

Nov.	3	Accounts Receivable—ABC Shop	4,417	
		Sales		4,417
	8	Accounts Receivable—Colt Enterprises	1,250	
		Sales		1,250
	11	Accounts Receivable—Red McKenzie	733	
		Sales		733

19	Sales Returns and Allowances	189	
	Accounts Receivable—Red McKenzie		189
28	Accounts Receivable—ABC Shop	2,606	
	Sales		2,606

Required

1. Open a General Ledger having T-accounts for Accounts Receivable, Sales, and Sales Returns and Allowances. Also, open a subsidiary Accounts Receivable Ledger having a T-account for each customer. Post the preceding entries to the General Ledger accounts and the customer accounts.
2. List balances of the accounts in the subsidiary ledger (schedule of accounts receivable), total the balances, and compare the total with the balance of the Accounts Receivable controlling account.

Exercise 10-4
Allowance for doubtful accounts entries
P1, P2

At the end of its annual accounting period, Bali Company estimated its bad debts as one-half of 1% of its $875,000 of credit sales made during the year. On December 31, Bali made an addition to its Allowance for Doubtful Accounts equal to that amount. On the following February 1, management decided the $420 account of Catherine Hicks was uncollectible and wrote it off as a bad debt. Four months later, on June 5, Hicks unexpectedly paid the amount previously written off. Give the journal entries required to record these events.

Exercise 10-5
Percent of accounts receivable method
P1, P2

At the end of each year, Deutch Supply Co. uses the percent of accounts receivable approach to estimate bad debts. On December 31, 2000, it has outstanding accounts receivable of $53,000 and estimates that 4% will be uncollectible. Give the entry to record bad debts expense for year 2000 under the assumption that the Allowance for Doubtful Accounts has a *(a)* $915 credit balance before the adjustment and *(b)* $1,332 debit balance before the adjustment.

Exercise 10-6
Dishonoring a note
P4

Prepare journal entries to record the following transactions of Madison Company:

Mar. 21 Accepted a $3,100, six-month, 10% note dated today from Bradley Brooks in granting a time extension on his past-due account.
Sept. 21 Brooks dishonored his note when it was presented for payment.
Dec. 31 After exhausting all legal means of collection, Madison Company wrote off Brooks' account against the Allowance for Doubtful Accounts.

Exercise 10-7
Honoring a note
P4

Prepare journal entries to record these transactions for Verona Company:

Oct. 31 Accepted a $5,000, six-month, 6% note dated today from Leann Grimes in granting a time extension on her past-due account.
Dec. 31 Adjusted the books for the interest due on the Grimes note.
Apr. 30 Grimes honored her note when presented for payment.

Exercise 10-8
Selling and pledging accounts receivable
C3

On July 31, Konrad International had $125,900 of accounts receivable. Prepare journal entries to record the following August transactions. Also, prepare any footnotes to the August 31 financial statements that should be reported as a result of these transactions.

Aug. 2 Sold merchandise to customers on credit, $6,295.
7 Sold $18,000 of accounts receivable to Fidelity Bank. Fidelity charges a 1.5% fee.
15 Received payments from customers, $3,436.
25 Borrowed $10,000 from Fidelity Bank, pledging $14,000 of accounts receivable as security for the loan.

Exercise 10-9
Accounts receivable turnover
A1

The following information is from the financial statements of Whimsy Company:

	2001	2000	1999
Net sales	$305,000	$236,000	$288,000
Accounts receivable (December 31)	22,900	20,700	17,400

Compute Whimsy's accounts receivable turnover for 2000 and 2001. Compare the two results and give a possible explanation for any significant change.

Exercise 10-10
Notes receivable transactions and entries
P3, P4

Prepare journal entries for the following transactions of Barnett Company:

1999

Dec. 16 Accepted a $8,600, 60-day, 7% note dated this day in granting Carmel Karuthers a time extension on her past-due account.
31 Made an adjusting entry to record the accrued interest on the Karuthers note.
31 Closed the Interest Earned account.

2000

Feb. 14 Received Karuthers' payment for the principal and interest on the note dated December 16.
Mar. 2 Accepted a $4,000, 8%, 90-day note dated this day in granting a time extension on the past-due account of ATW Company.
17 Accepted a $1,600, 30-day, 9% note dated this day in granting Leroy Johnson a time extension on his past-due account.
Apr. 16 Johnson dishonored his note when presented for payment.
May 1 Wrote off the Johnson account against Allowance for Doubtful Accounts.
June 10 Received ATW's payment for the principal and interest on the note dated March 2.

Problems

Problem 10-1
Short-term investment transactions and entries
C4, P5

Checkers Company had no short-term investments prior to 1999 but had the following transactions involving short-term investments in securities available-for-sale during 1999:

Mar. 16 Purchased 3,000 shares of Diamond Shamrock stock at $22\frac{1}{4}$ plus a $1,948 brokerage fee.
Apr. 1 Paid $100,000 to buy 90-day U.S. Treasury bills, $100,000 principal amount, 5%, dated April 1.
June 7 Purchased 1,800 shares of PepsiCo stock at $49\frac{1}{2}$ plus a $1,235 brokerage fee.
20 Purchased 700 shares of Xerox stock at $15\frac{3}{4}$ plus a $466 brokerage fee.
July 3 Received a check for the principal and accrued interest on the U.S. Treasury bills that matured on June 30.
15 Received a $0.95 per share cash dividend on the Diamond Shamrock stock.
28 Sold 1,500 shares of Diamond Shamrock stock at 26 less a $912 brokerage fee.
Sept. 1 Received a $2.10 per share cash dividend on the PepsiCo shares.
Dec. 15 Received a $1.35 per share cash dividend on the remaining Diamond Shamrock stock owned.
31 Received a $1.60 per share cash dividend on the PepsiCo shares.

Required

Prepare journal entries to record the preceding transactions.

Problem 10-2
Sales on credit and credit card sales
C1

Accessories Unlimited allows a few select customers to make purchases on credit. The other customers can use either of two credit cards. Express Bank deducts a 3% service charge for sales on its credit card but credits the checking accounts of its commercial customers immediately when credit card receipts are deposited. Accessories Unlimited deposits the Express Bank credit card receipts at the close of each business day.

When customers use UniCharge credit cards, Accessories Unlimited accumulates the receipts for several days before submitting them to UniCharge for payment. UniCharge deducts a 2% service charge and usually pays within one week of being billed. Accessories Unlimited completed the following transactions during the month of May:

May 4 Sold merchandise on credit to Anne Bismarck for $565. (The terms of all credit sales are 2/15, n/30, and all sales are recorded at the gross price.)
5 Sold merchandise for $5,934 to customers who used their Express Bank credit cards. Sold merchandise for $4,876 to customers who used their UniCharge cards.
8 Sold merchandise for $3,213 to customers who used their UniCharge credit cards.
10 The UniCharge card receipts accumulated since May 5 were submitted to the credit card company for payment.
13 Wrote off the account of Mandy Duke against Allowance for Doubtful Accounts. The $329 balance in Duke's account stemmed from a credit sale in October of last year.
17 Received the amount due from UniCharge.
18 Received Bismarck's check paying for the purchase of May 4.

Required

Prepare journal entries to record the preceding transactions and events.

Problem 10-3
Estimating bad debts
P1, P2

On December 31, 2000, SysComm Corporation's records show the following results for the year:

Cash sales	$1,803,750
Credit sales	3,534,000

In addition, the unadjusted trial balance includes the following items:

Accounts receivable	$1,070,100 debit
Allowance for doubtful accounts	15,750 debit

Required

1. Prepare the adjusting entry needed in SysComm's books to recognize bad debts under each of the following independent assumptions:
   a. Bad debts are estimated to be 2% of credit sales.
   b. Bad debts are estimated to be 1% of total sales.
   c. Analysis suggests 5% of outstanding accounts receivable at year-end are uncollectible.
2. Show how Accounts Receivable and the Allowance for Doubtful Accounts appear on the December 31, 2000, balance sheet given the facts in requirement 1*a*.
3. Show how Accounts Receivable and the Allowance for Doubtful Accounts appear on the December 31, 2000, balance sheet given the facts in requirement 1*c*.

Check Figure Bad Debts Expense (1a), $70,680 Dr.

Problem 10-4
Aging accounts receivable
P1, P2

Jewell Company had credit sales of $2.6 million in 1999. On December 31, 1999, the company's Allowance for Doubtful Accounts had a credit balance of $13,400. The accountant for Jewell has prepared a schedule of the December 31, 1999, accounts receivable by age and, on the basis of past experience, has estimated the percent of receivables in each age category that will become uncollectible. This information is summarized as follows:

December 31, 1999 Accounts Receivable	Age of Accounts Receivable	Expected Percent Uncollectible
$730,000	Not due (under 30 days)	1.25%
354,000	1 to 30 days past due	2.00
76,000	31 to 60 days past due	6.50
48,000	61 to 90 days past due	32.75
12,000	Over 90 days past due	68.00

Required

Preparation Component

1. Compute the amount in the December 31, 1999, balance sheet as the Allowance for Doubtful Accounts.
2. Prepare the journal entry to record bad debts expense for 1999.

Check Figure Bad Debts Expense. $31,625 Dr.

Analysis Component

3. On June 30, 2000, Jewell Company concluded that a customer's $3,750 receivable (created in 1999) is uncollectible and that the account should be written off. What effect will this action have on Jewell's 2000 net income? Explain your answer.

Problem 10-5
Recording accounts receivable transactions and bad debts adjustments
P1, P2

Harrell Industries began operations on January 1, 1999. During the next two years, the company completed a number of transactions involving sales on credit, accounts receivable collections, and bad debts. These transactions are summarized as follows:

1999

a. Sold merchandise on credit for $1,144,500, terms n/30.
b. Wrote off uncollectible accounts receivable in the amount of $17,270.
c. Received cash of $667,100 in payment of outstanding accounts receivable.
d. In adjusting the accounts on December 31, concluded that 1.5% of outstanding accounts receivable would become uncollectible.

2000

e. Sold merchandise on credit for $1,423,800, terms n/30.

f. Wrote off uncollectible accounts receivable in the amount of $26,880.

g. Received cash of $1,103,900 in payment of outstanding accounts receivable.

h. In adjusting the accounts on December 31, concluded that 1.5% of outstanding accounts receivable would become uncollectible.

Check Figure Year 2000 Bad Debts Expense, $31,275.30 Dr.

Required

Prepare journal entries to record Harrell's 1999 and 2000 summarized transactions and the adjustments to record bad debts expense at the end of each year.

Problem 10-6
Analysis and journalizing of notes receivable transactions
P3, P4

The following transactions are from The Perry-Finch Company:

1999

Dec. 16 Accepted a $9,600, 60-day, 9% note dated this day in granting Hal Krueger a time extension on his past-due account.

31 Made an adjusting entry to record the accrued interest on the Krueger note.

31 Closed the Interest Earned account.

2000

Feb. 14 Received Krueger's payment for principal and interest on the note dated December 16.

Mar. 2 Accepted a $5,120, 10%, 90-day note dated this day in granting a time extension on the past-due account of ARC Company.

17 Accepted a $1,600, 30-day, 9% note dated this day in granting Penny Bobek a time extension on her past-due account.

Apr. 16 Bobek dishonored her note when presented for payment.

21 Discounted, with recourse, the ARC Company note at BancFirst at a cost of $50. The transaction was considered to be a loan.

June 2 Received notice from BancFirst that ARC Company defaulted on the note due May 31. Paid the bank the principal plus interest due on the note. (Hint: Create an account receivable for the maturity value of the note.)

July 16 Received payment from ARC Company for the maturity value of its dishonored note plus interest for 45 days beyond maturity at 10%.

Aug. 7 Accepted a $5,440, 90-day, 12% note dated this day in granting a time extension on the past-due account of Mertz & Ivy.

Sept. 3 Accepted a $2,080, 60-day, 10% note dated this day in granting Cecile Duval a time extension on her past-due account.

18 Discounted, without recourse, the Duval note at BancFirst at a cost of $25.

Nov. 5 Received payment of principal plus interest from Mertz & Ivy for the note of August 7.

Dec. 1 Wrote off the Penny Bobek account against Allowance for Doubtful Accounts.

Required

Preparation Component

Prepare journal entries to record Perry-Finch's transactions.

Analysis Component

What reporting is necessary when a business discounts notes receivable with recourse and these notes have not reached maturity by the end of the fiscal period? Explain the reason for this requirement and what accounting principle is being satisfied.

Problem 10-7
Short-term investment transactions and entries
C4, P5

Franklin Security has relatively large idle cash balances and invests them in common stocks that it holds as available-for-sale securities. Following is a series of transactions and events relevant to the short-term investment activity of the company:

1999

Jan. 20 Purchased 900 shares of Johnson & Johnson at $18\frac{3}{4}$ plus a $590 commission.

Feb. 9 Purchased 2,200 shares of Sony Corp. at $46\frac{7}{8}$ plus a $2,578 commission.

Oct. 12 Purchased 500 shares of Mattel, Inc., at $55\frac{1}{2}$ plus an $832 commission.

2000

Apr. 15 Sold 900 shares of Johnson & Johnson at $21\frac{3}{4}$ less a $685 commission.
July 5 Sold 500 shares of Mattel at $49\frac{1}{8}$ less a $491 commission.
22 Purchased 1,600 shares of Sara Lee Corp. at $36\frac{1}{4}$ plus a $1,740 commission.
Aug. 19 Purchased 1,800 shares of Eastman Kodak Company at 28 plus a $1,260 commission.

2001

Feb. 27 Purchased 3,400 shares of Microsoft Corp. at $23\frac{5}{8}$ plus a $1,606 commission.
Mar. 3 Sold 1,600 shares of Sara Lee at $31\frac{1}{4}$ less a $1,750 commission.
June 21 Sold 2,200 shares of Sony at 40 less a $2,640 commission.
30 Purchased 1,200 shares of The Black & Decker Corp. at $47\frac{1}{2}$ plus a $1,995 commission.
Nov. 1 Sold 1,800 shares of Eastman Kodak at $42\frac{3}{4}$ less a $2,309 commission.

Required

Prepare journal entries to record the short-term investment activity for the years shown.

BEYOND THE NUMBERS

Reporting in Action

A1

Refer to the financial statements and related information for **NIKE** in Appendix A. Answer the following questions by analyzing information in its statements:

1. What is NIKE's total amount of cash and cash equivalents on May 31, 1997?
2. NIKE's most liquid assets include "cash and cash equivalents" and "accounts receivable." Express NIKE's most liquid assets as of May 31, 1997, as a percent of current liabilities. Do the same for May 31, 1996. Comment on the company's ability to satisfy current liabilities at the end of the fiscal year 1997 as compared to the end of fiscal year 1996.
3. What criteria did NIKE use to classify items as cash equivalents?
4. Compute NIKE's accounts receivable turnover as of May 31, 1997.

Swoosh Ahead

5. Obtain access to NIKE's annual report for fiscal years ending after May 31, 1997 at its web site **[www.nike.com]** or through the SEC's EDGAR database **[www.sec.gov]**. Recompute 2 and 4 above and comment on any changes since May 31, 1997.

Comparative Analysis

A1, P2

Both **NIKE** and **Reebok** design, produce, market, and sell sports footwear and apparel. Key comparative figures (in millions) for these two organizations follow:

	NIKE		Reebok	
Key figures*	**1997**	**1996**	**1996**	**1995**
Allowance for doubtful accounts	$ 57	$ 43	$ 44	$ 46
Accounts receivable, net	1,754	1,346	591	507
Net sales	9,187	6,471	3,479	3,481

*NIKE figures are from its annual reports for fiscal years ended May 31, 1997 and 1996. Reebok figures are from its annual reports for fiscal years ended December 31, 1996 and 1995.

Required

1. Compute the accounts receivable turnover for NIKE as of May 31, 1997, and Reebok as of December 31, 1996.
2. How many days does it take each company, *on average,* to collect its receivables?
3. Which company is more efficient in collecting the accounts receivable?
4. Which company has allowed for a higher percent of uncollectible accounts receivable?

Ethics Challenge

P1, P2

Randy Meyer is the chief executive officer of a medium-size company in Wichita, Kansas. Several years ago Randy persuaded the board of directors of his company to base a percent of his compensation on the net income the company earns each year. Each December Randy estimates year-end financial figures in anticipation of the bonus he will receive. If the bonus is not as high as he would like he offers several accounting recommendations to his controller for year-end adjustments. One of his favorite recommendations is for the controller to reduce the estimate of doubtful accounts. Randy has used this technique with success for several years.

1. What effect does lowering the estimate for doubtful accounts have on the income statement and balance sheet of Randy's company?
2. Do you think Randy's recommendation to adjust the allowance for doubtful accounts is within his right as CEO or do you think this action is an ethics violation? Justify your response.
3. What type of internal control might be useful for this company in overseeing the CEO's recommendations for accounting changes?

Communicating in Practice

P1, P2

As the accountant for Stephenson Distributing, you recently attended a sales managers' meeting devoted to a discussion of the company's credit policies. At the meeting, you reported that bad debts expense for the past year was estimated to be $59,000 and accounts receivable at the end of the year amounted to $1,750,000 less a $43,000 allowance for doubtful accounts. Sylvia Greco, one of the sales managers, expressed confusion over the fact that bad debts expense and the allowance for doubtful accounts were different amounts. You agreed to write a memorandum to her explaining why a difference in bad debts expense and the allowance for doubtful accounts is not unusual. The company estimates bad debts expense to be 2% of sales. Write the memorandum to Greco.

Taking It to the Net

P1

Visit the Web site "How to Collect Debts" at **www.insiderreports.com/BIZRPRTS/B2524.htm.** If you are unable to connect to the Web site listed here, then as an alternate exercise search the Web for five good business tips on effective management of credit customers.

Required

1. Identify four procedures that should routinely be included in dealing with credit customers.
2. What are the author's views in the report ("How to Collect Debts") about phone calls, use of collection agencies, and use of humor in collection letters?
3. Identify the recommended content for a collection letter.

Teamwork in Action

P2

Each member of a team is to participate in estimating uncollectibles based on the aging schedule and estimated percents shown in Problem 10-4A. The division of labor is up to the team. Your goal is to complete this task as soon as possible. After estimating uncollectibles, check your estimate with the instructor. If the team's estimate is correct, the team should proceed using the other information in the problem to prepare the adjusting entry and the presentation of net realizable accounts receivable as it should be shown on the December 31, 1999 Balance Sheet. Your team is to discuss these requirements and ensure all team members concur with and understand the team's solution.

Hitting the Road

C1

Most of us have seen television commercials that include a comment similar to the following: "Bring your **VISA** because we do not accept **American Express.**" Conduct your own research via interviews, phone calls, or the Internet to determine the reason why companies discriminate in their use of credit cards.

Business Week Activity

P1

Read the article "The Sherlock Holmes of Accounting" in the September 5, 1994 ***Business Week*** issue.

Required

1. Who is the "Sherlock Holmes of Accounting"?
2. How does "Sherlock" decide which companies are investigated?
3. Do companies suffer any consequences if investigated by "Sherlock"?
4. What is a forensic accountant?
5. What criticisms does "Sherlock" make of **Seitel** with respect to their accounting?

CHAPTER 11

Plant Assets, Natural Resources, and Intangible Assets

A Look Back

Chapters 9 and 10 focused on short-term assets: cash, cash equivalents, receivables, and short-term investments. We explained why they're known as liquid assets and described how companies account and report for them.

A Look at This Chapter

This chapter introduces us to long-term assets, including plant assets, natural resource assets, and intangible assets. We explain how to record a long-term asset's cost, the allocation of an asset's cost to periods benefiting from it, the recording of additional asset costs after an asset is purchased, and the disposal of an asset.

A Look Ahead

Chapter 12 emphasizes both current and long-term liabilities. We explain how they are computed, recorded, and reported in financial statements.

Chapter Outline

Bug Killer

ATLANTA, GA—Jenna Lee doesn't fancy herself a consumer crusader. "I'm no Ralph Nader," she says bluntly. But when the 19-year-old Atlanta student stumbled upon a serious glitch in the depreciation calculation in *PCaccount,* an accounting package for PCs, she complained to the program's developer, **Intech.** When the company rudely brushed her off, she got angry enough to take her story to the *Southern Chronicle*—a phone call that helped ignite a national firestorm of controversy.

Shortly after the *Chronicle*'s August 1 exposé, a "deeply distressed" Samuel Carter, Intech's chairman, confessed that his company's line of accounting software contained a "few bugs" in its depreciation and amortization schedules, producing inaccurate calculations. With customers already surly over problems with Intech's customer-service lines, Carter moved quickly. He offered to replace disks on request for Intech's 1 million customers.

The errors are no small problem—particularly to consumers who already used these depreciation programs to prepare their financial or tax reports. Management experts say Intech's aggressive response to the problems helped defuse a potential disaster. "The public loves a confessed sinner," notes Sherry Williams of Consumer Research. Along with the replacement offer, Carter penned an apology in a letter to the product's registered users: "We really let our customers down," he wrote. So far, Carter's willingness to publicly swallow a serving of humble pie appears to be working.

Not everyone is content, though. Even an apologetic telephone call from Intech's president and the offer of a replacement disk haven't managed to mollify Ms. Lee. "It shakes my faith in the whole industry," she says. "Next time, I'm doing my own depreciation calculations!"

Learning Objectives

Conceptual

C1 Describe plant assets and issues in accounting for them.

C2 Explain depreciation and the factors affecting its computation.

C3 Explain depreciation for partial years and changes in estimates.

C4 Identify cash flow impacts of long-term asset transactions.

Analytical

A1 Compare and analyze depreciation for different methods.

A2 Compute total asset turnover and apply it to analyze a company's use of assets.

Procedural

P1 Apply the cost principle to compute the cost of plant assets.

P2 Compute and record depreciation using the straight-line, units-of-production, and declining-balance methods.

P3 Distinguish between revenue and capital expenditures, and account for these expenditures.

P4 Account for asset disposal through discarding, selling, or exchanging an asset.

P5 Account for natural resource assets and their depletion.

P6 Account for intangible assets and their amortization.

CHAPTER PREVIEW

This chapter focuses on long-term assets used in the operation of a company. These assets can be grouped into plant assets, natural resource assets, and intangible assets. Plant assets are a major investment for most companies. They make up a large part of assets on the balance sheet and they yield depreciation, often one of the largest expenses on the income statement. They also affect the statement of cash flows when cash is spent to acquire plant assets or received from their sale. When companies acquire or build a plant asset, it is often referred to as a "capital expenditure." Capital expenditures are important news because they impact both the short- and long-term success of a company. Natural resource assets and intangible assets have similar impacts to plant assets. Because of this and other reasons it is important we understand accounting for each of these long-term assets. This chapter will describe the purchase and use of these assets. We also explain what distinguishes these assets from other types of assets, how to determine their cost, how to allocate their costs to periods benefiting from their use, and how we dispose of long-term assets. This knowledge can help us avoid blind reliance on software that might yield errors as evidenced in the opening article.

SECTION 1—PLANT ASSETS

Plant assets are tangible assets that are used in the operations of a company and have a useful life of more than one accounting period. Plant assets are also called *plant and equipment; property, plant, and equipment;* or *fixed assets.* For many companies, plant assets make up the single largest asset they own. Exhibit 11.1 shows plant assets as a percent of total assets for several companies. Not only do they make up a large percent of these companies' assets, but their dollar values are huge. **McDonald's** plant assets, for instance, are reported at more than $14 billion. Also, **Wal-Mart** and **Toys "Я" Us** report plant assets of more than $18 billion and $4 billion, respectively.

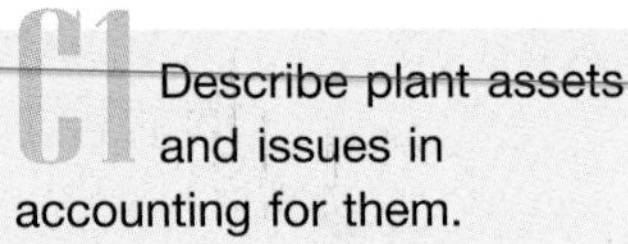

Describe plant assets and issues in accounting for them.

Plant assets are set apart from other assets by two important features. First, they are used in operations. This makes them different from, for instance, *inventory* that is held for sale and not used in operations. The distinctive feature here is use and not type of asset. A company that purchases a computer for purposes of reselling it reports it on the balance sheet as inventory. But if the same company purchases the same computer for

Exhibit 11.1

Plant Assets as Percent of Total Assets

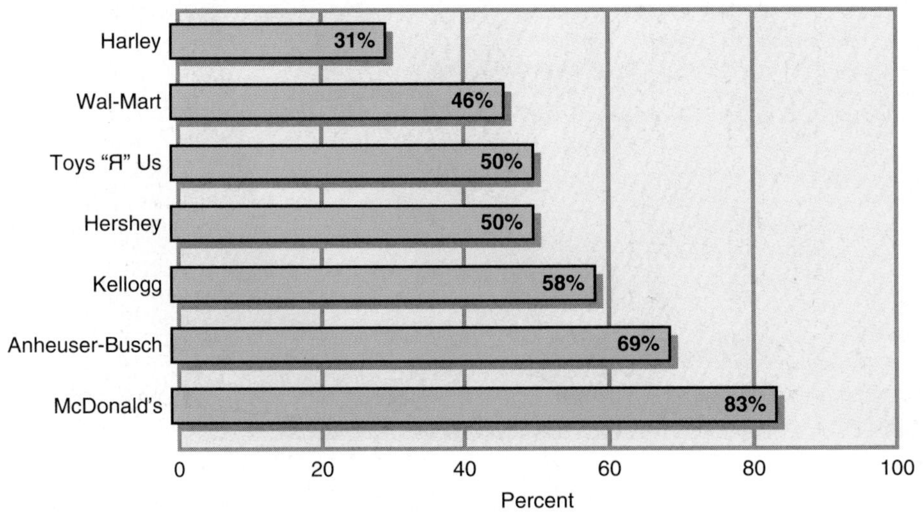

use in operations, it is a plant asset. Another example is *long-term investments* such as land held for future expansion. If this same land holds a factory used in operations, the land is part of plant assets. Still another example is *equipment* held for use in event of a breakdown or for use in peak periods of production. This equipment is reported in plant assets. But if this same equipment is removed from use and held for sale, it is not reported in plant assets.

The second important feature is plant assets have useful lives extending over more than one accounting period. This makes plant assets different from *current assets* such as *supplies* that are usually consumed in a short time after they are placed in use. The cost of current assets is assigned to a single period when they are used. Many *prepaid expenses* are distinguished from plant assets by the length of their useful lives.

The accounting for plant assets reflects these two important features. Since plant assets are used in operations, we try to match their costs against the revenues they generate. Also, since plant assets' useful lives extend over more than one period, our matching of costs and revenues must extend over several periods. We must measure plant assets (balance sheet focus) and allocate their cost to periods benefiting from their use (income statement focus).

Exhibit 11.2 shows the four main accounting issues with plant assets. They are:

1. Computing the costs of plant assets.
2. Allocating the costs of plant assets against revenues for the periods they benefit.
3. Accounting for expenditures such as repairs and improvements to plant assets.
4. Recording the disposal of plant assets.

Exhibit 11.2

Issues in Accounting for Plant Assets

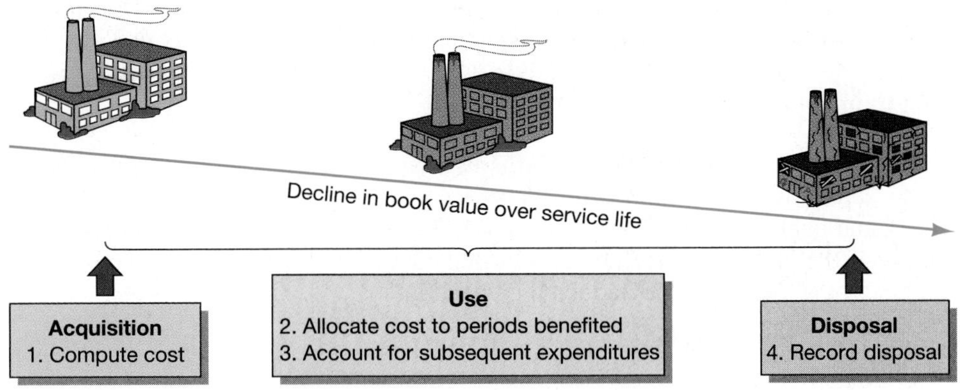

This chapter focuses on the decisions and factors surrounding these four important issues, and their accounting.

Cost of Plant Assets

P1 Apply the cost principle to compute the cost of plant assets.

Plant assets are recorded at cost when purchased. This is consistent with the *cost principle.* **Cost** includes all normal and reasonable expenditures necessary to get the asset in place and ready for its intended use. The cost of a factory machine, for instance, includes its invoice price less any cash discount for early payment, plus freight, unpacking, and assembling costs. The cost of a plant asset also includes the necessary costs of installing and testing a machine before placing it in use. Examples are the costs of building a base or foundation for a machine, of providing electrical hook-ups, and of adjusting the machine before using it in operations.

An expenditure must be normal, reasonable, and necessary in preparing an asset for its intended use for it to be charged to and reported as part of the cost of a plant asset. If a machine is damaged during unpacking, the repairs are not added to its cost. Instead, they are charged to an expense account. Also, a traffic fine paid for moving heavy machinery on city streets without a proper permit is not part of the machinery's cost. But payment for a proper permit is included in the cost of machinery. Charges in addition to the purchase price are sometimes incurred to modify or customize a new plant asset. These charges are added to the asset's cost. We explain how to determine the cost of plant assets in the remainder of this section for each of the four major classes of plant assets.

Land

When land is purchased for a building site, its cost includes the total amount paid for the land including any real estate commissions. Its cost also includes fees for insuring the title, legal fees, and any accrued property taxes paid by the purchaser. Payments for surveying, clearing, grading, draining, and landscaping also are included in the cost of land. Other costs of land include assessments by the local government, whether incurred at the time of purchase or later, for items such as roadways, sewers, and sidewalks. These assessments are included because they permanently add to the land's value.

Land purchased as a building site sometimes includes a building that must be removed. In such cases, the total purchase price is charged to the Land account. Also, the cost of removing the building, less any amounts recovered through sale of salvaged materials, is added to the Land account. To illustrate, assume The GAP bought land for a retail store for cash of $167,000. This land contains an old service garage that is removed at a net cost of $13,000 ($15,000 in costs less $2,000 proceeds from salvaged materials). Additional closing costs totaled $10,000, consisting of brokerage fees ($8,000), legal fees ($1,500), and title costs ($500). The cost of this land to The GAP is $190,000 and is computed as shown in Exhibit 11.3.

Computing Cost of Land

Net cash price of land	$167,000
Net cost of garage removal	13,000
Closing costs	10,000
Cost of land	**$190,000**

Land Improvements

Because land has an unlimited life and is not consumed when it is used, it is not subject to depreciation. But **land improvements** such as parking lot surfaces, driveways, fences, and lighting systems have limited useful lives. While these costs increase the usefulness of the land, they are charged to a separate Land Improvement account so their costs can be allocated to the periods they benefit.

Buildings

A Building account is charged for the costs of purchasing or constructing a building when it is used in operations. When purchased, the costs of a building usually include its purchase price, brokerage fees, taxes, title fees, and attorney costs. Its costs also include all expenditures to make it ready for its intended use. This includes any necessary repairs or renovations to prepare the building for use such as wiring, lighting, flooring, and wall coverings.

When a building, or any plant asset, is constructed by a company for its own use, its cost includes materials and labor plus a reasonable amount of indirect overhead cost. Overhead includes the costs of heat, lighting, power, and depreciation on machinery used to construct the asset. Cost of construction also includes design fees, building permits, and insurance during construction. But insurance costs for coverage *after* the asset is placed in use are an operating expense. **Wendy's** recently reported constructing plant assets for its own use. They disclosed the following building plans:

> . . . to open or have under construction about 400 new Wendy's restaurants . . . Capital expenditures could total as much as $170 million.

Machinery and Equipment

The cost of machinery and equipment consists of all costs normal and necessary to purchase them and prepare them for their intended use. It includes the purchase price, taxes, transportation charges, insurance while in transit, and the installing, assembling, and testing of machinery and equipment. **Sony,** for instance, disclosed in a recent annual report that:

> capital expenditures [much of this machinery and equipment] during the year under review increased 27.9% to . . . $2,817 million . . . Sony intends to further increase its capital expenditures.

Lump-Sum Asset Purchase

Plant assets sometimes are purchased in a group with a single transaction for a lump-sum price. This transaction is called a *lump-sum purchase,* also called *group,* or *basket, purchase.* When this occurs, we allocate the cost of the purchase among the different types of assets acquired based on their *relative market values.* Their market values can be estimated by appraisal or by using the tax-assessed valuations of the assets. To illustrate, Cola Company paid $90,000 cash to acquire land appraised at $30,000, land improvements appraised at $10,000, and a building appraised at $60,000. The $90,000 cost was allocated on the basis of appraised values as shown in Exhibit 11.4.

Exhibit 11.4

Computing Costs in a Lump-Sum Purchase

	Appraised Value	Percent of Total	Apportioned Cost
Land	$ 30,000	30% ($30,000/$100,000)	$27,000 ($90,000 × 30%)
Land improvements	10,000	10 ($10,000/$100,000)	9,000 ($90,000 × 10%)
Building	60,000	60 ($60,000/$100,000)	54,000 ($90,000 × 60%)
Totals	$100,000	100%	$90,000

Flash back

1. Identify the asset category for each of the following: *(a)* office supplies, *(b)* office equipment, *(c)* merchandise, *(d)* land held for future expansion, and *(e)* trucks used in operations.
2. Identify the account charged for each of the following expenditures: *(a)* purchase price of a vacant lot to be used in operations and *(b)* cost of paving that vacant lot.
3. What amount is recorded as the cost of a new machine given the following items related to its purchase: gross purchase price, $700,000; sales tax, $49,000; purchase discount taken, $21,000; freight to move machine to plant—terms FOB shipping point, $3,500; assembly costs, $3,000; cost of foundation for machine, $2,500; cost of spare parts used in maintaining the machine, $4,200?

Answers—p. 478

Depreciation

We explained in the prior section how plant assets are tangible assets purchased for use in operations for more than one period. It is helpful to think of a plant asset as an amount of "usefulness" contributing to the operations of a company throughout the asset's use-

C2 Explain depreciation and the factors affecting its computation.

ful life. Because the lives of all plant assets other than land are limited, the amount of usefulness expires as an asset is used. This expiration of a plant asset's amount of usefulness is called *depreciation.* **Depreciation** is the process of allocating the cost of a plant asset to expense in the accounting periods benefiting from its use.

When a company buys a delivery truck for use as a plant asset, for instance, it acquires an amount of usefulness in the sense that it obtains a quantity of transportation. The total cost of this transportation is the cost of the truck less the expected proceeds to be received when the truck is sold or traded in at the end of its useful life. This net cost is allocated to the accounting periods that benefit from the truck's use. This allocation of the truck's cost is depreciation.

Note that depreciation doesn't measure the decline in the truck's market value each period. Nor does it measure the physical deterioration of the truck. Depreciation is a process of allocating a plant asset's cost to expense over its useful life, nothing more. Because depreciation reflects the cost of using a plant asset, we do not begin recording depreciation charges until the asset is actually put into use providing services or producing products. This section describes the factors we need to consider in computing depreciation, the depreciation methods used, revisions in depreciation, and depreciation for partial periods.

Factors in Computing Depreciation

Three factors are relevant in determining depreciation: (1) cost, (2) salvage value, and (3) useful life.

Cost

The cost of a plant asset consists of all necessary and reasonable expenditures to acquire it and to prepare the asset for its intended use. We described the computation of cost earlier in this chapter.

Salvage Value

The total amount of depreciation to be charged off over an asset's benefit period equals the asset's cost minus its estimated salvage value. **Salvage value,** also called *residual value* or *scrap value*, is an estimate of the asset's value at the end of its benefit period. This is often viewed as the amount we expect to receive from selling the asset at the end of its benefit period. If we expect an asset to be traded in on a new asset, its salvage value is the expected trade-in value.

Useful (Service) Life

The **useful life** of a plant asset is the length of time it is productively used in a company's operations. Useful life, also called **service life,** may not be as long as the asset's total productive life. As an example, the productive life of a computer is often four to eight years or more. Yet some companies trade in old computers for new ones every two years. In this case, these computers have a two-year useful life. This means the costs of these computers (less their expected trade-in value) are charged to depreciation expense over a two-year period.

Several variables often make the useful life of a plant asset hard to predict. A major variable is the wear and tear from use in operations. But two other variables, inadequacy and obsolescence, also demand consideration. When a company grows more rapidly than expected, its assets sometimes don't meet the company's productive demands. **Inadequacy** refers to the condition where the capacity of a company's plant assets is too small to meet the company's productive demands. Obsolescence, like inadequacy, is hard to predict because the timing of new inventions and improvements normally can't be predicted. **Obsolescence** refers to a condition where, because of new inventions and improvements, a plant asset is no longer useful in producing goods or services with a competitive advantage. A company usually disposes of an obsolete asset before it wears out.

A company is often able to better predict the useful life of a new asset based on its past experience with a similar asset. When it has no experience with a type of asset, a company relies on the experience of others or on engineering studies and judgment. In note 4 of its annual report, **Coca-Cola Bottling** reported the following useful lives:

The principal categories and estimated useful lives of property, plant and equipment were as follows:

Buildings	10–50 years
Machinery and equipment	5–20 years
Transportation equipment	4–10 years
Furniture and fixtures	7–10 years
Vending equipment	6–13 years
Computer equipment and other	3–5 years

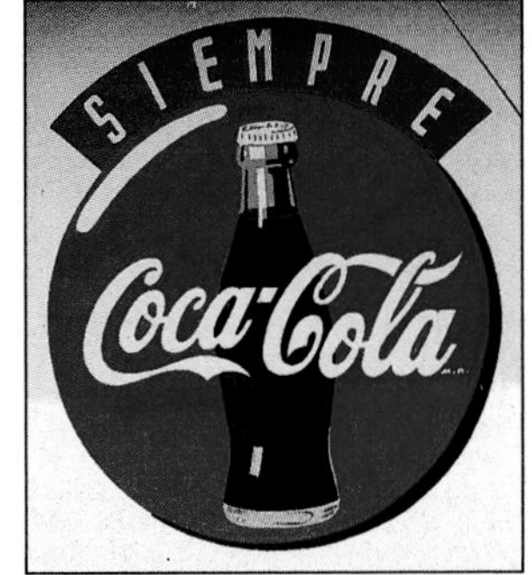

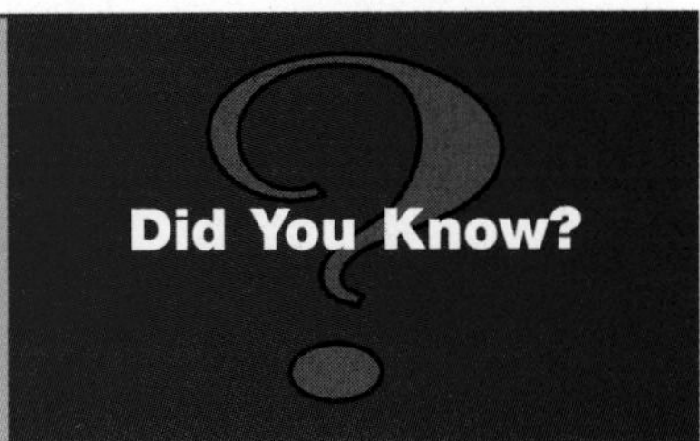

Life Expectancy
The life expectancy of plant assets is often in the eye of the beholder. Take **Converse** and **Stride Rite**, for instance. Both compete in the athletic shoe market, yet their buildings' life expectancies are quite different. Converse depreciates buildings over 5 to 10 years, but Stride Rite depreciates their buildings over 12 to 45 years. Such differences can dramatically impact financial statement numbers. [Source: 10K Reports.]

Depreciation Methods

P2 Compute and record depreciation using the straight-line, units-of-production, and declining-balance methods.

There are many *depreciation methods* for allocating a plant asset's cost over the accounting periods in its useful life. The most frequently used method of depreciation is the straight-line method. Another common depreciation method is the units-of-production method. We explain both of these methods in this section. This section also describes accelerated depreciation methods, with an emphasis on the declining-balance method.

The computations in this section use information from an athletic shoe manufacturer. In particular, we look at a machine used for inspecting athletic shoes before packaging. This machine is used by manufacturers such as **Converse, Reebok, Adidas,** and **L.A.Gear.** Data for depreciation of this machine are shown in Exhibit 11.5.

Exhibit 11.5

Data for Athletic Shoe-Inspecting Machine

Cost	$10,000
Salvage value	1,000
Depreciable cost	$ 9,000
Useful life:	
Accounting periods	5 years
Units inspected	36,000 shoes

Straight-Line Method

Straight-line depreciation charges the same amount to expense for each period of the asset's useful life. A two-step process is used to compute expense. We first compute the *depreciable cost* over the asset's life; this amount is also called the *cost to be depreciated.* It is computed by subtracting the asset's salvage value from its total cost. Second, depreciable cost is divided by the number of accounting periods in the asset's useful life.

The formula and computation for straight-line depreciation of the inspection equipment described above are shown in Exhibit 11.6.

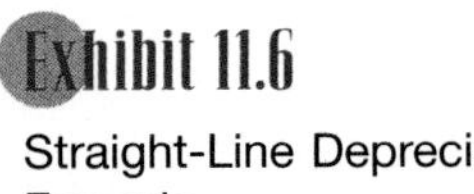

Exhibit 11.6

Straight-Line Depreciation Formula

$$\frac{\textbf{Cost} - \textbf{Salvage value}}{\textbf{Useful life in years}} = \frac{\$10{,}000 - \$1{,}000}{5 \text{ years}} = \$1{,}800 \text{ per year}$$

If this equipment is purchased on December 31, 1998, and used throughout its predicted useful life of five years, the straight-line method allocates an equal amount of depreciation to each of the years 1999 through 2003. We make the following adjusting entry at the end of each of these five years to record straight-line depreciation of this equipment:

Dec. 31	Depreciation Expense	1,800	
	Accumulated Depreciation, Equipment . . .		1,800
	To record annual depreciation over its 5-year useful life.		

Assets = Liabilities + Equity
−1,800 −1,800

The $1,800 Depreciation Expense appears on the income statement among operating expenses. This entry uses the common practice of crediting Accumulated Depreciation, a contra asset account to the Equipment account in the balance sheet.

The graph on the left in Exhibit 11.7 shows that the $1,800 per year expense amount is reported in each of these five years. The graph on the right shows the amounts reported on each of the six December 31 balance sheets while the company owns the asset.

Exhibit 11.7

Financial Statement Effects of Straight-Line Depreciation

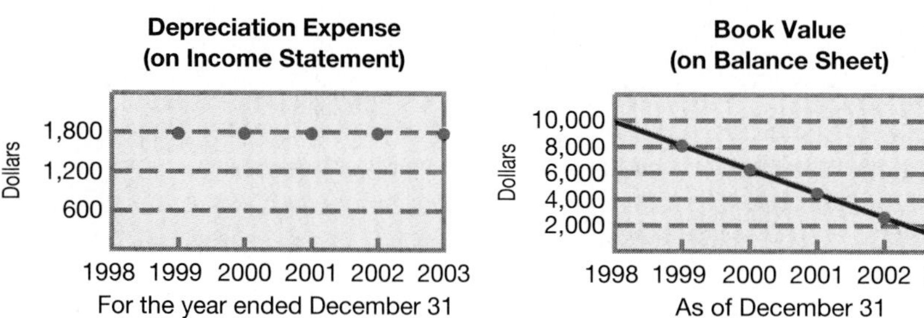

The net balance sheet amount is the asset's **book value** for each of those years and is computed as the asset's original cost less its accumulated depreciation. At the end of year two, its book value is $6,400 and is reported in the balance sheet as:

Equipment	$10,000	
Less accumulated depreciation	3,600	$6,400

The book value declines by $1,800 of depreciation each year. From the graphs we can see why this method is called straight line.

The *straight-line depreciation rate* is computed as 100% divided by the number of periods in the asset's useful life. In the case of our inspection machine, this rate is 20% (100% ÷ 5 years). We use this rate and other information on this machine to compute the machine's *straight-line depreciation schedule* shown in Exhibit 11.8.

Straight-Line Depreciation Schedule

	Depreciation for the Period			End of Period	
Period	**Depreciable Cost***	**Depreciation Rate**	**Depreciation Expense**	**Accumulated Depreciation**	**Book Value****
1998	—	—	—	—	$10,000
1999	$9,000	20%	$1,800	$1,800	8,200
2000	9,000	20	1,800	3,600	6,400
2001	9,000	20	1,800	5,400	4,600
2002	9,000	20	1,800	7,200	2,800
2003	9,000	20	1,800	9,000	**1,000**

*$10,000 − $1,000.
**Book value is cost minus accumulated depreciation.

Note three items in this schedule. First, depreciation expense is the same each period. Second, accumulated depreciation is the sum of current and prior periods' depreciation expense. Third, book value declines each period until it equals salvage value at the end of its useful life.

Straight line is by far the most frequently applied depreciation method. **Anheuser-Busch,** for instance, discloses its depreciation method in its annual report as follows:

> Depreciation is provided on the straight-line method over the estimated useful lives of the assets.

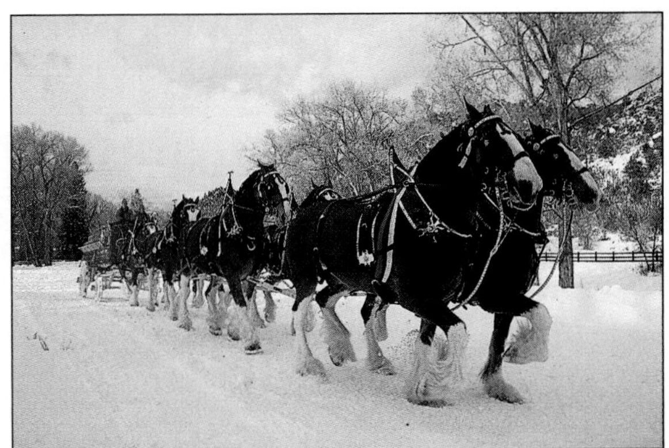

Units-of-Production Method

While many companies use straight-line depreciation, other methods are common in certain industries. The main purpose of recording depreciation is to provide relevant information about the cost of consuming an asset's usefulness. This means that each accounting period in which an asset is used is charged with a share of its cost. The straight-line method charges an equal share to each period. If plant assets are used about the same amount in each accounting period, this method produces a reasonable matching of expenses with revenues. Yet the use of some plant assets varies greatly from one accounting period to the next. A builder, for instance, may use a piece of construction equipment for a month and then not use it again for several months.

When use of equipment varies from period to period, the units-of-production depreciation method can provide a better matching of expenses with revenues than straight-line depreciation. **Units-of-production depreciation** charges a varying amount to expense for each period of an asset's useful life depending on its usage.

A two-step process is used to compute units-of-production depreciation. We first compute the *depreciation per unit.* It is computed by subtracting the asset's salvage value from its total cost and then dividing by the total number of units expected to be produced during its useful life. Units of production can be expressed in units of product or in any other unit of measure such as hours used or miles driven. This gives us the amount of depreciation per unit of service provided by the asset. The second step is to compute depreciation expense for the period by multiplying the units used in the period by the depreciation per unit.

The formula and computation for units-of-production depreciation for the testing machine described above are shown in Exhibit 11.9 (we expect 7,000 shoes inspected in its first year).

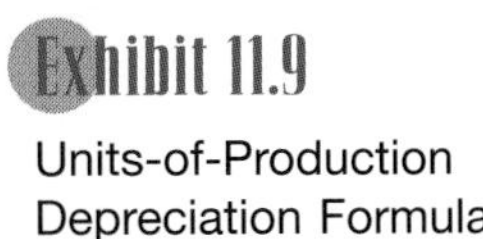

Units-of-Production Depreciation Formula

Step 1:

$$\textbf{Depreciation per unit} = \frac{\textbf{Cost} - \textbf{Salvage value}}{\textbf{Total units of production}} = \frac{\$10{,}000 - \$1{,}000}{36{,}000 \text{ units}} = \$0.25 \text{ per shoe}$$

Step 2:

$$\textbf{Depreciation expense} = \textbf{Depreciation per unit} \times \textbf{Units used in period}$$

$$\$0.25 \text{ per shoe} \times 7{,}000 \text{ shoes} = \$1{,}750$$

Using the production estimates for the machine, we compute the *units-of-production depreciation schedule* shown in Exhibit 11.10. If the machine inspects 7,000 shoes in its first year, depreciation for that first year is $1,750 (7,000 shoes at $0.25 per shoe). If the machine inspects 8,000 shoes in the second year, depreciation for the second year is 8,000 shoes times $0.25 per shoe, or $2,000.

Units-of-Production Depreciation Schedule

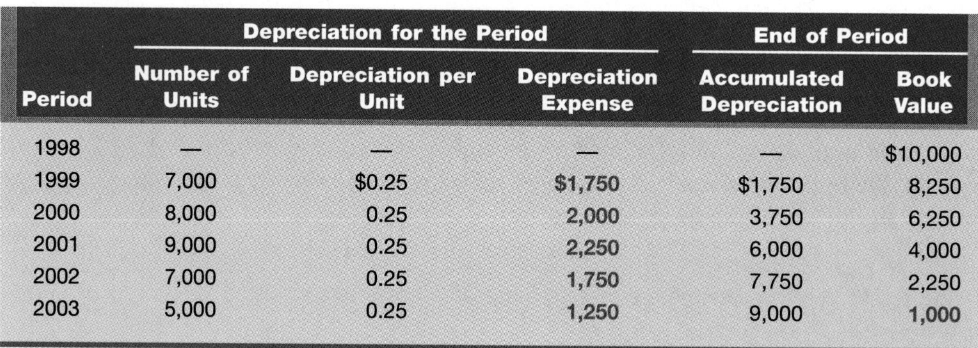

Period	Depreciation for the Period: Number of Units	Depreciation per Unit	Depreciation Expense	End of Period: Accumulated Depreciation	Book Value
1998	—	—	—	—	$10,000
1999	7,000	$0.25	$1,750	$1,750	8,250
2000	8,000	0.25	2,000	3,750	6,250
2001	9,000	0.25	2,250	6,000	4,000
2002	7,000	0.25	1,750	7,750	2,250
2003	5,000	0.25	1,250	9,000	1,000

Notice that depreciation expense depends on unit output, that accumulated depreciation is the sum of current and prior periods' depreciation expense, and book value declines each period until it equals salvage value at the end of the asset's useful life.

The units-of-production depreciation method is not as frequently applied as straight line. **Boise Cascade,** for instance, is one company using it and states in its annual report:

> Substantially all of the Company's paper and wood products manufacturing facilities determine depreciation by the units-of-production method.

Declining-Balance Method

An **accelerated depreciation method** yields larger depreciation expenses in the early years of an asset's life and smaller charges in later years. While there are several accelerated methods used in financial reporting, the most common is the declining-balance method. The **declining-balance method** of depreciation uses a depreciation rate of up to twice the straight-line rate and applies it to the asset's beginning-of-period book value. Because book value *declines* each period, the amount of depreciation also declines each period.

A common depreciation rate is twice the straight-line rate. This method is called the *double-declining-balance* method. The double-declining-balance method is applied as follows: (1) compute the asset's straight-line depreciation rate; (2) double it; and (3) compute depreciation expense by applying this rate to the asset's beginning-of-period book value. Salvage value is *not* used in these computations.

Let's return to the athletic shoe-testing machine and apply the double-declining-balance method to compute its depreciation expense. Exhibit 11.11 shows this formula and the first year computation for the machine. The three-step process is: (1) divide 100% by five years to determine the straight-line annual depreciation rate of 20% per year, (2) double this 20% rate to get a declining-balance rate of 40% per year, and (3) compute annual depreciation expense as the rate multiplied by the beginning period book value (see Exhibit 11.11).

Double-Declining-Balance Depreciation Formula

Step 1:

Straight-line rate = 100% ÷ Useful life = 100% ÷ 5 years = 20%

Step 2:

Double-declining-balance rate = 2 × Straight-line rate = 2 × 20% = 40%

Step 3:

Depreciation expense = Double-declining-balance rate × Beginning period book value

40% × $10,000 = $4,000

The *double-declining-balance depreciation schedule* is shown in Exhibit 11.12. The schedule follows the formula except in year 2003, when depreciation expense is $296. This is not equal to 40% × $1,296, or $518.40. The $296 is computed by subtracting the $1,000 salvage value from the $1,296 book value at the beginning of the fifth year. This is done because an asset is never depreciated below its salvage value. If we had used the $518.40 for depreciation expense in 2003, then ending book value would equal $777.60, which is less than the $1,000 salvage value.

Exhibit 11.12

Double-Declining-Balance Depreciation Schedule

	Depreciation for the Period			End of Period	
Period	**Beginning of Period Book Value**	**Depreciation Rate**	**Depreciation Expense**	**Accumulated Depreciation**	**Book Value**
1998	—	—	—	—	$10,000
1999	$10,000*	40%	$4,000	$4,000	6,000
2000	6,000	40	2,400	6,400	3,600
2001	3,600	40	1,440	7,840	2,160
2002	2,160	40	864	8,704	1,296
2003	1,296	40	296*	9,000	**1,000**

*Year 2003 depreciation is $1,296 − $1,000 = $296. This is because book value can't be less than salvage value.

Comparing Depreciation Methods

A1 Compare and analyze depreciation for different methods.

Exhibit 11.13 shows depreciation expense for the athletic shoe-inspecting machine under each of the three depreciation methods.

Depreciation Methods Compared

Period	Straight-Line	Units-of-Production	Double-Declining-Balance
1999	$1,800	$1,750	$4,000
2000	1,800	2,000	2,400
2001	1,800	2,250	1,440
2002	1,800	1,750	864
2003	1,800	1,250	296
	$9,000	$9,000	$9,000

While the amount of depreciation expense per period is different for different methods, total depreciation expense is the same for the machine's useful life. Each method starts with a total cost of $10,000 and ends with a salvage value of $1,000. The difference is the pattern in depreciation expense over the useful life. The book value of the asset when using straight line is always greater than book value from using double-declining-balance, except at the beginning and end of the asset's useful life. Also, the straight-line method yields a steady pattern of depreciation expense, while the units-of-production does not because it depends on the number of units produced. But both of these methods are acceptable as they allocate cost in a systematic and rational manner.[1]

[1] See FASB, *Statement of Financial Accounting Concepts No. 6*, "Elements of Financial Statements of Business Enterprises" (Norwalk, CT, 1985), par. 149.

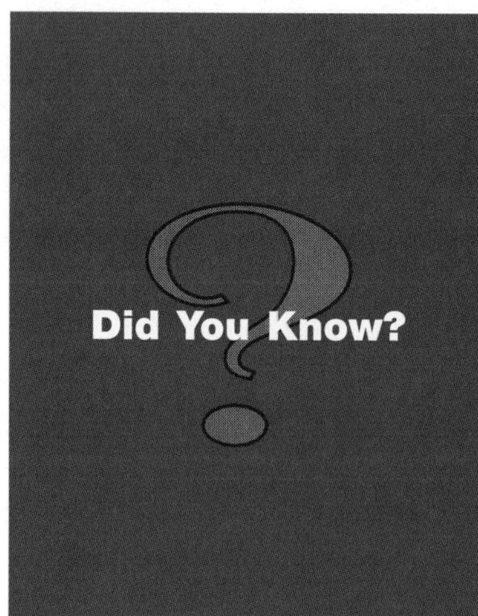

Trends in Depreciation
A recent survey suggests 80% of companies use straight-line depreciation for their plant assets, 7% use units-of-production, and 4% use declining balance. Another 8% of companies used an unspecified accelerated method, and probably most of these were declining balance. Accelerated depreciation is the preferred method of most companies for income tax reporting. [Source: *Accounting Trends & Techniques.*]
Used with permission from the American Institute of Certified Public Accountants, Inc.

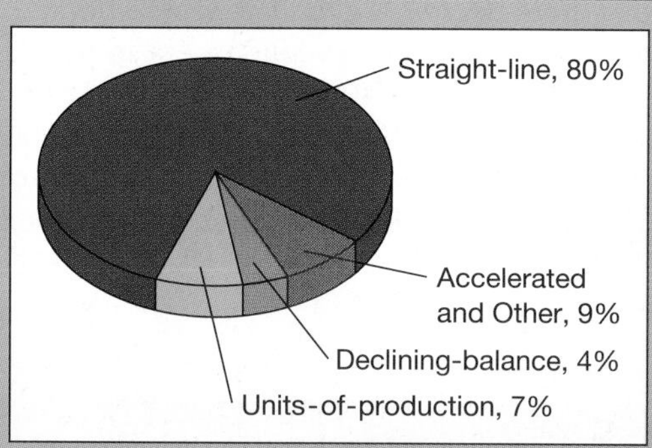

Depreciation for Tax Reporting

The records a company keeps for financial accounting purposes are usually different from the records it keeps for tax accounting purposes. Financial accounting aims to report useful information on financial performance and position, whereas tax accounting reflects government objectives in raising revenues. Differences between these two accounting systems are normal and expected. Depreciation is a common example.

Many companies use accelerated depreciation in computing taxable income. This reduces taxable income with higher depreciation expense in the early years of an asset's life. But taxable income is higher in the later years. A company's goal here is to postpone its tax payments. This means a company can use these resources now to earn additional profit before payment is due.

The United States federal income tax law has rules for depreciating assets. These rules are called the **Modified Accelerated Cost Recovery System (MACRS).** MACRS allows straight-line depreciation for some assets, but it requires accelerated depreciation for most kinds of assets. MACRS separates depreciable assets into different classes and defines the depreciable life and rate for each class. While MACRS is required for tax reporting, MACRS is not acceptable for financial reporting. This mainly is because it allocates costs over an arbitrary period often less than the asset's useful life.

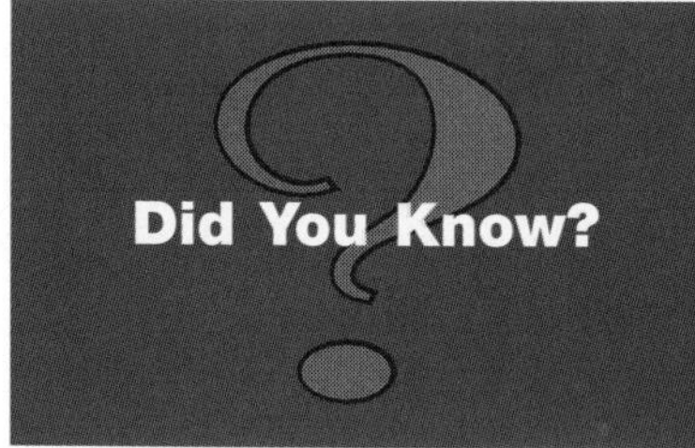

Depreciation Tech
Computer technology greatly simplifies depreciation computations and revisions. There are many inexpensive, off-the-shelf software packages and business calculators that allow a user to choose from a variety of depreciation methods for each asset entered. Detailed depreciation schedules for both financial reporting and income tax reporting are quickly and accurately generated.

Partial Year Depreciation

C3 Explain depreciation for partial years and changes in estimates.

Plant assets are purchased and disposed of at various times during a period. When an asset is purchased (or disposed of) at a time other than the beginning or end of an accounting period, depreciation is recorded for part of a year. This is so the year of purchase or the year of disposal is charged with its share of the asset's depreciation.

To illustrate, let's return to the athletic shoe-inspecting machine. Assume this machine is purchased and placed in service on October 8, 1999, and the annual accounting period ends on December 31. This machine costs $10,000, has a useful life of five years, and a salvage value of $1,000. Because this machine is purchased and used for nearly three months in 1999, the calendar year income statement should report depreciation expense on the machine for part of the year. The amount of depreciation reported usually is based on the assumption that an asset is purchased on the first day of the month nearest the actual date of purchase. In this case, since the purchase occurred on October 8, we assume an October 1 purchase date. This means three months' depreciation is recorded in 1999. If the purchase occurred anytime between October 16 through November 15, depreciation is computed as if the purchase is on November 1. Using straight-line depreciation, we compute three months' depreciation of $450 as follows:

$$\frac{\$10{,}000 - \$1{,}000}{5 \text{ years}} \times \frac{3}{12} = \$450$$

A similar computation is necessary when disposal of an asset occurs during a year. For example, let's suppose the machine described above is sold on June 24, 2004. Depreciation is recorded for the period January 1 through June 24 when it is disposed of. This partial year's depreciation, computed to the nearest whole month, is:

$$\frac{\$10{,}000 - \$1{,}000}{5 \text{ years}} \times \frac{6}{12} = \$900$$

Revising Depreciation Rates

Because depreciation is based on predictions of salvage value and useful life, depreciation expense is an estimate. During the useful life of an asset, new information may indicate the original predictions are inaccurate. If our estimate of an asset's useful life and/or salvage value changes, what should we do? The answer is to use the new estimate to compute depreciation for current and future periods. This means we revise depreciation expense computation by spreading the cost still to be depreciated over the revised useful life remaining. This approach is used for all depreciation methods.

Let's return to our athletic shoe-inspecting machine using straight-line depreciation. At the beginning of this asset's third year, its book value is $6,400, computed as:

Cost	$10,000
Less two years' accumulated depreciation	3,600
Book value	$ 6,400

At the beginning of its third year, the predicted number of years remaining in its useful life changes from three to four years *and* its estimate of salvage value changes from $1,000 to $400. Depreciation for each of the machine's four remaining years is computed as shown in Exhibit 11.14.

Computing Revised Depreciation Rates

$$\frac{\textbf{Book value} - \textbf{Revised salvage value}}{\textbf{Revised remaining useful life}} = \frac{\$6{,}400 - \$400}{4 \text{ years}} = \$1{,}500 \text{ per year}$$

This means $1,500 of depreciation expense is recorded for the machine at the end of the third through sixth years of its remaining useful life.

Since this asset was depreciated at the rate of $1,800 per year for the first two years, it is tempting to conclude that depreciation expense was overstated in the first two years. But these expenses reflected the best information available at that time. We don't go back and restate past years' financial statements in light of new information. Instead we adjust the current and future periods' statements to reflect this new information.

Revising an estimate of the useful life or salvage value of a plant asset is referred to as a **change in an accounting estimate.** A change in an accounting estimate results "from new information or subsequent developments and accordingly from better insight or improved judgment."[2] A change in an accounting estimate is reflected in future financial statements, and not in prior statements.

4. On January 1, 1999, a company pays $77,000 to purchase office furniture with a zero salvage value. The furniture's useful life is somewhere between 7 and 10 years. What is the 1999 straight-line depreciation on the furniture using a (a) 7-year useful life and (b) 10-year useful life?

Answer—p. 478

Reporting Depreciation on Assets

Both the cost and accumulated depreciation of plant assets are reported on the balance sheet. **Motorola,** for instance, reports the following in its balance sheet:

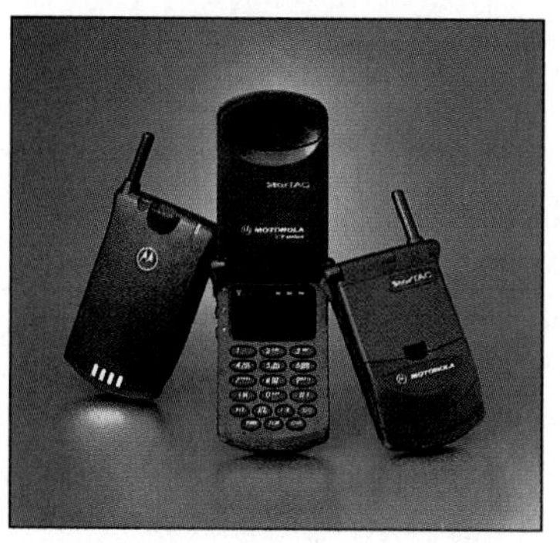

($ in millions)	1996	1995
Property, plant, and equipment:		
Land	$ 261	$ 201
Buildings	5,362	4,754
Machinery	13,975	12,511
	$19,598	$17,466
Less accumulated depreciation	(9,830)	(8,110)
Total	$ 9,768	$ 9,356

Many companies also show plant assets on one line with the net amount of cost less accumulated depreciation. When this is done, the amount of accumulated depreciation is disclosed in a note. **NIKE** reports only the net amount of its property, plant, and equipment in its balance sheet in Appendix A. To satisfy the *full-disclosure principle,* NIKE also describes its depreciation methods in note 1 and the individual amounts comprising plant assets in note 3.[3]

Reporting both the cost and accumulated depreciation of plant assets helps balance sheet readers compare the assets of different companies. For example, a company holding assets costing $50,000 and accumulated depreciation of $40,000 is likely in a situation different from a company with new assets costing $10,000. While the net undepreciated cost is the same in both cases, the first company may have more productive capacity available but likely is facing the need to replace older assets. These insights are not provided if the two balance sheets report only the $10,000 book values.

We emphasize that depreciation is a process of cost allocation. Plant assets are reported on a balance sheet at their remaining undepreciated costs (book value), not at market values. This emphasis on costs rather than market values is based on the *going-concern principle* described in Chapter 2. This principle states that, unless there is evidence to the contrary, we assume a company continues in business. This implies that plant assets are held and used long enough to recover their cost through the sale of products and services. Since plant assets are not sold, their market values are not reported in financial statements. Instead, assets are reported on a balance sheet at cost less accu-

[2] FASB, *Accounting Standards—Current Text* (Norwalk, CT, 1995), sec. A35.104 and sec. A06.130. First published as *APB Opinion No. 20*, par. 13 and par. 31.

[3] FASB, *Accounting Standards—Current Text* (Norwalk, CT, 1995), sec. D40.101. First published as *APB Opinion No. 12*, par. 5.

mulated depreciation. This is the remaining portion of the cost that is expected to be recovered in future periods.

Accumulated depreciation on a balance sheet doesn't reflect funds accumulated to buy new assets when the assets currently owned are replaced. Accumulated depreciation is a contra asset account with a credit balance that can't buy us anything. If a company has funds available to buy assets, the funds are shown on the balance sheet in liquid assets such as Cash.

Flash back

5. What is the meaning of the term *depreciation* in accounting?
6. A company purchases a new machine for $96,000 on January 1, 1999. Its predicted useful life is five years or 100,000 units of product, and its salvage value is $8,000. During 1999, 10,000 units of product are produced. Compute the book value of this machine on December 31, 1999, assuming *(a)* straight-line depreciation and *(b)* units-of-production depreciation.
7. In early January 1999, a company acquires equipment at a cost of $3,800. The company estimates this equipment to have a useful life of three years and a salvage value of $200. Early in 2001, the company changes its estimate to a total four-year useful life and zero salvage value. Using straight-line depreciation, what is depreciation expense on this equipment for the year ended 2001?

Answers—p. 478

Controller

You are the controller for Fascar Company. Fascar has struggled financially for more than two years, and there are no signs of improvement. Fascar's operations require major investments in equipment, and depreciation is a large item in computing income. Fascar's industry normally requires frequent replacements of equipment, and equipment is typically depreciated over three years. Your company's president recently instructed you to revise estimated useful lives of equipment from three to six years and to use a six-year life on all new equipment. You suspect this instruction is motivated by a desire to improve reported income. What actions do you take?

Answer—p. 478

Revenue and Capital Expenditures

P3 Distinguish between revenue and capital expenditures, and account for these expenditures.

When a plant asset is acquired and put into service, additional expenditures often are incurred to operate, maintain, repair, and improve it. In recording these added expenditures, we must decide whether they are capitalized or expensed. To capitalize an expenditure is to debit the asset account. A main issue is whether more useful information is provided by reporting these expenditures as current expenses or by adding them to the plant asset's cost and depreciating them over its remaining useful life.

Revenue expenditures are additional costs of plant assets that do not materially increase the asset's life or productive capabilities. They are recorded as expenses and deducted from revenues in the current period's income statement. Examples of revenue expenditures, also called *income statement expenditures,* are supplies, fuel, lubricants, and electric power. **Capital expenditures,** also called *balance sheet expenditures,* are additional costs of plant assets that provide material benefits extending beyond the current period. They are debited to asset accounts and reported on the balance sheet. Capital expenditures increase or improve the type or amount of service an asset provides. Examples are roofing replacement, plant expansion, and major overhauls of machinery and equipment.

Financial statements are affected for several years by the choice between recording costs as revenue expenditures or as capital expenditures. Managers must be careful in classifying them. This classification decision is helped by identifying costs as ordinary repairs, extraordinary repairs, betterments, or low cost asset purchases.

Ordinary Repairs

Ordinary repairs are expenditures to keep the asset in normal, good operating condition. They are necessary if an asset is to perform to expectations over its useful life. Ordinary repairs don't extend an asset's useful life beyond its original estimate and don't increase its productivity beyond original expectations. Examples are normal costs of cleaning, lubricating, adjusting, and replacing (small) parts of a machine. Ordinary repairs are treated as *revenue expenditures*. This means their costs are reported as expenses on the current income statement. Consistent with this rule, **America West Airlines** reports:

> Routine maintenance and repairs are charged to expense as incurred. The cost of major scheduled airframe, engine and certain component overhauls are capitalized . . . over the (future) periods benefited.

Extraordinary Repairs

Extraordinary repairs are expenditures extending the asset's useful life beyond its original estimate. Costs of extraordinary repairs are *capital expenditures* because they benefit future periods. They can be debited to the asset account. But historically they are debited to the asset's accumulated depreciation account to show they restore some effects of past years' depreciation.

Let's return to our inspecting machine purchased for $10,000 and depreciated over five years with a $1,000 salvage value. At the beginning of the machine's fourth year, when the machine's book value is $4,600 (see Exhibit 11.8), it is given a major overhaul at a cost of $2,400. This overhaul extends the machine's useful life by two additional years with no change in salvage value. This means the machine is expected to be used for four more years. The $2,400 cost of the extraordinary repair is recorded as:

Assets = Liabilities + Equity
+2,400
−2,400

Jan. 12	Accumulated Depreciation, Machinery	2,400	
	Cash		2,400
	To record extraordinary repairs.		

This entry increases the book value of the asset from $4,600 to $7,000. For the remaining four years of the asset's life, depreciation is based on this new book value. The effects of the extraordinary repairs are described in Exhibit 11.15.

Exhibit 11.15

Revised Depreciation Schedule from Extraordinary Repairs

	Before	Extraordinary Repair	After
Original cost	$10,000		$10,000
Accumulated depreciation	(5,400)	$2,400	(3,000)
Book value	$ 4,600		$ 7,000
Revised depreciation: ($7,000 − $1,000)/4 years			**$ 1,500**

Since the $2,400 cost of extraordinary repairs is part of the $7,000 book value computation, it is reflected in the revised depreciation for the asset's remaining life of four years.

Betterments

Betterments, also called *improvements*, are expenditures making a plant asset more efficient or productive. A betterment often involves adding a component to an asset or replacing one of its old components with a better component. A betterment doesn't always increase an asset's useful life. An example is replacing manual controls on a machine with automatic controls to reduce labor costs. This machine will still wear out just as fast as it would with manual controls.[4]

Because a betterment benefits future periods, it is debited to the asset account as a capital expenditure. The new book value (less salvage) is depreciated over the asset's remaining useful life. As an example, suppose a company pays $8,000 for a machine with an eight-year useful life and no salvage value. On January 2, after three years and $3,000 of depreciation, it adds an automated system to the machine at a cost of $1,800. This results in reduced labor cost in operating the machine in future periods. The cost of this betterment is added to the Machinery account with this entry:

Jan. 2	Machinery	1,800	
	Cash		1,800
	To record installation of automated system.		

Assets = Liabilities + Equity
+1,800
−1,800

After the betterment is added, the remaining cost to be depreciated is $6,800, computed as $8,000 − $3,000 + $1,800. Depreciation expense for the remaining five years is $1,360 per year, computed as $6,800/5 years.

Mechanic

You are a mechanic who recently opened your own auto service center. Because of a cash shortage, you are preparing financial statements in the hope of getting a short-term loan from the bank. A friend suggests you treat as many expenses as possible like capital expenditures. What are the impacts on financial statements of treating expenses as capital expenditures? What do you think is the aim of your friend's proposal?

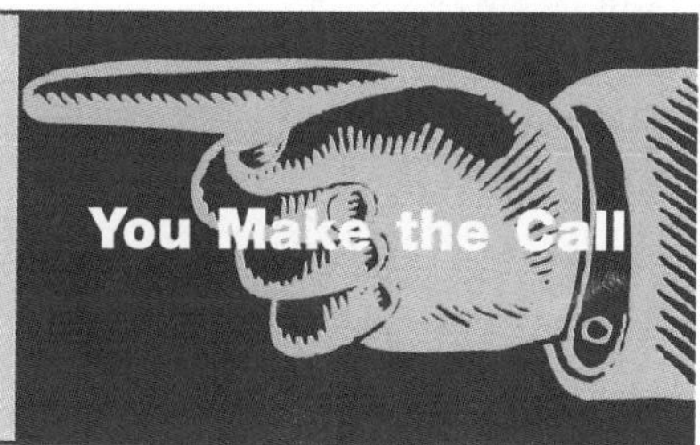

Answers—p. 478

Low Cost Asset Purchases

Maintaining individual plant asset records can be expensive, even in the most advanced system. For that reason, many companies don't keep detailed records for assets costing less than some minimum amount such as $100. Instead, these low cost plant assets are treated as a revenue expenditure. This means their costs are directly charged to an expense account at the time of purchase. This practice is acceptable under the *materiality principle.* Treating immaterial capital expenditures as revenue expenditures is unlikely to mislead users of financial statements. As an example, **Coca-Cola Bottling** discloses that it only capitalizes *major,* or material, betterments in its annual report:

> Additions and major replacements or betterments are added to the assets at cost. Maintenance and repair costs and minor replacements are charged to expense when incurred.

---

[4] One special type of betterment is an *addition.* Examples are a new wing to a factory or a new dock to a warehouse. All additions are capitalized.

Flash back

8. At the beginning of the fifth year of a machine's estimated six-year useful life, the machine is overhauled and its estimated useful life is extended to nine years in total. This machine originally cost $108,000 and the overhaul cost is $12,000. Prepare the entry recording the cost of this overhaul.
9. Explain the difference between revenue expenditures and capital expenditures and how they are recorded.
10. What is a betterment? How is a betterment recorded?

Answers—p. 479

Disposals of Plant Assets

P4 Account for asset disposal through discarding, selling, or exchanging an asset.

Plant assets are disposed of for several reasons. Many assets eventually wear out or become obsolete. Other assets are sold because of changing business plans. Sometimes an asset is discarded or sold because it is damaged by fire or accident. Regardless of the cause, disposals of plant assets occur in one of three ways: discarding, sale, or exchange. The accounting for each of these three types of disposals of plant assets is described in Exhibit 11.16.

Exhibit 11.16

Accounting for Disposals of Plant Assets

1. Record depreciation expense up to the date of disposal. This updates the Accumulated Depreciation account.
2. Remove the balances of the disposed asset and related Accumulated Depreciation accounts.
3. Record any cash (and other assets) received or paid in the disposal.
4. Record any gain or loss, computed by comparing the asset's book value with the fair value of assets received.*

*There is one exception to step 4 in the case of asset exchanges that we'll describe later in this section.

Discarding Plant Assets

A plant asset is *discarded* when it is no longer useful to the company and it has no market value. To illustrate, assume a machine costing $9,000 with accumulated depreciation of $9,000 is discarded on June 5. When accumulated depreciation equals the asset's cost it is said to be *fully depreciated* (zero book value). A fully depreciated asset usually doesn't yield a gain or loss on disposal. The entry to record the discarding of this asset is:

Assets	= Liabilities	+ Equity
+9,000		
−9,000		

June 5	Accumulated Depreciation, Machinery	9,000	
	Machinery		9,000
	To record the discarding of fully depreciated machinery.		

This entry reflects all four steps of Exhibit 11.16. Step 1 is not needed since the machine is fully depreciated. Step 2 is shown in the debit to Accumulated Depreciation and credit to Machinery. Since no cash is involved, step 3 is irrelevant. Also, since book value is zero and no cash is involved, no gain or loss is recorded in step 4.

How do we account for discarding an asset that isn't fully depreciated? Or one whose depreciation is not up to date? To answer this, consider equipment costing $8,000 with accumulated depreciation of $6,000 on December 31 of the prior fiscal year-end. This equipment is being depreciated using straight line over eight years with zero salvage value. On July 1 it is discarded. The first entry is to bring depreciation expense up to date:

Assets	= Liabilities	+ Equity
−500		−500

July 1	Depreciation Expense	500	
	Accumulated Depreciation, Equipment . . .		500
	To record the first six months' depreciation ($1,000 × 6/12).		

The second and final entry reflects steps 2–4 of Exhibit 11.16.

July 1	Accumulated Depreciation, Equipment	6,500	
	Loss on Disposal of Equipment	1,500	
	Equipment		8,000
	To record the discarding of machinery having a $1,500 book value.		

Assets	= Liabilities +	Equity
+6,500		−1,500
−8,000		

The loss is computed by comparing the equipment's $1,500 ($8,000 − $6,000 − $500) book value with the zero net cash proceeds. The loss on disposal is reported in the Other Expenses and Losses section of the income statement. An asset disposal can also sometimes require a cash payment instead of a receipt. Entries like those shown above are made in this case so that the income statement shows any gain or loss from disposal and the balance sheet reflects changes in the asset and accumulated depreciation accounts.

Selling Plant Assets

To illustrate the accounting for selling plant assets, we consider SportsWorld's March 1 sale of its delivery equipment. This equipment had cost $16,000 and had accumulated depreciation of $12,000 on December 31 of the prior calendar year-end. Annual depreciation on this equipment is $4,000 computed using straight-line depreciation. The entry to record depreciation expense and update accumulated depreciation to March 1 is:

March 1	Depreciation Expense	1,000	
	Accumulated Depreciation, Equipment . . .		1,000
	To record the first three months' depreciation ($4,000 × 3/12).		

Assets	= Liabilities +	Equity
−1,000		−1,000

The second entry to reflect steps 2–4 of Exhibit 11.16 depends on the amount received from the sale. We consider three different possibilities.

Sale at Book Value

If SportsWorld receives $3,000 cash, an amount equal to the equipment's book value, there is no gain or loss on disposal. The entry is:

March 1	Cash	3,000	
	Accumulated Depreciation, Equipment	13,000	
	Equipment		16,000
	To record sale of equipment for no gain or loss.		

Assets	= Liabilities +	Equity
+3,000		
+13,000		
−16,000		

Sale above Book Value

If SportsWorld receives $7,000 cash, an amount $4,000 above the equipment's book value, there is a gain on disposal. The entry is:

March 1	Cash	7,000	
	Accumulated Depreciation, Equipment	13,000	
	Gain on Disposal of Equipment		4,000
	Equipment		16,000
	To record sale of equipment for a $4,000 gain.		

Assets	= Liabilities +	Equity
+7000		+4,000
+13,000		
−16,000		

Sale Below Book Value

If SportsWorld receives $2,500 cash, an amount $500 below the equipment's book value, there is a loss on disposal. The entry is:

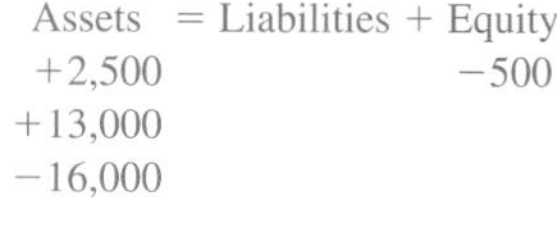

Assets	= Liabilities +	Equity
+2,500		−500
+13,000		
−16,000		

March 1	Cash	2,500	
	Loss on Disposal of Equipment	500	
	Accumulated Depreciation, Equipment	13,000	
	Equipment		16,000
	To record sale of equipment for a $500 loss.		

Companies at times restructure or downsize operations, which often involves selling plant assets. As part of its restructuring, **Woolworth** sold approximately 120 of its **Woolco** discount stores to **Wal-Mart.** Sale of its Woolco stores yielded a $168 million loss charged against the revenues of Woolworth.

Exchanging Plant Assets

Many plant assets such as machinery, automobiles, and office equipment are disposed of by exchanging them for new assets. In a typical exchange of plant assets, a trade-in allowance is received on the old asset and the balance is paid in cash. Accounting for the exchange of assets is similar to any other disposal unless the old and the new assets are similar in the functions they perform. Trading an old truck for a new truck is an exchange of similar assets, whereas trading a truck for a machine is an exchange of dissimilar assets. The recognition of gains and losses on exchanging plant assets is shown in Exhibit 11.17.

Gains and Losses on Plant Asset Exchanges

Assets Exchanged	Losses Recognized	Gains Recognized
Dissimilar	Yes	Yes
Similar	Yes	**No**

Losses on asset exchanges are always recognized. But gains are recognized only for dissimilar asset exchanges. The reason a gain from a similar asset exchange is not recognized is that the exchanged asset's earnings process is not considered complete. The decision to recognize a loss from a similar asset exchange is an application of *accounting conservatism.* This section explains the accounting for these cases.

Exchanging Dissimilar Assets

If a company exchanges a plant asset for another asset that is *dissimilar* in use or purpose, any gain or loss on the exchange is recorded. Any gain or loss is computed by comparing the book value of the asset given up with the fair market value of the asset received (or trade-in allowance).

Receiving More in Exchange: A Gain

Let's assume a company exchanges both an old machine and $16,500 in cash for land. The old machine originally cost $18,000 and has accumulated depreciation of $15,000 at the time of exchange. The land received has a fair market value of $21,000. Using the four steps outlined in Exhibit 11.16, the entry to record this exchange is:

Assets	= Liabilities +	Equity
+21,000		+1,500
+15,000		
−18,000		
−16,500		

Jan. 2	Land	21,000	
	Accumulated Depreciation, Machinery	15,000	
	Machinery		18,000
	Cash		16,500
	Gain on Exchange of Assets		1,500
	To record exchange of old machine and cash for land.		

We compute the gain on this transaction in the middle columns of Exhibit 11.18. The book value of the assets given totals $19,500. This includes the $16,500 cash and the $3,000 ($18,000 − $15,000) book value of the machine. The total $19,500 book value of assets given is compared to the fair market value of the land received ($21,000). This comparison yields a gain of $1,500 ($21,000 − $19,500).[5]

Exhibit 11.18

Computing Gain or Loss on *Dissimilar* Asset Exchanges

Dissimilar Plant Asset Exchange	Gain		Loss	
Fair market value of asset(s) received		$21,000		$16,000
Book value of asset(s) given:				
Machine	$ 3,000		$ 3,000	
Cash	16,500	19,500	16,500	19,500
Gain (loss) on exchange		**$ 1,500**		**($ 3,500)**

Receiving Less in Exchange: A Loss

Let's assume the same facts as in the exchange above *except* the land received has a fair market value of $16,000, not the $21,000 noted previously. The entry to record this exchange is:

Jan. 2	Land	16,000	
	Loss on Exchange of Assets	3,500	
	Accumulated Depreciation, Machinery	15,000	
	Machinery		18,000
	Cash		16,500
	To record exchange of old machine and cash for land.		

Assets	= Liabilities +	Equity
+16,000		−3,500
+15,000		
−18,000		
−16,500		

We compute the loss on this transaction in the far right columns of Exhibit 11.18. The $19,500 book value of assets given is compared to the fair market value of the land received ($16,000). This yields a loss of $3,500 ($16,000 − $19,500).

Exchanging Similar Assets

Accounting for exchanges of similar assets depends on whether the book value of the asset(s) given up is less or more than the fair market value of the asset(s) received.[6] When the fair market value of the asset(s) received is less than the book value of the asset(s) given, the difference is recognized as a loss. But when the value of the asset(s) received is more than the asset's book value given, the gain is *not* recognized.

Receiving Less in Exchange: A Loss

Let's assume a company exchanges both old equipment and $33,000 in cash for new equipment. The old equipment originally cost $36,000 and has accumulated depreciation of $20,000 at the time of exchange. The new equipment received has a fair market value of $42,000. These details are reflected in the middle columns of Exhibit 11.19.

[5] We can also compute a gain or loss by comparing the machine's book value with the trade-in allowance for the machine. Since the fair market value of the land is $21,000 and the cash paid is $16,500, the trade-in allowance for the machine is $4,500. The difference between the machine's $3,000 book value and its $4,500 trade-in allowance gives us the $1,500 gain on exchange.

[6] This rule applies to exchanges of similar assets when the exchange includes a cash payment or when no cash is received or paid. The accounting is slightly different when the exchange involves a cash *receipt.* See FASB, *Accounting Standards—Current Text* (Norwalk, CT, 1995), sec. N35.109. First published as *APB Opinion No. 29,* par. 22.

Exhibit 11.19

Computing Gain or Loss on *Similar* Asset Exchanges

Similar Plant Asset Exchange		Loss		Gain
Fair market value of asset(s) received		$42,000		$52,000
Book value of asset(s) given:				
Equipment	$16,000		$16,000	
Cash	33,000	49,000	33,000	49,000
Gain (loss) on exchange		**($ 7,000)**		**$ 3,000**

The entry to record this similar asset exchange is:

Assets = Liabilities + Equity
+42,000 −7,000
+20,000
−36,000
−33,000

Jan. 3	Equipment (**new**)	42,000	
	Loss on Exchange of Similar Assets	7,000	
	Accumulated Depreciation, Equipment	20,000	
	Equipment (**old**)		36,000
	Cash		33,000
	To record exchange of old equipment and cash for new equipment.		

The book value of the assets given totals $49,000. This includes the $33,000 cash and the $16,000 ($36,000 − $20,000) book value of the old equipment. The total $49,000 book value of assets given is compared to the fair market value of the new equipment received ($42,000). This yields a loss of $7,000 ($42,000 − $49,000).

Receiving More in Exchange: A Gain

Let's assume the same facts as in the similar asset exchange above *except* the new equipment received has a fair market value of $52,000, not the $42,000 noted previously. The entry to record this exchange is:

Assets = Liabilities + Equity
+49,000
+20,000
−36,000
−33,000

Jan. 3	Equipment (**new**)	49,000	
	Accumulated Depreciation, Equipment	20,000	
	Equipment (**old**)		36,000
	Cash		33,000
	To record exchange of old equipment and cash for new equipment.		

We compute a gain on this transaction shown in the far right columns of Exhibit 11.19. But it is *not* recognized in the entry because of the rule prohibiting recognizing a gain on similar asset exchanges.[7] The $49,000 recorded for the new equipment equals its cash price ($52,000) less the unrecognized gain ($3,000) on the exchange. The $49,000 cost recorded is called the *cost basis* of the new machine. This cost basis is the amount we use to compute depreciation and any gain or loss on its eventual disposal. The cost basis of the new asset also can be directly computed by summing book values for the assets given up as shown in Exhibit 11.20.

Exhibit 11.20

Cost Basis of New Asset when Gain Not Recognized

Cost of old equipment	$ 36,000
Less accumulated depreciation	20,000
Book value of old equipment	$ 16,000
Cash paid in the exchange	33,000
Cost recorded for new equipment	**$ 49,000**

[7] APB, "Accounting for Nonmonetary Transactions," *APB Opinion No. 29* (New York: AICPA, May 1973), par. 16.

The historical cost principle requires an asset be recorded at the cash or cash equivalent amount given in exchange. The $49,000 cost recorded for the new equipment equals the historical cost book value of the old equipment ($16,000) plus the cash paid in exchange ($33,000). We carry over the old equipment's book value because its earnings process is not considered complete in a similar asset exchange.

Flash back

11. A company acquires equipment on January 10, 1999, at a cost of $42,000. Straight-line depreciation is used, assuming a five-year life and $7,000 salvage value. On June 27, 2000, the company sells this equipment for $32,000. Prepare the entry or entries for June 27, 2000.

12. A company trades an old truck for a new truck. The original cost of the old truck is $30,000, and its accumulated depreciation at the time of the trade is $23,400. The new truck has a cash price of $45,000. Prepare entries to record the trade under two different assumptions: the company receives *(a)* a $3,000 trade-in allowance or *(b)* a $7,000 trade-in allowance.

Answers—p. 479

SECTION 2—NATURAL RESOURCES

Natural Resources

P5 Account for natural resource assets and their depletion.

Natural resources are assets that are physically consumed when used such as standing timber, mineral deposits, and oil and gas fields. Because they are consumed when used, they are often called *wasting assets.* The natural state of these assets represents inventories of raw materials that will be converted into a product by cutting, mining, or pumping. But until that conversion takes place, they are noncurrent assets and reported in a balance sheet using titles such as timberlands, mineral deposits, or oil reserves. These natural resources are reported under either plant assets or a separate category. **Alcoa,** for instance, reports its natural resources under the balance sheet title *Properties, plants and equipment.* In a note to the financial statements, Alcoa reports a separate amount for *Land and land rights, including mines.* **Weyerhaeuser,** on the other hand, reports its huge timber holdings in a separate balance sheet category titled *Timber and timberlands.*

Acquisition Cost and Depletion

Natural resources are initially recorded at cost. Cost includes all expenditures necessary to acquire the resource and prepare it for its intended use. **Depletion** is the process of allocating the cost of natural resources to periods when they are consumed, known as the resource's *useful life.* Natural resources are reported on the balance sheet at cost less *accumulated depletion.* The amount these assets are depleted each year by cutting, mining, or pumping is usually based on units extracted or depleted. This is similar to units-of-production depreciation. **Exxon** uses this approach to amortize the costs of discovering and operating its oil wells.

To illustrate depletion of natural resources, let's consider a mineral deposit with an estimated 500,000 tons of available ore. It is purchased for $500,000 and we expect zero salvage value. The depletion charge per ton of ore mined is $1, computed as $500,000 ÷ 500,000 tons. If 85,000 tons are mined and sold in the first year, the depletion charge for that year is $85,000. These computations are detailed in Exhibit 11.21.

Exhibit 11.21

Depletion Formula and Computations

Step 1:

$$\textbf{Depletion per unit} = \frac{\textbf{Cost} - \textbf{Salvage value}}{\textbf{Total units of capacity}} = \frac{\$500{,}000 - \$0}{500{,}000 \text{ tons}} = \$1 \text{ per ton}$$

Step 2:

$$\textbf{Depletion expense} - \textbf{Depletion per unit} \times \textbf{Units extracted in period}$$
$$= \$1 \times 85{,}000 = \$85{,}000$$

The depletion expense is recorded as:

Assets = Liabilities + Equity
−85,000 −85,000

Dec. 31	Depletion Expense, Mineral Deposit	85,000	
	Accumulated Depletion, Mineral Deposit . .		85,000
	To record depletion of the mineral deposit.		

The balance sheet at the end of this first year reports the deposit as shown in Exhibit 11.22.

Exhibit 11.22

Balance Sheet Presentation of Natural Resources

Mineral deposit	$500,000	
Less accumulated depletion	85,000	$415,000

Because the 85,000 tons of mined ore are sold in the year, the entire $85,000 depletion charge is reported on the income statement. But if some of the ore remains unsold at year-end, the depletion cost related to the unsold ore is carried forward on the balance sheet and reported as Unsold Ore Inventory, which is a current asset.

Plant Assets Used in Extracting Resources

The conversion of natural resources by mining, cutting, or pumping usually requires machinery, equipment, and buildings. When the usefulness of these assets is directly related to the depletion of the natural resource, their costs are depreciated over the life of the natural resource in proportion to the depletion charges. This means depreciation is computed using the units-of-production method. For example, if a machine is permanently installed in a mine and one-eighth of the mine's ore is mined and sold in the year, then one-eighth of the machine's cost (less salvage value) is charged to depreciation expense. The same procedure applies if the machine is abandoned once the resources are fully extracted. But if this machine will be moved to another site when extraction is complete, then it is depreciated over its useful life.

SECTION 3—INTANGIBLE ASSETS

Intangible Assets

P6 Account for intangible assets and their amortization.

Intangible assets are rights, privileges, and competitive advantages to the owner of long-term assets that have no physical substance and are used in operations. Examples are patents, copyrights, leaseholds, leasehold improvements, goodwill, and trademarks. Lack of physical substance isn't sufficient for an asset to be an intangible. Notes and accounts receivable, for instance, lack physical substance but aren't used in operations to produce products or services. Assets without physical substance that are not used in operations are reported as either current assets or investments. This section explains accounting for intangible assets and describes the more common types of intangible assets.

Accounting for Intangible Assets

Accounting for intangible assets is similar to that for plant assets. An intangible asset is recorded at cost when purchased. Its cost must be systematically allocated to expense over its estimated useful life through the process of **amortization.** The amortization period for an intangible asset must be 40 years or less.[8] Disposal of an intangible asset involves removing its book value, recording any asset received, and recognizing any gain or loss for the difference.

Amortization of intangible assets is similar to depreciation of plant assets and depletion of natural resources in that it is a process of cost allocation. But only the straight-line method is used for amortizing intangibles *unless* the company can show another method is preferred. Another difference is that the effects of depreciation and depletion are recorded in a contra account (Accumulated Depreciation or Accumulated Depletion), but amortization is usually credited directly to the intangible asset account. This means the original cost of intangible assets is rarely reported on the balance sheet. Instead, only the net amount of unamortized cost is reported.

Some intangibles have limited useful lives due to laws, contracts, or other characteristics of the asset. Examples are patents, copyrights, and leaseholds. Other intangibles such as goodwill, trademarks, and trade names have useful lives that can't be easily determined. The cost of intangible assets is amortized over the periods expected to be benefited by their use. But in no case can this be longer than their legal existence. Also, the amortization period of intangible assets must never be longer than 40 years even when the life of an asset (for example, goodwill) can continue indefinitely into the future.

Intangible assets are often shown in a separate section of the balance sheet immediately after plant assets. **Barnes & Noble,** for instance, follows this approach in reporting $90 million of *intangible assets, net* in its January 31, 1998, balance sheet. Companies also usually disclose the amortization periods they apply to intangibles. **Corning's** annual report, for instance, says it amortizes intangible assets over a maximum of 15 years except for goodwill that is amortized over 40 years. The remainder of our discussion focuses on accounting for specific types of intangible assets.

Patents

The federal government grants patents to encourage the invention of new machines, mechanical devices, and production processes. A **patent** is an exclusive right granted to its owner to manufacture and sell a patented machine or device, or to use a process, for 17 years. When patent rights are purchased, the cost of acquiring the rights is debited to an account called *Patents*. If the owner engages in lawsuits to effectively defend a patent, the cost of lawsuits is debited to the Patents account. The costs of research and development leading to a new patent are expensed when incurred.[9]

Drug War
Mention "drug war" and most people think of fighting cocaine or heroin use. But there's another drug war under way: brand-name drugmakers fight to stop generic copies of their products from hitting the market once their patents expire. Successfully delaying a generic rival means hundreds of millions of dollars in extra sales. [Source: *Business Week,* August 25, 1997.]

Did You Know?

[8] FASB, *Accounting Standards—Current Text* (Norwalk, CT, 1995), sec. I60.110. First published as *APB Opinion No. 17*, par. 29.

[9] FASB, *Accounting Standards—Current Text* (Norwalk, CT, 1995), sec. R50.108. First published as *Statement of Financial Accounting Standards No. 2*, par. 12.

While a patent gives its owner exclusive rights to it for 17 years, the cost of the patent is amortized over its estimated useful life but not to exceed 17 years. If we purchase a patent costing $25,000 with a useful life of 10 years, we make the following adjusting entry at the end of each of the 10 years to amortize one-tenth of its cost:

Dec. 31	Amortization Expense, Patents	2,500	
	Patents		2,500
	To write off patent costs over its 10-year useful life.		

Assets	= Liabilities +	Equity
−2,500		−2,500

The debit of $2,500 to Amortization Expense appears on the income statement as a cost of the product or service provided under the protection of the patent. This entry uses the common practice of crediting the Patents account rather than using a contra account.

Copyrights

A copyright is granted by the federal government or by international agreement. A **copyright** gives its owner the exclusive right to publish and sell a musical, literary, or artistic work during the life of the creator plus 50 years. Yet the useful life of most copyrights is much shorter. The costs of a copyright are amortized over its useful life. The only identifiable cost of many copyrights is the fee paid to the Copyright Office. If this fee is immaterial, it is charged directly to an expense account. But if the identifiable costs of a copyright are material, they are capitalized (recorded in an asset account) and periodically amortized by debiting an account called Amortization Expense, Copyrights.

Go PHISH

PHISH, a popular band, refused to give up copyrights to their first two independently produced CDs (under the label "The Dave Matthews Band") when signing with a recording company. This is unique for the recording industry. These two CDs generate more money for PHISH than some of their more recent recordings that sell more copies.

Leaseholds

Property is rented under a contract called a **lease.** The property's owner grants the lease and is called the **lessor.** The one who secures the right to possess and use the property is called the **lessee.** A **leasehold** refers to the rights granted to the lessee by the lessor under the terms of the lease. A leasehold is an intangible asset for the lessee.

Certain leases require no advance payment from the lessee but do require monthly rent payments. In this case, we don't need a Leasehold account. Instead, the monthly payments are debited to a Rent Expense account. But if a long-term lease requires the lessee to pay the final period's rent in advance when the lease is signed, the lessee records this advance payment with a debit to a Leasehold account. Because the usefulness of the advance payment is not used until the final period, the Leasehold account balance remains intact until that time. Then, its balance is transferred to Rent Expense.[10]

A long-term lease can increase in value when current rental rates for similar property increase while the required payments under the lease remain constant. This increase in the value of a lease is not reported on the lessee's balance sheet since no extra cost is incurred to acquire it. But if the property is subleased and the new tenant makes a cash payment to the original lessee for the rights under the old lease, the new tenant debits this payment to a Leasehold account. The balance of this Leasehold account is amortized to Rent Expense over the remaining life of the lease.

---

[10] Some long-term leases give the lessee essentially the same rights as a purchaser and result in tangible assets and liabilities reported by the lessee. Chapter 12 describes these leases.

To illustrate how the changing value of a lease can affect business decisions, we consider **La Côte Basque,** a historic restaurant in New York. Late in 1994, La Côte Basque sold the two years remaining on its lease to **Walt Disney Company.** La Côte Basque knew it couldn't renew the lease when it expired because Disney had negotiated a long-term lease of the property with the building owner, **Coca-Cola Company.** La Côte Basque had been operating in this location for 36 years but couldn't compete with the offer by Disney. This led the restaurant to sell the remainder of its lease for a sizable amount and relocate earlier than required.

Leasehold Improvements

Long-term leases sometimes require the lessee to pay for alterations or improvements to the leased property such as partitions, painting, and storefronts. These alterations and improvements are called **leasehold improvements,** and their costs are debited to a *Leasehold Improvements* account. Since leasehold improvements become part of the property and revert to the lessor at the end of the lease, the lessee amortizes these costs over the life of the lease or the life of the improvements, whichever is shorter. The amortization entry debits Rent Expense and credits Leasehold Improvements.

Goodwill

Goodwill has a special meaning in accounting. **Goodwill** is the amount by which the value of a company exceeds the fair market value of this company's net assets if purchased separately. This usually implies the company has certain valuable attributes not measured among its net assets. These can include superior management, skilled workforce, good supplier and customer relations, quality products or services, good location, or other competitive advantages.

Goodwill Illustration

Conceptually, a company has goodwill when its rate of expected future earnings is greater than the rate of normal earnings for its industry. To illustrate this concept, consider the information in Exhibit 11.23 for two competing companies (Winter Gear and Wild Sports). Both are of roughly equal size and compete in the snowboard industry.

Exhibit 11.23

Data for Goodwill Illustration

	Wild Sports	Winter Gear
Net assets (excluding goodwill)	$190,000	$190,000
Normal rate of return in this industry	10%	10%
Normal return on net assets	$19,000	$19,000
Expected net income	24,000	19,000
Expected net income above-normal	**$ 5,000**	**$ -0-**

The expected income for Wild Sports is $24,000. This is $5,000 higher than the norm (10%) for this industry. This implies Wild Sports has goodwill that yields above-normal net income. In contrast, Winter Gear's net income of $19,000 is the norm for this industry. This suggests zero goodwill for Winter Gear. What this means is we're willing to pay more for Wild Sports than for Winter Gear because goodwill is a valued asset.

Goodwill is usually recorded only when an entire company or a business segment is purchased. In determining the purchase price of a company, the buyer and seller can estimate the amount of goodwill in more than one way. For instance, how do we value Wild Sports' $5,000 per year above-normal net income? One way is to value goodwill at some *multiple* of above-normal net income. If we choose a multiple of 4, our goodwill estimate for Wild Sports is 4 times $5,000 (or $20,000). Another method is to assume the $5,000 above-normal net income continues indefinitely (often called *capitalizing* the above-normal net income). This is like an *annuity.* If we assume a 16% discount rate, our estimate of goodwill is $5,000/16%, or $31,250. We describe this computation in a later chapter. But whatever method we choose, the value of goodwill is confirmed only by the price the seller is willing to accept and the buyer is willing to pay.

Accounting for Goodwill

To keep financial statement information from being too subjective, goodwill isn't recorded unless it is purchased. Goodwill is measured by subtracting the fair market value of the purchased company's net assets (excluding goodwill) from the purchase price. Goodwill is a major part of many company purchases. For instance, **Procter & Gamble's** purchase of **Revlon's** worldwide Max Factor and Betrix lines of cosmetics for $1,025 million (net of cash acquired) included goodwill and other intangibles of $927 million.

Goodwill is amortized on a straight-line basis over its estimated useful life just like other intangible assets. Since estimating the useful life of goodwill is difficult, there is a wide range of estimates. Exhibit 11.24 shows us results from a recent survey on the goodwill amortization period. The most common amortization period is 40 years. Also, if we assume most of the companies that report "not exceeding 40" actually use 40 years, then we'd have nearly 60% of companies choosing the longest amortization period permitted. This is not surprising because it allows companies to spread goodwill costs over more years.

Exhibit 11.24

Goodwill Amortization Period

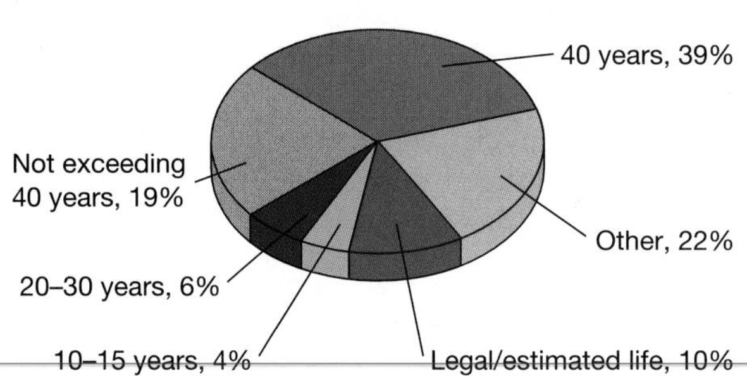

Trademarks and Trade Names

Companies often adopt unique symbols or select unique names and brands in marketing their products. A **trademark** or **trade name** is a symbol, name, phrase, or jingle identified with a company, product, or service. Examples are "I Can," NIKE's swoosh, Marlboro Man, Big Mac, Coca-Cola, and Corvette. Ownership and exclusive right to use a trademark or trade name is often established by showing that one company used it before another. But ownership is best established by registering a trademark or trade name with the government's Patent Office. The cost of developing, maintaining, or enhancing the value of a trademark or trade name by means such as advertising is charged to expense when incurred. But if a trademark or trade name is purchased, its cost is debited to an asset account and amortized.

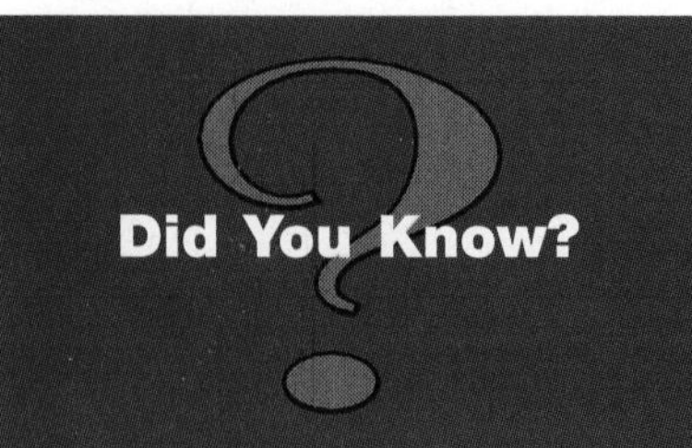

What's in a Name?

When it comes to brand building, nobody does it better than **NIKE.** Its swoosh is one of the best-known trademarks on the globe. It has helped NIKE pump out sales and earnings growth of nearly 40% for three years straight. Equally impressive is brand identity the "**Intel Inside**" campaign created for a product that consumers never see and few understand. [Source: *Business Week,* March 24, 1997.]

Flash back

13. Give an example of both a natural resource and an intangible asset.

14. A mining company pays $650,000 for an ore deposit. The deposit is estimated to have 325,000 tons of ore that will be fully mined over the next 10 years. During the current year, 91,000 tons are mined, processed, and sold. What is the current year's depletion expense?

15. On January 6, 1999, a company pays $120,000 for a patent with a 17-year legal life to produce a toy that is expected to be marketable for about three years. Prepare entries to record its acquisition and the December 31, 1999, adjustment.

Answers—p. 479

Cash Flow Impacts of Long-Term Assets

C4 Identify cash flow impacts of long-term asset transactions.

Acquisition and disposal transactions involving long-term assets impact the statement of cash flows. Acquisitions of long-term assets are investing activities and are reported in the investing section of the statement of cash flows. Most acquisitions are an immediate *use* of cash and the amount paid at acquisition is deducted in the statement. **NIKE,** for instance, reports the following in its statement of cash flows:

	1997
Cash provided (used) by investing activities ($ thousands):	
Additions to property, plant and equipment	($465,908)

Disposals of long-term assets usually create an immediate receipt of cash. When they do yield cash they are reported as a *source* of cash (an addition) in the investing section of the statement of cash flows. **NIKE** reports its disposals as:

	1997
Cash provided (used) by investing activities ($ thousands):	
Disposals of property, plant and equipment	$24,294

Gain or loss from disposal is the difference between an asset's book value and the value received, and it does not reflect any cash flows from investing activities.[11]

Total Asset Turnover

USING THE INFORMATION

A2 Compute total asset turnover and apply it to analyze a company's use of assets.

A company's assets are important in determining its ability to generate sales and earn profits. Managers devote a lot of attention to deciding what assets a company acquires, how much is invested in assets, and how assets can be used most efficiently and effectively. Decision makers and other users of financial statements are especially interested in evaluating a company's ability to use its assets in generating sales.

One measure of a company's ability in using its assets is **total asset turnover.** The formula for computing total asset turnover is shown in Exhibit 11.25.

[11] Also, depreciation and amortization of long-term assets do *not* impact cash (see Chapter 17).

Exhibit 11.25

Total Asset Turnover Formula

$$\text{Total asset turnover} = \frac{\text{Net sales}}{\text{Average total assets}}$$

Total asset turnover can be computed regardless of the type of company being evaluated. It can be applied to manufacturing and merchandising companies, and even to service companies. The numerator, net sales, reflects all operating revenues generated by the company. The denominator, average total assets, is usually measured by averaging total assets at the beginning of the period with total assets at the end of the period.

To illustrate, let's look at a company with total assets of $96,500 at the beginning of the year and $108,500 at the end of the year. Net sales for this company are $440,000 for the year. The company's total asset turnover for the current year is computed as:

$$\text{Total asset turnover} = \frac{\$440{,}000}{(\$96{,}500 + \$108{,}500)/2} = 4.3$$

We describe this company's use of assets in generating net sales by saying "it turned its assets over 4.3 times during the year." This means each $1.00 of assets produced $4.30 of net sales for the year.

Is a total asset turnover of 4.3 good or bad? It is safe to say all companies desire a high total asset turnover. But like many ratio analyses, a company's total asset turnover must be interpreted in comparison with prior years and with similar companies. Interpreting the total asset turnover also requires an understanding of the company's operations. Some operations are capital intensive, meaning a relatively large amount is invested in assets to generate sales. This suggests a relatively lower total asset turnover. Some other companies' operations are labor intensive, meaning sales are generated more by the efforts of people than the use of assets. In this case we expect a higher total asset turnover.[12]

To show how we analyze companies by using total asset turnover, we use data from the annual reports of two competing companies: **Coors** and **Anheuser-Busch.** Exhibit 11.26 shows results from computing total asset turnover for these two companies.

Exhibit 11.26

Analysis Using Total Asset Turnover

Company	Figure (in millions)	1996	1995
Coors	Net sales	$ 1,732	$ 1,680
	Average total assets	$ 1,374	$ 1,378
	Total asset turnover	**1.26**	**1.22**
Anheuser-Busch	Net sales	$10,884	$10,341
	Average total assets	$10,527	$10,569
	Total asset turnover	**1.03**	**0.98**

To show how we compute and use total asset turnover, let's look at the numbers for Coors in 1995–1996 as reported in Exhibit 11.26. We compute **Coors'** 1996 turnover as:

$$\text{Total asset turnover} = \frac{\$1{,}732}{\$1{,}374} = 1.26$$

This means Coors' average total asset balance is converted into sales 1.26 times in 1996. Another way to say this is Coors generated $1.26 of net sales for each $1 of assets. We also see Coors' turnover is steady over the period 1995–1996, and is su-

[12] There is a relation between total asset turnover and net profit margin. Companies with low total asset turnover require higher profit margins (examples are hotels and real estate), whereas companies with high total asset turnover can succeed with lower profit margins (examples are food stores and merchandisers).

perior to Anheuser-Busch. Is Coors' turnover high enough? Total asset turnover for Coors' other competitors, available in industry publications such as Dun & Bradstreet, is generally in the range of 1.0 to 1.1 over this same period. It appears Coors is competitive and possibly doing slightly better than its competitors on total asset turnover.

Environmentalist
You are an environmentalist battling a paper manufacturer on environmental concerns. The company claims it can't afford any additional controls. It points to its low total asset turnover of 1.9 and argues it can't compete with other companies where total asset turnover is much higher. Examples mentioned are food stores (5.5), wholesalers (4.0), and builders (3.5). The company suggests it might need to lay off workers to pay for any added costs. How do you respond?

Answers—p. 478

Summary

C1 Describe plant assets and issues in accounting for them. Plant assets are tangible assets used in the operations of a company and have a useful life of more than one accounting period. Plant assets are set apart from other tangible assets by two important features: use in operations and useful lives longer than one period. There are four main accounting issues with plant assets: (1) computing their costs, (2) allocating their costs to the periods they benefit, (3) accounting for subsequent expenditures, and (4) recording their disposal.

C2 Explain depreciation and the factors affecting its computation. Depreciation is the process of allocating to expense the cost of a plant asset over the accounting periods that benefit from the use of the plant asset. Depreciation doesn't measure the decline in a plant asset's market value, nor does it measure the asset's physical deterioration. Depreciation occurs as an asset is used to produce products or services. Three factors determine depreciation: cost, salvage value, and useful life. Salvage value is an estimate of the asset's value at the end of its benefit period. Useful (service) life is the length of time an asset is productively used in operations.

C3 Explain depreciation for partial years and changes in estimates. Partial years' depreciation is often required because assets are bought and sold throughout the year. Depreciation is revised when changes in estimates such as salvage value and useful life occur. If the useful life of a plant asset changes, for instance, the remaining cost to be depreciated is spread over the remaining (revised) useful life of the asset.

C4 Identify cash flow impacts of long-term asset transactions. Acquisition, depreciation, and disposal of long-term assets impact the statement of cash flows. Both acquisitions and disposals impact the investing section of this statement. Acquisitions are a use of cash, while disposals are a source of cash.

A1 Compare and analyze depreciation for different methods. The amount of depreciation expense per period is usually different for different methods. Yet total depreciation expense is the same for all methods. Each method starts with the same total cost and ends with the same salvage value. The difference is in the pattern of depreciation expense over the asset's useful life. The book value of an asset when using straight-line is always greater than when using double-declining-balance, except at the beginning and end. The straight-line method yields a steady pattern of depreciation expense, while the units-of-production does not because it depends on the number of units produced. Depreciation methods are acceptable if they allocate cost in a systematic and rational manner.

A2 Compute total asset turnover and apply it to analyze a company's use of assets. Total asset turnover measures a company's ability to use its assets to generate sales. Total asset turnover is defined as net sales divided by average total assets. The turnover measure is interpreted as the dollars of net sales generated for each dollar of assets. While all companies desire a high total asset turnover, it must be interpreted in comparison with prior years and with similar companies.

P1 Apply the cost principle to compute the cost of plant assets. Plant assets are recorded at cost when purchased. Cost includes all normal and reasonable expenditures necessary to get the asset in place and ready for its intended use. The cost of a lump-sum purchase is allocated among its individual assets based on their relative market values.

P2 Compute and record depreciation using the straight-line, units-of-production, and declining-balance methods. The straight-line method of depreciation divides the cost less salvage value by the number of periods in the asset's useful life to determine depreciation expense for each period. The units-of-production method divides the cost less salvage value by the estimated number of units the asset will produce to determine the depreciation per unit. The declining-balance method multiplies the asset's book value by a factor that is usually double the straight-line rate.

P3 Distinguish between revenue and capital expenditures, and account for these expenditures. Revenue expenditures expire in the current period. They are debited to expense accounts and matched with current revenues. Ordinary repairs are an example of revenue expenditures. Capital expenditures benefit future periods and are debited to asset accounts. Examples of capital expenditures include extraordinary repairs and betterments. Immaterial expenditures on plant assets are treated as revenue expenditures.

P4 Account for asset disposal through discarding, selling, or exchanging an asset. When a plant asset is discarded, sold, or exchanged, its cost and accumulated depreciation are removed from the accounts. Any cash proceeds from discarding or selling an asset are recorded and compared to the asset's book value to determine gain or loss. When dissimilar assets are exchanged, the new asset is recorded at its fair value, and any gain or loss on disposal is recognized. When similar assets are exchanged, losses are recognized but gains are not. When gains are not recognized, the new asset account is debited for the book value of the old asset plus any cash paid.

P5 Account for natural resource assets and their depletion. The cost of a natural resource is recorded in an asset account. Depletion of a natural resource is recorded by allocating its cost to expense using the units-of-production method. Depletion is credited to an Accumulated Depletion account.

P6 Account for intangible assets and their amortization. An intangible asset is recorded at the cost incurred to purchase the asset. Allocation of the cost of an intangible asset to expense is done using the straight-line method and is called *amortization*. Amortization is recorded with a credit made directly to the asset account instead of a contra account. Intangible assets include patents, copyrights, leaseholds, goodwill, and trademarks.

Guidance Answers to **You Make the Call**

Mechanic

Treating an expense as a capital expenditure means reported expenses will be lower and income higher in the short run. This is because, unlike an expense, a capital expenditure is not expensed immediately. Instead, the cost of a capital expenditure is spread out over the asset's useful life. Treating an expense as a capital expenditure also means asset and equity totals are reported at a larger amount. This continues until the asset is fully depreciated. Your friend is probably trying to help, but the suggestion hints at unethical behavior. You must remember that only an expenditure benefiting future periods is a capital expenditure. If an item is truly an expense not benefiting future periods, then it must not be treated as a capital expenditure.

Environmentalist

You need to point out that the company's comparison of its total asset turnover with food stores, wholesalers, and builders is misdirected. You must explain these other industries' turnovers are higher because their profit margins are lower (about 2%). Profit margins for the paper industry are usually 3% to 3.5%. You also need to collect data from competitors in the paper industry to show that a 1.9 total asset turnover is about right for this industry. You might even go further and collect data on this company's revenues and expenses, along with compensation data for this company's high-ranking officers and employees.

Guidance Answer to **Judgment and Ethics**

Controller

Before you conclude this instruction is unethical, you might tell the president of your concern that the longer estimate doesn't seem realistic in light of past experience with three-year replacements. You might ask if the change implies a new replacement plan. Depending on the president's response, such a conversation might eliminate your concern. It is possible the president's decision to change estimated useful life reflects an honest and reasonable prediction of the future. Since the company is struggling financially, the president may have concluded the normal pattern of replacing assets every three years can't continue. Perhaps the strategy is to avoid costs of frequent replacements and stretch use of the equipment a few years longer until financial conditions improve. Even if you doubt the company will be able to use the equipment six years, you should consider the possibility the president has a more complete understanding of the situation and honestly believes a six-year life is a good estimate.

On the downside, you may be correct in suspecting the president is acting unethically. If you conclude the president's decision is unethical, you might confront the president with your opinion that it is unethical to change the prediction just to increase income. This is a personally risky course of action and you may want to remind the president of her own ethical responsibility. Another possibility is to wait and see if the auditor will insist on not changing the estimate. You should always insist the statements be based on reasonable estimates.

Guidance Answers to Flash *backs*

1. (*a*) Office supplies—current assets
   (*b*) Office equipment—plant assets
   (*c*) Merchandise—current assets (inventory)
   (*d*) Land held for future expansion—long-term investments
   (*e*) Trucks used in operations—plant assets
2. (*a*) Land
   (*b*) Land Improvements
3. \$700,000 + \$49,000 − \$21,000 + \$3,500 + \$3,000 + \$2,500 = \$737,000
4. Straight-line with 7-year life: (\$77,000/7) = \$11,000
   Straight-line with 10-year life: (\$77,000/10) = \$7,700
5. Depreciation is a process of allocating and charging the cost of plant assets to the accounting periods that benefit from the assets' use.

6. (*a*) Book value using straight-line depreciation:
$96,000 − [($96,000 − $8,000)/5] = $78,400
(*b*) Book value using units of production:
$96,000 − [($96,000 − $8,000) × (10,000/100,000)] = $87,200

7. ($3,800 − $200)/3 = $1,200 (depreciation per year)
$1,200 × 2 = $2,400 (accumulated depreciation)
($3,800 − $2,400)/2 = $700 (revised depreciation)

8.

Accumulated Depreciation, Machinery	12,000	
Cash		12,000

9. A revenue expenditure benefits only the current period and should be charged to expense of the current period. A capital expenditure has a benefit that extends beyond the end of the current period and should be charged to an asset.

10. A betterment involves modifying an existing plant asset to make it more efficient, usually by replacing part of the asset with an improved or superior part. A betterment should be debited to the improved machine's account.

11.

Depreciation Expense	3,500	
Accumulated Depreciation		3,500
Cash	32,000	
Accumulated Depreciation	10,500	
Gain on Sale of Equipment		500
Equipment		42,000

12.

(*a*)	Truck	45,000	
	Loss on Trade-In	3,600	
	Accumulated Depreciation	23,400	
	Truck		30,000
	Cash ($45,000–$3,000)		42,000

(*b*)	Truck	44,600	
	Accumulated Depreciation	23,400	
	Truck		30,000
	Cash ($45,000–$7,000)		38,000

13. Examples of intangible assets are: patents, copyrights, leaseholds, leasehold improvements, goodwill, trademarks, and exclusive licenses.
Examples of natural resources are: timberlands, mineral deposits, and oil reserves.

14. ($650,000/325,000) × 91,000 = $182,000

15.

Jan. 6	Patents	120,000	
	Cash		120,000
Dec. 31	Amortization Expense . .	40,000*	
	Patents		40,000
	*Amortization computation: $120,000/3 years = $40,000		

Demonstration Problem

On July 14, 1999, Tulsa Company paid $600,000 to acquire a fully equipped factory. The purchase involved the following assets (we include additional facts related to each):

Asset	Appraised Value	Estimated Salvage Value	Estimated Useful Life	Depreciation Method
Land	$160,000			Not depreciated
Land improvements . . .	80,000	$ -0-	10 years	Straight-line
Building	320,000	100,000	10 years	Double-declining-balance
Machinery	240,000	20,000	10,000 units	Units-of-production*
Total	$800,000			

*The machinery is used to produce 700 units in 1999 and 1,800 units in 2000.

Required

1. Allocate the total $600,000 cost among the separate assets.
2. Compute the 1999 (six months) and 2000 depreciation expense for each type of asset and compute total depreciation expense each year for all assets.
3. On the first day of 2001, the machinery and $5,000 cash are exchanged for similar equipment with a fair value of $210,000. Journalize the exchange of similar assets.
4. Assume the exchange in (3) is for dissimilar, not similar, equipment. Journalize the dissimilar asset exchange.

5. On the last day of the fiscal year 2001, the company discards equipment that has been on the books for five years. The original cost of the equipment was $12,000 (estimated life of five years) and the salvage value was $2,000. No depreciation has been recorded for the fifth year before the disposal occurs. Journalize the fifth year of depreciation (straight-line method) and the asset disposal.
6. At the beginning of the year 2001, the company purchases with cash a patent right for $100,000. The company estimates the useful life of the patent to be 10 years. Journalize the patent acquisition and amortization for the year.
7. Late in the year 2001, the company makes its final addition to property and equipment with the acquisition for $600,000 cash of an ore deposit. Access roads and shafts are added for an additional cost of $80,000. Salvage value of the mine is estimated to be $20,000. The company estimates 330,000 tons of available ore. Only 10,000 tons of ore are mined and sold before the end of the year. Journalize the mine's acquisition and first year's depletion.

Planning the Solution

- Complete a three-column schedule showing these amounts for each asset: appraised value, percent of total value, and allocated cost.
- Using the allocated costs, compute the amount of depreciation for 1999 (only one-half year) and 2000 (full year) for each asset. Then summarize those computations in a table showing the total depreciation for each year.
- Remember that gains on exchanges of similar assets are not recognized. Make a journal entry to add the acquired machinery to the books and to remove the machinery, along with its accumulated depreciation, and the cash given in the exchange.
- Remember that gains on exchanges of dissimilar assets are recognized. Make a journal entry to add the acquired machinery to the books and to remove the machinery, along with its accumulated depreciation, and the cash given in the exchange. Also record the gain on the exchange in a separate account titled Gain on Exchange of Dissimilar Assets.
- Remember that all depreciation must be recorded before removing a disposed asset from the books. Calculate and record the depreciation expense for the fifth year using the straight-line method. Since salvage value has not been received at the end of the asset's life, the amount of the salvage value becomes a loss on disposal. Record the loss on the disposal as well as the removal of the asset and its related accumulated depreciation from the books.
- Record the patent as an intangible asset at its purchase price. Use straight-line amortization over the years of useful life to calculate amortization expense. Remember that no accumulated amortization account is used in recording amortization expense. The intangible asset account is credited directly.
- Record the ore deposit as a natural resource asset including all additional costs to ready the mine for use. Calculate depletion per ton using the depletion formula. Multiply the depletion amount per ton by the amount of tons mined since the acquisition to calculate the appropriate depletion expense for the current year.

Solution to Demonstration Problem

1. Allocation of the total cost of $600,000 among the assets:

Asset	Appraised Value	Percent of Total Value	Allocated Cost
Land	$160,000	20%	$120,000 ($600,000 × 20%)
Land improvements	80,000	10	60,000 ($600,000 × 10%)
Building	320,000	40	240,000 ($600,000 × 40%)
Machinery	240,000	30	180,000 ($600,000 × 30%)
Total	$800,000	100%	$600,000

2. Depreciation for each asset:

Land Improvements:	
Cost	$ 60,000
Salvage value	-0-
Net cost	$ 60,000
Useful life	10 years
Annual expense ($60,000/10)	$ 6,000
1999 depreciation ($6,000 × 6/12)	$ 3,000
2000 depreciation	$ 6,000
Building:	
Straight-line rate = 100%/10 = 10%	
Double-declining-balance rate = 10% × 2 = 20%	
1999 depreciation ($240,000 × 20% × 6/12)	$ 24,000
2000 depreciation [($240,000 − $24,000) × 20%]	$ 43,200
Machinery:	
Cost	$180,000
Salvage value	20,000
Net cost	$160,000
Total expected units	10,000
Expected cost per unit ($160,000/10,000)	$ 16
1999 depreciation ($16 × 700 units)	$ 11,200
2000 depreciation ($16 × 1,800 units)	$ 28,800

Total depreciation expense:

	2000	1999
Land improvements	$ 6,000	$ 3,000
Building	43,200	24,000
Machinery	28,800	11,200
Total	$78,000	$38,200

3. Recording the exchange of similar assets with a gain on the exchange:
The book value on the date of exchange is $240,000 (allocated cost) − $40,000 (accumulated depreciation). The book value of the machinery given in the exchange ($200,000) plus the $5,000 cash is less than the $210,000 value of the machine acquired in the exchange. The entry to record the exchange of similar assets does not recognize this $5,000 gain on exchange:

Machinery (new)	205,000*	
Accumulated Depreciation, Machinery (old)	40,000	
Machinery (old)		240,000
Cash		5,000
To record exchange of similar assets.		

*(Fair market value of acquired asset $210,000 minus $5,000 gain)

4. Recording the exchange of dissimilar assets with a gain on the exchange:

Machinery (new)	210,000	
Accumulated Depreciation, Machinery (old)	40,000	
Machinery (old)		240,000
Cash		5,000
Gain on exchange of dissimilar assets		5,000
To record exchange of dissimilar assets.		

5. Recording the depreciation on the discarded asset:

Depreciation Expense, Equipment	2,000	
Accumulated Depreciation, Equipment		2,000
To record depreciation to date of disposal: ($12,000 – $2,000)/5		

Recording the loss on disposal and the asset removal:

Accumulated Depreciation, Equipment	10,000	
Loss on Disposal of Equipment	2,000	
Equipment		12,000
To record the discarding of machinery with a $2,000 book value.		

6.

Patent	100,000	
Cash		100,000
To record patent acquisition.		

Amortization Expense, Patent	10,000	
Patent		10,000
To record amortization expense: $100,000/10 years = $10,000		

7.

Ore Deposit	680,000	
Cash		680,000
To record ore deposit acquisition and related costs.		

Depletion Expense, Ore Deposit	20,000	
Accumulated Depletion		20,000
To record depletion expense: ($680,000 – $20,000)/330,000 tons available = $2 per ton. $10,000 tons mined and sold × $2 = $20,000 depletion		

Glossary

Accelerated depreciation method depreciation method that produces larger depreciation charges during the early years of an asset's life and smaller charges in the later years. (p. 456).

Amortization a process of systematically allocating the cost of an intangible asset to expense over its estimated useful life. (p. 471).

Betterment an expenditure to make a plant asset more efficient or productive; also called *improvements.* (p. 463).

Book value the original cost of a plant asset less its accumulated depreciation (or depletion, or amortization). (p. 454).

Capital expenditure additional costs of plant assets that provides material benefits extending beyond the current period; also called *balance sheet expenditure.* (p. 461).

Change in an accounting estimate a change in a computed amount used in the financial statements that results from new information or subsequent developments and from better insight or improved judgment. (p. 459).

Copyright a right granted by the federal government or by international agreement giving the owner the exclusive privilege to publish and sell musical, literary, or artistic work during the life of the creator plus 50 years. (p. 472).

Cost includes all normal and reasonable expenditures necessary to get a plant asset in place and ready for its intended use. (p. 449).

Declining-balance depreciation a depreciation method in which a plant asset's depreciation charge for the period is determined by applying a constant depreciation rate (up to twice the straight-line rate) each year to the asset's book value at the beginning of the year. (p. 456).

Depletion the process of allocating the cost of natural resources to periods when they are consumed. (p. 469).

Depreciation the process of allocating the cost of a plant asset to expense in the periods benefiting from its use. (p. 452).

Extraordinary repairs major repairs that extend the useful life of a plant asset beyond original expectations; treated as a capital expenditure. (p. 462).

Goodwill the amount by which the value of a company exceeds the fair market value of the company's net assets if purchased separately. (p. 473).

Inadequacy a condition in which the capacity of the company's plant assets is too small to meet the company's productive demands. (p. 452).

Intangible assets rights, privileges, and competitive advantages to the owner of long-term assets that have no physical substance and are used in operations; examples include patents, copyrights, leaseholds, leasehold improvements, goodwill, and trademarks. (p. 470).

Land improvements assets that increase the usefulness of land but have a limited useful life and are subject to depreciation. (p. 450).

Lease a contract allowing property rental. (p. 472).

Leasehold a name for the rights granted to the lessee by the lessor under the terms of a lease. (p. 472).

Leasehold improvements alterations or improvements to leased property such as partitions, painting, and storefronts. (p. 473).

Lessee the party to a lease who secures the right to possess and use the property. (p. 472).

Lessor the party to a lease who grants the right to possess and use property to another. (p. 472).

Modified Accelerated Cost Recovery System (MACRS) the system of depreciation required by federal income tax law. (p. 450).

Natural resources assets that are physically consumed when used; examples include timber, mineral deposits, and oil and gas fields; also called *wasting assets.* (p. 469).

Obsolescence a condition in which, because of new inventions and improvements, a plant asset can no longer be used to produce goods or services with a competitive advantage. (p. 452).

Ordinary repairs repairs to keep a plant asset in normal, good operating condition; treated as a revenue expenditure. (p. 462).

Patent an exclusive right granted to its owner to manufacture and sell a machine or device, or to use a process, for 17 years. (p. 471).

Plant assets tangible assets that are used in the operations of a company and have a useful life of more than one accounting period. (p. 448).

Revenue expenditure an expenditure that should appear on the current income statement as an expense and be deducted from the period's revenues because it does not provide a material benefit in future periods. (p. 461).

Salvage value management's estimate of the amount that will be recovered at the end of a plant asset's useful life through a sale or as a trade-in allowance on the purchase of a new asset; also called *residual,* or *scrap, value.* (p. 452).

Straight-line depreciation a method that allocates an equal portion of the total depreciation for a plant asset (cost minus salvage) to each accounting period in its useful life. (p. 453).

Total asset turnover a measure of the ability of a company to use its assets to generate sales; computed by dividing net sales by average total assets. (p. 475).

Trademark or **trade name** symbol, name, phrase, or jingle identified with a company or service. (p. 474).

Units-of-production depreciation a method that charges a varying amount to expense for each period of an asset's useful life depending on its usage; expense is computed by taking the cost of the asset less its salvage value and dividing by the total number of units expected to be produced during its useful life. (p. 455).

Useful (or service) life the length of time a plant asset will be productively used in the operations of a business. (p. 452).

Questions

1. What characteristics of a plant asset make it different from other assets?
2. What is the balance sheet classification of land held for future expansion? Why is this type of land not classified as a plant asset?
3. In general, what is included in the cost of a plant asset?
4. What is the difference between land and land improvements?
5. Does the balance of the account, Accumulated Depreciation—Machinery, represent funds accumulated to replace the machinery when it wears out? What does the balance of accumulated depreciation represent?
6. Why is the Modified Accelerated Cost Recovery System not generally accepted for financial accounting purposes?
7. What is the difference between ordinary repairs and extraordinary repairs and how should they be recorded?

8. What accounting principle justifies charging low cost plant asset purchases immediately to an expense account?
9. What are some events that might lead to disposal of a plant asset?
10. Should a gain on an exchange of plant assets be recorded?
11. How does accounting for long-term property and equipment impact the statement of cash flows?
12. How is total asset turnover computed? Why would a financial statement user be interested in total asset turnover?
13. What is the name for the process of allocating the cost of natural resources to expense as natural resources are used?
14. What are the characteristics of an intangible asset?
15. Is the declining-balance method an acceptable means of computing depletion of natural resources?
16. What general procedures are followed in accounting for intangible assets?
17. When does a business have goodwill? Under what conditions can goodwill appear in a company's balance sheet?
18. A company bought an established business and paid for goodwill. If the company plans to incur advertising and promotional costs each year to maintain the value of the goodwill, must the company also amortize the goodwill?
19. Refer to the consolidated balance sheets for **NIKE** in Appendix A. What title does NIKE use to describe its plant assets? What is NIKE's book value of plant assets as of May 31, 1997, and May 31, 1996?
20. Refer to the consolidated balance sheet of **Reebok** in Appendix A. How are the property and equipment and intangibles of Reebok presented on its balance sheet?
21. Refer to the consolidated balance sheet of **America Online** in Appendix A. Identify two different intangible assets owned by American Online.

Quick Study

QS 11-1
Defining plant assets
C1

Explain the difference between *(a)* plant assets and current assets; *(b)* plant assets and inventory; and *(c)* plant assets and long-term investments.

QS 11-2
Cost of plant asset
C1

Starbuck Lanes installed automatic score-keeping equipment. The electrical work required to prepare for the installation was $18,000. The invoice price of the equipment was $180,000. Additional costs were $3,000 for delivery and $12,600 of sales tax. During the installation, a component of the equipment was damaged because it was carelessly left on a lane and hit by the automatic lane cleaning machine during a daily maintenance run. The cost of repairing the component was $2,250. What is the recorded cost of the automatic score-keeping equipment?

QS 11-3
Depreciation methods
P2

On January 2, 1999, Crossfire acquired sound equipment for concert performances at a cost of $55,900. The rock band estimated they would use this equipment for four years, during which time they anticipated performing about 120 concerts. They estimated at that point they could sell the equipment for $1,900. During 1999, the band performed 40 concerts. Compute the 1999 depreciation using *(a)* the straight-line method and *(b)* the units-of-production method.

QS 11-4
Computing revised depreciation
C3

Refer to the facts in QS 11–3. Assume that Crossfire chose straight-line depreciation but recognized during the second year that due to concert bookings beyond expectations, this equipment would only last a total of three years. The salvage value would remain unchanged. Compute the revised depreciation for the second year and the third year.

QS 11-5
Double-declining-balance method
P2

A fleet of refrigerated delivery trucks acquired on January 5, 1999, at a cost of $930,000 had an estimated useful life of eight years and an estimated salvage value of $150,000. Compute the depreciation expense for the first three years under the double-declining-balance method.

QS 11-6
Revenue and capital expenditures
P3

a. Classify the following expenditures as revenue or capital expenditures:
(1) Cost of annual tune-ups for delivery trucks.
(2) Cost of replacing a compressor for a refrigeration system that extends the estimated life of the system four years, $30,000.
(3) Cost of $220,000 for an addition of a new wing on an office building.
(4) Monthly cost of replacement filters on an air conditioning system, $175.

b. Prepare the journal entry to record items (2) and (3) of part *a*.

QS 11-7
Dissimilar asset exchanges
P4

Spectrum Flooring owned an automobile with a $15,000 cost and $13,500 accumulated depreciation. In a transaction with a neighboring computer retailer, Spectrum exchanged this auto for a computer with a fair market value of $4,500. Spectrum was required to pay an additional $3,750 cash. Prepare the entry to record this transaction for Spectrum.

QS 11-8
Similar asset exchange
P4

Mayes Co. owns an industrial machine that cost $38,400 and has accumulated depreciation of $20,400. Mayes exchanged the machine for a newer model that has a fair market value of $48,000. Record the exchange assuming cash paid of (*a*) $32,000 and then (*b*) $24,000.

QS 11-9
Cash impacts from acquisitions and disposals
C4

For each of the following investing activities, identify whether it is a source or use of cash.
Key: **A.** Source of cash from investing activities.
B. Use of cash for investing activities.

1. _____ Cash purchase of machinery
2. _____ Sale of patents for cash
3. _____ Purchase of productive timberland for cash
4. _____ Cash sale of factory warehouse

QS 11-10
Computing total asset turnover
A2

Eastman Kodak Company reported the following in its annual report: net sales of $13,557 million for 1994 and $12,670 million for 1993; total end-of-year assets of $14,968 million for 1994 and $18,810 million for 1993. Compute its total asset turnover for 1994.

QS 11-11
Natural resources and depletion
P5

Boise Industries acquired an ore mine at a cost of $1,300,000. It was necessary to incur additional costs of $200,000 to access the mine. The mine is estimated to hold 500,000 tons of ore, and the estimated value of the land after the ore is removed is $150,000.

a. Prepare the entry to record the cost of the ore mine.
b. Prepare the year-end adjusting entry assuming 90,000 tons of ore are mined and sold this year.

QS 11-12
Classifying assets
P6

Which of the following assets are reported on the balance sheet as intangible assets? Which are reported as natural resources? (*a*) Leasehold, (*b*) Salt mine, (*c*) Building, (*d*) Oil well, (*e*) Trademark.

QS 11-13
Intangible assets and amortization
P6

On January 4 of the current year, Amber's Boutique incurred a $95,000 cost to modernize its store. Improvements included new floors, lighting, and shelving for merchandise. It is estimated these improvements will last for 10 years. Amber's leases its retail space and has 8 years remaining on the lease. Prepare the entry to record the cost of modernization and the amortization entry at the end of the current year.

Exercises

Exercise 11-1
Cost of plant asset
C1

Santiago Co. purchased a machine for $11,500, terms 2/10, n/60, FOB shipping point. The seller prepaid the freight charges, $260, adding the amount to the invoice and bringing its total to $11,760. The machine required a special steel mounting and power connections costing $795, and another $375 was paid to assemble the machine and get it into operation. In moving the machine to its steel mounting, it was dropped and damaged. The repairs cost $190. Later, $30 of materials were consumed in adjusting the machine so that it would produce a satisfactory product. The adjustments were normal for this type of machine and were not the result of the damage. Prepare a computation to show the cost of this machine for accounting purposes. (Assume Santiago pays for the purchase within the discount period.)

Exercise 11-2
Lump-sum purchase of plant assets

Horizon Company paid $368,250 for real estate plus $19,600 in closing costs. The real estate included land appraised at $166,320; land improvements appraised at $55,440; and a building appraised at $174,240. Prepare a computation showing the allocation of the total cost among the three purchased assets and present the journal entry to record the purchase.

Exercise 11-3
Recording costs of real estate

Planning to build a new plant, Monarch Manufacturing purchased a large lot on which an old building was located. The negotiated purchase price for this real estate was $225,000 for the lot plus $120,000 for the old building. The company paid $34,500 to have the old building torn down and $51,000 for landscaping the lot. It paid a total of $1,440,000 in construction costs, which included the cost of a new building and $85,500 for lighting and paving a parking lot next to the building. Present a single journal entry to record these costs incurred by Monarch, all of which were paid in cash.

Exercise 11-4
Alternative depreciation methods
C2

On the first day of the year, Barrow Company installed a computerized machine in its factory at a cost of $42,300. The machine's useful life was estimated at 10 years, or 363,000 units of product, with a $6,000 trade-in value. During its second year, the machine produced 35,000 units of product. Determine the machine's second-year depreciation under the *(a)* straight-line, *(b)* units-of-production, and *(c)* double-declining-balance methods.

Exercise 11-5
Alternative depreciation methods; partial year's depreciation
C3

On April 1, 1999, Rodgers Backhoe Co. purchased a trencher for $250,000. The machine was expected to last five years and have a salvage value of $25,000. Compute depreciation expense for the year 2000, using the *(a)* straight-line method and *(b)* double-declining-balance method.

Exercise 11-6
Revising depreciation rates
C3

BodySmart Fitness Club used straight-line depreciation for a machine that cost $21,750, under the assumption it would have a four-year life and a $2,250 trade-in value. After two years, BodySmart determined that the machine still had three more years of remaining useful life, after which it would have an estimated $1,800 trade-in value. *(a)* Compute the machine's book value at the end of its second year. *(b)* Compute the amount of depreciation to be charged during each of the remaining three years in the machine's revised useful life.

Exercise 11-7
Income effects of alternative depreciation methods
A1

Shamrock Enterprises recently paid $235,200 for equipment that will last five years and have a salvage value of $52,500. By using the machine in its operations for five years, the company expects to earn $85,500 annually, after deducting all expenses except depreciation. Present a schedule showing income before depreciation, depreciation expense, and net income for each year and the total amounts for the five-year period, assuming *(a)* straight-line depreciation and *(b)* double-declining-balance depreciation.

Exercise 11-8
Alternate depreciation methods
P2

In January 1999, Labtech purchased computer equipment for $147,000. The equipment will be used in research and development activities for four years and then sold at an estimated salvage value of $30,000. Prepare schedules showing the depreciation and book values for the four years assuming *(a)* straight-line depreciation and *(b)* double-declining-balance.

Exercise 11-9
Ordinary repairs, extraordinary repairs, and betterments
P3

Archer Company paid $262,500 for equipment that was expected to last four years and have a salvage value of $30,000. Prepare journal entries to record the following costs related to the equipment:

a. During the second year of the equipment's life, $21,000 cash was paid for a new component that was expected to increase the equipment's productivity by 10% each year.

b. During the third year, $5,250 cash was paid for normal repairs necessary to keep the equipment in good working order.

c. During the fourth year, $13,950 was paid for repairs that were expected to increase the useful life of the equipment from four to five years.

Exercise 11-10
Extraordinary repairs; computations and entries
P3

Flemming Company owns a building that appeared on its prior year's balance sheet at its original $561,000 cost less $420,750 accumulated depreciation. The building has been depreciated on a straight-line basis under the assumption it has a 20-year life and no salvage value. During the first week in January of the current year, major structural repairs were completed on the building at a cost of $67,200. The repairs did not increase the building's capacity, but they did extend its expected life for 7 years beyond the 20 years originally estimated.

a. Determine the building's age as of the end of last year.

b. Give the entry to record the costs of major repairs, which are paid in cash.

c. Determine the book value of the building immediately after the repairs are recorded.

d. Give the entry to record the current year's depreciation.

Exercise 11-11
Partial year's depreciation; disposal of plant asset
P4

Levy Co. purchased and installed a machine on January 1, 1999, at a total cost of $92,750. Straight-line depreciation was taken each year for four years assuming a seven-year life and no salvage value. The machine was disposed of on July 1, 2003, during its fifth year of service. Prepare entries to record the partial year's depreciation on July 1, 2003, and to record the disposal under the following separate assumptions: *(a)* the machine is sold for $35,000 cash; and *(b)* Levy received an insurance settlement of $30,000 resulting from the total destruction of the machine in a fire.

Exercise 11-12
Exchanging similar assets
P4

Greenbelt Construction traded in an old tractor for a new tractor, receiving a $28,000 trade-in allowance and paying the remaining $82,000 in cash. The old tractor cost $95,000, and straight-line depreciation of $52,500 had been recorded under the assumption that it would last eight years and have an $11,000 salvage value. Answer the following questions:

a. What was the book value of the old tractor?

b. What is the loss on the exchange?

c. What amount should be debited to the new Tractor account?

Exercise 11-13
Recording plant asset disposals
P4

On January 2, 1999, Hammond Service Co. disposed of a machine that cost $42,000 and had been depreciated $22,625. Present the journal entries to record the disposal under each of the following unrelated assumptions:

a. Machine is sold for $16,250 cash.

b. Machine is traded in on a new machine of like purpose having a $58,500 cash price. A $20,000 trade-in allowance is received, and the balance is paid in cash.

c. A $15,000 trade-in allowance is received for the machine on a new machine of like purpose having a $58,500 cash price. The balance is paid in cash.

d. Machine is traded for vacant land next to the shop to be used as a parking lot. The land has a fair value of $37,500, and Hammond paid $12,500 cash in addition to giving up the machine.

Exercise 11-14
Cash flows related to plant assets
C4

Refer to the statement of cash flows for **America Online** in Appendix A for the year ended June 30, 1996, to answer the following:

a. What amount of cash is used to purchase property and equipment?

b. What amount of cash is received from sales of property and equipment?

c. How much depreciation and amortization is recorded?

d. What is the total amount of net cash used in investing activities?

e. Are there any gains or losses from sale of property and equipment?

Exercise 11-15
Evaluating efficient use of assets
A2

Atherton Co. reports net sales of $4,862,000 for 1999 and $7,542,000 for 2000. End-of-year balances for total assets were: 1998, $1,586,000; 1999, $1,700,000; and 2000, $1,882,000. Compute Atherton's total asset turnover for 1999 and 2000 and comment on the company's efficiency in using its assets.

Exercise 11-16
Depletion of natural resources
P5

On April 2, 1999, Cascade Mining Co. paid $3,633,750 for an ore deposit containing 1,425,000 tons. The company also installed machinery in the mine that cost $171,000, had an estimated seven-year life with no salvage value, and was capable of removing all the ore in six years. The machinery will be abandoned when the ore is completely mined. Cascade began operations on May 1, 1999, and mined and sold 156,200 tons of ore during the remaining eight months of the year. Give the December 31, 1999, entries to record the depletion of the ore deposit and the depreciation of the mining machinery. Depreciation of mining machinery should be in proportion to the mine's depletion.

Exercise 11-17
Amortization of intangible assets
P6

The Falstaff Gallery purchased the copyright on an oil painting for $236,700 on January 1, 1999. The copyright legally protects its owner for 19 more years. However, the company plans to market and sell prints of the original for only 12 years. Prepare journal entries to record the purchase of the copyright on January 1, 1999 and the annual amortization of the copyright on December 31, 1999.

Exercise 11-18
Estimating goodwill
P6

Corey Boyd has devoted years to developing a profitable business that earns an attractive return. Boyd is now considering the possibility of selling the business and is attempting to estimate the value of goodwill in the business. The fair value of the net assets of the business (excluding goodwill) is $437,000, and in a typical year net income is about $85,000. Most businesses of this type are expected to earn a return of about 10% on net assets. Estimate the value of the goodwill assuming *(a)* the value is equal to 10 times the amount that net income is above-normal, and *(b)* the value is computed by capitalizing the amount that net income is above-normal at a rate of 8%.

Problems

Problem 11-1
Real estate costs; partial year's depreciation

C1, C2, C3

S

In 1999, Lightscapes paid $2,800,000 for a tract of land and two buildings on it. The plan is to demolish Building One and build a new store in its place. Building Two is to be used as a company office and is appraised at a value of $641,300, with a useful life of 20 years and an $80,000 salvage value. A lighted parking lot near Building One has improvements (Land Improvements One) valued at $408,100 that are expected to last another 14 years and have no salvage value. Without considering the buildings or improvements, the tract of land is valued at $1,865,600. Lightscapes incurred the following additional costs:

Cost to demolish Building One	$ 422,600
Cost of additional landscaping	167,200
Cost to construct new building (Building Three), having a useful life of 25 years and a $390,100 salvage value	2,019,000
Cost of new land improvements near Building Two (Land Improvements Two) which have a 20-year useful life and no salvage value	158,000

Required

1. Prepare a schedule having the following column headings: Land, Building Two, Building Three, Land Improvements One, and Land Improvements Two. Allocate the costs incurred by Lightscapes to the appropriate columns and total each column.
2. Prepare a single journal entry to record all the incurred costs, assuming they are paid in cash on March 31, 1999.
3. Using the straight-line method, prepare December 31 adjusting entries to record depreciation for the nine months of 1999 during which the assets were in use.

Check Figure Accumulated depreciation, Land Improvements Two, $5,925 Cr.

Problem 11-2
Plant asset costs; partial year's depreciation; alternative methods

C1, C2, C3

Gunner Construction recently negotiated a lump-sum purchase of several assets from a company that was going out of business. The purchase is completed on March 1, 1999, at a total cash price of $787,500 and included a building, land, land improvements, and 12 vehicles. The estimated market values of the assets are: building, $408,000; land, $289,000; land improvements, $42,500; and vehicles, $110,500. The company's fiscal year ends on December 31.

Required

Preparation Component

1. Prepare a schedule to allocate the lump-sum purchase price to the separate assets purchased. Present the journal entry to record the purchase.
2. Compute the 1999 depreciation expense on the building using the straight-line method, assuming a 15-year life and a $25,650 salvage value.
3. Compute the 1999 depreciation expense on the land improvements assuming a five-year life and double-declining-balance depreciation.

Check Figure 1999 depreciation expense on land improvements, $13,125

Analysis Component

4. Defend or refute this statement: Accelerated depreciation results in less taxes being paid over the life of the asset.

Problem 11-3
Alternative depreciation methods; partial year's depreciation; disposal of plant asset

C3, P2

G

Part 1. A machine costing $210,000 with a four-year life and an estimated $20,000 salvage value is installed in Casablanca Company's factory on January 1. The factory manager estimates the machine will produce 475,000 units of product during its life. It actually produces the following units: year 1, 121,400; year 2, 122,400; year 3, 119,600; and year 4, 118,200. The total number of units produced by the end of year 4 exceeds the original estimate. The machine must not be depreciated below the estimated salvage value.

Required

Prepare a form with the following column headings:

Year	Straight-Line	Units-of-Production	Double-Declining-Balance

Check Figure Year 4, units-of-production depreciation expense, $44,640

Then show the depreciation for each year and the total depreciation for the machine under each depreciation method.

Part 2. Casablanca purchased a used machine for $167,000 on January 2. It is repaired the next day at a cost of $3,420 and installed on a new platform costing $1,080. The company predicts the machine will be used for six years and have a $14,600 salvage value. Depreciation is to be charged on a straight-line basis. A full year's depreciation is charged on December 31, the end of the first year of the machine's use. On September 30 of its sixth year in service, it is retired.

Required

a. Prepare journal entries to record the purchase of the machine, the cost of repairing it, and the installation. Cash is paid for all costs incurred.

b. Prepare entries to record depreciation at the machine at December 31 of its first year and on September 30 in the year of its disposal.

c. Prepare entries to record the retirement of the machine under each of the following unrelated assumptions: (i) it is sold for $13,500; (ii) it is sold for $36,000; and (iii) it is destroyed in a fire and the insurance company pays $24,000 in full settlement of the loss claim.

Problem 11-4
Partial year's depreciation; revising depreciation rates; revenue and capital expenditures
C3, P3

Crenshaw Contractors completed these transactions involving the purchase and operation of equipment:

1999

July 1 Paid $255,440 cash for a new loader plus $15,200 in sales tax and $2,500 for transportation charges. The loader is estimated to have a four-year life and a $34,740 salvage value. Loader costs are recorded in the Equipment account.

Oct. 2 Paid $3,660 to enclose the cab and install air conditioning in the loader. This increased the estimated salvage value of the loader by $1,110.

Dec. 31 Record straight-line depreciation on the loader.

2000

Feb. 17 Paid $920 to repair the loader after the operator backed it into a tree.

June 30 Paid $4,500 to overhaul the loader's engine. As a result, the estimated useful life of the loader is increased by two years.

Dec. 31 Record straight-line depreciation on the loader.

Required

Prepare journal entries to record these transactions.

Check Figure Dec. 31, 2000, Depr. Expense, Equipment, $48,674

Problem 11-5
Partial year's depreciation; revising depreciation rates; exchanging plant assets
C3, P4

ACT Company completed the following transactions involving delivery trucks:

1999

Mar. 26 Paid $19,415 cash for a new delivery truck plus $1,165 in sales tax. The truck is estimated to have a five-year life and a $3,000 trade-in value. Delivery truck costs are recorded in the Trucks account.

Dec. 31 Record straight-line depreciation on the truck.

2000

Dec. 31 Record straight-line depreciation on the truck. Due to new information obtained earlier in the year, the original estimated useful life of the truck is changed from five years to four years, and the original estimated trade-in value is increased to $3,500.

2001

July 7 Traded in the old truck and paid $13,565 in cash for a new truck. The new truck is estimated to have a six-year life and a $3,125 trade-in value. The invoice for the exchange shows:

Price of the new truck	$22,550
Trade-in allowance granted on the old truck	(9,750)
Balance of purchase price	$12,800
State sales tax	765
Total paid in cash	$13,565

Dec. 31 Record straight-line depreciation on the new truck.

Check Figure July 7, 2001, Loss on Exchange of Trucks, $1,527

Required

Prepare journal entries to record these transactions.

Problem 11-6
Partial year's depreciation; alternative methods; disposal of plant assets
C3, P2, P4

Wallingford Company completed the following transactions involving machinery:

Machine No. 15-50 is purchased for cash on May 4, 1999, at an installed cost of $158,700. Its useful life is estimated to be six years with a $12,900 trade-in value. Straight-line depreciation is recorded for the machine at the end of 1999, 2000, and 2001. On April 27, 2002, it is traded for Machine No. 17-95, a similar asset, for an installed cash price of $185,700. A trade-in allowance of $90,330 is received for Machine No. 15-50, and the balance is paid in cash.

Machine No. 17-95's life is predicted to be four years with a $24,600 trade-in value. Double-declining-balance depreciation on this machine is recorded each December 31. On November 5, 2003, it is traded for Machine No. BT-311, a dissimilar asset, for an installed cash price of $537,000. A trade-in allowance of $81,000 is received for Machine No. 17-95, and the balance is paid in cash.

It is estimated that Machine No. BT-311 will produce 600,000 units of product during its five-year useful life, after which it will have a $105,000 trade-in value. Units-of-production depreciation is recorded for the machine for 2003, a period in which it produces 93,000 units of product. Between January 1, 2004, and August 24, 2006, the machine produces 324,000 more units. On the latter date, it is sold for $243,600.

Check Figure 11/5/2003 Gain on Sale of Machinery, $10,545.

Required

Prepare journal entries to record: *(a)* the purchase of each machine, *(b)* the depreciation expense recorded on the first December 31 of each machine's life, and *(c)* the disposal of each machine. (Only one entry is needed to record the exchange of one machine for another.)

Problem 11-7
Intangible assets and natural resources
P5, P6

Part 1. In 1995, The Pullman Company leased space in a building for 15 years. The lease contract calls for annual rental payments of $70,000 to be made on each July 1 throughout the life of the lease and also provides that the lessee must pay for all additions and improvements to the leased property. In 2000, Pullman decided to sublease the space to Kidman & Associates for the remaining 10 years of the lease. On June 20, 2000, Kidman paid $185,000 to Pullman for the right to sublease the space and agreed to assume the obligation to pay the $70,000 annual rent to the building owner beginning July 1, 2000. After taking possession of the leased space, Kidman paid for improving the office portion of the leased space at a cost of $129,840. The improvements were paid for on July 5, 2000, and are estimated to have a life equal to the 16 years remaining in the life of the building.

Required

Prepare entries for Kidman to record *(a)* its payment to Pullman for the right to sublease the building space, *(b)* its payment of the 2000 annual rent to the building owner, and *(c)* its payment for the office improvements. Prepare Kidman's adjusting entries required at the end of 2000 to amortize *(d)* a proper share of the $185,000 cost of the sublease and *(e)* a proper share of the office improvements.

Part 2. On July 3 of the current year, Jackson Mining Co. paid $4,836,000 for land estimated to contain 7.8 million tons of recoverable ore of a valuable mineral. It installed machinery costing $390,000, which has a 10-year life and no salvage value, and is capable of exhausting the ore deposit in eight years. The machinery is paid for on July 25, nine days before mining operations began. The company removes 400,000 tons of ore during the first five months of operations. Depreciation of the machinery is in proportion to the mine's depletion (it will be abandoned after the ore is fully mined).

Required

Preparation Component

Prepare entries to record *(a)* the purchase of the land, *(b)* the installation of the machinery, *(c)* the first five months' depletion under the assumption the land is valueless after the ore is mined, and *(d)* the first five months' depreciation on the machinery.

Check Figure Depletion Expense, $248,000

Analysis Component

Describe the similarities and differences in amortization, depletion, and depreciation.

Problem 11-8
Goodwill estimation and amortization
P6

American Rental Co., an equipment rental business, has the following balance sheet on December 31, 1999:

Assets	
Cash	$ 93,930
Equipment	678,800
Accumulated depreciation, Equipment	(271,500)
Buildings	340,000
Accumulated depreciation, Buildings	(182,400)
Land	93,000
Total assets	$751,830
Liabilities and Equity	
Accounts payable	$ 18,650
Long-term note payable	337,250
J. Reynolds, capital	395,930
Total liabilities and owner's equity	$751,830

In this industry, net income averages 20% of owner's equity. American Rental regularly expects to earn $100,000 annually. The balance sheet amounts are reasonable estimates of fair market values for all assets except goodwill, which does not appear on the financial statement. In negotiations to sell the business, American Rental proposes that goodwill be measured by capitalizing the amount of above-normal net income at a rate of 15%. The potential buyer thinks that goodwill should be valued at five times the amount that net income is above the average for the industry.

Required

1. Compute the amount of goodwill as proposed by American Rental.
2. Compute the amount of goodwill according to the potential buyer.
3. The buyer purchases the business for the amount of the net assets reported on the December 31, 1999, balance sheet plus the amount proposed by American Rental for the goodwill. If the amount of expected net income (before amortization of goodwill) is obtained the first year, and the goodwill is amortized over the longest permissible time period, what amount of net income will be reported for the first year after the business is purchased?
4. What rate of return on the buyer's investment does the first year's net income represent?

Check Figure Goodwill, (1) $138,760, and (2) $104,070

BEYOND THE NUMBERS

Reporting in Action A1

Refer to the financial statements and related information for **NIKE** in Appendix A. Answer the following questions by analyzing the information in its annual report:

1. What percent of the original cost of NIKE's property and equipment remains to be depreciated as of May 31, 1997 and 1996? Assume these assets have no salvage value.
2. Over what periods of time is NIKE amortizing intangible assets and goodwill?
3. What is the net change in total property and equipment (before depreciation) for the year ended May 31, 1997? What is the amount of cash generated by (or used for) investment in property and equipment during the year ended May 31, 1997? What is one possible explanation for the difference between these two amounts?
4. Compute NIKE's total asset turnover for the year ended May 31, 1997.

Swoosh Ahead

5. Obtain access to NIKE's annual report for fiscal years ending after May 31, 1997. You can gain access to NIKE's annual report at its web site [**www.nike.com**] or through the SEC's EDGAR database [**www.sec.gov**]. Recompute NIKE's total asset turnover for the additional years' data you collect. Comment on any differences relative to the turnover computed in (4) above.

Comparative Analysis A2

Both **NIKE** and **Reebok** design, produce, market, and sell sports footwear and apparel. Key comparative figures ($ in millions) for these two companies follow:

	NIKE		Reebok	
Key Figures*	**1997**	**1996**	**1996**	**1995**
Total Assets	$5,361	$3,952	$1,786	$1,652
Net sales	9,187	6,471	3,479	3,481

*NIKE figures are from its annual reports for fiscal years ended May 31, 1997 and 1996. Reebok figures are from its annual reports for fiscal years ended December 31, 1996 and 1995.

Required

1. Compute NIKE's total asset turnover as of May 31, 1997. Compute Reebok's total asset turnover as of December 31, 1996.

Analysis Component

2. Which company is more efficient in generating net sales given the total assets employed?

Ethics Challenge C2

Marcia Diamond is a small business owner and handles all the books for her business. Her company just finished a year when a large amount of borrowed funds was invested into a new building addition as well as numerous equipment and fixture additions. Marcia's banker requires that she submit semi-annual financial statements so he can monitor the financial health of her business. He has warned her that if profit margins erode, he might raise the interest rate on the borrowed funds since this means the loan is riskier from the bank's point of view. Marcia knows profit margin is likely to decline in this current year. As she posts year-end adjusting entries, she decides to apply the following depreciation rule: all capital additions are considered put into service the first day of the following month.

Required

1. Identify decisions that managers like Ms. Diamond must make in applying depreciation methods.
2. Is Marcia's decision an ethical violation or is it a legitimate decision managers make in computing depreciation?
3. How will Marcia's depreciation rule affect the profit margin of her business?

Communicating in Practice

A2

The class is divided into teams. Teams are to select an industry, and each team member is to select a different company in that industry. Each team member is to acquire the annual report of the company selected. Annual reports can be obtained in many ways including accessing this book's Web page or through the SEC's EDGAR database **[www.sec.gov]**. Use the annual report to compute total asset turnover. Communicate with teammates via a meeting, e-mail, or telephone to discuss the meaning of this ratio, how different companies compare to each other, and the industry norm. The team must prepare a single memo reporting the ratios for each company and identify the conclusions reached during the team's discussion. The memo is to be duplicated and distributed to the instructor and all classmates.

Taking It to the Net

C1

Visit the Web site of the **U.S. Patent and Trademark Office** at http://patents.uspto.gov. Use the search function to look for any existing patents protecting some of your favorite products. For example, if you search "Coca Cola" you will find numerous patents protecting various aspects of the Coke product from its packaging, to its recipe, to products using it as a theme. Search three different products and note the range of patents protecting the product. (Note: If you have an idea for a new product you might also want to search the database to see if there are any preexisting patents on your idea.)

Teamwork in Action

C2, A1, P2

Each member of the team has the responsibility to become a resident expert on a specific depreciation method. This expertise is used to facilitate their teammates' understanding of the concepts relevant to the method he or she has chosen. Follow the procedure outlined below:

1. Each team member is to select an area for expertise by choosing one of the following depreciation methods: straight line, units of production, and declining balance. You have one minute to make your choices.
2. Learning teams are to disburse and expert teams are to be formed. Expert teams are made up of students who have all selected the same area of expertise. The instructor will identify the location where each expert team meets.
3. Using data below, expert teams are to collaborate and develop a presentation illustrating each of the relevant procedures and concepts required below. Expert team members must write up the presentation in a format they can show to their learning teams in the next step in the activity.

Data: On January 8, 1998, Whitewater Riders purchase a van to transport rafters back to the point of departure at the conclusion of the rafting adventure tours they run. The cost of the van is $44,000. It has an estimated salvage value of $2,000 and is expected to be used for 4 years and driven 60,000 miles. The van is expected to be driven: 12,000 miles in 1998; 18,000 miles in 1999; 21,000 in 2000; and 10,000 in 2001.

Procedures and concepts to illustrate in expert presentation:

- **a.** Compute annual depreciation expense for each year of the asset's estimated useful life.
- **b.** Explain when and how annual depreciation is recorded.
- **c.** Explain the impact of this method versus other methods on net income over the life of the asset.
- **d.** Identify the book value of the asset over each year of the asset's life and illustrate the reporting of this amount for any one year.

4. Re-form learning teams. In rotation, experts are to present to their teams the results from (3). Experts are to encourage and respond to questions.

Hitting the Road

C1

Team up with one or more classmates for this activity. You are to brainstorm and do any necessary research to identify companies in your community or your area of the country that have and must account for the following assets: natural resource; patent; lease; leasehold improvement; copyright; trademark; and goodwill. You might need to identify seven different companies given there are seven assets, or you might find a company having more than one type of asset. Once you have matched a company with the asset, identify the accounting this company must use for that asset to allocate its cost to the periods that benefited from its use.

Business Week Activity

C1

Read the article "Guardian of the Famous and the Dead" in the May 8, 1995, issue of ***Business Week***.

1. What is the purpose of the **Curtis Management Group** run by CEO Mark A. Roesler?
2. What is the difference between a trademark and rights of publicity?
3. Identify one famous person in each of the following categories represented by the Curtis Management Group: Hollywood, Music, Sports, and Historical.
4. What is the attitude of the U.S. Trade Representatives' office toward the work of the Curtis Management Group?

Current and Long-Term Liabilities

A Look Back

Chapter 11 focused on long-term assets including plant assets, natural resources, and intangible assets. We showed how to record their costs, allocate their costs to periods benefiting from them, and record their disposal.

A Look at This Chapter

This chapter emphasizes current liabilities, and also introduces long-term liabilities. We explain how these liabilities are identified, computed, recorded, and reported in financial statements.

A Look Ahead

Chapter 13 focuses on the corporate and partnership forms of organization. Important characteristics of both forms of organization are described along with some of their basic transactions.

Chapter Outline

Tax Cop

DETROIT, MI—Carmen Benish and her two comrades jump out of their battered Zhiguli and walk briskly to the door of a bicycle sales and services shop in the Moscow suburb of Podolsk. Ducking under bicycle frames hanging from the ceiling, they approach a salesclerk and flash their badges. A few days earlier, an undercover colleague made a purchase that wasn't reported. Benish, Mikail Nikolas, and Val Yaroslav are investigating whether the business is underreporting sales to avoid paying taxes. Two burly policemen in bulletproof vests stand guard as Benish and her fellow investigators confiscate Vladimir Zolov's records. "We pay our taxes on time. We are law-abiding citizens," he protests.

Benish is special. She grew up in a tough inner city environment. But she was determined to stay out of trouble. "I went to college and took accounting and criminal justice," say Benish. "I also joined an international club. I loved the cultural differences." When she graduated with her associate degree this past June, she faced a dilemma. "I like both accounting and criminal justice," says Benish. "I didn't know which way to go."

Fortunately for Benish, her counselor knew the IRS sometimes hires people with exactly the type of background she had. Benish is now an intern in a unique program for international tax investigators at the IRS. "It is a match made in heaven! I get to use my accounting and criminal justice background to help track the underreporting of international income to avoid taxes." Given the huge growth in international sales, this is a high priority at the IRS.

Benish is presently assigned to a one-month internship in Moscow. "Russia is a nightmare for us," says Peter Eastwood, Benish's supervisor at the IRS. "But our job is to ensure that U.S. companies and their affiliates doing business here pay their taxes." These investigators have considerable power. They can levy fines up to three times taxes owed and can seize taxpayers' property and freeze bank accounts during investigations.

But the job is dangerous. Last year in Russia alone, 26 tax officials were killed and 74 wounded, while another 18 tax offices were bombed or sprayed with gunfire. "Sure I'm sometimes scared. But I'm really having fun, and the odds of something bad happening are low," says Benish. "No green eyeshades and cushy desk job for me!"

Learning Objectives

Conceptual

C1 Describe current and long-term liabilities and their characteristics.

C2 Identify and describe known current liabilities.

C3 Explain how to account for contingent liabilities.

C4 Describe accounting for long-term liabilities.

Analytical

A1 Compute times interest earned ratio and use it to analyze liabilities.

Procedural

P1 Prepare entries to account for short-term notes payable.

P2 Compute and record *employee* payroll deductions and liabilities.

P3 Compute and record *employer* payroll expenses and liabilities.

P4 Account for estimated liabilities, including warranties and income taxes.

CHAPTER PREVIEW

Previous chapters introduced us to liabilities for accounts payable, notes payable, wages, and unearned revenues. In this chapter, we learn more about these liabilities and additional ones such as warranties, taxes, payroll, vacation pay, and leases. We also describe contingent liabilities and look at some long-term liabilities. This includes how we define, classify, and measure liabilities for the purpose of reporting useful information about them to decision makers. Understanding tax liabilities is important for Carmen Benish in her IRS work as described in the opening article.

Characteristics of Liabilities

C1 Describe current and long-term liabilities and their characteristics.

This section discusses important characteristics of liabilities, how they are classified, and how they are reported.

Defining Liabilities

A liability is a probable future payment of assets or services that a company is presently obligated to make as a result of past transactions or events.[1] This definition includes three crucial factors:

- Due to a past transaction or event
- Present obligation
- Future payment of assets or services

These three important elements are portrayed visually in Exhibit 12.1.

Exhibit 12.1

Characteristics of a Liability

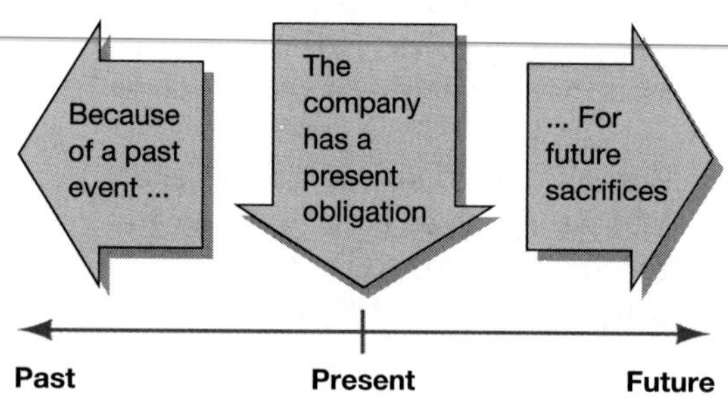

Liabilities do not include all expected future payments. For example, most companies expect to pay wages to its employees in upcoming months and years. But these future payments are not liabilities because there is no past event such as employee work resulting in a present obligation. Future liabilities will arise when employees perform their work and earn the wages.

Classifying Liabilities as Current or Long-Term

Information about liabilities is more useful when the balance sheet identifies them as either current or long-term. Decision makers need to know when obligations are due so they can plan for them and take appropriate action.

Current Liabilities

Current liabilities, also called *short-term liabilities,* are obligations expected to be paid using current assets or by creating other current liabilities.[2] Current liabilities are due within one year or the company's operating cycle, whichever is longer. Examples of current liabilities are accounts payable, short-term notes payable, wages payable, warranty liabilities, lease liabilities, payroll and other taxes payable, and unearned revenues.

[1] Financial Accounting Standards Board, *Statement of Financial Accounting Concepts No. 6,* "Elements of Financial Statements" (Norwalk, CT, 1985), par. 35.

[2] FASB, *Accounting Standards—Current Text* (Norwalk, CT, 1995), sec. B05.402. First published as *Accounting Research Bulletin No. 43,* Ch. 3A, par. 7.

Current liabilities are different for different companies. A company's current liabilities depend on its type of operations. **Harley-Davidson,** for instance, recently reported the following items related to its motorcycle operations in its current liabilities section ($ thousands):

Accrued Liabilities	
Warranty/recalls	$ 9,384
Dealer incentive programs	$29,220

Time Warner, the media and entertainment giant, reports a much different set of current liabilities. For instance, Time Warner reports more than $1 billion in current liabilities made up of items like television programming and royalties.

Long-Term Liabilities

A company's obligations not expected to be paid within one year (or a longer operating cycle) are reported as **long-term liabilities.** Long-term liabilities include long-term notes payable, warranty liabilities, lease liabilities, and bonds payable. They are sometimes reported on the balance sheet in a single long-term liabilities total. **The GAP,** for instance, reports a single total of $762 million long-term liabilities in its recent balance sheet. But many companies show them as two or more items such as *long-term debt* and *other liabilities.* **Dell,** for instance, reports long-term liabilities in its recent balance sheet of (in $ millions): long-term debt, $17; warranties, $225; other, $36. These are reported after current liabilities.

Many liabilities can be either current or long-term depending on their characteristics. A single liability also can be divided between these two sections if a company expects to make payments toward it in both the short and long-term. **Wal-Mart,** for instance, reports in its 1997 balance sheet ($ millions): long-term debt, $7,191; long-term debt due within one year, $1,039. The second item is reported in current liabilities. We also sometimes see liabilities that do not have a fixed due date but are payable on the creditor's demand. These are reported as current liabilities because of the possibility of payment within the year or the company's operating cycle, if longer. Exhibit 12.2 shows amounts of current and long-term liabilities for selected companies.

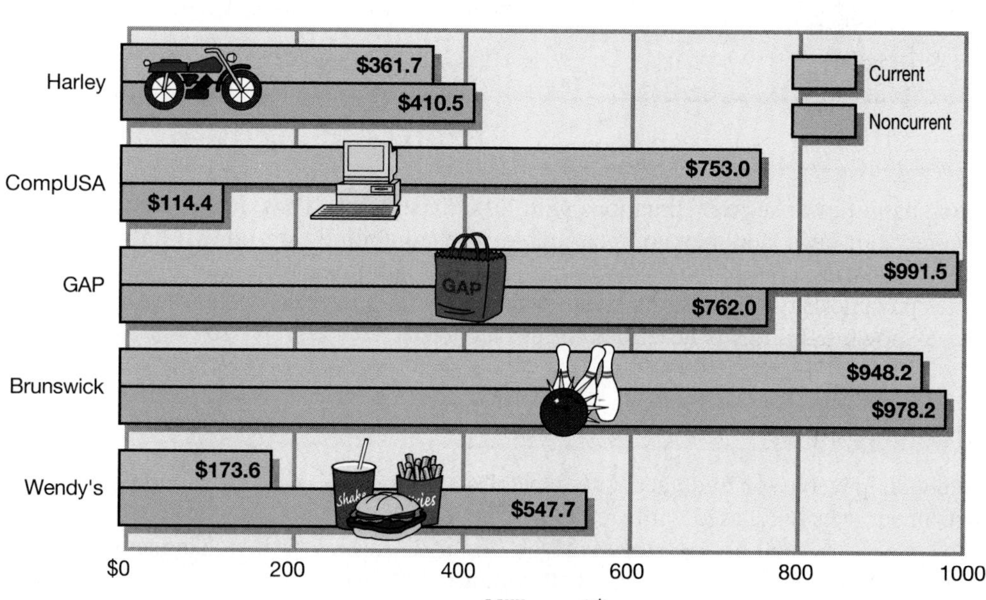

Exhibit 12.2

Current and Long-Term Liabilities

Uncertainty in Liabilities

Accounting for liabilities involves addressing three important questions: Whom to pay? When to pay? How much to pay? Answers to these questions often are decided when a liability is incurred. For example, if a company has an account payable to a specific individual for $100, payable on August 15, 1999, there is no uncertainty about the answers. The company knows whom to pay, when to pay, and how much to pay. But we do see liabilities with uncertainty in one or more of the answers to these three questions.

Uncertainty in Whom to Pay

Some liabilities involve uncertainty in whom to pay. For instance, a company creates a liability with a known amount when issuing a note that is payable to its holder. Although a specific amount is payable to the note's holder at a specified date, the company doesn't know who the holder is until that date. Despite this uncertainty, the corporation reports this liability on its balance sheet.

Uncertainty in When to Pay

A company can have an obligation of a known amount to a known creditor but not know when it must be paid. For example, a legal services firm can accept fees in advance from a client who expects to use its services in the future. This means the legal services firm has a liability that is settled by providing services at an unknown future date. Even though this uncertainty exists, the firm's balance sheet must report this liability. These types of obligations are reported as current liabilities because they are likely to be settled in the short term.

Uncertainty in How Much to Pay

A company can know it has an obligation but not know how much will be required to settle it. For example, a company using electrical power is billed only after the meter is read. This cost is incurred and the liability created before a bill is received. A liability to the power company is reported as an estimated amount if the balance sheet is prepared before a bill arrives.

Flash *back*

1. What is a liability?
2. Is every expected future payment a liability?
3. If a liability is payable in 15 months, is it classified as current or long-term?

Answers—p. 519

Known (Determinable) Liabilities

C2 Identify and describe known current liabilities.

Most liabilities arise from situations with little uncertainty. They are set by agreements, contracts, or laws, and they are measurable. These liabilities are **known liabilities,** also called *definitely determinable liabilities.* Known liabilities include accounts payable, notes payable, payroll, sales taxes, unearned revenues, and leases. How we account for these known liabilities is described in this section.

Accounts Payable

Accounts payable, or trade accounts payable, are amounts owed to suppliers for products or services purchased with credit. Accounting for accounts payable is explained and illustrated in several prior chapters. Much of our discussion of merchandising activities in Chapters 6 and 7, for instance, dealt with accounts payable.

Sales Taxes Payable

Nearly every state and many cities levy taxes on retail sales. Sales taxes are stated as a percent of selling prices. The retailer (seller) collects sales taxes from customers when sales occur and remits (often monthly) these collections to the proper government agency. Since retailers owe these collections to the government, this amount is a current liability for retailers. **Home Depot** reports sales taxes payable of $143 million in 1997. To illustrate, if Home Depot sells materials on August 31 worth $6,000 subject to a 5% sales tax, its entry is:

Aug. 31	Cash	6,300	
	Sales		6,000
	Sales Taxes Payable ($6,000 × 0.05)		300
	To record cash sales and 5% sales tax.		

Assets = Liabilities + Equity
+6,300 +300 +6,000

Sales Taxes Payable is debited and Cash credited when these collections are remitted to the government. Notice Sales Taxes Payable is not tied to any expense. Instead, it arises because laws require retailers to collect this cash from customers for the government.

Unearned Revenues

Unearned revenues (also called *deferred revenues, collections in advance,* and *prepayments*) are amounts received in advance from customers for future products or services. Advance ticket sales for sporting events or music concerts are examples of unearned revenues. The **Boston Celtics,** for instance, reported "deferred game revenues" including advance ticket sales of $6.2 million at March 31, 1998. For example, when the Celtics sell $5 million of season tickets, its entry is:

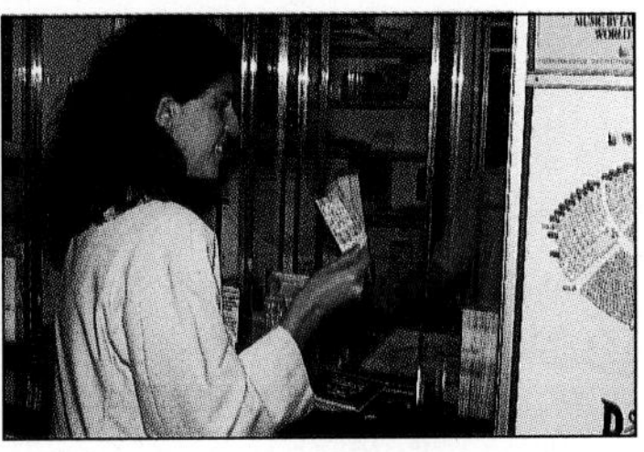

June 30	Cash	5,000,000	
	Unearned Season Ticket Revenue		5,000,000
	To record sale of of Celtic season tickets.		

Assets = Liabilities + Equity
+5,000,000 +5,000,000

When each game is played, the Celtics record revenue for the portion earned:

Oct. 31	Unearned Season Ticket Revenue	60,000	
	Season Ticket Revenue		60,000
	To record Celtic season ticket revenues earned.		

Assets = Liabilities + Equity
−60,000 +60,000

Unearned Season Ticket Revenue is an unearned revenue account and is reported as a current liability. Beyond sporting and music events, unearned revenues arise with airline ticket sales, magazine publishers, construction projects, hotel reservations, and custom orders.

Short-Term Notes Payable

P1 Prepare entries to account for short-term notes payable.

A **short-term note payable** is a written promise to pay a specified amount on a definite future date within one year or the company's operating cycle, whichever is longer. These promissory notes are negotiable (as are checks). This means they can be transferred from party to party by endorsement. The written documentation provided by notes is helpful in resolving disputes and for pursuing legal actions involving these liabilities.

Most notes payable are interest-bearing to compensate for the time until payment is made. Short-term notes payable arise from many transactions. A company purchases merchandise on credit and sometimes extends the credit period by signing a note to replace an account payable. They also arise when money is borrowed from a bank. We describe both of these cases in this section.

Note Given to Extend Credit Period

A company can create a note payable to replace an account payable. Most often, the creditor asks that an interest-bearing note be substituted for an overdue account payable that does not bear interest. A less common situation is where a debtor's weak financial condition encourages the creditor to obtain a note, sometimes for a lesser amount, and then close the account to ensure no additional credit sales are made to this customer.

Illustration of Note to Extend Credit Period

To illustrate, let's assume that on August 23 Wiley asks to extend its past-due $600 account payable to McGraw. After some negotiations, McGraw agrees to accept $100 cash and a 60-day, 12%, $500 note payable to replace the account payable. Wiley records this transaction with this entry:

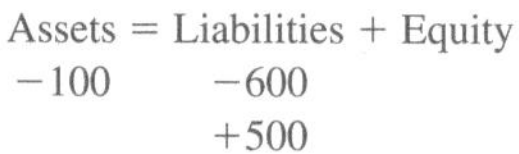

Aug. 23	Accounts Payable—McGraw Company	600	
	Cash		100
	Notes Payable		500
	Gave $100 cash and a 60-day, 12% note for payment on account.		

Signing the note does not pay off Wiley's debt. Instead, the form of debt is changed from an account payable to a note payable. McGraw prefers the note payable over the account payable because it earns interest and also because it is written documentation of the debt's existence, term, and amount.

When the note comes due, Wiley pays the note and interest by giving McGraw a check for $510. This payment is recorded with this entry:

Oct. 22	Notes Payable	500	
	Interest Expense	10	
	Cash		510
	Paid note with interest ($500 × 12% × 60/360).		

The interest expense is computed by multiplying the principal of the note ($500) by the annual interest rate (12%) for the fraction of the year the note is outstanding (60 days/360 days).

Note Given to Borrow from Bank

A bank nearly always requires a borrower to sign a promissory note when making a loan. When the note matures, the borrower repays the note with an amount larger than the amount borrowed. The difference between the amount borrowed and the amount repaid is *interest.* A note often states that the signer of the note promises to pay *principal* (the amount borrowed) plus interest. In this case the *face value* of the note equals principal. Face value is the value shown on the face of the note.

A bank sometimes has a borrower sign a note with a face value that includes both principal and interest. In this case, the signer of the note receives *less* than the note's face value. The difference between the borrowed amount and the note's face value is interest. Since the borrowed amount is less than the note's face value, the difference is sometimes called **discount on note payable.**

To illustrate these two different types of notes, let's assume a company needs $2,000 for a specific project and borrows this money from a bank at 12% annual interest. The loan is made on September 30, 1999, and is due in 60 days.

Face Value Equals Amount Borrowed

The bank in this case requires the company to sign a note with a face value equal to the $2,000 borrowed. The note includes a statement similar to: *"I promise to pay $2,000 plus interest at 12% within 60 days after September 30."* This note is shown in Exhibit 12.3.

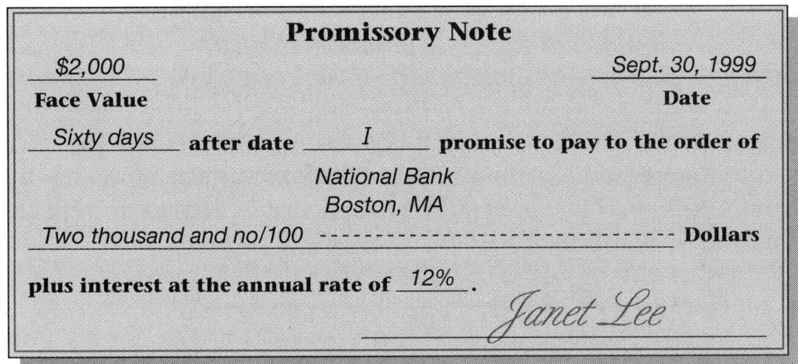
Promissory Note

$2,000 — Face Value | Sept. 30, 1999 — Date

Sixty days after date I promise to pay to the order of

National Bank
Boston, MA

Two thousand and no/100 ---------- Dollars

plus interest at the annual rate of 12%.

Janet Lee

Exhibit 12.3

Note with Face Value Equal to Amount Borrowed

The borrowing company records its receipt of cash and the new liability with this entry:

Sept. 30	Cash	2,000	
	Notes Payable		2,000
	Borrowed $2,000 cash with a 60-day, 12%, $2,000 note.		

Assets = Liabilities + Equity
+2,000 +2,000

When the note and interest are paid 60 days later, the borrowing company records payment with this entry:

Nov. 29	Notes Payable	2,000	
	Interest Expense	40	
	Cash		2,040
	Paid note with interest ($2,000 × 12% × 60/360).		

Assets = Liabilities + Equity
−2,040 −2,000 −40

Face Value Equals Amount Borrowed plus Interest

The bank in this case writes a note with the 12% interest in its face value. This type of note includes a promise similar to: *"I promise to pay $2,040 within 60 days after September 30."* This note is shown in Exhibit 12.4. The note does not refer to the rate used to compute the $40 of interest included in the $2,040 face value. In other respects, this note is identical to the one in Exhibit 12.3. Because this note lacks a stated interest rate, it is sometimes called a **noninterest-bearing note.** This term can be misleading since the note does bear interest, but interest is included in the face value.

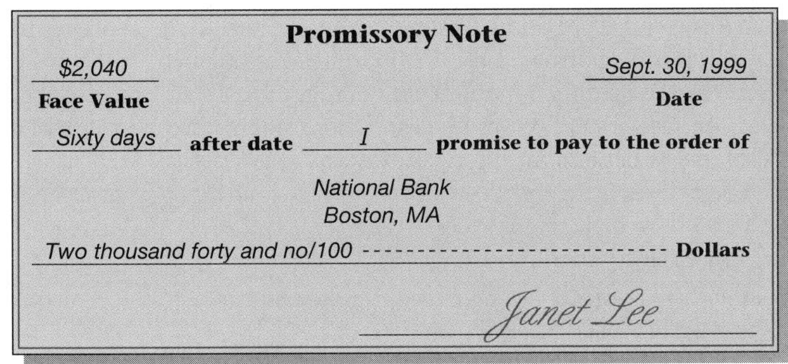
Promissory Note

$2,040 — Face Value | Sept. 30, 1999 — Date

Sixty days after date I promise to pay to the order of

National Bank
Boston, MA

Two thousand forty and no/100 ---------- Dollars

Janet Lee

Exhibit 12.4

Note with Face Value Equal to Amount Borrowed plus Interest

When the face value of the note includes principal and interest, the borrowing company usually records this note with an entry to credit Notes Payable for the face value of the note and record the discount in a *contra-liability* account. This entry is:[3]

Assets = Liabilities + Equity
+2,000 +2,040
−40

Sept. 30	Cash	2,000	
	Discount on Notes Payable	40	
	Notes Payable		2,040
	Borrowed $2,000 cash with a 60-day, 12%, $2,040 note.		

Discount on Notes Payable is a contra-liability account to the Notes Payable account. If a balance sheet is prepared after this transaction on September 30, the $40 discount is subtracted from the $2,040 balance in the Notes Payable account to reflect the $2,000 net amount borrowed as follows:[4]

Note payable	$2,040	
Less discount on note payable	40	$2,000

When this note matures 60 days later on November 29, the entry to record the company's $2,040 payment to the bank is:

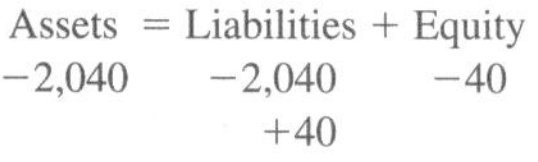
Assets = Liabilities + Equity
−2,040 −2,040 −40
+40

Nov. 29	Notes Payable	2,040	
	Interest Expense	40	
	Cash		2,040
	Discount on Notes Payable		40
	Paid note with interest.		

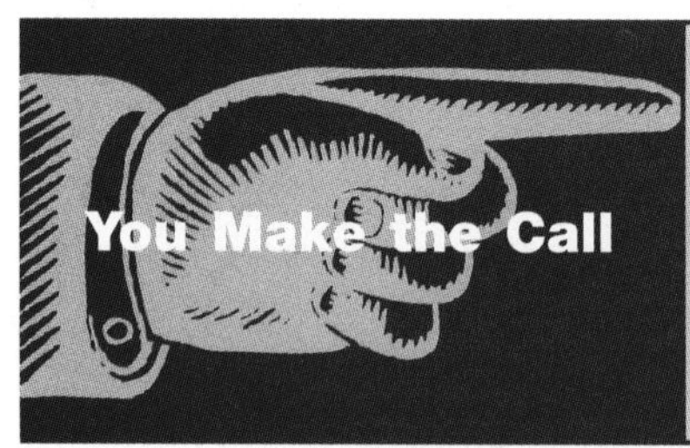

Rock Band

You are a member of a rock band. Your band needs $15,000 to upgrade equipment. You receive loan approvals for $15,000 cash at two banks. One bank's proposed loan contract reads: "Band promises to pay $15,000 plus interest at 14% within 6 months." The competing bank's contract reads: "Band promises to pay $16,000 within 6 months." Which loan do you prefer?

Answer—p. 519

End-of-Period Adjustments to Notes

When the end of an accounting period falls between the signing of a note payable and its maturity date, the *matching principle* requires us to record the accrued but unpaid interest on the note.

To illustrate these end-of-period adjustments, let's return to the short-term note above and assume the company borrowed the $2,000 on December 16, 1999, instead of September 30. This 60-day note then matures on February 14, 2000. Because the company's fiscal year ends on December 31, we need to record interest expense for the 15 days in December. The entries depend on the type of note.

---

[3] The discount is computed as $2,000 × 12% × 60/360.

[4] We approximate the annual interest rate on a short-term loan as: (Interest paid ÷ Amount received) × (360 days ÷ Loan period in days).

Face Value Equals Amount Borrowed

When the note's face value equals the amount borrowed, the accrued interest is charged to expense and credited to an Interest Payable account. To illustrate, we know that 15 days out of the 60-day loan period for the $2,000, 12% note have elapsed by December 31. This means one-fourth (15 days/60 days) of the $40 total interest is an expense of 1999. The borrowing company records this expense with the following adjusting entry at the end of 1999:

1999			
Dec. 31	Interest Expense	10	
	Interest Payable		10
	To record accrued interest on note ($2,000 × 12% × 15/360).		

Assets	= Liabilities	+ Equity
	+10	−10

When this note matures on February 14, the company records this entry:

2000			
Feb. 14	Interest Expense ($2,000 × 12% × 45/360)	30	
	Interest Payable	10	
	Notes Payable	2,000	
	Cash		2,040
	Paid note with interest.		

Assets	= Liabilities	+ Equity
−2,040	−10	−30
	−2000	

This entry recognizes 45 days of interest expense for year 2000 and removes the balances of the two liability accounts.

Face Value Equals Amount Borrowed plus Interest

We now assume the face value of the note *includes* interest. To illustrate, we assume the borrowing company signs a $2,040 noninterest-bearing note on December 15. When recording this note on December 15, the company credits the $2,040 face value to Notes Payable and debits the $40 discount to a contra-liability account. At year-end, the adjusting entry needed to record the accrual of 15 days of interest for 1999 is:

Dec. 31	Interest Expense	10	
	Discount on Notes Payable		10
	To record accrued interest on note ($2,000 × 12% × 15/360).		

Assets	= Liabilities	+ Equity
	+10	−10

Accrued interest is not credited to Interest Payable in this case. Instead, this entry reduces the balance of the contra-liability account from $40 to $30. This increases the net note liability to $2,010 ($2,040 note less $30 discount).

When this note matures, we need an entry both to accrue interest expense for the last 45 days of the note and to record its payment:

2000			
Feb. 14	Interest Expense	30	
	Notes Payable	2,040	
	Discount on Notes Payable		30
	Cash		2,040
	Paid note with interest ($2,000 × 12% × 45/360).		

Assets	= Liabilities	+ Equity
−2,040	−2,040	−30
	+30	

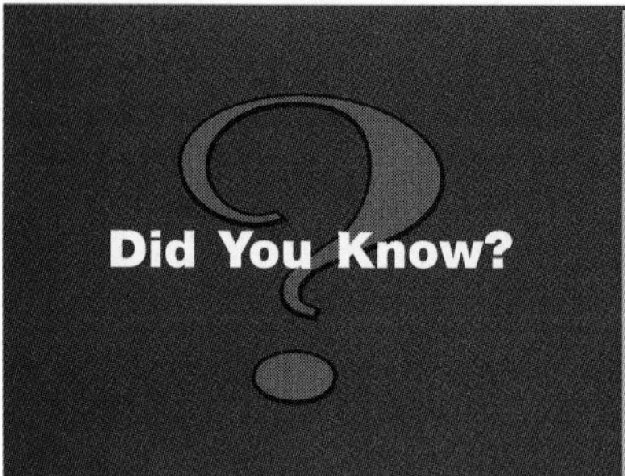

IHOP Notes
Many franchisors use notes to help entrepreneurs acquire its franchises. **International House of Pancakes** (IHOP) allows about 80% of its franchise fee to be paid with a note payable. Payments on these notes are usually collected weekly.

Flash back

4. Why does a creditor want a past-due account replaced by a note?
5. A company borrows money by signing a note payable promising to pay $1,050 in 6 months. In recording the transaction, the company correctly debits $50 to Discount on Notes Payable. How much is borrowed? What annual rate of interest is charged?

Answers—p. 519

Payroll Liabilities

An employer incurs several expenses and liabilities from having employees. These expenses and liabilities are often large and arise from salaries and wages earned, from employee benefits, and from payroll taxes levied on the employer. **Anheuser-Busch,** for instance, reports the following payroll related current liabilities:

Accrued salaries, wages and benefits (in millions)	$ 214.4

We discuss payroll liabilities and related accounts in this section. The appendix to this chapter describes important details about payroll reports, records, and procedures.

Employee Payroll Deductions

P2 Compute and record *employee* payroll deductions and liabilities.

Gross pay is the total compensation earned by an employee. It includes wages, salaries, commissions, bonuses, and any compensation earned before deductions such as taxes.[5] **Net pay,** also called "take home pay," is gross pay less all deductions.

Payroll deductions, commonly called *withholdings,* are amounts withheld from an employee's gross pay. They are either required or voluntary. Required deductions result from laws and include income taxes and Social Security taxes. Voluntary deductions are at the option of an employee and often include pension and health contributions, union dues, and charitable giving. Exhibit 12.5 shows the typical payroll deductions of an employee. Payroll deductions are withheld from employees' pay by the employer. The employer is obligated to transmit this money to the designated organization. The employer records payroll deductions as current liabilities until these amounts are transmitted. The major payroll deductions are discussed next.

---

[5] Wages usually refer to payments to employees at an hourly rate. Salaries usually refer to payments to employees at a monthly or yearly rate.

Payroll Deductions

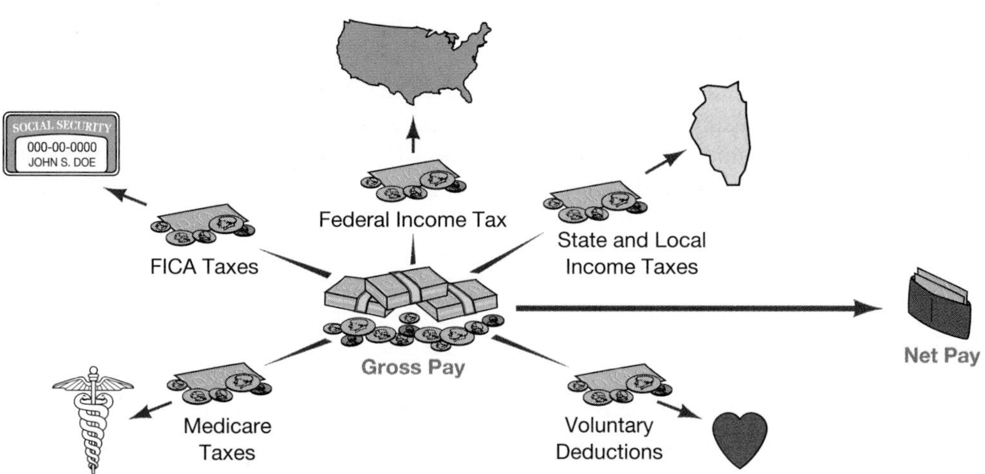

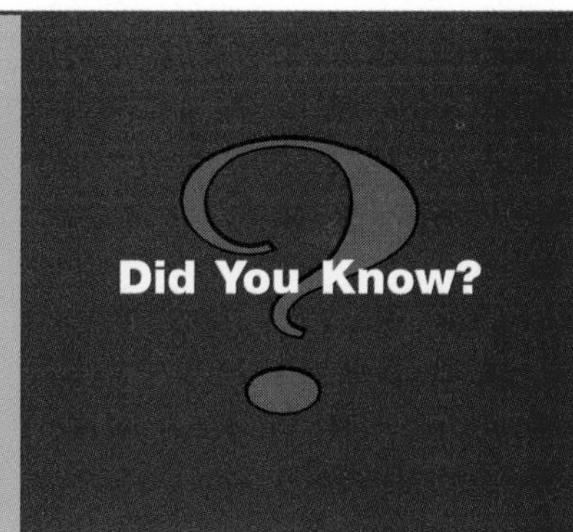

Pay or Else
Delay or failure to pay withholding taxes to government agencies has severe consequences. Fines, for instance, can be imposed at a rate of 5% of taxed owed for each month they're not paid. In severe cases, a 100% penalty can be levied, with interest, on the unpaid balance. The government can even close the company, take its assets, and pursue legal actions against individuals involved.

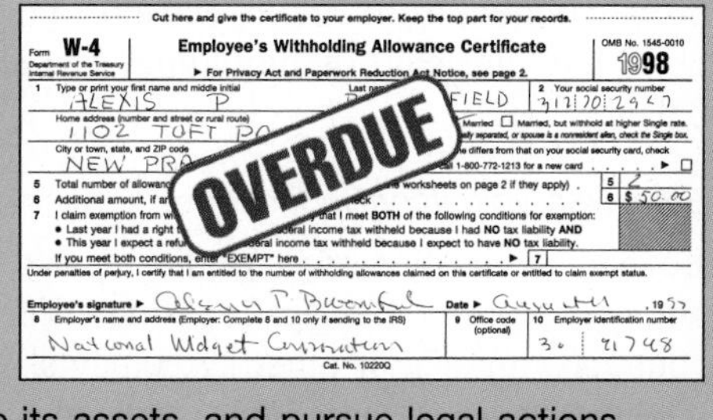

Employee FICA Taxes

The federal Social Security system provides qualified workers retirement, disability, survivorship, and medical benefits. Laws *require* employers to withhold **FICA taxes** from employees' pay to cover costs of the system.[6] Employers (and payroll programs) usually separate FICA taxes into two groups: (1) retirement, disability, and survivorship and (2) medical. We follow the same approach in our discussion.

For the first group, the Social Security system provides qualified workers retiring at age 62 or older (until 1999) with monthly cash payments for the rest of their lives. These payments are often called *Social Security benefits.* Starting in 1999, the age for collecting a full benefit begins to rise at a rate of nearly one month per year. The full-benefit retirement age continues increasing until it reaches age 67 in year 2027. The system also provides monthly payments to deceased workers' surviving families and to disabled workers who qualify for assistance.

For the second group, the system provides retirees *Medicare benefits* beginning at age 65. These benefits, like those in the first group, are paid with FICA taxes. Taxes related to the first group are often called *Social Security taxes,* whereas those in the second group (medical) are often called *Medicare taxes.*

Law requires employers to withhold FICA taxes from each employee's salary or wages on each payday. The taxes for Social Security and Medicare are computed separately. For 1998, the amount withheld from each employee's pay for Social Security tax is 6.2% of the first $68,400 earned by the employee in the calendar year, or a maximum of $4,240.80. The Medicare tax is 1.45% of *all* wages earned by the employee. There is no

[6] FICA is an abbreviation for the Federal Insurance Contributions Act, the legal source of these taxes.

maximum number for Medicare tax, as the government wants to maintain solvency of this program.

Employers must promptly pay withheld taxes to the Internal Revenue Service (IRS) on specific filing dates during the year. Substantial penalties can be levied against employers who fail to send the withheld taxes to the IRS on time. Until all these taxes are sent to the IRS, they are included in employers' current liabilities.

Employee Income Tax

Most employers are required to withhold federal income tax from each employee's paycheck. The amount withheld is computed using tables published by the IRS. The amount depends on the employee's annual earnings rate and the number of *withholding allowances* claimed by the employee. Allowances are items that reduce the amount of taxes one owes the government. The more allowances you claim, the less tax your employer will withhold. Employees can claim allowances for themselves and their dependents. They also can claim additional allowances if they expect major declines in their taxable income for medical expenses or other deductible items.[7] Most states and many local governments also require employers to withhold income taxes from employees' pay. Income taxes withheld from employees must be paid promptly to the proper government agency. Until they are paid, withholdings are reported as a current liability on the employer's balance sheet.

Employee Voluntary Deductions

Beyond Social Security, Medicare, and income taxes, employers often withhold other amounts from employees' earnings. These withholdings arise from employee requests, contracts, unions, or other agreements. They can include amounts for charitable giving, medical insurance premiums, pension contributions, and union dues. Until they are paid, these withholdings are current liabilities of employers.

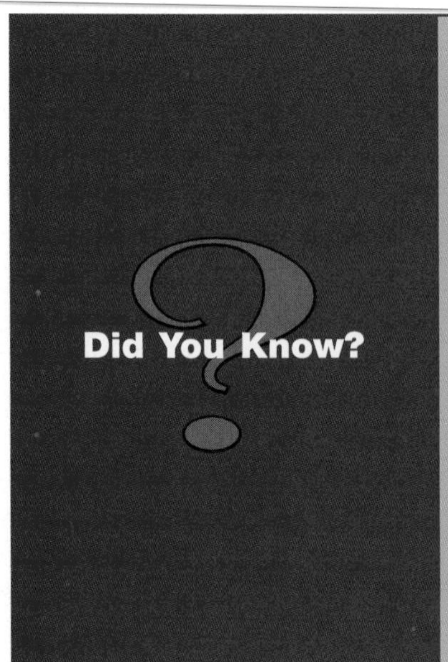

Pay Stats

Comparing pay is tricky business. **Mexico,** for example, has long been regarded as poor on the hourly base pay scale. But we must recognize that base pay makes up only 30% of a Mexican worker's total compensation as opposed to 70% for a U.S. worker. Mexican workers typically receive full pay 365 days a year—even though they take vacations and holidays, and usually work only 40 to 48 hours a week. They often receive profit-sharing plans, punctuality bonuses, saving plans, and 30 days' extra pay as a Christmas bonus. Even with these benefits, Mexican workers are still estimated to make about $10 less per hour than their U.S. counterparts. [Source: *Business Week,* October 31, 1994.]

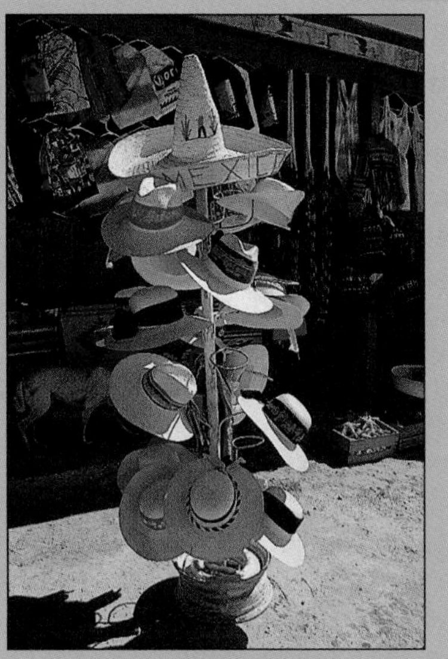

[7] An employee who claims more allowances than he or she is entitled to is subject to a stiff fine.

Recording Employee Payroll Deductions

Employers must accrue payroll expenses and liabilities at the end of each pay period. To illustrate, let's assume an employee earns a salary of $2,000 per month. At the end of January, the employer's entry to accrue payroll expenses and liabilities for this employee is:

Jan. 31	Salaries Expense	2,000	
	FICA—Social Security Taxes Payable (6.2%)		124
	FICA—Medicare Taxes Payable (1.45%) . .		29
	Employees' Federal Income Taxes Payable* .		213
	Employees' Medical Insurance Payable* . . .		85
	Employees' Union Dues Payable*		25
	Accrued Payroll Payable		1,524
	To record payroll for pay period ended January 31.		

**Amounts taken from the employer's accounting records.*

Assets	=	Liabilities	+	Equity
		+124		−2,000
		+29		
		+213		
		+85		
		+25		
		+1,524		

Salaries Expense (debit) indicates the employee earned a gross salary of $2,000. The first five payables (credits) record liabilities the employer owes on behalf of this employee to cover FICA taxes, income taxes, medical insurance, and union dues. The Accrued Payroll Payable account (credit) records the $1,524 net pay the employee receives from the $2,000 gross pay earned.

When the employee is paid, another entry (or a series of entries) is required to record the check written and distributed (or funds transferred). The entry to record cash payment to this employee is: Accrued Payroll Payable debited and Cash credited for $1,524.

Check Forgers
More than $600 million annually is estimated to be lost to check schemes. But now companies are fighting back with an internal control technique called **positive pay.** Here's how it works: Using accounting software, a company regularly sends the bank a "positive file" listing all checks written. When a check reaches the bank for payment, the bank compares the check against the positive file. This flags any forged checks, as well as authentic checks whose payee name or payment is altered. Discrepancies are reported to the company, who can stop payment. Many banks such as Texas Commerce Bank offer positive pay plans for free. [Source: *Business Week,* December 8, 1997.]

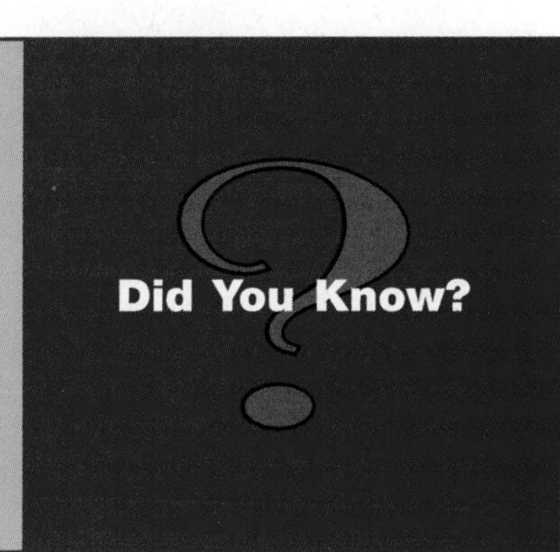

Employer Payroll Taxes

P3 Compute and record *employer* payroll expenses and liabilities.

Employers must pay payroll taxes in addition to those required of employees. These employer taxes include FICA and unemployment taxes.

Employer FICA Tax

Employers must pay FICA taxes *equal in amount* to the FICA taxes withheld from their employees. An employer's tax is credited to the same FICA Taxes Payable accounts used to record the Social Security and Medicare taxes withheld from employees.[8]

Federal and State Unemployment Taxes

The federal government participates with states in a joint federal-state unemployment insurance program. Under this joint program, each state administers its own program.

[8] A self-employed person has to pay both the employee and employer FICA taxes.

These programs provide unemployment benefits to covered workers. The federal government approves state programs and pays a portion of their administrative expenses.

Federal Unemployment Taxes (FUTA). Employers are subject to a federal unemployment tax on wages and salaries paid to their employees. For 1998, the Federal Unemployment Tax Act requires employers to pay a tax of as much as 6.2% of the first $7,000 in salary or wages paid to each employee. But this federal tax can be reduced by a credit of up to 5.4% for taxes paid to a state program. As a result, the net federal unemployment tax is usually only 0.8%.

State Unemployment Taxes (SUTA). All states support their unemployment insurance programs by placing a payroll tax on employers.[9] In most states, the basic rate is 5.4% of the first $7,000 paid each employee. This basic rate is adjusted according to an employer's merit rating. A **merit rating** is assigned by the state and reflects a company's stability or instability in employing workers. A good rating is based on high stability and means an employer can pay less than the basic 5.4% rate. A low rating reflecting high turnover or seasonal hiring and layoffs means an employer pays more. A favorable merit rating translates into cash savings from these taxes. To illustrate, an employer with 100 employees who each earn $7,000 or more per year saves $34,300 annually if it has a merit rating of 0.5% versus 5.4%. This is computed by comparing taxes of $37,800 at the 5.4% rate to only $3,500 at the 0.5% rate.

Tax Aid

Computer technology has reduced errors and increased speed in computing taxes as compared with manual use of tax tables. Tax tables can be stored on computer or downloaded off the Web and then used to accurately compute payroll taxes.

Recording Employer Payroll Taxes

Employer payroll taxes are an added expense beyond the wages and salaries earned by employees. These taxes are often recorded in a journal entry separate from the one recording payroll expenses and deductions (see previous page). To illustrate, assume the $2,000 recorded salaries expense illustrated above is earned by an employee whose earnings have not yet reached $7,000 for the year. Also assume the federal unemployment tax rate is 0.8% and the state unemployment tax rate is 5.4%.

The FICA portion of the employer's tax totals $153, computed by multiplying the 6.2% and 1.45% by the $2,000 gross pay. State unemployment (SUTA) taxes are $108, computed as 5.4% of the $2,000 gross pay. Federal unemployment (FUTA) taxes are $16, computed as 0.8% of $2,000. The entry to record the employer's payroll tax expense and related liabilities is:

Assets	= Liabilities	+ Equity
	+124	−277
	+29	
	+108	
	+16	

Jan. 31	Payroll Taxes Expense	277	
	FICA—Social Security Taxes Payable (6.2%)		124
	FICA—Medicare Taxes Payable (1.45%) . . .		29
	State Unemployment Taxes Payable		108
	Federal Unemployment Taxes Payable		16
	To record employer payroll taxes.		

The appendix to this chapter describes payroll reports, records, and procedures applied to a small company. It also illustrates use of accounting software in payroll accounting.

[9] A few states require employees to make a contribution. In this book and all its assignments, we assume this tax is only on the employer.

Flash back

6. A company pays its one employee $3,000 per month. This company's net FUTA rate is 0.8% on the first $7,000 earned by the employee, its SUTA rate is 4.0% on the first $7,000, its Social Security tax rate is 6.2% of the first $68,400, and its Medicare tax rate is 1.45% of all amounts earned by the employee. The entry to record this company's March payroll includes what amount for total payroll taxes expense?
7. Identify whether the employer or employee or both pays each of these taxes: *(a)* FICA taxes; *(b)* FUTA taxes; *(c)* SUTA taxes; and *(d)* withheld income taxes.

Answers—p. 519

Lawn Worker
You take a summer job working for a family friend who runs a small lawn mowing service. When the time arrives for your first paycheck, the owner slaps you on the back, gives you full payment in cash, winks, and adds: "No need to pay those high taxes, eh." What are your responsibilities in this case? Do you take any action?

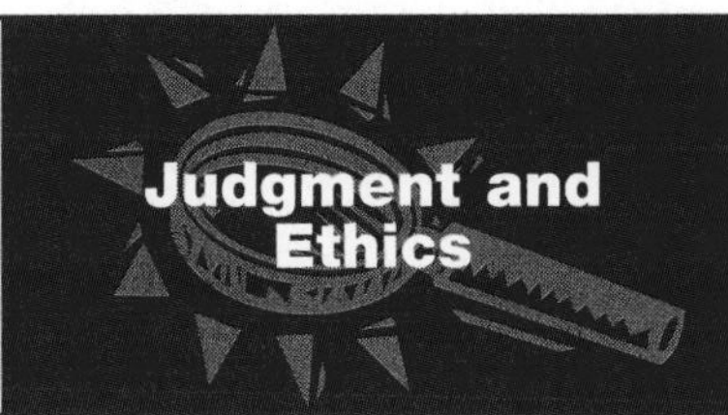

Answer—p. 519

Estimated Liabilities

P4 Account for estimated liabilities, including warranties and income taxes.

An **estimated liability** is a known obligation of an uncertain amount, but one that can be reasonably estimated. Common examples are warranties offered by a seller, income taxes, and employee benefits such as vacation pay, pensions, and health care. We discuss each of these in this section. Other examples of estimated liabilities include property taxes and certain contracts to provide future services.

Warranty Liabilities

A warranty is an estimated liability of the seller. A **warranty** obligates a seller to pay for replacing or repairing the product (or service) when it fails to perform as expected within a specified period. Most cars, for instance, are sold with a warranty covering parts for a specified period of time. **Ford** reported more than $4 billion in "dealer and customer allowances and claims" in its recent annual report.

To comply with the *full disclosure* and *matching principles,* the seller reports the expected expense of providing the warranty in the period when revenue from the sale of the product is reported. The seller reports this warranty obligation as a liability, even though there is uncertainty about the existence, amount, payee, and date of future sacrifices. The seller's warranty obligation does not require payments unless products fail and are returned for repairs. But future payments are probable and the amount of this liability can be estimated using, for instance, past experience with warranties.

Illustration of Warranty Liabilities

To illustrate, let's consider a dealer who sells a used car for $8,000 on December 1, 1999, with a one-year or 12,000-mile warranty covering parts. This dealer's experience shows warranty expense averages about 4% of a car's selling price. This means expense is expected to be $320 ($8,000 × 4%). The dealer records this estimated expense and liability with this entry:

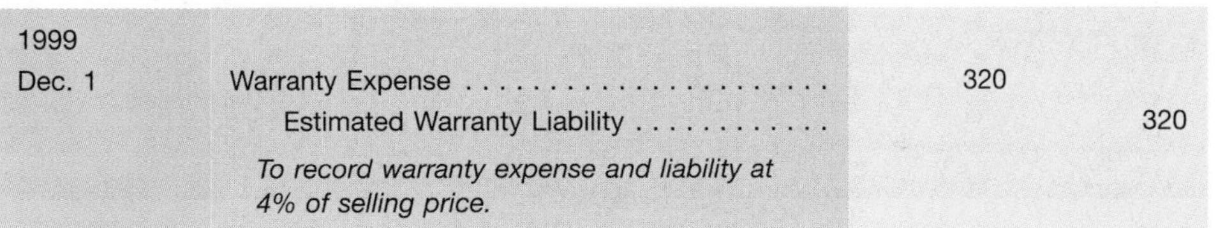

1999			
Dec. 1	Warranty Expense	320	
	Estimated Warranty Liability		320
	To record warranty expense and liability at 4% of selling price.		

Assets = Liabilities + Equity
+320 −320

This entry alternatively could be made as part of end-of-period adjustments. Either way, it causes the estimated warranty expense to be reported on the 1999 income statement. It also results in a warranty liability on the balance sheet for December 31, 1999.

To further extend our example, suppose the customer returns the car for warranty repairs on January 9, 2000. The dealer performs this work by replacing parts costing $200. The entry to record partial settlement of the estimated warranty liability is:

Assets = Liabilities + Equity
−200 −200

2000			
Jan. 9	Estimated Warranty Liability	200	
	Auto Parts Inventory		200
	To record costs of warranty repairs.		

This entry does not yield any additional recorded expense in year 2000. Instead, this entry reduces the balance of the estimated warranty liability. Warranty expense was previously recorded in 1999, the year the car was sold with the warranty.

What happens if total warranty costs turn out to be more or less than the estimated 4%, or $320? The answer is that management should monitor actual warranty costs to see whether the 4% rate is accurate. If experience reveals a large difference from estimates, the rate should be changed for future sales. This means while differences are expected, they should be small.

Employee Health and Pension Benefits

Many companies provide **employee benefits** beyond salaries and wages. An employer often pays all or part of medical, dental, life, and disability insurance. Many employers also contribute to pension plans and offer special stock purchase plans to employees. When payroll taxes and charges for employee benefits are added to the employees' basic earnings, employers often find that payroll cost exceeds employees' gross earnings by 25% or more.

To illustrate, we assume an employer agrees to (a) pay an amount for medical insurance equal to $8,000 and (b) to contribute an additional 10% of employees' $120,000 gross salary to a retirement program. The entry to record these benefits is:

Assets = Liabilities + Equity
+8,000 −20,000
+12,000

Jan. 31	Employee Benefits Expense	20,000	
	Employees' Medical Insurance Payable . . .		8,000
	Employees' Retirement Program Payable . .		12,000
	To record costs of employee benefits.		

Did You Know?

Post Game

Old timers are taking a swing at baseball. Several ex-players are suing major league baseball over a pension system they say unfairly excludes them and fails to reward their contributions to the game. Gripes include failure to extend pensions to players whose careers ended before 1947, were interrupted by World War II, or were spent in the Negro League. Current major leaguers need only play a quarter of a season to receive a pension. A full pension is about $113,000 a year. [Source: *Business Week,* June 9, 1997.]

Vacation Pay

Many employers offer paid vacation benefits. One example is where employees earn 2 weeks' vacation by working 50 weeks. This benefit increases employer's payroll expenses because employees are paid for 52 weeks but only work for 50 weeks. While total annual salary is the same, the cost per week worked is greater than the amount paid per week. To illustrate, if an employee is paid $20,800 for 52 weeks of employment but works only 50 weeks, then the weekly salary expense to the employer is $416 ($20,800/50 weeks) instead of the $400 paid weekly to the employee ($20,800/52 weeks). The $16 difference between these two amounts is recorded as salary expense and a liability for vacation pay. When the employee takes vacation, the employer reduces the vacation pay liability and does not record any additional expense.

Income Tax Liabilities for Corporations

Financial statements of both proprietorships and partnerships do not include income taxes because these organizations don't pay income taxes. Instead, taxable income for these organizations is carried to the owners' personal tax return and taxed at that level. But corporations are subject to income taxes and must estimate their income tax liability when preparing financial statements. We explain this process in this section. Then, in the next section, we discuss deferred income tax liabilities arising from temporary differences between GAAP and income tax rules.

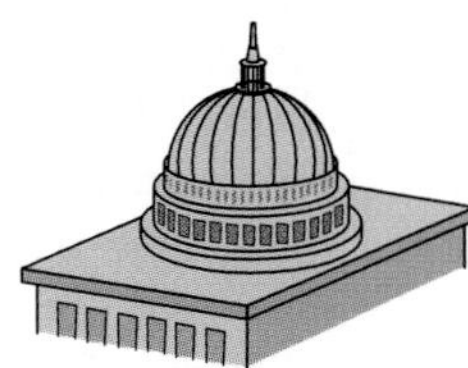

Income tax expense for a corporation creates a liability until payment is made to the government. Because this tax is created through earning income, a liability is incurred when income is earned. This tax must be paid quarterly under federal regulations.

Illustration of Income Tax Liabilities

To illustrate, let's consider a corporation that prepares monthly financial statements. Based on its income in January 1999, this corporation estimates that it owes income taxes of $12,100. The following adjusting entry records this estimate:

Jan. 31	Income Taxes Expense	12,100	
	Income Taxes Payable		12,100
	To accrue January income tax expense and liability.		

Assets = Liabilities + Equity
+12,100 −12,100

The tax liability is adjusted each month until the first quarterly payment is made. If estimated taxes for the first three months total $30,000, the entry to record its payment is:

Apr. 10	Income Taxes Payable	30,000	
	Cash		30,000
	Paid quarterly income taxes based on first quarter income.		

Assets = Liabilities + Equity
−30,000 −30,000

This process of accruing and then paying taxes continues through the year. By the time annual financial statements are prepared at year-end, the corporation knows its total earned income and the actual amount of income taxes it must pay. This information allows it to update the expense and liability accounts.

Suppose this corporation has a $22,000 credit balance in the Income Taxes Payable account at December 31, 1999, and year-end information shows the actual liability should be $33,500. The fourth quarter entry to record the final expense and liability adjustment is:

Assets = Liabilities + Equity
+11,500 −11,500

Dec. 31	Income Taxes Expense	11,500	
	Income Taxes Payable		11,500
	To record additional tax expense and liability.		

This liability is settled when the corporation makes its final quarterly payment early in year 2000.

Deferred Income Tax Liabilities for Corporations

An income tax liability also can arise when the amount of income before taxes that is reported on a corporation's income statement is not the same as the amount of income reported on its income tax return. This difference occurs because income tax laws and GAAP measure income differently.[10]

Some differences between tax laws and GAAP are temporary. *Temporary differences* arise when the tax return and the income statement report a revenue or expense in different years. As an example, companies are often able to deduct higher amounts of depreciation in the early years of an asset's life and smaller amounts in the later years for tax reporting. But for their income statements, they often report an equal amount of depreciation expense each year. This means in the early years, depreciation expense for tax reporting is more than depreciation expense on the income statement. But in later years, depreciation for tax reporting is less than depreciation on the income statement.

When there are temporary differences between taxable income on the tax return and income before taxes on the income statement, corporations are required to compute income tax expense based on the income reported on the income statement. In the above example involving depreciation, the result is that income taxes expense reported in the early years is more than the amount of income taxes payable. This difference is called a **deferred income tax liability.**

Illustration of Deferred Income Tax Liability

To illustrate, let's assume that in the process of recording its usual quarterly income tax payments, a corporation finds at the end of the year that an additional $25,000 of income tax expense should be recorded. But it also determines only $21,000 is currently due and $4,000 is deferred to future years (a timing difference). The entry to record the required end-of-year adjustment is:

Assets = Liabilities + Equity
+21,000 −25,000
+4,000

Dec. 31	Income Taxes Expense	25,000	
	Income Taxes Payable		21,000
	Deferred Income Tax Liability		4,000
	To record tax expense and deferred tax liability.		

The credit to Income Taxes Payable reflects the amount currently due to be paid. The credit to Deferred Income Tax Liability reflects tax payments deferred until future years when the temporary difference reverses.

Many corporations have deferred income tax liabilities. **Coca-Cola Bottling,** for instance, reports deferred income taxes of $108 million in its recent balance sheet.

Temporary differences also can cause a company to pay income taxes before they are reported on the income statement as expense. If so, the company often reports a *deferred income tax asset* on its balance sheet. This is similar to a prepaid expense. **Compaq,** for instance, reports deferred income taxes of $761 million as a current asset in its recent balance sheet.

---

[10] Differences between tax laws and GAAP arise because Congress uses tax laws to generate receipts, stimulate the economy, and influence behavior, whereas GAAP are intended to provide financial information useful for decision making.

Flash back

8. Estimated liabilities involve an obligation to pay:

a. An uncertain but reasonably estimated amount owed on a known obligation.

b. A known amount to a specific entity on an uncertain due date.

c. A known amount to an uncertain entity on a known due date.

d. All of the above.

9. A car is sold for $15,000 on June 1, 1999, with a one-year warranty covering parts. Warranty expense is estimated at 1.5% of selling price. On March 1, 2000, the car is returned for warranty repairs for parts costing $135. The amount recorded as warranty expense at the time of the March 1 repairs is: *(a)* $0; *(b)* $60; *(c)* $75; *(d)* $135; *(e)* $225.

10. Why does a corporation accrue an income tax liability for quarterly reports?

Answers—p. 520

Contingent Liabilities

C3 Explain how to account for contingent liabilities.

A **contingent liability** is a potential obligation that depends on a future event arising out of a past transaction or event. A typical example is a lawsuit pending in court. Here a past transaction or event leads to a lawsuit whose result depends on the court's decision. More generally, future payment of a contingent liability depends on whether an uncertain future event occurs.

Accounting for Contingent Liabilities

Accounting for contingent liabilities depends on the likelihood of a future event's occurring along with our ability to estimate the amount owed in the future if it occurs. Three categories are identified. (1) The first is where the future event is *probable* (likely) and the amount owed can be *reasonably estimated.* We record this amount as a liability.[11] Examples are the estimated liabilities described earlier in the chapter, such as warranties, vacation pay, and income taxes. (2) The second case is where the future event is *remote* (unlikely). We do not record or disclose any information regarding the contingent liability in this case. (3) The third category is where likelihood of the future event is between these two extremes. Here, if the future event is *reasonably possible* (could occur), then we disclose information about the contingent liability in notes to the financial statements.

The next section gives examples of contingent liabilities that often fall in the third category where the future event is reasonably possible. Disclosing information about contingencies in the third category (reasonably possible) is motivated by the *full-disclosure principle.* This principle requires the reporting of information relevant to decision makers.

Reasonably Possible Contingent Liabilities

This section discusses examples of reasonably possible contingent liabilities.

Potential Legal Claims

Many companies are sued or at risk of being sued. The accounting question is: Should the defendant recognize a liability on its balance sheet or disclose a contingent liability in its notes while a lawsuit is outstanding and not yet settled? The answer is that a potential claim is recorded in the accounts only if payment for damages is probable and the amount can be reasonably estimated. If the potential claim can't be reasonably esti-

[11] FASB, *Accounting Standards—Current Text* (Norwalk, CT, 1995), sec. C59.105. First published as *FASB Statement No. 5,* par. 8.

mated or it is less than probable but reasonably possible, then it is disclosed. **Ford,** for example, includes the following note in its recent annual report:

> Various legal actions, governmental investigations and proceedings and claims are pending . . . against the company . . . arising out of alleged defects in the company's products.

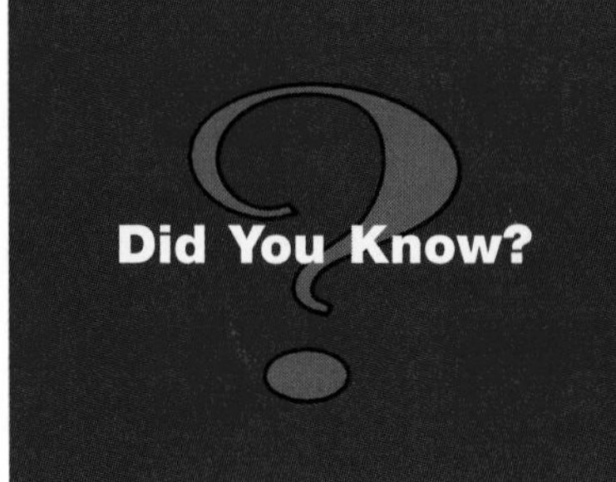

Boiling Mad

Remember the infamous lawsuit against **McDonald's** where an 81-year-old New Mexico woman was awarded $2.9 million—later reduced to $640,000—after spilling hot coffee in her lap? Well, copycat litigation is booming. Fast-food chains are beset by suits over hot-drink and food spills. Companies from **Burger King** to **Starbucks** now print cautions on coffee cups, signs at drive-throughs, and warnings on chili bowls. But restaurateurs continue to have a hard time in court with these claims and remain in hot water over potential legal claims.

Debt Guarantees

Sometimes a company guarantees the payment of debt owed by a supplier, customer, or another company. The guarantor usually discloses the guarantee in its financial statement notes as a contingent liability. But if it is probable the original debtor will default, the guarantor needs to record and report the guarantee in its financial statements as a liability. The **Boston Celtics** have an interesting type of guarantee when it comes to coaches and players as disclosed in its financial report:

> Certain of the contracts provide for guaranteed payments which must be paid even if the employee is injured or terminated.

Other Contingencies

Other examples of contingencies include environmental damages, possible tax assessments, insurance losses, and government investigations. **Sun,** for instance, reports:

> Federal, state, local and foreign laws . . . result in loss contingencies . . . at Sun's refineries, service stations, terminals, pipelines and truck transportation facilities.

Many of these contingencies require disclosure in notes to financial statements since they are reasonably possible. These contingencies sometimes carry characteristics that result in their being recorded as liabilities or omitted altogether.

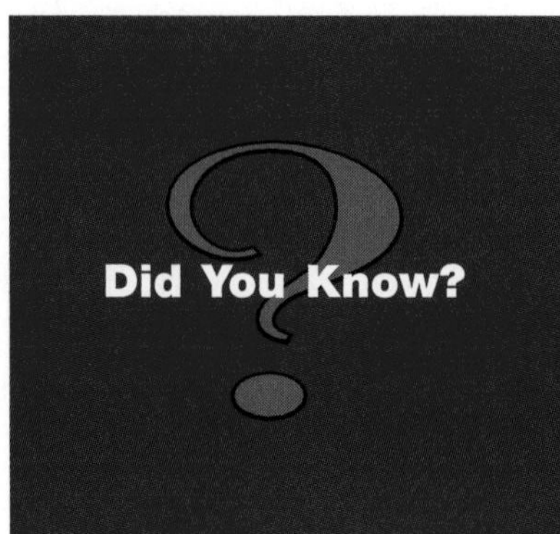

Eco Cops

What's it worth to see from one side of the Grand Canyon to the other? What's the cost when beaches are closed due to pollution? What's the life of a seal worth? These questions are part of measuring environmental liabilities of polluters. One method of measuring these liabilities is called **contingent valuation** by which people are surveyed and asked to answer questions like these. Their answers are used by regulators to levy fines, assess punitive damages, measure costs of clean-up, and assign penalties for damage to environmental intangibles.

Uncertainties

All organizations face uncertainties from future events such as natural disasters and the development of new competing products or services. If these events occur, they can damage a company's assets or drive it out of business. But these uncertainties are not contingent liabilities because they are future events *not* arising out of past transactions. Financial statements aren't useful if they unduly speculate about the effects of possible future uncertainties such as these.

Flash back

11. A future payment is reported as a liability on the balance sheet if payment is contingent on a future event that:
   a. Is not probable but is reasonably possible and the payment cannot be reasonably estimated.
   b. Is probable and the payment can be reasonably estimated.
   c. Is not probable but the payment is known.

12. Under what circumstances is a future payment reported in the notes to the financial statements as a contingent liability?

Answers—p. 520

Long-Term Liabilities

C4 Describe accounting for long-term liabilities.

Long-term liabilities are obligations of a company not requiring payment within one year or its longer operating cycle. Long-term liabilities are often identical to current liabilities except for the greater time interval until the obligation comes due.

Long-term liabilities arise from many different transactions and events. Probably their most common source is money borrowed from a bank or a note issued to buy an asset. They also commonly arise when a company enters into a multiyear lease agreement that is similar to buying the asset. We explain each of these long-term liabilities in the context of discussing known, estimated, and contingent long-term liabilities. A more complete discussion of accounting for long-term liabilities is in Chapter 15.

Known (Determinable) Long-Term Liabilities

Many known or determinable liabilities are long term. These include certain unearned revenues and notes payable. To illustrate, if ***Sports Illustrated*** sells a five-year magazine subscription, then it records amounts received for this subscription in an Unearned Subscription Revenues account. We know amounts in this account are liabilities, but are they current or long term? The answer is both. The portion of *Sports Illustrated's* Unearned Subscription Revenues account that will be fulfilled in the next year is reported as a current liability. But the remaining portion is reported as a long-term liability.

The same analysis applies to notes payable. The borrower, for instance, reports a two-year note payable as a long-term liability in the first year it is outstanding. But in the second year, the borrower reclassifies this note as a current liability since it is due within one year or the longer operating cycle. Certain other known liabilities are rarely, if ever, reported in long-term liabilities. These include accounts payable, sales taxes, and wages and salaries.

The remainder of this section discusses two additional known liabilities: leases and the current portion of long-term debt.

Lease Liabilities

Leasing is one alternative to purchasing an asset and, in certain situations, is reported like a known liability. A company can lease an asset by agreeing to make a series of rental payments to the property owner, called the *lessor.* Because a lease gives the asset's user (called the *lessee)* exclusive control over the asset's usefulness, the lessee can use it to earn revenues. A lease creates a liability for the lessee if it has essentially the same characteristics as a purchase of an asset on credit.

The lessee must report a leased asset and a lease liability if the lease qualifies as a capital lease. A **capital lease** is a lease agreement transferring the risks and benefits associated with ownership to the lessee. This type of lease spans a number of years and creates a long-term liability that is paid off in a series of payments. **Home Depot,** for instance, reports "certain retail locations are leased under capital leases." The net present value of these long-term capital lease liabilities is about $150 million.

When a capital lease is entered into, the lessee records a leased asset and depreciates it over its useful life. The lessee also records a lease liability and allocates interest expense to the years of the lease. This interest allocation process is the same as that for notes payable.

Leases that are not capital leases are called **operating leases.** The lessee does not record an operating lease as an asset nor as a liability. Instead, the lessee's income statement reports rent expense. It also doesn't report either interest or depreciation expense related to an operating lease. **Home Depot**'s rent expense on its operating leases totaled more than $262 million for the recent year reported.

Current Portion of Long-Term Debt

The **current portion of long-term debt** refers to the part of long-term debt that is due within one year or the longer operating cycle. While long-term debt is reported under long-term liabilities, the current portion due is *reported under current liabilities.* To illustrate, let's assume a $7,500 debt is paid in installments of $1,500 per year for five years. The $1,500 due within the year is reported as a current liability. No journal entry is necessary. Instead, we classify the amounts for debt as either current or long-term when the balance sheet is prepared.

Flash *back*

13. Which one of the following requires a lessee to record a liability? *(a)* Operating lease; *(b)* lessor; *(c)* contingent liability; *(d)* capital lease.

Answer—p. 520

Estimated Long-Term Liabilities

Estimated liabilities are both current and long-term. These include employee benefits and deferred income taxes. Pension liabilities to employees are long-term to those workers who will not retire within one year or the longer operating cycle. But for employees who are retired or will retire within the year, a portion of pension liabilities is current in nature. The same analysis applies to employee health benefits, deferred income taxes payable, and warranties. For example, many warranties are for 30 or 60 days in length. Estimated costs under these warranties are properly reported in current liabilities. Yet many automobile warranties are for three years or 36,000 miles. A portion of these warranties is reported as long-term.

Contingent Long-Term Liabilities

Contingent liabilities are both current and long-term in nature. This extends to nearly every contingent liability including litigation, debt guarantees, environmental, government investigation, and tax assessments.

Times Interest Earned

USING THE INFORMATION

A1 Compute times interest earned ratio and use it to analyze liabilities.

A company incurs interest expense on many of its current and long-term liabilities. Examples extend from its short-term notes and current portion of long-term liabilities to its long-term notes, bonds, and capital leases. Many of these liabilities are likely to remain obligations in one form or another for a substantial period of time even if a company experiences a decline in operations. Because of this, interest expense is often viewed as a *fixed cost.* This means the amount of interest is unlikely to fluctuate much from changes in sales or other operating activities.

While fixed costs can be advantageous when a company is growing, they create risk. This risk stems from the possibility a company might be unable to pay them if sales decline. Let's consider **X-Caliber**'s actual results for 1999 and two possible outcomes for the year 2000 shown in Exhibit 12.6 ($ in thousands). X-Caliber is a manufacturer of water sports equipment and remains a family owned operation.

Exhibit 12.6

X-Caliber's Actual and Projected Results

		Year 2000	
	Year 1999	If Sales Increase	If Sales Decrease
Sales	$600	$900	$300
Expense (75% of sales)	450	675	225
Income before interest	$150	$225	$ 75
Interest expense (fixed)	60	60	60
Net income	$ 90	$165	$ 15

Exhibit 12.6 shows expenses other than interest are projected to remain at 75% of sales. Expenses changing with sales volume are called *variable expenses.* But interest is expected to remain at $60,000 per year due to its fixed nature.

The middle number column of Exhibit 12.6 shows X-Caliber's income nearly doubles (100%) if sales increase by 50%. But the far right column shows that X-Caliber's profits fall sharply if sales decline by 50%. These numbers show a company's risk is affected by the amount of fixed interest charges it incurs each period.

The risk created by these fixed expenses is captured numerically with the **times interest earned** ratio. We use the formula in Exhibit 12.7 to compute this ratio.

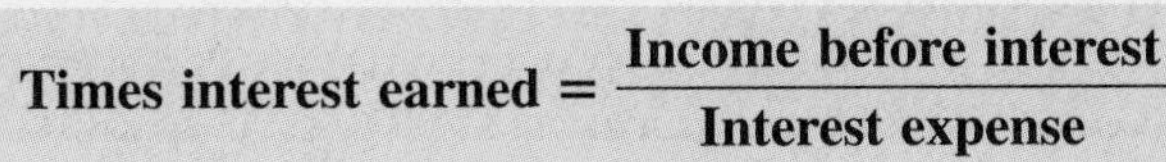

$$\textbf{Times interest earned} = \frac{\textbf{Income before interest}}{\textbf{Interest expense}}$$

Exhibit 12.7

Times Interest Earned Formula

For 1999, X-Caliber's income before interest is $150,000. This means its ratio is computed as $150,000/$60,000, or **2.5 times.** This ratio suggests X-Caliber faces relatively low risk. Its sales must decline sharply before it would be unable to cover its interest expenses. This result is comforting for the company's owners and creditors.

We must use care when computing the times interest earned ratio for a corporation. Since interest is deducted in determining taxable income for a corporation, the numerator for this ratio is adjusted for a **corporation** and expressed as:

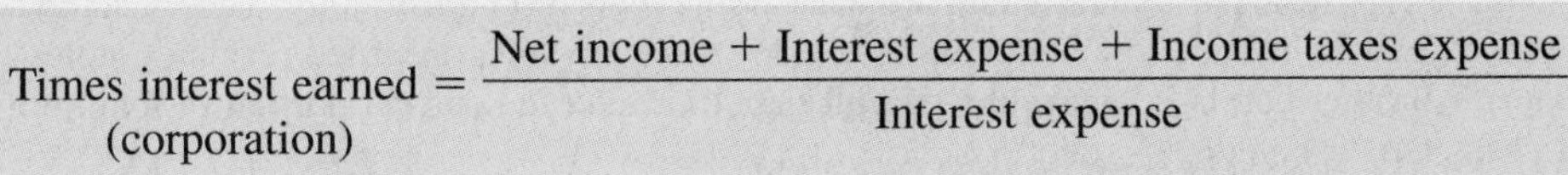

$$\text{Times interest earned (corporation)} = \frac{\text{Net income} + \text{Interest expense} + \text{Income taxes expense}}{\text{Interest expense}}$$

Best Buy's Times Interest Earned Ratio

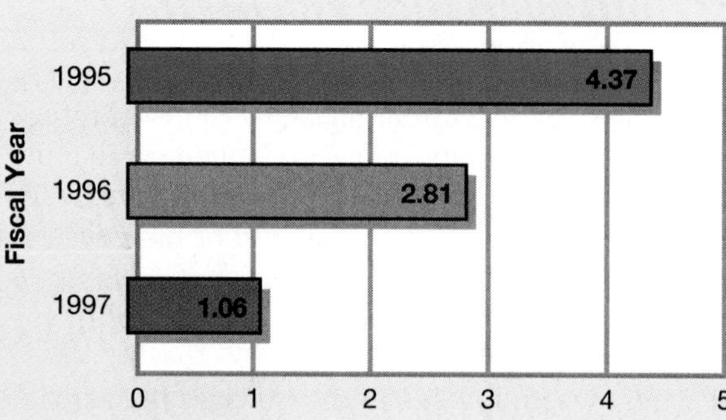

Best Buy's times interest earned ratio for 1995–1997 is shown in Exhibit 12.8. Best Buy's ratio has fallen sharply from 4.37 in 1995 to 1.06 in 1997. This results from a combination of several factors including reduced operating income and increased interest charges. Experience shows when this ratio falls below 1.5 and remains at that level or lower for several periods, the default rate on liabilities increases sharply. This implies increased risk for those decision makers involved with these companies and the creditors.

We must also interpret the times interest earned ratio in light of information about the variability of a company's net income before interest. If this amount is stable from year to year or is growing, the company can afford to take on added risk by borrowing. But if a company's income before interest varies greatly from year to year, fixed interest charges can increase the risk that an owner will not earn a positive return and be unable to pay interest charges.

Entrepreneur

You are an entrepreneur looking to invest in and operate a local franchise of a national chain. You narrow your alternatives to two. Each has an expected annual net income *after* interest of $100,000. Net income for the first franchise includes a regular fixed interest charge of $200,000. But fixed interest charge for the second franchise is $40,000. Which franchise is more risky to you if sales forecasts are not met? Does your decision change if the first franchise likely has more variability in its income before interest?

Answer—p. 519

Flash back

14. Times interest earned ratio:

a. Equals interest expense divided by net income.
b. Is larger as the amount of fixed interest charges gets larger.
c. Is best interpreted with information about the variability of income before interest.

Answer—p. 520

Summary

C1 **Describe current and long-term liabilities and their characteristics.** Liabilities are probable future payments of assets or services an entity is presently obligated to make as a result of past transactions or events. Current liabilities are due within one year or the operating cycle, whichever is longer. All other liabilities are long-term liabilities. Distinguishing characteristics among liabilities include uncertainty about the identity of the creditor, due date, and amount to be paid.

C2 **Identify and describe known current liabilities.** Known (or determinable) current liabilities are set by agreements or laws and are measurable with little uncertainty. They include accounts payable, sales taxes payable, unearned revenues, notes payable, payroll liabilities, and the current portion of long-term debt.

C3 **Explain how to account for contingent liabilities.** If an uncertain future payment depends on a probable future event and the amount can be reasonably estimated, the payment is recorded as a liability. But the future payment is reported as a contingent liability if *(a)* the future event is reasonably possible but not probable, or *(b)* the event is probable but the amount of the payment cannot be reasonably estimated.

C4 **Describe accounting for long-term liabilities.** Long-term liabilities are obligations not requiring payment within one year or the longer operating cycle. Long-term liabilities are similar to current liabilities with the exception being the length of time until payment and the likely use of present value concepts. Lease liabilities are one type of long-term liability often used as an alternative to asset purchases. Capital leases are recorded as assets and liabilities. Other leases, called *operating leases,* are recorded as rent expense when the asset is used.

A1 **Compute times interest earned ratio and use it to analyze liabilities.** Times interest earned is computed by dividing a company's net income before interest by the amount of fixed interest charges incurred. If this company is a corporation, the numerator is net income before interest and taxes. This ratio reflects the company's ability to pay interest and earn a profit for its owners against declines in sales.

P1 **Prepare entries to account for short-term notes payable.** Short-term notes payable are current liabilities and most bear interest. When a short-term note is interest-bearing, its face value equals the amount borrowed. This type of note also identifies a rate of interest to be paid at maturity. When a short-term note is noninterest-bearing, its face value equals the amount to be paid at maturity. This is because its face value includes interest.

P2 **Compute and record *employee* payroll deductions and liabilities.** Employee payroll deductions involve concepts of gross and net pay. Payroll deductions include FICA taxes, income tax, and voluntary deductions such as for pensions and charitable giving.

P3 **Compute and record *employer* payroll expenses and liabilities.** An employer's payroll expenses include gross earnings of the employees, additional employee benefits, and payroll taxes levied against the employer. Payroll liabilities include the net pay of employees, amounts withheld from the employees' wages, employee benefits, and the employer's payroll taxes. Payroll taxes are assessed for Social Security, Medicare, and unemployment programs.

P4 **Account for estimated liabilities, including warranties and income taxes.** Liabilities for warranties and income taxes are recorded with estimated amounts. Both warranties and income taxes are recognized as expenses when incurred. Deferred income tax liabilities are recognized if temporary differences between GAAP and tax rules result in recording more income tax expense than the amount to be currently paid.

Guidance Answers to **You Make the Call**

Rock Band

Both banks have agreed to give the band $15,000 cash, and both loans require repayment in 6 months. Provided terms in these contracts are similar, the only potential difference is in the amount of interest the band must pay. The second bank's contract makes this clear—since $15,000 is borrowed and the band must pay $16,000, the interest charged is $1,000. For the first bank, we must compute interest on the contract. It is $1,050, computed as $15,000 × 14% × 6/12. The band prefers the contract requiring less interest, which is the one reading: "Band promises to pay $16,000 within 6 months."

Entrepreneur

The risk is reflected by the ratio showing the number of times fixed interest charges are covered by net income *before* interest, known as the *times interest earned ratio.* This ratio for the first franchise is 1.5 [($100,000 + $200,000)/$200,000], whereas the ratio for the second franchise is 3.5 [($100,000 + $40,000)/$40,000]. This analysis shows the first franchise is more susceptible to the risk of incurring a loss if its sales decline and, therefore, is more risky. The second question asks about variability of income before interest. If income before interest varies greatly from year to year, this increases the risk an owner will not earn sufficient income to cover interest. Since the first franchise has the greater variability, it makes it an even worse investment.

Guidance Answer to **Judgment and Ethics**

Lawn Worker

You need to be concerned about being an accomplice to unlawful payroll activities. Not paying federal and state taxes on wages earned is illegal and unethical. Such payments also won't provide Social Security and some Medicare credits. The best course of action is to request payment by check. If this fails to change the owner's payment practices, you must consider quitting this job.

Guidance Answers to Flash *backs*

1. Liabilities are probable future payments of assets or services that an entity is presently obligated to make as a result of past transactions or events.
2. No, an expected future payment is not a liability unless an existing obligation was created by a past event or transaction.
3. In most cases, a liability due in 15 months is classified as long-term. But it is classified as a current liability if the company's operating cycle is 15 months or longer.
4. A creditor prefers a note payable instead of an account payable to *(a)* start charging interest and/or *(b)* have positive evidence of the debt and its terms for potential litigation.
5. The amount borrowed is $1,000 ($1,050 − $50). The rate of interest is 5% ($50/$1,000) for six months, which is an annual rate of 10%.
6. $1,000(.008) + $1,000(.04) + $3,000(.062) + $3,000(.0145) = $277.50

7. (a) FICA taxes are paid by both the employee and employer.
   (b) FUTA taxes are paid by the employer.
   (c) SUTA taxes are paid by the employer.
   (d) Withheld income taxes are paid by the employee.
8. *a*
9. *a*
10. A corporation accrues an income tax liability for its quarterly financial statements because income tax expense is incurred when income is earned, not just at the end of the year.
11. *b*
12. A future payment is reported as a contingent liability if *(a)* the uncertain future event is probable but the amount of payment cannot be reasonably estimated, and *(b)* the uncertain future event is not probable but has a reasonable possibility of occurring.
13. *d*
14. *c*

Demonstration Problem

The following series of transactions and events took place at the Kern Company during its recent calendar reporting year. Describe their effects on financial statements by presenting the journal entries described in each situation.

a. In September 1999, Kern sold $140,000 of merchandise covered by a 180-day warranty. Prior experience shows that costs of fulfilling the warranty equal 5% of sales revenue. Compute September's warranty expense and the increase in the warranty liability and show how it is recorded with a September 30 adjusting entry. Also show the journal entry on October 8 to record an expenditure of $300 cash to provide warranty service on an item sold in September.

b. On October 12, 1999, Kern arranged with a supplier to replace Kern's overdue $10,000 account payable by paying $2,500 cash and signing a note for the remainder. The note matures in 90 days and has a 12% interest rate. Show the entries recorded on October 12, December 31, and January 10, 2000 (when the note matures).

c. In late December, the company learns that it is facing a product liability suit filed by an unhappy customer. The company's lawyer is of the opinion that although the company will probably suffer a loss from the lawsuit it is not possible to estimate the amount of the damages at the present time.

d. Kern Company has made and recorded its quarterly income tax payments. In reviewing its end-of-year tax calculations, the company identifies an additional $50,000 of income tax expense that should be recorded. A portion of this additional expense, $10,000 is deferrable to future years. Record this year-end income tax expense adjusting entry.

e. Kern Company's net income for the year is $1,000,000. Its interest expense and income tax expense for the year are $275,000 and $225,000 respectively. Calculate times interest earned.

f. Sally Kline works for Kern Company. For the pay period ended November 30, her gross earnings were $3,000. Every paycheck Sally has $800 deducted for federal income taxes and $200 for state income taxes. Additionally, a $35 premium is deducted for her health care insurance and $10 as a donation for the United Way. Sally pays FICA Social Security taxes at a rate of 6.2% and FICA Medicare taxes at a rate of 1.45%. Sally has not earned enough this year to be exempt from FICA taxes. Journalize the payment of Sally's wages by Kern Company.

g. On November 1, Kern Company borrows $5,000 from the bank in return for a 60-day, 14% note. Record the issuance of the note on November 1 and repayment of the note with interest on December 31.

h. On December 16, Kern Company issues a noninterest-bearing note promising to pay $2,050 within 60 days. Record the issuance of the note, the interest accrual on December 31, and the repayment of the note on February 14 ($50 of interest is included in the note's face value of $2,050).

Planning the Solution

- For *(a)*, compute the warranty expense for September and record it with an estimated liability. Record the October expenditure as a decrease in the liability.
- For *(b)*, eliminate the liability for the account payable and create the liability for the note payable. Compute interest expense for the 80 days that the note is outstanding in 1999 and record it as an additional liability. Record the payment of the note, being sure to include the interest for the 10 days in 2000.

- For *(c)* decide if the contingent liability for the company needs to be disclosed or accrued (recorded) according to the two necessary criteria—probable loss and reasonably estimable.
- For *(d)* determine how much of the income tax expense is payable in the current year and how much needs to be deferred.
- For *(e)* calculate number of times interest charges are earned according to the formula given in the chapter. Remember that the numerator reflects income before interest and tax expense.
- For *(f)* set up payable accounts for all items in Sally's paycheck that require deductions. After all necessary items are deducted, credit the remaining amount to Accrued Payroll Payable.
- For *(g)* record the issuance of the note. Calculate 60 days' interest due using the 360-day convention in the interest formula.
- For *(h)* record the note as a noninteresting-bearing note. Use the contra account Discount on Notes Payable for the interest portion of the proceeds upon issuance. Make the year-end adjustment for 15 days' interest to Interest Expense and Discount on Notes Payable. Record the repayment of the note, being sure to include the interest for the 45 days in 2000.

Solution to Demonstration Problem

a. Warranty expense = 5% × $140,000 = $7,000

Sept. 30	Warranty Expense	7,000	
	Estimated Warranty Liability		7,000
	To record warranty expense and liability at 5% of sales for the month.		
Oct. 8	Estimated Warranty Liability	300	
	Cash		300
	To record the cost of the warranty service.		

b. Interest expense for 1999 = 12% × $7,500 × 80/360 = $200
Interest expense for 2000 = 12% × $7,500 × 10/360 = $25

Oct. 12	Accounts Payable	10,000	
	Notes Payable		7,500
	Cash		2,500
	Paid $2,500 cash and gave a 90-day, 12% note to extend the due date on the account.		
Dec. 31	Interest Expense	200	
	Interest Payable		200
	To accrue interest on note payable.		
Jan. 10	Interest Expense	25	
	Interest Payable	200	
	Notes Payable	7,500	
	Cash		7,725
	Paid note with interest, including accrued interest payable.		

c. The pending lawsuit should be disclosed in the financial statement notes. Although the loss is probable no liability can be accrued since the loss cannot be reasonably estimated.

d.

Dec. 31	Income Taxes Expense	50,000	
	Income Taxes Payable		40,000
	Deferred Income Tax Liability		10,000
	To record added income tax expense and the deferred tax liability.		

e.

$$\text{Times interest earned} = \frac{\text{Income before interest and taxes}}{\text{Interest expense}}$$

$$\text{Income before interest} = \text{Net income} + \text{Interest expense} + \text{Income taxes expense}$$

$$\text{Times interest earned} = \frac{\$1{,}000{,}000 + \$275{,}000 + \$225{,}000}{\$275{,}000} = \underline{\underline{5.45 \text{ times}}}$$

f.

Nov. 30	Salaries Expense	3,000.00	
	FICA Social Security Taxes Payable (6.2%)		186.00
	FICA Medicare Taxes Payable (1.45%)		43.50
	Employees' Federal Income Taxes Payable		800.00
	Employees' State Income Taxes Payable		200.00
	Employees' Medical Insurance Payable		35.00
	Employees' United Way Payable		10.00
	Accrued Payroll Payable		1,725.50
	To record Sally Kline's payroll for the pay period ended November 30.		

g.

Nov. 1	Cash	5,000	
	Notes Payable		5,000
	Borrowed cash with a 60-day, 14% note.		

When the note and interest are paid 60 days later, Kern Company records this entry:

Dec. 31	Notes Payable	5,000.00	
	Interest Expense	116.67	
	Cash		5,116.67
	Paid note with interest ($5,000 × 14% × 60/360).		

h.

Dec. 16	Cash	2,000.00	
	Discount on Notes Payable	50.00	
	Notes Payable		2,050.00
	Borrowed cash with a 60-day, noninterest-bearing note.		
Dec. 31	Interest Expense	12.50	
	Discount on Notes Payable		12.50
	To record accrued interest on note payable (15/60 days × $50).		

When the note matures on February 14, 2000, Kern Company records this entry:

2000			
Feb. 14	Interest Expense (45/60 days × $50)	37.50	
	Notes Payable	2,050.00	
	Cash		2,050.00
	Discount on Notes Payable		37.50
	Paid note with interest.		

Payroll Reports, Records, and Procedures

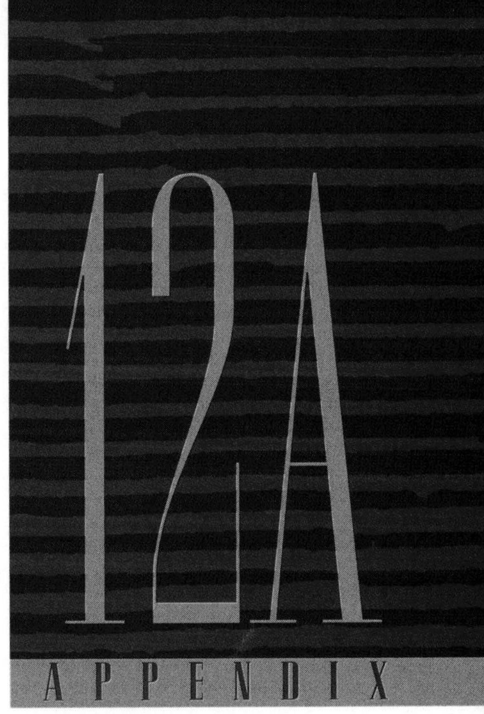

Learning Objectives

Conceptual

C5 Identify and describe payroll reporting.

C6 Identify and describe payroll records.

Procedural

P5 Compute payroll taxes.

P6 Record payment of payroll.

Understanding payroll procedures and keeping adequate payroll reports and records is essential to a company's success. Many companies now use accounting software to maintain their payroll records. This appendix focuses on payroll accounting and its reports, records, and procedures. We also show how accounting software helps with payroll reporting and analysis.

Payroll Reports

Most employees and employers are required to pay local, state, and federal payroll taxes. Payroll expenses involve liabilities to individual employees, to federal and state governments, and to other organizations such as insurance companies. Beyond paying these liabilities, employers are required to prepare and submit reports explaining how these payments are computed.

Reporting FICA Taxes and Income Tax

The Federal Insurance Contributions Act (FICA) requires each employer to file an Internal Revenue Service (IRS) **Form 941,** the **Employer's Quarterly Federal Tax Return.** Form 941 is filed within one month after the end of each calendar quarter. A Form 941 is shown in Exhibit 12A.1 for Phoenix Sales & Service, a landscape maintenance company.

Companies often use accounting software to maintain payroll records. We use an off-the-shelf program, **PeachTree Accounting for Windows,** to generate many of the reports in this section. But several other programs can produce the same reports. Accounting software is helpful in tracking payroll transactions and reporting the accumulated information on Form 941.

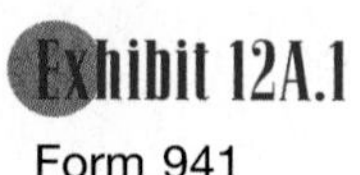
Exhibit 12A.1
Form 941

Form **941** (Rev. January 1996)
Department of the Treasury
Internal Revenue Service (O)

4141

Employer's Quarterly Federal Tax Return
▶ See separate instructions for information on completing this return.
Please type or print.

Enter state code for state in which deposits made ▶ (see page 3 of instructions).

Name (as distinguished from trade name): Phoenix Sales and Service
Date quarter ended: Dec. 31, 1998
Trade name, if any
Employer identification number: 86-3214587
Address (number and street): 1214 Mill Road, Phoenix, AZ 85621, USA
City, State, and ZIP code

OMB No. 1545-0029
T
FF
FD
FP
I
T

If address is different from prior return, check here ▶ ☐

IRS Use

If you do not have to file returns in the future, check here ▶ ☐ and enter date final wages paid ▶
If you are a seasonal employer, see Seasonal employers on page 1 of the instructions and check here ▶

Line	Description			Line	Amount
1	Number of employees (except household) employed in the pay period that includes March 12th ▶				
2	Total wages and tips, plus other compensation			2	36,599.00
3	Total income tax withheld from wages, tips and sick pay			3	3,056.47
4	Adjustment of withheld income tax for preceding quarters of calendar year			4	
5	Adjusted total of income tax withheld (line 3 as adjusted by line 4—see instructions)			5	3,056.47
6a	Taxable social security wages	$ 36,599.00	× 12.4% (.124) =	6a	4,538.28
b	Taxable social security tips	$	× 12.4% (.124) =	6a	
7	Taxable Medicare wages and tips	$ 36,599.00	× 2.9% (.029) =	7	1,061.36
8	Total social security and Medicare taxes (add lines 6a, 6b, and 7). Check here if wages are not subject to social security and/or Medicare tax ▶ ☐			8	5,599.64
9	Adjustment of social security and Medicare taxes (see instructions for required explanation) Sick Pay $ ____ ± Fractions of Cents $ ____ ± Other $ ____ =			9	
10	Adjusted total of social security and Medicare taxes (line 8 as adjusted by line 9—see instructions)			10	5,599.64
11	**Total taxes** (add lines 5 and 10)			11	8,656.11
12	Advance earned income credit (EIC) payments made to employees, if any			12	
13	Net taxes (subtract line 12 from line 11). **This should equal line 17, column (d) below** (or line D of Schedule B (Form 941))			13	8,656.11
14	Total deposits for quarter, including overpayment applied from a prior quarter			14	8,656.11
15	**Balance due** (subtract line 14 from line 13). See instructions			15	

16 **Overpayment,** if line 14 is more than line 13, enter excess here ▶ $ 0.00
and check if to be: ☐ Applied to next return **OR** ☐ Refunded.
- **All filers:** If line 13 is less than $500, you need not complete line 17 or Schedule B.
- **Semiweekly schedule depositors:** Complete Schedule B and check here ▶ ☐
- **Monthly schedule depositors:** Complete line 17, columns (a) through (d), and check here ▶ ☐

17 Monthly Summary of Federal Tax Liability.			
(a) First month liability	(b) Second month liability	(c) Third month liability	(d) Total liability for quarter
3,079.11	2,049.76	3,527.24	8,656.11

Sign Here — Under penalties of perjury, I declare that I have examined this return, including accompanying schedules and statements, and to the best of my knowledge and belief, it is true, correct, and complete.
Signature ▶ Print your Name and Title ▶ Date ▶

For Paperwork Reduction Act Notice, see page 1 of separate instructions. Cat. No. 17001Z Form **941** (Rev. 1-96)

On line 2 of Form 941 the employer reports the total wages and salaries subject to income tax withholding.[12] The income tax withheld is reported on lines 3 and 5. The combined amount of employees' and employer's FICA (Social Security) taxes for Phoenix Sales & Service is reported on line 6a: taxable Social Security wages, $36,599.00 × 12.4% = $4,538.28. The 12.4% is the sum of the Social Security tax withheld for 1998, computed as 6.2% tax withheld from the employees' wages for the quarter plus the 6.2% tax levied on the employer. The combined amount of employees' Medicare wages is reported on line 7. The 2.9% is the sum of 1.45% withheld from employees' wages for the quarter plus 1.45% tax levied on the employer. Total FICA taxes are reported on lines 8 and 10. They are added to total income taxes withheld of $3,056.47 to yield a total $8,656.11.

---

[12] For brevity, this appendix uses "wages" to refer to both "wages and salaries."

For 1998, income up to $68,400 is subject to Social Security tax. There is no income limit on amounts subject to Medicare tax. Congress sets annual limits on the amount owed for Social Security tax. The total of amounts deposited in a **federal depository bank** is subtracted to determine if a balance remains to be paid. Federal depository banks are authorized to accept deposits of amounts payable to the federal government.

Deposit requirements depend on the amount of tax owed. When the sum of FICA taxes plus the employees' income taxes is less than $500 for a quarter, the taxes can be paid when Form 941 is filed. Companies with large payrolls are often required to pay monthly or semiweekly. Also, if taxes owed are $100,000 or more at the end of any day, they must be paid by the end of the next banking day.

Reporting FUTA Taxes and SUTA Taxes

An employer's federal unemployment taxes (FUTA) are reported on an annual basis by filing an **Annual Federal Unemployment Tax Return,** IRS **Form 940.** It must be mailed on or before January 31 following the end of each tax year. Ten more days are allowed for filing if all required tax deposits are made on a timely basis and the full amount of the tax is paid on or before January 31. Payments of FUTA are made quarterly to a federal depository bank if the total amount due exceeds $100. If $100 or less is due, the taxes are remitted annually with Form 940.

Requirements for paying and reporting of state unemployment taxes (SUTA) vary depending on the laws of each state. But most states require filing quarterly payments and reports.

Reporting Wages and Salaries

Employers are required to give each employee an annual report of the employee's wages subject to FICA and federal income taxes along with the amounts of these taxes withheld. This report is called a **Wage and Tax Statement** or **Form W-2.** It must be given to employees before January 31 following the year covered by the report. Exhibit 12A.2 shows Form W-2 for Phoenix Sales & Service.

Copies of the W-2 Form must be sent to the Social Security Administration. Here they post to each employee's Social Security account the amount of an employee's wages subject to FICA tax and FICA tax withheld. These posted amounts become the basis for determining an employee's retirement and survivors' benefits. The Social Security Ad-

Exhibit 12A.2

Form W-2

a Control number	OMB No. 1545-0008		
AR101			
b Employer's identification number 86-3214587		1 Wages, tips, other compensation 4910.00	2 Federal income tax withheld 333.37
c Employer's name, address, and ZIP code Phoenix Sales and Service 1214 Mill Road Phoenix, AZ 85621 USA		3 Social security wages 4910.00	4 Social security tax withheld 304.42
		5 Medicare wages and tips 4910.00	6 Medicare tax withheld 71.20
		7 Social security tips	8 Allocated tips
d Employee's social security number 333-22-9999		9 Advance EIC payment	10 Dependent care benefits
e Employee's name, address, and ZIP code Robert Austin 18 Roosevelt Blvd., Apt C Tempe, AZ 86322		11 Nonqualified plans	12 Benefits included in box 1
		13	14 Other
		15 Statutory employee ☐ Deceased ☐ Pension plan ☐ Legal rep. ☐ Hshld. emp. ☐ Subtotal ☐ Deferred compensation ☐	

16 State	Employer's state I.D. No.	17 State wages, tips, etc.	18 State income tax	19 Locality name	20 Local wages, tips, etc.	21 Local income tax
AZ	13-902319	4910.00	26.68			

Department of the Treasury—Internal Revenue Service

Form **W-2** Wage and Tax Statement

Copy 1 For State, City, or Local Tax Department

ministration also transmits to the IRS the amount of each employee's wages subject to federal income tax and the amount of taxes withheld.

15. What determines the amount deducted from an employee's wages for federal income taxes?

Answer—p. 530

Payroll Records

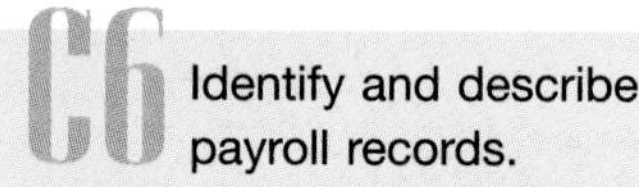

Identify and describe payroll records.

Employers must keep certain payroll records in addition to the reporting and paying of taxes. These records usually include a payroll register. Good records also require an individual earnings report for each employee.

Payroll Register

A **payroll register** shows the pay period dates, hours worked, gross pay, deductions, and net pay of each employee for every pay period. Exhibit 12A.3 shows a payroll register for Phoenix Sales & Service. There is a three-line heading and a one-line explanation of this report. The report is organized into nine columns:

Col. 1 Employee identification (ID); Employee name; Social Security number (SS No); Reference (check number); Date (date check issued)

Col. 2 Pay Type (regular or overtime hours)

Exhibit 12A.3

Payroll Register

Phoenix Sales and Service
Payroll Register
For the Period From Oct. 1, 1998 to Oct. 8, 1998

Employee ID Employee SS No Reference Date	Pay Type	Pay Hrs	Pay Amt	Amount	Gross State SUI_ER	Fed_Income Soc_Sec_ER	Soc_Sec Medicare_ER	Medicare FUTA_ER
AR101 Robert Austin 333-22-9999 9001 10/8/98	Regular	40.00	400.00	338.09	400.00 -2.32 -10.80	-28.99 -24.80	-24.80 -5.80	-5.80 -3.20
CJ102 Judy Cross 299-11-9201 9002 10/8/98	Regular Overtime	40.00 1.00	560.00 21.00	479.35	581.00 -4.24 -15.69	-52.97 -36.02	-36.02 -8.42	-8.42 -4.65
DJ103 John Diaz 444-11-9090 9003 10/8/98	Regular Overtime	40.00 2.00	560.00 42.00	503.75	602.00 -3.87 -16.25	-48.33 -37.32	-37.32 -8.73	-8.73 -4.82
KK104 Kay Keife 909-11-3344 9004 10/8/98	Regular	40.00	560.00	443.10	560.00 -5.49 -15.12	-68.57 -34.72	-34.72 -8.12	-8.12 -4.48
ML105 Lee Miller 444-56-3211 9005 10/8/98	Regular	40.00	560.00	480.18	560.00 -2.74 -15.12	-34.24 -34.72	-34.72 -8.12	-8.12 -4.48
SD106 Dale Sears 909-33-1234 9006 10/8/98	Regular	40.00	560.00	433.10	560.00 -5.49 -15.12	-68.57 -34.72	-34.72 -8.12	-8.12 -4.48
Summary Total 10/1/98 thru 10/31/98	Regular Overtime	240.00 3.00	3,200.00 63.00	2,687.57	3,263.00 -24.15 -88.10	-301.67 -202.30	-202.30 -47.31	47.31 -26.11

Col. 3 Pay Hrs (number of hours worked)[13]

Col. 4 Pay Amt (amount of gross pay)[14]

Col. 5 Amount (Net pay = Gross pay less amounts withheld)

Col. 6 Gross pay; State (state income tax withheld); SUI_ER (state unemployment tax withheld)

Col. 7 Fed_Income (federal income tax withheld); Soc_Sec-ER (Social Security tax withheld, employer)

Col. 8 Soc_Sec (social security tax withheld); Medicare_ER (Medicare tax withheld, employer)

Col. 9 Medicare (Medicare tax withheld); FUTA_ER (FUTA tax withheld, employer)

Exhibit 12A.3 shows separate columns for each type of payroll deduction and for expense accounts where payroll costs are charged. A payroll register includes all data necessary to record payroll in the General Journal. In some accounting software programs such as **PeachTree,** the entries to record payroll are made in a Payroll Journal.

Payroll Check

Payment of payroll is usually done by check or a funds transfer. Exhibit 12A.4 shows a *payroll check* for an employee of Phoenix Sales & Service. This check is accompanied with a detachable *statement of earnings* showing gross pay, deductions, and net pay.

Employee Earnings Report

An **employee earnings report** is a cumulative record of an employee's hours worked, gross earnings, deductions, and net pay. Payroll information on this report is taken from the payroll register. The employee earnings report for Phoenix Sales & Service is shown in Exhibit 12A.5.

Exhibit 12A.4

Check and Statement of Earnings

EMPLOYEE NO.	EMPLOYEE NAME	SOCIAL SECURITY NO.	PAY PERIOD END	CHECK DATE
AR101	Robert Austin	333-22-9999	10/8/98	10/8/98

ITEM	RATE	HOURS	TOTAL	ITEM	THIS CHECK	YEAR TO DATE
Regular	10.00	40.00	400.00	Gross	400.00	400.00
Overtime	15.00			Fed_Income	-28.99	-28.99
				Soc_Sec	-24.80	-24.80
				Medicare	-5.80	-5.80
				State	-2.32	-2.32

HOURS WORKED	GROSS THIS PERIOD	GROSS YEAR TO DATE	NET CHECK	CHECK No.
40.00	400.00	400.00	$338.09	9001

(Detach and retain for your records)

PHOENIX SALES AND SERVICE
1214 Mill Road
Phoenix, AZ 85621
602-555-8900

Phoenix Bank and Trust
Pheonix, AZ 85621
3312-87044

9001

CHECK NO.	DATE	AMOUNT
9001	Oct 8, 1998	**************$338.09*

Three Hundred Thirty–Eight and 9/100 Dollars

PAY TO THE ORDER OF Robert Austin
18 Roosevelt Blvd., Apt C
Tempe, AZ 86322

Mary Wills
AUTHORIZED SIGNATURE

[13] "Pay Hrs" column reports regular hours worked by each employee. If overtime hours apply, the Pay Hrs column shows a second line with overtime hours worked.

[14] The "Pay Amt" column shows regular hours worked on the first line multiplied by the regular pay rate. This equals regular pay. Overtime hours multiplied by the overtime premium rate equals overtime premium pay reported on the second line. If employers are engaged in interstate commerce, the federal law sets a minimum overtime rate of pay to employees. In 1998, this minimum wage is $5.15 per hour. For this company, the minimum overtime premium is 50% of the regular rate for hours worked in excess of 40 per week. This means workers earn at least 150% of their regular rate for hours in excess of 40 per week.

Exhibit 12A.5

Employee Earnings Report

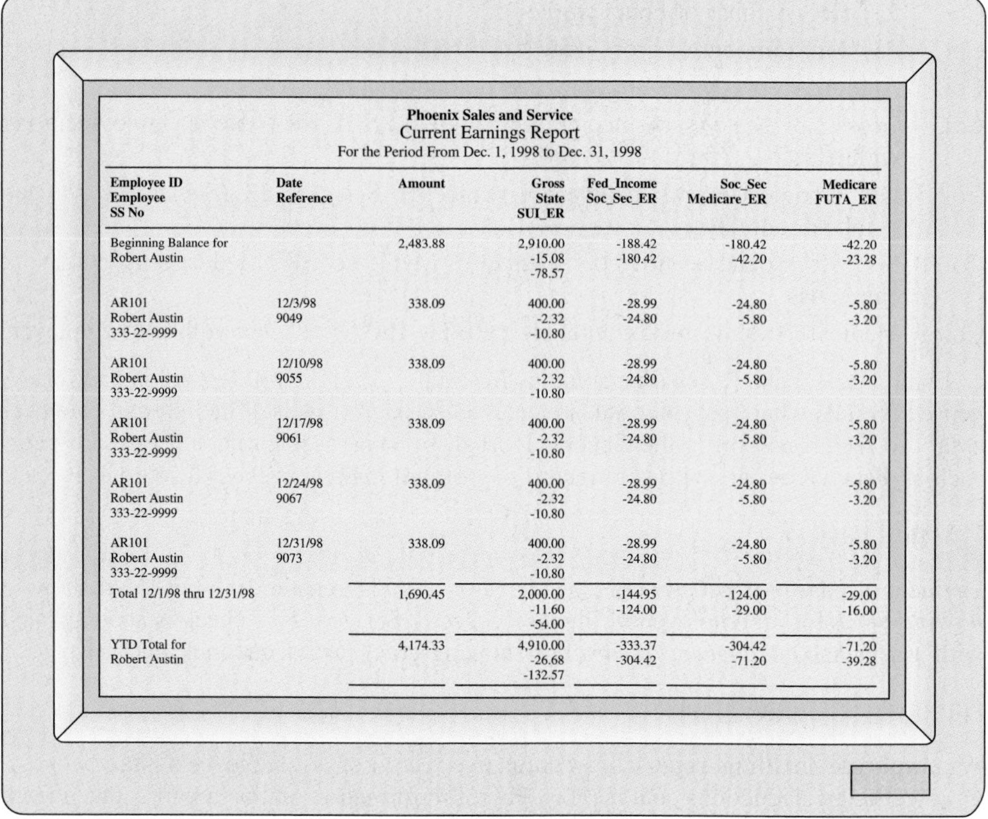

Phoenix Sales and Service
Current Earnings Report
For the Period From Dec. 1, 1998 to Dec. 31, 1998

Employee ID Employee SS No	Date Reference	Amount	Gross State SUI_ER	Fed_Income Soc_Sec_ER	Soc_Sec Medicare_ER	Medicare FUTA_ER
Beginning Balance for Robert Austin		2,483.88	2,910.00 -15.08 -78.57	-188.42 -180.42	-180.42 -42.20	-42.20 -23.28
AR101 Robert Austin 333-22-9999	12/3/98 9049	338.09	400.00 -2.32 -10.80	-28.99 -24.80	-24.80 -5.80	-5.80 -3.20
AR101 Robert Austin 333-22-9999	12/10/98 9055	338.09	400.00 -2.32 -10.80	-28.99 -24.80	-24.80 -5.80	-5.80 -3.20
AR101 Robert Austin 333-22-9999	12/17/98 9061	338.09	400.00 -2.32 -10.80	-28.99 -24.80	-24.80 -5.80	-5.80 -3.20
AR101 Robert Austin 333-22-9999	12/24/98 9067	338.09	400.00 -2.32 -10.80	-28.99 -24.80	-24.80 -5.80	-5.80 -3.20
AR101 Robert Austin 333-22-9999	12/31/98 9073	338.09	400.00 -2.32 -10.80	-28.99 -24.80	-24.80 -5.80	-5.80 -3.20
Total 12/1/98 thru 12/31/98		1,690.45	2,000.00 -11.60 -54.00	-144.95 -124.00	-124.00 -29.00	-29.00 -16.00
YTD Total for Robert Austin		4,174.33	4,910.00 -26.68 -132.57	-333.37 -304.42	-304.42 -71.20	-71.20 -39.28

This report accumulates information showing when an employee's earnings reach the tax-exempt points for FICA, FUTA, and SUTA taxes. It also gives data employers need to prepare Form W-2.

High-Tech Reports
Computer technology is used to produce many payroll reports including the (a) payroll register, (b) payroll checks, and (c) employee earnings report.

Payroll Procedures

Employers must be able to compute federal income tax in accounting for payroll. This section explains how we compute this tax and shows how to use a payroll bank account.

Computing Federal Income Tax

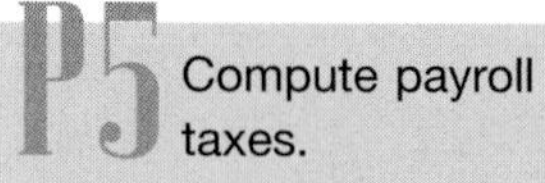

Compute payroll taxes.

To compute the amount of tax withheld from each employee's wages, we need to determine both the employee's wages earned and the employee's number of *withholding allowances.* Each employee records the number of withholding allowances claimed on a withholding allowance certificate, **Form W-4,** filed with the employer. When the number of withholding allowances increases, the amount of income tax withheld decreases.

Employers often use a **wage bracket withholding table** similar to the one shown in Exhibit 12A.6 to compute the federal income taxes withheld from each employee's gross pay. The table in Exhibit 12A.6 is for a single employee who is paid weekly. Tables are also provided for married employees and for biweekly, semimonthly, and monthly pay periods (most payroll software includes these tables). When using a wage bracket withholding table to compute federal income tax withheld from an employee's gross wages, we need to locate an employee's wage bracket within the first two columns of the table. We then find the amount withheld by looking in the withholding allowance column for that employee.

Exhibit 12A.6

Wage Bracket Withholding Table

SINGLE Persons—WEEKLY Payroll Period
(For Wages Paid in 1998)

If the wages are –		And the number of withholding allowances claimed is —										
At least	But less than	0	1	2	3	4	5	6	7	8	9	10
		The amount of income tax to be withheld is —										
$600	**$610**	95	80	68	60	52	44	36	29	21	13	5
610	**620**	97	83	69	61	53	46	38	30	22	15	7
620	**630**	100	86	71	63	55	47	39	32	24	16	8
630	**640**	103	88	74	64	56	49	41	33	25	18	10
640	**650**	106	91	77	66	58	50	42	35	27	19	11
650	**660**	109	94	79	67	59	52	44	36	28	21	13
660	**670**	111	97	82	69	61	53	45	38	30	22	14
670	**680**	114	100	85	70	62	55	47	39	31	24	16
680	**690**	117	102	88	73	64	56	48	41	33	25	17
690	**700**	120	105	91	76	65	58	50	42	34	27	19
700	**710**	123	108	93	79	67	59	51	44	36	28	20
710	**720**	125	111	96	82	68	61	53	45	37	30	22
720	**730**	128	114	99	84	70	62	54	47	39	31	23
730	**740**	130	116	102	87	73	64	56	48	40	33	25
740	**750**	134	119	105	90	76	65	57	50	42	34	26

Flash back

16. What amount of income tax is withheld from the salary of a single employee with 3 withholding allowances who earns $675 in a week? (*Hint:* Use the wage bracket withholding table in Exhibit 12A.6.)

Answer—p. 530

Payroll Bank Account

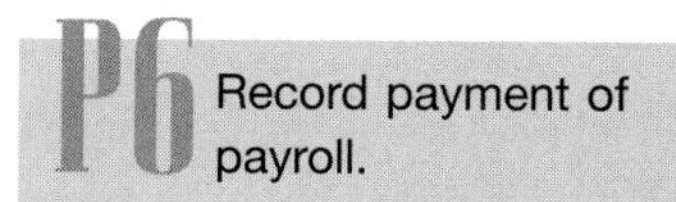
Record payment of payroll.

Companies with few employees often pay employees with checks drawn on the company's regular bank account. But a company with many employees often uses a special **payroll bank account** to pay employees. When this account is used, a company either (a) draws one check for total payroll on the regular bank account and deposits it in the payroll bank account or (b) executes an *electronic funds transfer* to the payroll bank account. The entry to record this transaction is:

Oct. 8	Accrued Payroll Payable	2,687.57	
	Cash		2,687.57
	To transfer cash to the payroll bank account.		

Assets	=	Liabilities	+	Equity
−2,687.57		−2,687.57		

Individual payroll checks are drawn on the company's payroll bank account. Because only one check for the total payroll is drawn on the regular bank account each payday, use of a special payroll bank account helps with internal control. It also helps with reconciling the regular bank account.

When companies use a payroll bank account, they usually include check numbers in the payroll register. Our **PeachTree**-generated payroll register shows check numbers in column 1. For instance, Exhibit 12A.3 reports that check no. 9001 is issued to Robert Austin. With this information, the payroll register serves as a supplementary record of wages earned by and paid to employees.

Flash back

17. Which of the following steps are executed when a company draws one check for total payroll and deposits it in a special payroll bank account?

a. Record information on the payroll register with a General Journal entry.
b. Write a check to the payroll bank account for the total payroll and record it with a debit to Accrued Payroll Payable and a credit to Cash.
c. Deposit a check for the total payroll in the payroll bank account.
d. Issue individual payroll checks drawn on the payroll bank account.
e. All of the above.

Answer—p. 530

Summary of Appendix 12A

C5 Identify and describe payroll reporting. Employers report FICA taxes and federal income tax withholdings using Form 941 on a quarterly basis. FUTA taxes are reported annually on Form 940. Annual earnings and deduction information are reported to each employee and to the federal government on Form W-2.

C6 Identify and describe payroll records. An employer's payroll records include a payroll register for each pay period, payroll checks and statements of earnings, and an employee earnings report for each employee. Many companies use accounting software to maintain payroll records. We showed certain reports generated by accounting software including: payroll register, employee earnings report, payroll check, Form 941, and Form W-2.

P5 Compute payroll taxes. Federal income tax deductions depend on the employee's earnings and the number of withholding allowances claimed. Wage bracket withholding tables are available for pay periods of different lengths and for several classes of employees such as single or married.

P6 Record payment of payroll. Employers with a large number of employees often use a separate payroll bank account. When this is done, the payment of employees is recorded with a single credit to Cash. This entry records the transfer of cash from the regular checking account to the payroll checking account.

Guidance Answers to  *backs*

15. An employees' gross earnings and number of withholding allowances determine the amount deducted for federal income taxes.

16. $70

17. e

Glossary

Capital lease a lease that gives the lessee the risks and benefits normally associated with ownership. (p. 516).

Contingent liability a potential liability that depends on a future event arising out of a past transaction. (p. 513).

Current liability obligations due within a year or the company's operating cycle, whichever is longer; paid using current assets or by creating other current liabilities. (p. 496).

Current portion of long-term debt the portion of long-term debt that is due within one year; reported under current liabilities on the balance sheet. (p. 516).

Deferred income tax liability payments of income taxes that are deferred until future years because of temporary differences between GAAP and tax rules. (p. 512).

Discount on note payable the difference between the face value of a note payable and the amount borrowed; represents interest that will be paid on the note over its life. (p. 500).

Employee benefits additional compensation paid to or on behalf of employees, such as premiums for medical, dental, life, and disability insurance; additional benefits include contributions to pension plans, stock purchase plans, and vacations. (p. 510).

Employee earnings report a record of an employee's net pay, gross pay, deductions, and year-to-date information. (p. 527).

Estimated liability obligation of an uncertain amount that can be reasonably estimated. (p. 509).

Federal depository bank a bank authorized to accept deposits of amounts payable to the federal government. (p. 525).

Federal Unemployment Taxes (FUTA) payroll taxes on employers assessed by the federal government to support the federal unemployment insurance program. (p. 508).

FICA taxes taxes assessed on both employers and employees under the Federal Insurance Contributions Act; these taxes fund Social Security and Medicare programs. (p. 505).

Form 940 IRS form used to report an employer's federal unemployment taxes (FUTA) on an annual filing basis. (p. 525).

Form 941 IRS form filed within one month after the end of each calendar quarter to report FICA taxes owed and remitted. (p. 523).

Form W-2 a yearly report given by an employer to each employee showing the employee's wages subject to FICA and federal income taxes along with the annual amounts of these taxes withheld. (p. 525).

Gross pay total compensation earned by an employee. (p. 504).

Known liabilities obligations of a company with little uncertainty; set by agreements, contracts, or laws; also called *definitely determinable liabilities.* (p. 498).

Long-term liability obligations of a company not requiring payment within one year or the company's operating cycle, if longer. (p. 497).

Merit rating a rating assigned to an employer by a state according to the employer's past record for creating or not creating unemployment. (p. 508).

Net pay gross pay less all deductions; also called *take home pay.* (p. 504).

Noninterest-bearing note a note that does not have a stated rate of interest; the interest is included in the face value of the note. (p. 501).

Operating lease a lease that is not a capital lease; costs of operating leases are reported as rent expense. (p. 516).

Payroll bank account a special bank account a company uses solely for paying employees, by depositing in the account each pay period an amount equal to the total employees' net pay and drawing the employees' payroll checks on that account. (p. 504).

Payroll deductions amounts withheld from an employee's gross pay; also called *withholdings.* (p. 504).

Payroll register a record for a pay period that shows the pay period dates and the regular and overtime hours worked, gross pay, net pay for each employee, and deductions. (p. 526).

Short-term note payable current obligation in the form of a written promissory note. (p. 499).

State Unemployment Taxes (SUTA) payroll taxes on employers assessed by states to support unemployment insurance programs. (p. 508).

Times interest earned the ratio of a company's income before interest divided by the amount of interest charges; used to evaluate the risk of being committed to make interest payments when income varies. (p. 517).

Wage bracket withholding table a table that shows the amounts of income tax to be withheld from employees' wages at various levels of earnings. (p. 528).

Warranty an agreement that obligates the seller or manufacturer to repair or replace a product when it breaks or otherwise fails to perform properly within a specified period. (p. 509).

The superscript letter [A] identifies assignment material based on Appendix 12A.

Questions

1. What is the difference between a current and a long-term liability?
2. What is an estimated liability?
3. What are the three important questions concerning the certainty of liabilities?
4. Suppose that a company has a facility located in an area where disastrous weather conditions often occur. Should it report a probable loss from a future disaster as a liability on its balance sheet? Why or why not?
5. Why are warranty liabilities usually recognized on the balance sheet as liabilities even when they are uncertain?
6. What is an employer's unemployment merit rating? Why are these ratings assigned to employers?
7. Which payroll taxes are the responsibility of the employee and which taxes are the responsibility of the employer?
8. How can a lease create an asset and a liability for the lessee?

9.[A] What determines the amount deducted from an employee's wages for federal income taxes?

10.[A] What is a wage bracket withholding table?

11.[A] What amount of income tax should be withheld from the salary of a single employee with two withholding allowances who earned $725 per week? What if the employee earned $625 and had no withholding allowances? (Use the wage bracket withholding table in Exhibit 12A.6 to find the answers.)

12.[A] List two IRS reports that can be generated using PeachTree Accounting for Windows.

13.[A] What is the 1998 income limit for Social Security tax?

14.[A] What is the combined amount of the employees' and employer's social security tax?

15. Identify the note on commitments and contingencies in the financial statements of **NIKE** in Appendix A. What are the amounts of minimum annual rental commitments under noncancelable operating leases in future years?
16. Refer to **Reebok**'s balance sheet in Appendix A. What accounts related to income taxes are on the balance sheet? Identify the meaning of each income tax account you identify.
17. Refer to **America Online**'s balance sheet in Appendix A. What account on America Online's balance sheet shows a liability to employees for future benefits?

Quick Study

QS 12-1
Distinguishing between current and long-term liabilities
C1, C2

Which of the following items are normally classified as a current liability for a company that has a 15-month operating cycle?

a. Salaries payable.
b. Note payable due in 18 months.
c. Bonds payable that mature in two years.
d. Note payable due in 11 months.
e. Portion of a long-term note that is due to be paid in 15 months.

QS 12-2
Recording warranty expenses
P4

On September 11, 1999, Valentine's Department Store sells a lawn mower for $400 with a one-year warranty that covers parts. Warranty expense is estimated at 5% of sales. On July 24, 2000, the mower is brought in for repairs covered under the warranty requiring $35 in parts. Prepare the July 24, 2000, entry to record the warranty repairs.

QS 12-3
Recording employer payroll taxes
P3

Yeager Co. has five employees, each of whom earns $2,600 per month. FICA Social Security taxes are 6.2% of gross pay and FICA Medicare taxes are 1.45% of gross pay. FUTA taxes are 0.8% and SUTA taxes are 2.8% of the first $7,000 paid to each employee. Prepare the March 31 journal entry to record March payroll taxes expense.

QS 12-4
Interest-bearing note transactions
P1

On November 7, 2000, the Eggemeyer Company borrowed $150,000 and signed a 90-day, 8% note payable with a face value of $150,000. Compute (a) the accrued interest payable on December 31, 2000, and (b) present the journal entry to record the paying of the note at maturity.

QS 12-5
Noninterest-bearing note transactions

Katie Company signs a noninterest-bearing note promising to pay $4,100 within 60 days after December 16. Record the signing of the note, the interest accrual on December 31, and the repayment of the note on February 14. ($100 of interest is included in the note's face value of $4,100.)

QS 12-6
Recording deferred income tax liability
P4

Longfellow Company has made and recorded its quarterly income tax payments. After a final review of taxes for the year, the company identifies an additional $30,000 of income tax expense that should be recorded. A portion of this additional expense, $8,000, is deferrable to future years. Record the year-end income tax expense adjusting entry for Longfellow Company.

QS 12-7
Accounting for contingent liabilities

The following legal claims exist for the CT Company. Identify the accounting treatment for each legal claim as either (a) a liability that is recorded or (b) an item described in the notes to the financial statements.

1. CT company estimates that this lawsuit could result in damages of $1,000,000; it is reasonably possible that the plaintiff will win the case.
2. CT faces a probable loss on a pending lawsuit; the amount of the judgment cannot be reasonably estimated.
3. CT company estimates damages of this case at $2,500,000 with a high probability of losing the case.

QS 12-8
Accounting for sales taxes
C2

Palm Computing sells $5,000 of merchandise for cash on September 30. The sales tax law requires Palm Computing to collect 4% sales tax on every dollar of merchandise sold. Record the entry for the $5,000 sale and its applicable sales tax. Also record the entry that shows the remittance of the 4% tax on this sale to the state government on October 15.

QS 12-9
Unearned revenue
C2

Ticketmaster receives $4,000,000 in advance cash ticket sales for a four date-tour for the Rolling Stones. Record the advance ticket sales as a lump sum as of October 31. Record the revenue earned for the first concert date played on November 5.

QS 12-10
Times interest earned
A1

Compute the times interest earned for Trevor Company, which has income after interest expense of $1,575,500 and interest expense of $137,000. Trevor Co. is a proprietorship.

Exercises

Exercise 12-1
Classifying liabilities
C1

The following items appear on the balance sheet of a company with a two-month operating cycle. Identify the proper classification of each item as follows: a *C* if it is a current liability, an *L* if it is a long-term liability, or an *N* if it is not a liability.

_____ **a.** Income taxes payable.
_____ **b.** Notes receivable (due in 30 days).
_____ **c.** Mortgage payable (due in 12 months).
_____ **d.** Notes payable (due in 6 to 12 months).
_____ **e.** Bonds payable (mature in 5 years).
_____ **f.** Notes payable (due in 13 to 24 months).
_____ **g.** Wages payable.
_____ **h.** Accounts receivable.
_____ **i.** Notes payable (due in 120 days).
_____ **j.** Mortgage payable (due after 13 months).

Exercise 12-2
Warranty expense and liability
P4

Mikado Co. sold a copier with a cost of $3,800 and a two-year parts warranty to a customer on August 16, 1999, for $5,500 cash. Mikado uses the perpetual system to account for inventories. Based on prior experience, Mikado expects to eventually incur warranty costs equal to 4% of this selling price. The liability expense is recorded with an adjusting entry at the end of the year. On November 22, 2000, the copier required on-site repairs that were completed the same day. The cost of the repairs consisted of $199 for the materials taken from the parts inventory. These were the only repairs required in 2000 for this copier.

a. How much warranty expense does the company report in 1999 for this copier?
b. How much is the warranty liability for this copier as of December 31, 1999?
c. How much warranty expense does the company report in 2000 for this copier?
d. How much is the warranty liability for this copier as of December 31, 2000?
e. Prepare the journal entries that are made to record (1) the sale; (2) the adjustment on December 31, 1999, to record the warranty expense; and (3) the repairs that occurred in November 2000. Mikado uses the perpetual method to account for merchandise inventories.

Exercise 12-3
Accounting for income taxes

Constructo Company prepares interim financial statements each month. As part of its accounting process, estimated income taxes are accrued each month for 30% of the current month's net income. The estimated income taxes are paid in the first month of each quarter for the amount accrued in the prior quarter. The following information is available for the last quarter of 1999:

a. October net income	$27,900
November net income	18,200
December net income	32,700

b. After tax computations are completed in early January, the accountant determines that the Income Taxes Payable account balance should be $29,100 on December 31.

Required

1. Determine the amount of the adjustment needed on December 31 to produce the proper ending balance in the Income Taxes Payable account.
2. Prepare journal entries to record the adjustment to the Income Taxes Payable account and to record the January 15 payment of the fourth-quarter taxes.

Exercise 12-4
Computing payroll taxes
P2, P3

Natkin Co. has one employee on its payroll. The employee and the company are subject to the following taxes:

Tax	Rate	Applied to
FICA—Social Security	6.20%	First $68,400
FICA—Medicare	1.45	Gross pay
FUTA	0.80	First $7,000
SUTA	2.90	First $7,000

Compute Natkin's amounts of these four taxes on the employee's gross earnings for September under each of three independent situations *a.* through *c.*:

	Gross Pay through August	Gross Pay for September
a.	$ 6,400	$ 800
b.	18,200	2,100
c.	60,600	7,900

Exercise 12-5
Payroll-related journal entries
P2, P3

Using the data in situation *a* of Exercise 12–4, prepare the employer's September 30 journal entries to record (a) the gross earnings and withholdings for the employee and (b) the employer's payroll taxes. The employee's federal income taxes withheld are $90.

Exercise 12-6
Interest-bearing and noninterest-bearing notes payable
P1

Portable Systems borrowed $94,000 on May 15, 1999, for 60 days at 12% interest by signing a note.

a. On what date will this note mature?

b. How much interest expense results from this note? (Assume a 360-day year.)

c. Suppose the face value of the note equals $94,000, the principal of the loan. Prepare the journal entries to record issuing the note and paying it at maturity.

d. Suppose the face value of the note is $95,880 which includes both the principal of the loan ($94,000) and the interest to be paid at maturity. Prepare the journal entries to record issuing the note and paying it at maturity.

Exercise 12-7
Interest-bearing and noninterest-bearing short-term notes payable with year-end adjustments

P1

Accura Co. borrowed $150,000 on November 1, 1999, for 90 days at 9% interest by signing a note.

a. On what date will this note mature?

b. How much interest expense results from this note in 1999? (Assume a 360-day year.)

c. How much interest expense results from this note in 2000? (Assume a 360-day year.)

d. Suppose the face value of the note equals $150,000, the principal of the loan. Prepare the journal entries to record issuing the note, to accrue interest at the end of 1999, and to record paying the note at maturity.

e. Suppose the face value of the note is $153,375 which includes both the principal of the loan ($150,000) and the interest to be paid at maturity. Prepare the journal entries to record issuing the note, to accrue interest at the end of 1999, and to record paying the note at maturity.

Exercise 12-8
Adjusting entries for liabilities

P4

Analysis of Lawrence Co. reveals the following information. Prepare any necessary adjusting entries at December 31, 2000, the company's year-end.

1. During December, Lawrence Company sold 3,000 units of a product that carries a 60-day warranty. December sales for this product total $120,000. The company expects 8% of the units to need repair under warranty, and it estimates that the average repair cost per unit will be $15.

2. The company is being sued by a disgruntled employee. Legal advisors believe it is probable that the company will have to pay damages, the amount of which cannot be reasonably estimated.

3. Employees earn vacation pay at a rate of one day per month. During December, 20 employees qualify for vacation pay. Their average daily wage is $120 per employee.

4. Lawrence Company has guaranteed the $5,000 debt of a supplier. It is not probable that the supplier will default on the debt.

5. The company records an adjusting entry for previously unrecorded cash sales and sales taxes payable at a rate of 5% on $2,000,000.

6. The company recognizes that $50,000 of $100,000 received in advance for products is now earned.

Exercise 12-9
Financial statement presentation—current liabilities

C2

Rashad Company has the following selected accounts after posting adjusting entries:

Accounts payable	$50,000
Notes payable, 6 month	10,000
Accumulated depreciation, Equipment	20,000
Accrued payroll payable	5,000
Estimated warranty liability	12,000
Discount on notes payable, 6 month	1,000
Payroll taxes expense	2,000
Mortgage payable	100,000

Prepare the current liability section of Rashad Company's balance sheet, assuming $10,000 of the mortgage payable is due within the next year.

Exercise 12-10
Computing and interpreting times interest earned

A1

Use the following information on proprietorships *a* through *f* to compute times interest earned:

	Net Income (Loss)	Interest Expense
a.	$140,000	$48,000
b.	140,000	15,000
c.	140,000	8,000
d.	265,000	12,000
e.	79,000	12,000
f.	(4,000)	12,000

Analysis Component

Which of the cases demonstrates the strongest ability to pay interest charges as they come due?

Exercise 12-11A
Computing gross and net pay
P5, P6

Norma Bailey, an unmarried employee of a company, worked 48 hours during the week ended January 12. Her pay rate is $12 per hour, and her wages are subject to no deductions other than FICA Social Security, FICA Medicare, and federal income taxes. She claims two withholding allowances. Compute her regular pay, overtime premium pay (overtime premium is 50% of regular rate for hours in excess of 40 per week), gross pay, FICA tax deduction at an assumed rate of 6.2% for the Social Security portion and 1.45% for the Medicare portion, income tax deduction (use the wage bracket withholding table of Exhibit 12A.6), total deductions, and net pay.

Exercise 12-12A
Payroll entry
P6

Using Exercise 12–11, show the journal entry to record the transfer of cash to the payroll bank account.

Exercise 12-13A
Computing net pay
P5

The payroll records of Press-A-Software show the following information about Jerry Wood, an employee, for the weekly pay period ending September 30, 1998:

Total earnings current pay period	$ 735
Cumulate earnings previous pay period	$9,700

Jerry Wood is single and claims one deduction. Compute his Social Security tax (6.2%), Medicare tax (1.45%), federal income tax withholding, and state income tax (0.5%). State income tax is 0.5 percent on $9,000 maximum.

Problems

Problem 12-1
Estimating product warranty expenses and liabilities
P4

On October 29, 1999, Sharp Products began to purchase electric razors for resale at $80 each. Sharp uses the perpetual method to account for inventories. The razors are covered under a warranty that requires the company to replace any nonworking razor within 90 days. When a razor is returned, the company simply throws it away and mails a new one from inventory to the customer. The company's cost for a new razor is $18. The manufacturer has advised the company to expect warranty costs to equal 7% of sales. The following transactions and events occurred in 1999 and 2000:

1999

Nov.	11	Sold 75 razors for $6,000 cash.
	30	Recognized warranty expense for November with an adjusting entry.
Dec.	9	Replaced 15 razors that were returned under the warranty.
	16	Sold 210 razors for $16,800 cash.
	29	Replaced 30 razors that were returned under the warranty.
	31	Recognized warranty expense for December with an adjusting entry.

2000

Jan.	5	Sold 130 razors for $10,400 cash.
	17	Replaced 50 razors that were returned under the warranty.
	31	Recognized warranty expense for January with an adjusting entry.

Required

1. How much warranty expense is reported for November and December 1999?
2. How much warranty expense is reported for January 2000?
3. What is the balance of the Estimated Warranty Liability account as of December 31, 1999?
4. What is the balance of the Estimated Warranty Liability account as of January 31, 2000?
5. Prepare journal entries to record these transactions and adjustments.

Check Figure 12/31/1999 estimated liability balance, $786 credit

Problem 12-2
Short-term notes payable transactions and entries

Langley Company entered into the following transactions involving short-term liabilities in 1999 and 2000:

1999

Apr. 20 Purchased merchandise on credit from Franken, Inc., for $38,500. The terms were 1/10, n/30. Langley uses a perpetual inventory system.

May 19 Replaced the account payable to Franken with a 90-day note bearing 9% annual interest. Langley paid $8,500 cash, with the result that the balance of the note was $30,000.

July 8 Borrowed $60,000 from North Bank by signing a 120-day interest-bearing note for $60,000. The note's annual interest rate is 10%.

? Paid the note to Franken, Inc., at maturity.

? Paid the note to North Bank at maturity.

Nov. 28 Signed a noninterest-bearing note with a face value of $21,280 from Crockett Bank that matures in 60 days. The face value includes a principal amount of $21,000.

Dec. 31 Recorded an adjusting entry for the accrual of interest on the note to Crockett Bank.

2000

? Paid the note to Crockett Bank at maturity.

Required

1. Determine the maturity dates of the three notes described above.

2. Determine the interest due at maturity for the three notes. (Assume a 360-day year.)

3. Determine the interest to be recorded in the adjusting entry at the end of 1999.

4. Determine the interest to be recorded in 2000.

5. Prepare journal entries for all the preceding transactions and events for years 1999–2000.

Check Figure Total interest for Crockett Bank note, $280

Problem 12-3
Payroll expenses, withholdings, and taxes

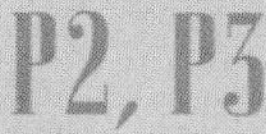

Legal Consultants pays its employees every week. The employees' gross earnings are subject to these taxes:

Tax	Rate	Applied To
FICA—Social Security	6.20%	First $68,400
FICA—Medicare	1.45	Gross pay
FUTA	0.80	First $7,000
SUTA	2.15	First $7,000

The company is preparing its payroll calculations for the week ended August 25. The payroll records show the following information for the company's four employees:

Name	Gross Pay Through 8/18	This Week Gross Pay	This Week Withholding Tax
Rose	$69,200	$1,800	$252
Chad	29,700	900	99
Mona	6,750	450	54
Jody	1,050	400	36

In addition to the gross pay, the company and each employee pay one-half of the weekly health insurance premium of $32 per employee. The company also contributes 8% of each employee's gross earnings to a pension fund.

Required

Use this information to compute the following for the week ended August 25 (round amounts to the nearest cent):

1. Each employee's FICA withholdings for Social Security.
2. Each employee's FICA withholdings for Medicare.
3. Employer's FICA taxes for Social Security.
4. Employer's FICA taxes for Medicare.
5. Employer's FUTA taxes.
6. Employer's SUTA taxes.
7. Each employee's take-home pay.
8. Employer's total payroll-related expense for each employee.

Check Figure Part 7: Total take-home pay, $2,885.02

Problem 12-4
Computing and analyzing times interest earned
A1

Here are condensed income statements for two different sole proprietorships:

Foxtrot Co.	
Sales	$500,000
Variable expenses (80%)	400,000
Net income before interest	$100,000
Interest expense (fixed)	30,000
Net income	$ 70,000

Tango Co.	
Sales	$500,000
Variable expenses (60%)	300,000
Net income before interest	$200,000
Interest expense (fixed)	130,000
Net income	$ 70,000

Required

Preparation Component

1. What is the times interest earned for Foxtrot Co.?
2. What is the times interest earned for Tango Co.?
3. What happens to each company's net income if sales increase by 30%?
4. What happens to each company's net income if sales increase by 50%?
5. What happens to each company's net income if sales increase by 80%?
6. What happens to each company's net income if sales decrease by 10%?
7. What happens to each company's net income if sales decrease by 20%?
8. What happens to each company's net income if sales decrease by 40%?

Check Figure Part 3: Net income for Foxtrot Co., $100,000 (a 43% increase)

Analysis Component

9. Comment on what you observe in relation to the fixed cost strategies of the two companies and the ratio values you computed in parts 1 and 2.

Problem 12-5[A]
Entries for payroll transactions
P5, P6

Vaughn Company has 10 employees, each of whom earns $2,600 per month and is paid on the last day of each month. All 10 have been employed continuously at this amount since January 1. Vaughn uses a payroll bank account and special payroll checks to pay its employees. On March 1, the following accounts and balances appeared in its ledger:

a. FICA—Social Security Taxes Payable, $3,224; FICA—Medicare Taxes Payable, $754. (The balances of these accounts represent the liabilities for both the employer's and employees' FICA taxes for the February payroll only.)
b. Employees' Federal Income Taxes Payable, $3,900 (liability for February only).
c. Federal Unemployment Taxes Payable, $416 (liability for January and February together).
d. State Unemployment Taxes Payable, $2,080 (liability for January and February together).

During March and April, the company had the following payroll transactions:

Mar. 15 Issued check payable to Union Bank, a federal depository bank authorized to accept employers' payments of FICA taxes and employee income tax withholdings. The $7,878 check is in payment of the February FICA and employee income taxes.

31 Prepared General Journal entries to record the March Payroll Record, which had the following column totals, and to transfer the funds from the regular bank account to the payroll bank account:

Salaries and Wages				Federal	Federal	
Office Salaries	Shop Wages	Gross Pay	FICA Taxes*	Income Taxes	Total Deductions	Net Pay
$10,400	$15,600	$26,000	$1,612 +$377	$3,900	$5,889	$20,111

*FICA taxes are Social Security and Medicare, respectively.

31 Issued checks payable to each employee in payment of the March payroll.

31 Prepared a General Journal entry to record the employer's payroll taxes resulting from the March payroll. The company has a merit rating that reduces its state unemployment tax rate to 4.0% of the first $7,000 paid each employee. The federal rate is 0.8%.

Apr. 15 Issued check payable to Union Bank in payment of the March FICA and employee income taxes.

15 Issued check to the State Tax Commission for the January, February, and March state unemployment taxes. Mailed the check along with the first quarter tax return to the State Tax Commission.

30 Issued check payable to Union Bank. The check is in payment of the employer's federal unemployment taxes for the first quarter of the year.

30 Mailed Form 941 to the IRS, reporting the FICA taxes and the employees' federal income tax withholdings for the first quarter.

Required

Prepare General Journal entries to record the transactions and events for March and April.

Problem 12-6^A^
Entries for payroll transactions

P5, P6

On January 8, the end of the first weekly pay period of the year, Prescott Company's Payroll Register showed that its employees had earned $11,380 of office salaries and $32,920 of sales salaries. Withholdings from the employees' salaries include FICA Social Security taxes at the rate of 6.2%, FICA Medicare taxes at the rate of 1.45%, $6,430 of federal income taxes, $670 of medical insurance deductions, and $420 of union dues. No employee earned more than $7,000.

Required

1. Calculate FICA Social Security taxes payable and FICA Medicare taxes payable. Prepare a General Journal entry to record Prescott Company's January 8 payroll.
2. Prepare a General Journal entry to record Prescott's payroll taxes resulting from the January 8 payroll. Prescott has a merit rating that reduces its state unemployment tax rate to 4.0% of the first $7,000 paid each employee. The federal unemployment tax rate is 0.8%.
3. Prescott Company uses a payroll bank account and special payroll checks in paying its employees. Prepare the General Journal entry to transfer funds equal to the payroll from the regular bank account to the payroll bank account.
4. After the entry in part 3 is journalized and posted, are additional journal entries required to record the payroll checks and pay all the employees?

Check Figure Part 3: Accrued Payroll Payable, $33,481.05 Dr.

Comprehensive Problem

Aardvark Exterminators

(Review of Chapters 1–12)

Aardvark Exterminators provides pest control services and sells extermination products manufactured by other companies. The following six-column table contains the company's unadjusted trial balance as of December 31, 2000.

AARDVARK EXTERMINATORS
December 31, 2000

	Unadjusted Trial Balance		Adjustments		Adjusted Trial Balance	
Cash	$ 17,000					
Accounts receivable	4,000					
Allowance for doubtful accounts		$ 828				
Merchandise inventory	11,700					
Trucks	32,000					
Accum. depreciation, Trucks		0				
Equipment	45,000					
Accum. deprec., Equipment		12,200				
Accounts payable		5,000				
Estimated warranty liability		1,500				
Unearned services revenue		0				
Long-term notes payable		15,000				
Discount on notes payable	3,974					
K. Jones, capital		59,600				
K. Jones, withdrawals	10,000					
Extermination services revenue		60,000				
Interest earned		872				
Sales		75,000				
Cost of goods sold	46,300					
Depreciation expense, Trucks	0					
Depreciation expense, Equip.	0					
Wages expense	35,000					
Interest expense	0					
Rent expense	9,000					
Bad debts expense	0					
Miscellaneous expenses	1,226					
Repairs expense	8,000					
Utilities expense	6,800					
Warranty expense	0					
Totals	$230,000	$230,000				

The following information applies to the company at the end of the current year:

a. The bank reconciliation as of December 31, 2000, includes these facts:

Balance per bank	$15,100
Balance per books	17,000
Outstanding checks	1,800
Deposit in transit	2,450
Interest earned	52
Service charges (miscellaneous expense)	15

Included with the bank statement was a canceled check that the company had failed to record. (The information in part *b* allows you to determine the amount of the check, which was a payment on account.)

b. An examination of customers' accounts shows that accounts totaling $679 should be written off as uncollectible. It is also determined that the ending balance of the Allowance for Doubtful Accounts should be $700.

c. A truck was purchased and placed in service on July 1, 2000. Its cost is being depreciated with the straight-line method using these facts and estimates:

Original cost	$32,000
Expected salvage value	8,000
Useful life (years)	4

d. Two items of equipment (a sprayer and an injector) were purchased and put into service early in January 1998. Their costs are being depreciated with the straight-line method using these facts and estimates:

	Sprayer	Injector
Original cost	$27,000	$18,000
Expected salvage value	3,000	2,500
Useful life (years)	8	5

e. On August 1, 2000, the company was paid $3,840 in advance to provide monthly service on an apartment complex for one year. The company began providing the services in August. When the cash was received, the full amount was credited to the Extermination Services Revenue account.

f. The company offers a warranty for the services it sells. The expected cost of providing warranty service is 2.5% of sales. No warranty expense has been recorded for 2000. All costs of servicing the warranties in 2000 were properly debited to the liability account.

g. The $15,000 long-term note is a five-year, noninterest-bearing note that was issued to First National Bank on December 31, 1998. The market interest rate on the date of the loan was 8% and interest expense (not yet recorded) is $882 for year 2000.

h. The ending inventory of merchandise was counted and determined to have a cost of $11,700. Aardvark uses a perpetual inventory system.

Required

1. Use the preceding information to determine amounts for the following items:
   a. Correct ending balance of Cash and the amount of the omitted check.
   b. Adjustment needed to obtain the correct ending balance of the Allowance for Doubtful Accounts.
   c. Annual depreciation expense for the truck that was acquired during the year (computed to the nearest month).
   d. Annual depreciation expense for the two items of equipment that were used during the year.
   e. Correct ending balances of the Extermination Services Revenue and Unearned Services Revenue accounts.
   f. Correct ending balances of the accounts for Warranty Expense and Estimated Warranty Liability.
   g. Correct ending balances of the accounts for Interest Expense and Discount on Notes Payable. (Round amounts to nearest whole dollar.)

2. Use the results of part 1 to complete the six-column table by first entering the appropriate adjustments for items *a* through *g* and then completing the adjusted trial balance columns. (Hint: Item *b* requires two entries.)

3. Present General Journal entries to record the adjustments entered on the six-column table. Assume that Aarkvark uses the closing entry approach to account for changes in Merchandise Inventory.

4. Prepare a single-step income statement, a statement of changes in owner's equity, and a classified balance sheet.

BEYOND THE NUMBERS

Reporting in Action

C3, A1

Refer to the financial statements and related information for **NIKE** in Appendix A. Answer the following questions by analyzing that information:

1. Compute times interest earned for the years ended May 31, 1997 and 1996. Comment on NIKE's ability to cover its interest expense.
2. Does NIKE's note on commitments provide information allowing one to determine whether the company has entered into any operating or capital leases?
3. What evidence would you look for as an indication that NIKE has any temporary differences between the income reported on the income statement and the income reported on its tax return? Can you find any evidence of these differences for NIKE?

Swoosh Ahead

4. Obtain access to NIKE's annual report for fiscal years ending after May 31, 1997. You can gain access to NIKE's annual report at its Web site **[www.nike.com]** or through the SEC's EDGAR database **[www.sec.gov].** Recompute NIKE's times interest earned for any additional years ending after May 31, 1997, that you have access to.

Comparative Analysis

A1

Reebok

Both **NIKE** and **Reebok** design, produce, market, and sell sports footwear and apparel. Key comparative figures ($ millions) for these two organizations follow:

	NIKE		Reebok	
Key Figures*	**1997**	**1996**	**1996**	**1995**
Net income	$796	$553	$139	$165
Income tax expense	499	346	84	100
Interest expense	52	39	42	26

*NIKE figures are from its annual reports for fiscal years ended May 31, 1997 and 1996.
Reebok figures are from its annual reports for fiscal years ended December 31, 1996 and 1995.

Required

1. Compute times interest earned using the two years' data shown for each company.
2. Comment on which company appears stronger in its ability to commit to interest payments if income should vary.

Communicating in Practice

C3

Mike Thatcher is a sales manager for an automobile dealership in Chicago. Mike earns a bonus each year based on revenue from the number of autos sold in the year less related warranty expenses. The quality of automobiles sold each year seems to vary since the warranty expenses for autos sold is highly variable. Actual warranty expenses have varied over the past 10 years from a low of 3% of an automobile's selling price to a high of 10%. In the past, Mike has tended toward estimating warranty expenses on the high end just to be conservative. It is the end of the year and once again he must work with the dealership's accountant in arriving at the warranty expense accrual for the cars sold this year.

1. Does the warranty accrual decision present any kind of ethical dilemma for Mike Thatcher?
2. Since warranty expenses are variable, what percent do you think Mike should choose for this year? Justify your response.

Ethics Challenge

P4

Norma Yager is the manager of accounting and finance for a manufacturing company. At the end of the year she must determine whether and how to describe the company's contingencies in financial statements. Her manager, Jonas Perlman, raised an objection to a specific contingency in Yager's proposal. Perlman objects to recognizing an expense and a liability for warranty service on units of a new product that was introduced in the company's fourth quarter. His comment was, "There is no way we can estimate this warranty cost. We don't owe anybody anything until the products break down and are returned for service. Let's report an expense if and when we do the repairs."

Required

Prepare a written response for Yager to send to Perlman addressing his objection in a one-page memorandum dated December 21.

Taking It to the Net

P2

Visit the **Social Security Administration's** Web site at **www.ssa.gov.** Find the link on the homepage to the *Social Security Handbook.* Once you have located the handbook consult the chapter "Wages." In the wages chapter look for information regarding the maximum earnings creditable in any one year. Maximum earnings serve as the threshold amount after which employees and employers do not owe tax during a given year. How does the 1997 level of maximum earnings compare to 1987, 1977, 1967, 1957, and 1947? How are yearly increases in earnings subject to the Social Security tax determined? Is it possible that *all* earnings of a given year will someday be subject to Social Security tax? Why or why not?

Teamwork in Action

P1, C2

Your team is in business and you need to borrow $6,000 for short-term needs. You have been shopping banks for a loan, and you have the following options:

(A) Sign a $6,000, 90-day, 11% interest-bearing note.

(B) Sign a $6,175.5, 90-day, noninterest-bearing note.

Required

1. Discuss these two options and determine the best choice. Ensure that all teammates concur with the decision and understand the rationale. Explain your decision to your instructor.
2. Each member of the team is to prepare *one* of the following entries:
   a. Option A—at date of issuance.
   b. Option B—at date of issuance.
   c. Option A—at maturity date.
   d. Option B—at maturity date.
3. In rotation, each member is to explain the entry prepared in (2) to the team. Ensure that all team members concur with and understand the entries.
4. Assume the funds are borrowed on December 1 and your business has a fiscal year that coincides with a calendar year. Each member of the team is to prepare *one* of the following entries:
   a. Option A—the year-end adjustment.
   b. Option B—the year-end adjustment.
   c. Option A—at maturity date.
   d. Option B—at maturity date.
5. In rotation, each member is to explain the entry prepared in (4) to the team. Ensure that all team members concur with and understand the entries.

Hitting the Road

P2

Check your local phone book or the **Social Security Administration** Web site **(www.ssa.gov)** to locate the Social Security office nearest to you. Visit the office to request a personal earnings and benefits estimate form. Fill out the form and mail according to the instructions. In several weeks, you will receive a statement from the Social Security Administration regarding your earnings history and future Social Security benefits you can receive. (Note: Formerly the request could be made online. The online request service has been discontinued and is now under review by the Social Security Administration due to security concerns.) It is good to request an earnings and benefit statement every 5 to 10 years to make sure you have received proper credit for all wages earned and for which you and your employer have paid taxes into the system.

Business Week Activity

P4

Read the article "Electronic Stores Get a Cruel Shock," in the January 14, 1991, issue of ***Business Week***.

Required

1. Describe the accounting guidelines companies must follow in recognizing revenue from the sale of extended warranties on consumer products.
2. Contrast the rules now in effect with former rules with respect to their effect on the income statements of companies selling extended warranties.
3. What accounting principle likely governed the FASB's decision to change the accounting rules for recognizing warranty revenue?
4. Is the rule on accounting for revenue from warranties consistent with the rules on accounting for expenses related to warranties?

CHAPTER 13

Partnerships and Corporations

A Look Back

Chapter 12 focused on current and long-term liabilities. We explained how liabilities are identified, computed, recorded, and reported in financial statements.

A Look at This Chapter

This chapter explains both the partnership and corporate forms of organization. Important characteristics of both forms of organization are described along with the accounting concepts and procedures for their most basic transactions.

A Look Ahead

Chapter 14 extends our discussion of corporate accounting to dividends and other equity transactions. We also explain how income, earnings per share, and retained earnings are reported.

Chapter Outline

Section 1—Partnerships

- **Partnership Form of Organization**
  - Characteristics of Partnerships
  - Organizations with Partnership Characteristics
- **Basic Partnership Accounting**
  - Organizing a Partnership
  - Dividing Income or Loss
  - Partnership Financial Statements
- **Admission and Withdrawal of Partners**
  - Admission of a Partner
  - Withdrawal of a Partner
  - Death of a Partner
- **Liquidation of a Partnership**
  - No Capital Deficiency
  - Capital Deficiency

Section 2—Corporations

- **Corporate Form of Organization**
  - Characteristics of Corporations
  - Organizing a Corporation
  - Management of a Corporation
  - Rights of Stockholders
  - Stock of a Corporation
  - Basics of Capital Stock
  - Stockholders' Equity
- **Common Stock**
  - Issuing Par Value Stock
  - Issuing No-Par Value Stock
  - Issuing Stated Value Stock
  - Issuing Stock for Noncash Assets
  - Issuing Stock through Subscriptions
- **Preferred Stock**
  - Issuing Preferred Stock
  - Dividend Preference
  - Convertible Preferred Stock
  - Callable Preferred Stock
  - Motivation for Preferred Stock
- **Using the Information—Book Value per Share**

Blue Fish

FRENCHTOWN, NJ—What do we say to a 17-year-old who wants some extra spending money? Maybe, check the "help wanted" at Wal-Mart, Kmart, McDonald's, or Sears. But do we ever say, "What do **you** want to do?" Well, Jennifer Paige Barclay did what she wanted to do. Barclay decided to block print cotton T-shirts and dresses in her parents' garage to be sold at craft shows and festivals. Hardly the recipe for immediate success.

But Barclay's efforts paid off. In her first full year of business, at the ripe old age of 18, her sales climbed to $110,000. In her second year, with a loan cosigned by her parents, she set up a small factory in a leased building in Frenchtown. Later that second year she incorporated her company and called it **Blue Fish.** Barclay has never looked back. The Junior Chamber of Commerce recently named her one of its "Ten Outstanding Young Americans."

Blue Fish's clothing is funky, flowing, and artsy. Each product is individually block-printed by hand with evocative designs and symbols and signed by the artist. Blue Fish's clothing isn't cheap—a T-shirt can cost $58 and a dress, $200 to $300—but the style holds up from year to year. Barclay says her clothing "is about something that has meaning" made from "products that are sourced responsibly." All clothing is made with natural dyes and uses only organic cotton. Also, in its recent 10K report, Blue Fish declares it "intends to donate up to 10% of its net income" to socially responsible organizations.

To finance growth of her company, Barclay recently sold common stock to the public. The idea, she says, is to "sell it to people who'd been supporting us so far as customers." Blue Fish's stock was priced at $5 per share. The stock issuance has raised more than a $4 million kitty for her to work with and expand her business. Barclay already has plans for new lines and new stores.

If all goes well, the biggest challenge will be "not losing our identity as we grow," says Barclay. For a company that swims against the mainstream, keeping its uniqueness should be easy.

Source: *Business Week,* December 22, 1997, and Blue Fish Clothing's *10K Report.*

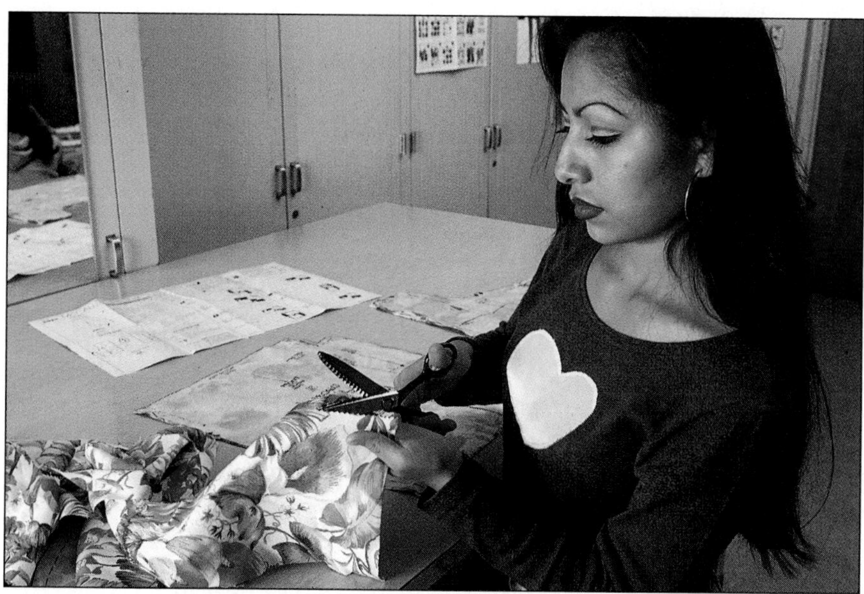

Learning Objectives

Conceptual

C1 Identify characteristics of partnerships and similar organizations.

C2 Identify characteristics of corporations and their organization.

C3 Describe the components of stockholders' equity.

C4 Explain characteristics of common and preferred stock.

Analytical

A1 Compute book value and explain its use in analysis.

Procedural

P1 Prepare entries when forming a partnership.

P2 Allocate and record income and loss among partners.

P3 Account for the admission and withdrawal of a partner.

P4 Prepare entries for partnership liquidation.

P5 Record the issuance of corporate stock.

P6 Distribute dividends between common stock and preferred stock.

CHAPTER PREVIEW

There are three common types of business organizations: corporations, partnerships, and proprietorships. Partnerships are similar to proprietorships, except they have more than one owner. This chapter explains partnerships and looks at several variations of them. These variations include limited partnerships, limited liability partnerships, "S" corporations, and limited liability companies. The chapter also looks at corporations. While corporations are fewest in number of the three types of organization, they transact more business than all the others combined. Corporations are very important players in our global economy, with dollar sales at least 10 times the combined sales of unincorporated companies. Understanding the advantages and disadvantages of these forms of business organization was important for Jennifer Barclay of **Blue Fish.** She chose to incorporate, but this is not always best. This chapter gives us information to make such a decision.

SECTION 1—PARTNERSHIPS

Partnership Form of Organization

C1 Identify characteristics of partnerships and similar organizations.

A **partnership** is an unincorporated association of two or more people to pursue a business for profit as co-owners. Many businesses are organized as partnerships. They are especially common in small retail and service businesses. Many professional practitioners also organize their practices as partnerships, including physicians, lawyers, and accountants.

Characteristics of Partnerships

Partnerships are an important type of organization because of certain advantages they offer with their unique characteristics. We describe these characteristics in this section.[1]

Voluntary Association

A partnership is a voluntary association between partners. Since joining a partnership involves increased risk to your personal financial position, your participation is voluntary.[2]

Partnership Agreement

Forming a partnership requires that two or more legally competent people (who are of age and of sound mental capacity) agree to be partners. Their agreement becomes a **partnership contract,** also called *articles of copartnership.* While it should be in writing, the contract is binding even if it is only expressed verbally.[3]

---

[1] Partnerships in which all partners have *mutual agency* and *unlimited liability* are called **general partnerships.** We explain these characteristics in this section.

[2] Some courts have ruled that partnerships are created by the actions of partners even when there is no expressed agreement to form one.

[3] Partnership agreements normally include details of the partners': (a) names and contributions, (b) rights and duties, (c) sharing of income and losses, (d) withdrawal arrangement, (e) dispute procedures, (f) admission and withdrawal of new partners, and (g) rights and duties in the event a partner dies.

Limited Life

The life of a partnership is limited. Death, bankruptcy, or any event taking away the ability of a partner to enter into or fulfill a contract ends a partnership. A partnership can also be terminated at will by any one of the partners.

Taxation

A partnership is not subject to taxes on its income. It has the same tax status as a proprietorship. The income or loss of a partnership is allocated to the partners according to the partnership agreement and is included for determining the taxable income on each partner's tax return. Allocation of partnership income or loss is done each year whether or not cash is distributed to partners.

Mutual Agency

The relationship between partners in a general partnership involves **mutual agency.** This means each partner is a fully authorized agent of the partnership. As its agent, a partner can commit or bind the partnership to any contract within the scope of the partnership's business. For instance, a partner in a merchandising business can sign contracts binding the partnership to buy merchandise, lease a store building, borrow money, or hire employees. These activities are all within the scope of business of a merchandising firm. But a partner in a law firm, acting alone, cannot bind the other partners to a contract to buy snowboards for resale or rent an apartment for parties. These actions are outside the normal scope of a law firm's business.

Partners can agree to limit the power of any one or more of the partners to negotiate contracts for the partnership. This agreement is binding on the partners and on outsiders who know it exists. But it is not binding on outsiders who don't know it exists. Outsiders unaware of the agreement have the right to assume each partner has normal agency powers for the partnership. Because mutual agency exposes all partners to the risk of unwise actions by any one partner, people should evaluate each partner before agreeing to join a partnership.

Unlimited Liability

When a general partnership can't pay its debts, the creditors usually can apply their claims to *personal* assets of partners. If a partner doesn't have enough assets to meet his or her share of the partnership debt, the creditors can apply their claims to the assets of the other partners. Because partners can be called on to pay the debts of a partnership, each partner is said to have **unlimited liability** for the partnership's debts. Mutual agency and unlimited liability are two main reasons why most partnerships have only a few members.

Co-Ownership of Property

Partnership assets are owned jointly by all partners. Any investment by a partner becomes the joint property of all partners. Partners have a claim on partnership assets based on their capital account.

Organizations with Partnership Characteristics

There exist organizations that combine certain characteristics of partnerships with other forms of organizations. We discuss several of these organizational forms in this section.

Limited Partnerships

Some individuals who want to invest in a partnership are unwilling to accept the risk of unlimited liability. Their needs may be met with a **limited partnership.** This type of organization is identified in its name with the words "Limited Partnership," or "Ltd.," or "L.P." A limited partnership has two classes of partners, general and limited. At least one partner must be a **general partner** who assumes management duties and unlimited liability for the debts of the partnership. The **limited partners** have no personal liability beyond the amounts they invest in the partnership. A limited partnership is managed by the general partner(s). Limited partners have no active role except as specified in the partnership agreement. A limited partnership agreement often specifies unique procedures for allocating income and losses between general and limited partners. The same basic accounting procedures are used for both limited and general partnerships.

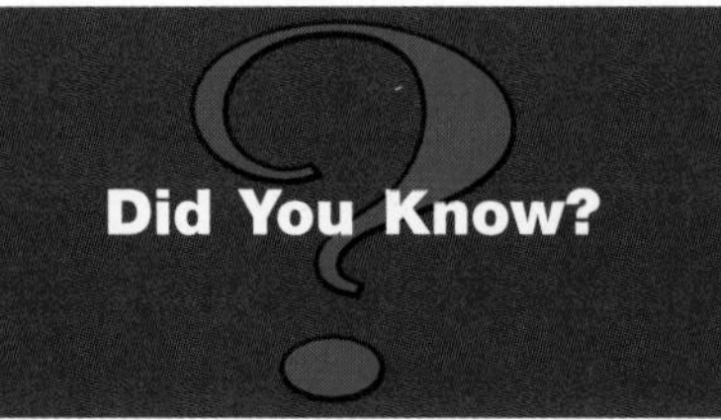

Celtic Partners

The **Boston Celtics** is organized as a limited partnership. It owns and operates the Boston Celtics NBA team. The general partner of the Boston Celtics is Celtics, Inc. The chairman of the board of Celtics, Inc., is Paul E. Gaston.

Limited Liability Partnerships

Most states allow professionals such as lawyers and accountants to form a **limited liability partnership.** This is identified in its name with the words "Limited Liability Partnership" or by "L.L.P." This type of partnership is designed to protect innocent partners from malpractice or negligence claims resulting from the acts of another partner. When a partner provides service resulting in a malpractice claim, that partner has personal liability for the claim. The remaining partners who were not responsible for the actions resulting in the claim are not personally liable for it. But most states hold all partners personally liability for other partnership debts. Accounting for a limited liability partnership is the same as for a general partnership.

"S" Corporations

Certain corporations with 75 or fewer stockholders can elect to be treated like a partnership for income tax purposes. These corporations are called Sub-Chapter S or simply **"S" corporations.** This distinguishes them from other corporations, called Sub-Chapter C or simply **"C" corporations.** "S" corporations provide stockholders with the same limited liability feature as "C" corporations. The advantage to an "S" corporation is that it doesn't pay income taxes. If stockholders work for an "S" corporation, their salaries are treated as expenses of the corporation. The remaining income or loss of the corporation is allocated to stockholders for inclusion on their personal tax returns. Except for "C" corporations having to account for income tax expenses and liabilities, the accounting procedures are the same for both "S" and "C" corporations.

Limited Liability Companies

A new, promising form of business organization is the **limited liability company.** The names of these businesses usually include the words "Limited Liability Company" or an abbreviation such as "L.L.C." or "L.C." This form of business has certain features like a corporation and others like a limited partnership. The owners, who are called members, are protected with the same limited liability feature as owners of corporations. While limited partners cannot actively participate in the management of a limited partnership, the members of a limited liability company can assume an active management role. A limited liability company usually has a limited life. For income tax purposes, the IRS usually classifies a limited liability company as a partnership. This classification depends on factors such as whether the members' equity interests are freely transferable and whether the company has continuity of life.

Tax Relief
New IRS rules let individuals set themselves up as LLCs. Previously, an LLC needed at least two people. There's also a PLLC for professionals. [Source: "You, Too, Can Be an LLC" *Business Week November 17, 1997.*]

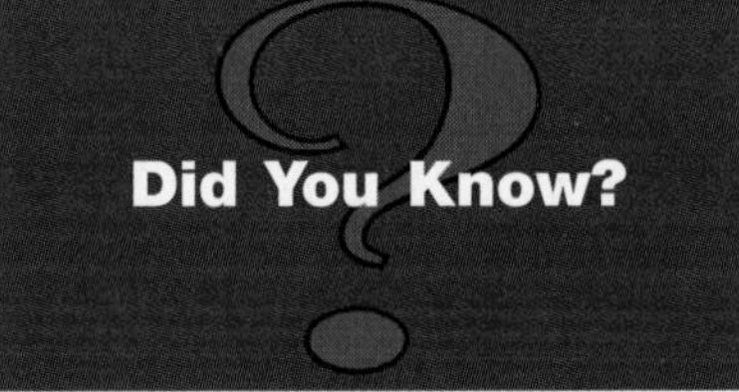
Did You Know?

A limited liability company's accounting system is designed to help management comply with the dictates of the articles of organization and company regulations adopted by its members. The accounting system also must provide information to support the company's compliance with state and federal laws, including taxation. This means the system usually has some features associated with corporate accounting and others associated with partnership accounting. For instance, depending on the articles of organization and company regulations, the allocation of income between members can be similar to either a corporation or a partnership.

Flash back

1. A partnership is terminated in the event: *(a)* a partnership agreement is not in writing; *(b)* a partner dies; *(c)* a partner exercises mutual agency.
2. What does the term *unlimited liability* mean when applied to a general partnership?
3. Which of the following forms of business organization do not provide limited liability to all of its owners: *(a)* "C" corporation; *(b)* "S" corporation; *(c)* limited liability company; *(d)* limited partnership?

Answers—p. 580

Basic Partnership Accounting

Accounting for a partnership is the same as accounting for a proprietorship except for transactions directly affecting partners' equity. Because ownership rights in a partnership are divided among partners, partnership accounting:

- Uses a capital account for each partner.
- Uses a withdrawals account for each partner.
- Allocates net income or loss to partners according to the partnership agreement.

This section describes partnership accounting for organizing a partnership, distributing income and losses, and preparing financial statements.

Organizing a Partnership

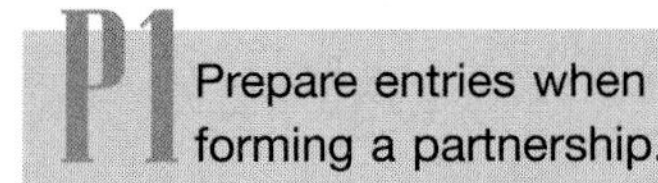
P1 Prepare entries when forming a partnership.

When partners invest in a partnership, their capital accounts are credited for the invested amounts. Partners can invest both assets and liabilities. Each partner's investment is recorded at an agreed-upon value, normally the fair market value of the assets and liabilities at their date of contribution.

To illustrate, in 1999 Kate Steeley and David Breck organized as a partnership called **BOARDS.** Their business offers year-round facilities for skateboarding and snowboarding. Steeley's initial net investment in BOARDS is $30,000, made up of cash ($7,000), boarding facilities ($33,000), and a note payable reflecting a bank loan for the business of ($10,000). Breck's initial investment is cash of $10,000. These amounts are the values agreed upon by both partners. The entries to record these investments are:

Assets = Liabilities + Equity
+7,000 +10,000 +30,000
+33,000

Steeley's Investment

Jan. 11	Cash	7,000	
	Boarding facilities	33,000	
	Note payable		10,000
	K. Steeley, Capital		30,000
	To record investment of Steeley.		

Assets = Liabilities + Equity
+10,000 +10,000

Breck's Investment

Jan. 11	Cash	10,000	
	D. Breck, Capital		10,000
	To record investment of Breck.		

After a partnership is formed, accounting for its transactions is similar to accounting for those of a proprietorship. Chapters 2 through 5 describe the basic accounting procedures for a proprietorship, and they apply here as well. The minor differences include:

1. Partners' withdrawals of assets are debited to their personal withdrawals accounts.
2. In closing the accounts at the end of a period, the partners' capital accounts are credited or debited for their shares of net income or loss.
3. The withdrawals account of each partner is closed to that partner's capital account.

These procedures are similar to those used for a single proprietorship, except that separate capital and withdrawals accounts are kept for each partner.

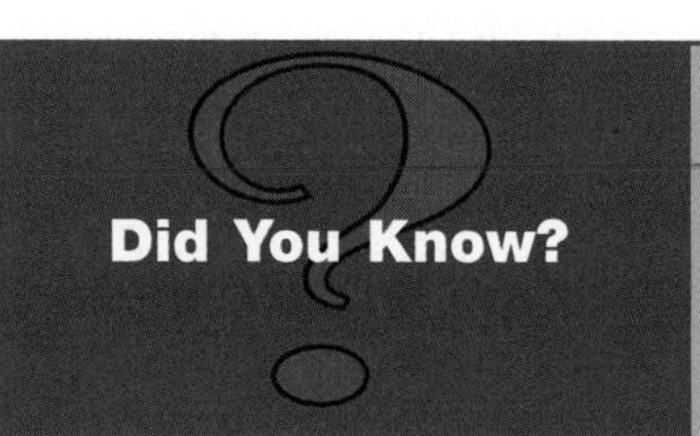

B-Ball Partners

The Boston Celtics' limited partnership for March 31, 1998 reported the following partners' capital balances ($ thousands):

General Partners	$315,339
Limited Partners	$271,037

Dividing Income or Loss

P2 Allocate and record income and loss among partners.

Partners are not employees of the partnership. They are its owners. If partners devote their time and services to their partnership, they are understood to do so for profit, not for salary. This means when partners compute the net income of a partnership, salaries to partners are not expenses on the income statement. But when net income or loss of a partnership is allocated among partners, the partners can agree to base part of their allocation on salary allowances reflecting the relative values of services they provide. Partners also can agree that division of partnership earnings includes a return based on the amount invested. For instance, since Steeley contributed three times the investment of Breck, it is only fair that this fact be considered when earnings are allocated between them. Their partnership agreement can also provide for interest allowances based on their capital balances. Like salary allowances, these interest allowances are not expenses on the income statement.

Partners can agree to any method of dividing income or loss. But in the absence of an agreement, the law says that income or loss of a partnership is shared equally by the partners. If partners agree on how they share income but say nothing about losses, then losses are shared in the same way as income. Several methods of sharing partnership income or loss are used. Three frequently used methods to divide income or loss use:

(1) a stated fractional basis, (2) the ratio of capital investments, or (3) salary and interest allowances and any remainder in a fixed ratio.

Allocated on a Stated Fractional Basis

One way to divide partnership income or loss is to give each partner a fraction of the total. Partners must agree on the fractional share each receives. Assume the partnership agreement of K. Steeley and D. Breck says Steeley receives two-thirds and Breck one-third of partnership income and loss. If their partnership's net income is $60,000, it is allocated to the partners, and the Income Summary account is closed, with the following entry:

Dec. 31	Income Summary	60,000	
	K. Steeley, Capital		40,000
	D. Breck, Capital		20,000
	To allocate income and close the Income Summary account.		

Assets = Liabilities + Equity
−60,000
+40,000
+20,000

Allocated on the Ratio of Capital Investments

Partners can also allocate income or loss on the ratio of the relative capital investments of each partner. If Steeley and Breck agreed to share earnings on the ratio of their capital investments—Steeley's $30,000 and Breck's $10,000—this means Steeley receives three-fourths of any income or loss ($30,000/$40,000) and Breck receives one-fourth ($10,000/$40,000).

Allocated Using Salaries, Interest, and a Fixed Ratio

Service contributions and capital contributions of partners often are not equal. Salary allowances can make up for differences in service contributions. Also, interest allowances can make up for unequal capital contributions. When both service and capital contributions are unequal, the allocation of income and loss can include both salary and interest allowances.

In Kate Steeley and David Breck's new partnership, assume both agree that Steeley's services are worth an annual salary of $36,000. Since Breck is less experienced in the business, his services are valued at $24,000 annually. To compensate Steeley and Breck fairly given these differences in service and capital contributions, they agree to share income or loss as follows:

1. Annual salary allowances of $36,000 to Steeley and $24,000 to Breck.
2. Interest allowances equal to 10% of each partner's beginning-of-year capital balance.
3. Any remaining balance of income or loss to be shared equally.

The provisions for salaries and interest in this partnership agreement are called *allowances.* Allowances are *not* reported as salaries and interest expense on the income statement. They are simply a means of dividing the income or loss of a partnership.

Illustration When Income Exceeds Allowance

If BOARDS has first year income of $70,000 and Steeley and Breck apply the partnership agreement above, they would allocate income or loss as shown in Exhibit 13.1. Steeley gets $42,000 and Breck gets $28,000 of the $70,000 total.

Illustration When Allowances Exceed Income

The method of sharing agreed to by Steeley and Breck must be followed even if net income is less than the total of the allowances. If BOARDS first year net income is $50,000 instead of $70,000, it is allocated to the partners as shown in Exhibit 13.2. Computations for salaries and interest are identical to those in Exhibit 13.1. When we apply the total allowances against net income, the balance of income is negative. This negative balance ($14,000) is allocated in the same manner as a positive balance. The equal shar-

Exhibit 13.1

Dividing Income When Income Exceeds Allowances

	Steeley	Breck	Total
Net income			$70,000
Salary allowances:			
Steeley	$36,000		
Breck		$24,000	
Interest allowances:			
Steeley (10% on $30,000)	3,000		
Breck (10% on $10,000)		1,000	
Total salaries and interest	39,000	25,000	64,000
Balance of income			**$ 6,000**
Balance allocated equally:			
Steeley	3,000		
Breck		3,000	
Total allocated equally			6,000
Balance of income			**$ 0**
Shares of each partner	$42,000	$28,000	

Exhibit 13.2

Dividing Income When Allowances Exceed Income

	Steeley	Breck	Total
Net income			**$50,000**
Total salaries and interest	39,000	25,000	64,000
Balance of income			**(14,000)**
Balance allocated equally:			
Steeley	(7,000)		
Breck		(7,000)	
Total allocated equally			14,000
Balance of income			**$ 0**
Shares of each partner	$32,000	$18,000	

ing agreement means a negative ($7,000) is allocated to each partner to determine the final allocation. In this case, Steeley ends up with $32,000 and Breck gets $18,000.

If BOARDS had experienced a loss, then it would have been shared by Steeley and Breck in the same manner as the $50,000 income. The only difference is they would have begun with a negative amount because of the loss. Specifically, the partners would still have been allocated their salary and interest allowances, further adding to the negative balance of the loss. This *total* negative balance *after* salary and interest allowances would have been allocated equally between the partners. These allocations would have been applied against the positive numbers from any allowances to determine each partner's share of the loss.

Flash back

4. Ben and Jerry form a partnership by contributing $70,000 and $35,000, respectively. They agree to an interest allowance equal to 10% of each partner's capital balance at the beginning of the year, with the remaining income shared equally. Allocate first-year income of $40,000 to each partner.

Answer—p. 580

Partnership Financial Statements

Partnership financial statements are very similar to those of a proprietorship. The **statement of changes in partners' equity** is one exception. It shows the capital balances at the beginning of the period, any additional investments made by the partners, the income or loss of the partnership, withdrawals by partners, and the ending capital balances. This statement, also called *statement of partners' capital,* usually shows these changes for each partner's capital account and includes the allocation of income among partners. To illustrate, Exhibit 13.3 shows the statement of changes in partners' equity for BOARDS prepared per the sharing agreement of Exhibit 13.1. Recall that BOARDS' first-year income was $70,000. Also, Steeley withdrew $20,000 and Breck $12,000 at the end of the first year.

Exhibit 13.3

Statement of Changes in Partners' Equity

BOARDS
Statement of Changes in Partners' Equity
For Year Ended December 31, 1999

	Steeley		Breck		Total
Beginning capital balances		$ 0		$ 0	$ 0
Plus:					
Investments by owners		30,000		10,000	40,000
Net income:					
Salary allowances	$36,000		$24,000		
Interest allowances	3,000		1,000		
Balance	3,000		3,000		
Total net income		42,000		28,000	70,000
Total		$72,000		$38,000	$110,000
Less partners' withdrawals		(20,000)		(12,000)	(32,000)
Ending capital balances		**$52,000**		**$26,000**	**$ 78,000**

The owner's equity section of the balance sheet of a partnership usually shows the separate capital account balance of each partner. In the case of BOARDS, both K. Steeley, Capital, and D. Breck, Capital, are listed in the owner's equity section along with their balances of $52,000 and $26,000, respectively. The **Boston Celtics'** recent year's statement of changes in partners' equity reports the following ($ thousands):

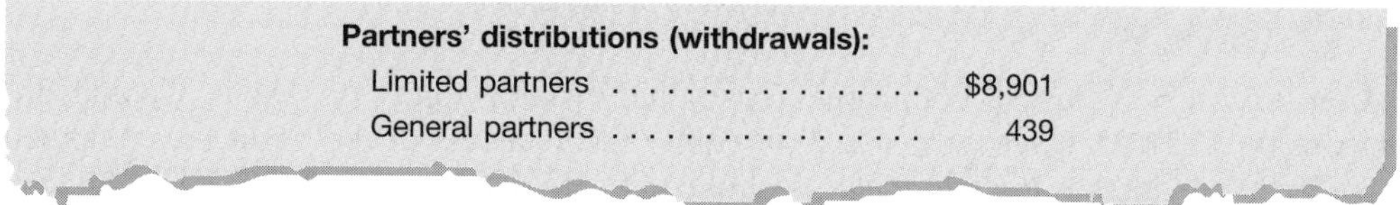

Partners' distributions (withdrawals):	
Limited partners	$8,901
General partners	439

Admission and Withdrawal of Partners

P3 Account for the admission and withdrawal of a partner.

A partnership is based on a contract between individuals. When a partner is added or a partner withdraws, the old partnership ends. Still, the business can continue to operate as a new partnership among the remaining partners. This section looks at how we account for the addition and withdrawal of a partner.

Admission of a Partner

There are two ways a new partner is admitted to a partnership. First, a new partner can purchase an interest from one or more current partners. Second, a new partner can invest cash or other assets.

Purchase of Partnership Interest

The purchase of partnership interest is a *personal transaction between one or more current partners and the new partner.* To become a partner, the purchaser must be accepted by the current partners. Accounting for the purchase of partnership interest involves a reallocation of current partners' capital to reflect the transaction.

To illustrate, at the end of BOARDS first year, David Breck sells one-half of his partnership interest to Cris Davis for $18,000. This means Breck gives up a $13,000 recorded interest ($26,000 × 1/2) in the partnership (see Exhibit 13.3). The partnership records this as:

Assets = Liabilities + Equity
−13,000
+13,000

Jan. 4	D. Breck, Capital	13,000	
	C. Davis, Capital		13,000
	To record admission of Davis by purchase.		

After this entry is posted, BOARDS's equity lists: K. Steeley, Capital; D. Breck, Capital; and C. Davis, Capital; along with their balances of $52,000, $13,000, and $13,000, respectively.

Two aspects of this transaction are important. First, the $18,000 Davis paid to Breck is *not* recorded by the partnership. This is regardless of the amount paid by Davis to Breck. The partnership's assets, liabilities, and total equity are unaffected by this transaction. Second, Steeley and Breck must agree if Davis is to become a partner. If they agree to accept Davis, a new partnership is formed and a new contract with a new income-and-loss-sharing agreement is prepared. If Steeley or Breck refuses to accept Davis as a partner, then (under the Uniform Partnership Act) Davis gets Breck's sold share of partnership income and loss. If the partnership is liquidated, Davis gets Breck's sold share of partnership assets. But Davis gets no voice in managing the company until being admitted as a partner.

Investing Assets in a Partnership

Admitting a partner by accepted assets is a *transaction between the new partner and the partnership.* The invested assets become partnership property. To illustrate, if Steeley (with a $52,000 interest) and Breck (with a $26,000 interest) agree to accept Davis as a partner in BOARDS with her investment of $22,000, the entry to record Davis's investment is:

Assets = Liabilities + Equity
+22,000 +22,000

Jan. 4	Cash	22,000	
	C. Davis, Capital		22,000
	To record admission of Davis by investment.		

After this entry is posted, both assets (cash) and owner's equity (C. Davis, Capital) increase by $22,000. Davis now has 22% equity in the assets of the business, computed as $22,000 divided by the entire partnership equity ($52,000 + $26,000 + $22,000). But she doesn't necessarily have a right to 22% of income. Dividing income and loss is a separate matter on which partners must agree.

Bonus to Old Partners

When the current value of a partnership is greater than the recorded amounts of equity, the partners usually require a new partner to pay a bonus for the privilege of joining. To illustrate, let's say Steeley and Breck agree to accept Davis as a partner with a 25% interest in BOARDS. But they require Davis to invest $42,000. Recall, the partnership's accounting records show Steeley's recorded equity in the business is $52,000 and Breck's recorded equity is $26,000 (see Exhibit 13.3). They agree to accept Davis's $42,000 investment in return for a 25% share in both the partnership's earnings and equity. Davis's equity is determined as follows:

Equities of existing partners ($52,000 + $26,000)	$ 78,000
Investment of new partner	42,000
Total partnership equity	$120,000
Equity of Davis (25% of total)	$ 30,000

Although Davis invests $42,000, her equity in the recorded net assets of the partnership is only $30,000. The $12,000 difference usually is called a bonus and allocated to existing partners (Steeley and Breck). The entry to record this is:

Jan. 4	Cash	42,000	
	Davis, Capital		30,000
	Steeley, Capital ($12,000 × 1/2)		6,000
	Breck, Capital ($12,000 × 1/2)		6,000
	To record admission of Davis and bonus to old partners.		

Assets = Liabilities + Equity
+42,000 +30,000
+6,000
+6,000

The $12,000 bonus is shared by Steeley and Breck according to their income-and-loss-sharing agreement. This bonus is always shared in this way because it is viewed as an increase in the value of the partnership that is not yet reflected in the accounts.

Bonus to New Partner

Existing partners can pay a bonus to a new partner. This usually occurs when they need additional cash or the new partner has exceptional talents. The new partner gets a larger share of equity than the amount invested. To illustrate, let's say Steeley and Breck agree to accept Davis as a partner with a 25% interest in both the partnership's earnings and equity, but they require Davis to only invest $18,000. Davis's equity is determined as:

Equities of existing partners ($52,000 + $26,000)	$78,000
Investment of new partner	18,000
Total partnership equity	$96,000
Equity of Davis (25% of total)	$24,000

The entry to record Davis's investment is:

Jan. 4	Cash	18,000	
	Steeley, Capital ($6,000 × 1/2)	3,000	
	Breck, Capital ($6,000 × 1/2)	3,000	
	Davis, Capital		24,000
	To record Davis's admission and bonus.		

Assets = Liabilities + Equity
+18,000 −3,000
−3,000
+24,000

Davis's bonus is contributed by the old partners in their income-and-loss-sharing ratio. Davis's 25% equity doesn't necessarily entitle her to 25% of any income or loss. This is a separate matter for agreement by the partners.

Withdrawal of a Partner

There are generally two ways a partner withdraws from a partnership. First, the withdrawing partner can sell his or her interest to another person who pays for it in cash or other assets. For this we need only debit the withdrawing partner's capital account and credit the new partner's capital account. The second case is when cash or other assets of the partnership are distributed to the withdrawing partner in settlement of his or her interest. This section explains the accounting for this second case.

To illustrate, let's assume in a future period that Breck withdraws from the partnership of BOARDS. The partners (Steeley, Breck, and Davis) share income and loss equally. Their partnership shows the following capital balances: Steeley, $84,000; Breck, $38,000; and Davis, $38,000. Accounting for the withdrawal depends on whether a bonus is paid or not. We describe three possibilities.

No Bonus

If Breck withdraws and takes cash equal to his equity, the entry is:

Assets = Liabilities + Equity
−38,000 −38,000

Oct. 31	Breck, Capital	38,000	
	Cash		38,000
	To record withdrawal of Breck from partnership with no bonus.		

Breck can take any combination of assets to which the partners agree to settle his equity. The withdrawal of Breck creates a new partnership between remaining partners. A new partnership contract and a new income-and-loss-sharing agreement is sometimes required.

Bonus to Remaining Partners

A withdrawing partner is sometimes willing to take less than the recorded value of his or her equity just to get out of the partnership or because the recorded value is overstated. Whatever the reason, when this occurs the withdrawing partner in effect gives to the remaining partners a bonus equal to the equity left behind. The remaining partners share this unwithdrawn equity in their income-and-loss-sharing ratio. To illustrate, if Breck withdraws and agrees to take $34,000 cash in settlement of his equity, the entry is:

Assets = Liabilities + Equity
−34,000 −38,000
+2,000
+2,000

Oct. 31	Breck, Capital	38,000	
	Cash		34,000
	Steeley, Capital		2,000
	Davis, Capital		2,000
	To record withdrawal of Breck and bonus to remaining partners.		

Breck withdrew $4,000 less than his recorded equity. This is divided between Steeley and Davis in their income-and-loss-sharing ratio.

Bonus to Withdrawing Partner

There are at least two reasons why a withdrawing partner may be able to receive more than his or her recorded equity. First, the recorded equity may be understated. Second, the remaining partners may agree to remove this partner by giving assets of greater value than this partner's recorded equity. When either case occurs, the withdrawing partner in effect receives a bonus. The remaining partners reduce their equity for this bonus using their income-and-loss-sharing ratio. To illustrate, if Breck withdraws and receives $40,000 cash in settlement of his equity, the entry is:

Assets = Liabilities + Equity
−40,000 −38,000
−1,000
−1,000

Oct. 31	Breck, Capital	38,000	
	Steeley, Capital	1,000	
	Davis, Capital	1,000	
	Cash		40,000
	To record Breck's withdrawal from partnership with bonus.		

Death of a Partner

A partner's death dissolves a partnership. A deceased partner's estate is entitled to receive his or her equity. The partnership contract should contain provisions for settlement in this case. These usually include provisions for *(a)* a closing of the books to determine income or loss since the end of the previous period and *(b)* a method for determining and recording current values for assets and liabilities. The remaining partners and the deceased partner's estate then must agree to a settlement of the deceased partner's equity. This can involve selling the equity to remaining partners or to an outsider, or it can involve withdrawing assets.

Lawyer

You are a lawyer hired by the two remaining partners of a three-member partnership. The third partner recently died. The three partners shared income and loss in the ratio of their capital balances, which were equal. The partnership agreement says a deceased partner's estate is entitled to the "partner's percent share of partnership assets." The estate argues it is entitled to one-third of the current value of the partnership's total assets. The remaining partners say the distribution should use the asset's book values, which are only 75% of current value. They also point to partnership liabilities, which equal 40% of the assets' book value, and 30% of current value. How would you resolve this situation?

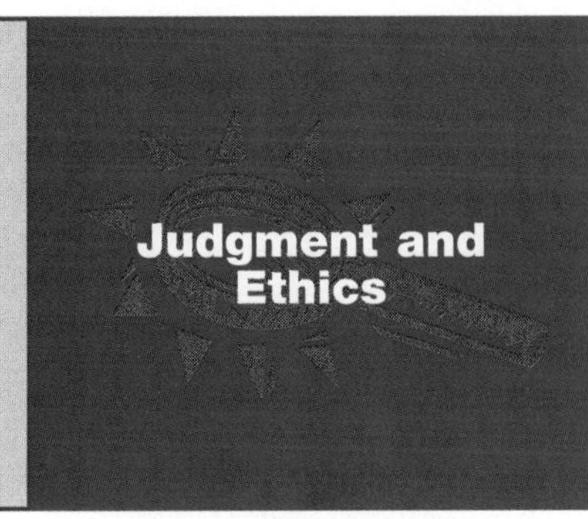

Answer—p. 580

Liquidation of a Partnership

P4 Prepare entries for partnership liquidation.

When a partnership is liquidated, its business is ended. Four steps are involved:

1. Noncash assets are sold for cash and a gain or loss on liquidation is recorded.
2. Gain or loss on liquidation is allocated to partners using their income-and-loss ratio.
3. Liabilities are paid.
4. Remaining cash is distributed to partners based on their capital balances.

Partnership liquidation often follows one of two different cases described below.

No Capital Deficiency

No capital deficiency means that all partners have a credit balance in their capital accounts for final distribution of cash. To illustrate, let's assume Steeley, Breck, and Davis operate their partnership in BOARDS for several years, sharing income and losses equally. The partners then decide to liquidate. On that date, the books are closed, and income from operations is transferred to the partners' capital accounts. The partners' recorded equity balances immediately prior to liquidation are: Steeley $70,000; Breck $66,000; and Davis $62,000.

In a liquidation, some gains or losses commonly result from the sale of noncash assets. These losses and gains are called *losses and gains from liquidation.* Just like any other net incomes or losses, partners share the losses and gains from liquidation in their income-and-loss-sharing ratio. Assume BOARDS sells its noncash assets for a net gain on realization of $6,000. This is shared by the partners using their income-and-loss-sharing agreement (equal for these partners) yielding the partners' revised equity balances of: Steeley, $72,000; Breck, $68,000; and Davis, $64,000.[4]

[4] The concepts behind these entries are not new. For example, assume BOARDS has two noncash assets recorded as: boarding facilities, $15,000, and land, $25,000. The entry to sell these assets for $46,000 is:

Jan. 15	Cash	46,000	
	Boarding facilities		15,000
	Land		25,000
	Gain from Liquidation		6,000
	Sold noncash assets at a gain.		

We then record the allocation of any loss or gain (a gain in this case) from liquidation according to the partners' income-and-loss sharing agreement as:

Jan. 15	Gain from Liquidation	6,000	
	Steeley, Capital		2,000
	Breck, Capital		2,000
	Davis, Capital		2,000
	To allocated liquidation gain to partners.		

After partnership assets are sold and the gain or loss shared, any liabilities must be paid. Because creditors have first claim, they are paid first. After creditors are paid, the remaining cash is divided among the partners according to their capital account balances. BOARDS's only liability at liquidation is $20,000 in accounts payable. The entries to record the payment to creditors and final distribution to partners is:

Assets = Liabilities + Equity
−20,000 −20,000

Assets = Liabilities + Equity
−204,000 −72,000
−68,000
−64,000

Jan. 15	Accounts Payable	20,000	
	Cash		20,000
	To pay claims of creditors.		
Jan. 15	Steeley, Capital	72,000	
	Breck, Capital	68,000	
	Davis, Capital	64,000	
	Cash		204,000
	To distribute remaining cash to partners.		

Remember the final cash payment is distributed to partners according to their capital account balances, whereas gains and losses from liquidation are allocated according to the income-and-loss-sharing ratio.

Capital Deficiency

Capital deficiency means that at least one partner has a debit balance in his or her capital account at the final distribution of cash. This can arise from liquidation losses, excessive withdrawals before liquidation, or recurring losses in prior periods. A partner with a capital deficiency must, if possible, cover the deficit by paying cash into the partnership.

To illustrate, let's assume Steeley, Breck, and Davis operate their partnership in BOARDS for several years, sharing income and losses equally. The partners then decide to liquidate. But, immediately prior to the final distribution of cash, the partners' recorded capital balances are: Steeley, $19,000; Breck, $8,000; and Davis, ($3,000). Davis's capital deficiency means she owes the partnership $3,000. Both Steeley and Breck have a legal claim against Davis's personal assets. The final distribution of cash in this case depends on how this capital deficiency is handled. Two possibilities exist.

Partner Pays Deficiency

Davis is obligated to pay $3,000 into the partnership to cover the deficiency. If Davis is willing and able to pay, the entry to record receipt of Davis's payment is:

Assets = Liabilities + Equity
+3,000 +3,000

Jan. 15	Cash	3,000	
	Davis, Capital		3,000
	To record payment of deficiency by Davis.		

After the $3,000 payment, the partners' capital balances are: Steeley, $19,000; Breck, $8,000; and Davis, $0. The entry to record the final cash distributions to partners is:

Assets = Liabilities + Equity
−27,000 −19,000
−8,000

Jan. 15	Steeley, Capital	19,000	
	Breck, Capital	8,000	
	Cash		27,000
	To distribute remaining cash to partners.		

Partner Can't Pay Deficiency

Because of unlimited liability in a partnership, a partner's unpaid deficiency is absorbed by the remaining partners with credit balances. To illustrate, if Davis is unable to pay the $3,000 deficiency, it is shared by Steeley and Breck based on their income-and-loss-sharing ratio. Since they share equally, Steeley and Breck each absorb $1,500 of the deficiency. This is recorded as:

Jan. 15	Steeley, Capital	1,500	
	Breck, Capital	1,500	
	Davis, Capital		3,000
	To transfer Davis's deficiency to Steeley and Breck.		

Assets = Liabilities + Equity
−1,500
−1,500
+3,000

After Davis's deficiency is absorbed by Steeley and Breck, the capital accounts of the partners are: Steeley, $17,500; Breck, $6,500; and Davis, $0. The entry to record the final cash distributions to the partners is:

Jan. 15	Steeley, Capital	17,500	
	Breck, Capital	6,500	
	Cash		24,000
	To distribute remaining cash to partners.		

Assets = Liabilities + Equity
−24,000 −17,500
−6,500

The inability of Davis to cover her deficiency does not relieve her of liability. If she becomes able to pay at some future date, Steeley and Breck can each collect $1,500 from her.

SECTION 2—CORPORATIONS

Corporate Form of Organization

A corporation is an entity that is created by law and is separate from its owners. It has most of the rights and privileges granted to individuals. Owners of corporations are called *stockholders* or *shareholders.* Corporations can be separated into privately held and publicly held corporations. A *privately held* corporation, also called *closely held,* does not offer its stock for public sale and usually has few stockholders. A *publicly held* corporation offers its stock for public sale and can have thousands of stockholders. *Public sale* usually refers to trading in an organized stock market.

Characteristics of Corporations

C2 Identify characteristics of corporations and their organization.

Corporations are an important type of organization because of the advantages offered by their unique characteristics. We describe these characteristics in this section.

Separate Legal Entity

A corporation is a separate legal entity. As a separate entity, a corporation conducts its affairs with the same rights, duties, and responsibilities as a person. A corporation takes actions through its agents, who are its officers and managers.

Limited Liability of Stockholders

Because a corporation is a separate legal entity, it is responsible for its own acts and its own debt. Its stockholders, also called *shareholders,* are not liable for either. From the viewpoint of a stockholder, this lack of liability is one of the most important advantages of the corporate form of business.

Ownership Rights Are Transferable

Ownership of a corporation is by shares of stock that are usually easily bought or sold. The transfer of shares from one stockholder to another usually has no effect on the corporation or its operations.[5] Many corporations have thousands or even millions of their shares bought and sold daily in major stock exchanges throughout the world. For example, *The Wall Street Journal* reports that on March 3, 1998, 2,053,300 shares of **NIKE** stock traded on the New York Stock Exchange.

Continuous Life

A corporation's life can continue indefinitely because it is not tied to the physical lives of its owners. A corporation's life can sometimes be initially limited by the laws of the state of its incorporation. But a corporation's charter can be renewed and its life extended when the stated time expires. This means a corporation can have a perpetual life as long as it continues to be successful.

Stockholders Are Not Corporate Agents

A corporation acts through its agents, who are the officers or managers of the corporation. Stockholders who are not officers or managers of the corporation do not have the power to bind the corporation to contracts. This is also referred to as *lack of mutual agency.* Instead, stockholders participate in the affairs of the corporation only by voting in the stockholders' meetings.

Ease of Capital Accumulation

Buying stock in a corporation often is attractive to investors because: (1) stockholders are not liable for the corporation's actions and debts, (2) stock usually is transferred easily, (3) the life of the corporation is unlimited, and (4) stockholders are not agents of the corporation. These advantages make it possible for some corporations to accumulate large amounts of capital from the combined investments of many stockholders. A corporation's capacity for raising capital is limited only by its ability to convince investors it can use their funds profitably.

Governmental Regulation

Corporations must meet requirements of a state's incorporation laws. These laws subject a corporation to state regulation and control. Single proprietorships and partnerships escape some of these regulations, and often avoid having to file some governmental reports required of corporations.

Corporate Taxation

Corporations are subject to the same property and payroll taxes as proprietorships and partnerships. But corporations are subject to *additional* taxes not levied on either of these other two forms. The most burdensome of these are federal and state income taxes that together can take 40% or more of a corporation's pretax income. Moreover, the income of a corporation is taxed twice, first as income of the corporation and again as personal income to stockholders when cash is distributed to them as dividends. This is called *double taxation.* It differs from proprietorships and partnerships, which are not subject to income taxes as business units. Their income is taxed only as the personal income of their owners. We described an "S" corporation earlier in this chapter and indicated that it has the same tax status as a partnership.

The tax situation of a corporation is usually a disadvantage. But in some cases it can be an advantage to stockholders because corporation and individual tax rates are progressive. A progressive tax means higher levels of income are taxed at higher rates and lower levels of income are taxed at lower rates. This suggests taxes can be saved or at

[5] A transfer of ownership can sometimes create significant effects if it brings about a change in who controls the company's activities.

least delayed if a large amount of income is divided among two or more tax-paying entities. A person who has a large personal income and pays taxes at a high rate can benefit if some of the income is earned by a corporation the person owns, as long as the corporation avoids paying dividends. By not paying dividends, the corporation's income is taxed only once at the lower corporate rate, at least temporarily until dividends are paid or the stock is sold.

Choosing a Business Form

Choosing the proper form of entity for a business is crucial and many factors should be considered, including: taxes, liability, tax and fiscal year-end, ownership structure, estate planning, business risks, and earnings and property distributions. The chart below gives a summary of several important characteristics of business organizations:

	Proprietorship	Partnership	LLP	Corporation	S Corporation	LLC
Business entity	yes	yes	yes	yes	yes	yes
Legal entity	no	no	no	yes	yes	yes
Limited liability	no	no	limited*	yes	yes	yes
Business taxed	no	no	no	yes	no	no
One owner allowed	yes	no	no	yes	yes (75 or less)	yes

*A partner's personal liability for LLP debts is limited. LLPs carry insurance to protect the public in case of malpractice.

We must remember this chart is a summary and not a detailed listing. There are many details underlying each of these business forms, and several are different across states. Also, state and federal laws change, and a body of law is still developing around LLCs. Business owners should look at these details and consider unique business arrangements such as organizing different parts of their businesses in different forms.

Organizing a Corporation

This section describes incorporation and treatment of the costs of organization.

Incorporation

A corporation is created by getting a charter from a state government. Requirements for a charter vary across states. Usually, a charter application must be signed by the prospective stockholders. They are called *incorporators* or *promoters.* The application is then filed with the proper state official. When the application process is completed and all fees are paid, the charter is issued and the corporation is formed. Investors then purchase the corporation's stock, meet as stockholders, and elect a board of directors. Directors are responsible for overseeing a corporation's affairs.

Netting Gold

Marc Andreessen cofounded **Netscape** at the age of 22, only four months after earning his degree in computer science. One year later, at the age of 23, Andreessen and friends issued Netscape shares to the public. Netscape's stock, offered at $28 a share, soared to nearly $75 before ending its first trading day at a less stratospheric $58. This made Andreessen a multimillionaire at 23. [Source: *Business Week* October 23, 1995, and Netscape's *10K Report.*]

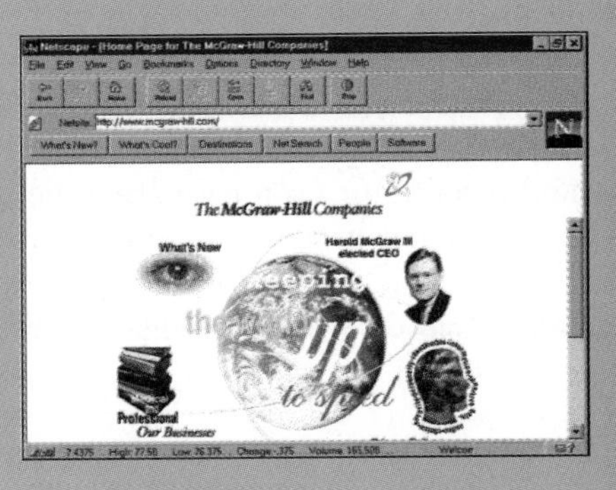

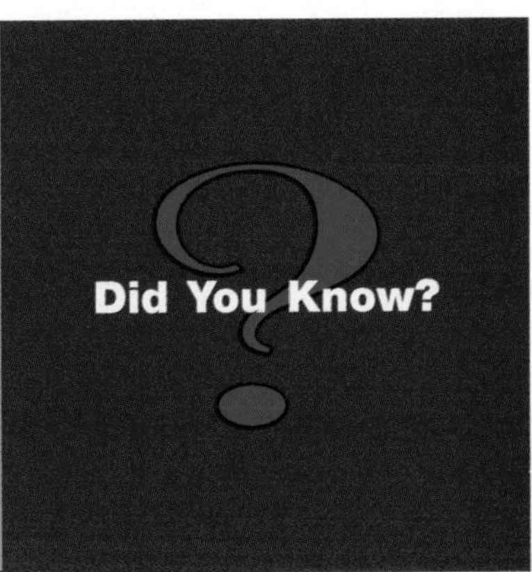

Organization Costs

Organization costs are the costs of organizing a corporation. They include legal fees, promoters' fees, and amounts paid to get a charter. The corporation records (debits) these costs to an asset account called Organization Costs. This intangible asset benefits the corporation throughout its life and its cost is amortized over a period no longer than 40 years.[6] Income tax rules permit a corporation to record organization costs as a tax deduction over a minimum of five years. This means many corporations use a five-year amortization period for financial reporting to ease recordkeeping. Because organization costs usually are small in amount, the *materiality principle* supports this arbitrary short amortization period.

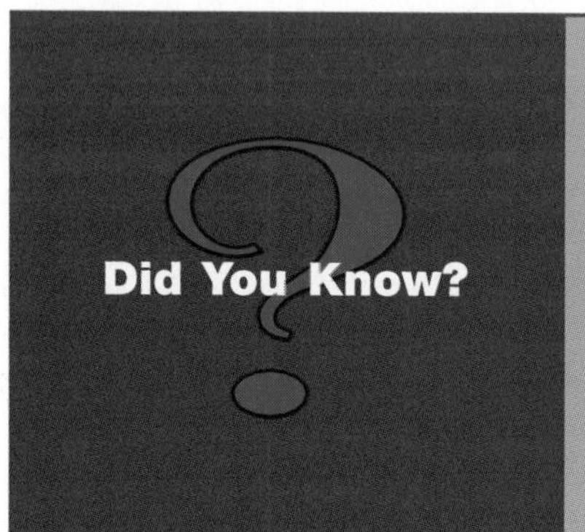

Startup Money

So you want to start a company but can't get the start-up money. Here are some ideas for getting started: (1) Hunt for "angel" investors—these are parents, siblings, friends, or anyone who believes in your company. (2) Run a bare-bones operation and pay employees, investors, and even suppliers with stock. (3) Seek out venture capitalists (special investors) who have a track record of success and giving advice. Also check out the National Venture Capital Assn. [www.nvca.org]. [Source: *Business Week,* October 13, 1997.]

Management of a Corporation

Corporations have different organizational structures. Yet ultimate control of a corporation rests with its stockholders. They control a corporation through election of the *board of directors,* or simply, *directors.* An individual stockholder's ability to affect management is limited to a vote in stockholders' meetings, where each stockholder has one vote for each share of stock owned. This control relation is shown in Exhibit 13.4. A corporation's board of directors is responsible for and has final authority for managing the corporation's activities. It can act only as a collective body. An individual director has no power to transact corporate business. Although the board has final authority, it usually limits its actions to establishing broad policy.

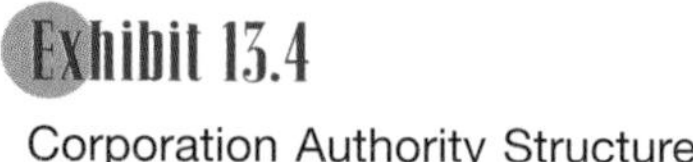

Corporation Authority Structure

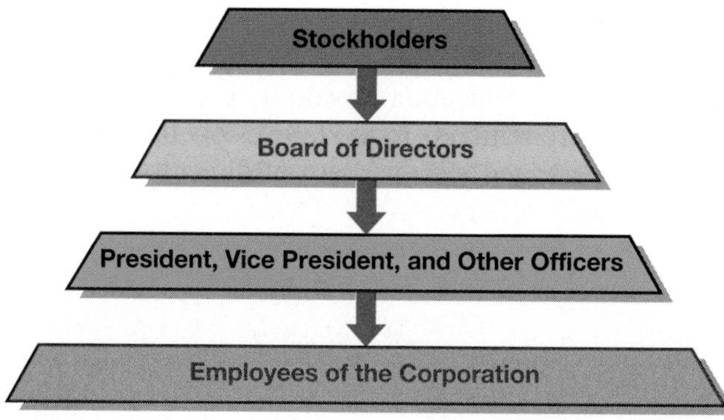

A corporation usually holds a stockholders' meeting once each year to elect directors and transact other business as required by its bylaws. A group of stockholders owning or controlling votes of more than a 50% share of a corporation's stock can elect the board and control the corporation. But in many corporations few stockholders attend the annual meeting or even care about getting involved in the voting process. This means a much smaller percent is often able to dominate the election of board members.

Stockholders who don't attend stockholders' meetings must be given an opportunity to delegate their voting rights to an agent. A stockholder does this by signing a docu-

[6] FASB, *Accounting Standards—Current Text* (Norwalk, CT, 1995), sec. I60.110. First published in *APB Opinion No. 17,* par. 29.

ment called a **proxy,** which gives a designated agent the right to vote the stock. Prior to a stockholders' meeting, a corporation's board of directors usually mails to each stockholder an announcement of the meeting and a proxy listing the existing board chairperson as the voting agent of the stockholder. The announcement asks the stockholder to sign and return the proxy.

Day-to-day direction of corporate business is delegated to executive officers appointed by the board. The chief executive officer (CEO) of a corporation is often its president. Several vice presidents, who report to the president, are commonly assigned specific areas of management responsibility such as finance, production, and marketing. The corporation secretary keeps minutes for meetings of stockholders and directors and ensures that all legal responsibilities are met. In a small corporation, the secretary is also responsible for keeping a record of current stockholders and amounts of their stock interest.

Another common corporate structure is the dual role of chairperson of the board of directors and CEO. In this case, the president is usually designated the chief operating officer (COO). The rest of the structure is similar.

Rights of Stockholders

When investors buy a corporation's stock they acquire all *specific* rights granted by the corporation's charter to those stockholders. They also acquire *general* rights granted stockholders by the laws of the state in which the company is incorporated. When a corporation has only one class of stock it is identified as **common stock.** Common stock represents *residual equity,* meaning that creditors and other stockholders (if any) rank ahead of common stockholders if a corporation is liquidated. State laws vary, but common stockholders usually have the general right to:

1. Vote at stockholders' meetings.
2. Sell or otherwise dispose of their stock.
3. Purchase additional shares of common stock later issued by the corporation. This right is called the **preemptive right.** It protects stockholders' proportionate interest in the corporation. For example, a stockholder who owns 25% of a corporation's common stock has the first opportunity to buy 25% of any new common stock issued. This enables the stockholder to maintain a 25% interest if desired.
4. Share equally with other common stockholders in any dividends. This means each common share receives the same dividend.
5. Share equally in any assets remaining after creditors are paid when the corporation is liquidated. This means each common share receives the same amount of remaining liquidated assets.

Stockholders also have the right to receive timely reports on the corporation's financial position and results of operations.

Stock of a Corporation

This section explains stock certificates, their transfer, and use of registrar and transfer agents.

Stock Certificates and Transfer

When investors buy a corporation's stock, they sometimes receive a *stock certificate* as proof they purchased shares.[7] In many corporations, only one certificate is issued for each block of stock purchased. A certificate can be for any number of shares. Exhibit 13.5 shows an actual stock certificate of one share of **Green Bay Packers** stock. A cer-

[7] Issuance of certificates is becoming less common. Instead, many stockholders maintain accounts with the corporation or their stockbrokers and never receive certificates.

Exhibit 13.5
Stock Certificate

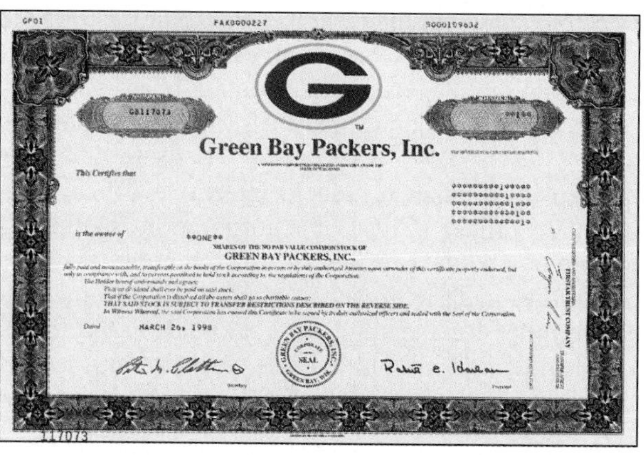

tificate shows the company name, stockholder name, number of shares, and other crucial information.

When selling stock, a stockholder completes and signs a transfer endorsement on the back of the certificate and sends it to the corporation's secretary or transfer agent. The secretary or agent cancels and files the old certificate and issues a new certificate to the new stockholder. If the old certificate represents more shares than were sold, the corporation issues two new certificates. One certificate goes to the new stockholder for the shares purchased and the other to the selling stockholder for the remaining unsold shares. Many stockholders have their shares held in the name of their stock brokerage. When this is done, the corporation's secretary or registrar keeps a record of who owns the shares and the stockholders don't receive stock certificates.

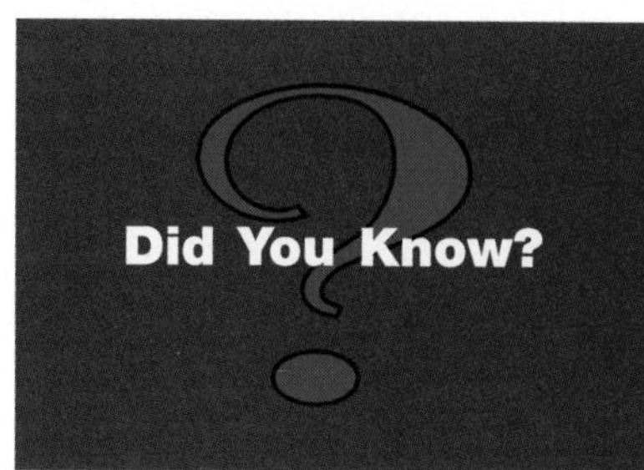

Online Trading

Thanks to the computing revolution, we can tap into a growing number of online brokerage services that plug buyers into the floors of the stock exchanges. Fee schedules begin as low as $5 to $10 per trade. These fees are a fraction of those charged by full-service firms such as Merrill Lynch. On-line brokerage firms say computers reduce their labor costs and eliminate most order-entry errors. They also say the Web has slashed their communications costs. [Source: *Business Week,* April 8, 1996.]

Registrar and Transfer Agents

If a corporation's stock is traded on a major stock exchange, the corporation must have a *registrar* and a *transfer agent.* A registrar keeps stockholder records and prepares official lists of stockholders for stockholders' meetings and dividend payments. A transfer agent assists purchases and sales of shares by receiving and issuing certificates as necessary. Registrars and transfer agents usually are large banks or trust companies having computer facilities and staff to do this work.

Basics of Capital Stock

C3 Describe the components of stockholders' equity.

Capital stock is a general term referring to a corporation's stock used in obtaining its capital (owner financing). This section introduces us to capital stock terminology and some of the basics in accounting for capital stock.

Authorized Stock

Authorized stock is the total amount of stock that a corporation's charter authorizes it to sell. Most corporations authorize more stock than they anticipate selling either initially or in the near future. This means the number of authorized shares usually exceeds the number of shares issued (and outstanding), and often by a large amount.[8] A corporation must apply to the state for a change in its charter if it wishes to issue more shares than previously authorized. Corporations disclose the number of shares authorized in the equity section of its balance sheet or notes. **Reebok**'s balance sheet in Appendix A reports authorized stock as ($ thousands):

---

[8] *Outstanding stock* refers to issued stock that is still held by stockholders. This distinction is important since corporations can buy back their issued stock (called *treasury stock*).

Stockholders' Equity	**1996**	**1995**
Common stock, par value $.01; authorized 250,000,000 shares; issued 92,556,295 shares in 1996, and 111,015,133 shares in 1995	$143,256	$142,756

No formal journal entry is required for authorization of stock.

Selling Stock

A corporation can issue stock in at least two ways. It can sell either directly or indirectly to stockholders. To *sell directly,* a corporation advertises its stock issuance to potential buyers. This type of issuance is most common with privately held corporations. To *sell indirectly,* a corporation pays a brokerage house (investment banker) to issue its stock. Some brokerage houses *underwrite* an indirect issuance of stock, meaning they buy the stock from the corporation and take all gains or losses from its resale to stockholders.

Sizing Up an IPO

A prospectus accompanies an initial public offering (IPO) of stock. It gives financial information about the company issuing the stock. Questions we look to answer in a prospectus include: (1) Is the underwriter well known? (2) Is there growth in revenues, profits, or cash flows? (3) What is management's view of operations? (4) Are current owners selling? (5) What are the risks? Answers to these questions help us size up an IPO. [Source: *Business Week* October 6, 1997.]

This announcement is neither an offer to sell nor a solicitation of an offer to buy these securities. The offer is made only by the Prospectus.

NEW ISSUE March 3, 1998

2,000,000 Shares

SurModics

Common Stock

Price $7.50 Per Share

Copies of the Prospectus may be obtained in any State from such dealers as may lawfully offer these securities in such State.

John G. Kinnard and Company, Incorporated

Cowen & Company Dain Rauscher Incorporated

EVEREN Securities, Inc. NationsBanc Montgomery Securities LLC

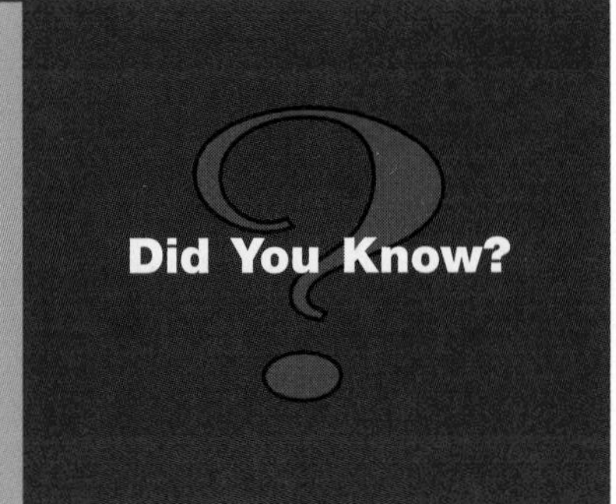

Market Value of Stock

Market value per share is the price at which a stock is bought or sold. Market value is influenced by a variety of factors, including expected future earnings, dividends, growth, and other company and economic events. Market values of frequently traded stocks are reported daily in newspapers such as *The Wall Street Journal* or are available immediately off the Web. Market values of stocks not actively traded are more difficult to determine. Several techniques are used to estimate the value of these and other stocks. Most all of these techniques use accounting information as an important input for this valuation process. We must always remember that the current market value of previously issued shares of a corporation (for example, the buying and selling of stock between investors) does not impact a corporation's stockholders' equity accounts.

Classes of Stock

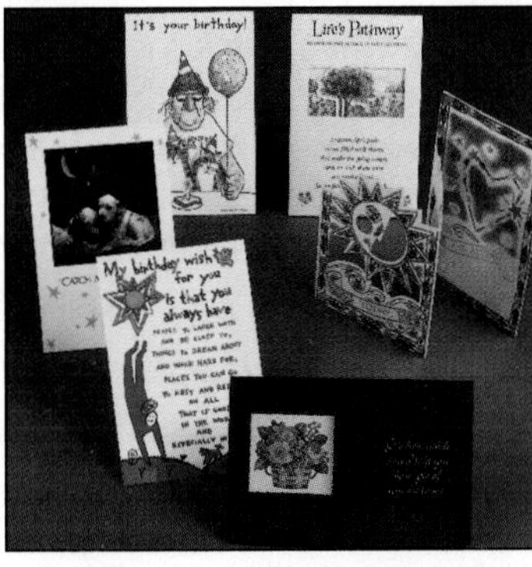

A corporation's charter authorizes it to issue a specified number of shares. If all authorized shares have the same rights and characteristics, the stock is called common stock. A corporation is sometimes authorized to issue more than one class of stock, including preferred stock and different classes of common stock. **American Greetings,** for instance, has two types of common stock outstanding; Class A stock has 1 vote per share and Class B stock has 10 votes per share. We discuss preferred stock later in this chapter.

Par Value Stock

Many stocks carry a value called a **par value** that is established at the time the stock is authorized. **Par value stock** is a class of stock assigned a par value per share by the corporation in its corporate charter. **Novell**'s common stock has a par value of $.10. Other widely used par values are $100, $25, $10, $5, $1 and $0.01. There is no restriction on the assigned par value. Par value stock has its par value printed on each certificate and is used in accounting for the stock.

In many states, the par value of a corporation's stock establishes the **minimum legal capital** for the corporation. Minimum legal capital normally means stockholders must invest assets equal to at least that amount. Minimum legal capital is usually defined as the par value of the issued stock. This means buyers of stock from a corporation must give the corporation assets equal in value to at least the par value of the stock or be subject to making up the difference later. For example, if a corporation issues 1,000 shares of $100 par value stock, the minimum legal capital of the corporation is $100,000. Minimum legal capital requirements often make it illegal to pay dividends if they reduce stockholders' equity below the minimum amount.

Minimum legal capital is intended to protect creditors of a corporation. Because a corporation's creditors cannot demand payment from the personal assets of stockholders, the creditors' claims must be satisfied by the corporation's assets. Minimum legal capital limits a corporation's ability to distribute its assets to stockholders. A corporation must maintain minimum legal capital until it is liquidated. At liquidation, all creditor claims are paid before any amounts are distributed to stockholders. Because par value determines the amount of minimum legal capital in many states, it is traditionally used in accounting for the part of stockholders' equity derived from the issuance of stock. But par value does not establish a stock's market value or its issue price. If buyers are willing to pay more, a corporation can sell and issue its stock at a price above par.

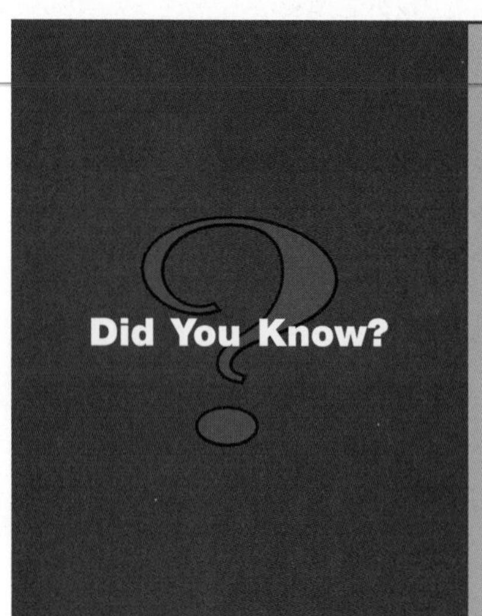

Stock Quotes

The **NIKE** stock quote below is interpreted as (left to right): **Hi,** highest price in the past 52 weeks; **Lo,** lowest price in the past 52 weeks; **Stock,** company name; **Sym,** exchange symbol; **Div,** dividends paid per share in the past year; **Yld %,** dividend divided by closing price; **PE,** ratio of stock price divided by earnings; **Vol 100s,** number of shares traded in 100s; **Hi,** highest price for the day; **Lo,** lowest price for the day; **Close,** closing price for the day; **Net Chg,** change in closing price from the prior day.

52 Weeks											
Hi	Lo	Stock	Sym	Div	Yld %	PE	Vol 100s	Hi	Lo	Close	Net Chg
76 3/8	37 3/4	Nike B	NKE	.48f	1.2	15	6848	40 1/4	39 7/8	40 1/8	. . .

No-Par Value Stock

No-par value stock, or simply no-par stock, is stock *not* assigned a value per share by the corporate charter. Nearly all states permit issuance of stock without par value. An advantage of no-par stock is that it can be issued at any price without the possibility of a discount as we explain later in the chapter. It also eliminates potential confusion by inexperienced investors who may try using par value in valuing a stock. The entire proceeds from sale of no-par stock becomes minimum legal capital in some states.

Frequency of Par, No-Par, and Stated Value Common Stock

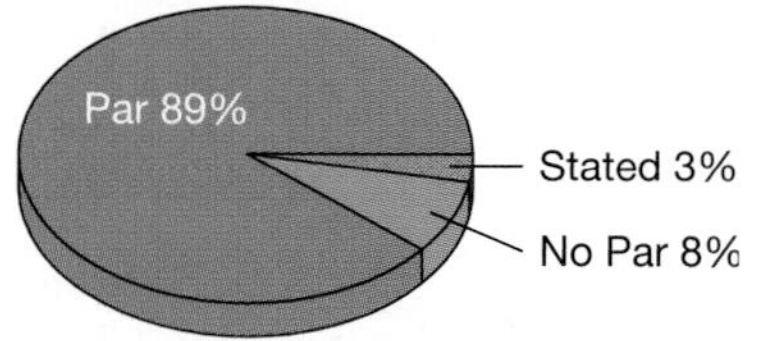

Stated Value Stock

Stated value stock is no-par stock that is assigned a value per share by the directors. Many states permit stated value stock. Stated value per share becomes the legal capital per share in these cases. The directors can change stated value at any time. Stated value stock normally doesn't have its assigned value printed on the stock certificate. The pie chart in the margin shows that most stock of companies carry a par value, while a much smaller percent are no-par or stated value stock.

Stockholders' Equity

The equity of a corporation is known as **stockholders' equity,** also called *shareholders' equity* or *corporate capital.* Stockholders' equity consists of (1) contributed (or paid-in) capital and (2) retained earnings. **Contributed capital** is the total amount of cash and other assets received by the corporation from its stockholders in exchange for common stock. **Retained earnings** is the cumulative net income retained in a corporation.

Exhibit 13.6 compares the equity accounts of a balance sheet for the three major forms of organizations: proprietorship, partnership, and corporation. Exhibits 2.4, 2.7, and 2.8 in Chapter 2 show actual equity sections for each of these three forms when applied to FastForward. Further details regarding the equity section of a corporation are described in this and the next chapter.

Exhibit 13.6

Equity Accounts by Organizational Form

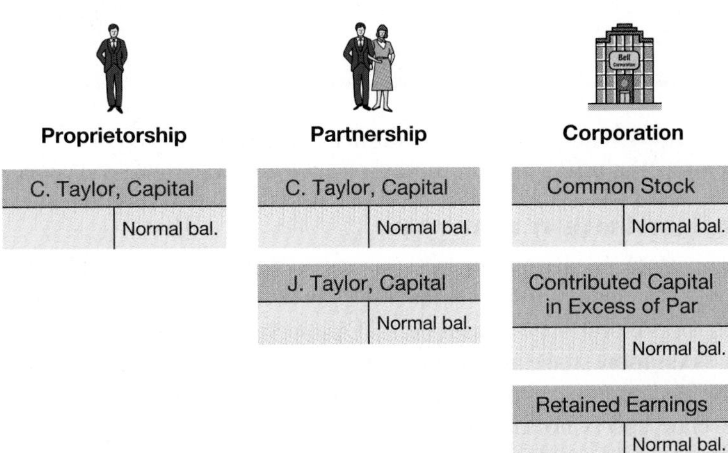

Flash back

5. Which of the following is *not* a characteristic of the corporate form of business? *(a)* Ease of capital accumulation. *(b)* Stockholder responsibility for corporate debts. *(c)* Easy transferability of ownership rights,
6. Why is income of a corporation said to be taxed twice?
7. What is a proxy?

Answers—p. 580

Common Stock

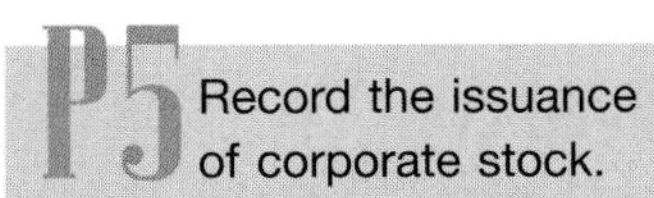

Accounting for the issuance of common stock involves (1) identifying the sources of contributed capital and (2) keeping contributed capital separate from retained earnings. Issuance of stock affects only contributed capital accounts; no retained earnings accounts are affected.

Issuing Par Value Stock

Par value stock can be issued at par, at a premium, or at a discount. In any of these transactions, the stock may be exchanged for either cash or noncash assets. This section covers these topics.

Issuing Par Value Stock at par

When we issue common stock at par value, we record amounts for both the asset(s) received and the par value stock issued. Stock is most commonly issued in exchange for cash. The entry to record Dillon Snowboards' immediate issuance of 30,000 shares of $10 par value stock for cash on June 5, 1999 is:

Assets = Liabilities + Equity
+300,000 +300,000

June 5	Cash	300,000	
	Common Stock, $10 Par Value		300,000
	Sold at par and issued 30,000 shares of $10 par value common stock.		

Exhibit 13.7 shows the stockholders' equity of Dillon Snowboards at the end of 1999 after earnings of $65,000 and no dividend payments.

Exhibit 13.7

Stockholders' Equity for Stock Issued at Par

Stockholders' Equity		
Contributed capital:		
Common Stock—$10 par value; 50,000 shares authorized;		
30,000 shares issued and outstanding	$300,000	
Retained earnings	65,000	
Total stockholders' equity		$365,000

The retained earnings balance can also be negative, reflecting losses. This is the case with **America Online**'s $7.767 million deficit in 1996 as shown in Appendix A.

Issuing Par Value Stock at a Premium

A **premium on stock** is an amount paid in excess of par by the purchasers of newly issued stock. When a corporation sells its stock for more than par value, the stock is said to be issued at a premium. For example, if Dillon Snowboards had sold and issued its $10 par value common stock at $12 per share, then the stock is sold at a $2 per share premium. This premium is reported on the balance sheet as part of stockholders' equity. It is not a revenue and is not listed on the income statement.

Accounting for stock sold at a price greater than its par value involves recording the premium separately from par value. This premium account is called *contributed capital in excess of par value.* The entry to record Dillon Snowboards' immediate issuance of 30,000 shares of $10 par value stock for $12 per share on June 5, 1999 is:

Assets = Liabilities + Equity
+360,000 +300,000
+60,000

June 5	Cash	360,000	
	Common Stock, $10 Par Value		300,000
	Contributed Capital in Excess of Par Value, Common Stock		**60,000**
	Sold and issued 30,000 shares of $10 par value common stock at $12 per share.		

The Contributed Capital in Excess of Par Value account is added to the par value of the stock in the equity section of the balance sheet for Dillon Snowboards as shown in Exhibit 13.8.

Exhibit 13.8

Stockholders' Equity for Stock Issued at a Premium

Stockholders' Equity		
Contributed capital:		
Common Stock—$10 par value; 50,000 shares authorized;		
30,000 shares issued and outstanding	$300,000	
Contributed capital in excess of par value, common stock	**60,000**	
Total contributed capital		$360,000
Retained earnings		65,000
Total stockholders' equity		$425,000

Issuing Par Value Stock at a Discount

A **discount on stock** is the difference between par value and issue price when the issue price is below par value. Most states prohibit the issuance of stock at a discount because stockholders would be investing less than minimum legal capital. In states that allow stock issued at a discount, its purchasers usually become contingently liable to the corporation's creditors for the amount of the discount. Because of this, stock is rarely issued at a discount. But if stock is issued at less than par, the discount is debited to a discount account. This account is a contra to the common stock account and its balance is subtracted from the par value of the stock on the balance sheet. A discount is not an expense, nor does it appear on the income statement.

Issuing No-Par Value Stock

When no-par stock is issued and not assigned a stated value, the amount received by the corporation becomes legal capital and is recorded as Common Stock. This means the entire proceeds are credited to a no-par stock account. To illustrate, if a corporation issues 1,000 shares of no-par stock for $40 per share, the transaction is recorded as:

Oct. 20	Cash	40,000	
	Common Stock, No-Par Value		40,000
	Sold and issued 1,000 shares of no-par value common stock at $40 per share.		

Assets = Liabilities + Equity
+40,000 +40,000

Issuing Stated Value Stock

When no-par stock is issued and assigned a stated value, it becomes legal capital and this stated value is credited to a no-par stock account. Assuming stock is issued at an amount in excess of stated value, this excess is credited to Contributed Capital in Excess of Stated Value, No-Par Common Stock. To illustrate, if a corporation issues 1,000 shares of no-par common stock with a stated value of $40 per share for cash of $50 per share, the entry is recorded as:

Oct. 20	Cash	50,000	
	Common Stock, No-Par Value		40,000
	Contributed Capital in Excess of Stated Value, No-Par Common Stock		10,000
	Sold 1,000 shares of no-par stock having a $40 per share stated value at $50 per share.		

Assets = Liabilities + Equity
+50,000 +40,000
+10,000

The Contributed Capital in Excess of Stated Value, No-Par Common Stock account is reported in the contributed capital part of the stockholders' equity section.

Issuing Stock for Noncash Assets

A corporation can receive assets other than cash in exchange for its stock.[9] The corporation records the assets acquired at the assets' fair market values as of the date of the transaction. The stock given in exchange is recorded at its par (or stated) value with any excess recorded in the Contributed Capital in Excess of Par account.[10]

---

[9] It can also assume liabilities on assets received such as a mortgage on property.

[10] If no-par stock is exchanged, then the stock is recorded at the assets' fair market value.

To illustrate, the entry to record receipt of land valued at $105,000 in return for immediate issuance of 4,000 shares of $20 par value common stock is:

Assets = Liabilities + Equity
+105,000 +80,000
+25,000

June 10	Land	105,000	
	Common Stock, $20 Par Value		80,000
	Contributed Capital in Excess of Par Value, Common Stock		25,000
	Exchanged 4,000 shares of $20 par value common stock for land.		

If reliable fair values for the assets received can't be determined, the fair market value of the stock given up is used to estimate the assets' values.

As another example, a corporation sometimes gives shares of its stock to promoters in exchange for their services in organizing the corporation. The corporation receives the intangible asset of Organization Costs in exchange for its stock. The entry to record receipt of services valued at $12,000 in organizing the corporation in return for immediate issuance of 600 shares of $15 par value common stock is:

Assets = Liabilities + Equity
+12,000 +9,000
+3,000

June 5	Organization Costs	12,000	
	Common Stock, $15 Par Value		9,000
	Contributed Capital in Excess of Par Value, Common Stock		3,000
	Gave promoters 600 shares of $15 par value common stock in exchange for services in organizing the corporation.		

While our examples use par value common stock, any type of stock can be issued for noncash assets.

Issuing Stock through Subscriptions

Stock is usually sold for cash and immediately issued. But corporations sometimes issue stock through stock subscriptions. A **stock subscription** involves selling stock where the investor agrees to buy a certain number of the shares at specified future dates and prices. The typical case is when a new corporation is formed and the organizers recognize both an immediate and future need for capital. The organizers can sell stock to investors who agree to contribute some cash now and to make additional contributions in the future.

Flash back

8. A company issues 7,000 shares of its $10 par value common stock in exchange for equipment valued at $105,000. The entry to record this transaction includes a credit to: *(a)* Contributed Capital in Excess of Par Value, Common Stock, for $35,000; *(b)* Retained Earnings for $35,000; *(c)* Common Stock, $10 Par Value, for $105,000.
9. What is a stock premium?
10. Who is intended to be protected by minimum legal capital?

Answers—p. 580

Preferred Stock

C4 Explain characteristics of common and preferred stock.

A corporation can issue two kinds of stock—common stock and preferred stock. **Preferred stock** has special rights that give it priority (or senior status) over common stock in one or more areas. Special rights typically include a preference for receiving dividends and for the distribution of assets if the corporation is liquidated. Preferred stock carries all the rights of common stock unless they are nullified in the corporate charter. Most preferred stock, for instance, does not have the right to vote. **NIKE,** for instance, has preferred stock outstanding without general voting rights (see Appendix A).[11] Exhibit 13.9 shows that preferred stock is issued by about one-fourth of large corporations. All corporations issue common stock.

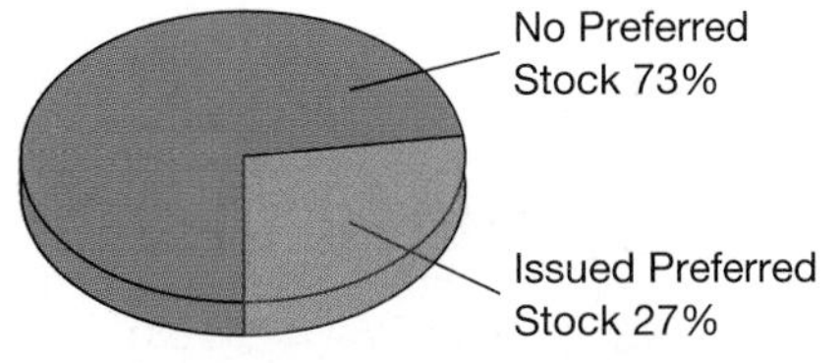

Exhibit 13.9

Corporations and Preferred Stock

Issuing Preferred Stock

Preferred stock usually has a par value. Like common stock, it can be sold at a price different from par. Separate contributed capital accounts are used to record preferred stock. To illustrate, if Dillon Snowboards also issued 50 shares of $100 par value preferred stock for $6,000 cash on July 1, 1999, the entry is:

July 1	Cash	6,000	
	Preferred Stock		5,000
	Contributed Capital in Excess of Par Value, Preferred Stock		1,000
	Issued preferred stock for cash.		

Assets = Liabilities + Equity
+6,000 +5,000
+1,000

The preferred stock accounts are included as part of contributed capital. The equity section of the year-end balance sheet for Dillon Snowboards, including preferred stock, appears as shown in Exhibit 13.10.[12]

Exhibit 13.10

Stockholders' Equity with Common and Preferred Stock

Stockholders' Equity		
Contributed capital:		
Common stock—$10 par value; 50,000 shares authorized; 30,000 shares issued and outstanding	$300,000	
Preferred stock—$100 par value; 1,000 shares authorized; 50 shares issued and outstanding	**5,000**	
Contributed capital in excess of par value, preferred stock	**1,000**	
Total contributed capital		$306,000
Retained earnings		65,000
Total stockholders' equity		$371,000

Issuing no-par preferred stock is similar to issuing no-par common stock. Also, the entries for issuing preferred stock for noncash assets are treated like similar entries for common stock.

Dividend Preference

P6 Distribute dividends between common stock and preferred stock.

Preferred stock usually carries a preference for dividends. This means preferred stockholders are allocated their dividends before any dividends are allocated to common stockholders. Simply put, a dividend cannot be paid to common stockholders unless preferred stockholders are allocated theirs when preferred stock carries a dividend preference. The dividends allocated to preferred stockholders are usually expressed as a dollar amount per share or as a percent applied to the par value.

[11] A corporation can also issue more than one class of stock. If two classes of common stock are issued, the primary difference between them usually involves voting rights. **NIKE,** for instance, has Class A and Class B common stock. Class B stock for NIKE has certain limitations in voting for directors.

[12] Common stock was issued at par.

As an example, the recent balance sheet of **Pitney Bowes** showed it had 4%, $50 par value, preferred stock outstanding. These shares require Pitney Bowes to pay quarterly dividends of $0.50 per share (an annual rate of $2, or 4% of par) before common shareholders can receive a dividend. A preference for dividends does *not* ensure dividends. If the directors don't declare a dividend, neither the preferred nor the common stockholders receive one.

Cumulative or Noncumulative Dividend

Most preferred stocks carry a cumulative dividend right. **Cumulative preferred stock** has a right to be paid both the current and all prior periods' unpaid dividends before any dividend is paid to common stockholders. When preferred stock is cumulative and the directors either don't declare a dividend to preferred stockholders or declare a dividend that doesn't cover the total amount of cumulative dividend, then the unpaid dividend amount is called **dividend in arrears.** Accumulation of dividends in arrears on cumulative preferred stock doesn't guarantee they will be paid. Also, some preferred stock is noncumulative. **Noncumulative preferred stock** has no right to prior periods' unpaid dividends if they were not declared.

To illustrate the difference between cumulative and noncumulative preferred stock, let's assume a corporation's outstanding stock includes (a) 1,000 shares of $100 par, 9% preferred stock and (b) 4,000 shares of $50 par common stock. During 1999, the first year of the corporation's operations, the directors declare cash dividends of $5,000. In year 2000, they declare $42,000. Allocations of total dividends are shown in Exhibit 13.11.

Exhibit 13.11

Allocation of Dividends (noncumulative vs. cumulative preferred stock)

	Preferred	Common
If noncumulative preferred:		
Year 1999	$ 5,000	$ 0
Year 2000:		
Step 1: Current year's preferred dividend	$ 9,000	
Step 2: Remainder to common		$33,000
If cumulative preferred:		
Year 1999	$ 5,000	$ 0
Year 2000:		
Step 1: Dividends in arrears	$ 4,000	
Step 2: Current year's preferred dividend	9,000	
Step 3: Remainder to common		$29,000
Totals for year 2000	$13,000	$29,000

Allocation of year 2000 dividends depends on whether the preferred stock is noncumulative or cumulative. With noncumulative preferred, the preferred stockholders never receive the $4,000 skipped in 1999. But if the preferred stock is cumulative, the $4,000 in arrears is paid in 2000 before any other dividends are paid.

Participating or Nonparticipating Dividend

Nonparticipating preferred stock has a feature where dividends are limited to a maximum amount each year. This maximum is often stated as a percent of the stock's par value or as a specific dollar amount per share. Once preferred stockholders receive this amount, the common stockholders receive any and all additional dividends.

Participating preferred stock has a feature where preferred stockholders share with common stockholders in any dividends paid in excess of the percent stated on the preferred stock. This participating feature doesn't apply until common stockholders receive dividends equal to the preferred stock's dividend percent. While many corporations are authorized to issue participating preferred stock, it is rarely issued and most managers never expect to issue it.

What then is the purpose of participating preferred stock? It is usually authorized as a defense against a possible *takeover* of the corporation by an "unfriendly" investor (or a group of investors) who intends to buy enough voting common stock to gain control. Taking a term from spy novels, the financial world refers to this kind of plan as a *poison pill* that a company swallows if it is threatened with capture by enemy investors.

A poison pill usually works as follows: A corporation's common stockholders on a given date are granted the right to purchase a large amount of participating preferred stock at a very low price. This right to purchase preferred shares is *not* transferable. This means if these stockholders sell their common shares, the buyers do *not* gain the right to purchase preferred shares. The right to purchase preferred shares is usually only exercised if the directors identify an investor of a large block of common shares as an unfriendly investor.

If an unfriendly investor buys a large block of common shares (whose right to purchase participating preferred shares did *not* transfer to this buyer), the board can issue preferred shares at a low price to the remaining common shareholders who retained the right to purchase. Future dividends must now be divided between the newly issued participating preferred shares and the common shares. This usually transfers a large value of the common shares to preferred shares. This means the common stock owned by the unfriendly investor loses much of its value, reducing the potential benefit of a hostile takeover.

Financial Statement Disclosure of Dividends

Dividends are not incurred as time passes. A liability for a dividend does not exist until a dividend is declared by the directors. This means if a preferred dividend date passes and the corporation's board fails to declare the dividend on its cumulative preferred stock, the dividend in arrears is not a liability. But when preparing financial statements, the *full-disclosure principle* requires the corporation to report the amount of preferred dividends in arrears as of the balance sheet date. This information is usually in a note.

Convertible Preferred Stock

Preferred stock is more attractive to investors if they carry a right to exchange preferred shares for a fixed number of common shares. **Convertible preferred stock** gives holders the option of exchanging their preferred shares for common shares at a specified rate. This feature offers holders of convertible preferred shares a higher potential return. When a company prospers and its common stock increases in value, convertible preferred stockholders can share in this success by converting their preferred stock into more valuable common stock. Also, these holders benefit from increases in the value of common stock without converting their preferred stock because the preferred stock's market value is impacted by changes in the value of common stock.

Callable Preferred Stock

Callable preferred stock gives the issuing corporation the right to purchase (retire) this stock from its holders at specified future prices and dates. Many issues of preferred stock are callable. The amount paid to call and retire a preferred share is its **call price,** or *redemption value.* This amount is set at the time the stock is issued. The call price normally includes the par value of the stock plus a premium giving holders additional return on their investment. When the issuing corporation calls and retires a preferred stock, it must pay the call price *and* any dividends in arrears.

Motivation for Preferred Stock

There are several reasons for a corporation to issue preferred stock. One reason is to raise capital without sacrificing control of the corporation. For example, let's suppose the organizers of a company have $100,000 cash to invest and wish to organize a corporation needing $200,000 of capital to get off to a good start. If they sold $200,000 worth of common stock, they'd have only 50% control and would need to negotiate extensively with other stockholders in making policy. But if they issue $100,000 worth of common stock to themselves and sell outsiders $100,000 of 8%, cumulative preferred stock with no voting rights, they retain control of the corporation.

A second reason for issuing preferred stock is to boost the return earned by common stockholders. To illustrate, let's suppose a corporation's organizers expect their new company to earn an annual after-tax income of $24,000 on an investment of $200,000. If they sell and issue $200,000 worth of common stock, this income produces a 12% return on the $200,000 of common stockholders' equity. But if they issue $100,000 of 8% preferred stock to outsiders and $100,000 of common stock to themselves, their own return increases to 16% per year as shown in Exhibit 13.12.

Exhibit 13.12

Return to Common Stockholders When Preferred Stock Is Issued

Net after-tax income	$24,000
Less preferred dividends at 8%	(8,000)
Balance to common stockholders	$16,000
Return to common stockholders ($16,000/$100,000)	16%

Common stockholders earn 16% instead of 12% because assets contributed by preferred stockholders are invested to earn $12,000 while the preferred dividend payment amounts to only $8,000.

Use of preferred stock to increase return to common stockholders is an example of **financial leverage.** Whenever the dividend rate on preferred stock is less than the rate the corporation earns on its assets, the effect of issuing preferred stock is to increase (or *lever)* the rate earned by common stockholders. Financial leverage also occurs when debt is issued and the interest rate paid on it is less than the rate earned from using the assets the creditors loaned to the corporation.

There are other reasons for issuing preferred stock. For example, a corporation's preferred stock may appeal to some investors who believe its common stock is too risky or that the expected return on common stock is too low. Also, if a corporation's management wants to issue common stock but believes the current market price for common stock is too low, the corporation may issue preferred stock that is convertible into common stock. If and when the price of common stock increases, the preferred stockholders can convert their shares into common shares.

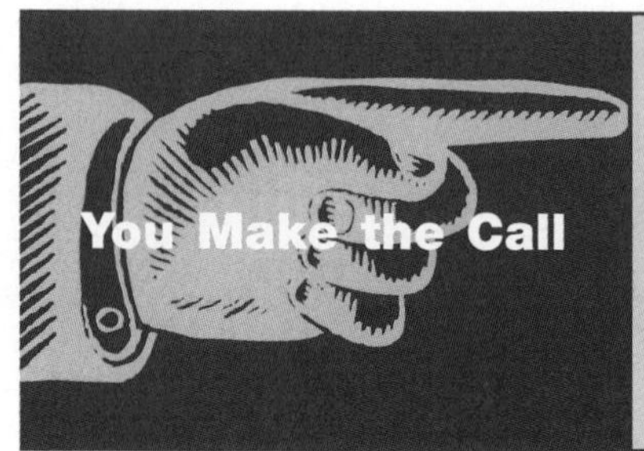

Concert Organizer

You organize music concerts for profit. You've recently decided to move away from concerts targeted at under 5,000 people to those targeted at between 10,000 to 50,000 people. This demands funding. You decide to incorporate because of the increased risk of lawsuits and your desire to issue stock to meet funding demands. It is important to you that you keep control of the company for decisions on whom to schedule and when. What type of stock issuance do you offer?

Answer—p. 580

Flash back

11. In what ways does preferred stock often have priority over common stock?
12. Increasing the return to common stockholders by issuing preferred stock is an example of: *(a)* financial leverage; *(b)* cumulative earnings; *(c)* dividends in arrears.
13. A corporation has *(a)* 9,000 shares of $50 par value, 10% cumulative and nonparticipating preferred stock and *(b)* 27,000 shares of $10 par value common stock issued and outstanding. No dividends have been declared for the past two years. During the current year, the corporation declares a $288,000 dividend. The amount paid to common shareholders is: *(a)* $243,000; *(b)* $153,000; *(c)* $135,000.

Answers—p. 580

Book Value per Share

USING THE INFORMATION

A1 Compute book value and explain its use in analysis.

This section explains how we compute book value and use it for analysis. We first focus on book value per share for corporations with only common stock outstanding and then look at book value per share when both common and preferred stock are outstanding.

Book Value per Share When Only Common Stock is Outstanding

Book value per share is the shareholders' recorded claim on the net assets (equity) of a corporation on a per share basis. **Book value per common share** is the recorded amount of stockholders' equity applicable to *common* shares on a per share basis. This ratio is defined in Exhibit 13.13.

$$\text{Book Value per Common Share} = \frac{\text{Stockholders' Equity Applicable to Common Share}}{\text{Number of Common Shares Outstanding}}$$

Exhibit 13.13

Book Value per Common Share Formula

We can compute the book value per common share for Dillon Snowboards at the end of 1999 using data in Exhibit 13.7. Dillon has 30,000 outstanding common shares and the stockholders' equity applicable to common shares is $365,000. Common shares are entitled to total stockholders' equity when there are no preferred shares outstanding. Dillon's book value per common share is $12.17, computed as $365,000 divided by 30,000 shares.

Book Value per Share When Both Common and Preferred Stock Are Outstanding

To compute book value when both common and preferred shares are outstanding, we must allocate total stockholders' equity between these two kinds of stock. The **book value per preferred share** is computed first, and its computation is shown in Exhibit 13.14.

$$\text{Book Value per Preferred Share} = \frac{\text{Stockholders' Equity Applicable to Preferred Shares}}{\text{Number of Preferred Shares Outstanding}}$$

Exhibit 13.14

Book Value per Preferred Share Formula

The stockholders' equity applicable to preferred shares equals the preferred share's call price (or par value if the preferred is not callable) plus any cumulative dividends in arrears. The remaining stockholders' equity is the portion applicable to common shares.

To illustrate, let's look at the stockholders' equity section of ***Music Live!*** as shown in Exhibit 13.15. The preferred stock of *Music Live!* is callable at $108 per share, and two years of cumulative preferred dividends are in arrears.

Exhibit 13.15

Stockholders' Equity with Preferred and Common Stock

Stockholders' Equity		
Preferred stock, $100 par value, 7% cumulative,		
2,000 shares authorized, 1,000 shares issued and outstanding	$100,000	
Contributed capital in excess of par value, preferred stock	5,000	
Total capital contributed by preferred stockholders		$105,000
Common stock, $25 par value, 12,000 shares authorized,		
10,000 shares issued and outstanding	$250,000	
Contributed capital in excess of par value, common stock	10,000	
Total capital contributed by common stockholders		260,000
Total contributed capital		$365,000
Retained earnings		82,000
Total stockholders' equity		$447,000

The book values of *Music Live!* preferred and common shares are computed in Exhibit 13.16. We need to first allocate equity to preferred shares before we compute the book value of common shares.

Exhibit 13.16

Computing Book Value per Share

Total stockholders' equity		$447,000
Less equity applicable to preferred shares:		
Call price (1,000 × $108)	$108,000	
Cumulative dividends in arrears ($100,000 × 7% × 2)	14,000	(122,000)
Equity applicable to common shares		$325,000
Book value per preferred share ($122,000/1,000 shares)	**$122.00**	
Book value per common share ($325,000/10,000 shares)	**$ 32.50**	

Book value per share is often used in the analysis of a company. It reflects the amount each share is worth if a company is liquidated at amounts reported on the balance sheet. Book value is also the starting point in many stock valuation methods. Other uses include merger negotiations, price-setting for public utilities, and loan contracts. The main limitation in using book value is the difference between book value and market value for both assets and liabilities. Professionals often adjust their analysis and the accounting numbers to reflect these differences.

Annual reports to stockholders sometimes disclose book value per share. **Anheuser-Busch's** common stock on December 31, 1996, carried a book value of $8.10, while its market (stock) value ranged from $32½ to $42⅞ in 1996. Book value and liquidation value per share can also be different because, at liquidation, the selling prices are often different from amounts reported on the balance sheet.

Investor

You are considering investing in **Ride,** a leading manufacturer of snowboards. Ride's current book value per common share is about $4, yet its common shares are priced at about $7 per share on the stock exchange. From this information, can you say whether Ride's net assets are priced higher or lower than their recorded values?

Answer—p. 580

Flash *back*

14. A corporation's outstanding stock includes (a) 1,000 shares of $90 par value cumulative preferred stock and (b) 12,000 shares of $20 par value common stock. Preferred stock has a call price of $90 and dividends of $18,000 in arrears. Total stockholders' equity is $630,000. What is the book value per common share?

15. The price at which a share of stock is bought or sold is the: *(a)* call price; *(b)* redemption value; *(c)* market value.

Answers—p. 580

Summary

C1 Identify characteristics of partnerships and similar organizations. Partnerships are voluntary associations, involve partnership agreements, have limited life, are not subject to income tax, include mutual agency, and have unlimited liability. Organizations that combine selected characteristics of partnerships and corporations include limited partnerships, limited liability partnerships, "S" corporations, and limited liability companies.

C2 Identify characteristics of corporations and their organization. Corporations are separate legal entities and their stockholders are not liable for corporate debts. Stock issued by corporations is easily transferred between stockholders. The life of a corporation does not end with the incapacity or death of a stockholder. A corporation acts through its agents, who are its officers and managers, not its stockholders. Corporations are regulated by the government and are subject to income taxes.

C3 Describe the components of stockholders' equity. Authorized stock is the total amount of stock that a corporation's charter authorizes it to sell. Issued stock is the portion of authorized shares sold to stockholders. Par value stock is a value per share assigned by the corporate charter. No-par value stock is stock *not* assigned a value per share by the corporate charter. Stated value stock is no-par stock that is assigned a value per share by the directors. Stockholders' equity is made up of (a) contributed capital and (b) retained earnings. Contributed capital consists of funds raised by stock issuances—both common and preferred. Retained earnings consists of current and prior periods' earnings not distributed to shareholders.

C4 Explain characteristics of common and preferred stock. Preferred stock has a priority (or senior status) relative to common stock in one or more areas. The usual areas include preference as to (a) dividends and (b) assets in case of liquidation. But they usually do not have voting rights. Preferred stock can also be convertible or callable. Convertibility permits the holder to convert preferred stock to common stock. Callability permits the issuer to buyback preferred stock under specified conditions.

A1 Compute book value and explain its use in analysis. Book value per common share is stockholders' equity applicable to common shares divided by the number of outstanding common shares. Book value per preferred share is stockholders' equity applicable to preferred shares divided by the number of outstanding preferred shares.

P1 Prepare entries when forming a partnership. A partner's initial investment is recorded at the fair market value of the assets contributed to the partnership.

P2 Allocate and record income and loss among partners. A partnership agreement should specify how to allocate partnership income or loss among partners. Allocation can be done on a percent (fractional) basis, or it can use salary and interest allowances to compensate partners for differences in their service and capital contributions.

P3 Account for the admission and withdrawal of a partner. When a new partner buys a partnership interest directly from one or more existing partners, the amount of cash paid from one partner to another does not affect the total recorded equity of the partnership. When a new partner purchases equity by investing additional assets in the partnership, the new partner's investment can yield a bonus either to existing partners or to the new partner. The entry to record a withdrawal can involve payment from either (a) the existing partners' personal assets or (b) partnership assets. The latter can yield a bonus to either the withdrawing or remaining partners.

P4 Prepare entries for partnership liquidation. When a partnership is liquidated, losses and gains from selling partnership assets are allocated to the partners according to their income-and-loss-sharing ratio. If a partner's capital account has a deficiency that the partner cannot pay, the other partners must share the deficit in their relative income-and-loss-sharing ratio.

P5 Record the issuance of corporate stock. When stock is issued, the par or stated value is credited to the stock account and any excess is credited to a separate contributed capital account. If the stock has no par or stated value, the entire proceeds are credited to the stock account. Stockholders must contribute assets equal to the minimum legal capital of a corporation or be potentially liable for the deficiency.

P6 Distribute dividends between common stock and preferred stock. Preferred stockholders usually hold the right to receive dividend distributions before common stockholders. This right is known as *dividend preference.* When preferred stock is cumulative and in arrears, the amount in arrears must be distributed to preferred stockholders before any dividends are distributed to common stockholders.

Guidance Answer to **Judgment and Ethics**

Lawyer

The partnership agreement apparently fails to mention liabilities or use the term *net assets.* Still, to give the estate one-third of total assets is not fair to the remaining partners. This is because if the partner had lived and the partners had decided to liquidate, the liabilities must be paid first. Also, a settlement based on the recorded equity of the deceased partner would fail to recognize excess of current value over book value. These value increases would be realized if the partnership was liquidated. A fair settlement would seem to be a payment to the estate for the balance of the deceased partner's equity based on the *current value of net assets.*

Guidance Answers to **You Make the Call**

Concert Organizer

Because you wish to maintain control of the company, you want to issue stock in a way that doesn't interfere with your ability to run the company the way you desire. You have two basic options: (1) different classes of common stock or (2) common and preferred stock. Your objective in this case is to issue stock to yourself that has all or a majority of the voting power. The other class of stock you issue would carry limited or no voting rights. In this way you maintain complete control and are able to raise your necessary funds.

Investor

Book value reflects recorded values. Ride's book value is about $4 per common share. Stock price reflects the market's expectation of current values. Ride's market value is about $7 per common share. Comparing these figures suggests the current values of Ride's net assets are higher than their recorded values (by the amount of $7 vs. $4 per share, respectively).

Guidance Answers to 

1. *b*
2. Unlimited liability means that the creditors of a partnership have the right to require each partner to be personally responsible for all partnership debts.
3. *d*
4.

	Ben	Jerry	Total
Net income			$40,000
Interest allowance	$ 7,000	$ 3,500	10,500
Remaining balance			**$29,500**
Balance allocated equally	14,750	14,750	29,500
Remaining balance			$ 0
Shares of partners	**$21,750**	**$18,250**	

5. *b*
6. A corporation must pay taxes on its income and its stockholders must pay personal income taxes on cash dividends received from the corporation.
7. A proxy is a legal document used to transfer a stockholder's right to vote to another person.
8. *a*
9. A stock premium is an amount in excess of par (or stated) value paid by purchasers of newly issued stock.
10. Creditors of the corporation are intended to be protected by minimum legal capital. Minimum legal capital intends to constrain a corporation from paying out excessive amounts to stockholders.
11. Typically, preferred stock has a preference in receiving dividends and in the distribution of assets in the case of a company's liquidation.
12. *a*
13. *b*

Total dividend	$288,000
To preferred shareholders	135,000*
Remainder to common shareholders	$153,000

*9,000 × $50 × .10 × 3 years = $135,000

14.

Total stockholders' equity		$630,000
Less equity applicable to preferred shares:		
Call price (1,000 × $90)	$90,000	
Dividends in arrears	18,000	108,000
Equity applicable to common shares		$522,000
Book value of common shares ($522,000/12,000)		$ 43.50

15. *c*

Demonstration Problem—Partnerships

Listed below are events that affect the partners' capital accounts in several successive partnerships. Prepare a table with six columns, one for each of the five partners along with a total column, to show the effects of the following events on the five partners' capital accounts.

Part 1

4/13/1999	Ries and Bax create R&B Company. Each invests $10,000, and they agree to share profits equally.
12/31/1999	R&B Co. earns $15,000 in its first year. Ries withdraws $4,000 from the partnership, and Bax withdraws $7,000.
1/1/2000	Royce is made a partner in RB&R Company after contributing $12,000 cash. The partners agree that a 10% interest allowance will be given on each partner's beginning capital balance. In addition, Bax and Royce are to receive $5,000 salary allowances. The remainder of the income is to be divided evenly.
12/31/2000	The partnership's income for the year is $40,000, and withdrawals at year-end are: Ries, $5,000; Bax, $12,500; and Royce, $11,000.
1/1/2001	Ries sells her interest to Murdock for $20,000, who is accepted by Bax and Royce as a partner in the new BR&M Co. The profits are to be shared equally after Bax and Royce each receive $25,000 salaries.
12/31/2001	The partnership's income for the year is $35,000, and year-end withdrawals are: Bax, $2,500; and Royce, $2,000.
1/1/2002	Elway is admitted as a partner after investing $60,000 cash in the new Elway & Associates partnership. Elway is given a 50% interest in capital after the other partners transfer $3,000 to his account from each of theirs. A 20% interest allowance (on the beginning-of-year capital balances) will be used in sharing profits, but there will be no salaries. Elway will get 40% of the remainder, and the other three partners will each get 20%.
12/31/2002	Elway & Associates earns $127,600 for the year, and year-end withdrawals are: Bax, $25,000; Royce, $27,000; Murdock, $15,000; and Elway, $40,000.
1/1/2003	Elway buys out Bax and Royce for the balances of their capital accounts, after a revaluation of the partnership assets. The revaluation gain is $50,000, which is divided in the previous 1:1:1:2 ratio. Elway pays the others from personal funds. Murdock and Elway will share profits on a 1:9 ratio.
2/29/2003	The partnership earns $10,000 of income since the beginning of the year. Murdock retires and receives partnership cash equal to her capital balance. Elway takes possession of the partnership assets in his own name, and the company is dissolved.

Part 2

Journalize the events affecting the partnership for the year ended December 31, 2000.

Planning the Solution

- Evaluate each transaction's effects on the capital accounts of the partners.
- Each time a new partner is admitted or a partner withdraws, allocate any bonus based on the income or loss sharing agreement.
- Each time a new partner is admitted or a partner withdraws, allocate subsequent net incomes or losses in accordance with the new partnership agreement.
- Make an entry to record Royce's initial investment. Make an entry to record the allocation of interest, salaries, and remainder. Make an entry to show the cash withdrawals from the partnership. Make an entry to close the withdrawal accounts on December 31, 2000.

Solution to Demonstration Problem

Part 1

Event	Ries	Bax	Royce	Murdock	Elway	Total
4/13/1999						
Initial investment	$10,000	$10,000				$20,000
12/31/1999						
Income (equal)	7,500	7,500				15,000
Withdrawals	(4,000)	(7,000)				(11,000)
Ending balance	$13,500	$10,500				$24,000
1/1/2000						
New investment			$12,000			$12,000
12/31/2000						
10% interest	1,350	1,050	1,200			3,600
Salaries		5,000	5,000			10,000
Remainder (equal)	8,800	8,800	8,800			26,400
Withdrawals	(5,000)	(12,500)	(11,000)			(28,500)
Ending balance	$18,650	$12,850	$16,000			$ 47,500
1/1/2001						
Transfer interest	(18,650)			$18,650		$ 0
12/31/2001						
Salaries		25,000	25,000			50,000
Remainder (equal)		(5,000)	(5,000)	(5,000)		(15,000)
Withdrawals		(2,500)	(2,000)			(4,500)
Ending balance	$ 0	$30,350	$34,000	$13,650		$ 78,000
1/1/2002						
New investment					$ 60,000	60,000
Bonuses to Elway		(3,000)	(3,000)	(3,000)	9,000	0
Adjusted balance		$27,350	$31,000	$10,650	$ 69,000	$138,000
12/31/2002						
20% interest beg. bal.		5,470	6,200	2,130	13,800	27,600
Remainder (1:1:1:2)		20,000	20,000	20,000	40,000	100,000
Withdrawals		(25,000)	(27,000)	(15,000)	(40,000)	(107,000)
Ending balance		$27,820	$30,200	$17,780	$ 82,800	$158,600
1/1/2003						
Gain (1:1:1:2)		10,000	10,000	10,000	20,000	50,000
Adjusted balance		$37,820	$40,200	$27,780	$102,800	$208,600
Transfer interests		(37,820)	(40,200)		78,020	0
Adjusted balance		$ 0	$ 0	$27,780	$180,820	$208,600
2/29/2003						
Income (1:9)				1,000	9,000	10,000
Adjusted balance				$28,780	$189,820	$218,600
Settlements				(28,780)	(189,820)	(218,600)
Final balance				$ 0	$ 0	$ 0

Part 2

2000			
Jan. 1	Cash	12,000	
	Royce, Capital		12,000
	To record investment of Royce.		
Dec. 31	Income Summary	40,000	
	Ries, Capital		10,150
	Bax, Capital		14,850
	Royce, Capital		15,000
	To allocate interest, salaries, and remainders.		
Dec. 31	Ries, Withdrawals	5,000	
	Bax, Withdrawals	12,500	
	Royce, Withdrawals	11,000	
	Cash		28,500
	To record cash withdrawals by partners.		
Dec. 31	Ries, Capital	5,000	
	Bax, Capital	12,500	
	Royce, Capital	11,000	
	Ries, Withdrawals		5,000
	Bax, Withdrawals		12,500
	Royce, Withdrawals		11,000
	To close withdrawal accounts.		

Demonstration Problem—Corporations

Barton Corporation began operations on January 1, 1999. The following transactions relating to stockholders' equity occurred during the first two years of the company's operations.

1. Prepare journal entries to record the transactions listed below.
2. Prepare the balance sheet presentation of stockholders' equity as of December 31, 1999, and December 31, 2000, related to the transactions listed below.
3. Prepare a schedule showing dividend allocations and dividends per share for 1999 and 2000. Barton Corporation declared the following cash dividends:

1999	$ 50,000
2000	$300,000

4. Prepare the journal entry for Barton's issuance of 200,000 shares of common stock for cash at $12 per share assuming:
   a. Common stock is no-par stock without a stated value.
   b. Common stock is no-par stock with a stated value of $10 per share.

Transactions

1999

Jan. 1	Authorized the issuance of 2 million shares of $5 par value common stock and 100,000 shares of $100 par value, 10% cumulative, preferred stock.
Jan. 2	Issued 200,000 shares of common stock for cash at $12 per share.
Jan. 3	Issued 100,000 shares of common stock in exchange for a building valued at $820,000 and merchandise inventory valued at $380,000.
Jan. 4	Paid cash to the company's founders for $100,000 of organization costs; these costs are to be amortized over 10 years.
Jan. 5	Issued 12,000 shares of preferred stock for cash at $110 per share.

2000

June 4	Issued 100,000 shares of common stock for cash at $15 per share.

Planning the Solution

- Record journal entries for the events in 1999 and 2000.
- Determine the balances for the 1999 and 2000 capital equity accounts for the balance sheet.
- Prepare the contributed capital portion of the 1999 and 2000 balance sheets.
- Prepare a schedule similar to Exhibit 13.11 that shows the dividend allocation for 1999 and 2000.
- Record the first issuance of common stock using the alternate specifications of no-par stock and no-par stock with a stated value.

Solution to Demonstration Problem

1. Journal entries:

Date	Account	Debit	Credit
1999			
Jan. 2	Cash	2,400,000	
	Common Stock		1,000,000
	Contributed Capital in Excess of Par Value, Common Stock		1,400,000
	Issued 200,000 shares of common stock.		
Jan. 3	Building	820,000	
	Merchandise Inventory	380,000	
	Common Stock		500,000
	Contributed Capital in Excess of Par Value, Common Stock		700,000
	Issued 100,000 shares of common stock.		
Jan. 4	Organization Costs	100,000	
	Cash		100,000
	Paid founders for organization costs.		
Jan. 5	Cash	1,320,000	
	Preferred Stock		1,200,000
	Contributed Capital in Excess of Par Value, Preferred Stock		120,000
	Issued 12,000 shares of preferred stock.		
2000			
June 4	Cash	1,500,000	
	Common Stock		500,000
	Contributed Capital in Excess of Par Value, Common Stock		1,000,000
	Issued 100,000 shares of common stock.		

2. Balance sheet presentations:

	As of December 31,	
	1999	2000
Stockholders' Equity		
Contributed capital:		
Preferred stock, $100 par value, 10% cumulative dividends, 100,000 shares authorized, 12,000 shares issued and outstanding	$1,200,000	$1,200,000
Contributed capital in excess of par value, preferred stock	120,000	120,000
Total capital contributed by preferred stockholders	$1,320,000	$1,320,000
Common stock, $5 par value, 2,000,000 shares authorized, 300,000 shares issued and outstanding in 1999, and 400,000 shares in 2000	$1,500,000	$2,000,000
Contributed capital in excess of par value, common stock	2,100,000	3,100,000
Total capital contributed by common stockholders	$3,600,000	$5,100,000
Total contributed capital	$4,920,000	$6,420,000

3. Dividend allocation schedule:

	Common	Preferred
1999 ($50,000):		
Preferred—normal (dividend due 12,000 sh. × $10 = $120,000)	$ 0	$ 50,000
Common—remainder (300,000 shares outstanding)	0	0
Total for the year	$ 0	$ 50,000
2000 ($300,000):		
Preferred—arrears from 1999 ($120,000 − $50,000)	$ 0	$ 70,000
Preferred—normal	0	120,000
Common—remainder (400,000 shares outstanding)	$110,000	0
Total for the year	$110,000	$190,000
Dividends per share		
1999	$ 0.00	$ 4.17
2000	$ 0.28	$ 15.83

4. Journal entries:

a.

1999			
Jan. 2	Cash	2,400,000	
	Common Stock, No-Par Value		2,400,000
	Issued 200,000 shares of no-par common stock at $12 per share.		

b.

1999			
Jan. 2	Cash	2,400,000	
	Common Stock, No-Par Value		2,000,000
	Contributed Capital in Excess of Stated Value, No-Par Common Stock		400,000
	Issued 200,000 shares of no-par common stock having a $10 per share stated value at $12 per share.		

Glossary

Authorized stock the total amount of stock that a corporation's charter authorizes it to sell. (p. 566).

Book value per common share the recorded amount of stockholders' equity applicable to common shares divided by the number of common shares outstanding. (p. 577).

Book value per preferred share the stockholders' equity applicable to preferred shares [equals the preferred share's call price (or par value if the preferred is not callable) plus any cumulative dividends in arrears] divided by the number of preferred shares outstanding. (p. 577).

"C" corporation a corporation that does not qualify for and elect to be treated like a partnership for income tax purposes and therefore is subject to income taxes. (p. 550).

Callable preferred stock preferred stock that the issuing corporation, at its option, may retire by paying a specified amount (the call price) to the preferred stockholders plus any dividends in arrears. (p. 575).

Call price the amount that must be paid to call and retire a preferred share. (p. 575).

Capital stock the general term referring to a corporation's stock used in obtaining its capital (owner financing). (p. 566).

Common stock stock of a corporation that has only one class of stock. (p. 565).

Contributed capital the total amount of cash and other assets received by the corporation from its stockholders in exchange for stock. (p. 569).

Convertible preferred stock a preferred stock that gives holders the option of exchanging their preferred shares for common shares at a specified rate. (p. 575).

Cumulative preferred stock preferred stock on which undeclared dividends accumulate until they are paid; common stockholders cannot receive a dividend until all cumulative dividends are paid. (p. 574).

Deficit a debit balance in Retained Earnings; occurs when a company's cumulative losses and dividends are greater than cumulative income.

Discount on stock the difference between the par value of stock and its issue price when it is issued at a price below par value. (p. 571).

Dividend in arrears an unpaid dividend on cumulative preferred stock; it must be paid before any regular dividends on the preferred stock and before any dividends on the common stock. (p. 574).

Financial leverage the earning of an increased return on common stock by paying dividends on preferred stock or interest on debt at a rate that is less than the rate of return earned with the assets invested in the corporation from issuing preferred stockholders or debt. (p. 576).

General partner a partner who assumes unlimited liability for the debts of the partnership; the general partner in a limited partnership is responsible for its management. (p. 550).

General partnership a partnership in which all partners have mutual agency and unlimited liability for partnership debts. (p. 548).

Limited liability company a form of business that has a combination of corporation and limited partnership features; provides limited liability to its members (owners) and may allow members to actively participate in management but generally does not have continuity of life. (p. 550).

Limited liability partnership a partnership in which each partner is not personally liable for malpractice or negligence claims unless the partner was responsible for providing the service that resulted in the claim. (p. 550).

Limited partners partners who have no personal liability for debts of the partnership beyond the amounts they have invested in the partnership. (p. 550).

Limited partnership a partnership that has two classes of partners, limited partners and general partners. (p. 549).

Market value per share the price at which stock is bought or sold. (p. 567).

Minimum legal capital an amount of assets defined by state law that stockholders must invest and leave invested in a corporation; usually defined as the par value of the stock; this provision is intended to protect the creditors of the corporation. (p. 568).

Mutual agency the legal relationship among the partners whereby each partner is an agent of the partnership and is able to bind the partnership to contracts within the apparent scope of the partnership's business. (p. 549).

Noncumulative preferred stock a preferred stock on which the right to receive dividends is lost for any year that the dividends are not declared. (p. 574).

Nonparticipating preferred stock a preferred stock on which dividends are limited to a maximum amount each year. (p. 574).

No-par value stock a class of stock that has not been assigned a par value by the corporate charter. (p. 568).

Organization costs the costs of bringing a corporation into existence, including legal fees, promoters' fees, and amounts paid to the state to secure the charter. (p. 564).

Par value an arbitrary value assigned to a share of stock by the corporate charter when the stock is authorized. (p. 568).

Par value stock a class of stock that has been assigned a par value by the corporate charter. (p. 568).

Participating preferred stock preferred stock with a feature that allows preferred stockholders to share with common stockholders in any dividends paid in excess of the percent stated on the preferred stock. (p. 574).

Partnership an unincorporated association of two or more persons to pursue a business for profit as co-owners. (p. 548).

Partnership contract the agreement between partners that sets forth the terms under which the affairs of the partnership will be conducted. (p. 548).

Partnership liquidation the dissolution of a business partnership by (1) selling noncash assets for cash and recording the gain or loss according to partners' income-and-loss ratio, (2) paying liabilities, and (3) distributing remaining cash to partners based on capital balances. (p. 559).

Preemptive right the right of common stockholders to protect their proportionate interest in a corporation by having the first opportunity to buy additional shares of common stock issued by the corporation. (p. 565).

Preferred stock stock that gives its owners a priority status over common stockholders in one or more ways, such as the payment of dividends or the distribution of assets on liquidation. (p. 572).

Premium on stock the difference between the par value of stock and its issue price when it is issued at a price above par value. (p. 570).

Proxy a legal document that gives an agent of a stockholder the power to exercise the voting rights of that stockholder's shares. (p. 565).

Retained earnings the cumulative net income retained by a corporation. (p. 569).

"S" corporation a corporation with 75 or fewer shareholders that meets all qualifications and elects to be treated like a partnership for income tax purposes. (p. 550).

Stated value of stock an arbitrary amount assigned to no-par stock by the corporation's board of directors; this amount is credited to the no-par stock account when the stock is issued. (p. 568).

Statement of changes in partners' equity a financial statement that shows the total capital balances at the beginning of the period, any additional investment by the partners, the net income or loss of the period, the partners' withdrawals during the period, and the ending capital balances; also called *statement of partners' capital.* (p. 555).

Stockholders' equity the equity of a corporation; also called *shareholders' equity* or *corporate capital.* (p. 569).

Stock subscription a contractual commitment by an investor to purchase unissued shares of stock at specific future dates and prices. (p. 572).

Unlimited liability of partners the legal relationship among general partners that makes each of them responsible for paying all the debts of the partnership if the other partners are unable to pay their shares. (p. 549).

Questions

1. Amey and Lacey are partners. Lacey dies, and her son claims the right to take his mother's place in the partnership. Does he have this right? Why?
2. If a partnership contract does not state the period of time the partnership is to exist, when does the partnership end?
3. As applied to a partnership, what does the term *mutual agency* mean?
4. Can partners limit the right of a partner to commit their partnership to contracts? Would the agreement be binding (a) on the partners and (b) on outsiders?
5. What does the term *unlimited liability* mean when it is applied to members of a partnership?
6. How does a general partnership differ from a limited partnership?
7. George, Burton, and Dillman have been partners for three years. The partnership is being dissolved. George is leaving the firm, but Burton and Dillman plan to carry on the business. In the final settlement, George places a $75,000 salary claim against the partnership. He contends that he has a claim for a salary of $25,000 for each year because he devoted all of his time for three years to the affairs of the partnership. Is his claim valid? Why?
8. The partnership agreement of Barnes and Ardmore provides for a two-thirds, one-third sharing of income but says nothing about losses. The first year of partnership operations resulted in a loss and Barnes argues that the loss should be shared equally because the partnership agreement said nothing about sharing losses. Is Barnes correct? Explain.
9. If the partners in Blume Partnership want the financial statements to show the procedures used to allocate the partnership income among the partners, on what financial statement should the allocation appear?
10. After all partnership assets are converted to cash and all liabilities have been paid, the remaining cash should equal the sum of the balances of the partners' capital accounts. Why?
11. Kay, Kat, and Kim are partners. In a liquidation, Kay's share of partnership losses exceeds her capital account balance. She is unable to meet the deficit from her personal assets, and the excess losses are shared by her partners. Does this relieve Kay of liability?

12. A partner withdraws from a partnership and receives assets of greater value than the book value of his equity. Should the remaining partners share the resulting reduction in their equities in the ratio of their relative capital balances or in their income-and-loss-sharing ratio?

13. Who is responsible for directing the affairs of a corporation?

14. What are organization costs? List several examples of these costs.

15. How are organization costs classified on the balance sheet?

16. List the general rights of common stockholders.

17. What is the preemptive right of common stockholders?

18. What is the difference between the par value and the call price of a share of stock?

19. Why would an investor find convertible preferred stock attractive?

20. Examine the balance sheet for **NIKE** in Appendix A at the end of the book and determine the classes of stock that the company has issued.

21. Refer to the balance sheet for **Reebok** in Appendix A at the end of the book. What is the par value of Reebok's common stock? Suggest a rationale for the amount of par value Reebok has chosen.

22. Refer to the financial statements for **America Online** in Appendix A at the end of the book. How many shares of preferred stock are outstanding as of June 30, 1996? What name does America Online use for its paid-in capital in excess of par value account?

23. What steps did Jennifer Barclay have to follow in order to receive a corporate charter for her **Blue Fish** corporation?

Quick Study

QS 13-1
Partnership liability
C1

Kurt and Ellen are partners in operating a store. Without consulting Kurt, Ellen enters into a contract for the purchase of merchandise for the store. Kurt contends that he did not authorize the order and refuses to take delivery. The vendor sues the partners for the contract price of the merchandise. Will the partnership have to pay? Why? Does your answer differ if Kurt and Ellen are partners in a public accounting firm?

QS 13-2
Liability in limited partnerships
P1

Furst organized a limited partnership and is the only general partner. Nexx invested $20,000 in the partnership and was admitted as a limited partner with the understanding that he would receive 10% of the profits. After two unprofitable years, the partnership ceased doing business. At that point, partnership liabilities were $85,000 larger than partnership assets. How much money can the creditors of the partnership obtain from the personal assets of Nexx in satisfaction of the unpaid partnership debts?

QS 13-3
Partnership income allocation
P2

Ace and Bud are partners who agree that Ace will receive a $50,000 salary allowance after which any remaining income or loss will be shared equally. If Bud's capital account is credited $1,000 as his share of the net income in a given period, how much net income did the partnership earn?

QS 13-4
Partnership income allocation
P2

Roger Bussey and Art Beery are partners in a business they started two years ago. The partnership agreement states that Bussey should receive a salary allowance of $30,000 and that Beery should receive $40,000. Any remaining income or loss is to be shared equally. Determine each partner's share of the current year's net income of $104,000.

QS 13-5
Admission of a partner
P3

Logan and Smythe are partners, each with $30,000 in their partnership capital accounts. Fontaine is admitted to the partnership by an investment of $30,000. Make the entry to show Fontaine's admission to the partnership.

QS 13-6
Partner admission through purchase of interest
P3

Fontaine agrees to pay Logan and Smythe $10,000 each for a one-third (33⅓%) interest in the Logan-Smythe partnership. At the time Fontaine is admitted, each partner has a $30,000 capital balance. Make the journal entry to record Fontaine's purchase of the partners' interest.

QS 13-7
Characteristics of corporations
C2

Of the following statements, which are true for the "C" corporation form of business?

a. Capital is more easily accumulated than with most other forms of organization.
b. It has a limited life.
c. Owners have unlimited liability for corporate debts.
d. Distributed income is taxed twice in normal circumstances.
e. It is a separate legal entity.
f. Ownership rights cannot be easily transferred.
g. Owners are not agents of the corporation.

QS 13-8
Issuance of common stock
P5

On February 1, Excel Corporation issued 37,500 shares of $5 par value common stock for $252,000 cash. Present the entry to record this transaction.

QS 13-9
Interpreting journal entries for stock issuances
P5

Each of these entries is recently recorded by a different corporation. Provide an explanation for the event or transaction described by each entry.

a. Apr. 1	Cash	60,000	
	Common Stock, No-Par Value		60,000
b. Apr. 3	Organization Costs	90,000	
	Common Stock, No-Par Value		66,000
	Contributed Capital in Excess of Stated Value, No-Par Common Stock		24,000
c. Apr. 5	Merchandise Inventory	90,000	
	Machinery	130,000	
	Notes Payable		144,000
	Common Stock, $25 Par Value		40,000
	Contributed Capital in Excess of Par Value, Common Stock		36,000

QS 13-10
Dividend allocation between classes of shareholders
P6

Holden Company's stockholders' equity includes (a) 75,000 shares of $5 par value, 8%, cumulative preferred stock and (b) 200,000 shares of $1 par value common stock. Holden did not declare any dividends during the prior year and now declares and pays a $108,000 cash dividend. Determine the amount distributed to each class of stockholders.

QS 13-11
Book value per common share
A1

The stockholders' equity section of Courtland Company's balance sheet follows:

Stockholders' Equity	
Preferred stock, 5% cumulative, $10 par value, 10,000 shares authorized, issued and outstanding	$100,000
Common stock, $5 par value, 100,000 shares authorized, 75,000 shares issued and outstanding	375,000
Retained earnings	445,000
Total stockholders' equity	$920,000

The call price of the preferred stock is $30. Determine the book value per share of the common stock.

Exercises

Exercise 13-1
Forms of organization
C1, C2

For each separate case below, recommend a form of business organization. Along with each recommendation explain how business profits would be taxed if the form of organization recommended is adopted by the owners. Also list several advantages that the owners will enjoy from the form of business organization that you recommend.

1. Keith, Scott, and Brian are new college graduates in computer science. They are thinking of starting a Web-page creation company. They all have college debts and currently do not own any of the computer equipment they will need to get the company started.
2. Dr. Marble and Dr. Sampson are new graduates from medical residency programs. They are both family practice physicians and would like to open a clinic in an underserved rural area. Although neither has any funds to bring to the new venture, a banker has expressed interest in making a loan to provide start-up funds for the practice.
3. Matt has been out of school for about five years and has become quite knowledgeable about the commercial real estate market. Matt would like to organize a company that buys and sells real estate. Matt believes he has the expertise to manage the company but needs funds to invest in commercial property.

Exercise 13-2
Journalizing partnership entries
P2

On March 1, 1999, Reed and Vaughn formed a partnership. Reed contributed $88,000 cash and Vaughn contributed land valued at $70,000 and a building valued at $120,000. Also, the partnership assumed responsibility for Vaughn's $80,000 long-term note payable associated with the land and building. The partners agreed to share profits as follows: Reed is to receive an annual salary allowance of $30,000, both are to receive an annual interest allowance of 10% of their original capital investment, and any remaining profit or loss is to be shared equally. On October 20, 1999, Reed withdrew cash of $32,000 and Vaughn withdrew $25,000. After the adjusting entries and the closing entries to the revenue and expense accounts, the Income Summary account had a credit balance of $79,000.

Required

a. Prepare General Journal entries to record the initial capital investments of the partners, their cash withdrawals, and the December 31 closing of the withdrawals accounts.
b. Determine the balances of the partners' capital accounts as of the end of 1999.

Exercise 13-3
Income allocation in a partnership
P2

Newton and Berry began a partnership by investing $50,000 and $75,000, respectively. During its first year, the partnership earned $165,000.

Required

Prepare calculations showing how the $165,000 income should be allocated to the partners under each of the following separate plans for sharing net incomes and losses:

a. Partners failed to agree on a method of sharing income.
b. Partners agreed to share incomes and losses in proportion to their initial investments.
c. Partners agreed to share income by allowing a $55,000 per year salary allowance to Newton, a $45,000 per year salary allowance to Berry, 10% interest on their initial investments, and the balance equally.

Exercise 13-4
Income allocation in a partnership
P2

Assume that the partners of Exercise 13-2 agreed to share net incomes and losses by allowing annual salary allowances of $55,000 to Newton and $45,000 to Berry, 10% interest allowances on their investments, and the balance equally.

Required

a. Determine the shares of Newton and Berry in a first-year net income of $94,400.
b. Determine the partners' shares in a first-year net loss of $15,700.

Exercise 13-5
Sale of partnership interest
P3

The partners in the Royal Partnership have agreed that partner Prince may sell his $90,000 equity in the partnership to Duke, for which Duke will pay Prince $75,000. Present the partnership's journal entry to record the sale of Prince's interest to Duke on September 30.

Exercise 13-6
Admission of new partner
P3

The E-O Partnership has total partners' equity of $510,000, which is made up of Elm, Capital, $400,000, and Oak, Capital, $110,000. The partners share net incomes and losses in a ratio of 80% to Elm and 20% to Oak. On November 1, Ash is admitted to the partnership and given a 15% interest in equity and incomes and losses. Prepare the journal entry to record the admission of Ash under each of the following separate assumptions: Ash invests cash of (a) $90,000; (b) $125,000; and (c) $60,000.

Exercise 13-7
Retirement of partner
P3

Holland, Flowers, and Wood have been partners sharing net incomes and losses in a 5:3:2 ratio. On January 31, the date Wood retires from the partnership, the equities of the partners are Holland, $350,000; Flowers, $240,000; and Wood, $180,000. Present General Journal entries to record Wood's retirement under each of the following separate assumptions:

a. Wood is paid $180,000 in partnership cash for his equity.
b. Wood is paid $200,000 in partnership cash for his equity.
c. Wood is paid $150,000 in partnership cash for his equity.

Exercise 13-8
Liquidation of partnership
P4

The Red, White & Blue partnership was begun with investments by the partners as follows: Red, $175,000; White, $220,000; and Blue, $205,000. The operations did not go well, and the partners eventually decided to liquidate the partnership, sharing all losses equally. On August 31, after all assets were converted to cash and all creditors were paid, only $60,000 in partnership cash remained.

Required

1. Compute the capital account balances of the partners after liquidation of assets and payment of creditors.

2. Any partner with a deficit agrees to pay cash to the partnership to cover the deficit. Present the General Journal entries on August 31 to record the cash receipt from the deficient partner(s) and the final disbursement of cash to the partners.

3. Assume that any partner with a deficit is not able to reimburse the partnership. Present journal entries (a) to transfer the deficit of any deficient partners to the other partners and (b) to record the final disbursement of cash to the partners.

Exercise 13-9
Liquidation of partnership
P4

Sandburg, McArthur, and Cox are partners who share incomes and losses in a 1:4:5 ratio. After lengthy disagreements among the partners and several unprofitable periods, the partners decided to liquidate the partnership. Before liquidation, the partnership balance sheet shows total assets, $116,000; total liabilities, $88,000; Sandburg, Capital, $1,200; McArthur, Capital, $11,700; and Cox, Capital, $15,100. The cash proceeds from selling the assets were sufficient to repay all but $24,000 to the creditors. Calculate the loss from selling the assets, allocate the loss to the partners, and determine how much of the remaining liability should be paid by each partner.

Exercise 13-10
Liquidation of limited partnership
P4

Assume that the Sandburg, McArthur, and Cox partnership of Exercise 13-9 is a limited partnership. Sandburg and McArthur are general partners and Cox is a limited partner. How much of the remaining $24,000 liability should be paid by each partner?

Exercise 13-11
Recording stock issuances
P5

Prepare the entries to record the following three separate issuances of stock:

a. Two thousand shares of no-par common stock are issued to the corporation's promoters in exchange for their efforts. Their efforts are estimated to be worth $30,000, and the stock has no stated value.

b. Two thousand shares of no-par common stock are issued to the corporation's promoters in exchange for their efforts. Their efforts are estimated to be worth $30,000, and the stock has a $1 per share stated value.

c. Four thousand shares of $10 par value common stock are issued for $70,000 cash.

d. One thousand shares of $100 par value preferred stock are issued for $120,000 cash.

Exercise 13-12
Accounting for par and no-par stock issuances
P5

Hanson, Inc., issued 6,000 shares of its common stock for $144,000 cash on February 2. Present the journal entries to record this event under each of the following separate situations:

a. The stock has no par or stated value.

b. The stock has a $20 par value.

c. The stock has a stated value of $8 per share.

Exercise 13-13
Dividends on common and noncumulative preferred stock
P6

The outstanding stock of Lipscomb includes (a) 40,000 shares of noncumulative preferred stock with a $10 par value and a 7.5% dividend rate, and (b) 100,000 shares of common stock with a $1 par value. During its first four years of operation, the corporation declared and paid the following total amounts of dividends:

1999	$10,000
2000	24,000
2001	100,000
2002	196,000

Determine the amount of dividends paid in each year to each class of stockholders. Also compute the total dividends paid to each class in the four years combined.

Exercise 13-14
Dividends on common and cumulative preferred stock
P6

Use the data in Exercise 13-13 to determine the amount of dividends paid in each year to each class of stockholders, assuming that the preferred stock is cumulative. Also determine the total dividends paid to each class in the four years combined.

Exercise 13-15
Using preferred stock for leverage
C3, C4

An entrepreneur is planning to start a new business and needs $312,500 of start-up capital. This person has $250,000 in personal assets that can be invested and needs to raise another $62,500 in cash. The person will buy 5,000 shares of common stock for $250,000 and has two alternative plans for raising the additional cash. Plan A is to sell 1,250 shares of common stock to one or more investors for $62,500 cash. Plan B is to sell 625 shares of cumulative preferred stock to one or more investors for $62,500 cash (this preferred stock would have a $100 par value, an annual 8% dividend rate, and would be issued at par).

1. If the business is expected to earn $45,000 of after-tax net income in the first year, what rate of return on beginning equity will this entrepreneur earn under each alternative? Which of the two plans will provide the higher return to the entrepreneur?
2. If the business is expected to earn $10,500 of after-tax net income in the first year, what rate of return on beginning equity will the entrepreneur earn under each alternative? Which of the two plans will provide the higher return to the entrepreneur?
3. Interpret differences between the results for parts (1) and (2).

Exercise 13-16
Identifying characteristics of preferred stock
C3, C4

Match each numbered description with the characteristic of preferred stock that it best describes. Indicate your answer by writing the letter for the characteristic in the blank next to each description.

a. Callable **b.** Convertible **c.** Cumulative
d. Noncumulative **e.** Nonparticipating **f.** Participating

____ **1.** Holders of the stock can exchange it for shares of common stock.
____ **2.** Issuing corporation can retire the stock by paying a prearranged price.
____ **3.** Holders of the stock are entitled to receive dividends in excess of the stated rate under some conditions.
____ **4.** Holders of the stock are not entitled to receive dividends in excess of the stated rate.
____ **5.** Holders of the stock lose any dividends that are not declared.
____ **6.** Holders of the stock are entitled to receive current and all past dividends before common stockholders receive any dividends.

Exercise 13-17
Characteristics of corporations and partnerships
C1, C2

Next to the following list of eight characteristics of business organizations, write a brief description of how each characteristic applies to C corporations and general partnerships.

	C Corporations	General Partnerships
1. Life		
2. Owners' liability		
3. Legal status		
4. Tax status of income		
5. Owners' authority		
6. Ease of formation		
7. Transferability of ownership		
8. Ability to raise large amounts of capital		

Exercise 13-18
Book value per share
A1

The balance sheet for Kuhn Corp. includes the following:

Stockholders' Equity	
Preferred stock, 6% cumulative, $25 par value, $30 call price, 5,000 shares issued and outstanding	$125,000
Common stock, $10 par value, 40,000 shares issued and outstanding	400,000
Retained earnings	267,500
Total stockholders' equity	$792,500

Determine the book value per share of the preferred and common stock under these two situations:

a. No preferred dividends are in arrears. **b.** Three years of preferred dividends are in arrears.

Problems

Problem 13-1
Methods of allocating partnership income

Tom Katz, Kaye Reeves, and Alice Troy invested $40,000, $56,000, and $64,000, respectively, in a partnership. During its first year, the firm earned $124,500.

Required

Prepare entries to close the firm's Income Summary account as of its December 31 year-end and to allocate the net income to the partners under each of the following separate assumptions:

a. The partners have no agreement on the method of sharing incomes and losses.

b. The partners agreed to share incomes and losses in the ratio of their beginning investments.

c. The partners agreed to share incomes and losses by providing annual salary allowances of $33,000 to Katz, $28,000 to Reeves, and $40,000 to Troy; allowing 10% interest on the partners' beginning investments; and sharing the remainder equally.

Check Figure (c) Troy, Capital, $48,900

Problem 13-2
Allocating partnership incomes and losses; sequential years

Linda Nuñez and Ray Parker are in the process of forming a partnership to which Nuñez will devote one-half time and Parker will devote full time. They have discussed the following alternative plans for sharing incomes and losses.

a. In the ratio of their initial investments, which they have agreed will be $21,000 for Nuñez and $31,500 for Parker.

b. In proportion to the time devoted to the business.

c. A salary allowance of $3,000 per month to Parker and the balance in accordance with the ratio of their initial investments.

d. A salary allowance of $3,000 per month to Parker, 10% interest on their initial investments, and the balance equally.

The partners expect the business to generate income as follows: Year 1, $18,000 net loss; Year 2, $45,000 net income; and Year 3, $75,000 net income.

Required

1. Prepare three schedules with the following column headings:

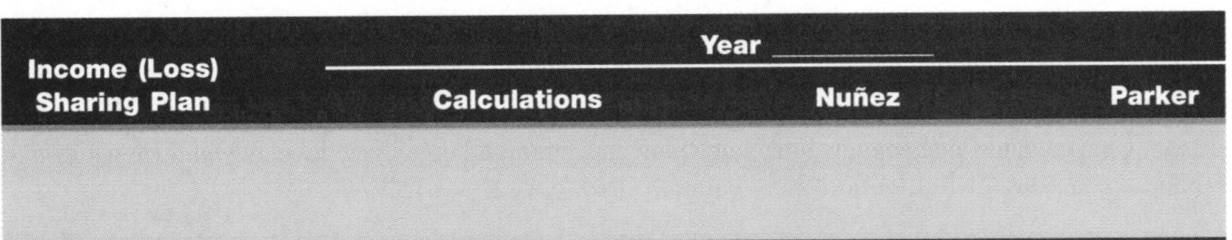

Income (Loss) Sharing Plan	Year ______		
	Calculations	Nuñez	Parker

2. Complete a schedule for each of the first three years by showing how partnership income or loss for each year would be allocated to the partners under each of the four plans being considered. Round answers to the nearest whole dollar.

Check Figure Plan (d), Year 1, Parker's share, $9,525

Problem 13-3
Partnership income allocation, statement of changes in partners' equity, and closing entries

Brad Marshall, Jon Spiller, and Leigh Rand formed the MSR Partnership by making capital contributions of $183,750, $131,250, and $210,000, respectively. They predict annual net incomes of $225,000 and are considering the following alternative plans of sharing incomes and losses: (a) equally; (b) in the ratio of their initial investments; or (c) salary allowances of $40,000 to Marshall, $30,000 to Spiller, and $45,000 to Rand; interest allowances of 10% on their initial investments; and the balance shared equally.

Required

1. Prepare a schedule with the following column headings:

Income (Loss) Sharing Plan	Calculations	Marshall	Spiller	Rand	Total

Use the schedule to show how net income of $225,000 for year 2000 would be distributed under each of the alternative plans being considered. Round answers to the nearest whole dollar.

Check Figure Part 2, Rand, Capital, $223,000

2. Prepare a statement of changes in partners' equity showing the allocation of income to the partners assuming they agree to use alternative (c), income earned is $104,500, and Marshall, Spiller, and Rand withdraw $17,000, $24,000, and $32,000, respectively, at year-end.
3. Prepare the December 31 journal entry to close Income Summary assuming they agree to use alternative (c) and the income is $104,500. Also, close the withdrawals accounts.

Problem 13-4
Withdrawal of a partner

Part 1. Godfrey, Gully, and Speck are partners with capital balances as follows: Godfrey, $84,000; Gully, $69,000; and Speck, $147,000. The partners share incomes and losses in a 3:2:5 ratio. Gully decides to withdraw from the partnership, and the partners agree to not have the assets revalued upon his retirement. Prepare General Journal entries to record the February 1 withdrawal of Gully from the partnership under each of the following separate assumptions:

a. Gully sells his interest to Goldman for $80,000 after Godfrey and Speck approve the entry of Goldman as a partner.
b. Gully gives his interest to a son-in-law, Swain. Godfrey and Speck accept Swain as a partner.
c. Gully is paid $69,000 in partnership cash for his equity.
d. Gully is paid $107,000 in partnership cash for his equity.
e. Gully is paid $15,000 in partnership cash plus computer equipment recorded on the partnership books at $35,000 less its accumulated depreciation of $11,600.

Check Figure (e) Speck, Capital, $19,125 credit

Part 2. Assume that Gully does not retire from the partnership described in Part 1. Instead, Hatch is admitted to the partnership on February 1 with a 25% equity. Prepare General Journal entries to record the entry of Hatch into the partnership under each of the following separate assumptions:

a. Hatch invests $100,000.
b. Hatch invests $72,500.
c. Hatch invests $131,000.

Problem 13-5
Liquidation of a partnership

Swanson, Chapel, and Page plan to liquidate their partnership. They share incomes and losses in a 3:2:1 ratio, and on the day of liquidation their balance sheet appears as follows:

SWANSON, CHAPEL, AND PAGE
Balance Sheet
May 31

Assets		Liabilities and Equity	
Cash	$ 90,400	Accounts payable	$122,750
Inventory	268,600	David Swanson, capital	46,500
		Annie Chapel, capital	106,250
		Maria Page, capital	83,500
Total assets	$359,000	Total liabilities and equity	$359,000

Required

Prepare the General Journal entries for the sale of inventory, the gain or loss allocation, and the distribution of cash in each of the following separate cases:

a. Inventory is sold for $300,000.
b. Inventory is sold for $250,000.
c. Inventory is sold for $160,000, and any partners with capital deficits pay in the amount of their deficits.
d. Inventory is sold for $125,000, and the partners have no assets other than those invested in the partnership.

Problem 13-6
Stockholders' equity transactions
C2, C3

Precision Products is incorporated at the beginning of the year and engages in a number of transactions. The following journal entries affected its stockholders' equity during its first year of operations:

a.	Cash	150,000	
	Common Stock, $25 Par Value		125,000
	Contributed Capital in Excess of Par Value, Common Stock		25,000
b.	Organization Costs	75,000	
	Common Stock, $25 Par Value		62,500
	Contributed Capital in Excess of Par Value, Common Stock		12,500
c.	Cash	21,500	
	Accounts Receivable	7,500	
	Office Equipment	10,750	
	Building	30,000	
	Accounts Payable		11,000
	Notes Payable		18,750
	Common Stock, $25 Par Value		25,000
	Contributed Capital in Excess of Par Value, Common Stock		15,000
d.	Cash	60,000	
	Common Stock, $25 Par Value		37,500
	Contributed Capital in Excess of Par Value, Common Stock		22,500

Required

1. Provide explanations for the journal entries labeled *a* through *d*.

2. Answer the following questions:

a. How many shares of common stock are outstanding at year-end?

b. What is the amount of minimum legal capital at year-end?

c. What is the total contributed capital at year-end?

d. What is the book value per share of the common stock at the end of the year if contributed capital plus retained earnings equals $347,500?

Check Figure (c) Contributed Capital, $325,000

Problem 13-7
Computing book values and dividend allocations
A1, P6

Segura Corporation's common stock is currently selling on a stock exchange at $170 per share. Segura's current balance sheet shows the following:

Stockholders' Equity	
Preferred stock, 5%, cumulative $ ___ par value, 1,000 shares authorized, issued, and outstanding	$100,000
Common stock, $___ par value, 4,000 shares authorized, issued, and outstanding	160,000
Retained earnings	300,000
Total stockholders' equity	$560,000

Required

Preparation Component

1. What is the market value of the corporation's common stock?

2. What are the par values of the corporation's preferred stock and its common stock?

3. If no dividends are in arrears, what are the book values per share of the preferred stock and the common stock?

4. If two years' preferred dividends are in arrears, what are the book values per share of the preferred stock and the common stock?

Check Figure (4) Book value of common, $112.50

5. If two years' preferred dividends are in arrears and the preferred stock is callable at $110 per share, what are the book values per share of the preferred stock and the common stock?
6. If two years' preferred dividends are in arrears and the board of directors declares dividends of $20,000, what total amount will be paid to the preferred and the common shareholders? What is the amount of dividends per share for the common stock?

Analysis Component

7. What are some factors that can contribute to a difference between the book value of common stock and its market value?

BEYOND THE NUMBERS

Reporting in Action

C3, A1

Refer to the financial statements and related information for **NIKE** in Appendix A. Answer the following questions by analyzing that information.

1. Has NIKE issued any preferred stock? If so, what are the features of its preferred stock?
2. How many shares of common stock are authorized? How many are issued as of May 31, 1997?
3. What is the par value of the common stock?
4. What is the book value of the common stock at May 31, 1997?

Swoosh Ahead

5. Obtain NIKE's annual report information for a fiscal year ending after May 31, 1997. You can get this information from either its Web site [**www.nike.com**] or the SEC's EDGAR database [**www.sec.gov**]. Is the redeemable preferred stock still outstanding? Has the number of common shares outstanding increased since May 31, 1997?

Comparative Analysis

A1

Key comparative figures ($ thousands) for **NIKE** and **Reebok** follow:

Key figures*	NIKE		Reebok	
	1997	1996	1996	1995
Total Stockholders' Equity	$3,155,838	$2,431,400	$381,234	$895,289
Equity applicable to preferred	$300	$300		
Common Shares Issued	289,270 (A&B)	287,258 (A&B)	92,557	111,015
Treasury Shares Repurchased			36,716	36,211

*NIKE figures are from its annual reports for fiscal years ended May 31,1997 and 1996.
Reebok figures are from its annual reports for fiscal years ended December 31, 1996 and 1995.

Required

1. Compute book value per common share for both Reebok and NIKE using these two years' data.
2. Identify causes of any changes in book value per share between the two years for each company.

Ethics Challenge

P2

Doctors Hall, Maben, and Sweet have been in a group practice for several years. Hall and Maben are family practice physicians and Sweet is a general surgeon. Sweet receives many referrals for surgery from his family practice partners. Upon the partnership's original formation, the three doctors agreed to a two-part formula to share income. Every month each doctor receives a salary allowance of $3,000. Additional income is divided according to a percent of patient charges the doctors generate for the month. In the current month Hall generated 10% of the billings, Maben 30%, and Sweet 60%. The group's income for this month is $50,000. Sweet has expressed dissatisfaction with the income-sharing formula and asks that income be split entirely on patient charge percents.

1. Compute income allocation for the current month using the original agreement.
2. Compute income allocation for the current month using Sweet's suggestion.
3. Identify the ethical components of this decision for the doctors.

Communicating in Practice A1

Investors use book value for investment decisions. Warren E. Buffett, one of the world's wealthiest individuals and a recognized investment expert, relies on book value for investment decisions. Read the article "Buffet Takes Stock" by L. J. Davis, *The New York Times,* April 1, 1990, and write a one-page report that includes the following:

1. Traditional definition of *book value* and formulas for its computation as shown in the chapter.
2. Buffet's definition of book value and its formula for computation. Who is the source of this alternative definition and what is the person's relationship to Buffett?
3. Compute book value per common share for a corporation of your choosing using (a) the traditional computation and (b) Buffet's computation. You will need an annual report which can be obtained in many ways, including accessing the SEC's database [**www.sec.gov**].
4. The market value of your chosen company's common stock on the date of the balance sheet in the annual report. (Research the financial press or on-line sites.)
5. An explanation of whether or not Buffett would have considered stock in the company you selected as a "sleeping beauty." (Hint: Guidance is in the article with a comparison of two sample numbers.)

Taking It to the Net P1

Visit the Edgar site (**www.sec.gov**), and search it using the word "Celtics". View the 1997 10K report filed by the **Boston Celtics** partnership and answer the following questions:

1. What are the Celtics' primary sources of revenue for the fiscal year ended June 30, 1997?
2. What is net income for the limited partnership for the fiscal year ended June 30, 1997?
3. Trace net income to the statement of partners' capital. What is the ending capital shown on the statement of partners' capital as of June 30, 1997?

Teamwork in Action C4

A. Using the facts below, **each** team member is to determine dividend allocation on a per share and per class basis for **one** of the assumptions that follow. Determine if this assumption results in arrears for future years. After determinations are complete, rotate around the team allowing each member to present his or her solution to the team. Do not proceed to the next team member until all team members express agreement with and understanding of the presentation. Be prepared to present your solution to the class if called on.

Facts

(a) 50,000 outstanding shares of $100 par value, 8% nonparticipating preferred stock. (b) 100,000 outstanding shares of $50 par value common stock.

Assumptions

1. Preferred is noncumulative and a $200,000 dividend is declared.
2. Preferred is cumulative, no dividends are in arrears, and a $600,000 dividend is declared.
3. Preferred is cumulative, dividend arrears of $5 per share, and a dividend of $500,000 is declared.
4. Preferred is cumulative, two full years of dividend arrears, and a dividend of $1,800,000 is declared.

B. After completing a team discussion of each member's solution for the above assumptions, the team is to collaborate and determine the dividend necessary to ensure that a common stockholder receives $3 per share if the preferred is cumulative and has two years of dividend arrears.

Hitting the Road C1, C2

Review the forms of business organization. Identify a business in your area that is organized as (a) sole proprietorship, (b) general partnership, (c) limited liability partnership, and (d) a corporation. You may need to confirm your identifications by placing a phone call to the various businesses. Speculate as to why the businesses identified are organized in their current form.

Business Week Activity

Visit the *Business Week* Web site [**www.businessweek.com**]. Explore this site as follows:

1. View the *Table of Contents* of the latest *Business Week* issue. Read an article that interests you.
2. Visit *Sign Up* and consider subscribing to a free BW Online Insider Newsletter.

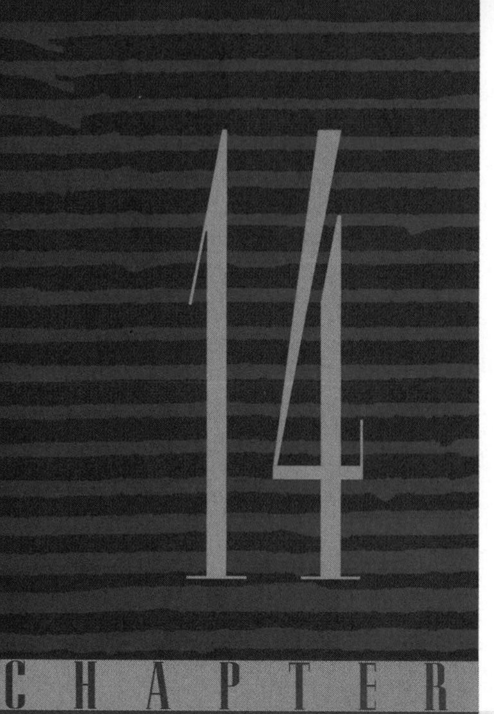

CHAPTER

Corporate Reporting: Dividends, Stock, and Income

A Look Back

Chapter 13 focused on both the partnership and corporate forms of organization. We described important characteristics of both forms of organization along with accounting for many of their important transactions.

A Look at This Chapter

This chapter extends our discussion of corporate accounting to dividends, treasury stock, income reporting, and retained earnings. We also explain earnings per share, dividend yield, and the price-earnings ratio.

A Look Ahead

Chapter 15 focuses on accounting for notes and bonds. This includes the characteristics of these liabilities and their implications to users of financial statements.

Chapter Outline

- **Dividends**
  - Cash Dividends
  - Stock Dividends
  - Stock Splits
- **Treasury Stock**
  - Purchasing Treasury Stock
  - Reissuing Treasury Stock
  - Retiring Stock
- **Reporting Income Information**
  - Continuing Operations
  - Discontinued Segments
  - Extraordinary Items
  - Changes in Accounting Principles
  - Earnings per Share
  - Stock Options
- **Retained Earnings**
  - Restricted Retained Earnings
  - Appropriated Retained Earnings
  - Prior Period Adjustments
  - Changes in Accounting Estimates
  - Statement of Changes in Stockholders' Equity
- **Using the Information—Dividend Yield and Price-Earnings Ratio**
  - Dividend Yield
  - Price-Earnings Ratio

To Be or Not to Be

NASHVILLE, TN—Nashville is the heart of country music. Yet just outside this all-American city is **The Shakespeare,** the brain-child of Peter "Buck" Owens, a farm boy from nearby Shelbyville.

"I always wanted to see England, and so my buddy and I took a $295 charter flight and our mountain bikes to Northern England after we finished our first year in college," says Owens. During their tour, they stopped over in Manchester for two days. "We hung out at a pub called The Shakespeare," recalls Owens. "While we drank our ale, I kept thinking a pub like this would be a hit back home."

Within two years, Owens was running an English-style pub in the land of Garth Brooks. But after three years, with a debt of $78,000, his dream was fading. "The first two years were great, and I was turning a hefty profit," boasted Owens. So what happened? "The next year the city took four months putting in a new sewer system on our street. At times, I was the only person in the pub. And then to top it off, we had an electrical fire closing us down for another two months."

To stay afloat, Owens needed cash. But who'd lend him money after such a disastrous year? "I thought I was finished," says Owens. But Owens, never the quitter, took the pub's records to the local bank officer. "He really understood the situation and explained things like continuing operations, unusual losses, and extraordinary items."

The bank officer agreed that the pub's poor performance was tied to the sewer work and the electrical fire. The pub's normal operations were highly profitable. "In the end, I got my loan and I'm back turning a nice profit." So the next time you're near Nashville, take in a little of England at The Shakespeare.

Learning Objectives

Conceptual

C1 Describe stock dividends and stock splits.

C2 Explain the form and content of a comprehensive income statement.

C3 Explain the items reported in retained earnings.

Analytical

A1 Compute earnings per share and describe this ratio's use.

A2 Compute dividend yield and explain its use in analysis.

A3 Compute price-earnings ratio and describe its use in analysis.

Procedural

P1 Record transactions involving cash dividends.

P2 Account for stock dividends and stock splits.

P3 Record purchases and sales of treasury stock and the retirement of stock.

CHAPTER PREVIEW

Corporations often enter into financing transactions involving changes in stockholders' equity. The first two major sections of this chapter focus on several of these transactions, including cash and stock dividends, stock splits, and a company's transactions in its own stock. The third section of this chapter describes the reporting of income information. Emphasis is placed on the form and content of a comprehensive income statement including earnings per share. The final section looks at accounting for retained earnings including prior period adjustments, retained earnings restrictions, and reporting guidelines. Understanding these topics aids us in reading, interpreting, and using financial statements for decision making. It is also useful to people like Peter Owens, as described in the opening article, for guidance in properly reporting income.

Dividends

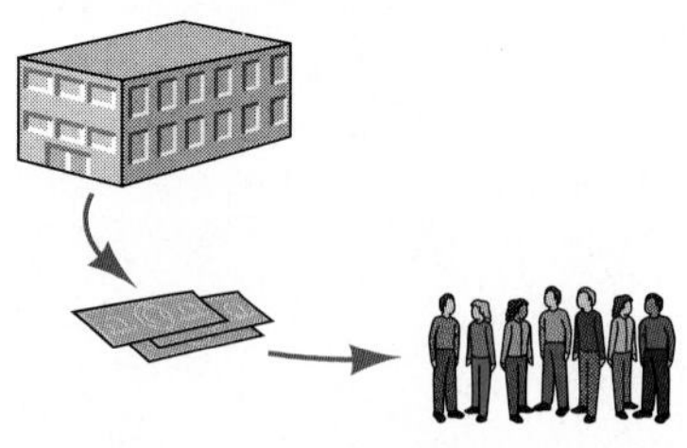

Dividends are normally paid out of retained earnings. A corporation's retained earnings is that part of stockholders' equity created by a company's income and loss activities. It equals the total cumulative amount of reported net income less any net losses and dividends declared since the company started operating. This section describes dividend transactions involving both cash and stock.

Cash Dividends

P1 Record transactions involving cash dividends.

Most state laws allow a corporation to pay cash dividends only if retained earnings exist. But to pay a cash dividend, a corporation must have cash in addition to retained earnings. The decision to pay cash dividends rests with the board of directors and involves more than evaluating retained earnings and cash. The directors, for instance, may decide to keep the cash and invest in the growth of the corporation. Other reasons to keep the cash include meeting emergencies, taking advantage of unexpected opportunities, or paying off debt.

Many corporations pay cash dividends to their stockholders in regular amounts at regular dates. These cash flows provide a return to investors and almost always affect the stock's market value. The graph in the margin shows the frequency of cash dividends to both common stock and preferred stock for large corporations.

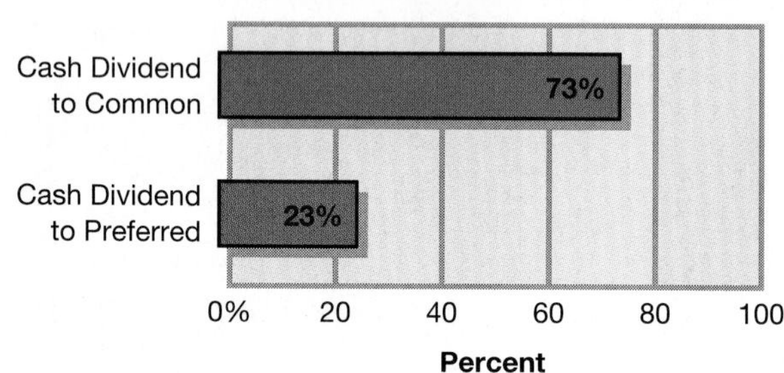

Entries for Cash Dividends

We sometimes assume for simplicity that dividends are declared and paid at the same time. But in practice the payment of dividends involves three important dates: declaration, record, and payment.

Date of declaration is the date the directors vote to pay a dividend. Stockholders receive a dividend only if the directors vote to declare one. Declaring a dividend creates a legal liability of the corporation to its stockholders. **Date of record** is the future date specified by the directors for identifying those stockholders listed in the corporation's records to receive dividends. The date of record usually follows the date of declaration by at least two weeks. Persons who own stock on the date of record receive dividends. **Date of payment** is the date when the corporation makes payment. This date follows the date of record by enough time to allow the corporation to arrange checks or other means to pay its stockholders dividends.

If a balance sheet is prepared between date of declaration and date of payment, a liability for the dividend is reported as a current liability. We record a legal liability when declaring a dividend. To illustrate, the entry to record a January 9 declaration of a $1 per share dividend by the directors of Z-Tech, Inc., with 5,000 outstanding shares is:

Date of Declaration

Jan. 9	Cash Dividends Declared	5,000	
	Common Dividend Payable		5,000
	Declared a $1 per share cash dividend on common stock.		

Assets = Liabilities + Equity
+5,000 −5,000

Cash Dividends Declared is a temporary (contra-equity) account that accumulates information about total dividends declared during the reporting period. It is *not* an expense account. Common Dividend Payable reflects the corporation's current liability to its stockholders.

The date of record is January 22. Those who own stock on this date will receive the dividend. No journal entry is needed at the date of record:

Date of Record

Jan. 22	No entry required		

The date of payment requires an entry to record distribution of the cash dividend. This entry to record both the settlement of the liability and the reduction of the cash balance on the date of payment is:

Date of Payment

Feb. 1	Common Dividend Payable	5,000	
	Cash		5,000
	Paid $1 per share cash dividend to common stockholders.		

Assets = Liabilities + Equity
−5,000 −5,000

At the end of the reporting period, the balance of the Cash Dividends Declared account is closed to Retained Earnings. For instance, if Z-Tech declared four quarterly dividends of $5,000, the account would have a $20,000 balance at the end of the year. The required year-end closing entry is:

Dec. 31	Retained Earnings	20,000	
	Cash Dividends Declared		20,000
	To close Cash Dividends Declared account.		

Assets = Liabilities + Equity
−20,000
+20,000

If one of the declared dividends remains unpaid on December 31, this closing entry is still recorded because the act of declaration reduces retained earnings. The Common Dividend Payable liability account continues to carry a balance until dividends are paid. Its balance is reported on the December 31 balance sheet.

Dividend Decline
There has been a major decline in cash dividends as a percent of stock prices in U.S. markets. Cash dividends are increasingly viewed as an inefficient way to reward shareholders. Dividend tax rates can be nearly 40%, and these taxes are inescapable. Companies are instead buying back shares, paying down debt, or expanding the business. [Source: "Are Stocks Overpriced—Or The Yardsticks Flawed?" *Business Week,* July 15, 1996.]

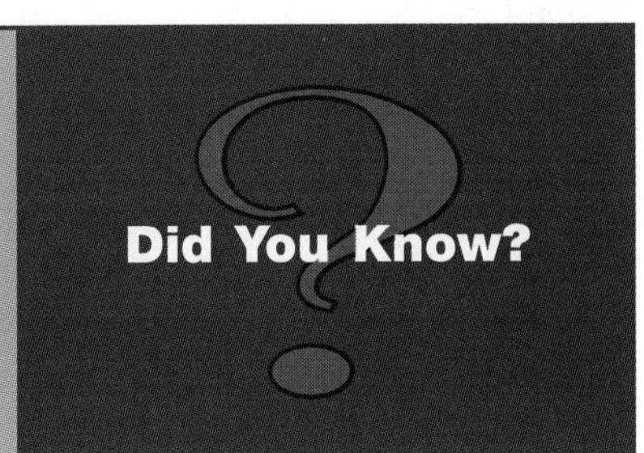

Deficits and Cash Dividends

A corporation with a debit (abnormal) balance for retained earnings is said to have a **deficit.** A deficit arises when a company incurs cumulative losses or pays dividends greater than total profits earned in other years. A deficit is deducted on a corporation's balance sheet as shown in Exhibit 14.1.

Exhibit 14.1

Stockholders' Equity with a Deficit

Common stock, $10 par value, 5,000 shares authorized and outstanding	$50,000
Retained earnings deficit	(6,000)
Total stockholders' equity	$44,000

A corporation with a deficit is not allowed to pay a cash dividend to its stockholders in most states. This legal restriction is designed to protect creditors of the corporation by preventing distribution of assets to stockholders at a time when the company is in financial difficulty.

America Online has a retained earnings deficit that's reported in its balance sheet in Appendix A as follows:

	1996	1995
Accumulated deficit	$(7,767)	$(36,623)

America Online has never paid cash dividends on its common stock.

Liquidating Cash Dividends

The Cash Dividends Declared account is normally closed to the Retained Earnings account. But some state laws allow cash dividends to be paid as a return of the capital contributed by stockholders. This means the Cash Dividends Declared account is closed with a debit entry to one of the contributed capital accounts instead of Retained Earnings. This kind of dividend is called a **liquidating cash dividend,** or simply *liquidating dividend,* because it returns a part of the original investment to the stockholders.

A liquidating dividend usually occurs when a company is completing a major downsizing, perhaps in preparation for a merger or even its closing. The equity from the par or stated value of outstanding stock cannot usually be used for a liquidating dividend unless all creditors are paid. This latter situation is typically limited to when a corporation is actually going out of business.

Flash back

1. The Cash Dividends Declared account is normally: *(a)* reported on the balance sheet as a liability; *(b)* closed to Income Summary; *(c)* closed to Retained Earnings.
2. What three dates are involved in the process of paying a cash dividend?
3. When does a dividend become a legal obligation of the company?

Answers—p. 624

Stock Dividends

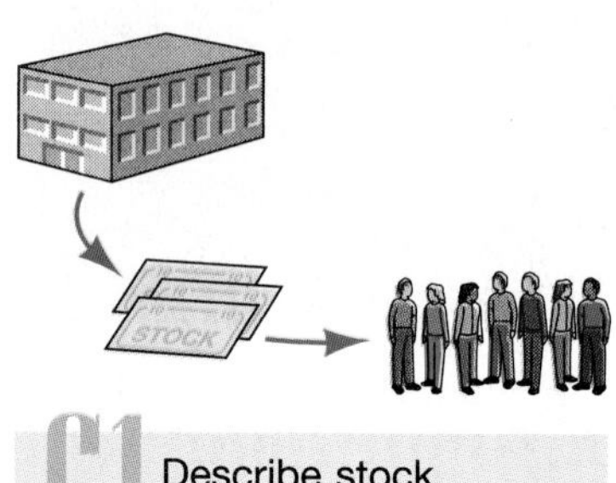

C1 Describe stock dividends and stock splits.

A corporation's directors can declare a stock dividend. A **stock dividend** is a distribution of additional shares of the corporation's own stock to its stockholders without the receipt of any payment in return. Stock dividends and cash dividends are different. A stock dividend does not reduce a corporation's assets and stockholders' equity, while a cash dividend does both. A stock dividend simply transfers a portion of equity from retained earnings to contributed capital.

Reasons for Stock Dividends

If stock dividends don't affect assets or total stockholders' equity, then why declare and distribute them? At least two reasons are suggested. First, directors are said to use stock dividends to keep the market price of the stock affordable. For example, if a corporation continues to earn profits and doesn't distribute these profits to shareholders through cash dividends, the price of its common stock likely increases. The price of such a share may become so high that it discourages some investors from buying the stock. When a corporation declares a stock dividend, it increases the number of outstanding shares and lowers the per share price of its stock. Another reason for declaring a stock dividend is to provide evidence of management's confidence that the company is doing well. The stock dividend may accomplish these goals without spending cash needed in the business.

Entries for Stock Dividends

A stock dividend does not affect a corporation's assets or total stockholders' equity, but it does affect the components of stockholders' equity. It does this by transferring part of retained earnings to contributed capital accounts. This is sometimes described as *capitalizing* retained earnings because it increases a company's contributed capital.

Accounting for a stock dividend depends on whether it is a small or large stock dividend. A **small stock dividend** is a distribution of less than or equal to 25% of the previously outstanding shares. It is unlikely to have a large effect on the stock's market price and is, therefore, sometimes viewed as similar to a cash dividend. A small stock dividend is recorded by capitalizing retained earnings for an amount equal to the market value of the shares to be distributed.

A **large stock dividend** is a distribution of more than 25% of the previously outstanding shares. A large stock dividend is likely to have a noticeable effect on the stock's market price. A large stock dividend is recorded by capitalizing retained earnings for the minimum amount required by the state law governing the corporation. Most states require capitalizing retained earnings equal to the par or stated value of the shares.

To illustrate both small and large stock dividends, we use the stockholders' equity section of X-Quest shown in Exhibit 14.2 just *before* its declaration of a stock dividend.

Exhibit 14.2

Stockholders' Equity before the Stock Dividend

X-QUEST Stockholders' Equity December 31, 2000	
Common stock—$10 par value, 15,000 shares authorized, 10,000 shares issued and outstanding	$100,000
Contributed capital in excess of par value, common stock	8,000
Total contributed capital	$108,000
Retained earnings	35,000
Total stockholders' equity	$143,000

Recording a Small Stock Dividend

P2 Account for stock dividends and stock splits.

Let's assume the directors of X-Quest declare a 10% stock dividend on December 31, 2000. This stock dividend of 1,000 shares, computed as 10% of its 10,000 outstanding shares, is to be distributed on January 20 to the stockholders of record on January 15. Since the market price of X-Quest's stock on December 31 is $15 per share, this small stock dividend declaration is recorded as:

Date of Declaration

Dec. 31	Stock Dividends Declared	15,000	
	Common Stock Dividend Distributable		10,000
	Contributed Capital in Excess of Par Value, Common Stock		5,000
	To record declaration of a 1,000-share common stock dividend.		

Assets = Liabilities + Equity
−15,000
+10,000
+5,000

The debit is recorded in the temporary (contra-equity) account called Stock Dividends Declared. This account serves the same purpose as the Cash Dividends Declared account. A complete chart of accounts includes separate accounts for cash and stock dividends because the financial statements must report stock and cash dividends as separate events. If stock dividends are not frequently declared, a company might not keep a separate account for Stock Dividends Declared. Instead, it can record the debit directly to Retained Earnings. This approach is acceptable as long as the information is reported correctly in financial statements.

In the stock dividend declaration entry, the $10,000 credit equals the par value of the dividend shares and goes to increase a contributed capital account called Common Stock Dividend Distributable. This account balance exists only until the shares are actually issued. The $5,000 credit equals the premium on the dividend shares and increases the Contributed Capital in Excess of Par Value account even though the shares are not yet issued. This account is used when the current market price is above par value.

A stock dividend is never a liability on a balance sheet because it will never reduce assets. Instead, any declared but undistributed stock dividend appears on the balance sheet as a part of contributed capital in stockholders' equity. In particular, a balance sheet changes in three ways when declaring a stock dividend. First, the amount of equity attributed to common stock increases from $100,000 to $110,000 because 1,000 additional shares are declared for issuance. Second, contributed capital in excess of par increases by $5,000, which equals the excess of the $15 per share market value over the $10 per share par value for 1,000 shares. Third, retained earnings decreases by $15,000 (from $35,000 to $20,000) reflecting the transfer of amounts to both common stock ($10,000) and contributed capital in excess or par ($5,000).

As part of the year-end closing process, X-Quest closes the Stock Dividends Declared account to Retained Earnings with this entry:

Assets = Liabilities + Equity
−15,000
+15,000

Dec. 31	Retained Earnings	15,000	
	Stock Dividends Declared		15,000
	To close the Stock Dividends Declared account.		

The stockholders' equity of X-Quest is shown in Exhibit 14.3 *after* the 10% stock dividend is declared on December 31.

Stockholders' Equity after Declaring a Stock Dividend

X-QUEST Stockholders' Equity December 31, 2000	
Common stock—$10 par value, 15,000 shares authorized, 10,000 shares issued and outstanding	$100,000
Common stock dividend distributable, 1,000 shares	10,000
Total common stock issued and to be issued	$110,000
Contributed capital in excess of par value, common stock	13,000
Total contributed capital	$123,000
Retained earnings	20,000
Total stockholders' equity	$143,000

No entry is made on the date of record for a stock dividend. On January 20, the date of payment, X-Quest distributes the new shares to stockholders and records it with this entry:

Date of Payment

Assets = Liabilities + Equity
−10,000
+10,000

Jan. 20	Common Stock Dividend Distributable	10,000	
	Common Stock		10,000
	To record distribution of a 1,000-share common stock dividend.		

The combined effect of these three stock dividend entries is to transfer (or capitalize) $15,000 of retained earnings to contributed capital. The amount of capitalized retained earnings equals the market value of the 1,000 issued shares ($15 × 1,000 shares). This stock dividend has no effect on X-Quest's assets or total stockholders' equity. Nor does it affect the ownership percent of individual stockholders.

To show this, assume we own 200 shares of X-Quest's stock prior to the 10% stock dividend. When X-Quest sends each stockholder one new share for each 10 shares held, we receive 20 new shares (10% × 200 shares). Exhibit 14.4 shows the effects of this 10% stock dividend for both X-Quest and our shares. There is no change in the book value of either X-Quest or our shares. Before the stock dividend, we owned 2% of X-Quest's stock, computed as 200 divided by 10,000 outstanding shares. After the dividend we hold 220 shares, but our holding still equals 2%, computed as 220 divided by 11,000 shares now outstanding. Total book value of our holding doesn't change and still equals $2,860. Before the stock dividend we owned 200 shares with a book value of $14.30 per share. After this dividend we hold 220 shares with a book value of $13.00 per share. The only change in our 2% investment is that it's now divided among 220 shares instead of 200 shares. Total stockholders' equity doesn't change. The only effect on stockholders' equity is a transfer of $15,000 from retained earnings to contributed capital.

Exhibit 14.4

Effects of X-Quest's 10% Stock Dividend

Before 10% stock dividend	
Stockholders' equity:	
Common stock (10,000 shares)	$100,000
Contributed capital in excess of par value, common stock	8,000
Retained earnings	35,000
Total stockholders' equity	**$143,000**
Book value per share = $143,000/10,000 shares = $14.30	
Book value of 200 shares = $14.30 × 200 = **$2,860**	
After 10% stock dividend is distributed	
Stockholders' equity:	
Common stock (11,000 shares)	$110,000
Contributed capital in excess of par value, common stock	13,000
Retained earnings	20,000
Total stockholders' equity	**$143,000**
Book value per share = $143,000/11,000 shares = $13	
Book value of 220 shares = $13 × 220 = **$2,860**	

Recording a Large Stock Dividend

A corporation capitalizes retained earnings equal to the minimum amount required by state law for a large stock dividend. For most states this amount is the par or stated value of the newly issued shares. To illustrate, suppose X-Quest's board declares a 30% stock dividend instead of 10% on December 31. Because this dividend is more than 25%, it is treated as a large stock dividend. This means the par value of the new 3,000 dividend shares is capitalized instead of its market value. X-Quest records this declaration with the entry:

Date of Declaration

Dec. 31	Stock Dividends Declared	30,000	
	Common Stock Dividend Distributable		30,000
	To record declaration of a 3,000-share stock dividend at par value.		

Assets = Liabilities + Equity
−30,000
+30,000

This transaction decreases retained earnings by the $30,000 par value of the dividend shares when the Stock Dividends Declared account is closed. It also increases contributed capital by $30,000. Subsequent entries related to a large stock dividend are the same as those for a small stock dividend. The effects on balance sheet accounts from a large stock dividend are similar to those for a small stock dividend except for the absence of any effect on contributed capital in excess of par.

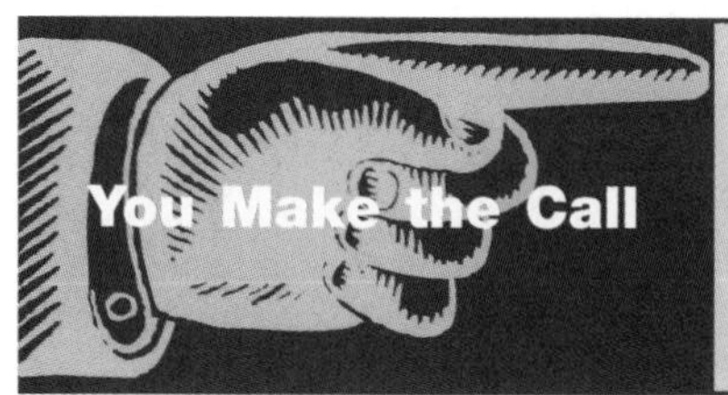

Engineer

You are an engineer with your savings invested in stocks. One of your stock investments announces a 50% stock dividend. Has the value of your stock investment increased?

Answer—p. 624

Stock Splits

We explained that a stock dividend can reduce a stock's market price and make it more marketable to investors. A stock dividend does this by dividing a company's shares into smaller pieces. The total value of the company is unchanged, but the price of each new share is smaller. We can accomplish the same thing with a stock split. A **stock split** is the distribution of additional shares of stock to stockholders according to their percent ownership. When a stock split occurs, the corporation calls in its outstanding shares and issues more than one new share in exchange for each old share.[1] Splits can be done in any ratio including two-for-one, three-for-one, or higher. It does this by reducing the par or stated value per share.

To illustrate, CompTec has 100,000 outstanding shares of $20 par value common stock with a current market value of $88 per share. A two-for-one stock split cuts par value in half from $20 to $10 per share. The split replaces 100,000 shares of $20 par value stock with 200,000 shares of $10 par value stock. Also, market value is reduced from $88 per share to about $44 per share.

A stock split does not affect the dollar amounts in stockholders' equity reported on CompTec's balance sheet. It also doesn't affect an individual stockholder's percent ownership of CompTec. The Contributed Capital and Retained Earnings accounts are unchanged by a split, and *no journal entry is made.* The only effect on the accounts is a change in the account description for common stock. CompTec's two-for-one split on its $20 par value stock means that after the split it changes its stock account title to Common Stock, $10 Par Value. Also, the description of this stock on its balance sheet is changed to reflect the additional authorized, issued and outstanding shares and the revised par value per share.

The difference between stock splits and large stock dividends is often blurred in practice. Many companies report stock splits in their financial statements without calling in the original shares and changing the par value of the common stock. This type of "split" is really a large stock dividend and results in additional shares issued to stockholders by capitalizing retained earnings or transferring other contributed capital to Common Stock. This approach avoids administrative costs of splitting the stock. **Harley-Davidson** recently declared a 2-for-1 stock split in the form of a 100% stock dividend by transferring additional paid-in capital to common stock.

A **reverse stock split** is the opposite of a stock split. It increases both the market value per share and the par or stated value per share. It does this by specifying the ratio to be less than one-for-one such as one-for-two. This means stockholders end up with fewer shares after a reverse stock split.

[1] To reduce administrative cost, most splits are done by issuing new certificates to stockholders for the additional shares they are entitled to receive. The stockholders keep the old certificates.

Flash back

4. Which of the following statements is correct?
   a. A large stock dividend is recorded by capitalizing retained earnings equal to the market value of the distributable shares.
   b. Stock dividends and stock splits have the same effect on the total assets and retained earnings of the issuing corporation.
   c. A stock dividend does not transfer corporate assets to the stockholders but does require retained earnings be capitalized.
5. What distinguishes a large stock dividend from a small stock dividend?
6. What amount of retained earnings is capitalized for a small stock dividend?

Answers—p. 624

Treasury Stock

Corporations acquire shares of their own stock for several reasons. First, they can use their shares to acquire control of another corporation. Second, they can repurchase shares to avoid a hostile takeover by an investor seeking to take control of the company. Third, they can buy shares and reissue them to employees as compensation. For example, **Hewlett-Packard** has a stock repurchase program to compensate employees. In 1996, more than 24 million shares were repurchased under this program. Fourth, they can buy shares to maintain a strong or stable market for the stock. This is often done when a stock quickly and markedly declines in price. By buying shares, management shows its confidence in the price of its shares.

A corporation's reacquired shares are called **treasury stock.** Treasury stock is similar to unissued stock in several ways. Neither treasury stock nor unissued stock is an asset. Neither receives cash dividends or stock dividends. Neither allows the exercise of voting rights. But treasury stock does have one potentially major difference from unissued stock. Specifically, the corporation can resell the stock at less than par without having the buyers incur a discount liability if the treasury stock was originally issued at par value or higher. As shown in the margin, a majority of larger corporations have reacquired some of their own stock.

Corporations and Treasury Stock

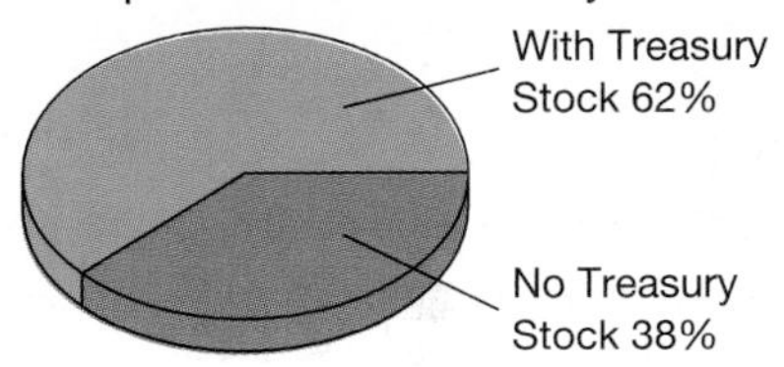

Treasury stock purchases require management to exercise ethical sensitivity. This is because corporate funds are being paid to specific stockholders instead of all stockholders. As a result, managers must be sure the purchase is in the best interest of all stockholders. These concerns cause most companies to fully disclose treasury stock transactions.

Manager and Director

You are a manager at Intex and a new member of its board of directors. The board is currently planning the agenda for its annual stockholders' meeting. The first item is whether to disclose a government contract Intex just signed. This contract will increase income and cash flows for current and future years. One officer said "the meeting should describe last year's activities, not future plans." After agreeing not to disclose the contract, the board moved to the next topic. It was a motion for stockholders to approve a compensation plan awarding managers options to acquire shares over the next two years. This plan gives managers a two-year option to buy shares at a fixed price equal to the stock price for 30 days after the stockholders' meeting. If stock price increases in the next two years, managers can earn considerable money. Can you see a potential problem here? What action do you take?

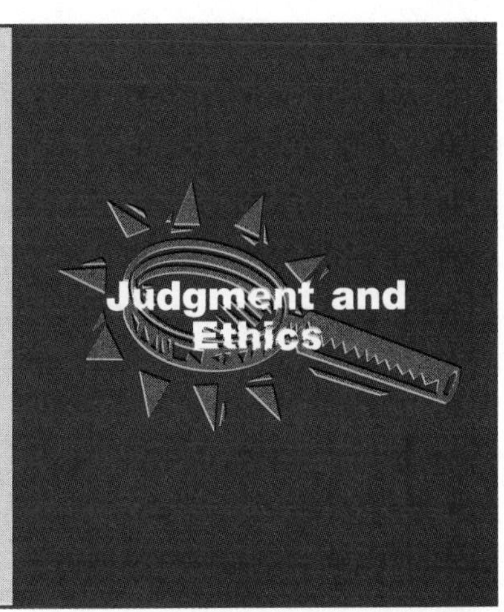

Answer—p. 624

P3 Record purchases and sales of treasury stock and the retirement of stock.

Purchasing Treasury Stock

Purchasing treasury stock reduces the corporation's assets and stockholders' equity by equal amounts.[2] We illustrate these effects on the balance sheet of Cyber Corporation. Exhibit 14.5 shows Cyber's account balances before any treasury stock purchase.

Exhibit 14.5

Balance Sheet before Purchasing Treasury Stock

CYBER CORP.
Balance Sheet
May 1, 1999

Assets		Stockholders' Equity	
Cash	$ 30,000	Contributed capital:	
Other assets	95,000	Common stock; $10 par; 10,000 shares authorized, issued and outstanding	$100,000
		Retained earnings	25,000
Total assets	$125,000	Total stockholders' equity	$125,000

On May 1, 1999, Cyber purchased 1,000 of its own shares for $11,500. The entry to record this purchase is:

Assets = Liabilities + Equity
−11,500 −11,500

May 1	Treasury Stock, Common	11,500	
	Cash		11,500
	Purchased 1,000 shares of treasury stock at $11.50 per share.		

This entry reduces stockholders' equity by debiting the Treasury Stock account, which is a contra-equity account. Exhibit 14.6 shows the effects of this transaction on Cyber's balance sheet.

Exhibit 14.6

Balance Sheet after Purchasing Treasury Stock

CYBER CORP.
Balance Sheet
May 1, 1999

Assets		Stockholders' Equity	
Cash	$ 18,500	Contributed capital:	
Other assets	95,000	Common stock; $10 par; 10,000 shares authorized and issued; 1,000 shares in treasury	$100,000
		Retained earnings, $11,500 restricted by treasury stock purchase	25,000
		Total	$125,000
		Less cost of treasury stock	**(11,500)**
Total assets	$113,500	Total stockholders' equity	$113,500

The treasury stock purchase reduces Cyber's cash, total assets, and total equity by $11,500. The equity reduction is reflected on the balance sheet by deducting the cost of treasury stock in the equity section. This purchase does not reduce the balance of either the Common Stock account or the Retained Earnings account. But two disclosures in this section describe the effects of the transaction. First, the stock description tells us 1,000 issued shares are in treasury, leaving only 9,000 shares outstanding. Second, the

[2] We describe the *cost method* of accounting for treasury stock. It is the method most widely used. The *par value* method is another method explained in advanced courses.

retained earnings description tells us it is partly restricted. We explain retained earnings restrictions later in this chapter.

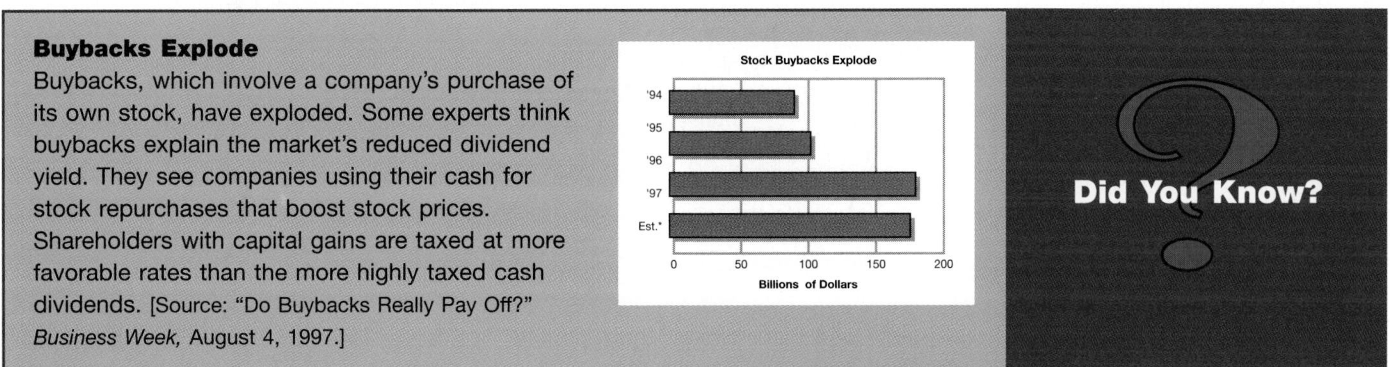

Buybacks Explode
Buybacks, which involve a company's purchase of its own stock, have exploded. Some experts think buybacks explain the market's reduced dividend yield. They see companies using their cash for stock repurchases that boost stock prices. Shareholders with capital gains are taxed at more favorable rates than the more highly taxed cash dividends. [Source: "Do Buybacks Really Pay Off?" Business Week, August 4, 1997.]
Stock Buybacks Explode
'94
'95
'96
'97
Est.*
0
50
100
150
200
Billions of Dollars
Did You Know?

Reissuing Treasury Stock

Treasury stock can be reissued by selling it at cost, above cost, or below cost. This section explains the accounting for reissuing treasury stock.

Selling Treasury Stock at Cost

If it is reissued at cost, the entry is the opposite of the entry made to record the purchase. For instance, if on May 21 Cyber reissues 100 of the treasury shares purchased on May 1 at the same $11.50 per share cost, the entry to record this sale is:

May 21	Cash	1,150	
	Treasury Stock, Common		1,150
	Received $11.50 per share for 100 treasury shares costing $11.50 per share.		

Assets = Liabilities + Equity
+1,150 +1,150

Selling Treasury Stock above Cost

If treasury stock is sold for more than cost, the amount received in excess of cost is credited to an account called Contributed Capital, Treasury Stock Transactions. For instance, if Cyber receives $12 cash per share for 400 treasury shares costing $11.50 per share, the entry to record this sale is:

June 3	Cash	4,800	
	Treasury Stock, Common		4,600
	Contributed Capital, Treasury Stock Transactions		**200**
	Received $12 per share for 400 treasury shares costing $11.50 per share.		

Assets = Liabilities + Equity
+4,800 +4,600
+200

The Contributed Capital, Treasury Stock Transactions account is reported as a separate item in the contributed capital section of stockholders' equity. No gain is ever reported from the sale of treasury stock.

Selling Treasury Stock below Cost

When treasury stock is sold below cost, the entry to record the sale depends on whether there is a credit balance in the Contributed Capital, Treasury Stock Transactions account. If there is no balance, the excess of cost over the sales price is debited to Retained Earnings. But if the contributed capital account has a credit balance, the excess of the cost over the sales price is debited for an amount up to the balance in this account. When the credit balance in the contributed capital account is eliminated, any remaining difference between the cost and the selling price is debited to Retained Earnings.

To illustrate, if Cyber sells its remaining 500 shares of treasury stock at $10 per share, the company's equity is reduced by $750 (500 shares × $1.50 per share excess of cost over selling price). This reissuance is recorded with the entry:

Assets	= Liabilities	+ Equity
+5,000		−200
		−550
		+5,750

July 10	Cash	5,000	
	Contributed Capital, Treasury Stock Transactions	**200**	
	Retained Earnings	**550**	
	Treasury Stock, Common		5,750
	Received $10 per share for 500 treasury shares costing $11.50 per share.		

This entry eliminates the $200 credit balance in the contributed capital account created on June 3 and then reduces the Retained Earnings balance by the remaining $550 excess of cost over selling price. This means the purchase and reissuance of treasury shares caused Cyber to incur a net $550 decrease in retained earnings and total stockholders' equity. A company never reports a loss from the sale of treasury stock.

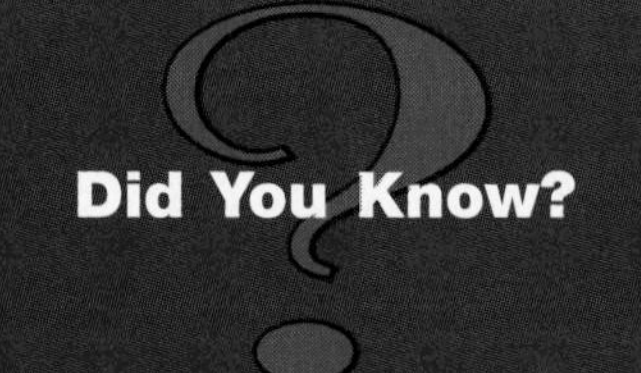

Online Stock Trading
The volume of on-line stock trading has skyrocketed. **Charles Schwab,** for instance, reported nearly $100 billion in on-line customer assets in January 1998. It also reported more than a million active on-line trading accounts and over a million daily on-line customer visits to its Web site.

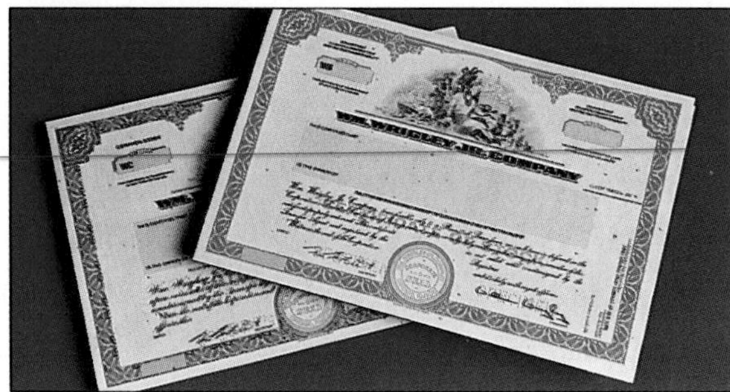

Retiring Stock

A corporation can purchase its own stock and retire it. For instance, **Wrigley Company** recently reported that "the Board of Directors adopted a resolution retiring the entire balance of shares of Common Stock held in the corporate treasury." Retiring stock reduces the number of issued shares. Stock that is retired is the same as authorized and unissued shares. Purchases and retirements of stock are permissible under state law only if they don't jeopardize the interests of creditors and stockholders.

When stock is purchased for retirement, we remove all the contributed capital amounts related to the retired shares. If the purchase price exceeds the net amount removed from contributed capital, this excess is debited to Retained Earnings. But if the net amount removed from contributed capital exceeds the purchase price, this excess is credited to the Contributed Capital from Retirement of Common Stock account. Retiring stock always reduces a company's assets and equity by the amount paid for the stock.

Flash back

7. Purchase of treasury stock: *(a)* has no effect on total assets; *(b)* reduces total assets and total stockholders' equity by equal amounts; *(c)* is recorded with a debit to Retained Earnings.

8. Southern Inc. purchases shares of Northern Corp. Should these shares be classified as treasury stock by either company?

9. How does treasury stock affect the number of authorized, issued, and outstanding shares of stock?

10. When a corporation purchases treasury stock: *(a)* retained earnings is restricted by the amount paid; *(b)* it's recorded with a credit to Appropriated Retained Earnings; *(c)* it's always retired.

Answers—p. 624

Reporting Income Information

C2 Explain the form and content of a comprehensive income statement.

When a company's revenue and expense transactions are from normal, continuing operations, a single-step income statement is adequate for describing its performance. This format shows revenues followed by a list of operating expenses and then net income. But a company's activities often include many income-related events that are not part of a company's normal, continuing operations. Companies need to provide useful information on these items in a format that helps users understand both current and past events and predict future performance.

To meet this objective, companies often separate the income statement into different sections. The most important sections are continuing operations, discontinued segments, extraordinary items, changes in accounting principles, and earnings per share. Exhibit 14.7 shows the entire 1999 income statement of **CompUS.**

Exhibit 14.7

Income Statement for a Corporation

CompUS
Income Statement
For Year Ended December 31, 1999

①	Net sales		$8,440,000
	Gain on sale of equipment		38,000
	Total revenues		$8,478,000
	Expenses:		
	Cost of goods sold	$5,950,000	
	Depreciation expense	35,000	
	Other selling, general, and administrative expenses	515,000	
	Interest expense	20,000	
	Income taxes expense	595,500	
	Total expenses		(7,115,500)
	Unusual loss on relocating a plant		(45,000)
	Infrequent gain on sale of surplus land		72,000
	Income from continuing operations		$1,389,500
②	**Discontinued segment**		
	Income from operating Division A (net of $180,000 taxes)	$ 420,000	
	Loss on disposal of Division A (net of $66,000 tax benefit)	(154,000)	266,000
	Income before extraordinary items and cumulative effect of change in accounting principle		$1,655,500
③	**Extraordinary items:**		
	Gain on sale of land taken by the state for a highway (net of $61,200 taxes)	$ 142,800	
	Loss from earthquake damage (net of $270,000 tax benefit)	(630,000)	(487,200)
④	**Cumulative effect of a change in accounting principle:**		
	Effect on prior years' income (through December 31, 1998) of changing to a different depreciation method (net of $24,000 taxes)		56,000
	Net income		$1,224,300
⑤	**Earnings per common share (200,000 outstanding shares):**		
	Income from continuing operations		$ 6.95
	Discontinued operations		1.33
	Income before extraordinary items and cumulative effect of change in accounting principle		$ 8.28
	Extraordinary items		(2.44)
	Cumulative effect of a change in accounting principle		0.28
	Net income (basic earnings per share)		$ 6.12

Continuing Operations

The first section of an income statement shows the revenues, expenses, and income generated by the company's continuing operations. This portion looks like the single-step income statement we first described in Chapter 6. Users rely on information in this section especially for predicting the results of future operations. This section is often viewed by users as the most important. Prior chapters have explained the nature of the items and measures included in income from continuing operations.

Discontinued Segments

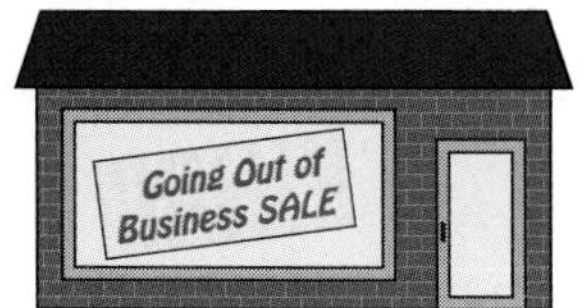

Many companies have several different lines of business and deal with different groups of customers. **IBM,** for instance, not only produces and sells computer hardware and software but also delivers systems design and repair services. Information about the segments of a company are of interest to users. A **segment of a business** is a part of a company's operations that serves a particular line of business or class of customers. A segment has assets, liabilities, and financial results of operations that can be distinguished from other parts of the company. Companies with operations in different segments are required to provide supplemental information about each of their major segments.

Reporting on Discontinued Segments

When a company incurs a gain or loss from selling or closing down a segment, this gain or loss is reported in a separate section of the income statement.[3] Section 2 of the income statement in Exhibit 14.7 includes this information. The purpose of reporting gains or losses from discontinued operations separately is to more clearly separate results of discontinued segments from continuing operations. Income from operating the discontinued segment prior to its disposal also is reported in section 2. When the income statement includes results of prior years side by side, we must go back and restate prior years' results to separate out the revenues and expenses of the discontinued segment.

Separating Operating Results from Gain or Loss on Disposal

Section 2 of Exhibit 14.7 reports both (a) income from operating the discontinued segment during the year and (b) the loss from disposing of the segment's net assets. The income tax effects of each are also reported. This means the tax effects from the discontinued segment are separate from the reporting of continuing operations in section 1. If the tax effects of the discontinued segment were not separate from the continuing operations, the information would be less useful.

Extraordinary Items

Section 3 of the income statement in Exhibit 14.7 reports **extraordinary gains and losses.** Extraordinary gains and losses are those that are both *unusual* and *infrequent.* An **unusual gain or loss** is abnormal or otherwise unrelated to the ordinary activities and environment of the business. An **infrequent gain or loss** is not expected to occur again in the company's operating environment.[4] Reporting extraordinary items in a separate category helps users predict future performance, absent the effects of extraordinary items.

Few items qualify as extraordinary items because they must meet both criteria of *unusual* and *infrequent.* For instance, the following items are *not* considered extraordinary:[5]

- Write-downs of inventories.
- Write-offs of receivables.

---

[3] FASB, *Accounting Standards—Current Text* (Norwalk, CT, 1995), sec. I13.105. Originally published as *APB Opinion No. 30,* par. 8.

[4] Ibid., sec. I17.107. Originally published as *APB Opinion No. 30,* par. 20.

[5] Ibid., sec. I17.110. Originally published as *APB Opinion No. 30,* par. 23.

- Gains or losses from exchanging foreign currencies.
- Gains and losses from disposing segments.
- Effects of labor strikes.
- Accrual adjustments on long-term contracts.

Items that are usually considered extraordinary include:

- Expropriation (taking away) of property by a foreign government.
- Condemning of property by a domestic government body.
- Prohibition against using an asset by a newly enacted law.
- Losses or gains from an unusual and infrequent calamity ("act of God").

Gains or losses that are neither unusual nor infrequent are reported as part of continuing operations. Gains or losses that are either unusual or infrequent, but *not* both, are not extraordinary and also are reported in the continuing operations *but* below the normal revenues, expenses, gains, and losses. For instance, **America Online**'s 1996 income statement in Appendix A reports nonrecurring "merger expenses" of $848,000 from its merger with **Johnson-Grace Company.** This item is separated from AOL's income from operations, but is still part of its $29.8 million net income from continuing operations. AOL has no extraordinary items or discontinued segments.

Section 1 of Exhibit 14.7 includes in total revenues a gain on sale of equipment that is neither unusual nor infrequent. Also note that both an unusual loss and an infrequent gain are reported at the *end* of section 1 below the normal revenues, gains, expenses, and losses. Proper classification of items demands examining the facts. Accounting principles require a few special items to be reported as extraordinary gains or losses to highlight their occurrence even when they don't meet the criteria. The one most frequently encountered is a gain or loss from retiring debt. For instance, **Chiquita** recently reported an extraordinary loss of $22.84 million from retirement of debt.

Farmer

You are a farmer with an orange grove outside Jacksonville, FL. This winter a bad frost wiped out about half your oranges. You are currently preparing an income statement for a bank loan. Can you claim the loss of oranges as extraordinary and separate from continuing operations?

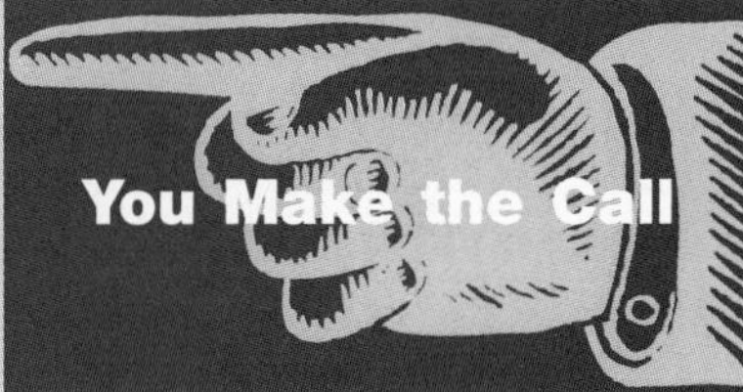

Answer—p. 624

Changes in Accounting Principles

The *consistency principle* requires a company to continue applying the same accounting principles once they are chosen. The phrase *accounting principles* in this context refers to accounting methods such as FIFO, LIFO, and straight-line depreciation. But a company can change from one acceptable accounting principle to another as long as the change improves the usefulness of information in its financial statements. A company will also have a change in accounting principles when they adopt new standards issued by the FASB.

Changes in accounting principles usually affect a company's reported income in more than one way. Let's look at CompUS's change in accounting principle reported in its income statement of Exhibit 14.7. CompUS purchased its only depreciable asset early in 1996 for $320,000. This asset has an 8 year useful life, a $40,000 salvage value, and has been depreciated using the double-declining balance method for the past three years. During 1999, CompUS decides its income statement would be more useful if depreciation is computed using the straight-line method instead of the double-declining balance method.

Exhibit 14.8 compares the results of applying these two depreciation methods to the initial three years of this asset's useful life. The accelerated method yielded $185,000 of depreciation from 1996 through 1998. But if the straight-line method had been used from

Exhibit 14.8

Computing Cumulative Effect of a Change in Accounting Principle

	Double-Declining Depreciation	Straight-Line Depreciation	Pretax Difference	After-Tax Cumulative Effect
Prior to change:				
1996	$ 80,000	$ 35,000		
1997	60,000	35,000		
1998	45,000	35,000		
Subtotal	**$185,000**	**$105,000**	**$80,000**	**$56,000***
Year of change:				
1999	33,750	35,000†		
After change:				
2000–2003		35,000		

*Reported on the 1999 income statement as the cumulative adjustment for differences in the three years prior to the change in 1999, net of $24,000 additional taxes to be paid (30% × $80,000).
†Reported on the 1999 income statement as depreciation expense.

1996 through 1998, only $105,000 of depreciation would have been reported. To adjust accounts to the balances they would be under the straight-line method, CompUS needs to decrease accumulated depreciation of this asset by $80,000 gross. Also, since CompUS is subject to a 30% income tax rate, we offset this gross debit with a credit of $24,000 (30% × $80,000) for deferred income taxes to be paid in the future. The $56,000 net is the resulting credit to equity. Since this credit increases equity (because straight line depreciation is less than that for double-declining balance for these years), CompUS adds it to income in 1999, the year the change is made.

Reporting on Changes in Accounting Principles

CompUS's income statement in Exhibit 14.7 shows how we report a change in an accounting principle. First, section 1 of the income statement reports $35,000 of depreciation using the straight-line method for 1999. This amount is shown in the straight-line method column in Exhibit 14.8. This means income for 1999 is computed using the new accounting principle. Straight-line depreciation also will be used in 2000 through 2003. The second effect on the income statement is the $56,000 catch-up adjustment reported in section 4. This item is the cumulative effect of the change in accounting principle.

The cumulative effect of changing accounting principles can be huge. Many companies report large cumulative effects when they changed their accounting for transactions and events. For example, **Deere** recently reported a $1,095 million reduction in net income when it changed its accounting for postretirement benefits.

Two additional points are important. First, a note should describe the change and why it is an improvement over the old principle. Second, the note should describe what 1999's income would have been under the old method if the change had not occurred. For CompUS, the note states 1999 depreciation of $33,750 would have been reported using double-declining balance instead of $35,000 under straight-line. This amount is in Exhibit 14.8 under the declining-balance column for 1999.

Flash back

11. Which of the following is an extraordinary item? *(a)* A settlement paid to a customer injured while using a company's product; *(b)* A loss to a plant from damages caused by a meteorite; *(c)* A loss from selling old equipment.

12. Identify the five major sections of the income statement that are potentially reported.

13. A company using FIFO for the past 15 years decides to switch to LIFO. The effect of this event on past years' net income is: *(a)* reported as a prior period adjustment to retained earnings; *(b)* ignored as it is a change in an accounting estimate; *(c)* reported on the current year's income statement.

Answers—p. 624

Earnings per Share

A1 Compute earnings per share and describe this ratio's use.

The final section of the income statement in Exhibit 14.7 reports earnings per share results. This information is included on the face of the income statement in accordance with accounting standards. The presentation in Exhibit 14.7 for CompUS is more complete than the minimum reporting requirements and shows the possible categories companies can and often do report.

Earnings per share is one of the most widely cited items of accounting information. **Earnings per share,** also called *net income per share,* is the amount of income earned by each share of a company's outstanding common stock. Investors find this ratio useful because it reports a company's earnings number in terms of a single common share. This aids investors in their valuation of common shares. This is especially helpful when compared with the stock market price per share discussed later in this chapter. Because of the importance and widespread use of earnings per share numbers, there are guidelines for computing it. The **basic earnings per share** formula is shown in Exhibit 14.9.

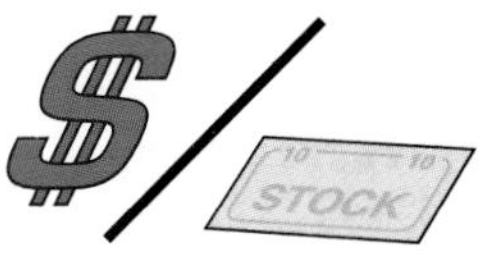

Exhibit 14.9

Basic Earnings per Share Formula

$$\textbf{Basic earnings per share} = \frac{\textbf{Net income} - \textbf{Preferred dividends}}{\textbf{Weighted-average common shares outstanding}}$$

This formula shows us that the basic earnings per share computation depends not only on net income but also on (1) preferred dividends and (2) weighted-average common shares outstanding. Our explanation begins by considering the simple case where there are no changes in shares outstanding during the period. We then look at what happens when the number of common shares outstanding changes.

No Changes in Common Shares Outstanding

Basic earnings per share is simple if (1) a company has only common stock and nonconvertible preferred stock outstanding and (2) the number of outstanding common shares does not change during the period. In this case, we take the amount of net income available to common stockholders and divide it by the number of common shares. The amount of income available to common stockholders depends on whether the preferred stock is cumulative or not. If preferred stock is *non*cumulative, the income available is the period's net income less any preferred dividends *declared* in that same period. If preferred stock is cumulative, the income available is the period's net income less the preferred dividends whether declared or not.

To illustrate, assume Quantum Co. earns $40,000 net income in 1999 and declares dividends of $7,500 on its noncumulative preferred stock. Quantum also had 5,000 common shares outstanding throughout 1999. This information allows us to compute Quantum's basic earnings per share as:

$$\text{Basic earnings per share} = \frac{\$40{,}000 - \$7{,}500}{5{,}000 \text{ shares}} = \$6.50$$

Changes in Common Shares Outstanding

The computation is more complex if the number of outstanding shares changes during the period. The number of shares outstanding may change for several reasons such as sales of additional shares, purchases of treasury stock, or stock dividends or splits. We consider each of these in this section.

Stock Sales or Purchases in the Period

When a company sells additional shares or purchases treasury shares during the period, the denominator of the basic earnings per share formula is adjusted to equal the weighted-average number of outstanding shares. The idea behind this computation is to compare earnings to the average number of shares outstanding during the period.

To illustrate, let's assume Quantum again earned $40,000 in year 2000, and it again declared preferred dividends of $7,500. But let's also assume Quantum sells 4,000 additional common shares on July 1, 2000, and purchases 3,000 treasury shares on November 1, 2000. This means there were 5,000 shares outstanding for the first six months, and 9,000 shares outstanding for July through October (four months), but only 6,000 shares outstanding for the final two months. Exhibit 14.10 shows us how we compute Quantum's weighted-average number of shares outstanding for year 2000.

Exhibit 14.10

Computing Weighted-Average Number of Shares

Time Period	Outstanding Shares		Fraction of Year		Weighted Average
January–June	5,000	×	6/12	=	2,500
July–October	9,000	×	4/12	=	3,000
November–December	6,000	×	2/12	=	1,000
Weighted-average shares outstanding					**6,500**

Using the weighted-average number of common shares outstanding, we compute Quantum's basic earnings per share as:

$$\text{Basic earnings per share} = \frac{\$40{,}000 - \$7{,}500}{6{,}500 \text{ shares}} = \$5$$

Quantum reports the $5 basic earnings per share number on the face of its December 31, 2000, income statement.

Stock Splits or Dividends in the Period

The number of outstanding shares is also affected by a stock split or stock dividend. These events don't produce additional assets, and don't affect the amount of earnings. This means the numerator of basic earnings per share is unaffected. But earnings for the year are now spread out over a larger (or smaller) number of shares. This affects our computation of the weighted-average number of shares outstanding. We handle a stock split or stock dividend by restating the number of shares outstanding during the period to reflect the stock split or dividend *as if it occurred at the beginning of the period.*

To illustrate, let's assume Quantum executed a two-for-one stock split on December 1, 2000. This split causes the percent ownership of each share to be cut in half while doubling the number of shares outstanding prior to December 1. The only change in computing weighted-average shares outstanding is the inclusion of an additional multiplication column reflecting the split as shown in Exhibit 14.11. The December outstanding shares reflect the split and do not require any adjustment.

Exhibit 14.11

Weighted-Average Number of Post-Split Shares

Time Period	Outstanding Shares		Effect of Split		Fraction of Year		Weighted Average
January–June	5,000	×	2	×	6/12	=	5,000
July–October	9,000	×	2	×	4/12	=	6,000
November	6,000	×	2	×	1/12	=	1,000
December	12,000	×	1	×	1/12	=	1,000
Weighted-average shares outstanding							**13,000**

Quantum's basic earnings per share for year 2000 under the assumption of the two-for-one stock split is then computed as:

$$\text{Basic earnings per share} = \frac{\$40{,}000 - \$7{,}500}{13{,}000 \text{ shares}} = \$2.50$$

We use the same computations when stock dividends occur. For instance, if the two-for-one stock split had been a 10% stock dividend, the numbers of old outstanding shares are multiplied by 1.1 instead of 2.0. This is because 110% (or 1.1) of the original number of shares are now outstanding, computed as 100% + 10%.

Great Expectations
A company's earnings per share is a major factor in determining its stock price. Even changes in earnings per share estimates can greatly affect a company's stock price. For instance, an analyst recently lowered Citicorp's earnings per share forecast by 5%. Citicorp's stock fell 7 points on this news. [Source: *Business Week,* January 19, 1998.]

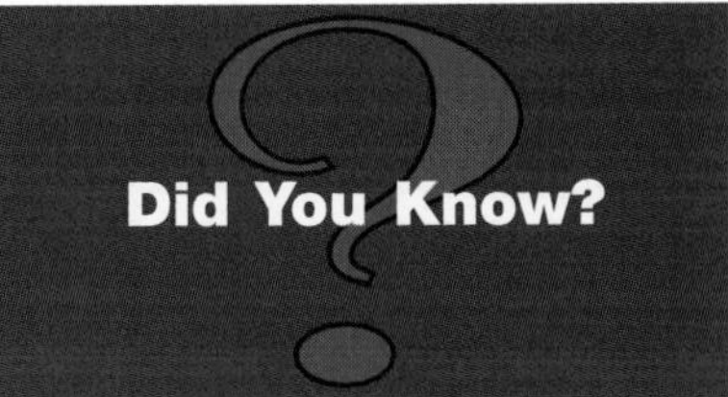

Complex Capital Structure

A company can be classified as having either a simple or complex capital structure. A **simple capital structure** refers to a company with only common stock and nonconvertible preferred stock outstanding. It is a structure that excludes dilutive securities. **Dilutive securities** include options, rights to purchase common stock, and any bonds or preferred stock convertible into common stock. These securities have the potential to increase the number of shares of common stock outstanding. A company with a simple capital structure needs only report basic earnings per share as described above.

A **complex capital structure** refers to companies with dilutive securities. A company with a complex capital structure must often report two earnings per share figures: basic earnings per share and diluted earnings per share. **Diluted earnings per share** is computed by adding all dilutive securities to the denominator of the basic earnings per share computation shown in Exhibit 14.9. Diluted earnings per share reflects the decrease in basic earnings per share if all dilutive securities were converted into common shares.

To illustrate, we show the prior three years' earnings per share figures in Exhibit 14.12 taken from the income statement of **K-Swiss,** the maker of high performance athletic footwear. For K-Swiss, basic earnings per share is nearly identical to diluted earnings per share for 1995 through 1997. This means K-Swiss has almost no dilutive securities. But this is not always the case. **Merrill Lynch,** for instance, announced fourth-quarter basic earnings per share of $1.37 per share in early 1998, while its diluted earnings per share was $1.17. This is a dilution of 20 cents a share, or nearly 15%.

Exhibit 14.12
Basic and Diluted Earnings per Share Disclosure

K-SWISS, INC.

	1997	1996	1995
Earnings per share			
Basic	$ .71	$ .11	$ .28
Diluted	$ .70	$ .11	$ .28

Corporations must report earnings per share figures on the face of their income statements. They also usually report the amount of earnings per share for each of the four subcategories of income (continuing operations, discontinued segments, extraordinary items, and the effect of accounting principle changes) when they exist. Exhibit 14.7 shows Cyber's earnings per share disclosure in section 5. Since Cyber has a simple capital structure, it reports only basic earnings per share.

Flash back

14. During 1999, FDI reports net income of $250,000 and pays preferred dividends of $70,000. On January 1, 1999, the company had 25,000 outstanding common shares and purchased 5,000 treasury shares on July 1. The 1999 basic earnings per share is: *(a)* $8; *(b)* $9; *(c)* $10.

15. How are stock splits and stock dividends treated in computing the weighted-average number of outstanding common shares?

16. What two earnings per share figures are reported for a company with a complex capital structure?

Answers—p. 624

Stock Options

The majority of corporations whose shares are publicly traded offer stock options. A **stock option** is a right to purchase common stock at a fixed price over a specified period of time. As the stock's price rises above the fixed price, the value of the option increases. Use of stock options is growing in popularity as a way to pay both managers and employees for performance. **Starbucks** and **Home Depot,** for instance, are leaders in offering stock options to both full- and part-time employees. Stock options are said to motivate managers and employees to: (1) focus on company performance, (2) take a long-run perspective, and (3) remain with the company. A stock option is like having an investment with no risk (or "a carrot with no stick").

To illustrate, let's say Quantum grants each of its employees the option to purchase 100 shares of its $1 par value common stock at its current market price of $50 per share any time within the next 10 years. This means if Quantum's stock price exceeds $50 per share, employees can exercise the option at a profit. For instance, if the stock price rises to $70 per share, an employee can exercise the option at a gain of $20 per share ($70 stock price less $50 option price). With 100 shares, a single employee has a total gain of $2,000, computed as $20 × 100 shares.

When options are granted, the difference between their estimated value and their exercise price is considered compensation expense. This expense is either recorded as compensation expense or is reported in notes to the financial statements. Most companies report this stock option compensation expense in their notes. **MCI** reported stock option compensation expense of nearly $100 million in 1996, while **Pepsico**'s was nearly $70 million.

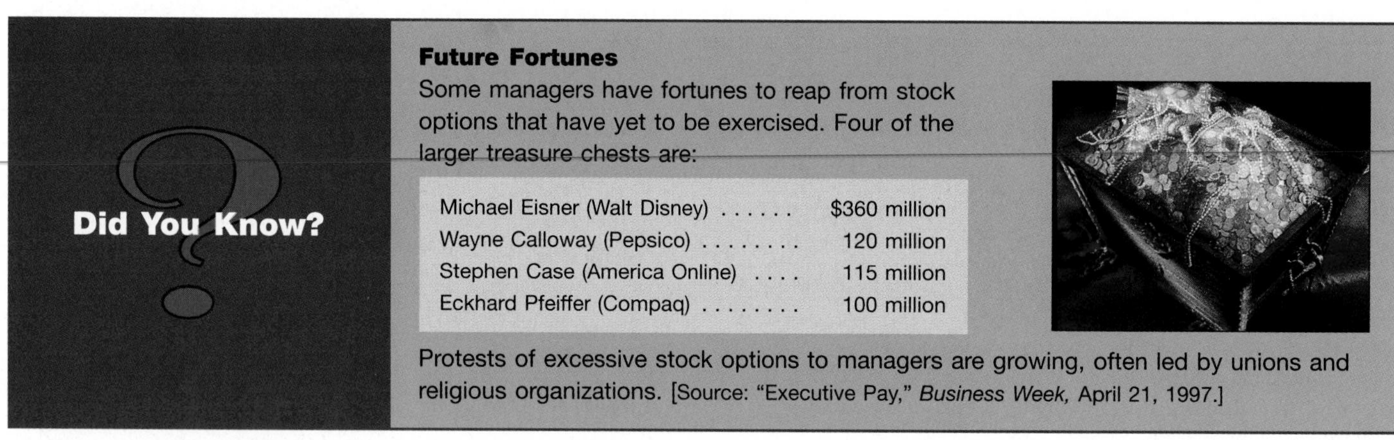

Did You Know?
Future Fortunes
Some managers have fortunes to reap from stock options that have yet to be exercised. Four of the larger treasure chests are:
Michael Eisner (Walt Disney) ...... $360 million
Wayne Calloway (Pepsico) .... 120 million
Stephen Case (America Online) .... 115 million
Eckhard Pfeiffer (Compaq) .... 100 million
Protests of excessive stock options to managers are growing, often led by unions and religious organizations. [Source: "Executive Pay," Business Week, April 21, 1997.]

Retained Earnings

C3 Explain the items reported in retained earnings.

Retained earnings are made up of a company's profits and losses retained in the business. It is the total cumulative amount of reported net income less any net losses and dividends declared since the company started operating. Retained earnings are part of the stockholders' claim on the company's net assets. Retained earnings do not imply that there is a certain amount of cash or other assets available to pay stockholders. This is highlighted in Exhibit 14.13 where we list the retained earnings, cash, and total assets of **NIKE, Reebok,** and **America Online.**

Exhibit 14.13

Retained Earnings, Cash, and Asset Balances

Company	Retained Earnings	Cash	Total Assets
NIKE	$2,974	$445	$5,361
Reebok	993	232	1,786
America Online	(8)	118	959

This section describes important events and transactions affecting retained earnings. It also explains how we report retained earnings in financial statements.

Restricted Retained Earnings

Retained earnings are usually available for dividends. But there are sometimes restrictions placed on retained earnings. These include both legal and contractual restrictions. For instance, most states restrict the amount of treasury stock purchases to the amount of retained earnings. This is called a *statutory restriction.* Purchasing treasury stock transfers cash to stockholders and reduces assets and equity. But a treasury stock purchase does not directly reduce the balance of the Retained Earnings account. Instead, the corporation discloses this type of restriction. The balance sheet in Exhibit 14.6 identifies the amount of **restricted retained earnings** created by treasury stock purchases.

Certain contracts such as loan agreements can also restrict retained earnings. These are called *contractual restrictions* and can include restrictions on paying dividends below a certain amount or percent of retained earnings. When important restrictions exist, they are often described in a note to the financial statements.

Appropriated Retained Earnings

In contrast to statutory or contractual retained earnings restrictions, a corporation's directors can voluntarily limit dividends because of a special need for cash such as the purchase of new facilities. When directors do this, management usually explains in the letter to shareholders or other means why dividends are being limited. They can also disclose this to users by setting up an amount of **appropriated retained earnings.** This appropriation is voluntary. It serves only to notify users of the directors' decision to not pay out cash dividends.

Prior Period Adjustments

Prior period adjustments refer to corrections of material errors in past years' financial statements. These errors include arithmetic mistakes, using unacceptable accounting principles, and ignoring relevant facts.[6] Examples are mistakenly omitting depreciation, applying an unacceptable depreciation method, and overlooking important facts in predicting an asset's useful life. Prior period adjustments are reported in the statement of retained earnings (or the statement of changes in stockholders' equity), net of any income tax effects. Prior period adjustments result in changing the beginning balance of retained earnings for events occurring prior to the earliest year reported in the current set of financial statements. They do not affect the current income statement.

To illustrate, let's assume CompUS makes an error in a 1997 journal entry for the purchase of land by incorrectly debiting an expense account. When this is discovered in 1999, the statement of retained earnings includes a prior period adjustment to correct this error as shown in Exhibit 14.14.

Exhibit 14.14

Prior Period Adjustment in Statement of Retained Earnings

CompUS Statement of Retained Earnings For Year Ended December 31, 1999	
Retained earnings, December 31, 1998, as previously stated	$4,745,000
Prior period adjustment:	
Cost of land incorrectly expensed (net of $63,000 income taxes)	**147,000**
Retained earnings, December 31, 1998, as adjusted	$4,892,000
Plus net income	1,162,500
Less cash dividends declared	(240,000)
Retained earnings, December 31, 1999	$5,814,500

[6] Ibid, sec. A35.104. Originally published as *APB Opinion No. 20,* par. 13.

Changes in Accounting Estimates

Many items reported in financial statements are based on estimates. Future events are certain to reveal that some of these estimates were inaccurate even when based on the best data available at the time. Because these inaccuracies are not the result of mistakes, they are *not* considered accounting errors. This means any corrections due to these estimates are *not reported as prior period adjustments.* Instead, they are identified as **changes in accounting estimates** and are accounted for in the current and future periods.

To illustrate, we know depreciation is based on estimated useful lives and salvage values. As time passes and new information becomes available, we may need to change these estimates and the amounts reported as depreciation expense. These types of changes in accounting estimates are not accounted for with a cumulative catch-up adjustment like a prior period adjustment. Instead, changes in accounting estimates are applied in determining revenues and expenses for the current and future periods. In Chapter 11, we explained one common change in an accounting estimate when we discussed revising depreciation rates.

Statement of Changes in Stockholders' Equity

Most companies don't report a separate statement of retained earnings. Instead, they provide a statement of changes in stockholders' equity. A **statement of changes in stockholders' equity** lists the beginning and ending balances of each equity account and describes the changes that occurred during the period. For instance, **NIKE, Reebok,** and **America Online** all report such a statement which is reproduced for each company in Appendix A. The usual format is to provide a column for each component of equity and use the rows to describe events occurring in the period. Exhibit 14.15 shows a condensed 1996 statement for **Intel.**

Exhibit 14.15

Statement of Changes in Stockholders' Equity

INTEL
Statement of Changes in Stockholders' Equity
December 28, 1996

	Common Stock and Capital in Excess of Par			
(In millions)	Shares	Amount	Retained Earnings	Total
Balance at December 30, 1995	**821**	**$2,583**	**$ 9,557**	**$12,140**
Stock sales	17	513	—	513
Stock repurchase and retirement	(17)	(269)	(925)	(1,194)
Cash dividends declared	—	—	(156)	(156)
Other, net	—	70	342	412
Net income	—	—	5,157	5,157
Balance at December 28, 1996	**821**	**$2,897**	**$13,975**	**$16,872**

USING THE INFORMATION

Dividend Yield and the Price-Earnings Ratio

This section looks at two important ratios in the analysis of common stock: dividend yield and the price-earnings ratio.

A2 Compute dividend yield and explain its use in analysis.

Dividend Yield

Investors buy shares of a company's stock in anticipation of receiving a return from either or both cash dividends and stock price increases. Stocks that pay large dividends on a regular basis are often called *income stocks.* They are attractive to investors who want dependable cash flows from their investments. In contrast, some stocks pay little or no dividends but are still attractive to investors because of their expected stock price increases. The stocks of companies that do not distribute cash but use their cash to finance expansion are often called *growth stocks.*

One way to help evaluate whether a stock is an income stock or a growth stock is to compute and analyze its dividend yield. **Dividend yield** tells us the annual amount of cash dividends distributed to common shareholders relative to the stock's market value (price). More generally, it tells us the amount of cash distributed from a company relative to its total market value. The dividend yield formula in Exhibit 14.16 shows it is a rate of return based on annual cash dividends and the stock's market value.

Exhibit 14.16

Dividend Yield Formula

$$\textbf{Dividend yield} = \frac{\textbf{Annual cash dividends per share}}{\textbf{Market value per share}}$$

Dividend yield can be computed for both current and prior periods using data on actual dividends and stock prices. It can also be computed for future periods using expected values. Exhibit 14.17 shows recent dividend and stock price data for **The GAP, Microsoft, Chevron,** and **Philip Morris.** Dividend yields are also reported.

Exhibit 14.17

Dividend and Stock Price Information

Company	Common Dividend per Share			Dividend Yield	
	1996	1995	1996 Stock Price	1996	1995
GAP	$0.30	$0.24	$ 30	1.0%	0.8%
Microsoft	0.00	0.00	112	0.0	0.0
Chevron	2.08	1.93	60	3.5	3.2
Philip Morris . .	4.40	3.65	105	4.2	3.5

We can compare dividend yields to assess the importance of dividends relative to earnings reinvestment for these companies' stock prices. Dividend yield is zero for **Microsoft,** and is very small for **The GAP.** Both of these stocks fall in the growth stock category. An investor who purchases these two stocks would look for increases in stock prices (and the eventual payment of dividends or cash from the sale of stock.)

Chevron and **Philip Morris** have substantial dividend yields of 3.2% to 4.2%. These stocks can be classed as income stocks. These stocks' dividend yields are less than we'd expect from investments in bonds but still high enough to conclude that dividends are a very important factor in assessing their values. While dividend yield is important to individuals in planning their personal cash flows (dividends now or stock sales later), it is only one of many factors that we look at in analyzing companies for investment.

Flash *back*

17. Which of the following produces an expected dividend yield of 10% on common stock?

a. Dividends of $100,000 are expected to be paid next year and expected net income is $1,000,000.

b. Dividends of $50,000 were paid during the prior year and net income was $500,000.

c. Dividends of $2 per share are expected to be paid next year and the current market value of the stock is $20 per share.

Answer—p. 624

Price-Earnings Ratio

A3 Compute price-earnings ratio and describe its use in analysis.

We explained in prior chapters how a stock's market value is affected by the stream of dividends expected to be paid out to stockholders. A stock's market value is also affected by expected growth in earnings, dividends, and other items. A comparison of a company's earnings per share and its market price per share reveals information about the stock market's expectations for a company's future growth in earnings, dividends, and opportunities.

It is possible to make this comparison as a rate of return by dividing earnings per share by the market price per share. However, the comparison is traditionally done the other way and computed as a **price-earnings (or PE) ratio,** expressed as *price-earnings* or *price-to-earnings* or *PE.* Some analysts interpret this ratio as what price the market is willing to pay for a company's current earnings. Price-earnings ratios can differ across companies with the same earnings because of either higher or lower expectations of future earnings.

The price-earnings ratio is defined as the market value (price) per share of a company's stock divided by its earnings per share as shown in Exhibit 14.18.

Exhibit 14.18

Price-Earnings Formula

$$\textbf{Price-earnings} = \frac{\textbf{Market value per share}}{\textbf{Earnings per share}}$$

This ratio is often computed using earnings per share from the most recent period. But many users compute this ratio using the expected earnings per share for the next period. To illustrate, let's assume a stock's current market price is $100 per share and its next year's earnings are expected to be $8 per share. Its price-earnings ratio is 12.5, computed as $100 divided by $8.

Some analysts apply the price-earnings ratio to search for over- or underpriced stocks. As a general rule, such analysts view stocks with high PE ratios (say, greater than 20 to 25) as more likely to be overpriced, while stocks with low PE ratios (say, less than 5 to 8) as more likely to be underpriced. These investors prefer to sell or avoid buying stocks with high PE ratios, while they prefer to buy or hold stocks with low PE ratios. The average PE ratio for the 1950–1995 period is about 14. But the PE ratio averages more than 16 when inflation is below 3.5%.

Investment decision making is rarely so simple as to rely on a single ratio. For instance, a stock with a high PE ratio may prove to be a good investment if its earnings continue to increase beyond current expectations. Similarly, a stock with a low PE ratio may prove to be a poor investment if its earnings decline below expectations. Like with dividend yield, the price-earnings ratio is important in users' decisions, but it is only one piece of information. This information along with analysis of other accounting and market data must be interpreted as part of a complete analysis and not viewed in isolation.

Flash *back*

18. Compute the price-earnings ratio when earnings per share is $4.25 and the stock price per share is $34.

19. Two companies in the same industry face similar levels of risk, have nearly the same level of earnings, and are expected to continue their historical record of paying $1.50 annual dividends per share. Yet one company has a PE ratio of 6 while the other has a PE ratio of 10. Which company reflects a more optimistic market expectation for future growth in earnings?

Answers—p. 624

Teacher
You are a teacher and receive regular payments to a pension fund as part of your compensation. You can't withdraw these funds until age 65, but you can and do choose where to invest them. You plan to invest in one of two companies that you've concluded as having identical future prospects. One has a PE of 19 and the other a PE of 25. Which do you invest in? Does it matter if your personal estimate of PE for these two companies is 29?

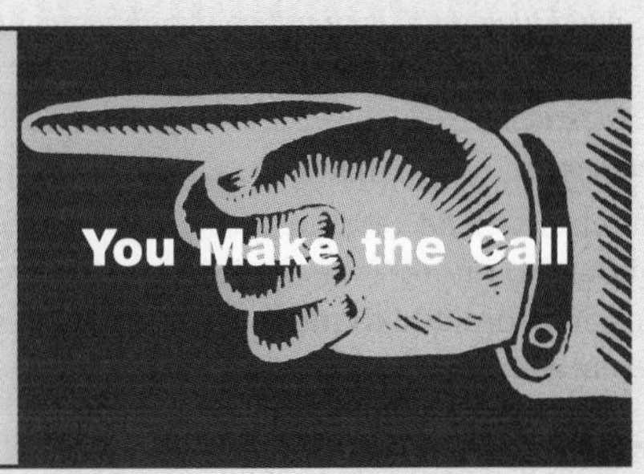

Answer—p. 624

Summary

C1 Describe stock dividends and stock splits. Both a stock dividend and a stock split divide a company's authorized and outstanding shares into smaller pieces. The total value of the company is unchanged, but the price of each new share is smaller. The distribution of additional shares of stock to stockholders is done according to individual stockholders' percent of ownership. Stock dividends and stock splits do not transfer any of the corporation's assets to stockholders. Stock dividends and stock splits do not affect assets, total stockholders' equity, or the equity attributed to each stockholder.

C2 Explain the form and content of a comprehensive income statement. Corporate income statements are similar to those for proprietorships and partnerships except for the inclusion of income taxes. A comprehensive income statement consists of five potential sections: (1) continuing operations, (2) discontinued segments, (3) extraordinary items, (4) changes in accounting principles, and (5) earnings per share. Many companies need only report income from continuing operations and earnings per share because the other three items are uncommon.

C3 Explain the items reported in retained earnings. Most states limit dividends and treasury stock purchases to the amount of retained earnings. Companies also enter into contracts that may limit the amount of dividends, even though the companies have both the cash and the retained earnings to pay them. Corporations may voluntarily appropriate retained earnings to inform stockholders why dividends are not larger. Prior period adjustments are corrections of material errors in past years' financial statements. They result in adjustments to retained earnings.

A1 Compute earnings per share and describe this ratio's use. A company with a simple capital structure is one with no outstanding securities convertible into common stock. These companies compute basic earnings per share by dividing net income less any preferred dividends by the weighted-average number of outstanding common shares. A company with a complex capital structure has outstanding securities convertible into common stock. This company must often report both basic earnings per share and diluted earnings per share.

A2 Compute dividend yield and explain its use in analysis. Dividend yield is the ratio of a stock's annual cash dividends per share to its market value (price) per share. It gives the rate of return to stockholders from the company's cash dividends. Dividend yield can be compared with the yield of other companies and kinds of investments to determine whether the stock is an income or growth stock.

A3 Compute price-earnings ratio and describe its use in analysis. The price-earnings ratio of a common stock is computed by dividing the stock's market value (price) per share by its earnings per share. Some analysts view a high ratio as suggesting the stock is overvalued, while a low ratio suggests a stock is undervalued. But a stock's market value is based on expectations that may prove to be better or worse than later performance. While the price-earnings ratio is important to many users of financial statements, it must be applied as only one part of a complete analysis and not viewed in isolation.

P1 Record transactions involving cash dividends. There are three important events involving cash dividends. The date of declaration is when the board of directors binds the company to pay the dividend. A dividend declaration reduces retained earnings and creates a current liability to stockholders. The date of record is when recipients of the dividend are identified. No entry is necessary on the date of record. The date of payment is when cash is paid to stockholders of record and the current liability is removed from the books.

P2 Account for stock dividends and stock splits. Small stock dividends (≤25%) are recorded by capitalizing retained earnings equal to the market value of the distributed shares. Large stock dividends (>25%) are recorded by capitalizing retained earnings equal to the par or stated value of the issued shares. Stock splits are not recorded with journal entries but do result in changes in the account description for common stock if it includes the par or stated value.

P3 Record purchases and sales of treasury stock and the retirement of stock. When a corporation purchases its own previously issued outstanding stock, it debits the cost of these shares to Treasury Stock. The balance of Treasury Stock is subtracted from total stockholders' equity in the balance sheet. If treasury stock is later reissued, the amount of any proceeds in excess of cost is credited to Contributed Capital, Treasury Stock Transactions. If the proceeds are less than cost, the difference is debited to Contributed Capital, Treasury Stock Transactions to the extent a credit balance exists in that account. Any remaining amount is debited to Retained Earnings. When stock is purchased for retirement, the corporation removes all the contributed capital amounts related to the retired shares.

Guidance Answers to **You Make the Call**

Engineer

The 50% stock dividend provides no direct income to you. But a stock dividend often reveals management's optimistic expectations about the future. It also can improve a stock's marketability by making it affordable to more investors. Accordingly, a stock dividend is usually good news.

Farmer

The frost loss is probably not extraordinary. Jacksonville experiences enough frost damage that it'd be difficult to argue this event is both unusual and infrequent. Nevertheless, you would want to highlight the frost loss and hope the bank would view this uncommon event separately from your continuing operations.

Teacher

If you've decided to invest in one of these two companies, and your analysis suggests they have identical future prospects, then you should pick the better deal. Since one requires a payment of $19 for each $1 of earnings, while the other requires $25, then you'd purchase the stock with the PE of 19 since it is a better deal. You'd also make sure these companies' earnings computations are roughly the same—for example, no extraordinary items, unusual events, and so forth. Also, it does matter what your estimate of PE is for these companies. If you're willing to pay $29 for each $1 of earnings for these companies, then both are solid investments because you obviously expect both to exceed current market expectations.

Guidance Answer to **Judgment and Ethics**

Manager and Director

This case deals with insider trading in a company's stock. The ethical conflict is between your responsibility to Intex's stockholders (and the public) and your own interest in increasing your personal wealth with the options. If information about the new contract is kept private until after the option plan is approved and the options are priced, then you are likely to make a lot of money. (Note, insider trading laws may make nondisclosure in this case a crime.) You should try to explain the ethical and legal concerns to the board. You might also consider whether staying on the board and working for this company is appropriate since it appears there was some intent to deceive outsiders even if not eventually implemented.

Guidance Answers to 

1. *c*
2. The three dates are the date of declaration, the date of record, and the date of payment.
3. A dividend is a legal liability at the date of declaration. It is also recorded on the date of declaration.
4. *c*
5. A small stock dividend is 25% or less of the previous outstanding shares. A large stock dividend is greater than 25%.
6. Retained earnings equal to the market value of the distributable shares should be capitalized.
7. *b*
8. No. The shares are an investment for Southern Inc. and are issued and outstanding shares for Northern Corp.
9. Treasury stock does not affect the number of either authorized or issued shares, but it reduces the amount of outstanding shares.
10. *a*
11. *b*
12. The five major sections are income from continuing operations, discontinued segments, extraordinary items, cumulative effects of changes in accounting principles, and earnings per share.
13. *c*
14. *a;* Weighted-average shares: (25,000 × 6/12) + (20,000 × 6/12) = 22,500.

    Earnings per share: ($250,000 − $70,000)/22,500 = $8.
15. The number of shares previously outstanding is retroactively restated to reflect the stock split or stock dividend as if it occurred at the beginning of the period.
16. The two types are (1) basic earnings per share and (2) diluted earnings per share.
17. *c*
18. $34/$4.25 = $8
19. The company with the higher PE ratio of 10.

Demonstration Problem

Precision Company began 1999 with the following balances in its stockholders' equity accounts:

Common stock, $10 par, 500,000 shares authorized	
200,000 shares issued and outstanding	$2,000,000
Contributed capital in excess of par	1,000,000
Retained earnings	5,000,000
Total	$8,000,000

All of the outstanding stock was issued for $15 when the company was created.

Part 1

Prepare journal entries to account for the following transactions during 1999:

Jan. 10	The board declared a $.10 cash dividend per share to shareholders of record Jan. 28.
Feb. 15	Paid the cash dividend declared on January 10.
Mar. 31	Declared a 20% stock dividend. The market value of the stock is $18 per share.
Apr. 15	Distributed the stock dividend declared on March 31.
June 30	Purchased 30,000 shares of treasury stock at $20 per share.
Aug. 31	Sold 20,000 treasury shares at $26 per share.
Nov. 30	Sold the remaining 10,000 shares of treasury stock at $7 per share.

Part 2

Use the following information to prepare a comprehensive income statement for 1999, including earnings per share results for each category of income.

Cumulative effect of a change in depreciation method (net of tax benefit)	$ (136,500)
Expenses related to continuing operations	(2,072,500)
Extraordinary gain on debt retirement (net of tax)	182,000
Gain on disposal of discontinued segment's assets (net of tax)	29,000
Gain on sale of stock investment	400,000
Loss from operating discontinued segment (net of tax benefit)	(120,000)
Income taxes on income from continuing operations	(225,000)
Prior period adjustment for error (net of tax benefit)	(75,000)
Sales	4,140,000
Infrequent loss	(650,000)

Planning the Solution

- Calculate the total cash dividend to be recorded by multiplying the cash dividend declared by the number of shares as of the date of record.
- Decide whether the stock dividend is a small or large dividend. Then analyze each event to determine the accounts affected and the appropriate amounts to be recorded.
- Based on shares of outstanding stock at the beginning of the year and the transactions during the year, compute the weighted-average number of outstanding shares for the year.
- Assign each of the listed items to an appropriate income statement category.
- Prepare an income statement similar to Exhibit 14.7, including appropriate earnings per share results.

Solution to Demonstration Problem

Part 1

Jan. 10	Cash Dividends Declared	20,000	
	Common Dividend Payable		20,000
	Declared a $.10 per share cash dividend on common stock.		
Feb. 15	Common Dividend Payable	20,000	
	Cash		20,000
	Paid $.10 per share cash dividend to common stockholders.		
Mar. 31	Stock Dividends Declared	720,000	
	Common Stock Dividend Distributable		400,000
	Contributed Capital in Excess of Par Value, Common Stock		320,000
	Declared a small stock dividend of 20% or 40,000 shares; market value is $18 per share.		

Apr. 15	Common Stock Dividend Distributable	400,000	
	Common Stock		400,000
	Distributed 40,000 shares of common stock.		
June 30	Treasury Stock, Common	600,000	
	Cash		600,000
	Purchased 30,000 shares of common stock at $20 per share.		
Aug. 31	Cash	520,000	
	Treasury Stock, Common		400,000
	Contributed Capital, Treasury Stock Transactions		120,000
	Sold 20,000 shares of treasury stock at $26 per share.		
Nov. 30	Cash	70,000	
	Contributed Capital, Treasury Stock Transactions	120,000	
	Retained Earnings	10,000	
	Treasury Stock, Common		200,000
	Sold 10,000 shares of treasury stock at $7 per share.		

Part 2

Computing the weighted-average number of outstanding shares:

Step 1:

Time Period	Original Shares	Effect of Dividend	Post-Dividend Shares
January–April 15	200,000	1.2	240,000

Step 2:

Time Period	Post-Dividend Shares		Fraction of Year		Weighted Average
January–June	240,000	×	6/12	=	120,000
July–August	210,000	×	2/12	=	35,000
September–November	230,000	×	3/12	=	57,500
December	240,000	×	1/12	=	20,000
Weighted-average shares outstanding					232,500

PRECISION COMPANY
Income Statement
For Year Ended December 31, 1999

Sales		$4,140,000
Expenses		(2,072,500)
Income taxes		(225,000)
Gain on sale of stock investment		400,000
Infrequent loss		(650,000)
Income from continuing operations		$1,592,500
Discontinued operations:		
Loss from operating discontinued segment (net of tax benefit)	$(120,000)	
Gain on disposal of discontinued segment's assets (net of tax)	29,000	
Loss from discontinued segment		(91,000)
Income before extraordinary items and cumulative effect of a change in accounting principle		$1,501,500
Extraordinary item:		
Extraordinary gain on debt retirement (net of tax)		182,000
Cumulative effect of a change in accounting principle:		
Cumulative effect of a change in depreciation method (net of tax benefit)		(136,500)
Net income		$1,547,000
Earnings per share (232,500 weighted-average shares):		
Income from continuing operations		$ 6.85
Discontinued operations		(0.39)
Income before extraordinary item and cumulative effect of change in accounting principle		$ 6.46
Extraordinary item		0.78
Cumulative effect of change in accounting principle		(0.59)
Net income (basic earnings per share)		$ 6.65

Glossary

Appropriated retained earnings retained earnings that are voluntarily restricted as a way of informing stockholders that dividends will be limited or not paid. (p. 619).

Basic earnings per share calculated with the formula: (Net income − Preferred dividends)/Weighted-average common shares outstanding. (p. 615).

Changes in accounting estimates corrections to previous estimates or predictions about future events and outcomes, such as salvage values and the useful lives of operating assets; the changes are accounted for in the current and future periods. (p. 620).

Complex capital structure a capital structure that includes outstanding rights or options to purchase common stock or securities that are convertible into common stock. (p. 617).

Date of declaration the date the directors vote to pay a dividend. (p. 600).

Date of payment the date when the corporation makes the dividend payment. (p. 600).

Date of record the date specified by the directors for identifying those stockholders listed in the corporation's records to receive dividends. (p. 600).

Deficit arises when a corporation has a debit (abnormal) balance for retained earnings. (p. 601).

Diluted earnings per share an earnings per share calculation that requires that the effect of dilutive securities be added to the denominator of the basic earnings per share calculation. (p. 617).

Dilutive securities securities having the potential to increase the number of common shares outstanding; examples are options, rights, and convertible bonds and preferred stocks. (p. 617).

Dividend yield a ratio that informs shareholders of the annual amount of cash dividends distributed to common shareholders relative to the stock's market value (price). (p. 621).

Earnings per share the amount of income earned by each share of a company's outstanding common stock; also called *net income per share.* (p. 615).

Extraordinary gain or loss a gain or loss that is reported separate from continuing operations because it is both unusual and infrequent. (p. 612).

Infrequent gain or loss a gain or loss that is not expected to occur again, given the operating environment of the business. (p. 612).

Large stock dividend a stock dividend that is more than 25% of the corporation's previously outstanding shares. (p. 603).

Liquidating cash dividend a distribution of corporate assets as a dividend that returns part of the original investment to the stockholders; these distributions are charged to contributed capital accounts. (p. 602).

Price-earnings ratio the ratio of a company's current market value per share and its earnings per share; used to gain understanding of the market's expectations for the stock. (p. 622).

Prior period adjustment a correction of a material error in a previous year that is reported in the statement of retained earnings (or statement of changes in stockholders' equity) net of any income tax effects. (p. 619).

Restricted retained earnings retained earnings that are not available for dividends because of legal or contractual limitations. (p. 619).

Reverse stock split an act by a corporation to call in its stock and replace each share with less than one new share; reverse splits are opposite of stock splits as they increase both the market value per share and the par or stated value per share. (p. 606).

Segment of a business a component of a company's operations that serves a particular line of business or class of customers and that has assets, activities, and financial results of operations that can be distinguished from other parts of the business. (p. 612).

Simple capital structure a capital structure that consists of only common stock and nonconvertible preferred stock; it cannot include any dilutive securities such as options or rights to purchase common stock or any convertible preferred stocks or bonds. (p. 617).

Small stock dividend a stock dividend that is 25% or less of the corporation's previously outstanding shares. (p. 603).

Statement of changes in stockholders' equity a financial statement that lists the beginning and ending balances of each equity account and describes all the changes that occurred during the period. (p. 620).

Stock dividend a corporation's distribution of its own stock to its stockholders without the receipt of any payment in return. (p. 602).

Stock option a right to purchase common stock at a fixed price over a specified period of time. (p. 618).

Stock split an act by a corporation to call in its stock and replace each share with more than one new share; a stock split will decrease the market value per share of stock and also the par or stated value per share. (p. 606).

Treasury stock a corporation's own stock that was reacquired and is still held by the issuing corporation. (p. 607).

Unusual gain or loss a gain or loss that is abnormal or otherwise unrelated to the ordinary activities and environment of the business. (p. 612).

Questions

1. Identify and explain the importance of the three dates relevant to corporate dividends.
2. Why is the term *liquidating dividend* used to describe cash dividends that are debited against contributed capital accounts?
3. What effects does declaring a stock dividend have on the corporation's assets, liabilities, and total stockholders' equity? What effects does the distribution of the stock have?
4. What is the difference between a stock dividend and a stock split?
5. Courts have ruled that a stock dividend is not taxable income to stockholders. What justifies this decision?
6. How does the purchase of treasury stock affect the purchaser's assets and total stockholders' equity?
7. Why do state laws place limits on purchases of treasury stock?
8. Where on the income statement would a company report an abnormal gain that is not expected to occur more often than once every two years?
9. After taking five years' straight-line depreciation expense for an asset that was expected to have an eight-year useful life, a company decides that the asset will last another six years. Is this decision a change in accounting principle? How do the financial statements describe this change?
10. How are earnings per share results computed for a corporation with a simple capital structure?
11. Refer to the financial statements for **Nike** in Appendix A at the end of the book. What amount was paid to purchase treasury stock during the year ended June 30, 1997? June 30, 1996?
12. Refer to the financial statements for **Reebok** in Appendix A. How many shares of treasury stock does Reebok report as having been repurchased as of December 31, 1996? Compute the average cost to Reebok of the shares in treasury as of December 31, 1996.
13. Refer to the financial statements for **America Online** in Appendix A. What is the balance of retained earnings as of June 30, 1996, and June 30, 1995?

14. Refer to the chapter's opening article. If you were consulting Owen in preparing documents to apply for a loan, would you recommend a single-step income statement or a comprehensive format such as in Exhibit 14.7? Explain.

Quick Study

QS 14-1
Accounting for cash dividends
P1

Prepare journal entries to record the following transactions for Desmond Corporation:

Apr. 15 Declared a $48,000 cash dividend payable to common stockholders.
June 30 Paid the dividend declared on April 15.
Dec. 31 Closed the Cash Dividends Declared account.

QS 14-2
Accounting for small stock dividend
P2

The stockholders' equity section of Jamestown Co.'s balance sheet as of April 1 follows:

Common stock, $5 par value, 375,000 shares authorized, 150,000 shares issued and outstanding	$ 750,000
Contributed capital in excess of par value, common stock	352,500
Total contributed capital	$1,102,500
Retained earnings	633,000
Total stockholders' equity	$1,735,500

On April 1, Jamestown declares and distributes a 10% stock dividend. The market value of the stock on April 1 is $25. Prepare the stockholders' equity section for Jamestown immediately after the stock dividend.

QS 14-3
Purchase and sale of treasury stock
P3

On May 3, Nicholson Corp. purchased 3,000 shares of its own stock for $27,000. On November 4, Nicholson reissued 750 shares of this treasury stock for $7,080. Prepare the November 4 journal entry Nicholson should make to record the sale of the treasury stock.

QS 14-4
Accounting for estimate changes and error adjustments
C2, C3

Answer the questions about each of the following items related to a company's activities for the year:

a. After using an expected useful life of seven years and no salvage value to depreciate its office equipment over the preceding three years, the company decided early this year that the equipment will last only two more years. How should the effects of this decision be reported in the current financial statements?

b. In reviewing the notes payable files, it was discovered that last year the company reported the entire amount of a payment (principal and interest) on an installment note payable as interest expense. The mistake had a material effect on the amount of income in the prior year. How should the correction be reported in the current year financial statements?

QS 14-5
Basic earnings per share
A1

Nelson Company earned a net income of $450,000. The number of common shares outstanding during the entire period was 200,000 and preferred shareholders received a dividend totaling $10,000. Compute Nelson Company's basic earnings per share.

QS 14-6
Weighted-average shares outstanding
A1

On January 1, Harmon Company had 100,000 shares of common stock outstanding. On February 1, Harmon issued 20,000 additional shares of common stock. On June 1, another 40,000 shares of common stock are issued. Compute Harmon Company's weighted-average shares outstanding for the year.

QS 14-7
Weighted-average shares outstanding
A1, P2

On January 1, Harrell Company had 150,000 shares of common stock outstanding. On April 1, it purchased 12,000 treasury shares and on June 2, declared a 20% stock dividend. Compute Harrell's weighted-average shares outstanding for the year.

QS 14-8
Dividend yield
A2

Cornerstone Company expects to pay out a $2.10 per share cash dividend this year on its common stock. The current market price per share is $28.50. Compute the expected dividend yield on the Cornerstone stock. Would you classify the Cornerstone stock as a growth stock or an income stock?

QS 14-9
Price-earnings ratio
A3

Compute Koehn Company's price-earnings ratio if its common stock has a market value of $30.75 per share and its earnings per share is $4.10. Would an analyst viewing this stock consider that it might be over- or underpriced?

Exercises

Exercise 14-1
Stock dividends and per share values
P2

The stockholders' equity of Brinkman Motors, Inc., on February 5 consisted of the following:

Common stock, $25 par value, 150,000 shares authorized, 60,000 shares issued and outstanding	$1,500,000
Contributed capital in excess of par value, common stock	525,000
Total contributed capital	$2,025,000
Retained earnings	675,000
Total stockholders' equity	$2,700,000

On February 5, the stock's market value is $40. On that date, the directors declare a 20% stock dividend distributable on February 28 to the February 15 stockholders of record. The stock's market value is $34 on March 2.

Required

1. Prepare entries to record the dividend declaration and distribution.
2. One stockholder owned 750 shares on February 5. Compute the book value per share and total book value of this stockholder's shares immediately before and after the stock dividend of February 5.
3. Compute the total market value of this investor's shares as of February 5 and March 2.

Exercise 14-2
Stock dividends and splits
P2

On June 30, 1999, Woodward Corporation's common stock was selling for $31 per share and the following information appeared in the stockholders' equity section of its balance sheet as of that date:

Common stock, $10 par value, 60,000 shares authorized, 25,000 shares issued and outstanding	$250,000
Contributed capital in excess of par value, common stock	100,000
Total contributed capital	$350,000
Retained earnings	330,000
Total stockholders' equity	$680,000

Required

1. Assume the company declares and immediately distributes a 100% stock dividend. This event is recorded by capitalizing the required minimum amount of retained earnings. Answer these questions about the stockholders' equity as it exists after issuing the new shares:
   a. What is the retained earnings balance?
   b. What is the total amount of stockholders' equity?
   c. How many shares are outstanding?
2. Assume the company implements a two-for-one stock split instead of the stock dividend in part 1. Answer these questions about the stockholders' equity as it exists after issuing the new shares:
   a. What is the retained earnings balance?
   b. What is the total amount of stockholders' equity?
   c. How many shares are outstanding?
3. Explain the difference, if any, to a stockholder from receiving new shares distributed under a large dividend versus a stock split.

Exercise 14-3
Reporting treasury stock purchase
P3

On October 10, the stockholders' equity of Affiliated Systems, Inc., consisted of the following:

Contributed capital:	
Common stock, $10 par value, 36,000 shares authorized, issued, and outstanding	$360,000
Contributed capital in excess of par value, common stock . .	108,000
Total contributed capital	$468,000
Retained earnings	432,000
Total stockholders' equity	$900,000

On October 11, the corporation purchased 4,500 shares of its own common stock at $30 per share. Explain how the equity section of Affiliated Systems changes after the purchase.

Exercise 14-4
Journal entries for treasury stock
P3

Use the information in Exercise 14-3 to prepare journal entries to record these events for Affiliated Systems:

1. Purchase of the treasury shares on October 11.
2. Sale of 1,200 treasury shares on November 1 for cash at $36 per share.
3. Sale of all the remaining treasury shares on November 25 for cash at $25 per share.

Exercise 14-5
Income statement categories
C2

During 1999, Burks Merchandise, Inc., sold its interest in a chain of wholesale outlets. This sale took the company out of the wholesaling business completely. The company still operates its retail outlets. Following is a lettered list of sections of an income statement:

a. Income from continuing operations
b. Income from operating a discontinued segment
c. Gain or loss from disposing of a discontinued segment
d. Extraordinary gain or loss
e. Cumulative effect of a change in accounting principle

Indicate where each of the nine income-related items for this company appears on its 1999 income statement by writing the letter of the appropriate section A through E in the blank beside each item.

		Debit	Credit
_____	1. Depreciation expense	$262,500	
_____	2. Gain on sale of wholesale segment (net of tax)		$ 675,000
_____	3. Loss from operating wholesale segment (net of tax)	555,000	
_____	4. Salaries expense	540,000	
_____	5. Sales		2,700,000
_____	6. Gain on state's condemnation of company property (net of tax)		330,000
_____	7. Cost of goods sold	1,380,000	
_____	8. Effect of change from declining-balance to straight-line depreciation (net of tax)		135,000
_____	9. Income taxes expense	207,000	

Exercise 14-6
Income statement presentation
C2

Use the data for Burks Merchandise, Inc., in Exercise 14-5 to prepare its income statement for 1999.

Exercise 14-7
Accounting for a change in accounting principle
C3

American Company put an asset in service on January 1, 1999. Its cost was $225,000, its predicted service life was six years, and its expected salvage value was $22,500. The company decided to use double-declining-balance depreciation and recorded these amounts of depreciation expense in the first two years of the asset's life:

1999	$75,000
2000	50,000

The scheduled depreciation expense for 2001 is $33,250. After consulting with the company's auditors, management decides to change to straight-line depreciation in 2001, without changing either the predicted service life or salvage value. Under this method, the annual depreciation expense for all years in the asset's life is $33,750. The company faces a 35% income tax rate.

1. Prepare a table like Exhibit 14.8 to analyze this change in accounting principle.
2. How much depreciation expense will be reported on the company's income statement for this asset in 2001 and in each of the remaining years of the asset's life?
3. What amount will be reported on the company's 2001 income statement as the after-tax cumulative effect of the change in accounting principle?

Exercise 14-8
Weighted-average shares outstanding and earnings per share
A1

ICM Company reported $1,350,000 of net income for 1999. It also declared $195,000 of dividends on preferred stock for the same year. At the beginning of 1999, the company had 270,000 outstanding shares of common stock. These two events changed the number of outstanding shares during the year:

Apr. 30 Sold 180,000 common shares for cash.
Oct. 31 Purchased 108,000 shares of its own common stock for the treasury.

a. What is the amount of net income available to common stockholders?
b. What is the weighted-average number of common shares outstanding for the year?
c. What is the company's basic earnings per share for the year?

Exercise 14-9
Weighted-average shares outstanding and earnings per share
A1

DQ Company reported $480,000 of net income for 1999. It also declared $65,000 of dividends on preferred stock for the same year. At the beginning of 1999, the company had 50,000 outstanding shares of common stock. These three events changed the number of outstanding shares during the year:

June 1 Sold 30,000 common shares for cash.
Aug. 31 Purchased 13,000 shares of its own common stock for the treasury.
Oct. 1 Completed a three-for-one stock split.

a. What is the amount of net income available to common stockholders?
b. What is the weighted-average number of common shares outstanding for the year?
c. What is the company's basic earnings per share for the year?

Exercise 14-10
Computing dividend yield
A2

Compute the dividend yield for each of these separate cases:

	Annual Dividend per Share	Market Price per Share
a.	$15.00	$216.00
b.	12.00	128.00
c.	6.00	61.00
d.	1.20	86.00
e.	11.00	130.00
f.	2.00	50.00

Which company's stock above would probably not be classified as an income stock?

Exercise 14-11
Computing the price-earnings ratio
A3

Use the information below to compute the price-earnings ratio for each separate case:

	Earnings per Share	Market Value per Share
a.	$10.00	$166.00
b.	9.00	86.00
c.	6.50	90.00
d.	1.50	36.00
e.	36.00	240.00

Which of the above stocks might an analyst investigate as being undervalued by the market?

Problems

Problem 14-1

Cash dividends and treasury stock transactions; statement of retained earnings

P1, P3

The balance sheet for Trellis Corporation reported the following components of stockholders' equity on December 31, 1999:

Common stock, $10 par value, 50,000 shares authorized, 20,000 shares issued and outstanding	$200,000
Contributed capital in excess of par value, common stock	30,000
Retained earnings	135,000
Total stockholders' equity	$365,000

In year 2000 the Trellis Company had the following transactions affecting stockholders and the stockholder equity accounts:

Jan. 1	Purchased 2,000 shares of its own stock as treasury stock at $20 per share.
Jan. 5	The directors declared a $2 per share cash dividend payable on Feb. 28 to the Feb. 5 stockholders of record.
Feb. 28	Paid the dividend declared on January 5.
July 6	Sold 750 of the treasury shares at $24 per share.
Aug. 22	Sold 1,250 of the treasury shares at $17 per share.
Sept. 5	The directors declared a $2 per share cash dividend payable on Oct. 28 to the Sept. 25 stockholders of record.
Oct. 28	Paid the dividend declared on September 5.
Dec. 31	Closed the $194,000 credit balance in the Income Summary account to Retained Earnings.
Dec. 31	Closed the Cash Dividends Declared account.

1. Prepare journal entries to record the transactions and closings for 2000.

2. Prepare a statement of retained earnings for the year ended December 31, 2000.

3. Prepare the stockholders' equity section of the company's balance sheet as of December 31, 2000.

Check Figure Retained earnings, Dec. 31, 2000, $252,250.

Problem 14-2

Describing equity changes with journal entries and account balances

P1, P2

At September 30, the end of the third quarter for Granger Co., the following balances exist in its stockholders' equity accounts:

Common stock, $12 par value	$720,000
Contributed capital in excess of par value	180,000
Retained earnings	640,000

During the company's fourth quarter, the following journal entries are recorded and affect the company's equity accounts:

Date	Account	Debit	Credit
Oct. 2	Cash Dividends Declared	120,000	
	Common Dividend Payable		120,000
Oct. 25	Common Dividend Payable	120,000	
	Cash		120,000
Oct. 31	Stock Dividends Declared	150,000	
	Common Stock Dividend Distributable		72,000
	Contributed Capital in Excess of Par Value, Common Stock		78,000
Nov. 5	Common Stock Dividend Distributable	72,000	
	Common Stock, $12 Par Value		72,000
Dec. 1	Memo—change the title of the common stock account to reflect the new par value of $4.		
Dec. 31	Income Summary	420,000	
	Retained Earnings		420,000
Dec. 31	Retained Earnings	270,000	
	Cash Dividends Declared		120,000
	Stock Dividends Declared		150,000

Required

1. Provide explanations for each of the journal entries.
2. Complete the following table showing the balances of the company's equity accounts (including the dividends declared accounts) at each of the indicated dates:

	Oct. 2	Oct. 25	Oct. 31	Nov. 5	Dec. 1	Dec. 31
Common stock	$____	$____	$____	$____	$____	$____
Common Stock dividend distributable	____	____	____	____	____	____
Contributed capital in excess of par	____	____	____	____	____	____
Retained earnings	____	____	____	____	____	____
Less: Cash dividends declared	____	____	____	____	____	____
Stock dividends declared	____	____	____	____	____	____
Combined balances of equity accounts	$____	$____	$____	$____	$____	$____

Check Figure Total equity, Dec. 31, $1,840,000

Problem 14-3
Analyzing changes in stockholders' equity accounts

C3

The equity sections from the 1999 and 2000 balance sheets of TRP Corporation appear as follows:

STOCKHOLDERS' EQUITY As of December 31, 1999	
Common stock, $4 par value, 50,000 shares authorized, 20,000 shares issued and outstanding	$ 80,000
Contributed capital in excess of par value, common stock	60,000
Total contributed capital	$140,000
Retained earnings	160,000
Total stockholders' equity	$300,000

STOCKHOLDERS' EQUITY As of December 31, 2000	
Common stock, $4 par value, 50,000 shares authorized, 23,700 shares issued, 1,500 in the treasury	$ 94,800
Contributed capital in excess of par value, common stock	89,600
Total contributed capital	$184,400
Retained earnings ($15,000 restricted)	200,000
Total	$384,400
Less cost of treasury stock	(15,000)
Total stockholders' equity	$369,400

The following events affecting equity accounts occurred during 2000:

Jan. 5	A $0.50 per share cash dividend is declared, and the date of record is Jan 10.
Mar. 20	Treasury stock is purchased.
Apr. 5	A $0.50 per share cash dividend is declared, and the date of record is April 10.
July 5	A $0.50 per share cash dividend is declared, and the date of record is July 10.
July 31	A 20% stock dividend is declared when the market value is $12 per share.
Aug. 14	The stock dividend is issued.
Oct. 5	A $0.50 per share cash dividend is declared, and the date of record is October 10.

Required

1. How many shares are outstanding on each of the cash dividend dates?
2. What are the amounts for each of the four cash dividends?
3. What is the amount of the capitalization of retained earnings for the stock dividend?

4. What is the price per share paid for the treasury stock?
5. How much income did the company earn during 2000?

Check Figure Net income, $124,000

Problem 14-4
Income statement presentation

The following schedule shows the balances from various accounts in the adjusted trial balance for Depew Corporation as of December 31, 1999:

	Debit	Credit
a. Interest earned		$ 12,000
b. Depreciation expense, Equipment	$ 36,000	
c. Loss on sale of equipment	24,750	
d. Accounts payable		42,000
e. Other operating expenses	97,500	
f. Accumulated depreciation, Equipment		73,500
g. Gain from settling a lawsuit		42,000
h. Cumulative effect of change in accounting principle (pre-tax)	63,000	
i. Accumulated depreciation, Buildings		163,500
j. Loss from operating a discontinued segment (pre-tax)	19,500	
k. Gain on retirement of debt (pre-tax)		28,500
l. Sales		970,500
m. Depreciation expense, Buildings	54,000	
n. Correction of overstatement of prior year's sales (pre-tax)	15,000	
o. Gain on sale of discontinued segment's assets (pre-tax)		33,000
p. Loss from settling a lawsuit	24,000	
q. Income taxes expense	?	
r. Cost of goods sold	487,500	

Required

Answer each of the following questions by providing detailed schedules:

1. Assume the company's income tax rate is 30% for all items, what are the tax effects and after-tax measures of the items labeled as pretax?
2. What is the amount of the company's income from continuing operations before income taxes? What is the amount of the company's income taxes expense? What is the amount of the company's income from continuing operations?
3. What is the amount of after-tax income associated with the discontinued segment?
4. What is the amount of income before extraordinary items and the cumulative effect of the change in principle?
5. What is the amount of net income for the year?

Check Figure Net income, $195,825

Problem 14-5
Changes in accounting principles and their disclosure

On January 1, 1999, Pohl, Inc., purchased equipment. Its cost was $600,000, and it was expected to have a salvage value of $30,000 at the end of its five-year useful life. Depreciation was allocated to 1999, 2000, and 2001 with the declining-balance method at twice the straight-line rate. Early in 2002, the company concluded that changing to the straight-line method would produce more useful financial statements and would be consistent with the practices of other firms in the industry.

Required

Preparation Component

1. Do generally accepted accounting principles allow Pohl to change depreciation methods in 2002?
2. Prepare a schedule that shows the amount of depreciation expense allocated to 1999 through 2001 under the declining-balance method.
3. Prepare a schedule that shows the amount of depreciation expense that would have been allocated to 1999 through 2001 under the straight-line method.
4. Combine the information from your answers to requirements 2 and 3 in a table like Exhibit 14.8 that computes the before- and after-tax cumulative effects of the change. The company's income tax rate is 30%. (Round answers to the nearest dollar.)

Check Figure After-tax cumulative effect, $89,880

5. How should the cumulative effect of the change in accounting principle be reported by the company? Does the cumulative effect increase or decrease net income?
6. How much depreciation expense will be reported on the company's income statement for 2002?

Analysis Component

7. Assume that Pohl makes the mistake of treating the change in depreciation methods as a change in an accounting estimate. Using your answers from requirements 2, 3, and 4, describe the effect this error would have on the 2002 financial statements.

Problem 14-6
Earnings per share calculations and presentation

A1

The income statements for Tennison, Inc., reported the following information when they were initially published in 2000, 2001, and 2002:

	2000	2001	2002
Sales	$370,000	$425,000	$412,500
Expenses	232,500	260,000	245,500
Income from continuing operations	$137,500	$165,000	$167,000
Loss on discontinued segment	(52,500)		
Income before extraordinary items	$ 85,000	$165,000	$167,000
Extraordinary gain (loss)		33,000	(70,000)
Net income	$ 85,000	$198,000	$ 97,000

The company also experienced changes in the number of outstanding shares from the following events:

Outstanding shares on December 31, 1999	40,000
2000:	
Treasury stock purchase on April 1	− 4,000
Issuance of new shares on June 30	+ 12,000
10% stock dividend on October 1	+ 4,800
Outstanding shares on December 31, 2000	52,800
2001:	
Issuance of new shares on July 1	+ 16,000
Treasury stock purchase on November 1	− 4,800
Outstanding shares on December 31, 2001	64,000
2002:	
Issuance of new shares on August 1	+ 20,000
Treasury stock purchase on September 1	− 4,000
Three-for-one split on October 1	+160,000
Outstanding shares on December 31, 2002	240,000

Required

Preparation Component

1. Compute the weighted-average of the common shares outstanding as of the end of 2000.
2. Compute the earnings per share amounts to report on the 2000 income statement for: income from continuing operations, loss on discontinued segment, and net income.
3. Compute the weighted-average of the common shares outstanding as of the end of 2001.
4. Compute the earnings per share amounts to report on the 2001 income statement for: income from continuing operations, the extraordinary gain, and net income.
5. Compute the weighted-average of the common shares outstanding as of the end of 2002.
6. Compute the earnings per share amounts to report on the 2002 income statement for: income from continuing operations, the extraordinary loss, and net income.

Check Figure 2001 earnings per share for net income, $3.30

Analysis Component

7. Explain how you would use the earnings per share data from requirement 6 in predicting earnings per share for 2003.

BEYOND THE NUMBERS

Reporting in Action

C2, A1, A2, A3

Refer to the financial statements and related information for **NIKE** in Appendix A. Answer the following questions by analyzing that information:

1. What is the per share amount of cash dividends paid on common stock for fiscal year 1997?
2. What is the total amount of cash dividends paid to preferred stockholders for fiscal year 1997?
3. How many shares of common stock are outstanding at the end of fiscal year 1997? How does this number compare with the weighted-average common shares outstanding at the end of fiscal year 1997?
4. Compare NIKE's May 31, 1997, net income per common share to the net income per common share as of May 31, 1996. Comment on any significant change.
5. Does NIKE hold any shares of treasury stock as of May 31, 1997?
6. Does NIKE report any changes in accounting principles or the occurrence of extraordinary items for fiscal years ended May 31, 1997, and May 31, 1996?
7. Did NIKE have any gains or losses on disposal of a business segment for fiscal year 1997?

Swoosh Ahead

8. Obtain NIKE's annual report information for a fiscal year ending after May 31, 1997. You can get this information from either its Web site [**nike.com**] or the SEC's EDGAR database [**sec.gov**]. Has NIKE increased the total amount of cash dividends paid compared to the fiscal year 1997?

Comparative Analysis

A1, A2, A3

Reebok

Both **NIKE** and **Reebok** design, produce, market, and sell sports footwear and apparel. Key comparative figures ($ thousands except for per share data) for these two organizations follow:

Key figures*	NIKE	Reebok
Net income	$795,822	$138,950
Dividends paid per share of common stock	$0.38	$0.225
Common shares outstanding	296,368	69,618
Market price per share	$57.50	$42.00

*NIKE figures are from its annual report for fiscal year ended May 31,1997.
Reebok figures are from its annual report for fiscal year ended December 31, 1996.

Required

1. Compute the earnings per share for each company using the data above.
2. Compute the dividend yield for each company using the data above. Does the dividend yield of either company characterize it as an income or growth stock?
3. Compute, compare, and interpret the price-earnings ratios for NIKE and Reebok from these data.

Ethics Challenge

C2

This chapter described CompUS's change in accounting principle from the double-declining-balance method of depreciation to the straight-line method. CompUS argued that its income statement would be more useful if depreciation were computed using the straight-line method instead of the double-declining-balance method. This change in accounting principle added $56,000 to net income for the current year.

As the auditor of this company, you must review the decision to make the change in accounting principle. You review the equipment in question and learn that it is a piece of high-tech equipment, and the risk of obsolescence in the near future is relatively high. You are also aware that all members of top management receive year-end bonuses based on net income.

Required

As the auditor, would you support the change in principle or ask management to continue using the declining-balance method? Justify your response.

Communicating in Practice

A3

Teams are to select an industry, and each team member is to select a different company in that industry. Each team member is to acquire the annual report of the company selected. Annual reports can be obtained in many ways including accessing this book's Web page. Use the annual report to determine the earnings per share of common stock. Use the financial press to determine the market price of this stock, and then compute the price-earnings ratio. Communicate with teammates via a meeting, e-mail, or telephone to discuss the meaning of these ratios, how different companies compare to each other, and the industry norms. The team must prepare a single memorandum reporting the ratios for each company and identifying the conclusions or consensus of opinion reached during the team's discussion. The memorandum is to be duplicated and distributed to the instructor and all classmates.

Taking it to the Net

A1, A2, A3

Visit the **Stockfever** Web site at **www.Stockfever.com.** Stockfever puts key financial data about companies at your fingertips. Using the stock symbols for **Nike** (NKE) and **Reebok** (RBK), search for the following information. (Hint: you may want to print out the various links for later reference.)

1. Under the sidebar category *Quote,* select the Yahoo detailed quote link. Record the market price per share, earnings per share, price-earnings ratio, and dividend per share for both companies.

2. Compute the dividend yield for each company using the data you collect in requirement 1.

3. Visit the sidebar category *Earnings.* View at least three of the earnings consensus links. How much difference do you find among the experts regarding the companies' future earnings prospects?

4. Under the sidebar category *Fundamentals,* select the dividends and splits link. Has either company's stock split recently?

Teamwork in Action

P3

This activity requires teamwork to reinforce understanding of accounting for treasury stock.

1. After a team discussion, write a brief team statement (a) generalizing what happens to a corporation's financial position when the entity engages in a stock "buyback" and (b) identifying reasons why a corporation would engage in this activity.

2. Assume an entity reacquired 100 shares of its $100 par value common stock at a cost of $134 per share. Discuss the entry to record this acquisition. After each member understands this entry, assign *each* team member the preparation of *one* of the following entries (assume each entry applies to all shares):

   a. Reissue at cost

   b. Reissue at $150 per share

   c. Reissue at $120 per share—assume the contributed capital account from treasury shares has a $1,500 balance.

   d. Reissue at $120 per share—assume the contributed capital account from treasury shares has a $1,000 balance.

   e. Reissue at $120 per share—assume the contributed capital account from treasury shares has a zero balance

3. In sequence, each member is to present his or her entry to the team and explain the *similarities* and *differences* between that entry and the previous entry. Encourage team members to ask questions and be sure concepts are understood before proceeding.

Hitting the Road

A1, A2, A3

Watch the **CNBC** financial news television station. While watching, take notes on company happenings that are catching the attention of analysts. You might hear reference to over- and under valuation of firms. You might also hear reports about PE ratios, dividend yields, and earnings per share. Be prepared to give a brief description in class of your observations of CNBC.

Business Week Activity

A1

Read the article "Worldcom: Paper Tiger?" in the October 20, 1997, issue of *Business Week*.

1. What is the "earnings magic" phenomenon referred to early in the article?
2. What reason is offered in the article for the upward trend in **Worldcom**'s stock price?
3. Historically, what has happened to the stock performance of companies in years subsequent to making acquisitions? Contrast the performance of stock-for-stock deals with acquisitions made with cash.

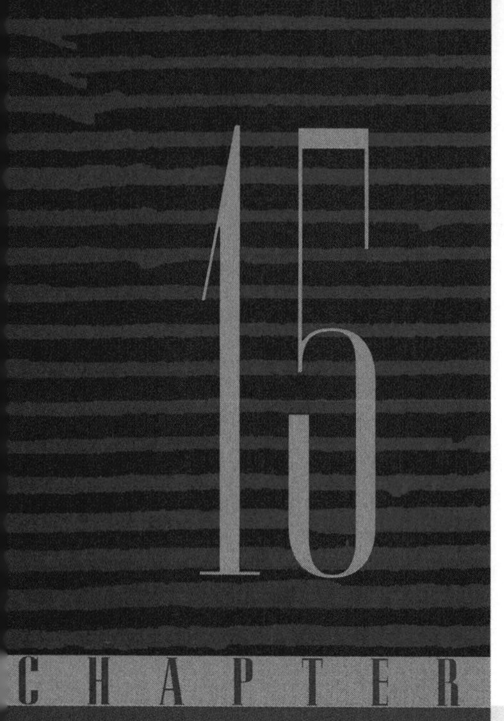

Bonds and Long-Term Notes Payable

A Look Back

Chapter 14 focused on corporate reporting including accounting for dividends, treasury stock, income reporting, earnings per share, and retained earnings.

A Look at This Chapter

This chapter describes the accounting for bonds and notes. We explain their characteristics, payment patterns, interest computations, retirement, and reporting requirements.

A Look Ahead

Chapter 16 focuses on long-term investments in securities. We explain how to identify, account for, and report for them. We also describe accounting for transactions listed in a foreign currency.

Chapter Outline

Get Real!

MEMPHIS, TN—Jessica Harris has overcome odds before. Three years ago she had a plan to open a natural foods store near Memphis. But she needed money. She took plans for her store to the local bank. "The banker ripped into my business plan and told me to get real," says Harris. "I've never forgotten that."

Harris then turned to her family and friends for start-up money. Motivated by the banker's remark, Harris named her new store **Get Real!** "I sell *real* food like farm-raised seafood and natural and organic produce. The name seemed to fit." Her store currently offers a line of more than 2,000 products.

But with success, Harris faced another obstacle. "I want to open two more stores. One in Birmingham and one in Jackson." Again, Harris had to meet with several bankers to get a loan. "Every bank wanted me to come to four meetings and prepare five sets of forecasts. Only then will they make a loan proposal, and none of them were acceptable to me. They viewed my plans as risky and I had little collateral."

Then Harris got an idea. "I remember when Ben & Jerry's was a tiny ice-cream parlor and advertised its stock on its ice cream cartons," said Harris. "But I didn't want the headache of stockholders." Instead, Harris decided to issue bonds on her own and got a lawyer to draw up papers. "I put up posters in the store and printed notices on my grocery bags offering bonds for sale. I also added the notice to my regular newspaper ads," says Harris. "For just the $25 par value, a person could buy one of my 8% bonds."

"I was flooded with requests. Some people viewed the bonds as an investment, others as a novelty. In the backroom, I typed in names and addresses and printed up bond certificates. When people sent me a check, I sent a bond." Harris ended up raising over $200,000. "I'm really fired up! I've already rented a location in Jackson, and I'm close to a deal in Birmingham." Thanks to the banker who told Harris to get real, **Get Real!** is a real success.

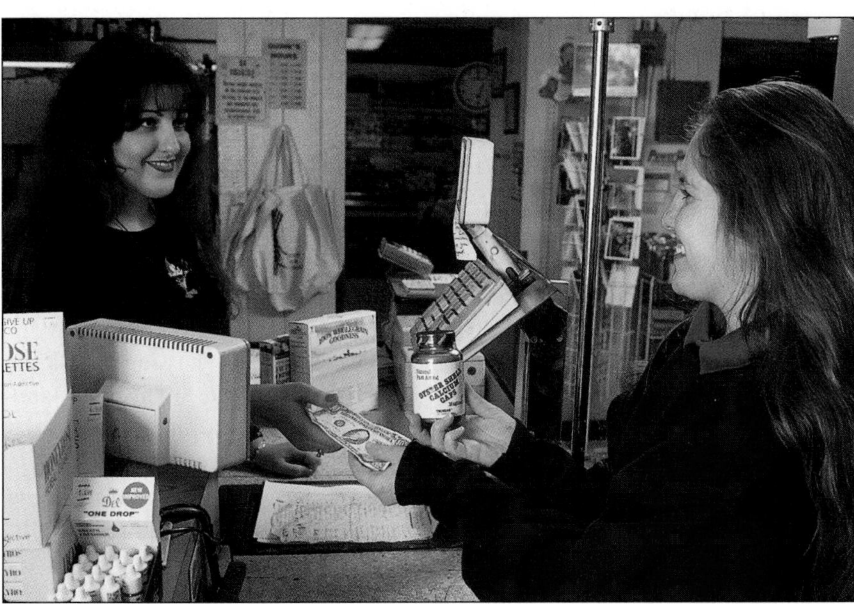

Learning Objectives

Conceptual

C1 Explain the types of bonds and the procedures for issuing them.

C2 Explain the types and payment patterns of notes.

Analytical

A1 Compare bond financing with stock financing.

A2 Explain collateral agreements and their effects on loan risk.

A3 Compute the ratio of pledged assets to secured liabilities and explain its use.

Procedural

P1 Prepare entries to record bond issuance and bond interest expense.

P2 Compute and record amortization of bond discount.

P3 Compute and record amortization of bond premium.

P4 Record the retirement of bonds.

P5 Prepare entries to account for notes.

CHAPTER PREVIEW

Bonds are issued by companies and governments to finance their activities. In return for money, bonds promise to repay the lender with interest. This chapter explains the basics of bonds and the accounting for their issuance and retirement. The chapter also describes long-term notes, including interest-bearing, noninterest-bearing, and installment notes. We explain how present value concepts impact both the accounting for and reporting of bonds and notes. An appendix to this chapter discusses important present value concepts in accounting for liabilities. Understanding how bonds and notes are used to the advantage of a company, as shown in the opening article, is an important goal of this chapter.

Basics of Bonds

Many companies finance operations and borrow money by issuing bonds. This section explains the basics of bonds and the companies' motivations for issuing them.

Bond Financing

Companies can finance their business activities in several ways, including issuing notes, leasing assets, and selling stock. But projects demanding large amounts of money often are funded from bond issuances.[1]

A1 Compare bond financing with stock financing.

A **bond** is a written promise to pay an amount identified as the par value of the bond along with interest at a stated annual rate. The **par value** of a bond, also called the *face amount* or *face value,* is paid at a specified future date known as the *maturity date* of the bond. Most bonds require the borrower to make semiannual interest payments. The amount of interest paid each year is determined by multiplying the par value of the bond by the stated rate of interest determined when the bonds are issued. This section explains both advantages and disadvantages of bond financing.

Advantages of Bonds

There are three main advantages of bond financing:

1. *Bonds do not affect stockholder control.* A share of stock reflects an ownership right in the corporation, whereas a bond does not. A person who owns 1,000 shares of a corporation's 10,000 outstanding shares controls one-tenth of all stockholders' votes. But a person who owns a $1,000, 11%, 20-year bond has no ownership right. This person, or bondholder, has a receivable from the bond issuer. The right of the bondholder is to receive 11% interest, or $110, each year the bond is outstanding and $1,000 when the bond matures in 20 years.

2. *Interest on bonds is tax deductible.* Bond interest is tax deductible, but cash dividends to stockholders are not. To illustrate the importance of this, let's assume a company earns $10,000 in income before paying taxes at a 40% tax rate. This company would have $10,000 available to pay interest on bonds. This same company, however, would only have $6,000 available to pay cash dividends on stock.

3. *Bonds can increase return on equity.* When a company earns a higher return with the borrowed funds than it is paying in interest, it increases its return on equity. This process is called *financial leverage* or *trading on the equity.*

[1] Bonds are issued by for-profit and nonprofit companies, as well as the federal government and other governmental units, such as cities, states, and school districts. Although the examples in this chapter deal with business situations, all issuers use the same practices to account for their bonds.

To illustrate the impact to return on equity, let's look at Magnum Skates. Magnum has $1 million in equity and is planning a $500,000 expansion to meet increasing demand for its product. Magnum predicts the $500,000 expansion will yield $125,000 in additional income before paying any interest. Magnum currently earns $100,000 per year and has no interest expense.

Magnum is considering three plans. Plan A is to not expand. Plan B is to expand and raise $500,000 from issuing stock. Plan C is to sell $500,000 worth of bonds paying 10% annual interest, or $50,000. Exhibit 15.1 shows us how these three plans affect Magnum's net income, equity, and return on equity (net income/equity).

Exhibit 15.1

Financing with Bonds or Stock

	Plan A Don't Expand	Plan B Issue Stock	Plan C Issue Bonds
Income before interest	$ 100,000	$ 225,000	$ 225,000
Interest	—	—	(50,000)
Net income	**$ 100,000**	**$ 225,000**	**$ 175,000**
Equity	$1,000,000	$1,500,000	$1,000,000
Return on equity	**10.0%**	**15.0%**	**17.5%**

Analysis of these plans shows the owners will earn a higher return on equity if expansion occurs. The preferred plan of expansion is by issuing bonds. Even though projected net income under Plan C ($175,000) is smaller than under Plan B ($225,000), the return on equity is larger because of less equity investment. This is an important result and yields a general rule: *return on equity increases when the expected rate of return from the new assets is greater than the rate of interest on the bonds.* Also, issuing bonds allows the current owners to remain in control.

Disadvantages of Bonds

There are two main disadvantages of bond financing:

1. *Bonds require payment of both periodic interest and the par value at maturity.* Bond payments can be especially burdensome when a company's income is low and when it is struggling to survive. Stock, on the other hand, does not require payment of dividends. Cash dividends on stock are paid at the discretion of the issuer.
2. *Bonds can decrease return on equity.* When a company earns a lower return with the borrowed funds than it is paying in interest, it decreases its return on equity. This is the downside risk of financial leverage. It is more likely to arise when a company has periods of low income.

A company must weigh the risks of these disadvantages against the advantages of bond financing when deciding on whether to issue bonds to finance operations.

C1 Explain the types of bonds and the procedures for issuing them.

Types of Bonds

There exist many different kinds of bonds with various characteristics. We describe the more common types of bonds in this section.

Secured and Unsecured Bonds

Secured bonds have specific assets of the issuing company pledged (or *mortgaged*) as collateral. This arrangement gives bondholders added protection against default by the issuer. If the issuing company fails to pay interest or par value, the secured bondholders can demand the collateral be sold and the proceeds used to pay the bond obligation.

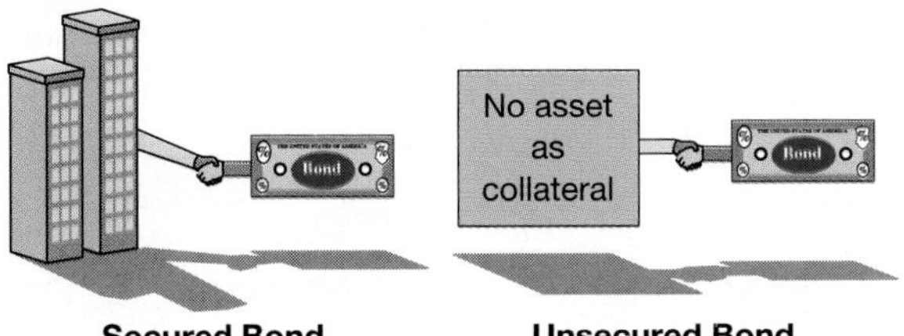

Unsecured bonds, also called *debentures,* are backed by the issuer's general credit standing. Unsecured bonds are almost always more risky than secured bonds. Because of this added risk, a company generally must be financially strong to successfully issue debentures at a favorable rate of interest.

Companies also can issue debentures whose claims on a company's assets are second to those of other unsecured liabilities. These debentures are called *subordinated debentures,* meaning these creditors' claims are subordinated to the claims of some others. **L.A. Gear** has issued subordinated debentures. In a liquidation, L.A. Gear's subordinated debentures are not repaid until the claims of the more senior, unsecured liabilities are first settled.

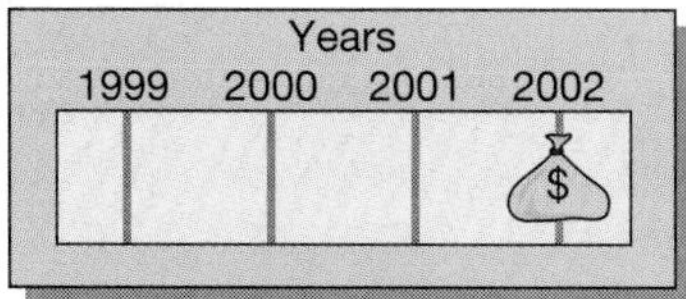

Term Bond

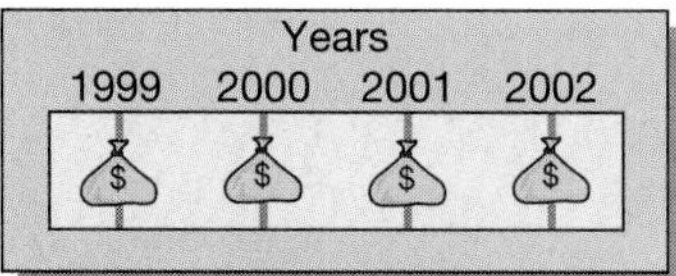

Serial Bond

Term and Serial Bonds

Term bonds are scheduled for payment (maturity) at a single specified date. **Serial bonds** mature at several different dates (in series). This means serial bonds are repaid over a number of periods. For instance, $1 million of serial bonds might mature at the rate of $100,000 each year from 6 to 15 years after the bonds are issued. This involves 10 groups (or series) of bonds of $100,000 each where one series matures after six years, another after seven years, and another each successive year until the final series is repaid.

Many bonds are also **sinking fund bonds.** To reduce the holder's risk, these bonds require the issuer to create a *sinking fund,* which is a group of assets used to repay the bonds at maturity. The issuer must set aside the assets to pay off these bonds before they mature.

Registered Bond

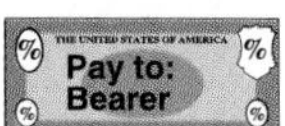

Bearer Bond

Registered Bonds and Bearer Bonds

Bonds issued in the names and addresses of their owners are **registered bonds.** The issuing company makes bond payments by sending checks to these registered owners. When one investor sells a bond to another investor, the issuer must be notified of the change. Registered bonds offer the issuer the practical advantage of not having to actually issue bond certificates to investors. This arrangement protects investors against loss or theft of bonds.

Bonds payable to whoever holds them (the *bearer)* are called **bearer bonds,** or *unregistered bonds.* Since there may be no record of sales or exchanges, the holder of a bearer bond is presumed to be its rightful owner. As a result, lost or stolen bearer bonds are difficult to replace.

Many bearer bonds are also **coupon bonds.** This term reflects interest coupons that are attached to these bonds. Each coupon matures on a specific interest payment date. The owner detaches each coupon when it matures and presents it to a bank or broker for collection. At maturity, the owner follows the same process and presents the bond certificate for collection. Because there is no readily available record of who actually receives the interest, the income tax law discourages companies from issuing new coupon bonds.

Convertible and Callable Bonds

Convertible Bond **Callable Bond**

Convertible bonds can be exchanged by bondholders for a fixed number of shares of the issuing company's common stock. Convertible bonds also offer bondholders the potential to participate in future increases in the stock's market value. But if the stock does not appreciate, bondholders continue to receive periodic interest and will receive the par value when the bond matures. In most cases, the bondholders decide whether and when to convert the bonds to stock. **Callable bonds** have an option exercisable by the issuer to retire them at a stated dollar amount prior to maturity.

Muni's

There are more than a million municipal bonds, or "munis," to choose from, and many are exempt from taxes. Munis are issued by all types of government agencies such as states, cities, towns, and counties. They are issued to pay for a variety of public projects including schools, roads, bridges, and stadiums.

Tax-Exempt Bonds

Representative prices for several active tax-exempt revenue and refunding bonds, based on institutional trades. Changes rounded to the nearest one-eighth. Yield is to maturity. n-New. Source: The Bond Buyer.

Issue	Coupon	Mat	Price	Chg	Bid Yld	Issue	Coupon	Mat	Price	Chg	Bid Yld
Ca Gen Obligate Bds	5.125	10-01-27	97 7/8	— 5/8	5.27	MD Hlth & Hgr Ed Au	5.000	07-01-27	96 7/8	— 3/8	5.21
Calif Hlth Fac	5.000	08-15-37	95 3/8	— 3/4	5.28	Miami-Dade FL Ser 97B	5.000	10-01-37	95 1/2	— 3/8	5.27
Calif Hlth Fac	5.375	08-15-30	100 5/8	— 5/8	5.33	Mich St Hsp Fin Auth	5.000	05-15-28	95 3/8	— 1/2	5.31
Chester Co Hth & Ed Pa	5.375	05-15-27	99 3/4	— 3/8	5.39	Mo Hlth & Ed Fac	5.000	11-15-37	95 1/2	— 1/2	5.27
Chicago Sch Refm BOT	5.250	12-01-27	98 1/2	— 3/8	5.35	Nashville-Davidson Co	4.875	11-01-28	93 5/8	— 1/2	5.29
Clv OH Arpt Sys Rev	5.125	01-01-27	97	— 3/8	5.33	NH Hghr Ed & Hlth	5.125	06-01-28	97 5/8	— 1/4	5.28
Denver Colo Arpt 97E	5.250	11-15-23	99 1/4	— 3/8	5.30	NY Lcl Gvt Asst Ser97B	4.875	04-01-20	95	— 5/8	5.26
Fulco Hsp Auth Ga	5.000	11-15-28	95 1/2	— 3/8	5.29	NY Lcl Gvt Asst Ser97B	5.000	04-01-21	96 1/2	— 5/8	5.26

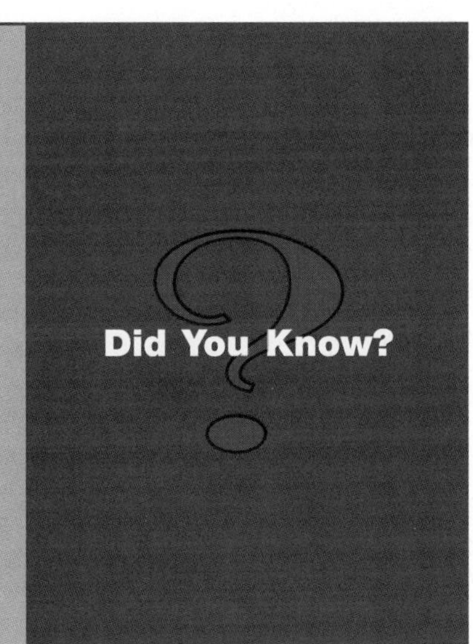

Bond Trading

Bonds are securities and can be readily bought and sold. A large number of corporate bonds trade on both the New York Exchange and the American Exchange. A bond issue consists of a large number of bonds, usually in denominations of $1,000 or $5,000, and are sold to many different lenders. After bonds are issued, they often are bought and sold by these investors, meaning any particular bond is probably owned by a number of people before it matures.

Because bonds are exchanged in the market, they have a market value (price). For convenience, bond market values are expressed as a percent of their par (face) value. For example, a company's bonds might be trading at 103½, which means they can be bought or sold for 103.5% of their par value. Bonds can also trade below par value. For instance, if a company's bonds are trading at 95, they can be bought or sold at 95% of their par value.

Bond Quotes

Bonds	Cur Yld	Vol	Close	Net Chg
CompUSA 9½ 00	9.2	145	103½	+⅛

The **CompUSA** bond quote shown here is interpreted as (left to right): **Bonds,** company name; **Rate,** contract interest rate (9½%) for this bond; **Maturity,** year (2000) in which bond's principal is paid (first two digits are either 19 or 20); **Cur Yld,** yield rate (9.2%) of bond at current price; **Vol,** dollars worth ($145,000) of bonds traded in 1000s; **Close,** closing price ($1,035) for the day as % of par value; **Net Chg,** change ($1.25) in closing price as a fraction of par from the prior day.

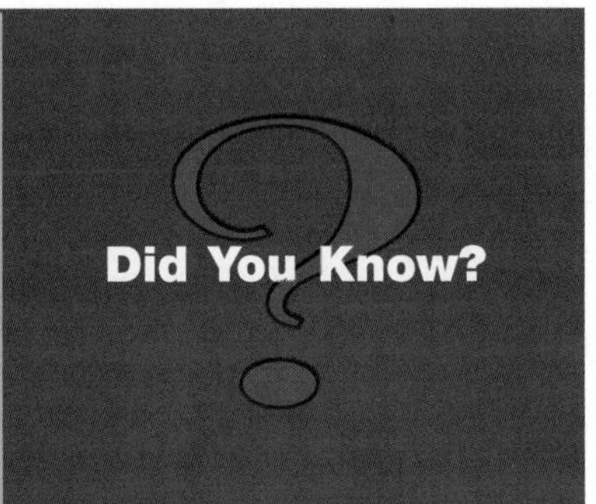

Bond Issuing Procedures

Bond issuances are governed by state and federal laws. Issuing company bonds usually requires approval by both the board of directors and stockholders. Authorization of bond issuances includes the number of bonds authorized, their par value, and the contract interest rate.

The legal document identifying the rights and obligations of both the bondholders and the issuer is called the **bond indenture.** The bond indenture acts as the legal contract be-

Exhibit 15.2

Bond Certificate

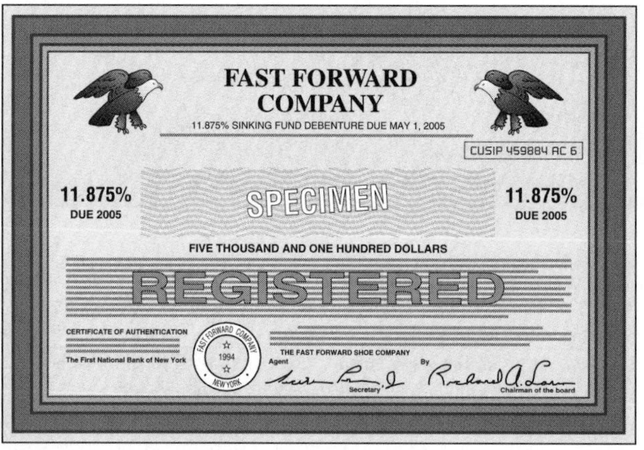

tween the issuer and the bondholders. A bondholder may also receive a bond certificate as evidence of the company's debt. A **bond certificate,** such as shown in Exhibit 15.2, includes specifics such as the issuer's name, the bond's par value, the contract interest rate, and the maturity date. Many companies reduce costs by not issuing certificates to registered bondholders.

The issuing company normally sells its bonds to an investment firm called an *underwriter.* The underwriter then resells them to the public. An issuing company can also sell bonds directly to investors. When an underwriter sells bonds to a large number of investors, the bondholders' interests are represented and protected by a *trustee.* The trustee monitors the issuer to ensure it complies with the obligations in the bond indenture. Most trustees are large banks or trust companies.

Terms of a bond indenture are drawn up and accepted by the trustee before bonds are issued. When bonds are offered to the public, called *floating an issue,* they must be registered with the Securities and Exchange Commission (SEC). SEC registration requires the issuer to file financial information in special reports. Most company bonds are issued in par value units of $1,000 or $5,000. A *baby bond* is a bond with less than a $1,000 par value such as $100.

Bond Issuances

This section explains accounting for bond issuances at par, below par (discount), and above par (premium). We also describe the amortization of a discount or premium, and how to record bonds issued between interest payment dates.

Issuing Bonds at Par

P1 Prepare entries to record bond issuance and bond interest expense.

To illustrate an issuance of bonds at par value, let's suppose Barnes Company receives authorization from the SEC to issue $800,000 of 9%, 20-year bonds. The bonds are dated January 1, 2000, and are due on December 31, 2019. They pay interest semiannually on each June 30 and December 31. After the bond indenture is accepted by the trustee on behalf of the bondholders, all or a portion of the bonds can be sold to an underwriter. If all bonds are sold at their par value, Barnes Company makes this entry to record the sale:

Assets = Liabilities + Equity
+800,000 +800,000

2000			
Jan. 1	Cash	800,000	
	Bonds Payable		800,000
	Sold bonds at par.		

This entry reflects increases in the company's cash and long-term liabilities.

Six months later, the first semiannual interest payment is made, and Barnes records its payment with this entry:

Assets = Liabilities + Equity
−36,000 −36,000

2000			
June 30	Bond Interest Expense	36,000	
	Cash		36,000
	Paid semiannual interest on bonds. (9% × $800,000 × ½ year)		

This entry is made every six months as Barnes pays its semiannual interest obligations until the bonds mature.

When the bonds mature 20 years later, Barnes Company records its payment of the maturity value with this entry:

2019			
Dec. 31	Bonds Payable	800,000	
	Cash		800,000
	Paid bonds at maturity.		

Assets = Liabilities + Equity
−800,000 −800,000

Ratings Game
Many bond buyers look to rating services for assessing the risk of bonds. The best known are **Standard and Poor's** and **Moody's.** These services focus on the financial strength of the issuer rather than the market attractiveness of the bond. Financial statements are a crucial part of the information these services rely on in setting ratings. Standard and Poor's ratings, from best quality to default, are: AAA, AA, A, BBB, BB, B, D.

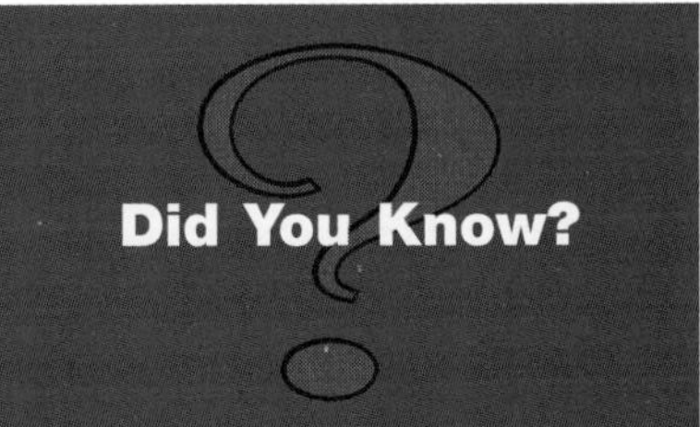

Bond Discount or Premium

The interest rate paid by the issuer of bonds is specified in the indenture and on the bond certificates. Because it is stated in the indenture, this rate is called the **contract rate** of the bonds. The contract rate is also called the *coupon rate,* the *stated rate,* or the *nominal rate.* The amount of interest paid each year is determined by multiplying the par value of the bonds by the contract rate.

The contract rate is usually stated on an annual basis, even if the interest is paid semiannually. For example, let's suppose a company issues a $1,000, 8% bond paying interest semiannually. This means the annual interest of $80 (8% × $1,000) is paid in two semiannual payments of $40 each.

The contract rate sets the amount of interest the issuer pays in *cash.* But the contract rate is not necessarily the rate of *bond interest expense* actually incurred by the issuer. Bond interest expense depends on the market value of the issuer's bonds, which is determined by market expectations on the risk of lending to this issuer. This expected risk, along with the supply of and demand for bonds, is reflected in the market rate of interest for the bond. The **market rate** is the rate that borrowers are willing to pay and that lenders are willing to earn for a particular bond and its risk level. A market rate changes in response to changes in both a bond's risk level and the supply of and demand for bonds.

Because factors that determine the market rate vary across companies, different companies face different market rates for their bonds. The market rate for a specific set of bonds depends on the level of risk investors assign to them. As the level of risk increases, the rate increases. The increased market rate compensates purchasers for the increased risk of bonds. Market rates also are affected by the length of the bonds' life. Long-term bonds generally have higher rates because they are more risky. This is because of the many things that can happen to a company over a long period of time.

Many bond issuers try to set a contract rate of interest equal to the market rate they expect as of the bonds' issuance date. When the contract rate and market rate are equal, the bonds sell at their par value. But when the contract does not equal the market rate, the bonds do not sell at their par value. Instead, they are sold at a *premium* above their par value or at a *discount* below their par value. Exhibit 15.3 shows the relation between the contract rate, market rate, and a bond's issue price.

Exhibit 15.3

Relation between Bond Issue Price, Contract Rate, and Market Rate

Contract rate is:		Bond sells:
Above market rate	➡	At a premium
Equal to market rate	➡	At par value
Below market rate	➡	At a discount

Some companies issue *zero-coupon bonds* that do not pay any periodic interest. This means the contract rate for zero-coupon bonds is zero. Because this 0% contract rate is always below the market rate, these bonds are always issued at a discount, meaning their prices are always less than their par values.

Flash back

1. Unsecured bonds backed only by the issuer's general credit standing are called: *(a)* serial bonds; *(b)* debentures; *(c)* registered bonds; *(d)* convertible bonds; or *(e)* bearer bonds.
2. How do you compute the amount of interest a bond issuer pays in cash each year?
3. When the contract rate is above the market rate, do bonds sell at a premium or a discount? Do purchasers pay more or less than the par value of the bonds?

Answers—p. 671

Issuing Bonds at a Discount

P2 Compute and record amortization of bond discount.

We described how a **discount on bonds payable** occurs when a company issues bonds with a contract rate less than the market rate. This means the issue price is less than the bonds' par value.

To illustrate this case, let's assume **Fila** announces an offer to issue bonds with a $100,000 par value, an 8% annual contract rate, and a five-year life. The market rate for Fila's bonds is 10%, meaning the bonds will sell at a discount since the contract rate is less than the market rate.[2] The exact issue price for these bonds is 97.277 (97.277% of par value).

These bonds obligate the issuer to pay out two different future cash flows:

1. $100,000 at the end of the bonds' five-year life.
2. $4,000 (4% × $100,000) at the end of each 6-month interest period of the bonds' five-year life.

The pattern of cash flows for Fila's bonds is shown in Exhibit 15.4.

Exhibit 15.4

Cash Flows of Fila's Bonds

								$100,000
	$4,000	$4,000	$4,000	$4,000		$4,000	$4,000	$4,000
0	6 mo.	12 mo.	18 mo.	24 mo.	. . .	48 mo.	54 mo.	60 mo.

If Fila accepts $92,277 cash for its bonds on the issue date of December 31, 2000, it records the sale with this entry:

Assets	=	Liabilities	+	Equity
+92,277		+100,000		
		−7,723		

2000			
Dec. 31	Cash	92,277	
	Discount on Bonds Payable	7,723	
	Bonds Payable		100,000
	Sold bonds at a discount on their issue date.		

[2] The difference between the contract rate and the market rate of interest on a new bond issue is usually a fraction of a percent. But we use a difference of 2% here to emphasize the effects.

These bonds are reported in the long-term liability section of the issuer's balance sheet as shown in Exhibit 15.5.

Exhibit 15.5

Balance Sheet Presentation of Bond Discount

Long-term liabilities:		
Bonds payable, 8%, due December 31, 2005	$100,000	
Less discount on bonds payable	7,723	$92,277

The discount is deducted from the par value of the bonds to produce the **carrying** (or **book**) **value** of the bonds payable. Discount on Bonds Payable is a contra-liability account.

Bond Rater
You are a bond rater. It is your job to assign a rating to a bond issue that reflects its riskiness to bondholders. Identify factors you look at in assigning risk to bonds. For the factors you identify, indicate their likely levels for a bond issue sold at a discount.

Answer—p. 670

Amortizing a Bond Discount

The issuer (Fila) received $92,277 for its bonds and will pay bondholders $100,000 after five years have passed (plus interest payments). Because the $7,723 discount is eventually paid to bondholders at maturity, it is part of the cost of using the $92,277 for five years. The upper portion of Exhibit 15.6 shows that total interest cost of $47,723 is the difference between the total amount repaid to bondholders ($140,000) and the amount borrowed from bondholders ($92,277).

Exhibit 15.6

Total Interest Expense for Bonds Issued at a Discount

Amount repaid to bondholders:	
Ten interest payments of $4,000	$ 40,000
Par value at maturity	100,000
Total repaid to bondholders	$140,000
Less amount borrowed from bondholders	(92,277)
Total interest expense	**$ 47,723**
Alternative Computation	
Ten payments of $4,000	$ 40,000
Plus discount	7,723
Total interest expense	**$ 47,723**

Alternatively, we can compute total bond interest expense as the sum of the interest payments and the bond discount. This alternative computation is shown in the lower portion of Exhibit 15.6.

Accounting for Fila's bonds must include two procedures. First, total bond interest expense of $47,723 must be allocated across the 10 six-month periods in the bonds' life. Second, the carrying value of the bonds must be updated at each balance sheet date. Two alternative methods accomplish these objectives: the straight-line and the effective interest methods of allocating interest. Both methods reduce the discount on the bonds over the life of the bonds. This process is often called *amortizing the bond discount.*

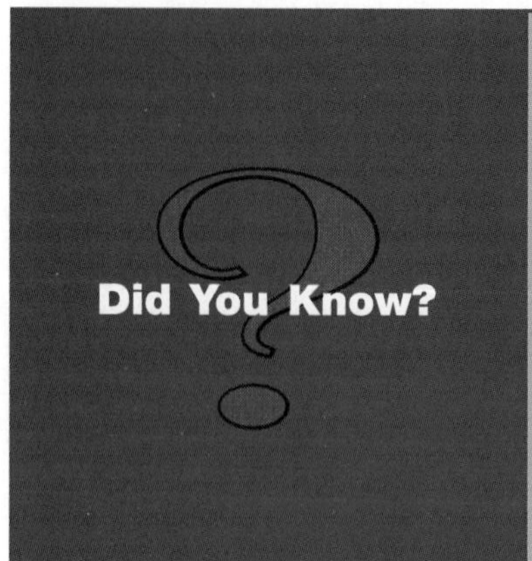

Junk Bonds

Junk bonds are company bonds with low credit ratings. Issuers of junk bonds are more likely than average to default on repayment. On the other hand, the high risk of junk bonds can yield high returns to their bondholders if the issuer survives and repays its debt. Junk bond issuances are running at over $100 billion a year. Also, the percent of junk bond issuances in default fell from 33% in 1984–90 to only 9% in 1991–97. [Source: *Business Week,* March 2, 1998.]

Straight-Line Method

The **straight-line method** of allocating interest is the simpler of the two methods of amortizing the bond discount. It allocates an equal portion of the total bond interest expense to each of the six-month interest periods.

To apply the straight-line method to Fila's bonds, we divide the five years' total interest expense of $47,723 by 10 (the number of semiannual periods in the bonds' life). This gives us a total bond interest expense of $4,772 per period.[3] Alternatively, we can find this number by first dividing the $7,723 original discount by 10. The resulting $772 is the amount of discount to be amortized in each interest period. When the $772 of amortized discount is added to the $4,000 cash payment, the total bond interest expense for each six-month period is $4,772.

The issuer records bond interest expense and updates the balance of the bond liability for each semiannual cash payment with this entry:

Assets	= Liabilities	+ Equity
−4,000	+772	−4,772

2001			
June 30	Bond Interest Expense	4,772	
	Discount on Bonds Payable		772
	Cash		4,000
	To record six months' interest and discount amortization (straight-line method).		

This is the entry made at the end of each of the 10 semiannual interest periods. The $772 credit to the Discount on Bonds Payable account *increases* the bonds' carrying value. This increase occurs because we *decrease* the balance of the Discount on Bonds Payable (contra) account which is subtracted from the Bonds Payable account. Exhibit 15.7 shows this pattern of decreases in the Discount on Bonds Payable account, along with increases in the bonds' carrying value.

We can summarize the following points in applying straight-line amortization to the discount on Fila's bonds over its life of 10 semiannual periods:

1. The $92,277 cash received from selling bonds equals the $100,000 par value of the bonds less the initial $7,723 discount from selling the bonds for less than par.

---

[3] For simplicity, all computations are rounded to the nearest whole dollar. Do the same when solving the exercises and problems at the end of the chapter.

2. Semiannual bond interest expense of $4,772 equals total bond interest expense of $47,723 divided by 10 semiannual periods (alternatively computed as the cash paid of $4,000 plus the periodic discount amortization of $772).
3. Semiannual credit to the Discount on Bonds Payable account equals the total discount of $7,723 divided by 10 semiannual periods.
4. Semiannual $4,000 interest payment equals the bonds' $100,000 par value multiplied by the 4% semiannual contract rate.
5. Carrying (or book) value of bonds continues to grow each period by the $772 discount amortization until it equals the par value of the bonds when they mature.

Exhibit 15.7

Bond Discount and Carrying Value under Straight-Line

Date	Bond Discount	Carrying Value
12/31/2000	$7,723	$ 92,277
6/30/2001	6,951	93,049
12/31/2001	6,179	93,821
6/30/2002	5,407	94,593
12/31/2002	4,635	95,365
6/30/2003	3,863	96,137
12/31/2003	3,091	96,909
6/30/2004	2,319	97,681
12/31/2004	1,547	98,453
6/30/2005	775*	99,225
12/31/2005	**0**	**100,000**

*Adjusted for rounding.

Fila incurs a $4,772 bond interest expense each period but pays only $4,000. The $772 unpaid portion of expense is added to the balance of the liability by decreasing the discount contra-liability account balance.

Effective Interest Method

The straight-line method yields changes in the bonds' carrying value (see Exhibit 15.7) while the amount for bond interest expense doesn't change (always equal to $4,772 for Fila bonds). This gives the impression of a changing interest rate when users divide a constant bond interest expense over a changing carrying value. As a result, accounting standards only allow use of straight-line when its results do not differ materially from those obtained using the effective interest method.[4]

The **effective interest method,** or simply *interest method,* allocates bond interest expense over the life of the bonds in a way that yields a constant rate of interest. This constant rate of interest is the market rate at the issue date. The effect of selling bonds at a premium or discount is that the issuer incurs the prevailing market rate of interest at issuance and not the contract rate. Bond interest expense for a period is found by multiplying the balance of the liability at the beginning of that period by the bonds' original market rate. An *amortization table* can be constructed to help us keep track of interest allocation and the balances of bond related accounts.

Exhibit 15.8 shows an effective interest amortization table for the Fila bonds. The key difference between the effective interest and straight-line methods lies in computation of bond interest expense. Instead of assigning an equal amount of interest to each interest period, the effective interest method assigns an increasing amount of interest over the Fila bonds' life because the balance of the liability increases over these five years. But both methods allocate the *same* $47,723 of total expense across the five years, but with different patterns.

The amortization table shows how the balance of the discount (column D) is amortized by the effective interest method until it reaches zero. The bonds' carrying value changes each period until it equals par value at maturity. Total bond interest expense is $47,723, composed of $40,000 of semiannual cash payments and $7,723 of the original discount below par value.

Except for differences in amounts, journal entries recording the expense and updating the liability balance are the same under the effective interest method and the straight-

[4] FASB, *Accounting Standards—Current Text* (Norwalk, CT, 1995), sec. I69.108. First published in *APB Opinion* No. 21, par. 15.

Exhibit 15.8

Effective Interest Amortization of Bond Discount

Bonds: $100,000 Par Value, Semiannual Interest Payments, 5-Year Life, 4% Semiannual Contract Rate, 5% Semiannual Market Rate

Semiannual Interest Period	(A) Cash Interest Paid	(B) Interest Expense	(C) Discount Amortization	(D) Unamortized Discount	(E) Carrying Value
12/31/2000				$7,723	$ 92,277
6/30/2001	$ 4,000	$ 4,614	$ 614	$7,109	92,891
12/31/2001	4,000	4,645	645	6,464	93,536
6/30/2002	4,000	4,677	677	5,787	94,213
12/31/2002	4,000	4,711	711	5,076	94,924
6/30/2003	4,000	4,746	746	4,330	95,670
12/31/2003	4,000	4,784	784	3,546	96,454
6/30/2004	4,000	4,823	823	2,723	97,277
12/31/2004	4,000	4,864	864	1,859	98,141
6/30/2005	4,000	4,907	907	952	99,048
12/31/2005	4,000	4,952	952	0	100,000
	$40,000	$47,723	$7,723		

Column **(A)** is the bonds' par value ($100,000) multiplied by the semiannual contract rate (4%).
Column **(B)** is the bonds' prior period carrying value multiplied by the semiannual market rate (5%).
Column **(C)** is the difference between interest paid and interest expense, or [(B) − (A)].
Column **(D)** is the prior period's unamortized discount less the current period's discount amortization.
Column **(E)** is the bonds' par value less unamortized discount, or [$100,000 − (D)].

line method. For instance, the entry to record the interest payment at the end of the first interest period is:

2001			
June 30	Bond Interest Expense	4,614	
	Discount on Bonds Payable		614
	Cash		4,000
	To record six months' interest and discount amortization (effective interest method).		

Assets = Liabilities + Equity
−4,000 +614 −4,614

We use the numbers in Exhibit 15.8 to make similar entries throughout the five-year life of the bonds.

Flash back

Five-year, 6% bonds with a $100,000 par value are issued at a price of $91,893. Interest is paid semiannually, and the market rate is 8% on the issue date. Use this information to answer the following questions:

4. Are these bonds issued at a discount or premium? Explain why.

5. What is the issuer's journal entry to record the sale?

6. What is the amount of bond interest expense recorded at the first semiannual cash payment using the (a) straight-line method and (b) effective interest method?

Answers—p. 671

Issuing Bonds at a Premium

P3 Compute and record amortization of bond premium.

When bonds carry a contract rate greater than the market rate, the bonds sell at a price greater than par value. The difference between par and market value is the **premium on bonds.** Buyers bid up the price of bonds above the bonds' par value until it reaches a level that will yield the lower market rate.

To illustrate, let's assume **Adidas** issues bonds with a $100,000 par value, a 12% annual contract rate, semiannual interest payments, and a five-year life. The market rate for Adidas's bonds is 10% on the issue date, meaning the bonds will sell at a premium because the contract rate is greater than the market rate. This means buyers of these bonds will bid up the market price until the yield equals the market rate. The issue price for these bonds is 107.72 (107.72% of par value).

These bonds obligate Adidas to pay out two different future cash flows:

1. $100,000 at the end of the bonds' five-year life.
2. $6,000 (6% × $100,000) at the end of each 6-month interest period of the bonds' five-year life.

The pattern of cash flows for Adidas's bonds is shown in Exhibit 15.9.

Exhibit 15.9

Cash Flows of Adidas's Bonds

0	6 mo.	12 mo.	18 mo.	24 mo.	. . .	48 mo.	54 mo.	60 mo.
	$6,000	$6,000	$6,000	$6,000		$6,000	$6,000	$6,000 $100,000

If Adidas accepts $107,720 cash for its bonds on the issue date of December 31, 2000, it records this transaction with the entry:

2000			
Dec. 31	Cash	107,720	
	Premium on Bonds Payable		7,720
	Bonds Payable		100,000
	Sold bonds at a premium on their issue date.		

Assets	=	Liabilities	+	Equity
+107,720		+100,000 +7,720		

These bonds are reported in the long-term liability section of the issuer's balance sheet as shown in Exhibit 15.10.

Exhibit 15.10

Balance Sheet Presentation of Bond Premium

Long-term liabilities:		
Bonds payable, 8%, due December 31, 2005	$100,000	
Plus premium on bonds payable	7,720	$107,720

The premium is added to the par value of the bonds to produce the carrying (book) value of the bonds payable. The Premium on Bonds Payable is an adjunct (also called *accretion*) liability account.

Amortizing a Bond Premium

The issuer (Adidas) receives $107,720 for its bonds and will pay bondholders $100,000 after five years have passed (plus semiannual interest payments). Because the $7,720 premium is not repaid to bondholders at maturity, it reduces the expense of using the $107,720 for five years.

The upper portion of Exhibit 15.11 shows that total bond interest expense of $52,280 is the difference between the total amount repaid to bondholders ($160,000) and the amount borrowed from bondholders ($107,720). Alternatively, we can compute total bond interest expense as the sum of the interest payments less the bond premium. The premium is subtracted because it will not be paid to the bondholders when the bonds mature. This alternative computation is shown in the lower portion of Exhibit 15.11. Total bond interest expense is allocated over the 10 semiannual periods with either the straight-line or the effective interest method.

Total Interest Expense for Bonds Issued at a Premium

Amount repaid to bondholders:	
Ten interest payments of $6,000	$ 60,000
Par value at maturity	100,000
Total repaid to bondholders	$160,000
Less amount borrowed from bondholders	(107,720)
Total interest expense	**$ 52,280**
Alternative Computation	
Ten payments of $6,000	$ 60,000
Less premium	(7,720)
Total interest expense	**$ 52,280**

Straight-Line Method

We explained how the straight-line method allocates an equal portion of total bond interest expense to each of the bonds' interest periods. To apply the straight-line method to Adidas's bonds, we divide the five years' total bond interest expense of $52,280 by 10 (the number of semiannual periods in the bonds' life). This gives us a total bond interest expense of $5,228 per period.

The issuer records bond interest expense and updates the balance of the bond liability for each semiannual cash payment with this entry:

2001			
June 30	Bond Interest Expense	5,228	
	Premium on Bonds Payable	772	
	Cash		6,000
	To record six months' interest and premium amortization (straight-line method).		

Assets = Liabilities + Equity
−6,000 −772 −5,228

This is the entry made at the end of each of the 10 semiannual interest periods. The $772 debit to the Premium on Bonds Payable account *decreases* the bonds' carrying value.

Effective Interest Method

Exhibit 15.12 shows the amortization table using the effective interest method for Adidas's bonds. Column A lists the semiannual cash payments. Column B shows the amount of expense, computed as the 5% market rate multiplied by the beginning carrying value. The amount of cash paid out in column A is larger than the bond interest expense because the cash payment is based on the higher 6% contract rate. The excess cash payment over the expense reduces the principal. These amounts are shown in column C. Column E shows the new carrying value after the amortized premium in column C is deducted from the prior period's carrying value. Column D shows how the premium is reduced by the amortization process over the life of the bonds.

The effect of premium amortization on bond interest expense and the bond liability is seen in the journal entry on June 30, 2001, when the issuer makes the first semiannual interest payment:

2001			
June 30	Bond Interest Expense	5,386	
	Premium on Bonds Payable	614	
	Cash		6,000
	To record six months' interest and premium amortization (effective interest method).		

Assets = Liabilities + Equity
−6,000 −614 −5,386

Similar entries are recorded at each payment date until the bonds mature at the end of 2005. The effective interest method yields decreasing amounts of bond interest expense and increasing amounts of premium amortization over the bonds' life.

Exhibit 15.12

Effective Interest Amortization of Bond Premium

Bonds: $100,000 Par Value, Semiannual Interest Payments, 5-Year Life, 6% Semiannual Contract Rate, 5% Semiannual Market Rate

Semiannual Interest Period	(A) Cash Interest Paid	(B) Interest Expense	(C) Premium Amortization	(D) Unamortized Premium	(E) Carrying Value
12/31/2000				$7,720	$107,720
6/30/2001	$ 6,000	$ 5,386	$ 614	7,106	107,106
12/31/2001	6,000	5,355	645	6,461	106,461
6/30/2002	6,000	5,323	677	5,784	105,784
12/31/2002	6,000	5,289	711	5,073	105,073
6/30/2003	6,000	5,254	746	4,327	104,327
12/31/2003	6,000	5,216	784	3,543	103,543
6/30/2004	6,000	5,177	823	2,720	102,720
12/31/2004	6,000	5,136	864	1,856	101,856
6/30/2005	6,000	5,093	907	949	100,949
12/31/2005	6,000	5,051*	949	0	100,000
	$60,000	$52,280	$7,720		

Column **(A)** is the bonds' par value ($100,000) multiplied by the semiannual contract rate (6%).
Column **(B)** is the bonds' prior period carrying value multiplied by the semiannual market rate (5%).
Column **(C)** is the difference between interest paid and interest expense, or [(A) − (B)].
Column **(D)** is the prior period's unamortized premium less the current period's premium amortization.
Column **(E)** is the bonds' par value plus unamortized premium, or [$100,000 + (D)].
*Adjusted for rounding.

Amortization Magic
Amortization tables are made easy by spreadsheet and accounting software such as **Excel, PeachTree,** and **Lotus.** We need only enter the bonds' par value, selling price, contract rate, market rate, and life to get a complete amortization table. All accounting entries and adjustments can be taken directly from the output.

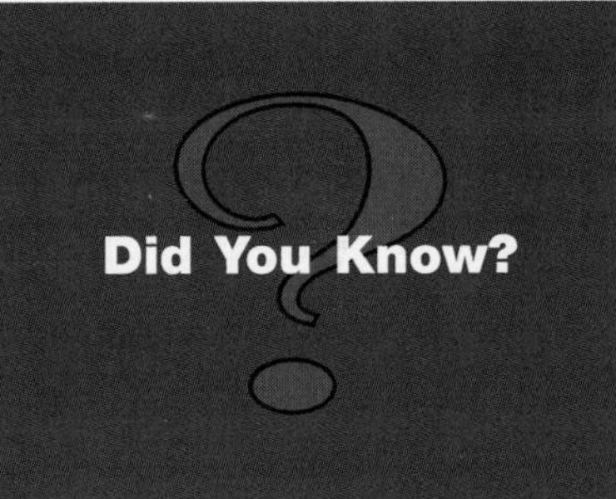

Issuing Bonds between Interest Dates

Many bonds are sold on an interest payment date. But a company can sell its bonds at a date other than an interest payment date. When this occurs, the purchasers normally pay the issuer the purchase price plus any interest accrued since the prior interest payment date. This accrued interest is then repaid to purchasers on the next interest date.

To illustrate, let's suppose **Avia** sells $100,000 of its 9% bonds at par on March 1, 1999, which is two months after the stated issue date. The interest on Avia's bonds is payable semiannually on each June 30 and December 31. Because two months have passed, the issuer collects two months' interest from the buyer at the time of the sale. This amount is $1,500 ($100,000 × 9% × 2/12 year). This case is reflected in Exhibit 15.13. Avia's entry to record the sale of its bonds on March 1 is:

		Debit	Credit
Mar. 1	Cash	101,500	
	Interest Payable		1,500
	Bonds Payable		100,000
	Sold $100,000 of bonds with two months' accrued interest.		

Assets	=	Liabilities	+ Equity
+101,500		+100,000	
		+1,500	

Accruing Interest between Interest Dates

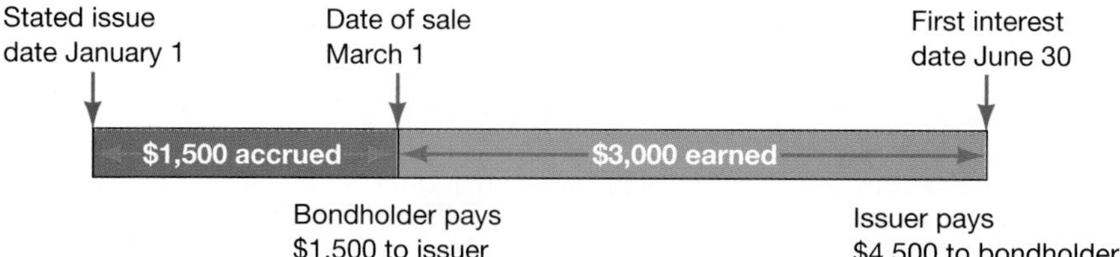

Liabilities for interest payable and bonds payable are recorded in separate accounts.

When the June 30 semiannual interest date arrives, Avia pays a full six months' interest of $4,500 ($100,000 × 9% × ½ year) to the bondholder. This payment includes the four months' interest of $3,000 earned by the bondholder from March 1 to June 30 *plus* the repayment of two months' accrued interest collected by Avia when the bonds were sold. Avia's entry to record this first interest payment is:

Assets = Liabilities + Equity
−4,500 −1,500 −3,000

June 30	Interest Payable	1,500	
	Bond Interest Expense	3,000	
	Cash		4,500
	Paid semiannual interest on the bonds.		

The practice of collecting and then repaying accrued interest with the first interest payment is done to simplify the bond issuer's administrative efforts. To understand this, suppose a company sells bonds on 15 or 20 different dates between the original issue date and the first interest payment date. If the issuer did not collect accrued interest from buyers, it would need to pay different amounts of cash to each of them according to the time passed since they purchased the bonds. This means the issuer would need to keep detailed records of purchasers and the dates they bought their bonds. Issuers avoid this extra recordkeeping by having each buyer pay accrued interest at the time of purchase. Issuers then pay a full six months' interest to all purchasers, regardless of when they bought the bonds.

Accruing Bond Interest Expense

If a bond's interest period does not coincide with the issuing company's accounting period, an adjusting entry is necessary to recognize bond interest expense accruing since the most recent interest payment.

To illustrate, let's assume the Adidas bonds described in Exhibit 15.12 are issued on September 1, 2000, instead of December 31, 2000. As a result, four months' interest (and premium amortization) accrue before the end of the 2000 calendar year. Because Adidas's reporting period ends on that date, an adjusting entry is needed to accurately convey information about the bonds.

Interest for the four months ended December 31, 2000, equals $3,591, which is ⁴⁄₆ of the first six months' interest of $5,386. The premium amortization is $409, which is ⁴⁄₆ of the first six months' amortization of $614. The sum of the bond interest expense and the amortization is $4,000 ($3,591 + $409), which also equals ⁴⁄₆ of the $6,000 cash payment due on March 1, 2001. We record these effects with this adjusting entry:

Assets = Liabilities + Equity
−409 −3,591
+4,000

2000			
Dec. 31	Bond Interest Expense	3,591	
	Premium on Bonds Payable	409	
	Interest Payable		4,000
	To record 4 months' accrued interest and premium amortization.		

Similar entries are made on each December 31 throughout the five-year life of the bonds.

When the $6,000 cash payment occurs on the next interest date, the journal entry recognizes the bonds' interest expense and amortization for January and February of 2001.

It must also eliminate the interest payable liability created by the December 31 adjusting entry. In this case we make the following entry to record payment on March 1, 2001:

2001			
Mar. 1	Interest Payable	4,000	
	Bond Interest Expense ($5,386 × 2/6)	1,795	
	Premium on Bonds Payable ($614 × 2/6)	205	
	Cash		6,000
	To record 2 months' interest and amortization and eliminate the accrued interest liability.		

Assets = Liabilities + Equity
−6,000 −4,000 −1,795
−205

The interest payments made each September are recorded as usual because the entire six-month interest period is included within a single fiscal year.

Bond Pricing

Prices for bonds that are traded on an organized exchange are published in newspapers and available through on-line services. This information includes the bond price (called *quote*), its contract rate, and its market (called *yield*) rate. But only a fraction of bonds outstanding are actually traded on an organized exchange. Many others are rarely traded. To compute the price of a bond, we need to apply present value concepts. This can be done using special bond pricing tables or by computing the present value of a bond's cash flows. This section explains how we use *present value concepts* to price the Fila discount bond and the Adidas premium bond.

Present Value of a Discount Bond

The issue price of bonds is found by computing the present value of the bond's cash payments, discounted at the market rate of interest. When computing the present value of the Fila bond, we work with *semiannual* compounding periods because this is the time between interest payments. This means the annual market rate of 10% is changed to a semiannual rate of 5%. Also, the five-year life of the bonds is changed to 10 semiannual periods.

Our computation is twofold: (1) find the present value of the $100,000 maturity payment and (2) find the present value of the series of 10 payments of $4,000 each; see Exhibit 15.4. These present values can be found by using present value tables.[5] Appendix C lists some present value tables and explains how to use them. Table C.1 in Appendix C is used to compute the single $100,000 maturity payment, and Table C.3 in Appendix C is used to compute the $4,000 series of interest payments.

We first go to Table C.1, row 10, and go across to the 5% column. The table value is 0.6139. Second, we go to Table C.3, row 10, and go across to the 5% column, where the table value is 7.7217. The bond price is computed by multiplying these cash flow amounts by their corresponding table values and adding them together. Exhibit 15.14 shows this result.

Exhibit 15.14
Computing Fila's Bond Price

Cash Flow	Table	Table Value	Amount	Present Value
$100,000 par value	C.1	0.6139	$100,000	$61,390
$4,000 interest payments	C.3	7.7217	4,000	30,887
Price of bond				$92,277

This analysis means if 5% is the semiannual market rate for Fila bonds, the maximum price that buyers will pay is $92,277. This amount is also the minimum price the issuer will accept.

[5] Many inexpensive calculators provide present value functions for easy computation of bond prices.

Present Value of a Premium Bond

We estimate the issue price of Adidas's bonds by using the market rate to compute the present value of its future cash flows. When computing the present value of this bond, we again work with *semiannual* compounding periods because this is the time between interest payments. This means the annual market rate of 10% is changed to a semiannual rate of 5%. Also, the five-year life of the bonds is changed to 10 semiannual periods.

Our computation is twofold: (1) find the present value of the $100,000 maturity payment and (2) find the present value of the series of 10 payments of $6,000 each; see Exhibit 15.9. These present values can be found by using present value tables. First, go to Table C.1, row 10, and go across to the 5% column. The table value is 0.6139. Second, go to Table C.3, row 10, and go across to the 5% column, where the table value is 7.7217. The bond price is computed by multiplying the cash flow amounts by their corresponding table values and adding them together. Exhibit 15.15 shows these computations.

Exhibit 15.15

Computing Adidas's Bond Price

Cash Flow	Table	Table Value	Amount	Present Value
$100,000 par value	C.1	0.6139	$100,000	$61,390
$6,000 interest payments	C.3	7.7217	6,000	46,330
Price of bond				$107,720

This analysis means if 5% is the semiannual market rate for Adidas's bonds, the maximum price that buyers will pay is $107,720. This amount is also the minimum price the issuer will accept.

Flash back

Use this information to solve Flashbacks 7 through 9: On December 31, 1999, a company issued 16%, 10-year bonds with a par value of $100,000. Interest is paid on June 30 and December 31. The bonds are sold to yield a 14% annual market rate at an issue price of $110,592.

7. Are these bonds issued at a discount or premium? Explain why.
8. Using the effective interest method of allocating bond interest expense, the issuer records the second interest payment (on December 31, 2000) with a debit to Premium on Bonds Payable in the amount of: *(a)* $7,470; *(b)* $7,741; *(c)* $259; *(d)* $530; or *(e)* $277.
9. How are the bonds reported in the long-term liability section of the issuer's balance sheet as of December 31, 2000?
10. On May 1, a company sells 9% bonds with a $500,000 par value that pays semiannual interest on each January 1 and July 1. The bonds are sold at par value plus interest accrued since January 1. The bond issuer's entry to record the first semiannual interest payment on July 1 includes: *(a)* a debit to Interest Payable for $15,000; *(b)* a debit to Bond Interest Expense for $22,500; or *(c)* a credit to Interest Payable for $7,500.

Answers—p. 671

Bond Retirements

P4 Record the retirement of bonds.

This section describes the retirement of bonds: (1) at maturity, (2) before maturity, and (3) by converting them to stock.

Bond Retirement at Maturity

The carrying value of bonds at maturity will always equal their par value. Both Exhibits 15.8 (a discount) and 15.12 (a premium) show the carrying value of these bonds at the end of their five-year life ($100,000) equals the bonds' par value.

The entry to record retirement of the Adidas bonds in Exhibit 15.12 at maturity, assuming interest is already paid and recorded, is:

2005			
Dec. 31	Bonds Payable	100,000	
	Cash		100,000
	To record retirement of bonds at maturity.		

Assets	=	Liabilities	+	Equity
−100,000		−100,000		

Bond Retirement before Maturity

Companies sometimes wish to retire some or all of their bonds prior to maturity. For instance, if interest rates decline significantly, a company may wish to replace old high-interest paying bonds with new low-interest bonds. Two common ways of retiring bonds before maturity are to (1) exercise a call option or (2) purchase them on the open market.

In the first instance, a company can reserve the right to retire bonds early by issuing callable bonds. This means the bond indenture gives the issuing company an option to *call* the bonds before they mature by paying the par value plus a *call premium* to the bondholders. In the second case, the issuer retires bonds by repurchasing them on the open market at their current price. Whether bonds are called or repurchased, the issuer is unlikely to pay a price that exactly equals the bonds' carrying value. When there is a difference between the bonds' carrying value and the amount paid in a bond retirement transaction, the issuer records a gain or loss equal to the difference.[6]

To illustrate the accounting for retiring callable bonds, let's assume a company has issued callable bonds with a par value of $100,000. The call option requires the issuer to pay a call premium of $3,000 to bondholders in addition to the par value. Immediately after the June 30, 2000, interest payment, the bonds have a carrying value of $104,500. On July 1, 2000, the issuer calls these bonds and pays $103,000 to bondholders. The issuer recognizes a $1,500 gain from the difference between the bonds' carrying value of $104,500 and the retirement price of $103,000. The entry to record this bond retirement is:

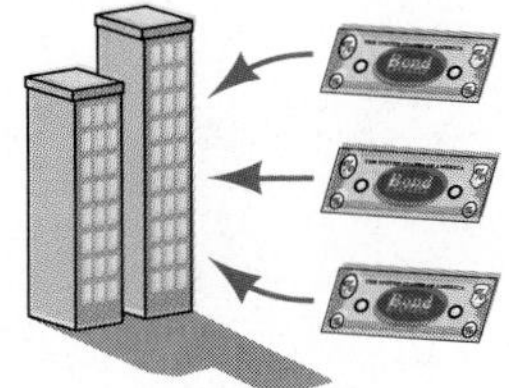

Callable Bond

July 1	Bonds Payable	100,000	
	Premium on Bonds Payable	4,500	
	Gain on Retirement of Bonds		1,500
	Cash		103,000
	To record retirement of bonds before maturity.		

Assets	=	Liabilities	+	Equity
−103,000		−100,000		+1,500
		−4,500		

A company generally must call all of its bonds when it exercises a call option. But a company can retire as many or as few bonds as it desires through open market transactions. If it retires less than the entire set of bonds, it recognizes a gain or loss for the difference between the carrying value of those bonds retired and the amount paid to acquire them.

Flash back

11. Six years ago, a company issued $500,000 of 6%, 8-year bonds at a price of 95. The current carrying value is $493,750. The company retired 50% of the bonds by buying them on the open market at a price of 102½. What is the amount of gain or loss on retirement of these bonds?

Answer—p. 671

[6] Gains and losses from retiring bonds or other debt must be reported on the debtor's income statement as an extraordinary gain or loss. FASB, *Accounting Standards—Current Text* (Norwalk, CT, 1995), sec. D14.105. First published in *FASB Statement of Financial Accounting Standards No. 4,* par. 8.

Bond Retirement by Conversion

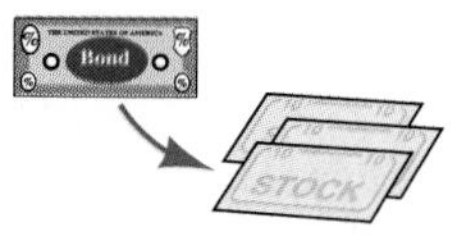

Convertible Bond

We described convertible bonds earlier in the chapter and explained how these bondholders have the right to convert their bonds to common stock. When conversion occurs, the carrying value of bonds is transferred to contributed capital accounts and no gain or loss is recorded.

To illustrate, let's assume on January 1 the $100,000 par value bonds of **Converse,** with a carrying value of $100,000, are converted to 15,000 shares of $2 par value common stock. The entry to record this conversion is:

Assets = Liabilities + Equity
−100,000 +30,000
+70,000

Jan. 1	Bonds Payable	100,000	
	Common Stock		30,000
	Contributed Capital in Excess of Par Value		70,000
	To record retirement of bonds by conversion.		

The market prices of the bonds and stock are not part of the entry for conversion.

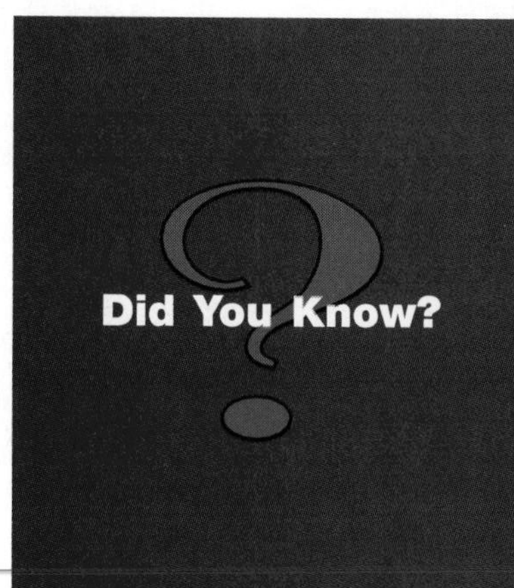

Cruising with Convertibles
When the stock market gets jumpy, convertible bonds can be a haven. Over the past decade, convertible funds have delivered about 80% of the returns of diversified stock funds but with only 66% of the price volatility (see returns in the margin). Convertibles also protect holders against stock price declines. Yet they give holders the chance to make money if share prices take off by converting bonds to stock. [Source: *Business Week,* February 9, 1998 and December 1, 1997.]

Bonds	1995–97 Annual Return
Convertibles	17.8%
Long-Term Gov.	12.1
Long-Term Corp.	11.3
Long-Term Muni	9.9
International Bond	9.9
All Bond Funds	9.4

Long-Term Notes Payable

C2 Explain the types and payment patterns of notes.

Like bonds, companies issue notes payable to borrow money to finance operations. But, unlike signing a bond, signing a note payable is typically a transaction with a single lender such as a bank. A note is initially measured and recorded at its selling price. Selling price is the note's face value minus any discount or plus any premium. Over the life of a note, the amount of interest expense allocated to each period is computed by multiplying the market interest rate at issuance of the note by the beginning-of-period balance of the note. The book balance of a note at any point in time equals its face value minus any unallocated discount or plus any unallocated premium.[7]

Interest-Bearing Notes

Let's assume **Taco Bell** buys service equipment on January 2 with a fair market value of $45,000 by issuing an 8%, three-year note with a face value of $45,000 to the equipment seller. The note pays all its interest at maturity. The company records this purchase with the entry:

Assets = Liabilities + Equity
+45,000 +45,000

Jan. 2	Service Equipment	45,000	
	Notes Payable		45,000
	Issued a $45,000, three-year, 8% note payable for equipment.		

[7] A note's book balance at any date is also computed as the present value of all remaining future payments, discounted at the original market interest rate.

The company (note issuer) reports annual interest expense equal to the original market interest rate times each year's beginning balance of the note over the life of the note. Exhibit 15.16 shows this interest expense computation and allocation.

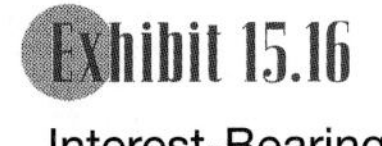

Exhibit 15.16

Interest-Bearing Note Where Interest Paid at Maturity

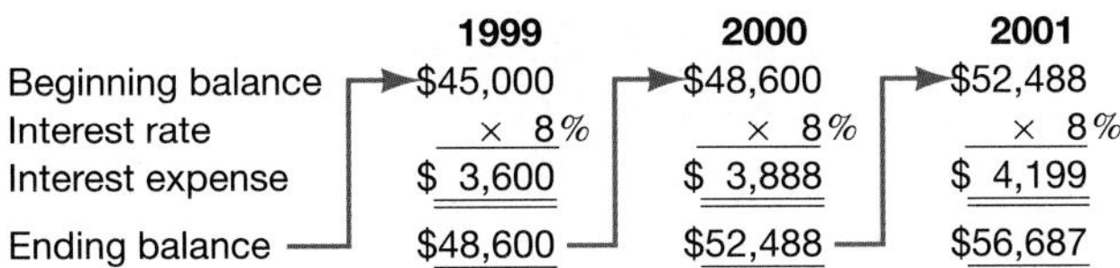

	1999	2000	2001
Beginning balance	$45,000	$48,600	$52,488
Interest rate	× 8%	× 8%	× 8%
Interest expense	$ 3,600	$ 3,888	$ 4,199
Ending balance	$48,600	$52,488	$56,687

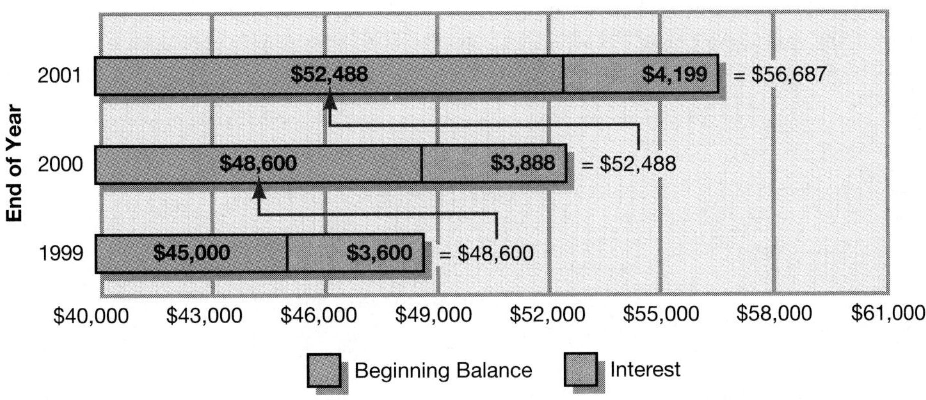

Interest is computed by multiplying each year's beginning balance by the original 8% market interest rate. Interest is then added to the beginning balance to find the ending balance. A period's ending balance becomes next period's beginning balance. Because the balance grows by compounding, the amount of interest allocated to each year increases over the life of the note. The final ending balance of $56,687 equals the original $45,000 borrowed plus total interest of $11,687. A note like this one that delays interest payments is more common for lower risk companies that wish to delay cash payments until some later period. It is often backed with assets as collateral.

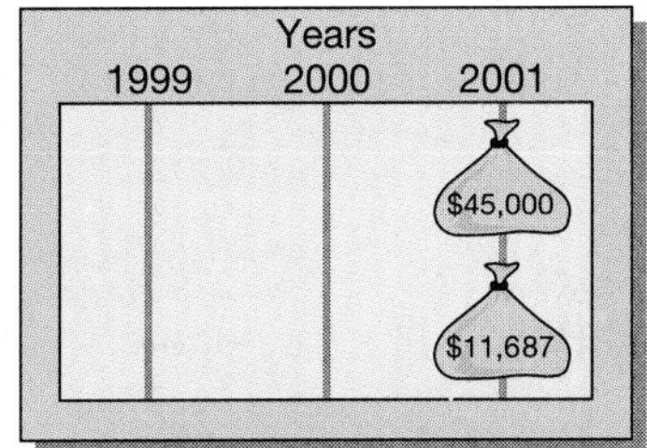

Retailer

You are a retailer in stereo components. You are planning a holiday sale on a quality stereo system, requiring no payments for two years. At the end of two years, buyers must pay the full amount. Your normal selling price is $4,100, but you are willing to sell it today for $3,000 cash. What is your holiday sale price if payment won't occur for two years and the market interest rate is 10%?

Answer—p. 670

Noninterest-Bearing Notes

A *noninterest-bearing note* includes interest in its face (maturity) value. When a noninterest-bearing note is used to purchase an asset, the note's face value (because it includes interest) is greater than the asset's fair value. This type of note is desired by issuers who wish to avoid periodic interest payments. The asset and the note are recorded at a carrying value of either the asset's fair value or the note's fair value, whichever is more clearly determinable.[8] A note's fair value, like that of a bond, is computed based on the market interest rate when it is issued. An asset's fair value is determined by current market transactions.

---

[8] FASB, *Accounting Standards—Current Text* (Norwalk, CT, 1995), sec. I69.105. First published as *APB Opinion No. 21,* par. 12.

To illustrate, let's assume **Disney** buys staging machinery on January 2, 1999, by issuing a noninterest-bearing, 5-year, $10,000 note payable. Exhibit 15.17 shows this note's cash flows.

Cash Flows of Noninterest-Bearing Note

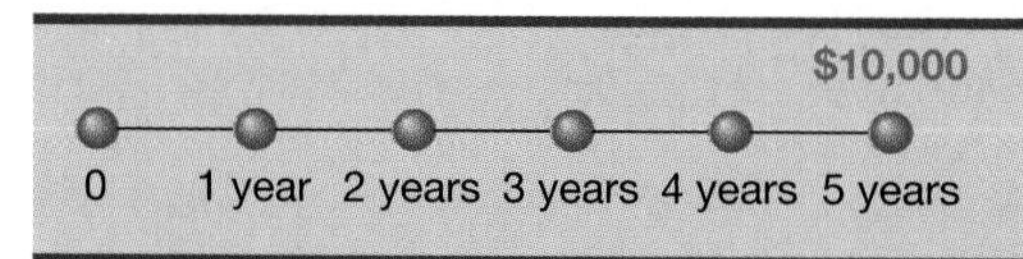

Disney decides its estimate of the machinery's fair value is less reliable than using the current 10% market interest rate available to Disney. The note's fair value when issued using a 10% rate is $6,209.[9] This also gives us the implied fair value of the machinery. The entry to record this purchase is:

Assets = Liabilities + Equity
+6,209 −3,791
+10,000

1999			
Jan. 2	Machinery	6,209	
	Discount on Notes Payable	3,791	
	Notes Payable		10,000
	Exchanged a 5-year noninterest-bearing note for machinery.		

By recording the face (maturity) value in one account and the discount in a separate liability contra account, this entry follows the usual practice in recording a noninterest-bearing note. The $3,791 debit to Discount on Notes Payable is the *total interest expense* to be allocated to the five years of the note's life.

Exhibit 15.18 shows each year's interest, the allocation of the discount, and the note's balance for its five-year life. The note's balance grows over the 5 years until it reaches its

Noninterest-Bearing Note

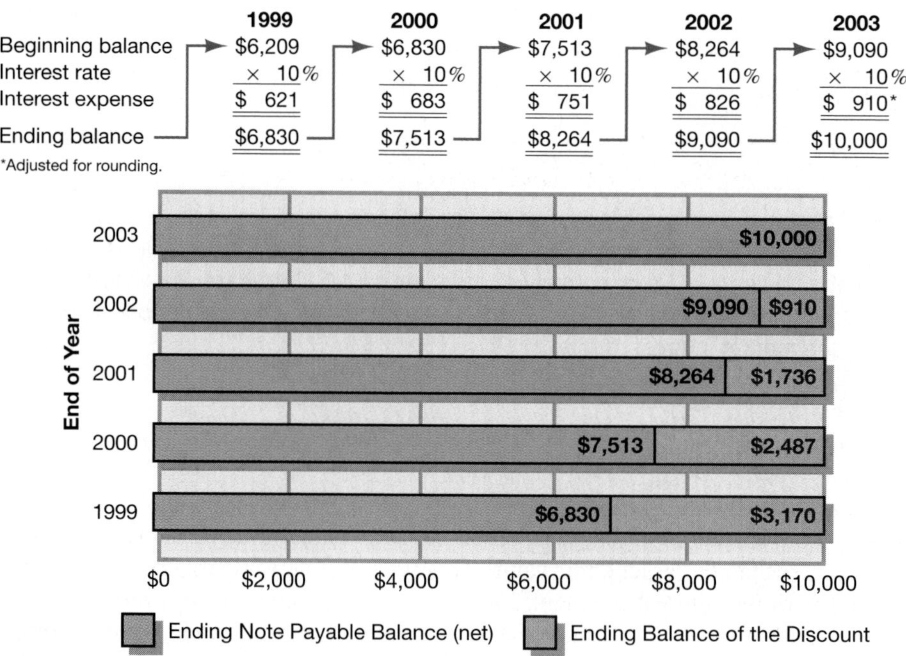

	1999	2000	2001	2002	2003
Beginning balance	$6,209	$6,830	$7,513	$8,264	$9,090
Interest rate	× 10%	× 10%	× 10%	× 10%	× 10%
Interest expense	$ 621	$ 683	$ 751	$ 826	$ 910*
Ending balance	$6,830	$7,513	$8,264	$9,090	$10,000

*Adjusted for rounding.

[9] The note's fair value is computed as the present value of the $10,000 payment due after 5 years discounted at the market rate of 10%. Table C.1 in Appendix C shows the present value of 1 discounted at 10% for 5 years is 0.6209. The present (fair) value of the note is $6,209, computed as $10,000 3 0.6209.

face value of $10,000 at the end of 5 years. The Discount on Notes Payable balance decreases from $3,791 at January 2, 1999 to $0 after 5 years. This pattern reflects the *amortizing of the discount.* The process of computing each year's interest is the same as in the previous example of the interest-bearing note. In particular, the note balance at the beginning of each year is multiplied by the 10% interest rate to determine interest for that year.

The first year's interest expense and discount amortization ($6,209 × 10%) are recorded when we make year-end adjusting entries as follows:

1999			
Dec. 31	Interest Expense	621	
	Discount on Notes Payable		621
	To record first year's interest expense accrued on noninterest-bearing note.		

Assets = Liabilities + Equity
+621 −621

Similar entries are recorded at the end of each year until the balance of the discount account equals $0 and the net note payable balance equals $10,000.

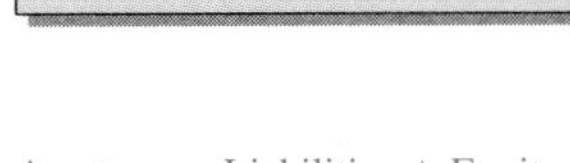

When the note payable matures on January 2, 2004, the issuer records its payment with the entry:

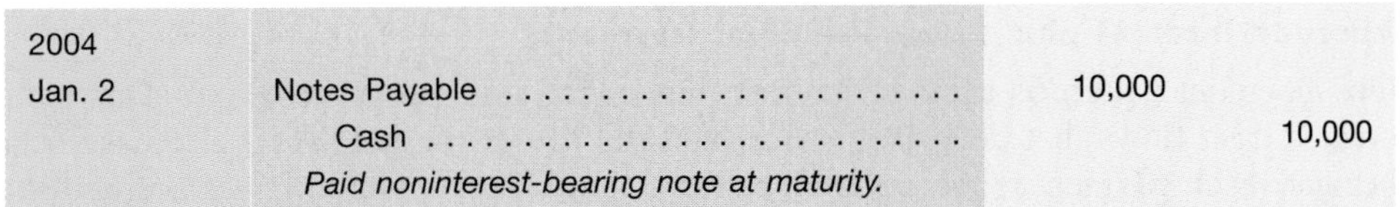

2004			
Jan. 2	Notes Payable	10,000	
	Cash		10,000
	Paid noninterest-bearing note at maturity.		

Assets = Liabilities + Equity
−10,000 −10,000

Flash back

12. On January 1, 1999, a company signs a $6,000 three-year note payable bearing 6% annual interest. The principal and all interest are paid on December 31, 2001. Interest is compounded annually. How much interest is allocated to year 2000? *(a)* $0; *(b)* $360; *(c)* $381.60; *(d)* $404.50.

13. A company promises to pay a lender $4,000 at the end of four years. The annual interest rate is 8% and interest is included in the $4,000 payments. This means the note's fair value is $2,940. Record this note's issuance.

Answers—p. 671

Installment Notes

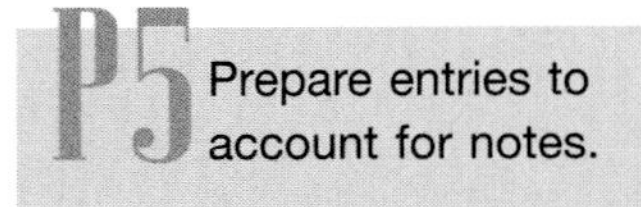

P5 Prepare entries to account for notes.

An **installment note** is an obligation requiring a series of periodic payments to the lender. Installment notes are common for franchises and other businesses where costs are large and the owner desires to spread these costs over several periods. When an installment note is used to borrow money or pay for assets, the borrower records the note with an entry similar to the one used for a single-payment note. This means the increase in cash or assets is recorded with a debit and the increase in the liability is recorded with a credit to Notes Payable.

To illustrate, let's assume SuperBowl, a bowling establishment, borrows $60,000 from a bank to purchase **AMF** and **Brunswick** bowling equipment. SuperBowl signs an 8% installment note with the bank, requiring six annual payments, and records the note's issuance as:

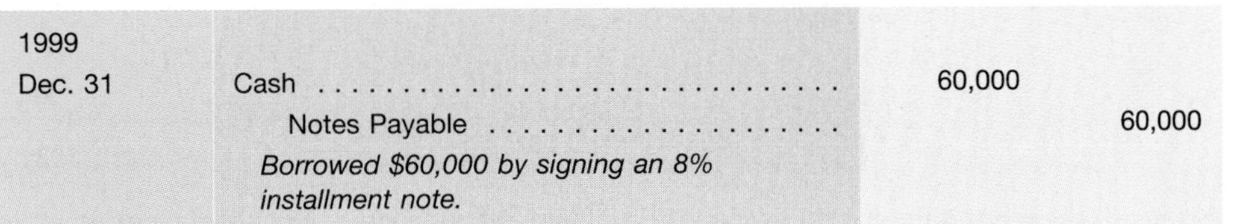

1999			
Dec. 31	Cash	60,000	
	Notes Payable		60,000
	Borrowed $60,000 by signing an 8% installment note.		

Assets = Liabilities + Equity
+60,000 +60,000

Alternatively, SuperBowl might have issued a note directly to the seller of the bowling equipment. In this case, SuperBowl would record the bowling equipment received instead of cash. One of these sellers, Brunswick Corp., often provides commitments to banks in the event of a buyer's default. **Brunswick**'s annual report states:

> The company has entered into agreements . . . that provide for the repurchase of its products from a financial institution in the event of repossession upon a dealer's default . . . [And] provide limited recourse on marine and bowling capital equipment sales.

Payments on an installment note normally include the interest expense accruing to the date of the payment plus a portion of the amount borrowed (the *principal*). Generally, we can identify two types of payment patterns: (1) accrued interest plus equal principal payments and (2) equal payments. The remainder of this section describes these two patterns and how we account for them.

Accrued Interest plus Equal Principal Payments

Years
2000 2001 2002 2003 2004 2005

One payment pattern is accrued interest plus equal amounts of principal. This pattern creates cash flows that decrease in size over the life of the note. This decrease occurs because each payment reduces the note's principal balance, yielding less accrued interest expense for the next period.

To illustrate, let's assume the $60,000, 8% note signed by SuperBowl requires it to make six payments at the end of each year equal to *accrued interest plus $10,000 of principal.* Exhibit 15.19 describes these payments, interest, and changes in the balance of this note. Column A lists the note's yearly beginning balance. Columns B, C, and D list each annual cash payment and how it is divided between interest and principal. Column B shows interest expense accruing in each year at 8% of the beginning balance. Column C shows each payment reduces principal with a $10,000 debit to the Notes Payable account. Column D is the total of B and C. Column E shows the ending balance of the note, which equals the beginning balance in column A minus the principal payment in column C. We include *debit* or *credit* in column headings to help understand their accounting effects. For instance, the credit to Cash equals the sum of debits to interest expense and principal.

This table shows total interest expense is $16,800 and total principal is $60,000. This means total cash payments for the 5 years are $76,800. The graph in the lower portion of Exhibit 15.19 captures these effects and highlights the decreasing total payment pattern, decreasing accrued interest, and constant principal payments of $10,000.

SuperBowl (borrower) records the effects of the first two payments with these entries:

Assets = Liabilities + Equity
−14,800 −10,000 −4,800

2000			
Dec. 31	Interest Expense	4,800	
	Notes Payable	10,000	
	Cash		14,800
	To record first installment payment.		

Assets = Liabilities + Equity
−14,000 −10,000 −4,000

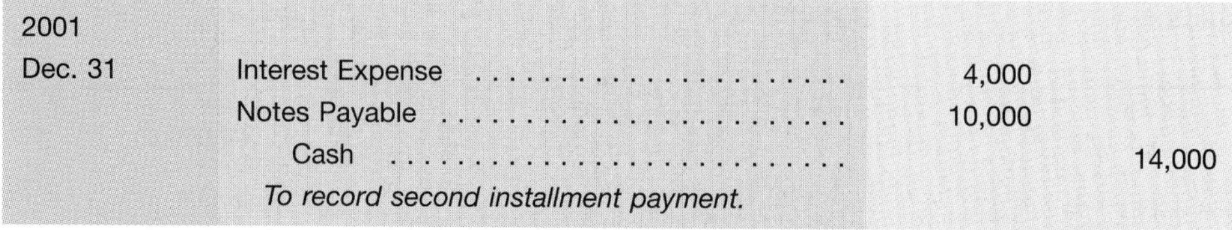

2001			
Dec. 31	Interest Expense	4,000	
	Notes Payable	10,000	
	Cash		14,000
	To record second installment payment.		

After all six payments are recorded, the balance of the Notes Payable account is zero.

Exhibit 15.19

Installment Note: Accrued Interest plus Equal Principal Payments

Period Ending	(A) Beginning Balance	(B) Debit Interest Expense 8% × (A)	+	(C) Debit Notes Payable $60,000/6	=	(D) Credit Cash (B) + (C)	(E) Ending Balance (A) − (C)
		Payments					
12/31/2000	**$60,000**	**$ 4,800**		**$10,000**		**$14,800**	**$50,000**
12/31/2001	50,000	4,000		10,000		14,000	40,000
12/31/2002	40,000	3,200		10,000		13,200	30,000
12/31/2003	30,000	2,400		10,000		12,400	20,000
12/31/2004	20,000	1,600		10,000		11,600	10,000
12/31/2005	10,000	800		10,000		10,800	0
		$16,800		**$60,000**		**$76,800**	

Principal
Interest
$10,000 Principal Payments
Decreasing Accrued Interest
Decreasing Total Payments
2005: $10,000 | $800
2004: $10,000 | $1,600
2003: $10,000 | $2,400
2002: $10,000 | $3,200
2001: $10,000 | $4,000
2000: $10,000 | $4,800
End of Year
0 $2,500 $5,000 $7,500 $10,000 $12,500 $15,000
Payment Pattern

Equal Total Payments

Many installment notes require the borrower to make a series of equal payments that consist of changing amounts of interest and principal.

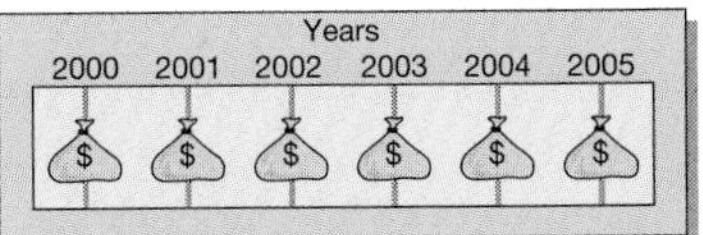

To illustrate, let's assume the above $60,000 note requires SuperBowl (borrower) to make a series of six *equal payments* of $12,979 at the end of each year.[10] The $12,979 includes both interest and principal, the amounts of which change with each payment. Exhibit 15.20 shows the equal total payments pattern and its effects on the note balance.

Exhibit 15.20 is very similar to Exhibit 15.19. Column A shows the note's beginning balance for each year. Column B shows accrued interest for each year at 8% of the

[10] The $60,000 equals the present value of an annuity of six annual payments of $12,979, discounted at 8% (we show this computation later in the section).

Exhibit 15.20

Installment Note: Equal Total Payments

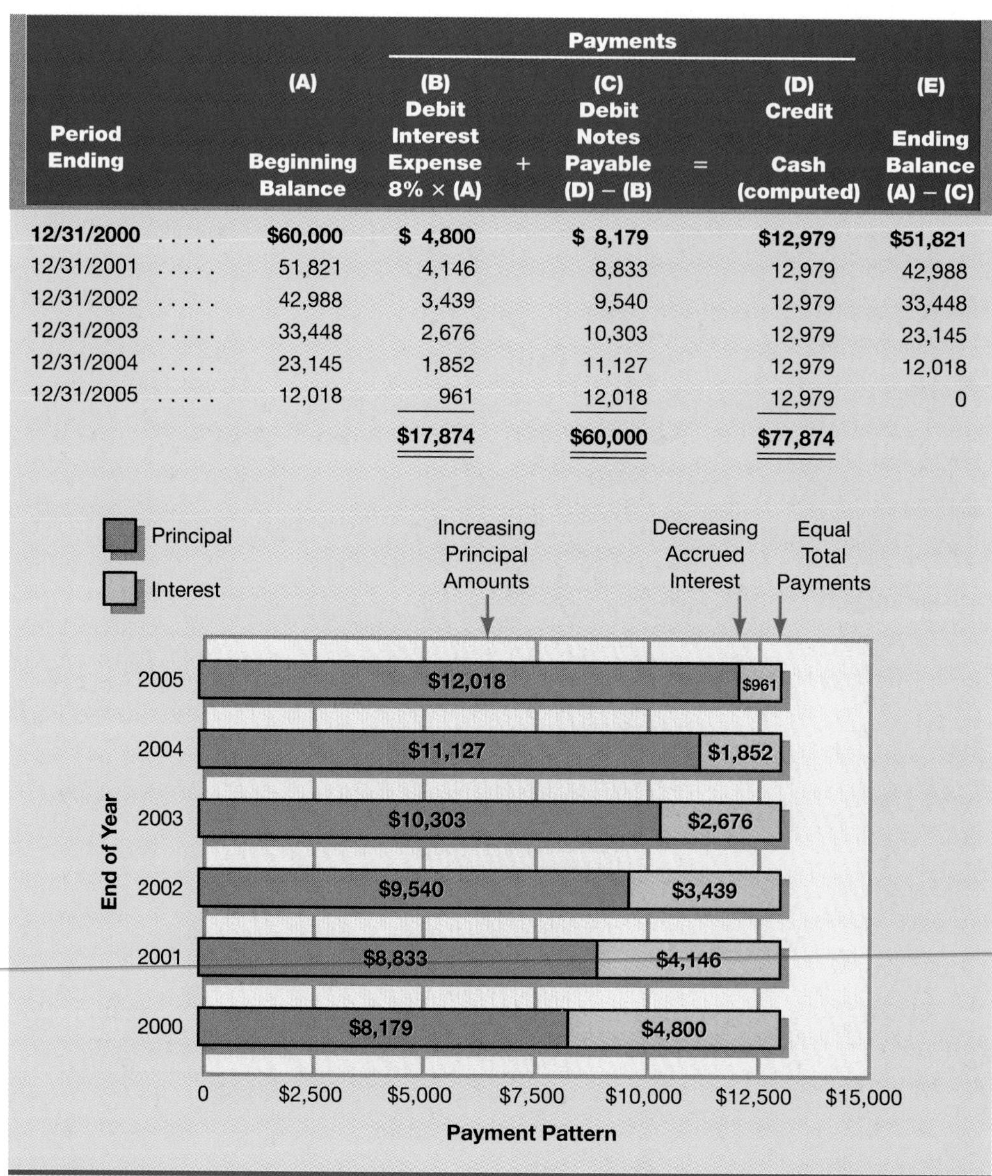

Period Ending	(A) Beginning Balance	(B) Debit Interest Expense 8% × (A)	+	(C) Debit Notes Payable (D) − (B)	=	(D) Credit Cash (computed)	(E) Ending Balance (A) − (C)
		Payments					
12/31/2000	**$60,000**	**$ 4,800**		**$ 8,179**		**$12,979**	**$51,821**
12/31/2001	51,821	4,146		8,833		12,979	42,988
12/31/2002	42,988	3,439		9,540		12,979	33,448
12/31/2003	33,448	2,676		10,303		12,979	23,145
12/31/2004	23,145	1,852		11,127		12,979	12,018
12/31/2005	12,018	961		12,018		12,979	0
		$17,874		**$60,000**		**$77,874**	

beginning balance. Column C shows the change in the principal of the note, which equals the difference between the total payment in column D and the interest expense in column B. Column E shows the ending balance after each payment.

While all six payments are equal, the accrued interest decreases each year because the principal balance of the note is declining. As the amount of interest decreases each year, the amount applied to the principal increases. This pattern is graphed in the lower portion of Exhibit 15.20.

The amounts in Exhibit 15.20 are used to show how we record the first two payments toward this note as reflected in the journal entries below:

Assets = Liabilities + Equity
−12,979 −8,179 −4,800

2000			
Dec. 31	Interest Expense	4,800	
	Notes Payable	8,179	
	Cash		12,979
	To record first installment payment.		

2001			
Dec. 31	Interest Expense	4,146	
	Notes Payable	8,833	
	Cash		12,979
	To record second installment payment.		

Assets = Liabilities + Equity
−12,979 −8,833 −4,146

The borrower records similar entries for each of the remaining four payments. After six years, the Notes Payable account balance is zero.

It is interesting to compare the two payment patterns in Exhibits 15.20 and 15.19. The series of equal total payments leads to a greater amount of interest expense over the life of the note. This is because the first three payments in Exhibit 15.20 are smaller and do not reduce the principal as quickly as the first three payments in Exhibit 15.19.[11]

Mortgage Notes

A **mortgage** is a legal agreement that helps protect a lender if a borrower fails to make the required payments on bonds or notes. A mortgage gives the lender the right to be paid out of the cash proceeds from the sale of a borrower's specific assets identified in the mortgage. A separate legal document, called a *mortgage contract,* describes the terms of a mortgage.

Mortgage notes include a mortgage contract pledging title to specific assets as security for the note. While less common, there also exist *mortgage bonds* backed by assets of the issuer. A mortgage contract is given to the lender who accepts a note or to the trustee for the bonds. This contract usually requires the issuer (borrower) to pay all property taxes on the mortgaged assets, to maintain them properly, and to carry adequate insurance against fire and other types of losses. These requirements are designed to keep the property from losing value and avoid diminishing the lender's security. Mortgage notes are especially popular in the purchase of homes and in the acquisition of plant assets by companies. For instance, more than 10% of **Musicland**'s long-term liabilities are in mortgage notes.

Accounting for mortgage notes and bonds is essentially the same as accounting for unsecured notes and bonds. The primary difference is that the mortgage agreement needs to be disclosed to users of financial statements. Musicland's disclosures include:

> The mortgage note payable is collateralized by land, buildings and certain fixtures of three of the Company's Media Play stores.

Musicland's note carries a variable interest rate, also called a *floating rate.* The contract rate on these types of notes and bonds can be periodically adjusted according to changes in interest rates and terms of the contract.

Most mortgage contracts grant the lender the right to *foreclose* on the property if the borrower fails to pay in accordance with the terms of the debt agreement. If foreclosure occurs, a court either orders the property to be sold or simply grants legal title to the

---

[11] Table C.3 in Appendix C is used to compute the amount of the 6 individual payments that are equal to the present value of the initial note balance of $60,000 at 8% interest. We go to Table C.3, row 6, and go across to the 8% column, where the table value is 4.6229. The present value is then equal to the payment amount multiplied by the table value as shown below:

Cash Flow	Table	Table Value	Amount	Present Value
$__?__ interest payment	C.3	4.6229	?	60,000

We solve for the payment by dividing $60,000 by 4.6229. When a note requires a series of equal payments, we can compute for the payment amount with a present value table or calculator.

mortgaged property to the lender. If the property is sold, the proceeds are first applied to court costs and then to the claims of the mortgage holder. If there are any additional proceeds, the borrower is entitled to receive them subject to any claims from the borrower's unsecured creditors.

Flash back

14. Which of the following is true for an installment note requiring a series of equal payments?

a. Payments consist of an increasing amount of interest and a decreasing amount of principal.

b. Payments consist of changing amounts of principal, but the interest portion remains constant.

c. Payments consist of a decreasing amount of interest and an increasing amount of principal.

15. How is the interest portion of an installment note payment computed?

16. When a borrower records an interest payment on an installment note, how are the balance sheet and income statement affected?

Answers—p. 671

USING THE INFORMATION Pledged Assets to Secured Liabilities

This section explains how lenders can reduce their risk of loss and how borrowers can achieve more favorable terms by entering into collateral agreements. We also describe an important measure of this risk.

Collateral Agreements for Bonds and Notes

A2 Explain collateral agreements and their effects on loan risk.

We already explained how some bonds are secured by collateral agreements. Other bonds, called *debentures,* are unsecured. We also explained how mortgage notes can be secured by collateral. Collateral agreements reduce the risk of loss for both bonds and notes. Unsecured bonds and notes are more risky because the issuer's obligation to pay interest and principal has the same priority as all other unsecured liabilities in the event of bankruptcy. If a company's financial troubles leave it unable to pay its debts in full, the unsecured creditors (including the holders of debentures) lose a proportion or all of their balances.

A company's ability to borrow money with or without collateral agreements depends on its credit rating. In some cases, debt financing is unavailable unless the borrower can provide security to creditors with a collateral agreement. Even if unsecured loans are available, the creditors are likely to charge a higher rate of interest to compensate for the added risk. To borrow funds at a more favorable rate, many bonds and notes are secured by collateral agreements in the form of mortgages.

Information about a company's security agreements with its lenders is important to users. Notes to financial statements sometimes describe the amounts of assets pledged as security against liabilities. We next describe a ratio used to assess a borrower's situation with respect to its security agreements.

Ratio of Pledged Assets to Secured Liabilities

A3 Compute the ratio of pledged assets to secured liabilities and explain its use.

Lenders reduce their risk with agreements that can force borrowers to sell specific assets to settle overdue debts. Buyers (investors) of a company's secured debt obligations need to determine whether the pledged assets of the debtor provide adequate security. One method of evaluating this is to compute the ratio of **pledged assets to**

secured liabilities. This is computed by dividing the book value of the company's assets pledged as collateral by the book value of the liabilities secured by these collateral agreements as shown in Exhibit 15.21.

Exhibit 15.21

Pledged Assets to Secured Liabilities

$$\textbf{Pledged assets to secured liabilities} = \frac{\textbf{Book value of pledged assets}}{\textbf{Book value of secured liabilities}}$$

To illustrate how we use this ratio, let's assume a company owns assets with a book value of $230,000 pledged against loans with a balance of $100,000. The pledged assets to secured liabilities ratio is 2.3 (often expressed as 2.3 to 1) and is computed as $230,000/$100,000. While there are no exact guidelines for interpreting the values for this ratio, the 2.3 value is sufficiently high to provide secured creditors with some comfort that their loans are covered by the borrower's assets.

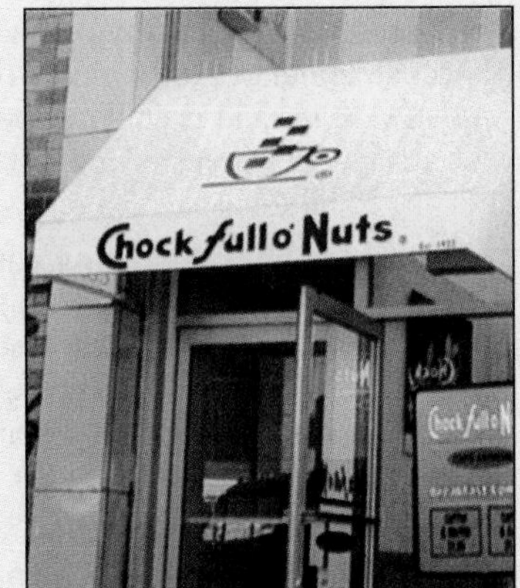

Chock Full O'Nuts provides us another example. Its recent annual report reveals that "borrowings under the Loan Agreements . . . are collateralized by . . . accounts receivable and inventories, and substantially all of the machinery and equipment and real estate." We can use this information to compute its pledged assets to secured liabilities ratio of 20.6, computed as $206 million/$10 million. This ratio implies there is more than $20 of collateral for each $1 of secured liabilities. This huge collateral commitment likely accounts for the low 8.5% interest that Chock Full O'Nuts pays on these secured liabilities.

The pledging of assets for the benefit of secured creditors also affects unsecured creditors. As an increasing portion of the assets are pledged, the unsecured creditors are less likely to receive a full repayment. In evaluating their position, unsecured creditors also gain information from the ratio of pledged assets to secured liabilities. A high ratio suggests that unsecured creditors are at greater risk for two reasons. Namely, secured creditors often demand a high ratio when they perceive (1) the values of the assets in liquidation are low and (2) the likelihood that the company will meet its obligations from operating cash flows is weak.

When we use this ratio we must be aware that reported book values of the company's assets are unlikely to exactly reflect their market values. This ratio is improved if we can determine the assets' current market values and then use them in the ratio instead of book values. Major lenders to a company can sometimes get this information directly by asking the borrower to provide recent appraisals or other evidence of the assets' market values. Many lenders do not have this option. Using the ratio also requires knowledge about secured liabilities and pledged assets—both how they're measured and reported. This requires analysis of information in both the financial statements and their notes.

Bond Investor

You are a bond investor. You're planning to purchase debenture bonds from one of two companies that operate in the same industry and are similar in size and performance. The first company has $350,000 of unsecured liabilities and $575,000 of secured liabilities. The book value of this company's pledged assets is $1,265,000. The second company has $1,200,000 of unsecured liabilities and $800,000 of secured liabilities, and its book value of pledged assets is $2,000,000. Using the ratio of pledged assets to secured liabilities, determine which company's debenture bonds are less risky.

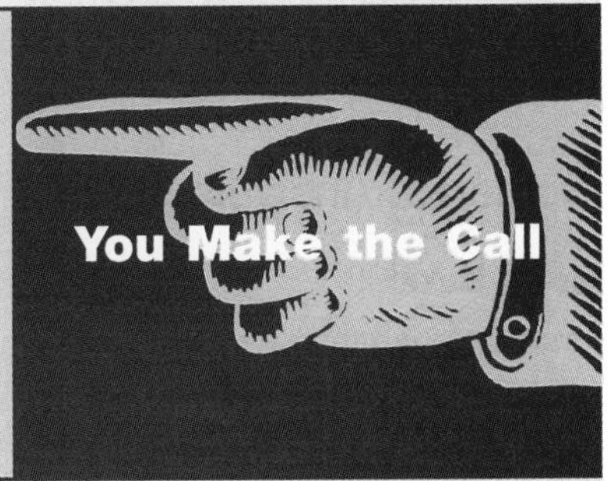

Answer—p. 671

Summary

C1 Explain the types of bonds and the procedures for issuing them. An issuer's bonds usually are sold to many investors. Certain bonds are secured by the issuer's assets while other bonds, called *debentures,* are unsecured. Serial bonds mature at different points in time, while term bonds mature at one time. Registered bonds have each bondholder's name and address recorded by the issuing company, while bearer bonds are payable to whoever holds the bonds. Convertible bonds are exchangeable by bondholders for shares of the issuing company's stock. Callable bonds can be retired by the issuer at a set price. Bonds are often issued by an underwriter, and a bond certificate is evidence of the issuer's obligation.

C2 Explain the types and payment patterns of notes. Notes are either interest-bearing or noninterest-bearing. Notes can require repayment of principal and interest (a) at the end of a period of time or (b) gradually over a period of time in either equal or unequal amounts. Notes repaid over a period of time are called *installment notes* and usually follow one of two payment patterns: (a) decreasing payments of interest plus equal amounts of principal or (b) equal total payments.

A1 Compare bond financing with stock financing. Bond financing is used to fund business activities. Advantages of bond financing versus common stock include (a) no effect on stockholders' control, (b) tax savings, and (c) increased earnings due to financial leverage. Disadvantages include (a) required interest and principal payments and (b) decreased earnings when operations turn less profitable.

A2 Explain collateral agreements and their effects on loan risk. Some bonds and notes are secured by collateral agreements. Collateral agreements reduce the risk of loss for both bonds and notes. Unsecured bonds and notes are more risky because the issuer's obligation to pay interest and principal has the same priority as all other unsecured liabilities in the event of bankruptcy. To borrow funds at a more favorable rate, many bonds and notes are secured by collateral agreements called *mortgages.*

A3 Compute the ratio of pledged assets to secured liabilities and explain its use. Both secured and unsecured creditors are concerned about the relation between the amounts of assets owned by the debtor and the amounts of secured liabilities. Secured creditors are safer when the ratio of pledged assets to secured liabilities is larger. But the risks of unsecured creditors are often increased when this ratio is high because their claims to assets are secondary to secured creditors.

P1 Prepare entries to record bond issuance and bond interest expense. When bonds are issued at par, Cash is debited and Bonds Payable is credited for the bonds' par value. At the bonds' interest payment dates, Bond Interest Expense is debited and Cash credited for an amount equal to the bonds' par value multiplied by the bonds' contract rate. The cash paid to bondholders on semiannual interest payment dates is computed as one-half of the result of multiplying the par value of the bonds by their contract rate.

P2 Compute and record amortization of bond discount. The issue price of a bond is computed using the market rate in solving for the present values of the bonds' interest payments and their par value. Bonds are issued at a discount when the contract rate is less than the market rate. This is the same as saying the issue (selling) price is less than par. When this occurs, the issuer records a credit to Bonds Payable (at par) and debits both to Discount on Bonds Payable and to Cash. The amount of bond interest expense assigned to each period is computed using either the straight-line or effective interest method. Straight-line can only be used if the results are not materially different from the effective interest method. Bond interest expense using the effective interest method equals the bonds' beginning-of-period carrying value multiplied by the original market rate at time of issuance.

P3 Compute and record amortization of bond premium. Bonds are issued at a premium when the contract rate is higher than the market rate. This means the issue (selling) price is greater than par. When this occurs, the issuer records a debit to Cash and credits both to Premium on Bonds Payable and to Bonds Payable (at par). The amount of bond interest expense assigned to each period is computed using either the straight-line or effective interest method. The balance of the Premium on Bonds Payable is allocated to reduce bond interest expense over the life of the bonds.

P4 Record the retirement of bonds. Bonds are retired at maturity with a debit to Bonds Payable and a credit to Cash for the par value of the bonds. Bonds can be retired early by the issuer by exercising a call option or by purchases on the open market. Alternatively, bondholders can retire bonds early by exercising a conversion feature on convertible bonds. The issuer recognizes a gain or loss for the difference between the amount paid out and the bonds' carrying value.

P5 Prepare entries to account for notes. Interest is allocated to each period in a note's life by multiplying its carrying value by its market rate at issuance. If a note is repaid with equal payments, the amount of payment is computed by dividing the borrowed amount by the present value of an annuity factor (taken from a present value table) using the market rate and the number of payments.

Guidance Answers to **You Make the Call**

Bond Rater

One factor in rating a bond is its payment pattern. Bonds that have longer repayment periods and smaller interest payments over the life of the bond have higher risk. Another factor is the competitive position of the company. Bonds issued by companies in financial difficulties or facing higher than normal uncertainties usually have higher risk. Still another factor is the financial health of the company. Companies with higher than normal debt and with large fluctuations in earnings are considered higher risk.

Retailer

This is a present value question where the market interest rate (10%) and present value ($3,000) are known, but the payment made two years later is not known. The amount we'd expect to receive at the end of two years (the holiday sale price) is $3,630. This is computed as $3,000 × 1.10 × 1.10. (This is similar to the computation in Exhibit 15.16.) Therefore, your sale price is $3,630 with no payments for two years. This $3,630 received two years from today is equivalent to $3,000 cash today.

Bond Investor

The first company's ratio of pledged assets to secured liabilities is 2.2 ($1,265,000/$575,000), and for the second company it is 2.5 ($2,000,000/$800,000). This suggests that secured creditors of the second company are at less risk than secured creditors of the first company. But *debenture bonds are unsecured.* Therefore, since the first company has fewer secured liabilities, it is of lower risk for unsecured debenture bonds. In addition, the first company has fewer liabilities and, since the companies are of equal size, the liabilities of the first company make up a smaller portion of total assets. Consequently, as a buyer of unsecured debenture bonds, you prefer the first company.

Guidance Answers to 

1. *b*
2. Multiply the par value of the bonds by the contract rate of interest.
3. The bonds sell at a premium when the contract rate exceeds the market rate, and the purchasers pay more than the par value of the bonds.
4. The bonds are issued at a discount, meaning issue price is less than par value. A discount occurs because the bonds' contract rate is less than their market rate.
5.

Cash	91,893	
Discount on Bonds Payable	8,107	
Bonds Payable		100,000

6. *a.* $3,811 (Total interest of $38,107 divided by 10 payments, or the $3,000 cash paid plus the $8,107 discount after dividing by 10 periods.)
   b. $3,676 (Beginning book balance of $91,893 multiplied by the 4% market interest rate.)
7. The bonds are issued at a premium, meaning issue price is greater than par value. A premium occurs because the bonds' contract rate is greater than their market rate.
8. *e.* (On 6/30/2000: $110,592 × 7% = $7,741 bond interest expense; $8,000 − $7,741 = $259 premium amortization; $110,592 − $259 = $110,333 bond ending balance. On 12/31/2000: $110,333 × 7% = $7,723 bond interest expense; $8,000 − $7,723 = $277 premium amortization.)
9.

Bonds payable, 16%, due 12/31/2009	$100,000	
Plus premium on bonds payable	10,056*	$110,056

*Beginning premium balance of $10,592 less $259 and $277 amortized on 6/30/2000 and 12/31/2000.

10. *a*
11. $9,375 loss. Computed as the difference between the repurchase price of $256,250 [50% of ($500,000 × 102.5%)] and the carrying value of $246,875 (50% of $493,750).
12. *c.* [$6,000 + ($6,000 × .06)] × .06 = $381.60
13.

Cash	2,940	
Discount on Notes Payable	1,060	
Notes Payable		4,000
Exchanged a 4-year noninterest-bearing note for cash.		

14. *c*
15. The interest portion of an installment payment equals the beginning balance for the period multiplied by the original market interest rate.
16. On the balance sheet, the balances of the liability (note payable) and cash are decreased. On the income statement, interest expense is increased.

Demonstration Problem

The Water Sports Company (WSC) patented and successfully test-marketed a new product. However, to expand its ability to produce and market the product, the company needed to raise $800,000 of financing. On January 1, 1999, the company obtained the money in two ways:

a. WSC signed a $400,000, 10% installment note to be repaid with five equal annual installments. The payments will be made on December 31 of 1999 through 2003.

b. WSC issued five-year bonds with a par value of $400,000. The bonds have a 12% annual contract rate and pay interest on June 30 and December 31. The annual market interest rate for the bonds is 10% on January 1, 1999.

Required

1. For the installment note, *(a)* compute the size of each payment, *(b)* prepare an amortization table, and *(c)* present the entry for the first payment.
2. For the bonds, *(a)* estimate the issue price of the bonds; *(b)* present the January 1, 1999, entry to record issuing the bonds; *(c)* prepare an amortization table using the interest method; *(d)* present the June 30, 1999, entry to record the first payment of interest; and *(e)* present an entry to record retiring the bonds at the call price of $416,000 on January 1, 2001.

Planning the Solution

- For the installment note, divide the borrowed amount by the annuity table factor (from Table C.3) for 10% and five payments. Prepare a table similar to Exhibit 15.20 and use the numbers in the first line for the entry.
- For the bonds, estimate the issue price by using the market rate to find the present values of the bonds' cash flows (use tables found in Appendix C). Then use this result to record issuing the bonds. Next, develop an amortization table like Exhibit 15.12 and use it to get the numbers that you need for the journal entry. Finally, use the table to find the carrying value as of the date of the retirement of the bonds that you need for the journal entry.

Solution to Demonstration Problem

Part 1: Installment Note

Payment = Note balance/Annuity table factor = $400,000/3.7908 = $105,519.
Annuity table factor is for 5 payments and an interest rate of 10%.

		Payments			
	(a)	(b) Debit	(c) Debit	(d) Credit	(e)
Period Ending	Beginning Balance	Interest Expense +	Notes Payable =	Cash	Ending Balance
1999	$400,000	$ 40,000	$ 65,519	$105,519	$334,481
2000	334,481	33,448	72,071	105,519	262,410
2001	262,410	26,241	79,278	105,519	183,132
2002	183,132	18,313	87,206	105,519	95,926
2003	95,926	9,593	95,926	105,519	0
Total		$127,595	$400,000	$527,595	

1999			
Dec. 31	Interest Expense	40,000	
	Notes Payable	65,519	
	Cash		105,519
	To record first installment payment.		

Part 2: Bonds

Estimated issue price of the bonds:

Cash Flow	Table	Table Value*	Amount	Present Value
Par value	App. C (PV of $1)	0.6139	$400,000	$245,560
Interest (annuity) payments	App. C (PV of annuity)	7.7217	24,000	185,321
Price of bond				$430,881

*Present value factors are for 10 payments and an interest rate of 5%.

1999			
Jan. 1	Cash	430,881	
	Premium on Bonds Payable		30,881
	Bonds Payable		400,000
	Sold bonds at a premium.		

Semiannual Interest Period	(A) Cash Interest Paid 6% × $400,000	(B) Interest Expense 5% × (E)	(C) Premium Amortization (A) − (B)	(D) Unamortized Premium Prior (D) − (C)	(E) Carrying Value $400,000 + (D)
1/1/1999				$30,881	$430,881
6/30/1999	$ 24,000	$ 21,544	$ 2,456	28,425	428,425
12/31/1999	24,000	21,421	2,579	25,846	425,846
6/30/2000	24,000	21,292	2,708	23,138	423,138
12/31/2000	24,000	21,157	2,843	20,295	420,295
6/30/2001	24,000	21,015	2,985	17,310	417,310
12/31/2001	24,000	20,866	3,134	14,176	414,176
6/30/2002	24,000	20,709	3,291	10,885	410,885
12/31/2002	24,000	20,544	3,456	7,429	407,429
6/30/2003	24,000	20,371	3,629	3,800	403,800
12/31/2003	24,000	20,200*	3,800	0	400,000
	$240,000	$209,119	$30,881		

*Adjusted for rounding.

1999			
June 30	Bond Interest Expense	21,544	
	Premium on Bonds Payable	2,456	
	Cash		24,000
	Paid semiannual interest on the bonds.		

2001			
Jan. 1	Bonds Payable	400,000	
	Premium on Bonds Payable	20,295	
	Cash		416,000
	Gain on Retirement of Bonds		4,295
	To record the retirement of bonds (carrying value determined as of December 31, 2000).		

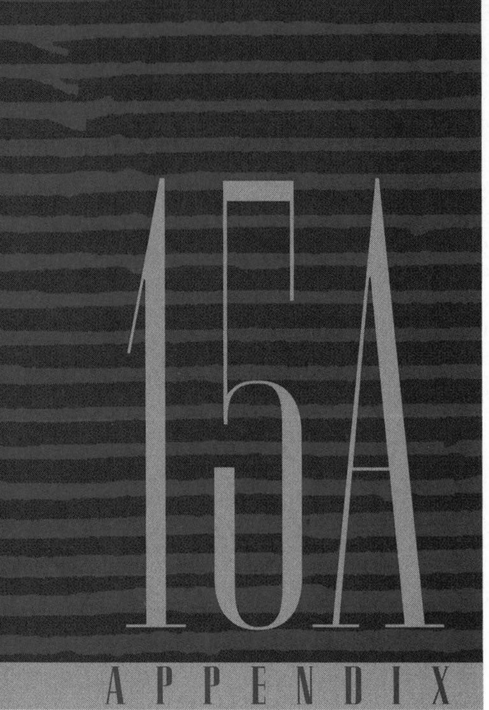

Present Values of Bonds and Notes

APPENDIX

Learning Objectives

Conceptual

C3 Explain and compute the present value of an amount to be paid at a future date.

C4 Explain and compute the present value of a series of equal amounts to be paid at future dates.

Accounting for long-term liabilities such as bonds and notes presents us with new challenges because of the extended time period until these obligations are settled. This appendix explains how we can apply present value techniques both to measure a long-term liability when it is created and to assign interest expense to the periods until it is settled. Appendix C provides additional discussion of present value concepts.

Present Value Concepts

The concept of *present value* affects accounting for liabilities. A focus on liabilities leads to a focus on the present value of future cash outflows, payables, and interest expense. But present value concepts also apply to future cash inflows, receivables, and interest income. The basic present value concept is the idea that cash paid (or received) in the future has less value now than the same amount of cash paid (or received) today.

To illustrate, if we must pay $1 one year from now, its present value is less than $1. To see this, let's assume we borrow $0.9259 today for one year at 8% interest. Our interest expense for this loan is computed as $0.9259 × 8%, or $0.0741. When the $0.0741 interest is added to the $0.9259 borrowed, we get the $1 payment necessary to repay our loan with interest. This is formally computed in Exhibit 15A.1.

Exhibit 15A.1

Components of a One-Year Loan

Amount borrowed	**$0.9259**
Interest for one year at 8%	0.0741
Amount owed after 1 year	$1.0000

The $0.9259 borrowed is the present value of the $1 future payment. More generally, an amount borrowed equals the present value of the future payment. This relation implies that a borrowed amount can yield interest at a given rate such that its future amount will repay the loan with interest.[12]

To extend this example, let's assume we must pay $1 two years from now instead of one, and the 8% interest is compounded annually. *Compounded* means interest during the second period is based on the total of the amount borrowed plus the interest accrued from the first period. The second period's interest is then computed as 8% multiplied by the sum of the amount borrowed plus interest earned in the first period. Exhibit 15A.2

Exhibit 15A.2

Components of a Two-Year Loan

Amount borrowed in first year	**$0.8573**
Interest for first year ($0.8573 × 8%)	0.0686
Amount borrowed in second year	$0.9259
Interest for second year ($0.9259 × 8%)	0.0741
Amount owed after 2 years	$1.0000

[12] This same interpretation applies to an investment. If $0.9259 is invested at 8%, it yields $0.0741 interest revenue in one year. This amounts to $1, made up of principal and interest.

shows how we compute the present value of $1 to be paid in two years. This amount is $0.8573.

The first year's interest of $0.0686 is added to the principal so that the second year's interest is based on $0.9259.[13] Total interest for this two year period is $0.1427, computed as $0.0686 plus $0.0741.

C3 Explain and compute the present value of an amount to be paid at a future date.

Present Value Tables

The present value of $1 that we must repay several periods into the future can be computed by using the formula: $1/(1 + i)^n$. The symbol i in the formula is the interest rate per period and n is the number of periods until the future payment must be made. Applying this formula to our two-year loan, we get: $\$1/(1.08)^2$, or $0.8573. This is the same value shown in Exhibit 15A.2.

We can use this formula to find any present value. But simpler methods are available. Perhaps the easiest is for us to use electronic calculators that are preprogrammed with present value formulas. But we can also use a present value table. A *present value table* lists present values computed with the formula for various interest rates and time periods. Many people find it helpful in learning present value concepts to first work with the table and then move to using a calculator.

Exhibit 15A.3 shows a present value table for a future payment of 1 for up to 10 periods at four different interest rates. Present values in this table are rounded to four decimal places.[14] This table is drawn from the larger and more complete Table C.1 in Appendix C at the end of the book.

Exhibit 15A.3

Present Value of 1

	Rate			
Periods	**4%**	**6%**	**8%**	**10%**
1	0.9615	0.9434	**0.9259**	0.9091
2	0.9246	0.8900	**0.8573**	0.8264
3	0.8890	0.8396	0.7938	0.7513
4	0.8548	0.7921	0.7350	0.6830
5	0.8219	0.7473	0.6806	0.6209
6	0.7903	0.7050	0.6302	0.5645
7	0.7599	0.6651	0.5835	0.5132
8	0.7307	0.6274	0.5403	0.4665
9	0.7026	0.5919	0.5002	0.4241
10	0.6756	0.5584	0.4632	0.3855

The first value in the 8% column is 0.9259. This is the value we computed above for the present value of a $1 loan for 1 year at 8% (see Exhibit 15A.1). Go down one row in the same 8% column and find the present value of 1 discounted at 8% for 2 years, or 0.8573. Again, this value of $0.8573 is the present value of our obligation to repay $1 after two periods at 8% interest (see Exhibit 15A.2).

Applying a Present Value Table

To illustrate how we measure a liability using a present value table, let's assume a company plans to borrow cash and repay it as follows:

Payment after 1 year	$ 2,000
Payment after 2 years	3,000
Payment after 3 years	5,000
Total payments	$10,000

[13] Benjamin Franklin is said to have described compounding as: "The money, money makes, makes more money."

[14] Four decimal places are sufficient for applications in this book. Some situations require more precision.

Exhibit 15A.4

Present Value of a Series of Unequal Payments

Years from Now	Expected Payments	Present Value of 1 at 10%	Present Value of Expected Payments
1	$2,000	0.9091	$1,818
2	3,000	0.8264	2,479
3	5,000	0.7513	3,757
Present value of all payments			**$8,054**

How much does this company receive today if the interest rate is 10% on this loan? To answer this question we need to compute the present value of the three future payments, discounted at 10%. This computation is shown in Exhibit 15A.4 using values from Exhibit 15A.3. It shows the company can borrow $8,054 today at 10% interest in exchange for its promise to make three payments at the scheduled dates.

Present Value of an Annuity

C4 Explain and compute the present value of a series of equal amounts to be paid at future dates.

The $8,054 present value of the loan in Exhibit 15A.4 equals the sum of the present values of the three payments. When payments are not equal, their combined present value is best computed by adding their individual present values as shown in Exhibit 15A.4. But sometimes payments follow an **annuity,** which is a series of equal payments at equal time intervals. The present value of an annuity is readily computed.

Exhibit 15A.5

Present Value of a Series of Equal Payments (Annuity) by Discounting Each Payment

Years from Now	Expected Payments	Present Value of 1 at 6%	Present Value of Expected Payments
1	$5,000	0.9434	$ 4,717
2	5,000	0.8900	4,450
3	5,000	0.8396	4,198
4	5,000	0.7921	3,961
Present value of all payments . .		**3.4651**	**$17,326**

To illustrate, let's take a company that must repay a 6% loan with a $5,000 payment at the end of each year for the next four years. The amount borrowed under this loan equals the present value of the four payments discounted at 6%. Exhibit 15A.5 shows how to compute its present value of $17,326 by multiplying each payment by its matching present value factor from Exhibit 15A.3. But since the series of $5,000 payments is an annuity, we can compute present value with either of two shortcuts. First, the third column of Exhibit 15A.5 shows that the sum of the present values of 1 at 6% for period 1 through 4 equals 3.4651. One shortcut is to multiply this total of 3.4651 by the $5,000 annual payment to get the combined present value of $17,326. It requires one multiplication instead of four.

The second shortcut uses an *annuity table* such as the one shown in Exhibit 15A.6.[15] Exhibit 15A.6 is drawn from the more complete Table C.3 in Appendix C. Instead of taking the sum of individual present values from Exhibit 15A.3, we go directly to the annuity table to get the present value factor for a specific number of payments and interest rate. We then multiply this factor by the amount of the payment to find the pres-

[15]The formula for finding this table's values is: $\dfrac{1 - \dfrac{1}{(1+i)^n}}{i}$. The present values in Exhibit 15A.6 are also found by adding the values of the individual payments from Exhibit 15A.3. (Since only four decimal places are shown, there are some ±0.0001 rounding differences between them.)

ent value of the entire annuity.

Specifically, look at Exhibit 15A.6 to find the row for 4 periods and go across to the column for 6%, where the factor is 3.4651. This factor equals the present value of an annuity with 4 payments of 1, discounted at 6%. We then multiply 3.4651 times $5,000 to get the $17,326 present value of our annuity.

	Rate			
Periods	**4%**	**6%**	**8%**	**10%**
1	0.9615	0.9434	0.9259	0.9091
2	1.8861	1.8334	1.7833	1.7355
3	2.7751	2.6730	2.5771	2.4869
4	3.6299	**3.4651**	3.3121	3.1699
5	4.4518	4.2124	3.9927	3.7908
6	5.2421	4.9173	4.6229	4.3553
7	6.0021	5.5824	5.2064	4.8684
8	6.7327	6.2098	5.7466	5.3349
9	7.4353	6.8017	6.2469	5.7590
10	**8.1109**	7.3601	6.7101	6.1446

Exhibit 15A.6

Present Value of an Annuity of 1

Compounding Periods Shorter than a Year

Our present value examples all involved periods of a year. But in many situations, interest is compounded over shorter periods. For example, the interest rate on bonds is usually stated as an annual rate but interest is often paid every six months. This means the present value of interest payments from these bonds must be computed using interest periods of six months.

To illustrate, let's assume a borrower wants to know the present value of a series of ten $4,000 *semiannual payments* made over five years at an *annual interest rate* of 8%. While the interest rate is stated as an annual rate of 8%, it is actually a rate of 4% per six-month interest period. To compute the present value of this series of $4,000 payments, enter Exhibit 15A.6 on row 10 and go across to the 4% column to find the factor 8.1109. The present value of this annuity is $32,444 (8.1109 × $4,000).

We recommend reading Appendix C to learn more about present value concepts. It includes more complete present value tables and provides a discussion of future value concepts and tables. It also includes assignment materials to help in understanding present value concepts.

Flash *back*

A1. A company enters into an agreement to make four annual payments of $1,000 each, starting one year from now. The annual interest rate is 8%. The present value of these four payments is: *(a)* $2,923; *(b)* $2,940; *(c)* $3,312; *(d)* $4,000; or *(e)* $6,733.

A2. Suppose a company has an option to pay either $10,000 after one year or $5,000 after six months and another $5,000 after one year. Which choice has the smaller present value?

Answers—p. 678

Summary of Appendix 15A

C3 Explain and compute the present value of an amount to be paid at a future date. The basic concept of present value is that an amount of cash to be paid or received in the future is worth less than the same amount of cash to be paid or received today. Another important present value concept is that interest is compounded. This means interest is added to the balance and used to determine interest for succeeding periods. The present value of an amount is computed using the present value table for a single amount (or calculator).

C4 Explain and compute the present value of a series of equal amounts to be paid at future dates. An annuity is a series of equal payments occurring at equal time intervals. The present value of an annuity can be computed as the sum of individual present values for each payment. Alternatively, and the preferred approach, is to compute the present value of the entire series using the present value table for an annuity (or a calculator).

Guidance Answers to 

A1. *c*. Computed as: 3.3121 × $1,000 = $3,312.

A2. The option of paying $10,000 after a year always has a lower present value. In effect, it postpones paying the first $5,000 by six months. As a result, the present value of the delayed payment is always less.

Glossary

Annuity a series of annual payments at equal time intervals. (p. 676).

Bearer bonds bonds that are made payable to whoever holds them (called the *bearer*); also called *unregistered bonds.* (p. 644).

Bond a written promise to pay an amount identified as the par (or face) value of the bond along with interest at a stated annual amount; usually issued in denominations of $1,000. (p. 642).

Bond certificate a document containing bond specifics such as the issuer's name, the bond's par value, the contract interest rate, and the maturity date. (p. 646).

Bond indenture the contract between the bond issuer and the bondholders; it identifies the rights and obligations of the parties. (p. 645).

Callable bonds bonds that give the issuer an option of retiring them at a stated dollar amount prior to maturity. (p. 644).

Carrying value the net amount at which bonds are reflected on the balance sheet; equals the par value of the bonds less any unamortized discount or plus any unamortized premium; also called the *book value* or *carrying amount* of the bonds. (p. 649).

Contract rate the interest rate specified in the bond indenture; it is multiplied by the par value of the bonds to determine the amount of interest to be paid each year; also called the *coupon rate,* the *stated rate,* or the *nominal rate.* (p. 647).

Convertible bonds bonds that can be exchanged by the bondholders for a fixed number of shares of the issuing company's common stock. (p. 644).

Coupon bonds bonds that have interest coupons attached to their certificates; the bondholders detach the coupons when they mature and present them to a bank or broker for collection. (p. 644).

Discount on bonds payable the difference between the par value of a bond and its lower issue price or carrying amount; arises when the contract rate is lower than the market rate. (p. 648).

Effective interest method allocates interest expense over the life of the bonds in a way that yields a constant rate of interest; interest expense for a period is found by multiplying the balance of the liability at the beginning of the period by the bonds' original market rate; also called *interest method.* (p. 651).

Installment note an obligation requiring a series of periodic payments to the lender (p. 663).

Market rate the interest rate that borrowers are willing to pay and that lenders are willing to earn for a particular bond at its risk level. (p. 647).

Mortgage a legal agreement that protects a lender by giving the lender the right to be paid out of the cash proceeds from the sale of a borrower's assets identified in the mortgage. (p. 667).

Par value of a bond the amount that the bond issuer agrees to pay at maturity and the amount on which interest payments are based; also called the *face amount* or *face value.* (p. 642).

Pledged assets to secured liabilities the ratio of the book value of a company's pledged assets to the book value of its secured liabilities. (p. 668).

Premium on bonds the difference between the par value of a bond and its higher issue price or carrying amount; arises when the contract rate is higher than the market rate. (p. 652).

Registered bonds bonds owned by investors whose names and addresses are recorded by the issuing company; the interest payments are made with checks to the registered owners. (p. 644).

Secured bonds bonds that have specific assets of the issuing company pledged as collateral. (p. 643).

Serial bonds bonds that mature at different dates with the result that the entire debt is repaid gradually over a number of years. (p. 644).

Sinking fund bonds bonds that require the issuing company to make deposits to a separate pool of assets; the bondholders are repaid at maturity from the assets in this pool. (p. 644).

Straight-line method a method that allocates an equal amount of interest to each accounting period in the life of bonds. (p. 650).

Term bonds bonds that are scheduled for payment (mature) at a single specified date. (p. 644).

Unsecured bonds bonds backed by the issuer's general credit standing; unsecured bonds are almost always more risky than secured bonds; also called *debentures.* (p. 644).

Questions

1. What is the main difference between notes payable and bonds payable?
2. What is the main difference between a common share and a bond?
3. What is the main advantage of issuing bonds instead of obtaining financing from the company's owners?
4. What is a bond indenture? What provisions are usually included in an indenture?
5. What are the duties of a trustee for the bondholders?
6. Why does a company that issues bonds between interest dates collect accrued interest from the bonds' purchasers?
7. What are the *contract* and *market* interest rates for bonds?
8. What factors affect the market interest rates for bonds?
9. If you know the par value of bonds, the contract rate, and the market rate, then how can you estimate the market value of the bonds?
10. Does the straight-line or effective interest method produce an allocation of interest that creates a constant rate of interest over a bond's life? Explain your answer.
11. What is the cash price of a $2,000 bond that is sold at 98¼? What is the cash price of a $6,000 bond that is sold at 101½?
12. Describe two alternative payment patterns for installment notes.
13. Explain why unsecured creditors should be alarmed when the pledged assets to secured liabilities ratio for a borrower has grown substantially.
14. Refer to the annual report for **Nike** in Appendix A. Is there any indication that the company has issued bonds?

15. Refer to the annual report for **Reebok** in Appendix A. For the fiscal year ended December 31, 1996, was Reebok in a net borrowing or net repayment position with respect to cash flows from notes payable to banks?
16. Refer to the annual report for **America Online** in Appendix A. For the fiscal year ended June 30, 1996, did America Online raise more cash by issuing common and preferred stock or by issuing debt?
17. What obligation does Jessica Harris, the owner of **Get Real!**, have to the investors that purchased $200,000 of bonds to finance her natural foods store?

Quick Study

QS 15-1
Bond terms and identifications
C1

Match the following terms and phrases by entering the letter of the description that best fits each term or phrase in the blank next to it.

1. _____ Debentures	5. _____ Sinking fund bonds
2. _____ Bearer bonds	6. _____ Serial bonds
3. _____ Registered bonds	7. _____ Secured bonds
4. _____ Bond indenture	8. _____ Convertible bonds

a. Issuer records the bondholders' names and addresses.
b. Unsecured; backed only by the issuer's general credit standing.
c. Varying maturity dates.
d. Identifies the rights and responsibilities of the issuer and bondholders.
e. Can be exchanged for shares of the issuer's common stock.
f. Unregistered; interest is paid to whoever possesses them.
g. Issuer maintains a separate pool of assets from which bondholders are paid at maturity.
h. Specific assets of the issuer are mortgaged as collateral.

QS 15-2
Quoted bond selling price and bond interest expense for bonds issued at a discount
A1, P2

Lyndon Industries issues 8%, 10-year bonds with a par value of $350,000 and semiannual interest payments. On the issue date, the annual market rate of interest for the bonds is 10%, and the selling price is 87½. The straight-line method is used to allocate the interest.

a. What are the proceeds of the bond?
b. What is the total amount of bond interest expense that will be recognized over the life of the bonds?
c. What is the amount of bond interest expense recorded on the first interest payment date?

QS 15-3
Quoted bond selling price and bond interest expense for bonds issued at a premium
A1, P3

Top Notch issues 10%, 15-year bonds with a par value of $120,000 and semiannual interest payments. On the issue date, the annual market rate of interest for the bonds is 8%, and they sold at 117¼. The effective interest method is used to allocate the interest.

a. What are the proceeds of the Top Notch bonds?

b. What is the total amount of bond interest expense that will be recognized over the life of the bonds?

c. What is the amount of bond interest expense recorded on the first interest payment date?

QS 15-4
Journalize bond issuance at a premium and at a discount
P1

Journalize the issuance of the bonds in QS 15-2 and QS 15-3. Assume that both bonds are issued on January 1, 1999.

QS 15-5
Computing bond proceeds from present values
P2, P3

Using the bond details in QS 15-2 and QS 15-3, confirm that the bond proceeds given in each problem are correct. Use the present value tables C.1 and C.3 in Appendix C.

QS 15-6
Issuing bonds between interest dates
P1

Lafrentz Company issues bonds on January 1, 1999. The total bond issue is $2,000,000 of 8% bonds. The company sells $1,800,000 of the bonds on the original issue date. The remaining $200,000 sell at par on March 1, 1999. The bonds pay interest semiannually as of June 30 and December 31. Record the entry for the March 1 sale of bonds.

QS 15-7
Retiring bonds before maturity
P4

On July 1, 1999, Geiger Company exercises a $4,000 call option (plus par value) on its outstanding bonds that have a carrying value of $208,000 and par value of $200,000. The company exercises the call option immediately after the semiannual interest is paid on June 30, 1999. Record the entry to retire the bonds.

QS 15-8
Bond retirement by stock conversion
P4

On January 1, 1999, the $1,000,000 par value bonds of Stephens Company with a carrying value of $1,000,000 are converted to 500,000 shares of $0.50 par value common stock. Journalize the conversion of the bonds.

QS 15-9
Installment note with equal payments
C2

West Corp. borrows $170,000 from a bank and signs an installment note that calls for five annual payments of equal size, with the first payment due one year after the note is signed. Use Table C.3 in Appendix C to compute the size of the annual payment for each of the following annual interest rates: (*a*) 4%, (*b*) 8%, and (*c*) 12%.

QS 15-10
Collateral agreements
A2

Footnote 2 of the **Collins Industries** annual report reads as follows:

> The credit facility [line] is collateralized by receivables, inventories, equipment and certain real property. Under the terms of the Agreement, the Company is required to maintain certain financial ratios and other financial conditions. The Agreement also prohibits the Company from incurring certain additional indebtedness, limits certain investments, advances or loans and restricts substantial asset sales, capital expenditures and cash dividends.

What restrictions are placed on Collins Industries by the bank that has granted the credit?

QS 15-11
Computing amount due on interest-bearing note
C2

On January 1, 1999, Deitrich Company borrows $75,000 in exchange for an interest-bearing note. The note plus compounded interest at an annual rate of 8% is due on December 31, 2001. Determine the amount that Deitrich will pay on the due date. (Round to the nearest dollar.)

QS 15-12
Ratio of pledged assets to secured liabilities
A3

Compute the ratio of pledged assets to secured liabilities for both companies below:

	Delta Co.	Sigma Co.
Pledged assets	$387,000	$172,000
Total assets	550,000	490,000
Secured liabilities	163,000	158,000
Unsecured liabilities	266,000	390,000

Which company appears to have the riskier secured liabilities?

Exercises

When solving exercises, round dollar amounts to the nearest whole dollar. Assume none of the companies use reversing entries.

Exercise 15-1
Journal entries for bond issuance and interest payments

On January 1, 1999, Maverick Enterprises issues $1,700,000 of 20-year bonds, dated January 1, 1999. The bonds have a $1,700,000 par value, mature in 20 years, and pay 9% interest semiannually on June 30 and December 31. The bonds are sold to investors at their par value.

a. How much interest will Maverick pay to the holders of these bonds every six months?

b. Show the journal entries that Maverick would make to record (1) the issuance of the bonds on January 1, 1999; (2) the first interest payment on June 30, 1999; and (3) the second interest payment on December 31, 1999.

c. Assume the Maverick Enterprises bonds are sold at (1) 98 and (2) 102. Journalize the issuance of the bonds at (1) 98 and (2) 102.

Exercise 15-2
Journal entries for bond issuance with accrued interest

On May 1, 1999, Maverick Enterprises issues bonds dated January 1, 1999. The bonds have a $1,700,000 par value, mature in 20-years, and pay 9% interest semiannually on June 30 and December 31. The bonds are sold to investors at their par value plus the four months' interest that has accrued since the original issue date.

a. How much accrued interest is paid to Maverick by the purchasers of these bonds on May 1, 1999?

b. Show the journal entries that Maverick would make to record (1) the issuance of the bonds on May 1, 1999; (2) the first interest payment on June 30, 1999; and (3) the second interest payment on December 31, 1999.

Exercise 15-3
Computing the present value of a bond and recording its issuance

Kloss Company issues bonds with a par value of $600,000 on their issue date. The bonds mature in 10 years and pay 6% annual interest in two semiannual payments. On the issue date, the annual market rate of interest for the bonds is 8%.

a. What is the amount of the semiannual interest payment for these bonds?

b. How many semiannual interest payments will be made on these bonds over their life?

c. Use the information about interest rates to determine whether the bonds are issued at par, a discount, or a premium.

d. Estimate the market value of the bonds as of the date they are issued.

e. Present the journal entry that would be made to record the bonds' issuance.

Exercise 15-4
Straight-line allocation of interest for bonds sold at a discount

Bailey's issues bonds with a par value of $90,000 on January 1, 2000. The annual contract rate on the bonds is 8%, and the interest is paid semiannually on June 30 and December 31. The bonds mature after three years. The annual market interest rate at the date of issuance is 10%, and the bonds are sold for $85,431.

a. What is the amount of the original discount on these bonds?

b. How much total bond interest expense will be recognized over the life of these bonds?

c. Present an amortization table like Exhibit 15.7 for these bonds; use the straight-line method of allocating the interest and amortizing the discount.

Exercise 15-5
Effective interest allocation of interest for bonds sold at a discount
P2

Profitt Corporation issues bonds with a par value of $250,000 on January 1, 2000. The annual contract rate on the bonds is 9%, and the interest is paid semiannually. The bonds mature after three years. The annual market interest rate at the date of issuance is 12%, and the bonds are sold for $231,570.

a. What is the amount of the original discount on these bonds?

b. How much total bond interest expense will be recognized over the life of these bonds?

c. Present an amortization table like Exhibit 15.8 for these bonds; use the effective interest method of allocating the interest and amortizing the discount.

Exercise 15-6
Computing present value of a bond and recording the issuance
P3

Innovention, Inc., issues bonds with a par value of $75,000 on their initial issue date. The bonds mature in five years and pay 10% annual interest in two semiannual payments. On the issue date, the annual market rate of interest for the bonds is 8%.

a. What is the amount of the semiannual interest payment for these bonds?

b. How many semiannual interest payments will be made on these bonds over their life?

c. Use the information about interest rates to determine whether the bonds are issued at par, a discount, or a premium.

d. Estimate the market value of the bonds as of the date they are issued.

e. Present the journal entry that would be made to record the bonds' issuance.

Exercise 15-7
Effective interest allocation of interest for bonds sold at a premium
P3

Great Plains Company issues bonds with a par value of $800,000 on January 1, 2000. The annual contract rate on the bonds is 13%, and interest is paid semiannually. The bonds mature after three years. The annual market interest rate at the date of issuance is 12%, and the bonds are sold for $819,700.

a. What is the amount of the original premium on these bonds?

b. How much total bond interest expense will be recognized over the life of these bonds?

c. Present an amortization table like Exhibit 15.12 for these bonds; use the effective interest method of allocating the interest and amortizing the premium.

Exercise 15-8
Accounting for retiring bonds payable
P4

On January 1, 1999, AeroFab, Inc., issues $350,000 of 10%, 15-year bonds at a price of 97¾. Six years later, on January 1, 2005, the corporation retires 20% of these bonds by buying them on the open market at 104½. All interest is properly accounted for and paid through December 31, 2004, the day before the purchase. The straight-line method is used to allocate the interest and amortize the original discount.

a. How much money does the company receive when it first issues the entire group of bonds?

b. What is the amount of the original discount on the entire group of bonds?

c. How much amortization does the company record on the entire group of bonds between January 1, 1999, and December 31, 2004?

d. What is the carrying value of the entire group of bonds as of the close of business on December 31, 2004? What is the carrying value of the retired bonds on this date?

e. How much money did the company pay on January 1, 2005, to purchase the bonds that it retired?

f. What is the amount of the gain or loss from retiring the bonds?

g. Prepare the journal entry that the company would make to record the retirement of the bonds.

Exercise 15-9
Straight-line amortization table and accrued interest
P2

Piccolo Corp. issues bonds with a par value of $50,000 and a four-year life on June 1, 1999. The contract interest rate is 7%. The bonds pay interest on November 30 and May 31. They are issued at a price of $47,974.

a. Prepare an amortization table (as shown in Exhibit 15.7) for these bonds that covers their entire life. Use the straight-line method of allocating interest.

b. Show the journal entries that the issuer would make to record the first two interest payments and to accrue interest as of December 31, 1999.

Exercise 15-10
Accounting for a noninterest-bearing note
P5

Kern Company acquired a machine on December 1 by giving a $60,000 noninterest-bearing note due in one year. The market rate of interest for this type of note is 10%. Prepare entries that would be made when the note *(a)* is issued on December 1, 1999, *(b)* accrues interest as of December 31, 1999, and *(c)* matures on December 1, 2000.

Exercise 15-11
Installment note with payments of accrued interest and equal amounts of principal
C2, P5

On December 31, 1999, JMS, Inc., borrows $25,000 by signing a four-year, 7% installment note. The note requires annual payments of accrued interest and equal amounts of principal on December 31 of each year from 2000 through 2003.

a. How much principal will be included in each of the four payments?

b. Prepare an amortization table for this installment note like the one presented in Exhibit 15.19.

Exercise 15-12
Journal entries for an installment note
C2, P5

Use the information in Exercise 15–11 to prepare journal entries that JMS, Inc., would make to record the loan on December 31, 1999, and the four payments starting on December 31, 2000, through the final payment on December 31, 2003.

Exercise 15-13
Installment note with equal payments
C2, P5

On December 31, 1999, Volks Corp. borrows $25,000 by signing a four-year, 7% installment note. The note requires four equal payments of accrued interest and principal on December 31 of each year from 2000 through 2003.

a. Compute the amount of each of the four equal payments.

b. Prepare an amortization table for this installment note like the one presented in Exhibit 15.20.

Exercise 15-14
Journal entries for an installment note
C2, P5

Use the information in Exercise 15-13 to prepare journal entries that Volks Corp. would make to record the loan on December 31, 1999, and the four payments starting on December 31, 2000, through the final payment on December 31, 2003.

Exercise 15-15
Computing ratio of pledged assets to secured liabilities
A2

An unsecured creditor of Telstar Corp. has been monitoring the company's financing activities. Two years ago, its ratio of pledged assets to secured liabilities was 1.7. One year ago, the ratio climbed to 2.3, and the most recent financial report shows that the ratio is now 3.1. Briefly describe what this trend may indicate about the company's activities, specifically from the point of view of this creditor.

Problems

When solving problems, round dollar amounts to the nearest whole dollar. Assume none of the companies use reversing entries.

Problem 15-1
Computing bond prices and recording issuances
P1, P2, P3

Abbey Research, Inc., issues bonds on January 1, 1999, that pay interest semiannually on June 30 and December 31. The par value of the bonds is $20,000, the annual contract rate is 10%, and the bonds mature in 10 years.

Required

For each of these three situations, *(a)* determine the issue price of the bonds and *(b)* show the journal entry that would record the issuance.

1. Market interest rate at the date of issuance is 8%.

2. Market interest rate at the date of issuance is 10%.

3. Market interest rate at the date of issuance is 12%.

Check Figure (1) Premium, $2,718

Problem 15-2
Straight-line method of amortizing interest for both a bond discount and a bond premium.
P1, P2, P3

Check Figure (3) Total bond interest expense, $2,071,776

Scofield Corporation issues $2,000,000 of bonds that pay 6% annual interest with two semiannual payments. The date of issuance is January 1, 1999, and the interest is paid on June 30 and December 31. The bonds mature after 15 years and are issued at a price of $1,728,224.

Required

1. Prepare a General Journal entry to record the issuance of the bonds.
2. Calculate *(a)* the cash payment, *(b)* the straight-line discount amortization amount, and *(c)* the bond interest expense to be recognized every six months.
3. Determine the total bond interest expense that will be recognized over the life of these bonds.
4. Prepare the first two years of an amortization table like Exhibit 15.7 based on the straight-line method of allocating the interest.
5. Present the journal entries that Scofield would make to record the first two interest payments.
6. Assume that the proceeds of the bond are $2,447,990. Repeat requirements 1–5.

Problem 15-3
Effective interest method of amortizing interest for a bond discount
P2

Check Figure Total bond interest expense, $195,639

Evans Corp. issues $650,000 of bonds that pay 5% annual interest with two semiannual payments. The date of issuance is January 1, 1999, and the interest is paid on June 30 and December 31. The bonds mature after four years and are issued at a price of $584,361. The market interest rate is 8%.

Required

Preparation Component

1. Prepare a General Journal entry to record the issuance of the bonds.
2. Determine the total bond interest expense that will be recognized over the life of these bonds.
3. Prepare the first two years of an amortization table like Exhibit 15.8 using the effective interest method.
4. Present the journal entries that Evans would make to record the first two interest payments.

Analysis Component

5. Assume the market interest rate on January 1, 1999, is 4% instead of 8%. Without providing numbers, describe how this change would affect the amounts presented on Evans's financial statements.

Problem 15-4
Effective interest method of amortizing interest for a bond premium; retiring bonds
P3, P4 S

Check Figure Bond interest expense for period ending 6/30/2000, $4,580

Phantom Industries issues $90,000 of bonds that pay 11% annual interest with two semiannual payments. The date of issuance is January 1, 1999, and the interest is paid on June 30 and December 31. The bonds mature after three years and are issued at a price of $92,283. The market interest rate is 10%.

Required

Preparation Component

1. Prepare a General Journal entry to record the issuance of the bonds.
2. Determine the total bond interest expense that will be recognized over the life of these bonds.
3. Prepare the first two years of an amortization table using the effective interest method as shown in Exhibit 15.12.
4. Present the journal entries that Phantom would make to record the first two interest payments.
5. Present the journal entry that would be made to record the retirement of these bonds on December 31, 2000, at a price of 98.

Analysis Component

6. Assume that the market interest rate on January 1, 1999, is 12% instead of 10%. Without presenting numbers, describe how this change would affect the amounts presented on the company's financial statements.

Problem 15-5
Amortize bond premium and find the present value of remaining cash flows
P3

Check Figure Balance as of 6/30/2001, $505,728

Ford Products issues bonds with a par value of $500,000 and a five-year life on January 1, 1999. The bonds pay interest on June 30 and December 31. The contract interest rate is 6.5%. The bonds are issued at a price of $510,666. The market interest rate is 6% on the original issue date.

Required

1. Calculate the total bond interest expense over the life of the bonds.
2. Prepare an effective interest amortization table like Exhibit 15.12 for these bonds that covers their entire life.

3. Show the journal entries that Ford Products would make to record the first two interest payments.
4. Use the original market interest rate to compute the present value of the remaining cash flows for these bonds as of December 31, 2001. Compare your answer with the amount shown on the amortization table as the balance for that date and explain your findings.

Problem 15-6
Installment notes
C2, P5

On October 31, 1999, Borghese Ltd. borrows $400,000 from a bank by signing a five-year installment note bearing interest at 8%. The terms of the note require equal payments each year on October 31.

Required

1. Compute the amount of each installment payment.
2. Complete an amortization schedule for this installment note similar to Exhibit 15.20.
3. Present the journal entries that Borghese would make to record accrued interest as of December 31, 1999 (the end of the annual reporting period) and the first yearly payment on the note.
4. Assume that the note does not require equal payments but instead requires five payments that include accrued interest and an equal amount of principal in each payment. Complete an amortization schedule for this installment note similar to Exhibit 15.19. Present the journal entries that Borghese would make to record accrued interest as of December 31, 1999 (the end of the annual reporting period) and the first yearly payment on the note.

Check Figure (2) Interest expense for period ending 10/31/2003, $14,292

Problem 15-7
Computing and analyzing the ratio of pledged assets to secured liabilities
A2, A3

On January 1, 2000, Dailey Company issues at par its 11%, four-year bonds with a $135,000 par value. The bonds are secured by a mortgage that specifies assets totaling $225,000 as collateral. On the same date, Weekley Company issues at par its 11%, four-year bonds with a par value of $60,000. Weekley is securing its bonds with a mortgage that includes $150,000 of pledged assets. The December 31, 1999, balance sheet information for both companies is shown below:

	Dailey Co.	Weekley Co.
Total assets	$900,000*	$450,000†
Liabilities:		
Secured	$210,000	$ 75,000
Unsecured	150,000	165,000
Stockholders' equity	540,000	210,000
Total liabilities and stockholders' equity	$900,000	$450,000

*43% are pledged.
†55% are pledged.

Required

Preparation Component

1. Compute the ratio of pledged assets to secured liabilities for each company at January 1, 2000.

Check Figure Dailey, 1.8 to 1

Analysis Component

2. Which company's bonds appear to offer the best security? What other information might be helpful in evaluating the risk of these companies' bonds?

BEYOND THE NUMBERS

Reporting in Action

A1, C1

Refer to the financial statements and related information for **NIKE** in Appendix A. Answer the following questions by analyzing that information:

1. Does NIKE have any bonds or long-term notes payable issued and outstanding?
2. How often is interest paid on its long-term notes payable?
3. Do any of NIKE's notes payable have a call provision?
4. How much cash is paid toward long-term debt during the fiscal year ended May 31, 1997?
5. Did NIKE issue any new long-term debt during fiscal year 1997?

Swoosh Ahead

6. Obtain NIKE's annual report information for a fiscal year ending after May 31, 1997. You can get this information from either its Web site [**www.nike.com**] or the SEC's EDGAR database [**www.sec.gov**]. Has NIKE issued additional long-term debt since the fiscal year ended May 31, 1997?

Comparative Analysis

A3

Reebok

Both **NIKE** and **Reebok** design, produce, market, and sell sports footwear and apparel. Key comparative figures ($ millions) for these two organizations follow:

Key Figures*	NIKE	Reebok
Accounts receivable, net	$1,754	$591
Inventory	1,339	545
Property and equipment, net	922	185
Long-term debt (includes current portion)	298	907

*NIKE figures are from its annual report for fiscal year ended May 31, 1997. Reebok figures are from its annual report for fiscal year ended December 31, 1996.

Required

1. Assume that both Nike and Reebok have pledged substantially all of their accounts receivable, inventories, and property and equipment to collateralize their long-term debt. Compute the ratio of pledged assets to secured liabilities for both companies.
2. Use the ratio you computed in (1) to determine which company's long-term debt is less risky.

Ethics Challenge

A1

The politicians in Brevard County, Florida, need a new building for the county government. The price tag for the building is $24 million. The politicians feel that it is unlikely that the voters would approve a bond issue to raise money for the building since approving the bond issue would cause taxes to increase. The politicians opt for a different approach. They are having a state bank issue $24 million worth of tax-exempt securities to pay for the construction of the building. The county then will make a yearly lease payment (of principal and interest) to repay the obligation. Unlike conventional municipal bonds, the lease payments are not binding obligations on the county government and, therefore, no voter approval is required.

Required

1. Do you think the actions of the politicians and the bankers are ethical in this situation?
2. How does the tax-exempt security issued to pay for the building compare in riskiness to a regular municipal bond issued by Brevard County?

Communicating in Practice

P3

Your business associate mentioned he is considering investing in the corporate bond market. He recently sent you an e-mail to say he is considering investing in bonds currently selling at a premium. He says that since the bonds are selling at a premium, they are highly valued and his investment will yield more than the going rate of return for the risk involved. Reply via e-mail (or memorandum) to confirm or correct your associate's analysis of premium bonds.

Taking It to the Net

A1

Visit the **Standard and Poor's** Rating Service Web site [**www.ratings.com**].

Required

1. Click on the link on the sidebar title Corporate Ratings. Next click on long-term debt link. Next click on the ratings definition link. Review the Standard and Poor's criteria and ratings for long-term debt issuers. Record the criteria used for long-term debt.
2. Return to the Corporate Ratings page. Click on the preferred stock link. Review the criteria and ratings definitions for preferred stock. Record the criteria used for preferred stock.
3. Return to the main page at www.ratings.com. Select the daily ratings link from the body of the main page. Record the names of several companies that have recently issued long-term debt along with the rating that Standard and Poor's assigned to the recently issued corporate debt.

Teamwork in Action

P2, P3

Break into teams and complete the following requirements.

1. Each team member is to independently prepare a blank table with the appropriate headings for amortization of a bond premium. When all members are done, compare tables and ensure all are in agreement.

Parts 2 and 3 require use of the following facts: On January 1, 1999, BC, Inc., issues $100,000, 9%, five-year bonds at a price of 104.1. The market rate at issuance is 8%. Interest is paid semiannually on June 30 and December 31.

2. In rotation, *each* member of the team must explain how to complete *one* line of the bond amortization table. Each member must completely verbalize any formula used and the specific numbers for their table line. (Round amounts to the nearest dollar.) All members are to fill in their tables during this process. You need not finish the table; stop when each member has an opportunity to explain a line.
3. In rotation, each team member is to identify one column of the table and indicate what the final number in that column will be. Each member must explain what that number is, and how it is known.
4. Reach a team consensus as to what the total bond interest expense on this bond issue will be if the bond is not retired before maturity.
5. As a team, you are to prepare a list of similarities and differences between the amortization table just prepared and the amortization table if the bond had been issued at a discount. You may again use a rotation system to identify these items.

Hitting the Road

A1

Visit your city library. Ask the librarian to help you locate the recent financial records of your city or county government. Examine the records of the municipality you choose.

Required

1. Determine the amount of long-term debt in the form of bonds that your municipality currently has outstanding.
2. Read the supporting information to your municipality's financial statements and record:
   a. The market interest rate the debt was issued at.
   b. When the debt will be mature.
   c. Whether the debt has received a rating from **Moody's, Standard and Poor's,** or another rating agency.

Business Week Activity

A1, C1

Read the article "The Bond Boom in the Former Soviet Bloc," in the September 15, 1997, issue of ***Business Week.***

Required

1. Historically, have companies in central and eastern Europe relied on debt financing?
2. How does the yield on a Eurobond issued by a Russian bank compare to a comparable U.S. Treasury bond?
3. Do experts feel the yields on bonds issued in central Europe compensate investors for the risks?
4. Refer to the chart in the article and list the top five eastern and central European countries in terms of Eurobond amounts issued in 1997.

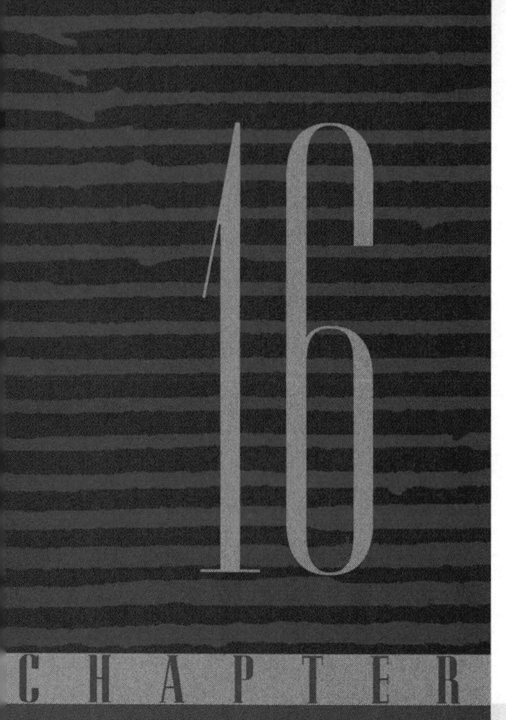

Long-Term Investments and International Accounting

A Look Back

Chapter 15 focused on a special group of long-term liabilities—notes payable and bonds. We described both of these liabilities and explained how to account for and report them.

A Look at This Chapter

This chapter emphasizes another special category, that of long-term investments in securities. We explain how to identify, account for, and report long-term investments in both debt and equity securities. We also introduce foreign exchange rates and describe accounting for transactions listed in a foreign currency.

A Look Ahead

Chapter 17 focuses on reporting and analyzing a company's cash flows. Special emphasis is directed at the statement of cash flows.

Chapter Outline

Investing: The Next Generation

LOS ANGELES—It was the worst day in Sara Brennan's young career as a financial analyst. She had just lost one of her clients and her boss removed her from a special analyst training program. Brennan's response? She quit. "Nothing fit," says Brennan. "Here I was, 23 years old, in a stuffy old-boys firm, advising clients twice my age on securities investments. I knew what I was doing, but no one believed in me."

That was five years ago. Today, Brennan is running her own investment firm, **Brennan & Brennan, LLP.** The other Brennan? "Well," laughs Brennan, "I asked my grandfather to sign on as joint partner because I thought I needed multiple names for the title of an investment firm." Adds Brennan, "Actually, he is the person who started me on my career. When he gave gifts to his grandchildren, he always tucked in some stock of the manufacturer of the gifts."

Grandpa must now be proud, for Brennan's upstart firm pulled in over $485,000 in commissions and consulting revenues this past year. And the current year is running 28% ahead of last year.

What's the secret? "Two things," says Brennan. "First, I work hard at knowing my investments and client needs. Second, I pursue a niche market for clients." What Brennan does is work tirelessly at attracting young investors, the twenty- and thirty-something crowd. "There is a large untapped market that I've only begun to break into," says Brennan. "Larger investment houses don't pursue these clients—I do." She also relies heavily on analysis of annual reports.

"My fundamental analysis is twofold," says Brennan. "I analyze the financial statements of potential investments to assess their strengths and weaknesses. Then I use their products and services and ask others about them." Brennan also usually insists on visiting a company before she invests, or recommends investment, in it. "If I'm looking at a camera company, I use its cameras. I ask other people for their opinions, too." Still, she cautions, "there is always a risk, but I try to minimize it through smart investing." Seems grandpa was a good teacher.

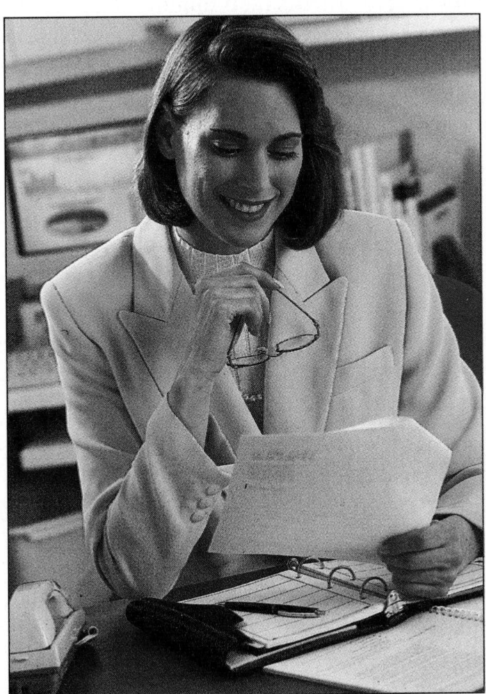

Learning Objectives

Conceptual

C1 Distinguish long-term investments from short-term investments.

C2 Identify classes of securities in long-term investments.

C3 Describe how equity securities with controlling influence are reported.

C4 Explain foreign exchange rates between currencies.

Analytical

A1 Compute and analyze the components of return on total assets.

Procedural

P1 Account for held-to-maturity securities.

P2 Account for available-for-sale securities.

P3 Account for equity securities with significant influence.

P4 Record transactions listed in a foreign currency.

CHAPTER PREVIEW

This chapter completes our study of assets by focusing on long-term investments. Many companies have long-term investments, and many of these are in the form of debt and equity securities issued by other companies. This chapter describes long-term investments in these securities and how they are accounted for. An increasing number of companies also invest in international operations. The financial statement effects of these investments are often very important. We explain how transactions listed in foreign currencies are accounted for and reported. Understanding the topics in this chapter is important for reading and interpreting financial statements. Sara Brennan, as described in the opening article, needed this understanding for her investment decisions and recommendations in stocks and bonds.

Classifying Investments

In this section, we first describe the distinction between short- and long-term investments, and then describe the different classifications of long-term investments.

Short-Term versus Long-Term Investments

C1 Distinguish long-term investments from short-term investments.

We explained in Chapter 10 how to account for short-term investments in debt and equity securities. Short-term investments are current assets and must meet two requirements. First, they are expected to be converted into cash within one year or the current operating cycle of the business, whichever is longer. Second, they are readily convertible to cash, sometimes called *marketable.*[1] Short-term investments are usually held as an investment of cash for use in current operations.

Long-term investments are investments not meeting the two requirements for short-term investments. This means long-term investments include investments in bonds and stocks that aren't marketable or, if marketable, aren't intended to be converted into cash in the short term. Long-term investments also include funds earmarked for a special purpose. Examples are bond sinking funds and investments in land or other assets not used in the company's operations. Long-term investments are reported in the noncurrent section of the balance sheet, often in its own separate section titled *Long-Term Investments.*

Classes of Long-Term Investments

C2 Identify classes of securities in long-term investments.

Accounting for investments depends on two major factors. The first factor is whether securities are classified as (1) *trading* securities, (2) debt securities *held-to-maturity,* or (3) debt and equity securities *available-for-sale.* Investments in trading securities always are short-term investments and are reported as current assets. The other two classes of investments are either long-term or short-term depending on what the company intends to do with them. The second factor in determining how to account for equity securities is a company's (investor's) percent ownership in the other company's (investee's) shares.

This chapter focuses on long-term investments, and Exhibit 16.1 classifies long-term securities on the basis of these two factors. The four classifications shown are: (1) debt securities *held-to-maturity,* (2) debt and equity securities *available-for-sale,* (3) equity securities with a significant influence over an investee, and (4) equity securities with control over an investee. We next describe each of these four classes of securities and how to account for them.

[1] It is helpful to review the section on short-term investments in Chapter 10 before studying this chapter.

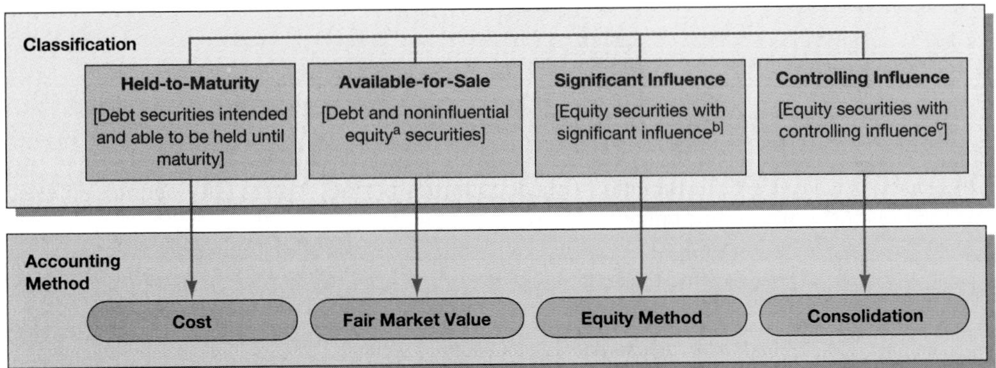

[a] Holding less than 20% of voting stock (equity securities only). [b] Holding 20% or more, but not more than 50%, of voting stock.
[c] Holding more than 50% of voting stock

Exhibit 16.1

Accounting for Long-Term Investments in Securities

Flash back

1. Give at least two examples of assets classified as long-term investments.
2. What are the requirements for a security to be classified as a long-term investment?

Answers—p. 704

Long-Term Investments in Securities

Similar to the accounting for short-term investments, a long-term investment is recorded at cost when purchased. Cost is defined as all necessary expenditures to acquire the investment, including any commissions or brokerage fees paid. But after the purchase, the accounting treatment for long-term investments depends on the class of investments.

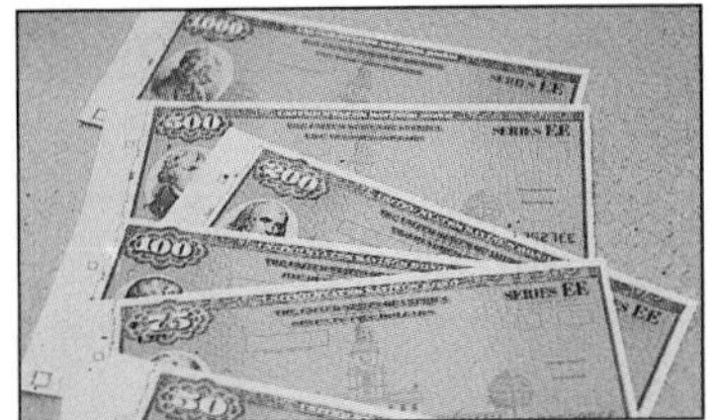

Held-to-Maturity Securities

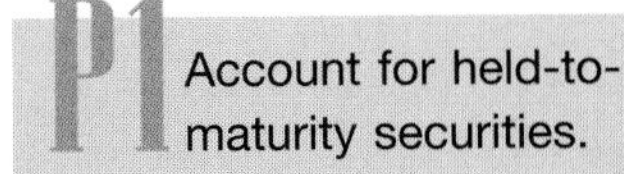

Held-to-maturity securities are *debt* securities a company intends and is able to hold until maturity.[2] Debt securities held to maturity can be short-term or long-term investments. In both cases these securities are recorded at cost when purchased. Interest revenue for long-term investments in held-to-maturity securities must be recorded as it accrues, while interest is not recorded for short-term investments.

The cost of an investment in a held-to-maturity debt security can be either higher or lower than the maturity value of the debt security. When the investment is long term, the difference between cost and maturity value is amortized over the remaining life of the security. Chapter 15 explains how we amortize this difference. For this chapter, we assume for ease of computations that the cost of a debt security equals its maturity value.

Illustration of a Held-to-Maturity Debt Security

Music City paid $29,500 plus a brokerage fee of $500 to buy Improv's 7%, two-year bonds payable with a $30,000 par value on August 31, 1998. The bonds pay interest semiannually on August 31 and February 28. The amount of each interest payment is $1,050, computed as $30,000 par value × 7% interest × 6/12 year. Music City intends to hold the bonds until they mature on August 31, 2000. The entry to record this purchase is:

[2] FASB, "Accounting for Certain Investments in Debt and Equity Securities," *Statement of Accounting Standards No. 115* (Norwalk, CT, 1995), par. 6.

Assets = Liabilities + Equity
+30,000
−30,000

1998			
Aug. 31	Investment in Improv Bonds	30,000	
	Cash		30,000
	Purchased bonds to be held to maturity.		

On December 31, 1998, at the end of its accounting period, Music City accrues interest receivable in the following entry:

Assets = Liabilities + Equity
+700 +700

Dec. 31	Interest Receivable	700	
	Interest Earned		700
	Accrue interest earned ($30,000 × 7% × 4/12).		

The $700 reflects 4/6 of the semiannual cash receipt of interest. This is the portion earned by Music City as of December 31. Relevant sections of Music City's financial statements at December 31, 1998, are shown in Exhibit 16.2.

Exhibit 16.2

Financial Statement Effects of Held-to-Maturity Securities

On the income statement for 1998:	
Interest earned	$ 700
On the December 31, 1998, balance sheet:	
Long-term investments:	
Investment in Improv bonds	$30,000

On February 28, 1999, Music City records receipt of semiannual interest as:

Assets = Liabilities + Equity
+1,050 +350
−700

1999			
Feb. 28	Cash	1,050	
	Interest Receivable		700
	Interest Earned		350
	Received 6 months' interest on Improv bonds.		

When the bonds mature, the entry to record proceeds from the matured bonds is:

Assets = Liabilities + Equity
+30,000
−30,000

2000			
Aug. 31	Cash	30,000	
	Investment in Improv Bonds		30,000
	Received cash from matured bonds.		

This illustration reflects the *cost method* for recording and reporting long-term investments in held-to-maturity debt securities. This method is required in practice.

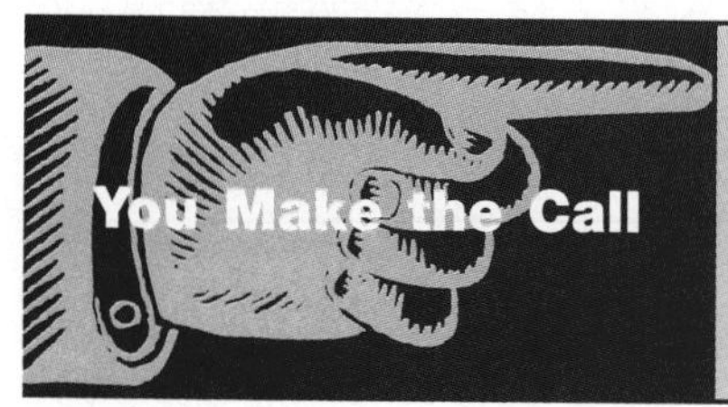

Money Manager

You are a money manager for a company. You currently manage a fund with large amounts of investments in other companies' fixed-rate bonds and notes. You expect interest rates to both sharply fall within a few weeks and remain at this lower rate. What is the strategy for your investments in fixed-rate bonds and notes?

Answer—p. 704

Available-for-Sale Securities

Available-for-sale securities are held with the intent of selling them in the future. If the intent is to hold the securities for at least the next year or operating cycle, they are classified as long-term investments. Exhibit 16.1 shows that long-term investments in available-for-sale securities can include both debt securities and noninfluential equity securities. This section describes the accounting for both of these available-for-sale securities.

Available-for-Sale Debt Securities

P2 Account for available-for-sale securities.

Accounting for **available-for-sale debt securities** is similar to accounting for held-to-maturity debt securities. First, debt securities are recorded at cost when purchased. Second, while debt securities are held, interest is recorded as it accrues.

The difference in accounting for held-to-maturity debt securities versus available-for-sale debt securities is with the amount reported on the balance sheet. Held-to-maturity debt securities are reported at cost, adjusted for the amortized amount of any difference between cost and maturity value. Available-for-sale debt securities are reported at fair market value.

Illustration of an Available-for-Sale Debt Security

To illustrate the accounting for an available-for-sale debt security, let's assume Music City did not intend to hold the Improv bonds to maturity in the prior case. The Improv bonds would then be classified as available-for-sale securities.

The entries in the prior section to record the purchase of the Improv bonds on August 31, the accrual of interest on December 31, 1998, and the receipt of interest on February 28, 1999, do not change provided the bonds are not yet sold. If Music City were to sell the bonds as planned (before they mature), any gain or loss on this sale is reported in the income statement. There is no amortization of any discount or premium.

Trading Secrets
Mutual fund companies keep secret their trading records for many reasons, including regulatory requirements and potential lawsuits. But a mystery arose when top-secret trading records of the $55 billion **Fidelity Magellan** fund appeared in the *Washington Post.* This resulted in several lawsuits filed against Fidelity. Fidelity's fund managers have since been barred from talking about individual stocks with the press, and the company has stopped its internal circulation of daily fund trading activities for security reasons. [Source: *Business Week,* May 27, 1996.]

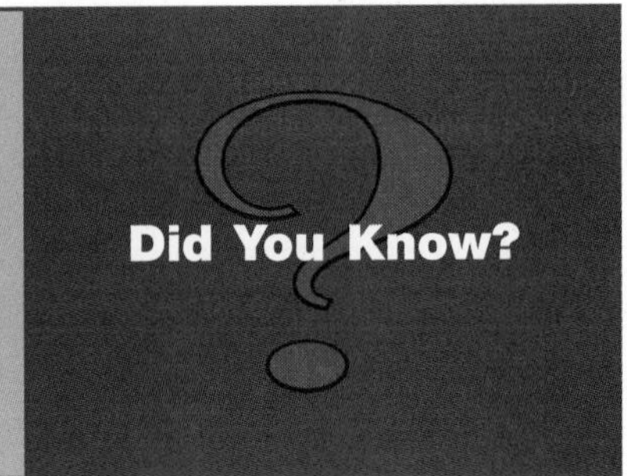

Available-for-Sale Equity Securities

The accounting is similar for short-term and long-term investments in **available-for-sale equity securities.** First, these investments are recorded at cost. Second, dividends received are credited to Dividends Earned and reported in the income statement. Third, when the shares are sold, proceeds from the sale are compared with the cost of the investment, and any gain or loss on the sale is reported in the income statement.

If a long-term investment in an equity security gives the investor significant influence over the investee, it cannot be classified as available-for-sale. Significant influence usually exists if the investor owns 20% or more of the investee company's voting stock.[3]

[3] The 20% limit is not an absolute rule. Other factors may overrule. FASB, *Accounting Standards—Current Text* (Norwalk, CT, 1995), sec. I82.107-8. First published in *FASB Interpretation No. 35,* pars. 3–4.

Illustration of an Available-for-Sale Equity Security

Music City purchases 1,000 shares of Intex's common stock at its par value of $86,000 on October 10, 1998. The entry to record this purchase is:

Assets = Liabilities + Equity
+86,000
−86,000

Oct. 10	Investment in Intex Common Stock	86,000	
	Cash		86,000
	Purchased 1,000 shares of Intex.		

On November 2, Music City receives a $1,720 quarterly cash dividend on the Intex shares. The entry to record the dividend receipt is:

Assets = Liabilities + Equity
+1,720 +1,720

Nov. 2	Cash	1,720	
	Dividends Earned		1,720
	Received dividend of $1.72 per share.		

On December 20, Music City sells 500 of the Intex shares for $45,000. The entry to record this sale is:

Assets = Liabilities + Equity
+45,000 +2,000
−43,000

Dec. 20	Cash	45,000	
	Investment in Intex Common Stock		43,000
	Gain on Sale of Long-Term Investment		2,000
	Sold 500 Intex shares (*$86,000/2*).		

Reporting Fair Market Value of Available-for-Sale Securities

Long-term investments in available-for-sale securities are reported at fair market value on the balance sheet. This applies to both debt and equity securities that are available-for-sale. Any unrealized holding gain or loss on the securities is not reported on the standard income statement. These items that bypass the income statement are referred to as *other comprehensive income.* All changes in equity for a period, except those from investments by and distributions to owners, make up *comprehensive income.* The items making up other comprehensive income are reported in the equity section of the balance sheet and as part of the statement of changes in stockholders' equity.[4]

Cash	41,000	
~~Loss on Sale of~~		
L-T Invest. ...	2,000	
Investment in		
Intex C. Stk.		43,000

Illustration of Reporting on Available-for-Sale Securities

Music City had no prior investments in available-for-sale securities other than the bonds purchased on August 31 and the stock purchased on October 10. Exhibit 16.3 shows both the book value and fair market value of these investments on December 31, 1998.

Exhibit 16.3

Book and Fair Market Value of Available-for-Sale Securities

	Book Value	Fair Market Value
Improv bonds	$30,000	$29,050
Intex common stock, 500 shares	43,000	45,500
Total	$73,000	$74,550

The entry to record the fair value of these investments is:

Assets = Liabilities + Equity
+1,550 +1,550

Dec. 31	Long-Term Investments, Fair Value Adjustment .	1,550	
	Unrealized Holding Gain		1,550
	To record change in fair value of available-for-sale securities.		

[4] Two other options are to report these items in a separate comprehensive income statement or in a combined statement of comprehensive income. These options are left for advanced courses.

It is common to combine the cost of investments with the balance in the Long-Term Investments, Fair Value Adjustment account and report the net as a single amount. Exhibit 16.4 shows this reporting approach for Music City's December 31, 1998, balance sheet.[5]

Exhibit 16.4

Balance Sheet Presentation of Available-for-Sale Securities

Assets:	
Long-term investments:	
Securities available-for-sale (at fair market value)	$74,550
Stockholders' equity:	
Unrealized holding gain	1,550

Flash back

3. Identify similarities and differences in accounting for long-term investments in debt securities that are (a) held-to-maturity and (b) available-for-sale.

Answer—p. 704

Mob on Wall Street

Today, the stock market is confronting a vexing problem. Call it what you will: organized crime, the Mafia, wiseguys. They are the stuff of tabloids and gangster movies. The Mob's activities seem confined to stocks traded in the over-the-counter "bulletin board" and NASDAQ small-cap markets. Its chief means of livelihood is ripping off investors by driving share prices upward—and dumping them on an unsuspecting public. Among stocks identified are **Affinity Entertainment, Hollywood Production, Innovative Medical Services,** and **Novatek International.** [Source: *Business Week,* December 16, 1996.]

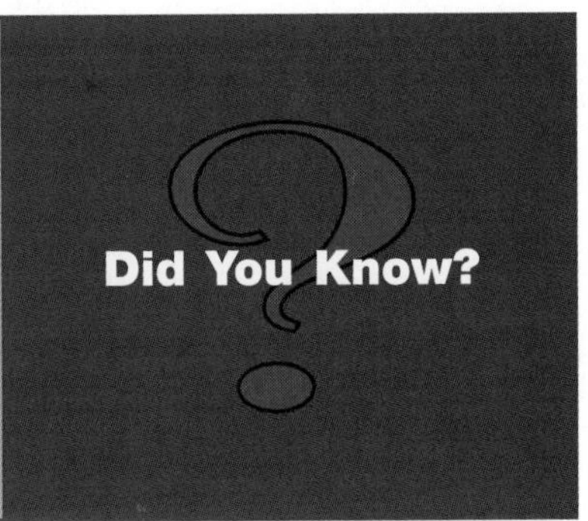
Did You Know?

Investment in Equity Securities with Significant Influence

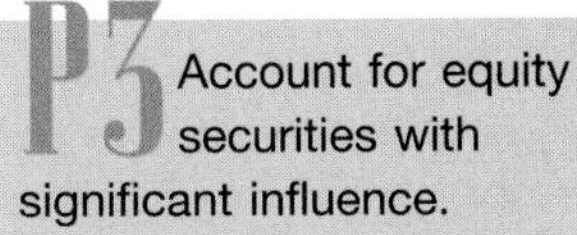
P3
Account for equity securities with significant influence.

A long-term investment in **equity securities with significant influence** is defined as an investor who is able to exert significant influence over the investee. This is usually the result of an investor buying a large block of a company's voting stock. An investor who owns 20% or more (but not more than 50%) of a company's voting stock is usually presumed to have a significant influence over the investee. Yet there are cases where the 20% test of significant influence is overruled by other, more persuasive, evidence. This evidence can either lower the 20% requirement or increase it. The **equity method** of accounting and reporting is used for long-term investments in equity securities with significant influence. We now illustrate this method.

You can influence, but NOT control me!

Illustration of an Investment in Equity Securities with Significant Influence

This section illustrates the equity method of accounting for long-term investments in equity securities with significant influence. An investor records the purchase of these securities at cost when acquired. To illustrate, Micron Company purchases 3,000 shares (30%) of JVT common stock for a total cost of $70,650 on January 1, 1998. The entry to record this purchase on Micron's books is:

---

[5] A recent study found that *other comprehensive income* items such as unrealized holding gains or losses from changes in security values are immaterial for most companies. It also showed these items are not significant in explaining prices or future cash and income flows (see D. Dhaliwal, K. R. Subramanyam, and R. Trezevant, *The Value Relevance of Comprehensive Income and Its Components, Journal of Accounting and Economics,* forthcoming).

Assets = Liabilities + Equity
+70,650
−70,650

Jan. 1	Investment in JVT Common Stock	70,650	
	Cash		70,650
	Purchased 3,000 JVT shares.		

Under the equity method, earnings of the investee (JVT) increase both the investee's net assets and the investor's (Micron) equity claims against the investee's net assets. This means when the investee closes its books and reports its earnings, the investor records its share of those earnings in its investment account. To illustrate, JVT reported net income of $20,000 for 1998. Micron's entry to record its 30% share of these earnings is:

Assets = Liabilities + Equity
+6,000 +6,000

Dec. 31	Investment in JVT Common Stock	6,000	
	Earnings from Investment in JVT		6,000
	To record 30% equity in investee's earnings of $20,000.		

The debit reflects the increase in Micron's equity in JVT. The credit means 30% of JVT's net income appears on Micron's income statement as earnings from the investment. As with all earnings, Micron closes these earnings to Income Summary.

If the investee incurs a net loss instead of a net income, the investor records its share of the loss and reduces (credits) its investment account. The investor closes this loss to Income Summary.

The receipt of cash dividends is not recorded as revenue when using the equity method. This is because the investor has already recorded its share of the earnings reported by the investee. Instead, cash dividends received from an investee convert the form of the investor's asset from a stock investment to cash. This means dividends reduce the balance of the investment account, but increase cash. To illustrate, JVT declares and pays $10,000 in cash dividends on its common stock. Micron's entry to record its 30% share of these dividends received on January 9, 1999 is:

Assets = Liabilities + Equity
+3,000
−3,000

Jan. 9	Cash	3,000	
	Investment in JVT Common Stock		3,000
	To record receipt of 30% of $10,000 dividend paid by JVT.		

The book value of an investment in equity securities when using the equity method is equal to the cost of the investment plus the investor's equity in the *undistributed* earnings of the investee. Once we record the above transactions for Micron, its investment account appears as shown in Exhibit 16.5.

Exhibit 16.5

Investment in JVT Common Stock (Ledger Account)

Date		Explanation	Debit	Credit	Balance
1998					
Jan.	1	Investment	70,650		70,650
Dec.	31	Share of earnings	6,000		76,650
1999					
Jan.	9	Share of dividend		3,000	73,650

Micron's account balance on January 9, 1999, for the investment in JVT is $73,650. This is the investment's cost *plus* Micron's equity in JVT's earnings since its purchase *less* Micron's equity in JVT's cash dividends since its purchase.

When an investment in equity securities is sold, the gain or loss is computed by comparing proceeds from the sale with the book value of the investment on the date of sale. If Micron sells its JVT stock for $80,000 on January 10, 1999, the entry to record the sale is:

Jan. 10	Cash	80,000	
	Investment in JVT Common Stock		73,650
	Gain on Sale of Investments		6,350
	Sold 3,000 shares of stock for $80,000.		

Assets = Liabilities + Equity
+80,000 +6,350
−73,650

Tinseltown Securities

Did you ever wish you could share in the profits of Hollywood films like *Independence Day, The Lost World, Titanic,* or *Speed*? Well, you can now. Both **Fox** and **Universal Studios** are selling equity shares in their upcoming movies to outside investors. **Citicorp,** which is handling these shares, forecasts a minimum annualized rate of return of 15%. But the possibility of big hits is what's drawing many investors. [Source: *Business Week,* August 11, 1997.]

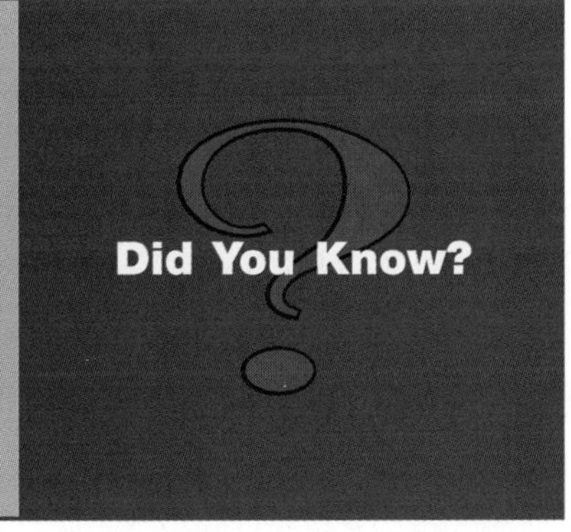

Investment in Equity Securities with Controlling Influence

C3 Describe how equity securities with controlling influence are reported.

A long-term investment in **equity securities with controlling influence** is defined as an investor who is able to exert a controlling influence over the investee. An investor who owns more than 50% of a company's voting stock has control over the investee. This investor can dominate all other shareholders in electing the corporation's board of directors and has control over the investee corporation's management.[6] There also are cases where controlling influence can extend to situations of under 50% ownership.

The equity method is used in accounting for long-term investments in equity securities with controlling influence. The investor also reports *consolidated financial statements* to the public when owning such securities. Exhibit 16.6 identifies the accounting for investments in equity securities by an investor's percent of ownership in the stock.

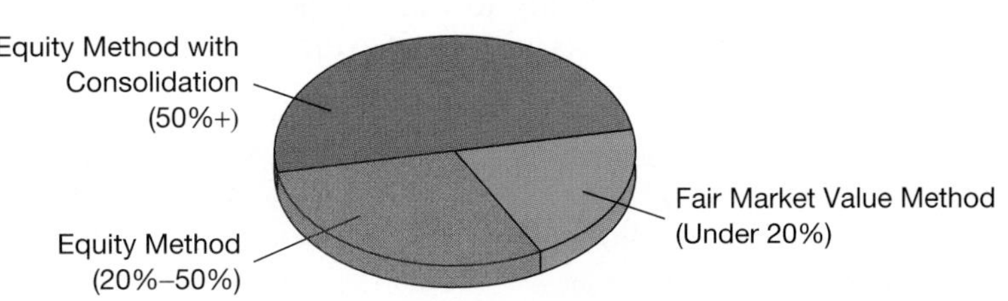

Exhibit 16.6

Accounting for Equity Investments by Percent of Ownership

Illustration of an Equity Security with Controlling Influence

This section describes how we account for long-term investments in equity securities with controlling influence. The equity method is used to account for transactions in these securities. In addition, the investor reports these securities investments with consolidated financial statements.

When an investor company owns more than 50% of the voting stock of an investee company, it has a controlling influence. The investor can elect the investee's board of directors and control its activities and resources. The controlling investor is called the **parent company** and the investee company is called the **subsidiary.** Many companies are parents with subsidiaries. Examples are (1) **McGraw-Hill,** the parent of *Business Week,* Standard and Poor's, and Compustat; (2) **The GAP,** the parent of Gap, Old Navy, and Banana Republic; and (3) **Brunswick,** the parent of Mercury Marine, Sea Ray, and U.S. Marine.

[6] Ibid., sec. C51.102. First published in *Statement of Financial Accounting Standards No. 94,* par. 13.

A company owning all the outstanding stock of a subsidiary can take over the subsidiary's assets, cancel the subsidiary's stock, and merge the subsidiary into the parent. But there often are financial, legal, and tax advantages if a business operates as a parent controlling one or more subsidiaries.

When a company operates as a parent with subsidiaries, separate accounting records are maintained by each separate entity. From a legal viewpoint, the parent and each subsidiary are separate entities with all the rights, duties, and responsibilities of individual companies. Yet the investors in the parent are indirect investors in the subsidiaries. To evaluate their investments, investors in the parent must consider the financial status and operations of the subsidiaries as well as the parent. This information is available in consolidated financial statements.

Consolidated financial statements show the financial position, results of operations, and cash flows of all companies under the parent's control, including all subsidiaries. These statements are prepared as if the company is organized as one entity. The parent uses the equity method in its accounts, but the investment account is *not* reported on the parent's financial statements. Instead, the individual assets and liabilities of the parent and its subsidiaries are combined on one balance sheet. Their revenues and expenses also are combined on one income statement and their cash flows are combined on one statement of cash flows. The detailed procedures for preparing consolidated financial statements are included in advanced courses.

Flash *back*

4. What are the three classes of long-term equity investments? Describe the criteria for each class and the method used to account for each.

Answer—p. 704

Accounting Summary for Investments in Securities

Exhibit 16.7 summarizes the accounting for investments in securities. Recall that many investment securities can be classified as either short term or long term depending on management's intent and ability to convert them in the future. Understanding the accounting for these investments enables us to draw better conclusions from financial statements in making decisions.

Exhibit 16.7

Accounting for Investments in Securities

Class of Investment Securities	Accounting Method
Short-term investment in securities:	
Held-to-maturity (debt) securities	Cost (without amortization)
Trading (debt and equity) securities	Fair market value (with market adjustment to income)
Available-for-sale (debt and equity) securities	Fair market value (with market adjustment to equity)
Long-term investment in securities:	
Held-to-maturity (debt) securities	Cost (with amortization)
Available-for-sale (debt and equity) securities	Fair market value (with market adjustment to equity)
Equity securities with significant influence	Equity method
Equity securities with controlling influence	Equity method (with consolidation)

Investments in International Operations

Many companies from small entrepreneurs to large corporations conduct business internationally. The operations of some large corporations take place in so many different countries that they're called **multinationals.** Many of us, for example, think of **Coca-Cola** and **McDonald's** as primarily U.S. companies. Yet both companies earn most of their sales from outside the U.S. Exhibit 16.8 shows the percent of sales and income earned from selected U.S. companies. Managing and accounting for companies with international operations present us with new challenges. This section describes some of these challenges and how we account for and report these activities.

Two major accounting challenges arise when companies have international operations. Both relate to transactions that occur using more than one currency. The two challenges can be described as (1) accounting for sales and purchases listed in a foreign currency and (2) preparing consolidated financial statements with international subsidiaries. For ease in this discussion, we use companies with a base of operations in the United States and with a need to prepare financial statements in U.S. dollars. This means the *reporting currency* of these companies is the U.S. dollar.

Exhibit 16.8

International Sales and Income as Percent of Total

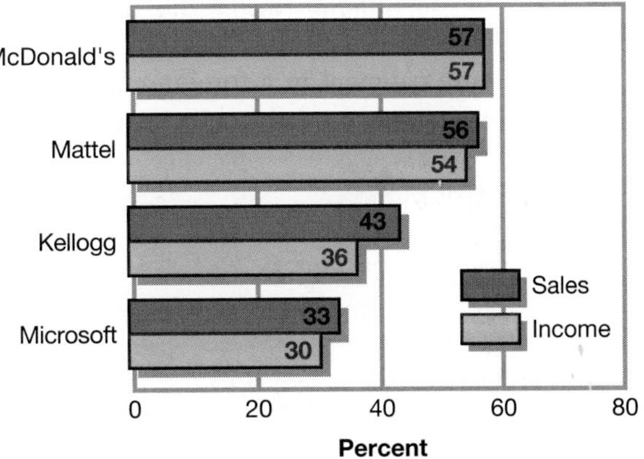

Exchange Rates between Currencies

C4 Explain foreign exchange rates between currencies.

Markets for the purchase and sale of foreign currencies exist all over the world. In these markets, U.S. dollars can be exchanged for Canadian dollars, British pounds, French francs, Japanese yen, or any other legal currencies. The price of one currency stated in terms of another currency is called a **foreign exchange rate.**

Exhibit 16.9 lists foreign exchange rates for selected currencies at January 1, 1998. We see the exchange rate for British pounds and U.S. dollars is $1.6508. This rate means one British pound can be purchased for $1.6508. On the same day, the exchange rate between German marks and U.S. dollars is $0.5562. This rate means one German mark can be purchased for $0.5562. Foreign exchange rates fluctuate due to changing economic and political conditions. These include the supply and demand for currencies and expectations about future events.

Exhibit 16.9

Foreign Exchange Rates for Selected Currencies*

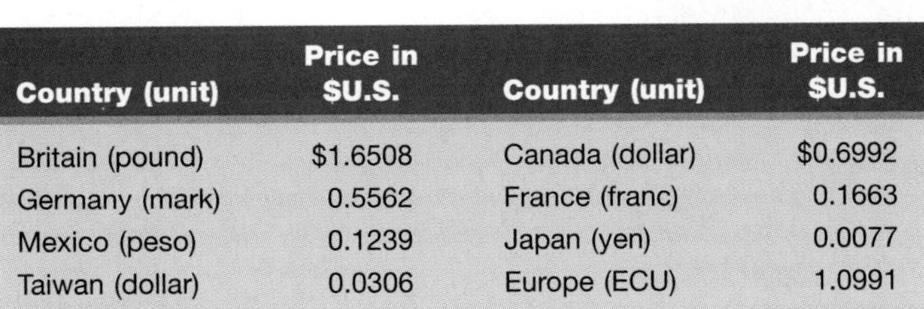

Country (unit)	Price in $U.S.	Country (unit)	Price in $U.S.
Britain (pound)	$1.6508	Canada (dollar)	$0.6992
Germany (mark)	0.5562	France (franc)	0.1663
Mexico (peso)	0.1239	Japan (yen)	0.0077
Taiwan (dollar)	0.0306	Europe (ECU)	1.0991

*Rates for January 1, 1998.

Rush to Russia

In New York, London, Frankfurt, and Tokyo, investors are swarming to buy Russian equities even in the face of rampant crime, corruption, and slow economic growth. Why? Many argue Russia remains a bargain-priced, if risky, bet on future growth. They focus on Russia not only as a way to buy into natural-resource companies for a song, but also as a play on growth. Some analysts argue resource-rich Russia is one of the cheapest emerging markets. [Source: *Business Week,* March 24, 1997.]

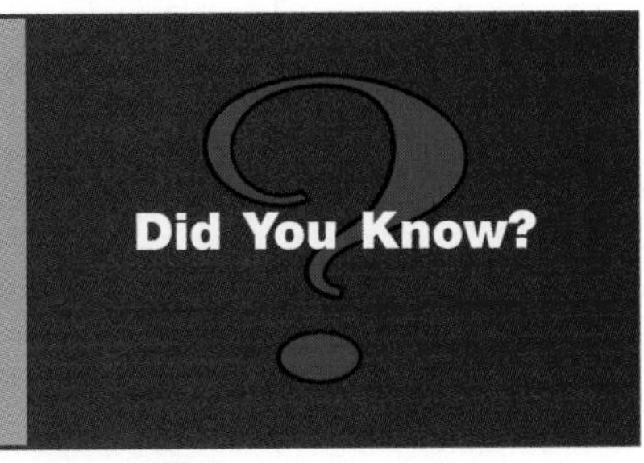

Sales and Purchases Listed in a Foreign Currency

P4 Record transactions listed in a foreign currency.

When a U.S. company makes a credit sale to an international customer, a question sometimes arises in accounting for the sale and the account receivable. If sales terms require the international customer's payment in U.S. dollars, no question arises. But if terms of the sale require payment in a foreign currency, the U.S. company must account for the sale and the account receivable in a special way.

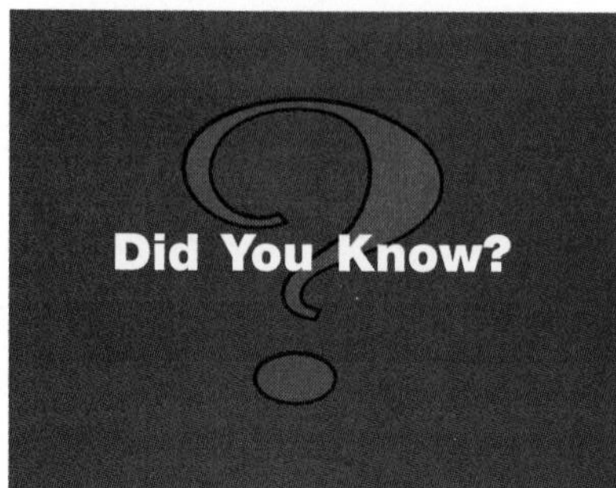

Greenback Effects
What do changes in foreign exchange rates mean? A recent decline in the price of the U.S. dollar against other currencies contributed to an 18% increase in international sales at **Caterpillar,** a 24% increase at **Upjohn,** and a 73% increase at **Parker Hannifin.** A weaker dollar allows U.S. companies to increase international sales without hiking prices or cutting costs and puts them on a stronger competitive footing abroad. At home, they can raise prices without fear that foreign rivals will undercut them.
[Source: *Business Week,* May 1, 1995.]

Consider the case of the U.S.-based manufacturer, **Boston Company,** who makes credit sales to **London Outfitters,** a British retail company. A sale occurred on December 12, 1998, for a price of £10,000 payment due on February 10, 1999. Boston Company keeps its accounting records in U.S. dollars. To record the sale, Boston Company must translate the sales price from pounds to dollars. This is done using the exchange rate on the date of the sale. Assuming the exchange rate on December 12, 1998, is $1.80, Boston records this sale as:

Assets = Liabilities + Equity
+18,000 +18,000

Dec. 12	Accounts Receivable—London Outfitters	18,000	
	Sales (£10,000 × $1.80)		18,000
	To record a sale at £10,000, when the exchange rate equals $1.80.		

Boston Company prepares its annual financial statements on December 31, 1998. On that date, the current exchange rate increases to $1.84. This means the current dollar value of Boston Company's receivable is $18,400 (10,000 × $1.84). This amount is $400 greater than the amount recorded on December 12. Accounting principles require a receivable to be reported in the balance sheet at its current dollar value. Boston Company must make the following entry to record the increase in the dollar value of this receivable at year-end:

Assets = Liabilities + Equity
+400 +400

Dec. 31	Accounts Receivable–London Outfitters	400	
	Foreign Exchange Gain or Loss		400
	To record the increased value of the British pound on the receivable.		

Boston Company receives London Outfitters' payment of £10,000 on February 10, 1999. Boston Company immediately exchanges the pounds for U.S. dollars. On this date, the exchange rate for pounds is $1.78. This means Boston Company receives only $17,800 (£10,000 × $1.78). It records the cash receipt and the loss associated with the decline in the exchange rate as follows:

Assets = Liabilities + Equity
+17,800 −600
−18,400

Feb. 10	Cash	17,800	
	Foreign Exchange Gain or Loss	600	
	Accounts Receivable—London Outfitters ..		18,400
	Received foreign currency payment of an account and converted it into dollars.		

Gains and losses from foreign exchange transactions are accumulated in the Foreign Exchange Gain or Loss account. After year-end adjustments, the balance in the Foreign Exchange Gain or Loss account is reported on the income statement and closed to the Income Summary account.[7]

Accounting for credit purchases from an international supplier is similar to the case of a credit sale to an international customer. In particular, if the U.S. company is required to make payment in a foreign currency, the account payable must be translated into dollars before the U.S. company can record it. If the exchange rate is different when preparing financial statements and when paying for the purchase, the U.S. company must recognize an exchange gain or loss at those dates.

Home Builder

You are a U.S. home builder that regularly purchases lumber from mills in both the U.S. and Canada. Lumber prices have been similar across both countries. But today the price of the Canadian dollar in terms of the U.S. dollar jumped from US$0.70 to US$0.80. Are you now more or less likely to buy lumber from Canadian or U.S. mills?

Answer—p. 704

Consolidated Statements with International Subsidiaries

A second challenge in accounting for international operations involves preparing consolidated financial statements when the parent company has one or more international subsidiaries. Consider the U.S.-based company, Classic Winery, which owns a controlling interest in a French subsidiary. The reporting currency of the U.S. parent is the dollar. The French subsidiary maintains its financial records in francs. Before preparing consolidated statements, the parent must translate financial statements of the French company into U.S. dollars. After this translation is complete, we prepare consolidated statements the same as with domestic subsidiaries.[8]

Procedures for translating an international subsidiary's account balances depend on the nature of the subsidiary's operations. The process requires the parent company to select appropriate foreign exchange rates and to apply those rates to the account balances of the foreign subsidiary.

Flash back

5. If a U.S. company makes a credit sale of merchandise to a French customer and the sales terms require payment in francs:

a. The U.S. company incurs an exchange loss if the exchange rate between francs and dollars increases from $0.199 at the date of sale to $0.189 at the date the account is settled.

b. The French company may eventually need to record an exchange gain or loss.

c. The U.S. company may be required to record an exchange gain or loss on the date of the sale.

Answer—p. 704

[7] Ibid., sec. F60.122. First published as FASB, *Statement of Financial Accounting Standards No. 52,* par. 15.

[8] The problem is more challenging when the accounts of the French subsidiary are maintained in accordance with the French version of GAAP. The French statements then must be converted to U.S. GAAP before consolidation.

USING THE INFORMATION — Components of Return on Total Assets

A1 Compute and analyze the components of return on total assets.

Chapter 1 described a company's **return on total assets** (or simply *return on assets*) and explained its importance in assessing financial performance. The return on total assets can be separated into two components to help us in analysis of financial statements. The two components are: net profit margin and total asset turnover. Net profit margin, or simply profit margin, was explained in Chapter 4 and total asset turnover in Chapter 11. Exhibit 16.10 shows how these two components determine return on total assets.

Exhibit 16.10

Components of Return on Total Assets

Return on Total Assets = Profit Margin × Total Asset Turnover

$$\frac{\textbf{Net Income}}{\textbf{Average Total Assets}} = \frac{\textbf{Net Income}}{\textbf{Net Sales}} \times \frac{\textbf{Net Sales}}{\textbf{Average Total Assets}}$$

Net profit margin (net income ÷ net sales) is the first component and reflects the percent of net income in each dollar of net sales. Total asset turnover (net sales ÷ average total assets) is the second component and reflects a company's ability to produce net sales from total assets. All companies desire a high return on total assets. By looking at these two components, we can often discover strengths and weaknesses not revealed by return on total assets. This improves our ability to assess future performance and company strategy.

To illustrate, we look at return on total assets and its components for **Reebok** and **NIKE.** Reebok's return on total assets and its components are shown in Exhibit 16.11.

Exhibit 16.11

Reebok's Components of Return on Total Assets

Year	Return on Total Assets	=	Profit Margin	×	Total Asset Turnover
1996	8.08%*	=	3.99%	×	2.02
1995	9.98%	=	4.73%	×	2.11
1994	16.74%*	=	7.76%	×	2.16

*Minor rounding differences.

At least three findings for Reebok emerge. First, Reebok's return on total assets declined from 1994 through 1996. Second, total asset turnover also declined over this period, but not significantly. And third, Reebok's net profit margin sharply fell between 1994 and 1996. These components show the dual role of net profit margin and total asset turnover for Reebok. More important, it shows the cause of Reebok's decline is not total asset turnover, but net profit margin. Reebok's costs and expenses have increased as a percent of sales, and cost management is necessary.

Generally, if a company is to maintain its return on total assets, then a decline in either profit margin or total asset turnover must be met with an increase in the other. If not, return on assets will decline. Companies look at these components in planning future strategies. A component analysis can also reveal where a company is weak and where changes are needed.

We especially study these two components when comparing competitors. If asset turnover is lower than the industry norm, for instance, a company should focus on getting asset turnover at least up to the norm. The same applies to profit margin. Exhibit 16.12 shows NIKE's components for its fiscal year ending May 31, 1997.

Exhibit 16.12

NIKE's Components of Return on Total Assets

Fiscal Year	Return on Total Assets	=	Profit Margin	×	Total Asset Turnover
1997	17.09%*	=	8.66%	×	1.97

*Minor rounding difference.

NIKE's most recent return on total assets is much higher than Reebok's. But the components show Reebok is slightly better than NIKE on total asset turnover. This highlights Reebok's sharp decline in net profit margin in recent years. One potential cause is Reebok's increased Cost of Goods Sold and Selling, General and Administrative Expenses as a percent of net sales (see its income statement in Appendix A). Reebok should focus on reducing these expenditures as a percent of sales.[9]

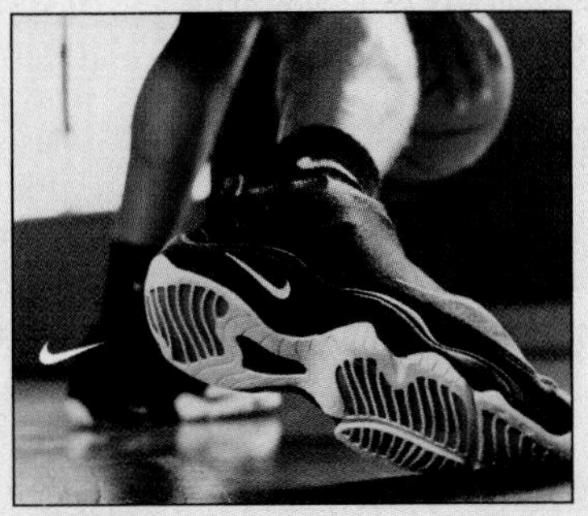

Retailer

You are an entrepreneur and owner of a retail sporting goods store. The store's recent year's performance reveals (industry norms in parentheses): return on total assets = 11% (11.2%); profit margin = 4.4% (3.5%); and total asset turnover = 2.5 (3.2). What does your analysis of these figures suggest?

Answer—p. 704

Summary

C1 Distinguish long-term investments from short-term investments. Short-term investments in securities are current assets that meet two criteria. First, they are expected to be converted into cash within one year or the current operating cycle of the business, whichever is longer. Second, they are readily convertible to cash, or *marketable.* All other investments in securities are long-term investments. Long-term investments also include assets not used in operations and those held for a special purpose, such as land for expansion.

C2 Identify classes of securities in long-term investments. Long-term investments in securities are classified into one of four groups: (1) debt securities held-to-maturity, (2) debt and equity securities available-for-sale, (3) equity securities where an investor has a significant influence over the investee, and (4) equity securities where an investor has a controlling influence over the investee.

C3 Describe how equity securities with controlling influence are reported. If an investor owns more than 50% of another company's voting stock and controls the investee, the investor's financial reports are prepared on a consolidated basis. These reports are prepared as if the company is organized as one entity. The individual assets and liabilities of the parent and its subsidiaries are combined on one balance sheet. Similarly, their revenues and expenses are combined on one income statement and their cash flows are combined on one statement of cash flows.

C4 Explain foreign exchange rates between currencies. A foreign exchange rate is the price of one currency stated in terms of another. A company with transactions in a foreign currency when the exchange rate changes between the time of the transactions and its settlement will experience an exchange gain or loss.

A1 Compute and analyze the components of return on total assets. Return on total assets is made up of two components that we can use to assess a company's ability in using its assets: net profit margin and total asset turnover. A decline in one component must be met with an increase in another if profits are to be maintained. The components are also helpful in assessing company performance compared to its competitors. For instance, if one component is worse than the industry norm, then a company should focus on getting its performance on this component at least up to the industry norm.

P1 Account for held-to-maturity securities. Debt securities held-to-maturity are reported at cost when purchased. Interest revenue is recorded as it accrues. The cost of held-to-maturity securities is adjusted for amortization of any difference between cost and maturity value.

P2 Account for available-for-sale securities. Debt and equity securities available-for-sale are recorded at cost when purchased. Available-for-sale securities are reported at their fair market values with unrealized holding gains or losses shown in the stockholders' equity section of the balance sheet. Gains and losses realized on the sale of these investments are reported in the income statement.

P3 Account for equity securities with significant influence. The equity method is used when an investor has a significant influence over an investee. This usually exists when an in-

[9] Another base of comparison is the average figures for manufacturers of athletic footwear and apparel. Industry averages are available through publications such as Dun & Bradstreet's *Industry Norms and Key Ratios.*

vestor owns 20% or more of the investee's voting stock, but not more than 50%. The equity method means an investor records its share of the investee's earnings with a debit to the investment account and a credit to a revenue account. Dividends received satisfy the investor's equity claims and reduce the investment account balance.

P4 **Record transactions listed in a foreign currency.** When a company makes a credit sale to a foreign customer and sales terms call for payment in a foreign currency, the company must translate the foreign currency into dollars to record the receivable. If the exchange rate changes before payment is received, foreign exchange gains or losses are recognized in the year they occur. The same treatment is used when a company makes a credit purchase from a foreign supplier and is required to make payment in a foreign currency. Also, a company with a foreign subsidiary that maintains its accounts in a foreign currency must translate these account balances into dollars before they are consolidated with the parent's accounts.

Guidance Answers to **You Make the Call**

Money Manager

If you have investments in fixed-rate bonds and notes when interest rates fall, then the value of your investments increases. This is because the bonds and notes you hold continue to pay the same (high) rate while the market is demanding a new lower interest rate. Your strategy is to continue holding your investments in bonds and notes, and, potentially, to increase these holdings through additional purchases.

Home Builder

You are now less likely to buy Canadian lumber. This is because it takes more U.S. money to buy a Canadian dollar (and lumber). For instance, the purchase of lumber from a Canadian mill with a $1,000 (Canadian dollars) price cost the U.S. builder $700 (U.S. dollars, computed as C$1,000 × US$0.70) before the rate change and $800 (US dollars, computed as C$1,000 × US$0.80) after the rate change.

Retailer

Your analysis of return on assets shows your store to be competitive. In particular, your store's return on assets is 11%, which is similar to the industry norm of 11.2%. However, disaggregation of return on assets reveals additional information. Your store's profit margin of 4.4% is much higher than the norm of 3.5%. But your total asset turnover of 2.5 is much lower than the norm of 3.2. These results suggest you are less efficient in using assets as compared with competitors. You need to focus on increasing sales or reducing your assets. You might wish to consider reducing prices to increase sales. You need to make sure such a strategy doesn't reduce your return on total assets. For instance, you could reduce your profit margin to 4% to increase sales. If total asset turnover increases to more than 2.75 when profit margin is lowered to 4%, then your overall return on total assets is improved.

Guidance Answers to Flash *backs*

1. Long-term investments include funds earmarked for a special purpose, bonds and stocks that do not meet the requirements of a current asset, and other assets that are not used in the regular operations of the business.
2. A stock investment is classified as a long-term investment if it is not marketable or, if marketable, it is not held as an available source of cash to meet the needs of current operations.
3. Debt securities held-to-maturity and debt securities available-for-sale are recorded at cost. Also, interest on both is accrued as earned. But only securities held-to-maturity require amortization of the difference between cost and maturity value. In addition, only securities available-for-sale require an end-of-period adjustment to fair market value.
4. Long-term equity investments are placed in one of three categories and accounted for as follows.
   a. **Available-for-Sale** (noninfluential, less than 20% of outstanding stock)—Fair Market Value.
   b. **Significant Influence** (20% to 50% of outstanding stock)—Equity Method.
   c. **Controlling Influence** (holding more than 50% of outstanding stock)—Consolidation.
5. *a*

Demonstration Problem

The following transactions relate to Brown Company's long-term investment activities during 1999 and 2000. Brown did not own any long-term investments prior to 1999. Show (a) the appropriate journal entries and (b) the portions of each year's balance sheet and income statement that describe these transactions for both 1999 and 2000.

1999

Sept. 9	Purchased 1,000 shares of Packard, Inc., common stock for $80,000 cash. These shares represent 30% of Packard's outstanding shares.
Oct. 2	Purchased 2,000 shares of AT&T common stock for $60,000 cash. These shares represent less than a 1% ownership in AT&T.
17	Purchased as a long-term investment 1,000 shares of Apple Computer common stock for $40,000 cash. These shares are less than 1% of Apple's outstanding shares.
Nov. 1	Received $5,000 cash dividend from Packard.
30	Received $3,000 cash dividend from AT&T.

Dec. 15	Received $1,400 cash dividend from Apple.
31	Packard's 1999 net income is $70,000.
31	Market values for the investments in marketable equity securities are Packard, $84,000; AT&T, $48,000; and Apple Computer, $45,000.
31	After closing the accounts, selected account balances on Brown Company's books are: Common Stock, $500,000; Retained Earnings, $350,000.

2000

Jan. 1	Packard, Inc., was taken over by other investors, and Brown sold its shares for $108,000.
May 30	Received $3,100 cash dividend from AT&T.
June 15	Received $1,600 cash dividend from Apple.
Aug. 17	Sold the AT&T stock for $52,000 cash.
19	Purchased 2,000 shares of Coca-Cola common stock for $50,000 as a long-term investment. The stock represents less than a 5% ownership in Coca-Cola.
Dec. 15	Received $1,800 cash dividend from Apple.
31	Market values of the investments in marketable equity securities are Apple, $39,000 and Coca-Cola, $48,000.
31	After closing the accounts, selected account balances on Brown Company's books are: Common Stock, $500,000; Retained Earnings, $410,000.

Planning the Solution

- Account for the investment in Packard under the equity method.
- Account for the investments in AT&T, Apple, and Coca-Cola as long-term investments in securities available-for-sale.
- Prepare the information for the two balance sheets by including the appropriate asset and stockholders' equity accounts.

Solution to Demonstration Problem

(a) Journal entries for 1999:

Date	Account	Debit	Credit
Sept. 9	Investment in Packard Common Stock	80,000	
	Cash		80,000
	Acquired 1,000 shares, representing a 30% equity in Packard, Inc.		
Oct. 2	Investment in AT&T Common Stock	60,000	
	Cash		60,000
	Acquired 2,000 shares as a long-term investment in securities available for sale.		
Oct. 17	Investment in Apple Common Stock	40,000	
	Cash		40,000
	Acquired 1,000 shares as a long-term investment in securities available for sale.		
Nov. 1	Cash	5,000	
	Investment in Packard Common Stock		5,000
	Received dividend from Packard, Inc.		
Nov. 30	Cash	3,000	
	Dividends Earned		3,000
	Received dividend from AT&T.		
Dec. 15	Cash	1,400	
	Dividends Earned		1,400
	Received dividend from Apple.		
Dec. 31	Investment in Packard Common Stock	21,000	
	Earnings from Investment in Packard		21,000
	To record our 30% share of Packard's annual earnings of $70,000.		

		Debit	Credit
Dec. 31	Unrealized Holding Gain or Loss	7,000	
	Long-Term Investments, Fair Value Adjustment*		7,000
	To record change in fair value of securities available-for-sale.		

*Fair value adjustment computations:

	Cost	Fair (Market) Value
AT&T	$ 60,000	$48,000
Apple	40,000	45,000
Total	$100,000	$93,000

Required credit balance of Long-Term Investments, Fair Value Adjustment account ($100,000 − $93,000)	$7,000
Existing balance	-0-
Necessary credit adjustment	$7,000

(b) December 31, 1999, balance sheet items:

Assets		
Long-term investments:		
Securities available-for-sale (at fair value)	$93,000	
Investment in Packard, Inc.	96,000	
Total		$189,000
Stockholders' Equity		
Common stock		$500,000
Retained earnings		350,000
Unrealized holding gain (loss)		(7,000)

Income statement items for the year ended December 31, 1999:

Dividends earned	$ 4,400
Earnings from equity method investment	21,000

(a) Journal entries for 2000:

		Debit	Credit
Jan. 1	Cash	108,000	
	Investment in Packard Common Stock		96,000
	Gain on Sale of Investments		12,000
	Sold 1,000 shares for cash.		
May 30	Cash	3,100	
	Dividends Earned		3,100
	Received dividend from AT&T.		
June 15	Cash	1,600	
	Dividends Earned		1,600
	Received dividend from Apple.		
Aug. 17	Cash	52,000	
	Loss on Sale of Investments	8,000	
	Investment in AT&T Common Stock		60,000
	Sold 2,000 shares for cash.		
Aug. 19	Investment in Coca-Cola Common Stock	50,000	
	Cash		50,000
	Acquired 2,000 shares as a long-term investment in securities available for sale.		
Dec. 15	Cash	1,800	
	Dividends Earned		1,800
	Received dividend from Apple.		

Dec. 31	Long-Term Investments, Fair Value Adjustment* .	4,000	
	Unrealized Holding Gain or Loss		4,000
	To record change in fair value of securities available-for-sale.		

*Fair value adjustment computations:

	Cost	Fair (Market) Value
Apple	$40,000	$39,000
Coca-Cola ..	50,000	48,000
Total	$90,000	$87,000

Required credit balance of Long-Term Investments, Fair Value Adjustment account ($90,000 − $87,000)	$3,000
Existing credit balance	7,000
Necessary debit adjustment	$4,000

(b) December 31, 2000, balance sheet items:

Assets	
Long-term investments:	
Securities available-for-sale (fair value)	$ 87,000
Stockholders' Equity	
Common stock	$500,000
Retained earnings	410,000
Unrealized holding gain (loss)	(3,000)

Income statement items for the year ended December 31, 2000:

Dividends earned	$ 6,500
Gain on sale of investments	12,000
Loss on sale of investments	(8,000)

Glossary

Available-for-sale debt securities long-term investments in debt securities that are held with the intent of selling them in the future. (p. 693).

Available-for-sale equity securities long-term investments in noninfluential equity securities. (p. 693).

Consolidated financial statements financial statements that show the results of all operations under the parent's control, including those of any subsidiaries; assets and liabilities of all affiliated companies are combined on a single balance sheet, revenues and expenses are combined on a single income statement, and cash flows are combined on a single statement of cash flows. (p. 698).

Equity method an accounting method used for long-term investments when the investor has significant influence over the investee. (p. 695).

Equity securities with controlling influence the definition for a long-term investment when the investor is able to exert controlling influence over the investee; investors owning 50% or more of a company's voting stock are presumed to exert controlling influence over the investee. (p. 697).

Equity securities with significant influence the definition for a long-term investment when the investor is able to exert significant influence over the investee; usually investors owning 20% or more of a company's voting stock are presumed to exert significant influence over the investee. (p. 695).

Foreign exchange rate the price of one currency stated in terms of another currency. (p. 699).

Held-to-maturity securities debt securities that the company has the intent and ability to hold until they mature. (p. 691).

Long-term investments investments in stocks and bonds that are not marketable or, if marketable, are not intended to be converted into cash in the short term; also funds earmarked for a special purpose, such as bond sinking funds, and land or other assets not used in the company's operations. (p. 690).

Multinational a company that operates in a large number of different countries. (p. 698).

Parent company a corporation that owns a controlling interest in another corporation (more than 50% of the voting stock is required). (p. 697).

Return on total assets a measure of a company's operating efficiency, computed by expressing net income as a percent of average total assets. (p. 703).

Subsidiary a corporation that is controlled by another corporation (the parent) because the parent owns more than 50% of the subsidiary's voting stock. (p. 697).

Questions

1. Under what conditions should investments be classified as current assets? As long-term assets?
2. Identify the classes for long-term investments.
3. On a balance sheet, what valuation must be reported for long-term debt securities classified as available-for-sale?
4. If a company purchases long-term investments in available-for-sale debt securities and their fair (market) values are below cost at the balance sheet date, what entry is required to recognize the amount of the unrealized loss?
5. For long-term investments in available-for-sale securities, how are unrealized holding gains and losses reported?
6. In accounting for investments in common stock, when should the equity method be used?
7. Under what circumstances would a company prepare consolidated financial statements?
8. Under what circumstances are long-term investments in debt securities reported at their original cost adjusted for amortization of any difference between cost and maturity value?
9. What are two major challenges in accounting for international operations?
10. If a U.S. company makes a credit sale to a foreign customer and the customer is required to make payment in U.S. dollars, can the U.S. company have an exchange gain or loss as a result of the sale?
11. A U.S. company makes a credit sale to a foreign customer, and the customer is required to make payment in a foreign currency. The foreign exchange rate is $1.40 on the date of the sale and is $1.30 on the date the customer pays the receivable. Will the U.S. company record an exchange gain or an exchange loss?
12. **NIKE** is a multinational company. Refer to the financial statements of NIKE in Appendix A. What percent of NIKE's total assets are non–United States assets as of May 31, 1997?
13. Refer to the balance sheet of **Reebok** in Appendix A. How can you tell that Reebok uses the consolidated method of accounting?

14. Refer to the financial statements of **America Online** in Appendix A. Compute the company's return on total assets for the year ended June 30, 1996.

15. In the chapter's opening article, how does Sara Brennan employ fundamental analysis of companies she invests in or makes recommendations on?

Quick Study

QS 16-1
Short- and long-term investments
C1, C2, C3

Complete the following descriptions by filling in the blanks.

1. Trading securities are classified as _____ assets.
2. Equity securities giving an investor significant influence are accounted for using the _____ _____.
3. Available-for-sale debt securities are reported on the balance sheet at _____ _____ _____.
4. Accrual of interest on bonds held as investments will require a credit to _____ _____.
5. The controlling investor is called the _____ _____ and the investee company is called the _____.

QS 16-2
Distinguishing short- and long-term investments
C1

Which of the following are true of long-term investments?

a. They are held as an investment of cash available for current operations.
b. They may include debt securities held-to-maturity.
c. They may include bonds and stocks that are not intended to serve as a ready source of cash.
d. They may include funds earmarked for a special purpose, such as bond sinking funds.
e. They may include investments in trading securities.
f. They are always easily sold and therefore qualify as being marketable.
g. They may include debt and equity securities available-for-sale.

QS 16-3
Debt securities
P1

On February 1, 2000, Tom LeJeune purchased 6% bonds issued by Aberdeen Utilities at a cost of $30,000, which equals their par value. The bonds pay interest semiannually on July 31 and January 31. Prepare the entries to record the July 31 receipt of interest and the December 31 year-end accrual.

QS 16-4
Equity securities
P2

On May 20, 1999, Castle Co. paid $750,000 to acquire 25,000 (10%) of S&P Corp.'s outstanding common shares as a long-term investment. On August 5, 2001, Castle sold half of the shares for $475,000. What method should be used to account for this stock investment? Prepare entries to record the acquisition of the stock and the stock sale.

QS 16-5
Equity method
P3

Assume the same facts as in QS 16-4, except assume that the stock acquired represents 40% of S&P Corp.'s outstanding stock. Also assume that S&P Corp. paid a $125,000 dividend on November 1, 1999, and reported a net income of $550,000 for 1999. Prepare the entry to record the receipt of the dividend and the December 31, 1999 year-end adjustment of the investment account.

QS 16-6
Fair value adjustment for securities
P2

During this year, Rose Consulting Group acquired long-term investment securities at a cost of $35,000. These securities were classified as available-for-sale. At December 31 year-end, these securities had a fair market value of $29,000. The consulting group owns no other long-term investments.

a. Prepare the necessary year-end adjustment.

b. Explain how each account used in requirement *a* would affect or be reported in the financial statements.

QS 16-7
Foreign currency transactions
P4

On March 1, 1999, a U.S. company made a sale with credit terms requiring payment in 30 days from a German company, Bittner Corp., in German marks. The amount of the sale was 20,000 marks. Assuming the exchange rate between German marks and U.S. dollars is $0.6811 on March 1 and $0.6985 on March 31, prepare the entries to record the sale on March 1 and the cash receipt on March 31.

QS 16-8
Foreign currency transactions
P4

A U.S. company sells a British company a product with the transaction listed in British pounds. On the date of the sale, the transaction of $16,000 was billed as 10,000 pounds, reflecting an exchange rate of 1.60 (that is, $1.60 per pound). Show the entry to record the sale and also the receipt of the payment when the exchange rate has fallen to 1.50.

QS 16-9
Return on total assets
A1

How is the return on total assets computed? What does this ratio evaluate?

QS 16-10
Component return on total assets
A1

State the formula to separate the return on total assets into its components. Explain how components of the return on total assets are useful to users of financial statements.

Exercises

Exercise 16-1
Transactions in short- and long-term investments
C1, P1, P2

Prepare journal entries to record the following transactions involving the short- and long-term investments of Morton Financial Corp., all of which occurred during 1999. Use an account titled "Short-Term Investments" for any transactions that you determine are short term.

a. On February 15, paid $150,000 to purchase American General's 90-day short-term notes at par, which are dated February 15 and pay 10% interest.

b. On March 22, bought 700 shares of Royal Industries common stock at 25½ plus a $250 brokerage fee.

c. On May 16, received a check from American General in payment of the principal and 90 days' interest on the notes purchased in transaction *a.*

d. On July 30, paid $50,000 to purchase OMB Electronics' 8% notes at par, dated July 30, 1999, and maturing on January 30, 2000.

e. On September 1, received a $0.50 per share cash dividend on the Royal Industries common stock purchased in transaction *b.*

f. On October 8, sold 350 shares of Royal Industries common stock for $32 per share, less a $175 brokerage fee.

g. On October 30, received a check from OMB Electronics for three months' interest on the notes purchased in transaction *d.*

Exercise 16-2
Recording fair values of long-term investments
P2

On December 31, 1999, Style, Inc., held the following long-term available-for-sale securities:

	Cost	Fair Value
Nintendo Co. common stock	$68,900	$75,300
Atlantic Richfield Co. bonds payable ..	24,500	22,800
Kellogg Co. notes payable	50,000	47,200
McDonald's Corp. common stock	91,400	86,600

Style, Inc., had no long-term securities investments prior to 1999. Prepare the December 31 year-end adjusting entry to record the change in fair value of these investments.

Exercise 16-3
Adjusting long-term securities accounts to reflect fair value
P2

Columbian Company's annual accounting period ends on December 31. The total cost and fair (market) value of the company's long-term investments in available-for-sale securities are as follows:

	Cost	Fair Value
Long-term investments in available-for-sale securities:		
On December 31, 1999	$79,483	$72,556
On December 31, 2000	85,120	90,271

Prepare Columbian's December 31, 2000, adjusting entry to record the fair values of these investments.

Exercise 16-4
Classifying investments in securities; recording fair values
P2

During 1999, GeoMass Company's investments in securities included five items. These securities, with their December 31, 1999, market values, are as follows:

a. Weller Company bonds: $418,500 cost; $455,000 market value. GeoMass intends and is able to hold these bonds until they mature in 2004.

b. Baybridge common stock: 29,500 shares; $332,450 cost; $361,375 market value. GeoMass owns 32% of Baybridge's voting stock and has a significant influence over Baybridge.

c. Carrollton common stock: 12,000 shares; $169,750 cost; $183,000 market value. The goal of this investment, which amounts to 3% of Carrollton's outstanding shares, is to earn dividends over the next few years.

d. Zetech common stock: 3,500 shares; $95,300 cost; $93,625 market value. The goal of this investment is an expected increase in market value of the stock over the next three to five years. Zetech has 30,000 common shares outstanding.

e. Flavius common stock: 16,300 shares; $102,860 cost; $109,210 market value. This stock is marketable and is held as an investment of cash available for operations.

State whether each of these investments should be classified as a current asset or as a long-term investment. For each of the long-term items, indicate in which of the four types of long-term investment classifications the item should be classified. Prepare a journal entry dated December 31, 1999, to record the fair value of the long-term investments in available-for-sale securities. Assume that GeoMass had no long-term investments prior to 1999.

Exercise 16-5
Fair value adjustments for available-for-sale securities
P2

Vallejo Services began operations in 1999 and regularly makes long-term investments in available-for-sale securities. The total cost and fair value of these investments for its most recent 4 years are:

	Cost	Market Value
On December 31, 1999	$374,000	$362,560
On December 31, 2000	426,900	453,200
On December 31, 2001	580,700	686,450
On December 31, 2002	875,500	778,800

Prepare journal entries to record the fair value of Vallejo's investments at the end of each year.

Exercise 16-6
Stock investment transactions; equity method
P3

Prepare journal entries to record the following events on the books of Kedgewick Company:

1999

Jan. 2 Purchased 30,000 shares of Lintex Co. common stock for $204,000 plus a broker's fee of $3,480. Lintex has 90,000 shares of common stock outstanding and admits its policies will be significantly influenced by Kedgewick.

Sept. 1 Lintex declared and paid a cash dividend of $3.10 per share.

Dec. 31 Lintex announced that net income for the year is $624,900.

2000

June 1 Lintex declared and paid a cash dividend of $3.60 per share.

Dec. 31 Lintex announced that net income for the year is $699,750.

Dec. 31 Kedgewick sold 10,000 shares of Lintex for $162,500.

Exercise 16-7
Receivables in a foreign currency
P4

On May 8, 1999, Jefferson Company (a U.S. company) made a credit sale to Devereaux (a French company). The terms of the sale required Devereaux to pay 800,000 francs on February 10, 2000. Jefferson prepares quarterly financial statements on March 31, June 30, September 30, and December 31. The foreign exchange rates for francs during the time the receivable is outstanding are:

May 8, 1999	$0.1984
June 30, 1999	0.2013
September 30, 1999	0.2029
December 31, 1999	0.1996
February 10, 1999	0.2047

Compute the foreign exchange gain or loss that Jefferson should report on each of its quarterly income statements for the last three quarters of 1999 and the first quarter of 2000. Also compute the amount reported on Jefferson's balance sheets at the end of each of its last three quarters of 1999.

Exercise 16-8
Foreign currency transactions
P4

Red Rover of New York sells its products to customers in the United States and in Great Britain. On December 16, 1999, Red Rover sold merchandise on credit to Bronson Ltd. of London, England, at a price of 17,000 pounds. The exchange rate on that day for 1 pound was $1.5238. On December 31, 1999, when Red Rover prepared its financial statements, the exchange rate was 1 pound for $1.4990. Bronson paid its bill in full on January 15, 2000, at which time the exchange rate was 1 pound for $1.5156. Red Rover immediately exchanged the 17,000 pounds for U.S. dollars. Prepare journal entries on December 16, December 31, and January 15 to account for the sale and account receivable on Red Rover's books.

Exercise 16-9
Return on total assets
A1

The following information is available from the financial statements of Rawhide Industries:

	1999	2000	2001
Total assets, December 31	$190,000	$320,000	$750,000
Net income	28,200	36,400	58,300

Compute Rawhide's return on total assets for 2000 and 2001. (Round answers to one decimal place.) Comment on the company's efficiency in using its assets in 2000 and 2001.

Problems

Problem 16-1
Entries and fair value adjustments for long-term investments

Franklin Security, Inc., has large idle cash balances that it invests in available-for-sale long-term securities. Following is a series of events and other facts relevant to the long-term investment activity of the company:

1999
Jan. 20 Purchased 900 shares of Johnson & Johnson at 18¾ plus a $590 commission.
Feb. 9 Purchased 2,200 shares of Sony at 46⅞ plus a $2,578 commission.
June 12 Purchased 500 shares of Mattel at 55½ plus an $832 commission.
Dec. 31 Per-share market values for stocks in the portfolio are: Johnson & Johnson, 20⅜; Mattel, 57¼; Sony, 39.

2000
Apr. 15 Sold 900 shares of Johnson & Johnson at 21¾ less a $685 commission.
July 5 Sold 500 shares of Mattel at 49⅛ less a $491 commission.
July 22 Purchased 1,600 shares of Sara Lee at 36¼ plus a $1,740 commission.
Aug. 19 Purchased 1,800 shares of Eastman Kodak at 28 plus a $1,260 commission.
Dec. 31 Per-share market values for stocks in the portfolio are: Kodak, 31¾; Sara Lee, 30; Sony, 36½.

2001
Feb. 27 Purchased 3,400 shares of Microsoft at 23⅝ plus a $1,606 commission.
June 21 Sold 2,200 shares of Sony at 40 less a $2,640 commission.
June 30 Purchased 1,200 shares of Black & Decker at 47½ plus a $1,995 commission.
Aug 3 Sold 1,600 shares of Sara Lee at 31¼ less a $1,750 commission.
Nov. 1 Sold 1,800 shares of Eastman Kodak at 42¾ less a $2,309 commission.

Dec. 31 Per-share market values for stocks in the portfolio are: Black & Decker, 56½; Microsoft, 28.

Required

Check Figure 12/31/2001 Long-Term Investments, Fair Value Adjustment, $53,727 Dr.

1. Prepare journal entries to record these events and any year-end adjustments needed to record the fair values of the long-term investments.
2. Prepare a schedule that shows the total cost, total fair value adjustment, and total fair value of the investments at the end of each year.
3. For each year, prepare a schedule that shows the realized gains and losses included in earnings and the total unrealized gains or losses at the end of each year.

Problem 16-2
Accounting for stock investments
P3 

Hammerman Steel Works is organized on January 4, 1999. The following investment transactions and events subsequently occurred:

1999

Jan. 5 Hammerman purchased 30,000 shares (20%) of Falcon's outstanding common stock for $780,000.

Oct. 23 Falcon declared and paid a cash dividend of $1.60 per share.

Dec. 31 Falcon announced its net income for 1999 is $582,000. Market value of the stock is $27.75 per share.

2000

Oct. 15 Falcon declared and paid a cash dividend of $1.30 per share.

Dec. 31 Falcon announced its net income for 2000 is $738,000. Market value of the stock is $30.45 per share.

2001

Jan. 2 Hammerman sold all of its investment in Falcon for $947,000 cash.

Part 1. Assume that Hammerman has a significant influence over Falcon with its 20% share.

Required

Check Figure Carrying value per share, $31.90

1. Give the entries to record the preceding transactions and events in Hammerman's books.
2. Compute the carrying value per share of Hammerman's investment as reflected in the investment account on January 1, 2001.
3. Compute the change in Hammerman's equity from January 5, 1999, through January 2, 2001, resulting from its investment in Falcon.

Part 2. Assume that even though Hammerman owns 20% of Falcon's outstanding stock, circumstances indicate that it does not have a significant influence over the investee.

Required

1. Give the entries to record the preceding transactions and events in Hammerman's books. Prepare an entry dated January 2, 2001, to remove any balances related to the fair value adjustment.
2. Compute the cost per share of Hammerman's investment as reflected in the investment account on January 1, 2001.
3. Compute the change in Hammerman's equity from January 5, 1999, through January 2, 2001, resulting from its investment in Falcon.

Problem 16-3
Accounting for long-term investments; unrealized and realized gains and losses
P2

Decker Co.'s long-term investment portfolio at December 31, 1999, consists of the following:

Available-for-Sale Securities	Cost	Fair Market Value
80,000 shares of Company A common stock	$1,070,600	$ 980,000
14,000 shares of Company B common stock	318,750	308,000
35,000 shares of Company C common stock	1,325,500	1,281,875

Decker entered into the following long-term investment transactions during 2000.

Jan. 29 Sold 7,000 shares of Company B common stock for $158,375 less a brokerage fee of $3,100.

Apr. 17 Purchased 20,000 shares of Company W common stock for $395,000 plus a brokerage fee of $6,800. The shares represent a 30% ownership in Company W.

July 6 Purchased 9,000 shares of Company X common stock for $253,125 plus a brokerage fee of $3,500. The shares represent a 10% ownership in Company X.

Aug. 22 Purchased 100,000 shares of Company Y common stock for $750,000 plus a brokerage fee of $8,200. The shares represent a 51% ownership in Company Y.

Nov. 13 Purchased 17,000 shares of Company Z common stock for $533,800 plus a brokerage fee of $6,900. The shares represent a 5% ownership in Company Z.

Dec. 9 Sold 80,000 shares of Company A common stock for $1,030,000 less a brokerage fee of $8,200.

The fair market values of Decker's investments at December 31, 2000, are: B, $162,750; C, $1,220,625; W, $382,500; X, $236,250; Y, $1,062,500; Z, $557,600.

Required

1. Determine what amount should be reported on Decker's December 31, 2000, balance sheet for its long-term investments in available-for-sale equity securities.
2. Prepare a December 31, 2000, adjusting entry, if necessary, to record the fair value adjustment of the long-term investments in available-for-sale equity securities.
3. What amount of gains or losses on transactions relating to long-term investments in available-for-sale equity securities should be reported on Decker's December 31, 2000, income statement?

Check Figure (2) Unrealized holding gain, $40,000 Cr.

Problem 16-4
Foreign currency transactions
P4

Savannah Co. is a U.S. corporation that has customers in several foreign countries. Following are some of Savannah's 1999 and 2000 transactions:

1999

Apr. 8 Sold merchandise to Salinas & Sons of Mexico for $7,938 cash. The exchange rate for pesos is $0.1323.

July 21 Sold merchandise on credit to Sumitomo Corp. located in Japan. The price of 1.5 million yen is to be paid 120 days from the date of sale. The exchange rate for yen is $0.009646 on this date.

Oct. 14 Sold merchandise for 19,000 pounds to Smithers Ltd. of Great Britain, payment in full to be received in 90 days. The exchange rate for pounds is $1.5181.

Nov. 18 Received Sumitomo's payment in yen for its purchase of July 21 and exchanged the yen for dollars. The current foreign exchange rate for yen is $0.009575.

Dec. 20 Sold merchandise for 17,000 marks to Schmidt Haus of Germany, payment in full to be received in 30 days. On this day, the foreign exchange rate for marks is $0.6852.

Dec. 31 Prepared adjusting entries to recognize exchange gains or losses on the annual financial statements. Rates for exchanging foreign currencies on this day are:

Pesos (Mexico)	$0.1335
Yen (Japan)	0.009551
Pounds (Britain)	1.5235
Marks (Germany)	0.6807

2000

Jan. 12 Received full payment in pounds from Smithers for the sale of October 14 and immediately exchanged the pounds for dollars. The exchange rate for pounds is $1.5314.

Jan. 19 Received Schmidt Haus's full payment in marks for the sale of December 20 and immediately exchanged the marks for dollars. The exchange rate for marks is $0.6771.

Required

Preparation Component

1. Prepare journal entries to account for these transactions on Savannah's books.
2. Compute the foreign exchange gain or loss to be reported on Savannah's 1999 income statement.

Check Figure 1999 total foreign exchange loss, $80.40

Analysis Component

3. What actions might Savannah consider to reduce its risk of foreign exchange gains or losses?

BEYOND THE NUMBERS

Reporting in Action

C3, C4

Refer to the financial statements and related information for **NIKE** in Appendix A. Answer the following questions by analyzing that information:

1. Are NIKE's financial statements consolidated? How can you tell?
2. Does NIKE have more than one subsidiary? How can you tell?
3. Does NIKE have any foreign operations? How can you tell?
4. Is there a foreign exchange gain or loss on the income statement (consolidated statement of operations)? Describe what you find or do not find.
5. Compute NIKE's reurn on total assets for the year ended May 31, 1997.

Swoosh Ahead

6. Obtain NIKE's annual report information for a fiscal year ending after May 31, 1997. You can get this information from either its Web site [**www.nike.com**] or the SEC's EDGAR database [**www.sec.gov**]. Recompute NIKE's return on total assets for the years subsequent to May 31, 1997, for which you have information.

Comparative Analysis

A1

Both **NIKE** and **Reebok** design, produce, market, and sell sports footwear and apparel. Key comparative figures ($ millions) for these two organizations follow:

	Nike		Reebok	
Key Figures*	**1997**	**1996**	**1996**	**1995**
Net income	$ 796	$ 553	$ 139	$ 165
Net sales	9,187	6,471	3,479	3,481
Total assets	5,361	3,952	1,786	1,652

*NIKE figures are from its annual reports for fiscal years ended May 31, 1997 and 1996. Reebok figures are from its annual reports for fiscal years ended December 31, 1996 and 1995.

Required

1. Compute return on total assets for NIKE as of May 31, 1997, and Reebok as of December 31, 1996.
2. Disaggregate the return on total assets computed in part (1) for both companies according to the formula given in the chapter.
3. Which company has the higher total return on assets? The higher profit margin? The higher total asset turnover? Compare your answers to the chapter's discussion of return on total assets which compared NIKE and Reebok.

Ethics Challenge

C2

Jack Phelps is the controller for Jayhawk Company. Jayhawk has numerous long-term investments in debt securities. During the past year, the company had idle cash invested in 10-year bonds. Jack is preparing the year-end financial statements. In accounting for long-term investments, he knows he must designate each long-term investment as a held-to-maturity or available-for-sale security. Since the bonds were purchased, interest rates have risen sharply, meaning the market values of the bonds have declined. The company does not necessarily intend to hold the bonds for the whole 10 years. Jack earns a bonus each year which is computed as a percent of net income.

Required

1. Will Jack's bonus depend in any way on the classification of the debt securities?
2. What criteria must Jack use to classify the securities as held-to-maturity or available-for-sale?
3. Is there any company oversight of Jack's classification of the securities?

Communicating in Practice

C2, P3

You are the accountant for Jackson Company. The owner of the company, Abel Terrio, has reviewed the financial statements you prepared for 2001 and questions the $6,000 loss reported on the sale of its investment in the common stock of Blackhawk Co. Jackson acquired 50,000 shares of Blackhawk's outstanding common stock on December 31, 1999, at a cost of $500,000. This stock purchase represented a 40% interest in Blackhawk. The 2000 income statement showed that earnings from all investments were $126,000. On January 3, 2001, Jackson Company sold the Blackhawk stock for $575,000. Blackhawk did not pay any dividends during 2000 and reported a net income of $202,500 for the year. Terrio believes that because the purchase price of the Blackhawk stock was $500,000 and it was sold for $575,000, the 2001 income statement should report a $75,000 gain on the sale.

Required

Draft a memo to Terrio explaining why the $6,000 loss on sale of Blackhawk stock is correctly reported.

Taking It to the Net C4

Visit the Web site **www.dna.lth.se/cgi-bin/kurt/rates.** This Web site affords the opportunity to convert 23 different currencies into any one of the other currencies. Use the Web site's currency converter and convert the U.S. dollar into at least five other currencies.

Teamwork in Action C1, C2, C3, P1, P2, P3

Each team member is to become an expert on a specific classification of long-term investments. This expertise will be used to facilitate other teammates' understanding of the concepts and procedures relevant to the classification chosen. Follow procedures outlined below:

1. Each team member is to quickly select an area for expertise by choosing one of the classifications of long-term investments listed below.
   a. Held-to-maturity debt securities
   b. Available-for-sale debt and equity securities
   c. Equity securities with significant influence
   d. Equity securities with controlling influence
2. Learning teams are to disburse and expert teams are to be formed. Expert teams are made up of all students who select the same area of expertise. The instructor will identify the location where each expert team will meet.
3. Expert teams will collaborate to develop a presentation following requirements listed below. Students must write up the presentation in a format they can show to their learning teams in step (4).

   Requirements for Expert Presentation

   a. Write a transaction for the acquisition of this investment. The transaction narrative is to include all necessary data to reflect the chosen classification.
   b. Prepare the journal entry to record the acquisition.
      [Note: The expert team on "Equity securities with controlling influence" will substitute requirements e–f below with a discussion of the reporting of these investments.]
   c. Identify information necessary to complete the end-of-period accounting for this investment.
   d. Design information that will allow your expert team to illustrate end-of-period accounting.
   e. Assuming this is the only investment owned, prepare any necessary year-end entries.
   f. Present relevant balance sheet section(s).
4. Re-form learning teams. In rotation, experts are to present to their teams the presentations they developed in 3. Experts are to encourage and respond to questions.

Hitting the Road C4

Assume that you are planning a spring break trip to Europe. Identify three different locations where you can find exchange rates for the dollar relative to European currencies.

***Business Week* Activity** C4

Read the article "A Garden Full of Hedges" in the April 14, 1993, issue of ***Business Week.***

1. What money-making export of Disney is highlighted in the article?
2. What percent of Disney's profits are from international activities for the time covered by the article?
3. What strategy might Disney use to counteract changes in foreign exchange rates?
4. Why are firms like Disney concerned the dollar might strengthen relative to foreign currencies?
5. Identify one reason automakers such as Mercedes Benz and BMW are building plants in the U.S.
6. What strategies do Renault and Merck use to manage foreign currency exchange risk?

CHAPTER 17

Reporting and Analyzing Cash Flows

A Look Back

Chapter 16 focused on long-term investments in securities. We explained how to identify, account for, and report them. We also described accounting for transactions listed in a foreign currency.

A Look at This Chapter

Chapter 17 focuses on reporting and analyzing cash inflows and cash outflows. We emphasize how to prepare and interpret the statement of cash flows.

A Look Ahead

Chapter 18 focuses on tools to help us analyze financial statements. We describe comparative analysis and the application of ratios for financial analysis.

Chapter Outline

Ginseng Rich, Cash Poor

MARATHON COUNTY, WI—Dennis Chen is a grower of ginseng, an herb whose root is valued for its health benefits. But this summer, high winds and hail swept through Chen's 20-acre plot of ginseng. Chen needed lumber and screening to repair the covering that protected his ginseng plants from nature's elements. But he had neither cash nor the sympathy of bankers.

"Every banker wanted to see my financial statements, especially my cash flows. But I tried to explain that I'd only been in business four years and had never received any cash from any customer," says Chen. "The bankers just didn't understand." What they didn't understand is that ginseng takes about five years to mature from planting until harvest. And since Chen began his business only four years ago, all of his cash flows were negative and large.

"When I finally showed them my statement of cash flows, there was a look of disbelief on their faces," says Chen. "One banker told me flat out he wouldn't touch my loan with a 10-foot pole!" Chen's income statement didn't help much either. Most accounting professionals won't accept recognition of revenue for agricultural products in their growth stage. Especially when growth extends over five years or more. So Chen's prospects were fading.

"I was lucky," says Chen. "I got an appointment with a small town bank. The loan officer grew up on a farm, and was familiar with ginseng. While they weren't the best terms, I got the loan." What Chen also got was cash to do the necessary repairs and save his ginseng and four years of work. Chen accepted a higher than average interest rate along with a collateral agreement giving the bank access to his ginseng if he defaulted.

"That loan officer really saved me," says Chen. "He looked beyond the numbers and the cash flows to see what was happening. I think it'll be a win-win situation for both of us." And ginseng lovers as well.

Learning Objectives

Conceptual

C1 Explain the purpose and importance of cash flow information.

C2 Distinguish among operating, investing, and financing activities.

C3 Identify and disclose noncash investing and financing activities.

C4 Describe the format of the statement of cash flows.

Analytical

A1 Analyze the statement of cash flows.

A2 Compute and apply the cash flow on total assets ratio.

Procedural

P1 Prepare a statement of cash flows.

P2 Compute cash flows from operating activities using the direct method.

P3 Compute cash flows from operating activities using the indirect method.

P4 Determine cash flows from both investing and financing activities.

HAPTER PREVIEW

Profitability is a primary goal of most managers. But it is not the only goal. A company cannot achieve or maintain profits without careful management of cash. Managers and other users of information pay close attention to a company's cash position and the events and transactions affecting cash. Information about these events and transactions is reported in the statement of cash flows. This chapter explains how we prepare, analyze, and interpret a statement of cash flows. It also discusses the importance of cash flow information for predicting future performance and making managerial decisions. Understanding the statement of cash flows is especially important in obtaining a small business loan and one with favorable terms. Dennis Chen's experience with the importance of this statement as described in the opening article is common.

Basics of Cash Flow Reporting

This section describes the basics of cash flow reporting including its purpose, measurement, classification, format, and preparation.

Purpose of the Statement of Cash Flows

C1 Explain the purpose and importance of cash flow information.

The purpose of the **statement of cash flows** is to report the major cash receipts (inflows) and cash payments (outflows) during a period. This includes separately identifying the cash flows related to operating, investing, and financing activities.

The statement of cash flows does more than simply report changes in cash. It is the detailed disclosure of individual cash flows that makes this statement useful to users. Information in this statement helps users answer questions such as:

- How does a company obtain its cash?
- Where does a company spend its cash?
- What is the change in the cash balance?

The statement of cash flows addresses these important questions by summarizing, classifying, and reporting a company's periodic cash inflows and outflows.

Importance of Cash Flows

Information about cash flows, and its sources and uses, can influence decision makers in important ways. For instance, we look more favorably at a company that is financing its expenditures with cash from operations than one that does it by selling its assets. Information about cash flows helps users decide whether a company has enough cash to pay its existing debts as they mature. It is also relied upon to evaluate a company's ability to meet unexpected obligations and pursue unexpected opportunities. External information users especially want to assess a company's ability to take advantage of new business opportunities. Internal users such as managers use cash flow information to plan day-to-day operating activities and make long-term investment decisions.

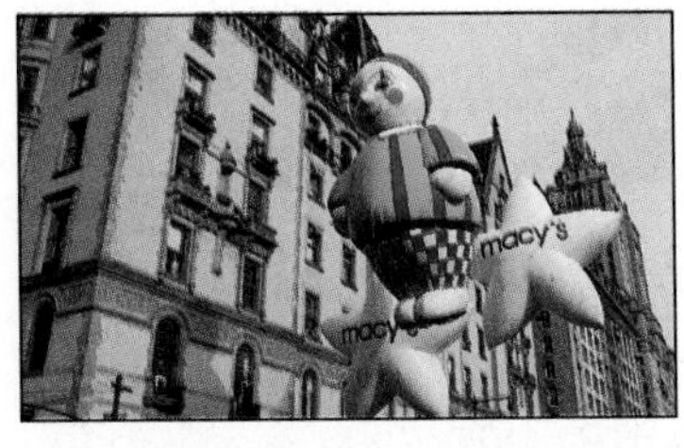

Macy's striking turnaround is an example of how careful analysis and management of cash flows can lead to improved financial stability. Macy's obtained temporary protection from bankruptcy in 1992 and desperately needed to improve its cash flows. It did so by engaging in aggressive cost-cutting measures. As a result of this effort, Macy's cash inflow rose to $210 million in fiscal 1993—up from a negative cash flow of $38.9 million in the prior year. Macy's eventually met its financial obligations and then merged with **Federated Department Stores.**

The case of **W. T. Grant Co.** is a classic example of why cash flow information is important in predicting a company's future performance and financial strength. Grant reported net income of more than $40 million per year for three consecutive years. At the same time, it was experiencing an alarming decrease in cash provided by operations. For instance, net cash outflow was more than $90 million by the end of that three-year period.[1] Grant soon went bankrupt. Users who relied solely on Grant's earnings numbers were unpleasantly surprised. This reminds us that cash flows as well as income statement and balance sheet information are crucial in making business decisions.

Cash Valuation
Some experts who value private companies do so on the basis of a multiple of operating cash flow. Medium-sized private companies usually sell for five to seven times operating cash flows. Larger companies can command even higher multiples. [Source: *Business Week*, January 26, 1998.]

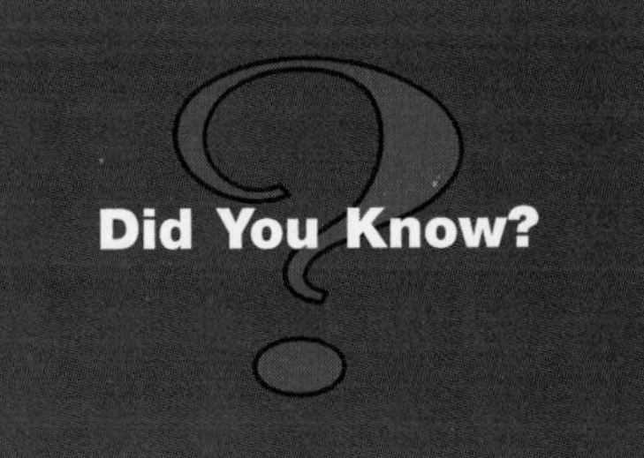

Measuring Cash Flows

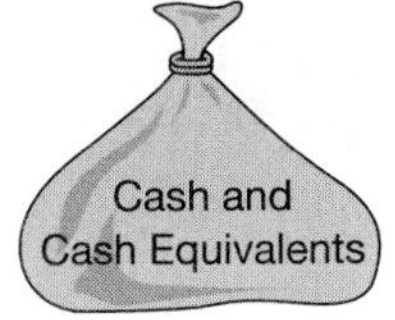

Cash flows are defined to include both *cash and cash equivalents* in the statement of cash flows. This means the statement explains the difference between the beginning and ending balances of cash and cash equivalents. While we continue to use the terms *cash flows* and the *statement of cash flows,* we must remember that both terms refer to cash and cash equivalents.

As we discussed in Chapter 9, a cash equivalent must satisfy two criteria:

1. It must be readily convertible to a known amount of cash.
2. It must be sufficiently close to its maturity date so its market value is unaffected by interest rate changes.

In most cases, securities must be within three months of their maturity dates to satisfy these criteria.[2] Classifying short-term, highly liquid investments as cash equivalents is based on the idea that companies make these investments to earn a return on idle cash balances.

Items meeting the criteria of cash equivalents are sometimes not held as short-term investments of idle cash. For instance, an investment company that specializes in the purchase and sale of securities often buys cash equivalents as part of its investing strategy. Companies in this situation are allowed to exclude these securities from the cash equivalents account. But these companies must follow a clear policy for determining the items to include and not include. These policies are disclosed in notes to their financial statements and must be followed consistently from period to period. **American Express,** for example, defines its cash equivalents as:

> . . . time deposits with original maturities of 90 days or less, excluding those that are restricted by law or regulation.

[1]J. Largay and C. Stickney, "Cash Flow, Ratio Analysis and the W. T. Grant Company Bankruptcy," *Financial Analysts Journal,* July-August 1980, pp. 51–56.

[2]FASB, *Accounting Standards—Current Text* (Norwalk, CT, 1995), sec. C25.106. First published in *Statement of Financial Accounting Standards No. 95,* par. 8.

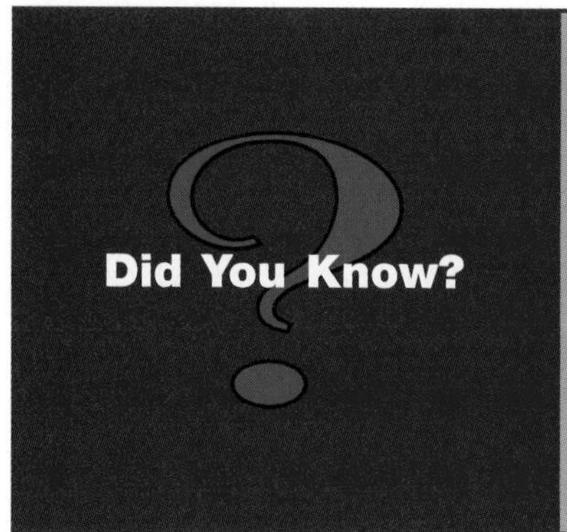

Cash, and Cash Alone

"A lender must have a complete understanding of a borrower's cash flows to assess both the borrowing needs and repayment sources. This requires information about the major types of cash inflows and outflows. Cash, and cash alone, is the source of repayment for all loans. I have seen many companies, whose financial statements indicate good profitability, experience severe financial problems because the owners or managers lacked a good understanding of the companies' cash flows."—Mary E. Garza, senior vice president, NationsBank of Texas

Classifying Cash Flows

C2 Distinguish among operating, investing, and financing activities.

Since we treat cash and cash equivalents as a single item on the statement of cash flows, transactions between cash and cash equivalents such as cash paid to purchase cash equivalents and cash received from selling cash equivalents are not reported in the statement. But all other cash receipts and payments are classified and reported on the statement as operating, investing, or financing activities. Individual cash receipts and payments within each of these three categories are labeled to identify their source transactions or events. Cash receipts and payments are then summarized for each category by netting them against each other. A net cash inflow (source) occurs when the receipts in a category exceed the payments. A net cash outflow (use) occurs when the payments in a category exceed receipts.

Operating Activities

Operating activities include the cash effects of transactions and events that determine net income. But not all items in income, such as unusual gains and losses, are operating activities. We discuss these exceptions later in the chapter.

Examples of operating activities are the production and purchase of merchandise, the sale of goods and services to customers, and expenditures toward administering the business. Exhibit 17.1 lists the more common cash inflows and outflows from operating activities.

Exhibit 17.1

Cash Flows from Operating Activities

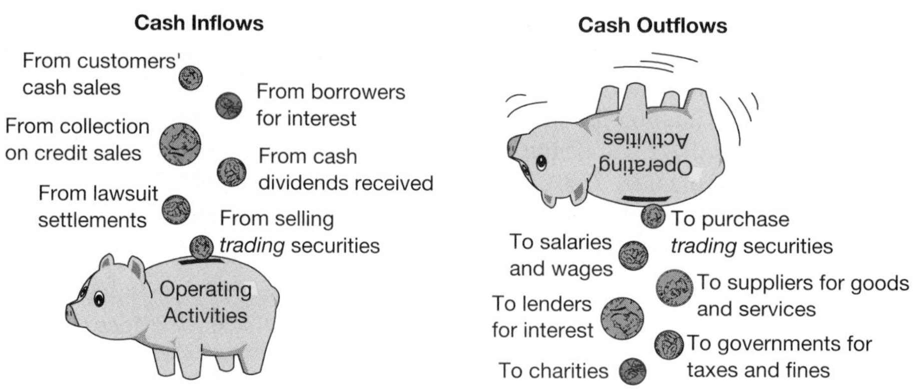

Investing Activities

Investing activities include the (a) purchase and sale of long-term assets, (b) the purchase and sale of short-term investments other than cash equivalents, and (c) lending and collecting loans. Exhibit 17.2 lists examples of cash flows from investing activities. Pro-

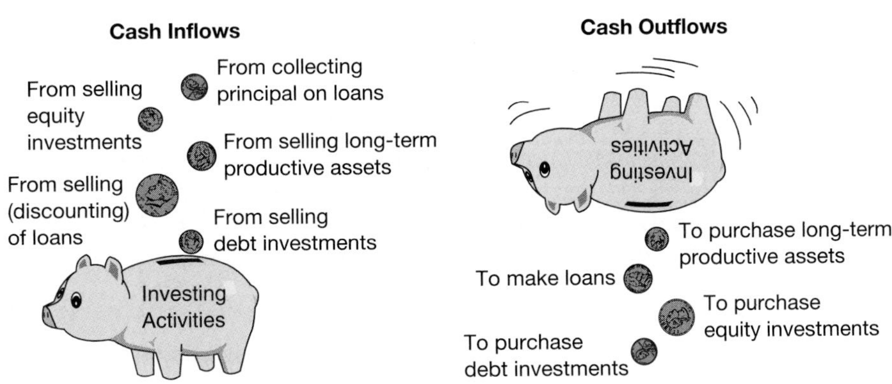

Exhibit 17.2

Cash Flows from Investing Activities

ceeds from collecting the principal amounts of loans deserve special attention. If the loan results from sales to customers, its cash receipts are classed as operating activities whether short term or long term. But if the loan results from a loan to another party, then its cash receipts from collecting the principal of the note are classed as an investing activity. The FASB does not consider collection of interest on a loan as an investing activity but rather as an operating activity.

Financing Activities

Financing activities include (a) obtaining cash from issuing debt and repaying the amounts borrowed, and (b) obtaining cash from or distributing cash to owners. These activities all involve transactions with a company's owners and creditors. They also involve the borrowing and repaying of principal amounts relating to both short- and long-term debt. But payments of interest expense are classified as operating activities. Also, cash payments to settle credit purchases of merchandise, whether on account or by note, are operating activities. Exhibit 17.3 lists examples of cash flows from financing activities.

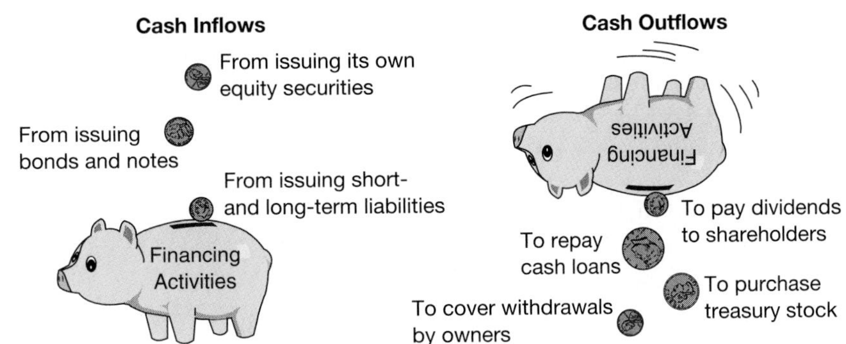

Exhibit 17.3

Cash Flows from Financing Activities

Noncash Investing and Financing Activities

C3 Identify and disclose noncash investing and financing activities.

There are often important investing and financing activities that do not affect cash receipts or payments. Yet because of their importance and the *full disclosure principle,* these important noncash investing and financing activities are disclosed at the bottom of the statement of cash flows or in a note to the statement. One example of such a transaction is the purchase of long-term assets by giving a long-term note payable. This transaction involves both investing and financing activities, but it does not affect any cash inflow or outflow and is not reported in any of the three sections of the statement of cash flows. Another example is investing and financing activities involving cash receipts or payments for only part of the entire transaction.

To illustrate, let's assume Burton purchases machinery for $12,000 by paying cash of $5,000 and trading in old machinery with a market value of $7,000. The statement of cash flows reports only the $5,000 cash outflow for purchase of machinery. This means the $12,000 investing transaction is only partially described in the body of the statement of cash flows. Yet this information is potentially important to users in that it changes the makeup of assets.

Companies use one of two ways to disclose noncash investing and financing activities not reported in the body of the statement of cash flows. They must be disclosed in either (1) a note or (2) a separate schedule attached to the statement. In the case of Burton, it could either describe the transaction in a note or include a small schedule at the bottom of its statement that lists the $12,000 asset investment along with financing of $5,000 and a $7,000 trade-in of old machinery.

We look at two cases to illustrate its application in practice. **Seagate Technology** gives us a note disclosure for a noncash investing and financing activity:

Receipt of note receivable for sale of building	$5,000,000

Union Camp provides an example of disclosure in a separate schedule of noncash investing and financing activity ($ in thousands):

Fair value of assets acquired	$8,345
Less: Cash paid	7,115
Liabilities incurred or assumed	$1,230

The Union Camp schedule attached to the statement describes an exchange of assets involving both cash and noncash aspects. The $7,115 cash payment is reported in Union Camp's statement of cash flows as an investing activity. But the note tells us that the purchase of certain assets involves a noncash aspect—that is, a liability to pay in the future. Exhibit 17.4 lists some transactions that are disclosed as noncash investing and financing activities.

Exhibit 17.4

Examples of Noncash Investing and Financing Activities

- Retirement of debt by issuing equity securities.
- Conversion of preferred stock to common stock.
- Leasing of assets in capital lease transaction.
- Purchase of long-term asset by issuing note payable.
- Exchange of noncash assets for other noncash assets.
- Purchase of noncash assets by issuing equity or debt.

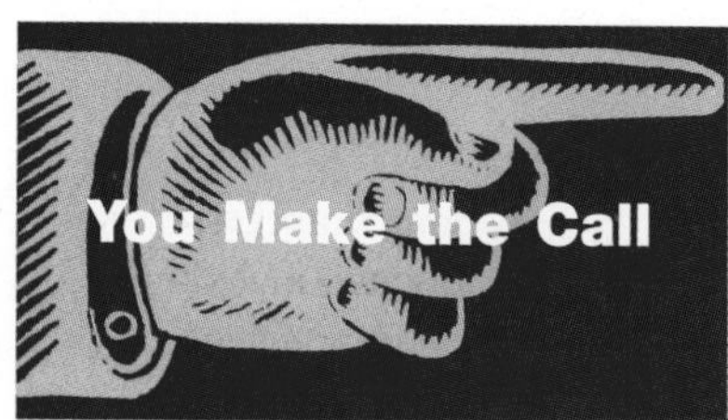

Community Activist

You are a community activist trying to raise public awareness of pollution emitted by a local manufacturer. The manufacturer complains about the high cost of pollution controls and points to its recent $4 million annual loss as evidence. But you also know its net cash flows were a positive $8 million this past year. How are these results possible?

Answer—p. 749

Format of the Statement of Cash Flows

C4 Describe the format of the statement of cash flows.

Accounting standards require companies to include a statement of cash flows in a complete set of financial statements. This statement must report information about a company's cash receipts and cash payments during the period.

Exhibit 17.5 shows us the usual format of the statement of cash flows. This exhibit shows that a company must report cash flows from three activities: operating, investing, and financing. Cash inflows and cash outflows are reported for each category. The statement explains how transactions and events impact the beginning-of-period cash (and cash equivalents) balance to produce its end-of-period balance.

Exhibit 17.5

Format of the Statement of Cash Flows

COMPANY NAME Statement of Cash Flows Period Covered	
Cash flows from operating activities:	
[List of individual inflows and outflows]	
Net cash provided (used) by operating activities	$ #
Cash flows from investing activities:	
[List of individual inflows and outflows]	
Net cash provided (used) by investing activities	#
Cash flows from financing activities:	
[List of individual inflows and outflows]	
Net cash provided (used) by financing activities	#
Net increase (decrease) in cash	**$ #**
Cash (and equivalents) balance at beginning of period	**#**
Cash (and equivalents) balance at end of period	**$ #**

Note: Separate schedule or note disclosure of "noncash investing and financing transactions" is required.

Flash *back*

1. Does a statement of cash flows disclose payments of cash to purchase cash equivalents? Does it disclose receipts of cash from selling cash equivalents?
2. Identify the categories of cash flows reported separately on the statement of cash flows.
3. Identify the category for each of the following cash flow activities: *(a)* purchase equipment for cash; *(b)* payment of wages; *(c)* sale of common stock for cash; *(d)* receipt of cash dividends from stock investment; *(e)* cash collection from customers; *(f)* issuance of bonds for cash.

Answers—p. 750

Preparing the Statement of Cash Flows

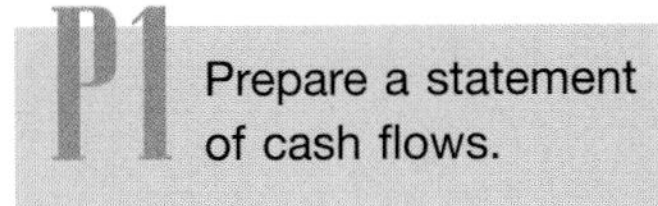

P1 Prepare a statement of cash flows.

Preparation of a statement of cash flows involves five steps: (1) compute the net increase or decrease in cash; (2) compute and report net cash provided (used) by operating activities (using either the direct or indirect method—both are explained in this chapter); (3) compute and report net cash provided (used) by investing activities; (4) compute and report net cash provided (used) by financing activities; and (5) compute net cash flow by combining net cash provided (used) by operating, investing, and financing activities and then *prove it* by adding it to the beginning cash balance to show it equals the ending cash balance. Noncash investing and financing activities are disclosed in either a note or in a separate schedule to the statement.

Step 1: Compute net increase or decrease in cash

Step 2: Compute net cash from operating activities

Step 3: Compute net cash from investing activities

Step 4: Compute net cash from financing activities

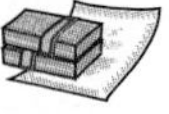

Step 5: Prove and report beginning and ending cash balances

The first step in preparing the statement—computing the net increase or decrease in cash—is a simple but crucial computation. It equals the current period's cash balance minus the prior period's cash balance. This is the *bottom line* figure for the statement of cash flows and is a helpful check on the accuracy of our work.

The information we need to prepare a statement of cash flows comes from a variety of sources. These include comparative balance sheets at the beginning and end of the period, an income statement for the period, and a careful analysis of each noncash balance sheet account in the general ledger. Because cash inflows and cash outflows are captured in our accounting system, we can also examine transactions affecting the Cash account.

The remaining sections of this chapter explain the important steps in preparing the statement of cash flows. But first we describe the two different approaches to preparing the statement: (1) analyzing the Cash account and (2) analyzing noncash accounts.

Analyzing the Cash Account

All of a company's cash receipts and cash payments are recorded in the Cash account in the General Ledger. The Cash account is therefore a natural place to look for information about cash flows from operating, investing, and financing activities.

To illustrate, let's look at the summarized Cash account of Genesis in Exhibit 17.6. Individual cash transactions are summarized in this Cash account according to the major types of cash receipts and cash payments. For instance, only the total of cash receipts from all customers is listed. Individual cash transactions underlying these totals can number into the thousands. Accounting software programs are available to provide us with summarized cash accounts similar to the one illustrated.

Exhibit 17.6

Summarized Cash Account

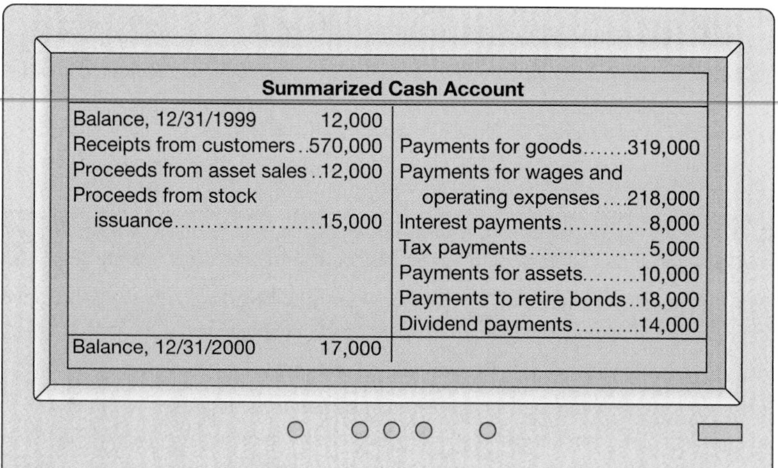

Summarized Cash Account			
Balance, 12/31/1999	12,000		
Receipts from customers	570,000	Payments for goods	319,000
Proceeds from asset sales	12,000	Payments for wages and operating expenses	218,000
Proceeds from stock issuance	15,000	Interest payments	8,000
		Tax payments	5,000
		Payments for assets	10,000
		Payments to retire bonds	18,000
		Dividend payments	14,000
Balance, 12/31/2000	17,000		

Preparing a statement of cash flows from Exhibit 17.6 requires us to determine whether the cash inflow or outflow is an operating, investing, or financing activity. We then list these individual cash flows according to their activity. This yields the statement shown in Exhibit 17.7.

Preparing the statement of cash flows from an analysis of the summarized Cash account presents two limitations. First, most companies have many individual cash receipts and payments, making it difficult to review them all. While accounting software greatly minimizes this burden, it is still a task requiring professional judgment. Second, the Cash account does not usually carry a description of each cash transaction. This makes it difficult to assign cash transactions according to activity.

Exhibit 17.7

Statement of Cash Flows—Direct Method

GENESIS Statement of Cash Flows For Year Ended December 31, 2000		
Cash flows from operating activities:		
Cash received from customers	$570,000	
Cash paid for merchandise	(319,000)	
Cash paid for wages and other operating expenses	(218,000)	
Cash paid for interest	(8,000)	
Cash paid for taxes	(5,000)	
Net cash provided by operating activities		$20,000
Cash flows from investing activities:		
Cash received from sale of plant assets	$ 12,000	
Cash paid for purchase of plant assets	(10,000)	
Net cash provided by investing activities		2,000
Cash flows from financing activities:		
Cash received from issuing stock	$ 15,000	
Cash paid to retire bonds	(18,000)	
Cash paid for dividends	(14,000)	
Net cash used in financing activities		(17,000)
Net increase in cash		$5,000
Cash balance at beginning of 2000		12,000
Cash balance at end of 2000		$17,000

Analyzing Noncash Accounts

The second approach to preparing the statement of cash flows is based on analyzing noncash accounts. This approach uses the fact that when a company records cash inflows and outflows with debits and credits to the Cash account (as reflected in the prior section), it also records credits and debits in other noncash accounts. Many of these noncash accounts are balance sheet accounts, for instance, the sale of land for cash. Others are revenue and expense accounts that are closed to Retained Earnings, also a balance sheet account. For instance, the sale of services for cash yields a credit to services revenue that is closed to Retained Earnings. In sum, *all cash transactions eventually affect noncash balance sheet accounts.* This means we can determine cash inflows and cash outflows by analyzing changes in noncash balance sheet accounts. We are not limited to analyzing the Cash account.

Exhibit 17.8 uses the accounting equation to show the important relation between the Cash account and noncash balance sheet accounts.

Exhibit 17.8

Relation between Cash and Noncash Accounts

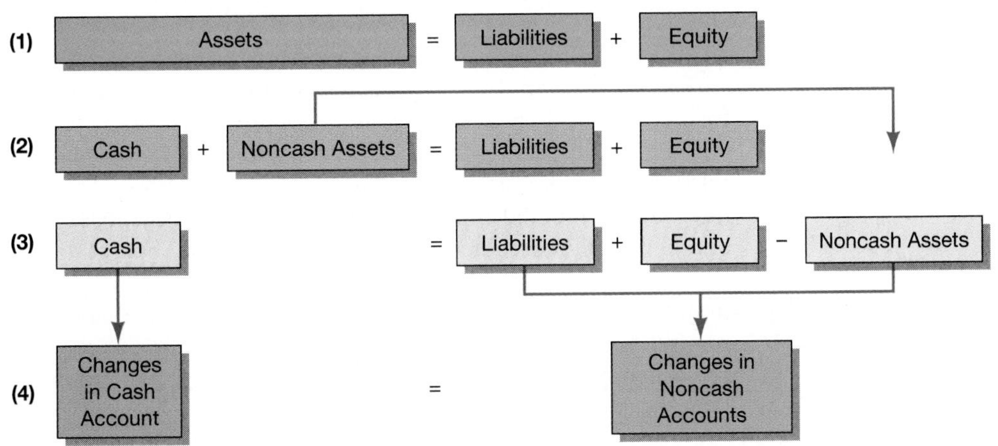

Exhibit 17.8 starts with the familiar accounting equation at the top. We then expand it in line (2) so that cash is separated from noncash asset accounts. Next, we move noncash asset accounts to the right-hand side of the equality in line (3) where they become a negative. This shows cash is equal to the sum of the liability and equity accounts *minus* the noncash asset accounts. Line (4) points out that *changes* in one side of the accounting equation are equal to *changes* on the other side. It also shows we can explain changes in cash by analyzing changes in the noncash accounts consisting of liabilities, equity accounts, and noncash assets. By analyzing all noncash balance sheet accounts and related income statement accounts, we have the information for preparing a statement of cash flows.

Information to Prepare the Statement

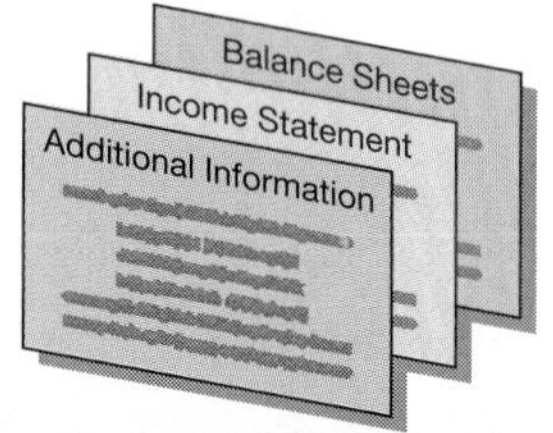

Information to prepare the statement of cash flows usually comes from three sources: (1) comparative balance sheets, (2) current income statement, and (3) additional information. Comparative balance sheets give us changes in noncash accounts from the beginning to the end of the period. The current income statement gives us details to help compute cash flows from operating activities. Additional information often includes details on transactions and events helping us explain both cash flows and noncash investing and financing activities.

Did You Know?

E-Cash

Every credit transaction on the net leaves a trail that a hacker, an aggressive marketer, or the government can pick up. Enter e-cash. E-cash is the electronic equivalent of cash—digital money that can be used as freely and anonymously as cash. With e-cash, the encryption not only protects your money from snoops and thieves but also obscures the identity of the owner. When you spend e-cash, it can't be traced back to you—not even by the issuing bank. [Source: *Business Week*, February 27, 1995.]

Cash Flows from Operating

This section describes the reporting of cash flows from operating activities using two different methods: direct method and indirect method. *These two different methods apply only to the operating activities section.*

Reporting Operating Cash Flows

The net cash flows provided (used) by operating activities can be reported in one of two ways: the *direct method* or the *indirect method*. The **direct method** separately lists each major item of operating cash receipts (such as cash received from customers) and each major item of operating cash payments (such as cash paid for merchandise). The cash payments are subtracted from cash receipts to determine the net cash provided (used) by operating activities. The operating activities section of Exhibit 17.7 is an example of the direct method of reporting operating cash flows.

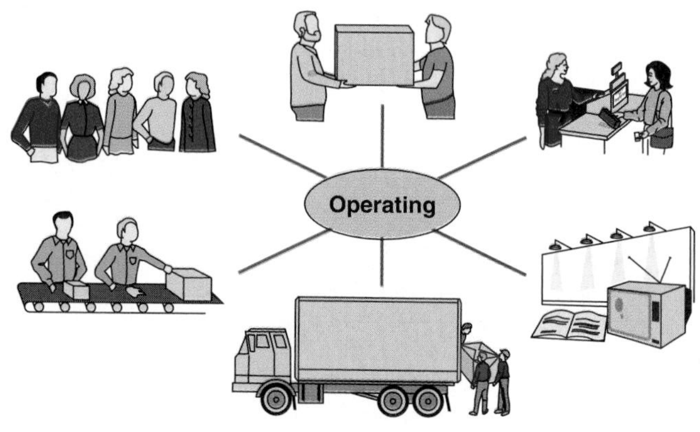

The **indirect method** reports net income and then adjusts it for items necessary to give us net cash provided (used) by operating activities. It does *not* report individual items of cash inflows and cash outflows from operating activities. Instead, the indirect method reports the necessary adjustments to reconcile net income to net cash provided (used) by operating activities. A common adjustment is a subtraction for depreciation. Since depreciation expense is not a current cash payment, we add depreciation expense back to net income in our process of adjusting net income to net cash provided (used) by operating activities.

The operating activities section prepared under the indirect method appears as shown in Exhibit 17.9.

Exhibit 17.9

Operating Activities Section—Indirect Method

Cash flows from operating activities:		
Net income	$38,000	
Adjustments to reconcile net income to net cash provided by operating activities:		
Increase in accounts receivable	(20,000)	
Increase in merchandise inventory	(14,000)	
Increase in prepaid expenses	(2,000)	
Decrease in accounts payable	(5,000)	
Decrease in interest payable	(1,000)	
Increase in income taxes payable	10,000	
Depreciation expense	24,000	
Loss on sale of plant assets	6,000	
Gain on retirement of bonds	(16,000)	
Net cash provided by operating activities		**$20,000**

It is important to see that the amount of net cash provided by operating activities is *identical* under both the direct and indirect methods. This equality always exists. The difference in these methods is with computation of this amount.

The indirect method of reporting operating cash flows does not provide as much detail as does the direct method. The direct method also is *recommended* by the FASB. But since the direct method is not required and the indirect method is arguably easier to compute, most companies report operating cash flows using the indirect method. We describe both methods in this chapter.

Since the direct method is the cash flow version of an income statement, many people find the direct method easier to understand when first learning about cash flow reporting. It allows decision makers to know the amount of revenues and costs that are actually received or paid in cash. It also follows the same format as the income statement. Many internal users such as managers and budget officers use the direct method to predict future cash requirements and availability.

To illustrate both methods, we prepare the operating activities section of the statement of cash flows for **Genesis, Inc.** The December 31, 1999, and 2000, balance sheets of Genesis along with its 2000 income statement are shown in Exhibit 17.10. Our objective is to prepare a statement of cash flows explaining the $5,000 increase in cash for year 2000 as seen from its balance sheets. This is computed as Cash of $17,000 at the end of year 2000 minus Cash of $12,000 at the end of 1999.

Genesis also discloses additional information about year 2000 transactions:

a. All accounts payable balances result from merchandise purchases.

b. Plant assets costing $70,000 are purchased by paying $10,000 cash and issuing $60,000 of bonds payable.

c. Plant assets with an original cost of $30,000 and accumulated depreciation of $12,000 are sold for $12,000 cash. This yields a $6,000 loss.

d. Proceeds from issuing 3,000 shares of common stock are $15,000.

e. Paid $18,000 to retire bonds with a book value of $34,000. This yields a $16,000 gain.

f. Cash dividends of $14,000 are declared and paid.

The next section describes the direct method. The section following this one describes the indirect method. An instructor may choose to cover either one or both methods for preparing a statement of cash flows. Neither section depends on the other.

Exhibit 17.10

Financial Statements

GENESIS Balance Sheet December 31, 2000 and 1999	2000	1999
Assets		
Current assets:		
Cash	$ 17,000	$ 12,000
Accounts receivable	60,000	40,000
Merchandise inventory	84,000	70,000
Prepaid expenses	6,000	4,000
Total current assets	$167,000	$126,000
Long term assets:		
Plant assets	$250,000	$210,000
Accum. depreciation	(60,000)	(48,000)
Total assets	$357,000	$288,000
Liabilities		
Current liabilities:		
Accounts payable	$ 35,000	$ 40,000
Interest payable	3,000	4,000
Income taxes payable	22,000	12,000
Total current liabilities	$ 60,000	$ 56,000
Long-term liabilities:		
Bonds payable	90,000	64,000
Total liabilities	$150,000	$120,000
Stockholders' Equity		
Contributed capital:		
Common stock, $5 par	$ 95,000	$ 80,000
Retained earnings	112,000	88,000
Total stockholders' equity	207,000	168,000
Total liabilities and equity	$357,000	$288,000

GENESIS Income Statement For Year Ended December 31, 2000		
Sales		$590,000
Cost of goods sold	$300,000	
Wages & other operating exp.	216,000	
Interest expense	7,000	
Income taxes expense	15,000	
Depreciation expense	24,000	(562,000)
Loss on sale of plant assets		(6,000)
Gain on retirement of debt		16,000
Net income		$ 38,000

Direct Method of Reporting

P2 Compute cash flows from operating activities using the direct method.

We compute cash flows from operating activities under the direct method by adjusting accrual based income statement items to a cash basis. The usual approach is to adjust income statement accounts related to operating activities for changes in their related balance sheet accounts as follows:

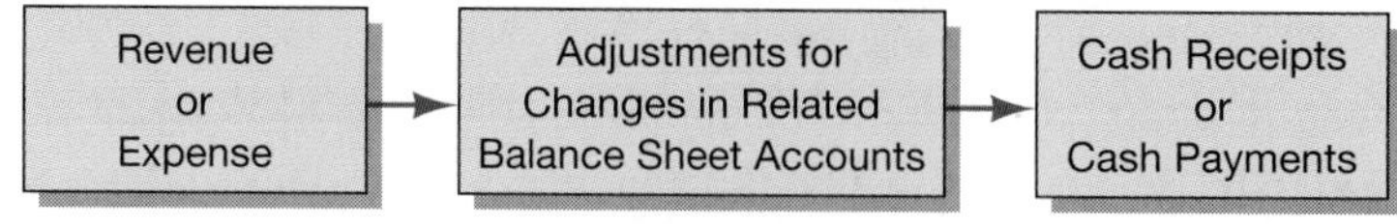

We follow this same approach in this section.

The framework for reporting major classes of cash receipts and cash payments is shown in Exhibit 17.11. This framework is for the operating section of the cash flow statement prepared using the direct method.

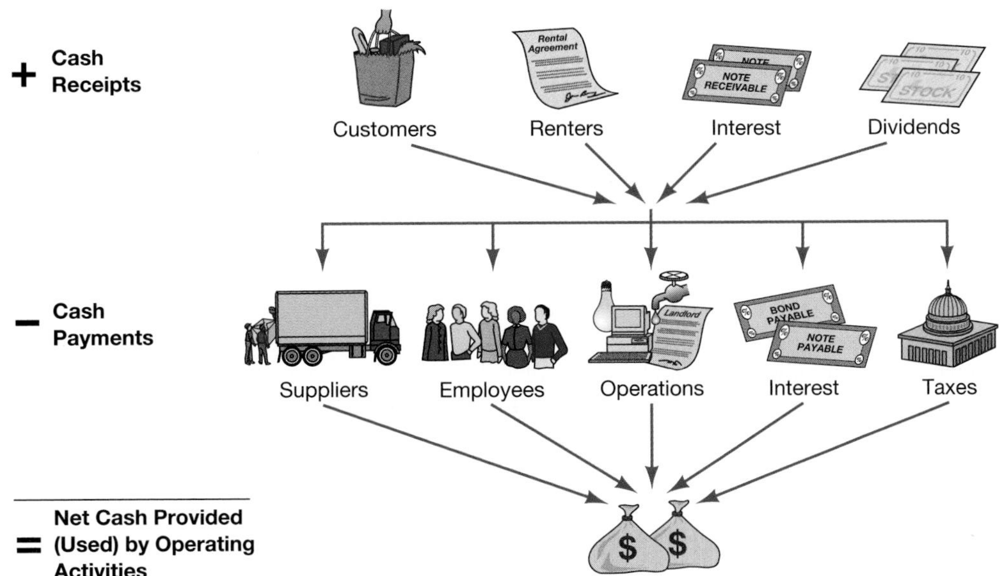

Exhibit 17.11

Major Classes of Operating Cash Flows

In preparing the operating section, we first look at cash receipts and then cash payments.

Operating Cash Receipts

Exhibit 17.10 and the additional information from Genesis identify only one potential cash receipt—that of sales to customers. This section starts with sales from the income statement and adjusts it as necessary to give us cash received from customers.

Cash Received from Customers

If all sales are for cash, the amount of cash received from customers is equal to sales. But when sales are on account, we must adjust the amount of sales revenue for the change in Accounts Receivable. It is often helpful to use *account analysis* for this purpose. This usually involves setting up a T-account and reconstructing its major entries, including its cash receipts and payments.

To illustrate, the T-account below reports accounts receivable balances on December 31, 1999, and 2000. The beginning balance is $40,000, and the ending balance is $60,000. The income statement shows sales is $590,000, and we enter it on the debit side of this account. With this information, we can reconstruct the Accounts Receivable account and determine the amount of cash received from customers.

Accounts Receivable			
Balance 12/31/1999	40,000		
Sales	590,000	**Collections =**	**570,000**
Balance 12/31/2000	60,000		

This T-account shows the balance of accounts receivable begins at $40,000 and increases to $630,000 from sales of $590,000. But then its ending balance is reported at only $60,000. This implies that cash receipts from customers are $570,000, computed as $40,000 + $590,000 − [?] = $60,000. This computation can be rearranged to express cash received as equal to sales of $590,000 plus a $20,000 increase in accounts receivable. This computation is summarized in Exhibit 17.12.

Exhibit 17.12

Formula to Compute Cash Received from Customers—Direct Method

$$\text{Cash received from customers} = \text{Sales} - \left[\begin{array}{c} -\text{ Increase in accounts receivable} \\ \text{or} \\ +\text{ Decrease in accounts receivable} \end{array}\right.$$

The statement of cash flows for Genesis in Exhibit 17.7 reports the $570,000 cash received from customers as a cash inflow from operating activities.

Other Cash Receipts

While cash receipts of Genesis are limited to collections from customers, we sometimes see other types of cash receipts. The most common are cash receipts involving rent, interest, and dividends. We compute cash received from these items by subtracting an increase in their respective account receivable or adding a decrease. For instance, if rent receivable increases in the period, it implies cash received is less than rent revenue reported on the income statement. But if rent receivable decreases, it implies cash received is more than reported rent revenue. The same logic applies to interest and dividends. The formulas for these computations are summarized in Exhibit 17.16 later in this section.

Operating Cash Payments

Exhibit 17.10 and the additional information from Genesis identify four operating expenses. We analyze each of these expenses to compute their operating cash payments for the statement of cash flows.

Cash Paid for Merchandise

We compute cash paid for merchandise by analyzing both cost of goods sold and merchandise inventory. If all merchandise purchases are for cash and the ending balance of Merchandise Inventory is unchanged from the beginning balance, then the amount of cash paid for merchandise equals cost of goods sold. But this situation is uncommon. We usually see some change in the Merchandise Inventory balance in a period. Also, merchandise purchases are often made on credit, and yield changes in the Accounts Payable balance.

When the balances of Merchandise Inventory and Accounts Payable change, we must adjust cost of goods sold for changes in both of these accounts to compute cash paid for merchandise. This adjustment has two steps. First, we use the change in the balance of Merchandise Inventory along with the amount of cost of goods sold to compute cost of purchases for the period. If inventory increases, it implies we bought more than was sold and we add the inventory change to cost of goods sold to compute cost of purchases. If inventory decreases, it implies we bought less than was sold and we subtract the inventory change from cost of goods sold to compute purchases.

The second step uses the change in the balance of Accounts Payable along with the amount of cost of purchases to compute cash paid for merchandise. If accounts payable decreases, it implies we paid for more goods than were acquired this period, and we add the accounts payable change to cost of purchases to compute cash paid for merchandise. If accounts payable increases, it implies we paid for less than the amount of goods acquired, and we subtract the accounts payable change from purchases to compute cash paid for merchandise.

We illustrate this two-step process for Genesis. First, we use account analysis of merchandise inventory to compute cost of purchases. We do this by reconstructing the Merchandise Inventory account:

Merchandise Inventory			
Balance, 12/31/1999	70,000		
Purchases =	**314,000**	Cost of goods sold	300,000
Balance, 12/31/2000	84,000		

The beginning balance is $70,000, and the ending balance is $84,000. The income statement shows cost of goods sold is $300,000, and we enter it on the credit side of this account. With this information, we determine the amount for cost of purchases at $314,000. This computation also can be rearranged to express cost of purchases as equal to cost of goods sold of $300,000 plus the $14,000 increase in inventory.

Our second step is to compute cash paid for merchandise by adjusting purchases for the change in accounts payable. This is done by reconstructing the Accounts Payable account:

Accounts Payable			
		Balance, 12/31/1999	40,000
Payments =	**319,000**	Purchases	314,000
		Balance, 12/31/2000	35,000

This account shows us that its beginning balance of $40,000 plus purchases of $314,000 minus an ending balance of $35,000 gives us cash paid of $319,000 (or $40,000 + $314,000 − [?] = $35,000). Alternatively, we can express cash paid for merchandise as equal to purchases of $314,000 plus the $5,000 decrease in accounts payable.

We summarize the two-step adjustment to cost of goods sold to compute cash paid for merchandise in Exhibit 17.13.

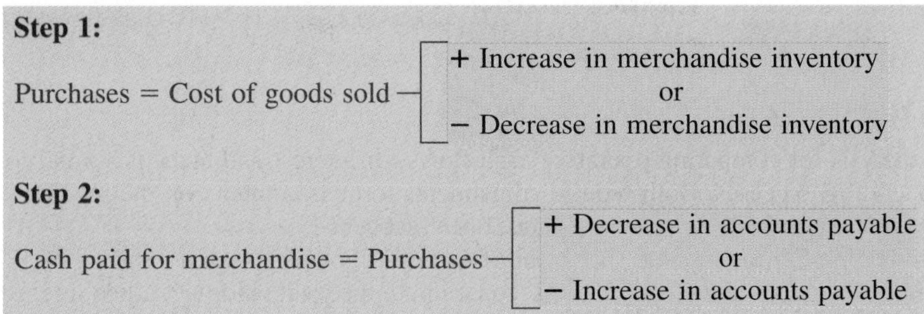
Step 1:

Purchases = Cost of goods sold + Increase in merchandise inventory or − Decrease in merchandise inventory

Step 2:

Cash paid for merchandise = Purchases + Decrease in accounts payable or − Increase in accounts payable

Exhibit 17.13

Two Steps to compute Cash Paid for Merchandise—Direct Method

Exhibit 17.7 shows the $319,000 cash paid by Genesis for merchandise is reported on the statement of cash flows as a cash outflow for operating activities.

Cash Paid for Wages and Operating Expenses (Excluding Depreciation)

The income statement of Genesis shows wages and other operating expenses of $216,000 (see Exhibit 17.10). To compute cash paid for wages and other operating expenses, we adjust this amount for changes in their related balance sheet accounts.

We begin by looking for prepaid expenses and accrued liabilities relating to wages and other operating expenses in the beginning and ending balance sheets of Genesis in Exhibit 17.10. These balance sheets show Genesis has prepaid expenses but no accrued liabilities. This means its adjustment is limited to the change in prepaid expenses. The amount of adjustment is computed by assuming all cash paid for wages and other operating expenses is initially debited to Prepaid Expenses. This assumption allows us to reconstruct the Prepaid Expenses account:

Prepaid Expenses			
Balance, 12/31/1999	4,000		
Payments =	**218,000**	Wages and other operating exp.	216,000
Balance, 12/31/2000	6,000		

This account shows prepaid expenses increase by $2,000 in the period. This means cash paid for wages and other operating expenses exceeds the reported expense by $2,000. Alternatively, we can express cash paid for wages and other operating expenses of Genesis as equal to its expenses of $216,000 plus the $2,000 increase in prepaid expenses.

Our analysis assumes all cash payments for wages and operating expenses are initially debited to Prepaid Expenses in reconstructing the Prepaid Expenses account. But this assumption is not necessary for our analysis to hold. If cash payments are debited directly to the expense account, the total amount of cash paid for wages and other operating expenses will still equal the $216,000 expense plus the $2,000 increase in prepaid expenses.

Exhibit 17.14 summarizes the adjustments to wages (including salaries) and other operating expenses. While the balance sheet of Genesis did not report accrued liabilities, we add these to the exhibit to explain the adjustment to cash when they do exist. If accrued liabilities decrease, it implies we paid for more goods or services than received this period, and we must add the change in accrued liabilities to the expense amount to get cash paid for these goods or services. If accrued liabilities increase, it implies we paid less than was acquired and we must subtract the change in accrued liabilities from the expense amount to get cash paid.

Exhibit 17.14

Formula to Compute Cash Paid for Wages and Operating Expenses—Direct Method

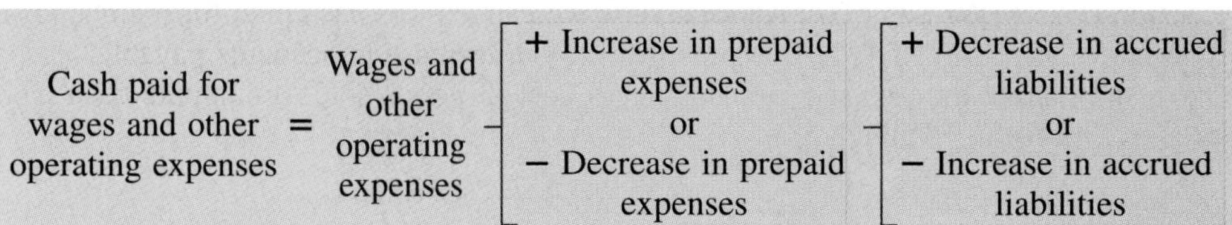

Cash Paid for Both Interest and Income Taxes

Our analysis for computing operating cash flows for interest and taxes is similar to that for operating expenses. Both require adjustments to their amounts on the income statement for changes in their related balance sheet accounts.

We begin with the income statement of Genesis showing interest expense of $7,000 and income taxes expense of $15,000. To compute the cash paid, we adjust interest expense for the change in interest payable and we adjust income taxes expense for the change in income taxes payable. These computations involve reconstructing both liability accounts:

Interest Payable			
		Balance, 12/31/1999	4,000
Interest paid =	8,000	Interest expense	7,000
		Balance, 12/31/2000	3,000

Income Taxes Payable			
		Balance, 12/31/1999	12,000
Income taxes paid =	5,000	Income taxes expense	15,000
		Balance, 12/31/2000	22,000

These accounts reveal cash paid for interest of $8,000 and cash paid for income taxes of $5,000. The formulas to compute these amounts are shown in Exhibit 17.15.

Formulas to Compute Cash Paid for both Interest and Taxes—Direct Method

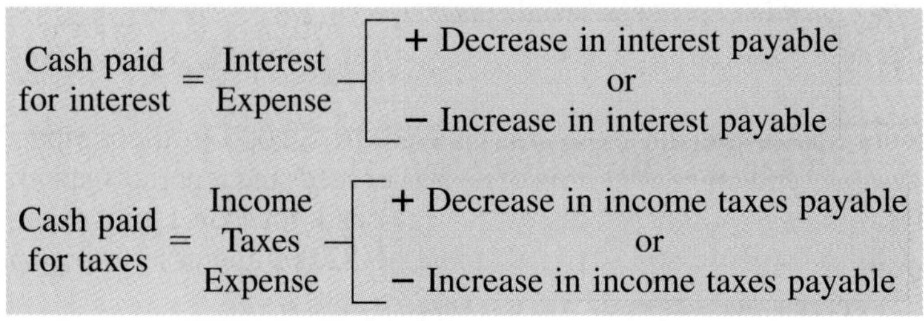

Both of these cash payments are reported as operating cash outflows on the statement of cash flows for Genesis in Exhibit 17.7.

Analysis of Other Operating Expenses

Genesis has three other operating expenses reported on its income statement: depreciation, loss on sale of assets, and gain on retirement of debt. We consider each of these for their potential cash effects.

Depreciation expense Depreciation expense for Genesis is $24,000. It is known as a *noncash expense* because there are no cash flows associated with depreciation. Depreciation expense is an allocation of the depreciable cost of a purchased asset. The cash outflow associated with a plant asset is reported as part of investing activities when it is paid for. This means depreciation expense is *never* reported on a statement of cash flows using the direct method. Depletion and amortization expenses are treated similarly.

Loss on sale of assets Sales of assets frequently result in gains and losses reported as part of net income. But the amount of recorded gain or loss does *not* reflect cash flows in these transactions. Asset sales result in cash inflow equal to the actual amount received, regardless of whether the asset was sold at a gain or a loss. This cash inflow is reported under investing activities. This means the loss or gain on a sale of assets is never reported on a statement of cash flows using the direct method.

Gain on retirement of debt Retirements of debt usually yield gains and losses reported as part of net income. But the amount of recorded gain or loss does *not* reflect cash flows in these transactions. Debt retirement results in cash outflow equal to the actual amount paid to settle the debt, regardless of whether the debt was retired at a gain or loss. This cash outflow is reported under financing activities. This means the loss or gain from retirement of debt is never reported on a statement of cash flows using the direct method.

Summary of Adjustments for Direct Method

Exhibit 17.16 summarizes the adjustments to the revenues and expenses making up net income to give us net cash provided (used) by operating activities under the direct method.

Exhibit 17.16

Summary of Selected Adjustments for Direct Method

Item	From Income Statement	Adjustments to get cash flow numbers	
Receipts:			
From customers	Sales Revenue	+ Decrease in Accounts Receivable − Increase in Accounts Receivable	
From rent	Rent Revenue	+ Decrease in Rent Receivable − Increase in Rent Receivable	
From interest	Interest Revenue	+ Decrease in Interest Receivable − Increase in Interest Receivable	
From dividends	Dividend Revenue	+ Decrease in Dividends Receivable − Increase in Dividends Receivable	
Payments:			
To suppliers	Cost of Goods Sold	+ Increase in Inventory − Decrease in Inventory	+ Decrease in Accounts Payable − Increase in Accounts Payable
For operations	Operating Expense	+ Increase in Prepaids − Decrease in Prepaids	+ Decrease in Accrued Liabilities − Increase in Accrued Liabilities
To employees	Wages (Salaries) Expense	+ Decrease in Wages (Salaries) Payable − Increase in Wages (Salaries) Payable	
For interest	Interest Expense	+ Decrease in Interest Payable − Increase in Interest Payable	
For income tax	Income Tax Expense	+ Decrease in Income Tax Payable − Increase in Income Tax Payable	

While computations for computing net cash provided (used) by operating activities are different for the direct and indirect methods, the result is identical. Both methods yield the same $20,000 amount for net cash provided (used) by operating activities; see Exhibits 17.7 and 17.17.

Direct Method Format of Operating Activities Section

Exhibit 17.7 shows the statement of cash flows for Genesis using the direct method. Major items of cash inflows and cash outflows are listed separately in the operating activities section. The format requires that operating cash outflows are subtracted from operating cash inflows to get net cash provided (used) by operating activities.

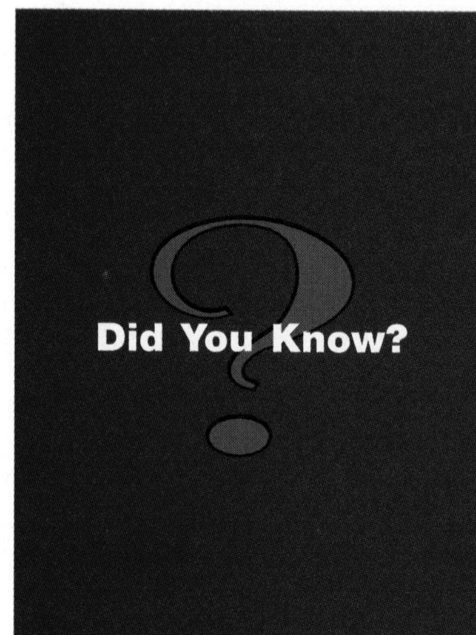

Celtic Green
The Boston Celtics report operating cash flows using the direct method. Its June 30, 1997, operating section from its annual statement of cash flows is shown here.

Basketball regular season receipts:	
Ticket sales	$33,132,256
Television and radio broadcast fees	22,009,139
Other, principally advertising	8,141,716
Costs and expenses:	
Basketball regular season expenditures:	
Team expenses	$34,390,240
Game expenses	2,273,709
General and administrative expenses	15,650,961
Selling and promotional expenses	3,730,578
Interest and income taxes	(475,655)
Payment of deferred compensation	(4,300,147)
Net Cash Flows From Operations	$ 2,461,821

Reconciling Net Income to Operating Net Cash Flows

The FASB recommends the operating activities section of the statement of cash flows be reported using the direct method. The direct method results in a listing of each major cash inflow and cash outflow from operating activities and is considered more useful to users of financial statements. *But the FASB requires a reconciliation of net income to net cash provided (used) by operating activities when the direct method is used.* This reconciliation is the same as preparing the operating section of the statement of cash flows using the indirect method. The next section describes this method.

Flash back

4. Is the direct or indirect method of reporting operating cash flows more informative? Explain. Which method is more common in practice?
5. Net sales in a period are $590,000, beginning accounts receivable are $120,000, and ending accounts receivable are $90,000. What amount is collected from customers in the period?
6. The Merchandise Inventory account balance decreases in a period from a beginning balance of $32,000 to an ending balance of $28,000. Cost of goods sold for the period is $168,000. If the Accounts Payable balance increases $2,400 in the period, what is the amount of cash paid for merchandise?
7. Reported wages and other operating expenses incurred total $112,000. At the end of the prior year, prepaid expenses totaled $1,200, and this year the balance is $4,200. The current balance sheet shows wages payable of $5,600, whereas last year's did not show any accrued liabilities. How much is paid for wages and other operating expenses this year?

Answers—p. 750

Indirect Method of Reporting

P3 Compute cash flows from operating activities using the indirect method.

Net income is computed using accrual accounting. Accrual accounting recognizes revenues when earned and expenses when incurred. But revenues and expenses do not necessarily reflect the receipt and payment of cash. The indirect method of computing and reporting net cash flows from operating activities involves adjusting the net income figure to get the net cash provided (used) by operating activities. This includes subtracting noncash credits from net income and adding noncash charges back to net income.

We again draw on the statements of Genesis in Exhibit 17.10 to illustrate application of the indirect method. The indirect method begins with net income of $38,000 for Genesis and then adjusts it to get net cash provided (used) by operating activities. Exhibit 17.17 shows the results of the indirect method of reporting operating cash flows for Genesis. The net cash provided by operating activities is $20,000. This amount is the same as that for the direct method of reporting operating cash flows (see Exhibit 17.7). *The two methods always yield the same net cash flow provided (used) by operating activities.* Only the computations and presentation are different.

The indirect method does not report individual operating cash inflows or cash outflows. Instead, the indirect method adjusts net income for three types of adjustments as shown in Exhibit 17.17. First, there are adjustments for changes in noncash current assets and current liabilities relating to operating activities. Second, there are adjustments to income statement items involving operating activities that do not affect cash

Exhibit 17.17

Statement of Cash Flows—Indirect Method

GENESIS
Statement of Cash Flows
For Year Ended December 31, 2000

	Cash flows from operating activities:		
	Net income	$38,000	
	Adjustments to reconcile net income to net cash provided by operating activities:		
①	Increase in accounts receivable	(20,000)	
①	Increase in merchandise inventory	(14,000)	
①	Increase in prepaid expenses	(2,000)	
①	Decrease in accounts payable	(5,000)	
①	Decrease in interest payable	(1,000)	
①	Increase in income taxes payable	10,000	
②	Depreciation expense	24,000	
③	Loss on sale of plant assets	6,000	
③	Gain on retirement of bonds	(16,000)	
	Net cash provided by operating activities		$20,000
	Cash flows from investing activities:		
	Cash received from sale of plant assets	$12,000	
	Cash paid for purchase of plant assets	(10,000)	
	Net cash provided by investing activities		2,000
	Cash flows from financing activities:		
	Cash received from issuing stock	$15,000	
	Cash paid to retire bonds	(18,000)	
	Cash paid for dividends	(14,000)	
	Net cash used in financing activities		(17,000)
	Net increase in cash		$ 5,000
	Cash balance at beginning of 1999		12,000
	Cash balance at end of 2000		$17,000

inflows or outflows in the period. Third, there are adjustments to eliminate gains and losses resulting from investing and financing activities (those not part of operating activities). This section describes each of these three types of adjustments in applying the indirect method.

① Adjustments for Changes in Current Assets and Current Liabilities

This section describes adjustments for changes in noncash current assets and current liabilities for determining operating cash flows using the indirect method.

Adjustments for Changes in Noncash Current Assets

Changes in noncash current assets are normally the result of operating activities. Examples are sales affecting accounts receivable and use of rented assets affecting prepaid rent expense. Our adjustments to net income in computing operating cash flows therefore include changes in noncash current assets. Under the indirect method for reporting operating cash flows:

Decreases in noncash current assets are added to net income

To see this logic, consider that a decrease in a noncash current asset such as accounts receivable suggests more available cash at the end of the period compared to the beginning of the period. This is because a decrease in accounts receivable implies greater cash receipts. We add these greater cash receipts from the decreases in noncash current assets to net income when computing net cash flow from operations.

Similarly, an increase in noncash current assets such as accounts receivable implies decreased cash receipts. For instance, an increase in prepaid rent expense suggests more cash was paid for rent than was deducted as rent expense. We must therefore subtract this increase in prepaid rent from net income in computing the amount of cash flow from operations. The indirect method for reporting operating cash flows requires:

Increases in noncash current assets are subtracted from net income

These adjustments to net income are a necessary part of the computations to get net cash provided by operating activities. We now turn to the individual noncash current assets of Genesis as shown in Exhibit 17.10.

Accounts receivable Accounts receivable of Genesis *increased* $20,000 in the period, from a beginning balance of $40,000 to an ending balance of $60,000. This increase implies Genesis collected less cash than its reported sales amount for this period. It also means some of these sales were in the form of accounts receivable, leaving accounts receivable with an increase. This lesser amount of cash collections compared with sales is reflected in the Accounts Receivable account as shown here:

Accounts Receivable			
Balance 12/31/1999	40,000		
Sales, 2000	590,000	Collections =	570,000
Balance 12/31/2000	60,000		

This $20,000 increase in accounts receivable is subtracted from net income as part of our adjustments to get net cash provided by operating activities. Subtracting it adjusts sales to the cash receipts amount.

Merchandise inventory Merchandise inventory *increased* $14,000 in the period, from a beginning balance of $70,000 to an ending balance of $84,000. This increase implies Genesis had a greater amount of cash purchases than goods sold this period. This greater amount of cash purchases ended up in the form of inventory, resulting in an inventory increase. This greater amount of cash purchases compared to the amount subtracted from income as cost of goods sold is reflected in the Merchandise Inventory account increase:

Merchandise Inventory			
Balance, 12/31/1999	70,000		
Purchases =	**314,000**	Cost of goods sold	300,000
Balance, 12/31/2000	84,000		

The $14,000 increase in inventory is subtracted from net income as part of our adjustments to get net cash provided by operating activities.

Prepaid expenses Prepaid expenses *increased* $2,000 in the period, from a beginning balance of $4,000 to an ending balance of $6,000. This increase implies Genesis's cash payments exceeded its operating expenses incurred this period. These larger cash payments ended up increasing the amount of prepaid expenses. This is reflected in the Prepaid Expenses account:

Prepaid Expenses			
Balance, 12/31/1999	4,000		
Payments =	**218,000**	Wages and other operating exp.	216,000
Balance, 12/31/2000	6,000		

This $2,000 increase in prepaid expenses is subtracted from net income as part of our adjustments to get net cash provided by operating activities. Subtracting it adjusts operating expenses to a cash payments amount.

Adjustments for Changes in Current Liabilities

Changes in current liabilities are normally the result of operating activities. An example is purchases affecting accounts payable. Our adjustments to net income in computing operating cash flows must therefore include changes in current liabilities. Under the indirect method for reporting operating cash flows:

Increases in current liabilities are added to net income

To see the logic, an increase in accounts payable suggests that cash payments are less than its related expense. As another example, an increase in wages payable implies that wages expense exceeded cash paid for the period. Because more was deducted as an expense than was paid in cash, we add the increase in wages payable to net income when computing net cash flow from operations.

When current liabilities decrease in the period, the indirect method for reporting operating cash flows requires:

Decreases in current liabilities are subtracted from net income

These adjustments to net income are a necessary part of the computations to get net cash provided by operating activities. We now analyze the individual current liabilities of Genesis as reported in Exhibit 17.10.

Accounts payable Accounts payable of Genesis *decreased* $5,000 in the period, from a beginning balance of $40,000 to an ending balance of $35,000. This decrease implies its cash payments exceeded its merchandise purchases by $5,000 for the period.

This larger amount for cash payments compared to purchases is reflected in the Accounts Payable account:

Accounts Payable			
		Balance, 12/31/1999	40,000
Payments =	319,000	Purchases	314,000
		Balance, 12/31/2000	35,000

The $5,000 decrease in accounts payable is subtracted from net income as part of our adjustments to get net cash provided by operating activities.

Interest payable Interest payable *decreased* $1,000 in the period, from a beginning balance of $4,000 to an ending balance of $3,000. This decrease indicates cash payments for interest exceeded interest expense for the period by $1,000. This larger cash payment compared to the reported interest expense is reflected in the Interest Payable account:

Interest Payable			
		Balance, 12/31/1999	4,000
Interest paid =	8,000	Interest expense	7,000
		Balance, 12/31/2000	3,000

The $1,000 decrease in interest payable is subtracted from net income as part of our adjustments to get net cash provided by operating activities.

Income taxes payable Income taxes payable *increased* $10,000 in the period, from a beginning balance of $12,000 to an ending balance of $22,000. This increase implies the amount owed for income taxes exceeded the cash payments for the period by $10,000. This smaller cash payment compared to income taxes owed is reflected in the Income Taxes Payable account:

Income Taxes Payable			
		Balance, 12/31/1999	12,000
Income taxes paid =	5,000	Income taxes expense	15,000
		Balance, 12/31/2000	22,000

The $10,000 increase in income taxes payable is added to net income as part of our adjustments to get net cash provided by operating activities.

② Adjustments for Operating Items Not Providing or Using Cash

The income statement usually includes certain expenses that do not reflect cash outflows in the period. Examples are depreciation, amortization of intangible assets, depletion of natural resources, and bad debts expense. The indirect method for reporting operating cash flows requires that:

Expenses with no cash outflows are added back to net income

To see this logic, recall that items such as depreciation, amortization, depletion, and bad debts are properly recorded with debits to expense accounts and credits to noncash accounts. There is *no* cash effect in these entries, and we need to add them back to net income when computing net cash flows from operations. Adding them back cancels their deductions.

Similarly, when net income includes revenues that do not reflect cash inflows in the period, the indirect method for reporting operating cash flows requires that:

Revenues with no cash inflows are subtracted from net income

Both types of adjustments to net income are a necessary part of the computations to get net cash provided by operating activities for the indirect method. We now look at the individual operating items of Genesis that fit this category and do not provide or use cash.

Depreciation

Depreciation expense is the only operating item for Genesis that does not affect cash flows in the period. Our discussion indicates we must add $24,000 depreciation expense back to net income as part of our adjustments to get net cash provided by operating activities. Later in the chapter we explain that the cash outflow for a plant asset is reported as an investing activity on the statement of cash flows when paid.

③ Adjustments for Nonoperating Items

The income statement sometimes includes losses that are not part of operating activities, and are classified as either investing or financing activities. Examples are a loss from sale of a plant asset and a loss from retirement of a bond payable. Under the indirect method for reporting operating cash flows:

Nonoperating losses are added back to net income

To see the logic, consider that items such as a plant asset sale and bond retirement are normally recorded by recognizing the cash, removing all plant asset or bond accounts, and recognizing the loss or gain. The cash received or paid is not part of operating activities. Instead it is recorded under either investing or financing activities. There is *no* operating cash flow effect. But because the nonoperating loss is a deduction in computing accrual income, we need to add it back to net income when computing the net cash flow effect from operations. Adding it back cancels the deduction.

Similarly, when net income includes gains that are not part of operating activities, the indirect method for reporting operating cash flows requires:

Nonoperating gains are subtracted from net income

These net income adjustments are part of computations to get net cash provided by operating activities. We now look at the individual nonoperating items of Genesis.

Loss on Sale of Plant Assets

Genesis reports a $6,000 loss on sale of plant assets in its income statement. This loss is a proper deduction in computing income, but it is *not part of operating activities.* Instead, a sale of plant assets is part of investing activities. This means the $6,000 nonoperating loss is added back to net income as part of our adjustments to get cash provided by operating activities. Adding it back cancels the recorded loss. Later in the chapter we explain how the cash inflow from the plant asset sale is reported in investing activities.

Gain on Retirement of Debt

There is a $16,000 gain on retirement of debt reported in the income statement of Genesis. This gain is properly included in net income, but it is *not part of operating activities.* This means the $16,000 nonoperating gain is subtracted from net income as part of our adjustments to get net cash provided by operating activities. Subtracting it cancels the recorded gain. Later in the chapter we describe how the cash outflow to retire debt is reported in financing activities.

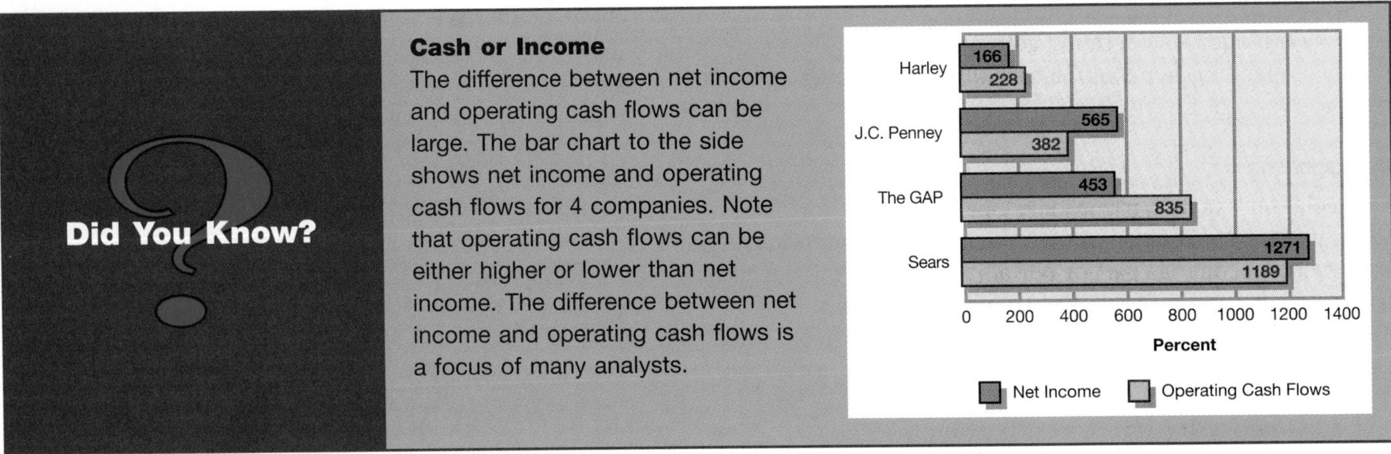

Did You Know?
Cash or Income
The difference between net income and operating cash flows can be large. The bar chart to the side shows net income and operating cash flows for 4 companies. Note that operating cash flows can be either higher or lower than net income. The difference between net income and operating cash flows is a focus of many analysts.
Harley
166
228
J.C. Penney
565
382
The GAP
453
835
Sears
1271
1189
0 200 400 600 800 1000 1200 1400
Percent
Net Income
Operating Cash Flows

Summary of Adjustments for Indirect Method

Exhibit 17.18 summarizes the adjustments to net income to get net cash provided (used) by operating activities for the indirect method.

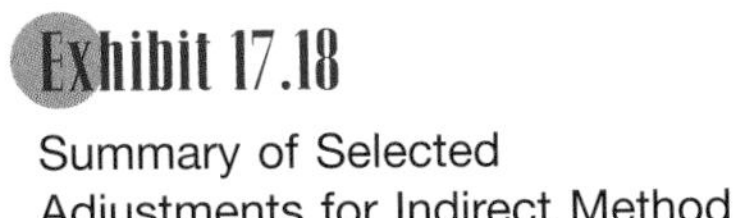

Summary of Selected Adjustments for Indirect Method

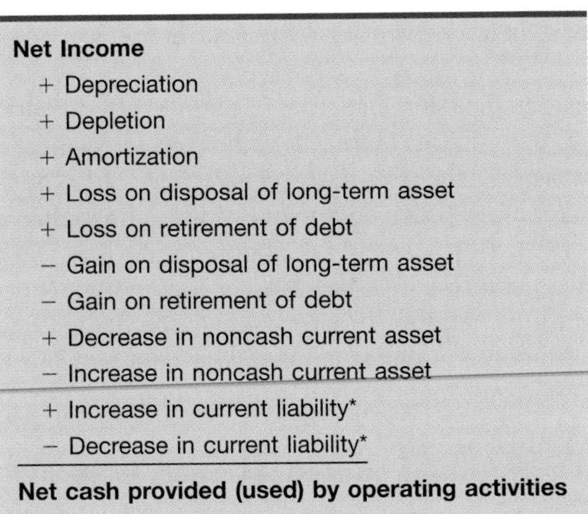

Net Income
+ Depreciation
+ Depletion
+ Amortization
+ Loss on disposal of long-term asset
+ Loss on retirement of debt
− Gain on disposal of long-term asset
− Gain on retirement of debt
+ Decrease in noncash current asset
− Increase in noncash current asset
+ Increase in current liability*
− Decrease in current liability*
Net cash provided (used) by operating activities

While the computations in determining net cash provided (used) by operating activities are different for the direct and indirect methods, the result is identical. Both methods yield the same $20,000 figure for net cash provided (used) by operating activities—see Exhibits 17.7 and 17.17.

8. Determine net cash provided (or used) by operating activities using the following data: Net income, $74,900; Decrease in accounts receivable, $4,600; Increase in inventory, $11,700; Decrease in accounts payable, $1,000; Loss on sale of equipment, $3,400; Payment of dividends, $21,500.
9. Why are expenses such as depreciation and amortization added to net income when cash flow from operating activities is computed by the indirect method?
10. A company reports net income of $15,000 that includes a $3,000 gain on the sale of plant assets. Why is this gain subtracted from net income in computing cash flow from operating activities using the indirect method?

Answers—p. 750

*Excludes current portion of long-term debt and any short-term notes payable if unrelated to sales. Both are financing activities.

Cash Flows from Investing

The third major step in preparing the statement of cash flows is to compute and report net cash flows from investing activities. We normally do this by identifying changes in all noncurrent asset accounts and both current and long-term notes receivable. These accounts include plant assets, intangible assets, investments, and notes. Changes in these accounts are then analyzed using available information to determine their effect, if any, on cash. Results of this analysis are reported in the investing activities section of the statement. *Reporting of investing activities is identical under the direct method and indirect method.*

Investing activities include transactions such as (a) the purchase and sale of long-term assets, (b) lending and collecting on notes receivable, and (c) the purchase and sale of short-term investments other than cash equivalents. Information to compute cash flows from investing activities is usually taken from beginning and ending balance sheets and from the income statement. Information provided earlier in the chapter about the transactions of Genesis reveals it both purchased and sold plant assets during the period. Both transactions are investing activities.

Plant Asset Transactions

P4 Determine cash flows from both investing and financing activities.

We use a three-step process in determining net cash provided (used) by investing activities: (1) identify changes in investing-related accounts; (2) explain these changes using reconstruction analysis; and (3) report cash flow effects.

For plant assets, we need to deal with both the plant asset account and its related accumulated depreciation account. Comparative balance sheet information for these accounts is in Exhibit 17.10. The first step reveals a $40,000 increase in plant assets from $210,000 to $250,000, and a $12,000 increase in accumulated depreciation from $48,000 to $60,000. We need to explain these changes.

The second step begins by reviewing ledger accounts and any additional information at our disposal. A plant asset account is affected by both purchases and sales of plant assets. An accumulated depreciation account is increased from depreciation and reduced by removing accumulated depreciation on asset sales. Items (b) and (c) of the additional information reported earlier for Genesis (page 727) are relevant for these accounts. To explain changes in these accounts and to help us understand the cash flows effects, we prepare *reconstructed entries.* A reconstructed entry is our reproduction of an entry from a transaction, *it is not the actual entry made by the preparer.* Item (b) reports Genesis purchased plant assets costing $70,000 by issuing $60,000 in bonds payable to the seller and paying $10,000 in cash. The reconstructed entry for our analysis of item (b) is:

Plant Assets	70,000	
Bonds Payable		60,000
Cash		**10,000**

Assets	=	Liabilities	+	Equity
+70,000		+60,000		
−10,000				

This entry reveals a $10,000 cash outflow for assets purchased. It also reveals a noncash investing and financing transaction involving $60,000 bonds given up for $60,000 of plant assets.

Item (c) reports Genesis sold plant assets costing $30,000 (with $12,000 of accumulated depreciation) for cash received of $12,000, resulting in a loss of $6,000. The reconstructed entry for item (c) is:

Cash	**12,000**	
Accumulated Depreciation	12,000	
Loss on Sale of Plant Assets	6,000	
Plant Assets		30,000

Assets	=	Liabilities	+	Equity
+12,000				−6,000
−30,000				
+12,000				

This entry reveals a $12,000 cash inflow for assets sold. The $6,000 loss is computed by comparing the asset book value to the cash received and does not reflect any cash inflow or outflow.

We also reconstruct the entry for depreciation expense using information from the income statement:

Assets = Liabilities + Equity
−24,000 −24,000

Depreciation Expense	24,000	
Accumulated Depreciation		24,000

This entry shows that depreciation expense results in no cash flow effects.

These reconstructed entries are reflected in the ledger accounts for both plant assets and accumulated depreciation.

Plant Assets			
Balance, 12/31/1999	210,000		
Purchase	**70,000**	**Sale**	**30,000**
Balance, 12/31/2000	250,000		

Accumulated Depreciation, Plant Assets			
		Balance, 12/31/1999	48,000
Sale	**12,000**	**Depr. expense**	**24,000**
		Balance, 12/31/2000	60,000

In performing an actual cash flow analysis, we have the entire ledger and additional information at our disposal. For brevity reasons, we are given the additional information for reconstructing accounts and verifying that our analysis of the investing-related accounts is complete.

The third step is to make the necessary disclosures on the statement of cash flows. Disclosure of the two cash flow effects in the investing section of the statement appears as (also see Exhibit 17.7 or 17.17):

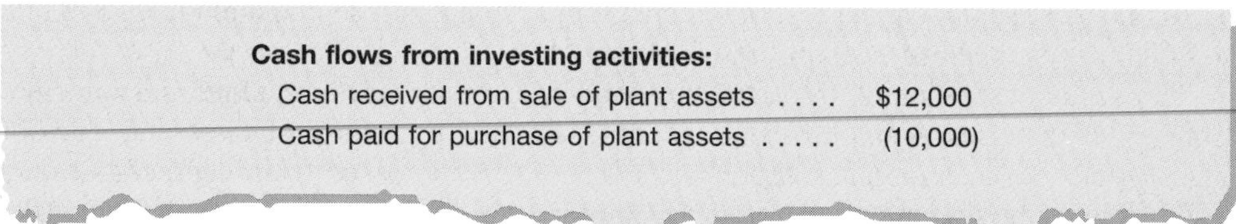

Cash flows from investing activities:	
Cash received from sale of plant assets	$12,000
Cash paid for purchase of plant assets	(10,000)

The $60,000 portion of the purchase described in item (b) and financed by issuance of the bonds is a noncash investing and financing activity. This can be reported in a note to the statement as:

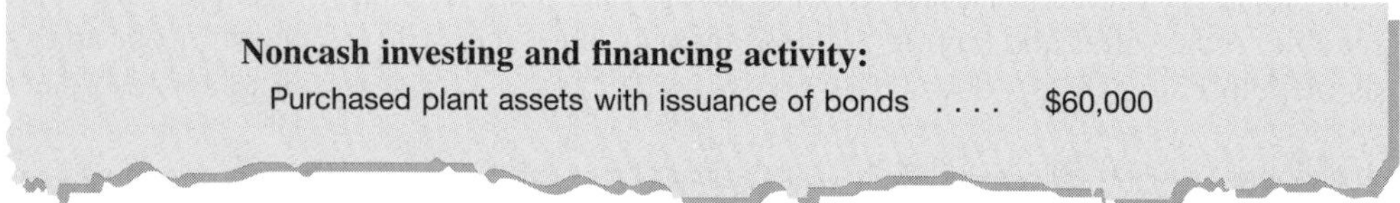

Noncash investing and financing activity:	
Purchased plant assets with issuance of bonds	$60,000

We have now reconstructed these accounts by explaining how the beginning balances of both accounts are affected by purchases, sales, and depreciation in yielding their ending balances. The change in plant assets from $210,000 to $250,000 is fully explained by the $70,000 purchase and the $30,000 sale. Also, the change in accumulated depreciation from $48,000 to $60,000 is fully explained by the sale of assets (with $12,000 of accumulated depreciation) and $24,000 of depreciation expense.

Flash *back*

11. Equipment costing $80,000 with accumulated depreciation of $30,000 is sold at a loss of $10,000. What is the cash receipt from the sale? In what category of the statement of cash flows is it reported?

Answer—p. 750

Cash Flows from Financing

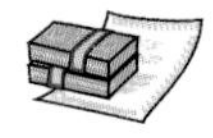

The fourth step in preparing the statement of cash flows is to compute and report net cash flows from financing activities. We normally do this by identifying changes in all note payable (current and noncurrent), noncurrent liability, and equity accounts. These accounts include long-term debt, notes payable, bonds payable, owner's capital, common stock, and retained earnings. Changes in these accounts are then analyzed using available information to determine their effect, if any, on cash. Results of this analysis are reported in the financing activities section of the statement. *Reporting of financing activities is identical under the direct method and indirect method.*

Financing activities include transactions such as (a) receiving cash from issuing debt and repaying the amounts borrowed and (b) receiving cash from or distributing cash to owners. Information provided earlier about the transactions of Genesis reveals four transactions involving financing activities. We already analyzed one of these, the $60,000 issuance of bonds payable to purchase plant assets as a noncash investing and financing activity. The remaining three transactions are retirement of bonds, issuance of common stock, and payment of cash dividends. We again use a three-step process in determining net cash provided (used) by financing activities: (1) identify changes in financing-related accounts; (2) explain these changes using reconstruction analysis; and (3) report cash flow effects.

Bonds Payable Transactions

Comparative balance sheet information from Exhibit 17.10 for bonds payable is our starting point. The first step reveals an increase in bonds payable from $64,000 to $90,000. We need to explain this change.

The second step is to review the bonds payable ledger account and any additional information available. Item (e) of the additional information given earlier for Genesis is relevant to bonds payable. Item (e) reports that bonds with a carrying value of $34,000 are retired for $18,000 cash, resulting in a $16,000 gain. The reconstructed entry for our analysis of item (e) is:

	Debit	Credit
Bonds Payable	34,000	
Gain on retirement of debt		16,000
Cash		**18,000**

Assets	= Liabilities	+ Equity
−18,000	−34,000	+16,000

This entry reveals an $18,000 cash outflow for retirement of bonds. It also shows a $16,000 gain from comparing the bonds payable carrying value with the cash received. This gain does not reflect any cash inflow or outflow.

Item (b) also involves bonds payable. It reports Genesis purchased plant assets costing $70,000 by issuing $60,000 in bonds payable to the seller and paying $10,000 in cash. We already reconstructed this entry for our analysis of investing activities. Recall it increased bonds payable by $60,000 and is reported as a noncash investing and financing transaction. These reconstructed entries are reflected in the ledger account for bonds payable:

Bonds Payable			
		Balance, 12/31/1999	64,000
Retired bonds	34,000	Issued bonds	60,000
		Balance, 12/31/2000	90,000

The third step is to make the necessary disclosures on the statement of cash flows. Disclosure of the cash flow effect from the bond retirement in the financing section of the statement appears as (also see Exhibit 17.7 or 17.17):

Cash flows from financing activities:

Cash paid to retire bonds	($18,000)

We have now reconstructed the bonds payable account by explaining how the change in bonds payable from $64,000 to $90,000 is fully explained by the $34,000 retirement and the $60,000 issuance.

Common Stock Transactions

We use comparative balance sheet information from Exhibit 17.10 for the first step in analyzing the common stock account. This first step reveals an increase in common stock from $80,000 to $95,000. We need to explain this change.

Our second step is to review the common stock ledger account and any additional information available. Item (d) of the additional information given earlier for Genesis reports it issued 3,000 shares of common stock at par for $5 per share. The reconstructed entry for our analysis of item (d) is:

Assets	= Liabilities	+ Equity
+15,000		+15,000

Cash	**15,000**	
Common Stock		15,000

This entry reveals a $15,000 cash inflow from stock issuance. This reconstructed entry is reflected in the ledger account for common stock:

Common Stock		
	Balance, 12/31/1999	80,000
	Issued stock	15,000
	Balance, 12/31/2000	95,000

The third step is to make the necessary disclosure on the statement of cash flows. Disclosure of the cash flow effect from stock issuance in the financing section of the statement appears as (also see Exhibit 17.7 or 17.17):

Cash flows from financing activities:

Cash received from issuing stock	$15,000

The $15,000 stock issuance fully explains the change in the Common Stock account.

Retained Earnings Transactions

The first step in analyzing the retained earnings account is to review comparative balance sheet information from Exhibit 17.10. The first step reveals an increase in retained earnings from $88,000 to $112,000. We need to explain this change.

Our second step is to analyze the retained earnings account and any additional information available. Item (f) of the additional information given earlier for Genesis reports it paid dividends of $14,000. The reconstructed entry for our analysis of item (f) is:

Assets	= Liabilities	+ Equity
−14,000		−14,000

Retained Earnings	14,000	
Cash		**14,000**

This entry reveals a $14,000 cash outflow to pay cash dividends. We must also remember retained earnings is affected by net income from the income statement. Net income was already dealt with under the operating section of the statement of cash flows. This reconstruction analysis is reflected in the ledger account for retained earnings:

Retained Earnings			
		Balance, 12/31/1999	88,000
Cash dividend	14,000	Net income	38,000
		Balance, 12/31/2000	112,000

The third step is to make the necessary disclosure on the statement of cash flows. Disclosure of the cash flow effect from the cash dividend appears in the financing section of the statement as (also see Exhibit 17.7 or 17.17):

Cash flows from financing activities:	
Cash paid for dividends	($14,000)

The $14,000 dividend payment along with the reported net income of $38,000 fully explains the change in Retained Earnings.

Proving Cash Balances

We have now explained all of the cash inflows and outflows of Genesis, along with one noncash investing and financing transaction. Our analysis has reconciled changes in all noncash balance sheet accounts. The fifth and final step in preparing the statement is to report the beginning and ending cash balances and prove that the *net change in cash* is explained by operating, investing, and financing net cash flows. This step is shown below for Genesis:

Net cash provided by operating activities	$ 20,000
Net cash provided by investing activities	2,000
Net cash used in financing activities	(17,000)
Net increase in cash	**$ 5,000**
Cash balance at beginning of 2000	12,000
Cash balance at end of 2000	$ 17,000

This schedule shows that the $5,000 net increase in cash from $12,000 at the beginning of the period to $17,000 at the end is reconciled by net cash flows from operating ($20,000 inflow), investing ($2,000 inflow), and financing ($17,000 outflow) activities. This is formally reported at the bottom of the statement of cash flows as shown in either Exhibit 17.7 or 17.17.

Reporter

You are a newspaper reporter covering a workers' strike. Management grants you an interview and complains about recent losses and negative cash flows. It shows you financial numbers revealing a recent $600,000 net loss which included a $930,000 extraordinary loss. It also shows you the company's total net cash outflow of $550,000 which included net cash outflows of $850,000 for investing activities and $350,000 for financing activities. What is your reaction to management's complaints?

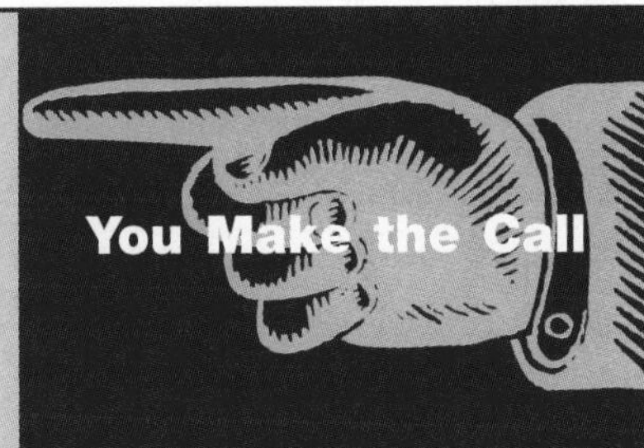

Answer—p. 749

USING THE INFORMATION — Cash Flow Analysis

Numerous ratios are used to analyze income statement and balance sheet data. By comparison, ratios related to the statement of cash flows are fewer in number. One of these ratios is cash flow per share. The FASB does not allow reporting cash flow per share, presumably because it might be misinterpreted as a measure of earnings.

Analyzing Cash Sources and Uses

A1 Analyze the statement of cash flows.

Most managers stress the importance of understanding and predicting cash flows. Many business decisions are based on cash flow evaluations. For instance, creditors evaluate a company's ability to generate cash before deciding whether to loan money. Many investors make similar evaluations before buying stock. Information in the statement of cash flows helps us address questions such as:

- How much cash is generated from or used in operations?
- What expenditures are made with cash from operations?
- How are dividends paid when losses occur?
- What is the source of cash for debt payments?
- What is the source of cash for distributions to owners?
- How is the increase in investments financed?
- What is the source of cash for new plant assets?
- Why is cash lower when income increased?
- What is the use of cash from financing?

While cash flows from investing and financing activities are important in these decisions, we pay special attention to operating cash flows. A statement of cash flows helps in this regard by separating investing, financing, and operating activities.

To illustrate the importance of separately analyzing cash flows by activities, we look at data from three different companies in Exhibit 17.19. These companies operate in the same industry and have been in business for several years.

Exhibit 17.19
Cash Flows of Competitors

(in thousands)	Fisher	Sprint	Tektron
Cash provided (used) by operating activities	$90,000	$40,000	$(24,000)
Cash provided (used) by investing activities:			
Proceeds from sale of operating assets			26,000
Purchase of operating assets	(48,000)	(25,000)	
Cash provided (used) by financing activities:			
Proceeds from issuance of debt			13,000
Repayment of debt	(27,000)		
Net increase (decrease) in cash	$15,000	$15,000	$ 15,000

These companies each generate a $15,000 net increase in cash flows. But their sources and uses of cash flows are very different. Fisher's operating activities provided net cash flows of $90,000. This allowed it to purchase additional operating assets for $48,000 and repay $27,000 of debt. Sprint's operating activities provided $40,000 of cash flows. This limited its purchase of operating assets to $25,000. Tektron's net cash increase is due to selling operating assets and incurring additional debt. Its operating activities yield a net cash outflow of $24,000.

Our analysis of these cash flow data reveals that Fisher is more capable of generating cash to meet its future obligations than is Sprint or Tektron. Also, the strong operating cash flows of Fisher bode well for future performance, while Tektron's operating outlook is poor. This evaluation is, of course, tentative and may be contradicted by other information, including data in the balance sheet or income statement.

Managers analyze cash flows for making many short-term and long-term decisions. A decision on the necessity of short-term borrowing is made using many of the procedures we discussed in this chapter. Short-term planning also can lead to decisions about investing idle cash balances. Managers' setting of sales prices is also influenced by cash flow data.

Managers' long-term decisions involving new investments are based on cash flow predictions. They estimate cash inflows and outflows over the life of the investment, often extending many years into the future. Other long-term decisions based on cash flow data include deciding whether a product is manufactured by the company or purchased from an outside supplier, and whether a product or a department is eliminated or retained.

Flash back

12. Refer to the statement of cash flows for America Online in Appendix A. What type and amount of investing activities took place during the year ended June 30, 1996? What is the largest source of cash from financing activities?

Answer—p. 750

Cash Flow on Total Assets

A2 Compute and apply the cash flow on total assets ratio.

We described the importance of return on total assets in both Chapters 1 and 16. Return on total assets is a valuable measure of financial performance and is computed as net income divided by average total assets. The numerator of return on total assets is net income based on accrual accounting.

Cash flow accounting is different from accrual accounting. Cash flow accounting recognizes cash inflows when received (not necessarily earned) and cash outflows when paid (not necessarily incurred). While cash flow information has limitations, it can help us measure a company's ability to meet its obligations, pay dividends, expand operations, and obtain financing.

Because of the importance of cash flows, users often look at a cash-based measure called cash flow on total assets. It is somewhat similar to return on total assets, but its numerator is net cash flows from operating activities (not net income). Specifically, the **cash flow on total assets** is computed as shown in Exhibit 17.20.

Exhibit 17.20

Cash Flow on Total Assets

$$\textbf{Cash flow on total assets} = \frac{\textbf{Operating cash flows}}{\textbf{Average total assets}}$$

This ratio can add to our analysis of company performance. The cash flow on total assets ratio reflects actual cash flows and is not affected by the accounting constraints of recognition and measurement for net income. It is important for companies to recognize their cash flow amounts and patterns in planning and analyzing operating activities. The cash flow on total assets ratio is one measure to help us assess cash flows.

To illustrate, we look at the cash flow on total assets for **NIKE** at May 31, 1997. It is computed as ($ in thousands):

$$\text{Cash flow on total assets} = \frac{\$323{,}120}{(\$5{,}361{,}207 + \$3{,}951{,}628)/2} = 6.94\%$$

Is a 6.94% cash flow on total assets good or bad for NIKE? To help answer this question and others like it, we can compare NIKE's ratio with its prior performance, the ratios of competitors, and with ratios of other noncompeting companies. As a first step, we show NIKE's cash flow on total assets ratio for each of the prior three years in the second column of Exhibit 17.21. Its return on total assets is provided for comparison purposes in the third column.

Exhibit 17.21

NIKE's Cash Flow on Total Assets

Year	Cash Flow on Total Assets	Return on Total Assets
1997	6.94%	17.09%
1996	9.58	15.60
1995	9.24	14.49

NIKE's cash flow on total assets has declined over the period 1995–97, while its return on total assets has grown. This result suggests NIKE's *earnings quality* has declined over this period. This decline in earnings quality for NIKE means less of its earnings is realized in the form of cash.

We also compare NIKE's cash flow on total assets to other companies' including PepsiCo, McDonald's, Wal-Mart, and Wendy's. A bar chart of these results is shown in Exhibit 17.22.

Exhibit 17.22

Cash Flow on Total Assets of Selected Companies

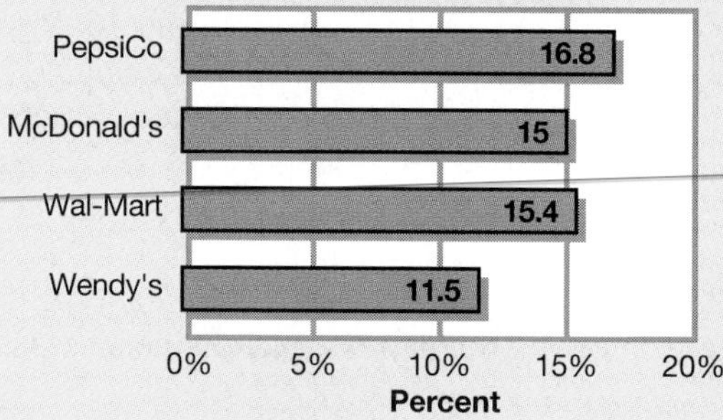

We see that NIKE's cash flow on total assets ratio is lower than the same ratio for these companies. This finding adds to our concern in the decline of the cash flow on total assets ratio as evidenced in Exhibit 17.21.

Overall, the statement of cash flows is an important bridge between the income statement and balance sheet, and valuable in financial analysis. The cash flow on total assets ratio is a useful part of this analysis and is an indicator of earnings quality.

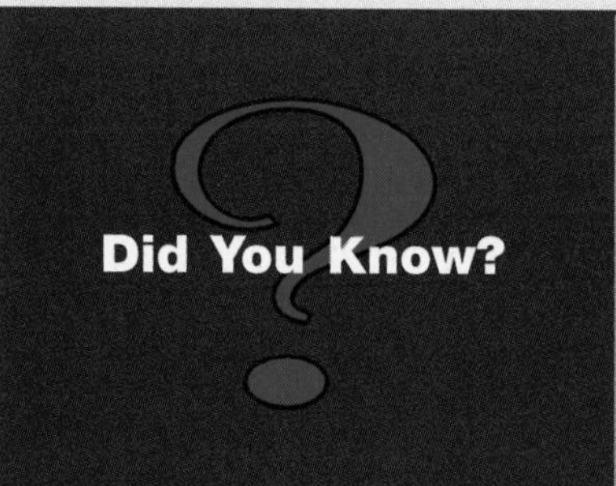

Free Cash Flow

Free cash flow is a common term in financial analysis. It refers to operating cash flows available after allowing for investing and financing requirements. Free cash flow is usually defined as operating cash flows minus capital expenditures and cash dividends. Growth and financial flexibility depend on adequate free cash flow.

Summary

C1 Explain the purpose and importance of cash flow information. The main purpose of the statement of cash flows is to report the major cash receipts and cash payments for a period. This includes identifying cash flows as relating to either operating, investing, or financing activities. Many business decisions involve evaluating cash flows. Examples are investor and creditor decisions to invest in or loan money to a company. Users' evaluations focus on the activities that provide or use cash.

C2 Distinguish among operating, investing, and financing activities. Operating activities include the transactions and events that determine net income. Investing activities include the (a) purchase and sale of long-term assets, (b) the purchase and sale of short-term investments other than cash equivalents, and (c) lending and collecting loans. Financing activities include (a) obtaining cash by issuing debt and repaying the amounts borrowed and (b) obtaining cash from or distributing cash to owners and giving owners a return on investment.

C3 Identify and disclose noncash investing and financing activities. For external reporting, a company must supplement its statement of cash flows with a description of its noncash investing and financing activities. These activities are disclosed in either a note to the statement or in a separate schedule usually reported at the bottom of the statement. Two examples of these activities are the retirement of debt by issuing equity securities and the exchange of a note payable for plant assets.

C4 Describe the format of the statement of cash flows. The statement of cash flows separates cash receipts and disbursements in one of three categories: operating, investing, or financing activities. Cash inflows and cash outflows are reported for each category.

A1 Analyze the statement of cash flows. To understand and predict cash flows, users stress the importance of separately identifying the sources and uses of cash flows by operating, investing, and financing activities. Special emphasis is placed on operating cash flows since they derive from a company's continuing operations.

A2 Compute and apply the cash flow on total assets ratio. The cash flow on total assets ratio is defined as operating cash flows divided by average total assets. Companies prefer to maintain a regular and positive level of net cash flows from operating activities. Analysis of current and past cash flow on total assets ratios is one measure of a company's success in achieving this goal. It is also viewed as a measure of earnings quality.

P1 Prepare a statement of cash flows. Preparation of a statement of cash flows involves five steps: (1) compute the net increase or decrease in cash; (2) compute net cash provided (used) by operating activities (using either the direct or indirect method); (3) compute net cash provided (used) by investing activities; (4) compute net cash provided (used) by financing activities; and (5) report the beginning and ending cash balance and prove it is explained by operating, investing, and financing net cash flows. Noncash investing and financing activities are disclosed in either a note or in a separate schedule to the statement.

P2 Compute cash flows from operating activities using the direct method. The direct method for reporting net cash provided (used) by operating activities involves listing separately the major classes of operating cash inflows and outflows. The operating cash outflows are then subtracted from operating cash inflows to get the net inflow or outflow from operating activities. The direct method is recommended by the FASB. The direct method must also include a separate schedule reporting the reconciliation between net income and net cash provided (used) by operating activities.

P3 Compute cash flows from operating activities using the indirect method. The indirect method for reporting net cash provided (used) by operating activities starts with net income and then adjusts it for three items: (a) changes in noncash current assets and current liabilities related to operating activities, (b) revenues and expenses not providing (using) cash, and (c) gains and losses from investing and financing activities.

P4 Determine cash flows from both investing and financing activities. Cash flows from both investing and financing activities are determined by identifying the cash flow effects of transactions and events affecting each balance sheet account related to these activities. All cash flows from these activities are identified when we can explain changes in these accounts from the beginning to the end of the period.

Guidance Answers to **You Make the Call**

Community Activist

Several reasons can explain an increase in net cash flows when a loss is reported. Possibilities include: (1) early recognition of expenses relative to revenues generated (such as research and development); (2) valuable long-term sales contracts not yet recognized in income; (3) issuances of debt or equity to finance expansion; (4) selling of assets; (5) delayed cash payments and (6) prepayment on sales. Your analysis of this manufacturer needs to focus on the components of both net income and net cash flows and their implications for future performance.

Reporter

Your initial course of action is to verify management's claims about poor performance. A $600,000 loss along with a $550,000 decrease in net cash flows seemingly supports its claim. But closer scrutiny reveals a different picture. You compute its cash flow from operating activities at a positive $650,000, computed as [?] − $850,000 − $350,000 = ($550,000). You also note net income *before* the extraordinary loss is a positive $330,000, computed as [?] − $930,000 = ($600,000). This is powerful information to use in confronting management. A serious and directed discussion is likely to reveal a far more positive picture of this company's financial performance.

Guidance Answers to Flash backs

1. No. The statement of cash flows reports changes in the sum of cash plus cash equivalents. It does not report transfers between cash and cash equivalents.
2. The three categories of cash inflows and outflows are operating activities, investing activities, and financing activities.
3. a. Investing
   b. Operating
   c. Financing
   d. Operating
   e. Operating
   f. Financing
4. The direct method is most informative because it separately lists each major item of operating cash receipts and each major item of operating cash payments. The indirect method is used most often.
5. $590,000 + ($120,000 − $90,000) = $620,000
6. $168,000 − ($32,000 − $28,000) − $2,400 = $161,600
7. $112,000 + ($4,200 − $1,200) − $5,600 = $109,400
8. $74,900 + $4,600 − $11,700 − $1,000 + $3,400 = $70,200
9. In the calculation of net income, expenses such as depreciation and amortization are subtracted. But these expenses do not require current cash outflows. Therefore, adding these expenses back to net income eliminates noncash items from the net income number, converting it to a cash basis.
10. In the process of reconciling net income to net cash provided (or used) by operating activities, a gain on the sale of plant assets is subtracted from net income because a sale of plant assets is not an operating activity; it is an investing activity.
11. $80,000 − $30,000 − $10,000 = $40,000
    The $40,000 cash receipt is reported as an investing activity.
12. Investing activities during the year ended June 30, 1996, used net cash of $79,066 (all amounts in thousands). Investing cash inflows (outflows) included: short-term investments, $7,960; purchase of property and equipment, ($50,262); product development costs, ($32,631); purchase costs of acquired business, ($4,133). The largest source of cash to finance these activities was $189,359 from issuing common stock.

Demonstration Problem

Umlauf's beginning and ending balance sheets, income statement, and related information follow.

UMLAUF COMPANY
Balance Sheet
December 31, 2000 and 1999

	2000	1999
Assets		
Cash	$ 43,050	$ 23,925
Accounts receivable	34,125	39,825
Merchandise inventory	156,000	146,475
Prepaid expenses	3,600	1,650
Equipment	135,825	146,700
Accum. depreciation, Equip.	(61,950)	(47,550)
Totals	$310,650	$311,025
Liabilities and Stockholders' Equity		
Accounts payable	$ 28,800	$ 33,750
Income taxes payable	5,100	4,425
Dividends payable	0	4,500
Bonds payable	0	37,500
Common stock, $10 par	168,750	168,750
Retained earnings	108,000	62,100
Totals	$310,650	$311,025

UMLAUF COMPANY Income Statement For Year Ended December 31, 2000		
Sales		$446,100
Cost of goods sold	$222,300	
Other operating expenses	120,300	
Depreciation expense	25,500	
Income taxes expense	13,725	(381,825)
Loss on sale of equipment		(3,300)
Loss on retirement of bonds		(825)
Net income		$ 60,150

Additional Information:

a. All sales are made on credit.

b. All merchandise purchases are on credit.

c. Accounts Payable balances result from merchandise purchases.

d. Prepaid expenses relate to other operating expenses.

e. Equipment costing $21,375 with accumulated depreciation of $11,100 was sold for cash.

f. Equipment was purchased for cash.

g. The change in the balance of Accumulated Depreciation resulted from depreciation expense and from the sale of equipment.

h. The change in the balance of Retained Earnings resulted from dividend declarations and net income.

Required

1. Prepare a statement of cash flows using the direct method for year 2000.

2. Prepare a statement of cash flows using the indirect method for year 2000.

Planning the Solution

- Prepare a blank statement of cash flows with sections for operating, investing, and financing activities using the direct method format.
- Compute cash received from customers, cash paid for merchandise, cash paid for other operating expenses and taxes as illustrated in the chapter.
- Compute the cash paid for equipment and the cash received from the sale of equipment using the additional information provided, the amount for depreciation expense, and the change in the balances of equipment and accumulated depreciation. Use a T-account to help chart the effects of the sale and purchase of the equipment on the balances of the equipment account and the accumulated depreciation account.
- Calculate the effect of net income on the change in the retained earnings balance. Ascribe the difference between the change in retained earnings and the amount of net income to dividends declared. Adjust the dividends declared amount for the change in the dividends payable balance.
- Enter the cash effects of the entry in the appropriate section of the statement.
- Total each section of the statement, determine the total change in cash, and add the beginning balance to get the ending balance.
- Now prepare a blank statement of cash flows with sections for operating, investing, and financing activities using the indirect method format.

Solution to Demonstration Problem

Supporting computations for cash receipts and cash payments:

(1) Sales	$446,100
Add decrease in accounts receivable	5,700
Cash received from customers	$451,800
(2) Cost of goods sold	$222,300
Plus increase in merchandise inventory	9,525
Purchases	$231,825
Plus decrease in accounts payable	4,950
Cash paid for merchandise	$236,775
(3) Other operating expenses	$120,300
Plus increase in prepaid expenses	1,950
Cash paid for other operating expenses	$122,250
(4) Income taxes expense	$ 13,725
Less increase in income taxes payable	(675)
Payments of income taxes	$ 13,050
(5) Cost of equipment sold	$ 21,375
Accumulated depreciation of equipment sold	(11,100)
Book value of equipment sold	$ 10,275
Loss on sale of equipment	(3,300)
Cash received from sale of equipment	$ 6,975
Cost of equipment sold	$ 21,375
Less decrease in the equipment account balance	(10,875)
Cash paid for new equipment	$ 10,500

Equipment			
Balance, 12/31/1999	146,700		
Purchase	10,500	Sale	21,375
Balance, 12/31/2000	135,825		

Accumulated Depreciation, Equipment			
		Balance, 12/31/1999	47,550
Sale	11,100	Depr. expense	25,500
		Balance, 12/31/2000	61,950

(6) Loss on retirement of bonds	$ 825
Carrying value of bonds retired	37,500
Cash paid to retire bonds	$ 38,325
(7) Net income	$ 60,150
Less increase in retained earnings	45,900
Dividends declared	$ 14,250
Plus decrease in dividends payable	4,500
Cash paid for dividends	$ 18,750

UMLAUF COMPANY
Statement of Cash Flows (Direct Method)
For Year Ended December 31, 2000

Cash flows from operating activities:		
Cash received from customers	$451,800	
Cash paid for merchandise	(236,775)	
Cash paid for other operating expenses	(122,250)	
Cash paid for income taxes	(13,050)	
Net cash provided by operating activities		$79,725
Cash flows from investing activities:		
Cash received from sale of equipment	$ 6,975	
Cash paid for equipment	(10,500)	
Net cash used in investing activities		(3,525)
Cash flows from financing activities:		
Cash paid to retire bonds payable	$ (38,325)	
Cash paid for dividends	(18,750)	
Net cash used in financing activities		(57,075)
Net increase in cash		$19,125
Cash balance at beginning of year		23,925
Cash balance at end of year		$43,050

UMLAUF COMPANY
Statement of Cash Flows (Indirect Method)
For Year Ended December 31, 2000

Cash flows from operating activities:		
Cash flows from operating activities:		
Net income	$ 60,150	
Adjustments to reconcile net income to net cash provided by operating activities:		
Decrease in accounts receivable	5,700	
Increase in merchandise inventory	(9,525)	
Increase in prepaid expenses	(1,950)	
Decrease in accounts payable	(4,950)	
Increase in income taxes payable	675	
Depreciation expense	25,500	
Loss on sale of plant assets	3,300	
Loss on retirement of bonds	825	
Net cash provided by operating activities		$79,725
Cash flows from investing activities:		
Cash received from sale of equipment	$ 6,975	
Cash paid for equipment	(10,500)	
Net cash used in investing activities		(3,525)
Cash flows from financing activities:		
Cash paid to retire bonds payable	$(38,325)	
Cash paid for dividends	(18,750)	
Net cash used in financing activities		(57,075)
Net increase in cash		$19,125
Cash balance at beginning of year		23,925
Cash balance at end of year		$43,050

Using a Spreadsheet to Prepare the Statement of Cash Flows

Learning Objectives

Procedural

P5 Illustrate use of a spreadsheet in preparing a statement of cash flows.

We compute net cash flows provided (or used) by operating activities under the indirect method by using balance sheets at the beginning and end of the period, the current period's income statement, and information about selected transactions. Exhibit 17.10 shows the income statement and balance sheet information for Genesis. Based on this information, Exhibit 17.17 presented the indirect method of reconciling net income to net cash provided by operating activities. This appendix explains how we can use a spreadsheet analysis to prepare the statement of cash flows using the indirect method.

Preparing the Indirect Method Spreadsheet

Analyzing noncash accounts can be challenging when a company has a large number of accounts and many operating, investing, and financing transactions. A *spreadsheet,* also called *work sheet* or *working paper,* can help us organize the information needed to prepare a statement of cash flows. A spreadsheet also makes it easier to check the accuracy of our work.

To illustrate how we use a spreadsheet, we return to the comparative balance sheets and income statement shown in Exhibit 17.10. Information needed for the spreadsheet in preparing the statement of cash flows is listed below along with identifying letters:

a. Net income is $38,000.
b. Accounts receivable increase by $20,000.
c. Merchandise inventory increases by $14,000.
d. Prepaid expenses increase by $2,000.
e. Accounts payable decrease by $5,000.
f. Interest payable decreases by $1,000.
g. Income taxes payable increase by $10,000.
h. Depreciation expense is $24,000.
i. Plant assets costing $30,000 with accumulated depreciation of $12,000 are sold for $12,000 cash. Loss on sale of assets is $6,000.
j. Bonds with a book value of $34,000 are retired with a cash payment of $18,000. Gain on retirement of bonds is $16,000.
k. Plant assets costing $70,000 are purchased with a cash payment of $10,000 and an issuance of bonds payable for $60,000.
l. Issued 3,000 shares of common stock for $15,000.
m. Paid cash dividends of $14,000.

Exhibit 17A.1 shows the indirect method spreadsheet for Genesis. Both beginning and ending balance sheets are recorded on the spreadsheet. We enter information in the

Exhibit 17A.1

Spreadsheet for Preparing Statement of Cash Flows—Indirect Method

GENESIS
Spreadsheet for Statement of Cash Flows–Indirect Method
For Year Ended December 31, 2000

	December 31, 1999	Analysis of Changes Debit		Analysis of Changes Credit		December 31, 2000
Balance sheet—debits:						
Cash	$ 12,000					$ 17,000
Accounts receivable	40,000	(b)	$20,000			60,000
Merchandise inventory	70,000	(c)	14,000			84,000
Prepaid expenses	4,000	(d)	2,000			6,000
Plant assets	210,000	(k1)	70,000	(i)	$30,000	250,000
	$336,000					$417,000
Balance sheet—credits:						
Accumulated depreciation	$ 48,000	(i)	$12,000	(h)	$24,000	$ 60,000
Accounts payable	40,000	(e)	5,000			35,000
Interest payable	4,000	(f)	1,000			3,000
Income taxes payable	12,000	(g)	10,000			22,000
Bonds payable	64,000	(j)	34,000	(k2)	60,000	90,000
Common stock, $5 par value	80,000			(l)	15,000	95,000
Retained earnings	88,000	(m)	14,000	(a)	38,000	112,000
	$336,000					$417,000
Statement of cash flows:						
Operating activities:						
Net income		(a)	$38,000			
Increase in accounts receivable				(b)	$20,000	
Increase in merchandise inventory				(c)	14,000	
Increase in prepaid expenses				(d)	2,000	
Decrease in accounts payable				(e)	5,000	
Decrease in interest payable				(f)	1,000	
Increase in income taxes payable		(g)	10,000			
Depreciation expense		(h)	24,000			
Loss on sale of plant assets		(i)	6,000			
Gain on retirement of bonds				(j)	16,000	
Investing activities:						
Receipts from sale of plant assets		(i)	12,000			
Payment for purchase of plant assets				(k1)	10,000	
Financing activities:						
Payments to retire bonds				(j)	18,000	
Receipts from issuing stock		(l)	15,000			
Payments of dividends				(m)	14,000	
Noncash investing and financing activities:						
Purchase of plant assets with bonds		(k2)	60,000	(k1)	60,000	
			$337,000		$337,000	

Analysis of Changes columns for the cash flows from operating, investing, and financing activities. We also include information about noncash investing and financing activities near the bottom. The spreadsheet does not reconstruct the income statement. Instead, net income is entered as the first item used in computing the amount of cash flows from operating activities.

Entering the Analysis of Changes on the Spreadsheet

The following sequence of procedures is used to complete the spreadsheet after the balance sheet accounts are entered:

① Enter net income as an operating cash inflow (debit) and as a credit to Retained Earnings.

② In the Statement of Cash Flows section, adjustments to net income are entered as debits if they increase cash inflows and as credits if they decrease cash inflows. Applying this rule, adjust net income for the change in each noncash current asset and current liability related to operating activities. For each adjustment to net income, the offsetting debit or credit helps reconcile the beginning and ending balances of a current asset or current liability.

③ Enter adjustments to net income for income statement items not providing or using cash in the period. For each adjustment, the offsetting debit or credit helps reconcile a noncash balance sheet account.

④ Adjust net income to eliminate any gains or losses from investing and financing activities. Because the cash from a gain must be excluded from operating activities, the gain is entered as a credit in the operating activities section. Losses are entered as debits. For each of these adjustments, the related debits and/or credits help reconcile balance sheet accounts and involve entries to show the cash flow from investing or financing activities.

⑤ After reviewing any unreconciled balance sheet accounts and related information, enter the reconciling entries for all remaining investing and financing activities. Examples are purchases of plant assets, issuances of long-term debt, sales of capital stock, and dividend payments. Some of these may require entries in the noncash investing and financing activities section of the spreadsheet.

⑥ Check accuracy by totaling the Analysis of Changes columns and by determining that the change in each balance sheet account has been explained.

We illustrate these steps in Exhibit 17A.1 for Genesis:

Step	Entries
①	*(a)*
②	*(b)* through *(g)*
③	*(h)*
④	*(i)* through *(j)*
⑤	*(k)* through *(m)*

Because adjustments *i, j,* and *k* are more challenging, we show them in the debit and credit format. These entries are for purposes of our understanding—they are *not* the entries actually made in the journals. The format we use is similar to the one used for General Journal entries, except that changes in the Cash account are identified as sources or uses of cash.

i.	Loss from sale of plant assets	6,000	
	Accumulated depreciation	12,000	
	Receipt from sale of plant assets (source of cash)	12,000	
	Plant assets		30,000
	To describe sale of plant assets.		
j.	Bonds payable	34,000	
	Payments to retire bonds (use of cash)		18,000
	Gain on retirement of bonds		16,000
	To describe retirement of bonds.		

k1. Plant assets	70,000	
Payment to purchase plant assets (use of cash)		10,000
Purchase of plant assets financed by bonds		60,000
To describe purchase of plant assets.		
k2. Purchase of plant assets financed by bonds	60,000	
Bonds payable		60,000
To issue bonds for purchase of assets.		

Summary

P5 **Illustrate use of a spreadsheet in preparing a statement of cash flows.** A spreadsheet is a useful tool in preparing a statement of cash flows. Six key steps (described in the appendix) are applied when using the spreadsheet. The result is a properly classified statement of cash flows.

Glossary

Cash flow on total assets ratio of operating cash flows to average total assets; is not affected by income recognition and measurement rules, and is an indicator of earnings quality. (p. 747).

Direct method a calculation of the net cash provided or used by operating activities that lists the major classes of operating cash receipts, and subtracts the major classes of operating cash disbursements. (p. 726).

Financing activities transactions with a company's owners and creditors that include obtaining cash from issuing debt and repaying the amounts borrowed, and obtaining cash from or distributing cash to owners and giving owners a return on investments. (p. 721).

Indirect method a calculation that reports net income and then adjusts the net income amount by adding and subtracting items that are necessary to yield net cash provided or used by operating activities. (p. 726).

Investing activities transactions that involve making and collecting loans or that involve purchasing and selling plant assets, other productive assets, or investments other than cash equivalents. (p. 720).

Operating activities activities that involve the production or purchase of merchandise and the sale of goods and services to customers, including expenditures related to administering the business. (p. 720).

Statement of cash flows a financial statement that reports the cash inflows and outflows for an accounting period and classifies those cash flows as operating activities, investing activities, and financing activities. (p. 718).

Questions

1. What are some examples of investing activities reported on a statement of cash flows?
2. What are some examples of financing activities reported on a statement of cash flows?
3. When a statement of cash flows is prepared by the direct method, what are some examples of cash flows from operating activities?
4. If a corporation pays cash dividends, where on the statement of cash flows is the payment reported?
5. A company purchases land for $100,000, paying $20,000 cash and borrowing the remainder on a long-term note payable. How should this transaction be reported on a statement of cash flows?
6. What is the direct method of reporting cash flows from operating activities?
7. What is the indirect method of reporting cash flows from operating activities?
8. Is depreciation a source of cash?
9. On June 3, a company borrowed $50,000 by giving its bank a 60-day, interest-bearing note. On the statement of cash flows, where should this item be reported?
10. If a company reports a net income for the year, is it possible for the company to show a net cash outflow from operating activities? Explain your answer.
11. Refer to **NIKE**'s consolidated statement of cash flows shown in Appendix A. *(a)* Which method is used to compute net cash provided by operating activities? *(b)* Although the consolidated balance sheet shows an increase in receivables from fiscal year 1996 to fiscal year 1997, why are receivables subtracted rather than added in computing net cash provided by operating activities for the May 31, 1997, fiscal year?
12. Refer to **Reebok**'s consolidated statement of cash flows shown in Appendix A. What activities make up Reebok's two major cash flows from financing activities for the fiscal year-end 1996?

13. Refer to **America Online**'s consolidated statement of cash flows shown in Appendix A. What three investing activities resulted in cash outflows for America Online for the year ended June 30, 1996?

14. What do the loan terms given to Dennis Chen in the opening article suggest regarding the banker's risk assessment of this loan to the ginseng farm?

Quick Study

QS 17-1
Statement of cash flows

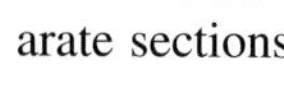

Describe the contents of a statement of cash flows, including identification of the statement's three separate sections.

QS 17-2
Classifying transactions by activity

Classify the following cash flows as operating, investing, or financing activities:

1. Issued common stock for cash.
2. Received interest on investment.
3. Paid interest on outstanding bonds.
4. Sold delivery equipment at a loss.
5. Paid property taxes on company offices.
6. Cash from sale of long-term investments.
7. Received payments from customers.
8. Paid wages.
9. Purchased merchandise for cash.
10. Paid dividends.

QS 17-3
Identifying noncash transactions

List three examples of transactions that are noncash financing and investing transactions.

QS 17-4
Computing cash received from customers

Use the balance sheet and income statement below to answer QS 17-4 through QS 17-9.

BRIGHTWELL CO., INC.
Comparative Balance Sheet
December 31, 2000

Assets	**2000**	**1999**
Cash	$ 95,800	$ 25,000
Accounts receivable (net)	42,000	52,000
Inventory	86,800	96,800
Prepaid expenses	6,400	5,200
Furniture	110,000	120,000
Accum. depreciation, Furniture	(18,000)	(10,000)
Total assets	$323,000	$289,000
Liabilities and Stockholders' Equity		
Accounts payable	$ 16,000	$ 22,000
Wages payable	10,000	6,000
Income taxes payable	2,400	3,600
Notes payable (long term)	30,000	70,000
Common stock, $5 par value	230,000	180,000
Retained earnings	34,600	7,400
Total liabilities and equity	$323,000	$289,000

BRIGHTWELL CO., INC. Income Statement For Year Ended June 30, 2000		
Sales		$468,000
Cost of goods sold		312,000
Gross profit		$156,000
Operating expenses:		
Depreciation expense	$38,600	
Other expenses	57,000	
Total operating expenses		95,600
Net income before taxes		$ 60,400
Income taxes		24,600
Net income		$ 35,800

How much cash is received from customers for fiscal year 2000?

QS 17-5
Computing cash paid for merchandise P2

Refer to the data in QS 17-4. How much cash is paid for merchandise for fiscal year 2000?

QS 17-6
Computing cash paid for expenses P2

Refer to the data in QS 17-4. How much cash is paid for operating expenses for fiscal year 2000?

QS 17-7
Computing cash from asset sales C3, P4

Refer to the data in QS 17-4 and assume that furniture costing $54,000 is sold at its book value and all furniture acquisitions are for cash. What is the cash inflow related to the sale of furniture?

QS 17-8
Computing cash paid for dividends P4

Refer to the data in QS 17-4 and assume that all stock is issued for cash. How much cash is paid toward dividends for fiscal year 2000?

QS 17-9
Computing cash from operations (indirect) P3

Refer to the data in QS 17-4. Using the indirect method, prepare a schedule to compute cash provided (or used) from operating activities.

QS 17-10
Analyzing sources and uses of cash
A1, A2

(in thousands)	Foxtail	Spiral	Tetris
Cash provided (used) by operating activities	$ 80,000	$ 70,000	$ (34,000)
Cash provided (used) by investing activities:			
Proceeds from sale of operating assets			36,000
Purchase of operating assets	(38,000)	(35,000)	
Cash provided (used) by financing activities:			
Proceeds from issuance of debt			33,000
Repayment of debt	(7,000)		
Net increase (decrease) in cash	$ 35,000	$ 35,000	$ 35,000
Average assets	$800,000	$650,000	$400,000

Required

1. Which of the three competitors is in the strongest position as shown by their cash flow statements?
2. Compare the strength of Foxtail's cash flow on total assets ratio to Spiral's.

AQS 17-11
Noncash accounts on a spreadsheet
P1

When a spreadsheet for a statement of cash flows is prepared, all changes in noncash balance sheet accounts are fully explained using the spreadsheet. Explain how we can use noncash balance sheet accounts to account for cash.

Exercises

Exercise 17-1
Classifying transactions on statement of cash flows (direct)
C2, C3

The following transactions and events occurred during the year. Assuming that the company uses the direct method of reporting cash provided by operating activities, indicate the proper accounting treatment for each item by placing an *x* in the appropriate column.

	Statement of Cash Flows			Noncash Investing and Financing Activities	Not Reported on Statement or in Note
	Operating Activities	Investing Activities	Financing Activities		
a. Borrowed cash from bank by signing a 9-month note payable.	____	____	____	____	____
b. Paid cash to purchase patent.	____	____	____	____	____
c. A 6-month note receivable is accepted in exchange for a building that had been used in operations.	____	____	____	____	____
d. Long-term bonds payable are retired by issuing common stock.	____	____	____	____	____
e. Depreciation expense is recorded on plant assets.	____	____	____	____	____
f. Cash dividend declared in a prior period is paid this period.	____	____	____	____	____
g. Inventory is sold for cash.	____	____	____	____	____

Exercise 17-2
Organizing the statement of cash flows and supporting note
C2, C3, C4

Use the following information about the cash flows of Ulrich Company to prepare a statement of cash flows (direct method) for the year ended December 31, 2000. Use a note disclosure for any noncash investing and financing activities.

Cash and cash equivalents balance, December 31, 1999	$ 25,000
Cash and cash equivalents balance, December 31, 2000	70,000
Cash received as interest	2,500
Cash paid for salaries	72,500
Bonds payable retired by issuing common stock (there is no gain or loss on retirement)	187,500
Cash paid to retire long-term notes payable	125,000
Cash received from sale of equipment	61,250
Cash borrowed on six-month note payable	25,000
Land purchased and financed by long-term note payable	106,250
Cash paid for store equipment	23,750
Cash dividends paid	15,000
Cash paid for other expenses	40,000
Cash received from customers	485,000
Cash paid for merchandise	252,500

Exercise 17-3
Computing cash flows
P2

For each of the following separate cases, use the information provided about the calendar year 2000 operations of Milwood Company to compute the required cash flow information:

Case A: Compute cash paid for salaries:	
Salaries expense	$ 51,000
Salaries payable, January 1	3,150
Salaries payable, December 31	3,750
Case B: Compute cash received from customers:	
Sales revenue	$510,000
Accounts receivable, January 1	25,200
Accounts receivable, December 31	34,800
Case C: Compute cash paid for insurance:	
Insurance expense	$ 68,400
Prepaid insurance, January 1	11,400
Prepaid insurance, December 31	17,100

Exercise 17-4
Computing cash flows
P2

For each of the following separate cases, use the information provided about the calendar year 2000 operations of Roche Company to compute the required cash flow information:

Case A: Compute cash received from interest:	
Interest revenue	$134,000
Interest receivable, January 1	3,000
Interest receivable, December 31	3,600
Case B: Compute cash paid for rent:	
Rent expense	$140,800
Rent payable, January 1	8,800
Rent payable, December 31	7,200
Case C: Compute cash paid for merchandise:	
Cost of goods sold	$528,000
Merchandise inventory, January 1	159,600
Accounts payable, January 1	67,800
Merchandise inventory, December 31	131,400
Accounts payable, December 31	84,000

Exercise 17-5
Cash flows from operating activities (direct)
P2

Use the following income statement and information about changes in noncash current assets and current liabilities to prepare the cash flows from operating activities section using the direct method:

RYLANDER COMPANY Income Statement For Year Ended December 31, 1999		
Sales		$1,818,000
Cost of goods sold		891,000
Gross profit from sales		$ 927,000
Operating expenses:		
Salaries expense	$248,535	
Depreciation expense	43,200	
Rent expense	48,600	
Amortization expense, Patents	5,400	
Utilities expense	19,125	364,860
Total		$ 562,140
Gain on sale of equipment		7,200
Net income		$ 569,340

Changes in current asset and current liability accounts for this calendar year, all of which relate to operating activities, are:

Accounts receivable	$40,500 increase	Accounts payable	13,500 decrease
Merchandise inventory	27,000 increase	Salaries payable	4,500 decrease

Exercise 17-6
Cash flows from operating activities (indirect)
P3

Refer to the information about Rylander Company in Exercise 17-5. Use the indirect method and compute the cash provided (or used) by operating activities.

Exercise 17-7
Cash flows from operating activities (indirect)
P3

Eden Company's 1999 income statement shows the following: net income, $364,000; depreciation expense, $45,000; amortization expense, $8,200; and gain on sale of plant assets, $7,000. An examination of the company's current assets and current liabilities reveals that the following changes occur because of operating activities: accounts receivable decrease, $18,100; merchandise inventory decrease, $52,000; prepaid expenses increase, $3,700; accounts payable decrease, $9,200; other payables increase, $1,400. Use the indirect method to compute cash flow from operating activities.

Exercise 17-8
Classifying transactions on statement of cash flows (indirect)
C2, P3

The following transactions and events occurred during the year. Assuming that the company uses the indirect method of reporting cash provided by operating activities, indicate the proper accounting treatment for each event listed by placing an *x* in the appropriate column.

	Statement of Cash Flows			Noncash Investing and Financing Activities	Not Reported on Statement or in Note
	Operating Activities	Investing Activities	Financing Activities		
a. Sold equipment at a loss.	____	____	____	____	____
b. Recorded depreciation expense.	____	____	____	____	____
c. Income taxes payable increased by 15% from prior year.	____	____	____	____	____
d. Declared and paid a cash dividend.	____	____	____	____	____
e. Paid cash to purchase inventory.	____	____	____	____	____
f. Land for a new plant is purchased by issuing common stock.	____	____	____	____	____
g. Accounts receivable decreased in the year.	____	____	____	____	____

Exercise 17-9
Preparation of statement of cash flows (direct)
P1, P2, A1

The following summarized journal entries show the total debits and total credits to the Pyramid Corporation's Cash account for calendar year 2000.

Part 1

Use the information to prepare a statement of cash flows for year 2000. The cash provided (or used) by operating activities should be presented using the direct method. In the statement, identify the entry that records each item of cash flow. The beginning balance of cash is $133,200.

		Debit	Credit
a.	Cash	1,440,000	
	Common Stock, $10 Par Value		360,000
	Contributed Capital in Excess of Par, Common Stock		1,080,000
	Issued common stock for cash.		
b.	Cash	2,400,000	
	Notes Payable		2,400,000
	Borrowed cash with a note payable.		
c.	Purchases	480,000	
	Cash		480,000
	Purchased merchandise for cash.		
d.	Accounts Payable	1,200,000	
	Cash		1,200,000
	Paid for credit purchases of merchandise.		
e.	Wages Expense	600,000	
	Cash		600,000
	Paid wages to employees.		
f.	Rent Expense	420,000	
	Cash		420,000
	Paid rent for buildings.		
g.	Cash	3,000,000	
	Sales		3,000,000
	Made cash sales to customers.		
h.	Cash	1,800,000	
	Accounts Receivable		1,800,000
	Collected accounts from credit customers.		
i.	Machinery	2,136,000	
	Cash		2,136,000
	Purchased machinery for cash.		
j.	Investments	2,160,000	
	Cash		2,160,000
	Purchased investments for cash.		
k.	Interest Expense	216,000	
	Notes Payable	384,000	
	Cash		600,000
	Paid notes and accrued interest.		
l.	Cash	206,400	
	Dividends Earned		206,400
	Collected dividends from investments.		
m.	Cash	210,000	
	Loss on Sale of Investments	30,000	
	Investments		240,000
	Sold investments for cash.		
n.	Cash	720,000	
	Accumulated Depreciation, Machinery	420,000	
	Machinery		960,000
	Gain on Sale of Machinery		180,000
	Sold machinery for cash.		
o.	Common Dividend Payable	510,000	
	Cash		510,000
	Paid cash dividends to stockholders.		
p.	Income Taxes Payable	480,000	
	Cash		480,000
	Paid income taxes owed for the year.		
q.	Treasury Stock, Common	228,000	
	Cash		228,000
	Acquired treasury stock for cash.		

Part 2

Consult the statement of cash flows you prepared for part (1) and answer the following questions:

1. Of the three activity sections (operating, investing, or financing), which section shows the largest cash flow for the year?
2. What is the purpose of the largest investing cash outflow for the year?
3. Are the proceeds larger from issuing debt or equity for the year?
4. Did the company have a net cash inflow or outflow from borrowing activity for the year?

Exercise 17-10
Preparation of statement of cash flows (direct)
P1, P2, A2

Part 1

Use the Benton, Inc., financial statements and supplementary information shown to prepare a statement of cash flows for the year ended June 30, 2000, using the direct method.

BENTON INC.
Comparative Balance Sheet
June 30, 2000

Assets	2000	1999
Cash	$ 85,800	$ 45,000
Accounts receivable (net)	70,000	52,000
Inventory	66,800	96,800
Prepaid expenses	5,400	5,200
Equipment	130,000	120,000
Accum. depreciation, Equip.	(28,000)	(10,000)
Total assets	$330,000	$309,000
Liabilities and Stockholders' Equity		
Accounts payable	$ 26,000	$ 32,000
Wages payable	7,000	16,000
Income taxes payable	2,400	3,600
Notes payable (long-term)	40,000	70,000
Common stock, $5 par value	230,000	180,000
Retained earnings	24,600	7,400
Total liabilities and equity	$330,000	$309,000

BENTON INC.
Income Statement
For Year Ended June 30, 2000

Sales		$668,000
Cost of goods sold		412,000
Gross profit		$256,000
Operating expenses:		
Depreciation expense	$58,600	
Other expenses	67,000	
Total operating expenses		125,600
Gain on sale of equipment		2,000
Net income before taxes		$132,400
Income taxes		45,640
Net income		$ 86,760

Additional information:

a. The note payable is retired at its carrying value.

b. The only changes affecting retained earnings are net income and cash dividends paid.

c. New equipment is acquired for $58,600.

d. Sold equipment costing $48,600 for a $2,000 gain.

e. Prepaid expenses and wages expense affect other expenses on the Income Statement.

f. All sales and purchases of merchandise are on credit.

Part 2

Compute the cash flow on total assets ratio for Benton, Inc., for the fiscal year 2000.

Problems

Problem 17-1
Statement of cash flows (direct method)

Infinity Corporation, a merchandiser, recently completed its year 2000 operations. During the year: (1) all sales were credit sales, (2) all credits to accounts receivable were receipts from customers, (3) all purchases of merchandise were on credit, (4) all debits to accounts payable were from payments for merchandise, (5) other operating expenses were cash expenses, and (6) the decrease in income taxes payable was for payment of taxes. Infinity's balance sheet and income statement are shown below:

INFINITY CORPORATION
Comparative Balance Sheet
December 31, 2000

	December 31	
	2000	1999
Assets		
Cash	$ 174,000	$117,000
Accounts receivable	93,000	81,000
Merchandise inventory	609,000	534,000
Equipment	333,000	297,000
Accum. depreciation, Equip.	(156,000)	(102,000)
Total assets	$1,053,000	$927,000
Liabilities and Stockholders' Equity		
Accounts payable	$ 69,000	$ 96,000
Income taxes payable	27,000	24,000
Common stock, $2 par value	582,000	558,000
Contributed capital in excess of par value, common stock	198,000	162,000
Retained earnings	177,000	87,000
Total liabilities and equity	$1,053,000	$927,000

INFINITY CORPORATION
Income Statement
For Year Ended December 31, 2000

Sales		$1,992,000
Cost of goods sold		1,194,000
Gross profit		$ 798,000
Operating expenses:		
Depreciation expense	$ 54,000	
Other expenses	501,000	
Total operating expenses		555,000
Income before taxes		$ 243,000
Income taxes		42,000
Net income		$ 201,000

Additional information on Infinity's transactions for year 2000:

a. Purchased equipment for $36,000 cash.

b. Issued 12,000 shares of stock for cash at $5 per share.

c. Declared and paid $111,000 of cash dividends.

Check Figure Cash from operating activities, $144,000

Required

Prepare a statement of cash flows that reports cash inflows and outflows from operating activities according to the direct method. Show supporting calculations.

Problem 17-2
Statement of cash flows (indirect method)
P1, P3

Refer to Infinity Corporation's financial statements and related information in Problem 17-1.

Required

Prepare a statement of cash flows that reports cash inflows and outflows from operating activities according to the indirect method.

Problem 17-3[A]
Cash flows spreadsheet (indirect method)
P3, P4

Refer to the information reported about Infinity Corporation in Problem 17-1.

Required

Prepare a statement of cash flows using a spreadsheet that follows the indirect method of reporting cash flows from operating activities. Identify the debits and credits in the Analysis of Changes columns with letters that correspond to the following list of transactions and events:

Check Figure Analysis of Changes column totals, $579,000

a. Net income is $201,000.
b. Accounts receivable increased.
c. Merchandise inventory increased.
d. Accounts payable decreased.
e. Income taxes payable increased.
f. Depreciation expense is $54,000.
g. Purchased equipment for $36,000.
h. Issued 12,000 shares at $5 per share.
i. Declared and paid $111,000 of cash dividends.

Problem 17-4
Statement of cash flows (direct method)
P1, P2, A1

Comptex Company, a merchandiser, recently completed its year 2000 operations. During the year: (1) all sales were credit sales, (2) all credits to accounts receivable were receipts from customers, (3) purchases of merchandise were on credit, (4) all debits to accounts payable were from payments for merchandise, (5) the decrease in income taxes payable was for payment of taxes, and (6) the other expenses were paid in advance and were initially debited to Prepaid Expenses. Comptex Company's balance sheet and income statement follow:

COMPTEX COMPANY
Comparative Balance Sheet
December 31, 2000

	December 31	
	2000	1999
Assets		
Cash	$ 53,875	$ 76,625
Accounts receivable	65,000	49,625
Merchandise inventory	273,750	252,500
Prepaid expenses	5,375	6,250
Equipment	159,500	110,000
Accum. depreciation, Equip.	(34,625)	(44,000)
Total assets	$522,875	$451,000
Liabilities and Stockholders' Equity		
Accounts payable	$ 88,125	$116,625
Short-term notes payable	10,000	6,250
Long-term notes payable	93,750	53,750
Common stock, $5 par value	168,750	156,250
Contributed capital in excess of par, common stock	32,500	
Retained earnings	129,750	118,125
Total liabilities and equity	$522,875	$451,000

COMPTEX COMPANY Income Statement For Year Ended December 31, 2000		
Sales		$496,250
Cost of goods sold		250,000
Gross profit		$246,250
Operating expenses:		
Depreciation expense	$ 18,750	
Other expenses	136,500	
Total operating expenses		155,250
Loss on sale of equipment		5,125
Income before taxes		$ 85,875
Income taxes		12,125
Net income		$ 73,750

Additional information on Comptex's transactions for year 2000:

a. Loss on sale of equipment is $5,125.

b. Sold equipment costing $46,875, with accumulated depreciation of $28,125, for $13,625.

c. Purchased equipment costing $96,375 by paying cash of $25,000 and signing a long-term note payable for the balance.

d. Borrowed $3,750 by signing a short-term note payable.

e. Paid $31,375 to reduce the long-term notes payable.

f. Issued 2,500 shares of common stock for cash at $18 per share.

g. Declared and paid cash dividends of $62,125.

Required

Preparation Component

1. Prepare a statement of cash flows that reports the cash inflows and outflows from operating activities according to the direct method. Show supporting calculations. Disclose any noncash investing and financing activities in a note.

Analysis Component

2. Analyze and discuss the cash flow information contained in your answer to part 1, giving special attention to the wisdom of the cash dividend payment.

Check Figure Cash from operating activities, $33,375

Problem 17-5 P1, P3
Statement of cash flows (indirect method)

Refer to Comptex Company's financial statements and related information in Problem 17-4.

Required

Prepare a statement of cash flows that reports cash inflows and outflows from operating activities according to the indirect method.

Check Figure Cash from operating activities, $33,375

Problem 17-6^A
Cash flows spreadsheet (indirect method)

Refer to the information reported about Comptex Company in Problem 17-4.

Required

Prepare a statement of cash flows using a spreadsheet that follows the indirect method of reporting cash flows from operating activities. Identify the debits and credits in the Analysis of Changes columns with letters that correspond to the following list of transactions and events:

a. Net income is $73,750.

b. Accounts receivable increased.

c. Merchandise inventory increased.

Check Figure Analysis of Changes column totals, $515,375

d. Prepaid expenses decreased.
e. Accounts payable decreased.
f. Depreciation expense is $18,750.
g. Sold equipment costing $46,875, with accumulated depreciation of $28,125, for $13,625 cash. This yields a loss of $5,125.
h. Purchased equipment costing $96,375 by paying cash of $25,000 and (**i.**) by signing a long-term note payable for the balance.
j. Borrowed $3,750 by signing a short-term note payable.
k. Paid $31,375 to reduce the long-term notes payable.
l. Issued 2,500 shares of common stock for cash at $18 per share.
m. Declared and paid cash dividends of $62,125.

BEYOND THE NUMBERS

Reporting in Action
A1, C4

Refer to the financial statements and related information for **NIKE** in Appendix A. Answer the following questions by analyzing that information.

1. Is NIKE's statement of cash flows prepared according to the direct method or the indirect method?
2. During each of the fiscal years 1997 and 1996, is the cash provided by operating activities more or less than the cash paid for dividends?
3. What is the largest item in reconciling the difference between net income and cash flow from operating activities in 1997? In 1996?
4. Describe major cash inflows and outflows from investing and financing activities during 1997.

Swoosh Ahead

5. Obtain NIKE's annual report information for a fiscal year ending after May 31, 1997. You can get this information from either its Web site [**www.nike.com**] or the SEC's EDGAR database [**www.sec.gov**]. Since May 31, 1997, what are NIKE's largest cash outflows and inflows in the investing and financing sections of the cash flow statement?

Comparative Analysis
A1, A2

Both **NIKE** and **Reebok** design, produce, market, and sell sports footwear and apparel. Key comparative figures ($ millions) for these two organizations follow:

	NIKE		Reebok	
Key figures*	**1997**	**1996**	**1996**	**1995**
Operating Cash Flows	$ 323.1	$ 339.7	$ 280.3	$ 171.7
Total Assets	5,361.2	3,951.6	1,786.2	1,651.6

*NIKE figures are from its annual reports for fiscal years ended May 31, 1997 and 1996. Reebok figures are from its annual reports for fiscal years ended December 31, 1996 and 1995.

Required

1. Compute the cash flow on total assets ratio for (a) NIKE for 1997 and (b) Reebok for 1996.
2. What does the cash flow on total assets ratio measure?
3. Which company has the higher cash flow on total assets ratio?
4. Does the cash flow on total assets ratio provide any information as to the quality of earnings?
5. What are the two largest sources of cash for Nike in 1997? For Reebok in 1996?

Ethics Challenge
C1, C2, A1

Wendy Geiger is working late in preparation for a meeting with her banker the next week. Her business is finishing its fourth year of operations. In the first year, the business experienced negative cash flows from operations. In the second and third years, cash flows from operations turned positive. Unfortunately, her inventory costs rose significantly in year four and her net income will probably be down about 25% once this year's adjusting entries are finalized. Wendy is hoping to secure a line of credit from her banker which will be a nice financing buffer. From prior experience, she knows a focus of the meeting will be cash flows from operations. The banker will scrutinize cash flows for years one through four and will want a projected number for year five. Wendy knows that a steady progression upward of cash flows in years one through four will help her case. Wendy decides to use her discretion as owner and considers several business actions that will turn her cash flow in year four from negative to positive.

Required

1. Identify two business actions Wendy might use to improve cash flows from operations on the statement of cash flows for year four.
2. Comment on the ethics and possible consequences of Wendy's decision to pursue these business actions for year four.

Communicating in Practice

C1, C4

Your friend, Maddy Massola, recently completed the second year in his own business, and just received annual financial statements from his accountant. Maddy says he finds the income statement and balance sheet informative, but he doesn't understand the statement of cash flows. He says the first section is especially confusing. He said it contained a lot of additions and subtractions that didn't make sense. Maddy added "I'm not concerned. It's probably one of those extra forms accountants are required to fill out. The income statement tells me the business is more profitable than last year and that is what's most important. If I want to know about cash or cash changes, I can look at the balance sheets from this year and last."

Required

Write a memorandum to your friend explaining the purpose of the statement of cash flows. Speculate on why the first section was so confusing and suggest how he might rectify this problem.

Taking It to the Net

A1

Use the Edgar database at **www.sec.gov** to access the 12/19/97 10K report filed by the **Walt Disney Company.** Locate Disney's consolidated comparative statement of cash flows showing cash flows for the fiscal years 1997, 1996, and 1995. Answer the following questions:

1. Which method, direct or indirect, does Disney use to prepare its statement of cash flows?
2. What is the largest adjustment needed to reconcile net income to cash flows from operations in each of the three years?
3. What is the largest investment activity requiring cash in each of the three years presented?
4. For fiscal year 1997, did Disney have a net cash inflow or outflow from borrowing activity?
5. Did Disney pay dividends in fiscal years 1995–1997?

Teamwork in Action

C1, C4, A1, P2, P3

Team members are to coordinate and independently answer one question in each of the three sections below. Team members should then report to the team and confirm or correct teammate's responses.

1. Prepare a response to ***one*** of the following questions about the statement of cash flows:
   a. What is this statement's reporting objectives?
   b. What two methods are used to prepare it? Identify similarities and differences between methods.
   c. What steps are followed to prepare the statement?
   d. What kinds of analysis are often made from this statement's information?
2. Prepare notes to identify and explain the formula for computing cash flows from operating activities using the direct method for ***one*** of the following items:
   a. Cash receipts from customers.
   b. Cash paid for merchandise.
   c. Cash paid for wages and operating expenses.
   d. Cash paid for interest and taxes.
3. Prepare notes to identify and explain the adjustment from net income to cash flows from operating activities using the indirect method for ***one*** of the following items:
   a. Noncash operating revenues and expenses.
   b. Gains and losses.
   c. Increases and decreases in current assets.
   d. Increases and decreases in current liabilities.

Hitting the Road

C1

Visit the **Motley Fool Investment** Web site at **www.fool.com.** Click on the sidebar link titled *School.* Identify and select the link *Valuation: Principles and Practice. (a)* How does the Fool's school define cash flow? *(b)* Per the school's instruction, why do analysts focus on earnings before interest and taxes (EBIT)? *(c)* Visit other links at the Web site that may interest you, such as "A Journey through the Balance Sheet," or find out what the "Fool's Ratio" is. Write a one-half page report on what you find.

Business Week Activity

A1

Read the article, "Are profits shakier than they look?" in the August 5, 1996, issue of ***Business Week.***

Required

1. How is the free cash flow number derived from cash flow from operations?

2. How does **Allied**'s explanation of their cash concerns differ from analyst Jeff Fotta's interpretation?

3. How does analyst Jeff Fotta conduct the dual cash flow analysis?

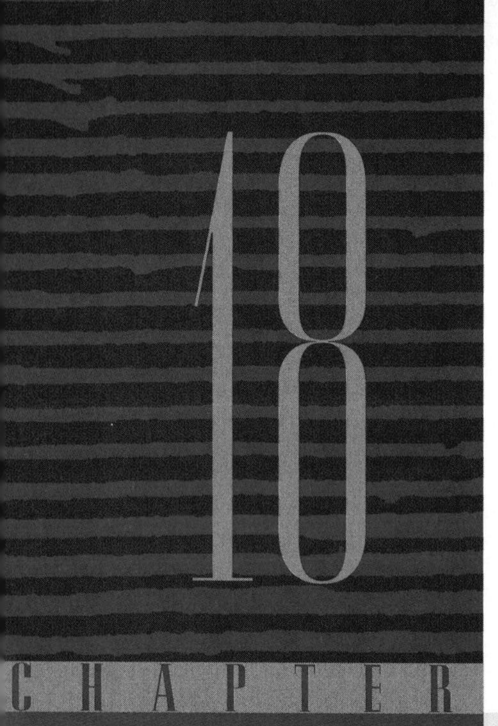

Analyzing Financial Statements

A Look Back

Chapter 17 focused on reporting and analyzing cash inflows and cash outflows. We explained how to prepare and interpret the statement of cash flows.

A Look at This Chapter

This chapter emphasizes the analysis and interpretation of financial statement information. We learn to apply horizontal, vertical, and ratio analyses to better understand company performance and financial condition.

A Look Ahead

Chapter 19 introduces us to managerial accounting. We discuss its purposes, concepts, and roles in helping managers gather and organize information for decision making. Management principles are also explained.

Chapter Outline

- **Basics of Analysis**
  - Purpose of Analysis
  - Building Blocks of Analysis
  - Information for Analysis
  - Standards for Comparisons
  - Tools of Analysis
- **Horizontal Analysis**
  - Comparative Statements
  - Trend Analysis
- **Vertical Analysis**
  - Common-Size Statements
  - Common-Size Graphics
- **Ratio Analysis**
  - Liquidity and Efficiency
  - Solvency
  - Profitability
  - Market
  - Summary of Ratios
- **Using the Information—Analysis Reporting**

Say It Ain't So!

BEARDSTOWN, ILL.—Is nothing sacred? The Beardstown Ladies, those homespun, grandmotherly investors whose supposed success created a mini-industry, are being called frauds. The ladies may have fudged the figures.

With three books to their name, the Beardstown Ladies are a fixture on the lecture circuit, riding a bull market in homespun advice. But their best advice might have been "know your accounting." The ladies' *Common-Sense Investment Guide* claims an annual return of 23.4% over the decade covered in the book. But this return is computed by averaging the ladies' two best years—1991 and 1992—and ignoring the other eight years.

Oops, that's not the way it's done. This would mean their total returns were nowhere near as great as claimed. The accounting firm Price Waterhouse, which did an audit of the ladies' books, says the actual return over the period covered is 9.1%. This figure is well below the 23.4% claimed by the ladies, and less than the 15% return of the overall stock market for the same period.

Experts in accounting and analysis are not surprised. The ladies' investment strategy was simple and not fundamentally sound. They pooled their money and bought shares of big, low-risk companies, then watched as the stock rose with the general increase in the stock market. An index fund would have returned about double that of the ladies' return over the same period.

Still, their apparent success and their folksiness make them popular guests on television shows and brought some work as money management experts. Their first book sold more than 800,000 copies. Senior partner Betty Sinnock says she is "just sick" about what's happened. A piece of homespun advice they didn't give—if it looks too good to be true, it probably is.

Sources: (1) *Fortune* Web site Paul Krugman, "There'll Always Be a Soros," March 30, 1998. (2) CNN Web site, *Moneyweek,* March 1, 1998. (3) CNN Web site, *Your Money,* February 28, 1998. (4) "Well! I never! Beardstown Ladies didn't mean to deceive," *Wisconsin State Journal,* February 28, 1998. (5) CNN Web, *Moneyline,* March 17, 1998.

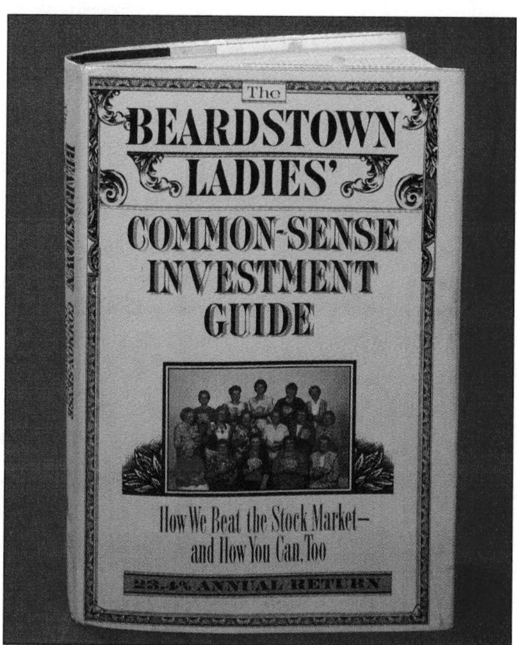

Learning Objectives

Conceptual

C1 Explain the purpose of analysis.

C2 Identify the building blocks of analysis.

C3 Describe standards for comparisons in analysis.

C4 Identify the tools of analysis.

Analytical

A1 Summarize and report results of analysis.

Procedural

P1 Explain and apply methods of horizontal analysis.

P2 Describe and apply methods of vertical analysis.

P3 Define and apply ratio analysis.

CHAPTER PREVIEW

This chapter shows us how to use information in financial statements to evaluate the financial performance and condition of a company. We describe the purpose of financial statement analysis, its basic building blocks, the information available, standards for comparisons, and tools of analysis. Three major analysis tools are emphasized—horizontal analysis, vertical analysis, and ratio analysis. We illustrate the application of each of these tools using **NIKE**'s financial statements. We also introduce comparative analysis using **Reebok**'s financial statements. This chapter expands and organizes the ratio analyses introduced at the end of each of the prior 17 chapters. Understanding financial statement analysis is crucial to sound business decision making. Its proper application avoids our reliance on the ladies from Beardstown.

Basics of Analysis

Financial statement analysis is the application of analytical tools to general-purpose financial statements and related data for making business decisions. It involves transforming data into useful information. Financial statement analysis reduces our reliance on hunches, guesses, and intuition. It reduces our uncertainty in decision making. But it does not lessen the need for expert judgment. Instead, it provides us an effective and systematic basis for business decisions. This section describes the purpose of financial statement analysis, its information sources, the use of comparisons, and some issues in computations.

Purpose of Analysis

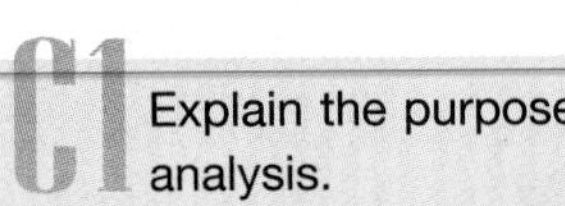

The purpose of financial statement analysis is to help users make better business decisions. These users include decision makers both internal and external to the company.

Internal users of accounting information are those individuals involved in managing and operating the company. They include managers, officers, internal auditors, consultants, and many other important internal decision makers. Internal users make the strategic and operating decisions of a company. The purpose of financial statement analysis for these users is to provide information helpful in improving the company's efficiency and effectiveness in providing products or services.

External users of accounting information are *not* directly involved in running the company. They include shareholders, lenders, directors, customers, suppliers, regulators, lawyers, brokers, and the press. Yet these users are affected by, and sometimes affect, the company's activities. External users rely on financial statement analysis to make better and more informed decisions in pursuing their own goals.

We can identify many examples of how financial statement analysis is used. Shareholders and creditors assess future company prospects for investing and lending decisions. A board of directors analyzes financial statements in monitoring management's decisions. Employees and unions use financial statements in labor negotiations. Suppliers use financial statements in establishing credit terms. Customers analyze financial statements in deciding whether to establish supply relationships. Public utilities set customer rates by analyzing financial statements. Auditors use financial statements in assessing the "fair presentation" of their clients' financial statement numbers. And analyst services such as **Dun & Bradstreet, Moody**'s, and **Standard & Poor**'s use financial statements in making buy-sell recommendations and setting credit ratings.

The common goal of all these users is to evaluate company performance. This includes evaluation of (1) past and current performance, (2) current financial position, and (3) future performance and risk.

Building Blocks of Analysis

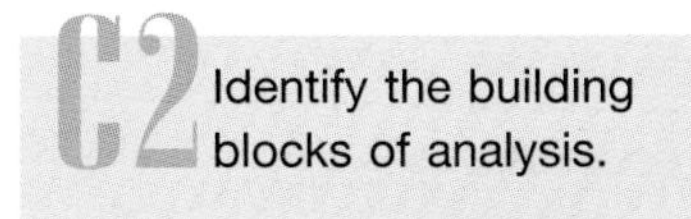

Financial statement analysis focuses on one or more elements of a company's financial condition or performance. Our analysis emphasizes four areas of inquiry—with varying degrees of importance. These four areas are described and illustrated in this chapter and are considered the *building blocks* of financial statement analysis.

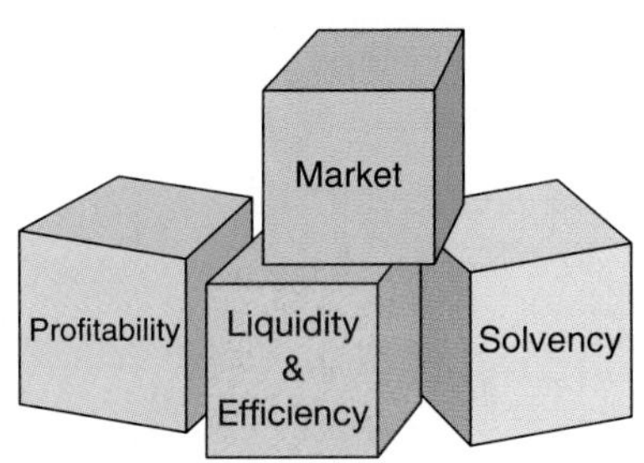

- **Liquidity** and **efficiency**—ability to meet short-term obligations and to efficiently generate revenues.
- **Solvency**—ability to generate future revenues and meet long-term obligations.
- **Profitability**—ability to provide financial rewards sufficient to attract and retain financing.
- **Market**—ability to generate positive market expectations.

Applying the building blocks of financial statement analysis involves determining (1) the objectives of analysis and (2) the relative emphasis among the building blocks. An investor, for instance, when evaluating the investment merit of a common stock often emphasizes earnings and returns analyses. This involves assessing profitability and efficiency. But a thorough analysis requires an investor to assess other building blocks, although with perhaps lesser emphasis. Attention to these other areas is necessary to assess risk exposure. This usually involves some analysis of liquidity and solvency. Further analysis can reveal important risks that outweigh earning power and may lead to major changes in the financial statement analysis of a company.

We distinguish among these four building blocks to emphasize the different aspects of a company's financial condition or performance. Yet we must remember these areas of analysis are interrelated. For instance, a company's operating performance is affected by availability of financing and short-term liquidity conditions. Similarly, a company's credit standing is not limited to satisfactory short-term liquidity, but depends also on its profitability and efficiency in using assets. Early in our analysis, we need to determine the relative emphasis of each building block and their order of analysis. Emphasis and analysis can later change due to evidence collected.

Chips and Brokers
The term *blue chips* is used to refer to stock of big, profitable companies. The term comes from poker—where the most valuable chips are the blue ones. *Brokers* execute orders to buy or sell stock. The term comes from wine retailers—individuals who broach (break) wine casks.

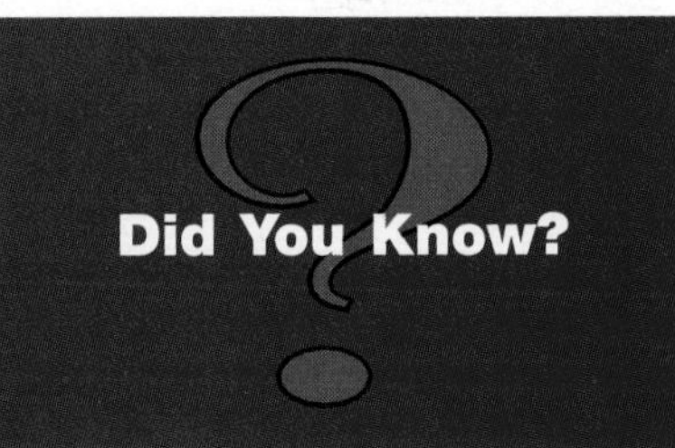

Information for Analysis

We explained how decision makers such as managers, employees, directors, customers, suppliers, current and potential owners, current and potential lenders, brokers, regulatory authorities, lawyers, economists, labor unions, analysts, and consultants need to analyze financial statements. Some of these people, such as managers and a few regulatory agencies, are able to receive special financial reports prepared to meet their needs. But most must rely on general-purpose financial statements that companies publish periodically. **General-purpose financial statements** include the (1) income statement, (2) balance sheet, (3) statement of changes in stockholders' equity (or statement of retained earnings), (4) statement of cash flows, and (5) notes related to the statements.

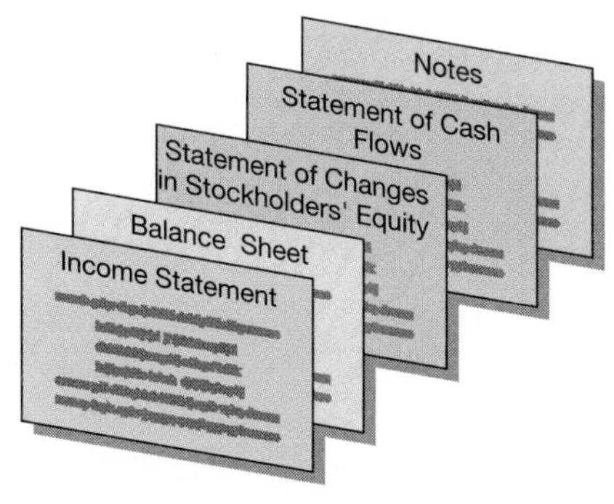

General-purpose financial statements are part of financial reporting. **Financial reporting** refers to the communication of relevant financial information to decision makers. It includes financial statements, but it also involves information from 10K or other filings with the Securities and Exchange Commission, news releases, shareholders' meetings, forecasts, management letters, auditors' reports, and analyses published in annual reports. Financial reporting broadly refers to information useful for decision makers in making investment, credit, and other decisions. It should help users assess the amounts, timing, and uncertainty of future cash inflows and outflows.

One example of useful information outside the traditional financial statements is the Management Discussion and Analysis (MD&A) section. **NIKE**'s annual report in Appendix A provides a typical example. The MD&A includes several parts. NIKE's begins with a listing of four main highlights: revenues, gross margins, costs, and net income. It then proceeds to compare operating activities for 1997 with 1996, and 1996 with 1995. This analysis includes a special breakdown of NIKE's revenues between footwear and apparel, and then domestic and international. The third and final part of its analysis examines liquidity and capital resources—roughly equivalent to investing and financing activities. While this analysis is not complete, it is an excellent starting point for us in understanding the business activities of a company.

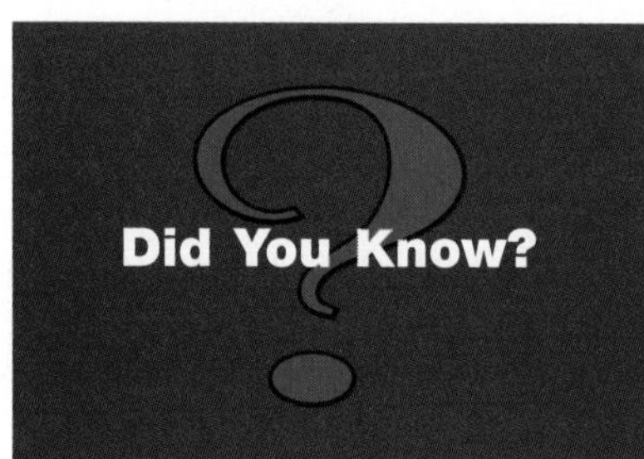

Data Web
Reviewing financial numbers used to involve mountains of paper in dark library basements. We can now do it from the convenience of our home via the Net. Many companies offer Web sites with free access and screening of numerous key financial numbers like earnings and sales. Most sites are updated daily with closing stock prices. For instance, **Standard & Poor**'s has information for more than 10,000 stocks [www.stockinfo.standardpoor.com]. [Source: *Business Week,* September 22, 1997.]

Standards for Comparisons

C3 Describe standards for comparisons in analysis.

When computing and interpreting analysis measures as part of our financial statement analysis, we need to decide whether these measures suggest good, bad, or average performance. To make these judgments, we need standards for comparisons. Standards for comparisons can include:

- *Intracompany* The company under analysis provides standards for comparisons based on prior performance and relations between its financial items. **NIKE**'s current net income, for instance, can be compared with prior years' net income and its relation to revenues.
- *Competitor* One or more direct competitors of the company under analysis can provide standards for comparisons. **Coca-Cola**'s profit margin, for instance, can be compared with the profit margin of **PepsiCo.**
- *Industry* Industry statistics can provide standards of comparisons. Published industry statistics are available from several services such as Dun & Bradstreet, Standard & Poor's, and Moody's.
- *Guidelines (rules of thumb)* General standards of comparisons can develop from past experiences. Examples are the 2-to-1 level for the current ratio or 1 to 1 level for the acid-test ratio. These guidelines, or rules of thumb, must be carefully applied since their context is often crucial.

All of these standards of comparisons are useful when properly applied; yet analysis measures taken from a selected competitor or group of competitors are often the best. Also, intracompany and industry measures are important parts of all analyses. Guidelines, or rules of thumb, should be applied with care, and then only if they seem reasonable in light of past experience and industry norms.

Flash back

1. Who are the intended users of general-purpose financial statements?
2. What statements are usually included in general-purpose financial statements published by corporations?
3. Which of the following are least useful as a basis for comparison when analyzing ratios and turnovers? *(a)* Companies operating in a different economy; *(b)* subjective standards from past experience; *(c)* rule-of-thumb standards; *(d)* averages within a trade or industry.
4. What basis of comparison for ratios is usually best?

Answers—p. 801

Tools of Analysis

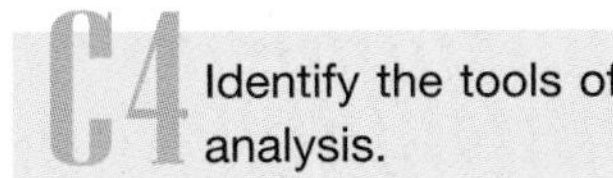

C4 Identify the tools of analysis.

There are several tools of financial statement analysis. Three of the most common tools are:

1. **Horizontal analysis** Comparison of a company's financial condition and performance across time.
2. **Vertical analysis** Comparison of a company's financial condition and performance to a base amount.
3. **Ratio analysis** Determination of key relations between financial statement items.

The remainder of this chapter describes these tools of analysis and how we apply them.

Ticker Prices

Ticker prices refer to a band of moving information on a computer or television screen carrying up-to-the-minute stock prices. The term comes from ticker tape—a one-inch wide strip of paper spewing stock prices and transactions from a printer that ticked as it ran. While most of today's investors have never actually seen ticker tape, the term survives.

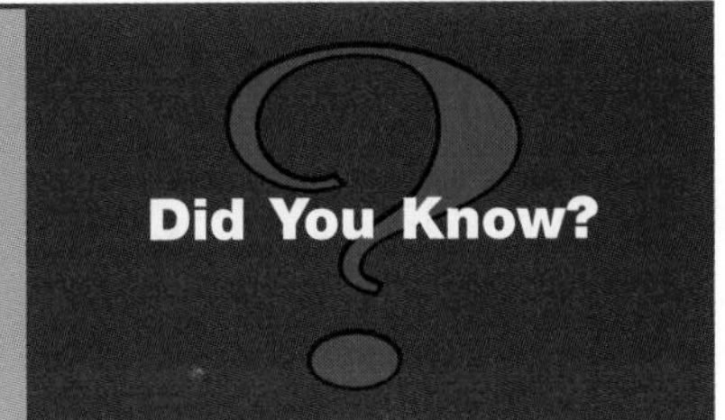

Horizontal Analysis

1999 Report ⟷ 2000 Report

Our analysis of a single financial item is important but is of limited value. Instead, important relations exist between items and across time, and our financial analysis needs to use this information. Much of financial statement analysis involves identifying and describing relations between items and groups of items and changes in those items. Horizontal analysis is a tool to evaluate changes in financial statement data *across time.*[1]

Comparative Statements

P1 Explain and apply methods of horizontal analysis.

Comparing amounts for two or more successive periods often helps in the analysis of financial statement data. **Comparative financial statements** facilitate this comparison by showing financial amounts in side-by-side columns on a single statement. Each financial statement can be presented in a *comparative format.* For instance, **NIKE**'s *Financial History* report in Appendix A is a comparative statement based on 10 years of financial performance. Using figures from NIKE's financial statements, this section explains how to compute dollar changes and percent changes in comparative statements.

Computation of Dollar Changes and Percent Changes

Comparing financial statements over relatively short time periods—two to three years—is often done by analyzing changes in line items. A change analysis usually includes an

[1] The term *horizontal analysis* arises from the left-to-right (or right-to-left) movement of our eyes as we review comparative financial statements across time.

analysis of absolute dollar amount changes as well as percent changes. Both analyses are relevant since dollar changes can sometimes yield large percent changes inconsistent with their importance. For instance, a 50% change from a base figure of $100 is less important than the same percent change from a base amount of $100,000 in the same statement. Reference to dollar amounts is necessary to retain a proper perspective and to assess the importance of changes.

We compute the *dollar change* for a financial statement item as:

Dollar change = Analysis period amount − Base period amount

where *analysis period* is the point or period of time for the financial statements under analysis, and *base period* is the point or period of time for the financial statements used for comparison purposes. We commonly use the prior year as the base period.

We compute the *percent change* by dividing the dollar change by the base period amount and then multiplying this quantity by 100:

$$\text{Percent change} = \frac{\text{Analysis period amount} - \text{Base period amount}}{\text{Base period amount}} \times 100\%$$

While we can always compute a dollar change, we must be aware of a few rules in working with percent changes. To illustrate, let's look at four separate cases in the chart below.

	Base	Analysis	Change Analysis	
Case No.	Period	Period	Dollar	Percent
A	$(4,500)	$ 1,500	$6,000)	—
B	2,000	(1,000)	(3,000)	—
C	—	8,000	8,000)	—
D	10,000	0	(10,000)	(100%)

When a negative amount appears in the base period and a positive amount in the analysis period (or vice versa), we cannot compute a meaningful percent change—see cases A and B. Also, when there is no value in the base period, no percent change is computable—see case C. Finally, when an item has a value in the base period and zero in the next period, the decrease is 100 percent—see case D.

It is also common for horizontal analysis to compare amounts to either average or median values from prior periods.[2] Comparing changes to average or median values computed over a number of years highlights unusual happenings, as average values smooth out erratic or unusual fluctuations. We also commonly round percents and ratios to one or two decimal places. But there is no uniform practice on this matter. Computations are as detailed as necessary. This is judged by whether or not they potentially affect users' decisions. Computations should not be so excessively detailed that important relations are lost among a mountain of decimal points.

Comparative Balance Sheet

One of the most useful comparative statements is the comparative balance sheet. It consists of amounts from two or more balance sheet dates arranged side by side. The usefulness of comparative financial statements is often improved by showing each item's

[2] *Median* is the middle value in a group of numbers. For instance, if five prior years' incomes are (in 000s) $15, $19, $18, $20, and $22, their median value is $18. When there are two middle numbers, we can take their average. For instance, if four prior years' sales are (in 000s) $84, $91, $96, and $93, then the median is $92 (computed as the average of $91 and $93).

dollar change and percent change. This type of presentation highlights large dollar and percent changes for decision makers. Exhibit 18.1 shows a comparative balance sheet for NIKE.

Exhibit 18.1

Comparative Balance Sheet

NIKE
Comparative Balance Sheet
May 31, 1997 and 1996

(in thousands)	1997	1996	Dollar Change	Percent* Change
Assets				
Current Assets				
Cash and equivalents	$ 445,421	$ 262,117	$ 183,304	69.9%
Accounts receivable, less allowance for doubtful accounts of $57,233 and $43,372	1,754,137	1,346,125	408,012	30.3
Inventories	1,338,640	931,151	407,489	43.8
Deferred income taxes	135,663	93,120	42,543	45.7
Prepaid expenses	157,058	94,427	62,631	66.3
Total current assets	$3,830,919	$2,726,940	$1,103,979	40.5%
Property, plant, and equipment, net	922,369	643,459	278,910	43.3
Identifiable intangible assets and goodwill	464,191	474,812	(10,621)	(2.2)
Deferred income taxes and other assets	143,728	106,417	37,311	35.1
Total assets	$5,361,207	$3,951,628	$1,409,579	35.7%
Liabilities and Shareholders' Equity				
Current Liabilities				
Current portion of long-term debt	$ 2,216	$ 7,301	$ (5,085)	(69.6)%
Notes payable	553,153	445,064	108,089	24.3
Accounts payable	687,121	455,034	232,087	51.0
Accrued liabilities	570,504	480,407	90,097	18.8
Income taxes payable	53,923	79,253	(25,330)	(32.0)
Total current liabilities	$1,866,917	$1,467,059	$ 399,858	27.3%
Long-term debt	296,020	9,584	286,436	2,988.7
Deferred income taxes and other liabilities	42,132	43,285	(1,153)	(2.7)
Commitments and contingencies	—	—		
Redeemable preferred stock	300	300	0	0.0
Shareholders' equity				
Common stock at stated value:				
Class A convertible—101,711 and 102,240 shares outstanding	152	153	(1)	(0.7)
Class B—187,559 and 185,018 shares outstanding	2,706	2,702	4	0.1
Capital in excess of stated value	210,650	154,833	55,817	36.0
Foreign currency translation adjustment	(31,333)	(16,501)	(14,832)	89.9
Retained earnings	2,973,663	2,290,213	683,450	29.8
Total shareholders' equity	$3,155,838	$2,431,400	$ 724,438	29.8%
Total liabilities and equity	$5,361,207	$3,951,628	$1,409,579	35.7%

*Percents are rounded to the first decimal point.

Our analysis of comparative financial statements begins by focusing on items that show large dollar or percent changes. We then try to identify the reasons for these changes and, if possible, determine whether they are favorable or unfavorable. We also follow up on items with small changes when we expected the changes to be large.

Regarding NIKE's comparative balance sheet, its first line item, "Cash and equivalents," in Exhibit 18.1 stands out and shows a $183.304 million increase (69.9%). The statement of cash flows in Appendix A reveals a substantial portion of this increase is due to cash flows from financing activities. To a large extent, this increase is related to cash received from issuing long-term debt and short-term notes payable as shown in the statement.

Our comparative analysis also reveals NIKE's total current liabilities increased by $399.858 million in 1997. Viewed in this light, the $183.304 million increase in cash and equivalents, together with the $1,103.979 million increase in current assets, does appear high. This is because we prefer a company that is not overly invested in highly liquid assets such as cash and equivalents since these assets earn a low return. The positive side of this situation is that NIKE is in a good position to respond to new opportunities and negative events.

The comparative balance sheet in Exhibit 18.1 also reveals a large increase in accounts payable. This increase in accounts payable is larger in magnitude than any increase in the current liability accounts. For instance, its percent increase of 51.0% is much larger than the percent increase in total current liabilities of 27.3%. This unusually large accounts payable increase is not a positive sign. We need to closely monitor its level and attempt to identify its cause.

Comparative Income Statement

A comparative income statement is prepared similar to the comparative balance sheet. Amounts for two or more periods are placed side by side, with additional columns for dollar and percent changes. Exhibit 18.2 shows NIKE's comparative income statement.

NIKE's rapid growth is reflected by its 42.0% increase in revenues for 1997. This increase in revenues continues a trend established in prior years as evident from its financial history section shown in Appendix A. For instance, revenues in 1996 were 35.9% higher than revenues in 1995. At least two reasons for this are NIKE's positive brand image and its commitment to product research and development. Its brand image plays

Exhibit 18.2

Comparative Income Statement

NIKE
Comparative Income Statement
For Years Ended May 31, 1997 and 1996

(in thousands, except per share data)	1997	1996	Dollar Change	Percent* Change
Revenues	$9,186,539	$6,470,625	$2,715,914	42.0%
Costs and expenses:				
Costs of sales	5,502,993	3,906,746	1,596,247	40.9
Selling and administrative	2,303,704	1,588,612	715,092	45.0
Interest expense	52,343	39,498	12,845	32.5
Other income/expense, net	32,277	36,679	(4,402)	(12.0)
Total costs and expenses	$7,891,317	$5,571,535	$2,319,782	41.6%
Income before income taxes	1,295,222	899,090	396,132	44.1
Income taxes	499,400	345,900	153,500	44.4
Net income	$ 795,822	$ 553,190	$ 242,632	43.9%
Net income per common share	$ 2.68	$ 1.88	$ 0.8	42.6%
Average number of common and common equivalent shares	297,000	293,608		

*Percents are rounded to the first decimal point.

off athletes like Tiger Woods and Michael Jordan. Its product research and development program is extensive with expenditures of $73.2 million in 1997, up from $46 million in 1996. NIKE wrote in its 10K report that it feels:

> research and development efforts are a key factor in its past and future success . . . to produce products that reduce or eliminate injury, aid athletic performance and maximize comfort. In addition . . . employee athletes wear-test and evaluate products.

Most income statement items, with the exception of "Other income/expense," reflect NIKE's current growth rate. The percent changes in Exhibit 18.2 range from 32.5% for interest expense to 45.0% for selling and administrative expenses. The large $715.092 million, or 45.0%, increase in selling and administrative is worth monitoring. It is the only operating expense that increased more than revenues. NIKE's management discussion and analysis section in Appendix A says this increase is due to brand expenses:

> brand expenses increased $353 in the U.S. and $355 million outside the U.S. Increases were largely driven by increased sales and marketing spending.

We must remember the ultimate payoff from sales and marketing spending is in revenues. While this spending may yield future benefits, we see its current spending increase exceeds the increase in revenue.

NIKE's only decrease in operating items of Exhibit 18.2 is in "Other income/expense." NIKE says:

> the reduction was attributable to increased interest income, higher gain on disposal of assets and income from a new promotional event staged in Japan.

This reasoning seems acceptable and does not warrant further analysis.

Output Made Easy
Today's accounting programs and spreadsheets can produce outputs with horizontal, vertical, and ratio analyses. These analyses include graphical depiction of financial relations. The key is being able to use this information properly and effectively for business decision making.

Trend Analysis

Trend analysis, also called *trend percent analysis* or *index number trend analysis,* is used to reveal patterns in data covering successive periods. It involves computing trend percents for a series of financial numbers. This method of analysis is a variation on the use of percent changes for horizontal analysis. The difference is that trend analysis does not subtract the base period amount in the numerator. To compute trend percents we need to:

1. Select a *base period* and assign each item in the base period statement a weight of 100%.
2. Express financial numbers from other periods as a percent of its base period number.

Specifically, a *trend percent,* also called an *index number,* is the amount in the analysis period divided by the amount of the same item in the base period, multiplied by 100 to get the percent form:

$$\textbf{Trend percent} = \frac{\textbf{Analysis period amount}}{\textbf{Base period amount}} \times 100$$

To illustrate trend analysis, we use selected NIKE data as reported in Exhibit 18.3.

Exhibit 18.3

Revenues and Expenses

	1997	1996	1995	1994	1993
Revenues	$9,186,539	$6,470,625	$4,760,834	$3,789,668	$3,930,984
Costs of sales	5,502,993	3,906,746	2,865,280	2,301,423	2,386,993
Selling and administrative	2,303,704	1,588,612	1,209,760	974,099	922,261

These data are from NIKE's financial history in Appendix A and its prior statements.

We select 1993 as the base period and compute the trend percent for each year and each item by dividing each year's dollar amount by its 1993 dollar amount. For instance, the revenue trend percent for 1997 is 233.7%, computed as $9,186,539/$3,930,984. The trend percents for the data from Exhibit 18.3 are shown in Exhibit 18.4.

Exhibit 18.4

Trend Percents of Revenues and Expenses

	1997	1996	1995	1994	1993
Revenues	233.7%	164.6%	121.1%	96.4%	100%
Costs of sales	230.5	163.7	120.0	96.4	100
Selling and administrative	249.8	172.3	131.2	105.6	100

Our analysis of trend percents is often aided by graphical depictions. Exhibit 18.5 presents the trend percents from Exhibit 18.4 in a *line graph.* A line graph can help us identify trends and detect changes in direction or magnitude. It reveals that through 1997, costs of sales increased at a rate almost identical to the increase in revenues. In particular, at no time do the revenues and costs of sales lines deviate by more than 5%. It also reveals that revenues and costs of sales were fairly flat from 1993–95, but that both markedly increased from 1995–97.

Exhibit 18.5

Trend Percent Lines for Revenues and Selected Expenses

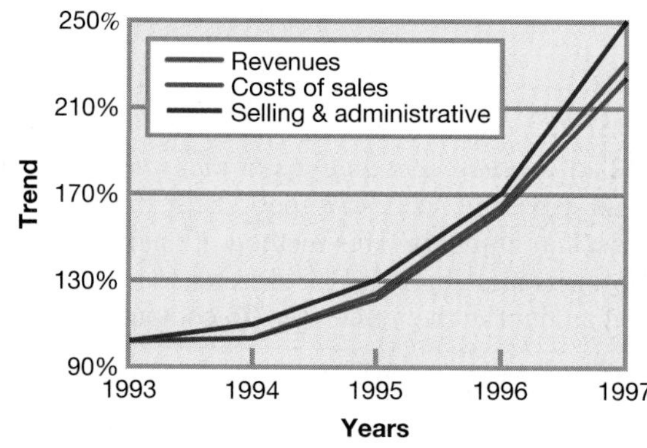

The line graph in Exhibit 18.5 also shows us that the increase in selling and administrative expenses has regularly exceeded the increase in revenues and cost of sales over this five-year period. Its trend line rises to nearly 250% in 1997 compared with 100% in 1993. As suggested from Exhibit 18.2, we should continue to monitor these expenses.

Exhibit 18.6 compares the revenue trend line of **NIKE** to the revenue trend line of **Reebok** for its most recent five-year period. While NIKE's revenues have continued to increase over this period, those of Reebok have not.

Trend analysis of financial statement items also can include comparisons of relations between items on different financial statements. For instance, Exhibit 18.7 shows a comparison of NIKE's revenues and total assets.

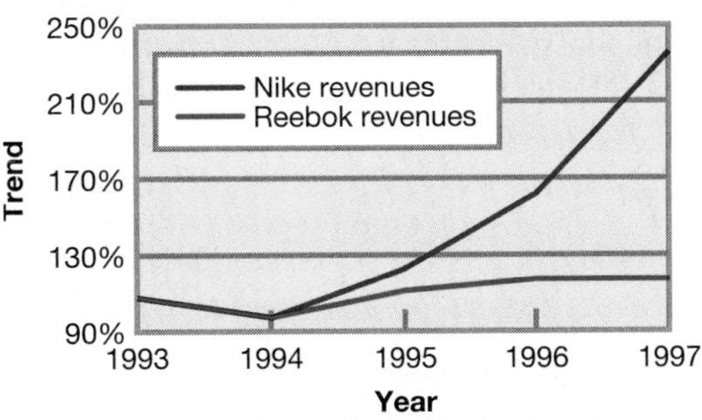

Exhibit 18.6

Trend Percent Lines—NIKE vs. Reebok

Exhibit 18.7

Revenues and Total Assets Data

	1997	1993	Trend Percent (1997 vs 1993)
Revenues	$9,186,539	$3,930,984	233.7%
Total assets (fiscal year-end)	5,361,207	2,186,269	245.2

The rate of increase in total assets is more than 10% larger than the increase in revenues. Is this change favorable? At first glance, it suggests NIKE is less able to use its assets as efficiently as in earlier years. If there is a positive, it is the potential for future revenues from increased assets. This relation is important to monitor to see if this increase in assets will generate future revenues or if it reveals a less efficient use of assets by NIKE. An important part of financial statement analysis is identifying questions and areas of concern such as these. They often direct us to important factors bearing on the future of the company under analysis.

Auditor

You are an auditor testing the "reasonableness" of a client's income. Your tests reveal a 3% increase in sales from $200,000 to $206,000, and a 4% decrease in expenses from $190,000 to $182,400. Both changes are within your reasonableness criterion of ±5% and, therefore, you don't pursue additional tests of the accounts. The partner in charge questions your lack of follow-up and notes the *joint relation* between sales and expenses. What is the partner referring to?

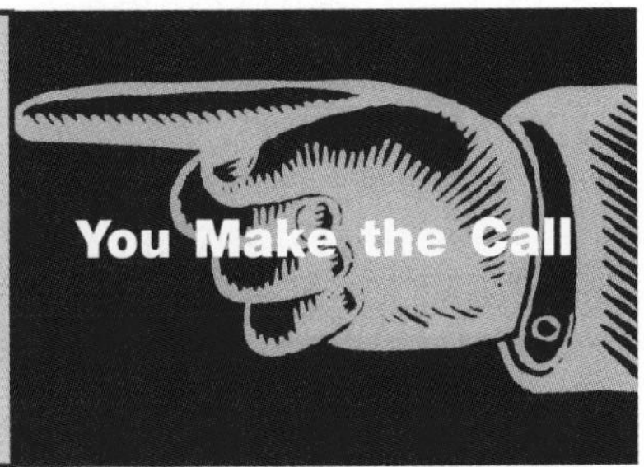

Answer—p. 801

Vertical Analysis

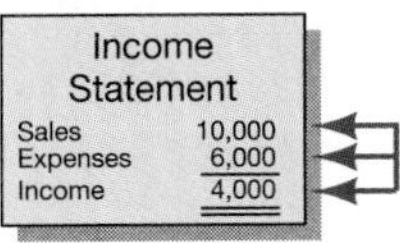

Vertical analysis is a tool to evaluate individual financial statement items or a group of items in terms of a specific base amount. We usually define a key aggregate figure as the base, and the base amount is commonly defined as 100%. For instance, an income statement's base is usually revenue and a balance sheet's base is usually total assets. Since the sum of individual items in vertical analysis is 100%, this analysis is also called *common-size analysis.* This section explains vertical analysis and applies it to NIKE's statements.[3]

[3] The term *vertical analysis* arises from the up-down (or down-up) movement of our eyes as we review common-size financial statements.

Common-Size Statements

P2 Describe and apply methods of vertical analysis.

The comparative statements in Exhibits 18.1 and 18.2 show how each item has changed over time, but they do not emphasize the relative importance of each item. We use **common-size statements** to reveal changes in the relative importance of each financial statement item. All individual amounts in common-size statements are redefined in terms of common-size percents. A *common-size percent* is measured by taking each individual financial statement amount under analysis and dividing it by its base amount:

$$\textbf{Common-size percent} = \frac{\textbf{Analysis amount}}{\textbf{Base amount}} \times 100\%$$

Common-Size Balance Sheet

Common-size statements express each item as a percent of a *base amount.* The base amount for a common-size balance sheet is usually total assets. It is assigned a value of 100%. This implies the total amount of liabilities plus equity equals 100% since this amount equals total assets. Next, we compute a common-size percent for each asset, liability, and stockholders' equity item where the base amount is total assets. When we present a company's successive balance sheets in this way, changes in the mixture of assets, liabilities, and equity are apparent.

Exhibit 18.8 shows a common-size comparative balance sheet for NIKE. Some relations that stand out include: (1) a decrease in accounts receivable (34.1% to 32.7%) and an increase in accounts payable (11.5% to 12.8%), (2) an increase in inventories (23.6% to 25.0%), (3) a decrease in intangible assets (12.0% to 8.7%), and (4) a sharp increase in long-term debt (0.2% to 5.5%). The increase in long-term debt is also evident in the decrease in total shareholders' equity (61.5% to 58.9%). None of these happenings are necessarily favorable to NIKE. In particular, increased inventory warrants special attention in our analysis. NIKE explains its increase in inventory as:

> representing growth in nearly all areas of the Company . . . The largest increases outside of the U.S. were in the European and Asia/Pacific regions with increases of $121 million (54%) and $119 million (134%).

This explanation from NIKE does not necessarily reconcile with our finding in Exhibit 18.2 showing a revenues increase of 42.0%, or with the total assets increase of 35.7% in Exhibit 18.1. Later in the chapter we will see that NIKE's inventory turnover ratio also unfavorably declined during this period.

Common-Size Income Statement

Our analysis also usually benefits from an examination of a common-size income statement. The amount of revenues is usually the base amount, and it is assigned a value of 100%. Each common-size income statement item appears as a percent of revenues. If we think of the 100% revenues amount as representing one sales dollar, the remaining items show how each revenue dollar is distributed among costs, expenses, and profit.

Exhibit 18.9 shows the comparative income statement for each dollar of NIKE's revenues. The exhibit shows that NIKE's expenses, as a percent of revenues, were stable from 1996 through 1997. The largest change is an increase in selling and administrative expenses, from 24.6 cents on the dollar to 25.1 cents. We previously identified and discussed our concern with this change.

Exhibit 18.8

Common-Size Comparative Balance Sheet

NIKE Common-Size Comparative Balance Sheet May 31, 1997 and 1996			Common-Size Percents*	
(in thousands)	1997	1996	1997	1996
Assets				
Current Assets				
Cash and equivalents	$ 445,421	$ 262,117	8.3%	6.6%
Accounts receivable, less allowance for doubtful accounts of $57,233 and $43,372	1,754,137	1,346,125	32.7	34.1
Inventories	1,338,640	931,151	25.0	23.6
Deferred income taxes	135,663	93,120	2.5	2.4
Prepaid expenses	157,058	94,427	2.9	2.4
Total current assets	$3,830,919	$2,726,940	71.5%	69.0%
Property, plant and equipment, net	922,369	643,459	17.2	16.3
Identifiable intangible assets and goodwill	464,191	474,812	8.7	12.0
Deferred income taxes and other assets	143,728	106,417	2.7	2.7
Total assets	$5,361,207	$3,951,628	100.0%	100.0%
Liabilities and Shareholders' Equity				
Current Liabilities				
Current portion of long-term debt	$ 2,216	$ 7,301	0.0%	0.2%
Notes payable	553,153	445,064	10.3	11.3
Accounts payable	687,121	455,034	12.8	11.5
Accrued liabilities	570,504	480,407	10.6	12.2
Income taxes payable	53,923	79,253	1.0	2.0
Total current liabilities	$1,866,917	$1,467,059	34.8%	37.1%
Long-term debt	296,020	9,584	5.5	0.2
Deferred income taxes and other liabilities	42,132	43,285	0.8	1.1
Commitments and contingencies	—	—		
Redeemable preferred stock	300	300	0.0	0.0
Shareholders' equity				
Common stock at stated value:				
Class A convertible—101,711 and 102,240 shares outstanding	152	153	0.0	0.0
Class B—187,559 and 185,018 shares outstanding	2,706	2,702	0.1	0.1
Capital in excess of stated value	210,650	154,833	3.9	3.9
Foreign currency translation adjustment	(31,333)	(16,501)	(0.6)	(0.4)
Retained earnings	2,973,663	2,290,213	55.5	58.0
Total shareholders' equity	$3,155,838	$2,431,400	58.9%	61.5%
Total liabilities and shareholders' equity	$5,361,207	$3,951,628	100.0%	100.0%

*Percents are rounded to the first decimal point.

Exhibit 18.9

Common-Size Comparative Income Statement

NIKE Common-Size Comparative Income Statement For Years Ended May 31, 1997 and 1996			Common-Size Percents*	
(in thousands, except per share data)	1997	1996	1997	1996
Revenues	$9,186,539	$6,470,625	100.0%	100.0%
Costs and expenses:				
Costs of sales	5,502,993	3,906,746	59.9	60.4
Selling and administrative	2,303,704	1,588,612	25.1	24.6
Interest expense	52,343	39,498	0.6	0.6
Other income/expense, net	32,277	36,679	0.4	0.6
Total costs and expenses	$7,891,317	$5,571,535	85.9%	86.1%
Income before income taxes	1,295,222	899,090	14.1	13.9
Income taxes	499,400	345,900	5.4	5.3
Net income	$ 795,822	$ 553,190	8.7%	8.5%
Net income per common share	$ 2.68	$ 1.88		
Average number of common and common equivalent shares	297,000	293,608		

*Percents are rounded to the first decimal point.

One of the advantages of computing common-size percents for successive income statements is that it helps uncover potentially important changes in a company's expenses. Evidence of no changes is also valuable information for our analysis.

Common-Size Graphics

There are several tools of common-size analysis. Two of the most common are trend analysis of common-size statements and graphical analysis. The trend analysis of common-size statements is similar to the trend analysis of comparative statements discussed under vertical analysis. Because the only difference is the substitution of common-size percents for percent changes, it is not illustrated here. Instead, this section discusses graphical analysis of common-size statements.

An income statement readily lends itself to common-size graphical analysis. Revenues affect nearly every item in an income statement. It is also usually helpful for our analysis to know what portion of revenues is taken up by various expenses. Exhibit 18.10 shows NIKE's common-size income statement in graphical form. This pie chart highlights the contribution of each component of revenues.

Exhibit 18.10

Common-Size Graphic of NIKE's Income Statement

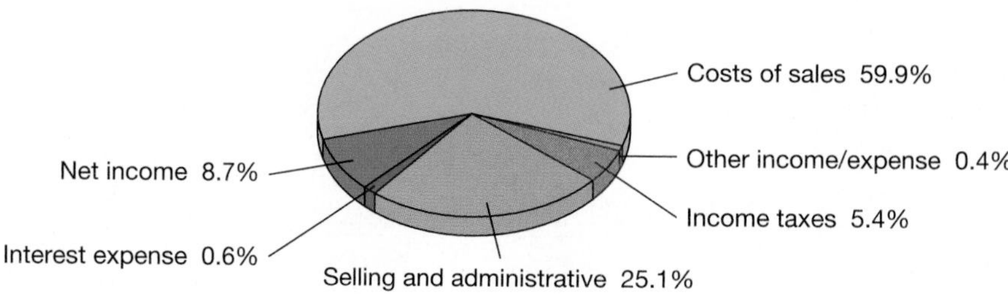

Exhibits 18.11 and 18.12 give a preview of more complex graphical analyses available and the insights they provide. The data for these graphs are taken from NIKE's financial history section in Appendix A. The bar chart in Exhibit 18.11 shows a graphi-

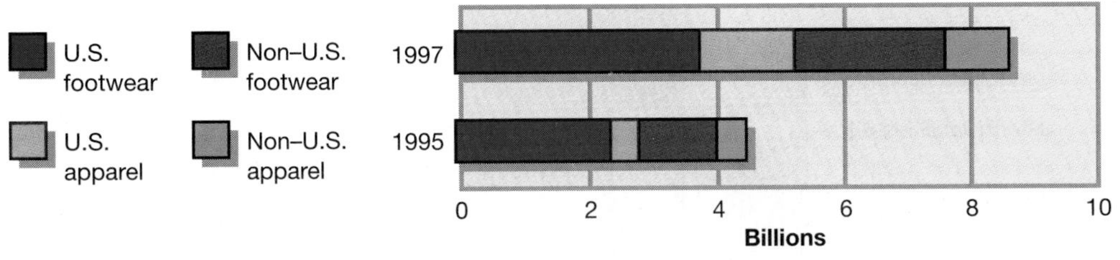

Exhibit 18.11

Revenue Breakdown in Dollars

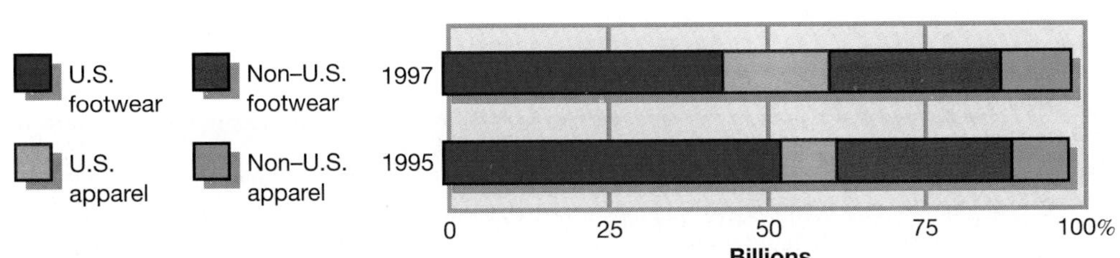

Exhibit 18.12

Revenue Breakdown as Percent of Total

cal breakdown of 1997 and 1995 revenues by apparel and footwear for both U.S. and non-U.S. revenues. It is immediately apparent from this chart that each segment's revenues increased from 1995 to 1997.

Exhibit 18.12 shows a bar chart measuring each segment's revenues as a percent of its yearly revenues. This presentation highlights the decline in magnitude of U.S. footwear revenues for NIKE. In particular, its U.S. footwear revenues were more than 50% of its total revenues in 1995, but by 1997 it had declined to under 45% of total revenues. The increase in non-U.S. revenues raises the risk exposure of NIKE to changes in the global economy. Also, NIKE's U.S. apparel business sharply increased from 1995 to 1997, but its non-U.S. apparel counterpart increased at a slower rate.

Graphical analysis is especially useful in evaluating a balance sheet. It is helpful in assessing two important elements: (1) sources of financing including the distribution among current liabilities, noncurrent liabilities, and equity capital and (2) identification of investing activities including distribution among current assets and noncurrent assets.

Common-size balance sheet analysis is often extended to examine the composition of subgroups. For instance, in assessing liquidity of current assets, it is often important to know what proportion of current assets is composed of inventories, and not simply what proportion inventories are of total assets. Exhibit 18.13 shows a common-size graphical display of the assets of NIKE.

Common-size financial statements are useful in comparing different companies. This is because financial statements of different companies are recast in common-size format. Exhibit 18.14 shows common-size graphics of both **NIKE** and **Reebok** regarding their financing sources. This graphic highlights the much larger percent of debt financing for Reebok compared to NIKE.

But common-size statements fail to reflect the relative sizes of companies under analysis. Comparison of a company's common-size statements with competitors' or industry common-size statistics alerts our attention to differences in the structure or distribution of its financial statements. Major differences should be explored and explained.

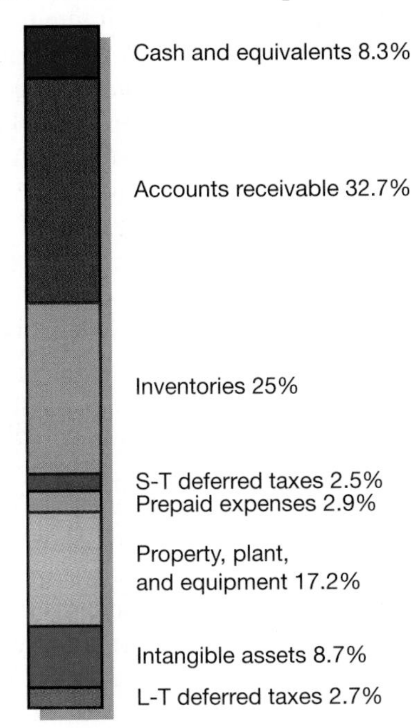

Exhibit 18.13

Common-Size Graphic of NIKE's Assets

Exhibit 18.14

Common-Size Graphic of Financing Sources—NIKE vs Reebok

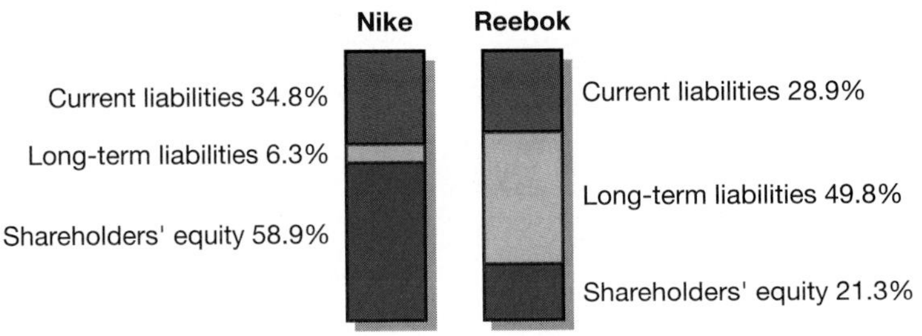

Flash back

5. On common-size comparative statements, which of the following is true? *(a)* Each item is expressed as a percent of a base amount. *(b)* Total assets is assigned a value of 100%. *(c)* Amounts from two or more successive periods are placed side by side. *(d)* All of the above are true.
6. What is the difference between the percents shown on a comparative income statement and those shown on a common-size comparative income statement?
7. Trend percents are: *(a)* shown on comparative income statements and comparative balance sheets; *(b)* shown on common-size comparative statements; or *(c)* also called index numbers.

Answers—p. 802

Ratio Analysis

P3 Define and apply ratio analysis.

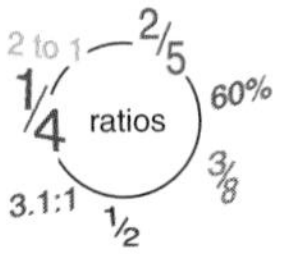

Ratios are among the most popular and widely used tools of financial analysis. They provide us with clues and symptoms of underlying conditions. Ratios, properly interpreted, identify areas requiring further investigation. A ratio can help us uncover conditions and trends difficult to detect by inspecting individual components making up the ratio. Ratios, like other analysis tools, are usually future oriented. This means they are often adjusted for their probable future trend and magnitude. Usefulness of ratios depends on our skillful interpretation of them, and is the most challenging aspect of ratio analysis.

A ratio expresses a mathematical relation between two quantities. It can be expressed as a percent, rate, or proportion. For instance, a change in an account balance from $100 to $250 can be expressed as: (1) 250%, (2) 2.5 times, or (3) 2.5 to 1 (or 2.5:1). While computation of a ratio is a simple arithmetic operation, its interpretation is not. To be meaningful, a ratio must refer to an economically important relation. For example, there is a direct and crucial relation between an item's sales price and its cost. Accordingly, the ratio of cost of goods sold to sales is a significant one. In contrast, there is no obvious relation between freight costs and the balance of marketable securities.

This section describes an important set of financial ratios and shows how to apply them. The selected ratios are organized into the four building blocks of financial statement analysis: (1) liquidity and efficiency, (2) solvency, (3) profitability, and (4) market. All of these ratios have been previously explained at relevant points in prior chapters. The purpose here is to organize and apply them under a summary framework.

Our focus is on **NIKE.** As we discussed earlier, there are four common standards for comparisons: intracompany, competitor, industry, and guidelines. Our analysis of NIKE uses three of the four standards in varying degrees—intracompany, competitor (Reebok), and guideline comparisons. Since there is no obvious industry comparison for NIKE, we do not use industry standards as we normally would. For instance, it might be useful to construct industry standards using Reebok, Adidas, and Fila. But since Adidas and Fila do not publish financial statements readily comparable to NIKE, this is not done.

Liquidity and Efficiency

Liquidity refers to the availability of resources to meet short-term cash requirements. A company's short-term liquidity is affected by the timing of cash inflows and outflows along with its prospects for future performance. Our analysis of liquidity is aimed at a company's capital requirements. *Efficiency* refers to how productive a company is in using its assets. Efficiency is usually measured relative to how much revenue is generated for a certain level of assets.

Both liquidity and efficiency are important and complementary in our analysis. If a company fails to meet its current obligations, its continued existence is doubtful. Viewed in this light, all other measures of analysis are of secondary importance. While accounting measurements assume indefinite existence of the company, our analysis must always assess the validity of this assumption using liquidity measures. Efficiency is how well a company uses its assets. Inefficient use of assets can yield liquidity problems.

For users, a lack of liquidity often precedes lower profitability and opportunity. It can foretell a loss of owner control or loss of investment. When a company's owners possess unlimited liability (proprietorships and certain partnerships), a lack of liquidity endangers their personal assets. To creditors of a company, lack of liquidity can yield delays in collecting interest and principal payments or the loss of amounts due them. A company's customers and suppliers of goods and services are affected by short-term liquidity problems. Implications include a company's inability to execute contracts and potential damage to important customer and supplier relationships. This section describes and illustrates ratios relevant to accessing liquidity and efficiency.

Working Capital and Current Ratio

The amount of current assets less current liabilities is called **working capital,** or *net working capital.* A company needs an adequate amount of working capital to meet current debts, carry sufficient inventories, and take advantage of cash discounts. A company that runs low on working capital is less likely to meet current obligations or continue operating.

When evaluating a company's working capital, we must look beyond the dollar amount of current assets less current liabilities. We also need to consider the relation between the amounts of current assets and current liabilities. Recall from Chapter 5 that the *current ratio* describes a company's ability to pay its short-term obligations. The current ratio relates current assets to current liabilities as follows:

$$\text{Current ratio} = \frac{\text{Current assets}}{\text{Current liabilities}}$$

Drawing on information in Exhibit 18.1, NIKE's working capital amounts and current ratios for both 1997 and 1996 are shown in Exhibit 18.15.

Exhibit 18.15

Working Capital and Current Ratio

(in millions)	May 31, 1997	May 31, 1996
Current assets	$3,830,919	$2,726,940
Current liabilities	1,866,917	1,467,059
Working capital	**$1,964,002**	**$1,259,881**
Current ratio:		
$3,830,919/$1,866,917	2.05 to 1	
$2,726,940/$1,467,059		1.86 to 1

Reebok's current ratio of 2.83 is shown in the margin. It is higher than NIKE's current ratio, but neither company appears in immediate danger of defaulting on loan payments.

Reebok
Current ratio = 2.83

A high current ratio suggests a strong liquidity position. A high ratio means a company should be able to meet its current obligations. But a company also can have a current ratio that is too high. An excessively high ratio means the company has invested too much in current assets compared to its current obligations. Since current assets don't normally generate much additional revenue, an excessive investment in current assets is not an efficient use of funds.

Many users apply a guideline of 2 to 1 for the current ratio in helping evaluate the debt-paying ability of a company. A company with a 2 to 1 or higher current ratio is generally thought to be a good credit risk in the short run. But this analysis is only one step in our process of assessing a company's debt-paying ability. We also need to analyze at least three additional factors:

1. Type of business.
2. Composition of current assets.
3. Turnover rate of current asset components.

Type of Business

The type of business a company operates affects our assessment of its current ratio. A service company that grants little or no credit and carries no inventories other than supplies can probably operate on a current ratio of less than 1 to 1 if its revenues generate enough cash to pay its current liabilities on time. On the other hand, a company selling high-priced clothing or furniture requires a higher ratio. This is because of difficulties in judging customer demand and other factors. For instance, if demand falls, this company's inventory may not generate as much cash as expected. A company facing these risks should maintain a current ratio of more than 2 to 1 to protect its creditors.

The importance of the type of business to our analysis implies that an evaluation of a company's current ratio should include a comparison with ratios of other successful companies in the same industry. Another important part of our analysis is to observe how the current ratio changes over time. We must also recognize that the current ratio is affected by a company's accounting methods, especially choice of inventory method. For instance, a company using LIFO tends to report a smaller amount of current assets than if it uses FIFO when costs are rising. These factors should be considered before we decide whether a given current ratio is adequate.

Composition of Current Assets

The composition of a company's current assets is important to our evaluation of short-term liquidity. For instance, cash, cash equivalents, and short-term investments are more liquid than accounts and notes receivable. Also, short-term receivables normally are more liquid than merchandise inventory. We know cash can be used to immediately pay current debts. But items such as accounts receivable and merchandise inventory normally must be converted into cash before payments can be made. An excessive amount of receivables and inventory weakens a company's ability to pay current liabilities. One way to take account of the composition of current assets is to evaluate the acid-test ratio. We discuss this in the next section.

Turnover Rate of Assets

Asset turnover measures the efficiency of a company's use of assets. One relevant measure of asset efficiency is the revenue generated. The general measure of asset turnover is revenues divided by total assets. But evaluation of turnover for individual assets is also useful in our analysis. We discuss total asset turnover along with both receivables and inventories turnover below.

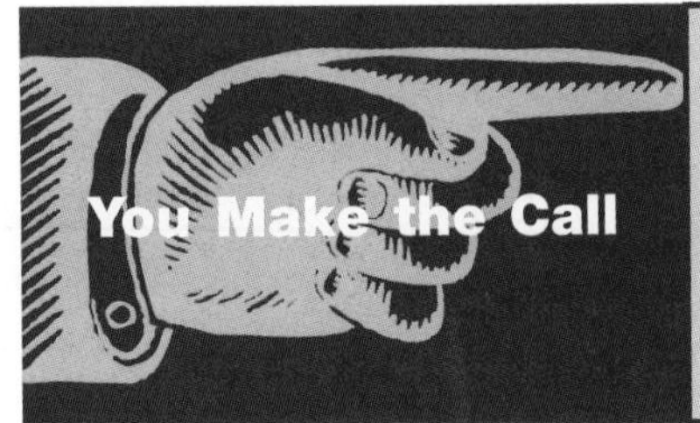

Banker

You are a banker, and a company calls on you for a 1-year, $200,000 loan to finance expansion. This company's current ratio is 4:1 with current assets of $160,000. Key competitors carry a current ratio of about 1.9:1. Using this information, do you approve the loan application? Does your decision change if the application is for a 10-year loan?

Answer—p. 801

Acid-Test Ratio

Chapter 6 introduced us to the *acid-test ratio,* also called *quick ratio.* This ratio focuses on current asset composition. Quick assets are cash, short-term investments, accounts receivable, and notes receivable. These are the most liquid types of current assets. We compute the acid-test ratio as:

$$\textbf{Acid-test ratio} = \frac{\textbf{Quick assets}}{\textbf{Current liabilities}}$$

Using information in Exhibit 18.1, we compute NIKE's acid-test ratios in Exhibit 18.16.

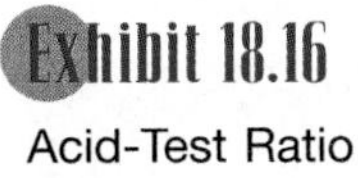

Acid-Test Ratio

(in millions)	May 31, 1997	May 31, 1996
Cash and equivalents	$ 445,421	$ 262,117
Accounts receivable, net of allowances	1,754,137	1,346,125
Total quick assets	$2,199,558	$1,608,242
Current liabilities	$1,866,917	$1,467,059
Acid-test ratio:		
$2,199,558/$1,866,917	1.18 to 1	
$1,608,242/$1,467,059		1.10 to 1

Reebok
Acid-test ratio = 1.59

NIKE's acid-test ratio is less than Reebok's, but it exceeds the common guideline for an acceptable acid-test ratio of 1 to 1. Similar to our analysis of the current ratio, we need to consider other factors. For instance, the working capital requirements of a company are affected by how frequently the company converts its current assets into cash. This implies our analysis of the company's short-term liquidity should also include analysis of receivables and inventories. We next look at these analyses.

Accounts Receivable Turnover

We can measure how frequently a company converts its receivables into cash by computing *accounts receivable turnover.* As explained in Chapter 10, this is computed as:

$$\textbf{Accounts receivable turnover} = \frac{\textbf{Net sales}}{\textbf{Average accounts receivable}}$$

While this ratio is called accounts receivable turnover, short-term receivables from customers are normally included in the denominator along with accounts receivable.

Accounts receivable turnover is more precise if credit sales are used for the numerator. But net sales (or revenues) are usually used by external users because information about credit sales is typically not reported.

NIKE's 1997 accounts receivable turnover is computed as:

$$\frac{\$9{,}186{,}539}{(\$1{,}754{,}137 + \$1{,}346{,}125)/2} = 5.9 \text{ times}$$

Reebok
Accounts receivable turnover = 6.34

NIKE's value of 5.9 is similar to Reebok's 6.34. If accounts receivable are collected quickly, then accounts receivable turnover is high. A high turnover is favorable because it means the company need not commit large amounts of capital to accounts receivable. But an accounts receivable turnover can be too high. This can occur when credit terms are so restrictive they negatively affect sales volume.

Ending accounts receivable is sometimes substituted for the average balance in computing accounts receivable turnover. This is acceptable if the difference between ending and average receivables is insignificant. Also, some users prefer using gross accounts receivable (before subtracting the allowance for doubtful accounts). But many balance sheets report only the net amount of accounts receivable.

Reebok
Merchandise turnover = 3.64

Merchandise Inventory Turnover

Working capital requirements are affected by how long a company holds merchandise inventory before selling it. One measure of this effect is the *merchandise inventory turnover,* or simply *merchandise* or *inventory turnover.* Merchandise turnover is defined in Chapter 7 as:

$$\textbf{Merchandise turnover} = \frac{\textbf{Cost of goods sold}}{\textbf{Average merchandise inventory}}$$

Using the costs of sales (NIKE's term for cost of goods sold) and inventories information in Exhibits 18.1 and 18.2, we compute NIKE's merchandise turnover for 1997 as:

$$\frac{\$5,502,993}{(\$1,338,640 + \$931,151)/2} = 4.8 \text{ times}$$

Average inventory is estimated by averaging the beginning and the ending inventories for 1997. If the beginning and ending inventories do not represent the amount normally on hand, an average of quarterly inventories may be used if available.

NIKE's merchandise turnover is 4.8 and is higher than Reebok's 3.64. A company with a high turnover requires a smaller investment in inventory than one producing the same sales with a lower turnover. But merchandise turnover can be too high if a company keeps such a small inventory on hand that it restricts sales volume.

Days' Sales Uncollected

We already described how accounts receivable turnover can be used to evaluate how frequently a company collects its accounts. Another measure of this activity is *days' sales uncollected,* defined in Chapter 9 as:

$$\textbf{Days' sales uncollected} = \frac{\textbf{Accounts receivable}}{\textbf{Net sales}} \times \textbf{365}$$

Any short-term notes receivable from customers are normally included in the numerator.

We illustrate this ratio's application by using NIKE's information in Exhibits 18.1 and 18.2. The days' sales uncollected on May 31, 1997, is:

Reebok
Days' sales uncollected = 62.0

$$\frac{\$1,754,137}{\$9,186,539} \times 365 = 69.7 \text{ days}$$

NIKE's days' sales uncollected of 69.7 days is slightly longer than the 62 days for Reebok. Days' sales uncollected is more meaningful if we know NIKE's and Reebok's credit terms. A rough guideline is days' sales uncollected should not exceed one and one-third times the days in its: *(a)* credit period, if discounts are not offered; or *(b)* discount period, if discounts are offered.

Days' Sales in Inventory

Chapter 7 explained how *days' sales in inventory* is a measure useful in evaluating the liquidity of a company's inventory. Days' sales in inventory is linked to inventory as days' sales uncollected is linked to receivables. Days' sales in inventory is computed as:

$$\textbf{Days' sales in inventory} = \frac{\textbf{Ending inventory}}{\textbf{Cost of goods sold}} \times \textbf{365}$$

We compute NIKE's 1997 days' sales in inventory as:

$$\frac{\$1{,}338{,}640}{\$5{,}502{,}993} \times 365 = 88.8 \text{ days}$$

Reebok
Days' sales in inventory = 92.7

If the products in NIKE's inventory are in demand by customers, this formula estimates that its inventory will be converted into receivables (or cash) in 88.8 days. If all of NIKE's sales are credit sales, the conversion of inventory to receivables in 88.8 days *plus* the conversion of receivables to cash in 69.7 days suggest that inventory will be converted to cash in about 158.5 days (88.8 + 69.7 = 158.5).

Total Asset Turnover

Total asset turnover describes the ability of a company to use its assets to generate sales. We explained in Chapter 11 that this ratio is computed as:

$$\textbf{Total asset turnover} = \frac{\textbf{Revenues}}{\textbf{Average total assets}}$$

In computing NIKE's total asset turnover for 1997, we follow the usual practice of averaging total assets at the beginning and the end of the year. Taking the information from Exhibits 18.1 and 18.2, this computation is:

$$\frac{\$9{,}186{,}539}{(\$5{,}361{,}207 + \$3{,}951{,}628)/2} = 1.97 \text{ times}$$

Reebok
Total asset turnover = 2.02

Total asset turnover is a basic component of operating efficiency. NIKE's performance on this factor is similar to Reebok's.

Flash back

8. The following information is from the 12/31/2000 balance sheet of Paff Company: cash, \$820,000; accounts receivable, \$240,000; inventories, \$470,000; plant and equipment, \$910,000; accounts payable, \$350,000; and income taxes payable, \$180,000. Compute the *(a)* current ratio and *(b)* acid-test ratio.

9. On 12/31/1999, Paff Company (in prior question) had accounts receivable of \$290,000 and inventories of \$530,000. During 2000, net sales amounted to \$2,500,000 and cost of goods sold was \$750,000. Compute the *(a)* accounts receivable turnover, *(b)* days' sales uncollected, *(c)* merchandise turnover, and *(d)* days' sales in inventory.

Answers—p. 802

Solvency

Solvency refers to a company's long-run financial viability and its ability to cover long-term obligations. All business activities of a company—financing, investing, and operating—affect a company's solvency. One of the most important components of solvency analysis is the composition of a company's capital structure. *Capital structure* refers to a company's sources of financing.

Analyzing solvency of a company is different from analyzing short-term liquidity. Analysis of solvency is long term and uses less precise but more encompassing measures. Analysis of capital structure is one key in evaluating solvency. Capital structure ranges from relatively permanent equity capital to more risky or temporary short-term financing. Assets represent secondary sources of security for lenders ranging from loans secured by specific assets to the assets available as general security to unsecured creditors. There are different risks associated with different assets and financing sources.

This section describes tools of solvency analysis. Our analysis is concerned with a company's ability to both meet its obligations and provide security to its creditors *over the long run.* Indicators of this ability include *debt* and *equity* ratios, the relation between *pledged assets and secured liabilities,* and the company's capacity to earn sufficient income to *pay fixed interest charges.*

Debt and Equity Ratios

One element of solvency analysis is to assess the portion of a company's assets contributed by its owners and the portion contributed by creditors. This relation is reflected in the debt ratio described in Chapter 3. Recall that the *debt ratio* expresses total liabilities as a percent of total assets. The **equity ratio** provides complementary information by expressing total stockholders' equity as a percent of total assets.

NIKE's debt and equity ratios are computed as:

	May 31, 1997	Ratios
Total liabilities	$2,205,369	41.1% [Debt ratio]
Total shareholders' equity	3,155,838	58.9 [Equity ratio]
Total liabilities and shareholders' equity	$5,361,207	100.0%

Reebok
Debt ratio = 78.7%
Equity ratio = 21.3%

NIKE's financial statements reflect less debt than equity. Also, NIKE's debt mainly comprises current liabilities. In particular, current liabilities make up nearly 85% of total liabilities, computed as $1,866,917/$2,205,369. A company is considered less risky if its capital structure (equity and long-term debt) comprises more equity. One risk factor is the required payments under debt contracts for interest and principal amounts. Another factor is the amount of financing provided by stockholders. The greater the stockholder financing, the more losses a company can absorb through its stockholders before the remaining assets become inadequate to satisfy the claims of creditors.

From the stockholders' point of view, including debt in the capital structure of a company is desirable so long as risk is not too great. If a company earns a return on borrowed capital that is higher than the cost of borrowing, the difference represents increased income to stockholders. Because debt can have the effect of increasing the return to stockholders, the inclusion of debt is described as *financial leverage.* Companies are said to be highly leveraged if a large portion of their assets is financed by debt.

Pledged Assets to Secured Liabilities

We explained in Chapter 15 how we use the ratio of pledged assets to secured liabilities to evaluate the risk of nonpayment faced by secured creditors. This ratio also is relevant to unsecured creditors. The ratio is computed as:

$$\textbf{Pledged assets to secured liabilities} = \frac{\textbf{Book value of pledged assets}}{\textbf{Book value of secured liabilities}}$$

The information needed to compute this ratio is not usually reported in published financial statements. This means the ratio is used primarily by persons who have the ability to obtain information directly from the company, such as bankers and certain lenders.

A generally agreed minimum value for this ratio is about 2 to 1. But the ratio needs careful interpretation because it is based on the *book value* of pledged assets. Book values are not necessarily intended to reflect amounts to be received for assets in event of liquidation. Also, the long-run earning ability of a company with pledged assets may be more important than the value of its pledged assets. Creditors prefer that a debtor be able to pay with cash generated by operating activities rather than with cash obtained by liquidating assets.

Times Interest Earned

Chapter 12 explained the *times interest earned* ratio. Its purpose is to reflect the riskiness of repayments with interest to creditors. The amount of income before the deduction of interest charges and income taxes is the amount available to pay interest charges. We compute this ratio as:

$$\textbf{Times interest earned} = \frac{\textbf{Income before interest and income taxes}}{\textbf{Interest expense}}$$

The larger this ratio, the less risky is the company for lenders. A guideline for this ratio says that creditors are reasonably safe if the company earns its fixed interest charges two or more times each year.

Exhibit 18.2 shows reported interest expense of $52,343 for NIKE. The times interest earned ratio for NIKE is computed as:

$$\frac{\$795{,}822 + 499{,}400 + 52{,}343}{\$52{,}343} = 25.7$$

Reebok
Times interest earned = 6.3

This ratio suggests there is little risk of repayment for NIKE's creditors.

Bears and Bulls
A *bear market* is a declining market. It comes from bear-skin jobbers who often sold bear skins before the bears were caught. The term *bear* was then used to describe investors who sold shares they didn't own in anticipation of a price decline. A *bull market* is a rising market. It comes from the once popular sport of bear and bull baiting. The term *bull* came to mean the opposite of *bear.*

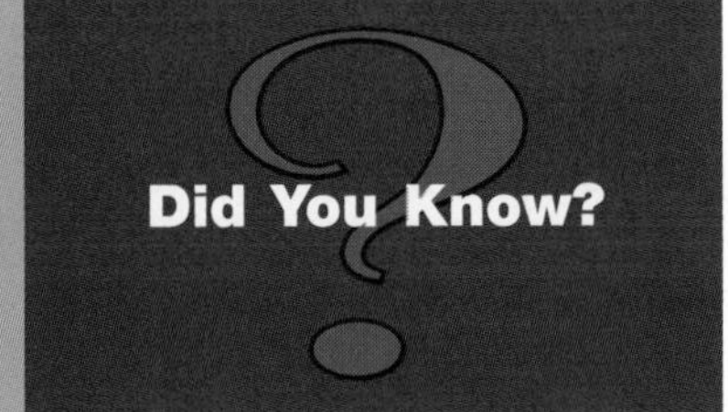

Profitability

We are especially interested in the ability of a company to use its assets efficiently to produce profits (and positive cash flows). *Profitability* refers to a company's ability to generate an adequate return on invested capital. Return is judged by assessing earnings relative to the level and sources of financing. Profitability is also relevant to solvency.

This section describes profitability measures and their importance to financial statement analysis. We also explain variations in return measures and their interpretation. We analyze the components of return on invested capital for additional insights into company performance.

Profit Margin

The operating efficiency and profitability of a company can be expressed in two components. The first is the company's *profit margin.* We explained in Chapter 4 how profit margin reflects a company's ability to earn a net income from sales. It is measured by expressing net income as a percent of revenues (sales and revenues are similar terms). We can use the information in Exhibit 18.2 to compute NIKE's 1995 profit margin as:

Reebok
Profit margin = 4.0

$$\textbf{Profit margin} = \frac{\textbf{Net income}}{\textbf{Revenues}} = \frac{\$795{,}822}{\$9{,}186{,}539} = 8.7\%$$

To evaluate the profit margin of a company, we must consider the industry in which it operates. For instance, a publishing company might be expected to have a profit margin between 10% and 15%, while a retail supermarket might have a normal profit margin of 1% or 2%.

The second component of operating efficiency is *total asset turnover.* We described this ratio earlier in this section. Both profit margin and total asset turnover make up the two basic components of operating efficiency. These ratios also reflect on management performance since managers are ultimately responsible for operating efficiency. The next section explains how we use both measures in analyzing return on total assets.

Return on Total Assets

The two basic components of operating efficiency, profit margin and total asset turnover, are used to compute a summary measure. This summary measure is the *return on total assets* we described in Chapters 1 and 16. It is computed as:

$$\textbf{Return on total assets} = \frac{\textbf{Net income}}{\textbf{Average total assets}}$$

NIKE's 1997 return on total assets is:

Reebok
Return on total assets = 8.1

$$\frac{\$795{,}822}{(\$5{,}361{,}207 + \$3{,}951{,}628)/2} = 17.1\%$$

NIKE's 17.1% return on total assets is favorable compared to most businesses, including Reebok's return of 8.1%. But we need comparisons with other competitors and alternative investment opportunities before reaching a conclusion. We also should evaluate the trend in the rate of return earned by the company in recent years.

The following computation shows the important relation between profit margin, total asset turnover, and return on total assets:

$$\textbf{Profit margin} \times \textbf{Total asset turnover} = \textbf{Return on total assets}$$

or

$$\frac{\textbf{Net income}}{\textbf{Revenues}} \times \frac{\textbf{Revenues}}{\textbf{Average total assets}} = \frac{\textbf{Net income}}{\textbf{Average total assets}}$$

Notice that both profit margin and total asset turnover contribute to overall operating efficiency, as measured by return on total assets. If we apply this formula to NIKE we get:

$$8.7\% \quad \times \quad 1.97 \quad = \quad 17.1\%$$

Reebok 4.0 × 2.02 = 8.1

This analysis shows NIKE and Reebok are similar on total asset turnover, but NIKE's profit margin greatly exceeds Reebok's.

Return on Common Stockholders' Equity

Perhaps the most important goal in operating a company is to earn net income for its owners. The *return on common stockholders' equity* measures the success of a company in reaching this goal. We explained in Chapter 2 how we compute this return measure:

$$\textbf{Return on common stockholders' equity} = \frac{\textbf{Net income} - \textbf{Preferred dividends}}{\textbf{Average common stockholders' equity}}$$

NIKE's statement of shareholders' equity and its notes show it paid \$30 in dividends on redeemable preferred stock in 1997. From this information and data in its statements, we compute NIKE's 1997 return on common stockholders' equity as:

$$\frac{\$795{,}822 - \$30}{(\$3{,}155{,}838 + \$2{,}431{,}400)/2} = 28.5\%$$

Reebok
Return on common stockholders' equity = 21.8

The denominator in this computation is the book value of common stock. In the numerator, the dividends on cumulative preferred stock are subtracted whether they are declared or are in arrears (NIKE's are cumulative as indicated in its *Note 7*). If preferred stock is not cumulative, its dividends are subtracted only if declared.

Wall Street
Wall Street is synonymous with financial markets and capitalism. It comes from the street location of the original New York Stock Exchange. The street's name derives from stockades built by early settlers to protect New York from pirate attacks.

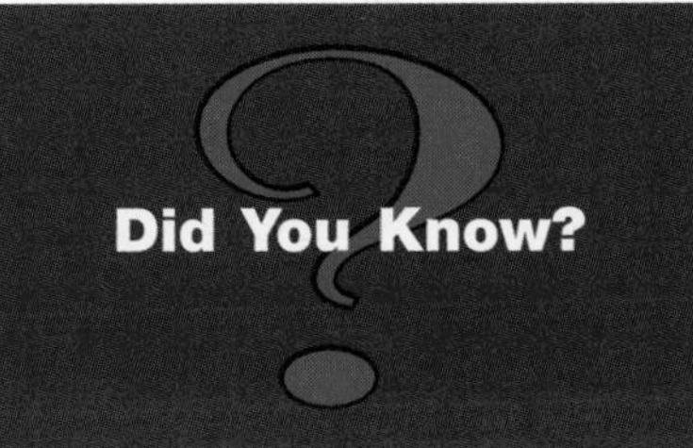

Market

Market measures are useful when analyzing corporations having publicly traded stock. These market measures use stock price in their computation. Stock price reflects what the market (public) expectations are for the company. This includes both the return and risk characteristics of a company as currently perceived by the market.

Price-Earnings Ratio

We explained in Chapter 14 how the *price-earnings ratio* is computed as:

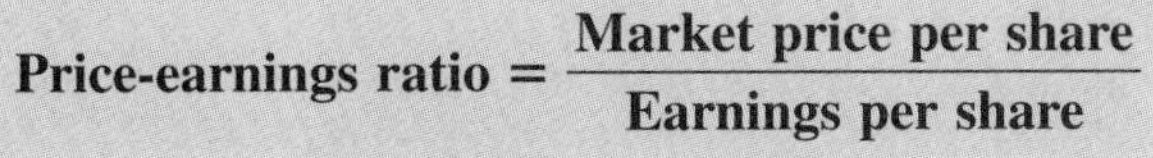

$$\textbf{Price-earnings ratio} = \frac{\textbf{Market price per share}}{\textbf{Earnings per share}}$$

We also described how the predicted earnings per share for the next period is often used in the denominator of this computation. Reported earnings per share for the most recent period is also commonly used. In both cases, the ratio is an indicator of the future growth of and risk related to a company's earnings as perceived by investors who establish the market price of the stock.

The market price of NIKE's common stock during 1997 ranged from a low of $47.875 to a high of $76.375 as shown in its financial history section of Appendix A. Using NIKE's $2.68 earnings per share reported in Exhibit 18.2, we compute its price-earnings ratios using both the low and high stock price:

$$\text{Low: } \frac{\$47.875}{\$2.68} = 17.9$$

$$\text{High: } \frac{\$76.375}{\$2.68} = 28.5$$

Reebok
PE (low) = 12.7
PE (high) = 22.6

NIKE's price-earnings ratios are higher than many companies'. Its higher ratios reflect the expectation of investors that the company will continue to grow at a rate faster than the typical company.

Dividend Yield

We explained in Chapter 14 how to use *dividend yield* as a means to compare the dividend-paying performance of different investment alternatives. Dividend yield is computed as:

$$\textbf{Dividend yield} = \frac{\textbf{Annual dividends per share}}{\textbf{Market price per share}}$$

NIKE's dividend yield, based on its end of fiscal-year market price per share of $57.625, is computed as:

$$\frac{\$0.38}{\$57.625} = 0.7\%$$

Some companies decide not to declare dividends because they prefer to reinvest the cash. Microsoft, for instance, does not pay cash dividends on its common stock.

Summary of Ratios

Exhibit 18.17 presents a summary of the major financial statement analysis ratios illustrated in this chapter and throughout the book. This summary includes each ratio's title, formula, and common use.

Flash *back*

10. Which ratio best reflects the ability of a company to meet immediate interest payments? *(a)* Debt ratio; *(b)* Equity ratio; *(c)* Times interest earned; *(d)* Pledged assets to secured liabilities.

11. Which ratio measures the success of a company in earning net income for its owners? *(a)* Profit margin; *(b)* Return on common stockholders' equity; *(c)* Price-earnings ratio; *(d)* Dividend yield.

12. If a company has net sales of $8,500,000, net income of $945,000, and total asset turnover of 1.8 times, what is its return on total assets?

Answers—p. 802

Financial Statement Analysis Ratios

Ratio	Formula	Measure of:
Liquidity and Efficiency		
Current ratio	$= \frac{\text{Current assets}}{\text{Current liabilities}}$	Short-term debt-paying ability
Acid-test ratio	$= \frac{\text{Cash + Short-term investments + Current receivables}}{\text{Current liabilities}}$	Immediate short-term debt-paying ability
Accounts receivable turnover	$= \frac{\text{Net sales}}{\text{Average accounts receivable}}$	Efficiency of collection
Merchandise turnover	$= \frac{\text{Cost of goods sold}}{\text{Average merchandise inventory}}$	Efficiency of inventory
Days' sales uncollected	$= \frac{\text{Accounts receivable}}{\text{Net sales}} \times 365$	Liquidity of receivables
Days' sales in inventory	$= \frac{\text{Ending inventory}}{\text{Cost of goods sold}} \times 365$	Liquidity of inventory
Total asset turnover	$= \frac{\text{Net sales}}{\text{Average total assets}}$	Efficiency of assets in producing sales
Solvency		
Debt ratio	$= \frac{\text{Total liabilities}}{\text{Total assets}}$	Creditor financing and leverage
Equity ratio	$= \frac{\text{Total stockholders' equity}}{\text{Total assets}}$	Owner financing
Pledged assets to secured liabilities	$= \frac{\text{Book value of pledged assets}}{\text{Book value of secured liabilities}}$	Protection to secured creditors
Times interest earned	$= \frac{\text{Income before interest and taxes}}{\text{Interest expense}}$	Protection in meeting interest payments
Profitability		
Profit margin	$= \frac{\text{Net income}}{\text{Net sales}}$	Net income in each sales dollar
Gross margin	$= \frac{\text{Net sales} - \text{Cost of goods sold}}{\text{Net sales}}$	Gross margin in each sales dollar
Return on total assets	$= \frac{\text{Net income}}{\text{Average total assets}}$	Overall profitability of assets
Return on common stockholders' equity	$= \frac{\text{Net income} - \text{Preferred dividends}}{\text{Average common stockholders' equity}}$	Profitability of owner's investment
Book value per common share	$= \frac{\text{Shareholders' equity applicable to common shares}}{\text{Number of common shares outstanding}}$	Liquidation at reported amounts
Basic earnings per share	$= \frac{\text{Net income} - \text{Preferred dividends}}{\text{Weighted-average common shares outstanding}}$	Net income on each common share
Market		
Price-earnings ratio	$= \frac{\text{Market price per common share}}{\text{Earnings per share}}$	Market value based on earnings
Dividend yield	$= \frac{\text{Annual dividends per share}}{\text{Market price per share}}$	Cash return to each common share

USING THE INFORMATION

Analysis Reporting

A1 Summarize and report results of analysis.

Understanding the purpose of our financial statement analysis is crucial to its usefulness. This understanding leads to efficiency of effort, effectiveness in application, and relevance in focus. Most analyses face constraints on availability of information, and decisions must be made using incomplete or inadequate information.

A goal of most financial statement analyses is reducing uncertainty through a rigorous and sound evaluation. A *financial statement analysis report* helps by directly addressing the building blocks of analysis. It also helps identify weaknesses in inference by requiring explanation, and it forces us to organize our reasoning and to verify the flow and logic of analysis. A report serves as our communication device with readers. The writing process reinforces our judgments and vice versa. It helps us to evaluate evidence and to refine conclusions on key building blocks.

A good report separates interpretations and conclusions of analysis from the information underlying them. This separation enables readers to see our process and rationale of analysis. It also enables the reader to draw personal conclusions and make modifications as appropriate. A good analysis report often consists of six sections devoted to:

1. **Executive summary** The executive summary is brief and focuses on important analysis results and conclusions.
2. **Analysis overview** Background material on the company, its industry, and its economic environment.
3. **Evidential matter** Financial statements and information used in the analysis. This includes ratios, trends, comparisons, statistics, and all analytical measures assembled. Often organized under the building blocks of analysis.
4. **Assumptions** Identification of important assumptions regarding a company's industry and economic environment, and other important assumptions for estimates.
5. **Important factors** Listing of important favorable and unfavorable factors, both quantitative and qualitative, for company performance—usually listed by areas of analysis.
6. **Inferences** Includes forecasts, estimates, interpretations, and conclusions drawing on all sections of the report.

We must remember that importance is defined by the user. This means our analysis report should include a brief table of contents to help readers focus on those areas most relevant to their decisions. All irrelevant matter must be eliminated. For example, decades-old details of the beginnings of a company and a detailing of the miscues of our analysis are irrelevant. Ambiguities and qualifications to avoid responsibility or the hedging of inferences should be eliminated. Finally, writing is important. Mistakes in grammar and errors of fact compromise the credibility of our analysis.

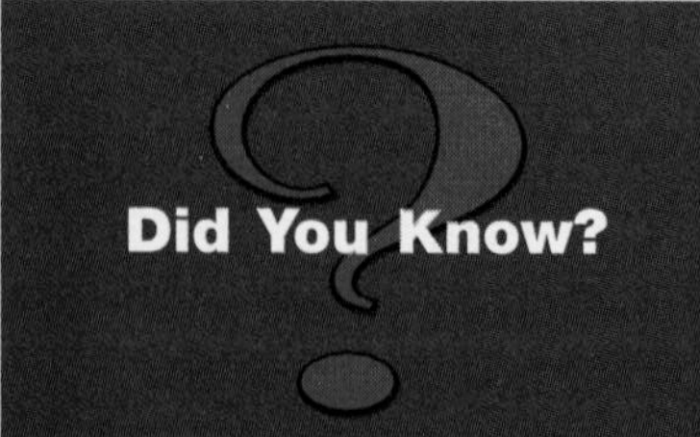

Short Selling

Short selling refers to selling stock before you buy it. Here's an example of how it works: You borrow 100 shares of NIKE stock, sell them in the market at $40 each, and receive money from their sale. You then wait. Your hope is that NIKE's stock price falls to, say, $35 each and you can replace the borrowed stock for less money than you sold it for—reaping a profit of $5 each less any transaction fees.

Summary

C1 **Explain the purpose of analysis.** The purpose of financial statement analysis is to help users make better business decisions. Internal users want information helpful in improving the company's efficiency or effectiveness in providing products or services. External users want information to make better and more informed decisions in pursuing their personal goals. The common goals of all users are to evaluate a company's (1) past and current performance, (2) current financial position, and (3) future performance and risk.

C2 **Identify the building blocks of analysis.** Financial statement analysis focuses mainly on four areas of inquiry. These four areas are the building blocks of analysis: (1) liquidity and efficiency—ability to meet short-term obligations and to efficiently generate revenues; (2) solvency—ability to generate future revenues and meet long-term obligations; (3) profitability—ability to provide financial rewards sufficient to attract and retain financing; and (4) market—ability to generate positive market expectations.

C3 **Describe standards for comparisons in analysis.** To make conclusions from analysis, we need standards for comparisons. Standards for comparisons include: (1) intracompany—prior performance and relations between financial items for the company under analysis; (2) competitor—one or more direct competitors of the company under analysis provides standards for comparisons; (3) industry—industry statistics can provide standards of comparisons; and (4) guidelines (rules of thumb)—general standards of comparisons can develop from past experiences and personal judgments.

C4 **Identify the tools of analysis.** The three most common tools of financial statement analysis are: (1) horizontal analysis—comparing a company's financial condition and performance across time; (2) vertical analysis—comparing a company's financial condition and performance to a base amount such as revenues or total assets; and (3) ratio analysis—using key relations among financial statement items.

A1 **Summarize and report results of analysis.** A financial statement analysis report is often organized around the building blocks of analysis. It serves as a communication device with readers. A good report separates interpretations and conclusions of analysis from the information underlying them. This separation enables readers to see the process and rationale of analysis. It also enables the reader to draw personal conclusions and make modifications as appropriate. An analysis report often consists of six sections: (1) executive summary; (2) analysis overview; (3) evidential matter; (4) assumptions; (5) important factors; and (6) inferences.

P1 **Explain and apply methods of horizontal analysis.** Horizontal analysis is a tool to evaluate changes in financial statement data across time. Two important tools of horizontal analysis are comparative statements and trend analysis. Comparative statements show amounts for two or more successive periods, often with changes disclosed in both absolute and percent terms. Trend analysis is used to reveal important changes occurring from one period to the next.

P2 **Describe and apply methods of vertical analysis.** Vertical analysis is a tool to evaluate each financial statement item or group of items in terms of a specific base amount. This base amount is commonly defined as 100%. Two important tools of vertical analysis are common-size statements and graphical analyses. In common-size statements, each item is expressed as a percent of a base amount. The base amount for the balance sheet is usually total assets, and the base amount for the income statement is usually net sales.

P3 **Define and apply ratio analysis.** Ratio analysis provides clues and symptoms of underlying conditions. Ratios, properly interpreted, identify areas requiring further investigation. A ratio expresses a mathematical relation between two quantities such as a percent, rate, or proportion. Ratios can be organized into the building blocks of analysis: (1) liquidity and efficiency, (2) solvency, (3) profitability, and (4) market.

Guidance Answers to **You Make the Call**

Auditor

The *joint relation* referred to here is where the increase in sales and the decrease in expenses yield a greater than 5% increase in income. In particular, both *individual* accounts (sales and expenses) yielded percent changes within the ±5% acceptable range. However, a joint analysis suggests a different picture. For example, consider a joint analysis using the profit margin ratio (net income/sales). The client's profit margin is 11.46% ($206,000 − $182,400 /$206,000) for the current year compared with 5.0% ($200,000 − $190,000 /$200,000) for the prior year—a 129% increase in profit margin! This is what the partner is concerned with, and it suggests expanding audit tests to verify or refute the client's figures.

Banker

Your decision on the loan application is positive for at least two reasons. First, the current ratio suggests a strong ability to meet short-term obligations. Second, current assets of $160,000 and a current ratio of 4:1 imply current liabilities of $40,000 (one-fourth of current assets) and a working capital excess of $120,000. This working capital excess is 60% of the loan amount. However, if the application is for a 10-year loan, our decision is less optimistic. While the current ratio and working capital suggest a good safety margin, there are indications of inefficiency in operations. In particular, a 4:1 current ratio is more than double its competitors' ratio. This is characteristic of inefficient asset use.

Guidance Answers to Flash*backs*

1. General-purpose financial statements are intended for the large variety of users who are interested in receiving financial information about a business but who do not have the ability to require the company to prepare specialized financial reports designed to meet their specific interests.

2. General-purpose financial statements include the income statement, balance sheet, statement of changes in stockholders' equity (or statement of retained earnings), and statement of cash flows, plus notes related to the statements.
3. *a*
4. Data from one or more direct competitors of the company under analysis are usually preferred for developing standards for comparisons.
5. *d*
6. Percents on a comparative income statement show the increase or decrease in each item from one period to the next. On a common-size comparative income statement, each item is shown as a percent of net sales for a specific period.
7. *c*
8. *a;* ($820,000 + $240,000 + $470,000)/($350,000 + $180,000) = 2.9 to 1.
   b; ($820,000 + $240,000)/($350,000 + $180,000) = 2 to 1.
9. *a;* $2,500,000/[($290,000 + $240,000)/2] = 9.43 times.
   b; ($240,000/$2,500,000) × 365 = 35 days.
   c; $750,000/[($530,000 + $470,000)/2] = 1.5 times.
   d; ($470,000/$750,000) × 365 = 228.7 days.
10. *c*
11. *b*
12.

$$\text{Profit margin} \times \text{Total asset turnover} = \text{Return on total assets}$$

$$\frac{\$945{,}000}{\$8{,}500{,}000} \times 1.8 = 20\%$$

Demonstration Problem

Use the financial statements of Precision Company to satisfy the following requirements:

1. Prepare a comparative income statement showing the percent increase or decrease for year 2000 in comparison to year 1999.
2. Prepare a common-size comparative balance sheet for years 2000 and 1999.
3. Compute and identify the appropriate building block of financial statement analysis for the following ratios as of December 31, 2000, or for the year ended December 31, 2000:
   - **a.** Current ratio
   - **b.** Acid-test ratio
   - **c.** Accounts receivable turnover
   - **d.** Days' sales uncollected
   - **e.** Merchandise turnover
   - **f.** Debt ratio
   - **g.** Pledged assets to secured liabilities
   - **h.** Times interest earned
   - **i.** Profit margin
   - **j.** Total asset turnover
   - **k.** Return on total assets
   - **l.** Return on common stockholders' equity

Selected Financial Statements

PRECISION COMPANY
Comparative Income Statement
For Years Ended December 31, 2000 and 1999

	2000	1999
Sales	$2,486,000	$2,075,000
Cost of goods sold	1,523,000	1,222,000
Gross profit from sales	$ 963,000	$ 853,000
Operating expenses:		
Advertising expense	$ 145,000	$ 100,000
Sales salaries expense	240,000	280,000
Office salaries expense	165,000	200,000
Insurance expense	100,000	45,000
Supplies expense	26,000	35,000
Depreciation expense	85,000	75,000
Miscellaneous expenses	17,000	15,000
Total operating expenses	$ 778,000	$ 750,000
Operating income	$ 185,000	$ 103,000
Less interest expense	44,000	46,000
Income before taxes	$ 141,000	$ 57,000
Income taxes	47,000	19,000
Net income	$ 94,000	$ 38,000
Earnings per share	$ 0.99	$ 0.40

PRECISION COMPANY Comparative Balance Sheet December 31, 2000, and December 31, 1999	2000	1999
Assets		
Current assets:		
Cash	$ 79,000	$ 42,000
Short-term investments	65,000	96,000
Accounts receivable (net)	120,000	100,000
Merchandise inventory	250,000	265,000
Total current assets	$ 514,000	$ 503,000
Plant and equipment:		
Store equipment (net)	$ 400,000	$ 350,000
Office equipment (net)	45,000	50,000
Buildings (net)	625,000	675,000
Land	100,000	100,000
Total plant and equipment	$1,170,000	$1,175,000
Total assets	$1,684,000	$1,678,000
Liabilities		
Current liabilities:		
Accounts payable	$ 164,000	$ 190,000
Short-term notes payable	75,000	90,000
Taxes payable	26,000	12,000
Total current liabilities	$ 265,000	$ 292,000
Long-term liabilities:		
Notes payable (secured by mortgage on building & land)	400,000	420,000
Total liabilities	$ 665,000	$ 712,000
Stockholders' Equity		
Contributed capital:		
Common stock, $5 par value	$ 475,000	$ 475,000
Retained earnings	544,000	491,000
Total stockholders' equity	$1,019,000	$ 966,000
Total liabilities and equity	$1,684,000	$1,678,000

Planning the Solution

- Set up a four-column income statement; enter the year 2000 and year 1999 amounts in the first two columns and then enter the dollar change in the third column and the percent change from 1999 in the fourth column.
- Set up a four-column balance sheet; enter the 2000 and 1999 year-end amounts in the first two columns and then compute and enter the amount of each item as a percent of total assets.
- Compute the required ratios using the provided numbers. Use the average of beginning and ending amounts where appropriate (see Exhibit 18.17 for definitions).

Solution to Demonstration Problem

1.

PRECISION COMPANY
Comparative Income Statement
For Years Ended December 31, 2000 and 1999

	2000	1999	Increase (Decrease) in 2000 Amount	Increase (Decrease) in 2000 Percent
Sales	$2,486,000	$2,075,000	$411,000	19.8%
Cost of goods sold	1,523,000	1,222,000	301,000	24.6
Gross profit from sales	$ 963,000	$ 853,000	$110,000	12.9
Operating expenses:				
Advertising expense	$ 145,000	$ 100,000	$ 45,000	45.0
Sales salaries expense	240,000	280,000	(40,000)	(14.3)
Office salaries expense	165,000	200,000	(35,000)	(17.5)
Insurance expense	100,000	45,000	55,000	122.2
Supplies expense	26,000	35,000	(9,000)	(25.7)
Depreciation expense	85,000	75,000	10,000	13.3
Miscellaneous expenses	17,000	15,000	2,000	13.3
Total operating expenses	$ 778,000	$ 750,000	$ 28,000	3.7
Operating income	$ 185,000	$ 103,000	$ 82,000	79.6
Less interest expense	44,000	46,000	(2,000)	(4.3)
Income before taxes	$ 141,000	$ 57,000	$ 84,000	147.4
Income taxes	47,000	19,000	28,000	147.4
Net income	$ 94,000	$ 38,000	$ 56,000	147.4
Earnings per share	$ 0.99	$ 0.40	$ 0.59	147.5

2.

PRECISION COMPANY
Common-Size Comparative Balance Sheet
December 31, 2000 and 1999

	December 31 2000	December 31 1999	Common-Size Percents 2000*	Common-Size Percents 1999*
Assets				
Current assets:				
Cash	$ 79,000	$ 42,000	4.7%	2.5%
Short-term investments	65,000	96,000	3.9	5.7
Accounts receivable (net)	120,000	100,000	7.1	6.0
Merchandise inventory	250,000	265,000	14.8	15.8
Total current assets	$ 514,000	$ 503,000	30.5	30.0
Plant and equipment:				
Store equipment (net)	$ 400,000	$ 350,000	23.8	20.9
Office equipment (net)	45,000	50,000	2.7	3.0
Buildings (net)	625,000	675,000	37.1	40.2
Land	100,000	100,000	5.9	6.0
Total plant and equipment	$1,170,000	$1,175,000	69.5	70.0
Total assets	$1,684,000	$1,678,000	100.0	100.0

[continued on next page]

Liabilities				
Current liabilities:				
Accounts payable	$ 164,000	$ 190,000	9.7%	11.3%
Short-term notes payable	75,000	90,000	4.5	5.4
Taxes payable	26,000	12,000	1.5	0.7
Total current liabilities	$ 265,000	$ 292,000	15.7	17.4
Long-term liabilities:				
Notes payable (secured by mortgage on building & land)	400,000	420,000	23.8	25.0
Total liabilities	$ 665,000	$ 712,000	39.4	42.4
Stockholders' Equity				
Contributed capital:				
Common stock, $5 par value	$ 475,000	$ 475,000	28.2	28.3
Retained earnings	544,000	491,000	32.3	29.3
Total stockholders' equity	$1,019,000	$ 966,000	60.5	57.6
Total liabilities and equity	$1,684,000	$1,678,000	100.0	100.0

*Columns may not precisely add up due to rounding.

3. Ratios for year 2000:

a. Current ratio: $514,000/$265,000 = 1.9 to 1 (Liquidity and efficiency)

b. Acid-test ratio: ($79,000 + $65,000 + $120,000)/$265,000 = 1.0 to 1 (Liquidity and Efficiency)

c. Average receivables: ($120,000 + $100,000)/2 = $110,000
Accounts receivable turnover: $2,486,000/$110,000 = 22.6 times (Liquidity and Efficiency)

d. Days' sales uncollected: ($120,000/$2,486,000) × 365 = 17.6 days (Liquidity and Efficiency)

e. Average inventory: ($250,000 + $265,000)/2 = $257,500
Merchandise turnover: $1,523,000/$257,500 = 5.9 times (Liquidity and Efficiency)

f. Debt ratio: $665,000/$1,684,000 = 39.5% (Solvency)

g. Pledged assets to secured liabilities: ($625,000 + $100,000)/$400,000 = 1.8 to 1 (Solvency)

h. Times interest earned: $185,000/$44,000 = 4.2 times (Solvency)

i. Profit margin: $94,000/$2,486,000 = 3.8% (Profitability)

j. Average total assets: ($1,684,000 + $1,678,000)/2 = $1,681,000
Total asset turnover: $2,486,000/$1,681,000 = 1.48 times (Liquidity and Efficiency)

k. Return on total assets: $94,000/$1,681,000 = 5.6% or 3.8% × 1.48 = 5.6% (Profitability)

l. Average total equity: ($1,019,000 + $966,000)/2 = $992,500
Return on common stockholders' equity: $94,000/$992,500 = 9.5% (Profitability)

Glossary

Common-size financial statement a statement in which each amount is expressed as a percent of a base amount. In the balance sheet, total assets is usually the base amount and is expressed as 100%. In the income statement, net sales is usually the base amount. (p. 784).

Comparative financial statement a statement with data for two or more successive periods placed in side-by-side columns, often with changes shown in dollar amounts and percents. (p. 777).

Efficiency a company's productivity in using its assets; usually measured relative to how much revenue is generated for a certain level of assets. (p. 775).

Equity ratio the portion of total assets provided by equity, computed as total equity divided by total assets. (p. 794).

Financial reporting the process of communicating information that is relevant to investors, creditors, and others in making investment, credit, and other decisions. (p. 776).

Financial statement analysis the application of analytical tools to general-purpose financial statements and related data for making business decisions. (p. 774).

General-purpose financial statements statements published periodically for use by a variety of interested parties; include the income statement, balance sheet, statement of changes in stockholders' equity (or statement of retained earnings), statement of cash flows, and notes related to the statements. (p. 775).

Horizontal analysis the comparison of a company's financial condition and performance across time. (p. 777).

Liquidity the availability of resources to meet short-term cash requirements. (p. 775).

Market expectations expectations (both good and bad) about the future performance of a company as assessed by financial statement users. (p. 775).

Profitability refers to a company's ability to generate an adequate return on invested capital. (p. 775).

Ratio analysis determination of key relations between financial statement items. (p. 777).

Solvency a company's long-run financial viability and its ability to cover long-term obligations. (p. 775).

Vertical analysis the evaluation of each financial statement item or group of items in terms of a specific base amount. (p. 777).

Working capital current assets minus current liabilities. (p. 789).

Questions

1. Explain the difference between financial reporting and financial statements.
2. What is the difference between comparative financial statements and common-size comparative statements?
3. Which items are usually assigned a value of 100% on a common-size comparative balance sheet and a common-size comparative income statement?
4. Why is working capital given special attention in the process of analyzing balance sheets?
5. What are three factors that would influence your decision as to whether a company's current ratio is good or bad?
6. Suggest several reasons why a 2 to 1 current ratio may not be adequate for a particular company.
7. What does a relatively high accounts receivable turnover indicate about a company's short-term liquidity?
8. What is the significance of the number of days' sales uncollected?
9. Why does merchandise turnover provide information about a company's short-term liquidity?
10. Why is the capital structure of a company, as measured by debt and equity ratios, of importance to financial statement analysts?
11. Why must the ratio of pledged assets to secured liabilities be interpreted with caution?
12. Why would a company's return on total assets be different from its return on common stockholders' equity?
13. What ratios would you compute for the purpose of evaluating management performance?
14. Using the financial statements for **NIKE** in Appendix A, compute NIKE's return on total assets for the fiscal year ended May 31, 1997.

15. Refer to the financial statements for **Reebok** in Appendix A. Compute Reebok's equity ratio as of December 31, 1996.

16. Refer to the financial statements for **America Online** in Appendix A. Compute AOL's profit margin for the fiscal year ended June 30, 1996.

17. Refer to the chapter's opening article about the **Beardstown Ladies**. Identify three factors that impact the return computation for a group of stocks and that may have contributed to the error made by Betty Sinnock.

Quick Study

QS 18-1
Financial reporting

Which of the following items are means of accomplishing the objective of financial reporting but are not included within general-purpose financial statements? *(a)* Income statements. *(b)* Company news releases. *(c)* Balance sheets. *(d)* Certain reports filed with the Securities and Exchange Commission. *(e)* Statements of cash flows. *(f)* Management discussions and analyses of financial performance.

QS 18-2
Common-size and trend percents
P1, P2

Use the following information for Heffington Corporation to determine *(a)* the common-size percents for gross profit from sales and *(b)* the trend percents for net sales, using 1999 as the base year.

	2000	1999
Net sales	$201,600	$114,800
Cost of goods sold	109,200	60,200

QS 18-3
Identifying ratios
C4

a. Which two short-term liquidity ratios measure how frequently a company collects its accounts?
b. Which two terms are used to describe the difference between current assets and current liabilities?
c. Which two ratios are the components in measuring a company's operating efficiency? Which ratio summarizes these two components?

QS 18-4
Comparing ratios
C3

What are four possible bases of comparison you can use when analyzing financial statement ratios? Which of these is generally considered to be the most useful? Which one is least likely to provide a good basis for comparison?

QS 18-5
Building blocks of analysis
C1, C4

Match the ratio to the building block of financial statement analysis to which it relates.

A. Liquidity and efficiency
B. Solvency
C. Profitability
D. Market

1. _____ Dividend yield
2. _____ Return on total assets
3. _____ Gross margin
4. _____ Acid-test ratio
5. _____ Equity ratio
6. _____ Times interest earned
7. _____ Pledged assets to secured liabilities
8. _____ Book value per common share
9. _____ Days' sales in inventory
10. _____ Accounts receivable turnover

QS 18-6
Interpreting ratios
P1, P3

For each ratio below, identify whether the change in the ratio from 1999 to 2000 is generally regarded as favorable or unfavorable.

Ratio	2000	1999	Ratio	2000	1999
1. Profit margin	8%	6%	5. Accounts receivable turnover	5.4	6.6
2. Debt ratio	45%	40%	6. Basic earnings per share	$1.24	$1.20
3. Gross margin	33%	45%	7. Merchandise turnover	3.5	3.3
4. Acid-test ratio	0.99	1.10	8. Dividend yield	1%	.8%

Exercises

Exercise 18-1
Computing trend percents
P1

Compute trend percents for the following items, using 1998 as the base year. Then state whether the situation shown by the trends appears to be favorable or unfavorable.

	2002	2001	2000	1999	1998
Sales	$283,880	$271,800	$253,680	$235,560	$151,000
Cost of goods sold	129,200	123,080	116,280	107,440	68,000
Accounts receivable	19,100	18,300	17,400	16,200	10,000

Exercise 18-2
Computing percent changes

Where possible, compute percents of increase and decrease for the following account balances:

	2000	1999
Short-term investments	$217,800	$165,000
Accounts receivable	42,120	48,000
Notes payable	57,000	-0-

Exercise 18-3
Computing common-size percents
P2

Express the following income statement information in common-size percents and assess whether the situation is favorable or unfavorable.

HARBISON CORPORATION Comparative Income Statement For Years Ended December 31, 2000 and 1999	2000	1999
Sales	$720,000	$535,000
Cost of goods sold	475,200	280,340
Gross profit from sales	$244,800	$254,660
Operating expenses	151,200	103,790
Net income	$ 93,600	$150,870

Exercise 18-4
Evaluating short-term liquidity
P3

Mixon Company's December 31 balance sheets include the following data:

	2001	2000	1999
Cash	$ 30,800	$ 35,625	$ 36,800
Accounts receivable, net	88,500	62,500	49,200
Merchandise inventory	111,500	82,500	53,000
Prepaid expenses	9,700	9,375	4,000
Plant assets, net	277,500	255,000	229,500
Total assets	$518,000	$445,000	$372,500
Accounts payable	$128,900	$ 75,250	$ 49,250
Long-term notes payable secured by mortgages on plant assets	97,500	102,500	82,500
Common stock, $10 par value	162,500	162,500	162,500
Retained earnings	129,100	104,750	78,250
Total liabilities and equity	$518,000	$445,000	$372,500

Required

Compare the short-term liquidity positions of the company at the end of 2001, 2000, and 1999 by computing: *(a)* the current ratio and *(b)* the acid-test ratio. Comment on any changes that occurred.

Exercise 18-5
Common-size percents
P2

Refer to Mixon Company's balance sheets in Exercise 18-4. Express the balance sheets in common-size percents. Round to the nearest one-tenth percent.

Exercise 18-6
Evaluating short-term liquidity
P3

Refer to the information in Exercise 18-4 about Mixon Company. The company's income statements for the years ended December 31, 2001 and 2000 include the following data:

	2001	2000
Sales	$672,500	$530,000
Cost of goods sold	$410,225	$344,500
Other operating expenses	208,550	133,980
Interest expense	11,100	12,300
Income taxes	8,525	7,845
Total costs and expenses	$638,400	$498,625
Net income	$ 34,100	$ 31,375
Earnings per share	$ 2.10	$ 1.93

Required

For the years ended December 31, 2001 and 2000, assume all sales were on credit and then compute the following: *(a)* days' sales uncollected, *(b)* accounts receivable turnover, *(c)* merchandise turnover, and *(d)* days' sales in inventory. Comment on any changes that occurred from 2000 to 2001.

Exercise 18-7
Evaluating risk and capital structure
P3

Refer to the information in Exercises 18-4 and 18-5 about Mixon Company. Compare the long-term risk and capital structure positions of the company at the end of 2001 and 2000 by computing the following ratios: *(a)* debt and equity ratios, *(b)* pledged assets to secured liabilities, and *(c)* times interest earned. Comment on any changes that occurred.

Exercise 18-8
Evaluating efficiency and profitability
P3

Refer to the financial statements of Mixon Company presented in Exercises 18-4 and 18-5. Evaluate the operating efficiency and profitability of the company by computing the following: *(a)* profit margin, *(b)* total asset turnover, and *(c)* return on total assets. Comment on any changes that occurred.

Exercise 18-9
Evaluating profitability
P3

Refer to the financial statements of Mixon Company presented in Exercises 18-4 and 18-5. The following additional information about the company is known:

Common stock market price, December 31, 2001	$15.00
Common stock market price, December 31, 2000	14.00
Annual cash dividends per share in 2001	0.30
Annual cash dividends per share in 2000	0.15

Required

To evaluate the profitability of the company, compute the following for 2001 and 2000: *(a)* return on common stockholders' equity, *(b)* price-earnings ratio on December 31, and *(c)* dividend yield.

Exercise 18-10
Determining income effects from common-size and trend percents
P1, P3

Common-size and trend percents for a company's sales, cost of goods sold, and expenses follow:

	Common-Size Percents			Trend Percents		
	2001	2000	1999	2001	2000	1999
Sales	100.0%	100.0%	100.0%	104.4%	103.2%	100.0%
Cost of goods sold	62.4	60.9	58.1	102.0	100.1	100.0
Expenses	14.3	13.8	14.1	94.0	90.0	100.0

Required

Determine whether net income increased, decreased, or remained unchanged in this three-year period.

Exercise 18-11
Analyzing short-term financial conditions
A1

Huff Company and Mesa Company are similar firms that operate within the same industry. The following information is available:

	Huff			Mesa		
	2001	2000	1999	2001	2000	1999
Current ratio	1.6	1.7	2.0	3.1	2.6	1.8
Acid-test ratio	0.9	1.0	1.1	2.7	2.4	1.5
Accounts receivable turnover	29.5	24.2	28.2	15.4	14.2	15.0
Merchandise turnover	23.2	20.9	16.1	13.5	12.0	11.6
Working capital	$60,000	$48,000	$42,000	$121,000	$93,000	$68,000

Required

Write a one-half page report comparing Huff and Mesa using the preceding information. Your discussion should include their relative ability to meet current obligations and to use current assets efficiently.

Exercise 18-12
Analyzing efficiency and financial leverage
A1

Kampa Company and Arbor Company are similar firms that operate within the same industry. Arbor began operations in 2005 and Kampa in 1999. In 2007, both companies pay 7% interest to creditors. The following additional information is available:

	Kampa Company			Arbor Company		
	2007	2006	2005	2007	2006	2005
Total asset turnover	3.0	2.7	2.9	1.6	1.4	1.1
Return on total assets	8.9%	9.5%	8.7%	5.8%	5.5%	5.2%
Profit margin	2.3%	2.4%	2.2%	2.7%	2.9%	2.8%
Sales	$400,000	$370,000	$386,000	$200,000	$160,000	$100,000

Required

Write a one-half page report comparing Kampa and Arbor using the preceding information. Your discussion should include their relative ability to use assets efficiently to produce profits. Also comment on their relative success in employing financial leverage in 2007.

Problems

Problem 18-1
Computing ratios and both common-size and trend percents
P1, P2, P3
S

The condensed financial statements of Thornhill Company follow:

THORNHILL COMPANY
Comparative Income Statement ($000)
For Years Ended December 31, 2001, 2000, and 1999

	2001	2000	1999
Sales	$444,000	$340,000	$236,000
Cost of goods sold	267,288	212,500	151,040
Gross profit	$176,712	$127,500	$ 84,960
Selling expenses	$ 62,694	$ 46,920	$ 31,152
Administrative expenses	40,137	29,920	19,470
Total expenses	$102,831	$ 76,840	$ 50,622
Income before taxes	$ 73,881	$ 50,660	$ 34,338
Income taxes	13,764	10,370	6,962
Net income	$ 60,117	$ 40,290	$ 27,376

THORNHILL COMPANY
Comparative Balance Sheet ($000)
December 31, 2001, 2000, and 1999

	2001	2000	1999
Assets			
Current assets	$ 48,480	$ 37,924	$ 50,648
Long-term investments	-0-	500	3,720
Plant and equipment	90,000	96,000	57,000
Total assets	$138,480	$134,424	$111,368
Liabilities and Stockholders' Equity			
Current liabilities	$ 20,200	$ 19,960	$ 19,480
Common stock	72,000	72,000	54,000
Other contributed capital	9,000	9,000	6,000
Retained earnings	37,280	33,464	31,888
Total liabilities and equity	$138,480	$134,424	$111,368

Required

Preparation Component

1. Compute each year's current ratio.
2. Express the income statement data in common-size percents.
3. Express the balance sheet data in trend percents with 1999 as the base year.

Check Figure 2001, Total assets, 124.34%

Analysis Component

4. Comment on any significant relations revealed by the ratios and percents.

Problem 18-2
Calculation and analysis of trend percents
P1

The condensed comparative financial statements of Cohorn Company follow:

COHORN COMPANY Comparative Income Statement ($000) For Years Ended December 31, 2005–1999							
	2005	2004	2003	2002	2001	2000	1999
Sales	$1,594	$1,396	$1,270	$1,164	$1,086	$1,010	$828
Cost of goods sold	1,146	932	802	702	652	610	486
Gross profit	$ 448	$ 464	$ 468	$ 462	$ 434	$ 400	$342
Operating expenses	340	266	244	180	156	154	128
Net income	$ 108	$ 198	$ 224	$ 282	$ 278	$ 246	$214

COHORN COMPANY Comparative Balance Sheet ($000) December 31, 2005–1999							
	2005	2004	2003	2002	2001	2000	1999
Assets							
Cash	$ 68	$ 88	$ 92	$ 94	$ 98	$ 96	$ 99
Accounts receivable, net	480	504	456	350	308	292	206
Merchandise inventory	1,738	1,264	1,104	932	836	710	515
Other current assets	46	42	24	44	38	38	19
Long-term investments	0	0	0	136	136	136	136
Plant and equipment, net	2,120	2,114	1,852	1,044	1,078	960	825
Total assets	$4,452	$4,012	$3,528	$2,600	$2,494	$2,232	$1,800
Liabilities and Equity							
Current liabilities	$1,120	$ 942	$ 618	$ 514	$ 446	$ 422	$ 272
Long-term liabilities	1,194	1,040	1,012	470	480	520	390
Common stock	1,000	1,000	1,000	840	840	640	640
Other contributed capital	250	250	250	180	180	160	160
Retained earnings	888	780	648	596	548	490	338
Total liabilities and equity	$4,452	$4,012	$3,528	$2,600	$2,494	$2,232	$1,800

Required

Preparation Component

1. Compute trend percents for the items of both statements using 1999 as the base year.

Check Figure 2005, Total assets, 247.3%

Analysis Component

2. Analyze and comment on the statements and trend percents from part (1).

Problem 18-3
Calculation of financial statement ratios

The December 31, 2000, financial statements of Hoffman Corporation follow:

HOFFMAN CORPORATION
Income Statement
For Year Ended December 31, 2000

Sales		$348,600
Cost of goods sold:		
Inventory, 12/31/1999	$ 32,400	
Purchases	227,900	
Goods available for sale	$260,300	
Inventory, 12/31/2000	31,150	
Cost of goods sold		229,150
Gross profit		$119,450
Operating expenses		52,500
Operating income		$ 66,950
Interest expense		3,100
Income before taxes		$ 63,850
Income taxes		15,800
Net income		$ 48,050

HOFFMAN CORPORATION
Balance Sheet
December 31, 2000

Assets		Liabilities and Stockholders' Equity	
Cash	$ 9,000	Accounts payable	$ 16,500
Short-term investments	7,400	Accrued wages payable	2,200
Accounts receivable, net	28,200	Income taxes payable	2,300
Notes receivable (trade)	3,500	Long-term note payable,	
Merchandise inventory	31,150	secured by mortgage on	
Prepaid expenses	1,650	plant assets	62,400
Plant assets, net	152,300	Common stock, $1 par value	90,000
		Retained earnings	59,800
Total assets	$233,200	Total liabilities and equity	$233,200

Assume that all sales are on credit. On the December 31, 1999, balance sheet, the assets totaled $182,400, common stock was $90,000, and retained earnings amounted to $31,300.

Required

Compute the following: *(a)* current ratio, *(b)* acid-test ratio, *(c)* days' sales uncollected, *(d)* merchandise turnover, *(e)* days' sales in inventory, *(f)* ratio of pledged assets to secured liabilities, *(g)* times interest earned, *(h)* profit margin, *(i)* total asset turnover, *(j)* return on total assets, and *(k)* return on common stockholders' equity.

Problem 18-4
Comparative analysis using financial statement ratios
P3

Two companies competing in the same industry are being evaluated by a bank that will lend money to only one of them. Summary information from the financial statements of the two companies follows:

	Datatech Company	Sigma Company
Data from the current year-end balance sheets:		
Assets		
Cash	$ 18,500	$ 33,000
Accounts receivable, net	36,400	56,400
Notes receivable (trade)	8,100	6,200
Merchandise inventory	83,440	131,500
Prepaid expenses	4,000	5,950
Plant and equipment, net	284,000	303,400
Total assets	$434,440	$536,450
Liabilities and Stockholders' Equity		
Current liabilities	$ 60,340	$ 92,300
Long-term notes payable	79,800	100,000
Common stock, $5 par value	175,000	205,000
Retained earnings	119,300	139,150
Total liabilities and equity	$434,440	$536,450

	Datatech Company	Sigma Company
Data from the current year's income statements:		
Sales	$660,000	$780,200
Cost of goods sold	485,100	532,500
Interest expense	6,900	11,000
Income tax expense	12,800	19,300
Net income	67,770	105,000
Earnings per share	1.94	2.56
Beginning-of-year data:		
Accounts receivable, net	$ 28,800	$ 53,200
Notes receivable (trade)	0	0
Merchandise inventory	54,600	106,400
Total assets	388,000	372,500
Common stock, $5 par value	175,000	205,000
Retained earnings	94,300	90,600

Required

1. Compute the current ratio, acid-test ratio, accounts (including notes) receivable turnover, merchandise turnover, days' sales in inventory, and days' sales uncollected for the two companies. Then identify the company that you consider to be the better short-term credit risk and explain why.
2. Compute the profit margin, total asset turnover, return on total assets, and return on common stockholders' equity for the two companies. Assuming that each company paid cash dividends of $1.50 per share and each company's stock can be purchased at $25 per share, compute their price-earnings ratios and dividend yields. Identify which company's stock you would recommend as the better investment and explain why.

Problem 18-5
Analysis of working capital

Providence Corporation began the month of May with $650,000 of current assets, a current ratio of 2.5 to 1, and an acid-test ratio of 1.1 to 1. During the month, it completed the following transactions:

May 2 Bought $75,000 of merchandise on account. (The company uses a perpetual inventory system.)
8 Sold merchandise that cost $58,000 for $103,000.
10 Collected a $19,000 account receivable.
15 Paid a $21,000 account payable.
17 Wrote off a $3,000 bad debt against the Allowance for Doubtful Accounts account.
22 Declared a $1 per share cash dividend on the 40,000 shares of outstanding common stock.
26 Paid the dividend declared on May 22.
27 Borrowed $75,000 by giving the bank a 30-day, 10% note.
28 Borrowed $90,000 by signing a long-term secured note.
29 Used the $175,000 proceeds of the notes and cash to buy additional machinery.

Required

Prepare a schedule showing Providence's current ratio, acid-test ratio, and working capital after each of the transactions. Round calculations to two decimal places.

Check Figure May 29 working capital, $310,000

BEYOND THE NUMBERS

Reporting in Action
P1, P2

Refer to the financial statements and related information for **NIKE** in Appendix A. Answer the following questions by analyzing that information.

Required

1. Using 1995 as the base year, compute trend percents for 1995–1997 for revenues, cost of sales, selling and administrative expenses, income taxes, and net income. (Round to the nearest whole percent.)
2. Compute common-size percents for 1997 and 1996 for the following categories of assets: (a) total current assets; (b) property, plant, and equipment—net of depreciation; (c) identifiable intangible assets and goodwill; and (d) deferred income taxes and other assets. (Round to the nearest tenth percent.)
3. Comment on any significant changes between years for the income statement trends computed in part (1) and balance sheet percents computed in part (2).

Swoosh Ahead

4. Obtain access to NIKE's annual report for fiscal years ending after May 31, 1997. This access can be through NIKE's Web site [**www.nike.com**] or through the SEC database [**www.sec.gov**]. Update your work for parts (1), (2), and (3) for any new information you have accessed.

Comparative Analysis
P2

Both **NIKE** and **Reebok** design, produce, market and sell sports footwear and apparel. Key comparative figures ($ thousands) for these two organizations follow:

Key Figures*	NIKE	Reebok	Key Figures*	NIKE	Reebok
Cash and equivalents	$ 445,421	$ 232,365	Income taxes	$ 499,400	$ 84,083
Accounts receivable	1,754,137	590,504	Revenues (Nike)	9,186,539	—
Inventory	1,338,640	544,522	Net sales (Reebok)	—	3,478,604
Retained earnings	2,973,663	992,563	Total assets	5,361,207	1,786,184
Cost of sales	5,502,993	2,144,422			

*NIKE figures are from its annual report for fiscal year ended May 31, 1997. Reebok figures are from its annual report for fiscal year ended December 31, 1996.

Required

1. Compute common-size percents for both companies for both years using the data provided.
2. Which company incurred a higher percent of their revenues or net sales as income tax expense?
3. Which company has retained a higher portion of total earnings in the company?
4. Which company has a higher gross margin on sales?
5. Which company is holding a higher percent of total assets as inventory?

Ethics Challenge
A1

As controller of Tallman Company, you are responsible for keeping the board of directors informed about the company's financial activities. At the board meeting, you present the following report:

	2004	2003	2002
Sales trend percent	147.0%	135.0%	100.0%
Selling expenses to net sales	10.1%	14.0%	15.6%
Sales to plant assets	3.8 to 1	3.6 to 1	3.3 to 1
Current ratio	2.9 to 1	2.7 to 1	2.4 to 1
Acid-test ratio	1.1 to 1	1.4 to 1	1.5 to 1
Merchandise turnover	7.8 times	9.0 times	10.2 times
Accounts receivable turnover	7.0 times	7.7 times	8.5 times
Total asset turnover	2.9 times	2.9 times	3.3 times
Return on total assets	9.1%	9.7%	10.4%
Return on stockholders' equity	9.75%	11.50%	12.25%
Profit margin	3.6%	3.8%	4.0%

After the meeting, the company's CEO holds a press conference with analysts in which she mentions the following ratios:

	2004	2003	2002
Sales trend percent	147.0%	135.0%	100.0%
Selling expenses to net sales	10.1%	14.0%	15.6%
Sales to plant assets	3.8 to 1	3.6 to 1	3.3 to 1
Current ratio	2.9 to 1	2.7 to 1	2.4 to 1

Required

1. Why do you think the CEO decided to report four ratios instead of the full 11 that you prepared?
2. Comment on the possible consequences of the CEO's reporting decision.

Communicating in Practice

A1, P3

The class should be divided into teams. Each team is to select a different industry, and each team member is to select a different company in that industry. Each team member is to acquire the annual report of the company selected. Use the annual report to analyze the company, using at least one ratio from each of the four categories presented in this chapter. Where necessary, use the financial press to determine the market price of the firm's stock. Communicate with teammates via a meeting, e-mail, or telephone to discuss how different companies compare to each other, and to industry norms. The team is to prepare a single memo reporting a comparison of the companies analyzed. The memo is to present the conclusions reached from the comparison. Duplicate the memo and distribute it to the instructor and all classmates.

Taking It to the Net

C1, C4

Both the financial press and the public often refer to the Dow Jones industrial average. While many people monitor the Dow Jones average, the majority may not know what stocks constitute the average. Visit the Web site **www.rapidresearch.com.** Click on the *Dow Jones Industrial Average* sidebar link under "Quote Central."

Required

1. Identify at least five companies included as part of the Dow Jones index.
2. How many different stocks constitute the Dow Jones average?
3. On the day you accessed this Web site, what stock was the most actively traded?
4. Which stock had the largest percent gain? And loss?

Teamwork in Action

C2, P1, P2, P3

A team approach to analyzing information in financial statements is often valuable.

Required

A. After a team discussion of the meaning of horizontal and vertical analysis, write up a description of each that all team members agree with and understand. Illustrate each description with an example.
B. **Each** member of the team is to select **one** of the categories of ratio analysis listed below. Explain what the ratios in that category measure. Choose one specific ratio from the category selected, present its formula, and explain what it measures.
   1. Liquidity and efficiency
   2. Solvency
   3. Profitability
   4. Market
C. Each member of the team is to report his or her notes from part (B) to the other teammates. Team members are to confirm or correct other teammates' presentation.

Hitting the Road C1

This course has given you tools to become a successful investor. Devise a savings/investment strategy whereby you are able to accumulate $1,000,000 by age 65. Start by making some assumptions about your salary. Next compute the percent of your salary that you will be able to save each year. If you will receive any lump-sum monies, you can also factor those amounts into your calculations. Historically, stocks have delivered average annual returns of 10–11%. Given this history, you should probably not assume that you will earn above 10% on the money you invest. It is not necessary to specify in this assignment exactly what types of assets you will buy for your investments; just make an assumption about a rate you expect to earn. Use the future value tables in Appendix C to calculate how your savings will grow. Experiment a bit with your figures to see how much less you have to save if you start at age 25 versus age 35 or 40. (For this assignment, do not factor inflation into your calculations.)

Business Week Activity C1

Read the article "You Can Do It" in the May 31, 1993, issue of ***Business Week.***

Required

1. What does a $10,000 investment grow to after 10 years if it earns an annual return of 11.9%? 15.6%?
2. What is the umbrella organization for investment clubs nationwide?
3. Where do some of the best ideas for stock selection come from for the individual investor?
4. What common flaw is shared by many investment clubs?
5. What should constitute an individual investor's plan of attack?

Managerial Accounting Concepts and Principles

A Look Back

Chapter 18 described the analysis and interpretation of financial statement information. We applied horizontal, vertical, and ratio analyses for a better understanding of company performance and financial condition.

A Look at This Chapter

We begin our study of managerial accounting by explaining its purpose and describing its major characteristics. We also discuss cost concepts and describe how they help managers in gathering and organizing information they need for making decisions. Important management principles are also introduced and discussed.

A Look Ahead

Chapters 20 through 26 discuss information that managers need and how they obtain it. We explain the types of decisions managers must make and how managerial accounting helps with these decisions. Chapter 20 looks at how we can measure costs assigned to certain types of processes.

Chapter Outline

Where Do I Start?

MILWAUKEE, WI—Sharon West thought she'd made it. A college graduate, four years' accounting experience, and a new job as manager of special projects at **Harley-Davidson.** Yet here she was, asking her supervisor "Where do I start?"

West's new job was to assist managers with accounting analysis. In her first week, she met with managers in marketing, sales, purchasing, and manufacturing. Purchasing needed help in setting criteria for selecting suppliers. Manufacturing needed help in planning equipment purchases. Marketing needed help measuring financial effects of promotion strategies. Sales needed help redesigning compensation plans.

West took notes, asked questions, and returned to her office. She reviewed financial statements, internal monthly reports, and strategic plans. Nowhere did she find the information she needed.

Discouraged, she went to the controller. "I'll never forget how helpless I felt," recalls West. "I looked him straight in the eyes, swallowed my pride, and said 'I don't know where to start.' I thought I knew where to look for answers. But the answers weren't in the usual accounting records."

West said the controller smiled and told her "Welcome to managerial accounting. The answers are in the future, not past, data." West's experience is common. Probably the most important skill of top managers is the ability to go beyond the numbers. Use it, yes. Depend on it, no.

Today, West believes one must precisely identify the question and only then gather relevant data. "But," stresses West, "You must go and learn about business operations." These days, West spends much of her time learning operating activities. Little time is spent in her office. And about that question—where do I start? West smiles, "Managerial accounting is a great beginning, but understanding operations is crucial. And," adds West, "don't let anyone tell you this is an office job!"

Learning Objectives

Conceptual

C1 Explain the purpose of managerial accounting.

C2 Describe major characteristics of managerial accounting.

C3 Explain differences in balance sheets of manufacturing and merchandising companies.

C4 Explain differences in income statements of manufacturing and merchandising companies.

C5 Describe accounting concepts useful in classifying costs.

C6 Define product and period costs and explain how they impact financial statements.

C7 Explain how a customer orientation in a global economy impacts business activities.

C8 Describe current manufacturing management principles.

Analytical

A1 Compute unit contribution margin and describe what it reveals about a company's cost structure.

Procedural

P1 Compute cost of goods sold for a manufacturer.

CHAPTER PREVIEW

Managerial accounting, like financial accounting, provides information to help users make better decisions. Yet there are important differences between managerial and financial accounting, which we explain. We also compare accounting and reporting practices used by manufacturing and merchandising companies. Both types of companies earn revenues by selling products.[1] A merchandising company sells products without changing their condition. A manufacturing company buys raw materials and turns them into finished products for sale to customers. We also explain important concepts useful in classifying costs. We conclude the chapter by identifying and describing four management principles. The implications of these principles on managerial accounting is discussed.

Managerial Accounting

Managerial accounting, also called **management accounting,** is an activity that provides financial and nonfinancial information to managers and other internal decision makers of an organization. This section explains the purpose of managerial accounting and compares it with financial accounting.

Purpose of Managerial Accounting

C1 Explain the purpose of managerial accounting.

Both managerial accounting and financial accounting share the common purpose of providing useful information to decision makers. They do this by collecting, managing, and reporting information in a manner useful to users of accounting data. Both areas of accounting also share the common practice of reporting monetary information.[2] They even report some of the same information. For instance, the financial statements of a company contain information useful for both the managers of a company (insiders) and other persons who are interested in the company (outsiders).

The remainder of this book takes a careful look at managerial accounting information, how accounting professionals gather it, and how managers use it. The main topic of this chapter and Chapters 20 and 21 is accounting for manufacturing activities. We look at the concepts and procedures used to determine the costs of products a company manufactures and sells. A company reports these costs on its balance sheet as inventory and on its income statement as cost of goods sold. Later chapters look at budgeting, break-even analysis, product costing, profit planning, cost analysis, and other managerial accounting topics.

Information about the costs of products is important for many decisions made by managers. These decisions include predicting the future costs of producing the same or similar items. Predicted costs are used in product pricing, profitability analysis, and even in deciding whether to make or buy a product or component. Much of managerial accounting is directed at gathering useful information about costs for planning and control decisions.

Planning is the process of setting goals and making plans to achieve them. Companies formulate long-term strategic plans that usually span a 5- to 10-year horizon and then refine them with medium-term and short-term plans. Strategic plans usually set the long-term direction of a firm by developing a road map for the future based on potential op-

[1] A service company is another type of company. It earns revenues by providing services rather than by selling products. The skills, tools, and techniques developed for measuring a manufacturing company's activities apply to service industries as well.

[2] Modern managerial accounting practices include the reporting of nonmonetary information in addition to monetary information.

portunities such as new products, new markets, and capital investments. The goals and objectives of a strategic plan are often broadly defined given its long-term orientation.

Medium- and short-term plans are more operational in nature. They translate the strategic plan into actions. These plans are more concrete and consist of objectives and goals that are better defined than in the strategic plan. A short-term plan often covers a one-year period which, when translated in monetary terms, is known as a budget.

Control is the process of monitoring planning decisions and evaluating an organization's activities and employees. Control includes measurement and evaluation of actions, processes, and outcomes. The feedback provided by the control function allows managers to revise their plans. The measurement of actions and processes also allows managers to take corrective actions to avoid undesirable outcomes. Exhibit 19.1 portrays these two important management functions.

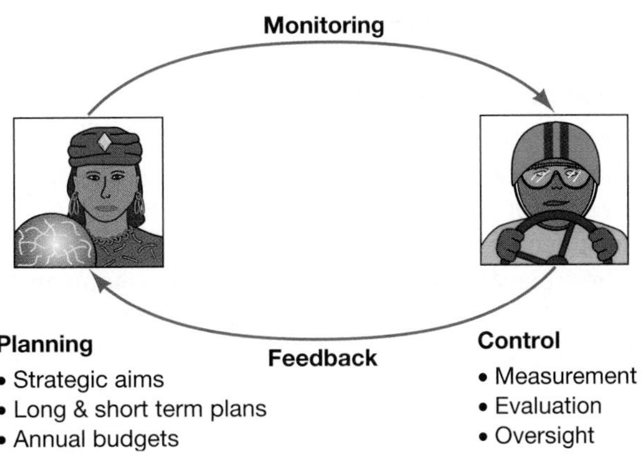

Exhibit 19.1

Planning and Control

Managers also use information to plan and control the production process. Information about manufacturing costs helps managers identify problems that require corrective actions. In later chapters, we explain more about how managers use cost information in controlling and planning business activities. This includes directing operating activities, improving business operations, and helping management's decision making.

Nature of Managerial Accounting

C2 Describe major characteristics of managerial accounting.

Managerial accounting has its own special characteristics. To understand these characteristics we compare managerial accounting to financial accounting. There are at least seven important differences. These are summarized in Exhibit 19.2.

Exhibit 19.2

Differences between Managerial Accounting and Financial Accounting

	Financial Accounting	Managerial Accounting
1. Users and decision makers	Investors, creditors, and other users external to the organization	Managers, employees, and decision makers internal to the organization
2. Purpose of information	Assist external users in making investment, credit, and other decisions	Assist managers in making planning and control decisions
3. Flexibility of practice	Structured and often controlled by GAAP	Relatively flexible (no GAAP)
4. Timeliness of information	Often available only after an audit is complete	Available quickly without the need to wait for an audit
5. Time dimension	Historical information with minimum predictions	Many projections and estimates; historical information also presented
6. Focus of information	Emphasis on whole organization	Emphasis on projects, processes, and subdivisions of an organization
7. Nature of information	Monetary information	Mostly monetary; some nonmonetary information

Users and Decision Makers

Companies accumulate, process, and report financial accounting and managerial accounting information for different groups of decision makers. Financial accounting information is primarily provided to external users. These users include investors, creditors, and regulators. External users rarely have a major role in managing the daily activities of a company. Managerial accounting information is primarily provided to internal users. Internal users are responsible for making and implementing decisions about a company's business activities.

Purpose of Information

Investors, creditors, and other external users of financial accounting information must often decide whether to invest in or lend to a company. They must choose the terms of investment or lending. If they have already invested in a company or loaned to it, they must decide whether to continue owning the company or carrying the loan. Internal decision makers must plan the future of a company. They look to take advantage of opportunities or to overcome obstacles. They also try to control activities and ensure they are being carried out efficiently. Managerial accounting information helps these internal users make both planning and control decisions.

Flexibility of Practice

Because external users make comparisons between companies and because external users need protection against false or misleading information, financial accounting practices rely on accepted principles. These principles are enforced through an extensive set of rules and guidelines, or GAAP.

Internal users need managerial accounting information for planning and controlling their company's activities rather than for external comparison. Different types of information are required depending on the activity. Because of this it is difficult to standardize managerial accounting systems across companies. Instead, managerial accounting systems are flexible. Also, since managers have access to most company data, they require less protection against false or misleading information compared to external users.

The design of a company's managerial accounting system largely depends on the nature of the business and the arrangement of the internal operations of the company. Managers can decide for themselves what information they want and how they want it reported. Even within a single company, different managers often design their own systems to meet their special needs. This flexibility allows managers to modify their systems quickly in response to changes in the environment.

Timeliness of Information

Formal financial statements reporting past transactions and events are not immediately available to outside parties. Independent certified public accountants often must audit the financial statements of a company before reporting to external users. Because audits can take one to three months to complete, annual financial reports to outsiders usually are not available to users until well after the end of the year.

Managerial accounting information can be forwarded to managers quickly. External auditors need not review it. Estimates and projections are acceptable. To get information quickly, managers often accept less precision in reports. As an example, an early internal report to management prepared right after the end of the year might say net income for the year is between $4.2 and $4.8 million. An audited income statement might later show net income for the year at $4.55 million. While the internal report is not precise, its information can be more useful because it is available earlier.

Although accounting reports to managers are available without waiting for completion of an audit, *internal auditing* plays an important role. The Foreign Corrupt Practices Act makes managers responsible for preventing and detecting fraudulent activities in their companies. Most companies responded by strengthening internal audit functions.

In a recent *Report to Shareholders,* the CEO and chief financial officer of **Chrysler Corporation** reports that:

> the company maintains a strong internal auditing program that independently assesses the effectiveness of the internal controls and recommends possible improvements.

Internal auditors evaluate the flow of information not only inside the company but also outside the company. Internal audits often help avoid situations as depicted in the following *Judgment and Ethics.*

Production Supervisor

You accept a new job as a production supervisor and invite three of your former classmates for a celebration at a restaurant. When the dinner check arrives, David, a self-employed entrepreneur, picks it up saying, "Here, let me pay. I'll deduct it as a business expense on my tax return. It won't cost me as much." Denise, a salesperson for a medium-size company, takes the check from David's hand and says, "I'll put this on my company's credit card. It won't cost us anything." Derek, a factory manager for a company, laughs and says, "Neither of you understands. I'll put this on my company's credit card and call it overhead on a cost-plus contract my company has with the government."* Adds Derek, "That way, my company pays for dinner *and* makes a profit on it too." Who should pay the bill?

*A cost-plus contract means the company receives its costs plus a percent of those costs.

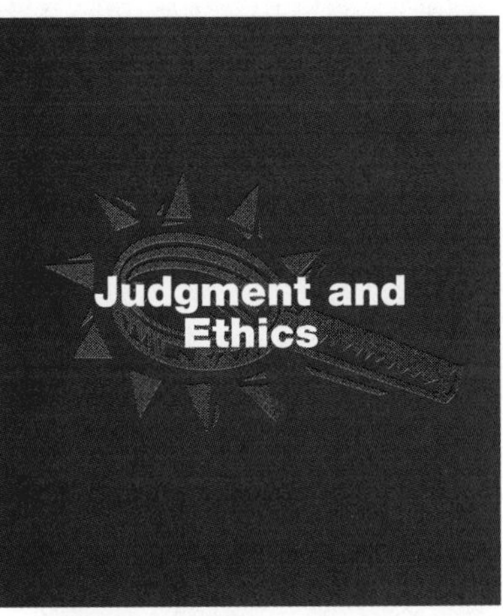

Answer—p. 840

Time Dimension

To protect external users from false expectations, financial reports deal primarily with results of both past activities and current conditions. While some predictions are necessary, such as service lives and salvage values of plant assets, financial accounting avoids predictions whenever possible. Managerial accounting regularly includes predictions of future conditions and events. As an example, one important managerial accounting report is a budget. A budget predicts revenues, expenses, and other items. If managerial accounting reports were restricted to the past and present, managers would be less able to plan activities and less effective in managing current activities.

Focus of Information

While companies often organize into divisions and departments, investors rarely can buy shares in one division or department. Neither do creditors lend money to a single division or department of a company. Instead, they own shares in or make loans to the whole company. Since external users need information about the whole company, financial accounting is focused primarily on a company as a whole as depicted in Exhibit 19.3.

Focus of External Reports

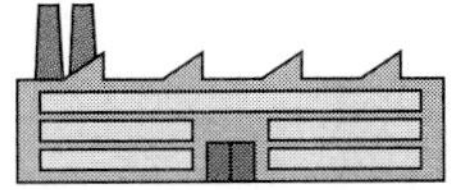

The focus of managerial accounting is different. Only top-level managers are responsible for managing the whole company. Most managers are responsible for much smaller sets of activities. These middle-level and lower-level managers need managerial accounting reports dealing with specific activities, projects, and subdivisions for which they are responsible. For instance, division sales managers are directly responsible only for the results achieved in their divisions. While they often want to see results for all divisions, they usually do not need a companywide sales report. Division sales managers need information about results achieved in their own divisions to improve their personnel's performance. This information includes the level of success achieved by each individual or department in each division as depicted by the many pieces in Exhibit 19.4.

Focus of Internal Reports

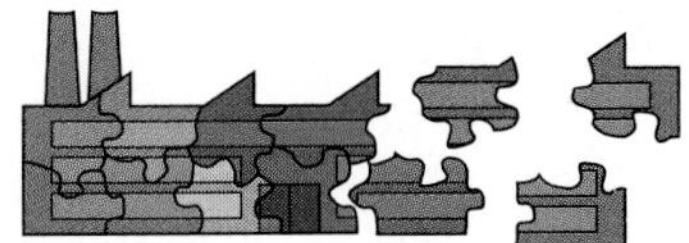

Nature of Information

Both financial and managerial accounting systems report monetary information. Yet for managerial accounting, the emphasis is less so. Managerial accounting systems report considerable nonmonetary information. In the chapter's opening article, we saw Sharon West helping with important decisions in purchasing, marketing, sales, and manufacturing departments. While monetary information is an important part of these decisions, nonmonetary information also plays a crucial role. This is especially so in cases where monetary effects are difficult to measure. One common example of nonmonetary information is the quality and delivery criteria of purchasing decisions.

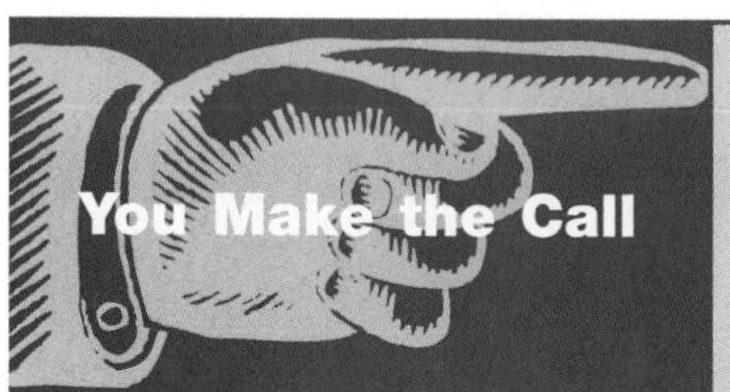

Division Manager
You are the manager of a division of a manufacturing company. At a recent executive meeting, you are asked to explore the manufacturing of a component that your division has been purchasing from an outside supplier for the past several years. What information do you collect in evaluating these two alternative sources?

Answer—p. 840

Decision Making Focus

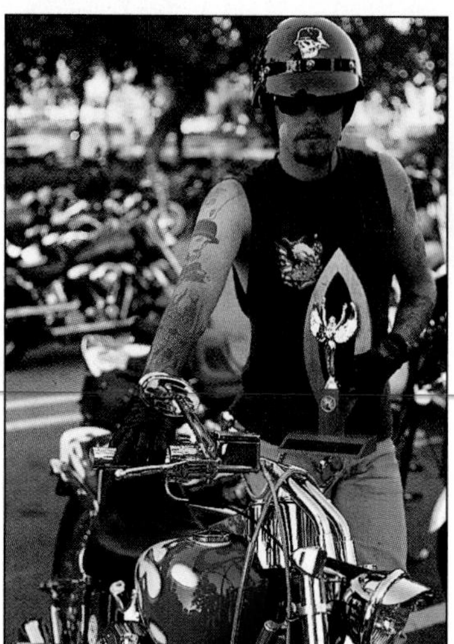

While the prior section emphasized differences between financial and managerial accounting, they are not entirely separate. Similar information is useful to both external and internal users. For instance, information about costs of manufacturing products is useful to all users in their decisions.

We must remember that both financial and managerial accounting can affect people's actions. In the chapter's opening article, West's job at **Harley-Davidson** demanded an understanding of accounting. West needed to quantify future costs and revenues associated with projects. But just as important was West's understanding of operations and the people making decisions using cost or revenue data.

Important managerial decisions often are related to each other and to people's behavior. For example, Harley's design of a sales compensation plan affects the behavior of its salesforce. Harley also must estimate the dual effects of promotion and sales compensation plans on buying patterns of customers. These estimates impact the equipment purchase decisions for manufacturing. It also can affect the supplier selection criteria established by purchasing. Financial and managerial accounting systems do more than measure, they affect people's decisions and actions.

Flash back

1. Managerial accounting produces information: (a) to meet the needs of internal users, (b) to meet specific needs of a user, (c) often focuses on the future, or (d) all of the above.
2. What is the difference between the intended users of financial and managerial accounting?
3. Do generally accepted accounting principles control the practice of managerial accounting?

Answers—p. 841

Reporting Manufacturing Activities

Companies with manufacturing activities are different from both merchandising and service companies. The main difference between merchandising and manufacturing companies is that merchandisers buy goods ready for sale while manufacturers produce goods from materials and labor. **Payless** is an example of a merchandising company. It buys and sells shoes without physically changing them. **NIKE** is a manufacturer of shoes. It purchases materials such as leather, cloth, plastic, rubber, glue, and laces. It then uses employees' labor to convert these materials to shoes. **Delta Air Lines** is a service company. It transports people and items.

Much of our focus in the book has been on the business activities of merchandising and service companies. We described these activities and how we account for them. Manufacturing activities are different from both selling merchandise and providing services. Also, the financial statements for manufacturing companies have unique features. This section looks at some of these features and compares them to accounting for a merchandising company.

Balance Sheet of a Manufacturer

C3 Explain differences in balance sheets of manufacturing and merchandising companies.

Manufacturers carry several unique kinds of assets. Manufacturers usually have three inventories instead of a single inventory as carried by merchandising companies. Exhibit 19.5 shows three different inventories in the current asset section of the balance sheet for **Rocky Mountain Bikes,** a manufacturer. The three inventories are: raw materials, goods in process, and finished goods.

Raw Materials Inventory

Raw materials inventory refers to the goods a company acquires to use in making products. It uses raw materials in two ways—directly and indirectly. Most raw materials physically become part of a product and are identified with specific units or batches of

Exhibit 19.5

Balance Sheet for a Manufacturer

ROCKY MOUNTAIN BIKES
Balance Sheet
December 31, 2000

Assets		
Current assets:		
Cash		$ 11,000
Accounts receivable	$32,000	
Allow. for doubtful accounts	(1,850)	30,150
Raw materials inventory		9,000
Goods in process inventory		7,500
Finished goods inventory		10,300
Supplies		350
Prepaid insurance		300
Total current assets		$ 68,600
Plant assets:		
Small tools		1,100
Delivery equipment	9,000	
Accumulated depreciation	(4,000)	5,000
Office equipment	1,700	
Accumulated depreciation	(400)	1,300
Factory machinery	72,000	
Accumulated depreciation	(6,500)	65,500
Factory building	90,000	
Accumulated depreciation	(3,300)	86,700
Land		9,500
Total plant assets		$169,100
Intangible assets:		
Patents		11,200
Total assets		$248,900

Liabilities and Stockholders' Equity		
Current liabilities:		
Accounts payable	$ 14,000	
Wages payable	540	
Interest payable	2,000	
Income taxes payable	32,600	
Total current liabilities	$ 49,140	
Long-term liabilities:		
Long-term notes payable	50,000	
Total liabilities		$ 99,140
Stockholders' equity:		
Common stock, $5 par	100,000	
Retained earnings	49,760	
Total stockholders' equity		$149,760
Total liabilities and equity		$248,900

a product. Raw materials used directly in a product are called **direct materials.** For example, the tires, seat, and frame of a mountain bike are direct materials. A mountain bike cannot be produced without direct materials. The costs of these materials are usually a significant portion of the total cost of producing the bike and therefore must be identified separately.

Other materials used in support of the production process are sometimes not as clearly identified with specific units or batches of product. Examples are lubricants needed for machinery and supplies for cleaning the factory. These materials are called **indirect materials** because they do not become a part of a product and are not clearly identified with specific units or batches of product. Items used as indirect materials often appear on a balance sheet as factory supplies. In other cases, they are included in raw materials.

In addition to the indirect materials as defined above, there may be some direct materials that are actually classified as indirect materials. These are classified this way because of their low (insignificant) values. Examples include screws and nuts used in assembling mountain bikes, or staples and glue used in manufacturing shoes. The costs of these materials are likely to be very low compared to the costs of other direct materials. Using the materiality principle, it does not make much economic sense to individually trace the costs of each of these materials and classify them separately as direct materials. For instance, it is not cost-beneficial to keep detailed records of the amount of glue used in manufacturing one unit of a shoe.

Inventories of Rocky Mountain Bikes

Finished goods $10,300
Goods in process $7,500
Raw materials $9,000

Goods in Process Inventory

Another inventory held by manufacturers is **goods in process inventory,** also called *work in process inventory.* It consists of products in the process of being manufactured but not yet complete. The amount of goods in process inventory depends on the type of production process. If the time required to produce a unit of product is short, the goods in process inventory is likely small. But if weeks or months are needed to produce a unit, the goods in process inventory is usually larger.

Finished Goods Inventory

A third inventory owned by a manufacturer is **finished goods inventory.** Finished goods inventory consists of completed products ready for sale. This inventory is similar to merchandise inventory owned by a merchandising company.

Manufacturers often carry unique plant assets such as small tools, factory buildings, and factory equipment. Patents are an intangible asset often owned by manufacturers. Companies use these assets to manufacture products. The balance sheet in Exhibit 19.5 shows Rocky Mountain Bikes owns all of these assets. Some manufacturers invest millions or even billions of dollars in production facilities and patents. **Caterpillar**'s recent balance sheet shows a net investment in land, buildings, machinery, and equipment of $3.8 billion, much of which involves production facilities.

Income Statement of a Manufacturer

C4 Explain differences in income statements of manufacturing and merchandising companies.

The main difference between the income statement of a manufacturer and merchandiser is the items making up cost of goods sold. Exhibit 19.6 compares the components of cost of goods sold for a manufacturer and a merchandiser. A merchandiser adds beginning merchandise inventory to cost of goods purchased and then subtracts ending merchandise inventory to get cost of goods sold. A manufacturer adds beginning finished goods inventory to cost of goods manufactured and then subtracts ending finished goods inventory to get cost of goods sold.

A merchandiser uses the term *merchandise* inventory while a manufacturer uses the term *finished goods* inventory. A manufacturer's inventories of raw materials and goods

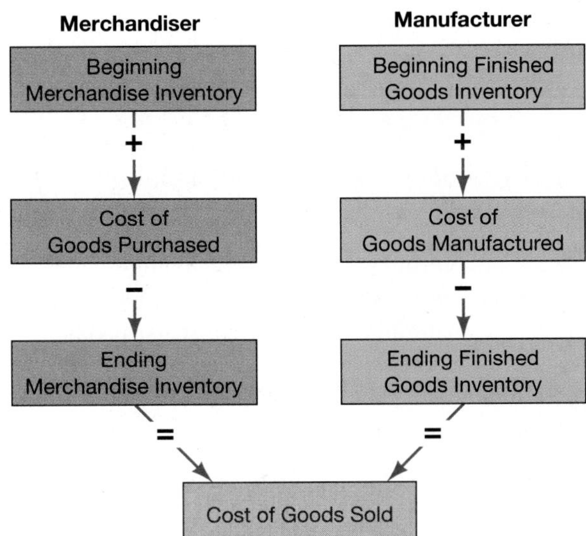

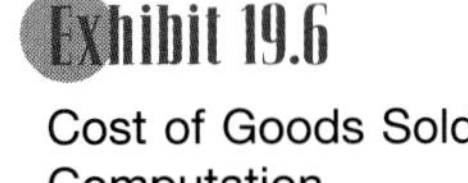

Cost of Goods Sold Computation

in process are not included in finished goods because they are not available for sale. A manufacturer also shows cost of goods *manufactured* instead of cost of goods *purchased.* This difference is because a manufacturer produces its goods instead of purchasing them ready for sale. We show in Chapter 20 how we derive cost of goods manufactured from the manufacturing statement.

P1 Compute cost of goods sold for a manufacturer.

We show cost of goods sold sections for a merchandiser (Tele-Mart) and a manufacturer (Rocky Mountain Bikes) in Exhibit 19.7 to highlight these differences. The remaining income statement sections are similar.

Cost of Goods Sold for a Merchandiser and Manufacturer

Merchandising Company		Manufacturing Company	
Cost of goods sold:		Cost of goods sold:	
Beginning *merchandise* inventory	$ 14,200	**Beginning *finished goods* inventory**	$ 11,200
Total cost of merchandise *purchased*	234,150	**Cost of goods *manufactured****	170,500
Goods available for sale	$248,350	Goods available for sale	$181,700
Ending *merchandise* inventory	12,100	**Ending *finished goods* inventory**	10,300
Cost of goods sold	$236,250	Cost of goods sold	$171,400

* The cost of goods manufactured amount is reported in the income statement of Exhibit 19.9.

Except for these differences, the cost of goods sold computations are the same. But we need to emphasize the numbers in these computations reflect different activities. A merchandiser's cost of goods purchased is the cost of buying products to be sold. A manufacturer's cost of goods manufactured is the sum of direct materials, direct labor, and factory overhead costs incurred in producing products. The remainder of this section explains these three manufacturing costs and also describes prime and conversion costs.

Direct Materials

Direct materials are tangible components of a finished product. **Direct material costs** are the expenditures for direct materials that are separately and readily traced through the manufacturing process to finished goods. Examples of direct materials in manufacturing a mountain bike include its tires, seat, frame, pedals, brakes, cables, gears, and handlebars. The pie chart in the margin shows us that direct materials generally make up about 45%

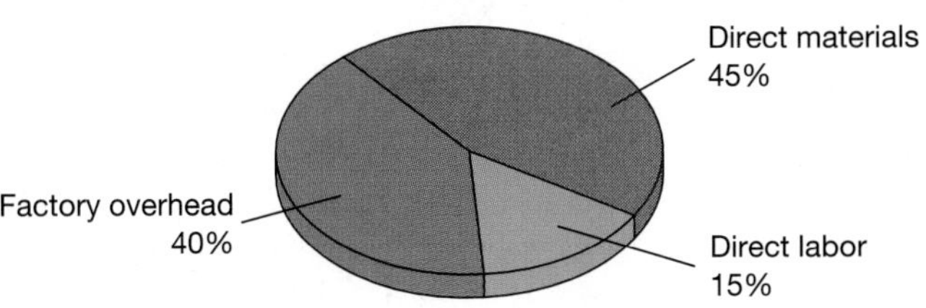

of manufacturing costs in today's products. But this amount varies considerably across industries and companies.

Direct Labor

Direct labor refers to the efforts of employees who physically convert materials to finished product. **Direct labor costs** are the wages and salaries for direct labor that are separately and readily traced through the manufacturing process to finished goods. Examples of direct labor in manufacturing a mountain bike include operators directly involved in converting raw materials into finished products (welding, painting, forming) and assembly workers who attach materials such as tires, seats, pedals, and brakes to mountain bike frames. Costs of other workers on the assembly line who assist direct laborers are classified as indirect labor. Efforts of indirect laborers are not linked to specific units or batches of the product.

Factory Overhead

Factory overhead involves components or activities that support the manufacturing process and are not direct materials or direct labor. **Factory overhead costs** are the expenditures for factory overhead that cannot be separately or readily traced to finished goods. These costs include indirect materials and indirect labor, costs not directly traceable to the product. Overtime paid to direct laborers is also included in overhead. This is because overtime is due to delays, interruptions, or constraints not necessarily identifiable to a specific product or batches of product.

Factory overhead costs also include maintenance of the mountain bike factory, supervision of its employees, repairing manufacturing equipment, factory utilities (water, gas, electricity), production manager's salary, factory rent, depreciation on factory buildings and equipment, factory insurance, property taxes on factory buildings and equipment, and factory accounting and legal services. Factory overhead does *not* include selling and administrative expenses. This is because they are not incurred in manufacturing products. These expenses are called *period costs* and are recorded as expenses on the income statement when incurred. We describe period costs later in the chapter.

Prime and Conversion Costs

Direct material costs and direct labor costs are also called **prime costs**—expenditures directly associated with the manufacturing of finished goods. Direct labor costs and overhead costs are called **conversion costs**—expenditures incurred in the process of converting raw materials to finished goods. Note that direct labor costs are considered both prime costs and conversion costs. Exhibit 19.8 conveys the relation between prime and conversion costs along with their components of direct material, direct labor, and factory overhead.

Exhibit 19.8

Prime and Conversion Costs

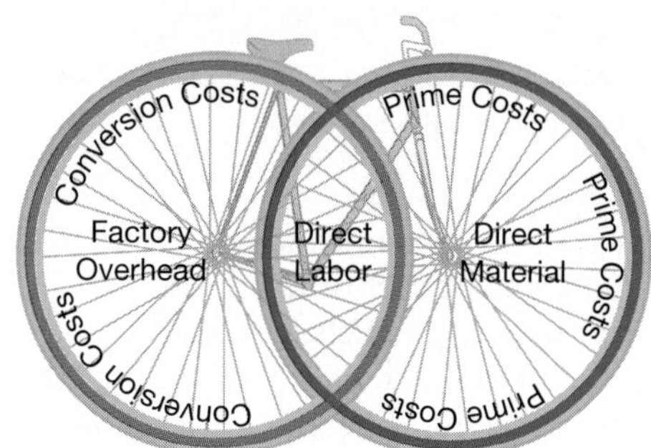

Reporting Performance

Exhibit 19.9 shows the income statement for Rocky Mountain Bikes. Its operating expenses include sales salaries, office salaries, and depreciation of delivery and office equipment. Operating expenses do not include manufacturing costs such as factory workers' wages and depreciation of production equipment and of the factory. These manufacturing costs are not reported as operating expenses. They are part of cost of goods manufactured and included in cost of goods sold. We explain why and how this is done in the next section under "Classification by Function."

Exhibit 19.9

Income Statement for a Manufacturer

ROCKY MOUNTAIN BIKES Income Statement For Year Ended December 31, 2000			
Sales			$310,000
Cost of goods sold:			
Finished goods inventory, December 31, 1999		$ 11,200	
Cost of goods manufactured		170,500	
Goods available for sale		$181,700	
Finished goods inventory, December 31, 2000		(10,300)	
Cost of goods sold			171,400
Gross profit			$138,600
Operating expenses:			
Selling expenses:			
Sales salaries expense	$ 18,000		
Advertising expense	5,500		
Delivery wages expense	12,000		
Shipping supplies expense	250		
Insurance expense, delivery equipment	300		
Depreciation expense, delivery equipment	2,100		
Total selling expenses		$38,150	
General and administrative expenses:			
Office salaries expense	$ 15,700		
Miscellaneous expense	200		
Bad debts expense	1,550		
Office supplies expense	100		
Depreciation expense, office equipment	200		
Interest expense	4,000		
Total general and administrative expenses		21,750	
Total operating expenses			59,900
Income before income taxes			$78,700
Less income taxes expense			(32,600)
Net income			$ 46,100
Net income per common share (20,000 shares)			$ 2.31

Flash back

4. What are the three types of inventory on a balance sheet of a manufacturing company?

5. What is the difference between cost of goods sold for merchandising versus manufacturing companies?

Answers—p. 841

Cost Accounting Concepts

We can classify costs on the basis of their (1) behavior, (2) traceability, (3) controllability, (4) relevance, and (5) function. This section explains each of these concepts in assigning costs to products and services.

C5 Describe accounting concepts useful in classifying costs.

Classification by Behavior

At a basic level, a cost can be classified as fixed or variable. A **fixed cost** does not change with changes in the volume of activity. Straight-line depreciation on a machine is a fixed cost. A **variable cost** changes in proportion to changes in the volume of activity. Sales commissions based on a percent of units sold is a variable cost. Additional examples of fixed and variable costs are provided in Exhibit 19.10. When cost items are combined, total cost can be fixed, variable, or mixed. Mixed means it is a combination of fixed and variable costs. Rent of equipment often includes a fixed cost for some minimum amount and a variable cost based on amount of usage. Classification of costs by behavior is helpful in cost-volume-profit analyses and short-term decision making. We discuss these in Chapters 23 and 26.

Exhibit 19.10

Fixed and Variable Costs

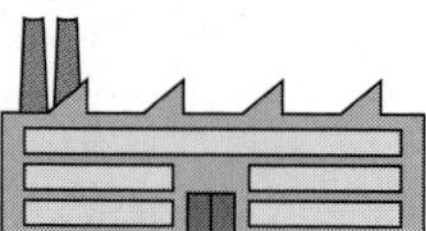

Fixed Cost: Rent for Rocky Mountain Bikes' factory is $22,000, and doesn't change with the number of bikes produced.

Variable Cost: Cost of tires is variable with the number of bikes produced—this cost is $15 per pair.

Classification by Traceability

A cost is often traced to a cost object. A **cost object** is a product, process, department, or customer to which costs are assigned. When a cost is traceable, it is classified as either a direct or indirect cost. **Direct costs** are those incurred for the benefit of one specific cost object. For example, if we use a product as a cost object, material and labor costs are usually directly traceable. **Indirect costs** are incurred for the benefit of more than one cost object. An example of an indirect traceable cost is a maintenance plan that benefits two or more departments. Exhibit 19.11 shows both direct and indirect costs in a manufacturing plant that arise from the maintenance department. Classification of costs by traceability is useful for cost allocation. This is discussed in Chapter 22.

Exhibit 19.11

Direct and Indirect Costs

Direct Costs:
- Salaries of maintenance department employees
- Equipment purchased by maintenance department
- Materials purchased by maintenance department
- Maintenance department equipment depreciation

Indirect Costs:
- Factory accounting
- Factory administration
- Factory rent
- Factory managers' salary
- Factory light and heat

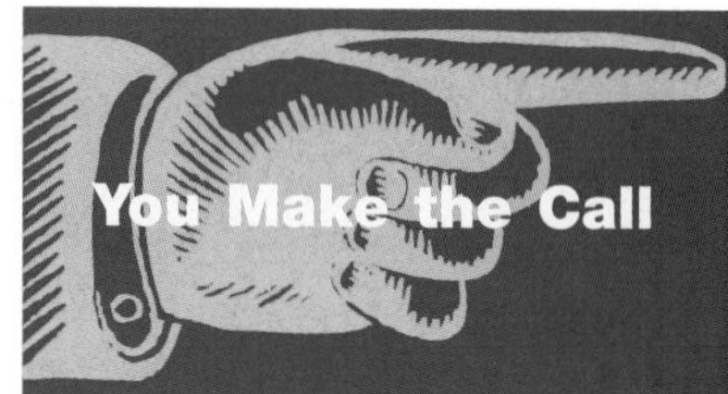

Budget Officer

You are the budget officer of a manufacturer. You are told by your boss to trace as many of the assembly department's direct costs as possible. You are able to trace 90% of direct costs in an economical manner. To trace the other 10%, you need a sophisticated and costly accounting software package. Do you purchase this package?

Answer—p. 840

Classification by Controllability

A cost can be defined as **controllable** or **not controllable.** Whether a cost is controllable or not depends on the employee's responsibilities, as shown in Exhibit 19.12. This is referred to as identifying hierarchical levels in management, or pecking order. For example, investments in machinery are controllable by upper level managers but not lower level managers. Many daily operating expenses such as overtime often are controllable by lower level managers. Classification of costs

Exhibit 19.12

Controllability of Costs

Senior Manager
Controls costs of investment in land, buildings, and equipment.

Supervisor
Controls daily expenses such as supplies, maintenance, and overtime.

by controllability is especially useful for evaluating managers.

Classification by Relevance

A cost can be classified by relevance. This is done by identifying a cost as either a sunk cost or an out-of-pocket cost. A **sunk cost** is one already incurred that cannot be avoided or changed. Sunk costs are irrelevant to future decisions. One example is the cost of production equipment previously purchased by a manufacturing company. An **out-of-pocket cost** requires a future outlay of cash and is relevant for decision making. Future purchases of production equipment involve out-of-pocket costs.

A discussion of relevant costs must consider opportunity costs. An **opportunity cost** is the potential benefit lost by choosing a specific action from two or more alternatives. One example is a student giving up wages from a job to attend summer school. Consideration of opportunity costs is important when, for example, a computer manufacturer must decide between internally manufacturing a chip versus buying it externally. This is discussed in Chapter 26.

Purchase Manager
You are the purchase manager of a motorcycle manufacturer. You are evaluating two potential suppliers of seats for your motorcycles. One supplier (A) quotes a price of $145 per seat and assures 100% quality standards and on-time delivery schedules. The second supplier (B) quotes a price of $115 per seat but does not give any written assurances on quality or delivery. You decide to award the contract to the second supplier (B), saving $30 per seat. Are there any opportunity costs of this decision?

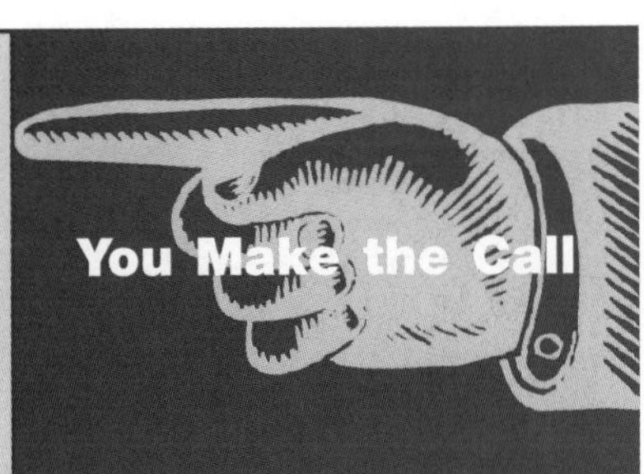

Answer—p. 840

Classification by Function

C6 Define product and period costs and explain how they impact financial statements.

Another classification of costs for manufacturers is one of capitalization as inventory or expense as incurred. Costs capitalized as inventory are called product costs. **Product costs** refer to expenditures that are necessary and integral to finished products. They include direct materials, direct labor, and overhead costs. Product costs pertain to activities carried out to manufacture the product.

Costs expensed are called period costs. **Period costs** refer to expenditures identified more with a time period than with finished products. They include selling and general administrative expenses. Period costs pertain to activities that are not part of the manufacturing process. A distinction between product and period costs is important. This is because it affects the amount of costs expensed in the income statement and the amount of costs assigned to inventory on the balance sheet.

Our ability to understand and identify product costs and period costs is crucial to using and understanding a *manufacturing statement.* This statement is described in the next chapter. Exhibit 19.13 shows the different effects of product and period costs incurred by Rocky Mountain Bikes. Period costs flow directly to its current income statement as expenses. They are not reported as assets.

Product costs for Rocky Mountain Bikes are first assigned to inventory. Final treatment of product costs depends on when inventory is sold or disposed of. Product costs assigned to finished goods that are sold in year 2000 are reported on Rocky Mountain Bikes' year 2000 income statement as part of cost of goods sold. Product costs assigned to unsold inventory are carried forward on Rocky Mountain Bikes' balance sheet at the end of year 2000. If this inventory is sold in year 2001, product costs assigned to it are reported in that year's income statement.

Period and Product Costs in Financial Statements

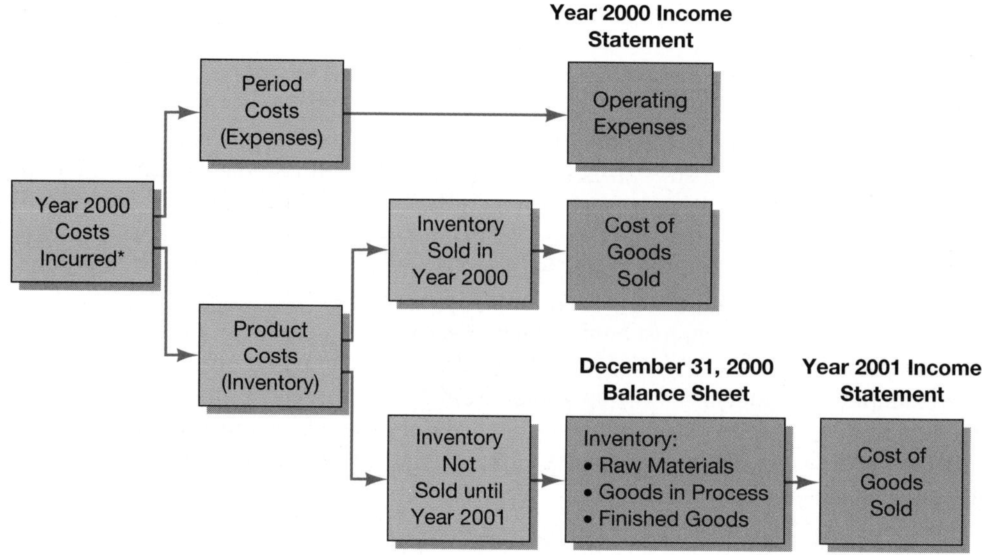

* We exclude from this diagram costs to acquire assets other than inventory, costs to retire debt, and costs of payments to owners.

This difference between period and product costs explains why the year 2000 income statement of Rocky Mountain Bikes does not report under operating expenses either factory workers' wages or depreciation on factory buildings and equipment. Instead, both these costs are combined with the cost of raw materials to compute the product cost of finished goods. A portion of these manufacturing costs is reported in the year 2000 income statement as part of cost of goods sold. The other portion is reported on the balance sheet at the end of that year as part of the cost of inventory. The portion assigned to inventory could be included in any or all of raw materials, goods in process, or finished goods inventories.

Identifying Cost Classification

It is important we understand that a cost can be classified using any of the five different methods described above. To do this, it is important we understand costs and operations. Using our five classifications, we must be able to identify the: *activity* for behavior, *cost object* for traceability, *management hierarchical level* for controllability, *opportunity cost* for relevance, and *benefit period* for functional. Factory rent, for instance, can be classified as a product cost and is fixed with respect to units produced, indirect with respect to products, and not controllable by a production supervisor. Potential multiple classifications are shown in Exhibit 19.14 using different cost items incurred in manufacturing mountain bikes. The finished bike is the cost object.

Examples of Multiple Cost Classifications

Cost item	By Behavior	By Traceability	By Function
Tires	Variable	Direct	Product
Wages of assembly worker	Variable	Direct	Product
Advertising	Fixed	Indirect	Period
Production manager's salary	Fixed	Indirect	Product
Office depreciation	Fixed	Indirect	Period

Proper allocation of these costs and managerial decisions made using cost data depend on our ability to correctly identify cost classifications.

Cost Concepts for Service Companies

The cost concepts described above are generally applicable to service organizations. We can consider **Delta Air Lines,** a service firm, as an example. Delta's cost of food for passengers is a variable cost based on the number of passengers. Yet the cost of leasing an aircraft is fixed with respect to the number of passengers. We can also trace a flight crew's salary to a specific flight whereas wages for ground crew are unlikely traceable to a specific flight. Classification by function (such as product versus period costs) is not relevant to service companies because services are not inventoried. Costs incurred by a service firm are expensed in the reporting period when incurred.

Understanding cost concepts is important to managers in service companies. They rely on accurate estimates of costs for many decisions. An airline manager must often decide between canceling or rerouting flights. A manager also must be able to estimate costs saved by canceling a flight versus rerouting. Knowledge of fixed costs is equally important. We explain more about the cost requirements for these and other managerial decisions in Chapter 26.

Service Costs

- food
- beverages
- cleaning
- pilots' salaries
- attendants' salaries
- fuel
- travel agents' fees
- ground crew's salaries

6. Which type of cost behavior causes total costs to increase when volume of activity increases?

7. How might traceability of costs improve managerial decisions?

Answers—p. 841

Manufacturing Management Principles

C7 Explain how a customer orientation in a global economy impacts business activities.

Two important factors have encouraged manufacturers to look for more effective and efficient ways to manage their business activities. First, there is increased emphasis on *customers* as the most important part of business. This has yielded a focus on quality, flexibility, and on-time delivery. Second, the expanding *global economy* has fostered greater competition and more opportunities.

The customer focus affects many business activities. Customers have little tolerance for poor quality. Today's goal is zero defects. Customers are demanding that manufacturers cater to their changing needs. This includes product design, features, and even order quantities. This requires manufacturers to adopt more flexible manufacturing practices. There is also increasing importance placed on time. Customers expect their orders delivered soon and on time.

These changes imply that companies accept the notion of customer orientation. **Customer orientation** means a company's managers and employees are in tune with the changing wants and needs of its consumers. They then align their management and manufacturing processes to respond to these wants and needs.

The global economy also produces changes in business activities. One notable case that reflects changes in customer demands and increased global competition is auto manufacturing. The top three Japanese auto manufacturers (**Honda, Nissan,** and **Toyota**) once controlled over 40% of the U.S. auto market. Customers perceived Japanese auto manufacturers as providing value not obtainable from other manufacturers. They were seen as high quality, flexible, responsive, and price competitive. Many North American and European auto manufacturers had to respond to consumer demands—and they did, with constructive changes in their manufacturing practices. In doing so they have recaptured a good portion of this lost market share.

Exhibit 19.15 shows the customer orientation in a global economy as the main focus of manufacturing management principles. This focus has led manufacturers to move away from traditional mass production techniques in response to consumer demands.

Exhibit 19.15

Manufacturing Management Principles in Action

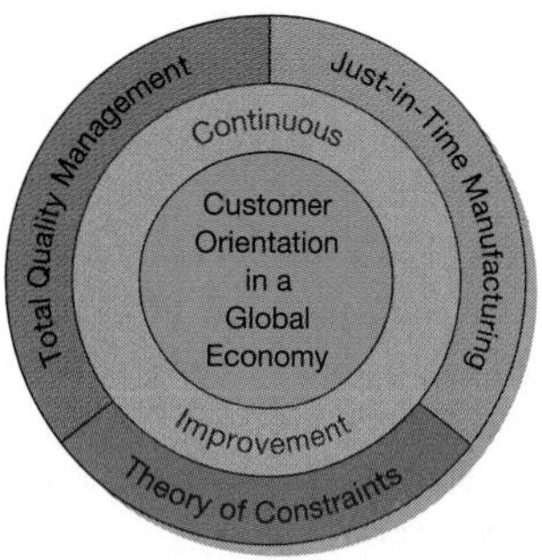

They've adopted improved approaches to manufacturing and production management. These approaches include total quality management (TQM), just-in-time (JIT) manufacturing, theory of constraints (TOC), and continuous improvement (CI). These modern manufacturing management principles apply to the production of both products and services. Customers look for flexibility and quality in services as much as they look for them in products. We describe each of these four principles in this section.

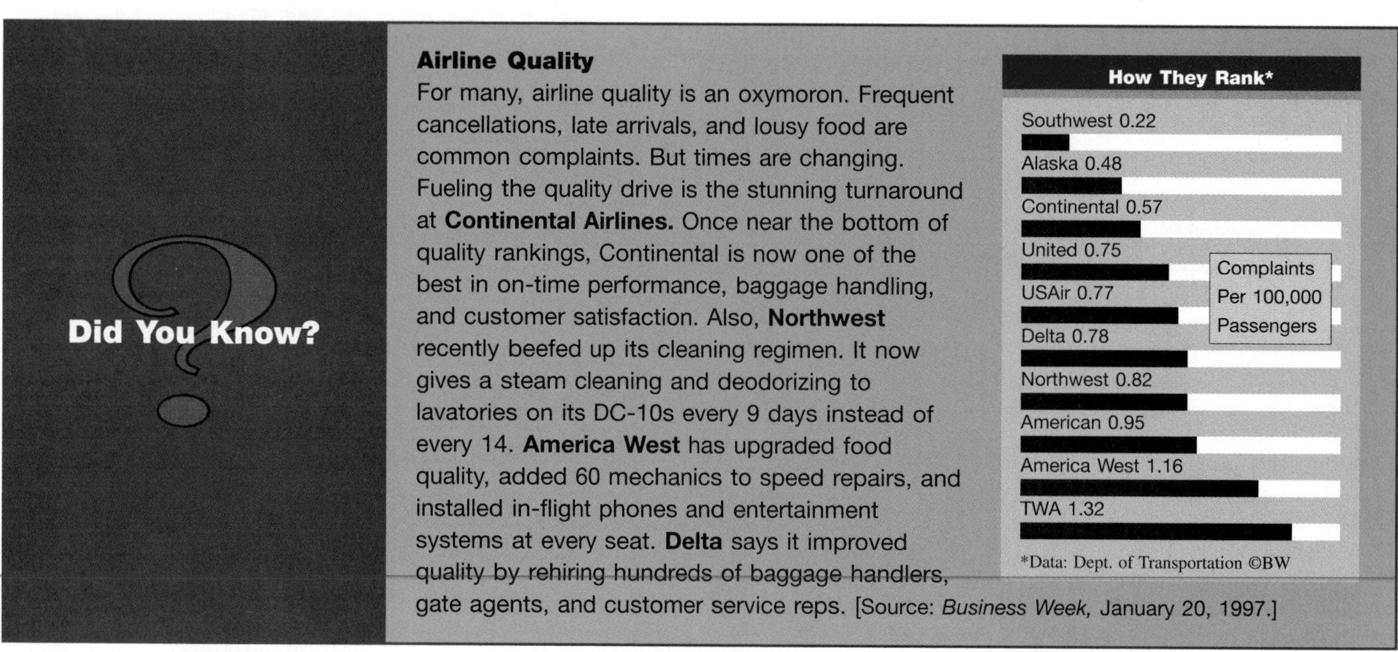

Airline Quality

For many, airline quality is an oxymoron. Frequent cancellations, late arrivals, and lousy food are common complaints. But times are changing. Fueling the quality drive is the stunning turnaround at **Continental Airlines.** Once near the bottom of quality rankings, Continental is now one of the best in on-time performance, baggage handling, and customer satisfaction. Also, **Northwest** recently beefed up its cleaning regimen. It now gives a steam cleaning and deodorizing to lavatories on its DC-10s every 9 days instead of every 14. **America West** has upgraded food quality, added 60 mechanics to speed repairs, and installed in-flight phones and entertainment systems at every seat. **Delta** says it improved quality by rehiring hundreds of baggage handlers, gate agents, and customer service reps. [Source: *Business Week,* January 20, 1997.]

Total Quality Management

C8 Describe current manufacturing management principles.

Total quality management (TQM) is based on having all managers and employees strive toward higher standards. These higher standards extend to their daily work and to the products and services offered to customers.

Traditional manufacturers tend to leave the responsibility for quality with an independent group of quality control inspectors. In this case the focus is on inspection of finished products. But TQM is different. TQM requires a focus on quality *throughout* the production process. Its strategy is to identify defective work when and where it occurs. This constant focus on quality reminds each employee of the need to eliminate defective work at all stages of production. The expected results are fewer defects in finished products and reduced costs from reworking rejected products.

A company using TQM rewards employees who find defects. With this reward, employees are unlikely to ignore defects in partially completed products arriving at their workstations. We all know pointing out problems can involve extra effort, paperwork, and hostile reactions from coworkers. An important part of TQM is changing attitudes of employees to encourage a new commitment to quality. TQM also encourages employees to try new methods to improve quality. With flexibility and rewards, managers committed to TQM try to tap the knowledge and abilities of people closest to the work.

Companies using TQM emphasize the value of reaching higher quality levels. A TQM company both sets quality standards and measures quality results at each stage of production. Many companies set maximum rejection rates as targets for each workstation. They encourage employees by rewarding those who reach their targets and by reporting actual rejection rates.

To encourage an emphasis on quality among companies, the U.S. Congress established the Malcolm Baldrige National Quality Award. The award's goals are to enhance U.S. competitiveness by promoting quality awareness, recognize quality and business achievements of U.S. companies, and publicize these companies' successful performance. Entrants must do a painstaking self-analysis using guidelines from the Baldrige committee. They must also submit to on-site review of operations.

Globe Metallurgical stands out as one of the smallest companies to win a Baldrige award. Using computer-controlled systems and statistical process control, Globe monitors and quantifies every aspect of its manufacturing process. This system advises workers whether processing targets are being met. It also identifies production steps most prone to failure. This system increased worker productivity by 50% in several areas and customer complaints fell 91%.

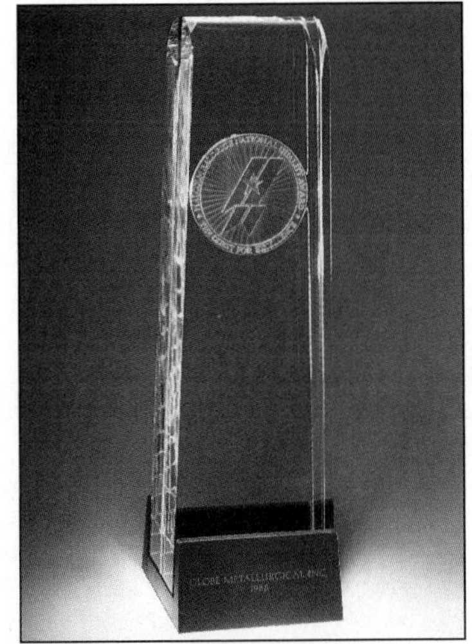

Another Baldrige winner is **IBM**'s division in Rochester, MN. IBM proudly proclaims:[3]

> IBM Rochester has created a quality policy, a vision, and a set of quality goals that are deployed throughout the site to individual departments. The quality policy is: *Customer—the final arbiter; Products and services—first with the best; Quality—excellence in education;* and *People—enabled, empowered, excited and rewarded.*

IBM Rochester's employees regularly score among the highest in morale across all its sites as measured by opinion surveys.

Duplicating Happiness
Xerox has had great success by focusing on its customers. Its *Customer Satisfaction Measurement System* tracks the behavior and preferences of some 200,000 Xerox equipment owners. This information is used to set benchmarks for quality improvements.

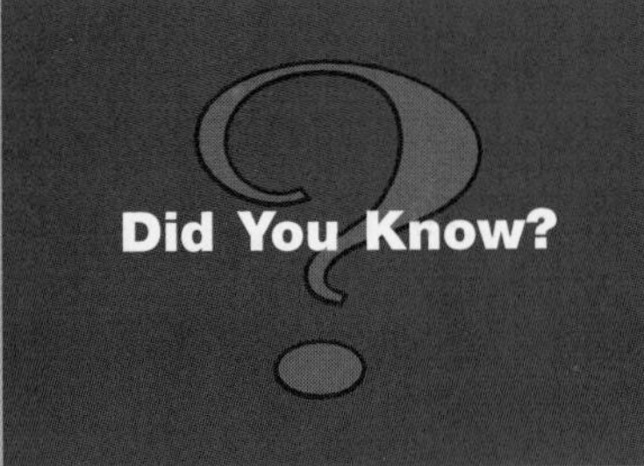

Just-in-Time Manufacturing

A commitment to customers and quality leads to profits only when a company's activities are carried out efficiently. A customer orientation demands efficiency. TQM promotes efficiency because it reduces the cost of reworking or repairing defects. Another means to increase efficiency is to use a just-in-time manufacturing system.

A **just-in-time (JIT)** system is where a company acquires or produces inventory only when needed. Manufacturing activities are planned so that finished products are produced just as they are needed for delivery to customers. Parts for the finished product are only completed as needed in the manufacturing process. Also, raw materials are acquired only when they are needed. A JIT system tries to stock the minimum amounts of finished goods, goods in process, and raw materials inventories.

---

[3] *The Quality Journey Continues . . .* , IBM, Second Edition, March 1991, © Copyright International Business Machines Corporation (IBM) 1990, 1991. Reprinted with permission.

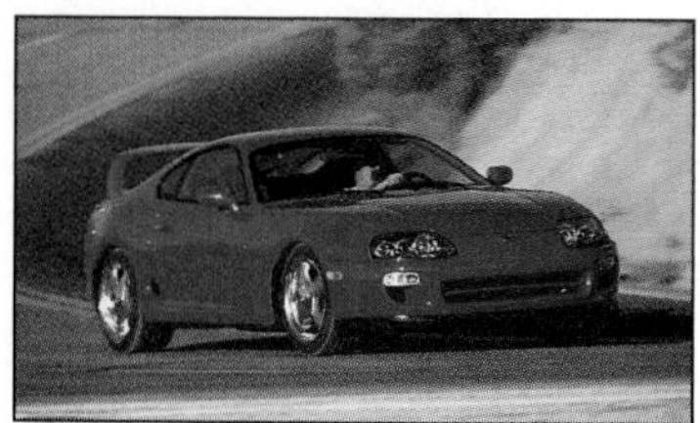

A JIT system can be directed to meet the needs of customers. This means companies manufacture products in response to predicted or actual customer wants and needs. A few years ago **Toyota** declared that all of its automobiles sold in Japan will be produced only when orders are received from customers. Customers would place orders through dealers and wait only two weeks to take delivery. The advantage to customers is getting exactly what they want after a relatively short wait. The advantage to Toyota and its dealers is the little investment in inventories of automobiles.

An important feature of JIT is the demand-pull system. A *demand-pull* system means products are pulled through the manufacturing process by orders from customers. A *supply-push* system is the old traditional system that pushes products through production by inserting raw materials and applying labor and overhead. It relies on marketing and sales forces to push finished goods to customers after the fact. A JIT system does not push but instead is pulled by customer needs. The demand-pull system requires a TQM philosophy and involvement of all employees.

A JIT system can be applied to raw materials and goods in process as well as finished products. To see this, look at the production process for a mountain bike in Exhibit 19.16. This process is split into 4 parts. Each part is performed in sequence as units move toward completion.

Exhibit 19.16

Production Process—Mountain Bike

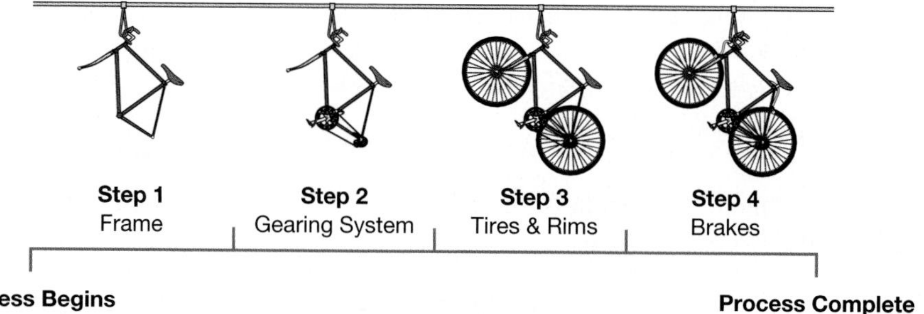

A traditional manufacturer allows inventories of mountain bikes to accumulate between workstations. This is to avoid shutting down the production line because of a shortage of any component. The JIT manufacturer aims to get each component to arrive at the production line *just in time* for its use. When successful, the JIT manufacturer needs fewer inventories and is able to use these freed up assets to reduce debt or invest in other profitable activities.

We must remember not all manufacturing processes can use JIT. To use JIT a company must be able to predict the timing and amount of customer orders. An effective TQM system must be in place to control the manufacturing process. This is because an unexpected number of defects can bring production to a stop. The use of JIT also requires dependable suppliers able to make frequent shipments of small quantities. Good computing and communication equipment are essential. Some JIT companies use systems that send orders directly from their production lines to the supplier's production lines.

The necessary requirements to using a JIT manufacturing system make it more susceptible to disruption than traditional systems. As one recent example, several U.S. plants of **General Motors** were temporarily shut down due to a strike at an assembly plant. These U.S. plants supplied components *just in time* to other assembly plants. Because of the lack of inventory, this worker strike had an immediate and major impact on several plants.

Theory of Constraints

Another means for improving a company's productive operations is the theory of constraints. The **theory of constraints (TOC)** focuses on identifying factors that constrain or limit a company's operations. Once constraints are identified, managers look for ways to overcome or relax these constraints.

A major emphasis of TOC is to increase throughput and reduce investment and operating expenses. **Throughput** is the added value a company brings to its finished products. We compute throughput as selling price minus costs of direct materials used in production. **Investment** refers to conversion costs and includes the cost of property, plant, equipment, and inventory for sale. While direct labor is a conversion cost, some companies choose to classify it as an operating expense along with other wages. *Operating expenses* are the cost of activities required to sell inventory. These include selling and general administrative expenses.

While TOC can be applied to the operations of an entire company—including production, sales, engineering, distribution, and administration—it is applied most often in production. Its aim is to synchronize and plan manufacturing operations to minimize processing time. Processing time is the time it takes to produce one item or one order. Shorter processing time helps a company better serve its customers with rapid deliveries.

TOC suggests that the key to decreasing processing time is to find the most binding constraint (bottleneck). A **constraint** is anything that prevents a company from achieving higher performance in terms of its goals. It can be part of the production process or a resource used in the process. We then manage this constraint to make it nonbinding. A solution may be to add more machinery or labor at the bottleneck of the process. It can also involve redesigning the production process itself.

To illustrate TOC, let's return to the production line for mountain bikes (see Exhibit 19.16). This line combines four components to produce finished goods. If the workstation for adding gearing systems (step 2) is the slowest of four workstations, then its output determines the output of the entire line. Workstations pertaining to steps 1, 3, and 4 have idle time while the workstation pertaining to step 2 catches up. One solution is to install more workstations pertaining to step 2 to balance the production flow. While this solution increases throughput because of increased production, it adds costs (more machinery). We should consider ways to increase throughput while minimizing added costs.

Binney & Smith is the manufacturer of Crayola Crayons®. It uses TOC to find and manage manufacturing bottlenecks, to rearrange plant layouts, and to decide the amount of goods in process used in its JIT inventory system. Binney & Smith has had great success with TOC. It decreased raw materials inventory by 40%, decreased goods in process inventory by 60%, improved on time shipping performance to 96%, and reduced shipping lead time from 12 to 5 days.

Applying the theory of constraints is a continuous process. After one constraint is identified and relaxed, we search for the next one. There is always some constraint that is binding and limiting throughput. We focus on identifying and relaxing this constraint. In this way, TOC is a system aimed at reaching a company's most effective and efficient production process.

Continuous Improvement

Continuous improvement is a management concept where every manager and employee continually looks for ways to improve operations. This extends to customer service, product quality, product features, production process, and employee relations. Continuous improvement rejects the view that an activity is "good enough." New ideas are tried and old ideas are challenged.

There is a relation between continuous improvement and the other manufacturing management principles. There is no place for resisting change with continuous improvement. Instead, managers and employees seek opportunities for growth and increased profitability. In today's global economy, a company is more likely to succeed if its employees are committed to continuous improvement.

Binney & Smith developed and implemented its version of continuous improvement by using both TOC and JIT principles. It is called *high velocity manufacturing.* It means encouraging employees to solve problems and accept responsibility for improving the process. Binney & Smith cut the time it takes to change from running one color of crayon to another. Remarkably, change-over time went from two hours to one-half hour. It shifted responsibility for quality control from end-of-the-line inspectors to machine operators. Again, defects decreased from 12% to 6%. It worked for Binney & Smith.

8. Describe the focus of the theory of constraints.
9. What factors encourage development of new ideas about production management?
10. What is the attitude in a company practicing total quality management?

Answers—p. 841

Implications of Manufacturing Management Principles

Adopting a new manufacturing management principle is challenging. Customer-oriented companies that apply one or more of these principles often end up making several changes to their manufacturing systems. The most common change is greater use of technology. This usually changes the cost structure in these companies. For instance, direct labor often becomes a smaller portion of total cost. It is replaced by machine costs and other overhead. This means total product cost now has a greater proportion of fixed and indirect costs rather than variable and direct costs. A good knowledge of the basic cost concepts discussed earlier in this chapter is essential in understanding the changes to the cost structure when a company's systems and processes are modified.

A customer orientation necessitates information for management decision making. Information on defects, returns, service calls, and on-time delivery is necessary. More accurate cost information is needed to compare different courses of action to satisfy customer needs. This means better methods to track information are required.

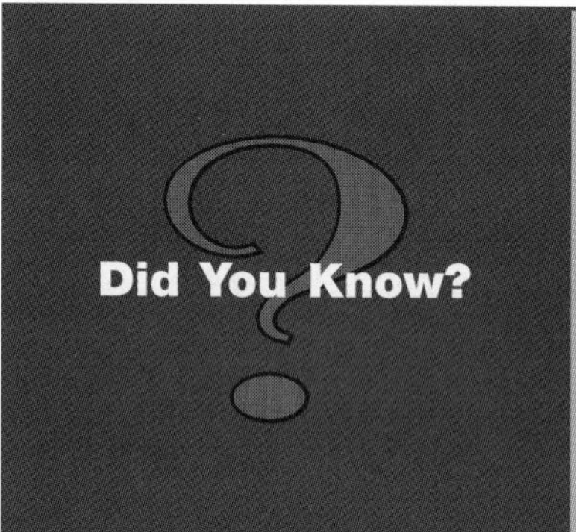

Overhead and Proud of It!

Our technology society may not eliminate direct labor, but it can banish us to overhead. We often pride ourselves on our work, a contribution to a product or service. But Roseville Networks Division (RND) of **Hewlett-Packard** now calls us overhead. RND found direct labor to be less than 2% of total manufacturing costs. They then decided to reclassify direct labor from a separate cost item to overhead. This reclassification eliminated about 30 minutes of direct labor per day spent on tracing labor time to products. But at least we're not "immaterial"—yet. [Source: D. Berlant, R. Browning and G. Foster, "How Hewlett-Packard Gets Numbers It Can Trust," *Harvard Business Review,* January-February 1990, pp. 178–183.]

USING THE INFORMATION

Unit Contribution Margin

A1 Compute unit contribution margin and describe what it reveals about a company's cost structure.

We explained in this chapter how managers classify costs by behavior. This means costs are either fixed or variable with respect to the volume of activity. In manufacturing companies, volume of activity frequently refers to the number of units produced. We then classify a cost as either fixed or variable depending on whether the total cost changes as the number of units produced changes.

Once we separate costs by behavior, we can then compute the contribution margin of a product. **Unit contribution margin**, or *contribution margin per unit,* is the amount a product's unit selling price exceeds its total unit variable cost. This excess amount contributes to covering fixed costs and generating profits on a per unit basis. Exhibit 19.17 shows the unit contribution margin formula.

Unit contribution margin = Sales price per unit − Total variable cost per unit

Exhibit 19.17

Unit Contribution Margin

Users often use contribution margin in the form of a contribution margin ratio. **Contribution margin ratio** is the percent of a unit's selling price that exceeds total unit variable cost. It can be interpreted as the percent of each sales dollar that remains after deducting total unit variable cost. Exhibit 19.18 shows the formula for the contribution margin ratio, defined as contribution margin divided by sales price.

$$\textbf{Contribution margin ratio} = \frac{\textbf{Unit Contribution margin}}{\textbf{Sales price per unit}}$$

Exhibit 19.18

Contribution Margin Ratio

We use Rocky Mountain Bikes' Tracker® product to show the usefulness of these measures. The selling price of a Tracker® mountain bike is $225, and the variable costs of its manufacturing and marketing are $100. The contribution margin per bike is computed as $125 ($225 − $100). This measure is useful to managers in determining the money contributed by each sale of a Tracker® bike to both (a) fixed costs and (b) profits. Specifically, each sale of a Tracker® bike yields a $125 contribution margin to cover fixed costs of Rocky Mountain Bikes. Once fixed costs are covered, what's left is profit.

We also compute the contribution margin ratio of the Tracker® mountain bike as 55.55% ($125/$225). This information is useful to managers when working with estimates of sales in dollars. Management now knows in the case of this product that approximately 56¢ (or 55.55%) of each sales dollar is available as contribution to fixed costs and profits. The contribution margin ratio is also useful in cost-volume-profit (CVP) analysis. CVP analysis is a method we use to assess the volume of activity necessary to achieve different performance levels (including profit, loss, and break-even points). We explain cost-volume-profit analysis in Chapter 23.

Salesperson

You are a salesperson involved with selling and taking customer orders. You are evaluating orders from two different customers, but you can accept only one of these orders because of your company's limited capacity. The first order is for 100 units of a product with a contribution margin ratio of 60% and a selling price of $1,000. The second order is for 500 units of a product with a contribution margin ratio of 20% and a selling price of $800. The incremental fixed costs are the same for both orders. Which order do you accept?

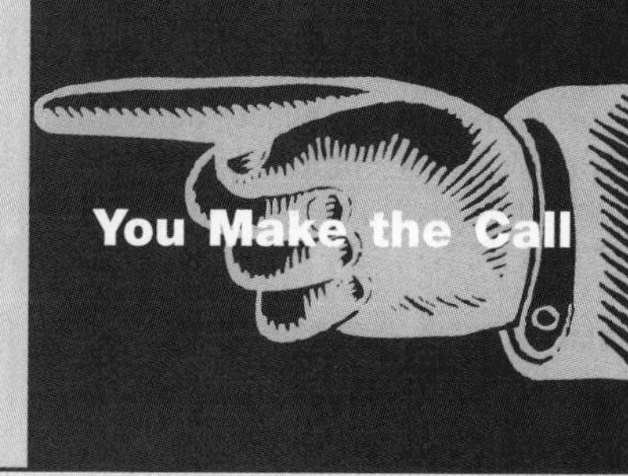

Answer—p. 841

Summary

C1 Explain the purpose of managerial accounting. The purpose of managerial accounting is to provide useful information to management and other internal decision makers. It does this by collecting, managing, and reporting both monetary and nonmonetary information in a manner useful to internal users.

C2 Describe major characteristics of managerial accounting. Major characteristics of managerial accounting include: (1) focus on internal decision makers, (2) emphasis on planning and control, (3) flexibility, (4) timeliness, (5) reliance on forecasts and estimates, (6) focus on segments and projects, and (7) reporting both monetary and nonmonetary information.

C3 Explain differences in balance sheets of manufacturing and merchandising companies. The main difference is that manufacturers usually carry three inventories instead of one inventory carried by merchandising companies. The three inventories are raw materials, goods in process, and finished goods.

C4 Explain differences in income statements of manufacturing and merchandising companies. The main difference between income statements of manufacturers and merchandisers is the items making up cost of goods sold. A merchandiser adds beginning merchandise inventory to cost of goods purchased and then subtracts ending merchandise inventory to get cost of goods sold. A manufacturer adds beginning finished goods inventory to cost of goods manufactured and then subtracts ending finished goods inventory to get cost of goods sold.

C5 Describe accounting concepts useful in classifying costs. We can classify costs on the basis of their (1) behavior—fixed vs. variable, (2) traceability—direct vs. indirect, (3) controllability—controllable vs. uncontrollable, (4) relevance—sunk vs. out of pocket, and (5) function—product vs. period. It is important to remember that a single cost can be classified in more than one way depending on the purpose for which the cost is being determined. These classifications are useful in understanding cost patterns, analyzing performance, and planning future operations.

C6 Define product and period costs and explain how they impact financial statements. Costs that are capitalized because they are expected to have value in the future are called *product costs,* whereas costs that are expensed are called *period costs.* This classification is important because it affects the amount of costs expensed in the income statement and the amount of costs assigned to inventory on the balance sheet. Product costs are commonly made up of direct materials, direct labor, and manufacturing overhead. Period costs include selling and administrative expenses.

C7 Explain how a customer orientation in a global economy impacts business activities. A customer orientation means an increased focus on quality, flexibility, and timeliness. An expanding global economy means both greater competition and more business opportunities. Business activities are increasingly designed to respond to and meet consumers' wants and needs.

C8 Describe current manufacturing management principles. Today's business environment emphasizes customer satisfaction. To satisfy the customer, companies increasingly focus on quality, flexibility, timely delivery, and cost. Several new manufacturing management principles have emerged to help in this process: total quality management, just-in-time manufacturing, theory of constraints, and continuous improvement.

P1 Compute cost of goods sold for a manufacturer. A manufacturer adds beginning finished goods inventory to cost of goods manufactured, and then subtracts ending finished goods inventory to get cost of goods sold.

A1 Compute unit contribution margin and describe what it reveals about a company's cost structure. Unit contribution margin is a product's sales price less its total variable costs, and the contribution margin ratio is a product's unit contribution margin divided by its sales price. Unit contribution margin is the amount received from each sale that is contributed to fixed costs and profits. The contribution margin ratio tells us what portion of each sales dollar is available as contribution to fixed costs and profits.

Guidance Answer to **Judgment and Ethics**

Production Supervisor

While someone must pay the bill, it appears that all three of your friends want to pay the bill with someone else's money. David is using money belonging to the tax authorities, Denise is taking money from her company, and Derek is defrauding the government. To prevent such practices, companies have internal audit mechanisms. Most companies precisely define the kinds of expenses that can be claimed. Many companies also set up ethical codes of conduct to help guide employees in making decisions. We must recognize that, depending on the circumstances, some entertainment expenses are justifiable and even encouraged. For example, the tax law allows certain deductions for entertainment that have a business purpose. Corporate policies also sometimes allow and encourage reimbursable spending for social activities, and government contracts sometimes include entertainment as allowable costs. Nevertheless, without further details, payment for this bill should be made from personal accounts.

Guidance Answers to **You Make the Call**

Division Manager

You need information from the managerial accounting system to help you decide between making the product in-house versus continuing to buy from outside. You need information pertaining to the costs of making it in-house: raw materials, direct labor, and overhead. You also need information about investments in machinery that are required to make the component. Regarding the possibility of continuing to buy from the outside, you need information about the purchase price of components and costs to place the order, along with costs of receiving and storing components. You must also consider nonfinancial factors such as quality of components currently supplied and the quality of in-house production.

Budget Officer

It is always desirable to trace all costs directly to cost objects. But you need to be able to trace costs in an economically feasible manner. In this case, you are able to trace 90% of costs directly to the assembly department. It may not be economical to spend added money on a new software to trace the final 10% of costs. You need to make a cost-benefit trade-off. Also, if the software offers benefits beyond tracing the remaining 10% of the assembly department's costs, your decision should take this into account.

Purchase Manager

Opportunity costs relate to the potential quality and delivery benefits given up by not choosing supplier (A) as the preferred supplier. Selecting supplier (B) might involve future costs of poor quality seats (inspection, repairs, and returns). Also, because of potential delivery delays, work might be interrupted and manufacturing costs increased. Your company might also incur sales losses if the product quality of supplier (B) is lower. As purchase manager, you are responsible for these costs and must consider them in making your decision.

Salesperson

The contribution margin for the first order is $600 per unit (60% of $1,000), whereas the contribution margin per unit for the second order is $160 (20% of $800). You are likely tempted to accept the first order based on its high contribution margin per unit. But you must compute total contribution margin based on the number of units sold for each order. Total contribution margin is $60,000 ($600 per unit × 100 units) and $80,000 ($160 per unit × 500 units) for the two orders respectively. The second order provides the largest return in absolute dollars, and is the order you would accept. Another factor you need to consider in your selection is the potential for a long-term relationship with these customers including repeat and increased sales.

Guidance Answers to 

1. *d.* Managerial accounting information is primarily used by internal users, is flexible to meet the needs of individual users, and often focuses on the future (e.g., budgets).
2. Financial accounting information is intended for users external to an organization such as investors, creditors, and government authorities. Managerial accounting, on the other hand, focuses on providing information to managers and other decision makers within the organization.
3. No, generally accepted accounting principles (GAAP) do not control the practice of managerial accounting. Unlike external users, the internal users need managerial accounting information for planning and controlling their organization's activities rather than for external comparison. Different types of information may be required depending on the managerial activity. Therefore, it is difficult to standardize managerial accounting systems across companies through use of GAAP or a similar structure.
4. The three different types of inventory on the balance sheet of a manufacturing company are raw materials inventory, goods in process inventory, and finished goods inventory.
5. The cost of goods sold for merchandising companies includes only the purchase price of the merchandise, whereas the cost of goods sold for manufacturing companies includes the three costs of manufacturing—direct materials, direct labor, and overhead.
6. Variable costs increase in total when volume of activity increases.
7. By being able to trace costs to cost objects (e.g., products, departments), managers have a better understanding of the total costs associated with a cost object. This information is useful when managers are considering making changes to the cost object (say dropping the product or expanding the department).
8. The theory of constraints focuses on factors limiting or constraining a company's operations.
9. The factors include: *(a)* increased demands by customers for higher quality products, custom-designed products, and faster delivery; *(b)* increased international competition; *(c)* improvements in computers and technology.
10. Under TQM, all managers and employees should strive toward higher standards in their work and in the products and services they offer to customers.

Demonstration Problem 1

The balance sheet and income statement for a manufacturing company are different than those for a merchandising or service company.

Required

1. Fill-in the [BLANKS] on the partial balance sheets for both the manufacturing company and the merchandising company. Explain why a different presentation is required.

Manufacturing Company

CHIP MAKING SYSTEMS Balance Sheet December 31, 2000	
Assets	
Current assets:	
Cash	$10,000
[BLANK]	8,000
[BLANK]	5,000
[BLANK]	7,000
Supplies	500
Prepaid insurance	500
Total current assets	$31,000

Merchandising Company

JOE'S SHOE OUTLET Balance Sheet December 31, 2000	
Assets	
Current assets:	
Cash	$ 5,000
[BLANK]	12,000
Supplies	500
Prepaid insurance	500
Total current assets	$18,000

2. Fill in the [BLANKS] on the income statements for the manufacturing company and the merchandising company. Explain why a different presentation is required.

3. The manufacturer's cost of good manufactured is the sum of (a) ________, (b) ________, and (c) ________ costs incurred in producing the product.

Manufacturing Company

CHIP MAKING SYSTEMS
Income Statement
For Year Ended December 31, 2000

Sales		$200,000
Cost of goods sold:		
Finished goods inventory, 12/31/1999	$ 10,000	
[BLANK]	120,000	
Goods available for sale	$130,000	
Finished goods inventory, 12/31/2000	(7,000)	
Cost of goods sold		123,000
Gross profit		$ 77,000

Merchandising Company

JOE'S SHOE OUTLET
Income Statement
For Year Ended December 31, 2000

Sales		$190,000
Cost of goods sold:		
Merchandise inventory, 12/31/1999	$ 8,000	
[BLANK]	108,000	
Net purchases	$116,000	
Merchandise inventory, 12/31/2000	(12,000)	
Cost of goods sold		104,000
Gross profit		$ 86,000

Solution to Demonstration Problem 1

1. Inventories for a manufacturer and for a merchandiser.

Manufacturing Company

CHIP MAKING SYSTEMS
Balance Sheet
December 31, 2000

Assets	
Current assets:	
Cash	$10,000
Raw materials inventory	8,000
Goods in process inventory	5,000
Finished goods inventory	7,000
Supplies	500
Prepaid insurance	500
Total current assets	$31,000

Merchandising Company

JOE'S SHOE OUTLET
Balance Sheet
December 31, 2000

Assets	
Current assets:	
Cash	$ 5,000
Merchandise inventory	12,000
Supplies	500
Prepaid insurance	500
Total current assets	$18,000

Explanation: A manufacturing company must control and measure three types of inventories—raw materials, goods in process, and finished goods. In the sequence of making a product, the raw materials move into production, labeled goods in process inventory, and then to finished goods. All raw materials and goods in process inventory at the end of each accounting period are considered current assets. All unsold finished inventory is considered a current asset at the end of each accounting period. The merchandising company must control and measure one type of inventory, the purchased goods.

2. Cost of goods sold for a manufacturer and for a merchandiser.

Manufacturing Company

CHIP MAKING SYSTEMS
Income Statement
For Year Ended December 31, 2000

Sales		$200,000
Cost of goods sold:		
Finished goods inventory, 12/31/1999	$ 10,000	
Cost of goods manufactured	**120,000**	
Goods available for sale	$130,000	
Finished goods inventory, 12/31/2000	(7,000)	
Cost of goods sold		123,000
Gross profit		$ 77,000

Merchandising Company

JOE'S SHOE OUTLET
Income Statement
For Year Ended December 31, 2000

Sales		$190,000
Cost of goods sold:		
Merchandise inventory, 12/31/1999	$ 8,000	
Cost of purchases	**108,000**	
Net purchases	$116,000	
Merchandise inventory, 12/31/2000	(12,000)	
Cost of goods sold		104,000
Gross profit		$ 86,000

Explanation: Different reporting terms are used for a manufacturing and merchandising company. In particular, the terms "finished goods" and "cost of goods manufactured" are used to reflect the production of goods. Yet the concepts and techniques of reporting cost of goods sold for a manufacturing company and merchandising company are similar.

3. A manufacturer's cost of goods manufactured is the sum of (a) **direct material,** (b) **direct labor,** and (c) **factory overhead** costs incurred in producing the product.

Demonstration Problem 2

It is important we understand the classification and assignment of costs. Consider the following company, **Chip Making Systems (CMS),** that manufactures computer chips. CMS incurs the following costs in manufacturing chips and in operating the company.

1. Plastic board used to mount the chip, $3.50 each.
2. Assembly worker pay of $15 per hour to attach chips to plastic board.
3. Salary for factory maintenance workers. These workers maintain factory equipment.
4. Factory foreman pay of $55,000 per year to supervise employees.
5. Real estate taxes paid on the factory, $14,500.
6. Real estate taxes paid on the company office, $6,000.
7. Depreciation costs on machinery used by workers, $30,000.
8. Salary paid to the chief financial officer, $95,000.
9. Advertising costs of $7,800 paid to promote products.
10. Salespersons' commissions of $.50 for each assembled chip sold.
11. Instead of producing and assembling chips, CMS could rent the manufacturing plant to store medical records for six local hospitals.

In the table below, classify each of these costs within the categories listed across the top of the chart. A cost can be classified under more than one category. The plastic board used to mount chips, for instance, is classified as a direct material product cost and as a direct unit cost.

	Period Costs	Product Costs			Unit Cost Classification		Sunk Cost	Opportunity Cost
Cost	Selling and Administrative	Direct Material (prime cost)	Direct Labor (prime and conversion cost)	Factory Overhead (conversion cost)	Direct	Indirect		
1. Plastic board used to mount the chip, $3.50 each		✔			✔			

Solution to Demonstration Problem 2

	Period Costs	Product Costs			Unit Cost Classification		Sunk Cost	Opportunity Cost
Cost*	Selling and Administrative	Direct Material (prime cost)	Direct Labor (prime and conversion cost)	Factory Overhead (conversion cost)	Direct	Indirect		
1.		✔			✔			
2.			✔		✔			
3.				✔		✔		
4.				✔		✔		
5.				✔		✔		
6.	✔							
7.				✔		✔	✔	
8.	✔							
9.	✔							
10.	✔							
11.								✔

* Costs 1–11 match the eleven cost items described above.

Glossary

Constraint anything that prevents a company from achieving higher performance in meeting its goals. (p. 837).

Continuous improvement a concept where every manager and employee continually looks for ways to improve operations. (p. 834).

Contribution margin a product's sale price less its total variable costs. (p. 838).

Contribution margin ratio a product's contribution margin divided by its sale price. (p. 839).

Control process of monitoring planning decisions, and evaluating the organization's activities and employees. (p. 821).

Controllable or not controllable cost a cost depending on the manager's responsibilities and whether or not he or she is in a position to make decisions on this cost. (p. 830).

Conversion costs expenditures incurred in the process of converting raw materials to finished goods—includes direct labor costs and factory overhead costs. (p. 828).

Customer orientation a company's managers and employees are in tune with the changing wants and needs of consumers. (p. 833).

Direct costs costs incurred for the benefit of one specific cost object. (p. 830).

Direct labor efforts of employees who physically convert materials to finished product. (p. 828).

Direct labor costs wages and salaries for direct labor that are separately and readily traced through the manufacturing process to finished goods. (p. 828).

Direct material raw material that physically becomes part of the product and is clearly identified with specific products or batches of product. (p. 826).

Direct material costs expenditures for direct material that are separately and readily traced through the manufacturing process to finished goods. (p. 827).

Factory overhead factory activities supporting the manufacturing process that are not direct material or direct labor. (p. 828).

Factory overhead costs expenditures for factory overhead that cannot be separately or readily traced to finished goods. (p. 828).

Finished goods inventory products that have completed the manufacturing process and are ready for sale. (p. 826).

Fixed cost cost that does not change with changes in the volume of activity. (p. 829).

Goods in process inventory products that are in the process of being manufactured but are not yet complete; also called *work in process inventory*. (p. 826).

Indirect costs costs incurred for the benefit of more than one cost object. (p. 830).

Indirect labor efforts of manufacturing employees who do not work specifically on converting direct materials into finished products and who are not clearly identified with specific units or batches of product. (p. 828).

Indirect material material used in support of the production process but not clearly identified with products or batches of product. (p. 826).

Just-in-time (JIT) manufacturing a company acquires or produces inventory only when needed. (p. 835).

Opportunity cost the potential benefit lost by choosing a specific action from two or more alternatives. (p. 831).

Out-of-pocket cost a cost requiring a future outlay of cash; relevant to current and future decisions. (p. 831).

Period costs expenditures identified more with a time period than with finished products costs—includes selling and general administrative expenses. (p. 831).

Planning process of setting goals and making plans to achieve them. (p. 820).

Prime costs expenditures directly identified with the manufacturing of finished goods—includes direct material costs and direct labor costs. (p. 828).

Product costs costs that are capitalized as inventory because they produce benefits that are expected to have future value—include direct materials, direct labor, and factory overhead. (p. 831).

Raw materials inventory goods a company acquires to use in making products. (p. 825).

Sunk cost a cost already incurred that cannot be avoided or changed. (p. 831).

Theory of constraints (TOC) practice of identifying factors that constrain, or limit, a company's operations. (p. 836).

Throughput the added value (selling price minus direct material costs) of finished products processed through the system. (p. 837).

Total quality management (TQM) a management concept under which all managers and employees at all stages of operations strive toward higher standards and a reduced number of defective units. (p. 834).

Variable cost cost that changes in proportion to changes in the volume of activity. (p. 829).

Questions

1. Discuss the role of the managerial accountant in business planning, control, and decision making.
2. Distinguish between managerial and financial accounting on:
   a. Users and decision makers
   b. Purposes of information
   c. Flexibility of practice
   d. Time dimension
   e. Focus of information
3. Explain differences in business activities and inventories between a manufacturing company, a merchandising company, and a service company.
4. Why does managerial accounting often involve working with numerous predictions and estimates?
5. How does an income statement and a balance sheet differ between a manufacturing company and a merchandising company?
6. Identify **NIKE**'s three inventory components (see NIKE's note 2) and reconcile this total to the amount reported on its balance sheet.
7. Besides inventories, what other assets often appear on balance sheets of manufacturers but not on balance sheets of merchandisers?
8. Why does a manufacturing company require three different inventory categories?
9. Distinguish between direct material and indirect material.
10. Distinguish between direct labor and indirect labor.
11. Distinguish between (a) factory overhead and (b) selling and administrative overhead.
12. What product cost is listed as both a prime cost and a conversion cost?
13. Assume you tour **Reebok**'s factory where they make basketball shoes for NBA teams. List three direct costs and three indirect costs you are likely to see.
14. Should we evaluate a manager's performance on the basis of controllable or noncontrollable costs? Why?
15. Explain why knowledge of cost behavior is useful in product performance evaluation.
16. Explain why product costs are capitalized but period costs are expensed in the current accounting period.
17. Identify changes a company must make when it adopts a customer orientation.
18. When a company employs total quality management throughout its operations, the responsibility for quality services and products shifts from ________ to ________. How does this shift relate to the concept of continuous improvement?
19. Explain why a traditional inventory system is labeled a *push* system and a just-in-time inventory system is labeled a *pull* system.
20. When managers apply the theory of constraints to a company's production process, what is their plan of action?
21. Define and describe unit contribution margin.
22. Define and explain the contribution margin ratio.
23. Describe the contribution margin ratio in layman's terms.
24. Why is the contribution margin ratio a useful measure for **NIKE** in deciding on what shoes to manufacture?

Quick Study

QS 19-1
Managerial accounting defined

Managerial accounting:

a. Must follow generally accepted accounting principles.
b. Provides information to aid management in the planning and controlling of business operations.
c. Is directed at reporting aggregate data on the company as a whole.
d. Provides information that is widely available to all interested parties.

QS 19-2
Managerial accounting versus financial accounting

Identify whether each description most likely applies to managerial or financial accounting:

a. ______ Its principles and practices are very flexible.
b. ______ Its primary users are company managers.
c. ______ Its primary focus is on the organization as a whole.
d. ______ Its information is often available only after an audit is complete.
e. ______ It's directed at external users in making investment, credit, and other decisions.

QS 19-3
Reporting inventory for manufacturers

Three inventory categories are reported on a manufacturing company's balance sheet: (1) raw materials, (2) goods in process, and (3) finished goods. Identify the usual order in which these inventory items are reported on a balance sheet.

a. (1)(2)(3) **b.** (2)(1)(3) **c.** (2)(3)(1) **d.** (3)(2)(1)

QS 19-4
Computing cost of goods sold

At year-end, a company has cost of goods manufactured of $4,000. It also has beginning finished goods inventory of $500, and ending finished goods inventory of $750. Its cost of goods sold is:

a. $4,250 **b.** $4,000 **c.** $3,750 **d.** $3,900

QS 19-5
Describing fixed and variable costs

Which one of these statements is true regarding fixed and variable costs?

a. Fixed and variable costs stay the same in total as volume increases.
b. Fixed and variable costs increase as volume increases.
c. Fixed costs stay the same and variable costs increase in total as volume increases.
d. Fixed costs increase and variable costs decrease in total as volume decreases.

QS 19-6
Describing product and period costs

Which one of these statements is true regarding product and period costs?

a. Sales commission is a product cost and factory rent is a period cost.
b. Factory wages is a product cost and direct material is a period cost.
c. Factory maintenance is a product cost and sales commission is a period cost.
d. Sales commission is a product cost and depreciation on factory equipment is a product cost.

QS 19-7
Describing management concepts

Match each management concept with its best description by entering its letter in the blank:

1. _____ Customer orientation	**a.** Focuses on factors that limit business operations.
2. _____ Total quality management	**b.** Inventory is acquired or produced only as needed.
3. _____ Just-in-time manufacturing	**c.** Flexible product designs that can be modified to accommodate customer choices.
4. _____ Theory of constraints	**d.** Every manager and employee constantly looks for ways to improve company operations.
5. _____ Continuous improvements	**e.** Focuses on quality throughout the production process.

QS 19-8
Contribution margin ratio

Compute and interpret the contribution margin ratio using the following data: Sales, $5,000; Total variable cost, $3,000.

QS 19-9
Computing cost of goods sold

Calculate cost of goods sold for year 2000 using the following information:

Finished goods inventory, December 31, 1999	$321,500
Goods in process inventory, December 31, 1999	74,550
Goods in process inventory, December 31, 2000	81,200
Cost of goods manufactured, year 2000	972,345
Finished goods inventory, December 31, 2000	297,200

Exercises

Exercise 19-1
Sources of accounting information

Both managerial accounting and financial accounting provide useful information to decision makers. Indicate in this chart the most likely source of information for each business decision (a decision can require major input from both sources):

Business decision	Primary Information Source:	
	Managerial	**Financial**
Estimate product cost for a new line of basketball shoes.		
Plan the budget for next quarter.		
Report financial performance to the board of directors.		
Measure profitability of all individual stores.		
Prepare financial reports according to GAAP.		
Determine amount of dividends to pay common stockholders.		
Determine location and size for a new plant.		
Evaluate a purchasing department's performance.		

Exercise 19-2
Planning and control descriptions

Complete the following statements by filling in the blanks:

1. __________ is the process of setting goals and making plans to achieve them.
2. __________ __________ usually covers a period of 5 to 10 years.
3. __________ __________ usually covers a period of one year.
4. __________ is the process of monitoring planning decisions and evaluating an organization's activities and employees.

Exercise 19-3
Characteristics of financial accounting and managerial accounting

C2

In the chart below compare financial accounting and managerial accounting by describing their differences on each of the seven items listed below. Be specific in your responses.

	Financial Accounting	**Managerial Accounting**
1. Users and decision makers		
2. Purpose of information		
3. Flexibility of practice		
4. Timeliness of information		
5. Time dimension		
6. Focus of information		
7. Nature of information		

Exercise 19-4
Identify and prepare balance sheets

C3

Current assets for two different companies at the end of calendar year 2000 are listed below. One is a manufacturer, Roller Blades Mfg., and the other, Wholesale Foods, is a grocery distribution company.

Required

1. Identify which set of numbers relates to the manufacturer and which to the merchandiser.
2. Prepare the current asset section for each company from the information below. Discuss why the current asset section is different for these two companies.

Account	Company 1	Company 2
Cash	$ 5,000	$ 7,000
Raw materials inventory		60,000
Merchandise inventory	40,000	
Goods in process inventory		50,000
Finished goods inventory		30,000
Accounts receivable	49,000	77,000
Prepaid expenses	2,000	1,000

Exercise 19-5
Identify and prepare income statements
C4, P1

Compute cost of goods sold for each of these two companies for the year ended December 31, 2000:

	The GAP Retail Company	GE Lighting Manufacturing
Beginning inventory:		
Merchandise	$250,000	
Finished goods		$500,000
Cost of Purchases	460,000	
Cost of goods manufactured		886,000
Ending inventory:		
Merchandise	150,000	
Finished goods		144,000

Exercise 19-6
Analyze and identify costs
C5, C6

The following costs are incurred by Procter & Gamble, a manufacturing company. (1) Classify each cost as either a product or a period cost. If a product cost, identify it as a prime and/or conversion cost. (2) Classify each cost as either a direct cost or an indirect cost using product as the cost object.

	Product Costs				
Cost	Prime	Conversion	Period Cost	Direct Cost	Indirect Cost
Direct materials used					
State and federal income taxes					
Payroll taxes for production supervisor					
Amortization of patents on factory machine . .					
Accident insurance on factory workers					
Wages to assembly workers					
Factory utilities					
Small tools used					
Bad debts expense					
Depreciation of factory building					
Advertising					
Office supplies used					

Exercise 19-7
Critical thinking about cost concepts
C5

Identify each of the 5 cost accounting concepts discussed in the chapter. Explain the purposes of identifying these separate cost accounting concepts.

Exercise 19-8
Analyze and categorize costs
C5

Listed below are product costs for the production of 1,000 soccer balls. Classify each cost as either fixed or variable, and as either direct or indirect. What pattern do you see regarding the relation between costs classified by behavior and costs classified by traceability?

	Cost by Behavior		Cost by Traceability	
Product Cost	Variable	Fixed	Direct	Indirect
Leather cover for soccer balls				
Lace to hold leather together				
Wages of assembly workers				
Taxes on factory				
Annual flat fee paid to a security company				
Water for cooling machinery				
Machinery depreciation				

Exercise 19-9
Customer orientation in practice
C7

Customer orientation means a company's managers and employees are responding to changing wants and needs of consumers. You are to stop at a restaurant, hotel, or other local business in your area and pick up a customer response card. On the right hand side of a sheet of paper write down the usual competitive forces: time, quality, cost, and flexibility of service. Attach the customer response card to the left side of the sheet. Draw arrows linking questions of the customer response card to the competitive forces. Identify how the response card provides information to management and employees to better meet competitive forces. Be prepared to form small groups to compare and contrast customer response cards across the types of businesses.

Exercise 19-10
Identify manufacturing management principles
C7, C8

The chart below lists 4 separate events affecting the managerial accounting systems for different companies. Match the manufacturing management principle(s) that is likely to be adopted by the company for the event identified. There is overlap in meaning between customer orientation and total quality management, and therefore, some responses can include more than one principle.

Event	Manufacturing Management Principle
_______ 1. The company starts measuring inventory turnover and discontinues elaborate inventory records. Its new focus is to pull inventory through the system.	a. Total quality management (TQM)
_______ 2. The company starts reporting measures on customer complaints and product returns from customers.	b. Just-in-time (JIT)
_______ 3. The company starts reporting measures such as the percent of defective products and the number of units scrapped.	c. Theory of constraints (TOC)
_______ 4. The company starts a program focusing on its bottlenecks.	d. Continuous improvement (CI)
	e. Customer orientation (CO)

Problems

Problem 19-1
Evaluate managerial accountant's role
C1, C8

This chapter includes a discussion of the objectives of managerial accounting along with a discussion on the current business environment. You are to look through the *automobile* section of your local newspaper—the Sunday paper is often best. Review advertisements of sport utility vehicles and take note of how many manufacturers offer these products and what factors they compete on.

Required

Discuss the potential contributions and responsibilities of the managerial accounting professional in helping an automobile manufacturer succeed. (*Hint:* Think about information and estimates a managerial accountant might provide new entrants into the sports utility market.)

Problem 19-2
Compute and evaluate ending inventory
C3, C8

Western Boot Company makes specialty boots for the rodeo circuit. On December 31, 1999, the company had (a) 500 boots in ending inventory valued at $100 per pair and (b) 1,500 heels valued at $5 each in raw materials inventory for boots to be made. During year 2000, the company purchased 50,000 heels at $5 each and manufactured 20,000 pairs of boots.

Required

Preparation Component

Check Figure Ending heel inventory, $57,500

1. Determine the unit and dollar amounts of raw materials inventory in heels at December 31, 2000.

Analysis Component

2. Write a one-page memorandum to the production manager explaining why a just-in-time inventory system for heels should be considered. Include in your memo the amount of working capital that can be reduced at December 31, 2000, if the ending heel raw material inventory is cut in half.

Problem 19-3
Computing and reporting inventory
C4, C5, P1
S

Shown below are the annual financial data at December 31, 2000, taken from two different companies.

	Sport World Retail	K2 Ski Manufacturing
Beginning inventory:		
Merchandise	$150,000	
Finished goods		$300,000
Cost of purchases	250,000	
Cost of goods manufactured		586,000
Ending inventory:		
Merchandise	100,000	
Finished goods		200,000

Required

1. Compute cost of goods sold at December 31, 2000, for each of the two companies. Include proper title and format in the solution.
2. Write a short memorandum to your instructor (a) identifying the inventory accounts and (b) describing where each is reported on the income statement and balance sheet.

Check Figure K2 Ski's cost of goods sold, $686,000

Problem 19-4
Explaining and contrasting costs
C5, C6

You must make a presentation to the marketing staff explaining the difference between product and period costs. Your supervisor tells you the marketing staff would also like clarification regarding prime and conversion costs and an explanation of how these terms fit with product and period cost. You are told that many on the staff are unable to identify with these terms in their merchandising activities.

Required

Write a one-page memorandum in proper form to your supervisor outlining your presentation to the marketing staff.

Problem 19-5
Compute, classify, and analyze costs
C5, A1

Listed below are costs for the production of 1,000 drum sets manufactured by Music Land. They sell for $300 each.

	Cost by Behavior		Cost by Function	
Costs	Variable	Fixed	Product	Period
Plastic for casing—$12,000	$12,000		$12,000	
Wages of assembly workers—$60,000				
Taxes on factory—$4,500				
Accounting staff's salary—$20,000				
Drum stands (1,000 stands outsourced)—$25,000				
Lease on equipment for sales staff—$7,000				
Upper management salaries—$100,000				
Annual flat fee for maintenance service—$9,000				
Sales commissions—$10 per unit				
Machinery deprecation—$10,000				

Required

Preparation Component

1. Classify costs and their amounts as (a) either fixed or variable and (b) either product or period (the first cost is completed as an example).

2. Compute the (a) contribution margin, and (b) contribution margin ratio by filling in the boxes in the table below.

Check Figure Total variable cost, $107,000

MUSIC LAND Contribution Margin Income Statement For the year ending December 31, 2000				
Sales ($300 × 1,000)		$[ ]		100%
Variable costs:				
Plastic for casing	$[ ]			
Wages of assembly	[ ]			
Drum stands	[ ]			
Sales commissions	[ ]			36%
Contribution margin		[ ]	Contribution margin ratio*	[ ]%

*Contribution margin ratio = (Contribution margin) Sales.

Analysis Component

3. What can we interpret from the contribution margin and the contribution margin ratio?

Problem 19-6
Projecting and estimating opportunity costs
C1, C5

Refer to *You Make the Call,* **Purchase Manager,** in this chapter. Assume you are the managerial accountant for the motorcycle manufacturer. The purchasing manager asks you about preparing an estimate of the related costs for buying motorcycle seats from supplier (B). She tells you this estimate is needed because unless dollar estimates are attached to nonfinancial factors, such as lost production costs, her supervisor will not give it full attention. The purchase manager also shows you the following information:

- Production output is 1,000 motorcycles per year based on 250 production days a year.
- Production time per day is 8 hours at a cost of $2,000 per hour to run the production line.
- Lost production time due to poor quality is 1%.
- Satisfied customers purchase, on average, three motorcycles during a lifetime.
- Satisfied customers recommend the product, on average, to 5 other people.
- Marketing estimates that using seat (B) will result in 5 lost customers per year from repeat business and referrals.
- Average contribution margin per motorcycle is $3,000.

Required

Check Figure Cost of lost production, $40,000

Estimate the costs of buying motorcycle seats from supplier (B). This problem requires you to think creatively and make reasonable estimates and, therefore, there is more than one correct answer. [*Hint:* Reread the answer to *You Make the Call* and think about costs of lost production time, repeat business, and similar factors.]

Problem 19-7
Projecting and estimating sales and costs; contribution margin analysis
C7, C8, A1

Food King grocery store chain, a market leader, is trying to increase sales to its existing customers by creating a customer orientation in meeting buyer needs and wants. Assume you're hired as a consultant by Food King to analyze its operations and suggest improvements. Food King wants to increase its contribution margin by $40,000.

Required

1. To increase sales and total contribution margin from existing customers of Food King, offer three improvements that you have observed in other stores and feel would be successful at Food King.
2. What level of increase in sales is necessary for Food King to increase total contribution margin by $40,000? (Hint: With each suggestion in part (1), identify the expected sales dollars and the contribution margin ratio to meet the $40,000 increase in contribution margin.)

Problem 19-8
Manufacturing management principles in practice

C8

A trip through a drive-up window of any leading fast food restaurant is useful in understanding manufacturing management principles such as total quality management (TQM), just-in-time (JIT), theory of constraints (TOC), and continuous improvement (CI). Each restaurant can be viewed as a small manufacturing plant. List two fast food restaurants you are familiar with in the first column of the table below (examples are McDonald's, Taco Bell, Burger King, and KFC). Record in the table how each company is putting each of these principles into action, both favorably and unfavorably.

Restaurant	TQM	JIT	TOC	CI

BEYOND THE NUMBERS

Reporting in Action

C1, C2

Managerial accounting is more than recording, maintaining, and reporting financial results. Managerial accountants must provide managers with both financial and nonfinancial information including estimates, projections, and forecasts. But looking into the future involves risk. **NIKE**'s managers, including its managerial accountants, must notify shareholders of this risk.

Required

1. Read the Management Discussion and Analysis in NIKE's annual report in Appendix A. What risks do NIKE's shareholders face as management and employees work to position the company for long-term success?
2. What is the managerial accountants' role and responsibilities in evaluating risk?

Swoosh Ahead

3. Obtain NIKE's annual report information for a fiscal year ending after May 31, 1997. You can get this information from either its Web site [**www.nike.com**] or the SEC's EDGAR database [**www.sec.gov**]. Answer the questions in (1) and (2) after reading the Management Discussion and Analysis section. Identify any major changes in this section for the report you collect compared with the one shown in Appendix A.

Comparative Analysis

C3, C8

NIKE and **Reebok** are primarily manufacturing companies. Answer the following questions using these companies' financial information reported in Appendix A.

Required

1. Review the balance sheets of each company and then identify and record clues indicating that each is a manufacturing company.
2. Search the notes to NIKE's financial statements for evidence that it is a manufacturing company. Record your evidence.
3. Compute inventory turnover (using ending inventory in the denominator) and days' sales in inventory for the most recent two years reported for each company. Interpret both ratios.
4. What likely impact would a just-in-time inventory system have on the turnover values in part (3)?

Ethics Challenge
C1, C5, C6

You are the managerial accountant at Music Production, a manufacturer of audio tapes, CDs, and record albums. The financial reporting year-end for this company is December 31. The chief financial officer is concerned about having enough cash to pay the expected corporate tax bill because of poor cash flow management. On November 15, the purchasing department purchased excess inventory of CD raw materials in anticipation of rapid growth of this product beginning in January. To decrease the company's tax liability, the chief financial officer tells you to record the purchase of this inventory as a supply and expense it in the current year. This action decreases tax liability by increasing expenses.

Required

1. Where should the purchase of CD raw materials be recorded?
2. How should you respond to this request?

Communicating in Practice

Write a memorandum to a prospective college student about salary expectations for graduates in business. Compare and contrast the expected salaries for accounting (including different subfields such as public, corporate, tax, audit, and so forth), marketing, management, and finance majors. Prepare a graph showing average starting salaries (and salaries for experienced professionals if available). To get this information, stop by your school's career services office; libraries also have this information. The following Web site can get you started: **http://jobsmart.org** (click on *Salary Info*).

Taking It to the Net
C1, C2

Managerial accounting professionals follow a code of ethics. As a member of the Institute of Management Accountants, the managerial accountant must comply with its Standards of Ethical Conduct. Identify and record the *Standards of Ethical Conduct for Management Accountants* posted on the following Web site: [**www.rutgers.edu/Accounting /raw/ima/imaethic.htm**].

Teamwork in Action
C3, C4, C5, C6, P1

Your team is to select a manufactured product that each is familiar with. The team is responsible for preparing a list of all product components and costs necessary to manufacture this product.

Required

1. Identify each of the product costs as direct materials, direct labor, or factory overhead. Provide an explanation for your classification.
2. Identify all period costs this manufacturer is likely to incur.
3. Prepare to report this cost information in class. Be prepared to explain where period and product costs are reported in financial statements. (Note: Each teammate can assume the responsibility for a different part of the presentation.)

Hitting the Road
C1, C5

Visit your favorite fast food restaurant. Observe its business operations. It may be helpful to introduce yourself to the manager and explain that you are doing field research for your class. You might request an opportunity to see business activities that customers do not normally observe.

Required

1. Describe all business activities from the time a customer arrives to the time a customer departs.
2. List all costs you can identify with the activities described in part (1).
3. Classify each cost from (2) as fixed or variable, and explain your classification.

Business Week Activity

C1, C2, C7, C8

The success or failure of many companies depends on the profits earned between October 15 and December 24 of any year. Read the article "Why Win98's Delay Is O.K." in the September 29, 1997, issue of ***Business Week.***

Required

1. Why are businesses—manufacturing, distribution, and retail—concerned about the release of Win98 by **Microsoft**? Does the managerial accounting professional need to know about the release of products and customer reactions to any products others than the ones his or her company sells?
2. Assume you make keyboards for **Dell Computer.** Write a one-page memorandum to your company's management outlining the possible impact on your product, knowing that Microsoft has delayed the release of its most recent operating system upgrade.

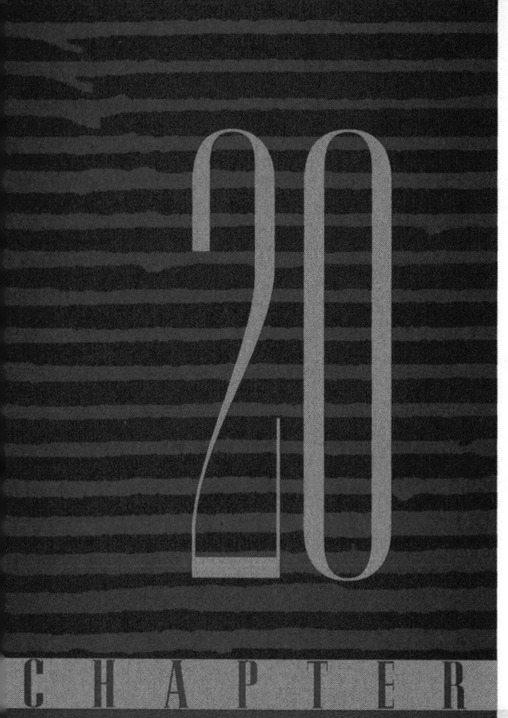

Manufacturing and Job Order Cost Accounting

A Look Back

Chapter 19 introduced us to managerial accounting. We compared it to financial accounting and explained basic cost concepts. We also described several modern manufacturing management principles that are changing the way companies conduct and account for business.

A Look at This Chapter

We begin this chapter by explaining the preparation of a manufacturing statement and describing the accounting system for manufacturing activities. We also explain how to measure costs in job order production companies and describe the procedures of a job order costing system.

A Look Ahead

Chapter 21 looks at how we measure costs in process production industries. We explain process production in detail, describe how to assign costs to processes, and compute and analyze the cost per equivalent unit.

Chapter Outline

Slippery Slopes

MEMPHIS, TN—Roger Worth thought he knew it all. He already had three years' experience with an on-line service provider as an executive assistant. Yet, since starting his new job as a junior manager with Dillon Snowboards, an upstart manufacturer of custom snowboards, he felt as if he was a rookie.

The worst occurred during Worth's second week at Dillon's. He was given two cost accounting projects termed "high priority" for use in setting prices of snowboards. One was to determine the cost of goods manufactured for the most recent six months of activity. The second was to compute the cost of producing an order of 90 custom snowboards for a mountain resort. Says Worth, "It was a chance to show off my quantitative skills."

Worth devoted much time and energy to both tasks. He obtained a mountain of manufacturing data from the production manager and presented a detailed report to his supervisor. After reading the report, his supervisor called Worth into her office, looked him straight in the eyes, and said: "This report is seriously incomplete. There's not even details on overhead and the allocation procedures used for our snowboards' manufacturing statement. And don't forget, we're a *custom snowboard manufacturer.*"

Worth returned to his office determined to address the supervisor's challenge. "I read everything I could get on custom manufacturing, job order manufacturing, and cost accounting," says Worth. "I learned that custom manufacturers require special accounting procedures and reports. I also learned about overhead and its potential impact for job order costing."

Two weeks later Worth submitted his revised report. "The supervisor said my new report was first rate. She said it'd be useful in making her case for some snowboard price adjustments." Added Worth, "I'm still learning. But I won't make the same mistake again." Somehow, one gets the feeling his supervisor will see to it!

Learning Objectives

Conceptual

C1 Explain manufacturing activities and the flow of manufacturing costs.

C2 Describe important features of job order manufacturing.

C3 Explain job cost sheets and how they are used in job order cost accounting.

Procedural

P1 Prepare a manufacturing statement and explain its purpose and links to financial statements.

P2 Describe and record the flow of materials costs in job order cost accounting.

P3 Describe and record the flow of labor costs in job order cost accounting.

P4 Describe and record the flow of overhead costs in job order cost accounting.

P5 Determine adjustments for overapplied and underapplied factory overhead.

Analytical

A1 Apply multiple overhead allocation rates in assigning overhead to products.

CHAPTER PREVIEW

We described managerial concepts and principles, along with differences between merchandising and manufacturing companies, in Chapter 19. In this chapter, we spend more time understanding how manufacturing activities are accounted for. We explain how to prepare a manufacturing statement and determine cost of goods manufactured. We also describe two different systems for assigning costs to the movement of goods through the production process. This is often called assigning cost flows to product flows. A *job order cost accounting system* provides information for decision making using a *perpetual inventory system.* A perpetual system provides a continuous record of materials, goods in process, and finished goods on hand. It is also increasingly popular in practice, especially by those companies benefiting from knowing current inventory levels. Job order costing is frequently used by manufacturers of custom products or small groups of custom products.

Manufacturing Activities and Information

C1 Explain manufacturing activities and the flow of manufacturing costs.

Manufacturing activities of a company are described in a special financial report called the **manufacturing statement.** This report is also called the *schedule of manufacturing activities* or the *schedule of cost of goods manufactured.* The manufacturing statement summarizes the types and amounts of costs incurred in a company's manufacturing process. To understand the manufacturing statement, we must first understand the flow of manufacturing costs and activities.

Flow of Manufacturing Activities

Exhibit 20.1 shows the flow of manufacturing activities for Rocky Mountain Bikes. This exhibit has three important sections: *materials activity, production activity* and *marketing activity.* We explain each of these activities in this section.

Exhibit 20.1

Activities and Cost Flows in Manufacturing

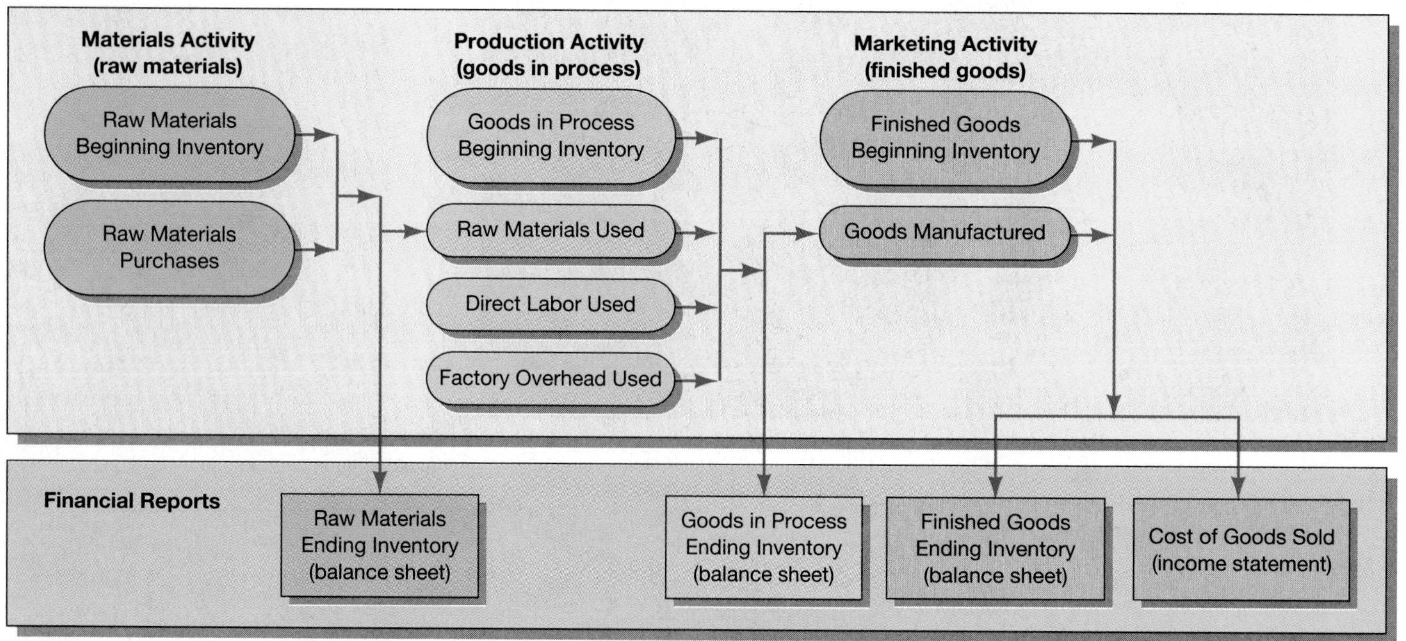

Materials Activity

The left column of Exhibit 20.1 shows the flow of raw materials. Rocky Mountain bikes, like most manufacturers, usually starts a period with some beginning raw materials inventory. This is shown as carried over from the previous period. During the current period, the company acquires additional raw materials. When these purchases are added to beginning inventory, we get total raw materials available for use in production. These raw materials are then either used in production in the current period or remain on hand at the end of the period for use in future periods.

Production Activity

The middle column of Exhibit 20.1 describes production activity. Four factors come together in production. They are beginning goods in process inventory, direct materials, direct labor, and overhead. Beginning goods in process inventory consists of partly assembled bikes from the previous period.

Production activity results in bikes that are either finished or remain unfinished. The cost of finished bikes makes up the cost of goods manufactured for the current period. Unfinished bikes are identified as ending goods in process inventory. The cost of unfinished bikes consists of direct materials, direct labor, and factory overhead. This cost is reported on the current period's balance sheet. The costs of both finished goods manufactured and goods in process are *product costs.*

Marketing Activity

The company's marketing activity is portrayed in the right column of Exhibit 20.1. Newly completed units are combined with beginning finished goods inventory to make up total finished goods available for sale in the current period. The cost of finished bikes sold is reported on the income statement as cost of goods sold. The cost of bikes not sold is reported on the current period's balance sheet as ending finished goods inventory.

Manufacturing Statement

> **P1** Prepare a manufacturing statement and explain its purpose and links to financial statements.

Exhibit 20.2 shows the manufacturing statement for Rocky Mountain Bikes. It reports costs of both materials and production activities as described in Exhibit 20.1. The statement is divided into four parts: *direct material, direct labor, overhead,* and *computation of cost of goods manufactured.* We describe each of these parts in this section.

① The manufacturing statement begins by computing direct materials used. We start by adding beginning raw materials inventory of $8,000 to the current period's purchases of $86,500. This yields $94,500 of total raw materials available for use. A physical count of inventory shows $9,000 of ending raw materials inventory. We then compute total cost of direct raw materials used during the period as $85,500. This is computed by subtracting the $9,000 ending inventory from the $94,500 total raw materials available for use.

② The second part of the manufacturing statement reports direct labor costs. Rocky Mountain Bikes had total direct labor cost of $60,000 for the period. This amount includes payroll taxes and fringe benefits.

③ The third part of the manufacturing statement reports overhead costs. The statement lists each important factory overhead item along with its cost. Total factory overhead cost for the period is $30,000. Some companies report only total factory overhead on the manufacturing statement and attach a separate schedule listing individual overhead costs. Total manufacturing costs for the period are $175,500, computed as $85,500 + $60,000 + $30,000. This is the sum of direct materials used, direct labor incurred, and overhead costs incurred.

④ The final section of the manufacturing statement computes and reports the *cost of goods manufactured.* First, total manufacturing costs are added to beginning goods in process inventory. This gives the total goods in process inventory of $178,000, computed as $175,500 plus $2,500. We then compute the current period's cost of goods manufactured of $170,500 by subtracting the cost of ending goods in process inventory of $7,500 from the total goods in process of $178,000. The amount of $7,500 assigned to the end-

Exhibit 20.2a

Manufacturing Statement

ROCKY MOUNTAIN BIKES Manufacturing Statement For Year Ended December 31, 2000			
①	**Direct materials:**		
	Raw materials inventory, December 31, 1999	$ 8,000	
	Raw materials purchases	86,500	
	Raw materials available for use	94,500	
	Raw materials inventory, December 31, 2000	(9,000)	
	Direct materials used		$ 85,500
②	**Direct labor**		60,000
③	**Factory overhead:**		
	Indirect labor	9,000	
	Factory supervision	6,000	
	Factory utilities	2,600	
	Repairs, factory equipment	2,500	
	Property taxes, factory building	1,900	
	Factory supplies used	600	
	Factory insurance expired	1,100	
	Small tools written off	200	
	Depreciation, factory equipment	3,500	
	Depreciation, factory building	1,800	
	Amortization, patents	800	
	Total factory overhead costs		30,000
④	Total manufacturing costs		$175,500
	Add goods in process inventory, December 31, 1999		2,500
	Total cost of goods in process		$178,000
	Deduct goods in process inventory, December 31, 2000		(7,500)
	Cost of goods manufactured		$170,500

ing goods in process inventory consists of direct materials, direct labor, and factory overhead. The cost of goods manufactured amount is also called *net cost of goods manufactured* or *cost of goods completed.* Exhibit 19.9 shows that this item and amount are listed in the cost of goods sold section of Rocky Mountain Bikes' income statement.

Since Rocky Mountain Bikes includes a detailed list of overhead costs in its manufacturing statement, we show the alternative use of a supporting schedule in Exhibit 20.2b. The manufacturing statement includes total factory overhead in its computation of cost of goods manufactured. Cost of goods manufactured is then carried to the income statement and shown as part of cost of goods sold.

Exhibit 20.2b

Overhead Cost Flows across Accounting Reports

Rocky Mountain Bikes Schedule of Overhead Items For Year Ended December 31, 2000	
Indirect labor	$ 9,000
Supervision	6,000
Other overhead items*	15,000
Total overhead	$30,000

*Overhead items are listed in Exhibit 20.2a.

Rocky Mountain Bikes Manufacturing Statement For Year Ended December 31, 2000	
Direct materials	$ 85,500
Direct labor	60,000
Factory overhead	30,000
Total Manuf. costs	$175,500
Beg. goods in process	2,500
Total goods in process	$178,000
End. goods in process	(7,500)
Cost of goods manuf.	$170,500

Rocky Mountain Bikes Income Statement For Year Ended December 31, 2000		
Sales		$310,000
Cost of goods sold:		
Beg. finished goods	$ 11,200	
Cost of goods manuf.	170,500	
End. finished goods	(10,300)	
Cost of goods sold		$171,400
Gross profit		$138,600
Expenses		(59,900)
Income taxes		(32,600)
Net income		$ 46,100

Information in the manufacturing statement is used by management in planning and controlling the company's manufacturing activities. To provide timely information for decision making, the statement is often prepared monthly, weekly, or even daily. While the manufacturing statement contains information useful to external users, it is not a general-purpose financial statement. Most companies view this information as proprietary and potentially harmful to the company if released to competitors. As a result companies rarely publish the manufacturing statement.

Flash back

1. A manufacturing statement: *(a)* computes cost of goods manufactured for the period, *(b)* computes cost of goods sold for the period, or *(c)* reports operating expenses incurred for the period.
2. Do GAAP require companies to report a manufacturing statement?
3. How are both beginning and ending goods in process inventories reported on a manufacturing statement?

Answers—p. 877

The Inventory System and Accounting for Costs

This section explains the accounting methods used to compile the costs reported in the manufacturing statement. We begin with a brief discussion of accounting for manufacturing activities using a general accounting system. But our main emphasis is describing accounting for manufacturing activities using a cost accounting system.

General Accounting System

A **general accounting system** records manufacturing activities using a *periodic* inventory system. A periodic inventory system measures costs of raw materials, goods in process, and finished goods from physical counts of quantities on hand at the end of each period. This information is used to compute amounts of the product used, finished, and sold during a period.

Some companies still use a general accounting system. But the frequency of a general accounting system in practice is declining. Competitive forces and customer demands have increased pressure on companies to better manage inventories. This means an increasing number of companies need more timely and precise information on inventories than is provided by a general accounting system.*

Cost Accounting System

An ever-increasing number of companies use a cost accounting system to generate timely and accurate inventory information. A **cost accounting system** records manufacturing activities using a *perpetual* inventory system. A perpetual system continuously updates records for costs of materials, goods in process, and finished goods inventories.

A cost accounting system gives us timely information about inventories and changes in inventories. It also gives us timely information about manufacturing costs per unit of product. This is especially helpful for managers in efforts to control costs and determine selling prices. There are two basic types of cost accounting systems: *job order cost accounting* and *process cost accounting.* We describe the first type, job order cost accounting, in this chapter. The second type, process cost accounting, is explained in the next chapter.

* Appendix 20A illustrates the closing process for a manufacturer using a general accounting system. The other parts of the accounting cycle are similar across the two accounting systems.

Job Order Cost Accounting

This section describes a job order manufacturing and cost accounting system. It is important for us to understand a job order manufacturing system and its activities before we can understand the accounting for them. We explain the costing system used by job order manufacturers in this section.

Job Order Manufacturing

C2 Describe important features of job order manufacturing.

Many companies manufacture products individually designed to meet the needs of each customer. Each of these unique products is manufactured separately and their production is called job order manufacturing. **Job order manufacturing,** also called *customized production,* is the production of products in response to special orders.

The production of a unique product is called a **job.** Items that might be produced as jobs include a special machine tool, a building, an airplane, and a piece of custom-made jewelry. They are made to meet the unique demands of specific customers. This type of manufacturing system is likely to be flexible in the number of different products it can produce.

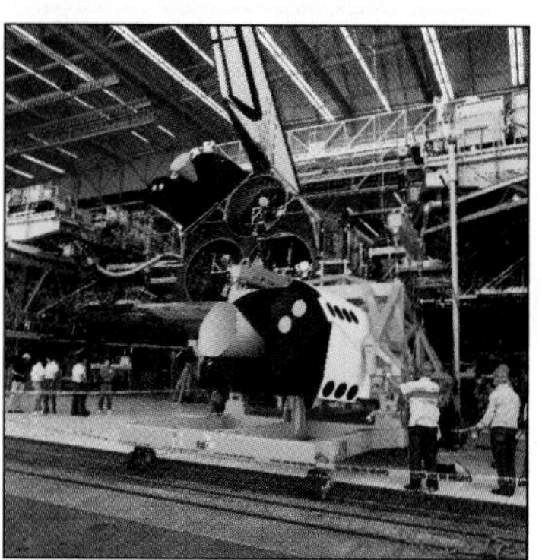

McDonnell Douglas's aerospace division is one example of a job order manufacturing system. Its primary business is twofold: (1) design, development, and integration of space carriers and (2) systems engineering and integration of Department of Defense (DoD) systems. Each order is usually unique.

When a job involves producing more than one unit of a unique product, it is often called a **job lot.** Products produced as job lots might include benches for a church, imprinted T-shirts for a 10K race or company picnic, and advertising signs for a chain of stores. Although these orders involve more than one unit, the volume of production is typically low. For example, 50 benches, 200 T-shirts, or 100 advertising signs.

Another feature of job order manufacturing is the diversity, often called *heterogeneity,* of the products manufactured. Each customer order is likely to be different from another in some respect. These variations can be minor or major. T-shirts for a 10K race, for instance, are different from those for a company or family picnic.

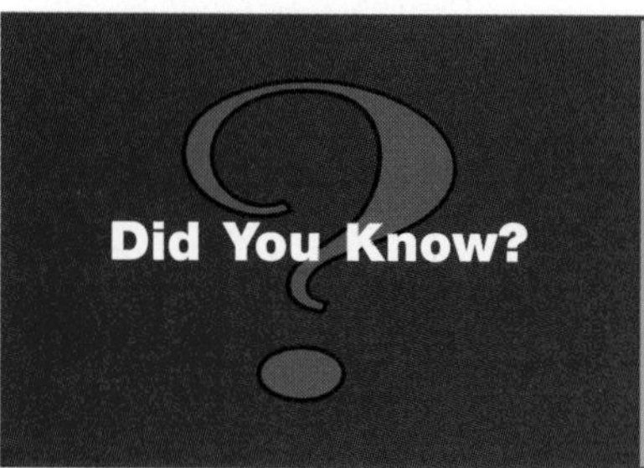

Build-to-Order Computers

Personal computers are often similar to one another. But **Dell Computer** broke with tradition and adopted a build-to-order strategy. Dell bypasses distributors and sells directly to customers. It builds a customized PC for every buyer and sells at below retailer prices. Dell's build-to-order strategy makes it one of the fastest growing companies. Other computer manufacturers, including Hewlett-Packard and Apple, are trying to copy Dell's strategy. [Source: *Business Week,* September 29, 1997.]

It is important to note that the job order system is equally applicable to both manufacturing *and* service companies. Most service companies meet customers' needs by performing a unique service for each customer. Examples of such services include an accountant's audit of a client's financial statements, an interior designer's remodeling of an office, a wedding consultant's planning and supervision of a reception, and a lawyer's defense of a client in a lawsuit. Whether the setting is manufacturing or services, job order operations involve meeting the needs of customers by producing or performing unique jobs.

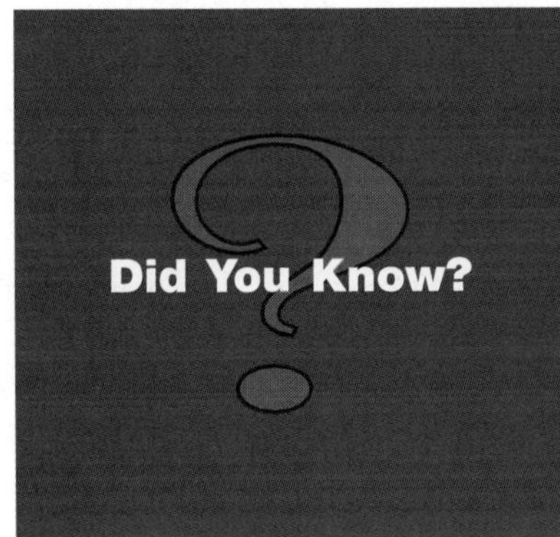

Job Order Colleges

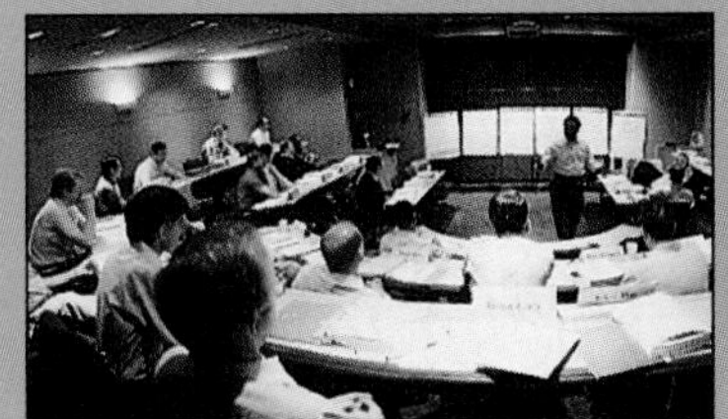

Demand for executive education is rising and colleges are developing customized educational programs for companies. These programs generate huge revenues for colleges. At **Babson College,** where customized programs are a focus, revenues have more than doubled in the past five years to more than $6.4 million. Custom programs offered by **Wharton, Babson, Harvard, Stanford,** and others create job order costs that must be traced to help colleges compute proper fees. [Source: *Business Week,* October 20, 1997.]

Events in Job Order Manufacturing

The initial event in a normal job order manufacturing operation is the receipt of a customer's order for a unique product. This causes the manufacturer to begin work on a job. A less common case is when management decides to begin work on a job before a contract is signed with a customer. This is referred to as *jobs manufactured on speculation.*

The first step in both cases is to predict the cost of completing the job. This cost depends on the design of the product—prepared by either the customer or the manufacturer. The second step is to negotiate a sales price and decide whether to pursue the job. Some jobs are priced on a *cost-plus basis.* This means the customer pays the manufacturer for costs incurred on the job plus a negotiated amount or rate of profit. The third step is for the manufacturer to schedule production of the job to meet the customer's needs and to fit within its own production capacity. This work schedule should take into account workplace facilities including tools, machinery, and supplies. Once this schedule is complete, the manufacturer can place orders for raw materials. Production occurs as materials and labor are applied to the job.

An overview of job order production activity is shown in Exhibit 20.3. This exhibit shows the March production activity of **Road Warriors.** Road Warriors manufactures security-equipped cars and trucks. They take any brand vehicle and give it a diversity of security items. These items include special alarms, reinforced exterior, bulletproof glass, and bomb detectors. The company began by catering to high profile celebrities but has grown dramatically as it now caters to anyone who wants added security in a vehicle.

Job Order Manufacturing Activities

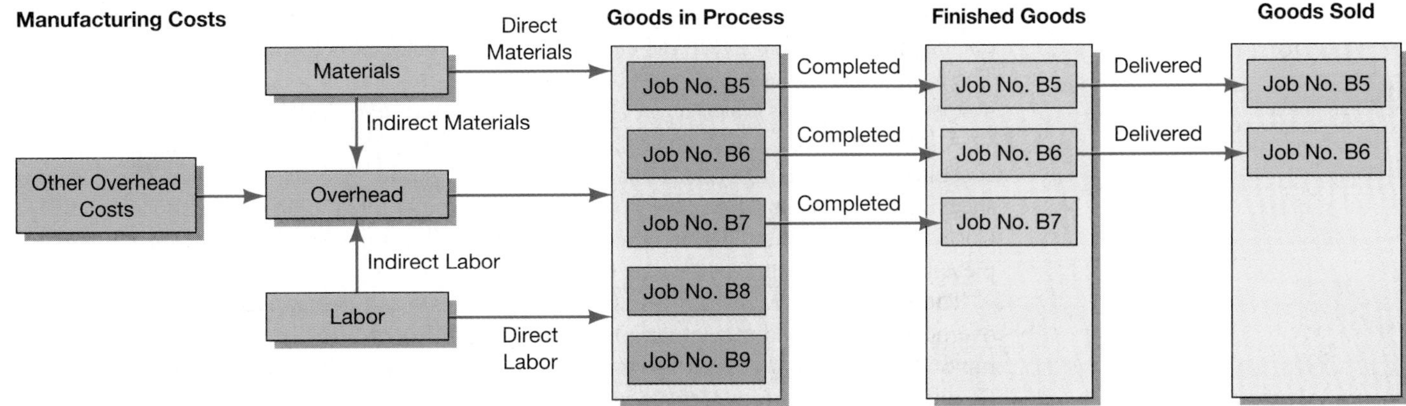

Job order manufacturing for Road Warriors requires materials, labor, and overhead costs. Recall that direct materials are goods used in manufacturing that are clearly identified with a particular job. Similarly, direct labor is efforts devoted to a particular job. Overhead costs support production of more than one job. Common overhead items are depreciation on factory buildings and equipment, factory supplies, supervision, maintenance, cleaning, and utilities.

Exhibit 20.3 shows materials, labor, and overhead are added to Job Numbers B5, B6, B7, B8, and B9 during March. Road Warriors completed Jobs B5, B6, and B7 in March, and delivered Jobs B5 and B6 to customers. At the end of March, Jobs B8 and B9 remain in goods in process inventory and Job B7 is in finished goods inventory. Labor and materials are also divided into their direct and indirect components. Their indirect costs are added to overhead. Total overhead cost is then allocated to the various jobs.

Flash back

4. Which of these products is likely to involve job order manufacturing? *(a)* Inexpensive watches; *(b)* Racing bikes; *(c)* Bottled soft drinks.
5. What is the difference between a job and a job lot?

Answers—p. 877

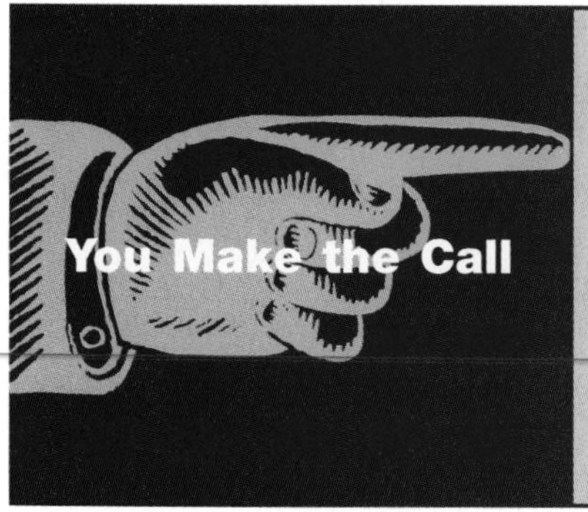

Management Consultant

You recently join a management consulting company. One of your first tasks is to control and manage costs for the consulting company. At the end of your first month, you find that three consulting jobs are completed and two are 60% complete. Each of the unfinished consulting jobs is estimated to cost $10,000 and to earn a revenue of $12,000. You are unsure about how to recognize goods in process inventory and record costs and revenues. First, do you expect to recognize any inventory? If yes, how much? Second, how much revenue is recorded for the unfinished jobs in your first month?

Answer—p. 876

Job Order Cost Sheet

C3 Explain job cost sheets and how they are used in job order cost accounting.

Much of the accounting information that managers of job order cost operations use to plan and control production activities is not stored in general ledger accounts. This is because the information often involves very detailed data. Instead it is usually stored in subsidiary records controlled by general ledger accounts. Subsidiary records can store information about raw materials, overhead costs, jobs in process, finished goods, and other items. This section describes use of these records with job order cost accounting.

A major aim of a **job order cost accounting system** is to determine the cost of producing each job or job lot. In the case of a job lot, it also aims to compute the cost per unit. The accounting system must include separate records for each job to accomplish this. The system must capture information about costs incurred and charge these costs to the jobs.

A **job cost sheet** is a separate record maintained for each job. Exhibit 20.4 shows a job cost sheet for an alarm system that Road Warriors produced for a customer. This job cost sheet identifies the customer, the number assigned to the job, the product, and various dates. Costs incurred on the job are immediately recorded on this sheet. When each job is complete, the supervisor enters the date of completion, records any remarks, and signs the sheet.

The job cost sheet in Exhibit 20.4 classifies costs as direct materials, direct labor, or overhead. It shows direct materials are added to Job B15 on four different dates totaling $600. The seven entries for direct labor costs total $1,000. Road Warriors allocates (applies, assigns, or charges) overhead costs of $1,600 to this job using an allocation rate of 160% of direct labor cost, computed as 160% × $1,000.

Exhibit 20.4
Job Cost Sheet

Road Warriors **Los Angeles, California**

•Job Cost Sheet•

Customer's Name: Carroll Connor Job No.: B15

Address: 1542 High Point Dr. City & State: Portland, Oregon

Job Description: Level I Alarm System on Ford Expedition

Date promised: March 15 Date started: March 3 Date completed: March 11

Direct Materials			Direct Labor			Manufacturing Overhead		
Date	Requisition	Cost	Date	Time Ticket	Cost	Date	Rate	Cost
3/3/2000	R-4698	100.00	3/3/2000	L-3393	120.00	3/11/2000	160% of Direct Labor Cost	1,600.00
3/7/2000	R-4705	225.00	3/4/2000	L-3422	150.00			
3/9/2000	R-4725	180.00	3/5/2000	L-3456	180.00			
3/10/2000	R-4777	95.00	3/8/2000	L-3479	60.00			
			3/9/2000	L-3501	90.00			
			3/10/2000	L-3535	240.00			
			3/11/2000	L-3559	160.00			
Total		600.00	Total		1,000.00	Total		1,600.00

REMARKS: Completed job on March 11, and shipped to customer on March 15. Met all specifications and requirements.

SUMMARY:	
Materials	600.00
Labor	1,000.00
Overhead	1,600.00
Total cost	3,200.00

Signed: C. Luther, Supervisor

While a job is being manufactured, its accumulated costs are kept in **goods in process inventory.** The collection of job cost sheets for all of the jobs in process make up a subsidiary ledger controlled by the Goods in Process Inventory account in the general ledger. Managers use job cost sheets to monitor costs incurred to date and to predict and control costs for each job.

When a job is finished, its job cost sheet is completed and moved from the file of jobs in process to the file of finished jobs awaiting delivery to customers. This latter file acts as a subsidiary ledger controlled by the **Finished Goods Inventory** account. When a finished job is delivered to the customer, the job cost sheet is moved to a permanent file supporting the total cost of goods sold. This permanent file contains records from both current and prior periods.

Flash back

6. Which of these statements is correct?
   a. The collection of job cost sheets for unfinished jobs makes up a subsidiary ledger controlled by the Goods in Process account.
   b. Job cost sheets are financial statements provided to investors.
   c. A separate job cost sheet is maintained in the General Ledger for each job in process.
7. What three costs are normally accumulated on job cost sheets?

Answers—p. 877

Materials Cost Flows and Documents

P2 Describe and record the flow of materials costs in job order cost accounting.

This section and the next two explain the flow of costs and related documents in a job order cost accounting system. We focus on the three cost components: (1) materials, (2) labor, and (3) overhead. Materials cost flows are described in this section, and labor and overhead costs in the following sections.

Materials

We begin our analysis of the flow of materials cost by looking at Exhibit 20.5. When materials are first received from suppliers, the employees count and inspect them. They record the quantity and cost of items on a receiving report. The receiving report serves as the *source document* for recording materials received in both the materials ledger card and in the general ledger. In nearly all job order cost systems, **materials ledger cards** are perpetual records that are updated each time units are purchased and each time units are issued for use in production.

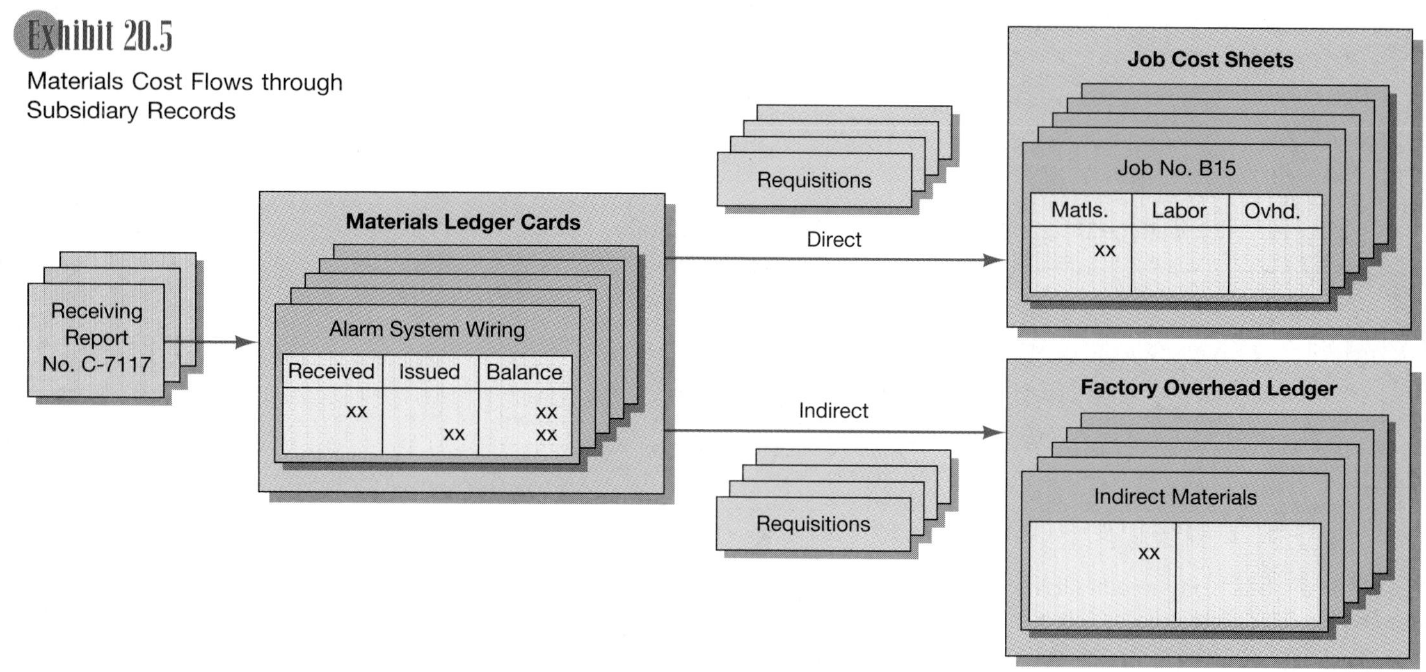

Materials Cost Flows through Subsidiary Records

Exhibit 20.5 shows that materials can be requisitioned for use either on a specific job (direct materials) or as overhead (indirect materials). Cost of direct materials flows from the materials ledger card to the job cost sheet. The cost of indirect materials flows from the materials ledger card to the Indirect Materials account in the factory overhead ledger. The factory overhead ledger is a subsidiary ledger controlled by the Factory Overhead account in the general ledger.

Exhibit 20.6 shows a materials ledger card for material used by Road Warriors. The card identifies the item as alarm system wiring. The card also shows the item's stock number, its location in the storeroom, information about the maximum and minimum quantities that should be on hand, and the reorder quantity. Notice that alarm system wiring is issued and recorded on March 7, 2000. The job cost sheet in Exhibit 20.4 shows this wiring is used in Job No. B15.

Materials Ledger Card

Road Warriors

Item *Alarm system wiring* Stock No. *M–347* Location in Storeroom *Bin 137*

Maximum quantity *5 units* Minimum quantity *1 unit* Quantity to reorder *2 units*

	Received				Issued				Balance		
Date	Receiving Report Number	Units	Unit Price	Total Price	Requisition Number	Units	Unit Price	Total Price	Units	Unit Price	Total Price
									1	225.00	225.00
3/ 4/2000	C-7117	2	225.00	450.00					3	225.00	675.00
3/ 7/2000					R–4705	1	225.00	225.00	2	225.00	450.00

When materials are needed in production, a production manager prepares a **materials requisition** and sends it to the materials manager. The requisition shows the job number, the type of material, the quantity needed, and the signature of the manager authorized to make the requisition. Exhibit 20.7 shows the materials requisition for alarm system wiring for Job No. B15. To see how this requisition ties to the flow of costs, compare the information on the requisition with the March 7, 2000, data in Exhibits 20.4 and 20.6.

Exhibit 20.7

Materials Requisition

Road Warriors

MATERIALS REQUISITION NUMBER R-4705

Job No.	B15	Date	3/7/2000
Material Stock No.	M-347	Material Description	Alarm system wiring
Quantity Requested	1	Requested By	C. Luther
Quantity Provided	1	Date Provided	3/7/2000
Filled By	M. Bateman	Material Received By	C. Luther
Remarks			

Use of alarm system wiring on Job No. B15 yields the following journal entry (locate this cost item in the job cost sheet shown in Exhibit 20.4):

Mar. 7	Goods in Process Inventory-Job No. B15	225	
	Raw Materials Inventory-M-347		225
	To record use of material on Job No. B15.		

Assets = Liabilities + Equity
+225
−225

This entry is posted to general ledger accounts and to subsidiary records. Posting to subsidiary records includes a debit to a job cost sheet and a credit to a materials ledger card.

An entry to record use of indirect materials is the same as that for direct materials *except* the debit is to Factory Overhead. In the subsidiary factory overhead ledger, this entry is posted to Indirect Materials.

Labor Cost Flows and Documents

P3 Describe and record the flow of labor costs in job order cost accounting.

Exhibit 20.8 shows the flow of labor costs from clock cards and the Factory Payroll account to subsidiary records of the job order cost accounting system. Recall that costs in subsidiary records give detailed information needed to manage and control operations.

Factory Labor

The flow of costs in Exhibit 20.8 begins with **clock cards.** These cards are commonly used by employees to record the number of hours worked. Clock cards serve as source documents for entries to record labor costs. Clock card data on the number of hours worked is used at the end of each pay period to determine total labor cost. This amount is then debited to the Factory Payroll account. Factory Payroll is a temporary account containing the total payroll cost (both direct and indirect). Payroll cost is later allocated to both specific jobs and overhead.

To assign labor costs to specific jobs and to overhead, we must know how each employee's time is used and how much it costs. Source documents called **time tickets** usually capture this data. Employees fill out time tickets each day to report how much time they spent on each job. An employee who works on several jobs during a day completes a separate time ticket for each job. Tickets are also prepared for time that is charged to overhead as indirect labor. A supervisor signs an employee's time ticket to confirm its accuracy.

Exhibit 20.8

Labor Cost Flows through Subsidiary Records

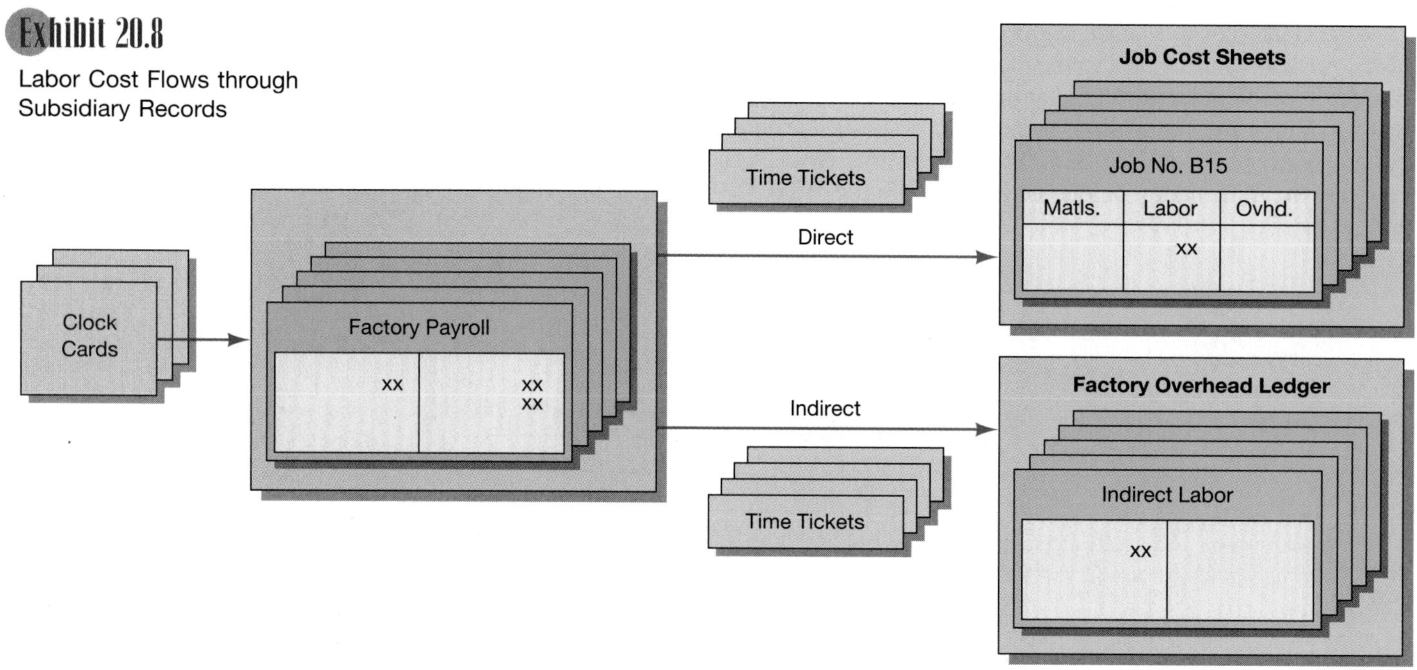

Exhibit 20.9 shows a time ticket reporting the time a Road Warrior employee spent working on Job No. B15. The employee's supervisor signed the ticket to confirm its accuracy. The hourly rate and total labor cost are computed after the time ticket is turned in. To see the effect of this time ticket on the job cost sheet, look at Exhibit 20.4 for the entry dated March 8, 2000.

Exhibit 20.9

Time Ticket

Road Warriors

TIME TICKET L–3479

Job No. *B15* Date *3/8/2000*

Employee Name *T. Zeller* Employee Number *3969*

TIME AND RATE INFORMATION:

Start Time *9:00* Finish Time *12:00*

Elapsed Time *3.0* Hourly Rate *$20.00* Total Cost *$60.00*

Approved By *C. Luther*

Remarks

When time tickets report labor used on a specific job, this cost is recorded as direct labor. The following entry records the data from time ticket number L-3479 shown in Exhibit 20.9:

Assets = Liabilities + Equity
+60 +60[1]

Mar. 8	Goods in Process Inventory—Job. No. B15 . . .	60	
	Factory Payroll		60
	To record direct labor used on Job No. B15.		

The debit in this entry is posted to both the general ledger account and to the appropriate job cost sheet.

[1] In the accounting equation, we treat accounts such as Factory Overhead and Factory Payroll as temporary accounts. These accounts hold various expenses until they are allocated to balance sheet or income statement accounts.

An entry to record indirect labor is the same as for direct labor *except* it debits Factory Overhead and credits Factory Payroll. In the subsidiary factory overhead ledger, the debit in this entry is posted to the Indirect Labor account.

Overhead Cost Flows and Documents

P4 Describe and record the flow of overhead costs in job order cost accounting.

Factory overhead (or simply overhead) cost flows are shown in Exhibit 20.10. Factory overhead includes all manufacturing costs other than direct materials and direct labor. Two of the four sources of overhead costs are indirect materials and indirect labor. These costs are recorded from requisitions for indirect materials and time tickets for indirect labor. The other two sources of overhead are (1) vouchers authorizing payments for items such as supplies or utilities and (2) adjusting entries for costs such as depreciation.

Exhibit 20.10

Overhead Cost Flows through Subsidiary Records

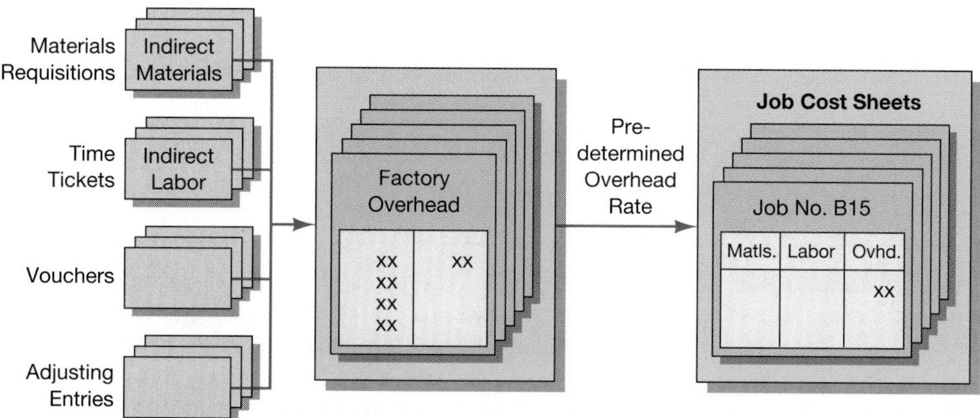

Because factory overhead usually includes many different costs, a separate account for each overhead cost is often maintained in a subsidiary factory overhead ledger. This ledger is controlled by the Factory Overhead account in the general ledger. Factory Overhead is a temporary account that accumulates costs until they are allocated to jobs.

Recall that manufacturing overhead costs are recorded with debits to the Factory Overhead account and credits to other accounts such as Cash, Accounts Payable, and Accumulated Depreciation—Equipment. In the subsidiary factory overhead ledger, the debits are posted to their proper accounts such as Depreciation on Factory Equipment, Insurance on Factory Equipment, or Amortization of Patents.

Exhibit 20.10 shows overhead costs flow from the Factory Overhead account to job cost sheets. Since overhead is made up of costs not directly associated with specific jobs or job lots, we cannot determine the dollar amount incurred on a particular job. But we know overhead costs are necessary in a manufacturing operation. If the cost of a job is to include all costs needed to manufacture the job, some amount of overhead must be included.

We already showed how to allocate overhead by linking it to another factor used in production, such as direct labor or machine hours. In Exhibit 20.4, for instance, overhead is expressed as 160% of direct labor. We then allocated overhead by multiplying 160% by the estimated amount of direct labor in both ending inventory and cost of goods sold.

But since perpetual inventory records are used in a job order cost accounting system, we cannot wait until the end of the period to allocate overhead to jobs. We must predict overhead in advance and assign it to jobs by using a **predetermined overhead allocation rate,** or simply *predetermined overhead rate.* This rate requires us to estimate total overhead cost and total direct labor cost (or another factor) before the start of the period. Exhibit 20.11 shows the formula for computing a predetermined overhead allocation rate. These estimates are usually based on annual amounts. We then use this rate during the period to allocate overhead to jobs.

Exhibit 20.11

Predetermined Overhead Allocation Rate Formula

$$\textbf{Predetermined overhead allocation rate} = \frac{\textbf{Estimated}}{\textbf{overhead costs}} \div \frac{\textbf{Estimated}}{\textbf{factor costs}}$$

Road Warriors, for instance, allocates overhead by linking it to direct labor. At the start of the current period, management predicted total direct labor costs of $125,000 and total overhead costs of $200,000. Using these estimates, management computed its predetermined overhead allocation rate as 160% of direct labor cost ($200,000 ÷ $125,000).

Look back to the job order cost sheet for Job No. B15 in Exhibit 20.4. See that $1,000 of direct labor is assigned to this job. We then use the predetermined overhead allocation rate of 160% to allocate $1,600 of overhead to the job. The journal entry to record this allocation is

Assets = Liabilities + Equity
+1,600 +1,600

Mar. 11	Goods in Process Inventory—Job. No. B15 . . .	1,600	
	Factory Overhead		1,600
	To assign overhead to Job No. B15.		

Because the allocation rate for overhead is estimated at the start of the period, the total amount assigned to jobs during the period is rarely equal to the amount actually incurred. We explain how this difference is treated at the end of the period later in this chapter.

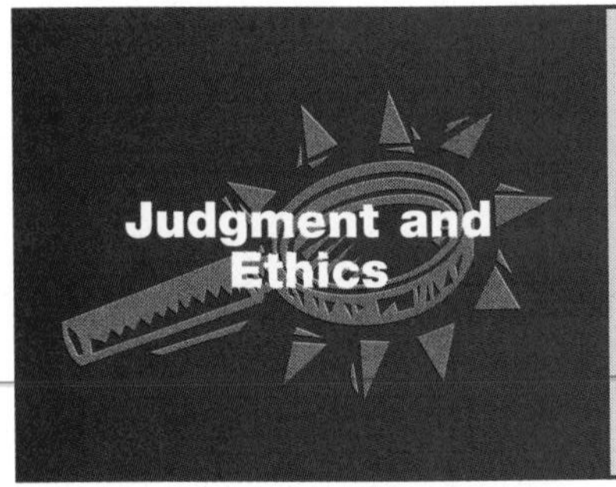

Systems Consultant

Your professional services firm is currently working on seven client engagements. In two of these engagements the clients reimburse your firm for actual costs plus a 10% markup. The other five pay a fixed fee for services. Your firm's costs include overhead allocated at $47 per labor hour. The partner of the firm instructs you to record as many labor hours as possible to the two markup engagements by transferring labor hours from the other engagements. She says "this will ensure we'll earn an added $47 markup for each added labor hour transferred." What do you do?

Answer—p. 876

Summary of Manufacturing Cost Flows

We showed journal entries for charging Goods in Process Inventory—Job No. B15 with the cost of (1) direct materials requisitions, (2) direct labor time tickets, and (3) factory overhead. While we entered separate entries for each of these costs, they are usually recorded in one entry. Specifically, materials requisitions are often collected for a day or a week and recorded with a single entry summarizing these requisitions. The same is done with labor time tickets. When summary entries are made, supporting schedules of the jobs charged and the types of materials used provide the basis for postings to subsidiary records.

To show all the manufacturing cost flows for a period and their related entries, we again look at Road Warriors' activities. Exhibit 20.12 shows costs linked to all of Road Warriors' manufacturing activities for March. Road Warriors did not have any jobs in process at the beginning of March, but it did apply materials, labor, and overhead costs to five new jobs in March. Job Nos. B15 and B16 are completed and delivered to customers in March, Job No. B17 is completed but not delivered, and Job Nos. B18 and B19 are still in process. Exhibit 20.12 shows purchases of raw materials for $2,750, labor costs incurred for $5,300, and overhead costs of $6,720.

Exhibit 20.13 shows the flow of these costs through general ledger accounts and the end-of-month balances in the subsidiary records. Arrow lines are numbered to show the flows of costs for March. Each numbered cost flow reflects several entries made in March.

The lower part of Exhibit 20.13 shows the status of job cost sheets at the end of March. The sum of costs assigned to the jobs in process ($1,970 + $1,810) equals the $3,780 balance in Goods in Process Inventory shown in Exhibit 20.12. Also, costs assigned to

Exhibit 20.12

Job Order Costs of All Manufacturing Activities

ROAD WARRIORS
Job Order Manufacturing Costs
For Month Ended March 31, 2000

Explanation	Materials	Labor	Overhead Incurred	Overhead Assigned	Goods in Process	Finished Goods	Cost of Goods Sold
Job B15	$ 600	$1,000		$1,600			$3,200
Job B16	300	800		1,280			2,380
Job B17	500	1,100		1,760		$3,360	
Job B18	150	700		1,120	$1,970		
Job B19	250	600		960	1,810		
Total job costs	$1,800	$4,200		$6,720	$3,780	$3,360	$5,580
Indirect materials ..	550		$ 550				
Indirect labor		1,100	1,100				
Other overhead ...			5,070				
Total costs used in production	$2,350	$5,300	$6,720				
Ending inventory ...	1,400						
Materials available .	$3,750						
Less beginning inv. .	(1,000)						
Purchases	$2,750						

Exhibit 20.13

Flow of All Job Order Costs and Ending Job Cost Sheets

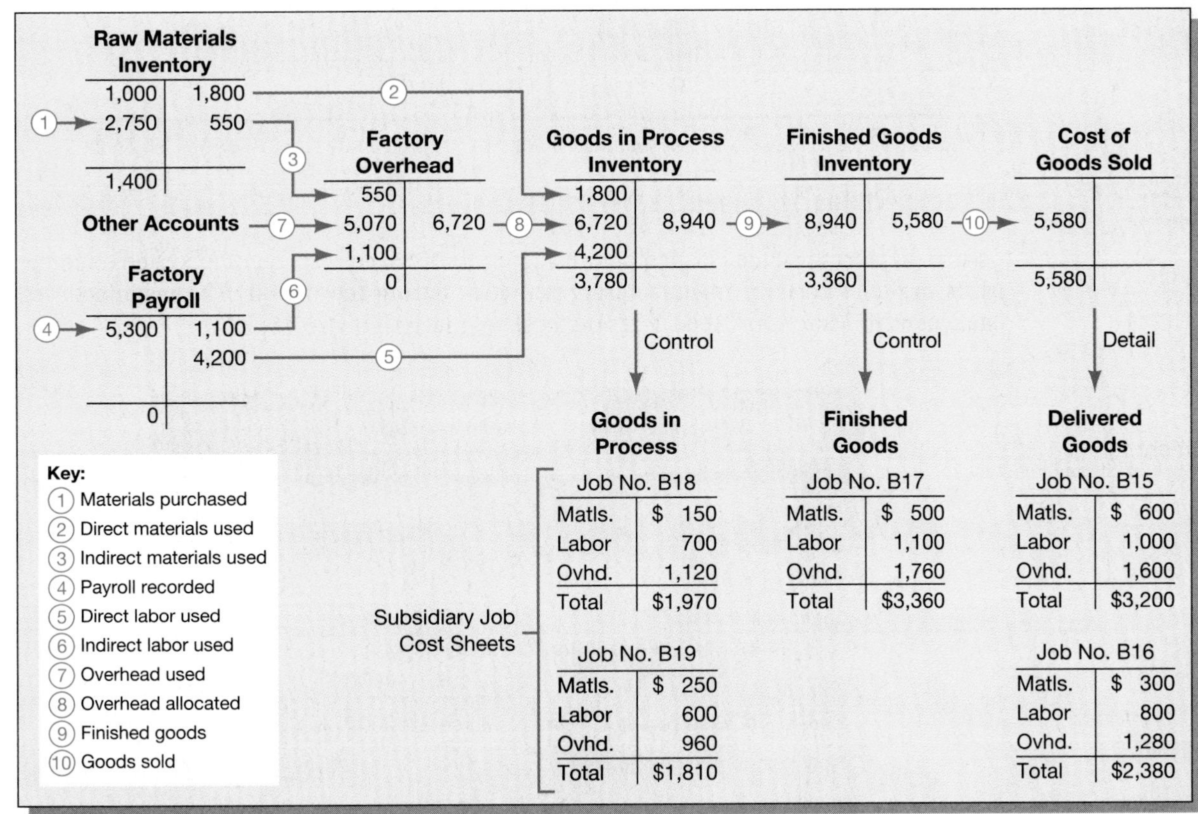

Job No. B17 equal the $3,360 balance in Finished Goods Inventory. The sum of costs assigned to Job Nos. B15 and B16 ($3,200 + $2,380) equals the $5,580 balance in Cost of Goods Sold.

Exhibit 20.14 shows each cost flow with a single entry summarizing the actual individual entries made in March. Each entry is numbered to link with the arrow lines in Exhibit 20.13.

Exhibit 20.14

Entries for Job Order Manufacturing Costs*

①	Raw Materials Inventory	2,750	
	Accounts Payable		2,750
	Acquired materials on credit for factory use.		
②	Goods in Process Inventory	1,800	
	Raw Materials Inventory		1,800
	To assign costs of direct materials used.		
③	Factory Overhead	550	
	Raw Materials Inventory		550
	To record use of indirect materials.		
④	Factory Payroll	5,300	
	Cash (and other accounts)		5,300
	To record salaries and wages of factory workers (including various payroll liabilities).		
⑤	Goods in Process Inventory	4,200	
	Factory Payroll		4,200
	To assign costs of direct labor used.		
⑥	Factory Overhead	1,100	
	Factory Payroll		1,100
	To record indirect labor costs as overhead.		
⑦	Factory Overhead	5,070	
	Cash (and other accounts)		5,070
	To record factory overhead costs such as insurance, utilities, rent, and depreciation.		
⑧	Goods in Process Inventory	6,720	
	Factory Overhead		6,720
	To apply overhead at 160% of direct labor.		
⑨	Finished Goods Inventory	8,940	
	Goods in Process Inventory		8,940
	To record completion of B15, B16, and B17.		
⑩	Cost of Goods Sold	5,580	
	Finished Goods Inventory		5,580
	To record sale of Job Nos. B15 and B16.		

*Transactions are numbered to be consistent with arrow lines in Exhibit 20.13.

Manufacturing Statement in Job Order Costing

A manufacturing statement prepared using a job order cost accounting system summarizes the total costs of manufacturing activities during the period. The manufacturing statement of March for Road Warriors is shown in Exhibit 20.15.

Exhibit 20.15

Manufacturing Statement for Road Warriors

ROAD WARRIORS Manufacturing Statement For Month Ended March 31, 2000	
Direct materials	$ 1,800
Direct labor	4,200
Factory overhead	6,720
Total manufacturing costs	$12,720
Add goods in process inventory, February 28, 2000	0
Total cost of goods in process	$12,720
Deduct goods in process inventory, March 31, 2000	(3,780)
Cost of goods manufactured	$ 8,940

Bits'n Pieces Accounting

Many job order companies maintain job cost records with computers. But software costs can be high. In response, some companies piece together less expensive off-the-shelf software. **Emerald Packaging,** for instance, expects to save $75,000 by piecing together its own programs rather than buying an entire customized software package. It bought accounting modules and an inventory system off the shelf and then developed its own job costing, sales order, pricing, and shop-floor programs. [Source: *Business Week,* April 28, 1997.]

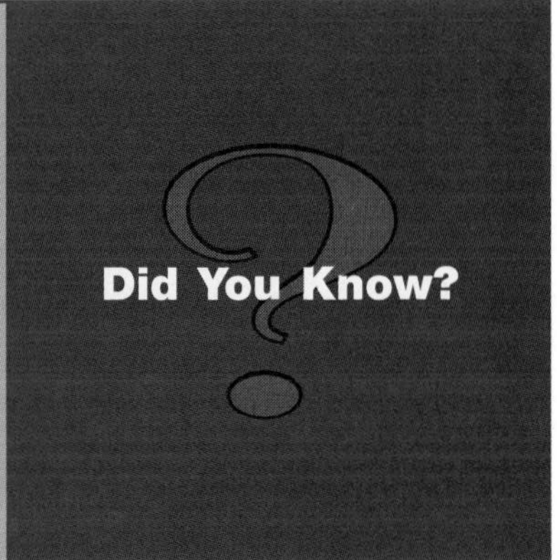

Flash *back*

8. In job order cost accounting, what account is debited in recording a raw materials requisition? *(a)* Raw Materials Inventory; *(b)* Raw Materials Purchases; *(c)* Goods in Process Inventory if for a job; *(d)* Goods in Process Inventory if they are indirect materials.
9. What are the 4 sources of information for recording costs in the Factory Overhead account?
10. Why does job order cost accounting use a predetermined overhead application rate?
11. What events result in a debit to Factory Payroll? What events result in a credit?

Answers—p. 877

Adjusting of Overapplied and Underapplied Overhead

Refer to the debits in the Factory Overhead account in Exhibit 20.13. The total cost of factory overhead incurred during March is $6,720, computed as $550 + $5,070 + $1,100. The $6,720 is exactly equal to the amount assigned to goods in process inventory (see arrow line ⑧). This means the overhead incurred is equal to the overhead applied in March. But the amount of overhead incurred is rarely equal to the amount of overhead applied. This is because a job order cost accounting system uses a predetermined overhead rate in applying factory overhead costs to jobs. This rate is determined using estimated amounts before the period begins, and estimates rarely are exactly equal to amounts actually incurred. This section explains what we do when too much or too little overhead is applied to jobs.

Underapplied Overhead

P5 Determine adjustments for overapplied and underapplied factory overhead.

When less overhead is applied than is actually incurred the remaining debit balance in the Factory Overhead account at the end of the period is called **underapplied overhead.** Let's assume Road Warriors actually incurred *other overhead costs* of $5,550 instead of the $5,070 shown in Exhibit 20.13. This yields a total overhead cost of $7,200 in March instead of the $6,720 applied. Since the amount of overhead applied was only $6,720, the Factory Overhead account would be left with a $480 debit balance as shown in the ledger account in Exhibit 20.16.

Exhibit 20.16

Underapplied Overhead in the Factory Overhead Ledger Account

Factory Overhead					Acct. No. 540
Date	Explanation	Debit	Credit	Balance	
2000					
Mar. 31	Indirect materials cost	550		550	
31	Indirect labor cost	1,110		1.650	
31	Other overhead costs	5,550		7,200	
31	Overhead costs applied to jobs		6,720	480	(debit)

The $480 debit balance reflects manufacturing costs not assigned to jobs. This means the balances in Goods in Process Inventory, Finished Goods Inventory, and Cost of Goods Sold don't include all manufacturing costs incurred. We technically should allocate this underapplied Factory Overhead balance to these accounts. But since the underapplied overhead amount is often immaterial, it often is entirely allocated (closed) to the Cost of Goods Sold account.[2] The adjusting entry to record this allocation is:

Assets = Liabilities + Equity
−480
+480

Mar. 31	Cost of Goods Sold	480	
	Factory Overhead		480
	To adjust for underapplied overhead costs.		

Overapplied Overhead

When the overhead applied in a period exceeds the overhead incurred the resulting credit balance in the Factory Overhead account is called **overapplied overhead.** We treat overapplied overhead at the end of the period in the same way we treat underapplied overhead, except that Factory Overhead is debited and Cost of Good Sold is credited.

When overhead is over- or underapplied, the manufacturing statement must be adjusted by the amount of the over- or underapplied overhead. This adjustment is necessary so that the manufacturing statement report the actual applied overhead. The adjustment for over- or underapplied overhead is normally reported as the final line item immediately above the total cost of goods manufactured figure in the manufacturing statement (where underapplied overhead is deducted and overapplied overhead is added to cost of goods manufactured). Demonstration Problem 2 at the end of the chapter illustrates this adjustment and its reporting. (Another common treatment for over- or underapplied overhead is to report it in the factory overhead section of the manufacturing statement.)

Flash back

12. In a job order cost accounting system, why does the Factory Overhead account usually have an overapplied or underapplied balance at the end of a period?

13. The Factory Overhead account has a debit balance at the end of a period. Does this reflect overapplied or underapplied overhead?

Answers—p. 877

[2] When the underapplied (or overapplied) overhead is significant, the amount is normally allocated to the Cost of Goods Sold, Finished Goods Inventory, and Goods in Process Inventory accounts. The preferred method of allocating underapplied overhead is one consistent with the allocation method used in the period. For Road Warriors this means underapplied overhead is allocated to jobs based on direct labor. Jobs B15 and B16, which are sold, account for 42.8% of the total direct labor cost in March. Also, 26.2% of direct labor was consumed by B16 which is in Finished Goods inventory, and the remaining 31% was consumed by jobs B17 and B18 which are in Goods in Process inventory. These percents are multiplied by $480 to compute the amount of underapplied overhead allocated to each account (for example, 42.8% of $480, or $205, is allocated to the Cost of Goods Sold account). An adjusting entry records this allocation:

Mar. 31	Goods in Process Inventory	149	
	Finished Goods Inventory	126	
	Cost of Goods Sold	205	
	Factory Overhead		480
	To adjust for underapplied overhead costs.		

Multiple Overhead Allocation Rates

USING THE INFORMATION

A1 Apply multiple overhead allocation rates in assigning overhead to products.

Overhead costs must be allocated to products or services in a reasonable manner. This chapter described the allocation of overhead using one allocation base (also called factor). We now explain how managers use more than one allocation base, and how this is useful in their managerial decisions.

The marketing manager, Samuel Moore, of the Denver plant of Rocky Mountain Bikes, requires accurate cost information for pricing purposes. Rocky Mountain Bikes usually computes product cost by allocating overhead as a percent of direct labor costs. Moore believes this allocation method distorts the cost of a bike and decisions on bike pricing. He also believes that allocation of costs is improved by using multiple overhead rates instead of a single rate.

To determine multiple rates, total overhead must first be separated in a meaningful way into its different components. It is then assigned to products using different allocation bases. The total factory overhead, for instance, at the Denver plant is $55,000 for the current year. This is separated into three components: (1) materials-related overhead: $20,000, (2) labor-related overhead: $15,000, and (3) machine-related overhead: $20,000. The overhead allocation rates are then determined as shown in Exhibit 20.17.

Overhead Type	Overhead Cost	Allocation Base	Overhead Rate
Materials-related	$20,000	$100,000 direct materials	20% of direct materials cost ($20,000 ÷ $100,000)
Labor-related	$15,000	5,000 direct labor hours	$3 per direct labor hour ($15,000 ÷ 5,000 hours)
Machine-related	$20,000	10,000 machine hours	$2 per machine hour ($20,000 ÷ 10,000 hours)

Exhibit 20.17
Computing Multiple Overhead Rates

To assign overhead to a job, we must then keep records of actual amounts of direct materials cost, direct labor hours, and machine hours consumed by a job.

To illustrate, one job order at the Denver plant required the following activities: direct materials cost of $1,000; 50 direct labor hours at $900; and 200 machine hours. If a single overhead allocation rate of 160% of direct labor cost is used to compute overhead, this job would be assigned total overhead of $1,440 (160% of $900). But when we use the multiple rates from Exhibit 20.17, the total overhead assigned amounts to $750, computed as (0.20 × $1,000) + ($3 × 50) + ($2 × 200). The difference in the overhead amount allocated is $690, a material amount in this case.

The cost figure based on allocation of overhead using multiple overhead rates gave Moore the information he needed to reduce the price of mountain bikes. Without this information, the bikes would not have been properly priced and the management of Rocky Mountain Bikes would be misinformed about the costs of its product.

Sales Director
You are the sales director of a product division. Your division's product is facing increasing price competition—competitors' prices are often lower than your product's price. You learn 53% of the total product cost used in setting prices is factory overhead allocated using direct labor hours. You believe product costs from your costing system are distorted, and you are wondering if there is a better means to allocate factory overhead and in setting product price. What do you suggest?

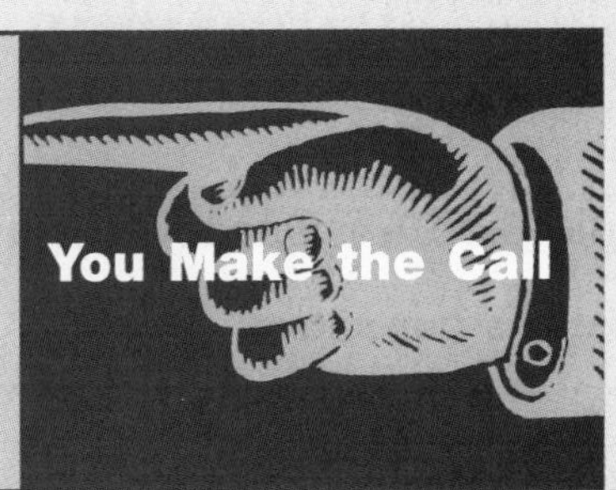

Answer—p. 876

Summary

C1 **Explain manufacturing activities and the flow of manufacturing costs.** Manufacturing activities consist of materials, production, and marketing activities. The materials activity consists of the purchase and issuance of materials to production. The production activity consists of converting materials into finished goods. At this stage in the process, the materials, labor, and overhead costs have been incurred and the manufacturing statement is prepared. The marketing activity consists of selling some or all of finished goods available for sale. At this stage in the process, the cost of goods sold is determined.

C2 **Describe important features of job order manufacturing.** Certain manufacturers produce unique products for customers and are called *job order manufacturers.* These unique or special products are manufactured in response to a customer's orders. The products produced by a job order manufacturer are usually different and, typically, manufactured in low volumes. The manufacturing systems of job order companies are flexible and are not highly standardized.

C3 **Explain job cost sheets and how they are used in job order cost accounting.** In a job order cost accounting system, the costs of producing each job are accumulated on a separate job cost sheet. Costs of direct materials, direct labor, and manufacturing overhead are accumulated separately on the job cost sheet and then added to determine the total cost of a job. Job cost sheets for jobs in process, finished jobs, and jobs that are sold make up subsidiary records that are controlled by general ledger accounts.

P1 **Prepare a manufacturing statement and explain its purpose and links to financial statements.** The manufacturing statement reports computation of cost of goods manufactured for the period. It begins by showing the period's costs for direct materials, direct labor, and overhead, and then adjusts these numbers for the beginning and ending inventories of goods in process to yield cost of goods manufactured.

P2 **Describe and record the flow of materials costs in job order cost accounting.** Costs of materials flow from receiving reports to materials ledger cards and then to either job cost sheets or the Indirect Materials account in the factory overhead ledger.

P3 **Describe and record the flow of labor costs in job order cost accounting.** Costs of labor flow from clock cards to the Factory Payroll account and then to either job cost sheets or the Indirect Labor account in the factory overhead ledger.

P4 **Describe and record the flow of overhead costs in job order cost accounting.** Manufacturing overhead costs are accumulated in the Factory Overhead account that controls the subsidiary factory overhead ledger. Then, using a predetermined overhead application rate, overhead costs are charged to jobs.

P5 **Determine adjustments for overapplied and underapplied factory overhead.** At the end of each period, the Factory Overhead account usually has a residual debit or credit balance. A debit balance reflects underapplied overhead and a credit balance reflects overapplied overhead. If the balance is not material, it is transferred to Cost of Goods Sold. If this balance is material, it is allocated to Goods in Process Inventory, Finished Goods Inventory, and Cost of Goods Sold.

A1 **Apply multiple overhead allocation rates in assigning overhead to products.** Total overhead is first separated into its different components—such as materials-related overhead, labor-related overhead, and machine-related overhead. Overhead is then assigned using these different components and their different overhead allocation rates.

Guidance Answers to **You Make the Call**

Management Consultant

Service companies do not recognize goods in process inventory or finished goods inventory. This is an important difference between service and manufacturing companies. As a result, you will not recognize any goods in process inventory at the end of the month.

For the two jobs that are 60% complete, you could recognize revenues and costs at 60% of the total expected amounts. This means you will recognize revenue of $7,200 (0.60 × $12,000) and costs of $6,000 (0.60 × $10,000), or net income of $1,200.

Sales Director

A faulty cost system can lead to distortions in product costs. The sales director should talk to the controller and ask to review factory overhead costs in detail. Once the different cost elements in the factory overhead account are known, they can be classified into several groups such as material-related, labor-related, or machine-related. Other groups can also be formed (we will discuss this in Chapter 22). Once overhead items are classified into groups, appropriate overhead allocation bases can be established and used to compute predetermined overhead rates. These multiple rates can then be used to assign overhead costs to products. This will likely improve product pricing.

Guidance Answer to **Judgment and Ethics**

Systems Consultant

There is a monetary incentive to *fudge* the numbers and make the two cost plus engagements look more costly. This would also reduce costs on the fixed price engagements. While there is an incentive to act in such a manner, it is unethical. As a professional and as an honest person, it is your responsibility to engage in ethical behavior. You must bring to your supervisor's attention the ethical concerns in this situation. You must not comply with the superior's instructions. If the supervisor insists you act in an unethical manner, you should report the matter to a higher authority in the organization.

Guidance Answers to 

1. *a*
2. No.
3. Beginning goods in process inventory is added to total manufacturing costs to yield total goods in process. Ending goods in process inventory is subtracted from total goods in process to yield cost of goods manufactured for the period.
4. *b*
5. A job is a special order for a unique product. A job lot consists of a quantity of identical, special order items.
6. *a*
7. The three costs normally accumulated are: direct materials, direct labor, and manufacturing overhead.
8. *c*
9. The four sources are: materials requisitions, time tickets, vouchers, and adjusting entries.
10. Because a job order cost accounting system uses perpetual inventory records, overhead costs must be assigned to jobs before the end of the period. This requires use of a predetermined overhead application rate.
11. Debits are recorded when wages and salaries of factory employees are paid or accrued. Credits are recorded when direct labor costs are assigned to jobs and when indirect labor costs are transferred to the Factory Overhead account.
12. Overapplied or underapplied overhead usually exists at the end of a period because application of overhead is based on estimates of overhead and another variable such as direct labor. Those estimates rarely equal the actual amounts incurred.
13. A debit balance reflects underapplied factory overhead.

General Accounting System for Manufacturing Activities

A general accounting system and a cost accounting system are different, yet they have many features in common. They both account for the three elements of manufacturing cost: *direct materials, direct labor,* and *factory overhead.* They also provide information about the three components of inventory—raw materials, goods in process, and finished goods. The difference is they do not keep records in the same way. The general accounting system uses a *periodic* inventory system in recording raw materials, goods in process, and finished goods. This appendix describes the closing process for a manufacturer using a general accounting system.

Journalizing in a General Accounting System

Journalizing for both the perpetual and periodic inventory systems of a merchandising company was described in Chapter 6, Appendix 6A. Except for the additional manufacturing inventories and expense accounts, the journalizing process is the same for a manufacturing company. However, the closing entries slightly change for a manufacturer using a general accounting (periodic) system.

To illustrate, let's assume Rocky Mountain Bikes uses the general accounting system and reports the information in Exhibit 20A.1 on inventories and manufacturing activities for year 2000.

Exhibit 20A.1

Manufacturing Transactions of Rocky Mountain Bikes for Year 2000

Beginning inventories:	
Raw materials	$ 8,000
Goods in process	2,500
Finished goods	11,200
Materials and production activity costs for year 2000:	
Raw materials purchases	$86,500
Direct labor	60,000
Factory overhead	30,000
Ending inventories:	
Raw materials	$ 9,000
Goods in process	7,500
Finished goods	10,300

C4 Describe the closing process for a manufacturer using a general accounting system.

A general accounting system uses a Manufacturing Summary account to close accounts that appear in the manufacturing statement. This temporary account is similar to the Income Summary account. The Manufacturing Summary account has a zero balance during each period. But during the closing process, all manufacturing costs are transferred to this account. The account balance is returned to zero when the costs in this account are allocated among the three ending inventory accounts and cost of goods sold.

The closing process for a manufacturer using a general accounting system can be done in 5 entries. We illustrate these for Rocky Mountain Bikes.

① This first closing entry is to close beginning raw materials, beginning goods in process, and the manufacturing cost accounts:

Dec. 31	Manufacturing Summary	187,000	
	Raw Materials Inventory		8,000
	Goods in Process Inventory		2,500
	Raw Materials Purchases		86,500
	Direct Labor		60,000
	Factory Overhead		30,000
	To close production accounts to Manufacturing Summary.		

When several factory overhead accounts are used, the above closing entry includes a credit to each of them.

② The second closing entry is to record ending raw materials inventory and ending goods in process inventory:

Dec. 31	Raw Materials Inventory	9,000	
	Goods in Process Inventory	7,500	
	Manufacturing Summary		**16,500**
	To update the raw materials and goods in process inventories.		

The $170,500 cost of completed units temporarily remains as the balance of Manufacturing Summary. Look at Exhibit 20.2a to find this amount as the last line of the Manufacturing Statement. We also see it in the Cost of Goods Sold section of the income statement in Exhibit 19.9.

③ The third closing entry is to close beginning finished goods inventory, the Manufacturing Summary account, and all expense accounts for Rocky Mountain Bikes. Balances of expense accounts are taken from the income statement in Exhibit 19.9.

Dec. 31	Income Summary	274,200	
	Manufacturing Summary		**170,500**
	Finished Goods Inventory		11,200
	Sales Salaries Expense		18,000
	Advertising Expense		5,500
	Delivery Wages Expense		12,000
	Shipping Supplies Expense		250
	Insurance Expense, Delivery Equipment		300
	Depreciation Expense, Delivery Equipment		2,100
	Office Salaries Expense		15,700
	Miscellaneous Expense		200
	Bad Debts Expense		1,550
	Office Supplies Expense		100
	Depreciation Expense, Office Equipment		200
	Interest Expense		4,000
	Income Taxes Expense		32,600
	To close the Manufacturing Summary and expense accounts, and to clear the Finished Goods Inventory account.		

④ The fourth closing entry records ending finished goods inventory and closes the sales account:

Dec. 31	Finished Goods Inventory	10,300	
	Sales	310,000	
	Income Summary		320,300
	To close the Sales account and update the Finished Goods Inventory account.		

After this entry is posted, the Income Summary account has a credit balance of $46,100. This equals net income for the year.

⑤ The fifth and final closing entry is to close the Income Summary account and update the Retained Earnings account:

Dec. 31	Income Summary	46,100	
	Retained Earnings		46,100
	To close Income Summary and update Retained Earnings.		

This last closing entry is the same whether the company is engaged in merchandising, manufacturing, or service activities.

After the closing process is complete, the T-accounts for the summary accounts appear as follows:

Manufacturing Summary			
① Dec. 31	187,000	Dec. 31	16,500 ②
		Dec. 31	170,500 ③

Income Summary			
③ Dec. 31	274,200	Dec. 31	320,300 ④
⑤ Dec. 31	46,100		

Both accounts have a zero balance indicating that all manufacturing activities are now closed to equity.

Summary of Appendix 20A

C4 Describe the closing process for a manufacturer using a general accounting system. After end-of-period adjustments are recorded in the closing process, all manufacturing costs are transferred to the Manufacturing Summary account. Next, the Manufacturing Summary balance is allocated to cost of goods manufactured (Income Summary) and to the ending inventories of materials and goods in process. At the same time, the beginning finished goods inventory balance is transferred to Income Summary. Another closing entry records the ending finished goods inventory.

Demonstration Problem 1—Manufacturing Activities and Reporting

The following account balances and other information are from the accounting records of SUNN Corporation for the year ended December 31, 2000. Use this information to prepare (1) a schedule of factory overhead costs, (2) a manufacturing statement (show only the total factory overhead cost), and (3) an income statement.

Advertising expense	$ 85,000	Goods in process inventory, 12/31/1999	8,000
Amortization of patents	16,000	Goods in process inventory, 12/31/2000	9,000
Bad debts expense	28,000	Income taxes	53,400
Depreciation expense, Office equipment	37,000	Indirect labor	26,000
Depreciation of factory building	133,000	Interest expense	25,000
Depreciation of factory equipment	78,000	Miscellaneous expense	55,000
Direct labor	250,000	Property taxes on factory equipment	14,000
Factory insurance expired	62,000	Raw materials inventory, 12/31/1999	60,000
Factory supervision	74,000	Raw materials inventory, 12/31/2000	78,000
Factory supplies used	21,000	Raw materials purchases	313,000
Factory utilities	115,000	Repairs on factory equipment	31,000
Finished goods inventory, 12/31/1999	15,000	Salaries expense	150,000
Finished goods inventory, 12/31/2000	12,500	Sales	1,630,000

Planning the Solution

- Analyze the account balances and select those that are part of factory overhead costs.
- Arrange these costs in a schedule of factory overhead costs for year 2000.
- Analyze the remaining costs and select the ones related to production activity for the year; the selected costs should include the materials and goods in process inventories and direct labor.
- Prepare a manufacturing statement for year 2000 showing the calculation of the cost of materials used in production, the cost of direct labor, and the total factory overhead cost. When presenting overhead cost on this statement, report only total overhead cost from the schedule of overhead costs for year 2000. Show the costs of beginning and ending goods in process inventory to determine cost of goods manufactured.
- Organize the remaining revenue and expense items into the income statement for year 2000. Combine cost of goods manufactured from the manufacturing statement with the finished goods inventory amounts to compute cost of goods sold for year 2000.

Solution to Demonstration Problem

SUNN CORPORATION
Schedule of Factory Overhead Costs
For Year Ended December 31, 2000

Amortization of patents	$ 16,000
Depreciation of factory building	133,000
Depreciation of factory equip.	78,000
Factory insurance expired	62,000
Factory supervision	74,000
Factory supplies used	21,000
Factory utilities	115,000
Indirect labor	26,000
Property taxes on factory equip.	14,000
Repairs on factory equipment	31,000
Total factory overhead	$570,000

SUNN CORPORATION
Manufacturing Statement
For Year Ended December 31, 2000

Direct materials:		
Raw materials inventory, 12/31/1999	$ 60,000	
Raw materials purchases	313,000	
Raw materials available for use	373,000	
Raw materials inventory, 12/31/2000	(78,000)	
Direct materials used		$ 295,000
Direct labor		250,000
Factory overhead		570,000
Total manufacturing costs		$1,115,000
Goods in process inventory, 12/31/1999		8,000
Total cost of goods in process		$1,123,000
Goods in process inventory, 12/31/2000		(9,000)
Cost of goods manufactured		$1,114,000

SUNN CORPORATION Income Statement For Year Ended December 31, 2000		
Sales		$1,630,000
Cost of goods sold:		
Finished goods inventory, December 31, 1999	$ 15,000	
Cost of goods manufactured	1,114,000	
Goods available for sale	1,129,000	
Finished goods inventory, December 31, 2000	(12,500)	
Cost of goods sold		(1,116,500)
Gross profit		$ 513,500
Operating expenses:		
Advertising expense	$ 85,000	
Bad debts expense	28,000	
Depreciation expense, Office equipment	37,000	
Interest expense	25,000	
Miscellaneous expense	55,000	
Salaries expense	150,000	
Total operating expenses		(380,000)
Income before income taxes		$ 133,500
Income taxes		(53,400)
Net income		$ 80,100

Demonstration Problem 2—Job Order Costing

The following information describes the job order manufacturing activities of Peak Manufacturing Company for May:

Raw materials purchases	$16,000
Factory payroll cost	15,400
Overhead costs incurred:	
Indirect materials	5,000
Indirect labor	3,500
Other factory overhead	9,500

The predetermined overhead rate is 150% of direct labor cost. These costs are allocated to the three jobs worked on during May as follows:

	Job 401	Job 402	Job 403
Balances on April 30:			
Direct materials	$3,600		
Direct labor	1,700		
Applied overhead	2,550		
Costs during May:			
Direct materials	3,550	$3,500	$1,400
Direct labor	5,100	6,000	800
Applied overhead	?	?	?
Status on May 31	**Finished (sold)**	**Finished (unsold)**	**In process**

Required

1. Determine the total cost of:

a. April 30 inventory of jobs in process.

b. Materials used during May.

c. Labor used during May.
d. Factory overhead incurred and applied during May and the amount of any over- or underapplied overhead on May 31.
e. Each job as of May 31, the May 31 inventories of goods in process and finished goods, and the goods sold during May.

2. Prepare summarized journal entries for the month to record:
   a. Materials purchases (on credit), the factory payroll (paid with cash), indirect materials, indirect labor, and the other factory overhead (paid with cash).
   b. Assignment of direct materials, direct labor, and overhead costs to the Goods in Process Inventory account. (Use separate debit entries for each job.)
   c. Transfer of each completed job to the Finished Goods Inventory account.
   d. Cost of goods sold.
   e. Removal of any underapplied or overapplied overhead from the Factory Overhead account. (Assume the amount is not material.)
3. Prepare a manufacturing statement for May.

Planning the Solution

- Determine the cost of the April 30 goods in process inventory by adding up the materials, labor, and applied overhead costs for Job 401.
- Compute the cost of materials used and labor by adding up the amounts assigned to jobs and to overhead.
- Compute the total overhead incurred by adding the amounts of the three components. Compute the amount of applied overhead by multiplying the total direct labor cost by the predetermined overhead rate. Compute the underapplied or overapplied amount as the difference between the actual cost and the applied cost.
- Determine the total cost charged to each job by adding the costs incurred in April to the materials, labor, and overhead applied during May.
- Group the costs of the jobs according to their status as completed.
- Record the direct materials costs assigned to the three jobs, using a separate Goods in Process Inventory account for each job; do the same thing for the direct labor and the applied overhead.
- Transfer costs of Jobs 401 and 402 from Goods in Process Inventory to Finished Goods.
- Record the costs of Job 401 as cost of goods sold.
- Record the transfer of underapplied overhead from the Factory Overhead account to the Cost of Goods Sold account.
- On the manufacturing statement, remember to include the beginning and ending in-process inventories, and to deduct the underapplied overhead.

Solution to Demonstration Problem

1. Total cost of:
   a. April 30 inventory of jobs in process (Job 401):

Direct materials	$3,600
Direct labor	1,700
Applied overhead	2,550
Total	$7,850

   b. Materials used during May:

Direct materials:	
Job 401	$ 3,550
Job 402	3,500
Job 403	1,400
Total direct materials	8,450
Indirect materials	5,000
Total materials	$13,450

c. Labor used during May:

Direct labor:	
Job 401	$ 5,100
Job 402	6,000
Job 403	800
Total direct labor	11,900
Indirect labor	3,500
Total labor	$15,400

d. Factory overhead incurred in May:

Indirect materials	$ 5,000
Indirect labor	3,500
Other factory overhead	9,500
Total actual overhead	18,000
Overhead applied (150% × $11,900)	17,850
Underapplied overhead	$ 150

e. Total cost of each job:

	401	402	403
From April:			
Direct materials	$ 3,600		
Direct labor	1,700		
Applied overhead*	2,550		
From May:			
Direct materials	3,550	$ 3,500	$1,400
Direct labor	5,100	6,000	800
Applied overhead*	7,650	9,000	1,200
Total costs	$24,150	$18,500	$3,400

*Equals 150% of the direct labor cost.

Total cost of the May 31 inventory of goods in process (Job 403) = $3,400

Total cost of the May 31 inventory of finished goods (Job 402) = $18,500

Total cost of goods sold during May (Job 401) = $24,150

2. Journal entries:

a.

	Debit	Credit
Raw Materials Inventory	16,000	
Accounts Payable		16,000
To record materials purchases.		
Factory Payroll	15,400	
Cash		15,400
To record factory payroll.		
Factory Overhead	5,000	
Raw Materials Inventory		5,000
To record indirect materials.		
Factory Overhead	3,500	
Factory Payroll		3,500
To record indirect labor.		
Factory Overhead	9,500	
Cash		9,500
To record other factory overhead.		

b. Assignment of costs to goods in process inventory:

Goods in Process Inventory (Job 401)	3,550	
Goods in Process Inventory (Job 402)	3,500	
Goods in Process Inventory (Job 403)	1,400	
Raw Materials Inventory		8,450
To assign direct materials to jobs.		
Goods in Process Inventory (Job 401)	5,100	
Goods in Process Inventory (Job 402)	6,000	
Goods in Process Inventory (Job 403)	800	
Factory Payroll		11,900
To assign direct labor to jobs.		
Goods in Process Inventory (Job 401)	7,650	
Goods in Process Inventory (Job 402)	9,000	
Goods in Process Inventory (Job 403)	1,200	
Factory Overhead		17,850
To apply overhead to jobs.		

c. Transfer of completed job to finished goods inventory:

Finished Goods Inventory	42,650	
Goods in Process Inventory (Job 401)		24,150
Goods in Process Inventory (Job 402)		18,500
To record completion of jobs.		

d.

Cost of Goods Sold	24,150	
Finished Goods Inventory		24,150
To record sale of Job 401.		

e.

Cost of Goods Sold	150	
Factory Overhead		150
To assign underapplied overhead.		

3.

PEAK MANUFACTURING COMPANY
Manufacturing Statement
For Month Ended May 31

Direct materials		$ 8,450
Direct labor		11,900
Factory overhead:		
Indirect materials	$5,000	
Indirect labor	3,500	
Other factory overhead	9,500	18,000
Total manufacturing costs		$38,350
Add goods in process, April 30		7,850
Total cost of goods in process		$46,200
Deduct goods in process, May 31		(3,400)
Deduct underapplied overhead		(150)
Cost of goods manufactured		$42,650

Glossary

Clock card a source document that is used to record the number of hours an employee works and to determine the total labor cost for each pay period. (p. 867).

Cost accounting system an accounting system for manufacturing activities based on the *perpetual* inventory system. (p. 861).

Finished goods inventory products that complete the manufacturing process and are ready to be sold by the manufacturer. (p. 865).

General accounting system an accounting system for manufacturing activities based on the *periodic* inventory system. (p. 861).

Goods in process inventory products that are in the process of being manufactured but are not yet complete. (p. 865).

Job the production of a unique product or service. (p. 862).

Job cost sheet a separate record maintained for each job. (p. 864).

Job lot producing more than one unit of a unique product or service. (p. 862).

Job order cost accounting system a cost accounting system designed to determine the cost of producing each job or job lot. (p. 864).

Job order manufacturing the production of special order products; also called *customized production.* (p. 862).

Manufacturing statement a report that summarizes the types and amounts of costs incurred in a company's manufacturing process for a period; also called *schedule of manufacturing activities* or *schedule of cost of goods manufactured.* (p. 858).

Materials ledger card a perpetual record that is updated each time units are both purchased and issued for use in production. (p. 866).

Materials requisition a source document that production managers use to request materials for manufacturing and that is used to assign materials costs to specific jobs or to overhead. (p. 867).

Overapplied overhead the amount by which the overhead applied to jobs in a period with the predetermined overhead allocation rate exceeds the overhead incurred in a period. (p. 874).

Predetermined overhead allocation rate the rate established prior to the beginning of a period that relates estimated overhead to another variable such as estimated direct labor and is used to assign overhead cost to jobs. (p. 869).

Time ticket a source document used to report how much time an employee spent working on a job or on overhead activities and then to determine the amount of direct labor to charge to the job or the amount of indirect labor to charge to overhead. (p. 867).

Underapplied overhead the amount by which overhead incurred in a period exceeds the overhead applied to jobs with the predetermined overhead allocation rate. (p. 873).

Questions

1. Manufacturing activities of a company are described in a special report called the __________. This statement summarizes the types and amounts of costs incurred in a company's manufacturing __________.
2. What are the three categories of manufacturing costs?
3. List several examples of factory overhead costs.
4. What is the difference between factory overhead and selling and administrative overhead?
5. List the four components of a manufacturing statement and provide specific examples of each for NIKE.

6. Prepare a proper title for the annual manufacturing statement of America Online. Does the date match the balance sheet or income statement? Why?

7. Describe the relations among the income statement, the manufacturing statement, and a detailed schedule of factory overhead costs.
8. A note to NIKE's financial statements identifies its inventory account values. What are the major components of NIKE's inventory?

9. Why must a company estimate the amount of factory overhead assigned to individual jobs or job lots?
10. The chapter used a percent of labor cost to assign factory overhead to jobs. Identify another factor (or base) a company may use to assign overhead costs.
11. What information is recorded on a job cost sheet? How are job cost sheets used by management and employees?
12. In a job order cost accounting system, what records serve as a subsidiary ledger for Goods in Process Inventory? For Finished Goods Inventory?
13. What journal entry is recorded when a materials manager receives a materials requisition and then issues materials for use in the factory?
14. How does the materials requisition slip help safeguard the company's assets?
15. What is the difference between a clock card and a time ticket?
16. What events cause debits to be recorded in the Factory Overhead account? What events cause credits to be recorded in the Factory Overhead account?
17. What account(s) are used to eliminate overapplied or underapplied overhead from the Factory Overhead account, assuming the amount is not material?
18. Reebok produced a batch of 300 football shoes, colored green and gold, for an NFL team. How do they account for this, as 300 individual jobs or a job lot? Why?

Reebok

19. Why must a company prepare a predetermined factory overhead rate when using job order cost accounting?
20. How would a hospital apply job order costing?

21[A]. In the general accounting system model, all manufacturing accounts are closed to the ______________ summary account.

Quick Study

QS 20-1
Identify manufacturing flows
C1

Identify the usual sequence of manufacturing activities by filling in the blank (1, 2, or 3) corresponding to its order: _____ Production activities; _____ Marketing activities; _____ Materials activities.

QS 20-2
Determine Cost of Goods Manufactured
P1

Determine the cost of goods manufactured for Max-It Company using the information shown:

Direct materials	$189,760
Direct labor	65,100
Factory overhead costs	24,720
Goods in process, December 31, 1999	299,400
Goods in process, December 31, 2000	234,210

QS 20-3
Determine factory overhead rates
P4

Secor Company incurred the following manufacturing costs this period: direct labor, $468,000; direct materials, $354,500; and factory overhead, $117,000. Compute overhead cost as a percent of *(a)* direct labor and *(b)* direct materials.

QS 20-4
Identifying jobs and job lots
C2

Determine which products are most likely to be manufactured as a job and which as a job lot:

1. Hats imprinted with company logo.
2. A hand-crafted table.
3. A custom-designed home.
4. A 90-foot motor yacht.
5. Little League trophies.
6. Wedding dresses for a chain of stores.

QS 20-5
Determine job cost
C3

The information below is from materials requisitions and time tickets for Job 9-1005, which was completed by Beaufort Boats for Redfish Rentals. The requisitions are identified by code numbers starting with the letter Q and the time tickets start with W:

Date	Document	Amount
7/ 1/2000	Q-4698	$1,250
7/ 1/2000	W-3393	600
7/ 5/2000	Q-4725	1,000
7/ 5/2000	W-3479	450
7/10/2000	W-3559	300

At the start of the year, management estimated that overhead cost would equal 140% of direct labor cost for each job. Determine the total cost on the job cost sheet for Job 9-1005.

QS 20-6
Prepare materials journal entries
P2

During the current month, a company that uses a job order cost accounting system purchases raw materials for $50,000 cash. It then uses $12,000 of raw materials indirectly as factory supplies and uses $32,000 of raw materials as direct materials. Prepare entries to record these transactions.

QS 20-7
Prepare labor journal entries
P3

During the current month, a company that uses a job order cost accounting system has a monthly factory payroll of $120,000, paid in cash. Of this amount, $30,000 is classified as indirect labor and the remainder as direct. Prepare entries to record these transactions.

QS 20-8
Prepare factory overhead entries
P4

During the current month, a company that uses a job order cost accounting system has a monthly factory payroll of $120,000, paid in cash. Of this amount, $30,000 is classified as indirect labor and the remainder as direct for the production of a job lot. Factory overhead is applied at 150% of direct labor. Prepare the entry to apply manufacturing overhead to this job lot.

QS 20-9
Prepare over- and underapplied overhead entry.

Relay Company allocates overhead at a rate of 150% of direct labor cost. Actual overhead cost for the current period is $950,000 and direct labor cost is $600,000. Prepare the closing entry of over- or underapplied overhead to cost of goods sold.

Exercises

Exercise 20-1
Computing cost of goods manufactured and cost of goods sold
P1

Using the data below, compute (a) the cost of goods manufactured and (b) the cost of goods sold for both Bean Company and Baby Company.

	Bean Company	Baby Company
Beginning finished goods inventory	$10,000	$15,800
Beginning goods in process inventory	12,400	22,000
Beginning raw materials inventory	6,400	8,240
Lease on factory equipment	24,000	35,000
Direct labor	15,000	16,000
Ending finished goods inventory	12,300	21,800
Ending goods in process inventory	15,400	19,000
Ending raw materials inventory	4,600	3,400
Factory utilities	8,000	6,400
Factory supplies used	5,600	2,800
General and administrative expenses	24,000	40,000
Indirect labor	1,300	1,920
Repairs, factory equipment	3,320	5,100
Raw materials purchases	27,000	32,600
Sales salaries	30,000	28,000

Exercise 20-2
Identifying components of financial statements

For each of the following account balances for a manufacturing company, indicate by a ✔ in the appropriate column whether it will appear on the balance sheet, the income statement, the manufacturing statement, or a detailed schedule of factory overhead costs. Assume that the income statement shows the calculation of cost of goods sold and the manufacturing statement shows only the total amount of factory overhead. (*An account balance may appear on more than one report.*)

Account	Balance Sheet	Income Statement	Manufacturing Statement	Overhead Schedule
Accounts receivable				
Computer supplies used in office				
Beginning finished goods inventory				
Beginning goods in process inventory				
Beginning raw materials inventory				
Cash				
Depreciation of factory building				
Depreciation of factory equipment				
Depreciation expense, Office building				
Depreciation expense, Office equipment				
Direct labor				
Ending finished goods inventory				
Ending goods in process inventory				
Ending raw materials inventory				
Factory maintenance wages				
Computer supplies used in factory				
Income taxes				
Insurance on factory building				
Rent on office building				
Office supplies used				
Property taxes on factory building				
Raw materials purchases				
Sales				

Exercise 20-3
Preparing a manufacturing statement
P1

Given the selected account balances of Packer Corp. shown below, prepare its manufacturing statement in proper form on December 31, 2000. Include the individual overhead account balances in this statement.

Sales	$1,000,000
Raw materials inventory, December 31, 1999	25,000
Goods in process inventory, December 31, 1999	45,525
Finished goods inventory, December 31, 1999	57,375
Raw materials purchases	120,825
Direct labor	136,650
Factory computer supplies used	13,800
Indirect labor	33,600
Repairs, factory equipment	6,000
Rent on factory building	49,500
Advertising expenses	86,400
General and administrative expenses	100,950
Raw materials inventory, December 31, 2000	35,625
Goods in process inventory, December 31, 2000	31,650
Finished goods inventory, December 31, 2000	53,475

Exercise 20-4
Preparing an income statement
P1

Use the information in Exercise 20-3 to prepare an income statement for Packer Corporation. Assume that the cost of goods manufactured is $363,625.

Exercise 20-5
Understanding cost flows in manufacturing
C1, P1

The following chart shows how costs flow through a business as a product is manufactured. Some boxes in the flowchart show cost amounts, while other boxes contain question marks. Compute the cost that should appear in each box containing a question mark.

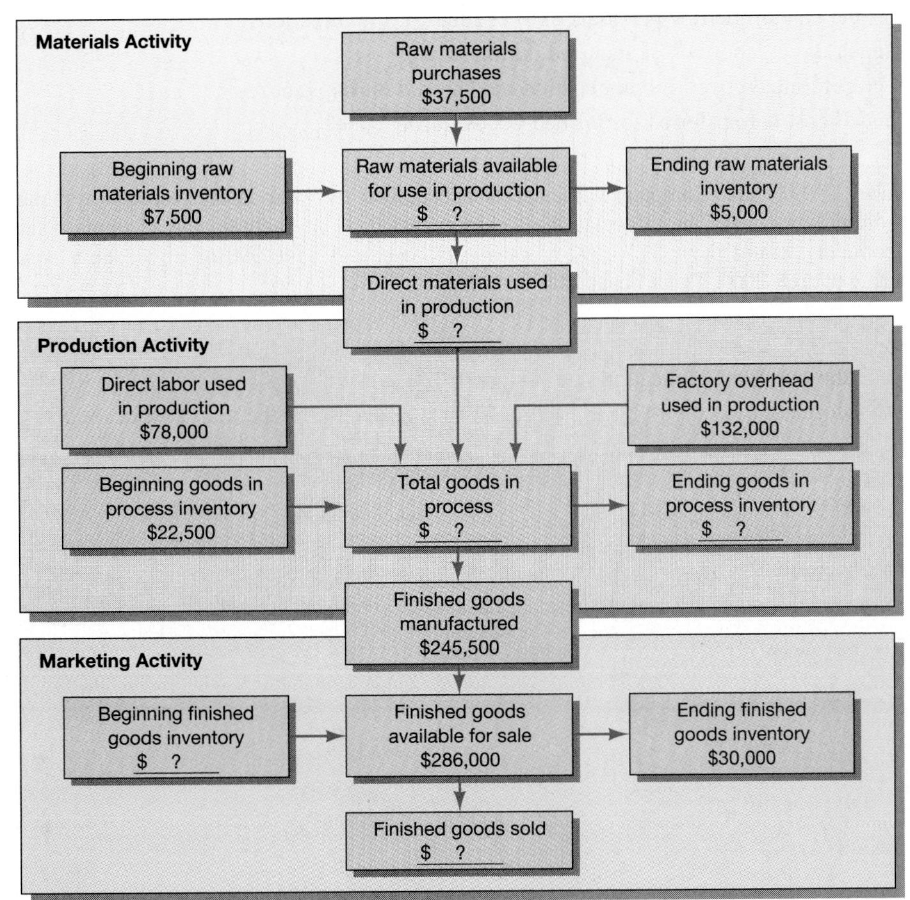

Exercise 20-6
Documents used in job order cost accounting
C2, C3, P2, P3, P4

The left column includes the titles of documents used in job order cost accounting. The right column presents short descriptions of the purposes of the documents. Match each of the documents in the left column to their numbered descriptions in the right column.

a. Factory Payroll account	______ **1.** Communicates the need for materials to complete a job.
b. Materials ledger card	______ **2.** Shows only total time an employee works each day.
c. Time ticket	______ **3.** Shows amount approved for payment of an overhead cost.
d. Voucher	______ **4.** Shows amount of time an employee works on a job.
e. Materials requisition	______ **5.** Temporarily accumulates the cost of incurred overhead until the cost is assigned to specific jobs.
f. Factory Overhead account	______ **6.** Temporarily accumulates incurred labor costs until they are assigned to specific jobs or to overhead.
g. Clock card	______ **7.** Perpetual inventory record of raw materials received, used, and on hand.

Exercise 20-7
Analysis of cost flows
C2, P3, P4, P5

As of the end of June, the job cost sheets at Skateboards-For-You, Inc., show the following total costs accumulated on three jobs:

	Job 102	Job 103	Job 104
Direct materials	$15,000	$33,000	$27,000
Direct labor	8,000	14,200	21,000
Overhead	4,000	7,100	10,500

Job 102 was started in production in May and the following costs were assigned to it in May: direct materials, $6,000; direct labor, $1,800; and overhead, $900. Jobs 103 and 104 are started in June. Overhead cost is applied with a predetermined rate based on direct labor cost. Jobs 102 and 103 are finished in June, and it is expected that Job 104 will be finished in July. No raw materials are used indirectly in June. Using this information, answer the following questions:

1. What is the cost of the raw materials used in June for the three jobs?
2. How much direct labor cost is incurred during June?
3. What predetermined overhead application rate is used during June?
4. How much cost is transferred to finished goods during June?

Exercise 20-8
Computing overhead application rate; assigning costs to jobs
P4

In December 1999, Dana Company's management establish the year 2000 overhead application rate based on direct labor cost. The information used in setting this rate includes the accountant's estimates that the company would incur $756,000 of overhead costs and $540,000 of direct labor cost in year 2000. During March 2000, Dana began and completed Job No. 13-56.

Required:

1. Compute the overhead application rate for year 2000.
2. Use the information on the following job cost sheet to determine the total cost of the job.

JOB COST SHEET

Customer's Name Keiser Co. **Job No.** 13-56
Job Description 5 two-page color monitors—21 inch

	Direct Materials		Direct Labor		Overhead Costs Applied	
Date	**Requisition No.**	**Amount**	**Time-Ticket No.**	**Amount**	**Rate**	**Amount**
Mar. 8	4-129	5,000	T-306	640		
Mar. 11	4-142	7,050	T-432	1,280		
Mar. 18	4-167	3,550	T-456	1,280		
Total						

Exercise 20-9
Analysis of costs assigned to goods in process
P4

Angus Company uses a job order cost accounting system that charges overhead to jobs on the basis of direct material. At year-end, the Goods in Process Inventory account shows the following:

	Goods in Process Inventory		Acct. No. 121	
Date	**Explanation**	**Debit**	**Credit**	**Balance**
2000				
Dec. 31	Direct materials cost	1,500,000		1,500,000
31	Direct labor cost	240,000		1,740,000
31	Overhead costs	450,000		2,190,000
31	To finished goods		2,100,000	90,000

Required

1. Determine the overhead application rate (based on direct material cost) used.
2. Only one job remained in the goods in process inventory at December 31, 2000. Its direct materials cost is $30,000. How much direct labor cost is assigned to it? How much overhead cost is assigned to it?

Exercise 20-10
Understanding cost flows in a job order cost accounting system
C1, C3, P4

The Security Company produces special order security products and uses a job order cost accounting system. The following information is available:

	April 30	May 31
Inventories:		
Raw materials	$40,000	$ 50,000
Goods in process	9,600	19,500
Finished goods	60,000	33,200
Information about May:		
Raw materials purchases (paid with cash)		$ 189,000
Factory payroll (paid with cash)		400,000
Factory overhead:		
Indirect materials		12,000
Indirect labor		75,000
Other overhead costs		100,500
Sales (received in cash)		1,200,000
Predetermined overhead rate based on direct labor cost		65%

Compute the following amounts for the month of May:

1. Cost of direct materials used.
2. Cost of direct labor used.
3. Cost of goods manufactured.
4. Cost of goods sold.
5. Gross profit.

Exercise 20-11
Recording journal entries for a job order cost accounting system
P2, P3, P4

Use information in Exercise 20-10 to prepare journal entries for the following events in May:

1. Raw materials purchases.
2. Direct materials usage.
3. Indirect materials usage.
4. Factory payroll costs.
5. Direct labor usage.

6. Indirect labor usage.
7. Factory overhead other than indirect materials and indirect labor (record credit to Other Accounts).
8. Application of overhead to goods in process.
9. Transfer of finished jobs to the finished goods inventory.
10. Sale and delivery of finished goods to customers.

Exercise 20-12
Computing, applying, and adjusting the factory overhead
P4, P5

In December 1999, Entertainment Inc. established its predetermined overhead application rate for movies produced during year 2000 by using the following cost predictions: overhead costs, $1,800,000; and direct labor costs, $450,000. At the end of year 2000, the company's records show that actual overhead costs for the year are $1,770,000. Actual direct labor cost had been assigned to jobs as follows:

Movies completed and released	$400,000
Movies still in production	45,000
Total actual direct labor cost	$445,000

Required

1. Compute the predetermined overhead application rate for year 2000.
2. Set up a T-account for Overhead and enter the overhead costs incurred and the amounts applied to movies during the year using the predetermined overhead rate.
3. Determine whether overhead is overapplied or underapplied during the year.
4. Prepare the adjusting entry to allocate any over- or underapplied overhead to cost of goods sold.

Exercise 20-13
Computing, applying, and adjusting the factory overhead
P4, P5

In December 1999, Setter Company established its predetermined overhead application rate for jobs produced during year 2000 by using the following cost predictions: overhead costs, $600,000; and direct labor costs, $500,000. At the end of year 2000, the company's records show that actual overhead costs for the year are $680,000. Actual direct labor cost had been assigned to jobs as follows:

Jobs completed and sold	$420,000
Jobs in finished goods inventory	84,000
Jobs in goods in process inventory	56,000
Total actual direct labor cost	$560,000

Required

1. Compute the predetermined overhead application rate for year 2000.
2. Set up a T-account for Factory Overhead and enter the overhead costs incurred and the amounts applied to jobs during the year using the predetermined overhead rate.
3. Determine whether overhead is overapplied or underapplied during the year.
4. Prepare the adjusting entry to allocate any over- or underapplied overhead to cost of goods sold.
5. Prepare the adjusting entry to allocate any over- or underapplied overhead to cost of goods sold and the various inventories.

Exercise 20-14[A]
Closing entries—general accounting
C4

Use the information provided in Exercise 20-3 and prepare closing entries for Packer Corporation, assuming it uses a general accounting system.

Exercise 20-15
Overhead rate calculation and analysis
P4

Cardinal Company uses the relation between factory overhead and direct labor costs to assign factory overhead to its inventories of goods in process and finished goods. The company incurred the following costs during 1999: direct materials used, $637,500; direct labor costs, $2,500,000; and factory overhead costs, $1,000,000.

1. Estimate the company's overhead application rate for year 2000.
2. Assuming that the company's $57,000 ending goods in process inventory for year 2000 had $18,000 of direct labor costs, determine the inventory's direct material costs.
3. Assuming that the company's $337,485 ending finished goods inventory for year 2000 had $137,485 of direct material costs, determine the inventory's direct labor cost and its overhead costs.

Exercise 20-16
Allocating costs to ending inventories

P4

Monarch Company's ending goods in process inventory consists of 4,500 units of partially completed product, and its finished goods inventory consists of 11,700 units of product. The factory manager determines that the goods in process inventory includes direct materials cost of $10 per unit and direct labor cost of $7 per unit. Finished goods are estimated to have $12 of direct materials cost per unit and $9 of direct labor cost per unit. During the period, the company incurred these costs: direct materials, $460,000; direct labor, $277,000; and factory overhead, $332,400. The company allocates factory overhead to its goods in process and finished goods inventories by relating overhead to direct labor cost.

1. Compute the overhead rate.
2. Compute the total cost of the two ending inventories.
3. Compute cost of goods sold for the year (assume no beginning inventories).

Problems

Problem 20-1
Preparing manufacturing and income statements; analysis of inventories

The following items are taken from the adjusted trial balance and other records of Floral Company before the calendar year-end closing entries are recorded:

Advertising expense	$ 16,200
Depreciation expense, Office equip.	6,750
Depreciation expense, Selling equip.	8,100
Depreciation of factory equipment	28,350
Direct labor	523,800
Factory supervision	97,200
Factory supplies used	4,850
Factory utilities	27,000
Income taxes expense	109,350
Indirect labor	47,250
Inventories:	
Raw materials, January 1	132,300
Raw materials, December 31	136,350
Goods in process, January 1	10,700
Goods in process, December 31	11,250
Finished goods, January 1	141,750
Finished goods, December 31	113,400
Miscellaneous production costs	6,750
Office salaries expense	56,700
Raw materials purchases	715,500
Rent expense, office space	18,900
Rent expense, selling space	21,600
Rent on factory building	74,800
Maintenance, factory equipment	24,300
Sales	3,431,350
Sales discounts	45,900
Sales salaries expense	236,250

Required

Preparation Component

Check Figure Cost of goods manufactured, $1,545,200

1. Prepare a manufacturing statement for the company.
2. Prepare an income statement for the company. The income statement should present separate categories for *(a)* selling expenses and *(b)* general and administrative expenses.

Analysis Component

3. Compute the (a) inventory turnover and (b) days' sales in inventory for Floral's raw materials inventory and its finished goods inventory (see Chapter 7). Discuss some possible reasons for differences between these ratios for the two inventories.

Problem 20-2
Computing and recording manufacturing costs and preparing reports
C1, C3, P1, P2, P3, P4

Lawn Co.'s March 31 inventory of raw materials is $150,000. Raw materials purchases in April are $400,000. Factory payroll cost in April is $220,000. Overhead costs incurred in April are: indirect materials, $30,000; indirect labor, $14,000; factory rent, $20,000; factory heat, $12,000; and factory equipment depreciation, $30,000. The predetermined overhead rate is 50% of direct labor cost. Job 306 is sold for $380,000 cash during April. Costs allocated to the three jobs worked on in April are:

	Job 306	Job 307	Job 308
Balances on March 31:			
Direct materials	$ 14,000	$ 18,000	
Direct labor	18,000	16,000	
Applied overhead	9,000	8,000	
Costs during April:			
Direct materials	100,000	170,000	$ 80,000
Direct labor	30,000	56,000	120,000
Applied overhead	?	?	?
Status on April 30	Finished (sold)	Finished (unsold)	In process

Required

Preparation Component

1. Determine the total of each manufacturing cost incurred for April (direct labor, direct materials, allocated overhead), and the total cost assigned to each of the three jobs (including the balances from March 31).
2. Prepare journal entries for the month to record:
   a. Materials purchases (on credit), factory payroll (paid in cash), and actual overhead costs including indirect materials and indirect labor. (Factory rent and utilities are paid in cash.)
   b. Assignment of direct materials, direct labor, and applied overhead costs to the Goods in Process Inventory.
   c. Transfer of Jobs 306 and 307 to the Finished Goods Inventory.
   d. Cost of goods sold for Job 306.
   e. Revenue from the sale of Job 306.
   f. Assignment of any underapplied or overapplied overhead to the Cost of Goods Sold account. (The amount is not material.)

Check Figure Cost of goods manufactured, $482,000

3. Prepare a manufacturing statement for April (use a single line presentation for direct materials and show the details of overhead cost).
4. Present a calculation of gross profit for April. Show how the inventories would be presented on the April 30 balance sheet.

Analysis Component

5. When the over- or underapplied overhead adjustment is made, we close Factory Overhead to Cost of Goods Sold. Discuss how this adjustment impacts business decision making regarding individual jobs or batches of jobs.

Problem 20-3
Source documents, journal entries, overhead and financial reports

P1, P2, P3, P4, P5

The following trial balance of the Scobey Company is generated by the computer system on the afternoon of December 31, 2000. The company's accountant knows something is wrong because the trial balance does not show any balance for goods in process inventory and it still shows balances for the Factory Payroll and Factory Overhead accounts:

	Debit	Credit
Cash	$ 48,000	
Accounts receivable	42,000	
Raw materials inventory	26,000	
Goods in process inventory	-0-	
Finished goods	9,000	
Prepaid rent	3,000	
Accounts payable		$ 10,500
Notes payable		13,500
Common stock		30,000
Retained earnings		87,000
Sales		180,000
Cost of goods sold	105,000	
Factory payroll	16,000	
Factory overhead	27,000	
Miscellaneous expenses	45,000	
Total	$321,000	$321,000

After searching various files, six source documents are found that need to be processed to bring the accounting records up to date:

Materials requisition 21–3010:	$4,600 direct materials to Job 402
Materials requisition 21–3011:	$7,600 direct materials to Job 404
Materials requisition 21–3012:	$2,100 indirect materials
Labor time ticket 6052:	$5,000 direct labor to Job 402
Labor time ticket 6053:	$8,000 direct labor to Job 404
Labor time ticket 6054:	$3,000 indirect labor

Jobs 402 and 404 are the only units in process at the end of the year. The predetermined overhead application rate is 200% of direct labor cost.

Required

Preparation Component

1. Use the information on the six source documents to prepare journal entries to assign the following costs:
    a. Direct material costs to goods in process inventory.
    b. Direct labor costs to goods in process inventory.
    c. Overhead costs to goods in process inventory.
    d. Indirect material costs to the overhead account.
    e. Indirect labor costs to the overhead account.
2. Determine the revised balance of the Factory Overhead account after making the entries in part (1). Determine whether there is any under- or overapplied overhead for the year. Prepare the adjusting entry to allocate any over- or underapplied overhead to cost of goods sold, assuming the amount is not material.
3. Prepare a revised trial balance.
4. Prepare an income statement for year 2000 and a balance sheet as of December 31, 2000.

Check Figure Net income, $23,900

Analysis Component

5. Assume that the $2,100 on materials requisition 21-3012 should have been direct materials charged to Job 404. Without providing specific calculations, describe what impact this error would have on Scobey's year 2000 income statement and balance sheet.

Problem 20-4
Source documents and journal entries in job order cost accounting
P4, P5

Skidoo Watercraft Co.'s predetermined overhead application rate for year 2000 is 200% of direct labor. The company's activities related to manufacturing during May 2000 are:

a. Purchased raw materials on account, $125,000.

b. Paid factory wages with cash, $84,000.

c. Paid $11,000 cash to computer consultant to reprogram factory equipment.

d. Materials requisitions for the month show that the following materials were used:

Job 136	$30,000
Job 137	20,000
Job 138	12,000
Job 139	14,000
Job 140	4,000
Total direct materials	$80,000
Indirect materials	12,000
Total materials used	$92,000

e. Labor time tickets for the month show the following labor was used:

Job 136	$ 8,000
Job 137	7,000
Job 138	25,000
Job 139	26,000
Job 140	2,000
Total direct labor	$68,000
Indirect labor	16,000
Total	$84,000

f. Overhead was applied to Jobs 136, 138, and 139.

g. Jobs 136, 138, and 139 were transferred to finished goods.

h. Jobs 136 and 138 were sold on account for a total price of $340,000.

i. Overhead costs incurred during the month are (credit Prepaid Insurance for expired factory insurance):

Depreciation of factory building	$37,000
Depreciation of factory equipment	21,000
Expired factory insurance	7,000
Accrued property taxes payable	31,000

j. At the end of the month, overhead is applied to the goods in process (Jobs 137 and 140) using the predetermined rate of 200% of direct labor cost.

Required

1. Prepare a job cost sheet for each job worked on during the month. Use the following simplified form of a job cost sheet:

Job No. ________	
Materials	$
Labor	
Overhead	
Total cost	$ ______

2. Prepare journal entries to record the events and transactions *a* through *j*.

3. Set up T-accounts for each of the following general ledger accounts, each of which started the month with a zero balance: Raw Materials Inventory; Goods in Process Inventory; Finished Goods Inventory; Factory Payroll; Factory Overhead; Cost of Goods Sold. Then, post the journal entries to these T-accounts and determine the balance of each account.

4. Prepare a schedule showing the total cost of each job in process and prove that the sum of their costs equals the Goods in Process Inventory account balance. Prepare similar schedules for the finished goods inventory and the cost of goods sold.

Check Figure Finished goods inventory, $92,000

Problem 20-5
Allocating overhead using predetermined overhead application rate
C3, P4, P5

In December 1999, Cantu Company's accountant estimated next year's direct labor using the cost of 50 persons, working an average of 2,000 hours each, at an average wage rate of $15 per hour. The accountant also estimated the following manufacturing overhead costs for year 2000:

Indirect labor	$159,600
Factory supervision	120,000
Rent on factory building	70,000
Factory utilities	44,000
Factory insurance expired	34,000
Depreciation of factory equipment	240,000
Repairs, factory equipment	30,000
Factory supplies used	34,400
Miscellaneous production costs	18,000
Total	$750,000

At the end of year 2000, records show the company incurred $725,000 of overhead costs. It completed and sold five jobs with the following direct labor costs: Job 201, $354,000; Job 202, $330,000; Job 203, $175,000; Job 204, $420,000; and Job 205, $184,000. In addition, Job 206 is in process at the end of year 2000 and had been charged $10,000 for direct labor. The company's predetermined overhead application rate is based on direct labor cost.

Required

1. Determine the:

a. Predetermined overhead application rate for year 2000.

b. Total overhead cost applied to each of the six jobs during year 2000.

c. Over- or underapplied overhead at year-end.

2. Assuming that any over- or underapplied overhead is not material, prepare the adjusting entry to allocate any over- or underapplied overhead to cost of goods sold at the end of year 2000.

Check Figure Factory overhead, $11,500 debit

Problem 20-6
Recording manufacturing transactions; subsidiary records; source documents
P2, P3, P4, P5

If the working papers that accompany this book are not available, do not attempt to solve this problem.

The Kaplan Company manufactures special variations of its product, a technopress, in response to special orders from its customers. On May 1, the company had no inventories of goods in process or finished goods but held the following raw materials:

Material M	120 units @ $200 =	$24,000
Material R	80 units @ 160 =	12,800
Paint	44 units @ 72 =	3,168
Total		$39,968

On May 4, the company began working on two technopresses: Job 102 for Grobe Company and Job 103 for Reynco Company.

Required

Follow the instructions in this list of activities and complete the materials provided in the working papers:

a. Purchased raw materials on credit and recorded the following information from receiving reports and invoices:

Receiving Report No. 426, Material M, 150 units at $200 each.
Receiving Report No. 427, Material R, 70 units at $160 each.

Instructions: Record the purchases with a single journal entry and post it to general ledger T-accounts, using the transaction letter to identify the entry. Enter the receiving report information on the materials ledger cards.

b. Requisitioned the following raw materials for production:

Requisition No. 35, for Job 102, 80 units of Material M.
Requisition No. 36, for Job 102, 60 units of Material R.
Requisition No. 37, for Job 103, 40 units of Material M.
Requisition No. 38, for Job 103, 30 units of Material R.
Requisition No. 39, for 12 units of paint.

Instructions: Enter amounts for direct materials requisitions only on the materials ledger cards and the job cost sheets. Enter the indirect material amount on the raw materials ledger card and record a debit to the Indirect Materials account in the subsidiary Factory Overhead Ledger. Do not record a journal entry at this time.

c. Employees turned in the following time tickets for work in May:

Time tickets Nos. 1 to 10 for direct labor on Job 102, $40,000.
Time tickets Nos. 11 to 30 for direct labor on Job 103, $32,000.
Time tickets Nos. 31 to 36 for equipment repairs, $12,000.

Instructions: Record direct labor reported on the time tickets only on the job cost sheets, and debit indirect labor to the Indirect Labor account in the subsidiary Factory Overhead Ledger. Do not record a journal entry at this time.

d. Paid cash for the following items during the month: factory payroll, $84,000; and miscellaneous overhead items, $36,000.
Instructions: Record these payments with journal entries and then post them to the general ledger accounts. Also record a debit in the Miscellaneous Overhead account in the subsidiary Factory Overhead Ledger.

e. Finished Job 102 and transferred it to the warehouse. The company assigns overhead to each job with a predetermined overhead application rate equal to 70% of direct labor cost.
Instructions: Enter the allocated overhead on the cost sheet for Job 102, fill in the cost summary section of the cost sheet, and then mark the cost sheet "Finished." Prepare a journal entry to record the job's completion and transfer to finished goods, and then post it to the general ledger accounts.

f. Delivered Job 102 and accepted the customer's promise to pay $290,000 within 30 days.
Instructions: Prepare journal entries to record the sale of Job 102 and the cost of goods sold. Post them to the general ledger accounts.

g. Applied overhead to Job 103 based on the job's direct labor to date.
Instructions: Enter overhead on the job cost sheet but do not make a journal entry at this time.

h. Recorded the total direct and indirect materials costs as reported on all the requisitions for the month.
Instructions: Prepare a journal entry to record these costs and post it to general ledger accounts.

i. Recorded the total direct and indirect labor costs as reported on all the time tickets for the month.
Instructions: Prepare a journal entry to record these costs and post it to general ledger accounts.

Check Figure Balance in Factory Overhead, $1,536 credit, overapplied

j. Recorded the total overhead costs applied to jobs.
Instructions: Prepare a journal entry to record the application of these costs and post it to general ledger accounts.

BEYOND THE NUMBERS

Reporting in Action

C1

NIKE's annual report indicates future growth potential from international sales.

Required

1. Predict the type of costs that will increase as a percent of sales with growth in international sales.
2. Explain why you think the types of costs identified for part (1) will increase for each company. (Hint: Think about why a cost increase is anticipated in the product and/or period cost category as international sales increase. You might evaluate the gross margin percent for further insight.)

Swoosh Ahead

3. Obtain NIKE's annual report information for a fiscal year ending after May 31, 1997. You can get this information from either its Web site [**www.nike.com**] or the SEC's EDGAR database [**www.sec.gov**]. Select no more than three accounts you identified in parts (1) and (2) and check your prediction.

Comparative Analysis

C1

Both **NIKE** and **Reebok** want to know the impact of a just-in-time inventory system for their operating cash flows. Review each company's statement of cash flows in Appendix A and answer the following:

Required

1. Identify the impact on operating cash flows (increase or decrease) for changes in inventory levels (increasing or decreasing) for each of the three most recent years data reported for both companies.
2. What impact would a JIT inventory system have on both NIKE's and Reebok's level of raw materials on hand and their operating cash flows? Link the answer to your response for part (1).
3. Would the move to a JIT system be a one time or recurring impact on operating cash flow?

Ethics Challenge

P4

An accounting professional requires at least two skill sets. The first is to be technically competent. Knowing how to capture, manage, and report information are necessary skills. The ability to anticipate management's and employees' biases is another skill. Knowing how a person is compensated, for instance, helps an accounting professional anticipate information biases. Draw on these two skills and write a one-half page memo to the financial officer on the practice of allocating overhead in your company. Information about your company follows:

Background: Your company sells portable housing to general contractors and the government. Jobs sold to contractors are won on a bid basis. A contractor will ask for three bids from different manufacturers. The combination of low bid and high quality wins the job. Jobs sold to the government are bid on a cost-plus basis. This means price is determined by adding all costs plus a profit based on cost at a specified percent, such as 10%. You observe that the amount of overhead allocated to government jobs is higher than that allocated to contract jobs. These allocations concern you and motivate your memo.

Communicating in Practice

C1, C2, C3

You are preparing for a second interview with a manufacturing company. The company is impressed with your credentials but has indicated they have several qualified applicants. You anticipate this second interview will necessitate that you exhibit how you can offer something special over other candidates. You learn the company currently uses a periodic inventory system and is not satisfied with the lack of timeliness of its information. The company manufactures special order holiday decorations and display items. To show your ability to improve the operation, you plan to recommend it use a cost accounting system.

Required

In preparation for the interview, you are to prepare notes outlining:

1. Your cost accounting system recommendation and why it is suitable for this company.
2. A general description of the documents that the cost accounting system requires.
3. How documents are used to facilitate the operation of the cost accounting system.

Taking It to the Net

C1, C2

Many manufacturing companies use job order cost accounting software to help measure the cost of jobs or job lots. As a consultant, you must find a good job order costing software package.

Required

Visit the Web site **www.comptrol.net** and click on *Job Cost.* Prepare a memo to the operating officer of a client company reporting information about job order costing software and a recommendation.

Teamwork in Action

C1, P1

The following items are taken from the adjusted trial balance and other records of Make-it-Better Company before the year-end closing entries are recorded:

Advertising expense	$ 15,300
Depreciation expense, Office equip.	7,000
Depreciation expense, Selling equip.	8,000
Depreciation of factory equipment	26,000
Direct labor	520,600
Factory supervision	98,000
Factory supplies used	12,600
Factory utilities	29,000
Indirect labor	48,000
Inventories:	
Raw materials, Jan. 1	142,000
Raw materials, Dec. 31	134,500
Goods in process, Jan. 1	12,700
Goods in process, Dec. 31	11,250
Finished goods, Jan. 1	131,500
Finished goods, Dec. 31	103,200
Miscellaneous production costs	6,800
Office salaries expense	60,700
Raw materials purchases	698,000
Rent expense, office space	16,900
Rent expense, selling space	20,600
Rent on factory building	63,800
Repairs, factory equipment	22,300
Sales	2,620,000
Sales discounts	46,000
Sales salaries expense	229,000

Required

1. **Each** member of the team is to assume the responsibility for computing **one** of the amounts listed below. You are not to duplicate your teammates' work. Get any necessary amounts from teammates. Each member is to explain the computation to the team in preparation for reporting to class.
   - **a.** Materials used.
   - **b.** Factory overhead.
   - **c.** Total manufacturing costs.
   - **d.** Total cost of goods in process.
   - **e.** Cost of goods manufactured.
2. Check your cost of goods manufactured with the instructor. If correct, proceed to part (3).
3. **Each** member of the team is to assume the responsibility for computing **one** of the amounts listed below. You are not to duplicate your teammates' work. Get any necessary amounts from teammates. Each member is to explain the computation to the team in preparation for reporting to class.
   - **a.** Net sales
   - **b.** Cost of goods sold
   - **c.** Gross profit
   - **d.** Total operating expenses
   - **e.** Net income or loss before taxes

Hitting the Road

C3, P2, P3, P4

Job order cost accounting is frequently used by builders.

Required

1. You (or your team) are to prepare a job order cost sheet for a single-family home under construction. List four items of both direct materials and direct labor. Explain how you think overhead should be applied.
2. Contact a builder and compare your job order cost sheet to the job cost sheet of this builder. If possible, speak to the accountant for that company. Write up your findings in a short report.

Business Week Activity

C1, C2

Managing materials in the production process is a challenging and crucial task for a company. Read the article "Porsche Is Back—And Then Some" in the September 15, 1997, issue of ***Business Week***.

Required

1. Explain how Wendelin Wiedeking used supply management to save Porsche.
2. Discuss what Wiedeking achieved in comparison to what we see in a successful grocery store.

Process Cost Accounting

A Look Back

Chapter 19 introduced managerial accounting, described cost concepts, and discussed modern manufacturing management principles. Chapter 20 introduced the manufacturing statement and how we account for cost flows. We also explained job order costing—an important cost accounting system.

A Look at This Chapter

This chapter focuses on how we measure and account for costs in process operations. We explain process production, describe how to assign costs to processes, and compute cost per equivalent unit for a process.

A Look Ahead

Chapter 22 describes managerial accounting reports useful in directing a company's activities. We explain how to allocate factory overhead costs to different products and describe the activity-based costing method of overhead allocation.

Chapter Outline

Cost of Tea Time

SAN FRANCISCO, CA—Christine Butler was about to confront her first on-the-job challenge. A recent business college graduate, she took her first job with Tasty Tea. **Tasty Tea** is a processor and distributor of tea products. It offers 15 different blends of tea to gourmet shops in one-pound bags.

After finishing her initial two-week training period, Butler and all other new employees had to prepare a report on Tasty Tea's process operations. "The company's expectations for us are high, and the competition is fierce," says Butler.

The report must include identifying the flow of information on product costs for Tasty Tea and estimating total product costs.

Butler's report identified three major processes: drying tea leaves, blending the different teas, and packaging the product. She explained that the drying and packaging processes are highly automated and computer controlled. But she described the blending process as much more labor intensive.

When Butler looked over her report, she was satisfied it covered all important processes and flows with one exception. "I just couldn't figure out how to come up with the cost of a pound of tea," says Butler. "It's a simple concept, but estimating actual costs is more difficult than I realized." Butler knows that cost estimation is crucial for setting selling prices and planning operations.

Butler recalled from her training course that companies with continuous processing, such as Tasty Tea, must use a costing system different from that used by custom manufacturers. She sought out colleagues and additional readings for help with process costing. "It took me about 40 hours of work to get my estimate," says Butler, "and I'm still not entirely confident with it."

Butler obtained her estimate using both process cost accounting methods and process cost summaries. Adds Butler, "Without training in managerial accounting it would have taken me twice as long, with twice as many questions!"

Learning Objectives

Conceptual

C1 Explain process operations and how they differ from job order operations.

C2 Define equivalent units and explain their use in process cost accounting.

C3 Explain the four steps in accounting for production activity in a period.

C4 Define a process cost summary and describe its purposes.

Analytical

A1 Compare process cost accounting and job order cost accounting.

A2 Analyze cost per equivalent unit with and without spoiled units of production.

Procedural

P1 Record the flow of direct materials costs in process cost accounting.

P2 Record the flow of direct labor costs in process cost accounting.

P3 Record the flow of factory overhead costs in process cost accounting.

P4 Compute equivalent units produced in a period.

P5 Prepare a process cost summary.

P6 Record the transfer of goods between departments.

P7 Record the transfer of completed goods to Finished Goods Inventory and Cost of Goods Sold.

CHAPTER PREVIEW

The type of product or service a company offers determines its cost accounting system. We focused on job order costing in Chapter 20. Companies use job order costing to account for manufacturing when a job consists of one unit (or a group of units) that is uniquely designed to meet the requirements of a particular customer. Each unit, or group of units, is a distinct product or job requiring unique applications of material, labor, and overhead. But not all products are manufactured in this way. Many products carry standard designs where one unit of product is no different than any other unit. This type of system often produces large numbers of products on a continuous basis, period after period. In this case, all units pass through similar manufacturing steps or processes. This chapter describes how to use a process cost accounting system to account for these types of products. We explain how manufacturing costs are accumulated for each process and then assigned to units passing through processes. This information helps in understanding and estimating the cost of each process. It also helps in finding ways to reduce costs and improve processes.

Process Operations

C1 Explain process operations and how they differ from job order operations.

There are many manufacturers engaged in continuous processing of similar, often called *homogeneous,* products. **Process manufacturing,** also called *process operations* or *process production,* is the mass production of products in a continuous flow of steps. This means products pass through a series of sequential processes.

Petroleum refining is a common example of process operations. Crude oil passes through a series of steps before it is processed into three grades of petroleum. The assembly line at the Ford Mustang plant in Dearborn, Michigan, reflects a process operation. An important characteristic of process operations is a high level of standardization. This is necessary if the system is to produce large volumes of products.

Other examples of products manufactured in a process manufacturing system are carpeting, hand tools, personal computers, furniture, skis, television sets, compact disks, building supplies (lumber, doors, paint), greeting cards, calculators, and small pleasure boats. **Dell Computer** uses a process manufacturing system and a process cost accounting system for a portion of its operations.

Process operations also extend to services. Examples include mail sorting in large post offices and order processing in large mail-order firms such as **L.L. Bean** and **Land's End.** The common feature in these service organizations is that operations are performed in a sequential manner using a series of standardized processes.

Each of these examples of products and services involves operations having a series of *processes,* or steps. Each process involves a different set of activities. A manufacturing operation that processes chemicals, for instance, might include the four steps shown in Exhibit 21.1. Understanding these processes is important for measuring their costs.

Exhibit 21.1

Process Manufacturing Operations: Chemicals

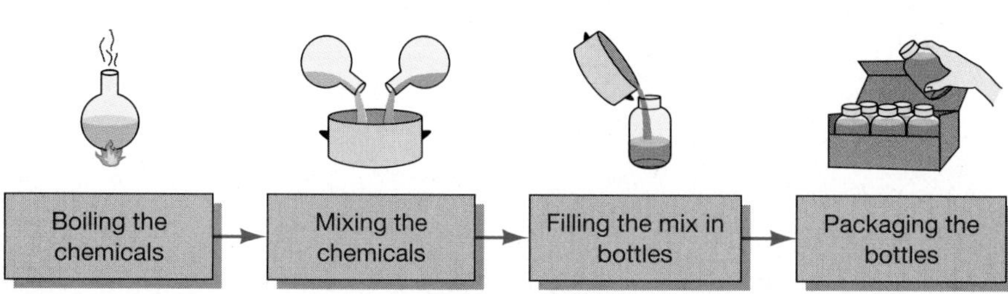

Comparing Job Order and Process Operations

A1 Compare process cost accounting and job order cost accounting.

Important features of both job order and process systems are shown in Exhibit 21.2. While we often describe job order and process operations with manufacturing examples, they also apply to service companies. In a job order costing system, the measurement focus is on the individual job or batch. In a process costing system, the measurement focus is on the process itself and the standardized units produced.

Exhibit 21.2
Comparing Job Order and Process Operations

Job Order Systems	Process Systems
• Custom orders	• Repetitive operations
• Heterogeneous products	• Homogeneous products
• Low production volume	• High production volume
• High product flexibility	• Low product flexibility
• Low to medium standardization	• High standardization

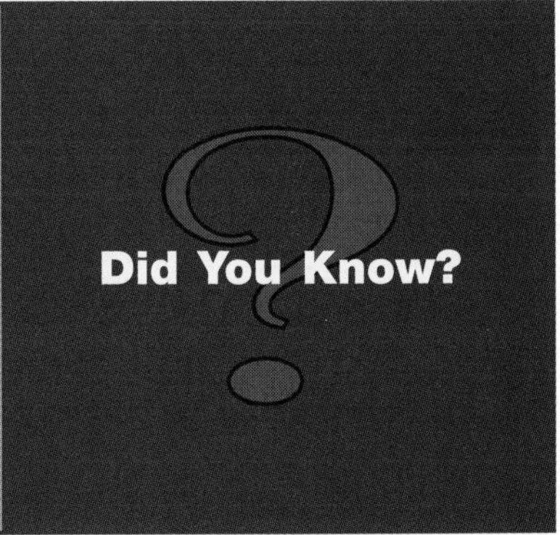

Mix and Match
A recent survey of 155 manufacturing companies show that 26.5% are organized as predominantly job order systems and 8.4% as predominantly process systems. Of the companies using either job order or process systems, 55.6% of these said they are adopting or using just-in-time manufacturing principles. [Source: M. Lindsay and S. Kalagnanam, *The Adoption of Just-in-Time Production Systems in Canada and Their Association with Management Control Practices,* Hamilton, Ontario: The SMAC, 1993.]

Organization of Process Operations

In a process manufacturing operation, each process is identified as a separate *production department, workstation,* or *work center.* A manager is usually responsible for one or more processes. With the exception of the first process or department, each receives the output from the prior department as a partially processed product. Depending on the nature of the process, a company applies direct labor, manufacturing overhead, and, perhaps, additional direct materials to move the product toward completion. Only the final process or department in the series produces finished goods ready for sale to customers.

Exhibit 21.3
Manufacturing Operations with Parallel and Sequential Processes

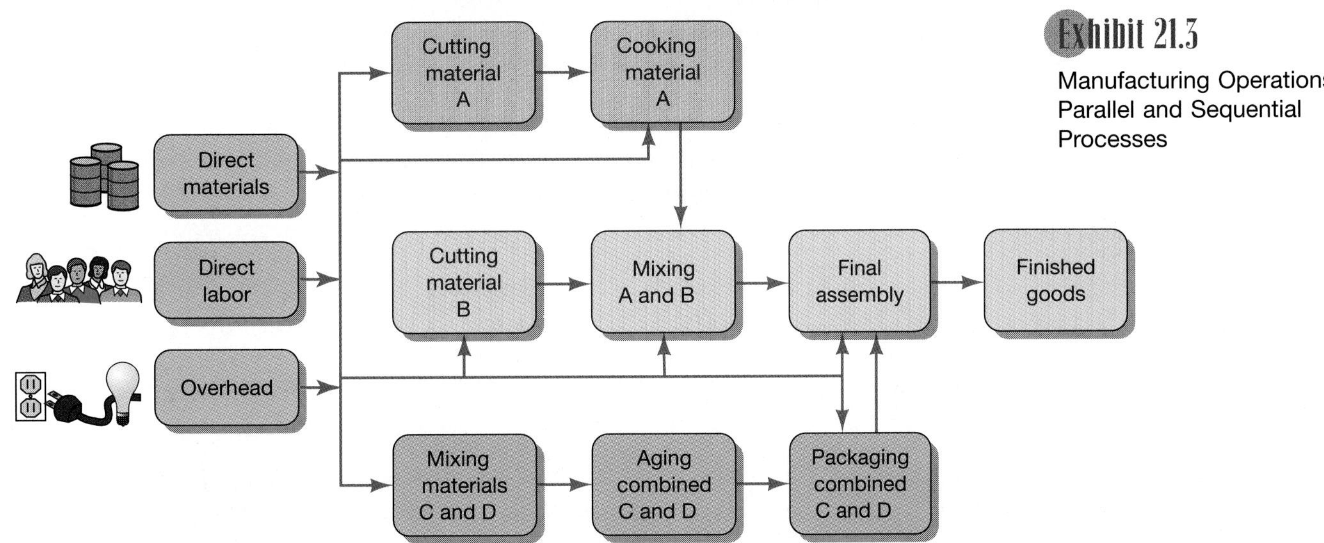

Exhibit 21.3 shows an operation in which components of a final product are manufactured in three parallel processes (shown in horizontal layout) and then combined at different stages of production. In addition to parallel processes, many manufacturing operations involve numerous components and related production processes.

GenX Company—An Illustration

We look at the **GenX Company** to illustrate process operations. GenX produces Profen®, an over-the-counter pain reliever for athletes. GenX sells Profen to wholesale distributors who in turn sell it to retailers.

Profen is produced in two steps. Step one uses a grinding process to pulverize blocks of its active ingredient, Profelene. Step two mixes the resulting powder with flavorings and preservatives and molds it into Profen tablets. Step two also includes packaging the Profen tablets.

Exhibit 21.4 shows a summary floor plan of the GenX factory, which has five rooms:

1. *Storeroom,* where materials are received and then distributed in response to requisitions.
2. *Production support office,* used by administrative and maintenance employees who support manufacturing operations.
3. *Locker rooms,* where workers change from street clothes into uniforms before working in the factory.
4. *Production floor,* divided into two areas for use by the grinding and mixing departments.
5. *Warehouse,* where finished products are stored before being shipped to wholesalers.

Floor Plan of GenX's Factory

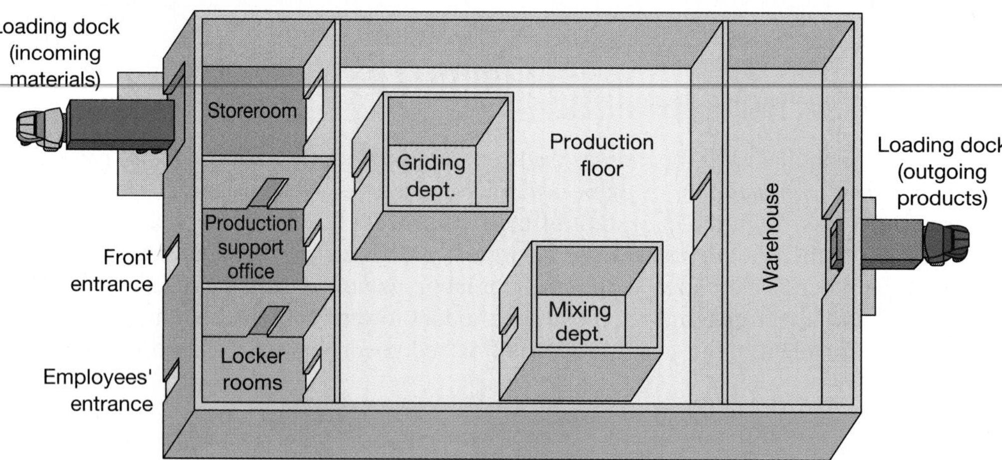

Even though GenX's manufacturing process is fairly simple, its factory operations can support five or more managers as shown in Exhibit 21.5.

Partial Organization Chart of GenX's Factory

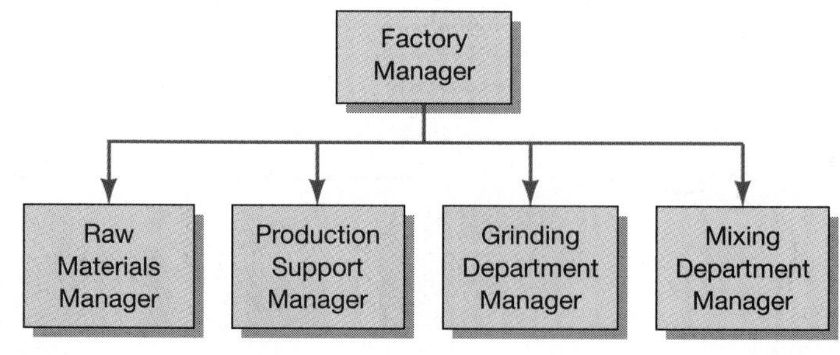

The first step in process manufacturing is the decision to produce a product. Management must determine the types and quantities of materials and labor needed and then schedule the work for departments. Based on these plans, production begins.

The flowchart in Exhibit 21.6 shows the production steps for GenX. The table in the lower portion of this exhibit summarizes GenX's cost of manufacturing inventories at the beginning of April, the manufacturing costs GenX incurred in April, and the application of these costs to the grinding and mixing departments. The following sections explain how GenX uses a process cost accounting system to obtain these costs. Many of the explanations refer back to this exhibit and its numbered cost flows.

Exhibit 21.6

Process Manufacturing Operations and Costs: GenX

A. Process Manufacturing Operations

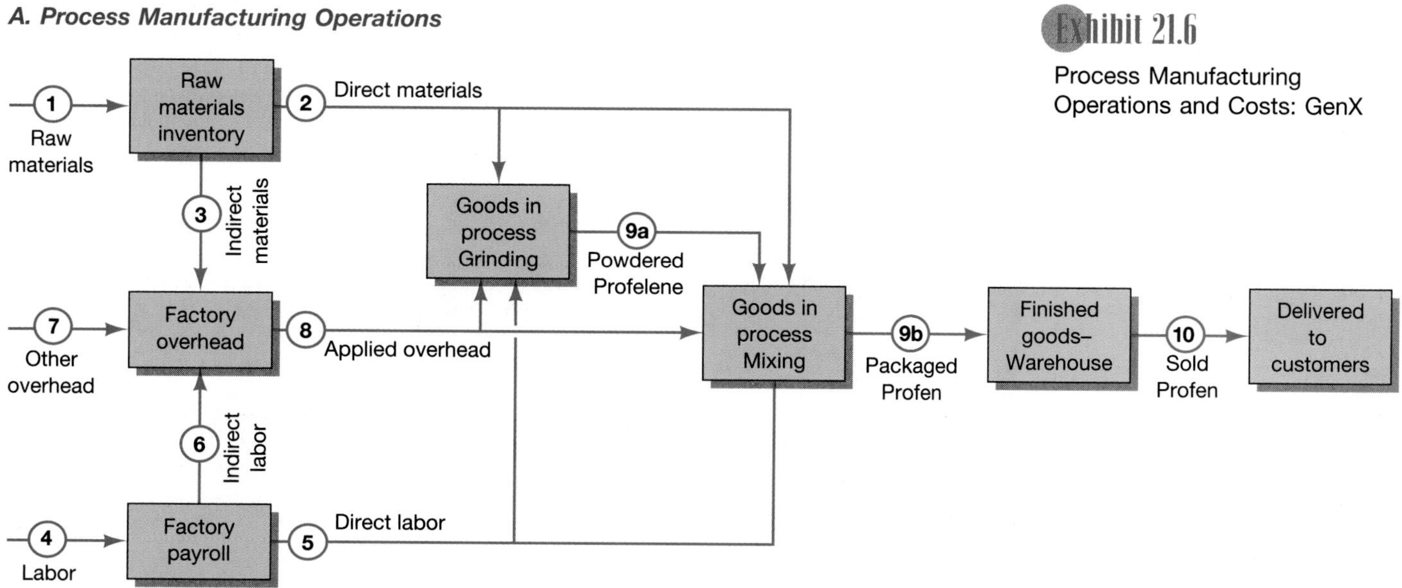

B. Manufacturing Costs in April

	Raw Materials	Factory Payroll	Factory Overhead	Grinding Department	Mixing Department
Beginning balance	$ 4,000			$ 4,250	$ 3,520
Purchases and costs incurred	14,135	$14,020	$ 880		
Application of costs:					
Direct materials	(11,940)			9,900	2,040
Indirect materials	(1,195)		1,195		
Direct labor		(10,800)		5,700	5,100
Indirect labor		(3,220)	3,220		
Overhead applied			(5,295)	4,275	1,020

Flash back

1. A process manufacturing operation: *(a)* is another name for a job order operation; *(b)* does not use the concepts of direct materials or direct labor; *(c)* usually assigns responsibility for each process to a manager.
2. Under what conditions is a process cost accounting system more suitable for measuring manufacturing costs than a job order cost accounting system?

Answers—p. 929

Process Cost Accounting

Process and job order manufacturing operations are similar in that they both combine materials, labor, and overhead in the process of producing products. Yet they differ in how they are organized and managed.

In job order operations, the **job order cost accounting** system assigns direct materials, direct labor, and overhead to specific jobs. The total job cost is then divided by the number of units to compute a cost per unit for that job.

In process manufacturing operations, the **process cost accounting system** assigns direct materials, direct labor, and overhead to specific processes. The total costs associated with each process are then divided by the number of units passing through that process to determine the cost per equivalent unit (defined later in the chapter) for that process. The cost per equivalent unit for each process is summed for all processes to determine the total cost per unit of a product.

The differences in how these two systems apply materials, labor, and overhead costs are highlighted in Exhibit 21.7. We explain how to compute unit costs later in the chapter.

Exhibit 21.7

Comparing Job Order and Process Cost Accounting

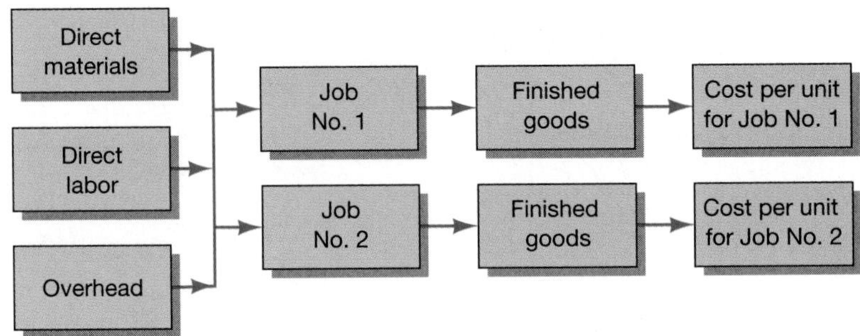

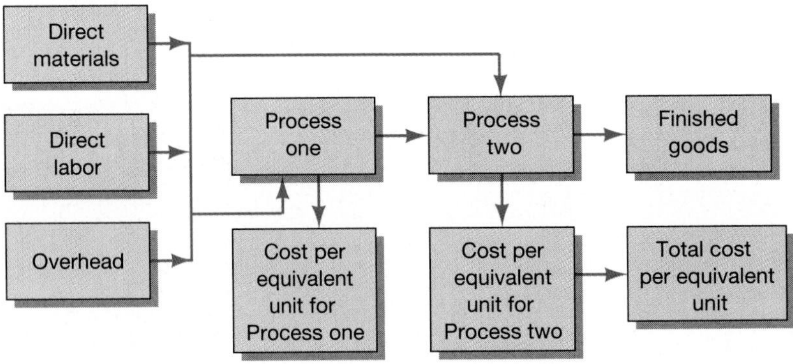

Direct and Indirect Costs

Chapter 19 explained that direct materials and direct labor costs are linked with specific units or batches of product. Manufacturing costs that cannot be clearly associated with specific units or batches of product are defined as manufacturing overhead. Chapter 20 explained how the concepts of direct and indirect costs are used in job order cost accounting. In particular, materials and labor used on jobs are charged to the jobs as direct costs. Materials and labor that contribute to manufacturing but that are not linked with specific jobs are indirect costs and are allocated to jobs as manufacturing overhead.

Process cost accounting systems also use the concepts of direct and indirect costs. Materials and labor that are clearly linked with specific processes are assigned to those processes as direct costs. Materials and labor that are not clearly linked with a specific process are indirect costs and are assigned to overhead. Some costs classified as overhead in a job order system may be classified as direct costs in process cost accounting. For example, depreciation of a machine used entirely by one process is a direct cost of that process. The next three subsections explain the accounting for materials, labor, and overhead in a process cost accounting system.

Factory Smarts
Robots, computers, and on-line information are all common in today's factory. This means more is expected of today's factory workers. The number of manufacturers putting a majority of their workers through training programs is triple what it was a decade ago. In addition, the roughly 20 million factory workers with a year or two of higher education has jumped to 25% from 17% a decade ago. Also, 19% have college degrees today, up from 16%. [Source: *Business Week,* September 30, 1996.]

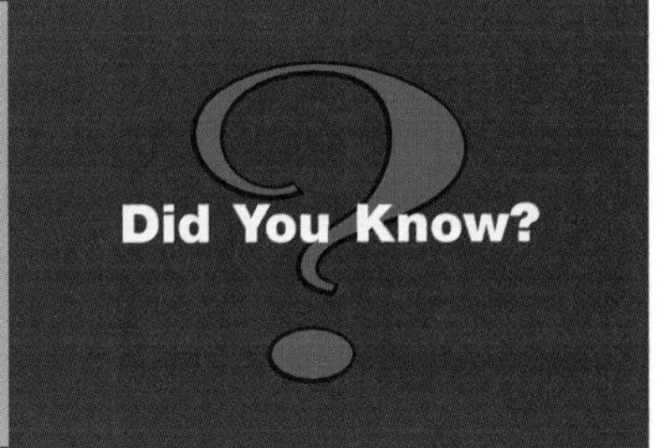

Accounting for Materials Costs

P1 Record the flow of direct materials costs in process cost accounting.

In Exhibit 21.6, arrow line ① reflects the arrival of materials at GenX's factory. These materials include Profelene, flavorings, preservatives, and packaging. It also includes supplies for the production support office. GenX uses a perpetual inventory system and makes all purchases on credit. The summary entry for receipts of raw materials in April is:[1]

①	Raw Materials Inventory	14,135	
	Accounts Payable		14,135
	Acquired materials on credit for factory use.		

Assets = Liabilities + Equity
+14,135 +14,135

The accounting department makes entries to record the receipt of materials when it receives copies of receiving reports from the storeroom.

Arrow line ② in Exhibit 21.6 reflects the flow of direct materials to the grinding and mixing departments, where they are used in producing Profen. Most direct materials are physically combined into the finished product. But in process cost accounting, direct materials also include supplies used in a specific process because they can be clearly linked with that process.

The manager of a process usually obtains material for use in a process by submitting a *materials requisition* to the raw materials storeroom manager. In some situations, materials move continuously from the raw materials inventory to a manufacturing process. **Coca-Cola Bottling,** for instance, uses a process in which inventory moves through the system continuously. In these cases, a **materials consumption report** summarizes the materials used by a department during a reporting period and replaces materials requisitions.

The entry to record the use of direct materials by GenX's two production departments in April is:

②	Goods in Process Inventory—Grinding	9,900	
	Goods in Process Inventory—Mixing	2,040	
	Raw Materials Inventory		11,940
	To assign costs of direct materials used in the grinding and mixing departments.		

Assets = Liabilities + Equity
+9,900
+2,040
−11,940

[1] We omit transaction dates in journal entries numbered ① through ⑩ for brevity.

Use of two goods in process inventory accounts allows the costs incurred by each process to be separately accumulated. Also, this entry doesn't increase or decrease the company's assets. It merely transfers costs from one asset account to two other asset accounts.

In Exhibit 21.6, the arrow line ③ shows the flow of indirect materials from the storeroom to factory overhead. These materials are not clearly linked with either the grinding or the mixing departments. They are used in support of overall production activity. The entry to record the cost of indirect materials used by GenX in April is:

Assets = Liabilities + Equity
−1,195 −1,195

③	Factory Overhead	1,195	
	Raw Materials Inventory		1,195
	To record indirect materials used in April.		

After the entries for both direct and indirect materials are posted, the Raw Materials Inventory account appears as shown in Exhibit 21.8.

Exhibit 21.8

Raw Materials Inventory Ledger Account

Raw Materials Inventory					Acct. No. 132
Date		**Explanation**	**Debit**	**Credit**	**Balance**
2000					
Mar.	31	Beginning balance			4,000
Apr.	30	Materials purchases	14,135		18,135
	30	Direct materials usage		11,940	6,195
	30	Indirect materials usage		1,195	5,000

The April 30 balance sheet reports a $5,000 Raw Materials Inventory account as a current asset.

P2 Record the flow of direct labor costs in process cost accounting.

Accounting for Labor Costs

Exhibit 21.6 shows factory payroll costs of GenX as reflected in arrow line ④. Total labor costs of $14,020 are paid in cash and are recorded in the Factory Payroll account with this entry:

Assets = Liabilities + Equity
−14,020 −14,020

④	Factory Payroll	14,020	
	Cash		14,020
	To record factory wages for April.		

This entry is triggered by time reports from the two production departments and the production support office. For simplicity, we do not separately identify withholdings and additional payroll taxes for employees.

In a process operation, the direct labor of a production department includes all labor used exclusively by that department. This is the case even if the labor is not applied to the product itself. If a production department in a process operation, for instance, has a full-time manager and a full-time maintenance worker, their salaries are direct labor costs, not factory overhead.

Arrow line ⑤ in Exhibit 21.6 shows GenX's use of direct labor in the grinding and mixing departments. The entry to transfer April's direct labor costs from the Factory Payroll account to the two goods in process inventory accounts is:

Assets = Liabilities + Equity
+5,700 +10,800
+5,100

⑤	Goods in Process Inventory—Grinding	5,700	
	Goods in Process Inventory—Mixing	5,100	
	Factory Payroll		10,800
	To assign costs of direct labor used in the grinding and mixing departments.		

Arrow line ⑥ in Exhibit 21.6 reflects the indirect labor costs of GenX. These employees provide the clerical, maintenance, and other services that help the grinding and mixing departments produce Profen more efficiently. For example, they order materials, deliver them to the factory floor, repair equipment, operate and program computers used in production, keep payroll and other production records, clean up, and move the finished goods to the warehouse. The entry to charge these indirect labor costs to factory overhead is:

⑥	Factory Overhead	3,220	
	Factory Payroll		3,220
	To record indirect labor as overhead.		

Assets = Liabilities + Equity
−3,220
+3,220

After these entries for both direct and indirect labor are posted, the Factory Payroll account appears as shown in Exhibit 21.9.

Exhibit 21.9

Factory Payroll Ledger Account

Factory Payroll					Acct. No. 530
Date		Explanation	Debit	Credit	Balance
2000					
Mar.	31	Beginning balance			-0-
Apr.	30	Total payroll for April	14,020		14,020
	30	Direct labor costs		10,800	3,220
	30	Indirect labor costs		3,220	-0-

The factory payroll account is now closed and ready to receive entries for May.

Full Service Accounting

Many service companies use process departments to perform specific tasks for consumers. Hospitals, for instance, have radiology and physical therapy facilities with special equipment and trained employees. When patients need services, they are processed through proper departments and receive prescribed care. In a different setting, **AT&T** uses a system similar to process cost accounting to accumulate costs for services such as directory assistance. Service companies need cost accounting information as much as manufacturers to estimate costs of providing services, to plan future operations, to control costs, and to determine charges to customers. The techniques of process cost accounting are applied equally well to service operations.

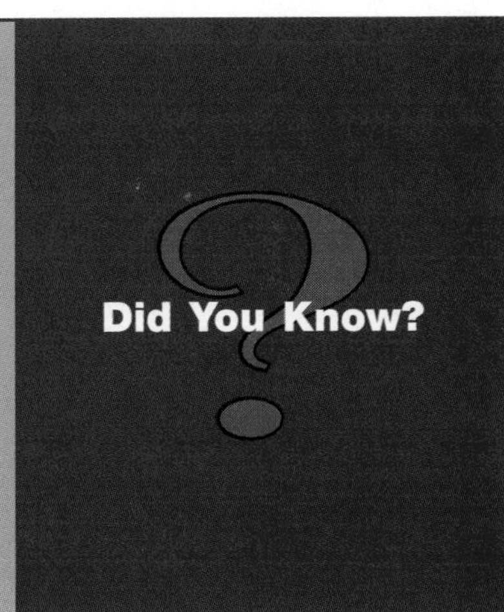

Accounting for Factory Overhead

P3 Record the flow of factory overhead costs in process cost accounting.

Overhead costs other than indirect materials and indirect labor are reflected by arrow line ⑦ in Exhibit 21.6. These overhead items include the costs of insuring manufacturing assets, renting the factory building, using factory utilities, and depreciating equipment not directly related to a specific process. The entry to record overhead costs for April is:

⑦	Factory Overhead	880	
	Prepaid Insurance		80
	Accrued Utilities Payable		200
	Cash		250
	Accumulated Depreciation, Factory Equipment		350
	To record overhead items incurred in April.		

Assets = Liabilities + Equity
−80 +200 −880
−250
−350

After this entry is posted, the Factory Overhead account balance is $5,295. This balance is comprised of indirect materials of $1,195, indirect labor of $3,220, and $880 of other overhead.

Arrow line ⑧ in Exhibit 21.6 reflects the application of factory overhead to the two production departments. Recall from Chapters 19 and 20 that factory overhead was applied to products or jobs by relating overhead cost to another variable such as direct labor hours or machine hours used in production. Process cost systems use a similar procedure along with predetermined application rates. For example, **Boeing** uses total labor hours for allocating its overhead costs to products.

In many situations, a single allocation basis such as direct labor hours (or a single rate for the entire plant) fails to provide useful allocations. As a result, management may use different rates for different production departments. Based on an analysis of each department's operations, GenX applies its April overhead on the basis of direct labor cost, but with different rates, as shown in Exhibit 21.10.

Exhibit 21.10

Applying Factory Overhead

Production Department	Direct Labor Cost	Predetermined Rate*	Overhead Applied
Grinding	$5,700	75%	$4,275
Mixing	5,100	20	1,020
Total			$5,295

* Predetermined overhead application rates are:
Grinding department . . . . 75% of direct labor cost
Mixing department . . . . . 20% of direct labor cost

GenX records its applied overhead with the following entry:

⑧	Goods in Process Inventory—Grinding	4,275	
	Goods in Process Inventory—Mixing	1,020	
	Factory Overhead		5,295
	Allocated overhead costs to grinding department at 75% of direct labor cost and to mixing department at 20% of direct labor cost.		

Assets = Liabilities + Equity
+4,275 +5,295
+1,020

After posting this entry, the Factory Overhead account appears as shown in Exhibit 21.11.

For GenX, the amount of overhead applied equals the actual overhead incurred during April. In most cases, using a predetermined overhead application rate leaves an over-

Exhibit 21.11

Factory Overhead Ledger Account

Factory Overhead					Acct. No. 540
Date		Explanation	Debit	Credit	Balance
2000					
Mar.	31	Beginning balance			-0-
Apr.	30	Indirect materials usage	1,195		1,195
	30	Indirect labor costs	3,220		4,415
	30	Other overhead costs	880		5,295
	30	Applied to production departments		5,295	-0-

applied or underapplied balance in the Factory Overhead account. At the end of the period, this overapplied or underapplied balance should be either closed to the Cost of Goods Sold account or allocated among the cost of goods sold, the goods in process inventory, and the finished goods inventory. Procedures for this allocation are the same as that described in Chapter 20 for job order cost accounting systems.

Budget Officer
You are working on identifying the direct and indirect costs of a new processing department containing several automated machines. The manager of this department instructs you to classify a majority of the costs as indirect to take advantage of the direct labor based overhead allocation method and to be charged with a lower amount of overhead (owing to the small direct labor component within the department). You know this penalizes other departments who will then be hit with higher allocations. It also means the performance ratings of managers in these other departments will suffer. What action(s) do you take?

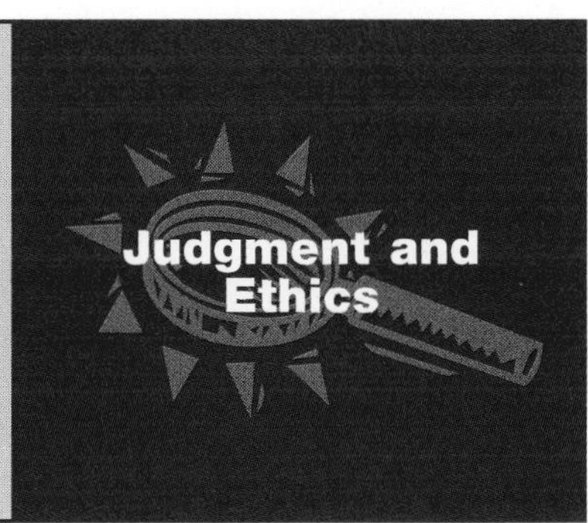

Answer—p. 928

Flash back

3. When direct materials are assigned and used in both Department X and Department Y, the entry that records the use of direct materials includes:
   a. A credit to Goods in Process Inventory—Department X.
   b. A debit to Goods in Process Inventory—Department Y.
   c. A credit to Goods in Process Inventory—Department Y.
4. What are the three categories of cost incurred by both job order and process manufacturing operations?
5. How many Goods in Process Inventory accounts are needed in a process cost accounting system?

Answers—p. 929

Equivalent Units of Production

C2 Define equivalent units and explain their use in process cost accounting.

We already explained how materials, labor, and overhead costs for a period are accumulated in separate Goods in Process Inventory accounts for each manufacturing process. But we have not explained the arrow lines labeled (9a), (9b) and (10) in Exhibit 21.6. These lines reflect the transfer of products from the grinding department to the mixing department, from the mixing department to finished goods inventory, and from finished goods inventory to cost of goods sold. To determine the costs recorded for these flows, we must first determine the cost per unit of product and then apply this result to the number of units transferred.

Accounting for Goods in Process

If a manufacturing process has no beginning and ending goods in process inventory, the unit cost computation is simple. The unit cost of goods transferred out of a process when there is no beginning and ending goods in process inventory is:

$$\frac{\textbf{Total cost assigned to the process (direct materials, direct labor, and overhead)}}{\textbf{Total number of units started and finished in the period}}$$

But if a process has a beginning or ending inventory of partially processed units, the total cost assigned to the process must be allocated to all units worked on during the period. This means the denominator must measure the entire production activity of the process for the period. This measure is called **equivalent units of production** (or **EUP**). Equivalent units of production refer to the number of units that would be completed if all effort during a period had been applied to only those units that were started and finished in a period. This measure is used in computing the cost per equivalent unit and to assign costs to finished goods and goods in process inventory (this is explained later in the chapter).

To illustrate, assume GenX adds (or introduces) 100 units of material into the grinding process during the period. Suppose at the end of the period, the production supervisor determines that the 100 units are 60% processed. The equivalent units of production for that period is 60 units, computed as 100 units × 60%. This means if we'd introduced 60 units into the process, we would've completely processed these 60 units.

Differences between Equivalent Units for Materials and for Labor and Overhead

P4 Compute the equivalent units produced in a period.

In many manufacturing processes, the equivalent units of production for materials is not the same as it is for labor and for overhead. To illustrate, consider the process operation shown in Exhibit 21.12:

Exhibit 21.12

Process Manufacturing: An Example

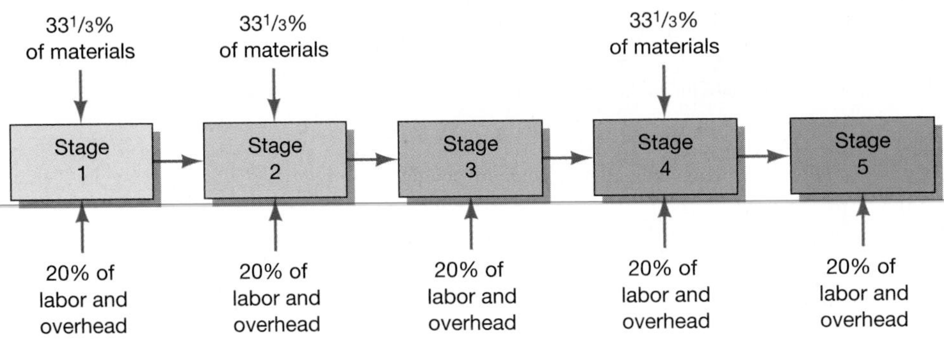

This exhibit shows a single production process consisting of five stages. One-third of the direct material cost is added at each of three stages: Stage 1, Stage 2, and Stage 4. One-fifth of the direct labor cost is added at each of the five stages. Because overhead is applied as a percent of direct labor, one-fifth of the overhead also is added at each of the five stages.

When units finish Stage 1, they are one-third complete with respect to materials but only one-fifth complete with respect to labor and overhead. When they finish Stage 2, they are two-thirds complete with respect to materials, but only two-fifths complete with respect to labor and overhead. When they finish Stage 3, they remain two-thirds complete with respect to materials, but are now three-fifths complete with respect to labor and overhead. When they finish Stage 4, they are 100% complete with respect to materials (all materials have been added) but only four-fifths complete with respect to labor and overhead.

As an example, if 300 units of product are started and processed through Stage 1 in Exhibit 21.12, they are one-third complete *with respect to materials.* Expressed in terms of equivalent finished units, the processing of these 300 units is equal to finishing 100 units, computed as 300 units × $33\frac{1}{3}\%$. But only one-fifth of direct labor and overhead are included in the 300 units at the end of Stage 1. The equivalent units of production *with respect to direct labor and overhead* is 60 units, computed as 300 units × 20%.

May I Help You?

Customer-interaction software is one of the hottest items in customer-service processes. Whether the business is insurance, long-distance phone service, or technology services, companies are finding this software can turn their customer-service process into an asset. How does it work? For starters, it cuts time spent on 800-service calls because a customer only describes a problem once. It also yields a database of customer questions and complaints that gives insights into needed improvements. It can also recognize incoming phone numbers and immediately direct them to the proper personnel along with data on previous dealings. [Source: *Business Week,* April 29, 1996.]

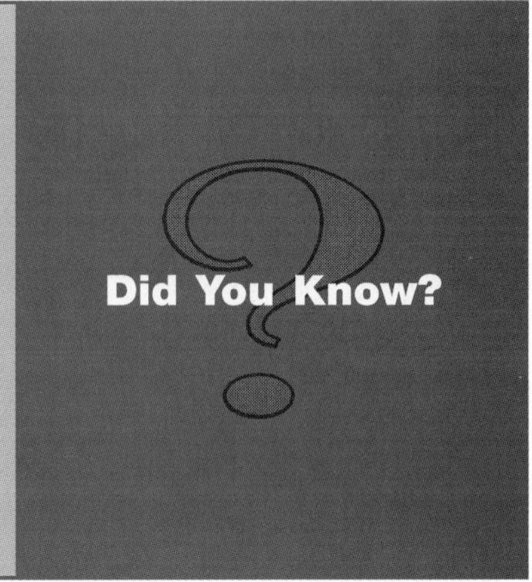

Accounting for First (Grinding) Department

Exhibit 21.13 shows the information necessary to compute equivalent units of production for GenX's grinding department for the month of April.

Exhibit 21.13

Production Data—Grinding Department

Beginning inventory (March 31):	
Units of product	30,000
Percentage of completion—direct materials	100%
Percentage of completion—direct labor	33⅓%
Units started in April	90,000
Units transferred from grinding to mixing in April	100,000
Ending inventory (April 30):	
Units of product	20,000
Percentage of completion—direct materials	100%
Percentage of completion—direct labor	25%

C3 Explain the four steps in accounting for production activity in a period.

In computing equivalent units, we assume each of GenX's production departments process units on a first-in, first-out basis.[2] Accounting for a period's activity includes four steps involving: (1) physical flow, (2) equivalent units, (3) cost per equivalent unit, and (4) cost reconciliation. Each of these steps is described in this section.

Physical Flow of Units

Physical flow is a reconciliation of (a) the physical units started in a period with (b) the physical units completed. A physical flow reconciliation is shown in Exhibit 21.14 for GenX for April.

Exhibit 21.14

Physical Flow—Grinding Department

Units to Account For:		Units Accounted For:	
Beginning inventory	30,000 units	Units transferred from grinding to mixing	100,000 units
Units started in April	90,000 units	Ending inventory	20,000 units
Total number of units	**120,000 units**	Total number of units	**120,000 units**

[2] We assume a FIFO flow for all related computations in this chapter. Weighted average and LIFO also can be used. But they are less useful for measuring how effectively costs are controlled during a period. When using a just-in-time inventory system, the different inventory methods will yield similar results because of minimal inventories carrying over from one period to the next.

The 100,000 units transferred from grinding to mixing during April include the 30,000 units from the beginning goods in process inventory (or simply beginning inventory). The remaining 70,000 units transferred out are from units started in April. A total of 90,000 units are started in April. Because 70,000 of these 90,000 units are completed, only 20,000 units remain unfinished at the end of the period.

Equivalent Units of Production

The second step is to compute equivalent units of production in the grinding department for direct materials, direct labor, and factory overhead for April. Overhead is applied using direct labor as an allocation base. This means the equivalent units are the same for both labor and overhead in this case.

Equivalent Units—Direct Materials

Direct materials (the Profelene blocks) are added at the beginning of the process. A unit of product is 100% complete with respect to materials as soon as it is started. This means beginning goods in process inventory for April received all its materials in March and is not assigned any additional materials. The 70,000 units started and completed in April and the 20,000 units in ending goods in process inventory (or simply ending inventory) on April 30 received all their materials in April. With respect to materials, the grinding department's equivalent units of production are computed as shown in Exhibit 21.15.

Exhibit 21.15

Equivalent Units of Production—Grinding Department's Direct Materials

	Units of Product		Percent Added This Period		Equivalent Units
Beginning goods in process	30,000	×	0%	=	-0-
Goods started and completed	70,000	×	100	=	70,000
Ending goods in process	20,000	×	100	=	20,000
Total units	120,000				90,000

Equivalent Units—Direct Labor and Factory Overhead

Direct labor and factory overhead, both considered conversion costs, are assigned uniformly throughout the process for GenX. Recall that beginning inventory of 30,000 units are partially completed in March. In April, additional labor and overhead are assigned to these units to complete them. Based on percent of completion, 33⅓% of labor and overhead was assigned in March. The remaining 66⅔% is assigned in April. The 70,000 units started and completed in April are assigned 100% of labor and overhead. The 20,000 units in ending inventory are assigned only 25% of labor at the end of April. Exhibit 21.16 shows us these computations.

Exhibit 21.16

Equivalent Units of Production—Grinding Department's Direct Labor and Overhead

	Units of Product		Percent Added This Period		Equivalent Units
Beginning goods in process	30,000	×	66⅔%	=	20,000
Goods started and completed	70,000	×	100	=	70,000
Ending goods in process	20,000	×	25	=	5,000
Total units	120,000				95,000

A summary of April's equivalent units of production for the grinding department is shown in Exhibit 21.17.*

* In Exhibits 21.17 and 21.19, the last two columns can be combined and termed *Conversion.* This practice of combining these two cost items must then be carried over to the other cost reports as well.

Activities during April	Direct Materials	Direct Labor	Factory Overhead
Units from beginning inventory processed in current period	0	20,000	20,000
Units started and completed in current period	70,000	70,000	70,000
Units in ending inventory at end of current period	20,000	5,000	5,000
Equivalent units of production for period	90,000	95,000	95,000

Exhibit 21.17

Equivalent Units of Production—Grinding Department Summary

Cost per Equivalent Unit

The third step is to compute the *cost per equivalent unit* for direct materials, direct labor, and factory overhead. Exhibit 21.6 reported that GenX's grinding department incurred $9,900 in direct materials and $5,700 in direct labor costs for April. Factory overhead of $4,275 is also applied to the grinding process. These costs are assigned to: the partially completed units from beginning inventory, the units started and completed during the current period, and the units in ending inventory at the end of the period. GenX's cost assignment of direct labor for April is illustrated in Exhibit 21.18. Similar cost assignments are made for materials and overhead.

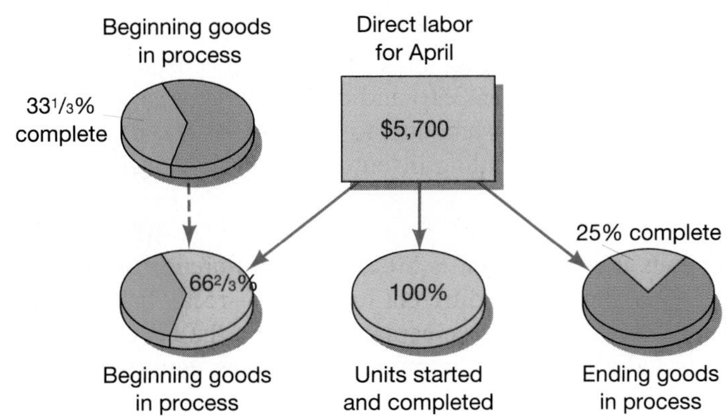

Exhibit 21.18

Grinding Department's Assignment of Direct Labor

These cost assignments along with the equivalent units computed in the prior section are used in determining the cost per equivalent unit for materials, labor, and overhead. These computations for April are shown in Exhibit 21.19.

Activities during April	Direct Materials	Direct Labor	Factory Overhead
Costs assigned to grinding in current period	$9,900	$5,700	$4,275
Equivalent units of production in current period	90,000	95,000	95,000
Cost per equivalent unit for period	$0.11	$0.06	$0.045

Exhibit 21.19

Cost per Equivalent Unit—Grinding Department

Total cost per equivalent unit for the grinding department amounts to $0.215, computed as $0.11 + $0.06 + $0.045.

Cost Reconciliation

The fourth and final step in this process is to reconcile the *costs to account for* with the *costs accounted for* in the period. We do this by identifying the costs to (1) process beginning inventory, (2) start and complete units transferred from grinding to mixing, and (3) process ending inventory. Exhibit 21.20 shows this cost reconciliation.

Exhibit 21.20

Cost Reconciliation—Grinding Department

Costs to Account for:		
From beginning inventory		$ 4,250
Assigned in April (direct materials, direct labor, and overhead)		19,875
Total costs		**$24,125**
Costs Accounted for:		
Beginning inventory completed in April:		
Costs from previous period		$ 4,250
Costs assigned in current period:		
Direct materials (0 units × $0.11)	$ 0	
Direct labor (20,000 units × $0.06)	1,200	
Factory overhead (20,000 units × $0.045)	900	2,100
Costs to process beginning inventory in April		$ 6,350
Cost of units started and completed in April (70,000 × $0.215)		$15,050
Ending inventory for April:		
Direct materials (20,000 units × $0.11)	$2,200	
Direct labor (5,000 units × $0.06)	300	
Factory overhead (5,000 units × $0.045)	225	
Costs of ending inventory in April		$ 2,725
Total costs		**$24,125**

The total *costs to account for* must equal the total *costs accounted for* in a cost reconciliation (minor differences can exist due to rounding). Also, the costs of units transferred out from grinding to mixing must include the costs of beginning inventory processed in the current period ($6,350) and the costs of units started and completed in the current period ($15,050). This amounts to $21,400 for 100,000 units transferred out, or $0.214 per unit. This leaves ending inventory, which is valued at $2,725, that is carried over to the next period.

Exhibit 21.19 showed that total cost per equivalent unit for April is $0.215. But the cost per unit for the units transferred out is $0.214. The difference of $0.001 exists because the total cost per equivalent unit is different for March—recall that $4,250 of the $21,400 is carried forward from March. As we explained earlier, the FIFO method uses only current period's costs and activities in computing the cost per equivalent unit for that period.

Flash back

6. Equivalent units are:

a. A measure of a production department's productivity in using direct materials, direct labor, or overhead.

b. Units of a product produced by a foreign competitor that are similar to units produced by a domestic company.

c. Generic units of a product similar to brand-name units of a product.

7. Interpret the meaning of a department's equivalent units with respect to direct labor?

8. A department began an accounting period with 8,000 units that were one-fourth complete. It also started and completed 50,000 units, and ended with 6,000 units that were one-third complete. How many equivalent units did it produce during the period?

Answers—p. 929

Process Cost Summary

C4 Define a process cost summary and describe its purposes.

An important managerial accounting report for a process cost accounting system is the **process cost summary.** A separate process cost summary is prepared for each process or production department. Three purposes of the summary are to: (1) help department managers control their departments; (2) help factory managers evaluate department managers' performances; and (3) provide cost information for financial statements. A process cost summary achieves these purposes by describing the costs charged to each department, computing the equivalent units of production achieved by each department, and determining the costs assigned to each department's output.

A summary report is prepared through a combination of Exhibits 21.14, 21.17, 21.19, and 21.20. A common format for the process cost summary is shown in Exhibit 21.21. The summary is divided into three sections. Section 1 lists the total costs charged to the department. This includes direct materials, direct labor, and overhead costs incurred. It also includes the cost of the beginning goods in process inventory.

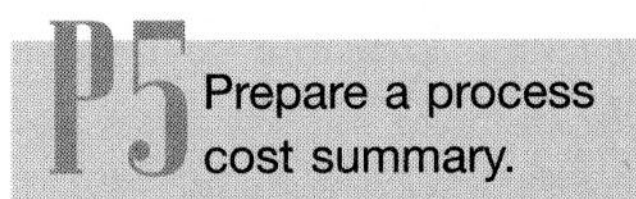

Prepare a process cost summary.

Section 2 describes the equivalent units of production for the department. Equivalent units for materials, labor, and overhead are often in separate columns. GenX reports equivalent units for labor and overhead in one column because it applies overhead using labor as the allocation base. Section 2 also shows direct materials, direct labor, and overhead costs per equivalent unit.

Section 3 allocates total costs among products worked on in the period. Costs of completing beginning inventory units are computed and added to the cost carried forward from March to get total processing cost of $6,350 for beginning inventory units. Also, costs of processing 70,000 units from start to finish are computed and added to get their total processing cost of $15,050. The $6,350 and $15,050 are added to give us $21,400 total cost of goods transferred out of the department. The final part of section 3 computes the $2,725 cost of partially processing the ending inventory units. The assigned costs are then added to show that the total $24,125 cost charged to the department in section 1 is now assigned to the units in section 3.

Flash back

9. A process cost summary for a department has three sections. What information is presented in each of them?

Answer—p. 929

General Manager

You are the general manager of a new company manufacturing two distinctly different types of tiny electronic components. Both components are produced in large quantities using the same process consisting of four departments. You are preparing for a meeting with the accountant to discuss whether to report the cost per equivalent unit for both products together or separately for each product. What do you advise?

Answer—p. 928

Transfers between Departments

P6 Record the transfer of goods between departments.

Arrow line (9) in Exhibit 21.6 reflects the transfer of units (powdered Profelene) from the grinding department to the mixing department. The $21,400 cost of this transfer, as computed in Section 3 of the process cost summary of Exhibit 21.21, is recorded with the following entry:

(9a)	Goods in Process Inventory—Mixing	21,400	
	Goods in Process Inventory—Grinding		21,400
	To record transfer of partially completed goods from the grinding department to the mixing department.		

Assets	= Liabilities + Equity
+21,400	
−21,400	

Exhibit 21.21

Process Cost Summary—Grinding Department

GENX COMPANY
Process Cost Summary for Grinding Department
For Month Ended April 30, 2000

①

Costs Charged to Department:	
Direct materials requisitioned	$ 9,900
Direct labor charged	5,700
Overhead allocated (at predetermined rate)	4,275
Total processing costs for the period	$19,875
Goods in process at the beginning of the period	4,250
Total costs to be accounted for	**$24,125**

②

		Equivalent Units	
Equivalent Unit Processing Costs:	**Units of Product**	**Direct Materials**	**Labor and Overhead**
Units processed:			
Beginning goods in process	30,000	0	20,000
Units started and completed	70,000	70,000	70,000
Ending goods in process	20,000	20,000	5,000
Total	120,000	90,000	95,000

Total direct materials cost for the period	$9,900
Direct materials cost per equivalent unit ($9,900/90,000 units)	$0.110
Total direct labor cost for the period	$5,700
Direct labor cost per equivalent unit ($5,700/95,000 units)	$0.060
Total overhead cost for the period	$4,275
Overhead cost per equivalent unit ($4,275/95,000 units)	$0.045

③

Assignment of Costs to Output of Department:	**Equivalent Units**	**Cost per Unit**	**Total Cost**
Goods in process, March 31, 2000, and completed in the period:			
Costs from prior period			$ 4,250
Direct materials added			0
Direct labor added	20,000	$0.060	1,200
Overhead applied	20,000	0.045	900
Total costs to process			$ 6,350
Goods started and completed in the period:			
Direct materials added	70,000	$0.110	$ 7,700
Direct labor added	70,000	0.060	4,200
Overhead applied	70,000	0.045	3,150
Total costs to process			$15,050
Total costs transferred to mixing department (unit cost = $21,400/100,000 units = $0.214)			$21,400
Goods in process, April 30, 2000:			
Direct materials added	20,000	$0.110	$ 2,200
Direct labor added	5,000	0.060	300
Overhead applied	5,000	0.045	225
Total costs to process			$ 2,725
Total costs accounted for			**$24,125**

After this entry is posted, the Goods in Process Inventory account for the grinding department appears as shown in Exhibit 21.22.

Goods in Process Inventory — Grinding					Acct. No. 133
Date		Explanation	Debit	Credit	Balance
2000					
Mar.	31	Beginning balance			4,250
Apr.	30	Direct materials usage	9,900		14,150
	30	Direct labor costs	5,700		19,850
	30	Applied overhead	4,275		24,125
	30	Transfer to mixing department		21,400	2,725

Exhibit 21.22

Goods in Process Inventory (Grinding) Ledger Account

The $2,725 ending balance in this Goods in Process Inventory account equals the cost assigned to partially completed units as shown in section 3 of the process cost summary.

Flash back

10. What effect does the transfer of a partially completed product from one production department to another have on the total assets of the company?

Answer—p. 929

Accounting for Second (Mixing) Department

The mixing department begins working on Profelene when it is received from the grinding department. Most of its costs are in the form of labor—for specialist in mixing the compounds and laborers for packaging the product. Direct labor and overhead are added at the same rate as direct materials.

Equivalent Units of Production

The mixing department requires only one computation of equivalent units of production. This is because direct materials, direct labor, and overhead are used at the same rate. Exhibit 21.23 provides the data needed to compute equivalent units of production for the mixing department for April.

Beginning inventory (March 31):	
Units of product	16,000
Percentage of completion—Direct materials, direct labor, and overhead	25%
Units received from grinding department	100,000
Units transferred to finished goods	101,000
Ending inventory (April 30):	
Units of product	15,000
Percentage of completion—direct materials, direct labor, and overhead	33⅓%

Exhibit 21.23

Production Data—Mixing Department

A total of 101,000 units are transferred from the mixing department to finished goods in the period. Based on a first-in, first-out assumption, 16,000 of these units came from beginning goods in process inventory and 85,000 are received and completed in the period. Because 100,000 units are received from the grinding department in the period and only 85,000 of these units are completed, the ending goods in process inventory is 15,000 units.

Exhibit 21.24 computes the mixing department's equivalent units of production for direct materials, direct labor, and overhead for the month of April.

Exhibit 21.24

Equivalent Units of Production—Mixing Department

	Units of Product		Percent Added This Period		Equivalent Units
Beginning goods in process	16,000	×	75%	=	12,000
Goods started and completed	85,000	×	100	=	85,000
Ending goods in process	15,000	×	33⅓	=	5,000
Total units	116,000				102,000

Process Cost Summary

Exhibit 21.25 shows the process cost summary for the mixing department. The costs charged to the department in section 1 include $21,400 transferred in from the grinding department. Section 2 shows the equivalent units of production for the direct materials, direct labor, and overhead for the mixing department. Section 2 also computes the costs per equivalent unit. Section 3 shows how costs charged to the department are assigned to the output of the department. The $29,470 cost of the units transferred to finished goods is computed as the combined cost of the beginning units in process and the units received and completed in the period.

The beginning goods in process inventory for the mixing department is 100% complete with respect to Profelene. None of the Profelene transferred in during April is used to complete the beginning inventory. Instead, the $21,400 cost transferred in during April relates to the 100,000 units that the mixing department began to process in April. In section 3 of Exhibit 21.25, $18,190 of the $21,400 is assigned to the 85,000 units received and completed in April (85,000 × $0.214). The remaining $3,210 is assigned to the 15,000 units in ending inventory of the mixing department (15,000 × $0.214).

Flash back

11. A ski manufacturer's total processing costs are $262,500 for its waxing department in the month of December. To complete beginning goods in process, this department added 20,000 equivalent units of materials, labor, and overhead. This department also started and completed 70,000 units during the month and had 15,000 equivalent units remaining in process at month-end. Costs transferred in from the sanding department for December total $300,000, of which 25% relates to units the waxing department hadn't finished by month-end. For the waxing department's process cost summary, what is reported as the total costs to process goods received and completed?

Answer—p. 929

Transfers to Finished Goods Inventory and Cost of Goods Sold

Arrow line ⑨b in Exhibit 21.6 reflects the transfer of completed products from the mixing department to Finished Goods Inventory. The process cost summary for the mixing department shows that the 101,000 units of finished Profen are assigned a cost of $29,470. The entry to record the transfer is:

Assets = Liabilities + Equity
+29,470
−29,470

⑨b	Finished Goods Inventory	29,470	
	Goods in Process Inventory—Mixing		29,470
	To record transfer of completed units of Profen.		

Exhibit 21.25

Process Cost Summary—Mixing Department

GENX COMPANY
Process Cost Summary for Mixing Department
For Month Ended April 30, 2000

Costs Charged to Department:	
Direct materials requisitioned	$ 2,040
Direct labor charged	5,100
Overhead allocated (at predetermined rate)	1,020
① Total processing costs for the period	$ 8,160
Goods in process at the beginning of the period	3,520
Costs transferred in from grinding department (100,000 units at $0.214 each)	21,400
Total costs to be accounted for	$33,080

Equivalent Unit Processing Costs:	Units of Product	Equivalent Units of Production
Units processed:		
Beginning goods in process	16,000	12,000
Units started and completed	85,000	85,000
Ending goods in process	15,000	5,000
② Total	116,000	102,000

Total direct materials cost for the period	$ 2,040
Direct materials cost per equivalent unit ($2,040/102,000 units)	$ 0.020
Total direct labor cost for the period	$ 5,100
Direct labor cost per equivalent unit ($5,100/102,000 units)	$ 0.050
Total overhead cost for the period	$ 1,020
Overhead cost per equivalent unit ($1,020/102,000 units)	$ 0.010

Assignment of Costs to Output of Department:	Equivalent Units	Cost per Unit	Total Cost
Goods in process, March 31, 2000, and completed in the period:			
Costs from prior period			$ 3,520
Direct materials added	12,000	$0.020	240
Direct labor added	12,000	0.050	600
Overhead applied	12,000	0.010	120
Total costs to process			$ 4,480
Goods started and completed in the period:			
Costs transferred in (85,000 × $0.214)			$18,190
Direct materials added	85,000	$0.020	1,700
③ Direct labor added	85,000	0.050	4,250
Overhead applied	85,000	0.010	850
Total costs to process			$24,990
Total costs transferred to finished goods (unit cost = $29,470/101,000 units = $0.2918)			$29,470
Goods in process, April 30, 2000:			
Costs transferred in (15,000 × $0.214)			$ 3,210
Direct materials added	5,000	$0.020	100
Direct labor added	5,000	0.050	250
Overhead applied	5,000	0.010	50
Total costs to process			$ 3,610
Total costs accounted for			$33,080

After this entry is posted, the mixing department's Goods in Process Inventory account appears as shown in Exhibit 21.26.

Exhibit 21.26

Goods in Process Inventory (Mixing) Ledger Account

Goods in Process Inventory—Mixing					Acct. No. 134
Date		Explanation	Debit	Credit	Balance
2000					
Mar.	31	Beginning balance			3,520
Apr.	30	Direct materials usage	2,040		5,560
	30	Direct labor costs	5,100		10,660
	30	Applied overhead	1,020		11,680
	30	Transfer from grinding department	21,400		33,080
	30	Transfer to warehouse		29,470	3,610

P7 Record the transfer of completed goods to Finished Goods Inventory and Cost of Goods Sold.

The ending balance of the Goods in Process Inventory—Mixing account equals the cost assigned to the partially completed units in section 3 of Exhibit 21.25.

GenX sells 106,000 units of Profen in April. The beginning inventory of finished goods consists of 23,000 units with a cost of $6,440. All of these 23,000 units are sold in April. The remaining 83,000 units sold are from the 101,000 units completed in April. Ending finished goods inventory amounts to the 18,000 units remaining.

Section 3 of Exhibit 21.25 shows that total cost per unit of finished goods in April is $0.2918 ($29,470/101,000 units). Using this information we can compute cost of goods sold for April as shown in Exhibit 21.27.

Exhibit 21.27

Cost of Goods Sold

23,000 units from beginning inventory*	$ 6,440
83,000 units manufactured in period (83,000 × $0.2918)	24,219
Total cost of goods sold	$30,659

*Computations assume a FIFO inventory system.

The entry to record cost of goods sold for April is:

Assets = Liabilities + Equity
−30,659 −30,659

⑩	Cost of Goods Sold	30,659	
	Finished Goods Inventory		30,659
	To record cost of goods sold for April.		

After this entry is posted, the Finished Goods Inventory account appears as shown in Exhibit 21.28.

Exhibit 21.28

Finished Goods Inventory Ledger Account

Finished Goods Inventory					Acct. No. 135
Date		Explanation	Debit	Credit	Balance
2000					
Mar.	31	Beginning balance			6,440
Apr.	30	Transfer from mixing department	29,470		35,910
	30	Cost of goods sold		30,659	5,251

Summary of Cost Flows

Exhibit 21.29 shows the manufacturing cost flows of GenX for April. Each of these cost flows and the entries to record them are explained in the prior sections. The flow of costs through the accounts reflects the flow of manufacturing activities and products in its operations.

Exhibit 21.29* Cost Flows through GenX

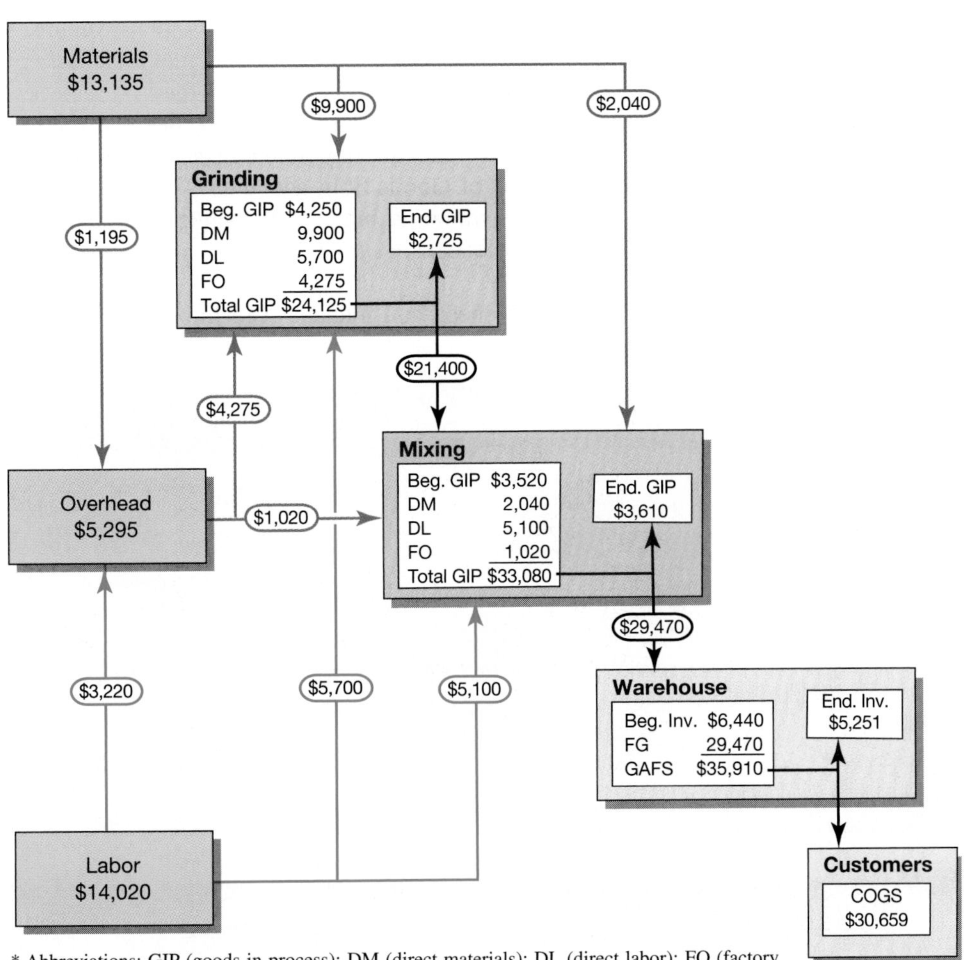

* Abbreviations: GIP (goods in process); DM (direct materials); DL (direct labor); FO (factory overhead); FG (finished goods); GAFS (goods available for sale); COGS (cost of goods sold).

Modern Manufacturing Management Principles and Process Operations

We described several modern manufacturing management principles in Chapter 19. Adopting these concepts brings about changes in some process manufacturing operations. Management concerns with throughput and just-in-time manufacturing, for instance, cause boundary lines between departments to become less distinct. In some cases, higher quality and better efficiency are obtained by entirely reorganizing production processes. Instead of producing different types of **Reebok** shoes in a series of departments, a separate work center for each shoe can be established in one department. When this rearrangement occurs, the process cost accounting system is changed to account for costs of each work center.

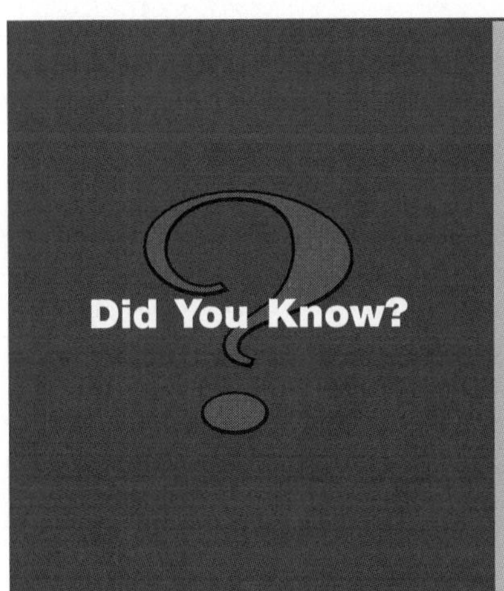

Best of Both Worlds

Customer orientation demands both flexibility and standardization to better serve customers. While flexibility allows companies to supply products or services to each customer's unique specifications such as in a job order setting, standardization helps achieve efficiencies and lower costs to customers such as in a process production operation. Both **Ford** and **Toyota** attempt to combine flexibility and standardization with breaks in their assembly line processes. This is done by using equipment to speed up the changeovers of jigs, tools, and fixtures for machines on the line. These companies get the best of both worlds and are better able to satisfy customers. [Source: P.F. Drucker, "The Emerging Theory of Manufacturing," *Harvard Business Review,* May-June 1990, pp. 94–102.]

When a company adopts just-in-time (JIT) manufacturing methods, the inventories described in this chapter can virtually disappear. For example, if raw materials are not ordered or received until needed, a Raw Materials Inventory account may be unnecessary. Instead, materials cost is immediately debited to the Goods in Process Inventory account. Similarly, a Finished Goods Inventory account may not be needed. Instead, cost of finished goods can be debited to the Cost of Goods Sold account.

When a company uses the theory of constraints to increase throughput, the cost accounting system helps managers locate bottlenecks. A bottleneck, for instance, can be seen by the presence of large upstream or downstream inventories. Based on analysis of inventories, managers can pinpoint the bottleneck and manage it to improve efficiency.

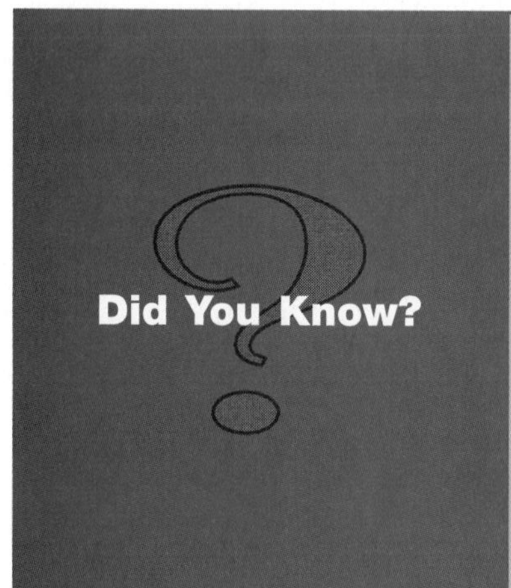

Gadgets at Work

Recent attention to customer orientation has led to a number of companies improving their processes. A manufacturer of control devices improved quality and reduced production time by forming teams to study processes and then to suggest improvements. Another manager reported the company set up "project groups [and] a steering committee that goes in and looks at everything we do, every process we undertake in manufacturing. Then we want to help organize the process." Still another manager uses statistical process control to identify problem areas and implement corrective actions. [Source: S. Kalagnanam, *The Use of Nonfinancial Performance Measures and Their Relationship to Strategy,* Ph.D Dissertation, University of Wisconsin—Madison, 1997.]

Flash back

12. A company successfully uses just-in-time manufacturing and essentially eliminates its goods in process inventories. How does this affect its computations of equivalent units of production?

Answer—p. 929

USING THE INFORMATION

Spoiled Units of Production

A2 Analyze cost per equivalent unit with and without spoiled units of production.

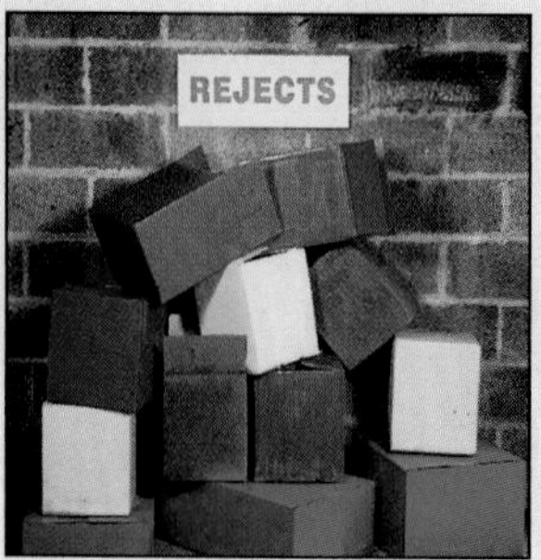

This chapter described how to compute product cost in process manufacturing companies. But this discussion assumes either that there are no *spoiled* units of production or that they are not considered in computing cost per unit. Managers, of course, prefer no spoiled units but recognize their likelihood. By not explicitly considering spoiled units in computing equivalent units of production (and the cost per equivalent unit), the good units are forced to *absorb* the cost of errors resulting from spoilage. This can impact decision making based on cost per equivalent unit.

Managers find it useful to know the actual cost per equivalent unit *without* the good units absorbing the cost of spoiled ones. This involves including the spoiled units when computing equivalent units of production.

To illustrate, let's assume a simple production process where *900 good units* and *100 spoiled units* are produced in year 2000. If there are zero goods in process inventories, the equivalent units of production are computed as either 900 units or 1,000 units. The answer depends on whether we ignore spoiled units or not. The greater the percent of spoiled units, the larger the impact on computing and using the equivalent units of production figure.

Let's extend this illustration and suppose the company has production costs in year 2000 equal to $18,000. The cost per equivalent unit of production is then determined in one of two ways as shown in Exhibit 21.30.

For calendar year 2000	Spoilage ignored	Spoilage considered
Production cost incurred	$18,000	$18,000
Equivalent units of production	900 units	1,000 units
Cost per equivalent unit	$20 per unit	$18 per unit

Exhibit 21.30

Costs per Equivalent Unit with and without Spoilage

There is a marked difference in the cost per equivalent unit depending on whether spoiled units are ignored or not.

Managers are often tempted to use the higher cost when pricing products. The thinking behind this approach is that using the higher cost allows them to determine a price to cover all expenses. The downside of using the information in this way is that companies can price themselves out of a market with too high of a price. It also reduces the likelihood of identifying and acting on the high cost of spoiled goods.

Process Manager
You are the manager of a crucial process in your company's manufacturing system. During the recent quarter, your process generated an unusually high percent of spoiled units. Yet the monthly process cost report doesn't show the cost of this spoilage. You want to submit a proposal to top management to obtain resources for implementing process improvement measures and need information on the cost of spoilage to include in your proposal. How do you proceed?

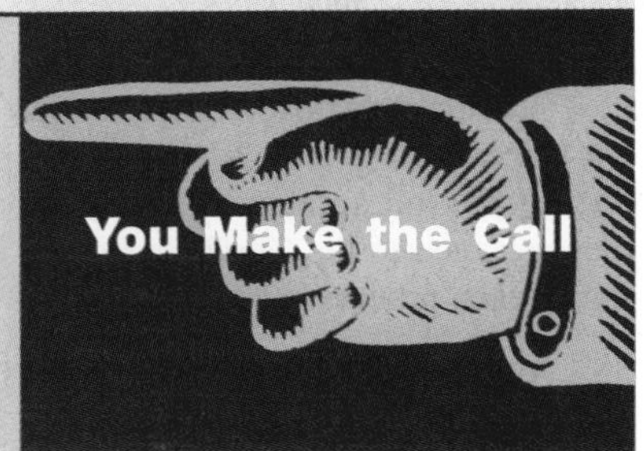

Answer—p. 928

Summary

C1 Explain process operations and how they differ from job order operations. Process operations produce large quantities of essentially identical products or services by passing them through a series of processes, or steps, in production. Like job order operations, they combine direct materials, direct labor, and overhead in the operations. Unlike job order operations that assign the responsibility for each job to a manager, process operations assign the responsibility for each process to a manager. The focus is on the series of processes, not jobs.

C2 Define equivalent units and explain their use in process cost accounting. Equivalent units of production measure the activity of a process as the number of units that would be completed if all effort during a period had been applied to units that were started and finished. This measure of production activity is used in computing the cost per equivalent unit. It is also used to assign costs to finished goods and goods in process inventory.

C3 Explain the four steps in accounting for production activity in a period. The four steps involved in accounting for production activity in a period are (1) recording the physical flow of units, (2) computing the equivalent units of production, (3) computing the cost per equivalent unit of production, and (4) reconciling costs. The last step involves assigning costs to finished goods and goods in process inventory for the period. These four steps are helpful in preparing the process cost summary report.

C4 Define a process cost summary and describe its purposes. A process cost summary is a managerial accounting report that summarizes the activity of a production process or department during a period. Three purposes of the report are to: (1) help department managers control their departments; (2) help factory managers evaluate department managers' performances; and (3) provide cost information for financial statements. A process cost summary achieves these purposes by describing the costs charged to the department, the equivalent units of production achieved by the department, and the costs assigned to the output.

A1 Compare process cost accounting and job order cost accounting. Process and job order manufacturing operations are similar in that they both combine materials, labor, and other factory overhead items in the process of producing products. They differ in the way they are organized and managed. In job order operations, the job order cost accounting system assigns materials, labor, and overhead to specific jobs. The total job cost is then divided by the number of units to compute a cost per unit for that job. In process manufacturing operations, the process cost accounting system assigns materials, labor, and overhead to specific manufacturing processes. The total costs associated with each process are then divided by the number of units passing through that process to determine the cost per equivalent unit for that process. The costs per equivalent unit for all processes are added to determine the total cost per unit of a product.

A2 **Analyze cost per equivalent unit with and without spoiled units of production.** Failure to consider spoiled units in computing both the equivalent units of production and the cost per equivalent unit means that good units are forced to absorb the cost of spoiled units. This can negatively impact decision making based on cost per equivalent unit. Decision makers should examine costs both with and without spoiled units.

P1 **Record the flow of direct materials costs in process cost accounting.** Materials purchased are debited to a Raw Materials Inventory account. As direct materials are issued to processes, they are separately accumulated in a Goods in Process Inventory account for that process.

P2 **Record the flow of direct labor costs in process cost accounting.** Direct labor costs are initially debited to the Factory Payroll account. The total amount in Factory Payroll is then assigned to the Goods in Process Inventory account pertaining to each process.

P3 **Record the flow of factory overhead costs in process cost accounting.** The different factory overhead items are first accumulated in the Factory Overhead account and then allocated, using a predetermined overhead rate, to the different processes. The allocated amount is debited to the Goods in Process Inventory account pertaining to each process.

P4 **Compute equivalent units produced in a period.** To compute equivalent units, determine the number of units that would have been finished if all of the materials (or labor or overhead) had been used to manufacture units that were started and completed during the period. The costs incurred by a process are divided by its equivalent units of production to determine cost per unit.

P5 **Prepare a process cost summary.** A process cost summary can be prepared by including the physical flow of units, equivalent units of production, costs per equivalent unit, and cost reconciliation in one summary report. The report shows the units and costs to account for during the period and how these were accounted for during the period. In terms of units, the report includes the beginning goods in process inventory and the units started during the month. These are accounted for in terms of goods completed and transferred out and ending goods in process inventory. With respect to costs, the report includes materials, labor, and overhead costs assigned to the process during the period. It shows how these costs are assigned to goods completed and transferred out and goods in process inventory at the end of the period.

P6 **Record the transfer of goods between departments.** As units of product are transferred from one process to the next, the accumulated cost of those units is transferred from one goods in process account to the next. Once the goods are completed in the preceding process, they are transferred out to the next process in the sequence. Costs associated with goods completed in the preceding process are then debited to the goods in process inventory of the next process. With this procedure, the costs of the preceding process are accumulated in the next process.

P7 **Record the transfer of completed goods to Finished Goods Inventory and Cost of Goods Sold.** As units complete the last manufacturing process and are eventually sold, their accumulated cost is transferred to Finished Goods Inventory and finally to Cost of Goods Sold.

Guidance Answer to **Judgment and Ethics**

Budget Officer

By instructing you to classify a majority of the costs as indirect, the manager is passing on some of his department's costs to a common overhead pool which will be partially absorbed by other departments within the company. Since overhead costs are allocated on the basis of direct labor for this company and the new department has a relatively low direct labor component, the new department will be assigned less overhead. Such action suggests unethical behavior by the department manager. You have a responsibility to bring this to the attention of the department manager. If this manager refuses to listen, you must then inform someone in a more senior position of authority.

Guidance Answers to **You Make the Call**

General Manager

Both components are produced using the same process. This means the conversion activity is likely very similar for both products. Therefore, the conversion cost per equivalent unit can be computed for both products combined. However, it is likely that the materials consumed by each component are different. If they are different, then the materials cost per equivalent unit must be computed and reported separately for each component; but the labor and overhead cost per equivalent unit can still be combined.

Process Manager

It is important for you to meet with the managerial accountant and explain the situation. Assuming you can collect information on spoilage, you should compute total equivalent units produced including spoilage and recompute cost per equivalent unit. The new cost per equivalent unit will be lower than what was previously computed. You can then multiply the new cost per equivalent unit by the number of spoiled units to determine the cost of spoilage. This spoilage cost information should be reported to top management to inform them about the financial implications of spoilage.

Guidance Answers to Flash backs

1. *c*
2. When a company produces large quantities of similar products/services, a process cost accounting system is more suitable.
3. *b*
4. The costs are direct materials, direct labor, and overhead.
5. One Goods in Process Inventory account is needed for each production department.
6. *a*
7. Equivalent units with respect to direct labor are the number of units that would have been produced if all of the labor had been used on units that were started and finished during the period.
8.

	Units of Product		Percent Added		Equivalent Units
Beginning inventory	8,000	×	75%	=	6,000
Units started and finished	50,000	×	100	=	50,000
Ending inventory	6,000	×	33⅓	=	2,000
Equivalent units					58,000

9. The first section shows the costs charged to the department. The second section describes the equivalent units produced by the department. The third section shows how the total costs are assigned to units worked on during the period.
10. The transfer decreases one Goods in Process Inventory account and increases another. Therefore, the transfer has no effect on total assets.
11. Equivalent unit processing cost:

$$\frac{\$262{,}500}{20{,}000 + 70{,}000 + 15{,}000} = \$2.50$$

Goods received and completed:

Costs transferred in	$225,000
Total costs added (70,000 × $2.50)	175,000
Total costs to process	$400,000

12. If goods-in-process inventories are eliminated, equivalent units of production is the number of units started and completed during the period.

Demonstration Problem

Pennsylvania Company produces a product by passing it through a molding process and then through an assembly process. Information related to its manufacturing activities for July follows:

Raw Materials:	
Beginning inventory	$100,000
Raw materials purchased on credit	300,000
Direct materials used in molding	(190,000)
Direct materials used in assembling	(88,600)
Indirect materials used	(51,400)
Ending inventory	$ 70,000
Factory Payroll:	
Direct labor used in molding	$ 42,000
Direct labor used in assembling	55,375
Indirect labor used	50,625
Total payroll cost (paid in cash)	$148,000
Factory Overhead:	
Indirect materials used	$ 51,400
Indirect labor used	50,625
Other overhead costs	71,725
Total factory overhead incurred	$173,750
Factory Overhead Applied:	
Molding (150% of direct labor)	$ 63,000
Assembling (200% of direct labor)	110,750
Total factory overhead applied	$173,750

Molding Department:	
Beginning goods in process inventory (units)	5,000
Percentage completed—materials	100%
Percentage completed—labor and overhead ..	60%
Units started and completed	17,000
Ending goods in process inventory (units)	8,000
Percentage completed—materials	100%
Percentage completed—labor and overhead ..	25%
Costs:	
Beginning goods in process inventory	$ 53,000
Direct materials added	190,000
Direct labor added	42,000
Overhead applied (150% of direct labor)	63,000
Total costs	$348,000
Assembling Department:	
Beginning goods in process inventory	$154,800
Ending goods in process inventory	108,325
Finished Goods Inventory:	
Beginning inventory	$ 96,400
Cost transferred in from assembling	578,400
Cost of goods sold	(506,100)
Ending inventory	$168,700

Required

1. Compute the equivalent units of production for the molding department for July and determine the costs per equivalent unit for direct materials, direct labor, and factory overhead.
2. Compute the cost of the units transferred from molding to assembling in July and the cost of the ending goods in process inventory for the molding department.
3. Prepare summary journal entries to record the transactions and events of July for *(a)* raw materials purchases, *(b)* direct materials usage, *(c)* indirect materials usage, *(d)* factory payroll costs, *(e)* direct labor usage, *(f)* indirect labor usage, *(g)* other overhead costs (credit Other Accounts), *(h)* application of overhead to the two departments, *(i)* transferring partially completed goods from molding to assembling, *(j)* transferring finished goods out of assembling, and *(k)* the cost of goods sold.

Planning the Solution

- Compute the molding department's equivalent units of production and cost per unit with respect to direct materials.
- Compute the molding department's equivalent units of production with respect to direct labor and overhead and determine the cost per unit for each.
- Compute the total cost of the goods transferred to the assembly department by using the equivalent units and unit costs to determine: *(a)* the cost of the beginning in-process inventory, *(b)* the materials, labor, and overhead costs added to the beginning in-process inventory, and *(c)* the materials, labor, and overhead costs added to the units that were started and completed in the month.
- Use the information to record the summary journal entries for July.

Solution to Demonstration Problem

1. Equivalent units of production—direct materials:

	Units of Product		Percent Added This Period		Equivalent Units
Beginning goods in process	5,000	×	0%	=	0
Goods started and completed	17,000	×	100	=	17,000
Ending goods in process	8,000	×	100	=	8,000
Total units	30,000				**25,000**

The direct materials used in molding total $190,000. Therefore:
Materials cost per equivalent unit = $190,000/25,000 units = $7.60 per unit

Equivalent units of production—direct labor and overhead:

	Units of Product		Percent Added This Period		Equivalent Units
Beginning goods in process	5,000	×	40%	=	2,000
Goods started and completed	17,000	×	100	=	17,000
Ending goods in process	8,000	×	25	=	2,000
Total units	30,000				**21,000**

The direct labor used in molding totals $42,000. Therefore:
Labor cost per equivalent unit = $42,000/21,000 units = $2 per unit

The overhead applied in molding totals 150% of direct labor cost. Therefore:
Overhead cost per equivalent unit = $63,000/21,000 units = $3 per unit

2. Cost of units transferred from molding to assembling in July:

	Equivalent Units	Cost per Unit	Total Cost
Beginning goods in process:			
Costs from prior month			$ 53,000
Direct materials added	0	$7.60	0
Direct labor added	2,000	2.00	4,000
Overhead applied	2,000	3.00	6,000
Total cost to process			$ 63,000
Goods started and completed:			
Direct materials added	17,000	$7.60	$129,200
Direct labor added	17,000	2.00	34,000
Overhead applied	17,000	3.00	51,000
Total cost to process			$214,200
Cost of transferred units			**$277,200**

Cost of the July ending goods in process inventory for the molding department:

	Equivalent Units	Cost per Unit	Total Cost
Direct materials added	8,000	$7.60	$60,800
Direct labor added	2,000	2.00	4,000
Overhead applied	2,000	3.00	6,000
Cost of ending good in process inventory			**$70,800**

3. Summary journal entries for the transactions and events in July:

a. Raw materials purchases:

Raw Materials Inventory	300,000	
Accounts Payable		300,000

b. Direct materials usage:

Goods in Process Inventory—Molding	190,000	
Goods in Process Inventory—Assembling	88,600	
Raw Materials Inventory		278,600

c. Indirect materials usage:

Factory Overhead	51,400	
Raw Materials Inventory		51,400

d. Factory payroll costs:

Factory Payroll	148,000	
Cash		148,000

e. Direct labor usage:

Goods in Process Inventory—Molding	42,000	
Goods in Process Inventory—Assembling	55,375	
Factory Payroll		97,375

f. Indirect labor usage:

Factory Overhead	50,625	
Factory Payroll		50,625

g. Other overhead costs:

Factory Overhead	71,725	
Other Accounts		71,725

h. Application of overhead:

Goods in Process Inventory—Molding	63,000	
Goods in Process Inventory—Assembling	110,750	
Factory Overhead		173,750

i. Transferring partially completed goods from molding to assembling:

Goods in Process Inventory—Assembling	277,200	
Goods in Process Inventory—Molding		277,200

j. Transferring finished goods out of assembling:

Finished Goods Inventory	578,400	
Goods in Process Inventory—Assembling		578,400

k. Cost of goods sold:

Cost of Goods Sold	506,100	
Finished Goods Inventory		506,100

Glossary

Equivalent units of production (EUP) the number of units that would be completed if all effort during a period had been applied to units that were started and finished. (p. 914).

Job order cost accounting a cost accounting system designed to determine the cost of producing each job or job lot. (p. 908).

Materials consumption report a document that summarizes the materials used by a department during a reporting period and replaces materials requisitions. (p. 909).

Process cost accounting system a system of assigning direct materials, direct labor, and overhead to specific manufacturing processes. The total costs associated with each process are then divided by the number of units passing through that process to determine the cost per equivalent unit. (p. 908).

Process cost summary a primary managerial accounting report for a process cost accounting system. The report describes the costs charged to a department, the equivalent units of production achieved by the department, and the costs assigned to the output. (p. 918).

Process manufacturing the processing of products in a continuous flow of steps (also called *process operations* or *process production*); this means products pass through a series of sequential processes. (p. 904).

Questions

1. Can services be delivered by means of process operations? Support your answer with an example.
2. The book has described two main types of cost accounting systems to this point: job order and process costing. What is the main factor for a company in selecting between these two cost accounting systems? Give two likely applications of each system.
3. Identify the control document for materials flow when a materials requisition slip is not used.

4. The focus in a job order costing system is the job or batch. Identify the two main focuses in process costing.
5. Are the journal entries that match cost flows to product flows in process costing primarily the same or much different than in job order costing? Explain.
6. Explain in layman terms the notion of equivalent units of production (EUP). Why is it necessary to use EUP in process costing?
7. Why is it possible for direct labor in a process operation to include the labor of employees who do not work directly on products or services?
8. Assume a manufacturing company produces a single product by processing it first through a mixing department and next through a cutting department. Direct labor costs flow through what accounts in this company's process cost system?
9. After all labor costs for a period are allocated, what balance should remain in the Factory Payroll account?
10. Is it possible to have underapplied or overapplied overhead costs in a process cost accounting system?
11. Explain why equivalent units of production for both direct labor and overhead can be the same and why they can differ from equivalent units for direct materials.
12. List the four steps in accounting for production activity in a period.
13. What purposes are served by a process cost summary?
14. Assume **NIKE** takes a special order to produce shoes for all employees of **The Walt Disney Company.** Outline NIKE's production process assuming three production departments: (1) cutting, (2) Disney design set to the material, and (3) assembly. Begin the outline with delivery of raw materials and finish with the shipment of goods (see Exhibit 21.6 for guidance).

Quick Study

QS 21-1
Matching product to cost accounting system
C1

For each of the following products and services, indicate whether it is most likely produced in a process operation or in a job order operation:

a. Door hinges
b. Wall clocks
c. Cut flower arrangements
d. Bolts and nuts
e. House paints
f. Folding chairs
g. Custom tailored suits
h. Sport shirts
i. Concrete swimming pools
j. Economical pianos

QS 21-2
Matching cost flows to product flows
P1, P2, P3

Texton Co. manufactures a product requiring two processes: cutting and sewing. During August, partially completed units with a cost of $297,500 are transferred from cutting to sewing. The sewing department requisitions $58,200 of direct materials and incurs direct labor of $96,000. Overhead is applied to the sewing department at 100% of direct labor. Units with a cost of $102,400 are completed and transferred to finished goods. Prepare entries to record these August activities of the sewing department.

QS 21-3
Computing equivalent units of production
C2, P4

Information below refers to units processed in the binding department of Lowe Printing in March:

	Units of Product	Percent of Labor Added
Beginning goods in process	150,000	25%
Goods started and completed	340,000	100
Ending goods in process	120,000	40

Compute the total equivalent units of production with respect to labor for March.

QS 21-4
Computing EUP cost
P5

The cost of beginning inventory plus the costs added during the period should equal the cost of units ____________________ plus the cost of ______________________.

Exercises

Exercise 21-1
Terminology in process cost accounting
C1, A1, P1, P2, P3

Match each of the following items *a* through *h* with the best description of its purpose:

a. Materials consumption report
b. Process cost summary
c. Equivalent units of production
d. Goods in process inventory—Dept. A
e. Raw materials inventory account
f. Materials requisition
g. Finished goods inventory account
h. Factory overhead account

_____ **1.** Holds costs of finished products until sold to customers.
_____ **2.** Holds costs of indirect materials, indirect labor, and similar costs until assigned to production.
_____ **3.** Describes the direct materials used in a production department.
_____ **4.** Notifies the materials manager that materials should be sent to a production department.
_____ **5.** Holds costs of materials until they are used in production departments or as factory overhead.
_____ **6.** Holds costs of direct materials, direct labor, and applied overhead until products are transferred from Department A.
_____ **7.** A periodic report that describes the activity and output of a production department.
_____ **8.** Partially completed units standardized to completed units.

Exercise 21-2
Journal entries in process cost accounting
P1, P2, P3

Model Toy Company manufactures products with two processes: sanding and painting. Prepare entries to record its following manufacturing activities for January:

a. Purchased raw materials on credit at a cost of $40,000.
b. Used direct materials costing $19,000 in the sanding department and $5,000 in the painting department.
c. Used indirect materials costing $20,500.
d. Incurred total labor cost of $75,000, all of which is paid in cash.
e. Used direct labor costing $30,000 in the sanding department and $24,000 in the painting department.
f. Used indirect labor costing $11,000.
g. Incurred other overhead costs of $24,000 (paid in cash).
h. Applied overhead at 125% of direct labor in the sanding department and at 75% of direct labor in the painting department.
i. Transferred partially completed products with a cost of $79,900 from the sanding department to the painting department.
j. Transferred completed products with a cost of $145,000 from the painting department to the finished goods inventory.
k. Sold products on credit for $300,000. Their accumulated cost is $150,000.

Exercise 21-3
Interpreting journal entries in process cost accounting
P1, P2, P3

The following journal entries are recorded in Sagrillo Co's process cost accounting system. The company produces clothing items by passing them through a cutting department and an assembly department. Overhead is applied to production departments based on direct labor cost for the period. Provide a brief explanation for each entry.

a.	Raw Materials Inventory	26,000	
	Accounts Payable		26,000
b.	Goods in Process Inventory—Cutting	12,000	
	Goods in Process Inventory—Assembly	9,000	
	Raw Materials Inventory		21,000
c.	Goods in Process Inventory—Cutting	8,000	
	Goods in Process Inventory—Assembly	5,000	
	Factory Payroll		13,000
d.	Factory Payroll	16,000	
	Cash		16,000
e.	Factory Overhead	5,000	
	Other Accounts		5,000

f.	Factory Overhead	5,000	
	Raw Materials Inventory		5,000
g.	Factory Overhead	3,000	
	Factory Payroll		3,000
h.	Goods in Process Inventory—Cutting	6,000	
	Goods in Process Inventory—Assembly	7,000	
	Factory Overhead		13,000
i.	Goods in Process Inventory—Assembly	30,000	
	Goods in Process Inventory—Cutting		30,000
j.	Finished Goods Inventory	44,000	
	Goods in Process Inventory—Assembly		44,000
k.	Accounts Receivable	125,000	
	Sales		125,000
	Cost of Goods Sold	50,000	
	Finished Goods Inventory		50,000

Exercise 21-4
Recording cost flows in a process cost system
P1, P2, P3

Kretz Lumber specializes in the production of shredded bark using a two-step process. The system begins by processing bark chips through the shredding department and then through the bagging department. The following information describes manufacturing operations for April:

	Shredding Department	Bagging Department
Direct materials used	$ 40,000	$ 460,000
Direct labor used	$ 45,000	$ 75,000
Predetermined overhead application rate (based on direct labor)	120%	200%
Goods transferred from shredding to bagging	$(145,000)	
Goods transferred from bagging to finished goods		$(403,000)

Revenue for the month totaled $900,000 from credit sales and cost of goods sold is $300,000.

Required

Prepare summary journal entries to record the April manufacturing activities.

Exercise 21-5
Computing equivalent units of production
C2, P4

During April, the production department of a process manufacturing system completed a number of units of a product and transferred them to finished goods. Of these units, 50,000 were in process in the department at the beginning of April and 220,000 were started and completed in April. April's beginning inventory units were 60% complete with respect to materials and 40% complete with respect to labor. At the end of April, 66,000 additional units were in process in the department and were 80% complete with respect to materials and 30% complete with respect to labor.

Required

Compute *(a)* the number of units transferred to finished goods and *(b)* the number of equivalent units both with respect to materials and with respect to labor produced in the department for April.

Exercise 21-6
Assigning costs to inventories
C3, P4, P5

The production department described in Exercise 21-5 had $700,000 of direct materials and $500,000 of direct labor cost charged to it during April. Compute the direct materials cost and the direct labor cost per equivalent unit in the department and allocate the costs among the units in the goods in process inventories and the units started and completed during April.

Exercise 21-7
Computing equivalent units
C2, P4, P5

The production department in a process manufacturing system completed 250,000 units of product and transferred them to finished goods during a recent week. Of these units, 75,000 were in process at the beginning of the week. The other 175,000 units were started and completed during the week. At the end of the period, 50,000 units were in process.

Required

Compute the department's equivalent units of production with respect to direct materials under each of the following separate assumptions:

a. All direct materials are added to products when processing begins.

b. Direct materials are added to products evenly throughout the process. Beginning goods in process inventory was 50% complete and ending goods in process inventory was 70% complete.

c. One-half of direct materials are added to products when the process begins and the other half is added when the process is 75% complete as to direct labor. Beginning goods in process inventory is 40% complete as to direct labor and ending goods in process inventory is 60% complete as to direct labor.

Exercise 21-8
Completing a flowchart for a process operation
P1, P2, P3, P6

The following flowchart shows the production activity of the punching and bending departments of the Cardboard Box Company for August. Use the amounts shown on the flowchart to compute the missing numbers identified by question marks.

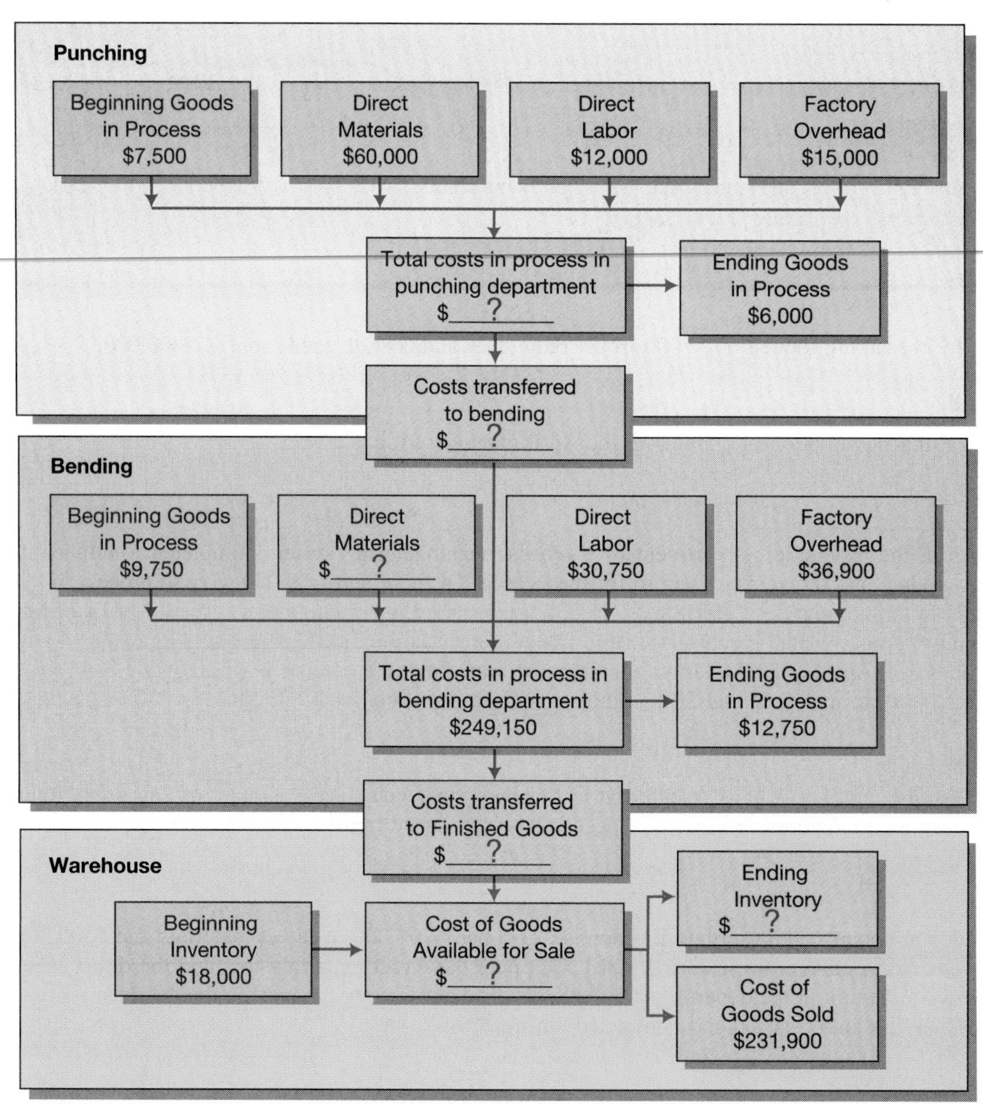

Exercise 21-9
Completing a process cost summary
P4

The following partially completed process cost summary describes the July activities of the slicing department of the Serranos Company. The output of the slicing department is sent to the canning department, which sends the finished goods to the warehouse for shipping.

Costs Charged to the Department:	
Direct materials requisitioned	$224,000
Direct labor charged	39,000
Overhead allocated (at 200% of direct labor)	78,000
Total processing costs for the month	341,000
Goods in process at the beginning of the month	24,000
Total costs to be accounted for	$365,000

		Equivalent Units	
Equivalent Unit Processing Costs:	**Units of Product**	**Direct Materials**	**Labor and Overhead**
Units processed:			
Beginning goods in process	1,600	0	1,200
Units started and completed	20,000	20,000	20,000
Ending goods in process	2,400	2,400	1,800
Total	24,000	22,400	23,000

Prepare the process cost summary for the slicing department by completing both the **Equivalent Unit Processing Costs** section and the **Assignment of Costs to the Output of Department** section.

Problems

Problem 21-1
Measuring production costs and preparing journal entries
P1, P2, P3, P6, P7

Lobo Company manufactures blankets by passing the products through a weaving department and a sewing department. The following information is available regarding its inventories for May:

	Beginning Inventory	Ending Inventory
Raw materials	$ 120,000	$ 100,000
Goods in process—Weaving	300,000	330,000
Goods in process—Sewing	570,000	700,000
Finished goods	1,266,000	1,206,000

The following additional information describes the company's manufacturing activities for May:

Raw materials purchases (on credit)	$ 500,000
Factory payroll cost (paid in cash)	3,060,000
Other overhead cost (credit Other Accounts)	156,000
Materials used:	
Direct—Weaving	$ 240,000
Direct—Sewing	75,000
Indirect	120,000
Labor used:	
Direct—Weaving	$1,200,000
Direct—Sewing	360,000
Indirect	1,500,000
Overhead rates as a percent of direct labor:	
Weaving	80%
Sewing	150%
Sales (on credit)	$4,000,000

Check Figure Cost of goods sold, $3,275,000

Required

1. Compute *(a)* the cost of products transferred from weaving to sewing, *(b)* the cost of products transferred from sewing to finished goods, and *(c)* the cost of goods sold.
2. Prepare summary journal entries to record the manufacturing activities during May.

Problem 21-2
Computing cost per equivalent unit and assigning costs to products
P4

Carver Company passes its product through several departments. The last of these is the carving department. Direct labor is added evenly throughout the process in the carving department. Also, one-fourth of direct materials are added at the beginning of the carving process and the remaining three-fourths are added when the process is 50% complete with respect to direct labor. During November, 575,000 units of product are transferred to finished goods from the carving department. Of these units, 100,000 units were 40% complete with respect to labor at the beginning of the period and 475,000 were started and completed during the period. At the end of November, the goods in process inventory consists of 300,000 units that are 25% complete with respect to labor. The carving department's direct labor cost for November is $1,220,000 and its direct materials cost is $1,875,000.

Required

Preparation Component

Check Figure Direct labor cost per equivalent unit, $2

1. Determine the carving department's equivalent units of production with respect to (a) direct labor and (b) direct materials.
2. Compute both the direct labor cost and the direct materials cost per equivalent unit.
3. Compute both direct labor cost and direct materials cost assigned to the (a) beginning goods in process inventory, (b) units started and completed, and (c) ending goods in process inventory.

Analysis Component

4. Carver sells and ships all units to customers as soon as they are completed. Assume an error is made in determining the percentage of completion for units in ending inventory. Instead of being 25% complete with respect to labor, they are actually 60% complete. Write a one-page memo to the plant manager describing how this error affects its November financial statements.

Problem 21-3
Journalizing in process cost accounting and using equivalent units
P1, P2, P3, P4

Walden Company produces a product in large quantities that goes through two processes—spinning and cutting. The following information is available on its factory's activities for March:

Raw materials:	
Beginning inventory	$ 32,000
Raw materials purchased (on credit)	221,120
Direct materials used in spinning	(160,000)
Direct materials used in cutting	(37,120)
Indirect materials used	(40,560)
Ending inventory	$ 15,440
Factory payroll:	
Direct labor used in spinning	$ 68,000
Direct labor used in cutting	55,680
Indirect labor used	36,320
Total payroll cost (paid in cash)	$160,000
Factory overhead incurred:	
Indirect materials used	$ 40,560
Indirect labor used	36,320
Other overhead costs	91,640
Total factory overhead incurred	$168,520
Factory overhead applied:	
Spinning (125% of direct labor)	$ 85,000
Cutting (150% of direct labor)	83,520
Total factory overhead applied	$168,520

Information about the inventory in the spinning department is reported below:

Units:		**Costs:**	
Beginning in process inventory	4,000	Beginning in process inventory	$ 41,000
Started and completed	12,000	Direct materials added	160,000
Ending in process inventory	8,000	Direct labor added	68,000
Beginning in process inventory:		Overhead applied (125% of direct labor)	85,000
Materials—percent complete	100%		
Labor and overhead—percent complete	25%	Total costs	$354,000
Ending in process inventory:		Transferred out to cutting department	(272,000)
Materials—percent complete	100%		
Labor and overhead—percent complete	25%	Ending in process inventory	$ 82,000

Information about the goods in process inventories for the cutting department follows: beginning in process inventory, $174,000; and ending in process inventory, $177,120. Also, these facts are available regarding finished goods:

Beginning inventory	$148,400
Cost transferred in from cutting	445,200
Cost of goods sold	(530,000)
Ending inventory	$ 63,600

During March, 10,000 units of finished goods are sold for cash at a price of $120 each.

Required

Preparation Component

1. Prepare journal entries to record the activities of March.
2. Compute equivalent units of production for the spinning department for March. Calculate the cost per equivalent unit for direct materials, direct labor, and overhead.
3. Compute the cost of ending goods in process inventory for the spinning department.

Check Figure Cost per equivalent unit: materials, $8; labor, $4; overhead, $5

Analysis Component

4. Walden provides incentives to managers of its processing departments by paying monthly bonuses based on their success in controlling costs per equivalent unit of production. Assume the spinning department underestimates the percentage of completion for units in ending inventory, with the result that its equivalent units of production in ending inventory for March are understated. What impact does this error have on bonuses paid to the manager of the spinning department and the manager of the cutting department? What impact, if any, does this error have on April bonuses?

Problem 21-4
Preparing a process cost summary
P4, P5

PraxAir Co. produces its product through a single processing department. Direct materials, direct labor, and overhead are added to the product evenly throughout the process. The company uses monthly reporting periods for its process cost accounting system. The Goods in Process Inventory account appears as follows after posting entries for direct materials, direct labor, and overhead costs for October:

Goods in Process Inventory					**Acct. No. 133**
Date		**Explanation**	**Debit**	**Credit**	**Balance**
Oct.	1	Beginning balance			40,800
	31	Direct materials	100,200		141,000
	31	Direct labor costs	400,500		541,500
	31	Applied overhead	123,000		664,500

During October, the company finished and transferred 150,000 units of the product to finished goods. Of these units, 30,000 were in process at the beginning of the month and 120,000 were started and completed during the month. The beginning goods in process inventory was 30% complete. At the end of the month, the goods in process inventory consisted of 20,000 units that are 80% complete.

Required

Check Figure Total cost transferred to finished goods, $600,570

1. Compute the number of equivalent units of production for October.
2. Prepare the department's process cost summary for October.
3. Prepare the journal entry to transfer the cost of the completed units to finished goods inventory.

Problem 21-5
Preparing a process cost summary
P4, P5, P6, A2

Manchu Co. manufactures a single product in one department. All direct materials are added at the beginning of the manufacturing process. Direct labor and overhead are added evenly throughout the process. The company uses monthly reporting periods for its process cost accounting system. During May, the company completed and transferred 22,200 units of product to finished goods inventory. The beginning goods in process inventory consisted of 3,000 units that were 100% complete with respect to direct materials and 40% complete with respect to direct labor and overhead. The other 19,200 completed units were started during the month. Also, 2,400 units are in process at the end of the month, and they are 100% complete with respect to direct materials and 80% complete with respect to direct labor and overhead. After posting entries to record direct materials, direct labor, and overhead for May, the company's Goods in Process Inventory account appears as follows:

Goods in Process Inventory					Acct. No. 133
Date		Explanation	Debit	Credit	Balance
May	1	Beginning balance			181,320
	31	Direct materials	496,800		678,120
	31	Direct labor costs	1,185,600		1,863,720
	31	Applied overhead	948,480		2,812,200

Required

1. Compute the equivalent units of production in May for direct materials and for direct labor and overhead.
2. Prepare the department's process cost summary for May.
3. Prepare the entry to transfer the cost of completed units to finished goods inventory.

Check Figure Cost transferred to finished goods, $2,578,230

Analysis Components

4. The accounting process depends on numerous estimates.
   a. Identify the two major estimates that determine the cost per equivalent unit.
   b. In what direction might you anticipate a bias from management for each estimate in part (a) (assume management compensation is based on maintaining low inventory values)? Explain.
5. Measurement of spoilage can impact the equivalent unit cost. Without providing computations, would the cost per equivalent unit increase or decrease if management only counted the good units of production? (Assume existence of spoiled units.) Explain why management needs to know the cost of spoiled units.

Comprehensive Problem

Corked Bat Company
(Review of Chapters 3, 6, 7, 19, 21)

Corked Bat Company manufactures baseball bats. The bats go through two processes: one cuts the wood into bats and drills a hole for the cork (Department One), and the other fills the hole with cork and stamps the company's logo on the bat (Department Two). All of Department One's output is transferred to Department Two. In addition to the goods in process inventories in Departments One and Two, the Corked Bat Company maintains inventories of raw materials and finished goods. The Corked Bat Company uses raw materials as direct materials in both Departments One and Two and also as indirect materials. Its factory payroll costs include direct labor for each department and indirect labor. All materials in each department are added at the beginning, and direct labor and factory overhead are applied uniformly throughout the process.

Required

You are to maintain records and produce measures of inventories to reflect the events of July. All computations of unit costs are rounded to the nearest penny and all other dollar amounts to the nearest whole dollar. Set up the following general ledger accounts and enter their June 30 balances: Raw Materials Inventory, $50,000; Goods in Process Inventory—Department One, $130,000; Goods in Process Inventory—Department Two, $50,000; Finished Goods Inventory, $220,000; Sales, $0; Cost of Goods Sold, $0; Factory Payroll, $0; and Factory Overhead, $0.

1. Prepare journal entries to record the following events in July:
   a. Purchased raw materials for $250,000 cash (use a perpetual inventory system).
   b. Used raw materials as follows: Department One, $60,000; Department Two, $45,000; and indirect materials, $20,000.
   c. Incurred factory payroll cost of $454,500 paid in cash (ignore taxes).
   d. Assigned factory payroll costs as follows: Department One, $270,000; Department Two, $134,500; and indirect labor, $50,000.
   e. Incurred additional factory overhead costs of $160,000 paid in cash.
   f. Allocated factory overhead to Departments One and Two at 50% of direct labor costs.
2. Information about the July inventories for the two departments is shown below:

	Department One	Department Two
Units:		
Beginning inventory	500	1,000
Started and finished	2,000	1,800
Ending inventory	1,000	1,600
Beginning inventory:		
Materials—percent complete	100%	100%
Labor and overhead—percent complete	20%	75%
Ending inventory:		
Materials—percent complete	100%	100%
Labor and overhead—percent complete	30%	40%

   Use this information along with that from part 1 to compute:
   a. Equivalent units of production in Department One along with its per unit costs for labor, materials, and overhead.
   b. Equivalent units of production in Department Two along with its per unit costs for labor, materials, and overhead.
3. Using results from part 2 along with the available information, make computations and prepare journal entries to record:
   a. Total costs transferred from Department One to Department Two for July (label entry *g*).
   b. Total costs transferred from Department Two to finished goods for July (label entry *h*).
   c. Sale of finished goods costing $531,400 for $1,250,000 in cash (label entry *i*).
4. Post entries from parts 1 and 3 to the ledger accounts set up at the beginning of the problem.
5. Compute the amount of gross profit from the sales in July.

BEYOND THE NUMBERS

Reporting in Action

C2, P7

A company must consider the costs and benefits to external reporting of precise estimates of the percentage complete for goods in process inventory. It must also consider whether reasonable estimates are acceptable. Look at NIKE's inventory note 2 in Appendix A and assume its work-in-process inventory value for 1997 is overstated by 10% and for 1996 is understated by 15% due to estimation errors.

Required

1. Compute the dollar amount that work-in-process inventory is (a) overstated for 1997 and (b) understated for 1996. Assume a 40% tax rate and compute the impact on net income for each year.

2. Compute the amount (in percent) that NIKE's net income increased or decreased for each of 1997 and 1996 due to the estimation errors. (*Hint: Work a simple example to see how an error in inventory impacts income.*)
3. Are amounts in part 2 material? Explain in reference to costs and benefits of decision makers.

Swoosh Ahead

4. Obtain access to NIKE's annual report to fiscal years ending after May 31, 1997, from its Web site [**www.nike.com**] or through the SEC's EDGAR database [**www.sec.gov**]. Take a look at NIKE's current period work-in-process inventory value and assume a 10% understatement and a 40% tax rate. Recompute answers for parts 1 through 3 using this current information.

Comparative Analysis

C1

Leading process manufacturers such as **NIKE** and **Reebok** usually work to maintain a high quality and low cost operation. One ratio routinely computed for this assessment is the cost of goods sold divided by total expenses. If this ratio declines, it can mean the company is spending too much on selling and administrative activities and not enough on production. If this ratio increases beyond a reasonable level, it can mean the company is spending too much on production or not enough on selling activities. (Assume for the analysis here that total expenses equal cost of goods sold plus selling and administrative expenses.)

Required

1. For both NIKE and Reebok, compute the ratio of cost of goods sold to total expenses for the 1996–97 and 1995–96 fiscal years, respectively, for each company.
2. Comment on the similarities or differences in the ratio results across years and companies.

Ethics Challenge

C1, C3

Many accounting and accounting-related professionals are skilled in financial analysis. But most are not skilled in the technical world of manufacturing. This is especially the case for process manufacturing environments (for example, a bottling plant or chemical factory). To provide professional accounting and financial services, we must understand the industry, product, and processes. We have an ethical responsibility to develop this understanding before offering services to clients in these areas.

Required

Write a one-page action plan, in memorandum format, on how you'd obtain an understanding of key business processes of a company that hires you to provide financial services. The memorandum should specify an industry, product, and one selected process. The memorandum should also draw on at least one reference, such as a professional journal or organization literature.

Communicating in Practice

A1, C1, P1, P2

You hire a new assistant production manager. His prior experience is with a company that produced goods to order. Your company engages in continuous production of homogeneous products that go through various manufacturing processes. Your new assistant sends you an e-mail questioning some cost classifications on an internal report. He questions why the costs of some materials that do not actually become part of the finished product, including some labor costs that are not directly associated with producing the product, are classified as direct costs. Respond to his question via memorandum or e-mail.

Taking It to the Net

C1, C3

Teamwork is essential for business success. The same is true for accounting software. Software products must work together to be useful in providing information in support of decision making. Check out the following Web site for **UEC** (UEC is the technology company of **USX**) and answer the following questions [**www.uec-usx.com/spts.htm**]:*

Required

1. Identify three systems that must work together to support the business information needs of a steel manufacturer such as USX.
2. Identify the role each system plays in coordinating the systems' applications and the information each system manages.

---

* If this site moves, then try accessing **www.uec-usx.com** and follow (in order): 1) Information Tech., 2) Applications, 3) Order Fulfillment System, and 4) Steel Process & Tracking System.

Teamwork in Action

C1, P1, P2, P3, P6, P7

The purpose of this team activity is to ensure that each team member understands process operations and the related accounting entries. Turn to Exhibit 21.6 and find the activities and flows identified with numbers ①–⑩. Pick a member of the team to start. This team member is to describe activity number ① in this exhibit, then verbalize the related journal entry, and describe how the amounts in the entry are computed. The other members of the team are to voice agreement or disagreement—discussion is to continue until all express understanding. Rotate to the next numbered activity and next team member until all activities and entries are discussed. If at any point a team member is uncertain about an answer, the team member may pass and get back in the rotation when he/she can contribute to the team's discussion.

Hitting the Road

C3

In process costing, the process is analyzed first and then a unit measure is computed in the form of equivalent units for direct materials, direct labor, overhead, and all three combined. The same analysis applies to both manufacturing and service processes.

Required

Visit your local U.S. Mail center. Look into the backroom and you will see several ongoing processes. Select one process, such as sorting, and list the costs associated with this process. Your list should include materials, labor, and overhead—be specific. Classify each cost as fixed or variable. At the bottom of your list, outline how overhead should be assigned to your identified process. The following format (with an example) is suggested:

Cost Description	Direct Material	Direct Labor	Overhead	Variable Cost	Fixed Cost
Manual sorting		X		X	
Overhead allocation suggestions:					

Business Week Activity

C1, C3

Does a change in company strategy result in changes to the process costing system? Read the article "Microprocessors Are for Wimps" in the December 15, 1997, issue of ***Business Week*** and answer the following questions in a one-page memorandum to your instructor.

1. Identify and describe the shift in **Motorola's** market focus regarding microprocessor production.

2. What changes can you suggest in the process costing system to support the new market focus?

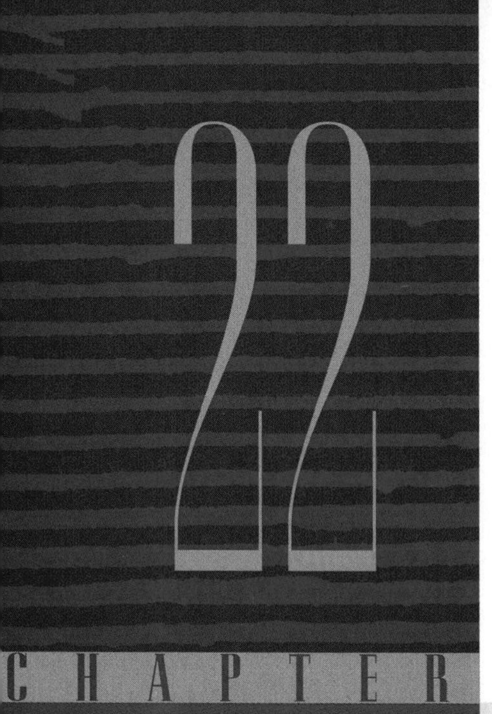

CHAPTER 22

Cost Allocation and Performance Measurement

A Look Back

Chapter 20 explained cost concepts and introduced the manufacturing statement and job order costing. Chapter 21 described process cost accounting and its implementation.

A Look at This Chapter

This chapter describes cost allocation and activity-based costing. It identifies managerial reports useful in directing a company's activities. It also describes responsibility accounting, measuring departmental performance, and allocating common costs across departments.

A Look Ahead

Chapter 23 looks at cost behavior and explains how its identification is useful to managers in performing cost-volume-profit analyses.

Chapter Outline

Chasing Costs, Finding Gold

SEATTLE, WA—Karla Sellers, a department manager for **AeroTech**—a small aerospace manufacturer—was recently confronted with several strategic initiatives launched by top management. These initiatives were directed at improving AeroTech's competitive position. Its managers pursue a policy of continuous improvement, but they aim to strategically identify specific areas for improvement. Says Sellers, "My department was the guinea pig, and I was leery, to put it politely."

To identify opportunities for improvement, Sellers's supervisors examined cost data based on an analysis of processes and activities. This required designing an accounting system to track cost information for the flow of materials, labor, and overhead in the processes at AeroTech. Management considered this necessary to obtain reliable data useful in targeting and implementing its policy of continuous improvement.

Sellers's department—the Small Aircraft Division—was the target of the process and activity analysis project. Its aim is to implement an activity-based cost system to meet management's information demands. Sellers and her team identified four main goals of their activity-based cost system:

- Identify costs, especially when processes cross departments.
- Identify major cost drivers for analysis and prediction of cost behavior.
- Improve tracing of overhead costs.
- Identify activities that add value to the product and those that do not.

"I felt uneasy about the whole project," says Sellers. "I'd never participated in such a major overhaul of an information system." Before beginning, Sellers needed to get a better understanding of how costs are traced to processes, how they're accumulated, and how costs per unit are computed for each process.

"It all eventually came together," says Sellers. She admits her team's lack of knowledge in activity-based costing slowed its progress. "In the end, we cut costs by nearly 12%, which drove price reductions. Our competitors didn't react and we gained 9% in market share." Sellers's reward? She's now vice president of strategic operations with a hefty salary to boot. Adds Sellers, "Our effective use of cost accounting data was the key."

Learning Objectives

Conceptual

C1 Explain departmentalization and the role of departmental accounting.

C2 Distinguish between direct and indirect expenses.

C3 Identify bases for allocating indirect expenses to departments.

C4 Explain controllable costs and responsibility accounting.

C5 Describe allocation of joint costs across products.

Analytical

A1 Analyze investment centers using return on total assets.

Procedural

P1 Assign overhead costs using two-stage cost allocation.

P2 Assign overhead costs using activity-based costing.

P3 Prepare departmental income statements.

P4 Prepare departmental contribution reports.

CHAPTER PREVIEW

The three prior chapters focused on measuring the costs of products or services, including reporting and analyzing the results in managerial reports. This chapter discusses further the issue of cost allocation. It describes how we allocate costs shared by more than one product across these different products, and how we allocate indirect costs of shared items such as utilities, advertising, and rent. The chapter then describes activity-based costing and its tracing of the costs of individual activities. This knowledge helps us better understand how resources are assigned as illustrated in the opening article. The chapter introduces additional managerial accounting reports useful in managing a company's activities. It also explains how and why management divides companies into departments.

Additional Methods of Overhead Cost Allocation

Chapter 20 explained how we allocated factory overhead costs to jobs by using a predetermined overhead allocation rate based on another activity such as direct labor cost. When a single overhead allocation rate is used on a plantwide basis, all overhead is lumped together and a predetermined overhead allocation rate is computed and used to assign overhead to jobs. This section considers additional cost allocation methods and issues.

Two-Stage Cost Allocation

P1 Assign overhead costs using two-stage cost allocation.

This section considers the situation where multiple overhead allocation rates are used to assign overhead. Multiple allocation rates were first introduced in Chapter 20 as part of *Using the Information* section. In this section we apply a two-stage cost allocation procedure to assign all direct and indirect costs.

In the first stage, costs are assigned to *operating departments,* also called *production departments.* An operating department usually performs at least one main function for the company. Operating departments are often production departments such as machining and assembly. Costs assigned to an operating department consist of both those directly incurred by the department and those allocated to it from one or more service departments within the company. A *service department* is one that supports the activities of more than one operating department.

The second stage involves computing a predetermined overhead allocation rate for each operating department. This rate is then used to assign overhead to jobs or processes.

Illustration of Two-Stage Cost Allocation

We use Exhibit 22.1 to explain the two-stage procedure. This exhibit illustrates cost allocation for **AutoGrand,** a custom automobile manufacturer. AutoGrand employs five manufacturing related departments: janitorial, maintenance, factory accounting, machining, and assembly. Expenses incurred by each department of AutoGrand are considered a product cost.

The three service departments—janitorial, maintenance, and factory accounting—expect to incur $10,000, $15,000, and $8,000 (total $33,000) of expenses, respectively, for a recent month that are not directly traceable to a department. Another $28,000 of service department expenses are directly traceable to the two operating departments (machining and assembly). This means a total of $61,000 of service department expenses, or overhead, must be allocated to processes or jobs.

The resources of the service departments are used by the two operating departments as shown in the exhibit. To illustrate the first stage of cost allocation, let's look at janitorial. Its costs are allocated to machining and assembly in the ratio 60:40. This means 60%, or $6,000, of janitorial costs are assigned to the machining department and 40%, or $4,000, to the assembly department.

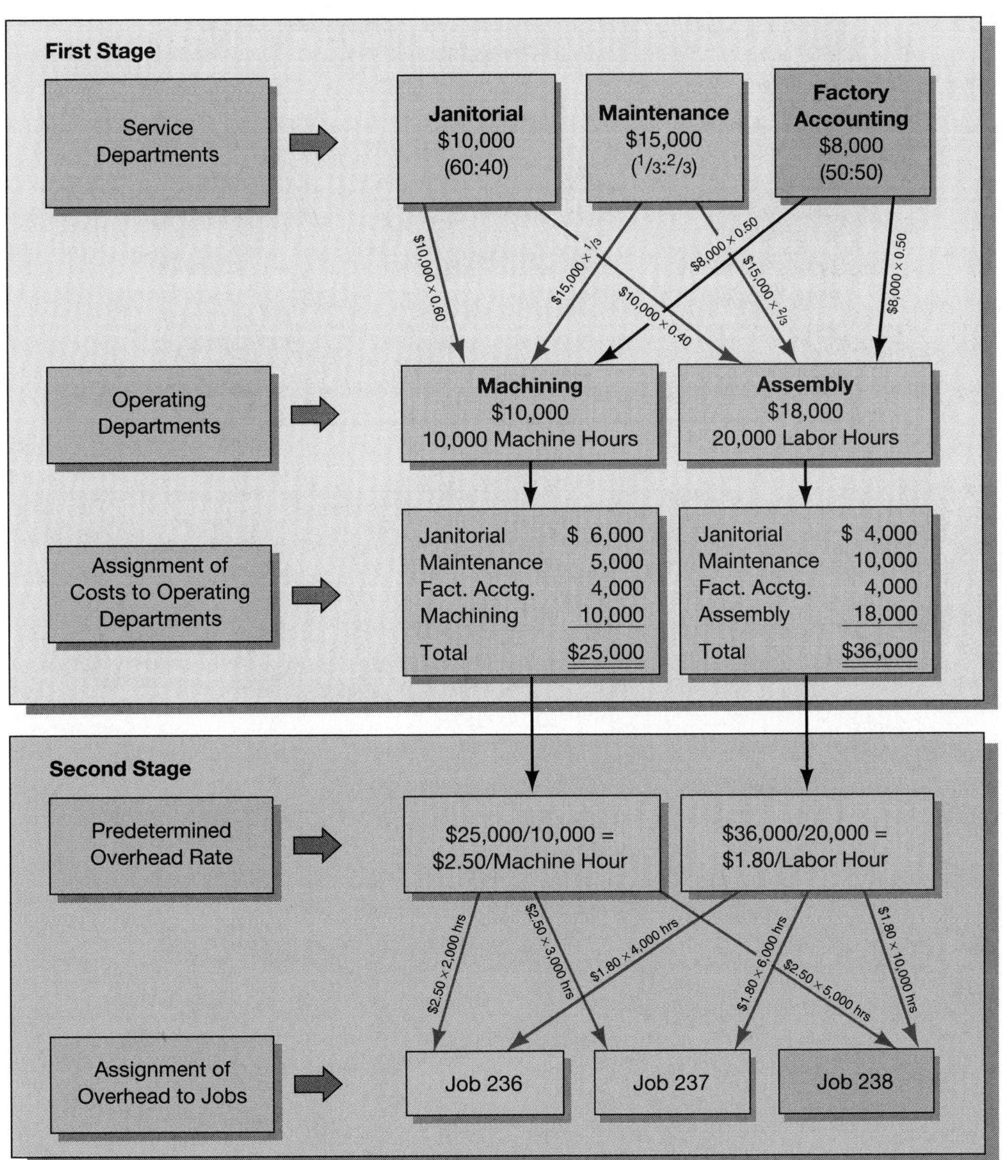

Exhibit 22.1

Two-Stage Cost Allocation

To determine total service department costs assigned to each operating department, the costs directly incurred by the operating department ($10,000 in the case of machining) are added to those assigned from service departments. This yields total costs of $25,000 assigned to machining and $36,000 to assembly.

In the second stage, predetermined overhead rates for each operating department are computed. For machining, this rate is computed using machine hours as the allocation base. For assembly, the rate is computed using labor hours as the allocation base. The predetermined overhead rates are computed as $2.50 per machine hour for machining and $1.80 per labor hour for assembly. The predetermined overhead rates are then used to assign overhead to jobs.

To illustrate, three jobs were started and finished in a recent month. These jobs consumed resources as follows: Job 236—2,000 machine hours in machining and 4,000 labor hours in assembly; Job 237—3,000 machine hours and 6,000 labor hours; Job 238—5,000 machine hours and 10,000 labor hours. The overhead assigned to these three jobs is computed and shown in Exhibit 22.2. Total overhead assigned to Jobs 236, 237, and 238, is $12,200, $18,300, and $30,500, respectively. This adds to $61,000, which is the total amount of overhead we started with.

Exhibit 22.2

Assignment of Overhead to Jobs

	Job 236	Job 237	Job 238
Machining:			
$2.50 × 2,000	$ 5,000		
$2.50 × 3,000		$ 7,500	
$2.50 × 5,000			$12,500
Assembly:			
$1.80 × 4,000	$ 7,200		
$1.80 × 6,000		10,800	
$1.80 × 10,000			18,000
Total overhead assigned	$12,200	$18,300	$30,500

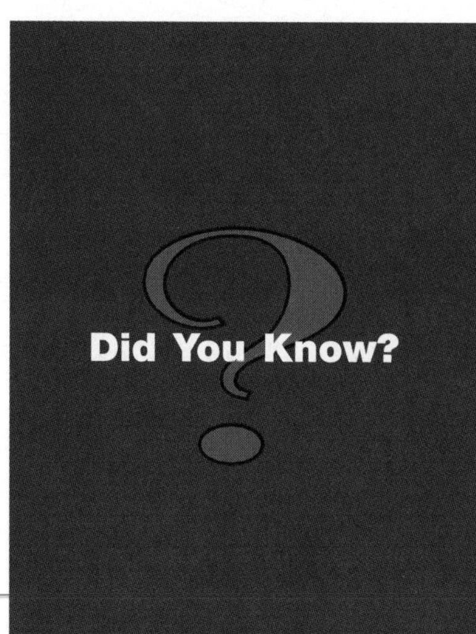

Overhead Can Kill

Futura Computer Co. recently outsourced 2 million units of a "money-losing" product to be manufactured by a Korean firm. Its domestic manufacturing facility was retooled to produce extra units of a "more profitable" product. The goal was to turn the company's current $11 million loss into a $17.5 million profit. But profits didn't materialize. Instead, losses grew to over $20 million! What went wrong? It turns out the better product was a loser, while the losing product was a winner. Futura's management didn't know this because fixed overhead items such as depreciation were allocated to products on the basis of direct labor cost. But where labor was being used, machinery wasn't. This meant labor intensive products were assigned too much overhead and, thus, messed up the identification of best and worst products. Bad cost allocation brought this company to its knees. [Source: "Overhead Can Kill You," *Forbes*, February 10, 1997.]

Activity-Based Costing

P2 Assign overhead costs using activity-based costing.

Overhead costs are usually too complex to be simply explained as the result of variation in one factor such as direct labor.[1] While computing multiple overhead rates, as in a two-stage allocation, is an improvement over allocation using simply direct labor, it has limitations. This is because the allocation bases used in the second stage are still volume-based (e.g., machine hours), whereas many overhead cost items are not driven by the volume of production or services.

Unfortunately, inappropriate allocations can distort unit costs. When the number of jobs, products, or departments increases, the possibility of improperly assigning costs increases. This can lead to poor decisions by managers and the eventual failure of a company.

Activity-based costing (ABC) attempts to better allocate costs to the proper users of overhead by focusing on *activities*. Companies are increasingly attracted by the potential benefits of activity-based costing. A recent survey found that most respondents feel

[1] Also, because technological advances have encouraged automated manufacturing, direct labor costs have declined as a percent of total production cost. In some companies, direct labor cost is such a small part of total cost that it is treated as overhead.

activity-based costing is worth the investment in terms of improving management decisions.[2]

Exhibit 22.3 shows the two-stage activity-based cost allocation method. The first step includes identifying activities involved in the different departments and forming activity cost *pools* by combining these activities into sets. The second step involves computing predetermined overhead cost allocation rates for each cost pool and then assigning costs to jobs.

Activity-Based Cost Allocation

First Stage

Set of Activities → Activity 1, Activity 2, ... (for each cost pool)

Cost Pools →

- **Janitorial** $10,000 10,000 Square Feet
- **Maintenance** $15,000 5,000 Maintenance Hours
- **Factory Accounting** $8,000 2,000 Transactions
- **Machining** $10,000 10,000 Machine Hours
- **Assembly** $18,000 20,000 Labor Hours

Second Stage

Predetermined Overhead Rate →

- $10,000/10,000 = $1/Square Foot
- $15,000/5,000 = $3/Maint. Hour
- $8,000/2,000 = $4/ Transaction
- $10,000/10,000 = $1/Machine Hour
- $18,000/20,000 = $0.90/Labor Hour

Assignment of Overhead to Jobs → Job 236, Job 237, Job 238

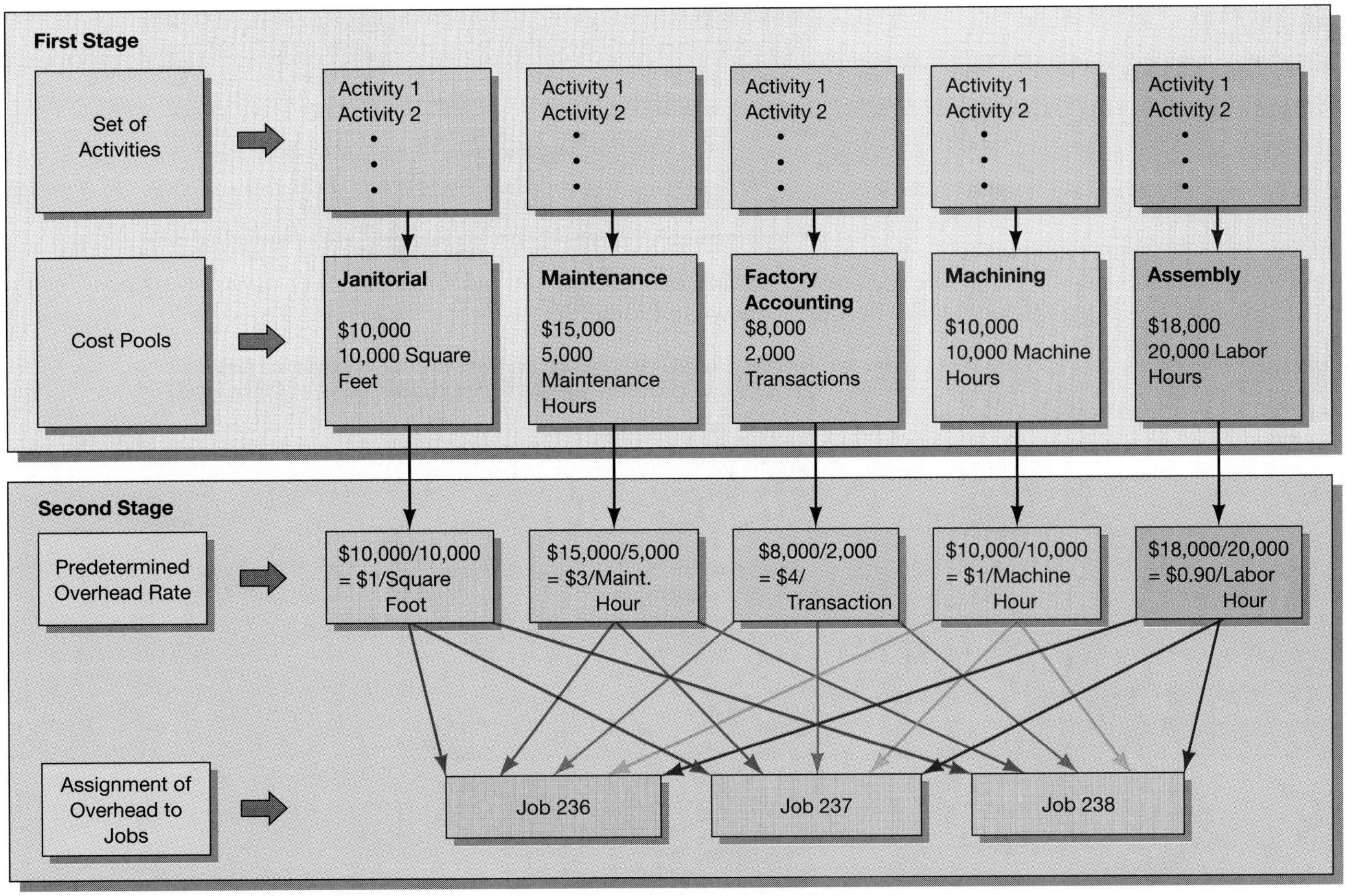

We begin our explanation at the top of Exhibit 22.3. Costs of individual activities of overhead items, or *resources,* are collected in separate temporary accounts. The cost of each activity is driven by what is called a cost driver. A **cost driver** causes the cost of an activity to go up or down. The cost driver for a purchase order processing activity, for instance, is the number of purchase orders processed.

Activities are then pooled in a logical manner into activity cost pools. An **activity cost pool** is a temporary account accumulating costs a company incurs to support an identified set of activities. Costs accumulated in an activity cost pool include variable and fixed costs of the activity. Variable costs pertain to resources acquired as needed (such as materials), whereas fixed costs pertain to resources acquired in advance (such as equipment).

---

[2] S. Jayson, "ABC *Is* Worth the Investment," *Management Accounting,* April 1994, p. 27. Another relevant article is "Does Your Company Need a New Cost System?" by Robin Cooper, *Harvard Business Review,* Spring 1987.

An activity cost pool account is handled like a manufacturing overhead account. After all activity costs are accumulated in an activity cost pool account, users of the activity, called *cost objects,* are assigned a portion of the total activity cost. This is done using a cost driver or allocation base.

Illustration of Activity-Based Costing

To illustrate, let's return to the three jobs of AutoGrand. Let's assume resources are used for completing Jobs 236, 237, and 238 as shown in Exhibit 22.4.

Exhibit 22.4

Activity Resource Consumption

Resource Use	Job 236	Job 237	Job 238
Square feet of space	5,000	3,000	2,000
Maintenance hours	2,500	1,500	1,000
Number of transactions	500	700	800
Machine hours	2,000	3,000	5,000
Direct labor hours	4,000	6,000	10,000

We then assign the $61,000 of total overhead costs to these three jobs using activity-based costing as shown in Exhibit 22.5.

Exhibit 22.5

Activity-Based Assignment of Overhead

	Job 236	Job 237	Job 238
Janitorial:			
$1.00 × 5,000 sq. ft.	$ 5,000		
$1.00 × 3,000 sq. ft.		$ 3,000	
$1.00 × 2,000 sq. ft.			$ 2,000
Maintenance:			
$3.00 × 2,500 hrs.	7,500		
$3.00 × 1,500 hrs.		4,500	
$3.00 × 1,000 hrs.			3,000
Factory Accounting:			
$4.00 × 500 trans.	2,000		
$4.00 × 700 trans.		2,800	
$4.00 × 800 trans.			3,200
Machining:			
$1.00 × 2,000 hrs.	2,000		
$1.00 × 3,000 hrs.		3,000	
$1.00 × 5,000 hrs.			5,000
Assembly:			
$0.90 × 4,000 hrs.	3,600		
$0.90 × 6,000 hrs.		5,400	
$0.90 × 10,000 hrs.			9,000
Total overhead assigned	$20,100	$18,700	$22,200

Comparing Exhibits 22.2 and 22.5 we see that the overhead amounts assigned to the three jobs vary markedly depending on whether two-stage cost allocation or activity-based costing is applied. Overhead assigned to Job 236 goes up from $12,200 using two-stage cost allocation to $20,100 under activity-based costing. But overhead assigned to Job 238 declines from $30,500 to $22,200. These differences in amounts assigned result from more accurate tracing of overhead costs to each job. This increase in accuracy results because activity-based costing uses allocation bases reflecting actual cost drivers.

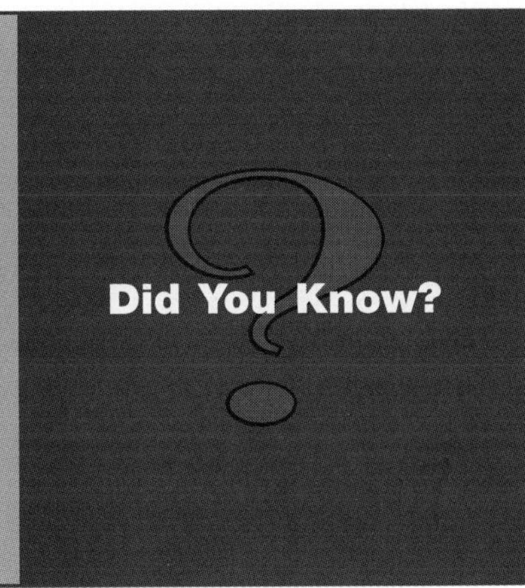

Your Health

Activity-based costing is used in many settings. Its only requirements are existence of overhead and a demand for reliable cost information. A recent study examined use of activity-based costing in a healthcare organization. Identifying cost drivers in a healthcare setting is challenging because activity drivers are less obvious than they are in manufacturing. The study found that activity-based costing offers major improvements in healthcare costing accuracy, enabling improved profitability analysis and decision making. [Source: T.D. West and D.A. West, "Applying ABC to Healthcare," *Management Accounting,* February 1997, pp. 22–33.]

Comparing Two-Stage and Activity-Based Cost Allocation Methods

Differences between traditional cost allocation methods and activity-based costing are mainly due to how many cost drivers are used and how many allocations are made. Traditional cost systems commonly accumulate overhead in one overhead account or a small number of overhead accounts. Companies then assign these overhead costs to jobs or products using a single allocation base such as direct labor. In addition, service department costs are often allocated to operating departments separately (see Exhibit 22.1).

Under activity-based costing, the costs of resources are assigned to the activities using the resources. These activities are then accumulated into activity cost pools. A company selects a cost driver (allocation base) for each activity pool. It uses this cost driver to assign the accumulated activity costs to cost objects (such as jobs or products) benefiting from the activity.

It is common for an activity-based costing system to involve 6 to 12 (or more) times as many allocations as a traditional cost system. As one example, a Chicago-based manufacturer currently uses nearly 20 different activity cost drivers to assign overhead costs to its products. An activity-based cost system was recently set up at **Perkin-Elmer,** a maker of analytical instruments. The company's controller reports that at first they tried to analyze too many cost drivers. Eventually, they set up cross-functional teams able to identify the important cost drivers for each pool.

Exhibit 22.6 lists examples of overhead cost pools and their cost drivers. We use these cost drivers to assign activity costs to cost objects and then to products produced.

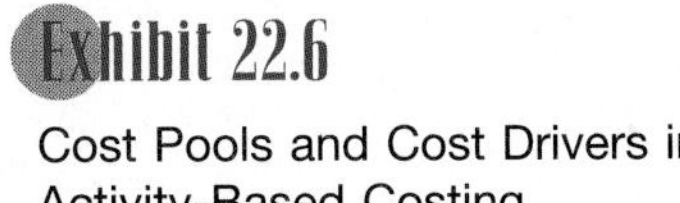
Exhibit 22.6

Cost Pools and Cost Drivers in Activity-Based Costing

Cost Pool	Cost Driver
Materials purchasing	Number of purchase orders
Materials handling	Number of materials requisitions
Personnel processing	Number of employees hired or laid off
Equipment depreciation	Number of products produced or hours of use
Quality inspection	Number of units inspected
Indirect labor in setting up equipment	Number of setups required
Engineering costs for product modifications	Number of modifications (engineering change orders)

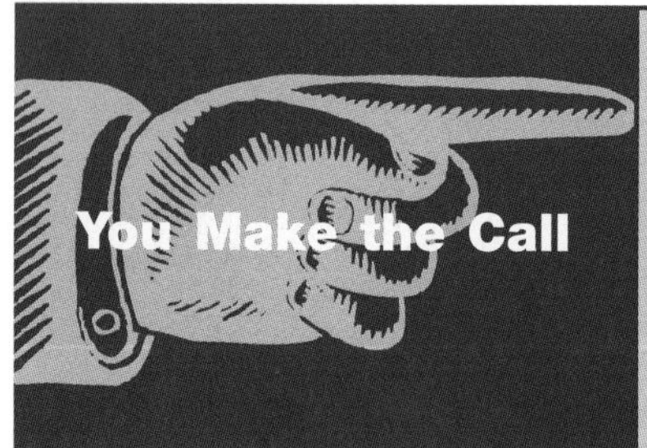

Director of Operations
You are the director of operations for a promotional company. Two department managers approach you with a complaint. Both feel they are unduly assigned high overhead costs. Overhead is currently assigned on the basis of labor hours for artwork designers. These managers argue overhead doesn't only depend on the designers' hours and that many overhead items are unrelated to these hours. How do you respond?

Answer—p. 970

Activity-based costing is especially effective when many different kinds of products are produced from the same department or departments. Some products produced in a department might be simple, while others are more complex. More complex products likely require more help from service departments such as engineering, maintenance, and materials handling. If the same amount of direct labor is applied to the complex and simple products, a traditional overhead allocation system assigns the same overhead cost to them. But with activity-based costing, the complex products are assigned a greater portion of overhead.

The difference in overhead assigned can affect product pricing, make-or-buy, and other managerial decisions. Activity-based costing allows production managers to focus on managing activities driving overhead cost instead of reducing allocated overhead by reducing direct labor cost. But managers cannot focus solely on activities. The contribution of an activity to the entire production process must be kept in mind.

Activity-based costing also causes managers to pay closer attention to all activities. If overhead costs are accumulated in one account, attention is less likely to be directed at controlling any individual item. Activity-based costing requires managers to look at each item. This encourages them to manage each cost to increase the benefit from each dollar spent. It also encourages managers to cooperate because it shows how their efforts are interrelated. This results in *activity-based management*.

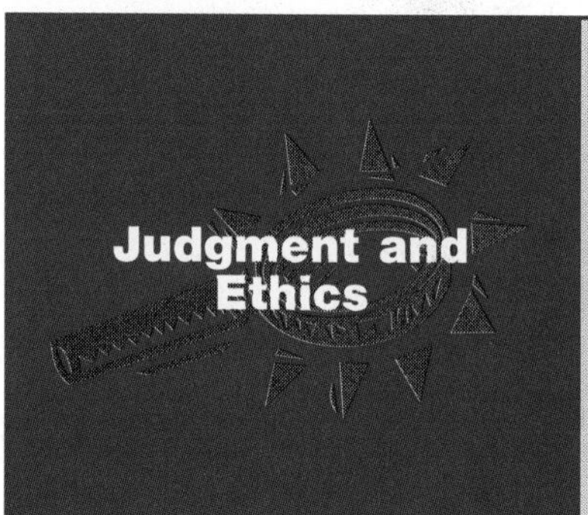

Accounting Officer
You are an accounting officer working for a company producing expensive women's footwear, the production of which involves many complex and specialized activities. The company's general manager recently learns about activity-based costing (ABC) and thinks it might be appropriate to use. But your current supervisor doesn't want to disturb the existing cost accounting system and instructs you to prepare a report stating "the implementation of ABC is a complicated process involving too many steps and may not be worth the effort." You actually believe ABC will help the company in identifying sources of costs and controlling them. What action do you take?

Answer—p. 970

Flash back

1. What is a cost driver?
2. When activity-based costing is used rather than traditional allocation methods:
   a. Managers must identify cost drivers for various items of overhead cost.
   b. Individual cost items in service departments are allocated to products manufactured or sold in operating departments.
   c. Managers can direct their attention to the activities that drive overhead cost.
   d. All of the above.

Answers—p. 970

Departmental Accounting

C1 Explain departmentalization and the role of departmental accounting.

When companies are too large to be managed effectively as a single unit, they are divided into *departments,* also called *subunits.* Accounting information about the performance of departments of a company is useful for managers. Our discussion of process cost accounting in Chapter 21 explained how manufacturing systems are sometimes divided into departments for better management.

Managerial accounting for departments has two main goals. The first is to provide information that managers can use to evaluate the profitability or cost effectiveness of each department's activities. This goal is met by a **departmental accounting system.** The second goal is to control costs and expenses and evaluate managers' performances by assigning costs and expenses to the managers who are responsible for controlling them. This goal is met by a *responsibility accounting system.* Departmental and responsibility accounting systems are related and share much information. We discuss departmental accounting in this and the next section. Responsibility accounting is described later in the chapter.

Motivation for Departmentalization

Many companies are sufficiently large and complex, requiring division into departments. When a company is departmentalized, each department is often placed under the direction of a manager. As a company grows, management often divides departments into new departments so that responsibilities for the activities of a department don't overwhelm a manager's ability to oversee and control them. A company also creates departments to take advantage of the skills of individual managers.

Basis of Departmentalization

The two basic categories of departments are (1) *operating (production)* and (2) *service.* In a manufacturer, operating departments engage directly in manufacturing. These operating departments are often organized to put each manufacturing process under the direction of one manager. The boundaries of an operating department are often defined by the types of activities it carries out or products it manufactures.

In a merchandiser, operating departments make sales directly to customers. Merchandisers often organize departments around the products they sell. For instance, each operating department often has the task of selling one or more lines of merchandise, and are usually referred to as *selling departments.*

Service departments help operating departments by providing support. Examples are advertising, purchasing, payroll, human resource management, and top management. Service departments do not directly manufacture products or generate revenues through services. Yet their support is crucial for the success of other departments.

Departmental Evaluation

When a company is divided into departments, managers need to know how each department is performing. The accounting system must supply information about resources used and outputs achieved by each department. This requires a system to measure and accumulate revenue and expense information for each department whenever possible.

Because of its potential usefulness to competitors, departmental information is rarely distributed publicly. Information about departments is prepared for internal managers to help control operations, appraise performance, allocate resources, and plan strategic actions. If a department is highly profitable, management may decide to expand its operations. Or, if a department is performing poorly, information about revenues and expenses can suggest useful changes.

More companies are emphasizing customer satisfaction as a main responsibility of each department. This has led to changes in the measures reported in responsibility

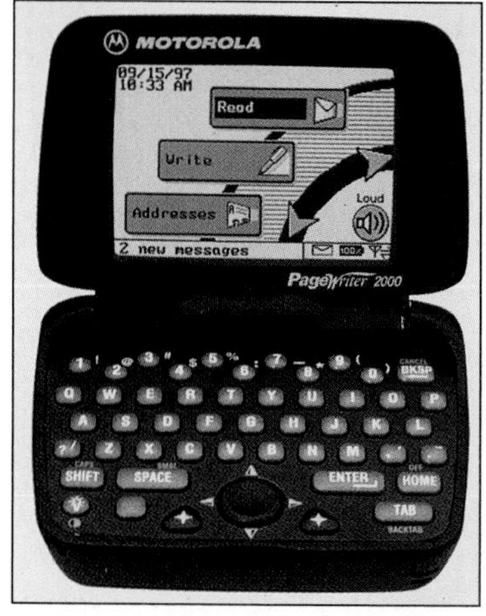

accounting systems. Increasingly, financial measurements are being supplemented with quality and customer satisfaction indexes. **Motorola,** for instance, uses two key measures: the number of defective parts per million parts produced and the percent of orders delivered on time to customers.

Financial information used to evaluate a department depends on whether it is a profit center or a cost center. A **profit center** incurs costs and generates revenues. Selling departments are often evaluated as profit centers. A **cost center** incurs costs or expenses without directly generating revenues. Manufacturing departments of a manufacturer, and service departments such as accounting, advertising, and purchasing, are all cost centers.

Evaluating the performance of managers depends on whether they are responsible for profit centers or cost centers. Managers of profit centers are judged on their ability to generate revenues in excess of the department's expenses. It is assumed they influence both revenue generation and cost incurrence. Managers of cost centers are judged on their ability to control costs by keeping them within a satisfactory range under an assumption they can only influence costs.

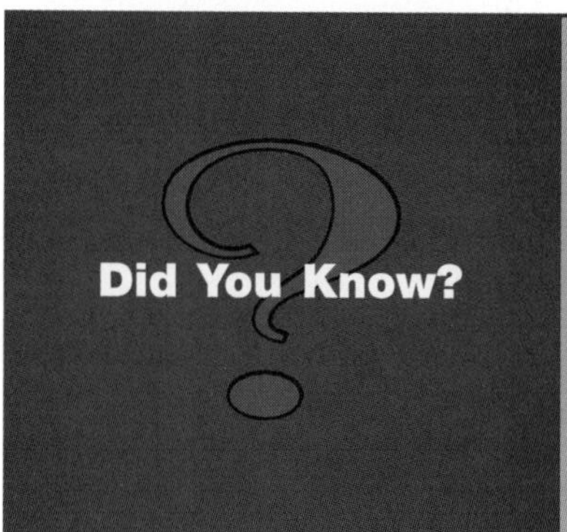

More than Profit!
A recent survey shows many companies use nonfinancial performance measures as part of the information reported to management. About 63% of companies indicated they use nonfinancial measures, and 87% indicated nonfinancial measures should be used even more. The nonfinancial measures used most often are: cycle time, defect rate, on-time deliveries, inventory turnover, customer satisfaction, and safety. Also, about one quarter of the companies said they are implementing activity-based management as part of their performance measurement system. [Source: Cost Management Group, "Companies Continue to Adjust Their Performance Measurement Systems," *Cost Management Update,* April 1997, p. 1.]

Departmental Reporting and Analysis

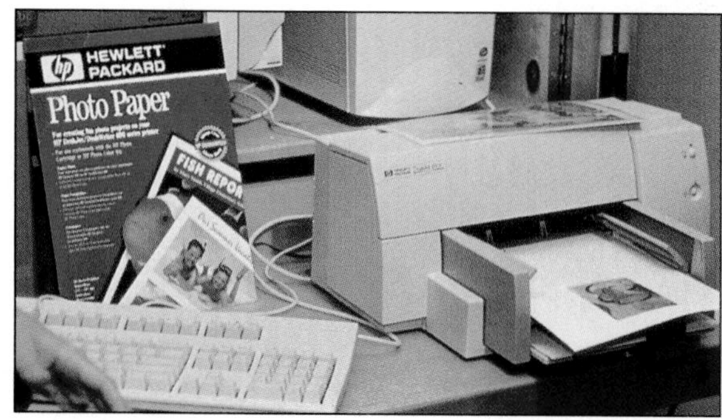

Companies use a variety of measurements and reporting formats in evaluating their departments. The type and form of information depend on the focus and philosophy of management. **Hewlett Packard**'s statement of corporate objectives, for instance, indicates its reason for existence is to satisfy customer needs. The challenge in its case is to set up managerial accounting systems to provide relevant feedback for evaluating performance in terms of its stated objectives. Also, the means of obtaining information about departments depend on how extensively a company uses computer and information technology.

Computerized Departmental Systems

Sophisticated cash registers allow managers of a merchandising company access to information about each department's sales, sales returns, and other crucial data. In a networked system, registers transfer this information directly to computers for reporting and analysis purposes.

Registers are also capable of more than accumulating sales information. They can print detailed information on a sales ticket given to a customer, total the ticket, and initiate journal entries to record credit sales in a customer's account. If information about goods sold is recorded at the register by a scanner or a keyboard, the system can produce detailed departmental summaries of items sold and those remaining in inventory.

Separate Accounts by Department

Sophisticated systems allow companies to compute total sales and sales returns for each department on a regular basis. More clerical effort is needed for less sophisticated systems. In less sophisticated systems, totals are often accumulated by one of two ways: (a) separate Sales and Sales Returns accounts in the general ledger for each department or (b) supplementary spreadsheet analysis of departmental sales and sales returns. Information systems can also accumulate information about purchases and purchases returns by departments.

If a company uses special journals and has separate Sales, Sales Returns, Purchases, and Purchases Returns accounts for each selling department, then its special journals often have separate columns for routine transactions by departments. Exhibit 22.7 shows a sales journal used to record information for three selling departments. The amounts debited to customers' accounts are entered in the Accounts Receivable Debit column and posted to these accounts daily. Less frequently, perhaps monthly, this column's total is posted to the Accounts Receivable controlling account. Amounts sold to a customer are identified by department and entered in one or more of the last three columns. Totals of these three columns are periodically posted to their ledger accounts.

Exhibit 22.7

Departmentalized Sales Journal

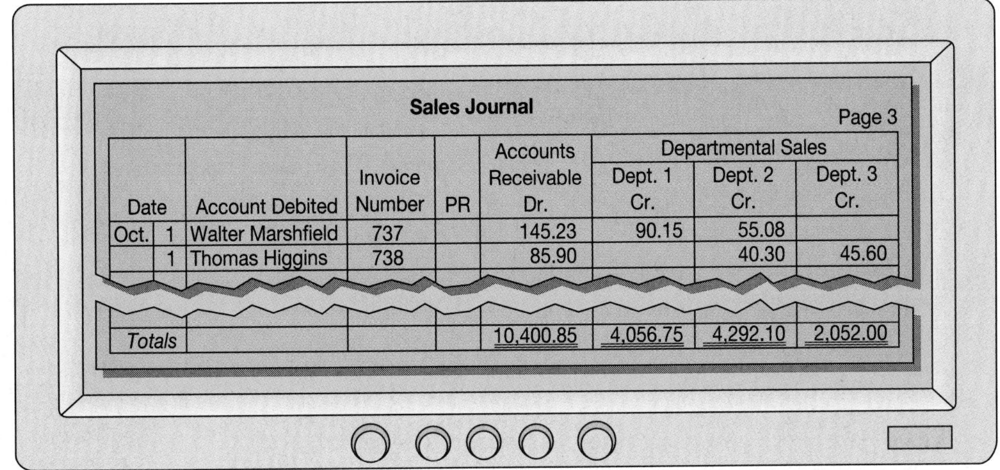

Sales Journal Page 3

Date		Account Debited	Invoice Number	PR	Accounts Receivable Dr.	Departmental Sales Dept. 1 Cr.	Dept. 2 Cr.	Dept. 3 Cr.
Oct.	1	Walter Marshfield	737		145.23	90.15	55.08	
	1	Thomas Higgins	738		85.90		40.30	45.60
Totals					10,400.85	4,056.75	4,292.10	2,052.00

Departmental Spreadsheet Analysis

If separate accounts aren't maintained in the general ledger by department, a company can create departmental information by using a supplemental spreadsheet analysis. In this case, a company records sales, sales returns, purchases, and purchases returns as if the company is not departmentalized. Then, it later identifies each department's transactions and enters these amounts on a spreadsheet.

To illustrate, after recording sales in its usual manner, a company can compute daily total sales by department and enter these totals on a sales spreadsheet. Exhibit 22.8 shows such a spreadsheet. At the end of a period, column totals of the spreadsheet show sales by department. The combined total of all columns equals the balance of the Sales account.

When a merchandiser uses a spreadsheet analysis of department sales, it often uses separate spreadsheets to accumulate sales, sales returns, purchases, and purchases returns by department. If each department keeps count of its inventory, it can also compute its gross profit. Accumulating information and computing gross profit by department is not difficult. Yet some companies don't measure profits by department because of difficulties in allocating expenses across departments. We consider these difficulties in the next section.

Exhibit 22.8

Departmental Sales Spreadsheet

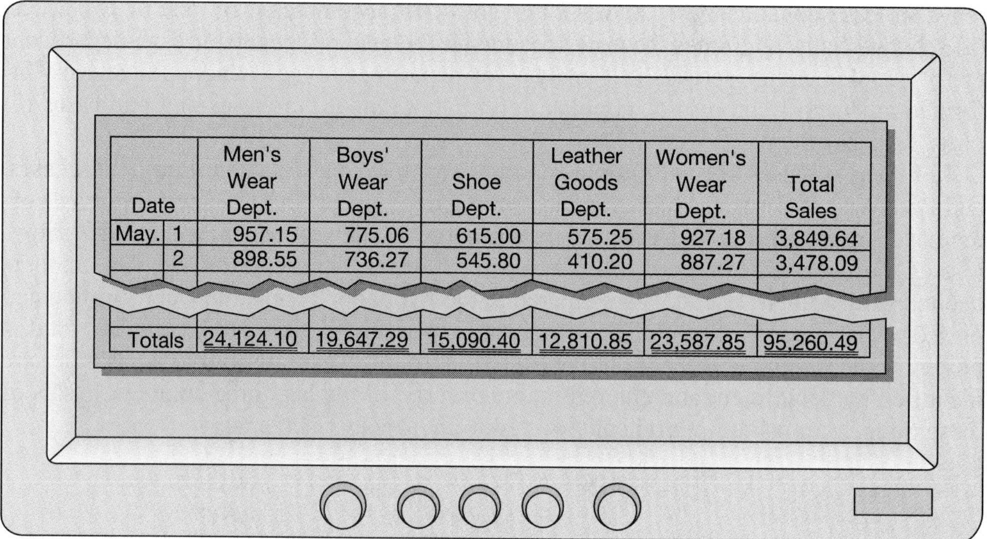

Date		Men's Wear Dept.	Boys' Wear Dept.	Shoe Dept.	Leather Goods Dept.	Women's Wear Dept.	Total Sales
May.	1	957.15	775.06	615.00	575.25	927.18	3,849.64
	2	898.55	736.27	545.80	410.20	887.27	3,478.09
Totals		24,124.10	19,647.29	15,090.40	12,810.85	23,587.85	95,260.49

Flash back

3. What is the difference between departmental accounting systems and responsibility accounting systems?
4. Service (support) departments: *(a)* manufacture products; *(b)* make sales directly to customers; *(c)* produce revenues; *(d)* assist operating departments.
5. Explain the difference between a cost center and a profit center and give an example of each.
6. A company that develops departmental information by using supplemental sales analysis spreadsheets would probably:
   a. Have a sophisticated computerized cash register system.
   b. Use separate spreadsheets to accumulate sales, sales returns, purchases, and purchases returns.
   c. Provide separate Sales accounts for each department in its general ledger.

Answers—p. 970

Departmental Expense Allocation

When a company computes departmental profits, it confronts some accounting challenges. These challenges involve allocating the company's expenses across its operating departments.

Direct Expenses

C2 Distinguish between direct and indirect expenses.

Direct expenses are readily traced to a department because they are incurred for the sole benefit of that department. They require no allocation across departments. For example, the salary of an employee who works in only one department is a direct expense of that one department.

The concept of direct expense is similar to the concept of direct cost introduced in Chapter 19. We used the term *direct cost* in the context of a manufacturer where all manufacturing costs are product costs that are assigned to products. This was different from period costs that are immediately expensed. In *non*manufacturing departments, costs are charged to expense as they are incurred. In these situations, the term *direct expense* is used instead of *direct cost.*

Indirect Expenses

A company's expenses include indirect expenses. **Indirect expenses** (like *indirect costs*) are incurred for the joint benefit of more than one department. For example, if two or more departments share a single building, they both enjoy the benefits of the expenses of renting, heating, and lighting. These expenses are indirect because they can't be readily traced to one department.

When we need information about departmental profits, indirect expenses are allocated across departments benefiting from them. Ideally we allocate indirect expenses by using a cause-effect relation. Identifying cause-effect relations is not always possible. In these latter situations, each indirect expense is allocated on a basis approximating the relative benefit received by each department. Measuring the benefit each department receives from an indirect expense can be difficult or sometimes impossible. Even when a reasonable allocation basis is chosen, considerable doubt sometimes exists regarding the amount charged to each department.

Illustration of Indirect Expense Allocation

To illustrate how an indirect expense is allocated, let's consider a jewelry store that purchases janitorial services from an outside company. Management allocates this cost across the store's three departments according to the floor space each occupies. Costs of janitorial services for a recent month are $300. Exhibit 22.9 shows the square feet of floor space occupied by each department. The store computes the percent of total square feet taken up by each department and then allocates the $300 cost using these percents.

Exhibit 22.9

Indirect Expense Allocation

Department	Square Feet	Percent of Total	Allocated Cost
Jewelry	2,400	60.0%	$180
Watch repair	600	15.0	45
China and silver	1,000	25.0	75
Total	4,000	100.0%	$300

The exhibit shows the jewelry department occupies 60% of the floor space in the store. This results in 60% of the total $300 cost being assigned to the jewelry department. When the allocation process is complete, these and other allocated costs are deducted from the gross profit for each department to determine net income for each.

We can apply the concepts of direct and indirect expenses (and costs) in a variety of cases. We can readily link direct expenses or costs with a *cost object*. Here, the relevant cost object is a department. Other cost objects may be relevant for other decisions. For job order cost systems in manufacturing operations (Chapter 20), the cost object is a job or job lot. For process cost systems (Chapter 21), the cost object is a process.

One consideration in allocating costs is to motivate managers and employees toward desired behavior. This means a cost incurred in one department might be best allocated to another department because the latter department caused the cost and can control it. For example, the controller of **AeroTech** (introduced in the opening article) captures the costs of reworking, delivering, and reinstalling aerospace components that are due to misspecifications in separate accounts. These costs are then allocated to individual salespersons who serviced the customers and provided the wrong component specifications. This process reassigns costs from manufacturing to those who best control them.

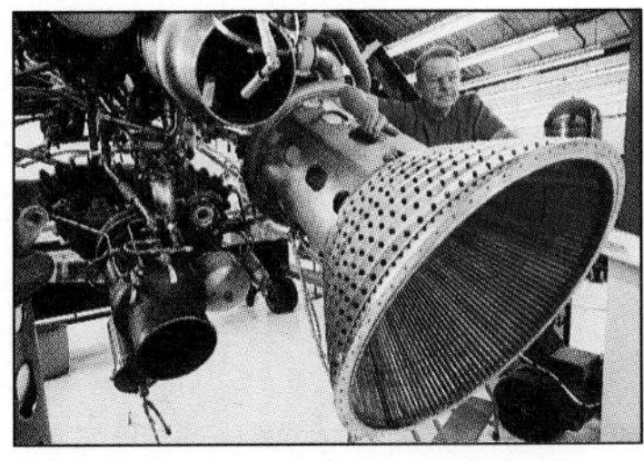

Allocation of Indirect Expenses

C3 Identify bases for allocating indirect expenses to departments.

This section describes how to allocate indirect expenses across departments and identify the bases used. There is no standard rule about what basis is best. This is because expense allocation involves several factors, and the relative importance of these factors varies across departments. Judgment is required, and people don't always agree. In our discussion, note the parallels between activity-based costing and the departmental expense allocation procedures described here.

Wages and Salaries

Employees' wages and salaries can be either direct or indirect expenses. If their time is spent entirely in one department, their wages are a direct expense of that department. But if employees work in more than one department, their wages are an indirect expense and must be allocated across the departments benefited. An employee's contribution to a department usually depends on the hours worked in that department. A reasonable basis then for allocating employees' wages and salaries is the *relative amount of time spent in each department*. But a supervisory employee often manages more than one department and it is sometimes not practical to record a supervisor's time spent in each department. In this case, a company can allocate supervisory salaries to departments on the basis of the number of employees in each department. This basis is reasonable if a supervisor's main task is managing people. Another basis of allocation is on sales across departments. This basis is reasonable if a supervisor's job reflects on departmental sales.

Rent and Related Building Expenses

Rent expense for a building is reasonably allocated to departments on the basis of floor space occupied by each department. But some floor space is often more valuable than other space because of location. If so, the allocation method charges departments with more valuable space a higher expense per square foot. Ground floor retail space, for instance, is often more valuable than basement or upper-floor space because all customers pass departments near the entrance while fewer go beyond the first floor. When there are no precise measures of floor space values, it is helpful to base allocations on data such as customer traffic and real estate assessments. When a company owns a building, then its expenses for depreciation, taxes, insurance, and other related building expenses are allocated like rent expense.

Advertising

Effective advertising of a department's products increases customer traffic and sales. Customers also often buy unadvertised products during their visit. This means advertising of products for some departments often helps sales of all departments, and therefore many stores treat advertising as an indirect expense. Advertising is often allocated on the basis of each department's proportion of total sales. For example, a department with 10% of a store's total sales is assigned 10% of advertising expense. Another method is to analyze each advertisement to compute the newspaper space or TV/radio time devoted to the products of a department. A department is then charged with the proportional costs of advertisements. Management must consider whether this more detailed and costly method is justified.

Equipment and Machinery Depreciation

Depreciation on equipment and machinery used only in one department is a direct expense of that department. Depreciation on equipment and machinery used by more than one department is an indirect expense to be allocated across departments. Accounting for each department's equipment depreciation expense requires a company to keep records showing which departments use specific assets. The number of hours equipment and machinery are used by departments is a reasonable basis for allocating depreciation.

Utilities

Utilities expenses such as heating and lighting are usually allocated on the basis of floor space occupied by departments. This practice assumes their use is uniform across departments. When this is not the case, a more involved allocation may be necessary. There is often a trade-off between the usefulness of more precise allocations and the effort in computing them.

Services

To generate product and service revenues, operating departments require services (support) by departments such as personnel, payroll, advertising, and purchasing. Because these service departments don't produce revenues, they are evaluated as cost centers. A departmental accounting system can accumulate and report costs incurred directly by each service department for this purpose. It then allocates a service department's indirect expenses and costs to operating departments benefiting from them. This is done, for example, using traditional two-stage cost allocation (see Exhibit 22.1). The costs of service departments are shared indirect expenses of operating departments. If management wants to evaluate operating departments as profit centers using net income instead of gross profit, service department costs are also allocated to them. Exhibit 22.10 shows some commonly used bases for allocating service department expenses and costs to operating departments.

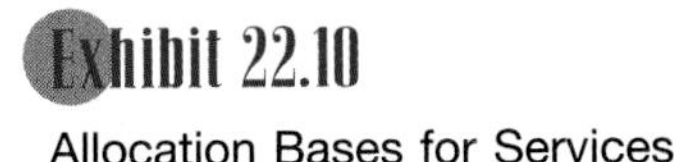
Exhibit 22.10
Allocation Bases for Services

Service Departments	Common Allocation Bases
Office	Number of employees or sales in each department
Personnel	Number of employees in each department
Payroll	Number of employees in each department
Advertising	Sales or amounts of advertising charged directly to each department
Purchasing	Dollar amounts of purchases or number of purchase orders processed
Cleaning	Square feet of floor space occupied
Maintenance	Square feet of floor space occupied

Departmental Income Statements

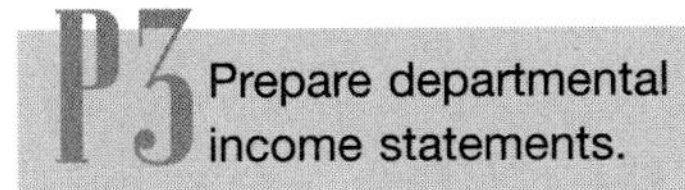
P3 Prepare departmental income statements.

Each department is assigned its expenses and costs to yield its own income statement. Its expenses include both direct expenses and those indirect expenses that are shared with other departments. For this purpose it is often useful to compile all expenses incurred in service departments before assigning them to operating departments.

To illustrate the steps in preparing departmental income statemens, let's look at **Ace Hardware** with five departments. Two of them (office and purchasing) are service departments and the other three (hardware, housewares, and appliances) are operating (selling) departments. There are four steps in allocating costs to its operating departments and preparing departmental income statements.

Step One

Step one is to accumulate direct expenses for each service and operating department as shown in Exhibit 22.11. Direct expenses include salaries, wages, and other expenses each department incurs but doesn't share with any other department. This information is accumulated in departmental expense accounts.

Step 1: Direct Expense Accumulation

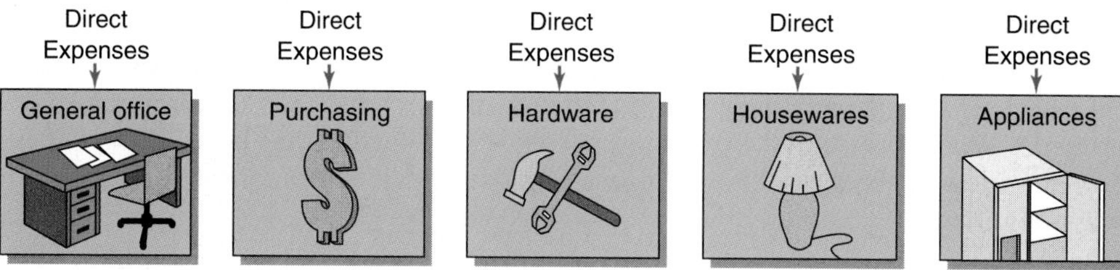

Step Two

Step two is to allocate indirect expenses across all departments using the allocation base identified for each expense. This step is shown in Exhibit 22.12.

Step 2: Indirect Expense Allocation

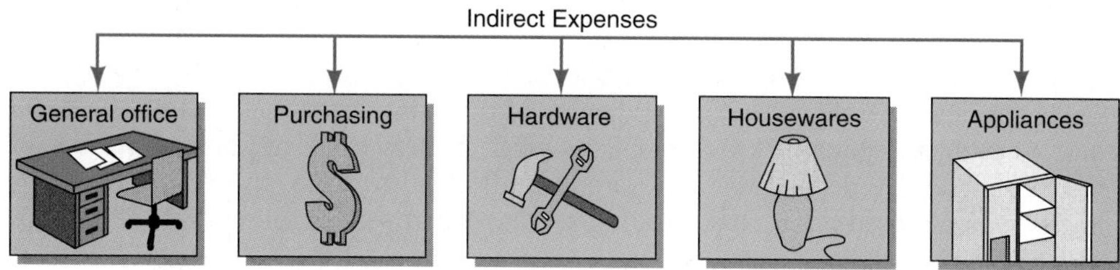

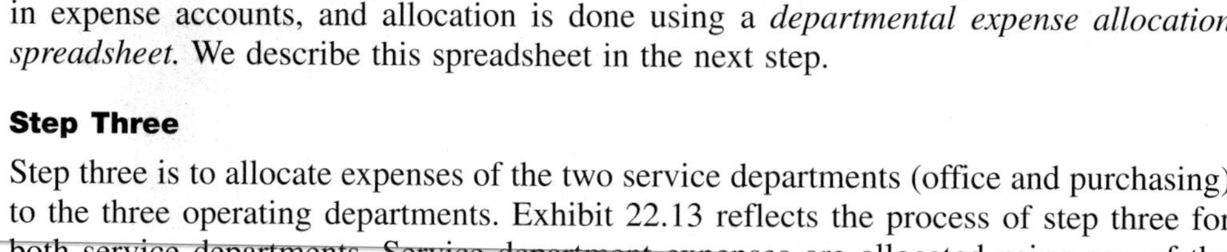

Indirect expenses can include items such as depreciation, rent, advertising, and any other expenses that cannot be directly assigned to a department. Indirect expenses are recorded in expense accounts, and allocation is done using a *departmental expense allocation spreadsheet.* We describe this spreadsheet in the next step.

Step Three

Step three is to allocate expenses of the two service departments (office and purchasing) to the three operating departments. Exhibit 22.13 reflects the process of step three for both service departments. Service department expenses are allocated using one of the bases described in the prior section. Computations for both steps two and three are commonly made on a departmental expense allocation spreadsheet as shown in Exhibit 22.14.[3]

Step 3: Service Department Expense Allocation

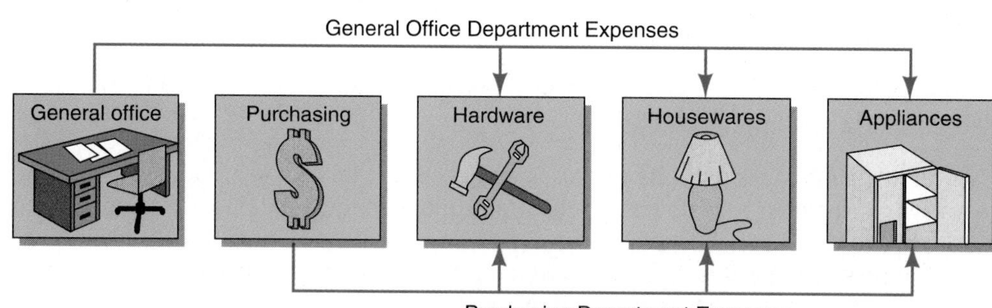

The top two-thirds of column one in Exhibit 22.14 lists both direct and indirect expenses. The lower part of column one lists service departments. The allocation bases are identified in the second column, and total expense amounts are reported in the third column.

[3] In some cases, we might allocate expenses of a service department to other service departments because they also use its services. For example, expenses of a payroll office benefit all service and operating departments and can be assigned to all departments. Nearly all examples and assignment materials in this book allocate service expenses only to operating departments for simplicity.

Exhibit 22.14

Departmental Expense Allocation Spreadsheet

ACE HARDWARE
Departmental Expense Allocations
For Year Ended December 31, 2000

	Allocation Base	Expense Account Balance	Allocation of Expenses to Departments: General Office Dept.	Purchasing Dept.	Hardware Dept.	Housewares Dept.	Appliances Dept.
Direct expenses:							
Salaries expense	Payroll records	$51,900	$13,300	$8,200	$15,600	$7,000	$7,800
Depreciation on equipment	Depreciation records	1,500	500	300	400	100	200
Supplies expense	Requisitions	900	200	100	300	200	100
Indirect expenses:							
Rent expense	Amount and value of space	12,000	600	600	4,860	3,240	2,700
Utilities expense	Floor space	2,400	300	300	810	540	450
Advertising expense	Sales	1,000			500	300	200
Insurance expense	Value of insured assets	2,500	400	200	900	600	400
Total department expenses		$72,200	$15,300	$9,700	$23,370	$11,980	$11,850
Service department expenses:							
General office department	Sales		$15,300		7,650	4,590	3,060
Purchasing department	Purchase orders			$9,700	3,880	2,630	3,190
Total expenses allocated to operating departments		$72,200			$34,900	$19,200	$18,100

The departmental expense allocation spreadsheet is useful in implementing the first three steps. First, the three direct expenses of salaries, depreciation, and supplies are accumulated in each of the five departments. Second, the four indirect expenses of rent, utilities, advertising, and insurance are allocated to all departments using the allocation bases identified. To illustrate how this is done, let's look at allocation of rent. Exhibit 22.15 lists the five departments' square footage of space occupied.

The two service departments (office and purchasing) occupy 25% of the total space (3,000 sq. feet/12,000 sq. feet). But they're located near the back of the building, which is of lower value than space near the front occupied by operating departments. Management estimates space near the back accounts for $1,200 of total rent expense of $12,000. Exhibit 22.16 shows how we allocate the $1,200 rent expense between these two service departments in proportion to their square footage.

Exhibit 22.15

Departments' Square Footages

General office	1,500
Purchasing	1,500
Hardware	4,050
Housewares	2,700
Appliances	2,250
Total	12,000

Exhibit 22.16

Allocating Indirect (Rent) Expense to Service Departments

Department	Square Feet	Percent of Total	Allocated Cost
General office	1,500	50.0%	$ 600
Purchasing	1,500	50.0	600
Total	3,000	100.0%	$1,200

Exhibit 22.17

Allocating Indirect (Rent) Expense to Operating Departments

Department	Square Feet	Percent of Total	Allocated Cost
Hardware	4,050	45.0%	$ 4,860
Housewares	2,700	30.0	3,240
Appliances	2,250	25.0	2,700
Total	9,000	100.0%	$10,800

We then allocate the remaining $10,800 of rent expense to the three operating departments as shown in Exhibit 22.17.

We continue step two in allocating the $2,400 of utilities expense to all departments based on the square footage occupied as shown in Exhibit 22.18.

Exhibit 22.18

Allocating Indirect (Utilities) Expense to All Departments

Department	Square Feet	Percent of Total	Allocated Cost
General office	1,500	12.50%	$ 300
Purchasing	1,500	12.50	300
Hardware	4,050	33.75	810
Housewares	2,700	22.50	540
Appliances	2,250	18.75	450
Total	12,000	100.00%	$2,400

The rows in Exhibit 22.14 for rent and utilities expenses show the amounts from Exhibits 22.16, 22.17, and 22.18. The allocations of the two other indirect expenses of advertising and insurance are similarly computed. Note that since advertising expense is allocated on the basis of sales, and since service departments don't have sales, it is allocated to only the three operating departments.

The third step allocates total expenses of the two service departments to the three operating departments using the allocation bases shown in the final three rows of Exhibit 22.14.

Step Four

When the departmental expense spreadsheet is complete, the amounts in the departmental columns are used to prepare departmental income statements as shown in Exhibit 22.19. This exhibit draws on the spreadsheet for its operating expenses. Information on sales and cost of goods sold is taken from departmental records.

Exhibit 22.19

Departmental Income Statements

ACE HARDWARE
Departmental Income Statements
For Year Ended December 31, 2000

	Hardware Department	Housewares Department	Appliances Department	Combined
Sales	$119,500	$71,700	$47,800	$239,000
Cost of goods sold	73,800	43,800	30,200	147,800
Gross profit	$ 45,700	$27,900	$17,600	$ 91,200
Operating expenses:				
Salaries expense	$ 15,600	$ 7,000	$ 7,800	$ 30,400
Depreciation expense, Equip.	400	100	200	700
Supplies expense	300	200	100	600
Rent expense	4,860	3,240	2,700	10,800
Utilities expense	810	540	450	1,800
Advertising expense	500	300	200	1,000
Insurance expense	900	600	400	1,900
Share of general office expenses	7,650	4,590	3,060	15,300
Share of purchasing expenses	3,880	2,630	3,190	9,700
Total operating expenses	$ 34,900	$19,200	$18,100	$ 72,200
Net income (loss)	**$ 10,800**	**$ 8,700**	**$ (500)**	**$ 19,000**
Partial analysis:				
Gross profit as percent of sales	38.2%	38.9%	36.8%	38.2%

Flash back

7. If a company has two operating (selling) departments (shoes and hats) and two service departments (payroll and advertising), which of the following statements is correct?
   a. Wages incurred in the payroll department are direct expenses of the shoe department.
   b. Wages incurred in the payroll department are indirect expenses of the operating departments.
   c. Advertising department expenses are allocated to the other three departments.
8. Which of the following bases can be used to allocate salaries of supervisors across operating departments?
   a. Hours spent in each department.
   b. Number of employees in each department.
   c. Sales achieved in each department.
   d. Any of the above, depending on which is most relevant.
9. What are the three steps in allocating expenses to operating departments?

Answers—p. 970

Departmental Contribution to Overhead

P4 Prepare departmental contribution reports.

Departmental income statements aren't always best for evaluating each department's performance. This is especially the case when indirect expenses are a large portion of total expenses, and when weaknesses in assumptions and decisions in allocating indirect expenses can markedly affect net income. In these and other cases we might look to evaluate department performance using departmental contributions to overhead. The **departmental contribution to overhead** is a report of the amount of revenues less *direct* expenses.[4]

Exhibit 22.20 shows a departmental contribution to overhead in the upper portion of the income statement for Ace Hardware. This type of presentation format is common when reporting departmental contributions to overhead.

Using the information in Exhibits 22.19 and 22.20, we can perform an evaluation of the profitability of the three operating departments. For instance, let's compare the performance of the appliances department as described in these two exhibits. Exhibit 22.19 shows a net loss of $500 resulting from this department's operations, whereas Exhibit 22.20 shows a positive contribution to overhead of $9,500, which is 19.9% of sales. While the contribution of the appliances department is not as large as the other selling departments, a $9,500 contribution to overhead is better than a $500 loss. This tells us that the appliances department is not a money loser. On the contrary, it is contributing $9,500 toward defraying total indirect expenses of $40,500.

Flash back

10. On an income statement showing the departmental and combined contribution to overhead: *(a)* indirect expenses are subtracted from each department's revenues; *(b)* only direct expenses are subtracted from each department's revenues; *(c)* net income is shown for each department.

Answer—p. 970

[4] A department's contribution is said to be "to overhead" because of the traditional practice of considering all indirect expenses as overhead. This means the excess of a department's revenues over direct expenses was a contribution to paying total overhead.

Departmental Contribution to Overhead

ACE HARDWARE
Income Statement Showing Departmental Contributions to Overhead
For Year Ended December 31, 2000

	Hardware Department	Housewares Department	Appliances Department	Combined
Sales	$119,500	$71,700	$47,800	$239,000
Cost of goods sold	73,800	43,800	30,200	147,800
Gross profit	$ 45,700	$27,900	$17,600	$ 91,200
Direct expenses:				
Salaries expense	$ 15,600	$ 7,000	$ 7,800	$ 30,400
Depreciation expense, Equip.	400	100	200	700
Supplies expense	300	200	100	600
Total direct expenses	$ 16,300	$ 7,300	$ 8,100	$ 31,700
Departmental contributions to overhead	$ 29,400	$20,600	$ 9,500	$ 59,500
Indirect expenses:				
Rent expense				$ 10,800
Utilities expense				1,800
Advertising expense				1,000
Insurance expense				1,900
General office department expense				15,300
Purchasing department expense				9,700
Total indirect expenses				$ 40,500
Net income				$ 19,000
Contribution as percent of sales	24.6%	28.7%	19.9%	24.9%

Responsibility Accounting

C4 Explain controllable costs and responsibility accounting.

Departmental accounting reports are often used to evaluate a department's performance. But are these reports useful in assessing how well a department *manager* performs? The answer is that neither departmental income nor its contribution to overhead may be useful because many expenses are outside the control of a manager. Instead, we often evaluate a manager's performance using responsibility accounting reports that describe a department's activities in terms of **controllable costs.**[5] Chapter 19 explained that a cost is controllable if a manager has the power to determine or at least strongly affect the amounts incurred. **Uncontrollable costs** are not within the manager's control or influence.

Controllable versus Direct Costs

Controllable costs aren't always the same as direct costs. Direct costs are readily traced to a department, but their amounts may or may not be under the control of the department manager. For example, department managers often have little or no control over depreciation expense because they can't affect the amount of equipment assigned to their departments. Department managers also usually have no control over their salaries. But department managers can control or influence items such as the cost of goods sold and supplies used in the department. When evaluating managers' performances, we should use data describing their departments' outputs along with their controllable costs and expenses. A manager's performance is then often judged by comparing current period's results with planned levels and those of prior periods.

[5] The terms *cost* and *expense* are often used interchangeably in managerial accounting. But they're not necessarily the same. *Cost* often refers to the monetary outlay of acquiring some resource that may have present and future benefit. *Expense* usually refers to an expired cost. This means that as the benefit of a resource expires, a portion of its cost is written off as an expense.

Identifying Controllable Costs

Controllable and uncontrollable costs are identified with a particular manager and a definite time period. Without defining these two reference points, we don't know whether a cost is controllable or not. For example, the cost of property insurance is usually not controllable at the department manager's level, but it is controllable by the executive responsible for obtaining the company's insurance coverage. Likewise, this executive may not have any control over costs resulting from insurance policies already in force. But, when a policy expires, this executive is free to renegotiate a replacement policy and now controls these costs. This means all costs are controllable at some level of management if the time period is sufficiently long. We must use good judgment in identifying controllable costs.

Responsibility Accounting System

The concept of controllable costs provides the basis for a responsibility accounting system. A **responsibility accounting system** assigns managers the responsibility for costs and expenses under their control. Prior to each reporting period, a company prepares plans that identify costs and expenses under the control of each manager. These plans are called **responsibility accounting budgets.** To ensure cooperation of managers and the reasonableness of budgets, managers should be involved in preparing their budgets.

A responsibility accounting system also prepares performance reports. A **responsibility accounting performance report** accumulates costs and expenses that a manager is responsible for. This report shows actual costs and expenses alongside budgeted amounts. Managers use performance reports to focus attention on differences between budgeted amounts and actual costs and expenses. This information often results in corrective or strategic actions. Upper-level management uses performance reports to evaluate the effectiveness of lower-level managers in controlling costs and expenses and keeping them within budgeted amounts. Chapter 25 further explains the nature and use of performance reports.

A responsibility accounting system must recognize that control over costs and expenses belongs to several levels of management. To illustrate, let's consider the organization chart in Exhibit 22.21. The lines in this chart connecting the managerial positions reflect channels of authority. This means while the three department managers for cutting, assembly, and service are responsible for controllable costs and expenses incurred in their departments, these same costs are subject to the overall control of the western plant manager. Similarly, the western plant's costs are subject to the control of the vice president of production, the president, and ultimately the board of directors.

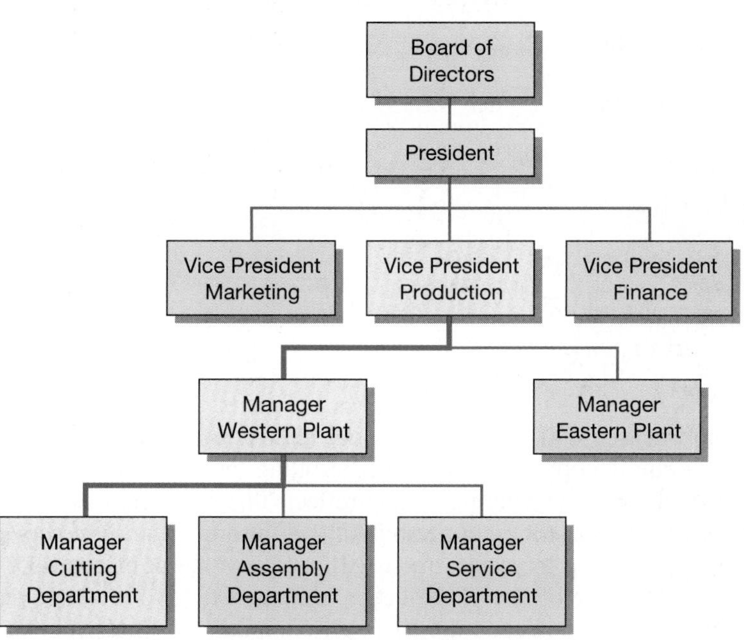

Exhibit 22.21
Organizational Responsibility

At lower levels, managers have limited responsibility and relatively little control over costs and expenses. Performance reports for this management level cover only the few controllable costs. Responsibility and control broaden at higher levels. Reports to higher-level managers therefore span a wider range of costs. But reports to higher-level managers often don't contain the details reported to their subordinates. These details are summarized for two reasons: (1) lower-level managers are often responsible for these detailed costs and (2) detailed reports can obscure important points. Detailed reports to higher-level managers can detract attention from the broader, more important issues facing a company.

Exhibit 22.22 shows summarized performance reports for the three management levels identified in Exhibit 22.21. Exhibit 22.22 shows that costs under the control of the cutting department manager are totaled and included among controllable costs of the western plant manager. Also, costs under the control of the plant manager are totaled and included among controllable costs of the vice president for production. In this way, a responsibility accounting system provides relevant information for each management level.

Responsibility Accounting Performance Reports

Vice President, Production	For July		
Controllable Costs	Budgeted Amount	Actual Amount	Over (Under) Budget
Salaries, Plant managers	$ 80,000	$ 80,000	$ 0
Quality control costs	21,000	22,400	1,400
Office costs	29,500	28,800	(700)
Western plant	**276,700**	**279,500**	**2,800**
Eastern plant	390,000	380,600	(9,400)
Total	$797,200	$791,300	$(5,900)

Manager, Western Plant	For July		
Controllable Costs	Budgeted Amount	Actual Amount	Over (Under) Budget
Salaries, Department managers	$ 75,000	$ 78,000	$3,000
Depreciation	10,600	10,600	0
Insurance	6,800	6,300	(500)
Cutting department	**79,600**	**79,900**	**300**
Assembly department	61,500	60,200	(1,300)
Service department 1	24,300	24,700	400
Service department 2	18,900	19,800	900
Total	**$276,700**	**$279,500**	**$2,800**

Manager, Cutting Department	For July		
Controllable Costs	Budgeted Amount	Actual Amount	Over (Under) Budget
Raw materials	$26,500	$25,900	$ (600)
Direct labor	32,000	33,500	1,500
Indirect labor	7,200	7,000	(200)
Supplies	4,000	3,900	(100)
Other controllable costs	9,900	9,600	(300)
Total	**$79,600**	**$79,900**	**$ 300**

We must recognize that technological advances increase our ability to produce vast amounts of information that often exceeds our ability to use information. Good managers select relevant data for planning and controlling the areas under their responsibility. A good responsibility accounting system reflects this need and makes every effort to get relevant information to the right person at the right time. The right person is the one who controls the cost, and the right time is before a cost is out of control.

Let's return to the case of **AeroTech** in the opening article to illustrate responsibility accounting. Its controller changed the basis for computing commissions paid to salespersons this past year. Sales revenues previously were the sole basis for computing commissions. But the new system reduced these sales revenues by the raw materials, direct labor, delivery, and reinstallation costs of reworking aerospace components. The new system combines the concepts of cost allocation, controllable costs, and responsibility accounting to motivate salespersons to control reworking costs. Because salespersons are now rewarded on sales net of the cost of controllable errors, their behavior changed. They verified specifications before submitting component orders. This led to reduced costs and a net income increase of more than 20%.

Flash back

11. Are departmental net income and contribution to overhead reports useful when assessing the performance of a department manager? Explain.

12. Performance reports used to evaluate managers should: *(a)* include data about controllable expenses; *(b)* compare actual results with budgeted levels; *(c)* both *a* and *b*.

Answers—p. 970

Joint Costs

C5 Describe allocation of joint costs across products.

Most manufacturing processes involve joint costs. A **joint cost** is a single cost incurred in producing or purchasing two or more essentially different products at the same time. A joint cost is like an indirect expense in the sense it is shared across more than one cost object. For example, a petroleum refining company incurs a joint cost when it buys crude oil that it separates into gasoline, lubricating oil, kerosene, paraffin, ethylene, and other products as shown in Exhibit 22.23. The joint cost includes the crude oil (raw material) and its refining (conversion). Likewise, a sawmill incurs joint costs when it buys a log and cuts it into boards classified as Clear, Select, No. 1 Common, No. 2 Common, No. 3 Common, and other types of lumber and by-products.

When a joint cost is incurred, a question arises as to whether its amount should be allocated to different products produced from it. The answer is that when management wishes to estimate the total cost of a product, joint costs are included in the computation. But when management needs information to help decide whether to sell a product at a certain point in the production process or process it further, joint costs are ignored. For example, many managerial decisions, such as whether to continue buying logs and cutting lumber, are based on unallocated cost information.

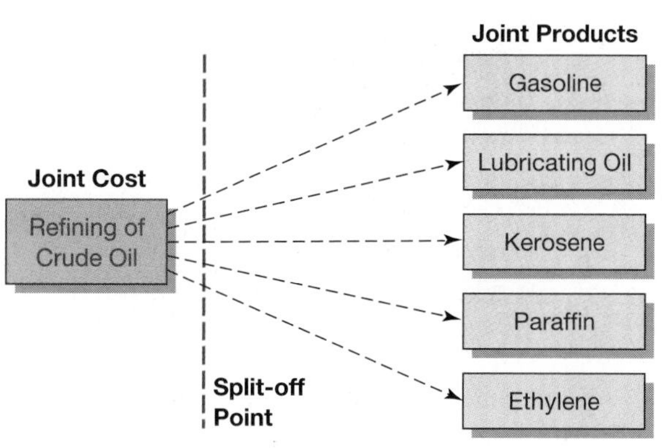

Exhibit 22.23

Joint Products from Petroleum Refining

Financial statements prepared according to GAAP must assign joint costs to products. This includes deciding how to allocate joint costs across products resulting from the costs. Also, if some products are sold and others remain in inventory, allocating joint costs involves assigning costs to both cost of goods sold and ending inventory.

There are two usual methods to allocate joint costs: physical basis or value basis. The physical basis typically involves allocating joint cost using physical characteristics, such as the ratio of pounds, cubic feet, or gallons of each joint product to the total pounds, cubic feet, or gallons of all joint products flowing from the cost. But this method is not usually applied because the resulting cost allocations don't reflect the relative market values generated from the joint cost. A better approach is the value basis, which allocates joint cost in proportion to the sales value of the output produced by the process at the split-off point.

Illustrating Physical Basis Allocation of Joint Cost

To illustrate the physical basis of allocating a joint cost, let's consider a sawmill that bought logs for $30,000. When cut, these logs produce 100,000 board feet of lumber in the grades and amounts shown in Exhibit 22.24. The logs produce 20,000 board feet of No. 3 Common lumber, which is 20% of the total. With physical allocation, the No. 3 Common lumber is assigned 20% of the $30,000 cost of the logs, or $6,000 ($30,000 × 20%). Because this low-grade lumber sells for $4,000, this allocation gives a $2,000 loss from its production and sale. The physical basis for allocating joint costs does not reflect the extra value flowing into some products or the inferior value flowing into others. The portion of a log that produces Structural grade lumber is worth more than the portion used to produce the three grades of Common lumber.

Exhibit 22.24

Allocating Joint Costs on a Physical Basis

Grade of Lumber	Board Feet Produced	Percent of Total	Allocated Cost	Sales Value	Gross Profit
Structural	10,000	10.0%	$ 3,000	$12,000	$ 9,000
No. 1 Common	30,000	30.0	9,000	18,000	9,000
No. 2 Common	40,000	40.0	12,000	16,000	4,000
No. 3 Common	20,000	20.0	6,000	4,000	(2,000)
Total	100,000	100.0%	$30,000	$50,000	$20,000

Illustrating Value Basis Allocation of Joint Cost

Exhibit 22.25 reflects the value basis method of allocation. Here, the percents of the total costs allocated to each grade are determined by the ratio of each grade's sales value to the total sales value of $50,000 (sales value is the unit selling price multiplied by the number of units produced). The Structural grade lumber receives 24% of the total cost ($12,000/$50,000) instead of the 10% portion using a physical basis. The No. 3 Common lumber receives only 8% of the total cost, or $2,400, which is much less than the $6,000 assigned to it using the physical basis.

Exhibit 22.25

Allocating Joint Costs on a Value Basis

Grade of Lumber	Sales Value	Percent of Total	Allocated Cost	Gross Profit
Structural	$12,000	24.0%	$ 7,200	$ 4,800
No. 1 Common	18,000	36.0	10,800	7,200
No. 2 Common	16,000	32.0	9,600	6,400
No. 3 Common	4,000	8.0	2,400	1,600
Total	$50,000	100.0%	$30,000	$20,000

An outcome of value basis allocation is that *every* grade produces exactly the same 40% gross profit at the split-off point. This 40% rate equals the gross profit rate from selling all the lumber made from the $30,000 logs for a combined price of $50,000.

Flash back

13. A company produces three products: B1, B2, and B3. The joint cost incurred for the current month for these products is $180,000. The following data relate to this month's production:

Product	Units Produced	Unit Sales Value
B1	96,000	$3.00
B2	64,000	6.00
B3	32,000	9.00

The amount of joint cost allocated to product B3 using the value basis allocation is: *(a)* $30,000; *(b)* $54,000; *(c)* $90,000.

Answer—p. 970

Return on Total Assets by Investment Centers

USING THE INFORMATION

A1 Analyze investment centers using return on total assets.

Large companies are often broken into several divisions that are evaluated as investment centers. An **investment center** acquires assets in a desire to generate income. The investment center manager is responsible for its revenues and expenses along with the cost of the investment in assets.

A measure often used to evaluate the performance of an investment center manager is the center's *return on total assets,* also called *return on investment.* This measure is computed as a center's net income divided by its average total assets. Net income is for the center, and average total assets reflects the center's asset investment level. To illustrate, if a center with an average investment of $1 million yields a net income of $210,000, its return on total assets is 21%.

A center's return on total assets provides top management with an assessment of how well a center manager has utilized the center's assets to generate returns for the company. Top management can also compare performance across divisions using this same measure. Many companies establish a center's target return on total assets and reward managers depending on whether the targets are met. In addition, center managers often use the center's current return on total assets to decide whether they want to invest additional resources in new center opportunities.

Center Manager
You are a center manager and your center's usual return on total assets is 19%. You are considering two new investing opportunities for your center. The first requires a $250,000 average investment and is expected to yield annual net income of $50,000. The second requires a $1 million average investment with an expected annual net income of $175,000. Do you pursue either opportunity?

Answer—p. 970

Summary

C1 **Explain departmentalization and the role of departmental accounting.** Companies are divided into departments whenever they become too large to be effectively managed as a single unit. Operating departments either manufacture products in a factory, sell products in a store, or provide services. Service departments support the activities of operating departments. Departmental accounting systems provide information for evaluating departments' performances.

C2 **Distinguish between direct and indirect expenses.** Direct expenses are traced to a specific department and are incurred for the sole benefit of one department. Indirect expenses benefit more than one department. If departmental net incomes are measured, indirect expenses are allocated to the departments on some reasonable basis.

C3 **Identify bases for allocating indirect expenses to departments.** There is no standard rule about what allocation base is best to allocate indirect expenses to departments. Ideally we allocate indirect expenses by using a cause-effect relation. But identifying cause-effect relations is not always possible. In these situations, each indirect expense is allocated on a basis approximating the relative benefit received by each department.

C4 **Explain controllable costs and responsibility accounting.** A controllable cost is one influenced by a specific level of management and a specific time period. The total expenses of operating a department often include some items not controllable by the department manager. Responsibility accounting systems provide information for evaluating the performance of department managers. Performance reports produced by a responsibility accounting system for evaluating department managers should include only the expenses (and revenues) controllable by the managers.

C5 **Describe allocation of joint costs across products.** A joint cost is a single cost incurred in producing or purchasing two or more different products at the same time. When income statements are prepared, joint costs are usually allocated to the resulting joint products using either a physical or value basis of the joint products at the split-off point.

A1 **Analyze investment centers using return on total assets.** A measure often used to evaluate an investment center manager is the center's return on total assets, also called return on investment. This measure is computed as the center's net income divided by the center's average total assets.

P1 **Assign overhead costs using two-stage cost allocation.** In the traditional two-stage cost allocation procedure, costs are first assigned to operating departments such as machining and assembly. Then in the second stage, a predetermined overhead allocation rate is computed for each operating department, which is used to assign overhead to jobs.

P2 **Assign overhead costs using activity-based costing.** In activity-based costing, the costs of separate activities of overhead items, or resources, are first collected in separate temporary accounts. Then the activities are pooled together in some logical manner into activity cost pools. After all activity costs are accumulated in an activity cost pool account, users of the activity, termed cost objects, are assigned a portion of the total activity cost using a cost driver or allocation base.

P3 **Prepare departmental income statements.** Each profit center (department) is assigned its applicable expenses to yield its own income statement. These costs include its own direct expenses and its share of indirect expenses. The departmental income statement begins by listing its revenues and costs of goods sold to determine gross profit. The operating expenses (direct expenses and indirect expenses allocated to the departments) are deducted from gross profit to yield the department's net income.

P4 **Prepare departmental contribution reports.** The departmental contribution report is similar to the departmental income statement in terms of computing the gross profit for each department. But then the direct operating expenses for each department are deducted from gross profit to determine the contribution generated by each department. The indirect operating expenses are not allocated to individual departments. Instead, they are deducted in total from the combined contribution of the company.

Guidance Answers to **You Make the Call**

Director of Operations

You should collect details on the overhead items and review them to see if direct labor does indeed drive these costs. If it does not, then the department managers are correct in pointing out that overhead may be unduly assigned to their departments. The situation also provides an opportunity to consider other overhead allocation bases, including the use of activity-based costing.

Center Manager

We must first realize that the two investment opportunities are not comparable on the basis of absolute dollars of income. For instance, the second investment provides a higher income in absolute dollars but requires a greater investment. This shows the need to compute return on total assets for each alternative: (1) $50,000 ÷ $250,000 = 20%, and (2) $175,000 ÷ $1 million = 17.5%. Alternative 1 has the higher return and is preferred over alternative 2. But do you pursue one, both, or neither? Given that alternative 1's return is higher than the center's usual return of 19%, it should be pursued, assuming its risks are acceptable. Also, since alternative 1 requires a small investment, the top management is likely to be more agreeable to pursuing it. Alternative 2's return is lower than the usual 19% and is not likely to be acceptable.

Guidance Answer to **Judgment and Ethics**

Accounting Officer

You should not write a report as requested by your supervisor if you disagree with it. It also appears the report may be misrepresenting the situation. It is your responsibility to ascertain all the facts regarding activity-based costing (the implementation procedure to be followed, advantages and disadvantages of ABC, and costs involved). You should then approach your supervisor with all the facts and suggest that you would like to modify the report to request, for example, a pilot implementation of the system. The pilot test will allow you to further assess the suitability of ABC in your company. You should realize your suggestion may be rejected, at which time you may wish to speak to some other person with more senior authority.

Guidance Answers to 

1. A cost driver is a factor that affects the amount of an overhead cost item. In activity-based costing, cost drivers are the allocation bases used to assign overhead costs to products and processes.
2. *d*
3. Departmental accounting systems provide information used to evaluate the performance of *departments*. Responsibility accounting systems provide information used to evaluate the performance of *department managers*.
4. *d*
5. A cost center, such as a service department, incurs costs without directly generating revenues. A profit center, such as a selling department, incurs costs but also generates revenues.
6. *b*
7. *b*
8. *d*
9. 1. Assign the direct expenses to each department. 2. Allocate indirect expenses to all departments. 3. Allocate the service department expenses to the operating departments.
10. *b*
11. No, because many of the expenses that enter into these calculations are beyond the control of the manager, and managers should not be evaluated using costs they do not control.
12. *c*
13. *b;* $180,000 × ($288,000/$960,000).

Demonstration Problem

Use the information below to prepare departmental income statements for Hacker's Haven, a computer store. The store has five departments. Three of them are operating departments (hardware, software, and repairs), and two are service departments (general office and purchasing).

	General Office	Purchasing	Hardware	Software	Repairs
Sales	—	—	$960,000	$600,000	$840,000
Cost of goods sold	—	—	500,000	300,000	200,000
Direct expenses:					
Payroll	$60,000	$45,000	80,000	25,000	325,000
Depreciation	6,000	7,200	33,000	4,200	9,600
Supplies	15,000	10,000	10,000	2,000	25,000

Several indirect expenses are incurred by the departments. In preparing departmental income statements, these indirect expenses are allocated across the five departments. Then the expenses of the two service departments are allocated to the three selling departments. Total cost amounts and the allocation bases for each indirect expense are as follows:

Indirect Expense	Total Cost	Allocation Basis
Rent	$150,000	Square footage occupied
Utilities	50,000	Square footage occupied
Advertising	125,000	Dollars of sales
Insurance	30,000	Value of assets insured
Service departments:		
General office	?	Number of employees
Purchasing	?	Dollars of cost of goods sold

The information below is needed for indirect expense allocations:

Department	Square Feet	Sales	Insured Assets	Employees	Cost of Goods Sold
General office	500		$ 60,000		
Purchasing	500		72,000		
Hardware	4,000	$ 960,000	330,000	5	$ 500,000
Software	3,000	600,000	42,000	5	300,000
Repairs	2,000	840,000	96,000	10	200,000
Total	10,000	$2,400,000	$600,000	20	$1,000,000

Required:

1. Prepare a departmental expense allocation spreadsheet for Hacker's Haven.
2. Prepare a departmental income statement reporting net income for each operating department and for all operating departments combined.

Planning the Solution

- Set up and complete four schedules to allocate the indirect expenses of rent, utilities, advertising, and insurance.

- Allocate the departments' indirect expenses using a spreadsheet like the one in Exhibit 22.14. Enter the given amounts of the direct expenses for each department. Then enter the allocated amounts of the indirect expenses that you computed.
- Complete two schedules for allocating the general office and purchasing department costs to the three operating departments. Enter these amounts on the spreadsheet and determine the total expenses allocated to the three operating departments.
- Prepare departmental income statements like the one in Exhibit 22.19. Show sales, cost of goods sold, gross profit, individual direct and indirect expenses, and net income for each of the three operating departments and for the combined company.

Solution to Demonstration Problem

Allocations of the four indirect expenses across the five departments:

Rent	Square Feet	Percent of Total	Allocated Cost
General office	500	5.0%	$ 7,500
Purchasing	500	5.0	7,500
Hardware	4,000	40.0	60,000
Software	3,000	30.0	45,000
Repairs	2,000	20.0	30,000
Total	10,000	100.0%	$150,000

Utilities	Square Feet	Percent of Total	Allocated Cost
General office	500	5.0%	$ 2,500
Purchasing	500	5.0	2,500
Hardware	4,000	40.0	20,000
Software	3,000	30.0	15,000
Repairs	2,000	20.0	10,000
Total	10,000	100.0%	$50,000

Advertising	Sales Dollars	Percent of Total	Allocated Cost
Hardware	$ 960,000	40.0%	$ 50,000
Software	600,000	25.0	31,250
Repairs	840,000	35.0	43,750
Total	$2,400,000	100.0%	$125,000

Insurance	Assets Insured	Percent of Total	Allocated Cost
General office	$ 60,000	10.0%	$ 3,000
Purchasing	72,000	12.0	3,600
Hardware	330,000	55.0	16,500
Software	42,000	7.0	2,100
Repairs	96,000	16.0	4,800
Total	$600,000	100.0%	$30,000

Allocations of service department expenses to the three operating departments:

General Office Allocations to:	Employees	Percent of Total	Allocated Cost
Hardware	5	25.0%	$23,500
Software	5	25.0	23,500
Repairs	10	50.0	47,000
Total	20	100.0%	$94,000

Purchasing Allocations to:	Cost of Goods Sold	Percent of Total	Allocated Cost
Hardware	$ 500,000	50.0%	$37,900
Software	300,000	30.0	22,740
Repairs	200,000	20.0	15,160
Total	$1,000,000	100.0%	$75,800

HACKER'S HAVEN
Departmental Expense Allocations
For Year Ended December 31, 2000

	Allocation Base	Expense Account Balance	General Office Dept.	Purchasing Dept.	Hardware Dept.	Software Dept.	Repairs Dept.
Direct expenses:							
Payroll		$ 535,000	$60,000	$45,000	$ 80,000	$ 25,000	$325,000
Depreciation		60,000	6,000	7,200	33,000	4,200	9,600
Supplies		62,000	15,000	10,000	10,000	2,000	25,000
Indirect expenses:							
Rent	Square ft.	150,000	7,500	7,500	60,000	45,000	30,000
Utilities	Square ft.	50,000	2,500	2,500	20,000	15,000	10,000
Advertising	Sales	125,000	—	—	50,000	31,250	43,750
Insurance	Assets	30,000	3,000	3,600	16,500	2,100	4,800
Total expenses		$1,012,000	$94,000	$75,800	$269,500	$124,550	$448,150
Service department expenses:							
General office	Employees		$94,000		23,500	23,500	47,000
Purchasing	Goods sold			$75,800	37,900	22,740	15,160
Total expenses allocated to operating departments		$1,012,000			$330,900	$170,790	$510,310

2. Departmental income statements for Hacker's Haven:

HACKER'S HAVEN
Departmental Income Statements
For Year Ended December 31, 2000

	Hardware	Software	Repairs	Combined
Sales	$960,000	$600,000	$840,000	$2,400,000
Cost of goods sold	500,000	300,000	200,000	1,000,000
Gross profit	$460,000	$300,000	$640,000	$1,400,000
Expenses:				
Payroll	$ 80,000	$ 25,000	$325,000	$ 430,000
Depreciation	33,000	4,200	9,600	46,800
Supplies	10,000	2,000	25,000	37,000
Rent	60,000	45,000	30,000	135,000
Utilities	20,000	15,000	10,000	45,000
Advertising	50,000	31,250	43,750	125,000
Insurance	16,500	2,100	4,800	23,400
General office	23,500	23,500	47,000	94,000
Purchasing	37,900	22,740	15,160	75,800
Total expenses	$330,900	$170,790	$510,310	$1,012,000
Net income	$129,100	$129,210	$129,690	$ 388,000

Glossary

Activity-based costing (ABC) a type of two-step allocation system: (1) identify activities involved in the manufacturing (or service) process and form cost pools by combining activities, and (2) compute the predetermined overhead cost allocation rate for each cost pool and assign costs. (p. 948).

Activity cost pool a temporary account that accumulates costs a company incurs to support an activity. (p. 949).

Controllable costs costs that a manager has the power to determine or at least strongly influence. (p. 964).

Cost center a department or unit that incurs costs alone, such as the accounting or legal department. (p. 954).

Cost driver a variable that causes the cost of an activity to go up or down; a causal factor. (p. 949).

Departmental accounting system an accounting system that provides information useful in evaluating the profitability or cost effectiveness of a department's activities. (p. 953).

Departmental contribution to overhead the amount by which a department's revenues exceed its direct expenses. (p. 963).

Direct expenses expenses traced to a specific department that are incurred for the sole benefit of that department. (p. 956).

Indirect expenses expenses incurred for the joint benefit of more than one department. (p. 957).

Investment center a center in which a manager is responsible for revenues, costs, and asset investments. (p. 969).

Joint cost a single cost incurred in producing or purchasing two or more different products at the same time. (p. 967).

Profit center a unit of a business that incurs costs and generates revenues. (p. 954).

Responsibility accounting budget a plan that specifies the expected costs and expenses under the control of a manager. (p. 965).

Responsibility accounting performance report a responsibility accounting report that compares actual costs and expenses for a department with budgeted amounts. (p. 965).

Responsibility accounting system an accounting system that provides information that management can use to evaluate the performance of a department's manager. (p. 965).

Uncontrollable costs costs that a manager does not have the power to determine or at least strongly influence. (p. 964).

Questions

1. Why are businesses divided into departments?
2. Identify the two stages in a two-stage allocation system by completing the following: In the first stage, costs are assigned to _____ departments such as machining and assembly. In the second stage, a predetermined overhead allocation rate is computed for each operating department which is used to assign overhead to _____.
3. What is the difference between operating departments and service departments?
4. What is activity-based costing?
5. Identify five typical cost pools for activity-based costing.
6. In activity-based costing, costs in a cost pool are allocated to _____.
7. What company circumstances motivate use of activity-based costing?
8. What are the two primary goals for managerial accounting for departments?
9. Is it possible to evaluate the profitability of a cost center? Explain?
10. How is a departmental sales analysis spreadsheet used in determining sales by departments?
11. What is the difference between direct and indirect expenses?
12. Suggest a reasonable basis for allocating each of the following indirect expenses to departments: (*a*) salary of a supervisor who manages several departments, (*b*) rent, (*c*) heat, (*d*) electricity used for lighting, (*e*) janitorial services, (*f*) advertising, (*g*) expired insurance on equipment, and (*h*) property taxes on equipment.
13. How is a department's contribution to overhead measured?
14. What are controllable costs?
15. Controllable and uncontrollable costs must be identified with a particular _____ and a definite _____ period.
16. Why should managers be closely involved in preparing their responsibility accounting budgets?
17. In responsibility accounting, who is the proper person to be given timely reports and specific cost information?
18. What is a joint cost? How are joint costs usually allocated among the products produced from them?
19. Give two examples of products with joint costs.
20. NIKE receives orders for merchandise sold in different types of stores, such as sporting goods super stores and specialty running shoe stores. Why is it useful to (*a*) collect information for each particular store category and (*b*) treat each category as a profit center?
21. Reebok delivers its products to many different locations around the world. List three controllable and three uncontrollable costs for Reebok's delivery department.

Quick Study

QS 22-1
Activity-based costing
P2

The following is taken from Fost Co.'s internal records of its factory with two operating departments:

	Direct Labor	Hours of Machine Use
Department 1	$ 9,400	1,200
Department 2	6,600	2,000
Totals	$16,000	3,200
Factory overhead:		
Rent and utilities		$ 6,100
Indirect labor		2,700
General office expense		1,700
Equipment depreciation		1,500
Supplies		900
Total overhead		$12,900

Compute the total amount of overhead cost that is allocated to Department 1 if activity-based costing is used. The cost driver for indirect labor and supplies is direct labor, and the cost driver for the remaining overhead items is hours of machine use.

QS 22-2
Allocation and measurement terms
C1, C2, C3, C4, A1

In each of the blanks next to the following terms, place the identifying letter of its best description.

1. _____ Cost center
2. _____ Investment center
3. _____ Departmental accounting system
4. _____ Operating department
5. _____ Profit center
6. _____ Responsibility accounting system
7. _____ Service department

a. Provides information used to evaluate the performance of a department.
b. Provides information used to evaluate the performance of a department manager.
c. Does not directly manufacture products but contributes to the profitability of the entire company.
d. Engages directly in manufacturing or in making sales directly to customers.
e. Incurs costs without directly generating revenues.
f. Incurs costs and also generates revenues.
g. Manager is responsible for revenues, costs, and investments.

QS 22-3
Basis for cost allocation
C3

For each of the following types of indirect and service department expenses, identify one possible allocation basis that could be used to distribute it to the departments indicated:

a. Computer services expenses for the scheduling of factory production: ______________________________.
b. Electric utility expenses to all departments: ______________________________.
c. Maintenance department expenses to the operating departments: ______________________________.
d. General office department expenses to the operating departments: ______________________________.

QS 22-4
Departmental contribution to overhead
P4

Use the information in the schedule to compute each department's contribution to overhead (both in dollars and as a percent). Which department contributes the highest dollar amount to total overhead? Which department's contribution percent is the highest?

	Dept. A	Dept. B	Dept. C
Sales	$53,000	$170,000	$84,000
Cost of goods sold	34,185	103,700	49,560
Gross profit	18,815	66,300	34,440
Total direct expenses	6,360	37,060	8,736
Contribution to overhead	$	$	$
Contribution percent	%	%	%

QS 22-5
Joint cost allocation
C5

A 10,020 square foot commercial building is purchased for $325,000. An additional $50,000 is spent to split the space into two separate rental units and to get it ready to rent. Unit A, which has the desirable location on the corner and contains 3,340 square feet, will be rented out for $1.00 per square foot. Unit B contains 6,680 square feet and will be rented out for $0.75 per square foot. How much of the joint cost should be assigned to Unit B using the value basis of allocation?

QS 22-6
Investment center analysis
A1
Reebok

Compute return on assets for each of the Reebok shoe divisions below (each is an investment center). Comment on the relative performance of the investment centers.

Division	Net Income	Average Assets	Return on Assets
Basketball	$4,000,000	$20,000,000	
Soccer	$1,500,000	$15,000,000	
Cross-trainer	$ 750,000	$10,000,000	

Exercises

Exercise 22-1
Allocating rent expense to departments
P1, C3

National Auto Club pays $128,000 rent every year for its two-story building. The space in this building is occupied by five departments as specified below:

Paint department	1,390 square feet of first-floor space
Engine department	3,410 square feet of first-floor space
Window department	2,040 square feet of second-floor space
Electrical department	960 square feet of second-floor space
Accessory department	1,800 square feet of second-floor space

The company allocates 65% of total rent expense to the first floor and 35% to the second floor. It then allocates rent expense for each floor to the departments on that floor on the basis of space occupied. Determine the rent to be allocated to each department. (Round percents to the nearest one-tenth and dollar amounts to the nearest whole dollar.)

Exercise 22-2
Departmental expense allocations
P1, C3

Pembroke Co. has four departments: materials, personnel, manufacturing, and packaging. In a recent month, the four departments incurred three shared indirect expenses. The amounts of these indirect expenses and the bases used to allocate them are:

Indirect Expense	Cost	Allocation Base
Supervision	$ 75,000	Number of employees
Utilities	60,000	Square feet occupied
Insurance	16,500	Value of assets in use
Total	$151,500	

The departmental data below are to be used in allocating these indirect expenses for the month:

Department	Employees	Square Feet	Asset Values
Materials	18	27,000	$ 6,000
Personnel	6	4,500	1,200
Manufacturing	66	45,000	37,800
Packaging	30	13,500	15,000
Total	120	90,000	$60,000

Use the information above to prepare allocations of each of the three indirect expenses across the four departments. Then prepare a table that shows total indirect expenses assigned to the four departments.

Exercise 22-3
Activity-based costing
P2

Glass Company manufactures two types of glass shelving—rounded-edge and squared-edge—on the same production line. For the current month, the company recorded the following data:

	Rounded-Edge	Squared-Edge	Total
Direct materials	$ 9,500	$21,600	$ 31,100
Direct labor	6,100	11,900	18,000
Overhead (300% of labor)	18,300	35,700	54,000
Total cost	$33,900	$69,200	$103,100
Quantity produced	10,500	14,100	
Average cost per unit	$3.23	$4.91	

Several managers ask the accounting department for help in understanding activity-based costing (ABC). Their request is that ABC be applied to the production results to see whether average cost per unit is significantly changed. For this purpose, additional information is obtained from the production records for the current month:

- Overhead cost for supervision is $2,160. The cost driver for supervision is direct labor cost.
- Overhead cost for machinery depreciation is $28,840. The cost driver for depreciation is machine hours of use. The machinery is used 300 hours for rounded-edge shelves and 700 hours for squared-edge shelves.
- Overhead cost for preparing the line to manufacture products is $23,000. The cost driver for this preparation cost is the number of times equipment is set up. The line is set up 31 times to produce different kinds of rounded-edge shelves, and 94 times to produce different kinds of squared-edge shelves.

Required

a. Assign these three overhead costs to products using activity-based costing.

b. Determine average cost per unit of the two products from direct materials, direct labor, and overhead allocated using ABC.

c. Compare and explain the average cost per unit under ABC to the average cost per unit recorded in the data reported above.

Exercise 22-4
Allocating service department expenses to operating departments
P3

Shown below is a partially completed lower section of a departmental expense allocation spreadsheet for Early Bird Bookstore. It reports the total amounts of direct and indirect expenses that are allocated to the five departments:

	Allocation Base	Expense Account Balance	Allocation of Expenses to Departments				
			Advertising Dept.	Purchasing Dept.	Book Dept.	Magazine Dept.	Newspaper Dept.
Total dept. expenses		$654,000	$22,000	$30,000	$425,000	$86,000	$91,000
Service dept. expenses:							
Advertising	Sales		?		?	?	?
Purchasing	Purchase orders			?	?	?	?
Total expenses allocated to operating departments		?			?	?	?

Complete the spreadsheet by allocating the two service departments' expenses (advertising and purchasing) to the three operating departments. Information about the allocation bases for the three operating departments is listed below:

	Sales	Purchase Orders
Books	$448,000	424
Magazines	144,000	312
Newspapers	208,000	264
Total	$800,000	1,000

Exercise 22-5
Allocating indirect payroll expense to departments
C3

Jenna Short works in both the jewelry department and the hosiery department of Fine's Department Store. Short assists customers in both departments and also arranges and stocks merchandise in both departments. The store allocates Short's annual wages of $30,000 between the two departments based on a sample of the time worked in the two departments. The sample is obtained from a diary that Short kept of hours worked in a randomly chosen two-week period. The diary showed the following hours and activities spent in the two departments:

Selling in jewelry department	64
Arranging and stocking merchandise in jewelry department	6
Selling in hosiery department	14
Arranging and stocking merchandise in hosiery department	12
Idle time spent waiting for a customer to enter one of the selling departments	4

Required

Allocate Short's wages between the two departments. (Round percents to the nearest tenth of a percent and dollar amounts to the nearest whole dollar.)

Exercise 22-6
Departmental expense allocation spreadsheet
C3, P1

ProCycle Shop has two service departments (advertising and administrative) and two selling departments (cycles and clothing). During year 2000, the departments had the following direct expenses: Advertising department, $16,000; Administrative department, $18,500; Cycle department, $101,600; and Clothing department, $11,900. The departments occupy the following square feet of floor space: Advertising department, 1,088; Administrative department, 1,152; Cycle department, 6,336; and Clothing department, 4,224. The advertising department developed and distributed 100 ad pieces during the year. Of these, 76 promoted cycles and 24 promoted clothing. The store sold $300,000 of merchandise during the year. Of this amount, $225,000 is from the cycle department while the remainder is from the clothing department.

Required

Prepare a departmental expense allocation spreadsheet for the ProCycle Shop. The spreadsheet should assign (a) direct expenses to each of the four departments, (b) the year's $64,000 of utilities expense to the four departments on the basis of floor space occupied, (c) the advertising department expenses on the basis of the number of ads placed, and (d) the administrative department expenses based on the amount of sales. Provide supplemental schedules showing how you compute the expense allocations. (Round percents to the nearest one-tenth and dollar amounts to the nearest whole dollar.)

Exercise 22-7
Evaluating managerial performance
C4

Cathy Shore manages the auto service department of an auto dealership. Shown below is the calendar year 2000 income statement for her department:

Revenues:		
Sales of parts	$ 72,000	
Sales of services	105,000	$177,000
Costs and expenses:		
Cost of parts sold	$ 30,000	
Building depreciation	9,300	
Income taxes allocated to department	8,700	
Interest on long-term debt	7,500	
Manager's salary	12,000	
Payroll taxes	8,100	
Supplies	15,900	
Utilities	14,400	
Wages (hourly)	6,000	
Total costs and expenses		111,900
Departmental net income		$ 65,100

Analyze the items on the income statement to identify those that definitely should be included on a performance report used to evaluate Cathy's performance. List them and explain why you have chosen them. Then list and explain the items that should definitely be excluded. Finally, list the items that are not definitely included or excluded and explain why they fall into that category.

Exercise 22-8
Assigning joint real estate costs
C5

Capital Properties is developing a subdivision that includes 400 home lots. The 300 lots in the Canyon section are below a ridge and do not have views of the neighboring canyons and hills, while the 100 lots in the Hilltop section offer unobstructed views. The Canyon lots are expected to sell for $50,000 each, while the Hilltop lots are expected to sell for $90,000 each. The developer acquired the land for $2,500,000 and spent another $2,500,000 on street and utilities improvements. Assign the joint land and improvement costs to the lots using the value basis of allocation and determine the average cost per lot. (Round percents to the nearest one-tenth and dollar amounts to the nearest whole dollar.)

Exercise 22-9
Assigning joint product costs
C5

Tasty Seafood Company purchases lobsters and processes them into tails and flakes. It then sells the lobster tails for $21 per pound and sells the flakes for $14 per pound. On average, 100 pounds of lobster are processed into 52 pounds of tails and 22 pounds of flakes, with 26 pounds of waste. Assume 2,400 pounds of lobster are purchased for $4.50 per pound. The lobsters are then processed with an additional labor cost of $1,800. No materials or labor costs are assigned to the waste. If 1,096 pounds of tails and 324 pounds of flakes are sold, what is the allocated cost of the sold items and the cost of the remaining inventory?

Exercise 22-10
Investment center analysis
A1

You must prepare a return on investment analysis for the regional manager of King Burgers. This growing chain is trying to decide which outlet to open among two alternatives. The first location (A) requires a $500,000 investment and is expected to yield annual net income of $80,000. The second location (B) requires a $200,000 investment and is expected to yield annual net income of $38,000.

Required

1. Compute the return on investment for each King Burgers alternative.
2. Write up your recommendation in a one-half page memorandum to the regional manager. Be prepared to explain your reasoning in class.

Problems

Problem 22-1
Allocating building occupancy costs
P1, C3

Music City Co. has several departments that occupy both floors of a two-story building. The departmental accounting system has a single account in the ledger called Building Occupancy Cost. The types and amounts of costs recorded in this account for the current calendar year are:

Depreciation—Building	$18,000
Interest—Building mortgage	27,000
Taxes—Building and land	8,000
Gas (heating) expense	2,500
Lighting expense	3,000
Maintenance expense	5,500
Total	$64,000

The building has 4,000 square feet on each floor. For simplicity, the accountant merely divides the $64,000 occupancy cost by 8,000 square feet to find an average cost of $8 per square foot. Then each department is charged with a building occupancy cost equal to this rate times the number of square feet that it occupies.

Joan French manages a first-floor department that occupies 1,000 square feet and Leo Perry manages a second-floor department that occupies 1,800 square feet of floor space. In discussing the departmental reports, they question whether using the same rate per square foot for all departments makes sense because the first-floor space is of greater value. The two managers also check a recent real estate study of average rental costs for similar space. They find that first-floor space is worth $30 per square foot while second-floor space is worth only $20 per square foot (these amounts do not include costs for heating, lighting, and cleaning).

Required

Preparation Component

1. Allocate occupancy cost to the two departments by the accountant's simple method.

2. Allocate occupancy cost to the two departments in proportion to the relative market values of the space, except for heating, lighting, and cleaning costs, which are allocated on an equal basis per square foot occupied. (Round costs per square foot to the nearest cent.)

Check Figure Part 2. Total occupancy cost to French, $9,330

Analysis Component

3. If you were a manager of a second-floor department, explain which allocation method you'd prefer.

Problem 22-2
Activity-based costing
P2

Surgery Care is an outpatient surgical center that has enjoyed excess profits for many years. But Medicare has recently cut reimbursement by as much as 50%. As a result, the center wants a better understanding of its costs. You are to prepare an activity-based cost analysis using the data below. It also is important to estimate the average cost of both general surgery and orthopedic surgery. The company's three cost centers and their cost drivers are:

Cost Center	Cost	Cost Driver	Quantity
Professional salaries	$1,500,000	Professional hours	10,000
Service patients/supplies	25,000	Number of patients	500
Building cost	150,000	Square feet	1,500

The two main surgical units and their related data are:

Service	Hours	Square Feet*	Patients
General surgery	2,500	500	400
Orthopedic surgery	7,500	1,000	100

*Orthopedic surgery requires more space for patients, supplies, and equipment.

Required

Preparation Component

1. Compute the cost per driver.
2. Compute the average cost for (a) general surgery and (b) orthopedic surgery.

Check Figure Average cost of general surgery, $1,113

Analysis Component

3. Without computations, would the average cost of general surgery be more or less if center costs are allocated on the number of patients? Explain.

Problem 22-3
Departmental income statements
P3

Looking-At-You Co. began operating in January 2000 with two operating (selling) departments and one service (office) department. Departmental income statements are shown below:

LOOKING-AT-YOU CO.
Departmental Income Statements
For Year Ended December 31, 2000

	Clocks	Mirrors	Combined
Sales	$122,500	$ 52,500	$175,000
Cost of goods sold	60,000	32,000	92,000
Gross profit	$ 62,500	$ 20,500	$ 83,000
Direct expenses:			
Sales salaries	20,000	7,000	27,000
Advertising	1,200	500	1,700
Store supplies used	900	400	1,300
Depreciation of equipment	1,500	300	1,800
Total direct expenses	$ 23,600	$ 8,200	$ 31,800
Allocated expenses:			
Rent expense	7,020	3,780	10,800
Utilities expense	2,600	1,400	4,000
Share of office department expenses	10,500	4,500	15,000
Total allocated expenses	$ 20,120	$ 9,680	$ 29,800
Total expenses	$ 43,720	$ 17,880	$ 61,600
Net income	$ 18,780	$ 2,620	$ 21,400

Looking-At-You plans to open a third department in January 2001 that will sell paintings. Management predicts the new department will generate $35,000 in sales with a 55% gross profit margin, and that it will require the following direct expenses: sales salaries, $8,000; advertising, $800; store supplies, $500; and equipment depreciation, $200. The company currently rents space in a building. It will be possible to fit the new department into the current space by taking some square footage from the other two departments. When the new painting department is opened, it will fill one-fifth of the space presently used by the clock department and one-sixth of the space used by the mirror department. Management does not predict any increase in utilities costs, which are allocated to the departments in proportion to occupied space (or rent expense). The company allocates office department expenses to the selling departments in proportion to their sales. It expects the painting department to increase total office department expenses by $7,000. Because the painting department will bring new customers into the store, management expects sales in both the clock and mirror departments to increase by 7%. Those departments' gross profit percents are not expected to change. Also, no changes are expected in their direct expenses, except for store supplies used, which will increase in proportion to sales.

Required

Prepare departmental income statements that show the company's predicted results of operations for calendar year 2001 with the three operating (selling) departments. (Round percents to the nearest one-tenth and dollar amounts to the nearest whole dollar.)

Check Figure Forecasted combined net income, $29,815

Problem 22-4
Responsibility accounting performance reports

C4, P4

Terry Wald, the manager of Royal Co.'s Indiana plant, is responsible for all costs of the plant's operations other than her own salary. The plant has two operating departments and one service department. The camper and trailer operating departments manufacture different products and have their own managers. The office department provides services equally to the two operating departments. Wald also manages the office department. A budget is prepared for each operating department and the office department. The responsibility accounting system must assemble information to present budgeted and actual costs in performance reports for each of the operating department managers and the plant manager. Each performance report includes only those costs that a particular manager can control. The operating department managers control the costs of raw materials, wages, supplies used, and equipment depreciation. The plant manager is responsible for the department managers' salaries, utilities, building rent, office salaries other than her own, other office costs, plus all the costs controlled by the two operating department managers. The annual departmental budgets and cost accumulations for the two operating departments are:

	Budget			Actual		
	Campers	Trailers	Combined	Campers	Trailers	Combined
Raw materials	$160,000	$250,000	$ 410,000	$159,400	$246,500	$ 405,900
Wages	99,000	191,000	290,000	102,300	193,700	296,000
Dept. manager salary	40,000	44,000	84,000	41,000	47,000	88,000
Supplies used	34,000	83,000	117,000	31,900	84,600	116,500
Equipment depreciation	58,000	110,000	168,000	58,000	110,000	168,000
Utilities	2,800	4,200	7,000	2,700	3,800	6,500
Building rent	5,000	8,000	13,000	4,800	7,200	12,000
Office department costs	56,000	56,000	112,000	54,450	54,450	108,900
Total	$454,800	$746,200	$1,201,000	$454,550	$747,250	$1,201,800

The office department budget and its actual costs are shown below:

	Budget	Actual
Plant manager salary	$ 60,000	$ 62,000
Other office salaries	30,000	27,700
Other office costs	22,000	19,200
Total	$112,000	$108,900

Required

Preparation Component

Prepare responsibility accounting performance reports that list costs controlled by the following:

1. Manager of camper department.

2. Manager of trailer department.

3. Manager of the Indiana plant.

In each report, include the budgeted and actual costs and show the amount that each actual cost is over or under the budgeted amount.

Check Figure Part 3. Indiana plant controllable costs, $1,200 under budget

Analysis Component

4. Did the plant manager or the operating department managers better manage costs? Explain.

Problem 22-5
Allocating joint costs
C5

SunRipe Orchards produces a good crop of peaches this year. But after preparing its income statement below, SunRipe feels it should have given its No. 3 peaches to charity and saved its money and efforts.

SUNRIPE ORCHARDS Income Statement For Year Ended December 31, 2000	No. 1	No. 2	No. 3	Combined
Sales (by grade):				
No. 1: 300,000 lbs. @ $1.50	$450,000			
No. 2: 300,000 lbs. @ $1.00		$300,000		
No. 3: 750,000 lbs. @ $0.20			$ 150,000	
Total sales				$900,000
Costs:				
Tree pruning and care @ $0.20/lb	60,000	60,000	150,000	270,000
Picking, sorting, and grading @ $0.12/lb	36,000	36,000	90,000	162,000
Delivery costs @ $0.03/lb	9,000	9,000	22,500	40,500
Total costs	$105,000	$105,000	$ 262,500	$472,500
Net income (loss)	$345,000	$195,000	$(112,500)	$427,500

In preparing this statement, SunRipe allocated joint costs among the grades on a physical basis as an equal amount per pound. Records on delivery costs show that $30,000 of the $40,500 relates to the cost of crating the No. 1 and No. 2 peaches and hauling them to the buyer. The remaining $10,500 of delivery costs is the cost of crating the No. 3 peaches and hauling them to the cannery where they are used to make preserves.

Required

Preparation Component

1. Prepare allocation schedules showing how costs would be allocated on a sales value basis to the three grades of peaches. Separate delivery costs into the amounts directly identifiable to each grade. Then allocate any shared delivery costs on the basis of the relative sales value of each grade. (Round percents to the nearest one-tenth and dollar amounts to the nearest whole dollar.)
2. Using your answers to part 1, prepare an income statement using the joint costs allocated on a sales value basis.

Check Figure Part 2. Net income from No. 1 peaches, $216,000

Analysis Component

3. Do you think delivery costs fit the definition of a joint cost? Explain.

BEYOND THE NUMBERS

Reporting in Action
C4

A careful review of **NIKE's** financial statements in Appendix A offers clues as to growth in sales revenue. In particular, you should read NIKE's note 15.

Required

1. Compute the growth in percent for "Revenues from unrelated entities" using 1995 as the base for 1996 and 1996 as the base for 1997. Do this for each of the four geographic areas listed.
2. What geographic area from part 1 is growing the fastest for NIKE?
3. How can NIKE's managers use this information?

Swoosh Ahead

4. Obtain NIKE's annual report information for a fiscal year ending after May 31, 1997. You can get this information from its Web site **[www.nike.com]** or the SEC's EDGAR database **[www.sec.gov]**. Compute growth in "Revenues from unrelated entities" by geographic areas for the most recent reporting period. Compare results to those from part 1. What growth patterns, if any, do you observe?

Comparative Analysis

P3

Reebok and NIKE compete in several sporting goods markets. The most common competitive markets for these two companies are sports footwear and apparel.

Required

1. Design a three-level responsibility accounting performance report assuming you have available internal information for both companies. Exhibit 22.22 can be used as an example (also see Exhibit 22.21). The goal of this assignment is to design a reporting framework for the companies; numbers are not required. Limit your reporting framework to sales activity only. Prepare to share your answers in a class discussion regarding responsibility accounting.
2. Explain why it is important to have similar performance reports when comparing performance within a company and across different companies. Be specific in your response.

Ethics Challenge

P3

Creative Services (CS) offers a range of services involving security for senior citizens. Each type of service is considered within a separate department. Carl Stone, the overall manager, is compensated partly on the basis of departmental performance by staying within the quarterly cost budget. Stone often revises his plans to make sure he stays within budget. "I can't afford to go over budget even if it means slightly compromising the level and quality of service. But these are minor compromises and don't significantly affect my clients, at least in the short term."

Required

1. Is there an ethical concern in this situation? Which parties are affected?
2. Can Stone take action to eliminate or reduce any ethical concerns?
3. What is CS's ethical responsibility in offering professional services?

Communicating in Practice

C4, C5, P3

Home Improvements is a national home improvement chain with more than 100 stores throughout the country. The manager of each store receives a salary as well as a bonus equal to a percent of the store's net income for the reporting period. The following net income calculation is reported on the Denver store manager's performance report for the recent three-month period:

Sales	$2,500,000
Cost of goods sold	800,000
Wages expense	500,000
Utilities expense	200,000
Home office expense	75,000
Net income	$ 925,000
Manager's bonus (5%)	$ 46,250

In previous periods, the bonus had also been 5%, but the performance report had not included any charges for the home office expense. The home office expense is now assigned to each store as a percent of its sales.

Required

Assume you are the national office manager. Write a one-half page memorandum to your store managers explaining why "home office expense" is in the new performance report.

Taking It to the Net

A1

This chapter described and used spreadsheets to prepare various managerial reports. You can download from Web sites various tutorials showing how spreadsheets are used in business applications.

Required

1. Check out this Web site: **www.lacher.com.** Open up its table of contents (TOC). Select "Business Solutions" under "Tutorials" and identify three tutorials for review.
2. Describe in a one-half page memorandum to your instructor how the applications described in each of the three tutorials are helpful in business decision making.

Teamwork in Action
C1, C2

Activity-based costing is increasingly popular as a useful managerial tool in (1) measuring the cost of resources consumed and (2) assigning cost to individual products. Yet, this managerial tool has been available to accounting and business decision makers for more than 30 years.

Required

Break into teams and prepare a list of at least three reasons why activity-based costing has gained popularity in recent years. Be prepared to present your answers in a class discussion. (Hint: What changes occurred in products and services over the past 30 years?)

Hitting the Road
P3

Visit a local movie theater and check out both its concession area and its showing areas. The manager of a theater must confront questions such as:

- How much return do we earn on concessions?
- What types of movies generate the greatest sales?
- What types of movies generate the greatest net income?

Required

You are the new accounting manager for a 16-screen movie theater. You are to set up a responsibility accounting reporting framework for the theater.

1. Recommend how to segment the different departments of a movie theater for responsibility reporting.
2. Propose an expense allocation system for heat, rent, insurance, and maintenance costs of the theater.

Business Week Activity
C4

You are the manager of a truck division of a Ford dealership in Seattle, WA. The owner of the dealership asks you to read "AUTO—Prognosis 1998" in the January 12, 1998, issue of *Business Week*, pp. 102–3, and make any necessary revisions to the dealership's 1998 budget prepared in late 1997.

Required

Listed below are the controllable items in your 1998 budget. Identify whether you plan to increase, decrease, or make no change in modifying this budget given the auto industry prognosis described in *Business Week.* Explain. Be prepared to present your answers in a class discussion.

Description	Amount	I = increase; D = decrease; NC = no change
Sales	$10,000,000	
Commissions	500,000	
Advertising	2,500,000	
Training	750,000	
Heat and lights	1,000,000	
Maintenance	500,000	
Projected income	$ 4,750,000	

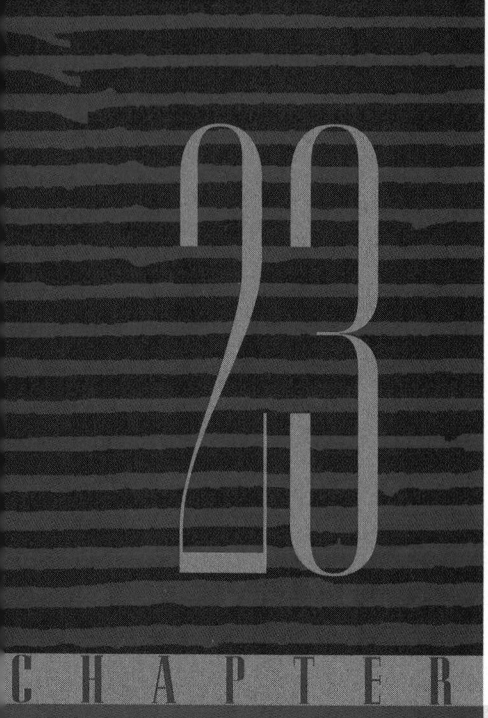

Cost-Volume-Profit Analysis

A Look Back

Chapter 22 focused on cost allocation, activity-based costing, and performance measurement. We identified several managerial reports useful in measuring and analyzing a company's activities.

A Look at This Chapter

This chapter shows how information on both cost and sales behavior is useful to managers in performing cost-volume-profit analysis. This analysis is an important part of successful management.

A Look Ahead

Chapter 24 introduces and describes the budgeting process and its importance. It also explains the master budget and its usefulness to the planning of future company activities.

Chapter Outline

Staying Afloat

CHARLESTON, S.C.—Cara McKey is the marketing manager for **Maxum,** a leading manufacturer of sealant for water sports equipment and gear. This past year, McKey helped close one of the company's biggest deals ever. But the big deal came close to being the big bust.

Maxum had been working with **Sport Marine** over the past two years, supplying goods and services to its water sports division. "Then," says McKey, "they asked about a long-term contract that'd nearly double our yearly sales. I was ecstatic." McKey quickly put things in motion. But McKey then got a call from Maxum's controller. He wanted to go over the proposed contract with her.

"I knew he was a numbers person," says McKey, "So I prepared and came armed with accounting reports." She pointed out the new contract wouldn't impact any current business, and that the new business would require no added advertising or unusual servicing costs. "Then, to top it off," adds McKey, "I proposed we offer Sport Marine a contract price 10% to 12% lower than normal. And, I showed him we'd cover current inventory costs and maintain our 15% gross profit margin."

Now it was the controller's turn. McKey says he pointed out that current inventory product cost was an average of current manufacturing costs at today's sales level. He said that such a major shift in sales would result in many changes in cost behavior.

"The next thing I knew," adds McKey, "he and I are running cost-volume-profit analyses on the contract." In the end, Maxum got the contract. But not at the price cut McKey originally proposed. Maxum did slice about 3% off the price and still maintained its 15% margin. "If it wasn't for cost-volume-profit analysis, I'd be looking at about a 5% gross margin today and," adds McKey, "a new job!"

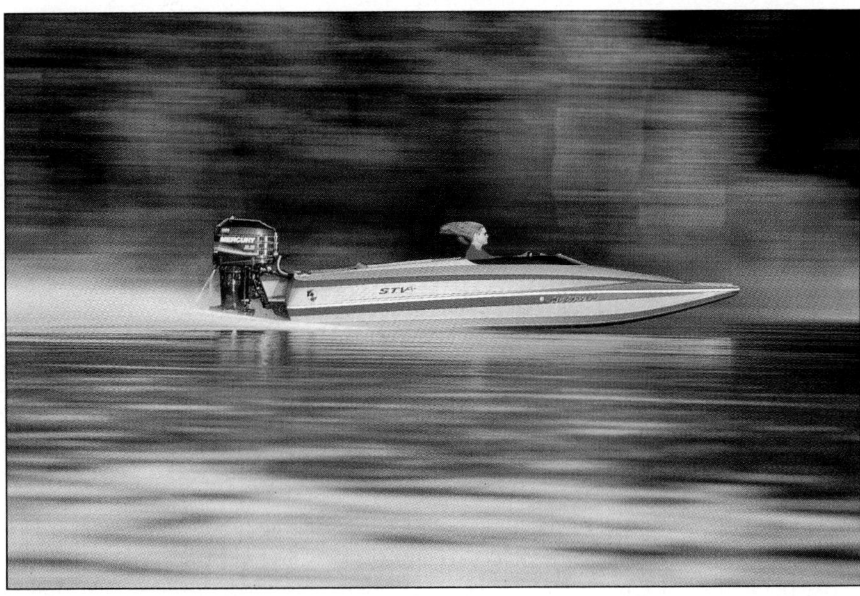

Learning Objectives

Conceptual

C1 Describe different types of cost behavior in relation to production and sales volume.

C2 Identify assumptions in cost-volume-profit analysis and explain their impact.

C3 Describe several applications of cost-volume-profit analysis.

Analytical

A1 Compare the scatter diagram, high-low, and regression methods of estimating costs.

A2 Analyze changes in sales using the degree of operating leverage.

Procedural

P1 Determine cost estimates using three different methods.

P2 Compute break-even point for a single product company.

P3 Graph costs and revenues for a single product company.

P4 Compute break-even point for a multiproduct company.

CHAPTER PREVIEW

This chapter describes different types of costs and shows how they are affected by changes in the operating volume of a business. The chapter also analyzes the costs and revenues of a company to understand how different operating strategies affect profit or loss. Managers use this kind of analysis to forecast what will happen if changes are made in costs, sales volume, selling prices, or product mix. They then use these forecasts to select the best strategy for the future such as whether to price a special order below the usual selling price, as seen with **Maxum** in the opening article.

Identifying Cost Behavior

Planning a company's future activities and events is a crucial phase in successful management. One of the first steps in planning is predicting the volume of activity, the costs to be incurred, revenues to be received, and income (or profit) to be earned. An important tool to help managers carry out this step is **cost-volume-profit (CVP) analysis.**

Cost-volume-profit analysis helps managers predict how income is affected by changes in costs and sales levels. In its basic form, CVP analysis involves computing the sales level at which a company neither earns an income nor incurs a loss. This is called the break-even point. For this reason, this basic form of cost-volume-profit analysis is often called *break-even analysis.* But managers use many other applications of CVP analysis to answer questions like:

- What sales volume is needed to earn a target income?
- What is the change in income if selling prices decline and sales volume increases?
- How much does income increase if we install a new machine to reduce labor costs?
- What is the income effect if we change the sales mix of our products?

The phrase *cost-volume-profit analysis* is better than *break-even analysis* as a description of this tool when it is used to address questions like these.

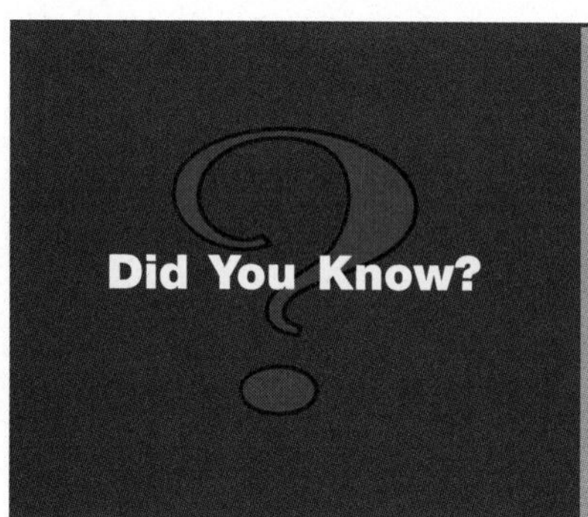

Breaking Even
Compaq Computer got its start when Rod Canion, Jim Harris, and Bill Murto, all prior senior managers at **Texas Instruments,** had a good plan and a solid product. They eventually raised start-up capital of $20 million using cost-volume-profit analysis showing break-even volumes attainable within the first year after product development. Compaq's first year sales totaled more than $100 million.

Conventional cost-volume-profit analysis requires management to classify all costs as either *fixed* or *variable* with respect to production or sales volume. We introduced different cost behaviors in Chapter 19. The remainder of this section extends that discussion of cost behavior as it relates to CVP analysis.

C1 Describe different types of cost behavior in relation to production and sales volume.

Fixed Costs

The amount of a **fixed cost** incurred each period remains unchanged even when production volume varies from period to period within a relevant range. For example, $5,000 monthly rent paid for a factory building remains the same whether the factory operates with a single eight-hour shift or around the clock with three shifts. This also means rent cost is the same each month at any level of output from zero on up to the full production capacity of the plant.

While *total* fixed cost remains constant as the level of production changes, the fixed cost *per unit* of product decreases as volume increases. For instance, if 20 units are produced when monthly rent is $5,000, the average factory building rent cost per unit is $250 (computed as $5,000 ÷ 20 units). When production increases to 100 units per month, the average cost per unit decreases to $50 (computed as $5,000 ÷ 100 units). The average cost decreases to $10 per unit if production increases to 500 units per month. Other common examples of fixed costs include depreciation, property taxes, office salaries, and many service department costs.

When production volume and costs are graphed, units of product are usually plotted on the *horizontal axis* and dollars of cost are plotted on the *vertical axis*. This means fixed costs are represented as a horizontal line because its total amount remains constant at all levels of production. The graph in Exhibit 23.1 shows this fixed cost behavior. Fixed costs remain at $32,000 at all production levels up to the factory's monthly capacity of 2,000 units of output. The *relevant range* for fixed costs in Exhibit 23.1 is 0 to 2,000 units. If the relevant range changes (i.e., production capacity increases or decreases), it is likely the amount of fixed costs will change.

Exhibit 23.1

Relations of Fixed and Variable Costs to Volume

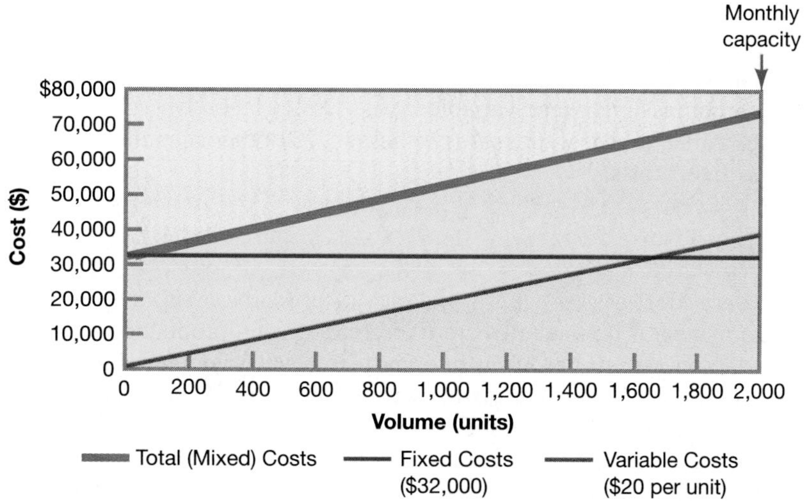

Car Deals

Fixed costs were a driving force behind the **Daimler-Benz** and **Chrysler** merger. The automobile business is one of huge fixed costs, primarily in plant and equipment. This means the higher the sales volume, the more units you have to spread those fixed costs over. This in turn lowers your fixed cost per automobile.

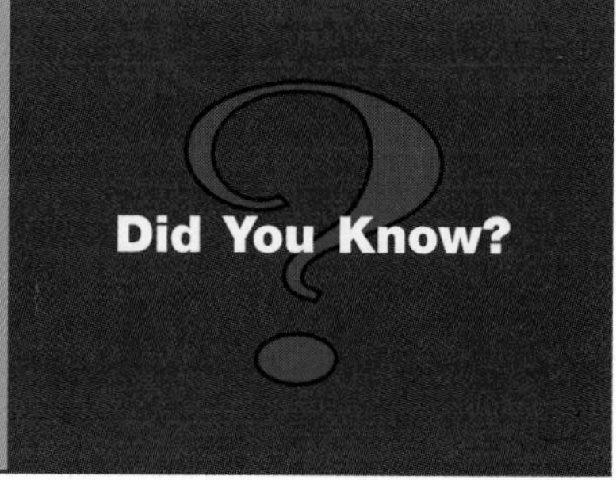

Variable Costs

The total amount of a **variable cost** changes in proportion to changes in volume. The direct material cost of a product is one example of a variable cost. If one unit of product requires material costing $20, total material costs are $200 when 10 units of product are manufactured, $400 for 20 units, $600 for 30 units, and so on. The variable cost *per unit* produced remains constant while the *total* amount of variable cost changes with the level of production. Other variable costs include direct labor (if workers are paid for completed units), some overhead costs, selling commissions, and shipping costs.

When variable costs are plotted on a graph of cost and volume, it appears as a straight line starting at the zero cost level. This straight line is upward (positive) sloping. The line rises as production volume increases. The variable cost line using a $20 per unit cost is graphed in Exhibit 23.1.

Mixed Costs

Mixed costs are those that reflect both fixed and variable costs. Compensation for sales representatives often includes a fixed monthly salary and a variable commission based on sales. The total cost line in Exhibit 23.1 is a mixed cost. Like a fixed cost, it is greater than zero when volume is zero. But unlike a fixed cost, it increases steadily in proportion to increases in volume. The mixed cost line in Exhibit 23.1 starts on the vertical axis at the $32,000 fixed cost point. This means at the zero volume level, total cost equals only the fixed costs. But total cost increases as the activity level increases. The amount of the increase equals the variable cost per unit for each additional unit produced and is the highest when production volume is 2,000 units (the end point of our graph).

The simplest way to include mixed costs in a CVP analysis is to separate them into fixed and variable components. The fixed component is added to other fixed costs for the planning period, and the variable component is added to other variable costs.

Recall the opening article involving **Maxum.** In analyzing the potential sales order, the controller's first course of action was to separate all manufacturing and selling costs into variable and fixed cost categories. The controller concluded that only raw materials and sales commissions were variable costs. Direct labor was added in eight-hour shifts and was called a *step-wise cost* (see below). All other manufacturing costs were categorized as fixed costs.

Step-Wise Costs

Step-wise costs reflect a step pattern. Salaries of production supervisors often behave in a step-wise manner. Their salaries are fixed for a certain production volume, whether it be zero or the maximum produced in a shift. But when another shift is added to increase production, additional supervisors must be hired. Then the total cost for supervisory salaries goes up by a lump-sum amount. Total supervisory salaries remain fixed at this new, higher level until a third shift is added. A third shift increases cost by another lump sum. This behavior reflects step-wise costs, also known as *stair-step costs.*

A step-wise cost is graphed in Exhibit 23.2. See how it is flat within narrow ranges (steps). Then it jumps up to the next higher level and stays there over another range (step). In a conventional CVP analysis, a step-wise cost is treated as either a fixed cost or a variable cost. This treatment involves judgment on the part of the manager and mostly depends on the width of the range and the expected volume level.

To illustrate, suppose after the production of every 25 snowboards, an operator must add a special oil to the finishing machine. The cost of this oil reflects a step-wise pat-

Exhibit 23.2

Step-Wise and Curvilinear Costs

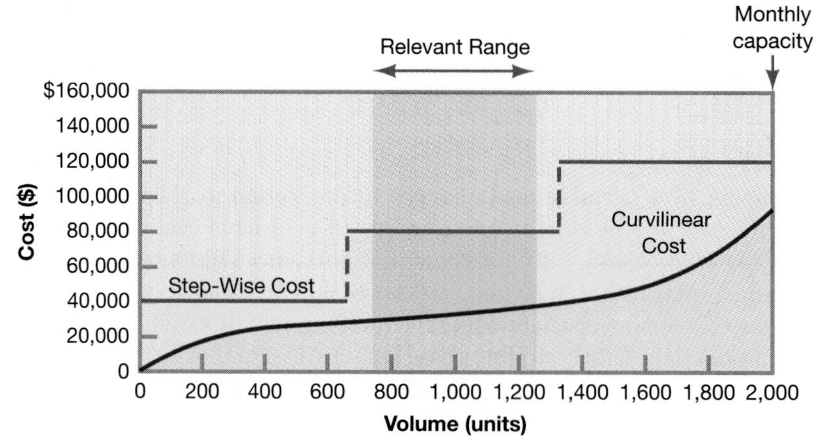

tern. Also suppose that after the production of every 1,000 units, a maintenance person must replace the snowboard cutting tool. Again, this is a step-wise cost. But note the range of 25 snowboards is much narrower than the range of 1,000 snowboards. This means some managers might treat the cost of the oil as a variable cost and the cost of the cutting tool as a fixed cost.

Curvilinear Costs

A variable cost, as explained above, is a *linear* cost. This means it increases at a constant rate as production volume increases. **Curvilinear costs,** also called *nonlinear costs,* increase as volume increases but not at a constant rate like variable costs. When graphed, curvilinear costs appear as a curved line. Exhibit 23.2 shows a curvilinear cost beginning at zero when production is zero and then increasing at different rates. Its highest rate is when sales volume reaches the maximum for the month.

An example of a curvilinear cost is total direct labor cost when workers are paid by the hour. At low levels of production, adding more workers allows each of them to specialize by doing the same task over and over again instead of doing several different tasks. The work crew becomes more efficient and able to produce additional units for lower costs. But a point is eventually reached where adding more workers begins to create inefficiencies. For instance, a large crew may demand more time and effort in communicating or coordinating their efforts. While adding workers increases output, the labor cost per unit increases and the total labor cost goes up with a steeper slope. This pattern is seen in Exhibit 23.2 where the curvilinear cost curve starts at zero, rises, flattens out, and then increases at a faster rate as output nears the maximum for the month.

Flash *back*

1. Which of the following statements is typically true?
   a. Variable cost per unit increases as volume increases.
   b. Fixed cost per unit decreases as volume increases.
   c. A curvilinear cost includes both fixed and variable elements.
2. Describe the behavior of a fixed cost.
3. If a raw material cost per unit remains constant (fixed), why is it called a variable cost?

Answers—p. 1006

Measuring Cost Behavior

Identifying and measuring cost behavior requires careful analysis and judgment. We first want to identify individual costs that can be classified as either fixed or variable. When it is difficult to identify a cost as either fixed or variable, an analysis of past cost behavior is often useful.

Three methods are usually used in analyzing past costs: scatter diagrams, high-low, and least-squares regression. Each method is discussed in this section using the sales and cost data shown in Exhibit 23.3 taken from a start-up company. Sales volume in dollars is used here as the activity base in estimating cost behavior.

Exhibit 23.3

Data for Estimating Cost Behavior

Month	Sales Volume ($)	Total Cost ($)
January	$17,500	$20,500
February	27,500	21,500
March	25,000	25,000
April	35,000	21,500
May	47,500	25,500
June	22,500	18,500
July	30,000	23,500
August	52,500	28,500
September	37,500	26,000
October	57,500	26,000
November	62,500	31,000
December	67,500	29,000

Scatter Diagrams

Scatter diagrams display data about past costs in graphical form. In preparing a scatter diagram, sales

P1 Determine cost estimates using three different methods.

volume in dollars or units is plotted on the horizontal axis and cost is plotted on the vertical axis. Each individual point on a scatter diagram reflects the cost and sales levels for a prior period.

In Exhibit 23.4, the prior 12 months' cost and sales figures are graphed. Each point reflects total costs incurred and sales volume for one of those months. For instance, the point labeled March had sales of $25,000 and costs of $25,000.

Exhibit 23.4

Scatter Diagram

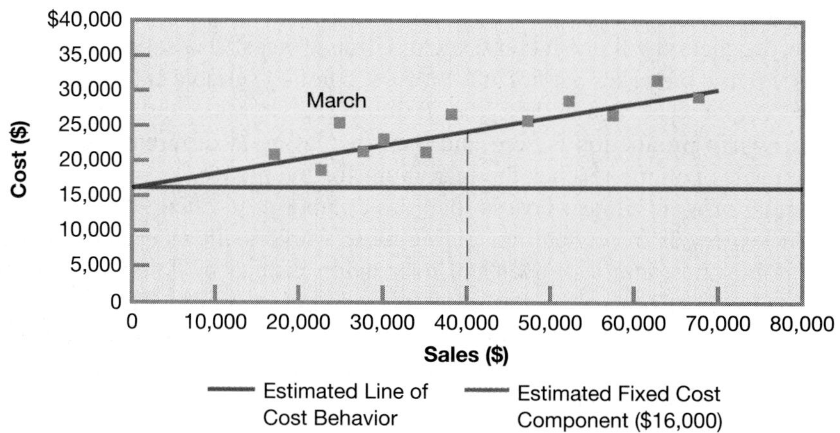

The **estimated line of cost behavior** is drawn on a scatter diagram to reflect the past relation between cost and sales volume. This line best "fits" visually the points in a scatter diagram. Fitting this line demands judgment. The line drawn in Exhibit 23.4 intersects the vertical axis at approximately $16,000. This amount reflects the fixed cost estimate.

To compute variable cost per unit, or the slope, we perform three steps. First, we select any two points on the horizontal axis (sales), say $0 and $40,000. Second, we draw a vertical line from the $40,000 point to intersect the estimated line of cost behavior. The point on the vertical axis (cost) corresponding to the intersection point on the estimated line is roughly $24,000. Similarly, the cost corresponding to zero sales is $16,000 (the fixed cost point). Third, we compute the slope of the line, or variable cost, as the change in cost divided by the change in sales. Exhibit 23.5 shows this computation.

Exhibit 23.5

Variable Cost per Unit (Scatter Diagram)

$$\frac{\textbf{Change in cost}}{\textbf{Change in sales}} = \frac{\$24{,}000 - \$16{,}000}{\$40{,}000 - \$0} = \frac{\$8{,}000}{\$40{,}000} = \$0.20 \text{ per sales dollar}$$

Variable cost is $0.20 per sales dollar. This means the cost equation used by management to predict costs for different sales levels is: $16,000 plus $0.20 per sales dollar.

High-Low Method

The **high-low method** is another means to estimate the cost equation. To apply this method, we connect the two cost amounts in the diagram representing the highest and lowest sales volumes. In our case, the lowest sales volume is $17,500 and the highest is $67,500, and the costs corresponding to these sales volumes are $20,500 and $29,000 (see data in Exhibit 23.3). The estimated line of cost behavior for the high-low method is then drawn by connecting these two points on the scatter diagram corresponding to the lowest and highest sales volumes as follows:

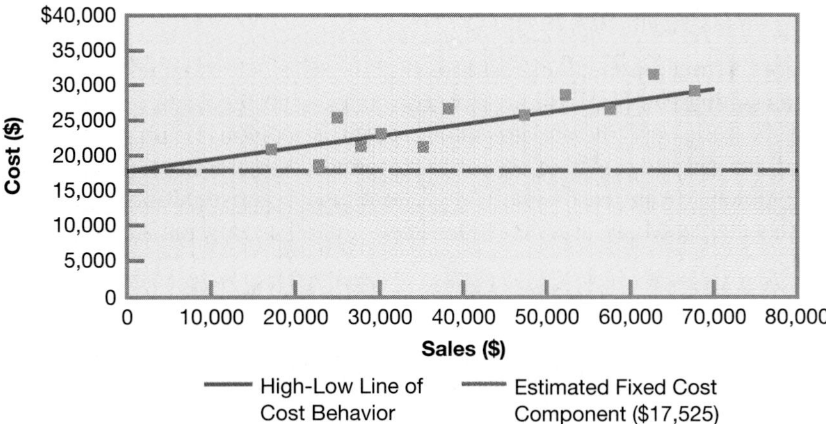

If we extend this line to the vertical axis, it intersects the vertical axis at a cost of about $17,525. This amount is the fixed cost. The variable cost per unit is determined as the change in cost divided by the change in sales and uses the data from Exhibit 23.3 corresponding to the high and low sales volumes. This results in a slope, or variable cost per sales dollar, of $0.17 as computed in Exhibit 23.6.

$$\frac{\textbf{Change in cost}}{\textbf{Change in sales}} = \frac{\$29{,}000 - \$20{,}500}{\$67{,}500 - \$17{,}500} = \frac{\$8{,}500}{\$50{,}000} = \$0.17 \text{ per sales dollar}$$

Exhibit 23.6

Variable Cost per Unit (High-Low Method)

The cost equation used to estimate costs at different sales levels is: $17,525 plus $0.17 per sales dollar. This cost equation is slightly different from that determined using the scatter diagram method. One deficiency of the high-low method is that it ignores all sales points except the highest and lowest. The result is less precise because it uses the most extreme points rather than the more usual conditions that are likely to occur in future periods.

Least-Squares Regression

Least-squares regression is a statistical method of identifying cost behavior. For our purposes we will use the cost equation estimated from this method but leave the details for more advanced cost accounting courses. The computations for least-squares regression are easily made on most spreadsheet programs and calculators.

The regression cost equation for the data presented in Exhibit 23.3 is: $16,947 plus $0.19 per sales dollar. This means fixed cost is estimated as $16,947 and variable cost is $0.19 per sales dollar. Both costs are reflected in the graph below:

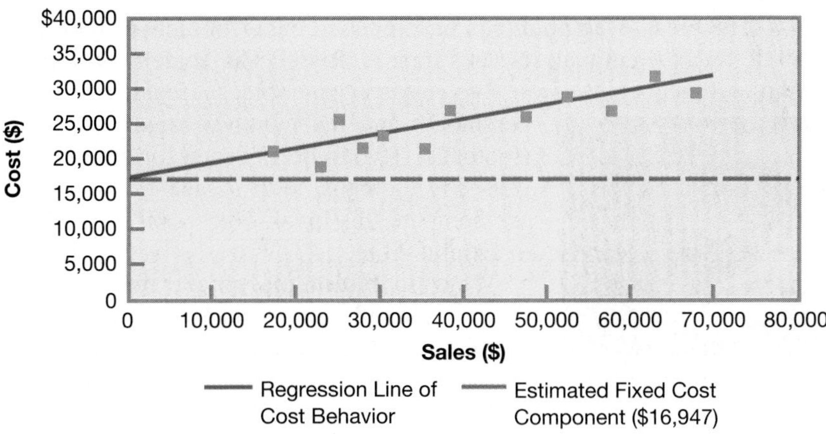

Comparing Cost Estimation Methods

A1 Compare the scatter diagram, high-low, and regression methods of estimating costs.

The three cost estimation methods result in slightly different estimates of fixed and variable costs as summarized in Exhibit 23.7. Estimates from the scatter diagram are based on a visual fit of the cost line and are subject to interpretation. Estimates from the high-low method use only two sets of values corresponding to the lowest and highest sales volumes. Estimates from least-squares regression use a statistical technique and all the data points available. Many users consider least-squares regression superior to the other two methods.

Exhibit 23.7

Comparison of Cost Estimation Methods

Estimation Method	Fixed Cost	Variable Cost
Scatter diagram	$16,000	$0.20 per sales dollar
High-low	$17,525	$0.17 per sales dollar
Least-squares regression	$16,947	$0.19 per sales dollar

We must remember all three methods use *past data.* This means cost estimates resulting from either of the methods are only as good as the data used for estimation. Managers must establish that the data are reliable and can be used to derive cost estimates useful in predicting future costs.

Flash *back*

4. Which of the following methods is likely to yield the most precise estimated line of cost behavior? (a) High-low; (b) least-squares regression; (c) scatter diagram.
5. What is the primary weakness of the high-low method?
6. Using conventional CVP analysis, a mixed cost should be: *(a)* Disregarded; *(b)* treated as a fixed cost; *(c)* separated into fixed and variable components.

Answers—p. 1006

Break-Even Analysis

Break-even analysis is a special case of cost-volume-profit analysis. This section describes break-even analysis including computation of the break-even point and preparing a CVP (or break-even) chart.

Computing Break-Even Point

P2 Compute break-even point for a single product company.

The **break-even point** is the sales level at which a company neither earns a profit nor incurs a loss. The break-even point can be expressed either in units or dollars of sales.

To illustrate break-even analysis, let's look at **Rydell Co.** Rydell sells footballs for $100 per unit and incurs $70 of variable costs per unit sold. Its fixed costs are $24,000 per month and the monthly capacity is 1,800 units (footballs). Rydell breaks even for the month when it sells 800 footballs, with a sales volume of $80,000. We compute this break-even point using the formula in Exhibit 23.8.

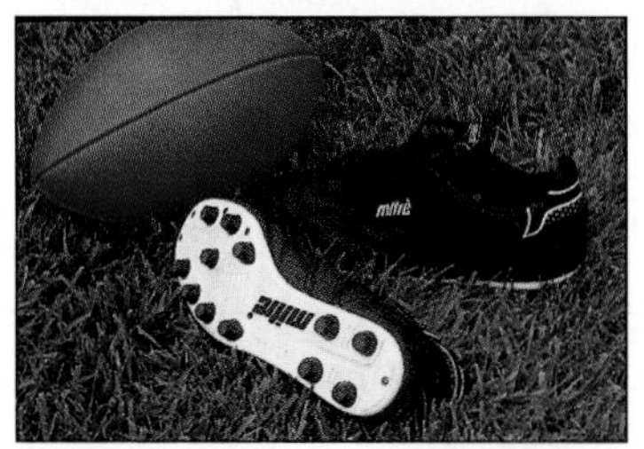

The **contribution margin per unit** is the difference between the selling price and the variable cost per unit (see Chapter 19). For Rydell, the contribution margin per unit is $30 ($100 − $70). This means break-even sales volume is computed as

$24,000 ÷ $30, or 800 units per month. At a price of $100 per unit, monthly sales of 800 units generate revenues of $80,000 (break-even sales dollars).

$$\textbf{Break-even point in units} = \frac{\textbf{Fixed costs}}{\textbf{Contribution margin per unit}}$$

Exhibit 23.8

Formula for Computing Break-Even Sales (in units)[1]

The break-even sales volume of $80,000 can be computed directly, without computing sales units. This involves using the formula shown in Exhibit 23.9.

$$\textbf{Break-even point in dollars} = \frac{\textbf{Fixed costs}}{\textbf{Contribution margin ratio}}$$

Exhibit 23.9

Formula for Computing Break-Even Sales (in dollars)[2]

The **contribution margin ratio** is the *proportion* of a unit's selling price that exceeds total unit variable cost. It is computed as the unit contribution margin divided by the unit selling price (see Chapter 19).

For Rydell, the contribution margin ratio is 30%, computed as $30 ÷ $100. Break-even sales dollars is then computed as $24,000 ÷ 0.30, or $80,000 of monthly sales.

To verify that Rydell's break-even point equals $80,000 (or 800 units), we prepare a simple income statement as shown in Exhibit 23.10. It shows the $80,000 revenue from sales of 800 units exactly equals the sum of variable and fixed costs.

Exhibit 23.10

Income Statement for Break-Even Sales

RYDELL COMPANY Income Statement at Break-Even	
Sales (800 units @ $100 each)	$80,000
Variable costs (800 units @ $70 each)	56,000
Contribution margin	$24,000
Fixed costs	24,000
Net income	$ 0

Exhibit 23.10 shows the *contribution margin income statement.* This statement only differs in format from the conventional income statement. First, it separately classifies costs and expenses as variable or fixed. Second, it reports contribution margin, which is sales less variable costs and expenses. Because of its usefulness in CVP analysis, the contribution margin income statement format is used in this chapter and its assignment materials.

---

[1] To obtain this formula, we define: S = Sales in units; R = Revenue per unit; F = Fixed costs per period; V = Variable cost per unit; $S \times R$ = Dollar sales; $S \times V$ = Total variable cost. Then recall that: contribution margin per unit = $R - V$. At break-even, net income is zero, so therefore:

$$\begin{aligned}
\text{Sales} &= \text{Fixed costs} + \text{Variable costs}\\
(S \times R) &= F + (S \times V)\\
(S \times R) - (S \times V) &= F\\
S \times (R - V) &= F\\
S &= F/(R - V)\\
S &= F/\text{Contribution margin per unit}
\end{aligned}$$

[2] To obtain this formula, recall that: Contribution margin ratio = $(R - V)/R$. Then, at break-even:

$$\begin{aligned}
S &= F/(R - V) \text{ [from prior footnote]}\\
S \times R &= (F \times R)/(R - V)\\
S \times R &= F \times [R/(R - V)]\\
S \times R &= F/[(R - V)/R]\\
S \times R &= F/\text{Contribution margin ratio}
\end{aligned}$$

Preparing a Cost-Volume-Profit Chart

P3 Graph costs and revenues for a single product company.

Exhibit 23.11 is a graph of the cost-volume-profit relations for Rydell. This graph is called a **cost-volume-profit (CVP) chart,** also called a *break-even chart* or *break-even graph.* The horizontal axis is the number of units sold and the vertical axis is dollars of sales and costs. The lines in the chart depict both costs and revenues.

Exhibit 23.11

Cost-Volume-Profit Chart

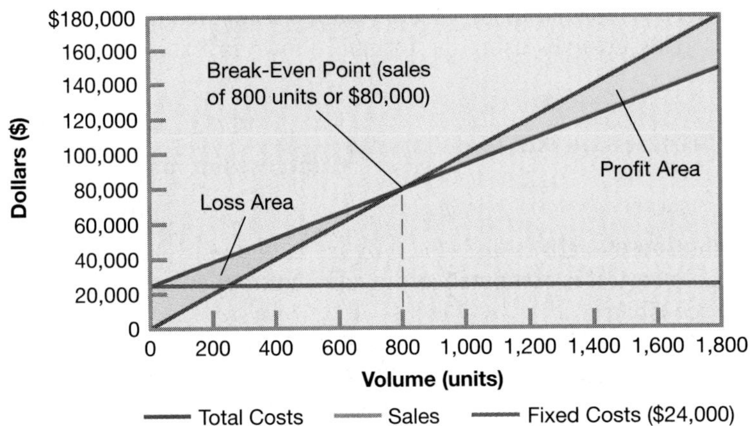

To prepare a CVP chart, we follow 3 steps:[3]

1. Plot fixed costs on the vertical axis ($24,000 for Rydell). Draw a horizontal line at this level to show that fixed costs remain unchanged regardless of sales volume (the fixed cost line is not essential to the chart).
2. Draw a line reflecting total costs (variable costs plus fixed costs). For any sales level, this line shows the sum of both fixed and variable costs for that level. This line starts at the fixed costs level on the vertical axis because total costs equal fixed costs at zero sales level. The slope of the total cost line equals the variable cost per unit ($70). To draw the line, compute the total costs for any sales level, and connect this point with the vertical axis intercept ($24,000). Do not draw this line beyond the productive capacity for the planning period (1,800 units for Rydell).
3. Draw a sales line starting at the origin (zero units and zero dollars of sales). The slope of this line equals the selling price per unit ($100). To draw the line, compute the total revenues for any sales level and connect this point with the origin. Do not extend this line beyond the productive capacity for the planning period. The total revenue is at its highest level at maximum capacity. It is likely that the relevant range is somewhere near the middle of the graph.

The total cost line and the sales line intersect at 800 units of product in Exhibit 23.11. This intersection is the break-even point. It is the point where total sales revenue of $80,000 equals the sum of both fixed and variable costs ($80,000).

On either side of the break-even point, the vertical distance between the sales line and the total cost line at any specific sales volume measures the profit or loss expected at that volume. At volume levels to the left of the break-even point, this vertical distance is the amount of the loss because the total cost line is above the total sales line. At volume levels to the right of the break-even point, the vertical distance represents the amount of profit because the total sales line is above the total cost line.

[3] These instructions are provided to guide you through a manual drafting process. The graph can also be drawn with computer assistance, including spreadsheet programs that can convert numeric data to graphs.

Manager of Operations
You are the manager of operations for a new manufacturing plant set up to produce a variety of gift articles. One of your immediate and important tasks is to coordinate with the accountant to identify the behavior of manufacturing costs to develop a production cost budget. You know three methods can be used to identify cost behavior from past data. But past data is not available as this is a new plant. What do you do?

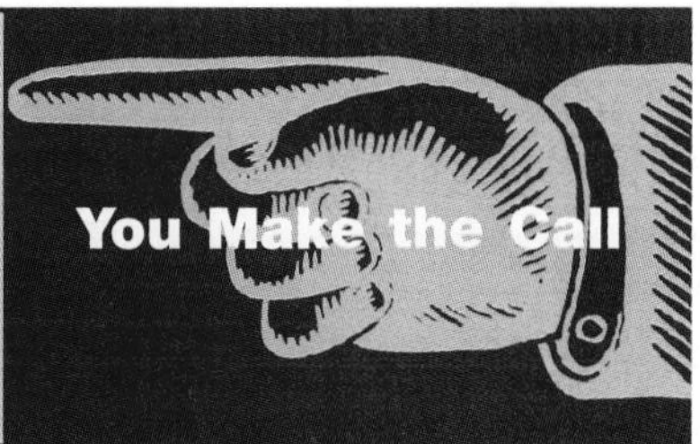

Answer—p. 1005

Assumptions of Cost-Volume-Profit Analysis

C2 Identify assumptions in cost-volume-profit analysis and explain their impact.

Cost-volume-profit analysis assumes relations can be expressed as straight lines similar to those in Exhibits 23.1 and 23.11. This assumption allows users of CVP to classify all costs as either fixed or variable. CVP analysis also treats revenues as variable, with all units of a product being sold at the same unit price. These assumptions allow users to answer several important questions. But the usefulness of the answers depends on the validity of at least three of these assumptions for the planning period:

1. Selling price per unit is constant.
2. Variable costs per unit are constant.
3. Fixed costs are constant.

While these assumptions are not always realistic, they don't necessarily limit the usefulness of CVP analysis as a first step in forecasting the effects of an operating plan. This section discusses these and other assumptions for CVP analysis.

Production Output versus Sales Volume

We normally define variable costs and fixed costs in terms of the level of *output produced.* But CVP analysis usually describes the planning period's level of activity in terms of *sales volume* rather than production output. Sales volume can be described as either the number of units sold or the dollars of sales.

To simplify analysis, we often assume the level of production is the same as the level of sales. This means we don't have to be concerned with costs flowing into inventory instead of being sold or with costs flowing into cost of goods sold from the prior period's inventory. This assumption is usually justified because CVP analysis provides only rough estimates.

Working with Assumptions

The behavior of individual costs and revenues often is not perfectly consistent with CVP assumptions. If the expected cost and revenue behavior are different from the assumptions, the results of a CVP analysis may be limited. Still, there are several reasons why we can perform useful analyses using these assumptions.

Summing Costs Can Offset Deviations

Deviations from assumptions with individual costs are often minor when these costs are summed. For instance, while individual variable cost items may not be perfectly variable, when we sum all variable costs their individual deviations can offset each other. This means the assumption of variable cost behavior may be proper for total variable costs even when it is not for individual variable cost items. Similarly, an assumption that total fixed costs are constant may be proper even when individual fixed cost items are not exactly constant.

Relevant Range of Operations

Revenues, variable costs, and fixed costs often are reasonably reflected in straight lines on a graph when the assumptions are applied only over a relevant range of operations. The

relevant range of operations is the normal operating range for a business. Except for unusually difficult or prosperous times, management typically plans for operations within a range of volume neither close to zero nor maximum capacity. The relevant range for planning excludes extremely high and low operating levels that are unlikely to occur. The validity of assuming a specific cost is fixed or variable is more acceptable when operations are within the relevant range. As shown in Exhibit 23.2, a curvilinear cost can be treated as variable and linear if the relevant range covers volumes where it has a near constant slope.

A relevant range may not be applicable to all cost items. For example, production supervisory salaries will increase as more production shifts are added. If production in each shift is 1,000 units, the initial relevant range for supervisory salaries is 0 to 1,000 and increases in steps of 1,000. But factory rent increases only when a company rents more space. Rental cost remains the same up to a production level of, say, 3,000 units from the three shifts. The initial relevant range for this cost item is then 0 to 3,000 units of production and increases in steps of 3,000. A company cannot keep track of all these different relevant ranges. Management must plan according to the normal relevant range of activity. If the normal range of activity changes, some costs may need reclassification.

Estimates from Cost-Volume-Profit Analysis

CVP analysis yields approximate answers to questions about costs, volumes, and profits. These answers don't have to be precise because the analysis makes rough estimates about the future. As long as managers understand that CVP analysis gives estimates, it can be a useful tool for starting the planning process.

Recall the opening article and the decision by the controller at **Maxum** to use CVP analysis. While Maxum's variable costs per unit appeared to be stable, the proposed volume was well beyond the current relevant range of its production capacity. Maxum was already near capacity during its peak months. After including the new fixed costs necessary to expand production capacity, Maxum set a rough price to recover all relevant costs and contribute 15% to overhead and income.

CVP analysis is only a starting point. Other qualitative factors must be considered. The large capital outlay for a second manufacturing facility would increase Maxum's fixed costs. These fixed costs would leverage the company and make it vulnerable in a business downturn. This is because fixed costs don't decline if volume does. Also, the proposal would mean about 50% of Maxum's business is with one buyer. Maxum could end up being a captive supplier for Sport Marine. This would make it vulnerable to pressure for future price concessions.

Flash *back*

7. Fixed cost divided by the contribution margin ratio yields the:

a. Break-even point in dollars.

b. Contribution margin per unit.

c. Break-even point in units.

8. A company sells a product for $90 per unit with variable costs of $54 per unit. What is the contribution margin ratio?

9. Refer to *Flashback* no. 8 above. If fixed costs for the period are $90,000, what is the break-even point in dollars?

10. What are the three basic assumptions used in CVP analysis?

Answers—p. 1006

Applying Cost-Volume-Profit Analysis

Managers consider a variety of strategies in planning business operations. These strategies often affect costs and revenues for the company. Cost-volume-profit analysis is useful in helping managers evaluate the likely effects of these strategies. This section explains several applications of cost-volume-profit analysis.

Computing Income from Sales

C3 Describe several applications of cost-volume-profit analysis.

An important question managers often need an answer to is, "What is the predicted amount of income from a predicted level of sales?" To answer this, we look at four variables in CVP analysis. These variables and their relations to income (pre-tax) are shown in Exhibit 23.12. We use these relations to compute income from predicted sales and cost levels.

Exhibit 23.12
Income Relations in CVP Analysis

Income (pre-tax) = Sales − [Variable costs + Fixed costs]

or

Income (pre-tax) = Sales − Variable costs − Fixed costs

To illustrate, let's assume the management of Rydell expects to sell 1,500 product units this month. What is the amount of income if this sales level is achieved? At this level, revenues are $150,000, computed as 1,500 units × $100. Rydell's fixed costs are $24,000 per month. Its variable costs per unit are $70, and total variable costs for 1,500 units are $105,000 (1,500 units × $70). Using the relations from Exhibit 23.12 and substituting these amounts, we compute Rydell's expected income as shown in Exhibit 23.13.

Exhibit 23.13
Computing Expected Income from Expected Sales

Income (pre-tax) = [1,500 units × $100] − [1,500 units × $70] − $24,000
= $21,000

The $21,000 income does not include the effects of income taxes. Recall that corporations must pay income taxes. If management wants to find the amount of *after-tax* income from selling 1,500 units, they must apply the proper tax rate to the $21,000. If the tax rate is 25%, then income tax is $5,250 and net income is $15,750. Management would then determine whether this net income is an adequate return on assets invested. Management should also look at whether sales and income can be increased by raising or lowering prices. CVP analysis is a good tool for addressing these kinds of "what if" questions.

"How many
units must I sell
to earn $50,000?"

Computing Sales for a Target Income

Many companies' annual plans are based on certain income targets. Rydell's income target for year 2000 is to increase 1999 income by 10%. When 1999 income is known, Rydell easily computes its target income for 2000. CVP analysis helps in determining the sales level needed to achieve the target income. Computing this sales level is important because planning for the year is then based on this level. We use the formula shown in Exhibit 23.14 to compute sales for a target after-tax income.

Exhibit 23.14
Computing Sales (Dollars) for a Target Income[4]

$$\textbf{Dollar sales at target income} = \frac{\textbf{Fixed costs} + \textbf{Target income} + \textbf{Income taxes}}{\textbf{Contribution margin ratio}}$$

[4] To obtain this formula, we define: S = Sales in units; R = Revenue per unit; F = Fixed costs per period; V = Variable cost per unit; N = Target net income; T = Income taxes; $S \times R$ = Dollar sales; $S \times V$ = Total variable cost. Then recall that: Contribution margin ratio = $(R - V)/R$. The after-tax target net income is then defined as:

$$(S \times R) - F - (S \times V) - T = N$$
$$(S \times R) - (S \times V) = F + N + T$$
$$S \times (R - V) = F + N + T$$
$$S = (F + N + T)/(R - V)$$
$$S \times R = [(F + N + T) \times R]/(R - V)$$
$$S \times R = (F + N + T) \times [R/(R - V)]$$
$$S \times R = (F + N + T)/[(R - V)/R]$$
$$S \times R = (F + N + T)/\text{Contribution margin ratio}$$

To illustrate, we return to Rydell, which has monthly fixed costs of \$24,000 and a 30% contribution margin ratio. Let's assume it sets a target monthly after-tax income of \$9,000 when the tax rate is 25%. This means the before-tax income is targeted at \$12,000 [\$9,000/(1 − .25)] with a tax expense of \$3,000. Using the formula in Exhibit 23.14 we find \$160,000 of sales are needed to produce an \$18,000 net income after taxes. We show this computation in Exhibit 23.15.

Exhibit 23.15

Rydell's Dollar Sales for a Target Income

$$\text{Dollar sales at target income} = \frac{\$24{,}000 + \$9{,}000 + \$3{,}000}{30\%} = \$120{,}000$$

We can alternatively use a formula to compute *unit sales* instead of dollar sales. To do this we need only substitute the *contribution margin* in place of the contribution margin ratio in the denominator. This gives us the number of units needed to be sold to reach the target after-tax income level. Exhibit 23.16 illustrates this application to Rydell Company. The two computations in Exhibits 23.15 and 23.16 are equivalent because sales of 1,200 units at \$100 per unit equals \$120,000 of sales.

Exhibit 23.16

Computing Sales (Units) for a Target Income

$$\textbf{Unit sales at target income} = \frac{\textbf{Fixed costs} + \textbf{Target income} + \textbf{Income taxes}}{\textbf{Contribution margin}}$$

$$= \frac{\$24{,}000 + \$9{,}000 + \$3{,}000}{\$30} = 1{,}200 \text{ units}$$

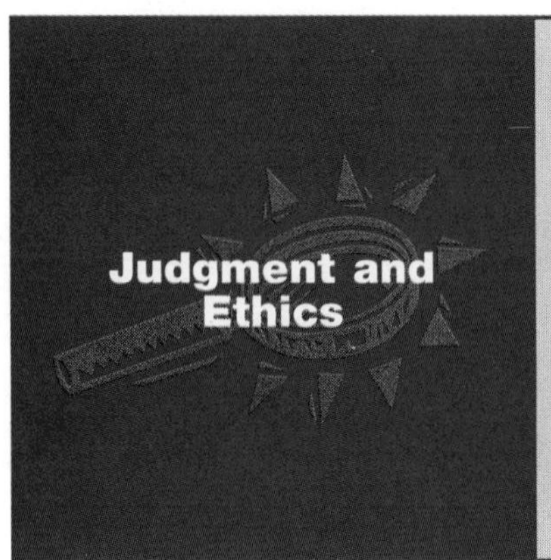

Management Trainee

You are part of a management trainee group debating a proposed product launch. A crucial factor is the range of income levels from different sales projections. Sales projections are subjective given the product has not been produced before. One team member suggests they pick numbers producing favorable income numbers because any estimate is "as good as any other." Another crucial factor is fixed and variable cost predictions that are being estimated from a scatter diagram of 20 months' production on a comparable product. But these cost predictions do not support the investment. A team member asks whether less favorable data points can be dropped from the analysis to see if the cost picture is improved. Your role is to conduct a cost-volume-profit analysis to reflect these suggestions. What do you do?

Answer—p. 1005

Computing the Margin of Safety

All companies desire to sell more than the break-even number of units and earn income. The excess of expected sales over the break-even sales level is called a company's **margin of safety.** The margin of safety is the amount that sales can drop before the company incurs a loss. It can be expressed in units, in dollars, or even as a percent of the predicted level of sales.

To illustrate, if Rydell's expected sales are \$100,000, the margin of safety is \$20,000 above break-even sales of \$80,000. As a percent, the margin of safety is 20% of expected sales as shown in Exhibit 23.17.

$$\textbf{Margin of safety (in percent)} = \frac{\textbf{Expected sales} - \textbf{Break-even sales}}{\textbf{Expected sales}} = \frac{\$100{,}000 - \$80{,}000}{\$100{,}000} = 20\%$$

Exhibit 23.17
Computing Margin of Safety (in Percent)

Management needs to assess whether this margin of safety is adequate in light of various factors. These factors include sales variability, competition, consumer tastes, and economic conditions.

Paging Out of Business!
Just a few years ago, the paging industry buzzed with promise. As the rage to page swept the nation, beeper operators saw subscriber rolls triple. But recently, the messages beeped to paging executives are coming from concerned stockholders. Determined to outdo competitors, operators spent freely to expand their networks, and many relied on low-margin paging to grab market share. Price competition led to paging companies giving business to resellers—companies that lease services at a discount and then resell them to subscribers. But many paging companies are charging resellers less than $3 a month, compared with the $9 they charge consumers. **Paging Network,** the biggest carrier, charged some resellers under $1, less than a third of what is needed to break even. Its CEO now admits the low-price strategy was flawed, and claims "We don't want to be in that (price-cutting) business." [Source: "Scary Signals on Pagers," *Business Week,* December 29, 1997.]

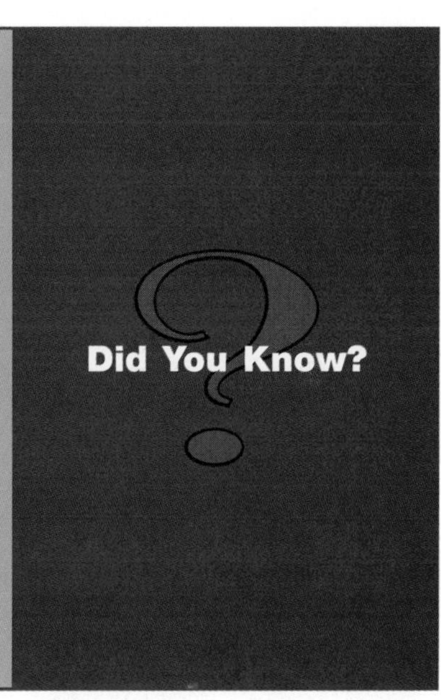

Sensitivity Analysis

It is often useful for us to know the effects of changing some estimates used in CVP analysis. This is because they are *estimates* and not actual values. For instance, we may want to know what happens if we reduce a product's selling price to increase sales. Or, we may want to know what happens to income if we install a new machine that increases fixed costs but reduces variable costs. If we can describe how these changes affect a company's fixed costs, variable costs, selling price, and volume, we can use CVP analysis to predict income.

To illustrate, let's assume Rydell Company is looking into buying a new machine that would increase monthly fixed costs from $24,000 to $30,000, but decrease variable costs from $70 per unit to $60 per unit. The product's selling price will remain unchanged at $100. This also results in increases in both the unit contribution margin and the contribution margin ratio. The new contribution margin per unit is $40 ($100 − $60) and the new contribution margin ratio is 40% of selling price ($40/$100). The manager wants to know what the break-even point would be if this machine is bought.

We use CVP analysis to help answer that question. If Rydell buys the machine, its new break-even point in dollars would be $75,000. This is computed as shown in Exhibit 23.18.

$$\textbf{New break-even point in dollars} = \frac{\textbf{New fixed costs}}{\textbf{New contribution margin ratio}} = \frac{\$30{,}000}{40\%} = \$75{,}000$$

Exhibit 23.18
Computing Break-Even When Changes Occur

The new fixed costs and the new contribution margin ratio can also be used to address other issues including computation of (a) expected income for a given sales level and (b) the sales level needed to earn a target income. Another use of sensitivity analysis is to generate three different sets of revenue and cost estimates that are: *optimistic, pessimistic,* and *most likely.* Different CVP analyses based on these estimates provide management with different scenarios that they can analyze and use in planning business strategy.

Flash back

11. A company has fixed costs of $50,000 and a 25% contribution margin ratio. How many dollars of sales are necessary for the company to achieve an after-tax net income of $120,000 if the tax rate is 20%? *(a)* $800,000; *(b)* $680,000; *(c)* $600,000.

12. If the contribution margin ratio decreases from 50% to 25%, what can be said about unit sales needed to achieve the same target income level?

13. What is a company's margin of safety?

Answers—p. 1006

Computing Multiproduct Break-Even Point

P4 Compute break-even point for a multiproduct company.

To this point we have looked only at cases where the company produces a single product. This was to keep the basic CVP analysis simple. But many companies produce multiple products. We can modify the CVP analysis for use when a company produces and sells several products.

An important assumption in a multiproduct setting is that the sales mix of different products is known and remains constant during the planning period. **Sales mix** is the ratio (proportion) of the sales volume for the various products. For instance, if a company normally sells 10,000 footballs, 5,000 baseballs, and 4,000 basketballs per month, then its sales mix can be expressed as 10:5:4 for footballs, baseballs, and basketballs.

To apply multiproduct CVP analysis, we need to estimate the break-even point by using a composite unit. A **composite unit** consists of a specific number of units of each product in proportion to their expected sales mix. Multiproduct CVP analysis treats this composite unit like a single product.

To illustrate, let's look at **Hair-Today,** a stylist salon, that offers three cuts: basic, ultra, and budget in the ratio of 4 units of basic to 2 units of ultra to 1 unit of budget (expressed as 4:2:1). Management wants to estimate its break-even point for next year. Unit selling prices for these three cuts are: basic, $10; ultra, $16; and budget, $8. Using the 4:2:1 sales mix, the selling price of a composite unit of the three products is computed as:

4 units of basic @ $10 per unit	$40
2 units of ultra @ $16 per unit	32
1 unit of budget @ $8 per unit	8
Selling price of a composite unit	**$80**

The fixed costs of Hair-Today are $96,000 per year and its variable costs of the three products are: basic, $6.50; ultra, $9.00; and budget, $4.00. This means that variable costs for a composite unit of these products are:

4 units of basic @ $6.50 per unit	$26
2 units of ultra @ $9.00 per unit	18
1 unit of budget @ $4.00 per unit	4
Variable costs of a composite unit	**$48**

Once we determine the variable costs and the selling price of a composite unit of the company's products, we can compute Hair-Today's contribution margin for a composite unit. This is computed as $32, by subtracting the variable costs ($48) of a composite unit from its selling price ($80).

We can, for instance, use the $32 contribution margin to determine Hair-Today's break-even point in composite units as shown in Exhibit 23.19.

Break-Even Point in Composite Units

$$\textbf{Break-even point in composite units} = \frac{\textbf{Fixed costs}}{\textbf{Contribution margin per composite unit}}$$

$$= \frac{\$96{,}000}{\$32} = 3{,}000 \text{ composite units}$$

This computation implies Hair-Today breaks even when it sells 3,000 composite units of its products. To determine how many units of each product must be sold to break even, we multiply the number of units of each product in the composite by 3,000:

Basic: 4 × 3,000	12,000 units
Ultra: 2 × 3,000	6,000 units
Budget: 1 × 3,000	3,000 units

The schedule in Exhibit 23.20 verifies these results by showing Hair-Today's revenues and costs at this break-even point.

Exhibit 23.20

Multiproduct Break-Even Income Statement

HAIR-TODAY
Forecasted Income Statement at Break-Even Point

	Basic	Ultra	Budget	Combined
Revenues:				
Basic (12,000 @ $10)	$120,000			
Ultra (6,000 @ $16)		$96,000		
Budget (3,000 @ $8)			$24,000	
Total revenues				$240,000
Variable costs:				
Basic (12,000 @ $6.5)	78,000			
Ultra (6,000 @ $9)		54,000		
Budget (3,000 @ $4)			12,000	
Total variable costs				144,000
Contribution margin	$ 42,000	$42,000	$12,000	$ 96,000
Fixed costs				96,000
Net income				$ 0

A CVP analysis using composite units can be used to answer a variety of planning questions. Once a product mix is set, all answers are based on the assumption that it remains constant at all sales levels, just like other factors in the analysis. But we also can vary the sales mix to see what happens under alternative strategies.

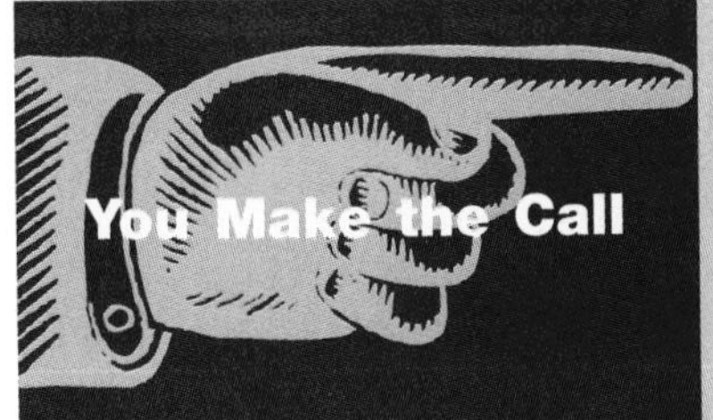

Marketing Manager
You are the marketing manager of a communications firm, responsible for marketing cellular phones and accessories. A CVP analysis indicates that with the current sales mix and price levels, the product line will just break even. You want to earn at least 10% more income than you earned last year. What alternatives do you have for achieving the desired income level?

Answer—p. 1005

Flash back

14. The sales mix of a company's two products, X and Y, is 2:1. Unit price and variable cost data are:

	X	Y
Unit sales price	$5	$4
Unit variable cost	2	2

What is the contribution margin per composite unit? *(a)* $5; *(b)* $10; *(c)* $8.

15. What additional assumption about sales mix must be made in doing a conventional CVP analysis for a company that produces and sells more than one product?

Answers—p. 1006

USING THE INFORMATION

Operating Leverage

A2 Analyze changes in sales levels using the degree of operating leverage.

CVP analysis is especially useful when management begins the planning process and wishes to predict outcomes of alternative strategies. These strategies can involve changes in selling prices, fixed costs, variable costs, sales volume, and product mix. Managers are interested in looking at the effects of changes in some or all of these factors.

One goal of all managers is to get maximum benefits from their fixed costs Managers would like to use 100% of their production capacity so that fixed costs are spread over the largest possible number of units. This would decrease fixed cost per unit and increase income.

The extent, or relative size, of fixed costs in the total cost structure is known as **operating leverage.** Companies having a greater proportion of fixed costs in their total cost structure are said to have higher operating leverage. An example of this would be a company that chooses to automate its processes instead of using direct labor. This would increase its fixed costs and lower its variable costs.

A useful managerial tool for assessing the effect on income of changes in the level of sales is the **degree of operating leverage (DOL).** The DOL is computed by taking a **ratio of total contribution margin (in dollars) to pre-tax income.**

To illustrate, let's return to Rydell Company. At a sales level of 1,200 units, the total contribution margin for Rydell is $36,000 (1,200 units × $30 contribution margin per unit). Its pre-tax income, after subtracting fixed costs of $24,000, is $12,000 (computed as $36,000 minus $24,000). This means the degree of operating leverage for Rydell at this sales level is 3.0, computed as contribution margin divided by pre-tax income (or $36,000 ÷ $12,000).

We can use DOL to measure the effect of changes in the level of sales for pre-tax income. For instance, suppose Rydell expects sales to increase by 10%. If this increase is within the relevant range of operations, we can expect this 10% increase in sales to result in a 30% increase in pre-tax income. This is computed as DOL multiplied by the increase in sales, or 3.0 × 10%. Similar analyses can be done for expected decreases in sales.

Summary

C1 Describe different types of cost behavior in relation to production and sales volume. A cost's behavior is described in terms of how its amount changes in relation to production or sales volume changes in a relevant range. Fixed costs remain constant to changes in sales volume. Total variable costs change in direct proportion to sales volume changes. Mixed costs display the effects of both fixed and variable components. Stepwise costs remain constant over a small volume range, then change by a lump sum and remain constant over another volume range, and so on. Curvilinear costs change in a nonlinear relation to volume changes.

C2 Identify assumptions in cost-volume-profit analysis and explain their impact. Conventional cost-volume-profit analysis is based on assumptions that the selling price of the product remains constant and that variable and fixed costs behave in a manner consistent with their variable and fixed classifications. These assumptions are not likely to hold at volume levels outside the relevant range of operations. If the assumptions do not apply, CVP analysis is less useful.

C3 Describe several applications of cost-volume-profit analysis. Cost-volume-profit analysis can be used to develop predictions of what can happen under alternative strategies concerning sales volume, selling prices, variable costs, or fixed costs. Applications include "what if" analysis, computing sales for a target income, and break-even analysis.

A1 Compare the scatter diagram, high-low, and regression methods of estimating costs. Cost estimates from the scatter diagram are based on a visual fit of the cost line and are subject to interpretation. Estimates from the high-low method are based only on two sets of values corresponding to the lowest and highest sales volumes. The least-squares regression method is a statistical technique and uses all the data points. The regression method usually is considered superior to the other two methods.

A2 Analyze changes in sales using the degree of operating leverage. The extent, or relative size, of fixed costs in a company's total cost structure is known as operating leverage. One tool useful in assessing the effect of changes in sales on income is the degree of operating leverage, or DOL. DOL is the ratio of the contribution margin divided by pre-tax income. This ratio can be used to determine the expected percent change in income given a percent change in sales.

P1 Determine cost estimates using three different methods. The three different methods used to estimate costs are the scatter diagram, the high-low method, and least-squares regression. All three methods use past data to estimate costs.

P2 Compute break-even point for a single product company. A company's break-even point for a period is the sales volume at which total revenues equal total costs. To compute a break-even point in terms of sales units, divide total fixed costs by the contribution margin per unit. To compute a break-even point in terms of sales dollars, divide total fixed costs by the contribution margin ratio.

P3 Graph costs and revenues for a single product company. The costs and revenues for a company can be graphically illustrated. This type of presentation is called a CVP chart. In this chart, the horizontal axis represents the number of units sold and the vertical axis represents dollars of sales or costs. Straight lines are used to depict both costs and revenues on the CVP chart.

P4 Compute break-even point for a multiproduct company. CVP analysis can be applied to a multiproduct company by expressing the predicted sales volume in terms of composite units of product. A composite unit consists of a specific number of units of each product in proportion to their expected sales mix. Multiproduct CVP analysis treats this composite unit like a single product.

Guidance Answers to **You Make the Call**

Manager of Operations

Without the availability of past data, none of the three methods described in the chapter can be used to measure cost behavior. In this situation, the manager must investigate if s/he can get access to data from similar manufacturing systems, such as from other plants within the company. If not, the manager can attempt to obtain this information from other companies. But this is difficult due to the sensitive nature of the data. In the absence of any data, the manager should develop a list of the different production inputs and identify input-output relations. This understanding provides preliminary guidance to the manager in measuring cost behavior. After several months, actual cost data are available for analysis.

Marketing Manager

You must first compute the level of sales required to achieve the desired net income. Then you must conduct sensitivity analysis by varying the price, sales mix, and cost estimates. Results from the sensitivity analysis provide you with information you can use to assess the possibility of reaching the target sales level based on the price and sales mix estimates. For instance, you may have to pursue aggressive marketing strategies to push the high margin products, or you may have to cut prices to increase sales and profits, or some other suggested strategy may emerge.

Guidance Answer to **Judgment and Ethics**

Management Trainee

Your dilemma is whether to go along with the suggestion to "manage" the numbers to make the project look like it will achieve sufficient profits to allow it to be approved. You should not succumb to this suggestion. Many people will likely be affected negatively if you manage the predicted numbers and the project eventually is unprofitable. Moreover, if it does fail, it is likely an investigation would reveal that data in the proposal were "fixed" to make it look good. Probably the only benefit from managing the numbers is the short-term payoff of pleasing the manager who proposed the project. One way to deal with this dilemma and comply with one's professional responsibilities is to prepare several analyses showing results under different assumptions, and then let senior management decide whether to go ahead in light of the information about the uncertainties of success. A point to remember is that it seldom makes sense for groups within an organization to attempt to deceive each other. Major decisions often affect many people in addition to those who make them, and their effects can linger for a long time. You might also recall the Institute of Management Accountants' *Standards of Ethical Conduct* (at the end of the book) include several provisions that apply to this situation.

Guidance Answers to 

1. *b*
2. A fixed cost remains unchanged in total amount regardless of production levels.
3. The cost of raw materials is a variable cost because the total cost changes in proportion to volume changes.
4. *b*
5. The high-low method ignores all of the costs and sales volume data points except the costs corresponding to the highest and lowest sales volume.
6. *c*
7. *a*
8. ($90 − $54)/$90 = 40%
9. $90,000/40% = $225,000
10. The three basic assumptions are: (1) selling price per unit is constant; (2) variable costs per unit are constant; and (3) fixed costs are constant.
11. *a;* Two steps are required:
    (1) Before-tax income = $120,000/(1 − .20) = $150,000
    (2) $\frac{\$50{,}000 + \$120{,}000 + (\$150{,}000 \times 20\%)}{25\%} = \$800{,}000$
12. If the contribution margin ratio decreases from 50% to 25%, unit sales would have to double.
13. A company's margin of safety is the excess of the predicted sales level over its break-even sales level.
14. *c;* Selling price of a composite unit:

2 units of X @ $5 per unit	$10
1 unit of Y @ $4 per unit	4
Selling price of a composite unit	$14

Variable costs of a composite unit:

2 units of X @ $2 per unit	$4
1 unit of Y @ $2 per unit	2
Variable costs of a composite unit	$6

Therefore, contribution margin per composite unit is $8.

15. It must be assumed that the sales mix remains unchanged at all sales levels in the relevant range.

Demonstration Problem

Sport Caps Co. manufactures and sells sporting caps for different sports activities. The fixed costs of operating the company are $150,000 per month, and the variable costs for caps are $5 per unit. The caps are sold at $8 per unit. The fixed costs provide a production capacity of up to 100,000 caps per month.

Required

1. Use the formulas in the chapter to compute the:
   a. Contribution margin per cap.
   b. Break-even point in terms of the number of caps produced and sold.
   c. Amount of net income at 30,000 caps sold per month (ignore taxes).
   d. Amount of net income at 85,000 caps sold per month (ignore taxes).
   e. Quantity of caps to be produced and sold to provide $45,000 of after-tax income, assuming an income tax rate of 25%.
2. Draw a CVP chart for the company, showing cap output on the horizontal axis. Identify the break-even point and the amount of pre-tax income when the level of cap production is 75,000. (Omit the fixed cost line.)
3. Use the formulas in the chapter to compute the:
   a. Contribution margin ratio.
   b. Break-even point in terms of sales dollars.
   c. Amount of net income at $250,000 of sales per month (ignore taxes).
   d. Amount of net income at $600,000 of sales per month (ignore taxes).
   e. Dollars of sales needed to provide $45,000 of after-tax income, assuming an income tax rate of 25%.

Planning the Solution

- Identify the formulas in the chapter for the required items expressed in units and solve them using the data given in the problem.
- Draw a CVP chart that reflects the facts in the problem. The horizontal axis should plot the volume in units up to 100,000, and the vertical axis should plot the total dollars up to $800,000. Plot the total cost line as upward-sloping, starting at the fixed cost level ($150,000) on the vertical axis and increasing until it reaches $650,000 at the maximum volume of 100,000 units. Verify that the break-even point (where the two lines cross) equals the amount you computed in (1).
- Identify the formulas in the chapter for the required items expressed in dollars and solve them using the data given in the problem.

Solution to Demonstration Problem

1. a. Contribution margin per cap = Selling price per unit − Variable cost per unit = $8 − $5 = $3

b. Break-even point in caps $= \dfrac{\text{Fixed costs}}{\text{Contribution margin per cap}} = \dfrac{\$150{,}000}{\$3} = \underline{\underline{50{,}000 \text{ caps}}}$

c. Net income at 30,000 caps sold = (Units × Contribution margin per unit) − Fixed costs = (30,000 × $3) − $150,000 = −$60,000 (loss)

d. Net income at 85,000 caps sold = (Units × Contribution margin per unit) − Fixed costs = (85,000 × $3) − $150,000 = $105,000 profit

e. Pre-tax income = $45,000 / (1 − .25) = $60,000
Income taxes = $60,000 × 25% = $15,000
Units needed for $45,000 income

$$= \frac{\text{Fixed costs} + \text{Target income} + \text{Income taxes}}{\text{Contribution margin per cap}}$$

$$= \frac{\$150{,}000 + \$45{,}000 + \$15{,}000}{\$3} = \underline{\underline{70{,}000 \text{ caps}}}$$

2. CVP chart:

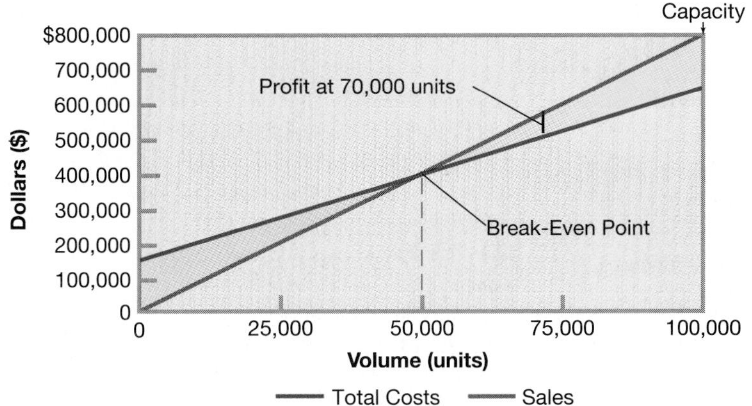

3. a. Contribution margin ratio $= \dfrac{\text{Contribution margin per unit}}{\text{Selling price per unit}} = \dfrac{\$3}{\$8} = \underline{\underline{.375}}, \text{ or } \underline{\underline{37.5\%}}$

b. Break-even point in dollars $= \dfrac{\text{Fixed costs}}{\text{Contribution margin ratio}} = \dfrac{\$150{,}000}{37.5\%} = \underline{\underline{\$400{,}000}}$

c. Net income at sales of $250,000 = (Sales × Contribution margin ratio) − Fixed costs = ($250,000 × 37.5%) − $150,000 = −$56,250 (loss)

d. Net income at sales of $600,000 = (Sales × Contribution margin ratio) − Fixed costs = ($600,000 × 37.5%) − $150,000 = $75,000 income

e. Dollars of sales to yield $45,000 income

$$= \frac{\text{Fixed costs} + \text{Target income} + \text{Income taxes}}{\text{Contribution margin ratio}}$$

$$= \frac{\$150{,}000 + \$45{,}000 + \$15{,}000}{37.5\%} = \underline{\underline{\$560{,}000}}$$

Glossary

Break-even point the sales level at which a company neither earns a profit nor incurs a loss. (p. 994).

Composite unit consists of a specific number of units of each product in proportion to their expected sales mix. (p. 1002).

Contribution margin per unit the amount that the sale of one unit contributes toward recovering fixed costs and earning profit. (p. 994).

Contribution margin ratio the contribution margin per unit expressed as a percent of the product's selling price. (p. 995).

Cost-volume-profit (CVP) analysis an early step in business planning; includes predicting the volume of activity, the costs incurred, revenues received, and profits earned. (p. 988).

Curvilinear cost a cost that changes with volume but not at a constant rate such as with pure variable costs. (p. 991).

CVP chart a graphic representation of cost-volume-profit relations. (p. 996).

Degree of operating leverage (DOL) the ratio of contribution margin divided by pre-tax income; used in assessing the effect on income of changes in sales. (p. 1004).

Estimated line of cost behavior a line on a scatter diagram drawn to fit the past relation between cost and sales volume. (p. 992).

Fixed cost a cost that remains unchanged in total amount even when production volume varies. (p. 988).

High-low method a means to draw an estimated line of cost behavior by connecting costs associated with the highest and lowest sales volume with a straight line. (p. 992).

Least-squares regression a statistical method for deriving an estimated line of cost behavior that is more precise than the high-low method and a scatter diagram. (p. 993).

Margin of safety the excess of expected sales over the level of break-even sales. (p. 1000).

Mixed cost a cost that behaves like a combination of a fixed and a variable cost. (p. 990).

Operating leverage the extent, or relative size, of fixed costs in the total cost structure. (p. 1004).

Relevant range of operations a company's normal operating range; excludes extremely high and low volumes that are not likely to be encountered. (p. 998).

Sales mix the ratio of the sales volumes for the various products sold by a company. (p. 1002).

Scatter diagram a graph used to display data about past cost behavior and sales volumes as points on a diagram. (p. 991).

Step-wise cost a cost that remains fixed over limited ranges of volumes but changes by a lump sum when volume changes occur beyond these limited ranges. (p. 990).

Variable cost a cost that changes in proportion to changes in production volume. (p. 989).

Questions

1. What is the usefulness of cost-volume-profit analysis?
2. What is a variable cost? Identify two variable costs.
3. When volume increases, do variable costs per unit increase, decrease, or stay the same within the relevant range of activity? Explain.
4. When volume increases, do fixed costs per unit increase, decrease, or stay the same within the relevant range of activity? Explain.
5. How do step-wise costs and curvilinear costs differ?
6. In performing CVP analysis for a manufacturing company, what simplifying assumption is usually made about the volume of production and the volume of sales?
7. What two arguments tend to justify classifying all costs as either fixed or variable even though individual costs might not behave perfectly consistently with these classifications?
8. How does assuming that operating activity occurs within a relevant range affect cost-volume-profit analysis?
9. List three methods to measure cost behavior.
10. How is a scatter diagram used in identifying and measuring the behavior of a company's costs?
11. In cost-volume-profit analysis, what is the estimated profit at the break-even point?
12. Assume a straight line on a CVP chart intersects the vertical axis at the level of fixed costs and has a positive slope, such that it rises with each additional unit of volume by the amount of the variable costs per unit. What does this line represent?
13. Why are fixed costs depicted as a horizontal line on a CVP chart?
14. Two similar companies each have sales of $20,000 and total costs of $15,000 for a month. Company A's total costs include $10,000 of variable costs and $5,000 of fixed costs. If Company B's total costs include $4,000 of variable costs and $11,000 of fixed costs, which company will enjoy a greater profit if sales double?
15. _____ of _____ measures the expected sales in excess of the level of break-even sales.
16. NIKE manufactured hats for sale during the Olympic games. Identify some of the variable and fixed product costs associated with that process. [Hint: Limit costs to product costs.]
17. Reebok is thinking of expanding production of its most popular walking shoe by 65%. Do you expect its variable and fixed costs to stay within the relevant range? Explain.

Quick Study

QS 23-1
Identifying cost behavior

Listed below are four series of separate costs measured at various volume levels. Examine each series and identify whether it is best described as a fixed, variable, step-wise, or curvilinear cost.

Volume (Units)	Series 1	Series 2	Series 3	Series 4
0	$ 0	$450	$ 800	$100
100	800	450	800	105
200	1,600	450	800	120
300	2,400	450	1,600	145
400	3,200	450	1,600	190
500	4,000	450	2,400	250
600	4,800	450	2,400	320

QS 23-2
Identifying cost behavior

For each of the following, determine whether it is best described as a fixed, variable, or mixed cost:

a. Maintenance of factory machinery.
b. Packaging expense.
c. Wages of an assembly-line worker paid on the basis of acceptable units produced.
d. Factory supervisor's salary.
e. Taxes on factory building.
f. Rubber used to manufacture athletic shoes.

QS 23-3
Estimating cost behavior

This scatter diagram reflects past maintenance hours and their corresponding maintenance costs:

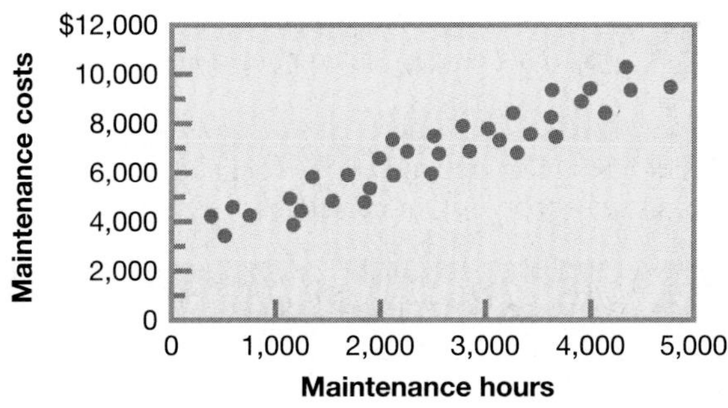

a. Draw an estimated line of cost behavior.
b. Estimate the fixed and variable components of maintenance costs.

QS 23-4
Identifying CVP assumptions

Which one of the following is an assumption that underlies cost-volume-profit analysis?

a. Selling price per unit must change in proportion to the number of units sold in the planning period.
b. All costs have approximately the same relevant range.
c. For costs classified as variable, the costs per unit of output must change constantly.
d. For costs classified as fixed, the costs per unit of output must remain constant.

QS 23-5
Contribution margin and break-even units P2

ATI Phone Company sells its cordless phone for $100 per unit. Fixed costs total $180,000 and variable costs are $40 per unit. Determine *(a)* contribution margin per unit and *(b)* break-even point in units.

QS 23-6
Contribution margin ratio and break-even P2

Refer to QS 23-5. Determine *(a)* contribution margin ratio and *(b)* break-even point in dollars.

QS 23-7
CVP analysis and target income C3, P2

Refer to QS 23-5. Assume ATI Phone Co. is subject to an income tax rate of 30%. Compute the units of product that must be sold to earn after-tax income of $140,000.

QS 23-8
Multiproduct break-even P4

Beeper Company manufactures and sells two products, green beepers and gold beepers, in the ratio of 5:3. Fixed costs are $85,000 and the contribution margin per composite unit is $170. What amounts of both green beepers and gold beepers are sold at the break-even point?

QS 23-9
Analyzing operating leverage A2

A high proportion of Company A's total costs are variable with respect to units sold whereas a high proportion of Company B's total costs are fixed with respect to units sold. Which company is likely to have a higher degree of operating leverage (DOL)? Explain.

Exercises

Exercise 23-1
Defining cost behavior C1

The left column lists several categories of costs. The right column presents short definitions of those costs. In the blank space beside each of the numbers in the right column, write the letter of the cost best described by the definition.

a. Total cost
b. Mixed cost
c. Variable cost
d. Curvilinear cost
e. Step-wise cost
f. Fixed cost

_____ **1.** This cost remains constant over a limited range of volume; when it reaches the end of its limited range, it changes by a lump sum and remains at that level until another limited range is exceeded.
_____ **2.** This cost has a component that remains the same over all volume levels and another component that increases in direct proportion to increases in volume.
_____ **3.** This cost increases when volume increases, but the increase is not constant for each unit produced.
_____ **4.** This cost remains constant over all volume levels within the productive capacity for the planning period.
_____ **5.** This cost increases in direct proportion to increases in volume; its amount is constant for each unit produced.
_____ **6.** This cost is the combined amount of all the other costs.

Exercise 23-2
Identifying cost behavior C1

Shown below are five series of costs measured at various volume levels. Examine each series and identify which is fixed, variable, mixed, step-wise, or curvilinear:

Volume (Units)	Series A	Series B	Series C	Series D	Series E
0	$ 0	$2,200	$ 0	$1,000	$3,000
400	3,200	2,700	6,000	1,000	3,000
800	6,400	3,200	6,600	2,000	3,000
1,200	9,600	3,700	7,200	2,000	3,000
1,600	12,800	4,200	8,200	3,000	3,000
2,000	16,000	4,700	9,600	3,000	3,000
2,400	19,200	5,200	13,500	4,000	3,000

Exercise 23-3
Identifying cost behavior in graphs C1

Shown below are five graphs representing various cost behaviors.

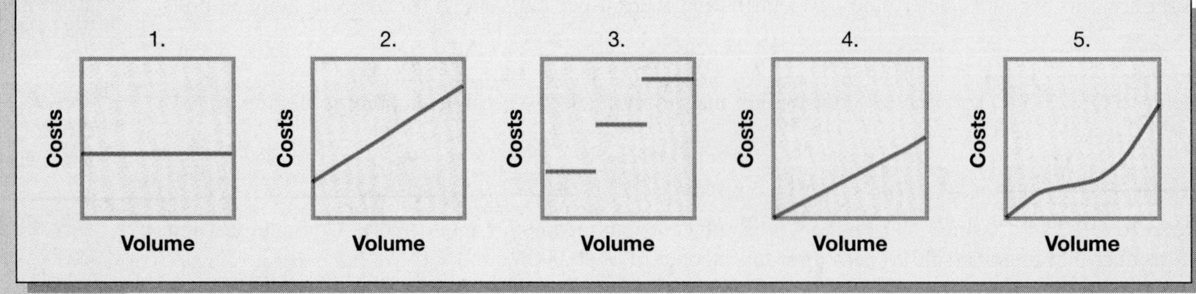

Required

a. Identify the cost behavior in each graph: mixed, step-wise, fixed, variable, or curvilinear.

b. Identify the graph (by number) that best illustrates the cost behavior described below:

(1) Factory policy requires one supervisor for every 30 factory workers.

(2) Real estate taxes on factory.

(3) Electricity charge that includes the standard monthly charge plus a charge for each kilowatt hour.

(4) Commissions to salespersons.

(5) Costs of hourly paid workers that provide substantial gains in efficiency when a few workers are added, but gradually smaller gains in efficiency when more workers are added.

Exercise 23-4
Measuring cost behavior using a scatter diagram
P1

A company's accounting system provides the following information about its monthly sales and the amount of cost in those months. Each unit sells for $500.

Month	Sales	Cost
1	$15,000	$10,100
2	11,500	7,500
3	10,500	7,000
4	7,500	5,500
5	9,000	6,000
6	12,500	9,500

Use this data to prepare a scatter diagram. Draw an estimated line of cost behavior and determine whether the cost appears to be variable, fixed, or mixed.

Exercise 23-5
Scatter diagram and measuring cost behavior
P1

Use the following information about monthly sales volume and its costs to prepare a scatter diagram. Draw a cost line that reflects the behavior displayed by this cost. Determine whether the cost is variable, step-wise, fixed, mixed, or curvilinear.

Period	Sales	Cost	Period	Sales	Cost
1	$380	$295	9	290	$195
2	400	280	10	160	120
3	100	115	11	120	115
4	200	200	12	360	275
5	240	195	13	140	130
6	310	275	14	222	205
7	340	295	15	190	130
8	270	215			

Exercise 23-6
Computing contribution margin and break-even point
P2, P3

Pace Company manufactures a single product that sells for $168 per unit. Total variable costs of the product are $126 per unit and the company's annual fixed costs are $630,000.

1. Use this information to compute the company's:

a. Contribution margin.

b. Contribution margin ratio.

c. Break-even point in units.

d. Break-even point in dollars of sales.

2. Draw a CVP chart for the company.

Exercise 23-7
Income reporting and break-even analysis
C3

Refer to Exercise 23-6 and prepare an income statement for Pace Company showing sales, variable costs, and fixed costs at the break-even point. Next, if Pace's fixed costs increase by $135,000, what amount of sales (in dollars) would be needed to break even?

Exercise 23-8
Computing sales to achieve target income
C3

The management of Pace Company (in Exercise 23-6) targets an annual after-tax income of $840,000. The company is subject to an income tax rate of 20%. Compute the:

a. Units of product that must be sold to earn the target after-tax net income.

b. Dollars of sales that must be achieved to earn the target after-tax net income.

Exercise 23-9
Forecasted income statement
C3

The sales manager of Pace Company (in Exercise 23-6) predicts that annual sales of the company's product will soon reach 40,000 units even though its price will increase to $200 per unit. According to the production manager, the variable costs are expected to increase to $140 per unit but fixed costs will remain at $630,000. The company's tax adviser expects the income tax rate to remain at 20%. What amounts of pre-tax and after-tax income can the company expect to earn from these expected changes? (*Hint:* Prepare forecasted income statement.)

Exercise 23-10
Unit and dollar sales using contribution margin
C3

The management of Grant Company thinks it will incur a total of $500,000 of variable costs and $800,000 of fixed costs while earning a pre-tax income of $100,000 in the next quarter. Management also predicts that the contribution margin per unit will be $60. Use this information to compute the *(a)* total expected dollar sales for the quarter and *(b)* number of units expected to be sold in the quarter.

Exercise 23-11
Computing variable and fixed costs
P3

Snap Company expects to sell 100,000 units of its product next year, which would generate total revenues of $12 million. Management predicts that pre-tax net income for next year will be $3,000,000 and that the contribution margin per unit will be $40.

Required

1. Use this information to compute next year's total expected *(a)* variable costs and *(b)* fixed costs.

2. Prepare a CVP chart from this information.

Exercise 23-12
Computing sales and variable costs using contribution margin
C3

The management of Waterloo Company predicts that it will incur fixed costs of $250,000 next year and that pre-tax income will be $350,000. The expected contribution margin ratio is 60%. Use this information to compute the amounts of *(a)* total dollar sales and *(b)* total variable costs.

Exercise 23-13
CVP analysis using composite units
P4

Home Company sells windows and doors in the ratio of 8:2 (8 windows for every 2 doors). The selling price of each window is $100 and the selling price of each door is $450. The variable cost of a window is $60 and the variable cost of a door is $300. Next year's fixed costs are expected to be $750,000. Use this information to determine the:

a. Selling price per composite unit

b. Variable costs per composite unit.

c. Break-even point in composite units.

d. Number of units of each product that will be sold at the break-even point.

Exercise 23-14
Computing and applying operating leverage
A2

Company A is a manufacturer with current sales of $1,000,000 and a 65% contribution margin. Its fixed costs equal $500,000. Company B is a consulting firm with current service revenues of $1,000,000 and a 25% contribution margin. Its fixed costs equal $100,000. Compute the degree of operating leverage (DOL) for each company. Identify which company benefits more from a 20% increase in sales and explain why.

Problems

Problem 23-1
Scatter diagram and estimating cost behavior
P1

Bricks Co.'s monthly sales and cost data for its operating activities of the past year are shown below. The management of the company wants to use these data to predict future fixed and variable costs.

Period	Sales	Total Cost
1	$160,000	$ 80,000
2	80,000	50,000
3	140,000	110,000
4	100,000	50,000
5	150,000	115,000
6	100,000	60,000
7	170,000	110,000
8	140,000	80,000
9	10,000	40,000
10	80,000	70,000
11	50,000	50,000
12	55,000	40,000

Required

1. Prepare a scatter diagram with sales volume (in $) plotted on the horizontal axis and total cost plotted on the vertical axis for Bricks Co.
2. Estimate the line of cost behavior by a visual inspection and draw it on the scatter diagram. (Assume a linear relation, which means that you should draw a straight cost line on the graph.)
3. Using the estimated line of cost behavior and the assumption that the future will be like the past, predict an amount of monthly fixed costs for Brick Co. Also, predict future variable costs per sales dollar.
4. Use the estimated line of cost behavior to predict future total costs when the sales volume is *(a)* $100,000 and *(b)* $150,000.

Check Figure Approximate slope of cost line, $0.50 per sales dollar

Problem 23-2
CVP analysis and chart
P2, P3

Long Co. manufactures and markets a number of rope products. Management is considering the future of Product XT, a special rope for hang gliding, which has not been as profitable as planned. Because this product is manufactured and marketed independently from the other products, its total costs can be precisely measured. Next year's plans call for a selling price of $150 per 100 yards. Its fixed costs for the year are expected to be $200,000, up to the maximum capacity of 550,000 yards. Forecasted variable costs are $100 per every 100 yards.

Required

1. Predict the break-even point for Product XT in terms of *(a)* sales units and *(b)* sales dollars.
2. Prepare a CVP chart for Product XT. Use 550,000 yards as the maximum number of sales units on the graph and $900,000 as the maximum number of dollars.
3. Prepare an income statement showing sales, variable costs, and fixed costs for Product XT at the break-even point.

Check Figure Break-even sales, $600,000

Problem 23-3
Targeting and forecasting income
C3

Little Co. sold 20,000 units of its only product and incurred a $50,000 loss (ignoring taxes) for the year as shown below:

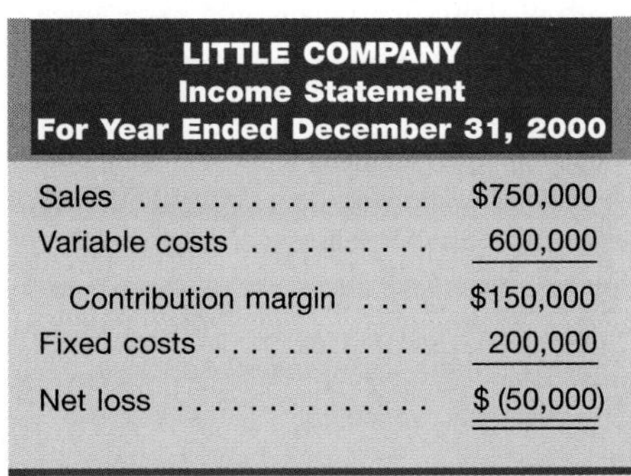

LITTLE COMPANY
Income Statement
For Year Ended December 31, 2000

Sales	$750,000
Variable costs	600,000
Contribution margin	$150,000
Fixed costs	200,000
Net loss	$ (50,000)

During a planning session for year 2001's activities, the production manager points out that variable costs can be reduced 50% by installing a machine that automates several operations. To obtain these savings, the company must increase its annual fixed costs by $150,000. The maximum capacity of the system would be 40,000 units per year.

Required

1. Compute break-even point in dollar sales for year 2000.
2. Compute break-even point in dollar sales for year 2001 assuming the machine is installed.
3. Prepare a forecasted income statement for 2001 that shows the expected results with the machine installed. Assume there will be no change in the selling price and no change in the number of units sold. The income tax rate is 30%.
4. Compute the sales level required to earn $140,000 of after-tax income in 2001 with the machine installed and with no change in the selling price.
5. Prepare a forecasted income statement that shows the results at the sales level computed in part (4).

Check Figure Required sales, 24,445 units

Problem 23-4
Break-even analysis and different cost structures

Beach Co. produces and sells two products, T and O. These products are manufactured in separate factories and marketed through different channels. They do not have any shared costs. This year, Beach sold 50,000 units of each product. The following income statements describe the financial results:

	Product T	Product O
Sales	$800,000	$800,000
Variable costs	560,000	100,000
Contribution margin	$240,000	$700,000
Fixed costs	100,000	560,000
Income before taxes	$140,000	$140,000
Income taxes (32% rate)	44,800	44,800
Net income	$ 95,200	$ 95,200

Required

Preparation Component

1. Compute the break-even point in dollars for each product.
2. Assume the company expects sales of each product to decline to 33,000 units next year, even though the price will remain unchanged. Prepare a forecasted income statement that shows the expected net income from the two products (assume a 32% tax rate for next year). Follow the format of the preceding statement and assume that any loss before taxes results in a tax savings.
3. Assume the company expects sales of each product to increase to 64,000 units next year, even though the price will remain unchanged. Prepare a forecasted income statement that shows the expected net income from the two products (assume a 32% tax rate for next year). Follow the format of the preceding statement.

Check Figure Part 3: After-tax income, Product O, $228,480

Analysis Component

4. If sales greatly decrease, which of these products would experience the greater loss? Explain.
5. Describe some factors that might have created the different cost structures for these two products.

Problem 23-5
Analyzing price and volume changes on profits

This year Clark Company sold 35,000 units of product at $16 per unit. Manufacturing and selling the product required $120,000 of fixed manufacturing costs and $180,000 of fixed selling and administrative expenses. This year's variable costs and expenses per unit are:

Material	$4.00
Direct labor (paid on the basis of completed units)	3.00
Variable manufacturing overhead costs	0.40
Variable selling and administrative expenses	0.20

Next year the company will use new material that is easier to work with than the old material. Also, a switch to the new material will reduce material costs by 60% and direct labor costs by 40%. The new material will not affect the product's quality or marketability. Because the factory's output is nearing its annual capacity of 40,000 units, some consideration is being given to increasing the selling price to reduce the number of units sold. At this point, two strategies are being considered. Under Plan 1, the company will keep the price at the current level and sell the same volume as last year. This plan increases profits because of the material change. Under Plan 2, the product's price will be increased by 25%, but unit sales volume will fall by 10%. Under both Plan 1 and Plan 2, the total fixed costs and variable costs per unit will remain the same.

Required

1. Compute the break-even point in dollars for *(a)* Plan 1 and *(b)* Plan 2.
2. Prepare side-by-side forecasted income statements showing the expected results of Plan 1 and Plan 2. The statements should show sales, total variable costs and expenses, total fixed costs, income before taxes, income taxes (30% rate), and net income.

Check Figure Net income under Plan 1, $84,000

Problem 23-6
Break-even analysis with composite units
P4, C3

Peabody Co. manufactures and sells three products: Red, White, and Blue. Their selling prices are: Red, $55 per unit; White, $85 per unit; and Blue, $110 per unit. The variable costs of manufacturing and selling these products are: Red, $40 per unit; White, $60 per unit; and Blue, $80 per unit. Their sales mix is reflected in a ratio of 5:4:2 (Red:White:Blue). Annual fixed costs shared by all three products are $150,000. One item of raw materials is used in manufacturing all three products. The company has developed a new material that is of equal quality and less costly. The new material would reduce variable costs per unit as follows: Red by $10; White by $20; and Blue by $10. But the new material requires new equipment, which will increase annual fixed costs by $20,000. (Round answers to the nearest whole composite unit.)

Required

1. If the company continues to use the old material, determine the company's break-even point in both sales dollars and sales units of each individual product.
2. If the company uses the new material, determine the company's new break-even point in both sales dollars and sales units of each individual product.

Check Figure New plan break-even, 442 composite units

Analysis Component

3. What insight does this analysis offer management in long-term planning?

BEYOND THE NUMBERS

Reporting in Action
C1

NIKE has expanded its product line from running shoes to a full assortment of athletic shoes and apparel in the past decade. You are assigned to head up NIKE's new product, snowboards, to be sold through its sporting goods distribution channels. You are given permission to use all existing resources in getting the product to market, such as NIKE's purchasing department, legal department, and buildings and equipment.

Required

1. What costs, variable or fixed, are your most immediate concern and why?
2. Identify direct costs of snowboards and where they are primarily reflected in financial reports.
3. Assume the contribution margin is 60% and you anticipate sales of $5 million this year. Explain why gross margin on the income statement will not fully reflect your success. (Hint: Consider the difference between gross margin and contribution margin.)

Comparative Analysis

P2, C3, A2

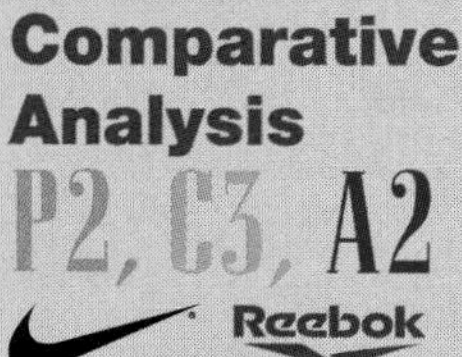

Both **NIKE** and **Reebok** make basketball shoes. Yet one company is often more profitable than the other with their shoes. We know each company makes decisions about purchasing plant assets to produce basketball shoes. We also know the fixed costs along with the variable costs of manufacturing and selling determine break-even point and profitability of these companies.

Required

1. Using the data below, compute the total cost per each pair (or unit) of basketball shoes for NIKE and Reebok. (Assume sales volume equals production volume.)

	NIKE	Reebok
Estimated sales and price	10,000 @ $60/unit	10,000 @ $60/unit
Direct material per unit	$10/unit	$10/unit
Direct labor per unit	$30/unit	$34/unit
Factory rent per month	$30,000	$10,000
Factory equipment (depreciation)	$50,000	$60,000

2. Compare these companies using the data and the results of your analysis of part (1). Explain why one company is more profitable than the other.
3. If sales decline to very low levels, which company will be more profitable (computations are unnecessary)?

Ethics Challenge

C1

Labor costs of an auto mechanic to repair our cars are not usually based on actual hours worked. Instead, the amount paid to a mechanic is based on an industry average amount of time estimated to complete a repair job. The repair shop bills the customer for the industry average amount of time at the repair center's billable cost per hour. This means a customer can pay, for example, $120 for 2 hours of work on a car, when the actual time worked may be only 1 hour. Many experienced mechanics can complete repair jobs well under the industry average. The average data are compiled by engineering studies and surveys conducted in the auto repair business.

Assume you are an expert in the area and are asked to complete such a survey for a repair center. The survey calls for objective input and many questions require detailed cost data and analysis. The mechanics and owners know you have the survey and are encouraging you to complete the survey in a way that increases the average billable cost per hour for repair work.

Required

Write a one-page memorandum to the mechanics and owners describing the direct labor analysis you will undertake in completing this survey.

Communicating in Practice

C2

Several important assumptions underlie CVP analysis. Assumptions often help simplify and focus our analysis of costs. A common application of CVP analysis is as a tool to forecast revenues and costs.

Required

Assume you are actively searching for a job. You are to prepare a one-half page report identifying three assumptions relating to your expected revenue (salary) and three assumptions relating to your expected costs for the first year of your new job. Be prepared to present and discuss your assumptions in class.

Taking It to the Net

C1, C3

Creativity is a skill we must build and maintain. CVP analysis demands creativity in several respects, including its application in projecting revenues and costs. Locate the following Web site: [**www.ozemail.com.au/caveman/Creative/Basics**]. Click on and read: "*What can I do to increase my creativity?*"

Required

Identify and explain activities that can help build and maintain our creativity.

Teamwork in Action

C2

The owner of a local movie theater explains to you that ticket sales on weekends and evenings are strong, but attendance during the weekdays, Monday–Thursday, is poor. The owner proposes to offer to the local grade school a contract to have educational materials shown at the theater for a set charge per student during school hours. The owner asks your help to prepare a CVP analysis listing the cost and revenue projections for the proposal. The owner must propose to the school's administration a charge per child. At a minimum, the charge per child needs to be sufficient for the theater to break even.

Required

Your team is to prepare a list of questions that must be answered by *(a)* the school's administration and *(b)* the owner of the movie theater for you to complete a reliable CVP analysis.

Hitting the Road

P4

Multiproduct break-even analysis is often viewed differently when actually applied in practice. You are to visit a local fast food restaurant and count the number of items on the menu. To apply multiproduct break-even analysis to the restaurant, similar menu items must often be fit into groups. A reasonable approach is to classify menu items into approximately five categories—for example, a typical group is drinks. We then estimate average selling price and average variable cost to compute average contribution margin. (*Hint:* The contribution margin ratio on drinks is about 90%.)

Required

1. Prepare a one-year multiproduct break-even analysis for the restaurant you visit. You must begin by establishing groups. Next, estimate the volume and contribution margin for each group. These estimates are necessary to compute the contribution margin for each group. Assume that annual fixed costs in total are $500,000 per year. (Hint: You must develop your own estimates on volume and contribution margin for each group to obtain the break-even point and sales.)
2. Prepare a one-page report on the results of your analysis. Comment on the volume of sales necessary to break even at a fast food restaurant.

Business Week Activity

C3

We normally applaud deflation in the prices we pay for products and services. But is this good news for the business world? Read "The Zero Inflation Economy" in the January 19, 1998, issue of ***Business Week***, pp. 28–31 and answer the following questions to see the impact deflation has on a company when making decisions about cost behavior and CVP analysis.

Required

1. Define price stability.
2. List advantages of price stability in predicting revenue and cost behavior within the relevant range.
3. Explain why the metal industry discussed in this article is negatively impacted by deflation.
4. What impact does deflation have on companies in the metal industry when preparing a CVP analysis?

Master Budgets and Planning

A Look Back

Chapter 23 looked at cost behavior and described its relevance for managers in performing cost-volume-profit analysis. The chapter also explained and illustrated the application of cost-volume-profit analysis.

A Look at This Chapter

This chapter explains the importance of budgeting and describes the master budget. It discusses the value of the master budget to the planning of future company activities.

A Look Ahead

Chapter 25 focuses on flexible budgets, standard costs, and variance reporting.

Chapter Outline

Easy Rider

ST. LOUIS—**BIKER** is a high-tech and unconventional manufacturer of coil springs. Its customers are domestic and international manufacturers of sports bikes, both bicycles and motorcycles. BIKER is recognized in the sports world for having developed and patented a unique spring design that substantially cushions the jolts of on- and off-road biking. The growth in mountain bikes has further fueled its double-digit sales growth over the past five years.

Candy Bergman, with brother Michael, launched the company from her parents' garage only eight short years ago. "Dad loved off-road biking and really got us hooked," says Bergman, now 29. "But the ride was horrible, and we started tinkering with the springs. Dad was an auto mechanic and got us on the right track."

But BIKER came close to folding. "We didn't run a profit until our fourth year," complains Bergman. "Both Michael and I had other jobs, and the money demands were almost too much."

It wasn't until BIKER's fourth year that they turned a profit. Bergman points to several problems, but one was budgeting. "Our goal is to give our customers a better ride, at less cost," says Bergman. "But this demands careful budgeting and planning. And we didn't do either well."

But Bergman learned fast. "We now run budgets for everything," says Bergman. "Estimates of the demand for sports bikes, and our sales in particular, enable us to forecast sales and prepare budgets for the next three years. We know things change, but at least we know what happens when they change."

While Bergman is far from a numbers person, she knows the importance of income and cash flow. She points to the sales budget as the starting point. "I don't pay employees, customers do. If we don't serve customers, none of us gets paid." Adds Bergman, "What's the use of other budgets or plans if there's no sales? The sales budget is key." For now, BIKER's ride is smooth and fast.

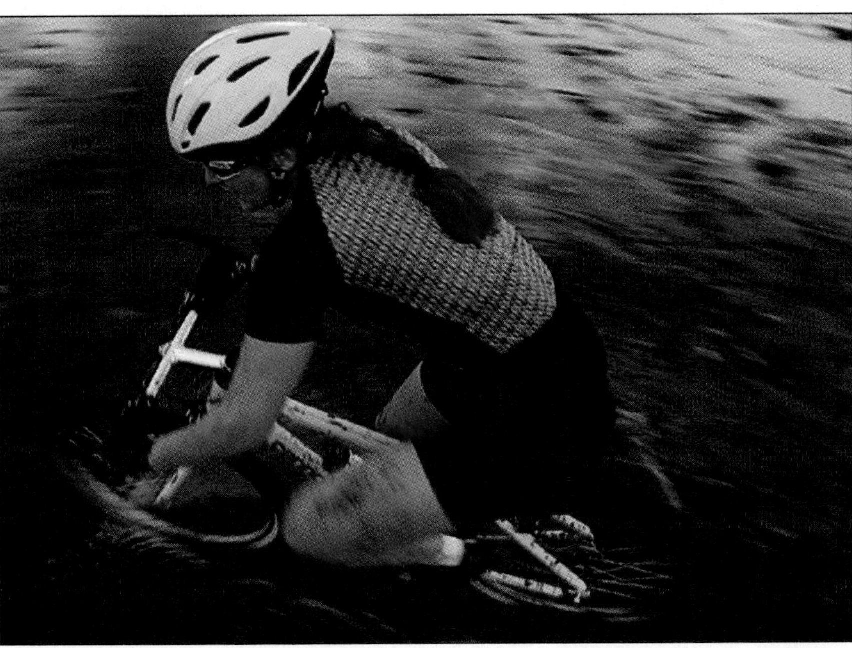

Learning Objectives

Conceptual

C1 Describe the importance and benefits of budgeting.

C2 Explain the process of budget administration.

C3 Describe a master budget and the process of preparing it.

Analytical

A1 Analyze expense planning using zero-based budgeting.

Procedural

P1 Prepare each component of a master budget and link them to the budgeting process.

P2 Link both operating and capital expenditure budgets to budgeted financial statements.

CHAPTER PREVIEW

After management applies cost-volume-profit analysis or other techniques in devising a strategy for future periods, it then looks to turn this strategy into action plans. These action plans are usually compiled in a master budget. The budgeting process serves several purposes. This includes motivating employees and effectively communicating with them. The budget process also helps coordinate a company's activities toward common goals, and is useful for evaluating actual results and management performance.

In this chapter, we explain how to prepare a master budget and use it as a formal plan for the future activities of a company. One's ability to prepare this kind of formal plan is of enormous help in starting and operating a company. It gives us a glimpse into the future and attempts to translate plans into actions. As described in the opening article, this kind of planning is crucial to the success of **BIKER.**

Budgeting Process

C1 Describe the importance and benefits of budgeting.

Management often must carefully plan a company's activities for weeks, months, and even years ahead to successfully achieve its goals. Managers then monitor and control activities so that they conform to the plan. In many situations, particularly in a continuous improvement environment, management will update the plan to reflect new information. This revised plan then serves as the basis for controlling current company activities.

Budgeting is the process of planning future business actions and expressing them as formal plans. The **budget** is a formal statement of a company's future plans. Because the economic or financial aspects of the business are the primary factors driving management's decisions, budgets are usually expressed in monetary terms.

All managers should be involved in planning. Managers who plan carefully and formalize plans in a budgeting process increase the likelihood of both personal and company success.

Analysis and Future Focus

When management plans the future with the care and attention to detail needed for preparing a budget, it requires thorough analysis. A good budgeting process leads to both well-conceived plans and careful analysis. The process also promotes good decision making.

The relevant focus of a budgetary analysis is the future. It directs management's attention to future events and the opportunities available. A focus on the future is important because the pressures of daily operating problems often divert management's attention and take precedence over planning. A good budgeting system counteracts this tendency by formalizing the planning process and demanding relevant input. Budgeting makes planning an explicit management responsibility.

Basis for Evaluation

The control function requires management to evaluate business operations against some norm. Evaluation involves comparing actual results against one of two usual alternatives: (1) past performance or (2) expected performance. An evaluation assists management in taking corrective actions if necessary.

Evaluation using expected, or budgeted, performance is potentially superior to past performance in deciding whether actual results trigger a need for corrective actions. This is because past performance is often inferior as a standard for evaluation as it fails to take into account several changes that may affect current activities. Changes in economic conditions, shifts in competitive advantages within the industry, new product developments, increased or decreased advertising, and other factors all reduce the usefulness of comparisons with past results. In the computer industry, for instance, increasing competition and technological advances often reduce the usefulness of performance comparisons across different years.

Budgeted performance levels are computed after careful analysis and research attempting to anticipate and adjust for changes in important company, industry, and economic factors. This usually means budgets provide an excellent basis for evaluating performance. This yields management a more effective control and monitoring system.

Employee Motivation

Because budgeting provides standards for evaluating performance, it can affect the attitudes of employees who are evaluated. The budgeting process can be used to have a positive effect on employees' attitudes, but it can also yield a negative one without care. Budgeted levels of performance, for instance, must be realistic to avoid discouraging employees. Also, personnel who will be evaluated should be consulted and involved in preparing the budget to increase their commitment to meeting it. Evaluations of performance must allow the affected employees to explain the reasons for apparent performance deficiencies. Accounting reports don't tell the whole story.

We can identify three important guidelines in the budgeting process:

1. Employees affected by a budget should be consulted when it is prepared.
2. Goals reflected in a budget should be attainable.
3. Evaluations should be made carefully with opportunities to explain any failures.

Budgeting can be a positive motivating force when these guidelines are followed. Budgeted performance levels can provide goals for employees to attain or even exceed as they carry out their responsibilities.

Coordination of Activities

An important management objective in larger companies is to make certain that activities of all departments contribute to meeting a company's overall goals. This requires coordination. Budgeting provides a way to achieve this coordination. We describe later in this chapter how a company's budget, or operating plan, is based upon its objectives. This operating plan starts with the sales budget, which drives all other budgets including production, materials, labor, and overhead. The budgeting process coordinates the activities of these various departments to meet the company's overall goals.

Soccer Budgeting

France Telecom failed to properly budget and coordinate its efforts to sell tickets for the 1998 World Cup. According to France Telecom, 60 of its operators were assigned to take orders for the several thousand tickets available to UK citizens. In the first 5 minutes after the phone lines opened, **British Telecom** says its system logged an amazing 250,000 calls. That figure soared to four million call attempts within the first 60 minutes. Estimates suggest as many as 20 million call attempts were made on the first day. Experts say the odds of a UK soccer fan getting through to the ticket hotline were around one in two million.

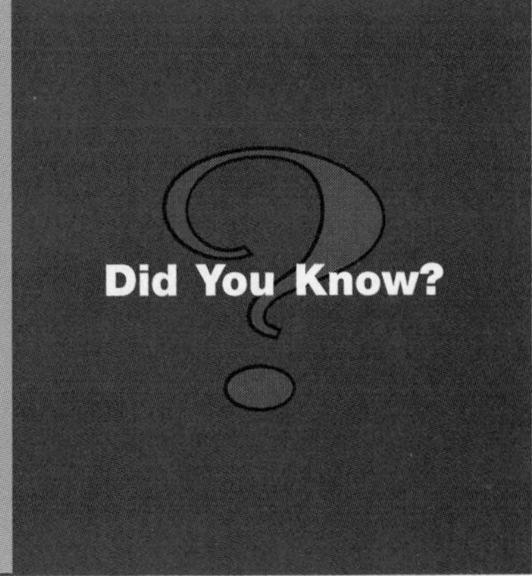

Communication of Plans

A manager can adequately explain business plans directly to employees in smaller companies. This can occur through conversations and other informal communications. But conversations can create uncertainty and confusion if not supported by clear documentation of the plans. A written budget is preferred and can inform employees in all types of organizations about management's plans. The budget can also communicate management's specific action plans for the employees in the budget period.

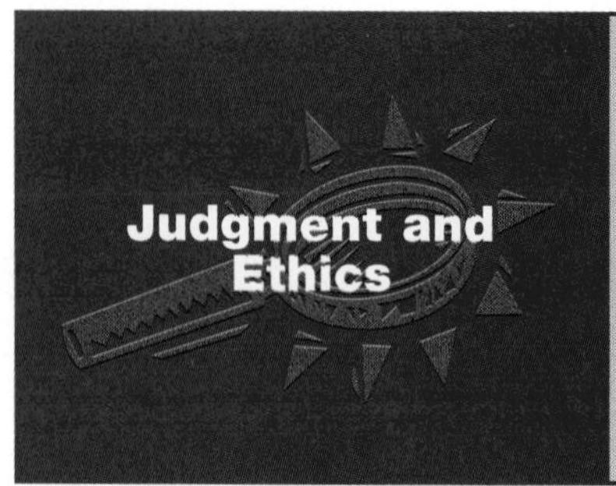

Budgeting Staffer
You are working in the budget office of a company. You learn that earnings for the current quarter are going to be far below the budgeted amount reported in the press. You also know that one of your superiors, who is also aware of the impending news of the earnings shortfall, has decided to accept a management position with a competitor. This superior is in the process of selling her shares of the company that you and she are working for. Her departure will further hurt your company's ability to improve earnings. Does this situation present ethical concerns or responsibilities for you?

Answer—p. 1038

Budget Administration

C2 Explain the process of budget administration.

Budgeting is an important and detailed activity that must be properly administered. This section explains the details of budget administration.

Budget Committee

The task of preparing a budget should not be the sole responsibility of any one department. Similarly, the budget should not be simply handed down as top management's final word. Instead, budget figures and budget estimates usually are more useful if developed through a *bottom-up* process. This includes, for instance, involving the sales department in preparing sales estimates. Likewise, the production department should have initial responsibility for preparing its own expense budget. Without active employee involvement in preparing budget figures, there is a risk these employees will feel as if the numbers fail to reflect their special problems and needs.

While most budgets should be developed by a bottom-up process, the budgeting system requires central guidance. This guidance is supplied by a budget committee of department heads and other executives responsible for seeing that budgeted amounts are realistic and coordinated. If a department submits initial budget figures not reflecting efficient performance, the budget committee should return them with explanatory comments on how to improve them. Then the originating department must either adjust its proposals or explain why they are acceptable. Communication between the originating department and the budget committee should continue as needed to ensure that both parties accept the budget as reasonable, attainable, and desirable.

The concept of continuous improvement applies to budgeting as well as production. **Amoco** recently streamlined its monthly budget reporting package from a one-inch-thick stack of monthly control reports to a tidy, two-page flash report on monthly earnings and key production statistics. The key to this efficiency gain was the integration of new budgeting and cost allocation processes with Amoco's strategic planning process. Amoco's controller explained the new role of the finance department with respect to the budgetary control process as follows:[1]

> . . . there's less of an attitude that finance's job is to control. People really have come to see that our job is to help attain business objectives.

[1] Stephen Barr, "Grinding It Out," *CFO Magazine,* January 1995.

Budget Reporting

We explained in Chapter 19 how most companies prepare long-term strategic plans spanning 5 to 10 years. These are then fine tuned in preparing medium-term and short-term plans. Strategic plans usually set the long-term direction of a company. They provide a road map for the future about potential opportunities such as new products, markets, and investments. The strategic plan can be rough, given its long-term focus. Medium- and short-term plans are more operational and translate strategic plans into actions. These action plans are fairly concrete and consist of defined objectives and goals.

Short-term plans are usually called *budgets* and cover a one-year period. For convenience, the budget period usually coincides with the accounting period. This means most companies prepare at least an annual budget. An annual budget reflects the objectives for the next year. To provide specific guidance, the annual budget usually is separated into quarterly or monthly budgets. These short-term budgets allow management to quickly evaluate performance and take corrective action. Managers can compare actual results to budgeted amounts in a report such as that shown in Exhibit 24.1. This report shows actual results, budgeted results, and any differences. A difference is called a *variance,* which we discuss in detail in Chapter 25. Management examines variances to identify areas for improvement and corrective action.

Exhibit 24.1

Comparing Actual Performance with Budgeted Performance

ECCENTRIC MUSIC
Income Statement with Variations from Budget
For Month Ended April 30, 2000

	Actual	Budget	Variance
Sales	$63,500	$60,000	$+3,500
Less: Sales returns and allowances	1,800	1,700	+100
Sales discounts	1,200	1,150	+50
Net sales	$60,500	$57,150	$+3,350
Cost of goods sold:			
Merchandise inventory, April 1, 2000	$42,000	$44,000	$−2,000
Purchases, net	39,100	38,000	+1,100
Transportation-in	1,250	1,200	+50
Goods available for sale	$82,350	$83,200	$ −850
Merchandise inventory, April 30, 2000	41,000	44,100	−3,100
Cost of goods sold	$41,350	$39,100	$+2,250
Gross profit	$19,150	$18,050	$+1,100
Operating expenses:			
Selling expenses:			
Sales salaries	$ 6,250	$ 6,000	$ +250
Advertising	900	800	+100
Store supplies	550	500	+50
Depreciation, Store equipment	1,600	1,600	
Total selling expenses	$ 9,300	$ 8,900	$ +400
General and administrative expenses:			
Office salaries	$ 2,000	$ 2,000	
Office supplies used	165	150	$ +15
Rent	1,100	1,100	
Insurance	200	200	
Depreciation, Office equipment	100	100	
Total general and admin. expenses	$ 3,565	$ 3,550	$ +15
Total operating expenses	$12,865	$12,450	$ +415
Income from operations	$ 6,285	$ 5,600	$ +685

Budget Timing

Many companies apply **continuous budgeting** by preparing **rolling budgets.** As each monthly or quarterly budget period goes by, these companies revise their entire set of budgets for the months or quarters remaining, and add new monthly or quarterly budgets to replace the ones that have lapsed. This means at any point in time, monthly or quarterly budgets are available for the next 12 months or four quarters.

Exhibit 24.2 shows five rolling budgets. The first set of budgets is prepared in December 1999 and covers the four calendar quarters of the year 2000. In March 2000, the company prepares another rolling budget for the next four quarters through March 2001. This same process is repeated every three months. As a result, management is continuously planning ahead.

Exhibit 24.2

Rolling Budgets

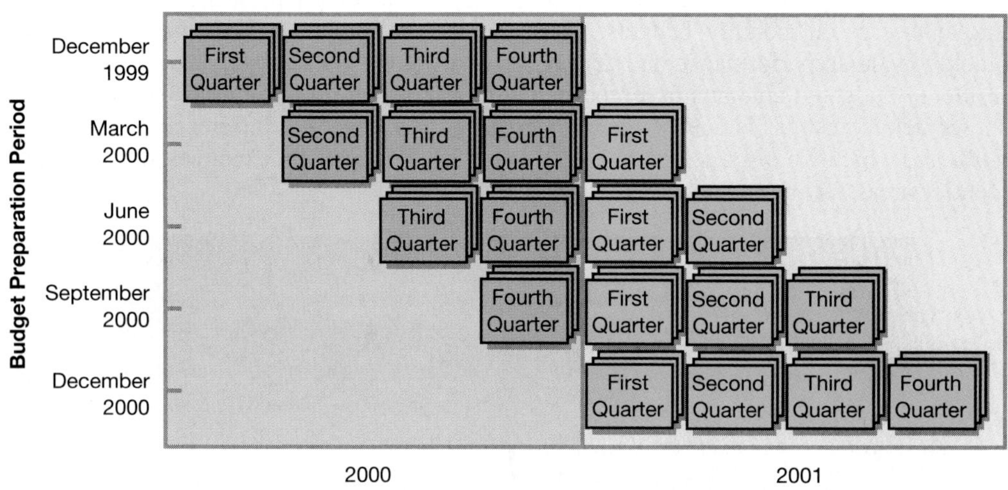

Exhibit 24.2 reflects an annual budget composed of 4 quarters that is drawn up four times per year using the most recent information available. For example, the budget for the fourth quarter of 2000 is prepared in December 1999 and revised in March, June, and September of 2000. When continuous budgeting is not used, the fourth-quarter budget is nine months old and, perhaps, out of date when applied.

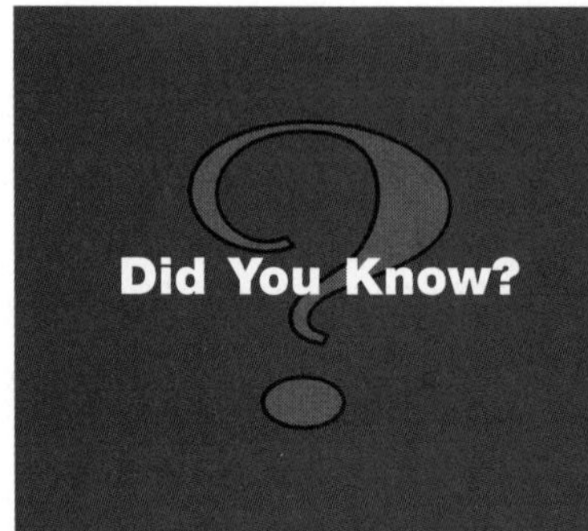

Budget Calendar

Penn Fuel Gas (PFG), a public utility, initiated its first annual, long-range operating budget process in early 1995. Three stakeholder groups influenced the creation of its budgeting system: bankers, board of directors, and management. All three are interested in cash flow projections and future earnings potential. PFG's budgeting process begins six months before the budget is due to the board of directors. Its budget calendar, shown below, provides information on the activities of the budget group during this period. [Source: R.N. West and A.M. Snyder, "How to Set Up a Budgeting and Planning System," *Management Accounting,* January 1997, pp. 20–26.]

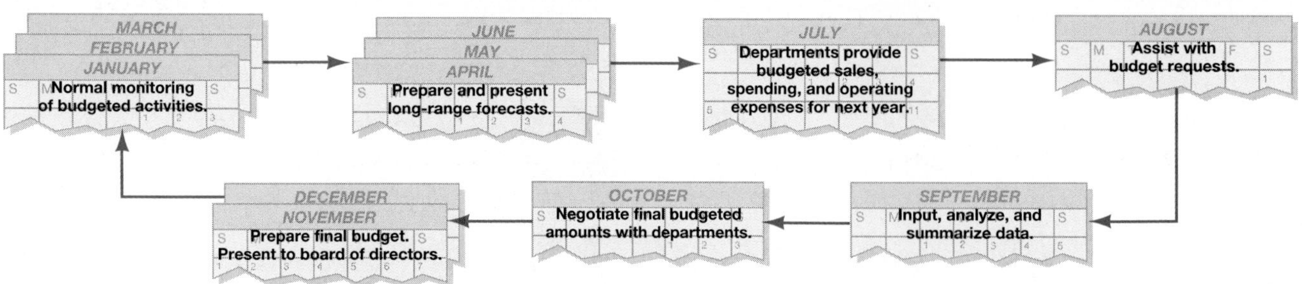

Flash back

1. What are the major benefits of budgeting?
2. What is the responsibility of the budget committee?
3. What is the usual time period covered by a budget?
4. What are rolling budgets?

Answers—p. 1038

Master Budget

A **master budget** is a formal, comprehensive plan for the future of a company. To include definite plans for all activities, a master budget contains several individual budgets. These individual budgets are linked with each other to form a coordinated plan for the company.

Master Budget Components

C3 Describe a master budget and the process of preparing it.

The master budget typically includes individual budgets for sales, purchases, production, various expenses, capital expenditures, and cash. Managers often express the expected financial results of these planned activities with both a budgeted income statement for the budget period and a budgeted balance sheet for the end of the budget period.

The usual number and types of budgets included in a master budget depend on the size and complexity of the company. A master budget should include, at a minimum, the budgets listed in Exhibit 24.3. In addition to these individual budgets, managers often include supporting calculations and schedules along with the master budget.

Exhibit 24.3

Basic Components of a Master Budget

- **Operating budgets**
  - *Sales budget*
    For merchandisers: *Merchandise purchases budget* (specifying units to be purchased)
    For manufacturers: *Production budget* (specifying units to be produced)
    Manufacturing budget (specifying manufacturing costs)
  - *Selling expense budget*
  - *General and administrative expense budget*
- **Capital expenditures budget** (specifying expenditures for plant assets)
- **Financial budgets**
  - *Cash budget* (specifying cash receipts and disbursements)
  - *Budgeted income statement*
  - *Budgeted balance sheet*

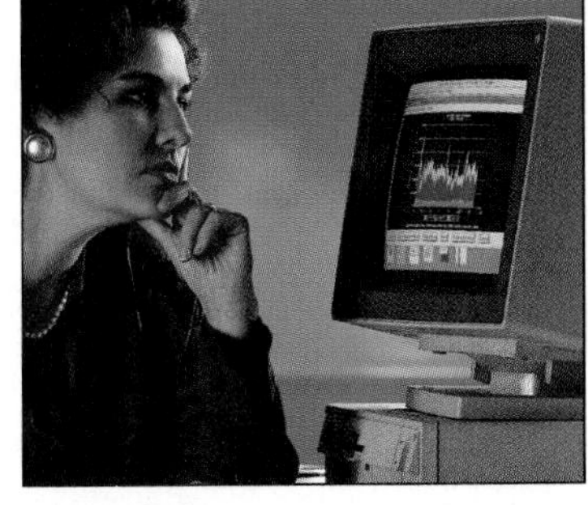

Some budgets require the input of other budgets. For example, the merchandise purchases budget can't be prepared until after the sales budget. This is because the number of units to be purchased depends on how many units are expected to be sold. As a result, we must prepare budgets within the master budget in a sequence. A typical sequence is that followed by **HON Company,** an office products manufacturer, in its quarterly budgeting process.[2] Its quarterly budget consists of five steps as shown in Exhibit 24.4, which is completed over a six-week period.

At any stage in this budgeting process, undesirable outcomes might be revealed. This means changes often must be made to prior budgets and the previous steps repeated. For instance, an early version of the cash budget might show an insufficient amount of cash

[2] R. Drtina, S. Hoeger, and J. Schaub, "Continuous Budgeting at the HON Company," *Management Accounting,* January 1996, pp. 20–24.

Master Budget Sequence

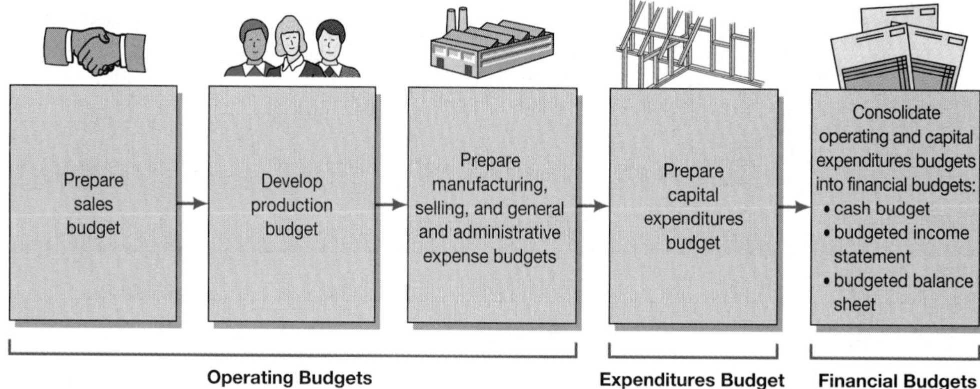

unless cash outlays are reduced. This might yield a reduction in planned equipment purchases. Or a preliminary budgeted balance sheet may reveal too much debt from an ambitious expenditures budget. These findings often result in revised plans.

The remainder of this section explains how the master budget for **Hockey Den (HD),** a retailer of youth hockey sticks, is prepared. The company's master budget includes operating, capital expenditures, and cash budgets for each month in a quarter. It also includes a budgeted income statement for each quarter and a budgeted balance sheet as of the last day of each quarter. We will show how HD's budgets are prepared for October, November, and December of 1999. Exhibit 24.5 presents HD's balance sheet at the start of this budgeting period. We will often refer to it as we prepare the component budgets.

Exhibit 24.5

Balance Sheet Prior to the Budgeting Periods

HOCKEY DEN
Balance Sheet
September 30, 1999

Assets		
Cash		$ 20,000
Accounts receivable		42,000
Inventory (900 units @ $60)		54,000
Equipment*	$200,000	
Less accumulated depreciation	(36,000)	164,000
Total assets		$280,000
Liabilities and Stockholders' Equity		
Liabilities:		
Accounts payable	$ 58,200	
Income taxes payable (due 10/31/1999)	20,000	
Note payable to bank	10,000	$ 88,200
Stockholders' equity:		
Common stock	$150,000	
Retained earnings	41,800	191,800
Total liabilities and equity		$280,000

*Equipment is depreciated on a straight-line basis over 10 years where salvage value is $20,000.

Budgeting Acquisitions

Budgeting is a crucial part of management's analysis at **Koch Industries** for potential acquisitions. Analysis begins by projecting annual sales volume, prices, and total revenues. It then estimates cost of sales for each revenue item along with selling, general, and administrative expenses. These are combined to form projected net income of the potential acquisition for the next several years. It also predicts expenditures and other costs. By comparing the budgeted cost of a potential acquisition with its expected future income, it decides the price to offer for the potential acquisition.

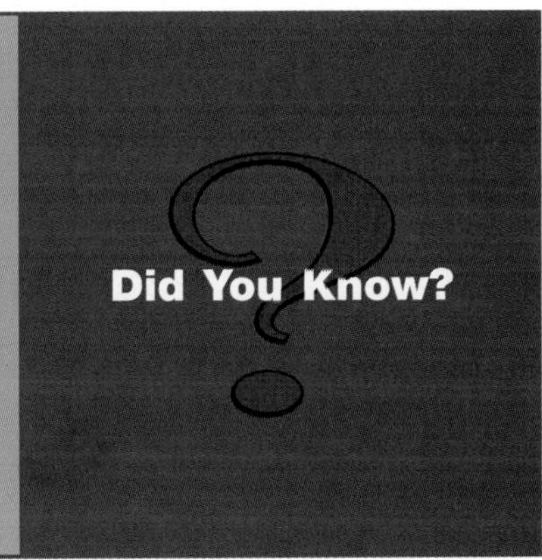

Flash back

5. What is a master budget?
6. A master budget:
   a. Always includes a manufacturing budget specifying the units to be produced.
   b. Is prepared with a process starting with the operating budgets and continues with the expenditures budget, and then financial budgets.
   c. Is prepared with a process ending with the sales budget.
7. What are the three primary categories of budgets in the master budget?

Answers—p. 1038

Operating Budgets

P1 Prepare each component of a master budget and link them to the budgeting process.

This section explains the preparation of operating budgets for Hockey Den. Operating budgets consist of the sales budget, merchandise purchases budget, selling expense budget, and general and administrative expense budget. Hockey Den does not prepare production and manufacturing budgets because it is a merchandiser. The preparation of a production budget and related manufacturing budgets is described in Appendix 24A.

There's No Business Like Snow Business

While many of us spend money to clear away snow, ski resorts pay for snow. Estimates of the costs of manmade snow to ski resorts are in the tens of millions of dollars for snowmaking equipment alone. Snowmaking involves spraying droplets of water into the air, causing them to freeze and come down as snow. It can cost up to $2,000 an hour to make snow. For many ski resorts, snowmaking accounts for 40 to 50 percent of their operating budget.

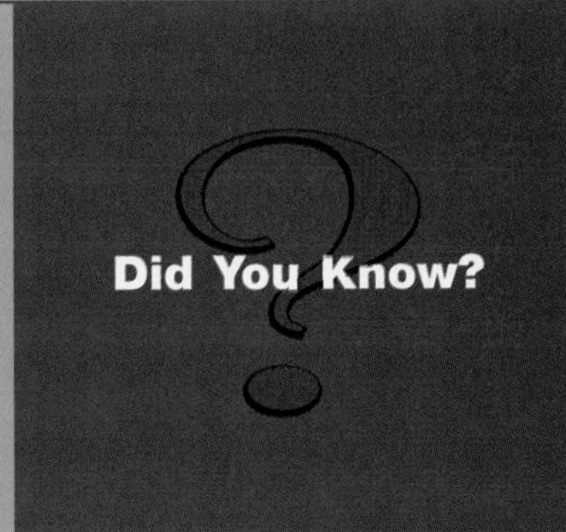

Sales Budget

The first step in preparing the master budget is planning the **sales budget.** This budget shows the planned sales units and the revenue derived from these sales. The sales budget is the starting point in the budgeting process because plans for most departments are linked to sales. The sales budget should emerge from a careful analysis of forecasted economic and market conditions, plant capacity, proposed selling expenses (such as advertising), and predictions of unit sales. Because people normally feel a greater commitment to goals they have had a hand in setting, the sales personnel of a company are usually asked to develop predictions of sales for each territory and department. Another advantage of using this *participatory budgeting* approach is that it draws on knowledge and experience of people involved in the activity.

In September 1999, Hockey Den sold 700 hockey sticks at $100 per unit. After considering sales predictions and market conditions, Hockey Den's sales budget is prepared for the next quarter (three months) plus one extra month see Exhibit 24.6. The sales budget includes January 2000 because the purchasing department relies on estimated January sales in deciding on December 1999 purchases.

Exhibit 24.6

Sales Budget Showing Planned Unit and Dollar Sales

HOCKEY DEN
Monthly Sales Budget
October 1999–January 2000

	Budgeted Unit Sales	Budgeted Unit Price	Budgeted Total Sales
September 1999 (actual)	700	$100	$ 70,000
October 1999	1,000	$100	$100,000
November 1999	800	100	80,000
December 1999	1,400	100	140,000
Total for the quarter	3,200	$100	$320,000
January 2000	900	$100	$ 90,000

The sales budget in Exhibit 24.6 includes forecasts of both unit sales and unit prices. While some companies prepare a sales budget expressed only in total sales dollars, most sales budgets are more detailed. Management finds it useful to know budgeted units and unit prices for many different products, regions, departments, and sales representatives.

This chapter's opening article described budgets and planning at **BIKER.** In prior years, BIKER had classified its sales budget by the type of coil (steel vs. titanium). This past year it expanded the classifications by type of bike. It used the planning process to identify industries other than sports bikes that can benefit from the high tensile strength and lightweight properties of titanium coil springs. It identified and successfully marketed a new coil spring to **NASCAR** racing vehicles. Both strength and weight are crucial in this sport and important enough to justify the added expense of titanium coil springs. By using the budgeting and planning process, BIKER successfully increased its sales. Projections for the next two years have titanium coil spring sales increasing by 30% to 50%. The majority of this growth is from NASCAR parts.

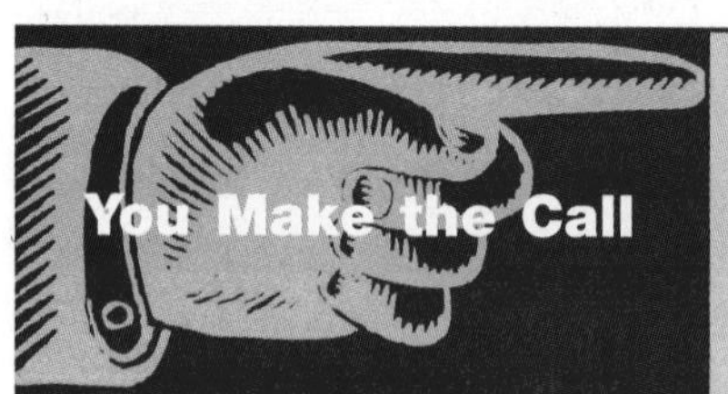

Sales Manager

You are a sales manager for a designer clothes manufacturer. Business is highly seasonal and you find that fashions and designs are continuously changing. How do you prepare annual sales budgets?

Answer—p. 1038

Merchandise Purchases Budget

Various methods are used to help managers make inventory purchasing decisions. These methods all recognize that the number of units added to inventory depends on budgeted sales volume. Whether a company manufactures or purchases the product it sells, budgeted future sales volume is the primary factor in most inventory management decisions.

Just-in-Time Inventory Systems

Managers of *just-in-time* (JIT) inventory systems use sales budgets covering short periods (often as few as one or two days) to order just enough merchandise or materials to satisfy the immediate sales demand. As a result, the level of inventory on hand is held to a minimum (or zero in an ideal situation). A just-in-time system minimizes the costs of maintaining inventory. But just-in-time systems are practical only if customers are content to order in advance or if managers can accurately determine short-term sales demand. Also, suppliers must be able and willing to ship small quantities regularly and promptly.

Safety Stock Inventory Systems

Market conditions and manufacturing processes for many products may not allow a just-in-time system to be used. Instead, many companies keep enough inventory on hand to reduce the risk of running short. This practice requires enough purchases to satisfy the budgeted sales amounts and to maintain an additional quantity of inventory as a **safety stock.** The safety stock provides protection against lost sales caused by unfulfilled demands from customers or delays in shipments from suppliers.

Merchandise Purchases Budget Preparation

Companies usually express a **merchandise purchases budget** in both units and dollars. Exhibit 24.7 shows the general layout for this budget in equation form. If this formula is expressed in units and only one product is involved, we can compute the number of dollars of inventory to be purchased for our budget by multiplying the units to be purchased by the cost per unit.

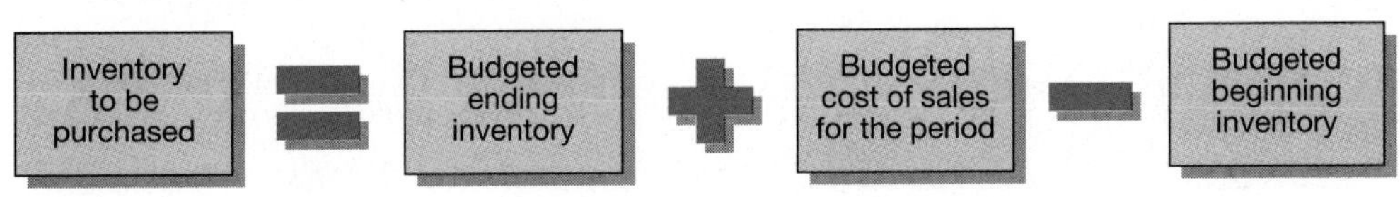

Exhibit 24.7

Formula for a Merchandise Purchases Budget

After Hockey Den assessed the cost of keeping inventory along with the risk of a temporary inventory shortage, it decided the number of units in its inventory at the end of each month should equal 90% of next month's predicted sales. For example, inventory at the end of October should equal 90% of budgeted November sales, and the November ending inventory should equal 90% of budgeted December sales, and so on.

Hockey Den's suppliers expect the September 1999 per unit cost of $60 to remain unchanged through January 2000. This information, along with knowing 900 units are on hand at September 30 (see Exhibit 24.5), allows the company to prepare the merchandise purchases budget shown in Exhibit 24.8.

Exhibit 24.8

Merchandise Purchases Budget

HOCKEY DEN
Merchandise Purchases Budget
October 1999–December 1999

	October	November	December
Next month's budgeted sales (units)	800	1,400	900
Ratio of inventory to future sales	× 90%	× 90%	× 90%
Budgeted ending inventory (units)	720	1,260	810
Add budgeted sales for the month (units)	1,000	800	1,400
Required units of available merchandise	1,720	2,060	2,210
Deduct beginning inventory (units)	(900)	(720)	(1,260)
Number of units to be purchased	820	1,340	950
Budgeted cost per unit	$60	$60	$60
Budgeted cost of merchandise purchases	$49,200	$80,400	$57,000

The first three lines of Hockey Den's merchandise purchases budget determine the required ending inventories. Budgeted unit sales are then added to the desired ending inventory to give us the required units of available merchandise. We then subtract beginning inventory to determine the budgeted number of units to be purchased. The last line is the budgeted cost of the purchases, computed by multiplying the units to be purchased by the predicted cost per unit.

We already indicated that some budgeting systems describe only the total dollars of budgeted sales. Likewise, a system can express a merchandise purchases budget only in terms of the total cost of merchandise to be purchased, omitting the number of units to be purchased. This method assumes a constant relation between sales and cost of goods sold. Hockey Den, for instance, might assume the expected cost of goods sold to be 60% of sales, computed from the budgeted unit cost of $60 and the budgeted sales price of $100. Here its cost of goods sold can be budgeted in dollars on the basis of budgeted sales without requiring information on the number of units involved. But it is still necessary to consider the effects of beginning and ending inventories in determining the amounts to be purchased.

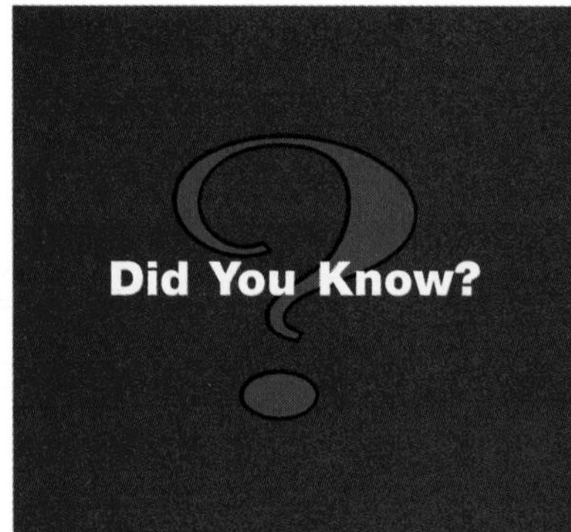

Activity/Process Based Budgeting

Paul Sharman, president of **Focused Management Information** [www.FocusedManagement.com], says companies that use activity-based costing and analysis of processes should consider activity/process-based budgeting. He says activity-based costing information is useful for strategic goal setting, and process analysis is useful for process goal setting. Both are followed by activity analysis and the preparation of budgets for each major process. Sharman claims activity/process based budgeting "offers a most powerful device to . . . organizations in driving change and human behavior." [Source: P. Sharman, "Activity/Process Budgets: A Tool for Change Management," *CMA Magazine,* March 1996, pp. 21–24.]

Selling Expense Budget

The **selling expense budget** is a plan listing the types and amounts of selling expenses expected during the budget period. Its initial responsibility usually rests with the vice president of marketing or an equivalent sales manager. The selling expense budget is normally created to provide sufficient selling expenses to meet sales goals reflected in the sales budget. Predictions of selling expenses are based on both the sales budget and the experience of previous periods. After some or all of the master budget is prepared, management may decide that projected sales volume is inadequate. If so, subsequent adjustments in the sales budget may require corresponding adjustments in the selling expense budget.

Hockey Den's selling expense budget is shown in Exhibit 24.9. Hockey Den's selling expenses consist of commissions paid to sales personnel and a $2,000 monthly salary paid to the sales manager. Sales commissions equal 10% of total sales and are paid in the month sales occur. Sales commissions are variable with respect to sales volume, whereas the sales manager's salary is fixed. No advertising expenses are budgeted for this particular quarter.

General and Administrative Expense Budget

The **general and administrative expense budget** is a plan showing the predicted operating expenses not included in the selling expenses budget. General and administrative expenses may consist of items that are variable or fixed with respect to sales volume. The office manager, or the person responsible for general administration, often is responsible for preparing the initial general and administrative expense budget.

Exhibit 24.9

Selling Expense Budget

HOCKEY DEN Selling Expense Budget October 1999–December 1999	October	November	December	Total
Budgeted sales	$100,000	$80,000	$140,000	$320,000
Sales commission percent	× 10%	× 10%	× 10%	× 10%
Sales commissions	$ 10,000	$ 8,000	$ 14,000	$ 32,000
Salary for sales manager	2,000	2,000	2,000	6,000
Total selling expenses	$ 12,000	$10,000	$ 16,000	$ 38,000

While interest expense and income tax expense are often classified as general and administrative expenses in published income statements, they normally can't be planned for at this stage of the budgeting process. The prediction of interest expense follows the preparation of the cash budget and the decisions regarding debt. The predicted income tax expense depends on the budgeted amount of pre-tax income. Also, both interest and income taxes are usually beyond the control of the office manager. As a result, they are not used in evaluating that person's performance in comparison to the budget.

Exhibit 24.10 shows the general and administrative expense budget for Hockey Den. General and administrative expenses include salaries of $54,000 per year, or $4,500 per month. Salaries are paid each month when they are earned. Using information in Exhibit 24.5, the depreciation on equipment is computed as $18,000 per year [($200,000 − $20,000)/10 years], or $1,500 per month ($18,000/12 months).

Exhibit 24.10

General and Administrative Expense Budget

HOCKEY DEN General and Administrative Expense Budget October 1999–December 1999	October	November	December	Total
Administrative salaries	$4,500	$4,500	$4,500	$13,500
Depreciation of equipment	1,500	1,500	1,500	4,500
Total general and admin. expenses	$6,000	$6,000	$6,000	$18,000

Flash back

8. In preparing monthly budgets for the third quarter, a company budgeted 120 unit sales for July and 140 unit sales for August. The June 30 finished goods inventory consists of 50 units and management wants each month's ending inventory to be 60% of next month's sales. How many units of product should the merchandise purchases budget for the third quarter specify for July acquisition? *(a)* 84; *(b)* 120; *(c)* 154; *(d)* 204.

9. What is the difference between operating budgets for merchandising and manufacturing companies?

10. How does a just-in-time inventory system differ from a safety stock system?

Answers—p. 1038

Capital Expenditures Budget

The **capital expenditures budget** lists dollar amounts both to be received from disposing of equipment and to be spent on purchasing additional equipment if the budgeted business activities are carried out. It is usually prepared after the operating budgets. Because productive capacity is limited by the company's plant and equipment, this budget is usually affected by long-range plans for the business instead of short-term sales budgets for the next year or quarter. But still the process of preparing a sales or purchases budget can reveal that the company needs more capacity and additional equipment is necessary.

Capital budgeting is the process of evaluating and planning for capital (plant and equipment) expenditures. Planning for capital expenditures is an important task of management because these expenditures often involve long-run commitments of large amounts. Also, capital expenditures often have a major effect on predicted cash flows and the company's need for debt or equity financing. This means the capital expenditures budget is often linked with management's evaluation of the company's ability to take on more debt. We discuss capital budgeting in detail in Chapter 26.

In the case of Hockey Den, it doesn't anticipate any disposals of equipment through December 1999. But it does plan to acquire additional equipment for $25,000 cash near the end of December 1999. Since this is the only budgeted capital expenditure from October 1999 through January 2000, no separate budget is shown. The cash budget in Exhibit 24.11 reflects this $25,000 planned expenditure.

Financial Budgets

P2 Link both operating and capital expenditure budgets to budgeted financial statements.

After preparing the operating and capital expenditures budgets, a company uses information from these budgets to prepare at least three financial budgets: cash budget, budgeted income statement, and budgeted balance sheet.

Cash Budget

After developing budgets for sales, merchandise purchases, expenses, and capital expenditures, the next step is preparing the cash budget. The **cash budget** shows expected cash inflows and outflows during the budget period. It is especially important to maintain a cash balance necessary to meet a company's obligations. By preparing a cash budget, management can prearrange loans to cover any anticipated cash shortages before they are needed. A cash budget also helps management avoid a cash balance that is too large. Too much cash is undesirable because it earns a relatively low rate of return.

When preparing a cash budget, we add expected cash receipts to the beginning cash balance and deduct expected cash disbursements. If the expected final cash balance is inadequate, any additional cash requirements appear in the budget as planned increases from short-term loans. If the expected final cash balance exceeds the desired balance, the excess is used to repay loans or to acquire short-term investments. Information for preparing the cash budget is primarily taken from the operating and capital expenditures budgets. But further data and calculations are sometimes necessary to compute the final amounts.

Exhibit 24.11 presents the cash budget for Hockey Den. The beginning cash balance for October is taken from the September 30, 1999, balance sheet in Exhibit 24.5. The remainder of this section describes the computations in the cash budget.

Budgeted sales of Hockey Den are shown in Exhibit 24.6. Analysis of past sales indicates 40% of Hockey Den's sales are for cash. The remaining 60% are credit sales and these customers are expected to pay in full in the month following the sales. We can compute the budgeted cash receipts from customers as shown in Exhibit 24.12.

Exhibit 24.11

Cash Budget

HOCKEY DEN Cash Budget October 1999–December 1999	October	November	December
Beginning cash balance	$ 20,000	$ 20,000	$ 22,272
Cash receipts from customers (Exhibit 24.12)	82,000	92,000	104,000
Total cash available	$102,000	$112,000	$126,272
Cash disbursements:			
Payments for merchandise (Exhibit 24.13)	$ 58,200	$ 49,200	$ 80,400
Sales commissions (Exhibit 24.9)	10,000	8,000	14,000
Salaries:			
Sales (Exhibit 24.9)	2,000	2,000	2,000
Administrative (Exhibit 24.10)	4,500	4,500	4,500
Income taxes payable (Exhibit 24.5)	20,000		
Dividends ($150,000 × 2%)		3,000	
Interest on bank loan:			
October ($10,000 × 1%)	100		
November ($22,800 × 1%)		228	
Purchase of equipment			25,000
Total cash disbursements	$ 94,800	$ 66,928	$125,900
Preliminary balance	$ 7,200	$ 45,072	$ 372
Additional loan from bank	12,800		19,628
Repayment of loan from bank		(22,800)	
Ending cash balance	$ 20,000	$ 22,272	$ 20,000
Loan balance, end of month	$ 22,800	$ -0-	$ 19,628

Exhibit 24.12

Computing Budgeted Cash Receipts

	September	October	November	December
Sales	$70,000	$100,000	$80,000	$140,000
Ending accounts receivable (60%)	$42,000	$ 60,000	$48,000	$ 84,000
Cash receipts from:				
Cash sales (40%)		$ 40,000	$32,000	$ 56,000
Collections of prior month's receivables		42,000	60,000	48,000
Total cash receipts		$ 82,000	$92,000	$104,000

Exhibit 24.12 shows October's budgeted cash receipts consist of $40,000 from expected cash sales ($100,000 × 40%) plus the anticipated collection of $42,000 of accounts receivable from the end of September. Each month's cash receipts from customers are listed on the second line of Exhibit 24.11.

Hockey Den's purchases of merchandise are entirely on account. Full payments are made during the month following these purchases. This means cash disbursements for purchases are computed from the September 30, 1999, balance sheet (Exhibit 24.5) and from the merchandise purchases budget (Exhibit 24.8). This computation is shown in Exhibit 24.13.

Exhibit 24.13

Computing Cash Disbursements for Purchases

October payments (September 30 balance)	$58,200
November payments (October purchases)	49,200
December payments (November purchases)	80,400

Because sales commissions and all salaries are paid monthly, the budgeted cash disbursements for these expenses come from the selling expense budget (Exhibit 24.9) and the general and administrative expense budget (Exhibit 24.10). The cash budget is unaffected by depreciation reported in the general and administrative expenses budget.

As shown in the September 30, 1999, balance sheet (Exhibit 24.5), income taxes are due and payable in October. The cash budget in Exhibit 24.11 shows this $20,000 expected payment in October. Predicted income tax expense for the quarter ending December 31 is 40% of net income and is due in January 2000. It is therefore not reported in the October–December 1999 cash budget. But it does appear in the budgeted income statement as income tax expense and on the budgeted balance sheet as income tax liability.

Hockey Den also pays a cash dividend equal to 2% of the par value of common stock in the second month of each quarter. The cash budget in Exhibit 24.11 shows a November payment of $3,000 for this purpose (2% of $150,000; see Exhibit 24.5).

Hockey Den has an agreement with its bank that promises additional loans at the end of each month if necessary to keep a minimum cash balance of $20,000. Interest is paid at the end of each month at the rate of 1% of the beginning balance of these loans. If the cash balance exceeds $20,000 at the end of a month, the company uses the excess to repay loans. The interest payments in Exhibit 24.11 equal 1% of the prior month's ending loan balance. For October, this payment is 1% of the $10,000 amount reported in the balance sheet of Exhibit 24.5. For November, the company expects to pay interest of $228, computed as 1% of the $22,800 expected loan balance at October 31. No interest is budgeted for December because the company expects to repay the loans in full at the end of November.

Exhibit 24.11 shows the October 31 cash balance declines to $7,200 (before any loan-related activity). This amount is less than the $20,000 minimum. Hockey Den expects to bring this balance up to the minimum by borrowing $12,800 with a short-term note. At the end of November, the budget shows an expected cash balance of $45,072 before any loan activity. This means the company expects to repay the $22,800 debt. The equipment purchase budgeted for December reduces the expected cash balance to $372, far below the $20,000 minimum. This means the company expects to borrow $19,628 in that month to reach the minimum desired ending balance.

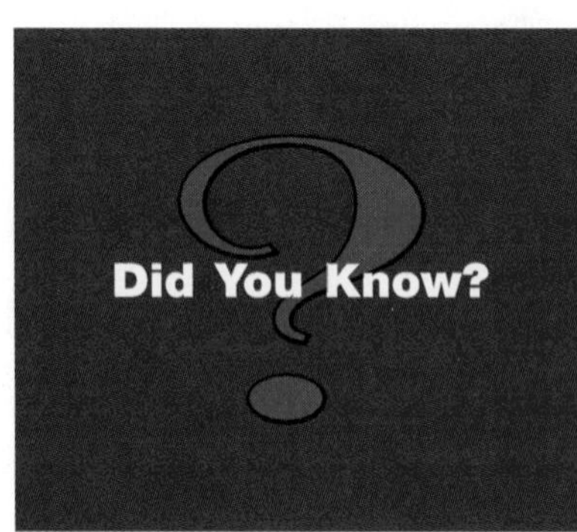

Managing Cash

Harley-Davidson's net cash flows from investing activities were negative (outflows) and averaged $150 million per year from 1994–1996. This was due mainly to increases in capital expenditures. Harley said it "is pursuing a long-term manufacturing strategy to increase its motorcycle production capacity." During this time period, Harley's cash balance fell by more than 50%. [Source: Annual Report, Harley-Davidson.]

Budgeted Income Statement

One of the final steps in preparing the master budget is summarizing the income effects of the plans. The **budgeted income statement** is a managerial accounting report showing predicted amounts of revenues and expenses for the budget period. Information needed for preparing a budgeted income statement comes primarily from already prepared budgets.

The volume of information summarized in the budgeted income statement is so large for some companies that spreadsheets are often used to accumulate the budgeted transactions and classify them by their effects on income. We condense the budgeted income statement for Hockey Den and show it in Exhibit 24.14. All information in this exhibit is taken from earlier budgets.

HOCKEY DEN Budgeted Income Statement For Three Months Ended December 31, 1999		
Sales (Exhibit 24.6, 3,200 units @ $100)		$320,000
Cost of goods sold (3,200 units @ $60)		192,000
Gross profit		$128,000
Operating expenses:		
Sales commissions (Exhibit 24.9)	$32,000	
Sales salaries (Exhibit 24.9)	6,000	
Administrative salaries (Exhibit 24.10)	13,500	
Depreciation on equipment (Exhibit 24.10)	4,500	
Interest expense (Exhibit 24.11)	328	(56,328)
Net income before income taxes		$ 71,672
Income tax expense ($71,672 × 40%)		(28,669)
Net income		$ 43,003

Exhibit 24.14

Budgeted Income Statement

From this budget, we can predict the amount of income tax expense for the quarter, computed as 40% of the budgeted pre-tax net income. This amount is included in the cash budget and/or the budgeted balance sheet as necessary.

Planning Ahead
Most companies allocate dollars based on budgets submitted by department managers. These managers need to be sure the numbers are correct, and then monitor the budget during the period for discrepancies. But managers must remember that a budget is judged by its success in helping achieve the organization's mission. One analogy is airplane piloting. A pilot must know the destination to properly plan a flight. So too must a department manager know the desired company destination to properly plan a budget. [Source: S.M. Rehnberg, "Keep Your Head Out of the Cockpit," *Management Accounting,* July 1995.]

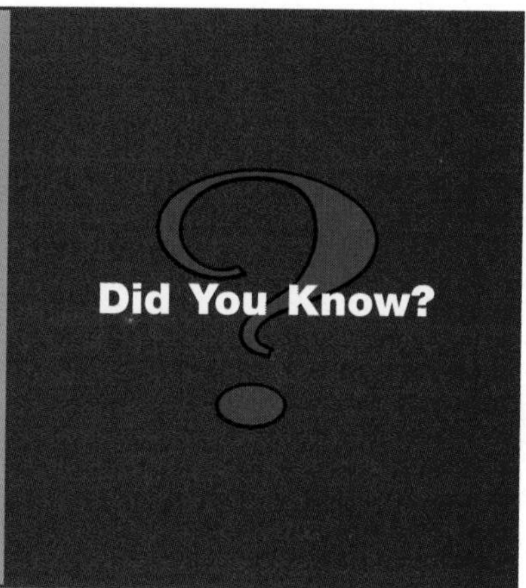

Budgeted Balance Sheet

The final step in preparing the master budget is summarizing the company's financial position. The **budgeted balance sheet** shows predicted amounts for the company's assets, liabilities, and equity as of the end of the budget period. The budgeted balance sheet of Hockey Den is prepared using information from the other budgets. The sources of amounts shown in its budgeted balance sheet are listed in Exhibit 24.15.

The resulting budgeted balance sheet is shown in Exhibit 24.16. An eight-column spreadsheet, or work sheet, can be used to prepare the budgeted balance sheet (and income statement). The first two columns would show the post-closing trial balance as of the last day of the period prior to the budget period. The budgeted transactions and adjustments are entered in the third and fourth columns in the same manner as end-of-period adjustments are entered on an ordinary work sheet. After all budgeted transactions and adjustments are entered, the post-closing trial balance amounts in the first two columns are combined with the budget amounts in the third and fourth columns and sorted to the proper Income Statement (fifth and sixth columns) and Balance Sheet columns (seventh and eighth columns). Balances in these columns are used to prepare the budgeted income statement and balance sheet.

Exhibit 24.15

Sources of Amounts in Budgeted Balance Sheet

Item	Amount	Explanation
Cash	$ 20,000	Ending balance for December from the cash budget in Exhibit 24.11.
Accounts receivable	$ 84,000	60% of $140,000 sales budgeted for December from the sales budget in Exhibit 24.6.
Inventory	$ 48,600	810 units in budgeted December ending inventory at the budgeted cost of $60 per unit (from the purchases budget in Exhibit 24.8).
Equipment	$225,000	September 30 balance of $200,000 from the beginning balance sheet in Exhibit 24.5 plus $25,000 cost of new equipment from the cash budget in Exhibit 24.11.
Accumulated depreciation	$ 40,500	September 30 balance of $36,000 from the beginning balance sheet in Exhibit 24.5 plus $4,500 expense from the general and administrative expense budget in Exhibit 24.10.
Accounts payable	$ 57,000	Budgeted cost of purchases for December from the purchases budget in Exhibit 24.8.
Income taxes payable	$ 28,669	Income tax expense from the budgeted income statement for the fourth quarter in Exhibit 24.14.
Bank loan payable	$ 19,628	Budgeted December 31 balance from the cash budget in Exhibit 24.11.
Common stock	$150,000	Unchanged from the beginning balance sheet in Exhibit 24.5.
Retained earnings	$ 81,803	September 30 balance of $41,800 from the beginning balance sheet in Exhibit 24.5 plus budgeted net income of $43,003 from the budgeted income statement in Exhibit 24.14 minus budgeted cash dividends of $3,000 from the cash budget in Exhibit 24.11.

Exhibit 24.16

Budgeted Balance Sheet

HOCKEY DEN
Budgeted Balance Sheet
December 31, 1999

Assets		
Cash		$ 20,000
Accounts receivable		84,000
Inventory (810 units @ $60)		48,600
Equipment	$225,000	
Less accumulated depreciation	(40,500)	184,500
Total assets		$337,100
Liabilities and Stockholders' Equity		
Liabilities:		
Accounts payable	$ 57,000	
Income taxes payable	28,669	
Bank loan payable	19,628	$105,297
Stockholders' equity:		
Common stock	150,000	
Retained earnings	81,803	231,803
Total liabilities and equity		$337,100

Flash back

11. In preparing a budgeted balance sheet:

a. Plant assets are determined by analyzing the capital expenditures budget and the balance sheet from the beginning of the budget period.

b. Liabilities are determined by analyzing the general and administrative expense budget.

c. Retained earnings are determined from information contained in the cash budget and the balance sheet from the beginning of the budget period.

12. What sequence is followed in preparing the budgets that constitute the master budget?

Answers—p. 1038

Zero-Based Budgeting

USING THE INFORMATION

A1 Analyze expense planning using zero-based budgeting.

This chapter focused on the preparation of budgets. In most cases, annual budgets are based on figures from the previous year and are adjusted for changes in business conditions. But in some cases companies encounter totally new circumstances that demand a different budgeting process.

Consider, for example, the marketing department of a company that plans to promote its products for the very first time at a trade show. How does it prepare a budget for the trade show? One solution to this situation is zero-based budgeting.

Companies using zero-based budgeting start each budgeting period at "ground zero." They assume no previous history for the set of activities being planned. Instead, they prepare a detailed list of activities to be carried out, the resources required to carry out these activities, and the expenses of acquiring these resources. This type of expense planning requires managers to justify the amounts budgeted for each activity.

Environmental Manager
You are the new manager responsible for environmental control of a chemical company. This is a new position within the company. You are asked to develop a budget for your job and its responsibilities. How do you proceed?

Answer—p. 1038

Summary

C1 Describe the importance and benefits of budgeting. Planning is a management responsibility of crucial importance to business success. Budgeting is the process used by management to formalize its plans. Budgeting promotes analysis by management and focuses its attention on the future. Budgeting also provides a basis for evaluating performance, serves as a source of motivation, is a means of coordinating business activities, and communicates management's plans and instructions to employees.

C2 Explain the process of budget administration. Budgeting is a detailed activity that requires administration. At least three aspects are important: budget committee, budgeting reporting, and budget timing. A budget committee oversees the preparation of the budget. The budget period pertains to the time period for which the budget is prepared such as a year, quarter, or month.

C3 Describe a master budget and the process of preparing it. A master budget is a formal overall plan for a company. It consists of specific plans for business operations, capital expenditures, and the financial results of those activities. The budgeting process begins with preparing a sales budget. Based on expected sales volume, merchandisers can budget merchandise purchases, selling expenses, and administrative expenses. Next, the capital expenditures budget is prepared, followed by the cash budget, and budgeted financial statements. Manufacturers also must budget production quantities, direct materials purchases, direct labor costs, and overhead.

A1 Analyze expense planning using zero-based budgeting. Companies often budget for the next year based on the current year's budgets. This may not be possible if there is no historical data available as a base. In such situations, zero-based budgeting can be used for expense planning. Managers following the zero-based budgeting approach must prepare a detailed list of the activities to be carried out, the resources required to carry out these activities, and the expenses of acquiring these resources.

P1 Prepare each component of a master budget and link them to the budgeting process. In the process of preparing a master budget, each component budget is designed to provide guidance for persons responsible for activities covered by that budget. The master budget shows how much revenue is to be received from sales and how much expense is to be incurred. Budgets are designed to reflect the activities of one area (such as merchandising) impacting the activities of others (such as marketing). The various components of a company are directed to pursue activities consistent with and supportive of its overall objectives.

P2 Link both operating and capital expenditures budgets to budgeted financial statements. The operating budgets, capital expenditures budget, and cash budget contain much of the information to prepare a budgeted income statement for the budget period and a budgeted balance sheet at the end of the budget period. Budgeted financial statements show the expected financial consequences of the planned activities described in the budgets.

Guidance Answer to **Judgment and Ethics**

Budget Staffer

The action of your superior is unethical. This is because she is using private information for personal gain. Her actions also hurt the company and its shareholders. As a budget staffer, you are low in the company's hierarchical structure and probably unable to directly confront this superior. Yet you should inform an individual with a position of authority within the organization about your discovery. You might also enlist the support of a colleague to explain the situation. The information might be more credible if it comes from two staffers rather than one.

Guidance Answers to **You Make the Call**

Sales Manager

There are two issues you must deal with. First, given that fashions and designs are constantly changing, you cannot rely heavily on previous budgets because they may be irrelevant. As a result, you must carefully analyze the market to understand what designs are in vogue and how long they will last. This information will help you plan the product mix of designs you are willing to offer and help you estimate demand for your designs. The second issue is one of the budgeting period. Because of continuous change, you may not be able to prepare an annual sales budget. Your best bet may be to prepare monthly and quarterly sales budgets that you continuously monitor and revise as necessary.

Environmental Manager

Given that yours is a new position, you are unlikely to have historical data to draw on in preparing your budget. In this situation, you must use zero-based budgeting to develop your budget. This requires you to develop a list of activities you plan to conduct, the resources required to carry out these activities, and the expenses associated with these resources. You should challenge yourself to be absolutely certain that the listed activities are necessary and that the listed resources are required. This process will strengthen your budget and its likelihood of funding.

Guidance Answers to

1. Major benefits include: (1) promoting a focus on the future; (2) providing a basis for evaluating performance; (3) providing a source of motivation; (4) coordinating the departments of a business; and (5) communicating plans and instructions.
2. The budget committee's responsibility is to provide central guidance to ensure that budget figures are realistic and coordinated.
3. Budget periods usually coincide with accounting periods and therefore cover a month, quarter, or a year. Budgets can also be prepared to cover a long-range period, such as five years.
4. Rolling budgets are budgets that are periodically revised in the process of continuous budgeting.
5. A master budget is a comprehensive or overall plan for the company that is generally expressed in monetary terms.
6. *b*
7. The master budget includes operating budgets, the capital expenditures budget, and financial budgets.
8. *c;* Computed as: $(.60 \times 140) + 120 - 50 = 154$.
9. Merchandisers prepare merchandise purchases budgets while manufacturers prepare production and manufacturing budgets.
10. With a just-in-time system, the level of inventory is kept to a minimum and orders for merchandise or materials are intended to meet immediate sales demand. A safety stock system maintains an inventory that is large enough to meet sales demands plus an amount to satisfy unexpected sales demands and an amount to cover delayed shipments from suppliers.
11. *a*
12. (1) Sales budget (and any other operating budgets), (2) capital expenditures budget, (3) financial budgets—cash budget, budgeted income statement, and budgeted balance sheet.

Demonstration Problem

The management of Wild Wood Co. asks you to prepare a master budget for the company using the following information. The budget is to cover the months of April, May, and June 1999.

WILD WOOD COMPANY
Balance Sheet
March 31, 1999

Assets			**Liabilities and Stockholders' Equity**		
Cash	$ 50,000		Accounts payable	$156,000	
Accounts receivable	175,000		Short-term notes payable	12,000	
Inventory	126,000		Total current liabilities		$168,000
Total current assets		$351,000	Long-term note payable		200,000
Equipment	480,000		Total liabilities		$368,000
Accumulated depreciation	(90,000)	390,000	Common stock	235,000	
Total assets		$741,000	Retained earnings	138,000	
			Total stockholders' equity		373,000
			Total liabilities and equity		$741,000

Additional Information

a. Unit sales for March are 10,000 units. Each month's sales are expected to exceed the prior month's results by 5%. The selling price of the product is $25 per unit.

b. Company policy calls for ending inventory of a given month to equal 80% of next month's expected unit sales. The March 31 inventory is 8,400 units, which is in compliance with the policy. The purchase price is $15 per unit.

c. Sales representatives' commissions are 12.5% and are paid in the month of the sales. The sales manager's salary will be $3,500 in April and $4,000 thereafter.

d. General and administrative expenses include: administrative salaries of $8,000 per month, depreciation of $5,000 per month, and 0.9% monthly interest on the long-term note payable.

e. Thirty percent of the company's sales are expected to be for cash and the remaining 70% will be on credit. Receivables are collected in full in the month following the sale (none is collected in the month of the sale).

f. All purchases of merchandise are on credit, and no payables arise from any other transactions. The purchases of one month are fully paid in the next month.

g. The minimum ending cash balance for all months is $50,000. If necessary, the company will borrow enough cash to reach the minimum. The resulting short-term note will require an interest payment of 1% at the end of each month. If the ending cash balance exceeds the minimum, the excess will be applied to repaying the short-term notes payable.

h. Dividends of $100,000 are to be declared and paid in May.

i. No cash payments for income taxes are to be made during the second calendar quarter. Income taxes will be assessed at 35% in the quarter.

j. Equipment purchases of $55,000 are scheduled for June.

Required

Prepare the following budgets and other financial information as required:

1. Sales budget, including sales for July.
2. Purchases budget, the budgeted cost of goods sold for each month and quarter, and the cost of the June 30 budgeted inventory.

3. Selling expense budget.
4. General and administrative expense budget.
5. Expected cash receipts from customers and the expected June 30 balance of accounts receivable.
6. Expected cash payments for purchases and the expected June 30 balance of accounts payable.
7. Cash budget.
8. Budgeted income statement.
9. Budgeted statement of retained earnings.
10. Budgeted balance sheet.

Planning the Solution

- The sales budget shows expected sales for each month in the quarter. Start by multiplying March sales by 105%, and do the same for the remaining months. July's sales are needed for the purchases budget. To complete the budget, multiply the expected unit sales by the selling price of $25 per unit.
- Use these results and the 80% inventory policy to budget the size of ending inventory for April, May, and June. Add the budgeted sales to these numbers and subtract the actual or expected beginning inventory for each month. The result will be the number of units to be purchased each month. Multiply these numbers by the per unit cost of $15. Find the budgeted cost of goods sold by multiplying the unit sales in each month by the $15 cost per unit. Compute the cost of the June 30 ending inventory by multiplying the units expected to be on hand at that date by the $15 cost per unit.
- The selling expense budget has only two items. Find the amount of the sales representatives' commissions by multiplying the expected dollar sales in each month by the 12.5% commission rate. Then include the sales manager's salary of $3,500 in April and $4,000 in May and June.
- The general and administrative expense budget should show three items. Administrative salaries are fixed at $8,000 per month, and depreciation is to be $5,000 per month. Budget the monthly interest expense on the long-term note by multiplying its $200,000 balance by the 0.9% monthly interest rate.
- Determine the amounts of cash sales in each month by multiplying the budgeted sales by 30%. Add to this amount the credit sales of the prior month, which you can compute as 70% of the prior month's sales. April's cash receipts from collecting receivables will equal the March 31 balance of $175,000. The expected June 30 accounts receivable balance equals 70% of June's total budgeted sales.
- Determine expected cash payments on accounts payable for each month by making them equal to the merchandise purchases in the prior month. The payments for April equal the March 31 balance of accounts payable shown on the beginning balance sheet. The June 30 balance of accounts payable equals merchandise purchases for June.
- Prepare the cash budget by combining the given information and the amounts of cash receipts and cash payments on account that you just computed. Complete the cash budget for each month by either borrowing enough to raise the preliminary balance up to the minimum or paying off the short-term note as much as the balance will allow without falling below the minimum. Show the ending balance of the short-term note in the budget.
- Prepare the budgeted income statement by combining the budgeted items for all three months. Determine the income before income taxes and multiply it by the 35% rate to find the quarter's income tax expense.
- The budgeted statement of retained earnings should show the March 31 balance plus the quarter's net income minus the quarter's dividends.
- The budgeted balance sheet includes updated balances for all the items that appear in the beginning balance sheet and an additional liability for unpaid income taxes. Amounts for all asset, liability, and equity accounts can be found either in the budgets and schedules or by adding amounts found there to the beginning balances.

Solution to Demonstration Problem

1. Sales budget

	April	May	June	July
Prior month's sales	10,000	10,500	11,025	11,576
Plus 5% growth	500	525	551	579
Projected unit sales	10,500	11,025	11,576	12,155

	April	May	June	Quarter
Projected unit sales	10,500	11,025	11,576	
Selling price per unit	× $25	× $25	× $25	
Projected sales revenue	$262,500	$275,625	$289,400	$827,525

2. Purchases budget:

	April	May	June	Quarter
Next month's unit sales (*part 1*)	11,025	11,576	12,155	
Ending inventory percent	× 80%	× 80%	× 80%	
Desired ending inventory	8,820	9,261	9,724	
This month's unit sales (*part 1*)	10,500	11,025	11,576	
Units to be available	19,320	20,286	21,300	
Beginning inventory	(8,400)	(8,820)	(9,261)	
Units to be purchased	10,920	11,466	12,039	
Budgeted cost per unit	$15	$15	$15	
Projected purchases	$163,800	$171,990	$180,585	$516,375

Budgeted cost of goods sold:

	April	May	June	Quarter
This month's unit sales (*part 1*)	10,500	11,025	11,576	
Budgeted cost per unit	× $15	× $15	× $15	
Projected cost of goods sold	$157,500	$165,375	$173,640	$496,515

Budgeted inventory for June 30:

Units (*part 1*)	9,724
Cost per unit	× $15
Total	$145,860

3. Selling expense budget:

	April	May	June	Quarter
Budgeted sales (*part 1*)	$262,500	$275,625	$289,400	$827,525
Commission percent	× 12.5%	× 12.5%	× 12.5%	× 12.5%
Sales commissions	$ 32,813	$ 34,453	$ 36,175	$103,441
Manager's salary	3,500	4,000	4,000	11,500
Projected selling expenses	$ 36,313	$ 38,453	$ 40,175	$114,941

4. General and administrative expense budget:

	April	May	June	Quarter
Administrative salaries	$ 8,000	$ 8,000	$ 8,000	$24,000
Depreciation	5,000	5,000	5,000	15,000
Interest on long-term note payable (0.9% × $200,000)	1,800	1,800	1,800	5,400
Projected expenses	$14,800	$14,800	$14,800	$44,400

5. Expected cash receipts from customers:

	April	May	June	Quarter
Budgeted sales (*part 1*)	$262,500	$275,625	$289,400	
Ending accounts receivable (70%)	$183,750	$192,938	$202,580	
Cash receipts:				
Cash sales (30%)	$ 78,750	$ 82,687	$ 86,820	$248,257
Collections of prior month's receivables	175,000	183,750	192,938	551,688
Total cash to be collected	$253,750	$266,437	$279,758	$799,945

6. Expected cash payments to suppliers:

	April	May	June	Quarter
Cash payments (equal to prior month's purchases)	$156,000	$163,800	$171,990	$491,790
Expected June 30 balance of accounts payable (June purchases)			$180,585	

7. Cash budget:

	April	May	June
Beginning cash balance	$ 50,000	$ 89,517	$ 50,000
Cash receipts (*part 5*)	253,750	266,437	279,758
Total cash available	$303,750	$355,954	$329,758
Cash payments:			
Payments for merchandise (*part 6*)	$156,000	$163,800	$171,990
Sales commissions (*part 3*)	32,813	34,453	36,175
Salaries:			
Sales	3,500	4,000	4,000
Administrative	8,000	8,000	8,000
Interest on long-term note	1,800	1,800	1,800
Dividends		100,000	
Equipment purchase			55,000
Interest on short-term notes:			
April ($12,000 × 1.0%)	120		
June ($6,099 × 1.0%)			61
Total	$202,233	$312,053	$277,026
Preliminary balance	$101,517	$ 43,901	$ 52,732
Additional loan		6,099	
Loan repayment	(12,000)		(2,732)
Ending cash balance	$ 89,517	$ 50,000	$ 50,000
Ending short-term notes	$ 0	$ 6,099	$ 3,367

8.

WILD WOOD COMPANY
Budgeted Income Statement
Quarter Ended June 30, 1999

Sales (*part 1*)		$827,525
Cost of goods sold (*part 2*)		(496,515)
Gross profit		$331,010
Operating expenses:		
Sales commissions (*part 3*)	$103,441	
Sales salaries (*part 3*)	11,500	
Administrative salaries (*part 4*)	24,000	
Depreciation (*part 4*)	15,000	
Interest on long-term note (*part 4*)	5,400	
Interest on short-term notes (*part 7*)	181	
Total operating expenses		(159,522)
Income before income taxes		$171,488
Income taxes (35%)		(60,021)
Net income		$111,467

9.

WILD WOOD COMPANY
Budgeted Statement of Retained Earnings
For Quarter Ended June 30, 1999

Beginning retained earnings (*given*)	$138,000
Net income (*part 8*)	111,467
Total	$249,467
Dividends (*given*)	(100,000)
Ending retained earnings	$149,467

10.

WILD WOOD COMPANY
Budgeted Balance Sheet
June 30, 1999

Assets		
Cash (*part 7*)	$ 50,000	
Accounts receivable (*part 5*)	202,580	
Inventory (*part 2*)	145,860	
Total current assets		$398,440
Equipment (*given plus purchase*)	535,000	
Accumulated depreciation (*given plus expense*)	(105,000)	430,000
Total assets		$828,440
Liabilities and Equity		
Accounts payable (*part 6*)	$180,585	
Short-term notes payable (*part 7*)	3,367	
Income taxes payable (*part 8*)	60,021	
Total current liabilities		$243,973
Long-term note payable (*given*)		200,000
Total liabilities		$443,973
Common stock (*given*)	235,000	
Retained earnings (*part 9*)	149,467	
Total stockholders' equity		384,467
Total liabilities and equity		$828,440

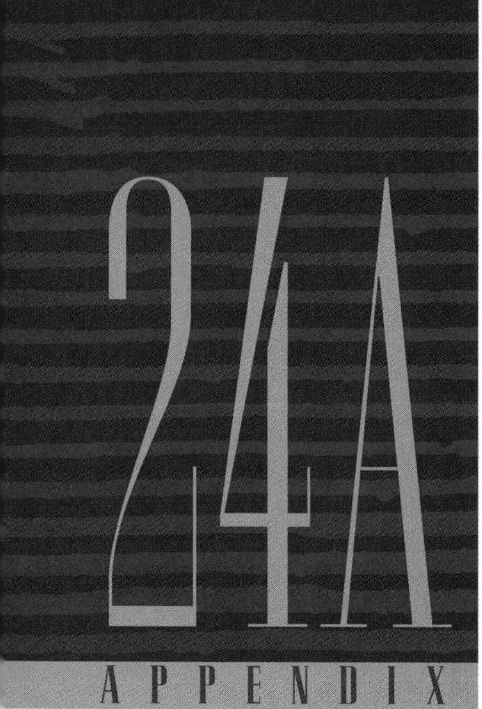

Production and Manufacturing Budgets

APPENDIX

Learning Objective

Procedural

P3 Prepare production and manufacturing budgets.

Unlike a merchandising company, a manufacturer must prepare a **production budget** instead of a merchandise purchases budget. A production budget shows the number of units to be produced each month. Production budgets are similar to merchandise purchases budgets except the number of units to be purchased each month (as shown in Exhibit 24.8) is replaced by the number of units to be manufactured each month. A production budget doesn't show costs because it is *always expressed in units of product.* Exhibit 24A.1 shows the production budget for **Toronto Supply Company (TSC)**, a manufacturer of hockey sticks and exclusive supplier of hockey sticks to Hockey Den. This means TSC uses the same budgeted sales figures from Hockey Den (Exhibit 24.6) to determine its production and manufacturing budgets.

Exhibit 24A.1

Production Budget

TSC
Production Budget
October 1999–December 1999

	October	November	December
Next month's budgeted sales (units)	800	1,400	900
Ratio of inventory to future sales	× 90%	× 90%	× 90%
Budgeted ending inventory (units)	720	1,260	810
Add budgeted sales for the month (units)	1,000	800	1,400
Required units of available production	1,720	2,060	2,210
Deduct beginning inventory (units)	(900)	(720)	(1,260)
Number of units to be produced	820	1,340	950

A **manufacturing budget** shows the budgeted costs for direct materials, direct labor, and manufacturing overhead. It is based on the budgeted production volume from the production budget. The manufacturing budget for most companies consists of three individual budgets: direct materials budget, direct labor budget, and overhead budget. Exhibits 24A.2–24A.4 show these three manufacturing budgets for TSC. These budgets show the total cost of goods to be manufactured in the budget period.

The *direct materials budget* begins by computing the budgeted materials needed to satisfy each month's production requirement. We must also add the desired ending inventory requirements. The desired ending inventory of direct materials as shown in Exhibit 24A.2 is 50% of next month's budgeted material requirements of wood. For instance, in the month of October 1999, an ending inventory of 335 units of material is desired (50% of November's 670 units). The desired ending inventory for December 1999 is 225 units, computed from the direct material requirement of 450 units for a production level of 900 units in January 2000.

The total material requirements are computed by adding the desired ending inventory figures to that month's budgeted production material requirements. For October 1999, the total material requirement is 745 units (335 + 410). From the total material

TSC Direct Materials Budget October 1999–December 1999	October	November	December
Budget production (units)	820	1,340	950
Material requirements per unit	× 0.5	× 0.5	× 0.5
Materials needed for production (units)	410	670	475
Add desired ending inventory (units)	335	237.5	225
Total materials requirements (units)	745	907.5	700
Deduct beginning inventory (units)	(205)	(335)	(237.5)
Units of materials to be purchased	540	572.5	462.5
Material price per unit	$20	$20	$20
Total cost of direct materials purchases	$10,800	$11,450	$9,250

Exhibit 24A.2

Direct Materials Budget

requirement we then subtract the units of materials available in beginning inventory. For October 1999, the materials available from September 1999 are computed as 50% of October's material requirements to satisfy production, or 205 units (50% of 410). This means the direct materials purchases in October 1999 are budgeted at 540 units (745 − 205). See Exhibit 24A.2.

The *direct labor budget* for TSC is shown in Exhibit 24A.3. About 15 minutes of labor time is required to produce one unit for TSC. Labor is paid at the rate of $12 per hour. Budgeted labor hours are computed by multiplying the budgeted production level for each month by one quarter (0.25) of an hour. Direct labor cost is then computed by multiplying budgeted labor hours by the labor rate of $12 per hour.

TSC Direct Labor Budget October 1999–December 1999	October	November	December
Budgeted production (units)	820	1,340	950
Labor requirements per unit (hours)	× 0.25	× 0.25	× 0.25
Total labor hours needed	205	335	237.5
Labor rate (per hour)	$ 12	$ 12	$ 12
Labor dollars	$2,460	$4,020	$2,850

Exhibit 24A.3

Direct Labor Budget

The *manufacturing overhead budget* for TSC is shown in Exhibit 24A.4. The variable portion of overhead is assigned at the rate of $2.50 per unit of production for TSC. The fixed portion stays constant at $15,000 per month for TSC. We show a condensed manufacturing overhead budget in Exhibit 24A.4. Most overhead budgets are more detailed, listing each overhead cost item.

TSC Manufacturing Overhead Budget October 1999–December 1999	October	November	December
Budgeted production (units)	820	1,340	950
Variable manufacturing overhead rate	×$2.50	×$2.50	×$2.50
Budgeted variable overhead	$2,050	$3,350	$2,375
Budgeted fixed overhead	1,500	1,500	1,500
Budgeted total overhead	$3,550	$4,850	$3,875

Exhibit 24A.4

Manufacturing Overhead Budget

Glossary

Budget a formal statement of future plans, usually expressed in monetary terms. (p. 1020).

Budgeted balance sheet an accounting report that presents predicted amounts of the company's assets, liabilities, and equity balances as of the end of the budget period. (p. 1035).

Budgeted income statement an accounting report that presents predicted amounts of the company's revenues and expenses for the budget period. (p. 1034).

Budgeting the process of planning future business actions and expressing them as formal plans. (p. 1020).

Capital expenditures budget a plan that lists dollar amounts to be received from disposing of plant assets and dollar amounts to be spent on purchasing plant assets if the proposed business activities are carried out. (p. 1032).

Cash budget a plan that shows the expected cash inflows and outflows during the budget period, including receipts from loans needed to maintain a minimum cash balance and repayments of such loans. (p. 1032).

Continuous budgeting the practice of preparing budgets for each of several future periods and revising those budgets as each period is completed; as one period is completed, a new budget is added, with the result that the budget always covers the same number of future periods. (p. 1024).

General and administrative expense budget a plan that shows the predicted operating expenses not included in the selling expenses budget. (p. 1030).

Manufacturing budget a plan that shows the predicted costs for direct materials, direct labor, and overhead costs to be incurred in manufacturing units in the production budget. (p. 1044).

Master budget a comprehensive, or overall, formal business plan that includes specific plans for expected sales, the units of product to be produced, the merchandise (or materials) to be purchased, the expenses to be incurred, the long-term assets to be purchased, and the amounts of cash to be borrowed or loans to be repaid, as well as a budgeted income statement and balance sheet. (p. 1025).

Merchandise purchases budget a plan that shows the units or costs of merchandise to be purchased by a merchandising company during the budget period. (p. 1029).

Production budget a plan showing the number of units to be produced each month. (p. 1044).

Rolling budgets as each budget period goes by, a firm adds a new set of budgets for the next period to replace the ones that have lapsed. (p. 1024).

Safety stock inventory on hand to reduce the risk of running out; a quantity of merchandise or materials over the minimum needed to satisfy budgeted demand. (p. 1029).

Sales budget a plan showing the units of goods to be sold and the revenue to be derived from the sales; the starting point in the budgeting process because the plans for most departments are related to sales. (p. 1027).

Selling expense budget a plan that lists the types and amounts of selling expenses expected in the budget period. (p. 1030).

The superscript letter A identifies assignment material based on Appendix 24A.

Questions

1. Identify at least three roles budgeting plays in helping managers control a business.
2. Budgeting promotes good decision making by requiring managers to conduct __________ and by focusing their attention on the __________.
3. What two alternative norms or objectives can be used to evaluate actual performance? Which of the two is generally more useful?
4. What is the benefit of continuous budgeting?
5. Identify the three typical short-term planning time horizons for budgets.
6. Why should each department participate in preparing its own budget?
7. How does budgeting help management coordinate business activities?
8. Why is the sales budget so important to the budgeting process?
9. What is a selling expense budget? What is a capital expenditures budget?
10.[A] What is the difference between a production budget and a manufacturing budget?
11. What is a cash budget? Why do operating budgets and the capital expenditures budget need to be prepared before the cash budget?
12. Assume **NIKE's** athletic apparel division is charged with the responsibility of preparing a master budget. Identify the participants—for example, the sales manager for the sales budget—and describe the information each person would provide in preparing the master budget.
13. Does the manager of a local fast food restaurant participate in long-term budgeting?

Quick Study

QS 24-1
Budget motivation 

What are three guidelines that should be followed if budgeting is to serve effectively as a source of motivation?

QS 24-2
Identifying components of a master budget
C3

Which of the following items make up the master budget?

a. Sales budget, operating budgets, and historical financial budgets.
b. Operating budgets, historical income statement, and budgeted balance sheet.
c. Operating budgets, financial budgets, and capital expenditures budget.
d. Prior sales reports, capital expenditures budget, and financial budgets.

QS 24-3
Purchases budget
P1

The July sales budget of Loop Company calls for sales of $400,000. The store expects to begin July with $40,000 of inventory and to end the month with $50,000 of inventory. Cost of goods sold is typically about 70% of sales. Determine the cost of goods that should be purchased during July.

QS 24-4
Cash budget
P1, P2

Use the information below to prepare a cash budget for MC Company. The budget should show expected cash receipts and cash disbursements for the month of March and the balance expected on March 31.

a. Beginning cash balance on March 1, $82,000.
b. Cash receipts from sales, $300,000.
c. Budgeted cash disbursements for purchases, $120,000.
d. Budgeted cash disbursements for salaries, $80,000.
e. Other budgeted cash expenses, $55,000.
f. Repayment of bank loan, $30,000.

QS 24-5[A]
Production budget
P3

Time Company manufactures watches and has a policy that ending inventory equals 20% of the next month's sales. Time estimates that October's actual ending inventory will consist of 95,000 watches. Sales for November and December are estimated to be 350,000 and 400,000, respectively. Calculate the number of watches to be produced that would appear on Time's production budget for November.

QS 24-6
Computing budgeted accounts receivable
P2

Light Company anticipates total sales for June and July of $420,000 and $398,000, respectively. Cash sales are normally 60% of total sales. Of the credit sales, 10% are collected in the same month as the sale, 70% are collected during the first month after the sale, and the remaining 20% are collected in the second month. Determine the amount of accounts receivable that should be reported on Light's budgeted balance sheet as of July 31.

QS 24-7
Budgeting process
C2

Explain why the bottom-up approach to budgeting is considered more successful than a top-down approach. Provide an example.

QS 24-8
Zero-based budgeting
A1

Why is zero-based budgeting usually more time-consuming for management and employees?

Exercises

Exercise 24-1[A]
Preparing production budgets for two periods
P3

UVW Company manufactures an innovative automobile transmission for electric cars. Management predicts that ending inventory for the first quarter will be 90,000 units. The following unit sales of the transmissions are expected during the rest of the year: second quarter, 300,000 units; third quarter, 500,000 units; and fourth quarter, 400,000 units. Management's policy calls for the ending inventory of a quarter to equal 30% of the next quarter's budgeted sales.

Required

Prepare a production budget showing the transmissions that should be manufactured during this year's second and third quarters.

Exercise 24-2
Computing and preparing merchandise purchases budgets for three periods
C3, P1

In-Line Skates Company prepares monthly budgets. The current budget plans for a September ending inventory of 15,000 units. The company follows a policy of ending each month with merchandise inventory on hand equal to a specified percent of budgeted sales for the following month. Budgeted sales and merchandise purchases for the three most recent months are:

	Sales (Units)	Purchases (Units)
July	120,000	138,000
August	210,000	204,000
September	180,000	159,000

1. Use this information to compute the following amounts:
   a. Policy (percent relation) between a month's ending inventory and sales budgeted for September.
   b. Units budgeted to be sold in October.
   c. Units budgeted for July's beginning inventory.
2. Show the merchandise purchases budgets for July, August, and September.

Exercise 24-3
Preparing cash budgets for three periods
C3, P2

Keller Co. budgeted the following cash receipts and cash disbursements for the first 3 months of next year:

	Cash Receipts	Cash Disbursements
January	$500,000	$450,000
February	300,000	250,000
March	400,000	500,000

According to a credit agreement with the company's bank, Keller promises to have a minimum cash balance of $30,000 at the end of each month. In return, the bank has agreed that the company can borrow up to $150,000 with interest of 12% per year, paid on the last day of each month. The interest is computed on the beginning balance of the loan for the month. The company has a cash balance of $30,000 and a loan balance of $60,000 on January 1.

Required

Prepare monthly cash budgets for the first 3 months of next year.

Exercise 24-4
Preparing a cash budget from transaction data
C3, P2

Use the information below to prepare a cash budget for Multimedia, Inc. It should show expected cash receipts and cash disbursements for the month of July and the cash balance expected on July 31.

a. Beginning cash balance on July 1: $50,000.
b. Cash receipts from sales: 30% is collected in the month of sale, 50% in the next month, 18% in the second month after sale, and 2% is uncollectible. The following actual and budgeted amounts of sales are: May (actual), $1,720,000; June (actual), $1,200,000; and July (budgeted), $1,400,000.
c. Payments on purchases: 60% in the month of purchase and 40% in the month following purchase. The following actual and budgeted amounts of merchandise purchases are: June (actual), $430,000; and July (budgeted), $600,000.
d. Budgeted cash disbursements for salaries in July: $211,000.
e. Budgeted depreciation expense for July: $12,000.
f. Other cash expenses budgeted for July: $150,000.
g. Accrued income taxes due in July: $80,000.
h. Bank loan interest due in July: $6,600.

Exercise 24-5
Preparing a budgeted income statement and balance sheet
C3, P2

Use the information in Exercise 24-4 and the additional information below to prepare a budgeted income statement for the month of July and a budgeted balance sheet for July 31:

a. Cost of goods sold is 44% of sales.

b. Inventory at the end of June is $80,000 and at the end of July is $64,000.

c. Salaries payable on June 30 are $50,000 and are expected to be $40,000 on July 31.

d. Equipment account balance is $1,600,000 on July 31. On June 30, accumulated depreciation is $280,000.

e. The $6,600 cash payment of interest represents the 1% monthly expense on a bank loan of $660,000.

f. Income taxes payable on July 31 are $115,920, and the income tax rate applicable to the company is 30%. Use this information to check the net income value.

g. Ending July 31 balances of Accounts Receivable and the Allowance for Doubtful Accounts are $1,220,000 and $52,000 respectively. The 2% of sales that prove to be uncollectible are debited to Bad Debts Expense and credited to Allowance for Doubtful Accounts in the month of sale.

h. The only other balance sheet accounts are: Common Stock, with a balance of $600,000 on June 30; and Retained Earnings, with a balance of $1,013,600 on June 30.

Exercise 24-6
Computing budgeted cash payments
C3, P2

Handle Company's cost of goods sold is consistently 60% of sales. The company plans to carry merchandise inventory at the beginning of each month with a cost equal to 40% of that month's budgeted cost of goods sold. All merchandise is purchased on credit, and 50% of the purchases made during a month are paid for in that month. Another 35% are paid for during the first month after purchase, and the remaining 15% are paid for during the second month after purchase. Use the following sales budgets to compute the expected cash payments on accounts in October: August, $150,000; September, $350,000; October, $200,000; and November, $300,000.

Exercise 24-7
Computing budgeted purchases and costs of goods sold
C3, P1, P2

Camping World Company purchases all of its camping merchandise on credit. It has recently budgeted the following accounts payable balances and merchandise inventory balances:

	Accounts Payable	Merchandise Inventory
May 31	$120,000	$250,000
June 30	170,000	400,000
July 31	200,000	300,000
August 30	160,000	330,000

Cash payments on accounts payable during each month are expected to be: May, $1,300,000; June, $1,450,000; July, $1,350,000; and August, $1,400,000.

a. Complete budgeted amounts of merchandise purchases for June, July, and August.

b. Compute budgeted amounts of cost of goods sold for June, July, and August.

Exercise 24-8
Computing budgeted accounts payable and purchases
P1, P2

All-Tec, a merchandising company specializing in home computer speakers, budgets its monthly cost of goods sold to equal 70% of sales. The inventory policy calls for a beginning inventory in each month equal to 25% of the budgeted cost of goods sold for that month. All purchases are on credit, and 20% of the purchases in any month are paid for in the same month. Another 50% are paid for during the first month after purchase, and the remaining 30% are paid for in the second month after purchase. The following sales budgets are established: July, $300,000; August, $240,000; September, $270,000; October, $240,000; and November, $210,000.

a. Compute budgeted merchandise purchases for July, August, September, and October.

b. Compute budgeted payments on accounts payable for September and October.

c. Compute budgeted ending balances of accounts payable for September and October.

Exercise 24-9
Comparing zero-based and continuous budgeting
C2, A1

Jimmy John's foot-long, ball park franks are sold at sporting events around the country. Each year management and employees begin preparing the master budget in October and present the final budget in late December. The process requires the budget committee to merge several hundred regional budgets into one consolidated budget to begin production planning at the manufacturing plant. This is a challenging process because new regions are added and other regions dropped each year.

Required

As the chair of the budget committee you are to identify your preferred budgeting process (continuous or zero-based) and justify your selection for preparing the budgets for each region. Regions are defined as new or existing. A new region represents a new customer base, where the market size must be estimated from available data. An existing region is one that has a stable, predictable market.

Region	Budget Process (Continuous or Zero-Based)	Justification
New region		
Existing region		

Problems

Problem 24-1A
Preparing production and materials purchases budgets
C3, P3

Check Figure Cost of carbon fiber purchases, $2,748,000

Sport World Company produces snow skis. Each ski requires two pounds of carbon fiber. The company's management predicts there will be 7,000 skis and 10,000 pounds of carbon fiber in inventory on June 30 of the current year, and that 120,000 skis will be sold during the next quarter. Management wants to end the third quarter with 4,000 skis and 5,000 pounds of carbon fiber in inventory. Carbon fiber can be purchased for $12 per pound.

Required

1. Prepare the third-quarter production budget for skis.
2. Prepare the third-quarter carbon fiber purchases budget (include the dollar cost of purchases).

Problem 24-2
Preparing and analyzing merchandise purchases budgets
C3, P1

Check Figure Shoe purchases for May, 31,200 units

Tennis-One retails three products that it buys ready for sale. The company's February 28 inventories are: shoes, 15,500 units; equipment, 70,000 units; and apparel, 40,000 units. Management feels that excessive inventories have accumulated for all three products. As a result, a new policy dictates that ending inventory in any month should equal 40% of the expected unit sales for the following month. Expected sales in units for March, April, May, and June are:

	Budgeted Sales in Units			
	March	April	May	June
Shoes	10,000	20,000	30,000	33,000
Equipment	66,000	85,000	90,000	80,000
Apparel	36,000	30,000	30,000	18,000

Required

Preparation Component

1. Prepare separate purchases budgets (in units) for each of the products for March, April, and May.

Analysis Component

2. The purchases budgets should reflect fewer purchases of all three products in March compared to April and May. What factor caused these fewer purchases to be planned? Suggest business conditions that would cause this factor to both occur and affect Tennis-One as it has.

Problem 24-3
Preparing and analyzing cash budgets with supporting inventory and purchases schedules
C3, P2

DVD Company has a cash balance of $60,000 on June 1. The company's product sells for $125 per unit, and its actual and projected sales are:

	Units	Dollars
April (actual)	8,000	$1,000,000
May (actual)	4,000	500,000
June (budgeted)	12,000	1,500,000
July (budgeted)	6,000	750,000
August (budgeted)	7,600	950,000

All of its sales are on credit. Recent experience shows that 20% of its sales are collected in the month of the sale, 30% in the month after the sale, 48% in the second month after the sale, and 2% prove to be uncollectible. The purchase price of the product is $100 per unit. All purchases are payable within 12 days. This means 60% of purchases made in a month are paid in that month and the other 40% are paid in the next month. DVD's management has a policy of maintaining an ending monthly inventory of 25% of the next month's unit sales plus a safety stock of 100 units. The March 31 and May 31 actual inventory levels are consistent with this policy. Selling and administrative expenses for the year are $1,200,000 and are paid evenly throughout the year in cash. The company's minimum cash balance for the end of a month is $60,000. This minimum is maintained, if necessary, by borrowing cash from the bank. If the balance goes over $60,000, the company repays as much of the loan as it can without going below the minimum. This type of loan carries an annual 9% interest rate. On May 31, the balance of the loan is $32,000.

Required

Preparation Component

1. Prepare a schedule that shows cash to be collected in June and July from customers.
2. Prepare a schedule that shows budgeted ending inventories (in units) for April, May, June, and July.
3. Prepare a schedule showing the purchases budgets for the product for May, June, and July. Present calculations in units and then show the dollar amount of purchases for each month.
4. Prepare a schedule showing the cash to be paid in June and July for product purchases.
5. Prepare monthly cash budgets for June and July, including any loan activity and interest expense. Compute the loan balance at the end of each month.

Check Figure Budgeted ending loan balance for June, $72,240

Analysis Component

6. Refer to your answer for part (5). DVD's cash budget indicates the company will need to borrow over $40,000 in June and over $60,000 in July. Suggest some reasons why knowing this information in May would be helpful to DVD's management.

Problem 24-4
Preparing cash budgets for three periods
C3, P2

During the last week of August, the owner of Jazz Company approaches the bank for a $80,000 loan to be made on September 1 and repaid on November 30 with annual interest of 12%, or a total of $2,400. The owner plans to increase the store's inventory by $60,000 during September and needs the loan to pay for merchandise acquired in October and November. The bank's loan officer needs more information about Jazz's ability to repay the loan and asks the owner to forecast the store's November 30 cash position. On September 1, Jazz is expected to have a $3,000 cash balance, $120,000 of accounts receivable, and $100,000 of accounts payable. Its budgeted sales, purchases, and cash disbursements for the next three months are:

	September	October	November
Sales	$220,000	$300,000	$380,000
Merchandise purchases	210,000	180,000	220,000
Payroll	16,000	17,000	18,000
Rent	6,000	6,000	6,000
Other cash expenses	64,000	8,000	7,000
Repayment of bank loan			80,000
Interest on the bank loan			2,400

The budgeted September purchases include the inventory increase. All sales are on account. The company's past experience shows that 25% of its sales are collected in the month of the sale, 45% in the month following the sale, 20% in the second month, 9% in the third, and the remainder is uncollectible. Applying these percents to the September 1 accounts receivable balance, for example, shows that $81,000 of the $120,000 will be collected in September, $36,000 in October, and $16,200 in November. All merchandise is purchased on credit. Eighty percent of the balance is paid in the month following a purchase and the remaining 20% is paid in the second month. For example, of the $100,000 of accounts payable at the end of August, $80,000 will be paid in September and $20,000 in October.

Check Figure Budgeted total cash disbursements for November, $299,400

Required

Prepare cash budgets for September, October, and November for the Jazz Company. Show supplemental schedules as needed.

Problem 24-5
Preparing and analyzing budgeted income statements
C3, P2

Talbert Co., a one product mail-order firm, buys graduation rings at $60 per unit and sells them at $130 per unit. The company's sales staff receives a 10% commission on each sale. Its December income statement is shown below:

TALBERT COMPANY
Income Statement
For Month Ended December 31, 2000

Sales	$1,300,000
Cost of goods sold	600,000
Gross profit	$ 700,000
Expenses:	
Sales commissions (10%)	$ 130,000
Advertising	200,000
Store rent	24,000
Administrative salaries	40,000
Depreciation	50,000
Other	12,000
Total expenses	$ 456,000
Net income	$ 244,000

The company's management believes that the December results will be repeated in January, February, and March without any changes in strategy. Management also believes that unit sales will increase at a rate of 10% each month during the next quarter (including January) if the item's selling price is reduced to $115 per unit and if advertising expenses are increased by 25% and remain at that level for all three months. Whatever changes are made, the purchase price will remain at $60 per ring, the sales staff would continue to earn a 10% commission, and the remaining expenses would stay the same.

Required

Preparation Component

Check Figure Budgeted net income for February, $150,350

1. Using a three-column format (one column for each month), prepare budgeted income statements for January, February, and March that show the expected results of implementing the proposed changes.

Analysis Component

2. Use the budgeted income statements to recommend whether management should implement the changes.

Problem 24-6
Preparing a complete master budget
C2, C3, P1, P2

The management of Sports Cooler Co. prepared the following budgeted balance sheet for December 31, 2000:

SPORTS COOLER
Budgeted Balance Sheet
As of December 31, 2000

Assets		
Cash		$ 36,000
Accounts receivable		525,000
Inventory		150,000
Total current assets		$ 711,000
Equipment	$540,000	
Accumulated depreciation	67,500	472,500
Total assets		$1,183,500
Liabilities and Equity		
Accounts payable	$360,000	
Loan from bank	15,000	
Taxes payable (due 3/15/2001)	90,000	
Total liabilities		$ 465,000
Common stock	472,500	
Retained earnings	246,000	
Total stockholders' equity		718,500
Total liabilities and equity		$1,183,500

For preparing a master budget for January, February, and March of 2001, management gathers the following information:

a. Sports Cooler's single product is purchased for $30 per unit and resold for $45 per unit. The expected inventory level on December 31, 2000, of 5,000 units is greater than management's desired level for year 2001 of 25% of the next month's expected sales (in units). Budgeted sales are: January, 6,000 units; February, 8,000 units; March, 10,000 units; and April, 9,000 units.

b. Cash sales are 25% of total sales and credit sales are 75% of total sales. Of the credit sales, 60% are collected in the first month after the sale and 40% in the second month after the sale. For example, 60 percent of the December 31, 2000, balance of accounts receivable will be collected in January and 40% will be collected in February.

c. Merchandise purchases are paid for as follows: 20% in the month after purchase, and 80% in the second month after purchase. For example, 20 percent of the Accounts Payable balance on December 31, 2000, will be paid in January, and 80% will be paid in February.

d. Sales commissions of 20% of sales are paid each month. Additional sales salaries are $90,000 per year.

e. General and administrative salaries are $144,000 per year. Repairs expense equals $3,000 per month and is paid in cash.

f. Equipment reported in the December 31, 2000, balance sheet is purchased in January 2000. It is being depreciated over eight years under the straight-line method with no salvage value. The following new purchases of equipment are planned in the coming quarter: January, $72,000; February, $96,000; and March, $28,800. This equipment will be depreciated under the straight-line method over eight years with no salvage value. A full month's depreciation is taken for the month in which equipment is purchased.

g. The company plans to acquire land at the end of March at a cost of $150,000. The purchase price will be paid with cash on the last day of the month.

h. Sports Cooler has a working arrangement with the bank to obtain additional loans as needed. The interest rate is 12% per year, and the interest is paid at the end of each month based on the beginning balance. Partial or full payments on these loans can be made on the last day of the month. The company has agreed to maintain a minimum ending cash balance of $36,000 in every month.

i. The income tax rate for the company is 40%. Income taxes on the first quarter's income will not be paid until April 15.

Required

Prepare a master budget for the first quarter of 2001, including the following component budgets (show supplemental schedules as needed, and round amounts to the nearest dollar):

1. Monthly sales budgets (showing both budgeted unit sales and dollar sales).
2. Monthly merchandise purchases budgets.
3. Monthly selling expense budgets.
4. Monthly general and administrative expense budgets.
5. Monthly capital expenditures budgets.
6. Monthly cash budgets.
7. Budgeted income statement for the first quarter.
8. Budgeted balance sheet as of March 31, 2001.

Check Figure Budgeted total assets at March 31, $1,346,875

BEYOND THE NUMBERS

Reporting in Action

P2, C2, C3

Financial statements often serve as a starting point for information on the upcoming budget period. You are assigned the task of determining **NIKE's** cash paid for dividends in the current year and the budgeted cash needed to pay out next year's dividend.

Required

1. Which financial statement(s) reports the amount of (a) cash dividends paid and (b) annual cash dividends declared? Explain where on the statement(s) this information is reported.
2. Indicate the amount of cash dividends (a) paid in the year ended May 31, 1997, and (b) to be paid (budgeted for) next year under the assumption that next year's dividends equal 20% of current year's net income.

Swoosh Ahead

3. Obtain NIKE's annual report information for a fiscal year ending after May 31, 1997. You can get this information from either its Web site [**www.nike.com**] or the SEC's EDGAR database [**www.sec.gov**]. Compare your answer for part (2) with actual cash dividends paid for the year ended May 31, 1998. Compute the error, if any, in your estimate.

Comparative Analysis

P2

One source of cash savings for a company is improved management of ending inventory. To illustrate, assume **NIKE** and **Reebok** each have $2,000,000 per month in shoe sales in Virginia, and each forecasts this level of sales per month for the next 24 months. Also assume both NIKE and Reebok have a 20% contribution margin, equal fixed costs, and that cost per shoe is the only variable cost. The difference between NIKE and Reebok is the shoe distribution system. NIKE has a well-established shoe distribution system and requires an ending inventory of only 10% of next month's sales in inventory at the end of each month. Reebok is building a new distribution system and requires 40% of next month's sales in inventory at the end of each month.

Required

1. Compute the amount by which Reebok can reduce its inventory level if it can match NIKE's system of maintaining an inventory equal to 10% of next month's sales.
2. Explain how the analysis in part (1) that shows ending inventory levels for both the 40% and 10% required inventory policies can help justify a just-in-time inventory system. You can assume a 15% interest cost for resources that are tied up in ending inventory.

Ethics Challenge

C1, C2

Both the budget process and the budgets impact management performance. For instance, a common practice among not-for-profit organizations and government agencies is for management to spend any amounts remaining in a budget at the end of the budget period. This practice is often called "use it or lose it." The view is if a department manager doesn't spend the budgeted amount, top management reduces next year's budget by the amount not spent. To avoid losing budget dollars, department managers often spend all budgeted amounts regardless of the value added to products or services. All of us pay for the costs associated with this budget system.

Required

You are to prepare a one-page report to a local not-for-profit organization or government agency offering a solution to this budgeting problem.

Communicating in Practice
P1

The sales budget is usually the first and most crucial of the component budgets in a master budget. This is because all other budgets use it in planning.

Required

Assume your company's sales staff provides information on expected sales and selling prices for items making up the sales budget. Prepare a one-page memorandum to your supervisor outlining concerns with the sales staff's input in the sales budget when its compensation is at least partly tied to these budgets. Explain the importance of assessing any potential bias in information provided to the budget process.

Taking It to the Net
C2, P1, P2

The software industry provides budgeting templates to meet the needs of many different users. This software provides a structured framework to input financial information.

Required

1. Use the **Yahoo** (or another) search engine and search on the word *budgeting*. Identify at least four different industries or companies that provide budgeting spreadsheet templates.
2. Select one company offering budgeting spreadsheet templates. List three functions offered in this template that are helpful to users. You will find that many of its competitors offer similar features.

Teamwork in Action
A1

Your team is to prepare a budget report outlining the costs of attending college (full time) for the next two semesters (30 hours) or three quarters (45 hours). The focus of this budget is solely on attending college—do not include personal items in the team's budget. Your budget must include tuition, books, supplies, club fees, food, housing, and all costs associated with travel to and from college. This budgeting exercise is similar to the initial phase in zero-based budgeting. Include a list of any assumptions you use in completing the budget. Be prepared to present your budget in class.

Hitting the Road
C3, P1

To help understand the factors impacting a sales budget, you are to visit three businesses with the same ownership or franchise membership. Record the selling prices of two identical products at each location, such as regular and premium gas sold at Texaco stations. You are likely to find a difference in prices for at least one of the three locations you visit.

Required

1. Identify at least three external factors that must be considered when setting the sales budget. (*Note:* There is a difference between internal and external factors that impact the sales budget.)
2. What factors might explain any differences identified in the prices of the businesses you visited?

***Business Week* Activity**
C2, A1

Commercial credit cards are an increasingly important business tool for small businesses. A commercial credit card is similar to a charge card used by individuals. Read "Pick a Card, Not Any Card" in the November 17, 1997, issue of ***Business Week*** to answer the following questions.

Required

1. List the advantages of a commercial credit card to a company and its employees.
2. Identify how a commercial credit card helps a company budget expenses (be specific).

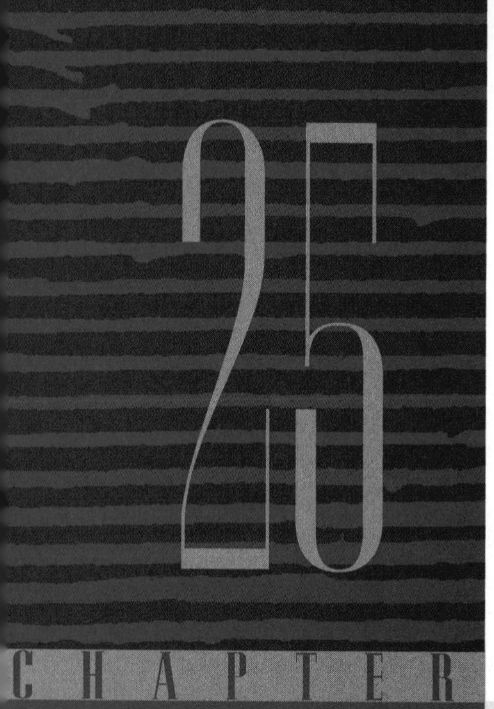

Flexible Budgets and Standard Costs

A Look Back

Chapter 24 explained the importance of budgeting. It also described the master budget, its component budgets, and its usefulness for planning future company activities.

A Look at This Chapter

This chapter describes flexible budgets, variance analysis, and standard costs. It explains how each is used for purposes of controlling and monitoring business activities.

A Look Ahead

Chapter 26 focuses on capital budgeting decisions. It also explains procedures used in evaluating many short-term managerial decisions.

Chapter Outline

A Hole in One

PHOENIX, AZ—In the shadow of Superstition Mountain just outside Phoenix, **G-Max** could be just another trinket shop for wandering tourists. But rolls of twine, fabrication equipment, and a driving range make it clear that this is a local success story with a difference. This collection is all part of the G-Max manufacturing facility.

G-Max makes specialty golf equipment and accessories for individual consumers and organizations. It specializes in golf balls that are customized, from simple color changes to an entirely new design. In six years, G-Max has made a name for itself and is quickly becoming the leader in this quirky market. For its most recent fiscal year, earnings are up more than 23%, to $455,000.

Nancy Stricker, 25, is the founder of G-Max. "When I was in high school, I caddied at a golf course in Mesa. I was amazed at what golfers would do to dazzle friends and clients," says Stricker. "They were always looking for that special item or gag gift." Stricker began by taking golf balls and dressing them up to a buyer's liking. "Names, colors, logos, whatever. I'd fix them up anyway they liked."

Stricker was soon overwhelmed by more than 100 requests that led her to set up a small manufacturing facility in an old service garage. "People requested all kinds of things. And they were willing to pay for it." Stricker quickly launched into specialty manufacturing of golf balls. "But within a year I was losing control of costs and revenues," says Stricker. "The business was growing so fast that I didn't know what I was doing right and what I was doing wrong. I needed a way to assess how I was doing."

With help from a financial advisor, Stricker implemented an accounting system with budgets and standard costs. "It literally saved my business. It gave me information I needed to make good decisions. Budget reports and cost variances quickly identified problems," says Stricker. "And I quickly moved to solve them."

And the strangest order? "That's easy," says Stricker. "Square, pink golf balls! A consulting firm ordered them for its clients for one of those 'think out of the box' sessions. I guess the firm wanted to make a point."

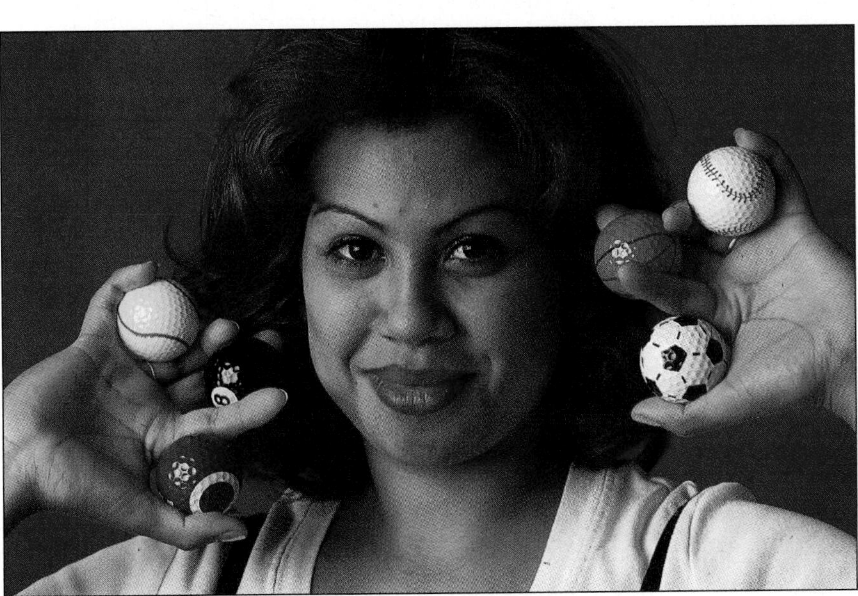

Learning Objectives

Conceptual

C1 Define standard costs and explain their computation and uses.

C2 Describe variances and what they reveal about performance.

C3 Explain how standard cost information is useful for management by exception.

Analytical

A1 Compare fixed and flexible budgets.

A2 Analyze changes in sales from expected amounts.

Procedural

P1 Prepare a flexible budget and interpret a flexible budget performance report.

P2 Compute materials and labor variances.

P3 Compute overhead variances.

P4 Record journal entries for standard costs and account for price and quantity variances.

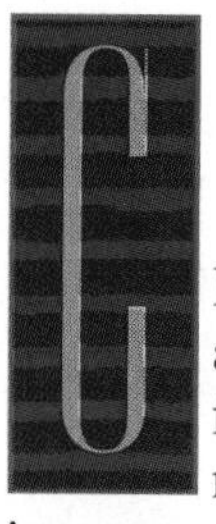

HAPTER PREVIEW

In Chapter 24 we explained how budgeting helps organize and formalize management's planning activities. We also explained how budgets provide a basis for evaluating actual performance. This chapter extends that discussion to look more closely at how budgets are used to evaluate performance. Evaluations are important for controlling and monitoring business activities. We also describe and illustrate the use of standard costs and variance analyses. This includes explanation of revenue variances. These managerial tools are useful for both evaluation and control of organizations and for the planning of future activities. Application of these tools can greatly impact the performance of a company as evidenced by **G-Max** in the opening article.

ECTION 1—FLEXIBLE BUDGETS

Section 1 introduces fixed budgets and fixed budget performance reports. It then introduces flexible budgets and flexible budget performance reports. The advantages of flexible budgets and reports are illustrated with comparisons to fixed budgets and reports.

Budgetary Process

A master budget reflects management's planned objectives for a future period. We explained in Chapter 24 how a master budget is prepared based on a predicted level of activity such as sales volume for the budget period. This section discusses the effects on the usefulness of budget reports when the actual level of activity is different from the predicted level.

Budgetary Control and Reporting

Budgetary control is the use of budgets by management to monitor and control the operations of a company. This includes use of budgets to see that planned objectives are met.

Budget reports contain relevant information that compares actual results to planned objectives. This comparison is motivated by a need to both monitor performance and control activities. Budget reports are sometimes viewed as progress reports, or *report cards,* on management's performance in achieving planned objectives. These reports can be prepared at any time and for any period. Three common periods for a budget report are a month, quarter, and year.

The process of budgetary control involves at least four steps: (1) develop the budget from planned objectives; (2) compare actual results to budgeted amounts and analyze differences; (3) take corrective and strategic actions; and (4) establish new planned objectives and prepare a new budget. Exhibit 25.1 shows this continual process of budgetary control.

Budget reports and related documents are effective tools for managers in getting the greatest benefits from this budgetary process.

Exhibit 25.1
Process of Budgetary Control

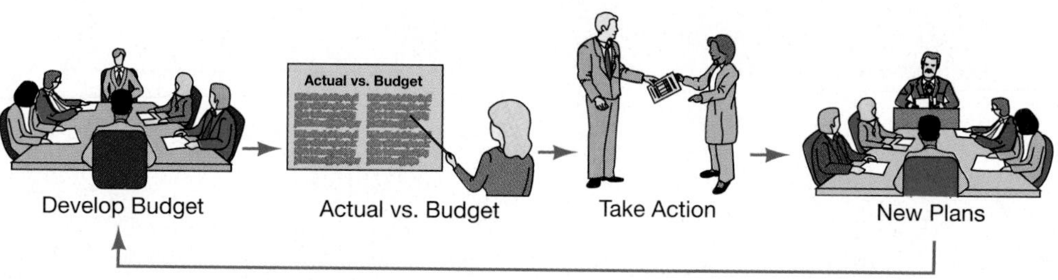

Fixed Budget Performance Report

In a fixed budgetary control system, the master budget is based on a single prediction for sales volume or other activity level. The budgeted amount for each cost essentially assumes that a specific (or *fixed*) amount of sales will occur. A **fixed budget,** also called *static budget,* is one based on a single predicted amount of sales or production volume.

We explained in Chapter 24 that one benefit of a budget is its usefulness in comparing actual results with planned activities. Information useful for analysis is often presented for comparison in a performance report. A **fixed budget performance report** is shown in Exhibit 25.2. This report compares the actual results of Optel for November 1999 with the results expected under its fixed budget that predicted 10,000 (composite) units of sales. Optel is a manufacturer of inexpensive eyeglasses, frames, contact lens, and related supplies. For this report, its production volume equals sales volume (meaning the amount of inventory did not change).

Exhibit 25.2

Fixed Budget Performance Report

OPTEL
Fixed Budget Performance Report
For Month Ended November 30, 1999

	Fixed Budget	Actual Results	Variances*
Sales: In units	10,000	12,000	
In dollars	$100,000	$125,000	$25,000 F
Cost of goods sold:			
Direct materials	10,000	13,000	3,000 U
Direct labor	15,000	20,000	5,000 U
Overhead:			
Factory supplies	2,000	2,100	100 U
Utilities	3,000	4,000	1,000 U
Depreciation of machinery	8,000	8,000	
Supervisory salaries	11,000	11,000	
Selling expenses:			
Sales commissions	9,000	10,800	1,800 U
Shipping expenses	4,000	4,300	300 U
General and administrative expenses:			
Office supplies	5,000	5,200	200 U
Insurance expense	1,000	1,200	200 U
Depreciation of office equipment	7,000	7,000	
Administrative salaries	13,000	13,000	
Total expenses	$ 88,000	$ 99,600	$11,600 U
Income from operations	$ 12,000	$ 25,400	$13,400 F

* F = Favorable variance; and U = Unfavorable variance.

This type of performance report designates differences between budgeted and actual results as variances. We see the letters *F* and *U* located beside the numbers in the third column of this report. Their meanings are:

F = **Favorable variance** When compared to budget, the actual cost or revenue contributes to a *higher* income. This means actual revenue (cost) is greater (lower) than budgeted revenue (cost).

U = **Unfavorable variance** When compared to budget, the actual cost or revenue contributes to a *lower* income. This means actual revenue (cost) is lower (greater) than budgeted revenue (cost).

This convention is common in practice and is used throughout this chapter.

Budget Reports for Evaluation

The primary use of budget reports is for management in monitoring and controlling operations. A main part of this activity is the use of budget reports in evaluation. In the case of Optel's report, management's evaluation is likely to focus on a variety of questions. These questions might include:

- Why is actual income from operations $13,400 higher than budgeted?
- Are amounts paid for each expense item too high?
- Is manufacturing using too much direct material?
- Is manufacturing using too much direct labor?

The performance report in Exhibit 25.2 provides little help in answering these questions. This is because actual sales volume is 2,000 units higher than budgeted. A manager doesn't know if this higher level of sales activity is the driving force behind variations in total dollar sales and expenses or if other factors have influenced these amounts.

This inability of fixed budget reports to adjust for changes in activity levels is a major limitation of a fixed budget performance report. It fails to show whether actual costs are out of line due to a change in actual sales volume or some other factor.

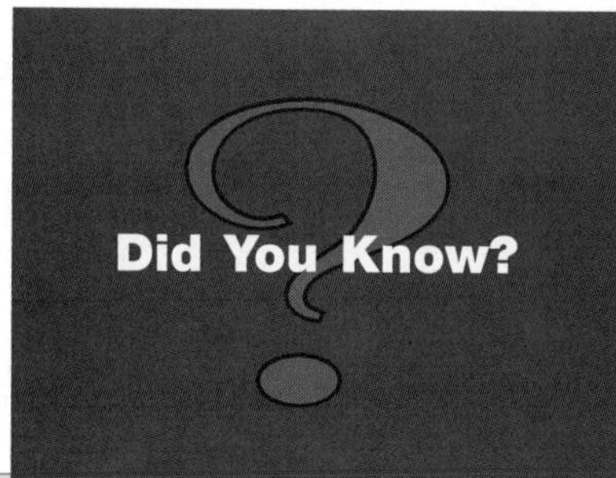
Did You Know?

Budgeting for a Better World
Budget reporting and evaluation are used at the **Environmental Protection Agency (EPA).** The EPA's goal is to improve human health and the environment. It regularly prepares performance plans and budget requests that describe performance goals, measures of outputs and outcomes, and various activities aimed at achieving performance goals. This process promotes budgetary control in that its annual plan sets forth in measurable form the levels of performance for each objective in the budget period.

Flexible Budget Reports

This section explains the purposes of both a flexible budget and a flexible budget performance report. We also describe the preparation of the flexible budget and the presentation of the flexible budget performance report.

Purpose of Flexible Budgets

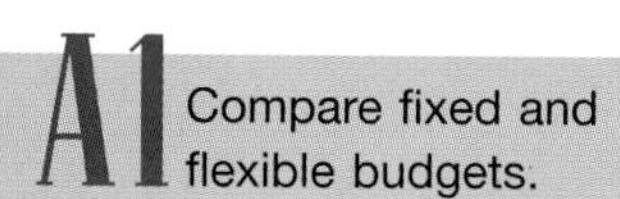
A1 Compare fixed and flexible budgets.

To help management address questions that arise with the fixed budget performance report, we look to a flexible budget. A **flexible budget,** also called a *variable budget,* is a report based on predicted amounts of revenues and expenses corresponding to the actual level of output. Unlike fixed budgets, a flexible budget is prepared after a period's activities are complete. A flexible budget can be viewed as a fixed budget prepared at the activity level corresponding to the actual level of activity. Many companies prepare and use flexible budgets.

The primary purpose of a flexible budget is to help managers evaluate past performance. A flexible budget is especially useful for evaluations because it reflects the different levels of activities in different amounts of revenues and costs. This means comparisons of actual results with budgeted performance are more likely to identify the reasons for any differences. This also helps managers focus attention on problem areas and to implement corrective actions. This is in contrast to a fixed budget, whose primary purpose is to assist managers in planning future activities and whose numbers are based on one expected amount of budgeted sales or production.

Preparing Flexible Budgets

A flexible budget is designed to reveal the effects of volume on the level of revenues and costs. To prepare a flexible budget, management relies on the distinctions between fixed and variable costs. Fixed and variable costs are described under cost-volume-profit analysis in Chapter 23 and also in Chapter 19. Recall that the cost per unit of activity remains constant for variable costs. This means the total amount of a variable cost changes in direct proportion to a change in level of activity. For fixed costs, the total amount of cost remains unchanged regardless of changes in the level of activity within a relevant (normal) operating range.[1]

P1 Prepare a flexible budget and interpret a flexible budget performance report.

When we create the numbers constituting a flexible budget, we need to express each variable cost as either a constant amount per unit of sales or as a percent of a sales dollar. In the case of a fixed cost, we need to express its budgeted amount as the total amount expected to occur at any sales volume within the relevant range.

Exhibit 25.3 shows a set of flexible budgets for Optel in November 1999. Seven of its expenses are classified as variable costs. Its remaining five expenses are fixed costs. These classifications result from management's investigation of each of the company's expenses using the cost estimation methods we explained in Chapter 23. Variable and fixed expense categories are *not* the same for every company, and we must avoid drawing conclusions from specific cases. For example, depending on the nature of a company's operations, office supplies expense can be either fixed or variable with respect to sales.

Exhibit 25.3
Flexible Budgets

OPTEL
Flexible Budgets
For Month Ended November 30, 1999

	Flexible Budget		Flexible Budget for Unit Sales of 10,000	Flexible Budget for Unit Sales of 12,000	Flexible Budget for Unit Sales of 14,000
	Variable Amount per Unit	Total Fixed Cost			
Sales	$10.00		$100,000	$120,000	$140,000
Variable Costs:					
Direct materials	1.00		10,000	12,000	14,000
Direct labor	1.50		15,000	18,000	21,000
Factory supplies	0.20		2,000	2,400	2,800
Utilities	0.30		3,000	3,600	4,200
Sales commissions	0.90		9,000	10,800	12,600
Shipping expenses	0.40		4,000	4,800	5,600
Office supplies	0.50		5,000	6,000	7,000
Total variable costs	$ 4.80		$ 48,000	$ 57,600	$ 67,200
Contribution margin	$ 5.20		$ 52,000	$ 62,400	$ 72,800
Fixed Costs:					
Depreciation, Machinery		$ 8,000	8,000	8,000	8,000
Supervisory salaries		11,000	11,000	11,000	11,000
Insurance expense		1,000	1,000	1,000	1,000
Depreciation, Office equip.		7,000	7,000	7,000	7,000
Administrative salaries		13,000	13,000	13,000	13,000
Total fixed costs		$40,000	$ 40,000	$ 40,000	$ 40,000
Income from operations			$ 12,000	$ 22,400	$ 32,800

[1] We assume here that costs can be reasonably classified as either variable or fixed within a relevant range.

The layout for the flexible budgets in Exhibit 25.3 reports sales followed by variable costs and then fixed costs. Both individual and total variable costs are reported and then subtracted from sales. As we explained in Chapter 23, the difference between sales and variable costs equals contribution margin. The expected amounts of fixed costs are listed next, followed by the expected income from operations before taxes.

The first and second columns of Exhibit 25.3 show the flexible budget amounts for variable costs per unit and the fixed costs for any volume of sales in the relevant range. The third, fourth, and fifth columns show the flexible budget amounts computed for three different sales volumes. For instance, the third column's flexible budget is based on 10,000 units. These numbers are the same as those in the fixed budget of Exhibit 25.2 because the expected volumes are the same for these two budgets.

Recall that Optel's actual sales volume for November is 12,000 units. This sales volume is 2,000 units more than the 10,000 units originally predicted in the master budget. When differences arise between actual and predicted volume, the usefulness of a flexible budget is apparent. For instance, compare the flexible budget for 10,000 units in the third column (which is the same as the fixed budget in Exhibit 25.2) with the flexible budget for 12,000 units in the fourth column. The higher levels for both sales and variable costs reflect nothing more than the increase in sales activity. Any budget analysis comparing actual with planned results that ignores this information is less useful to management.

To illustrate, when we evaluate the performance of Optel, we need to prepare a flexible budget showing actual and budgeted values at 12,000 units. As part of a complete profitability analysis, managers could compare the actual income of $25,400 (from Exhibit 25.2) with the $22,400 income expected at the actual sales volume of 12,000 units (from Exhibit 25.3). This results in a total income variance of $3,000 to be explained and understood. This variance is markedly different from the $13,400 variance identified in Exhibit 25.2 using a fixed budget. After receiving the flexible budget based on November's actual volume, management's next step is to determine what caused this $3,000 difference. The next section describes a flexible budget performance report that provides guidance for answering this and similar questions.

Flexible Budget Performance Report

A **flexible budget performance report** lists differences between actual performance and budgeted performance based on actual sales volume or other level of activity. This report helps direct management's attention to those costs or revenues that differ substantially from budgeted amounts.

Exhibit 25.4 shows the flexible budget performance report of Optel for November. We prepare this report after the actual volume is known to be 12,000 units.

This report shows a $5,000 favorable variance in total dollar sales. Because actual and budgeted volumes are both 12,000 units, the $5,000 sales variance must have resulted from a selling price that was higher than expected. Further analysis of the facts surrounding this $5,000 sales variance reveals a favorable sales variance per unit of nearly $0.42 as shown here:

Actual average price per unit (rounded to cents)	$125,000/12,000 =	$10.42
Budgeted price per unit	$120,000/12,000 =	10.00
Favorable sales variance per unit	$5,000/12,000 =	$ 0.42

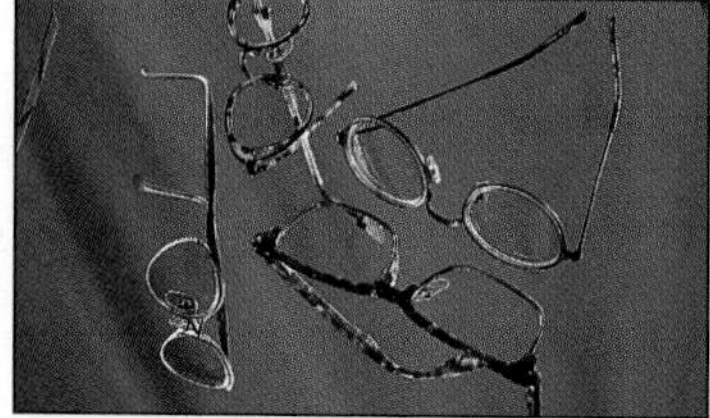

The other variances computed in Exhibit 25.4 also direct management's attention to areas where corrective actions can help them control Optel's operations. Each variance is analyzed like the previous sales variance. We can think of each expense as the joint result of using a given number of units of an expense item and paying a specific price per unit.

Each variance in Exhibit 25.4 is due in part to a difference between *actual price* per unit of input and *budgeted price* per unit of input. This is a **price variance.** A

OPTEL Flexible Budget Performance Report For Month Ended November 30, 1999	Flexible Budget	Actual Results	Variances*
Sales (12,000 units)	$120,000	$125,000	$5,000 F
Variable Costs:			
Direct materials	$ 12,000	$ 13,000	$1,000 U
Direct labor	18,000	20,000	2,000 U
Factory supplies	2,400	2,100	300 F
Utilities	3,600	4,000	400 U
Sales commissions	10,800	10,800	
Shipping expenses	4,800	4,300	500 F
Office supplies	6,000	5,200	800 F
Total variable costs	$ 57,600	$ 59,400	$1,800 U
Contribution margin	$ 62,400	$ 65,600	$3,200 F
Fixed Costs:			
Depreciation of machinery	$ 8,000	$ 8,000	
Supervisory salaries	11,000	11,000	
Insurance expense	1,000	1,200	$ 200 U
Depreciation of office equipment	7,000	7,000	
Administrative salaries	13,000	13,000	
Total fixed costs	$ 40,000	$ 40,200	$ 200 U
Income from operations	$ 22,400	$ 25,400	$3,000 F

* F = Favorable variance; and U = Unfavorable variance.

Exhibit 25.4

Flexible Budget Performance Report

variance also can be due in part to a difference between *actual quantity* of input used and *budgeted quantity* of input. This is a **quantity variance.** We explain more about this breakdown, known as **variance analysis,** in the section on standard costs later in the chapter.

Budget Officer
You are the budget officer for a management consulting firm. The heads of both the strategic consulting and tax consulting divisions complain to you about the unfavorable variances on their performance reports. "We worked on more consulting assignments than planned. It's not surprising our costs are higher than expected. But this report characterizes our work as *poor*!" How do you respond?

Answer—p. 1081

Flash back

1. A flexible budget:
   a. Shows fixed costs as constant amounts of cost per unit of activity.
   b. Shows variable costs as constant amounts of cost per unit of activity.
   c. Is prepared based on one expected amount of budgeted sales or production.
2. What is the initial step in preparing a flexible budget?
3. What is the difference between a fixed and a flexible budget?
4. What is contribution margin?

Answers—p. 1082

SECTION 2—STANDARD COSTS

We described job order and process cost accounting systems in Chapters 20 and 21. The costs described in these prior chapters are historical costs. Historical costs are the dollar amounts paid by a company in past transactions. These historical (or actual) costs provide useful information for many analyses.

C1 Define standard costs and explain their computation and uses.

To decide whether these historical cost-based amounts are reasonable or excessive, management needs a measure of comparison. Standard costs offer one basis for these comparisons. **Standard costs** are preset costs for delivering a product or service under normal conditions. These costs are established through personnel, engineering, and accounting studies using past experiences and data. They are used by management to assess the reasonableness of actual costs incurred for producing the product or service. When actual costs vary from standard costs, management follows up to identify potential problems and take corrective actions.

Standard costs are often used in preparing budgets because they are the anticipated cost incurred under normal conditions. Terms such as *standard materials cost, standard labor cost,* and *standard overhead cost* are often used to refer to amounts budgeted for direct materials, direct labor, and overhead.

Materials and Labor Standards

This section explains how we set materials and labor standards. It also shows us how to prepare a standard cost card.

Identifying Standard Costs

Managerial accountants, engineers, personnel administrators, and other managers combine their efforts in setting standard costs. To identify standards for direct labor costs, we can conduct time and motion studies for each labor operation in the process of providing a product or service. From these studies, management can learn the best way to perform the operation. It then sets the standard labor time required for the operation under normal conditions. In a similar way, standards for materials are set by studying the quantity, grade, and cost of each material used. Standards for overhead costs are explained later in the chapter.

Regardless of the care used in setting standard costs and in revising them as conditions change, actual costs frequently differ from standard costs. These differences often are due to more than one factor.

For instance, the actual quantity of material used may differ from the standard, and the price paid per unit of material also may differ from the standard. Quantity and price differences from standard amounts can also occur for labor. For instance, the actual labor time and actual labor rate may vary from what was expected. Additional factors can cause actual overhead cost to differ from its standard.

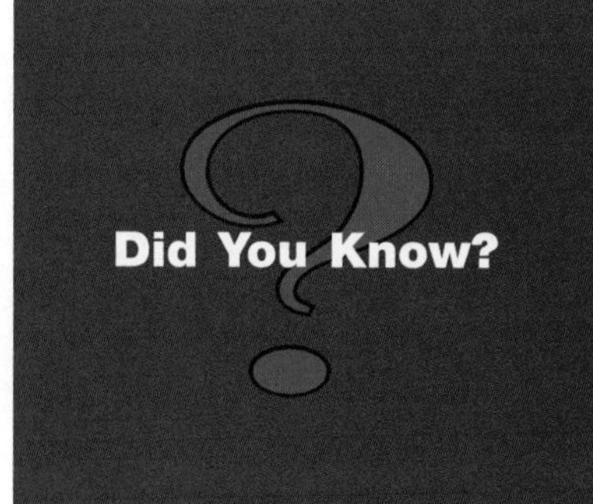

Standard in Vans

Chrysler Canada builds over 1,000 minivans per day in its Windsor, Ontario, plant. Each minivan requires about 3,500 parts purchased from more than 600 suppliers. This Chrysler plant has about 1,500 employees. Imagine the task of setting standard costs for each and every one of the minivan's parts, the different grades of labor, and its factory overhead!

Setting Standard Costs

To illustrate the setting of a standard cost, we consider the case of a baseball bat manufactured by **ProBat.** Engineers of ProBat have determined that the manufacturing of one bat requires 0.90 kgs. of high-grade wood. They also expect some loss of material as part of the process, due to inefficiencies and waste. This results in adding an *allowance* of 0.10 kgs. This means the standard requirement is 1.0 kg. of wood for each bat.

The 0.90 kgs. portion is called an ideal standard. An *ideal standard* is the quantity of material required if the process is 100% efficient without any loss or waste. Reality suggests there is usually some loss of material associated with any process. The revised standard of 1.0 kg. is known as the practical standard. A *practical standard* is the quantity of material required under normal application of the process.

High-grade wood can be purchased at a standard price of $25 per kilogram. This is the price the purchasing department determines as the expected price for the budget period. To determine this price, the purchasing department considers factors such as the quality of materials, future economic conditions, supply factors (shortages and excesses), and any available discounts.

The engineers also decide that two hours of labor time (after including allowances) are required to manufacture a bat. The wage rate is $20 per hour (better than average skilled labor is required). ProBat assigns all overhead at the rate of $10 per labor hour. The standard costs of direct materials, direct labor, and overhead for one bat are as shown in Exhibit 25.5 in what's called a *standard cost card.*

Exhibit 25.5

Standard Cost Card

STANDARD COST CARD

Production factor	Cost factor	Total
Direct materials (wood)	*1 kg. @ $25 per kg.*	*$25*
Direct labor	*2 hours @ $20 per hour*	*40*
Overhead	*2 labor hours @ $10 per hour*	*20*
	Total cost	*$85*

These cost amounts are used to prepare manufacturing budgets for a budgeted level of production.

Flash back

5. Standard costs:

a. Change in direct proportion to changes in the level of activity.

b. Are amounts incurred at the actual level of production for the period.

c. Are amounts incurred under normal conditions to provide a product or service.

Answer—p. 1082

Cost Variances

A **cost variance,** also called simply a *variance,* is the difference between actual and standard costs. A cost variance can be favorable or unfavorable. A variance from standard cost is considered favorable if actual cost is less than standard cost. It is considered un-

C2 Describe variances and what they reveal about performance.

favorable if actual cost is more than standard cost. This section discusses variance analysis and its computation.[2]

Cost Variance Analysis

Variances are usually identified in performance reports. When a variance occurs, management wants to determine the factors causing it. This often involves analysis, evaluation, and explanation. The results of these efforts should allow management to assign responsibility for the variance. It can then take actions to correct the situation.

To illustrate, Optel's standard materials cost for producing 12,000 units of its product is $12,000. But its actual materials cost for November proved to be $13,000. The $1,000 unfavorable variance raises questions. These questions call for answers that, in turn, can lead to changes designed to correct the situation and eliminate this variance in the next period. A performance report can often identify the existence of a problem, but we must follow up with further investigation to see what can be done to improve future results.

Exhibit 25.6 shows the flow of events in the effective management of variance analysis. Four steps are shown: (1) preparation of a standard cost performance report; (2) computation and analysis of variances; (3) identification of questions and their explanations; and (4) corrective and strategic actions.

Exhibit 25.6

Variance Analysis

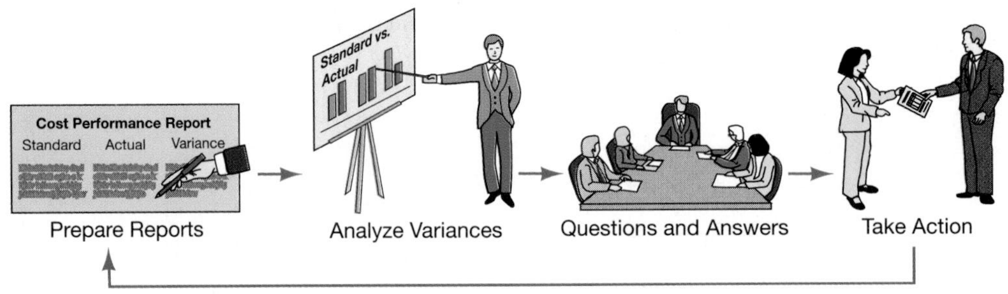

These variance analysis steps are interrelated and are applied frequently in good organizations.

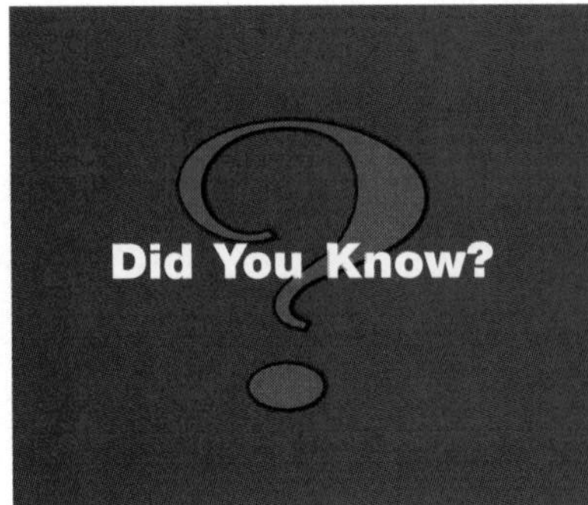

Strategic Partnerships

Strategic partnerships are in vogue. They are roughly defined as a joint effort by the supplier and the manufacturing customer to improve the quality and the delivery of an end product. This joint partnership requires trust, communication, and sharing in financial rewards. It is based on the idea that there is less revenue for both partners without the sharing arrangement. In practice, a supplier-manufacturer partnership often falls short of the ideal because the reward system focuses on the purchase price variance. One solution is multiple suppliers and a mentality of minimizing cost versus maximizing revenues.

Computing Cost Variances

Management needs information about the factors causing a cost variance. But it must first know how to compute a variance. In its most simple form, a cost variance (CV) is computed as the difference between actual cost (AC) and standard cost (SC) as shown in Exhibit 25.7.

[2] Short-term favorable variances can sometimes lead to long-term unfavorable variances. For instance, if management spends less than the budgeted amount on maintenance or insurance, the performance report would show a favorable variance. But cutting these expenses can lead to major losses in the long run if machinery wears out prematurely or insurance coverage proves inadequate.

Cost Variance (CV) = **Actual Cost** (AC) − **Standard Cost** (SC)

where:

Actual Cost (AC) = **Actual Quantity** (AQ) × **Actual Price** (AP)

Standard Cost (SC) = **Standard Quantity** (SQ) × **Standard Price** (SP)

Exhibit 25.7

Cost Variance Formulas

A cost variance is further defined by its components. Actual quantity (AQ) is the input (material or labor) used in manufacturing the quantity of output. Standard quantity (SQ) is the input expected for the quantity of output. Actual price (AP) is the amount paid for acquiring the input (material or labor), and standard price (SP) is the expected price.

Two main factors cause a cost variance. (1) The difference between actual price and standard price results in a *price* (or rate) *variance*. (2) The difference between actual quantity and standard quantity results in a *quantity* (or usage or efficiency) *variance*.

To assess the impacts of these two factors on a cost variance, we use the formula in Exhibit 25.8.

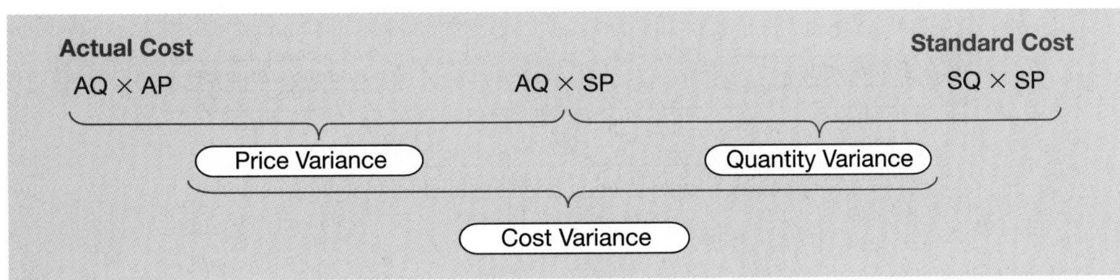

Exhibit 25.8

Price Variance and Quantity Variance Formulas

These formulas precisely identify the sources of the cost variance. Managers sometimes find it useful to apply an alternative computation for the price and quantity variances as shown in Exhibit 25.9.

Price Variance (PV) = [**Actual Price** (AP) − **Standard Price** (SP)] × **Actual Quantity** (AQ)

Quantity Variance (QV) = [**Actual Quantity** (AQ) − **Standard Quantity** (SQ)] × **Standard Price** (SP)

Exhibit 25.9

Alternative Price Variance and Quantity Variance Formulas

The results from applying the formulas in Exhibits 25.8 and 25.9 are identical.

Materials and Labor Variances

P2 Compute materials and labor variances.

We illustrate computation of the materials and labor cost variances using data from **G-Max,** the company described in the chapter's opening article. This company has set the following standard quantities and prices for materials and labor per unit for its hand-crafted golf clubhead:

Direct materials (1 lb. per unit at $1 per lb.)	$1.00
Direct labor (1 hr. per unit at $6 per hr.)	6.00
Total standard direct cost per unit	$7.00

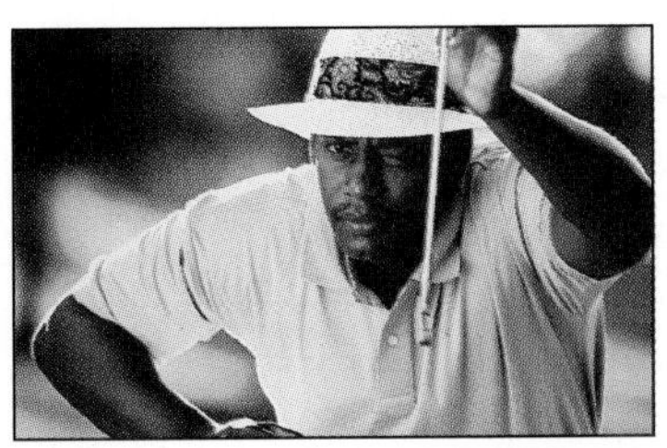

Materials Cost Variances

During May 2000, G-Max budgeted to produce 4,000 clubheads (units). It actually produced only 3,500 units. It used 3,600 pounds of direct materials (titanium) costing $1.05

per pound. This means its total materials cost was $3,780. This information allows us to compute both actual and standard direct materials costs for G-Max's 3,500 units along with its direct materials cost variance:

Actual cost	3,600 lbs. @ $1.05 per lb.	= $3,780
Standard cost	3,500 lbs. @ $1.00 per lb.	= 3,500
Direct materials cost variance (unfavorable)		= $ 280

The materials price and quantity variances for these G-Max clubheads are computed and shown in Exhibit 25.10.

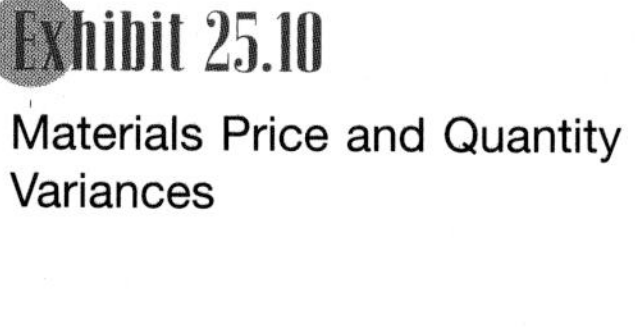

Materials Price and Quantity Variances

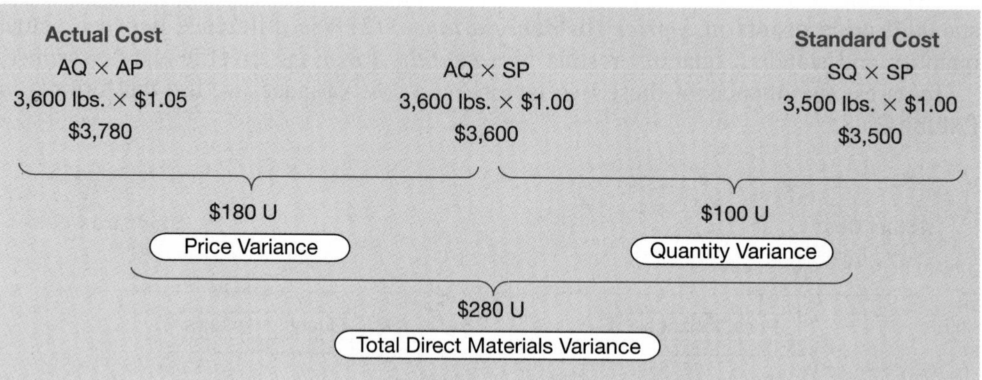

The unfavorable price variance of $180 is caused by the company paying 5 cents more than the standard price, computed as 3,600 lbs × $0.05. The unfavorable quantity variance of $100 is due to the company using 100 lbs more than the standard quantity, computed as 100 lbs × $1. The total direct materials variance is $280 and is unfavorable. This information allows management to go to the responsible individuals for explanations and corrective actions.

The purchasing department is usually responsible for the price paid for materials. Responsibility for explaining the situation rests with the purchasing manager if the variance is caused by a price higher than standard. The production department is usually responsible for the amount of material used. The production department manager is responsible for explaining why the process used more than the standard amount of materials.

But variance analysis can present challenges. For instance, the production department may have used more than the standard amount of material because the quality of material didn't meet specifications and led to excessive waste. In this case the purchasing manager is responsible for explaining why inferior materials were acquired. But the production manager is responsible for explaining what happened if our analysis shows that waste was due to inefficiencies and not poor quality material.

In evaluating price variances, managers must recognize that a favorable price variance may indicate a problem with poor product quality. **Redhook Ale,** the largest micro brewery in the Pacific Northwest, can probably save 10% to 15% in material prices by buying six-row barley malt instead of the better two-row from Washington's Yakima valley. But Redhook's chief financial officer doesn't like to gamble on quality. He proclaims:[3]

> "We don't cut costs when it comes to the taste and quality of our ale."

[3] Chris Barnett, "Just the Right Brew," *CFO Magazine,* vol. 6, no. 6, June 1992.

This implies that purchasing activities at Redhook are judged on both the quality of the materials and the purchase price variance. Redhook's stand on quality is having an impact. Sales have increased more than 35% per year for five years, and its gross margin has also increased.

Labor Cost Variances

Labor cost for a specific product or service depends on the number of hours worked (quantity) and the wage rate paid to employees (price). This means when actual amounts for a task differ from standard, the labor cost variance can be divided into a rate (price) variance and an efficiency (quantity) variance.

To illustrate, G-Max's direct labor standard for 3,500 units of its hand-crafted clubheads is one hour per unit, or 3,500 hours at $6 per hour. Since only 3,400 hours at $6.30 per hour were actually used to complete the units, the actual and standard labor costs are:

Actual cost	3,400 hrs. @ $6.30 per hr. =	$21,420
Standard cost	3,500 hrs. @ $6.00 per hr. =	21,000
Direct labor cost variance (unfavorable)		$ 420

This analysis shows actual cost is merely $420 over the standard and suggests no immediate concern. But computing both the labor rate and efficiency variances reveals a different picture as shown in Exhibit 25.11.

Exhibit 25.11

Labor Rate and Efficiency Variances*

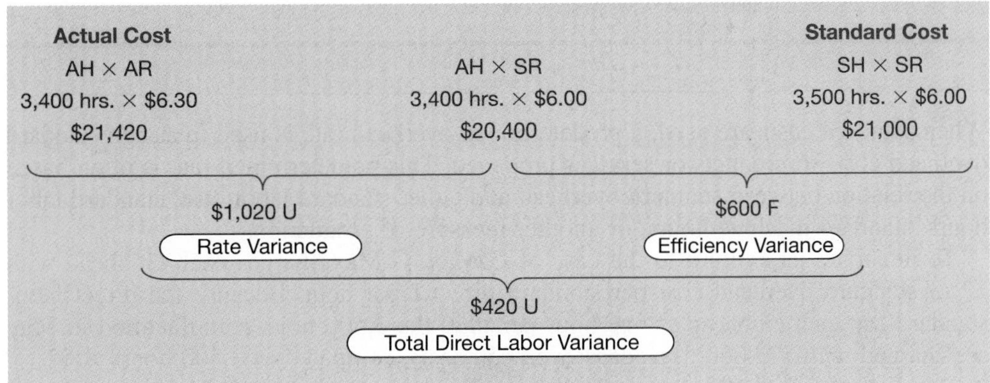

* Where AH is actual direct labor hours; AR is actual wage rate; SH is standard direct labor hours allowed for actual output; SR is standard wage rate.

The analysis in Exhibit 25.11 shows that the favorable efficiency variance of $600 results from using 100 fewer direct labor hours than standard for the units produced. But this favorable variance is more than offset by a wage rate that is $0.30 more than standard. The personnel administrator, or possibly the production manager, needs to explain why the wage rate is higher than expected. Also, the production manager should explain how the labor hours were reduced. If this experience can be repeated and transferred to other departments, more savings are possible.

One possible explanation of these labor rate and efficiency variances might be the use of workers with different skill levels. If so, it is the responsibility of the production manager to assign each task to workers with the appropriate skill level. In this case, an investigation might show higher skilled workers were used to produce 3,500 units of hand-crafted clubheads. As a result, fewer labor hours were required for the work. But the wage rate paid to such workers would be higher than standard because of their greater skills. In G-Max's situation, the effect of this strategy would be a higher than standard total cost. This would require actions to remedy the situation or adjust the standard.

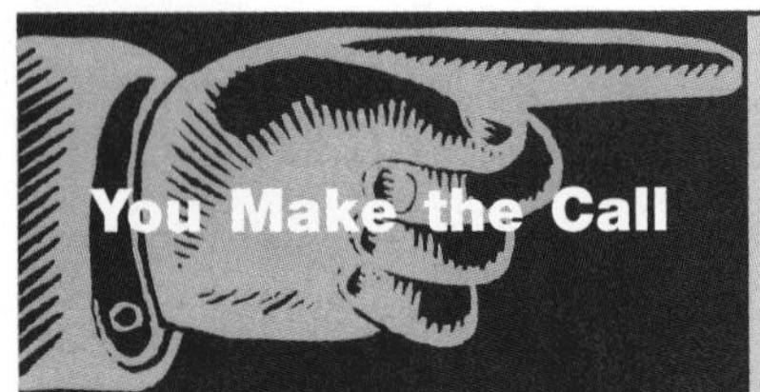

Human Resource Manager

You are the human resource manager of an electronics plant. You receive the manufacturing variance report for June and discover a large unfavorable labor efficiency variance. What factors do you investigate to identify possible causes of this variance?

Answer—p. 1081

Flash back

6. What is a cost variance?
7. The following information is available for York Co.:

Actual hours worked per unit	2.5
Standard direct labor hours per unit	2.0
Actual production (units)	2,500
Budgeted production (units)	3,000
Actual rate per hour	$3.10
Standard rate per hour	$3.00

The labor efficiency variance is: *(a)* $3,750 U; *(b)* $3,750 F; *(c)* $3,875 U; *(d)* $3,875 F.

8. Refer to the prior *Flashback* (No. 7); the labor rate variance is: *(a)* $500 U; *(b)* $500 F; *(c)* $625 F; *(d)* $625 U.
9. If a material quantity variance is favorable and a material price variance is unfavorable, can the total material cost variance be favorable?

Answers—p. 1082

Overhead Standards and Variances

When standard costs are used, a predetermined overhead rate is used to assign standard overhead costs to products or services produced. This predetermined rate is often based on the relation between standard overhead and either standard labor cost, standard labor hours, standard machine hours, or another measure of production.

To illustrate, let's return to the case of G-Max. G-Max charges each clubhead with $2 of standard overhead cost per standard direct labor hour. Because the direct labor standard for each clubhead is one hour per unit, the 3,500 units manufactured in May are charged with $7,000 of standard overhead costs, computed as 3,500 hours × $2.

Recall that only 3,400 actual direct labor hours were used by G-Max in producing these units. Yet overhead costs are assigned to units on the basis of standard labor hours, not on the basis of actual labor hours. Standard labor hours are used because the total amount of overhead charged to all units produced should equal the total flexible budget overhead cost for the period. While this is true for variable overhead, the fixed overhead assigned will be equal to the budget only when actual production equals expected production. A difference between actual and expected production will result in what we term *fixed overhead volume variance,* which we discuss later in the chapter.

Setting Overhead Standards

Standard overhead costs are the amounts expected to occur at a certain level of activity. Unlike direct materials and direct labor, overhead includes both variable and fixed costs. This results in the average overhead cost per unit changing as the predicted volume changes.

Because standard costs are also budgeted costs, they must be established before the reporting period begins. This means standard overhead costs are average per unit costs based on the predicted level of activity.

To establish the standard overhead cost rate, management uses the same cost structure that is used to construct a flexible budget at the end of a period. This cost structure identifies the different overhead cost components and classifies them as variable or fixed. To get the standard overhead rate, management selects a level of activity (volume) and predicts total overhead cost. It then divides this total by the allocation base to get the standard rate. Standard direct labor hours expected to be used to produce the predicted volume is a common allocation base and is used in this section.

Exhibit 25.12 shows the overhead cost structure used in developing flexible overhead budgets of May 1999 for G-Max. It sets the predetermined standard overhead rate for May before the month begins. The first column lists the per-unit amounts of variable costs and the monthly amounts of fixed costs. The next four columns show the total costs expected to occur at four different levels of activity. The predetermined overhead rate per labor hour gets smaller as volume of activity increases. This occurs because fixed costs remain constant.

Flexible Overhead Budgets

G-MAX
Flexible Overhead Budgets
For Month Ended May 31, 1999

	Flexible Budget					
	Variable Amount per Unit	Total Fixed Cost	Flexible Budget at 70% Capacity	Flexible Budget at 80% Capacity	Flexible Budget at 90% Capacity	Flexible Budget at 100% Capacity
Production in units	1 unit		3,500	4,000	4,500	5,000
Factory overhead:						
Variable costs (per unit):						
Indirect labor	$0.40		$1,400	$1,600	$1,800	$2,000
Indirect materials	0.30		1,050	1,200	1,350	1,500
Power and lights	0.20		700	800	900	1,000
Maintenance	0.10		350	400	450	500
Total	$1.00		$3,500	$4,000	$4,500	$5,000
Fixed costs (per month):						
Building rent		$1,000	1,000	1,000	1,000	1,000
Depreciation, machinery		1,200	1,200	1,200	1,200	1,200
Supervisory salaries		1,800	1,800	1,800	1,800	1,800
Total		$4,000	$4,000	$4,000	$4,000	$4,000
Total factory overhead			$7,500	$8,000	$8,500	$9,000
Standard direct labor hours	1 hr./unit		3,500	4,000	4,500	5,000
Predetermined overhead rate per standard direct labor hour			$2.14	$2.00	$1.89	$1.80

In setting the standard overhead budget for May, managers of G-Max predicted an 80% activity level. This yields a predicted production volume of 4,000 clubheads. At this volume, they budget $8,000 as the total overhead for May. This choice implies a $2 per unit (labor hour) average overhead cost, computed as $8,000 divided by 4,000 units.

Since G-Max has a standard of one direct labor hour for each unit, the predetermined standard overhead application rate for May is $2 per standard direct labor hour. The variable overhead rate remains constant at $1 per direct labor hour regardless of the budgeted production level. The fixed overhead rate changes according to the budgeted production volume. For instance, for the predicted level of 4,000 units of production, the fixed rate is \$1 per hour–computed as \$4,000 fixed costs divided by 4,000 units. But for a production level of 5,000 units, the fixed rate is \$0.80 per hour.

When choosing the predicted activity level for a company, management looks at many factors. The level can be set as high as 100% of capacity. But this is rare. Factors causing the activity level to be less than full capacity include difficulties in scheduling work, equipment under repair or maintenance, and insufficient product demand. Good long-run management practices often call for some plant capacity in excess of current operating needs to allow for special opportunities and demand changes.

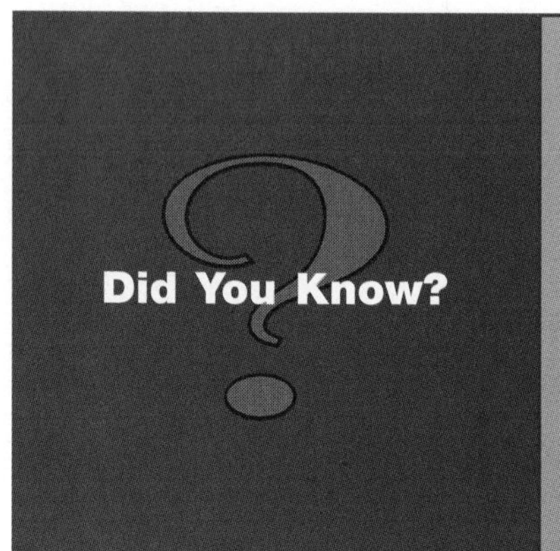

Measuring Up

In the spirit of continuous improvement, leading companies are setting new standards (benchmarks) for performance. Competitors are comparing their processes and performance standards against benchmarks established by the industry leaders. This implies continuous revision of standards in all areas of an organization to improve productivity. Corporate giants such as **Xerox, Motorola,** and **AT&T** use benchmarking to stay one step ahead of competitors.

Overhead Cost Variance Analysis

P3 Compute overhead variances.

When standard costs are used, the cost accounting system applies overhead to the good units produced using the predetermined standard overhead rate. At the end of the period, the difference between the total overhead cost applied to products and the total overhead cost actually incurred is called an **overhead cost variance.** This variance is computed as shown in Exhibit 25.13.

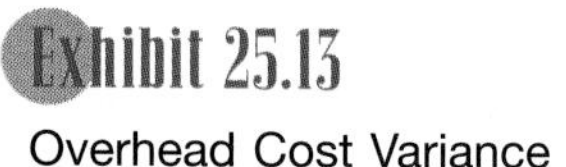
Exhibit 25.13

Overhead Cost Variance

Overhead cost variance (OCV) = Actual overhead incurred (AOI) − Standard overhead applied (SOA)

To help management identify factors causing the overhead cost variance, we analyze this variance separately for variable and fixed overhead. The results provide information useful to management for taking strategic actions to improve company performance.

Similar to our analysis of direct materials and direct labor variances, both the variable and fixed overhead variances can be separated into useful components as shown in Exhibit 25.14.

A **spending variance** occurs when management pays an amount different than the standard price to acquire an item. For instance, the actual wage rate paid to indirect labor might be higher than the standard rate. Similarly, actual supervisory salaries might be different than expected. Spending variances such as these cause management to investigate the reasons why the amount paid is different than the standard. Both variable and fixed overhead costs can yield their own spending variances.

The analysis of variable overhead includes computation of an efficiency variance. An **efficiency variance** occurs when standard direct labor hours (the allocation base) expected for actual production are different from the actual direct labor hours used. This efficiency variance is unrelated to whether variable overhead is used efficiently. Instead, this variance results from whether or not the overhead allocation base is used efficiently.

Exhibit 25.14

Variable and Fixed Overhead Variances

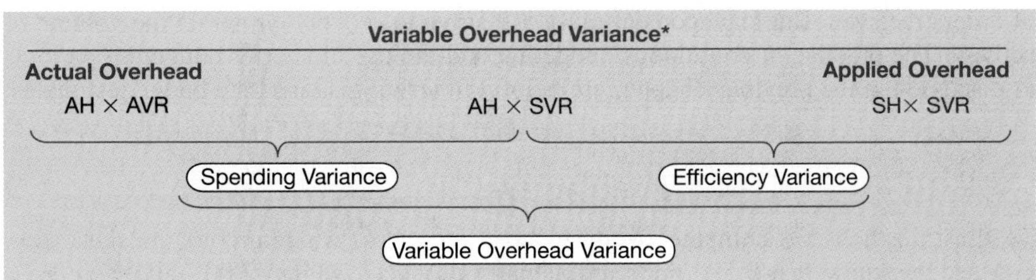

*Where: AH = actual hours; AVR = actual variable overhead rate; SH = standard hours; SVR = standard variable overhead rate.

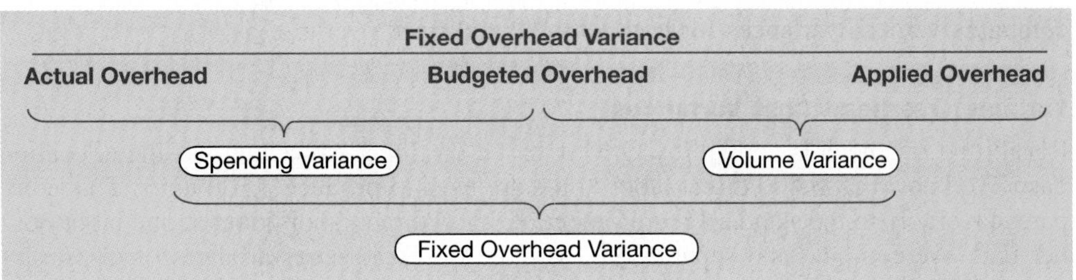

We can combine the variable overhead spending variance, the fixed overhead spending variance, and the variable overhead efficiency variance to get **controllable variance;** see Exhibit 25.15. The controllable variance is so named because it's usually under the control of management.

Exhibit 25.15

Framework for Understanding Total Overhead Variance

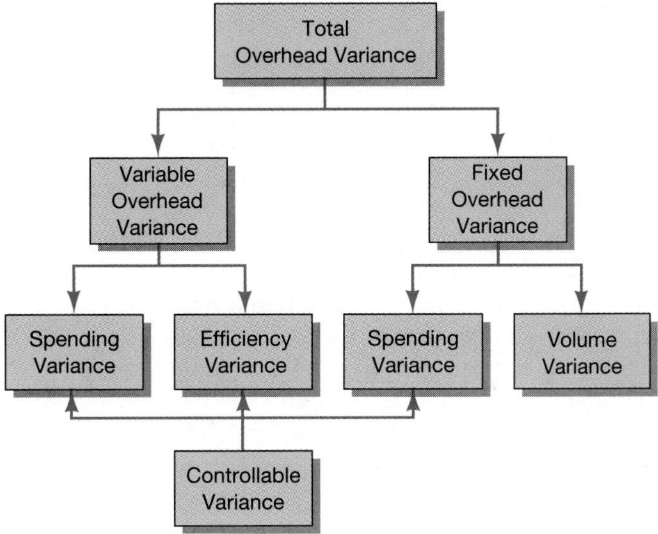

A **volume variance** occurs when there is a difference between the actual volume of production and the standard volume of production. The budgeted fixed overhead amount remains the same regardless of the actual volume of production (within the relevant range). This budgeted amount is computed based on standard direct labor hours that are allowed for with the budgeted production volume. But the applied overhead is based on the standard direct labor hours allowed for with the actual volume of production. This means if there is a difference between budgeted and actual production volumes, there is a difference in the standard direct labor hours allowed for these two production levels. Such a situation yields a volume variance different from zero.

A volume variance is not included as part of controllable variance. The actual production level depends on many factors after a budget is established, such as the number of orders received. But management must still strive to accurately predict the volume of activity. The practice of continuous budgeting and the use of shorter budgeting periods, as discussed in the previous chapter, are helpful in arriving at accurate budget estimates.

Computing Overhead Cost Variances

To illustrate how we compute overhead cost variances, we return to the data from G-Max. We know that 3,500 units are actually produced while 4,000 units were budgeted. Additional data from G-Max show that actual overhead cost incurred is $7,650, with the variable portion totaling $3,650 of the $7,650. Using this information we can compute overhead variances for both variable and fixed overhead.

Variable Overhead Cost Variances

Recall that overhead is applied by G-Max based on direct labor hours as the allocation base. We know that 3,400 direct labor hours are used to produce 3,500 units. This compares favorably to the standard requirement of 3,500 direct labor hours at one labor hour per unit. We compute and separate the variable overhead cost variances of G-Max as shown in Exhibit 25.16.

Exhibit 25.16

Computing Variable Overhead Cost Variances

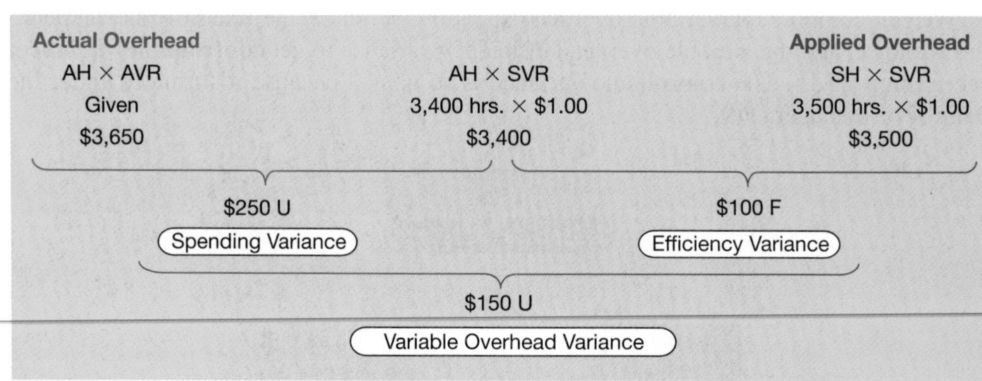

The actual variable overhead amount of $3,650 is available from G-Max's cost records. We use this amount to compute the actual variable overhead rate of $1.07 per direct labor hour, computed as $3,650 divided by 3,400 units. This reveals that, on average, G-Max incurred $0.07 more per direct labor hour in variable overhead, compared to the standard rate. The middle column of Exhibit 25.16 is computed by multiplying the actual direct labor hours (3,400) with the standard rate of $1 per direct labor hour. The right-hand column is the applied overhead. It is computed by multiplying the standard hours allowed for actual production (3,500) with the standard rate of $1 per direct labor hour.

Fixed Overhead Cost Variances

G-Max reports that it incurred $4,000 in actual fixed overhead, computed as $7,650 minus $3,650 of variable overhead cost. This $4,000 amount is equal to the budgeted fixed overhead for May 1999 (see Exhibit 25.12). G-Max's budgeted fixed overhead application rate is $1 per hour, computed as $4,000 divided by 4,000 direct labor hours. But the actual production level for G-Max is only 3,500 units. Using this information, we can compute the fixed overhead cost variances.

The applied fixed overhead is computed by multiplying standard hours allowed for the actual production (3,500) by the fixed overhead allocation rate ($1). Exhibit 25.17 reveals the fixed overhead spending variance is zero and the volume variance is $500. The volume variance occurs because 500 less units are produced than budgeted. This is because 80% of the manufacturing capacity is budgeted but only 70% is used.

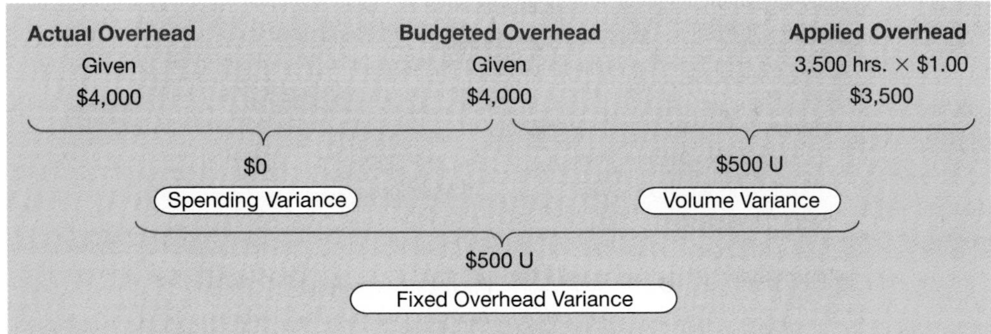

Exhibit 25.17

Computing Fixed Overhead Cost Variances

We also show the volume variance graphically in Exhibit 25.18. The upward-sloping line reflects the amount of fixed overhead costs applied to the units produced in May using the predetermined fixed overhead rate. The uppermost horizontal line reflects the $4,000 of total fixed costs budgeted for May. These two lines cross at the planned operating volume of 4,000 units. When unit volume is 3,500 units, the overhead-costs-applied line falls $500 below the budgeted fixed overhead line. This shortfall is the volume variance.

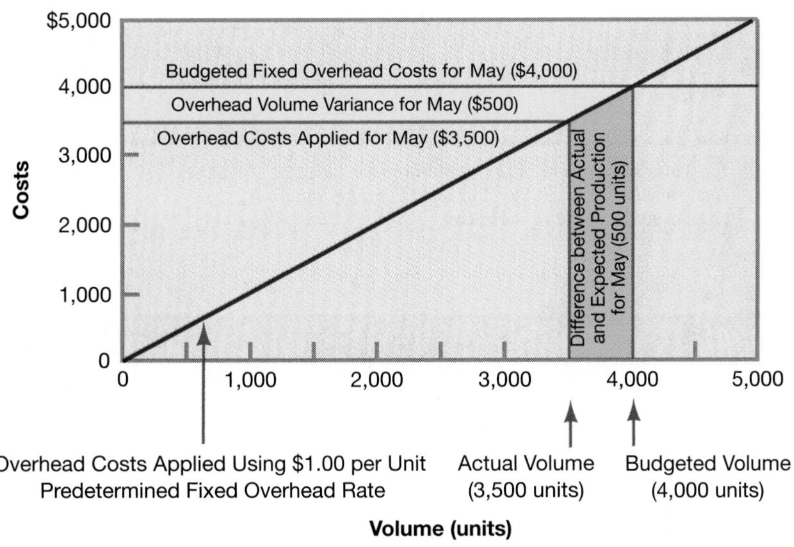

Exhibit 25.18

Fixed Overhead Volume Variance

An unfavorable volume variance implies the company did not reach its predicted operating level. Of course, management would already know this result. More important, management needs to know why the actual level of performance is different from the expected level. The main purpose of the volume variance is that it identifies what portion of the total variance is caused by failing to meet the expected level. This permits management to then focus on the controllable variance.

A complete overhead variance report provides managers with information about specific overhead costs and how they differ from budgeted amounts. Exhibit 25.19 shows G-Max's overhead variance report for May. It reveals that: (1) fixed costs and the maintenance cost were incurred as expected; (2) costs for indirect labor and power and lights were higher than expected; and (3) indirect materials cost was less than expected.

Using information from Exhibits 25.16 and 25.17, we compute the total controllable variance as $150 unfavorable ($250 U + $100 F + $0). This amount also can be computed from the variances for the variable overhead costs; see Exhibit 25.19. The overhead variance report shows the total volume variance as $500 unfavorable (shown at the top). The sum of the controllable variance and the volume variance equals the total (fixed and variable) overhead variance of $650 unfavorable.

Exhibit 25.19

Overhead Variance Report

G-MAX
Overhead Variance Report
For Month Ended May 31, 1999

Volume Variance

Expected production level	80% of capacity
Production level achieved	70% of capacity
Volume variance	$500 (unfavorable)

Controllable Variance	**Flexible Budget**	**Actual Results**	**Variances***
Variable overhead costs:			
Indirect labor	$1,400	$1,525	$125 U
Indirect materials	1,050	1,025	$ 25 F
Power and lights	700	750	50 U
Maintenance	350	350	
Total variable costs	$3,500	$3,650	$150 U†
Fixed overhead costs:			
Building rent	$1,000	$1,000	
Depreciation, Machinery	1,200	1,200	
Supervisory salaries	1,800	1,800	
Total fixed costs	$4,000	$4,000	$ 0¶
Total overhead costs	$7,500	$7,650	$150 U

* F = Favorable variance; and U = Unfavorable variance.
† Total variable overhead (spending and efficiency) variance.
¶ Fixed overhead spending variance.

10. Under what conditions is the overhead volume variance considered favorable?

Answer—p. 1082

Extending Standard Costs

This section extends the application of standard costs for use in control systems, for use by service companies, and for use in the accounting system.

Standard Costs for Control

C3 Explain how standard cost information is useful for management by exception.

To control business activities, top management must be able to affect the actions of lower-level managers responsible for the company's revenues, costs, and expenses. After a budget is prepared and standard costs are established, management should take actions to gain control when actual costs differ from the standard or budgeted amounts.

Reports like the ones illustrated in this chapter call management's attention to variances from business plans and other standards. When managers use these reports to focus on problem areas, the budgeting process contributes to the control function. In using budgeted performance reports, it is often useful for management to practice management by exception.

Management by exception means that managers focus attention on the most significant variances and give less attention to areas where performance is reasonably close to the standard. This practice leads management to concentrate on the exceptional or irregular situations. It also means deferring any serious analysis of areas showing actual results that are reasonably close to the plan. Management by exception is especially useful when directed at controllable items.

Internal Auditor
You are an internal auditor reviewing your company's records. You discover one manager who always spends exactly what is budgeted for supplies and equipment. You also find about 30% of this manager's annual budget is spent just before the end of the period. A talk with this manager reveals she always spends what is budgeted, whether or not supplies and equipment are needed. She offers three reasons for her actions. First, she doesn't want her budget cut. Second, the company's practice of management by exception calls attention to deviations from the budget. Third, she feels the money is budgeted to be spent. Do you mention these findings in your report?

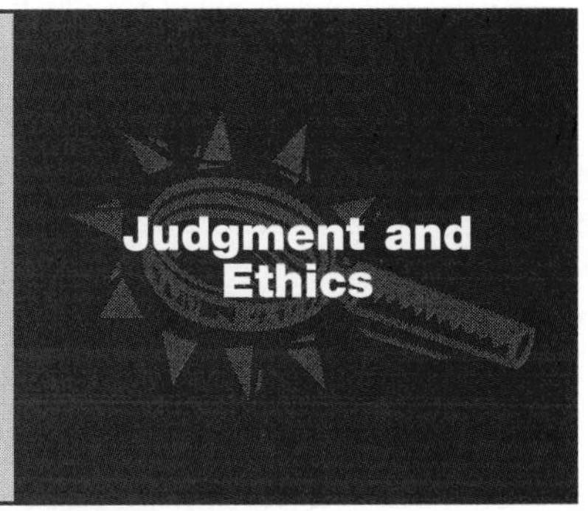

Answer—p. 1082

Standard Costs for Services

Many managers use standard costs and variance analysis for manufacturing costs. There are also many managers who recognize that standard costs and variances can help them control *non*manufacturing costs. Companies providing services to customers instead of products can especially benefit from use of standard costs.

Our explanation and application of standard costs and variances can be readily adapted to these nonmanufacturing situations. To illustrate, many hospitals use standard costs to help control expenses. First, standard costs are used as a basis for budgeting throughout the hospital. Second, periodic performance reports compare actual results to standards. Third, these reports are used to identify significant variances within specific areas of responsibility. Fourth, appropriate control procedures are implemented.

Flash back

11. To use management by exception with standard costs:

a. A company must record standard costs in its accounts.

b. Variances from flexible budget amounts should be computed to allow management to focus its attention on significant differences between actual and budgeted results.

c. Only variances for direct materials and direct labor should be analyzed.

Answer—p. 1082

Standard Cost Accounting System

P4 Record journal entries for standard costs and account for price and quantity variances.

We've shown how companies use standard costs in management reports. Most standard cost systems also record these costs and variances in accounts. This practice simplifies recordkeeping and helps in preparation of reports.

We don't need knowledge of standard cost accounting practices to understand standard costs and how they are used. But we do need to know how to interpret accounts in which standard costs and variances are recorded. The entries in this section briefly illustrate the important aspects of this process for G-Max's standard costs and variances for May.

The first of these entries is the one to record standard materials cost incurred in May. It is recorded in the Goods in Process Inventory account. This part of the entry is similar to the usual accounting entry. But the amount of the debit equals the standard cost ($3,500) instead of the actual cost ($3,780). Yet this entry credits Raw Materials Inventory for actual cost. This difference between standard and actual costs is recorded with debits to two separate materials variance accounts (recall Exhibit 25.10). Both the materials price and quantity variances are recorded as debits because they reflect additional costs greater than the standard cost (if actual costs were less than the standard, they would be recorded as credits). This treatment reflects their unfavorable effect because they represent higher costs and lower income.

Assets	= Liabilities	+ Equity
+3,500		−100
−3,780		−180

May 31	Goods in Process Inventory	3,500	
	Direct Materials Price Variance*	**100**	
	Direct Materials Quantity Variance	**180**	
	Raw Materials Inventory		3,780
	To charge production for standard quantity of materials used (3,500 lbs.) at the standard price ($1 per lb.) and to record material price and material quantity variances.		

The second entry is to debit Goods in Process Inventory for the standard labor cost of the goods manufactured during May ($21,000). Actual labor cost ($21,420) is recorded with a credit to the Factory Payroll account. The difference between standard and actual labor costs is explained by two variances (see Exhibit 25.11). The direct labor rate variance is unfavorable and is debited to that account. The direct labor efficiency variance is favorable and is credited.

Assets	= Liabilities	+ Equity
+21,000		+21,420
		− 1,020
		+ 600

May 31	Goods in Process Inventory	21,000	
	Direct Labor Rate Variance	**1,020**	
	Direct Labor Efficiency Variance		**600**
	Factory Payroll		21,420
	To charge production with 3,500 standard hours of direct labor at the standard $6 per hour rate and to record the labor rate and efficiency variances.		

The direct labor efficiency variance is favorable because it represents a lower cost and a higher net income.

The entry to assign standard predetermined overhead to the cost of goods manufactured must debit the predetermined amount ($7,000) to the Goods in Process Inventory account. The actual overhead costs incurred of $7,650 are debited to the Factory Overhead account. This means when Factory Overhead is applied to Goods in Process Inventory, the amount applied is debited to the Goods in Process Inventory account and credited to the Factory Overhead account. To account for the difference between actual and standard costs, the entry includes a debit of $250 to the Variable Overhead Spending Variance, a credit of $100 to the Variable Overhead Efficiency Variance, and a debit of $500 to the Volume Variance (recall Exhibits 25.16 and 25.17). An alternative (simpler) approach, which we show here, is to record the difference with a debit of $150 to the Controllable Variance account and a debit of $500 to the Volume Variance account (recall from Exhibit 25.15 that controllable variance is the sum of both variable overhead variances and the fixed overhead spending variance).

Assets	= Liabilities	+ Equity
+7,000		+7,650
		− 150
		− 500

May 31	Goods in Process Inventory	7,000	
	Controllable Variance	**150**	
	Volume Variance	**500**	
	Factory Overhead		7,650
	To apply overhead at the standard rate of $2 per standard direct labor hour (3,500 hours) and to record overhead variances.		

* Many companies record the materials price variance when materials are purchased. For simplicity, we record both the materials price and quantity variances when materials are issued into production.

The balances of these six different variance accounts accumulate until the end of the accounting period. This can result in unfavorable variances of some months offsetting favorable variances of others.

These account balances, which reflect results of various transactions and events in the period, are closed at the end of the period. Since their balances represent differences between actual and standard costs, they must be added to or subtracted from the materials, labor, and overhead costs recorded in the period. In this way the recorded costs equal the actual costs incurred in the period.

A company must use actual cost amounts in external financial statements prepared in accordance with generally accepted accounting principles. If the variances are material, they need to be added to or subtracted from the balances of the Goods in Process Inventory, the Finished Goods Inventory, and the Cost of Goods Sold accounts. If the amounts are immaterial, they are usually added to or subtracted from the balance of the Cost of Goods Sold account.[4]

Flash back

12. A company uses a standard cost accounting system. Prepare the journal entry to record these material variances:

Direct material cost actually incurred	$73,200
Direct material quantity variance (favorable)	3,800
Direct material price variance (unfavorable)	1,300

13. If standard costs are recorded in the manufacturing accounts, how are recorded variances treated at the end of an accounting period?

Answers—p. 1082

Sales Variances

USING THE INFORMATION

A2 Analyze changes in sales from expected amounts.

This chapter explained the computation and analysis of cost variances. A similar variance analysis can be applied to sales.

To illustrate, consider the following sales data of G-Max from two of its golf products for May—fluorescent Excel balls and Big Bert® drivers.

	Budgeted	Actual
Sales of Excel golf balls (units)	1,000	1,100
Sales price per Excel golf ball	$10	$10.50
Sales of Big Bert drivers (units)	150	140
Sales price per Big Bert driver	$200	$190

Using this information, we compute both the *sales price variance* and the *sales volume variance* as shown in Exhibit 25.20. The total sales price variance is $850 unfavorable, and the total sales volume variance is $1,000 unfavorable. Neither variance implies anything positive about these two products.

Further analysis of these total sales variances reveals that both the sales price and sales volume variances for Excel golf balls are favorable. This means that both the unfavorable total sales price variance and the unfavorable total sales volume variance are due to the Big Bert driver.

[4] This process is similar to that shown in Chapter 20 for eliminating an underapplied or overapplied balance in the Factory Overhead account.

Computing Sales Variances

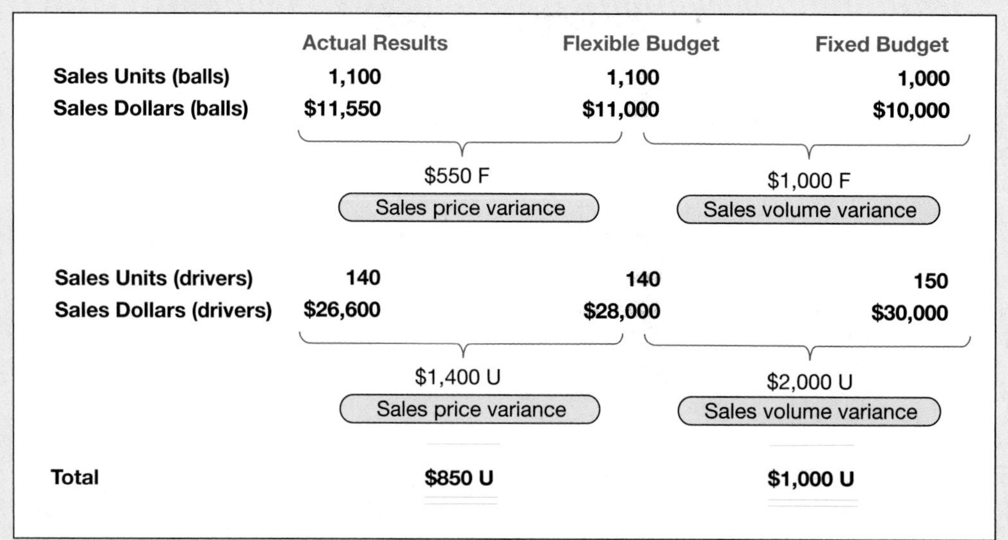

	Actual Results		Flexible Budget		Fixed Budget
Sales Units (balls)	**1,100**		**1,100**		**1,000**
Sales Dollars (balls)	**$11,550**		**$11,000**		**$10,000**
		$550 F Sales price variance		$1,000 F Sales volume variance	
Sales Units (drivers)	**140**		**140**		**150**
Sales Dollars (drivers)	**$26,600**		**$28,000**		**$30,000**
		$1,400 U Sales price variance		$2,000 U Sales volume variance	
Total		**$850 U**		**$1,000 U**	

Sales managers usually find sales variance information useful, especially when multiple products are involved. With multiple products, the sales volume variance can be further separated into a *sales mix variance* and a *sales quantity variance*. The sales mix variance is the difference between the actual and budgeted sales mix of the products. The sales quantity variance is the difference between the total actual and total budgeted quantity of units sold.

Managers use sales variances for planning and control purposes. With respect to planning, the sales variance information is used to plan future actions so as to avoid unfavorable variances. G-Max sold a total of 90 combined units (both balls and drivers) more than planned. But the added 90 units were not sold in the proportion budgeted. G-Max sold less than the budgeted quantity of the higher margin driver which contributed to the unfavorable total sales variances. This detail is used by managers to ask questions about what caused the company to sell more golf balls and fewer drivers.

With respect to control, managers use this information to evaluate and even reward their salespeople. Extra compensation is spent on salespeople who contribute to a higher profit margin.

Regional Sales Manager
You are the sales manager for a three-product company. A recent performance report from your company's office reveals a large favorable sales volume variance but an unfavorable sales price variance. You are confused because you didn't expect to see a large increase in sales volume. What steps do you take to analyze this situation?

Answer—p. 1081

Summary

C1 **Define standard costs and explain their computation and uses.** Standard costs are the normal costs that should be incurred to produce a product or perform a service. Standard costs are budgeted before the period and used in evaluations. They should be based on a careful examination of the processes used to produce a product or perform a service along with the quantities and prices that should be incurred in carrying out those processes. On a performance report, standard costs (which are flexible budget amounts) are compared to actual costs and the differences are presented as variances.

C2 **Describe variances and what they reveal about performance.** Variances can be used by management to monitor and control activities. They are also used to identify problem areas. Total cost variances can be broken into price and quantity variances to direct management's attention to the actions of lower-level managers responsible for quantities used or prices paid.

C3 Explain how standard cost information is useful for management by exception. Standard cost accounting provides management with information about costs that differ from budgeted (expected) amounts. Performance reports disclose the costs or areas of operations that have significant variances from budgeted amounts. This disclosure of differences from expected levels allows managers to devote attention to the exceptions and pay less attention to areas in which operations are proceeding normally.

A1 Compare fixed and flexible budgets. A fixed budget shows the revenues, costs, and expenses expected to occur at a specified production and sales volume. But if the actual production and sales volume is at some other level, the amounts in the fixed budget do not provide a reasonable basis for evaluating actual performance. A flexible budget expresses variable costs in per unit terms so that it can be used to develop budgeted amounts for any production and sales volume within the relevant range. This means managers compute budgeted amounts after a period for the volume that actually occurred. A flexible budget is more useful in evaluating actual performance.

A2 Analyze changes in sales from expected amounts. As in the case of costs, actual sales can be different from budgeted sales. Managers can further investigate this difference by computing both the sales price and sales volume variances. The sales price variance refers to that portion of the total variance resulting from a difference between the actual and budgeted selling prices. The sales volume variance refers to that portion of the total variance resulting from a difference between the actual and budgeted sales quantities.

P1 Prepare a flexible budget and interpret a flexible budget performance report. To prepare a flexible budget, management depends on the distinctions between fixed and variable costs. In generating the numbers to be used in preparing a flexible budget, we express each variable cost as a constant amount per unit of sales (or as a percent of a sales dollar). In contrast, the budgeted amount of each fixed cost is expressed as a total amount expected to occur at any sales volume within the relevant range. The flexible budget is then prepared using these computations and amounts for fixed and variable costs at the expected sales volume.

P2 Compute materials and labor variances. Materials and labor variances are due to differences between the actual costs incurred and the budgeted costs. The price (or rate) variance is computed by comparing the actual cost with the flexible budget amount that should have been incurred to acquire the actual quantity of resources. The quantity (or efficiency) variance is computed by comparing the flexible budget amount that should have been incurred to acquire the actual quantity of resources versus the flexible budget amount that should have been incurred to acquire the standard quantity of resources.

P3 Compute overhead variances. Overhead variances are due to differences between the actual overhead costs incurred and the overhead applied to production. An overhead spending variance arises when the actual amount incurred is different than the budgeted amount of overhead. An overhead efficiency (or volume) variance arises when the flexible overhead budget amount is different than the overhead applied to production. It is important to realize that overhead is not directly traced to a cost object. Instead, it is assigned using an overhead allocation base. This means an efficiency variance (in the case of variable overhead) is a result of the overhead application base being used more or less efficiently than planned.

P4 Record journal entries for standard costs and account for price and quantity variances. When a company records standard costs in its accounts, the standard costs of materials, labor, and overhead are debited to the Goods in Process Inventory account. Based on an analysis of the material, labor, and overhead costs, each quantity variance, price variance, volume variance, and controllable variance is recorded in a separate account. At the end of the period, if the variances are material, they are allocated among the balances of the Goods in Process Inventory, Finished Goods Inventory, and Cost of Goods Sold accounts. If they are not material, they are simply debited or credited to the Cost of Goods Sold account.

Guidance Answers to **You Make the Call**

Budget Officer

From the complaints, it appears that this performance report compared actual results with a fixed budget. While this comparison is useful in determining whether the amount of work actually performed was more or less than what was planned, it is not useful in determining whether the divisions were more or less efficient than planned. If the two consulting divisions worked on more assignments than expected, some of their costs will increase. Therefore, the budgeting department should prepare a flexible budget using the actual number of consulting assignments and compare the actual performance to the flexible budget.

Human Resource Manager

As the HR manager, you may not be directly responsible for labor efficiency variance. However, you should still investigate the causes for any labor related variances because labor issues generally fall under human resource management. An unfavorable labor efficiency variance occurs because more labor hours than standard are used during the period. There are at least three possible reasons for this. First, materials quality may be poor, resulting in more labor consumption due to rework. Second, there could have been unplanned interruptions during the period (e.g., strike, breakdowns, accidents). Third, a different labor mix may have been used by the production manager to expedite orders. This new labor mix may have consisted of a larger proportion of untrained labor which resulted in more labor hours.

Regional Sales Manager

The unfavorable sales price variance suggests that actual prices were lower than budgeted prices. As the regional sales manager, you certainly want to know the reasons for a lower than expected price. Perhaps your salespersons lowered the price of certain products by offering quantity discounts. You may then want to know what prompted these individuals to offer the quantity discounts (e.g., perhaps the main competitors were offering similar discounts). With respect to the sales volume variance, you may want to break it down further into both the sales mix and sales quantity variances. You may find that although the sales quantity variance is favorable, the sales mix variance may not be. Then you need to investigate further as to why the actual sales mix is different from the budgeted sales mix.

Guidance Answer to **Judgment and Ethics**

Internal Auditor

This is a situation where the manager of the department is "playing it safe" with regard to the practice of management by exception. It may not be appropriate to classify this manager's action as unethical. However, this action is undesirable and senior management should be informed about it. It is the internal auditor's role to bring to management's attention such behavior. Perhaps a good way in which the internal auditor can deal with the situation is to mention this behavior in an indirect manner in the report. In addition, the internal auditor can recommend that for the purchase of such discretionary items, the individual department managers must provide a report once every three years and any future budgetary requests must be done using a zero-based budgeting process. The internal auditor must be given full authority to verify this budget request.

Guidance Answers to 

1. *b*
2. The first step is classifying each cost as variable or fixed.
3. A fixed budget is prepared using an expected volume of sales or production. A flexible budget is prepared using the actual volume of activity.
4. Contribution margin equals sales less variable costs.
5. *c*
6. It is the difference between actual cost and standard cost.
7. *a;* Total actual hours: 2,500 × 2.5 = 6,250
   Total standard hours: 2,500 × 2.0 = 5,000
   Efficiency variance = (6,250 − 5,000) × $3.00 = $3,750 U
8. *d;* Rate variance = ($3.10 − $3.00) × 6,250 = $625 U
9. Yes, this will occur when the materials quantity variance is greater than the materials price variance.
10. The overhead volume variance is favorable when the actual operating level is greater than the expected level.
11. *b*
12.

Goods in Process Inventory	75,700	
Direct Materials Price Variance	1,300	
Direct Materials Quantity Variance		3,800
Raw Materials Inventory		73,200

13. If the variances are material, they should be prorated among the Goods in Process Inventory, Finished Goods Inventory, and Cost of Goods Sold accounts. If they are not material, they can be closed to Cost of Goods Sold.

Demonstration Problem

The Pacific Company provides the following information about its budgeted and actual results for June 1999. Although the expected volume for June was 25,000 units produced and sold, the company actually produced and sold 27,000 units as detailed below:

	Budget (25,000 units)	Actual (27,000 units)
Selling price	$5.00 per unit	$5.23 per unit
Variable costs (per unit):		
Direct materials	1.24 per unit	1.12 per unit
Direct labor	1.50 per unit	1.40 per unit
Factory supplies*	0.25 per unit	0.37 per unit
Utilities*	0.50 per unit	0.60 per unit
Selling costs	0.40 per unit	0.34 per unit
Fixed costs (per month):		
Depreciation of machinery*	$3,750	$3,710
Depreciation of building*	2,500	2,500
General liability insurance	1,200	1,250
Property taxes on office equipment	500	485
Other administrative expense	750	900

*Indicates factory overhead item.

Standard costs based on expected output of 25,000 units:

	Per Unit of Output	Quantity to Be Used	Total Cost
Direct materials, 4 oz. @ $0.31/oz.	$1.24/unit	100,000 oz.	$31,000
Direct labor, 0.25 hrs. @ $6.00/hr.	1.50/unit	6,250 hrs.	37,500
Overhead	1.00/unit		25,000

Actual costs incurred to produce 27,000 units:

	Per Unit of Output	Quantity Used	Total Cost
Direct materials, 4 oz. @ $0.28/oz.	$1.12/unit	108,000 oz.	$30,240
Direct labor, 0.20 hrs. @ $7.00/hr.	1.40/unit	5,400 hrs.	37,800
Overhead	1.20/unit		32,400

Standard costs based on expected output of 27,000 units:

	Per Unit of Output	Quantity to Be Used	Total Cost
Direct materials, 4 oz. @ $0.31/oz.	$1.24/unit	108,000 oz.	$33,480
Direct labor, 0.25 hrs. @ $6.00/hr.	1.50/unit	6,750 hrs.	40,500
Overhead			26,500

Required

1. Prepare flexible budgets for June showing expected sales, costs, and net income under assumptions of 20,000, 25,000, and 30,000 units of output produced and sold.

2. Prepare a flexible budget performance report that compares actual results with the amounts budgeted if the actual volume had been expected.

3. Apply variance analyses for direct materials, direct labor, and overhead.

Planning the Solution

- Prepare a table showing the expected results at the three specified levels of output. Compute the variable costs by multiplying the per unit variable costs by the expected volumes. Include fixed costs at the given amounts. Combine the amounts in the table to show total variable costs, contribution margin, total fixed costs, and income from operations.
- Prepare a table showing the actual results and the amounts that should be incurred at 27,000 units. Show any differences in the third column and label them with either an *F* for favorable if they increase income or a *U* for unfavorable if they decrease income.
- Using the variance format from the chapter, compute these total variances and the individual variances requested:
  - Total materials variance (including the direct materials quantity variance and the direct materials price variance).
  - Total direct labor variance (including the direct labor efficiency variance and the direct labor rate variance).
  - Total overhead variance (including both variable and fixed overhead variances and their component variances).

Solution to Demonstration Problem

1.

PACIFIC COMPANY
Flexible Budgets
For Month Ended June 30, 1999

	Flexible Budget		Flexible Budget for Unit Sales of 20,000	Flexible Budget for Unit Sales of 25,000	Flexible Budget for Unit Sales of 30,000
	Variable Amount per Unit	Total Fixed Cost			
Sales	$5.00		$100,000	$125,000	$150,000
Variable costs:					
Direct materials	1.24		24,800	31,000	37,200
Direct labor	1.50		30,000	37,500	45,000
Factory supplies	0.25		5,000	6,250	7,500
Utilities	0.50		10,000	12,500	15,000
Selling costs	0.40		8,000	10,000	12,000
Total variable costs	$3.89		$ 77,800	$ 97,250	$116,700
Contribution margin	$1.11		$ 22,200	$ 27,750	$ 33,300
Fixed costs:					
Depreciation of machinery		$3,750	3,750	3,750	3,750
Depreciation of building		2,500	2,500	2,500	2,500
General liability insurance		1,200	1,200	1,200	1,200
Property taxes on office equip.		500	500	500	500
Other administrative expense		750	750	750	750
Total fixed costs		$8,700	$ 8,700	$ 8,700	$ 8,700
Income from operations			$ 13,500	$ 19,050	$ 24,600

2.

PACIFIC COMPANY
Flexible Budget Performance Report
For Month Ended June 30, 1999

	Flexible Budget	Actual Results	Variance*
Sales (27,000 units)	$135,000	$141,210	$ 6,210 F
Variable costs:			
Direct materials	$ 33,480	$ 30,240	$ 3,240 F
Direct labor	40,500	37,800	2,700 F
Factory supplies	6,750	9,990	3,240 U
Utilities	13,500	16,200	2,700 U
Selling costs	10,800	9,180	1,620 F
Total variable costs	$105,030	$103,410	$ 1,620 F
Contribution margin	$ 29,970	$ 37,800	$ 7,830 F
Fixed costs:			
Depreciation of machinery	$ 3,750	$ 3,710	$ 40 F
Depreciation of building	2,500	2,500	
General liability insurance	1,200	1,250	50 U
Property taxes on office equipment	500	485	15 F
Other administrative expense	750	900	150 U
Total fixed costs	$ 8,700	$ 8,845	$ 145 U
Income from operations	$ 21,270	$ 28,955	$ 7,685 F

* F = Favorable variance; and U = Unfavorable variance.

3. Variance analysis of materials, labor, and overhead costs:

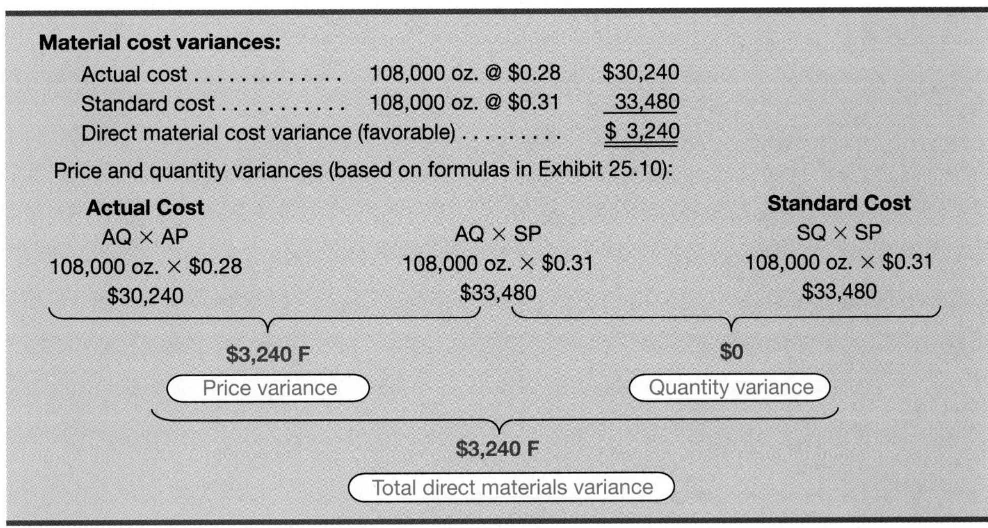

Material cost variances:
Actual cost . . . . 108,000 oz. @ $0.28 $30,240
Standard cost . . . . 108,000 oz. @ $0.31 33,480
Direct material cost variance (favorable) . . . . $ 3,240
Price and quantity variances (based on formulas in Exhibit 25.10):
Actual Cost
AQ × AP
108,000 oz. × $0.28
$30,240
AQ × SP
108,000 oz. × $0.31
$33,480
Standard Cost
SQ × SP
108,000 oz. × $0.31
$33,480
$3,240 F
Price variance
$0
Quantity variance
$3,240 F
Total direct materials variance

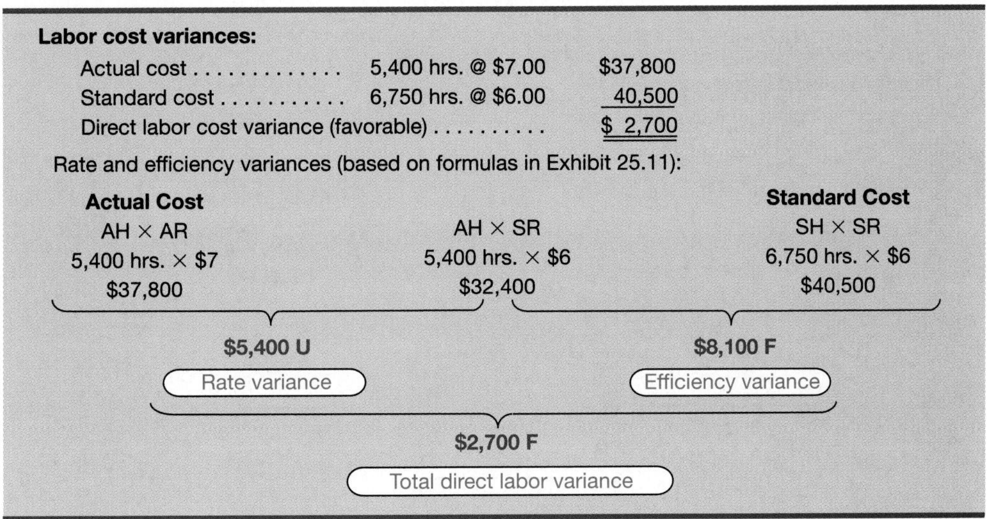

Labor cost variances:
Actual cost . . . . 5,400 hrs. @ $7.00 $37,800
Standard cost . . . . 6,750 hrs. @ $6.00 40,500
Direct labor cost variance (favorable) . . . . $ 2,700
Rate and efficiency variances (based on formulas in Exhibit 25.11):
Actual Cost
AH × AR
5,400 hrs. × $7
$37,800
AH × SR
5,400 hrs. × $6
$32,400
Standard Cost
SH × SR
6,750 hrs. × $6
$40,500
$5,400 U
Rate variance
$8,100 F
Efficiency variance
$2,700 F
Total direct labor variance

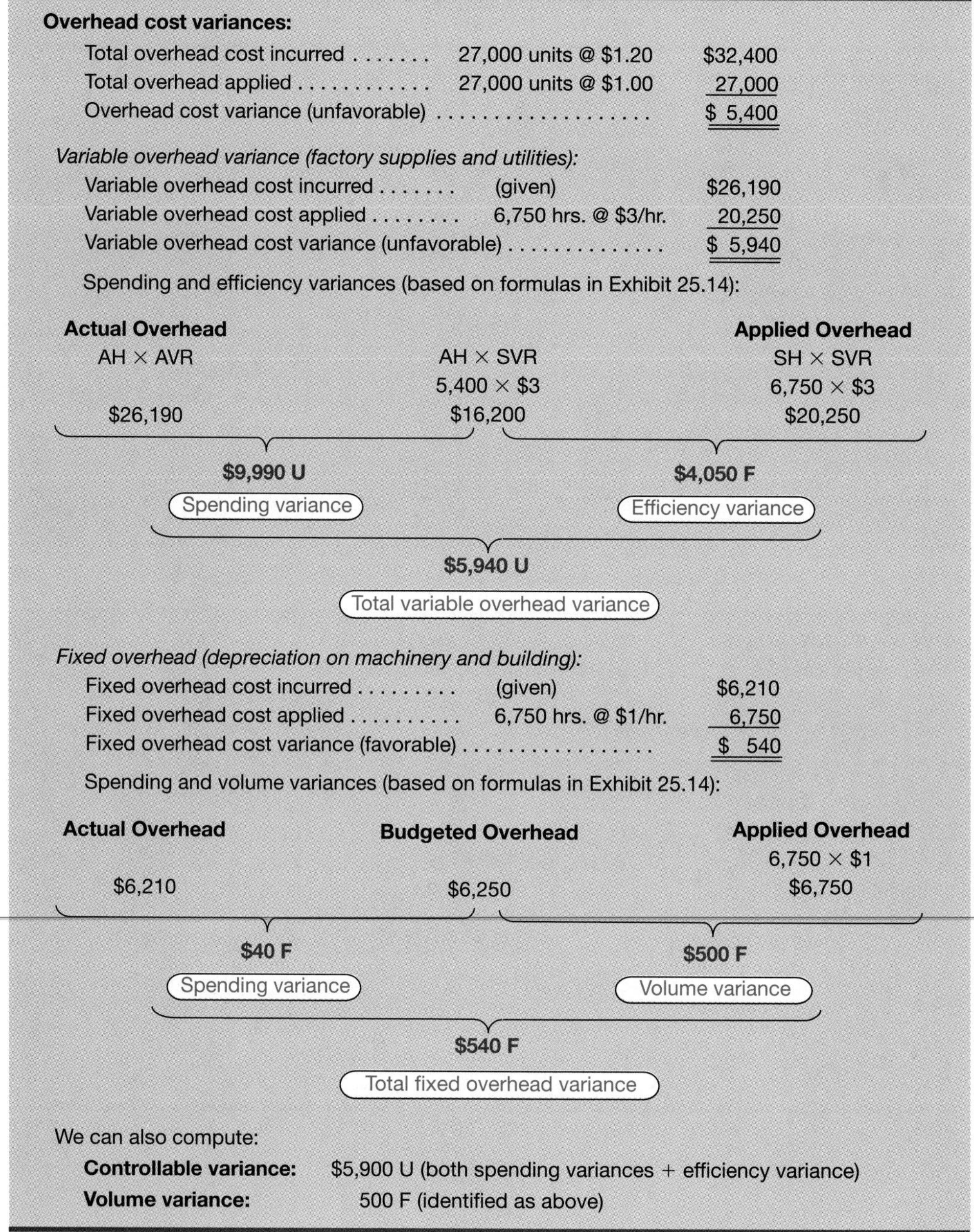

Overhead cost variances:

Total overhead cost incurred	27,000 units @ $1.20	$32,400
Total overhead applied	27,000 units @ $1.00	27,000
Overhead cost variance (unfavorable)		$ 5,400

Variable overhead variance (factory supplies and utilities):

Variable overhead cost incurred	(given)	$26,190
Variable overhead cost applied	6,750 hrs. @ $3/hr.	20,250
Variable overhead cost variance (unfavorable)		$ 5,940

Spending and efficiency variances (based on formulas in Exhibit 25.14):

Fixed overhead (depreciation on machinery and building):

Fixed overhead cost incurred	(given)	$6,210
Fixed overhead cost applied	6,750 hrs. @ $1/hr.	6,750
Fixed overhead cost variance (favorable)		$ 540

Spending and volume variances (based on formulas in Exhibit 25.14):

We can also compute:

Controllable variance: $5,900 U (both spending variances + efficiency variance)

Volume variance: 500 F (identified as above)

Glossary

Budgetary control use of budgets by management to monitor and control the operations of a company. (p. 1058).

Budget report report comparing actual results to planned objectives; sometimes used as a progress report (p. 1058).

Controllable variance both overhead spending variances (variable and fixed) and the variable overhead efficiency variance combined. (p. 1073).

Cost variance the difference between the actual incurred cost and the standard amount. (p. 1065).

Efficiency variance the difference between the actual quantity of an input and the standard quantity of that input. (p. 1072).

Favorable variance difference in revenues or costs, when the actual value is compared to the budgeted value, that contributes to a higher income. (p. 1059).

Fixed budget a planning budget based on a single predicted amount of sales or production volume; unsuitable for evaluations if the actual volume differs from the predicted volume. (p. 1059).

Fixed budget performance report an internal report that compares actual revenue and cost amounts with fixed budgeted amounts and identifies the differences between them as favorable or unfavorable variances. (p. 1059).

Flexible budget a budget prepared after an operating period is complete to help managers evaluate past performance; uses fixed and variable costs in determining total costs. (p. 1060).

Flexible budget performance report an internal report that compares actual revenue and cost amounts with their variable budgeted amounts based on the actual sales volume (or other level of activity); identifies differences between actual and budgeted amounts as variances. (p. 1062).

Management by exception a process used by management to focus on the most significant variances and give less attention to areas where performance is close enough to the standard to be satisfactory. (p. 1076).

Overhead cost variance the difference between the total overhead cost applied to products and the total overhead cost actually incurred. (p. 1072).

Price variance a difference between actual and budgeted revenue or cost caused by the difference between the actual price per unit and the budgeted price per unit. (p. 1062).

Quantity variance the difference between actual and budgeted revenue or cost caused by the difference between the actual number of units sold or used and the budgeted number of units. (p. 1063).

Spending variance the difference between the actual price of an item and its standard price. (p. 1072).

Standard costs the costs that should be incurred under normal conditions to produce a specific product or component or to perform a specific service. (p. 1064).

Unfavorable variance difference in revenues or costs, when the actual value is compared to the budgeted value, that contributes to a lower income. (p. 1059).

Variance analysis a process of examining differences between actual and budgeted revenues or costs and describing them in terms of the amounts that resulted from price and quantity differences. (p. 1063).

Volume variance difference between two dollar amounts of fixed overhead cost. One amount is the total budgeted overhead cost. The other amount is the overhead cost allocated to products using the predetermined fixed overhead rate. (p. 1073).

Questions

1. What limits the usefulness of fixed budget performance reports?
2. Prepare the title (in proper form) for a flexible budget performance report of Spalding Company for the calendar year 1999. Why is a proper title important for this or any report?
3. Identify the primary purpose of a flexible budget.
4. In what sense can a variable cost be considered constant?
5. What type of analysis does a flexible budget performance report help management conduct?
6. What is a price variance? What is a quantity variance?
7. What is the purpose of using standard costs?
8. What department is usually responsible for a direct labor rate variance? What department is usually responsible for a direct labor efficiency variance?
9. What is the predetermined standard overhead rate? How is it computed?
10. In an analysis of fixed overhead cost variances, what is the volume variance?
11. In an analysis of overhead cost variances, what is the controllable variance and what causes it?
12. If a company is budgeted to operate at 80% of capacity and actually operates at 75% of capacity, what effect will the 5% reduction have on the controllable variance? The volume variance?
13. Generally, it is said that variance analysis provides information about _________ and _________ variances.
14. If a company's overhead costs consist of only variable costs and its actual sales volume is 10% higher than the budgeted sales volume, what kind of volume variance would the company experience?
15. What is the relation among standard costs, flexible budgets, variance analysis, and management by exception?
16. Assume NIKE has a standard cost for a special line of women's running shoes. List several factors that might cause the actual cost incurred to vary from the standard cost.

Quick Study

QS 25-1
Preparing a flexible budget performance report

Milestone Company reports the following results for May:

Sales (150,000 units) . .	$1,275,000
Variable costs	712,500
Fixed costs	300,000

For the level of production achieved in May, sales were budgeted at $1,400,000, variable costs at $800,000, and fixed costs at $300,000. Prepare a flexible budget performance report for May.

QS 25-2
Computing materials cost
C2, P2

Clawson Company's output for the current period involved a standard direct materials cost of $150,000. For this same period, the direct materials variances included a favorable price variance of $12,000 and a favorable quantity variance of $4,000. What is the actual total direct materials cost for this period?

QS 25-3
Computing labor cost
C2, P2

Neely Company's output for the current period results in an unfavorable direct labor rate variance of $20,000 and an unfavorable direct labor efficiency variance of $10,000. The products produced for this same period involved a standard direct labor cost of $400,000. What is the actual total direct labor cost incurred for this period?

QS 25-4
Computing materials used
C2, P2

For the current period, Holloway Company's manufacturing operations yield a favorable price variance of $4,000 on its direct materials usage. The actual price per pound of material is $77 while the standard price is $77.50. How many pounds of material are used in the current period?

QS 25-5
Computing actual overhead
P3

Trek Company's output for the current period yields a favorable overhead volume variance of $30,000 and an unfavorable overhead controllable variance of $50,400. Standard overhead charged to production for the period amounts to $225,000. What is the actual total overhead cost incurred for the period?

QS 25-6
Management by exception
C3

Describe the concept of management by exception. Explain how standard costs help managers apply this concept.

QS 25-7
Preparing overhead journal entries
P4

Refer to the information in QS 25-5. Trek records standard costs in its accounts. Prepare the journal entry to charge overhead costs to the Goods in Process Inventory account and to record any variances.

QS 25-8
Computing sales variances
A2

Minivans, Inc., specializes in selling used minivans. During the first six months of 1999, the dealership sold 50 minivans at an average price of $9,000 each. The budget for the first six months of 1999 was to sell 45 minivans at an average price of $9,500 each. Compute the sales price variance and sales volume variance for the first six months of 1999 for the dealership.

Exercises

Exercise 25-1
Classifying costs as fixed or variable
P1

TKD Company manufactures and sells mountain bikes. It normally operates 8 hours a day, 5 days per week. Using this information, classify each of the following costs as fixed or variable. If additional information would affect your decision, describe what information would cause you to change your answer.

a. Bike frames
b. Direct labor
c. Screws
d. Repair expense for tools
e. Management salaries
f. Incoming shipping expenses
g. Office supplies
h. Depreciation on tools
i. Taxes on property
j. Pension cost
k. Gas used for heating

Exercise 25-2
Preparing flexible budgets
P1

Malone Company prepared the following fixed budget for the first quarter of calendar year 2000.

Sales (10,000 units)		$3,000,000
Cost of goods sold:		
Direct materials	$320,000	
Direct labor	680,000	
Production supplies	264,000	
Plant manager's salary	60,000	1,324,000
Gross profit		$1,676,000
Selling expenses:		
Sales commissions	$120,000	
Packaging	210,000	
Advertising	100,000	430,000
Administrative expenses:		
Administrative salaries	$ 80,000	
Depreciation, Office equip.	30,000	
Insurance	18,000	
Office rent	24,000	152,000
Income from operations		$1,094,000

Following the format of Exhibit 25.3, prepare flexible budgets that show variable costs per unit, fixed costs, and three different flexible budgets for sales volumes of 7,500, 10,000, and 12,500 units.

Exercise 25-3
Preparing a flexible budget performance report
A1

Land Company's fixed budget performance report for July shows this information:

	Fixed Budget	Actual Results	Variances
Sales (in units)	6,000	4,800	
Sales (in dollars)	$480,000	$422,400	$57,600 U
Total expenses	440,000	394,000	46,000 F
Income from operations	$ 40,000	$ 28,400	$11,600 U

The budgeted expenses of $440,000 include $300,000 of variable expenses and $140,000 of fixed expenses. The actual expenses include $130,000 of fixed expenses. Prepare a flexible budget performance report that shows any variances between budgeted results and actual results. (List fixed and variable expenses separately.)

Exercise 25-4
Preparing a flexible budget performance report
A1

Barnes Company's fixed budget performance report for June shows this information:

	Fixed Budget	Actual Results	Variances
Sales (in units)	8,400	10,800	
Sales (in dollars)	$840,000	$1,080,000	$240,000 F
Total expenses	630,000	756,000	126,000 U
Income from operations	$210,000	$ 324,000	$114,000 F

The budgeted expenses of $630,000 include $588,000 of variable expenses and $42,000 of fixed expenses. The actual expenses include $54,000 of fixed expenses. Prepare a flexible budget performance report that shows any variances between budgeted results and actual results. (List fixed and variable expenses separately.)

Exercise 25-5
Computing and interpreting materials variances
C2, P2

AMP Company made 6,000 bookshelves using 88,000 board feet of wood costing $607,200. The company's direct materials standards for one bookshelf are 16 board feet of wood at $7 per board foot.

Required

1. Compute the direct materials variances incurred in manufacturing these bookshelves.
2. Interpret the direct materials variances.

Exercise 25-6
Computing and interpreting labor variances
C2, P2

After evaluating Zeron Company's manufacturing process, management decides to establish standards of 1.5 hours of direct labor per unit of product and $11 per hour for the labor rate. During October, the company uses 3,780 hours of direct labor at a total cost of $45,360 to produce 2,700 units of product. In November, the company uses 4,480 hours of direct labor at a total cost of $47,040 to produce 2,800 units of product.

Required

1. Compute the rate variance, the efficiency variance, and the total direct labor cost variance for each of these two months.
2. Interpret the October direct labor variances.

Exercise 25-7
Computing and interpreting overhead variances
C2, P3

Sharp Company set the following standard costs for one unit of its product for 1999:

Direct material (20 lbs. @ $2.50 per lb.)	$ 50.00
Direct labor (15 hrs. @ $8.00 per hr.)	120.00
Factory variable overhead (15 hrs. @ $2.50 per hr.)	37.50
Factory fixed overhead (15 hrs. @ $0.50 per hr.)	7.50
Standard cost	$215.00

The $3.00 ($2.50 + $0.50) total overhead rate per direct labor hour is based on an expected operating level equal to 75% of the factory's capacity of 50,000 units per month. The following monthly flexible budget information is also available:

	Operating Levels		
	70%	75%	80%
Budgeted output (units)	35,000	37,500	40,000
Budgeted labor (standard hours)	525,000	562,500	600,000
Budgeted overhead:			
Variable overhead	$1,312,500	$1,406,250	$1,500,000
Fixed overhead	281,250	281,250	281,250
Total overhead	$1,593,750	$1,687,500	$1,781,250

During the current month, the company operated at 70% of capacity, employees worked 500,000 hours, and the following actual overhead costs are incurred:

Variable overhead costs	$1,267,500
Fixed overhead costs	285,000
Total overhead costs	$1,552,500

Required

1. Show how the company computed its predetermined overhead application rates per hour for total overhead, variable overhead, and fixed overhead.
2. Compute the variable overhead spending and efficiency variances and interpret each.
3. Compute the fixed overhead spending and volume variances and interpret each.

Exercise 25-8
Computing volume and controllable overhead variances
P3

Earth Company expected to operate last month at 80% of its productive capacity of 25,000 units per month. At this planned level, the company expected to use 40,000 standard hours of direct labor. Overhead is allocated to products using a predetermined standard rate based on direct labor hours. At the 80% level of operation, the total budgeted cost includes $40,000 of fixed overhead cost and $280,000 of variable overhead cost. During the current month, the company incurred $340,000 of actual overhead and 39,000 actual hours while producing 19,500 units of product. Compute (1) the total overhead variance, (2) the overhead volume variance, and (3) the overhead controllable variance.

Exercise 25-9
Recording materials variances in the accounts
C3, P4

Refer to Exercise 25-5 in working this exercise. AMP Company records standard costs in its accounts. It also records its material variances in separate accounts when it assigns materials costs to the Goods in Process Inventory account.

Required

1. Show the journal entry that both charges the direct materials costs to the Goods in Process Inventory account and records the materials variances in their accounts.
2. Assume AMP's material variances are the only variances accumulated in the accounting period and that they are considered immaterial. Show the adjusting journal entry that is made to close the variance accounts at the end of the period.
3. Which variance should be investigated according to the management by exception concept? Explain.

Exercise 25-10
Computing and interpreting sales variances
A2

Computer Outlet, Inc., specializes in selling computers. During May 1999, the company sold 500 computers at an average price of $900 each. The budget for May 1999 included sales of 550 computers at an average price of $850 each. Compute the sales price variance and the sales volume variance for May 1999. Interpret the findings.

Problems

Problem 25-1
Preparing and analyzing a flexible budget
P1, A1

Penn Company's master budget for 1999 included the following fixed budget performance report. It is based on expected production and sales volume of 20,000 units.

PENN COMPANY
Fixed Budget Performance Report
For Year Ended December 31, 1999

Sales		$3,000,000
Cost of goods sold:		
Direct materials	$1,200,000	
Direct labor	260,000	
Machinery repairs (variable cost)	57,000	
Depreciation on plant equipment (annual)	250,000	
Utilities (variable cost is 25%)	200,000	
Plant management salaries	140,000	(2,107,000)
Gross profit		$ 893,000
Selling expenses:		
Packaging	$ 80,000	
Shipping	116,000	
Sales salary (fixed annual amount)	160,000	(356,000)
General and administrative expenses:		
Advertising expense	$ 81,000	
Salaries	241,000	
Entertainment expense	90,000	(412,000)
Income from operations		$ 125,000

Required

1. Classify all items in the fixed budget as either variable or fixed. Also, determine their amounts per unit or their amounts for the year, as appropriate.

Check Figure Budgeted income at 24,000 units, $372,400

2. Prepare flexible budgets (see Exhibit 25.3) for the company at sales and production volumes of 18,000 and 24,000 units.
3. The company's business conditions are improving and one possible effect could be a sales volume of approximately 28,000 units. The president of the company is confident that this volume is within the relevant range of existing capacity. How much would operating income increase over the 1999 budgeted amount if this level is reached without increasing capacity?
4. There is a remote possibility of an unfavorable change, in which case production and sales volume for 1999 could fall to 14,000 units. How much income (or loss) from operations would occur if sales volume falls to this level?

Problem 25-2
Preparing and analyzing a flexible budget performance report
P1, A2
S

Refer to information in Problem 25-1. Penn Company's actual income statement for 1999 follows:

PENN COMPANY
Statement of Income from Operations
For Year Ended December 31, 1999

Sales (24,000 units)		$3,648,000
Cost of goods sold:		
Direct materials	$1,400,000	
Direct labor	360,000	
Machinery repairs (variable cost)	60,000	
Depreciation on plant equipment (annual)	250,000	
Utilities (fixed cost is $154,000)	218,000	
Plant management salaries	155,000	(2,443,000)
Gross profit		$1,205,000
Selling expenses:		
Packaging	$ 90,000	
Shipping	124,000	
Sales salary (annual)	162,000	(376,000)
General and administrative expenses:		
Advertising expense	$ 104,000	
Salaries	232,000	
Entertainment expense	100,000	(436,000)
Income from operations		$ 393,000

Required

Preparation Component

Check Figure Total variance in income, $20,600 favorable

1. Prepare a flexible budget performance report for 1999.

Analysis Component

2. Analyze and interpret both *(a)* the sales variance and *(b)* the direct materials variance.

Problem 25-3
Computing and reporting materials, labor, and overhead variances
C2, P2, P3

Peach Company has set the following standard costs per unit for the product it manufactures:

Direct material (10 lbs. @ $3 per lb.)	$30.00
Direct labor (4 hrs. @ $6 per hr.)	24.00
Overhead (4 hrs. @ $2.50 per hr.)	10.00
Total standard cost	$64.00

The predetermined overhead rate is based on a planned operating volume of 80% of the productive capacity of 10,000 units per month. The following flexible budget information is available:

	Operating Levels		
	70%	80%	90%
Production in units	7,000	8,000	9,000
Standard direct labor hours	28,000	32,000	36,000
Budgeted overhead:			
Variable costs:			
Indirect materials	$ 8,750	$10,000	$11,250
Indirect labor	14,000	16,000	18,000
Power	3,500	4,000	4,500
Maintenance	1,750	2,000	2,250
Total variable costs	$28,000	$32,000	$36,000
Fixed costs:			
Rent of factory building	$12,000	$12,000	$12,000
Depreciation, Machinery	20,000	20,000	20,000
Taxes and insurance	2,400	2,400	2,400
Supervisory salaries	13,600	13,600	13,600
Total fixed costs	$48,000	$48,000	$48,000
Total overhead costs	$76,000	$80,000	$84,000

During May of this year, the company operated at 90% of capacity and produced 9,000 units. The following actual costs are incurred:

Direct material (92,000 lbs. @ $2.95 per lb.)		$271,400
Direct labor (37,600 hrs. @ $6.05 per hr.)		227,480
Overhead costs:		
Indirect materials	$10,000	
Indirect labor	16,000	
Power	4,500	
Maintenance	3,000	
Rent of factory building	12,000	
Depreciation, Machinery	19,200	
Taxes and insurance	3,000	
Supervisory salaries	14,000	81,700
Total costs		$580,580

Required

1. Compute the direct materials variance, including its price and quantity variances.

2. Compute the direct labor variance, including its rate and efficiency variances.

3. Compute (*a*) the variable overhead spending and efficiency variances, (*b*) the fixed overhead spending and volume variances, and (*c*) the total overhead controllable variance.

4. Prepare a detailed overhead variance report (as in Exhibit 25.19) that shows the variances for individual items of overhead.

Check Figure Total overhead controllable variance, $2,300 favorable

Problem 25-4
Computing materials, labor, and overhead variances
C2, P2, P3

Tuna Company set the following standard unit costs for its single product:

Direct material (25 lbs. @ $4 per lb.)	$100.00
Direct labor (6 hrs. @ $8 per hr.)	48.00
Factory overhead—variable (6 hrs. @ $5 per hr.)	30.00
Factory overhead—fixed (6 hrs. @ $7 per hr.)	42.00
Total standard cost	$220.00

The predetermined overhead rate is based on a planned operating volume of 80% of the productive capacity of 60,000 units per quarter. The following flexible budget information is available:

	Operating Levels		
	70%	80%	90%
Production in units	42,000	48,000	54,000
Standard direct labor hours	252,000	288,000	324,000
Budgeted overhead:			
Fixed factory overhead	$2,016,000	$2,016,000	$2,016,000
Variable factory overhead	1,260,000	1,440,000	1,620,000

During the current quarter, the company operated at 70% of capacity and produced 42,000 units of product; actual direct labor totaled 250,000 hours. Units produced are assigned the following standard costs:

Direct material (1,050,000 lbs. @ $4 per lb.)	$4,200,000
Direct labor (252,000 hrs. @ $8 per hr.)	2,016,000
Factory overhead (252,000 hrs. @ $12 per hr.)	3,024,000
Total standard cost	$9,240,000

Actual costs incurred during the current quarter are:

Direct material (1,000,000 lbs. @ $ 4.25)	$4,250,000
Direct labor (250,000 hrs. @ $7.75)	1,937,500
Fixed factory overhead costs	1,960,000
Variable factory overhead costs	1,200,000
Total actual costs	$9,347,500

Required

1. Compute the direct materials cost variance, including its price and quantity variances.

2. Compute the direct labor variance, including its rate and efficiency variances.

Check Figure Labor rate variance, $62,500 favorable

3. Compute (*a*) the variable overhead spending and efficiency variances, (*b*) the fixed overhead spending and volume variances, and (*c*) the total overhead controllable variance.

Problem 25-5
Preparing a flexible budget, computing variances, and preparing an overhead report
P1, P2, P3, C2

Hard Drive Company has set the following standard costs for one unit of its product:

Direct material (4.5 lbs. @ $6 per lb.)	$27.00
Direct labor (1.5 hrs. @ $12 per hr.)	18.00
Overhead (1.5 hrs. @ $16 per hr.)	24.00
Total standard cost	$69.00

The predetermined overhead rate ($16.00 per direct labor hour) is based on an expected volume of 75% of the factory's capacity of 20,000 units per month. Following are the company's budgeted overhead costs per month at the 75% level:

Overhead Budget (75% capacity)		
Variable costs:		
Indirect materials	$22,500	
Indirect labor	90,000	
Power	22,500	
Repairs and maintenance	45,000	
Total variable costs		$180,000
Fixed costs:		
Depreciation, Building	$24,000	
Depreciation, Machinery	72,000	
Taxes and insurance	18,000	
Supervision	66,000	
Total fixed costs		180,000
Total overhead costs		$360,000

The company incurred the following actual costs when it operated at 75% of capacity in October:

Direct material (69,000 lbs. @ $6.10)		$ 420,900
Direct labor (22,800 hrs. @ $12.30)		280,440
Overhead costs:		
Indirect materials	$21,600	
Indirect labor	82,260	
Power	23,100	
Repairs and maintenance	46,800	
Depreciation, Building	24,000	
Depreciation, Machinery	75,000	
Taxes and insurance	16,500	
Supervision	66,000	355,260
Total costs		$1,056,600

Required

1. Classify all items in the overhead budget as either variable or fixed. Also, determine their amounts per unit or their amounts for the month, as appropriate.
2. Prepare flexible overhead budgets (as in Exhibit 25.12) for October showing the amounts of each variable and fixed cost at the 65%, 75%, and 85% capacity levels.
3. Compute the direct materials cost variance, including its price and quantity variances.
4. Compute the direct labor cost variance, including its rate and efficiency variances.
5. Compute (*a*) the variable overhead spending and efficiency variances, (*b*) the fixed overhead spending and volume variances, and (*c*) the total overhead controllable variance.
6. Prepare a detailed overhead variance report (as in Exhibit 25.19) that shows the variances for individual items of overhead.

Check Figure Total overhead controllable variance, $4,740 favorable

Problem 25-6
Recording and analyzing materials, labor, and overhead variances
C3, P4

Best Company's standard cost accounting system recorded the following information from its operations for December:

Standard direct material cost	$130,000
Direct material quantity variance (unfavorable)	5,000
Direct material price variance (favorable)	1,500
Actual direct labor cost	65,000
Direct labor efficiency variance (favorable)	7,000
Direct labor rate variance (unfavorable)	500
Actual overhead cost	250,000
Volume variance (unfavorable)	12,000
Controllable variance (unfavorable)	8,000

Required

Preparation Component

1. Prepare December 30 journal entries to record the company's costs and variances for the month.

Check Figure Goods in Process Inventory (for overhead), $230,000 debit

Analysis Component

2. Identify areas that would attract the attention of a manager who uses management by exception. Explain what action the manager should take.

BEYOND THE NUMBERS

Reporting in Action

C1

Analysis of flexible budgets and standard costs emphasizes that the unit of measure must be the same to make meaningful comparisons and evaluations. When **NIKE** compiles its financial reports in compliance with GAAP, it applies the same unit of measurement, U.S. dollars, for most measures of business operations. Without this practice, comparisons with other companies and across time are meaningless. One issue for NIKE is how to best adjust account values for its subsidiaries that compile financial reports in currencies other than the U.S. dollar.

Required

1. Read NIKE's Note 1 in Appendix A and identify the financial statement where NIKE reports its foreign currency translation.
2. Record the annual amount of NIKE's foreign currency translation adjustment and its ending balance for the three fiscal years 1995–1997.

Swoosh Ahead

3. Obtain NIKE's annual report information for a fiscal year ending after May 31, 1997. You can get this invormation from either its Web site [**www.nike.com**] or the SEC's EDGAR database [**www.sec.gov**]. (*a*) Identify the May 31, 1998, foreign currency translation adjustment. (*b*) Does this adjustment increase or decrease net income? Explain.

Comparative Analysis

A2

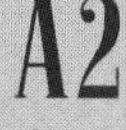

The usefulness of budgets, variances, and subsequent related analyses often depends on the accuracy of management's estimates of future sales activity.

Required

1. Identify and record the prior 3 years' sales (in dollars) for both **NIKE** and **Reebok** using their financial statements in Appendix A.
2. Using the data in part (1), predict both companies' future sales activity for the next two years. (If possible, compare your predictions to actual sales figure for these years.)

Ethics Challenge

C1

Setting materials, labor, and overhead standards is challenging. If standards are set too low, companies may purchase inferior products and employees may not work to their full potential. If standards are set too high, companies may be unable to offer a quality product at a profitable rate and employees may be overworked. The ethical challenge is to set a standard that is reasonable. Assume you are a manager at Computer Chips. You are asked to set the standard materials price and quantity for the new 1,000 CKB Mega-Max chip. This is a technically advanced product. To properly set the price and quantity standards, you need to assemble a team of specialists to provide information.

Required

Identify a team of four specialists you would assemble to provide information to set the materials price and quantity standards. Briefly explain why you have chosen each individual.

Communicating in Practice

P4, C2

Why use the words *favorable* or *unfavorable* when evaluating variances? The reason is clear when we look at the closing of accounts. To see this, consider: (1) all variance accounts are closed at the end of each period (temporary accounts); (2) a favorable variance is always a credit balance; and (3) an unfavorable variance is always a debit balance. (Assume variance accounts are closed to Cost of Goods Sold.) Write a one-half page memorandum to your instructor with three parts that answer the three questions below.

Required

1. Does Cost of Goods Sold increase or decrease when closing a favorable variance? Does gross margin increase or decrease when a favorable variance is closed to Cost of Goods Sold?
2. Does Cost of Goods Sold increase or decrease when closing an unfavorable variance? Does gross margin increase or decrease when an unfavorable variance is closed to Cost of Goods Sold?
3. Explain the meaning of a favorable variance and an unfavorable variance.

Taking It to the Net

C1

Compliance with standards is important to the success of a company. A customer will pay a higher price for a product that meets certain standards. This is why the UL label, Underwriters Laboratories, is important. This label implies the product meets certain standards. Visit the Web site [**www.ul.com**]. Click on (1st) Services and (2nd) Testing and Certification, then answer the following questions.

Required

1. Identify one product category that is certified by Underwriters Laboratories. Record specific examples of products in this category.
2. Why would a company pay for the UL certification?

Teamwork in Action

C2

This chapter links labor rate and time (quantity) standards with products and manufacturing processes. The service industry also uses standard labor rate and time measurements. One example is the standard time to board an aircraft. The reason time plays such an important role in the service industry is that it is viewed as a competitive advantage–best service in the shortest amount of time. Although the labor rate component is difficult to observe, the time component of a service delivery standard is often readily apparent—for example, "lunch to be served in less than five minutes, or it is free."

Required

Break into teams and select two industries for your analysis. Identify and describe all the time elements used to create a competitive advantage for each industry.

Hitting the Road

C1

Training employees to use standard amounts of materials in production is common. Large companies typically invest in this training. Small organizations typically do not. One can observe these different practices in a trip to two different pizza businesses. Visit both a local pizza business and a national pizza chain business and then complete the following.

Required

1. Observe and record the number of raw material items used to make a typical cheese pizza. Also observe how the person making the pizza applies each item when making the pizza.
2. Record any differences in how items are applied between the two businesses.
3. Estimate which business is more profitable from your observations. Explain.

Business Week Activity

C1

In Germany, labor unions are influential in setting both the wage rate and the standard amount of hours worked in a week. This influence impacts the German economy. Read "The German Worker Is Making a Sacrifice" in the July 28, 1997, issue of ***Business Week*** and answer the following questions.

Required

1. Identify the concerns linked to labor unions in terms of the health of the German economy.
2. Identify how German labor unions are supporting the country's economic recovery in the setting of wage rates and hours worked. Identify three companies and their unions as examples.

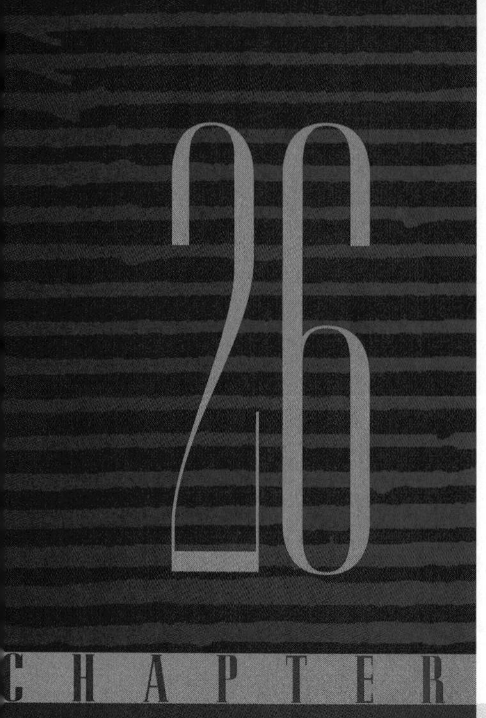

Capital Budgeting and Managerial Decisions

A Look Back

Chapter 25 discussed flexible budgets, variance analysis, and standard costs. It explained how each is used by management for controlling and monitoring business activities.

A Look at This Chapter

This chapter focuses on evaluating capital budgeting decisions. It also explains procedures used in evaluating many short-term managerial decisions.

Chapter Outline

Gee-Whiz

BALTIMORE, MD—At the end of 10th grade, Greg Cass left school to work as an auto mechanic. He learned he hated mechanical work, but he loved electronics. "I found myself tinkering with circuits and other gadgets on cars after work hours," says Cass. He eventually went back to school and earned his high school equivalency and then a diploma in computer electronics.

What Cass is now doing is running **Gee-Whiz,** a small computer electronics manufacturer. "It's really tough competing in this industry. With all the changes in prices and what customers want, it's amazing I have any hair left at all." But Gee-Whiz is bucking the odds and making a name for itself by living on the edge. "We try to be the company with the newest hip thing," says Cass.

While he admits getting burned once or twice, such as with his video pager, he is getting it right more times than not. Cass mixes computer savvy with sound business methods to analyze potential opportunities. These methods include capital budgeting, payback period, and net present value.

"I needed some structure in making decisions," says Cass. "There are a lot of methods out there to help me. If the numbers don't add up, I don't do it."

Gee-Whiz Jeans—a jeans manufacturing company in Washington is the new project for Cass. "I'm creating wearable computers woven into jeans," says Cass. "If this works, I'll be merging two industries—electronics and jeans manufacturing." But he admits the development is slow. "I'm over budget, and when I'll make a profit is anyone's guess. But I will cut my losses if I have to. I can't hide from the numbers." But don't count Cass out. So far the numbers for Gee-Whiz are pretty rosy.

Learning Objectives

Conceptual

C1 Explain the importance of capital budgeting.

C2 Describe selection of a hurdle rate for an investment.

C3 Describe the importance of relevant costs for short-term decisions.

Analytical

A1 Evaluate short-term managerial decisions using relevant costs.

A2 Analyze a capital investment project using break-even time.

Procedural

P1 Compute the payback period and describe its use.

P2 Compute accounting rate of return and explain its use.

P3 Compute net present value and describe its use.

P4 Compute internal rate of return and explain its use.

CHAPTER PREVIEW

Business decisions involve choosing between alternative courses of action. Although many factors affect business decisions, our analysis typically begins by looking for the alternative that offers the highest return on investment or the greatest reduction in costs. Some decisions are based on little more than an intuitive understanding of the situation because available information is too limited to allow a more systematic analysis. In other cases, intangible factors such as convenience, prestige, and environmental considerations are more important than strictly quantitative factors. But even in these situations, we can reach a more sound decision if we identify the consequences of alternative choices in financial terms. This chapter explains several methods of analysis that can help managers such as Greg Cass (see opening article) make long-term and short-term decisions.

SECTION 1—CAPITAL BUDGETING

We described the capital expenditures budget in Chapter 24. It is management's plan for acquiring and selling plant assets. **Capital budgeting** is the process of analyzing alternative long-term investments and deciding which assets to acquire or sell. These decisions can involve developing a new product or process, buying a new machine or a new building, or acquiring an entire company. An objective for all of these decisions is to earn a satisfactory return on investment.

C1 Explain the importance of capital budgeting.

Capital budgeting decisions require careful analysis because they are usually the most difficult and risky decisions that managers make. These decisions are difficult because they require predictions of events that won't occur until well into the future. Many of these predictions are tentative and potentially unreliable. Specifically, a capital budgeting decision is risky because (1) the outcome is uncertain, (2) large amounts of money are usually involved, (3) the investment involves a long-term commitment, and (4) the decision may be difficult or impossible to reverse, no matter how poor it turns out to be.

Capital budgeting covers a wide range of decisions. Managers use several methods in evaluating capital budgeting decisions. Nearly all of these methods involve predicting cash inflows and cash outflows of proposed investments, assessing the riskiness of and returns on those flows, and then choosing the investments to be made.

A capital investment is expected to provide benefits over more than one period. To decide whether to invest or not, management must decide at the present time whether to make such an investment. Given that the cash flows are generated in the future, management often restates future cash flows in terms of their present value. This approach applies the time value of money—a dollar today is worth more than a dollar tomorrow. Similarly, a dollar tomorrow is worth less than a dollar today. The process of restating future cash flows in terms of their present value is called *discounting*. While it is important to consider the time value of money when evaluating capital investments, managers sometimes apply evaluation methods that do not explicitly consider it.

This chapter describes four methods for comparing alternative investments. These methods call for computing the *payback period,* the *accounting rate of return,* the *net present value,* and the *internal rate of return*. The first two methods do not consider the *time value of money,* whereas the latter two methods do.

Methods Not Using Time Value of Money

All investments, whether they involve the purchase of a machine or another long-term asset, are expected to produce cash inflows and cash outflows. *Net cash flow* is the cash inflows minus the cash outflows for a period. There are methods available for management to perform simple analyses of the financial feasibility of an investment without using the time value of money. This section explains two of the most common methods in this category: (1) payback period and (2) accounting rate of return.

Payback Period

The **payback period (PBP)** of an investment is the expected time period it will take to recover the initial investment amount. Managers prefer investing in assets with shorter payback periods to reduce the risk of an unprofitable investment over the long run. Acquiring assets with short payback periods reduces a company's risk due to potentially inaccurate long-term predictions of future cash flows.

P1 Compute the payback period and describe its use.

Computing Payback Period

This section explains how we compute the payback period with either equal or unequal cash flows.[1]

Equal Cash Flows

To illustrate use of the payback period with equal cash flows, we look at data from **FasTrac,** a manufacturer of exercise equipment and supplies. FasTrac is considering several different capital investments, one of which is the purchase of a machine for use in manufacturing a new product. This machine costs $16,000 and is expected to have an eight-year life with no salvage value. Management predicts this machine will produce 1,000 units of product each year and that the new product will be sold for $30 per unit.

Exhibit 26.1 shows the annual net cash flows this asset is expected to generate over its life. It also shows the expected annual revenues and expenses (including depreciation and income taxes) from investing in this machine.

Exhibit 26.1
Cash Flow Analysis

FASTRAC
Cash Flow Analysis—New Machinery
January 15, 1999

	Expected Net Accrual Figures	Expected Net Cash Flows
Annual sales of new product	$30,000	$30,000
Deduct annual expenses:		
Cost of materials, labor, and overhead (except depr.)	(15,500)	(15,500)
Depreciation of machinery	(2,000)	
Additional selling and administrative expenses	(9,500)	(9,500)
Annual pretax income	$ 3,000	
Income taxes (30%)	(900)	(900)
Annual net income	$ 2,100	
Annual net cash flow		$ 4,100

The amount of net cash flows from the machinery is computed by subtracting expected cash outflows from expected cash inflows. The cash flow column excludes all noncash revenues and expenses. For FasTrac, depreciation is the only noncash item. Alternatively, some managers adjust the projected net income for revenue and expense items that do

[1] Equal cash flows means cash flows are the same each and every year. Unequal cash flows means not all cash flows are equal in amount.

not affect cash flows. For FasTrac this means taking the net income of $2,100 and adding back the $2,000 depreciation.

The formula for computing the payback period of an investment yielding equal net cash flows is shown in Exhibit 26.2.

Exhibit 26.2

Payback Period Formula with Equal Cash Flows

$$\textbf{Payback period} = \frac{\textbf{Cost of investment}}{\textbf{Annual net cash flow}}$$

The payback period reflects the time it will take the investment to generate enough net cash flow to return (or pay back) the cash initially invested to purchase it.

In the case of FasTrac, the payback period for this machine is just under four years as computed below:

$$\text{Payback period} = \frac{\$16{,}000}{\$4{,}100} = 3.9 \text{ years}$$

This means the initial investment is fully recovered in 3.9 years, or just before we reach the halfway point of this machinery's useful life of eight years.

Unequal Cash Flows

Computation of the payback period in the prior section assumes equal net cash flows. But what if the net cash flows are unequal? In this case the payback period is computed using the *cumulative total of net cash flows. Cumulative* refers to the addition of each additional period's net cash flows as we progress through time.

To illustrate, let's look at data for another potential investment that FasTrac is considering. This machine is predicted to produce unequal, or uneven, net cash flows over the next eight years. The relevant data along with computation of the payback period are shown in Exhibit 26.3.

Exhibit 26.3

Payback Period Calculation with Unequal Cash Flows

Period*	Expected Net Cash Flows	Cumulative Net Cash Flows
Year 0	$(16,000)	$(16,000)
Year 1	3,000	(13,000)
Year 2	4,000	(9,000)
Year 3	4,000	(5,000)
Year 4	4,000	(1,000)
Year 5	5,000	4,000
Year 6	3,000	7,000
Year 7	2,000	9,000
Year 8	2,000	11,000
		Payback period = 4.2 years

* All cash flows occur at the end of the year indicated.

Year 0 refers to the period of initial investment and is reflected in the $16,000 cash outflow to acquire the machinery. By the end of Year 1, the cumulative net cash flow is reduced to $(13,000)—computed as the $(16,000) initial cash outflow plus Year 1's $3,000 cash inflow. This process continues throughout the asset's life.

The cumulative net cash flow amount changes from negative to positive in Year 5. Specifically, at the end of Year 4, the cumulative net cash flow is $(1,000). This means that as soon as FasTrac receives a net cash inflow of $1,000 in the fifth year, the investment is fully recovered. If we assume cash flows are received uniformly *within* each year, then receipt of the $1,000 occurs about one-fifth of the way through the year. This

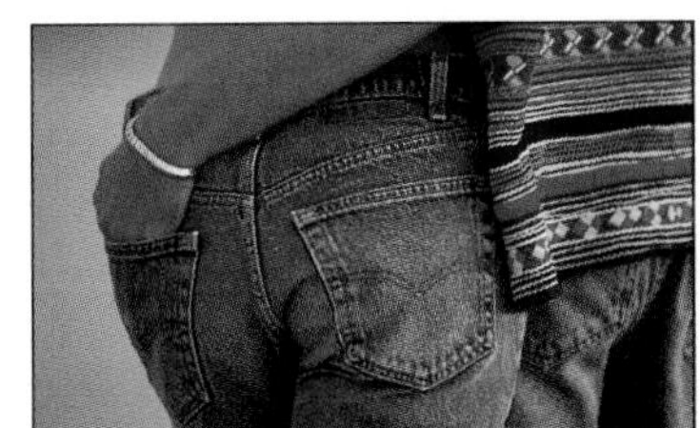

is computed as $1,000 divided by Year 5's total net cash flow of $5,000, or 0.20. This gives us our payback period of 4.2 years, computed as 4 years plus 0.20 of Year 5.

Let's return to the opening article and the decision by **Gee-Whiz** to acquire a jeans fabric processing plant. Gee-Whiz put together a five-year forecast of cash flows for this acquisition. While a major reason to acquire it was for the processing technology, Gee-Whiz continued the plant's current operations. Revenue was projected to grow annually based on an assumed increasing market share and stable prices for the current mix of products. Projected cash outflows reflected an increasing advertising budget believed necessary to increase market share and sales. Projected outflows also assumed stable raw material costs with modest increases in plant, administrative, and sales costs. Gee-Whiz assumed the fabric could be sold and administered by the existing sales and administrative staff. It then compared these cash flows with estimated net cash flows from investing in a start-up fabric processing plant. Cash flows of this start-up alternative were used to set a ceiling on the amount to be paid for the plant.

Using the Payback Period

Companies desire a short payback period to increase return and reduce risk. The more quickly cash is received, the sooner it is available for other uses, and the less time its cash investment is at risk of loss. A shorter payback period also improves the company's ability to respond to unanticipated changes and lessens its risk of having to keep an unprofitable investment.

Payback period should never be the only consideration in evaluating investments. This is because it ignores at least two important factors. First, it fails to reflect differences in the timing of net cash flows within the payback period. In Exhibit 26.3, FasTrac's net cash flows in the first five years were $3,000, $4,000, $4,000, $4,000, and $5,000. If another asset had predicted cash flows of $9,000, $3,000, $2,000, $1,800, and $1,000 in these five years, its payback period would also be 4.2 years. But this second alternative may be more desirable because it provides cash more quickly.

The second important factor is that the payback period ignores *all* cash flows after the point where its costs are fully recovered. For example, one investment may pay back its cost in 3 years but stop producing cash after 4 years. But a second investment might require 5 years to pay back its cost yet continue to produce net cash flows for another 15 years. A focus on only the payback period would mistakenly lead one to choose the first investment over the second.

Flash back

1. Capital budgeting is:
   - **a.** Concerned with analyzing alternative sources of capital, including debt and equity.
   - **b.** An important activity for companies when considering what assets to acquire or sell.
   - **c.** Best done by intuitive assessments of the value of assets and their usefulness.
2. Why are capital budgeting decisions often difficult?
3. A company is considering the purchase of equipment costing $75,000. Annual net cash flows from this equipment are $30,000, $25,000, $15,000, $10,000, and $5,000. The payback period is: *(a)* 4 years, *(b)* 3.5 years, or *(c)* 3 years.
4. If depreciation is an expense, why is it added back to net income from an investment to compute the net cash flow from the investment?
5. If two investments have the same payback period, are they equally desirable? Explain.

Answers—p. 1123

Accounting Rate of Return

P2 Compute accounting rate of return and explain its use.

Another method used by managers in capital budgeting decisions is to compute and apply the accounting rate of return. This section explains that method.

Computing Accounting Rate of Return

The **accounting rate of return,** also called *return on average investment,* is computed by dividing the after-tax net income from a project by the average amount invested in the project. To illustrate, let's return to the $16,000 machinery investment by FasTrac described in Exhibit 26.1. Our first step is to compute (1) the after-tax net income and then (2) the average amount invested. The after-tax net income of $2,100 is already available from Exhibit 26.1. We then must compute the average amount invested.

We begin by assuming net cash flows are received evenly throughout each year. This means the average investment for each year is computed as the average of its beginning and ending book values. If FasTrac's $16,000 machine is depreciated $2,000 each year, then the average amount invested in the machine for each year is computed as shown in Exhibit 26.4. The average for any year is the average of the beginning and ending book values.

Exhibit 26.4

Computing Average Amount Invested

	Beginning Book Value	Annual Depreciation	Ending Book Value	Average Book Value
Year 1	$16,000	$ 2,000	$14,000	$15,000
Year 2	14,000	2,000	12,000	13,000
Year 3	12,000	2,000	10,000	11,000
Year 4	10,000	2,000	8,000	9,000
Year 5	8,000	2,000	6,000	7,000
Year 6	6,000	2,000	4,000	5,000
Year 7	4,000	2,000	2,000	3,000
Year 8	2,000	2,000	0	1,000
				$64,000/8 years

Next, we need the average book value for the asset's entire life. This amount is computed by taking the average of the individual yearly averages. This average equals $8,000, computed as $64,000 (the sum of the individual years' averages) divided by 8 years (see last column of Exhibit 26.4).

If a company uses straight-line depreciation, we can find the average amount invested by using the formula in Exhibit 26.5. Since FasTrac uses straight-line depreciation, its average amount invested for the eight years is the sum of the beginning and ending book values (for the 8 year period) divided by 2 as shown in Exhibit 26.5.

Exhibit 26.5

Computing Average Amount Invested under Straight-Line Depreciation

$$\text{Annual average investment} = \frac{\text{Beginning book value} + \text{Ending book value}}{2}$$

$$= \frac{\$16{,}000 + \$0}{2} = \$8{,}000$$

If an investment carries a salvage value, then the average amount invested when using straight-line depreciation is computed as (Beginning book value + Salvage value)/2.

Once we determine the after-tax net income and the average amount invested, the accounting rate of return on the investment can be computed. This is done by dividing the annual after-tax net income by the average amount invested as shown in Exhibit 26.6.

Exhibit 26.6

Accounting Rate of Return Formula

$$\text{Accounting rate of return} = \frac{\text{Annual after-tax net income}}{\text{Annual average investment}}$$

This yields an accounting rate of return for FasTrac of:

$$\text{Accounting rate of return} = \frac{\$2{,}100}{\$8{,}000} = 26.25\%$$

Using Accounting Rate of Return

Management's use of the accounting rate of return is to decide whether or not 26% is a satisfactory rate of return. To make this decision we must factor in the riskiness of the investment. For instance, we can't say an investment with a 26% return is preferred over one with a lower return unless we recognize differences in risk. This means an investment's return is satisfactory or unsatisfactory only when it is related to returns from other investments with similar lives and risk.

When accounting rate of return is used to select between capital investments, the one with the least risk, the shortest payback period, and the highest return for the longest time is often identified as the best. But this analysis is sometimes challenging because different investments often yield different rankings depending on the measure used.

Perhaps because accounting rate of return is readily computed, it is often used in evaluating investment opportunities. But its usefulness is limited because its use of the amount invested is based on book values for future periods. Depreciation methods are used to allocate costs among years, not to predict market values of assets. The accounting rate of return is also limited when an asset's net incomes are expected to vary from year to year. This requires that the rate be computed using *average* annual net incomes. Yet this accounting rate of return fails to distinguish between two investments that have the same average annual net income but one yields higher amounts in early years and the other in later years.

Flash *back*

6. The following data relate to a company's decision to purchase a machine or not:

Cost	$180,000
Salvage value	15,000
Annual after-tax net income	40,000

The machine's accounting rate of return, assuming its net cash flows are received evenly throughout the year and straight-line depreciation is used, equals: *(a)* 22%, *(b)* 41%, or *(c)* 21%.

7. Is a 15% accounting rate of return for a machine a good rate?

Answers—p. 1123

Methods Using Time Value of Money

This section describes methods that help managers with capital budgeting decisions and that also use the time value of money. The two methods described are (1) net present value and (2) internal rate of return.

To apply the methods in this section, we need a basic understanding of the concept of present value. An expanded explanation of present value concepts is in Appendix C near the end of the book. We can use the present value tables at the end of Appendix C to solve many of the assignments at the end of this chapter.

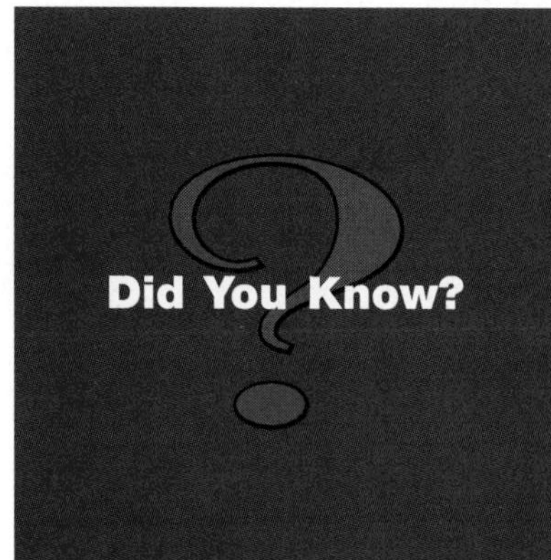

And the Winner Is . . .

How do we choose among the methods for evaluating capital investments? Management surveys consistently show the internal rate of return (IRR) as the most popular method. This is followed by the payback period and net present value (NPV). The internal rate of return measures the return of a project and is easily understood, while payback period is a quick measure of when an investment is fully recovered. Few companies use the accounting rate of return (ARR). Nearly all companies use more than one of these methods.

Net Present Value

P3 Compute net present value and describe its use.

An investment in a plant asset is expected to produce future positive net cash flows. A company should not acquire an asset unless its expected net cash flows are sufficient to provide a satisfactory return on investment and recover the amount initially invested. One way to make this decision is to compare the cost of the asset to the projected cash flows at a single point in time. Net present value (NPV) is one such method that compares costs to projected cash flows.

Computing Net Present Value

An NPV analysis uses the time value of money applied to future cash inflows and cash outflows so that management can evaluate the benefit and cost of a project at one point in time. To illustrate, let's return to the proposed machinery purchase by FasTrac described in Exhibit 26.1. Does this machine provide a satisfactory return while recovering the amount invested? Recall that this machine requires a $16,000 investment. Its annual net cash inflows are expected to be $4,100 for the next eight years. If we know the annual return that FasTrac requires on its investments, we then can compute the net present value of this investment.

Net present value is computed by discounting the future net cash flows from the investment at the required rate of return and then subtracting the initial amount invested as shown in Exhibit 26.7. We assume net cash flows from this machine are received at the end of each year and that FasTrac requires a 12% annual return.[2]

Exhibit 26.7

Net Present Value Calculation with Equal Cash Flows

	Net Cash Flows	Present Value of 1 at 12%*	Present Value of Net Cash Flows
Year 1	$ 4,100	0.8929	$ 3,661
Year 2	4,100	0.7972	3,269
Year 3	4,100	0.7118	2,918
Year 4	4,100	0.6355	2,606
Year 5	4,100	0.5674	2,326
Year 6	4,100	0.5066	2,077
Year 7	4,100	0.4523	1,854
Year 8	4,100	0.4039	1,656
Total	$32,800		$20,367
Amount invested			(16,000)
Net present value			$ 4,367

*Present value of 1 factors are taken from Table C.1 in Appendix C.

[2] The assumption of end-of-year cash flows simplifies computations and is common in practice.

The first column of Exhibit 26.7 shows the annual net cash flows. Present value of 1 factors, also called *discount factors,* are shown in the second column. They are taken from Table C.1 in Appendix C and they assume net cash flows are received at the end of each year. *To simplify present value computations and for assignment material at the end of this chapter, we assume net cash flows are received at the end of each year.*

Annual net cash flows from the first column of Exhibit 26.7 are multiplied by the discount factors in the second column to give present values shown in the third column. The last three lines of this exhibit show the final net present value computations. The asset's $16,000 initial cost is deducted from the $20,367 total present value of all future net cash flows to give us this asset's net present value of $4,367. This means the machine is expected to (1) recover its cost, (2) provide a 12% compounded return, and (3) generate $4,367 above cost. We can summarize this analysis by saying the present value of this machine's future net cash flows to FasTrac exceeds the $16,000 investment by $4,367.

Net Present Value Decision Rule

The decision rule in applying net present value is: When the expected cash flows from an asset are discounted at the required rate and yield a *positive* net present value, the asset should be acquired. This decision rule is reflected in the following chart:

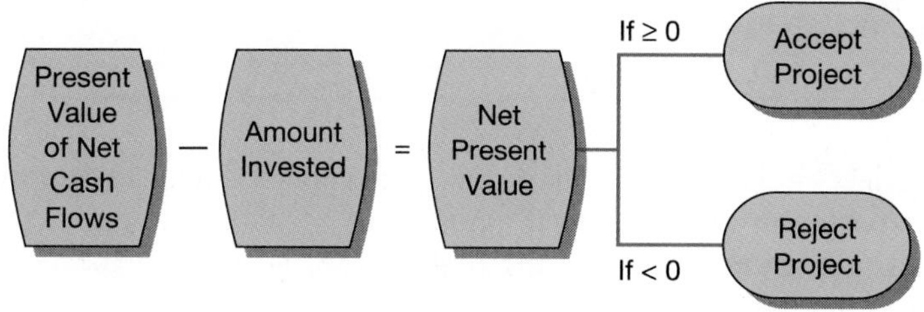

When comparing several investment opportunities of about the same cost and the same risk, the one with the highest positive net present value is preferred.

Systems Manager
You are a systems manager. Top management recently adopted new policies to control equipment purchases. The new policy says all proposals for purchases in excess of $5,000 must be submitted with cash flow predictions to the financial analysis group for capital budget analysis. This group has authority to approve or disapprove a proposal. Another systems manager, who is a friend, wants to upgrade his department's computers at a $25,000 cost. Your friend is considering submitting several purchase orders all under $5,000 to avoid the proposal process. He says the computers will increase profits, and he wants to avoid a delay. How do you advise your friend?

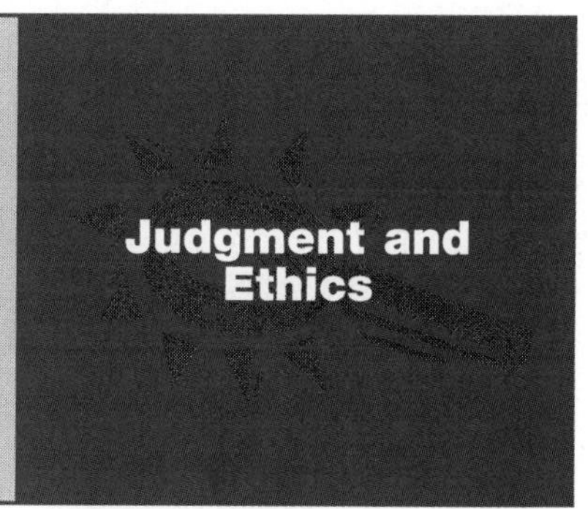

Answer—p. 1123

Simplifying Computations

The computations in Exhibit 26.7 use separate present value of 1 factors for each of the eight years. Each year's net cash flow is multiplied by its present value of 1 factor to determine its present value. The individual present values for each of the eight net cash flows are added to give us the total present value of the asset.

This computation can be simplified in two ways if annual net cash flows are equal in amount. One simplification is to add the eight annual present value of 1 factors for a total of 4.9676. This amount is then multiplied by the annual net cash flow of $4,100 to get the $20,367 total present value of net cash flows.[3] A second simplification is to use a calculator with compound interest functions or a spreadsheet program. But whatever procedure is chosen, it is important we understand the concepts behind these computations. The actual procedure we use doesn't matter as long as we apply it properly.

Unequal Cash Flows

Net present value analysis can also be applied when net cash flows are unequal. To illustrate, let's assume FasTrac can choose only one capital investment from among Projects A, B, and C. Each project requires the same $12,000 initial investment. Future net cash flows for each project are shown in the first three columns of Exhibit 26.8.

Exhibit 26.8

Net Present Value Calculation with Unequal Cash Flows

	Net Cash Flows			Present Value of 1 at 10%	Present Value of Net Cash Flows		
	-A-	-B-	-C-		-A-	-B-	-C-
Year 1	$ 5,000	$ 8,000	$ 1,000	0.9091	$ 4,546	$ 7,273	$ 909
Year 2	5,000	5,000	5,000	0.8264	4,132	4,132	4,132
Year 3	5,000	2,000	9,000	0.7513	3,757	1,503	6,762
Total	$15,000	$15,000	$15,000		$12,435	$12,908	$11,803
Amount invested					(12,000)	(12,000)	(12,000)
Net present value					$ 435	$ 908	$ (197)

All three projects in Exhibit 26.8 have the same expected total cash flow of $15,000. Project A is expected to produce equal amounts of $5,000 each year. Project B is expected to produce a larger amount in the first year. Project C is expected to produce a larger amount in the third year.

The fourth column of Exhibit 26.8 shows the present value of 1 factors from Table C.1. Since the patterns of net cash flows are different, we expect these projects to yield different net present values.

Computations in the right-most columns show that Project A has a $435 positive net present value. Project B has the largest net present value of $908 because it brings in cash more quickly. Project C has a $197 *negative* net present value because its larger cash inflows are delayed. If FasTrac requires a 10% return, then Project C should be rejected because its net present value implies a return *under* 10%. If only one project can be accepted, then Project B appears best because it yields the highest net present value.

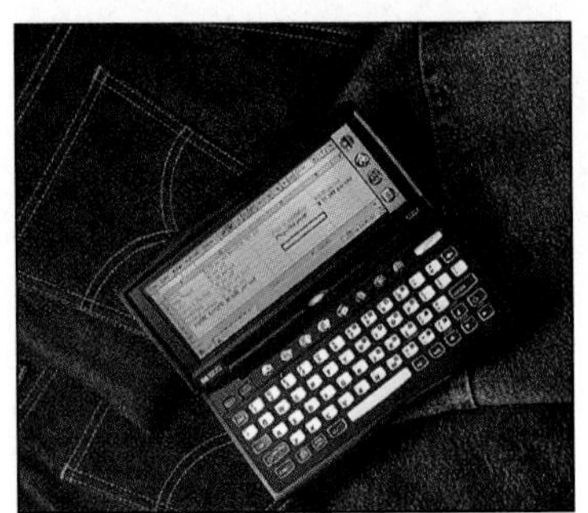

Salvage Value and Accelerated Depreciation

FasTrac predicted the $16,000 machine to have zero salvage value at the end of its useful life (recall Exhibit 26.1). But in many cases an asset is expected to have a salvage value. If so, this amount is an additional net cash inflow received at the end of the final year of the asset's life. All other computations remain the same.

Let's again return to the opening article's discussion of **Gee-Whiz**'s acquisition of a jeans processing plant. Gee-Whiz's analysis used predicted cash flows *and* assumed the ability to sell the processing plant at about 10 times earnings at the end of five years. In this analysis, the plant's expected selling price was treated like salvage value.

Depreciation computations also affect net present value analysis. FasTrac computes depreciation using the straight-line method. But accelerated depreciation is also com-

[3] We can simplify this computation even further using Table C.3, which gives the present value of 1 to be received periodically for a number of periods. To determine the present value of these eight annual receipts discounted at 12%, go down the 12% column of Table C.3 to the factor on the eighth line. This factor is 4.9676. We then compute the $20,367 present value for these eight annual $4,100 receipts, computed as 4.9676 × $4,100.

monly used, especially for income tax reports. Accelerated depreciation produces larger depreciation deductions in the early years of an asset's life and smaller deductions in later years. This pattern results in smaller income tax payments in early years and larger payments in later years.

Accelerated depreciation does not change the basics of a present value analysis, but it can change the result. Using accelerated depreciation for tax reporting affects the net present value of an asset's cash flows because it produces larger net cash inflows in the early years of the asset's life and smaller ones in later years. Because early cash flows are more valuable than later ones, being able to use accelerated depreciation for tax reporting always makes an investment more desirable.

Using Net Present Value

In deciding whether to proceed with a capital investment project, we go ahead if the NPV is positive but reject the proposal if the NPV is negative. If there are several projects of similar investment amounts and risk levels, we can compare the net present values of the different projects and rank them on the basis of their NPVs. But if the amount invested differs substantially across projects, then NPV is of limited value for comparison purposes.

To illustrate, suppose Project X requires an investment of $1 million and provides a NPV of $100,000. But Project Y requires an investment of only $100,000 and returns a NPV of $75,000. Ranking on the basis of NPV puts Project X ahead of Y. Yet X's NPV is only 10% of the initial investment whereas Y's NPV is 75% of its investment.

We must also remember that when reviewing projects with different risks, the NPVs of individual projects are computed using different discount rates. The greater the risk, the higher the discount rate.

Internal Rate of Return

P4 Compute internal rate of return and explain its use.

Another means to evaluate capital investments is to use the internal rate of return. The **internal rate of return (IRR)** is a rate used to evaluate the acceptability of an investment. It equals the rate that yields a net present value of zero for an investment. This means if we compute the total present value of a project's net cash flows using the IRR as the discount rate and then subtract the initial investment from this total present value, we get a zero NPV.

Computing Internal Rate of Return

To illustrate, we use the data for Project A of FasTrac from Exhibit 26.8 to compute its IRR. Exhibit 26.9 shows the two-step process in computing IRR.

Exhibit 26.9

Computing Internal Rate of Return

Step 1: Compute present value factor for FasTrac's three-year project.

$$\text{Present value factor} = \frac{\text{Amount invested}}{\text{Net cash flows}} = \frac{\$12{,}000}{\$5{,}000} = 2.4000$$

Step 2: Identify present value factor of 2.4000 in Table C.3 for the three-year row. The factor is approximately equal to the 12% discount rate factor of 2.4018. This implies the IRR is approximately 12%.*

*Since the present value factor of 2.4000 is not exactly equal to the 12% factor of 2.4018, we can more precisely estimate the IRR as follows:

Discount rate	Present value factor
12%	2.4018
15%	2.2832
	0.1186 = difference

$$\text{Then, IRR} = 12\% + \left[(15\% - 12\%) \times \frac{2.4018 - 2.4000}{0.1186}\right] = \underline{\underline{12.05\%}}$$

When cash flows are equal, such as with Project A, we compute the present value factor by dividing the initial investment by its annual net cash flows. We then use an annuity table to determine the discount rate equal to this present value factor. For Project A of FasTrac, we look across the 3-period row of Table C.3 and find that the discount rate corresponding to the present value factor of 2.4000 is roughly equal to the 2.4018 value for the 12% rate. This row is reproduced here:

Present Value of an Annuity of 1 for Three Periods

	Rate				
Periods	**1%**	**5%**	**10%**	**12%**	**15%**
3	2.9410	2.7232	2.4869	2.4018	2.2832

The 12% rate is the Project's IRR. A more precise estimate of the IRR can be computed following the procedure shown in the note to Exhibit 26.9. Spreadsheet software and calculators can also compute this IRR.

Unequal Cash Flows

If net cash flows are unequal, we must use trial and error to compute the IRR. We do this by selecting any reasonable discount rate and computing the NPV. If the amount is positive (negative), we recompute the NPV using a higher (lower) discount rate. We continue these steps until we reach a point where two consecutive computations result in NPVs having different signs (positive and negative). Since the NPV is zero using IRR, we know that the IRR lies between these two discount rates. We can then estimate its value. Spreadsheet programs and calculators can do these computations for us.

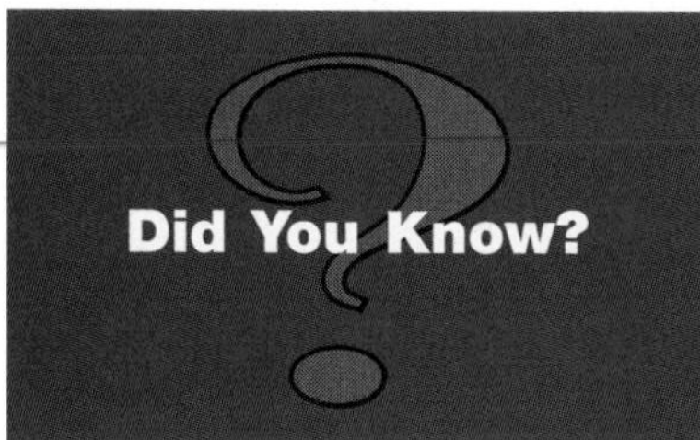

Deciding What's New
Cyto Technologies is a rapidly growing bio-tech company using both financial and nonfinancial criteria to evaluate its investments in new products. The use of IRR is a major part of its evaluation of investment opportunities. [Source: S. Kalagnanam and S. Schmidt, "Analyzing Capital Investments in New Products," *Management Accounting,* January 1996, pp. 31–36.]

C2 Describe selection of a hurdle rate for an investment.

Using Internal Rate of Return

When we use the IRR to evaluate a project, we compare the IRR with a predetermined hurdle rate. A **hurdle rate** is a minimum acceptable rate of return and is applied as follows:

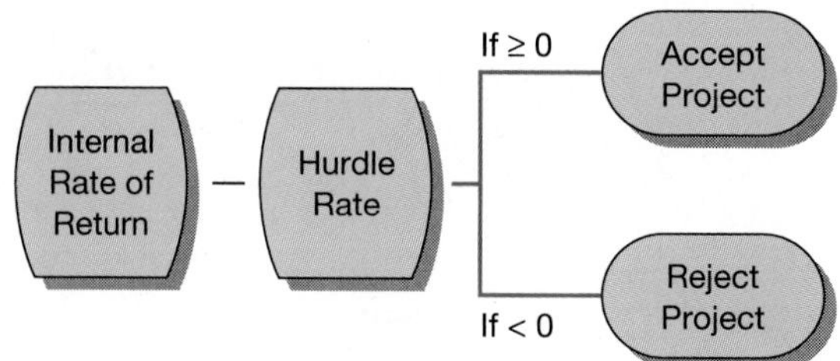

Top management selects the rate used as the hurdle in evaluating capital investments. While financial formulas aid in this selection, the choice of a minimum rate is subjective and left to management.

In the case of projects financed from borrowed funds, the hurdle rate must exceed the interest rate paid on these funds. This is because the return on an investment must cover interest and provide an additional profit to reward the company for its risk. For instance, if money is borrowed at 10%, a required after-tax return of 15% (or 5% above the borrowing rate) is often required by the management of industrial companies with average risk. We must remember that lower risk investments require a lower rate of return compared with higher risk investments.

If the project is internally financed, the hurdle rate is often based on actual returns from comparable projects. If the IRR is higher than the hurdle rate, the project is accepted. In the case of multiple projects, they are often ranked by the extent to which IRR exceeds the hurdle rate. The hurdle rate for individual projects is often different depending on the risk involved. Also, IRR is not subject to the limitations of NPV when comparing projects with different amounts invested. This is because the IRR is expressed as a percent rather than an absolute dollar value as in NPV.

In analyzing its jeans processing plant acquisition, **Gee-Whiz** used an 18% required return on investment. Based on this rate, the bid price was accepted by its competitor and the processing plant became Gee-Whiz Jeans.

Capital budgeting decisions involve estimates, not certainties. This became apparent to Gee-Whiz Jeans less than two years after acquisition when it admitted that it failed to fully take into account changes in customer and distribution channels. This led to higher administrative, delivery, and sales costs than anticipated. The expected increase in market share also had not occurred. Its share actually had declined, as it had under previous ownership. This was despite increased advertising and marketing.

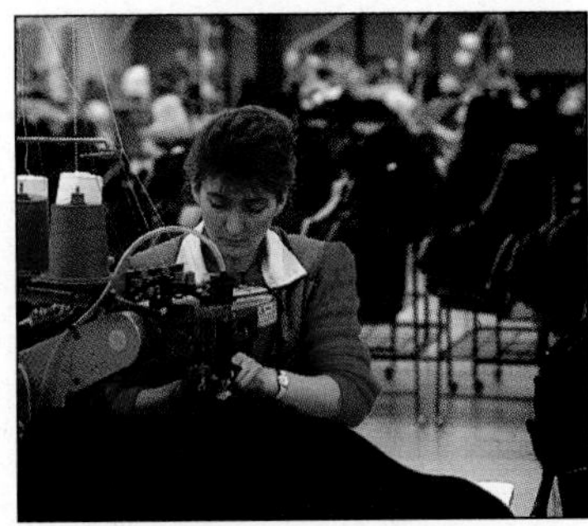

R&D Manager
You are the research and development manager of a technology company. For a new product being developed under your management, you decide to use a 12% discount rate to compute its NPV. The controller expresses concern that your discount rate is too low. How do you respond?

Answer—p. 1123

Comparing Capital Budgeting Methods

We explained four methods managers use to evaluate capital investment projects. But how do they compare with each other? This section addresses that question.

Both the payback period and the accounting rate of return do not consider the time value of money. On the other hand, both the net present value and the internal rate of return do. Exhibit 26.10 identifies this and other differences.

The payback period is probably the simplest method. It gives managers an estimate of how soon they will recover their initial investment. Managers sometimes use this method when they have limited cash to invest and a number of projects to choose from.

The accounting rate of return yields a percent measure. It is computed using accrual income instead of cash flows. The accounting rate of return is an average rate for the entire investment period.

Net present value considers all estimated net cash flows for the expected life of the project. It can be applied to equal and unequal cash flows and can reflect changes in the level of risk over the life of a project. But because it is a dollar measure, a comparison of projects of unequal sizes is more difficult.

The internal rate of return considers all cash flows from a project. It is readily computed when the cash flows are equal but requires some trial and error estimation when cash flows are unequal. Since the internal rate of return is a percent measure, it is readily used to compare projects with different investment amounts. But changes in risk over the life of a project are not reflected in the internal rate of return.

Exhibit 26.10

Comparing Capital Budgeting Methods

	Payback Period	Accounting Rate of Return	Net Present Value	Internal Rate of Return
Measurement Basis	• Cash flows	• Accrual income	• Cash flows • Profitability	• Cash flows • Profitability
Measurement Unit	• Years	• Percent	• Dollars	• Percent
Strengths	• Easy to understand • Allows comparison of projects	• Easy to understand • Allows comparison of projects	• Reflects time value of money • Reflects varying risks over project's life	• Reflects time value of money • Allows comparisons of dissimilar projects
Limitations	• Ignores time value of money • Ignores cash flows after payback period	• Ignores time value of money • Ignores annual rates over life of project	• Difficult to compare dissimilar projects	• Ignores varying risks over life of project

Flash back

8. A company can invest in only one of two projects, A or B. Each project requires a $20,000 investment and is expected to generate end-of-period, annual cash flows as follows:

	Year 1	Year 2	Year 3	Total
Project A	$12,000	$8,500	$ 4,000	$24,500
Project B	4,500	8,500	13,000	26,000

Assuming a discount rate of 10%, which project has the greater net present value?

9. Two investment alternatives are expected to generate annual cash flows with the same net present value (assuming the same discount rate applied to each). Using this information, can you conclude the two alternatives are equally desirable?

10. When two investment alternatives have the same total expected cash flows but differ in the timing of those flows, which method of evaluating those investments is superior? *(a)* Accounting rate of return or *(b)* net present value.

Answers—p. 1123

SECTION 2—MANAGERIAL DECISIONS

This section focuses on the use of accounting information for several important managerial decisions. The emphasis is on the use of quantitative measures to help managers make decisions. Most of these involve short-term decisions. Methods for long-term managerial decisions are described in the first section of this chapter and in several other chapters of this book. A primary goal of this section is to explain what costs and other financial factors are most relevant to short-term decisions. We provide a framework to help structure our analysis of these decision situations.

Decisions and Information

This section explains how managers make decisions and the information relevant to these decisions.

Decision Making

Managerial decision making involves five steps: (1) define the decision task; (2) identify alternative courses of action; (3) collect relevant information to evaluate each alternative; (4) select the preferred course of action; (5) analyze and assess decisions made. These five steps are illustrated in Exhibit 26.11.

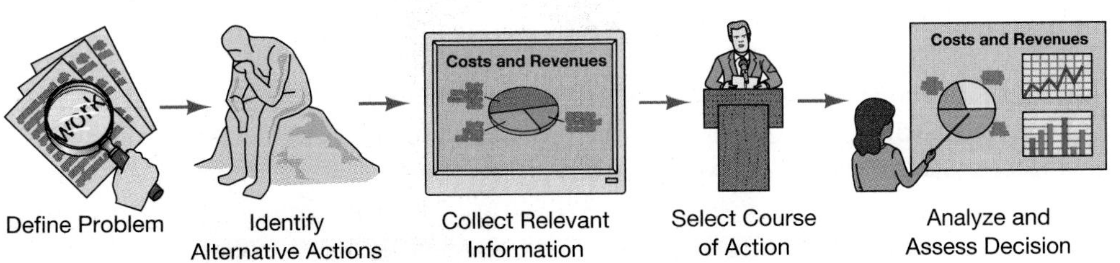

Exhibit 26.11
Managerial Decision Making

Both managerial and financial accounting information play an important role in most management decisions. The accounting system is expected to provide primarily *financial* information such as performance reports and budget analyses for decision making. But *nonfinancial* information is also relevant. This includes information on environmental effects, political sensitivities, and social responsibility.

Relevant Costs

C3 Describe the importance of relevant costs for short-term decisions.

Most financial measures of revenues and costs from cost accounting systems are based on historical costs. While historical costs are important and useful for many tasks such as product pricing and the control and monitoring of business activities, we sometimes find that *relevant costs,* or *avoidable costs,* are especially useful for certain managerial decisions. Three types of costs were identified in Chapter 19 that are pertinent to our discussion of relevant costs: sunk costs, out-of-pocket costs, and opportunity costs.

A **sunk cost** arises from a past decision and cannot be avoided or changed. Sunk costs are irrelevant to future decisions. An example is the cost of production equipment previously purchased by a company. Most of a company's allocated costs, including fixed overhead items such as depreciation and administrative expenses, are sunk costs.

An **out-of-pocket cost** requires a future outlay of cash and is relevant for current and future decision making. These costs are usually the direct result of management's decisions. For instance, future purchases of production equipment involve out-of-pocket costs.

Analysis of relevant costs must consider opportunity costs. An **opportunity cost** is the potential benefit lost by taking a specific action when two or more alternative choices are available. An example is a student giving up wages from a job to attend summer school. Companies are continually faced with alternative courses of action from which they must choose. For instance, a company making standardized products might be approached by a customer with a request to supply a special (nonstandard) product. A decision to accept or not accept the special order must consider not only the profit to be made from the special order but also the profit given up by devoting time and resources to this order instead of pursuing an alternative project. The profit given up is an opportunity cost.

Consideration of opportunity costs is important. The implications extend to internal resource allocation decisions. For instance, a computer manufacturer must decide between internally manufacturing a chip versus buying it externally. In another case, management of a multidivision company must decide whether to continue operating or discontinue a particular division.

Besides relevant costs, management must also consider the relevant benefits associated with a decision. **Relevant benefits** refer to the additional or *incremental* revenue that is generated by selecting a particular course of action over another. For instance, a student must decide the relevant benefits of taking one course over another course. In sum, both relevant costs and relevant benefits are crucial to managerial decision making.

Managerial Decision Tasks

Managers confront many different types of tasks that require analyzing alternative actions and making a decision. We describe several different types of decision tasks in this section. We set these tasks in the context of FasTrac, the exercise supplies and equipment manufacturer introduced earlier. *We treat each of these decision tasks as separate from another.*

A1 Evaluate short-term managerial decisions using relevant costs.

Additional Business

FasTrac is operating at its normal level of 80% of full capacity. At this level it produces and sells approximately 100,000 units of product annually. FasTrac's per unit and annual total costs are shown in Exhibit 26.12.

Exhibit 26.12

Current Accounting Performance Report

	Per Unit	Annual Total
Sales (100,000 units)	$10.00	$1,000,000
Direct materials	$ 3.50	$ 350,000
Direct labor	2.20	220,000
Overhead	1.10	110,000
Selling expenses	1.40	140,000
Administrative expenses	0.80	80,000
Total costs and expenses	$ 9.00	$ 900,000
Operating income	$ 1.00	$ 100,000

A current buyer of FasTrac's products wants to buy additional units of FasTrac's product and export them to another country. This buyer offers to buy 10,000 units of the product at $8.50 per unit, or $1.50 less than the current price. While the offer price is low, FasTrac is considering the proposal because this sale would be several times larger than any single previous sale made by the company. Also, the units will be exported, and this new business will not affect its current sales.

To determine whether this order should be accepted or rejected, management needs to know whether net income will increase if the offer is accepted. The analysis in Exhibit 26.13 shows that if management relied on per unit historical costs, the sale would be rejected because it yields a loss.

Exhibit 26.13

Analysis of Additional Business Using Historical Costs

	Per Unit	Total
Sales (10,000 units)	$8.50	$85,000
Direct materials	$3.50	$35,000
Direct labor	2.20	22,000
Overhead	1.10	11,000
Selling expenses	1.40	14,000
Administrative expenses	0.80	8,000
Total costs and expenses	$9.00	$90,000
Operating loss	$(0.50)	$ (5,000)

But historical costs are *not* relevant to this decision. Instead, the relevant costs are the additional costs called incremental costs. **Incremental costs,** also called *differential costs,* are the additional costs incurred if a company pursues a certain course of action. FasTrac's incremental costs are those related to the added volume that this new order would bring.

To make its decision, FasTrac must analyze the costs of this new business in a different manner. The following information is available regarding the order:

- Manufacturing 10,000 additional units requires direct materials of $3.50 per unit and direct labor of $2.20 per unit (same as all other units).
- 10,000 additional units can be manufactured with $5,000 of incremental overhead costs for power, packaging, and indirect labor (all variable costs).
- Incremental commissions and selling expenses from this sale of 10,000 additional units would be $2,000 (all variable costs).

- Incremental administrative expenses of $1,000 for clerical efforts are needed (all fixed costs) with the sale of 10,000 additional units.

We use this information, as shown in Exhibit 26.14, to assess how accepting this new business will affect FasTrac's income.

Exhibit 26.14

Analysis of Additional Business Using Relevant Costs

	Current Business	Additional Business	Combined
Sales	$1,000,000	$85,000	$1,085,000
Direct materials	$ 350,000	$35,000	$ 385,000
Direct labor	220,000	22,000	242,000
Overhead	110,000	5,000	115,000
Selling expenses	140,000	2,000	142,000
Administrative expense	80,000	1,000	81,000
Total costs and expenses	$ 900,000	$65,000	$ 965,000
Operating income	$ 100,000	$20,000	$ 120,000

The analysis of relevant costs in Exhibit 26.14 suggests the additional business should be accepted. The additional business would provide $85,000 of added revenue while incurring only $65,000 of added costs. This would yield $20,000 of additional pretax income, or a pretax profit margin of 23.5%. Specifically, FasTrac would increase its income with any price that exceeded $6.50 per unit. The $6.50 amount is computed from the $65,000 incremental cost divided by the 10,000 additional units.

An analysis of incremental costs of additional volume is always relevant for this type of decision. But we must proceed cautiously when the additional volume approaches or exceeds the existing available capacity of the factory. If the additional volume requires the company to expand its capacity by obtaining more equipment, more space, or more personnel, the incremental costs could quickly exceed the incremental revenue.

Another cautionary note is the effect on existing sales. For FasTrac, all new units are sold outside its normal domestic sales channels. But if accepting additional business causes existing sales to decline, then this information must be included in our analysis. The contribution margin lost from a decline in sales is an opportunity cost. Also, if future cash flows over several time periods are affected, then their net present value must be computed and used in making this analysis.

The key point is that management must not blindly use historical costs, especially allocated overhead costs. Instead, the accounting system needs to provide information about the incremental costs to be incurred if the additional business is accepted.

Production Supervisor
You are the production supervisor for a custom manufacturer. A customer inquires about a special product that is currently not manufactured by your company. The controller asks you for information relevant to this decision. What information do you provide?

Answer—p. 1123

Make or Buy

Incremental costs are used in deciding whether to make or buy a component of a product. To illustrate, FasTrac has excess productive capacity that can be used to manufacture Part #417. This part is a component of the main product it sells. The component is currently purchased and delivered to the plant at a cost of $1.20 per unit. FasTrac estimates that to make Part #417 would cost $0.45 for direct materials, $0.50 for direct labor, and an undetermined amount for overhead.

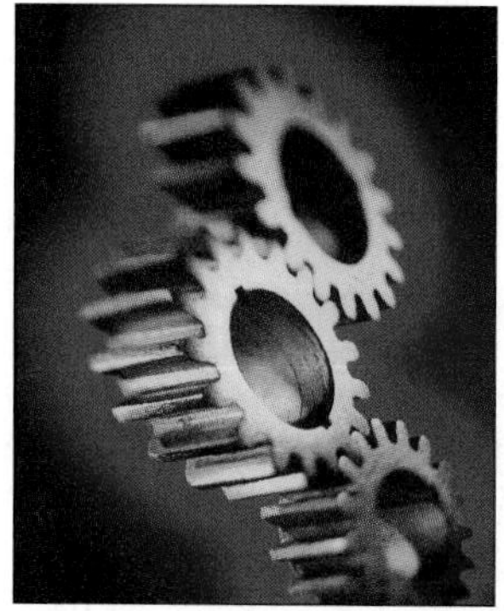

Our task is to figure out how much overhead should be added to these costs so we can decide whether to make or buy Part #417. If FasTrac's normal predetermined overhead application rate is 100% of direct labor cost, we might be tempted to conclude that overhead cost is $0.50 per unit, computed as 100% of the $0.50 direct labor cost. We would then mistakenly conclude that total cost is $1.45, computed as $0.45 of materials plus $0.50 of labor plus $0.50 of overhead. Our decision in this case would be that the company is better off buying the part at $1.20 each than making it for $1.45 each.

But as we explained earlier, only incremental overhead costs are relevant in this situation. This means we must compute an *incremental overhead rate*. Incremental overhead costs might include, for example, power for operating machines, extra supplies, added cleanup costs, materials handling, and quality control. We can prepare a per unit analysis in this case such as the following:

Make or Buy Analysis

	Make	Buy
Direct materials	$0.45	—
Direct labor	0.50	—
Overhead costs	[?]	—
Purchase price	—	$1.20
Total incremental costs	$0.95 + [?]	$1.20

If incremental overhead costs are less than $0.25 per unit, then the total cost of making the component is less than the purchase price of $1.20. This implies FasTrac should make the part.

FasTrac's decision rule in this case is any amount of overhead less than $0.25 per unit yields a total cost for Part #417 that is less than the $1.20 purchase price. But FasTrac must consider several factors in deciding whether to make or buy the part. These include product quality, timeliness of delivery (especially in a just-in-time setting), reactions of customers and suppliers, and other intangibles such as employee morale and workload. It must also consider whether making the part requires incremental fixed costs to expand plant capacity. When these added factors are considered, small cost differences may not matter.

A key point is that historical costs provided by the accounting system are not always the most relevant to a make or buy decision. Instead, incremental costs are most relevant.

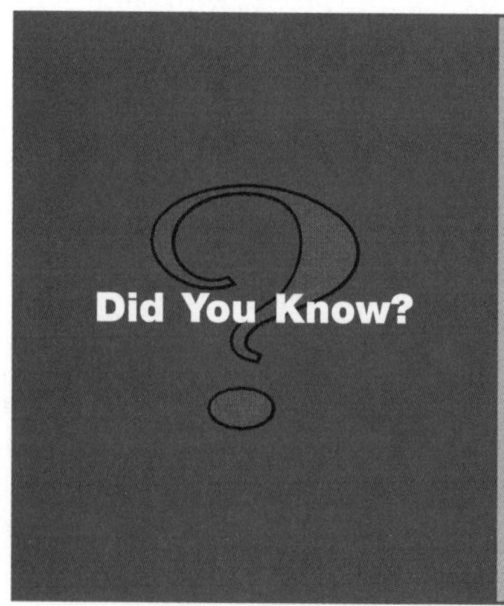

Make or Buy Services

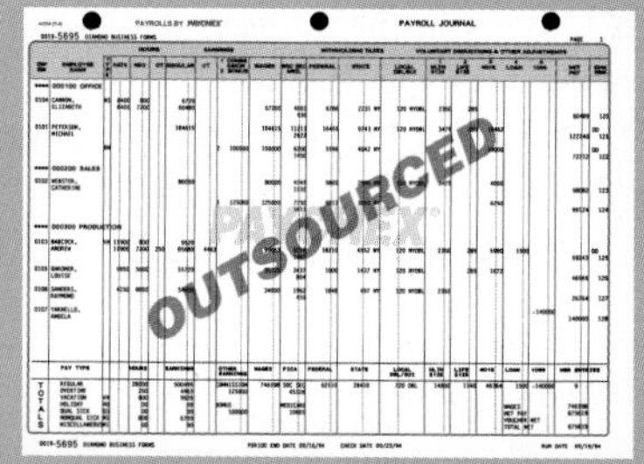

Just as companies apply make or buy decisions to manufacturing, they can apply them to services as well. **Marine & Restaurant Fabricators (MRF)** in San Diego now outsources its payroll activities to **Paychex,** a payroll service, after finding itself at the wrong end of an IRS notice. While the price paid for the service is close to what it costs to do it, the absence of headaches is worth it. "I couldn't be happier," says MRF's office manager. "There's security in knowing that it's being done right—they know all the rules." A tax manager at **Ernst & Young** says that because "there is so much risk [doing it in-house] that it is just easier to outsource it." [Source: *Business Week,* February 9, 1998.]

Scrap or Rework

Costs already incurred in manufacturing the units of a product that do not meet quality standards are sunk costs. This means these costs have been incurred and cannot be changed. These costs are irrelevant in any decision on whether to sell the substandard units as scrap or rework them so they meet quality standards.

To illustrate, let's assume FasTrac has 10,000 defective units of a product that has already cost $1 per unit to manufacture. These units can be sold as is, or scrap, for $0.40 each. Alternatively, they can be reworked for $0.80 per unit, and then sold for their full price of $1.50 each. Should FasTrac sell the units as scrap or rework them?

To make this decision, management must recognize the original manufacturing costs of $1 per unit are sunk, or unavoidable. This means these costs are *entirely irrelevant* to the decision. In addition, we must be certain that all costs of reworking defects, including interfering with normal operations, are accounted for in our analysis. For instance, reworking the defects means FasTrac is unable to manufacture 10,000 *new* units with an incremental cost of $1 per unit and a selling price of $1.50 per unit. This means it incurs an opportunity cost equal to the lost $5,000 net return from making and selling new units. This opportunity cost is the difference between the $15,000 revenue (10,000 units × $1.50) from selling these new units and their $10,000 manufacturing costs (10,000 units × $1). Our analysis of this entire situation is reflected in Exhibit 26.16.

Exhibit 26.16
Scrap or Rework Analysis

	Scrap	Rework
Sale of scrapped/reworked units	$4,000	$15,000
Less rework of defects		(8,000)
Less opportunity cost of not making new units		**(5,000)**
Incremental net income	$4,000	$ 2,000

The analysis yields a $2,000 difference in favor of scrapping the defects, yielding a net incremental return of $4,000. If we had failed to include the opportunity costs of $5,000, the rework option would show a return of $7,000 instead of $2,000. This would mistakenly make reworking appear more favorable than scrapping.

Flash back

11. A company receives a special order for 200 units of its product. This order requires the buyer's name be stamped on each unit, yielding an additional fixed cost of $400 above its normal manufacturing costs. Without the order, the company is operating at 75% of capacity and produces 7,500 units of product at the following costs:

Direct materials	$37,500
Direct labor	60,000
Overhead (30% variable)	20,000
Selling expenses (60% variable)	25,000

The special order will not affect normal unit sales and will not increase fixed overhead and selling expenses. Variable selling expenses on the special order are reduced to one-half the normal amount. The price per unit necessary to earn $1,000 on this order is: *(a)* $14.80, *(b)* $15.80, *(c)* $19.80, *(d)* $20.80, or *(e)* $21.80.

12. What are the incremental costs of accepting additional business?

Answers—p. 1124

Sell or Process

Relevant costs are an important part of the decision to sell partially completed products as is or to process them further for sale. To illustrate, let's suppose FasTrac has 40,000 units of partially finished Product Q. FasTrac has already spent $0.75 per unit to manufacture these 40,000 units of Product Q at a total cost of $30,000. The 40,000 units can be sold to another manufacturer as raw material for $50,000. Alternatively, FasTrac can process them further and produce finished products X, Y, and Z at an incremental cost of $2 per unit. The added processing yields the products and revenues shown in Exhibit 26.17. FasTrac must decide whether the added revenues from selling finished products X, Y, and Z exceed the costs of finishing them.

Exhibit 26.17

Revenues from Processing Further

Product	Price	Units	Revenues
Product X	$4.00	10,000	$ 40,000
Product Y	6.00	22,000	132,000
Product Z	8.00	6,000	48,000
Spoilage	—	2,000	0
Total		40,000	$220,000

Exhibit 26.18 shows the two-step analysis for this decision. First, FasTrac needs to compute its incremental revenue from further processing Q into products X, Y, and Z. This amount is the difference between the $220,000 revenue from the further processed products and the $50,000 FasTrac will give up from not selling Q as is (the $50,000 is an opportunity cost). Second, FasTrac needs to compute its incremental costs from further processing Q into X, Y, and Z. This amount is $80,000, computed as 40,000 units × $2 incremental cost. The analysis shows FasTrac can earn incremental net income of $90,000 from a decision to further process Q.

Exhibit 26.18

Sell or Process Analysis

Revenue if processed	$220,000
Revenue if sold as is	(50,000)
Incremental revenue	$170,000
Cost if processed	(80,000)
Incremental net income	$ 90,000)

The earlier $30,000 manufacturing cost for the 40,000 units of Product Q does not appear in Exhibit 26.18. This cost is a sunk cost and is irrelevant to the decision because it has already been incurred.

Flash *back*

13. A company has already incurred a cost of $1,000 in partially producing its four products. Selling prices for these products when partially and fully processed are listed below. Also shown are additional costs necessary to finish these partially processed units:

Product	Unfinished Selling Price	Finished Selling Price	Further Processing Costs
Alpha	$300	$600	$150
Beta	450	900	300
Gamma	275	425	125
Delta	150	210	75

Which product(s) should not be processed further? *(a)* Alpha, *(b)* Beta, *(c)* Gamma, or *(d)* Delta

14. Under what conditions is a sunk cost relevant to decision making?

Answers—p. 1124

Selecting Sales Mix

When a company sells a mix of products, some are likely to be more profitable than others. Management is often wise to concentrate sales efforts on more profitable products. But if production facilities or other factors are limited, an increase in the production and sale of one product usually requires a company to reduce the production and sale of others. In this case, management must identify the most profitable combination, or *sales mix,* of products. Attention is then focused on selling this sales mix of products.

To identify the best sales mix, management must know the contribution margin of each product. It must also know what facilities are required to produce these products, any constraints on these facilities, and the markets for the products.

To illustrate, let's assume FasTrac makes and sells two products, A and B. The same machines are used to produce both products. The products have the following selling prices and variable costs per unit:

	Product A	Product B
Selling price	$5.00	$7.50
Variable costs	3.50	5.50
Contribution margin	$1.50	$2.00

The variable costs are included in the analysis because they are the incremental costs of producing these products within the existing capacity of 100,000 machine hours per month. Three separate cases are considered.

Case 1: Assume (a) each product requires 1 machine hour per unit for production and (b) the markets for these products are unlimited. Under these conditions, FasTrac should produce as much of Product B as it can because of its larger contribution margin per unit. At full capacity, FasTrac would produce $200,000 of total contribution margin per month, computed as $2 per unit times 100,000 machine hours.

Case 2: Assume (a) Product A requires 1 machine hour per unit, (b) Product B requires 2 machine hours per unit, and (c) the markets for these products are unlimited. Under these conditions, FasTrac should produce as much of Product A as it can because it produces a contribution margin of $1.50 per machine hour while Product B produces only $1 per machine hour. Exhibit 26.19 shows the relevant analysis.

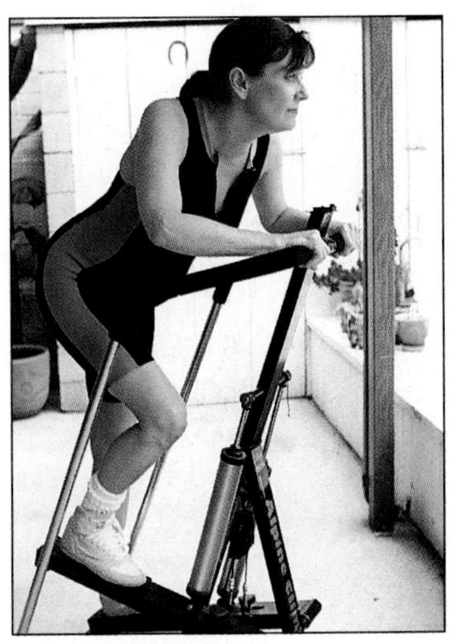

Exhibit 26.19

Sales Mix Analysis

	Product A	Product B
Selling price	$5.00	$7.50
Variable costs	3.50	5.50
Contribution margin	$1.50	$2.00
Machine hours per unit	1.0	2.0
Contribution margin per machine hour	**$1.50**	**$1.00**

At its full capacity of 100,000 machine hours, FasTrac would produce 100,000 units of Product A. This would yield $150,000 of total contribution margin per month. In contrast, if all 100,000 hours are used to produce Product B, only 50,000 units would be produced with a contribution margin of $100,000. These results suggest that when a company has no excess capacity, only the most profitable product per input should be manufactured.

Case 3: The need for a mix of different products arises when market demand is not sufficient to allow a company to sell all that it produces. For instance, assume (a) Product A requires 1 machine hour per unit, (b) Product B requires 2 machine hours per unit, and (c) the market for Product A is limited to 80,000 units. Under these conditions, FasTrac should produce no more than 80,000 units of Product A. This would leave another 20,000 machine hours of capacity for making Product B. FasTrac should use this spare capacity to produce 10,000 units of Product B. This sales mix would maximize FasTrac's total contribution margin per month at $140,000.[4]

Eliminating a Segment

When a segment such as a department or division is performing poorly, management must consider eliminating it. But segment information on either net income (loss) or its contribution to overhead is not sufficient for this decision. Instead, we must look at the segment's avoidable expenses and unavoidable expenses. **Avoidable expenses,** also called *escapable expenses,* are deductions that would not be incurred if the segment is eliminated. **Unavoidable expenses,** also called *inescapable expenses,* are deductions that would continue even if the segment is eliminated.

To illustrate, FasTrac is considering eliminating its treadmill division because total expenses of $48,300 are greater than its sales of $47,800. Classification of this division's operating expenses into avoidable or unavoidable expenses is shown in Exhibit 26.20.

Exhibit 26.20

Classification of Segment Operating Expenses for Analysis

	Total	Avoidable Expenses	Unavoidable Expenses
Cost of goods sold	$30,200	$30,200	—
Direct expenses:			
Salaries expense	7,900	7,900	—
Depreciation expense, Equipment	200	—	$ 200
Indirect expenses:			
Rent and utilities expense	3,150	—	3,150
Advertising expense	200	200	—
Insurance expense	400	300	100
Service department costs:			
Share of office department expenses	3,060	2,200	860
Share of purchasing expenses	3,190	1,000	2,190
Total	$48,300	$41,800	$6,500

FasTrac's analysis shows it can avoid expenses of $41,800 if it eliminates the treadmill division. Since this division's sales are $47,800, it also means FasTrac will lose $6,000 of income if it eliminates the segment. *Our decision rule is that a segment is a candidate for elimination if its revenues are less than its avoidable expenses.* Avoidable expenses can be viewed as the costs of generating this segment's revenues.

When considering elimination of a segment we must assess its impact on other segments. While a segment may be unprofitable on its own, it might still contribute to the revenues and profits of other segments. This means it's possible to continue a segment even when its revenues are less than its avoidable expenses. Similarly, a profitable segment might be discontinued if its space, assets, or staff can be more profitably used by expanding existing segments or by creating new ones. Our decision to keep or eliminate a segment requires a more complex analysis than simply looking at a segment's performance report. While such reports provide useful information, they do not provide all the information necessary for this decision.

Flash back

15. What is the difference between avoidable and unavoidable expenses?

16. A segment is a candidate for elimination if: *(a)* Its revenues are less than its avoidable expenses; *(b)* it has a net loss; *(c)* its unavoidable expenses are greater than its revenues.

Answers—p. 1124

[4] A method called *linear programming* is useful for finding the optimal sales mix for several products subject to many market and production constraints. This method is described in advanced courses.

Qualitative Decision Factors

Managers must consider qualitative factors in making managerial decisions. To illustrate, let's consider a make or buy decision where a manager is considering buying from an outside supplier instead of continuing to make a component. Several qualitative decision factors must be considered. For example, the quality, delivery, and reputation of the proposed supplier is important. Also, the effects from discontinuing the making of the component can include potential layoffs and impaired worker morale.

Consider another situation where a company is examining a one-time additional sale to a new customer at a special low price. Qualitative factors to consider include the effects of a low price on the image of the company and the threat of regular customers demanding a similar price. The company must also consider whether this customer is really a one-time customer. If not, can it continue to offer this low price in the long run? Management cannot rely solely on financial data to make managerial decisions.

Break-Even Time

USING THE INFORMATION

A2 Analyze a capital investment project using break-even time.

The first section of this chapter explained several methods to evaluate capital investments. One of these methods was payback period. Our computation of payback period did not require us to use the time value of money. We explained how this is a limitation of the method.

Break-even time of an investment project is a variation on the payback period that overcomes the limitation of not using the time value of money. **Break-even time (BET)** is a time-based measure that is used to evaluate the acceptability of a capital investment. It equals the expected time before the *present value* of the net cash flows from an investment equals its initial cost. Break-even time is computed by first restating future cash flows in terms of their present values. We then compute the payback period using these present values of future cash flows.

To illustrate, let's return to the case of FasTrac described in Exhibit 26.1. This involved a $16,000 investment in machinery. The annual net cash flows from this investment are projected at $4,100 for eight years. Exhibit 26.21 shows the computation of break-even time for this investment decision.

Exhibit 26.21

Break-Even Time Analysis*

Year	Cash Flows	Present Value of 1 at 10%	Present Value of Cash Flows	Cumulative Present Value of Cash Flows
0	$(16,000)	1.0000	$(16,000)	$(16,000)
1	4,100	0.9091	3,727	(12,273)
2	4,100	0.8264	3,388	(8,885)
3	4,100	0.7513	3,080	(5,805)
4	4,100	0.6830	2,800	(3,005)
5	4,100	0.6209	2,546	(459)
6	4,100	0.5645	2,314	1,855
7	4,100	0.5132	2,104	3,959
8	4,100	0.4665	1,913	5,872

* Analysis occurs at the start of Year 1 (same as end of Year 0). All cash flows occur at the end of each year.

The right-hand column of this exhibit shows that break-even time is between 5 and 6 years, or about 5.2 years. This is the time it takes for the project to break even after considering the time value of money. Cash flows earned after 5.2 years contribute to generating a positive net present value that, in this case, eventually amounts to $5,872.

Break-even time is a useful measure for managers because it informs them as to when they can start expecting the cash flows to yield net positive returns. It also tells us that if break-even time is less than the estimated life of the investment, management can expect a positive net present value from the investment. The method allows managers to compare and rank alternative investments, where the project with the lowest break-even time gets the highest rank.

Investment Manager
You are an investment manager for a company. Management asks you to evaluate three alternative investments. Investment recovery time is crucial because cash is scarce. Also, the time value of money is important. Which capital budgeting method(s) do you use to evaluate these investments?

Answers—p. 1123

Summary

C1 Explain the importance of capital budgeting. Capital budgeting is the process of analyzing alternative investments and deciding which assets to acquire or sell. Generally, capital budgeting involves predicting the cash flows to be received from alternative possibilities, evaluating their merits, and then choosing which ones to pursue.

C2 Describe selection of a hurdle rate for an investment. Top management should select the hurdle (discount) rate to be used for evaluating capital investments. Although financial formulas can aid this selection, the choice of a satisfactory (minimum) rate is largely subjective. The required hurdle rate should be at least higher than the rate at which money can be borrowed because the return on an investment must cover the interest and provide an additional profit to reward the company for its risk.

C3 Describe the importance of relevant costs for short-term decisions. In the case of short-term decision making, a company must rely on relevant costs pertaining to alternative courses of action rather than historical costs. Out-of-pocket expenses and opportunity costs are relevant because these are avoidable, whereas sunk costs are irrelevant because they result from past decisions and are therefore unavoidable. In addition to relevant costs, managers must also consider the relevant benefits associated with alternative courses of action.

A1 Evaluate short-term managerial decisions using relevant costs. Examples of these decisions are accepting additional business, make or buy, and sell as is or process further. Relevant costs are useful in making these decisions. For example, in deciding whether to produce and sell additional units of product, the relevant factors are the incremental costs and incremental revenues from the additional volume.

A2 Analyze a capital investment project using break-even time. Break-even time (BET) is a method for evaluating capital investment projects. It is computed by first restating future cash flows in terms of their present values (i.e., discounting the cash flows) and then calculating the payback period using these present values of cash flows. This method is superior to the payback period method because it considers the time value of money.

P1 Compute the payback period and describe its use. One method of comparing potential investments computes and compares their payback periods. The payback period is an estimate of the expected time before the cumulative net cash inflow from the investment equals its initial cost. A payback period analysis is limited because it fails to reflect the riskiness of the cash flows, differences in the timing of cash flows within the payback period, and all cash flows that occur after the payback period.

P2 Compute accounting rate of return and explain its use. A project's accounting rate of return is computed by dividing the expected annual after-tax net income by the average amount of investment in the project. When the net cash flows are received evenly throughout each period and straight-line depreciation is used, the average investment is computed as the average of the investment's initial book value and its salvage value. One major limitation of the accounting rate of return is its dependence on predictions of future value derived from depreciation methods. It also fails to reflect year-to-year variations in expected incomes.

P3 Compute net present value and describe its use. The net present value of an investment is determined by predicting the future cash flows that it is expected to generate, discounting them at a rate that represents an acceptable return, and then subtracting the initial cost of the investment from the sum of the present values. This technique can deal with any pattern of expected cash flows and applies a superior concept of return on investment. It is limited by the subjectivity in predicting future cash flows and in selecting the discount rate.

P4 Compute internal rate of return and explain its use. The internal rate of return (IRR) is the discount rate that results in a zero net present value. When the cash flows are equal, we can compute the present value factor corresponding to the IRR by dividing the initial investment by the annual cash flows. We then look up in the annuity tables to determine the discount rate corresponding to our present value factor. If the cash flows are uneven, we must use trial and error to compute the IRR.

Guidance Answer to **Judgment and Ethics**

Systems Manager

The dilemma faced by your friend and fellow manager is whether to abide by rules that are designed to prevent abuse or to bend those rules to acquire an investment that he believes will benefit the firm. This situation is realistic and representative of the business world. Because breaking up the entire order into small components is fundamentally dishonest, you should advise your friend against this action. You should point out the consequences of being caught at a later stage, particularly the potential embarrassment in front of peers and subordinates. You should encourage your friend to develop a proposal for the entire package and then do all that he can to expedite its processing, particularly by pointing out the significant benefits associated with the investment. When faced with an internal control system that isn't working, there is virtually never a legitimate reason to overcome its shortcomings by dishonesty. Rather, a direct assault on those limitations is more sensible, and is the ethical thing to do.

Guidance Answers to **You Make the Call**

R&D Manager

The controller is probably concerned that new products are risky and should therefore be evaluated using a higher rate of return. As the R&D manager, you should conduct a thorough technical analysis and obtain detailed market data and information about any similar products available in the market. These factors might provide sufficient information to support the use of a lower return. You must be able to convince the controller (and yourself) that the risk level is consistent with the discount rate used. You should also be confident that the company has the capacity and the resources to handle the new product.

Production Supervisor

As the person who will most likely be responsible for the production of the new product (if the order is accepted), you should identify as much detail as possible regarding the production implications of the order. You must provide details pertaining to the estimated direct costs of the product, requirements of any special equipment or processing (handling, packaging, etc.), and the costs associated with them. You must also identify any manufacturing capacity constraints which may affect the production of currently manufactured products if this order is accepted. All these details will allow the controller to identify and compute the relevant costs that must be considered in determining a price to be quoted.

Investment Manager

Given that the time value of money is crucial, you want to use methods that reflect the time value of money. Also, since recovery time is important, your attention should probably be directed at either the payback period or break-even time. The latter method is superior because it accounts for the time value of money, which is an important consideration in this decision.

Guidance Answers to 

1. *b*
2. A capital budgeting decision is difficult because (1) the outcome is uncertain, (2) large amounts of money are usually involved, (3) it involves a long-term commitment, and (4) the decision may be difficult or impossible to reverse.
3. *b*
4. Depreciation expense is subtracted from revenues in computing net income. However, it does not use cash and should be added back to net income to compute net cash flows.
5. Not necessarily. One investment may continue to generate cash flows beyond the payback period for a longer time period than the other. Also, the timing of their cash flows within the payback period may differ.
6. *b*; Annual average investment = ($180,000 + $15,000)/2 = $97,500

   Accounting rate of return = $40,000/$97,500 = 41%
7. It cannot be conclusively determined without comparing it to the returns expected from alternative investments with similar risk.
8. Project A has the greater net present value as shown below:

		Project A		Project B	
Year	Present Value of 1 at 10%	Net Cash Flows	Present Value of Net Cash Flows	Net Cash Flows	Present Value of Net Cash Flows
1	.9091	$12,000	$10,909	$ 4,500	$ 4,091
2	.8264	8,500	7,024	8,500	7,024
3	.7513	4,000	3,005	13,000	9,767
Total		$24,500	$20,938	$26,000	$20,882
Amount invested			(20,000)		(20,000)
Net present value			$ 938		$ 882

9. No, the information is too limited to draw that conclusion. For example, one investment may have more risk than the other, or one may require a substantially larger initial investment.
10. *b*; Net present value.

11. *e*; Variable costs per unit for this order of 200 units are:

Direct materials ($37,500/7,500)	$ 5.00
Direct labor ($60,000/7,500)	8.00
Variable overhead [(.30 × $20,000)/7,500]	.80
Variable selling expenses [(.60 × $25,000 × .5)/7,500]	1.00
Total variable costs per unit	$14.80

Cost to produce special order: (200 × $14.80) + $400 = $3,360.
Price per unit to earn $1,000: ($3,360 + $1,000)/200 = $21.80.

12. They are the additional costs that result from accepting new business.

13. *d*

14. A sunk cost is never relevant because it results from a past decision and is already incurred.

15. Avoidable expenses are those that a company will not incur if a segment is eliminated, whereas unavoidable expenses are those that will continue even after a segment is eliminated.

16. *a*

Demonstration Problem

Determine the appropriate action in each of the following managerial decision situations:

a. Packer Company is operating at 80% of its manufacturing capacity of 100,000 product units per year. A chain store has offered to buy an additional 10,000 units at $22 each and sell them in an area where Packer Co. currently has no outlet. The following facts are available:

Costs at 80% capacity	Per Unit	Total
Direct materials	$ 8.00	$ 640,000
Direct labor	7.00	560,000
Overhead (fixed and variable)	12.50	1,000,000
Total	$27.50	$2,200,000

In producing 10,000 additional units, fixed overhead costs would remain at their current level but incremental variable overhead costs of $3 per unit would be incurred. Should the company accept or reject this order?

b. Green Company uses Part JR3 in manufacturing its products. In the past, it has always purchased this part from a supplier at $40 each. It recently upgraded its own manufacturing capabilities and has enough excess capacity (including trained workers) to begin manufacturing Part JR3 instead of buying it. The accountant has prepared the following cost projections of making the part, assuming overhead is allocated to the part at the normal predetermined rate of 200% of direct labor cost.

Direct materials	$11.00
Direct labor	15.00
Overhead (fixed and variable)—(200% of direct labor)	30.00
Total	$56.00

The required volume of output to produce the part will not require any incremental fixed overhead. Incremental variable overhead cost will be $17 per unit. Should the company make or buy this part?

c. Gold Company's manufacturing process causes a relatively large number of defective parts to be produced. The defective parts can be (1) sold for scrap, (2) melted down to recover the recycled metal for reuse, or (3) reworked to be good units. If defective parts are reworked, the output of other good units is reduced because there is no excess capacity. Each unit reworked means that one new unit cannot be produced. The following information is available about 500 defective parts currently on hand:

Proceeds of selling as scrap	$2,500
Additional cost of melting down defective parts	$ 400
Cost of purchases avoided by using recycled metal from defects	$4,800
Cost to rework 500 defective parts:	
Direct materials	$ 0
Direct labor	1,500
Incremental overhead	1,750
Cost to produce 500 new parts:	
Direct materials	$6,000
Direct labor	5,000
Incremental overhead	3,200
Selling price of good unit	$40

Should the company melt down the parts, sell them as scrap, or rework them?

d. White Company can invest in one of two projects, TD1 or TD2. Each project requires an initial investment of $100,000 and produces the following end-of-year cash inflows:

	TD1	TD2
Year 1	$ 20,000	$ 40,000
Year 2	30,000	40,000
Year 3	70,000	40,000
Total	$120,000	$120,000

Use net present values to determine which project, if any, should be acquired. Assume the company requires a 10% return from its investments.

Planning the Solution

- Determine whether the Packer Company should accept the additional business by finding the incremental costs of materials, labor, and overhead that will be incurred if the order is accepted. Leave out fixed costs that will not be increased by the order. If the incremental revenue exceeds the incremental cost, then accept the order.
- Determine whether Green Company should make or buy the component by finding the incremental cost of making each unit. If the incremental cost exceeds the purchase price, the component should be purchased. If the incremental cost is less than the purchase price, the component should be made.
- Determine whether the Gold Company should sell the defective parts, melt them down and recycle the metal, or rework them. To compare the three choices, examine all costs incurred and benefits received from the alternatives in working with the 500 defective units to the production of 500 new units. For the scrapping alternative, include the costs of producing 500 new units and subtract the $2,500 proceeds from selling the old ones. For the melting alternative, include the costs of melting the defective units, add the net cost of new materials in excess over those obtained from recycling, and add the direct labor and overhead costs. For the reworking alternative, add the costs of direct labor and incremental overhead. Select the alternative that has the lowest cost. The cost assigned to the 500 defective units is sunk and not relevant in choosing among the three alternatives.
- Compute the net present value of each investment using a 10% discount rate.

Solution to Demonstration Problem

a. This decision concerns accepting additional business. Because current unit costs are $27.50, it initially appears as if the offer to sell for $22 should be rejected. But the $27.50 cost includes fixed costs. When the analysis includes only *incremental* costs, the per unit cost is:

Direct materials	$ 8.00
Direct labor	7.00
Variable overhead (given)	3.00
Total incremental cost	$18.00

The offer should be accepted because it will produce $4 of additional profit per unit (computed as $22 price less $18 incremental cost), which yields a total profit of $40,000 for the 10,000 additional units.

b. This is a make or buy decision. The analysis must not include the nonincremental overhead of $13 per unit (computed as $30 less $17). When only the incremental overhead of $17 is included, the relevant unit cost of manufacturing the part is:

Direct materials	$11.00
Direct labor	15.00
Variable overhead	17.00
Total incremental cost	$43.00

It would be better to continue buying the part for $40 instead of making it for $43.

c. This is a scrap or rework decision. The goal is to identify the alternative that produces the greatest net benefit to the company. To compare the alternatives, we determine the net cost of obtaining 500 marketable units as follows:

Incremental Cost to Produce 500 Marketable Units	Sell as Is	Melt and Recycle	Rework Units
Direct material:			
New materials	$ 6,000	$6,000	
Recycled (metal) materials		(4,800)	
Net materials cost		$1,200	
Melting costs		400	
Total direct materials cost	$ 6,000	$1,600	
Direct labor	5,000	5,000	$1,500
Incremental overhead	3,200	3,200	1,750
Cost to produce 500 marketable units	$14,200	$9,800	$3,250
Less proceeds of selling defects as scrap	(2,500)		
Opportunity costs*			$5,800
Net cost	$11,700	$9,800	$9,050

*The opportunity cost of $5,800 is the lost contribution margin from not being able to produce and sell 500 units because of reworking, computed as ($40 − $28.40) × 500 units.

The incremental cost of 500 marketable parts is smallest if the defects are reworked.

d. **TD1:**

	Net Cash Flows	Present Value of 1 at 10%	Present Value of Net Cash Flows
Year 1	$ 20,000	0.9091	$ 18,182
Year 2	30,000	0.8264	24,792
Year 3	70,000	0.7513	52,591
Total	$120,000		$ 95,565
Amount invested			$(100,000)
Net present value			$ (4,435)

TD2:

	Net Cash Flows	Present Value of 1 at 10%	Present Value of Net Cash Flows
Year 1	$ 40,000	0.9091	$ 36,364
Year 2	40,000	0.8264	33,056
Year 3	40,000	0.7513	30,052
Total	$120,000		$ 99,472
Amount invested			$(100,000)
Net present value			$ (528)

White Co. should not invest in either project. Both are expected to yield a negative net present value, and only positive net present projects should be considered.

Glossary

Accounting rate of return a rate used to evaluate the acceptability of an investment; equals the after-tax periodic income from a project divided by the average investment in the asset; also called *rate of return on average investment.* (p. 1104).

Avoidable expense an expense (or cost) that is relevant for decision making; an expense that is not incurred if a department, product, or service is eliminated. (p. 1120).

Break-even time (BET) a time-based measurement used to evaluate the acceptability of an investment; equals the time expected to pass before the *present value* of the net cash flows from an investment equals its initial cost. (p. 1121).

Capital budgeting the process of analyzing alternative investments and deciding which assets to acquire or sell. (p. 1100).

Hurdle rate a minimum acceptable rate of return (set by management) for an investment. (p. 1111).

Incremental cost an additional cost incurred only if a company pursues a specific course of action. (p. 1114).

Internal rate of return (IRR) a rate used to evaluate the acceptability of an investment; equals the rate that yields a net present value of zero for an investment. (p. 1109).

Net present value (NPV) a dollar estimate of an asset's value to the company that is used to evaluate the acceptability of an investment; computed by discounting future cash flows from the investment at a satisfactory rate and then subtracting the initial cost of the investment. (p. 1106).

Opportunity cost a cost that represents the potential benefits lost by choosing an alternative course of action. (p. 1113).

Out-of-pocket cost a cost incurred or avoided as a result of management's decisions. (p. 1113).

Payback period (PBP) a time-based measurement used to evaluate the acceptability of an investment; equals the time expected to pass before the net cash flows from an investment equal its initial cost. (p. 1101).

Relevant benefits additional or incremental revenue generated by selecting a particular course of action over another. (p. 1113).

Sunk cost a cost that cannot be avoided or changed because it arises from a past decision; irrelevant to current and future decisions. (p. 1113).

Unavoidable expense an expense (or cost) that is not relevant for decision making; an expense that would continue even if a department, product, or service is eliminated. (p. 1120).

Questions

1. What is capital budgeting?
2. Capital budgeting decisions require careful analysis because they are generally the ____________ ____________ and ____________ decisions that management faces.
3. Identify four reasons why capital budgeting decisions are risky.
4. Why is an investment more attractive if it has a shorter payback period?
5. Identify two disadvantages of using the payback period for comparing investments.
6. What is the average amount invested in a machine during its life if it costs $200,000 and has a predicted five-year life with a $20,000 salvage value? Assume that net income is received evenly throughout each year and straight-line depreciation is used.
7. Why is the present value of $100 that you expect to receive one year from now worth less than $100 received today? What is the present value of $100 that you expect to receive one year from now, discounted at 12%?
8. If the present value of the expected net cash flows from a machine, discounted at 10%, exceeds the amount to be invested, what can you say about the expected rate of return on the investment? What can you say about the expected rate of return if the present value of the net cash flows, discounted at 10%, is less than the amount of the investment?
9. Why is the value of an investment increased by using an accelerated depreciation method (instead of straight line) for income tax reporting?
10. Why should the required rate of return always be higher than the rate at which money can be borrowed when making a typical capital budgeting decision?
11. A company manufactures and sells 500,000 units of product at $30 per unit in domestic markets. The product costs $20 per unit to manufacture ($13 variable cost per unit, $7 fixed cost per unit). Can you describe a situation under which the company may be willing to sell an additional 25,000 units of the product in an international market at $15 per unit?
12. What is an out-of-pocket cost? What is an opportunity cost? Are opportunity costs recorded in the accounting records?
13. Why are sunk costs irrelevant in deciding whether to sell a product in its present condition or to make it into a new product through additional processing?
14. Identify the incremental costs incurred by NIKE for shipping one additional pair of running shoes to a retail sporting goods store along with the store's normal order of 1,000 pairs of running shoes.

Quick Study

QS 26-1
Payback period
P1

Brooks Company is considering investment that requires immediate payment of $18,000 and provides expected cash inflows of $6,000 annually for four years. What is the investment's payback period?

QS 26-2
Analyzing payback alternatives
P1

Freeman Company is considering two alternative investments. Investment A has a payback period of 3.5 years and Investment B has a payback period of 4 years. Why might Freeman's analysis of these two alternatives lead to the selection of B over A?

QS 26-3
Computing accounting rate of return
P2

Pad Company is considering an investment expected to generate an average net income after taxes of $1,300 for three years. The investment cost $30,000 and has an estimated $4,000 salvage value. Compute the accounting rate of return for this investment.

QS 26-4
Computing net present value
P3

If Fox Company invests $50,000 now, it can expect to receive $10,000 at the end of each year for seven years plus an extra $6,000 at the end of the seventh year. What is the net present value of this investment, assuming Fox requires a 10% return on its investments?

QS 26-5
Analyzing incremental costs
C3, A1

Marker Company incurs $6 per unit costs for Product A, which it currently manufactures and sells for $9 per unit. Instead of manufacturing and selling this product, Marker can purchase Product B for $5 and sell it for $8. If this is done, unit sales would remain unchanged and $5 of the $6 per unit costs assigned to Product A would be eliminated. Should Marker continue to manufacture Product A or purchase Product B for resale?

QS 26-6
Selecting a sales mix
C3, A1

Byte Company can sell all the units it can produce of computer memory X and Y, but it has limited production capacity. It can produce two units of X per hour or three units of Y per hour, and it has 4,000 production hours available. Product X has a contribution margin of $5 and Product Y has a contribution margin of $4. What is the most profitable sales mix for Byte Company?

QS 26-7
Computing break-even time
A2

Cut-To-Fit, a shoe manufacturer, is evaluating the costs and benefits of new equipment that would custom fit each pair of athletic shoes. The customer would have his/her foot scanned by digital computer equipment and this information would be used to cut the raw materials to provide a perfect fit to the customer. The new equipment costs $100,000 and is expected to generate an additional $35,000 in cash flows for five years. A bank will make a $100,000 loan to Cut-To-Fit at a 10% interest rate for this equipment's purchase. Use the table below to determine the break-even time for this equipment.

Year	Cash Flows	Present Value of 1 at 10%	Present Value of Cash Flows	Cumulative Present Value of Cash Flows
0	$(100,000)	1.0000		
1	35,000	0.9091		
2	35,000	0.8264		
3	35,000	0.7513		
4	35,000	0.6830		
5	35,000	0.6209		

Exercises

Exercise 26-1
Computing payback period; equal cash flows
P1

Compute the payback period for each of these two separate investments:

a. A new control system for an existing machine is expected to cost $260,000 and have a useful life of five years. The system yields an incremental after-tax income of $75,000 each year, after deducting its straight-line depreciation. The predicted salvage value of the system is $10,000.

b. A machine costs $190,000, has a $10,000 salvage value, is expected to last nine years, and will generate an after-tax income of $30,000 per year after straight-line depreciation.

Exercise 26-2
Computing payback period; unequal cash flows
P1

Champ Company is considering the purchase of an asset for $90,000. The asset is expected to produce the following net cash inflows:

	Year 1	Year 2	Year 3	Year 4	Year 5	Total
Net cash flows	$30,000	$20,000	$30,000	$60,000	$19,000	$159,000

The cash flows occur evenly throughout each year. Compute the payback period for this investment.

Exercise 26-3
Computing payback period; declining-balance depreciation
P1

A machine can be purchased for $300,000 and used for 5 years, yielding the following net incomes:

	Year 1	Year 2	Year 3	Year 4	Year 5
Net incomes	$20,000	$50,000	$100,000	$75,000	$200,000

In projecting net incomes, double-declining balance depreciation is deducted, using a 5-year life and a $50,000 salvage value. Compute the machine's payback period. Ignore taxes.

Exercise 26-4
Accounting rate of return
P2

A machine costs $500,000 and is expected to yield an after-tax net income of $15,000 each year. Management predicts this machine has a 10-year service life and a $100,000 salvage value. Compute the accounting rate of return for this machine.

Exercise 26-5
Payback and return on average investment
P1, P2

Link Co. is considering the purchase of equipment that would allow the company to add a new product to its line. The equipment is expected to cost $240,000 with a six-year life and no salvage value. It will be depreciated on a straight-line basis. The company expects to sell 96,000 units of the equipment's product each year. The expected end-of-year income related to the equipment is as follows:

Sales	$150,000
Costs:	
Materials, labor, and overhead (except depreciation)	$ 80,000
Depreciation on new equipment	20,000
Selling and administrative expenses	15,000
Total costs and expenses	$115,000
Pre-tax income	$ 35,000
Income taxes (30%)	10,500
Net income	$ 24,500

Compute the *(a)* payback period and *(b)* accounting rate of return for this equipment.

Exercise 26-6
Computing net present value
P3

After evaluating the risk of the investment described in Exercise 26-5, the Link Co. concludes that it must earn at least an 8% return on this investment. Compute the net present value of this investment.

Exercise 26-7
Computing and interpreting net present value and internal rate of return
P3, P4

Badger Company can invest in each of three cheese-making projects: C1, C2, and C3. Each project requires an initial investment of $190,000 and would yield the following annual cash flows:

	C1	C2	C3
Year 1	$ 10,000	$ 80,000	$150,000
Year 2	90,000	80,000	50,000
Year 3	140,000	80,000	40,000
Total	$240,000	$240,000	$240,000

Required

1. Assuming the company requires a 12% return from its investments, use net present value to determine which projects, if any, should be acquired.
2. Using the answer from part (1), is the internal rate of return greater than or less than 12% for project C2? Compute the internal rate of return for project C2.

Exercise 26-8
Decision to accept additional business
C3, A1

Camp Co. expects to sell 200,000 units of its product in the next period with the following results:

Sales (200,000 units)	$3,000,000
Costs and expenses:	
Direct materials	$ 400,000
Direct labor	800,000
Overhead	200,000
Selling expenses	300,000
Administrative expenses	514,000
Total costs and expenses	$2,214,000
Net income	$ 786,000

The company has an opportunity to sell 20,000 additional units at a price of $12 per unit. The additional sales would not affect current sales. Direct materials and labor costs would be the same for additional units as they are for regular units. The additional volume would create the following incremental costs: (1) total overhead would increase by 15%; and (2) administrative expenses would increase by $86,000. Prepare an analysis to determine whether the company should accept or reject the offer to sell the additional units at the reduced price.

Exercise 26-9
Make or buy decision
C3, A1

Green Company currently manufactures one of its crucial parts at a cost of $3.40 per unit. This cost is based on a normal production rate of 50,000 units per year. Variable costs are $1.50 per unit, fixed costs related to making this part are $50,000 per year, and allocated fixed costs are $45,000 per year. Allocated fixed costs are unavoidable whether or not the company makes or buys the part. Green is considering buying the part from a supplier that has quoted a price of $2.70 per unit. This price would be guaranteed for a three-year period. Should the company continue to manufacture the part or should it buy the part from the outside supplier? Support your answer with analyses.

Exercise 26-10
Sell or process decision
C3, A1

Newton Company has 20,000 units of Product A that are already manufactured for a total cost of $20 per unit. The 20,000 units can be sold at this stage for $500,000. Alternatively, they can be further processed at a total additional cost of $300,000 and be converted into 4,000 units of Product B and 8,000 units of Product C. Product B can be sold for $75 per unit and Product C can be sold for $50 per unit. Prepare an analysis that shows whether the 20,000 units of Product A should be processed further or not.

Exercise 26-11
Analyzing and determining sales mix
C3, A1

Dial Company owns a machine that can produce two specialized products. Product TLX can be produced at the rate of two units per hour and Product MTV can be produced at the rate of five units per hour. The capacity of the machine is 2,200 hours per year. Both products are sold to a single customer who has agreed to buy all of the company's output up to a maximum of 3,750 units of Product TLX and 2,000 units of Product MTV. Selling prices and variable costs per unit to produce the products are:

	Product TLX	Product MTV
Selling price	$12.50	$7.50
Variable costs	3.75	4.50

Determine *(a)* the most profitable sales mix for the company and *(b)* the contribution margin that results from that sales mix.

Exercise 26-12
Analyzing income effects of eliminating departments
C3, A1

Suresh Co. expects its five departments to produce the following income results for next year:

	Dept. M	Dept. N	Dept. O	Dept. P	Dept. T
Sales	$63,000	$ 35,000	$56,000	$ 42,000	$ 28,000
Expenses:					
Avoidable	9,800	36,400	22,400	14,000	37,800
Unavoidable	51,800	12,600	4,200	29,400	9,800
Total expenses	$61,600	$ 49,000	$26,600	$ 43,400	$ 47,600
Net income (loss)	$ 1,400	$(14,000)	$29,400	$ (1,400)	$(19,600)

Required

Prepare a combined income statement for the company under each of the following scenarios:

a. Management does not eliminate any department.

b. Management eliminates departments with expected net losses. Explain.

c. Management eliminates departments with less sales dollars than avoidable expenses.

Exercise 26-13
Comparing payback and BET
P1, A2

This chapter explained two methods to evaluate investments using recovery time, the payback period and break-even time. Refer to QS 26-7 and compute *(a)* the payback period and *(b)* break-even time.

Required

1. Report the recovery time for each method.
2. Discuss the advantage(s) of break-even time over the payback period.
3. List two conditions where payback period and break-even time are similar.

Problems

Problem 26-1
Computing payback period, accounting rate of return, and net present value
P1, P2, P3

Emerson Company is planning to add a new product to its line. To manufacture this product, the company needs to buy a new machine at a cost of $300,000. This asset is expected to have a four-year life and a $20,000 salvage value. All sales are for cash and all costs are out-of-pocket, except for depreciation on the new machine. Additional information includes the following:

Expected annual sales of new product	$1,150,000
Expected costs:	
Direct materials	300,000
Direct labor	420,000
Overhead excluding straight-line depreciation on new machine	210,000
Selling and administrative expenses	100,000
Income taxes	30%

Required

1. Compute straight-line depreciation for each year of this asset's life.
2. Determine expected net income and net cash flow for each year of this asset's life.
3. Compute payback period for this asset, assuming that cash flows occur evenly throughout each year.
4. Compute accounting rate of return for the asset, assuming income is earned evenly throughout each year.
5. Compute net present value for this asset using a discount rate of 7% and assuming cash flows occur at the end of each year. (Hint: Salvage value is a cash inflow at the end of the asset's life.)

Check Figure Net present value, $70,915

Problem 26-2
Analyzing and computing payback period, accounting rate of return, and net present value
P1, P2, P3

Pentium Company has an opportunity to invest in one of two new projects. Project Y requires an investment of $240,000 for new machinery having a four-year life and no salvage value. Project Z requires an investment of $240,000 for new machinery having a three-year life and no salvage value. The two projects yield the following predicted annual results:

	Project Y	Project Z
Sales	$250,000	$200,000
Expenses:		
Direct materials	$ 35,000	$ 25,000
Direct labor	50,000	30,000
Overhead including depreciation	90,000	90,000
Selling and administrative expenses	18,000	18,000
Total expenses	$193,000	$163,000
Pretax income	$ 57,000	$ 37,000
Income taxes (30%)	17,100	11,100
Net income	$ 39,900	$ 25,900

The company uses straight-line depreciation, and assume that cash flows occur evenly throughout each year. For part 4 only, assume cash flows occur at the end of each year.

Required

Preparation Component

Check Figure Accounting rate of return for Project Y, 33.25%

1. Compute the annual expected net cash flows for each project.
2. Determine the payback period for each project.
3. Compute the accounting rate of return for each project.
4. Determine the net present value for each project using 8% as the discount rate.

Analysis Component

5. Identify the project you would recommend to management and explain your choice.

Problem 26-3
Computing cash flows and net present values with alternative depreciation methods
P3

Flight Corporation is considering a new project that would require a $30,000 investment in special test equipment with no salvage value. The project would produce $12,000 of pretax income before depreciation at the end of each year for six years. The company's income tax rate is 40%. In compiling its tax return and computing its income tax payments, the company can choose between these two alternative depreciation schedules:

	Straight-Line Depreciation	MACRS Depreciation*
Year 1	$ 3,000	$ 6,000
Year 2	6,000	9,600
Year 3	6,000	5,760
Year 4	6,000	3,456
Year 5	6,000	3,456
Year 6	3,000	1,728
Total	$30,000	$30,000

* The modified accelerated cost recovery system (MACRS) for depreciation is discussed in Chapter 11.

Required

Preparation Component

1. Produce a five-column table that reports amounts for each of the following items for each of the six years: *(a)* income before depreciation, *(b)* straight-line depreciation expense, *(c)* taxable income, *(d)* income taxes, and *(e)* net cash flow. Net cash flow equals the amount of income before depreciation minus the income taxes.
2. Produce a five-column table that reports amounts for each of the following items for each of the six years: *(a)* income before depreciation, *(b)* MACRS depreciation expense, *(c)* taxable income, *(d)* income taxes, and *(e)* net cash flow. Net cash flow equals the amount of income before depreciation minus the income taxes.

3. Compute the net present value of the investment if straight-line depreciation is used. Use 10% as the discount rate.

4. Compute the net present value of the investment if MACRS depreciation is used. Use 10% as the discount rate.

Check Figure Net present value (using straight-line), $10,041

Analysis Component

5. Explain why the MACRS depreciation method increases the net present value of this project.

Problem 26-4
Analyzing income effects of additional business
C3, A1 S

Design Products manufactures underwater markers that it sells to wholesalers at $4 per package. The company manufactures and sells approximately 300,000 packages of markers each year to deep-sea treasure hunting teams. Annual costs for the production and sale of this quantity are:

Direct materials	$384,000
Direct labor	96,000
Overhead	288,000
Selling expenses	120,000
Administrative expenses	80,000
Total costs and expenses	$968,000

A new wholesaler has offered to buy 50,000 packages of markers for $3.44 each. These markers would be marketed under the wholesaler's name and would not affect Design Products' sales through its normal channels. A study of the costs of this additional business reveals the following:

- Direct material costs are 100% variable.
- Per unit direct labor costs for the additional units would be 50% greater than normal because their production would require overtime pay at one-and-one-half times the usual labor rate.
- One-fourth of the normal annual overhead costs are fixed at any production level from 250,000 to 400,000 units. The remaining three-fourths of the annual overhead cost is variable with volume.
- There will be no additional selling costs if the new business is accepted.
- Accepting the new business would increase administrative expenses by a fixed amount of $4,000.

Required

Prepare a three-column comparative income statement that shows:

1. Annual operating income without the special order (column 1).

2. Annual operating income that would be received from the new business (column 2).

3. Combined annual operating income from normal business and the new business (column 3).

Check Figure Operating income from new business, $44,000

Problem 26-5
Analyzing sales mix strategies
C3, A1

Packer Company is capable of producing two products, G and B, with the same machine in its factory. The following per unit facts are known:

	Product G	Product B
Selling price	$60	$80
Variable costs	20	45
Contribution margin	$40	$35
Machine-hours to produce 1 unit	0.4	1.0
Maximum unit sales per month	550	175

The company presently operates the machine for a single eight-hour shift for 22 working days each month. Management is thinking about operating the machine for two shifts, which will increase the machine's availability by another eight hours per day for 22 days per month. This change would require additional fixed costs of $3,250 per month.

Required

1. Determine the contribution margin per machine hour that each product generates.

2. How many units of G and B should the company produce if it continues to operate with only one shift? How much total contribution margin is produced each month with this mix?

Check Figure (3) Units of B to be produced, 132 units

3. If the company adds another shift, how many units of G and B should the company produce? How much total contribution margin would be produced each month with this mix? Should the company add the new shift?
4. Suppose the company determines it can increase the maximum sales of Product G to 675 units per month by spending $4,500 per month in marketing efforts. Should the company pursue this strategy along with the double shift?

Problem 26-6
Analyzing elimination of a department
C3, A1

The management of Home Appliance Company is trying to decide whether to eliminate Department 200, which has produced losses or low profits for several years. The company's 1999 departmental income statement shows the following:

HOME APPLIANCE COMPANY
Departmental Income Statement
For Year Ended December 31, 1999

	Dept. 100	Dept. 200	Combined
Sales	$436,000	$290,000	$726,000
Cost of goods sold	262,000	207,000	469,000
Gross profit	$174,000	$ 83,000	$257,000
Operating expenses:			
Direct expenses:			
Advertising	$ 17,000	$ 12,000	$ 29,000
Store supplies used	4,000	3,800	7,800
Depreciation of store equipment	5,000	3,300	8,300
Total direct expenses	$ 26,000	$ 19,100	$ 45,100
Allocated expenses:			
Sales salaries	$ 65,000	$ 39,000	$104,000
Rent expense	9,440	4,720	14,160
Bad debts expense	9,900	8,100	18,000
Office salary	18,720	12,480	31,200
Insurance expense	2,000	1,100	3,100
Miscellaneous office expenses	2,400	1,600	4,000
Total allocated expenses	$107,460	$ 67,000	$174,460
Total expenses	$133,460	$ 86,100	$219,560
Net income (loss)	$ 40,540	$ (3,100)	$ 37,440

In analyzing whether to eliminate Department 200, management considers the following items:

a. The company has one office worker who earns $600 per week, or $31,200 per year, and four salesclerks who each earn $500 per week, or $26,000 per year.
b. The full salaries of two sales clerks are charged to Department 100. The full salary of one sales clerk is charged to Department 200. Because the fourth clerk works half-time in both departments, her salary is divided evenly between the two departments.
c. The sales salaries and the office salary currently assigned to Department 200 are avoidable if the department were eliminated. However, management prefers another plan. Two sales clerks have indicated that they will be quitting soon. Management thinks that their work can be done by the other two clerks if the one office worker works in sales half-time. The office worker's schedule will allow this shift of duties if Department 200 is eliminated. If this change is implemented, half the office worker's salary would be reported as sales salaries and half would be reported as office salary.
d. The store building is rented under a long-term lease that cannot be changed. Therefore, the space presently occupied by Department 200 will have to be used by the current Department 100. The equipment used by Department 200 will be used by the current Department 100.
e. Closing Department 200 will eliminate its expenses for advertising, bad debts, and store supplies. It will also eliminate 70% of the insurance expense allocated to the department for coverage on its merchandise inventory. In addition, 25% of the miscellaneous office expenses presently allocated to Department 200 will be eliminated.

Required

Preparation Component

1. Prepare a three-column schedule that lists *(a)* the company's total expenses (including cost of goods sold), *(b)* the expenses that would be eliminated by closing Department 200, and *(c)* the expenses that will continue.
2. Prepare a forecasted income statement for the company reflecting the elimination of Department 200 under the assumption that sales and the gross profit for Department 100 will not be affected. The statement should reflect the reassignment of the office worker to one-half time as a salesclerk.

Check Figure Forecasted net income without Department 200, $31,510

Analysis Component

3. Prepare a reconciliation of the company's combined net income with the forecasted net income assuming Department 200 is eliminated. Analyze the reconciliation and explain why you think the department should or should not be eliminated.

BEYOND THE NUMBERS

Reporting in Action

C1, A1, P3

Locate the notes for **NIKE's** annual report in Appendix A and answer the following questions.

Required

1. Locate note 1 and identify depreciation methods used by NIKE for property, plant, and equipment.
2. Locate the note that reports the percent of gross property, plant, and equipment that consists of machinery and equipment for May 1997 and 1996. Report these amounts.
3. Using your answers to parts (1) and (2), why do you think NIKE uses declining-balance depreciation for its machinery and equipment when this method reduces NIKE's reported earnings in the early years of the investment period? (Hint: Consider taxes and cash flows.)

Swoosh Ahead

4. Obtain NIKE's annual report information for a fiscal year ending after May 31, 1997. You can get this information from either its Web site **[www.nike.com]** or the SEC's EDGAR database **[www.sec.gov].** If the tax laws don't change for depreciation, do you expect NIKE to follow the same depreciation method in subsequent years for machinery and equipment? Check your response with NIKE's current statements.

Comparative Analysis

C3

Reebok

Reebok and **NIKE** sell several different products. Some are profitable and others are not. Teams of employees in each company make advertising, investment, and product mix decisions. For both companies, a certain portion of advertising is done on a local basis to a target audience.

Required

1. Find one major advertisement of a product or group of products for each company in your local newspaper. Contact the newspaper and ask them the approximate cost of this ad space (for example, cost of one page or one-half page of advertising).
2. Estimate how many products must be sold from this advertisement for it to justify the cost of the advertisement. Begin by taking the selling price of the product advertised for each company and assume a 20% contribution margin.
3. Prepare a one-half page memorandum describing the importance of effective advertising when making a product mix decision. Be prepared to present your ideas in class.

Ethics Challenge

P3

A consultant commented that "Too often the numbers look good, but feel bad." This comment stems from estimation errors commonly found in capital budgeting proposals relating to the number of years that a project is assumed to generate cash flows. This error is often linked to three reasons. First, it is very difficult to reliably predict cash flow several years into the future. Second, the present value of cash flows many years into the future (say, beyond 10 years) is often very small. Third, it is difficult for personal biases and expectations not to unduly influence present value computations.

Required

1. Record the value today of $100 to be received in 10 years, at a 12% discount rate.
2. Why is having an understanding of the three reasons mentioned above for estimation errors important when evaluating investment projects? Link this response to your answer for part (1).

Communicating in Practice

P1, P2, P3, P4

Payback period, accounting rate of return, net present value, and internal rate of return are common techniques used in evaluating capital investment opportunities. Assume your manager asks you to identify the type of measurement basis each perspective offers and to list the advantages and disadvantages of each. Present your response in memorandum format of less than one page.

Taking It to the Net

More companies are using the Web to search for employees. Our knowledge of the Web as a job search tool can potentially help us obtain that "special opportunity." Check out the following Web site and read how to prepare a resume: Go to **[www.resumix.com]** and click on *Materials* to help create your resume. Prepare a draft of your resume following the Web advice provided.

Teamwork in Action

P1, P3

Break into teams and identify four reasons why an international airline company such as United, Delta, or American Airlines would make an investment in a project when its direct analysis using both payback period and net present value indicate it would be a poor investment. (Hint: Think about qualitative factors.) Provide an example of an investment project supporting your answer.

Hitting the Road

C1, P3

Visit or call a local auto dealership and inquire about leasing a car. Ask about the down payment and the required monthly payments. You are likely to find the salesperson does not discuss the cost of purchasing this car. The sales focus will be on the affordability of the monthly payments. This chapter gives you the tools to compute the cost of this car using the lease payment schedule, in present dollars, and to estimate the profit from leasing for an auto dealership.

Required

1. Compare the cost of leasing the car to the buy decision in present dollars. Use the information given to you by the dealership you contact. (Assume you will make a final payment at the end of the lease and own the car upon completion of the lease.)
2. Is it more costly to lease or buy the car? Support your answer with computations.

Business Week Activity

C1

Office equipment a decade ago included products like ink blotters, adding machines, and thermal faxes. Today's office equipment is quick to change and often more expensive. It is not uncommon for today's office equipment manager to require a three-year payback on all office equipment investments. But quantifying the benefits of office equipment is often difficult. Read "The Digital Copier Comes of Age" in ***Business Week***, December 8, 1997.

Required

1. List three advantages of the new digital copier.
2. How would you measure these advantages in justifying the current price?

Financial Statement Information

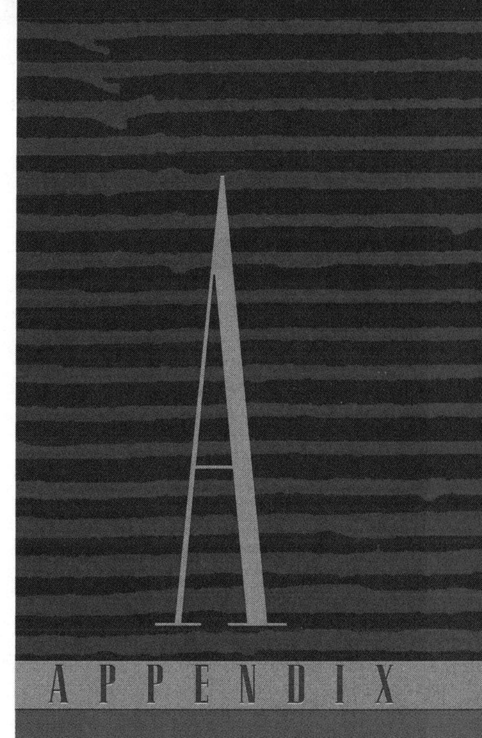

This appendix includes financial statement information for (a) **NIKE** (b) **Reebok** and (c) **America Online.** All of this information is taken from their annual reports. An **annual report** is a summary of the financial results of a company's operations for the year and its future plans. It is directed at external users of financial information, but also affects the actions and decisions of internal users.

An annual report is also used by a company to showcase itself and its products. Many include attractive pictures, diagrams and illustrations related to the company. But the *financial section* is its primary objective. The financial section communicates much information about a company, with most data drawn from the accounting information system.

The layout of the financial section of an annual report is fairly standard and usually includes:

- Letter to Shareholders
- Financial History and Highlights
- Management Discussion and Analysis
- Management's Report
- Report of Independent Accountants (Auditor's Report)
- Financial Statements
- Notes to Financial Statements
- List of Directors and Managers

This appendix provides most of the financial information for NIKE that is contained in its annual report. It also includes the financial statements for Reebok and America Online. The appendix is organized as follows:

Many assignments at the end of each chapter refer to information in this appendix. We encourage readers to spend extra time with these assignments as they are especially useful in reinforcing and showing the relevance and diversity of financial accounting and reporting.

FINANCIAL HISTORY

(in thousands, except per share data and financial ratios)

YEAR ENDED MAY 31,	1997	1996	1995	1994
Revenues	$9,186,539	$6,470,625	$4,760,834	$3,789,668
Gross margin	3,683,546	2,563,879	1,895,554	1,488,245
Gross margin %	40.1%	39.6%	39.8%	39.3%
Net income	795,822	553,190	399,664	298,794
Net income per common share	2.68	1.88	1.36	0.99
Average number of common and common equivalent shares	297,000	293,608	294,012	301,824
Cash dividends declared per common share	0.38	0.29	0.24	0.20
Cash flow from operations	323,120	339,672	254,913	576,463
Price range of common stock				
High	76.375	52.063	20.156	18.688
Low	47.875	19.531	14.063	10.781
At May 31:				
Cash and equivalents	$ 445,421	$ 262,117	$ 216,071	$ 518,816
Inventories	1,338,640	931,151	629,742	470,023
Working capital	1,964,002	1,259,881	938,393	1,208,444
Total assets	5,361,207	3,951,628	3,142,745	2,373,815
Long-term debt	296,020	9,584	10,565	12,364
Redeemable Preferred Stock	300	300	300	300
Common shareholders' equity	3,155,838	2,431,400	1,964,689	1,740,949
Year-end stock price	57.500	50 .188	19.719	14.750
Market capitalization	16,633,047	14,416,792	5,635,190	4,318,800
Financial Ratios:				
Return on equity	28.5%	25.2%	21.6%	17.7%
Return on assets	17.1%	15.6%	14.5%	13.1%
Inventory turns	4.8	5.0	5.2	4.3
Current ratio at May 31	2.1	1.9	1.8	3.2
Price/Earnings ratio at May 31	21.5	26.6	14.5	14.9
Geographic Revenues:				
United States	$5,529,132			$2,432,684
Europe	1,833,722			927,269
Asia/Pacific	1,245,217			283,421
Canada, Latin America, and other	578,468			146,294
Total Revenues	$9,186,539	$6,470,625	$4,760,834	$3,789,668

All per common share data has been adjusted to reflect the 2-for-1 stock splits paid October 23, 1996, October 30, 1995 and October 5, 1990. The Company's Class B Common Stock is listed on the New York and Pacific Exchanges and trades under the symbol NKE. At May 31, 1997, there were approximately 300,000 shareholders. Years 1993 and prior have been restated to reflect the implementation of Statement of Financial Accounting Standard No. 109 – Accounting for Income Taxes (see Notes 1 and 6 to the Consolidated Financial Statements).

972 1973 1974 1975 1976 1977 1978 1980 1981 1982 1983 1984 198
999 2000 2001 2002 2003 2004 2005 2006 2007 2008 2009 201

1993	1992	1991	1990	1989	1988
$3,930,984	$3,405,211	$3,003,610	$2,235,244	$1,710,803	$1,203,440
1,543,991	1,316,122	1,153,080	851,072	635,972	400,060
39.3%	38.7%	38.4%	38.1%	37.2%	33.2%
365,016	329,218	287,046	242,958	167,047	101,695
1.18	1.07	0.94	0.80	0.56	0.34
308,252	306,408	304,268	302,672	300,576	301,112
0.19	0.15	0.13	0.10	0.07	0.05
265,292	435,838	11,122	127,075	169,441	19,019
22.563	19.344	13.625	10.375	4.969	3.313
13.750	8.781	6.500	4.750	2.891	1.750
$ 291,284	$ 260,050	$ 119,804	$ 90,449	$ 85,749	$ 75,357
592,986	471,202	586,594	309,476	222,924	198,470
1,165,204	964,291	662,645	561,642	419,599	295,937
2,186,269	1,871,667	1,707,236	1,093,358	824,216	707,901
15,033	69,476	29,992	25,941	34,051	30,306
300	300	300	300	300	300
1,642,819	1,328,488	1,029,582	781,012	558,597	408,567
18.125	14.500	9.938	9.813	4.750	3.031
5,499,273	4,379,574	2,993,020	2,942,679	1,417,381	899,741
24.5%	27.9%	31.7%	36.3%	34.5%	27.4%
18.0%	18.4%	20.5%	25.3%	21.8%	16.7%
4.5	3.9	4.1	5.2	5.1	5.0
3.6	3.3	2.1	3.1	2.9	2.2
15.3	13.5	10.5	12.2	8.6	9.0
$2,528,848	$2,270,880	$2,141,461	$1,755,496	$1,362,148	$ 900,417
1,085,683	919,763	664,747	334,275	241,380	233,402
178,196	75,732	56,238	29,332	32,027	21,058
138,257	138,836	141,164	116,141	75,248	48,563
$3,930,984	$3,405,211	$3,003,610	$2,235,244	$1,710,803	$1,203,440

NIKE

FINANCIAL HIGHLIGHTS

(in thousands, except per share data and financial ratios)

YEAR ENDED MAY 31,	1997	1996	% CHG
Revenues	$9,186,539	$6,470,625	42.0%
Gross margin	3,683,546	2,563,879	43.7%
Gross margin %	40.1%	39.6%	
Net income	795,822	553,190	43.9%
Net income per common share	2.68	1.88	42.6%
Return on equity	28.5%	25.2%	13.1%
Stock price at May 31	57.500	50.188	14.6%

SELECTED QUARTERLY FINANCIAL DATA (UNAUDITED)

34

(in thousands, except per share data)	1st Quarter		2nd Quarter		3rd Quarter		4th Quarter	
	1997	1996*	1997	1996*	1997	1996*	1997	1996*
Revenues	$2,281,926	$1,700,020	$2,107,034	$1,356,758	$2,423,648	$1,582,039	$2,373,931	$1,852,067
Gross margin	919,807	686,641	829,406	528,629	988,221	628,723	946,112	731,514
Gross margin %	40.3%	40.4%	39.4%	39.0%	40.8%	39.7%	39.9%	39.5%
Net income	226,063	182,098	176,872	97,812	237,133	133,874	155,754	133,727
Net income per common share	0.76	0.62	0.60	0.34	0.80	0.45	0.52	0.45
Average number of common and common equivalent shares	296,368	291,704	297,022	293,988	297,368	294,212	297,252	295,466
Cash dividends declared per common share	0.08	0.06	0.10	0.08	0.10	0.08	0.10	0.07
Price range of common stock								
High	55.625	24.188	64.000	31.313	76.375	35.688	73.125	52.063
Low	47.875	19.531	51.625	22.656	51.500	28.938	51.250	32.688

* For comparable purposes with 1997, quarterly figures for 1996 have been adjusted to reflect the elimination of the one month lag in reporting by certain of the Company's non-U.S. operations. See further discussion in Note 1 to the Consolidated Financial Statements.

972 1973 1974 1975 1976 1977 1978 1980 1981 1982 1983 1984 198
999 2000 2001 2002 2003 2004 2005 2006 2007 2008 2009 201

MANAGEMENT DISCUSSION AND ANALYSIS

HIGHLIGHTS

Fiscal year 1997 saw record revenues and earnings. Revenues and net income have now increased 13 and 11 consecutive comparable quarters, respectively.

- Revenues grew 42%, an increase of $2.7 billion, compared to the previous year increase of 36%.
- Gross margins established a new record, surpassing 40% of revenues for the first time.
- Selling and administrative costs increased 0.5%, as a percent of revenues, over the previous year.
- Net income was $795.8 million, an increase of 44%.

RESULTS OF OPERATIONS

FISCAL 1997 COMPARED TO FISCAL 1996

Significant growth in worldwide revenues and improved gross margin percentage were the primary factors contributing to record earnings for fiscal 1997 as compared to 1996. In the United States, footwear revenues increased $1 billion, or 36%, demonstrating continued market share gains and industry growth. U.S. apparel exceeded $1 billion in revenues for the first time, increasing $588.5 million, or 70%, over the previous year. Revenues from international (non-U.S.) markets increased 49% over the previous year, and now represent 38% of total revenues. Markets outside the U.S. in which the Company operates, continue to offer tremendous opportunity for growth. The Company continues to invest in infrastructure and local marketing and advertising to capitalize on these opportunities. Through aggressive worldwide marketing efforts and global infrastructure spending, the Company is positioning itself to maintain and to expand markets and gain market share on a worldwide basis.

The Company experienced revenue growth in fiscal 1997 in all breakout categories (see chart). U.S. footwear represents the largest increase in total dollars, improving by almost $1 billion, or 36%, as a result of 28% more pairs sold and a 6% increase in average selling price. The increase in average selling price was due to a change in product mix as well as increased prices in effect during the second half of the fiscal year in certain categories. Men's basketball, men's running, men's cross training, kids, and women's fitness comprise approximately 79% of the total U.S. footwear business, and individually increased 35%, 59%, 26%, 53% and 51%, respectively. Brand Jordan and Golf categories increased significantly over the prior year, improving 133% and 111%, respectively. Two categories experienced revenue reductions, men's court and outdoor, down 22% and 24%, respectively. U.S. apparel experienced growth in all categories, demonstrating the strength of the NIKE brand. Brand revenues outside of the U.S. increased $1.1 billion, or 49%. The U.S. dollar strengthened against nearly all currencies. Had the U.S. dollar remained constant with that of the prior year, non-U.S. revenues would have increased $1.4 billion, or 59%. By region, Asia Pacific increased $511 million, or 70% (84% on a constant dollar basis), Europe increased $497 million, or 38% (48% on a constant dollar basis) and the Americas (which includes Canada and Latin America) increased $137 million, or 44% (46% on a constant dollar basis). The most significant increases were in Japan, Korea, United Kingdom, Italy, and Canada. Other Brands, which includes Bauer Inc., Cole Haan, Sports Specialties, Corp., and Tetra Plastics, Inc., decreased 3% to $504 million. The Company expects revenue growth in fiscal 1998 to be affected by strong demand for the NIKE brand on a global scale, and reduced growth rates in the U.S. given the significance of the existing market share.

The breakdown of revenues follows:

(in thousands)

YEAR ENDED MAY 31,	1997	% CHG	1996	% CHG	1995	% CHG
United States footwear	$3,770,600	36%	$2,772,500	20%	$2,309,400	24%
United States apparel	1,431,000	70	842,500	99	423,900	25
Total United States	5,201,600	44	3,615,000	32	2,733,300	24
Non-U.S. footwear	2,391,000	42	1,682,300	35	1,244,300	25
Non-U.S. apparel	1,089,800	67	651,400	38	472,700	32
Total Non-U.S.	3,480,800	49	2,333,700	36	1,717,000	27
Other brands	504,100	(3)	521,900	68	310,600	38
Total NIKE	$9,186,500	42%	$6,470,600	36%	$4,760,900	26%

Gross margins increased to 40.1% of revenues in fiscal 1997, exceeding 40% for the first time in Company history. The improved percentage was principally driven by price increases in certain U.S. footwear categories in effect the second half of the year. This was offset by slight reductions in gross margin percentages from increased close-out sales as a percentage of total sales, most predominately at Bauer, due to the softening of the in-line skate market and liquidation of non-Bauer brand product to consolidate to a single Bauer brand. Global fiscal 1998 margins could be affected negatively by increasing product costs, added infrastructure to support higher levels of operations, and increased sales of lower priced product including close-outs.

Selling and administrative expenses represented 25.1% of revenues compared with 24.6% in the prior year. NIKE brand expenses increased $353 in the U.S. and $355 million outside the U.S. Increases were largely driven by increased sales and marketing spending, as well as infrastructure-related costs to support growth outside the U.S. The Company intends to continue to invest in growth opportunities and worldwide marketing and advertising in order to ensure the successful sell-through of orders discussed below.

Interest expense increased $12.8 million due to increased short-term and new long-term borrowings needed to fund the increased level of operations, including increased working capital requirements and infrastructure. See further discussion under liquidity and capital resources.

Other income/expense was a net expense of $32.3 million in fiscal 1997, compared with $36.7 million in 1996. The majority of the reduction was attributable to increased interest income, higher gain on disposal of assets and income from a new promotional event staged in Japan, offset by an one-time Bauer restructuring charge of $18 million, which includes, among other things, moving certain products to offshore production and the closing of certain facilities.

Worldwide futures and advance orders for NIKE brand athletic footwear and apparel, scheduled for delivery from June through November, 1997, were approximately $4.9 billion, 18% higher than such orders booked in the comparable period of the prior year. These orders and the percentage growth in these orders are not necessarily indicative of the growth in revenues which the Company will experience for the subsequent periods. This is because the mix of advance/futures and orders at once has shifted significantly toward advance/futures orders as the NIKE brand and futures program become more established in all areas, specifically in the non-U.S. regions. The mix of orders will continue to vary as the non-U.S. operations continue to account for a greater percentage of total revenues and place a greater emphasis on futures programs. Finally, exchange rates can cause differences in comparisons.

Since the Company operates globally, it is exposed to market risks from changes in foreign currency exchange rates. In order to minimize the effect of fluctuations on the Company's foreign currency transactions, the Company uses highly liquid foreign currency spot, forward and purchased options with high credit quality financial institutions. The Company transacts in foreign exchange contracts to hedge underlying economic exposures and does not transact in derivatives for trading or speculative purposes. Where possible, the Company nets its foreign exchange exposures to take advantage of natural offsets that occur in the normal course of business. Firmly committed transactions and the related receivables and payables may be hedged with forward exchange contracts or purchased options. Anticipated, but not yet firmly committed transactions, may be hedged through the use of purchased options. Additional information concerning the Company's hedging activities is presented in Note 14 to the Consolidated Financial Statements.

The Company's non-U.S. operations are subject to the usual risks of doing business abroad, such as the imposition of import quotas or anti-dumping duties. In 1995, the EU Commission, at the request of the European footwear manufacturers, initiated two anti-dumping investigations covering certain footwear imported from the People's Republic of China, Indonesia and Thailand. In January 1997, the Commission imposed significant provisional anti-dumping duties on textile upper shoes imported from China and Indonesia. The Commission has not yet adopted permanent measures nor measures for leather/synthetic shoes, and the Company is unable to determine whether the Commission will do so.

Nevertheless, the investigations and the anti-dumping duties expressly exclude "footwear designed for a sporting activity", and the Company does not currently believe that the Commission will change the exclusion. While the exclusion is subject to interpretation and/or amendment by customs authorities, the Company believes that most of its footwear sourced in the target countries for sale in the EU fits within the exclusion and, therefore, the Company will not be materially affected by the results of the anti-dumping investigations. If the Company's footwear were not covered by the exclusion, the Company would consider, in addition to its possible legal remedies, shifting the production of such footwear to other countries in order to maintain competitive pricing. The Company believes that it is prepared to deal effectively with any such anti-dumping measures that may arise and that any adverse impact would be of a short-term nature. The Company continues to closely monitor international trade restrictions and to adopt its multi-country sourcing strategy and contingency plans. The Company believes that its major competitors would be similarly impacted by any such restrictions.

As further explained in Note 1 to the Consolidated Financial Statements, prior to fiscal year 1997, certain of the Company's non-U.S. operations reported their results of operations on a one month lag which allowed more time to compile results. Beginning in the first quarter of fiscal year 1997, the one month lag was eliminated and the May 1996 charge from operations for these entities of $4.1 million was recorded to retained earnings. This change did not have a material effect on the annual results of operations, however, quarterly results changed as certain reporting periods shifted one month. The Selected Quarterly Data section includes adjusted quarterly data for fiscal year 1996 as if the change had been in effect.

FISCAL 1996 COMPARED TO FISCAL 1995

Significant growth in worldwide revenues and improved leverage of selling and administrative costs were the primary factors contributing to record earnings for fiscal year 1996 as compared to 1995.

The Company experienced revenue growth in fiscal 1996 in all breakout categories. The most significant increase in absolute dollars was U.S. footwear, which grew $463.2 million, or 20.1%, as a result of 19% more pairs shipped and a 0.9% increase in average selling price per pair. Men's basketball, women's fitness and men's training comprised approximately half of the U.S. footwear category in terms of total revenues, and individually increased 7%, 29% and 25%, respectively, over the prior year. U.S. apparel increased $418.6 million, or 99%, experiencing growth in all categories and demonstrating the strength of the NIKE brand. Non-U.S. brand revenues also increased significantly, growing $616.7 million, or 35.9%, as a result of increases of $438.0 million (35.2%) and $178.7 million (37.8%) in footwear and apparel, respectively, over the prior year. Non-U.S. revenues were increased 1.2% as a result of the foreign currency translation impact. All NIKE regions outside the U.S. experienced revenue increases greater than 30%. Europe increased 33%, Asia Pacific, 41%, and the Americas, 35%. The most significant increases were in Japan, Italy, United Kingdom, Korea and Canada. Other brands increased $211.3 million, or 68%, over the prior year. Bauer, which was acquired at the end of the Company's third quarter of fiscal 1995, contributed $173.7 million of the increase.

Gross margins were 39.6% in fiscal 1996 compared to 39.8% in 1995. The slight reduction in gross margins compared with 1995 was primarily driven by increased costs of air freight to meet delivery dates on increasing customer orders, and increased footwear product costs not fully recovered through the selling price. These higher expenses were partially offset by improved apparel margins due to significant increases in revenues and a reduction in close-outs as a percentage of total revenues.

Total selling and administrative expenses as a percentage of revenues decreased to 24.6% as compared to 25.4% in 1995. The reduction can be attributed primarily to significant increases in revenues. The increase in absolute dollars was $378.9 million, or 31%. U.S. operations increased $160.5 million and non-U.S. increased $176.3 million, largely a result of increased sales and marketing spending as well as infrastructure to support growth outside the U.S. Bauer accounted for $33 million of the increase.

Interest expense increased $15.3 million due primarily to the higher levels of short term borrowings needed to fund current operations. In 1995, average cash and equivalents were higher, as available cash was used to fund the acquisition of Bauer.

Other income/expense rose $25 million in expense over 1995, primarily as a result of increased goodwill amortization from the acquisition of Bauer, a reduction in interest income due to a net lower cash position compared with the prior year, and increased profit share expense due to increased earnings. These were partially offset by the absence of non-recurring specific obligations which occurred in the prior year related to the shutdown for certain facilities in conjunction with the consolidation of European warehouses.

LIQUIDITY AND CAPITAL RESOURCES

The Company's financial position was very strong at May 31, 1997. Compared to May 31, 1996, total assets grew 36%, or $1.4 billion, to $5.4 billion, and shareholders' equity increased 30%, or $724 million, to $3.2 billion. Working capital increased $704 million, and the Company's current ratio increased to 2.1 at May 31, 1997 from 1.9 at 1996 fiscal year-end.

Cash provided by operations decreased slightly to $323 million for the year ended May 31, 1997, primarily due to improved operating results offset by increased working capital requirements, given the global growth of the Company. Specifically, inventories increased $417 million, representing growth in nearly all areas of the Company. U.S. footwear and apparel inventories increased $71 million (31%) and $52 million (29%), respectively. The largest increases outside of the U.S. were in the European and Asia/Pacific regions with increases of $121 million (54%) and $119 million (134%), respectively, due primarily to the significant increase in operations. Inventory turns on a consolidated basis reduced to approximately 4.8 times, as compared with 5.0 in fiscal 1996. Accounts receivable increased $486 million due, in part, to the higher level of fourth quarter revenues compared with the previous year.

Additions to property, plant and equipment for fiscal 1997 were $466 million, an increase of $250 million over 1996. Additions in the U.S. totaled $266 million for the year due to continued overall expansion of U.S. operations which includes warehouse locations, management information systems, world headquarters expansion and the continued development of NIKETOWN retail locations. Outside the U.S., additions totaled $172 million, compared to $154 million for fiscal 1996, and relates to the continued expansion of infrastructure, investments in information systems and new NIKE retail locations. The remaining additions relate to other brands. Expected capital expenditures for fiscal 1998 approximate $680 million, with the primary components consisting of the continued expansion of the world headquarters, new NIKETOWN retail locations and warehouse expansion in the U.S., Japan and Korea.

Additions to long-term debt of approximately $300 million in fiscal 1997, were used to fund the significant increase in property, plant and equipment, as well as increased working capital requirements. In June 1996, the Company's Japanese subsidiary borrowed 10.5 billion Yen (approximately $100 million) in a private placement, maturing June 26, 2011, to fund construction of a warehouse and distribution center and for other corporate purposes. Additionally, during December 1996 the Company filed a shelf

972 1973 1974 1975 1976 1977 1978 1980 1981 1982 1983 1984 198
999 2000 2001 2002 2003 2004 2005 2006 2007 2008 2009 201

registration statement with the Securities and Exchange Commission for the sale of up to $500 million of debt securities. The filing will enable the Company to issue debt from time to time during the next several years. Under this program, the Company issued $200 million seven-year notes in December 1996, maturing December 1, 2003, and subsequent to May 31, 1997, an additional $100 million medium-term notes were issued, maturing in three to five years. The proceeds were swapped into Dutch Guilders to obtain long-term fixed rate financing to support the growth of the Company's European operations.

Management believes that significant funds generated by operations, together with access to sufficient sources of funds, will adequately meet its anticipated operating, global infrastructure expansion and capital needs. Significant short and long-term lines of credit are maintained with banks which, along with cash on hand, provide adequate operating liquidity. Liquidity is also provided by the Company's commercial paper program under which there was $0 outstanding at both May 31, 1997 and 1996.

Dividends per share of common stock for fiscal 1997 rose $.09 over fiscal 1996 to $.38 per share. Dividend declaration in all four quarters has been consistent since February 1984. Based upon current projected earnings and cash flow requirements, the Company anticipates continuing a dividend and reviewing its amount at the November Board of Directors meeting. The Company's policy continues to target an annual dividend in the range of 15% to 25% of trailing twelve-month earnings.

During fiscal 1994, the Company announced that the Executive Committee of its Board of Directors, acting within limits set by the Board, authorized a plan to repurchase a maximum of $450 million NIKE Class B Common Stock over a period of up to three years. During fiscal 1996, the Board of Directors voted to extend the 1994 stock repurchase program until July 1, 1999. Funding has, and is expected to continue to, come from operating cash flow in combination with occasional short or medium-term borrowings. The timing and the amount of shares purchased will be dictated by working capital needs and stock market conditions. The Company did not repurchase any shares during fiscal 1997 and, as of May 31, 1997, the Company had repurchased 20.6 million shares at a total cost of $301.7 million.

Special Note Regarding Forward-Looking Statements and Analyst Reports

Certain written and oral statements made or incorporated by reference from time to time by NIKE or its representatives this report, other reports, filings with the Securities and Exchange Commission, press releases, conferences, or otherwise, are "forward-looking statements" within the meaning of the Private Securities Litigation Reform Act of 1995 ("the Act"). Forward-looking statements include, without limitation, any statement that may predict, forecast, indicate, or imply future results, performance, or achievements, and may contain the words "believe," "anticipate," "expect," "estimate," "project," "will be," "will continue," "will likely result," or words or phrases of similar meaning. Forward-looking statements involve risks and uncertainties which may cause actual results to differ materially from the forward-looking statements. The risks and uncertainties are detailed from time to time in reports filed by NIKE with the S.E.C., including Forms 8-K, 10-Q, and 10-K, and include, among others, the following: international, national and local general economic and market conditions; the size and growth of the overall athletic footwear, apparel, and equipment markets; intense competition among designers, marketers, distributors and sellers of athletic footwear, apparel, and equipment for consumers and endorsers; demographic changes; changes in consumer preferences; popularity of particular designs, categories of products, and sports; seasonal and geographic demand for NIKE products; the size, timing and mix of purchases of NIKE's products; fluctuations and difficulty in forecasting operating results, including, without limitation, the fact that advance "futures" orders may not be indicative of future revenues due to the changing mix of futures and at-once orders; the ability of NIKE to sustain, manage or forecast its growth; new product development and introduction; the ability to secure and protect trademarks, patents, and other intellectual property; performance and reliability of products; customer service; adverse publicity; the loss of significant customers or suppliers; dependence on distributors; business disruptions; increased costs of freight and transportation to meet delivery deadlines; changes in business strategy or development plans; general risks associated with doing business outside the United States, including, without limitation, import duties, tariffs, quotas and political instability; changes in government regulations; liability and other claims asserted against NIKE; the ability to attract and retain qualified personnel; and other factors referenced or incorporated by reference in this report and other reports. The risks included here are not exhaustive. Other sections of this report may include additional factors which could adversely impact NIKE's business and financial performance. Moreover, NIKE operates in a very competitive and rapidly changing environment. New risk factors emerge from time to time and it is not possible for management to predict all such risk factors, nor can it assess the impact of all such risk factors on NIKE's business or the extent to which any factor, or combination of factors, may cause actual results to differ materially from those contained in any forward-looking statements. Given these risks and uncertainties, investors should not place undue reliance on forward-looking statements as a prediction of actual results.

FINANCIAL REPORTING

Management of NIKE, Inc. is responsible for the information and representations contained in this report. The financial statements have been prepared in conformity with the generally accepted accounting principles we considered appropriate in the circumstances and include some amounts based on our best estimates and judgments. Other financial information in this report is consistent with these financial statements.

The Company's accounting systems include controls designed to reasonably assure that assets are safeguarded from unauthorized use or disposition and which provide for the preparation of financial statements in conformity with generally accepted accounting principles. These systems are supplemented by the selection and training of qualified financial personnel and an organizational structure providing for appropriate segregation of duties.

An Internal Audit department reviews the results of its work with the Audit Committee of the Board of Directors, presently consisting of three outside directors of the Company. The Audit Committee is responsible for recommending to the Board of Directors the appointment of the independent accountants and reviews with the independent accountants, management and the internal audit staff, the scope and the results of the annual examination, the effectiveness of the accounting control system and other matters relating to the financial affairs of the Company as they deem appropriate. The independent accountants and the internal auditors have full access to the Committee, with and without the presence of management, to discuss any appropriate matters.

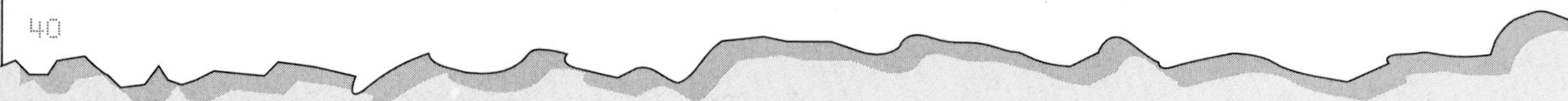

REPORT OF INDEPENDENT ACCOUNTANTS

Portland, Oregon
June 27, 1997
To the Board of Directors and
Shareholders of NIKE, Inc.

In our opinion, the accompanying consolidated balance sheet and the related consolidated statements of income, of cash flows and of shareholders' equity present fairly, in all material respects, the financial position of NIKE, Inc. and its subsidiaries at May 31, 1997 and 1996, and the results of their operations and their cash flows for each of the three years in the period ended May 31, 1997, in conformity with generally accepted accounting principles. These financial statements are the responsibility of the Company's management; our responsibility is to express an opinion on these financial statements based on our audits. We conducted our audits of these statements in accordance with generally accepted auditing standards which require that we plan and perform the audit to obtain reasonable assurance about whether the financial statements are free of material misstatement. An audit includes examining, on a test basis, evidence supporting the amounts and disclosures in the financial statements, assessing the accounting principles used and significant estimates made by management, and evaluating the overall financial statement presentation. We believe that our audits provide a reasonable basis for the opinion expressed above.

Price Waterhouse LLP

NIKE, INC. CONSOLIDATED STATEMENT OF INCOME

(in thousands, except per share data)

YEAR ENDED MAY 31,	1997	1996	1995
Revenues	$9,186,539	$6,470,625	$4,760,834
Costs and expenses:			
Costs of sales	5,502,993	3,906,746	2,865,280
Selling and administrative	2,303,704	1,588,612	1,209,760
Interest expense (Notes 4 and 5)	52,343	39,498	24,208
Other income/expense, net (Notes 1, 9 and 10)	32,277	36,679	11,722
	7,891,317	5,571,535	4,110,970
Income before income taxes	1,295,222	899,090	649,864
Income taxes (Note 6)	499,400	345,900	250,200
Net income	$ 795,822	$ 553,190	$ 399,664
Net income per common share (Note 1)	$ 2.68	$ 1.88	$ 1.36
Average number of common and common equivalent shares (Note 1)	297,000	293,608	294,012

The accompanying notes to consolidated financial statements are an integral part of this statement.

972 1973 1974 1975 1976 1977 1978 1980 1981 1982 1983 1984 198
999 2000 2001 2002 2003 2004 2005 2006 2007 2008 2009 201

NIKE, INC. CONSOLIDATED BALANCE SHEET

(in thousands)

MAY 31,	1997	1996
Assets		
Current Assets:		
Cash and equivalents	$ 445,421	$ 262,117
Accounts receivable, less allowance for doubtful accounts of $57,233 and $43,372	1,754,137	1,346,125
Inventories (Note 2)	1,338,640	931,151
Deferred income taxes (Note 6)	135,663	93,120
Prepaid expenses (Note 1)	157,058	94,427
Total current assets	3,830,919	2,726,940
Property, plant and equipment, net (Notes 3 and 5)	922,369	643,459
Identifiable intangible assets and goodwill (Note 1)	464,191	474,812
Deferred income taxes and other assets (Notes 1 and 6)	143,728	106,417
Total assets	$5,361,207	$3,951,628
Liabilities and Shareholders' Equity		
Current Liabilities:		
Current portion of long-term debt (Note 5)	$ 2,216	$ 7,301
Notes payable (Note 4)	553,153	445,064
Accounts payable (Note 4)	687,121	455,034
Accrued liabilities	570,504	480,407
Income taxes payable	53,923	79,253
Total current liabilities	1,866,917	1,467,059
Long-term debt (Notes 5 and 13)	296,020	9,584
Deferred income taxes and other liabilities (Notes 1 and 6)	42,132	43,285
Commitments and contingencies (Notes 11 and 14)	—	—
Redeemable Preferred Stock (Note 7)	300	300
Shareholders' equity (Note 8):		
Common Stock at stated value:		
Class A convertible – 101,711 and 102,240 shares outstanding	152	153
Class B – 187,559 and 185,018 shares outstanding	2,706	2,702
Capital in excess of stated value	210,650	154,833
Foreign currency translation adjustment	(31,333)	(16,501)
Retained earnings	2,973,663	2,290,213
Total shareholders' equity	3,155,838	2,431,400
Total liabilities and shareholders' equity	$5,361,207	$3,951,628

The accompanying notes to consolidated financial statements are an integral part of this statement.

NIKE, INC. CONSOLIDATED STATEMENT OF CASH FLOWS

(in thousands)

YEAR ENDED MAY 31,	1997	1996	1995
Cash provided (used) by operations:			
Net income	$795,822	$553,190	$399,664
Income charges (credits) not affecting cash:			
Depreciation	138,038	97,179	71,113
Deferred income taxes and purchased tax benefits	(47,146)	(73,279)	(24,668)
Amortization and other	30,291	32,685	14,966
Changes in certain working capital components:			
Increase in inventories	(416,706)	(301,409)	(69,676)
Increase in accounts receivable	(485,595)	(292,888)	(301,648)
Increase in other current assets	(56,928)	(20,054)	(10,276)
Increase in accounts payable, accrued liabilities and income taxes payable	365,344	344,248	175,438
Cash provided by operations	323,120	339,672	254,913
Cash provided (used) by investing activities:			
Additions to property, plant and equipment	(465,908)	(216,384)	(154,125)
Disposals of property, plant and equipment	24,294	12,775	9,011
Increase in other assets	(43,829)	(26,376)	(9,499)
(Decrease) increase in other liabilities	(10,833)	(9,651)	3,239
Acquisition of subsidiaries:			
Identifiable intangible assets and goodwill	—	—	(345,901)
Net assets acquired	—	—	(84,119)
Cash used by investing activities	(496,276)	(239,636)	(581,394)
Cash provided (used) by financing activities:			
Additions to long-term debt	300,500	5,044	2,971
Reductions in long-term debt including current portion	(5,190)	(30,352)	(39,804)
Increase in notes payable	92,926	47,964	263,874
Proceeds from exercise of options	26,282	21,150	6,154
Repurchase of stock	—	(18,756)	(142,919)
Dividends – common and preferred	(100,896)	(78,834)	(65,418)
Cash provided (used) by financing activities	313,622	(53,784)	24,858
Effect of exchange rate changes on cash	(166)	(206)	(1,122)
Effect of May 1996 cash flow activity for certain subsidiaries (Note 1)	43,004	—	—
Net increase (decrease) in cash and equivalents	183,304	46,046	(302,745)
Cash and equivalents, beginning of year	262,117	216,071	518,816
Cash and equivalents, end of year	$445,421	$262,117	$216,071
Supplemental disclosure of cash flow information:			
Cash paid during the year for:			
Interest (net of amount capitalized)	$ 44,000	$ 32,800	$ 20,200
Income taxes	543,100	359,300	285,400

The accompanying notes to consolidated financial statements are an integral part of this statement.

NIKE, INC. CONSOLIDATED STATEMENT OF SHAREHOLDERS' EQUITY

	Common Stock				Capital In	Foreign		
	Class A		Class B		Excess	Currency		
(in thousands)	Shares	Amount	Shares	Amount	Of Stated Value	Translation Adjustment	Retained Earnings	Total
Balance at May 31, 1994	26,679	$159	46,521	$2,704	$108,284	$(15,123)	$1,644,925	$1,740,949
Stock options exercised			241	2	8,954			8,956
Conversion to Class B Common Stock	(784)	(4)	784	4				—
Repurchase of Class B Common Stock			(2,130)	(13)	(4,801)		(138,106)	(142,920)
Stock issued pursuant to contractual obligations			134	1	9,999			10,000
Translation of statements of non-U.S. operations						16,708		16,708
Net income							399,664	399,664
Dividends on Redeemable Preferred Stock							(30)	(30)
Dividends on Common Stock							(68,638)	(68,638)
Balance at May 31, 1995	25,895	155	45,550	2,698	122,436	1,585	1,837,815	1,964,689
Stock options exercised				3	32,848			32,851
Conversion to Class B Common Stock	(655)	(2)		2				—
Repurchase of Class B Common Stock				(1)	(451)		(18,304)	(18,756)
Two-for-one Stock Split October 30, 1995	25,880							
Translation of statements of non-U.S. operations						(18,086)		(18,086)
Net income							553,190	553,190
Dividends on Redeemable Preferred Stock							(30)	(30)
Dividends on Common Stock							(82,458)	(82,458)
Balance at May 31, 1996	51,120	153	92,509	2,702	154,833	(16,501)	2,290,213	2,431,400
Stock options exercised			1,475	3	55,817			55,820
Conversion to Class B Common Stock	(279)	(1)	279	1				—
Two-for-one Stock Split October 23, 1996	50,870		93,296					
Translation of statements of non-U.S. operations						(14,832)		(14,832)
Net income							795,822	795,822
Dividends on Redeemable Preferred Stock							(30)	(30)
Dividends on Common Stock							(108,249)	(108,249)
Net income for the month ended May 1996, due to the change in fiscal year-end of certain non-U.S. operations (Note 1)							(4,093)	(4,093)
Balance at May 31, 1997	101,711	$152	187,559	$2,706	$210,650	($31,333)	$2,973,663	$3,155,838

The accompanying notes to consolidated financial statements are an integral part of this statement.

NIKE, INC. NOTES TO CONSOLIDATED FINANCIAL STATEMENTS

NOTE 1 – SUMMARY OF SIGNIFICANT ACCOUNTING POLICIES:

Basis of consolidation:

The consolidated financial statements include the accounts of the Company and its subsidiaries. All significant intercompany transactions and balances have been eliminated. Prior to fiscal year 1997, certain of the Company's non-U.S. operations reported their results of operations on a one month lag which allowed more time to compile results. Beginning in the first quarter of fiscal year 1997, the one month lag was eliminated. As a result, the May 1996 charge from operations for these entities of $4,093,000 was recorded to retained earnings in the first quarter of the current year.

Recognition of revenues:

Revenues recognized include sales plus fees earned on sales by licensees.

Advertising:

Advertising production costs are expensed the first time the advertisement is run. Media (TV and print) placement costs are expensed in the month the advertising appears. Total advertising and promotion expenses were $978,251,000, $642,498,000 and $495,006,000 for the years ended May 31, 1997, 1996 and 1995, respectively. Included in prepaid expenses and other assets was $111,925,000 and $69,340,000 at May 31, 1997 and 1996, respectively, relating to prepaid advertising and promotion expenses.

Cash and equivalents:

Cash and equivalents represent cash and short-term, highly liquid investments with original maturities three months or less.

Inventory valuation:

Inventories are stated at the lower of cost or market. Cost is determined using the last-in, first-out (LIFO) method for substantially all U.S. inventories. Non-U.S. inventories are valued on a first-in, first-out (FIFO) basis.

Property, plant and equipment and depreciation:

Property, plant and equipment are recorded at cost. Depreciation for financial reporting purposes is determined on a straight-line basis for buildings and leasehold improvements and principally on a declining balance basis for machinery and equipment, based upon estimated useful lives ranging from two to thirty years.

Identifiable intangible assets and goodwill:

At May 31, 1997 and 1996, the Company had patents, trademarks and other identifiable intangible assets with a value of $219,186,000 and $209,586,000, respectively. The Company's excess of purchase cost over the fair value of net assets of businesses acquired (goodwill) was $326,252,000 and $327,555,000 at May 31, 1997 and 1996, respectively.

Identifiable intangible assets and goodwill are being amortized over their estimated useful lives on a straight-line basis over five to forty years. Accumulated amortization was $81,247,000 and $62,329,000 at May 31, 1997 and 1996, respectively. Amortization expense, which is included in other income/expense, was $19,765,000, $21,772,000 and $13,176,000 for the years ended May 31, 1997, 1996 and 1995, respectively. Intangible assets are periodically reviewed by the Company for impairments where the fair value is less than the carrying value.

Other liabilities:

Other liabilities include amounts with settlement dates beyond one year, and are primarily composed of long-term deferred endorsement payments of $15,815,000 and $21,674,000 at May 31, 1997 and 1996, respectively. Deferred payments to endorsers relate to amounts due beyond contract termination, which are discounted at various interest rates and accrued over the contract period.

972 1973 1974 1975 1976 1977 1978 1980 1981 1982 1983 1984 198
999 2000 2001 2002 2003 2004 2005 2006 2007 2008 2009 201

Endorsement contracts:

Accounting for endorsement contracts is based upon specific contract provisions. Generally, endorsement payments are expensed uniformly over the term of the contract after giving recognition to periodic performance compliance provisions of the contracts. Contracts requiring prepayments are included in prepaid expenses or other assets depending on the length of the contract.

Foreign currency translation:

Adjustments resulting from translating foreign functional currency financial statements into U.S. dollars are included in the foreign currency translation adjustment in shareholders' equity.

Derivatives:

The Company enters into foreign currency contracts in order to reduce the impact of certain foreign currency fluctuations. Firmly committed transactions and the related receivables and payables may be hedged with forward exchange contracts or purchased options. Anticipated, but not yet firmly committed, transactions may be hedged through the use of purchased options. Premiums paid on purchased options and any gains are included in prepaid expenses or accrued liabilities and are recognized in earnings when the transaction being hedged is recognized. Gains and losses arising from foreign currency forward and option contracts, and cross-currency swap transactions are recognized in income or expense as offsets of gains and losses resulting from the underlying hedged transactions. Cash flows from risk management activities are classified in the same category as the cash flows from the related investment, borrowing or foreign exchange activity. See Note 14 for further discussion.

Income taxes:

Income taxes are provided currently on financial statement earnings of non-U.S. subsidiaries expected to be repatriated. The Company intends to determine annually the amount of undistributed non-U.S. earnings to invest indefinitely in its non-U.S. operations.

The Company accounts for income taxes using the asset and liability method. This approach requires the recognition of deferred tax liabilities and assets for the expected future tax consequences of temporary differences between the carrying amounts and the tax bases of other assets and liabilities. See Note 6 for further discussion.

Net income per common share:

Net income per common share is computed based on the weighted average number of common and common equivalent (stock option) shares outstanding for the periods reported.

On October 23, 1996 and October 30, 1995, the Company issued additional shares in connection with two-for-one stock splits effected in the form of a 100% stock dividend on outstanding Class A and Class B common stock. The per common share amounts in the Consolidated Financial Statements and accompanying notes have been adjusted to reflect these stock splits.

Management estimates:

The preparation of financial statements in conformity with generally accepted accounting principles requires management to make estimates, including estimates relating to assumptions that affect the reported amounts of assets and liabilities and disclosure of contingent assets and liabilities at the date of financial statements and the reported amounts of revenues and expenses during the reporting period. Actual results could differ from these estimates.

Reclassifications:

Certain prior year amounts have been reclassified to conform to fiscal 1997 presentation. These changes had no impact on previously reported results of operations or shareholders' equity.

NOTE 2 – INVENTORIES:

Inventories by major classification are as follows:

(in thousands)

MAY 31,	1997	1996
Finished goods	$1,248,401	$874,700
Work-in-progress	50,245	28,940
Raw materials	39,994	27,511
	$1,338,640	$931,151

The excess of replacement cost over LIFO cost was $20,716,000 at May 31, 1997, and $16,023,000 at May 31,1996.

NOTE 3 – PROPERTY, PLANT AND EQUIPMENT:

Property, plant and equipment includes the following:

(in thousands)

MAY 31,	1997	1996
Land	$ 90,792	$ 75,369
Buildings	241,062	246,602
Machinery and equipment	735,739	572,396
Leasehold improvements	206,593	83,678
Construction in process	151,561	69,660
	1,425,747	1,047,705
Less accumulated depreciation	503,378	404,246
	$ 922,369	$ 643,459

Capitalized interest expense was $2,765,000, $858,000 and $261,000 for the fiscal years ended May 31, 1997, 1996 and 1995 respectively.

972 1973 1974 1975 1976 1977 1978 1980 1981 1982 1983 1984 198
999 2000 2001 2002 2003 2004 2005 2006 2007 2008 2009 201

NIKE

NOTE 4 – SHORT-TERM BORROWINGS AND CREDIT LINES:

Notes payable to banks and interest bearing accounts payable to Nissho Iwai American Corporation (NIAC) are summarized below:

(in thousands)

MAY 31,	1997 Borrowings	1997 Interest Rate	1996 Borrowings	1996 Interest Rate
Banks:				
Non-U.S. Operations	$553,153	4.08%	$445,064	4.38%
	$553,153		$445,064	
NIAC	$414,132	6.14%	$237,413	5.80%

The Company has outstanding loans at interest rates at various spreads above the banks' cost of funds for financing non-U.S. national operations. Certain of these loans can be secured by accounts receivable and inventory.

The Company purchases through Nissho Iwai American Corporation ("NIAC") substantially all of the athletic footwear and apparel it acquires from non-U.S. suppliers. Accounts payable to NIAC are generally due up to 120 days after shipment of goods from the foreign port. Interest on such accounts payable accrues at the ninety day London Interbank Offered Rate (LIBOR) as of the beginning of the month of the invoice date, plus .30%.

At May 31, 1997 and 1996, the Company had no outstanding borrowings under its $500 million unsecured multiple option facility with ten banks, which matures on October 31, 2001. This agreement contains optional borrowing alternatives consisting of a committed revolving loan facility and a competitive bid facility. The interest rate charged on this agreement is determined by the borrowing option and, under the committed revolving loan facility, is either the LIBOR plus .19% or the higher of the Fed Funds rate plus .50% or the Prime Rate. The agreement provides for annual fees of .07% of the total commitment. Under the agreement, the Company must maintain, among other things, certain minimum specified financial ratios with which the Company was in compliance at May 31, 1997.

Ratings for the Company to issue commercial paper, which is required to be supported by committed and uncommitted lines of credit, are A1 by Standard and Poor's Corporation and P1 by Moody's Investor Service. There were no amounts outstanding at May 31, 1997 or May 31, 1996 under these arrangements.

NOTE 5 – LONG-TERM DEBT:

Long-term debt includes the following:

(in thousands)

MAY 31,	1997	1996
6.375% Medium term notes, payable December 1, 2003	$199,211	$ —
4.30% Japanese yen notes, payable June 26, 2011	92,373	—
9.43% capital warehouse lease	—	7,485
Other	6,652	9,400
Total	298,236	16,885
Less current maturities	2,216	7,301
	$296,020	$ 9,584

In December of 1996, the Company filed a $500 million shelf registration with the Securities and Exhange Commission and issued $200 million seven-year notes, maturing December 1, 2003. The proceeds were subsequently exchanged for Dutch Guilders and loaned to a European subsidiary. Interest on the loan is paid semi-annually. The Company entered into swap transactions reducing the effective interest rate to 5.64% as well as to hedge the foreign currency exposure related to the repayment of the intercompany loan. In June of 1997, the Company issued an additional $100 million medium term notes under this program with maturities of June 16, 2000 and June 17, 2002.

In June of 1996, the Company's Japanese subsidiary borrowed 10.5 billion yen in a private placement with a maturity of June 26, 2011. Interest is paid semi-annually. The agreement provides for early retirement after year ten.

The Company's long-term debt ratings are A+ by Standard and Poor's Corporation and A1 by Moody's Investor Service.

Amounts of long-term maturities in each of the five fiscal years 1998 through 2002, respectively, are $2,216,000, $1,891,000, $2,187,000, $188,000 and $47,000.

972 1973 1974 1975 1976 1977 1978 1980 1981 1982 1983 1984 198
999 2000 2001 2002 2003 2004 2005 2006 2007 2008 2009 201

NIKE

NOTE 6 – INCOME TAXES:

Income before income taxes and the provision for income taxes are as follows:

(in thousands)

YEAR ENDED MAY 31,	1997	1996	1995
Income before income taxes:			
United States	$1,008,023	$ 644,755	$ 467,548
Foreign	287,199	254,335	182,316
	$1,295,222	$ 899,090	$ 649,864
Provision for income taxes:			
Current:			
United States			
Federal	$ 359,408	$ 247,526	$ 172,127
State	74,716	42,622	34,764
Foreign	112,679	127,345	75,964
	546,803	417,493	282,855
Deferred:			
United States			
Federal	(21,097)	(33,003)	(25,689)
State	(5,062)	(7,657)	(2,430)
Foreign	(21,244)	(30,933)	(4,536)
	(47,403)	(71,593)	(32,655)
	$ 499,400	$ 345,900	$ 250,200

51

During fiscal 1994 the Company permanently reinvested approximately $56,000,000 of its undistributed non-U.S.earnings in certain subsidiaries.

A benefit has been recognized for foreign loss carry forwards of $138,500,000 and $96,600,000 at May 31, 1997 and 1996, respectively, which have no expiration. As of May 31, 1997, the Company has utilized all foreign tax credits.

1985 1986 1987 1988 1989 1990 1991 1992 1993 1994 1996 1997 1998
2010 2011 2012 2013 2014 2015 2016 2017 2018 2019 2020 2021 2022

Deferred tax liabilities (assets) are comprised of the following:

(in thousands)

MAY 31,	1997	1996
Undistributed earnings of foreign subsidiaries	$ 3,026	$ 3,220
Other	13,017	12,040
Gross deferred tax liabilities	16,043	15,260
Allowance for doubtful accounts	(16,092)	(9,050)
Inventory reserves	(30,347)	(20,796)
Deferred compensation	(26,659)	(17,583)
Reserves and accrued liabilities	(50,738)	(42,870)
Tax basis inventory adjustment	(19,263)	(12,363)
Depreciation	(8,379)	(2,594)
Foreign loss carry forwards	(32,100)	(25,162)
Other	(9,582)	(12,978)
Gross deferred tax assets	(193,160)	(143,396)
Net deferred tax assets	$(177,117)	$(128,136)

A reconciliation from the U.S. statutory federal income tax rate to the effective income tax rate follows:

YEAR ENDED MAY 31,	1997	1996	1995
U.S. Federal statutory rate	35.0%	35.0%	35.0%
State income taxes, net of federal benefit	3.5	2.6	3.2
Other, net	.1	.9	.3
Effective income tax rate	38.6%	38.5%	38.5%

NOTE 7 – REDEEMABLE PREFERRED STOCK:

NIAC is the sole owner of the Company's authorized Redeemable Preferred Stock, $1 par value, which is redeemable at the option of NIAC at par value aggregating $300,000. A cumulative dividend of $.10 per share is payable annually on May 31 and no dividends may be declared or paid on the Common Stock of the Company unless dividends on the Redeemable Preferred Stock have been declared and paid in full. There have been no changes in the Redeemable Preferred Stock in the three years ended May 31, 1997. As the holder of the Redeemable Preferred Stock, NIAC does not have general voting rights but does have the right to vote as a separate class on the sale of all or substantially all of the assets of the Company and its subsidiaries, on merger, consolidation, liquidation or dissolution of the Company or on the sale or assignment of the NIKE trademark for athletic footwear sold in the United States.

972 1973 1974 1975 1976 1977 1978 1980 1981 1982 1983 1984 198
999 2000 2001 2002 2003 2004 2005 2006 2007 2008 2009 201

NOTE 8 – COMMON STOCK:

The authorized number of shares of Class A Common Stock no par value and Class B Common Stock no par value are 110,000,000 and 350,000,000, respectively. The Company announced a two-for-one stock split which was effected in the form of a 100% stock dividend on outstanding Class A and Class B Common Stock, paid October 23, 1996. In the previous year a similar two-for-one stock split was announced, paid October 30, 1995. Each share of Class A Common Stock is convertible into one share of Class B Common Stock. Voting rights of Class B Common Stock are limited in certain circumstances with respect to the election of directors.

The Company's Employee Incentive Compensation Plan (the "1980 Plan") was adopted in 1980 and expired on December 31, 1990. The 1980 Plan provided for the issuance of up to 13,440,000 shares of the Company's Class B Common Stock in connection with the exercise of stock options granted under such plan. No further grants will be made under the 1980 Plan.

In 1990, the Board of Directors adopted, and the shareholders approved, the NIKE, Inc. 1990 Stock Incentive Plan (the "1990 Plan"). The 1990 Plan provides for the issuance of up to 16,000,000 shares of Class B Common Stock in connection with stock options and other awards granted under such plan. The 1990 Plan authorizes the grant of incentive stock options, non-statutory stock options, stock appreciation rights, stock bonuses, and the sale of restricted stock. The exercise price for incentive stock options may not be less than the fair market value of the underlying shares on the date of grant. The exercise price for non-statutory stock options and stock appreciation rights, and the purchase price of restricted stock, may not be less than 75% of the fair market value of the underlying shares on the date of grant. No consideration will be paid for stock bonuses awarded under the 1990 Plan. The 1990 Plan is administered by a committee of the Board of Directors. The committee has the authority to determine the employees to whom awards will be made, the amount of the awards, and the other terms and conditions of the awards. As of May 31, 1997, the committee has granted substantially all non-statutory stock options at 100% of fair market value on the date of grant under the 1990 Plan.

In addition to the option plans discussed above, the Company has several agreements outside of the plans with certain directors, endorsers and employees. As of May 31, 1997, 7,754,000 options with exercise prices ranging from $0.417 per share to $53.625 per share had been granted. The aggregate compensation expenses related to these agreements is $9,530,000 and is being amortized over vesting periods from October 1980 through September 2000. The outstanding agreements expire from December 1998 through September 2006.

During 1995, the Financial Accounting Standards Board issued SFAS 123, "Accounting for Stock Based Compensation," which defines a fair value method of accounting for an employee stock option or similar equity instrument and encouraged, but does not require, all entities to adopt that method of accounting. Entities electing not to adopt the fair value method of accounting must make pro forma disclosures of net income and earnings per share, as if the fair value based method of accounting defined in this statement has been applied.

The Company has elected not to adopt the fair value method; however, as required by SFAS 123, the Company has computed for pro forma disclosure purposes the value of options granted during fiscal years 1997 and 1996 using the Black-Scholes option pricing model. The weighted average assumptions used for stock option grants for 1997 and 1996 were a dividend yield of 1%, expected volatility of the market price of the Company's common stock of 30%, a weighted-average expected life of the options of approximately five years, and interest rates of 6.42 and 6.56 for fiscal 1997 and 5.92 and 5.97 for fiscal 1996. These interest rates are reflective of option grant dates made throughout the year.

Options were assumed to be exercised over the 5 year expected life for purposes of this valuation. Adjustments for forfeitures are made as they occur. For the years ended May 31, 1997 and 1996, the total value of the options granted, for which no previous expense has been recognized, was computed as approximately $29,074,000 and $18,167,000, respectively, which would be amortized on a straight line basis over the vesting period of the options. The weighted average fair value per share of the options granted in 1997 and 1996 are $17.39 and $7.15, respectively.

If the Company had accounted for these stock options issued to employees in accordance with SFAS 123, the Company's net income and pro forma net income and net income per share and pro forma net income per share would have been reported as follows:

YEAR ENDED MAY 31,	1997		1996	
	Net Income	EPS	Net Income	EPS
As Reported	$795,822	$2.68	$553,190	$1.88
Pro Forma	788,692	2.66	550,426	1.87

The pro forma effects of applying SFAS 123 may not be representative of the effects on reported net income and earnings per share for future years since options vest over several years and additional awards are made each year.

The following summarizes the stock option transactions under plans discussed above (adjusted for all applicable stock splits):

	Shares (in thousands)	Weighted Average Option Price
Options outstanding May 31, 1995	11,916	$10.87
Exercised	(2,281)	7.90
Surrendered	(66)	17.07
Granted	2,690	21.25
Options outstanding May 31, 1996	12,259	13.67
Exercised	(2,012)	11.28
Surrendered	(55)	23.50
Granted	1.692	48.93
Options outstanding May 31, 1997	11,884	19.05
Options exercisable at May 31,		
1996	4,225	8.35
1997	5,219	11.33

The following table sets forth the exercise prices, the number of options outstanding and exercisable, and the remaining contractual lives of the Company's stock options at May 31, 1997:

Exercise Price	Number of Options Outstanding (thousands)	Weighted Average Exercise price	Weighted Average Contractual Life Remaining (years)	Number of Options Exercisable (thousands)	Weighted Average Exercise price
$ 3.125 – $ 9.563	2,841	$ 7.56	2.90	2,841	$ 7.56
11.250 – 14.188	3,027	13.73	5.76	1,108	14.00
14.219 – 21.000	4,132	18.40	7.65	1,263	17.35
22.813 – 71.875	1,884	46.32	8.68	7	32.78

NOTE 9 – BENEFIT PLANS:

The Company has a profit sharing plan available to substantially all employees. The terms of the plan call for annual contributions by the Company as determined by the Board of Directors. Contributions of $18,500,000, $15,500,000 and $11,200,000 to the plan are included in other expense in the consolidated financial statements for the years ended May 31, 1997, 1996 and 1995, respectively.

The Company has a voluntary 401(k) employee savings plan. The Company matches with Common Stock a portion of employee contributions, vesting that portion over 5 years. Company contributions to the savings plan were $6,349,000, $4,660,000 and $3,363,000 for the years ended May 31, 1997, 1996 and 1995, respectively.

NOTE 10 – OTHER INCOME/EXPENSE, NET:

Included in other income/expense for the years ended May 31, 1997, 1996 and 1995, is interest income of $20,089,000, $16,083,000 and $26,094,000, respectively. During the year, the Company's subsidiary, Bauer Inc, recognized a one-time restructuring charge of $18,096,000 for a plan which includes, among other things, moving certain products to offshore production and the closing of certain facilities. The Company recognized $11,412,000 in non-recurring specific obligations associated with the
55 shutdown of certain facilities in conjunction with the consolidation of European warehouses for the year ended May 31, 1995.

NOTE 11 – COMMITMENTS AND CONTINGENCIES:

The Company leases space for its offices, warehouses and retail stores under leases expiring from one to twenty years after May 31, 1997. Rent expense aggregated $84,109,000, $52,483,000 and $43,506,000 for the years ended May 31, 1997, 1996 and 1995, respectively. Amounts of minimum future annual rental commitments under non-cancellable operating leases in each of the five fiscal years 1998 through 2002 are $76,319,000, $65,315,000, $53,776,000, $46,125,000, $42,274,000, respectively, and $326,198,000 in later years.

Lawsuits arise during the normal course of business. In the opinion of management, none of the pending lawsuits will result in a significant impact on the consolidated results of operations or financial position.

NOTE 12 – ACQUISITION OF BAUER INC.:

During the third quarter of fiscal 1995, NIKE acquired all the outstanding shares of Bauer Inc. (formerly Canstar Sports Inc.), the world's largest hockey equipment manufacturer. The acquisition was accounted for using the purchase method of accounting. The cash purchase price, including acqusition costs, was approximately $409 million.

Bauer's assets and liabilities have been recorded in the Company's consolidated balance sheet at their fair values at the acquisition date. Identifiable intangible assets and goodwill relating to the purchase approximated $336 million with estimated useful lives ranging from 5 to 40 years. The amortization period is based on the Company's belief that the combined company has substantial potential for achieving long-term appreciation of the fully integrated global company. Bauer will permit the continued expansion of the current lines of business, as well as the development of new businesses, which can be used to strategically exploit the companies' brand names and products on an accelerated basis. NIKE believes that the combined company will benefit from the acquisition for an indeterminable period of time of at least 40 years and that therefore a 40-year amortization period is appropriate. The proforma effect of the acquisition on the combined results of operations in fiscal 1995 was not significant.

NOTE 13 – FAIR VALUE OF FINANCIAL INSTRUMENTS:

The carrying amounts reflected in the consolidated balance sheet for cash and equivalents and notes payable approximate fair value as reported in the balance sheet because of their short maturities. The fair value of long-term debt is estimated using discounted
56 cash flow analyses, based on the Company's incremental borrowing rates for similar types of borrowing arrangements. The fair value of the Company's long-term debt, including current portion, is approximately $295,863,000, compared to a carrying value of $298,236,000 at May 31, 1997 and $16,840,000, compared to a carrying value of $16,885,000 at May 31, 1996. See Note 14 for fair value of derivatives.

NOTE 14 – FINANCIAL RISK MANAGEMENT AND DERIVATIVES:

The purpose of the Company's foreign currency hedging activities is to protect the Company from the risk that the eventual dollar cash flows resulting from the sale and purchase of products in foreign currencies will be adversely affected by changes in exchange rates. In addition, the Company seeks to manage the impact of foreign currency fluctuations related to the repayment of intercompany borrowings. The Company does not hold or issue financial instruments for trading purposes. It is the Company's policy to utilize derivative financial instruments to reduce foreign exchange risks where internal netting strategies cannot be effectively employed. Fluctuations in the value of hedging instruments are offset by fluctuations in the value of the underlying exposures being hedged.

The Company uses forward exchange contracts and purchased options to hedge certain firm purchases and sales commitments and the related receivables and payables including other third party or intercompany foreign currency transactions. Purchased currency options are used to hedge certain anticipated but not yet firmly committed transactions expected to be recognized within one year. Cross-currency swaps are used to hedge foreign currency denominated payments related to intercompany loan agreements. Hedged transactions are denominated primarily in European currencies, Japanese yen and Canadian dollar. Premiums paid on purchased options and any realized gains are included in prepaid expenses or accrued liabilities and recognized in earnings when the transaction being hedged is recognized. Deferred option premiums paid, net of realized gains, were $14,500,000 and $5,100,000 at May 31, 1997 and 1996, respectively. Gains and losses related to hedges of firmly committed transactions and the related receivables and payables are deferred and are recognized in income or as adjustments of carrying amounts when the offsetting gains and losses are recognized on the hedged transaction. Net realized and unrealized gains on forward contracts deferred at May 31, 1997 and 1996 were $28,000,000 and $20,700,000, respectively.

The estimated fair values of derivatives used to hedge the Company's risks will fluctuate over time. The fair value of the forward exchange contracts is estimated by obtaining quoted market prices. The fair value of option contracts is estimated using option pricing models widely used in the financial markets. These fair value amounts should not be viewed in isolation, but rather in relation to the fair values of the underlying hedged transactions and the overall reduction in the Company's exposure to adverse fluctuations in foreign exchange rates. The notional amounts of derivatives summarized below do not necessarily represent amounts exchanged by the parties and, therefore, are not a direct measure of the exposure to the Company through its use of derivatives. The amounts exchanged are calculated on the basis of the notional amounts and the other terms of the derivatives, which relate to interest rates, exchange rates or other financial indices.

The following table presents the aggregate notional principal amounts, carrying values and fair values of the Company's derivative financial instruments outstanding at May 31, 1997 and 1996.

(in millions)

MAY 31,	1997			1996		
	Notional Principal Amounts	Carrying Values	Fair Values	Notional Principal Amounts	Carrying Values	Fair Values
Currency Swaps	$ 200.0	$19.4	$13.7	$ —	$ —	$ —
Forward Contracts	2,328.5	14.8	47.4	1,422.8	(2.1)	14.5
Purchased Options	413.7	9.7	9.4	280.2	2.6	.5
Total	$2,942.2	$43.9	$70.5	$1,703.0	$ .5	$15.0

5 1986 1987 1988 1989 1990 1991 1992 1993 1994 1996 1997 199
0 2011 2012 2013 2014 2015 2016 2017 2018 2019 2020 2021 202

At May 31, 1997 and May 31, 1996, the Company had no contracts outstanding with maturities beyond one year except the currency swaps which have maturity dates consistent with the maturity dates of the related debt. All realized gains/losses deferred at May 31, 1997 will be recognized within one year.

The counterparties to derivative transactions are major financial institutions with investment grade or better credit ratings and, additionally, counterparties to derivatives three years or greater are all AAA rated. However, this does not eliminate the Company's exposure to credit risk with these institutions. This credit risk is generally limited to the unrealized gains in such contracts should any of these counterparties fail to perform as contracted and is immaterial to any one institution at May 31, 1997 and 1996. To manage this risk, the Company has established strict counterparty credit guidelines which are continually monitored and reported to Senior Management according to prescribed guidelines. The Company utilizes a portfolio of financial institutions either headquartered or operating in the same countries the Company conducts its business. As a result, the Company considers the risk of counterparty default to be minimal.

NOTE 15 – INDUSTRY SEGMENT AND OPERATIONS BY GEOGRAPHIC AREAS:

The Company operates predominantly in one industry segment, that being the design, production, marketing and selling of sports and fitness footwear, apparel and accessories. During 1997, 1996 and 1995, sales to one major customer amounted to approximately 12%, 12% and 14% of total sales, respectively. The geographic distributions of the Company's identifiable assets, operating income and revenues are summarized in the following table.

(in thousands)

YEAR ENDED MAY 31,	1997	1996	1995
Revenues from unrelated entities:			
United States	$5,529,132	$3,964,662	$2,997,864
Europe	1,833,722	1,334,340	980,444
Asia/Pacific	1,245,217	735,094	515,652
Latin America/Canada and other	578,468	436,529	266,874
	$9,186,539	$6,470,625	$4,760,834
Total revenues:			
United States	$5,531,957	$3,972,815	$3,004,260
Europe	1,833,722	1,341,738	985,882
Asia/Pacific	1,245,217	735,094	515,652
Latin America/Canada and other	730,046	503,591	298,323
Less inter-geographic revenues	(154,403)	(82,613)	(43,283)
	$9,186,539	$6,470,625	$4,760,834
Operating income:			
United States	$ 968,993	$ 697,094	$ 501,685
Europe	170,612	145,722	113,800
Asia/Pacific	174,997	123,585	64,168
Latin America/Canada and other	71,342	55,851	37,721
Less corporate, interest and other income (expense) and eliminations	(90,722)	(123,162)	(67,510)
	$1,295,222	$ 899,090	$ 649,864
Assets:			
United States	$2,994,017	$2,371,991	$1,659,522
Europe	1,272,918	941,522	771,752
Asia/Pacific	665,776	386,485	306,390
Latin America/Canada and other	328,681	188,839	209,389
Total identifiable assets	5,261,392	3,888,837	2,947,053
Corporate cash and eliminations	99,815	62,791	195,692
Total assets	$5,361,207	$3,951,628	$3,142,745

NIKE

DIRECTORS

William J. Bowerman
Deputy Chairman of the Board of Directors
Eugene, Oregon

Thomas E. Clarke (1)
President and Chief Operating Officer, NIKE, Inc.
Beaverton, Oregon

Jill K. Conway (4) (5)
Visiting Scholar
Massachusetts Institute of Technology
Boston, Massachusetts

Ralph D. DeNunzio (3) (4)
President, Harbor Point Associates, Inc., private investment and consulting firm
New York, New York

Richard K. Donahue
Vice Chairman of the Board
Lowell, Massachusetts

Delbert J. Hayes (2) (3)
Newberg, Oregon

Douglas G. Houser (2)
Assistant Secretary, NIKE, Inc.
Partner – Bullivant, Houser, Bailey, Pendergrass & Hoffman, Attorneys
Portland, Oregon

John E. Jaqua (4)
Secretary, NIKE, Inc.
Partner – Jaqua & Wheatley, P.C., Attorneys
Eugene, Oregon

Philip H. Knight (1)
Chairman of the Board and Chief Executive Officer, NIKE, Inc.
Beaverton, Oregon

Kenichi Ohmae
Former Chairman of the Board
McKinsey & Company
Tokyo, Japan

Charles W. Robinson (3)
President, Robinson & Associates, venture capital
Santa Fe, New Mexico

A. Michael Spence (2)
Dean, Graduate School of Business
Stanford University
Palo Alto, California

John R. Thompson, Jr. (4)
Head Basketball Coach
Georgetown University
Washington, D.C.

(1) Member – Executive Committee
(2) Member – Audit Committee
(3) Member – Finance Committee
(4) Member – Personnel Committee
(5) Member – Compensation Plan Subcommittee

OFFICERS

Philip H. Knight
Chairman of the Board and Chief Executive Officer

Thomas E. Clarke
President and Chief Operating Officer

Jeffrey M. Cava
Vice President

Martin P. Coles
Vice President

Gary M. DeStefano
Vice President

Elizabeth G. Dolan
Vice President

Robert S. Falcone
Vice President, Chief Financial Officer

Stephen D. Gomez
Vice President

Mark G. Parker
Vice President

Lindsay D. Stewart
Vice President, and Assistant Secretary

David B. Taylor
Vice President

Marcia A. Stilwell
Treasurer

Douglas G. Houser
Assistant Secretary

John E. Jaqua
Secretary

A. Thomas Niebergall
Assistant Secretary

ADVISORY COUNCIL

Michael Jordan
President
The Michael Jordan Foundation
Chicago, Illinois

Gareth C.C. Chang
Senior Vice President – Marketing
GM Hughes Electronics
President and CEO
Hughes International
Los Angeles, California

DIVISION VICE PRESIDENTS

Alexander Bodecker
Beaverton, Oregon

Charlie Denson
Hilversum, The Netherlands

Shelley K. Dewey
Beaverton, Oregon

Dr. Joseph Ha
Beaverton, Oregon

Anders Hanson
Solna, Sweden

Tinker Hatfield
Beaverton, Oregon

Timothy J. Joyce
Beaverton, Oregon

Robert Kreinberg
Beaverton, Oregon

Gary Kurtz
Beaverton, Oregon

Larry Miller
Beaverton, Oregon

Andrew P. Mooney
Beaverton, Oregon

Anthony Peddie
Hong Kong

Kirk T. Stewart
Beaverton, Oregon

Gordon Thompson III
Beaverton, Oregon

Sharon S. Tunstall
Beaverton, Oregon

Matthew F. Wolff
Beaverton, Oregon

Robert C. Wood
Beaverton, Oregon

Craig Zanon
Beaverton, Oregon

972 1973 1974 1975 1976 1977 1978 1980 1981 1982 1983 1984 198
999 2000 2001 2002 2003 2004 2005 2006 2007 2008 2009 201

CONSOLIDATED BALANCE SHEETS

Amounts in thousands, except share data

DECEMBER 31,	1996	1995
ASSETS		
Current assets:		
Cash and cash equivalents	$ 232,365	$ 80,393
Accounts receivable, net of allowance for doubtful accounts (1996, $43,527; 1995, $46,401)	590,504	506,563
Inventory	544,522	635,012
Deferred income taxes	69,422	65,484
Prepaid expenses and other current assets	26,275	45,418
Total current assets	1,463,088	1,332,870
Property and equipment, net	185,292	192,033
Non-current assets:		
Intangibles, net of amortization	69,700	64,436
Deferred income taxes	7,850	5,455
Other	60,254	56,825
	137,804	126,716
Total Assets	$1,786,184	$1,651,619
LIABILITIES AND STOCKHOLDERS' EQUITY		
Current liabilities:		
Notes payable to banks	$ 32,977	$ 66,682
Current portion of long-term debt	52,684	946
Accounts payable	196,368	166,037
Accrued expenses	169,344	144,585
Income taxes payable	65,588	47,956
Dividends payable		5,742
Total current liabilities	516,961	431,948
Long-term debt, net of current portion	854,099	254,178
Minority interest	33,890	31,081
Commitments and contingencies		
Outstanding redemption value of equity put options		39,123
Stockholders' equity:		
Common stock, par value $.01; authorized 250,000,000 shares; issued 92,556,295 shares in 1996, 111,015,133 shares in 1995	926	1,096
Retained earnings	992,563	1,487,006
Less 36,716,227 shares at December 31, 1996 and 36,210,902 at December 31, 1995 in treasury at cost	(617,620)	(603,241)
Unearned compensation	(283)	(1,208)
Foreign currency translation adjustment	5,648	11,636
	381,234	895,289
Total Liabilities and Stockholders' Equity	$1,786,184	$1,651,619

The accompanying notes are an integral part of the consolidated financial statements.

CONSOLIDATED STATEMENTS OF INCOME

Amounts in thousands, except per share data

YEAR ENDED DECEMBER 31,	1996	1995	1994
Net sales	$3,478,604	$3,481,450	$3,280,418
Other income	4,325	3,126	7,165
	3,482,929	3,484,576	3,287,583
Costs and expenses:			
Cost of sales	2,144,422	2,114,084	1,966,138
Selling, general and administrative expenses	1,065,792	999,731	889,590
Special charges		72,098	
Amortization of intangibles	3,410	4,067	4,345
Interest expense	42,246	25,725	16,515
Interest income	(10,609)	(7,103)	(6,373)
	3,245,261	3,208,602	2,870,215
Income before income taxes and minority interest	237,668	275,974	417,368
Income taxes	84,083	99,753	153,994
Income before minority interest	153,585	176,221	263,374
Minority interest	14,635	11,423	8,896
Net income	$ 138,950	$ 164,798	$ 254,478
Net income per common share	$ 2.00	$ 2.07	$ 3.02
Dividends per common share	$ 0.225	$ 0.300	$ 0.300
Weighted average common and common equivalent shares outstanding	69,618	79,487	84,311

The accompanying notes are an integral part of the consolidated financial statements.

Reebok

CONSOLIDATED STATEMENTS OF STOCKHOLDERS' EQUITY

Dollar amounts in thousands	*Common Stock*		*Additional Paid-in Capital*	*Retained Earnings*	*Treasury Stock*	*Unearned Compensation*	*Foreign Currency Translation Adjustment*
	Shares	*Par Value*					
BALANCE, DECEMBER 31, 1993	119,902,298	$1,199	$266,890	$1,198,190	$(603,241)	$(3,276)	$(13,145)
Net income				254,478			
Adjustment for foreign currency translation							12,306
Issuance of shares to certain employees	19,293		611			(611)	
Amortization of unearned compensation						827	
Shares repurchased and retired	(3,261,200)	(33)	(112,105)				
Shares retired	(16,000)		(462)			462	
Shares issued under employee stock purchase plans	158,965	2	4,082				
Shares issued upon exercise of stock options	352,255	4	6,172				
Income tax reductions relating to exercise of stock options			2,765				
Dividends declared				(24,610)			
BALANCE, DECEMBER 31, 1994	117,155,611	1,172	167,953	1,428,058	(603,241)	(2,598)	(839)
Net income				164,798			
Adjustment for foreign currency translation							12,475
Issuance of shares to certain employees	43,545		1,558			(1,558)	
Amortization of unearned compensation						1,008	
Shares repurchased and retired	(6,639,600)	(66)	(182,569)	(42,835)			
Shares retired	(67,200)	(1)	(1,385)	(554)		1,940	
Shares issued under employee stock purchase plans	161,377	2	4,253				
Shares issued upon exercise of stock options	361,400	4	6,004				
Put option contracts outstanding		(15)		(39,108)			
Premium received from unexercised equity put options			3,233				
Income tax reductions relating to exercise of stock options			953				
Dividends declared				(23,353)			
BALANCE, DECEMBER 31, 1995	111,015,133	1,096	0	1,487,006	(603,241)	(1,208)	11,636
Net income				138,950			
Adjustment for foreign currency translation							(5,988)
Treasury shares repurchased					(14,379)		
Issuance of shares to certain employees	43,278			1,505		(55)	
Amortization of unearned compensation						292	
Shares repurchased and retired	(18,931,403)	(190)		(672,900)		688	
Shares issued under employee stock purchase plans	157,134	2		4,042			
Shares issued upon exercise of stock options	272,153	3		6,930			
Put option contracts expired		15		39,825			
Income tax reductions relating to exercise of stock options				2,385			
Dividends declared				(15,180)			
BALANCE, DECEMBER 31, 1996	92,556,295	$ 926	$ 0	$ 992,563	$ (617,620)	$ (283)	$ 5,648

The accompanying notes are an integral part of the consolidated financial statements.

CONSOLIDATED STATEMENTS OF CASH FLOWS

Amounts in thousands

YEAR ENDED DECEMBER 31,	1996	1995	1994
Cash flows from operating activities:			
Net income	$ 138,950	$ 164,798	$ 254,478
Adjustments to reconcile net income to net cash provided by operating activities:			
Depreciation and amortization	42,927	39,579	37,400
Minority interest	14,635	11,423	8,896
Deferred income taxes	(6,333)	(1,573)	(13,332)
Special charges		62,743	
Changes in operating assets and liabilities, exclusive of those arising from business acquisitions:			
Accounts receivable	(107,082)	16,157	(64,786)
Inventory	77,286	(29,531)	(81,948)
Prepaid expenses	22,650	7,841	(7,752)
Other	11,042	(18,830)	(13,648)
Accounts payable and accrued expenses	67,769	(25,327)	35,211
Income taxes payable	18,419	(55,553)	20,236
Total adjustments	141,313	6,929	(79,723)
Net cash provided by operating activities	280,263	171,727	174,755
Cash flows from investing activities:			
Payments to acquire property and equipment	(29,999)	(63,610)	(61,839)
Proceeds (payments) for business acquisitions and divestitures	6,887		(4,297)
Net cash used for investing activities	(23,112)	(63,610)	(66,136)
Cash flows from financing activities:			
Net borrowings (payments) of notes payable to banks	(36,947)	2,426	37,148
Proceeds from issuance of common stock to employees	13,362	11,216	13,025
Dividends paid	(20,922)	(23,679)	(24,827)
Repayments of long-term debt	(1,290)	(112,445)	(2,585)
Net proceeds from long-term debt	632,108	230,000	
Proceeds from premium on equity put options	717	3,233	
Dividends to minority shareholders	(7,426)	(2,885)	(2,141)
Repurchases of common stock	(686,266)	(225,470)	(112,138)
Net cash used for financing activities	(106,664)	(117,604)	(91,518)
Effect of exchange rate changes on cash	1,485	5,944	(12,512)
Net increase (decrease) in cash and cash equivalents	151,972	(3,543)	4,589
Cash and cash equivalents at beginning of year	80,393	83,936	79,347
Cash and cash equivalents at end of year	$232,365	$ 80,393	$ 83,936
Supplemental disclosures of cash flow information:			
Interest paid	$ 38,738	$ 23,962	$ 19,135
Income taxes paid	101,975	152,690	135,060

The accompanying notes are an integral part of the consolidated financial statements.

Reebok

America Online, Inc.

Consolidated Statements of Operations

(Amounts in thousands, except per share data)	Year ended June 30, 1996	1995	1994
Revenues:			
Online service revenues	**$ 991,656**	$ 344,309	$ 98,497
Other revenues	**102,198**	49,981	17,225
Total revenues	**1,093,854**	394,290	115,722
Costs and expenses:			
Cost of revenues	**627,372**	229,724	69,043
Marketing	**212,710**	77,064	23,548
Product development	**53,817**	14,263	5,288
General and administrative	**110,653**	42,700	13,667
Acquired research and development	**16,981**	50,335	–
Amortization of goodwill	**7,078**	1,653	–
Total costs and expenses	**1,028,611**	415,739	111,546
Income (loss) from operations	**65,243**	(21,449)	4,176
Other income (expense), net	**(2,056)**	3,074	1,810
Merger expenses	**(848)**	(2,207)	–
Income (loss) before provision for income taxes	**62,339**	(20,582)	5,986
Provision for income taxes	**(32,523)**	(15,169)	(3,832)
Net income (loss)	**$ 29,816**	$ (35,751)	$ 2,154
Earnings (loss) per share:			
Net income (loss)	**$ 0.28**	$ (0.51)	$ 0.03
Weighted average shares outstanding	**108,097**	69,550	69,035

See accompanying notes.

America Online, Inc.

Consolidated Balance Sheets

(Amounts in thousands, except share data)	June 30, 1996	1995
Assets		
Current assets:		
Cash and cash equivalents	**$118,421**	$ 45,877
Short-term investments	**10,712**	18,672
Trade accounts receivable	**42,939**	32,176
Other receivables	**29,674**	11,381
Prepaid expenses and other current assets	**68,832**	25,527
Total current assets	**270,578**	133,633
Property and equipment at cost, net	**101,277**	70,919
Other assets:		
Product development costs, net	**44,330**	18,949
Deferred subscriber acquisition costs, net	**314,181**	77,229
License rights, net	**4,947**	5,579
Other assets	**35,878**	9,121
Deferred income taxes	**135,872**	35,627
Goodwill, net	**51,691**	54,356
	$958,754	$405,413
Liabilities and Stockholders' Equity		
Current liabilities:		
Trade accounts payable	**$105,904**	$ 84,640
Other accrued expenses and liabilities	**127,898**	23,509
Deferred revenue	**37,950**	20,021
Accrued personnel costs	**15,719**	2,863
Current portion of long-term debt	**2,435**	2,329
Total current liabilities	**289,906**	133,362
Long-term liabilities:		
Notes payable	**19,306**	17,369
Deferred income taxes	**135,872**	35,627
Other liabilities	**1,168**	2,243
Total liabilities	**446,252**	188,601
Stockholders' equity:		
Preferred stock, $.01 par value; 5,000,000 shares authorized, 1,000 shares issued and outstanding at June 30, 1996	**1**	–
Common stock, $.01 par value; 300,000,000 and 100,000,000 shares authorized, 92,626,000 and 76,728,268 shares issued and outstanding at June 30, 1996 and 1995, respectively	**926**	767
Additional paid-in capital	**519,342**	252,668
Accumulated deficit	**(7,767)**	(36,623)
Total stockholders' equity	**512,502**	216,812
	$958,754	$405,413

See accompanying notes.

America Online, Inc.

Consolidated Statements of Changes in Stockholders' Equity

(Amounts in thousands, except share data)	Preferred Stock Shares	Preferred Stock Amount	Common Stock Shares	Common Stock Amount	Additional Paid-in Capital	Accumulated Deficit	Total
Balances at June 30, 1993	–	–	49,562,136	$495	$ 26,992	$ (3,550)	$ 23,937
Common stock issued:							
Exercise of options and warrants	–	–	2,827,280	28	1,836	–	1,864
Sale of stock, net	–	–	10,713,760	107	66,149	–	66,256
Tax benefit related to stock options	–	–	–	–	4,590	–	4,590
Net income	–	–	–	–	–	2,154	2,154
Balances at June 30, 1994	–	–	63,103,176	630	99,567	(1,396)	98,801
Effect of immaterial poolings	–	–	2,062,756	21	1,032	524	1,577
Balances as Restated	–	–	65,165,932	651	100,599	(872)	100,378
Common stock issued:							
Exercise of options	–	–	2,905,256	29	4,655	–	4,684
Business acquisitions	–	–	4,785,354	48	75,653	–	75,701
Sale of stock, net	–	–	3,871,726	39	56,998	–	57,037
Tax benefit related to stock options	–	–	–	–	14,763	–	14,763
Net loss	–	–	–	–	–	(35,751)	(35,751)
Balances at June 30, 1995	–	–	76,728,268	767	252,668	(36,623)	216,812
Effect of pooling restatement	–	–	–	–	–	(960)	(960)
Balances as Restated	–	–	76,728,268	767	252,668	(37,583)	215,852
Common stock issued:							
Exercise of options and warrants	–	–	10,370,338	104	47,885	–	47,989
Business acquisitions	–	–	465,502	5	16,632	–	16,637
Sale of stock, net	–	–	5,061,892	50	141,320	–	141,370
Sale of preferred stock, net	1,000	$1	–	–	28,314	–	28,315
Tax benefit related to stock options	–	–	–	–	32,523	–	32,523
Net income	–	–	–	–	–	29,816	29,816
Balances at June 30, 1996	**1,000**	**$1**	**92,626,000**	**$926**	**$519,342**	**$(7,767)**	**$512,502**

See accompanying notes.

America Online, Inc.

Consolidated Statements of Cash Flows

(Amounts in thousands)	Year ended June 30, 1996	1995	1994
Cash flows from operating activities:			
Net income (loss)	**$ 29,816**	$ (35,751)	$ 2,154
Adjustments to reconcile net income to net cash (used in) provided by operating activities:			
Depreciation and amortization	**33,366**	12,266	2,822
Amortization of subscriber acquisition costs	**126,072**	60,924	17,922
Loss on sale of property and equipment	**44**	37	5
Charge for acquired research and development	**16,981**	50,335	–
Changes in assets and liabilities:			
Trade accounts receivable	**(10,435)**	(14,373)	(4,266)
Other receivables	**(18,293)**	(9,086)	(626)
Prepaid expenses and other current assets	**(43,305)**	(19,635)	(2,873)
Deferred subscriber acquisition costs	**(363,024)**	(111,761)	(37,424)
Other assets	**(26,938)**	(6,051)	(2,542)
Trade accounts payable	**21,150**	60,805	10,224
Accrued personnel costs	**12,856**	1,850	397
Other accrued expenses and liabilities	**104,531**	5,747	9,474
Deferred revenue	**17,929**	7,190	2,322
Deferred income taxes	**32,523**	14,763	3,832
Total adjustments	**(96,543)**	53,011	(733)
Net cash (used in) provided by operating activities	**(66,727)**	17,260	1,421
Cash flows from investing activities:			
Short-term investments	**7,960**	5,380	(18,947)
Purchase of property and equipment	**(50,262)**	(59,255)	(18,010)
Product development costs	**(32,631)**	(13,054)	(5,131)
Sale of property and equipment	**–**	180	95
Purchase costs of acquired businesses	**(4,133)**	(20,523)	–
Net cash used in investing activities	**(79,066)**	(87,272)	(41,993)
Cash flows from financing activities:			
Proceeds from issuance of common stock, net	**189,359**	61,721	68,120
Proceeds from issuance of preferred stock, net	**28,315**	–	–
Principal and accrued interest payments on line of credit and long-term debt	**(935)**	(3,045)	(7,795)
Proceeds from line of credit and issuance of long-term debt	**3,000**	13,488	14,260
Principal payments under capital lease obligations	**(1,402)**	(368)	(83)
Net cash provided by financing activities	**218,337**	71,796	74,502
Net increase in cash and cash equivalents	**72,544**	1,784	33,930
Cash and cash equivalents at beginning of period	**45,877**	44,093	10,163
Cash and cash equivalents at end of period	**$ 118,421**	$ 45,877	$ 44,093
Supplemental cash flow information			
Cash paid during the period for:			
Interest	**$ 1,659**	$ 1,076	$ 577
Income taxes	**–**	–	–

See accompanying notes.

Accounting Concepts and Alternative Valuations

B

APPENDIX

Appendix Outline

Section 1—Accounting Concepts

- **Accounting Concepts and Principles**
- **Descriptive and Prescriptive Concepts**
- **Conceptual Framework**
  - Objectives of Financial Reporting
  - Qualitative Characteristics
  - Elements of Financial Statements
  - Recognition and Measurement

Section 2—Alternative Accounting Valuations

- **Historical Cost Accounting and Price Changes**
  - Impact of Price Changes on the Balance Sheet
  - Impact of Price Changes on the Income Statement
- **Valuation Alternatives to Historical Cost**
  - Constant Dollar Accounting
  - Current Cost Accounting
  - Mark to Market Accounting

Learning Objectives

Conceptual

C1 Explain both descriptive and prescriptive concepts and their development.

C2 Describe the conceptual framework for accounting.

C3 Explain how price changes impact conventional financial statements.

C4 Discuss valuation alternatives to historical cost.

APPENDIX PREVIEW

Accounting concepts are broad ideas developed as a way of *describing* current accounting practices and *prescribing* new and improved practices. In this appendix we explain the accounting concepts the FASB developed in an effort to guide future changes and improvements in accounting. We also discuss alternatives to the historical cost measurements reported in financial statements. Understanding these alternatives helps us with interpreting information in financial statements.

SECTION 1 ACCOUNTING CONCEPTS

Accounting Concepts and Principles

C1 Explain both descriptive and prescriptive concepts and their development.

Accounting concepts are the ideas guiding the selection of transactions and events to be accounted for, the measurement of those transactions and events, and the methods to summarize and report them to users.[1] Accounting concepts serve two main purposes. First, they provide descriptions of existing accounting practices that help us understand and use accounting information. Knowing how concepts are applied enables us to effectively use accounting information in different situations. Also, understanding accounting concepts is more useful than memorizing a list of procedures. Second, accounting concepts are important for the Financial Accounting Standards Board (FASB), which is charged with developing acceptable practices for financial reporting in the United States and with improving the quality of such reporting. They are important because they are used in establishing current and future accounting standards.

We previously defined and illustrated several important accounting *principles* in this book. Several of these major principles are listed in Exhibit B.1. Accounting principles describe in general terms the practices as currently applied. We first explained these principles in Chapter 2, but we referred to them frequently in the book. The term *concepts* includes both these principles and other accounting practices. The FASB also uses the term *concepts* in this way.

Exhibit B.1

Partial List of Accounting Principles

Business Entity
Conservatism
Consistency
Cost
Full Disclosure
Going-Concern
Matching
Materiality
Objectivity
Revenue Recognition
Time Period

As business practices evolved in recent years, accounting concepts were sometimes difficult to apply in dealing with new and different types of transactions. Because they were intended as general descriptions of current accounting practices, these concepts did not necessarily describe what *should* be done. Since these concepts didn't identify weaknesses in accounting practices, they did not lead to major changes or improvements in accounting practices.

The FASB, however, is charged with improving financial reporting. It decided a new set of concepts needed to be developed for this purpose. They also decided this new set of concepts should not merely *describe* what is being done in current practice. Instead, the new concepts should *prescribe* (or guide) what ought to be done to improve things. The project to develop a new set of prescriptive concepts was called the *conceptual framework project.* Before we describe the conceptual framework, we look more closely at the differences between descriptive and prescriptive uses of accounting concepts.

Descriptive and Prescriptive Concepts

Concepts differ in how they are developed and used. Generally, when concepts are intended to describe current practice, they are developed by looking at accepted practices and then making rules to encompass them. This bottom-up, or *descriptive,* approach is shown in Exhibit B.2. It shows arrows going from specific practices to concepts. The outcome of this process is a set of concepts that summarize practice. This process, for instance, leads us to the concept that asset purchases are recorded at cost.

[1] FASB, *Scope and Implications of the Conceptual Framework Project* (Stamford, Conn.: FASB, 1976).

Exhibit B.2

Bottom-Up Development of Descriptive Concepts

Descriptive Concepts

Specific Practices | Specific Practices | Specific Practices

Descriptive concepts often fail to show how new problems might be solved. For example, the concept that assets are recorded at cost doesn't provide direct guidance for situations where assets have no cost because they are donated to a company by a local government. The bottom-up approach is based on the presumption that current practices are adequate. They don't lead to development of new and improved accounting methods. The concept that assets are initially recorded at cost doesn't encourage asking the question of whether they should always be carried at that amount.

Exhibit B.3

Top-Down Development of Prescriptive Concepts

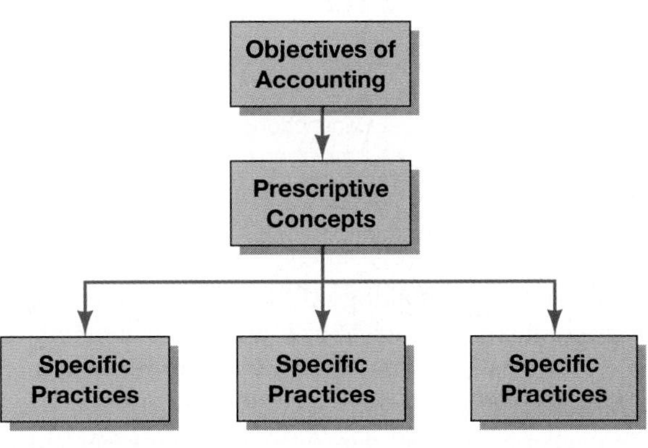

When concepts are intended to *prescribe* (or guide) improvements in accounting practice, they are likely to be designed by a top-down approach as shown in Exhibit B.3. The top-down approach starts with broad accounting objectives. The process then generates concepts about the types of information that should be reported. These concepts lead to specific practices that ought to be used. The advantage of this approach is that these concepts are good for solving new problems and evaluating old answers. Its disadvantage is the concepts may not be very descriptive of current practice. The suggested practices may not even be in current use.

Since the FASB uses accounting concepts to prescribe accounting practices, the Board used a top-down approach to develop its conceptual framework. The Board's concepts are not necessarily perfect. But the new concepts are intended to provide better guidelines for developing new and improved accounting practices. The FASB declares it will continue to use them as a basis for future actions and already has used them to justify many important changes in financial reporting.

It is crucial in setting accounting standards that the issues be properly identified and described. The conceptual framework helps the FASB do this by providing common objectives and terms. The conceptual framework also helps the Board focus on the important factors in accounting standard-setting and reduces some of the political aspects of policymaking.

Flash back

1. What is the starting point in a top-down approach to developing accounting concepts?
2. What is the starting point in a bottom-up approach to developing accounting concepts?

Answers—p. B-8

Conceptual Framework

C2 Describe the conceptual framework for accounting.

The Financial Accounting Standards Board's approach to developing a conceptual framework is diagrammed in Exhibit B.4. The Board has issued six *Statements of Financial Accounting Concepts (SFAC).* These concepts statements are not the same as the FASB's *Statements of Financial Accounting Standards (SFAS).* The *SFAS*s are authoritative statements of generally accepted accounting principles, whereas the *SFAC*s are guidelines the Board uses in developing new standards. Accounting professionals are not required to follow the *SFACs* in practice.

Conceptual Framework

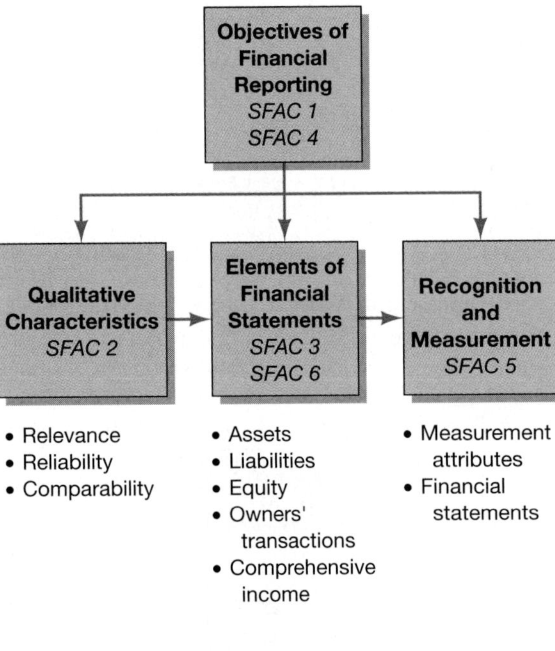

Objectives of Financial Reporting

The first *SFAC* identifies the broad objectives of financial reporting (see Exhibit B.4). The initial and most general objective in *SFAC 1* is to "provide information that is useful to present and potential investors and creditors and other users in making rational investment, credit, and similar decisions."[2] From this starting point, the Board expressed other more specific objectives. These objectives recognize that (1) financial reporting should help users predict future cash flows, and (2) information about a company's resources and obligations is useful in making these predictions.

The concepts making up the conceptual framework are intended to be consistent with these objectives. Current accounting practice already provides information about a company's resources and obligations that are presumably useful for decision makers. While this conceptual framework is intended to be prescriptive of new and improved practices, its concepts are also descriptive of many current practices.

Did You Know?

On-line Concepts

The FASB has a Web site [www.rutgers.edu/Accounting/raw/fasb] where we can access current FASB documents, planned FASB projects, and summaries and status of all FASB statements. This site also provides access to many current standards and happenings in accounting.

Qualitative Characteristics

Exhibit B.4 shows the next step in the conceptual framework is to identify the qualities (or qualitative characteristics) that financial information should have if it is to be useful in decision making. The Board recognized that information is useful only if it is understandable to users. But the Board assumed users have the training, experience, and motivation to analyze financial reports. With this decision, the Board indicated financial reporting should not try to meet the needs of unsophisticated or casual users.

In *SFAC 2,* the Board stated information is useful if it is (1) relevant, (2) reliable, and (3) comparable. Information is *relevant* if it can make a difference in a decision. Information has this quality when it helps users predict the future or evaluate the past and is received in time to affect their decisions.

Information is *reliable* if users can depend on it to be free from bias and error. Reliable information is verifiable and faithfully represents what is intended to be described. Users can depend on information only if it is neutral. This means the rules used to produce information are not designed to lead users to accept or reject any specific decision.

[2] FASB, *Statement of Financial Accounting Concepts No. 1,* "Objective of Financial Reporting by Business Enterprises" (Norwalk, CT, 1978), par. 34.

Information is *comparable* if users can use it to identify differences and similarities between companies. Complete comparability is possible only if companies follow uniform practices. But even if all companies uniformly follow the same practices, comparable reports do not result if the practices are inappropriate. For example, comparable information is not provided if all companies ignored the useful lives of their assets and depreciate them over two years.

Comparability also requires consistency (see Chapter 7). This means a company should not change its accounting practices unless the change is justified as a reporting improvement. Another important concept discussed in *SFAC 2* is materiality (see Chapter 10). An accounting item is material if it affects decisions of users. Items not material are often accounted for in the easiest way possible using cost-benefit criteria.

Elements of Financial Statements

The Board's discussion of financial statement elements, an important part of the conceptual framework, identified and defined categories such as assets, liabilities, equity, revenues, expenses, gains, and losses. In earlier chapters, we drew on many of those definitions. As shown in Exhibit B.4, the Board's original pronouncement on financial statement elements is *SFAC 3*. *SFAC 3* was replaced by *SFAC 6,* which modified the discussion of financial statement elements to include several elements for not-for-profit accounting entities.[3]

Recognition and Measurement

In *SFAC 5,* the Board established concepts for deciding (1) when items should be presented (or recognized) in financial statements and (2) how to assign numbers to (or measure) those items. The Board generally concluded that an item should be recognized in financial statements if it meets the following criteria:

Definable	Meets the definition of an element of financial statements.
Measurable	Has a relevant attribute that's measurable with reliability.
Relevant	Is capable of making a difference in user decisions.
Reliable	Is representationally faithful, verifiable, and neutral.

The question of how an item is measured raises a fundamental question of whether financial statements should be based on cost or on current value. The Board's discussion of this issue is more descriptive of current practice than it is prescriptive of new measurement methods.

In *SFAC 5,* the Board stated that a full set of financial statements should show:

1. Financial position at the end of the period.
2. Earnings for the period. (This is similar to net income reported in current practice.)
3. Comprehensive income for the period. (This concept is broader than earnings and includes all changes in owner's equity other than those that result from transactions with owners. Some changes in asset values are included here but excluded from earnings.)
4. Cash flows during the period.
5. Investments by and distributions to owners during the period.

SFAC 5 is the first pronouncement to call for a statement of cash flows. The statement of cash flows is now required under *SFAS 95,* issued two years after *SFAC 5.*

[3] Among the six *Statements of Financial Accounting Concepts* issued by the FASB, one (*SFAC 4*) is directed toward accounting by not-for-profit organizations. Although *SFAC 4* is important, it is beyond the scope of this course.

Flash back

3. The FASB's conceptual framework is intended to:
   a. Provide a historical analysis of accounting practice.
   b. Describe current accounting practice.
   c. Provide concepts that are prescriptive of what should be done in accounting practice.
4. The notion that accounting practices should be consistent from year to year most directly relates to the FASB's concept that information reported in financial statements should be: *(a)* relevant, *(b)* material, *(c)* reliable, or *(d)* comparable.
5. What characteristics of accounting information make it reliable?
6. What do the *elements of financial statements* refer to?

Answers—p. B-8

SECTION 2 ALTERNATIVE ACCOUNTING VALUATIONS

Historical Cost Accounting and Price Changes

Most agree that conventional (historical cost based) financial statements provide useful information to users. But some also believe conventional financial statements inadequately account for the impact of changing prices. When prices change, users often look for alternative valuations along with the conventional statements when making decisions.

C3 Explain how price changes impact conventional financial statements.

Impact of Price Changes on the Balance Sheet

Conventional financial statements reflect transactions recorded using historical costs. Amounts in these statements are usually not adjusted even though subsequent price changes alter their values.[4] As an example, consider Company X, which purchases 10 acres of land for $25,000. At the end of each accounting period, Company X reports a balance sheet showing "Land . . . $25,000." Several years later, after sharp price increases, Company Y purchases 10 acres of land next to and nearly identical to Company X's land. But Company Y paid $60,000 for its land. Exhibit B.5 shows the conventional balance sheet disclosures of these two companies for the land account.

Exhibit B.5
Conventional Balance Sheet Comparison

	Company X	Company Y
Land	$25,000	$60,000

Without detailed disclosures, a user is likely to conclude that either Company Y has more land than Company X or that Company Y's land is more valuable. In reality, both companies own 10 acres that are identical. The difference is due to price changes.

Impact of Price Changes on the Income Statement

The inability of a conventional balance sheet to reflect price changes also shows up in the income statement. As an example, consider two companies that purchase identical machines but at different times. Company A purchases the machine for $10,000 in 1998,

---

[4] One exception to this is the reporting of certain investments in debt and equity securities at their fair (market) values. We explain this exception in Chapters 10 and 16.

while Company Z purchases the machine in 2000 when its price is $18,000. Both machines are depreciated on a straight-line basis over a 10-year period with no salvage value. Exhibit B.6 shows depreciation expense in the conventional annual income statements for these two companies.

	Company A	Company Z
Depreciation expense, Machinery	$1,000	$1,800

Conventional Income Statement Comparison

Although identical assets are being depreciated, the income statement shows a much higher depreciation expense for Company Z.

Valuation Alternatives to Historical Cost

C4 Discuss valuation alternatives to historical cost.

This section discusses three alternatives to historical cost valuation in financial statements.

Constant Dollar Accounting

One alternative to conventional financial statements is to adjust the dollar amounts of cost incurred in earlier years for changes in the general price level. This means a specific dollar amount of cost in a previous year is restated in terms of current purchasing power. Restating accounting numbers into dollars of equal purchasing power yields *constant dollar* financial statements. Constant dollar accounting changes the unit of measurement, but it is still based on historical cost.

Current Cost Accounting

All prices do not change at the same rate. When the general price level is rising, some specific prices may be falling. *Current cost* accounting measures financial statement elements at current values. It is not based on historical cost. The result of measuring expenses in current costs is that revenue is matched with current costs of the resources used to earn the revenue (at the time revenue is earned). This means operating profit is not positive unless revenues are large enough to replace all of the resources consumed in the process of producing those revenues. Those who argue for current cost believe that operating profit measured in this fashion provides an improved basis for evaluating the effectiveness of operating activities. On the balance sheet, current cost accounting reports assets at amounts needed to purchase them as of the balance sheet date. Liabilities are reported at amounts needed to satisfy the liabilities as of the balance sheet date.

Mark to Market Accounting

We can also report assets (and liabilities) at current selling prices. On the balance sheet, this means assets are reported at amounts received if the assets were sold. Liabilities are reported at amounts needed to settle the liabilities. This method of valuation is called the *current selling price method* or, more commonly, *mark to market* accounting.

One argument supporting current selling prices of assets is that the alternative to owning an asset is to sell it. This means the sacrifice a business makes to hold an asset is the amount it would receive if the asset were sold. Also, the benefit derived from holding a liability is the amount the business avoids paying by not settling it. Equity in this case represents the net amount of cash from liquidating the company. This net liquidation value is the amount that can be invested in other projects if the company were liquidated. It is a relevant basis for evaluating whether the income the company earns is enough to justify remaining in business.

Some proponents of current selling price believe it should be applied to assets but not liabilities. Others argue it applies equally well to both. Still others believe it should be applied only to assets held for sale. As Chapters 10 and 16 explain, companies use the current selling price approach to value some investments. Investments in trading securities are reported at their fair (market) values, with the related changes in fair values reported on the income statement. Investments in securities available for sale are also reported at their fair values, but the related changes in fair values are not reported on the conventional income statement. Instead, they are reported as part of stockholders' equity.

Summary

C1 **Explain both descriptive and prescriptive concepts and their development.** Descriptive accounting concepts provide general descriptions of current accounting practices. Prescriptive accounting concepts guide us in the practices that should be followed. These prescriptive concepts are most useful in developing accounting procedures for new types of transactions and making improvements in accounting practice. A bottom-up (descriptive) approach to developing concepts begins by examining the practices currently in use. Then, concepts are developed that provide general descriptions of those practices. A top-down (prescriptive) approach begins by stating the objectives of accounting. From these objectives, concepts are developed that guide us in identifying the types of accounting practices one should follow.

C2 **Describe the conceptual framework for accounting.** The FASB's conceptual framework begins by stating the broad objectives of financial reporting. Next, it identifies the qualitative characteristics accounting information should possess. The elements contained in financial reports are then defined, followed by recognition and measurement criteria.

C3 **Explain how price changes impact conventional financial statements.** Conventional financial statements report transactions in terms of historical dollars received or paid. The statements usually are not adjusted to reflect general price level changes or changes in the specific prices of the items reported. Items on financial statements that do not reflect current values can lead to errors in judgment by uninformed users.

C4 **Discuss valuation alternatives to historical cost.** Constant dollar accounting involves multiplying cost by a factor reflecting the change in the general price level since the cost was incurred. Current cost accounting involves reporting (a) on the balance sheet the dollar amounts needed to purchase the assets or settle the liabilities at the balance sheet date, and (b) on the income statement the amounts needed to acquire operating assets on the date they are used. Mark to market accounting involves reporting current selling prices of assets and liabilities.

Guidance Answers to 

1. A top-down approach to developing accounting concepts begins by identifying appropriate objectives of accounting reports.
2. A bottom-up approach to developing accounting concepts starts by examining existing accounting practices and determining the general features that characterize those procedures.
3. *c*
4. *d*
5. To have the qualitative characteristic of being reliable, accounting information should be free from bias and error, should be verifiable, should faithfully represent what it is intended to describe, and should be neutral.
6. The elements of financial statements are the objects and events that financial statements should describe; for example, assets, liabilities, revenues, and expenses.

Questions

1. Can a concept be used descriptively and prescriptively?
2. Explain the difference between the FASB's *Statements of Financial Accounting Concepts* and the *Statements of Financial Accounting Standards.*
3. Which three qualitative characteristics of accounting information did the FASB identify as being necessary if the information is to be useful?
4. What is implied by saying that financial information should have the qualitative characteristic of relevance?
5. What are the four criteria an item should satisfy to be recognized in financial statements?
6. Some people argue that conventional financial statements fail to adequately account for inflation. What problem with conventional financial statements generates this argument?
7. What is the fundamental difference in the adjustments made under current cost accounting and under constant dollar accounting?
8. What are three alternatives to historical cost valuation for financial statements?

Quick Study

QS B-1
Understanding accounting concepts
C1, C2

Identify the following statements as true or false:

1. _____ Accounting concepts are good examples of laws of nature.
2. _____ There are really no viable alternatives to historical cost measurements for financial statement reporting.
3. _____ Specific practices suggested by applying FASB's conceptual framework must be in current use.
4. _____ Accounting professionals are not required to follow the *SFAC*s in practice.
5. _____ *SFAC*s and *SFAS*s are acronyms that both describe authoritative generally accepted accounting principles.
6. _____ Relevance, as an important quality of financial information, is placed above reliability in the conceptual framework hierarchy.
7. _____ When concepts are intended to prescribe improvements in accounting practice, they are likely to be designed by a top-down approach.

QS B-2
Qualities of accounting information
C2

Match the desired qualities of financial information to their most appropriate characteristics. Use the following codes: **A.** Relevant **B.** Reliable **C.** Comparable

1. _____ Timely
2. _____ Neutral
3. _____ Verifiable
4. _____ Requires consistency
5. _____ Makes a difference in decision making
6. _____ Useful in identifying differences between companies
7. _____ Faithful representation
8. _____ Free from bias and error
9. _____ Predictive

QS B-3
Impact of price changes on the balance sheet
C3

Identify *four* accounts from the following list whose account balances you feel are most likely to mislead users when prices change:

a. Accounts receivable
b. Inventories
c. Land
d. Equipment
e. Accounts payable
f. Cash
g. Long-term stock investments
h. Prepaid expenses
i. Income taxes payable

Exercises

Exercise B-1
Reviewing accounting principles
C1

Match the accounting principle to its best description.

Principle

1. _____ Business entity principle
2. _____ Going-concern principle
3. _____ Objectivity principle
4. _____ Revenue recognition principle
5. _____ Matching principle
6. _____ Time period principle

Description

A. Requires that financial statement information be supported by something other than someone's opinion or imagination.
B. Requires that revenue be recognized at the time it is earned.
C. Assumes the business will continue operating instead of being closed or sold.
D. Requires expenses to be reported in the same period as the revenues earned as the result of the expenses.
E. Requires every business to be accounted for separately and distinctly from its owners.
F. Requires identifying the activities of a business with specific time periods such as quarters or years.

Exercise B-2
Descriptive and prescriptive concepts
C1, C2

Write a one-page report explaining the difference between descriptive and prescriptive concepts. Indicate why the FASB's conceptual framework is designed to be prescriptive and discuss the issue of whether specific concepts can be both descriptive and prescriptive.

Exercise B-3
Mark to market valuation C4

Review **NIKE**'s balance sheet in Appendix A. Identify four account balances that would likely change if its balance sheet were prepared on a mark to market basis rather than using generally accepted accounting principles.

Exercise B-4
Mark to market valuation C4

Your employer asks you to prepare the company's balance sheet using mark to market accounting. You realize that some accounts have valuations that don't differ from the historical cost basis, such as cash, accounts receivable, accounts payable, and prepaid expenses. However, there are four accounts that you need to locate market values for. These accounts are inventory, land, equipment, and short-term stock investments. Identify possible sources you may need to consult for these market values.

Present and Future Values

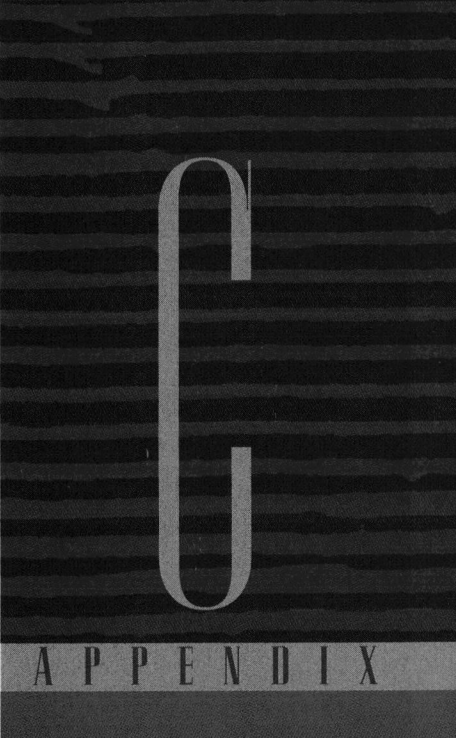

Appendix Outline

- **Present and Future Value Concepts**
- **Present Value of a Single Amount**
- **Future Value of a Single Amount**
- **Present Value of an Annuity**
- **Future Value of an Annuity**

Learning Objectives

Conceptual

C1 Describe the earning of interest and the concepts of present and future values.

Procedural

P1 Apply present value concepts to a single amount by using interest tables.

P2 Apply future value concepts to a single amount by using interest tables.

P3 Apply present value concepts to an annuity by using interest tables.

P4 Apply future value concepts to an annuity by using interest tables.

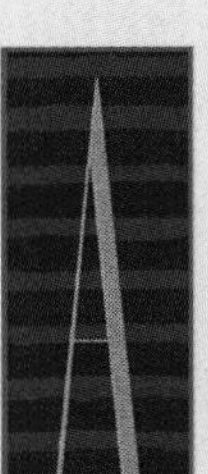

APPENDIX PREVIEW

The concepts of present value are described and applied in Chapter 15. This appendix helps to supplement that discussion with added explanations, illustrations, computations, present value tables, and additional assignments. We also give attention to illustrations, definitions, and computations of future values.

Present and Future Value Concepts

C1 Describe the earning of interest and the concepts of present and future values.

There's an old saying, *time is money.* This saying reflects the notion that as time passes, the assets and liabilities we hold are changing. This change is due to interest. *Interest* is the payment to the owner of an asset for its use by a borrower. The most common example of this type of asset is a savings account. As we keep a balance of cash in our accounts, it earns interest that is paid to us by the financial institution. An example of a liability is a car loan. As we carry the balance of the loan, we accumulate interest costs on this debt. We must ultimately repay this loan with interest.

Present and future value computations are a way for us to estimate the interest component of holding assets or liabilities over time. The present value of an amount applies when we either lend or borrow an asset that must be repaid in full at some future date, and we want to know its worth today. The future value of an amount applies when we either lend or borrow an asset that must be repaid in full at some future date, and we want to know its worth at a future date.

The first section focuses on the present value of a single amount. Later sections focus on the future value of a single amount, and then both present and future values of a series of amounts (or annuity).

Present Value of a Single Amount

We graphically express the present value (p) of a single future amount (f) received or paid at a future date in Exhibit C.1.

Exhibit C.1

Present Value of a Single Amount

P1 Apply present value concepts to a single amount by using interest tables.

The formula to compute the present value of this single amount is shown in Exhibit C.2 where: p = present value; f = future value; i = rate of interest per period; and n = number of periods.

Exhibit C.2

Present Value of a Single Amount Formula

$$p = \frac{f}{(1 + i)^n}$$

To illustrate the application of this formula, let's assume we need $220 one period from today. We want to know how much must be invested now, for one period, at an interest rate of 10% to provide for this $220.[1] For this illustration the p, or present value, is the unknown amount. In particular, the present and future values, along with the interest rate, are shown graphically as:

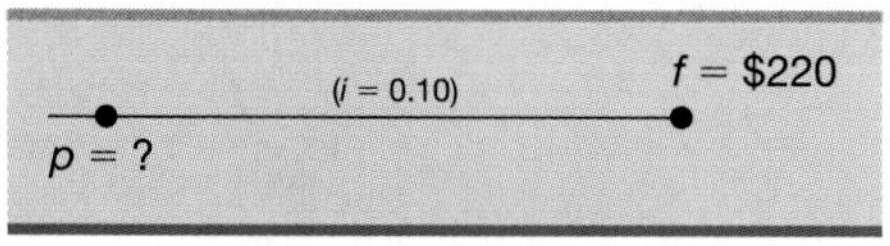

$(i = 0.10)$ $f = \$220$

$p = ?$

[1] Interest is also called a *discount,* and an interest rate is also called a *discount rate.*

Conceptually, we know p must be less than \$220. This is obvious from the answer to the question: Would we rather have \$220 today or \$220 at some future date? If we had \$220 today, we could invest it and see it grow to something more than \$220 in the future. Therefore, if we were promised \$220 in the future, we would take less than \$220 today. But how much less?

To answer that question we can compute an estimate of the present value of the \$220 to be received one period from now using the formula in Exhibit C.2 as:

$$p = \frac{f}{(1+i)^n} = \frac{\$220}{(1+.10)^1} = \$200$$

This means we are indifferent between \$200 today or \$220 at the end of one period.

We can also use this formula to compute the present value for *any number of periods.* To illustrate this computation, we consider a payment of \$242 at the end of two periods at 10% interest. The present value of this \$242 to be received two periods from now is computed as:

$$p = \frac{f}{(1+i)^n} = \frac{\$242}{(1+.10)^2} = \$200$$

These results tells us we are indifferent between \$200 today, or \$220 one period from today, or \$242 two periods from today.

I will pay your allowance at the end of the month. Do you want to wait or receive its present value today?

The number of periods (n) in the present value formula does not have to be expressed in years. Any period of time such as a day, a month, a quarter, or a year can be used. But, whatever period is used, the interest rate (i) must be compounded for the same period. This means if a situation expresses n in months, and i equals 12% per year, then we can assume 1% of an amount invested at the beginning of each month is earned in interest per month and added to the investment. In this case, interest is said to be compounded monthly.

A present value table helps us with present value computations. It gives us present values for a variety of interest rates (i) and a variety of periods (n). Each present value in a present value table assumes the future value (f) is 1. When the future value (f) is different than 1, we can simply multiply present value (p) by that future amount to give us our estimate.

The formula used to construct a table of present values of a single future amount of 1 is shown in Exhibit C.3.

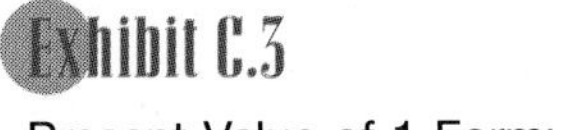

Present Value of 1 Formula

$$p = \frac{1}{(1+i)^n}$$

This formula is identical to that in Exhibit C.2 except that f equals 1. Table C.1 at the end of this appendix is a present value table for a single future amount. It is often called a **present value of 1 table.** A present value table involves three factors: p, i, and n.[2] Knowing two of these three factors allows us to compute the third. To illustrate, consider the three possible cases.

Case 1 (solve for p when knowing i and n). Our example above is a case in which we need to solve for p when knowing i and n. To illustrate how we use a present value table, let's again look at how we estimate the present value of \$220 (f) at the end of one period (n) where the interest rate (i) is 10%. To answer this we go to the present value

[2] A fourth is f, but as we already explained, we need only multiple the "1" used in the formula by f.

table (Table C.1) and look in the row for 1 period and in the column for 10% interest. Here we find a present value *(p)* of 0.9091 based on a future value of 1. This means, for instance, that $1 to be received 1 period from today at 10% interest is worth $0.9091 today. Since the future value is not $1, but is $220, we multiply the 0.9091 by $220 to get an answer of $200.

Case 2 (solve for *n* when knowing *p* and *i*). This is a case in which we have, say, a $100,000 future value *(f)* valued at $13,000 today *(p)* with an interest rate of 12% *(i)*. In this case we want to know how many periods *(n)* there are between the present value and the future value. A case example is when we want to retire with $100,000, but have only $13,000 earning a 12% return. How long will it be before we can retire? To answer this we go to Table C.1 and look in the 12% interest column. Here we find a column of present values *(p)* based on a future value of 1. To use the present value table for this solution, we must divide $13,000 *(p)* by $100,000 *(f)*, which equals 0.1300. This is necessary because **a present value table defines *f* equal to 1, and *p* as a fraction of 1.** We look for a value nearest to 0.1300 *(p)*, which we find in the row for 18 periods *(n)*. This means the present value of $100,000 at the end of 18 periods at 12% interest is $13,000 or, alternatively stated, we must work 18 more years.

Case 3 (solve for *i* when knowing *p* and *n*). This is a case where we have, say, a $120,000 future value *(f)* valued at $60,000 *(p)* today when there are nine periods *(n)* between the present and future values. Here we want to know what rate of interest is being used. As an example, suppose we want to retire with $120,000, but we only have $60,000 and hope to retire in nine years. What interest rate must we earn to retire with $120,000 in nine years? To answer this we go to the present value table (Table C.1) and look in the row for nine periods. To again use the present value table we must divide $60,000 *(p)* by $120,000 *(f)*, which equals 0.5000. Recall this is necessary because a present value table defines *f* equal to 1, and *p* as a fraction of 1. We look for a value in the row for nine periods that is nearest to 0.5000 *(p)*, which we find in the column for 8% interest *(i)*. This means the present value of $120,000 at the end of nine periods at 8% interest is $60,000 or, in our example, we must earn 8% annual interest to retire in nine years.

1. A company is considering an investment expected to yield $70,000 after six years. If this company demands an 8% return, how much is it willing to pay for this investment?

Answer—p. C-8

Future Value of a Single Amount

We use the formula for the present value of a single amount and modify it to obtain the formula for the future value of a single amount. To illustrate, we multiply both sides of the equation in Exhibit C.2 by $(1 + i)^n$. The result is shown in Exhibit C.4.

Exhibit C.4

Future Value of a Single Amount Formula

$$f = p \times (1 + i)^n$$

P2 Apply future value concepts to a single amount by using interest tables.

Future value *(f)* is defined in terms of *p, i,* and *n*. We can use this formula to determine that $200 invested for 1 period at an interest rate of 10% increases to a future value of $220 as follows:

$$\begin{aligned} f &= p \times (1 + i)^n \\ &= \$200 \times (1 + .10)^1 \\ &= \$220 \end{aligned}$$

This formula can also be used to compute the future value of an amount for *any number of periods* into the future. As an example, assume $200 is invested for three periods at 10%. The future value of this $200 is $266.20 and is computed as:

$$f = p \times (1 + i)^n$$
$$= \$200 \times (1 + .10)^3$$
$$= \$266.20$$

It is also possible to use a future value table to compute future values *(f)* for many combinations of interest rates *(i)* and time periods *(n)*. Each future value in a future value table assumes the present value *(p)* is 1. As with a present value table, if the future amount is something other than 1, we simply multiply our answer by that amount. The formula used to construct a table of future values of a single amount of 1 is shown in Exhibit C.5.

$$f = (1 + i)^n$$

Exhibit C.5

Future Value of 1 Formula

Table C.2 at the end of this appendix shows a table of future values of a single amount of 1. This type of table is called a **future value of 1 table.**

It is interesting to point out some items in Tables C.1 and C.2. Note in Table C.2 for the row where $n = 0$, that the future value is 1 for every interest rate. This is because no interest is earned when time does not pass. Also notice that Tables C.1 and C.2 report the same information in a different manner. In particular, one table is simply the *inverse* of the other.

To illustrate this inverse relation let's say we invest $100 annually for a period of five years at 12% per year. How much do we expect to have after five years? We can answer this question using Table C.2 by finding the future value *(f)* of 1, for five periods from now, compounded at 12%. From the table we find $f = 1.7623$. If we start with $100, the amount it accumulates to after five years is $176.23 ($100 × 1.7623).

We can alternatively use Table C.1. Here we find the present value *(p)* of 1, discounted five periods at 12%, is 0.5674. Recall the inverse relation between present value and future value. This means $p = 1/f$ (or equivalently $f = 1/p$).[3] Knowing this we can compute the future value of $100 invested for five periods at 12% as:

$$f = \$100 \times (1 / 0.5674) = \$176.24$$

A future value table involves three factors: *f, i,* and *n*. Knowing two of these three factors allows us to compute the third. To illustrate, consider the three possible cases.

Case 1 (solve for *f* when knowing *i* and *n*). Our example above is a case in which we need to solve for *f* when knowing *i* and *n*. We found that $100 invested for five periods at 12% interest accumulates to $176.24.

Case 2 (solve for *n* when knowing *f* and *i*). This is a case where we have, say, $2,000 *(p)* and we want to know how many periods *(n)* it will take to accumulate to $3,000 *(f)* at 7% *(i)* interest. To answer this, we go to the future value table (Table C.2) and look in the 7% interest column. Here we find a column of future values *(f)* based on a present value of 1. To use a future value table, we must divide $3,000 *(f)* by $2,000 *(p)*, which equals 1.500. This is necessary because **a future value table defines *p* equal to 1, and *f* as a multiple of 1.** We look for a value nearest to 1.50 *(f)*, which we find in the row for six periods *(n)*. This means $2,000 invested for six periods at 7% interest accumulates to $3,000.

[3] Proof of this relation is left for advanced courses.

Case 3 (solve for i when knowing f and n). This is a case where we have, say, \$2,001 (p) and in nine years (n) we want to have \$4,000 (f). What rate of interest must we earn to accomplish this? To answer this, we go to Table C.2 and search in the row for nine periods. To use a future value table, we must divide \$4,000 (f) by \$2,001 (p), which equals 1.9990. Recall this is necessary because a future value table defines p equal to 1, and f as a multiple of 1. We look for a value nearest to 1.9990 (f), which we find in the column for 8% interest (i). This means \$2,001 invested for nine periods at 8% interest accumulates to \$4,000.

Flash back

2. Assume you're a winner in a \$150,000 cash sweepstakes. You decide to deposit this cash in an account earning 8% annual interest and you plan to quit your job when the account equals \$555,000. How many years will it be before you can quit working?

Answer—p. C-8

Present Value of an Annuity

An annuity is a series of equal payments occurring at equal intervals. One example is a series of three annual payments of \$100 each. The present value of an *ordinary annuity* is defined as the present value of equal payments at equal intervals as of one period before the first payment. An ordinary annuity of \$100 and its present value (p) is illustrated in Exhibit C.6.

Exhibit C.6

Present Value of an Ordinary Annuity

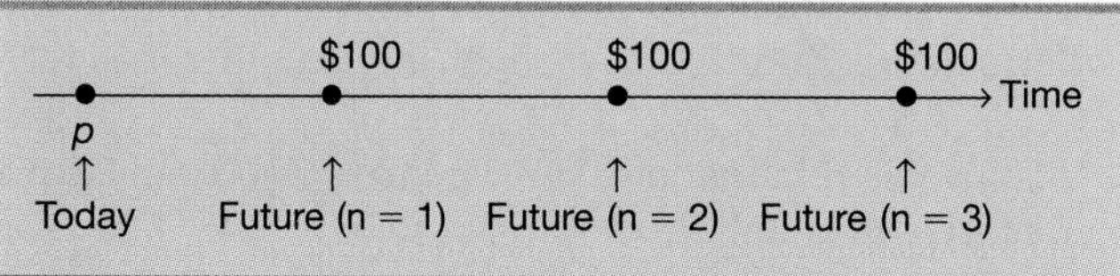

P3 Apply present value concepts to an annuity by using interest tables.

One way for us to compute the present value of an ordinary annuity is to find the present value of each payment using our present value formula from Exhibit C.3. We then would add up each of the three present values. To illustrate, let's look at three, \$100 payments at the end of each of the next three periods with an interest rate of 15%. Our present value computations are:

$$p = \frac{\$100}{(1 + .15)^1} + \frac{\$100}{(1 + .15)^2} + \frac{\$100}{(1 + .15)^3} = \$228.32$$

This computation also is identical to computing the present value of each payment (from Table C.1) and taking their sum or, alternatively, adding the values from Table C.1 for each of the three payments and multiplying their sum by the \$100 annuity payment.

A more direct way is to use a present value of annuity table. Table C.3 at the end of this appendix is one such table. This table is called a **present value of an annuity of 1 table.** If we look at Table C.3 where $n = 3$ and $i = 15\%$, we see the present value is 2.2832. This means the present value of an annuity of 1 for 3 periods, with a 15% interest rate, is 2.2832.

A present value of annuity formula is used to construct Table C.3. It can also be constructed by adding the amounts in a present value of 1 table.[4] To illustrate, we use Tables C.1 and C.3 to confirm this relation for the prior example:

---

[4] The formula for the present value of an annuity of 1 is: $p = \frac{1 - \frac{1}{(1 + i)^n}}{i}$

From Table C.1		From Table C.3	
$i = 15\%, n = 1$	0.8696		
$i = 15\%, n = 2$	0.7561		
$i = 15\%, n = 3$	0.6575		
Total	2.2832	$i = 15\%, n = 3$	2.2832

We can also use business calculators or spreadsheet computer programs to find the present value of an annuity.

Flash back

3. A company is considering an investment paying $10,000 every 6 months for 3 years. The first payment would be received in six months. If this company requires an annual return of 8%, what is the maximum amount they are willing to invest?

Answer—p. C-8

Fish'n Pell Lake

Frank and Shirley Capaci went fishing in Pell Lake, Wisconsin, a village of 1,200 people—fishing for money that is. They purchased a ticket in the powerball lottery system and hit the jackpot. The Capaci's had to choose between a $196 million annuity over 25 years or a single amount of $104 million. They chose the latter making it the largest one-time payment in U.S. lottery history. Mr. Capaci, a retired electrician, said they plan to spend the money on their children.

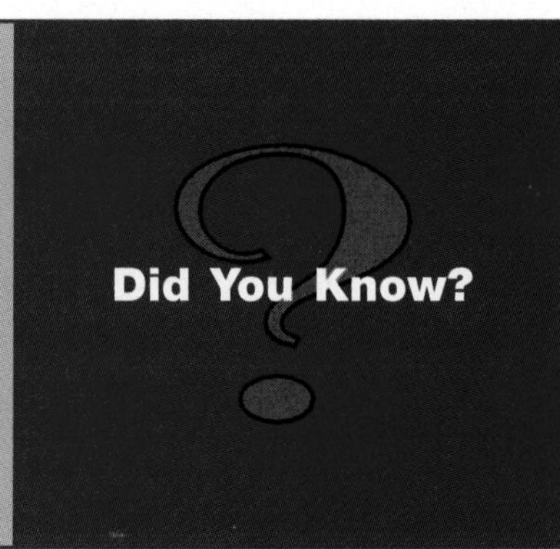

Future Value of an Annuity

We can also compute the future value of an annuity. The future value of an *ordinary annuity* is the accumulated value of each annuity payment with interest as of the date of the final payment. To illustrate, let's consider the earlier annuity of three annual payments of $100. Exhibit C.7 shows the point in time for the future value *(f)*. The first payment is made two periods prior to the point where future value is determined, and the final payment occurs on the future value date.

Exhibit C.7

Future Value of an Ordinary Annuity

Today	Future (n = 1)	Future (n = 2)	Future (n = 3)
	$100	$100	$100 (*f*) → Time

P4 Apply future value concepts to an annuity by using interest tables.

One way to compute the future value of an annuity is to use the formula to find the future value of *each* payment and add them together. If we assume an interest rate of 15%, our calculation is:

$$f = \$100 \times (1 + .15)^2 + \$100 \times (1 + .15)^1 + \$100 \times (1 + .15)^0 = \$347.25$$

This is identical to using Table C.2 and finding the sum of the future values of each payment, or adding the future values of the three payments of 1 and multiplying the sum by $100.

A more direct way is to use a table showing future values of annuities. Such a table is called a **future value of an annuity of 1 table.** Table C.4 at the end of this appendix is one such table. We should note in Table C.4 that when $n = 1$, the future values are equal to 1 ($f = 1$) for all rates of interest. That is because the annuity consists of only one payment and the future value is determined on the date of that payment—no time passes between the payment and its future value.

A formula is used to construct Table C.4.[5] We can also construct it by adding the amounts from a future value of 1 table. To illustrate, we use Tables C.2 and C.4 to confirm this relation for the prior example:

From Table C.2		From Table C.4	
i = 15%, n = 0	1.0000		
i = 15%, n = 1	1.1500		
i = 15%, n = 2	1.3225		
Total	3.4725	i = 15%, n = 3	3.4725

Note the future value in Table C.2 is 1.0000 when $n = 0$, but the future value in Table C.4 is 1.0000 when $n = 1$. Is this a contradiction? No. When $n = 0$ in Table C.2, the future value is determined on the date where a single payment occurs. This means no interest is earned, since no time has passed, and the future value equals the payment. Table C.4 describes annuities with equal payments occurring at the end of each period. When $n = 1$, the annuity has one payment, and its future value equals 1 on the date of its final and only payment. Again, no time passes from the payment and its future value date.

Flash back

4. A company invests $45,000 per year for five years at 12% annual interest. Compute the value of this annuity investment at the end of five years.

Answer—p. C-8

Summary

C1 Describe the earning of interest and the concepts of present and future values. Interest is payment to the owner of an asset for its use by a borrower. Present and future value computations are a way for us to estimate the interest component of holding assets or liabilities over a period of time.

P1 Apply present value concepts to a single amount by using interest tables. The present value of a single amount to be received at a future date is the amount that can be invested now at the specified interest rate to yield that future value.

P2 Apply future value concepts to a single amount by using interest tables. The future value of a single amount invested at a specified rate of interest is the amount that would accumulate at a future date.

P3 Apply present value concepts to an annuity by using interest tables. The present value of an annuity is the amount that can be invested now at the specified interest rate to yield that series of equal periodic payments.

P4 Apply future value concepts to an annuity by using interest tables. The future value of an annuity to be invested at a specific rate of interest is the amount that would accumulate at the date of the final equal periodic payment.

Guidance Answers to  backs

1. $70,000 × 0.6302 = $44,114 (using Table C.1, i = 8%, n = 6).
2. $555,000/$150,000 = 3.7000; Table C.2 shows this value is not achieved until after 17 years at 8% interest.
3. $10,000 × 5.2421 = $52,421 (using Table C.3, i = 4%, n = 6).
4. $45,000 × 6.3528 = $285,876 (using Table C.4, i = 12%, n = 5).

[5] The formula for the future value of an annuity of 1 is: $f = \frac{(1 + i)^n - 1}{i}$

Quick Study

QS C-1
Identifying interest rates in tables
C1

You are asked to make future value estimates using the *future value of 1 table* (Table C.2). Which interest rate column do you use when working with the following rates?

a. 8% compounded quarterly
b. 12% compounded annually
c. 6% compounded semiannually
d. 12% compounded monthly

QS C-2
Present value of an amount
P1

Flaherty is considering an investment which, if paid for immediately, is expected to return $140,000 five years hence. If Flaherty demands a 9% return, how much is she willing to pay for this investment?

QS C-3
Future value of an amount
P2

CII, Inc., invested $630,000 in a project expected to earn a 12% annual rate of return. The earnings will be reinvested in the project each year until the entire investment is liquidated 10 years hence. What will the cash proceeds be when the project is liquidated?

QS C-4
Present value of an annuity
P3

Beene Distributing is considering a contract that will return $150,000 annually at the end of each year for six years. If Beene demands an annual return of 7% and pays for the investment immediately, how much should it be willing to pay?

QS C-5
Future value of an annuity
P4

Claire Fitch is planning to begin an individual retirement program in which she will invest $1,500 annually at the end of each year. Fitch plans to retire after making 30 annual investments in a program that earns a return of 10%. What will be the value of the program on the date of the last investment?

QS C-6
Interest rate on an investment.
P1

Ken Francis has been offered the possibility of investing $2,745 for 15 years, after which he will be paid $10,000. What annual rate of interest will Francis earn? (Use Table C.1.)

QS C-7
Number of periods of an investment
P1

Megan Brink has been offered the possibility of investing $6,651. The investment will earn 6% per year and will return Brink $10,000 at the end of the investment. How many years must Brink wait to receive the $10,000? (Use Table C.1.)

Exercises

Exercise C-1
Using present and future value tables
C1

For each of the following situations identify (1) it as either (a) present or future value and (b) single amount or annuity case, (2) the table you would use in your computations (but don't solve the problem), and (3) the interest rate and time periods you would use.

a. You need to accumulate $10,000 for a trip you wish to take in four years. You are able to earn 8% compounded semiannually on your savings. You only plan on making one deposit and letting the money accumulate for four years. How would you determine the amount of the one-time deposit?
b. Assume the same facts as in (a), except you will make semiannual deposits to your savings account.
c. You hope to retire after working 40 years with savings in excess of $1,000,000. You expect to save $4,000 a year for 40 years and earn an annual rate of interest of 8%. Will you be able to retire with more than $1,000,000 in 40 years?
d. A sweepstakes agency names you a grand prize winner. You can take $225,000 immediately or elect to receive annual installments of $30,000 for 20 years. You can earn 10% annually on investments you make. Which prize do you choose to receive?

Exercise C-2
Number of periods of an investment
P2

Bill Thompson expects to invest $10,000 at 12% and, at the end of the investment, receive $96,463. How many years will elapse before Thompson receives the payment? (Use Table C.2.)

Exercise C-3
Interest rate on an investment
P2

Ed Summers expects to invest $10,000 for 25 years, after which he will receive $108,347. What rate of interest will Summers earn? (Use Table C.2.)

Exercise C-4
Interest rate on an investment
P3

Betsey Jones expects an immediate investment of $57,466 to return $10,000 annually for 8 years, with the first payment to be received in one year. What rate of interest will Jones earn? (Use Table C.3.)

Exercise C-5
Number of periods of an investment
P3

Keith Riggins expects an investment of $82,014 to return $10,000 annually for several years. If Riggins is to earn a return of 10%, how many annual payments must he receive? (Use Table C.3.)

Exercise C-6
Interest rate on an investment
P4

Steve Algoe expects to invest $1,000 annually for 40 years and have an accumulated value of $154,762 on the date of the last investment. If this occurs, what rate of interest will Algoe earn? (Use Table C.4.)

Exercise C-7
Number of periods of an investment
P4

Katherine Beckwith expects to invest $10,000 annually that will earn 8%. How many annual investments must Beckwith make to accumulate $303,243 on the date of the last investment? (Use Table C.4.)

Exercise C-8
Present value of an annuity
P3

Sam Weber financed a new automobile by paying $6,500 cash and agreeing to make 40 monthly payments of $500 each, the first payment to be made one month after the purchase. The loan bears interest at an annual rate of 12%. What was the cost of the automobile?

Exercise C-9
Future value of an amount
P2

Mark Welsch deposited $7,200 in a savings account that earns interest at an annual rate of 8%, compounded quarterly. The $7,200 plus earned interest must remain in the account 10 years before it can be withdrawn. How much money will be in the account at the end of the 10 years?

Exercise C-10
Future value of an annuity
P4

Kelly Malone plans to have $50 withheld from her monthly paycheck and deposited in a savings account that earns 12% annually, compounded monthly. If Malone continues with her plan for 2 1/2 years, how much will be accumulated in the account on the date of the last deposit?

Exercise C-11
Present value of bonds
P1, P3

Spiller Corp. plans to issue 10%, 15-year, $500,000 par value bonds payable that pay interest semiannually on June 30 and December 31. The bonds are dated December 31, 1999, and are to be issued on that date. If the market rate of interest for the bonds is 8% on the date of issue, what will be the cash proceeds from the bond issue?

Exercise C-12
Future value of an amount plus an annuity
P2, P4

Starr Company has decided to establish a fund that will be used 10 years hence to replace an aging productive facility. The company will make an initial contribution of $100,000 to the fund and plans to make quarterly contributions of $50,000 beginning in three months. The fund is expected to earn 12%, compounded quarterly. What will be the value of the fund 10 years hence?

Exercise C-13
Present value of an amount
P1

McAdams Company expects to earn 10% per year on an investment that will pay $606,773 six years hence. Use Table C.1 to compute the present value of the investment.

Exercise C-14
Future value of an amount
P2

Catten, Inc., invests $163,170 at 7% per year for nine years. Use Table C.2 to compute the future value of the investment nine years hence.

Exercise C-15
Present value of an amount and annuity
P1, P3

Compute the amount that can be borrowed under each of the following circumstances:

a. A promise to pay $90,000 in seven years at an interest rate of 6%.

b. An agreement made on February 1, 2000, to make three payments of 20,000 on February 1 of 2001, 2002, and 2003. The annual interest rate is 10%.

Exercise C-16
Present value of an amount
P1

On January 1, 2000, a company agrees to pay $20,000 in three years. If the annual interest rate is 10%, determine how much cash the company can borrow with this promise.

Exercise C-17
Present value of an amount
P1

Find the amount of money that can be borrowed with each of the following promises:

Case	Single Future Payment	Number of Years	Interest Rate
a.	$40,000	3	4%
b.	75,000	7	8
c.	52,000	9	10
d.	18,000	2	4
e.	63,000	8	6
f.	89,000	5	2

Exercise C-18
Present values of annuities
P3

C&H Ski Club recently borrowed money and agreed to pay it back with a series of six annual payments of $5,000 each. C&H subsequently borrowed more money and agreed to pay it back with a series of four annual payments of $7,500 each. The annual interest rate for both loans is 6%.

a. Use Table C.1 to find the present value of these two annuities. (Round amounts to the nearest dollar.)

b. Use Table C.3 to find the present value of these two annuities.

Exercise C-19
Present value with semiannual compounding
C1, P3

Otto Co. borrowed cash on April 30, 2000, by promising to make four payments of $13,000 each on November 1, 2000, May 1, 2001, November 1, 2001, and May 1, 2002.

a. How much cash is Otto able to borrow if the interest rate is 8%, compounded semiannually?

b. How much cash is Otto able to borrow if the interest rate is 12%, compounded semiannually?

c. How much cash is Otto able to borrow if the interest rate is 16%, compounded semiannually?

Table C.1

Present Value of 1 Due in *n* Periods

Periods	Rate 1%	2%	3%	4%	5%	6%	7%	8%	9%	10%	12%	15%
1	0.9901	0.9804	0.9709	0.9615	0.9524	0.9434	0.9346	0.9259	0.9174	0.9091	0.8929	0.8696
2	0.9803	0.9612	0.9426	0.9246	0.9070	0.8900	0.8734	0.8573	0.8417	0.8264	0.7972	0.7561
3	0.9706	0.9423	0.9151	0.8890	0.8638	0.8396	0.8163	0.7938	0.7722	0.7513	0.7118	0.6575
4	0.9610	0.9238	0.8885	0.8548	0.8227	0.7921	0.7629	0.7350	0.7084	0.6830	0.6355	0.5718
5	0.9515	0.9057	0.8626	0.8219	0.7835	0.7473	0.7130	0.6806	0.6499	0.6209	0.5674	0.4972
6	0.9420	0.8880	0.8375	0.7903	0.7462	0.7050	0.6663	0.6302	0.5963	0.5645	0.5066	0.4323
7	0.9327	0.8706	0.8131	0.7599	0.7107	0.6651	0.6227	0.5835	0.5470	0.5132	0.4523	0.3759
8	0.9235	0.8535	0.7894	0.7307	0.6768	0.6274	0.5820	0.5403	0.5019	0.4665	0.4039	0.3269
9	0.9143	0.8368	0.7664	0.7026	0.6446	0.5919	0.5439	0.5002	0.4604	0.4241	0.3606	0.2843
10	0.9053	0.8203	0.7441	0.6756	0.6139	0.5584	0.5083	0.4632	0.4224	0.3855	0.3220	0.2472
11	0.8963	0.8043	0.7224	0.6496	0.5847	0.5268	0.4751	0.4289	0.3875	0.3505	0.2875	0.2149
12	0.8874	0.7885	0.7014	0.6246	0.5568	0.4970	0.4440	0.3971	0.3555	0.3186	0.2567	0.1869
13	0.8787	0.7730	0.6810	0.6006	0.5303	0.4688	0.4150	0.3677	0.3262	0.2897	0.2292	0.1625
14	0.8700	0.7579	0.6611	0.5775	0.5051	0.4423	0.3878	0.3405	0.2992	0.2633	0.2046	0.1413
15	0.8613	0.7430	0.6419	0.5553	0.4810	0.4173	0.3624	0.3152	0.2745	0.2394	0.1827	0.1229
16	0.8528	0.7284	0.6232	0.5339	0.4581	0.3936	0.3387	0.2919	0.2519	0.2176	0.1631	0.1069
17	0.8444	0.7142	0.6050	0.5134	0.4363	0.3714	0.3166	0.2703	0.2311	0.1978	0.1456	0.0929
18	0.8360	0.7002	0.5874	0.4936	0.4155	0.3503	0.2959	0.2502	0.2120	0.1799	0.1300	0.0808
19	0.8277	0.6864	0.5703	0.4746	0.3957	0.3305	0.2765	0.2317	0.1945	0.1635	0.1161	0.0703
20	0.8195	0.6730	0.5537	0.4564	0.3769	0.3118	0.2584	0.2145	0.1784	0.1486	0.1037	0.0611
25	0.7798	0.6095	0.4776	0.3751	0.2953	0.2330	0.1842	0.1460	0.1160	0.0923	0.0588	0.0304
30	0.7419	0.5521	0.4120	0.3083	0.2314	0.1741	0.1314	0.0994	0.0754	0.0573	0.0334	0.0151
35	0.7059	0.5000	0.3554	0.2534	0.1813	0.1301	0.0937	0.0676	0.0490	0.0356	0.0189	0.0075
40	0.6717	0.4529	0.3066	0.2083	0.1420	0.0972	0.0668	0.0460	0.0318	0.0221	0.0107	0.0037

Table C.2

Future Value of 1 Due in *n* Periods

Periods	Rate 1%	2%	3%	4%	5%	6%	7%	8%	9%	10%	12%	15%
0	1.0000	1.0000	1.0000	1.0000	1.0000	1.0000	1.0000	1.0000	1.0000	1.0000	1.0000	1.0000
1	1.0100	1.0200	1.0300	1.0400	1.0500	1.0600	1.0700	1.0800	1.0900	1.1000	1.1200	1.1500
2	1.0201	1.0404	1.0609	1.0816	1.1025	1.1236	1.1449	1.1664	1.1811	1.2100	1.2544	1.3225
3	1.0303	1.0612	1.0927	1.1249	1.1576	1.1910	1.2250	1.2597	1.2950	1.3310	1.4049	1.5209
4	1.0406	1.0824	1.1255	1.1699	1.2155	1.2625	1.3108	1.3605	1.4116	1.4641	1.5735	1.7490
5	1.0510	1.1041	1.1593	1.2167	1.2763	1.3382	1.4026	1.4693	1.5386	1.6105	1.7623	2.0114
6	1.0615	1.1262	1.1941	1.2653	1.3401	1.4185	1.5007	1.5869	1.6771	1.7116	1.9738	2.3131
7	1.0721	1.1487	1.2299	1.3159	1.4071	1.5036	1.6058	1.7138	1.8280	1.9487	2.2107	2.6600
8	1.0829	1.1717	1.2668	1.3686	1.4775	1.5938	1.7182	1.8509	1.9926	2.1436	2.4760	3.0590
9	1.0937	1.1951	1.3048	1.4233	1.5513	1.6895	1.8385	1.9990	2.1719	2.3579	2.7731	3.5179
10	1.1046	1.2190	1.3439	1.4802	1.6289	1.7908	1.9672	2.1589	2.3674	2.5937	3.1058	4.0456
11	1.1157	1.2434	1.3842	1.5395	1.7103	1.8983	2.1049	2.3316	2.5804	2.8531	3.4785	4.6524
12	1.1268	1.2682	1.4258	1.6010	1.7959	2.0122	2.2522	2.5182	2.8127	3.1384	3.8960	5.3503
13	1.1381	1.2936	1.4685	1.6651	1.8856	2.1329	2.4098	2.7196	3.0658	3.4523	4.3635	6.1528
14	1.1495	1.3195	1.5126	1.7317	1.9799	2.2609	2.5785	2.9372	3.3417	3.7975	4.8871	7.0757
15	1.1610	1.3459	1.5580	1.8009	2.0789	2.3966	2.7590	3.1722	3.6425	4.1772	5.4736	8.1371
16	1.1726	1.3728	1.6047	1.8730	2.1829	2.5404	2.9522	3.4259	3.9703	4.5950	6.1304	9.3576
17	1.1843	1.4002	1.6528	1.9479	2.2920	2.6928	3.1588	3.7000	4.3276	5.0545	6.8660	10.7613
18	1.1961	1.4282	1.7024	2.0258	2.4066	2.8543	3.3799	3.9960	4.7171	5.5599	7.6900	12.3755
19	1.2081	1.4568	1.7535	2.1068	2.5270	3.0256	3.6165	4.3157	5.1417	6.1159	8.6128	14.2318
20	1.2202	1.4859	1.8061	2.1911	2.6533	3.2071	3.8697	4.6610	5.6044	6.7275	9.6463	16.3665
25	1.2824	1.6406	2.0938	2.6658	3.3864	4.2919	5.4274	6.8485	8.6231	10.8347	17.0001	32.9190
30	1.3478	1.8114	2.4273	3.2434	4.3219	5.7435	7.6123	10.0627	13.2677	17.4494	29.9599	66.2118
35	1.4166	1.9999	2.8139	3.9461	5.5160	7.6861	10.6766	14.7853	20.4140	28.1024	52.7996	133.176
40	1.4889	2.2080	3.2620	4.8010	7.0400	10.2857	14.9745	21.7245	31.4094	45.2593	93.0510	267.864

Table C.3

Present Value of an Annuity of 1 per Period

Periods	Rate 1%	2%	3%	4%	5%	6%	7%	8%	9%	10%	12%	15%
1	0.9901	0.9804	0.9709	0.9615	0.9524	0.9434	0.9346	0.9259	0.9174	0.9091	0.8929	0.8696
2	1.9704	1.9416	1.9135	1.8861	1.8594	1.8334	1.8080	1.7833	1.7591	1.7355	1.6901	1.6257
3	2.9410	2.8839	2.8286	2.7751	2.7232	2.6730	2.6243	2.5771	2.5313	2.4869	2.4018	2.2832
4	3.9020	3.8077	3.7171	3.6299	3.5460	3.4651	3.3872	3.3121	3.2397	3.1699	3.0373	2.8550
5	4.8534	4.7135	4.5797	4.4518	4.3295	4.2124	4.1002	3.9927	3.8897	3.7908	3.6048	3.3522
6	5.7955	5.6014	5.4172	5.2421	5.0757	4.9173	4.7665	4.6229	4.4859	4.3553	4.1114	3.7845
7	6.7282	6.4720	6.2303	6.0021	5.7864	5.5824	5.3893	5.2064	5.0330	4.8684	4.5638	4.1604
8	7.6517	7.3255	7.0197	6.7327	6.4632	6.2098	5.9713	5.7466	5.5348	5.3349	4.9676	4.4873
9	8.5660	8.1622	7.7861	7.4353	7.1078	6.8017	6.5152	6.2469	5.9952	5.7950	5.3282	4.7716
10	9.4713	8.9826	8.5302	8.1109	7.7217	7.3601	7.0236	6.7101	6.4177	6.1446	5.6502	5.0188
11	10.3676	9.7868	9.2526	8.7605	8.3064	7.8869	7.4987	7.1390	6.8052	6.4951	5.9377	5.2337
12	11.2551	10.5753	9.9540	9.3851	8.8633	8.3838	7.9427	7.5361	7.1607	6.8137	6.1944	5.4206
13	12.1337	11.3484	10.6350	9.9856	9.3936	8.8527	8.3577	7.9038	7.4869	7.1034	6.4235	5.5831
14	13.0037	12.1062	11.2961	10.5631	9.8986	9.2950	8.7455	8.2442	7.7862	7.3667	6.6282	5.7245
15	13.8651	12.8493	11.9379	11.1184	10.3797	9.7122	9.1079	8.5595	8.0607	7.6061	6.8109	5.8474
16	14.7179	13.5777	12.5611	11.6523	10.8378	10.1059	9.4466	8.8514	8.3126	7.8237	6.9740	5.9542
17	15.5623	14.2919	13.1661	12.1657	11.2741	10.4773	9.7632	9.1216	8.5436	8.0216	7.1196	6.0472
18	16.3983	14.9920	13.7535	12.6593	11.6896	10.8276	10.0591	9.3719	8.7556	8.2014	7.2497	6.1280
19	17.2260	15.6785	14.3238	13.1339	12.0853	11.1581	10.3356	9.6036	8.9501	8.3649	7.3658	6.1982
20	18.0456	16.3514	14.8775	13.5903	12.4622	11.4699	10.5940	9.8181	9.1285	8.5136	7.4694	6.2593
25	22.0232	19.5235	17.4131	15.6221	14.0939	12.7834	11.6536	10.6748	9.8226	9.0770	7.8431	6.4641
30	25.8077	22.3965	19.6004	17.2920	15.3725	13.7648	12.4090	11.2578	10.2737	9.4269	8.0552	6.5660
35	29.4086	24.9986	21.4872	18.6646	16.3742	14.4982	12.9477	11.6546	10.5668	9.6442	8.1755	6.6166
40	32.8347	27.3555	23.1148	19.7928	17.1591	15.0463	13.3317	11.9246	10.7574	9.7791	8.2438	6.6418

Table C.4

Future Value of an Annuity of 1 per Period

Periods	Rate 1%	2%	3%	4%	5%	6%	7%	8%	9%	10%	12%	15%
1	1.0000	1.0000	1.0000	1.0000	1.0000	1.0000	1.0000	1.0000	1.0000	1.0000	1.0000	1.0000
2	2.0100	2.0200	2.0300	2.0400	2.0500	2.0600	2.0700	2.0800	2.0900	2.1000	2.1200	2.1500
3	3.0301	3.0604	3.0909	3.1216	3.1525	3.1836	3.2149	3.2464	3.2781	3.3100	3.3744	3.4725
4	4.0604	4.1216	4.1836	4.2465	4.3101	4.3746	4.4399	4.5061	4.5731	4.6410	4.7793	4.9934
5	5.1010	5.2040	5.3091	5.4163	5.5256	5.6371	5.7507	5.8666	5.9847	6.1051	6.3528	6.7424
6	6.1520	6.3081	6.4684	6.6330	6.8019	6.9753	7.1533	7.3359	7.5233	7.7156	8.1152	8.7537
7	7.2135	7.4343	7.6625	7.8983	8.1420	8.3938	8.6540	8.9228	9.2004	9.4872	10.0890	11.0668
8	8.2857	8.5830	8.8923	9.2142	9.5491	9.8975	10.2598	10.6366	11.0285	11.4359	12.2997	13.7268
9	9.3685	9.7546	10.1591	10.5828	11.0266	11.4913	11.9780	12.4876	13.0210	13.5795	14.7757	16.7858
10	10.4622	10.9497	11.4639	12.0061	12.5779	13.1808	13.8164	14.4866	15.1929	15.9374	17.5487	20.3037
11	11.5668	12.1687	12.8078	13.4864	14.2068	14.9716	15.7835	16.6455	17.5603	18.5312	20.6546	24.3493
12	12.6825	13.4121	14.1920	15.0258	15.9171	16.8699	17.8885	18.9771	20.1407	21.3843	24.1331	29.0017
13	13.8093	14.6803	15.6178	16.6268	17.7130	18.8821	20.1406	21.4953	22.9534	24.5227	28.0291	34.3519
14	14.9474	15.9739	17.0863	18.2919	19.5986	21.0151	22.5505	24.2149	26.0192	27.9750	32.3926	40.5047
15	16.0969	17.2934	18.5989	20.0236	21.5786	23.2760	25.1290	27.1521	29.3609	31.7725	37.2797	47.5804
16	17.2579	18.6393	20.1569	21.8245	23.6575	25.6725	27.8881	30.3243	33.0034	35.9497	42.7533	55.7175
17	18.4304	20.012	21.7616	23.6975	25.8404	28.2129	30.8402	33.7502	36.9737	40.5447	48.8837	65.0751
18	19.6147	21.4123	23.4144	25.6454	28.1324	30.9057	33.9990	37.4502	41.3013	45.5992	55.7497	75.8364
19	20.8109	22.8406	25.1169	27.6712	30.5390	33.7600	37.3790	41.4463	46.0185	41.1591	63.4397	88.2118
20	22.0190	24.2974	26.8704	29.7781	33.0660	36.7856	40.9955	45.7620	51.1601	57.2750	72.0524	102.444
25	28.2432	32.0303	36.4593	41.6459	47.7271	54.8645	63.2490	73.1059	84.7009	98.3471	133.334	212.793
30	34.7849	40.5681	47.5754	56.0849	66.4388	79.0582	94.4608	113.283	136.308	164.494	241.333	434.745
35	41.6603	49.9945	60.4621	73.6522	90.3203	111.435	138.237	172.317	215.711	271.024	431.663	881.170
40	48.8864	60.4020	75.4013	95.0255	120.800	154.762	199.635	259.057	337.882	442.593	767.091	1,779.09

Selections from the AICPA Code of Professional Conduct*

PRINCIPLES

Article I—Responsibilities In carrying out their responsibilities as professionals, members should exercise sensitive professional and moral judgments in all their activities.

Article II—The Public Interest Members should accept the obligation to act in a way that will serve the public interest, honor the public trust, and demonstrate commitment to professionalism.

Article III—Integrity To maintain and broaden public confidence, members should perform all professional responsibilities with the highest sense of integrity.

Article IV—Objectivity and Independence A member should maintain objectivity and be free of conflicts of interest in discharging professional responsibilities. A member in public practice should be independent in fact and appearance when providing auditing and other attestation services.

Article V—Due Care A member should observe the professional's technical and ethical standards, strive continually to improve competence and the quality of services, and discharge professional responsibility to the best of the member's ability.

Article VI—Scope and Nature of Services A member in public practice should observe the Principles of the *Code of Professional Conduct* in determining the scope and nature of services to be provided.

RULES

The Bylaws of the AICPA require that members adhere to the Rules of the *Code of Professional Conduct.* Departures from the Rules must be justified. The current Rules are:

Rule 101—Independence
Rule 102—Integrity and Objectivity
Rule 201—General Standards
Rule 202—Compliance with Standards
Rule 203—Accounting Principles
Rule 301—Confidential Client Information
Rule 302—Contingent Fees
Rule 501—Acts Discreditable
Rule 502—Advertising and Other Forms of Solicitation
Rule 503—Commissions
Rule 505—Form of Practice and Name

Compliance with the AICPA *Code of Professional Conduct* depends primarily on a member's understanding and voluntary actions. There are provisions for reinforcement by peers and the public through public opinion, and ultimately by disciplinary proceedings. Adherence to the *Code* helps ensure ethical behavior by CPAs.

* See, AICPA, *Code of Professional Conduct* (New York: American Institute of Certified Public Accountants, Inc., 1988).

Ethical Standards for Management Accountants

Management accountants have an obligation to the organizations they serve, their profession, the public, and themselves to maintain the highest standards of ethical conduct. In recognition of this obligation, the Institute of Management Accountants has promulgated the following standards of ethical conduct for management accountants. Adherence to these standards is integral to achieving the Objectives of Management Accounting. Management accountants shall not commit acts contrary to these standards, nor shall they condone the commission of such acts by others within their organizations.

Competence

Management accountants have a responsibility to:

- Maintain an appropriate level of professional competence by ongoing development of their knowledge and skills.
- Perform their professional duties in accordance with relevant laws, regulations, and technical standards.
- Prepare complete and clear reports and recommendations after appropriate analyses of relevant and reliable information.

Confidentiality

Management accountants have a responsibility to:

- Refrain from disclosing confidential information acquired in the course of their work except when authorized, unless legally obligated to do so.
- Inform subordinates as appropriate regarding the confidentiality of information acquired in the course of their work and monitor their activities to assure the maintenance of that confidentiality.
- Refrain from using or appearing to use confidential information acquired in the course of their work for unethical or illegal advantage either personally or through third parties.

Integrity

Management accountants have a responsibility to:

- Avoid actual or apparent conflicts of interest and advise all appropriate parties of any potential conflict.

Source: *Statements on Management Accounting,* No. 1C. "Standards of Ethical Conduct for Management Accountants" (New York: Institute of Management Accountants, 1983), pp. 1–2. Reprinted with permission.

- Refrain from engaging in any activity that would prejudice their ability to carry out their duties ethically.
- Refuse any gift, favor, or hospitality that would influence or would appear to influence their actions.
- Refrain from either actively or passively subverting the attainment of the organization's legitimate and ethical objectives.
- Recognize and communicate professional limitations or other constraints that would preclude responsible judgment or successful performance of an activity.
- Communicate unfavorable as well as favorable information and professional judgments or opinions.
- Refrain from engaging in or supporting any activity that would discredit the profession.

Objectivity

Management accountants have a responsibility to:

- Communicate information fairly and objectively.
- Disclose fully all relevant information that could reasonably be expected to influence an intended user's understanding of the reports, comments, and recommendations presented.

Resolution of Ethical Conflict

In applying the standards of ethical conduct, management accountants may encounter problems in identifying unethical behavior or in resolving an ethical conflict. When faced with significant ethical issues, management accountants should follow the established policies of the organization bearing on the resolution of such conflict. If these policies do not resolve the ethical conflict, management accountants should consider the following course of action:

- Discuss such problems with the immediate superior except when it appears that the superior is involved, in which case the problem should be presented initially to the next higher managerial level. If satisfactory resolution cannot be achieved when the problem is initially presented, submit the issues to the next higher managerial level.

  If the immediate superior is the chief executive officer, or equivalent, the acceptable reviewing authority may be a group such as the audit committee, executive committee, board of directors, board of trustees, or owners. Contact with levels about the immediate superior should be initiated only with the superior's knowledge, assuming the superior is not involved.
- Clarify relevant concepts by confidential discussion with an objective advisor to obtain an understanding of possible courses of action.
- If the ethical conflict still exists after exhausting all levels of internal review, the management accountant may have no other recourse on significant matters than to resign from the organization and to submit an informative memorandum to an appropriate representative of the organization.

Except where legally prescribed, communication of such problems to authorities or individuals not employed or engaged by the organization is not considered appropriate.

Chart of Accounts

Assets

Current Assets

101 Cash
102 Petty cash
103 Cash equivalents
104 Short-term investments
105 Short-term investments, fair value adjustment
106 Accounts receivable
107 Allowance for doubtful accounts
108 Legal fees receivable
109 Interest receivable
110 Rent receivable
111 Notes receivable
115 Subscriptions receivable, common stock
116 Subscriptions receivable, preferred stock
119 Merchandise inventory
120 __________ inventory
121 __________ inventory
124 Office supplies
125 Store supplies
126 ______ supplies
128 Prepaid insurance
129 Prepaid interest
131 Prepaid rent
132 Raw materials inventory
133 Goods in process inventory, ______
134 Goods in process inventory, ______
135 Finished goods inventory

Long-Term Investments

141 Investment in ______ stock
142 Investment in ______ bonds
143 Long-term investments, fair value adjustment
144 Investment in ______
145 Bond sinking fund

Plant Assets

151 Automobiles
152 Accumulated depreciation, Automobiles
153 Trucks
154 Accumulated depreciation, Trucks
155 Boats
156 Accumulated depreciation, Boats
157 Professional library
158 Accumulated depreciation, Professional library
159 Law library
160 Accumulated depreciation, Law library
161 Furniture
162 Accumulated depreciation, Furniture
163 Office equipment
164 Accumulated depreciation, Office equipment
165 Store equipment
166 Accumulated depreciation, Store equipment
167 ______ equipment
168 Accumulated depreciation, ______ equipment
169 Machinery
170 Accumulated depreciation, Machinery
173 Building ______
174 Accumulated depreciation, Building ______
175 Building ______
176 Accumulated depreciation, Building ______
179 Land improvements ______
180 Accumulated depreciation, Land improvements ______
181 Land improvements ______
182 Accumulated depreciation, Land improvements ______
183 Land

Natural Resources

185 Mineral deposit
186 Accumulated depletion, Mineral deposit

Intangible Assets

191 Patents
192 Leasehold
193 Franchise
194 Copyrights
195 Leasehold improvements
196 Organization costs

Liabilities

Current Liabilities

201 Accounts payable
202 Insurance payable
203 Interest payable
204 Legal fees payable
207 Office salaries payable
208 Rent payable
209 Salaries payable
210 Wages payable
211 Accrued payroll payable
214 Estimated warranty liability
215 Income taxes payable
216 Common dividend payable
217 Preferred dividend payable
218 State unemployment taxes payable
219 Employees' federal income taxes payable
221 Employees' medical insurance payable
222 Employees' retirement program payable
223 Employees' union dues payable
224 Federal unemployment taxes payable
225 FICA taxes payable
226 Estimated vacation pay liability

Unearned Revenues

230 Unearned consulting fees
231 Unearned legal fees
232 Unearned property management fees
233 Unearned ______ fees
234 Unearned ______ fees
235 Unearned janitorial revenue
236 Unearned ________ revenue
238 Unearned rent

Notes Payable

240 Short-term notes payable
241 Discount on short-term notes payable
245 Notes payable
251 Long-term notes payable
252 Discount on notes payable

Long-Term Liabilities

253 Long-term lease liability
255 Bonds payable
256 Discount on bonds payable
257 Premium on bonds payable
258 Deferred income tax liability

Equity

Owners' Equity

301 __________, capital
302 __________, withdrawals
303 __________, capital
304 __________, withdrawals
305 __________, capital
306 __________, withdrawals

Contributed Capital

307 Common stock, $ ___ par value
308 Common stock, no par
309 Common stock subscribed
310 Common stock dividend distributable
311 Contributed capital in excess of par value, common stock
312 Contributed capital in excess of stated value, no-par common stock
313 Contributed capital from retirement of common stock
314 Contributed capital, treasury stock transactions
315 Preferred stock
316 Contributed capital in excess of par value, preferred stock
317 Preferred stock subscribed

Retained Earnings

318 Retained earnings
319 Cash dividends declared
320 Stock dividends declared

Other Equity Accounts

321 Treasury stock, common
322 Unrealized holding gain (loss)

Revenues

401 __________ fees earned
402 __________ fees earned
403 __________ services revenue
404 __________ services revenue
405 Commissions earned
406 Rent earned
407 Dividends earned
408 Earnings from investment in ______
409 Interest earned
410 Sinking fund earnings
413 Sales
414 Sales returns and allowances
415 Sales discounts

Cost of Sales

Cost of Goods Sold

502 Cost of goods sold
505 Purchases
506 Purchases returns and allowances
507 Purchases discounts
508 Transportation-in

Manufacturing

520 Raw materials purchases
521 Freight-in on raw materials
530 Factory payroll
531 Direct labor
540 Factory overhead
541 Indirect materials
542 Indirect labor
543 Factory insurance expired
544 Factory supervision
545 Factory supplies used
546 Factory utilities
547 Miscellaneous production costs
548 Property taxes on factory building
549 Property taxes on factory equipment
550 Rent on factory building
551 Repairs, factory equipment
552 Small tools written off
560 Depreciation of factory equipment
561 Depreciation of factory building

Standard Cost Variance

580 Direct material quantity variance
581 Direct material price variance
582 Direct labor quantity variance
583 Direct labor price variance
584 Factory overhead volume variance
585 Factory overhead controllable variance

Expenses

Amortization, Depletion, and Depreciation

601 Amortization expense, ______
602 Amortization expense, ______
603 Depletion expense, ______
604 Depreciation expense, Boats
605 Depreciation expense, Automobiles
606 Depreciation expense, Building ______
607 Depreciation expense, Building ______
608 Depreciation expense, Land improvements ______
609 Depreciation expense, Land improvements ______
610 Depreciation expense, Law library
611 Depreciation expense, Trucks
612 Depreciation expense, ______ equipment
613 Depreciation expense, ______ equipment
614 Depreciation expense, ______
615 Depreciation expense, ______

Employee-Related Expenses

620 Office salaries expense
621 Sales salaries expense
622 Salaries expense
623 ______ wages expense
624 Employees' benefits expense
625 Payroll taxes expense

Financial Expenses

630 Cash over and short
631 Discounts lost
632 Factoring fee expense
633 Interest expense

Insurance Expenses

635 Insurance expense, Delivery equipment
636 Insurance expense, Office equipment
637 Insurance expense, ______

Rental Expenses

640 Rent expense
641 Rent expense, Office space
642 Rent expense, Selling space
643 Press rental expense
644 Truck rental expense
645 ______ rental expense

Supplies Expenses

650 Office supplies expense
651 Store supplies expense
652 ______ supplies expense
653 ______ supplies expense

Miscellaneous Expenses

655 Advertising expense
656 Bad debts expense
657 Blueprinting expense
658 Boat expense
659 Collection expense
661 Concessions expense
662 Credit card expense
663 Delivery expense
664 Dumping expense
667 Equipment expense
668 Food and drinks expense
669 Gas, oil, and repairs expense
671 Gas and oil expense
672 General and administrative expense
673 Janitorial expense
674 Legal fees expense
676 Mileage expense

677 Miscellaneous expenses
678 Mower and tools expense
679 Operating expense
681 Permits expense
682 Postage expense
683 Property taxes expense
684 Repairs expense, ______
685 Repairs expense, ______
687 Selling expense
688 Telephone expense
689 Travel and entertainment expense
690 Utilities expense
691 Warranty expense
695 Income taxes expense

Gains and Losses

701 Gain on retirement of bonds
702 Gain on sale of machinery
703 Gain on sale of short-term investments
704 Gain on sale of trucks
705 Gain on ______
706 Foreign exchange gain or loss
801 Loss on disposal of machinery
802 Loss on exchange of equipment
803 Loss on exchange of ______
804 Loss on sale of notes
805 Loss on retirement of bonds
806 Loss on sale of investments
807 Loss on sale of machinery
808 Loss on sale of ______
809 Loss on ______

Clearing Accounts

901 Income summary
902 Manufacturing summary

Alternate Problems

Problem 1-1A
Determining profits, sales, costs and returns
A1, A3, A4

Klondike Company manufactures, markets, and sells snowmobile equipment. The companies that constitute the recreational vehicle industry earn an average return on investment of 9.5%. The average amount invested, or average total assets, in Klondike Company is $2,000,000. In its most recent year, Klondike earned a profit of $100,000 on sales of $1,200,000.

Required

1. What is Klondike Company's return on investment?
2. Does return on investment seem satisfactory for Klondike given competitors' return on investment?
3. What are the total costs for Klondike Company in its most recent year?
4. What is the average total amount of financing (liabilities and equity) for Klondike Company?

Problem 1-2A
Computing and interpreting return on investment
A4

AT&T and GTE produce and market telecommunications products and are direct competitors. Key financial figures (in $ millions) for these businesses over the past year follow:

Key figures	AT&T	GTE
Sales	$79,609	$19,957
Profit	$ 139	$ 2,538
Average invested (assets)	$87,261	$37,019

Required

1. Compute return on investment for (a) AT&T and (b) GTE.
2. Which company is more successful in sales to consumers?
3. Which company is more successful in earning profits from its amount invested?
4. Write a brief memo explaining which company you would invest your money.

Problem 1-3A
Identifying risk and return
A2

All business decisions involve risk and return.

Required

Identify the risk and return in the following activities:

1. Stashing $1,000 under your mattress.
2. Placing a $500 bet on the Kentucky Derby.
3. Investing $10,000 in NIKE stock.
4. Investing $10,000 in U.S. Savings Bonds.

Problem 1-4A
Describing organizational activities
C3

Prepare an outline of an organization's major activities.

Problem 1-5A
Describing organizational activities.
C3

A new company will engage in the following activities during their first year of operation. Categorize the activities listed by the following letters:

A. Financing **B.** Investing **C.** Operating

_____ **1.** Checking compliance with local laws
_____ **2.** Obtaining a bank loan.
_____ **3.** Purchasing machinery.
_____ **4.** Researching products.
_____ **5.** Supervising workers.
_____ **6.** Contributing personal savings to the business.
_____ **7.** Renting office space.

2 CHAPTER

Problem 2-1A

Analyzing effects of transactions and calculating return on equity

C5, A1, A2

Judith Grimm started a new business called Southwest Consulting and completed the following transactions during its first year of operations:

a. Invested $50,000 cash and office equipment valued at $5,000 in the business.

b. Paid $120,000 for a small building to be used as an office. Paid $10,000 in cash and signed a note payable promising to pay the balance over several years.

c. Purchased $9,000 of office equipment for cash.

d. Purchased $2,000 of office supplies and $3,200 of office equipment on credit.

e. Paid a local newspaper $1,500 for an announcement of the office's opening.

f. Completed a financial plan on credit and billed the client $3,000 for the service.

g. Designed a financial plan for another client and collected a $5,400 cash fee.

h. Withdrew $2,750 cash from the company bank account to pay personal expenses.

i. Received $1,200 from the client described in transaction *f.*

j. Made a $900 payment on the equipment purchased in transaction *d.*

k. Paid $1,900 cash for the office secretary's wages.

Required

Preparation component

1. Create a table like the one presented in Exhibit 2.14, using the following headings for the columns: Cash; Accounts Receivable; Office Supplies; Office Equipment; Building; Accounts Payable; Notes Payable; and Judith Grimm, Capital. Leave space for an explanation column to the right of the Capital column. Identify revenues and expenses by name in the explanation column.

2. Use additions and subtractions to show the effects of the above transactions on the elements of the equation. Show new totals after each transaction. Also, indicate next to each change in the owner's equity whether it was caused by an investment, a revenue, an expense, or a withdrawal.

3. Once you have completed the table, determine the company's net income.

Analysis component

4. Determine the return on Grimm's average owner's equity. Next, assume that Grimm could have earned $3,000 for the period from another job and determine the modified return on equity for the period. State whether you think the business is a good use of Grimm's money if an alternative investment would have returned 10% for the same period.

Problem 2-2A

Preparing a balance sheet, an income statement, and a statement of changes in owner's equity

C1, A1, P1

Andrew Martin began a new business called Universal Maintenance Co. and began operations on June 1. The following transactions were completed during the month:

June 1 Invested $120,000 in the business.
1 Rented a furnished office of a maintenance company that was going out of business and paid $4,500 cash for the month's rent.
4 Purchased cleaning supplies for $2,400 cash.
6 Paid $1,125 cash for advertising the opening of the business.
8 Completed maintenance services for a customer and immediately collected $750 cash.
14 Completed maintenance services for First Union Center on credit, $6,300.
16 Paid $900 cash for an assistant's salary for the first half of the month.
20 Received payment in full for the services completed for First Union Center on June 14.
21 Completed maintenance services for Skyway Co. on credit, $3,500.
22 Purchased additional cleaning supplies on credit, $750.
24 Completed maintenance services for Comfort Motel on credit, $825.
29 Received full payment from Skyway Co. for the work completed on June 21.
29 Made a partial payment of $375 for the cleaning supplies purchased on June 22.
30 Paid $120 cash for the month's telephone bill.
30 Paid $525 cash for the month's utilities.
30 Paid $900 cash for an assistant's salary for the second half of the month.
30 Purchased insurance protection for the next 12 months (beginning
July 1 by paying a $3,600 premium. Because none of this insurance protection had been used up, it was considered to be an asset called Prepaid Insurance.
30 Martin withdrew $2,000 from the business for personal use.

Required

1. Arrange the following asset, liability, and owner's equity titles in an equation like Exhibit 2.14: Cash; Accounts Receivable; Cleaning Supplies; Prepaid Insurance; Accounts Payable; Andrew Martin, Capital. Include an explanation column for changes in owner's equity. Identify revenues and expenses by name in the explanation column.
2. Show the effects of the transactions on the elements of the equation by recording increases and decreases in the appropriate columns. Do not determine new totals for the items of the equation after each transaction. Next to each change in owner's equity, state whether it was caused by an investment, a revenue, an expense, or a withdrawal. Determine the final total for each item and verify that the equation is in balance.
3. Prepare a June income statement, a June statement of changes in owner's equity, and a June 30 balance sheet.

Problem 2-3A
Calculating and interpreting net income, preparing a balance sheet, and calculating return on equity
C1, A2, P1

The accounting records of Stiller Co. show the following assets and liabilities as of the end of 1999 and 2000:

	December 31	
	1999	**2000**
Cash	$14,000	$ 10,000
Accounts receivable	25,000	30,000
Office supplies	10,000	12,500
Office equipment	60,000	60,000
Machinery	30,500	30,500
Building		260,000
Land		65,000
Accounts payable	5,000	15,000
Note payable		260,000

Late in December 2000 (just before the amounts in the second column were calculated), Joseph Stiller, the owner, purchased a small office building and moved the business from rented quarters to the new building. The building and the land it occupies cost $325,000. The business paid $65,000 in cash and a note payable was signed for the balance. Stiller had to invest an additional $25,000 to enable it to pay the $65,000. The business earned a satisfactory net income during 2000, which enabled Stiller to withdraw $1,000 per month from the business for personal use.

Required

1. Prepare balance sheets for the business as of the end of 1999 and the end of 2000. (Remember that owner's equity equals the difference between the assets and the liabilities.)
2. By comparing the owner's equity amounts from the balance sheets and using the additional information presented in the problem, prepare a calculation to show how much net income was earned by the business during 2000.
3. Calculate the 2000 return on equity for the business. Also, calculate the modified return on equity, assuming that Stiller's efforts were worth $25,000 for the year.

Problem 2-4A
Analyzing transactions, preparing financial statements, and calculating return on equity
C1, A1, A2, P1

Cantu Excavating Co., owned by Robert Cantu, began operations in July and completed these transactions during the month:

July	1	Invested $60,000 cash in the business.
	1	Rented office space and paid the month's rent of $500.
	1	Purchased excavating equipment for $4,000 by paying $800 in cash and agreeing to pay the balance in six months.
	6	Purchased office supplies by paying $500 cash.
	8	Completed work for a customer and immediately collected $2,200 for doing the work.
	10	Purchased $3,800 of office equipment on credit.
	15	Completed work for a customer on credit in the amount of $2,400.
	17	Purchased $1,920 of office supplies on credit.
	23	Paid for the office equipment purchased on July 10.

25 Billed a customer $5,000 for completed work; the balance is due in 30 days.
28 Received $2,400 for the work completed on July 15.
31 Paid an assistant's salary of $1,260.
31 Paid the monthly utility bills of $260.
31 Withdrew $1,200 from the business to pay personal expenses.

Required

Preparation Component

1. Arrange the following asset, liability, and stockholders' equity titles in an equation like Exhibit 2.14: Cash; Accounts Receivable; Office Supplies; Office Equipment; Excavating Equipment; Accounts Payable; and Robert Cantu, Capital. Leave space for an explanation column to the right of the Robert Cantu, Capital column. Identify revenues and expenses by name in the explanation column.
2. Use additions and subtractions to show the effects of each transaction on the items in the equation. Show new totals after each transaction. Next to each change in owner's equity, state whether the change was caused by an investment, a revenue, an expense, or a withdrawal.
3. Use the increases and decreases in the last column of the equation to prepare an income statement and a statement of changes in owner's equity for the month. Also, prepare a balance sheet as of the end of the month.
4. Calculate the return on average owner's equity for the month, using the initial investment as the beginning balance of equity.

Analysis Component

5. Assume that Cantu invested $4,000 cash in the business to obtain the excavating equipment on July 1 instead of the purchase conditions described in the transaction. Explain the effect of this change on total assets, total liabilities, owner's equity, and return on equity.

Computing Problem 2-5A
Computing missing information using accounting knowledge
C1, C2

The following financial statement information is known about five unrelated companies:

	Company V	Company W	Company X	Company Y	Company Z
December 31, 1999:					
Assets	$45,000	$70,000	$121,500	$82,500	$124,000
Liabilities	30,000	50,000	58,500	61,500	?
December 31, 2000:					
Assets	49,000	90,000	136,500	?	160,000
Liabilities	26,000	?	55,500	72,000	52,000
During 2000:					
Owner investments	6,000	10,000	?	38,100	40,000
Net income	?	30,000	16,500	24,000	32,000
Withdrawals	4,500	2,000	0	18,000	6,000

Required

1. Answer the following questions about Company V:
   a. What was the owner's equity on December 31, 1999?
   b. What was the owner's equity on December 31, 2000?
   c. What was the net income for 2000?
2. Answer the following questions about Company W:
   a. What was the owner's equity on December 31, 1999?
   b. What was the owner's equity on December 31, 2000?
   c. What was the amount of liabilities owed on December 31, 2000?
3. Calculate the amount of owner investments in Company X made during 2000.
4. Calculate the amount of assets owned by Company Y on December 31, 2000.
5. Calculate the amount of liabilities owed by Company Z on December 31, 1999.

Problem 2-6A
Identifying effects of transactions on financial statements
C1, C2

CHAPTER 2

You are to identify how each of the following transactions affects the company's financial statements. For the balance sheet, you are to identify how each transaction affects total assets, total liabilities, and stockholders' equity. For the income statement, you are to identify how each transaction affects net income. For the statement of cash flows, you are to identify how each transaction affects cash flows from operating activities, cash flows from financing activities, and cash flows from investing activities. If there is an increase, place a "+" in the column or columns. If there is a decrease, place a "−" in the column or columns. If there is both an increase and a decrease, place "+/−" in the column or columns. The line for the first transaction is completed as an example.

		Balance Sheet			Income Stmt.	Statement of Cash Flows		
	Transaction	Total Assets	Total Liab.	Equity	Net Income	Operating	Financing	Investing
1	Invests cash	+		+			+	
2	Pays wages with cash							
3	Acquires services on credit							
4	Buys store equipment for cash							
5	Borrows cash with note payable							
6	Sells services for cash							
7	Sells services on credit							
8	Pays rent with cash							
9	Withdraw cash							
10	Collects receivable from (7)							

Problem 2A-7
Constructing a statement of cash flows
C1

A new business, Surfnet, has the following cash balance and cash flows for the month of December:

Cash balance, December 1	$ 0
Withdrawals by owner	1,000
Cash received from customers	7,800
Repayment of debt	1,800
Cash paid for store supplies	5,000
Purchase of equipment	40,000
Cash paid for rent	2,000
Cash paid to employee	1,400
Investment by owner	60,000

Required

Prepare a statement of cash flows for the month of December.

Problem 3-1A
Recording transactions in T-accounts; preparing a trial balance
A1, P2

CHAPTER 3

West Consulting completed these transactions during June:

a. Susan West, the sole proprietor, invested $23,000 cash and office equipment valued at $12,000 in the business.

b. Purchased land and a small office building. The land was worth $8,000 and the building was worth $33,000. The purchase price was paid with $15,000 cash and a long-term note payable for $26,000.

c. Purchased $600 of office supplies on credit.

d. Susan West transferred title of her personal automobile to the business. The automobile had a value of $7,000 and is to be used exclusively in the business.

e. Purchased $1,100 of additional office equipment on credit.
f. Paid $800 salary to an assistant.
g. Provided services to a client and collected $2,700 cash.
h. Paid $430 for this month's utilities.
i. Paid account payable created in transaction *c*.
j. Purchased $4,000 of new office equipment by paying $2,400 cash and trading in old equipment with a recorded net cost of $1,600.
k. Completed $2,400 of services for a client. This amount is to be paid within 30 days.
l. Paid $800 salary to an assistant.
m. Received $1,000 payment on the receivable created in transaction *k*.
n. Susan West withdrew $1,050 cash from the business for personal use.

Required

1. Open the following T-accounts: Cash; Accounts Receivable; Office Supplies; Automobiles; Office Equipment; Building; Land; Accounts Payable; Long-Term Notes Payable; Susan West, Capital; Susan West, Withdrawals; Fees Earned; Salaries Expense; and Utilities Expense.
2. Record the transactions above by entering debits and credits directly in T-accounts. Use the transaction letters to identify each debit and credit entry.
3. Determine the balance of each account and prepare a trial balance as of June 30.

Problem 3-2A
Recording transactions in T-accounts; preparing a trial balance; computing a debt ratio
A1, A2, P2

At the beginning of June, Avery Wilson created a custom computer programming company called Softouch. The company had the following transactions during the month:

a. Avery Wilson invested $45,000 cash, office equipment with a value of $4,500, and $28,000 of computer equipment.
b. Purchased land for an office. The land was worth $24,000, and is paid with $4,800 cash and a long-term note payable for $19,200.
c. Purchased a portable building with $21,000 cash and moved it onto the land.
d. Paid $6,600 cash for the premiums on two one-year insurance policies.
e. Provided services to a client and collected $3,200 cash.
f. Purchased additional computer equipment for $3,500. Paid $700 cash and signed a long-term note payable for the $2,800 balance.
g. Completed $3,750 of services for a client. This amount is to be paid within 30 days.
h. Purchased $750 of additional office equipment on credit.
i. Completed client services for $9,200 on credit.
j. Received a bill for rent of a computer testing device that was used on a completed job. The $320 rent must be paid within 30 days.
k. Collected $4,600 from the client described in transaction *i*.
l. Paid $1,600 wages to an assistant.
m. Paid the account payable created in transaction *h*.
n. Paid $425 cash for some repairs to an item of computer equipment.
o. Avery Wilson withdrew $3,875 cash from the business for personal use.
p. Paid $1,600 wages to an assistant.
q. Paid $800 cash to advertise in the local newspaper.

Required

1. Open the following T-accounts: Cash; Accounts Receivable; Prepaid Insurance; Office Equipment; Computer Equipment; Building; Land; Accounts Payable; Long-Term Notes Payable; Avery Wilson, Capital; Avery Wilson, Withdrawals; Fees Earned; Wages Expense; Computer Rental Expense; Advertising Expense; and Repairs Expense.
2. Record the transactions by entering debits and credits directly in T-accounts. Use the transaction letters to identify each debit and credit. Prepare a trial balance as of June 30.
3. Calculate the company's debt ratio. Use $108,000 as the ending total assets. Are the assets of the company financed more by debt or equity?

Problem 3-3A
Preparing and posting general journal entries; preparing a trial balance
A1, P1, P2

Leonard Management Services completed these transactions during November:

Nov. 1 Arthur Leonard, the owner, invested $28,000 cash and office equipment valued at $25,000 in the business.
2 Prepaid $10,500 cash for three months' rent for an office.
4 Made credit purchases of office equipment for $9,000 and office supplies for $1,200.
8 Completed work for a client and immediately received $2,600 cash.
12 Completed a $13,400 project for a client, who will pay within 30 days.
13 Paid the account payable created on November 4.
19 Paid $5,200 cash as the annual premium on an insurance policy.
22 Received $7,800 as partial payment for the work completed on November 12.
24 Completed work for another client for $1,900 on credit.
28 Arthur Leonard withdrew $5,300 from the business for personal use.
29 Purchased $1,700 of additional office supplies on credit.
30 Paid $460 for the month's utility bill.

Required

1. Prepare general journal entries to record the transactions.
2. Open the following accounts (use the balance column format): Cash (101); Accounts Receivable (106); Office Supplies (124); Prepaid Insurance (128); Prepaid Rent (131); Office Equipment (163); Accounts Payable (201); Arthur Leonard, Capital (301); Arthur Leonard, Withdrawals (302); Service Fees Earned (401); and Utilities Expense (690).
3. Post entries to the accounts and enter the balance after each posting.
4. Prepare a trial balance as of the end of the month.

Problem 3-4A
Interpreting journals; posting; correcting a trial balance
A1, P1, P2

Damon Oleson started a business called Knot Board on June 1 and completed several transactions during the month. His accounting skills are weak and he needs some help gathering information at the end of the month. Presented below are the journal entries that he recorded during June:

June	1	Cash	11,000	
		Store Equipment	9,000	
		Damon Oleson, Capital		20,000
	2	Prepaid Insurance	400	
		Cash		400
	6	Accounts Receivable	1,800	
		Fees Earned		1,800
	9	Office Supplies	700	
		Office Equipment	4,200	
		Accounts Payable		4,900
	11	Cash	2,100	
		Fees Earned		2,100
	14	Accounts Payable	120	
		Office Supplies		120
	20	Cash		1,500
		Accounts Receivable		1,500
	21	Accounts Payable	4,780	
		Cash		4,780
	23	Automobile	8,000	
		Damon Oleson, Capital		8,000
	28	Damon Oleson, Withdrawals	1,000	
		Cash		1,000
	29	Salaries Expense	1,400	
		Cash		1,400
	30	Office Supplies	390	
		Accounts Payable		390

3 CHAPTER

Based on these entries, Oleson prepared the following trial balance:

KNOT BOARD Trial Balance For Month Ended June 30		
	Debit	**Credit**
Cash	$ 7,200	
Accounts receivable	400	
Office supplies	790	
Prepaid insurance	4,000	
Automobiles	8,000	
Office equipment		$ 4,200
Store equipment		9,000
Accounts payable		930
Damon Oleson, capital		28,000
Damon Oleson, withdrawals		1,000
Fees earned		3,900
Salaries expense	1,500	
Total	$21,890	$47,030

Required

Preparation Component

1. Oleson remembers something about trial balances and realizes the preceding one has at least one error. To help him find the mistakes, set up the following balance column accounts and post entries to them: Cash (101); Accounts Receivable (106); Office Supplies (124); Prepaid Insurance (128); Automobiles (151); Office Equipment (163); Store Equipment (165); Accounts Payable (201); Damon Oleson, Capital (301); Damon Oleson, Withdrawals (302); Fees Earned (401); and Salaries Expense (622).

Analysis Component

2. Although Oleson's journal entries are correct, he forgot to provide explanations. Analyze each entry and present a reasonable explanation of what happened.
3. Prepare a correct trial balance and describe the errors that Oleson made.

Problem 3-5A
Analyzing account balances and reconstructing transactions
A1, P2

Cass Consulting's first seven transactions resulted in the following accounts, which have normal balances:

Cash	$12,485
Office supplies	560
Prepaid rent	1,500
Office equipment	11,450
Accounts payable	11,450
Stephanie Cass, capital	10,000
Stephanie Cass, withdrawals	6,200
Consulting fees earned	16,400
Operating expenses	5,655

Required

Preparation Component

1. Prepare a trial balance for the business.

Analysis Component

2. Analyze the accounts and their balances and prepare a list that describes each of the seven most likely transactions that resulted in the previous account balances.
3. Present a schedule that shows how the seven transactions in *2* resulted in the $12,485 Cash balance.

Problem 3-6A
Classifying accounts in financial statements

A1

3 CHAPTER

Rachel Rohr operates a computer programming company specializing in "html" programming and Web site construction. For the first few months of the company's life (through April), the accounting records were maintained by an outside accounting service. According to those records, Rohr's owner's equity balance was $18,500 as of May 1. To save on expenses, Rohr decided to keep the records herself. She managed to record May's transactions properly, but she had problems properly classifying accounts in financial statements. Her first versions of the balance sheet and income statement follow. Using the information contained in these financial statements, prepare revised statements, including a statement of changes in owner's equity, for the month of May.

R^2 Consulting
Income Statement
May 31

Revenue:		
Investments by owner		$ 4,000
Unearned programming fees		9,000
Total revenues		$ 13,000
Operating expenses:		
Rent expense	$4,100	
Telephone expense	700	
Office equipment	6,500	
Advertising expense	4,300	
Utilities expense	400	
Insurance expense	800	
Withdrawals by owner	7,000	
Total operating expenses		23,800
Net income (loss)		$(10,800)

R^2 CONSULTING
Balance Sheet
For Month Ended May 31

Assets		Liabilities	
Cash	$ 4,900	Accounts payable	$ 1,400
Accounts receivable	2,800	Programming fees earned	30,000
Prepaid insurance	1,900	Short-term notes payable	18,000
Prepaid rent	4,100	Total liabilities	$49,400
Office supplies	400	**Owner's Equity**	
Computer equipment	40,000		
Salaries expense	3,000	Rachel Rohr, Capital	7,700
Total assets	$57,100	Total liabilities and owner's equity	$57,100

Problem 4-1A
Adjusting and subsequent journal entries

A1, P1, P2, P5

4 CHAPTER

The Perfecto Company's annual accounting period ends on October 31, 2005. Perfecto follows the practice of recording prepaid expenses and unearned revenues in balance sheet accounts. The following information concerns the adjusting entries that need to be recorded as of that date:

a. The Office Supplies account started the fiscal year with a $500 balance. During the fiscal year, the company purchased supplies at a cost of $3,650, which was added to the Office Supplies account. The inventory of supplies on hand at October 31 had a cost of $700.

b. An analysis of the company's insurance policies provided these facts:

Policy	Date of Purchase	Years of Coverage	Total Cost
1	April 1, 2004	2	$3,000
2	April 1, 2005	3	3,600
3	August 1, 2005	1	660

4 CHAPTER

The total premium for each policy was paid in full at the purchase date, and the Prepaid Insurance account was debited for the full cost.

c. The company has 4 employees who earn a total of $800 for every working day. They are paid each Monday for their work in the five-day workweek ending on the previous Friday. October 31, 2005, falls on Monday, and all 4 employees worked the first day of the week. They will be paid salaries for five full days on Monday, November 7, 2005.

d. The company purchased a building on August 1, 2005. The building cost $155,000, and is expected to have a $20,000 salvage value at the end of its predicted 25-year life.

e. Because the company is not large enough to occupy the entire building, it arranged to rent some space to a tenant at $600 per month, starting on September 1, 2005. The rent was paid on time on September 1, and the amount received was credited to the Rent Earned account. However, the tenant has not paid the October rent. The company has worked out an agreement with the tenant, who has promised to pay both October's and November's rent in full on November 15. The tenant has agreed not to fall behind again.

f. On September 1, the company rented space to another tenant for $525 per month. The tenant paid five months' rent in advance on that date. The payment was recorded with a credit to the Unearned Rent account.

Required

1. Use the information to prepare adjusting entries as of October 31, 2005.

2. Prepare journal entries to record the first subsequent cash transactions for parts *c* and *e*.

Problem 4-2A
Adjusting entries; financial statements; profit margin
P1, P2, P4, A1, A2

Presented below is the unadjusted trial balance for Design Institute as of December 31, 1999. Design Institute follows the practice of initially recording prepaid expenses and unearned revenues in balance sheet accounts. The institute provides one-on-one training to individuals who pay tuition directly to the business and also offers extension training to groups in off-site locations. Shown after the trial balance are items that will require adjusting entries as of December 31, 1999.

DESIGN INSTITUTE
Unadjusted Trial Balance
December 31, 1999

Account	Debit	Credit
Cash	$ 50,000	
Accounts receivable		
Teaching supplies	60,000	
Prepaid insurance	18,000	
Prepaid rent	2,600	
Professional library	10,000	
Accumulated depreciation—Professional library		$ 1,500
Equipment	30,000	
Accumulated depreciation—Equipment		16,000
Accounts payable		12,200
Salaries payable		
Unearned training fees		27,600
Jay Stevens, capital		68,500
Jay Stevens, withdrawals	20,000	
Tuition fees earned		105,000
Training fees earned		62,000
Depreciation expense—Equipment		
Depreciation expense—Professional library		
Salaries expense	43,200	
Insurance expense		
Rent expense	28,600	
Teaching supplies expense		
Advertising expense	18,000	
Utilities expense	12,400	
Totals	$292,800	$292,800

Additional Items

a. An analysis of the company's insurance policies shows that $6,400 of coverage has expired.

b. An inventory shows that teaching supplies costing $2,500 are on hand at the end of the year.

c. Annual depreciation on the equipment is $4,000.

d. Annual depreciation on the professional library is $2,000.

e. On November 1, the company agreed to do a special four-month course for a client. The contract calls for a $4,600 monthly fee, and the client paid the first two months' fees in advance. When the cash was received, the Unearned Training Fees account was credited.

f. On October 15, the school agreed to teach a four-month class to an individual for $2,200 tuition per month payable at the end of the class. The services are being provided as agreed, and no payment has been received.

g. The school's only employee is paid weekly. As of the end of the year, three days' wages have accrued at the rate of $180 per day.

h. The balance in the Prepaid Rent account represents rent for December.

Required

1. Prepare T-accounts with the balances listed from the unadjusted trial balance.

2. Prepare adjusting journal entries for items *a* through *h* and post them to the T-accounts.

3. Update the balances in T-accounts for the adjusting entries and prepare an adjusted trial balance.

4. Prepare Design Institute's income statement and the statement of changes in owner's equity for 1999, and prepare its balance sheet as of December 31, 1999.

5. Calculate the company's profit margin for the year. The owner was not actively involved in managing the company.

Problem 4-3A[B]
Interpreting unadjusted and adjusted trial balances; preparing financial statements; calculating profit margin

P1, P2, P4, A1, A2

A six-column table for Personal Consulting Company is shown below. The first two columns contain the unadjusted trial balance for the company as of July 31, 2000, and the last two columns contain the adjusted trial balance as of the same date.

	Unadjusted Trial Balance		Adjustments		Adjusted Trial Balance	
Cash	$ 48,000				$ 48,000	
Accounts receivable	70,000				76,660	
Office supplies	30,000				7,000	
Prepaid insurance	13,200				8,600	
Office equipment	150,000				150,000	
Accumulated depreciation—Office eq.		$ 30,000				$ 40,000
Accounts payable		36,000				42,000
Interest payable						1,600
Salaries payable						11,200
Unearned consulting fees		30,000				17,800
Long-term notes payable		80,000				80,000
Dick Persons, capital		70,200				70,200
Dick Persons, withdrawals	10,000				10,000	
Consulting fees earned		264,000				282,860
Depreciation expense—Office eq.					10,000	
Salaries expense	115,600				126,800	
Interest expense	6,400				8,000	
Insurance expense					4,600	
Rent expense	24,000				24,000	
Office supplies expense					23,000	
Advertising expense	43,000				49,000	
Totals	$510,200	$510,200			$545,660	$545,660

4 CHAPTER

Required

Preparation Component

1. Prepare this company's income statement and its statement of changes in owner's equity for the year ended July 31, 2000.
2. Prepare the company's balance sheet as of July 31, 2000.
3. Calculate the company's modified profit margin for the year, assuming the value of the owner's services to the business during the year was $30,000.

Analysis Component

4. Analyze the differences between the unadjusted and adjusted trial balances to determine the adjustments that must have been made. Show the results of your analysis by inserting amounts from the adjusting journal entries that must have been recorded by the company in the two middle columns. Label each entry with a letter and provide a short description of the purpose for recording it.

Problem 4-4A
Computing accrual income from cash income
C3

The records for Craven Products are kept on the cash basis instead of the accrual basis. But the company is now applying for a loan and the bank wants to know what its net income for year 2000 is under generally accepted accounting principles. Here is the income statement for year 2000 under the cash basis:

CRAVEN PRODUCTS Income Statement (Cash Basis) For Year Ended December 31, 2000	
Revenues	$165,000
Expenses	66,000
Net income	$ 99,000

Additional information was gathered to help convert the income statement to the accrual basis:

	As of 12/31/1999	As of 12/31/2000
Accrued revenues	$11,100	$3,600
Unearned revenues	7,050	7,800
Accrued expenses	4,800	11,400
Prepaid expenses	6,300	3,300

All prepaid expenses from the beginning of the year are consumed or expired, all unearned revenues from the beginning of the year are earned, and all accrued expenses and revenues from the beginning of the year are paid or collected.

Required

Prepare an accrual basis income statement for this company for year 2000. Provide schedules that explain how you converted from cash revenues and expenses to accrual revenues and expenses.

Problem 4-5A
Identifying adjusting and subsequent entries
C4, P5

For these adjusting and transaction entries, enter the letter of the explanation that most closely describes the adjustment or transaction in the space beside each entry. (You can use letters more than once.)

a. To record receipt of accrued revenue.
b. To record payment of an accrued expense.
c. To record payment of a prepaid expense.
d. To record this period's depreciation expense.
e. To record the earning of previously unearned revenue.
f. To record this period's use of a prepaid expense.
g. To record an accrued revenue.
h. To record receipt of unearned revenue.
i. To record an accrued expense.

_____	1.	Salaries Payable	8,000	
		Cash		8,000
_____	2.	Depreciation Expense	6,000	
		Accumulated Depreciation		6,000

			Debit	Credit
_____	3.	Unearned Professional Fees	3,500	
		Professional Fees Earned		3,500
_____	4.	Interest Receivable	1,500	
		Interest Earned		1,500
_____	5.	Cash	5,000	
		Accounts Receivable		5,000
_____	6.	Interest Expense	9,000	
		Interest Payable		9,000
_____	7.	Cash	4,000	
		Unearned Professional Fees		4,000
_____	8.	Insurance Expense	3,000	
		Prepaid Insurance		3,000
_____	9.	Rent Expense	6,500	
		Prepaid Rent		6,500
_____	10.	Prepaid Rent	7,000	
		Cash		7,000
_____	11.	Salaries Expense	1,000	
		Salaries Payable		1,000
_____	12.	Cash	2,000	
		Interest Receivable		2,000

Problem 4-6A
Preparing financial statements from the adjusted trial balance; calculating profit margin
P4, A1, A2

The adjusted trial balance below is for Horizon Courier as of December 31, 2000:

	Debit	Credit
Cash	$ 48,000	
Accounts receivable	110,000	
Interest receivable	6,000	
Notes receivable (due in 90 days)	200,000	
Office supplies	12,000	
Trucks	124,000	
Accumulated depreciation—Trucks		$ 48,000
Equipment	260,000	
Accumulated depreciation—Equipment		190,000
Land	90,000	
Accounts payable		124,000
Interest payable		22,000
Salaries payable		30,000
Unearned delivery fees		110,000
Long-term notes payable		190,000
K. Ainesworth, capital		115,000
K. Ainesworth, withdrawals	40,000	
Delivery fees earned		580,000
Interest earned		24,000
Depreciation expense—Trucks	24,000	
Depreciation expense—Equipment	46,000	
Salaries expense	64,000	
Wages expense	290,000	
Interest expense	25,000	
Office supplies expense	33,000	
Advertising expense	26,400	
Repairs expense, trucks	34,600	
Total	$1,433,000	$1,433,000

4 CHAPTER

Required

1. Use the information in the trial balance to prepare *(a)* the income statement for the year ended December 31, 2000, *(b)* the statement of changes in owner's equity for the year ended December 31, 2000, and *(c)* the balance sheet as of December 31, 2000.
2. Assume the services of the owner during year 2000 are valued at \$30,000. Calculate the modified profit margin for year 2000.

Problem 4-7A[A]
Recording prepaid expenses and unearned revenues
P1, P2, P6

Werthman Company had the following transactions in the last two months of its fiscal year ended July 31:

Apr.	1	Paid \$3,450 for future consulting services.
	1	Paid \$2,700 for insurance through March 31 of the following year.
	30	Received \$7,500 for future services to be provided to a customer.
May	1	Paid \$3,450 for future newspaper advertising.
	23	Received \$9,450 for future services to be provided to a customer.
	31	Of the consulting services paid for on April 1, \$1,500 worth had been received.
	31	Part of the insurance paid for on April 1 had expired.
	31	Services worth \$3,600 had not yet been provided to the customer who paid on April 30.
	31	Of the advertising paid for on May 1, \$1,050 worth had not been published yet.
	31	The company has performed \$4,500 of services that the customer paid for on May 23.

Required

Preparation Component

1. Prepare entries for the above transactions under the method that records prepaid expenses and unearned revenues in balance sheet accounts. Also, prepare adjusting entries at the end of the year.
2. Prepare entries for the above transactions under the method that records prepaid expenses and unearned revenues in income statement accounts. Also, prepare adjusting entries at the end of the year.

Analysis Component

3. Explain why the alternative sets of entries in requirements 1 and 2 do not result in different financial statement amounts.

5 CHAPTER

Problem 5-1A
Closing entries, financial statements, and current ratio
C3, A1, P1

Western Shoe Shops' adjusted trial balance on December 31, 2000, is shown below:

WESTERN SHOE SHOPS
Adjusted Trial Balance
December 31, 2000

	Account Title	Debit	Credit
101	Cash	\$ 13,450	
125	Store supplies	4,140	
128	Prepaid insurance	2,200	
167	Equipment	33,000	
168	Accumulated depreciation—Equipment		\$ 9,000
201	Accounts payable		1,000
210	Wages payable		3,200
301	Pearl Jones, capital		31,650
302	Pearl Jones, withdrawals	16,000	
401	Repair fees earned		62,000
612	Depreciation expense—Equipment	3,000	
623	Wages expense	28,400	
637	Insurance expense	1,100	
640	Rent expense	2,400	
651	Store supplies expense	1,300	
690	Utilities expense	1,860	
	Totals	\$106,850	\$106,850

Required

Preparation Component

1. Prepare an income statement and a statement of changes in owner's equity for the year 2000 and a classified balance sheet at the end of the year. There were no owner investments during the year.
2. Enter the adjusted trial balance in the first two columns of a 6-column table that has middle columns for closing entries and the last two columns for a post-closing trial balance. Insert an Income Summary account as the last item in the trial balance.
3. Enter closing entries in the six-column table and prepare journal entries for them.
4. Determine the company's current ratio.

Analysis Component

5. Assume we collect the following two additional information items related to the adjusted trial balance shown above:
   a. None of the $1,100 insurance expense had expired during the year. Instead, it is a prepayment of future insurance protection.
   b. There were no earned and unpaid wages at the end of the year.
   Describe the changes in financial statements that would result from these two information items.

Problem 5-2A
Closing entries, financial statements, and ratios
C3, A1, P1

The adjusted trial balance for Canner Co. as of December 31, 2000 is shown below:

CANNER CO.
Adjusted Trial Balance
December 31, 2000

No.	Account Title	Debit	Credit
101	Cash	$ 6,400	
104	Short-term investments	10,200	
126	Supplies	3,600	
128	Prepaid insurance	800	
167	Equipment	18,000	
168	Accumulated depreciation—Equipment		$ 3,000
173	Building	90,000	
174	Accumulated depreciation—Building		9,000
183	Land	28,500	
201	Accounts payable		2,500
203	Interest payable		1,400
208	Rent payable		200
210	Wages payable		1,180
213	Property taxes payable		2,330
233	Unearned professional fees		650
251	Long-term notes payable		32,000
301	Joe Canner, capital		91,800
302	Joe Canner, withdrawals	6,000	
401	Professional fees earned		47,000
406	Rent earned		3,600
407	Dividends earned		500
409	Interest earned		1,120
606	Depreciation expense—Building	2,000	
612	Depreciation expense—Equipment	1,000	
623	Wages expense	17,500	
633	Interest expense	1,200	
637	Insurance expense	1,425	
640	Rent expense	1,800	
652	Supplies expense	900	
682	Postage expense	310	
683	Property taxes expense	3,825	
684	Repairs expense	579	
688	Telephone expense	421	
690	Utilities expense	1,820	
	Totals	$196,280	$196,280

An analysis of other information reveals that Canner Company is required to make a $6,400 payment on its long-term note payable during 2001. Also, J. Canner invested $30,000 cash at the beginning of year 2000.

Required

1. Prepare the income statement, statement of changes in owner's equity, and classified balance sheet.
2. Prepare the closing entries at the end of the year 2000.
3. Use the information in the financial statements to calculate these ratios:
   a. Return on equity.
   b. Modified return on equity, assuming the owner's efforts are valued at $15,000 per year.
   c. Debt ratio.
   d. Profit margin (use total revenues as the denominator).
   e. Current ratio.

Problem 5-3A
Applying the accounting cycle
C2, P1, P2

On July 1, 2000, Cindy Tucker created a new self-storage business called Lockit Co. These transactions occurred during the company's first month:

July	1	Tucker invested $20,000 cash and buildings worth $120,000.
	2	Rented equipment by paying $1,800 rent for the first month.
	5	Purchased $2,300 of office supplies for cash.
	10	Paid $5,400 for the premium on a one-year insurance policy.
	14	Paid an employee $900 for two weeks' salary.
	24	Collected $8,800 of storage fees from customers.
	28	Paid another $900 for two weeks' salary.
	29	Paid the month's $300 telephone bill.
	30	Paid $850 cash to repair a leaking roof.
	31	Tucker withdrew $1,600 cash from the business for personal use.

The company's chart of accounts included these accounts:

101	Cash	401	Storage Fees Earned
106	Accounts Receivable	606	Depreciation Expense—Buildings
124	Office Supplies	622	Salaries Expense
128	Prepaid Insurance	637	Insurance Expense
173	Buildings	640	Rent Expense
174	Accumulated Depreciation—Buildings	650	Office Supplies Expense
209	Salaries Payable	684	Repairs Expense
301	Cindy Tucker, Capital	688	Telephone Expense
302	Cindy Tucker, Withdrawals	901	Income Summary

Required

1. Use the balance-column format to create each of the listed accounts.
2. Prepare journal entries to record the transactions for July and post them to the accounts. Record prepaid and unearned items in balance sheet accounts.
3. Prepare an unadjusted trial balance as of July 31.
4. Use the following information to journalize and post adjusting entries for the month:
   a. Two-thirds of one month's insurance coverage was consumed.
   b. There were $1,550 of office supplies on hand at the end of the month.
   c. Depreciation on the buildings was estimated to be $1,200.
   d. The employee had earned $180 of unpaid and unrecorded salary.
   e. The company had earned $950 of storage fees that had not yet been billed.
5. Prepare an income statement, a statement of changes in owner's equity, and a balance sheet.
6. Prepare journal entries to close the temporary accounts and post them to the accounts.
7. Prepare a separate post-closing trial balance.

Problem 5-4A
Balance sheet classifications
C3

In the blank space beside each numbered balance sheet item, enter the letter of its balance sheet classification. If the item should not appear on the balance sheet, enter a *z* in the blank.

a. Current assets
b. Investments
c. Plant and equipment
d. Intangible assets
e. Current liabilities
f. Long-term liabilities
g. Owner's equity
h. Stockholders' equity

_____ **1.** Office supplies
_____ **2.** Owner, capital
_____ **3.** Common stock
_____ **4.** Notes receivable—due in 120 days
_____ **5.** Accumulated depreciation—Trucks
_____ **6.** Salaries payable
_____ **7.** Commissions earned
_____ **8.** Retained earnings
_____ **9.** Office equipment
_____ **10.** Notes payable—due in three years
_____ **11.** Building
_____ **12.** Prepaid insurance
_____ **13.** Current portion of long-term note payable
_____ **14.** Interest receivable
_____ **15.** Short-term investments
_____ **16.** Land (used in operations)
_____ **17.** Copyrights
_____ **18.** Owner, withdrawals
_____ **19.** Depreciation expense—Trucks
_____ **20.** Investment in Ford common stock (long-term holding)

Problem 5-5A
Work sheet, journal entries, financial statements, and current ratio
C3, A1, P3

Shown below is the unadjusted trial balance of Boomer Demolition Company as of the end of its June 30 fiscal year. The beginning balance of the owner's capital balance was $36,900 and the owner invested another $30,000 cash in the company during the year.

BOOMER DEMOLITION COMPANY
Unadjusted Trial Balance
June 30, 2000

No.	Account Title	Debit	Credit
101	Cash	$ 9,000	
126	Supplies	18,000	
128	Prepaid insurance	14,600	
167	Equipment	140,000	
168	Accumulated depreciation—Equipment		$ 10,000
201	Accounts payable		16,000
203	Interest payable		
208	Rent payable		
210	Wages payable		
213	Property taxes payable		
251	Long-term notes payable		20,000
301	R. Boomer, capital		66,900
302	R. Boomer, withdrawals	24,000	
401	Demolition fees earned		177,000
612	Depreciation expense—Equipment		
623	Wages expense	51,400	
633	Interest expense	2,200	
637	Insurance expense		
640	Rent expense	8,800	
652	Supplies expense		
683	Property taxes expense	8,400	
684	Repairs expense	6,700	
690	Utilities expense	6,800	
	Totals	$289,900	$289,900

Required

Preparation Component

1. Prepare a 10-column work sheet for year 2000, starting with the unadjusted trial balance and including these additional facts:
   a. The supplies on hand at the end of the year had a cost of $8,100.
   b. The cost of expired insurance for the year is $11,500.
   c. Annual depreciation on equipment is $18,000.
   d. The June utilities expense of $700 is not included in the unadjusted trial balance because the bill arrived after it was prepared. The $700 amount owed needs to be recorded.
   e. The company's employees have earned $2,200 of accrued wages.
   f. The lease for the office requires the company to pay total rent for each fiscal year equal to 8% of the company's annual revenues. Rent has been estimated and is being paid to the building owner with monthly payments of $800. If the annual rent owed exceeds the total monthly estimated payments, the company must pay the excess before July 31. If the total owed is less than the amount previously paid, the building owner will refund the difference by July 31.
   g. Additional property taxes of $450 have been assessed on the equipment but have not been paid or recorded in the accounts.
   h. The long-term note payable bears interest at 1% per month, which the company is required to pay by the 10th of the following month. The balance of the Interest Expense account equals the amount paid for the first 11 months of the year. The interest for June has not yet been paid or recorded. In addition, the company is required to make a $4,000 payment on the note on August 30, 2000.
2. Use the work sheet to journalize the adjusting and closing entries.
3. Prepare an income statement, a statement of changes in owner's equity and a classified balance sheet. Calculate the company's current ratio.

Analysis Component

4. Analyze the following separate errors and describe how each would affect the 10-column work sheet. Explain whether the error is likely to be discovered in completing the work sheet and, if not, the effect of the error on the financial statements.
   a. The adjustment for expiration of the insurance coverage credited the Prepaid Insurance account for $3,100 and debited the same amount to the Insurance Expense account.
   b. When completing the adjusted trial balance in the work sheet, the $6,700 Repairs Expense account balance is extended to the Debit column for the balance sheet.

Problem 5-6A[A]
Adjusting, reversing, and subsequent entries
P3, P4

This six-column table for Machine Rental Co. includes the unadjusted trial balance as of December 31, 2000:

MACHINE RENTAL CO.
December 31, 2000

Account Title	Unadjusted Trial Balance		Adjustments		Adjusted Trial Balance	
Cash	$ 9,000					
Accounts receivable						
Supplies	6,600					
Machinery	40,100					
Accumulated depreciation—Machinery		$15,800				
Interest payable						
Salaries payable						
Unearned rental fees		5,200				
Notes payable		20,000				
Kara Smith, capital		13,200				
Kara Smith, withdrawals	10,500					
Rental fees earned		37,000				
Depreciation expense—Machinery						
Salaries expense	23,500					
Interest expense	1,500					
Supplies expense						
Totals	$91,200	$91,200				

5 CHAPTER

Required

1. Complete the six-column table by entering adjustments that reflect the following information:

a. As of December 31, employees have earned $420 of unpaid and unrecorded wages. The next payday is January 4, and the total wages to be paid are $1,250.

b. The cost of supplies on hand at December 31 is $2,450.

c. The note payable requires an interest payment to be made every three months. The amount of unrecorded accrued interest at December 31 is $500, and the next payment is due on January 15. This payment will be $600.

d. An analysis of the unearned rental fees shows that $3,100 remains unearned at December 31.

e. In addition to the machinery rental fees included in the revenue account balance, the company has earned another $2,350 in fees that will be collected on January 21. The company is also expected to collect $4,400 on the same day for new fees earned during that month.

f. Depreciation expense for the year is $3,800.

2. Prepare journal entries for the adjustments entered in the six-column table.

3. Prepare journal entries to reverse the effects of the adjusting entries that involve accruals.

4. Prepare journal entries to record the cash payments and collections that are described for January.

Problem 6-1A
Journal entries for merchandising activities (perpetual system)
P1, P2

Prepare journal entries to record the following perpetual system merchandising transactions of Minchew Company. (Use a separate account for each receivable and payable; for example, record the purchase on May 2 in Accounts Payable—Mobley Co.)

May 2 Purchased merchandise from Mobley Co. for $9,000 under credit terms of 1/15, n/30, FOB shipping point.
4 Sold merchandise to Cornerstone Co. for $1,200 under credit terms of 2/10, n/60, FOB shipping point. The merchandise had cost $750.
5 Paid $150 for freight charges on the purchase of May 2.
9 Sold merchandise that cost $1,800 for $2,400 cash.
10 Purchased merchandise from Richter Co. for $3,450 under credit terms of 2/15, n/60, FOB destination.
12 Received a $300 credit memorandum acknowledging the return of merchandise purchased on May 10.
14 Received the balance due from Cornerstone Co. for the credit sale dated May 4, net of the discount.
17 Paid the balance due to Mobley Co. within the discount period.
20 Sold merchandise that cost $1,350 to Harrill Co. for $1,875 under credit terms of 2/15, n/60, FOB shipping point.
22 Issued a $225 credit memorandum to Harrill Co. for an allowance on goods sold on May 20.
23 Received a debit memorandum from Harrill Co. for an error that overstated the total invoice by $75.
25 Paid Richter Co. the balance due after deducting the discount.
31 Received the balance due from Harrill Co. for the credit sale dated May 20, net of the discount.
31 Sold merchandise that cost $4,800 to Cornerstone Co. for $7,500 under credit terms of 2/10, n/60, FOB shipping point.

Problem 6-2A
Journal entries for merchandising activities (perpetual system)
P1, P2

Prepare journal entries to record the following perpetual system merchandising transactions of Treadwell Company. (Use a separate account for each receivable and payable; for example, record the purchase on July 3 in Accounts Payable—CMP Corp.)

July 3 Purchased merchandise from CMP Corp. for $15,000 under credit terms of 1/10, n/30, FOB destination.
4 At CMP's request, paid $250 for freight charges on the July 3 purchase, reducing the amount owed to CMS.
7 Sold merchandise to Harbison Co. for $10,500 under credit terms of 2/10, n/60, FOB destination. The merchandise had cost $7,500.
10 Purchased merchandise from Cimarron Corporation for $13,250 under credit terms of 1/10, n/45, FOB shipping point, plus $600 shipping charges. The invoice showed that at Treadwell's request, Cimarron had paid the $600 shipping charges and added that amount to the bill.
11 Paid $300 shipping charges related to the July 7 sale to Harbison Co.
12 Harbison returned merchandise from the July 7 sale that had cost $1,250 and been sold for $1,750. The merchandise was restored to inventory.
14 After negotiations with Cimarron Corporation concerning problems with the merchandise purchased on July 10, received a credit memorandum from Cimarron granting a price reduction of $2,000.
17 Received balance due from Harbison Co. for the July 7 sale less the return on July 12.

20 Paid the amount due Cimarron Corporation for the July 10 purchase less the price reduction granted.
21 Sold merchandise to Hess for $9,000 under credit terms of 1/10, n/30, FOB shipping point. The merchandise had cost $6,250.
24 Hess requested a price reduction on the July 21 sale because the merchandise did not meet specifications. Sent Hess a credit memorandum for $1,500 to resolve the issue.
31 Received Hess's payment of the amount due from the July 21 purchase.
31 Paid CMP Corp. the amount due from the July 3 purchase.

Problem 6-3A
Income statement calculations and formats
P4, A1

Reyna Company's adjusted trial balance as of May 31, 2000, the end of its fiscal year, is shown below:

	Debit	Credit
Merchandise inventory	$ 46,500	
Other assets	192,600	
Liabilities		$ 52,500
Paul Reyna, capital		176,475
Paul Reyna, withdrawals	24,000	
Sales		318,000
Sales discounts	4,875	
Sales returns and allowances	21,000	
Cost of goods sold	123,900	
Sales salaries expense	43,500	
Rent expense—Selling space	15,000	
Store supplies expense	3,750	
Advertising expense	27,000	
Office salaries expense	39,750	
Rent expense—Office space	3,900	
Office supplies expense	1,200	
Totals	$546,975	$546,975

On May 31, 1999, the company's merchandise inventory amounted to $37,500. Supplementary records of merchandising activities during the 2000 fiscal year disclose the following:

Cost of merchandise purchases	$136,500
Purchase discounts received	2,850
Purchase returns and allowances received	6,600
Cost of transportation-in	5,850

Required

1. Calculate the company's net sales for the year.
2. Calculate the company's total cost of merchandise purchased for the year.
3. Present a classified, multiple-step income statement (see Exhibit 6.18) that lists the company's net sales, cost of goods sold, and gross profit, as well the components and amounts of selling expenses and general and administrative expenses.
4. Prepare a condensed single-step income statement that lists these costs: cost of goods sold, selling expenses, and general and administrative expenses.
5. Accounts receivable increased by $50,000 during the period. Calculate cash received from customers.

Problem 6-4A
Closing entries and interpreting information about discounts and returns
P3

Use the data for Reyna Company in Problem 6-3A to meet the following requirements:

Required

Preparation Component

1. Prepare closing entries for Reyna Company as of May 31, 2000.

Analysis Component

2. All of the company's purchases were made on credit and its suppliers uniformly offer a 3% sales discount. Does it appear that the company's cash management system is accomplishing the goal of taking all available discounts? Explain.

3. In prior years, the company experienced a 4% return and allowance rate on its sales, which means approximately 4% of its gross sales were for items that were eventually returned outright or that caused the company to grant allowances to customers. How does this year's results compare to prior years' results?

6 CHAPTER

Problem 6-5A
Adjusting entries, income statements, and acid-test ratio
A2, P3, P4

The following unadjusted trial balance is prepared at the end of the fiscal year for Resource Products Company:

RESOURCE PRODUCTS COMPANY Unadjusted Trial Balance October 31, 2000		
Cash	$ 6,400	
Merchandise inventory	23,000	
Store supplies	9,600	
Prepaid insurance	4,600	
Store equipment	83,800	
Accumulated depreciation—Store equipment		$ 30,000
Accounts payable		16,000
Jan Smithers, capital		70,400
Jan Smithers, withdrawals	6,400	
Sales		208,000
Sales discounts	2,000	
Sales returns and allowances	4,000	
Cost of goods sold	74,800	
Depreciation expense—Store equipment		
Salaries expense	62,000	
Insurance expense		
Rent expense	28,000	
Store supplies expense		
Advertising expense	19,800	
Totals	$324,400	$324,400

Rent and salaries expense are equally divided between the selling and the general and administrative functions. Resource Products Company uses a perpetual inventory system.

Required

1. Prepare adjusting journal entries for the following:
   a. Store supplies on hand at year-end amount to $3,300.
   b. Expired insurance, an administrative expense, for the year is $3,000.
   c. Depreciation expense, a selling expense, is $2,800 for the year.
   d. A physical count of the ending merchandise inventory shows $22,200 of goods on hand.

2. Prepare a multiple-step (not classified) income statement (see Exhibit 6.19).

3. Prepare a single-step income statement (see Exhibit 6.20).

4. Compute the company's current and acid-test ratios as of October 31, 2000.

Clinton Company has the following inventory purchases during the fiscal year ended December 31, 2000:

Problem 7-1A
Alternative cost flows—perpetual

P1

7 CHAPTER

Beg.	600 units	$55/unit
1/10	450 units	56/unit
2/13	200 units	57/unit
7/21	230 units	58/unit
8/5	345 units	59/unit

7 CHAPTER

Clinton Company employs a perpetual inventory system. It had two sales during the period, and the units had a selling price of $90 per unit. The specific units sold are the entire beginning inventory plus 165 units of the 2/13 purchase:

2/15 sales	430 units
8/10 sales	335 units

Required

Preparation Component

1. Calculate cost of goods available for sale and units available for sale.
2. Calculate units remaining in ending inventory.
3. Calculate the dollar value of ending inventory using (a) FIFO, (b) LIFO, (c) specific identification, and (d) weighted average.
4. Calculate the gross profit earned by Hall Company under each of the cost methods in (3).

Analysis Component

5. If the Clinton Company's manager earns a bonus based on a percent of gross profit, which method of inventory costing will be preferred?

Problem 7-2A[A]
Alternative cost flows—periodic
P4

Sea Blue Co. began year 2000 with 6,300 units of Product B in its January 1 inventory that cost $35 each, and it made successive purchases of the product as follows:

January 4	10,500 units @ $33 each
May 18	13,000 units @ $32 each
July 9	12,000 units @ $29 each
November 21	15,500 units @ $26 each

The company uses a periodic inventory system. On December 31, 2000, a physical count disclosed that 16,500 units of Product B remained in inventory.

Required

1. Prepare a calculation showing the number and total cost of the units available for sale during the year.
2. Prepare calculations showing the amounts assigned to the ending inventory and to cost of goods sold assuming *(a)* a FIFO basis, *(b)* a LIFO basis, and *(c)* a weighted average basis.

Problem 7-3A[A]
Income comparisons and cost flows—periodic
A1, P4

The Denney Company sold 2,500 units of its product at $98 per unit during year 2000, and incurred operating expenses of $14 per unit in selling the units. It began the year with 740 units and made successive purchases of units of the product as follows:

January 1 (beginning inventory) ...	740 units costing $58 per unit
Purchases:	
April 2	700 units @ $59 per unit
June 14	600 units @ $61 per unit
August 29	500 units @ $64 per unit
November 18	800 units @ $65 per unit
	3,340 units

Required

Preparation Component

1. Prepare a comparative income statement for the company, showing in adjacent columns the net incomes earned from the sale of the product, assuming the company uses a periodic inventory system and prices its ending inventory on the basis of: *(a)* FIFO, *(b)* LIFO, and *(c)* weighted average. Assume an income tax rate of 25%.

Analysis Component

2. How would the results from the three alternative inventory costing methods change if Denney had been experiencing decreasing prices in the acquisition of additional inventory?
3. What specific advantages and disadvantages are offered by using LIFO and by using FIFO, assuming a continuing trend of increasing costs?

Problem 7-4A
Analysis of inventory errors
A2

The following amounts were reported in Matchstick Company's financial statements:

	Financial Statements for Year Ended December 31		
	1999	2000	2001
(a) Cost of goods sold	$205,200	$212,800	$196,030
(b) Net income	174,800	211,270	183,910
(c) Total current assets	266,000	276,500	262,950
(d) Owner's equity	304,000	316,000	336,000

In making physical counts of inventory, Matchstick made the following errors:

Inventory on December 31, 1999:	Overstated $17,000
Inventory on December 31, 2000:	Understated $25,000

Required

Preparation Component

1. For each of the preceding financial statement items—(a), (b), (c), and (d)—prepare a schedule similar to the following and show the adjustments necessary to correct the reported amounts.

	1999	2000	2001
Cost of goods sold:			
Reported			
Adjustments: 12/31/1999 error			
12/31/2000 error			
Corrected			

Analysis Component

2. What is the error in aggregate net income for the three-year period that results from the inventory errors? Explain why this result occurs.

7 CHAPTER

Problem 7-5A
Lower of cost or market
P2

A physical inventory of Office Outfitters taken at December 31 reveals the following:

Item	Units on Hand	Per Unit Cost	Per Unit Market
Office furniture:			
Desks	436	$261	$305
Credenzas	295	227	256
Chairs	587	49	43
Bookshelves	321	93	82
Filing cabinets:			
Two-drawer	214	81	70
Four-drawer	398	135	122
Lateral	175	104	118
Office equipment:			
Fax machines	430	168	200
Copiers	545	317	288
Typewriters	352	125	117

Required

Calculate the lower of cost or market *(a)* for the inventory as a whole, *(b)* for the inventory by major category, and *(c)* for the inventory applied separately to each item.

Problem 7-6A
Retail inventory method
P3

The records of The R.E. McFadden Co. provide the following information for the year ended December 31:

	At Cost	At Retail
January 1 beginning inventory	$ 81,670	$114,610
Cost of goods purchased	492,250	751,730
Sales		786,120
Sales returns		4,480

Required

1. Prepare an estimate of the company's year-end inventory by the retail method.
2. The company took a year-end physical inventory at marked selling prices that totaled $78,550. Prepare a schedule showing the store's loss from shrinkage at cost and at retail.

Problem 7-7A
Gross profit method
P3

Four Corners Equipment Co. wants to prepare interim financial statements for the first quarter of year 2000. The company would like to avoid making a physical count of inventory each quarter. During the last five years, the company's gross profit rate has averaged 30%. The following information for the first quarter is available from its records:

January 1 beginning inventory	$ 752,880
Net cost of goods purchased	2,159,630
Sales	3,710,250
Sales returns	74,200

Required

Use the gross profit method to prepare an estimate of the company's March 31, 2000, inventory.

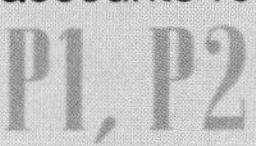

Problem 8-1A
Special journals, subsidiary ledgers, schedule of accounts receivable
P1, P2

Eldridge Industries completed these transactions during July of the current year:

July 1 Purchased merchandise on credit from Beech Company, invoice dated June 30, terms 2/10, n/30, $6,300.
3 Issued Check No. 300 to *The Weekly Journal* for advertising expense, $575.
5 Sold merchandise on credit to Karen Harden, Invoice No. 918, $18,400. (The terms of all credit sales are 2/10, n/30.)
6 Sold merchandise on credit to Paul Kane, Invoice No. 919, $7,500.
7 Purchased store supplies on credit from Blackwater Inc., $1,050. Invoice dated July 7, terms n/10 EOM.
8 Received a $150 credit memorandum from Blackwater Inc. for store supplies received on July 7 and returned for credit.
9 Purchased store equipment on credit from Poppe's Supply, invoice dated July 8, terms n/10 EOM, $37,710.
10 Issued Check No. 301 to Beech Company in payment of its June 30 invoice, less the discount.
13 Sold merchandise on credit to Kelly Grody, Invoice No. 920, $8,350.
14 Sold merchandise on credit to Karen Harden, Invoice No. 921, $4,100.
15 Received payment from Karen Harden for the July 5 sale, less the discount.
15 Issued Check No. 302, payable to Payroll, in payment of sales salaries for the first half of the month, $30,620. Cashed the check and paid employees.
15 Cash sales for the first half of the month were $121,370. (Cash sales are usually recorded daily from the cash register readings. They are recorded only twice in this problem to reduce repetitive transactions.)
16 Received payment from Paul Kane for the July 6 sale, less the discount.
17 Purchased merchandise on credit from Sprague Company, invoice dated July 17, terms 2/10, n/30, $8,200.
20 Purchased office supplies on credit from Poppe's Supply, $750. Invoice dated July 19, terms n/10 EOM.
21 Borrowed $20,000 from College Bank by giving a long-term note payable.
23 Received payment from Kelly Grody for the July 13 sale, less the discount.
24 Received payment from Karen Harden for the July 14 sale, less the discount.
24 Received a $2,400 credit memorandum from Sprague Company for defective merchandise received on July 17 and returned to Sprague.
26 Purchased merchandise on credit from Beech Company, invoice dated July 26, terms 2/10, n/30, $9,770.
27 Issued Check No. 303 to Sprague Company in payment of its July 17 invoice, less the return and the discount.
29 Sold merchandise on credit to Paul Kane, Invoice No. 922, $28,090.
30 Sold merchandise on credit to Kelly Grody, Invoice No. 923, $15,750.
31 Issued Check No. 304, payable to Payroll, in payment of the sales salaries for the last half of the month, $30,620.
31 Cash sales for the last half of the month were $79,020.

Required

Preparation Component

1. Prepare a Sales Journal like Exhibit 8.5 and a Cash Receipts Journal like Exhibit 8.9. Number both journals as page 3.
2. Review the transactions of Eldridge Industries and enter those transactions that should be journalized in the Sales Journal and those that should be journalized in the Cash Receipts Journal. Ignore any transactions that should be journalized in a Purchases Journal, a Cash Disbursements Journal, or a General Journal.
3. Open the following general ledger accounts: Cash, Accounts Receivable, Long-Term Notes Payable, Sales, and Sales Discounts. Also open subsidiary accounts receivable ledger accounts for Karen Harden, Kelly Grody, and Paul Kane.
4. Post the items that should be posted as individual amounts from the journals. (Normally, such items are posted daily; but since they are few in number in this problem you are asked to post them only once.)
5. Foot and crossfoot the journals and make the month-end postings.
6. Prepare a trial balance of the General Ledger and test the accuracy of the subsidiary ledger by preparing a schedule of accounts receivable.

8 CHAPTER

Analysis Component

7. Assume the sum of the account balances on the schedule of accounts receivable does not equal the balance of the controlling account in the General Ledger. Describe steps you would take to discover the error(s).

Problem 8-2A
Special journals; subsidiary ledgers; schedule of accounts payable
P1, P2

The July transactions of Eldridge Industries are listed in Problem 8-1A.

Required

1. Prepare a General Journal, a Purchases Journal like Exhibit 8.11, and a Cash Disbursements Journal like Exhibit 8.13. Number all journal pages as page 3.

2. Review the July transactions of Eldridge Industries and enter those transactions that should be journalized in the General Journal, the Purchases Journal, or the Cash Disbursements Journal. Ignore any transactions that should be journalized in a Sales Journal or Cash Receipts Journal.

3. Open the following General Ledger accounts: Cash, Office Supplies, Store Supplies, Store Equipment, Accounts Payable, Long-Term Notes Payable, Purchases, Purchases Returns and Allowances, Purchases Discounts, Sales Salaries Expense, and Advertising Expense. Enter the June 30 balances of Cash ($165,500) and Long-Term Notes Payable ($165,600). Also open subsidiary Accounts Payable Ledger accounts for Poppe's Supply, Beech Company, Sprague Company, and Blackwater Inc.

4. Post items that should be posted as individual amounts from the journals. (Normally, such items are posted daily; but since they are few in number in this problem you are asked to post them only once.)

5. Foot and crossfoot the journals and make the month-end postings.

6. Prepare a trial balance of the General Ledger and a schedule of accounts payable.

Problem 8-3A
Special journals; subsidiary ledgers; trial balance

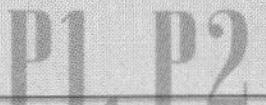

(If the Working Papers that accompany this text are not being used, omit this problem.)
It is December 16 and you have just taken over the accounting work of Starshine Products, whose annual accounting period ends December 31. The company's previous accountant journalized its transactions through December 15 and posted all items that required posting as individual amounts (see the journals and ledgers in the working papers). The company completed these transactions beginning on December 16:

Dec. 16 Purchased office supplies on credit from Green Supply Company, $765. Invoice dated December 16, terms n/10 EOM.

16 Sold merchandise on credit to Heather Flatt, Invoice No. 916, $4,290. (Terms of all credit sales are 2/10, n/30.)

18 Issued a credit memorandum to Amy Izon for defective merchandise sold on December 15 and returned for credit, $200.

19 Received a $640 credit memorandum from Walters Company for merchandise received on December 15 and returned for credit.

20 Received a $143 credit memorandum from Green Supply Company for office supplies received on December 16 and returned for credit.

20 Purchased store equipment on credit from Green Supply Company, invoice dated December 19, terms n/10 EOM, $7,475.

21 Sold merchandise on credit to Jan Wildman, Invoice No. 917, $5,520.

22 Received payment from Heather Flatt for the December 12 sale less the discount.

25 Received payment from Amy Izon for the December 15 sale less the return and the discount.

25 Issued Check No. 623 to Walters Company in payment of its December 15 invoice less the return and the discount.

25 Issued Check No. 624 to Sunshine Company in payment of its December 15 invoice less a 2% discount.

28 Received merchandise with an invoice dated December 28, terms 2/10, n/60, from Sunshine Company, $6,030.

28 Sold a neighboring merchant a carton of calculator tape (store supplies) for cash at cost, $58.

29 Marlee Levin, the owner of Starshine Products, used Check No. 625 to withdraw $4,000 cash from the business for personal use.

30 Issued Check No. 626 to Midwest Electric Company in payment of the December electric bill, $990.

30 Issued Check No. 627 to Jamie Ford, the company's only sales employee, in payment of her salary for the last half of December, $2,620.

31 Cash sales for the last half of the month were $66,128. (Cash sales are usually recorded daily but are recorded only twice in this problem to reduce the repetitive transactions.)

Required

1. Record the transactions listed above in the journals provided in the working papers.
2. Post to the customer and creditor accounts and also post any amounts that should be posted as individual amounts to the General Ledger accounts. (Normally, these amounts are posted daily, but they are posted only once in this problem because they are few in number.)
3. Foot and crossfoot the journals and make the month-end postings.
4. Prepare a December 31 trial balance and test the accuracy of the subsidiary ledgers by preparing schedules of accounts receivable and accounts payable.

Problem 8-4A
Special journals; subsidiary ledgers; trial balance
P1, P2

Crystal Company completed these transactions during November of the current year:

Nov. 1 Purchased office equipment on credit from Jett Supply, invoice dated November 1, terms n/10 EOM, $5,062.
2 Borrowed $86,250 by giving Jefferson Bank a long-term promissory note payable.
4 Received merchandise and an invoice dated November 3, terms 2/10, n/30, from Defore Industries, $11,400.
5 Purchased store supplies on credit from Atlas Company, $1,020. Invoice dated November 5, terms n/10 EOM.
8 Sold merchandise on credit to Leroy Holmes, Invoice No. 439, $6,350. (Terms of all credit sales are 2/10, n/30.)
10 Sold merchandise on credit to Sam Spear, Invoice No. 440, $12,500.
11 Received merchandise and an invoice dated November 10, terms 2/10, n/30, from The Welch Company, $2,887.
12 Sent Defore Industries Check No. 633 in payment of its November 3 invoice less the discount.
15 Issued Check No. 634, payable to Payroll, in payment of sales salaries for the first half of the month, $8,435. Cashed the check and paid the employees.
15 Cash sales for the first half of the month were $27,170. (Normally, cash sales are recorded daily; however, they are recorded only twice in this problem to reduce the number of repetitive entries.)
15 Post to the customer and creditor accounts and also post any amounts that should be posted as individual amounts to the General Ledger accounts. (Normally, such items are posted daily; but you are asked to post them on only two occasions in this problem because they are few in number.)
15 Sold merchandise on credit to Marjorie Cook, Invoice No. 441, $4,250.
16 Purchased office supplies on credit from Atlas Company, $559. Invoice dated November 16, terms n/10 EOM.
17 Received a credit memorandum from The Welch Company for unsatisfactory merchandise received on November 10 and returned for credit, $487.
18 Received payment from Leroy Holmes for the November 8 sale less the discount.
19 Received payment from Sam Spear for the November 10 sale less the discount.
19 Issued Check No. 635 to The Welch Company in payment of its invoice of November 10 less the return and the discount.
22 Sold merchandise on credit to Sam Spear, Invoice No. 442, $2,595.
24 Sold merchandise on credit to Marjorie Cook, Invoice No. 443, $3,240.
25 Received payment from Marjorie Cook for the sale of November 15 less the discount.
26 Received a credit memorandum from Jett Supply for office equipment received on November 1 and returned for credit, $922.
30 Issued Check No. 636, payable to Payroll, in payment of sales salaries for the last half of the month, $8,435. Cashed the check and paid the employees.
30 Cash sales for the last half of the month were $35,703.
30 Post to the customer and creditor accounts and post any amounts that should be posted as individual amounts to the General Ledger accounts.
30 Foot and crossfoot the journals and make the month-end postings.

Required

1. Open the following General Ledger accounts: Cash, Accounts Receivable, Office Supplies, Store Supplies, Office Equipment, Accounts Payable, Long-Term Notes Payable, Sales, Sales Discounts, Purchases, Purchases Returns and Allowances, Purchases Discounts, and Sales Salaries Expense. Open the following Accounts Receivable Ledger accounts: Marjorie Cook, Leroy Holmes, and Sam Spear. Open the following Accounts Payable Ledger accounts: Atlas Company, Defore Industries, Jett Supply, and The Welch Company.

CHAPTER

2. Enter the transactions listed above in a Sales Journal like Exhibit 8.5, a Purchases Journal like Exhibit 8.11, a Cash Receipts Journal like Exhibit 8.9, a Cash Disbursements Journal like Exhibit 8.13, and a General Journal. Post when instructed to do so.
3. Prepare a trial balance of the General Ledger and test the accuracy of the subsidiary ledgers by preparing schedules of accounts receivable and accounts payable.

9 CHAPTER

Problem 9-1A
Establishing, reimbursing, and increasing petty cash fund
P3

Dodge & Sons had the following petty cash transactions in July of the current year:

July 5 Drew a $200 check, cashed it, and turned the proceeds and the petty cash box over to Jackie Boone, the petty cashier.
6 Paid $14.50 COD charges on merchandise purchased for resale, terms FOB shipping point. Dodge & Sons uses the perpetual inventory method to account for merchandise inventory.
11 Paid $8.75 delivery charges on merchandise sold to a customer, terms FOB destination.
12 Purchased file folders, $12.13.
14 Reimbursed Collin Dodge, the manager of the business, $9.65 for office supplies purchased.
18 Purchased paper for printer, $22.54.
27 Paid $47.10 COD charges on merchandise purchased for resale, terms FOB shipping point.
28 Purchased stamps, $16.
30 Reimbursed Dodge $58.80 for business car mileage.
31 Boone sorted the petty cash receipts by accounts affected and exchanged them for a check to reimburse the fund for expenditures. There was $11.53 cash in the fund, and she could not account for the overage. The dollar amount of the petty cash fund was increased to $250.

Required

1. Prepare the general journal entry to record establishing the petty cash fund.
2. Prepare a petty cash payments report that has these categories: delivery expense, mileage expense, postage expense, merchandise inventory (transportation-in), and office supplies. Sort the payments into the appropriate categories and total the expenses in each category.
3. Prepare the general journal entry to record the reimbursement and the increase of the fund.

Problem 9-2A
Establishing, reimbursing, and adjusting petty cash fund; accounting adjustments
P3

The accounting system used by The Thrifty Company requires that all entries be journalized in a General Journal. To facilitate payments for small items, Thrifty established a petty cash fund. The following transactions involving the petty cash fund occurred in February (the last month of the company's fiscal year).

Feb. 3 A company check for $150 was drawn and made payable to the petty cashier to establish the petty cash fund.
14 A company check was drawn to replenish the fund for the following expenditures made since February 3 and to increase the fund to $175.
a. Purchased office supplies, $16.29.
b. Paid $17.60 COD charges on merchandise purchased for resale, terms FOB shipping point. Thrifty uses the perpetual method to account for merchandise inventory.
c. Paid $36.57 to Data Services for minor repairs to a computer.
d. Paid $14.82 for items classified as miscellaneous expenses.
e. Counted $62.28 remaining in the petty cash box.
28 The petty cashier noted that $17.35 remained in the fund and decided that the February 14 increase in the fund was not large enough. A company check was drawn to replenish the fund for the following expenditures made since February 14 and to increase it to $250.
f. Paid $40 to *The Smart Saver* for an advertisement in a monthly newsletter.
g. Paid $28.19 for office supplies.
h. Paid $58 to Best Movers for delivery of merchandise to a customer, terms FOB destination.

Required

Preparation Component

1. Prepare journal entries to record the establishment of the fund on February 3 and its replenishment on February 14 and February 28 along with any increases or decreases in the fund balance.

Analysis Component

2. Explain how the company's financial statements are affected if the petty cash fund is not replenished and no entry is made on February 28. (Hint: The amount of Office Supplies that appears on a balance sheet is determined by a physical count of the supplies on hand.)

Problem 9-3A
Preparing a bank reconciliation and recording adjustments
P5

The following information is available to reconcile Bohannon Co.'s book cash balance with its bank statement balance as of December 31, 2000:

a. After posting is complete, the December 31 cash balance according to the accounting records is $31,743.70, and the bank statement balance for that date is $45,091.80.

b. Check No. 1273 for $1,084.20 and Check No. 1282 for $390, both written and entered in the accounting records in December, were not among the canceled checks returned. Two checks, No. 1231 for $2,289 and No. 1242 for $370.50, were outstanding on November 30 when the bank and book statement balances were last reconciled. Check No. 1231 was returned with the December canceled checks, but Check No. 1242 was not.

c. When the December checks were compared with entries in the accounting records, it was found that Check No. 1267 had been correctly drawn for $2,435 to pay for office supplies but was erroneously entered in the accounting records as $2,453.

d. Two debit memoranda were included with the returned checks and were unrecorded at the time of the reconciliation. One of the debit memoranda was for $749.50 and dealt with an NSF check for $732 that had been received from a customer, Tork Industries, in payment of their account. It also assessed a $17.50 fee for processing. The second debit memorandum covered check printing and was for $79. These transactions were not recorded by Bohannon before receiving the statement.

e. A credit memorandum indicated that the bank had collected a $20,000 note receivable for the company, deducted a $20 collection fee, and credited the balance to the company's account. This transaction was not recorded by Bohannon before receiving the statement.

f. The December 31 cash receipts of $7,666.10 were placed in the bank's night depository after banking hours on that date and did not appear on the bank statement.

Required

Preparation Component

1. Prepare a bank reconciliation for the company as of December 31.

2. Prepare the journal entries necessary to bring the company's book balance of cash into conformity with the reconciled balance.

Analysis Component

3. Explain the nature of the communications conveyed by a bank to one of its depositors when the bank sends a debit memo and a credit memo to the depositor.

Problem 9-4A
Preparing a bank reconciliation and recording adjustments

Safety Systems most recently reconciled its bank balance on April 30 and showed two checks outstanding at that time, No. 1771 for $781 and No. 1780 for $1,325.90. The following information is available for the May 31, 1999, reconciliation:

From the May 31 bank statement:

BALANCE OF PREVIOUS STATEMENT ON 04/30/99	18,290.70
5 DEPOSITS AND OTHER CREDITS TOTALING	16,416.80
9 CHECKS AND OTHER DEBITS TOTALING	12,898.90
CURRENT BALANCE AS OF THIS STATEMENT	21,808.60

CHECKING ACCOUNT TRANSACTIONS

DATE	AMOUNT	DESCRIPTION	DATE	AMOUNT	DESCRIPTION
5/4	2,438.00	+Deposit	5/25	7,200.00	+Credit Memo
5/14	2,898.00	+Deposit	5/26	2,079.00	+Deposit
5/18	431.80	−NSF check	5/31	12.00	−Service charge
5/22	1,801.80	+Deposit			

DATE	CHECK NO	AMOUNT	DATE	CHECK NO	AMOUNT
5/01	1771*	781.00	5/26	1785	157.20
5/04	1782	1,285.50	5/25	1787*	8,032.50
5/02	1783	195.30	5/29	1788	554.00
5/11	1784	1,449.60			

*Indicates a skip in check sequence.

From Safety Systems' accounting records:

Cash Receipts Deposited

Date			Cash Debit
May	4		2,438.00
	14		2,898.00
	22		1,801.80
	26		2,079.00
	31		2,526.30
			11,743.10

Cash Disbursements

Check No.		Cash Credit
1782		1,285.50
1783		195.30
1784		1,449.60
1785		157.20
1786		353.10
1787		8,032.50
1788		544.00
1789		639.50
		12,656.70

Cash **Acct. No. 101**

Date		Explanation	PR	Debit	Credit	Balance
Apr.	30	Balance				16,183.80
May	31	Total receipts	R7	11,743.10		27,926.90
	31	Total disbursements	D8		12,656.70	15,270.20

Check No. 1788 was correctly drawn for $554 to pay for May utilities; however, the recordkeeper misread the amount and entered it in the accounting records with a debit to Utilities Expense and a credit to Cash as though it were for $544. The bank paid and deducted the correct amount. The NSF check was originally received from a customer, Goldie Mayer, in payment of her account. Its return was unrecorded. The credit memorandum resulted from a $7,300 note that the bank had collected for the company. The bank deducted a $100 collection fee and deposited the remainder in the company's account. The collection and fee have not been recorded.

9 CHAPTER

Required

Preparation Component

1. Prepare the May 31 bank reconciliation for Safety Systems.
2. Prepare the journal entries to adjust the book balance of cash to the reconciled balance.

Analysis Component

3. The bank statement discloses two places where the canceled checks returned with the bank statement are not numbered sequentially. This means some of the prenumbered checks in the sequence are missing. Several possible situations might explain why canceled checks returned with a bank statement are not numbered sequentially. Describe three of these situations.

Problem 9-5A
Analyzing internal control
C2

For the following five scenarios, identify the principle of internal control that is violated. Make a recommendation of what the business should do to ensure adherence to principles of internal control.

1. Tamerick Company is a fairly small organization but has segregated the duties of cash receipts and cash disbursements. However, the employee responsible for cash disbursements also reconciles the monthly bank account.
2. Stan Spencer is the most computer literate employee in his company. His boss has recently asked him to put password protection on all the office computers. Stan's main job at the company is to process payroll. Stan has put a password in place that only allows his boss access to the file where pay rates are changed and personnel are added/or deleted from the company payroll.
3. Starlight Theater has a computerized order-taking system for its tickets. The system is active all week and backed up every Friday night.
4. Trek There Company has two employees handling acquisitions of inventory. One employee places purchase orders and pays vendors. The second employee receives the merchandise.
5. The owner of Holiday Helper uses a check protector to perforate checks, making it difficult for anyone to alter the amount of the check. The check protector sits on the owner's desk in an office that houses company checks and is often unlocked.

Problem 10-1A
Short-term investment transactions and entries
C4, P5

McLean Systems had no short-term investments on December 31, 1999, but had the following transactions involving short-term investments in securities available-for-sale during 2000:

Feb. 6 Purchased 3,400 shares of The Walt Disney Co. stock at $29\frac{1}{2}$ plus a $2,500 brokerage fee.
15 Paid $20,000 to buy six-month U.S. Treasury bills with a principal amount of $20,000, paying 5%, dated February 15.
Apr. 7 Purchased 1,200 shares of The Gillette Co. stock at $13\frac{1}{4}$ plus a $477 brokerage fee.
June 2 Purchased 2,500 shares of Zenith Electronics stock at $32\frac{3}{4}$ plus a $2,865 brokerage fee.
30 Received a $1.75 per share cash dividend on the Disney shares.
Aug. 11 Sold 850 shares of Disney stock at 25 less a $531 brokerage fee.
16 Received a check for the principal and accrued interest on the U.S. Treasury bills purchased February 15.
24 Received a $0.20 per share cash dividend on the Gillette shares.
Nov. 9 Received a $1.00 per share cash dividend on the remaining Disney shares.
Dec. 18 Received a $0.45 per share cash dividend on the Gillette shares.

Required

Prepare General Journal entries to record the preceding transactions.

Problem 10-2A
Sales on credit and credit card sales

Ace Office Supply Co. allows a few select customers to make purchases on credit. The other customers can use either of two credit cards. Commerce Bank deducts a 3% service charge for sales on its credit card but immediately credits the checking account of its commercial customers when credit card receipts are deposited. Ace deposits the Commerce Bank credit card receipts at the close of each business day.

10 CHAPTER

When customers use the Fortune card, Ace accumulates the receipts for several days and then submits them to the Fortune Credit Company for payment. Fortune deducts a 2% service charge and usually pays within one week of being billed. Ace completed the following transactions in July:

July 2 Sold merchandise on credit to J.R. Lacey for $2,780. (Terms of all credit sales are 2/10, n/30; all sales are recorded at the gross price.)

8 Sold merchandise for $3,248 to customers who used their Commerce Bank credit cards. Sold merchandise for $1,114 to customers who used their Fortune cards.

12 Received Lacey's check paying for the purchase of July 2.

13 Sold merchandise for $2,960 to customers who used their Fortune cards.

16 The Fortune card receipts accumulated since July 8 were submitted to the credit card company for payment.

20 Wrote off the account of River City Rentals against Allowance for Doubtful Accounts. The $398 balance in River City's account stemmed from a credit sale in November of last year.

23 Received the amount due from Fortune Credit Company.

Required

Prepare journal entries to record the preceding transactions.

On December 31, 2000, Genie Service Corp's records show the following results for the year:

Cash sales	$1,015,000
Credit sales	1,241,000

In addition, the unadjusted trial balance includes the following items:

Accounts receivable	$475,000 debit
Allowance for doubtful accounts	5,200 credit

Required

1. Prepare the adjusting entry on the books of Genie Service Corp. to estimate bad debts under each of the following independent assumptions:
   a. Bad debts are estimated to be 2.5% of credit sales.
   b. Bad debts are estimated to be 1.5% of total sales.
   c. Analysis suggests 6% of outstanding accounts receivable at year-end are uncollectible.

2. Show how Accounts Receivable and the Allowance for Doubtful Accounts appear on the December 31, 2000, balance sheet given the facts in requirement 1*a*.

3. Show how Accounts Receivable and the Allowance for Doubtful Accounts appear on the December 31, 2000, balance sheet given the facts in requirement 1*c*.

Problem 10-4A
Aging accounts receivable
P1, P2

NutraMade Company had credit sales of $3.5 million in 1999. On December 31, 1999, the company's Allowance for Doubtful Accounts had a debit balance of $4,100. The accountant for NutraMade has prepared a schedule of the December 31, 1999, accounts receivable by age and, on the basis of past experience, has estimated the percent of receivables in each age category that will become uncollectible. This information is summarized as follows:

December 31, 1999 Accounts Receivable	Age of Accounts Receivable	Expected Percent Uncollectible
$296,400	Not due (under 30 days)	2.0%
177,800	1 to 30 days past due	4.0
58,000	31 to 60 days past due	8.5
7,600	61 to 90 days past due	39.0
3,700	Over 90 days past due	82.5

Required

Preparation Component

1. Compute the amount in the December 31, 1999, balance sheet as the Allowance for Doubtful Accounts.
2. Prepare the journal entry to record bad debts expense for 1999.

Analysis Component

3. On July 31, 2000, NutraMade concluded that a customer's $2,345 receivable (created in 1999) is uncollectible and that the account should be written off. What effect will this action have on NutraMade's 2000 net income? Explain your answer.

Problem 10-5A
Recording accounts receivable transactions and bad debts adjustments
P1, P2

Spring Products Co. began operations on January 1, 1999, and completed a number of transactions during 1999 and 2000 that involved sales on credit, accounts receivable collections, and bad debts. These transactions are summarized as follows:

1999

a. Sold merchandise on credit for $673,490, terms n/30.
b. Received cash of $437,250 in payment of outstanding accounts receivable.
c. Wrote off uncollectible accounts receivable in the amount of $8,330.
d. In adjusting the accounts on December 31, concluded that 1% of outstanding accounts receivable would become uncollectible.

2000

e. Sold merchandise on credit for $930,100, terms n/30.
f. Received cash of $890,220 in payment of outstanding accounts receivable.
g. Wrote off uncollectible accounts receivable in the amount of $10,090.
h. In adjusting the accounts on December 31, concluded that 1% of outstanding accounts receivable would become uncollectible.

Required

Prepare journal entries to record the 1999 and 2000 summarized transactions of Spring Products Co. and the adjustments to record bad debts expense at the end of each year.

Problem 10-6A
Analyzing and journalizing notes receivable transactions
P3, P4

The following transactions are from Metro, Inc.:

1999

Nov. 16 Accepted a $3,700, 90-day, 12% note dated this day in granting Bess Parker a time extension on her past-due account.
Dec. 31 Made an adjusting entry to record the accrued interest on the Parker note.
31 Closed the Interest Earned account.

2000

Feb. 14 Received Parker's payment for principal and interest on the note dated November 16.
28 Accepted a $12,400, 9%, 30-day note dated this day in granting a time extension on the past-due account of The Simms Co.
Mar. 1 Accepted a $5,100, 60-day, 10% note dated this day in granting Bedford Holmes a time extension on his past-due account.
23 Discounted, without recourse, the Holmes note at Security Bank at a cost of $50.
30 The Simms Co. dishonored its note when presented for payment.
June 15 Accepted a $1,900, 60-day, 9% note dated this day in granting a time extension on the past-due account of Sarah Mayfield.
21 Accepted a $9,300, 90-day, 12% note dated this day in granting Vince Soto a time extension on his past-due account.
July 5 Discounted, with recourse, the Soto note at Security Bank at a cost of $200. The transaction was considered to be a loan.
Aug. 14 Received payment of principal plus interest from Mayfield for the note of June 15.
Sept 25 Received notice from Security Bank that the Soto note had been paid.
Nov 30 Wrote off The Simms Co.'s account against Allowance for Doubtful Accounts.

Required

Preparation Component

Prepare journal entries to record Metro's transactions.

Analysis Component

What reporting is necessary when a business discounts notes receivable with recourse and these notes have not reached maturity by the end of the fiscal period? Explain the reason for this requirement and what accounting principle is being satisfied.

Problem 10-7A
Short-term investment transactions and entries
C4, P5

Dayton Enterprises has idle cash balances and invests them in common stocks that it holds as available-for-sale securities. Following is a series of transactions and events relevant to the short-term investment activity of the company:

1999

Mar. 10	Purchased 2,400 shares of Apple Computer, Inc., at $33\frac{1}{4}$ plus $1,995 commission.
May 7	Purchased 5,000 shares of Ford Motor Co. at $17\frac{1}{2}$ plus $2,625 commission.
Sept. 1	Purchased 1,200 shares of Polaroid Corp. at 49 plus $1,176 commission

2000

Apr. 26	Sold 5,000 shares of Ford at $16\frac{3}{8}$ less $2,237 commission.
27	Sold 1,200 shares of Polaroid at 52 less $1,672 commission.
June 2	Purchased 3,600 shares of Duracell Int'l., Inc., at $18\frac{7}{8}$ plus $2,312 commission.
14	Purchased 900 shares of Sears, Roebuck & Co. at $24\frac{1}{2}$ plus $541 commission.

2001

Jan. 28	Purchased 2,000 shares of The Coca-Cola Co. at 41 plus $3,280 commission.
31	Sold 3,600 shares of Duracell at $16\frac{5}{8}$ less $1,496 commission.
Aug. 22	Sold 2,400 shares of Apple at $29\frac{3}{4}$ less $2,339 commission.
Sept. 3	Purchased 1,500 shares of Motorola, Inc., at 29 plus $870 commission.
Oct. 9	Sold 900 shares of Sears at $27\frac{1}{2}$ less $619 commission.

Required

Prepare journal entries to record the short-term investment activity for the years shown.

Problem 11-1A
Real estate costs; partial year's depreciation
C1, C2, C3

In 1999, Spicewood Technologies paid $1,350,000 for a tract of land with two buildings on it. The plan is to demolish Building A and build a new shop in its place. Building B is to be used as a company office and is appraised at a value of $472,770, with a useful life of 15 years and a $90,000 salvage value. A lighted parking lot near Building B has improvements (Land Improvements B) valued at $125,145 that are expected to last another six years and have no salvage value. Without considering the buildings or improvements, the tract of land is valued at $792,585. AutoTech incurred the following additional costs:

Cost to demolish Building A	$ 117,000
Cost of additional landscaping	172,500
Cost to construct new building (Building C), having a useful life of 20 years and a $295,500 salvage value	1,356,000
Cost of new land improvements near Building C (Land Improvements C), which have a 10-year useful life and no salvage value	101,250

Required

1. Prepare a schedule having the following column headings: Land, Building B, Building C, Land Improvements B, and Land Improvements C. Allocate the costs incurred by AutoTech to the appropriate columns and total each column.
2. Prepare a single journal entry to record all the incurred costs, assuming they are paid in cash on October 1, 1999.
3. Using the straight-line method, prepare December 31 adjusting entries to record depreciation for the three months of 1999 during which the assets were in use.

Problem 11-2A
Plant asset costs; partial year's depreciation; alternative methods
C1, C2, C3

Timberline Company recently negotiated a lump-sum purchase of several assets from a contractor who was planning to change locations. The purchase is completed on September 30, 1999, at a total cash price of $1,610,000 and included a building, land, land improvements, and six trucks. The estimated market values of the assets are: building, $784,800; land, $540,640; land improvements, $226,720; and trucks, $191,840. The company's fiscal year ends on December 31.

Required

Preparation Component

1. Prepare a schedule to allocate the lump-sum purchase price to the separate assets purchased. Present the journal entry to record the purchase.
2. Compute the 1999 depreciation expense on the building using the straight-line method, assuming a 12-year life and a $100,500 trade-in value.
3. Compute the 1999 depreciation expense on the land improvements assuming a 10-year life and double-declining-balance depreciation.

Analysis Component

4. Defend or refute this statement: Accelerated depreciation results in more taxes being paid over the life of the asset.

Problem 11-3A
Alternative depreciation methods; partial year's depreciation; disposal of plant assets
C3, P2

Part 1. On January 2, Brodie Co. purchased and installed a new machine costing $312,000, with a five-year life and an estimated $28,000 salvage value. Management estimates the machine will produce 1,136,000 units of product during its life. Actual production of units is as follows: Year 1, 245,600; Year 2, 230,400; Year 3, 227,000; Year 4, 232,600; and Year 5, 211,200. The total number of units produced by the end of Year 5 exceeds the original estimate. The machine must not be depreciated below the estimated salvage value.

Required

Prepare a schedule with the following column headings:

Year	Straight-Line	Units-of-Production	Double-Declining-Balance

Show depreciation for each year and the total depreciation for the machine under each depreciation method.

Part 2. On January 1, Brodie purchased a used machine for $130,000. The next day, it is repaired at a cost of $3,390 and mounted on a new platform costing $4,800. Management estimates the machine will be used for seven years and have a $18,000 salvage value. Depreciation is to be charged on a straight-line basis. A full year's depreciation is charged on December 31 of the first through the fifth years of the machine's use. On April 1 of its sixth year of use, the machine is retired.

Required

a. Prepare journal entries to record the purchase of the machine, the cost of repairing it, and the installation. Cash is paid for all costs incurred.
b. Prepare entries to record depreciation on the machine at December 31 of its first year and on April 1 in the year of its disposal.
c. Prepare entries to record the retirement of the machine under each of the following unrelated assumptions: (i) it is sold for $30,000; (ii) it is sold for $50,000; and (iii) it is destroyed in a fire and the insurance company pays $20,000 in full settlement of the loss claim.

11 CHAPTER

Problem 11-4A
Partial year's depreciation; revising depreciation rates; revenue and capital expenditures
C3, P3

Rush Delivery Service completed these transactions involving the purchase and operation of delivery equipment:

1999

Mar. 25 Paid cash for a new delivery van, $24,950 plus $1,950 in sales tax. The van is estimated to have a five-year life and a $3,400 salvage value. Van costs are recorded in the Equipment account.

Sept. 30 Paid $1,550 to replace the manual transmission in the van with an automatic transmission. This increased the estimated salvage value of the van by $200.

Dec. 31 Record straight-line depreciation on the van.

2000

May 10 Paid $600 to repair the van after the driver backed it into a loading dock.

Oct. 1 Paid $1,970 to overhaul the van's engine. As a result, the estimated useful life of the van is increased by two years.

Dec. 31 Record straight-line depreciation on the van.

Required

Prepare journal entries to record these transactions.

Problem 11-5A
Partial year's depreciation; revising depreciation rates; exchanging plant assets
C3, P4

Precision Machine Shop completed the following transactions involving machinery:

1999

June 24 Paid $106,600 cash for a new machine plus $6,400 in sales tax. The machine is estimated to have a six-year life and a $9,800 trade-in value.

Dec. 31 Record straight-line depreciation on the machinery.

2000

Dec. 31 Record straight-line depreciation on the machine. Due to new information obtained earlier in the year, the original estimated useful life of the machinery is changed from six years to four years, and the original estimated trade-in value is increased to $13,050.

2001

Nov. 4 Traded in the old machine and paid $79,500 in cash for a new, similar machine. The new machine is estimated to have an eight-year life and a $10,380 trade-in value. The invoice for the exchange shows:

Price of the new machine	$123,000
Trade-in allowance granted on the old machine	(48,000)
Balance of purchase price	$ 75,000
State sales tax	4,500
Total paid in cash	$ 79,500

Dec. 31 Record straight-line depreciation on the new machine.

Required

Prepare journal entries to record these transactions.

Problem 11-6A
Partial year's depreciation; alternative methods; disposal of plant assets
C3, P2, P4

Central Printing Co. completed the following transactions involving printing equipment:

Printing press A is purchased for cash on April 3, 1995, at an installed cost of $169,400. Its useful life is estimated to be seven years with a $25,200 trade-in value. Straight-line depreciation is recorded for the press at the end of 1995, 1996, and 1997. On July 2, 1998, it is traded for printing press B, a similar asset, for an installed cash price of $206,400. A trade-in allowance of $112,000 is received for printing press A, and the balance is paid in cash.

Printing press B's life is predicted to be 10 years with a $22,000 trade-in value. Double-declining-balance depreciation is recorded on each December 31 of its life. On March 31, 2000, it is traded for a color laser copier, a dissimilar asset, for an installed cash price of $153,000. A trade-in allowance of $138,000 is received for printing press B, and the balance is paid in cash.

It is estimated that the copier will produce 1,000,000 copies during its four-year useful life, after which it will have a $13,000 trade-in value. Units-of-production depreciation is recorded for the copier for 2000, a period in which it produces 190,000 copies. Between January 1, 2001, and February 10, 2003, the copier produces 640,000 more copies. On the latter date, it is sold for $40,000.

Required

For each item of equipment, prepare journal entries to record: *(a)* its purchase, *(b)* the depreciation expense recorded on the first December 31 of its life, and *(c)* its disposal. (Only one entry is needed to record the exchange of one item of equipment for another.)

Problem 11-7A
Intangible assets and natural resources
P5, P6

Part 1. In 1994, Granite Co. entered into a 12-year lease on a building. The lease contract requires: (1) $26,400 annual rental payments to be made each May 1 throughout the life of the lease and (2) all additions and improvements to the leased property to be paid for by the lessee. In 2000, Granite decided to sublease the space to Magnolia Service Co. for the remaining five years of the lease. On April 25, 2001, Magnolia paid $30,000 to Granite for the right to sublease the space and agreed to assume the obligation to pay the $26,400 annual rent to the building owner beginning May 1, 2001. After taking possession of the leased space, Magnolia paid for improving the office portion of the leased space at a cost of $18,000. The improvements were paid for on May 6, 2001, and are estimated to have a life equal to the 13 years remaining in the life of the building.

Required

Prepare entries for Magnolia to record *(a)* its payment to Granite for the right to sublease the building space, *(b)* its payment of the 2001 annual rent to the building owner, and *(c)* its payment for the office improvements. Prepare Magnolia's adjusting entries required on December 31, 2001, to amortize *(d)* a proper share of the $30,000 cost of the sublease and *(e)* a proper share of the office improvements.

Part 2. On February 19 of the current year, Wayman Industries paid $4,450,000 for land estimated to contain 5 million tons of recoverable ore of a valuable mineral. It installed machinery costing $200,000, which has a 16-year life and no salvage value and is capable of exhausting the ore deposit in 12 years. The machinery is paid for on March 21, 11 days before mining operations began. The company removes 352,000 tons of ore during the first nine months of operations. Depreciation of the machinery is in proportion to the mine's depletion (it will be abandoned after the ore is fully mined).

Required

Preparation Component

Prepare entries to record *(a)* the purchase of the land, *(b)* the installation of the machinery, *(c)* the first nine months' depletion under the assumption the land is valueless after the ore is mined, and *(d)* the first nine months' depreciation on the machinery.

Analysis Component

Describe the similarities and differences in amortization, depletion, and depreciation.

Problem 11-8A
Goodwill estimation and amortization
P6

Kudos Casual Wear has the following balance sheet on December 31, 2001:

Assets	
Cash	$ 138,700
Merchandise inventory	607,950
Buildings	451,500
Accumulated depreciation	(210,800)
Land	192,400
Total assets	$1,179,750
Liabilities and Equity	
Accounts payable	$ 98,325
Long-term note payable	414,050
N. Pursley, capital	667,375
Total liabilities and owner's equity	$1,179,750

In this industry, net income averages 32% of owner's equity. Kudos regularly expects to earn $230,000 annually. The balance sheet amounts are reasonable estimates of fair market values for all assets except goodwill, which does not appear on the financial statements. In negotiations to sell the business, Kudos proposes that goodwill be measured by capitalizing the amount of above-normal net income at a rate of 10%. The potential buyer thinks that goodwill should be valued at eight times the amount that net income is above the average for the industry.

Required

1. Compute the amount of goodwill as proposed by Kudos.
2. Compute the amount of goodwill according to the potential buyer.
3. The buyer purchases the business for the amount of the net assets reported on the December 31, 2001, balance sheet plus the amount proposed by Kudos for the goodwill. If the amount of expected net income (before amortization of goodwill) is obtained the first year, and the goodwill is amortized over the longest permissible time period, what amount of net income will be reported for the first year after the business is purchased?
4. What rate of return on the buyer's investment does the first year's net income represent?

12 CHAPTER

Problem 12-1A
Estimating product warranty expenses and liabilities

P4

On November 10, 1999, Gourmet Co. began to purchase electric coffee grinders for resale at $35 each. Gourmet uses the perpetual method to account for inventories. The grinders are covered under a warranty that requires the company to replace any nonworking coffee grinder within 60 days. When a grinder is returned, the company simply throws it away and mails a new one from inventory to the customer. The company's cost for a new grinder is $14. The manufacturer has advised the company to expect warranty costs to equal 10% of sales. The following transactions and events occurred in 1999 and 2000:

1999

Nov. 16	Sold 50 coffee grinders for $1,750 cash.
30	Recognized warranty expense for November with an adjusting entry.
Dec. 12	Replaced six grinders that were returned under the warranty.
18	Sold 150 coffee grinders for $5,250 cash.
28	Replaced 17 grinders that were returned under the warranty.
31	Recognized warranty expense for December with an adjusting entry.

2000

Jan. 7	Sold 60 coffee grinders for $2,100 cash.
21	Replaced 38 grinders that were returned under the warranty.
31	Recognized warranty expense for January with an adjusting entry.

Required

1. How much warranty expense is reported for November and December 1999?
2. How much warranty expense is reported for January 2000?
3. What is the balance of the Estimated Warranty Liability account as of December 31, 1999?
4. What is the balance of the Estimated Warranty Liability account as of January 31, 2000?
5. Prepare journal entries to record these transactions and adjustments.

Problem 12-2A
Short-term notes payable transactions and entries

Palermo Company entered into the following transactions involving short-term liabilities in 1999 and 2000:

1999

Apr. 22	Purchased merchandise on credit from Omni Products for $4,000. The terms were 1/10, n/30. Palermo uses a perpetual inventory system.
May 23	Replaced the account payable to Omni Products with a 60-day note bearing 15% annual interest. Palermo paid $400 cash, with the result that the balance of the note was $3,600.

July 15 Borrowed $9,000 from the Liberty Bank by signing a 120-day interest-bearing note for $9,000. The note's annual interest rate is 10%.
? Paid the note to Omni Products at maturity.
? Paid the note to Liberty Bank at maturity.
Dec. 6 Signed a noninterest-bearing note with a face value of $16,180 from Metro Bank that matures in 45 days. The principal amount on the note is $16,000.
31 Recorded an adjusting entry for the accrual of interest on the note to the Metro Bank.

2000
? Paid the note to Metro Bank at maturity.

Required

1. Determine the maturity dates of the three notes described above.
2. Determine the interest due at maturity for the three notes. (Assume a 360-day year.)
3. Determine the interest to be recorded in the adjusting entry at the end of 1999.
4. Determine the interest to be recorded in 2000.
5. Prepare journal entries for all the preceding transactions and events for years 1999–2000.

Problem 12-3A
Payroll expenses, withholdings, and taxes
P2, P3

Jordanaire Company pays its employees every week. The employees' gross earnings are subject to these taxes:

Tax	Rate	Applied To
FICA—Social Security	6.20%	First $68,400
FICA—Medicare	1.45%	Gross pay
FUTA	0.80%	First $7,000
SUTA	1.75%	First $7,000

The company is preparing its payroll calculations for the week ended September 30. The payroll records show the following information for the company's four employees:

		This Week	
Name	Gross Through 9/23	Gross Pay	Withholding Tax
Abel	$69,000	$1,650	$149
Barney	59,085	1,515	182
Crystal	6,650	475	52
Dionne	22,200	600	48

In addition to the gross pay, the company and each employee pay one-half of the weekly health insurance premium of $44 per employee. The company also contributes 5% of each employee's gross earnings to a pension fund.

Required

Use this information to compute the following for the week ended September 30 (round amounts to the nearest cent):

1. Each employee's FICA withholdings for Social Security.
2. Each employee's FICA withholdings for Medicare.
3. Employer's FICA taxes for Social Security.
4. Employer's FICA taxes for Medicare.
5. Employer's FUTA taxes.
6. Employer's SUTA taxes.
7. Each employee's take-home pay.
8. Employer's total payroll-related expense for each employee.

12 CHAPTER

Problem 12-4A
Computing and analyzing times interest earned
A1

Here are condensed income statements for two different sole proprietorships:

Solstice Co.	
Sales	$120,000
Variable expenses (50%)	60,000
Net income before interest	$ 60,000
Interest expense (fixed)	45,000
Net income	$ 15,000

Equinox Co.	
Sales	$120,000
Variable expenses (75%)	90,000
Net income before interest	$ 30,000
Interest expense (fixed)	15,000
Net income	$ 15,000

Required

Preparation Component

1. What is the times interest earned for Solstice?
2. What is the times interest earned for Equinox?
3. What happens to each company's net income if sales increase by 10%?
4. What happens to each company's net income if sales increase by 40%?
5. What happens to each company's net income if sales increase by 90%?
6. What happens to each company's net income if sales decrease by 20%?
7. What happens to each company's net income if sales decrease by 50%?
8. What happens to each company's net income if sales decrease by 80%?

Analysis Component

9. Comment on what you observe in relation to the fixed cost strategies of the two companies and the ratio values you computed in parts 1 and 2.

Problem 12-5A[A]
Entries for payroll transactions
P5, P6

Capital Company has five employees, each of whom earns $1,200 per month and is paid on the last day of each month. All five have been employed continuously at this amount since January 1. Capital uses a payroll bank account and special payroll checks to pay its employees. On June 1, the following accounts and balances appeared in its ledger:

a. FICA—Social Security Taxes Payable, $744; FICA—Medicare Taxes Payable, $174. (The balances of these accounts represent liabilities for both the employer and employees' FICA taxes for the May payroll only.)
b. Employees' Federal Income Taxes Payable, $900 (liability for May only).
c. Federal Unemployment Taxes Payable, $96 (liability for April and May together).
d. State Unemployment Taxes Payable, $480 (liability for April and May together).

During June and July, the company had the following payroll transactions:

June 15 Issued check payable to First Bank, a federal depository bank authorized to accept employers' payments of FICA taxes and employee income tax withholdings. The $1,818 check is in payment of the May FICA and employee income taxes.

30 Prepared General Journal entries to record the June Payroll Record, which had the following column totals, and to transfer funds from the regular bank account to the payroll bank account:

Salaries and Wages						
Office Salaries	Shop Wages	Gross Pay	FICA Taxes*	Federal Income Taxes	Total Deductions	Net Pay
$2,000	$4,000	$6,000	$372 +$ 87	$900	$1,359	$4,641

*FICA taxes are Social Security and Medicare, respectively.

12 CHAPTER

30 Issued checks payable to each employee in payment of the June payroll.

30 Prepared a General Journal entry to record the employer's payroll taxes resulting from the June payroll. The company has a merit rating that reduces its state unemployment tax rate to 4.0% of the first $7,000 paid each employee. The federal rate is 0.8%.

July 15 Issued check payable to First Bank in payment of the June FICA and employee income taxes.

15 Issued check to the State Tax Commission for the April, May, and June state unemployment taxes. Mailed the check along with the second quarter tax return to the State Tax Commission.

31 Issued check payable to First Bank. The check is in payment of the employer's federal unemployment taxes for the second quarter of the year.

31 Mailed Form 941 to the IRS, reporting the FICA taxes and the employees' federal income tax withholdings for the second quarter.

Required

Prepare the General Journal entries to record the transactions and events for June and July.

Problem 12-6A[A]
Entries for payroll transactions
P5, P6

Watson Company's first weekly pay period of the year ended on January 8. On that date, the column totals in Watson's Payroll Register indicated its sales employees had earned $69,490, its office employees had earned $42,450, and its delivery employees had earned $2,060. The employees are to have withheld from their wages: FICA Social Security taxes at the rate of 6.2%, FICA Medicare taxes at the rate of 1.45%, $17,250 federal income taxes, $2,320 of medical insurance deductions, and $275 of union dues. No employee earned more than $7,000.

Required

1. Calculate FICA Social Security taxes payable and FICA Medicare taxes payable. Prepare a General Journal entry to record Watson Company's January 8 payroll.
2. Prepare a General Journal entry to record Watson's payroll taxes resulting from the January 8 payroll. Watson has a merit rating that reduces its state unemployment tax rate to 3.4% of the first $7,000 paid each employee. The federal unemployment tax rate is 0.8%.
3. Watson Company uses special payroll checks and a payroll bank account in paying its employees. Prepare the General Journal entry to transfer funds equal to the payroll from the regular bank account to the payroll bank account.
4. After the entry in part 3 is journalized and posted, are additional journal entries required to record the payroll checks and pay the employees?

Problem 13-1A
Methods of allocating partnership income
P2

Paul Jones, Will Rogers, and Anne Thompson invested $82,000, $49,200, and $32,800, respectively, in a partnership. During its first year, the firm earned $135,000.

Required

Prepare entries to close the firm's Income Summary account as of its December 31 year-end and to allocate the net income to the partners under each of the following separate assumptions. (Round answers to whole dollars.)

a. The partners have no agreement on the method of sharing incomes and losses.
b. The partners agreed to share incomes and losses in the ratio of their beginning investments.
c. The partners agreed to share incomes and losses by providing annual salary allowances of $48,000 to Jones, $36,000 to Rogers, and $25,000 to Thompson; allowing 10% interest on the partners' beginning investments; and sharing the remainder equally.

Problem 13-2A
Allocating partnership incomes and losses; sequential years

Jacob Jackson and K. D. Fletcher are in the process of forming a partnership to which Jackson will devote one-third time and Fletcher will devote full time. They have discussed the following alternative plans for sharing incomes and losses.

a. In the ratio of their initial investments, which they have agreed will be $52,000 for Jackson and $78,000 for Fletcher.
b. In proportion to the time devoted to the business.
c. A salary allowance of $2,000 per month to Fletcher and the balance in accordance with the ratio of their initial investments.

d. A salary allowance of $2,000 per month to Fletcher, 10% interest on their initial investments, and the balance equally.

The partners expect the business to generate income as follows: Year 1, $18,000 net loss; Year 2, $38,000 net income; and Year 3, $94,000 net income.

Required

1. Prepare three schedules with the following column headings:

Income (Loss) Sharing Plan	Year ______ Calculations	Jackson	Fletcher

2. Complete a schedule for each of the first three years by showing how partnership income or loss for each year would be allocated to the partners under each of the four plans being considered. Round answers to the nearest whole dollar.

Problem 13-3A
Partnership income allocation, statement of changes in partners' equity, and closing entries
P2

Ella Phillips, Chet Fong, and Lou Campos formed the PFC Partnership by making capital contributions of $72,000, $108,000, and $60,000, respectively. They predict annual net incomes of $120,000 and are considering the following alternative plans of sharing incomes and losses: *(a)* equally; *(b)* in the ratio of their initial investments; or (*c*) salary allowances of $20,000 to Phillips, $15,000 to Fong, and $40,000 to Campos; interest allowances of 12% on their initial investments; and the balance shared equally.

Required

1. Prepare a schedule with the following column headings:

Income (Loss) Sharing Plan	Calculations	Phillips	Fong	Campos	Total

Use the schedule to show how net income of $120,000 for year 2000 would be distributed under each of the alternative plans being considered. Round answers to the nearest whole dollar.

2. Prepare a statement of changes in partners' equity showing the allocation of income to the partners assuming they agree to use alternative *(c)*, income earned is $43,800, and Phillips, Fong, and Campos withdraw $9,000, $19,000, and $12,000, respectively, at year-end.

3. Prepare the December 31 journal entry to close Income Summary assuming they agree to use alternative *(c)* and the income is $43,800. Also, close the withdrawals accounts.

Problem 13-4A
Withdrawal of partner
P3

Part 1. Soltani, Sugimoto, and Suza are partners with capital balances as follows: Soltani, $303,000; Sugimoto, $74,000; and Suza, $223,000. The partners share incomes and losses in a 5:1:4 ratio. Soltani decides to withdraw from the partnership, and the partners agree to not have the assets revalued upon her retirement. Prepare general journal entries to record the April 30 withdrawal of Soltani from the partnership under each of the following separate assumptions:

a. Soltani sells her interest to Samba for $250,000 after Sugimoto and Suza approve the entry of Samba as a partner.

b. Soltani gives her interest to a daughter-in-law, Shulak. Sugimoto and Suza accept Shulak as a partner.

c. Soltani is paid $303,000 in partnership cash for her equity.

d. Soltani is paid $175,000 in partnership cash for her equity.

e. Soltani is paid $100,000 in partnership cash plus manufacturing equipment recorded on the partnership books at $269,000 less its accumulated depreciation of $168,000.

Part 2. Assume that Soltani does not retire from the partnership described in Part 1. Instead, Sung is admitted to the partnership on April 30 with a 20% equity. Prepare general journal entries to record the entry of Sung under each of the following separate assumptions:

a. Sung invests $150,000.

b. Sung invests $98,000.

c. Sung invests $213,000.

Problem 13-5A
Liquidation of a partnership
P4

Huggins, Hart, and Love, who share incomes and losses in a 2:1:2 ratio, plan to liquidate their partnership. At liquidation, their balance sheet appears as follows:

HUGGINS, HART, AND LOVE
Balance Sheet
January 18

Assets		Liabilities and Equity	
Cash	$174,300	Accounts payable	$171,300
Equipment	308,600	C.J. Huggins, capital	150,200
		D.C. Hart, capital	97,900
		J.D. Love, capital	63,500
Total assets	$482,900	Total liabilities and equity	$482,900

Required

Prepare general journal entries for the sale of inventory, the gain or loss allocation, and the distribution of cash in each of the following separate cases:

a. Equipment is sold for $325,000.

b. Equipment is sold for $265,000.

c. Equipment is sold for $100,000, and any partners with capital deficits pay in the amount of their deficits.

d. Equipment is sold for $75,000, and the partners have no assets other than those invested in the partnership.

Problem 13-6A
Stockholders' equity transactions
C2, C3

Livingston Company is incorporated at the beginning of the year and engages in a number of transactions. The following journal entries affected its stockholders' equity during its first year of operations:

a.	Cash	60,000	
	Common Stock, $1 Par Value		1,500
	Contributed Capital in Excess of Par Value, Common Stock		58,500
b.	Organization Costs	20,000	
	Common Stock, $1 Par Value		500
	Contributed Capital in Excess of Par Value, Common Stock		19,500
c.	Cash	6,650	
	Accounts Receivable	4,000	
	Office Equipment	6,000	
	Building	12,500	
	Accounts Payable		2,000
	Notes Payable		7,150
	Common Stock, $1 Par Value		400
	Contributed Capital in Excess of Par Value, Common Stock		19,600
d.	Cash	30,000	
	Common Stock, $1 Par Value		600
	Contributed Capital in Excess of Par Value, Common Stock		29,400

13 CHAPTER

Required

1. Provide explanations for the journal entries labeled *a* through *d*.
2. Answer the following questions:
   a. How many shares of common stock are outstanding at year-end?
   b. What is the amount of minimum legal capital at year-end?
   c. What is the total contributed capital at year-end?
   d. What is the book value per share of the common stock at the end of the year if contributed capital plus retained earnings equals $141,500?

Problem 13-7A
Computing book values and dividend allocations
A1, P6

Longhorn, Inc.'s common stock is currently selling on a stock exchange at $45 per share. Longhorn's current balance sheet shows the following:

Stockholders' Equity	
Preferred stock, Cumulative, 8%, $ ___ par value, 1,500 shares authorized, issued, and outstanding	$ 187,500
Common stock, $ ___ par value, 18,000 shares authorized, issued, and outstanding	450,000
Retained earnings	562,500
Total stockholders' equity	$1,200,000

Required

Preparation Component

1. What is the market value of the corporation's common stock?
2. What are the par values of the corporation's preferred stock and its common stock?
3. If no dividends are in arrears, what are the book values per share of the preferred stock and the common stock?
4. If two years' preferred dividends are in arrears, what are the book values per share of the preferred stock and the common stock?
5. If two years' preferred dividends are in arrears and the preferred stock is callable at $140 per share, what are the book values per share of the preferred stock and the common stock?
6. If two years' preferred dividends are in arrears and the board of directors declares dividends of $50,000, what total amount will be paid to the preferred and the common shareholders? What is the amount of dividends per share for the common stock?

Analysis Component

7. Discuss why the book value of common stock may not always be a good estimate of its market value.

14 CHAPTER

Problem 14-1A
Cash dividends and treasury stock transactions; statement of retained earnings
P1, P3

The balance sheet for Caldwell Corp. reported the following components of stockholders' equity on December 31, 1999:

Common stock, $1 par value, 160,000 shares authorized, 100,000 shares issued and outstanding	$ 100,000
Contributed capital in excess of par value, common stock	700,000
Retained earnings	1,080,000
Total stockholders' equity	$1,880,000

The company completed these transactions during 2000:

Jan. 10	Purchased 20,000 shares of its own stock as treasury stock at $12 per share.
Mar. 2	The directors declared a $1.50 per share cash dividend payable on March 31 to the March 15 stockholders of record.
Mar. 31	Paid the dividend declared on March 2.
Nov. 11	Sold 12,000 of the treasury shares at $13 per share.

Nov. 25 Sold 8,000 of the treasury shares at $9.50 per share.
Dec. 1 The directors declared a $2.50 per share cash dividend payable on January 2, 2001, to the December 10 stockholders of record.
Dec. 31 Closed the $536,000 credit balance in the Income Summary account to Retained Earnings.
Dec. 31 Closed the Cash Dividends Declared account.

Required

1. Prepare general journal entries to record the transactions and closings for 2000.
2. Prepare a statement of retained earnings for the year ended December 31, 2000.
3. Prepare the stockholders' equity section of the company's balance sheet as of December 31, 2000.

Problem 14–2A
Describing equity changes with journal entries and account balances
P1, P2

At December 31, the end of the third quarter for Hixton Co., the following balances exist in its stockholders' equity accounts:

Common stock, $10 par value	$480,000
Contributed capital in excess of par value	192,000
Retained earnings	800,000

During the company's fourth quarter, the following journal entries are recorded and affect the company's equity accounts:

Date	Account	Debit	Credit
Jan. 17	Cash Dividends Declared	48,000	
	Common Dividend Payable		48,000
Feb. 5	Common Dividend Payable	48,000	
	Cash		48,000
Feb. 28	Stock Dividends Declared	126,000	
	Common Stock Dividend Distributable		60,000
	Contributed Capital in Excess of Par Value, Common Stock		66,000
Mar. 14	Common Stock Dividend Distributable	60,000	
	Common Stock, $10 Par Value		60,000
Mar. 25	Memo—change the title of the common stock account to reflect the new par value of $5.		
Mar. 31	Income Summary	360,000	
	Retained Earnings		360,000
Mar. 31	Retained Earnings	174,000	
	Cash Dividends Declared		48,000
	Stock Dividends Declared		126,000

Required

1. Provide explanations for each of the journal entries.
2. Complete the following table showing the balances of the company's equity accounts (including the dividends declared accounts) at each of the indicated dates:

	Jan. 17	Feb. 5	Feb. 28	Mar. 14	Mar. 25	Mar. 31
Common stock	$____	$____	$____	$____	$____	$____
Common stock dividend distributable	____	____	____	____	____	____
Contributed capital in excess of par	____	____	____	____	____	____
Retained earnings	____	____	____	____	____	____
Less: Cash dividends declared	____	____	____	____	____	____
Stock dividends declared	____	____	____	____	____	____
Combined balance of equity accounts	$____	$____	$____	$____	$____	$____

14 CHAPTER

Problem 14-3A
Analyzing changes in stockholders' equity accounts
C3

The equity sections from the 1999 and 2000 balance sheets of Thornhill Corporation appear as follows:

STOCKHOLDERS' EQUITY As of December 31, 1999	
Common stock, $20 par value, 15,000 shares authorized, 8,500 shares issued and outstanding	$170,000
Contributed capital in excess of par value, common stock	30,000
Total contributed capital	$200,000
Retained earnings	135,000
Total stockholders' equity	$335,000

STOCKHOLDERS' EQUITY As of December 31, 2000	
Common stock, $20 par value, 15,000 shares authorized, 9,500 shares issued, 500 in the treasury	$190,000
Contributed capital in excess of par value, common stock	52,000
Total contributed capital	$242,000
Retained earnings ($20,000 restricted)	147,600
Total	$389,600
Less cost of treasury stock	(20,000)
Total stockholders' equity	$369,600

The following events affecting equity accounts occurred during 2000:

Feb. 15	A $0.40 per share cash dividend is declared, and the date of record is 5 days later.
Mar. 2	Treasury stock is purchased.
May 15	A $0.40 per share cash dividend is declared, and the date of record is 5 days later.
Aug. 15	A $0.40 per share cash dividend is declared, and the date of record is 5 days later.
Oct. 4	A 12.5% stock dividend is declared when the market value is $42 per share.
Oct. 20	The stock dividend is issued.
Nov. 15	A $0.40 per share cash dividend is declared, and the date of record is 5 days later.

Required

1. How many shares are outstanding on each of the cash dividend dates?
2. What are the amounts for each of the four cash dividends?
3. What is the amount of the capitalization of retained earnings for the stock dividend?
4. What is the price per share paid for the treasury stock?
5. How much income did the company earn during 2000?

Problem 14-4A
Income statement presentation
C2

The following schedule shows the balances from various accounts in the adjusted trial balance for Barbour Corp. as of December 31, 1999:

	Debit	Credit
a. Accumulated depreciation, Buildings		$ 200,000
b. Interest earned		10,000
c. Cumulative effect of change in accounting principle (pretax)		46,000
d. Sales		1,320,000
e. Income taxes expense	$?	
f. Loss on retirement of debt (pretax)	32,000	
g. Accumulated depreciation, Equipment		110,000
h. Other operating expenses	164,000	
i. Depreciation expense, Equipment	50,000	
j. Loss from settling a lawsuit	18,000	
k. Gain from settling a lawsuit		34,000
l. Loss on sale of equipment	12,000	

m. Loss from operating a discontinued segment (pretax)	60,000	
n. Depreciation expense, Buildings	78,000	
o. Correction of overstatement of prior year's expense (pretax)		24,000
p. Cost of goods sold	520,000	
q. Loss on sale of discontinued segment's assets (pretax)	90,000	
r. Accounts payable		66,000

Required

Answer each of the following questions by providing detailed schedules:

1. Assume the company's income tax rate is 25% for all items. What are the tax effects and after-tax measures of the items labeled as "pretax"?

2. What is the amount of the company's income from continuing operations before income taxes? What is the amount of the company's income taxes expense? What is the amount of the company's income from continuing operations?

3. What is the amount of after-tax income associated with the discontinued segment?

4. What is the amount of income before extraordinary items and the cumulative effect of the change in principle?

5. What is the amount of net income for the year?

Problem 14-5A
Changes in accounting principles and their disclosure

On January 1, 1999, Fricke Co. purchased equipment. Its cost was $200,000 and it was expected to have no salvage value at the end of its five-year useful life. Depreciation was allocated to 1999, 2000, and 2001 with the declining-balance method at twice the straight-line rate. Early in 2002, the company concluded that changing to the straight-line method would produce more useful financial statements and would be consistent with the practices of other firms in the industry.

Required

Preparation Component

1. Do generally accepted accounting principles allow Fricke Co. to change depreciation methods in 2002?

2. Prepare a schedule that shows the amount of depreciation expense that was allocated to 1999 through 2001 under the declining-balance method.

3. Prepare a schedule that shows the amount of depreciation expense that would have been allocated to 1999 through 2001 under the straight-line method.

4. Combine the information from your answers to parts 2 and 3 in a table like Exhibit 14.8 that computes the before- and after-tax cumulative effect of the change. The company's income tax rate is 25%.

5. How should the cumulative effect of the change in accounting principle be reported by the company? Does the cumulative effect increase or decrease net income?

6. How much depreciation expense will be reported on the company's income statement for 2002?

Analysis Component

7. Assume that Fricke Co. makes the mistake of treating the change in depreciation methods as a change in an accounting estimate. Using your answers from parts 2, 3, and 4, describe the effect this error would have on the 2002 financial statements.

Problem 14-6A
Earnings per share calculations and presentation

A1

The income statements for Titus, Inc., reported the following information when they were initially published in 2000, 2001, and 2002:

	2000	2001	2002
Sales	$250,000	$300,000	$400,000
Expenses	160,000	215,000	270,000
Income from continuing operations	$ 90,000	$ 85,000	$130,000
Loss on discontinued segment	(26,145)		
Income before extraordinary items	$ 63,855	$ 85,000	$130,000
Extraordinary gain (loss)		14,100	(37,125)
Net income	$ 63,855	$ 99,100	$ 92,875

The company also experienced changes in the number of outstanding shares from the following events:

Outstanding shares on December 31, 1999	10,000
2000	
Treasury stock purchase on July 1	− 1,000
Issuance of new shares on September 30	+ 3,500
20% stock dividend on December 1	+ 2,500
Outstanding shares on December 31, 2000	15,000
2001	
Issuance of new shares on March 31	+ 4,000
Treasury stock purchase on October 1	− 1,500
Outstanding shares on December 31, 2001	17,500
2002	
Issuance of new shares on July 1	+ 3,000
Treasury stock purchase on October 1	− 1,750
2-for-1 split on November 1	+18,750
Outstanding shares on December 31, 2002	37,500

Required

Preparation Component

1. Compute the weighted-average of the common shares outstanding as of the end of year 2000.
2. Compute the earnings per share amounts to report on the year 2000 income statement for: income from continuing operations, loss on discontinued segment, and net income.
3. Compute the weighted-average of the common shares outstanding as of the end of year 2001.
4. Compute the earnings per share amounts to report on the year 2001 income statement for: income from continuing operations, the extraordinary gain, and net income.
5. Compute the weighted-average of the common shares outstanding as of the end of year 2002.
6. Compute the earnings per share amounts to report on the year 2002 income statement for: income from continuing operations, the extraordinary loss, and net income.

Analysis Component

7. Explain how you would use the earnings per share data from part 6 in predicting earnings per share for year 2003.

15 CHAPTER

Problem 15-1A
Computing bond prices and recording issuances
P1, P2, P3

Strata Systems, Inc., issues bonds on January 1, 1999, that pay interest semiannually on June 30 and December 31. The par value of the bonds is $45,000, the annual contract rate is 12%, and the bonds mature in 5 years.

Required

For each of these three situations, *(a)* determine the issue price of the bonds and *(b)* show the journal entry that would record the issuance.

1. Market interest rate at the date of issuance is 10%.
2. Market interest rate at the date of issuance is 12%.
3. Market interest rate at the date of issuance is 14%.

Problem 15-2A
Straight-line method of amortizing interest for both a bond discount and a bond premium
P1, P2, P3

Poole Corporation issues $1,700,000 of bonds that pay 10% annual interest with two semiannual payments. The date of issuance is January 1, 1999, and the interest is paid on June 30 and December 31. The bonds mature after 10 years and are issued at a price of $1,505,001.

Required

1. Prepare a journal entry to record the issuance of the bonds.
2. Calculate *(a)* the cash payment, *(b)* the straight-line discount amortization amount, and *(c)* the bond interest expense to be recognized every six months.

3. Determine the total bond interest expense that will be recognized over the life of these bonds.
4. Prepare the first two years of an amortization table like Exhibit 15.7 based on the straight-line method of allocating the interest.
5. Present the journal entries that Poole would make to record the first two interest payments.
6. Assume that the proceeds on the bond are $2,096,466. Repeat requirements 1–5.

Problem 15-3A
Effective interest method of amortizing interest for a bond discount
P2

Joseph Manufacturing Corp. issues $120,000 of bonds that pay 6% annual interest with two semiannual payments. The date of issuance is January 1, 1999, and the interest is paid on June 30 and December 31. The bonds mature after 15 years and are issued at a price of $99,247. The market interest rate is 8%.

Required

1. Prepare a general journal entry to record the issuance of the bonds.
2. Determine the total bond interest expense that will be recognized over the life of these bonds.
3. Prepare the first four lines of an amortization table like Exhibit 15.8 using the effective interest method.
4. Present the journal entries that Joseph Manufacturing would make to record the first two interest payments.

Problem 15-4A
Effective interest method of amortizing interest for a bond premium; retiring bonds
P3, P4

Adams Brothers, Inc., issues $900,000 of bonds that pay 13% annual interest with two semiannual payments. The date of issuance is January 1, 1999, and the interest is paid on June 30 and December 31. The bonds mature after four years and are issued at a price of $987,217. The market interest rate is 10%.

Required

Preparation Component

1. Prepare a general journal entry to record the issuance of the bonds.
2. Determine the total bond interest expense that will be recognized over the life of these bonds.
3. Prepare the first two years of an amortization table like Exhibit 15.12 using the effective interest method.
4. Present the journal entries that Adams Brothers would make to record the first two interest payments.
5. Present the journal entry that would be made to record the retirement of these bonds on December 31, 2000, at a price of 106.

Analysis Component

6. Assume that the market interest rate on January 1, 1999, is 14% instead of 10%. Without presenting numbers, describe how this change would affect the amounts presented on the company's financial statements.

Problem 15-5A
Amortize bond premium and find the present value of remaining cash flows
P3

LaRue Company issues bonds with a par value of $160,000 and a five-year life on January 1, 1999. The bonds pay interest on June 30 and December 31. The contract interest rate is 9%. The bonds are issued at a price of $166,494. The market interest rate is 8% on the original issue date.

Required

1. Calculate the total bond interest expense over the life of the bonds.
2. Prepare an effective interest amortization table like Exhibit 15.12 for these bonds that covers their entire life.
3. Show the journal entries that LaRue would make to record the first two interest payments.
4. Use the original market interest rate to compute the present value of the remaining cash flows for these bonds as of December 31, 2001. Compare your answer with the amount shown on the amortization table as the balance for that date and explain your findings.

Problem 15-6A
Installment notes
C3, P5

On September 30, 1999, Rome Enterprises borrows $300,000 from a bank by signing a three-year installment note bearing interest at 10%. The terms of the note require equal payments each year on September 30.

Required

1. Compute the amount of each installment payment. (Use Exhibit 15A.6.)
2. Complete an amortization schedule for this installment note similar to Exhibit 15.20.
3. Present the journal entries that Rome would make to record accrued interest as of December 31, 1999 (the end of the annual reporting period) and the first yearly payment on the note.

15 CHAPTER

4. Assume that the note does not require equal payments but instead requires three payments that include accrued interest and an equal amount of principal in each payment. Complete an amortization schedule for this installment note similar to Exhibit 15.19. Present the journal entries that Rome would make to record accrued interest as of December 31, 1999 (the end of the annual reporting period) and the first yearly payment on the note.

Problem 15-7A
Computing and analyzing the ratio of pledged assets to secured liabilities
A2

On January 1, 2002, Spruce Company issues $45,000 of its 12%, 10-year bonds at par that are secured by a mortgage that specifies assets totaling $120,000 as collateral. On the same date, Willow Company issues its 12%, 10-year bonds at par that have a par value of $150,000. Willow's bonds are secured by a mortgage that includes $225,000 of pledged assets. The December 31, 2001, balance sheet information for both companies is shown below:

	Spruce Co.	Willow Co.
Total assets	$180,000*	$750,000†
Liabilities:		
Secured	$ 39,000	$ 57,000
Unsecured	42,000	505,500
Owners' equity	99,000	187,500
Total liabilities and owners' equity	$180,000	$750,000

*59% are pledged.
†10% are pledged.

Required

Preparation Component

1. Compute the ratio of pledged assets to secured liabilities for each company at January 1, 2002.

Analysis Component

2. Which company's bonds appear to offer the best security? What other information would be helpful in evaluating the risk of these companies' bonds?

16 CHAPTER

Problem 16-1A
Entries and fair value adjustments for long-term investments
P2

Dayton Enterprises has idle cash balances that it invests in available-for-sale long-term securities. Following is a series of events and other facts relevant to the long-term investment activity of the company:

1999

Mar. 10	Purchased 2,400 shares of Apple Computer at 33¼ plus $1,995 commission.
Apr. 7	Purchased 5,000 shares of Ford at 17½ plus $2,625 commission.
Sept. 1	Purchased 1,200 shares of Polaroid at 49 plus $1,176 commission.
Dec. 31	Per share market values for stocks in the portfolio are: Apple, 35½; Ford, 17; Polaroid, 51¾.

2000

Apr. 26	Sold 5,000 shares of Ford at 16⅜ less $2,237 commission.
June 2	Purchased 3,600 shares of Duracell at 18⅞ plus $2,312 commission.
June 14	Purchased 900 shares of Sears at 24½ plus $541 commission.
Nov. 27	Sold 1,200 shares of Polaroid at 52 less $1,672 commission.
Dec. 31	Per share market values for stocks in the portfolio are: Apple, 36¼; Duracell, 18⅛; Sears, 26.

2001

Jan. 28	Purchased 2,000 shares of Coca-Cola Co. at 41 plus $3,280 commission.
Aug. 22	Sold 2,400 shares of Apple at 29¾ less $2,339 commission.
Sept. 3	Purchased 1,500 shares of Motorola at 29 plus $870 commission.
Oct. 9	Sold 900 shares of Sears at 27½ less $619 commission.
Oct. 31	Sold 3,600 shares of Duracell at 16⅝ less $1,496 commission.
Dec. 31	Per share market values for stocks in the portfolio are: Coca-Cola, 46⅞; Motorola, 22½.

Required

1. Prepare journal entries to record these events and any year-end adjustments needed to record the fair values of the long-term investments.
2. Prepare a schedule that shows the total cost, total fair value adjustment, and total fair value of the investments at the end of each year.
3. For each year, prepare a schedule that shows the realized gains and losses included in earnings and the total unrealized gains or losses at the end of each year.

Problem 16-2A
Accounting for stock investments
P3

Main Street Company is organized on January 3, 1999. The following investment transactions and events subsequently occurred:

1999

Jan. 5 Main Street purchased 15,000 shares (25%) of Cornerstone's outstanding common stock for $187,500.

Aug. 1 Cornerstone declared and paid a cash dividend of $0.95 per share.

Dec. 31 Cornerstone announced its net income for 1999 is $92,000. Market value of the stock is $12.90 per share.

2000

Aug. 1 Cornerstone declared and paid a cash dividend of $1.25 per share.

Dec. 31 Cornerstone announced its net income for 2000 is $76,000. Market value of the stock is $13.55 per share.

2001

Jan. 8 Main Street sold all of its investment in Cornerstone for $204,750 cash.

Part 1. Assume that Main Street has a significant influence over Cornerstone with its 25% share.

Required

1. Give the entries to record the preceding transactions and events in Main Street's books.
2. Compute the carrying value per share of Main Street's investment as reflected in the investment account on January 7, 2001
3. Compute the change in Main Street's equity from January 5, 1999, through January 8, 2001, resulting from its investment in Cornerstone.

Part 2. Assume that even though Main Street owns 25% of Cornerstone's outstanding stock, circumstances indicate that it does not have a significant influence over the investee.

Required

1. Give the entries to record the preceding transactions and events in Main Street's books. Prepare an entry dated January 8, 2001, to remove any balances related to the fair value adjustment.
2. Compute the cost per share of Main Street's investment as reflected in the investment account on January 7, 2001.
3. Compute the change in Main Street's equity from January 5, 1999, through January 8, 2001, resulting from its investment in Cornerstone.

Problem 16-3A
Accounting for long-term investments; unrealized and realized gains and losses

Certifax Co.'s long-term investment portfolio at December 31, 1999, consists of the following:

Available-for-Sale Securities	Cost	Fair Market Value
45,000 shares of Company R common stock	$1,118,250	$1,198,125
17,000 shares of Company S common stock	616,760	586,500
22,000 shares of Company T common stock	294,470	303,600

Certifax entered into the following long-term investment transactions during 2000:

Jan. 13 Sold 4,250 shares of Company S common stock for $144,500 less a brokerage fee of $2,390.

Mar. 24 Purchased 31,000 shares of Company U common stock for $565,750 plus a brokerage fee of $9,900. The shares represent a 62% ownership in Company U.

Apr. 5 Purchased 85,000 shares of Company V common stock for $267,750 plus a brokerage fee of $4,500. The shares represent a 10% ownership in Company V.

Sept. 2 Sold 22,000 shares of Company T common stock for $313,500 less a brokerage fee of $5,400.

Sept. 27 Purchased 5,000 shares of Company W common stock for $101,000 plus a brokerage fee of $2,100. The shares represent a 25% ownership in Company W.

Oct. 30 Purchased 10,000 shares of Company X common stock for $97,500 plus a brokerage fee of $2,340. The shares represent a 13% ownership in Company X.

The fair market values of Certifax's investments at December 31, 2000, are: R, $1,136,250; S, $420,750; U, $545,600; V, $269,875; W, $109,375; X, 91,250.

Required

1. Determine what amount should be reported on Certifax's December 31, 2000, balance sheet for its long-term investments in available-for-sale equity securities.
2. Prepare a December 31, 2000, adjusting entry, if necessary, to record the fair value adjustment of the long-term investments in available-for-sale equity securities.
3. What amount of gains or losses on transactions relating to long-term investments in available-for-sale equity securities should be reported on Certifax's December 31, 2000, income statement?

Problem 16-4A
Foreign currency transactions
P4

Ben Franklin Co. is a United States corporation that has customers in several foreign countries. Following are some of Ben Franklin's 1999 and 2000 transactions:

1999

May 26 Sold merchandise for 6.5 million yen to Fuji Company of Japan, payment in full to be received in 60 days. On this day, the foreign exchange rate for yen is $0.009412.

June 1 Sold merchandise to Fordham Ltd. of Great Britain for $72,613 cash. The foreign exchange rate for pounds is $1.5277.

July 25 Received Fuji's payment in yen for its purchase of May 26 and exchanged the yen for dollars. The current exchange rate for yen is $0.009368.

Oct. 15 Sold merchandise on credit to Martinez Brothers of Mexico. The price of 373,000 pesos is to be paid 90 days from the date of sale. On this date, the foreign exchange rate for pesos is $0.1341.

Dec. 6 Sold merchandise for 242,000 francs to LeFevre Company of France, payment in full to be received in 30 days. The exchange rate for francs is $0.1974.

Dec. 31 Prepared adjusting entries to recognize exchange gains or losses on the annual financial statements. Rates of exchanging foreign currencies on this day are:

Yen (Japan)	$0.009447
Pounds (Britain)	1.5318
Pesos (Mexico)	0.1562
Francs (France)	0.1998

2000

Jan. 5 Received LeFevre's full payment in francs for the sale of December 6 and immediately exchanged the francs for dollars. The exchange rate for francs is $0.2063.

Jan. 13 Received full payment in pesos from Martinez Brothers for the sale of October 15 and immediately exchanged the pesos for dollars. The exchange rate for pesos is $0.1419.

Required

Preparation Component

1. Prepare journal entries to account for these transactions on Ben Franklin's books.
2. Compute the foreign exchange gain or loss to be reported on Ben Franklin's 1999 income statement.

Analysis Component

3. What actions might Ben Franklin consider to reduce its risk of foreign exchange gains or losses?

Problem 17-1A
Statement of cash flows (direct method)
P1, P2

Tanaka Company, a merchandiser, recently completed its year 2000 operations. During the year: (1) all sales were credit sales, (2) all credits to accounts receivable were receipts from customers, (3) purchases of merchandise were on credit, (4) all debits to accounts payable were from payments for merchandise, (5) the other operating expenses were cash expenses, and (6) the decrease in income taxes payable was for payment of taxes. Tanaka's balance sheet and income statement are shown below:

TANAKA COMPANY
Comparative Balance Sheet
December 31, 2000

	December 31	
Assets	**2000**	**1999**
Cash	$ 53,925	$ 31,800
Accounts receivable	19,425	23,250
Merchandise inventory	175,350	139,875
Equipment	105,450	76,500
Accum. depreciation, Equip.	(48,300)	(30,600)
Total assets	$305,850	$240,825
Liabilities and Stockholders' Equity		
Accounts payable	$ 38,475	$ 35,625
Income taxes payable	4,500	6,750
Common stock, $5 par	165,000	150,000
Contributed capital in excess of par, common stock	42,000	15,000
Retained earnings	55,875	33,450
Total liabilities and equity	$305,850	$240,825

TANAKA COMPANY
Income Statement
For Year Ended December 31, 2000

Sales		$609,750
Cost of goods sold		279,000
Gross profit		$330,750
Operating expenses:		
Depreciation expense	$ 17,700	
Other expenses	179,775	
Total operating expenses		197,475
Income before taxes		$133,275
Income taxes		44,850
Net income		$ 88,425

Additional information on Tanaka's transactions for year 2000:

a. Purchased equipment for $28,950 cash.

b. Issued 3,000 shares of stock for cash at $14 per share.

c. Declared and paid $66,000 of cash dividends.

Required

Prepare a statement of cash flows that reports cash inflows and outflows from operating activities according to the direct method. Show supporting calculations.

Problem 17-2A
Statement of cash flows (indirect method)
P1, P3

Refer to Tanaka Company's financial statements and related information in Problem 17-1A.

Required

Prepare a statement of cash flows that reports cash inflows and outflows from operating activities according to the indirect method.

Problem 17-3A[A]
Cash flows spreadsheet (indirect method)
P3, P4

Refer to the information reported about Tanaka Company in Problem 17-1A.

Required

Prepare a statement of cash flows using a spreadsheet that follows the indirect method of reporting cash flows from operating activities. Identify the debits and credits in the Analysis of Changes columns with letters that correspond to the following list of transactions and events:

a. Net income is $88,425.

b. Accounts receivable decreased.

c. Merchandise inventory increased.

d. Accounts payable increased.

e. Income taxes payable decreased.

f. Depreciation expense is $17,700.

g. Purchased equipment for $28,950 cash.

h. Issued 3,000 shares at $14 per share.

i. Declared and paid $66,000 of cash dividends.

17 CHAPTER

Problem 17-4A
Statement of cash flows (direct method)
P1, P2, A1

Kirby Corporation, a merchandiser, recently completed its year 2000 operations. During the year: (1) all sales were credit sales, (2) all credits to accounts receivable were receipts from customers, (3) purchases of merchandise were on credit, (4) all debits to accounts payable were from payments for merchandise, (5) the decrease in income taxes payable was for payment of taxes, and (6) the other expenses were paid in advance and were initially debited to prepaid expenses. Kirby Corporation's balance sheet and income statement follow:

KIRBY CORPORATION
Comparative Balance Sheet
December 31, 2000

	December 31	
Assets	**2000**	**1999**
Cash	$136,500	$ 71,550
Accounts receivable	74,100	90,750
Merchandise inventory	454,500	490,200
Prepaid expenses	17,100	19,200
Equipment	278,250	216,000
Accum. depreciation, Equip.	(108,750)	(93,000)
Total assets	$851,700	$794,700
Liabilities and Stockholders' Equity		
Accounts payable	$117,450	$123,450
Short-term notes payable	17,250	11,250
Long-term notes payable	112,500	82,500
Common stock, $5 par	465,000	450,000
Contributed capital in excess of par, common stock	18,000	
Retained earnings	121,500	127,500
Total liabilities and equity	$851,700	$794,700

KIRBY CORPORATION
Income Statement
For Year Ended December 31, 2000

Sales		$1,083,000
Cost of goods sold		585,000
Gross profit		$ 498,000
Operating expenses:		
Depreciation expense	$ 36,600	
Other expenses	392,850	
Total operating expenses		429,450
Loss on sale of equipment		2,100
Income before taxes		$ 66,450
Income taxes		9,450
Net income		$ 57,000

Additional information on Kirby's transactions for year 2000:

a. Loss on sale of equipment is $2,100.
b. Sold equipment costing $51,000, with accumulated depreciation of $20,850, for $28,050.
c. Purchased equipment costing $113,250 by paying cash of $38,250 and signing a long-term note payable for the balance.
d. Borrowed $6,000 by signing a short-term note payable.
e. Paid $45,000 to reduce the long-term notes payable.
f. Issued 3,000 shares of common stock for cash at $11 per share.
g. Declared and paid cash dividends of $63,000.

Required

Preparation Component

1. Prepare a statement of cash flows that reports cash inflows and outflows from operating activities according to the direct method. Show supporting calculations. Disclose any noncash investing and financing activities in a note.

Analysis Component

2. Analyze and discuss the cash flow information contained in your answer to part 1, giving special attention to the wisdom of the cash dividend payment.

Problem 17-5A
Statement of cash flows (indirect method)
P1, P3

Refer to Kirby Corporation's financial statements and related information reported in Problem 17-4A.

Required

Prepare a statement of cash flows that reports cash inflows and outflows from operating activities according to the indirect method.

Problem 17-6A[A]
Cash flows spreadsheet (indirect method)
P3, P4

17 CHAPTER

Refer to the information reported about Kirby Corporation in Problem 17-4A.

Required

Prepare a statement of cash flows using a spreadsheet that follows the indirect method of reporting cash flows from operating activities. Identify the debits and credits in the Analysis of Changes columns with letters that correspond to the following list of transactions and events:

a. Net income is $57,000.
b. Accounts receivable decreased.
c. Merchandise inventory decreased.
d. Prepaid expenses decreased.
e. Accounts payable decreased.
f. Depreciation expense is $36,600.
g. Sold equipment costing $51,000, with accumulated depreciation of $20,850, for $28,050 cash. This yields a loss of $2,100.
h. Purchased equipment costing $113,250 by paying cash of $38,250 and
i. by signing a long-term note payable for the balance.
j. Borrowed $6,000 by signing a short-term note payable.
k. Paid $45,000 to reduce the long-term notes payable.
l. Issued 3,000 shares of common stock for cash at $11 per share.
m. Declared and paid cash dividends of $63,000.

Problem 18-1A
Computing ratios and both common-size and trend percents
P1, P2, P3

The condensed financial statements of Temptron Corporation follow:

TEMPTRON CORPORATION
Comparative Income Statement ($000)
For Years Ended December 31, 2001, 2000, and 1999

	2001	2000	1999
Sales	$199,800	$167,000	$144,800
Cost of goods sold	109,890	87,175	67,200
Gross profit	$ 89,910	$ 79,825	$ 77,600
Selling expenses	$ 23,680	$ 20,790	$ 19,000
Administrative expenses	17,760	15,610	16,700
Total expenses	$ 41,440	$ 36,400	$ 35,700
Income before taxes	$ 48,470	$ 43,425	$ 41,900
Income taxes	5,050	4,910	4,300
Net income	$ 43,420	$ 38,515	$ 37,600

TEMPTRON CORPORATION
Comparative Balance Sheet ($000)
December 31, 2001, 2000, and 1999

	2001	2000	1999
Assets			
Current assets	$ 55,860	$ 33,660	$ 37,300
Long-term investments	0	2,700	11,600
Plant and equipment	113,810	114,660	80,000
Total assets	$169,670	$151,020	$128,900
Liabilities and Stockholders' Equity			
Current liabilities	$ 23,370	$ 20,180	$ 17,500
Common stock	47,500	47,500	38,000
Other contributed capital	14,850	14,850	12,300
Retained earnings	83,950	68,490	61,100
Total liabilities and equity	$169,670	$151,020	$128,900

Required

Preparation Component

1. Compute each year's current ratio.
2. Express the income statement data in common-size percents.
3. Express the balance sheet data in trend percents with 1999 as the base year.

Analysis Component

4. Comment on any significant relations revealed by the ratios and percents.

Problem 18-2A
Calculation and analysis of trend percents
P1

The condensed comparative financial statements of Hensley Company follow:

HENSLEY COMPANY
Comparative Income Statement ($000)
For Years Ended December 31, 2005–1999

	2005	2004	2003	2002	2001	2000	1999
Sales	$660	$710	$730	$780	$840	$870	$960
Cost of goods sold	376	390	394	414	440	450	480
Gross profit	$284	$320	$336	$366	$400	$420	$480
Operating expenses	184	204	212	226	240	244	250
Net income	$100	$116	$124	$140	$160	$176	$230

HENSLEY COMPANY
Comparative Balance Sheet ($000)
December 31, 2005–1999

	2005	2004	2003	2002	2001	2000	1999
Assets							
Cash	$ 34	$ 36	$ 42	$ 44	$ 50	$ 52	$ 58
Accounts receivable, net	120	126	130	134	140	144	150
Merchandise inventory	156	162	168	170	176	180	198
Other current assets	24	24	26	28	28	30	30
Long-term investments	26	20	16	100	100	100	100
Plant and equipment, net	410	414	420	312	320	328	354
Total assets	$770	$782	$802	$788	$814	$834	$890
Liabilities and Equity							
Current liabilities	$138	$146	$176	$180	$200	$250	$270
Long-term liabilities	82	110	132	138	184	204	250
Common stock	150	150	150	150	150	150	150
Other contributed capital	60	60	60	60	60	60	60
Retained earnings	340	316	284	260	220	170	160
Total liabilities and equity	$770	$782	$802	$788	$814	$834	$890

Required

Preparation Component

1. Compute trend percents for the items of both statements using 1999 as the base year.

Analysis Component

2. Analyze and comment on the statements and trend percents from part (1).

Problem 18-3A
Calculation of financial statement ratios
P3

The December 31, 2000, financial statements of Nowland Corporation follow:

NOWLAND CORPORATION
Income Statement
For Year Ended December 31, 2000

Sales		$215,500
Cost of goods sold:		
Inventory, 12/31/1999	$ 16,400	
Purchases	132,200	
Goods available for sale	$148,600	
Inventory, 12/31/2000	12,500	
Cost of goods sold		136,100
Gross profit		$ 79,400
Operating expenses		50,200
Operating income		$ 29,200
Interest expense		1,200
Income before taxes		$ 28,000
Income taxes		2,200
Net income		$ 25,800

NOWLAND CORPORATION
Balance Sheet
December 31, 2000

Assets		Liabilities and Stockholders' Equity	
Cash	$ 5,100	Accounts payable	$ 10,500
Short-term investments	5,900	Accrued wages payable	2,300
Accounts receivable, net	11,100	Income taxes payable	1,600
Notes receivable (trade)	2,000	Long-term note payable,	
Merchandise inventory	12,500	secured by mortgage	
Prepaid expenses	1,000	on plant assets	25,000
Plant assets, net	72,900	Common stock, $5 par value	41,000
		Retained earnings	30,100
Total assets	$110,500	Total liabilities and equity	$110,500

Assume that all sales are on credit. On the December 31, 1999, balance sheet, the assets totaled $95,900, common stock was $41,500, and retained earnings were $19,800.

Required

Compute the following: *(a)* current ratio, *(b)* acid-test ratio, *(c)* days' sales uncollected, *(d)* merchandise turnover, *(e)* days' sales in inventory, *(f)* ratio of pledged assets to secured liabilities, *(g)* times interest earned, *(h)* profit margin, *(i)* total asset turnover, *(j)* return on total assets, and *(k)* return on common stockholders' equity.

Problem 18-4A
Comparative analysis using ratios

Two companies competing in the same industry are being evaluated by a bank that will lend money to only one of them. Summary information from the financial statements of the two companies follows:

18 CHAPTER

	Lutz Company	Highland Company
Data from the current year-end balance sheets:		
Assets		
Cash	$ 22,000	$ 38,500
Accounts receivable, net	79,100	72,500
Notes receivable (trade)	13,600	11,000
Merchandise inventory	88,800	84,000
Prepaid expenses	11,700	12,100
Plant and equipment, net	178,900	254,300
Total assets	$394,100	$472,400
Liabilities and Stockholders' Equity		
Current liabilities	$ 92,500	$ 99,000
Long-term notes payable	95,000	95,300
Common stock, $5 par value	135,000	143,000
Retained earnings	71,600	135,100
Total liabilities and equity	$394,100	$472,400

	Lutz Company	Highland Company
Data from the current year's income statements:		
Sales	$395,600	$669,500
Cost of goods sold	292,600	482,000
Interest expense	7,900	12,400
Income tax expense	7,700	14,300
Net income	35,850	63,700
Earnings per share	$1.33	$2.23
Beginning-of-year data:		
Accounts receivable, net	$ 74,200	$ 75,300
Notes receivable (trade)	0	0
Merchandise inventory	107,100	82,500
Total assets	385,400	445,000
Common stock, $5 par value	135,000	143,000
Retained earnings	51,100	111,700

Required

1. Compute the current ratio, acid-test ratio, accounts (including notes) receivable turnover, merchandise turnover, days' sales in inventory, and days' sales uncollected for the two companies. Then identify the company that you consider to be the better short-term credit risk and explain why.
2. Compute the profit margin, total asset turnover, return on total assets, and return on common stockholders' equity for the two companies. Assuming that each company paid cash dividends of $3 per share and each company's stock can be purchased at $25 per share, compute their price-earnings ratios and dividend yields. Identify which company's stock you would recommend as the better investment and explain why.

Problem 18-5A
Analysis of working capital
P3

Resource Corporation began the month of June with $280,000 of current assets, a current ratio of 2.80 to 1, and an acid-test ratio of 1.2 to 1. During the month, it completed the following transactions:

June 1 Sold merchandise that cost $62,000 for $101,000.
3 Collected a $78,000 account receivable.
5 Bought $130,000 of merchandise on account. (The company uses a perpetual inventory system.)
7 Borrowed $90,000 by giving the bank a 60-day, 10% note.
10 Borrowed $180,000 by signing a long-term secured note.
12 Used $280,000 cash to buy additional machinery.
15 Declared a $1 per share cash dividend on the 60,000 shares of outstanding common stock.
19 Wrote off a $7,000 bad debt against Allowance for Doubtful Accounts.
22 Paid a $11,000 account payable.
31 Paid the dividend declared on June 15.

Required

Prepare a schedule showing the company's current ratio, acid-test ratio, and working capital after each of the transactions. Round computations to two decimal places.

19 CHAPTER

Problem 19-1A
Evaluate managerial accountant's role
C1, C8

This chapter includes a discussion of the objectives of managerial accounting along with a discussion on the current business environment. You are to look through the *home electronics* section of your local newspaper — the Sunday paper is often best. Review advertisements of home electronics and take note of how many manufacturers offer these products and what factors they compete on.

Required

Discuss the potential contributions and responsibilities of the managerial accounting professional in helping a home electronics manufacturer succeed? (*Hint:* Think about information and estimates a managerial accountant might provide new entrants into the home electronics market.)

Problem 19-2A
Compute and evaluate ending inventory
C3, C8

Candle Skate, Inc., makes specialty skates for the ice skating circuit. On December 31, 1999, the company had (a) 1,500 skates in ending inventory valued at $200 per pair and (b) 2,000 blades valued at $15 each in raw materials inventory for skates to be made. During year 2000, Candle Skate, Inc., purchased 45,000 blades at $15 each and manufactured 20,000 pairs of skates.

Required

Preparation Component

1. Determine the units and dollar amounts of raw materials inventory in blades at December 31, 2000.

Analysis Component

2. Write a one-page memorandum to the production manager explaining why a just-in-time inventory system for blades should be considered. Include in your memo the amount of working capital that can be reduced at December 31, 2000, if the ending blade raw material inventory is cut in half.

Problem 19-3A
Computeing and reporting inventory
C4, C5, P1

Shown below are the annual financial data at December 31, 2000, taken from two different companies.

	Cardinal CD Retail	Van Conversion Inc. Manufacturing
Beginning inventory:		
Merchandise	$50,000	
Finished goods		$200,000
Cost of purchases	350,000	
Cost of goods manufactured		686,000
Ending inventory:		
Merchandise	25,000	
Finished goods		300,000

Required

1. Compute cost of goods sold at December 31, 2000, for each of the two companies. Include proper title and format in the solution.
2. Write a short memorandum to your instructor *(a)* identifying the inventory accounts and *(b)* describing where each is reported on the income statement and balance sheet.

Problem 19-4A
Explaining and contrasting costs
C5, C6

You must make a presentation to a client explaining the difference between prime and conversion costs. The client makes and sells bread for 200,000 customers per week. The client tells you that the sales staff also would like a clarification regarding product and period costs. She tells you that many on the staff have financial accounting training but lack training in managerial accounting topics.

Required

Write a one-page memorandum in proper form to your client outlining your planned presentation to her sales staff.

Problem 19-5A
Compute, classify, and analyze costs
C5, A1

Listed below are costs for the production of 12,000 CDs manufactured by Music City. They sell for $15 each.

	Cost by Behavior		Cost by Function	
Costs	Variable	Fixed	Product	Period
Plastic for CDs—$1,000	$1,000		$1,000	
Wages of assembly workers—$20,000				
Rent on factory—$4,500				
Systems staff's salary—$10,000				
Labeling (12,000 outsourced)—$2,500				
Lease on office equipment—$700				
Upper management salaries—$100,000				
Annual fees for cleaning service—$3,000				
Sales commissions—$0.50 per CD				
Machinery depreciation—$15,000				

19 CHAPTER

Required

Preparation Component

1. Classify costs and their amounts as *(a)* either fixed or variable and *(b)* either product or period.
2. Compute the *(a)* contribution margin and *(b)* contribution margin ratio by filling in the boxes in the table below.

Check Figure Total variable cost, $29,500

MUSIC CITY Contribution Margin Income Statement For the Year Ending December 31, 2000			
Sales ($15 × 12,000)		$☐	100%
Variable costs:			
Plastic for CDs	$☐		
Wages of assembly	☐		
Labels outsourced	☐		
Sales commissions	☐		16%
Contribution margin		☐	Contribution margin ratio* ☐%

*Contribution margin ratio = Contribution margin/Sales.

Analysis Component

3. What can we interpret from the contribution margin and the contribution margin ratio?

Problem 19-6A
Projecting and estimating opportunity costs
C1, C5

Refer to *You Make the Call,* **Purchase Manager,** in this chapter. Assume you are the managerial accountant for the motorcycle manufacturer. The purchasing manager asks you about preparing an estimate of the related costs for buying motorcycle seats from supplier (B). She tells you this estimate is needed because unless dollar estimates are attached to nonfinancial factors such as lost production costs, her supervisor will not give it full attention. The purchase manager also shows you the following information:

- Production output is 1,000 motorcycles per year based on 250 production days a year.
- Production time per day is 8 hours at a cost of $1,500 per hour to run the production line.
- Lost production time due to poor quality is 1%.
- Satisfied customers purchase, on average, three motorcycles during a lifetime.
- Satisfied customers recommend, on average, the product to 4 other people.
- Marketing estimates that using seat (B) will result in 4 lost customers per year from repeat business and referrals.
- Average contribution margin per motorcycle is $4,000.

Required

Estimate the costs of buying motorcycle seats from supplier (B). This problem requires you think creatively and make reasonable estimates and, therefore, there is more than one correct answer. [*Hint:* Reread the answer to *You Make The Call,* and think about costs of lost production time, repeat business, and similar factors.]

Problem 19-7A
Projecting and estimating sales and costs; contribution margin analysis
C7, C8, A1

American Bagel Store chain, a market leader, is trying to increase sales to its existing customers by creating a customer orientation in meeting buyer needs and wants. Assume you are hired as a consultant by American Bagel to analyze its operations and suggest improvements. American Bagel wants to increase its contribution margin by $10,000.

Required

1. To increase sales and total contribution margin from existing customers of American Bagel, offer three improvements that you have observed in other stores and feel would be successful at American Bagel.
2. What level of increase in sales is necessary for American Bagel to increase total contribution margin by $10,000? (Hint: With each suggestion in (1), identify the expected sales dollars and contribution margin ratio to meet the $10,000 increase in contribution margin.)

Problem 19-8A Manufacturing management principles in practice C8

19 CHAPTER

A trip to the photography store is useful in understanding manufacturing management principles such as total quality management (TQM), just-in-time (JIT), theory of constraints (TOC), and continuous improvement (CI). List two photography stores you are familiar with in the first column of the table below. Record in the table how each store is putting each of these principles into action, both favorably and unfavorably. (Hint: To prepare a response to this question you may want to watch how film is processed and prints prepared within 1 hour.)

Photography Store	TQM	JIT	TOC	CI

Problem 20-1A Preparing manufacturing and income statements; analysis of inventories P1

20 CHAPTER

The following items are taken from the adjusted trial balance and other records of Home Building, Inc., before the calendar year-end closing entries are recorded:

Advertising expense	$ 16,200	Direct labor	450,000
Depreciation expense, Office equip.	6,750	Income taxes expense	109,350
Depreciation expense, Selling equip.	8,100	Indirect labor	47,250
Depreciation of factory equipment	28,350	Miscellaneous production costs	6,750
Factory supervision	97,200	Office salaries expense	56,700
Factory supplies used	4,850	Raw materials purchases	715,500
Factory utilities	30,000	Rent expense, office space	18,900
Inventories:		Rent expense, selling space	21,600
Raw materials, January 1	32,300	Rent on factory building	74,800
Raw materials, December 31	136,350	Maintenance, factory equipment	24,300
Goods in process, January 1	10,000	Sales	4,000,000
Goods in process, December 31	11,250	Sales discounts	45,900
Finished goods, January 1	141,750	Sales salaries expense	236,250
Finished goods, December 31	113,400		

Required

Preparation Component

1. Prepare a manufacturing statement for the company.
2. Prepare an income statement for the company. The income statement should present separate categories for *(a)* selling expenses and *(b)* general and administrative expenses.

Analysis Component

3. Compute the *(a)* inventory turnover and *(b)* days' sales in inventory for raw materials inventory and its finished goods inventory (see Chapter 7). Discuss some possible reasons for differences between these ratios for the two inventories.

Check Figure Cost of goods manufactured, $1,373,700

Problem 20-2A Computing and recording manufacturing costs and preparing reports C1, C3, P1, P2, P3, P4

Alliance Co.'s March 31 inventory of raw materials is $16,000. Raw materials purchases in April are $60,000. Factory payroll cost in April is $68,000. Overhead costs incurred in April are: indirect materials, $6,000; indirect labor, $4,000; factory rent, $24,000; factory utilities, $22,000; and factory equipment depreciation, $25,000. The predetermined overhead rate is 130% of direct labor cost. Job 114 is sold for $100,000 cash during April. Costs allocated to the three jobs worked on in April are:

	Job 114	Job 115	Job 116
Balances at March 31:			
Direct materials	$ 4,000	$ 6,000	
Direct labor	2,000	2,200	
Applied overhead	2,600	2,860	
Costs during April:			
Direct materials	10,000	30,000	$16,000
Direct labor	16,000	28,000	20,000
Applied overhead	?	?	?
Status at April 30	Finished (sold)	Finished (unsold)	In process

Required

Preparation Component

1. Determine the total of each manufacturing cost incurred for April (direct labor, direct materials, allocated overhead), and the total cost assigned to each of the three jobs (including the balances from March 31).
2. Prepare journal entries for the month to record:
   a. Materials purchases (on credit), factory payroll (paid in cash), and actual overhead costs including indirect materials and indirect labor. (Factory rent and utilities are paid in cash.)
   b. Assignment of direct materials, direct labor, and applied overhead costs to Goods in Process Inventory.
   c. Transfer of Jobs 114 and 115 to the Finished Goods Inventory.
   d. Cost of Job 114 in the Cost of Goods Sold account.
   e. Revenue from the sale of Job 114.
   f. Assignment of any underapplied or overapplied overhead to the Cost of Goods Sold account. (The amount is not material.)
3. Prepare a manufacturing statement for April (use a single line presentation for direct materials and show the details of overhead cost).
4. Present a calculation of gross profit for April. Show how the inventories would be presented on the April 30 balance sheet.

Analysis Component

5. When the over- or underapplied overhead adjustment is made, we close Factory Overhead to Cost of Goods Sold. Discuss how this adjustment impacts business decision making regarding individual jobs or batches of jobs.

Problem 20-3A
Source documents, journal entries, overhead and financial reports
P1, P2, P3, P4, P5

The following trial balance of the Velcro Company is generated by the computer system on the afternoon of December 31, 2000. The company's accountant knows that is wrong because the trial balance does not show any balance for the goods in process inventory and it still shows balances for the Factory Payroll and Factory Overhead accounts:

	Debit	Credit
Cash	$ 40,000	
Accounts receivable	80,000	
Raw materials inventory	24,000	
Goods in process inventory	-0-	
Finished goods	50,000	
Prepaid rent	4,000	
Accounts payable		$ 16,000
Notes payable		30,000
Common stock		60,000
Retained earnings		33,800
Sales		250,000
Cost of goods sold	140,000	
Factory payroll	20,000	
Factory overhead	9,800	
Miscellaneous expenses	22,000	
Total	$389,800	$389,800

After searching various files, six source documents are found that need to be processed to bring the accounting records up to date:

Materials requisition 94-231:	$ 5,000 direct materials to Job 603
Materials requisition 94-232:	8,000 direct materials to Job 604
Materials requisition 94-233:	1,500 indirect materials
Labor time ticket 765:	6,000 direct labor to Job 603
Labor time ticket 766:	12,000 direct labor to Job 604
Labor time ticket 777:	2,000 indirect labor

Jobs 603 and 604 are the only units in process at the end of the year. The predetermined overhead application rate is 80% of direct labor cost.

Required

Preparation Component

1. Use the information on the six source documents to prepare journal entries to assign the following costs:
   a. Direct materials costs to goods in process inventory.
   b. Direct labor costs to goods in process inventory.
   c. Overhead costs to goods in process inventory.
   d. Indirect materials costs to the overhead account.
   e. Indirect labor costs to the overhead account.
2. Determine the revised balance of the Factory Overhead account after making the entries in part (1). Determine whether there is under- or overapplied overhead for the year. Prepare the adjusting entry to allocate any over- or underapplied overhead to cost of goods sold, assuming the amount is not material.
3. Prepare a revised trial balance.
4. Prepare an income statement for year 2000 and a balance sheet as of December 31, 2000.

Analysis Component

5. Assume that the $1,500 indirect materials on materials requisition 94–233 should have been direct materials charged to Job 604. Without providing specific calculations, describe what impact this error would have on Velcro's year 2000 income statement and balance sheet.

Problem 20-4A
Source documents and journal entries in job order cost accounting
P4, P5

Back Pack Company's predetermined overhead application rate is 90% of direct labor. The company's activities related to manufacturing during April 2000 are:

a. Purchased raw materials on account, $57,000.
b. Paid factory wages with cash, $99,750.
c. Paid miscellaneous factory overhead costs with cash, $11,250.
d. Materials requisitions for the month show that the following materials were used:

Job 487	$13,500
Job 488	9,000
Job 489	12,000
Job 490	10,500
Job 491	1,500
Total direct materials	$46,500
Indirect materials	3,750
Total materials used	$50,250

e. Labor time tickets for the month show the following labor was used:

Job 487	$16,500
Job 488	19,500
Job 489	25,500
Job 490	18,000
Job 491	7,500
Total direct labor	$87,000
Indirect labor	12,750
Total	$99,750

f. Jobs 487, 489, and 490 were completed, and overhead was allocated to them.
g. Jobs 487, 489, and 490 were transferred to finished goods.

h. Jobs 487 and 489 were sold on account for a total price of $225,000.

i. Overhead costs incurred during the month are (credit Prepaid Insurance for expired factory insurance):

Depreciation of factory building	$24,750
Depreciation of factory equipment	18,750
Expired factory insurance	2,250
Accrued property taxes payable	5,250

j. At the end of the month, overhead is applied to the goods in process (Jobs 488 and 491) using the predetermined rate of 90% of direct labor cost.

Required

1. Prepare a job cost sheet for each job worked on during the month. Use the following simplified form of a job cost sheet:

Job No. ________	
Materials	$
Labor	
Overhead	
Total cost	$

2. Prepare journal entries to record the events and transactions *a* through *j*.

3. Set up T-accounts for each of the following general ledger accounts, each of which started the month with a zero balance: Raw Materials Inventory, Goods in Process Inventory, Finished Goods Inventory, Factory Payroll, Factory Overhead, Cost of Goods Sold. Then post the journal entries to these T-accounts and determine the balance of each account.

4. Prepare a schedule showing the total cost of each job in process and prove that the sum of their costs equals the Goods in Process Inventory account balance. Prepare similar schedules for the finished goods inventory and the cost of goods sold.

Problem 20-5A
Allocating overhead using predetermined overhead application rate
C3, P4, P5

In December 1999, Watson Company's accountant estimated next year's direct labor using the cost of 40 persons, working an average of 1,500 hours each, at an average wage rate of $50 per hour. The accountant also estimated the following manufacturing overhead costs for year 2000:

Indirect labor	$ 540,000
Factory supervision	450,000
Rent on factory building	360,000
Factory computer system	200,000
Factory insurance expired	60,000
Depreciation of factory equipment	300,000
Repairs, factory equipment	180,000
Factory supplies used	110,000
Miscellaneous production costs	200,000
Total	$2,400,000

At the end of year 2000, records show the company incurred $2,200,000 of overhead costs. It completed and sold five jobs with the following direct labor costs: Job 625, $300,000; Job 626, $225,000; Job 627, $975,000; Job 628, $240,000; and Job 629, $375,000. In addition, Job 630 is in process at the end of year 2000 and had been charged $75,000 for direct labor. The company's predetermined overhead application rate is based on direct labor cost.

Required

1. Determine the:
   a. Predetermined overhead application rate for year 2000.
   b. Total overhead cost applied to each of the six jobs during year 2000.
   c. Over- or underapplied overhead at year-end.
2. Assuming that any over- or underapplied overhead is not material, prepare the adjusting entry to allocate any over- or underapplied overhead to cost of goods sold at the end of year 2000.

Problem 20-6A
Recording manufacturing transactions; subsidiary records; source documents
P2, P3, P4

If the working papers that accompany this book are not available, do not attempt to solve this problem. Natkin Company manufactures special variations of its product, a megatron, in response to special orders from its customers. On March 1, the company had no inventories of goods in process or finished goods but held the following raw materials:

Material M	150 units @ $ 40 =	$ 6,000
Material R	50 units @ 160 =	8,000
Paint	20 units @ 20 =	400
Total		$14,400

On March 3, the company began working on two megatrons: Job 450 for Ancira Company and Job 451 for Montero, Inc.

Required

Follow instructions in the list of activities below and complete the materials provided in the working papers.

a. Purchased raw materials on credit and recorded the following information from receiving reports and invoices:

> Receiving Report No. 20, Material M, 150 units at $40 each.
> Receiving Report No. 21, Material R, 200 units at $160 each.

Instructions: Record the purchases with a single journal entry and post it to general ledger T-accounts, using the transaction letter to identify the entry. Enter the receiving report information on the materials ledger cards.

b. Requisitioned the following raw materials for production:

> Requisition No. 223, for Job 450, 60 units of Material M.
> Requisition No 224, for Job 450, 100 units of Material R.
> Requisition No. 225, for Job 451, 30 units of Material M.
> Requisition No. 226, for Job 451, 75 units of Material R.
> Requisition No. 227, for 10 units of paint.

Instructions: Enter amounts for direct materials requisitions only on the materials ledger cards and the job cost sheets. Enter the indirect material amount on the raw materials ledger card and record a debit to the Indirect Materials account in the subsidiary Factory Overhead Ledger. Do not record a journal entry at this time.

c. Employees turned in the following time tickets for work in March:

> Time tickets Nos. 1 to 10 for direct labor on Job 450, $24,000.
> Time tickets Nos. 11 to 20 for direct labor on Job 451, $20,000.
> Time tickets Nos. 21 to 24 for equipment repairs, $4,000.

Instructions: Record direct labor reported on the time tickets only on the job cost sheets, and debit indirect labor to the Indirect Labor account in the subsidiary Factory Overhead Ledger. Do not record a journal entry at this time.

d. The company paid cash for the following items during the month: factory payroll, $48,000; and miscellaneous overhead items, $47,000.
Instructions: Record these payments with journal entries and post them to the general ledger accounts. Also record a debit in the Miscellaneous Overhead account in the subsidiary Factory Overhead Ledger.

e. Finished Job 450 and transferred it to the warehouse. The company assigns overhead to each job with a predetermined overhead application rate equal to 120% of direct labor cost.
Instructions: Enter the allocated overhead on the cost sheet for Job 20, fill in the cost summary section of the cost sheet, and then mark the cost sheet "Finished." Prepare a journal entry to record the job's completion and transfer to finished goods, and then post it to the general ledger accounts.

f. Delivered Job 450 and accepted the customer's promise to pay $130,000 within 30 days.
Instructions: Prepare journal entries to record the sale of Job 450 and the cost of goods sold. Post them to the general ledger accounts.

g. At month-end, apply overhead cost to Job 451 based on the direct labor cost used on the job for that date.
Instructions: Enter overhead on the job cost sheet but do not make a journal entry at this time.

h. Recorded the total direct and indirect materials costs as reported on all the requisitions for the month.
Instructions: Prepare a journal entry to record these costs and post it to general ledger accounts.

i. Recorded the total direct and indirect labor costs as reported on all the time tickets for the month.
Instructions: Prepare a journal entry to record these costs, and post it to general ledger accounts.

j. Recorded the total overhead costs applied to jobs.
Instructions: Prepare a journal entry to record the application of these costs and post it to general ledger accounts.

21 CHAPTER

Problem 21-1A
Measuring production costs and preparing journal entries
P1, P2, P3, P6, P7

Tots Toys Company manufactures dolls by passing the products through a molding department and an assembly department. The following information is available regarding its inventories for June:

	Beginning Inventory	Ending Inventory
Raw materials	$ 36,000	$ 45,000
Goods in process—molding	12,000	21,000
Goods in process—assembly	66,000	54,000
Finished goods	78,000	99,000

The following additional information describes the company's manufacturing activities for June:

Raw materials purchases (on credit)	$100,000
Factory payroll cost (paid in cash)	200,000
Other overhead cost (credit Other Accounts)	50,000
Materials used:	
Direct—molding	$ 6,000
Direct—assembly	54,000
Indirect	21,000
Labor used:	
Direct—molding	$100,000
Direct—assembly	75,000
Indirect	25,000
Overhead rates as a percent of direct labor:	
Molding	80%
Assembly	75%
Sales (on credit)	$500,000

Required

1. Compute *(a)* the cost of products transferred from molding to assembly, *(b)* the cost of products transferred from assembly to finished goods, and *(c)* the cost of goods sold.
2. Prepare journal entries to record the manufacturing activities during June.

Problem 21-2A
Computing cost per equivalent unit and assigning costs to products
P4

Penbrook Company passes its product through several departments. The last of these is the bagging department. Direct materials are added evenly throughout the process in the bagging department. Also, one-half of the direct labor is added at the beginning of the bagging process and the other half is added when the process is 50% complete with respect to materials. During September, 80,000 units of product are transferred to finished goods from the bagging department. Of these units, 18,000 units were 60% complete at the beginning of the period and 62,000 were started and completed during the period. At the end of September, the goods in process inventory consists of 8,000 units that are 25% complete with respect to materials. The bagging department's direct materials cost for September is $712,000 and its direct labor cost is $1,980,000.

Required

Preparation Component

1. Determine the bagging department's equivalent units of production with respect to *(a)* direct labor and *(b)* direct materials.
2. Compute both the direct labor cost and the direct materials cost per equivalent unit.
3. Compute the amounts of both direct labor cost and direct materials cost assigned to the *(a)* beginning goods in process inventory, *(b)* units started and completed, and *(c)* ending goods in process inventory.

Check Figure
Direct labor cost per equivalent unit, $30

Analysis Component

4. Penbrook sells and ships all units to customers as soon as they are completed. Assume an error is made in determining the percentage of completion for units in ending inventory. Instead of being 25% complete with respect to materials, they are actually 75% complete. Write a one-page memo to the plant manager describing how this error affects Penbrook's September financial statements.

Problem 21-3A
Journalizing in process cost accounting and using equivalent units
P1, P2, P3, P4

Trimble Company produces a product in large quantities that goes through two processes—tooling and machining. The following information is available on its factory activities for May:

Raw materials:	
Beginning inventory	$ 84,000
Raw materials purchased (on credit)	500,000
Direct materials used in tooling	(248,200)
Direct materials used in machining	(178,200)
Indirect materials used	(101,600)
Ending inventory	$ 56,000
Factory payroll:	
Direct labor used in tooling	$318,000
Direct labor used in machining	35,640
Indirect labor used	46,360
Total payroll cost (paid in cash)	$400,000
Factory overhead incurred:	
Indirect materials used	$101,600
Indirect labor used	46,360
Other overhead costs	50,520
Total factory overhead incurred	$198,480
Factory overhead applied:	
Tooling (40% of direct labor)	$127,200
Machining (200% of direct labor)	71,280
Total factory overhead applied	$198,480

Information about the inventory in the tooling department is reported below:

Units:	
Beginning in process inventory	40,000
Started and completed	120,000
Ending in process inventory	20,000
Beginning in process inventory:	
Materials—percent complete	80%
Labor and overhead—percent complete	40%
Ending in process inventory:	
Materials—percent complete	90%
Labor and overhead—percent complete	75%
Costs:	
Beginning in process inventory	$ 99,200
Direct materials added	248,200
Direct labor added	318,000
Overhead applied (40% of direct labor)	127,200
Total costs	$792,600
Transferred out to machining department	(720,000)
Ending in process inventory	$ 72,600

Information about the goods in process inventories for the machining department follows: beginning in process inventory, $249,000; and ending in process inventory, $229,320. Also, these facts are available regarding finished goods:

Beginning inventory	$ 36,600
Cost transferred in from machining	1,024,800
Cost of goods sold	(1,000,400)
Ending inventory	$ 61,000

During May, 80,000 units of finished goods are sold for cash at a price of $20 each.

Required

Preparation Component

1. Prepare journal entries to record the activities of May.

2. Compute the tooling department's equivalent units of production for May. Calculate the cost per equivalent unit for direct materials, direct labor, and overhead, assuming all product costs are added evenly throughout the process.

3. Compute the cost of ending goods in process inventory for the tooling department.

Analysis Component

4. Trimble provides incentives to managers of its processing departments by paying monthly bonuses based on their success in controlling costs per equivalent unit of production. Assume the tooling department overestimates the percentage of completion for units in ending inventory, with the result that its equivalent units of production in ending inventory for May are overstated. What impact does this error have on bonuses paid to the manager of the tooling department and the manager of the machining department? What impact, if any, does this error have on these managers' June bonuses?

Problem 21-4A
Preparing a process cost summary
P4, P5

Osorio Company produces its product through a single processing department. Direct materials, direct labor, and overhead are added to the product evenly throughout the process. The company uses monthly reporting periods for its process cost accounting system. The Goods in Process Inventory account appears as follows after posting entries for direct materials, direct labor, and overhead costs for November:

Goods in Process Inventory					Acct. No. 133
Date		**Explanation**	**Debit**	**Credit**	**Balance**
Nov.	1	Beginning balance			70,000
	30	Direct materials	115,000		185,000
	30	Direct labor costs	425,000		610,000
	30	Applied overhead	600,000		1,210,000

During November, the company finished and transferred 100,000 units of the product to finished goods. Of these units, 7,500 were in process at the beginning of the month, and 92,500 were started and completed during the month. The beginning goods in process inventory was 80% complete. At the end of the month, the goods in process inventory consisted of 12,000 units that are 25% completed.

Required

1. Compute the number of equivalent units of production for November.
2. Prepare the department's process cost summary for November.
3. Prepare the journal entry to transfer the cost of the completed units to Finished Goods Inventory.

Problem 21-5A
Preparing a process cost summary

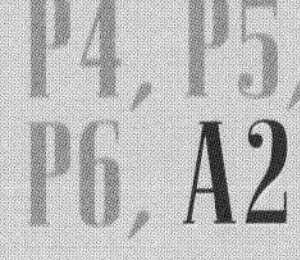

Jiffy Manufacturing Co. manufactures a single product in one department. Direct labor and overhead are added evenly throughout the process. Direct materials are added as needed. The company uses monthly reporting periods for its process cost accounting system. During January, the company completed and transferred 220,000 units of product to finished goods inventory. The beginning goods in process inventory consisted of 20,000 units that were 75% complete with respect to direct materials and 60% complete with respect to direct labor and overhead. The other 200,000 completed units were started during the month. Also, 40,000 units are in process at the end of the month, and they are 50% complete with respect to direct materials and 30% complete with respect to direct labor and overhead. After posting entries for direct materials, direct labor, and overhead for January, the company's Goods in Process Inventory account appears as follows:

Goods in Process Inventory					Acct. No. 133
Date		**Explanation**	**Debit**	**Credit**	**Balance**
Jan.	1	Beginning balance			41,100
	31	Direct materials	112,500		153,600
	31	Direct labor costs	176,000		329,600
	31	Applied overhead	440,000		769,600

Required

1. Compute the equivalent units of production for direct materials and for direct labor and overhead.
2. Prepare the department's process cost summary for January.
3. Prepare the entry to transfer the cost of completed units to finished goods inventory.

Analysis Components

4. The accounting process depends on several estimates.
   a. Identify the two major estimates that affect the cost per equivalent unit.
   b. In what direction might you anticipate a bias from management for each estimate in part (a) (assume management compensation is based on maintaining low inventory values)? Explain.
5. Measurement of spoilage can impact the equivalent unit cost. Without providing computations, would the cost per equivalent unit increase or decrease if management only counted the good units of production? (Assume existence of spoiled units.) Explain why management needs to know the cost of spoiled units.

22 CHAPTER

Problem 22-1A
Allocating building occupancy costs
C3, P1

DuPree's has several departments that occupy all three floors of a two-story building with a basement. The store has rented this building under a long-term lease negotiated when rental rates were lower. The departmental accounting system has a single account in the ledger called Building Occupancy Cost. The types and amounts of costs recorded in this account for the current calendar year are:

Building rent	$300,000
Lighting expense	24,000
Cleaning expense	16,000
Total	$340,000

The building has 7,500 square feet on each floor but only 5,000 square feet in the basement. For simplicity, the accountant merely divides the $340,000 occupancy cost by 20,000 square feet to find an average cost of $17 per square foot. Then each department is charged with a building occupancy cost equal to this rate times the number of square feet that it occupies.

Manny Malone manages a department that occupies 2,000 square feet of floor space in the basement. In discussing the departmental reports with other managers, Malone questions whether using the same rate per square foot for all departments makes sense because different floor space has different values. Malone checked a recent real estate report of average rental costs for similar space. The report shows that first-floor space is worth $40 per square foot while second-floor space is worth $20 per square foot and basement space is worth only $10 per square foot (amounts do not include costs for lighting and cleaning).

Required

Preparation Component

1. Allocate occupancy cost to Malone's department by the accountant's simple method.
2. Allocate occupancy cost to Malone's department in proportion to the relative market value of the space, except for lighting and cleaning costs, which are allocated on an equal basis per square foot occupied.

Analysis Component

3. If you were a manager of a basement department, explain which allocation method you'd prefer.

Problem 22-2A
Activity-based Costing
P2

Bill's Landscaping is a landscaping business that has enjoyed excess profits for many years. But new competition has cut service revenue by as much as 30%. As a result, the company wants a better understanding of its costs. You are to prepare an activity-based cost analysis using the data below. It also is important to estimate the average cost of both general landscaping services and custom design landscaping services. The company's three cost centers and their cost drivers are:

Cost Center	Cost	Cost Driver	Quantity
Professional salaries	$500,000	Professional hours	10,000
Customer supplies	125,000	Number of customers	500
Building cost	150,000	Square feet	1,500

The two main landscaping units and their related data are:

Service	Hours	Square Feet*	Customers
General landscaping	2,500	500	400
Custom design landscaping	7,500	1,000	100

*Custom design landscaping requires more space for equipment, supplies, and planning.

Required

Preparation Component

1. Compute the cost per driver.
2. Compute the average cost for *(a)* general landscaping and *(b)* custom design landscaping.

Analysis Component

3. Without computations, would the average cost of general landscaping be more or less if center costs are allocated on the number of customers? Explain.

Problem 22-3A
Departmental income statements
P3

Crane Entertainment, Inc., began operating in January 2000 with two operating (selling) departments and one service (office) department. Departmental income statements are shown below:

CRANE ENTERTAINMENT, INC.
Departmental Income Statements
For Year Ended December 31, 2000

	Movies	Video Games	Combined
Sales	$540,000	$180,000	$720,000
Cost of goods sold	378,000	138,600	516,600
Gross profit	$162,000	$ 41,400	$203,400
Direct expenses:			
Sales salaries	35,000	14,000	49,000
Advertising	10,500	5,500	16,000
Store supplies used	3,300	700	4,000
Depreciation of equipment	4,200	2,800	7,000
Total direct expenses	$ 53,000	$ 23,000	$ 76,000
Allocated expenses:			
Rent expense	29,520	6,480	36,000
Utilities expense	4,100	900	5,000
Share of office department expenses	39,000	14,000	53,000
Total allocated expenses	$ 72,620	$ 21,380	$ 94,000
Total expenses	$125,620	$ 44,380	$170,000
Net income (loss)	$ 36,380	$ (2,980)	$ 33,400

Crane plans to open a third department in January 2001 that will sell compact discs. Management predicts the new department will generate $250,000 in sales with a 35% gross profit margin, and that it will require the following direct expenses: sales salaries, $18,000; advertising, $10,000; store supplies, $1,500; and equipment depreciation, $1,000. The company currently rents space in a building. It will be possible to fit the new department into the current space by taking some square footage from the other two departments. When the new compact disc department is opened, it will fill one-fourth of the space presently used by the movie department and one-third of the space used by the video game department. Management does not predict any increase in utilities costs, which are allocated to the departments in proportion to occupied space (or rent expense). The company allocates office department expenses to the selling departments in proportion to their sales. It expects the compact disc department to increase total office department expenses by $8,000. Because the compact disc department will bring new customers into the store, management expects sales in both the movie and video game departments to increase by 10%. Those departments' gross profit percents are not expected to change. Also, no changes are expected in their direct expenses, except for store supplies used, which will increase in proportion to sales.

Required

Prepare departmental income statements that show the company's predicted results of operations for calendar year 2001 with the three operating (selling) departments. (Round percents to the nearest one-tenth and dollar amounts to the nearest whole dollar.)

22 CHAPTER

Problem 22-4A
Responsibility accounting performance reports
C4, P4

Margaret Penny, the manager of AMP Co.'s Chicago plant, is responsible for all costs of the plant's operations other than her own salary. The plant has two operating departments and one service department. The refrigerator and dishwasher operating departments manufacture different products and have their own managers. The office department provides services equally to the two operating departments. Penny also manages the office department. A monthly budget is prepared for each operating department and the office department. The responsibility accounting system must assemble information to present budgeted and actual costs in performance reports for each of the operating department managers and the plant manager. Each performance report includes only those costs that a particular manager can control. The operating department managers control the costs of raw materials, wages, supplies used, and equipment depreciation. The plant manager is responsible for the department managers' salaries, utilities, building rent, office salaries other than her own, other office costs, plus all the costs controlled by the two operating department managers. The April departmental budgets and cost accumulations for the two operating departments are:

	Budget			Actual		
	Refrigerators	Dishwashers	Combined	Refrigerators	Dishwashers	Combined
Raw materials	$400,000	$200,000	$ 600,000	$375,000	$200,000	$ 575,000
Wages	172,000	80,000	252,000	174,700	76,800	251,500
Dept. mgr. salary	55,000	49,000	104,000	55,000	46,500	101,500
Supplies used	15,000	9,000	24,000	14,000	10,000	24,000
Equipment depr.	53,000	37,000	90,000	53,000	37,000	90,000
Utilities	30,000	18,000	48,000	34,500	20,700	55,200
Building rent	63,000	17,000	80,000	61,000	15,000	76,000
Office dept. costs	70,500	70,500	141,000	75,000	75,000	150,000
Total	$858,500	$480,500	$1,339,000	$842,200	$481,000	$1,323,200

The office department budget and its actual costs for April are shown below:

	Budget	Actual
Plant manager salary	$ 80,000	$ 85,000
Other office salaries	40,000	35,200
Other office costs	21,000	29,800
Total	$141,000	$150,000

Required

Preparation Component

Prepare responsibility accounting performance reports that list costs controlled by the following:

1. Manager of refrigerator department.

2. Manager of dishwasher department.

3. Manager of Chicago plant.

In each report, include the budgeted and actual costs for the month and show the amount by which each actual cost is over or under the budgeted amount.

Check Figure
3. Chicago plant controllable costs, $20,800 under budget

Analysis Component

4. Did the plant manager or the operating department managers better manage costs? Explain.

Problem 22-5A
Allocating joint costs
C5

22 CHAPTER

Kathy and Ken Vine own and operate a tomato grove. After preparing the income statement below, Kathy feels they should have offered the No. 3 tomatoes to the public for free and saved themselves money and efforts.

KATHY AND KEN VINE
Income Statement
For Year Ended December 31, 2000

	No. 1	No. 2	No. 3	Combined
Sales (by grade):				
No. 1: 400,000 lbs. @ $1.50	$600,000			
No. 2: 300,000 lbs. @ $1.00		$300,000		
No. 3: 100,000 lbs. @ $0.30			$ 30,000	
Total sales				$930,000
Costs:				
Land preparation, seeding, and cultivating @ $0.5/lb . . .	200,000	150,000	50,000	400,000
Harvesting, sorting, and grading @ $0.02/lb	8,000	6,000	2,000	16,000
Delivery costs @ $0.01/lb.	4,000	3,000	1,000	8,000
Total costs	$212,000	$159,000	$ 53,000	$424,000
Net income (loss)	$388,000	$141,000	$(23,000)	$506,000

In preparing this statement, Kathy and Ken allocated joint costs among the grades on a physical basis as an equal amount per pound. Records on delivery costs show that $7,000 of the $8,000 relates to the cost of crating the No. 1 and No. 2 tomatoes and hauling them to the buyer. The remaining $1,000 of delivery costs is the cost of crating the No. 3 tomatoes and hauling them to the cannery where they are stewed and canned.

Required

Preparation Component

1. Prepare allocation schedules showing how costs would be allocated on a sales value basis to the three grades of tomatoes. Separate delivery costs into the amounts directly identifiable to each grade. Then allocate any shared delivery costs on the basis of the relative sales value of each grade. (Round percents to the nearest one-tenth and dollar amounts to the nearest whole dollar.)
2. Using your answers to part 1, prepare an income statement using the joint costs allocated on a sales value basis.

Analysis Component

3. Do you think delivery costs fit the definition of a joint cost? Explain.

Problem 23-1A
Scatter diagram and estimating cost behavior

P1

23 CHAPTER

Inland Co.'s monthly sales and costs data for its operating activities of the past year are shown to the side. The management of the company wants to use these data to predict future fixed and variable costs.

Period	Sales	Total Costs
1	$390	$194
2	250	174
3	210	146
4	310	178
5	190	162
6	430	220
7	290	186
8	370	210
9	270	170
10	170	130
11	350	190
12	230	158

Required

1. Prepare a scatter diagram with sales volume (in $) plotted on the horizontal axis and total costs plotted on the vertical axis.
2. Estimate the line of cost behavior by a visual inspection and draw it on the scatter diagram. (Assume a linear relation, which means that you should draw a straight cost line on the graph.)
3. Use the estimated line of cost behavior and the assumption that the future will be like the past to predict an amount of monthly fixed costs for Inland. Also, predict future variable costs per sales dollar.
4. Use the estimated line of cost behavior to predict future total costs when the sales volume is *(a)* $150 and *(b)* $250.

23 CHAPTER

Problem 23-2A
CVP analysis and chart
P2, P3

Washington Co. manufactures and markets a number of products. Management is considering the future of one product, electronic keyboards, which has not been as profitable as planned. Because this product is manufactured and marketed independently from the other products, its total costs can be precisely measured. Next year's plans call for a selling price of $225 per unit. The fixed costs for the year are expected to be $30,000, up to the maximum capacity of 700 units. Forecasted variable costs are $150 per unit.

Required

1. Predict the break-even point for keyboards in terms of *(a)* sales units and *(b)* sales dollars.
2. Prepare a CVP chart for keyboards. Use 700 keyboards as the maximum number of sales units on the graph and $180,000 as the maximum number of dollars.
3. Prepare an income statement showing sales, variable costs, and fixed costs for keyboards at the break-even point.

Problem 23-3A
Targeting and forecasting income
C3

Capital Co. sold 50,000 units of its only product and incurred a $200,000 loss (ignoring taxes) for the year as shown below:

CAPITAL COMPANY Income Statement For Year Ended December 31, 2000	
Sales	$ 800,000
Variable costs	900,000
Contribution margin	$(100,000)
Fixed costs	100,000
Net loss	$(200,000)

During a planning session for year 2001's activities, the production manager points out that variable costs can be reduced 72.22% by installing a machine that automates several operations. To obtain these savings, the company must increase its annual fixed costs by $200,000. The maximum capacity of the system would be 80,000 units per year.

Required

1. Compute break-even point in dollars sales for year 2000.
2. Compute break-even point in dollar sales for year 2001 assuming the machine is installed. (Round the change in variable costs to a whole number.)
3. Prepare a forecasted income statement for 2001 that shows the expected results with the machine installed. Assume there will be no change in the selling price and no change in the number of units sold. The income tax rate is 40%.
4. Compute the sales level required to earn $300,000 of after-tax income in 2001 with the machine installed and with no change in the selling price.
5. Prepare a forecasted income statement that shows the results at the sales level computed in part (4).

Check Figure
Required sales, 72,728 units

Problem 23-4A
Break-even analysis and different cost structures
C3

Model Co. produces and sells two products, BB and TT. These products are manufactured in separate factories and marketed through different channels. They do not have any shared costs. This year, Model Co. sold 120,000 units of each product. The following income statements describe the financial results:

	Product BB	Product TT
Sales	$3,000,000	$3,000,000
Variable costs	1,800,000	600,000
Contribution margin	$1,200,000	$2,400,000
Fixed costs	600,000	1,800,000
Income before taxes	$ 600,000	$ 600,000
Income taxes (35% rate)	210,000	210,000
Net income	$ 390,000	$ 390,000

Required

Preparation Component

1. Compute the break-even point in dollars for each product.
2. Assume the company expects sales of each product to decline to 104,000 units next year, even though the price will remain unchanged. Prepare a forecasted income statement that shows the expected net income from the two products (assume a 35% tax rate). Follow the format of the preceding statement.
3. Assume the company expects sales of each product to increase to 190,000 units next year, even though the price will remain unchanged. Prepare a forecasted income statement that shows the expected net income from the two products (assume a 35% tax rate). Follow the format of the preceding statement.

Analysis Component

4. If sales greatly increase, which of these products would experience the greater increase in profit? Explain.
5. Describe some factors that might have created the different cost structures for these two products.

Problem 23-5A
Analyzing price and volume changes on profits
C3

This year White Company earned a disappointing 4.2% after-tax return on sales from marketing 100,000 units of its only product, watch bands. The company buys watch bands in bulk and repackages them for resale at the price of $25 per unit. White incurred these costs this year:

Cost of bulk product of 100,000 packages	$1,000,000
Variable packaging materials and costs	100,000
Fixed costs	1,250,000
Income tax rate	30%

The marketing manager claims that next year's results will be the same as this year's unless some changes are made. The manager predicts the company can increase the number of units sold by 80% if it reduces the selling price by 20% and upgrades the packaging. This change would increase variable packaging costs by 25%. Increased sales would allow the company to take advantage of a 20% quantity purchase discount on the cost of the bulk product price. Neither the packaging nor the volume change would affect fixed costs, which provide an annual capacity of 200,000 units.

Required

1. Compute the break-even point in dollars for selling watch bands under the *(a)* existing business strategy and *(b)* new strategy that alters both selling price and variable costs.
2. Prepare side-by-side forecasted income statements showing the expected results of *(a)* continuing the existing strategy and *(b)* changing to the new strategy. The statements should report sales, variable costs (separately for product and packaging), fixed costs, income before taxes, income taxes, and net income. Determine whether the after-tax return on sales will be changed by the new strategy.

Check Figure Net income under new strategy, $479,500

Problem 23-6A
Break-even analysis with composite units
P4, C3

Unity Co. manufactures and sells three products: Product 1, Product 2, and Product 3. Their selling prices are: Product 1, $40 per unit; Product 2, $30 per unit; and Product 3, $14 per unit. The variable costs of manufacturing and selling these products are: Product 1, $30 per unit; Product 2, $20 per unit; and Product 3, $8 per unit. Their sales mix is reflected in a ratio of 6:3:5. Annual fixed costs shared by all three products are $200,000. One item of raw materials is used in manufacturing Products 1 and 2. The company has developed a new material that is of equal quality and less costly. The new material would reduce variable costs per unit as follows: Product 1 by $10; and Product 2 by $5. But the new material requires new equipment, which will increase annual fixed costs by $50,000.

Required

1. If the company continues to use the old material, determine the company's break-even point in both sales dollars and sales units of each individual product.
2. If the company uses the new material, determine the company's new break-even point in both sales dollars and sales units of each individual product.

Check Figure New plan break-even, 1,282 composite units

Analysis Component

3. What insight does this analysis offer management in long-term planning?

24 CHAPTER

Problem 24-1A
Preparing production and materials purchases budgets
C3, P3

Osborne Company produces baseball bats. Each bat requires four pounds of aluminum alloy. The company's management predicts there will be 10,000 bats and 28,000 pounds of aluminum alloy on hand on March 31 of the current year, and that 100,000 bats will be sold during this year's second quarter. Management wants to end the second quarter with 3,000 finished bats and 2,000 pounds of aluminum alloy in inventory. Aluminum alloy can be purchased for $3 per pound.

Required

1. Prepare the second-quarter production budget for bats.
2. Prepare the second-quarter aluminum alloy purchases budget (include the dollar cost of purchases).

Problem 24-2A
Preparing and analyzing merchandise purchases budgets
C3, P1

FMR Corporation retails three products that it buys ready for sale. The company's June 30 inventories are: Product X, 40,000 units; Product Y, 90,000 units; and Product Z, 250,000 units. Management feels that excessive inventories have accumulated for all three products. As a result, a new policy dictates that ending inventory in any month should equal 10% of the expected unit sales for the following month. Expected sales in units for July, August, September, and October are:

	Budgeted Sales in Units			
	July	August	September	October
Product X	70,000	90,000	130,000	140,000
Product Y	100,000	90,000	110,000	100,000
Product Z	300,000	260,000	310,000	260,000

Required

Preparation Component

1. Prepare separate purchases budgets (in units) for each of the products for July, August, and September.

Analysis Component

2. The purchases budgets should reflect fewer purchases of all three products in July compared to August and September. What factor caused these fewer purchases to be planned? Suggest business conditions that would cause this factor to both occur and affect FMR as it has.

Problem 24-3A
Preparing and analyzing cash budgets with supporting inventory and purchases schedules
C3, P2

Galaxy Company has a cash balance of $45,000 on March 1. The company's product sells for $20 per unit, and its actual and projected sales are:

	Units	Dollars
January (actual)	18,000	$360,000
February (actual)	27,000	540,000
March (budgeted)	15,000	300,000
April (budgeted)	27,000	540,000
May (budgeted)	33,000	660,000

All of its sales are on credit. Recent experience shows that 40% of its sales are collected in the month of the sale, 30% in the month after the sale, 25% in the second month after the sale, and 5% prove to be uncollectible. The purchase price of the product is $12 per unit. All purchases are payable within 21 days. This means 30% of purchases made in a month are paid in that month and the other 70% are paid in the next month. Galaxy Co.'s management has a policy of maintaining an ending monthly inventory of 30% of the next month's unit sales plus a safety stock of 300 units. The January 31 and February 28 actual inventory levels are consistent with this policy. Selling and administrative expenses for the year are $1,440,000 and are paid evenly throughout the year in cash. The company's minimum cash balance for the end of a month is $45,000. This minimum is maintained, if necessary, by borrowing cash from the bank. If the balance goes over $45,000, the company repays as much of the loan as it can without going below the minimum. This type of loan carries an annual 12% interest rate. At February 28, the balance of the loan is $12,000.

Required

Preparation Component

1. Prepare a schedule that shows cash to be collected in March and April from customers.

2. Prepare a schedule showing budgeted ending inventories (units) for January, February, March, and April.

3. Prepare a schedule showing the purchases budgets for the product for February, March, and April. Present calculations in terms of units and then show the dollar amount of purchases for each month.

4. Prepare a schedule showing the cash to be paid in March and April for product purchases.

5. Prepare monthly cash budgets for March and April, including any loan activity and interest expense. Compute the loan balance at the end of each month.

Analysis Component

6. Refer to your answer for part (5). Galaxy's cash budget indicates the company will need to borrow nearly $12,000 in March, but that it will be able to repay that new loan plus a prior loan of $12,000 in April. Suggest some reasons why knowing this information in February would be helpful to Galaxy's management.

Problem 24-4A
Preparing cash budgets for three periods
C3, P2

During the last week of March, the owner of Buy-Right Stereo approaches the bank for a $125,000 loan to be made on April 1 and repaid on June 30 with annual interest of 8% plus bank charges, or a total of $3,375. The owner plans to increase the store's inventory by $100,000 in April and needs the loan to pay for merchandise acquired in May and June. The bank's loan officer needs more information about Buy-Right Stereo's ability to repay the loan and asks the owner to forecast the store's June 30 cash position. On April 1, Buy-Right Stereo is expected to have a $12,000 cash balance, $135,000 of accounts receivable, and $90,000 of accounts payable. Its budgeted sales, purchases, and cash disbursements for the next three months are:

	April	May	June
Sales	$350,000	$500,000	$550,000
Merchandise purchases	250,000	200,000	190,000
Payroll	22,500	30,000	37,500
Rent	12,000	12,000	12,000
Other cash expenses	9,000	13,500	16,500
Repayment of bank loan			125,000
Interest on the loan plus bank charges			3,375

The budgeted April purchases include the inventory increase. All sales are on account. The company's past experience shows that 10% of its sales are collected in the month of the sale, 60% in the month following the sale, 25% in the second month, 3% in the third, and the remainder is uncollectible. Applying these percents to the April 1 accounts receivable balance, for example, shows that $81,000 of the $135,000 will be collected in April, $33,750 in May, and $4,050 in June. All merchandise is purchased on credit. Eighty percent of the balance is paid in the month following a purchase and the remaining 20% is paid in the second month. For example, of the $90,000 of accounts payable at the end of March, $72,000 will be paid in April and $18,000 in May.

Required

Prepare cash budgets for April, May, and June for Buy-Right Stereo. Show supplemental schedules as needed.

24 CHAPTER

Problem 24-5A
Preparing and analyzing budgeted income statements
C3, P2

Spencer Co. buys one kind of computer graphics chip at $20 and sells it at $50 per chip. The company's sales staff receives a 10% commission on each sale. Its June income statement is shown below:

SPENCER COMPANY Income Statement For Month Ended June 30, 2000	
Sales	$1,000,000
Cost of goods sold	400,000
Gross profit	$ 600,000
Expenses:	
Sales commissions (10%)	$ 100,000
Advertising	100,000
Store rent	10,000
Administrative salaries	20,000
Depreciation	12,000
Other	24,000
Total expenses	$ 266,000
Net income	$ 334,000

The company's management believes that the June results will be repeated in July, August, and September without any changes in strategy. Management also believes that unit sales will increase at a rate of 10% each month during the next quarter (including June) if the item's selling price is reduced to $45 per unit and if advertising expenses are increased by 20% and remain at that level for all three months. Whatever changes are made, the purchase price will remain at $20 per chip, the sales staff would continue to earn a 10% commission, and the remaining expenses would stay the same.

Required

Preparation Component

1. Using a three-column format (one column for each month), prepare budgeted income statements for July, August, and September that show the expected results of implementing the proposed changes.

Analysis Component

2. Use the budgeted income statements to recommend whether management should implement the plan.

Problem 24-6A
Preparing a complete master budget
C2, C3, P1, P2

The management of Chain Corp. prepared the following budgeted balance sheet for December 31, 2000:

CHAIN CORPORATION Budgeted Balance Sheet As of December 31, 2000		
Assets		
Cash		$ 160,000
Accounts receivable		400,000
Inventory		180,000
Total current assets		$ 740,000
Equipment	$1,200,000	
Accumulated depreciation	120,000	1,080,000
Total assets		$1,820,000
Liabilities and Equity		
Accounts payable	$ 300,000	
Loan from bank	20,000	
Taxes payable (due 3/15/2001)	200,000	
Total liabilities		$ 520,000
Common stock	1,500,000	
Retained earnings (deficit)	(200,000)	
Total stockholders' equity		1,300,000
Total liabilities and equity		$1,820,000

For preparing a master budget for January, February, and March of 2001, management gathers the following information:

a. Chain Corporation's single product is purchased for $10 per unit and resold for $24 per unit. The expected inventory level on December 31, 2000 (18,000 units) is greater than management's desired level for year 2001 of 40% of the next month's expected sales (in units). Budgeted sales are: January, 30,000 units; February, 24,000 units; March, 40,000 units; and April, 50,000 units.

b. Cash sales are 40% of total sales and credit sales are 60% of total sales. Of the credit sales, 70% are collected in the first month after the sale and 30% in the second month after the sale. For example, 70 percent of the December 31, 2000, balance of accounts receivable will be collected in January and 30% will be collected in February.

c. Merchandise purchases are paid for as follows: 80% in the month after purchase, and 20% in the second month after purchase. For example, 80 percent of the Accounts Payable balance on December 31, 2000, will be paid in January, and 20% will be paid in February.

d. Sales commissions of 10% of sales are paid each month. Additional sales salaries are $288,000 per year.

e. General and administrative salaries are $336,000 per year. Repairs expense equals $6,000 per month and is paid in cash.

f. Equipment reported in the December 31, 2000, balance sheet is purchased in January 2000. It is being depreciated over 10 years under the straight-line method with no salvage value. The following new purchases of equipment are planned in the coming quarter: January, $240,000; February, $120,000; and March, $96,000. This equipment will be depreciated using the straight-line method over 10 years with no salvage value. A full month's depreciation is taken for the month in which equipment is purchased.

g. The company plans to acquire land at the end of March at a cost of $232,000. The purchase price will be paid with cash on the last day of the month.

h. Chain Corporation has a working arrangement with the bank to obtain additional loans as needed. The interest rate is 12% per year, and the interest is paid at the end of each month based on the beginning balance. Partial or full payments on these loans can be made on the last day of the month. Chain Corporation has agreed to maintain a minimum ending cash balance of $160,000 in every month.

i. The income tax rate for the company is 30%. Income taxes on the first quarter's income will not be paid until April 15.

Required

Prepare a master budget for the first quarter of 2001, including the following component budgets (show supplemental schedules as needed, and round amounts to the nearest dollar):

1. Monthly sales budgets (showing both budgeted unit sales and dollar sales).
2. Monthly merchandise purchases budgets.
3. Monthly selling expense budgets.
4. Monthly general and administrative expense budgets.
5. Monthly capital expenditures budgets.
6. Monthly cash budgets.
7. Budgeted income statement for the first quarter.
8. Budgeted balance sheet as of March 31, 2001.

Problem 25-1A
Preparing and analyzing a flexible budget
P1, A1

Ranch Company's master budget for 1999 included the following fixed budget performance report. It is based on expected production and sales volume of 10,000 units.

25 CHAPTER

RANCH COMPANY Fixed Budget Performance Report For Year Ended December 31, 1999		
Sales		$250,000
Cost of goods sold:		
Direct materials	$100,000	
Direct labor	20,000	
Patent royalties paid (based on units)	3,000	
Depreciation of machinery (annual)	11,920	
Utilities (variable cost is 80%)	8,000	
Supervisory salaries	6,000	(148,920)
Gross profit		$101,080
Selling expenses:		
Commissions	$ 9,000	
Shipping	30,000	
Sales salary (fixed annual amount)	18,000	(57,000)
General and administrative expenses:		
Property taxes	$ 4,000	
Salaries	9,360	
Rent expense	10,000	(23,360)
Income from operations		$ 20,720

Required

1. Classify all items in the fixed budget as either variable or fixed. Also, determine their amounts per unit or their amounts for the year, as appropriate.
2. Prepare flexible budgets (see Exhibit 25.3) for the company at sales and production volumes of 8,000 and 12,000 units.
3. The company's business conditions are improving, and one possible effect could be a sales volume of approximately 14,400 units. The president of the company is confident that this volume is within the relevant range of existing capacity. How much would operating income increase over the 1999 budgeted amount if this level is reached without increasing capacity?
4. There is a remote possibility of an unfavorable change, in which case production and sales volume for 1999 could fall to 5,000 units. How much income (or loss) from operations would occur if sales volume falls to this level?

Problem 25-2A
Preparing and analyzing a flexible budget performance report
P1, A2

Refer to information in Problem 25-1A. Ranch Company's actual income statement for 1999 follows:

RANCH COMPANY Statement of Income from Operations For Year Ended December 31, 1999		
Sales (12,000 units)		$288,000
Cost of goods sold:		
Direct materials	$95,000	
Direct labor	16,000	
Patent royalties paid (based on units)	3,300	
Depreciation of machinery (annual)	11,920	
Utilities (variable cost is $7,160)	8,520	
Supervisory salaries	6,720	(141,460)
Gross profit		146,540
Selling expenses:		
Commissions	$10,800	
Shipping	37,200	
Sales salary (annual)	19,200	(67,200)
General and administrative expenses:		
Property taxes	$ 4,200	
Salaries	9,360	
Rent expense	10,000	(23,560)
Income from operations		$ 55,780

Required

Preparation Component

1. Prepare a flexible budget performance report for 1999.

Analysis Component

2. Analyze and interpret both *(a)* the sales variance and *(b)* the direct materials variance.

Problem 25-3A
Computing and reporting materials, labor, and overhead variances
C2, P2, P3

Challenger Company has set the following standard costs per unit for the product it manufactures:

Direct material (40 oz. @ $0.75 per oz.)	$ 30.00
Direct labor (2 hr. @ $20 per hr.)	40.00
Overhead (2 hr. @ $53.50 per hr.)	107.00
Total standard cost	$177.00

The predetermined overhead rate is based on a planned operating volume of 60% of the productive capacity of 3,000 units per month. The following flexible budget information is available:

	Operating Levels		
	50%	60%	70%
Production in units	1,500	1,800	2,100
Standard direct labor hours	3,000	3,600	4,200
Budgeted overhead:			
Variable costs:			
Indirect materials	$ 18,000	$ 21,600	$ 25,200
Indirect labor	10,500	12,600	14,700
Power	7,500	9,000	10,500
Maintenance	4,500	5,400	6,300
Total variable costs	$ 40,500	$ 48,600	$ 56,700
Fixed costs:			
Rent of factory building	$ 48,000	$ 48,000	$ 48,000
Depreciation, Machinery	44,000	44,000	44,000
Taxes and insurance	20,000	20,000	20,000
Supervisory salaries	32,000	32,000	32,000
Total fixed costs	$144,000	$144,000	$144,000
Total overhead costs	$184,500	$192,600	$200,700

During March of this year, the company operated at 70% of capacity and produced 2,100 units. The following actual costs are incurred:

Direct material (88,000 ozs. @ $ 0.70 per oz.)		$ 61,600
Direct labor (4,000 hrs. @ $19.50 per hr.)		78,000
Overhead costs:		
Indirect materials	$23,600	
Indirect labor	14,800	
Power	10,000	
Maintenance	3,200	
Rent of factory building	48,000	
Depreciation, Machinery	44,000	
Taxes and insurance	24,000	
Supervisory salaries	31,600	199,200
Total costs		$338,800

Required

1. Compute the direct materials cost variance, including its price and quantity variances.
2. Compute the direct labor variance, including its rate and efficiency variances.
3. Compute *(a)* the variable overhead spending and efficiency variances, *(b)* the fixed overhead spending and volume variances, and *(c)* the total overhead controllable variance.
4. Prepare a detailed overhead variance report (as in Exhibit 25.19) that shows the variances for individual items of overhead.

Problem 25-4A
Computing materials, labor, and overhead variances
C2, P2, P3

Titletown Company set the following standard unit costs for its single product:

Direct material (5 lbs. @ $10 per lb.)	$ 50.00
Direct labor (3 hrs. @ $15 per hr.)	45.00
Variable factory overhead (3 hrs. @ $5 per hr.)	15.00
Fixed factory overhead (3 hrs. @ $3 per hr.)	9.00
Total standard cost	$119.00

The predetermined overhead rate is based on a planned operating volume of 90% of the productive capacity of 40,000 units per quarter. The following flexible budget information is available:

	Operating Levels		
	80%	90%	100%
Production in units	32,000	36,000	40,000
Standard direct labor hours	96,000	108,000	120,000
Budgeted overhead:			
Fixed factory overhead	$324,000	$324,000	$324,000
Variable factory overhead	480,000	540,000	600,000

During the current quarter, the company operated at 80% of capacity and produced 32,000 units of product; direct labor hours worked were 96,000. Units produced are assigned the following standard costs:

Direct material (160,000 lbs. @ $10 per lb.)	$1,600,000
Direct labor (96,000 hrs. @ $15 per hr.)	1,440,000
Factory overhead (96,000 hrs. @ $8.00 per hr.)	768,000
Total standard cost	$3,808,000

Actual costs incurred during the current quarter are:

Direct material (155,000 lbs. @ $10.20)	$1,581,000
Direct labor (100,000 hrs. @ $14)	1,400,000
Fixed factory overhead costs	370,000
Variable factory overhead costs	480,000
Total actual costs	$3,831,000

Required

1. Compute the direct materials cost variance, including its price and quantity variances.
2. Compute the direct labor variance, including its rate and efficiency variances.
3. Compute *(a)* the variable overhead spending and efficiency variances, *(b)* the fixed overhead spending and volume variances, and *(c)* the total overhead controllable variance.

Problem 25-5A
Preparing a flexible budget, computing variances, and preparing an overhead report
P1, P2, P3, C2

Tropical Company has set the following standard costs for one unit of its product:

Direct material (48 kgs. @ $4 per kg.)	$192.00
Direct labor (12 hrs. @ $9 per hr.)	108.00
Overhead (12 hrs. @ $4.50 per hr.)	54.00
Total standard cost	$354.00

The predetermined overhead rate ($4.50 per direct labor hour) is based on an expected volume of 50% of the factory's capacity of 10,000 units per month. Following are the company's budgeted overhead costs per month at the 50% level:

Overhead Budget (50% capacity)		
Variable costs:		
Indirect materials	$40,000	
Indirect labor	80,000	
Power	20,000	
Repairs and maintenance	30,000	
Total variable costs		$170,000
Fixed costs:		
Depreciation, Building	$20,000	
Depreciation, Machinery	30,000	
Taxes and insurance	10,000	
Supervision	40,000	
Total fixed costs		100,000
Total overhead costs		$270,000

The company incurred the following actual costs when it operated at 40% of capacity in December:

Direct material (196,000 kgs. @ $4.00)		$ 784,000
Direct labor (46,000 hrs. @ $9.15)		420,900
Overhead costs:		
Indirect materials	$30,000	
Indirect labor	66,000	
Power	15,600	
Repairs and maintenance	21,000	
Depreciation, Building	20,000	
Depreciation, Machinery	30,000	
Taxes and insurance	9,600	
Supervision	39,600	231,800
Total costs		$1,436,700

Required

1. Classify all items in the overhead budget as either variable or fixed. Also, determine their amounts per unit or their amounts for the month, as appropriate.
2. Prepare flexible overhead budgets (as in Exhibit 25.12) for December showing the amounts of each variable and fixed cost at the 40%, 50%, and 60% capacity levels.
3. Compute the direct materials cost variance, including its price and quantity variances.
4. Compute the direct labor cost variance, including its rate and efficiency variances.

25 CHAPTER

5. Compute *(a)* the variable overhead spending and efficiency variances, *(b)* the fixed overhead spending and volume variances, and *(c)* the total overhead controllable variance.
6. Prepare a detailed overhead variance report (as in Exhibit 25.19) that shows the variances for individual items of overhead.

Problem 25-6A
Recording and analyzing materials, labor, and overhead variances
C3, P4

Kraft Company's standard cost accounting system recorded the following information from its operations for June:

Standard direct material cost	$220,500
Direct material quantity variance (favorable)	20,250
Direct material price variance (favorable)	14,500
Actual direct labor cost	335,000
Direct labor efficiency variance (favorable)	26,700
Direct labor rate variance (unfavorable)	3,500
Actual overhead cost	359,000
Volume variance (unfavorable)	1,650
Controllable variance (unfavorable)	32,500

Required

Preparation Component

1. Prepare journal entries dated June 30 to record the company's costs and variances for the month.

Analysis Component

2. Identify areas that would attract the attention of a manager who uses management by exception. Describe what action the manager should take.

26 CHAPTER

Problem 26-1A
Computing payback period, accounting rate of return, and net present value
P1, P2, P3

Continental Company is planning to add a new product to its line. To manufacture this product, the company needs to buy a new machine at a cost of $100,000. This asset is expected to have a five-year life and a $25,000 salvage value. All sales are for cash and all costs are out-of-pocket, except for depreciation on the new machine. Additional information includes the following:

Expected annual sales of new product	$350,000
Expected costs:	
Direct materials	150,000
Direct labor	50,000
Overhead excluding straight-line depreciation on new machine	100,000
Selling and administrative expenses	23,000
Income taxes	20%

Required

1. Compute straight-line depreciation for each year of this asset's life.
2. Determine expected net income and net cash flow for each year of this asset's life.
3. Compute payback period for this asset, assuming that cash flows occur evenly throughout each year.
4. Compute accounting rate of return for this asset, assuming income is earned evenly throughout each year.
5. Compute net present value for this asset using a discount rate of 12% and assuming cash flows occur at the end of each year. (Hint: Salvage value is a cash inflow at the end of the asset's life.)

Problem 26-2A
Analyzing and computing payback period, accounting rate of return, and net present value
P1, P2, P3

Green Company has an opportunity to invest in one of two projects. Project A requires an investment of $480,000 for new machinery having a three-year life and no salvage value. Project B also requires an investment of $480,000 for new machinery having a four-year life and no salvage value. The two projects yield the following predicted annual results:

	Project A	Project B
Sales	$750,000	$800,000
Expenses:		
Direct materials	$125,000	$250,000
Direct labor	130,000	80,000
Overhead including depreciation	330,000	276,000
Selling and administrative expenses	120,000	120,000
Total expenses	$705,000	$726,000
Pretax income	$ 45,000	$ 74,000
Income taxes (30%)	13,500	22,200
Net income	$ 31,500	$ 51,800

The company uses straight-line depreciation. Assume that cash flows occur evenly throughout each year. For part 4 only, assume cash flows occur at the end of each year.

Required

Preparation Component

1. Compute the annual expected net cash flows for each project.
2. Determine the payback period for each project.
3. Compute the accounting rate of return for each project.
4. Determine the net present value for each project, using 10% as the discount rate.

Analysis Component

5. Identify the project you would recommend to management and explain your choice.

Problem 26-3A
Computing cash flows and net present values with alternative depreciation methods
P3

Grill Corporation is considering a new project that would require a $25,000 investment in an asset having no salvage value. The project would produce $15,000 of pretax income before depreciation at the end of each year for six years. The company's income tax rate is 30%. In compiling its tax return and computing its income tax payments, the company can choose between these two alternative depreciation schedules:

	Straight-Line Depreciation	MACRS Depreciation*
Year 1	$ 2,500	$ 5,000
Year 2	5,000	8,000
Year 3	5,000	4,800
Year 4	5,000	2,880
Year 5	5,000	2,880
Year 6	2,500	1,440
Total	$25,000	$25,000

* The modified accelerated cost recovery system (MACRS) for depreciation is discussed in Chapter 11.

Required

Preparation Component

1. Produce a five-column table that reports amounts for each of the following items for each of the six years: *(a)* income before depreciation, *(b)* straight-line depreciation expense, *(c)* taxable income, *(d)* income taxes, and *(e)* net cash flow. Net cash flow equals the amount of income before depreciation minus the income taxes.

26 CHAPTER

2. Produce a five-column table that reports amounts for each of the following items for each of the six years: *(a)* income before depreciation, *(b)* MACRS depreciation expense, *(c)* taxable income, *(d)* income taxes, and *(e)* net cash flow. Net cash flow equals the amount of income before depreciation minus the income taxes.
3. Compute the net present value of the investment if straight-line depreciation is used. Use 15% as the discount rate.
4. Compute the net present value of the investment if MACRS depreciation is used. Use 15% as the discount rate.

Analysis Component

5. Explain why the MACRS depreciation method increases the net present value of this project.

Problem 26-4A
Analyzing income effects of additional business
C3, A1

Wire Company manufactures bottled water that it sells to wholesalers in the local area at $1 per bottle. The company manufactures and sells approximately 200,000 bottles each month. Monthly costs for the production and sale of this quantity are:

Direct materials	$ 30,000
Direct labor	12,000
Overhead	50,000
Selling expenses	7,500
Administrative expenses	31,500
Total costs and expenses	$131,000

A new out-of-state distributor has offered to buy 20,000 bottles next month for $.80 each. These bottles would be marketed in other states and would not affect Wire's sales through its normal channels. A study of the costs of this new business reveals the following:

- Direct material costs are 100% variable.
- Per unit direct labor costs for the additional units would be 100% greater than normal because their production would require special double overtime pay to meet the distributor's deadline.
- Eighty percent of the normal annual overhead costs are fixed at any production level from 120,000 to 300,000 units. The remaining 20% of the annual overhead cost is variable with volume.
- There will be no additional selling costs if the new business is accepted.
- Accepting the new business would increase administrative expenses by a fixed amount of $750.

Required

Prepare a three-column comparative income statement that shows:

1. Monthly operating income without the special order (column 1).
2. Monthly operating income that would be received from the new business (column 2).
3. Combined monthly operating income from the usual business and the new business (column 3).

Problem 26-5A
Analyzing sales mix strategies
C3, A1

Branck Company is capable of producing two products, Product 22 and Product 47, with the same machine in its factory. The following per unit facts are known:

	Product 22	Product 47
Selling price	$175	$200
Variable costs	100	150
Contribution margin	$ 75	$ 50
Machine-hours to produce 1 unit	0.8	0.5
Maximum unit sales per month	525	450

The company presently operates the machine for a single eight-hour shift for 23 working days each month. Management is thinking about operating the machine for two shifts, which will increase the machine's availability by another eight hours per day for 23 days per month. This change would require additional fixed costs of $5,000 per month.

Required

1. Determine the contribution margin per machine hour that each product generates.
2. How many units of Product 22 and Product 47 should the company produce if it continues to operate with only one shift? How much total contribution margin is produced each month with this mix?
3. If the company adds another shift, how many units of Product 22 and Product 47 should the company produce? How much total contribution margin would be produced each month with this mix? Should the company add the new shift?
4. Suppose the company determines it can increase the maximum sales of Product 47 to 500 units per month by spending $500 per month in marketing efforts. Should the company pursue this strategy along with the double shift?

Problem 26-6A
Analyzing elimination of a department
C3, A1

The management of TeeTime Company is trying to decide whether to eliminate Department Z, which has produced low profits or losses for several years. The company's year 2000 departmental income statement shows the following:

THE TEETIME COMPANY
Departmental Income Statement
For Year Ended December 31, 2000

	Dept. A	Dept. Z	Combined
Sales	$700,000	$175,000	$875,000
Cost of goods sold	461,300	125,100	586,400
Gross profit	$238,700	$ 49,900	$288,600
Operating expenses:			
Direct expenses:			
Advertising	$ 27,000	$ 3,000	$ 30,000
Store supplies used	5,600	1,400	7,000
Depreciation of store equipment	14,000	7,000	21,000
Total direct expenses	$ 46,600	$ 11,400	$ 58,000
Allocated expenses:			
Sales salaries	$ 70,200	$ 23,400	$ 93,600
Rent expense	22,080	5,520	27,600
Bad debts expense	21,000	4,000	25,000
Office salary	20,800	5,200	26,000
Insurance expense	4,200	1,400	5,600
Miscellaneous office expenses	1,700	2,500	4,200
Total allocated expenses	$139,980	$ 42,020	$182,000
Total expenses	$186,580	$ 53,420	$240,000
Net income (loss)	$ 52,120	$ (3,520)	$ 48,600

In analyzing whether to eliminate Department Z, management considers the following items:

a. The company has one office worker who earns $500 per week or $26,000 per year and four salesclerks who each earn $450 per week or $23,400 per year.
b. The full salaries of three salesclerks are charged to Department A. The full salary of one salesclerk is charged to Department Z.
c. The sales salaries and the office salary currently assigned to Department Z are avoidable if the department were to be eliminated. However, management prefers another plan. Two salesclerks have indicated that they will be quitting soon. Management thinks that their work can be done by the two remaining clerks if

the one office worker works in sales half time. The office worker's schedule will allow this shift of duties if Department Z is eliminated. If this change is implemented, half the office worker's salary would be reported as sales salaries and half would be reported as office salary.

d. The store building is rented under a long-term lease that cannot be changed. Therefore, the space presently occupied by Department Z will have to be used by the current Department A. The equipment used by Department Z will be used by the current Department A.

e. Closing Department Z will eliminate its expenses for advertising, bad debts, and store supplies. It will also eliminate 65% of the insurance expense allocated to the department for coverage on its merchandise inventory. In addition, 30% of the miscellaneous office expenses presently allocated to Department Z will be eliminated.

Required

Preparation Component

1. Prepare a three-column schedule that lists *(a)* the company's total expenses (including cost of goods sold), *(b)* the expenses that would be eliminated by closing Dept. Z, and *(c)* the expenses that will continue.

2. Prepare a forecasted income statement for the company reflecting the elimination of Dept. Z under the assumption that sales and the gross profit will not be affected. The statement should reflect the reassignment of the office worker to one-half time as a salesclerk.

Analysis Component

3. Prepare a reconciliation of the company's combined net income with the forecasted net income assuming Department Z is eliminated. Analyze the reconciliation and explain why you think the department should or should not be eliminated.

Credits

Page 3 © Mira
Page 5 © Ralph Mercer: Tony Stone Images
Page 10 Courtesy of America Online, Inc.
Page 15 Courtesy of Nike
Page 18 Courtesy of Converse, Inc.
Page 25 © Nicholas Communications, Inc.
Page 37 © Rob Lewine: The Stock Market
Page 37 © Harold Pfeiffer: Tony Stone Images
Page 39 Courtesy of McDonald's Corporation
Page 48 © Bill Bachmann: PhotoEdit
Page 53 © Kathleen Campbell: Tony Stone Images
Page 54 © GM Media Archives
Page 59 Courtesy of Delta Airlines
Page 61 © David Madison: Tony Stone Images
Page 81 © David Young-Wolff: PhotoEdit
Page 85 Courtesy of ShowBiz Pizza
Page 86 Courtesy of Reader's Digest Association
Page 87 © Ralf Schultheiss: Tony Stone Images
Page 88 Courtesy of Boston Celtics
Page 102 © Tony Stone Images
Page 107 Courtesy of Nike
Page 108 Courtesy of Converse, Inc.
Page 129 © PhotoDisc
Page 131 © Nicholas Communications, Inc.
Page 131 © Nicholas Communications, Inc.
Page 133 © Photofest
Page 139 © Nicholas Communications, Inc.
Page 148 Courtesy of Sun Microsystems
Page 175 © Terry Vine: Tony Stone Images
Page 181 Courtesy of Hershey Foods Corporation
Page 192 © Phill Matt
Page 194 © Ron Chapple: FPG International
Page 195 © Oliver Tennent: Tony Stone Images
Page 221 © PhotoDisc
Page 221 © StockFood America/Wondrasch
Page 222 © Nicholas Communications, Inc.
Page 224 Courtesy of Dayton-Hudson
Page 231 Courtesy of WMS Industries
Page 235 © James Mejuto
Page 246 Courtesy of J.C. Penney
Page 275 © 97 and Mouse Shutter: The Stock Market
Page 282 © Major League Baseball Photos
Page 282 Courtesy of Motorola
Page 284 © Nicholas Communications, Inc.
Page 286 © Michael Newman: PhotoEdit
Page 289 Courtesy of Best Buy
Page 295 Courtesy of Toys "R" Us
Page 312 © Dwight Cendrowski
Page 320 Courtesy of Grand Ol' Opry/Donnie Beauchamp
Page 321 Courtesy of Microsoft
Page 324 Courtesy of Nike
Page 335 © Michael Rosenfeld: Tony Stone Images
Page 337 Courtesy of Federal Express
Page 339 Courtesy of Foot Locker
Page 363 Courtesy of University of Michigan
Page 370 Courtesy of Ford Motor Company
Page 371 Courtesy of Mattel, Inc.
Page 373 © PhotoDisc
Page 373 © Helena Soopail: PhotoEdit
Page 391 Courtesy of Mattel, Inc.
Page 405 © PhotoDisc
Page 408 © Shaun Egan: Tony Stone Images
Page 424 © Nicholas Communications, Inc.
Page 426 Courtesy of Pennzoil
Page 427 Courtesy of Intel
Page 428 Courtesy of Dairy Queen International, Inc.
Page 447 © Tony Freeman: PhotoEdit
Page 451 Courtesy of Sony Electronics
Page 453 © Bill Aron: PhotoEdit
Page 455 Courtesy of Anheuser Busch
Page 460 Courtesy of Motorola
Page 462 Courtesy of America West
Page 471 © Nicholas Communications, Inc.
Page 495 © Ron Chapple: FPG International
Page 495 © Vladimir Pcholkin: FPG International
Page 499 © Michael Newman: PhotoEdit
Page 504 Courtesy of International House of Pancakes
Page 506 © Chris Mooney: FPG International
Page 510 © Tony Freeman: PhotoEdit
Page 514 © Travelpix: FPG International
Page 517 © Warren Bolster: Tony Stone Images
Page 547 © Michael Newman: PhotoEdit
Page 550 © Roger Allyn Lee: Tony Stone Images
Page 563 Courtesy of The McGraw-Hill Companies
Page 564 © Thomas Del Brase: Tony Stone Images
Page 567 Courtesy of SurModics
Page 567 Courtesy of American Greetings
Page 574 Courtesy of Pitney Bowes
Page 599 © Christopher Bissell: Tony Stone Images
Page 610 Courtesy of Wm. Wrigley Jr. Company
Page 613 Courtesy of America Online
Page 613 © James Mejuto

Page 617 Courtesy of K-Swiss
Page 618 © Nick Vedros: Tony Stone Images
Page 641 © Michael Newman: PhotoEdit
Page 644 © Nicholas Communications, Inc.
Page 650 © David Sacks: FPG International
Page 669 Courtesy of Chock Full O'Nuts
Page 689 © Michael A. Keller: The Stock Market
Page 691 © Susan Van Etten: PhotoEdit
Page 691 © James Mejuto
Page 693 Courtesy of the New York Stock Exchange
Page 697 © Photofest
Page 699 © Michael Simpson: FPG International
Page 703 Courtesy of Nike
Page 717 © Andy Whale: Tony Stone Images
Page 717 © Rob Lewine: The Stock Market
Page 718 © A. Ramey: PhotoEdit
Page 719 © John Akhtar: Vivid Images Photography, Inc.
Page 720 Courtesy of Mary E. Garza
Page 726 Courtesy of E-Cash
Page 748 © Jean Miele: The Stock Market
Page 773 © James Mejuto
Page 775 © James Mejuto
Page 781 © James Mejuto
Page 792 © Nicholas Communications, Inc.
Page 797 © Vic Bider: PhotoEdit
Page 819 © Jeff Greenberg: Unicorn Stock Photos
Page 819 © Michael Newman: PhotoEdit
Page 824 © Michael Newman: PhotoEdit
Page 826 Courtesy of Caterpillar
Page 833 Courtesy of Delta Airlines
Page 835 Courtesy of Xerox Corporation
Page 835 Courtesy of Globe Metallurgical, Inc.
Page 836 Courtesy of Toyota Motor Sales
Page 837 Courtesy of Binney & Smith Inc.
Page 857 © David Young Wolff: PhotoEdit
Page 862 Courtesy of the National Aeronautics and Space Administration
Page 863 Courtesy of Babson College
Page 863 © Amy C. Etra: PhotoEdit
Page 873 © Don Smetzer: Tony Stone Images
Page 875 © ChromoSohm: PhotoEdit
Page 903 © James Mejuto
Page 903 Courtesy of L.L. Bean
Page 905 © Sylvain Coffie: Tony Stone Images
Page 909 © Phil Matt
Page 911 Property of AT&T Archives
Page 912 Courtesy of Boeing Commercial Airplane Group
Page 915 © Jon Riley: Tony Stone Images
Page 925 Courtesy of Toyota
Page 926 © David Joel: Tony Stone Images
Page 926 © James Mejuto
Page 945 © Chris Sorensen: The Stock Market
Page 948 © Bonnie Kamin: PhotoEdit
Page 951 © Michael Newman: PhotoEdit
Page 951 Courtesy of Perkin-Elmer
Page 954 Courtesy of Motorola
Page 954 Courtesy of Hewlett-Packard Company
Page 957 © Tom Carroll: FPG International
Page 987 © Donald Johnston: Tony Stone Images
Page 988 © Phil Matt
Page 989 © Michael Newman: PhotoEdit
Page 990 Courtesy of Mercedes-Benz of North America, Inc.
Page 994 © David Young Wolff: PhotoEdit
Page 1001 © David Young Wolff: Tony Stone Images
Page 1002 © Jeff Greenberg: PhotoEdit
Page 1019 © David Brownell
Page 1021 AP/Wide World Photos
Page 1022 © Nicholas Communications, Inc.
Page 1025 © Tim Brown: Tony Stone Images
Page 1026 © Richard Buring: Tony Stone Images
Page 1027 © Jack Affleck
Page 1028 Courtesy of the Renton Coil Spring Company
Page 1034 © Michael Newman: PhotoEdit
Page 1035 © Mark Wagner: Tony Stone Images
Page 1057 © Michael Newman: PhotoEdit
Page 1059 © John Madere: The Stock Market
Page 1062 © Barry Rosenthal: FPG International
Page 1064 Courtesy of Chrysler Corporation
Page 1066 Logos courtesy of US Web & National Broadcasting Company
Page 1067 © Bruce Ayres: Tony Stone Images
Page 1069 Courtesy of the Redhook Ale Brewery
Page 1072 Courtesy of Motorola
Page 1077 © Lori Adamski Peek: Tony Stone Images
Page 1099 Courtesy of Paychex
Page 1101 © Tony Freeman: PhotoEdit
Page 1103 © John Running: Tony Stone Images
Page 1108 © Phil Matt
Page 1111 © Steven Weinberg: Tony Stone Images
Page 1119 © Amy C. Etra: PhotoEdit
C-7 © AP/Wide World Photos

Index

FUNDAMENTALS

① Accounting Equation

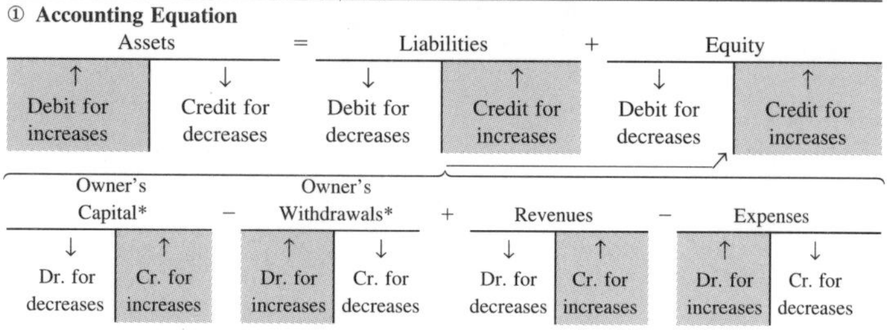

Indicates normal balance.

*Comparable corporate accounts are Contributed Capital and Cash Dividends.

② Accounting Cycle

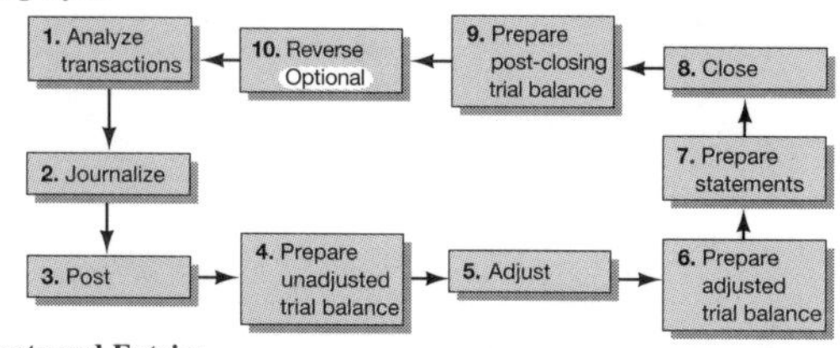

③ Adjustments and Entries

Type	Adjusting Entry	
Prepaid Expense	Dr. Expense	Cr. Asset
Depreciation	Dr. Expense	Cr. Contra-Asset
Unearned Revenues	Dr. Liability	Cr. Revenue
Accrued Expenses	Dr. Expense	Cr. Liability
Accrued Revenues	Dr. Asset	Cr. Revenue

④ 4-Step Closing Process

<1>Transfer revenue account balances to Income Summary.
<2>Transfer expense account balances to Income Summary.
<3>Transfer Income Summary balance to Owner's Capital.
<4>Transfer Withdrawals balance to Owner's Capital.

⑤ Accounting Concepts

Characteristics	Assumptions	Principles	Constraints
Relevance	Business entity	Historical cost	Cost-benefit
Reliability	Going concern	Revenue recognition	Materiality
Comparability	Monetary unit	Matching	Industry practice
Consistency	Periodicity	Full disclosure	Conservatism

⑥ Ownership of Inventory

	Ownership transfers when goods passed to	Transportation costs paid by
FOB Shipping Point	Carrier	Buyer
FOB Destination	Buyer	Seller

⑦ Inventory Costing Methods

Specific Identification
First-In, First-Out (FIFO)
Last-In, First-Out (LIFO)
Weighted-Average

⑧ Depreciation and Depletion

Straight-Line: $\frac{\text{Cost} - \text{Salvage value}}{\text{Useful life in periods}} \times \text{Periods expired}$

Units-of-Production: $\frac{\text{Cost} - \text{Salvage value}}{\text{Useful life in units}} \times \text{Units produced}$

Declining Balance: Rate* × Beginning of period book value

*Rate is often double the straight-line rate, or 2x(1/useful life)

Depletion: $\frac{\text{Cost} - \text{Salvage value}}{\text{Total capacity in units}} \times \text{Units extracted}$

⑨ Interest Computation

Interest = Principal (face) × Rate × Time

⑩ Costing Terminology

Variable cost: Cost changes in proportion to volume of activity.
Fixed cost: Cost does not change in proportion to volume of activity.
Relevant range: Company's normal range of operating activity.
Direct cost: Cost incurred for the benefit of one cost object.
Indirect cost: Cost incurred for the benefit of more than one cost object.
Product cost: Cost that is necessary and integral to finished products.
Period cost: Cost identified more with a time period than with finished products.
Overhead cost: Cost not separately or directly traceable to a cost object.
Relevant cost: Cost that is pertinent to a decision.
Opportunity cost: Benefit lost by choosing an action from two or more alternatives.
Sunk cost: Cost already incurred that cannot be avoided or changed.
Standard cost: Cost computed using standard price and standard quantity.
Cost variance: Difference between actual cost and budgeted (standard) cost.
Budget: Formal statement of a company's future plans.
Break-even point: Sales level at which a company earns zero profit.
Incremental cost: Cost incurred only if the company undertakes certain action.

ANALYSES

① Liquidity and Efficiency

$$\text{Current ratio} = \frac{\text{Current assets}}{\text{Current liabilities}}$$

$$\text{Acid-test ratio} = \frac{\text{Cash} + \text{Short-term investments} + \text{Current receivables}}{\text{Current liabilities}}$$

$$\text{Accounts receivable turnover} = \frac{\text{Net sales}}{\text{Average accounts receivable}}$$

$$\text{Merchandise turnover} = \frac{\text{Cost of goods sold}}{\text{Average merchandise inventory}}$$

$$\text{Days' sales uncollected} = \frac{\text{Accounts receivable}}{\text{Net sales}} \times 365^*$$

$$\text{Days' sales in inventory} = \frac{\text{Ending inventory}}{\text{Cost of goods sold}} \times 365^*$$

$$\text{Total asset turnover} = \frac{\text{Net sales}}{\text{Average total assets}}$$

*360 days is also commonly used.

② Solvency

$$\text{Debt ratio} = \frac{\text{Total liabilities}}{\text{Total assets}} \qquad \text{Equity ratio} = \frac{\text{Total equity}}{\text{Total assets}}$$

$$\text{Pledged assets to secured liabilities} = \frac{\text{Book value of pledged assets}}{\text{Book value of secured liabilities}}$$

$$\text{Times interest earned} = \frac{\text{Income before interest and taxes}}{\text{Interest expense}}$$

③ Profitability

$$\text{Profit margin} = \frac{\text{Net income}}{\text{Net sales}} \qquad \text{Gross margin} = \frac{\text{Net sales} - \text{Cost of goods sold}}{\text{Net sales}}$$

$$\text{Return on total assets} = \frac{\text{Net income}}{\text{Average total assets}}$$

$$\text{Return on common stockholders' equity} = \frac{\text{Net income} - \text{Preferred dividends}}{\text{Average common stockholders' equity}}$$

$$\text{Book value per common share} = \frac{\text{Stockholders' equity applicable to common shares}}{\text{Number of common shares outstanding}}$$

$$\text{Basic earnings per share} = \frac{\text{Net income} - \text{Preferred dividends}}{\text{Weighted-average common shares outstanding}}$$

$$\text{Cash flow on total assets} = \frac{\text{Operating cash flows}}{\text{Average total assets}}$$

④ Market

$$\text{Price-earnings ratio} = \frac{\text{Market price per common share}}{\text{Earnings per share}} \qquad \text{Dividend yield} = \frac{\text{Annual dividends per share}}{\text{Market price per share}}$$

⑤ Ratio Adjustments for Noncorporations*

$$\text{Profit margin} = \frac{\text{Net income} - \text{Value of owner's efforts}}{\text{Net sales}}$$

$$\text{Return on total assets} = \frac{\text{Net income} - \text{Value of owner's efforts}}{\text{Average total assets}}$$

$$\text{Return on equity} = \frac{\text{Net income} - \text{Value of owner's efforts}}{\text{Average equity}}$$

***Notes:** 1. Taxes are zero for nearly all proprietorships and partnerships. 2. Sales are also called revenues. 3. Costs of goods sold are also called costs of sales.

⑥ Costing Ratios

Contribution margin ratio = (Net Sales − Variable costs) / Net Sales
Predetermined overhead rate = Estimated overhead costs / Estimated "factor" costs
Costs per unit = Material, labor, and overhead costs per unit

⑦ Planning and Control

Break-even point = Fixed costs / Contribution margin per unit
Cost variance = Actual cost − Budgeted cost
Revenue variance = Actual sales − Budgeted sales
Payback period = Time expected to recover initial investment
Net present value = Present value of cash flows − Initial investment

REPORTS*

Income Statement
For _period_ Ended _date_

Total net sales (revenues)		$ #
Cost of goods sold:		
Beginning inventory	$ #	
Cost of purchases	#	
Goods available for sale	$ #	
Ending inventory	#	
Cost of goods sold		#
Gross margin (gross profit)		$ #
Operating expenses:		
Examples: Depreciation, salaries,	$ #	
wages, rent, utilities, interest,	#	
amortization, advertising, taxes	#	
Total operating expenses		#
Nonoperating gains and losses		#
Net income (net profit or earnings)		$ #

*A chart of accounts near the end of the book classifies accounts by financial statement categories.